ENCYCLOPEDIC DICTIONARY OF ACCOUNTING & FINANCE

JAE K. SHIM • JOEL G. SIEGEL

MJF BOOKS
NEW YORK

Published by MJF Books
Fine Communications
Two Lincoln Square
60 West 66th Street
New York, NY 10023

Library of Congress Catalog Card Number 95-82181
ISBN 1-56731-112-1

This edition is reprinted by arrangement with Prentice-Hall Inc./Career & Personal Development.

Manufactured in the United States of America

MJF Books and the MJF colophon are trademarks of Fine Creative Media, Inc.

10 9 8 7 6 5 4 3 2 1

To

Chung Shim,
dedicated wife

and

Roberta Siegel,
loving and wonderful wife

David F. Hawkins,
noted scholar, leading intellectual, and dear friend

Philip E. Levine,
dear and precious friend

ACKNOWLEDGMENTS

We wish to express our deep gratitude to Bette Schwartzberg for her outstanding editorial assistance during this project. Her input and efforts are recognized and greatly appreciated. Much thanks and appreciation goes to Christina Burghard for her highly professional and superb production editorial work.

We also thank Roberta M. Siegel for her help in preparing the data base of entries to be included in the book, as well as her reading of the computer topics and offering suggestions.

ABOUT THE AUTHORS

Jae K. Shim, Ph.D., is Professor of Accounting and Finance at California State University, Long Beach. He received his MBA and Ph.D. degrees from the University of California at Berkeley.

Dr. Shim, an accounting and financial consultant, has published numerous referred articles in such journals as *Financial Management, Econometrica, Decision Sciences, Management Science, Long Range Planning, OMEGA, Journal of Operational Research Society,* and *Advances in Accounting.* He has sixteen college and professional books to his credit, including *Handbook of Financial Analysis, Forecasting and Modeling; Accountants' Microcomputer Handbook; The Vest Pocket MBA;* and *The Vest Pocket CPA.*

Dr. Shim is the recipient of the 1982 Credit Research Foundation for his article on financial modeling.

Joel G. Siegel, Ph.D., CPA, is Professor of Accounting and Finance at Queens College of the City University of New York. He is an accounting and financial consultant.

Dr. Siegel was previously a member of the staff of Coopers and Lybrand, CPAs, and a faculty resident with Arthur Andersen, CPAs. He has acted as a consultant in accounting and financial issues to many organizations, including International Telephone & Telegraph, Citicorp, and Person-Wolinsky Associates.

Dr. Siegel is the author of 21 books and about 150 articles on accounting and financial topics. His books have been published by Prentice Hall, McGraw-Hill, John Wiley, Barron's, and the American Institute of CPAs.

He has been published in numerous accounting and financial journals, including *The CPA Journal, Computers in Accounting, National Public Accountant, Financial Executive,* and *The Financial Analysts Journal.*

In 1972, he was the recipient of the Outstanding Educator of America Award. He is listed in *Who's Where Among Writers* and *Who's Who in the World.*

WHAT THIS BOOK WILL DO FOR YOU

The *Encyclopedic Dictionary of Accounting and Finance* is written and compiled in such a way that working professionals engaged in the fields of accounting, finance, investment, and banking may use it in both their day-to-day practice and for technical research. The Encyclopedic Dictionary is a practical reference of proven techniques, strategies, and approaches that are successfully used by professionals to diagnose accounting and financial problems. The book covers virtually all important topics dealing with financial accounting, financial statement analysis, managerial/cost accounting, auditing, managerial finance, investments, financial planning, financial economics, and money and banking. It also covers such topics as computers, quantitative techniques and models, and economics as applied to accounting and finance. The Encyclopedic Dictionary will benefit practicing accountants, financial analysts and planners, financial managers, investment analysts, and professional bankers, among others.

The subjects are explained with

- Clear definitions and explanations, including step-by-step instructions
- Checklists
- Practical applications
- Tables and statistical data, as needed
- Charts, exhibits, and diagrams, where appropriate

The Encyclopedic Dictionary will enlighten the practitioner by presenting the most current information, offer important directives, and explain the technical procedures involved in the aforementioned dynamic business disciplines. This reference book will help you diagnose and evaluate accounting and financial situations you face daily. This library of accounting and finance will answer every question you may have. Real-life examples are provided, along with suggestions for handling everyday problems. The Encyclopedic Dictionary applies to large, medium, or small companies. It will help you to make smart decisions in all areas of accounting and finance. It should be used as an *advanced guide* for working professionals, rather than as a reference guide for laymen or a glossary of accounting and finance terms.

The Encyclopedic Dictionary is a handy reference for today's busy accountant and financial executive. It is a working guide to help you quickly pinpoint

- What to look for
- What to watch out for
- What to do
- How to do it
- How to apply it in the complex world of business

You'll find ratios, formulas, examples, applications, tables, charts, and rules of thumb to help you analyze and evaluate any business-related situation. New up-to-date methods and techniques are included. Throughout, you'll find this Encyclopedic Dictionary practical, comprehensive, quick, and useful. In short, this is a veritable cookbook of guidelines, illustrations, and how-to's for you, the modern decision maker. The uses of this handbook are as varied as the topics presented. Keep it handy for easy reference throughout your busy day.

There are approximately 500 major topics in accounting and finance covered in the Encyclopedic Dictionary, as well as about 100 related entries. Where appropriate, there is a cross-reference to another entry to explain the topic in greater detail. The entries are listed in alphabetical order for easy reference. The Encyclopedic Dictionary is so comprehensive that any subject area of interest to accountants and financial executives, as well as other interested parties, can be found.

CREDIT LINES

Permission to reprint Example 1 of Appendix C (pages 44–51) of *FASB Statement 95—Statement of Cash Flows* and the example on page 32 of *FASB Statement 96—Accounting for Income Taxes* were received from the Financial Accounting Standards Board, High Ridge Park, Stamford, Connecticut, 06905, U.S.A. Reprinted with permission. Copies of the complete document are available from the Financial Accounting Standards Board.

The CPA System and The Client System are trademarks of ICON Interactive Concepts. ATOM 1–3, Plus Plan, Statistical Techniques, and Estimation Sampling are trademarks of Deloitte, Haskins and Sells. Enterprise System is a trademark of BPI Corp. Crystal Payroll is a trademark of Crystal Software. Stock-Master is a trademark of Applied Micro Business Systems. Taxadvisor is a trademark of R. Michaelson. Auditor is a trademark of C. Dungan. TICOM is a trademark of A. Bailey, A. Whinston, and M. Gagle. Arborist Decision Tree, Natural Link, and Personal Consultant/Plus are trademarks of Texas Instruments. Audit Cube is a trademark of Blackman, Kallick & Co. Automated Workpapers is a trademark of Linton Shafer. Pre-Audit is a trademark of Coopers and Lybrand. dBase III+ and Framework are trademarks of Ashton-Tate. Sidekick is a trademark of Borland International. Expert Ease is a trademark of Human Edge Software. Planpower is a trademark of Applied Expert System. Expert Strategist is a trademark of Unitek Technologies. Interactive Easy Flow is a trademark of Haven Tree Software. PC Storyboard and Topview are trademarks of IBM. Harvard Presentation Graphics is a trademark of Software Publishing. Market Analyzer, Market Manager, Market Microscope, and Investment Evaluator are trademarks of Dow Jones. Value Pac is a trademark of Value Line. Winning on Wall Street is a trademark of Samna Software. Stockpac II is a trademark of Standard and Poor's. Option Strategy Calculation and Reporting is a trademark of ATS Software. Portfolio is a trademark of Software Option. Real Estate Analyzer is a trademark of Howard Software. Real Estate and Financial Software is a trademark of Taft Cameron. Property Management Plus is a trademark of Realty Software. Property Management is a trademark of Yardi Systems. Local Net is a trademark of Sytek. Managing Your Money is a trademark of Andrew Tobias. Scratch Pad is a trademark of SuperSoft. Note It is a trademark of Turner Hall Publishing. Spreadsheet Auditor is a trademark of Consumers Software. Spreadsheet Analyst is a trademark of Cambridge Software. SPSS/PC is a trademark of SPSS Inc. Strategic Management Game is a trademark of Strategic Management Group. Windows is a trademark of Microsoft. GEM Desktop is a trademark of Digital Research. Desqview is a trademark of Quarterback Office Systems. Amps Tax is a trademark of Amps Software. Volts Tax Software Pack is a trademark of Hanover Software. Micro-Tax is a trademark of Microcomputers Tax Systems. Tax-Plan is a trademark of Ernst and Whinney. A-plus Tax is a trademark of Arthur Andersen. The Tax Planning Template is a trademark of Permar Associates. Security Modem is a trademark of ITT. Think Tank is a trademark of Living Videotext. Time Management and Billing System is a trademark of Systematic Data Marketing Corp. Professional Time and Billing is a trademark of UniLink. Crosstalk is a trademark of Microstuf. Smartcom is a trademark of Hayes. SideTalk is a trademark of Lattice. Lotus 1-2-3 is a trademark of Lotus Development Corp.

A

ABC INVENTORY METHOD This is a method that categorizes items according to importance. Hence, greater attention is given to higher dollar merchandise (A's) than lower cost items (B's). The least essential items (C's) are lowest in priority order in terms of control and attention. Under this method, inventory evaluation is performed often. The steps involved follow:

1. A segregation is made of merchandise into components (e.g., varying models) based on dollar value.

2. Annual dollar usage is computed by inventory type (anticipated annual usage times unit cost).

3. A ranking is given to inventory in terms of dollar usage, ranging from high to low (e.g., A's in top 30%, B's in next 50%, and C's in last 20%.

4. Inventory is tagged with the appropriate classification so proper emphasis may be placed on them. A recording is made in the inventory records of the classifications.

See also Inventory Control and Management; Inventory Planning and Control.

ACCEPTANCE SAMPLING This involves an accept–reject decision, such as for inventory items and documents. It necessitates a precise advance decision regarding the error incidence mandating rejection. For example, if a company's internal control system is rejected after sampling, the entire system will be closely scrutinized.

In acceptance sampling, a group of data are examined to ascertain whether the number of sampled items possessing a specified attribute is greater than a stated percentage. One objective is not to reject acceptable batches. It is a useful approach for the internal auditor in gauging the quality of clerical work. Acceptance sampling tables are used to formulate a sampling plan to assure that errors will not exceed a stated percentage of the batch (tolerable error rate). However, a complete examination of rejected batches must be made. Also, documents may be examined for such things as mathematical computations. Acceptance sampling is primarily an internal audit technique rather than an external audit tool. For example, it is quite difficult to come up with a sampling plan that while rejecting, say, 95% of deficient batches does not also reject many good batches. Three considerations in a sampling plan are batch size, sample size, and maximum number of defects before rejection of the whole batch. *See also* Sampling.

ACCOUNTING CHANGES The types of accounting changes provided for in APB 20 are principle, estimate, and reporting entity. Proper disclosure of accounting changes is necessary.

Change in Accounting Principle

Once adopted, it is presumed that an accounting principle should not be changed for events or transactions of a similar nature. A method used for a transaction that is being terminated or was a single nonrecurring event in the past should not be changed. Only where necessary should a change in principle be made.

A change in accounting principle is accounted for in the current year's income statement in an account called cumulative effect of a change in accounting principle. The amount equals the difference between retained earnings at the beginning of the year with the old method versus what retained earnings would have been at the beginning of the year if the new method had been used in prior years. The account is shown net of tax with EPS on it. The new principle is used in the current and future years. Consistency is needed to make proper user comparisons. The cumulative effect account is shown after extraordinary items and before net income in the income statement. Note that a change in depreciation method for a *new* fixed asset is *not* a change in principle. Footnote disclosure should be made of the nature and justification of a change in principle, including an explanation of why the new principle is preferred. Proper justification may take the form of a new FASB pronouncement, new tax law, new AICPA recommended practice, change in circumstances, and to conform more readily to industry practice. According to FASB 32, specialized accounting practices and principles included in the AICPA Statements of Position (SOPs) and Guides are "preferable accounting principles" for the application of APB 20.

In the case where summaries of financial data for several years are presented in financial reports, APB 20 applies to them.

Indirect effects are included in the cumulative effect only if they are to be recorded on the books as a result of a change in accounting principle. The cumulative effect does *not* include nondiscretionary adjustments based on earnings (e.g., employee bonuses), which would have been recognized if the new principle had been used in prior years.

If comparative financial statements are not shown, *pro forma* disclosures (recalculated figures) should be made between the body of the financial statements and the footnotes of what earnings would have been in prior years if the new principle had been used in those prior years, along with showing the actual amounts for those years. If income statements are presented for comparative purposes, they should reflect the change on a pro forma basis as if the change had been in effect in each of such years. Financial statements of prior years, presented for comparative purposes, are presented *as previously reported*. But income before extraordinary items, net income, and earnings per share for previous years presented are *recalculated* and disclosed on the face of the prior periods' income statements as if the new principle had been in use in those periods. If space does not allow, this information may be presented in separate schedules showing both the original and recalculated figures. If only the current period's income statement is presented, the actual and pro forma (recalculated) figures for the immediate preceding period should be disclosed.

In exceptional cases, pro forma amounts are not determinable for prior years even though the cumulative effect on the opening retained earnings balance can be computed. The cumulative effect of a change in principle is presented in the usual fashion, with reasons given for omitting pro forma figures. In a similar vein, when the cumulative effect of a change in principle is impossible to calcu-

late, disclosure is given for the effect of the change on income data of the current period and explaining the reason for omitting the cumulative effect and pro forma amounts for prior periods. An example of a situation where the cumulative effect is not determinable is a switch from the FIFO to LIFO inventory pricing method.

If an accounting change in principle is deemed immaterial in the current year but it is anticipated to be material in later years, disclosure is necessary.

Certain types of changes in accounting principle instead of being shown in a cumulative effect account require the restatement of prior years as if the new principle had been used in those years. These changes are

• Change from LIFO to another inventory method.

• Change in accounting for long-term construction contracts (e.g., changing from the completed contract method to the percentage of completion method).

• Change to or from the full cost method used in the extractive industry. The full cost method is where both successful and unsuccessful exploration costs are deferred to the asset account and amortized. An alternative method is successful efforts where only successful costs are deferred while unsuccessful ones are immediately expensed.

Exempt from the requirements of APB Opinion 20 is a *closely held* business that for the *first time* registers securities, obtains equity capital, or effects a business combination. Such company *may* restate prior year financial statements.

Not considered a change in accounting principle are

• A principle adopted for the first time on new or previously immaterial events or transactions

• A principle adopted or changed due to events or transactions clearly different in substance

As per Interpretation 1, an *accounting principle* is not only an accounting principle or

practice, but also includes the methods used to apply such principles and practices. *Changing the composition* of the cost elements (e.g., material, labor, and overhead) of inventory qualifies as an accounting change. Changing the composition must be reported and justified as preferable. The basis of preferability among the different accounting principles is established in terms of whether the new principle improves the financial reporting function. Preferability is not determinable considering income tax effect alone.

■ **Example**

X Company changed from double declining balance to straight-line depreciation in 19X7. It uses ACRS depreciation for tax purposes, which results in depreciation higher than the double declining balance method for each of the three years. The tax rate is 34%. Relevant data follow:

Year	Double Declining Balance Depreciation	Straight-Line Depreciation	Difference
19X5	$250,000	$150,000	$100,000
19X6	200,000	150,000	50,000
19X7	185,000	150,000	35,000

The entries to reflect the change in depreciation in 19X7 follow:

Depreciation	150,000	
Accumulated depreciation		150,000
(For current year depreciation under the straight-line method.)		
Accumulated depreciation (100,000 + 50,000)	150,000	
Deferred income tax credit (150,000 × 0.34)		51,000
Cumulative effect of a change in accounting principle		99,000

Change in Accounting Estimate

A change in accounting estimate is caused by new circumstances or events requiring a revision in the estimates, such as a change in salvage value or life of an asset. A change in accounting estimate is accounted for pro-

spectively over current and future years. There is *no* restatement of prior years. A footnote should describe the nature of the change. Disclosure is required in the period of the change for the effect on income before extraordinary items, net income, and earnings per share. However, such disclosure is *not* required for estimate changes in the ordinary course of business when immaterial. Examples are revising estimates of uncollectible accounts or inventory obsolescence. If a change in estimate is coupled with a change in principle and the effects cannot be distinguished, it is accounted for as a change in estimate. For instance, a change may be made from deferring and amortizing a cost to expensing it as incurred because future benefits may be doubtful. This should be accounted for as a change in estimate.

■ Example

Equipment was bought on 1/1/19X2 for $40,000 having an original estimated life of 10 years with a salvage value of $4,000. On 1/1/19X6, the estimated life was revised to 8 more years remaining with a new salvage value of $3,200. The journal entry on 12/31/19X6 for depreciation expense is

Depreciation	2,800	
Accumulated depreciation		2,800

Computations follow:
Book value on 1/1/19X6:

Original cost		$40,000
Less: Accumulated depreciation		
$\frac{\$40,000 - \$4,000}{10} = \$3,600 \times 4$		14,400
Book value		$25,600

Depreciation for 19X6:

Book value	$25,600
Less: New salvage value	3,200
Depreciable cost	$22,400

$$\frac{\text{Depreciable cost}}{\text{New life}} \quad \frac{\$22,400}{8} = \$2,800$$

Change in Reporting Entity

A change in reporting entity (e.g., two previously separate companies combine) is accounted for by restating prior years' financial statements as if both companies were always combined. Restatement for a change in reporting entity is necessary to show proper trends in comparative financial statements and historical summaries. The effect of the change on income before extraordinary items, net income, and per share amounts is reported for all periods presented. The restatement process does not have to go back more than 5 years. Footnote disclosure should be made of the nature of and reason for the change in reporting entity only in the year of change. Examples of changes in reporting entity are

• Presenting consolidated statements instead of statements of individual companies

• Change in subsidiaries included in consolidated statements or those included in combined statements

• A business combination accounted for under the pooling-of-interests method

ACCOUNTING INFORMATION SYSTEM (AIS)

AIS is a subsystem of management information system (MIS) that processes financial transactions to provide scorekeeping, attention-directing, and decision-making information to management. The AIS is therefore the set of activities of the firm responsible for the preparation of financial information and the information obtained from transaction data for the purposes of (1) internal reporting to managers for use in planning, controlling, and decision making and (2) external reporting to outside parties such as stockholders, creditors, and government. *See also* Financial Information System; Management Information System (MIS).

ACCOUNTING POLICIES
Accounting policies of a business entity are the specific accounting principles and methods of applying them that are selected by management. Accounting policies used should be those that are most appropriate in the circumstances to fairly

present financial position and results of operations for the period. Accounting policies can relate to reporting and measurement methods as well as disclosures. They include
• A selection from generally accepted accounting principles
• Practices unique to the given industry
• Unusual applications of generally accepted accounting principles

The first footnote or a section preceding the notes to the financial statements should be a description of the accounting policies followed by the company.

The application of GAAP requires the use of *judgment* where alternative acceptable principles exist and where varying methods of applying a principle to a given set of facts exist. Disclosure of these principles and methods is vital to the full presentation of financial position and operations so that rational economic decisions can be made.

Examples of accounting policy disclosures are the depreciation method used, consolidation bases, amortization period for goodwill, construction contract method, and inventory pricing method.

Some types of financial statements need not describe the accounting policies followed. Examples are quarterly unaudited statements when there has not been a policy change since the last year-end and statements solely for internal use.

ACCOUNTING PRINCIPLES
These are guidelines, laws, or rules used in accounting practice to prepare financial statements. GAAP curtails the differences in accounting practice so that usefulness and comparability of financial statements are improved. GAAP is formulated by authoritative bodies, such as the Financial Accounting Standards Board. Applying accounting principles to a particular situation may require the accountant's judgment. Sources of GAAP include
• FASB pronouncements
• AICPA Interpretations, Audit Guides, Accounting Guides, and Statements of Position
• SEC regulations
• IRS regulations
• Accounting literature

ACCOUNTING SOFTWARE
An accounting package must be selected given the client's circumstances and needs. Accounting modules include general ledger, accounts receivable, accounts payable, payroll, inventory, and fixed assets. The first four modules are the most common. There are many accounting packages on the market, with a wide range in cost, quality, features, applications, and sophistication. Select the one that best meets your needs as well as your client's requirements.

The client may acquire individual modules or an integrated package. A small business may find that a general ledger module is adequate. A large corporation would need several modules. *Note*: Integrated accounting software links a number of modules performing related tasks; data from one module are transferred to another module. With integrated accounting packages, you do not have to continually reenter information because the different modules communicate with each other, updating the data base. For example, updating accounts payable automatically updates the general ledger. Integrated accounting software centers around the general ledger and includes other modules for specific accounting purposes, plus spreadsheet and word processing. You can go from accounting programs and other software to answering questions even if you're in the middle of a batch of transactions. Compatibility, efficiency, expeditious learning, integration, and lower cost dictate purchasing an integrated package from one vendor. It would be a mistake to acquire individual packages from different vendors.

The better accounting software works in different business situations and on different

types of computers. This kind of package is needed to meet changing circumstances. Lower priced general ledger software having such key features as accounts receivable, accounts payable, and report writing can be bought. However, inexpensive packages have fewer features and look only at the broadest accounting problems. Although the number of accounts might be restricted, there is still an automatic interface to the general ledger, along with adequate audit trails and controls.

ICON Interactive Concepts™ has compatible systems for CPAs and their clients. The CPA System™ includes audit, client write-up, tax preparation and planning, and practice management. The Client System™ includes general ledger, inventory control, accounts receivable/accounts payable, order entry/billing, sales analysis, and office automation. There is an instant rescue package to solve problems. Client data may be transferred to the CPA's computer automatically.

Deloitte, Haskins and Sells' ATOM 1-3™ has modules for trial balance, financial statements, and financial analysis. It maintains trial balance and financial statement information for many years. Items prepared include adjusting and reclassifying entries, working papers, ratio analysis, and financial statements. Information can be transferred to other programs such as Lotus 1-2-3.™

BPI's Enterprise Series™ generates an income statement for the company and income statements for departments. There are modules for accounts receivable, accounts payable, payroll, and inventory. It updates the control account and individual accounts automatically for a single transaction. Standard adjusting entries are made in the general ledger with a single command. Using information in the cash disbursements journal, checks may be written automatically. It has the ability to customize financial statements and produce ledgers with a full year's transactions.

Consolidation packages exist to prepare consolidations or foreign currency translations; an example is Deloitte, Haskins and Sell's Plus Plan.™

While there are specialized accounting programs for specific industries (e.g., Bristol Information Systems is a manufacturer of industry-specific software), general-purpose programs usually fit the bill.

The implementation of a new computerized system usually takes 6 to 12 months. Typically, one module is implemented at a time.

General Ledger Module

The general ledger module is central to the entire accounting system. It alone is sufficient for a small company. The general ledger module typically produces a chart of accounts, journals, trial balance, general ledger, and financial statements. The package should be flexible, allowing you to customize the system and report formats to the particular business requirements and preferences.

General ledger and financial statement programs should be used for client write-ups, whether for compilations, reviews, or audits, as well as to keep the practitioner's records. General ledger programs set up the chart of accounts and allow for entering beginning balances, budget amounts, and comparative prior period amounts. From a control point of view, these programs should also generate batch totals for input verification; display cumulative totals for both sides of a transaction, warning of any out-of-balance situation; and search for and reject any erroneous account numbers.

Accounts Receivable

An accounts receivable module is needed where there are significant amounts of sales transactions. The accounts receivable module assists cash flow and credit policy. Receiv-

ables from customers are tracked, reconciled, invoiced, and aged.

Desirable features in an accounts receivable package include
- Types of receivables accommodated
- Number of customers and general ledger accounts
- Highest transaction amount
- Number of invoices and payments
- Verification of customer information before transaction processing
- Proper adjustments to accounts receivable accounts
- Aging analysis
- Comparison of individual accounts to credit limits
- Sales analysis by salesperson, customer, and territory
- Sales tax reports

Accounts Payable

An accounts payable module is needed only when numerous checks are written. The frequency of the system may be weekly, semimonthly, or monthly, depending on the availability of cash discounts and the number of transactions. The accounts payable package makes out checks to vendors, assures the receipt of discounts, and prepares an aging of payables.

A quality accounts payable package should
- Accommodate many vendors, vouchers, checks, and invoices.
- Alphabetically list vendors
- Provide highest invoice amount allowed
- Calculate discounts and finance charges
- Pinpoint frequency and amount of payments and payables
- List recurring checks
- Show a due date register of payables along with their terms
- Analyze vendors
- Track lost discounts
- Compare receiving reports to supplier invoices

- List open purchase orders by vendor and item number

Payroll

A payroll package is feasible only if there are enough employees to justify the cost. Payroll software aids in determining the payroll deposit and offers needed payroll data at tax reporting time. Various packages exist. For example, Crystal Software's Crystal Payroll™ has user-defined pay types for hourly, salary, dollar, bonus, commission, tips, piece wage rates, expenses, and voluntary reductions, including 401Ks. There are multiple pay and deduction rates as well as allocation to multigeneral ledger accounts and departments. Quarterly and year-end reports are prepared.

Inventory

In evaluating an inventory package's quality, consideration should be given to
- Master files for inventory, customer, and vendor
- Number of inventory items handled
- Inventory records, including balances by item and category
- Inventory transactions for receipts, issuances, returns, and adjustments
- Interfacing with purchase orders and sales orders
- Comparing packing slips to purchase orders for quantity and part verification
- Processing adjustments to inventory quantities and price
- Reconciliation of promised date for delivery to actual delivery date
- Warehouse information
- Pricing determined by product, such as by using preestablished pricing methods
- Comparison of book to physical amounts
- Entry error-rejection capability
- Variance analysis for inventory discrepancies

• Calculation of economic order quantity and economic order point

• Calculation of lead time in receiving inventory

• Determination of safety stock

• Shortage reports

• Inventory turnover rates

• Actual inventory amounts compared with preestablished limits

• Back-order report

• ABC inventory classification

• Sales data by item for a given period

• Gross profit data by customer, item, and sales territory

An example of an inventory package is Applied Micro Business Systems' Stock-Master™, which provides stock status, trend analysis, purchase order tracking, quality control reporting, detail analysis, and Bill of Materials.

Fixed Assets

A good fixed asset package may provide the following features

• Description and categorization of assets

• Number and amount of assets accommodated

• Cost, life, and salvage value for fixed assets

• Allowance for different depreciation methods

• Pro rata depreciation calculations

• Fixed asset cost center

Best Programs' PC/Fixed Asset System™ manages fixed assets and provides necessary record keeping. Three sets of books are maintained for each fixed asset for the IRS, state, and internal use. Voluminous assets can be managed at once. It calculates depreciation, tracks asset location and "class," and indicates warranty expiration.

ACCOUNTS RECEIVABLE FINANCING (INCLUDING ASSIGNMENT AND FACTORING) Accounts receivable may be financed either through an assignment or factoring arrangement.

Assignment

When accounts receivable are assigned, the owner of the receivables borrows cash from a lender in the form of a note payable. The accounts receivable acts as collateral. New receivables substitute for receivables collected.

At a particular date, the transferor's equity in the assigned receivables equals the difference between the accounts receivable assigned and the balance of the line ($5,000). When payments on the receivables are received, they are remitted by the company to the lending institution to reduce the liability. Assignment is on a nonnotification basis to customers. It is made with recourse, where the company has to make good for uncollectable customer accounts.

■ Example

On 4/1/19X1, X Company assigns accounts receivable totaling $600,000 to A Bank as collateral for a $400,000 note. X Company will continue to receive customer remissions since the customers are not notified of the assignment. There is a 2% finance charge of the accounts receivable assigned. Interest on the note is 13%. Monthly settlement of the cash received from assigned receivables is made. During the month of April, there were collections of $360,000 of assigned receivables less cash discounts of $5,000. Sales returns were $10,000. On 5/1/19X1, April remissions were made plus accrued interest. In May the balance of the assigned accounts receivable was collected less $4,000 that were uncollectable. On 6/1/19X1, the balance due was remitted to the bank plus interest for May. The journal entries follow:

4/1/19X1

Cash	388,000	
Finance charge		
(2% × $600,000)	12,000	
Accounts receivable assigned	600,000	
Notes payable		400,000
Accounts receivable		600,000

During April:

Cash	355,000	
Sales discount	5,000	
Sales returns	10,000	
Accounts receivable assigned		370,000

5/1/19X1

Interest expense	4,333*	
Notes payable	355,000	
Cash		359,333

During May:

Cash	226,000	
Allowance for bad debts	4,000	
Accounts receivable assigned ($600,000 − $370,000)		230,000

6/1/19X1

Interest expense	488†	
Notes payable ($400,000 − $355,000)	45,000	
Cash		45,488

* $400,000 \times 0.13 \times 1/12 = \$4,333$
† $45,000 \times 0.13 \times 1/12 = \$488$

Factoring

In a factoring of accounts receivable, the receivables are in effect sold to a finance company. The factor buys the accounts receivable at a discount from face value, usually at a discount of 6%. Customers are typically notified. Factoring is usually done without recourse, where the risk of uncollectability of the customer's account rests with the financing institution. Billing and collection is typically done by the factor. On a factoring arrangement, the factor charges a commission of from 3/4% to 1½% of the net receivables acquired. The entry is

Cash (proceeds)
Loss on sale of receivables
Due from factor (proceeds kept by factor to cover possible adjustments such as sales discounts, sales returns, and allowances)
Accounts receivable (face amount of receivables)

Factoring is normally a continuous process. The seller of the goods receives orders and transmits the purchase orders to the factor for approval; on approval, the goods are shipped; the factor advances the money to the seller; the buyers pay the factor when payment is due; and the factor periodically remits any excess reserve to the seller of the goods. Once a routine is established, a continuous circular flow of goods and funds takes place among the seller, the buyers, and the factor. Once the agreement is in force, funds from this source are spontaneous.

■ Example

T Company factors $200,000 of accounts receivable. There is a 4% finance charge. The factor retains 6% of the accounts receivable. Appropriate journal entries are

Cash	180,000	
Loss on sale of receivables (4% × $200,000)	8,000	
Due from factor (6% × $200,000)	12,000	
Accounts receivable		200,000

Factors provide a needed and dependable source of income for small manufacturers and service businesses.

■ Example

You need an additional $100,000. You are considering a factoring arrangement. The factor is willing to buy the accounts receivable and advance the invoice amount less a 4% factoring commission on the receivables purchased. Sales are on 30-day terms. A 14% interest rate will be charged on the total invoice price and deducted in advance. With the factoring arrangement, the credit department will be eliminated, reducing monthly credit expenses by $1,500. Also, bad debt losses of 8% on the factored amount will be avoided.

To net you $100,000, the amount of accounts receivable to be factored is

$$\frac{\$100,000}{1 - (0.04 + 0.14)} = \frac{\$100,000}{0.82} = \$121,951$$

The effective interest rate on the factoring arrangement is

$$\frac{0.14}{0.82} = 17.07\%$$

The annual total dollar cost is

Interest (0.14 × $121,951)	$17,073
Factoring (0.04 × $121,951)	4,878
Total cost	$21,951

ACCOUNTS RECEIVABLE MANAGEMENT

In managing accounts receivable, the financial manager should consider that there is an opportunity cost associated with holding receivables. Means to expedite collection should be explored. A key concern is the amount and credit terms given to customers. Receivable management bears on the bottom line.

Means of Managing Accounts Receivable

• "Cycle bill" to produce greater uniformity in the billing process.

• Mail customer statements within 24 hours of the close of the accounting period.

• Send an invoice to customers when the order is processed at the warehouse instead of when merchandise is shipped.

• Bill for services periodically when work is performed or charge a retainer. *Tip*: Bill large sales immediately.

• Use seasonal datings. *Recommendation*: When business is slow, sell to customers with delayed payment terms to stimulate demand for customers who are unable to pay until later in the season. *What to do*: Compare profitability on incremental sales plus the reduction in inventory carrying costs, which have to exceed the opportunity cost on the additional investment in average accounts receivable.

• Carefully analyze customer financial statements before giving credit. Also, obtain ratings from financial advisory sources such as Dun and Bradstreet.

• Avoid typically high-risk receivables (e.g., customers in a financially troubled industry).

• Modify credit limits based on changes in customer's financial health.

• Ask for collateral in support of question-able accounts. *Tip*: The collateral value should equal or exceed the account balance.

• Factor accounts receivable when net savings ensue.

• Use outside collection agencies where warranted.

• Consider marketing factors, since a stringent credit policy might result in a loss of business.

• Consumer receivables have greater risk of default than corporate receivables.

• Age accounts receivable to spot delinquent customers. Aged receivables can be compared to prior years, industry norms, and competitive norms. *Note*: Bad debt losses are typically higher for smaller companies than for larger ones.

• Accelerate collections from customers currently having financial problems.

• Have credit insurance to guard against unusual bad debt losses. *What to consider*: In deciding whether to get this insurance, take into account expected average bad debt losses, financial capability of the firm to withstand the losses, and the cost of insurance.

Attributes of a Good Credit System

• Clear, quick, and uniform in application.

• Does not intrude on customer's privacy.

• Inexpensive (e.g., centralization of credit decisions by experienced staff).

• Based upon past experience, considering characteristics of good, questionable, and bad accounts. *Tip*: Determine the correlation between customer characteristics and future uncollectability.

The financial executive often has to determine the dollar investment tied up in accounts receivable.

■ Example

A company sells on terms of net/30. The accounts are on average 20 days past due. Annual credit sales are $600,000. The investment in accounts receivable is

$$\frac{50}{360} \times \$600,000 = \$83,333.28$$

■ Example

The cost of a product is 30% of selling price and the cost of capital is 10% of selling price. On average, accounts are paid 4 months after sale. Average sales are $70,000 per month.

The investment in accounts receivable from this product is

Accounts receivable	
(4 months × $70,000)	$280,000
Investment in accounts receivable	
[$280,000 × (0.30 + 0.10)]	112,000

Should customers be offered a discount for the early payment of account balances? Compare the return on freed cash resulting from customers' paying sooner to the cost of the discount.

■ Example

The following data are provided

Current annual credit sales	$14,000,000
Collection period	3 months
Terms	net/30
Minimum rate of return	15%

The company is considering offering a 3/10, net/30 discount. We expect 25% of the customers to take advantage of it. The collection period will decline to two months.

The discount should be offered, as indicated in the calculations shown below.

Should the company give credit to marginal customers? Compare the earnings on sales obtained to the added cost of the receivables. *Note*: If the company has idle capacity, the additional earnings is the contribution margin on the incremental sales because fixed costs are constant. The additional cost on the additional receivables results from the greater number of bad debts and the opportunity cost of tying up funds in receivables for a longer time period.

■ Example

Sales price per unit	$120
Variable cost per unit	80
Fixed cost per unit	15
Annual credit sales	$600,000
Collection period	1 month
Minimum return	16%

If you liberalize the credit policy, you project that
- Sales will increase by 40%.
- The collection period on total accounts will be 2 months.
- Bad debts on the increased sales will be 5%.

Preliminary calculations:

Current units ($600,000/$120)	5,000
Additional units (5,000 × 0.4)	2,000

Advantage

Increased profitability:	
Average accounts receivable balance before a change in policy	
$\dfrac{\text{Credit sales}}{\text{Accounts receivable turnover}} \quad \dfrac{\$14,000,000}{4}$	$3,500,000
Average accounts receivable balance after change in policy	
$\dfrac{\text{Credit sales}}{\text{Average receivable turnover}} \quad \dfrac{\$14,000,000}{6}$	$2,333,333
Reduction in average accounts receivable balance	$1,116,667
Rate of return	× 0.15
Return	$ 175,000

Disadvantage

Cost of the discount 0.30 × 0.25 × $14,000,000	$ 105,000
Net advantage of discount	$ 70,000

The new average unit cost is now calculated:

	Units × Unit Cost = Total Cost		
Current units	5,000 ×	$95	$475,000
Additional units	2,000 ×	$80	160,000
Total	7,000		$635,000

New average unit cost =
$$\frac{\text{Total cost}}{\text{Units}} = \frac{\$635,000}{7,000} = \$90.71$$

Note that at idle capacity, fixed cost remains constant. Thus, the incremental cost is only the variable cost of $80 per unit. This will cause the new average unit cost to drop.

Advantage

Additional profitability:

Incremental sales volume ×	2,000 units
Contribution margin per unit (Selling price − variable cost) $120 − $80	× $40
Incremental profitability	$ 80,000

Disadvantage

Incremental bad debts:

Incremental units × Selling price 2,000 × $120	$240,000
Bad debt percentage	× 0.05
Additional bad debts	$ 12,000

Opportunity cost of funds tied up in accounts receivable: Average investment in accounts receivable after change in policy:

$$\frac{\text{Credit sales}}{\text{Accounts receivable turnover}} \times \frac{\text{Unit cost}}{\text{Selling price}}$$

$$\frac{\$840,000 \ @}{6} \times \frac{\$90.71}{\$120} \qquad \$105,828$$

@7,000 units × $120 = $840,000

Current average investment in accounts receivable:

$\frac{\$600,000}{12} \times \frac{\$ 95}{\$120}$	39,583
Additional investment in accounts receivable	$66,245
Minimum return	× 0.16
Opportunity cost of funds tied up	$10,599
Net advantage of relaxation in credit standards:	
Additional earnings	$80,000
Less:	
Additional bad debt losses	$12,000
Opportunity cost	10,599
	22,599
Net savings	$57,401

The company may have to decide whether to extend full credit to presently limited credit customers or no-credit customers. Full credit should be given only if net profitability occurs.

■ **Example**

In deciding on a credit policy, the financial manager is appraising for different categories of customers what the percentage of uncollectability will be as well as the collection pool.

Category	Bad Debt Percentage	Collection Period	Credit Policy	Increase in Annual Sales if Credit Restrictions Are Relaxed
X	2%	30 days	Unlimited	$ 80,000
Y	5%	40 days	Restricted	600,000
Z	30%	80 days	No credit	850,000

Gross profit is 25% of sales. The minimum return on investment is 12%.

	Category Y	Category Z
Gross profit		
$600,000 × 0.25	$150,000	
$850,000 × 0.25		$212,500
Less bad debts		
$600,000 × 0.05	−30,000	
$850,000 × 0.30		−255,000
Incremental average investment in accounts receivable		
$\frac{40}{360}$ × (0.75 × $600,000)	$50,000	
$\frac{80}{360}$ × (0.75 × $850,000)		$141,667
Opportunity cost of incremental investment in accounts receivable	× 0.12 − 6,000	× 0.12 − 17,000
Net earnings	$114,000	$(59,500)

Credit should be extended to Category Y.

■ Example

The company is planning a sales campaign in which it will offer credit terms of 3/10, net/45. We expect the collection period to increase from 60 days to 80 days. Relevant data for the contemplated campaign follow.

	Percent of Sales Before Campaign	Percent of Sales During Campaign
Cash sales	40	30
Payment from		
1–10	25	55
11–100	35	15

The proposed sales strategy will probably increase sales from $8 million to $10 million. There is a gross margin rate of 30%. The rate of return is 14%. Sales discounts are given on cash sales.

	Without Sales Campaign	With Sales Campaign
Gross margin (0.3 × $8,000,000)	$2,400,000	0.3 × $10,000,000 $3,000,000
Sales subject to discount		
0.65 × $8,000,000	$5,200,000	
0.85 × $10,000,000		$8,500,000
Sales discount	× 0.03 − 156,000	× 0.03 − 255,000
Investment in average accounts receivable		
$\frac{60}{360}$ × $8,000,000 × 0.7	$933,333	
$\frac{80}{360}$ × $10,000,000 × 0.7		$1,555,555
Return rate	× 0.14 − 130,667	× 0.14 −217,778
Net profit	$2,113,333	$2,527,222

The company should undertake the sales campaign, because earnings will increase by $413,889 ($2,527,222 − $2,113,333).

ACCRUAL BASIS   This is an accounting method that recognizes revenue and expenses when earned or incurred rather than at the time of cash flow. The accrual basis is employed in the case of a manufacturer or dealer in inventory. *See also* Cash Basis.

ACCUMULATED BENEFIT OBLIGATION   The accumulated benefit obligation is the actuarial present value of future benefits to be paid to retired employees for services performed prior to a specified date and based on employee service and salary up to that date. The *existing* salary levels are used in the computation. *See also* Pension Plans.

ACTUARIAL COST METHOD   The actuarial cost method is a technique that actuaries use to compute annual employer contribution to the pension so that plan sufficient monies exist at employee retirement. An actuarial cost method is needed for pension expense and funding computation. Two general approaches are based on *cost* or *benefit*. The cost technique estimates total retirement benefit and then computes the adequate cost level (including expected interest) sufficient to provide retirement benefits. The benefit technique computes pension benefits applicable to service to date and then derives the present value of these benefits. *See also* Pension Plans.

ACTUARIAL GAINS AND LOSSES   These represent the difference between actual experience and estimates applicable to the pension plan. If, for instance, the actual return on pension assets is less than the estimated return rate, there is an actuarial loss. Actuarial gains and losses are deferred and amortized as an adjustment to pension expense. An actuarial gain decreases pension expense whereas an actuarial loss increases it. However, if an actuarial gain or loss arises from an occurrence not applicable to the pension plan (e.g., closing a plant), it is immediately recognized in the current year's income statement. *See also* Pension Plans.

ADDING OR DROPPING A PRODUCT LINE   The decision whether to drop an old product line or add a new one must take into account both qualitative and quantitative factors. Ultimately, however, any final decision should be based primarily on the impact the decision will have on contribution margin or net income.

■ **Example**

The ABC grocery store has three major product lines: produce, meats, and canned goods. The store is considering the decision to drop the meat line because the income statement shows it is being sold at a loss. Note the income statement for these product lines below:

	Produce	Meats	Canned Food	Total
Sales	$10,000	$15,000	$25,000	$50,000
Less: Variable costs	6,000	8,000	12,000	26,000
CM	$ 4,000	$ 7,000	$13,000	$24,000
Less: Fixed costs:				
Direct	$ 2,000	$ 6,500	$ 4,000	$12,500
Allocated	1,000	1,500	2,500	5,000
Total	$ 3,000	$ 8,000	$ 6,500	$17,500
Net income	$ 1,000	($ 1,000)	$ 6,500	$ 6,500

In this example, direct fixed costs are those costs that are identified directly with each of the product lines, whereas allocated fixed costs are the amount of common fixed costs allocated to the product lines using some base such as space occupied. The amount of common fixed costs typically continue regardless of the decision and thus cannot be saved by dropping the product line to which it is distributed.

The following calculations show the effects on the company as a whole with and without the meat line:

	Keep Meats	Drop Meats	Difference
Sales	$50,000	$35,000	($15,000)
Less:			
Variable cost	26,000	18,000	(8,000)
CM	$24,000	$17,000	($ 7,000)
Less:			
Fixed cost:			
Direct	$12,500	$ 6,000	($ 6,500)
Allocated	5,000	5,000	—
Total	$17,500	$11,000	($ 6,500)
Net income	$ 6,500	$ 6,000	($ 500)

We see that by dropping meats the store will lose an additional $500. Therefore, the meat product line should be kept. One of the great dangers in allocating common fixed costs is that such allocations can make a product line look less profitable than it really is. Because of such an allocation, the meat line showed a loss of $1,000, but it in effect contributes $500 ($7,000 − $6,500) to the recovery of the store's common fixed costs.

ADJUSTABLE RATE MORTGAGE (ARM)   An ARM is a mortgage where the interest rate is not fixed but changes over the life of the loan. ARMs are often called *variable* or *flexible rate mortgages*. Adjustable rate mortgages often feature attractive starting interest rates and monthly payments. But there is the risk that payments will rise. Pluses of ARMs include:

1. Lower initial interest (often 2 or 3 percentage points below that of a fixed rate) and lower initial payments, which can mean considerable savings. This means that ARMs are easier to qualify for.
2. Payments come down if interest rates fall.
3. Loans are more readily available and their processing time is quicker than fixed-rate mortgages.
4. Many adjustables are assumable by a borrower, which can help when it comes time to sell.
5. Many ARMs allow one to prepay the loan without penalty.

Some of the pitfalls of ARMs include:
1. Monthly payments can go up if interest rates rise.
2. Negative amortization can occur. Negative amortization occurs when the monthly payments do not cover all of the interest cost. The interest cost that is not covered is added to the unpaid principal balance. This means after making many payments one could owe more than at the beginning of the loan balance.
3. The initial interest rates last only until the first adjustment, typically 6 months or 1 year. And the promotional or tease rate is often not distinguished from the true contract rate, which is based on the index to which the loan is tied.

ARMs vs. Fixed Rate

A borrower should consider a fixed rate loan over an ARM if he or she
• Plans to be in the same home for a long time. It pays to get an ARM if buying a starter home or expecting to move or be transferred in 2 to 3 years.
• Does not expect income to rise.
• Plans to take sizable debts, like auto or educational loans.
• Prizes the security of constant payments.

Checklist for ARMs

When shopping for an ARM (or for any other adjustable rate loan), the following checklist of questions to ask lenders is helpful:
• What is the initial loan rate and the annual percentage rate (APR)? What costs besides interest does the APR reflect? What are the points?
• What is the monthly payment?
• What index is the loan tied to? How has the index moved in the past? Will the rate always move with the index?

• What is the lender's margin above the index? The margin is an important consideration when comparing ARM loans because it never changes during the life of the loan. Note that index rate + margin = ARM interest rate.

■ Example

You are comparing ARMs offered by two different lenders. Both ARMs are for 30 years and amount to $65,000. Both lenders use the 1-year Treasury index, which is 10%. But Lender A uses a 2% margin and Lender B uses a 3% margin. Here is how the difference in margin would affect the initial monthly payment:

	Lender A	Lender B
ARM interest rate	12% (10% + 2%)	13% (10% + 3%)
Monthly payment	$668.60 at 12%	$719.03 at 13%

• How long will the initial rate be in effect? Will there be an automatic increase at the first adjustment period even if the index has not changed? What effect will this have on monthly payments?
• How often can the rate change?
• Is there a limit on each rate change and how will the limit affect monthly payments?
• What is the "cap," or ceiling on the rate change over the life of the loan?
• Does the loan require private mortgage insurance (PMI) and how much does it cost per month?
• Is negative amortization possible?
• Is the loan assumable?
• Is there a prepayment penalty?

AFTER-TAX RATE OF RETURN The after-tax rate of return is the return on an investment that has to be considered in after-tax dollars.

■ Example

An individual earns 12% interest and is in the 28% tax bracket. The after-tax return rate is

$$12\% \times 72\% = 8.64\%$$

Inflation can be incorporated into the analysis. Assuming an inflation rate of 4%, the real rate of return after taxes and inflation is

$$\begin{array}{r} 8.64\% \\ -\ 4.0\ \% \\ \hline 4.64\% \end{array}$$

AGENCY THEORY This is a branch of law and economics applying to the contractual relationship between principals and their agents. An example of a principal is the owner, and his agent is the manager. The principal delegates authority for action to the agent.

AGING SCHEDULE An aging schedule shows the length of time an item has been outstanding or held. Examples are aging of accounts receivable, accounts payable, and inventory. For example, an aging of accounts receivable reveals how many days receivables have been outstanding. The longer receivables are uncollected, the greater is the likelihood for uncollectability. Thus, there are varying bad debt percentages applied to the various categories of receivables. The percentages used are based on prior experience.

■ Example

X Company
AGING SCHEDULE

Customer's Name	12/31/19X1 Balance	Under 60 Days	61–90 Days	91–120 Days	Over 120 Days
ABC Co.	$ 85,000	$ 60,000	$ 20,000	$ 5,000	
XYZ Co.	160,000	160,000			
TEL Co.	120,000	70,000	25,000	10,000	$15,000
Total	$365,000	$290,000	$ 45,000	$15,000	$15,000

AGING SCHEDULE—Continued

Age	Amount	Bad Debt Percentage	Needed Balance in Allowance Account
Under 60 days	$290,000	1%	$ 2,900
61–90 days	45,000	4%	1,800
91–120 days	15,000	8%	1,200
Over 120 days	15,000	10%	1,500
	$365,000		$ 7,400

ALLOCATION OF SERVICE DEPARTMENT COSTS TO PRODUCTION DEPARTMENTS   There are two basic types of departments in a manufacturing company: production departments and service departments. A production department (such as assembly and machining) is where the production or conversion occurs. A service department (such as engineering and maintenance) provides support to production departments. Before departmental overhead rates are developed for product costing, the costs of a service department should be allocated to the appropriate production department (as part of factory overhead). There are three basic methods of allocation:
1. Direct allocation method
2. Step down method
3. Reciprocal service method

Direct Allocation Method

Direct allocation method, also called *direct method*, is a method of allocating the costs of each service department directly to the production departments. Under this method, no consideration is given to services performed by one service department for another. This is perhaps the most widely used method because of its simplicity and ease of use.

■ Example

Assume the following data:

	Production Departments		Service Departments	
	A Machining	B Assembly	General Plant (GP)	Engineering (E)
Overhead costs before allocation	$30,000	$40,000	$20,000	$10,000
Engineering hours by Engineering	50,000	30,000	5,000	4,000
Direct labor hours by General Plant	60,000	40,000	15,000	20,000

Using the direct method yields:

	Service Departments		Production Departments	
	GP	E	A	B
Overhead costs	$20,000	$10,000	$30,000	$40,000
Reallocation:				
GP(60%, 40%)[a]	($20,000)		12,000	8,000
E(5/8, 3/8)[b]		($10,000)	6,250	3,750
			$48,250	$51,750

[a] Base is (60,000 + 40,000 = 100,000); 60,000/100,000 = 0.6; 40,000/100,000 = 0.4.
[b] Base is (50,000 + 30,000 = 80,000); 50,000/80,000 = 5/8; 30,000/80,000 = 3/8.

Step Allocation Method

This is a method of allocating services rendered by service departments to other service departments using a sequence of allocation; also called the *step-down* method and the *sequential* method. The sequence normally begins with the department that renders service to the greatest number of other service departments; the sequence continues in step-by-step fashion and ends with the allocation of costs of service departments that provide the least amount of service. But no *reciprocal* service is considered. Using the same data, the step allocation method yields:

| | Service Departments | | Production Departments | |
	GP	E	A	B
Overhead costs	$20,000	$10,000	$30,000	$40,000
Reallocation:				
GP(1/2, 1/3, 1/6)	($20,000)	3,333	10,000	6,667
E(5/8, 3/8)		($13,333)	8,333	5,000
			$48,333	$51,667

Reciprocal Allocation Method

Reciprocal allocation method, also known as the *reciprocal* method, the *matrix* method, the *double-distribution* method, the *cross-allocation* method and the *simultaneous equation* method, is a method of allocating service department costs to production departments, where *reciprocal* services are allowed between service departments. The method sets up simultaneous equations to determine the allocable cost of each service department.

Using the same data, we set up the following equations:

$$GP = \$20,000 + 50/85\ E$$
$$E = \$10,000 + 1/6\ GP$$

Substituting M from the second equation into the first:

$$GP = \$20,000 + 5/85\ (\$10,000 + 1/6\ GP)$$

Solving for *GP* gives *GP* = $20,791. Substituting *GP* = $20,791 into the second equation and solving for *E* gives *E* = $13,465.

| | Service Departments | | Production Departments | |
	GP	E	A	B
Overhead costs	$20,000	$10,000	$30,000	$40,000
Reallocation:				
GP(1/2, 3/1, 1/6)	($20,791)	3,465	10,396	6,930
E(50/85, 30/85, 5/85)	791	($13,465)	7,921	4,753
	0	0	$48,317	$51,683

ALPHA VALUE Alpha value of a security is the excess return that would be expected on the security if the excess return on the market portfolio were zero. It is also called *average differential return*. In the context of a mutual fund, an alpha value is the value representing the difference between the return on a fund and a point on the market line that corresponds to a beta equal to the fund, where the market line describes the relationship between excess returns and the portfolio beta. It has been used to evaluate performance of mutual funds. Generally, a positive alpha (excess return) indicates superior performance, whereas a negative value leads to the opposite conclusion. "Keep your alpha high and your beta low" is a basic strategy for those who wish to generate good investment performance. *See also* Beta Coefficient; Mutual Fund; Portfolio Theory and Capital Asset Pricing Model (CAPM).

AMORTIZATION This is the periodic reduction of an amount over time. It can apply to the gradual write-down of an asset and the gradual extinguishment of a debt. Examples are periodically reducing an intangible asset or deferred charge and reducing loan principal by making monthly payments.

Assets having a limited life must be reduced gradually over the period benefited. In the case of intangibles, amortization is over a period not exceeding 40 years using the straight-line method. In the case of some intangibles, a legal life may exist, such as with patents that have to be amortized over a period not exceeding 17 years. *Note*: If an intangible asset is suddenly deemed worthless, it is immediately written off, reflecting a nonrecurring loss.

■ Example

During 19X2 and 19X3 research costing $300,000 to discover a new product was incurred. On 1/1/19X4, a patent is registered for $20,000 on the product. The useful life of the patent is estimated at 10 years. On 1/3/19X6, legal costs incurred in the successful defense of the patent is $5,000. The amortization expense for 19X6 is computed below:

Initial cost of 1/1/19X4	$20,000	
Less: Accumulated amortization ($20,000/10) × 2	4,000	
Book value on 1/1/19X6		$16,000
Add: Legal costs on 1/3/19X6		5,000
Book value on 1/3/19X6		$21,000
Amortization expense for 19X6 ($21,000/8)		$ 2,625

ANALYTICAL PROCEDURES AICPA Statement on Auditing Standards No. 56 deals with auditor involvement with analytical review. The auditor is required to employ analytical review procedures in the planning and final review stages of an audit. Analytical techniques at the planning stage typically employ data at a high level. The procedures employed will vary depending on the complexity associated with the client's operations and reporting system. Examples of procedures are appraising the trend in account balances over the years and careful evaluation of quarterly financial statements.

Analytical review procedures are a type of substantive testing relating to the study and comparison of the relationships among data. It is helpful in alerting the auditor to the possibility of certain kinds of material irregularities. When significant fluctuations exist that are unexpected or unusual, the auditor should determine the reasons therefore. For example, the auditor may compare total wages to the number of employees to identify unauthorized payments. If a relationship does not make sense, detailed evaluation is required.

Analytical review procedures may be based on dollars, quantities, percentages, and ratio analysis comparing current period financial information with prior period financial data, anticipated amounts, predictable pattern information, intra-industry information, and nonfinancial data. In looking at nonfinancial data, the auditor may consider sales volume (e.g., if volume declines, there may exist merchandise quality problems), area of selling space occupied in square footage, and number of employees.

Professional judgment is exercised in deciding on specific analytical review procedures to be employed in a particular client setting.

There is greater assurance and predictability to relationships in a stable environment relative to one in an unstable environment. There is more assurance associated with income statement account relationships relative to balance sheet items. The former involves transactions over a time period. On the other hand, balance sheet items are static as of the end of the accounting period. If management discretion exists, the relationship associated with the transaction is more uncertain. For instance, management may cut back on repairs instead of buying new fixed assets. *See also* Substantive Test.

ANNUAL PERCENTAGE RATE (APR) Different types of investments use different compounding periods. For example, most bonds pay interest semiannually. Some banks pay interest quarterly. If an investor wishes to compare investments with different compounding periods, he needs to put them on a common basis. The annual percentage rate (APR), or effective annual rate, is used for this purpose and is computed as follows:

$$APR = (1 + r/m)^m - 1.0$$

where r = the stated, nominal, or quoted rate,

m = the number of compounding periods per year.

■ Example

Assume that a bank offers 6% interest, compounded quarterly, then the APR is

$$APR = (1 + 0.06/4)^4 - 1.0 = (1.015)^4 - 1.0$$
$$= 1.0614 - 1.0 = 0.0614 = 6.14\%$$

This means that if one bank offered 6% with quarterly compounding while another offered 6.14% with annual compounding, they would both be paying the same effective rate of interest.

Annual percentage rate (APR) also is a measure of the cost of credit, expressed as a yearly rate. It includes interest as well as other financial charges such as loan origination and certain closing fees. The lender is required to tell a borrower the APR. It provides him with a good basis for comparing the cost of loans, including mortgage plans.

ANNUAL REPORT　A report prepared by a business entity at the end of its calendar or fiscal year. It presents a company's financial position and operating results for use by interested parties, including potential investors, creditors, stockholders, and employees. An audit report is prepared by an independent CPA to determine whether the financial statements fairly present the company's financial health. In addition, the president's letter appears outlining current status and future prospects. There is a section on "Management's Discussion and Analysis of the Summary of Earnings," in which management explains the reasons for material changes in revenue and expenses.

ANNUITY　An annuity is a series of equal receipts or payments. It is also called rent. Examples of an annuity are cash dividends from a preferred stock, semiannual interest receipts from a bond investment, and a retirement annuity from an insurance company. There are different types of an annuity, including
1. Ordinary annuity (or annuity in arrears), where receipts or payments are made at the end of the period
2. Annuity due, where receipts or payments are made at the beginning of the period
3. Deferred annuity, where receipts or payments do not start until two or more periods have elapsed
4. Perpetuity, which is an annuity that continues for an indefinite period
　See also Retirement and Pension Planning; Time Value of Money and Its Applications.

APPROPRIATION

1. Restricting retained earnings for a designated purpose, such as appropriation for retirement of bonds or appropriation for plant expansion.
2. Authorization of a municipality to expend money subject to legal restrictions. The appropriate account is credited when a budget is adopted and debited when the budget is closed. It is a nominal account.
　See also Governmental Accounting.

ARBITRAGE　This applies to earning a profit arising from the price difference of the identical stock, bond, commodity, or currency that is traded in more than one market. Arbitrage tends to equalize prices of the items in different markets, except for differences in the costs of transportation, risk, and so on.

■ Example

An arbitrageur buys one security in the New York market for $40,000 and sells that security in the Chicago market for $41,000, making a profit of $1,000 since the price of the security at that exact time is different in the two markets. Brokerage commissions will reduce the profit.

What some arbitrageurs do is purchase stock of a company that may be acquired by another and sell short the stock of the acquiring company. If the acquisition occurs, a profit will be made. If not, a loss may be incurred.

ARITHMETIC AVERAGE RETURN VERSUS GEOMETRIC AVERAGE RETURN

It is one thing to measure the return over a single holding period and quite another to describe a series of returns over time. When an investor holds an investment for more than one period, it is important to understand how to compute the average of the successive rates of return. There are two types of multiperiod average (mean) returns. They are *arithmetic average return* and the *geometric average return*. The arithmetic return is simply the arithmetic average of successive one-period rates of return. It is defined as

$$\text{Arithmetic return} = 1/n \sum_{t=1}^{n} r_t$$

where n = the number of time periods and r_t = the single holding period return in time t.

The arithmetic average return, however, can be quite misleading in multiperiod return calculations.

A more accurate measure of the actual return generated by an investment over multiple periods is the geometric average return. The geometric return over n periods is computed as follows:

$$\text{Geometric return} = \sqrt[n]{(1 + r)(1 + r) \ldots (1 + r)} - 1$$

Since it is cumbersome to calculate the nth root (although there is a formula for approximation), we will illustrate only the two-period return calculation ($n = 2$).

■ Example

Consider the following data where the price of a stock doubles in one period and depreciates back to the original price. Assume no dividend.

	Time Periods		
	$t = 0$	$t = 1$	$t = 2$
Price (end of period)	$50	$100	$50
HPR	—	100%	-50%

The holding period return (HPR) for periods 1 and 2 are computed as follows:

Period 1 (t = 1)

$$\text{HPR} = \frac{\$0 + (\$100 - \$50)}{\$50} = \frac{\$50}{\$50} = 100\%$$

Period 2 (t = 2)

$$\text{HPR} = \frac{\$0 + (\$50 - \$100)}{\$100} = \frac{-\$50}{\$100} = -50\%$$

Therefore, the arithmetic average return is the average of 100% and -50%, which is 25%, as shown below:

$$\frac{100\% + (-50\%)}{2} = 25\%$$

Obviously, the stock purchased for $50 and sold for the same price two periods later did not earn 25%; it earned *zero* return. The geometric average return provides a correct return.

Note that $n = 2$, $r_1 = 100\% = 1$, and $r_2 = -50\% = -0.5$
Then:

$$\text{Geometric return} = \sqrt[2]{(1 + 1)(1 - 0.5)} - 1$$
$$= \sqrt[2]{(2)(0.5)} - 1$$
$$= \sqrt{1} - 1 = 1 - 1 = 0\%$$

See also Mean.

ARM'S-LENGTH TRANSACTION

In an arm's-length transaction, the seller and buyer attempt to maximize their best interest without any restrictions being placed. Some transactions do not satisfy this criteria, such as transactions between related parties and affiliated businesses. Arm's-length transactions are the basis for a fair market value determination in connection with recording the acquisition cost of an asset.

ARTIFICIAL INTELLIGENCE (AI)

Artificial intelligence software enhances the thinking process of accountants and financial executives so that optimum decisions can be made. In effect, microcomputers evaluate and solve

problems requiring human imagination and intelligence that involve known and unknown information. Reasons for difficulties can be uncovered and expert advice furnished. *Note*: There is imitation of intelligent human behavior and learning from experience. Significant data are evaluated and relevant relationships, such as the determination of a warranty reserve, uncovered. The computer learns which kinds of answers are reasonable and which are not. AI performs complicated strategies that assist in determining the best or worst way to accomplish a task or avoid an undesirable result. Applications of AI include

• Tax preparation and planning, such as tax shelter options, given the client's financial status

• Financial ratio analysis, including what-if analysis for the effect of alternative assumptions on an outcome

• Planning and audit analysis, including testing, internal control, attestation of EDP systems, appraising evidence, formulating an audit opinion, scheduling and monitoring the audit engagement, and uncovering illogical relationships (e.g., promotion expense to sales)

• Management services, including providing pension plan advice

• Practice management involving making decisions about staff development and assignment

• Analyzing delinquent accounts receivable along with probabilities of collection

An expert system for estate planning called Taxadvisor™ was developed by R. Michaelson of the University of Illinois. A package called Auditor™ is for the examination of bad debts and was formulated by C. Dungan of the same school. For internal control evaluation, a package referred to as TICOM™ was developed by A. Bailey of the University of Minnesota and A. Whinston and M. Gagle of Purdue.

Artificial intelligence programming languages include LISP, PROLOG, OPS5, ESIE, and POPLOG. Artificial intelligence software basically searches a data base for certain characteristics and then extracts them. Inference and reasoning functions exist. LISP programs change nonnumeric symbols like words to present useful and meaningful associations and interrelationships. When the program lists are correctly integrated in terms of facts and associations, a rational solution to a problem can be generated. LISP packages can modify themselves and create new data lists. INTERLISP is a version of LISP containing many packaged routines.

Backward chaining is involved where the system begins with a hypothesis, finds a rule whose premise supports the hypothesis, and then attempts to verify the knowledge base for a relevant fact. The process verifies or disproves the hypothesis.

■ Example

Lightyear™ is a decision software package that has the manager put into the microcomputer alternative solutions to a problem and evaluating criteria. Lightyear then ranks the alternatives from good to bad according to user weights. The manager can then go backward through the problem to reappraise the criteria. Comparison of decisions among different executives can also be made. The software permits the management and organization of decisions. Although the software does not make decisions, it has the financial executive organize and give the reasons supporting the decision already made. The user can also get a detailed evaluation for any of the alternatives.

■ Example

TIMM-PC™ logically considers alternative ways to solve problems when essential data are missing or inadequate. A pattern-matching technique permits differentiation between statements that vary continuously and those that have an all-or-nothing quality. Solutions are provided to problems, with probabilities assigned. Various types of statistical forecasting formulas are provided in the model.

The user can specify the rules to be followed by the micro to solve the problem via interaction with it. Once the particular problem is solved, the micro is trained to solve similar problems with fewer indicators.

▪ Example

Texas Instruments' Natural Link™ provides the financial executive with a selection of phrases at each point, representing possible alternatives. The executive chooses from the available options until a sentence has been constructed indicating what the program is supposed to do.

▪ Example

Texas Instruments' Personal Consultant/ Plus™ has a frames feature allowing a complex problem to be segregated into smaller, related subproblems. There is an external program interface so that other programs (e.g., spreadsheet, data base) can be used in the consultation process.

ASCII (AMERICAN STANDARD CODE FOR INFORMATION INTERCHANGE)

ASCII is a standard code for the conversion of a character to a binary number so that it is understandable by many microcomputers and on-line information systems. Because of this uniform code, varying models of microcomputers are capable of communication. Most computer terminals, microcomputers, and printers utilize ASCII. Included are control characters that are used by on-line data bases. Reference should be made to software and microcomputer books that contain a description of ASCII characters. ASCII aids in permitting information files produced by one kind of software (i.e., spreadsheet) to be used in a different kind of software (i.e., data base management, word processing).

▪ Example

Information is downloaded from an on-line data base (i.e., AICPA NAARS) in ASCII and then loaded into word processing software. It is then modified, and data may also be transferred to a distant computer at another office via telecommunications. ASCII is also used for electronic mail so that letters may be sent among executives at different locations.

▪ Example

A client may upload accounting files to his CPA in ASCII via MCI for audit-testing purposes.

ASSET MANAGEMENT OF BANKS

A commercial bank earns profits for stockholders by having a positive spread in lending and through leverage. A positive spread results when the average yield on earning assets exceeds the average cost of deposit liabilities. A high-risk asset portfolio can increase profits since the greater the risk position of the borrower, the larger the risk premium charged. On the other side of the coin, a high-risk portfolio can reduce profits because of the increased chance that it could become "nonperforming" assets. Favorable use of leverage (the bank's capital-asset ratio is falling) can increase the return on owners' equity. A mix of a high-risk portfolio and high leverage could result, however, in insolvency and bank failure. It is extremely important for banks to find an optimal mix. A bank is also threatened with insolvency if it has to liquidate its asset portfolio at a loss to meet large withdrawals. It can happen because, historically, a large proportion of banks' liabilities come from demand deposits—and therefore can easily be withdrawn. For this reason, commercial bank asset management theory focuses on the need for liquidity. There are three theories:

1. *The commercial loan theory*—contends that commercial banks should make only short-term self-liquidating loans (e.g., short-term seasonal inventory loans). In this way, loans could be repaid and cash could be readily available to meet deposit outflows. This theory lost much of its credibility as a certain source of liquidity since there is no guarantee

that even seasonal working capital loans can be repaid.

2. *The shiftability theory*—an extension of the commercial loan theory and states that by holding money market instruments, a bank could sell such assets without capital loss in the event of a deposit outflow.

3. *The anticipated-income theory*—holds that intermediate-term installment loans are liquid because they generate continuous cash inflows. The focus is not on short-term asset financing but on cash flow lending.

It is important to note that contemporary asset management hinges primarily on the shiftability theory, anticipated-income theory, and liability management. *See also* Liability Management of Banks.

ASSIGNMENT OF ACCOUNTS RECEIVABLE
See Accounts Receivable Financing.

ATTESTATION STANDARDS
The auditor may be engaged to prepare reports other than for historical cost financial statements, such as for supplementary financial data, compliance with regulatory requirements, statistical data on investment results, and evaluation of internal control. The guidelines for auditor involvement are contained in the AICPA's *Statement on Standards for Attestation Engagements*. The Statement defines an attest engagement as one when the CPA will express in writing an opinion on the reliability of specified information. The two types of attest assurance are

• *Positive assurance* contained in reports involving an *examination* engagement

• *Negative assurance* contained in reports based on a *review*

Attestation may be in accordance with agreed-upon procedures provided the report is limited to the individuals agreeing on such procedures.

The attestation standards are classified into general standards, standards of fieldwork, and standards of reporting.

1. General Standards
   a. The practitioner should have technical training and knowledge in order to perform the attest function.
   b. An engagement should be undertaken if the following conditions are present: (1) reasonable criteria exist to conduct an evaluation and (2) reasonable estimation or measurement can be made.
   c. The practitioner is independent.
   d. The practitioner shall conduct himself or herself with due professional care.

2. Standards of Fieldwork
   a. The engagement should be properly planned and staff adequately supervised.
   b. Sufficient evidence should exist as a basis to express an opinion.

3. Standards of Reporting
   a. The assertion being reported on should be stated along with the nature of the engagement.
   b. The practitioner should provide his or her conclusion as to whether the assertion is presented in accordance with established criteria.
   c. The practitioner's reservations should be given in the report.
   d. If the engagement is to apply agreed-upon criteria, there should be a statement in the report restricting its use to individuals who have agreed upon those criteria.

See also Audit.

ATTRIBUTE SAMPLING
An attribute is defined as a characteristic that a component of the population has or does not have. For instance, a customer's account is either past due or not. Authorization to pay a vendor has either been given or not.

In attribute sampling, an estimate is made of the proportion of the population that contains a particular characteristic. It can apply to a random sample of physical units or to a systemic sample that approximates a ran-

dom sample. A sample item possesses or does not possess the specific characteristic. No consideration is given to the magnitude of the characteristic. Based on the sample result, it is found if the true occurrence rate in the population is not greater than a specified percentage expressed at a given reliability level. The auditor may test for several different attributes in a sample.

Attribute sampling is based on a binomial distribution. An estimation may be made of the probable occurrence rates of particular characteristics in a population, where each characteristic has two mutually exclusive outcomes. Software for attribute-sampling purposes is available from time-sharing vendors.

An application of attribute sampling is the auditor's substantiation of breakdown of control procedures. Examples are the measurement of the degree of breakdown of control procedures related to cash disbursements, cash receipts, sales, payroll, and the extent of incorrect entries and incorrect postings.

Attribute sampling of physical units cannot be employed to estimate the total of a variable characteristic (e.g., values).

In determining sample size, the auditor should select an acceptable risk level. In practical terms, auditors select either a 5% or a 10% risk because these levels will furnish the auditor with a 95% or a 90% confidence, respectively, that the sample is representative of the population. The lower the risk the auditor selects, the greater will be the sample size.

A tolerable error rate will have to be selected. It is the maximum rate of deviation the auditor is willing to tolerate and still be able to rely on the control. The tolerable rate depends on professional judgment and the extent of reliance placed on the control or procedure. The following guidelines exist:

Degree of Reliance	Tolerable Rate
Little	11–20%
Moderate	6–12%
Substantial	2–7%

An evaluation should be made of the anticipated deviation rate which may be based on deviations in prior years, taking into account corrective changes in the current year.

The actual deviation rate in the sample equals:

$$\frac{\text{Number of deviations}}{\text{Sample size}}$$

The auditor should ascertain whether the deviations are due to errors or irregularities (intentional). When the sample deviation is in excess of the tolerable rate, no reliance may be placed on the control.

In examining the population, the population should be complete so that representative testing is possible. For instance, in testing purchase transactions, unpaid as well as paid invoices should be included.

The auditor should define the period covered by the examination. If interim testing is involved, the period after testing to the end of the year should be reviewed. Consideration should be given to the nature and amount of transactions and balances, and the length of the remaining period. The working papers should contain definitions of attributes and occurrences.

Attribute sampling is helpful in tests of controls. An example is evaluating the appropriateness of accounting controls through transaction testing.

Tables are referred to in determining sample size given the risk of overreliance, tolerable occurrence rate, and anticipated occurrence rate.

▪ Example

In ascertaining if the credit department is performing well, a CPA uses attribute sampling in examining sales orders through compliance testing. The CPA determines that (1) the deviation condition is the failure of the credit manager's initials on a sales order; (2) the population is comprised of the duplicate sales orders for the whole year; (3) the

sampling unit is the sales order; (4) random number selection is used; (5) a 5% risk of overreliance on internal control is used; (6) the tolerable rate of deviation is 6%; and (7) the anticipated population deviation rate is 2%.

Using Table 1, 127 is the sample size. The CPA uses a random number table (Table 5) to select the sample. Because the population is comprised of sales orders numbered 1 to 500, the CPA decides to use the first three digits of items selected from the random number table. With a blind start at column 5, row 6, the auditor selects the following sales orders: 277, 188, 174, 496, 482, 312, and so on.

After carrying out the sampling plan, the auditor discovers that four sales orders are missing the credit manager's signature (apparently an error on the part of the credit manager). The sample deviation rate is thus 4/127, or 3.1%. The upper occurrence limit, determined by referring to Table 3, is 7.2. In evaluating the results, 127 is used for the sample size for conservative reasons. Because the upper occurrence limit exceeds the tolerable rate of 7%, the auditor rejects the control and attempts to identify a compensating control for further tests of compliance. *See also* Sampling.

AUDIT

1. Examination of accounting records by an independent CPA for the purpose of expressing an auditor opinion on the fairness of presentation of a company's financial statements in conformity with GAAP. It includes tests of transactions as well as analysis of records and supporting documents. Confirmation requests may be sent to outside parties (i.e., customers) for verification of account balances. Inspection and counting of assets is typically involved (i.e., inventory count). 2. Investigation and appraisal of an entity's operations and procedures by an internal auditor in order to ascertain conformity with prescribed criteria.

See also Audit Opinion; Audit Procedure; Auditing Standard.

AUDITING ACCOUNTING ESTIMATES Statement on Auditing Standard No. 57 relates to the auditor's responsibilities with regard to accounting estimates. The auditor has to obtain and evaluate evidential matter dealing with significant accounting estimates. Although management makes the estimates, the auditor must assure himself of their reasonableness. The auditor must follow professional skepticism in examining the objective and subjective factors in the estimation process.

There is greater risk of an estimate being incorrect as the complexity and subjectivity of the situation increases. The estimation process is also more difficult when information is not readily available or is unreliable. If assumptions are significant, the estimate is more prone to the possibility of an error resulting in misleading financial statements. When estimation factors are difficult, a specialist in the area may be retained by management.

The auditor should examine and test the management process of making the estimate, consider events occurring after the estimate but before the audit report date, and determine whether he or she would come up with the same estimate that management did.

In appraising the management process, the auditor does the following:

• Analyzes the consistency of the assumptions

• Evaluates supporting information (e.g., documentation for estimates)

• Compares corporate data to industry information

• Compares previous estimates to current estimates

• Determines the effect of changes in the industry or business based on assumptions and estimates used

• Ascertains if alternative assumptions exist

Table 1

5 Percent Risk of Overreliance

Statistical Sample Sizes for Tests of Controls (for large populations)

Expected Population Deviation Rate	TOLERABLE OCCURRENCE RATE								
	2%	3%	4%	5%	6%	7%	8%	9%	10%
0.00%	149	99	74	59	49	42	36	32	29
.50	•	157	117	93	78	66	58	51	46
1.00	•	•	156	93	78	66	58	51	46
1.50	•	•	192	124	103	66	58	51	46
2.00	•	•	•	181	127	88	77	68	46
2.50	•	•	•	•	150	109	77	68	61
3.00	•	•	•	•	195	129	95	84	61
4.00	•	•	•	•	•	•	146	100	89
5.00	•	•	•	•	•	•	•	158	116
6.00	•	•	•	•	•	•	•	•	179

Table 2

10 Percent Risk of Overreliance

Expected Population Deviation Rate	TOLERABLE OCCURRENCE RATE								
	2%	3%	4%	5%	6%	7%	8%	9%	10%
0.00%	114	76	57	45	38	32	28	25	22
.50	194	129	96	77	64	55	48	42	38
1.00	•	176	96	77	64	55	48	42	38
1.50	•	•	132	105	64	55	48	42	38
2.00	•	•	198	132	88	75	48	42	38
2.50	•	•	•	158	110	75	65	58	38
3.00	•	•	•	•	132	94	65	58	52
4.00	•	•	•	•	•	149	98	65	65
5.00	•	•	•	•	•	•	160	115	78
6.00	•	•	•	•	•	•	•	182	116

•Sample size is too large to be cost effective.

Table 3

5 Percent Risk of Overreliance

Statistical Sample Results Evaluation Table for Tests of Controls

Upper Occurrence Limit
(for large populations)

Sample Size	ACTUAL NUMBER OF OCCURRENCES FOUND								
	0	1	2	3	4	5	6	7	8
25	11.3	17.6	•	•	•	•	•	•	•
30	9.5	14.9	19.5	•	•	•	•	•	•
35	8.2	12.9	16.9	•	•	•	•	•	•
40	7.2	11.3	14.9	18.3	•	•	•	•	•
45	6.4	10.1	13.3	16.3	19.2	•	•	•	•
50	5.8	9.1	12.1	14.8	17.4	19.9	•	•	•
55	5.3	8.3	11.0	13.5	15.9	18.1	•	•	•
60	4.9	7.7	10.1	12.4	14.6	16.7	18.8	•	•
65	4.5	7.1	9.4	11.5	13.5	15.5	17.4	19.3	•
70	4.2	6.6	8.7	10.7	12.6	14.4	16.2	18.0	19.7
75	3.9	6.2	8.2	10.0	11.8	13.5	15.2	16.9	18.4
80	3.7	5.8	7.7	9.4	11.1	12.7	14.3	15.8	17.3
90	3.3	5.2	6.8	8.4	9.9	11.3	12.7	14.1	15.5
100	3.0	4.7	6.2	7.6	8.9	10.2	11.5	12.7	14.0
125	2.4	3.7	4.9	6.1	7.2	8.2	9.3	10.3	11.3
150	2.0	3.1	4.1	5.1	6.0	6.9	7.7	8.6	9.4
200	1.5	2.3	3.1	3.8	4.5	5.2	5.8	6.5	7.1

Table 4

10 Percent Risk of Overreliance

Sample Size	ACTUAL NUMBER OF OCCURRENCES FOUND								
	0	1	2	3	4	5	6	7	8
20	10.9	18.1	•	•	•	•	•	•	•
25	8.8	14.7	19.9	•	•	•	•	•	•
30	7.4	12.4	16.8	•	•	•	•	•	•
35	6.4	10.7	14.5	18.1	•	•	•	•	•
40	5.6	9.4	12.8	15.9	19.0	•	•	•	•
45	5.0	8.4	11.4	14.2	17.0	19.6	•	•	•
50	4.5	7.6	10.3	12.9	15.4	17.8	•	•	•
55	4.1	6.9	9.4	11.7	14.0	16.2	18.4	•	•
60	3.8	6.3	8.6	10.8	12.9	14.9	16.9	18.8	•
70	3.2	5.4	7.4	9.3	11.1	12.8	14.6	16.2	17.9
80	2.8	4.8	6.5	8.3	9.7	11.3	12.8	14.3	15.7
90	2.5	4.3	5.8	7.3	8.7	10.1	11.4	12.7	14.0
100	2.3	3.8	5.2	6.6	7.8	9.1	10.3	11.5	12.7
120	1.9	3.2	4.4	5.5	6.6	7.6	8.6	9.6	10.6
160	1.4	2.4	3.3	4.1	4.9	5.7	6.5	7.2	8.0
200	1.1	1.9	2.6	3.3	4.0	4.6	5.2	5.8	6.4

•over 20%

Table 5

Random Number Table

Line	(1)	(2)	(3)	(4)	(5)	(6)	(7)	(8)	(9)	(10)	(11)	(12)	(13)	(14)
							Column							
1	10480	15011	01536	02011	81647	91646	69179	14194	62590	36207	20969	99570	91291	90700
2	22368	46573	25595	85393	30995	89198	27982	53402	93965	34095	52666	19174	39615	99505
3	24130	48360	22527	97265	76393	64809	15179	24830	49340	32081	30680	19655	63348	58629
4	42167	93093	06243	61680	07856	16376	39440	53537	71341	57004	00849	74917	97758	16379
5	37570	39975	81837	16656	06121	91782	60468	81305	49684	60672	14110	06927	01263	54613
6	77921	06907	11008	42751	27756	53498	18602	70659	90655	15053	21916	81825	44394	42880
7	99562	72905	56420	69994	98872	31016	71194	18738	44013	48840	63213	21069	10634	12952
8	96301	91977	05463	07972	18876	20922	94595	56869	69014	60045	18425	84903	42508	32307
9	89579	14342	63661	10281	17453	18103	57740	84378	25331	12566	58678	44947	05585	56941
10	85475	36857	53342	53988	53060	59533	38867	62300	08158	17983	16439	11458	18593	64952
11	28918	69578	88231	33276	70997	79936	56865	05859	90106	31595	01547	85590	91610	78188
12	63553	40961	48235	03427	49626	69445	18663	72695	52180	20847	12234	90511	33703	90322
13	09429	93969	52636	92737	88974	33488	36320	17617	30015	08272	84115	27156	30613	74952
14	10365	61129	87529	85689	48237	52267	67689	93394	01511	26358	85104	20285	29975	89868
15	07119	97336	71048	08178	77233	13916	47564	81056	97735	85977	29372	74461	28551	90707
16	51085	12765	51821	51259	77452	16308	60756	92144	49442	53900	70960	63990	75601	40719
17	02368	21382	52404	60268	89368	19885	55322	44819	01188	63255	64835	44919	05944	55157
18	01011	54092	33362	94904	31273	04146	18594	29852	71585	85030	51132	01915	92747	64951
19	52162	53916	46369	58586	23216	14513	83149	98736	23495	64350	94738	17752	35156	35749
20	07056	97628	33787	09998	42698	06691	76988	13602	51851	46104	88916	19509	25625	58104
21	48663	91245	85828	14346	09172	30168	90229	04734	59193	22178	30421	61666	99904	32812
22	54164	58492	22421	74103	47070	25306	76468	26384	58151	06646	21524	15227	96909	44592
23	32639	32363	05597	24200	13363	38005	94342	28728	35806	06912	17012	64161	18296	22851
24	29334	27001	87637	87308	58731	00256	45834	15398	46557	41135	10367	07684	36188	18510
25	02488	33062	28834	07351	19731	92420	60952	61280	50001	67658	32586	86679	50720	94953
26	81525	72295	04839	96423	24878	82651	66566	14778	76797	14780	13300	87074	79666	95725
27	29676	20591	68086	26432	46901	20849	89768	81536	86645	12659	92259	57102	80428	25280
28	00742	57392	39064	66432	84673	40027	32832	61362	98947	96067	64760	64584	96096	98253
29	05366	04213	25669	26422	44407	44048	37937	63904	45766	66134	75470	66520	34693	90449
30	91921	26418	64117	94305	26766	25940	39972	22209	71500	64568	91402	42416	07844	69618
31	00582	04711	87917	77341	42206	35126	74087	99547	81817	42607	43808	76655	62028	76630
32	00725	69884	62797	56170	86324	88072	76222	36086	84637	93161	76038	65855	77919	88006
33	69011	65795	95876	55293	18988	27354	26575	08625	40801	59920	29841	80150	12777	48501
34	25976	57948	29888	80604	67917	48708	18912	82271	65424	69774	33611	54262	85963	03547
35	09763	83473	73577	12908	30883	18317	28290	35797	05998	41688	34952	37888	38917	80050
36	91567	42595	29758	30134	04024	86385	29880	99730	55536	84855	29080	09250	79656	73211
37	17955	56349	90999	49127	20044	59931	06115	20542	18059	02008	73708	83517	36103	42791
38	46503	18584	18845	49618	02304	51038	20655	58727	28168	15475	56942	53389	20562	87338
39	92157	89634	94824	78171	84610	82834	09922	25417	44137	48413	25555	21246	35509	20468
40	14577	62765	35605	81263	39667	47358	56873	56307	61607	49518	89656	20103	77490	18062
41	98427	07523	33362	64270	01638	92477	66969	98420	04880	45585	46565	04102	46880	45709
42	34914	63976	88720	82765	34476	17032	87589	40836	32427	70002	70663	88863	77775	69348
43	70060	28277	39475	46473	23219	53416	94970	25832	69975	94884	19661	72828	00102	66794
44	53976	54914	06990	67245	68350	82948	11398	42878	80287	88267	47363	46634	06541	97809
45	76072	29515	40980	07391	58745	25774	22987	80059	39911	96189	41151	14222	60697	59583
46	90725	52210	83974	29992	65831	38857	50490	83765	55657	14361	31720	57375	56228	41546
47	64364	67412	33339	31926	14883	24413	59744	92351	97473	89286	38931	04110	23726	51900
48	08962	00358	31662	25388	61642	34072	81249	35648	56891	69352	48373	45578	78547	81788
49	95012	68379	93526	70765	10592	04542	76463	54328	02349	17247	28865	14777	62730	92277
50	15664	10493	20492	38391	91132	21999	59516	81652	27195	48223	46751	22923	32261	85653

• Appraises the controls over the estimation process

• Ascertains the relevance and reliability of the estimates

• Tests management computations in translating assumptions to estimates

• Examines goals and plans of the entity to determine how they tie into the estimates used

AUDITING STANDARDS These provide guidance in assuring that audit performance is of high quality. CPAs have to conform to ten generally accepted auditing standards (GAAS), as promulgated by the AICPA. Interpretations of the standards are issued in the form of Statements on Auditing Standards (SAS). Audit Guides for specific industries are also issued by the AICPA.

GAAS consist of ten standards in the following three groupings: general standards, standards of fieldwork, and reporting standards. SASs are interpretations of these standards. The SASs are often called GAAS themselves. The ten standards are

General Standards

1. The examination must be conducted by individuals with sufficient audit training and expertise.
2. The auditor must be independent in performing his activities.
3. Due professional care must be exercised in conducting the audit and in preparing the audit report.

Standards of Fieldwork

1. The engagement must be properly planned and assistants adequately supervised.
2. There must be an adequate understanding of the internal control structure so that the audit may be properly planned and a determination made of the nature, timing, and degree of tests to be conducted.
3. Sufficient competent evidential matter must be obtained through observation, inspection, inquiries, and confirmations so that a proper basis exists for an audit opinion.

Standards of Reporting

1. The report should state if the financial statements are prepared in accordance with GAAP.
2. The report should identify those circumstances in which accounting principles have not been consistently observed in the current year relative to the preceding period.
3. Footnote disclosures should be deemed sufficient unless indicated otherwise in the audit report.
4. The report should contain an audit opinion or an assertion that no opinion can be expressed. If not, the reasons should be given. The nature of the audit examination and the degree of responsibility assumed should be contained in the audit report.

A brief summary of a few important SASs issued by the Auditing Standards Board of the AICPA follow:

SAS No. 42—Reporting on Condensed Financial Statements and Selected Financial Data This statement applies to reporting on a client-prepared document containing (1) condensed financial statements that are derived from audited financial statements and/or (2) selected financial data derived from audited financial statements.

The auditor's report on condensed financial statements should include

• A statement that the auditor has examined, in accordance with GAAS, the complete set of financial statements

• An indication that an opinion has been expressed on the complete set of financial statements

• The date of the auditor's report on the complete set of financial statements

• The type of opinion expressed on the complete set of financial statements

• An opinion as to whether the information

contained in the condensed financial statements is presented fairly in all material respects in relation to the complete set of financial statements

SAS No. 46—Consideration of Omitted Procedures After the Report Date In certain cases, such as peer review, the auditor may conclude after the issuance of an audit report that he or she omitted one or more auditing procedures. In these instances, the auditor has the responsibility to assess the importance of the omitted procedure(s) to his or her present ability to support the previously expressed opinion. In making this assessment, the auditor should consider any alternative auditing procedures performed. If the auditor still feels that the omitted procedure(s) impairs the present ability to support the audit report, he or she should undertake to apply the omitted procedure(s) or alternative procedures. If the auditor is unable to apply the necessary procedures, he or she should contact legal counsel in order to discuss the appropriate course of action to be taken.

SAS No. 50—Reports on the Application of Accounting Principles An accountant may be asked to prepare a written report on (1) the application of accounting principles to specified transactions; (2) the type of opinion that may be expressed on an entity's financial statements; or (3) the application of accounting principles not involving facts or circumstances of a particular principal (i.e., a hypothetical transaction).

The accountant's report should include
• The appropriate address (i.e., it should be addressed to the principal to the transaction or to the intermediary).
• A statement describing the engagement.
• An indication that the engagement was conducted in accordance with the relevant standards of the AICPA.
• A description of the transaction and its related facts, circumstances, and assumptions (including their source). Furthermore, an identification of the principals to the transaction should be made.

• A description of the relevant accounting principles.
• A statement fixing the responsibility for the proper accounting treatment with the preparers of the financial statements, who should consult with their continuing accountants.
• A warning that the report may change if differences of facts, circumstances, or assumptions are altered.

SAS No. 51—Reporting on Financial Statements Prepared for Use in Other Countries Generally accepted auditing standards as developed in the United States should be adhered to when examining financial statements of a U.S. entity prepared in conformity with accounting principles accepted in another country. Under certain circumstances the auditor may also have to adhere to the auditing standards of the foreign country.

If the financial statements are for use only in a foreign country, the auditor may issue (1) a U.S.-style report modified for reporting on the foreign country's accounting principles or (2) a report based on the foreign country's standards.

AUDIT OPINION AICPAs' Statement on Auditing Standards No. 58 deals with the audit report. The standard audit report takes the following form:

> We have audited the accompanying balance sheet of X Company as of December 31, 19XX, and the related statements of income, retained earnings, and cash flows for the year then ended. These financial statements are the responsibility of the Company's management. Our responsibility is to express an opinion on these financial statements based on our audit.
>
> We conducted our audit in accordance with generally accepted auditing standards. Those standards require that we plan and perform the audit to obtain reasonable assurance about whether the financial statements are free of material misstatement. An audit includes examining, on a test basis, evidence supporting the amounts and disclosures in the financial statements. An

audit also includes assessing the accounting principles used and significant estimates made by management, as well as evaluating the overall financial statement presentation. We believe that our audit provides a reasonable basis for our opinion.

In our opinion, the financial statements referred to above present fairly, in all material respects, the financial position of X Company as of [at] December 31, 19XX, and the results of its operations and its cash flows for the year then ended in conformity with generally accepted accounting principles.

In the introductory paragraph, there is mention of management's responsibility for the financial statements. In the scope paragraph (second paragraph), it is stated that an audit furnishes reasonable assurance within the context of materiality that the financial statements are free of material misstatement. An explanation of what an audit involves is also stated. The opinion paragraph provides the audit opinion. Note that the reference to consistency is no longer made. But if there is a lack of consistency, an additional explanatory paragraph should be given of that fact.

An unqualified opinion means that the financial statements present fairly the financial position and operating results of the company in conformity with GAAP.

A qualified opinion occurs in the following cases:

• A scope limitation exists where the auditor was not
  • Able to obtain sufficient evidential matter for an unqualified opinion.
  • Able to apply a necessary auditing procedure. (If the scope limitation is not severe, an "except for" qualified opinion may be issued instead of a disclaimer.)

• The financial statements have a departure from GAAP and the client refuses to make the needed modifications. In this case, an "except for" qualified opinion is rendered (assuming the effects are not so severe as

to require an adverse opinion). Departures from GAAP include an inappropriate accounting method that does not reflect the theoretical substance of a transaction and inadequate disclosure.

Statements on Auditing Standards Nos. 58 and 59 have eliminated "subject to" opinion qualifications. In disclaiming an opinion, the auditor is saying that he or she is unable to form an opinion on the fairness of the financial statements. One is allowed to disclaim an opinion on some of the financial statements while at the same time expressing an opinion on the other statements.

An adverse opinion occurs when the financial statements do *not* fairly present a company's financial position and operating results. The financial statements are therefore misleading.

AUDIT PROCEDURES   These comprise detailed steps in performing an audit that change by audit engagement. The auditor obtains evidence to support recorded figures in the financial statements. The audit procedures followed depend on the complexity of the tasks to be performed, the type of client's accounting system, characteristics of the records, and nature of the company. Examples of procedures include confirming accounts receivable balances, physically inspecting assets, and testing the system of internal control. *See also* Audit Program; Workpapers.

AUDIT PROGRAM

1. Procedures carried out in the performance of an audit
2. Description and outline of work to be conducted in an audit

The audit program typically includes the estimated time for each task as well as the personnel to perform it. It gives an indication of the scope of the examination and provides guidance for staff. It serves for planning and control purposes as well as to document functions performed. Information is given on who performed the audit and when.

AUDIT RISK Statement on Auditing Standards No. 47, titled "Audit Risk and Materiality in Conducting an Audit," deals with the steps to take when to reduce audit risk when planning and conducting an examination. Audit risk refers to the possibility that the auditor may unintentionally fail to modify the audit opinion on materially misstated financial statements. Audit risk must be taken into account in ascertaining the nature, timing, and degree of audit techniques to be employed on the particular engagement. Also, an analysis of audit results must be carefully performed.

The auditor is required to

• Aggregate likely errors

• Compare estimates made by management to what the auditor believes is reasonable

• Take into account that undetected errors may exist even though proper audit procedures have been undertaken and, as a result, the financial statements may be materially misstated

• Preliminarily estimate materiality for the financial statements so that audit procedures may be properly planned

• Minimize audit risk through a thorough examination

• Conduct substantive tests based on evaluating control risks

In considering audit risk, the CPA must be aware of inherent risk, control risk, and detection risk.

Inherent risk is the "built-in" susceptibility of an account balance or class of transactions to errors, irrespective of the internal control system. For example, cash has greater risk due to its liquidity.

Control risk is the risk that an account balance or class of transactions may contain errors that may be undetected or prevented by the internal control system.

Detection risk is the risk that the auditor may fail to spot material errors. *Note*: There is no guarantee that a statistical sample will detect all errors that may exist.

There is an inverse relationship between detection risk and inherent and control risks. For example, the less the inherent and control risks, the more is the detection risk the auditor should accept.

The auditor can minimize detection risk through the application of necessary auditing procedures. On the other hand, it is management's responsibility to curtail control risk by formulating and maintaining a sound internal control system. *See also* Audit.

AUDIT SAMPLING Statement on Auditing Standard No. 39 provides recommendations as to planning, performing, and analyzing audit samples. Also, the AICPA has issued a related guide called "Audit Sampling." Audit sampling is the use of an audit procedure to part of the population being examined (e.g., similar transactions, account balances, documents, entries, lines in a voucher register) to derive a conclusion regarding characteristics of the population.

The two acceptable alternative approaches to audit sampling are nonstatistical (judgmental) and statistical. The prime distinction is that the former does not provide for a quantitative measure of sampling risk, whereas the latter does. The selection of the appropriate type depends on the particular circumstances, typically taking into account cost and effectiveness.

However, that choice (nonstatistical or statistical sampling) does not directly impact decisions regarding the audit approach to be used (systems-reliance or substantive) or particular audit procedures to be applied, the competence of evidential matter obtained with respect to sampled items, or the actions that might be taken when errors or irregularities are uncovered.

Some important sampling terms from the auditor's perspective are

• *Sampling risk*—The risk that sample results do not accurately reflect the population. A particular sample may contain proportionately more or less monetary errors or

compliance deviations than in the balance or class as a whole. Sampling risk varies inversely with sample size. If sampling risk is unacceptable to undertake, the population should be tested in full.

• *Tolerable error*—an estimate of the maximum amount of error that may exist so that the financial statements are not materially misstated.

In determining sample size, the following factors should be considered:

• Purpose of the sample.
• Desired efficiency level.
• Tolerable error. A higher acceptable error rate will require a lower sample size.
• Frequency or size of expected errors. As more errors are anticipated, the sample size increases for a fixed tolerable error rate.
• Risk of improper acceptance.
• Population characteristics such as variation in items comprising the population. Wide variability requires a larger sample. Sample size can be reduced, however, through stratification (breaking down the population into subgroups).
• Extent of other audit procedures performed for the item under scrutiny. A lower sample size is needed if other audit techniques are being used in conjunction with the sample.

Computer software may be used to compute sample size and appraise sample results.

The auditor must be on guard against the possibility of reaching an incorrect conclusion regarding the population based on the sample result. For example, the sample may indicate that the population is correct when in fact it is not. The degree of risk of improper acceptance of a population varies depending on the appropriateness of the internal control structure or other substantive tests (e.g., analytical procedures) performed for the same particular audit objective.

In examining deviations, the auditor should consider the following:

• Frequency of errors.
• Nature and reason for errors, including whether they were intentional (irregularities).
• Effect of deviations on other aspects of the audit.

In reviewing audit sampling, consideration should be given to:

• Satisfaction of the audit objective.
• Appropriateness in defining the sampling unit.
• Whether the reported amounts in the financial statements were verified.
• Whether the sample selection is from the correct population.
• Whether internal control structure was supported by tests of controls. If not, substantive tests may have to be adjusted.

When engaging in audit sampling, items or groups are identified as having significance. For example, when evaluating accounts receivable, testing may be done of accounts with significant balances, unusual balances, or out-of-the-ordinary activity.

An acceptable method to project the results of a nonstatistical sample is

$$\frac{\text{Dollar amount of errors}}{\text{Total dollars tested}}$$

■ Example

The sample of a population being examined is \$300,000. The sample results indicate \$20,000 being in error. The incidence rate of error is therefore

$$\frac{\$20,000}{\$300,000} = 6.7\%$$

This should now be compared to the tolerable rate of error that was deemed acceptable.

With regard to tests of controls, the auditor should

• Take into account in the planning stage population the characteristics and deviation from prescribed controls.
• Formulate the objectives of the test and conditions of deviation.
• Determine a sampling method and appropriate sample size.
• Derive a representative sample so that

all items in the population have an equal chance for inclusion.

• Evaluate the sample results.

If sample results will not support the desired level of confidence in controls, substantive tests must be expanded to provide assurance.

In tests of controls, the following should be documented in the working papers:

• Prescribed control procedures being tested.

• Sampling method and means of selection.

• Application objectives.

• Relationship of tests of controls to planned substantive testing.

• Definition of the population, sampling unit, and deviation condition.

• Risk of overreliance.

• Tolerable deviation rate.

• Anticipated population deviation rate.

• Description of sampling procedure.

• Enumeration of compliance deviations found, including their nature.

• Appraisal of sample results, including sample errors found and whether the sample results indicate good controls in existence.

• Impact on planned substantive tests.

In substantive testing, the following items should be documented in the working papers:

• Objectives of the test.

• Description of audit procedures to meeting objectives.

• Sampling technique and method of sample selection.

• Description of the population sampling unit.

• Definition of the error.

• Rationale for the risk of (1) incorrect acceptance, (2) tolerable error, and (3) expected population error.

• Enumeration of errors found.

• Appraisal of sample results, including a projection of the errors uncovered in the sample and the population. Qualitative aspects of the errors should be considered.

• Sampling risk.

• Overall conclusion concerning the population.

See also Sampling.

AUDIT SOFTWARE Audit software assists in examining and testing client accounting data. The packages combine general accounting, spreadsheet, and word processing to aid in the accounting, analysis, and reporting elements of the audit. Audit reports, footnote data, compilation and review reports, management letters, and other related auditing schedules and analyses are prepared.

Audit programs carry out mathematical and logical operations: sampling data from a population, comparing actual data to predetermined criteria and printing out exceptions (e.g., excessive inventory balances), appraising accounting data, reading and extracting information, comparing financial data on different files for consistency, integrating data from one file to another, sending out confirmations, and analytical review of the logic in reported figures.

Is the audit software performing correctly? Test the software periodically to assure reasonable results. Is the programming proper for the objectives to be accomplished? Current auditing pronouncements must be incorporated. *Warning*: Make sure the package is the one actually being used. Audit controls must exist over any modifications to the program or documentation.

Audit software should provide for preventing and correcting errors, including error messages. Does the error message suggest the cause and the appropriate corrective action? Audit software also exists to ask internal control questions to derive an audit program.

Audit software exists for flow chart preparation showing the movement of transactions in processing and control. As the need occurs, revised flow charts are prepared to assist in internal control evaluation.

Audit software should display control to-

tals for checking purposes. Software should have processing checks. An example is the "next file version" on the file header. There should be sequential numbers in the control field such as 1/19 and then 1/20.

The CPA must check what each program does and how it impacts files. Files can be printed to assure correct processing. Updates and amendments to audit software must be tested to assure there has been no deterioration in internal control.

Packaged (canned) audit software exists for a particular application (e.g., general ledger). If the packed software cannot satisfy the application, a customized program should be written.

Canned packages can be employed to test transactions, appraise data processing, and examine records. Deloitte, Haskins and Sells has an appropriate package called Auditape.™ Packaged audit software may be used for different clients in terms of file data and characteristics. *Problem*: A canned package may not be able to access information from a data base management system. *Solution*: Put information on the data base to tape and then use the packaged program or utilize the querying ability of DBMS to conduct the audit function.

If a packaged audit program will not satisfy client needs, the auditor is forced to go the customization route. Some programming knowledge is thus essential to assure that the programmer is doing the right job in terms of logical flow. *Recommendation*: Consider customization in the following instances:

• Excessive limitations exist to the canned program.

• "Tailored" confirmations are required.

• There is a need to identify an unusual item.

• Client application is difficult.

• Integration with a data base management system is called for.

When compliance and substantive tests are being performed, utility programs can assist. For example, a useful utility function is changing and sequencing file data. The use of a utility program will reduce tests needed with audit software.

■ Example

Blackman, Kallick and Company's Audit Cube™ handles mechanical, computational, and sorting procedures on an audit. With the aid of a portable computer, the auditor can prepare a fully documented audit in the field. Statements and reports are printed automatically.

■ Example

Linton Shafer's Automated Workpapers™ has a main program and optional modules. It is structured for CPAs using the lead schedule approach for workpapers on audit engagements for clients who maintain their own general ledger.

■ Example

Coopers and Lybrand's Pre-Audit™ prepares financial statements, footnotes, and audit reports.

■ Example

Deloitte, Haskins and Sells' Statistical Techniques for Analysis Review™ program utilizes linear regression in conducting analytical review procedures. It identifies and quantifies the relationship between a dependent variable of audit interest and independent variables. The program computes the amount by which estimates differ from recorded values. Excessive differences require audit attention.

■ Example

Deloitte, Haskins and Sells' Estimation Sampling™ helps in designing, selecting, and appraising samples. Conclusions are drawn about the population based on sample results. Applications include valuing receivables, in-

ventory, and estimated liabilities. Also, the auditor can evaluate the impact of employing alternative GAAP.

Workpaper information and analysis can be facilitated. Audit codes should be assigned to accounts to encourage later grouping for audit purposes. Computerized lead sheets should be used in the audit so that workpapers may be cross-referenced. The lead sheets can also serve as documentation of adjusted balances. Permanent workpaper information is carried forward, such as description of business activities and the accounting system. If data are altered, modifications may easily be made.

An audit program may be processed with the auditor's computer, on the client's premises, or with an outside service bureau. If it is on the client's premises, an appraisal must be made of the client's general controls to guard against unauthorized access to programs. Stringent audit control is needed. *Recommendation*: If the client's facilities are not adequate (e.g., bad geographic location, control problems), the service bureau may be the route to go.

Software can be used for analytical review by comparing corporate information with industry standards noting deviations, comparing the company's current year figures with prior years, and deriving financial ratios. *See also* Accounting Software.

AUDIT TRAIL This is the total recording and documentation associated with a transaction (journal entry or posting) to source backup (i.e., document). A sound audit trail makes it easy and time efficient to trace a transaction to a source.

AUTOCORRELATION (OR SERIAL CORRELATION) This is one of the assumptions required in a *regression* in order to make it reliable. It means that the error terms are independent of each other. The deviation of one point about the line (i.e., the error $= y - y'$) is unrelated to the deviation of any other point. When autocorrelation exists (i.e., the error terms are not independent), the standard errors of the regression coefficients are seriously underestimated. The problem of autocorrelation is usually detected by the Durbin-Watson statistic. *See also* Durbin-Watson Statistic; Regression Analysis.

B

"BAIT RECORD" A bait record is a fictitious record. If it is manually or electronically processed, it is indicative of a problem in internal control, which requires the attention of the external auditor. A determination should be made of when, how, and by whom this dummy record has been processed.

■ **Example**

There is a change in the account balance of a nonexistent supplier, such as that due to a recorded cash payment.

■ **Example**

A "dummy" inventory item has the balance changed by an employee. *See also* Internal Control Structure.

BALANCE OF PAYMENTS AND BALANCE OF TRADE The *balance of payments* is a statistical tabulation of all kinds of a nation's transactions with all other countries during a given period, such as a year. These transactions consist of exports and imports of goods and services, and movements of short-term and long-term investments, currency, gold, and gifts. The transactions may be classified into several categories, of which the two major ones are the current account and the capital account. The *balance of trade* (*trade balance*) is that portion of a country's balance of payments covering merchandise trade. A favorable balance of trade results when the value of exports exceeds the value of imports. An unfavorable balance of trade, more often called *trade deficit* results when the opposite is the case. A large number of trade deficits could drive interest rates higher and stocks and a country's currency lower as the country increases its reliance on foreign capital to finance the budget deficit.

BALANCE SHEET ANALYSIS In analyzing the balance sheet, the financial analyst is primarily concerned with the realizability of the assets, turnover, and earning potential. The evaluation of liabilities considers arbitrary adjustments and understatement.

Assets

If assets are overstated, net income will be overstated because the earnings do not include necessary charges to reduce earnings to their proper valuations. Asset quality depends on the amount of timing of the realization of assets. Assets should be categorized by risk category. Useful ratios are the percentage of high-risk assets to total assets and

high-risk assets to sales. High asset realization risk points to poor quality of earnings due to possible future write-offs. For instance, the future realization of accounts receivable is better than that of goodwill. Multipurpose assets are of better quality than single-purpose assets resulting from readier salability. Assets lacking separable value cannot be sold easily and as such have low realizability. An example is work-in-process and intangibles.

In appraising realization risk in assets, the effect of changing government policies on the entity has to be taken into account. Risk may exist with chemicals and other products deemed hazardous to health. Huge inventory losses may have to be taken.

■ Example

Company A presents total assets of $6 million and sales of $10 million. Included in total assets are the following high-risk assets as perceived by the credit and investment analyst.

Deferred moving costs	$300,000
Deferred plant rearrangement costs	100,000
Receivables for claims under a government contract	200,000
Goodwill	150,000

Applicable ratios are:

$$\frac{\text{High-risk assets}}{\text{Total assets}} = \frac{\$750,000}{\$6,000,000} = 12.5\%$$

$$\frac{\text{High-risk assets}}{\text{Sales}} = \frac{\$750,000}{\$10,000,000} = 7.5\%$$

Cash

A high ratio of sales to cash may indicate inadequate cash leading to financial problems if additional financing is not available at reasonable interest rates. A low turnover ratio, on the other hand, indicates excessive cash being held.

A determination should be made as to whether part of the cash is restricted and unavailable for use. An example is a compensating balance that does not constitute "free" cash. Also, cash in a politically unstable foreign country may have remission restrictions.

Accounts Receivable

Realization risk in receivables can be appraised by studying the nature of the receivable balance. Examples of high-risk receivables include amounts from economically unstable foreign countries, receivables subject to offset provisions, and receivables due from a company experiencing severe financial problems. Further, companies dependent on a few customers have greater risk than those with a large number of important accounts. Receivables due from industry are typically safer than receivables arising from consumers. Fair trade laws are more protective of consumers.

A significant increase in accounts receivable compared to the prior year may indicate higher realization risk. The firm may be selling to more risky customers. The trends in accounts receivable to total assets and accounts receivable to sales should be evaluated.

The financial analyst should appraise the trends in the ratios of bad debts to accounts receivable and bad debts to sales. An unwarranted decrease in bad debts lowers the quality of earnings. This may happen when there is a decline in bad debts even though the company is selling to less credit-worthy customers and/or actual bad debt losses are increasing.

A company may purposely overstate bad debts to provide accounting cushions to report understated profits. Also, companies may have substantial bad debt provisions in the current period because improper provisions were made in prior years, distorting the earnings trend. A sudden write-off of accounts receivable may arise from prior understated bad debt provisions. Earnings may be managed by initially increasing and then lowering the bad debt provision.

Receivables are of low quality if they arose from loading customers up with unneeded merchandise by giving generous credit terms. "Red flags" as to this happening include
• A significant increase in sales in the final quarter of the year
• A substantial amount of sales returns in the first quarter of the next year
• A material decrease in sales for the first quarter of the next year

In a *seasonal* business, the accounts receivable turnover (credit sales/average accounts receivable) may be based on monthly or quarterly sales figures so that a proper averaging takes place.

The trend in sales returns and allowances is often a good reflection of the quality of merchandise sold to customers. A significant decrease in a firm's sales allowance account as a percentage of sales is not in conformity with reality when a greater liability for dealer returns exist. This will result in lower earnings quality.

■ Example

Company X's sales and sales returns for the period 19X3 to 19X5 are shown below.

The reduction in the ratio of sales returns to sales from 19X4 to 19X5 indicates that less of a provision for returns is being made by the company. This would appear unrealistic if there is a greater liability for dealer returns and credits on an expanded sales base.

Inventory

An inventory buildup may point to greater realization risk. The buildup may be at the plant, wholesaler, or retailer. A sign of buildup is when the increase in inventory is at a faster rate than the increase in sales.

A production slowdown may be indicated when there is a reduction in raw materials coupled with an increase in work-in-process and finished goods. Further, greater obsolescence risk exists with work-in process and finished goods due to major buildups. Raw materials have the best realizability because of greater universality and multipurpose.

Computation should be made of the turnover rate by each major inventory category and by department. A low turnover rate may be indicative of overstocking, obsolescence, or problems with the product line or marketing effectiveness. But there are cases where a low inventory rate is appropriate. For example, a higher inventory level may arise because of expected future increases in price.

A high inventory turnover rate may point to inadequate inventory possibly leading to a loss in business. At the "natural year-end" the turnover rate may be unusually high because at that time the inventory balance may be very low.

Computation should also be made of the number of days inventory is held. The age of inventory should be compared to industry averages and to prior years of the company.

High realization risk applies with specialized, technological, fad, luxurious, perishable, and price-sensitive merchandise. The credit analyst must be on guard that the company has not assigned values to unsalable and obsolete merchandise. If there is a sudden inventory write-off, the financial analyst may be suspicious of the firm's deferral policy. Low realization risk applies to standardized, staple, and necessity goods due to their better salability.

	19X5	19X4	19X3
Balance in sales returns account at year-end	$ 2,000	$ 3,800	$ 1,550
Sales	240,000	215,000	100,000
Percentage of sales returns to sales	0.0083	0.0177	0.0155

Collateralized inventory has greater risk because creditors can retain it in the event of nonpayment of an obligation. Also, inventory can have political risk associated with it. An example is increased gas prices due to a shortage situation making it unfeasible to purchase large cars.

Inventory may be overstated due to mistakes in quantities, costing, pricing, and valuation of work-in-process. The more technical the product and the more dependence on internally developed cost records, the greater is the susceptibility of the cost estimates to misstatement.

If adequate insurance cannot be obtained at reasonable rates due to an unfavorable geographic location of the merchandise (e.g., high crime area, flood susceptibility), a problem exists.

The investment analyst should note the appropriateness of a change in inventory. Is it required by a new FASB pronouncement, SEC release, or IRS tax ruling?

Investments

Are there any decreases in portfolio market values that have not been recognized in the accounts? An indication of the fair value of investments may be the revenue (dividend income, interest income) obtained from them. Higher realization risk exists where there is a declining trend in the percentage of earnings derived from investments to their carrying value. Also check subsequent event disclosures for unrealized losses in the portfolio occurring after year-end.

■ Example

Company X presents the following information:

	19X1	19X2
Investments	$50,000	$60,000
Investment income	7,000	5,000

The percentage of investment income to total investments decreased from 14% in 19X1 to 8.3% in 19X2, pointing to higher realization risk in the portfolio.

If a company is buying securities in other companies for diversification purposes, this will reduce overall risk. Risk in an investment portfolio can be ascertained by computing the standard deviation of its rate of return.

When an investment portfolio has a market value above cost, it constitutes an undervalued asset.

An investment portfolio of securities fluctuating widely in price is of higher realization risk than a portfolio that is diversified by industry and economic sector. But the former portfolio will show greater profitability in a bull market. The investment analyst should appraise the extent of diversification and stability of the investment portfolio. There is less risk when securities are negatively correlated (price goes in opposite directions) or not correlated, compared to a portfolio of positively correlated securities (price goes in same direction).

The financial analyst should be on guard against a dubious reclassification of a marketable security to long-term investment in order to avoid showing a future unrealized loss on the security portfolio in the income statement. The unrealized loss on a long-term portfolio is presented in the stockholders' equity section of the balance sheet.

The investment analyst should also note a case where debt securities have a cost in excess of market value.

Fixed Assets

Inadequate provision for the maintenance of property, plant, and equipment detracts from the long-term earning power of the firm. If obsolete assets are not replaced and repairs not properly made, breakdowns and detracted operational efficiency will result. Failure to write down obsolete fixed assets results in overstated earnings.

The financial analyst should determine the age and condition of each major asset along

with its replacement cost. The trend in fixed asset acquisitions to total gross assets should be reviewed. This trend is particularly revealing for a technological company that has to keep up to date. A decrease in the trend points to the failure to replace older assets on a timely basis. Inactive and unproductive asests put a drain on the firm. Asset efficiency may be reviewed by evaluating production levels, downtime, and discontinuances. Assets that have not been used for a long period of time may have to be written down.

Pollution-causing equipment may necessitate replacement or modification to meet governmental ecology requirements.

■ Example

Company T presents the following information regarding its fixed assets:

	19X1	19X2
Fixed assets	$120,000	$105,000
Repairs and maintenance	6,000	4,500
Replacement cost	205,000	250,000

The company has inadequately maintained its assets as indicated by (1) the reduction in the ratio of repairs and maintenance to fixed assets from 5% in 19X1 to 4.3% in 19X2; (2) the material variation between replacement cost and historical cost; and (3) the reduction in fixed assets over the year.

When a company's rate of return on assets (e.g., net income to fixed assets) is poor, the firm may be justified in not maintaining fixed assets. If there is a declining industry, fixed asset replacement and repairs may have been restricted.

The fixed asset turnover ratio (net sales to average fixed assets) aids in appraising a company's ability to use its asset base efficiently to obtain revenue. A low ratio may mean that investment in fixed assets is excessive relative to the output generated.

A company having specialized or risky fixed assets has greater vulnerability to asset obsolescence. Examples include machinery used to manufacture specialized products and fad items.

A depreciation method should be used that most realistically measures the expiration in asset usefulness. For example, the units-of-production method may result in a realistic charge for machinery. Unrealistic book depreciation may be indicated when depreciation for stockholder reporting is materially less than depreciation for tax return purposes.

The investment analyst should examine the trend in depreciation expense as a percentage of both fixed assets and net sales. A reduction in the trend may point to inadequate depreciation charges for the potential obsolescence of fixed assets. Another indication of inadequate depreciation charges is a concurrent moderate rise in depreciation coupled with a material increase in capital spending.

■ Example

The following information applies to X Company:

	19X1	19X2
Depreciation expense to fixed assets	5.3%	4.4%
Depreciation expense to sales	4.0%	3.3%

The previous declining ratios indicate improper provision for the deterioration of assets.

A change in classification of newly acquired fixed assets to different depreciation categories from the older assets (e.g., accelerated depreciation to straight-line) will result in lower earnings quality. A vacillating depreciation policy will distort continuity in earnings. Also, if there is a reduction in depreciation expense caused by an unrealistic change in the lives and salvage values of property, plant, and equipment, there will be overstated earnings.

An inconsistency exists when there is a material decline in revenue coupled with a major increase in capital expenditures. It may be indicative of overexpansion and later write-offs of fixed assets.

Intangibles

High realization risk is indicated when there are high ratios of (1) intangible assets to total assets and (2) intangible assets to net worth. Intangibles may be overstated compared to their market value or future earning potential. For example, a firm's goodwill may be overstated or worthless in a recessionary environment. A 40-year amortization period may be excessive. Also, intangibles acquired before 1970 may be retained on the books without amortization.

Leasehold improvements are improvements made to rented property, such as paneling and fixtures. Leasehold improvements are amortized over the life of the rented property or the life of the improvement, whichever is shorter. Leasehold improvements have no cash realizability.

A company's goodwill account should be appraised to ascertain whether the firm acquired has superior earning potential to justify the excess of cost over fair market value of net assets paid for it. If the acquired company does not have superior profit potential, the goodwill has no value because excess earnings do not exist relative to other companies in the industry. However, internally developed goodwill is expensed and not capitalized. It represents an undervalued asset, such as the good reputation of McDonald's.

Patents may be undervalued. Patents are recorded at the registration cost plus legal fees to defend them, which may be far below the present value of future cash flows to be derived from the patents. Patents are less valuable when they may easily be infringed upon by minor alteration or when they apply to high-technological-oriented items. Also considered is the financial condition of the company, because it may have to incur significant legal costs in defending patents. What is the expiration dates of the patents and the degree to which new patents are coming on stream?

The change in intangible assets to the change in net income should also be examined. A rising trend may mean this net income has been relieved of appropriate charges.

An unwarranted lengthening in the amortization period for intangibles overstates earnings. An example of an unjustified change is when the company's reputation has been worsened due to political bribes and environmental violations.

Deferred Charges

Deferred expenses depend to a greater extent on estimates of future probabilities than do other assets. The estimates may be overly optimistic. Is the company deferring an item having no future benefit just to defer costs so as not to burden net income? Deferred charges are not cash-realizable assets and cannot be used to meet creditor claims. Examples of questionable deferred charges are moving costs, start-up costs, plant rearrangement costs, merger expenses, and promotional costs.

A company may try to hide declining profitability by deferring costs that were expensed in prior years. The CPA should be on the outlook for such a situation.

The financial analyst should examine the trend in deferred charges to sales, deferred charges to net income, and deferred charges (e.g., deferred promotion costs) to total expenditures. Increasing trends may be indicative of a more liberal accounting policy.

■ Example

Company G presents the following information:

	19X1	19X2
Deferred charges	$ 70,000	$150,000
Total assets	500,000	590,000
Sales	800,000	845,000
Net income	200,000	215,000
Computed ratios are		
Deferred costs to total assets	14%	25.4%
Deferred costs to sales	8.8%	17.8%
Deferred costs to net income	35%	69.8%

The higher ratios of deferred charges to (1) total assets, (2) sales, and (3) net income indicate more realization risk in assets. Further, 19X2's earnings quality may be lower because deferred costs may include in it items that should have been expensed.

A high ratio of intangible assets and deferred charges to total assets points to an asset structure of greater realization risk. Overstated assets in terms of realizability may necessitate later write-off.

Unrecorded Assets

The investment analyst should note the existence of unrecorded assets representing resources of the business or items expected to have future economic benefit. Unrecorded assets are positive aspects of financial position even though they are not shown on the balance sheet. Examples of unrecorded assets are tax loss carry forward benefit and a purchase commitment where the company has a contract to buy an item at a price materially less than the going rate.

Liabilities

If liabilities are understated, net income is overstated because it does not include necessary charges to reflect the proper valuation of liabilities.

The credit analyst should examine trends in current liabilities to total liabilities, current liabilities to stockholders' equity, and current liabilities to sales. Rising trends may point to liquidity problems.

Are liabilities patient or pressing? A supplier with a long relationship may postpone or modify the debt payable for a financially troubled company. Pressing debts include taxes and loans payable. These have to be paid without excuse. A high ratio of pressing liabilities to patient liabilities points to greater liquidity risk.

■ Example

Company A reports the following information shown in the table below.

The company has greater liquidity risk in 19X2, as reflected by the higher ratios of current liabilities to total liabilities, current liabilities to sales, and pressing current liabilities to patient current liabilities.

Arbitrary adjustments of estimated liabilities should be eliminated in deriving corporate earning power. For instance, profits derived from a recoupment of prior year reserves may necessitate elimination. If the credit analyst finds that reserves are used to manage earnings, he or she should add back the amounts charged to earnings and deduct the amounts credited to earnings. Estimated liability provisions should be realistic given the nature of the circumstances.

A firm having an unrealistically low provi-

Current Liabilities	19X1	19X2
Accounts payable	$ 30,000	$ 26,000
Short-term loans payable	50,000	80,000
Commercial paper	40,000	60,000
Total current liabilities	$ 120,000	$ 166,000
Total noncurrent liabilities	300,000	308,000
Total liabilities	$ 420,000	$ 468,000
Sales	$1,000,000	$1,030,000
Relevant ratios follow:		
Current liabilities to total liabilities	28.6%	35.5%
Current liabilities to sales	12.0%	16.1%
Pressing current liabilites to patient current liabilities (short-term loans payable plus commercial paper/accounts payable)	3.01	5.4

sion for future costs has understated earnings. For example, it is inconsistent for a company to have a lower warranty provision when prior experience points to a deficiency in product quality.

An overprovision in estimated liabilities is sometimes made when profits are too high and management wants to bring them down. In effect, the company is providing for a reserve for a rainy day.

Poor earnings quality is indicated when more operating expenses and losses are being charged to reserve accounts compared to prior years.

Unrecorded liabilities are not reported on the financial statements but do require future payment or services. Examples are lawsuits and noncapitalized leases.

Useful disclosures of long-term obligations is mandated by FASB 47. The credit analyst may want to review commitments applicable to unconditional purchase obligations and future payments on long-term debt and redeemable stock.

FASB Interpretation 34 requires disclosure of indirect guarantees of indebtedness. Included are contracts in which a company promises to advance funds to another if financial problems occur, as when sales drop below a stipulated level.

Preferred stock with a maturity date or subject to sinking fund requirements is more like debt than equity. However, convertible bonds with an attractive conversion feature are more like equity than debt since there is an expectation of conversion. *See also* Income Statement Analysis.

BANKRUPTCY This involves a discharge of the debtor's obligations through court order. The purpose of bankruptcy is to provide the debtor with a fresh start and to have an equitable distribution of the debtor's assets among creditors. A major federal law concerning bankruptcy is the Bankruptcy Reform Act of 1978. Chapter 7 deals with corporate bank-

ruptcy; Chapter 9 provides procedures for municipal bankruptcy; and Chapter 13 pertains to individual bankruptcy. *See also* Business Failure.

BARRON'S CONFIDENCE INDEX This looks at the trading pattern of bond investors to determine the timing of buying or selling stocks. The index is based on the belief that bond traders are more sophisticated than stock traders and thus identify stock market trends sooner. *See also* Technical Analysis.

BARTER Many companies are turning to barter as a way of improving efficiency and increasing profits. But barter may not be for everyone. The substance of the arrangement must be evaluated to see if it is economically advantageous. Appropriate accounting measures are needed to ensure that the transaction conforms to financial and tax-reporting requirements. Financial management should study the pros and cons of entering into barter deals, weighing the possible effects on both the short- and long-term financial health of the business. On average, 8% of U.S. export sales are bartered. Counter trade is in excess of $100 billion a year.

What Is Barter?

Various kinds of barter arrangements are possible. The simplest is when two firms exchange services or products in a transaction involving no cash. There is a contract for a given quantity of items specifying what constitutes complete payment. When possible, it is recommended that two companies make an exchange *directly* to avoid the commission charged by a barter middleman. It may be best for the firm to make public a listing of the items it has available and a corresponding list describing what merchandise or services it needs.

Examples of bartering contracts are infinite. Only a few are cited here. An airline exchanges seats for advertising space and

time. A manufacturer barters a product with a carrier in return for lower shipping rates.

Middlemen—act as intermediaries between companies. Often there is a barter club that prepares a catalog of commodities and services that are available among its members. There also may be a broker who can prepare a contract between companies entering into a barter arrangement.

When goods or services are transferred between members, there is a trade credit for the issuer and a trade charge for the receiver. Mainframe, minicomputer, or microcomputer systems may be used to keep abreast of dealings between parties.

When using a middleman, there are several factors to consider:

• What is the middleman charging and is it reasonable?
• Is there an initiation fee?
• What is the commission rate?
• How reliable is the middleman?

Accounts of member firms may be settled in cash from companies having goods not yet traded at period-end. Financial management should attempt cash-settlement arrangements so it does not have to accept unneeded merchandise or services.

Some barter firms where transaction information is available include Business Exchange Inc. and Universal Trading Exchange.

"You owe me." This is when one company delivers a product or service to another in return for the other company's promise to reciprocate later. Sometimes there is even a third company involved.

Buyback—when a United States entity provides goods or services to a foreign country to be paid back from the output generated from the plant it is helping to construct.

Counter trade—possible between both domestic or international companies. An example of such an arrangement is a business providing a machine in exchange for a certain commodity.

Bilateral clearing arrangements between central banks—used by certain countries. An even-netting effect occurs without the need for a company to use currency for settlement of a transaction with a company in a foreign country.

Favorable Bartering Conditions

Financial management may be more prone to employ bartering arrangements during the following circumstances:

• Difficulties with foreign currency
• Slow economic conditions
• High inflation
• Monetary problems in international markets or trade
• Rising interest rates
• A credit crunch
• High inventory balances
• The dollar is high priced
• A debt crisis exists in the world market

Advantages of Bartering

The reasons for opting to enter into barter arrangements are many. Barter can

• Attract cash customers who are satisfied with a product or service.
• Lessen cash flow problems by trading goods at wholesale for their full market value. For example, an accountant charges $3,000 for accounting work. He is paid by a company in merchandise having a market value of $3,000 but costing $2,500 wholesale. The accountant may not actually take the merchandise but instead obtains credits from a barter company.
• Minimize the production risk because it creates a greater market for a product or service.
• Get rid of excess inventory and do so at a higher price than in a liquidation.
• Improve the profit margin.
• Cover fixed costs in an idle-capacity situation.
• Generate new and sometimes innovative advertising channels.

• Help dispose of unattractive, discontinued, or surplus product lines without having to drastically lower prices.

• Help in starting new product lines, which is especially attractive for firms experiencing seasonal sales.

Limitations to Bartering

There are limitations and disadvantages to entering into barter arrangements, which financial management should carefully consider. Some disadvantages are

• The company giving the goods to another may not learn what the market for the product is really like and what manufacturing and marketing improvements can be made.

• Possible lower profitability on the bartered item compared to a normal sale.

• Unattractive or even unneeded items may be received in exchange (e.g., products lacking marketability).

• Commission fees may be high, often ranging from 2% to 12%.

• Merchandise received may be of inferior quality or lack marketability.

• A foreign government may restrict export of a good under a bartering contract.

• In the case of a firm with financial problems, the trader has a lien after secured creditors when the merchandise has been collateralized.

• Dumping bartered goods on the market may lower the selling price of goods in normal distribution channels, which may have a negative effect on overall earnings.

• Inefficiencies may be compounded by manufacturing excessive merchandise.

A Word of Caution

Before getting involved in a barter network, investigate the reliability of the broker, the companies involved, and the availability and desirability of the goods or services:

• Does the network or broker offer promises that can't be kept?

• What is the quality of the services or goods?

• What is the prior record of the broker or barter club you are considering?

• Is the barter network financially healthy to meet its commitments?

• Have club members withdrawn after receiving benefits but before reciprocating?

Financial management should get assurances that its company's products will not ultimately go into its own normal distribution channels, because that, in effect, will cause the company to be competing with itself. The bartered items often are sold at a lower price than nonbartered items. To protect itself, a legal contract with the broker or barter network should be entered into to restrict where the merchandise may be sold. For example, if a good is now sold only in New York, the contract might allow sales only to other states. The same holds true for sales in a given foreign geographic location. Similarly, merchandise currently distributed in the United States could be limited to bartering done overseas.

An accountant should advise his client that counter trade can be utilized for debt collection from a problem company. For example, assume an Italian company does not have sufficient dollars to pay a U.S. company. A trading company can be employed and the debt renegotiated in lira with the customer giving the lira to the trading company's Italian subsidiary. When the Italian subsidiary buys Italian commodities and sells them in the market, dollars can be transferred to the U.S.

The accountant should be involved in the selection process for an experienced barter middleman to handle barter arrangements for the client since financial aspects are crucial to the deal.

Authoritative Accounting Requirements

Accounting pronouncements are virtually silent regarding the accounting, financial reporting, and disclosures involving barter transactions. For such a growing area of busi-

ness activity, clarification and mandates are necessary.

Some accounting guidelines in the area are APB 29 and FASB 63. According to APB 29, Accounting for Nonmonetary Transactions, barter transactions should be reported at the estimated fair market value of the product or service received. This requirement is consistent with the tax law that provides for each party to recognize as revenue the fair market value of the exchange.

FASB 63, Financial Reporting by Broadcasters, defines barter as the exchange of unsold advertising time for products or services. The broadcaster benefits (providing the exchange does not interfere with its cash sales) by exchanging unsold time for other products or services (i.e., fixed asset, merchandise, travel, and entertainment). Barter revenue is to be reported when commercials are broadcast. Merchandise or services received should be reported when received or used. If merchandise or services are received before the commercial is broadcast, a liability should be reported. Similarly, if the commercial is broadcast first, a receivable should be reported.

Recommended Accounting and Reporting

Accountants must assure themselves that their clients have reported all income from barter activities at their fair market value, in accordance with tax and financial reporting requirements. Is the fair market value assigned to the exchange realistic? Will the client be able to sell goods received at the price in the market or will a price cut be required? Has fair market value been manipulated to reduce the tax obligation?

The accountant must carefully determine the method used and relevant assumptions applicable to fair market value. Is it based on an objective appraisal, the present value of future cash flows, replacement cost, or some other approach?

Are there sham and unrealistically priced exchange transactions? Some swaps are not clear-cut and are subject to abuse. But the accountant must be assured the client is obtaining full tax benefits. For instance, a restaurant providing a meal for advertising space may recognize the revenue and the expense for the full amount since advertising is a business expense. Accountants must be assured the client never loses his tax benefit when rightfully due.

The accountant must watch out for unreported income through such means as examining inventory figures (an unexplained reduction in inventory may arise from bartering) because misrepresentation by the client may result in IRS attack. The IRS can trace unreported revenue from the other barter party who has reported it.

The accountant must assure himself that his client's counter trade party is not padding the price for the item in question by examining available price lists. Note that the fair market value of items to be exchanged may be less than current cash prices received due to excess supply on the market.

Audit difficulties occur because bartering may be abused. For example, a broadcaster may receive a credit card from a credit card company in exchange for broadcast time. The assumption is that the card will be used for proper travel and entertainment expenses to lower current cash flow problems. However, because the credit card company will be absorbing the charge in return for broadcast time, the audit trail is not clear. The possibility is present that the credit card will be used partly for nonbusiness purposes.

The accountant must evaluate situations where the terms of the barter are unrealistic.

■ Example

An exchange of a foreign product may be such that the foreign government demands an inflated price. This may cause both companies involved to appear as if they are going along with this by formulating a fictitious transaction to justify the outrageous price.

Assume two letters of credit are made up—one for the inflated value and one for the reasonable price. The letter of credit for the overstated amount is canceled by the exchange. The U.S. exporter obtains cash for the merchandise value from the bank, which obtains that cash by marketing the foreign country's product.

■ Example

Obsolete inventory may be given to a barter dealer for credit of $100,000. The credit is treated as a receivable on the company's books so a loss is not recognized. If television time is given in exchange for cash at a discount rate of 60% of the going price, the $100,000 credit is reduced by 40% of the spread between the price paid to the barter dealer and the normal price.

Hence, if the manufacturer draws down $30,000 worth of time, it pays $18,000 cash and has its credit reduced by the barter dealer for $12,000. When the receivable is totally eliminated, the manufacturer will have incurred $150,000 in cash for television time represented by the $100,000 credit. While the manufacturer has not had to show a write-down loss, it has unrealistically enhanced earnings and thus paid additional tax. The net effect has been detrimental to stockholders.

Conclusion

Financial management should take full advantage of all the positive aspects of the rapidly growing trend toward bartering. Bartering is especially advantageous to a firm that can dispose of surplus merchandise or services that cannot be sold on favorable terms via ordinary distribution channels.

Selecting the right bartering arrangement can lower risk, improve efficiency, and enhance the bottom line. If it is done correctly, it can satisfy the short- and long-term objectives of a business.

BASIC FORMS OF BUSINESS ORGANIZATION

The three basic forms are (1) the sole proprietorship, (2) the partnership, and (3) the corporation.

A *sole proprietorship* is a business owned by one individual. Of the three forms of business organizations, sole proprietorships are the greatest in number.

The advantages of this form are
• No formal charter required
• Minimal organizational costs
• Profits and control not shared with others
The disadvantages are
• Limited ability to raise large sums of money
• Unlimited liability for the owner
• Limited to the life of the owner

A *partnership* is similar to the sole proprietorship except that the business has more than one owner.

Its advantages are
• Minimal organizational effort and costs
• Free from governmental regulations
Its disadvantages are
• Unlimited liability for the individual partners
• Limited ability to raise large sums of money
• Dissolved upon the death or withdrawal of any of the partners
There is a special form of partnership, called *limited partnership,* where one or more partners but not all have limited liability up to their investment, to creditors in the event of failure of the business. The *general partner* manages the business. *Limited partners* are not involved in daily activities. The return to limited partners is in the form of income and capital gains. Often, tax benefits are involved. Examples of limited partnerships are in real estate and oil and gas exploration.

A *corporation* is a legal entity that exists apart from its owners, better known as stockholders. Ownership is evidenced by possession of shares of stock. In terms of types of businesses, the corporate form is not the

greatest in number but is the most important in terms of total sales, assets, profits, and contribution to national income.

The advantages of a corporation are
• Unlimited life
• Limited liability for its owners
• Ease of transfer of ownership through transfer of stock
• Ability to raise large sums of capital
Its disadvantages are
• Difficult and costly to establish because a formal charter is required
• Subject to double taxation—on its earnings and dividends paid to stockholders
See also Going Public; Limited Partnership.

BAYESIAN PROBABILITY   This is revised prior estimates of probabilities, based on additional experience and information. An example of Bayesian probability applied to accounting is when the estimated bad debt percentage has to be revised because of such considerations as recent uncollectability experience of customer defaults, sales to more marginal customers, or poor economic conditions.

BETA COEFFICIENT   Many investors hold more than one financial asset. The portion of a security's risk, called *unsystematic risk*, can be controlled through diversification. This type of risk is unique to a given security. Business, liquidity, and default risks fall in this category. Nondiversifiable risk, more commonly referred to as *systematic risk,* results from forces outside of the firm's control and are therefore not unique to the given security. Purchasing power, interest rate, and market risks fall into this category. This type of risk is measured by *beta*. A particular stock's beta is useful in predicting how much the security will go up or down, provided that financial analysts and investors know which way the market will go. It does help them to figure out risk and expected return. Most of the unsystematic risk affecting a

security can be diversified away in an efficiently constructed portfolio. Therefore, this type of risk does not need to be compensated with a higher level of return. The only relevant risk is *systematic risk* or *beta risk* for which they can expect to receive compensation. Investors are compensated for taking this type of risk, which cannot be controlled.

In general, there is a relationship between a stock's expected (or required return) and its beta. The following formula, known as the Capital Asset Pricing Model (CAPM), is very helpful in determining a stock's expected return.

$$r_j = r_f + b\,(r_m - r_f)$$

where r_f = risk-free rate (the rate on a security such as a T-bill),

b = beta, the index of systematic risk,

r_m = expected market return (such as Standard & Poor's 500 Stock Composite Index),

$(r_m - r_f)$ = the market risk premium, the expected market return minus risk-free rate.

In words,

Expected return = risk-free rate + (beta × market risk premium)

The relevant measure of risk is the risk of the individual security, or its beta. The higher the beta for a security, the greater the return expected (or demanded) by the investor.

■ **Example**

Assume that r_f (the risk-free rate) = 6%, and r_m (the expected return for the market) = 10%. If a stock has a beta of 2.0, its risk premium $(r_m - r_f)$ should be 4% (10% − 6%). Therefore:

$$2.0 \times (10\% - 6\%) = 2.0 \times 4\% = 8\%$$

This means that an investor would expect (or demand) an extra 8% (risk premium) on this stock on top of the risk-free return of

6%. Therefore, the total expected (required) return on the stock should be 14%:

$$6\% + 8\% = 14\%$$

How to Read Beta

Beta measures a security's volatility relative to an average security. Put another way, it is a measure of a security's return over time to that of the overall market. For example, if Paine Webber's beta is 2.0, it means that if the stock market goes up 10%, Paine Webber's common stock goes up 20%; if the market goes down 10%, Paine Webber goes down 20%. Here is a guide for how to read betas:

Beta	What It Means
0	The security's return is independent of the market. An example is a risk-free security such as a T-bill.
0.5	The security is only half as responsive as the market.
1.0	The security has the same responsive, or risk, as the market (i.e., average risk). This is the beta value of the market portfolio such as Standard & Poor's 500 or Dow Jones 30 Industrials.
2.0	The security is twice as responsive, or risky, as the market.

How to Measure Beta

In measuring an asset's systematic risk, beta, an indication is needed of the relationship between the asset's returns and the market returns (such as returns on the Standard & Poor's 500 Stock Composite Index or Dow Jones 30 Industrials). This relationship can be statistically computed by determining the regression coefficient between asset and market returns. The equation is presented above.

$$b = \frac{Cov(r_j, r_m)}{\sigma_m^2}$$

where $Cov(r_j, r_m)$ is the covariance of the returns of the assets with the market returns, and σ_m^2 is the variance (standard deviation squared) of the market returns.

An easier way to compute beta is to determine the slope of the least-square's linear regression line $(r_j - r_f)$, where the excess return of the asset $(r_j - r_f)$ is regressed against the excess return of the market portfolio $(r_m - r_f)$. The formula for b is

$$b = \frac{\Sigma MK - n \bar{M}\bar{K}}{\Sigma M^2 - n \bar{M}^2}$$

where $M = (r_m - r_f)$,

$K = (r_j - r_f)$,

n = number of years,

$\bar{M}$ = average of M,

$\bar{K}$ = average of K.

■ Example

Compute the beta coefficient, b, using the following data for stock x and the market portfolio:

Historic Rates of Return

Year	r_j (%)	r_m (%)
19X5	−5	10
19X6	4	8
19X7	7	12
19X8	10	20
19X9	12	15

Assume that the risk-free rate is 6%. For easy computation, it is convenient to set up the following table:

Year	r_j	r_m	r_f	$(r_j - r_f) = K$	$(r_m - r_f) = M$	M^2	MK
19X5	−0.05	0.10	0.06	−0.11	0.04	0.0016	−0.0044
19X6	0.04	0.08	0.06	−0.02	0.02	0.0004	−0.0004
19X7	0.07	0.12	0.06	0.01	0.06	0.0036	0.0006
19X8	0.10	0.20	0.06	0.04	0.14	0.0196	0.0056
19X9	0.12	0.15	0.06	0.06	0.09	0.0081	0.0054
				−0.02	0.35	0.0333	0.0068

$$\bar{K} = -0.004 \quad \bar{M} = 0.07$$

Therefore, beta is

$$b = \frac{\Sigma MK - n\bar{M}\bar{K}}{\Sigma M^2 - n\bar{M}^2}$$

$$= \frac{0.0068 - (5)(-0.004)(0.07)}{0.0333 - (5)(0.07)^2}$$

$$= \frac{0.0082}{0.0088} = 0.93$$

See also Portfolio Theory; Capital Asset Pricing Model (CAPM).

BID AND ASKED This is the terminology used for a price quotation on an over-the-counter security. The highest price to be paid for a security by a prospective buyer is the bid price. The lowest price that a seller will accept for that security is the asked price. The differential between bid and asked is the spread that goes to the brokerage house, making a market in the security.

"BIG EIGHT" This refers to the eight largest CPA firms in the United States. In alphabetical order, they are Arthur Andersen & Co.; Coopers and Lybrand; Deloitte, Haskins and Sells; Ernst and Whinney; Peat, Marwick, Main and Co.; Price Waterhouse & Co.; Touche Ross & Co.; and Arthur Young & Co. Different bases exist to rank the CPA firms, such as by gross revenue, net income, number of staff, number of partners, and number of accounts. Also, firm ranking may change over time.

BLOCK SAMPLING This is a method of choosing sampling units (e.g., accounts, documents) in sequential sequence. Once the first item in the block is selected, the remainder of the block is automatically chosen. An example of a limited block, or cluster, from a given population is testing only a week of sales invoices for control deviations in April and May for the purpose of formulating a conclusion about the 6 months ended June 30. *See also* Sampling.

BOND ACCOUNTING The two methods of amortizing bond discount or bond premium are

• *Straight-line method*, which results in a constant dollar amount of amortization but a different effective rate each period.

• *Effective interest method*, which results in a constant rate of interest but different dollar amounts each period. This method is preferred over the straight-line method. The amortization entry is

Interest Expense (Yield × Carrying value of bond at the beginning of the year)
    Discount
    Cash (Nominal interest × Face value of bond)

In the early years, the amortization amount under the effective interest method is lower relative to the straight-line method (either for discount or premium).

■ Example

On 1/1/19X1, a $100,000 bond is issued at $95,624. The yield rate is 7% and the nominal interest rate is 6%. The schedule (shown below) is the basis for the journal entries to be made.

The entry on 12/31/19X1 is

Interest Expense	6,694	
Cash		6,000
Discount		694

At maturity, the bond will be worth its face

Date	Debit Interest Expense	Credit Cash	Credit Discount	Carrying Value
1/1/19X1				$95,624
12/31/19X1	$6,694	$6,000	$694	96,318
12/31/19X2	6,742	6,000	742	97,060

value of $100,000. When bonds are issued between interest dates, the entry is

Cash
  Bonds Payable
  Premium (or debit Discount)
  Interest Expense

■ Example

A $100,000, 5% bond having a life of 5 years is issued at 110 on 4/1/19X0. The bonds are dated 1/1/19X0. Interest is payable on 1/1 and 7/1. Straight-line amortization is used. The journal entries are

4/1/19X0	Cash (110,000 + 1,250)	111,250	
	Bonds Payable		100,000
	Premium on Bonds Payable		10,000
	Bond Interest Expense (100,000 × 5% × 3/12)		1,250
7/1/19X0	Bond Interest Expense	2,500	
	Cash		2,500

100,000 × 5% × 6/12

| | Premium on Bonds Payable | 526.50 | |
| | Bond Interest Expense | | 526.50 |

4/1/19X0 − 1/1/19X5   4 years, 9 months = 57 months

$$\frac{\$10,000}{57} = \$175.50 \text{ per month}$$

$175.50 × 3 months = $526.50

12/31/19X0	Bond Interest Expense	2,500	
	Interest Payable		2,500
	Premium on Bonds Payable	1,053	
	Bond Interest Expense		1,053
1/1/19X1	Interest Payable	2,500	
	Cash		2,500

Bonds Payable is shown on the balance sheet at its present value in the following manner:
- Bonds Payable
- Add: Premium
- Less: Discount
- Carrying Value

Bond issue costs are the expenditures incurred in issuing the bonds, such as legal, registration, and printing fees. Preferably, bond issue costs are deferred and amortized over the life of the bond. They are shown as a Deferred Charge.

In determining the price of a bond, the face amount is discounted using the present value of $1 table. The interest payments are discounted using the present value of annuity of $1 table. The yield rate is used as the discount rate.

■ Example

A $50,000, 10-year bond is issued with interest payable semiannually at an 8% nominal interest rate. The yield rate is 10%. The present value of $1 table factor for $n = 20$, $i = 5\%$ is 0.37689. The present value of annuity of $1 table factor for $n = 20$, $i = 5\%$ is 12.46221. The price of the bond should be

Present value of principal $50,000 × 0.37689	$18,844.50
Present value of interest payments $20,000 × 12.46221	24,924.42
	$43,768.92

In converting a bond into stock, there are three alternative methods that can be used: book value of bond, market value of bond, and market value of stock. Under the book value of bond method, no gain or loss on bond conversion will result because the book value of the bond is the basis to credit equity. Under the market value methods, gain or loss will result because the book value of the bond will be different from the market value of bond or market value of stock which is the basis to credit the equity accounts.

■ Example

A $100,000 bond with unamortized premium of $8,420.50 is converted to common stock.

There are 100 bonds ($100,000/$1,000). Each bond is converted into 50 shares of stock. Thus, 5,000 shares of common stock are involved. Par value is $15 per share. The market value of the stock is $25 per share. The market value of the bond is 120. Using the bond value method, the entry for the conversion is

Bonds Payable	100,000	
Premium on Bonds Payable	8,420.50	
Common Stock (5,000 × $15)		75,000
Premium on Common Stock		33,420.50

Using the market value of stock method, the entry is

Bonds Payable	100,000	
Premium on Bonds Payable	8,420.50	
Loss on Conversion	16,579.50	
Common Stock		75,000
Premium on Common Stock 5,000 × $25 = $125,000		50,000

Using the market value of the bond method, the entry is

Bonds Payable	100,000	
Premium on Bonds Payable	8,420.50	
Loss on Conversion	11,579.50	
Common Stock		75,000
Premium on Common Stock $100,000 × 120% = $120,000		45,000

BOND RATINGS These reflect the probability that a bond issue will go into default. They can influence investors' perceptions of risk and therefore have an impact on the interest rate. Bond investors tend to place more emphasis on independent analysis of quality than do common stock investors. Bond analysis and ratings are done, among others, by Standard & Poor's and Moody's. Below is an actual listing of the designations used by these well-known independent agencies. Descriptions on ratings are summarized. For original versions of descriptions, see Moody's *Bond Record* and Standard & Poor's *Bond Guide*.

Description of Bond Ratings

Moody's	Standard & Poor's	Quality Indication
Aaa	AAA	Highest quality
Aa	AA	High quality
A	A	Upper medium grade
Baa	BBB	Medium grade
Ba	BB	Contains speculative elements
B	B	Outright speculative
Caa	CCC & CC	Default definitely possible
Ca	C	Default, only partial recovery likely
C	D	Default, little recovery likely

Bond investors pay careful attention to ratings because they can affect not only potential market behavior but relative *yields* as well. Specifically, the higher the rating, the lower the yield of a bond, other things being equal. It should be noted that the ratings do change over time and the rating agencies have "credit watch lists" of various types.

BOND REFUNDING Bonds may be refunded by the firm prior to maturity through either the issuance of a serial bond or exercising a call privilege on a straight bond. The issuance of serial bonds allows the company to refund the debt over the life of the issue. A call feature in a bond enables the issuer to retire it before the expiration date. The call feature is included in many corporate bond issues.

When future interest rates are expected to decline, a call provision in the bond issue is recommended. Such a provision enables the company to buy back the high-interest

bond and issue a low-interest one. The timing for the refunding depends on expected future interest rates. A call price is usually established in excess of the face value of the bond. The resulting call *premium* equals the difference between the call price and the maturity value. The issuer pays the premium to the bondholder in order to acquire the outstanding bonds before the maturity date. The call premium is generally equal to one year's interest if the bond is called in the first year, and it declines at a constant rate each year thereafter. Also involved in selling a new issue are flotation costs. Both the call premium and flotation costs are tax-deductible expenses.

A bond with a call provision typically will be issued at an interest rate higher than one without the call provision. The investor prefers not to have a situation where the company can buy back the bonds early and issue lower interest bonds when interest rates de-

■ Example

Cypress Corporation is considering calling a $20 million, 30-year bond that was issued 10 years ago at 97 at a nominal interest rate of 14%. The call price on the bond is 104. The initial flotation cost was $200,000. The firm is considering issuing $20 million, 12%, 20-year bonds in order to net proceeds and retire the old bonds. The new bonds will be issued at 100. The flotation costs for the new issue are $225,000. The tax rate is 34%. The after-tax cost of new debt ignoring flotation costs is 7.92% (12% × 66%). With the flotation costs, the after-tax cost of new debt is anticipated to be 9%. There is a 2-month overlap in which interest must be paid on the old and new bonds. To determine whether refunding should take place, we need to compute the *net* initial cash outlay and net annual cash savings as follows:

The initial cash outlay is

Cost to call old bonds ($20,000,000 × 104%)	$20,800,000
Cost to issue new bond	225,000
Interest on old bonds for overlap period ($20,000,000 × 14% × 2/12)	466,667
Initial cash outlay	$21,491,667

The initial cash inflow is

Proceeds from selling new bond		$20,000,000
Tax-deductible items:		
Call premium	$ 800,000	
Unamortized discount ($600,000 × 20/30)	400,000	
Unamortized issue cost of old bond ($200,000 × 20/30)	133,333	
Overlap interest ($20,000,000 × 14% × 2/12)	466,667	
Total tax-deductible items	$1,800,000	
Tax rate	× 0.34	
Tax savings		612,000
Initial cash inflow		$20,612,000

cline. The investor would obviously want to hold onto a high-interest bond when prevailing rates are low.

The desirability of refunding a bond requires discount flow analysis.

The *net* initial cash outlay is therefore:

Initial cash outlay	$21,491,667
Inital cash inflow	20,612,000
Net initial cash outlay	$ 879,667

The annual cash flow for the old bond is

Interest (14% × $20,000,000)		$2,800,000
Less: Tax-deductible items		
Interest	$2,800,000	
Amortization of discount ($600,000/30)	20,000	
Amortization of issue cost ($200,000/30)	6,667	
Total tax-deductible items	$2,826,667	
Tax rate	× 0.34	
Tax savings		961,067
Annual cash outflow with old bond		$1,838,933

The annual cash flow for the new bond is

Interest (12% × $20,000,000)		$2,400,000
Less: Tax-deductible items		
Interest	$2,400,000	
Amortization of discount ($225,000/20)	11,250	
Total tax-deductible items	$2,411,250	
Tax rate	× 0.34	
Tax savings		819,825
Annual cash outflow with old bond		$1,580,175

The net annual cash savings with the new bond compared to the old bond is

Annual cash outflow with old bond	$1,838,933
Annual cash outflow with new bond	1,580,175
Net annual cash savings	$ 258,758

The net present value (NPV) with the refunding is

	Calculations	Present Value
Year 0	−$879,667 × 1	−$ 879,667
Year 1–20	$258,758 × 9.129*	+ 2,362,202
		$1,482,535

* PVIFA(9%, 20 years) = 9.129 from Table 4 in the Appendix.

Since a positive NPV exists, the refunding should take place.

BOND VALUATION   The process of determining security valuation involves finding the present value of an asset's expected future cash flows using the investor's required rate of return. Thus, the basic security valuation model can be defined mathematically as shown:

$$V = \sum_{t=1}^{n} \frac{C_t}{(1 + r)^t}$$

where V = intrinsic value or present value of an asset,

C_t = expected future cash flows in period $t = 1, \ldots, n$,

r = investor's required rate of return.

The valuation process for a bond requires a knowledge of three basic elements: (1) the amount of the cash flows to be received by the investor, which is equal to the periodic interest to be received and the par value to be paid at maturity; (2) the maturity date of the bond; and (3) the investor's required rate of return.

Incidentally, the periodic interest can be received annually or semiannually. The value of a bond is simply the present value of these cash flows. Two versions of the bond valuation model are presented below:

If the interest payments are made annually, then:

$$V = \sum_{t=1}^{n} \frac{I}{(1 + r)^t} + \frac{M}{(1 + r)^n}$$

$$= I(PVIFA_{r,n}) + M(PVIF_{r,n})$$

where I = interest payment each year = coupon interest rate × par value,

M = par value, or maturity value, typically $1,000,

r = investor's required rate of return,

n = number of years to maturity,

$PVIFA$ = present value interest factor of an annuity of $1 (which can be found in Table 4 in the Appendix)

$PVIF$ = present value interest factor of $1 (which can be found in Table 3 in the Appendix)

■ Example 1

Consider a bond maturing in 10 years and having a coupon rate of 8%. The par value is $1,000. Investors consider 10% to be an appropriate required rate of return in view of the risk level associated with this bond. The annual interest payment is $80 (8% × $1,000). The present value of this bond is

$$V = \sum_{t=1}^{n} \frac{I}{(1+r)^t} + \frac{M}{(1+r)^n} = I(PVIFA_{r,n})$$
$$+ M(PVIF_{r,n})$$

$$= \sum_{t=1}^{10} \frac{\$80}{(1+0.1)^t} + \frac{\$1,000}{(1+0.1)^{10}}$$

$$= \$80 \, (PVIFA_{10\%,10}) + \$1,000 \, (PVIF_{10\%,10})$$

$$= \$80 \, (6.145) + \$1,000 \, (0.386)$$

$$= \$491.60 + \$386.00 = \$877.60$$

If the interest is paid semiannually, then:

$$V = \sum_{t=1}^{2n} \frac{I/2}{(1+2/r)^t} + \frac{M}{(1+r/2)^{2n}}$$

$$= \frac{I}{2}(PVIFA_{r/2,2n}) + M(PVIF_{r/2,2n})$$

■ Example 2

Assume the same data as in Example 1, except the interest is paid semiannually.

$$V = \sum_{t=1}^{2n} \frac{I/2}{(1+r/2)^t} + \frac{M}{(1+r/2)^{2n}}$$

$$= \frac{I}{2}(PVIFA_{r/2,2n}) + M(PVIF_{r/2,2n})$$

$$= \sum_{t=1}^{20} \frac{\$40}{(1+0.05)^t} + \frac{\$1,000}{(1+0.05)^{20}}$$

$$= \$40(PVIFA_{5\%,20}) + \$1,000(PVIF_{5\%,20})$$

$$= \$40(12.462) + \$1,000(0.377)$$

$$= \$498.48 + \$377.00 = \$875.48$$

BOND YIELD—EFFECTIVE RATE OF RETURN ON A BOND

Bonds are evaluated on many different types of returns, including current yield, yield to maturity, yield to call, and realized yield.

Current Yield

The current yield is the annual interest payment divided by the current price of the bond. This is reported in *The Wall Street Journal*, among others.

■ Example 1

Assume a 12% coupon rate $1,000 par value bond is selling for $960. The current yield is

$$\$120/\$960 = 12.5\%$$

The problem with this measure of return is that it does not take into account the maturity date of the bond. A bond with 1 year to run and another with 15 years to run would have the same current yield quote if interest payments were $120 and the price were $960. Clearly, the 1-year bond would be preferable under this circumstance because you would not only get $120 in interest, but also a gain of $40 ($1,000 − $960) with a 1-year time period, and this amount could be reinvested.

Yield to Maturity

The yield to maturity takes into account the maturity date of the bond. It is the real return to be received from interest income plus capital gain, assuming the bond is held to maturity. There are two ways to calculate this measure: the exact method and the approximate method.

The Exact Method

Under the exact method, a bond's yield to maturity is the internal rate of return on investment in the bond. It is calculated by solving the bond valuation model for r:

$$V = \sum_{t=1}^{n} \frac{I}{(1 + r)^t} + \frac{M}{(1 + r)^n}$$
$$= I\,(PVIFA_{r,n}) + M(PVIF_{r,n})$$

where V is the market price of the bond, I is the interest payment, and M is the maturity value, usually $1,000. *PVIFA* and *PVIF* are found in Tables 4 and 3, respectively, in the Appendix.

Finding the bond's yield, r, involves trial and error. It is best explained by example.

■ Example 2

Suppose you are offered a 10-year, 8% coupon, $1,000 par value bond at a price of $877.60. What rate of return could you earn if you bought the bond and held it to maturity?

First, set up the bond valuation model:

$$V = \$877.60 = \sum_{t=1}^{10} \frac{\$80}{(1 + r)^t} + \frac{\$1,000}{(1 + r)^{10}}$$
$$= \$80(PVIFA_{r,10}) + \$1,000(PVIF_{r,10})$$

Since the bond is selling at a discount, the bond's yield is above the going coupon rate of 8%. Therefore, try a rate of 9%. Substituting factors for 9% in the equation, we obtain: $V = \$80(6.418) + \$1,000(0.422) = \$513.44 + \$422.00 = \$935.44$. The calculated bond value, $935.44, is above the actual market price of $877.60, so the yield is not 9%. To lower the calculated value, the rate must be raised. Trying 10%, we obtain: $V = \$80(6.145) + \$1,000(0.386) = \$491.60 + \$386.00 = \$877.60$. This calculated value is exactly equal to the market price of the bond; thus, 10% is the bond's yield to maturity.

The Approximate Method

$$Yield = \frac{I + (M - V)/n}{(M + V)/2}$$

here V = the market value of the bond,
I = dollars of interest paid per year,
M = maturity value, usually $1,000,
n = number of years to maturity.

■ Example 3

Using the same data in Example 2,

$$Yield = \frac{\$80 + (\$1,000 - \$877.60)/10}{(\$1,000 + \$877.60)/2}$$
$$= \frac{\$80 + \$12.24}{\$938.80} = \frac{\$92.24}{\$938.80} = 9.8\%$$

which came out to very close to 10%.

Yield to Call

Not all bonds are held to maturity. If the bond may be called prior to maturity, the yield to maturity formula will have the call price in place of the par value ($1,000).

■ Example 4

Assume a 20-year bond was initially issued at a 13.5% coupon rate and after two years rates have dropped. Assume further that the bond is currently selling for $1,180, the yield to maturity on the bond is 11.15%, and the bond can be called in 5 years after issue at $1,090. Thus if you buy the bond two years after issue, your bond may be called back after 3 more years at $1,090. The yield to call can be calculated as follows:

$$\frac{\$135 + (\$1,090 - \$1,180)/3}{(\$1,090 + \$1,180)/2} = \frac{\$135 + (-90/3)}{\$1,135}$$
$$= \frac{\$105}{\$1,135} = 9.25\%$$

The yield to call figure of 9.25% is 190 basis points less than the yield to maturity of 11.15%. Clearly, you need to be aware of the differential because a lower return is earned.

Realized Yield

You may trade in and out of a bond long before it matures. You obviously need a measure of return to evaluate the investment appeal of any bonds you intend to buy and sell. Realized yield is used for this purpose. This measure is simply a variation of yield to maturity, as only two variables are changed in the yield to maturity formula. Future price

is used in place of par value ($1,000), and the length of the holding period is substituted for the number of years to maturity.

■ Example 5

In Example 2, assume that you anticipate holding the bond only 3 years and that you have estimated interest rates will change in the future so that the price of the bond will move to about $925 from its present level of $877.60. Thus you will buy the bond today at a market price of $877.60 and sell the issue 3 years later at a price of $925. Given these assumptions, the realized yield of this bond would be

$$\text{Realized yield} = \frac{\$80 + (\$925 - \$877.70)/3}{(\$925 + \$877.70)/2}$$
$$= \frac{\$80 + \$15.80}{\$901.30} = \frac{\$95.80}{\$901.30} = 10.63\%$$

Fortunately, a bond table is available to find the value for various yield measures. A source is *Thorndike Encyclopedia of Banking and Financial Tables*, by Warren, Gorham & Lamont, Boston.

Equivalent Before-Tax Yield

Yield on a municipal bond needs to be looked at on an equivalent before-tax yield basis, because the interest received is not subject to federal income taxes. The formula used to equate interest on municipals to other investments is

Tax equivalent yield = Tax-exempt yield/(1 − tax rate)

■ Example 6

If you have a marginal tax rate of 28% and are evaluating a municipal bond paying 10% interest, the equivalent before-tax yield on a taxable investment would be

$$10\%/(1 - 0.28) = 13.9\%$$

Thus, you could choose between a taxable investment paying 13.9% and a tax-exempt bond paying 10% and be indifferent between the two.

BOOK VALUE PER SHARE   The book value per share is the amount each share would obtain in the event the company was liquidated based on the historical cost valuation in the financial statements. However, the ratio has limited utility because the fair market value of the balance sheet accounts are not taken into account. Book value per share is computed for both preferred stock and common stock as follows. Book value per share for preferred stock equals:

$$\frac{\text{(Liquidation value of preferred stock} + \text{Preferred dividends in arrears)}}{\text{Preferred stock outstanding}}$$

Book value per share for common stock equals:

$$\frac{\text{Total stockholders' equity} - \text{(Liquidation value of preferred stock} + \text{Preferred dividends in arrears)}}{\text{Common stock outstanding}}$$
$$\frac{\text{Common stockholders' equity}}{\text{Common stock outstanding}}$$

■ Example

The stockholders' equity section of the balance sheet for XYZ Company is as follows:

Capital stock:	
Preferred stock, cumulative, 10,000 shares, $10 par value, liquidation value $12, 6% dividend rate	$100,000
Common stock, 20,000 shares, $15 par value	300,000
Total capital stock	$400,000
Paid-in-capital	150,000
Retained earnings	200,000
Total stockholders' equity	$750,000

Preferred dividends in arrears is $12,000. Book value per share for preferred stock:

$$\frac{(\$120,000 + \$12,000)}{10,000 \text{ shares}} = \frac{\$132,000}{10,000} = \$13.20$$

Book value per share for common stock:

$$\frac{(\$750,000 - \$132,000)}{20,000 \text{ shares}} = \frac{\$618,000}{20,000} = \$30.90$$

Excerpts From Bond Table
Four Years Interest Payable Semiannually

Effective Rate of Return (Yield) Percent Per Annum	Nominal Rate 3%	3½%	4%	4½%	5%	6%	7%
4.00	96.31	98.17	100.00	101.83	103.66	107.33	110.99
4.10	95.98	97.81	99.63	101.46	103.29	106.94	110.60
4.125	95.89	97.72	99.54	101.37	103.20	105.85	110.50
4.20	95.62	97.45	99.27	101.09	102.92	106.56	110.21
4.25	95.45	97.27	99.00	100.91	102.73	106.38	110.02
4.30	95.27	97.09	98.91	100.73	102.55	106.19	109.83
4.375	95.00	96.82	98.64	100.45	102.27	105.90	109.54
4.40	94.92	96.73	98.55	100.36	102.18	105.81	100.44
4.50	94.56	96.38	98.19	100.00	101.81	105.44	109.06
4.60	94.21	96.02	97.83	99.64	101.45	105.06	108.68
4.625	94.13	95.93	97.74	99.55	101.36	104.97	108.58
4.70	93.87	95.67	97.47	99.28	101.08	104.69	108.30
4.75	93.69	95.49	97.30	99.10	100.90	104.51	108.11
4.80	93.52	95.32	97.12	98.92	100.72	104.32	107.92
4.875	93.26	95.06	96.85	98.65	100.45	104.04	107.64
4.90	93.17	94.97	96.77	98.56	100.36	103.95	107.54
5.00	92.83	94.62	96.41	98.21	100.00	103.59	107.17
5.10	92.49	94.28	96.06	97.85	99.64	103.22	106.80
5.125	92.40	94.19	95.98	97.77	99.55	103.13	106.70
5.20	92.15	93.93	95.72	97.50	99.29	102.86	106.43
5.25	91.98	93.76	95.54	97.33	99.11	102.67	106.24
5.30	91.81	93.59	93.37	97.15	98.93	102.49	106.06
5.375	91.55	93.33	95.11	96.89	98.67	102.22	105.78
5.40	91.47	93.25	95.02	96.80	98.58	102.13	105.69
5.50	91.13	92.91	94.68	96.45	98.23	101.77	105.32
5.625	90.71	92.48	94.25	96.02	97.79	101.33	104.86
5.75	90.30	92.06	93.83	95.59	97.35	100.38	104.41
5.875	89.88	91.64	93.40	95.16	96.92	100.44	103.96
6.00	89.47	91.23	92.98	94.74	96.49	100.00	103.51

Example: A $1,000, 4-year, 6% bond purchased at $104.69 (=$1,046.90) yields 4.70% effective interest. Interest is payable semiannually. To purchase this bond to yield 4.70% effective interest, an investor should pay $1,046.90.

BRANCH ACCOUNTING This is a separate accounting system for each branch of an organization. The home office opens an account in its general ledger entitled Branch, Branch Control, Investment in Branch, or some other similar name. Frequently, one account will be used to show the long-term investment in a branch while another account (such as Branch Current) will be used for more common accounts. In the home office ledger, this account or group of accounts is charged for everything sent to the branch or for services rendered to or for the branch, and it is credited for amounts received from the branch. In a similar manner, the branch ledger maintains an equity account entitled Home Office, Home Office Control, Home Office Current, or some other similar names. This account is credited for all assets received by the branch from the home office. It is also credited for all debts incurred for merchandise acquired or for services rendered by the home office for the branch. Such an account would also be credited as a result of expenses incurred by the home office for the benefit of the branch. It is debited for amounts sent by the branch to the home office. In operation, the branch account on the home office books will be debited when the home office account on the branch books is

credited, and vice versa. Thus, the balance of each of such pair of accounts should be equal in dollar amount, but the balances should be the opposite sides of the respective accounts. Two accounts that have such relationship are often referred to as *reciprocal*.

BREADTH INDEX The Breadth Index computes each trading day the net advances or declines in stocks on the New York Stock Exchange. When there are net advances, a strong market exists. The magnitude of strength depends on the spread between the number of advancing and declining issues. The Breadth Index equals the number of net advances or declines in securities divided by the number of securities traded.

Advances and declines typically go in the same direction as a standard market average (e.g., Dow Jones Industrial Average). But they may go in the opposite direction at a market peak or bottom.

Change instead of level is emphasized in breadth analysis. The computed Breadth Index should be compared to popular market averages. Usually, consistency exists in their movement. In a bull market, the security analyst should watch out for an extended disparity of the two. An example is when the Breadth Index moves downward gradually to new lows while the Dow Jones Industrial Average goes to new highs. A comparison may also be made of the Breadth Index over a number of years.

■ **Example**

Net declining issues are 58. Securities traded are 1,475. The Breadth Index equals:

$$\frac{\text{Declining issues}}{\text{Number of issues traded}} = \frac{58}{1,475} = -3.9$$

The Breadth Index may be compared to a base year or included in a 150-day moving average.

Market strength is indicated when the Breadth Index and Dow Jones Industrial Av-

erage are increasing. Market weakness is pointed to when they are declining. *See also* Technical Analysis.

BREADTH OF MARKET INDICES Indices of market breadth apply to the dispersion of general price increases or decreases in the stock market. It acts as a valuable indicator of a major turn in stock prices. *See also* Technical Analysis.

BUDGETING FOR PROFIT PLANNING A comprehensive (master) budget is a formal statement of management's expectation regarding sales, expenses, volume, and other financial transactions of an organization for the coming period. Simply put, a budget is a set of *pro forma* (*projected* or *planned*) financial statements. It consists basically of a pro forma income statement, pro forma balance sheet, and cash budget.

A budget is a tool for both planning and control. At the beginning of the period, the budget is a plan or standard; at the end of the period it serves as a control device to help management measure its performance against the plan so that future performance may be improved.

The budget is classified broadly into two categories:

1. *Operating budget*, reflecting the results of operating decisions
2. *Financial budget*, reflecting the financial decisions of the firm

The operating budget consists of:
• Sales budget
• Production budget
• Direct materials budget
• Direct labor budget
• Factory overhead budget
• Selling and administrative expense budget
• Pro forma income statement

The financial budget consists of:
• Cash budget
• Pro forma balance sheet

The major steps in preparing the budget are

1. Prepare a sales forecast.
2. Determine expected production volume.
3. Estimate manufacturing costs and operating expenses.
4. Determine cash flow and other financial effects.
5. Formulate projected financial statements.

Figure 1 (p. 62) shows a simplified diagram of the various parts of the comprehensive budget, the master plan of the company.

Illustration

To illustrate how all these budgets are put together, we will focus on a manufacturing company called the Johnson Company, which produces and markets a single product. We will assume that the company develops the master budget in *contribution* format for 19B on a quarterly basis. We will highlight the variable cost-fixed cost breakdown throughout the illustration.

The Sales Budget

The sales budget is the starting point in preparing the master budget, since estimated sales volume influences nearly all other items appearing throughout the master budget. The sales budget ordinarily indicates the quantity of each product expected to be sold. After sales volume has been estimated, the sales budget is constructed by multiplying the expected sales in units by the expected unit sales price. Generally, the sales budget includes a computation of expected cash collections from credit sales, which will be used later for cash budgeting.

■ Example 1

Refer to table presented at bottom of the page.

The Production Budget

After sales are budgeted, the production budget can be determined. The number of units expected to be manufactured to meet budgeted sales and inventory requirements is set forth in the production budget. The expected volume of production is determined by subtracting the estimated inventory at the beginning of the period from the sum of the units expected to be sold and the desired inventory at the end of the period. The production budget is illustrated in Example 2, found on p. 63.

Example 1
The Johnson Company
Sales Budget for the Year Ending December 31, 19B

	Quarter				
	1	*2*	*3*	*4*	*Total*
Expected sales in units	800	700	900	800	3,200
Unit sales price	×$80	×$80	×$80	×$80	×$80
Total sales	$64,000	$56,000	$72,000	$64,000	$256,000

Schedule of Expected Cash Collections

Accounts receivable, 12/31/19A	$ 9,500[a]				$ 9,500
1st quarter sales ($64,000)	$44,800[b]	$17,920[c]			62,720
2nd quarter sales ($56,000)		39,200	$15,680		54,880
3rd quarter sales ($72,000)			50,400	$20,160	70,560
4th quarter sales ($64,000)				44,800	44,800
Total cash collections	$54,300	$57,120	$66,080	$64,960	$242,460

[a] All $9,500 accounts receivable balance is assumed to be collectable in the first quarter.
[b] 70% of a quarter's sales are collected in the quarter of sale.
[c] 28% of a quarter's sales are collected in the quarter following, and the remaining 2% are uncollectable.

Figure 1 Comprehensive Budget

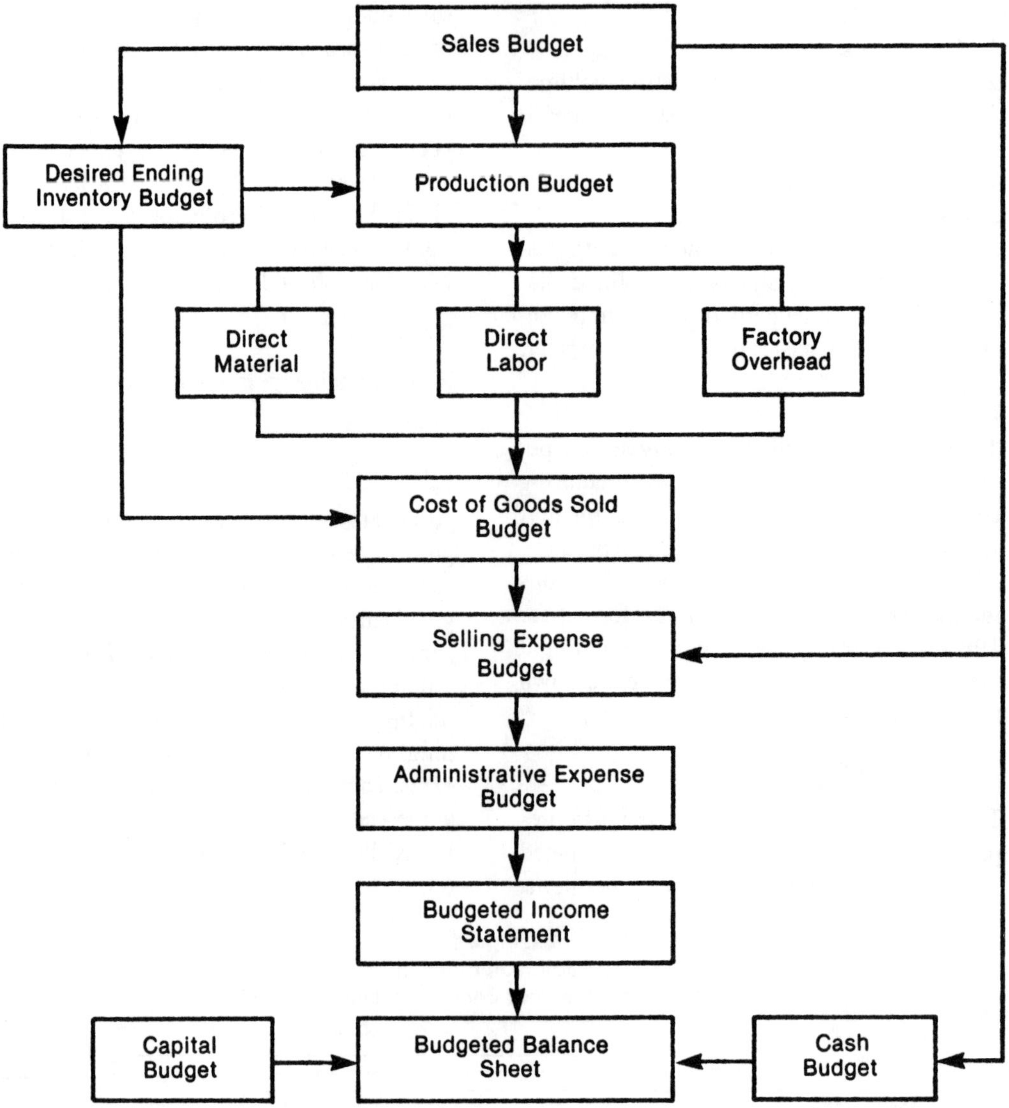

■ Example 2

Example 2
The Johnson Company
Production Budget for the Year Ending December 31, 19B

	Quarter				
	1	*2*	*3*	*4*	*Total*
Planned sales (Example 1)	800	700	900	800	3,200
Desired ending inventory[a]	70	90	80	100[b]	100
Total needs	870	790	980	900	3,300
Less: Beginning inventory[c]	80	70	90	80	80
Units to be produced	790	720	890	820	3,220

[a] 10% of the next quarter's sales
[b] Estimated
[c] The same as the previous quarter's ending inventory

The Direct Material Budget

When the level of production has been computed, a direct material budget should be constructed to show how much material will be required for production and how much material must be purchased to meet this production requirement. The purchase will depend on both expected usage of materials and inventory levels. The formula for computation of the purchase is

Purchase in units = Usage + Desired ending material inventory units − Beginning inventory units

The direct material budget is usually accompanied by a computation of expected cash payments for materials.

■ Example 3

Example 3
The Johnson Company
Direct Material Budget for the Year Ending December 31, 19B

	Quarter				
	1	*2*	*3*	*4*	*Total*
Units to be produced (Example 2)	790	720	890	820	3,220
Material needs per unit (lbs)	× 3	× 3	× 3	× 3	× 3
Material needs	2,370	2,160	2,670	2,460	9,660
Desired ending inventory of materials[a]	216	267	246	250[b]	250
Total needs	2,586	2,427	2,916	2,710	9,910
Less: Beginning inventory of materials[c]	237	216	267	246	237
Materials to be purchased	2,349	2,211	2,649	2,464	9,673
Unit price	× $2	× $2	× $2	× $2	× $2
Purchase cost	$4,698	$4,422	$5,298	$4,928	$19,346

Schedule of Expected Cash Disbursements

Accounts payable, 12/31/19A[a]	$2,200				$ 2,200
1st quarter purchases ($4,698)	2,349	$2,349[d]			4,698
2nd quarter purchases ($4,422)		2,211	$2,211		4,422
3rd quarter purchases ($5,298)			2,649	$2,649	5,298
4th quarter purchases ($4,928)				2,464	2,464
Total disbursements	$4,549	$4,560	$4,860	$5,113	$19,082

[a] 10% of the next quarter's units needed for production
[b] Estimated
[c] The same as the prior quarter's ending inventory.
[d] 50% of a quarter's purchases are paid for in the quarter of purchase; the remainder are paid for in the following quarter.

The Direct Labor Budget

The production requirements as set forth in the production budget also provide the starting point for the preparation of the direct labor budget. To compute direct labor requirements, expected production volume for each period is multiplied by the number of direct labor hours required to produce a single unit. The direct labor hours required to meet production requirements is then multiplied by the direct labor cost per hour to obtain budgeted total direct labor costs.

■ Example 4

See table below.

The Factory Overhead Budget

The factory overhead budget should provide a schedule of all manufacturing costs other than direct materials and direct labor. Using the contribution approach to budgeting requires the development of a predetermined overhead rate for the variable portion of the factory overhead. In developing the cash budget, we must remember that depreciation does not entail a cash outlay and therefore must be deducted from the total factory overhead in computing cash disbursement for factory overhead.

■ Example 5

To illustrate the factory overhead budget, we will assume that
• Total factory overhead budgeted = $6,000 fixed (per quarter) plus $2 per hour of direct labor.
• Depreciation expenses are $3,250 each quarter.
• All overhead costs involving cash outlays are paid for in the quarter incurred.
See table below.

The Ending Inventory Budget

The desired ending inventory budget provides us with the information required for the construction of budgeted financial statements. Specifically, it will help compute the cost of goods sold on the budgeted income statement. Secondly, it will give the dollar value of the ending materials and finished goods inventory to appear on the budgeted balance sheet.

Example 4
The Johnson Company
Direct Labor Budget for the Year Ending December 31, 19B

| | Quarter | | | | |
	1	2	3	4	Total
Units to be produced (Example 2)	790	720	890	820	3,220
Direct labor hours per unit	× 5	× 5	× 5	× 5	× 5
Total hours	3,950	3,600	4,450	4,100	16,100
Direct labor cost per hour	× $5	× $5	× $5	× $5	× $5
Total direct labor cost	$19,750	$18,000	$22,250	$20,500	$80,500

Example 5
The Johnson Company
Factory Overhead Budget for the Year Ending December 31, 19B

| | Quarter | | | | |
	1	2	3	4	Total
Budgeted direct labor hours (Example 4)	3,950	3,600	4,450	4,100	16,100
Variable overhead rate	× $2	× $2	× $2	× $2	× $2
Variable overhead budgeted	7,900	7,200	8,900	8,200	32,200
Fixed overhead budgeted	6,000	6,000	6,000	6,000	24,000
Total budgeted overhead	13,900	13,200	14,900	14,200	56,200
Less: Depreciation	3,250	3,250	3,250	3,250	13,000
Cash disbursement for overhead	10,650	9,950	11,650	10,950	43,200

■ Example 6

Example 6
The Johnson Company
Ending Inventory Budget for the Year Ending December 31, 19B

	Ending Inventory Units	Unit Cost	Total
Direct materials	250 pounds (Example 3)	$2	$ 500
Finished goods	100 units (Example 2)	41[a]	4,100

[a] The unit variable cost of $41 is computed as follows:

	Unit Cost	Units	Total
Direct materials	$2	3 pounds	$ 6
Direct labor	5	5 hours	25
Variable overhead	2	5 hours	10
Total variable manufacturing cost			$41

The Selling and Administrative Expense Budget

The selling and administrative expense budget lists the operating expenses involved in selling the products and in managing the business. In order to complete the budgeted income statement in contribution format, variable selling and administrative expense per unit must be computed.

■ Example 7

See table presented below.

The Cash Budget

The cash budget is prepared for the purpose of cash planning and control. It presents the expected cash inflow and outflow for a designated time period. The cash budget helps management keep cash balances in reasonable relationship to its needs. It aids in avoiding unnecessary idle cash and possible cash shortages. The cash budget consists typically of four major sections:

1. The receipts section, which is the beginning cash balance, cash collections from customers, and other receipts
2. The disbursements section, which comprises all cash payments made by purpose
3. The cash surplus or deficit section, which simply shows the difference between the cash receipts section and the cash disbursements section
4. The financing section, which provides a detailed account of the borrowings and repayments expected during the budgeting period

Example 7
The Johnson Company
Selling and Administrative Expense Budget for the Year Ending December 31, 19B

	Quarter				
	1	2	3	4	Total
Expected sales in units	800	700	900	800	3,200
Variable selling and administrative expense per unit[a]	× $4	× $4	× $4	× $4	× $4
Budgeted variable expense	$ 3,200	$ 2,800	$ 3,600	$ 3,200	$12,800
Fixed selling and administrative expenses:					
Advertising	1,100	1,100	1,100	1,100	4,400
Insurance	2,800				2,800
Office salaries	8,500	8,500	8,500	8,500	34,000
Rent	350	350	350	350	1,400
Taxes			1,200		1,200
Total budgeted selling and administrative expenses[b]	$15,950	$12,750	$14,750	$13,150	$56,600

[a] Includes sales agents' commissions, shipping, and supplies
[b] Paid for in the quarter incurred

■ Example 8

To illustrate, we will make the following assumptions:

• The company desires to maintain a $5,000 minimum cash balance at the end of each quarter.

• All borrowing and repayment must be in multiples of $500 at an interest rate of 10% per annum. Interest is computed and paid as the principal is repaid. Borrowing takes place at the beginning of each quarter and repayment at the end of each quarter.

See table presented below.

The Budgeted Income Statement

The budgeted income statement summarizes the various component projections of revenue and expenses for the budgeting period. However, for control purposes the budget can be divided into quarters or even months, depending on the need.

See Example 9 on p. 67.

Example 8
The Johnson Company
Cash Budget for the Year Ending December 31, 19B

		Quarter				
	Example	1	2	3	4	Total
Cash balance, beginning	Given	$10,000	$ 9,401	$ 5,461	$ 9,106	$ 10,000
Add: Receipts—Collections from customers	1	54,300	57,120	66,080	64,960	242,460
Total cash available		64,300	66,521	71,541	74,066	252,460
Less: Disbursements						
Direct materials	3	4,549	4,560	4,860	5,113	19,082
Direct labor	4	19,750	18,000	22,250	20,500	80,500
Factory overhead	5	10,650	9,950	11,650	10,950	43,200
Selling and administration	7	15,950	12,750	14,750	13,150	56,600
Machinery purchase	Given	—	24,300	—	—	24,300
Income tax	Given	4,000	—	—	—	4,000
Total disbursements		54,899	69,560	53,510	49,713	227,682
Cash surplus (deficit)		9,401	(3,039)	18,031	24,353	24,778
Financing:						
Borrowing		—	8,500	—	—	8,500
Repayment		—	—	(8,500)	—	(8,500)
Interest		—	—	(425)	—	(425)
Total financing		—	8,500	(8,925)	—	(425)
Cash balance, ending		$ 9,401	$ 5,461	$ 9,106	$24,353	$ 24,353

■ **Example 9**

Example 9
The Johnson Company
Budgeted Income Statement for the Year Ending December 31, 19B

	Example No.		
Sales (3,200 units @ $80)	1		$256,000
Less: Variable expenses			
Variable cost of goods sold (3,200 units @ $41)	6	$131,200	
Variable selling and administration	7	12,800	144,000
Contribution margin			112,000
Less: Fixed expenses			
Factory overhead	5	24,000	
Selling and administration	7	43,800	67,800
Net operating income			44,200
Less: Interest expense	8		425
Income before taxes			43,775
Less: Income taxes (20%)			8,755
Net income			35,020

The Budgeted Balance Sheet

The budgeted balance sheet is developed by beginning with the balance sheet for the year just ended and adjusting it, using all the activities that are expected to take place during the budgeting period. Some of the reasons that the budgeted balance sheet must be prepared are

• It could disclose some unfavorable financial conditions that management might want to avoid.

• It serves as a final check on the mathematical accuracy of all the other schedules.

• It helps management perform a variety of ratio calculations.

• It highlights future resources and obligations.

■ **Example 10**

To illustrate, we will use the following balance sheet for the year 19A.

Example 10
The Johnson Company
Balance Sheet as of December 31, 19A

Assets		Liabilities and Stockholders' Equity	
Current assets:		Current liabilities:	
Cash	$10,000	Accounts payable	$ 2,200
Accounts receivable	9,500	Income tax payable	4,000
Material inventory	474	Total current liabilities	$ 6,200
Finished goods inventory	3,280	Stockholders' equity:	
Total current assets	$23,254	Common stock, no-par	70,000
Fixed assets:		Retained earnings	37,054
Land	$ 50,000		
Building and equipment	100,000		
Accumulated depreciation	(60,000)		
Total fixed assets	$ 90,000		
Total assets	$113,254	Total liabilities and stockholders' equity	$113,254

The Johnson Company
Budgeted Balance Sheet as of December 31, 19A

Assets			*Liabilities and Stockholders' Equity*	
Current assets:			Current Liabilities:	
Cash	$24,353	(a)	Accounts payable	$ 2,464 (h)
Accounts receivable	23,040	(b)	Income tax payable	8,755 (i)
Material inventory	500	(c)	Total current liabilities	$11,219
Finished goods inventory	4,100	(d)	Stockholders' equity:	
Total current assets	$51,993		Common stock, no-par	70,000 (j)
Fixed assets:			Retained earnings	72,074 (k)
Land	$ 50,000	(e)		
Buildings and equipment	124,300	(f)		
Accumulated depreciation	(73,000)	(g)		
Total fixed assets	101,300			
Total assets	$153,293		Total liabilities and stockholders' equity $153,293	

Computations:
  (a) From Example 8 (cash budget)
  (b) $9,500 + $256,000 sales − $242,460 receipts = $23,040
  (c) and (d) From Example 6 (ending inventory budget)
  (e) No change
  (f) $100,000 + $24,300 (from Example 8) = $124,300
  (g) $60,000 + $13,000 (from Example 5) = $73,000
  (h) $2,200 + $19,346 − $19,082 = $2,464 (all accounts payable relate to material purchases), or 50% of 4th quarter
       purchases = 50% ($4,928) = 2,464
  (i) From Example 9 (budgeted income statement)
  (j) No change
  (k) $37,054 + $35,020 net income = $72,074

A Shortcut Approach to Formulating the Budget

In actual practice use of a shortcut approach is very widely used in formulating a budget. The approach can be summarized as follows:

1. A *pro forma income statement* is developed using past percentage relationships between certain expense and cost items and the firm's sales and applying these percentages to the firm's projected sales. The income statement can be set up in a traditional or contribution format.

2. A *pro forma balance sheet* is estimated using the *percentage-of-sales method,* which involves the following steps:

(a) Express balance sheet items that vary directly with sales as a percentage of sales. Any item that does not vary with sales (such as long-term debt) is designated not applicable (n.a.).

Multiply these percentages by the sales projected to obtain the amounts for the future period.

(b) Where no percentage applies (such as long-term debt, common stock, and paid-in-capital), simply insert the figures from the present balance sheet or their desired level in the column for the future period.

(c) Compute the projected retained earnings as follows:

Projected retained earnings = Present retained earnings + Projected net income − Cash dividend to be paid

(d) Sum the asset accounts and the liability and equity accounts to see if there is any difference. The difference, if any, is a *shortfall,* which is the amount of financing the firm has to raise externally.

Computer-Based Models for Budgeting

More and more companies are developing computer-based models for financial planning and budgeting, using powerful yet easy-to-use financial modeling languages such as Execum's *Interactive Financial Planning System (IFPS)*™ and Social Systems' *SIMPLAN.*™ The models help not only to build a budget for profit planning but answer a variety of what-if scenarios. The resultant calculations provide a basis for choice among alternatives under conditions of uncertainty. Financial modeling can be accomplished using spreadsheet programs such as Lotus 1-2-3™ and SuperCalc.™ *See also* Budgeting Models; Financial Forecasting and the Percentage-of-Sales Method; Financial Models; Simulation Models.

BUDGETING MODELS These are quantitative models that generate a budget. The models help accountants and budget analysts answer what-if questions. There are primarily two approaches to modeling in the corporate budgeting process: *simulation* and *optimization*. *See also* Financial Models; Simulation Models.

BUSINESS COMBINATIONS A business combination occurs before a consolidation. Business combinations may be accounted for under the pooling-of-interests method and the purchase method. Criteria for pooling and purchase, accounting and reporting requirements, and disclosures are dealt with.

The purchase method is used when cash or other assets are given or liabilities incurred to effect the combination. An acquisition of a minority interest is always a purchase at a later date even if the original acquisition was accounted for as a pooling.

The pooling-of-interests method is used when there is an exchange of voting common stock and *all* the twelve criteria for a pooling

are satisfied. In a pooling, it is assumed for accounting purposes that both companies were always combined. No purchase or sale is assumed to have taken place. A pooling is a union of the ownership interests of the two previously separated groups of stockholders.

Pooling-of-Interests Method

The criteria for a pooling-of-interests deal with independence of the combining companies, time period for consummation of the combination, voting rights, consideration given in the exchange, purchase of treasury stock, ownership interests, and absence of planned transactions. The accounting for a pooling is based on recognizing net assets at book value with earnings recognized for the entire year. Footnote disclosure describes the terms of the agreement and accounting adjustments made.

Criteria for a Pooling

The twelve criteria, all of which must be met, for a pooling are indicated following. When more than one company is acquired in a combination plan, each pooling consideration must be met by each company.

1. The combining companies are autonomous, meaning that a combining company must not have been a subsidiary or division of any other combining company within 2 years before the initiation date. *Note:* A new company incorporated within 2 years qualifies unless it is in any respect a successor to a company not considered autonomous.

2. The combining companies are independent, meaning that a combining company does not own 10% or more of another combining company's voting common stock at the initiation or consummation dates or at any time in between. *Note:* A change in the exchange ratio results in a new initiation date.

The *consummation* date is the date when the net assets are transferred to the acquiring company. However, temporary assets (e.g., cash, marketable securities) may be held to settle liabilities and contingent items.

3. The combining companies come together in a single transaction or within 1 year after the initiation date. A delay is allowed for litigation or governmental action. For instance, if the combination took 15 months but 4 months involved a delay because of antitrust litigation, this criteria is still satisfied.

4. The acquiring company issues voting common stock in exchange for 90% or more of the voting common stock of the acquired company.

The following shares of the combiners are excluded from the 90% minimum.

• Shares owned by the issuing company or its subsidiaries prior to the initiation date

• Shares acquired by the initiating company other than by issuing its own common stock

• Shares outstanding subsequent to the consummation date

In determining if 90% of the stock of the combiner has been transferred to the issuing corporation, the number of shares transferred must be reduced by the equivalent number of shares of the issuing corporation owned by the combiner before combination. This reduced number of shares is then compared to 90% of the *total* outstanding shares of the combiner company, to determine if the requirement is satisfied.

An acquiring company may give cash or common stock for debt or preferred stock of an acquired business and qualify as a pooling, but only if the debt securities and preferred stock were not issued in an exchange for voting common stock of the acquired business within 2 years before the initiation date.

A combination plan may not provide for a pro rata cash distribution but may within certain restrictions have a cash distribution for fractional shares. Cash may also be used in a combination plan to retire or redeem callable debt and equity securities.

5. None of the combining companies alters the equity interest of voting common stock within 2 years before the combination in contemplation of it. The voting interest is deemed changed for abnormal dividends based on taking into account profits and prior dividends.

6. Treasury stock is acquired by a combining company for reasons other than the business combination between the initiation and consummation dates. Treasury stock may be acquired for purposes of a stock option plan, compensation plan, and similar recurring transactions.

7. The relative ownership percentage of each stockholder in the combined entity remains the same as before. For example, if Mr. A and Mr. B owned 2% of XYZ Company, they should still own the same percentage in the newly formed entity (e.g., 1.5%).

8. There is no restriction in voting rights among stockholders by the combined entity (e.g., delayed voting rights).

9. The combination is finalized at the consummation date with no pending provisions of any kind related to the combination. For instance, no contingently issuable shares or distribution of assets to the former stockholders of the combining companies are allowed.

There is an absence of planned or subsequent transactions related to the combination as follows:

10. Repurchase of stock issued to effect the combination.

11. Financial arrangements benefiting former stockholders of the combining companies. An example is guarantying loans secured by stock issued in the combination which in substance negates the exchange of equity securities.

12. Sale of a significant part of the combined entity's assets within two years subsequent

to the combination, such as the disposal of a division. However, the disposal of a duplicate warehouse would be in the ordinary course of business.

Accounting Under Pooling-of-Interests

• Net assets of the acquired company are brought forth at book value.

• Retained earnings and paid-in-capital of the acquired company are brought forth at book value. There is no change in *total* stockholders' equity, but the equity components do change. Any necessary adjustments are made to paid-in-capital. In the event that paid-in-capital is insufficient to absorb the difference, retained earnings would next be reduced. However, retained earnings could never be increased. If there is a deficit in retained earnings for a combining entity, it is continued in the combined entity.

• Net income of the acquired company is brought forth for the entire year regardless of the date of acquisition.

• Expenses of the pooling are charged against earnings as incurred. Examples are registration fees, finders' fees, and consultants' fees.

• A gain or loss from the sale of a major part of the assets of the acquired business within 2 years subsequent to combination is considered an extraordinary item.

■ Example

The mechanics of a pooling follow:

	Company X	Company Y	Combined
Assets	$300	$100	$200
Liabilities	50	20	30
Equity	250	80	*

* Addition of:
—Capital stock of Company X before
—Capital stock issued in the pooling
—Retained earnings of both
—Paid-in-capital absorbs the difference.

Note: There can be no new assets from a pooling. In the year of pooling, recurring

intercompany transactions should be eliminated to the degree possible from the beginning of the period. But nonrecurring intercompany transactions relating to long-term assets and liabilities do not have to be eliminated.

An issuing company may effect a pooling by distributing treasury stock (acquired prior to 2 years before combination). The transfer of this stock is accounted for as if the stock had been *retired* and then reissued to effect the combination. The reissuance of this stock is accounted the same as the issuance of new shares.

Combining companies may hold investments in the common stock of each other. The accounting treatment follows:

• Investment of a combiner in the common stock of the *issuing* corporation. (The stock is in effect returned to the resulting combined entity and hence should be accounted for as treasury stock.)

• Investments in the common stock of the *other* combining companies. (This is an investment in the type of stock that is exchanged for the new shares issued. It should be accounted for as *retired* stock.)

Where one combining company employs a different GAAP than another (e.g., straight-line vs. double declining balance depreciation), the company is permitted to change to the GAAP used by the other combiner(s) and to record the cumulative effect of a change in accounting principle. Prior year financial statements when issued on a pooled basis should be restated for accounting principle changes.

Disclosures Under Pooling

Footnote disclosure of a pooling follows:

• Name and description of combined companies

• A statement that it is a pooling

• Description and number of shares issued to effect the pooling

• Net income of the previously separate companies

• Accounting method used for intercompany transactions

• Adjustments required to net assets so the combining companies are employing the same accounting methods and the related effects on earnings

• Particulars of changes in retained earnings due to a change in fiscal year of a combining company

• Reconciliation of profits previously reported by the issuing company

Advantages and Disadvantages of Pooling

An advantage of pooling is the retention of historical cost. A disadvantage from a financial reader's perspective is the possible overstated earnings (e.g., picking up net income for the whole year regardless of acquisition date, lower depreciation charges related to purchase method, and sale of low-cost basis assets at a gain).

Purchase Method

If any one of the 12 criteria is not satisfied for a pooling, the business combination is accounted for as a purchase. A purchase typically involves either the payment of assets or incurrence of liabilities for the other business. To effect a purchase, more than 50% of voting common stock has to be acquired.

Accounting Under Purchase Method

The accounting followed for a purchase is indicated below:

• Net assets of the acquired company are brought forth at fair market value.

Guidelines in assigning values to individual assets acquired and liabilities assumed (except goodwill) follow:

  • *Marketable securities*—current net realizable values.

  • *Receivables*—Present value of net receivables using present interest rates.

• *Inventories—finished goods* at estimated net realizable value less a reasonable profit allowance (lower limit). *Work-in-process* at estimated net realizable value of finished goods less costs to complete and profit allowance. *Raw materials* at current replacement cost.

• *Plant and equipment*—if to be employed in operations, show at replacement cost. If to be sold, reflect at net realizable value. If to be used temporarily, show at net realizable value recognizing depreciation for the period.

• *Identifiable intangibles*—at appraisal value.

• *Other assets* (including land and noncurrent securities)—at appraised values.

• *Payables*—at estimated present value.

• *Liabilities and accruals*—at estimated present value.

• *Other liabilities and commitments*—at estimated present value. However, a deferred income tax credit account of the acquired company is not brought forth.

• The excess of cost paid over book value of assets acquired is attributed to the identifiable net assets. The remaining balance not attributable to specific assets is of an unidentifiable nature and is assigned to goodwill. The identifiable assets are depreciated. Goodwill is amortized over the period benefited, not exceeding 40 years. Note that adjustments for fair value and amortization of goodwill are factors used just in preparing consolidated financial statements.

• Goodwill of the acquired company is not brought forth.

• None of the equity accounts of the acquired business (e.g., retained earnings) appear on the acquirer's books. Ownership interests of the acquired company stockholders are not continued subsequent to the merger.

• Net income of the acquired company is brought forth from the date of acquisition to year-end.

• Direct costs of the purchase are a deduction from the fair value of the securities issued, whereas indirect costs are expensed as incurred.

When stock is issued in a purchase transaction, quoted market price of stock is typically a clear indication of asset cost. Consideration should be given to price fluctuations, volume, and issue price of stock.

If liabilities are assumed in a purchase, the difference between the fixed rate of the debt securities and the present yield rate for comparable securities is reflected as a premium or discount.

Following is the step-by-step acquisition procedure:

• If control is not accomplished on the initial purchase, the subsidiary is not includable in consolidation until control has been accomplished.

• Once the parent owns in excess of 50% of the subsidiary, a retroactive restatement should be made including all of the subsidiary's earnings in consolidated retained earnings on a step-by-step fashion commencing with the initial investment.

• The subsidiary's earnings are included for the ownership years at the appropriate ownership percentage.

• After control is accomplished, fair value and adjustments for goodwill will be applied retroactively on a step-by-step basis. Each acquisition is separately determined.

The acquiring company cannot generally record a net operating loss carry forward of the acquired company since there is no assurance of realization. However, if realized in a later year, recognition will be a retroactive adjustment of the purchase transaction allocation, thus causing the residual purchase cost to be reallocated to the other assets acquired. In effect, there will be a reduction of a goodwill or the other assets.

FASB 38 provides guidelines for recording preacquisition contingencies during the allocation period as a part of allocating the cost of an investment in an enterprise acquired under the purchase method. A preacquisition contingency is a contingency of a business that is acquired with the purchase method and that exists prior to the consummation date. Examples of preacquisition contingencies are a contingent asset, a contingent liability, or a contingent impairment of an asset. The allocation period is the one required to identify and quantify the acquired assets and liabilities assumed. The allocation period ceases when the acquiring company no longer needs information it has arranged to obtain and that is known to be available. Hence, the existence of a preacquisition contingency for which an asset, a liability, or an impairment of an asset cannot be estimated does not, of itself, extend the allocation period. Although the time required depends on the circumstances, the *allocation period* typically is not greater than one year from the consummation date.

Preacquisition contingencies (except for tax benefits of NOL carry forwards) must be included in the allocation of purchase cost. The allocation basis is determined in the following manner:

• The *fair value* of the preacquisition contingency, assuming a fair value can be determined during the allocation period.

• If fair value is not determinable, the following criteria are used:

1. Information available before the termination of the allocation period indicates that it is probable that an asset existed, a liability had been incurred, or an asset had been impaired at the consummation date. It must be probable that one or more future events will occur confirming the existence of the asset, liability, or impairment.

2. The amount of the asset or liability can be reasonably estimated.

Adjustments necessitated from a preacquisition contingency occurring after the end of the allocation period must be included in income in the year the adjustment is made.

Disclosures Under Purchase

Footnote disclosures under the purchase method include:
- Name and description of companies combined.
- A statement that the purchase method is being used.
- The period in which earnings of the acquired company is included.
- Cost of the acquired company, including the number and value of shares issued, if any.
- Amortization period of goodwill.
- Contingencies arising under the acquisition agreement.
- Earnings for the current and prior periods as if the companies were combined at the beginning of the period. This pro forma disclosure is to make the purchase method comparable to that of pooling.

Advantages and Disadvantages of Purchase Method

An advantage of the purchase method is that fair value is used to recognize the acquired company's assets just as in the case of acquiring a separate asset. Disadvantages are the difficulty in determining fair value, the amortization period to use, and mixing fair value of acquired company's assets and historical cost for the acquiring company's assets.

BUSINESS CYCLE The business cycle is the regular pattern of expansion (recovery) and contraction (recession) in aggregate economic activity around the path of trend growth, with effects on growth, employment, and inflation. At the peak of the cycle, economic activity is high relative to trend, whereas at the trough (valley) of the cycle, the low point in economic activity is reached. The business cycle tends to have an impact on corporate earnings, cash flow, and expansion. *See also* Recession.

BUSINESS FAILURE In technical insolvency, the business is unable to meet current obligations even if total assets exceed total liabilities. In bankruptcy, liabilities exceed the fair market value of assets. A negative real net worth exists. According to law, business failure can be either technical insolvency or bankruptcy.

Voluntary Settlement

A voluntary settlement with creditors allows the company to save many of the costs that would exist in bankruptcy. The settlement is accomplished out of court. The voluntary settlement permits the company to either continue or be liquidated and is initiated to permit the debtor to recover some of its investment.

A creditor committee may allow the business to continue to operate if it is anticipated that the entity will recover. Creditors may also continue to do business with the company. In sustaining the firm's existence, there may be
- An extension
- A composition
- Creditor control
- Integration of each of the above

Extension

In an extension, creditors will receive the balances due but over a longer time period. Current purchases are made with cash. Creditors may also agree to subordinate their claims to suppliers giving credit to the company during the extension period. The creditors believe the debtor will be able to eventually handle the problems.

The creditor committee may require certain controls, including legal control over the entity's assets or common stock, getting a security interest in assets and approval of all cash payments.

Creditors objecting to the extension arrangement may be paid immediately to prevent them from having the business declared bankrupt.

Composition

In a composition, a voluntary reduction is made in the amount the debtor owes the creditor. The creditor receives a specified percentage of the balance owed in *full* settlement of the account. The creditor may try to work with the debtor in resolving financial difficulties. The advantages of a composition are the avoidance of court costs and the stigma of a bankrupt company.

If dissenting creditors exist, they may be paid in full or allowed to recover a higher percentage so they do not force the business to close.

In order that an extension or composition will work, the following should exist:
• The debtor is ethical so that company assets will not be used for personal use.
• The debtor is expected to recover.
• Current business conditions are favorable, enhancing the debtor's recovery.

Creditor Control

A creditor committee may decide to take control of the business if they are not pleased with current management. They will operate the business in order to satisfy their claims. Once paid, the creditors may recommend that new management replace the old before further credit is given. A drawback is the possibility of mismanagement lawsuits brought by stockholders against the creditors.

Integration

The creditors and the company negotiate a plan that involves a combination of extension, composition, and creditor control. For example, the agreement may provide for a 20% cash payment of the balance owed plus 5 future payments of 12%, typically in the form of notes. The total payment is thus 80%.

The advantages of negotiated settlements are that:

• They are less formal than bankruptcy proceedings.
• They cost less (thus reducing legal expenses).
• They are easier to implement than bankruptcy proceedings.
• They typically give creditors a better return.

The following disadvantages may arise:
• Although creditors implement controls, it is still possible that further decline in asset values may occur.
• Unrealistic small creditors may make the negotiating process difficult by demanding full payment.

Bankruptcy Reorganization

If there is no voluntary settlement, the creditors may place the firm into bankruptcy. The bankruptcy proceeding may either reorganize or liquidate the business.

Legal bankruptcy may be declared if the company cannot meet its bills or when liabilities exceed the fair market value of assets. A company may file for reorganization, under which it will develop a plan for continued existence.

Chapter 7 of the Bankruptcy Reform Act of 1978 outlines the steps in liquidation. This chapter is used when reorganization is not practical. Chapter 11 deals with reorganization. If reorganization is not possible under Chapter 11, the company will be liquidated under Chapter 7.

The two types of reorganization petitions are

• *Voluntary*—the company petitions for its own reorganization. The entity need not be insolvent to file for voluntary reorganization.

• *Involuntary*—creditors file for an involuntary reorganization of the entity. The petition must establish either that the debtor firm is not satisfying its debts when due or that a creditor or another party has taken control over the debtor's assets.

Reorganization involves the following steps:

- A reorganization petition is filed under Chapter 11 in court.
- A judge approves the petition and either appoints a trustee or allows the creditors to elect one to manage asset disposition.
- The trustee presents an equitable reorganization plan to the court.
- The plan is given to the creditors and stockholders for approval.
- The debtor pays the expenses associated with the reorganization.

The trustee in a reorganization values the company, recapitalizes it, and exchanges outstanding debts for new securities.

Valuation

In valuing the business, the trustee estimates its liquidation value relative to its value as a going concern. Liquidation is recommended when the liquidation value is greater than the continuity value. If the entity is more valuable when operating, reorganization is suggested. Future earnings must be estimated when determining the value of the reorganized company. The going concern value represents the present value of future earnings.

Recapitalization

A plan has to be formulated for the reorganization. The debts may be extended or equity securities may be issued in place of the obligations. Recapitalization is the process of exchanging liabilities for other types of liabilities or equity securities. In recapitalizing the business, the objective is to provide a combination of debt and equity that will allow the firm to satisfy its debt and provide reasonable earnings for the owners.

Exchange of Obligations

In exchanging obligations to derive the optimal capital structure, priorities are followed.

Senior claims come before junior claims. Senior debt holders must receive a claim on new capital equal to their prior claims. The last priority goes to common stockholders in receiving new securities. A debt holder typically receives a combination of different securities. Preferred and common stockholders may receive nothing. Typically, however, they keep some small ownership. Subsequent to the exchange, the debt holders may become the firm's new owners.

Liquidation Arising From Bankruptcy

If a company is declared bankrupt, creditors have to meet between 10 and 30 days after that declaration. A judge or referee presides over the meeting. The creditors appoint a trustee. The trustee manages the property of the defaulted company, liquidates the business, keeps suitable records, appraises the claims of creditors, makes payments, and gives applicable information about the liquidation process. Claim priority in bankruptcy follows:

1. *Secured claims.* Secured creditors receive the value of the secured assets in support of their claims. If the value of the secured assets is inadequate to meet their claims in full, the balance reverts to general creditor status.

2. *Bankruptcy administrative costs.* These costs include any expenses applicable to handling bankruptcy, such as legal and trustee expenses.

3. *Unsecured salaries and commissions.* These claims are limited to $2,000 per individual and must have been incurred within 90 days of the bankruptcy petition.

4. *Unsecured customer deposit claims.* The maximum per claim is $900.

5. *Taxes.* Tax claims relate to unpaid taxes due the government.

6. *General creditor claims.* General creditors have loaned the business money without

specific collateral. Included are debentures and accounts payable.

7. *Preferred stockholders*.

8. *Common stockholders*.

Usually, after creditor claims have been settled with the remaining assets, nothing is left for stockholders.

After the assets of the business are distributed in accordance with the priority order above, the business may be *discharged* from any legitimate debts still remaining (except for debts immune to discharge). Provided a debtor has not been discharged within the previous 6 years and was not bankrupt because of fraud, the debtor may begin a new business.

■ Example

The balance sheet of Ace Corporation for the year ended December 31, 19X4, follows:

The liquidation value is $625,000. Instead of liquidation, there could be a reorganization with an investment of an additional $320,000. The reorganization is anticipated to provide earnings of $115,000 each year. A multiplier of 7.5 is appropriate. If the $320,000 is obtained, long-term debt holders will obtain 40% of the common stock in the reorganized business in place of their present claims.

If the $320,000 of additional investment is made, the company's going concern value is $862,500 (7.5 × $115,000). The liquidation value is given at $625,000. Because the reorganization value is in excess of the liquidation value, reorganization is recommended.

■ Example

The balance sheet of the Oakhurst Company is presented below.

Balance Sheet of the Ace Corporation

Current assets	$400,000	Current liabilities	$475,000
Fixed assets	410,000	Long-term liabilities	250,000
		Common stock	175,000
		Retained earnings	(90,000)
Total assets	$810,000	Total liabilities and stockholders' equity	$810,000

Balance Sheet of the Oakhurst Company
Assets

Current assets		
Cash	$ 9,000	
Marketable securities	6,000	
Receivables	1,100,000	
Inventory	3,000,000	
Prepaid expenses	4,000	
Total current assets		$4,119,000
Noncurrent assets		
Land	1,800,000	
Fixed assets	2,000,000	
Total noncurrent assets		3,800,000
Total assets		$7,919,000

Balance Sheet of the Oakhurst Company—*Continued*
Liabilities and Stockholders' Equity

Current liabilities		
Accounts payable	$ 180,000	
Bank loan payable	900,000	
Accrued salaries	300,000[a]	
Employee benefits payable	70,000[b]	
Customer claims—unsecured	80,000[c]	
Taxes payable	350,000	
Total current liabilities		$1,880,000
Noncurrent liabilities		
First mortgage payable	$1,600,000	
Second mortgage payable	1,100,000	
Subordinated debentures	700,000	
Total noncurrent liabilities		3,400,000
Total liabilities		$5,280,000
Stockholders' equity		
Preferred stock (3,500 shares)	$ 350,000	
Common stock (8,000 shares)	480,000	
Paid-in-capital	1,600,000	
Retained earnings	209,000	
Total stockholders' equity		2,639,000
Total liabilities and stockholders' equity		$7,919,000

[a] The salary owed to each employee is less than $2,000 and was incurred within 90 days of the bankruptcy petition.
[b] Employee benefits payable have the same limitations as unsecured wages and are eligible in bankruptcy distribution.
No customer claim exceeds $900.

Additional data follows:

1. The mortgages relate to the firm's total noncurrent assets.

2. The subordinated debentures are subordinated to the bank loan payable. Thus, they come after the bank loan payable in liquidation.

3. The company's current assets and noncurrent assets have been sold for $2.1 million and $1.9 million, respectively.

Hence, the trustee received $4.0 million.

4. The company is bankrupt, since the total liabilities of $5.28 million exceed the $4 million of the fair value of the assets.

5. The administrative expense for handling the bankrupt company is $900,000. This liability is not reflected in the previous balance sheet.

The allocation of the $4 million to the creditors follows:

Proceeds		$4,000,000
Available to secured creditors		
First mortgage—payable from $1,900,000 proceeds of noncurrent assets	$1,600,000	
Second mortgage—payable from the balance of proceeds of noncurrent assets	300,000	1,900,000
Balance after secured creditors		$2,100,000
Next priority		
Administrative expenses	$ 900,000	
Accrued salaries	300,000	
Employee benefits payable	70,000	
Customer claims—unsecured	80,000	
Taxes payable	350,000	1,700,000
Proceeds available to general creditors		$ 400,000

Now that the claims on the proceeds from liquidation have been satisfied, general creditors receive the residual on a proportionate basis. The distribution of the $400,000 is shown below.

BYPRODUCT ACCOUNTING A byproduct is an incidental occurrence from the manufacturing process. The byproduct has little value relative to the main product. Byproduct income (selling price less completion and disposal costs) can be accounted for in any of the following ways:

- Reduce the cost of the main product
- Other revenue
- Reduce total costs

■ Example

Work-in-process has been charged with the cost of making furniture amounting to $60,000. Sawdust resulted, which was sold netting $200. The entry is

Cash	200	
Work-in-Process		200

See also Joint Product Accounting.

General Creditor	Amount	Pro Rata Allocation for Balance to Be Paid
Second-mortgage balance ($1,100,000–$300,000)	$ 800,000	$124,031
Accounts payable	180,000	27,907
Bank loan payable	900,000	248,062[a]
Subordinated debentures	700,000	0
Total	$2,580,000	$400,000

[a] Because the debentures are subordinated, the bank loan payable has to be met in full before any amount can be distributed to the subordinated debentures. The subordinated debenture holders thus receive nothing.

C

CALLABLE OBLIGATIONS BY THE CREDITOR

Included as a current liability is a long-term debt callable by the creditor because of the debtor's violation of the debt agreement except if one of the following conditions exist:

• The creditor waives or lost his right to require repayment for a period in excess of one year from the balance sheet date.

• There is a grace period in the terms of the long-term debt issue that the debtor may cure the violation, which makes it callable, and it is probable that the violation will be rectified within the grace period.

CAPITAL ASSET PRICING MODEL (CAPM)

A security risk consists of two components—diversifiable risk and nondiversifiable risk. Diversifiable risk, sometimes called controllable risk or *unsystematic* risk, represents the portion of a security's risk that can be controlled through diversification. This type of risk is unique to a given security. Business, liquidity, and default risks fall into this category. Nondiversifiable risk, sometimes referred to as noncontrollable risk or *systematic* risk, results from forces outside of the firm's control and is therefore not unique to the given security. Purchasing power, interest rate, and market risks fall into this category.

Nondiversifiable risk is assessed relative to the risk of a diversified portfolio of securities, or the market portfolio. This type of risk is measured by the beta coefficient.

The capital asset pricing model (CAPM) relates the risk measured by beta to the level of expected or required rate of return on a security. The model, also called the security market line (SML), is given as follows:

$$r_j = r_f + b\,(r_m - r_f)$$

where r_j = the expected (or required) return on security j,

r_f = the risk-free security (such as a T-bill),

r_m = the expected return on the market portfolio (such as Standard & Poor's 500 Stock Composite Index or Dow Jones 30 Industrials),

b = Beta, an index of nondiversifiable (noncontrollable, systematic) risk.

In words, the CAPM or (SML) equation shows that the required (expected) rate of return on a given security (r_j) is equal to the return required for securities that have no risk (r_f) plus a risk premium required by investors for assuming a given level of risk.

The higher the degree of systematic risk (*b*), the higher the return on a given security demanded by investors. *See also* Beta Coefficient; Capital Asset Pricing Model (CAPM); Portfolio Theory.

CAPITAL BUDGETING This is the process of deciding whether or not to commit resources to a project whose benefits will be spread over several time periods. There are typically two types of investments:

1. Selection decisions in terms of obtaining new facilities or expanding existing facilities. Examples include:
   (a) Investments in long-term assets such as property, plant, and equipment.
   (b) Resource commitments in the form of new product development, market research, refunding of long-term debt, introduction of a computer, and so on.
2. Replacement of decisions in terms of replacing existing facilities. Examples include replacing a manual bookkeeping system with a computerized system and replacing an inefficient lathe with one that is numerically controlled.

As such, capital budgeting decisions are a key factor in the long-term profitability of a firm. To make wise investment decisions, managers need tools at their disposal that will guide them in comparing the benefits and costs of various investment alternatives.

Capital Budgeting Techniques

Many techniques for evaluating investment proposals are widely available. They include:

1. Payback period
2. Accounting rate of return (ARR) (also called *simple rate of return*)
3. Net present value (NPV)
4. Internal rate of return (IRR) (also called *time-adjusted rate of return*)
5. Profitability index (also called the excess present value index)

The NPV method and the IRR method are called discounted cash flow (DCF) methods since they both recognize the time value of money and thus discount future cash flows. Each of the methods is discussed below.

Payback Period

Payback period measures the length of time required to recover the amount of initial investment. The payback period is determined by dividing the amount of initial investment by the cash inflow through increased revenues or cost savings.

■ Example 1

Assume:

Cost of investment	$18,000
Annual cash savings	3,000

Then, the payback period is

$$\frac{\$18,000}{\$3,000} = 6 \text{ years}$$

When cash inflows are not even, the payback period is determined by trial and error. When two or more projects are considered, the rule for making a selection decision is as follows:

Decision rule: Choose the project with the shorter payback period. The rationale behind this is: The shorter the payback period, the less risky the project and the greater the liquidity.

■ Example 2

Consider two projects whose cash inflows are not even. Assume each project costs $1,000.

Year	A	B
1	$100	$500
2	200	400
3	300	300
4	400	100
5	500	—
6	600	—

Based on trial and error, the payback period of project A is 4 years ($100 + $200 + $300 + $400 = $1,000 in 4 years). The payback period of project B is

$$2 \text{ years} + \frac{\$100}{\$300} = 2\frac{1}{3} \text{ years}$$

Therefore, according to this method, choose project B over project A.

Advantages of the payback period method:
1. It is simple to compute and easy to understand.
2. It handles investment risk effectively.

Shortcomings of the payback period method:
1. It does not recognize the time value of money.
2. It ignores the impact of cash inflows after the payback period which determines profitability of an investment.

Accounting (Simple) Rate of Return

Accounting rate of return (ARR) measures profitability from the conventional accounting standpoint by relating the required investment to the future annual net income. Sometimes the former is the average investment.

Decision rule: Under the ARR method, choose the project with the higher rate of return.

■ Example 3

Consider the investment:

Initial investment	$10,000
Estimated life	20 years
Cash inflows per year	$2,000
Depreciation by straight line	$ 500

then:

$$ARR = \frac{\$2,000 - \$500}{10,000} = 15.0\%$$

Using the average investment, which is usually assumed to be one half of the original investment, the resulting rate of return will be doubled:

$$ARR = \frac{\$2,000 - \$500}{\frac{1}{2}(\$10,000)} = \frac{\$1,500}{\$5,000} = 30.0\%$$

The justification for using the average investment is that each year the investment amount is decreased by $500 through depreciation, and therefore the average is computed as one half of the original cost.

Advantages: The method is easily understandable and simple to compute, and recognizes the profitability factor.

Shortcomings:
1. It fails to recognize the time value of money.
2. It uses accounting data instead of cash flow data.

Net Present Value

Net present value (NPV) is the excess of the present value (PV) of cash inflows generated by the project over the amount of the initial investment (I). Simply, *NPV = PV − I*. The present value of future cash flows is computed using the so-called *cost of capital* (or minimum required rate of return) as the discount rate.

Decision rule: If NPV is positive, accept the project. Otherwise, reject it.

■ Example 4

Initial investment	$4,356
Estimated life	6 years
Annual cash inflows	$1,000
Cost of capital (minimum required rate of return)	8%

Present value of cash inflows (*PV*):

$1,000 × *PV* of annuity of $1, 6 years and 8% $PVIFA_{8\%, 6 \text{ years}}$ [=$1,000(4.623)]	$4,623
Initial investment (*I*)	4,356
Net present value (*NPV = PV − I*)	$ 267

Since the investment's NPV is positive, the investment should be accepted.

Advantages: The NPV method obviously recognizes the time value of money and is easy to compute, whether the cash flows form an annuity or vary from period to period.

Disadvantage: It requires detailed long-term forecasts of incremental cash flow data.

Internal Rate of Return (or Time-Adjusted Rate of Return)

Internal rate of return (IRR) is defined as the rate of interest that equates I with the PV of future cash inflows. In other words, at IRR, $I = PV$, or $NPV = 0$.

Decision rule: Accept if IRR exceeds the cost of capital; otherwise, reject it.

■ Example 5

Assume the same data given in Example 4. We will set up the following equality ($I = PV$):

$$\$4,356 = \$1,000 \times PVIFA_{i,6}$$

$$PVIFA_{i,6} = \frac{\$4,356}{\$1,000} = 4.356$$

which gives exactly 10% in the 6-year line. (See Table 4 in the Appendix.) Since the investment's IRR (10%) is greater than the cost of capital (8%), the investment should be accepted.

Advantages: It considers the time value of money and is therefore more exact and realistic than ARR.

Shortcomings:
1. It is difficult to compute, especially when the cash inflows are not even.
2. It fails to recognize the varying size of investment in competing projects and their respective dollar profitability.

The trial-and-error method for computing IRR when cash inflows are not even is summarized, step by step, as follows:
1. Compute NPV at the cost of capital, denoted here as r_1.
2. See if NPV is positive or negative.
3. If NPV is positive, then pick another rate (r_2) much higher than r_1. If NPV is negative, then pick another rate (r_2) much smaller than r_1. The true IRR at which $NPV = 0$ must be somewhere in between these two rates.
4. Compute NPV using r_2.
5. Use interpolation for the exact rate.

■ Example 6

Consider the following investment whose cash flows are different from year to year:

Year	Cash Inflows
1	$1,000
2	2,500
3	1,500

Assume that the amount of initial investment is $3,000 and the cost of capital is 14%.
Step 1   NPV at 14%.

		$PVIF_{14\%,n}$	
Year	Cash Inflows	PV Factor at 14%	Total PV
1	$1,000	0.877	$ 877
2	2,500	0.769	1,923
3	1,500	0.675	1,013
			$3,813

Thus: $NPV = \$3,813 - \$3,000 = \$813$

Step 2   We see that $NPV = \$813$ is positive at $r_1 = 14\%$.
Step 3   Pick, say, 30% to play safe as r_2.
Step 4   Computing NPV at $r_2 = 30\%$:

		$PVIF_{30\%,n}$	
Year	Cash Inflows	PV Factor at 30%	Total PV
1	$1,000	0.769	$ 769
2	2,500	0.592	1,480
3	1,500	0.455	683
			$2,932

Thus: $NPV = \$2,932 - \$3,000 = \$(68)$

Step 5   Interpolate:

	NPV	
14%	$813	$813
IRR		0
30%	−68	
Difference	$881	$813

Therefore:

$$IRR = 14\% + \frac{\$813}{\$881}(30\% - 14\%)$$

$$= 14\% + 0.923(16\%)$$

$$= 14\% + 14.77\% = 28.77\%$$

Profitability Index (*Excess Present Value Index*)

The profitability index is the ratio of the total PV of future cash inflows to the initial investment, that is, *PV/I*. This index is used as a means of ranking projects in descending order of attractiveness. If the profitability index is greater than 1, then accept it.

■ Example 7

Using the data in Example 4, the profitability index, *PV/I*, is $4,623/$4,356 = 1.06. Since this project generates $1.06 for each dollar invested (or its profitability index is greater than 1), you should accept the project.

Income Tax Factors—Determining After-Tax Cash Flow

Income taxes make a difference in many capital budgeting decisions. In other words, the project that is attractive on a pre-tax basis may have to be rejected on an after-tax basis. Income taxes typically affect both the amount and the timing of cash flows. Since net income, not cash inflows, is subject to tax, after-tax cash inflows are not usually the same as after-tax net income.

Let us define: S = sales,
E = cash operating expenses,
d = depreciation,
t = tax rate.

Then, before-tax cash inflows $= S - E$, and net income $= S - E - d$. By definition,

After-tax cash inflow
   = Before-tax cash inflow − Taxes

After-tax cash inflow
   $= (S - E) - (S - E - d)(t)$

Rearranging, give the shortcut formula:

After-tax cash inflow $= (S - E)(1 - t) + (d)(t)$ [or after-tax cash inflow $= (S - E - d)(1 - t) + d$]

As can be seen, the deductibility of depreciation from sales in arriving at net income subject to taxes reduces income tax payments and thus serves as a tax shield.

Tax shield = Tax savings of depreciation = $(d)(t)$

■ Example 8

Assume: S = $12,000,
E = $10,000,
d = $500/year by straight line,
t = 40%.

Then:

After-tax cash inflow = ($12,000 − $10,000) (1 −0.4) + ($500) (0.4) = $1,200 + $200 = $1,400

Note that:

Tax shield = Tax savings on depreciation = $(d)(t)$
= ($500)(0.4) = $200.

After-tax cash outflow would be similarly computed by simply dropping S in the previous formula. Therefore:

After-tax cash outflow = $(-E)(1 - t) + (d)(t)$

■ Example 9

Assume: E = $6,000,
d = $800/year by straight line,
t = 40%.

Then:

After-tax cash outflow = (−$6,000) (1 − 0.4) + ($800) (0.4) = − $3,600 + $320 = −$3,280, which is a cash outflow of $3,280.

Since the tax shield is $d \times t$, the higher the depreciation deduction, the higher the tax savings on depreciation.

■ Example 10

XYZ Corporation has provided its revenues and cash operating costs (exluding depreciation) for the old and the new machine, as follows:

	Revenue	Annual Cash Operating Costs	Net Profits Before Depreciation and Taxes
Old machine	$150,000	$70,000	$ 80,000
New machine	180,000	60,000	120,000

Assume that the annual depreciation of the old machine and the new machine will be $30,000 and $50,000, respectively. Assume further that the tax rate is 46%.

To arrive at net profits after taxes, we first have to deduct depreciation expenses from the net profits before depreciation and taxes, see below.

Subtracting the after-tax cash inflows of the old machine from the cash inflows of the new machine results in the relevant, or incremental, cash inflows for each year.

Therefore, in this example the relevant or incremental cash inflows for each year are $87,800 − $57,000 = $30,800.

Alternatively, the incremental cash inflows after taxes can be computed using the following simple formula:

After-tax incremental cash inflows = (Increase in revenues) (1 − Tax rate) − (Increase in cash charges) (1 − Tax rate) + (Increase in depreciation expenses) (Tax rate)

■ Example 11

Using the data in Example 10, after-tax incremental cash inflows for each year are

Increase in revenue × (1 − Tax rate):
($180,000 − $150,000) (1 − 0.46) $16,200
− Increase in cash charges × (1 − Tax rate): ($60,000 − $70,000) (1 − 0.46)   −(−5,400)
+ Increase in depreciation expense × Tax rate: ($50,000 − $30,000) (0.46)   9,200
                                          ―――――
                                          $30,800

CAPITAL BUDGETING AND INFLATION   The accuracy of capital budgeting decisions depends on the accuracy of the data regarding cash inflows and outflows. For example, failure to incorporate price-level changes due to inflation in capital budgeting situations can result in errors in the predicting of cash flows and thus in incorrect decisions. Typically, an analyst has two options dealing with a capital budgeting situation with inflation: Either restate the cash flows in nominal terms and discount them at a nominal *cost of capital* (minimum required rate of return) *or* restate both the cash flows and cost of capital in *constant* terms and discount the constant cash flows at a constant cost of capital. The two methods are basically equivalent.

■ Example

A company has the following projected cash flows estimated in real terms:

Period	Real Cash Flows (000s)			
	0	1	2	3
	−100	35	50	30

The nominal cost of capital is 15%. Assume that inflation is projected at 10% a year. Then the first cash flow for year 1, which is $35,000 in current dollars, will be $35,000 × 1.10 = $38,500 in year 1 dollars. Similarly, the cash flow for year 2 will be $50,000 × (1.10)^2 = $60,500 in year 2 dollars, and so on. If we discount these nominal cash flows at the 15% nominal cost of capital, we have the net present value (NPV) shown on p. 86:

	Net Profits After Taxes	Add Depreciation	After-Tax Cash Inflows
Old machine	($80,000 − $30,000) (1 − 0.46) = $27,000	$30,000	$57,000
New machine	($120,000 − $50,000) (1 − 0.46) = $37,800	50,000	87,800

Period	Cash Flows	PVIF (Table 3)	Present Values
0	−100	1.000	−100
1	38.5	0.870	33.50
2	60.5	0.756	45.74
3	39.9	0.658	26.25
		NPV =	5.49, or $5,490

Instead of converting the cash-flow forecasts into nominal terms, we could convert the cost of capital into real terms by using the following formula:

$$\text{Real cost of capital} = \frac{1 + \text{Nominal cost of capital}}{1 + \text{Inflation rate}} - 1$$

In the example, this gives

Real cost of capital = (1 + 0.15)/(1 + 0.10)
= 1.15/1.10 = 0.045 or 4.5%

We will obtain the same answer except for rounding errors ($5,490 vs. $5,580). Refer to table below.

CAPITAL EXPENDITURE
A capital expenditure is one that will benefit one year or more. It can increase the quantity or quality of services to be derived from an asset. It is charged to an asset account. An example is an addition to a fixed asset that is then depreciated. Rearrangement and relocation costs of existing assets may also be deferred if they have future benefit. *Note:* An *immaterial* expenditure even though benefiting more than one year (e.g., door knob) may be expensed.

In taxation, a capital expenditure has to be added to the cost basis of the asset. *See also* Revenue Expenditure.

CAPITAL INTENSIVE
This is a business with substantial investment in property, plant, and equipment. The auto industry, for instance, is capital intensive in nature. There is much downside risk with a capital intensive firm because if revenue declines, earnings will drastically fall since in the short run, fixed cost cannot be cut to adjust to reduction in demand. However, there does exist upside potential since an increase in revenue, with fixed costs being constant, results in a sharp increase in profits. The following diagram is revealing:

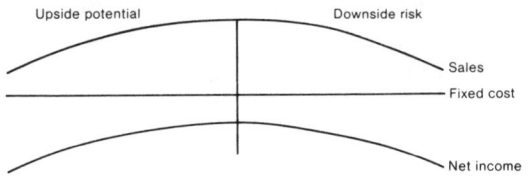

See also Labor Intensive.

CAPITALIZATION OF INTEREST
This refers to interest incurred on debt funds needed to self-construct an asset (e.g., machine) or to construct an asset intended for sale or lease that is a discrete project (e.g., real estate, ship). The interest is capitalized to the asset account involved and amortized over the life of the asset. Capitalized interest applies to the firm's actual borrowings and interest incurrence. The applicable interest rate for computational purposes is the interest on the particular borrowing for that asset. If not ascertainable, the weighted-average interest rate on the entity's obligations would be employed.

The capitalization period commences when *all* of the following are satisfied:

Period	Cash Flows	PVIF = $1/(1 + 0.045)^n$	Present Values
0	−100	1.000	−100
1	35	1/(1 + 0.045) = 0.957	33.50
2	50	1/(1.045)² = 0.916	45.80
3	30	1/(1.045)³ = 0.876	26.28
		NPV =	5.58 or $5,580

• Expenditures have been made.
• Activities required to get the asset ready for intended use are in progress.
• Interest is being incurred.

■ **Example**

A company acquires land for the construction of a new facility through construction loans. The interest cost incurred on the loans would be capitalized for each accounting period as long as it does not exceed the total interest cost incurred by the enterprise in that period. Capitalization ceases when the facility is substantially complete and ready for use.

CAPITAL LEASE Although the lessee does not legally own rental property, such property is theoretically acquired and recorded as an asset with the related liability. *See also* Leases.

CAPITAL MARKETS These are the markets for long-term debt and corporate stocks. The New York Stock Exchange (NYSE), which trades the stocks of many of the larger corporations, is a prime example of a capital market. The American Stock Exchange and regional stock exchanges are also examples. In addition, securities are issued and traded through the thousands of brokers and dealers on the *over-the-counter* market. *See also* Financial Institutions and Markets.

CAPITAL RATIONING Many firms specify a limit on the overall budget for capital spending. Capital rationing is concerned with the problem of selecting the mix of acceptable projects that provides the highest overall NPV. The *profitability index* is used widely in ranking projects competing for limited funds.

■ **Example**

A company with a fixed budget of $250,000 needs to select a mix of acceptable projects from the table shown at bottom of the page.

The ranking resulting from the profitability index shows that the company should select projects A, B, and D.

	I	*PV*
A	$ 70,000	$112,000
B	100,000	145,000
D	60,000	79,000
	$230,000	$336,000

The overall profitability index for the best combination is

$$\$336,000/\$230,000 = 1.46$$

Therefore:

$$NPV = \$336,000 - \$230,000 = \$106,000$$

Unfortunately, the profitability index method has some limitations. One of the more serious is that it breaks down whenever more than one resource is rationed. In this case, the use of zero–one programming is suggested. *See also* Project Selection and Zero–One Programming.

CASH BASIS This is an acceptable accounting method that recognizes revenue and expenses at the time of cash receipt or payment. The

Projects	*I*	*PV*	*NPV*	Profitability Index	Ranking
A	$ 70,000	$112,000	$42,000	1.6	1
B	100,000	145,000	45,000	1.45	2
C	110,000	126,500	16,500	1.15	5
D	60,000	79,000	19,000	1.32	3
E	40,000	38,000	−2,000	0.95	6
F	80,000	95,000	15,000	1.19	4

cash basis may be used in the case where a company deals in inventory *only* if there is an uncertain realization of the sale. If inventory is not involved, such as a service-oriented business, the cash basis may be chosen. In the preparation of a tax return for an individual, the cash basis is typically used. *See also* Accrual Basis.

CASH BREAK-EVEN POINT

If a firm has a minimum of available cash or the opportunity cost of holding excess cash is high, management may want to know the volume of sales that will cover all cash expenses during a period. This is known as the cash break-even point.

Not all fixed operating costs involve cash payments. For example, depreciation expense is a noncash charge. To find the cash break-even point, the noncash charges must be subtracted from total fixed operating costs. Therefore, the cash break-even point is lower than the usual break-even point. The formula is

$$x = \frac{FC - d}{p - v}$$

where p = selling price per unit,
v = unit variable cost,
FC = fixed operating costs,
and d = depreciation expense.

▪ Example

The XYZ Company manufactures and sells doors to home builders. The doors are sold for $25 each. Variable costs are $15 per door, and fixed operating costs total $50,000, which includes depreciation in the amount of $2,000. Then the company's cash break-even point is

$$x = \frac{FC - d}{p - v}$$

$$= \frac{\$50,000 - \$2,000}{\$25 - \$15} = \frac{\$48,000}{\$10} = 4,800 \text{ doors}$$

The company has to sell 4,800 doors to cover only the fixed costs involving cash payments of $48,000 and to break even. *See also* Cost-Volume-Profit (CVP) and Break-Even Analysis; Leverage.

CASH BUDGET

This is a budget for cash planning and control presenting expected cash inflow and outflow for a designated time period. The cash budget helps management keep cash balances in reasonable relationship to its needs. It aids in avoiding idle cash and possible cash shortages. To meet its main objective, sound projections of cash collections from customers and cash expenditures are necessary. *See also* Budgeting for Profit Planning.

CASH MANAGEMENT

The purpose of cash management is to invest excess cash for a return and at the same time have adequate liquidity to meet future needs. The proper cash balance should exist, neither excessive nor deficient. Do you know how much cash you need, how much you have, and where the cash is? Proper cash forecasting is needed to determine (1) the optimal time to incur and pay back debt and (2) the amount to transfer daily between accounts. *Recommendation:* Analyze each bank account as to type, balance, and cost. Do not have an excessive cash balance because no return is earned. When quick liquidity is needed, invest in marketable securities.

Factors in Determining the Amount of Cash to Be Held

• Your utility preferences regarding liquidity risk
• Proper use of cash management
• Expected future cash flows, considering the probabilities of different cash flows under alternative circumstances
• Maturity period of debt
• Your ability to borrow on short notice and on favorable terms
• Probability of different cash flows under varying circumstances

What to Watch Out for: Having an "excessive" line of credit with the bank, which involves a commitment fee. Watch the amount of the compensating balance, since the portion of a loan that serves as collateral is restricted and unavailable for your use. Is cash unnecessarily tied up in other accounts (e.g., loans to employees, insurance deposits)? *Warning:* Liquid asset holdings are required during a downturn in a company's cycle, when funds from operations decline.

Recommendation: Do not seek to fund peak seasonal cash requirements internally. Rather, borrow on a short-term basis to enable internal funds to be used more profitably throughout the year, such as by investing in plant and equipment.

Acceleration of Cash Inflow

You should evaluate the causes and take corrective action for delays in having cash receipts deposited. *What to Do:* Ascertain how and where cash receipts come, how cash is transferred from outlying accounts to the main corporate account, and banking policy regarding availability of funds.

Types of Delays in Processing Checks

• *Mail float*—the time required for a check to move from debtor to creditor.

• *Processing float*—the time needed for the creditor to enter the payment.

• *Deposit collection float*—the time for a check to clear.

Means of Accelerating Cash Receipts

• Lockbox arrangement, where the collection point is placed near customers. Customer payments are mailed to strategic post office boxes geographically situated to hasten mailing and depositing time. Banks collect from these boxes several times a day and make deposits to the corporate account. *Recommendation:* Undertake a cost-benefit analysis to ensure that instituting a lockbox arrange-

ment will result in net savings. Determine the average face value of checks received, cost of operations eliminated, reducible overhead, reduction in mail float days, and per-item processing cost. *Tip:* Compare the returned earned on freed cash to the cost of the lockbox arrangement.

• Concentration banking, where funds are collected in local banks and transferred to a main concentration account.

• Transfer funds between banks by wire.

• Accelerate billing.

• Send customers preaddressed, stamped envelopes.

• Require deposits on large or custom orders or progress billings as the work progresses.

• Charge interest on accounts receivable after a certain amount of time.

• Use personal collection efforts.

• Offer discounts for each payment.

• Have postdated checks from customers.

• Have cash-on-delivery terms.

• Deposit checks immediately.

■ Example

You are determining whether to initiate a lockbox arrangement that will cost $150,000 annually. Its average daily collections are $700,000. The system will reduce mailing and processing time by 2 days. Your rate of return is 14%.

Return on freed cash (14% × 2 × $700,000)	$196,000
Annual cost	150,000
Net advantage of lockbox system	$ 46,000

■ Example

You presently have a lockbox arrangement with bank A in which it handles $5 million a day in return for an $800,000 compensating balance. You are thinking of canceling this arrangement and further dividing your western region by entering into contracts with two other banks. Bank B will handle $3 mil-

lion a day in collections with a compensating balance of $700,000, and bank C will handle $2 million a day with a compensating balance of $600,000. Collections will be half a day quicker than the current situation. Your return rate is 12%.

Accelerated cash receipts ($5 million per day × 0.5 day)	$2,500,000
Increased compensating balance	500,000
Improved cash flow	$2,000,000
Rate of return	× 0.12
Net annual savings	$ 240,000

Delay of Cash Outlay

You should delay cash payments to earn a greater return on your money. Evaluate who your payees are and to what extent you can reasonably stretch time limits.

Ways of Delaying Cash Payments

• Centralize the payables operation so that debt may be paid at the most profitable time and so that the amount of disbursement float in the system may be ascertained.

• Make partial payments.

• Use payment drafts, where payment is *not* made on demand. Instead, the draft is presented for collection to the bank, which in turn goes to the issuer for acceptance. When approved, the company deposits the funds. *Net Result:* Less of a required checking balance.

• Draw checks on remote banks (e.g., a New York company can use a Texas bank).

• Mail from post offices with limited service or where mail has to go through numerous handling points. *Tip:* If you utilize float properly, you can maintain higher bank balances than the actual lower book balances. For instance, if you write checks averaging $200,000 per day and three days are necessary for them to clear, you will have a $600,000 checking balance less than the bank's records.

• Use probability analysis to determine the expected date for checks to clear. *Suggestion:* Have separate checking accounts (e.g., payroll, dividends) and monitor check-clearing dates. For example, payroll checks are not all cashed on the payroll date, so funds can be deposited later to earn a return.

• Use a computer terminal to transfer funds between various bank accounts at opportune times.

• Use a charge account to lengthen the time between buying goods and paying for them.

• Stretch payments as long as possible as long as there is no associated finance charge or impairment in credit rating.

• Do not pay bills before due dates.

• Utilize noncash compensation and remuneration methods (e.g., stock).

• Delay the frequency of your company payrolls.

• Disburse commissions on sales when the receivables are collected rather than when they are made.

■ Example

Every 2 weeks you disburse checks that average $500,000 and take 3 days to clear. You want to find out how much money you can save annually if you delay transfer of funds from an interest-bearing account that pays 0.0384% per day (annual rate of 14%) for those 3 days.

$$\$500,000 \times (0.000384 \times 3) = \$576$$

The savings per year is $576 × 26 (yearly payrolls) = $14,976.

Cash Models

William Baumol developed a model to determine the optimum amount of transaction cash under conditions of certainty. The objective is to minimize the sum of the fixed costs associated with transactions *and* the opportu-

nity cost of holding cash balances. These costs are expressed as

$$F \cdot \left(\frac{T}{C}\right) + i\left(\frac{C}{2}\right)$$

where F = the fixed cost of a transaction,

T = the total cash needed for the time period involved,

i = the interest rate on marketable securities,

C = cash balance.

The optimal level of cash is determined using the following formula:

$$C^* = \sqrt{\frac{2FT}{i}}$$

A helpful graph follows:

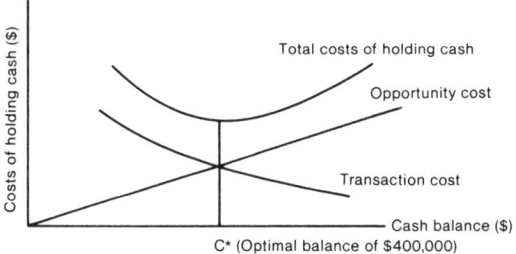

■ Example

You estimate a cash need for $4,000,000 over a 1-month period where the cash account is expected to be disbursed at a constant rate. The opportunity interest rate is 6% per annum, or 0.5% for a 1-month period. The transaction cost each time you borrow or withdraw is $100.

The optimal transaction size (the optimal borrowing or withdrawal lot size) and the number of transactions you should make during the month follow:

$$C^* = \sqrt{\frac{2FT}{i}} = \sqrt{\frac{2(100)(4,000,000)}{0.005}} = \$400,000$$

The optimal transaction size is $400,000.

The average cash balance is

$$\frac{C^*}{2} = \frac{\$400,000}{2} = \$200,000$$

The number of transactions required are

$$\frac{\$4,000,000}{\$400,000} = 10 \text{ transactions during the month}$$

You can use a stochastic model for cash management where major uncertainty exists regarding cash payments. The Miller-Orr model places an upper and lower limit for cash balances. When the upper limit is reached, a transfer of cash to marketable securities is made. When the lower limit is reached, a transfer from securities to cash takes place. A transaction will not occur as long as the cash balance falls within the limits.

Factors taken into account in the Miller-Orr model are the fixed costs of a securities transaction (F), assumed to be the same for buying as well as selling, the daily interest rate on marketable securities (i), and the variance of daily net cash flows (σ^2). The objective is to meet cash requirements at the lowest possible cost. A major assumption is the randomness of cash flows. The two control limits in the Miller-Orr model may be specified as d dollars as an upper limit and zero dollars at the lower limit. When the cash balance reaches the upper level, d less z dollars of securities are bought and the new balance becomes z dollars. When the cash balance equals zero, z dollars of securities are sold and the new balance again reaches z. Of course, practically speaking you should note that the minimum cash balance is established at an amount greater than zero due to delays in transfer as well as to having a safety buffer.

The optimal cash balance z is computed as follows:

$$z = \sqrt[3]{\frac{3F\sigma^2}{4i}}$$

The optimal value for d is computed as $3z$.

The average cash balance will approximate $\frac{(z + d)}{3}$.

■ Example

You wish to use the Miller-Orr model. The following information is supplied:

Fixed cost of a securities transaction	$10
Variance of daily net cash flows	50
Daily interest rate on securities (10%/360)	0.0003

The optimal cash balance, the upper limit of cash needed, and the average cash balance follow:

$$z = \sqrt[3]{\frac{3(10)(50)}{4(0.0003)}} = \sqrt[3]{\frac{3(10)(50)}{0.0012}}$$

$$= \sqrt[3]{\frac{1,500}{0.0012}} = \sqrt[3]{1,250,000} = \$102$$

The optimal cash balance is $102.
The upper limit is $306 (3 × $102).
The average cash balance is $136 $\frac{(\$102 + \$306)}{3}$.

A brief elaboration on these findings is needed for clarification. When the upper limit of $306 is reached, $204 of securities ($306 − $102) will be purchased to bring you to the optimal cash balance of $102. When the lower limit of zero dollars is reached, $102 of securities will be sold to again bring you to the optimal cash balance of $102.

An informative graph follows:

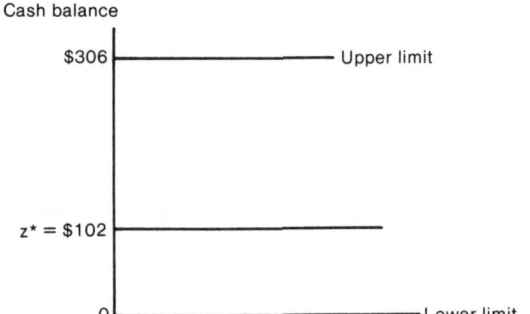

Cash balance

$306 ——————— Upper limit

z* = $102

0 ——————— Lower limit

CASH SURRENDER VALUE OF LIFE INSURANCE
This is the sum payable upon cancellation of the policy by the insured; the insured will of course receive less than the premiums paid in. Cash surrender value is classified under long-term investments. It applies to ordinary life and limited payment policies. It is *not* usually applicable to term insurance. The insurance premium payment consists of two elements—expense and cash surrender value.

■ Example

A premium of $6,000 is paid that increases the cash surrender value by $2,000. The appropriate entry is

Life Insurance Expense	4,000	
Cash Surrender Value of Life Insurance	2,000	
Cash		6,000

The gain on a life insurance policy is *not* typically considered an extraordinary item since it is in the ordinary course of business. *See also* Insurance Programs.

CASUALTY INSURANCE
This covers such items as fire loss and water damage. The premiums are usually paid in advance and debited to Prepaid Insurance, which is then amortized over the policy period. Casualty insurance reimburses the holder for the fair market value of property lost. Insurance companies typically have a coinsurance clause so that the insured bears part of the loss. The insurance reimbursement formula follows (assumes an 80% coinsurance clause):

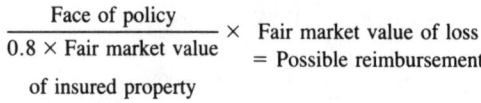

$$\frac{\text{Face of policy}}{0.8 \times \text{Fair market value}} \times \text{Fair market value of loss}$$
$$\text{of insured property} = \text{Possible reimbursement}$$

Insurance reimbursement is based on the lower of the face of the policy, fair market value of loss, or possible reimbursement.

■ **Example**

Case	Face of Policy	Fair Market Value of Property	Fair Market Value of Loss
A	$ 4,000	$10,000	$ 6,000
B	6,000	10,000	10,000
C	10,000	10,000	4,000

Insurance reimbursement follows:

Case A:

$$\frac{\$4,000}{0.8 \times \$10,000} \times \$6,000 = \boxed{\$ 3,000}$$

Case B:

$$\frac{\boxed{\$6,000}}{0.8 \times \$10,000} \times \$10,000 = \$7,500$$

Case C:

$$\frac{\$10,000}{0.8 \times \$10,000} \times \boxed{\$4,000} = \$5,000$$

A blanket policy covers several items of property. The face of the policy is allocated based upon the fair market values of the insured assets.

■ **Example**

A blanket policy of $15,000 applies to equipment I and equipment II. The fair values of equipment I and II are $30,000 and $15,000, respectively. Equipment II is partially destroyed, resulting in a fire loss of $3,000.

The policy allocation to equipment II is computed below:

	Fair Market Value	Policy
Equipment I	$30,000	$10,000
Equipment II	15,000	5,000
	$45,000	$15,000

The insurance reimbursement is

$$\frac{\$5,000}{0.8 \times \$15,000} \times \$3,000 = \boxed{\$1,500}$$

When a fire loss occurs, the asset destroyed has to be removed from the accounts, with the resulting fire loss recorded based on book value. The insurance reimbursement

reduces the fire loss. The fire loss is an extraordinary item (net of tax).

■ **Example**

The following fire loss information exists for ABC Company. Merchandise costing $5,000 is fully destroyed. There is no insurance for it. Furniture costing $10,000 with accumulated depreciation of $1,000 and having a fair market value of $7,000 is entirely destroyed. The policy is for $10,000. Building costing $30,000 with accumulated depreciation of $3,000 and having a fair market value of $20,000 is 50% destroyed. The face of the policy is $15,000. The journal entries to record the book loss follow:

Fire Loss	5,000	
Inventory		5,000
Fire Loss	9,000	
Accumulated Depreciation	1,000	
Furniture		10,000
Fire Loss	13,500	
Accumulated Depreciation	1,500	
Building		15,000

Insurance reimbursement totals $16,375, computed as follows:

Furniture:

$$\frac{\$10,000}{0.8 \times \$7,000} \times \boxed{\$7,000} = \$12,500$$

Building:

$$\frac{\$15,000}{0.8 \times \$20,000} \times \$10,000 = \boxed{\$9,375}$$

The journal entry for the insurance reimbursement is

Cash	16,375	
Fire Loss		16,375

The net fire loss is $11,125 ($27,500 − $16,375), which will typically be shown as an extraordinary item. *See also* Insurance Programs.

CASUALTY LOSS This is the loss due to fire, theft, or other casualty. The loss after insurance reimbursement is reported in the income statement as an extraordinary item (net of tax effect). The loss account is based on the book value of the assets destroyed. If insurance reimbursement, which is based on appraised value, exceeds the book value of assets destroyed or damaged, a net gain will occur. *See also* Insurance Programs.

CERTAINTY EQUIVALENTS Certainty equivalent is the amount of cash (or rate of return) that a decision maker would require *with certainty* to make the recipient indifferent between this certain sum and a particular *uncertain*, *risky* sum. Multiplying the expected cash inflow by the certainty cash equivalent coefficient results in an *equivalent certain* cash inflow.

CHARTING Investment analysts can use charts to appraise volume and price behavior of the overall market as well as individual securities. Charting information for many stocks may be gotten from Standard and Poor's *Trendline*. The interpretation of charts requires an evaluation of formations and identifying buy and sell signs. *Caution*: Analysts may differ somewhat in their interpretations even though they are looking at a particular chart pattern. *See also* Technical Analysis.

CHECK DIGIT The check digit is appended to a number in order for the auditor to determine if that number is accurate when read or written. The digit involves a computation performed to that number. When the number is used in processing, a recalculation is made to assure that the computed check digit is identical to the original number. If the numbers do not match, there is an error indicated, perhaps arising from transposition or omission.

CLASSICAL VARIABLES SAMPLING This is comprised of a family of three statistical techniques (mean per unit approach, difference sampling, and ratio sampling) that use normal distribution theory and are concerned with ascertaining whether account balances are properly stated. The method estimates the statistical range within which the true account balance being tested falls. It requires an estimate of population variability (population standard deviation) and necessitates the use of a computer. The technique predicts what the value of a particular variable in the population will be. Audit-related variables are usually the total population or the arithmetic mean. For example, an auditor may estimate the cost of a group of inventory components. The approach may also be used to estimate the dollar amount of error in a population. *See also* Probability Proportional to Size (PPS) Sampling; Sampling.

CLOSELY HELD CORPORATION This is a corporation that has only a few stockholders. It contrasts with a privately held corporation in that a closely held corporation is public although most of the shares are not traded. The so-called corporate pocketbooks may become subject to the additional personal holding company tax on income not distributed. For example, deductions and losses in transactions between a major stockholder and the corporation may be disallowed under certain circumstances.

CLUSTER SAMPLING Cluster sampling generally applies to samples of physical units in the case where a dollar-value estimate is needed. Groups (clusters) rather than individual items are selected at a random starting point in the population.

■ Example

Twenty-five groups of 10 consecutively numbered invoices are selected, starting

with each of 15 randomly selected invoices.

Selection can be made of more than one item at a time. Each cluster becomes a sampling unit. Once the suitable number of clusters is chosen, the auditor may audit all items in the cluster (one-stage) or a random number of items in the cluster (two-stage). The mean for the individual sampling units is determined and is multiplied by the number of units in the population to arrive at the population's estimated value. A precision limit on this estimate must also be determined. With cluster sampling, there is a reduction in sampling cost because sample selection is facilitated. On the negative side, there is less statistical efficiency. Cluster sampling can be used to measure a variable (e.g., inventory value, accounts receivable balance). Attributes may also be measured. *See also* Sampling.

CODE OF PROFESSIONAL ETHICS
The Code of Professional Ethics are the rules of conduct for certified public accountants in conducting their responsibilities to the public. Ethical regulations are published by the American Institute of CPAs and each state society. An example of an ethical violation is when a CPA issues an audit opinion even though he or she lacks independence. A lack of independence occurs, for example, when the CPA owns stock in the client or is associated with the company as a director. Another ethical violation is when the CPA fails to exercise due professional care in the audit engagement. GAAS must be followed in performing the attest function. Further, the CPA is not permitted to accept a contingent fee based on the findings of his or her services. If the accountant is in violation of an ethical standard, he or she faces disciplinary action.

COEFFICIENT OF DETERMINATION
This is a statistical measure of how good the estimated regression equation is, designated as r^2 (read as r-squared). Simply put, it is a measure of "goodness of fit" in the regression. Therefore, the higher the r-squared, the more confi-

dence we have in our equation. Statistically, the coefficient of determination represents the proportion of the total variation in the dependent variable that is explained by the regression equation. It has the range of values between 0 and 1.

■ Example

The statement "price/earnings ratio is a function of sales with $r^2 = 0.30$," can be interpreted as "only 30% of the total variation in the price/earnings ratio is explained by sales and the remaining 70% is still unexplained." This suggests inclusion of more explanatory variables (e.g., beta and asset size) in the regression equation in order to improve predictive power of the relationship. *See also* Regression Analysis.

COEFFICIENT OF VARIATION
This is a measure of relative dispersion, or relative risk. It is computed by dividing the standard deviation (σ) by the expected value ($\bar{x}$). *See also* Decision Making Under Uncertainty.

COINCIDENT INDICATORS
These are the types of economic indicator series that tend to move up and down in line with the aggregate economy and therefore are measures of current economic activity. Examples are gross national product (GNP), retail sales, and industrial production. *See also* Economic Indicators.

COLLECTIBLES
These include art, rare stamps, valuable coins, antiques, and books. They provide profit potential and aesthetic enjoyment. To invest in collectibles, one must know well current market conditions and the factors affecting price. Purchase of collectibles may be made through dealers, auction, or directly from prior owners. Disadvantages to owning collectibles are high insurance costs, lack of immediate marketability, high transaction costs, and possible forgeries. Information regarding collectibles may be found in *Money, Collector/Investor,* and *Antique Monthly.*

COMMITMENT An expected expenditure supported by a purchase order or contract given to an external party. A commitment is not reflected in the accounting records. Footnote disclosure is required of the nature of the commitment and amount.

COMMODITIES FUTURES CONTRACTS The seller of a commodity contract guarantees to deliver a particular commodity by a specified date at a predetermined price. The contract indicates the item, price, expiration date (up to 1 year), and the standardized unit to be traded (e.g., 100,000 lbs). The investor has to closely monitor the financial impact of market price changes in the commodity as it affects the contract's value.

Assume one purchases a futures contract for delivery of 1,000 units of a commodity 6 months from now at $5 per unit. The seller of the contract need not take physical possession of the item, and the contract buyer does not have to take custody of the commodity at the "delivery" date. Usually, there is reversal of commodity contracts or termination before their consummation. For example, as an initial buyer of 1,000 bushels of corn, one may engage in a similar contract to sell the same quantity so that the position is effectively closed out.

The following table reveals the unit size of some commodity contracts:

Unit Size of Some Commodity Contracts

Contract	Contract Stated in
Cattle	40,000 lbs
Coffee	37,500 lbs
Cotton	50,000 lbs
Sugar	112,000 lbs
Wheat	5,000 bushels

The investor can directly acquire a commodity or have indirect ownership via a mutual fund. Another possibility is purchasing a limited partnership dealing in commodity investments. The more conservative approaches are mutual fund and partnership involvement because of diversification and management expertise.

An investor may undertake commodity trading to obtain high return or hedge against inflation. In inflation, commodities do well because they are tied into economic trends. *Warning*: There exists high risk and uncertainty due to the variability in commodity prices and the small down payment. *Caution*: The investor should have significant cash in reserve in case of a margin call to cover losses. Minimization of risk can be achieved by diversification. *Recommendation*: Be sure to ascertain the honesty and reliability of the commodities representatives (e.g., salespeople).

The purchaser of a commodity may terminate the contract or let it continue to obtain more profits. Alternatively, the investor may use profits earned to put up margin on another futures contract. The latter is termed an inverse pyramid in a futures contract.

Commodity futures exchanges permit buyers and sellers to negotiate cash (spot) prices. Cash is paid for immediately receiving physical possession of a commodity. Prices in the cash market are based to some extent on prices in the futures market. In fact, cash prices for commodities are close to prices in the short-term futures market. There may exist higher prices for the commodity over time, incorporating holding costs and expected inflation.

Commodity and financial futures are traded in the Chicago Board of Trade, which is the largest exchange. There exist other exchanges (e.g., Amex Commodities Exchange), some specializing in particular commodities. An example is the New York Cotton Exchange. Because of the possibility of significant gain and loss in commodities, there are exchange limitations on the highest price change for a commodity in a given day. The federal government's Commodity Futures Trading Commission regulates the commodities exchanges.

The financial pages of many newspapers (e.g., *The Wall Street Journal*) give the starting, high, low, and closing (settle) prices for the day, as well as the commodity's price change. In addition, the all-time high and low are given. Open interest refers to the number of outstanding futures contracts for the commodity and the expiration dates. An illustrative table is presented below.

The return on a futures contract is derived from capital gain (selling price less purchase price) because no current income is involved. There is significant capital gain potential because of price variability in the commodity and the effect of leverage arising from a low margin requirement. *Warning*: There also exists the possibility of losing all the margin put down quickly if commodity prices go against you. The return on investment equals:

$$\frac{\text{Selling price} - \text{Purchase price}}{\text{Margin deposit}}$$

■ Example

An investor buys a contract on a commodity for $70,000 giving an initial deposit of $7,000. The contract is subsequently sold for $75,000. The return equals:

$$\frac{\$75,000 - \$70,000}{\$7,000} = \frac{\$5,000}{\$7,000} = 71.4\%$$

Margin requirements for commodity contracts are relatively low, typically ranging from 5% to 10% of the contract's value. In commodities trading, no funds are being borrowed so there is no interest charge.

An initial margin is necessary as a deposit on the futures contract. The reason for the deposit is to cover a price decline on the contract. The amount of the deposit varies with the type of contract and the commodity exchange involved.

There is also a maintenance deposit that is lower than the initial deposit and provides the minimum margin that has to be kept in the account. It typically is about 80% of the initial margin.

■ Example

On July 1, an investor enters into a contract to purchase 37,500 pounds of coffee at $6 a pound to be delivered by October 1. The contract has a total value of $225,000. The initial margin requirement is 10%, or $22,500. The margin maintenance requirement is 60%, or $13,500. If a contract loss of $2,000 occurs, an additional $2,000 has to be remitted to cover the margin position. If not, the contract is terminated with the ensuing loss.

■ Example

An investor makes an initial deposit of $10,000 on a contract and a maintenance deposit of $7,500. If the market value of the contract does not decrease by more than $2,500, there is no problem. But if the market value of the contract declines by $4,500, the margin or deposit will go to $5,500, and the investor will have to deposit another $5,500 in order to keep the sum at the initial deposit level. If the investor does not come up with the additional $5,500, the contract will be canceled.

There are different forms of commodity

Commodity Quotes

Open	High	Low	Settle	Change	Lifetime High	Lifetime Low	Open Interest
Cotton (CTN)—50,000 lbs, cents per lb							
July 65.32	65.32	64.55	64.62	−0.64	79.85	63.86	5887
Oct. 63.80	63.80	63.51	63.53	−0.20	77.50	63.51	1555
Dec. 63.75	63.78	63.50	63.60	−0.15	73.00	63.50	6247

trading, including hedging, speculating, and spreading.

Hedging is used to protect a position in a commodity. For example, a fruit grower (seller) will hedge to obtain a higher price for his products, whereas a processor (or buyer) of the item will hedge to obtain a lower price. Although hedging is a conservative strategy that reduces the risk of loss, it also restricts gain potential.

■ Example

A commodity is presently selling for $120 a pound, but a potential buyer (manufacturer) anticipates a future price increase. To protect against higher prices, the buyer acquires a futures contract selling at $135 a pound. Six months later, the price of the commodity reaches $180 a pound. The futures contract price will similarly rise to, say $210. The buyer's profit is $75 a pound. If 5,000 pounds are involved, the total profit is $375,000. At the same time, the cost of the market increased by only $60 per pound, or $300,000. In effect, the manufacturer hedged his position, coming out with a profit of $75,000, and has controlled the increasing costs of the commodity.

Speculators also invest in commodities.

■ Example

An investor buys an October futures contract for 37,500 pounds of coffee at $5 a pound. If the price increases to $5.40, he will gain $0.40 a pound for a total gain of $15,000. The percentage gain, considering the initial margin requirement, is 80%. If the transactions occurred over a 2-month period, the annual gain would be 480%. This arose from only a 7.4% gain in the price of coffee.

In spreading, there is an attempt to profit from swings in price and at the same time limit loss exposure. The investor engages in two or more contracts to get some profit while restricting loss. The investor buys one contract and sells the other, expecting to ob-

tain a minimal but reasonable profit. In the worst case scenario, the spread will reduce the investor's loan.

■ Example

An investor buys Contract 1 for 10,000 pounds of Commodity Z at $500 a pound. At the same time, he sells short Contract 2 for 10,000 pounds of the same commodity at $535 a pound. Later, he sells Contract 1 for $520 a pound and buys Contract 2 for $543 a pound. Contract 1 yields a profit of $20 a pound, while Contract 2 involves a loss of $8 a pound. On net, however, the investor earns a profit of $12 a pound, so the total gain is $120,000.

COMMON-SIZE FINANCIAL STATEMENT A common-size financial statement is one expressed in percentages of a base, instead of in dollars. The base for the income statement is net sales, whereas for the balance sheet it is either total assets or total liabilities plus stockholders' equity. The percentages permit relative comparisons among companies of varying sizes. Also indicated are abnormal variations of a particular company's statistics to industry norms. *See also* Vertical Analysis.

COMMON STOCK EQUIVALENT A common stock equivalent is a security that can become common stock at a later date and as such is included in the computation of earnings per share. Examples are stock options, stock warrants, and convertible securities whose yield at the time of issuance is less than 66⅔% of the Aa corporate bond yield. *See also* Earnings per Share.

COMMON STOCK VALUATION The process of determining security valuation involves finding the present value of an asset's expected future cash flows using the investor's required rate of return. Thus, the basic security valuation model can be defined mathematically as follows:

$$V = \sum_{t=1}^{n} \frac{C_t}{(1+r)^t}$$

where V = intrinsic value or present value of an asset,

C_t = expected future cash flows in period $t = 1, \ldots, n,$

r = investor's required rate of return.

Like bonds, the value of a common stock is the present value of all future cash inflows expected to be received by the investor. The cash inflows expected to be received are dividends and the future selling price. For an investor holding a common stock for only 1 year, the value of the stock would be the present value of both the expected cash dividend to be received in 1 year (D_1) and the expected market price per share of the stock at year-end (P_1).

If r represents an investor's required rate of return, the value of common stock (P_o) would be:

$$P_o = \frac{D_1}{(1+r)^1} + \frac{P_1}{(1+r)^1}$$

■ Example 1

Assume an investor is considering the purchase of stock A at the beginning of the year. The dividend at year-end is expected to be $1.50, and the market price by the end of the year is expected to be $40. If the investor's required rate of return is 15%, the value of the stock would be:

$$P_o = \frac{D_1}{(1+r)^1} + \frac{P_1}{(1+r)^1} = \frac{\$1.50}{(1+0.15)} + \frac{\$40}{(1+0.15)}$$

$$= \$1.50(0.870) + \$40(0.870) = \$1.31 + \$34.80$$

$$= \$36.11$$

Since common stock has no maturity date and is held for many years, a more general, multiperiod model is needed. The general common stock valuation model is defined as follows:

$$P_o = \sum_{t=1}^{\infty} \frac{D_1}{(1+r)^t}$$

The model is based on the concept that a common stock is worth the present value of future dividends. However, future dividends may grow with three different patterns, as follows:

1. Zero growth
2. Constant growth
3. Nonconstant, or supernormal, growth

Zero growth. If dividends are expected to remain unchanged, i.e.,

$$D_o = D_1 = \ldots = D$$

then the above model reduces to the formula:

$$P_o = \frac{D}{r}$$

This is the case with a perpetuity. This model is most applicable to the valuation of preferred stocks or the common stocks of very mature companies such as big municipal utilities.

■ Example 2

Assuming D equals $2.50 and r equals 10%, then the value of the stock is

$$P_o = \frac{\$2.50}{0.1} = \$25$$

Constant growth. If we assume that dividends grow at a constant rate of g every year [i.e., $D_t = D_o(1 + g)^t$], then the previous model is simplified to

$$P_o = \frac{D_1}{r - g}$$

This formula is known as the Gordon's growth model. This model is most applicable to the valuation of the common stock of very large or broadly diversified companies.

■ Example 3

Consider a common stock that paid a $3 dividend per share at the end of the last year and is expected to pay a cash dividend every year at a growth rate of 10%. Assume the investor's required rate of return is 12%. The value of the stock would be

$$D_1 = D_o(1 + g) = \$3(1 + 0.10) = \$3.30$$

$$P_o = \frac{D_1}{r - g} = \frac{\$3.30}{0.12 - 0.10} = \$165$$

Nonconstant, or supernormal, growth. Firms typically go through life cycles, during part of which their growth is faster than that of the economy and then falls sharply.

The value of stock during such supernormal growth can be found by taking the following steps: (1) compute the dividends during the period of supernormal growth and find their present value; (2) find the price of the stock at the end of the supernormal growth period and compute its present value; and (3) add these two *PV* figures to find the value (P_o) of the common stock.

■ Example 4

Consider a common stock whose dividends are expected to grow at a rate of 25% for 2 years, after which the growth rate is expected to fall to 5%. The dividend paid last period was $2. The investor desires a 12% return. To find the value of this stock, take the following steps:
1. Compute the dividends during the supernormal growth period and find their present value. Assuming D_o is $2, g is 15%, and r is 12%:

$$D_1 = D_o(1 + g) = \$2(1 + 0.25) = \$2.50$$

$$D_2 = D_o(1 + g)^2 = \$2(1.563) = \$3.126$$

or $\quad D_2 = D_1(1 + g) = \$2.50(1.25) = \$3.126$

Therefore,

$$PV \text{ of dividends} = \frac{D_1}{(1 + r)^1} + \frac{D_2}{(1 + r)^2}$$

$$= \frac{\$2.50}{(1 + 0.12)^1} + \frac{\$3.125}{(1 + 0.12)^2}$$

$$= \$2.50(PVIF_{12\%,1})$$
$$+ \$3.125(PVIF_{12\%,2})$$

$$= \$2.50(0.893) + \$3.125(0.797)$$

$$= \$2.23 + \$2.49 = \$4.72$$

2. Find the price of the stock at the end of the supernormal growth period. The dividend for the third year is

$$D_3 = D_2(1 + g'), \text{ where } g' = 5\%$$
$$= \$3.125(1 + 0.05) = \$3.28$$

The price of the stock is therefore:

$$P_2 = \frac{D_3}{r - g'} = \frac{\$3.28}{0.12 - 0.05} = \$46.86$$

$$PV \text{ of stock price} = \$46.86$$
$$(PVIF_{12\%,2}) = \$46.86(0.797) = \$37.35$$

3. Add the two *PV* figures obtained in steps 1 and 2 to find the value of the stock.

$$P_o = \$4.72 + \$37.35 = \$42.07$$

Expected Rate of Return on Common Stock

The formula for computing the expected rate of return on common stock can be derived easily from the valuation models.

The single-period return formula is derived from

$$P_o = \frac{D_1}{(1 + r)} + \frac{P_1}{(1 + r)}$$

Solving for *r* gives:

$$r = \frac{D_1 + (P_1 - P_o)}{P_o}$$

In words,

$$\text{Rate of return} = \frac{\text{Dividends} + \text{Capital gain}}{\text{Beginning price}}$$

$$= \text{Dividend yield} + \text{Capital gain yield}$$

■ Example 5

Consider a stock that sells for $50. The company is expected to pay a $3 cash dividend at the end of the year, and the stock market price at the end of the year is expected to be $55 a share. Thus the expected return would be

$$r = \frac{D_1 + (P_1 - P_o)}{P_o} = \frac{\$3 + (\$55 - \$50)}{\$50}$$

$$= \frac{\$3 + \$5}{\$50} = 16\%$$

or:

$$\text{Dividend yield} = \frac{\$3}{\$50} = 6\%$$

$$\text{Capital gain yield} = \frac{\$5}{\$50} = 10\%$$

r = Dividend yield + Capital gain yield

= 6% + 10% = 16%

Assuming a constant growth in dividend, the formula for the expected rate of return on an investment in stock can be derived as follows:

$$P_o = \frac{D_1}{r - g}$$

$$r = \frac{D_1}{P_o} + g$$

■ Example 6

Suppose that ABC Company's dividend per share was $4.50, expected to grow at a constant rate of 6%. The current market price of the stock is $30. Then the expected rate of return is

$$r = \frac{D_1}{P_o} + g = \frac{\$4.50}{\$30} + 6\% = 15\% + 6\% = 21\%$$

The Price-Earnings Ratio—A Pragmatic Approach

The dividend valuation models discussed so far are best suited for those companies that are at the expansion or maturity stage of their life cycle. A more pragmatic approach to valuing a common stock is to use the P/E ratio (or multiple). Many common stock analysts use the simple formula:

Forecasted price at the end of year
= Estimated EPS in year t × Estimated P/E ratio

■ Example 7

The XYZ Corporation had EPS of $5. The EPS is expected to grow at 20%. The company's normal P/E ratio is estimated to be 7, which is used as the multiplier. The value of the stock is

Estimated EPS = $5(1 + 0.20) = $6.00

Therefore, the expected price of the stock is $6 × 7 = $42.

Of course, for this method to be effective in forecasting the future value of a stock, earnings need to be correctly projected and the appropriate P/E multiple must be applied.

Forecasts of EPS

Forecasting EPS is not an easy task. Many security analysts use a simple method of forecasting EPS. They use a sales forecast combined with an after-tax profit margin, as follows:

Estimated earnings in year t
= Estimated sales in year t
× After-tax profit margin expected in year t

Estimated EPS in year t
= Estimated earnings in year t/
Number of common shares outstanding in year t

More sophisticated methods of forecasting sales and earnings, such as linear regression, are available.

■ Example 8

Assume that in the year just ended, the XYZ Corporation reported sales of $60 million, and it is estimated that revenues will grow at a 4% annual rate, while the after-tax profit margin should amount to about 8%, and the number of common shares outstanding is 400,000 shares. Then:

Estimated earnings in year t
= $60 million × 0.04 = $2.4 million

Estimated EPS in year t
= $2.4 million/400,000 shares = $6 per share

Determinants of the P/E Ratio

What determines the P/E multiple is very complex. Empirical evidence seems to suggest the following factors:
- Historical growth rate in earnings
- Forecasted earnings
- Average dividend payout ratio
- Beta coefficient measuring the firm's systematic risk

- Instability of earnings
- Financial leverage
- Other factors such as competitive position, management ability, and economic conditions

COMMUNICATION WITH AUDIT COMMITTEES

According to Statement on Auditing Standards No. 61, the auditor must bring to the attention of the client's audit committee certain results of the audit, such as problems with the internal control structure and the occurrence of illegal acts. The communication may be written or oral. In the case of the latter, the auditor must have documentation such as workpaper references or relevant memoranda. The following areas should be communicated to the audit committee:

- Internal control weaknesses
- Material misstatements in the financial statements
- Degree of audit responsibility assumed
- Audit tests conducted
- Accounting policies used and changes therein
- Method used to reflect unusual material transactions
- Approach management uses in deriving sensitive accounting estimates, and the auditor's opinion as to the reasonableness of the estimates
- Significant audit objectives required, impacting the company's financial reporting process
- Auditor responsibility for other data included in documents containing audited financial statements
- Audit procedures undertaken and results thereof
- Disagreements between the auditor and management, and whether they have been resolved

COMPENSATED ABSENCES   These include sick leave, holiday, and vacation time. The employer shall accrue a liability for employee's compensation for future absences when *all* of the following criteria are met:

- Employee services have already been performed.
- Employee rights to pay have vested.
- Probable payment exists.
- Amount of estimated liability can reasonably be determined.

If the criteria are satisfied except that the amount is not determinable, only a footnote can be made since an accrual is not possible.

Accrual for sick leave is required only when the employer permits employees to take accumulated sick leave days off irrespective of actual illness. But no accrual is required if employees can only take accumulated days off for actual illness, since losses for these are typically immaterial.

FASB 43 is not applicable to

- Severance or termination pay
- Deferred compensation
- Post retirement benefits
- Stock option plans
- Other long-term fringe benefits (e.g., insurance, disability)

■ Example

Estimated compensation for future absences is $30,000. The entry is

Expense	30,000	
Estimated Liability		30,000

If at a later date a payment of $28,000 is made, the entry is

Estimated Liability	28,000	
Cash		28,000

■ Example

Employees are entitled to 2 weeks vacation each year. Mr. X began work on July 1, 19X1. He is entitled to the equivalent of 1 week of vacation, which will be accrued on 12/31/19X1.

COMPILATION   In a compilation, presented financial statement information is the representation of management or owners. There is

no audit opinion or other form of assurance given to the financial statements. As a result, the procedures conducted are very limited. In a compilation engagement, the practitioner should

- Obtain a letter of engagement.
- Obtain a knowledge of the accounting policies prevalent in the industry.
- Obtain an understanding of the nature of the client's transactions and accounting records.
- Evaluate the competency of client accounting personnel.
- Ascertain the basis of accounting used (e.g., accrual basis, cash basis).
- Determine if the client's books have to be adjusted.
- Obtain satisfaction regarding management representations that seem unsatisfactory and incorrect. *Note*: The practitioner does *not* have to verify management representations that appear logical.
- Modify the accountant's report if the client fails to prepare needed adjustments.
- Read the financial statements to assure that obvious errors do not exist, including departures from GAAP, insufficient footnotes, or mathematical errors.

The compilation report includes the following:

- Identification of the financial statements
- Statement that the compilation was conducted in accord with standards established by the AICPA
- Definition of a compilation, in that it is restricted to presenting in the form of financial statements information that is the representation of management (owners)
- Statement that the financial statements have *not* been audited or reviewed, and as such there is *no* opinion or any other form of assurance involved
- Date the compilation was completed
- Signature of accountant

Each page of the financial statements should be labeled, ''See accountant's compi-lation report.'' If desired, the accountant may expand the label to include the footnotes to the financial statements. Further, to eliminate any possible misinterpretation, the practitioner may mark each page of the financial statements, ''unaudited.'' *See also* Review.

COMPLIANCE AUDIT   A compliance audit examines specific activities for the purpose of ascertaining whether performance has been conducted as prescribed by a particular statute, contract, or specified purpose. An example is an audit of a physician's records to assure that proper charges have been made to the government.

COMPLIANCE TEST   Subsequent to the review of a client's system of internal control, compliance testing is performed, which is necessary so that the auditor is satisfied that prescribed internal controls are in proper operation. The results of compliance testing are obtained by inquiry, observation, and inspection. Compliance testing is necessary only for the internal controls that reliance is needed for. Often, attribute sampling is used to conduct compliance testing to result in economies of cost and time. The objective of the compliance test is to obtain reasonable assurance that a given control is performing properly. An example is verifying that the individual making out a check is different from the one who approves the payment after examining supplier invoices for accuracy. The auditor should be on the lookout for departures from prescribed controls. An example is the failure of a receiving department employee to verify that the quantity received agrees with the purchase order and, accordingly, failing to sign the receiving report. As a result of this departure in policy, an error may occur since substantiation has not taken place.

In appraising compliance-testing results, the auditor should take into account

• Potential and actual errors and irregularities.

• Controls and procedures to guard against errors and irregularities.

• Sufficiency of internal controls. A weakness in internal control exists when there does not exist reasonable reliance on a prescribed procedure to prevent or detect errors or irregularities.

Note: For audits of financial statements for periods beginning on or after January 1, 1990, the term *test of controls* will replace *compliance test*. *Test of controls* is a broader concept than *compliance tests*. Tests of controls is not only used to evaluate the effectiveness of policies and procedures in preventing or detecting material misstatements of assertions but is also used in obtaining an understanding of the client's internal control structure. Thus, *test of controls* relates to what SAS 1 previously referred to as review of the client's system, as well as test of compliance. *See also* Substantive Test.

COMPOSITE BREAK-EVEN POINT This is a break-even sales when a company sells more than one product or service. A break-even point for all the products or services combined can be determined, based on the expected *sales mix* and the composite or weighted average unit contribution margin. *See also* Cost-Volume-Profit (CVP); Break-Even Analysis.

COMPOSITION This is a voluntary reduction in the balance the debtor owes a creditor. *See also* Business Failure.

COMPREHENSIVE ANNUAL FINANCIAL REPORT (CAFR) CAFR is the annual report of a government. Financial reporting includes a combined, combining (showing information for all funds), and individual balance sheet. The following are shown as applicable on a combined, combining, and individual basis:

• Statement of revenues, expenditures, and changes in fund balance (all funds)

• Statement of revenues, expenditures, and changes in fund balance, budget and actual (general and special revenue funds)

• Statement of revenues, expenses, and changes in retained earnings (proprietary funds)

• Statement of changes in financial position (for proprietary funds)

See also Governmental Accounting.

COMPREHENSIVE INCOME This is the change in equity occurring from transactions and other events with nonowners. It excludes investment (disinvestment) by owners. Items included in comprehensive income but excluded from net income are

• Cumulative effect of a change in accounting principle

• Unrealized losses and gains on long-term investments

• Foreign currency translation gains and losses

Comprehensive income is subdivided into revenues and gains, as well as expenses and losses. These are further classified as either recurring or extraordinary.

COMPUTER CONFERENCING This occurs when financial executives located at distances apart are brought together for the purpose of giving and receiving information and to discuss corporate problems in order to develop strategy and solutions. Participants may become involved in discussions whenever desired through the use of their computers or terminals. Numerous on-line services exist, including GEnies's Business Real Time Conferencing and CompuServe. Computer conferencing allows for the quick dissemination and evaluation of corporate data to facilitate the decision-making process.

CONFIRMATION This is when the auditor makes a request in writing or orally asks a third party to a client to verify the existence and/or amount of a financial item. In a positive confirmation, the auditor seeks a reply

even if the item is correct. In a negative confirmation, a reply is given only in the case of a disagreement.

■ **Example**

A company sends to its sampled customers a form on behalf of the CPA firm asking them to respond to the auditor if a discrepancy in the account balance exists.

Negative confirmations also may be used in confirming accounts payable and bank balances.

CONSIGNMENT In a consignment, the consignor transfers goods to the consignee. The consignor retains legal title and includes the goods in his inventory. The consignee is acting as an agent in an attempt to sell the goods. Although the consignee is temporarily holding the goods, the inventory is not an asset on his books. If a sale occurs, the consignee deducts from the selling price his commission and related expenses, remitting the balance to the consignor. *See also* Inventory Valuation.

CONSOLIDATION This occurs when the parent owns in excess of 50% of the voting common stock of the subsidiary. The major objective of consolidation is to present as one economic unit the financial position and operating results of a parent and subsidiaries. It shows the group as a single company (with one or more branches or divisions), rather than separate companies. It is an example of theoretical substance over legal form. The companies making up the consolidated group keep their individual legal identity. Adjustments and eliminations are for the sole purpose of financial statement reporting. Consolidation is still appropriate even if the subsidiary has a material amount of debt. Disclosure in footnotes or by explanatory headings should be made of the firm's consolidation policy.

A consolidation is negated, even if more than 50% of voting common stock is owned by the parent, in the following cases:

• Parent is not in actual control of subsidiary (e.g., subsidiary is in receivership, subsidiary is in a politically unstable foreign country).

• Parent has sold or contracted to sell subsidiary shortly after year-end. The subsidiary is a temporary investment.

• Minority interest is very large in comparison to the parent's interest, thus individual financial statements are more meaningful.

Intercompany eliminations include that for intercompany payables and receivables, advances, and profits. But for certain regulated companies, intercompany profit does not have to be eliminated to the extent the profit represents a reasonable return on investment. Subsidiary investment in the parent's shares is not consolidated outstanding stock in the consolidated balance sheet. Consolidated statements do not reflect capitalized earnings in the form of stock dividends by subsidiaries subsequent to acquisition.

Minority interest in a subsidiary is the stockholders' equity of those outside of the parent's controlling interest in the partially owned subsidiaries. Minority interest should be shown as a separate component of stockholders' equity. When losses applicable to the minority interest in a subsidiary exceed the minority interest's equity capital, the excess and any subsequent losses related to the minority interest are charged to the parent. If profit subsequently occurs, the parent's interest is credited to the degree of prior losses absorbed.

If a parent acquires a subsidiary in more than one block of stock, each purchase is on a step-by-step basis and consolidation does not occur until control exists.

In case the subsidiary is acquired within the year, the subsidiary should be included in consolidation as if it had been bought at the beginning of the year, with a subtraction for the preacquisition part of earnings applicable to each block of stock. An alternative, but less preferable, approach is to include

in consolidation the subsidiary's earnings subsequent to the acquisition date.

The retained earnings of a subsidiary at the acquisition date is not included in the consolidated financial statements.

When the subsidiary is disposed of during the year, the parent should present its equity in the subsidiary's earnings prior to the sale date as a separate line item consistent with the equity method.

A subsidiary whose major business activity is leasing to a parent should always be consolidated.

Consolidation is still permissible without adjustments when the fiscal year-ends of the parent and subsidiary are 3 months or less apart. But footnote disclosure is needed of material events occurring during the intervening period.

The equity method of accounting is used for unconsolidated subsidiaries unless there is a foreign investment or a temporary investment. In a case where the equity method is not used, the cost method is followed. The cost method recognizes the difference between the cost of the subsidiary and the equity in net assets at the acquisition date. Depreciation is adjusted for the difference as if consolidation of the subsidiary was made. There is an elimination of intercompany gain or loss for unconsolidated subsidiaries to the extent the gain or loss exceeds the unrecorded equity in undistributed earnings. Unconsolidated subsidiaries accounted for with the cost method should have adequate disclosure of assets, liabilities, and earnings. Such disclosure may be in footnote or supplementary schedule form.

There may be instances when combined rather than consolidated financial statements are more meaningful, such as where a person owns a controlling interest in several related operating companies (brother-sister corporation).

There are cases where besides consolidated statements, parent company statements are required to properly provide information to creditors and preferred stockholders. In this event, *dual columns* are needed—one column for the parent and other columns for subsidiaries.

CONSTANT GROWTH MODEL The constant growth model for stock valuation, also called Gordon's model, is used to value the market price of a company's stock. It assumes dividends grow each year at a constant rate, g.

$$\text{Common stock value} = \frac{D_1}{r - g}$$

where D_1 = dividend in year 1,
         r = required rate of return,
         g = growth rate.

■ Example

Dividends per share for the current year is $10, required rate of return is 12%, and the constant growth rate in dividends is 2%. The value of the stock is

$$\frac{\$10}{0.12 - 0.02} = \frac{\$10}{0.10} = \$100$$

See also Common Stock Valuation.

CONSTRUCTION CONTRACT ACCOUNTING The two methods to account for construction contracts are the *completed contract method* and the *percentage of completion method*. Under the former method, profit on the contract is recognized in full in the year of completion, whereas under the latter method, profit on the contract is recognized gradually each year as work is performed. *See also* Revenue Recognition Methods.

CONSUMER PRICE INDEX (CPI) CPI is the measure of price level computed by the Bureau of Labor Statistics. It is the ratio of the cost of specific consumer items in any one year to the cost of those items in the

base year, 1967. Because the CPI includes things consumers buy regularly, it is frequently called the *cost-of-living index*. The so-called market basket, covered by the index, includes items such as food, clothing, automobiles, homes, and doctor fees. *See also* Price Indices.

CONTRIBUTION APPROACH TO PRICING

This is an approach to pricing a special order. This situation occurs because a company often receives a nonroutine, special order for its products at lower prices than usual. In normal times, the company may refuse such as order since it will not yield a satisfactory profit. If times are bad or when there is idle capacity, an order should be accepted if the incremental revenue exceeds the incremental costs involved. Such a price, one lower than the regular price, is called a *contribution price*. This approach to pricing is called the contribution approach to pricing, also called the *variable pricing model*.

■ Example

Assume that a company with 100,000-unit capacity is currently producing and selling only 90,000 units of product each year with a regular price of $2. If the variable cost per unit is $1 and the annual fixed cost is $45,000, the income statement looks as follows:

		Per Unit
Sales (90,000 units)	$180,000	$2.00
Less: Variable cost	90,000	1.00
Contribution margin	$ 90,000	$1.00
Less: Fixed cost	45,000	0.50
Net income	$ 45,000	$0.50

The company has just received an order that calls for 10,000 units @ $1.20, for a total of $12,000. The acceptance of this special order will not affect regular sales. Management is reluctant to accept this order because the $1.20 price is below the $1.50 factory unit cost ($1.50 = $1.00 + $0.50). Is it advisable? The answer to this question is no. The company can add to total profits by accepting this special order even though the price offered is below the unit factory cost. At a price of $1.20, the order will contribute $0.20 (CM per unit = $1.20 − $1.00 = $0.20) toward fixed cost, and profit will increase by $2,000 (10,000 units × $0.20). Using the contribution approach to pricing, the variable cost of $1.00 will be a better guide than the full unit cost of $1.50. Note that the fixed costs will not increase because of the presence of idle capacity.

The same result can be seen using the *total project approach* shown below. *See also* Incremental Analysis; Relevant Costing; Total Project Approach.

CONTRIBUTION APPROACH VERSUS TRADITIONAL APPROACH TO THE INCOME STATEMENT

The traditional approach to the income statement shows the functional classification of costs; that is, manufacturing costs vs. nonmanufacturing expenses (or operating expenses). It is not organized according to cost behavior. The contribution approach, however, looks at cost behavior. That is, it shows the relationship of variable costs and fixed costs, regardless of the functions a given cost item is associated with. The contribution

	Per Unit	Without Special Order (90,000 Units)	With Special Order (100,000 Units)	Difference
Sales	$2.00	$180,000	$192,000	$12,000
Less: VC	1.00	90,000	100,000	10,000
CM	$1.00	$ 90,000	$ 92,000	$ 2,000
Less: FC	0.50	45,000	45,000	—
Net income	$0.50	$ 45,000	$ 47,000	$ 2,000

approach to income determination provides data that are useful for managerial planning and decision making. It is not acceptable, however, for income tax or external reporting purposes. A contribution income statement highlights the concept of *contribution margin*, which is the difference between sales and variable costs. The traditional format, on the other hand, emphasizes the concept of *gross margin*, which is the difference between sales and cost of goods sold. These two concepts are independent and have nothing to do with each other. Gross margin is available to cover nonmanufacturing expenses, whereas contribution margin is available to cover fixed costs. The concept of contribution margin has numerous applications for internal management. A comparison between the traditional format and the contribution format follows.

Traditional Format

Sales		$15,000
Less: Cost of goods sold		7,000
Gross margin		$ 8,000
Less: Operating expenses		
Selling	$2,100	
Administrative	1,500	3,600
Net income		$ 4,400

Contribution Format

Sales		$15,000
Less: Variable expenses		
Manufacturing	$4,000	
Selling	1,600	
Administrative	500	6,100
Contribution margin		$ 8,900
Less: Fixed expenses		
Manufacturing	$3,000	
Selling	500	
Administrative	1,000	4,500
Net income		$ 4,400

See also Contribution Income Statement.

CONTRIBUTION INCOME STATEMENT This is an income statement that organizes the cost by behavior. It shows the relationship of vari-

able costs and fixed costs, regardless of the functions a given cost item is associated with. A contribution income statement highlights the concept of *contribution margin* (*CM*). This format provides data that are useful for internal management. An illustrative format of the contribution margin income statement follows:

- Sales
- Less: Variable Cost of Sales
  Variable selling and administrative expenses
- Contribution margin (CM)
- Less: Fixed overhead
  Fixed selling and administrative expenses
- Net income

Disadvantages of the contribution income statement are

1. It is not acceptable for external reporting purposes. It is only an internal measure.
2. It ignores fixed overhead as an inventoriable product cost.

See also Contribution Approach Versus Traditional Approach to the Income Statement; Contribution Margin.

CONTRIBUTION MARGIN (CM) Contribution margin, or marginal income, is the difference between sales and the variable costs of the product or service. It is the amount of money available to cover fixed costs and generate profits.

■ Example

If sales are $12,000 and variable costs are $5,000, contribution margin is $7,000 ($12,000 less $5,000).

The concept of contribution margin (CM) has many applications. A company can sell an item below the normal selling price when idle capacity exists as long as there is a contribution margin since it will help to cover the fixed costs or add to profits. The CM calculation requires the segregation of fixed and variable costs, which is needed in *break-even*

analysis. Further, CM analysis is effective in evaluating the performance of the department as a whole and its manager. *See also* Contribution Income Statement.

CONTRIBUTION MARGIN (CM) VARIANCE   The CM variance is the difference between actual contribution margin per unit and the budgeted contribution margin per unit multiplied by the actual number of units sold. If the actual CM is greater than the budgeted CM per unit, a variance is favorable; otherwise, it is unfavorable.

CM variance = (Actual CM per unit
              − Budgeted CM per unit) × Actual sales

See also Contribution Margin; Profit Variance Analysis.

CORPORATE PLANNING MODELS   Today more and more companies are using, developing, or experimenting with some form of corporate planning model. This is primarily due to development of planning and modeling software packages that make it possible to develop the model without much knowledge of computer coding and programming. For the accountant and financial analyst, the attractive features of corporate modeling are the formulation of budgets, budgetary planning and control, and financial analyses that can be used to support management decision making. However, corporate modeling involves much more than the generation of financial statements and budgets. Depending on the structure and breadth of the modeling activity, a variety of capabilities, uses, and analyses are available. A corporate planning model is an integrated business planning model in which marketing and production models are linked to the financial model.

More specifically, a corporate model is a description, explanation, and interrelation of the functional areas of a firm (accounting, finance, marketing, production, and others) expressed in terms of a set of mathematical and logical relationships so as to produce a variety of reports, including financial statements. The ultimate goals of a corporate planning model are to improve quality of planning and decision making; reduce decision risk; and, more importantly, influence or even shape the future environment favorably.

Generally speaking, a corporate model can be used to:

1. Simulate an alternative strategy by evaluating its impact on profits.
2. Help establish corporate and divisional goals.
3. Measure the interactive effect of parts within the firm.
4. Help management better understand the business and its functional relationships and help improve decision-making ability.
5. Link the firm's goals and strategies to its master budgets.
6. Assess critically the assumptions underlying environmental constraints.

Types of Analysis

The type of the corporate model that management is looking for would depend on what types of analysis it wishes to perform. There are typically three types of model investigations.

The first type of questions to be raised are "What is" or "What has been" questions, such as the relationship between variables of the firm and external macroeconomic variables such as GNP or inflation. The goal of this type of model investigation is to obtain a specific answer based on the stipulated relationship. For example, what is or has been the firm's profit when the price of raw material was $12.50?

The second type of investigation focuses on "What-if" questions. This is done through *simulation* or *sensitivity analysis*. This analysis often takes the following form: "What happens under a given set of assumptions if the decision variable(s) is changed in a prescribed manner?" For example,

"What is going to happen to the company's cash flow and net income if it is contemplating a reduction in price by 10% and an increase in advertising budget by 25%?

The third type of question that can be addressed by way of corporate-planning modeling takes the following form: "What has to be done in order to achieve a particular objective?" This type of analysis is often called *goal seeking*. It usually requires the use of optimization models such as linear programming and goal programming.

Typical Questions Addressed Via Corporate Modeling

The following is a list of questions management addresses itself using corporate modeling. (For greater detail, see F. Rosenkranz, *An Introduction to Corporate Modeling*, Duke University Press, Durham, NC, 1979.)

• What are the effects of different pricing policies?
• What is the effect of different interest rates and current exchange rates on the income statement and balance sheet of the firm?
• What will be the demand for the end products of the firm at various locations and different times?
• What is and will be the unit contribution margin for certain production, transportation, and sales allocations?
• What will the absence and turnover rates of the employees of the firm be and what effect will they have?
• What is the effect of advertising and distribution expenditures on sales?
• What marketing strategy can and should the firm follow?
• What do price-demand or supply relations on the output or input side of the firm look like? What are the effects of price/cost changes on sales?
• How do certain states of the national or world economy influence sales of the firm

on the one side and purchase price of the production factors on the other?
• What is the nature of the conditions that must be fulfilled if the total sales of the firm at a certain time are supposed to be higher than a certain budget value?
• Should the firm produce and sell a certain product, purchase and sell the product, or not get involved at all?
• What is the range of the return on investment on various projects and units?
• How will the income statement, the balance sheet, and the cash flow statement develop for several operating divisions? What will their contributions be?
• What effects with respect to the financial position of the firm could an acquisition or merger with another firm have?

Benefits derived from the corporate planning models include
• The ability to explore more alternatives
• Better quality decision making
• More effective planning
• A better understanding of the business
• Faster decision making
• More timely information
• More accurate forecasts
• Cost savings

Types of Models

Corporate planning models can be categorized according to two approaches: simulation and optimization. *Simulation models* are attempts to mathematically represent the operations of the company or of the conditions in the external economic environment. By adjusting the values of controllable variables and assumed external conditions, the future implications of present decision making can be estimated. Probabilistic simulation models incorporate probability estimates into the forecast sequence, whereas deterministic models do not. *Optimization models* are intended to identify the best decision, given specific constraints.

Current Trend in Corporate Modeling

Interactive computing facilities allow for faster and more meaningful input/output sequences for modelers; trial-and-error adjustments of inputs and analyses are possible while on-line to the central computer or to an outside time-sharing service. The advent of corporate simulation languages enables analysts with little experience to write modeling programs in an Englishlike programming language—for example, to name a few, IFPS™, SIMPLAN™, and XSIM™. In addition, a number of spreadsheet programs, such as Lotus 1–2–3™ and SuperCalc™, have become available for use by corporate planning modelers. By 1979, nearly every Fortune 1000 company was using a corporate simulation model. This statistic will definitely increase to cover small and medium-sized firms. *See also* Financial Models.

CORRELATION COEFFICIENT (r)   A measure of the degree of correlation between the two variables. The range of values it takes is between -1 and $+1$. A negative value of r indicates an inverse relationship; a positive value of r indicates a direct relationship; a zero value of r indicates that the two variables are independent of each other; an r of 1 indicates that the two variables are perfectly correlated; the closer r is to $+1$ or -1, the stronger the relationship between the two variables. *See also* Regression Analysis; Simple Regression.

COST BEHAVIOR ANALYSIS—ANALYSIS OF MIXED COSTS   Depending on how a cost will react or respond to changes in the level of activity, costs may be viewed as variable, fixed, or mixed (semivariable). (Reference should be made to Figure 1.) A mixed cost is one that contains both variable and fixed elements. For planning, control, and decision-making purposes, mixed costs need to be separated into their variable and fixed

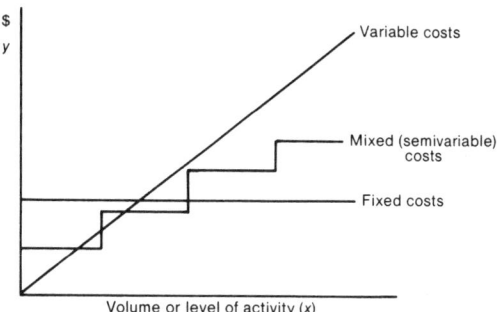

Figure 1   Cost Behavior Patterns

components, using such methods as the high-low method, the scattergraph method, and regression analysis. They are discussed following.

The High-Low Method

The high-low method, as the name indicates, uses two extreme data points to determine the values of a (the fixed cost portion) and b (the variable rate) in the equation $y = a + bx$. The extreme data points are the highest representative $x-y$ pair and the lowest representative $x-y$ pair. The activity level x, rather than the mixed cost item y, governs their selection.

The high-low method is explained, step by step, as follows:

• Step 1   Select the highest pair and the lowest pair.

• Step 2   Compute the variable rate, b, using the formula:

$$\text{Variable rate} = \frac{\text{Difference in cost } y}{\text{Difference in activity } x}$$

• Step 3   Compute the fixed cost portion as:

$$\text{Fixed cost portion} = \text{Total semivariable cost} - \text{Variable cost}$$

■ Example 1

Flexible Manufacturing Company decided to relate total factory overhead costs to direct labor hours (DLH) to develop a cost-volume formula in the form of $y' = a + bx$. Twelve

Table 1

Month	Direct Labor Hours (x) (000 omitted)	Factory Overhead (y) (000 omitted)
January	9 hours	$ 15
February	19	20
March	11	14
April	14	16
May	23	25
June	12	20
July	12	20
August	22	23
September	7	14
October	13	22
November	15	18
December	17	18
Total	174 hours	$225

monthly observations are collected. They are given in Table 1.

The high-low points selected from the monthly observations are

	x		y	
High	23	hours	$25	(May pair)
Low	7		14	(September pair)
Difference	16	hours	$11	

Thus:

Variable rate b

$$= \frac{\text{Difference in } y}{\text{Difference in } x} = \frac{\$11}{16 \text{ hours}}$$

$$= \$0.6875 \text{ per DLH}$$

The fixed cost portion is computed as

	High	Low
Factory overhead (y)	$25	$14
Variable expense ($0.6875/DLH)	(15.8125)	(4.8125)
	$ 9.1875	$ 9.1875

Therefore, the cost-volume formula for factory overhead is $9.1875 fixed, plus $0.6875 per DLH.

Or, alternatively:

$$y' = \$9.1875 + \$0.6875x$$

where y' = estimated factory overhead,

$$x = \text{DLH}.$$

Note that the reason for using a new symbol y' (read y-prime) is that the cost volume for-

mula just obtained gives an estimated value of y.

The high-low method is simple and easy to use. It has the disadvantage, however, of using two extreme data points, which may not be representative of normal conditions. The method may yield unreliable estimates of a and b in our formula. In such a case, it would be wise to drop them and choose two other points that are more representative of normal situations.

The Scattergraph Method

In this method, a semivariable expense is plotted on the vertical axis (or y axis) and activity measure is plotted on the horizontal axis (or x axis). Then a regression line is fitted by visual inspection of the plotted $x-y$ data. The method is best explained by the following example.

■ Example 2

For purposes of illustration, let us use the data in Example 1. The factory overhead and direct labor hours are plotted in Figure 2.

Since the regression line obtained by visual inspection strikes the factory overhead axis at the $6 point, that amount represents the fixed cost component. The variable cost component is computed as

Factory overhead at 23 hours of direct labor	$25
Less: Fixed cost component	6
Variable cost component	$19

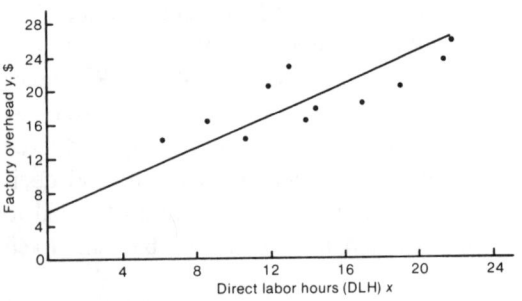

Figure 2 The Scattergraph Method

Therefore, the variable rate per hour is $19/23 hours = $0.8261 per DLH.

In summary, based on the scattergraph method, we obtain

$$y' = \$6 + \$0.8261x$$

where y' = estimated factory overhead,

x = DLH.

The scattergraph method is relatively easy to use and simple to understand. However, it should be used with extreme caution because it does not provide an objective test for assuring that the regression line drawn is the most accurate fit for the underlying observations.

Regression Analysis

One popularly used method for estimating the cost-volume formula is regression analysis. Regression analysis is a statistical procedure for estimating mathematically the average relationship between the dependent variables and the independent variable(s). Simple regression involves one independent variable (e.g., DLH or machine hours alone), whereas multiple regression involves two or more activity variables. We will assume simple linear regression, which means that we will maintain the $y = a + bx$ relationship.

Unlike the high-low method, in estimating the variable rate and the fixed cost portion, the regression method does include all the observed data and attempts to find a line of best fit. To find the line of best fit, a technique called the *method of least squares* is used.

To explain the least-squares method, we define the error as the difference between the observed value and the estimated value of some semivariable cost and denote it with u.

Symbolically,

$$u = y - y'$$

where y = observed value of a semivariable expense,

y' = estimated value based on $y' = a + bx$.

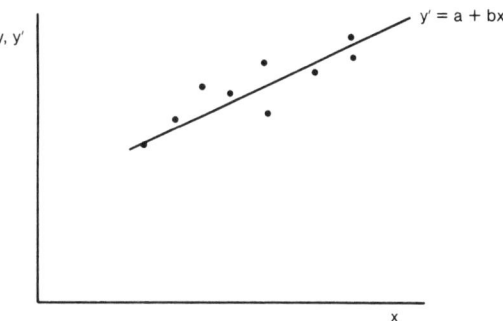

Figure 3 y and y'

The least-squares criterion requires that the line of best fit be such that the sum of the squares of the errors (or the vertical distance in Figure 3 from the observed data points to the line) is a minimum, that is,

$$\text{minimum:} \quad \Sigma u^2 = \Sigma(y - y')^2$$

Using differential calculus we obtain the following equations, called normal equations:

$$\Sigma y = na + b\Sigma x$$
$$\Sigma xy = a\Sigma x + b\Sigma x^2$$

solving the equations for b and a yields

$$b = \frac{n\Sigma xy - (\Sigma x)(\Sigma y)}{n\Sigma x^2 - (\Sigma x)^2}$$

$$a = \bar{y} - b\bar{x}$$

where $\bar{y} = \Sigma y/n$ and $\bar{x} = \Sigma x/n$.

■ Example 3

To illustrate the computations of b and a, we will refer to the data in Table 1. All the sums required are computed and shown below.

Direct Labor Hours x	Factory Overhead y	xy	x^2	y^2
9 hours	$ 15	135	81	225
19	20	380	361	400
11	14	154	121	196
14	16	224	196	256
23	25	575	529	625
12	20	240	144	400
12	20	240	144	400
22	23	506	484	529
7	14	98	49	196
13	22	286	169	484
15	18	270	225	324
17	18	306	289	324
174 hours	$225	3,414	2,792	4,359

From the previous table:

$\Sigma x = 174$ $\Sigma y = 225$ $\Sigma xy = 3,414$ $\Sigma x^2 = 2,792$

$\bar{x} = \Sigma x/n = 174/12 = 14.5$

$\bar{y} = \Sigma y/n = 225/12 = 18.75$

Substituting these values into the formula for b first:

$$b = \frac{n\Sigma xy - (\Sigma x)(\Sigma y)}{n\Sigma x^2 - (\Sigma x)^2}$$

$$= \frac{(12)(3,414) - (174)(225)}{(12)(2,792) - (174)^2}$$

$$= \frac{1,818}{3,228} = 0.5632$$

$a = \bar{y} - b\bar{x} = 18.75 - (0.5632)(14.5)$

$= 18.75 - 8.1664 = 10.5836$

The cost formula then is:

$$y' = \$10.5836 + 0.5632x$$

Note that Σy^2 is not used here but rather is computed for future use.

Regression Statistics

Unlike the high-low method, regression analysis is a statistical method. It uses a variety of statistics that tell us about the accuracy and reliability of the regression results. They include:

1. Correlation coefficient (r) and coefficient of determination (r^2)
2. Standard error of the estimate (S_e)
3. Standard error of the regression coefficient (S_b) and t-statistic

Correlation Coefficient (r) and Coefficient of Determination (r²)

The correlation coefficient r measures the degree of correlation between y and x. The range of values it takes on is between -1 and $+1$. More widely used, however, is the coefficient of determination, designated r^2 (read as r-squared). Simply put, r^2 tells us how good the estimated regression equation is. In other words, it is a measure of "goodness of fit" in the regression. Therefore, the higher the r^2, the more confidence we can have in our estimated cost formula.

More specifically, the coefficient of determination represents the proportion of the total variation in y that is explained by the regression equation. It has the range of values between 0 and 1.

■ Example 4

The statement, "Factory overhead is a function of machine hours with $r^2 = 70\%$," can be interpreted as, "70% of the total variation of factory overhead is explained by the regression equation or the change in machine hours, and the remaining 30% is accounted for by something other than machine hours."

The coefficient of determination is computed as

$$r^2 = 1 - \frac{\Sigma(y - y')^2}{\Sigma(y - \bar{y})^2}$$

In a simple regression situation, however, there is a shortcut method available:

$$r^2 = \frac{[n\Sigma xy - (\Sigma x)(\Sigma y)]^2}{[n\Sigma x^2 - (\Sigma x)^2][n\Sigma y^2 - (\Sigma y)^2]}$$

Comparing this formula with the one for b in Example 3, we see that the only additional information we need to compute r^2 is Σy^2.

■ Example 5

From the table prepared in Example 3, $\Sigma y^2 = 4,359$. Using the shortcut method for r^2,

$$r^2 = \frac{(1,818)^2}{(3,228)[(12)(4,359) - (225)^2]}$$

$$= \frac{3,305,124}{(3,228)(52,308 - 50,625)} = \frac{3,305,124}{(3,228)(1,683)}$$

$$= \frac{3,305,124}{5,432,724} = 0.6084 = 60.84\%$$

This means that about 60.84% of the total variation in total factor overhead is explained by DLH and the remaining 39.16% is still unexplained. A relatively low r^2 indicates that there is a lot of room for improvement in our estimated cost-volume formula ($y' = \$10.5836 + \$0.5632x$). Machine hours or a combination of DLH and machine hours might improve r^2.

Standard Error of the Estimate (S_e)

The standard error of the estimate, designated S_e, is defined as the standard deviation of the regression. It is computed as

$$S\hat{e} = \sqrt{\frac{\Sigma(y - y')^2}{n - 2}} = \sqrt{\frac{\Sigma y^2 - a\Sigma y - b\Sigma xy}{n - 2}}$$

The statistics can be used to gain some idea of the accuracy of our predictions.

■ Example 6

Going back to our example data, S_e is calculated as

$$S_e = \sqrt{\frac{4{,}359 - (10.5836)(225)}{12 - 2} - (0.5632)(3{,}414)} = \sqrt{\frac{54.9252}{10}} = 2.3436$$

If a manager wants the prediction to be 95% confident, the confidence interval would be the estimated cost $\pm$ 2(2.3436).

Standard Error of the Regression Coefficient (S_b) and the t-Statistic

The standard error of the regression coefficient, designated S_b, and the t-statistic are closely related. S_b gives an estimate of the range where the true coefficient will "actually" fall. The t-statistic shows the statistical significance of an independent variable x in explaining the dependent variable y. It is determined by dividing the estimated regression coefficient b by its standard error S_b. Thus

the t-statistic measures how many standard errors the coefficient is away from zero. Generally, any t value greater than $+2$ or less than -2 is acceptable. The higher the t value, the greater the confidence we have in the coefficient as the predictor.

COST BEHAVIOR PATTERNS Not all costs behave in the same way. There are certain costs that vary in proportion to change in activity, called *variable costs*. There are other costs that do not change regardless of the volume, called *fixed costs*. (See Figures 1 and 2 below.) An understanding of costs by behavior is very useful:
1. For break-even and cost-volume-profit (CVP) analysis
2. To analyze short-term, nonroutine decisions such as the make-or-buy decision and the sales mix decision
3. For appraisal of profit center performance by means of the contribution approach and for flexible capital budgeting
    See also Cost Behavior Analysis.

COST-BENEFIT ANALYSIS The cost-benefit, or benefit-cost, analysis is an analysis to determine whether the favorable results of an alternative are sufficient to justify the cost of taking that alternative. This analysis is widely used in connection with capital expend-

Figure 1 Variable Costs

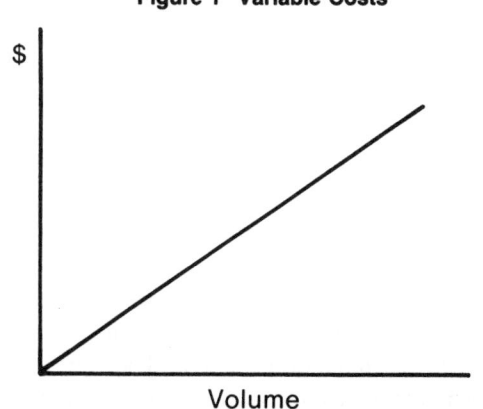

Figure 2 Fixed Costs

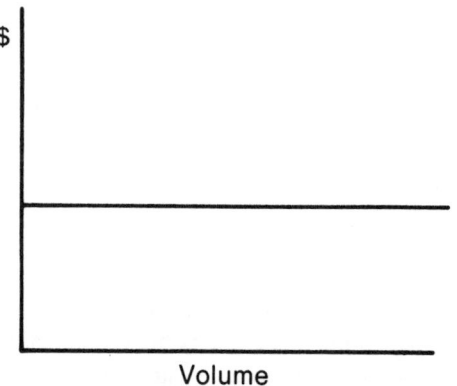

iture projects. An example of cost-benefit analysis is where the cost incurred to uncover the reasons for a variance outweigh the benefit to be derived. Cost-benefit ratio or *profitability* index is widely used for capital expenditure decisions. *See also* Capital Rationing; Profitability Index.

COST FUNCTION This describes the relationship between cost and activity. A cost function may be either linear or nonlinear. A simple example of a cost function is a *cost-volume formula* which is in the form of $y = a + bx$, where y is the estimated value of a cost item for any specified value of x (activity). The constant a is the intercept; b is the slope. The fixed cost element is a, whereas b is the variable rate per unit of x. *See also* Cost Behavior Analysis—Analysis of Mixed Costs; Cost Behavior Patterns; Cost-Volume Formula.

COST METHOD FASB No. 12 covers accounting under the cost method. It does *not* apply to not-for-profit organizations, mutual life insurance companies, or employee benefit plans.

A security is usually classified as current if it is liquid and used for temporary excess cash. A security is usually classified as long term if the intent is to hold for one year or more, it is for capital appreciation purposes, dividend income is desired, possible eventual control is involved, there is a lack of market price quotations, and restricted marketability exists. "Restricted" stock is noncurrent except if it qualifies for sale within one year of the balance sheet date and there are readily available price quotations.

The cost method of accounting for investments is used when the holder owns less than 20% of the voting common stock of the company. However, the cost method could be used instead of the equity method when the holder owns between 20% to 50% of the voting common stock but *lacks* significant influence (effective control).

Significant influence may be indicated by one or more of the following:
• Involvement in decision making of owned company.
• Material intercompany transactions.
• Representation on the Board of Directors of the investee company.
• Investor owns a high percentage of investee's shares relative to other stockholders.
• Managerial personnel are interchanged between the investor and investee.
• Investor provides investee with technological expertise.

Indicators of a lack of significant influence follow:
• Concentration of majority ownership of investee among a limited number of stockholders, especially when the group operates the investee in disregard of the investor's viewpoints.
• Investor is unable to obtain the financial data needed from the investee to use the equity method.
• Investor and investee sign an agreement (called "standstill") in which the investor surrenders material shareholder rights. The standstill agreement is typically employed to settle disputes between the investor and investee.
• Investee opposes the investment (e.g., a lawsuit or complaint is filed).

The cost method must be used for equity securities. Although it is not required for debt securities, debt securities in practice are usually reflected in the entire investment portfolio at the lower of cost or market value. *Note:* The cost method is used to account for preferred stock since it is nonvoting irrespective of the percentage of shares owned.

The investment portfolio is broken down into current and noncurrent. Current securities are shown as marketable securities under current assets. Noncurrent securities are shown as noncurrent assets. The lower of cost or market value is applied to each portfolio separately.

If market value is in excess of cost, the securities are shown at cost with market value either disclosed in parentheses or in a footnote. If market value is less than cost, the securities portfolio is written down to market value, reflecting an unrealized loss due to conservatism. Thus, a temporary decline in value of the portfolio is reflected. The portfolio is shown on the balance sheet at the lower of total cost or total market value. The following entry is made at the end of the year:

Unrealized Loss
Allowance to Reduce Securities
from Cost to Market Value

For short-term securities, the unrealized loss is shown in the income statement. For long-term securities, the unrealized loss is shown as a separate item in the stockholders' equity section. The allowance account is a contra account to Investments to derive the net amount. The only time the allowance account is entered into is at the end of the year.

In the following year, if there is a partial or full recovery from cost to market value, the entry is

Allowance to Reduce Securities
from Cost to Market Value
Unrealized Gain

However, in recording the recovery from cost to market value, the portfolio can never be written up at an amount in excess of the original cost.

If securities are sold during the year, a realized loss or realized gain will occur. The realized loss or gain is shown in the income statement irrespective of whether the portfolio is current or noncurrent. The same realized loss or gain on sale is reflected for tax return preparation purposes.

The entry to record the sale of securities is

Cash (proceeds received)
Loss
    Securities (at cost)
    Gain

Either a loss or gain will be involved in the previous entry.

A security cannot be recorded at more than cost since that will lack conservatism. The only time market value can be used for valuation is the case of a *permanent* increase in value. However, accountants are very reluctant to state that a permanent increase has occurred because of legal liability exposure.

If a balance sheet is unclassified, the investment security portfolio is considered to be noncurrent.

A permanent decline in value of a particular security is immediately recognized with a realized loss being booked shown in the income statement even if it is a noncurrent portfolio. The investment account is credited directly. The new market value becomes the new cost basis, which means it cannot later be written up.

A permanent decline in market price of stock may be indicated when the company has several years of losses, is in a very weak financial condition, and has issued a liquidating dividend. For example, if the company sells some of its major divisions and distributes the proceeds to stockholders, a writedown of the investment may be appropriate.

■ **Example**

In a long-term investment portfolio, one stock in ABC Company has suffered a permanent decline in value from cost of $6,000 to market value of $5,000. The entry is

Realized Loss   1,000
Long-term Investment   1,000

The new cost now becomes $5,000 (the market value). If in a later period the market value increased above $5,000, the stock would *not* be written up above $5,000.

If a particular stock is reclassified from noncurrent to current, or vice versa, it is transferred at the lower of cost or market value at the transfer date. If market value exceeds cost, it is transferred at cost intact, with no unrealized gain being recorded. If

market value is below cost, a realized loss in the income statement is booked and the investment account is credited. The new cost basis becomes the market value, which means the portfolio cannot be written up above cost.

▪ Example

XYZ stock is reclassified from noncurrent to current. If cost is $3,000 and market value is $2,700, the entry for the reclassification is

Short-term Securities	2,700	
Realized Loss	300	
Long-term Investment		3,000

If a later recovery occurs and market value becomes $2,900, no entry will be made.

If market value of a portfolio substantially drops below cost between year-end and the audit report date, subsequent event footnote disclosure is required.

Income tax allocation occurs with investments due to resulting temporary differences. A deferred tax credit will arise because unrealized losses and gains on securities are not reflected for tax return preparation purposes.

▪ Example

On 1/1/19X1, Company X purchases long-term securities of $480,000 plus brokerage commissions of $20,000. On 5/12/19X1, a cash dividend of $15,000 is received. On 12/31/19X1, the market value of the portfolio is $490,000. On 2/6/19X2 securities costing $50,000 are sold for $54,000. On 12/31/19X2, the market value of the portfolio is $447,000. The journal entries follow:

1/1/19X1 Long-term Invest- ments	500,000	
Cash		500,000
5/12/19X1 Cash	15,000	
Dividend Revenue		15,000
12/31/19X1		
Unrealized Loss	10,000	
Allowance		10,000

The balance sheet presentation of the long-term investments is

Long-term Investments	$500,000
Less: Allowance	10,000
Net Balance	$490,000

If market value were $510,000 instead of $490,000, the securities portfolio would remain intact at $500,000 with the market value of $510,000 being disclosed.

2/2/19X2 Cash	54,000	
Long-term Investments		50,000
Gain		4,000
12/31/19X2		
Allowance	7,000	
Unrealized Loss		7,000

The balance sheet presentation of the long-term securities is

Long-term Investments	$450,000
Less: Allowance	3,000
Net Balance	$447,000

If instead the market value was $435,000, the entry would have been

Unrealized Loss	5,000	
Allowance		5,000

If instead the market value was $452,000, the entry would have been

Allowance	10,000	
Unrealized Loss		10,000

If two or more securities are purchased at one price, the cost is allocated among the securities based on their relative fair market value. In the exchange of one security for another, the new security received in the exchange is valued at its fair market value.

▪ Example

Preferred stock costing $10,000 is exchanged for 1,000 shares of common stock having a market value of $15,000. The entry is

Investment in Common Stock	15,000	
Investment in Preferred Stock		10,000
Gain		5,000

A stock dividend involves a memo entry reflecting more shares at no additional cost. As a result, the cost per share decreases.

■ Example

Assume 50 shares at $12 per share for a total cost of $600 is owned. A 20% stock dividend is declared amounting to 10 shares. A memo entry is made reflecting the additional shares as follows:

		Investment	°
50	$12	$600	
10		0	
60	($10)	$600	

If 10 shares are later sold at $15, the entry is

Cash	150	
Long-term Investment		100
Gain		50

A stock split has the effect of increasing the shares and reducing the cost basis on a proportionate basis. A memo entry is made. Assume 100 shares costing $20 per share is owned. A 2 for 1 split would result in 200 shares at a cost per share of $10. Total cost remains at $2,000. *See also* Equity Method.

COST OF CAPITAL This is defined as the rate of return that is necessary to maintain the market value of the firm (or price of the firm's stock). Financial managers must know the cost of capital (the minimum required rate of return) in (1) making capital budgeting decisions; (2) helping to establish the optimal capital structure; and (3) making decisions such as leasing, bond refunding, and working capital management. The cost of capital is computed as a weighted average of the various capital components, which are items on the right-hand side of the balance sheet, such as debt, preferred stock, common stock, and retained earnings.

Computing Individual Costs of Capital

Each element of capital has a component cost that is identified by the following:

k_i = before-tax cost of debt,

$k_d = K_i (1 - t)$ = after-tax cost of debt, where t = tax rate,

k_p = cost of preferred stock,

k_s = cost of retained earnings (or internal equity),

k_e = cost of external equity, or cost of issuing new common stock,

k_o = firm's overall cost of capital, or a weighted average cost of capital.

Cost of Debt

The before-tax cost of debt can be found by determining the internal rate of return (or yield to maturity) on the bond cash flows.

However, the following shortcut formula may be used for approximating the yield to maturity on a bond:

$$k_i = \frac{I + (M - V)/n}{(M + V)/2}$$

where I = annual interest payments in dollars,

M = par value, usually $1,000 per bond,

V = value or net proceeds from the sale of a bond,

n = term of the bond n years.

Since the interest payments are tax-deductible, the cost of debt must be stated on an after-tax basis. The after-tax cost of debt is

$$k_d = k_i (1 - t)$$

where t is the tax rate.

■ Example 1

Assume that the Carter company issues a $1,000, 8%, 20-year bond whose net proceeds are $940. The tax rate is 40%. Then, the before-tax cost of debt, k_i, is

$$k_i = \frac{I + (M - V)/n}{(M + V)/2}$$

$$= \frac{\$80 + (\$1,000 - \$940)/20}{(\$1,000 + \$940)/2}$$

$$= \frac{\$83}{\$970} = 8.56\%$$

Therefore, the after-tax cost of debt is

$$k_d = k_i (1 - t)$$
$$= 8.56\% \ (1 - 0.4) = 5.14\%$$

Cost of Preferred Stock

The cost of preferred stock, k_p, is found by dividing the annual preferred stock dividend, d_p, by the net proceeds from the sale of the preferred stock, p, as follows:

$$k_p = \frac{d_p}{p}$$

Since preferred stock dividends are not a tax-deductible expense, these dividends are paid out after taxes. Consequently, no tax adjustment is required.

■ Example 2

Suppose that the Carter company has preferred stock that pays a $13 dividend per share and sells for $100 per share in the market. The flotation (or underwriting) cost is 3% or $3 per share. Then the cost of preferred stock is

$$k_p = \frac{d_p}{p}$$
$$= \frac{\$13}{\$97} = 13.4\%$$

Cost of Equity Capital

The cost of common stock, k_e, is generally viewed as the rate of return investors require on a firm's common stock. Three techniques for measuring the cost of common stock equity capital are available: (1) the Gordon's growth model; (2) the capital asset pricing model (CAPM) approach; and (3) the bond plus approach.

The Gordon's Growth Model

The Gordon's model is

$$P_o = \frac{D_1}{r - g}$$

where P_o = value of common stock,
D_1 = dividend to be received in 1 year,
r = investor's required rate of return,
g = rate of growth (assumed to be constant over time).

Solving the model for r results in the formula for the cost of common stock:

$$r = \frac{D_1}{P_o} + g \quad \text{or} \quad k_e = \frac{D_1}{P_o} + g$$

Note that the symbol r is changed to k_e to show that it is used for the computation of cost of capital.

■ Example 3

Assume that the market price of the Carter Company's stock is $40. The dividend to be paid at the end of the coming year is $4 per share and is expected to grow at a constant annual rate of 6%. Then the cost of this common stock is

$$k_e = \frac{D_1}{P_o} + g = \frac{\$4}{\$40} + 6\% = 16\%$$

The cost of new common stock, or external equity capital, is higher than the cost of existing common stock because of the flotation costs involved in selling the *nw* common stock.

If f is flotation cost in percent, the formula for the cost of new common stock is

$$k_e = \frac{D_1}{P_o(1 - f)} + g$$

■ Example 4

Assume the same data as in Example 3, except the firm is trying to sell new issues of stock A and its flotation cost is 10%. Then:

$$k_e = \frac{D_1}{p_o(1 - f)} + g$$
$$= \frac{\$4}{\$40(1 - 0.1)} + 6\% = \frac{\$4}{\$36} + 6\%$$
$$= 11.11\% + 6\% = 17.11\%$$

The CAPM Approach

An alternative approach to measuring the cost of common stock is to use the CAPM, which involves the following steps:

1. Estimate the risk-free rate, r_f, generally taken to be the United States Treasury bill rate.

2. Estimate the stock's beta coefficient, b, which is an index of systematic (or nondiversifiable market) risk.

3. Estimate the rate of return on the market portfolio such as the Standard & Poor's 500 Stock Composite Index or Dow Jones 30 Industrials.

4. Estimate the required rate of return on the firm's stock, using the CAPM (or SML) equation:

$$k_e = r_f + b(r_m - r_f)$$

Again, note that the symbol r_j is changed to k_e.

■ Example 5

Assuming that r_f is 7%, b is 1.5, and r_m is 13%, then:

$$k_e = r_f + b(r_m - r_f) = 7\% + 1.5(13\% - 7\%) = 16\%$$

This 16% cost of common stock can be viewed as consisting of 7% risk-free rate plus a 9% risk premium, which indicates that the firm's stock price is 1.5 times more volatile than the market portfolio to the factors affecting nondiversifiable, or systematic, risk.

The Bond Plus Approach

Still another simple but useful approach to determining the cost of common stock is to add a risk premium to the firm's own cost of long-term debt, as follows:

$$k_e = \text{long-term bond rate} + \text{risk premium}$$
$$= k_i (1 - t) + \text{risk premium}$$

A risk premium of about 4% is commonly used with this approach.

■ Example 6

Using the data found in Example 1, the cost of common stock using the bond plus approach is

$$k_e = \text{long-term bond rate} + \text{risk premium}$$
$$= k_i (1 - t) + \text{risk premium}$$
$$= 5.14\% + 4\% = 9.14\%$$

Cost of Retained Earnings

The cost of retained earnings, k_s, is closely related to the cost of existing common stock, since the cost of equity obtained by retained earnings is the same as the rate of return investors require on the firm's common stock. Therefore:

$$k_e = k_s$$

Measuring the Overall Cost of Capital

The firm's overall cost of capital is the weighted average of the individual capital costs, with the weights being the proportions of each type of capital used. Let k_o be the overall cost of capital.

$$k_o = \sum \begin{pmatrix} \% \text{ of total capital} & \text{Cost of capital} \\ \text{structure supplied by} \times \text{for each source} \\ \text{each type of capital} & \text{of capital} \end{pmatrix}$$
$$= w_d \cdot k_d + w_p \cdot k_p + w_e \cdot k_e + w_s \cdot k_s$$

where w_d = % of total capital supplied by debt

w_p = % of total capital supplied by preferred stock.

w_e = % of total capital supplied by external equity,

w_s = % of total capital supplied by retained earnings (or internal equity).

The weights can be historical, target, or marginal.

Historical Weights

Historical weights are based on a firm's existing capital structure. The use of these weights is based on the assumption that the firm's existing capital structure is optimal and therefore should be maintained in the future. Two types of historical weights can be used—book value weights and market value weights.

Book Value Weights

The use of book value weights in calculating the firm's weighted cost of capital assumes that new financing will be raised using the same method the firm used for its present capital structure. The weights are determined by dividing the book value of each capital component by the sum of the book values of all the long-term capital sources. The computation of overall cost of capital is illustrated in the following example.

■ Example 7

Assume the following capital structure for the Carter Company:

Mortgage bonds ($1,000 par)	$20,000,000
Preferred stock ($100 par)	5,000,000
Common stock ($40 par)	20,000,000
Retained earnings	5,000,000
Total	$50,000,000

The book value weights and the overall cost of capital are computed as follows:

Source	Book Value	Weights	Cost	Weighted Cost
Debt	$20,000,000	40%	5.14%	2.06%
Preferred stock	5,000,000	10%	13.40%	1.34%
Common stock	20,000,000	40%	17.11%	6.84%
Retained earnings	5,000,000	10%	16.00%	1.60%
	$50,000,000	100%		11.84%

Overall cost of capital = k_o = 11.84%

Market Value Weights

Market value weights are determined by dividing the market value of each source by the sum of the market values of all sources. The use of market value weights for computing a firm's weighted average cost of capital

is theoretically more appealing than the use of book value weights because the market values of the securities closely approximate the actual dollars to be received from their sale.

■ Example 8

In addition to the data from Example 7, assume that the security market prices are as follows:

Mortgage bonds = $1,100 per bond
Preferred stock = $90 per share
Common stock = $80 per share

The firm's number of securities in each category is

$$\text{Mortgage bonds} = \frac{\$20,000,000}{\$1,000} = 20,000$$

$$\text{Preferred stock} = \frac{\$5,000,000}{\$100} = 50,000$$

$$\text{Common stock} = \frac{\$20,000,000}{\$40} = 500,000$$

Therefore, the market value weights are

Source	Number of Securities	Price	Market Value
Debt	20,000	$1,100	$22,000,000
Preferred stock	50,000	90	4,500,000
Common stock	500,000	80	40,000,000
			$66,500,000

The $40 million common stock value must be split in the ratio of 4 to 1 (the $20 million common stock versus the $5 million retained earnings in the original capital structure) since the market value of the retained earnings has been impounded into the common stock.

The firm's cost of capital is as follows:

Source	Market Value	Weights	Cost	Weighted Average
Debt	$22,000,000	33.08%	5.14%	1.70%
Preferred stock	4,500,000	6.77%	13.40%	0.91%
Common stock	32,000,000	48.12%	17.11%	8.23%
Retained earnings	8,000,000	12.03%	16.00%	1.92%
	$66,500,000	100.00%		12.76%

Overall cost of capital = k_o = 12.76%

Target Weights

If the firm has determined the capital structure it believes most consistent with its goal, the use of that capital structure and associated weights is appropriate.

Marginal Weights

The use of marginal weights involves weighting the specific costs of various types of financing by the percentage of the total financing expected to be raised using each method. In using target weights, the firm is concerned with what it believes to be the optimal capital structure or target percentage. In using marginal weights, the firm is concerned with the actual dollar amounts of each type of financing to be needed for a given investment project.

■ Example 9

The Carter Company is considering raising $8 million for plant expansion. Management

estimates using the following mix for financing this project:

Debt	$4,000,000	50%
Common stock	2,000,000	25%
Retained earnings	2,000,000	25%
	$8,000,000	100%

The company's cost of capital is computed as shown below.

Level of Financing and the Marginal Cost of Capital (MCC)

Because external equity capital has a higher cost than retained earnings due to flotation costs, the weighted cost of capital increases for each dollar of new financing. Therefore, the lower cost capital sources are used first. In fact, the firm's cost of capital is a function of the size of its total investment. A schedule or graph relating the firm's cost of capital to the level of new financing is called the weighted marginal cost of capital (MCC). Such a schedule is used to determine the

Source	Marginal Weights	Cost	Weighted Cost
Debt	50%	5.14%	2.57%
Common stock	25%	17.11%	4.28%
Retained earnings	25%	16.00%	4.00%
	100%		10.85%

Overall cost of capital = k_o = 10.85%

discount rate to be used in the firm's capital budgeting process. The steps to be followed in calculating the firm's marginal cost of capital are summarized below.

1. Determine the cost and the percentage of financing to be used for each source of capital (debt, preferred stock, common stock equity).

2. Compute the break points on the MCC curve where the weighted cost will increase. The formula for computing the break points is

$$\text{Break point} = \frac{\begin{array}{c}\text{Maximum amount of the} \\ \text{lower cost source of capital}\end{array}}{\begin{array}{c}\text{Percentage of financing} \\ \text{provided by the source}\end{array}}$$

3. Calculate the weighted cost of capital over the range of total financing between break points.

4. Construct an MCC schedule or graph that shows the weighted cost of capital for each level of total new financing. This schedule will be used in conjunction with the firm's available investment opportunities schedule (IOS) in order to select the investments. As long as a project's IRR is greater than the marginal cost of new financing, the project should be accepted. Also, the point at which the IRR intersects the MCC gives the optimal capital budget.

■ Example 10

A firm is contemplating three investment projects, A, B, and C, whose initial cash outlays and expected IRR are shown below. IOS for these projects is

Project	Cash Outlay	IRR
A	$2,000,000	13%
B	$2,000,000	15%
C	$1,000,000	10%

If these projects are accepted, the financing will consist of 50% debt and 50% common stock. The firm should have $1.8 million in earnings available for reinvestment (internal common). The firm will consider only the effects of increases in the cost of common stock on its marginal cost of capital.

1. The costs of capital for each source of financing have been computed and are given following:

Source	Cost
Debt	5%
Common stock ($1.8 million)	15%
New common stock	19%

If the firm uses only internally generated common stock, the weighted cost of capital is

$k_o = \Sigma$ percentage of the total capital structure supplied by each source of capital $\times$ Cost of capital for each source

In this case the capital structure is composed of 50% debt and 50% internally generated common stock. Thus:

$$k_o = (0.5)5\% + (0.5)15\% = 10\%$$

If the firm uses only new common stock, the weighted cost of capital is

$$k_o = (0.5)5\% + (0.5)19\% = 12\%$$

Range of Total New Financing (in millions of dollars)	Type of Capital	Proportion	Cost	Weighted Cost
$0–$3.6	Debt	0.5	5%	2.5%
	Internal common	0.5	15%	7.5
				10.0%
$3.6 and up	Debt	0.5	5%	2.5%
	New common	0.5	19%	9.5
				12.0%

2. Next compute the break point, which is the level of financing at which the weighted cost of capital increases.

$$\text{Break point} = \frac{\begin{array}{c}\text{Maximum amount of source}\\\text{of the lower cost}\\\text{source of capital}\end{array}}{\begin{array}{c}\text{Percentage financing}\\\text{provided by the source}\end{array}}$$

$$= \frac{\$1,800,000}{0.5} = \$3,600,000$$

3. That is, the firm may be able to finance $3.6 million in new investments with internal common stock and debt without having to change the current mix of 50% debt and 50% common stock. Therefore, if the total financing is $3.6 million or less, the firm's cost of capital is 10%.

4. Construct the MCC schedule on the IOS graph to determine the discount rate to be used in order to decide in which project to invest and to show the firm's optimal capital budget. See Figure 1.

The firm should continue to invest up to the point where the IRR equals the MCC. From the graph in Figure 1, note that the firm should invest in projects B and A, since each IRR exceeds the marginal cost of capital. The firm should reject project C since its cost of capital is greater than the IRR. The optimal capital budget is $4 million,

since this is the sum of the cash outlay required for projects A and B.

COST OF PREDICTION ERRORS There is always a cost involved with a failure to predict a certain variable accurately. For example, assume that a company has been selling a toy doll having a cost of $0.60 for $1.00 each. The fixed cost is $300. The company has no privilege of returning any unsold dolls. It has predicted sales of 2,000 units. However, unforeseen competition has reduced sales to 1,500 units. Then the cost of its prediction error—that is, its failure to predict demand accurately—would be calculated as follows:

1. Initial predicted sales = 2,000 units.
Optimal decision: purchase 2,000 units.
Expected net income = $500 [(2,000 units × $0.40 contribution) − $300 fixed costs]

2. Alternative parameter value = 1,500 units.
Optimal decision: purchase 1,500 units.
Expected net income = $300 [(1,500 units × $0.40 contribution) − $300 fixed costs]

3. Results of original decision under alternative parameter value.
Expected net income:
Revenue (1,500 units × $1.00) − Cost of dolls (2,000 units × $0.60) − $300 fixed costs = $1,500 − $1,200 − $300 = $0.

4. Cost of prediction error, (2) − (3) = $300.

COST-PLUS PRICING This is a widely used pricing technique that involves: (1) defining an appropriate cost base and (2) adding the markup. There are two primary approaches to cost-plus pricing: the *absorption* or *full cost approach* and the *contribution approach*.

1. The absorption (or full) cost approach defines the cost base as the full unit manufacturing cost. Selling and administrative costs are provided for through the markup that is added

Figure 1 MCC Schedule and IOS Graph

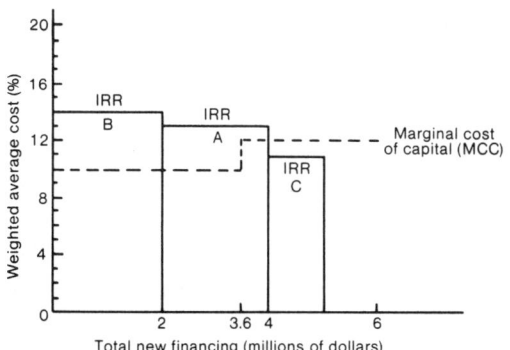

Total new financing (millions of dollars)

to the cost base. This approach is also called *full-cost-plus pricing*.

2. The contribution approach defines the cost base as the unit variable cost. Fixed costs are provided for through the markup that is added to this base. This approach is also called the *contribution approach to pricing*.

■ Example

XYZ Company has accumulated the following cost data on its regular product:

	Per Unit	Total
Direct materials	$6	
Direct labor	4	
Variable overhead	4	
Fixed overhead (based on 20,000 units)	6	$120,000
Variable selling and administrative expenses	1	
Fixed selling and administrative expenses (based on 20,000 units)	2	

Assume that in order to obtain its desired selling price, the company has a general policy of adding a markup equal to 50% of the full unit cost or 100% of the unit variable cost.

Under the absorption approach, the desired unit selling price is

Direct materials	$ 6
Direct labor	4
Factory overhead	10 ($4 + $6)
Full (or absorption) cost per unit	$20
Markup to cover selling and administrative expenses and desired profit —50% of full cost per unit	10
Desired selling price	$30

Using the contribution approach, the desired selling price is determined as follows:

Direct materials	$ 6
Direct labor	4
Variable costs (overhead, selling, and administration)	5
Variable cost per unit	$15
Markup to cover fixed costs and desired profit —100% of variable cost per unit	15
Desired selling price	$30

COST-VOLUME FORMULA A cost-volume formula, also called a *flexible budget formula*, is a cost function in the form of

$$y = a + bx$$

where y = mixed (semivariable) costs to be broken up,

x = any given measure of activity such as machine or labor hours,

a = the fixed cost component,

b = the variable rate per unit of x.

For example, the cost-volume formula for factory overhead is $y = \$100 + \$5x$ where y = estimated factory overhead and x = direct labor hours, which means that the factory overhead is estimated to be $100 fixed, plus $5 per hour of direct labor. Cost accountants use the formula for *cost estimation* and *flexible budgeting* purposes. *See also* Cost Function; Flexible Budgets and Performance Reports.

COST-VOLUME-PROFIT (CVP) AND BREAK-EVEN ANALYSIS CVP analysis, together with cost behavior information, helps managers perform many useful analyses. CVP analysis deals with how profit and costs change with a change in volume. More specifically, it looks at the effects on profits of changes in such factors as variable costs, fixed costs, selling prices, volume, and mix of products sold. By studying the relationships of costs, sales, and net income, management is better

able to cope with many planning decisions. Break-even analysis, a branch of CVP analysis, determines the break-even sales, which is the level of sales where total costs equal total revenue.

Questions Answered by CVP Analysis

1. What sales volume is required to break even?
2. What sales volume is necessary in order to earn a desired profit?
3. What profit can be expected on a given sales volume?
4. How would changes in selling price, variable costs, fixed costs, and output affect profits?
5. How would a change in the mix of products sold affect the break-even and target income volume and profit potential?

Concepts of Contribution Margin (CM)

For accurate CVP analysis, a distinction must be made between costs as being either variable or fixed. Semivariable costs (or mixed costs) must be separated into their variable and fixed components.

In order to compute the break-even point and perform various CVP analyses, note the following important concepts.

Contribution margin (CM). The contribution margin is the excess of sales (S) over the variable costs (VC) of the product. It is the amount of money available to cover fixed costs (FC) and to generate profits. Symbolically, $CM = S - VC$.

Unit CM. The unit CM is the excess of the unit selling price (p) over the unit variable cost (v). Symbolically, unit $CM = p - v$.

CM ratio. The CM ratio is the contribution margin as a percentage of sales, that is

$$CM \text{ ratio} = \frac{CM}{S} = \frac{S - VC}{S} = 1 - \frac{VC}{S}$$

The CM ratio can also be computed using per-unit data as follows:

$$CM \text{ ratio} = \frac{\text{Unit } CM}{p} = \frac{p - v}{p} = 1 - \frac{v}{p}$$

Note that the CM ratio is 1 minus the variable cost ratio. For example, if variable costs account for 70% of the price, the CM ratio is 30%.

■ Example 1

To illustrate the various concepts of CM, consider the following data for Company Z:

	Per Unit	Total	Percentage
Sales (1,500 units)	$25	$37,500	100
Less: Variable costs	10	15,000	40
Contribution margin	$15	$22,500	60
Less: Fixed costs		15,000	
Net income		$ 7,500	

From the data just listed, CM, unit CM, and the CM ratio are computed as:

$$CM = S - VC = \$37,500 - \$15,000 = \$22,500$$
$$\text{Unit } CM = p - v = \$25 - \$10 = \$15$$
$$CM \text{ ratio} = \frac{CM}{S} = \frac{\$22,500}{\$37,500}$$
$$= 60\% \text{ or } 1 - \frac{VC}{S} = 1 - 0.4 = 0.6 = 60\%$$

Break-Even Analysis

The break-even point, the point of no profit and no loss, provides managers with insights into profit planning. It can be computed in three different ways:
1. The equation approach
2. The contribution approach
3. The graphical approach

The *equation approach* is based on the cost-volume equation, which shows the relationships among sales, variable and fixed costs, and net income: $S = VC + FC +$ Net income. At the break-even volume, $S = VC + FC + 0$.

Defining x = volume in units, this relationship can be rewritten in terms of x: $px = vx + FC$. To find the break-even point in units, simply solve the equation for x.

■ Example 2

In Example 1, $p = \$25$, $v = \$10$, and $FC = \$15,000$. Thus, the equation is

$$\$25x = \$10x + \$15,000$$
$$\$25x - \$10x = \$15,000$$
$$(\$25 - \$10)x = \$15,000$$
$$\$15x = \$15,000$$
$$x = \$15,000/\$15 = 1,000 \text{ units}$$

Therefore, Company Z breaks even at a sales volume of 1,000 units.

The *contribution margin approach*, another technique for computing the break-even point, is based on solving the cost-volume equation. Solving the equation $px = vx + FC$ for x yields:

$$x_{BE} = \frac{FC}{p - v}$$

where $p - v$ is the unit CM by definition, and x_{BE} = break-even unit sales volume. In words,

$$\text{Break-even point in units} = \frac{\text{Fixed costs}}{\text{Unit } CM}$$

If the break-even point is desired in terms of dollars, then:

Break-even point in dollars = Break-even point
in units ×
unit sales price = $x_{BE} \cdot p$

Or, alternatively,

$$\text{Break-even point in dollars} = \frac{\text{Fixed costs}}{\text{CM ratio}}$$

■ Example 3

Using the same date given in Example 1, where unit $CM = \$25 - \$10 = \$15$ and CM ratio = 60%, we get:

Break-even point in units = \$15,000/\$15
= 1,000 units

Break-even point in dollars = 1,000 units
× \$25 = \$25,000

or, alternatively:

$$\$15,000/0.6 = \$25,000$$

The *graphical approach* is based on the so-called break-even chart, as shown in Figure 1. Sales revenue, variable costs, and fixed costs are plotted on the horizontal axis. The break-even point is the point where the total sales revenue line intersects the total cost line. The chart can also effectively report profit potentials over a wide range of activity. The profit-volume $(P - V)$ chart, as shown in Figure 2, focuses more directly on how profits vary with changes in volume. Profits are plotted on the vertical axis, whereas units of output are shown on the horizontal axis. Note that the slope of the chart is the unit CM.

Figure 1 Break-Even Chart

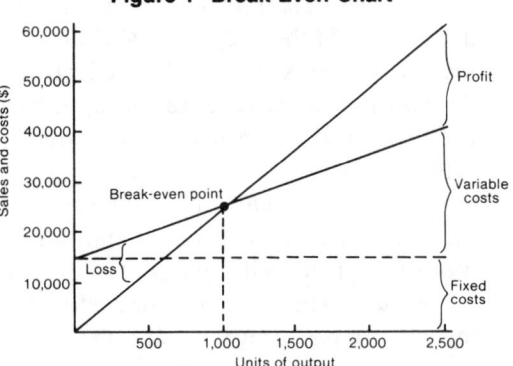

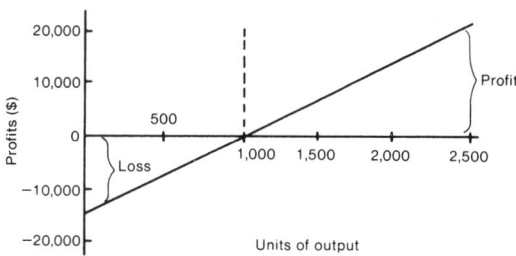

Figure 2   Profit-Volume (P/V) Chart

Determination Target Income Volume

Besides being able to determine the break-even point, *CVP* analysis determines the sales required to attain a particular income level or target net income. There are two ways target net income can be expressed:

Case 1—as a specific dollar amount.

Case 2—as a percentage of sales.

Case 1—as a specific dollar amount. The cost-volume equation specifying target net income is

$$px = vx + FC + \text{Target income}$$

Solving the equation for x yields:

$$x_{TI} = \frac{FC + \text{Target income}}{p - v}$$

where x_{TI} = sales volume required to achieve a given target income.

In words,

Target income sales volume
$$= \frac{\text{Fixed costs plus target income}}{\text{Unit } CM}$$

Case 2—specifying target income as a percentage of sales, the cost-volume equation is

$$px = vx + FC + \%(px)$$

Solving this for x yields:

$$x_{TI} = \frac{FC}{p - v - \%(p)}$$

In words,

Target income sales volume
$$= \frac{\text{Fixed costs}}{\text{Unit } CM - \% \text{ of unit sales price}}$$

■ Example 4

Using the same data given in Example 1, assume that Company Z wishes to attain:

• Case 1—a target income of $15,000 before tax

• Case 2—a target income of 20% sales

In Case 1, target income sales volume (in units) required would be

$$x_{TI} = \frac{FC + \text{Target income}}{p - v}$$
$$= \frac{\$15,000 + \$15,000}{\$25 - \$10} = 2,000 \text{ units}$$

In Case 2, the target income volume required would be

$$x_{TI} = \frac{FC}{p - v - \%(p)}$$
$$= \frac{\$15,000}{\$15 - (20\%)(\$25)}$$
$$= \frac{\$15,000}{\$15 - \$5} = 1,500 \text{ units}$$

To prove:

Sales (1,500 units)	$37,500	(100%)
VC (1,500 units)	−15,000	
CM	$22,500	(60%)
FC	−15,000	
Net income	$ 7,500	(20%)

Impact of Income Taxes

If target income is given on an after-tax basis, the target income volume formula becomes:

Target income volume = $\dfrac{\text{Fixed costs} + [\text{Target after-tax income}/(1\text{-tax rate})]}{\text{Unit } CM}$

■ Example 5

Assume in Example 1 that Company Z wants to achieve an after-tax income of $6,000. An income tax is levied at 40%. Then:

Target income volume

$$= \frac{\$15,000 + [\$6,000/(1 - 0.4)]}{\$15}$$

$$= \frac{\$15,000 + \$10,000}{\$15} = 1,667 \text{ units}$$

Margin of Safety

The margin of safety is a measure of difference between the budgeted level of sales and the break-even sales. It is the amount by which sales revenue may drop before losses begin, and is expressed as a percentage of budgeted sales:

Margin of safety

$$= \frac{\text{Budgeted sales} - \text{Break-even sales}}{\text{Budgeted sales}}$$

The margin of safety is often used as a measure of risk. The larger the ratio, the safer is the situation, since there is less risk of reaching the break-even point.

■ Example 6

Assume Company Z projects sales of $30,000 with a break-even sales level of $25,000. The expected margin of safety is

$$\frac{\$30,000 - \$25,000}{\$30,000} = 16.7\%$$

Some Applications of CVP Analysis and What-If Analysis

The concepts of contribution margin have many applications in profit planning and short-term decision making. Some applications are illustrated in Examples 7 to 11 using the same data as in Example 1.

■ Example 7

Recall from Example 1 that Company Z has a *CM* of 60% and fixed costs of $15,000 per period. Assume that the company expects sales to go up by $10,000 for the next period. How much will income increase?

Using the *CM* concepts, we can quickly compute the impact of a change in sales on profits. The formula for computing the impact is

Change in net income

$$= \text{Dollar change in sales} \times CM \text{ ratio}$$

Thus, in this question,

Increase in net income $- \$10,000 \times 60\% - \$6,000$

Therefore, the income will go up by $6,000, assuming there is no change in fixed costs.

If we are given the change in sales in units instead of dollars, then the formula becomes:

Change in net income

$$= \text{Change in unit sales} \times \text{Unit } CM$$

■ Example 8

What before-tax income is expected on sales of $47,500? The answer is the difference between the *CM* and the fixed costs:

CM: $47,500 × 60%	$28,500
Less: Fixed costs	15,000
Net income	$13,500

■ Example 9

Company Z is considering increasing the advertising budget by $5,000, which would increase sales revenue by $8,000. Should the advertising budget be increased?

The answer is no, since the increase in the *CM* is less than the increased cost:

Increase in *CM*: $8,000 × 60%	$4,800
Increase in advertising	5,000
Decrease in net income	$ (200)

■ Example 10

Company Z's sales manager is considering a $3,000 increase in sales salaries. What additional sales are required to cover the higher cost?

The increase in fixed cost must be matched by an equal increase in *CM*:

Increase in *CM* = Increase in fixed cost

0.60 sales = $3,000

Sales = $5,000

■ Example 11

Consider the original data. Assume again that Company Z is currently selling 1,500 units per period. In an effort to increase sales, management is considering cutting its unit price by $5 and increasing the advertising budget by $1,000. If these two steps are taken, management feels that unit sales will go up by 60%. Should the two steps be taken?

A $5 reduction in the selling price will cause the unit *CM* to decrease from $15 to $10. Thus:

Proposed *CM*: 2,400 units × $10	$24,000
Present *CM*: 1,500 units × $15	22,500
Increase in *CM*	$ 1,500
Increase in advertising outlay	1,000
Increase in net income	$ 500

The answer, therefore, is yes.

Sales Mix Analysis

Break-even and cost-volume-profit analysis require some additional computations and assumptions when a company produces and sells more than one product. Different selling prices and different variable costs result in different unit *CM* and *CM* ratios. As a result, break-even points vary with the relative proportions of the products sold, called the sales mix. In break-even and CVP analysis, it is necessary to predetermine the sales mix and then compute a weighted average *CM*. It is also necessary to assume that the sales mix does not change for a specified period. The break-even formula for the company as a whole is

$$\text{Company-wide break-even in units (or in dollars)} = \frac{\text{Fixed costs}}{\text{Average unit } CM \text{ (or average } CM \text{ ratio)}}$$

■ Example 12

Assume that Company X has two products with the following *CM* data:

	A	B
Selling price	$15	$10
Variable cost	12	5
Unit *CM*	$ 3	$ 5
Sales mix	60%	40%
Fixed costs	$76,000	

The weighted average unit *CM* = ($3)(0.6) + ($5)(0.4) = $3.80. Therefore, the company's break-even point in units is

$$\$76,000 / \$3.80 = 20,000 \text{ units}$$

which is divided as follows:

A: 20,000 units × 60% = 12,000 units
B: 20,000 units × 40% = 8,000
20,000 units

■ Example 13

Assume that Company Y produces and sells three products with the following data:

	A	B	C	Total
Sales	$30,000	$60,000	$10,000	$100,000
Sales mix	30%	60%	10%	100%
Less: VC	24,000	40,000	5,000	69,000
CM	$ 6,000	$20,000	$ 5,000	$ 31,000
CM ratio	20%	33⅓%	50%	31%

Total fixed costs are $18,600.
The *CM* ratio for Company Y is $31,000/$100,000 = 31%. Therefore, the break-even point in dollars is

$$\$18,600/0.31 = \$60,000$$

which will be split in the mix ratio of 3:6:1 to give us the following break-even points for the individual products A, B, and C:

A: $60,000 × 30% = $18,000
B: $60,000 × 60% = 36,000
C: $60,000 × 10% = 6,000
$60,000

One of the most important assumptions underlying CVP analysis in a multiproduct firm is that the sales mix will not change during the planning period. But if the sales

mix changes, the break-even point will also change.

■ Example 14

Assume that total sales from Example 13 remain unchanged at $100,000 but that a shift is expected in mix from product B to product C, as shown below.

Note that the shift in sales mix toward the more profitable line C has caused the *CM* ratio for the company as a whole to go up from 31% to 36%. The new break-even point will be $18,600/0.36 = $51,667. The break-even dollar volume has decreased from $60,000 to $51,667.

Break-Even and CVP Analysis Assumptions

The CVP models are subject to several limiting assumptions:
1. The behavior of both sales revenue and expenses is linear throughout the entire relevant range of activity.
2. There is only one product or a constant sales mix.
3. Volume is the only factor affecting variable costs.
4. Inventories do not change significantly from period to period.

CRITICAL PATH METHOD   CPM is a technique for project management that uses a single time estimate for each activity, rather than three time estimates (optimistic, most likely, and pessimistic). The primary objective of CPM is to identify the critical path for a project. *See also* Program Evaluation and Review Technique (PERT).

CURRENCY FUTURES CONTRACT   The holder of the contract has the right to a given amount of foreign currency at a later date. Standardized contracts exist, and there is a secondary market. The contract is expressed in terms of dollars or cents per unit of the related foreign currency. The delivery date is usually no more than 1 year.

Trading Units of Different Currencies

Currency	Trading Unit
British pound	25,000
Canadian dollar	100,000
Swiss franc	125,000
West German mark	125,000

Currency futures may be used for hedging or speculation purposes. A banker might hedge in a currency to lock in the best money exchange possible.

■ Example

A financial manager agrees to obtain pounds in 6 months. If the pound declines relative to the dollar, there is less value to the manager. To hedge his exposure, the manager can sell a futures contract in pounds by going short. If the pound declines in value, there will be a gain in the futures contract offsetting the loss when the manager receives the pounds.

	A	B	C	Total
Sales	$30,000	$30,000	$40,000	$100,000
Sales mix	30%	30%	40%	100%
Less: VC	24,000	20,000*	20,000	64,000
CM	$ 6,000	$10,000	$20,000	$ 36,000
CM ratio	20%	33⅓%	50%	36%

* $20,000 = $30,000 × 66⅔%

■ Example

There is a standardized contract of 50,000 pounds. In April, a currency futures contract is bought for delivery in August. The contract price is $1 equals 2.5 pounds. The contract's value is $20,000, and the margin requirement is $3,000. The pound becomes more valuable in the currency market equaling 2 pounds to $1. Thus, the value of the contract increases to $25,000, providing a return of 167%. In the event of a weakening pound, a loss would have been incurred.

CURRENT SERVICE COST   This is the actuarial present value of benefits derived from the pension benefit formula for employee services rendered in the current year. It is a component of pension expense. *See also* Pension Plans.

CURTAILMENT IN PENSION PLAN   An occurrence significantly *reducing* employees' future service years or eliminating for many the accrual of benefits for future services. *See also* Pension Plans.

D

DATA BASE MANAGEMENT SYSTEMS (DBMS)

A data base package is an organized collection of readily accessible related information used on a recurring basis by the financial manager and/or accounting practitioner. There are numerous examples where this package can be used (e.g., accounts receivable and inventory monitoring). DBMS acts as an administration aid by enabling the accessing of data items in many different, logically related files (e.g., a master file contains permanent information updated by transactional file data). Data base systems also provide answers to numerous questions from the same data file. The DBMS integrates data in one place so that it can be shared by all systems. Thus, any change automatically can impact all relevant and interrelated systems. It also allows cross-referencing of data among files to eliminate data repetition.

Data base programs allow practitioners to enter, manipulate, retrieve, display, extract, select, sort, edit, and index data. DBMS packages define the structure of collected data, design screen formats for input information, handle files, and generate reports. In creating a data base, the user has to name the fields and describe the type of data in each field. DBMS permits the creation of financial statement formats and the performance of numerical calculations. In essence, it is an electronic filing cabinet providing a common core of information accessible by a program. DBMS allows the accountant or auditor to formulate custom programs and applications by stipulating what data must be entered into the microcomputer and what should be done to it to accomplish the desired output.

Data base packages can be used for specific purposes and general applications. The first may only be utilized for the particular objective for which it was designed (e.g., accounting module for accounts receivable). The second type lets the CPA set up the objective and design of the data base. The types of general application data base programs include file managers and relational data base systems. Differences primarily exist in the capacity to use information from more than one file concurrently. File managers can support many individual files, but only one file may be accessed and manipulated at a time. A File Management System is software permitting the user to describe file, processing, and report formats to produce a data processing system without the need to write computer programs. Relational

Exhibit 1   Hierarchical Data Base Model for Staff Assignments

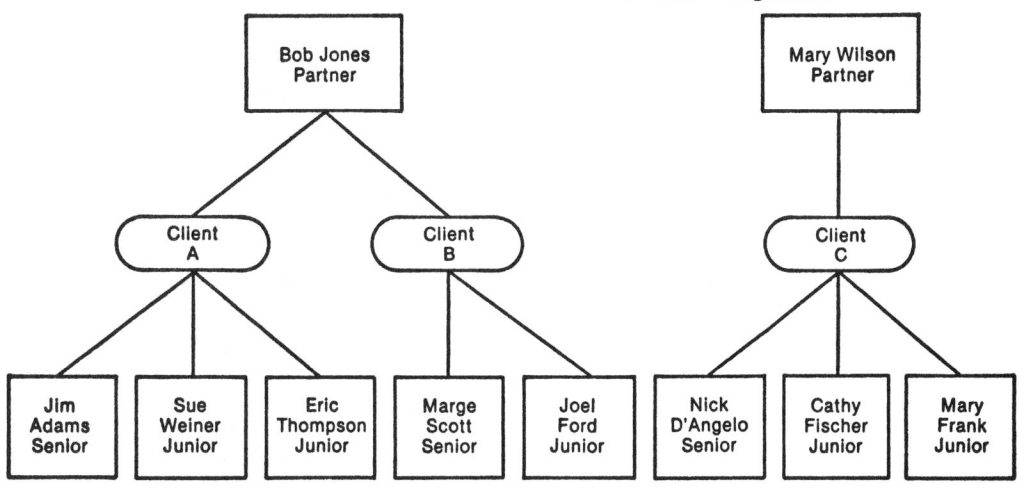

data bases can access data from two or more files concurrently. This ability varies depending on the particular program.

Data Base Models

Data bases relate data sets into one of three models comprising hierarchical, network, and relational.

In a hierarchical data base manager (tree-structured), one data set is subservient to another (i.e., parent–child relationship). For example, data may be put in a standard input form and then taken from that form to prepare reports. The finalized reports represent modifications of data included in one master information form. A filer puts data in any order desired. Here, data are stored in discrete records. A real-life example is a "tree" model for staff assignments for audit engagements. As can be seen in Exhibit 1, a one-to-one relationship exists. That is one path is followed by the individual data elements.

Modification of the hierarchical data base to include multipath relationships converts

Exhibit 2   Network Data Base Model for Staff Assignments

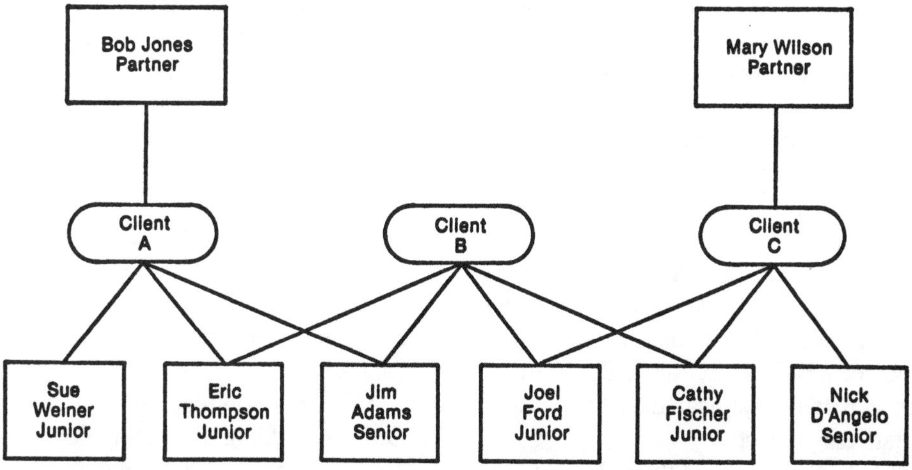

Exhibit 3 Partial Relational Data Base Model for Staff Assignments

COLUMNS

Partner	Client	Staff Member
Bob Jones	A	Jim Adams
Bob Jones	B	Jim Adams
Bob Jones	C	Jim Adams
Mary Wilson	A	Jim Adams
Mary Wilson	B	Jim Adams
Mary Wilson	C	Jim Adams
Bob Jones	A	Sue Weiner
Bob Jones	B	Sue Weiner
Bob Jones	C	Sue Weiner
Mary Wilson	A	Sue Weiner
Mary Wilson	B	Sue Weiner
Mary Wilson	C	Sue Weiner
, ,	,	, ,
, ,	,	, ,
, ,	,	, ,

(R O W S)

the DBMS into a network data base. Such a relationship exists in Exhibit 2.

A relational data base manager has data sets of information in a table of rows and columns (matrix) with no parent–child relationship. Information is stored in two-dimensional data sets or tables similar to a traditional file-processing system, and there is an integration of several different files. The reports produced from this can have greater complexity and they could be more useful than is the case with a hierarchical system. A relational data base allows for the access of data fields by enabling the accountant to ignore the traditional one-to-one relationship by permitting access to a particular grid or cell. For example, if a relational data base includes first and last names of clients as well as their area codes, telephone numbers, street address, city, state, and zip code, data can be accessed by stipulating any one of the parameters for selection. Exhibit 3 illustrates a partial relational data base system for staff assignments.

dBASE III+™, by Ashton-Tate, is one of the more powerful and popular data base models that makes use of this type of system.

Features

An appraisal should be made by the accountant or financial person of a particular DBMS package in terms of

• Compatibility with other packages and applications in terms of ascertaining whether data formatted with other data base packages can be imported and translated into the format your program utilizes. Also, how many other programs can the DBMS package exchange data with?

• Commands that make sense in describing the operation to be performed.

• Search capabilities.

• The number of fields that can be edited at a time.

• Permitting an enumerated field that allows for specifying all of a field's possible values.

• Flexibility in field type and record structure (i.e., adding or deleting fields even subsequent to entering information on records).

• Types and limitations of data field. It

is crucial that the program have the ability to handle the types of fields the practitioner requires and that the fields are sufficient to permit expansion should the need arise.

• Ability to hide selected facts.

• Ability to generate derived or computed fields. A derived field is one that performs mathematical calculations on data sorted in other fields.

• Processing of multiple files simultaneously.

• Available formats for reporting purposes.

• Report features in terms of graphics and formatting.

• Reformatting ease (allowing for changing a format at any time).

• Error-catching ability (i.e., existence of unique fields to prevent erroneous duplication of records).

• Error messages along with an indexed listing of all errors at the end of the manual.

• Number and size of records that can be contained in one file, including maximum records to be accommodated. Care must be exercised in selection to ensure that the program is capable of handling more records than your present needs mandate. For instance, if the DBMS is to be used for billing, the maximum number of records capable of being accommodated should be greatly in excess of your present client or customer list.

• Linkage of files, where a change in one automatically changes another.

• Creation of a new data base representing a subset of a parent file.

• Ability to peek into unopened files of the data base. For example, while looking at the inventory file, a view command allows for the calling of an unrelated file onto the screen.

• Capability to sort data. Sorting can be on the basis of numeric or alphabetic relationships. More sophisticated programs like dBASE III+™ have the ability to sort data utilizing a "conditional sort" command. For example, client customers can be selected

for accounts receivable confirmations "if" their balances exceed a prescribed limit. Sorting based on "multiple key fields" is a further extension of the capabilities of many DBMS. Thus, telephone numbers can be arranged in ascending or descending order, firstly by area code and then by the first three digits of the number.

• Calculational ability, including present value, future value, growth rate, log, exponential notation, square root, and absolute value. If a derivation is changed, the program automatically recomputes the data throughout the data base.

• Ability to work with many files at once.

• Available templates for different applications. A template is a preformatted setup that comes ready for use. The practitioner merely inputs data relevant to a specific application. For example, a template may exist for the maintenance of perpetual inventory records relevant to fixed asset additions and deletions.

• Window features. This enables the accountant to simultaneously use and view different files and/or programs. This is especially useful for integrating data base files with word processing applications.

Applications

Financial managers and accountants may utilize DMBS for the following applications:

• Retrieving information based on varied criteria. In a general ledger formatted data base, the accountant has the ability to recall or retrieve information based upon varied criteria; that is, based upon (a) the date a check was issued, (b) the payee, (c) the amount paid, or (d) the account to which an amount was posted. If the "payee" criteria is selected, a listing may be generated of all checks written over a specified period. This assists in the audit attest function.

• Searching for accounting records having a key word or amount such as listing accounts that are 90 days past due.

• Establishing upper and lower limits. This may be utilized by clients in establishing credit limits. From the accountant's point of view, this can assist in the selection of accounts receivable to be confirmed positively and negatively. Similarly, assistance is available for the confirmation of other accounts, such as accounts payable.

• Field calculations. A client's DBMS with this ability facilitates the footings and extensions of inventory listings. Further, in applying the lower-of-cost-or-market rule, field calculations can prove most useful.

• Existence of utility functions to assist accountants in conducting common functions. A good data base program should provide the more common utility functions so as to enable the practitioner to (a) rename existing files without destroying its contents, (b) copy or transport the contents of a particular file to another file, and (c) erase files permanently.

• Asking what-if questions and their effect on client financial data. This feature, most commonly found in spreadsheets, enables the practitioner to recalculate the effects of changing one or more variables. One application is in the use of forecasting.

• Audit aspects such as performing entry validation procedures. Also, it can be used in analytical review in terms of performing ratio analysis of selected accounts of interest to the auditor. A data base showing a schedule of expenses and revenue by type and data may be made for audit analysis, where warranted. Further, asset listings may be made to evaluate the adequacy of insurance coverage.

• Preparation of listings by client, customer, supplier, and so on. The tax practitioner utilizing a relational data base can format and generate schedules and reports to control the preparation of client tax returns by fiscal year-end, initial due date, and due date after any extensions. Tax returns may be for federal and local reporting, including payroll tax returns.

• Client mailing list along with telephone numbers.

• Payroll. Users of DBMS may keep track of all payroll information required by both federal and state governments.

• Inventory management. Keeping track of individual items by description, vendor, or price is no longer an involved process. Determination of reorder points, possibly using the economic order quantity (EOQ), can be built into data base application. Obsolescence can be determined when the inventory control system generates lists of items based upon given criteria.

• General ledger. Perhaps the most useful application of DBMS programs for the accountant is the preparation of client general ledgers.

• Tax preparation and planning. A data base may be established for tax information of a repetitive nature that will be used for several years. An example is the management of a stock portfolio involving acquisition dates and cost. Tax projections may be used to minimize the overall tax liability of the client considering different variables. For example, projections may be made for oil and gas shelters and the timing of the sale of securities.

DEBT FINANCING This may be short-term, intermediate-term, and long-term. Short-term and intermediate-term financing sources include trade credit, bank loan, finance company loan, commercial paper, inventory financing, and leasing. Long-term financing includes the issuance of mortgages and bonds.

Trade Credit

Trade credit is the amount owed to suppliers on account. Advantages are easy to obtain, no collateral is required, there is little or no interest, and trade creditors are more lenient than other creditors. However, trade credit is limited to certain types of items. Further, the opportunity cost of not taking

a discount on early payment should be determined, since it may be very costly.

■ Example

A $10,000 purchase is made on terms of 2/20, net/60. The opportunity cost of not taking the discount is

$$\frac{\text{Discount foregone}}{\text{Proceeds from use of}} \times \frac{360}{\text{Days use of the money}}$$

$$\frac{\$200}{\$9,800} \times \frac{360}{40} = 18.37\%$$

You could most likely borrow at a lower rate than 18.37% in order to take advantage of the discount.

Bank Loan

Types of Bank Credit

• *Unsecured loans*—recommended for financing projects that have immediate cash flow or for interim financing for a long-term project. *Suggestion*: Use for seasonal cash shortfalls, desired inventory buildups, or any situation in which you need immediate cash flow and can repay the loan quickly or shortly obtain longer term financing. Disadvantages are its short term, higher interest rate, and the fact that it is repaid in a lump sum.

• *Line of credit*—a continuing agreement for loans up to a specified amount. *Recommendation*: Use if you work on large individual projects for a long time period and obtain minimal or no payments until the job is completed. Advantages are easy access to funds in tight money periods and ability to borrow only when needed, with quick repayment possibility. Disadvantages are that collateral is required and there are greater limitations (e.g., restrictions on capital expenditures). Determine whether your line of credit is adequate for your present and immediate future needs.

• *Revolving credit*—notes are short term (typically 90 days). You may renew the loan or borrow additional funds up to a maximum amount. Advantages are readily available credit and fewer restrictions relative to the line-of-credit agreement. A disadvantage is the bank restrictions.

• *Intermediate-term loans*—recommended for financing fixed assets, acquiring another business, and to retire long-term debt. An advantage is that they may be adjusted more easily than a bond indenture or a preferred stock agreement. Disadvantages are possible collateral requirements, restrictive covenants (e.g., dividend restrictions), and periodic submission of financial reports.

• *Installment loans*—necessitate monthly payments. As the loan principal is lowered, refinancing may take place at lower interest rates. *Suggestion*: Tailor the loan to satisfy seasonal financing requirements.

The cost of a short-term loan equals

$$\frac{\text{Interest}}{\text{Proceeds Received}}$$

A bank typically discounts a loan, meaning that interest is deducted from the face of the loan to obtain the proceeds. A compensating balance also reduces the proceeds. As a result, the effective (real) interest rate on the loan exceeds the face interest, since the proceeds received are less than the face of the loan.

■ Example

You take out a $320,000, 1-year, 11% loan with a compensating balance of 15%. The loan is made on a discount basis. The effective interest rate is

$$\frac{11\% \times \$320,000}{\$236,800*} = \frac{\$35,200}{\$236,800} = 14.9\%$$

* Proceeds received equals

Face of loan	$320,000
Less:	
Interest	(35,200)
Compensating balance (15% × $320,000)	(48,000)
Proceeds	$236,800

Vital Question: If your bank chose to call your demand loans, could you obtain alterna-

tive financing without impairing your business?

Finance Company Loan

If you cannot obtain bank financing because of credit risks, you may be able to borrow from a finance company. Such borrowings are secured (collateral usually exceeds the loan balance) and they have higher interest rates than bank loans.

Commercial Paper

Commercial paper is unsecured and represents short-term notes issued by the highest quality companies. Advantages are that the interest rate is lower than the bank borrowing rate and no security is required.

■ Example

You need $300,000 for the month of November. Your options are
1. A 1-year line of credit for $300,000 with a bank. The commitment fee is 0.5%, and the interest charge on the used funds is 12%.
2. Issue 2-month commercial paper at 10% interest. Because the funds are required for only 1 month, the excess funds ($300,000) can be invested in 8% marketable securities for December. The total transaction fee for the marketable securities is 0.3%.
1. The line of credit costs:

Commitment fee for unused period (0.005) (300,000) (11/12)	$1,375
Interest for 1 month (0.12) (300,000) (1/12)	3,000
Total cost	$4,375

2. The commercial paper costs:

Interest charge (0.10) (300,000) (2/12)	$5,000
Transaction fee (0.003) (300,000)	900
Less:	
Interest earned on marketable securities (0.08) (300,000) (1/12)	(2,000)
Total cost	$3,900

Note: The commerical paper arrangement is less costly.

Inventory Financing

Inventory financing usually occurs when you have already made full use of your ability to borrow on receivables. It requires that inventory be marketable, have a high turnover rate, not be perishable, and not be subject to rapid obsolescence. Raw materials and finished goods will typically be financed at about 75% of their value. The interest rate is typically several points in excess of the prime interest rate.

■ Example

You need $500,000 for a 3-month period. An insurance company has agreed to lend you the money at an 8% per annum interest rate using the inventory as collateral. A field warehouse agreement would be used, costing $1,300 per month.

For 3 months:

$$\text{Effective interest rate} = \frac{(3 \times 1,300) + (0.08 \times 500,000 \times 3/12)}{500,000}$$

$$\frac{13,900}{500,000} = 0.028$$

For 1 year:

$$0.028 \text{ (3 months)} \times 4 = 0.112$$

Leasing

Advantages of leasing are the absence of an immediate substantial cash payment, the possibility of a bargain purchase option, the availability of the lessor's service capability, fewer financing restrictions, protection from technological obsolescence, and the fact that the obligation to pay does not necessarily have to be reported as a liability on the balance sheet. Disadvantages of leasing are higher cost than outright purchase, the necessity of paying current prices at lease termination to enter into a new lease or acquire prop-

erty, and having to use property no longer usable or suitable.

Comparing Short-term to Long-term Financing

Short-term financing is easier to arrange, has lower cost, and is more flexible than long-term financing. However, short-term financing makes the borrower more susceptible to interest rate changes, requires refinancing more quickly, and is more difficult to repay. *Recommendation*: Use short-term financing as additional working capital, to finance short-lived assets, or as interim financing on long-term projects. Long-term financing is more suitable to finance long-term assets or construction projects.

Advice: If there are financial problems, attempt to refinance short-term loans on a long-term basis, such as by extending the maturity date.

Mortgages

Mortgages are notes payable to banks, which are secured by real property and are used to finance long-term requirements (e.g., buying fixed assets, plant construction and renovation). Positive aspects are attractive interest rates, less financing restrictions than other long-term sources, long payment schedules, and availability. On the negative side, there is a collateral requirement.

Bonds

In a private placement, bonds are issued to a few investors (typically institutional investors) without a public offering. Advantages are the elimination of underwriter fees and no need for SEC registration.

Reasons to issue debt rather than equity securities are the tax deductibility of interest and the fact that you will be paying back in cheaper dollars during inflation, there is no dilution of voting control, and flexibility in financing is possible due to a call provision

in the bond indenture. Drawbacks are the required repayment of principal and fixed interest charges and indenture restrictions.

Factors Favoring Long-Term Debt Issuance

- High profits
- Stability in revenue and earnings
- Low debt to equity ratio
- Presently depressed market price of stock

Financial leverage should be employed when the entity's profits are sufficient to meet preferred stock dividends. However, when the debt position is high, the business should attempt to reduce other risks (e.g., product risk). A bond issue usually requires the establishment of a sinking fund. *Recommendation*: If you expect declining interest rates in the future, it is advisable to include a call provision.

Convertible bonds offer several positive aspects including marketability, lower interest rates, and nonrepayment because of conversion to stock.

Warning: If the maturity structure of debt requires large repayments to be due, stock issuance is recommended.

DECISION MAKING UNDER CERTAINTY

A management accountant or financial manager is often faced with a decision situation where for each decision alternative there is only one event and therefore only one outcome for each action.

■ Example

Assume there is only one possible event for the two possible actions: "Buy" a facility at a future cost of $5 per unit for 10,000 units, or "lease" it at a future cost of $4.80 for the same number of units. We can set up the following table:

Actions	Possible Outcome With Certainty
Buy	$50,000 (10,000 units × $5)
Lease	48,000 (10,000 units × $4.80)

Since there is only one possible outcome for each action (with certainty) the decision is obviously to choose the action that will result in the most desirable outcome (least cost); that is, to "lease."

DECISION MAKING UNDER UNCERTAINTY

When decisions are made in a world of uncertainty, it is often helpful to make the following computations:
1. Expected value
2. Standard deviation
3. Coefficient of variation

Expected Value

Expected value is a weighted average using the probabilities as weights. For decisions involving *uncertainty*, the concept of expected value provides a rational means for selecting the best course of action. The expected value ($E(x)$) is found by multiplying the probability of each outcome by its *payoff*.

$$E(x) = \sum_{i=1} x_i p_i$$

where x_i is the outcome for ith possible event and p_i is the probability of occurrence of that outcome.

■ Example 1

Consider two investment proposals, A and B, with the following probability distribution of cash flows in each of the next 5 years:

Cash Inflows

Probability	(0.2)	(0.3)	(0.4)	(0.1)
A	$50	200	300	400
B	$100	150	250	850

The expected value of the cash inflow in proposal A is

$50(0.2) + 200(0.3) + 300(0.4) + 400(0.1) = \$230$

The expected value of the cash inflow in proposal B is

$100(0.2) + 150(0.3) + 250(0.4) + 850(0.1) = \$250$

Standard Deviation

Standard deviation is a measure of the dispersion of a probability distribution. It is the square root of the mean of the squared deviations from the *expected value E(x)*.

$$\sigma = \sqrt{\Sigma \, (x_i - E(x))^2 p_i}$$

It is commonly used as an absolute measure of risk. The higher the standard deviation, the higher the risk.

■ Example 2

Consider the two investment proposals, A and B, in Example 1.

The standard deviations of proposals A and B are computed as follows:

For A: $= \sqrt{\begin{array}{l}(\$50 - 230)^2 \,(0.2) + (200 - 230)^2 \,(0.3) \\ + \,(300 - 230)^2 \,(0.4) + (400 - 230)^2 \\ (0.1)\end{array}} = \$107.70$

For B: $= \sqrt{\begin{array}{l}(\$100 - 250)^2 \,(0.2) + (150 - 250)^2 \,(0.3) \\ + \,(250 - 250)^2 \,(0.4) + (850 - 250)^2 \\ (0.1)\end{array}} = \$208.57$

Proposal B is more risky than proposal A, since its standard deviation is greater.

Coefficient of Variation

Coefficient of variation is a measure of relative dispersion, or relative risk. It is computed by dividing the standard deviation (σ) by the expected value $E(x)$.

■ Example 3

From Examples 1 and 2, we note:

Proposal	Expected Value	Standard Deviation
A	$230	$107.70
B	250	208.57

The coefficient of variation for each proposal is

For A: $107.70/\$230 = 0.47$

For B: $208.57/\$250 = 0.83$.

Therefore, because the coefficient is a relative measure of risk, B is considered more risky than A.

DECISION SUPPORT SYSTEMS (DSS) DSS software furnishes support to the accountant in the decision-making processes. They analyze a specific situation and can be modified as the practitioner wishes. Models are constructed and decisions analyzed. Planning and forecasting are facilitated.

Financial modeling systems such as Execum's IFPS™ (Interactive Financial Planning System) and Social Systems' SIMPLAN™ are widely used for decision support. They have a column and row format similar to a spreadsheet, but they are really multifile systems. It is important to note that financial modeling software is superior to spreadsheets because they can carry out complex modeling and evaluation. More specifically, they are designed to

• Perform what-if analysis. That is, they provide a picture of the current financial position and allow the accountant to see the effect of changes in variables upon outcome.

• Perform goal seeking (opposite of what-if) to calculate the effect required to generate a specific outcome in another variable (e.g., how much should service A be billed out to earn a certain net income?).

• Evaluate risk of the alternatives being considered.

• Perform statistical functions, including regression analysis, trend analysis, and econometrics.

• Generate graphics to illustrate accounting and financial matters.

There are special purpose packages that are widely used for decision support. They include

• Infordata Systems' INQUIRE™ for query, data retrieval, and report generation.

• SPSS™ (Statistical Package for Social Scientists) and SAS™ (Statistical Analysis System) for extensive statistical analysis and forecasting.

• Various packages handling inventory planning, material requirement planning (MRP), project management, and linear programming. *See also* Management Information System.

DECISION THEORY Although the statistics such as expected value and standard deviation are essential for choosing the best course of action under uncertainty, the decision problem can best be approached using what is called decision theory. Decision theory is a systematic approach to making decisions especially under uncertainty. Decision theory utilizes an organized approach such as a *decision matrix* (*payoff table*), which is characterized by: (1) the *row* representing a set of alternative *courses of action* available to the decision maker; (2) the *column* representing the *state of nature* or conditions that are likely to occur that the decision maker has no control over; and (3) the *entries* in the body of the table representing the outcome of the decision, known as *payoffs*, which may be in the form of costs, revenues, profits, or cash flows. By computing expected value of each action, we will be able to pick the best one.

■ Example 1

Assume the following probability distribution of daily demand for strawberries:

Daily demand	0	1	2	3
Probability	0.2	0.3	0.3	0.2

Also assume that unit cost = \$3, selling price = \$5 (i.e., profit on sold unit = \$2), and salvage value on unsold units = \$2 (i.e., loss on unsold units = \$1). We can stock either 0, 1, 2, or 3 units. The question is, How many units should be stocked each day? Assume that units from one day cannot be sold the next day. Then the payoff table can be constructed as follows:

	State of Nature				
Demand	0	1	2	3	Expected value
Stock (probability)	(0.2)	(0.3)	(0.3)	(0.2)	
0	$0	0	0	0	$0
Actions 1	−1	2	2	2	1.40
2	−2	1[a]	4	4	1.90[b]
3	−3	0	3	6	1.50

[a] Profit for (stock 2, demand 1) equals (no. of units sold) (profit per unit) − (no. of units unsold) (loss per unit) = (1) ($5 − 3) − (1) ($3 − 2) = $1

[b] Expected value for (stock 2) is −2 (0.2) + 1 (0.3) + 4 (0.3) + 4 (0.2) = $1.90.

The optimal stock action is the one with the highest *expected monetary value*; that is, stock 2 units.

Expected Value of Perfect Information

Suppose the decision maker can obtain a perfect prediction of which event (state of nature) will occur. The *expected value with perfect information* would be the total expected value of actions selected on the assumption of a perfect forecast. The *expected value of perfect information* can then be computed as: expected value with perfect information *minus* the expected value with existing information.

■ Example 2

From the payoff table in Example 1 above, the analysis at the bottom of the page yields the expected value *with* perfect information.
   Alternatively:

$0 (0.2) + 2 (0.3) + 4 (0.3) + 6 (0.2) = $3.00

With existing information, the best that the decision maker could obtain was select stock 2 and obtain $1.90. With perfect information (forecast), the decision maker could make as much as $3. Therefore, the expected value of perfect information is $3.00 − $1.90 = $1.10. This is the maximum price the decision maker is willing to pay for additional information.

DECISION TREE This is another approach used in *decision making under uncertainty*. It is a pictorial representation of a decision situation. As in the case of the *decision matrix* (*payoff table*) approach, it shows decision alternatives, states of nature, probabilities attached to the state of nature, and conditional benefits and losses. The decision tree approach is most useful in a sequential decision situation.

■ Example

Assume ABC Corporation wishes to introduce one of two products to the market this year. The probabilities and present values (PV) of projected cash inflows are given on the following page:

		State of Nature				
	Demand	0	1	2	3	Expected value
	Stock	(0.2)	(0.3)	(0.3)	(0.2)	
	0	$0				$0
Actions	1		2			0.6
	2			4		1.2
	3				6	1.2
						$3.00

Products	Initial Investment	PV of Cash Inflows	Probabilities
A	$225,000		1.00
		$450,000	0.40
		200,000	0.50
		−100,000	0.10
B	80,000		1.00
		320,000	0.20
		100,000	0.60
		−150,000	0.20

A decision tree analyzing the two products follows.

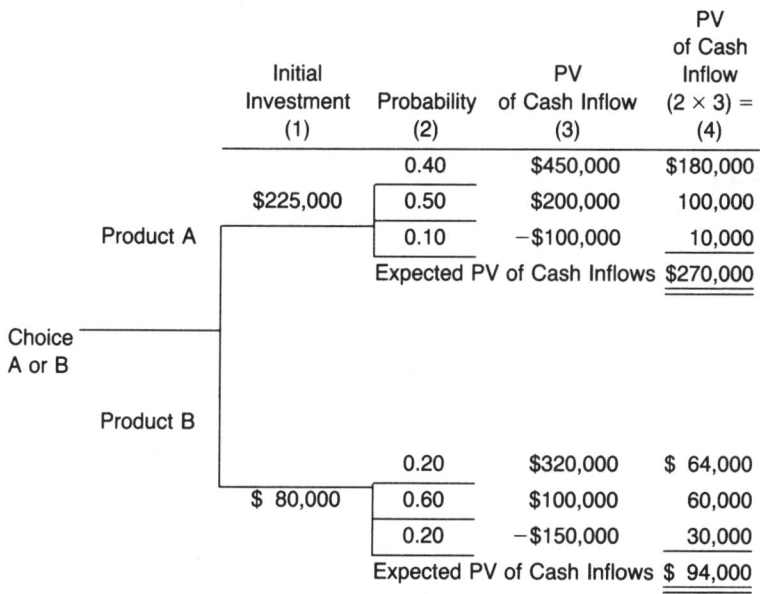

				PV of Cash Inflow
	Initial Investment (1)	Probability (2)	PV of Cash Inflow (3)	(2 × 3) = (4)
Product A	$225,000	0.40	$450,000	$180,000
		0.50	$200,000	100,000
		0.10	−$100,000	10,000
			Expected PV of Cash Inflows	$270,000
Product B	$ 80,000	0.20	$320,000	$ 64,000
		0.60	$100,000	60,000
		0.20	−$150,000	30,000
			Expected PV of Cash Inflows	$ 94,000

For Product A:

Expected NPV = expected PV − I = $270,000 − $225,000 = $45,000

For Product B:

Expected NPV = $94,000 − $80,000 = $14,000

Based on the expected net present value, the company should choose product A over product B.

DEFICIT FINANCING AND CROWDING OUT

Deficit financing refers to borrowing by a government to cover a revenue shortfall. This can stimulate the economy for a time but dampen the economy in the long run by put-ting upward pressure on interest rates. Government borrowing can create the situation of "crowding out" consumers and businesses out of credit markets. *Crowding out* means that large increases in government spending and the resultant deficit financing are likely to reduce personal consumption and business investment spending for the following reasons:

1. Financial resources that may otherwise be used by the consumer and business sectors are diverted to public use.

2. Interest rates may be pushed up due to competition between the private and public sectors, which increases the costs of borrowing by the private sector and drives it out of their financial markets.

For these reasons, private incentives to work and invest may be diminished, thereby dampening the economy.

DEFLATION This is a general decrease in prices. It is the opposite of *inflation* and distinguished from *disinflation*, which is a reduction in the rate of price increases. Deflation is caused by a reduction in the money stock of the economy. *See also* Inflation.

DEPLETION This is the physical exhaustion of a natural resource (wasting asset). Examples of wasting assets are minerals, petroleum, and timber. Natural resources are consumed physically over the years of use and do not keep their physical characteristics. Typically, depletion expense is determined using the units of production method.

■ Example

A coal mine costs $150,000. Estimated salvage value is $30,000. The estimated total tons to be extracted are 10,000. In the first year, 1,500 tons are extracted. Depletion expense is

$$\frac{\text{Cost} - \text{Salvage value}}{\text{Estimated total tons}} = \frac{\$150,000 - \$30,000}{10,000}$$

$$= \frac{\$120,000}{10,000}$$

$$= \$12 \text{ per ton}$$

Depletion equals: 1,500 tons × $12 per ton = $18,000

The entry is

| Depletion Expense | 18,000 | |
| Accumulated Depletion | | 18,000 |

DEPRECIATION This is the allocation of the historical cost of a fixed asset into expense over the period benefited to result in matching expense against revenue.

Fractional year depreciation is computing depreciation when the asset is acquired during the year. A proration is required.

■ Example

On 10/1/19X7, a fixed asset costing $10,000 with a salvage value of $1,000 and a life of 5 years is acquired.

Depreciation expense for 19X8 using the sum-of-the-years' digits method is

1/1/19X8 − 9/30/19X8 5/15 × $9,000 × 9/12 $2,250
10/1/19X8 − 12/31/19X8 4/15 × $9,000 × 3/12   600
                                                    $2,850

Depreciation expense for 19X8 using double declining balance is shown in the table at the bottom of this page.

Group and composite depreciation methods involve similar accounting. The group method is used for similar assets, whereas the composite method is used for dissimilar assets. Both methods are generally accepted. There is one accumulated depreciation account for the entire group. The depreciation rate equals

$$\frac{\text{Depreciation}}{\text{Gross cost}}$$

Depreciation expense for a period equals:

$$\text{Depreciation rate} \times \text{Gross cost}$$

The depreciable life equals:

$$\frac{\text{Depreciable cost}}{\text{Depreciation}}$$

Year	Computation	Depreciation	Book Value
0			$10,000
10/1/19X7 − 12/31/19X7	3/12 × $10,000 × 40%	$1,000	9,000
1/1/19X8 − 12/31/19X8	$9,000 × 40%	3,600	5,400

When an asset is sold in the group, the entry is

Cash (proceeds received)
Accumulated Depreciation (plug figure)
Fixed Asset (cost)

Note that upon sale of a fixed asset in the group the difference between the proceeds received and the cost of the fixed asset is plugged to accumulated depreciation. No gain or loss is recognized upon the sale. The only time a gain or loss would be recognized is if the entire assets were sold.

▪ Example

Calculations for composite depreciation appear in the table at the bottom of this page.
Composite rate:

$$\frac{\$17,600}{\$117,000} = 15.04\%$$

Composite life:

$$\frac{\$106,000}{\$17,600} = 6.02 \text{ years}$$

The entry to record depreciation is

Depreciation	17,600	
Accumulated Depreciation		17,600

The entry to sell asset B for $36,000 is

Cash	36,000	
Accumulated Depreciation	4,000	
Fixed Asset		40,000

DEPRESSION This represents a bottom phase of a business cycle in which the economy is operating with substantial unemployment of its resources (such as labor) and a depressed rate of business investment and con-

sumer spending. *See also* Business Cycle; Recession.

DESKTOP SOFTWARE In an attempt to get rid of the clutter on the accountant's or financial executive's desk, organizer software exists. Desktop software operates in windows that overlay the accountant's main application. When a desk accessory is called up, the practitioner is temporarily exiting the main program. Some accessories let the user transfer information to and from the main application. Applications cover almost all office activities. An evaluation must be made of the compatibility of the desk software to the main programs being used.

Features of Desktop Software

• Appointment calendar. When an appointment time occurs, a beep sounds.
• Telling and setting time.
• Recording time spent with specific files.
• Notepad, including a place for memos and reminders.
• Directory for mail and telephone, including names, addresses, and telephone numbers.
• Telephone dialing as well as keeping track of important calls.
• Card filing.
• Performing calculator functions.
• Dating stamps.
• Preparation of custom forms.
• Voice and modem communications.
• Ability to access and execute major DOS commands. There should also be commands to customize screens and windows.

Disk organization software enables the practitioner who has many different things

Asset	Cost	Salvage	Depreciable Cost	Life	Depreciation
A	$ 25,000	$ 5,000	$ 20,000	10	$ 2,000
B	40,000	2,000	38,000	5	7,600
C	52,000	4,000	48,000	6	8,000
	$117,000	$11,000	$106,000		$17,600

to do at one time to press some keys and become familiar with a given situation. The micro in effect can handle paperwork difficulties that come up.

■ Example

Borland International's Sidekick™ is designed to complement a word processor, data base, or spreadsheet. The windows include notepad for typing comments and memos and taking notes of telephone conversations, calculator, appointment calendar, automatic telephone dialer, and on-screen help. The windows can be moved around the screen, enlarged, and contracted. Multiple windows overlay each other, but you can change the order at any time. It has a report generator.

DEVELOPMENT STAGE ENTERPRISE A development stage entity is one concentrating on establishing a new business and either major operations have not begun or principal operations have started but no significant revenue has been derived. Some types of activities of a development stage enterprise are establishing sources of supply, developing markets, obtaining financing, financial and production planning, research and development, buying capital assets, and recruiting staff. The *same* generally accepted accounting principles for an established company must be followed by a development stage enterprise. A balance sheet, income statement, and statement of cash flows are prepared. The balance sheet shows the accumulated net losses as a deficit. The income statement presents cumulative amounts of revenues and expenses since inception of the business. Similarly, the Statement of Cash Flows presents the cumulative amount of cash. The stockholders' equity statement shows for each equity security from inception: (1) date and number of shares issued and (2) dollar figures per share applicable to cash and non-

cash consideration. The nature and basis to determine amounts for noncash consideration must also be provided.

Financial statements must be headed "Development Stage Enterprise." A footnote should describe the development stage activities. In the first year that the entity is no longer in the development stage, it should disclose that in previous years it was.

DIF (DATA INTERCHANGE FORMAT) FILE In a computer system, the DIF feature allows for the transfer of files among programs. An example is the transfer of files from a data base management system to a spreadsheet. DIF is the suffix to the file name. The accountant can import files generated on other systems (e.g., client) into the practitioner's spreadsheet or data base. Many spreadsheet and data base programs allow for the DIF format. Numerous accounting packages (e.g., BPI) enable the creation of DIF files. A financial manager can take a Lotus 1–2–3™ spreadsheet and place it into another spreadsheet or word processing program. A drawback, however, is that a DIF file requires extra storage space.

DIRECT COSTING VERSUS ABSORPTION COSTING Direct costing is a costing method where the costs to be inventoried include only the *variable* manufacturing costs. The fixed factory overhead is treated as a period cost—it is deducted along with the selling and administrative expenses in the period incurred. That is,

Direct materials	$xx
Direct labor	xx
Variable factory overhead	xx
Product cost	$xx

Under *absorption costing*, the cost to be inventoried includes all manufacturing costs, both variable and fixed. Nonmanufacturing

(operating) expenses—that is, selling and administrative expenses—are treated as period expenses and thus are charged against the current revenue.

Direct materials	$xx
Direct labor	xx
Variable factory overhead	xx
Fixed factory overhead	xx
Product cost	$xx

Two important facts are noted:
1. Effects of the two costing methods on net income:
   a. When production exceeds sales, a larger net income will be reported under absorption costing.
   b. When sales exceed production, a larger net income will be reported under direct costing.
   c. When sales and production are equal, net income will be the same under both methods.
2. Reconciliation of the direct and absorption costing net income figures:
   a. The difference in net income can be reconciled as follows:

$$\frac{\text{Difference in}}{\text{net income}} = \frac{\text{Change in}}{\text{inventory}} \times \frac{\text{Fixed factory}}{\text{overhead rate}}$$

   b. The previous formula works only if the fixed overhead rate per unit does not change between the periods.

■ Example

Given:

	19x1
Inventory	
Beginning balance	0
Production	10,000
Available for sale	10,000
Units sold	6,500
Ending balance	3,500
Other data	
Sales (6,500 × @ $2)	$13,000
Variable manufacturing costs	
(10,000 × @ $0.75)	7,500
Fixed manufacturing costs	5,000
Selling and administrative expenses	4,500

Assuming that selling and administrative expenses are 50% variable and 50% fixed, income statements for 19x1 using both *direct costing* and *absorption costing* can be constructed as shown in Figure 1 below.

We can prove:
1. Difference in net income: $375 − ($1,375) = $1,750. Absorption costing shows a larger net income.
2. Reconciliation of difference in net income:

$$\frac{\text{Change in}}{\text{inventory}} \times \frac{\text{Fixed factory}}{\text{overhead rate}} = \frac{\text{Difference in}}{\text{net income}}$$

$$3,500 \times \$0.5 \ (\$5,000/10,000) = \$1,750$$

It is important to realize that direct costing is used for internal management only. It highlights the concept of *contribution margin* and focuses on the costs by behavior rather than by function. Its managerial uses include:

Figure 1

19x1

Direct			Absorption		
Sales		$13,000	Sales		$13,000
Less: VC			Less: CGS		
VMC (6,500 × $0.75)	4,875		VMC (6,500 × $0.75)	4,875	
VS&A (4,500 × 0.5)	2,250		FMC (6,500 × $0.5)	3,250	
CM		$ 5,875	Gross margin		$ 4,875
Less: FC			Less:		
FMC	5,000		VS&A	2,250	
FS&A	2,250		FS&A	2,250	
Net income (loss)		($ 1,375)	Net income		$ 375

1. Relevant cost analysis
2. Break-even and cost-volume-profit (CVP) analyses
3. Short-term decision making

Direct costing is, however, not acceptable for external reporting or income tax reporting. Companies that use direct costing for internal reporting must convert to absorption costing for external reporting. *See also* Contribution Income Statement; Contribution Margin (CM); Relevant Costing.

DIRECT FINANCING LEASE   The lessor is *not* a manufacturer or dealer in the rented property. The lessor records interest revenue over the life of the lease. *See also* Leases.

DISCLOSURE   This is required for any information that if not disclosed would mislead a reader of the financial statements. Disclosure may be made in the footnotes, a separate schedule, or body to the financial statements. Examples of disclosures are accounting policies employed, litigation, lease information, and pension plan particulars.

According to AICPA Statement on Auditing Standards No. 32, if the auditor concludes that audited financial statements omit information required by GAAP, the auditor should express either an "except for" qualified opinion or an adverse opinion. If practical, the auditor should provide the omitted information in a middle explanatory paragraph of the audit report. Practical means in this context that the data is obtainable from the client's records and that the auditor is not put in the position of a preparer of the information.

DISCLOSURE OF LONG-TERM OBLIGATIONS
An unconditional purchase obligation is an obligation to provide funds for goods or services at a determinable future date. An example is a take-or-pay contract making the buyer obligated to pay specified periodic amounts for products or services. Even in the case where the buyer does not take delivery of the goods, periodic payments must still be made.

When unconditional purchase obligations are recorded in the balance sheet, disclosure is still made of the following:

• Payments made for recorded unconditional purchase obligations

• Maturities and sinking fund requirements for long-term borrowings

Unconditional purchase obligations that are not reflected in the balance sheet should usually be disclosed if they meet the following criteria:

• Noncancellable but may be cancellable upon a remote contingency

• Negotiated to arrange financing to provide contracted goods or services

• A term in excess of one year

The disclosure needed for unconditional purchase obligations when not recorded in the accounts are

• Nature and term

• Fixed and variable amounts

• Total amount for the current year and for the next 5 years

• Purchases made under the obligation for each year presented

Optional disclosure exists of the amount of imputed interest required to reduce the unconditional purchase obligation to present value.

DISCONTINUED OPERATION   A discontinued operation is a business segment that has ceased operation or will shortly be liquidated after year-end. Income from discontinued operations are shown separately in the income statement. *See also* Income Statement Format.

DISCOUNTED PAYBACK PERIOD   This is the length of time required to recover the initial cash outflow from the discounted future cash inflows. This is obtained at the point where the present values of cash inflows are accumulated until they equal the initial investment.

■ Example

Assume a machine purchased for $18,000 yields cash inflows of $4,000, $5,000, $6,000, $6,000, and $8,000. The cost of capital is 10%. Then we have

Year	Cash Flow	$PVIF_{10\%,n}$	PV of Cash Flow
1	$4,000	0.909	$3,636
2	5,000	0.826	4,130
3	6,000	0.751	4,506
4	6,000	0.683	4,098
5	8,000	0.621	4,968

The number of years required to recoup the $18,000 investment is

Year 1	$ 3,636
2	4,130
3	4,506
4	4,098
	$16,370

Balance in year 5: ($18,000 − $16,370) = $1,630

Therefore, the discounted payback period is 4 years + $1,630/$4,968 = 4 + 0.33 = 4.33 years. *See also* Payback Period.

DISCOVERY SAMPLING This is usually used in a search for critical deviations such as when the audit suggests the existence of irregularities. This sampling technique may be employed when the auditor wants to determine if an acceptable error rate in the population has been exceeded. If the error rate is not excessive, no additional audit testing is required. If it is exceeded, alternative audit procedures are necessary. An attribute estimate may also be required. In discovery sampling, there is a minimum sample size that would include at least one error if the population errors are greater than a given rate. Hence, if one error is found in the sample, the test is resolved. Because discovery sampling is based on a minimum sample size to uncover only one error, the sample size has to be increased in the event a useful attribute estimate is needed, such as the real error rate in the population.

In using discovery sampling, a determination has to be made regarding population size, minimum unacceptable error rate, and confidence level. Sample size is determined from a sampling table. In the event that none of the random samples show an error, it is concluded that the actual error rate is less than the minimum unacceptable error rate at the desired confidence level. Typically, the technique is used to spot groups of documents needing thorough testing.

■ Example

The auditor wants to assure the accuracy of pricing documents from 15 branches. Discovery sampling can be used to identify those batches having, for instance, a 95% probability of an error rate less than 1%. The auditor accepts those batches as satisfactory and appraises fully the remaining batches.

Discovery sampling is a sound approach in testing the correctness of clerical work. When there is not much time available in the final couple of months at the end of the reporting year, discovery sampling can provide the auditor with confidence that error incidence is below a specified percentage using a small sample size. Another benefit of this sampling method is to test auditor reliability.

■ Example

Even though the auditor used a random sample, an error was not uncovered. But once the error has been identified, the auditor can arrive at the probability of having found this error. The auditor may have examined n random units furnishing a 95% confidence level that the error rate in the population was less than 1%. Assume the incorrect units are, say 0.1% of the population. Thus, the method and assumptions employed were appropriate.

■ Example

The auditor wants to examine for inventory items, quantity, unit cost, and total cost. Cost/benefit makes it not practical for the CPA to verify all pricings and extensions for the inventory listing. Discovery sampling can be used to obtain a 90% confidence level that the error rate in pricing and extension is less than 1%. According to the sampling table, for 2,000 inventory items, a random sample size of 220 is needed. If no mistakes exist in the sample, it is concluded that all inventory items are correct. In the event a single error is found, the CPA stops sampling and examines extensions for all inventory items.

Discovery sampling has a pitfall in the possible rejection of some acceptable batches. Using a level of significance of 0.05, one is willing to reject on acceptable batch 5% of the time. It is appropriate for use by the internal auditor as a final check. But the external auditor should employ it only as a *preliminary* scanning procedure in examining the quality of population data. *See also* Sampling.

DIVIDENDS   These represent distributions paid out by the company to stockholders. After the date of declaration of a dividend is the date of record. In order to qualify to receive a dividend, a person must be registered as the owner of the stock on the date of record. Several days prior to the date of record, the stock will be selling "ex-dividend." This is done to alert investors that those owning the stock before the record date are eligible to receive the dividend, and that those selling the stock before the record date will lose their rights to the dividend.

A dividend is usually in the form of cash or stock. A dividend is based on the outstanding shares (issued shares less treasury shares).

■ Example

Issued shares are 5,000, treasury shares are 1,000, and outstanding shares are therefore 4,000. The par value of the stock is $10 per share. If a $0.30 dividend per share is declared, the dividend is

$$4,000 \times \$.30 = \$1,200$$

If the dividend rate is 6%, the dividend is

$$4,000 \text{ shares} \times \$10 \text{ par value} = \$40,000$$
$$\times .06$$
$$\overline{\$ \ 2,400}$$

Assuming a cash dividend of $2,400 is declared, the entry is

Retained Earnings	2,400	
Cash Dividend Payable		2,400

No entry is made at the record date.
The entry at the payment date is

Cash Dividend Payable	2,400	
Cash		2,400

In the case of a property dividend, the entry at the declaration date at the fair market value of the asset is

Retained Earnings	
Asset	

Gain or loss arising between the carrying value and fair market value of the asset is recorded at the time of declaration.

A stock dividend is issued in the form of stock. Stock dividend distributable is shown in the capital stock section of stockholders' equity. It is *not* a liability. If the stock dividend is less than 20% to 25% of outstanding shares at the declaration date, retained earnings is reduced at the market price of the shares. If the stock dividend is in excess of 20% to 25% of outstanding shares, retained earnings is charged at par value. Between 20% to 25% is a gray area.

■ Example

A stock dividend of 10% is declared on 5,000 shares of $10 par value common stock having a market price of $12. The entry at the declaration and issuance dates follow:

Retained Earnings (500 shares × $12)	6,000	
Stock Dividend Distributable		
(500 shares × $10)		5,000
Paid-in-capital		1,000
Stock Dividend Distributable	5,000	
Common Stock		5,000

Assume instead that the stock dividend was 30%. The entries would be

Retained Earnings (500 × $10)	5,000	
Stock Dividend Distributable		5,000
Stock Dividend Distributable	5,000	
Common Stock		5,000

A liability dividend (scrip dividend) is payable in the form of a liability (e.g., notes payable). A liability dividend sometimes occurs when a company has financial problems.

■ Example

On 1/1/19X2, a liability dividend of $20,000 is declared in the form of a 1-year, 8% note. The entry at the declaration date is

Retained Earnings	20,000	
Scrip Dividend Payable		20,000

When the scrip dividend is paid, the entry is

Scrip Dividend Payable	20,000	
Interest Expense	1,600	
Cash		21,600

A liquidating dividend can be deceptive because it is not actually a dividend. It is a return of capital and not a distribution of earnings. The entry is to debit paid-in-capital and credit dividends payable. The recipient of a liquidating dividend pays no tax on it.

DIVISIONAL PERFORMANCE EVALUATION

The ability to measure performance is essential in developing management incentives and controlling the operation toward the achievement of organizational goals. A typical decentralized subunit is an *investment center* that is responsible for an organization's invested capital (operating assets) and the related operating income. There are two widely used measurements of performance for the investment center: the rate of return on investment (ROI) and residual income (RI).

Rate of Return on Investment (ROI)

ROI relates net income to invested capital. Specifically,

$$ROI = \frac{\text{Operating income}}{\text{Operating assets}}$$

■ Example 1

Consider the following financial data for a division:

Operating assets	$100,000
Operating income	18,000
ROI = $18,000/$100,000 = 18%	

Residual Income (RI)

Another approach to measuring performance in an investment center is residual income (RI). RI is the operating income that an investment center is able to earn above some minimum rate of return on its operating assets. RI, unlike ROI, is an absolute amount of income rather than a specific rate of return. When RI is used to evaluate divisional performance, the objective is to maximize the total amount of residual income, not to maximize the overall ROI figure.

RI = Operating income
    − (Minimum required rate of return
                × Operating assets)

■ Example 2

In Example 1, assume the minimum required rate of return is 13%. Then the residual income of the division is

$18,000 − (13% × $100,000)
                = $18,000 − $13,000 = $5,000

RI is regarded as a better measure of performance than ROI because it encourages investment in projects that would be rejected under ROI. A major disadvantage of RI, however, is that it cannot be used to compare divisions of different sizes. RI tends to favor the larger divisions due to the larger amount of dollars involved.

Investment Decisions Under ROI and RI

The decision whether to use ROI or RI as a measure of divisional performance affects financial managers' investment decisions. Under the ROI method, division managers tend to accept only the investments whose returns exceed the division's ROI; otherwise, the division's overall ROI would decrease. Under the RI method, on the other hand, division managers would accept an investment as long as it earns a rate in excess of the minimum required rate of return. The addition of such an investment will increase the division's overall RI.

■ Example 3

Consider the same data given in Examples 1 and 2:

Operating assets	$100,000
Operating income	18,000
Minimum required rate of return	13%
ROI = 18% and RI = $5,000	

Assume that the division is presented with a project that would yield 15% on a $10,000 investment. The division manager would not accept this project under the ROI approach since the division is already earning 18%. Acquiring this project will bring down the present ROI to 17.73%, as shown below:

	Present	New Project	Overall
Operating assets (a)	$100,000	$10,000	$110,000
Operating income (b)	18,000	1,500*	19,500
ROI (b / a)	18%	15%	17.73%

* $10,000 × 15% = $1,500

Under the RI approach, the manager would accept the new project since it provides a higher rate than the minimum required rate of return (15% vs. 13%). Accepting the new project will increase the overall residual income to $5,200, as shown following:

	Present	New Project	Overall
Operating assets (a)	$100,000	$10,000	$110,000
Operating income (b)	18,000	1,500	19,500
Minimum required income at 13% (c)	13,000	1,300*	14,300
RI (b − c)	$ 5,000	$ 200	$ 5,200

* $10,000 × 13% = $1,300

See also Du Pont Formula.

DOLLAR-COST AVERAGING This may be used for stock deemed to be a good long-term investment. A constant dollar amount of stock or stocks is bought at regularly spaced intervals. The strategy represents time diversification. By investing a fixed amount each time, more shares are purchased at a low price and less shares are bought at a high price. It typically results in a lower average cost per share because the investor buys more shares of stock with the same dollars. The technique is advantageous when a stock price moves within a narrow range. If there is a decrease in stock price, the investor will incur less of a loss than ordinarily. If there is an increase in stock price, the investor will gain, but less than usual. Drawbacks to dollar-cost averaging are (1) higher transaction costs and (2) it will not work when stock prices are in a continuous downward direction. *Tip*: Dollar-cost averaging is a conservative investment strategy since it avoids whims when the investor may be tempted to buy when the market is high or sell when the market is low. A conservative stock may be acquired with relatively little risk benefiting from long-

term price appreciation. Further, the investor is not stuck with too many shares at high prices. In addition, in a bear market many shares are purchased at very depressed prices.

■ Example

An investor makes a $100,000 investment per month in ABC Company and engages in the following transactions:

Date	Investment	Market Price Per Share	Shares Purchased
6/1	$100,000	$40	2,500
7/1	100,000	35	2,857
8/1	100,000	34	2,941
9/1	100,000	38	2,632
10/1	100,000	50	2,000

The investor has purchased fewer shares at the higher price and more shares at the lower price. The average price per share is

$$\frac{\$197}{5} = \$39.40$$

However, with the $500,000 investment, 12,930 shares have been bought, resulting in a cost per share of $38.67. At 10/1, the market price of the stock of $50 exceeded the average cost of $38.67, reflecting an attractive gain.

DOLLAR UNIT SAMPLING (DUS) DUS is useful when the auditor wishes to confirm if a population value is materially correct. Under dollar unit sampling, an examination is made of sample units of $1 to ascertain whether an error exists. Random samples of monetary units not physical units are involved. An estimate is made of the maximum proportion or amount of dollars in error in the population.

There is a separate analysis for understatement and overstatement errors. When sample errors are uncovered, various analytical methods may be used (e.g., combined attributes-variables) to adjust the simple attribute result to take into account the magnitude of the errors. But as additional errors are uncov-

ered, the estimates become overly conservative, thus, it is recommended to use dollar-unit sampling only for cases where few or no errors are anticipated. In other words, there is a low error rate. A possible statistical statement to use is, There are overstatement errors not exceeding $300,000 in the population at a particular confidence level. Another statement might be, The population is overstated not in excess of $150,000 and understated by no more than $100,000.

■ Example

A maximum error rate of 4% in a population of $200,000 results in a maximum error of $8,000 (4% × $200,000).

Dollar unit sampling is a probability proportionate to size sampling of audit units having an upper precision level of possible error based on dollar mistakes found in the sample combined with an attribute resulting from a probability determination. For instance, a supplier account with a carrying value of $500 represents 500 *dollar units*. The auditor performs a random sample of the dollar units with probabilities proportionate to size. The auditor then audits the sample dollar units. In the event a dollar error is found in a sampled item, it is converted on a "per dollar" basis. Sample results are projected to the population. In essence, this sampling approach converts into dollars the conclusion that a given attribute has been exceeded. *See also* Sampling.

DOLLAR VALUE LIFO This is an acceptable method in which price indices are used in determining the value of ending inventory. Inventory is restated in base dollars. The change in inventory for the period in base dollars is then multiplied by the price index for the current year. *See also* Inventory Valuation.

DOW THEORY The Dow Theory applies to specific stocks and the overall market. It is based on the movements in the Dow Jones Industrial

Average and the Dow Jones Transporation Average. Stock market direction has to be substantiated by both averages. *See also* Technical Analysis.

DU PONT FORMULA The Du Pont formula combines the income statement and balance sheet into either of two summary measures of performance, *return on investment* (ROI) and *return on equity* (ROE).

The first version of the Du Pont formula breaks down the return on investment (ROI) into *net profit margin* and *total asset turnover,* as shown below.

$$ROI = \frac{\text{Net profit after taxes}}{\text{Total assets}}$$

$$= \frac{\text{Net profit after taxes}}{\text{Sales}} \times \frac{\text{Sales}}{\text{Total assets}}$$

= Net profit margin × Total asset turnover

■ Example 1

Consider the following financial data:

Total assets	$200,000
Net profit after taxes	20,000
Sales	$400,000

Then;

ROI = $20,000/$200,000 = 10%

Net profit margin = $20,000/$400,000 = 5%

Total asset turnover = $400,000/$200,000 = 2 times

Therefore:

ROI = 10% = 5% × 2 times = 10%

The breakdown provides a lot of insights to financial managers on how to improve profitability of the company and investment strategy. Specifically, it has several advantages over the original formula (i.e., net profits after taxes/total asset) for profit planning. They are

1. The importance of turnover as a key to overall return on investment is emphasized in the breakdown. In fact, turnover is just as important as profit margin in enhancing overall return.

2. The importance of sales is explicitly rec-

ognized, which is not there in the original formula.

3. The breakdown stresses the possibility of trading one off for the other. The margin and turnover complement each other. In other words, a low turnover can be made up for by a high margin and vice versa.

The breakdown of ROI into its two components shows that a number of combinations of margin and turnover can yield the same rate of return, as shown below:

	Margin	×	Turnover	= ROI
(1)	5%	×	2 times	= 10%
(2)	4	×	2.5	= 10
(3)	3	×	3.33	= 10
(4)	2	×	5	= 10
(5)	1	×	10	= 10

The turnover-margin relationship and its resulting ROI follow.

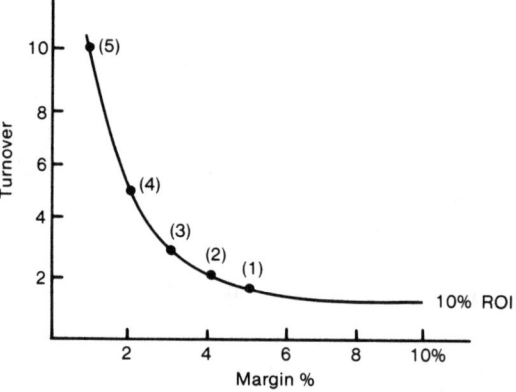

The previous figure indicates that the total asset turnover and net profit margin factors complement each other. Weak margin can be complemented by a strong turnover, and vice versa. It also shows how important turnover is as a key to profit making. In effect, these two factors are equally important in overall profit performance.

4. The formula indicates where your weaknesses are: margin or turnover, or both. Various actions can be taken to enhance ROI. They include:

    a. Reduce expenses (e.g., improve productivity, automate, or cut down on

discretionary expenses), thereby increasing net profit.

b. Reduce assets (e.g., improve inventory control, speed up receivable collections, etc.) without decreasing sales.

c. Increase sales while maintaining profit margin.

The second version of the Du Pont formula, also called the *modified Du Pont formula*, ties together the ROI and the degree of financial leverage as measured using the *equity multiplier*, which is the ratio of total assets to stockholders' equity to determine the *return on equity* (ROE):

$$\text{ROE} = \frac{\text{Net profit after taxes}}{\text{Stockholders' equity}}$$

$$= \frac{\text{Net profit after taxes}}{\text{Total assets}} \times \frac{\text{Total assets}}{\text{Stockholders' equity}}$$

$$= \quad\text{ROI} \quad\times\quad \text{Equity multiplier}$$

The use of the equity multiplier to convert the ROI to the ROE reflects the impact of the leverage (use of debt) on stockholders' return.

▪ Example 2

In Example 1, assume stockholders' equity of $90,000. Then, equity multiplier = $200,000/$90,000 = 2.22

ROE = $20,000/$90,000 = 22.2%, or

ROE = ROI × Equity multiplier
$$= 10\% \times 2.22 = 22.2\%$$

If the company used only equity, the 10% ROI would equal ROE. However, 55% of the firm's capital is supplied by creditors ($90,000/$200,000 = 45% is the equity-to-asset ratio). Since the 10% ROI all goes to stockholders, who put up only 45% of the capital, the ROE is higher than 10%. This example indicates the company was using the leverage (debt) positively (favorably). (If the assets in which the funds are invested are able to earn a return greater than the fixed rate of return required by the creditors, the leverage is positive and the common stockholders benefit.)

The advantage of this formula is that it enables the company to break its ROE into a profit margin portion (net profit margin), an efficiency-of-asset-utilization portion (total asset turnover), and a use-of-leverage portion (equity multiplier). Financial managers have the task of determining just what combination of asset return and leverage will work best in its competitive environment. Most companies try to keep at least a level equal to what is considered to be "normal" within the industry.

The Du Pont and Modified Du Pont Formulas

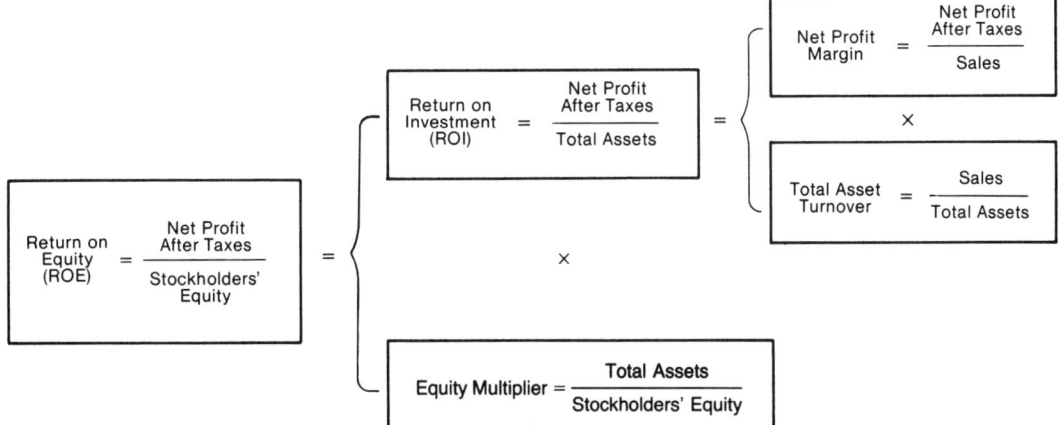

DURBIN-WATSON STATISTIC This is a summary measure of the amount of *autocorrelation* in the error terms of the *regression*. Roughly speaking, if the statistic approaches a value of 2, there is no autocorrelation. If the error terms are highly positively correlated, the statistic would be less than 1 and could get near 0. If the error terms are highly negatively correlated, the statistic would be greater than 3 and could get near the upper limit of 4. *See also* Autocorrelation; Regression Analysis.

DYNAMIC PROGRAMMING This is a form of mathematical programming. It is a programming technique that divides the problem to be solved into a number of subproblems and then solves each subproblem in such a way that the overall solution is optimal to the original problem. For example, a firm may wish to make a series of accounting and financial decisions over time that will provide it with the highest possible cash inflow. *See also* Mathematical Programming.

E

EARLY EXTINGUISHMENT OF DEBT Long-term debt may be called back early when new debt can be issued at a lower interest rate. It can also occur when the company has excess cash and wants to avoid paying interest charges and having the debt on its balance sheet. The gain or loss on the early extinguishment of debt is an extraordinary item shown net of tax. Extraordinary classification occurs whether the extinguishment is early, at scheduled maturity, or later. An exception exists in that the gain or loss on extinguishment is an ordinary item if it satisfies a sinking fund requirement that has to be met within one year of the date of extinguishment. But serial bonds do not have characteristics of sinking fund requirements.

Debt may be construed as being extinguished in the case where the debtor is relieved of the principal liability and it is probable the debtor will not have to make future payments.

■ Example

A $100,000 bond payable with an unamortized premium of $10,000 is called at 85. The entry is

Bonds Payable	100,000	
Premium on Bonds Payable	10,000	
Cash (85% × 100,000)		85,000
Extraordinary Gain		25,000

Footnote disclosures regarding extinguishment of debt follow:

• Description of extinguishment transaction including the source of funds used

• Per share gain or loss net of tax

If convertible debt is converted to stock in connection with an "inducement offer" where the debtor alters conversion privileges, the debtor recognizes an expense rather than an extraordinary item. The amount is the fair value of the securities transferred in excess of the fair value of securities issuable according to the original conversion terms. This fair market value is measured at the earlier of the conversion date or date of the agreement. An inducement offer may be accomplished by giving debt holders a higher conversion ratio, payment of additional consideration, or other favorable changes in terms.

According to FASB 76, if the debtor puts cash or other assets in a trust to be utilized only for paying interest and principal on debt on an irrevocable basis, disclosure should be made of the particulars, including a de-

scription of the transaction and the amount of debt considered to be extinguished. *See also* Bond Accounting.

EARNINGS PER SHARE
APB 15 requires that earnings per share must be computed by publicly held companies. It is not required for nonpublic companies. In a simple capital structure, no potentially dilutive securities exist. (Potentially dilutive means the security will be converted into common stock at a later date reducing EPS). Thus, only one EPS figure is necessary. In a complex capital structure, dilutive securities exist requiring dual presentation. The dual presentation of EPS for all periods presented is

$$\text{Primary EPS} = \frac{\text{Net income} - \text{Preferred dividend}}{\substack{\text{Weighted} - \text{average common stock} \\ \text{outstanding} + \text{Common} \\ \text{stock equivalents}}}$$

$$\text{Fully diluted EPS} = \frac{\text{Net income} - \text{Preferred dividend}}{\substack{\text{Weighted-average common stock} \\ \text{outstanding} + \text{Common stock} \\ \text{equivalents} + \text{Other fully} \\ \text{diluted securities}}}$$

Fully diluted EPS reflects the *maximum* potential dilution per share on a prospective basis.

Weighted-average common stock shares outstanding takes into account the number of months in which those shares were outstanding.

■ Example

On 1/1/19X1, 10,000 shares were issued. On 4/1/19X1, 2,000 of those shares were bought back by the company. The weighted-average common stock outstanding is

$$(10{,}000 \times 3/12) + (8{,}000 \times 9/12) = 8{,}500 \text{ shares}$$

The inclusion of common stock equivalents in determining EPS is an example of theoretical substance over legal form. Although the common stock equivalent (e.g., stock option) is not legally common stock, it is treated as such since in theoretical substance the common stock equivalent is common stock. Common stock equivalents are securities that can become common stock at a later date and are shown in both primary EPS and fully diluted EPS.

Common stock equivalents include
- Stock options.
- Stock warrants.
- Subscribed stock.
- Two-class common stock.
- Contingent shares only related to the passage of time.
- Convertible securities (convertible bonds, convertible preferred stock) when the yield at the time of issuance is less than ⅔ of the average Aa bond yield at the time of issuance. Once a convertible security is defined as a common stock equivalent, it continues as such. Aa bonds are defined by Standard and Poor's and Moody's as of the highest quality. For zero-coupon bonds, the effective yield is the interest rate necessary to discount the maturity value of the bond to its present value. This rate is then used to determine common stock equivalent by company by comparing it to the ⅔ average yield. In the situation where convertible securities are issued in a foreign country, we use the most comparable long-term yield in that country in performing the cash yield test.

Note: Although stock options are *always* deemed a common stock equivalent, they are only included in computing EPS if the market price of common stock is greater than the option price for substantially all of the last 3 months of the year. In this case, we assume the stock options were exercised at the *beginning* of the year (or at time of issuance, if later). Although convertible securities are classified as common stock equivalents based on the circumstances at time of issue, warrants are classified according to the conditions at each period.

In computing EPS, common stock equivalents are included if they have a dilutive effect. Dilutive effect means that the inclusion of a common stock equivalent reduced EPS by 3% or more in the aggregate and is applied

by type of security. The 3% dilution also applies to presenting fully diluted EPS. Fully diluted EPS is also shown if it reduces primary EPS by 3% or more. Antidilutive securities that increase EPS are not shown in the EPS computation because they will increase EPS, which violates conservatism.

When shares are issued because of a stock dividend or stock split, the computation of weighted-average common stock shares outstanding mandates retroactive adjustment as if the shares were outstanding at the beginning of the year.

In computing the common stock equivalent in shares of options and warrants, the *treasury stock method* is used. Options and warrants are assumed to have been exercised at the beginning of the year (or at time of issuance, if later). The proceeds received from the options and warrants are assumed to:

• First, buy back common stock at the average market price for the period not exceeding 20% of common stock outstanding at year-end.

• Second, reduce long- or short-term borrowing.

• Third, invest in U.S. government securities or commerical paper.

Assumption of exercise of options exists only when market price of stock is greater than exercise price for 3 consecutive months ending with the year-end month.

In computing fully diluted EPS, the treasury stock method is modified in that the market price at the end of the accounting period is used if it is higher than the average market price for the period.

■ Example

Assume 100 shares are under option at an option price of $10. The average market price of stock is $25. The common stock equivalent is 60 shares, as calculated below:

Issued shares from option 100 shares × $10 = $1,000
Less: Treasury shares   40 shares × $25 = $1,000
Common stock equivalent   60 shares

Convertible securities are accounted for using the "if converted method." The convertible securities are assumed converted at the beginning of the earliest year presented or date of security issuance. Interest or dividends on them are added back to net income since the securities are considered part of equity in the denominator of the EPS calculation.

Other fully diluted securities are defined as convertible securities that did not meet the ⅔ test. They are included only in the calculation of fully diluted EPS. Thus, fully diluted EPS will be a lower figure than primay EPS because of the greater shares in the denominator. Contingent issuance of shares in computing fully diluted EPS is assumed to have occurred at the beginning of the year or at the time of issuance if later. Fully diluted EPS is a pro forma presentation showing what EPS would be if *all* potential contingencies of common stock issuances having a dilutive effect took place.

To accomplish the fullest dilution in arriving at fully diluted EPS, an assumption is made that all common stock issuances on exercise of options or warrants during the period were made at the start of the year. The *higher* of the closing price or the average price of common stock is used in determining the number of shares of treasury stock to be purchased from the proceeds received upon issuance of the options. If the ending market price exceeds the average market price, the assumed treasury shares acquired will be lessened, resulting in higher assumed outstanding shares with the resulting decrease in EPS.

Net income less preferred dividends is in the numerator of the EPS fraction, representing earnings available to common stockholders. On cumulative preferred stock, preferred dividends for the current year are subtracted out whether or not paid. Further, preferred dividends are only subtracted out for the current year. Thus, if preferred dividends in arrears were for 5 years all of which were

paid plus the sixth year dividend, only the sixth year dividend (current year) is deducted. Note that preferred dividends for each of the prior years would have been deducted in those years.

In computing EPS, preferred dividends are only subtracted out on preferred stock that was not included as a common stock equivalent. If the preferred stock is a common stock equivalent, the preferred dividend would *not* be subtracted out since the equivalency of preferred shares into common shares are included in the denominator.

If convertible bonds are included in the denominator of EPS, they are considered as equivalent to common shares. Thus, interest expense (net of tax) has to be added back in the numerator.

Disclosure of EPS should include information on the capital structure, explanation of the computation of EPS, identification of common stock equivalents, assumptions made, and number of shares converted. Rights and privileges of the securities should also be disclosed. Such disclosure includes dividend and participation rights, call prices, conversion ratios, and sinking fund requirements.

A stock conversion occurring during the year or between year-end and the audit report date may have materially affected EPS if it had taken place at the beginning of the year. Thus, supplementary footnote disclosure should be made reflecting on an "as-if" basis what the effects of these conversions would have had on EPS if they were made at the start of the accounting period.

If a subsidiary has been acquired under the *purchase accounting method* during the year, the weighted-average shares outstanding for the year is used from the purchase date. But if a *pooling of interests* occurred, the weighted-average shares outstanding for all the years are presented.

If common stock or a common stock equivalent are sold during the year and the monies obtained to buy back debt or retire preferred stock, there should be a presentation of supplemental EPS figures.

When comparative financial statements are presented, there is a retroactive adjustment for stock splits and stock dividends. Assume in 19X5 a 10% stock dividend occurs. The weighted-average shares used for previous years' computations has to be increased by 10% to make EPS data comparable.

When a prior period adjustment occurs that causes a restatement of previous years' earnings, EPS should also be restated.

■ Example

The stockholders' equity section of ABC Company's balance sheet as of 12/31/19X3 appears at the bottom of the page.

On 5/1/19X3, ABC Company acquired XYZ Company in a pooling-of-interest. For each of XYZ Company's 800,000 shares, ABC issued one of its own shares in the exchange.

On 4/1/19X3, ABC Company issued 500,000 shares of convertible preferred stock at $38 per share. The preferred stock is con-

$1.20 cumulative preferred stock (par value of $10 per share, issued 1,200,000 shares of which 500,000 were converted to common stock and 700,000 shares are outstanding)	$ 7,000,000
Common stock (par value of $2.50 issued and outstanding 6,000,000 shares)	15,000,000
Paid-in-capital	20,000,000
Retained earnings	32,000,000
Total stockholders' equity	$74,000,000

vertible to common stock at the exchange rate of 2 shares of common for each share of preferred. On 9/1/19X3, 300,000 shares and on 11/1/19X3, 200,000 shares of preferred stock were converted into common stock. The market price of the convertible preferred stock is $38 per share.

During August, ABC Company granted stock options to executives to buy 100,000 shares of common stock at an option price of $15 per share. The market price of stock at year-end was $20.

ABC Company has 8%, $10,000,000 convertible bonds payable issued at fair value in 19X1. The conversion rate is 4 shares of common stock for each $100 bond. No conversions have occurred yet.

The Aa corporate bond yield is 10%. The tax rate is 34%. Net income for the year is $12,000,000.

The convertible bonds are not common stock equivalents because the interest rate of 8% is more than ⅔ of the Aa bond yield of 10%.

The convertible preferred stock is a common stock equivalent because its yield of 3.16% ($1.20/$38.00) is less than ⅔ of the Aa bond yield of 10%.

Stock options are always considered common stock equivalents.

Shares outstanding from 1/1/19X3 (including 800,000 shares issued upon acquisition of XYZ Company):		
6,000,000 − 1,000,000		5,000,000
Shares issued upon conversion of 500,000 shares of preferred stock to common stock:		
Issued 9/1/19X3 600,000 × 4/12	200,000	
Issued 11/1/19X3 400,000 × 2/12	66,667	266,667
Total shares of common stock		5,266,667
Common stock equivalents:		
Convertible preferred stock:		
500,000 shares of convertible preferred issued on 4/1/19X3		
500,000 × 2 × 9/12	750,000	
Less: Common shares applicable to 500,000 preferred shares converted during the year	266,667	
Common stock equivalents of convertible preferred stock		483,333
Common stock equivalents of stock options:		
Option	100,000 × $15 = $1,500,000	
Less: Treasury stock	75,000 × $20 = 1,500,000	
Common stock equivalent of stock options	25,000	25,000
Weighted-average common stock outstanding plus common stock equivalents for primary EPS		5,775,000
Convertible bonds payable assumed converted at 1/1/19X3 ($10,000,000/$100) = 100,000 bonds		
100,000 bonds × 4 shares per bond		400,000
Weighted-average common stock outstanding plus common stock equivalents plus other fully diluted securities for fully diluted EPS		6,175,000

Primary EPS equals:

$$\frac{\$12,000,000}{5,775,000 \text{ shares}} = \$2.08$$

Fully diluted EPS equals:

$$\frac{\$12,000,000 + \$528,000^*}{6,175,000 \text{ shares}} = \$2.03$$

* $10,000,000 × 8% = $800,000 × 66% = $528,000

EBIT—EPS APPROACH TO CAPITAL STRUCTURE

This is a practical tool for use by financial managers in order to evaluate alternative financing plans. This is a practical effort to move toward achieving an optimal capital structure that results in the lowest overall cost of capital.

The use of financial leverage has two effects on the earnings that go to the firm's common stockholders: (1) an increased risk in earnings per share (EPS) due to the use of fixed financial obligations and (2) a change in the level of EPS at a given EBIT associated with a specific capital structure.

The first effect is measured by the degree of financial leverage. The second effect is analyzed by means of EBIT-EPS analysis. This analysis is a practical approach that enables the financial manager to evaluate alternative financing plans by investigating their effect on EPS over a range of EBIT levels. Its primary objective is to determine the *EBIT break-even, or indifference, points* between the various alternative financing plans. The indifference points between any two methods of financing can be determined by solving for EBIT in the following equality:

$$\frac{(EBIT - I)(1 - t) - PD}{S_1} = \frac{(EBIT - I)(1 - t) - PD}{S_2}$$

where t = tax rate,
PD = preferred stock dividends,
S_1 and S_2 = number of shares of common stock outstanding after financing for plan 1 and plan 2, respectively.

■ Example

Assume that ABC Company, with long-term capitalization consisting entirely of $5 million in stock, wants to raise $2 million for the acquisition of special equipment by (1) selling 40,000 shares of common stock at $50 each; (2) selling bonds, at 10% interest; or (3) issuing preferred stock with an 8% dividend. The present EBIT is $8 million, the income tax rate is 50%, and 100,000 shares of common stock are now outstanding. In order to compute the indifference points, we begin by calculating EPS at a projected EBIT level of $1 million as shown in the table below.

Now connect the EPS at the level of EBIT of $1 million with the EBIT for each financing alternative on the horizontal axis to obtain the EPS-EBIT graphs. We plot the EBIT necessary to cover all fixed financial costs for each financing alternative on the horizontal axis. For the common stock plan, there are no fixed costs, so the intercept on the horizontal axis is zero. For the debt plan, there must be an EBIT of $200,000 to cover interest charges. For the preferred stock plan, there must be an EBIT of $320,000 [$160,000/(1 − 0.5)] to cover $160,000 in preferred stock dividends at a 50% income tax rate; so $320,000 becomes the horizontal axis intercept. See Figure 1.

	All Common	All Debt	All Preferred
EBIT	$1,000,000	$1,000,000	$1,000,000
Interest		200,000	
Earnings before taxes (EBT)	$1,000,000	$ 800,000	$1,000,000
Taxes	500,000	400,000	500,000
Earnings after taxes (EAT)	$ 500,000	$ 400,000	$ 500,000
Preferred stock dividend			$ 160,000
EAC	$ 500,000	$ 400,000	$ 340,000
Number of shares	140,000	100,000	100,000
EPS	$3.57	$4.00	$3.40

Figure 1 EBIT/EPS Graph

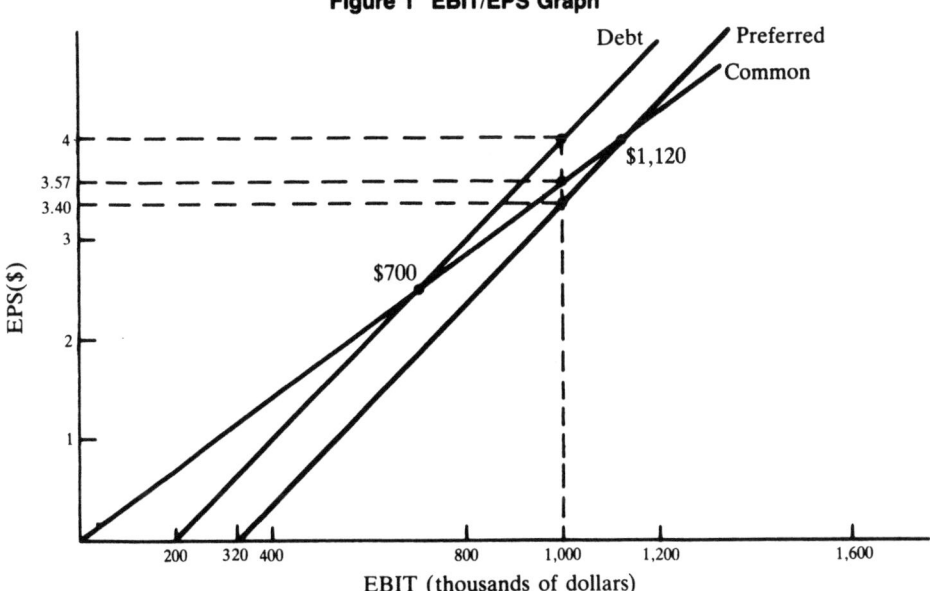

In this example, the indifference point between all common and all debt is:

$$\frac{(EBIT - I)(1 - t) - PD}{S_1} = \frac{(EBIT - I)(1 - t) - PD}{S_2}$$

$$\frac{(EBIT - 0)(1 - 0.5) - 0}{140,000}$$

$$= \frac{(EBIT - 200,000)(1 - 0.5) - 0}{100,000}$$

Rearranging yields:

$$0.5 \, (EBIT) \, (100,000) = 0.5 \, (EBIT) \, (140,000)$$
$$- 0.5 \, (200,000)(140,000)$$
$$20,000 \, EBIT = 14,000,000,000$$
$$EBIT = \$700,000$$

Similarly, the indifference point between all common and all preferred would be

$$\frac{(EBIT - I)(1 - t) - PD}{S_1} = \frac{(EBIT - I)(1 - t) - PD}{S_2}$$

$$\frac{(EBIT - 0)(1 - 0.5) - 0}{140,000}$$

$$= \frac{(EBIT - 0)(1 - 0.5) - 160,000}{100,000}$$

Rearranging yields:

$$0.5(EBIT)(100,000) = 0.5(EBIT)(140,000)$$
$$- 160,000(140,000)$$
$$20,000 \, EBIT = 22,400,000,000$$
$$EBIT = \$1,120,000$$

Based on the previous computations, we can draw the following conclusions:

1. At any level of EBIT, debt is better than preferred stock.

2. At a level of EBIT above $700,000, debt is better than common stock. If EBIT is below $700,000, the reverse is true.

3. At a level of EBIT above $1,120,000, preferred stock is better than common. At or below that point, the reverse is true.

See also Cost of Capital; Leverage.

ECONOMETRICS This is concerned with empirical testing of economic theory using various statistical methods such as *regression analysis*. Econometric analysis involves four basic phases:

1. Specification of the model, which utilizes economic theory and economic reality

2. Estimation of the model, using statistical methods such as regression analysis

3. Verification of the model, which involves economic interpretation and statistical tests

4. Applications, which include testing economic theorems and forecasting economic variables

Econometrics have been used widely both by accountants and financial analysts for forecasting purposes. Examples include projection of earnings and analysis of mixed costs. *See also* Cost Behavior Analysis; Regression Analysis.

ECONOMIC INDICATORS These attempt to size up where the economy seems to be headed and where it's been. Each month government agencies, including the Federal Reserve, and several economic institutions publish economic indicators. These may be broken down into six broad categories:

1. *Measures of overall economic performance*—include gross national product (GNP), personal income, plant and equipment expenditures, corporate profits, and inventories.

2. *Price indices*—designed to measure the rate of inflation of the economy. The Consumer Price Index (CPI), the most well-known inflation gauge, is used as the cost-of-living index, to which labor contracts and social security are tied. The Producer Price Index (PPI) covers raw materials and semifinished goods and measures prices at the early stage of the distribution system. It is the one that signals changes in the general price level, or the CPI, some time before they actually materialize. The GNP *implicit deflator* is the third index of inflation that is used to separate price changes in GNP calculations from real change in economic activity.

3. *Indices of labor market conditions*—unemployment rate, average workweek of production workers, applications for unemployment compensation, and hourly wage rates.

4. *Money and credit market indicators*—most widely reported in the media are money supply, consumer credit, the Dow Jones industrial average, and the Treasury bill rate.

5. *Index of leading indicators*—most widely publicized signal caller made up of 12 data series. They are money supply, business formation, stock prices, vendor performance, average workweek, new orders, contracts, building permits, inventory change, layoff rate, change in sensitive prices, and change in total liquid assets. They monitor certain business activities that can signal a change in the economy.

6. *Measures for major product markets*—designed to be indicators for segments of the economy such as housing, retail sales, steel, and automobile. Examples are 10-day auto sales, advance retail sales, housing starts, and construction permits.

How to Use Economic Indicators

It is important to note that indicators are only signals. They tell you something about the economic conditions in the country, a particular area, an industry, and, over time, the trends that seem to be shaping up. Here are some tips for using the indicators:

1. Choose indicators closely related to the line of business, its specific aspects, and the geographical area. Home insurance business should monitor building permits as an indicator of future demand for homeowners' policies. Suppliers to the auto industry should closely watch average workweek and new orders as indicators appropriate to their business, rather than looking at money supply or stock prices.

2. Systematically trace the movement of the indicators chosen and assess their appropriateness for the business.

3. Use combinations of important economic indicators for best results—to avoid overreliance on one indicator.

4. Select a price index related to a specific business activity. Effective business planning and budgeting require selecting appropriate price indices. Remember there is no one all-purpose price index. Review separate price indices for products and markets, unit labor costs, raw material costs, and energy costs.

See also Index of Leading Economic Indicators.

ECONOMIC ORDER QUANTITY (EOQ)
The economic order quantity (EOQ) model determines the order size that minimizes the sum of carrying and ordering costs. EOQ is computed as follows:

$$EOQ = \sqrt{\frac{2(\text{Annual demand})(\text{Ordering cost})}{\text{Carrying cost per unit}}}$$

See also Inventory Planning and Control.

ECONOMIC PRODUCTION RUN SIZE
This is an optimum production run quantity that minimizes the sum of carrying and setup costs. The way it is computed is exactly the same as economic order quantity (EOQ), except that the ordering cost in the EOQ formula is replaced by the setup cost. The setup cost is the cost incurred each time a batch is produced. It includes the engineering cost of setting up the production runs or machines, paperwork cost of processing the work order, and ordering cost to provide raw materals for the batch. *See also* Economic order Quantity (EOQ); Inventory Planning and Control.

EFFECTIVE INTEREST RATE
1. The true (real) interest rate on a loan computed as:

$$\frac{\text{Nominal interest}}{\text{Loan proceeds}}$$

■ Example

A borrower took out a $30,000 1-year 12% discounted loan (interest is subtracted at the time of loan in deriving loan proceeds). A compensating balance of 6% is also required. The effective interest rate is

$$\frac{\$3,600}{\$30,000 - \$3,600 - \$1,800} = \frac{\$3,600}{\$24,600} = 14.6\%$$

Note: A discounted loan and compensating balance both act to increase the real interest rate.
2. Yield to maturity.
   See also Yield.

EFFICIENT MARKET
An efficient market is one in which the market price of a stock is identical to its real (intrinsic) value. In an efficient market, all data are fully and immediately reflected in price. A price change is equally possible to be positive or negative. The hypothesis applies most directly to large companies trading on the New York and American Stock Exchanges. An efficient market may be of the weak, semistrong, or strong type.

In the weak form, no relationship exists between prior and future stock prices. Independence exists over time between prices. The value of historical information already lies in the current price. Therefore, there is no importance associated with reviewing past prices. This puts into question the very nature of technical analysis.

In the semistrong type, stock prices immediately reflect new information. Therefore, action after a known event produces random results. All public information is incorporated in a stock's value. Therefore, fundamental analysis is not helpful in ascertaining whether a stock is over- or undervalued. Investors quickly consider information.

The storng form suggests that stock prices reflect *all* information, whether it be public or private (insider). A perfect market exists. There is no individual who has sole access to information. Hence, a superior return cannot be earned by one individual or group of individuals. *See also* Random Walk Theory.

EFFICIENT PORTFOLIO
This combines assets so as to minimize the risk for a given level of return. *See also* Portfolio Theory and Capital Asset Pricing Model (CAPM).

ELASTICITY OF DEMAND
One of the most important concepts in demand is elasticity, which is the sensitivity of change in quantity demanded to a change in a factor in the demand function. The principal variables involved with demand elasticity are
1. The price of the good (in the case of price elasticity)

2. Income (in the case of income elasticity)
3. The price of a substitute-product (in the case of cross elasticity)
4. Advertising (in the case of promotional elasticity)

We discuss only the price elasticity here in detail since other elasticity concepts are much the same with respect to their calculations and implications.

Price Elasticity of Demand

Price elasticity, denoted with e_p, is the ratio of a percentage change in quantity demanded (Q) to a percentage change in price (p).

$$e_p = \frac{dQ/Q}{dp/p} = dQ/dp \cdot p/Q$$

where dQ/dp is simply the slope of the demand function $Q = (p)$. We classify the price elasticity demand into three categories:

If $e_p = 1$, elastic

$e_p = 1$, unitary

$e_p < 1$, inelastic

■ Example

The demand function is given as $Q = 200 - 6p$. The price elasticity at $p = 4$ is computed as follows:

First, $Q = 200 - 6(4) = 176$

Since $dQ/dp = -6$, the e_p at $p = 4$ is

$$e_p = -6 \times (4/176) = -0.136$$

which means that a 1% change in price will bring about a 0.14% change in demand. The product under study is considered price inelastic, since the e_p is less than 1 in absolute value.

Economists have established the following relationships between price elasticity (e_p) and total revenue (TR), which can aid a firm in setting its price.

Price	$e_p > 1$	$e_p = 1$	$e_p < 1$
Price rises	TR falls	No change	TR rises
Price falls	TR rises	No change	TR falls

Firms need to be aware of the eleasticity of their own demand curves when they set product prices.

■ Example

A profit maximizing firm would never choose to lower its price in the inelastic range of its demand curve—such a price decrease would only decrease total revenue (see the previous chart) and at the same time increase costs, since output would be rising. The result would be a drastic decrease in profits. In fact, when costs are rising and the product is inelastic, the firm would have no difficulty passing on the increases by raising the price to the customer.

On the other hand, when there are many substitutes and demand is quite elastic, increasing prices may lead to a reduction in total revenue rather than an increase. The result may be lower profits rather than higher profits.

Similarly, managers are sometimes surprised by a lack of success of price reductions, this merely being a reflection of the fact that demand is relatively inelastic. In such a case, they may have to rely on other marketing efforts such as advertising and sales promotion in an effort to increase their market share.

ELECTRONIC MAIL   This is a document transmitted electronically from the user's computer or terminal to an on-line data base or other information service. Examples of transmitted documents are spreadsheets, records, reports, letters, and memos. Accountants and financial executives use electronic mail to send and receive timely and important messages from or to clients or others within the organization. There is a "mailbox" for each individual within the system, where messages are received, held, and sent to others. Many services exist, including AT&T and MCI.

ELIMINATIONS Transactions that occur between a parent and its subsidiaries are not considered to reflect arms-length actions; thus, the resulting account balances have to be eliminated in consolidation. An example of an item that would be eliminated in consolidation is the unrealized intercompany profit on the sale of inventory. This would result from the sale of products between parent and subsidiary at a price that is higher than the cost to the transferor. At the end of the reporting period a determination has to be made of the inventory on hand that was bought in this manner. An elimination in the consolidation process is then made for the amount of profit on the company's books applicable to the remaining inventory. Other items that have to be eliminated include profit related to the intercompany sale of fixed assets, the elimination of bonds issued by one company and purchased by another member of the consolidated group, along with related interest expense and income and the shifting of a subsidiary's retained earnings to its common stock account in consolidation in a year when a subsidiary declares a stock dividend on its common stock which is payable in the same class of stock. This entry would take place even though the stock dividend does not affect relative ownership interests and only requires a memo entry on the parent's books. *See also* Consolidation.

EMBEZZLEMENT This occurs when an employee of an entity is involved with theft of money or assets of that business over which he has been given responsibility. For example, an employee who has custody of inventory steals some merchandise. A sound internal control system is needed to guard against improprieties. *See also* Internal Control Structure.

EMPLOYEE STOCK OWNERSHIP PLAN (ESOP)
An ESOP is a stock bonus plan that encourages employees to invest in the employer's stock. Employees may participate in the management of a company and even take control of the company, which would otherwise go bankrupt. The ESOP, however, is an inappropriate instrument for retirement savings. Because most of the funds are concentrated in the stock of one company, it does not provide any safety through diversification.

ENCUMBRANCE
1. In the case of accounting for governmental funds, encumbrances are contractual commitments or purchase orders for merchandise or goods. An encumbrance is established to prevent additional expenditures from being made so that adequate funds exist to meet the commitments that have already been made. When a contractual commitment occurs, encumbrances is debited and reserve for encumbrances credited for the estimated amount. (Reserve for encumbrances represents a reservation of fund equity.) When the actual amount of the encumbered item is known, the initial entry is reversed. A second entry is made, debiting expenditures and crediting vouchers payable.

■ **Example**

On 6/2/19X1, a contractual commitment is made for an estimated $10,000. The items are received on 7/1/1X1, and the actual cost is $10,200. The entries are

6/2/19X1	Encumbrances	10,000	
	Reserve for Encumbrances		10,000
7/1/19X1	Reserve for Encumbrances	10,000	
	Encumbrances		10,000
	Expenditures	10,200	
	Vouchers Payable		10,200

Since encumbrances is a nominal account, it is credited and fund balance debited at the end of the budget year.
2. An obligation collateralized by a lien on assets.
See also Governmental Accounting.

EQUATION OF EXCHANGE Basically, this is a statement of the fundamental principle that the aggregate amount spent by buyers is equal

to the total value of the goods and services sold. Mathematically, the equation is an identity, expressed as follows:

$$MV = PQ$$

where M = money supply,
         V = income velocity of money,
         P = average price of final goods and services produced during the year,
         Q = physical quantity of those goods and services.

▪ Example

If the supply of money is $300 billion and each of these dollars on the average is spent five times a year for currently produced goods and services, total expenditures for currently produced goods and services will be $1,500 billion. If producers turn out 750 billion "units" of goods and services and these are subsequently sold at an average price of $2 per unit, then the value of these currently produced goods and services, or GNP, is $1,500 billion. In other words,

$$MV = PQ$$
(\$300 billion) (5) = (\$2) (750 billion units)
$1,500 billion = $1,500 billion

The equation of exchange is very important because it provides insights into what will happen to output (Q) and prices (P) when the money supply (M) changes. For example, assume that the velocity of money (V) is constant. If M increases, then either P or Q or both must increase. The effects of P and Q will depend on the state of the economy.

1. If the economy is operating well below the full employment level, Q will tend to rise relatively more than P as unemployed resources are reemployed.

2. If the economy is at full employment, P will tend to rise more than Q; that is, the increase in M will be purely inflationary.

If it is assumed that both V and Q remain constant, then P depends directly on M. This theory is called the *quantity theory of money*. The theory states, for example, that a 5% increase in money supply will cause a 5% increase in P. Similarly, a 5% decrease in M will cause a 5% decrease in P.

EQUILIBRIUM PRICE AND QUANTITY Equilibrium is a state of balance between opposing forces. *Equilibrium price* is the price of a commodity (good and service) determined by the intersection of the market forces of demand and supply (Figure 1). It is also the price that maximizes a firm's profit (Figure 2). *Equilibrium quantity* is the quantity that corresponds to the equilibrium price. The *Capital Asset Pricing Model (CAPM)* provides an equilibrium price on capital assets (Figure 3).

Figure 1 Demand and Supply

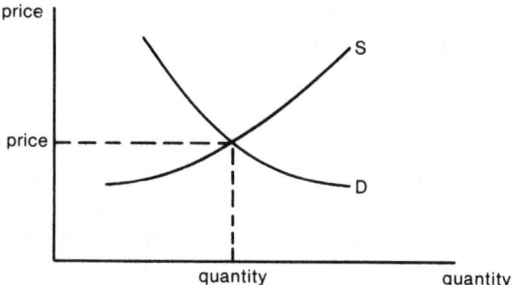

Figure 2 Profit Maximization

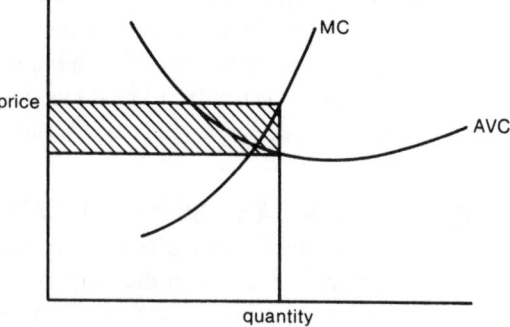

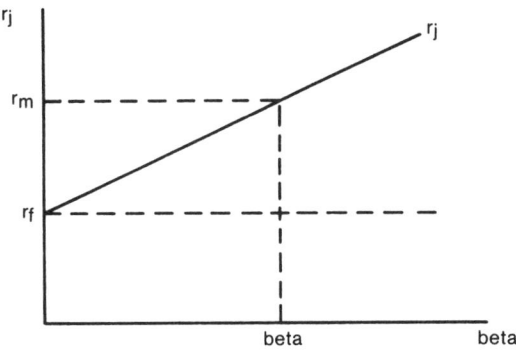

Figure 3 Capital Asset Pricing Model (CAPM)

See also Capital Asset Pricing Model (CAPM).

EQUITY FINANCING Equity issuance may be in the form of common stock or preferred stock. The company obtains cash, other assets, or services. When debt levels are excessive, equity financing is preferred. *Suggestion*: If you are materially affected by outside forces, you need more stability and reliability in your financing.

If stock price is *temporarily low* (e.g., after a stock market crash such as October 1987), funds should be obtained on a short-term debt basis. After stock prices rebound, equity financing may be made and the debt repaid.

Small businesses can obtain equity financing economically by going to venture capital groups that take a position in a small business. A "finder" may act as an intermediary between the company and investing group. Alternatively, an ad may be placed in a newspaper. Another possibility is direct private placement to an institutional investor or a key customer or supplier. *Warning*: Avoid stringent restrictions that will curtail your freedom (e.g., minimum working capital requirement).

Common stock is the real ownership interest in the company, since it carries voting rights. Advantages are that there are no fixed charge payments, no maturity date, no sinking fund requirements, no dividends to pay in times of financial distress, and they improve the debt-equity ratio. Disadvantages are that you give up voting rights, ownership interest is diluted, there are higher flotation costs, investors receive dividends after preferred stockholders, investors come after preferred stockholders in the event of liquidation, dividend payments are not tax deductible (unlike interest), and the cost is higher because greater risk exists with common stock than with preferred stocks and bonds.

Preferred stock comes after debt but before common stock in liquidation and in the distribution of earnings. With cumulative preferred stock, preferred dividends in arrears must be paid before any dividends can be paid to common stockholders. *Suggestion*: To avoid SEC disclosures and reduce issuance costs, private placement may be made.

The advantages of preferred stock relative to bonds are that you can omit a dividend but not interest and there is no maturity date and no sinking fund requirement. Compared to common stock, there is no ownership dilution with preferred stock. Disadvantages of preferred stock relative to debt are that dividends are not tax deductible and there is a higher yield because of the greater risk to the holder. *Recommendation*: Issue preferred stock where debt is already excessive and issuing common stock will result in control problems for the ownership group.

The cost of preferred stock usually follows changes in interest rates. Hence, the cost of preferred stock will most likely be low when interest rates are low. When the cost of common stock is high, preferred stock issuance may be achieved at a lower cost.

Suggestion: If you want to issue preferred stock at a lower cost with fewer restrictions, warrants may be given as "sweeteners." Warrants are rights to buy common stock at a certain price at a later date.

EQUITY METHOD The investor company is the owner and the investee company is being owned. If an investor owns between 20%–50% of the voting common stock of an investee, the equity method is used. The equity method would also be employed if the holder owned less than 20% of the voting common stock but possessed significant influence (effective control). The equity method is also used if more than 50% of the voting common stock is owned but one of the negating factors for consolidation exists. Investments in joint ventures have to be accounted for under the equity method.

The accounting under the equity method can be illustrated by examining the following "T-accounts," which will be described in more detail shortly:

Investment in Investee

Cost	Dividends
Ordinary profit	Amortization expense on goodwill
Extraordinary gain	Depreciation on excess of fair market value less book value of specific assets
	Permanent decline

Equity in Earnings of Investee

Amortization expense	Ordinary profit
Depreciation	

Loss

Permanent decline	

Extraordinary Gain

	Extraordinary gain

The cost of the investment includes brokerage fees. The investor recognizes his percentage ownership interest in the ordinary profit of the investee by debiting investment in investee and crediting equity in earnings of investee. The investor's share in investee's earnings is computed after deducting cumulative preferred dividends, whether or not declared. Investor's share of investee's profit should be based on the investee's most recent income statement applied on a consistent basis. Extraordinary gains or losses as well as prior period adjustments are also picked up as shown on the investee's books. Dividends reduce the carrying value of the investment account.

The excess paid by the investor for the investee's net assets is first assigned to the specific assets and liabilities and depreciated. The unidentifiable portion of the excess is considered goodwill, which is amortized over the period benefited, not exceeding 40 years. The amortization expense on goodwill and depreciation on excess value of assets reduce the investment account and are charged to equity in earnings. Temporary decline in price of the investment in the investee is ignored. Permanent decline in value of the investment is reflected by debiting loss and crediting investment in investee.

When the investor's share of the investee's losses is greater than the balance in the investment account, the equity method should be discontinued at the zero amount unless the investor has guaranteed the investee's obligations or where immediate profitability is assured. A return to the equity method is made only after offsetting subsequent profits against losses not recorded.

When the investee's stock is sold, a realized gain or loss will arise for the difference between selling price and the cost of the investment account.

The mechanics of consolidation essentially apply with the equity method. For example, intercompany profits and losses are eliminated. Investee capital transactions impacting the investor's share of equity should be accounted for as in a consolidation. Investee's capital transactions should be accounted for as if the investee were a consolidated subsidiary. For example, when the investee issues its common stock to third parties at a price in excess of book value, there will be an increase in the value of the investment and a related increase in the investor's paid-in-capital.

Interperiod income tax allocation will occur because the investor shows the investee's profits for book reporting but dividends for tax reporting. This results in a deferred income tax credit account.

If the ownership goes below 20% or the investor for some reason is unable to control the investee, the investor should cease recognizing the investee's earnings. The equity method is discontinued but the balance in the investment account is maintained. The cost method should then be applied.

If the investor increases his ownership in the investee to 20% or more, the equity method should be used for current and future years. Further, the effect of using the equity method rather than the cost method on prior years at the old percentage (e.g., 15%) should be recognized as an adjustment to retained earnings and other accounts so affected, such as investment in investee. The retroactive adjustment on the investment, earnings, and retained earnings should be applied in the same manner as a step-by-step acquisition of a subsidiary.

Disclosures should be made by the investor in footnotes, separate schedules, or parenthetically of the following: percent owned, name of investee, investor's accounting policies employed, material effects of possible conversions and exercises of investee common stock, and quoted market price (for investees not qualifying as subsidiaries). Further, summarized financial data as to assets, liabilities, and earnings should be given in footnotes or separate schedules for material investments in unconsolidated subsidiaries. Material realized and unrealized gains and losses relating to the subsidiary's portfolio occurring between the dates of the financial statements of the subsidiary and parent must also be disclosed.

▪ Example

On 1/1/19X5, X Company bought 30,000 shares at $25 per share for a 40% interest in the common stock of AB Company. Bro-

kerage commissions were $10,000. During 19X5, AB's net income was $140,000 and dividends received were $30,000. On 1/1/19X6, X Company received 15,000 shares of common stock as a result of a stock split by AB Company. On 1/4/19X6, X Company sold 2,000 shares of AB stock at $16 per share. The journal entries follow:

1/1/19X5	Investment in Investee	760,000	
	Cash		760,000
12/31/19X5	Investment in Investee	56,000	
	Equity in Earnings of Investee 40% × $140,000 = $56,000		56,000
	Cash	30,000	
	Investment in Investee		30,000
1/1/19X6	Memo entry for stock split		
1/4/19X6	Cash (2,000 × $16)	32,000	
	Loss on Sale of Investment	2,940	
	Investment in Investee (2,000 × $17.47)		34,940

$$\frac{\$786,000}{45,000} = \$17.47 \text{ per share}$$

Investment in Investee

1/1/19X5	760,000	12/31/19X5	30,000
12/31/19X5	56,000		
	816,000		
	786,000		

▪ Example

On 1/1/19X6, the investor purchased 100,000 shares of investee's 400,000 shares outstanding for $3,000,000. The book value of net assets acquired was $2,500,000. Of the $500,000 excess paid over book value, $300,000 is attributable to undervalued tangible assets and the remainder is attributable to unidentifiable assets. The depreciation period is 20 years and the maximum period is used to amortize goodwill. In 19X6, investee's net income was $800,000, including an extraordinary loss of $200,000. Dividends of $75,000 were paid on June 1, 19X6. The following journal entries are necessary for the acquisition of investee by investor accounted for under the equity method.

1/1/19X6	Investment in Investee	3,000,000	
	Cash		3,000,000
6/1/19X6	Cash	18,750	
	Investment in Investee 25% × $75,000		18,750
12/31/19X6	Investment in Investee	250,000	
	Equity in Earnings of Investee $1,000,000 × 25% = $250,000		250,000
	Extraordinary Loss from Investment	50,000	
	Investment in Investee $200,000 × 25% = $50,000		50,000
	Equity in Earnings of Investee	20,000	
	Investment in Investee		20,000

Computation follows:

Undervalued depreciable assets $300,000/20 years	$15,000
Unrecorded goodwill $200,000/40 years	5,000
	$20,000

See also Cost Method.

EQUIVALENT TAXABLE YIELD

This is what the return would be on a nontaxable security if it were taxable given the individual's tax rate.

■ Example

A client owns a municipal bond that pays an interest rate of 7%. The client's tax rate is 28%. The equivalent rate on a taxable instrument is

$$\frac{0.07}{1 - 0.28} = \frac{0.07}{0.72} = 9.7\%$$

See also Bond Yield—Effective Rate of Return on a Bond.

ERRORS AND IRREGULARITIES

The AICPAs' Statement on Auditing Standard No. 53 titled ''The Auditor's Responsibility to Detect and Report Errors and Irregularities'' specifies the auditor's responsibility to uncover material misstatements (material errors and irregularities). The auditor must evaluate the risk that errors and irregularities may result in the material misstatement of the financial statements. Based on his evaluation, the auditor has to design the audit to obtain reasonable assurance of uncovering significant errors. However, certain irregularities (e.g., forgery, collusion) may reasonably go undetected by the auditor even with a properly designed and executed audit.

ESTATE

An estate consists of the real and personal assets of an individual at the time of death. The distribution of the assets to the heirs is based on the will. If no will exists, the distribution is in accordance with a court order. It is a liquidation process. Court-supervised probate achieves the following purposes:

- Determine ownership of property
- Ascertain who is to receive benefits
- Assure the proper transfer of property
- Provide for the payment of debts and taxes

The executor of a will is the individual chosen by the decedent during his lifetime to fulfill the terms of the will. Some activities of the executor are

- Collect estate assets
- Manage property
- Pay creditors
- Distribute remaining property

In general, expenses applicable to settle a decedent's estate reduce principal. Expenses to operate, preserve, and manage income-producing property are charged against income.

Accounting for a fiduciary to the court is in the form of Charge-and-Discharge Statements showing the fiduciary's activities relating to principal and income.

The following table shows an illustrative Charge-and-Discharge Statement as to Principal.

Mr. X, Executor
Estate of Mr. A
Charge-and-Discharge Statement as to Principal
Feb. 1, 19X1, to June 30, 19X1

I charge myself with:		
Assets per inventory	$200,000	
Assets discovered	10,000	
Total charges		$210,000
I credit myself with:		
Debts paid	$ 35,000	
Legacies paid or delivered	100,000	
Loss on realization of principal assets	1,000	
Administration expenses	20,000	
Funeral expenses	4,000	
Devise distributed	30,000	
Total credits		190,000
Balance as to principal		$ 20,000
Consisting of:		
Principal cash		$ 5,000
Savings accounts		11,000
Securities		4,000
Total		$ 20,000

The "I charge myself with" section shows the assets the fiduciary is accountable for. The "I credit myself with" section reveals the way in which the fiduciary conducted his responsibilities.

ESTATE PLANNING   This involves deriving the most favorable tax consequences for wealth that has been accumulated. This would assume that any inheritance is passed on to the beneficiaries with the least amount given over to taxes.

The tax-planning aspects for estates include:

• Determining what financial strategy could be developed, taking into account the particular assets being considered.

• The transfer of assets before the taxpayer's death. For example, title to property should be transferred to those who would benefit the most from their lower income tax brackets. *Note*: When property will ultimately be transferred to children, it's best to start with gradual transfers at an early age through judicious use of the $10,000 gift tax annual exclusion.

• The attorney should draft a will considering the tax and asset transfer ramifications. For instance, property can be transferred between spouses without any tax because of the unlimited marital deduction.

• Consideration must be given to the terms of any life insurance policies. Will the proceeds go to the estate? If so, how much will it be? Did the insured possess any incidents of ownership? With some policies, the insured will collect if he or she outlives the life expectancy. However, if the insured then dies, the size of the taxable estate will increase, thus increasing the amount of the estate tax.

Estate tax planning begins with the calculation of the consequences of shifting property at some point in the future. Estate tax rates are graduated—the higher the incremental value of the estate, the higher is the incremental tax. To calculate the estate tax, start with determining the gross estate (generally, the taxable estate plus adjusted taxable gifts). Subtract from that figure the allowable deductions, such as administrative expenses, debts, and the marital and charitable deductions. Then compute the tax. Subtract from the tax any credits allowable. Perhaps the most valuable credit is the unified credit. Like other credits, it's a direct reduction of the computed tax. However, because of its size ($192,800), it can allow some estates (those up to $600,000) to pass tax free. Note that the effect of the full unified credit may be diminished if lifetime gifts were made by the decedent that exceeded the $10,000 annual gift tax exclusion.

On-line data bases can provide accurate and cost-effective estate data to the tax accountant or attorneys. Examples are Lexis™, Westlaw™, and PHINet™. The practitioner enters key words for the estate-planning item and the relevant information is downloaded.

ESTIMATED LIABILITIES (CONTINGENCIES)   A loss contingency should be accrued if *both* of the following criteria exist:

• At year-end, it is *probable* (likely to occur) that an asset was impaired or a liability was incurred.

• The amount of loss is subject to reasonable estimation.

The loss contingency is booked because of the principle of conservatism. The entry for a probable loss is

Expense (Loss)
  Estimated Liability

A probable loss that cannot be estimated should be footnoted.

■ Example

On 12/31/19X6, warranty expenses are estimated at $20,000. On 3/15/19X7, actual warranty costs paid for were $16,000. The journal entries are

12/31/19X6	Warranty Expense	20,000	
	Estimated Liability		20,000
3/15/19X7	Estimated Liability	16,000	
	Cash		16,000

If a loss contingency exists at year-end but no asset impairment or liability incurrence exists (e.g., uninsured equipment), footnote disclosure may be made.

A probable loss occurring after year-end but before the audit report date only requires subsequent event disclosure.

Examples of probable loss contingencies may be

• Warranties
• Lawsuits
• Claims and assessments
• Expropriation of property by a foreign government
• Casualties and catastrophes (e.g., fire)

If the amount of loss is within a range, the accrual is based on the best estimate within that range. However, if no amount within the range is better than any other amount, the *minimum amount* (not maximum amount) of the range is booked. The exposure to additional losses should be disclosed.

In the case of a reasonably possible loss (more than remote but less than likely), no accrual is made but rather footnote disclosure is required. The disclosure includes the nature of the contingency and the estimate of probable loss or range of loss. If an estimate of loss is not possible, that fact should be stated.

A remote contingency (slight chance of occurring) is usually ignored and no disclosure is made. There are exceptions when a remote contingency would be disclosed in the case of guarantees of indebtedness, standby letters of credit, and agreements to repurchase receivables or properties.

General (unspecified) contingencies are not accrued. Examples are self-insurance and possible hurricane losses. Disclosure and/or an appropriation of retained earnings can be made for general contingencies. To be booked as an estimated liability, the future loan must be *specific* and *measurable*, such as parcel post and freight losses.

Gain contingencies cannot be booked because it violates conservatism. However, footnote disclosure can be made.

ESTIMATING CASH COLLECTION RATES (PAYMENT PROPORTIONS) FOR CASH BUDGETING   A forecast of cash collections and potential write-offs of accounts receivable is essential in cash budgeting and in judging the appropriateness of current credit and discount policies.

The critical step in making such a forecast is estimating the cash collection rates (or payment proportions) to be applied to sales or accounts receivable. Two methods are discussed following. They are the probability matrix approach and the lagged regression approach.

The Probability Approach

The probability matrix (or Markov) approach has been around for a long time. This ap-

proach has been successfully applied by Cyert and others to accounts receivable analysis, specifically to the estimation of that portion of the accounts receivable that will eventually become uncollectable. The method requires classification of outstanding accounts receivable according to age categories that reflect the stage of account delinquency; for example, current accounts, accounts 1 month past due, accounts 2 months past due, and so forth.

■ Example

XYZ department store divides its accounts receivable into two classifications: 0–60 days old and 61–120 days old. Accounts that are more than 120 days old are declared uncollectable by XYZ. XYZ currently has $10,000 in accounts receivable: $7,000 from the 0–60 day-old category and $3,000 from the 61–120 day-old category. Based on an analysis of its past records, we can formulate with what is known as the matrix of transition probabilities. The matrix is given, as shown in Table 1.

Transition probabilities are nothing more than the probabilities that an account receivable moves from one age stage category to another. We will note three basic features of this matrix. First, notice the squared element, 0 in the matrix. This indicates that $1 in the 0–60 day-old category *cannot* become a bad debt in 1 month's time. Now look at the two circled elements; each of these is 1, indicating that, in time, all the accounts receivable dollars will either be paid

or become uncollectable. Eventually, all the dollars do wind up either as collected or uncollected, but XYZ is interested in knowing the probability that a dollar of 0–60 day-old or 61–120 day-old receivable would eventually find its way into either paid bills or bad debts. It is convenient to partition the matrix of transition probabilities into four submatrices as follows:

$$\left[\begin{array}{c|c} I & O \\ \hline R & Q \end{array}\right]$$

so that

$$I = \begin{bmatrix} 1 & 0 \\ 0 & 1 \end{bmatrix} \quad O = \begin{bmatrix} 0 & 0 \\ 0 & 0 \end{bmatrix}$$

$$R = \begin{bmatrix} 0.3 & 0 \\ 0.5 & 0.1 \end{bmatrix} \quad Q = \begin{bmatrix} 0.5 & 0.2 \\ 0.3 & 0.1 \end{bmatrix}$$

Now we are in a position to illustrate the procedure used to determine

1. Estimated collection and bad debt percentages by age category
2. Estimated allowance for doubtful accounts

Step by step, the procedure is as follows:

Step 1. Set up the matrix $[I - Q]$.

$$[I - Q] = \begin{bmatrix} 1 & 0 \\ 0 & 1 \end{bmatrix} - \begin{bmatrix} 0.5 & 0.2 \\ 0.3 & 0.1 \end{bmatrix} = \begin{bmatrix} 0.5 & -0.2 \\ -0.3 & 0.9 \end{bmatrix}$$

Step 2. Find the inverse of this matrix, denoted by N.

$$N = [I - Q]^{-1} = \begin{bmatrix} 2.31 & 0.51 \\ 0.77 & 1.28 \end{bmatrix}$$

Step 3. Multiply this inverse by matrix R.

Table 1

From \ To	Collected	Uncollectable	0–60 days old	61–120 days old
Collected	①	0	0	0
Uncollectable	0	①	0	0
0–60 days old	0.3	⓪	0.5	0.2
61–120 days old	0.5	0.1	0.3	0.1

$$NR = \begin{bmatrix} 2.31 & 0.51 \\ 0.77 & 1.28 \end{bmatrix} \begin{bmatrix} 0.3 & 0 \\ 0.5 & 0.1 \end{bmatrix} = \begin{bmatrix} 0.95 & 0.05 \\ 0.87 & 0.13 \end{bmatrix}$$

NR gives us the probabilities that an account will eventually be collected or become a bad debt. Specifically, the top row in the answer is the probability that \$1 of XYZ's accounts receivable in the 0–60 day-old category will end up in the collected and bad debt categories. There is a 0.95 probability that \$1 currently in the 0–60 day-old category will be paid, and a 0.05 probability that it will eventually become a bad debt. Turning to the second row, the two entries represent the probabilities that \$1 now in the 61–120 day-old category will end up in the collected and bad debt categories. We can see from this row that there is a 0.87 probability that \$1 currently in the 61–120 day-old category will be collected and a 0.13 probability that it will eventually become uncollectable.

If XYZ wants to estimate the future of its \$10,000 accounts receivable, it must set up the following matrix multiplication:

$$[7,000 \quad 3,000] \begin{bmatrix} 0.95 & 0.05 \\ 0.87 & 0.13 \end{bmatrix} = [9,260 \quad 740]$$

Hence, of the \$10,000 accounts receivable, it expects to collect \$9,260 and to lose \$740 to bad debts. Therefore, the estimated allowances for uncollectable accounts is \$740.

The variance of each component is equal to

$$A = be(cNR - (cNR)_{sq})$$

where $c_i = b_i \bigg/ \sum_{i=1}^{2} b_i$ and e is the unit vector.

In our example, $b = (7,000 \quad 3,000)$, $c = (0.7 \quad 0.3)$.

Therefore:

$$A = [7,000 \quad 3,000] \begin{bmatrix} 1 \\ 1 \end{bmatrix} \left[[0.7 \quad 0.3] \begin{bmatrix} 0.95 & 0.05 \\ 0.87 & 0.13 \end{bmatrix} \right.$$

$$\left. - [0.7 \quad 0.3] \begin{bmatrix} 0.95 & 0.05 \\ 0.87 & 0.13 \end{bmatrix}_{sq} \right]$$

$$= 10,000 \left[[0.926 \quad 0.074] \right.$$

$$\left. - [0.857476 \quad 0.005476] \right] = [685.24 \quad 685.24]$$

which makes the standard deviation equal to \$26.18 ($\sqrt{685.24}$). If we want to be 95% confident about our estimate of collections, we would set the interval estimate at \$9,260 ± 2(26.18), or \$9,207.64 – \$9,312.36, assuming $t = 2$ as a rule of thumb. We would also be able to set the allowance to cover the bad debts at \$740 + 2(26.18), or \$792.36.

The Lagged Regression Approach

Credit sales affect cash collections with time lags. In other words, there is a time lag between the point of credit sale and realization of cash. More specifically, the lagged effect of credit sales and cash inflows is distributed over a number of periods as follows:

$$C_t = b_1 S_{t-1} + b_2 S_{t-2} + \cdots + b_i S_{t-i}$$

where C_t = cash collections,
S_t = credit sales made in period t,
$b_1, b_2, \ldots b_i$ = collection percentages,
i = number of periods lagged.

By using the regression method, we will be able to estimate these collection rates (or payment proportions). We can utilize /Data Regression of Lotus 1-2-3™ or special packages such as STATPACK™ and SAS™.

It should be noted that the cash collection percentages, $(b_1, b_2, \ldots, b_i)$ may not add up to 100% because of the possibility of bad debts. Once we estimate these percentages by using the method, we should be able to compute the bad debt percentage with no difficulty.

Table 2 shows the regression results using actual monthly data on credit sales and cash inflows for a real company. Equation I can be written as follows:

$$C_t = 60.6\%(S_{t-1}) + 24.3\%(S_{t-2}) + 8.8\%(S_{t-3})$$

This result indicates that the receivables generated by the credit sales are collected at the following rates: first month after sale, 60.6%; second month after sale, 24.3%; and third month after sale, 8.8%. The bad debt

Table 2 Regression Results for Cash Collection (C_t)

Independent Variables	Equation I	Equation II
S_{t-1}	0.606[a]	0.596[a]
	(0.062)[b]	(0.097)
S_{t-2}	0.243[a]	0.142
	(0.085)	(0.120)
S_{t-3}	0.088	0.043
	(0.157)	(0.191)
S_{t-4}		0.136
		(0.800)
$\bar{R}^2$	0.754	0.753
Durbin-Watson	2.52[c]	2.48[c]
Standard error of the estimate	11.63	16.05
# of monthly observations	21	20
Bad debt percentages	0.063	0.083

[a] Statistically significant at the 5% significance level
[b] The figure in the parentheses is the standard error of the estimate for the coefficient.
[c] No autocorrelation present at the 5% significance level

percentage is computed as 6.3% (100% − 93.7%).

It is very important to note, however, that these collection and bad debt percentages are probabilistic variables; that is, variables whose values cannot be known with precision. However, the standard error of the regression coefficient and the t-value permit us to assess a probability that the true percentage is between specified limits. The confidence interval takes the following form:

$$b \pm t \text{ (standard error)}$$

■ **Example**

To illustrate, assuming $t = 2$ as a rule of thumb at the 95% confidence level, the true collection percentage from the prior month's sales will be

$$60.6\% \pm 2(6.2\%)$$
$$= 60.6\% \pm 12.4\%$$

Turning to the estimation of cash collections and allowance for doubtful accounts, we will use the following values for illustrative purposes:

$S_{t-1} = \$77.6$, $S_{t-2} = \$58.5$, $S_{t-3} = \$76.4$,
and forecast average monthly net credit sales = \$75.2

Then, (*i*) the forecast cash collection for period t would be

$C_t = 60.6\%(77.6) + 19.3\%(58.5)$
$\qquad\qquad + 8.8\%(76.4) = \$65.04$

If the financial planner wants to be 95% confident about this forecast value, then he or she would set the interval as follows:

$$C_t \pm t\text{(standard error of the estimate)}$$

To illustrate, using $t = 2$ as a rule of thumb at the 95% confidence level, the true value for cash collections in period t will be

$$\$65.04 \pm 2(11.63)$$
$$= \$65.04 \pm 23.26$$

See also Budgeting for Profit Planning; Cash Budget.

EXPECTED VALUE The expected value ($E(x)$) is found by multiplying the probability of each outcome by its *payoff*.

$$E(x) = x_i\, p_i$$

where x_i is the outcome for ith possible event and p_i is the probability of occurrence of that outcome. *See also* Decision Making Under Uncertainty.

EXPERT SYSTEM An expert system refers to a computer-oriented information system employing knowledge about a difficult area to serve as an advisor to you. The expert system includes a knowledge base and software modules that carry out logical inferences on the knowledge and give appropriate answers to problems faced. The software is also able to explain the reasons for answers. Knowledge refiner programs reduce significant amounts of data to more meaningful knowledge. The result can then be transferred to an expert system in helping you solve a problem.

Special Note: Expert systems simulate the human reasoning process. They codify the knowledge and guidelines used to derive con-

clusions. Knowledge is used to answer complex questions. The system has programmed in it rules for reasoning (inference or logical functions). Information received is compared to the stored knowledge base and a recommended solution offered along with supporting rationale. There is an interface representing interaction between the user and expert system. The system can be used for financial and managerial decision making such as portfolio management. The knowledge base must be updated for new information and trends and hence will have to be tied into an on-line data base.

What goes on? The computer ascertains what data are necessary for a decision and asks appropriate sequential questions. It then searches, retrieves, and derives relevant data to make that decision. For example, in an acquisition and merger setting, the program determines the appropriate information from the data base and communicates the information in quantitative terms, including analysis.

Many practitioner benefits exist with the use of expert systems, including:

- Reduction of CPA firm staff time.
- Use of ''real-situation'' simulation for the instruction of accounting, audit, and tax staff.
- Transmittal of knowledge from the partners to lower staff levels, including associated reasoning. It can provide a confirming opinion to that initially selected by the partner or manager for a particular problem.

■ Example

Human Edge Software's Expert Ease™ induces rules and a knowledge base based on the expert information including examples given to it. The rules permit decisions and diagnoses via an inquiry interface. It appraises a range of factors relative to a particular objective and ignores irrelevant variables.

It can perform complicated financial analysis models.

■ Example

Applied Expert Systems' Planpower™ provides expert assistance to professional financial planners. It emulates the knowledge of planning experts in the firm, evaluates and plans, and prepares the actual plan, including recommendations. It has many decision rules in its knowledge base. Reasoning behind recommendations is given and recommendations are tested against all alternatives.

■ Example

Unitek Technologies' Expert Strategist™ interprets financial statements transferred from a conventional accounting package. In effect, financial statement analysis is performed. It also reveals the impact of different management actions on the financial ratios.

EXPONENTIAL SMOOTHING This is a popular technique for short-run forecasting by financial managers. It uses a weighted average of past data as the basis for a forecast. The procedure gives heaviest weight to more recent information and lesser weights to observations in the more distant past. The reason for this is that the future is more dependent upon the recent past than on the distant past. In connection with sales forecasting, the method is known to be effective when there is random demand and no seasonal fluctuations in the sales data. One disadvantage of the method, however, is that it does not include industrial or economic factors such as market conditions, prices, or the effects of competitors' actions.

The Model

The formula for exponential smoothing is

$$\hat{y}_{t+1} = \alpha \, y_t + (1 - \alpha) \, \hat{y}_t$$

or in words,

$$\hat{y}_{new} = \alpha\, y_{old} + (1 - \alpha)\, \hat{y}_{old}$$

where $\hat{y}_{new}$ = exponentially smoothed average to be used as the forecast,
y_{old} = most recent actual data,
$\hat{y}_{old}$ = most recent smoothed forecast,
α = smoothing constant.

The higher the α, the higher the weight given to the more recent information.

Data on sales follow.

Time Period (t)	Actual Sales (000) (y_t)
1	$60.0
2	64.0
3	58.0
4	66.0
5	70.0
6	60.0
7	70.0
8	74.0
9	62.0
10	74.0
11	68.0
12	66.0
13	60.0
14	66.0
15	62.0

To initialize the exponential smoothing process, we must have the initial forecast. The first smoothed forecast to be used can be

1. First actual observations.
2. An average of the actual data for a few periods.

For illustrative purposes, let us use a six-period average as the initial forecast ($\hat{y}_7$) with a smoothing constant of $\alpha = 0.40$.

Then $\hat{y}_7 = (y_1 + y_2 + y_3 + y_4 + y_5 + y_6)/6$
$= (60 + 64 + 58 + 66 + 70 + 60)/$
$6 = 63$

Note that $y_7 = 70$. Then $\hat{y}_8$ is computed as follows:

$$\hat{y}_8 = \alpha\, y_7 + (1 - \alpha)\, \hat{y}_7$$
$$= (0.40)\,(70) + (0.60)\,(63)$$
$$= 28.0 + 37.80 = 65.80$$

Similarly:

$$\hat{y}_9 = \alpha\, y_8 + (1 - \alpha)\, \hat{y}_8$$
$$= (0.40)\,(74) + (0.60)\,(65.80)$$
$$= 29.60 + 39.48 = 69.08$$

and:

$$\hat{y}_{10} = \alpha\, y_9 + (1 - \alpha)\, \hat{y}_9$$
$$= (0.40)\,(62) + (0.60)\,(69.08)$$
$$= 24.80 + 41.45 = 66.25$$

By using the same procedure, the values of $\hat{y}_{11}, \hat{y}_{12}, \hat{y}_{13}, \hat{y}_{14}$, and $\hat{y}_{15}$ can be calculated. The table on page 182 shows a comparison between the actual sales and predicted sales by the exponential smoothing method.

Due to the negative and positive differences between actual sales and predicted sales, the forecaster can use a higher or lower smoothing constant α, in order to adjust his/her prediction as quickly as possible to large fluctuations in the data series. For example, if the forecast is slow in reacting to increased sales, (that is to say, if the difference is negative), he/she might want to try a higher value. For practical purposes, the *optimal* α may be picked by minimizing what is known as the *mean squared error* (MSE).

$$MSE = \sum_{t=1}^{n} (y_t - \hat{y}_t)^2/(n - i)$$

where i = the number of observations used to determine the initial forecast (in our example, $i = 6$).

In our example,

$$MSE = 307.27/(15 - 6) = 307.27/9 = 34.14$$

The idea is to select the α that minimizes MSE, which is the average sum of the variations between the historical sales data and the forecast values for the corresponding periods.

Comparison of Actual Sales and Predicted Sales

Time Period (t)	Actual Sales (y_t)	Predicted Sales ($\hat{y}_t$)	Difference ($y_t - \hat{y}_t$)	Difference^2 ($y_t - \hat{y}_t$)^2
1	$60.0			
2	64.0			
3	58.0			
4	66.0			
5	70.0			
6	60.0			
7	70.0	63.00	7.00	49.00
8	74.0	65.80	8.20	67.24
9	62.0	69.08	−7.08	50.13
10	74.0	66.25	7.75	60.06
11	68.0	69.35	−1.35	1.82
12	66.0	68.81	−2.81	7.90
13	60.0	67.69	−7.69	59.14
14	66.0	64.61	1.39	1.93
15	62.0	65.17	−3.17	10.05
				307.27

EXTRAORDINARY ITEMS These items are *both* unusual in nature and infrequent in occurrence. They are presented net of tax separately in the income statement. *See also* Income Statement Format.

F

FACTORING OF ACCOUNTS RECEIVABLE *See* Accounts Receivable Financing.

FACTORY OVERHEAD APPLICATION Regardless of the cost accumulation system used (i.e., job order, process, or standard costing), factory overhead is applied to a job or process using a *predetermined overhead rate*, which is determined based on budgeted factory overhead cost and budgeted activity. The rate is calculated as follows:

Predetermined overhead rate =

$$\frac{\text{Budgeted yearly total factory overhead costs}}{\text{Budgeted yearly activity (direct labor hours, etc.)}}$$

Budgeted activity units used in the denominator of the formula, more often called the *denominator level*, are measured in direct labor hours, machine hours, direct labor costs, production units, or any other representative surrogate of production activity.

■ Example

Assume that two companies have prepared the budgeted data shown in the table at the bottom of this page for the year 19A. Now assume that actual overhead costs and the actual level of activity for 19A for each firm are shown as follows:

	Company X	Company Y
Actual overhead costs	$198,000	$256,000
Actual machine hours	96,000	
Actual direct labor cost		176,000

Note that for each company the actual cost and activity data differ from the budgeted figures used in calculating the predetermined overhead rate. The computation of the resulting *underapplied* and *overapplied* overhead for each company follows on page 184.

	Company X	Company Y
Predetermined rate based on	Machine hours	Direct labor cost
Budgeted overhead	$200,000 (1)	$240,000 (1)
Budgeted machine hours	100,000 (2)	
Budgeted direct labor cost		$160,000(2)
Predetermined overhead rate (1)/(2)	$2 per machine hours	150% of direct labor cost

183

	Company X	Company Y
Actual overhead costs	$198,000	$256,000
Factory overhead applied to work-in-process during 19A:		
96,000 actual machine hours × $2	192,000	
$176,000 actual direct labor cost × 150%		264,000
Underapplied (overapplied) factory overhead	$ 6,000	($ 8,000)

See also Job Order Cost Accounting.

FEDERAL FUNDS   These are unsecured loans that commercial banks make to one another, usually overnight and over-the-counter by telephone or telegraph, out of their excessive reserve. The *federal fund market* is one in which commercial banks trade deposit balances at the Federal Reserve banks. Banks that are deficient to meet the Federal Reserve requirements borrow or "buy" federal funds. Banks that have more than enough to meet requirements lend or "sell" federal funds. The interest rate involved—the *federal fund rate*—is a highly sensitive and widely quoted money market yield. In general, the lower the volume of excess reserves, the higher will be the rate. Therefore, the federal fund rate is an important indicator that the Fed watches to decide whether it should add to banks' reserves or take them away. As part of its policy-making function, the Fed attempts to maintain a federal fund rate that is consistent with other monetary goals. *See also* Monetary Policy; Money Supply.

FEDERAL RESERVE SYSTEM   This is the system, created by an act of Congress in 1913, that is made up of 12 *Federal Reserve District Banks*, their 25 branches, and all national and state banks (about 5,700 member banks) that are part of the system scattered throughout the nation. It is headed by a seven-member Board of Governors. (see Figure 1.) The primary function of the Board is to establish and conduct the nation's monetary policy. The system manages the nation's monetary policy by exercising control over the money stock. (See Figure 2.) It controls the money supply primarily in three ways: (1) by raising or lowering the reserve requirement; (2) by setting the *discount rate* for loans to commercial banks; and (3) by purchasing and selling the government securities, mainly 3-month bills and notes issued by the U.S. Treasury. The system also serves as the central bank of the United States and a banker's bank that offers banks many of the same services that banks provide their customers. It performs many other functions. It sets margin requirements, regulates member banks, and acts as fiscal agent in the issuance of U.S. Treasury and U.S. government agency securities. *See also* Monetary Policy.

FIDUCIARY   A fiduciary is an individual who holds something in trust for another. The fiduciary is typically responsible for investing money prudently for the benefit of the beneficiary. Examples of fiduciaries are executors of estates, administrators of trusts, and receivers in bankruptcy. Fiduciaries are very often restricted as to what they are allowed to do with a beneficiary's assets. The term is also used to refer to corporate directors, trustees of nonprofit entities, and agencies. *See also* Estate; Trust.

FINANCIAL ANALYSIS   This involves the use and transformation of financial data into a form that can be used to monitor and evaluate the firm's financial position, to plan future financing, and to designate the size of the firm and its rate of growth. Financial analysis includes the use of *financial statement analysis* and *cash flow analysis*. *See also* Financial Statement Analysis; Z Scores.

Figure 1 Organization and Map of the Federal Reserve System

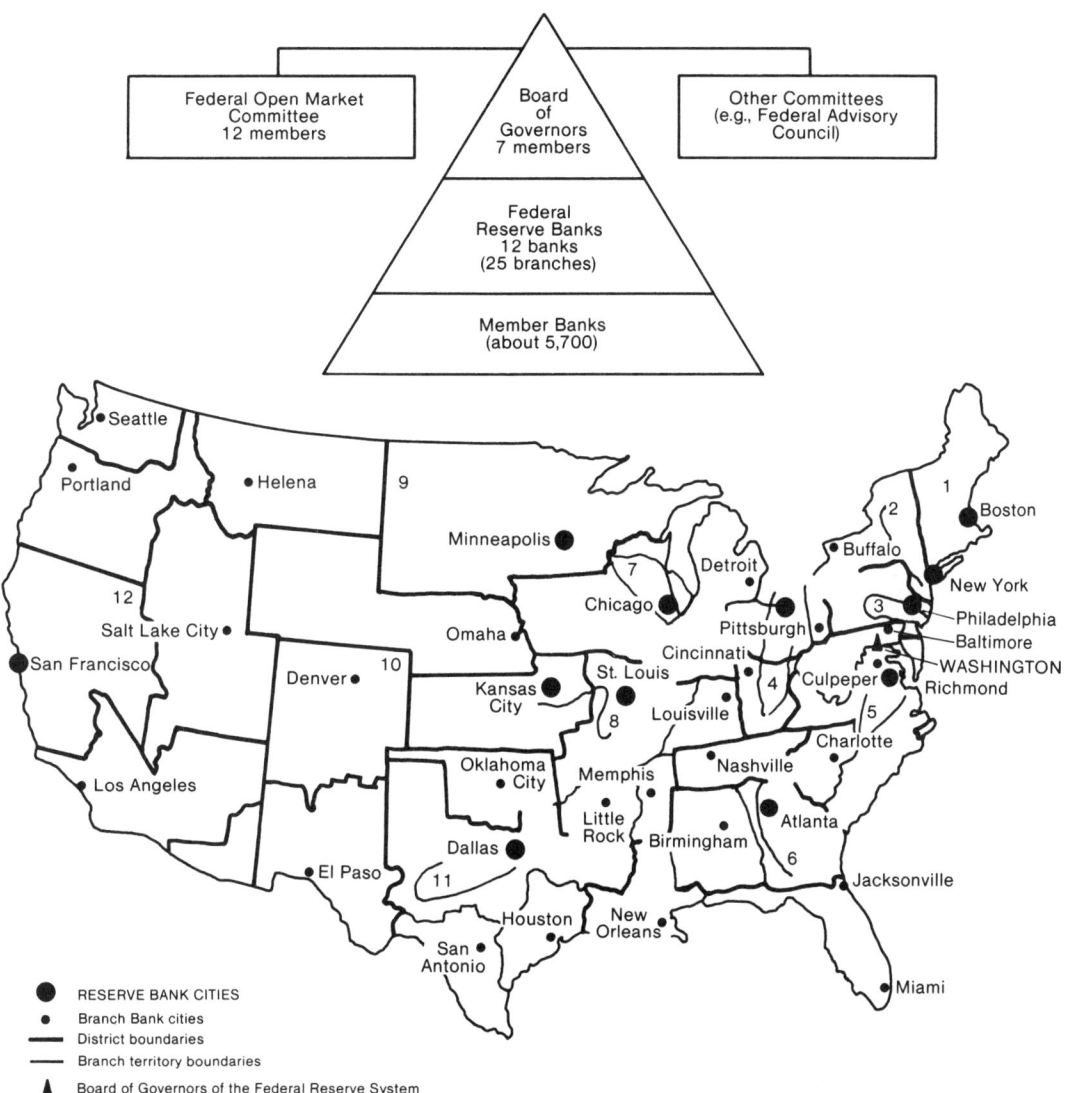

FINANCIAL FORECASTING AND THE PERCENTAGE-OF-SALES METHOD

Financial forecasting, an essential element of planning, is the basis for budgeting activities. It is also needed where future financing needs are being estimated. Basically, forecasts of future sales and their related expenses provide the firm with the information needed to project its future needs for financing.

The basic steps involved in projecting those financing needs are

1. Project the firm's sales. The sales forecast is the initial most important step. Most other forecasts (budgets) follow the sales forecast.
2. Project additional variables such as expenses.
3. Estimate the level of investment in current and fixed assets that are required to support the projected sales.
4. Calculate the firm's financing needs.

The most widely used method for projecting the company's financing needs is the *per-*

Figure 2 Flow of Federal Reserve System Influence

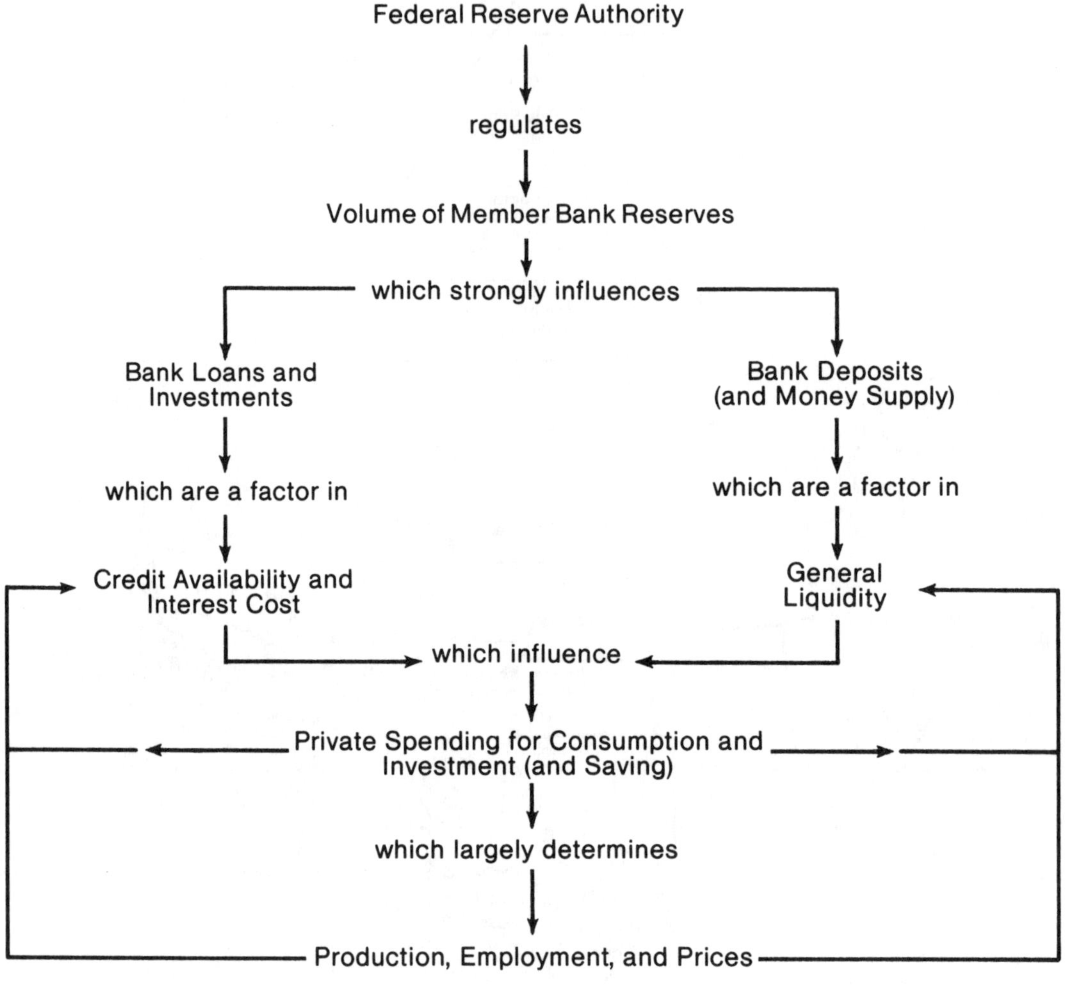

Federal Reserve Authority

↓

regulates

↓

Volume of Member Bank Reserves

↓

which strongly influences

| Bank Loans and Investments | Bank Deposits (and Money Supply) |

↓   ↓

which are a factor in   which are a factor in

↓   ↓

Credit Availability and Interest Cost   General Liquidity

which influence

↓

Private Spending for Consumption and Investment (and Saving)

↓

which largely determines

↓

Production, Employment, and Prices

Source: Board of Governors of the Federal Reserve System. Adapted.

cent-of-sales method. This method involves estimating the various expenses, assets, and liabilities for a future period as a percentage of the sales forecast and then using these percentages, together with the projected sales, to construct *pro forma* balance sheets. The following example illustrates how to develop a pro forma balance sheet and determine the amount of external financing needed.

■ Example 1

Assume that sales for 19x1 = $20, projected sales for 19x2 = $24, net income = 5% of sales, and the dividend payout ratio = 40%.

The steps for the computations are outlined as follows:

Step 1. Express those balance sheet items *that vary directly with sales* as a percentage

of sales. Any item such as long-term debt that does not vary directly with sales is designated "n.a.," or "not applicable."

Step 2. Multiply these percentages by the 19x2 projected sales = $2.4 to obtain the projected amounts, as shown in the last column.

Step 3. Simply insert figures for long-term debt, common stock, and paid-in capital from the 19x1 balance sheet.

Step 4. Compute 19x2 retained earnings as shown in (b).

Step 5. Sum the asset accounts, obtaining a total projected assets of $7.2, and also add the projected liabilities and equity to obtain $7.12, the total financing provided. Since liabilities and equity must total $7.2 but only $7.12 is projected, we have a shortfall of $0.08 "external financing needed."

Although the forecast of additional funds required can be made by setting up pro forma balance sheets, as described previously, it is often easier to use the following formula:

$$
\begin{array}{llll}
\text{External} & \text{Required} & \text{Spontaneous} & \text{Increase in} \\
\text{funds} & = \text{increase} & - \text{increase in} & - \text{retained} \\
\text{needed} & \text{in assets} & \text{liabilities} & \text{earnings} \\
\text{(EFN)} & & &
\end{array}
$$

$$\text{EFN} = (A/S)\,\Delta S - (L/S)\,\Delta S - (PM)(PS)(1-d)$$

where A/S = assets that increase spontaneously with sales as a percentage of sales,

L/S = liabilities that increase spontaneously with sales as a percentage of sales,

ΔS = change in sales,

PM = profit margin on sales,

PS = projected sales,

d = dividend payout ratio.

Figure 1   Projecting Balance Sheet Using Percentage-of-Sales Method

**Pro Forma Balance Sheet
(in millions of dollars)**

	Present (19x1)	% of Sales (19x1 sales = $20)	Projected (19x2 sales = $24)	
Assets				
Current assets	2	10	2.4	
Fixed assets	4	20	4.8	
Total assets	6		7.2	
Liabilities and stockholder's equity				
Current liabilities	2	10	2.4	
Long-term debt	2.5	n.a.	2.5	
Total liabilities	4.5		4.9	
Common stock	0.1	n.a.	0.1	
Paid-in-capital	0.2	n.a.	0.2	
Retained earnings	1.2		1.92[a]	
Total equity	1.5		2.22	
Total liabilities and stockholders' equity	6		7.12	Total financing provided
			0.08[b]	External financing needed
			7.2	Total

[a] 19x2 retained earnings = 19x1 retained earnings + projected net income − cash dividends paid = $1.2 + 5%($24) − 40%[5%($24)] = $1.2 + $1.2 − $0.48 = $2.4 − $0.48 = $1.92

[b] External financing needed = projected total assets − (projected total liabilities + projected equity) = $7.2 − ($4.9 + $2.22) = $7.2 − $7.12 = $0.08

■ Example 2

In Example 1,
$$A/S = \$6/\$20 = 30\%,$$
$$L/S = \$2/\$20 = 10\%,$$
$$\Delta S = (\$24 - \$20) = \$4,$$
$$PM = 5\% \text{ on sales},$$
$$PS = \$24,$$
$$d = 40\%.$$

Plugging these figures into the formula yields:

$$\text{EFN} = 0.3(\$4) - 0.1(\$4) - (0.05)(\$24)(1 - 0.4)$$
$$= \$1.2 - \$0.4 - \$0.72 = \$0.08$$

Thus, the amount of external financing needed is $800,000, which can be raised by issuing notes payable, bonds, stocks, or any combination of these financing sources.

The major advantage of the precent-of-sales method of financial forecasting is that it is simple and inexpensive to use. To obtain a more precise projection of the firm's future financing needs, however, the preparation of a *cash budget* is required. One important assumption behind the use of the method is that the firm is operating at full capacity. This means that the company has no sufficient productive capacity to absorb a projected increase in sales and thus requires additional investment in assets. *See also* Cash Budget.

FINANCIAL FUTURES

These may be utilized to hedge for the variability in interest and exchange rates. They may also be employed as speculative investments due to the potential for significant price fluctuation. Further, financial futures involve a lower margin requirement than commodities. For instance, the margin on a U.S. Treasury bill may be as low as 2%. Some places where financial futures may be traded are the New York Futures Exchange and the Chicago Board of Trade. Financial futures are mostly for fixed income debt securities designed to hedge or speculate on changes in interest rates or foreign currency. *See also* Interest Rate Futures Contract; Currency Futures Contract.

FINANCIAL GAMES

These focus on middle management decisions and emphasize particular areas of the firm. Financial games deal with the finance function of the firm. For example, a popular financial game, known as *FINANSIM: A Financial Management Simulation*™ (by Greenlaw and Frey), is a computerized functional game that emphasizes capital cost and budgeting, cash utilization and acquisition, and the asset structure of the firm. Marketing decisions are excluded; demand and price are considered exogeneous factors. Typically, there is no interaction in many functional games between player decisions. They bear strong resemblance to *simulation models*. *See also* Management Games; Simulation Models.

FINANCIAL INFORMATION SYSTEM

The financial information system is a subsystem of a *management information system (MIS)*. The financial information system is concerned with the financial resources of the firm and their acquisition, management, and expenditure in line with the overall objectives of the firm. Its primary objective is to meet the firm's financial obligations as they become due, using the minimum amount of minimum resources consistent with an established margin of safety. The financial information system typically has two input subsystems and four output systems. Internal accounting data and external sources such as information on the firm's stockholders and money and credit markets are fed into the input subsystems—*the accounting information system (AIS)* and the financial intelligence subsystem. The four output subsystems—the forecasting subsystem, funds management subsystem, financial control subsystem, and financial decision support system—are concerned with forecasting the future financial condition of the firm, managing the flow of funds in and out of the firm, controlling disbursements, and facilitating financial decision making. *See also* Account-

Figure 1 General Flow of Funds Among Financial Institutions and Financial Markets

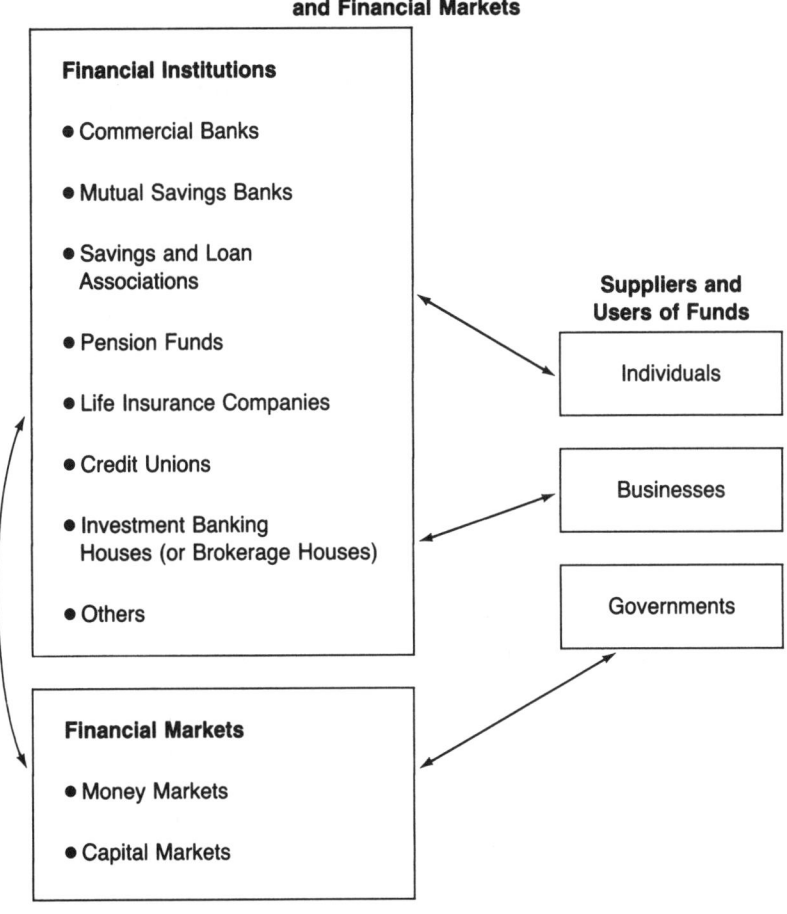

Financial Institutions

- Commercial Banks
- Mutual Savings Banks
- Savings and Loan Associations
- Pension Funds
- Life Insurance Companies
- Credit Unions
- Investment Banking Houses (or Brokerage Houses)
- Others

Suppliers and Users of Funds

Individuals

Businesses

Governments

Financial Markets

- Money Markets
- Capital Markets

ing Information System (AIS); Decision Support System (DSS); Financial Model; Management Information System (MIS).

FINANCIAL INSTITUTIONS AND MARKETS A healthy economy depends heavily on efficient transfer of funds from savers to the individuals, businesses, and governments who need capital. Most transfers occur through specialized *financial institutions* (see Figure 1) that serve as intermediaries between suppliers and users of funds. *Financial intermediaries* are firms that serve as middlemen between lenders and borrowers. In general, they are wholesalers and retailers of funds. It is in the *financial markets* that entities demanding funds are brought together with those having

surplus funds. Financial markets provide a mechanism through which the financial manager may obtain funds from a wide range of sources, including financial institutions. Figure 1 depicts the general flow of funds among financial institutions and financial markets.

The financial markets are composed of money markets and capital markets. *Money markets* (credit markets) are the markets for short-term (less than 1 year) debt securities. Examples of money market securities include U.S. Treasury bills, federal agency securities, bankers' acceptances, commercial paper, and negotiable certificates of deposit issued by government, business, and financial institutions. The money market securities are

characterized by their highly liquid nature and a relatively low default risk.

Capital markets are the markets in which long-term securities issued by the government and corporations are traded. Unlike the money market, both debt instruments (bonds) and equities (common and preferred stocks) are traded. Relative to money market instruments, those of the capital market often carry greater default and market risks but return a relatively high yield in compensation for the higher risks. The New York Stock Exchange, which handles the stock of many of the larger corporations, is a prime example of a capital market. The American Stock Exchange and the regional stock exchanges are still another example. These exchanges are organized markets. In addition, securities are traded through the thousands of brokers and dealers on the *over-the-counter (or unlisted) market*, a term used to denote an informal system of telephone contacts among brokers and dealers. There are other markets that include (1) the commodity markets, which handle various commodity futures; (2) the foreign exchange market, which involves international financial transactions between the U.S. and other countries; and (3) the insurance, shipping, and other markets handling short-term credit accommodations in their operations. A *primary market* refers to the market for new issues, whereas a *secondary market* is a market in which previously issued, "secondhand" securities are exchanged. The New York Stock Exchange is an example of a secondary market.

FINANCIAL LEVERAGE This is a portion of a firm's assets financed with debt instead of equity and therefore involves contractual interest and principal obligations. Financial leverage benefits common stockholders as long as the borrowed funds generate a return in excess of the cost of borrowing, although the increased risk can offset the general cost of capital. For this reason, financial leverage

is popularly called *trading on equity. See also* Leverage; Trading on Equity.

FINANCIAL MODELS A financial model is a system of mathematical equations, logic, and data that describe the relationships among financial and operating variables. A financial model can be viewed as a subset of broadly defined *corporate planning models* or a standalone functional system that is essentially used to generate *pro forma* financial statements and financial ratios. It is the basic tool for budgeting and profit planning. Also, the financial model is a technique for risk analysis and what-if experiments. In the face of uncertainty about the future, financial management is particularly interested in obtaining the best possible course of action under a given circumstance. The model is used as a tool to help minimize risk and uncertainty and develop the best corporate strategy. For example, a company is able to examine the effects of proposed mergers and acquisitions with much less uncertainty and to estimate with more confidence the potential profits from new markets. The financial model is also needed for day-to-day operational and tactical decisions for immediate planning problems. A financial model is one in which:
1. One or more financial variables appear (expenses, revenues, investment, cash flow, taxes, earnings, and so on).
2. The model user can manipulate (set and alter) the value of one or more financial variables.
3. The purpose of the model is to influence strategic decisions by revealing to the decision maker the implications of alternative values of these financial variables.

Financial models fall into two types: *simulation*, better known as *what-if*, models and *optimization* models. *What-if models* are models that attempt to simulate the effects of alternative management policies and assumptions about the firm's external environment. They are basically a tool for manage-

ment's laboratory. *Optimization models* are those in which the goal is to maximize or minimize an objective such as present value of profit or cost. Multiobjective techniques such as *goal programming* are being experimented.

Models can be deterministic or probabilistic. Deterministic models do not include any random or probabilistic variables, whereas probabilistic models incorporate random numbers and/or one or more probability distributions for variables such as sales, costs, and so on.

Financial models can be solved and manipulated computationally to derive from them the current and projected future implications and consequences. Due to technological advances in computers (such as spreadsheets, financial modeling languages, graphics, data base management systems, and networking), more and more companies are using modeling.

Applications and Uses of Financial Models

Basically, a financial model is used to generate projected financial statements such as the income statement, balance sheet, and cash flow statement. Such a model can be called a budgeting model, since we are essentially developing a master budget with such a model. Applications and uses of the model are numerous. They include:

• Projection of financial statements or development of budgets
  • Financial forecasting and analysis
  • Cash budgeting
  • Capital expenditure analysis
  • Tax planning
  • Exchange rate analysis
  • Analysis for mergers and acquisitions
  • Labor contract negotiations
  • Capacity planning
  • Cost-volume-profit analysis
  • New venture analysis
  • Lease/purchase analysis

• Evaluation of performance by segments
• Market analysis
• New product analysis
• Development of long-term strategy
• Planning for financial requirements
• Risk analysis
• Cash flow analysis
• Cost and price projections

Development of Financial Models

Development of financial models essentially involves two steps: (1) definition of variables and input parameters and (2) model specification. As far as model specification goes, we will explain only the simulation-type model here.

Generally speaking, the model consists of three important ingredients:
• Variables
• Input parameter values
• Definitional and/or functional relationships

Definition of Variables and Input Parameters

Fundamental to the specification of a financial model is the definition of the variables to be included in the model. There are basically three types of variables: policy variables (Z), external variables (X), and performance variables (Y).

Policy variables—the variables over which financial management can exert some degree of control. The policy variables are often called control variables. Among these we may list, in the area of finance, such variables as cash management policy, working capital policy, debt management policy, depreciation policy, tax policy, merger-acquisition decisions, the rate and direction of the firm's capital investment programs, the extent of its equity and external debt financing and the financial leverage represented thereby, and the size of its cash balances and liquid assets position. Policy variables are denoted by the symbol Z in Figure 1.

Figure 1   Variables in a Financial Model

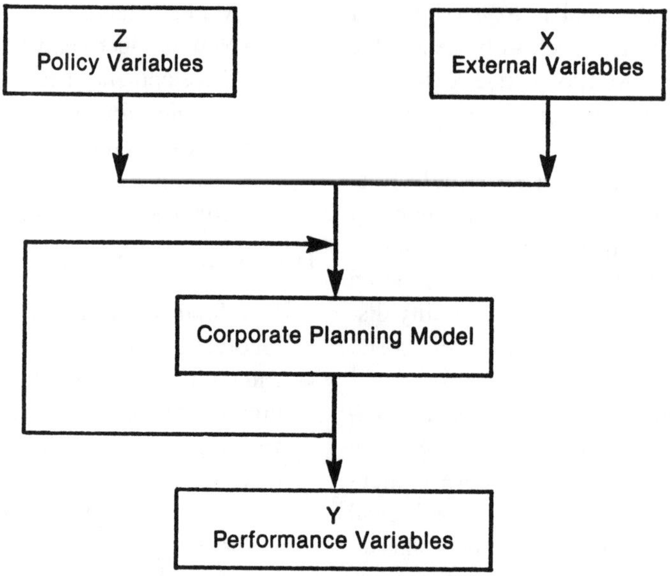

External variables—the environmental variables that are external to the company and that influence the firm's decisions from outside of the firm, generally exogeneous in nature. Generally speaking, the firm is embedded in an industry environment. This industry environment, in turn, is influenced by overall general business conditions. General business conditions exert influences upon particular industries in several ways. Total volume of demand, product prices, labor costs, material costs, money rates, and general expectations are among the industry variables affected by the general business conditions. The symbol X represents the external variables in the figure.

Performance variables—measure the firm's economic and financial performance, which are usually endogenous. We use the symbol Y in the diagram. The Y's are often called output variables. The output variables of a financial model would be the line items of the balance sheet, cash budget, income statement, or statement of cash flows. How to define the output variables of the firm will depend on the goals and objectives of

financial management. They basically indicate how financial officers measure the performance of the organization or some segments of it. Financial management is likely to be concerned with: (1) the firm's level of earnings; (2) growth in earnings; (3) projected earnings; (4) growth in sales; and (5) cash flow.

Frequently when we attempt to set up a financial model we face risk or uncertainty associated with particular projections. In a case such as this, we treat some of these variables such as sales as *random* variables with given probability distributions. The inclusion of random variables in the model transforms it from a *deterministic* model to a *risk analysis* model. However, the use of the risk analysis model in practice is rare because of the difficulty involved in modeling and computation.

Input parameter values—the model as a major part includes various input parameter values. For example, in order to generate the balance sheet, the model needs to input beginning balances of various asset, liability, and equity accounts. These input and parame-

ter values are supplied by management. The ratio between accounts receivable and sales and financial decision variables such as the maximum desired debt-equity ratio would be good examples of parameters.

Model Specification—Functional Relationships

Once we define various variables and input parameters for our financial model, we must then specify a set of mathematical and logical relationships linking the input variables to the performance variables. The relationships usually fall into two types of equations: definition equations and behavioral equations. Definitional equations take the form of accounting identities. Behavioral equations involve theories or hypotheses about the behavior of certain economic and financial events. They must be empirically tested and validated before they are incorporated into the financial model.

Definitional Equations

Definitional equations are exactly what the term refers to—mathematical or accounting definitions. For example,

$$\text{Assets} = \text{Liabilities} + \text{Equity}$$
$$\text{Net income} = \text{Revenues} - \text{Expenses}$$

These definitional equations are fundamental definitions in accounting for the balance sheet and income statement, respectively. Two more examples follow:

$$\text{CASH} = \text{CASH}(-1) + \text{CC}$$
$$+ \text{OCR} + \text{DEBT} - \text{CD} - \text{LP}$$

This equation is a typical cash equation in a financial model. It states that ending cash balance (CASH) is equal to the beginning cash balance (CASH(-1)) plus cash collections from customers (CC) plus other cash receipts (OCR) plus borrowings (DEBT) minus cash disbursements (CD) minus loan payments (LP).

$$\text{INV} = \text{INV}(-1) + \text{MAT} + \text{DL} + \text{OVER} - \text{CGS}$$

This equation states that ending inventory (INV) is equal to the beginning inventory (INV(-1)) plus cost of materials used (MAT) plus cost of direct labor (DL) plus manufacturing overhead (OVER) minus the cost of goods sold (CGS).

Behavioral Equations

Behavioral equations describe the behavior of the firm regarding the specific activities that are subject to empirical testing and validation. The classical demand function in economics is

$$Q = f(P) \text{ or more specifically } Q = a - bP$$

It simply says that the quantity demanded is negatively related to the price. That is to say, the higher the price, the lower the demand. However, the firm's sales are more realistically described as follows:

$$\text{SALES} = f(P, ADV., I, GNP, Pc, \text{etc.}) \text{ or}$$

assuming linear relationship among these variables, we can specify the model as follows:

$$\text{SALES} = a + bP + cADV + dI + eGNP + fPc + u$$

which says that the sales are affected by such factors as price (P), advertising expenditures (ADV), consumer income (I), gross national product (GNP), prices of competitive goods (Pc), and so on. The error term is u. With the data on SALES, P, ADV, I, GNP, and Pc, we will be able to estimate parameter values a, b, c, d, e, and f, using linear regression. We can test the statistical significance of each of the parameter estimates and evaluate the overall explanatory power of the model, measured by the t-statistic and r-squared, respectively. This way we will be able to identify most influential factors that affect the sales of a particular product. With the best model chosen, financial management can simulate the effects on sales of alternative pricing and advertising strategies. We can also experiment with alternative assumptions regarding the external economic factors such

as GNP, consumer income, and prices of competitive goods.

Model Structure

A majority of financial models that have been in use are recursive and/or simultaneous models. *Recursive* models are the ones in which each equation can be solved one at a time by substituting the solution values of the preceding equations into the right-hand side of each equation. An example of a financial model of recursive type follows.

(1) SALES   = $A - B$*PRICE + C*ADV
(2) REVENUE = SALES*PRICE
(3) CGS   = 0.70*REVENUE
(4) GM   = SALES − CGS
(5) OE   = $10,000 + 0.2*SALES
(6) EBT   = GM − OE
(7) TAX   = 0.46*EBT
(8) EAT   = EBT − TAX

In this example, the selling price (PRICE) and advertising expenses (ADV) are given. A, B, and C are parameters to be estimated and

SALES = sales volume in units
REVENUE = sales revenue
CGS = cost of goods sold
GM = gross margin
OE = operating expenses
EBT = earnings before taxes
TAX = income taxes
EAT = earnings after taxes

Simultaneous models are frequently found in econometric models which require a higher level of computational methods such as matrix inversion. An example of a financial model of this type follows:

(1) INT   = 0.10*DEBT
(2) EARN = REVENUE − CGS − OE
            − INT − TAX − DIV
(3) DEBT = DEBT(−1) + BOW
(4) CASH = CASH(−1) + CC + BOW
            + EARN − CD − LP
(5) BOW = MBAL − CASH

Note that earnings (EARN) in Equation (2) is defined as sales revenue minus CGS, OE, interest expense (INT), TAX, and dividend

payment (DIV). But INT is a percentage interest rate on total debt in Equation (1). Total debt in Equation (3) is equal to the previous period's debt (DEBT(−1)) plus new borrowings (BOW). New debt is the difference between a minimum cash balance (MBAL) minus cash. Finally, the ending cash balance in Equation (5) is defined as the sum of the beginning balance (CASH(−1)), cash collection, new borrowings and earnings *minus* cash disbursements and loan payments of the existing debt (LP). Even though the model presented here is a simple variety, it is still simultaneous in nature, which requires the use of a method capable of solving simultaneous equations. Very few of the financial modeling languages have the capability to solve this kind of system.

Decision Rules

The financial model may, in addition to those previously discussed—that is, definitional equations and behavioral equations—include basic decision rules specified in a very general form. The decision rules are not written in the form of conventional equations. They are described algebraically using *conditional operations*, consisting of statements of the type: "IF . . . THEN . . . ELSE." For example, suppose that we wish to express the following decision rule: "If X is greater than 0, then Y is set equal to O."

Then we can express the rule as follows:

Y = IF X GT O THEN X*5 ELSE 0

Suppose the company wishes to develop the financing decision problem, which is based upon alternative sales scenarios. To attempt to determine an optimal financing alternative, financial managers might want to incorporate some decision rules into the model for a what-if or sensitivity analysis. Some examples of these decision rules are as follows:

• The amount of dividends paid are determined on the basis of targeted earnings avail-

able to common stockholders and a maximum dividend payout ratio as specified by financial management.

• After calculating the external funds needed to meet changes in assets as a result of increased sales, dividends, and maturing debt, the amount of long-term debt to be floated is selected on the basis of a prespecified leverage ratio.

• The amount of equity financing to be raised is chosen on the basis of funds needed, which are not financed by new long-term debt but are constrained by the responsibility to meet minimum dividend payments.

In the model just described, *simultaneity* is quite evident. A sales figure is used to generate earnings, and this in turn leads to, among other items, the level of long-term debt required. Yet the level of debt affects the interest expense incurred within the current period and, therefore, earnings. Furthermore, as earnings are affected, so is the price at which new shares are issued, the number of shares to be sold, and thus earnings per share. Earnings per share then "feeds back" into the stock price calculation.

Lagged Model Structure

Lagged model structure is common in financial modeling. Virtually all balance sheet equations or identities are of this type. For example,

Capital = Capital(−1) + Net income
                           + Contributions − Cash dividends

More interestingly,

$$CC = a*SALES + b*SALES(-1) + c*SALES(-2)$$

where CC = cash collections from customers,
            a = percentage received within the current period,
            b = percentage received with one period lag,
            c = percentage received with two period lag.

Figure 2 (page 196) shows the basic structure of a corporate financial model. *See also* Corporate Planning Models.

FINANCIAL PLANNER A financial planner is the one who is engaged in providing *personal financial planning* service to individuals. He or she may be an independent professional or may be affiliated with a large investment, insurance, accounting, or other institution. Financial planners come from a variety of backgrounds and, therefore, may hold a variety of degrees and licenses. Currently, there are no state or federal regulations for the financial planning industry. However, some take specialized training in financial planning and earn credentials such as Certified Financial Planner (CFP) or Chartered Financial Consultant (ChFC). Others may hold degrees or registrations such as attorney (JD), Chartered Life Underwriter (CLU), or, of course, Certified Public Accountant (CPA).

To become a CFP conferred by the Institute of Certified Financial Planners (ICFP), a candidate must take a two year course that consists of six parts, each capped by a three-hour test: introduction to financial planning; risk management (insurance); investments; tax planning and management; retirement planning and employee benefits; and estate planning. To become a CLU or ChFC, designations granted by the American College of the American Society of Chartered Life Underwriters, a person must pass a ten-course program and have three years' professional experience.

A handful of colleges award degrees and certificates in financial planning or "family financial counseling." Adelphi University offers a certificate in financial planning. Golden Gate University offers master degrees in both financial planning and services. The American College also grants a master's degree in financial services. Baylor, Brigham Young, Drake, Georgia State, San Diego State, University of California extensions,

Figure 2 Corporate Financial Model

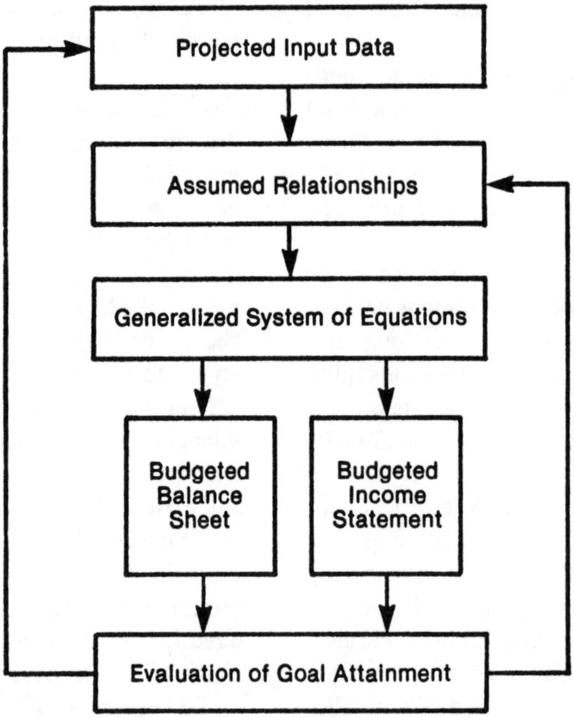

Sarasota, and other colleges offer certificates or degree programs with either a concentration or major in financial planning.

A financial planner should assist the client in the following ways:

1. Assess the client's financial history, such as tax returns, investments, retirement plans, wills, and insurance policies.

2. Help the client decide on a financial plan based on his or her personal and financial goals, history, and preferences.

3. Identify financial areas where the client may need help, such as building up retirement income or improving investment returns.

4. Prepare a financial plan based upon the client's individual situation and discuss it thoroughly with the client in plain English.

5. Help the client implement the financial plan, including referring the client to specialists such as attorneys, investment counselors, bankers, and certified financial planners, if necessary.

6. Review the client's situation and financial plan periodically and suggest changes in the program when needed.

See also Personal Financial Planning.

FINANCIAL RATIO   A financial ratio is the relationship of one account or category to another account or category. Financial statement analysis involves the computation of ratios to evaluate a company's financial position and results of operations. Examples of major classifications of ratios are

• *Liquidity ratios*—evaluate short-term ability to meet maturing debt.

• *Activity ratios*—determine effectiveness of the company to use assets in generating revenue.

• *Profitability ratios*—appraise a company's earning power ability.

• *Coverage ratios*—look at the extent long-term creditors and investors are protected.

A ratio should be examined over time to evaluate direction. The ratio should also be compared to that of competing companies and industry averages. *See also* Balance Sheet Analysis; Income Statement Analysis; Financial Statement Analysis.

FINANCIAL STATEMENT ANALYSIS This involves appraising the financial statements and related footnotes of an entity. This may be done by accountants, investment analysts, credit analysts, management, and other interested parties. The financial statements to be evaluated are the balance sheet, income statement, and statement of cash flows. Financial statement analysis includes an appraisal of a company's previous financial performance and its future potential.

The CPA analyzes financial statements of clients for a number of important reasons, including:

• They indicate areas requiring audit attention. The CPA can look at the percentage change in an account over the years or relative to some base year to identify inconsistencies. For example, if promotion and entertainment expense to sales last year was 2% and this year shot up to 16%, the auditor would want to uncover the reasons. This would be especially disturbing if other companies in the industry still have a percentage relationship of 2%. The auditor would be quite suspicious that the promotion and entertainment expense account may contain some personal rather than business charges. Supporting documentation for the charges would be requested and carefully reviewed by the CPA.

• They indicate the financial health of the client, which is of interest to the CPA for the following reasons:

• A determination has to be made if the client is financially sound to pay the accounting fees.

• The CPA wants to ascertain whether poor financial condition exists regarding a qualified audit opinion as to a going-concern problem.

• The CPA wants to know his potential legal exposure. If the client has a poor financial condition, corporate failure may occur, resulting in lawsuits by creditors and others. If financial problems exist, the auditor would have to take proper audit and reporting steps, including suitable references in the audit report.

• They provide vital information to be included in the management letter.

• They assist in identifying areas of financial problems and means of corrective action for the client.

• They aid the client in determining appropriateness of mergers and acquisitions.

The investor evaluates financial statements to see if the company would be a good investment. The investor is interested in earning a good return in the form of dividends and appreciation in market price of stock. Emphasis is focused on corporate profitability and utility ratios (return on assets, return on sales, and so on).

Creditors are primarily concerned with getting their money from the company. Therefore, emphasis is placed on the company's liquidity position as a basis to pay off the account balance. Cash flow analysis is important.

Management analyzes the financial statements to see how the company looks to the financial community and what corrective steps can be made to minimize liquidity and solvency problems. Areas of risk are identified. Means to efficiently utilize assets and earn greater returns are concentrated on.

A company's financial health has a bearing upon its price-earnings ratio, bond rating, cost of financing, and availability of financing. Financial analysts should especially watch out for the "high accounting risk" companies, including

• "Glamour" companies known for earnings growth

• Companies in the public eye

• Companies having difficulty obtaining future financing

• Companies whose management previously committed dishonest acts

To obtain worthwhile conclusions from financial ratios, the financial analyst has to make two comparisons:

1. *Industry comparison*—the financial analyst should compare the company's ratios to those of competing companies in the industry or with industry standards. Industry norms can be obtained from such services as Dun and Bradstreet, Robert Morris Associates, Standard and Poor, and Value Line. For example, Dun and Bradstreet computes 14 ratios for each of 125 lines of business. They are published annually in *Dun's Review* and *Key Business Ratios*. Robert Morris Associates publishes *Annual Statement Studies*. Sixteen ratios are computed for more than 300 lines of business, as well as a percentage distribution of items, on the balance sheet and income statement (common size financial statements). In analyzing a company, the CPA should appraise the trends in the particular industry. What is the pattern of expansion or contraction in the industry? The profit dollar is worth more if earned in a healthy, expanding industry than a declining one.

2. *Trend analysis*—a company's ratio may be compared over several years to identify direction of financial health or operational performance.

The optimum value for any given ratio usually varies across industry lines, through time, and even within different companies in the same industry. In other words, a ratio deemed optimum for one company may be inadequate for another. A particular ratio is typically deemed optimum within a given range of values, and an increase or decrease beyond this range points to weakness or inefficiency. For instance, while a low current ratio may indicate poor liquidity, a very high current ratio may indicate inefficient utilization of assets (e.g., excessive inventory) or

inability to use short-term credit to the firm's advantage.

In appraising a seasonal business, the financial analyst may find that year-end financial data are not representative. Thus, averages based on quarterly or monthly information may be used to level out seasonality effects.

FLEXIBLE BUDGETS AND PERFORMANCE REPORTS

A flexible budget is a tool that is extremely useful in cost control. In contrast to a *static budget*, the flexible budget is characterized as follows:

1. It is geared toward a range of activity rather than a single level of activity.

2. It is dynamic in nature rather than static. By using the *cost-volume formula* (or *flexible budget formula*), a series of budgets can easily be developed for various levels of activity.

The static (*fixed*) budget is geared for only one level of activity and has problems in cost control. Flexible budgeting distinguishes between fixed and variable costs, thus allowing for a budget that can be automatically adjusted (via changes in variable cost totals) to the particular level of activity *actually* attained. Thus, variances between actual costs and budgeted costs are adjusted for volume ups and downs before differences due to price and quantity factors are computed.

The primary use of the flexible budget is for accurate measure of performance by comparing actual costs for a given output with the budgeted costs for the *same level of output*.

■ Example 1

To illustrate the difference between the static budget and the flexible budget, assume that the Assembly Department of Company Y is budgeted to produce 6,000 units during June. Assume further that the company was able to produce only 5,800 units. The budget

for direct labor and variable overhead costs is as follows:

Company Y
The Direct Labor and Variable Overhead Budget
Assembly Department
for the Month of June

Budgeted production	6,000 units
Actual production	5,800 units
Direct labor	$39,000
Variable overhead costs:	
Indirect labor	6,000
Supplies	900
Repairs	300
	$46,200

If a static budget approach is used, the performance report will appear as follows:

Company Y
The Direct Labor and Variable Overhead Budget
Assembly Department
for the Month of June

	Budget	Actual	Variance (U or F)*
Production in units	6,000	5,800	200 U
Direct labor	$39,000	$38,500	$500 F
Variable overhead costs:			
Indirect labor	6,000	5,950	50 F
Supplies	900	870	30 F
Repairs	300	295	5 F
	$46,200	$45,615	$585 F

* A variance represents the deviation of actual cost from the standard or budgeted cost. U and F stand for "unfavorable" and "favorable," respectively.

These cost variances are useless in that they are comparing oranges with apples. The problem is that the budget costs are based on an activity level of 6,000 units, whereas the actual costs were incurred at an activity level below this (5,800 units). From a control standpoint, it makes no sense to try to compare costs at one activity level with costs at a different activity level. Such comparisons would make a production manager look good as long as the actual production is less than the budgeted production. Using the cost-volume formula and generating the budget based on the 5,800 actual units gives the performance report appearing at the bottom of the page. Notice that all cost variances are unfavorable (U), as compared to the favorable cost variances on the performance report based on the static budget approach.

FORECASTING EARNINGS PER SHARE Dividends and market price of stock depend upon future earnings per share.

Estimated earnings at the end of the year = Estimated sales at the end of the year × After-tax profit margin

$$\frac{\text{Estimated earnings at the end of the year}}{\text{Estimated outstanding shares at the end of the year}}$$

Company Y
Peformance Report
Assembly Department
For the Month of June

Budgeted production	6,000 units	
Actual production	5,800 units	

	Cost-volume formula	Budget 5,800 units	Actual 5,800 units	Variance (U or F)
Direct labor	$6.50 per unit	$37,700	$38,500	$800 U
Variable overhead:				
Indirect labor	1.00	5,800	5,950	150 U
Supplies	.15	870	870	0
Repairs	.05	290	295	5 U
	$7.70	$44,660	$45,615	$955 U

■ Example

You expect the sales for ABC Company to be $2,000,000 based on financial projections you read in a brokerage report and/or reading management's discussion in the annual report. The company's tax rate is 34%. After-tax profit is therefore:

$$\$2,000,000 \times 66\% = \$1,320,000$$

Assume expected shares outstanding are 1,000,000.

Estimated earnings per share

$$= \frac{\$1,320,000}{1,000,000 \text{ shares}} = \$1.32$$

If the price/earnings ratio is 10, the estimated market price of stock is

Estimated EPS × Estimated P/E ratio
$$= \$1.32 \times 10 = \$13.20$$

FOREIGN CORRUPT PRACTICES ACT

According to the act, management and independent auditors for publicly held companies must maintain internal controls to assure the reliability of accounting records. Further, it is a crime to offer a bribe to a foreign official to obtain business. *See also* Internal Control.

FOREIGN CURRENCY TRANSLATION AND TRANSACTIONS

FASB 52 applies to foreign currency transactions such as exports and imports denominated in other than a company's functional currency. It also relates to foreign currency financial statements of branches, divisions, and other investees incorporated in the financial statements of a U.S. company by combination, consolidation, or the equity method.

A purpose of translation is to furnish data of expected impacts of rate changes on cash flow and equity. Also, it provides data in consolidated financial statements relative to the financial results of each individual foreign consolidated entity.

Covered in FASB 52 are the translation of foreign currency statements and gains and

losses on foreign currency transactions. Translation of foreign currency statements is typically needed when the statements of a foreign subsidiary or equity-method investee having a functional currency other than the U.S. dollar are to be included in the financial statements of a domestic enterprise (e.g., through consolidation or using the equity method). Generally, the foreign currency statements should be translated using the exchange rate at the end of the reporting year. Resulting translation gains and losses are shown as a separate item in the stockholders' equity section.

Also important is the accounting treatment of gains and losses emanating from transactions denominated in a foreign currency. These are presented in the current year's income statement.

Foreign Currency Terminology

Key definitions to be understood by the practitioner follow:

• *Conversion*—an exchange of one currency for another.

• *Currency swap*—an exchange between two companies of the currencies of two different countries as per an agreement to re-exchange the two currencies at the same rate of exchange at a specified future date.

• *Denominate*—pay or receive in that *same* foreign currency. It can only be denominated in one currency (e.g., pounds). It is a real account (asset or liability) fixed in terms of a foreign currency irrespective of exchange rate.

• *Exchange rate*—ratio between a unit of one currency and that of another at a particular time. If there is a *temporary lack of exchangeability* between two currencies at the transaction date or balance sheet date, the *first rate available* thereafter at which exchanges could be made is used.

• *Foreign currency*—a currency other than the functional currency of the business (for instance, the dollar could be a foreign currency for a foreign entity).

• *Foreign currency statements*—financial statements using as the unit of measure a functional currency that is not the reporting currency of the business.

• *Foreign currency transactions*—transactions whose terms are denominated in a currency other than the entity's functional currency. Foreign currency transactions take place when a business (a) buys or sells on credit goods or services whose prices are denominated in foreign currency; (b) borrows or lends funds, and the amounts payable or receivable are denominated in foreign currency; (c) is a party to an unperformed forward exchange contract; or (d) acquires or disposes of assets, or incurs or settles liabilities denominated in foreign currency.

• *Foreign currency translation*—expressing in the reporting currency of the company those amounts that are denominated or measured in a different currency.

• *Foreign entity*—an operation (e.g., subsidiary, division, branch, joint venture) whose financial statements are prepared in a currency other than the reporting currency of the reporting entity.

• *Functional currency*—an entity's functional currency is the currency of the *primary economic environment* in which the business operates. It is typically the currency of the environment in which the business primarily obtains and uses cash. This is usually the foreign country. The functional currency of a foreign operation may be the same as a related affiliate in the case where the foreign activity is an essential component or extension of the related affiliate.

Prior to translation, the foreign country figures are remeasured in the functional currency. For instance, if a company in Italy is an independent entity and received cash and incurred expenses in Italy, the Italian currency is the functional currency. However, in the event the Italian company was an extension of a Canadian parent, the functional currency is the Canadian currency. The functional currency should be consistently used except if material economic changes necessitate a change. However, previously issued financial statements are not restated for an alteration in the functional currency.

If a company's books are *not* kept in its functional currency, remeasurement into the functional currency is mandated. The remeasurement process occurs before translation into the reporting currency takes place. When a foreign entity's functional currency is the reporting currency, remeasurement into the reporting currency obviates translation. The remeasurement process is intended to generate the same result as if the entity's books had been kept in the functional currency.

Guidelines are referred to in determining the functional currency of a foreign operation. The benchmarks apply to selling price, market, cash flow, financing, expense, and intercompany transactions. A detailed discussion follows:

1. *Selling price*. The functional currency is the foreign currency when the foreign operation's selling price of products or services are primarily because of local factors such as government law and competition. It is *not* due to changes in exchange rate. The functional currency is the parent's currency when foreign operation's sales prices mostly apply in the short-run to fluctuation in the exchange rate resulting from international factors (e.g., worldwide competition).

2. *Market*. The functional currency is the foreign currency when the foreign activity has a strong local sales market for products or services, even though a significant amount of exports may exist. The functional currency is the parent's currency when the foreign operation's sales market is mostly in the parent's country.

3. *Cash flow*. The functional currency is the foreign currency when the foreign operation's cash flows are primarily in foreign currency not directly affecting the parent's cash flow. The functional currency is the parent's currency when the foreign operation's cash flows directly impact the parent's cash flows. They

are usually available for remittance via intercompany accounting settlement.

4. *Financing*. The functional currency is the foreign currency if financing the foreign activity is in foreign currency and funds obtained by the foreign activity are sufficient to meet debt obligations. The functional currency is the parent's currency when financing foreign activity is provided by the parent or occurs in U.S. dollars. Funds obtained by the foreign activity are insufficient to satisfy debt requirements.

5. *Expenses*. The functional currency is the foreign currency when foreign operation's production costs or services are usually incurred locally. However, some foreign imports may exist. The functional currency is the parent's currency when the foreign operation's production and service costs are primarily component costs obtained from the parent's country.

6. *Intercompany transactions*. The functional currency is the foreign currency when minor interrelationship occurs between the activities of the foreign entity and parent except for competitive advantages (e.g., patents). There is a restricted number of intercompany transactions. The functional currency is the parent's currency when material interrelationship exists between the foreign entity and parent. Many intercompany transactions exist.

Consistent use of the functional currency of the foreign entity must exist over the years except if there are changes in circumstances warranting a change. If a change in the functional currency takes place, it is accounted for as a change in estimate.

• *Local currency*—the currency of the particular foreign country.

• *Measure*—translation into a currency other than the original reporting currency. Foreign financial statements are measured in U.S. dollars by using the applicable exchange rate.

• *Reporting currency*—the currency the

business prepares its financial statements in. It is usually U.S. dollars.

• *Spot rate*—exchange rate for immediate delivery of currencies exchanged.

• *Transaction gain or loss*—occur due to a change in exchange rates between the functional currency and the currency in which a foreign currency transaction is denominated. They represent an increase or decrease in (a) the actual functional currency cash flows realized upon settlement of foreign currency transactions and (b) the expected functional currency cash flows on unsettled foreign currency transactions.

• *Translation adjustments*—arise from translating financial statements from the entity's functional currency into the reporting one.

Translation Process

Translation of Foreign Currency Statements When the U.S. Dollar Is the Functional Currency

The foreign entity's financial statements in a highly *inflationary* economy is not stable enough and should be remeasured as if the functional currency were the reporting currency. Thus, the financial statements of those entities should be remeasured into the reporting currency (the U.S. dollar becomes the functional currency). In effect, the reporting currency is used directly.

A *highly inflationary environment* is one that has cumulative inflation of about *100% or more over a 3-year period*. In other words, the inflation rate must be increasing at a rate of about 35% a year for 3 consecutive years. *Tip*: The International Monetary Fund of Washington, DC, publishes monthly figures on international inflation rates.

Translation of Foreign Currency Statements When the Foreign Currency Is the Functional Currency

Balance sheet items are translated via the *current exchange rate*. For assets and liabilities, use the rate at the balance sheet date.

If a current exchange rate is not available at the balance sheet date, use the first exchange rate available after that date. The *current exchange rate* is also used to translate the *Statement of Cash Flows* except for those items found in the Income Statement, which are translated using the weighted-average rate. For income statement items (revenues, expenses, gains, and losses), use the exchange rate at the dates those items are recognized. Since translation at the exchange rates at the dates the many revenues, expenses, gains, and losses are recognized is almost always impractical, use a *weighted-average exchange rate* for the period in translating *income statement items*.

A material change occurring between the date of the financial statements and the audit report date should be disclosed as a subsequent event. Disclosure should also be made of the effects on unsettled balances pertaining to foreign currency transactions.

Translation Adjustments

There are several steps in translating the foreign country's financial statements into U.S. reporting requirements. They are
1. Conform the foreign country's financial statements to U.S. GAAP.
2. Determine the functional currency of the foreign entity.
3. Remeasure the financial statements in the functional currency, if necessary. Gains or losses from remeasuremnt are includable in remeasured current net income.
4. Convert from the foreign currency into U.S. dollars (reporting currency).

If a company's functional currency is a foreign currency, *translation adjustments* arise from translating that company's financial statements into the reporting currency. Translation adjustments are unrealized and should not be included in the income statement but should be reported separately and accumulated in a *separate component of equity*. However, if remeasurement from the

recording currency to the functional currency is required before translation, the gain or loss is reflected in the income statement.

Upon sale or liquidation of an investment in a foreign entity, the amount attributable to that entity and accumulated in the translation adjustment component of equity is removed from the stockholders' equity section and considered a part of the gain or loss on sale or liquidation of the investment in the income statement for the period during which the sale or liquidation occurs.

As per Interpretation 37, a sale of an investment in a foreign entity may include a partial sale of an ownership interest. In that case, a pro rata amount of the cumulative translation adjustment reflected as a stockholders' equity component is includable in arriving at the gain or loss on sale. For example, if a business sells a 40% ownership interest in a foreign investment, 40% of the translation adjustment applicable to it is included in calculating gain or loss on sale of that ownership interest.

Foreign Currency Transactions

Foreign currency transactions are those denominated in a currency other than the company's functional currency. Foreign currency transactions may result in receivables or payables fixed in terms of the amount of foreign currency to be received or paid.

A foreign currency transaction requires settlement in a currency other than the functional currency: A change in exchange rates between the functional currency and the currency in which a transaction is denominated increases or decreases the expected amount of functional currency cash flows upon settlement of the transaction. This change in expected functional currency cash flows is a *foreign currency transaction gain or loss* that typically is included in arriving at earnings in the *income statement* for the period in which the exchange rate is altered. An example of a transaction gain or loss is when a

British subsidiary has a receivable denominated in pounds from a French customer.

Similarly, a transaction gain or loss (measured from the *transaction date* or the most recent intervening balance sheet date, whichever is later) realized upon settlement of a foreign currency transaction usually should be included in determining net income for the period in which the transaction is settled.

■ Example

An exchange gain or loss occurs when the exchange rate changes between the purchase date and sale date.

Merchandise is bought for 100,000 pounds. The exchange rate is 4 pounds to 1 dollar. The journal entry is

Purchases	$25,000	
Accounts Payable		$25,000
100,000/4 = $25,000		

When the merchandise is paid for, the exchange rate is 5 to 1. The journal entry is

Accounts Payable	$25,000	
Cash		$20,000
Foreign Exchange Gain		$5,000
100,000/5 = $20,000		

The $20,000 using an exchange rate of 5 to 1 can buy 100,000 pounds. The transaction gain is the difference between the cash required of $20,000 and the initial liability of $25,000.

Note that a foreign transaction gain or loss has to be determined at each balance sheet date on all recorded foreign transactions that have not been settled.

■ Example

A U.S. company sells goods to a customer in England on 11/15/X7 for 10,000 pounds. The exchange rate is 1 pound to 75 cents. Thus, the transaction is worth $7,500 (10,000 pounds × 0.75). Payment is due 2 months later. The entry on 11/15/X7 is

Accounts Receivable—England	$7,500	
Sales		$7,500

Accounts receivable and sales are measured in U.S. dollars at the transaction date employing the spot rate. Even though the accounts receivable is measured and reported in U.S. dollars, the receivable is fixed in pounds. Thus, there can occur a transaction gain or loss if the exchange rate changes between the transaction date (11/15/X7) and the settlement date (1/15/X8).

Since the financial statements are prepared between the transaction date and settlement date, receivables that are denominated in a currency other than the functional currency (U.S. dollar) have to be restated to reflect the spot rate on the balance sheet date. On December 31, 19X7, the exchange rate is 1 pound equals 80 cents. Hence, the 10,000 pounds are now valued at $8,000 (10,000 × $0.80). Therefore, the accounts receivable denominated in pounds should be upwardly adjusted by $500. The required journal entry on 12/31/X7 is

Accounts Receivable—England	$500	
Foreign Exchange Gain		$500

The income statement for the year-ended 12/31/X7 shows an exchange gain of $500. Note that sales is not affected by the exchange gain since sales relates to operational activity.

On 1/15/X8, the spot rate is 1 pound = 78 cents. The journal entry is

Cash	$7,800	
Foreign Exchange Loss	200	
Accounts Receivable—England		$8,000

The 19X8 income statement shows an exchange loss of $200.

Transaction Gains and Losses to be Excluded from Determination of Net Income

Gains and losses on the following foreign currency transactions are not included in earnings but rather reported as translation adjustments:

• Foreign currency transactions designated as *economic hedges* of a net investment in a foreign entity, beginning as of the designation date

• Intercompany foreign currency transactions of a *long-term investment* nature (settlement is not planned or expected in the foreseeable future), when the entities to the transaction are consolidated, combined, or accounted for by the equity method in the reporting company's financial statements

A gain or loss on a forward contract or other foreign currency transaction that is intended to *hedge* an identifiable foreign currency commitment (e.g., an agreement to buy or sell machinery) should be deferred and included in the measurement of the related foreign currency transaction. Losses should *not* be deferred if it is anticipated that deferral would cause recognizing losses in subsequent periods. A foreign currency transaction is considered a hedge of an identifiable foreign currency commitment provided both of the following criteria are satisfied:

1. The foreign currency transaction is designated as a hedge of a foreign currency commitment.

2. The foreign currency commitment is firm.

Forward Exchange Contracts

A forward exchange contract is an agreement to exchange different currencies at a given future date and at a specified rate (forward rate). A forward contract is a foreign currency transaction. A gain or loss on a forward contract that does not meet the conditions described following are includable in net income. *Note*: Currency swaps are accounted for in a similar fashion.

A gain or loss (whether or not deferred) on a forward contract, except a speculative forward contract, should be computed by multiplying the foreign currency amount of the forward contract by the difference between the *spot rate* at the balance sheet date

and the spot rate at the date of inception of the forward contract.

The *discount or premium on a forward contract* (i.e., the foreign currency amount of the contract multiplied by the difference between the contracted forward rate and the spot rate at the date of inception of the contract) should be accounted for separately from the gain or loss on the contract and typically should be included in computing net income over the life of the forward contract.

A gain or loss on a *speculative forward contract* (a contract that does not hedge an exposure) should be computed by multiplying the foreign currency amount of the forward contract by the difference between the forward rate available from the remaining maturity of the contract and the contracted forward rate (or the forward rate last used to measure a gain or loss on that contract for an earlier period). *No separate accounting recognition is given to the discount or premium on a speculative forward contract.*

Hedging

Foreign currency transactions gains and losses on assets and liabilities denominated in a currency other than the functional currency can be hedged if the U.S. company engages into a forward exchange contract.

A hedge can occur even if there does not exist a forward exchange contract. For instance, a foreign currency transaction can serve as an economic hedge offsetting a parent's net investment in a foreign entity when the transaction is entered into for hedging purposes and is effective.

■ Example

A U.S. parent completely owns a French subsidiary having net assets of $3 million in francs. The U.S. parent can borrow $3 million francs to hedge its net investment in the French subsidiary. Also assume the French franc is the functional currency and

the $3 million obligation is denominated in francs. Variability in the exchange rate for francs does *not* have a net impact on the parent's consolidated balance sheet since increases in the translation adjustments balance arising from translation of the net investment will be netted against decreases in this balance emanating from the adjustment of the liability denominated in francs.

FOREIGN EXCHANGE RATES

Foreign exchange is the instrument used for international payments. Such instruments consist not only of currency, but also of checks, drafts, and bills of exchange. A *foreign exchange market* is available for trading foreign exchanges. A *foreign exchange rate* is the price of one currency in terms of another. For example, 1 American dollar is 125 yens in Japanese currency. Foreign exchange rates are determined in various ways:

1. *Fixed exchange rates*—an international financial arrangement in which governments directly intervene in the foreign exchange market to prevent exchange rates from deviating more than a very small margin from some central or parity value.

2. *Flexible (floating exchange) rates*—an arrangement by which exchange rate levels are allowed to change daily in response to market demand and supply. Arrangements may vary from *free float* (i.e., absolutely no government intervention) to *managed float* (i.e., limited but sometimes aggressive government intervention in the foreign exchange market).

3. *Forward exchange rate*—the exchange rate in contract for receipt of and payment for foreign currency at a specified date, usually 30 days, 90 days, or 180 days in the future, at a stipulated current or "spot" price. By buying and selling forward exchange, importers and exporters can protect themselves against the risks of fluctuations in the current exchange market.

See also Financial Institutions and Markets.

401 (K) PLAN This is a company-sponsored retirement plan that allows an employee to defer up to $7,000, under the new tax law, of the employee's gross salary withheld and invested in stocks, bonds, or money market funds, also called *salary reduction plan*. This amount is indexed for inflation using the Consumer Price Index, beginning in 1988. The employee's contributions and all earnings arising therefrom go tax free until withdrawn at the request of the employee or until the employee retires or leaves the company. Usually the employer provides a choice of investment vehicles into which the funds may be placed while earning tax-deferred returns. Furthermore, many employers offer matching contributions. The $7,000 limitation of annual deferrals to 401(k) plans applies only to an employee's elective deferrals—not the employer's matching funds. The employee's contributions plus the employer's may total, annually, the lesser of $30,000 or 25% of earnings. These contributions plus the current reduction in income taxes typically make 401(k) salary reduction plans an excellent long-term investment. *See also* Retirement and Pension Planning.

FRACTIONAL SHARE WARRANTS These may be issued when less than a full share is involved.

▪ Example

There are 1,000 shares of $10 par value common stock. The common stock has a market price of $15. A 20% dividend is declared, resulting in 200 shares (20% × 1,000). Included in the 200 shares are fractional share warrants. Each warrant equals 1/5 of a share of stock. There are 100 warrants resulting in 20 shares of stock (100/5). Thus, 180 regular shares and 20 fractional shares are involved.

The journal entries follow:

At the declaration date:

Retained Earnings (200 shares × $15	3,000	
Stock Dividends Distributable (180 shares × $10)		1,800
Fractional Share Warrants (20 shares × $10)		200
Paid-in-Capital		1,000

At time of issuance:

Stock Dividend Distributable	1,800	
Common Stock		1,800
Fractional Share Warrants	200	
Common Stock		200

If instead of all the fractional share warrants being turned in, only 80% were turned in the entry is

Fractional Share Warrants	200	
Common Stock		160
Paid-in-Capital		40

FRANCHISE FEE REVENUE According to FASB 45, the franchisor can record revenue only from the initial sale of the franchise when all significant services and obligations applicable to the sale have been substantially performed. Substantial performance is indicated by

• Absence of intent to give cash refunds or relieve the accounts receivable due from the franchisee.

• Nothing material remains to be done by the franchisor.

• Initial services have been rendered.

The earliest date that substantial performance can occur is the franchisee's commencement of operations unless special circumstances can be shown to exist. In the case where it is probable that the franchisor will ultimately repurchase the franchise, the initial fee must be deferred and treated as a reduction of the repurchase price.

If revenue is deferred, the related expenses must be deferred for later matching in the year in which the revenue is recognized. This is illustrated following.

Year of initial fee:
Cash
  Deferred Revenue
Deferred Expenses
  Cash
Year when substantial performance takes place:
Deferred Revenue
  Revenue
Expenses
  Deferred Expenses

In case the initial fee includes both initial services and property (real or personal), there should be an appropriate allocation based on fair market values.

When part of the initial franchise fee applies to *tangible property* (e.g., equipment, signs, inventory), revenue recognition is based on the fair value of the assets. Revenue recognition may take place prior to or after recognizing the portion of the fee related to initial services. For instance, part of the fee for equipment may be recognized at the time title passes, with the balance of the fee being recorded as revenue when future services are performed.

Recurring franchise fees are recognized as earned and receivable. Related costs are expensed. An exception does exist to this revenue recognition practice. If the price charged for the continuing services or goods to the franchisee is below the price charged to third parties, it indicates that the initial franchise fee was in essence a partial *prepayment* for the recurring franchise fee. In this situation, part of the initial fee has to be deferred and recognized as an adjustment of the revenue from the sale of goods and services at bargain prices.

When probability exists that continuing franchise fees will not cover the cost of the continuing services and provide for a reasonable profit to the franchisor, the part of the initial franchise fee should be deferred to satisfy the deficiency and amortized over the life of the franchise. The deferred amount should be adequate to meet future costs and

generate an adequate profit on the recurring services. This situation may occur if the continuing fees are minimal relative to services provided or the franchisee has the privilege of making bargain purchases for a particular time period.

Unearned franchise fees are recorded at present value. Where a part of the initial fee constitutes a nonrefundable amount for services already performed, revenue should be recognized accordingly.

The initial franchise fee is *not* typically allocated to specific franchisor services before all services are performed. This practice can be done only if actual transaction prices are available for individual services.

If the franchisor sells equipment and inventory to the franchisee at no profit, a receivable and payable is recorded. *No* revenue or expense recognition is given.

In the case of a repossessed franchise, refunded amounts to the franchisee reduce current revenue. If there is no refund, the franchisor books additional revenue for the consideration retained that was not previously recorded. In either situation, *prospective* accounting treatment is given for the repossession. *Warning*: Do *not* adjust previously recorded revenue for the repossession.

Indirect costs of an operating and recurring nature are expensed immediately. Future costs to be incurred are accrued no later than the period in which related revenue is recognized. Bad debts applicable to expected uncollectability of franchise fees should be recorded in the year of revenue recognition.

Installment or cost recovery accounting may be employed to account for franchisee fee revenue *only* if a long collection period is involved and future uncollectability of receivables cannot be accurately predicted.

Footnote disclosure is required of

• Outstanding obligations under agreement

• Segregation of franchise fee revenue between initial and continuing. *See also* Revenue Recognition Methods.

FRAUD The auditor should distinguish between negligence (belief in the absence of adequate basis), constructive fraud (not believing in a position), and fraud (known to be wrong). Fraud is a legal concept, in which the person falsifies with knowledge and intent to deceive. Fraud can occur through a false representation of a material fact that results in damage to a party relying on that information. An example of fraud is the theft of corporate assets while falsifying records.

Management fraud relates to employing improper practices to overstate net income or to prevent insolvency. Fraud may be perpetrated by engaging in fictitious transactions, transactions lacking substance, and purposely not applying GAAP. Employee fraud typically involves theft.

The auditor is obligated to uncover fraud, including intentional errors and irregularities, by exercising due professional care.

The auditor must examine significant transactions to ascertain if management is involved in fraudulent activities. He or she should withdraw from an engagement if confidence in management's integrity is lacking. Investigation of fraud should take into account the following:

• Special audit engagements are less likely to detect fraud than audits.

• A standard audit procedure may not in all cases detect fraud, such as where customers returning confirmations are in collusion with management.

• A prospective or existing client may be dishonest.

• Extent to which internal control prevents the detetion of fraud.

• The nature of the client's business and the industry to which it is a part.

• Clients with severe financial problems are more desperate and as a result more prone to engage in fraudulent activity.

Tax fraud may either be civil or criminal. In civil fraud, the IRS can charge a penalty of 50% of a tax underpayment. In criminal

fraud, fines and/or imprisonment can be involved, depending upon the nature of the fraud. Conviction requires that the taxpayer intended to *evade* the tax payment through the preparation of an intentional misstatement of the tax return. The burden of proof is on the IRS. *See also* Internal Control.

FUNDAMENTAL ANALYSIS This appraises a company's stock based on an examination of the financial statements. It considers overall financial health, economic and political conditions, industry factors, and future outlook of the company. The analysis attempts to determine if a security is overpriced, underpriced, or priced in proportion to its market value. A stock is valuable only if one can predict the future financial performance of the business. Financial statement analysis provides much data needed to predict earnings and dividends. *See also* Balance Sheet Analysis; Income Statement Analysis; Financial Ratios; Financial Statement Analysis.

FUTURES CONTRACT Futures trading can relate to commodities and financial instruments. A future is a contract to buy or sell a specified amount of an item for a certain price by a given date. The seller of a futures contract agrees to deliver the item to the buyer of the contract, who agrees to purchase the item. The contract stipulates an amount, valuation, method, quality, month, means of delivery, and exchange to be traded on. The expiration date is the month of delivery of the commodity or financial instrument. *Commodity contracts* are assurances by a seller to deliver a commodity. *Financial contracts* are commitments by sellers to deliver a financial instrument (e.g., a Treasury bill) or a specified amount of foreign currency. *Beware*: Futures contracts are a risky investment.

A *long position* is buying a contract expecting the price to rise. A *short position* is selling the contract anticipating the price

to decrease. The position may be terminated by reversing the transaction. For example, the long buyer can subsequently take a short position of the same amount of the commodity or financial instrument. Most futures contracts are canceled out prior to delivery. Rarely does delivery settle the future contract.

Futures trading may be performed by hedgers and speculators. Hedgers protect themselves with futures contracts in the commodity they produce or in the financial instrument they own. For example, if a cotton producer expects a drop in price, he can sell a futures contract to assure a higher current price. Then at the time of the future delivery he will obtain a higher price. Speculators employ futures contracts to get capital gain on price increases of the commodity, financial instrument, or currency.

Commodity futures trading may be done by auction. A futures contract can be traded in the futures market. Trading is accomplished through specialized brokers and some commodity firms dealing only in futures. Fees for futures contracts depend on the amount of the contract and the price of the item. There is a varying commission based on the amount and nature of the contract. An investor has to have a commodity trading account. Contracts are typically bought on margin. The investor can buy or sell a contract with specified terms.

A futures contract assists in keeping pace with inflation. But futures contracts are a high-risk specialized area due to the many variables involved (e.g., international economic instability). Further, there may be wide vacillation in contract prices. *See also* Commodities Futures Contracts; Financial Futures Contracts.

FUTURES CONTRACTS ACCOUNTING A futures contract is a legal arrangement entered into by the purchaser or seller and a regulated futures exchange in the U.S. or overseas.

However, FASB 80 does not apply to foreign currencies futures, which are dealt with in FASB 82. Futures contracts involve

• A buyer or seller receiving or making a delivery of a commodity or financial instrument (e.g., stocks, bonds, commercial paper, mortgages) at a given date. Cash settlement rather than delivery often exists (e.g., stock index future).

• A futures contract may be eliminated prior to the delivery date by engaging in an offsetting contract for the particular commodity or financial instrument involved. For instance, a futures contract to buy 100,000 pounds of a commodity by December 31, 19X1, may be canceled by entering into another contract to sell 100,000 pounds of that same commodity on December 31, 19X1.

• Changes in value of open contracts are settled regularly (e.g., daily). The usual contract provides that when a decrease in the contract value occurs, the contract holder has to make a cash deposit for such decline with the clearinghouse. If the contract increases in value, the holder may withdraw the increased value.

The change in market value of a futures contract involves a gain or loss that should be recognized in earnings. An exception exists that for certain contracts the timing of income statement recognition relates to the accounting for the applicable asset, liability, commitment, or transaction. This accounting exception applies when the contract is designed as a hedge against price and interest rate fluctuation. When the criteria noted following are satisfied, the accounting for the contract relates to the accounting for the hedged item. Thus, a change in market value is recognized in the same accounting period that the effects of the related changes in price or interest rate of the hedged item is reflected in income.

The *hedge* exists when both of the following criteria are met:

• The hedged item places price and interest rate risk on the firm. Risk means the sensitivity of corporate earnings to market price changes or rates of return of existing assets, liabilities, commitments, and expected transactions. This criteria is *not* met in the case where other assets, liabilities, commitments, and anticipated transactions *already* offset the risk.

• The contract lowers risk exposure and is entered into as a hedge. High correlation exists between the change in market value of the contract and the fair value of the hedged item. In effect, the market price change of the contract offsets the price and interest rate changes on the exposed item. An example is when there exists a futures contract to sell silver that offsets the changes in the price of silver.

A change in market value of a futures contract that meets the hedging criteria of the related asset or liability should adjust the carrying value of the hedge item. For instance, a company has an investment in a government bond that it anticipates to sell at a later date. The company can reduce its susceptibility to changes in fair value of the bonds by engaging in a futures contract. The changes in the market value of the futures contract adjusts the book value of the bonds.

A change in market value of a futures contract that is for the purpose of hedging a firm commitment is included in measuring the transaction satisfying the commitment. An example is when the company hedges a firm purchase commitment by using a futures contract. When the acquisition takes place thus satisfying the purchase commitment, the gain or loss on the futures contract is an element of the cost of the acquired item. Assume ABC Company has a purchase commitment for 30,000 pounds of a commodity at $2 per pound, totaling $60,000. At the time of the consummation of the transaction, the $60,000 cost is *decreased* by any gain

(e.g., $5,000) arising from the "hedged" futures contract. The net cost is shown as the carrying value (e.g., $55,000).

A futures contract may apply to transactions the company *expects* to conduct in the ordinary course of business. It is not obligated to do so. These expected transactions do not involve existing assets or liabilities, or transactions applicable to *existing* firm commitments. For instance, a company may *anticipate* buying a certain commodity in the future but has not made a formal purchase commitment. The company may minimize risk exposure to price changes by entering into a futures contract. The change in market value of this "anticipatory hedge contract" is included in measuring the subsequent transaction. The change in market value of the futures contract adjusts the cost of the acquired item. The following criteria must be met for "anticipatory hedge accounting":

1. and 2. are the same as the criteria for regular hedge contracts related to *existing* assets, liabilities, or firm commitments.

3. Identification exists of the major terms of the contemplated transaction. Included are the type of commodity or financial instrument, quantity, and expected transaction date. If the financial instrument carries interest, the maturity date should be given.

4. It is probable that the expected transaction will take place.

Probability of occurrence depends on the following:
- Time period involved
- Monetary commitment for the activity
- Financial capability to conduct the transaction

- Frequency of previous transactions of a similar nature
- Possibility that other types of transactions may be undertaken to accomplish the desired goal
- Adverse operational effects of not engaging in the transaction

The accounting applicable for a "hedge type" futures contract related to an expected asset acquisition or liability incurrence should be consistent with the company's accounting method employed for those assets and liabilities. For instance, the firm should book a loss for a futures contract that is a hedge of an expected inventory acquisition if the amount will not be recovered from the sale of inventory.

If a "hedged" futures contract is closed prior to the expected transaction, the accumulated value change in the contract should be carried forward to be included in measuring the related transaction. If it is probable that the quantity of an expected transaction will be less than the amount initially hedged, recognize a gain or loss for a pro rata portion of futures results that would have been included in the measurement of the subsequent transaction.

A "hedged" futures contract requires disclosure of
- Firm commitments
- Nature of assets and liabilities
- Accounting method used for the contract, including a description of events or transactions resulting in recognized changes in contract values
- Expected transactions that are hedged with futures contracts

G

GAIN CONTINGENCY A gain contingency is the future possibility that the business will obtain a favorable financial development. Examples are winning a lawsuit, or contract renegotiation with another company or government. Due to conservatism, a gain contingency cannot be recorded in the accounts. Instead, footnote disclosure is made.

GAME THEORY This is an *operations research* technique that deals with competitive situations where two or more participants pursue conflicting objectives. The theory attempts to provide optimal strategies for the participants. In games, the participants are competitors; the success of one is usually at the expense of the other. Each person selects and executes those strategies that he believes will result in winning the game. There are many different types of games that reflect different conflict situations. A two-person, zero sum game is an example.

GOAL PROGRAMMING (GP) GP is a special case of *linear programming (LP)*, that attempts to find a solution to resource allocation. LP, however, has one important drawback in that it is limited primarily to solving problems where the objectives of manage-

ment can be stated in a single goal such as profit maximization or cost minimization. But financial management must now deal with multiple goals, which are often incompatible and conflict with each other. GP gets around this difficulty. In GP, unlike LP, the objective function may consist of multiple, incommensurable, and conflicting goals. Rather than maximizing or minimizing the objective criterion, the deviations from these set goals are minimized, often based on the priority factors assigned to each goal. The fact that financial management will have multiple goals that are in conflict with each other means that instead of maximizing or minimizing financial executives attempt to *satisfice*. In other words, they will look for a satisfactory solution rather than an optimal solution.

Examples of Multiple Conflicting Goals

For example, consider an investor who desires investments that will have a maximum return and minimum risk. These goals are generally incompatible and therefore unachievable. Other examples of multiple conflicting goals can be found in businesses that want to

1. Maximize profits and increase wages paid to employees

2. Upgrade product quality and reduce product costs

3. Pay larger dividends to shareholders and retain earnings for growth

4. Increase control of channels of distribution and reduce working capital requirements

5. Reduce credit losses and increase sales

GOING CONCERN QUALIFICATION AICPAs' Statement on Auditing Standards No. 59 applies to the auditor's consideration of an entity's ability to continue as a going concern. The auditor must appraise the client's going concern potential, and if a substantial doubt exists, the auditor must provide an explanatory paragraph in the audit report. The auditor looks at the client's "going concern" ability for a reasonable time period, not to exceed one year beyond the date of the audited financial statements. An example follows:

> The accompanying financial statements have been prepared assuming that Company Y will continue as a going concern. As discussed in Note X to the financial statements, Company Y has suffered recurring losses from operations and has a net capital deficiency that raises substantial doubt about the entity's ability to continue as a going concern. Management's plans in regard to these matters are also described in Note X. The financial statements do not include any adjustments that might result from the outcome of this uncertainty.

Note that the absence of a reference of substantial doubt in the audit report cannot be construed as providing assurance of continued existence.

GOING PUBLIC This refers to selling formerly privately held shares to new investors on the over-the-counter market for the first time. For the individual company, going public marks a historic moment. It often is the springboard for greater growth and success. There are the advantages and disadvantages of raising capital through a public offering.

The Pros of Going Public

• Going public raises money. If it is common stock, it does not have to be repaid.

• The use of proceeds from the sale of the issue is generally unrestricted.

• Management often experiences an increase in prestige and reputation.

• Public companies can acquire other businesses with stock without depleting cash reserves.

• Other financing alternatives may improve.

The Cons of Going Public

• Much jealously guarded information must be disclosed. The guarded items include management salaries, competitive position, transactions between the company and its management, and the identity of significant customers and suppliers.

• Corporate decision making becomes more cumbersome as the company attempts to move from a tightly controlled entrepreneurially oriented company to a professionally managed one where ownership and management are divorced. Any decision, long-term or short-term, may be manifested promptly in the company's stock price. The company may worry constantly about improving quarterly earnings (and stock prices) instead of trying to take a longer perspective in developing its strategy.

• Since the number of shares outstanding increases when the company goes public, greater earnings must be achieved to avoid reducing earnings per share.

• If the market price declines, many problems may result: management is usually personally blamed; the flexibility of issuing stock to make acquisitions may be hampered; if the decline occurs soon after the offering, litigation against everyone involved may take place; and other financing alternatives may evaporate.

• Preparation of various reports and financial statements may be costly.

How to Avoid the Drawbacks of Going Public

Here are some tips for avoiding the pitfalls of going public.

• Assemble the proper team. This involves selecting an underwriter, accountant, counsel, and perhaps some new directors.

• When choosing an underwriter, distribution capacity is important. An underwriter appropriate for one company or one industry may be inappropriate for another. In addition to technical ability, personalities and confidence in each also should be considered.

• The selection of accountants and lawyers need careful examination. The registration process is complex, coupled with absolute liability for the company for material misstatements or omissions—regardless of good faith or motive. It is important to remember that malpractice insurance in the securities field is the most expensive of any specialty. That carries a message. It is good to hire a "Big Eight" or nationally prominent accounting firm for the reasons that it enhances marketability and may be viewed by the underwriter as insurance in the event of litigation. *See also* Private Placement.

GOLDEN PARACHUTE   A golden parachute is an agreement giving very significant financial benefit to corporate officers in terms of money (e.g., severance pay, bonus), stock options, and so on in the event the firm is bought out by another and the officers are not retained in the new entity. This is particularly done when the business is a target of acquisition.

GOVERNMENTAL ACCOUNTING   This is the accounting policies, reporting requirements, and disclosures required for government units. There is an absence of private ownership. The government provides goods and services to the public without a profit motive. According to the fund theory, assets equal restrictions on assets. The purpose of financial reporting is accountability to the public.

Funds assure accountability and expenditure for specified purposes. Revenues are obtained and used in accordance with special regulations and restrictions. They should be classified by source. Expenditures should be classified by function, activity, character, and principal classes of objectives. Depreciation is not recorded in governmental funds (except for proprietary funds and certain trust funds). Budgets are adopted and recorded in the accounts of the applicable fund. Recording both the budget and actual transactions aid in identifying responsibility and maintaining control. The journal entry to record the budget at the beginning of the year is

Estimated Revenue (authorization to raise funds)
Fund Balance
Appropriation (authorization to spend)

The journal entry to close the budget at the end of the reporting period is

Appropriations
Revenue
   Estimated Revenue
   Expenditures
   Encumbrances
   Fund Balance

Fund balance is the difference between assets and liabilities and reserve for encumbrances. Fund balance is affected by budgetary (nominal) accounts and actual accounts. Nominal accounts of governmental units relate to controlling accounts that support detailed (subsidiary) ledgers. Nominal accounts are closed out at the end of the accounting period. Examples are appropriations, estimated revenues, expenditures, and encumbrances.

Some funds follow GAAP employing accrual accounting just as commercial enterprises. They include the proprietary funds (enterprise fund and internal service fund) since their operations are similar to those of profit-oriented organizations. The users of the services pay for them. Thus, proprietary funds have profit and loss attributes. Examples of enterprise funds are utilities,

airports, transportation systems, hospitals, and port authority. An internal service fund provides services or goods to other funds on a cost reimbursement basis. Examples are maintenance and data processing. Proprietary funds record depreciation.

A fund is a fiscal and accounting entity with a self-balancing set of accounts recording assets, liabilities, and fund balance. Each fund has its own self-contained double-entry set of accounts.

The various types of governmental funds that follow the modified accrual basis of accounting include

• *General fund*—accounts for all financial resources, except those accounted for in another fund.

• *Special revenue fund*—accounts for the proceeds of specific revenue sources that are restricted to expenditure for specified projects. Examples are financing libraries, schools, and parks.

• *Capital projects fund*—accounts for resources used to buy or construct capital facilities. There has to be a capital projects fund for each authorized project to assure that the proceeds of a bond issue are expended only as authorized.

• *Debt service fund*—accounts for the accumulation of resources for and the payment of principal and interest on long-term debt. Three types of long-term debt are term or sinking fund bonds, serial bonds, and note or time warrants having a maturity of more than one year.

Fiduciary funds relate to trust and agency funds, which account for assets held by the governmental body acting as trustee or agent for individuals, organizations, or other governmental units. The funds do *not* own the assets held. The difference between agency and trust is that agency transactions cancel out while trust transactions reflect custody over assets in a more permanent sense. All agency fund assets are owed to another party. Fiduciary funds may be nonexpendable (can-

not expend principal) and expendable (can use principal). Nonexpendable fiduciary funds use accrual accounting, while those that are expendable use modified accrual. An example of a nonexpendable fund is a loan fund in which the original amount must remain intact. Examples of expendable funds are pension and retirement funds.

There are also account groups that are *not* funds but are accounting entities. Account groups are presented in the balance sheet only. There are *no* revenue or expenditures for account groups. They are self-balancing sets of accounts. They furnish double-entry control in memorandum form. The two types are

• *General fixed asset account group*—accounts for all fixed assets that are not shown in another fund. The funds that do show fixed assets are proprietary and trust. The fixed assets are maintained at original cost. Property records are kept for each piece of property and equipment held.

• *General long-term debt account group*—accounts for principal on long-term debt except that payable from a proprietary or trust fund. Under GAAP the proper valuation for the long-term liability is the sum of the discounted value of the principal and interest payments. At maturity, funds are transferred to the debt service fund. There is multiple recording of transactions where two or more funds record that transaction.

■ Example

The general fund expends $1,000,000 to buy fixed assets. The entry in the general fund is

Expenditures	1,000,000	
Vouchers Payable		1,000,000

A memo is made of the $1,000,000 fixed assets being held in the general fixed asset account group.

Interfund transactions may be loans and advances. They are temporary shifts of resources that will be repaid later. They are

recorded in "due to" and "due from" accounts.

The name of the annual report for a government is "comprehensive annual financial report." The basic financial statements are prepared in conformity with GAAP as applied to governmental units. The reporting standards are provided in Statement No. 1, "Governmental Accounting and Financial Reporting Principles," of the National Council on Governmental Accounting.

While legal provisions come before accounting principles, there should exist adequate records to allow for GAAP-based reporting. Differences between legal provisions and governmental accounting principles should be disclosed in the footnotes to the financial statements.

There is a combined financial statement with columns for each fund and a total column for all funds. In addition, to a combined, combining (assembling data for all funds within a type), and individual balance sheet, the following is also shown:

• Statement of revenues, Expenditures, and Changes in fund balance (all funds)

• Statement of revenues, Expenditures, and Changes in fund balance, Budget and actual (General and special revenue funds)

See also Encumbrance; Modified Accrual; Not-for-Profit Accounting, Other Than Governmental.

GRAPHICAL METHOD OF LP The graphical method in *linear programming* (LP) is a solution procedure used when an LP problem has usually no more than two decision variables. The graphical method follows the steps:

1. Change inequalities to equalities.
2. Graph the equalities.
3. Identify the correct side for the original inequalities.
4. After all this, determine the *feasible region*, the area of feasible solutions.

5. Evaluate the *corner points* (*basic feasible solution*) of the feasible region.
6. Pick the one that maximizes (or minimizes) the objective function, which is an *optimal solution*.

See also Linear Programming; Simplex Method of LP.

GRAPHIC SOFTWARE Graphic software put numeric data in graphic form, including charts, diagrams, and signs. Graphs can be turned into photographic slides, overhead transparencies, and images on paper. Absolute amounts (i.e., totals, increases), percentages, dollars, and units can be of multiple color. Software that allows free-style drawing is more beneficial for imaginative enhancements. Structured programs clarify a simple chart. *Note*: Better quality can be gotten with stand-alone graphic packages rather than programs that are part of an integrated package.

Accounting graphics can capture complex data collection, show relationships between different numbers, and present them dramatically. Graphics can be used by financial executives to appraise trends and make superior managerial decisions. Presentation graphic packages can produce slides, transparencies, and hard-copy output to accompany presentations and reports at meetings. Audit uses of graphic software include analytical review, reports, and proposals.

Graphic hardware and software are able to accommodate both standard charts and special charts. IBM's Enhanced Graphics Adapter™ card is a graphic interface. Graphic boards provide high resolution and hundreds of colors.

Types of graphics include bar charts (stacked, horizontal, and three-dimensional), line graphs, area graphs, pie shapes, high-low-close charts, bubble charts (depict the relative values of items by size and position of circles in a coordinate range), surface area

charts, scatter diagrams, and spherical diagrams.

Graphics may display the following accounting and financial applications:

• Charting revenue and/or costs by product line, market share, and customer

• Break-even analysis

• Trends in major expense categories such as promotion and entertainment expense

• Depicting the variance between actual and budget costs and sales

• Backlog information on orders

• Trends in capital expenditures

• Showing personnel statistics, such as number of employees, sales per employee, and productivity measures

In looking at graphic programs under consideration, the following should be taken into account:

• Compatibility with other packages and applications

• Maximum number of actions and symbols

• Maximum number of columns and rows in chart, automatic overlapped column specifications, and three-dimensional columns

• Maximum number of bars

• Image libraries, which let the financial person merge a picture with a chart or with another image

• Formatting aspects, such as screen resolution display and multiple graph sizes

• Ability to modify predefined or drawn images

• Editing abilities, such as titles, labels, and modification of graph type

• Ability to adjust plot orientation and page size

• Ability to generate graphs with different y axes

• Printing features such as bold type, pattern handling, and multiple copies

• Availability of chart legends

• Degree of color selection

• Ability of a graphics enhancement program to accept charts from a standardized business graphics package

Remember: Often, graphics come after data are gotten from an integrated spreadsheet. For example, a chart may depict alternative earnings derived from altering the sales base.

In the case of project management, Gantt charts may be utilized. These are boxes that "float," showing the starting and ending dates of some activity. Haven Tree Software's Interactive Easy Flow™ is a graphics program dedicated to flow charts and organization charts.

■ Example

IBM's PC Storyboard™ is a graphics program having four separate elements. It gives the financial manager the ability to create, edit, and combine business graphics and freehand drawings. Whatever is on the screen can be put into the final design.

■ Example

Software Publishing's Harvard Presentation Graphics™ integrates text, graphs, and charts into a full feature package.

GREENMAIL This refers to "pay-off" payments made by a targeted takeover company to the suitor (prospective acquiring company) so as to cease the takeover attempt. Usually, the targeted company purchases its shares of stock back from the acquirer at materially higher than the current market price. In exchange, the prospective acquirer stops the takeover effort. Existing stockholders in the targeted company may suffer since the company is paying more than the prevailing price for the stock, which ultimately comes out of the stockholders' pockets.

GRETHAM'S LAW This law is popularly phrased as "bad money drives good money out of circulation." More accurately, the law

asserts that when an item has a use as both a commodity and money, it will be used where its value is greater. The rapid disappearance of silver certificates is an example of Gretham's law. If a one dollar silver certificate entitles the holder to more than a dollar's worth of silver, the certificate will be hoarded, melted down, exported, or exchanged for silver bullion, thereby disppearing from circulation.

GROSS NATIONAL PRODUCT (GNP) GNP is the current market value in dollars of all final goods and services produced in the economy in a given period. It is normally stated in annual terms, though data are compiled and released quarterly. GNP consists of personal consumption expenditures, gross private domestic investment, government spending, and net exports (exports minus imports).

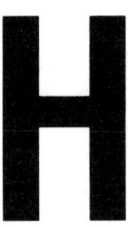

H

HASH TOTAL This is adding numbers without practical meaning but done for audit control, mainly in computer applications. The objective is to uncover a lost or omitted file during processing.

■ **Example**

A hash total may be made of sales invoice numbers. A lack of agreement between processed sales invoices and the hash total indicates an error mandating investigation. *See also* Internal Control.

HEDGING

1. Financing assets with liabilities of similar maturity. In this way, there are sufficient funds to satisfy debt when due. For example, permanent assets should be financed with long-term debt rather than short-term debt. 2. Entering into a futures contract to buy or sell an item at a future date at the *current* price. This strategy is recommended when price increases are anticipated, such as that due to inflation or expected shortage situations.

■ **Example**

A company wants to buy 1,000 units of an item having a current price of $25 each but does not need the goods until 3 months from now. By entering into a futures contract to take delivery 3 months later at $25 each, the company has protected itself from possible price increases (e.g., $40 price).

HIGH-LOW METHOD The high-low method is an algebraic procedure used to separate a *mixed (semivariable) cost* into the fixed and the variable portion. The high-low method, as the name indicates, uses two extreme data points to determine the values of a (the fixed-cost portion) and b (the variable rate) in the *cost-volume formula* $y = a + bx$. The extreme data points are the highest and lowest cost-volume pairs. The high-low method is simple and easy to use. It has the disadvantage, however, of using two extreme data points, which may not be representative of normal conditions. The method may yield unreliable estimates of a and b in the formula. In such a case, it would be wise to drop them and choose two other points that are more representative of normal situations. *See also* Cost Behavior Analysis.

HOLDING COMPANY A holding company has the sole objective of owning the stock of other firms. A holding company can buy a small percentage of another business (e.g., 10%), which may be enough to get effective

control over the other, particularly if stock ownership is widely disbursed. A holding company that desires to obtain voting control of a business may make a direct market purchase or a tender offer to obtain additional shares. What would encourage the officers of a company to turn it into a holding company? A company in a declining industry, for instance, may decide to move out of its basic operations by liquidating assets and use the funds obtained to invest in other companies that have good growth potential.

Because the operating companies held by the holding company are distinct legal entities, the obligations of any one are isolated from the others. If one of them goes bankrupt, there is no claim on the assets of another. However, a loan officer that lends to one company may require a guarantee by the other companies. This will, in effect, join the assets of the companies. In any event, a major financial setback involving one company is not the responsibility of the others.

Advantages of Holding Company Arrangement

• The ability of the holding company to buy a large amount of assets with a small investment. In effect, the holding company can control more assets than it could acquire through a merger.

• Risk protection since the failure of one of the companies does not cause the failure of the holding company. The most the holding company would lose is its investment in the failed business.

• Easy to obtain control of another firm because all that is required is purchasing enough stock. Unlike a merger in which stockholder or management approval is required, no approval is needed for a holding company.

Disadvantages of Holding Company Arrangement

• Multiple taxation exists because the income of the holding company that it receives from subsidiaries is in the form of cash. Before paying dividends, the subsidiary must pay taxes on its earnings. When the earnings are distributed to the holding company as dividends, it must pay tax on the dividends received less the 80% dividend exclusion. But if the holding company owns 80% or more of the subsidiary's stock, there will be a 100% dividend exemption. There is no multiple taxation for a subsidiary that is part of a merged company.

• Usually more costly to administer than a single company resulting from a merger. The increased costs result since economies of scale accomplished from a merger do not typically occur.

• The U.S. Department of Justice may construe the holding company as a monopoly and force dissolution.

• By acquiring stock ownership in other companies with debt, a deterioration in financial leverage ratios may occur, as well as magnifying earnings changes. A greater debt position means more risk, with the resulting effect of fluctuating earnings.

A holding company can get a large amount of control for a small investment by obtaining voting control in a company for a minimal amount and then using that firm to gain voting control in another, and so on.

HOME EQUITY LOAN   The home equity loan comes in two forms: a second trust deed (mortgage) and an equity line of credit.
1. *Second trust deed*—similar to a first trust deed (mortgage) except that in the event of foreclosure, the holder of the first mortgage has priority in payment over the holder of the second mortgage.
2. *Line of credit*—under the line of credit provision, a check may be written whenever funds are needed. Interest is charged only on the amount borrowed. Under the Tax Reform Act of 1986, interest incurred on the first and second homes is deductible for tax purposes. However, limitations exist on the deductibility of other types of interest—especially interest on consumer loans. As a result,

it is a good idea to convert your consumer loan interest to interest on a home equity loan in order to continue the full tax-deductibility of interest expense.

Advantages of Home Equity Loan

1. Low interest rates because (a) the loan is secured by a house and (b) it usually bears variable rates.
2. No loan-processing fees. There is no need to go through a loan application and incur fees each time money is borrowed.
3. Convenience. A check may be written only when money is needed. Interest is charged only on the amount borrowed.

Pitfalls of Home Equity Loan

1. *High points*. Points imposed on an equity loan are based on the amount of the credit line, not on the amount actually borrowed. Many home equity loans have no caps on interest rates.
2. *Long payback period*. It is convenient to have to pay a small minimum amount each month, but stretching out the loan payback period usually means higher interest rates over the period.
3. *High balloon payments*. Some loans require a large balloon payment of the principal at the end of the loan period.
4. *Risk of home loss*. Unlike other loans, there is risk in losing a home. It may be

difficult to sell the home fast enough and at fair market price to be able to meet the balloon.
5. *Frivolous spending habit*. One may get into the habit of spending on unnecessary things.

HOMOSCEDASTICITY (or constant variance)

This is one of the assumptions required in a *regression* in order to make valid statistical inferences about population relationships. Homoscedasticity requires that the standard deviation and variance of the error terms be constant for all x's and that the error terms are drawn from the same population. This indicates that there is a uniform scatter or dispersion of data points about the regression line (see figures below). If the assumption does not hold, the accuracy of the regression coefficient(s) is open to question. *See also* Regression Analysis.

HUMAN RESOURCE ACCOUNTING (HRA) A

positive relationship exists between an entity's success and the quality of its employees. Companies' annual reports often state that their employees are their most valuable assets. Why, then, if the employees are valuable assets, is their value not seen on the accompanying financial statements?

Acceptance of human resource accounting involves a decision to accept the notion that

Constant Variance of Error Term (*u*) (Homoscedasticity)

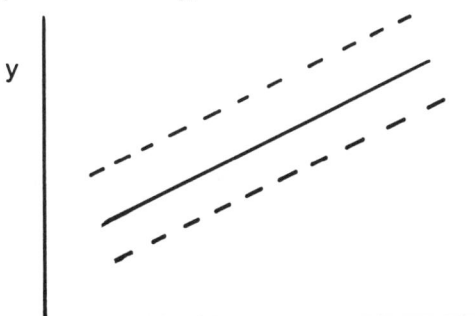

Nonconstant Variance of Error Term (*u*)

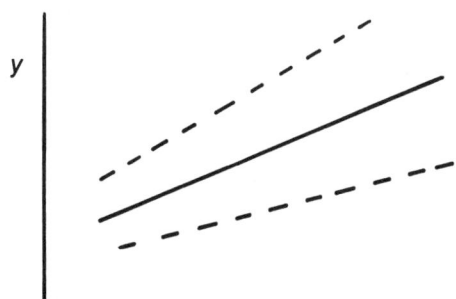

employees are assets and have a value in monetary terms to the firm's future performance. Employee valuation should be considered in management decisions. HRA can provide data that gives the relative value of employee groups and can relate employees to their effects on the long-term performance of the entity. Human resources can be accounted for much like intangible prepaid expenses.

The objectives of HRA are to provide

• Quantitative information on an entity's human resources that management and investors can utilize in their decision-making process

• Methods of appraising management's utilization of its human resources such as the funds spent on personnel turnover

• Methods to value people, identify relevant variables, and develop models for the management of human resources

The two major valuation approaches are recording human resource expenditures as assets and recording human resources at their value (i.e., present value or future value). The advantage of the former approach is that expenditures (costs) are how assets are measured under GAAP.

The cost approach to human resource valuation is perhaps the most acceptable to traditional accountants, but it is a diluted form of the basic premise of human resource accounting; namely, what are the entity's human resources worth? Worth is a value and not a cost, but value judgments are not acceptable by GAAP.

Historical cost valuation is probably the most widely accepted approach. Costs includable in the human resource asset account would be the actual costs incurred to hire, train, and develop employees. These costs are capitalized and amortized for each employee over the employee's expected period of working with the firm. If the employee leaves earlier than expected, the unamortized balance in the assets would be immediately written off as a loss.

Another cost approach is to use replacement cost, where the employee is valued according to the expense that would be incurred to replace him or her. The costs would include the costs of recruiting and training a replacement. An advantage of this approach is that the replacement cost will be adjusted to price changes in the labor market and hence better approximate the employee's worth to the business.

The economic value approach is in conflict with GAAP but may come up with a more realistic measure. A calculation is made of the present value of the contribution to future profits and the amount is capitalized. This discounted value of future earnings provided by the employee is debited to human resources (asset account) and credited to stockholders' equity.

A macro-economic model may be used employing the discounted value of future salary payments for 5 years. This is multiplied by the efficiency ratio, which is the entity's rate of return relative to industry norms. The final outcome is the present value of the human resources.

Another approach is unpurchased goodwill. The nonhuman assets are valued, net income determined (using assets' market values), and the net income is then compared to the industry average. Differences are then capitalized. Such differences presumably reflect corporate earning power.

For a large number of service organizations, the only product being offered is the professional talents (an intangible product) of their human resources (e.g., law firms with lawyers, hospitals with doctors and nurses).

I

IF-CONVERTED METHOD If convertible securities are deemed to be common stock equivalents for the purpose of computing primary or fully diluted EPS, the if-converted method is used. Under this method, there is an assumption that conversion of convertible securities were made as of the beginning of the earliest period reported (or at time of issuance, if later). Applicable dividends and interest on the convertible securities are added back to net income, if either was previously deducted. *See also* Earnings per Share.

ILLEGAL ACTS Under Statement on Auditing Standard No. 54, an illegal act is the violation of a governmental regulation or law. The illegal act may be perpetrated by management or the employees representing it. The following audit procedures and analysis of findings may indicate that an illegal act has occurred.

- Questionable disbursements to employees, outside parties, and government representatives
- Absence of the filing of government forms (e.g., tax returns, compliance reports)
- Unusually high payments for services that have not been documented (e.g., consulting fees)
- Unusual penalties and fines assessed by federal or local authorities

- Government investigation of corporate activities
- Enforcement proceedings against the entity
- Documented violations of regulations and laws
- Excessive commissions and finders' fees
- Material payments in cash
- Significant checks payable to bearer
- Improperly executed and recorded transactions
- Excessive time delays in record keeping or exercising controls

The auditor should attempt to comprehend the nature of the illegal act, the circumstances surrounding it, and its impact upon the financial statements. Inquiry should be made of one level of management above that committing the illegal act. In the event that management does not furnish acceptable assurance that an illegal act has not occurred, the auditor should ask the client's legal counsel about applicable laws and regulations, and the impact the illegal act will have upon the financial statements. The meeting between the auditor and the client's attorney should be made by the client.

The auditor should extend his audit procedures to gather additional relevant information, including

• Ascertaining the proper authorization of transactions

• Obtaining confirmations of essential data from external parties (e.g., attorneys, banks)

• Reviewing documentation in support of the transaction (e.g., canceled checks, invoices, freight bills)

• Comparing how similar transactions were accounted for in the past

The auditor must appraise the impact of an illegal act on financial statement figures, including contingent monetary amounts (e.g., damages, penalties). Contingencies that may occur because of illegality are expropriations, litigation, and bankruptcy. Disclosure of significant revenue obtained from illegal activities is needed. Further, the additional risks forthcoming from illegal acts and relationships should be mentioned.

If a material act has taken place that has not been satisfactorily reflected in the body or notes to the financial statements, a qualified or adverse opinion is necessitated based on the significance of the act or the financial statements.

The auditor should disclaim an opinion when the client prevents the auditor from obtaining competent evidential matter regarding the materiality of the illegal act on the client's financial position.

IMPUTING INTEREST ON NOTES In the case where the face amount of a note does not represent the present value of the consideration given or received in the exchange, imputation of interest is needed to avoid the misstatement of profit. Interest is imputed on noninterest-bearing notes, notes that provide for an unrealistically low interest rate, and notes for which the face value is significantly different from the "going" selling price of the property or market value of the note.

If a note is issued only for cash, the note should be recorded at the cash exchanged, irrespective of whether the interest rate is reasonable or the amount of the face value of the note. The note has a present value at issuance equal to the cash transacted. When a note is exchanged for property, goods, or services, a presumption exists that the interest rate is fair and reasonable. Where the stipulated interest rate is not fair and adequate, the note has to be recorded at the fair value of the merchandise or services or at an amount that approximates fair value. If fair value is not determinable for the goods or services, the discounted present value of the note has to be used.

The imputed interest rate is one that would have resulted if an independent borrower or lender had negotiated a similar transaction. For example, it is the prevailing interest rate the borrower would have paid for financing. The interest rate is based on economic circumstances and events.

Factors to be considered in deriving an appropriate discount rate include

• Prime interest rate

• "Going" market rate for similar quality instruments

• Issuer's credit standing

• Collateral

• Restrictive convenants and other terms in the note agreement

• Tax effects of the arrangement

APB 21 applies to long-term payables and receivables. Short-term payables and receivables are typically recorded at face value since the extra work of amortizing a discount or premium on a short-term note is not worth the information benefit obtained. APB 21 is *not* applicable to

• Security deposits

• Usual lending activities of banks

• Amounts that do not mandate repayment

• Receivables or payables occurring within the ordinary course of business

• Transactions between parent and subsidiary

The difference between the face value of the note and the present value of the note

represents discount or premium that has to be accounted for as an element of interest over the life of the note. Present value of the payments of the note is based on an imputed interest rate.

The interest method is used to amortize the discount or premium on the note. The interest method results in a constant rate of interest. Under the method, amortization equals

Interest rate × Present value of the liability/
            Receivable at the beginning of the year

Interest expense is recorded for the borrower, whereas interest revenue is recorded for the lender. Issuance costs are treated as a deferred charge.

The note payable and note receivable are presented in the balance sheet as follows:

Notes payable (principal plus interest)
Less: Discount (interest)
Present value (principal)

Notes receivable (principal plus interest)
Less: Premium (interest)
Present value (principal)

■ Example

On 1/1/19X1, equipment is acquired in exchange for a 1-year note payable of $1,000 maturing on 12/31/19X1. The imputed interest rate is 10%, resulting in the present value factor for $n = 1$, $i = 10\%$ of 0.91. Relevant journal entries follow:

1/1/19X1	Equipment	910	
	Discount	90	
	Notes payable		1,000
12/31/19X1	Interest Expense	90	
	Discount		90
	Notes Payable	1,000	
	Cash		1,000

■ Example

On 1/1/19X1, a machine is bought for cash of $10,000 and the incurrence of a $30,000, 5-year, noninterest-bearing note payable. The imputed interest rate is 10%. The present value factor for $n = 5$, $i = 10\%$ is 0.62. Appropriate journal entries follow:

1/1/19X1

Machine ($10,000 + $18,600)	28,600	
Discount	11,400	
Notes Payable		30,000
Cash		10,000

Present value of note equals $30,000 × 0.62 = $18,600. On 1/1/19X1, the balance sheet shows:

Notes payable	$30,000
Less: Discount	11,400
Present value	$18,600

12/31/19X1

Interest Expense	1,860	
Discount		1,860

10% × $18,600 = $1,860

1/1/19X2

Notes payable	$30,000
Less: Discount (11,400 − 1,860)	9,540
Present value	$20,460

12/31/19X2

Interest Expense	2,046	
Discount		2,046

10% × $20,460 = $2,046

INCOME SMOOTHING   This is a form of income manipulation that results in earnings that do not reflect economic reality but rather what the company desires them to be. This masks the inherent cyclical irregularities that are part of the reality of the entity's experience and, thus, detracts from the quality of earnings. Additionally, a firm's taking a "financial bath" causes a lowering in current period earnings while relieving future income of these charges. Improper revenue recognition, either belatedly or prematurely, lowers earnings quality. For instance, the recognition of revenue before it is reasonably assured to be collected may cause the reporting of earnings in one year and its reversal, and an ensuing loss, in a later year. Net income is improperly stated for both periods.

The financial analyst should restate net income for profit increases or decreases arising from income-smoothing attempts.

The quality of earnings depends on the extent to which profits stand on their own for the current period, as well as on the degree to which they borrow from the future or benefit from the past. Earnings are of lower quality if they do not portray the economic performance of the business entity for the period.

INCOME STATEMENT ANALYSIS

The analysis of the income statement indicates a company's earning power, quality of earnings, and operating performance. Net income backed up by cash is important for corporate liquidity. The accounting policies employed should be realistic in reflecting the substance of the transactions. Accounting changes should be made only for proper reasons. Further, a high degree of estimation in the income measurement process results in uncertainty in reported figures. Earnings stability enhances the predictability of future results based on currently reported profits.

Cash Flow From Operations

Cash flow from operations equals net income plus noncash expenses less noncash revenue. Net income is of higher quality if it is backed up by cash. The trend in the ratio of cash flow from operations to net income should be evaluated.

The closer a transaction is to cash, the more objective is the evidence supporting revenue and expense recognition. As the proximity to cash becomes less, the less objective is the transaction and the more subjective are the interpretations. Higher earnings quality relates to recording transactions close to cash realization.

In appraising the cash adequacy of a company, the CPA should compute the following:
• Cash flow generated from operations before interest expense
• Cash flow generated from operations less cash payments to meet debt principal, dividends, and capital expenditures

■ Example

A condensed income statement for Company A follows:

Sales		$1,000,000
Less: Cost of sales		300,000
Gross margin		$ 700,000
Less: Operating expenses		
Salary	$100,000	
Rent	200,000	
Telephone	50,000	
Depreciation	80,000	
Amortization expense	60,000	
Total operating expenses		490,000
Income before other items		$ 210,000
Other revenue and expense		
Interest expense	$ 70,000	
Amortization of deferred credit	40,000	
Total other revenue and expense		30,000
Net income		$ 180,000

The ratio of cash flow from operations to net income is 1.55, calculated as follows:

Cash flow from operations		$180,000
Add: Noncash expenses		
Depreciation	$80,000	
Amortization expense	60,000	140,000
Less: Noncash revenues		
Amortization of deferred credit		(40,000)
Cash flow from operations		$280,000

$$\frac{\text{Cash flow from operations}}{\text{Net income}} = \frac{\$280,000}{\$180,000} = 1.55$$

Discretionary Costs

Discretionary costs may easily be changed by management decision. They include advertising, repairs and maintenance, and research and development. Discretionary costs may be decreased when a company is having problems or wants to show a stable earnings trend. A pullback in discretionary costs results in overstated earnings and a long-term negative effect because management is starving the company of needed expenses. Cost reduction programs may lower earnings quality when material cutbacks are made in dis-

cretionary costs. However, the CPA cannot always conclude that any reduction in discretionary costs is improper. The reduction may be necessary when the prior corporate strategy is deficient and ill-conceived.

The CPA should determine if the present level of discretionary costs is in conformity with the company's prior trends and with current and future requirements. Index numbers may be utilized to make a comparison of current discretionary expenditures with base year expenditures. A vacillating trend in discretionary costs to revenue may indicate the company is smoothing earnings by altering its discretionary costs. A substantial increase in discretionary costs may have a positive impact on corporate earning power and future growth.

A declining trend in discretionary costs to net sales may indicate lower earnings quality. Also to be reviewed is the relationship of discretionary costs to the assets to which they apply.

■ Example

The following relationship exists between advertising and sales:

	19X1	19X2	19X3
Sales	$120,000	$150,000	$100,000
Advertising	11,000	16,000	8,000

19X1 is the most typical year.
Increasing competition is expected in 19X4.
Advertising to sales equals:

19X1	19X2	19X3
9.2%	10.7%	8%

In terms of base dollars, 19X1 is assigned 100. In 19X2, the index number is 145.5 ($16,000/$11,000) and in 19X3 it is 72.7 ($8,000/$11,000).

The indicators regarding 19X3 are negative. Advertising is of a lower level than in previous years. In fact, advertising should have risen due to expected increased competition.

Accounting Policies

Conservatively determined net income is of higher quality than liberally determined net income. Conservatism applies to the accounting methods and estimates used. A comparison should be made between the company's accounting policies and the prevailing accounting policies in the industry. If the firm's policies are more liberal, earnings quality may be lower. The CPA should take into account the company's timing of revenue recognition and the deferral of costs relative to prevailing industry practices.

The accounting policies employed should be realistic in reflecting the economic substance of the firm's transactions. The underlying business and financial realities of the company and industry have to be taken into account. For example, the depreciation method should most approximately measure the decline in usefulness of the asset. The CPA may question the reasonableness of a company's accounting estimates when prior estimates have been materially different from what actually occurred. Examples of realistic accounting policies are cited in AICPA Industry Audit Guides and in accounting policy guides published by various CPA firms. If the use of realistic policies would have resulted in substantially lower earnings than the policies used, earnings quality is lower.

The artificial shifting of earnings from one year to another results in poor earnings quality. This encompasses bringing future revenue into the current year (or its converse), shifting earnings from good years to bad years, or shifting expenses and losses among the years.

It is questionable when a company immediately recognizes revenue even though services still have to be performed. An example is a magazine publisher recognizing subscription income immediately when payment is received even though the subscription period may be for 3 years.

The unrealistic deferral of revenue recognition results in poor earnings quality because profits are unjustifiably understated. When there is a reversal of previously recorded profits, the CPA may question the company's revenue recognition policies.

If expenses are underaccrued or overaccrued, lower earnings quality results. An example of an underaccrued expense is the failure of a computer manufacturer to provide for normal maintenance service for rented computers because they are being used by lessees. An example of an overaccrued expense is when a company with high earnings decides to accrue for possible sales returns that are highly unlikely to materialize. The CPA should try to ascertain what these normal charges are and adjust reported earnings accordingly.

Accounting changes made to conform with new FASB Statements, AICPA Industry Audit Guides, and IRS Regulations are justifiable. However, an unjustified accounting change causes an earnings increment of low quality. Unwarranted changes may be made in accounting principles, estimates, and assumptions.

Are accounting changes being made to create artificial earnings growth? If there are numerous accounting changes, it will be more difficult to use current profits as a predictor for future earnings.

Degree of Certainty in Accounting Estimates

The more subjective accounting estimates and judgments are in arriving at earnings, the more uncertain is the net income figure. For example, a firm engaged in long-term activity (e.g., a shipbuilder using the percentage of completion contract method) has more uncertainty regarding earnings due to the material estimates involved. A higher percentage of assets subject to accounting estimates (intangibles) to total assets means uncertain earnings.

The CPA may want to determine the difference between estimated reserves and actual losses for previous years. A significant difference between the two may point to lower earnings quality. Further, substantial gains and losses on the sale of assets may point to inaccurate depreciation estimates being originally used.

The CPA should segregate cash expenses versus estimated expenses. Trends should be determined in

- Cash expenses to net sales
- Estimated expenses to net sales
- Estimated expenses to total expenses
- Estimated expenses to net income

■ Example

The CPA assembles the following information for Company B for the period 19X1 and 19X2:

	19X1	19X2
Cash and near-cash (conversion period to cash is short) revenue items	$100,000	$110,000
Noncash revenue items (long-term receivables arising from credit sales to the government, revenue recognized under the precentage of completion method)	150,000	200,000
Total revenue	$250,000	$310,000
Cash and near-cash expenses (salaries, rent, telephone)	$ 40,000	$ 60,000
Noncash expenses (depreciation, depletion, amortization, bad debts)	70,000	120,000
Total expenses	$110,000	$180,000
Net income	$140,000	$130,000

Estimated revenue items to total revenue was 60% ($150,000/$250,000) in 19X1 and 65% ($200,000/$310,000) in 19X2. Estimated revenue to net income was 107% ($150,000/$140,000) in 19X1 and 154% ($200,000/$130,000) in 19X2.

Estimated expense items to total expenses was 64% ($70,000/$110,000) in 19X1 and 67% ($120,000/$180,000) in 19X2. Estimated expenses to total revenue was 28% ($70,000/$250,000) in 19X1 and 39% ($120,000/$310,000) in 19X2. Estimated expenses to net income was 50% ($70,000/$140,000) in 19X1 and 92% ($120,000/$130,000) in 19X2.

Uncertainty exists with respect to the earnings of 19X1 and 19X2 arising from the high percentages of estimated income statement items. Also, a greater degree of estimation exists with regard to 19X2's income measurement process.

Residual Income

An increasing trend in residual income to net income points to a strong degree of corporate profitability because the company is earning enough to meet its imputed cost of capital.

Taxable Income

If a company reports significant stockholder earnings and a substantial tax loss, the CPA may want to evaluate the quality of reported results.

A company having a significant deferred income tax credit account will have book profits in excess of taxable earnings. An increase in the deferred tax credit account may indicate the company is moving toward more liberal accounting policies. This is because a widening gap in the deferred tax credit account indicates a greater disparity between book earnings and taxable earnings.

A decline in the effective tax rate because of a nonrecurring source (e.g., a loss carry forward that will shortly expire) results in an earnings increment of low quality. The tax benefits will not continue in the future. However, the effective tax rate may be stable when it results from a recurring source (e.g., foreign tax credit, interest on municipal bonds).

Lower earnings quality exists if there is a high percentage of foreign earnings that will not be repatriated to the U.S. for a long time.

Foreign Operations

The CPA should consider the following in evaluating the effect of foreign operations on the company's financial health:

- Degree of intercountry transactions
- Different year-ends of foreign subsidiaries
- Foreign restrictions on the transfer of funds
- Tax structure of the foreign country
- Economic and political stability of the foreign country

An erratic foreign exchange rate results in instability. The CPA can measure the degree of vacillation of the foreign exchange rate by determining its percentage change over time and/or its standard deviation. The CPA should look at the trend in the ratio of foreign translation gains and losses (reported in the stockholders' equity section) to net income to evaluate the degree of stability.

Discontinued Operations

Income from discontinued operations is usually of a one-time nature and should be ignored when forecasting future earnings. Further, a discontinued operation implies a company is in a state of decline or that a poor management decision is the cause for the firm's entering the discontinued line of

business in the first place. *See also* Balance Sheet Analysis.

INCOME STATEMENT FORMAT

The format of the income statement starting with income from continuing operations follows:

Income from continuing operations before tax
Less: Taxes
Income from continuing operations after tax
Discontinued operations:
 Income from discontinued operations (net of tax)
 Loss or gain on disposal of a division (net of tax)
Income before extraordinary items
Extraordinary items (net of tax)
Cumulative effect of a change in accounting principle
 (net of tax)
Net income

Note that earnings per share is shown on the previous items as well.

Extraordinary Items

Extraordinary items are those that are *both* unusual in nature and infrequent in occurrence. Unusual in nature means the event is abnormal and not related to the typical operations of the entity. The environment of a company includes consideration of industry characteristics, geographic location of operations, and extent of government regulation. Infrequent in occurrence means the transaction is not anticipated to take place in the foreseeable future, taking into account the corporate environment. Materiality is considered by judging the items individually and not in the aggregate. However, if arising from a single specific event or plan they should be aggregated. Extraordinary items are shown net of tax between income from discontinued operations and cumulative effect of a change in accounting principle. Extraordinary items include

• Casualty losses
• Losses on expropriation of property by a foreign government
• Gain on life insurance proceeds

• Loss or gain on the early extinguishment of debt
• Gain on troubled debt restructuring
• Loss from prohibition under a newly enacted law or regulation
• Gain or loss on disposal of a major part of the assets of a previously separate company in a business combination when sale is made within 2 years subsequent to the combination date

Losses on receivables and inventory occur in the normal course of business and therefore are not extraordinary. There is an exception, however, that losses on receivables and inventory are extraordinary if they relate to a casualty loss (e.g., earthquake) or governmental expropriation (e.g., banning of a product because of a health hazard).

Nonrecurring Items

Nonrecurring items are items that are *either* unusual in nature or infrequent in occurrence. They are shown as a separate line item before tax in arriving at income from continuing operations. An example is the gain or loss on the sale of a fixed asset.

Discontinued Operations

A business segment is a major line of business or customer class. A discontinued operation is an operation that has been discontinued during the year or will be discontinued shortly after year-end. A discontinued operation may be a segment that has been sold, abandoned, or spun off. Even though it may be operating, there exists a formal plan to dispose. Footnote disclosure regarding the discontinued operation should include an identification of the segment, disposal date, the manner of disposal, and description of remaining net assets of the segment at year-end.

The two components of discontinued operations are (1) income or loss from operations and (2) loss or gain on disposal of division.

Income or Loss From Operations. In a year that includes the measurement date, it is the income from the beginning of the year to the measurement date. The measurement date is the one on which management commits itself to a formal plan of action. Applicable estimates may be required.

If comparative financial statements are presented, including periods before the measurement date, discontinued operations should be separately shown from continuing operations.

Loss or Gain on Disposal of Division. Income or loss from activities subsequent to the measurement date and before the disposal date is an element of the gain or loss on disposal. The disposal date is the date of closing by sale or the date activities cease because of abandonment. The gain or loss is shown in the disposal year. However, if losses are expected, such losses are recorded in the year of the measurement date even if disposal is not completed in that year. Loss or gain should include estimated net losses from operations between the measurement date and the disposal date. If the loss cannot be estimated, a footnote is required. Loss on disposal includes the costs directly associated with the disposal decision. On the other hand, if a gain is expected, it should be recognized at the disposal date. The estimated gain or loss is determined at the measurement date and includes consideration of the net realizable value of the segment's assets. Also, loss or gain on disposal includes costs and expenses *directly* applicable to the disposal decision. These costs include severance pay, additional pension costs, employment relocation, and future rentals on long-term leases where subrentals are not possible. *Note*: Normal business adjustments (e.g., routinely writing down accounts receivable) are not includable in the loss on disposal. These ordinary adjustments apply to the discontinued segment's operation rather than

to the disposal of the segment. Typically, disposal is expected within one year of the measurement date. *See also* Accounting Changes.

INCOME TAX ACCOUNTING   FASB No. 96 provides that income taxes should be allocated to financial periods using the *liability method.* Tax allocation is required when *temporary differences* rather than permanent differences exist.

The deferred tax liability or asset is measured at the tax rate under existing law that will be in effect when the temporary difference reverses itself. Further, the deferred tax liability or asset must be adjusted for changes in tax law or in tax rate. The liability method is balance sheet oriented since emphasis is placed on asset and liability recognition.

Comprehensive deferred tax accounting is followed where tax expense equals taxes payable plus the tax effects of all temporary differences.

Income tax is accounted for on the *accrual basis.*

Interperiod tax allocation is employed to recognize current (or deferred) tax liability or asset for the current (or deferred) tax effect of events that have taken place at year-end. Tax effects of future events should be reflected in the year they take place.

Temporary Differences

Temporary differences are differences between periods in which transactions affect taxable income and accounting income. They originate in one period and subsequently reverse in another. Temporary differences are created by four types of transactions, the nature of which (and examples) are as follows:

1. Income included in taxable income after being included in accounting income (e.g., installment sales)

2. Expenses deducted for taxable income after being deducted for accounting income (e.g., warranty provision)

3. Income included in taxable income before being included in accounting income (e.g., rents received in advance)

4. Expenses deducted for taxable income before being deducted for accounting income (e.g., accelerated depreciation)

A temporary difference may result from increases in the tax basis of assets because of indexing for inflation.

If tax rates are graduated based on taxable income, aggregate calculations may be made using an estimated average rate.

Permanent Differences

Permanent differences do not reverse (turn around) and as such do not require tax allocation. Examples of nontax-deductible expenses are goodwill amortization, premiums on officers' life insurance, and fines. An example of income that is not taxable is interest on municipal bonds.

Financial Statement Presentation

In the balance sheet, deferred charges and credits are netted against each other and shown net current and net noncurrent. However, offset is not permitted for deferred tax liabilities or assets that apply to different tax jurisdictions.

Deferred taxes are classified as current or noncurrent based on the expected reversal dates of the temporary differences. Temporary differences reversing within one year are current, whereas those reversing in greater than one year are noncurrent.

In the income statement, disclosure is made of (1) income tax expense currently payable (the liability) and (2) the *deferred portion* of the expense (the portion of the expense based on temporary differences). (The total expense provision is based on financial reporting income, excluding permanent differences.)

Presentation of these two expense portions (with numbers and a 40% tax rate assumed) would be as follows:

Income before income taxes		$200
Income tax expense:		
Amount currently payable	$400	
Deferred portion	(320)	80
Net income		$120

Intraperiod tax allocation is when tax expense is shown in different parts of the financial statements for the current year. The income statement shows the tax allocated to (1) income from continuing operations; (2) income from discontinued operations; (3) extraordinary items; and (4) cumulative effect of a change in accounting principle. Note that in the retained earnings statement, prior period adjustments are shown net of tax.

Loss Carry Backs and Loss Carry Forwards

The tax effects of net operating *loss carry backs* should be allocated to the loss period. An entity may carry back a net operating loss 3 years and obtain a refund for taxes paid in those years. The loss is first applied to the earliest year. Any residual loss is carried forward up to 15 years.

Presentation of *loss carry back* with recognition of refund during loss year:

Loss before refundable income taxes	$1,000
Refund of prior year's income taxes arising from carry back of operating loss	485
Net loss	$ 515

(*Note*: The refund should be computed at the amount actually refundable, regardless of current tax rates).

The tax effects of net operating *loss carry forwards* and tax credits (e.g., alternative minimum tax credit) generally cannot be recognized until the year realized (the year in

which the tax liability is reduced). A journal entry typically *cannot* be made in the loss year for any possible tax benefits because of the uncertainty of future earnings. Recognition is given only in the year realized.

When the tax benefit of a loss carry forward is recognized when realized in a later year, it is classified in the same way as the income enabling recognition (typically reducing tax expense).

Presentation of the loss carry forward with recognition of benefit in year realized (numbers and 50% rate assumed):

Income before income taxes		$1,000
Income tax expense:		
Without carry forward	$500	
Reduction of income taxes arising from carry forward of prior year's operating losses	(300)	200
Net income		$800

An exception exists to the general rule of not permitting the recognition of a net operating loss carry forward in the current year. The net operating loss carry forward may be recognized to the extent of net taxable amounts in the carry forward period (deferred tax liabilities now exist to absorb them).

Disclosure should be made of the amounts and expiration dates of operating loss carry forwards.

Deferred Tax Liability vs. Deferred Tax Asset

If book income exceeds taxable income, tax expense exceeds tax payable so a deferred tax liability results. If book income is less than taxable income, tax expense is less than tax payable so a deferred tax asset results.

Deferred Tax Liability

■ Example

Assume book income and taxable income are $1,000. Depreciation for book purposes is $50 based on the straight-line method and $100 for tax purposes based on the accelerated cost recovery system. Assuming a tax rate of 34%, the entry is

Income Tax Expense ($950 × 34%)	323	
Income Tax Payable ($900 × 34%)		306
Deferred Tax Liability		17

At the end of the asset's life, the deferred tax liability of $17 will be fully reversed.

■ Example*

At the end of year 1, future recovery of the reported amount of an enterprise's installment receivables will result in taxable amounts totaling $240,000 in years 2–4. Also, a $20,000 liability for estimated expenses has been recognized in the financial statements in year 1, and those expenses will be deductible for tax purposes in year 4 when the liability is expected to be paid. Those temporary differences are estimated to result in net taxable amounts in future years as presented at bottom of this page.

This example assumes that the enacted tax rates for years 2–4 are 20% for the first $50,000 of taxable income, 30% for the next $50,000, and 40% for taxable income over $100,000. The liability for deferred tax consequences is measured at top of page 234.

	Year 2	Year 3	Year 4
Taxable amounts	$70,000	$110,000	$60,000
Deductible amount	—	—	(20,000)
Net taxable amounts	$70,000	$110,000	$40,000

* *Source*: Financial Accounting Standards Board, FASB No. 96, "Accounting for Income Taxes," Stamford, CT, December 1987, p. 32.

	Year 2	Year 3	Year 4
20% tax on first $50,000	$10,000	$10,000	$8,000
30% tax on next $50,000	6,000	15,000	—
40% tax on over $100,000	—	4,000	—
	$16,000	$29,000	$8,000

A deferred tax liability is recognized for $53,000 (the total of the taxes payable for years 2–4) at the end of year 1.

Deferred Tax Asset

A deferred tax asset results in a future deductible amount (for tax purposes) that can only be recognized as an asset in the current year if the entity is certain to have taxable income in the future. Thus, a deferred tax asset can be booked only for the amount of the certain future deductibility of the item for tax purposes (e.g., resulting from temporary differences due to deferred tax liabilities already existing).

■ Example

In 19X8, a company sold a fixed asset reporting a gain of $70,000 for book purposes which was deferred for tax purposes (installment method) until 19X9. In addition, in 19X8, $40,000 of subscription income was received in advance. The income was recognized for tax purposes in 19X8 but was deferred for book purposes until 19X9.

The deferred tax asset may be recorded because the deductible amount in the future ($40,000) offsets the taxable amount ($70,000). Assuming a 34% tax rate and income taxes payable of $100,000, the entry in 19X8 is

Income Tax Expense	110,200	
Deferred Tax Asset ($40,000 × 34%)	13,600	
Deferred Tax Liability ($70,000 × 34%)		23,800
Income Taxes Payable		100,000

Note: The deferred tax asset can be recognized only up to the later years' deferred tax liabilities caused from temporary differences. Thus, if the gain on the sale of fixed assets was $25,000, the maximum amount of deferred revenue that could be recognized as a deferred tax asset would be $25,000. In this case, the entry is

Income Tax Expense	100,000	
Deferred Tax Asset (maximum up to deferred liability)	8,500	
Deferred Tax Liability ($25,000 × 34%)		8,500
Income Taxes Payable		100,000

A deferred tax asset can also be recognized for the tax benefit of deductible amounts realizable by carrying back a loss from future years to reduce taxes paid in the current or a prior year.

The restrictions on the recording of the deferred tax asset is based on *conservatism*.

Tax Rates

Tax rates in later years may be different. Further, a change in tax law may occur.

Different Tax Rates in the Future

Deferred taxes are reflected at the amounts of settlement when the temporary differences reverse.

■ Example

Assume in 19X3 a cumulative temporary difference of $200,000 that will reverse in the future generating the following taxable amounts and tax rate:

	19X4	19X5	19X6	Total
Reversals	$60,000	$90,000	$50,000	$200,000
Tax rate	×0.34	×0.30	×0.25	
Deferred tax liability	$20,400	$27,000	$12,500	$ 59,900

On December 31, 19X3, the deferred tax liability is recorded at $59,900.

A future tax rate can be used *only* if it has been enacted by law.

While there may be graduated tax rates, the highest tax rate may be used when the difference is not material.

Change in Tax Rate

Immediately reflect the impact of a change in tax rate on the accounts. Tax expense and deferred tax are appropriately adjusted in the year of change.

■ Example

Assume at the end of 19X2, a law is passed reducing the tax rate from 34% to 30% starting in 19X4. In 19X2, there was deferred profit of $100,000, showing a deferred tax liability of $34,000 as of 19X2. The gross profit is to be reflected equally in 19X3, 19X4, 19X5, and 19X6. Thus, the deferred tax liability at the end of 19X2 is $31,000, as shown at the bottom of this page.

The appropriate entry in 19X2 is

Deferred Tax Liability	3,000	
Income Tax Expense		3,000

Purchase Combination

In a purchase combination, the net assets acquired are reflected at their gross fair values with a separate deferred tax balance for the applicable tax effects. Further, a temporary difference will occur for the difference between the financial reporting and tax basis of assets and liabilities acquired. If the acquired company has an operating loss or tax credit carry forward, it may be used to reduce the deferred tax liability of the acquired company.

Disclosures

Disclosure should be made of the types of temporary differences that have occurred causing a material deferred tax liability or asset. An example is the disclosure that ACRS is used for tax and straight-line depreciation is used for books.

If a deferred tax liability is *not* recognized, disclosure should be made of the following:

• Description of the kinds of temporary differences for which *no* recognition has been given to a deferred tax liability and the types of events that would result in tax recognition of the temporary differences

• Cumulative amount of each kind of temporary difference

A reconciliation should exist between the reported amount of tax expense and the tax expense that would have occurred using federal statutory tax rates. The reconciliation should be in terms of percentages or dollar amounts. If statutory tax rates do not exist, use the regular tax rates for alternative tax systems. Disclosure should be given of the estimated amount and the nature of each material reconciling item.

Disclosure should be made of the provisions of intercorporate tax-sharing arrangements and tax-related balances due to or from affiliates.

Extensions of Tax Allocation

In accordance with APB Opinions No. 23 and 24, undistributed earnings (parent/investor share of subsidiary/investee income less dividends received) are considered to be temporary differences.

The rationale for this treatment is based on the basic presumption that such earnings will eventually be transferred.

	19X3	19X4	19X5	19X6	Total
Reversals	$25,000	$25,000	$25,000	$25,000	
Tax rate	×0.34	×0.30	×0.30	×0.30	
Deferred tax liability	$ 8,500	$ 7,500	$ 7,500	$ 7,500	$31,000

Temporary Difference

Income taxes related to temporary differences should be accounted for in accordance with FASB No. 96. In the case of investee income arising from the application of APB No. 18, if evidence indicates eventual realization by disposition of investment, income taxes should be determined at capital gains or other appropriate rates.

Indefinite Reversal

There is no interperiod tax allocation in the case of indefinite reversal. Indefinite reversal is when undistributed earnings in a foreign subsidiary will indefinitely be postponed or when earnings will be remitted in a tax-free liquidation.

If there is a change in circumstances and the presumption of indefinite reversal no longer holds, there should be an adjustment to tax expense.

Disclosure should be made of the declaration to reinvest indefinitely or to remit tax free, and the cumulative amount of undistributed earnings.

Amount of Temporary Difference

Of the dividends received from affiliated corporations 80% are generally exempt from tax. Consequently, the temporary difference is equal to 20% of the undistributed earnings (parent/investor interest less dividends received).

INCREMENTAL ANALYSIS Incremental (differential) analysis is an approach to choosing the best decision alternative that utilizes the concept of *relevant* costs. Under this approach, the decision involves the following steps:

1. Gather all revenue and cost data for each decision alternative.
2. Drop the *sunk* costs, since they are past costs and therefore are irrelevant to the decision.

3. Drop those costs that do not differ between alternatives. Only consider incremental revenue and cost data.
4. Select the best alternative based on the remaining data.

■ Example

A company produces three products, X, Y, and Z, from a joint process. Joint manufacturing costs for the year were $100,000. Product Z may be sold at the point of separation, called the *split-off point*, or processed further for more revenue. Specific data for product Z are as follows:

		Additional Cost and Sales Value After Further Processing	
Units Produced	Sales Value at Split-off	Sales	Cost
50,000	$250,000	$300,000	$25,500

The decision as to whether product Z should be sold at split-off or processed further can be analyzed using the incremental approach, under which incremental revenue is compared with incremental cost, as shown following.

Incremental sales revenue	$50,000 ($300,000 − $250,000)
Incremental costs, additional processing	25,500
Incremental gain	$24,500

The analysis shows that it pays to extend processing. Note that the joint production cost of $100,000 is not included in the analysis, since it is a sunk cost and therefore irrelevant to the decision. *See also* Relevant Costing; Sell-or-Process-Further Decision.

INDEXATION This refers to the assignment of escalator clauses to long-term contracts where wages, incomes, social security payments, and even the tax system can be readjusted automatically in order to prevent infla-

tion from distorting real income or other real values. This way an individual's gains are not taxed away, thereby reducing real income. *Escalator clause* is a provision in a long-term contract whereby these payments are tied to a comprehensive measure of price-level and cost-of-living changes. The consumer price index (CPI) and GNP deflator (implicit price index) are the measures most commonly used for indexation. Indexation may be partial or comprehensive in nature.

■ Example

Assume an employee's income goes up by 5% while prices go up by 5%. That means he/she has no more purchasing power than before, although the income tax will rise because a higher income will push one into a higher tax bracket. Indexation can avoid this situation by correcting the income for inflation. *See also* Inflation; Price Indices.

INDEX OF LEADING ECONOMIC INDICA-TORS
The index of leading economic indicators (economic indicator series) are the economic series of indicators that tend to predict future changes in economic activity; officially called *Composite Index of 12 Leading Indicators*. This series is the government's main barometer for forecasting business trends. Each of the series has shown a tendency to change before the economy makes a major turn—hence, the term "leading indicators." This series is published monthly by the U.S. Department of Commerce, consisting of:
• *Average workweek of production workers in manufacturing*
Employers find it a lot easier to increase the number of hours worked in a week than to hire more employees.
• *Initial claims for unemployment insurance*
The number of people who sign up for unemployment benefits signals changes in present and future economic activity.
• *Vendor performance*

Vendor performance represents the percentage of companies reporting slower deliveries. As the economy grows, firms have more trouble filling orders.
• *Change in total liquid assets*
This indicates changes in the amount of buying power readily available.
• *Percentage change in prices of sensitive crude materials*
Rises in prices of such critical materials as steel and iron usually mean factory demands are going up, which means factories plan to step up production.
• *Contracts and orders for plant and equipment*
Heavier contracting and ordering usually lead economic upswings.
• *Net business formation*
More businesses are created in anticipation of profit prospects. This usually leads rebounds by several months.
• *Stock prices*
A rise in the common stock index indicates expected profits and lower interest rates. Stock market advances usually precede business upturns by 3 to 8 months.
• *Money supply*
A rising money supply means easy money that sparks brisk economic activity. This usually leads recoveries by as much as 14 months.
• *New orders for manufacturers of consumer goods and materials*
New orders mean more workers hired, more materials and supplies purchased, and increased output. Gains in this series usually lead recoveries by as much as 4 months.
• *Residential building permits for private housing*
Gains in building permits signal business upturns.
• *Change in inventories*
Expected higher sales means the building up of inventories on the part of companies. Rises usually lead upswings by up to 8 months.

These 12 components of the index are adjusted for inflation. Rarely do these components of the index all go in the same direction at once. Each factor is weighted. The composite figure is designed to tell only in which direction business will go. It is not intended to forecast the magnitude of future ups and downs.

INFLATION This means a general rise in the price level. When inflation is present, a dollar today can buy more than a dollar in the future. Although the causes of inflation are diverse, a frequent source of inflationary pressures is the excess demand for goods and services which pulls product prices upward—*demand-pull inflation*. Rising wages and material costs may lead to the upward pressure on prices—*cost-push inflation*. Furthermore, excessive spending and/or heavy borrowing due to a budget deficit by the federal government can be inflationary. All of these sources may be intermingled at a particular point in time, making it difficult to pinpoint the cause for inflation.

There are numerous ways in which financial management can counteract the adverse effects of inflation upon the business, including:

1. *Selling price considerations*. Inflation risks can be passed on to consumers, as by increasing selling prices at short intervals (e.g., monthly). Further, the company can swiftly modify price catalogs and sales literature. Price quotations should be held only for short periods of time (e.g., 2 months).

Sales pricing policy should be determined on a next-in, first-out basis so that replacement costing is taken into account. Pricing ahead of inflation is a key weapon.

In sales agreements, a provision should exist that prices may be increased up to the point of actual shipment when a long lead time exists between the time an order is received and the goods are shipped. Further, in such cases, progress billings should be received as work is performed. Long-term contracts should include a "cost plus" provision, possibly tied into a Consumer Price Index.

2. *Control over costs*. Product components that typically experience excessive increases should be deemphasized. The company should contract for long-term purchase agreements and encourage suppliers to quote firm prices. A change in suppliers may be advisable if they give more liberal credit or easier terms.

When inflation is anticipated to worsen, the company should engage in future contracts in order to lock itself into buying raw materials at current lower prices.

It is recommended that competitive bids from insurance companies be periodically received and carriers changed when costs are beneficial.

A redesign of truck logistics may be made to accomplish economies of petroleum products.

3. *Marketing aspects*. Deemphasis should be on products significantly impacted by inflation (production, promotion). Inflation-resistant product substitutes should be emphasized.

4. *Labor implications*. Companies with automated facilities and a minimal labor force do better during inflation.

5. *Financial matters*. A good hedge against inflation is a tangible asset such as gold, silver, or real estate. Another is to borrow from insurance companies against the cash surrender value of life insurance. The rates provided for the policies are most likely less than the prevailing interest rate.

See also Price Indices.

INSTABILITY INDEX OF EARNINGS This is a measure of the variation between actual earnings and trend earnings. It equals:

$$I = \sqrt{\frac{\Sigma(y - y^T)^2}{n}}$$

where y = net income,
y^T = trend earnings,
n = number of periods.

Trend earnings is computed through the use of a trend equation solved by the computer. A low index indicates stability in the entity's profitability. A high index points to unstable earnings.

INSURANCE PROGRAMS provide a vital means of meeting the financial objectives of individuals. The type and amount of insurance depends on the age, assets, income, and needs of an individual. Insurance is basically replacement: life insurance provides income lost at the death of the wage earner; disability insurance assures income when the insured is not able to work full time; health insurance covers medical bills; and homeowners/casualty policies pay most of the costs of theft, accident, or fire.

Life Insurance

Life insurance is the most important tool of estate planning and one of the most valuable aids to financial planning. There are two basic types of life insurance policies—term insurance and whole life insurance. All other kinds of policies are variations on one or more of the two basic types.

1. *Term insurance*—protection for the client for a specified period of time. It pays a benefit only if the insured dies during the period covered by the policy. It provides for a level premium rate for a set period, after which the policy ceases and becomes void, except when renewed or changed to some other form of policy. It is the cheapest form of life insurance because it provides the most coverage for the least money.

2. *Whole life insurance* (cash value insurance or straight life insurance)—provides insurance protection by the payment of a fixed premium throughout the lifetime of the insured. However, in addition to death protec-

tion, whole life insurance has a savings element called "cash value." As the policies mature, they develop cash values representing the early surplus plus investment earnings. There are many variations of whole life insurance: universal life, variable life, single-premium whole life, adjustable life, and adjustable-premium life.

Aspects of term insurance:
• Protection for a specified period of time.
• Low initial premium.
• May be renewable and/or convertible.
• Premium rises with each new term.
• You or your dependents get nothing back if you survive the term.

Aspects of whole life insurance:
• Protection for life.
• Fixed premium.
• Growing cash value.
• Higher initial premium than term.
• You or your dependents always receive benefits.
• Available as universal, variable, single-premium whole life, adjustable life, and adjustable-premium life.
• Should be purchased with the intention of keeping for life or for a long period of time.

Disability Insurance

This insurance provides a regular cash income when an insured person is unable to work as a result of a covered illness, injury, or disease. Most disability payments are tax exempt as long as the individual policyholder pays the premium.

Health Insurance

For most people, health insurance is provided by the employer as a major fringe benefit. Otherwise, individual policies can be purchased. There are three kinds of medical or health insurance: basic hospitalization, basic medical/surgical, and major medical.

Property and Liability Insurance

Property and liability insurance is important to an individual's personal financial security. He or she can be successful in the job, investments, and the like, and yet be almost destroyed financially by an accident, disaster, or lawsuit for which there is not adequate property and liability insurance. It is wise to carry such insurance to protect family assets and future income from a catastrophic event. *See also* Personal Financial Planning.

INTANGIBLE ASSETS These are assets having a life of one year or more and lack physical substance (e.g., goodwill) or represent a right granted by the government (e.g., patent) or another company (e.g., franchise fee). APB 17 covers accounting for intangible assets, whether purchased or internally developed. The costs of intangibles *acquired* from others should be reported as assets. The cost equals the cash or fair market value of the consideration given. The individual intangibles that can be separately identified must be costed separately. If not separately identified, the intangibles are assigned a cost equal to the difference between the total purchase price and the cost of identifiable tangible and intangible assets. *Note*: Goodwill does not include identifiable assets.

The cost of developing and maintaining intangibles should be charged against earnings if the assets are not specifically identifiable, have indeterminate lives, or are inherent in the continuing business (e.g., goodwill). An example of internally developed goodwill that is expensed are the costs incurred in developing a name (e.g., Burger King).

All intangible assets are amortized over the period benefited using the straight-line method not exceeding a 40-year life. Factors in estimating useful lives include

•Legal, contractual, and regulatory provisions.

•Renewal or extension provisions. If a renewal occurs, the life of the intangible may be increased.

•Obsolescence and competitive factors.

•Product demand.

•Service lives of essential employees within the organization.

For example, an intangible may be enhanced because of good public relations staff.

Intangibles on the books before 1970 need *not* be amortized.

Footnote disclosure is made of the amortization period and method.

If a firm buys, on a step-by-step basis, an investment using the equity method, the fair value of the acquired assets and the goodwill for each step purchased must be separately identified.

When the purchase of assets results in goodwill, later sale of a separable portion of the entity acquired mandate a proportionate reduction of the goodwill account. A portion of the unamortized goodwill is included in the cost of assets sold.

Goodwill is recorded only in a business combination accounted for under the purchase method when the cost to the acquirer exceeds the fair market value of the net identifiable assets acquired. Goodwill may be determined by an individual appraiser, a purchase audit done by the acquiring company's public accounting firm, and so on. Goodwill is then amortized using the straight-line method over the period benefited, not exceeding 40 years. If the cost to the acquirer is less than the fair market value of the net identifiable assets acquired, a credit arises which reduces the noncurrent assets acquired on a proportionate basis (excluding long-term investments). If a credit still remains, it is treated as a deferred credit not to be amortized over more than 40 years under the straight-line method.

Goodwill is theoretically equal to the present value of future excess earnings of a company over other companies in the industry. However, it is difficult to predict the length of time superior earnings will occur. Some

factors involved in the makeup of goodwill are superior salesforce, outstanding management talent, effective advertising, strategic location, and dependable suppliers.

In buying a new business, a determination must often be made as to the estimated value of the goodwill. Two possible methods that can be used are (1) capitalization of earnings and (2) capitalization of excess earnings.

■ Example

The following information is available for a business that we are contemplating acquiring:

Expected average annual earnings	$10,000
Expected future value of net assets exclusive of goodwill	$45,000
Normal rate of return	20%

Using the capitalization-of-earnings approach, goodwill is estimated at:

Total asset value implied ($10,000/20%)	$50,000
Estimated fair value of assets	45,000
Estimated goodwill	$ 5,000

Assuming the same facts except a capitalization rate of excess earnings of 22% and using the capitalization of excess earnings method, goodwill is estimated at:

Expected average annual earnings	$10,000
Return on expected average assets ($45,000 × 20%)	9,000
Excess earnings	$ 1,000

Goodwill ($1,000/0.22) = $4,545

■ Example

The net worth of ABC Company excluding goodwill is $800,000, and profits for the last 4 years were $750,000. Included in the later figure are extraordinary gains of $50,000 and nonrecurring losses of $30,000. It is desired to determine a selling price of the business. A 12% return on net worth is deemed typical for the industry. The capitalization of excess earnings is 45% in determining goodwill.

Net income for 4 years	$750,000
Less: Extraordinary gains	50,000
Add: Nonrecurring losses	30,000
Adjusted 4-year earnings	$730,000
Average earnings ($730,000/4)	$182,500
Normal earnings ($800,000 × 0.12)	96,000
Excess annual earnings	$ 86,500

Excess earnings capitalized at 45%:

$$\frac{\$86,500}{0.45} = \$192,222$$

The determination of goodwill and its amortization can have a large impact on the balance sheet and financial position of a company. A good example of this is when Turner Broadcasting attempted to take over CBS. Turner assigned the difference of what he would pay for CBS and its book value entirely to goodwill and amortized this amount over 40 years. CBS claimed a smaller amount should be assigned to goodwill and their assets revalued, which would have lowered the net income of the combined Turner–CBS Company. Here, the valuation of goodwill was extremely important in this takeover battle.

Internally generated costs to derive a patented product are expensed such as R&D incurred in developing a new product. The patent is recorded at the registration fees to secure and register it, legal fees in successfully defending it in court, and the cost of acquiring competing patents from outsiders. The patent account is amortized over its useful life, not exceeding 17 years. If an intangible asset is deemed worthless, it should be written off, recognizing an extraordinary item.

Organization costs are the costs incurred to incorporate a business (e.g., legal fees). They are deferred and amortized.

Leaseholds are rent paid in advance and are amortized over the life of the lease.

If the amortization expense of an intangible is not tax deductible (e.g., amortization of goodwill), a permanent difference arises. Thus, no interperiod tax allocation is involved.

INTEGER PROGRAMMING This is a form of mathematical programming. It is really a special case of *linear programming* where all (or some) variables are restricted to being integers (whole numbers). For example, quantities like 5.25 cars, 32.75 tables, and 1½ persons may be unrealistic. Simply rounding off the linear programming solution to the nearest whole numbers may not produce a feasible solution. The integer programming method allows managers to find the optimal *integer* solution to a problem without violating any of the constraints. *See also* Linear Programming; Mathematical Programming.

INTEGRATED SOFTWARE Integrated software comprises two or more modules that perform together. Integrated packages permit moving data between several programs. *Remember*: They utilize common, comprehendable commands (instructions) and file structures for all applications. In effect, you have multiple applications in memory simultaneously.

Integrated software may combine functions like word processing, spreadsheets, data base management, telecommunications, and graphics. In effect, different processing tasks are carried out with the same data file. For example, data derived from spreadsheets or data base management files may be graphed. Word processing software can merge text with data from other records. From a data base of client names you could print labels for mailing of overdue balance letters.

When should an integrated package be used? If identical source information is to be used for varying purposes and activities, an integrated package is recommended. It is superior to an individual package, which requires the practitioner to load each program and data file each time another package is required. With integrated software, a sequence of applications is accomplished without the need to go from separate, distinct programs. Also, some canned software will not perform with files derived from other programs.

Questions to Ask When Selecting an Integrated Package

• Are all applications in the package necessary?

• What is the quality of individual tasks within each program that will be used the most?

• Does the integration work satisfactorily?

• Does one of the programs in the integrated package duplicate already existing software?

• Is there a possibility of modifying applications?

• Does the integrated package run well on the present computer? If not, what additional hardware must be acquired?

With an integrated package, one function is transferred to another. Windows depict the contents of each on the monitor.

■ Example

ABC Company's integrated software:

• Generates an accounting file via data base management systems

• Has an electronic worksheet perform what-if calculations

• Graphs the options with a graphics package

• Prints out a report, schedule, and management letter with the word processing program

• Sends the letter by electronic mail to the client via a data communications package

You can use integrated software to accomplish the following accounting applications:

• Develop a model to test various scenarios (e.g., effect of tax law changes on the operations and accounts)

• Prepare consolidated worksheets and statements

• Prepare reports and related graphical information

• Make an appraisal of business segments

- Prepare and analyze financial data
- Evaluate trends

■ Example

Ashton-Tate's Framework™ is an integrated package of word processing, spreadsheet, graphics, data base management, and communications.

INTEREST METHOD OF AMORTIZATION (SCIENTIFIC AMORTIZATION)   Interest expense (or interest revenue) equals the interest rate times the carrying value of the liability (or receivable) at the beginning of the period. It is the preferred method of amortizing bond discount or bond premium. *See also* Bond Accounting.

INTEREST RATE FUTURES CONTRACT   This contract gives the holder the right to a specified amount of the related debt security at a future time (typically, no more than 3 years). It may cover Treasury bills, commercial paper, GNMA certificates, and certificates of deposit.

Interest rate futures are stated in percentage terms of the par value of the related obligation. The contract's value is directly related to interest rates. For example, contract value will increase when interest rates decrease, and vice versa. As the contract's price increases, the buyer of the contract profits while the seller loses. A change of one basis point in interest rates results in a price change. A basis point equals $\frac{1}{100}$ of 1%.

The buyer of the contract will not typically take possession of the financial instrument. The contract is basically employed either for hedging or speculation purposes on future interest rates and security prices. For instance, the banker may utilize the contract to hedge the bank's position in financial instruments.

■ Example

Company XYZ will issue bonds in 4 months. Terms of the underwriting are now being made up. There is an anticipation that interest rates will increase in the next 4 months. Investors can hedge by selling short the Treasury bills. An increase in interest rates will cause a lower price to reacquire the interest rate future with the resulting profit. This profit reduces the higher interest cost of the debt.

Financial futures may attract speculators due to the significant return possible on a small investment. With a large contract (e.g., $500,000 Treasury bill), a small change in the contract's price may generate a substantial profit. *Caution*: Do not forget the risk involved. Volatile securities may exist, resulting in substantial loss. A speculator anticipating rising interest rates will desire to sell an interest rate future because it will shortly decline in value.

INTERIM REPORTING   Interim periods are essential parts of the annual period. Interim reports may be issued at appropriate reporting intervals, such as quarterly or monthly. Complete financial statements or summarized data may be given. Interim financial statements do not have to be certified. It is recommended that interim balance sheets and funds flow data be provided. If not presented, material changes in liquid assets, working capital, long-term debt, and stockholders' equity should be disclosed.

Usually, interim reports include results of the current interim period and the cumulative year-to-date figures. Typically, comparisons are made to results of comparable interim periods for the prior year.

Interim results should be based on the accounting principles used in the last year's annual report unless a change has been made in the current year.

A gain or loss cannot be deferred to a later interim period except if such deferral would have been permissible for annual reporting.

Revenue from merchandise sold and services performed should be accounted for as earned in the interim period in the same way

as accounted for in annual reporting. If an advance is received in the first quarter and benefits the entire year, it should be allocated ratably to the interim periods affected.

Costs and expenses should be matched to related revenue in the interim period. If a cost cannot be associated with revenue in a future interim period, it should be expensed in the current period. Yearly expenses such as administrative salaries, insurance, pension plan expense, and year-end bonuses should be allocated to the quarters. The allocation basis may be based on such factors as time expired, benefit obtained, and activity.

The gross profit method can be used to estimate interim inventory and cost of sales. Disclosure should be made of the method, assumptions made, and material adjustments by reconciliations with the annual physical inventory.

A permanent inventory loss should be reflected in the interim period it occurs. A subsequent recovery is treated as a gain in the later interim period. However, if the change in inventory value is temporary, no recognition is given in the accounts.

When there is a temporary liquidation of the LIFO base with replacement expected by year-end, cost of sales should be based on replacement cost.

▪ Example

The historical cost of an inventory item is $10,000 with replacement cost expected at $15,000. The entry is

Cost of Sales	15,000	
Inventory		10,000
Reserve for Liquidation of LIFO Base		5,000

Note the Reserve for Liquidation of LIFO Base account is shown as a current liability.

When replenishment is made at year-end the entry is

Reserve for Liquidation of LIFO Base	5,000	
Inventory	10,000	
Cash		15,000

Volume discounts given to customers tied into annual purchases should be apportioned to the interim period based on the ratio of:

$$\frac{\text{Purchases for the interim period}}{\text{Total estimated purchases for the year}}$$

When a standard cost system is used, variances expected to be reversed by year-end may be deferred to an asset or liability account.

With regard to income taxes, the income tax provision includes current and deferred taxes. Federal and local taxes are provided for. The tax provision for an interim period should be cumulative (e.g., total tax expense for a 9-month period is shown in the third quarter based on a 9-month income). The tax expense for the 3-month period based on 3 months of revenue may also be presented (e.g., third quarter tax expense based on only the third quarter). In computing tax expense, the estimated annual effective tax rate should be used. The effective tax rate should be based on income from continuing operations. If a reliable estimate is not practical, the actual year-to-date effective tax rate should be used.

At the end of each interim period, a revision to the effective tax rate may be necessary, employing the best current estimates of the annual effective tax rate. The projected tax rate includes adjustment for net deferred credits. Adjustments should be contained in deriving the maximum tax benefit for year-to-date figures.

The estimated effective tax rate should incorporate all available tax credits (e.g., foreign tax credit) and available alternative tax methods in determining ordinary earnings. A change in tax legislation is reflected only in the interim period affected.

Income statement items after income from continuing operations (e.g., income from discontinued operations, extraordinary items, cumulative effect of a change in accounting principle) should be presented net of the tax

effect. The tax effect on these unusual line items should be reflected only in the interim period in which they actually occur. For example, we should not predict items before they occur. Prior period adjustments in the retained earnings statement are also shown net of tax when they take place.

The tax implication of an interim loss is recognized *only* when realization of the tax benefit is assured beyond reasonable doubt. If a loss is expected for the remainder of the year and carry back is not possible, the tax benefits typically should not be recognized.

The tax benefit of a previous year operating loss carry forward is recognized as an extraordinary item in each interim period to the extent that income is available to offset the loss carry forward.

When a change in principle is made in the first interim period, the cumulative effect of a change-in-principle account should be shown net of tax in the first interim period. If a change in principle is made in a quarter other than the first (e.g., third quarter), we assume the change was made at the beginning of the first quarter, showing the cumulative effect in the first quarter. The interim periods will have to be *restated* using the new principle (e.g., first, second, and third quarters).

When interim data for previous years is presented for comparative purposes, data should be restated to conform with newly adopted policies. Alternatively, disclosure can be made of the effect on prior data had the new practice been applied to that period.

For a change in principle, disclosure should be made of the nature and justification in the interim period of change. The effect of the change on per share amounts should be given.

Disclosure should be made of seasonality aspects affecting interim results. Also disclose contingencies. When a change in the estimated effective tax rate occurs, it should be disclosed. Further, if a fourth quarter is not presented, any material adjustments to that quarter must be commented upon in the footnotes to the annual report. If an event is immaterial on an annual basis but material in the interim period, it should be disclosed. Purchase or pooling transactions should be noted.

The financial statement presentation for prior period adjustments follow:

• Include in net income for the current period the portion of the effect related to current operations.

• Restate earnings of impacted prior interim periods of the current year to include the portion related thereto.

• If the prior period adjustment affects prior years, include it in the earnings of the first interim period of the current year.

The criteria to be met for prior period adjustments in interim periods follow:

• Materiality

• Estimable

• Identified to a prior interim period

Examples of prior period adjustments for interim reporting are

• Error corrections

• Settlement of litigation or claims

• Adjustment of income taxes

• Renegotiation proceedings

• Utility revenue under rate-making processes

Earnings per share are computed for interim purposes the same way as for annual purposes.

Segmental disposal is separaely shown in the interim period it occurs.

INTERNAL AUDIT An internal audit is performed by auditors working for the business entity itself. They independently perform an audit review and appraisal of the firm's accounting records, controls, and operations. In addition, a determination is made as to whether assets are being properly safeguarded. It is also ascertained whether management policies and procedures are being

followed throughout the entity. Often, the internal auditors report directly to the Audit Committee of the Board of Directors so that they may objectively provide their viewpoints of management's performance. Recommendations for improvement in the accounting system are made.

INTERNAL CONTROL STRUCTURE Probably, this is the most important aspect of the auditor's examination. As per Statement on Auditing Standards No. 55, the auditor must consider the internal control structure when planning the audit and incorporate internal control considerations in gathering audit evidence. The major elements of internal control are the control environment, accounting system, and control procedures. All must be understood by the auditor to plan the audit. The CPA must be familiar with relevant policies, procedures, and records, and whether they have been put into operation. Control risk should be appraised in relation to financial statement assertions. This evaluation at the assertion level should be at the maximum (highest control risk) when an inadequate internal control structure exists.

The internal control system of a client is comprised of an organizational plan, accounting records, procedures, and controls to reasonably assure that the entity's assets are safeguarded and reliability exists in the financial records to fairly present financial position and opeating results.

An adequate internal control system should have the following attributes:
- Restricted access to assets
- Proper authorization of transaction
- Agreement between the amount per the books and the physical existence of the assets
- Segregation of duties, including a separation between individuals resonsible for keeping the books and those having physical custody of assets
- Technically competent individuals performing accounting tasks

- Recording transactions so that they reflect their substance

An examination of internal controls is necessary so that the auditor can determine his or her reliance on it in order to formulate the degree and timing of necessary substantive tests. Under the second fieldwork standard of GAAS, the auditor must perform an adequate evaluation of the client's internal control structure. In conducting the internal control analysis, the auditor should use the cycle approach, involving the selection of broad areas of activity so that specific transactions may be tested. The major cycles are for revenue (e.g., credit approval, invoicing, cash receipts), expenditure (e.g., purchasing, receiving, and cash payments), production (e.g., inventories and fixed assets), financing (e.g., notes receivable, leases), and external reporting (e.g., GAAP, financial statement preparation).

The preliminary review of internal control structure gives the auditor an overall understanding of the client's control environment, transaction flow, and means of data processing. This review encompasses the following aspects:
- Prior experience with the client and inquiry of client personnel
- Observing client activities
- Referring to previous years' workpapers
- Evaluation of relevant client material such as accounting manuals

In completing the review, documentation must exist, such as in the form of flow charts and questionnaires.

When the internal control structure may be relied upon, compliance tests will be performed and results evaluated.

As per AICPA Statement on Auditing Standards No. 60, the auditor must report deficiencies in the control environment, accounting system, and control procedures to the audit committee of the company. To be reported are matters representing material deficiencies in the design or operation of the

internal control structure that could negatively impact the company's ability to record, process, summarize, and report financial data in the financial statements. *See also* Compliance Test; Substantive Test.

INTERNAL RATE OF RETURN (IRR)
IRR, also called time adjusted rate of return (TARR), is the rate of interest that equates the initial investment (I) with the present value (PV) of future cash inflows. That is, at IRR, $I = PV$, or NPV (net present value) $= 0$. Under the internal rate of return method, the decision rule is: Accept the project if IRR exceeds the cost of capital; otherwise, reject the proposal.

■ Example

Consider the following data:

Initial investment	$12,950
Estimated life	10 years
Annual cash inflows	$ 3,000
Cost of capital (minimum required return)	12%

We will set up the following equality ($I = PV$):

$$\$12,950 = \$3,000 \times PVIFA$$

Then $PVIFA = \$12,950/\$3,000 = 4.317$, which stands somewhere between 18% and 20% in the 10-year line of Table. The interpolation follows:

	PV Factor	
18%	4.494	4.494
IRR		4.317
20%	4.192	
Difference	0.302	0.177

Therefore, $IRR = 18\% + (0.177/0.302)$
$(20\% - 18\%)$
$= 18\% + 0.586(2\%)$
$= 18\% + 1.17\% = 19.17\%$

Since the investment's IRR (19.17%) is greater than the cost of capital (12%), the investment should be accepted.

The IRR method is easy to use as long as cash inflows are even from year to year. Where the cash flows are uneven, the IRR must be determined by trial and error. Assume, for example, that a company is considering an investment project that promises cash inflows of $400,000, $600,000, and $1,000,000 for each of the next 3 years for a given investment of $800,000. The IRR is found by selecting a rate and discounting the cash inflows. If the PV is greater than I, select a higher rate until one is found that equates the PV of the cash inflows with I. In this example, the IRR is approximately 20%, determined as follows:

Present Values (Based on Table 3) = PVIF

Annual Cash Inflows	20%	22%
$ 400,000	$333,200	$328,000
600,000	416,400	403,200
1,000,000	57,900	55,100
	$807,500	$786,300

An advantage of the IRR method is that it considers the *time value of money* and is therefore more exact and realistic than *the simple (or accounting) rate of return*. Disadvantages are (1) it fails to recognize the varying size of investment in competing projects and their respective dollar profitabilities; and (2) in limited cases, where there are multiple reversals in the cash-flow streams, the project could yield more than one internal rate of return.

INVENTORY CONTROL AND MANAGEMENT
This is maintaining the optimum inventory level through inventory records. This is done to maximize profits by creating a good balance between inventory investment and smooth, continuous production, for a profit-oriented firm. For a nonprofit entity, this means minimizing costs.

Maintaining excessive inventories may mean risk of carrying obsolete items and high carrying costs. Maintaining inadequate in-

ventories may mean losing sales and poor production control. Maintaining adequate inventory means some hedge against sudden price increases and being able to serve customers promptly, in order to satisfy their needs. By maintaining a functional inventory supply, a company will be able to protect itself against unplanned changes in supply and demand.

An optimal safety stock level should exist. It requires a balancing of expected costs of stockouts against the costs of carrying the additional inventory.

Good internal control over inventory is necessary to guard against theft and other irregularities. A surprise inventory count should periodically occur to assure agreement between the book inventory and physical inventory.

Major shortages may take place and go unnoticed for a long time period if satisfactory control is lacking. Inventory is an area in which many frauds take place. Good control is needed in the acquisition and handling phases. Segregation should exist in purchasing, receiving, storing, and shipping of inventories. There should be a separation of the accounting for and the custody of merchandise.

An inventory control system should accomplish the following objectives: (1) proper record keeping; (2) implementing inventory decision models; (3) reporting exceptions; (4) aiding in forecasting usage and needs; and (5) maintaining proper safeguards to prevent misuse. *See also* ABC Inventory Method; Economic Order Quantity (EOQ); Inventory Planning and Control.

INVENTORY PLANNING AND CONTROL One of the most common problems that faces managerial accountants is that of inventory planning and control. This is understandable because inventory usually represents a sizable portion of a firm's total assets. Excess funds tied up in inventory is a drag on profitability.

The purpose of inventory planning and control is to develop policies that will achieve an optimal investment in inventory. This objective is achieved by determining the optimal level of inventory necessary to minimize inventory-related costs.

Inventory costs fall into three categories:
1. Order costs include all costs associated with preparing a purchase order.
2. Carrying costs include storage costs for inventory items plus opportunity cost (i.e., the cost incurred by investing in inventory).
3. Shortage (stockout) costs include those costs incurred when an item is out of stock. These include the lost contribution margin on sales plus lost customer goodwill.

There are many inventory planning and control models available that try to answer basically the following questions:
1. How much to order?
2. When to order?

They include the basic economic order quantity (EOQ) model, the reorder point, and the determination of safety stock.

Economic Order Quantity (EOQ)

The economic order quantity (EOQ) model determines the order size that minimizes the sum of carrying and ordering costs. Demand is assumed to be constant throughout the year. EOQ is computed as

$$EOQ = \sqrt{2OD/C}$$

where O = cost of placing an order.
D = annual demand (usage) in units,
and C = cost of carrying one unit in stock.
If the carrying cost is expressed as a percentage of average inventory value (say, 12% per year to hold inventory), then the denominator value in the EOQ formula would be 12% times the price of an item.

■ Example 1

Assume ABC store buys sets of steel at $40 per set from an outside vendor. ABC will sell 6,400 sets evenly throughout the year.

ABC desires a 16% return (cost of borrowed money) on its inventory investment. In addition, rent, taxes, and so on for each set in inventory is $1.60. The ordering cost is $100 per order. Then the carrying cost per dozen is 16%($40) + $1.60 = $8.00. Therefore:

$$EOQ = \sqrt{\frac{2(6,400)(\$100)}{\$8.00}} = \sqrt{160,000} = 400 \text{ sets}$$

Total inventory costs = Carrying cost per unit × $\frac{EOQ}{2}$

+ Ordering cost per order

× $\frac{\text{Annual demand}}{EOQ}$

= ($8.00)(400/2)
+ ($100)(6,400/400)

= $1,600 + $1,600 = $3,200

Total number of orders per year
= Annual demand/EOQ = 6,400/400
= 16 orders

The EOQ model is depicted graphically in Figure 1.

There are some basic assumptions underlying the EOQ model. They are
1. Demand is constant and known with certainty.
2. Depletion of stock is linear and constant.
3. No discount is allowed for quantity purchases.
4. *Lead time*, which is the time interval between placing an order and receiving delivery, is a constant (i.e., stockout is not possible).

Reorder Point (ROP)

Reorder point (economic order point), which answers *when* to place a new order, requires a knowledge about the lead time. Reorder point (ROP) can be calculated as follows:

Reorder point = Average usage per unit of lead time
× Lead time + Safety stock

First, multiply average daily (or weekly) usage by the lead time in days (or weeks) yielding the lead time demand. Then add safety stock to this to provide for the variation in lead time demand to determine the reorder point. If average usage and lead time are both certain, no safety stock is necessary and should be dropped from the formula.

■ Example 2

Assume in Example 1, lead time is constant at 1 week and there are 50 working weeks in a year. Then reorder point is 128 sets = (6,400 sets/50 weeks) × 1 week. Therefore, when the inventory level drops to 128 sets, the new order should be placed. Figure 2 shows this inventory system when the order quantity is 400 sets and the reorder point is 128 sets.

Figure 1

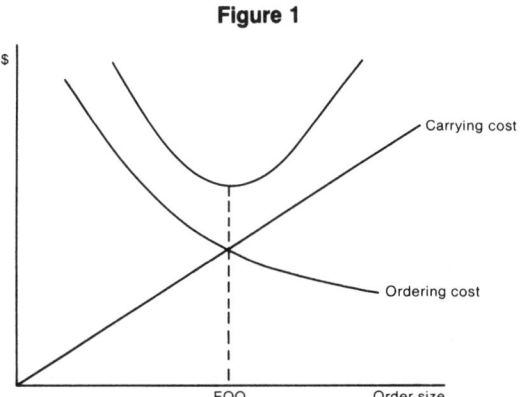

Figure 2 Basic Inventory System With EOQ and Reorder Point

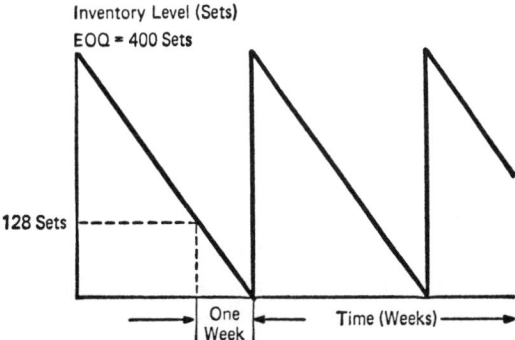

Computation of Safety Stock

Safety Stock Levels in Units	Stockout and Probability	Average Stockout in Units	Average Stockout Costs	No. of Orders	Total Annual Stockout Cost	Carrying Costs	Total
0	50 with 0.2 100 with 0.1 150 with 0.1	35[a]	$420[b]	16	$6,720[c]	0	$7,140
50	50 wlth 0.1 100 with 0.1	15	180	16	2,880	400[d]	3,280
100	50 with 0.1	5	60	16	960	800	1,760
150	0	0	0	16	0	1,200	1,200

[a] 50(.2) + 100(.1) + 150(.1) = 10 + 10 + 15 = 35 units
[b] 35 units × $12 = $420
[c] $420 × 16 times = $6,720
[d] 50 units × $8 = $400

Assumptions and Applications

The EOQ model described here is appropriate for a pure inventory system; that is, for single-item, single-stage inventory decisions for which joint costs and constraints can be ignored. They assume that both lead time and demand rates are constant and known with certainty. This may be unrealistic; however, these models have proved to be useful in inventory planning for many firms.

Many situations exist where such an assumption holds or nearly holds. Subcontractors who must supply parts on a regular basis to a primary contractor face a constant demand. Even where demand varies, the assumption of uniform usage is not unrealistic. Demand for automobiles, for example, varies from week to week but, over a season, the weekly fluctuations tend to cancel each other out so that seasonal demand can be assumed constant.

Safety Stock and Reorder Point

When lead time and demand are not certain, the firm must carry extra units of inventory, called *safety stock*, as protection against possible stockouts. Stockouts can be quite expensive. Lost sales and disgruntled customers are examples of external costs. Idle machines and disrupted production scheduling are ex-

amples of internal costs. We will illustrate the probability approach to show how the optimal size of safety stock can be determined in the presence of stockout costs.

■ Example 3

Recall from Example 2 that the reorder point is 128 sets. If either lead time or demand is variable, the store needs to carry an extra stock as safety. Suppose that the total usage over a 1-week period is expected to be

Total Usage	Probability
78	0.2
128	0.4
178	0.2
228	0.1
278	0.1
	1.00

Suppose further that a stockout cost is estimated at $12 per set. Recall that the carrying cost is $8 per set. The computation at the top of the page shows that the total costs are minimized at $1,200, when a safety stock of 150 sets is maintained. Therefore, the reorder point is 128 sets + 150 sets = 278 sets.

INVENTORY VALUATION Inventory may be valued at the lower of cost or market value. Specialized inventory methods may be used

such as retail, retail lower of cost or market, retail LIFO, and dollar value LIFO. Losses on purchase commitments should be recognized in the accounts.

If ending inventory is overstated, cost of sales is understated, and net income is overstated. If beginning inventory is overstated, cost of sales is overstated and net income is understated.

Lower of cost or market value method—inventories are recorded at the lower of cost or market value for conservatism purposes applied on a total basis, category basis, or individual basis. The method used must be consistently applied.

If cost is below market value (replacement cost), cost is taken. If market value is below cost, we start with market value. However, market value cannot exceed the ceiling, which is net realizable value (selling price less costs to complete and dispose). If it does, the cost is chosen. Further, market value cannot be less than the floor, which is net realizable value less a normal profit margin. If market value is less than the floor, the floor value is used. Of course, market value is used when it lies between the ceiling and floor. The following diagram may be helpful:

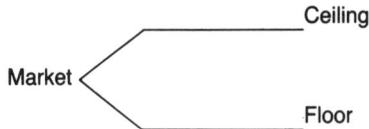

Ceiling

Market

Floor

■ Example

The lower of cost or market value method is being applied on an item-by-item basis. The circled figure is the appropriate valuation.

Product	Cost	Market	Ceiling	Floor
A	($5)	$7	$9	$6
B	14	12	(11)	7
C	18	(15)	16	12
D	20	12	18	(16)
E	(6)	5	12	7

Note that in case E, market value of $5 was originally selected. The market value of $5 exceeded the floor of $7, so the floor value would be used. However, if after applying the lower of cost or market value rule the valuation derived ($7) exceeds the cost ($6), the cost figure is more conservative and thus is used.

Note that if market (replacement cost) is below the original cost but the selling price has not likewise declined, no loss should be recognized. To do so would create an abnormal profit margin in the future period.

The lower of cost or market value method is not used with LIFO, since under LIFO current revenue is matched against current costs.

Retail method—used by department stores and other large retail businesses. These businesses usually carry inventory items at retail selling price. The retail method is used to estimate the ending inventory at cost by employing a cost to retail (selling price) ratio. The ending inventory is first determined at selling price and then converted to cost. Markups and markdowns are both considered in arriving at the cost to retail ratio resulting in a higher ending inventory than the retail lower of cost or market value method.

Retail lower of cost or market value method (conventional retail)—a modification of the retail method and preferable to it. In computing the cost to retail ratio, markups but not markdowns are considered, resulting in a lower inventory figure.

The following example illustrates the accounting difference between the retail method and the retail lower of cost or market value method.

■ Example   Retail Method vs. Retail Lower of Cost or Market Value Method

		Cost	Retail	
Inventory—1/1		16,000	30,000	
Purchases		30,000	60,000	
Purchase returns		(5,000)	(10,000)	
Purchase discount		(2,000)		
Freight in		1,000		
Markups	25,000			
Markup cancellations	5,000			
Net markups			20,000	
Total		40,000	100,000	(40%)
Markdowns	22,000			
Markdown cancellations	2,000			
Net markdowns			20,000	
Cost of goods available		40,000	80,000	(50%)
Deduct:				
Sales	55,000			
Sales returns	5,000		50,000	
Inventory—retail			30,000	
Retail method:				
At cost 50% × 30,000			15,000	
Retail lower of cost or market method:				
40% × 30,000			12,000	

Retail LIFO—in computing ending inventory, the mechanics of the retail method are basically followed. Beginning inventory is *excluded* and both markups and markdowns are *included* in computing the cost to retail ratio. A decrease in inventory during the period is deducted from the most recently added layer and then subtracted from layers in the inverse order of addition. A retail price index is used in restating inventory.

■ Example

Retail LIFO

Retail price indices follow:

19X7	100
19X8	104
19X9	110

19×8	Cost	Retail	
Inventory—Jan. 1 (base inv.)	80,000	130,000	
Purchases	240,000	410,000	
Markups		10,000	
Markdowns		(20,000)	
Total (exclude beg. inv.)	240,000	400,000	60%
Total (include beg. inv.)	320,000	530,000	
Sales		389,600	
19X8 inv.—end—retail		140,400 ◄	

Cost Basis	Cost	Retail		
19X8 Inventory in forms of				
19X7 prices 140,400 ÷ 1.04		135,000		
19X7 Base	80,000	130,000	130,000 × 1.04	135,200
19X8 Layer in 19X7 prices		5,000		
19X8 Layer in 19X8 prices		5,200	5,000 × 1.04	5,200
				140,400
19X8 LIFO cost 60% × 5,200	3,120			
	83,120	140,400		

19X9	Cost	Retail	
Inventory—Jan. 1	83,120	140,400	
Purchases	260,400	430,000	
Markups		20,000	
Markdowns		(30,000)	
Total (exclude beg. inv.)	260,400	420,000	62%
Total (include beg. inv.)	343,520	560,400	
Sales		408,600	
19X9 Inventory—end of retail		151,800	

Cost Basis	Cost	Retail		
19X9 Inventory in 19X7 prices 151,800 ÷ 1.10		138,000		
19X7 base	80,000	130,000	130,000 × 1.10	143,000
Excess over base year		8,000		
19X8 layer in 19X8 prices	3,120	5,000	5,000 × 1.10	5,500
19X9 layer in 19X7 prices		3,000		
19X9 layer in 19X9 prices		3,300	3,000 × 1.10	3,300
19X9 Increase in 19X9 prices				
LIFO cost 62% × 3,300	2,046			
	85,166	151,800		151,800

Dollar value LIFO—an extension of the historical cost principle. The method aggregates dollars instead of units into homogeneous groupings. The method assumes that an inventory decrease came from the last year.

The procedures under dollar value LIFO follow:

1. Restate ending inventory in the current year into base dollars by applying a price index.

2. Subtract the year 0 inventory in base dollars from the current year's inventory in base dollars.

3. Multiply the incremental inventory in the current year in base dollars by the price index to obtain the incremental inventory in current dollars.

4. Obtain the reportable inventory for the current year by adding to the year 0 inventory in base dollars the incremental inventory for the current year in current dollars.

■ Example

At 12/31/19X1, the ending inventory is $130,000 and the price index is 1.30. The base inventory on 1/1/19X1 was $80,000. The 12/31/19X1 inventory is computed following:

12/31/19X1 inventory in base dollars	
$130,000/1.30	$100,000
1/1/19X1 beginning base inventory	80,000
19X1 Increment in base dollars	$ 20,000
19X1 Increment in current year	
dollars	× 1.3
	$ 26,000
Inventory in base dollars	$ 80,000
Increment in current year dollars	26,000
Reportable inventory	$106,000

Losses on purchase commitments—significant net losses on purchase commitments should be recognized at the end of the reporting period.

■ Example

In 19X8, ABC Company committed itself to buy raw materials at $1.20 per pound. At the end of the year, before fulfilling the purchase commitment, the price of the materials dropped to $1 per pound. Conservatism dictates that a loss on purchase commitment of $0.20 per pound be recognized in 19X8. Loss on Purchase Commitment is debited and Allowance for Purchase Commitment Loss is credited.

Inventory valuation difficulties—while the basics of inventory cost measurement is easily stated, difficulties arise because of cost allocation problems. For example, idle capacity costs and abnormal spoilage costs may have to be written off immediately in the current year instead of being allocated as an element of inventory valuation. Furthermore, general and administrative expenses are inventoriable when they specifically relate to production activity.

Inventory stated at market value in excess of cost—in unusual circumstances, inventories may be stated in excess of cost. This may occur when there is no basis for cost apportionment (e.g., meat-packing industry). Market value may also be used when immediate marketability exists at quoted prices (e.g., certain precious metals or agricultural prod-ucts). Disclosure is necessary when inventory is stated above cost.

INVESTMENT BANKING involves public flotation, or sale, of a security issue. The investment banker acts as the intermediary between the issuing company and the security purchaser. Investment bankers conduct the following activities.

• *Underwriting*—the investment banker purchases a new security issue, pays the issuer, and markets the securities. The underwriter's compensation is the difference between the price at which the securities are sold to the public and the price paid to the issuing company.

• *Distributing*—the investment banker markets the security issue.

• *Giving advice*—the investment banker provides advice to the company regarding the optimal means of raising funds. The investment banker is knowledgeable regarding the alternative sources of long-term funds, debt and equity markets, and SEC regulations.

• *Providing funds*—the investment banker provides funds to the issuing company during the distribution period.

A *syndicate* is a group of investment bankers dealing with a particular issue. One investment banker among the group will be the manager, called *originating house*. The originating house underwrites the major amount of the issue. One bid price for the issue is made on behalf of the group, but the terms and features of the issue are set by the company.

Two kinds of underwriting syndicates are *divided* and *undivided*. In a *divided account*, each member's liability is limited in terms of participation. Once a member sells the securities assigned, that investment banker has no further obligation, regardless of whether the other members are able to sell their part of the security issue. In an *undivided account*, each member is obligated for unsold

securities up to the amount of the percentage participation, regardless of the number of securities that investment banker has sold. Most syndicates are of the undivided type.

In another approach to investment banking, the investment banker contracts to sell securities on a best-efforts basis, or as an agent for the issuer. The investment banker is not acting as an underwriter but instead sells the stock and obtains a commission on the sale. The investment banker may opt for this arrangement when he or she is not sure about the successful issuance of that security in the marketplace. *See also* Going Public.

INVESTMENT CENTER An investment center is a responsibility center within an organization that has control over revenue, cost, and investment funds. It is a *profit center* whose performance is evaluated on the basis of the return earned on invested capital. The corporate headquarters or division in a large decentralized organization would be an example of an investment center. *Return on investment* and *residual income* are two key performance measures of an investment center. *See also* Divisional Performance Evaluation; Profit Center; Responsibility Accounting.

INVESTMENT MANAGEMENT The maturity dates of investment should be staggered. For instance, if all the securities mature on one date, reinvestment may be subject to low returns if interest rates are low at the time.

Risk should be examined. You should analyze the degree of diversification and stability of the portfolio. It is best if securities are negatively correlated with each other. In this way, as one security goes up in price, another decreases in price. Positively correlated securities are risky since they all move in the same direction. Examples are auto, steel, and tire stocks.

Note whether declines in portfolio market values have been reflected in the accounts.

Use the ratio of revenue (dividend revenue, interest income) to the book value as a clue. The footnotes should be examined for subsequent event disclosure regarding any unrealized losses that have taken place in the portfolio. You may wish to adjust downward the extent to which an investment account can be realized in the event of such declines. You should also evaluate the riskiness of the portfolio by computing the standard deviation of its rate of return.

■ Example

Travis Company reports the following data for year-ends 19X1 and 19X2:

	19X1	19X2
Investments	$30,000	$33,000
Income from investments	4,000	3,200

The 19X2 annual report has a footnote titled "Subsequent Events," which indicates a $5,000 decline in the portfolio as of March 5, 19X3. The ratio of investment income to total investments went from 0.133 in 19X1 to 0.097 in 19X2, indicating a higher realization risk in the portfolio. Further, the post balance sheet disclosure of a $5,000 decline in value should prompt you to adjust downward the amount to which the year-end portfolio can be realized.

When formulating an optimal investment strategy, tax aspects must be taken into account. For instance, interest income on bonds is fully taxable, whereas dividend income has an 80% tax exclusion.

An investment portfolio that has a market value in excess of cost represents an undervalued asset.

By scrutinizing the investment portfolio, one may see signs of a company's attempt to gain a controlling interest in another. Such expansion may have positive or negative implications, depending on the reader's viewpoint. For example, expansion for diversification purposes tends to curtail operating risk.

INVESTMENT PLANNING   This involves formulating an investment strategy based on an individual's goals and financial characteristics. Investment planning should be aimed at arriving at a good mix of risk and reward. It should first outline the types of investments available, including their return potential and riskiness. It should take into account the general risks of investing, including those related to stock market price variability, inflation, and money market conditions. Investing is an integral part of all personal financial planning. Realistically, it can be done only with money left over after paying expenses, having proper insurance, and making pension contributions. The person with capital has a wide choice of investments.

Types of Investments

Investments can be classified into two forms: fixed dollar and variable dollar. Simply stated, fixed-income investments promise the investor a stated amount of income periodically. These include corporate bonds and preferred stocks, U.S. government securities, municipal bonds, and other savings instruments (savings accounts, certificates of deposit). On the other hand, variable-dollar investments are those where neither the principal nor the income is contractually set in advance in terms of dollars. That is, both the value and income of variable-dollar investments can change in dollar amount, either up or down, with changes in internal or external economic conditions. These include common stocks, mutual funds, real estate, variable annuities, and other tax-sheltered investments.

Factors to Be Considered in Investment-Planning Decisions

Consideration should be given to safety, return rate, stability of income and dividends, and liquidity.

Security of principal—the degree of risk involved in a particular investment. There should not be a loss of part or all of the initial investment.

Rate of return—the primary purpose of investing is to earn a return on the investor's capital in the form of interest, dividends, rental income, and capital appreciation. However, increasing total investment returns would entail greater investment risks. Thus, yield and degree of risk are directly related. An investor has to choose the priority that fits his or her circumstances and objectives.

Stability of income—when steady income is an important consideration, bond interest or stock dividends should be emphasized. This might be the situation for retired people or individuals who need to supplement their earned income on a regular basis with income from their outside investment.

Marketability and liquidity—the ability of an investor to find a ready market to dispose of the investment at the right price. *See also* Personal Financial Planning.

INVESTMENT SOFTWARE   The investment analyst is called upon to render investment advice to clients. Included are the tax ramifications of buy-and-sell decisions, selection of securities based on the client's tax rate and risk preferences, and keeping track of portfolio performance. Familiarity is required with available software so the analyst can best help the client in deriving the right portfolio and accurately monitoring security performance.

How Is the Portfolio? Investment maintenance software keeps track of investments in terms of shares, cost, and revenue. Some programs also include the price and dividend history of securities. Comparisons can be made with major market indicators.

Dow Jones Market Analyzer™ uses information from Dow Jones News/Retrieval to construct price and volume charts of securi-

ties, moving averages, and support and resistance lines.

Dow Jones Market Manager™ accesses Dow Jones News/Retrieval and enables the immediate valuation of a portfolio. There is a Tax Lot™ accounting system that records all transactions and assists in matching sell transactions with existing positions to lower the tax liability. Dow Jones Market Manager Plus™ handles all security types, stock splits, dividend distributions, and fractional shares. It separately totals federal, state, and municipal exempt funds.

Dow Jones Market Microscope™ uses fundamental analysis techniques. It obtains fundamental data from Media General Financial Services and Corporate Earnings Estimator available on line from Dow Jones News/ Retrieval. By preestablishing financial indicators, you can employ the data to generate screening reports and warnings. The program identifies securities meeting criteria standards and improves the timing of buys and sells.

Dow Jones Investment Evaluator™ is a basic portfolio management product. It permits the formulation of multiple portfolios comprising stocks, bonds, mutual funds, options, and other securities. It automatically values issue positions in terms of current value, unrealized gain or loss, and daily price change.

Value Line's Value Pac™ provides financial data and ratios on companies.

The Winning on Wall Street™ program by Samna Software permits the maintenance of a data base of securities, allows for technical analysis, and keeps track of the investment portfolio. It produces charts and graphs, allowing for technical analysis to properly time buys and sells. It shows points where a stock price exceeds or goes below price trend lines.

Standard and Poor's Stockpac II™ allows for the screening of takeover candidates for investment purposes.

Lotsoff Systems™ has several packages designed for financial institutions to keep track of commodity future transactions and to assist investors in hedging.

Option Strategy Calculation and Reporting™ software by ATS Software allows traders to analyze option trading strategies using price data. The program enables traders to appraise strategies on every object or combination. It prescreens trades based on the user's trading criteria and ranks them.

Software Option's Portfolio™ keeps track of foreign exchange positions. It handles forward contacts and options simultaneously.

A detailed listing of investment management and financial analysis software appears in the American Association of Individual Investor's newsletter.

Regarding real estate investment, HowardSoft's Real Estate Analyzer™ allows you to make projections considering changes in interest rates, rental payments, and inflation. There is an after-tax analysis of cash flows and profitability. Taft Cameron Company's Real Estate and Financial Software™ series determines property worth, compares different offers, amortization schedule, present value and internal rate of return analysis, and considers IRS compliance rules. Some real estate management programs include Realty Software Company's Property Management Plus™ and Yardi's Systems' Property Management™

Datext Inc. offers corporate financial information on compact disks, including financial statements, SEC documents, and investment analysts' reports for many companies.

INVOLUNTARY CONVERSION   There may exist an involuntary conversion of nonmonetary assets into monetary assets and the later replacement of the involuntarily converted assets. For example, a warehouse destroyed by a fire and the insurance proceeds received are used to purchase a similar warehouse.

As per Interpretation 30, gain or loss is recognized for the difference between the insurance recovery and the book value of the destroyed asset. The new warehouse is recorded at its purchase price.

A contingency results if the old fixed asset is damaged in one period but the insurance recovery is not received until a later period. A contingent gain or loss is reported in the period the old fixed asset was damaged. The gain or loss may be recognized for book and tax purposes in different years, causing a temporary difference requiring interperiod income tax allocation.

J

JOB ORDER COST ACCOUNTING is the cost accumulation system under which costs are accumulated by specific jobs, contracts, or orders. This costing method is appropriate when direct costs can be identified with specific units of production. Job order costing is widely used by custom manufacturers such as printing, aircraft, construction, auto repair, and professional services. Job order costing keeps track of costs as follows: direct material and direct labor are traced to a particular job. Costs not directly traceable—factory overhead—are applied to individual jobs using a *predetermined overhead (application) rate*. The overhead rate is determined as follows:

Overhead rate = Budgeted annual overhead/
        Budgeted annual activity units
        (direct labor hours, machine hours, etc.)

At the end of the year, the difference between actual overhead and overhead applied is closed to cost of goods sold, if an immaterial difference. On the other hand, if a material difference exists, work-in-process, finished goods, and cost of goods sold are adjusted on a proportionate basis based on units or dollars at year-end for the deviation between actual and applied overhead.

A job cost sheet is used to record various production costs for work-in-process inventory. A separate cost sheet is kept for each identifiable job, accumulating the direct materials, direct labor, and factory overhead assigned to that job as it moves through production. The form varies according to the needs of the company. A sample job cost sheet follows on page 260.

Job Cost Sheet
XYZ Company

Job No. _____

For Stock _____ Customer _____
Product _____ Date Started _____ Date Completed _____

Direct Material			Direct Labor			Overhead	
Date	Reference	Amount	Date	Reference	Amount	Date	Amount
	(Stores requisition number)			(work ticket number)			(based on predetermined overhead rate)

Summary of Costs

Direct materials	xx
Direct labor	xx
Factory overhead applied	xx
Total	xxx

Typical journal entries required to account for job order costing transactions are as follows:

1. To apply direct material and direct labor to, say, job X

Work-in-process (WIP)—job X	xx	
Stores Control		xx
Accrued Payroll		xx

2. To *apply* overhead to the job in process

WIP—job X	xx	
Overhead Applied		xx

3. To record *actual* overhead

Overhead Control	xx	
Stores Control, Accrued Payroll, Other Sundries		xx

4. To transfer completed goods

Finished Goods—job X	xx	
WIP—job X		xx

5. To record sale of finished goods

Cost of Goods Sold	xx	
Finished Goods		xx
Accounts Receivable	xx	
Sales		xx

JOINT PRODUCT ACCOUNTING Joint products are two or more products manufactured simultaneously by a common processing operation. The joint cost is allocated to the joint products based on sales values or physical measures (e.g., pounds, feet, units). Commonly used sales value methods are

• Relative sales value at the split-off point.
• Relative sales value attached to all production, whether or not sold. Any costs incurred after the split-off point (called separable costs) are subtracted from the sales value.
• Total sales price.

■ **Example**

The joint cost to manufacture products X and Y was $63,000. The following information relates to both products:

	Product X	Product Y
Production	10,000 units	50,000 units
Selling price	$3.00	$1.20
Separable costs	$2,000	$5,000

The relative sales value method is used. The joint cost allocations are

Product	Sales Value −	Separable Costs =	Sales Value	Joint Cost
X	$30,000	$2,000	$28,000	$21,253
Y	60,000	5,000	55,000	41,747
Total	$90,000	$7,000	$83,000	$63,000

If instead the allocation was based on volume, the joint cost assigned to each product would be

Product X 10,000/60,000 × $63,000 = $10,500
Product Y 50,000/60,000 × $63,000 = 52,500
                                               $63,000

See also Byproduct Accounting.

JOINT VENTURE   A joint venture occurs when two or more entities join together for a particular purpose. A joint venture is typically restricted to one project. An example is when IBM and Intel had a joint undertaking with regard to computer activities. The objectives of a joint venture may be to
• Reduce risk applicable to an activity
• Limit liabilities
• Obtain capital
• Add management talent
• Attract investors
• Accomplish synergistic effects
The equity method is typically used to account for joint ventures. *See also* Equity Method.

JUDGMENT SAMPLING   This occurs when an auditor uses his prior experience and knowledge with a particular client and industry to compute the number of sampling units and specific items to be studied from the population. The sample takes into account the nature of the business and the unique characteristics that may exist. The CPA must be objective in carrying out the sample and performing a detailed analysis to assure the sampled units are correct. This approach may be advisable when a particular area of the population is being carefully examined or immediate results and feedback are needed. *Note*: A judgment sample does *not* involve random selection. There is no computation made of sampling error, precision, or confidence level. Thus, there is an absence of statistical techniques and conclusions. *See also* Sampling.

K

KEYNESIAN ECONOMICS This is a body of economic thought and principles that originated with the British economist John Maynard Keynes (1882–1946) in the 1930s. It has since been modified, extended, and empirically tested to the point where many of its basic prescriptions, ideas, and tools are now an integral part of general economic theory and governmental economic policy. Through his book *The General Theory of Employment, Interest and Money* (1936), he contends that an economy may be in equilibrium at any level of employment, not necessarily at full employment, and therefore active fiscal and monetary policies are needed to seek full employment and economic growth with price stability. In addition, Keynesian economics focuses on stimulating aggregate demand and thus has been referred to as demand-side economics. Features of Keynesian economics include

1. The dependency of consumption on income, called the consumption function
2. The *multiplier* effect of an autonomous spending on GNP
3. The marginal efficiency of investment as a measure of business demand for investment

    See also Multipliers; Supply-Side Economics vs. Demand-Side Economics.

KITING This is a form of fraud that conceals a poor cash position and overstates cash receipts. The company keeps the bank from uncovering an overdraft in the account by exploiting the time needed for check clearance.

■ Example

Travis Company's main office is in Stamford and a branch office is in Dallas. The firm has a bank account with banks in both cities. A shortage of $80,000 exists in the Stamford bank. The bookkeeper covers up the cash deficiency by preparing a check on December 30, 19X4, on the Dallas bank that is deposited in the Stamford bank on December 30th. The check is listed as a cash payment in the cash disbursements book on January 2, 19X5. On January 4, 19X5, the check clears the Dallas bank. Note that the balance per bank and balance per book of the Stamford bank will be in agreement on December 31, 19X4, but not on January 2, 19X5. This impropriety may be detected by the auditor through an examination of bank transfers before and subsequent to December 31, 19X4, to assure that a book entry has been made in the same year that the check was dated

and the deposit in the Stamford bank was made.

When transfers exist between bank accounts, a schedule should be prepared of interbank transfers showing data of withdrawal and deposit as per bank and books. The auditor must trace transfer checks in transit at the year-end date to outstanding checks and deposits in transit when examining bank reconciliations. The deposit date of a transfer may be substantiated by tracing the deposit to the cutoff bank statements for the receiving bank. *See also* Internal Control.

LABOR INTENSIVE Labor intensive describes an industry or business entity that primarily employs labor in its activities. Relative to capital intensive businesses, those that are labor intensive have more stability in profit due to the greater emphasis on variable costs to total costs. Labor cost is a variable cost that changes with production activity. Thus, if a downturn in business occurs, variable costs may be slashed. However, the fixed cost emphasis of capital intensive companies prevents reducing costs for business downturns since by definition fixed costs remain constant regardless of production activity. For example, you cannot fire a machine. A problem, however, with labor intensive companies is more vulnerability to union actions, such as strikes and slowdowns. Further, during inflationary periods employees will demand greater wage increases. This problem is acute if the company is unable to pass along higher wage rates by raising selling prices due to competitive factors. *See also* Capital Intensive.

LAFFER CURVE The Laffer curve shows a hypothetical relationship between the marginal tax rate and tax revenues. As Figure 1 indicates, as the tax rate increases from 0 to 100%, tax revenues rise from 0 to some maximum level and then declines to 0. The optimum tax rate is of course the one that reaches the maximum revenue. Rates that are lower than optimum are regarded "normal" since tax revenues can be increased by raising the rate. Rates that are above optimum are viewed as prohibitive because they dampen incentives on the part of businesses and individuals and are thus counterproductive. Therefore, when the rate is in the prohibitive range, reductions in tax are needed to provide *incentives*, stimulate production, and bring higher, not lower, tax revenues. There is no empirical evidence to support this relationship and it still remains a hypothesis. Profes-

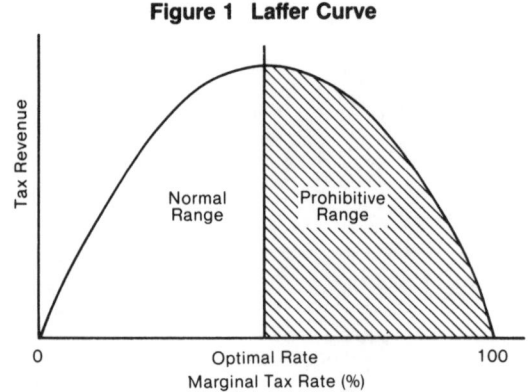

Figure 1 Laffer Curve

sor Laffer, who originated this curve, is considered the principal advocate of the controversial *supply-side economics*. *See also* Supply-Side Economics vs. Demand-Side Economics.

LAGGING INDICATORS These are the economic series of indicators that follow or trail behind aggregate economic activity. There are currently six lagging indicators published by the government, comprising unemployment rate, business expenditures, labor cost per unit, loans outstanding, bank interest rates, and book value of manufacturing and trade inventories. *See also* Index of Leading Economic Indicators.

LAPPING This is a form of fraud in which a customer's payment is misappropriated. A customer's account is credited when cash is received from another customer at a later date. It involves repeated misappropriations and posting delays to customer accounts. It is also possible that the cashier may transfer shortages to other accounts (i.e., inventory) for temporary concealment. Lapping may occur if a bookkeeper who receives customer collections also records transactions to customer accounts. Lapping may be prevented by having a separation of the handling of cash receipts and the posting to accounts. The auditor should also be on guard against the alteration of duplicate deposit tickets. A comparison should be made between the duplicate copy and the original one retained at the bank. The auditor should compare the entries in the cash receipts journal, postings to accounts receivable, listing of cash receipts from the mailroom, and deposit slips for the bank. *See also* Internal Control.

LEARNING CURVE The learning curve is based on the proposition that labor hours decrease in a definite pattern as labor operations are repeated. More specifically, it is based on the statistical findings that as the cumulative output doubles, the cumulative average labor

input time required per unit will be reduced by some constraint percentage, ranging between 10 and 40%. The curve is usually designated by its complement. If the rate of reduction is 20%, the curve is referred to as an *80% learning curve*.

The following data illustrate the 80% learning curve relationship:

Quantity (*In Units*)		Time (*In Hours*)	
Per Lot	Cumulative	Total Cumulative	Average Time Per Unit
15	15	600	40.0
15	30	960	32.0(40.0 × 0.8)
30	60	1,536	25.6(32.0 × 0.8)
60	120	2,460	20.5(25.6 × 0.8)
120	240	3,936	16.4(20.5 × 0.8)

As can be seen, as production quantities double, the average time it takes per unit goes down by 20% of its immediate previous time. Figure 1 depicts a learning curve.

■ Example

Stanley Electronics Products, Inc., finds that new-product production is affected by an 80% learning effect. The company has just produced 50 units of output at 100 hours per unit. Costs were as follows:

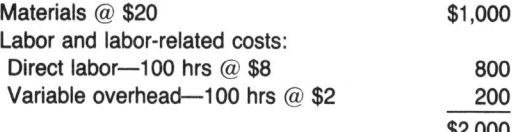

Materials @ $20	$1,000
Labor and labor-related costs:	
Direct labor—100 hrs @ $8	800
Variable overhead—100 hrs @ $2	200
	$2,000

Figure 1   Learning Curve

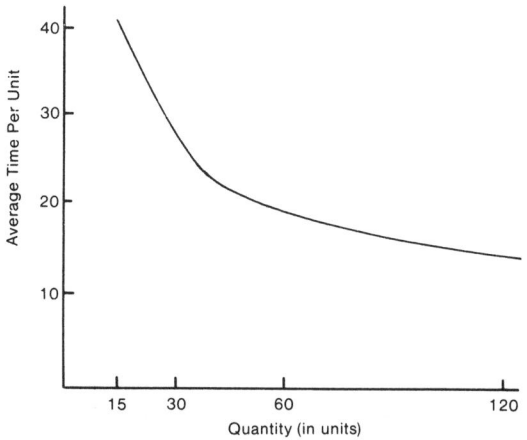

The company has just received a contract calling for another 50 units of production. It wants to add a 50% markup to the cost of materials and labor and labor-related costs. Let us determine the price for this job.

Building up the table yields:

Quantity	Total Time (In Hours)	Average Time (Per Unit)
50 units	100 hours	2 hours
100	160	1.6 (80% × 2 hrs)

Thus, for the new 50-unit job, it takes 60 hours total.

Materials @ $20	$1,000
Labor and labor-related costs:	
Direct labor—60 hrs @ $8	480
Variable overhead—60 hrs @ $2	120
	$1,600
50% markup	800
Contract price	$2,400

Other applications of learning curve theory include

1. Scheduling labor requirements
2. Capital budgeting decisions
3. Setting incentive wage rates

LEASE-PURCHASE DECISION The lease-purchase decision is one commonly confronting firms considering the acquisition of new assets. It is a hybrid *capital budgeting* decision which forces a company to compare the leasing and purchasing alternatives. To make an intelligent decision, an after-tax, cash outflow, present value comparison is needed. There are special steps to take when making this comparison. When considering a lease, take the following steps:

1. *Find the annual lease payment.* Since the annual lease payment is typically made in advance, the formula to be used is

Amount of lease

$$= A + A(PVIFA_{i,n-1}) \text{ or}$$

$$A = \frac{\text{Amount of lease}}{1 + PVIFA_{i,n-1}}$$

Notice we use $n - 1$ rather than n.

2. Find the after-tax cash outflows.
3. Find the present value of the after-tax cash outflows.

When considering a purchase, take the following steps:

1. Find the annual loan amortization by using:

$$A = \frac{\text{Amount of loan for the purchase}}{PVIFA_{i,n}}$$

This step may not be necessary since this amount is usually available.

2. *Calculate the interest.* The interest is segregated from the principal in each of the annual loan payments because only the interest is tax deductible.

3. Find the cash outflows by adding interest and depreciation (plus any maintenance costs) and then compute the after-tax outflows.

4. Find the present value of the after-tax cash outflows.

■ **Example**

A firm has decided to acquire an asset costing $100,000 that has an expected life of 5 years, after which the asset is not expected to have any residual value. The asset can be purchased by borrowing or it can be leased. If leasing is used, the lessor requires a 12% return. As is customary, lease payments are to be made in advance, that is, at the end of the year prior to each of the 10 years. The tax rate is 50% and the firm's cost of capital, or after-tax cost of borrowing, is 8%.

First compute the present value of the after-tax cash outflows associated with the leasing alternative.

1. Find the annual lease payment:

$$A = \frac{\text{Amount of lease}}{1 + PVIFA_{i,n-1}}$$

$$= \frac{\$100,000}{1 + PVIFA_{12\%,4 \text{ years}}} = \frac{\$100,000}{1 + 3.3073}$$

$$= \frac{\$100,000}{4.3073} = \$23,216 \text{ (rounded)}$$

Steps 2 and 3 can be done in the same schedule, as follows:

	(1)	(2)	(3) = (1) − (2)	(4)	(5) = (3) × (4)
	Lease	Tax	After-Tax	PV	PV of Cash Out-
Year	Payment ($)	Savings($)	Cash Outflow ($)	at 8%	flow ($, Rounded)
0	23,216		23,216	1.000	23,216
1–4	23,216	11,608[a]	11,608	3.312[b]	38,445
5		11,608	(11,608)	0.681[c]	(7,905)
					53,756

[a] $23,216 × 50%
[b] From Table 4 in the Appendix
[c] From Table 3 in the Appendix

If the asset is purchased, the firm is assumed to finance it entirely with a 10% unsecured term loan. Straight-line depreciation is used with no salvage value. Therefore, the annual depreciation is $20,000 ($100,000/5 years). In this alternative, first find the annual loan payment by using:

$$A = \frac{\text{Amount of loan}}{PVIFA_{i,n}}$$

$$A = \frac{\$100,000}{PVIFA_{10\%,5 \text{ years}}}$$

$$= \frac{\$100,000}{3.7906} = \$26,381 \text{ (rounded)}$$

2. Calculate the interest by setting up a loan amortization schedule.

The sum of the present values of the cash outflows for leasing and purchasing by borrowing shows that purchasing is preferable because the PV of borrowing is less than the PV of leasing ($52,090 versus $53,756). The incremental savings is $1,664.

LEASES These are typically long-term noncancelable commitments. In a lease, the lessee acquires the right to use property owned by the lessor. Even though no legal transfer of title occurs, many leases transfer substantially all the risks and ownership benefits. Theoretical substance governs over legal form in accounting resulting in the lessee

	(1)	(2)			(5) = (2) − (4)
	Loan	Beginning-of-Year	(3) = (2)(10%)	(4) = (1) − (3)	End-of-Year
Year	Payment ($)	Principal ($)	Interest ($)	Principal ($)	Principal
1	26,381	100,000	10,000	16,381	83,619
2	26,381	83,619	8,362	18,019	65,600
3	26,381	65,600	6,560	19,821	45,779
4	26,381	45,779	4,578	21,803	23,976
5	26,381	23,976[a]	2,398	23,983[a]	

[a] Because of rounding errors, there is a slight difference between (2) and (4)

Steps 3 (cash outflows) and 4 (present values of those outflows) can be done as follows:

recording an asset and liability for a capital lease.

A lease may be between related parties.

	(1)			(4) = (2) + (3)	(5) = (4) × 40%	(6) = (1) − (5)	(7)	(8) = (6) × (7)
	Loan	(2)	(3)	Total	Tax	Cash	PV at	PV of
Year	Payment ($)	Interest	Depreciation ($)	Deductions ($)	Savings ($)	Outflow ($)	8%	Cash Outflow
1	26,381	10,000	20,000	30,000	15,000	11,381	0.926	10,538
2	26,381	8,362	20,000	28,362	14,181	12,200	0.857	10,455
3	26,381	6,560	20,000	26,560	13,280	13,101	0.794	10,402
4	26,381	4,578	20,000	24,578	12,289	14,092	0.735	10,357
5	26,381	2,398	20,000	22,398	11,199	15,182	0.681	10,338
								$52,090

This occurs when an entity has significant influence over operating and financial policies of another entity.

The *date of inception* of a lease is the time of lease *agreement or commitment*, if earlier. A commitment has to be in writing, signed, and provide principal provisions. If any major provisions are to be negotiated later, there is *no* committed agreement.

Lessee

The two methods to account for a lease by the lessee are the operating method and capital method.

Operating lease—a regular rental of property. As rental payments become payable, rent expense is debited and cash and/or payables credited. The lessee does not show anything on the balance sheet. Rent expense is reflected on a straight-line basis unless another method is more appropriate under the circumstances. Accrual basis accounting is followed.

Capital lease—the lessee uses the capital lease method if any *one* of the following four criteria are met:

• The lessee obtains ownership to the property at the end of the lease term.

• There is a bargain purchase option where either the lessee can acquire the property at a nominal amount or renew the lease at nominal rental payments.

• The life of the lease is 75% or more of the life of the property.

• The present value of minimum lease payments at the inception of the lease equals or is greater than 90% of the fair market value of the property. Minimum lease payments exclude executory costs to be paid by the lessor, such as maintenance, insurance, and property taxes.

If criteria 1 or 2 are met, the depreciation period is the life of the property. If criteria 3 or 4 are satisfied, the depreciation period is the life of the lease.

It should be noted that the third and fourth criteria do not apply when the beginning of the lease term falls within the last 25% of the total economic life of the property, including earlier years of use.

The asset and liability are recorded at the present value of the minimum lease payments plus the present value of the bargain purchase option. The expectation is that the lessee will take advantage of the nominal purchase price. If the present value of the minimum lease payments plus the bargain purchase option is greater than the fair value of the leased property at the time of lease inception, the asset should be capitalized at the fair market value of the property. The discount rate used by the lessee is the *lower* of the lessee's incremental borrowing rate (the rate at which the lessee would have to borrow to be able to buy the asset) or the lessor's implicit interest rate. The lessor's implicit interest rate is the one implicit in the recovery of the fair value of the property at lease inception through the present value of minimum lease payments, including the lessee's guarantee of salvage value. The liability is broken down between current and noncurrent.

The lessee's minimum lease payments (MLP) usually include MLP over the lease term plus any residual value guaranteed by the lessee. The guarantee is the determinable amount for which the lessor has the right to require the lessee to buy the property at the lease termination. It is the stated amount when the lessee agrees to satisfy any dollar deficiency below a stated amount in the lessor's realization of the residual value. MLP also includes any payment lessee must pay due to failure to extend or renew the lease at expiration. If there exists a bargain purchase option, MLP includes *only* MLP over the lease term and exercise option payment. MLP does *not* include contingent rentals, lessee's guarantee of lessor's debt, and lessee's obligation for executory costs.

Each minimum lease payment is allocated as a reduction of principal (debiting the liabil-

ity) and as interest (debiting interest expense). The interest method is used to result in a constant periodic rate of interest. Interest expense equals the interest rate times the carrying value of the liability at the beginning of the year.

The balance sheet shows the Asset under lease less Accumulated depreciation. The income statement shows interest expense and depreciation expense. In the first year, the expenses under a capital lease (interest expense and depreciation) are greater than the expenses under an operating lease (rent expense).

As per Interpretation 26, when a lessee buys a leased asset during the lease term that has been originally capitalized, the transaction is considered an *extension* of a capital lease rather than a termination. Thus, the difference between the purchase price and the carrying amount of the lease obligation recorded is an *adjustment* of the carrying amount of the asset. *No loss recognition* is required on an *extension* of a capital lease.

■ Example

On 1/1/19X1, the lessee enters into a capital lease for property. The minimum rental payment is $20,000 a year for 6 years to be made at the end of the year. The interest rate is 5%. The present value of an ordinary annuity factor for $n = 6$, $i = 5\%$ is 5.0757. The journal entries for the first 2 years follow:

1/1/19X1 Asset	101,514	
Liability		101,514
12/31/19X1		
Interest Expense	5,076	
Liability	14,924	
Cash		20,000

$5\% \times \$101,514 = \$5,076$

| Depreciation | 16,919 | |
| Accumulated Depreciation | | 16,919 |

$$\frac{\$101,514}{6} = \$16,919$$

The liability as of 12/31/19X1 follows:

Liability

| 12/31/19X1 | 14,924 | 1/1/19X1 | 101,514 |
| | | 12/31/19X1 | 86,590 |

12/31/19X2		
Interest Expense	4,330	
Liability	15,670	
Cash		20,000

$5\% \times \$86,590 = \$4,330$

| Depreciation | 16,919 | |
| Accumulated Depreciation | | 16,919 |

Footnote disclosures under a capital lease include

- Assets under lease by class
- Future minimum lease payments in total and for each of the next five years
- Contingent rentals (rentals based on other than time, such as based on sales)
- Total future sublease rentals
- Description of leasing arrangements, including renewal terms, purchase options, escalation options, and restrictions in the lease agreement

Lessor

The three methods of accounting for leases by the lessor are the operating, direct-financing, and sales-type methods.

Operating method—a regular rental by the lessor. An example is Avis renting automobiles. Under the operating method, the lessor records rental revenue less related expenses, including depreciation and maintenance expense. The income statement shows rental revenue less expenses to obtain profit. The balance sheet presents the asset under lease less accumulated depreciation to derive book value.

Rental income is recognized as earned using the straight-line basis over the lease term except if there is another preferable method. Initial direct costs are deferred and amortized over the lease term on a pro rata basis based on rental income recognized. However, if immaterial relative to the allocation amount, the initial direct costs may be expensed.

■ Example

Hall Corporation produced machinery costing $5,000,000 which it held for resale from January 1, 19X1, to June 30, 19X1, at a price to Travis Company under an operating lease. The lease is for 4 years with equal monthly payments of $85,000 due on the first of the month. The initial payment was made on July 1, 19X1. The depreciation period is 10 years, with no salvage value.

Lessee's rental expense for 19X1:

$85,000 × 6	$510,000

Lessor's income before taxes for 19X1:

Rental income	$510,000
Less: Depreciation $\dfrac{\$5,000,000}{10} \times \dfrac{6}{12}$	250,000
Income before taxes	$260,000

Direct-financing method—satisfies one of the four criteria for a capital lease by the lessee plus both of the following two criteria for the lessor:

• Collectibility of lease payments is assured.

• No important uncertainties exist regarding future costs to be incurred.

The lessor is *not* a manufacturer or dealer. The lessor acquires the property for the sole purpose of leasing it out. An example is a bank leasing computers. The carrying value and fair value of the leased property are the same at the inception of the lease.

The lessor uses as the discount rate the interest rate implicit in the lease.

Interest income is only recognized in the financial statements over the life of the lease using the interest method. Unearned interest income is amortized as income over the lease term to result in a constant rate of interest. Interest revenue equals the interest rate times the carrying value of the receivable at the beginning of the year.

Contingent rentals are recognized in earnings as earned.

The lessor's MLP includes the (1) MLP made by the lessee (net of any executory costs together with any profit thereon) and (2) any guarantee of the salvage value of the leased property or of rental payments after the lease term made by a third party unrelated to either party in the lease provided the third party is financially able to satisfy the commitment. A guarantee by a third party related to the lessor makes the residual value unguaranteed. A guarantee by a third party related to the lessee infers a guaranteed residual value by the lessee.

A change in lease provisions, which would have resulted in a different classification had they taken place at the beginning of the lease, mandate that the lease be considered a new agreement and classified under the new terms. However, exercise of existing renewal options are not deemed lease changes. A change in estimate does not result in a new lease.

A provision for escalation of the MLP during a construction or preacquisition period may exist. The resulting increase in MLP is considered in determining the fair value of the leased property at the lease inception. There may also exist a salvage value increase that takes place from an escalation clause.

Initial direct costs are incurred by the lessor and are directly applicable with negotiating and consummating *completed* leasing transactions such as legal fees, commissions, document preparation and processing for new leases, credit investigation, and the relevant portion of salespersons' and other employees' compensation. It does *not* include costs for *leases not consummated* nor supervisory, administrative, or other indirect expenses. Initial direct costs of the lease are expensed as incurred. A portion of the unearned income equal to the initial direct costs shall be recognized as income in the same accounting period.

If the lease agreement contains a penalty for failure to renew and becomes inoperative due to lease renewal or other extension of time, the unearned interest income account

must be adjusted for the difference between the present values of the old and revised agreements. The present value of the future minimum lease payments under the new agreement should be computed employing the original rate used for the initial lease.

Lease termination is accounted for by the lessor through eliminating the net investment, recording the leased property at the lower of cost or fair value, and charging the net adjustment against earnings.

The lessor shows on his balance sheet as the gross investment in the lease the total minimum lease payments plus salvage value of the property accruing to the lessor. This represents lease payments receivable. Deducted from lease payments receivable is unearned interest revenue. The balance sheet presentation follows:

• Lease payments receivable (principal + interest)
• Less: Unearned interest revenue (interest)
• Net receivable balance (principal)

The income statement shows:

• Interest revenue
• Less: Initial direct costs
• Less: Executory costs
• Net income

Footnote disclosure should include assets leased out by category, future lease payments in total and for each of the next 5 years, contingent rentals, and the terms of the lease.

Sales-type method—must satisfy the same criteria as the direct-financing method. The only difference is that the sales-type method involves a lessor who is a manufacturer or dealer in the leased item. Thus, a manufacturer or dealer profit results. Although legally there is no sale of the item, theoretical substance governs over legal form and a sale is assumed to have taken place. *Note*: The distinction between a sales-type lease and a direct-financing lease affects only the lessor; as to lessee, either type would be a capital lease.

If there is a renewal or extension of an existing sales-type or financing lease, it shall *not* be classified as a sales-type lease. There is an *exception* which may exist when the renewal occurs toward the end of the lease term.

In a sales-type lease, profit on the assumed sale of the item is recognized in the year of lease as well as interest income over the life of the lease. The cost and fair value of the leased property are different at the inception of the lease.

An annual appraisal should be made of the salvage value and where necessary reduce the net investment and recognize a loss but do not adjust the salvage value.

The cost of the leased property is matched against the selling price in determining the assumed profit in the year of lease. Initial direct costs of the lease are expensed.

Except for the initial entry to record the lease, the entries are the same for the direct-financing and sales-type methods.

■ Example

Assume the same facts as in the capital lease example. The accounting by the lessor assuming a direct-financing lease and a sales-type lease appear on the top of page 272.

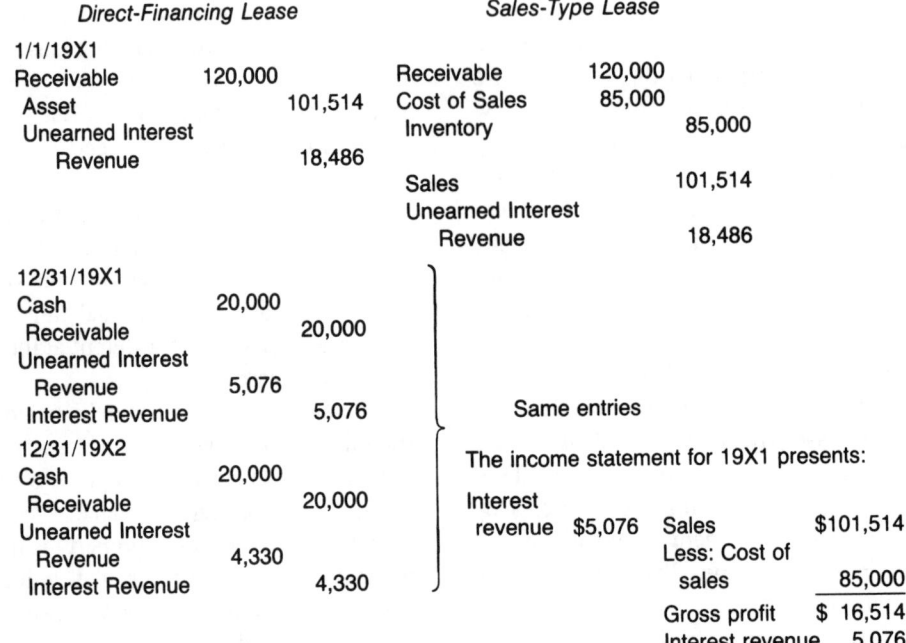

Direct-Financing Lease			Sales-Type Lease		
1/1/19X1					
Receivable	120,000		Receivable	120,000	
Asset		101,514	Cost of Sales	85,000	
Unearned Interest			Inventory		85,000
Revenue		18,486			
			Sales		101,514
			Unearned Interest		
			Revenue		18,486
12/31/19X1					
Cash	20,000				
Receivable		20,000			
Unearned Interest					
Revenue	5,076				
Interest Revenue		5,076	Same entries		
12/31/19X2			The income statement for 19X1 presents:		
Cash	20,000				
Receivable		20,000	Interest		
Unearned Interest			revenue $5,076	Sales	$101,514
Revenue	4,330			Less: Cost of	
Interest Revenue		4,330		sales	85,000
				Gross profit	$ 16,514
				Interest revenue	5,076

■ Example

Jones leased equipment to Tape Company on October 1, 19X1. It is a capital lease to the lessee and a sales-type lease to the lessor. The lease is for 8 years, with equal annual payments of $500,000 due on October 1 each period. The first payment was made on October 1, 19X1. The cost of the equipment to Tape Company is $2,500,000. The equipment has a life of 10 years with no salvage value. The appropriate interest rate is 10%.

Tape reports the following in its income statement for 19X1:

Asset cost ($500,000 × 5.868 = $2,934,000)

Depreciation $\left(\dfrac{\$2,934,000}{10} \times \dfrac{3}{12}\right)$ $73,350

Interest expense:

Present value of lease pay-	
ments	$2,934,000
Less: Initial payment	500,000
Balance	$2,434,000

Interest expense $2,434,000 \times 10\% \times \dfrac{3}{12}$ 60,850

Total expenses $134,200

Jones' income before tax is

Interest revenue		$ 60,850
Gross profit on assumed sale of property:		
Selling price	$2,934,000	
Less: Cost	2,500,000	
Gross profit		434,000
Income before tax		$494,850

Sales-Leaseback Arrangement

A sales-leaseback is when the lessor sells the property and then leases it back. The lessor may do this when he is in need of funds.

The profit or loss on the sale is deferred and amortized as an adjustment on a proportionate basis to depreciation expense in the

case of a capital lease or in proportion to rental expense in the case of an operating lease. However, if the fair value of the property at the time of the sales-leaseback is below its book value, a loss is immediately recognized for the difference between book value and fair value.

■ Example

The deferred profit on a sales-leaseback is $50,000. An operating lease is involved where rental expense in the current year is $10,000 and total rental expense is $150,000. Rental expense is adjusted as follows:

Rental expense $10,000
Less: Amortization of deferred gross profit
$50,000 × $\frac{\$10,000}{\$150,000}$ 3,333
                                                       $6,667

Subleases and Similar Transactions

There are three types of transactions. In a *sublease*, the original lessee leases the property to a third party. The lease agreement of the original parties remains intact. Another possibility is where a new lessee is substituted under the original agreement. The original lessee may still be secondarily liable. Finally, the new lessee is substituted in a new agreement. There is a cancellation of the original lease.

In accounting by the original lessor, he continues his present accounting method if the original lessee subleases or sells to a third party. If the original lease is replaced by a new agreement with a new lessee, the lessor terminates the initial lease and accounts for the new lease in a separate transaction.

In accounting by the original lessee, if the original lessee is relieved of primary obligation by a transaction other than a sublease, terminate the original lease:
• If original lease was a capital lease remove the asset and liability; recognize a gain or loss for the difference, including any additional consideration paid or received; and

accrue a loss contingency where secondary liability exists.
• If the original lease was an operating one and the initial lessee is secondarily liable, recognize a loss contingency accrual.

If the original lessee is not relieved of *primary* obligation under a sublease, the original lessee (now sublessor) accounts in the following manner:
• If original lease met lessee criteria 1 or 2, classify the new lease per normal classification criteria by lessor. If sublease is sales-type or direct-financing lease, the unamortized asset balance becomes the cost of the leased property. Otherwise, it is an operating lease. Continue to account for the original lease obligation as before.
• If original lease met only lessee criteria 3 or 4, classify the new lease using lessee criteria 3 and lessor criteria 1 and 2. Classify as a direct-financing lease. The unamortized balance of the asset becomes the cost of the leased property. Otherwise, it is an operating lease. Continue to account for the original lease obligation as before.

If the original lease was an *operating lease,* account for old and new leases as operating leases.

Leveraged Leases

A leveraged lease occurs when the lessor (equity participant) finances a small part of the acquisition (retaining total equity ownership) while a third party (debt participant) finances the balance. The lessor maximizes his leveraged return by recognizing lease revenue and income tax shelter (e.g., interest deduction, rapid depreciation).

A leveraged lease meets *all* of the following:
• It satisfies the tests for a direct-financing lease. Sales-type leases are not leveraged leases.
• It involves at least three parties: lessee, long-term creditor (debt participant), and lessor (equity participant).

• The long-term creditor provides nonrecourse financing as to the general credit of the lessor. The financing is adequate to give the lessor significant leverage.

• The lessor's net investment (see following) decreases during the initial lease years, then increases in the subsequent years just before its liquidation by sale. These increases and decreases in the net investment balance may take place more than once during the lease life.

The lessee classifies and accounts for leveraged leases in the same way as nonleveraged leases.

The lessor records investment in the leveraged lease net of the nonrecourse debt. The net of the following balances represent the initial and continuing investment: rentals receivable (net of the amount applicable to principal and interest on the nonrecourse debt), estimated residual value, and unearned and deferred income. The initial entry to record the leveraged lease is

> Lease receivable
> Residual value of asset
>   Cash investment in asset
>   Unearned income

The lessor's net investment in the leveraged lease for computing net income is the investment in the leveraged lease less deferred income taxes. *Periodic net income* is determined in the following manner employing the net investment in the leveraged lease:

• Determine annual cash flow equal to the following:

Gross lease rental (plus residual value of asset in last year of lease term)
Less: Loan interest payments
Less: Income tax charges (or add income tax credits)
Less: Loan principal payments
Annual cash flow

• Determine the return rate on the net investment in the leveraged lease. The rate of return is the one when applied to the net investment in the years when it is positive will distribute the net income (cash flow) to those positive years. The net investment will be positive (but declining rapidly due to accelerated depreciation and interest expense) in the early years; it will be negative during the middle years; and it will again be positive in the later years (because of the declining tax shelter).

LEAST-SQUARES METHOD The least-squares method is a technique of developing a regression equation that relates the dependent variable (such as a company's price-earnings ratio) to one or more independent (explanatory) variables (such as growth in earnings, dividend payout ratio, beta, and so on). This method is mathematically contrived in such a way that the resulting combination of explanatory variables produces the smallest error between the observed values and those fitted by the regression. *See also* Regression Analysis.

LEGAL LIABILITY This refers to litigation against an accountant because he or she is guilty of an improper act, including fraud or gross negligence. Significant monetary damages may be assessed to plaintiffs who suffered losses as a result of relying upon the accountant's work. These parties may include investors, stockholders, and creditors. In addition, the accountant may be faced with disciplinary action by the American Institute of CPAs. The accountant may not have complied with GAAS, GAAP, or other professional standards. An ethical violation may have occurred, such as the expression of an audit opinion when a lack of independence existed. As a result of increased lawsuits against accounting firms, the premiums for malpractice insurance have skyrocketed.

LEVERAGE This is the portion of the fixed costs that represents a risk to the firm. *Operating leverage*, a measure of operating risk, refers to the fixed operating costs found in the firm's

income statement. *Financial leverage*, a measure of financial risk, refers to financing a portion of the firm's assets, bearing fixed financing charges in hopes of increasing the return to the common stockholders. The higher the financial leverage, the higher the financial risk, and the higher the cost of capital. Cost of capital rises because it costs more to raise funds for a risky business. *Total leverage* is a measure of total risk.

To determine the degrees of operating, financial, and total leverage, let us define:

$$x = \text{sales volume in units,}$$
$$p = \text{selling price per unit,}$$
$$v = \text{unit variable cost,}$$
$$FC = \text{fixed operating costs.}$$

Operating Leverage

Operating leverage is a measure of operating risk and arises from fixed operating costs. A simple indication of operating leverage is the effect that a change in sales has on earnings. The formula is

Operating leverage at a given level of sales (x)

$$= \frac{\text{Percentage change in EBIT}}{\text{Percentage change in sales}} = \frac{(p-v)x}{(p-v)x - FC}$$

where:

$$\text{EBIT} = \text{earnings before interest and taxes}$$
$$= (p-v)x - FC$$

■ Example 1

The Wayne Company manufactures and sells doors to home builders. The doors are sold for $25 each. Variable costs are $15 per door, and fixed operating costs total $50,000. Assume further that the Wayne Company is currently selling 6,000 doors per year. Its operating leverage is

$$\frac{(p-v)x}{(p-v)x - FC}$$

$$= \frac{(\$25 - \$15)(6,000)}{(\$25 - \$15)(6,000) - \$50,000}$$

$$= \frac{\$60,000}{\$10,000} = 6$$

which means if sales increase by 10%, the company can expect its EBIT to increase by six times that amount, or 60%.

Financial Leverage

Financial leverage is a measure of financial risk and arises from fixed financial costs. One way to measure financial leverage is to determine how earnings per share are affected by a change in EBIT (or operating income).

Financial leverage at a given level of sales (x)

$$= \frac{\text{Percentage in change in EPS}}{\text{Percentage in change in EBIT}}$$

$$= \frac{(p-v)x - FC}{(p-v)x - FC - IC}$$

where EPS is earnings per share, and IC is fixed finance charges; that is, interest expense or preferred stock dividends. [Preferred stock dividend must be adjusted for taxes; that is, preferred stock dividend/$(1 - t)$.]

■ Example 2

Using the data in Example 1, the Wayne Company has total financial charges of $2,000, half in interest expense and half in preferred stock dividend. The corporate tax rate is 40%. First, the fixed financial charges are

$$IC = \$1,000 + \frac{1,000}{(1 - 0.4)}$$

$$= \$1,000 + \$1,667 = \$2,667$$

Therefore, Wayne's financial leverage is computed as follows:

$$\frac{(p-v)x - FC}{(p-v)x - FC - IC}$$

$$= \frac{(\$25 - \$15)(6,000) - \$50,000}{(\$25 - \$15)(6,000) - \$50,000 - \$2,667}$$

$$= \frac{\$10,000}{\$7,333} = 1.36$$

which means that if EBIT increases by 10%, Wayne can expect its EPS to increase by 1.36 times, or by 13.6%.

Total Leverage

Total leverage is a measure of total risk. The way to measure total leverage is to determine how EPS is affected by a change in sales.

Total leverage at a given
level of sales (X)

$$= \frac{\text{Percentage in change in EPS}}{\text{Percentage in change in sales}}$$

$$= \text{Operating leverage} \times \text{Financial leverage}$$

$$= \frac{(p - v)x}{(p - v)x - FC} \cdot \frac{(p - v)x - FC}{(p - v)x - FC - IC}$$

$$= \frac{(p - v)x}{(p - v)x - FC - IC}$$

■ Example 3

From Examples 1 and 2, the total leverage for Wayne company is

Operating leverage × financial leverage = 6 × 1.36
$$= 8.16$$

or

$$\frac{(p - v)X}{(p - v)x - FC - IC}$$

$$= \frac{(\$25 - \$15)(6,000)}{(\$25 - \$15)(6,000) - \$50,000 - \$2,667}$$

$$= \frac{\$60,000}{\$7,333} = 8.18 \text{ (due to rounding error)}$$

See also Cost-Volume-Profit (CVP); Break-Even Analysis.

LEVERAGED BUYOUT
A leveraged buyout occurs when an entity primarily borrows money in order to buy another company. Typically, the acquiring company uses as collateral the assets of the acquired business. Generally, repayment of the debt will be made from the funds flow of the acquired company. A leveraged buyout may also be made when the acquiring company uses its own assets as security for the loan. It may also be used if a firm wishes to go *private*. In most cases, the stockholders of the acquired company will receive an amount greater than the current market price of the stock. A leveraged buyout involves more risk than an acquisition done through the issuance of equity securities. *See also* Going Public.

LEVERAGED LEASES
In a leveraged lease, the lessor finances part of the purchase of property with a third party financing the balance. *See also* Leases.

LEVERAGE IN REAL ESTATE INVESTING
Leverage means use of other people's money (OPM) in an effort to increase the reward for investing. To a lot of people, it means risk. The fact of the matter is, using leverage in real estate investing is an exciting way to earn big yields on small dollars. When building real estate wealth, leverage will help one grow quickly without involving too much risk. High-leveraged investing in real estate is especially powerful when inflation is in full swing. High-leverage investors have numbers going for them because property values rise faster than the interest charges on their borrowed money. To see the full power of high-leverage investing, an example is given below.

■ Example 1

You pay a seller $100,000 cash for a piece of property. During the next 12 months, the property appreciates 5% and grows in resale value to $105,000. The $5,000 gain equals a 5% yield on your investment. But suppose you had put down only 10% ($10,000) on the property and mortgaged the balance. Now, your return on investment leaps to an astonishing 50% ($5,000/$10,000)! Another way of looking at the result is: Since you only put down $10,000 on $100,000 worth of property, you actually control the asset ten times the value of your actual cash outlay. This means 5% × 10 times = 50%. (In this example, for simplicity, we've omitted mortgage interest costs as well as the return on the $10,000 you would have invested somewhere else plus any rental income you would have earned from the property.)

■ Example 2

Instead of putting 100% down ($100,000), you put down 10% ($10,000) and bought nine more pieces of property, each costing $100,000, and each bought with 10% down ($10,000). Again assume that they appreciate at the rate of 5%. Therefore, your wealth increases: $5,000 a piece × 10 pieces = $50,000. All that in one year. Tying up your wealth in one property ($100,000) cost you $45,000 ($50,000 − $5,000). Conversely, by spreading your funds over more properties and leveraging the balance, you would multiply your earnings ten times.

The lower the amount of cash invested, the higher your return (from value appreciation and/or rental income). On the other hand, the larger your cash investment, the lower your return. Also, a higher appreciation will greatly increase earnings on your leveraged investment.

Pitfalls of High-Leverage Real Estate Investing

High-leverage real estate investing sounds really good as long as an investor watches out for some of the pitfalls. They are

• Property values can go down as well as up. Some types of real estate in some parts of the country are experiencing value declines.

• Select the property carefully.

• Anticipate a rising market due to a lower mortgage rate or a high inflation rate before jumping in a high-leverage world.

• Look out for negative cash flow. Income from highly leveraged property may be insufficient to cover operating expenses and debt payments. Do not overpay for property and underestimate costs. Buying for little or nothing down is easy. The difficult part is making the payments. Try to avoid negative cash flow (losses are tax deductible, however).

• Watch out for deferred maintenance. Deferred maintenance can create lots of problems down the road. One can avoid hidden costs and potential future expenditure by bargaining for a fair (or less than market) price and reasonable terms. In any case, overrepair is poison to the high-leverage investor.

See also Leverage.

LIABILITY MANAGEMENT OF BANKS Traditionally, banks have taken the liability side of the balance sheet pretty much as outside of their control in the short run. They have taken liabilities as given and have been concerned with *asset management. Liability management* involves actions taken by banks and other depositary institutions to actively obtain funds at their own initiative by issuing negotiable certificates of deposit (CDs), borrowing federal funds, and other procedures. It means altering the bank's liability structure (mix of demand deposits, time deposits, and so on) by changing the interest paid on nontransaction liabilities (such as CDs). The technique of liability management is certainly an important discretionary source of bank funds. However, the excessive use of the technique would make them vulnerable in future liquidity crises. The example of the Continental Illinois Bank is a case in point. *See also* Asset Management of Banks.

LIMIT ORDER *See* Stock Orders.

LIMITED AUDIT

1. Audit covering all accounts for a short time period
2. Audit restricted to specific accounts or transactions
3. Audit in which an agreement is reached to exclude specified typical features

LIMITED PARTNERSHIP A limited partnership is one in which one or more partners but not all have limited liability up to their investment to creditors in the event of the failure of the business or activity. The general partner manages the business. Limited partners

are not involved in daily activities. The return to limited partners is in the form of income and capital gains. Often, tax benefits are involved. Examples of limited partnerships are in real estate and oil and gas exploration. In general, public limited partnerships are sold by brokerage firms in $5,000 minimums. Typically, private limited partnerships consist of less than 35 limited partners. *See also* Basic Forms of Business Organization; Real Estate Syndicate.

LINEAR PROGRAMMING (LP)   LP concerns itself with the problem of allocating limited resources among competing activities in an optimal manner. Specifically, it is a technique used to maximize a revenue, contribution margin, or profit function, or minimize a cost function subject to constraints. Linear programming consists of two important ingredients:

1. Objective function
2. Constraints (including nonnegativity constraints), which are typically inequalities

■ Example 1

A firm wishes to find an optimal product mix so as to maximize its total contribution without violating restrictions imposed upon the availability of resources. Or it may want to determine a least cost combination of input materials while satisfying production requirements, maintaining required inventory levels, staying within production capacities, and using available employees. The objective function is to minimize production cost, and the constraints are production requirements, inventory levels, production capacity, and available employees.

Applications

Other managerial applications include
  • Selecting an investment mix
  • Blending chemical products
  • Scheduling flight crews
  • Assigning jobs to machines
  • Determining transportation routes
  • Determining distribution or allocation pattern

Formulation of Linear Programming

To formulate the LP problem, the first step is to define what are called *decision variables* for which you are trying to solve. The next step is to express the objective function and constraints in terms of these decision variables. Notice, however, that, as in the name of *linear* programming, all the expressions must be of *linear* form.

■ Example 2

A firm produces two products, A and B. Both products require time in two processing departments, Assembly Department and Finishing Department. Data on the two products are as follows:

Processing	Products A	B	Available Hours
Assembly	2	4	100
Finishing	3	2	90
Contribution margin per unit	$25	$40	

The firm wants to find the most profitable mix of these two products. First, define the decision variables as follows:

A = the number of units of product A to be produced.

B = the number of units of product B to be produced.

Then, the objective function that is to minimize total contribution margin (*CM*) is expressed as:

$$\text{Total } CM = \$25A + \$40B$$

Then formulate the constraints as inequalities:

$$2A + 4B \leq 100 \quad \text{(Assembly constraint)}$$
$$3A + 2B \leq 90 \quad \text{(Finishing constraint)}$$

and do not forget to add the nonnegativity constraints:

$$A, B \geq 0$$

Our LP model is

$$\text{maximize} \quad \text{Total } CM = 25A + 40B$$
$$\text{subject to} \quad 2A + 4B \leq 100$$
$$3A + 2B \leq 90$$
$$A, B \geq 0$$

Computational Methods of LP

There are several solution methods available to solve LP problems. They include (1) the simplex method and (2) the graphical method.

The *simplex* method is the technique most commonly used to solve LP problems. It is an algorithm, which is an iteration method of computation, to move from one solution to another until it reaches the best solution. The graphical solution is easier to use but limited to the LP problems involving two (or at most three) decision variables. The graphical method follows the steps:
1. Change inequalities to equalities.
2. Graph the equalities.
3. Identify the correct side for the original inequalities.
4. After all this, identify the feasible region, the area of feasible solutions. *Feasible solutions* are values of decision variables that satisfy all the restrictions simultaneously.
5. Determine the contribution margin at all of the corners in the feasible region.

■ Example 3

In Example 2, after having gone through steps 1 to 4, we obtain the following feasible region (shaded area):

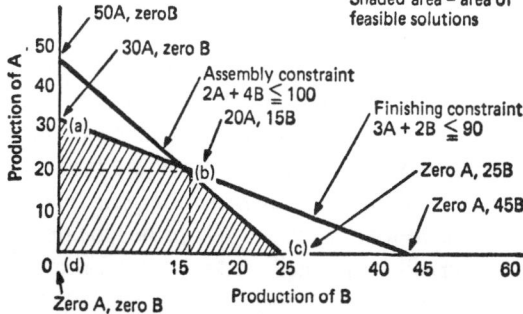

Then we evaluate all of the corner points in the feasible region in terms of their CM, as follows:

Corner Points		Contribution Margin
A	B	$25A + $40B
(a) 30	0	$25(30) + $40(0) = $ 750
(b) 20	15	25(20) + 40(15) = 1,100
(c) 0	25	25(0) + 40(25) = 1,000
(d) 0	0	25(0) + 40(0) = 0

The corner, $20A$, $15B$ produces the most profitable solution.

Shadow Prices (Opportunity Costs)

A decision maker who has solved an LP problem might wish to know whether it pays to add capacity in hours in a particular department. He or she would be interested in the monetary value to the firm of adding, say, an hour per week of assembly time. This monetary value is the additional contribution margin that could be earned. This amount is called the *shadow price* of the given resource. A shadow price is in a way an opportunity cost—the contribution margin that would be lost by not adding an additional hour of capacity. To justify a decision in favor of a short-term capacity expansion, the decision maker must be sure that the shadow price (or opportunity cost) exceeds the actual price of that expansion. Shadow prices are computed, step by step, as follows:
1. Add 1 hour (preferably, more than 1 hour to make it easier to show graphically) to the constraint under consideration.
2. Resolve the problem and find the maximum CM.
3. Compute the difference between the CM of the original LP problem and the CM determined in step 2, which is the shadow price.

Other methods, such as using the dual problem, are available to compute shadow prices.

■ Example 4

Using the data in Example 3, we shall compute the shadow price of the assembly capacity. To make it easier to show graphically, we shall add 8 hours of capacity to the assembly department, rather than 1 hour. The new assembly constraint is shown in the graph that follows.

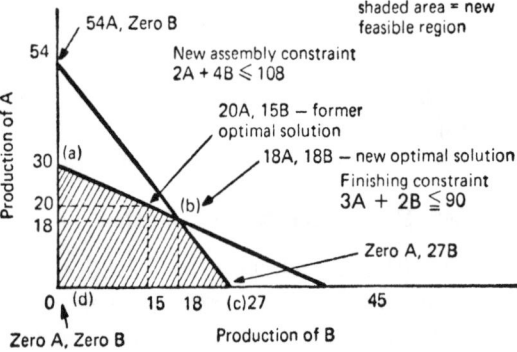

Corner Points		Contribution Margin		
	A	*B*	$25A + $40B	
(a)	30	0	$25(30) + $40(0)	= $ 750
(b)	18	18	25(18) + 40(18)	= 1,170
(c)	0	27	25(0) + 40(27)	= 1,080
(d)	0	0	25(0) + 40(0)	= 0

The new optimal solution of 18A, and 18B has a total *CM* of $1,170 per week. Therefore, the shadow price of the assembly capacity is $70 ($1,170 − $1,100 = $70). The firm would be willing to pay up to $70 to obtain an additional 8 hours per week, or $8.75 *per hour* per week.

LIQUIDATION *Corporation*: An insolvent corporation decides to liquidate under Chapter 7 of the Bankruptcy Reform Act of 1978. The objective of the liquidation is to sell assets and pay off liabilities in order to cease activities rather than remaining in business as a reorganization. Proceeds remaining are distributed to creditors in priority order. A discharge of the unsatisfied debts is received by the debtor.

Partnership: A partnership liquidates its assets and settles partnership affairs. After assets are sold and liabilities are paid, the residual left over is distributed to the partners.

See also Business Failure.

LIQUIDITY This is the ability of a company to meet short-term debt out of current assets. A company's liquidity is primarily of interest to short-term creditors. In analyzing liquidity, funds flow is a major consideration. Liquidity measures include:

• *Current ratio*—equal current assets divided by current liabilities.

• *Quick ratio*—equals cash plus marketable securities plus receivables divided by current liabilities. It is a stringent test of liquidity.

• *Working capital*—equals current assets less current liabilities. A high working capital is needed when the company may have difficulty borrowing on short notice. Working capital should be compared to other financial statement items such as sales and total assets. For example, working capital to sales indicates if the company is optimally employing its liquid balance. To identify changes in the composition of working capital, the financial analyst should ascertain the trend in the percentage of each current asset to total current assets. A movement from cash to inventory, for instance, points to less liquidity.

• *Sales to current assets*—a high turnover rate indicates inadequate working capital. Maybe current liabilities will be due prior to inventories and receivables turning into cash.

• *Working capital provided from operations* (net income plus nonworking capital expenses minus nonworking capital revenue) *to net income*—liquidity is enhanced when net income is backed up by liquid funds.

• *Working capital provided from operations to total liabilities*—indicates the extent internally generated working capital is available to meet debt.

• *Cash plus marketable securities to current liabilities*—indicates the immediate amount of cash available to satisfy short-term obligations.

• *Cost of sales, operating expenses, and taxes to average total current assets*—the trend in this ratio indicates the adequacy of current assets in meeting ongoing business-related expenses.

• *Quick assets to year's cash expenses*—indicates the days of expenses the highly liquid assets could support.

• *Sales to short-term trade liabilities*—indicates whether the firm can partly finance by cost-free funds. A decline in trade credit means creditors have less faith in the financial strength of the business.

• *Net income to sales*—a decline in the profit margin of the business indicates financial deterioration.

• *Fixed assets to short-term debt*—a company financing long-term assets with short-term obligations has a problem satisfying debt when due because the return and proceeds from the fixed asset will not be realized prior to the maturity date of the current liabilities.

• *Short-term debt to long-term debt*—a higher ratio points to greater liquidity risk because debt is of a current nature.

• *Accounts payable to average daily purchases*—indicates the number of days required for the company to pay creditors.

• *Liquidity index*—indicates the days in which current assets are removed from cash.

■ Example

	Amount	Days Removed From Cash	Total
Cash	$10,000 ×	—	—
Accounts receivable	40,000 ×	25	$1,000,000
Inventory	60,000 ×	40	2,400,000
	$110,000		$3,400,000

$$\text{Index} = \frac{\$3,400,000}{\$110,000} = 30.9 \text{ days}$$

■ Example

Company B provides the following financial information:

Current assets	$ 400,000
Fixed assets	800,000
Current liabilities	500,000
Noncurrent liabilities	600,000
Sales	5,000,000
Working capital provided from operations	100,000
Industry norms are	
Fixed assets to current liabilities	4.0 times
Current liabilities to noncurrent liabilities	45.0%
Sales to current assets	8.3 times
Working capital provided from operations to total liabilities	30.5%
Company B's ratios are	
Fixed assets to current liabilities	1.6 times
Current liabilities to noncurrent liabilities	83.3%
Sales to current assets	12.5 times
Working capital provided from operations to total liabilities	9.1%

Company B's liquidity ratios are all unfavorable compared to industry standards. There is a high level of short-term debt as well as deficiency in current assets. Also, working capital provided from operations to satisfy total debt is inadequate.

A company's failure to take cash discounts raises a question as to management's financial astuteness because a high opportunity cost is involved.

■ Example

Company C bought goods for $300,000 on terms of 2/10, net/60. It failed to take advantage of the discount. The opportunity cost is

$$\frac{\text{Discount foregone}}{\text{Proceeds use of}} \times \frac{360}{\text{Days delayed}}$$

$$\frac{\$6,000}{\$294,000} \times \frac{360}{50} = 14.7\%$$

The firm would have been better off financially paying within the discount period by taking out a loan since the prime interest rate is below 14.7%.

LOCAL AREA NETWORKS One of the more recent innovations in the area of data communications systems is the concept of local area networking. The overall objective of a local area network, known as a LAN, is to link computer devices and systems in the same geographical area, typically in a building. Local area networking (LAN) consists of a collection of microcomputers and expensive peripherals such as hard disk drives and laser printers linked together by connections that provide a cost effective means of sharing data and hardware among all linked users. This concept not only permits a centralizing control over policies and processing, but also provides for the flexibility of decentralization. In addition, they permit the sharing of information in an office building in an efficient and timely manner. LANs are fast, flexible, and provide ease of informational flow. One micro, for example, may easily communicate with another to transfer data among locations.

In its most basic form, the LAN, physically speaking, is nothing more than a group of microcomputers, printers, and other peripherals connected by twisted-pair wires or coaxial cables. However, fiber optics—the up and coming technology—is quickly replacing these more traditional connecting media. An important part of the LAN technology is the server, which can be a microcomputer or a peripheral that handles all the requests of the interconnected microcomputers making up the network. The server usually takes the form of a hard disk drive that is available to all participating PCs. Frequently, it is partitioned so that each computer can access a specific, private storage area. However, many systems allow certain areas to be accessed by all computer work stations. Thus, data files, such as data bases and spreadsheets, can be shared by all users making up the network. Optimally, the LAN should allow any user access to any computer resource that he or she is authorized to access

within the system, irrespective of its location. More will be said on this topic later.

In general, LANs provide the practitioner with immeasurable benefits enhancing profitability, accuracy and timeliness. In addition, they are relatively easy to install, expandable, and overall not expensive.

LAN Configurations

There are three basic LAN configurations, consisting of star, ring, and bus (tree). A description of each of these follows.

Star Network

In a star network, there is a linking of subsidiary micros or terminals to a central (host) computer whose task is to link all system micros together and route data and transmission among terminals and satellite micros. Clearly, all micros must be wired to the central controller. It is this resulting pattern of connecting micros to the central computer that produces the starlike shape that gives this configuration its name.

In this system, all information must pass through the central controller for direction to their final destination. This centralization predicates the performance of this network system on the performance of the central controller. In fact, failure of the central computer impairs the entire network. This is a major weakness of this configuration. The central controller, which regulates all communication in the system, should have adequate controls that are reviewed and tested periodically.

A star network is best utilized when it is necessary to enter and process data at many locations with distributions to different remote users, for example, shared data bases. Star networks are most frequently designed with a polling technology to communicate to all introcomponental PCs. In this technology the central controller waits for a signal from one of the microcomputers and then processes it. Another star communications

technology, called reservation, permits the transmission of signals at preset times. These reservations occur several times per second.

Ring Networks

The ring network configuration was developed as a result of attempting to eliminate the dependence of the central controller in the star network. A ring network has multiple computers connected together through a continuous communications cable. The network frequency does not involve a central computer. It does, however, offer the fastest response time of any LAN configuration. In this system the sending PC originates a message with the address of the intended receiver PC. The message is then passed on to the next PC in the ring. If this PC determines that this message was not intended for it (incorrect address), it passes the message along to the next PC. This process continues in an orderly sequential fashion until the message is accepted by the correct PC.

The ring network basically represents a communications system in which all stations constantly monitor the system. For example, the ring configuration is frequently used when several users at different locations have to access updated information on a continual basis. In this situation, more than one data transmission occurs simultaneously, keeping the system current on an ongoing basis. A ring network, for example, permits accountants within the firm to create and update shared data bases (e.g., general ledger, accounts receivable, accounts payable).

Given the fact that data are accessed or processed by many users in a ring configuration, it is important that controls be established to ensure that all messages and information have been communicated correctly. One such control requires that a message that has been delivered to a receiver continues on to the sender PC so that it may be determined that the data has remained intact. Another control requires that the receiving PC

remove the message from the ring and replace it with a verification that the message has been delivered.

In general, although a ring network is reliable, it is difficult to service and expand. In addition, loss of one station may cause the entire system to crash.

Bus Networks

A bus network consists of a series of microcomputers or peripherals at different locations attached to a central cable. The PCs and peripherals tap directly to the main cable, which may be installed over floors in an office building with drop cables running to the micros. As a result of this configuration, it is very easy to expand the system by just tapping into the central line. In addition, if a single PC work station malfunctions, the LAN will continue to operate.

One of two types of communication technologies may be utilized in most bus networks. Each is based on a first come, first serve assumption. The first, termed Common Sense Multiple Access/Carrier Avoidance, has the sending micro first determine whether any other station is sending. If not, it starts to transmit. However, if two stations transmit at the same time, the signals are sent garbled, preventing the sending stations from receiving a verification that the messages were received. As a result, retransmission occurs. Another related technology, called the Common Sense Multiple Access/Collision Detection, is comparable to the first technology except that when two micros transmit at the same time, they both immediately stop and will singularly start to retransmit again only after waiting for a short period of time.

Which Network Should Be Acquired?

In deciding which network is best given the particular circumstances of the accountant's office or that of the client, the following questions must be answered. How many users are involved, and what is the nature of their

work? What kind of accounting and internal controls exist? How often must data be updated, and what processing speed is required? Is the cost/benefit relationship attractive? Does the "right" software exist for desired network applications? What is the maximum data storage possible? Can the system be maintained in an efficient and cost-effective manner?

It should be noted that a network can consist of multivendor equipment where a proper protocal is used. An example is Sytek's Local Net™.

It is possible to combine two networks to enhance performance and obtain desirable features.

Be careful! IBMs DOS 3.1 NETBIOS™ operating system appears to be the standard for LANs. You are taking a risk if you select another operating system.

Software Considerations

Currently the choice of network software is limited by the network system purchased. However, it is hoped that this incompatibility restrictiveness will diminish in the future. Network software consists of data communications packages typically termed communications monitors or teleprocessing monitors. Included are communications access programs formulating a connection between terminals and computer systems, and the link between application programs and the network. Also involved are network control programs managing the communications network functions.

Communications monitors perform many processing and controlling activities that accounting practitioners should be aware of. These include such activities as establishing the amount of waiting in the system for transfer and processing; connecting and disconnecting links; polling terminals; establishing the direction for message transfer; identifying, keeping track, and correcting errors in the network process; and editing and executing of programs and varied data base activities.

Of course, the practicing accountant should carefully examine and review all network-related software to make sure that the network activity will run reasonably with adequate controls. He or she should make sure that there are proper communications links and transfers, that the terminals and micros work correctly, that reasonable waiting time exists to send and receive data, and that all system errors that occur are capable of being identified, documented, corrected, and disposed of.

For several networks, there exist multiuser packages. Examples of software for networking systems include dBASE PLUS™, Lotus' Symphony™, and IBM's Business Management Series™. A specialist in networking software is Torus Systems of England. Accounting software for LANs is also available.

Internal Control Considerations That Must Be Evaluated by the Accountant

The accountant must consider important internal control considerations related to a networking system to assure that data integrity and security exist. Clearly, errors must be minimized since the reliability and communicability of the financial reporting system is effected.

The accountant must make sure that the proposed network system is viable, especially when different types of computers are used, to assure there is appropriate data communication. Standard protocols, communications hardware and software interfaces should exist. In addition, there should be a uniform multilevel interface between the central system and users.

To ensure the overall quality of the proposed system the CPA should compare the network to the International Standards Organization's Open System Interconnection reference model for quality control design in seven categories. The areas covered by the

model include data routing and transmissions and user applications.

Parity checking provides the system with a means of controlling errors in transmitting and routing. In this control, the system ascertains whether there exists an odd or even number of digits in a character of information being sent. Communications control units should be used to control errors in data transmissions.

As was previously noted, the server is that part of the LAN (a microcomputer or peripheral) that handles all information requests of the member work station. It usually takes the form of a hard disk drive that is available to all participating PCs. As was noted, this hard disk drive should be partitioned so that each micro has its own storage segment. From a control point of view, this provides for segregation to isolate the responsibility for specific processing. Also, it is clear from this segregation that one micro will not improperly effect information going to others. Where segments of the hard disk are accessed equally by all network micros, only one work station may do the accessing at a time.

For data files that contain more confidential information, good internal control dictates that there be higher level security measures in effect to prevent unauthorized access of information. For example, determination must be made of the specific people who have the authority to access and update files. Logs should be kept of who altered and used files as well as the amount of time spent in the system. Additional control considerations include

• Making sure that adjacent work stations are properly connected, both physically and electrically.

• Safeguards should be established to make sure that unauthorized personnel have not accessed data transferred over communication lines. Passwords and voice recognition may be used.

• Checks should be made of information stored in the storage areas and devices within the network system. This includes assurance that data have not been lost in processing or tampered with.

• The adequacy of network communications should be reviewed. The quality of the protocol management scheme to gain access to the network, uniform rules, and procedures should be periodically reviewed.

• Data sent between adjacent micro work stations should be monitored for accuracy.

• Procedures should exist for avoiding and detecting signal collisions immediately. The effect of the collision on the network should be ascertained.

• Volume locking should be available so that when an accountant uses a file, client personnel are unable to access it.

• "Read-only" configurations should enable the reading of a file but not writing to it.

• "Redundant" cables should be used to prevent a break in the network link.

• Encryption, which is a form of difficult coding, should be used for data transmission. Data are decoded when received. National Data Encryption Standards exist.

• Use of a polynomial equation instead of an arithmetic addition should be used to obtain a check answer for transmission reliability.

• Block coding should exist for putting bytes in a matrix.

• Security controls should be enhanced as files become more confidential.

LONG-FORM REPORT   This is a detailed audit report by the independent CPA. It is addressed to management or the board of directors. It may be prepared in addition to or in substitution of the short-form report. Typically, the long-form report includes information regarding the audit scope, comments on financial condition, operating results and cash flow statement, trends over the years, and recommendations.

M

MAKE-OR-BUY DECISION This is a decision whether to produce a component part internally or to buy it externally from an outside supplier. This decision involves both quantitative and qualitative factors. The qualitative considerations include ensuring product quality and the necessity for long-run business relationships with the subcontractors. The quantitative factors deal with cost. The quantitative effects of the make-or-buy decision are best seen through *incremental analysis*.

■ Example

Assume a firm has prepared the cost estimates (above right) for the manufacture of a subassembly component based on an annual production of 8,000 units:

	Per Unit	Total
Direct materials	$ 5	$ 40,000
Direct labor	4	32,000
Variable overhead applied	4	32,000
Fixed overhead applied (150% of direct labor cost)	6	48,000
Total cost	$19	$152,000

The supplier has offered to provide the subassembly at a price of $16 each. Two thirds of fixed factory overhead—which represents executive salaries, rent, depreciation, and taxes—continue regardless of the decision. Should the company buy or make the product? The key to the decision lies in the investigation of those relevant costs that change between the make-or-buy alternatives. Assuming that the productive capacity will be idle if not used to produce the subassembly, the analysis takes the following form:

	Per Unit		Total of 8,000 units	
	Make	Buy	Make	Buy
Purchase price		$16		$128,000
Direct materials	$ 5		$40,000	
Direct labor	4		32,000	
Variable overhead	4		32,000	
Fixed overhead that can be avoided by *not* making	2		16,000	
Total relevant costs	$15	$16	$120,000	$128,000
Difference in favor of making	$1		$8,000	

The make-or-buy decision must be investigated in the broader perspective of available facilities. The alternatives are

1. Leaving facilities idle
2. Buying the parts and renting out idle facilities
3. Buying the parts and using unused facilities for other products

MANAGEMENT ADVISORY SERVICES (MAS)

MAS are performed by accountants to aid the management of a company. Types of services performed can be to assist in computer use, budgeting, controls, operations, planning, personnel, and other management decision-making purposes. The objective is to enhance a company's financial posture and operating performance as well as to reduce corporate risk. There exist standards to be followed in conducting MAS engagements. Independence must be maintained by CPAs involved in MAS activities. Reference should be made to the AICPA Statements for Management Advisory Services (SSMAS).

MANAGEMENT AUDIT
In a management audit, an evaluation is done of the ability of management to conduct operational activities. An appraisal is made of the nature and quality of management decisions in generating profit and controlling risk. *See also* Operational Audit.

MANAGEMENT GAMES
These offer a unique means of teaching business managers and financial executives financial and managerial concepts and developing strategic abilities. More and more companies as well as virtually all MBA programs across the nation are using management games as a basic teaching tool for industrial training programs.

The management game is a form of simulation. The distinction between a game and a simulation is a subtle one. Both are mathematical models, but they differ in purpose and mode of use. *Simulation models* are designed to simulate a system and to generate a series of quantitative and financial results regarding system operations. Games are also a form of simulation, except that in games human beings play a significant part. In games, participants make decisions at various stages; thus, games are distinguished by the idea of play. The major goals of the game play can be summarized as follows:

1. Improve decision-making and analytical skills
2. Facilitate an understanding of the external environment simulated on the part of the participants
3. Integratively apply the knowledge, concepts, and skills acquired in various business courses
4. Develop awareness of the need to make decisions lacking complete information
5. Improvise appropriately and adapt constructively from previously learned concepts, theories, and techniques
6. Develop ability to recognize the need for additional factual material
7. Develop an understanding of the interrelationships of the various functions within the firm and how these interactions affect overall performance
8. Learn about the effects of present decisions on future decisions
9. Develop an understanding of the fact of uncertainty and the impact of competitive environment on the firm
10. Have an understanding of the necessity for good communications, teamwork, leadership, and the organization
11. Develop ability to function cooperatively and effectively in a group situation

The basic structure of a typical executive management game is given in Figure 1 (page 288).

Executive Games Versus Functional Games

Management games generally fall into two categories: executive games and functional games. *Executive games* are general management games and cover all functional areas

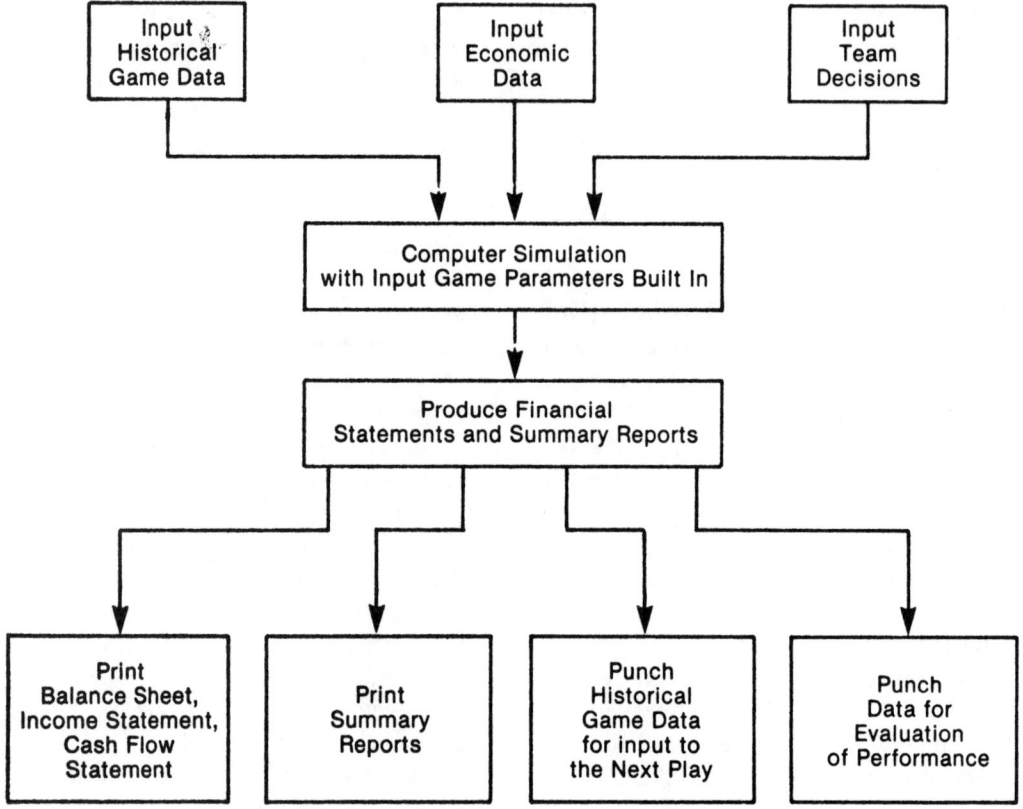

Figure 1   Structure of a Typical Executive Game

of business and theory interactions and dynamics. Executive games are designed to train general executives.

Following is a partial list of some well-known executive management games.

- XGAME™ by Jackson and Henshaw
- The IMAGINIT MANAGEMENT GAME™ by R. Barton
- COGITATE™ by Carnegie Mellon University
- The Business Policy Game™ by Cotter and Fritzsche
- Top Management Decision Game™ by Schrieber
- Harvard Business Game™ by Harvard University
- Management Accounting Game™ by K. Goosen

Functional games, on the other hand, focus on middle management decisions and emphasize particular functional areas of the firm. They cover such areas as:

- Resource allocation in general
- Production planning and scheduling
- Manpower requirements and allocation
- Logistics systems
- Material management
- Maintenance scheduling
- Sales management
- Advertising and promotion
- Stock transactions
- Investment analysis
- Research and development management

The objective in the play of functional games is usually to minimize cost by achieving efficient operations or to maximize reve-

nues by allocating limited resources efficiently. With emphasis on efficiency in specific functional areas rather than competition in a marketplace, found in executive management games, there is little or no interaction in many functional games between player decisions. From that standpoint, functional games are very similar to simulation models. Here is a partial list of some well-known functional games:

Name of Functional Game	Area(s) They Cover
• The Westinghouse Plant Scheduling™ Warehouse Simulation Exercise™	Distribution and logistics
• Greene and Sisson's Materials™ Inventory Management Game™	Inventory planning
• Greene and Sisson's Production™ Scheduling Management Game™	Production scheduling
• X-Otol™	Distribution
• IBM Production Manpower Decision Model™	Production and manpower scheduling decisions
• MARKSIM™	Marketing decision simulation
• FINASIM™	Financial management simulation
• PERT-SIM™	Project planning and control

See also Corporate Planning Models; Financial Games; Financial Models.

MANAGEMENT INFORMATION SYSTEM (MIS)

MIS is a manual or a computer-based system that transforms data into information useful in the support of planning, control, and decision making. MIS can be classified as performing three functions:

1. MIS that generates reports. These reports can be financial statements, inventory status reports, performance reports, or financial analysis reports that are needed for routine and nonroutine purposes. *Accounting infor-*

mation system (*AIS*) and *financial information system* are two subsystems of MIS.

2. MIS that answer what-if kinds of questions asked by financial management. For example, questions such as "What would happen to cash flow if the company grants a lenient cash discount term?" can be answered by MIS. This type of MIS can be called *simulation*.

3. MIS that supports decision making. This type of MIS is appropriately called *Decision Support System* (*DSS*). DSS attempts to integrate the decision maker, the data base, and the quantitative models being used. Financial modeling packages such as *IFPS* can be used for this kind of purpose.

See also Accounting Information System (AIS); Decision Support System (DSS); Financial Information System; Simulation.

MARGIN TRADING   This involves buying securities on credit. An investor opening a margin account signs a margin agreement, similar to an agreement signed to obtain a bank loan. This document states the annual rate of interest, its method of computation, and specific conditions under which interest rates can be changed. The Federal Reserve Board sets rules specifying the minimum percentage of the purchase price that a margin customer must pay in cash, known as a margin requirement. This requirement is currently for at least 50% of the current market value of the security. (Some securities may not be purchased on margin.) A 60% margin requirement means that 100 shares of a stock selling for $200 a share can be purchased by putting up, in cash, only 60% of the total purchase price; that is, $12,000 and borrowing the remaining $8,000. The stockbroker lends the margin purchaser the money, retaining custody of the stock as collateral. This is a form of leverage that, whether used in a long position or a short position, magnifies the gains and losses from a given percentage of price fluctuation in securities.

MARGINAL ANALYSIS

This is a key principle of microeconomics that can be applied to financial and investment decisions. The analysis suggests that financial and investment decisions should be made and actions taken only when *marginal revenues* exceed *marginal costs*. If this condition exists, a given decision should maximize the firm's profits.

MARGINAL COST (MC)

MC is the change in total cost associated with a unit change in quantity. For example, the marginal cost of the five hundredth unit of output can be calculated by finding the difference in total cost at 499 units of output and total cost at 500 units of output. MC is thus the additional cost of one more unit of output. It is calculated as:

$$MC = \text{change in total cost/change in quantity}$$

MC is also the change in total variable cost associated with a unit change in output. This is because total cost changes, whereas total fixed cost remains unchanged. MC may also be thought of as the rate of change in total cost as the quantity (Q) of output changes and is simply the first derivative of the total cost (TC) function.

Thus:

$$MC = dTC/dQ$$

In *accounting* and actual applications of this concept, MC is viewed as being equivalent to *incremental cost*, which is the increment in cost between the two alternatives or two discrete volumes of output. *See also* Marginal Revenue.

MARGINAL REVENUE

This is the rate of change of total revenue with respect to quantity sold. Marginal revenue indicates to a firm how total sales revenues will change if there is a change in the quantity of a firm's product sold. In economics, marginal revenue must equal marginal cost in order for profit to be maximized. In a discrete range of activity, marginal revenue is equivalent to incremental revenue.

MARKET (STOCK) INDEXES AND AVERAGES

These are market gauges used to track performance for stocks and bonds. At least in theory, an average is the simple arithmetic mean, whereas an index is an average expressed relative to a preestablished market value. In practice, the distinction is not all that clear. There are many stock market indexes and averages available. Each market has several indexes published by Dow Jones, Standard & Poor's, and other financial services. Different investors prefer different indexes. Indexes and averages are also used as the underlying value of index futures and index options.

Dow Jones Averages

Dow Jones averages are the most widely used and watched market indexes published by *The Wall Street Journal*. The *Dow Jones Industrial Average (DJIA)* is one of the four stock averages compiled by the *Journal*. This average consists of 30 large companies and is considered a blue chip index (stocks of very high quality). There are three other Dow Jones averages: the transportation (composed of 20 transportation issues), the 15 utilities, and a composite of the total 65 stocks. The DJIA would be a simple average of 30 blue chip stocks, but when a firm splits its stock price, the average has to be adjusted in some manner. In fact, the divisor is changed from time to time to maintain continuity of the average. The Dow Jones averages are designed to serve as indicators of broad movements in the securities markets. The *Dow Jones Composite*, also called *65 Stock Average*, combines all three Dow Jones averages.

Barron's Indexes

Barron's, which is also a publication of Dow Jones, compiles *Barron's 50 Stock Average* and an index of low-priced securities that meets the needs of small investors. Barron's

also publishes a weekly average called *Barron's Group Stock Averages*, covering 32 industry groups.

Standard & Poor's Indexes

Standard & Poor's Corporation publishes several indexes, including two most widely used indexes—the *S&P 400 Industrials* and the *S&P 500 Stock Index*. The S&P 400 is composed of 400 industrial common stocks of companies listed on the New York Stock Exchange, and the S&P 500 Stock Index consists of the 400 industrials and utilities and transportation stocks. They are used as broad measures of the market direction. They are also frequently used as proxies for market return when computing the systematic risk measure (*"beta"*) of individual stocks and portfolios. The S&P 500 Stock Index is one of the U.S. Commerce Department's 12 leading economic indicators. This index represents some 80% of the market value of all issues traded on the NYSE.

The *Standard & Poor's 100 Stock Index* consists of stocks for which options are listed on the Chicago Board Option Exchange (CBOE).

Value Line Average

The Value Line average is a simple average of 1,685 companies from the NYSE, AMEX, and the over-the-counter market.

Other Market Indexes

Different exchanges publish their market indexes. The NYSE publishes a composite index as well as industrial, utility, transportation, and financial indexes. The American Stock Exchange (AMEX) compiles two major indexes—the *AMEX Market Value Index* (*AMVI*) and the *AMEX Major Market Index*. The National Association of Securities Dealers also publishes several indexes to represent the companies in the over-the-counter mar-

ket. It publishes the *NASDAQ OTC* composite, insurance, industrial, and banking indexes. *Wilshire 5000 Equity Index*, published by the Wilshire Associates of Santa Monica, California, represents the market value of 5,000 NYSE, AMEX, and over-the-counter issues.

Bond Averages

Barron's publishes an index of 20 bonds, 10 utility bonds, and 10 industrial bonds as an average of the bond market. Dow Jones publishes two major bond averages—the *Dow Jones 40 Bond Average*, representative of six different bond groups, and the *Dow Jones Municipal Bond Yield Average*.

Mutual Fund Averages

Lipper Analytical Services compiles the Lipper Mutual Fund Investment Performance Averages. It publishes three basic fund indexes for growth funds, growth income funds, and balanced funds. *See also* Beta Coefficient; Index of Leading Economic Indicators.

MARKOV ANALYSIS This is an *operations research* technique. It is a technique that attempts to analyze the current behavior of some variable to predict the future behavior of that variable. It can be used to estimate the percentages of cash collections (payment proportions) from customers for cash-budgeting purposes. It can also be used to estimate the amount of bad debt allowance required. *See also* Budgeting Models.

MATERIALITY An item is material if the absence to disclose it would mislead readers of the financial statements. Disclosure may be made in the body of the financial statements, footnotes, or separate schedule. Materiality is difficult to measure. In SEC Accounting Series Release No. 159, the SEC requires disclosure by management of a

change in a revenue or expense item by 10% or more than the prior year. Some CPA firms have a more stringent requirement to guard against possible litigation. Some use a conservative 5% figure. In APB Opinion No. 15, a common stock equivalent is only included in the EPS calculation if it decreases EPS by 3% or more.

MATHEMATICAL PROGRAMMING This is a branch of *Operations Research/Management Science* whose primary objective is to search for an optimal solution to a decision problem. It is an optimization model. It typically consists of two ingredients in its model formulation: objective function and constraints. Mathematical programming covers a wide range of techniques, including linear programming, integer programming, dynamic programming, zero–one programming, quadratic programming, and other forms of nonlinear programming. *See also* Operations Research/Management Science; Optimization Models.

MATURITY VALUE 1. The face amount of an obligation payable on the maturity date. The maturity value will differ from the issuance price if a security is sold at a discount (below face value) or premium (above face value). Maturity value equals issuance price only if the security was issued at par.

■ Example 1

A $100,000 bond is issued at 97%, or $97,000. The bond was issued at a discount. At maturity, the company will retire the bond by paying its maturity value of $100,000.

2. On a note receivable that is discounted at the bank before the maturity date, maturity value equals

Face value of note
Plus: Interest to maturity
Maturity value

■ Example 2

A $10,000, 6%, 90-day note is received from a customer. It is discounted at the bank with 60 days still remaining. The bank discount rate is 7%.

Face value of note	$10,000
Interest to maturity ($10,000 × 6% × 90/360)	150
Maturity value	$10,150
Bank discount ($10,150 × 7% × 60/360)	118
Proceeds	$10,032

MEAN The mean gives us the average, or central value, of our data. Typically, there are three measures of central tendency: (1) arithmetic mean, (2) weighted mean, and (3) geometric mean. Each of these means is described following.

1. Arithmetic Mean($\bar{x}$)

The arithmetic mean is a simple average. To find it, we sum the value in our data and divide by the number of observations. Symbolically:

$$\bar{x} = \frac{\Sigma x}{n}$$

where n = number of observations.

■ Example 1

John Jay Lamp Company has a revolving credit agreement with a local bank. The loan showed the following ending monthly balances last year:

Jan	$18,500
Feb	21,000
Mar	17,600
Apr	23,200
May	18,600
Jun	24,500
Jul	60,000
Aug	40,000
Sep	25,850
Oct	33,100
Nov	41,000
Dec	28,400

Then the mean monthly balance for the loan last year is computed as follows:

Arithmetic mean balance

$$= \frac{\begin{array}{c} \$18,500 + \$21,000 + \$17,600 + \$23,200 \\ + \$18,600 + \$24,500 + \$60,000 \\ + \$40,000 + \$25,850 + \$33,100 + \$41,000 + \$28,400 \end{array}}{12}$$

$$= \frac{\$351,750}{12} = \$29,312.50$$

2. Weighted Mean

The arithmetic mean is an unweighted average. It assumes equal likelihood of each value in one data. When our observations have different degrees of importance or frequency, we use the *weighted mean*. The weighted average enables us to take into account the importance of each value in the overall total. Symbolically, the formula for calculating the weighted average is

$$\text{Weighted mean} = \Sigma\, w \cdot x$$

where w = weight (in percentage or in relative frequency) assigned to each observation.

■ Example 2

Consider the company that uses three grades of labor to produce a finished product. The company wants to know the average cost of labor per hour for this product.

Grade of Labor	Labor Hours per Unit of Output	Hourly Wages (x)
Skilled	6	$10
Semiskilled	3	8
Unskilled	1	6

Using the arithmetic mean, the labor wage rates would be

$$\text{Arithmetic mean} = \frac{\$10 + \$8 + \$6}{3} = \frac{\$24}{3}$$

$$= \$8/\text{hour}$$

which implicitly assumes that the same amounts of each grade of labor were used to produce the output. More specifically,

$$\frac{\$10 + \$8 + \$6}{3} = \$10(\tfrac{1}{3}) + \$8(\tfrac{1}{3}) + \$6(\tfrac{1}{3})$$

$$= \$8/\text{hour}$$

This is simply not true. We have to consider different amounts of each grade of labor in calculating the average cost of labor per hour. The correct way is to take a weighted average, as follows:

$$\text{Weighted mean} = \$10(\tfrac{6}{10}) + \$8(\tfrac{3}{10})$$
$$+ \$6(\tfrac{1}{10})$$
$$= \$9/\text{hour}$$

Note that we weight the hourly wage for each grade by its proportion of the total labor required to produce the product.

3. Geometric Mean

Sometimes we are dealing with quantities that change over a period of time. In such a case, we need to know an average rate of change, such as an average rate of return on investment or an average rate of growth in earnings over a period of several years. The formula for finding the geometric mean over n periods is

Geometric mean
$$= \sqrt[n]{(1 + x_1)(1 + x_2)\ldots(1 + x_n)} - 1$$

where x's represent the percentage rate of change or percentage return on investment. Since it is cumbersome to calculate the nth root (although most scientific calculators have a key to compute this), we will illustrate only the two-period return calculation ($n = 2$).

■ Example 3

Consider the following, which shows the inadequacy of the arithmetic mean return when the price of a stock doubles in one period and then depreciates back to the original price.

	Time Periods		
	$t = 0$	$t = 1$	$t = 2$
Price (end of period)	$80	$160	$80
Rate of return	—	100%	−50%

The rate of return for periods 1 and 2 are computed as follows:

$$\text{Period 1 } (t = 1) \frac{(\$160 - \$80)}{\$80} = \frac{\$80}{\$80} = 100\%$$

$$\text{Period 2 } (t = 2) \frac{(\$80 - \$160)}{\$160} = \frac{-\$80}{\$160} = -50\%$$

Therefore, the arithmetic mean return over the two periods is the average of 100% and −50%, which is 25%, as shown following:

$$\frac{100\% + (-50\%)}{2} = 25\%$$

As can be easily seen, the stock purchased for $80 and sold for the same price two periods later did not earn 25%; it clearly earned a *zero* return. This can be shown by computing the geometric mean return, as follows:

Note that $n = 2$, $x_1 = 100\% = 1$, and $x_2 = -50\% = -0.5$

Geometric mean return

$$= \sqrt[n]{(1 + 1)(1 - 0.5)} - 1$$
$$= \sqrt[n]{(2)(0.5)} - 1$$
$$= \sqrt{1} - 1 = 1 - 1 = 0\%$$

MICROECONOMICS VERSUS MACROECONOMICS

Microeconomics is the study of the individual units of the economy—individuals, households, firms, and industries, whereas macroeconomics is concerned with the workings of the whole economy or large sectors of it. Microeconomics zeros in on such economic variables as the prices and outputs of specific firms and industries, the expenditures of consumers, wage rates, competition, and markets. The focus is on the trees, not the forest. Questions that can be addressed by microeconomics include

• What determines the price and output of individual goods and services?

• What are the factors that determine supply and demand of a particular good?

• How can government policies such as price controls, subsidies, and excise taxes affect the price and output levels of individual markets?

Macroeconomics is the study of the national economy as a whole, or of its major

sectors. It deals with national price, output, unemployment, inflation, and international trade. It looks at the forest, not the trees. Typical macroeconomic questions include

• What determines national income and employment levels?

• What determines the general price level or rate of inflation?

• What are the policies that combat typical economic problems such as inflation, unemployment, and recession?

MINIMUM PENSION LIABILITY The minimum pension liability equals the excess of the accumulated benefit obligation over the fair value of pension plan assets. *See also* Pension Plans.

MINORITY INTEREST Minority interest in a subsidiary, whether acquired in a purchase or pooling-of-interests, refers to the equity of the shareholders outside the parent's controlling interest in partially owned subsidiaries. The preferable presentation in the balance sheet is to show the minority interest as a separate item in stockholders' equity. If two or more subsidiaries exist, a supplementary schedule may be prepared summarizing the external ownership equities.

■ Example

An external group owns 7% of the voting common stock of a subsidiary company that is controlled by a parent. The outside group represents a minority interest. *See also* Consolidation.

MODIFIED ACCRUAL This is the accounting method used by most funds in government. Under it there is recognition given to revenue when it is available and measurable. An example would be property taxes delayed beyond the normal time of receipt. Expenditures are usually reflected in the accounting period in which the liability is incurred, with the expectation that: (1) encumbrances are re-

corded; (2) interest on long-term debt is booked on the due date; (3) inventories of materials and supplies may be deemed expenditures when bought or consumed; and (4) prepaid items are immediately shown as expenditures.

Note: Proprietary governmental funds (e.g., enterprise, internal service) follow accrual accounting since they have profit and loss attributes.

MONETARY POLICY This is a deliberate exercise of the Federal Reserve's power to induce changes in the money supply in order to achieve price stability, to help smooth out business cycles, and to bring the economy's employment and output to desired levels. Monetary policy is essentially directed at regulating the economy's overall money supply; credit availability; and, to a lesser degree, the level of interest rates by the Federal Reserve System. The Federal Reserve System has three major devices that it can use to control the money supply: (1) changes in the required reserve ratio; (2) changes in the discount rate; and (3) open market operations—that is, purchase and sale of government securities.

MONEY MARKETS (CREDIT MARKETS) The money markets are for short-term debt instruments, such as certificates of deposit, commercial paper, Treasury bills, and bankers' acceptances. Also included are bank loans, trade credit, federal funds borrowing between banks, and bank borrowings from the Federal Reserve. Money market instruments are liquid and secure. *See also* Capital Markets; Financial Institutions and Markets.

MONEY SUPPLY This is the level of funds available at a given time for conducting transactions in an economy. The Federal Reserve System can influence the money supply through its monetary policy measures. There are many definitions of the money supply. For example, $M1$, a broadly used measure of money supply, currency in circulation, demand deposits, traveler's checks, and those in interest-bearing NOW accounts. Other definitions of money supply, that is, $M2$, $M3$, and L are given below.

$L = M3$ + LIQUID AND NEAR-LIQUID ASSETS
  Treasury obligations, including bills and bonds
  Term Eurodollars, high-grade commercial paper, and banker's acceptances

$M3 = M2$ + WIDE-RANGE MONEY
  Large-denomination time deposits
  Term repurchase agreements

$M2 = M1$ + MEDIUM-RANGE MONEY
  Savings (time) deposits
  Repurchase agreements (overnight)
  Money market mutual fund shares
  Eurodollars (overnight)

$M1 =$ NARROW-TRANSACTIONS MONEY, BASIC MONEY SUPPLY
  Traveler's checks
  Other checkable deposits
    (NOW, share draft, and other accounts)
  Demand deposits
  Currency

Other checkable deposits
Demand deposits
Currency

See also Federal Reserve System; Monetary Policy.

MONTE CARLO SIMULATION   This is a special type of *simulation* in which the variables of a given system are subject to uncertainty. The technique gets its name from the famous Mediterranean resort associated with games of chance. In fact, the chance element is an important aspect of Monte Carlo simulation. The method can be used only when a system has a *random*, or chance, component. Under this approach, a probability distribution is developed that reflects the random component of the system under study. Random samples taken from this distribution are analogous to observations made on the system itself. As the number of observations increases, the results of the simulation will tend to more closely approximate the random behavior of the real system, provided a proper model has been developed. Sampling is done by the use of random numbers. Business applications of simulation include testing alternative credit policies and inventory policies. *See also* Simulation.

MORTGAGES   These are liens securing notes payable that have as collateral real assets and require periodic payments. For personal property, such as machines or equipment, the lien is called a *chattel mortgage*. Mortgages can be issued to finance the acquisition of assets, construction of plants, and modernization of facilities. The bank will require that the value of the property exceed the mortgage on that property. Mortgages have a number of advantages over other debt instruments, including favorable interest rates, less financing restrictions, and extended maturity date for loan repayment.

MOVING AVERAGE   A moving average is an average that is updated as new information is received. With the moving average, an accountant employs the most recent observations to calculate an average, which is used as the forecast for the next period. For example, assume that the accountant has the following cash inflow data.

Month	Cash Collections (000)
May	20
June	24
July	22
August	26
September	25

Using a four-period moving average, predicted cash collection for October is computed as follows:

$$(24 + 22 + 26 + 25)/4 = 97/4 = 24.25, \text{ or } \$24,250$$

MULTICOLLINEARITY   This is the condition that exists when the independent variables are highly correlated with each other. In the presence of multicollinearity, the estimated regression coefficients may be unreliable. The presence of multicollinearity can be tested by investigating the correlation between the independent variables. One way to correct for multicollinearity is to keep one variable and drop the rest of the variables that are highly correlated. *See also* Regression Analysis.

MULTIPLE DISCRIMINANT ANALYSIS (MDA)   MDA is a statistical classificatory technique, similar to *regression analysis*, that has a wide number of applications in financial analysis. In general, MDA uses any quantifiable factor to help classify populations. For example, in the case of consumer credit, loan applicants may be divided into those with a high probability of becoming default and those unlikely to default, based on such factors as annual income, job security, and the like. This is referred to as *a credit scoring system*. Lenders, mortgage companies, credit card service companies, and retailers use MDA to make a credit-granting decision. MDA is used to classify firms into two groups; those with a high chance of experiencing failure and those

that are unlikely to go bankrupt, based on each firm's characteristics as measured by its financial ratios. Altman's Z score model (bankruptcy prediction model) is a classic use of MDA. MDA is also used to develop a bond-rating scheme.

MDA involves the following three steps:
1. Estimate the discriminant function.
2. Select the cutoff point for the discriminant function.
3. Investigate the predictive capability of the model on the validation sample.

There are two MDA methods: *linear* discriminant analysis and *quadratic* discriminant analysis. *See also* Bond Ratings; Regression Analysis; Z Scores; Forecasting Business Failures.

MULTIPLE REGRESSION This attempts to estimate statistically the average relationship between the dependent variable (e.g., sales) and two or more independent variables (e.g., price, advertising, income, and so on). It takes the following form:

$$y = b_0 + b_1x_1 + b_2x_2 \ldots b_kx_k + u$$

where y = dependent variable,
  x's = independent (explanatory) variables,
  b's = regression coefficients,
  u = error term.
See also Regression Analysis.

MULTIPLIERS These generally refer to the fact that changes in an economic variable can bring about magnified changes in another performance-related economic variable. There are various multipliers in economics, depending on what we try to measure. They are

1. *Expenditure* (*simple or investment*) *multiplier*—refers to the fact that any change in spending—whether by households, businesses, or government and whether for consumption or for investment—can have a mag-

nified effect on income. The expenditure multiplier is calculated as:

$$\text{Multiplier} = 1/ (1 - \text{MPC}) = 1/\text{MPS}$$

where MPC = the marginal propensity to consume and MPS = the marginal propensity to save.

■ Example

Assume that MPC = 4/5 and hence MPS = 1/5. Then the multiplier is 5. An increase in business investment (or government spending) of $5 billion will bring about an increase in income of $25 billion, as shown following.

Change in income (or GNP)
  = Multiplier × Change in Spending
  $25 billion = 5 × $5 billion

2. *Tax multiplier*—shows the relationship between a change in income taxes and the change in GNP. It is computed as:

$$\text{MPC} \times (1/\text{MPS})$$

■ Example

Assume that MPC = 4/5 and MPS = 1/5. Then the tax multiplier is 4. A $1 increase in taxes will reduce GNP by $4.

3. *Balanced-budget multiplier*—under this principle, if government spending and taxes are changed simultaneously by equal amounts, income (or GNP) will be changed by the same amount.

■ Example

An equal increase (decrease) in government spending and taxes of $10 billion will raise (lower) GNP by 1 × $10 billion = $10 billion.

4. *Foreign-trade multiplier*—a principle that states that fluctuations in net exports (exports − imports) can generate magnified changes in GNP. It is calculated as:

$$1/(\text{MPS} + \text{MPM})$$

where MPM = the fraction of any increase in income that "leaks" into imports.

■ Example

Assume MPS = 0.2 and MPM = 0.05. The foreign-trade multiplier is 1/(0.2 + 0.05) = 1/0.25 = 4.

5. *Deposit multiplier*—tries to determine the maximum multiple by which the banking system's deposits can expand as a result of an initial increase in excess reserve. It is the reciprocal of the required-reserve ratio (1/r).

■ Example

If r = 10%, or 1/10, the deposit multiplier is 10. For example, excess reserves of, say, $5,000 can generate a new increase in newly created money of as much as $50,000 (10 × $5,000).

6. *Money multiplier*—implies that the money supply, such as $M1$, is some multiple, m, of the monetary base, B. That is $M1 = mB$, where m = the money multiplier (m can be derived from regularly published data from $M1$ and B).

■ Example

If in a given year $M1$ = $850 billion and B = $400 billion, then m = 2.25. Over the long run, m has ranged between 2 and 3 in value.

MULTISTAGE SAMPLING
This consists of sampling at multilevels where an estimate of the total dollars of the population that is in groups over a wide area is required. For example, if an estimate of the total dollar value of inventory of a chain store with widely distributed outlets is required, the multistage technique would be appropriate. Selections at any level may be accomplished using alternative sampling methods (e.g., random, stratified, systematic).

Multistage sampling will necessitate a larger sample size and more sophisticated evaluation formulas than is the case with simple or stratified sampling methods. *See also* Sampling.

MUTUAL FUNDS
These are popular investment vehicles that represent ownership in a professionally managed portfolio of securities. Major advantages of investing in mutual funds are

1. *Diversification*—each share of a fund gives an investor an interest in a cross section of stocks, bonds, or other investments.

2. *Small minimum investment*—an investor with a small amount of money (as little as $50) can achieve diversification through the large number of securities in the portfolio. A handful of funds have no minimums.

3. *Automatic reinvestment*—most funds allow investors to automatically reinvest dividends and any capital gains that may arise from the fund's buying and selling activities. Funds typically do not charge a sales fee on automatic reinvestments.

4. *Automatic withdrawals*—most funds will allow shareholders to withdraw money on a regular basis.

5. *Liquidity*—an investor is allowed to redeem the shares owned.

6. *Switching*—an investor may want to make changes in his investments. His long-term goals may remain the same, but the investment climate does not. To facilitate switching among funds, such companies as Fidelity and Vanguard have introduced "families" of funds. The investor may move among them with relative freedom, usually at no fee.

Net Asset Value (NAV)

The value of a mutual fund share is measured by net asset value (NAV), which equals

$$\frac{\text{Fund's total assets} - \text{Liabilities}}{\text{Number of shares outstanding in the fund}}$$

■ Example

For simplicity, assume that a fund owns 100 shares each of GM, Xerox, and IBM. Assume also that on a particular day, the following

market values existed. Then NAV of the fund is calculated as follows (assume the fund has no liabilities):

(a) GM—$90 per share × 100 shares	=	$ 9,000
(b) Xerox—$100 per share × 100 shares	=	10,000
(c) IBM—$160 per share × 100 shares	=	16,000
(d) Value of the fund's portfolio		$35,000
(e) Number of shares outstanding in the fund		1,000
(f) Net asset value (NAV) per share = (d)/(e)		$ 35

If an investor owns 5% of the fund's outstanding shares, or 50 shares (5% × 1,000 shares), then the value of the investment is $1,750 ($35 × 50).

It is important to note at this point that there are three ways to make money in mutual funds. NAV is only one of the three. NAV only indicates the current market value of the underlying portfolio. An investor also receives capital gains and dividends. Therefore, the performance of a mutual fund must be judged on the basis of these three, which will be discussed later.

Types of Mutual Funds

Mutual funds may be classified into different types, according to organization, the fees charged, methods of trading funds, and their investment objectives. In *open-end* funds, investors buy from and sell their shares back to the fund itself. On the other hand, *closed-end* funds operate with a fixed number of shares outstanding, which trade among individuals in secondary markets like common stocks. All open- and closed-end funds charge management fees. A major point of closed-end funds is the size of discount or premium, which is the difference between their market prices and their net asset values (NAVs). Many funds of this type sell at discounts, which enhances their investment appeal. Funds that charge sales commissions are called *load* funds. *No-load funds* do not charge sales commissions.

Load funds perform no better than no-

loads. Many experts believe investors should buy only no-load or low-load funds. They should have no trouble finding such funds that meet their investment requirements. The prospectus contains such information as the fund's investment objective, method of selecting securities, performance figures, sales charges, and other expenses.

Depending on their investment philosophies, mutual funds generally fall into ten major categories:

1. *Money market funds*—mutual funds that invest exclusively in debt securities maturing within 1 year, such as government securities, commercial paper, and certificates of deposit. These funds provide a safety valve for many investors because the price never changes. They are known as dollar funds, which means investors always buy and sell shares at $1.00 each.

2. *Aggressive growth funds*—go for big future capital gains instead of current dividend income. They invest in the stocks of upstart and high-tech-oriented companies. Return can be great but so can risk. These funds are suited for investors who are not particularly concerned with short-term fluctuations in return but with long-term gains. Aggressive growth funds are also called *maximum capital gain, capital appreciation,* and *small company growth funds*.

3. *Growth funds*—seek long-term gains by investing in the stocks of established companies that are expected to rise in value faster than inflation. These stocks are best for investors who wish steady growth over a long-term period but feel little need for income in the meantime.

4. *Income funds*—best suited for investors who seek a high level of dividend income. Income funds usually invest in high-quality bonds and stocks with consistently high dividends.

5. *Growth and income funds*—seek both current dividend income and capital gains. The goal of these funds is to provide long-term

growth without much variation in share value.

6. *Balanced funds*—combine investments in common stock and bonds and often preferred stock, and attempt to provide income and some capital appreciation. Balanced funds tend to underperform all-stock funds in strong bull markets.

7. *Bond and preferred stock funds*—invest in both bonds and preferred stock, with the emphasis on income rather than growth. The funds that invest exclusively in bonds are called *bond funds*. There are two types of bond funds: bond funds that invest in corporate bonds and *municipal bond funds* that provide tax-free income and a diversified portfolio of municipal securities. In periods of volatile interest rates, bond funds are subject to price fluctuations. The value of the shares will fall when interest rates rise.

8. *Index funds*—invest in a portfolio of corporate stocks, the composition of which is determined by the Standard & Poor's 500 or some other market index.

9. *Sector funds*—funds that invest in one or two fields or industries. These funds are risky in that they rise and fall depending on how the individual fields or industries do. They are also called *specialized funds*.

10. *International funds*—invest in the stocks and bonds of corporations traded on foreign exchanges. These funds make significant gains when the dollar is falling and foreign stock prices are rising.

How to Read Mutual Fund Quotations

The following are quotations of mutual funds shown in a newspaper.

Funds	NAV	Offer Price	NAV Chg.
Acorn Fund	30.95	N.L.	+0.38
. . . . .	. . . .	. . . . . .	. . .
American Growth	8.52	9.31	+0.05

In a *load fund*, the price you pay for a share is called the *offer price*, and it is higher than net asset value (NAV), the difference being the commission. American Growth is a load fund. As shown, American Growth has a load of $0.79 ($9.31 − $8.52), or 8.49% ($0.79/$9.31). Acorn Fund is a *no-load* fund, as "N.L." indicates. In a no-load fund, the price you pay is NAV.

In the case of a *closed-end* fund, the following is a typical listing shown in a newspaper.

Funds	NAV	Strike Price	% Diff
Claremont	35.92	29⅜	−18.2
. . . . .	. . . .	. . . .	. . .
Nautilus	34.41	34½	+0.2

In the "% Diff" column, negative difference means the shares sell at a discount; positive difference means they sell at a premium.

Performance of Mutual Funds

Generally, mutual funds provide returns to investors in the form of (1) change in share value (or net asset value); (2) dividend income; and (3) capital gain distribution. The return for mutual funds is calculated as follows:

$$\frac{(\text{Dividends} + \text{Capital gain distributions}) + (\text{Ending NAV} - \text{Beginning NAV})}{\text{Beginning NAV}}$$

■ Example

Assume XYZ mutual fund paid dividends of $0.50 and capital gain distributions of $0.25 per share over the course of the year and had a price (NAV) at the beginning of the year of $8.50 that rose to $9.50 per share by the end of the year. The return is

$$\frac{(\$0.50 + \$0.25) + (\$9.50 - \$8.50)}{\$8.50} = \frac{\$1.75}{\$8.50} = 20.59\%$$

In assessing fund performance, investors must also resort to the published *beta* of the funds being considered in order to determine the amount of risk involved. Beta is a measure of risk. It is based on the price swings of a fund compared with the market as a whole, measured by the Standard & Poor's 500 Stock

Index. The higher the beta, the greater the risk.

Beta	What It Means
1.0	A fund moves up and down just as much as the market.
>1.0	The fund tends to climb higher in bull markets and dip lower in bear markets than the S&P index.
<1.0	The fund is less volatile (risky) than the market.

Betas for individual funds are widely available in many investment newsletters and directories. An example is *Value Line Investment Survey*.

Mutual Fund Ratings

Investors can get help in selecting mutual funds from a number of sources, including investment advisory services that charge fees. More readily available sources, however, include *Money*, *Forbes*, *Barron's*, and *Personal Finance*. *Money* has a "Fund Watch" column appearing in each monthly issue. In addition, it ranks about 450 funds twice a year in terms of fund performance and risk. *Forbes* has an annual report covering each fund's performance in both up and down markets. *Value Line Investment Survey* shows the makeup of the fund's portfolio *beta* values. Information about no-load funds is contained in *The Individual Investor's Guide to No Load Mutual Funds* (American Association of Individual Investors, 612 N. Michigan Ave., Chicago, IL 60611).

In summary, investors should not choose a fund only on the basis of its performance rating. They should consider *both performance and risk (beta)*.

How to Choose a Mutual Fund

What mutual fund to choose is not an easy question and there is no sure answer. It will be advisable to take the following steps:
1. Develop a list of funds that appear to meet investment goals.

2. Obtain a prospectus. The prospectus contains the fund's investment objectives. Read the statement of objectives as well as risk factors and investment limitations. Also request the Statement of Additional Information, which includes the details of fees and lists the investments; a copy of the annual report; and the most recent quarterly report.
3. Make sure the fund's investment objectives and investment policies meet investment goals.
4. Analyze the fund's past performance in view of its set objectives, in both *good* markets and *bad* markets. The quarterly and annual statements issued by the fund will show results for the previous year and probably a comparison with the S&P 500. Look at historical performance over a 5- or 10-year period. Look for *beta* figures in investment newsletters and directories. Also, read the prospectus summary section for per-share and capital changes. *Money*, *Forbes*, and other investment periodicals publish semiannual or annual performance data on mutual funds.
5. From the prospectus, try to determine some clues to management's ability to accomplish the fund's investment objectives. Emphasize the record, experience, and capability of the management company.
6. Note what securities comprise the fund's portfolio to see how they look to you. Not all mutual funds are fully diversified. Not all mutual funds invest in high-quality companies.
7. Compare various fees (such as redemption, management, and sales charges, if any) and various shareholder services offered by the funds being considered (such as the right of accumulation, any switch privilege within fund families, available investment plans, and a systematic withdrawal plan).

See also Beta Coefficient.

MUTUALLY EXCLUSIVE INVESTMENTS A project is said to be mutually exclusive if the acceptance of one project automatically

excludes the acceptance of one or more other projects. In the case where one must choose between mutually exclusive investments, the NPV and IRR methods may result in contradictory indications. The conditions under which contradictory rankings can occur are

1. Projects that have different life expectancies.

2. Projects that have different sizes of investment.

3. Projects whose cash flows differ over time. For example, the cash flows of one project increase over time, while those of another decrease.

The contradictions result from different assumptions with respect to the reinvestment rate on cash flows from the projects.

1. The NPV method discounts all cash flows at the cost of capital, thus implicitly assuming that these cash flows can be reinvested at this rate.

2. The IRR method implies a reinvestment rate at IRR. Thus, the implied reinvestment rate will differ from project to project.

The NPV method generally gives correct ranking, since the cost of capital is a more realistic reinvestment rate.

▪ Example

Assume the following:

	Cash Flows					
	0	1	2	3	4	5
A	(100)	120	–	–	–	–
B	(100)	–	–	–	–	201.14

Figure 1   NPV Profile

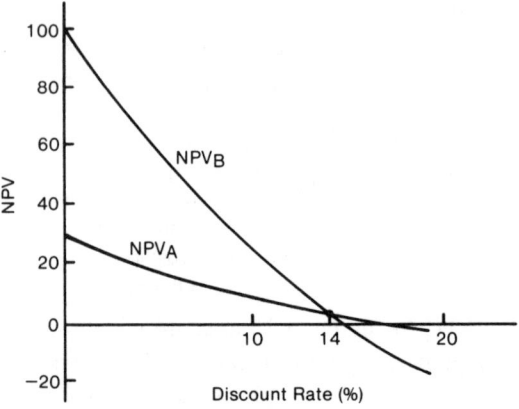

Computing IRR and NPV at 10% gives the following different rankings:

	IRR	NPV at 10%
A	20%	9.01
B	15%	24.90

The NPVs plotted against the appropriate discount rates form a graph called an NPV profile (Figure 1).

At a discount rate larger than 14%, A has a higher NPV than B. Therefore, A should be selected. At a discount rate less than 14%, B has the higher NPV than A and thus should be selected. The correct decision is to select the project with the higher NPV, since the NPV method assumes a more realistic reinvestment rate, that is, the cost of capital.

N

NATIONAL INCOME ACCOUNTING This is the accounting system for macroeconomics. It is a necessary step in learning how macroeconomic variables—such as the economy's total output, the price level, the level of employment, interest rates, and others—are determined. The national income accounts give us regular estimates of gross national product (GNP), the basic measure of the performance of the economy in producing goods and services. They are also useful because they provide us with a conceptual framework for describing the relationships among three key macroeconomic variables: output, income, and spending.

NEGATIVE ASSURANCE This is when the CPA indicates to financial statement users (usually underwriters and bankers) that nothing came to his or her attention that has a detrimental effect upon the financial statements and related data. Negative assurance is typically requested by investment bankers in connection with an equity or debt issuance. It may also be expressed if the CPA is requested to comment on financial statements that were audited in a prior year and for which an audit opinion was given. Negative assurance cannot be given if a certifying audit in conformity with GAAS has been made. It may also not be given unless an examination has been made in accordance with GAAP for the prior year. An expression of negative assurance gives confidence to the user that nothing was found by the auditor to give the opinion that the financial statements do not fairly present financial position in conformity with GAAP consistently applied.

■ Example

If a company wants to issue securities to the public, it has to file a registration statement with the SEC that typically includes unaudited financial statements besides the audited statements. Usually, the underwriters will ask the independent CPA to furnish a *comfort letter* covering the accountant's independence, compliance of the format of audited financial statements with SEC requirements, unaudited financial statements, material subsequent events after the date of the financial statements, and other financial data. The CPA will state in giving negative assurance that nothing was found in the course of applying procedures that would make him or her believe that the statements are in violation of accounting requirements.

NEGLIGENCE This refers to the auditor's failure to exercise due care in the performance of the attest function. *Ordinary negligence*, which is unintentional, occurs from judgmental mistakes due to such factors as inexperience, inadequate training, or poor supervision. *Gross negligence* arises from reckless disregard for promulgated accounting, reporting, and auditing standards. Legal liability exists to a greater degree for gross negligence.

NEGOTIATED PRICE The negotiated price is the *transfer* price that is established through meetings between the buying and supplying divisions. Negotiated transfer prices, like *market price*-based transfer prices, are believed to preserve divisional autonomy. In case divisions cannot agree on a transfer price, some companies establish arbitrary procedures to help settle disputes between divisions. However, an intervention by an arbitrator reduces divisional autonomy. *See also* Transfer Pricing.

NET PRESENT VALUE METHOD (NPV) This is a method widely used for evaluating investment projects. Under the NPV method, the present value (PV) of all cash inflows from the project is compared against the initial investment (I). The net present value (NPV), which is the difference between the present value and the initial investment (i.e., NPV = PV − I), determines whether or not the project is an acceptable investment. Under the method, if the net present value is positive (NPV > 0 or PV > I), the project should be accepted. *See also* Capital Budgeting.

NONMONETARY EXCHANGE OF ASSETS Nonmonetary transactions covered under APB Opinion 29 primarily deal with exchanges or distributions of fixed assets.

In an exchange of similar assets (e.g., truck for truck), the new asset received is recorded at the book value of the old asset plus the cash paid. Since book value of the old asset is the basis to charge the new asset, no gain is possible. However, a loss is possible because in no case can the new asset exceed the fair market value of the new asset.

In an exchange of dissimilar assets (e.g., truck for machine), the new asset is recorded at the fair market value of the old asset plus the cash paid. Thus, a gain or loss may arise because the fair market value of the old asset will be different from the book value of the old asset. However, the new asset cannot be shown at more than its fair market value. Fair market value in a nonmonetary exchange may be based upon

- Quoted market price
- Appraisal
- Cash transaction for similar items

■ Example

An old fixed asset costing $10,000 with accumulated depreciation of $2,000 is traded in for a new fixed asset having a fair market value of $22,000. Cash paid on the exchange is $4,000. The fair market value of the old asset is $5,000.

If a similar exchange is involved, the entry is

Fixed Asset ($8,000 + $4,000)	12,000	
Accumulated Depreciation	2,000	
Fixed Asset		10,000
Cash		4,000

Assume instead that the fair market value of the new asset was $11,000, resulting in the exception where the new fixed asset must be recorded at $11,000. Note the new fixed asset cannot be shown at more than its fair market value. In this case, the entry is

Fixed Asset	11,000	
Accumulated Depreciation	2,000	
Loss	1,000	
Fixed Asset		10,000
Cash		4,000

Assume the original facts except that a dissimilar exchange is involved. The entry is

Fixed Asset ($5,000 + $4,000)	9,000	
Accumulated Depreciation	2,000	
Fixed Asset		10,000
Gain		1,000

In a nonmonetary exchange, the entity receiving the monetary payment (boot) recognizes a gain to the degree the monetary receipt is greater than the proportionate share of the book value of the asset given up.

$$\text{Gain} = \frac{\text{Monetary}}{\text{receipt}} - \left(\frac{\text{Monetary receipt}}{\begin{array}{c}\text{Fair market value of}\\ \text{total consideration}\\ \text{received}\end{array}} \right)$$

$$\times \left(\begin{array}{c}\text{Book value of asset}\\ \text{given up}\end{array} \right)$$

The company receiving the boot records the asset acquired at the carrying value of the asset surrendered minus the portion considered sold.

The company paying the boot records the asset purchased at the carrying value of the asset surrendered plus the boot paid.

NONROUTINE DECISIONS These are usually short-term, nonrecurring types of decisions such as the following:
1. Acceptance or rejection of a special order
2. Make or buy a certain subassembly
3. Sell or process further
4. Keep or drop a certain business segment
In these types of decisions, a choice is typically made considering *relevant costs* and *contribution margin*. *See also* Contribution Margin (CM); Relevant Costing.

NONSTATISTICAL SAMPLING Nonstatistical sampling occurs when an auditor uses his prior experience and knowledge with a particular client and industry to compute the number of sampling units and specific items to be studied from the population. The sample takes into account the nature of the business and unique characteristics that may exist. The CPA must be objective in carrying out the sample and perform detailed analysis to assure the sampled units are correct. This approach may be advisable when a particular area of the population is being carefully examined or immediate results and feedback are needed. *Note*: A nonstatistical sample does *not* involve random selection. There is no computation made of sampling error, precision, or confidence level. Thus, there is an absence of statistical techniques and conclusions.

The auditor in using nonstatistical sampling considers the same factors in determining sample size and in evaluating sample results as in statistical sampling. The difference is that in nonstatistical sampling, the auditor does not quantify or explicitly enumerate values for these factors. In statistical sampling, however, they are explicitly quantified. That is, in nonstatistical sampling, the auditor determines the sample size, selects a sample, and evaluates the sample results entirely on the basis of subjective criteria and his own experience, that is, judgment. In addition, it is important to note that a properly designed nonstatistical sample may be just as effective as a statistical sample. *See also* Sampling.

NORMAL DISTRIBUTION This is the most popular probability distribution that is used for statistical decision making in business. It has the following important characteristics:
1. The curve has a single peak.
2. It is bell-shaped.
3. The mean (average) lies at the center of the distribution and the distribution is symmetrical around the mean.
4. The two tails of the distribution extend indefinitely and never touch the horizontal axis.
5. The shape of the distribution is determined by its *mean* (μ) and *standard deviation* (σ).
Normal distribution is pictured in Figure 1. Since it is a symmetric distribution, it has the nice property that a known percentage

Figure 1 Normal Distribution

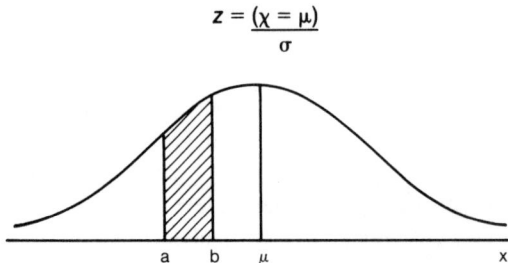

$$z = \frac{(x = \mu)}{\sigma}$$

Figure 3 Standard Normal Variate

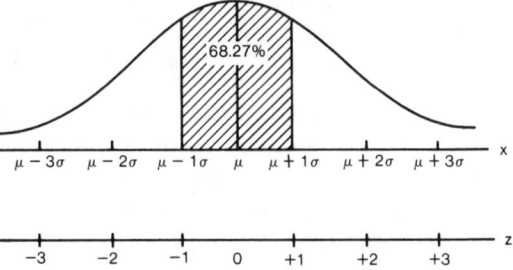

of all possible values of x lie within $\pm$ a certain number of standard deviations of the mean, as illustrated by Figure 2. For example, 68.27% of the values of any normally distributed variable lie within the interval $(\mu - 1\sigma, \mu + 1\sigma)$.

Figure 2 Area Under the Curve

%	99.73%	99%	95.45%	95%	90%	68.27%
No. of $\pm\sigma$'s	3.00	2.58	2.00	1.96	1.645	1.00

The probability of the normal distribution, as just given, is difficult to work with in determining areas under the curve, and each set of x values generates another curve (as long as the means and standard deviations are different). To facilitate computations, every set of x values is translated to a new axis, a z axis, with the translation defined as

$$z = \frac{x - \mu}{\sigma}$$

The resulting values, called z-values, are the values of a new variable called the *standard normal variate*, z. The translation process is depicted in Figure 3.

The new variable z is normally distributed with a mean of zero and a standard deviation of 1. Tables of areas (See Table 5 in the Appendix) under this standard normal distribution have been compiled and widely published so that areas under any normal distribution can be found by translating the x values

to z values and then using the tables for the standardized normal.

■ Example

Assume the total book value of an inventory is normally distributed with $\mu = \$5,000$ and $\sigma = \$1,000$. What percentage of the population lies between \$3,000 and \$7,000? To answer, we first translate these two x-values to z-values using the z formula:

$$z_1 = (\$3,000 - \$5,000)/\$1,000 = -2$$
$$z_2 = (\$7,000 - \$5,000)/\$1,000 = +2$$

Referring to Figure 2, we see that 95.45% of the population lies between these two values. This means that total book value will lie between \$3,000 and \$7,000 with 95.45% chance.

Applications of a normal distribution in accounting and finance are numerous, including

1. Capital budgeting under risk
2. Probability of meeting a delivery date
3. Determination of safety stock

NOT-FOR-PROFIT ACCOUNTING, OTHER THAN GOVERNMENTAL This applies to universities, voluntary hospitals, and voluntary health and welfare organizations. The *accrual basis* of accounting is required. There exists segregation of activities by fund. A fund is an accounting entity established with the objective of accounting for resources considered to meet specified activities in conformity with legal restrictions and regulations. Funds may

be restricted or unrestricted. Restricted funds are limited in activity by outside parties (e.g., agencies). Unrestricted funds are not limited through external restrictions or terms of activity. Fund balance is the residual of assets over liabilities. Budgetary accounting and encumbrance accounting are *not* followed. Fixed assets are reported in the balance sheet and depreciated. Investments may be valued at lower of cost or market, or just market value. Pledges are reflected as receivables and income when they are received. Donations of service, materials, and facilities are recorded at their fair market value. There is a functional reporting of expenses, meaning that expenses are accumulated by pro-gram purpose instead of by object of expenditure.

The not-for-profit institutions present a balance sheet with a distinction between restricted and unrestricted resources by type of fund. The activity statement shows the results of support, revenue, expenses, and expenditures. The activity statement is referred to differently depending upon the type of organization. For instance, it is termed "statement of current funds revenue and expenditures" by colleges and universities. The statement of changes in fund balance is prepared by all entities, either by itself or as a part of the activity statement. *See also* Governmental Accounting.

O

OBSERVATION TEST An observation test is performed by the auditor who *visually* evaluates operations occurring at the client. A substantive test would be observing the quantity and quality of inventory. A compliance procedure would be to see if the person who has physical custody over inventory records is someone different from the one who has responsibility for physical custody.

ODD LOT An odd-lot transaction is one involving less than 100 shares of a stock. *See also* Stock Orders.

ODD-LOT THEORY In odd-lot trading, the investment analyst can see popular opinion. According to the theory, the rule of contrary opinion holds that whatever small investors are doing, the opposite is the correct choice. *See also* Technical Analysis.

OFF-BALANCE SHEET ASSET An unrecorded asset is a financial resource of the company for which future benefit may be received. Although it is not listed on the balance sheet as an asset, it represents a favorable attribute of financial position. For analytical purposes, the credit or investment analyst may consider it as an asset in evaluating a company. Examples are a tax loss carryforward benefit, purchase commitment where the price to be paid for the contract is currently less than its market value, value of human resources, worth of a mailing list, expected rebate, a contingent asset in which payment will be received in the event a certain occurrence takes place, and a long-term lease at low rental payments. *See also* Off-Balance Sheet Liability.

OFF-BALANCE SHEET LIABILITY An unrecorded obligation is not shown on the balance sheet as a liability, but it may require later payment or the rendering of services. For analytical purposes, the analyst may consider it as a liability of the entity. Examples are many, including a lawsuit, tax dispute, cosigning of a loan for a problem borrower, dispute under a government contract, long-term lease at a higher rental in an undesirable location (e.g., warehouse located in a high crime area), projected benefit obligation exceeds the accumulated benefit obligation in a pension plan, and unrecognized health insurance benefits to be paid in the future for retired employees. *See also* Off-Balance Sheet Asset.

OKUN'S LAW This describes the relationship between changes in the rate of economic growth (measured by changes in GNP) and changes in the unemployment rate. This law is attributed to Arthur Okun, chairman of the Council of Economic Advisors under President Johnson. The law states that for every 2½ percentage points of growth in real GNP above the trend rate that is sustained for a year, the unemployment rate declines by·1 percentage point.

It means that the economy must continue to grow considerably faster than its trend (long-term average) rate in order to achieve a substantial reduction in the unemployment rate.

■ Example

Suppose that the trend rate of growth is 3% per year and the unemployment rate is currently 9%. How many years would it take to return to a target rate of, say, 6% unemployment? The answer depends on how fast the economy grows in the recovery. Assume that the growth rate of potential output is 3% per year. One possible path to achieve the target is for output to grow at 5½% per year for 3 years. On this path, each year the economy is growing 2½% above trend, and thus each year it takes 1 percentage point off the unemployment rate.

ON-LINE DATA BASES An accountant or financial manager must know the existing data bases and what they contain to obtain relevant accounting, audit, tax, financial, and legal information. A listing of data bases is provided in the *Directory of On-Line Data Bases* and *Data Pro Directory of On-Line Services*. Also, reference can be made to Mike Cane's books on on-line services (e.g., *The Computer Phone Book: Directory of On-Line Systems* published by New American Library).

Before using a new data base, you should ask the following questions:
• Is a data base demonstration available?

• Will the data base meet your information needs?
• Is the data base updated on a regular basis and at what cost?
• Is the data base easy to use?
• Is there an index of terms to facilitate data base use?
• Does the data base provide numeric codes for industries or geographic locations?

When using an on-line data base, there may be several ways to search in order to obtain an answer to a question, including by key word or phrase, code section, citation or case name, and document type.

In using an accounting data base, a search may be made by key word or phrase, Financial Accounting Standards Board Number, Statement on Auditing Standards Number, and Securities and Exchange Commission Release Number.

When accessing a legal data base for a legislative item or document, the search may be made by bill number, public law number, tax act, or originating committee.

After the search is completed and the information found, the result may be output in various ways, such as (1) sorting the documents in order (e.g., chronologically), ranking documents by relevance, displaying the documents, listing the items, and printing the output.

Dialog Information Services' Dialoglink Communications Manager™ is communications software that saves the tax practitioner money by reducing the connect time when accessing on-line data bases. It facilitates the data base search for tax-related items.

Available data bases for accounting and tax needs are cited in *Computers in Accounting* and the *The CPA Journal*.

Easy Net™ allows the accountant and tax practitioner without special software to use an 800 telephone number to access 600 data bases. For information, call (800) 841-9553. Compuserve Information Service™ allows the attorney and accountant to access up to

700 domestic and international data bases through the Iquest on-line search and retrieve.

Lockheed's Dialog™ contains over 150 different data bases covering areas of interest to accountants and attorneys as Securities and Exchange Commission filings. The American Institute of CPA's time-sharing library has accounting and tax information, including Internal Revenue Service codes and regulations, proposed regulations, and Supreme Court decisions.

On-line data bases of interest to accountants and tax practitioners are

• *Prentice Hall's Information Network* (*PHINet*)—contains tax information included in Prentice Hall's looseleaf tax services. Included in the data base are Prentice Hall's daily tax update, articles written by tax experts, tax court case rulings, editorial explanations of tax requirements, annotations, announcements, Internal Revenue Code sections, tax regulations, new legislation, committee reports, revenue rulings and procedures, news releases, and private letter rulings. Covered in the data base are federal income tax, estate tax, gift tax, and excise tax questions. There is a pension and profit sharing service as well. The data base also contains selected Internal Revenue Service numbered publications that interpret code sections, regulations, and court decisions. Documents related to tax shelters are also provided.

• *American Institute of CPAs' NAARS*—contains recommended accounting practices and footnote references, answers practice questions, and furnishes proper accounting for a transaction or event. NAARS has about 4,200 companies in each annual report file.

• *West's Westlaw*—contains legal cases and information for attorneys. It comes in handy for the tax attorney who wants to search for legal precedents relating to a tax case.

• *Mead Data Central's Legal Exchange Information Service* (*Lexis*)—covers diverse areas of law such as tax and bankruptcy.

• *Legal Source*—contains federal and state court procedures along with a full text data base manager for lawyers.

• *Mead Data Central's News Exchange Information Service* (*Nexis*)—covers authoritative pronouncements, preferred practice, and industry information. Data are presented regarding different types of business situations, including litigation, acquisitions, and bankruptcy.

• *Source Telecomputing's The Source*—provides answers to tax questions and the option of reading IRS publications.

• *Business/Professional Software Data Base*—describes software packages for accounting functions, including inventory control.

• *Western Union's InfoMaster*—includes corporate descriptions, legal references, and financial statements and analysis.

• *Predicasts*—contains acquisition/merger information.

• *American Institute of CPAs' Accountant's Index*— lists accounting and tax articles and books.

See also Electronic Mail.

OPERATING LEASE This is a lease accounted for by the lessee or lessor as a regular rental of property. The lessee charges rental expense while the lessor credits rental revenue. *See also* Leases.

OPERATING LEVERAGE This is a measure of *operating risk* and arises from fixed operating costs. A simple indication of operating leverage is the effect that a change in sales has an operating income. The formula is

$$\text{Operating leverage at a given level of sales} = \frac{\text{Percentage change in EBIT (or operating income)}}{\text{Percentage change in sales}}$$

Another measure of operating leverage (risk) is the ratio of fixed costs to total costs. High fixed costs in a company's cost structure is indicative of risk because fixed costs cannot be slashed in the short run to meet declining demand for the product or service. *See also* Leverage.

OPERATIONAL AUDIT
An operational audit is conducted on a recurring basis by internal auditors of the business entity. A review is made of the efficiency and appropriateness of the company's operations and organization in meeting goals. Additionally, irregularities and errors are searched out. Management's performance and ability to conform to stated procedures and budgets are examined. Areas evaluated include policies, processes, structure, and controls. The subject of an operational audit may be a business segment (e.g., division, product line) and specific task (activity). Management is the major user of the operational audit results. The typical operational audit report specifies the success in which functions are being carried out, deficiencies in the process, recommendations for improvement, and overall conclusions. *See also* Internal Audit.

OPERATIONS RESEARCH/MANAGEMENT SCIENCE
Operations research (OR), which is very often used interchangeably with management science, is a scientific method of providing the decision maker with a quantitative basis for decisions regarding the operations under his or her control. It is divided broadly into two categories of techniques (models): optimization models (mathematical programming) and simulation models. *Optimization models* attempt to provide an optimal solution (or prescriptive solution) to a problem, whereas *simulation models* produce a descriptive (or what-if type of) solution. Operations research, for example, covers such quantitative techniques as inventory

models, linear programming, queuing theory, program evaluation and review technique (PERT), and Monte Carlo simulation. *See also* Mathematical Programming; Optimization Models.

OPPORTUNITY COST APPROACH
This is where the concept of *opportunity cost* is applied to solve a decision problem. Opportunity cost represents the net benefit lost by rejecting some alternative course of action. Its significance in decision making is that the best decision is always sought, since it considers the cost of the best available alternative *not* taken. The opportunity cost does not appear on formal accounting statements.

■ Example

If $1 million can be invested in a CD earning 9%, the opportunity cost of using that money for a particular business venture would be computed to be $90,000 ($1 million $\times$ 0.09). *See also* Incremental Analysis; Total Project Approach.

OPTIMAL REORDER POINT
This is the inventory level at which it is appropriate to replenish stock. Reorder point is calculated as follows:

Reorder point = Average usage per unit of lead time
$\times$ Lead time + Safety stock

First, multiply average daily (or weekly) usage by the lead time in days (or weeks), yielding the lead time demand. Then add safety stock to this to provide for the variation in lead time demand to determine the reorder point. If aveage usage and lead time are both certain, no safety stock is necessary and should be dropped from the formula. *See also* Inventory Planning and Control.

OPTIMIZATION MODELS
These are quantitative models (such as operations research/management science) that attempt to provide an optimal (profit-maximizing or cost-mini-

mizing) solution to a resource allocation problem. They typically consist of two important ingredients in their formulation: (1) objective function to be maximized or minimized and (2) constraints. Optimization models include *linear programming* (*LP*), *integer programming*, *quadratic programming*, and *dynamic programming*. *See also* Mathematical Programming; Simulation Models.

OPTIONS: CALLS AND PUTS Options provide the investor with the right to buy a security at a given price for a specified time period. Options have their own inherent value and are traded in secondary markets. Option prices are tied into the market price of the common stock to which they apply. High risk is involved when investing in options.

Calls and puts are types of stock options. They are bought and sold in 100-share denominations.

When a *call* is bought, the investor has the right to purchase a stock at a stated price for a given time frame. The expectation is that the company's market price of stock will increase. There is an opportunity for a substantial gain from a small investment, but significant risk exists because if the market price does not increase sufficiently, the entire investment will be lost.

When a *put* is bought, the investor has the right to sell stock at a given price for a stated time horizon. A put is bought when there is an expectation of a declining stock price. There is an opportunity for substantial gain from a small investment, but significant risk exists because the entire investment will be lost if stock price does not fall sufficiently.

Calls and puts are in bearer negotiable form with a life ranging between 1 month to 9 months. They are usually written for widely held, actively traded companies. Brokerage fees are based on the amount and value of the option contract.

Calls do *not* give the holder ownership rights in the stock and thus dividend and voting rights do not exist. But options are adjusted for stock dividends and stock splits.

The life of calls and puts is longer than for stock rights but shorter than for stock warrants. Calls and puts are speculative and provide leverage. They are an alternative to investments in common stock.

Calls and puts are not issued by the company with the common stock but rather by option writers. The option writer receives the price paid for the call or put less commission costs. Options are traded on the open market. Calls and puts are written and can be bought through brokers and dealers. The writer buys or delivers the stock when requested.

To earn a return, the holder of a call or put does not have to exercise it. The option can be sold in the secondary market for its market price. The value of a call rises as the related common stock increases. The call may be sold prior to its expiration date.

Calls and puts are traded on listed option exchanges (e.g., Chicago Board Options Exchange, American Stock Exchange, Philadelphia Stock Exchange). They are also traded on the over-the-counter market. Option exchanges deal solely with the buying and selling of calls and puts. *Listed options* are traded on organized exchanges. *Conventional options* are traded in the over-the-counter market.

The Options Clearing Corporation issues calls listed on the options exchanges. Orders are placed with this corporation, which then issues the calls or closes the position. When a call is exercised, the holder goes through the Clearing Corporation, which picks at random a writer from member accounts. A call writer must sell 100 shares of common stock at the exercise price.

The price per share for 100 shares, which the buyer may buy at, is called the *striking price* (exercise price). For a put, it is the

price at which the stock may be sold. The purchase or sale of the stock is to the writer of the option. The striking price is fixed for the life of the option. When a change in stock price occurs, new strike prices may be introduced for trading to reflect new value.

In the case of conventional calls, there are *no* restrictions as to what the striking price should be. But it is typically near the market price of the stock to which it applies. For listed calls, stocks having a price below $50 per share must have striking prices in $5 increments, stocks between $50 and $100 have striking prices in $10 increments, and stocks selling at more than $100 per share have striking prices in $20 increments.

The expiration date of an option is the last day it can be exercised. In the case of conventional options, it can be any business day. A listed option has a standardized expiration date.

Premium is the term used to connote the cost of the option. It is the price the buyer of the call or put pays the option writer.

Factors Determining the Premium

• Trading volume of the option. The greater the trading volume, the greater the price.

• Direction of the stock market and the particular security itself. An upward market usually means a higher premium for a call.

• Dividend trend of the security.

• Fluctuation in stock price of the company. Wider vacillation in price means a higher premium since there is more speculative appeal to the option.

• Exchange on which the option is listed. A more reputable exchange means a higher premium for a call.

• Going interest rates.

• Change in market price of the underlying security.

• The spread between the market price of the stock and the option's exercise price. A greater differential means a higher price.

• The period still left before expiration of the option. A longer period justifies a higher premium.

A call is *in-the-money* when market price is greater than the strike price. A call is *out-of-the-money* when market price is less than the strike price. Call options in-the-money have intrinsic value equal to:

Value of call = (Market price of stock
$$- \text{Exercise price of call}) \times 100$$

■ Example

The market price of stock is $30 and the strike price is $27. The value of the call is

$$(\$30 - \$27) \times 100 = \$300$$

There is no intrinsic value to out-of-the-money calls. Typically, the investor can earn a higher return at lower risk with out-of-the-money calls. A problem however is that the price consists only of the investment premium which is lost if the stock price does not increase.

If the total premium (option price) of an option is $8 and the intrinsic value is $5, the difference of $3 is for other factors. The amount of the premium equals the intrinsic value plus speculative premium (time value), considering such items as variability, risk, expected future prices, leverage, expiration date, and dividend.

Total premium = Intrinsic value
$$+ \text{Speculative premium}$$

The meaning of in-the-money and out-of-the-money is different for puts since they allow the owner to sell stock at the strike price. When strike price is greater than market price of stock, an in-the-money put option exists. Its value equals:

Value of put = (Exercise price of put
$$- \text{Market price of stock}) \times 100$$

■ Example

The market price of a stock is $60 and the strike price of the put is $67. The value of the put equals:

$$(\$67 - \$60) \times 100 = \$700$$

An out-of-the-money put exists when the market price of stock is greater than the strike price. Since a stock owner can sell it for a greater amount in the market than he could obtain by exercising the put, no intrinsic value exists for an out-of-the-money put.

	ABC Calls at $70 Strike Price	ABC Puts at $70 Strike Price
	Stock Price	Stock Price
In the money	over $70	under $70
At the money	$70	$70
Out of the money	under $70	over $70

The theoretical value for calls and puts indicates the price at which the options should be traded. However, they are usually traded at prices in excess of true value when a long expiration period exists. This difference is termed the investment premium.

Investment premium
$$= \frac{\text{Option premium} - \text{Option value}}{\text{Option value}}$$

■ Example

A put has a theoretical value of $2,000 and a price of $2,400. The investment premium equals:

$$\frac{\$2,400 - \$2,000}{\$2,000} = \frac{\$400}{\$2,000} = 20\%$$

Calls

The call purchaser gains if the market price of the stock increases.

■ Example

An investor buys a 3-month call option to purchase 1,000 shares of ABC Company at $15 per share. When the stock price reaches $22, the option is exercised. The gain is

$$\$7 \times 1,000 \text{ shares} = \$7,000$$

If the market price had declined below $15, the cost of the option would be lost.

The advantage of a call is that the investor owns common stock for a fraction of the cost of purchasing regular shares. Leverage exists since a little change in the price of the common stock can cause a significant change in the option price of the call.

■ Example

The market price of stock is $40. A call can be bought for $350, permitting the acquisition of 100 shares at $40 each. The market price of the stock rises to $58. The gain is $18 per share, or a total of $1,800 on an investment of $350. This translates to a 414% return after considering the cost of the option:

$$\frac{\text{Gain} - \text{Cost of option}}{\text{Cost of option}} = \frac{\$1,800 - \$350}{\$350}$$

$$= \frac{\$1,450}{\$350} = 414\%$$

In effect, when the investor exercises the call at $40, he can sell the stock at $58. *Note*: The investor could have earned the same gain of $1,800 but would have had to invest $4,000 so the rate of return would have been only 45% ($1,800/$4,000).

■ Example

A call gives an investor the right to buy 100 shares of $30 stock at $27. The call will trade at a price of about $3 a share. The call option may be used if the investor believes the stock price will increase in the future but has a cash flow problem and is unable to buy the stock. However, the investor will have adequate cash to do so later. In this case, the investor can buy a call so as not to lose a good investment opportunity. For instance, on February 6, the investor purchases a $32 June call option for $3 a share. If the stock price is $34½, the speculative premium is $½. In June, the investor exercises the call option when the stock price

is $37. The cost of the 100 shares of stock for tax reporting is the strike price ($32) plus the option premium ($3), or $35.

Puts

A put holder may sell 100 shares at the strike price to a put writer prior to the expiration date.

■ Example

The market price of a stock is $45 per share. A put is bought at $45 per share. The cost of the put is $400. When the market price of the stock reaches $30, the put is exercised, realizing a profit of $15 per share, or a total of $1,500. You buy on the market 100 shares at $30 and sell them to the writer of the put for $45. The net gain equals:

$$\text{Gain} - \text{Cost of put} = \text{Net gain}$$
$$\$1,500 - \$400 = \$1,100$$

This translates into a percentage gain of 275% computed as follows:

$$\frac{\text{Gain} - \text{Cost of put}}{\text{Cost of put}} = \frac{\$1,500 - \$400}{\$400}$$
$$= \frac{\$1,100}{\$400} = 275\%$$

If the put is not exercised, a loss of $400 equal to the cost of the put is lost.

■ Example

A company's stock price was $55 on March 2. An investor buys a $56 June put for $4. The speculative premium is therefore $3. On June 7, the stock price falls to $47 and the price of the June $56 put to $8. The intrinsic value is $9 and the speculative premium is $1. As the put holder, the investor has a gain of $4.

Hedging

An owner of a call and put option may *hedge* by holding on to two or more securities to reduce risk and at the same time to earn a

profit. It may relate to buying a stock and subsequently purchasing an option on it. For instance, a stock may be acquired along with writing a call on it. Further, a holder of stock that has increased in price may buy a put in order to obtain downside risk protection.

■ Example

An investor buys 100 shares of ABC Company at $25 each and a put for $175 with a strike price of $25. If the stock remains static, a $175 loss is incurred. If the price decreases, the loss on the stock is offset by the gain on the put. If stock price rises, there is a gain on the stock and a loss on the put. In effect, to accomplish the benefit of a hedge, a loss on the put has to be incurred. *Careful*: At the expiration of the put, a loss is incurred with no further hedge.

A put may also be bought to hedge a position after earning a profit on the stock. Assume you buy 100 shares of ABC Company at $70 per share. The stock is now at $85, for a profit of $15 per share. To assure a profit, a put costing $250 is purchased with an $85 strike price. Regardless of what transpires in the future, there is a minimum gain of $1,250 ($1,500 − $250).

If the stock price drops, the minimum profit of $1,700 will be earned. If the stock price increases, an additional profit will be earned.

A call may be bought to protect a short sale from the risk of an increasing stock price. In this hedging strategy, the short seller will not incur a loss above a stated amount. But profit will be decreased by the cost of the call.

Speculation

Calls and puts may be employed as an alternative to investing in the common stock itself. While a higher return is possible from the leverage effect, speculation is involved, since all the invested funds may be lost.

▪ Example

A speculator purchases an option contract to buy 100 shares at $25 a share. The option costs $150. Assume a rise in stock price to $33 a share. The speculator exercises the option and sells the shares in the market, realizing a gain of $650 ($33 − $25 − $1.50 = $6.50 × 100 shares). Now the speculator can sell the option in the market and make a profit because of its increased value. However, if there is a decline in stock price, the loss to the holder is limited to $150 (the option's cost). Of course, brokerage fees are involved. In effect, this call option permitted the speculator to purchase 100 shares worth $2,500 for $150 for a short period. *See also* Stock Right; Stock Warrant.

OPTION WRITING   The writer of a call agrees to sell shares at the strike price paid for the call option. Call option writers do the opposite of what buyers do. An option is written because it is believed that a price increase in the stock will be less than what the call purchaser expects. The writer may even anticipate a static or decreasing price in the security. Option writers receive the option premium less related transaction costs. If the option is not exercised, the writer earns the price paid for it. If the option is exercised, the writer incurs a loss, which may be substantial.

If the writer of the option decides to sell shares, he has to come up with stock at the agreed-upon price if the option is exercised. In either case, the option writer receives income from the premium. The option is in 100-share denominations. The writer sells the option because he feels it will not be exercised. The risk of option writing is that the writer if uncovered has to buy the stock or if covered loses the gain.

The writer can elect to buy back the option to eliminate his exposure.

▪ Example

There is a strike price of $30 and the premium for the option is $4. If the stock is at less than $30, the call will not be exercised and the writer earns the $4 premium. If the stock goes above $30, the call may be exercised and the writer will have to come up with 100 shares at $30. But the call writer only incurs a loss if the stock goes beyond $34.

Options may be naked (uncovered) or covered. In a naked option, the writer does not own the underlying stock. The investor writes the call or put for the premium and will retain it if the price change is in his favor or insignificant in amount. However, there is unlimited loss exposure to the writer. In a covered option, the writer already owns the underlying stock and thus less risk is involved. For example, a call can be written for stock the writer owns or a put can be written for stock sold short. This is a conservative strategy to obtain positive returns. The goal is to write an out-of-the-money option, keep the premium paid, and have the market price of the stock be equal but not greater than the option exercise price. Writing a covered call option is similar to hedging a position, since if stock price drops, the writer's loss on the stock is in part netted against the option premium.

OVER-THE-COUNTER MARKET   The over-the-counter market is not a specific institution but instead a means of trading securities. Although it is not an auction market, it furnishes a forum where new unlisted issues are traded. Traders (dealers) utilize a telecommunications network referred to as the National Association of Security Dealers Automated Quotation System (NASDAQ) for transactions in these securities. The NASDAQ index is comprised of about 2,300 companies. The over-the-counter market trades a higher dollar volume of securities than the national and regional exchanges.

Each over-the-counter trader makes a market in specified securities by offering to buy or sell them at specified prices. Dealers are the second party to a transaction. The *bid price* is the maximum price the dealer offers for a security. The *ask price* is the lowest price at which the dealer will sell the security. The dealer's profit is the spread between the bid price and the ask price.

Advantages of Buying Stocks in the Over-the-Counter Market

• Some securities are traded only in this market.

• Some securities have potential for substantial return but possess high risk.

• Through the NASDAQ communications network, there is much marketability for stocks and a good reflection of accurate stock price.

A disadvantage of buying over-the-counter stocks is that the companies whose stocks are sold there are often lower quality firms than those listed on the organized exchanges.

P

PARALLEL PROCESSING This applies to the simultaneous performance of two or more activities in a computer. For example, one task may be running at the same time another task is being read from memory.

PARITY CHECK A parity check is a test performed by checking a unit of information (i.e., word, byte) for even or odd parity to determine if an error has occurred in reading, writing, or transferring data. For example, if information is written, the computed parity bit is compared to the parity bit already appended to that information. Correctness exists if the parity bits agree. Otherwise, a mistake has occurred.

PARTNERSHIP ACCOUNTING According to the Uniform Partnership Act, a partnership is an association of two or more individuals as co-owners carrying on a business for profit. There are separate capital and drawing accounts for each partner. When a noncash asset is invested, it should be recorded at its fair market value at the date of transfer to the partnership. An obligation assumed by the partnership is credited to the specific liability account involved. If it is a long-term liability, it is recorded at the present value of future payments.

■ Example

Enright and Geller form a partnership. Enright, who was previously the sole proprietor, brings the following into the partnership:

	Book Value	Fair Market Value
Cash	$12,000	$12,000
Accounts receivable	7,000	7,000
Inventory	20,000	18,000
Auto	7,000	
Accumulated depreciation, auto	2,000	
Accounts payable	9,000	9,000
Allowance for uncollectible accounts	600	600

The following entry is made to record Enright's initial investment:

Cash	12,000	
Accounts receivable	7,000	
Inventory	18,000	
Auto	5,500	
Allowance for uncollectible accounts		600
Accounts payable		9,000
Enright, Capital		32,900

318

Depreciation on the auto on the partnership books will be based on the assigned value of $5,500.

Allocating Net Income or Loss to Partners

Partnership profit or loss is allocated according to the partnership agreement. Typically, the division is based upon the proportionate capital interest of each partner.

Division Based on Capital Interest

In this approach, profit is assigned based upon the ratio of the partners' capital balances.

■ Example

Nelson and Loft have capital balances of $40,000 and $10,000, respectively. The profit is $5,000. The entry is

Income Summary	5,000	
Nelson, Capital		4,000
Loft, Capital		1,000

Division Based Equally

In the absence of a stipulation in the partnership agreement, profits are assigned equally to the partners. Assuming the same facts as the previous example, each partner would receive $2,500.

Division Partially Based on Salary

Under this approach, partners are given credit for work performed and the remaining profit is allocated on some specific basis.

■ Example

Nelson and Loft have capital balances of $40,000 and $10,000, respectively. The net income is $5,000. Nelson and Loft are given salary allowances of $2,000 and $8,000, respectively. The remaining net income is to be allocated based on their capital balances.

The computation is

	Nelson	Loft	Total
Salary	$2,000	$ 800	$2,800
Balance	1,760[a]	440[b]	2,200
Total	$3,760	$1,240	$5,000

[a] $\frac{\$40,000}{\$50,000} \times \$2,200 = \$1,760$

[b] $\frac{\$10,000}{\$50,000} \times \$2,200 = \$440$

Division Partially Based on Interest

In this case, each partner receives interest on his or her capital balance and the remaining net income is allocated on some specified basis.

■ Example

Nelson and Loft have capital balances of $40,000 and $10,000, respectively. The net income for the year is $5,000. Each partner is to receive 8% interest on his or her capital balance and the remaining earnings are to be divided equally. The computation is

	Nelson	Loft	Total
Interest on capital balance	$3,200	$ 800	$4,000
Balance	500	500	1,000
Total	$3,700	$1,300	$5,000

Division Partially Based on Salary and Interest

Each partner may get a salary, interest on the capital balance, and the remainder of the profit on some basis.

■ Example

Nelson and Loft have capital balances of $40,000 and $10,000, respectively. The net income for the year is $5,000. Nelson and Loft receive salaries of $1,000 and $600, respectively, receive 5% interest on capital, and divide the remainder of the profit equally. The computation is

	Nelson	Loft	Total
Salary	$1,000	$ 600	$1,600
Interest	2,000	500	2,500
Balance	450	450	900
Total	$3,450	$1,550	$5,000

If the net income is less than the salary and/or interest allowances for the partners, the remaining negative balance should be allocated to the partners as if it were a loss.

Admitting a New Partner

According to the Uniform Partnership Act, a partner has the option to sell all or a portion of his or her interest without the consent of the others. The person buying the selling partner's interest obtains the right to share in profits. However, unless admitted to the firm, the individual cannot vote or participate in partnership affairs.

Admission by Acquiring an Interest

A new partner who purchases an interest from an old partner pays the purchase price directly to the old partner. An entry is made on the partnership books to transfer only the capital from the old partner to the new one. All other accounts remain intact.

■ Example

Simon and Davis have capital balances of $60,000 and $40,000, respectively. Smith buys half of Simon's interest for $33,000. The entry to transfer the capital balances is

Simon, Capital	30,000	
Smith, Capital		30,000

Note that $30,000, half of Simon's capital, has been transferred to Smith. The extra $3,000 paid by Smith to Simon is not reflected in the partnership books. Instead the $3,000 is in the nature of a *personal* benefit to Simon.

Admission by Contributing Assets

If the new partner contributes assets to the firm, the entry is to debit assets and credit capital.

■ Example

Assume the same facts as the prior example except that Smith contributes $25,000 for a one-fifth interest in the new partnership. The entry is

Cash	25,000	
Smith, Capital		25,000

Smith now has a one-fifth interest ($25,000/$125,000).

In the previous two examples, we assumed that the book value of the assets of the partnership reflected their fair market value when Smith was admitted. Thus, no adjustments to the recorded values were needed. But, in many instances, partnership assets must be revalued or goodwill recognized before the admission of a new partner.

Asset revaluation—before admitting a new partner, certain assets of the partnership have to be adjusted from book value to fair market value. The net effect of this revaluation is allocated to the existing partners based on the profit-sharing ratio.

■ Example

Simon and Davis share profits equally. Prior to the admission of Smith, it is decided that equipment having a book value of $6,000 is worth $7,500. The entry for the revaluation is

Equipment	1,500	
Simon, Capital		750
Davis, Capital		750

Recording goodwill—if a partnership earns excess earnings over other similar firms, there exists goodwill. When a new partner is admitted, he or she may have to pay for that goodwill. The goodwill account is debited and the capital accounts of the

old partners credited based on the profit-and-loss ratio.

■ **Example**

Smith and Davis have capital balances of $60,000 and $40,000, respectively. Net income is shared equally. Smith gains admission to the partnership by contributing $30,000 for a one-fifth interest. Although the total capital of the partnership before Smith's admission is $100,000, the parties agree that the firm is worth $120,000. The $20,000 excess constitutes goodwill that has to be divided equally between the old partners. The journal entry to record goodwill is

Goodwill	20,000	
Simon, Capital		10,000
Davis, Capital		10,000

The entry to admit the new partner is

Cash	30,000	
Smith, Capital		30,000

Note that Smith now has a one-fifth interest in the partnership ($30,000/$150,000).

Goodwill may be associated with the incoming partner. If the old partners agree to give the new partner recognition for his or her goodwill, the goodwill account is debited and the new partner's capital account is credited.

■ **Example**

Simon and Davis have capital balances of $60,000 and $40,000, respectively. Smith obtains admittance by making an investment of $40,000. Smith is granted goodwill recognition of $10,000. The entry is

Cash	40,000	
Goodwill	10,000	
Smith, Capital		50,000

Liquidating a Partnership

In liquidating a partnership, the following steps are involved: (1) the accounts are adjusted and closed; (2) assets are sold; (3)

liabilities are paid; and (4) the remaining cash is distributed to the partners based on their remaining capital balances.

■ **Example**

Tyler, Simpson, and White discontinue their partnership. The partnership books have been adjusted and all the accounts have been closed. The following is the post-closing trial balance:

Cash	$40,000	
Noncash assets	25,000	
Liabilities		$15,000
Tyler, capital		5,000
Simpson, capital		10,000
White, capital		35,000
	$65,000	$65,000

The partners share net income equally. Noncash assets are sold for $40,000. Appropriate journal entries follow:

(a) For the sale of assets

Cash	40,000	
Noncash Assets		25,000
Tyler, Capital		5,000
Simpson, Capital		5,000
White, Capital		5,000

(b) For the payment to creditors

Liabilities	15,000	
Cash		15,000

(c) For the cash distribution

Tyler, Capital	10,000	
Simpson, Capital	15,000	
White, Capital	40,000	
Cash		65,000

Note that the final cash distribution is based on the partners' ending capital balances.

PAYBACK PERIOD This is the length of time required to recover the initial amount of a capital investment. If the cash inflows occur at a uniform rate, it is the ratio of the amount of initial investment over expected annual cash inflows, or

Payback period = Initial investment/Annual cash inflows

■ Example

Assume projected annual cash inflows are expected to be $4,500 a year for 5 years from an investment of $18,000. The payback period on this proposal is 4 years, which is calculated as follows:

Payback period = $18,000/$4,500 = 4 years

If annual cash inflows are not even, the payback period would have to be determined by trial and error. Assume instead that the cash inflows are $4,000 in the first year, $5,000 in the second year, $6,000 in the third year, $6,000 in the fourth year, and $8,000 in the fifth year. The payback period would then be 3.5 years. In 3 years, all but $3,000 has been recovered. It takes one-half year ($3,000/$6,000) to recover the balance. When two or more projects are considered, the rule for making a selection decision is as follows: Choose the project with the shorter payback period. The rationale behind this is that the shorter the payback period, the greater the liquidity and the less risky the project. Advantages of the method include (1) it is simple to compute and easy to understand and (2) it handles investment risk effectively. Disadvantages of the method include (1) it ignores profitability of an investment and (2) it does not recognize the *time value of money*. To take into account the time value of money, the discounted payback period may be used. *See also* Discounted Payback Period.

PAYBACK RECIPROCAL Payback reciprocal is the reciprocal of the payback time. This often gives a quick, accurate estimate of the *internal rate of return (IRR)* on an investment when the project life is more than twice the payback period and the cash inflows are uniform every period.

■ Example

ABC Company is contemplating three projects, each of which would require an initial investment of $10,000 and each of which is expected to generate a cash inflow of $2,000 per year. The payback period is 5 years ($10,000/$2,000), and the payback reciprocal is 1/5, or 20%. The table of the present value of an annuity of $1 (see Table 4 in the Appendix) shows that the factor of 5.00 applies to the following useful lives and internal rates of return:

Useful Life	IRR
10 years	15%
15	18
20	19

It can be observed that the payback reciprocal is 20% as compared with the IRR of 18% when the life is 15 years and 20% as compared with the IRR of 19% when the life is 20 years. This shows that the payback reciprocal gives a reasonable approximation of the IRR if the useful life of the project is at least twice the payback period.

PEER REVIEW This is an analysis conducted by one CPA firm of the quality of another CPA firm's performance in the accounting and auditing processes. At a minimum, the review takes place every 3 years. An objective is to make certain that quality controls exist in accord with AICPA Quality Control Standards. Included in the review is an appraisal of the quality of working papers and accounting procedures employed. Peer review includes consideration of (1) firm organization; (2) administrative and personnel files; (3) quality of issued reports and statements; and (4) existence of appropriate documentation for findings. Once peer review has been completed, the reviewer and reviewee discuss the findings and an evaluation report is prepared. Poor quality work by the CPA firm may necessitate additional training, fines, censures, and in an extreme case suspension.

A typical peer review would be performed in the following manner. An accounting firm

is usually chosen to do the review from among the members of the Division for CPA Firms. When a firm review is to be performed, the Public Oversight Board must be appointed to meet SEC standards. The board oversees the review process. This board was enacted in response to criticisms by the SEC, which felt that it would be difficult for a CPA firm to give another firm a bad review. The audit team chosen to do the review must be independent of the firm to be reviewed. Any information obtained during the review is confidential and should not be communicated to anyone not involved with the review. The firm supplies the review team with documents of the firm's quality control policies and procedures. With these documents the review team does a study and evaluation of the firm's quality control system. They test to see whether the firm is complying with its quality control policies and procedures. The review team then communicates its conclusions to the firm. At this time the review team will often make recommendations for improvement of the firm's controls. A written report is then prepared, stating the findings of the review. If the review team finds no irregularities in the firm's quality controls, a standard unqualified report will be issued. If the firm did not comply with quality control policies and procedures, a qualified report will be issued.

PENSION PLANS A company does not have to have a pension plan. If it does, the firm must conform to FASB and governmental rules regarding the accounting and reporting for the pension plan. FASB 87 requires accounting for pension costs on the accrual basis. Pension expense is reflected in the service periods using a method that considers the benefit formula of the plan. On the income statement, pension expense is presented as a single amount. The pension plan relationship between the employer, trustee, and employee is diagramed below.

The two types of pension plans are

• *Defined contribution*—the annual contribution amount by the employer is specified instead of the benefits to be paid.

• *Defined benefit*—the determinable pension benefit to be received by participants upon retirement is specified. In determining amounts, consideration is given to such factors as age, salary, and service years. The employer has to provide plan contributions so that sufficient assets are accumulated to pay for the benefits when due. Typically, an annuity of payments is made. Pension expense applicable to administrative staff is expensed. Pension expense related to factory personnel is inventoriable.

The following pension plan terminology should be understood:

• *Actuarial assumptions*—actuaries make assumptions as to variables in determining pension expense and related funding. Examples of estimates are mortality rate, employee turnover, compensation levels, and rate of return.

• *Actuarial cost (funding) method*—the method used by actuaries in determining the employer contribution to assure sufficient funds will be available at employee retirement. The method used determines the pension expense and related liability.

Figure 1 Pension Plan Relationship

Pension Expense

Pension Plan Assets on Books of Trustee

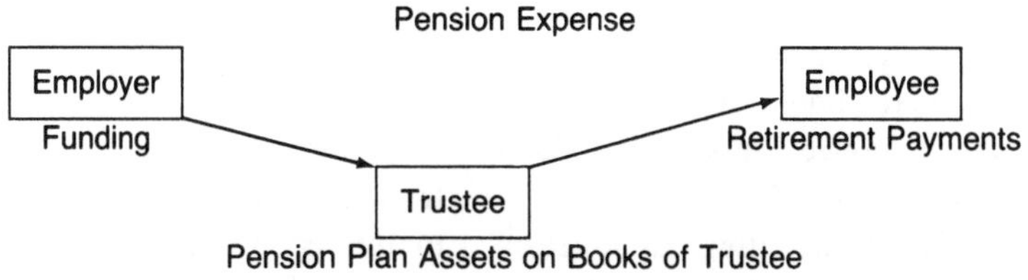

• *Actuarial present value of accumulated plan benefits*—the discounted amount of money that would be required to satisfy retirement obligations for active and retired employees.

• *Benefit information date*—the date the actuarial present value of accumulated benefits is presented.

• *Vested benefits*—employee vests when he or she has accumulated pension rights to receive benefits upon retirement. The employee no longer has to remain in the company to receive pension benefits.

• *Projected benefit obligation*—the year-end pension obligation based on *future* salaries. It is the actuarial present value of vested and nonvested benefits for services performed before a particular actuarial valuation date based on expected future salaries.

• *Accumulated benefit obligation*—the year-end obligation based on *current* salaries. It is the actuarial present value of benefits (vested and nonvested) attributable to the pension plan based on services performed before a specified date based on current salary levels.

The accumulated and projected benefit obligation figures will be the same in the case of plans having flat-benefit or nonpay-related pension benefit formulas.

• *Net assets available for pension benefits*—represent plan assets less plan liabilities. The plan's liabilities exclude participants' accumulated benefits.

Defined Contribution Pension Plan

Pension expense equals the employer's cash contribution for the year. There is no deferred charge or deferred credit arising. If the defined contribution plan stipulates contributions are to be made for years subsequent to an employee's rendering of services (e.g., after retirement), there should be an accrual of costs during the employee's service period.

Footnote disclosure includes

• Description of plan, including employee groups covered

• Basis of determining contributions

• Nature and effect of items affecting interperiod comparability

• Cost recognized for the period

Defined Benefit Pension Plan

The components of pension expense in a defined benefit pension plan follow:

• Service cost

• Prior service cost

• Expected return on plan assets (reduces pension expense)

• Interest on projected benefit obligation

• Actuarial gain or loss

Service cost is based on the present value of future payments under the benefit formula for employee services of the current period. It is recognized in full in the current year. The calculation involves actuarial assumptions.

Prior service cost is the pension expense applicable to services rendered before the adoption or amendment date of a pension plan. The cost of the retroactive benefits is the increase in the projected benefit obligation at the date of amendment. It involves the allocation of amounts of cost to future service years. Prior service cost determination involves actuarial considerations. The total pension cost is *not* booked but rather there are periodic charges based on actuarial determinations. Amortization is accomplished by assigning at the amendment date an equal amount to each service year of these active employees who are expected to receive plan benefits. The amortization of prior service cost may take into account future service years, change in the projected benefit obligation, the period in which employees will receive benefits, and decrement in employees receiving benefits each year.

▪ Example

X Company changes its pension formula from 2% to 5% of the last 3 years of pay multiplied by the service years on January 1, 19X1. This results in the projected benefit

obligation being increased by $500,000. Employees are anticipated to receive benefits over the next 10 years.

Total future service years equals:

$$\frac{n(n+1)}{2} \times P$$

where n = the number of years services are to be made,

P = the population decrement each year.

$$\frac{10(10+1)}{2} \times 9 = 495$$

Amortization of prior service cost in 19X1 equals:

$$\$500,000 \times \frac{10 \times 9}{495} = \$90,909$$

The expected return on plan assets (e.g., stocks, bonds) reduces pension expense. Plan assets are valued at the moving average of asset values for the accounting period.

Interest is on the projected benefit obligation at the beginning of the year. The settlement rate is employed representing the rate for which pension benefits could be settled. Interest equals:

Interest rate × Projected benefit obligation
　　　　　　　　　　　at the beginning of the year

Actuarial gains and losses are the difference between estimates and actual experience. For example, if the assumed interest rate is 10% and the actual interest rate is 12%, an actuarial gain results. There may also be a change in actuarial assumptions regarding the future. Actuarial gains and losses are deferred and amortized as an adjustment to pension expense over future years. Actuarial gains and losses related to a single event *not* related to the pension plan and not in the ordinary course of business are immediately recognized in the current year's income statement. Examples are plant closing and segment disposal.

Pension expense will not usually equal the employer's funding amount. Pension expense is typically based on the unit credit method. Under this approach, pension expense and related liability is based on estimating future salaries for total benefits to be paid.

If Pension expense > Cash paid
= Deferred pension liability

If Pension expense < Cash paid
= Deferred pension charge

Interest on the deferred pension liability reduces future pension expense. On the other hand, interest on the deferred pension charge increases pension expense.

Note: The "unit credit" method is used for flat-benefit plans (benefits are stated as a constant amount per year of service). In the case of final-pay plans, the projected unit credit method is used.

Minimum pension liability—must be recognized when the accumulated benefit obligation exceeds the fair value of pension plan assets. However, no minimum pension assets are recognized because it violates conservatism. When there is an accrued pension liability, an additional liability is booked up to the minimum pension liability.

When an additional liability is recorded, the debit is to an intangible asset under the pension plan. However, the intangible asset cannot exceed the unamortized prior service cost. If it does, the excess is reported as a separate component of stockholders' equity shown net of tax. While these items may be adjusted periodically, they are not amortized.

▪ Example

Accumulated benefit obligation	$500,000
Less: Fair value of pension plan assets	200,000
Minimum pension liability	$300,000
Less: Accrued pension liability	120,000
Additional liability	$180,000

Note that if instead of there being an accrued pension liability there was an accrued pension asset of $120,000, the additional liability would have been $420,000.

Assume unamortized prior service cost is $100,000. The entry is

New Intangible Asset Under		
Pension Plan	100,000	
Stockholders' Equity	80,000	
Additional Liability		180,000

■ Example

Mr. A has 6 years prior to retirement. The estimated salary at retirement is $50,000. The pension benefit is 3% of final salary for each service year payable at retirement. The retirement benefit is computed below:

Final annual salary	$50,000
Formula rate	× 3%
	$ 1,500
Years of service	× 6
Retirement benefit	$ 9,000

■ Example

On 1/1/19X1, a company adopts a defined benefit pension plan. Expected return and interest rate are both 10%. Service cost for 19X1 and 19X2 are $100,000 and $120,000, respectively. The funding amount for 19X1 and 19X2 are $80,000 and $110,000, respectively.

The entry for 19X1 is

Pension Expense	100,000	
Cash		80,000
Pension Liability		20,000

The entry in 19X2 is

Pension Expense	122,000	
Cash		110,000
Pension Liability		12,000

Computation:

Service cost	$120,000
Interest on projected benefit obligation 10% × $100,000	10,000
Expected return on plan assets 10% × $80,000	(8,000)
	$122,000

At 12/31/19X2:

Projected benefit obligation $230,000 ($100,000 + $120,000 + $10,000).

Pension plan assets $198,000 ($80,000 + $110,000 + $8,000).

■ Example

Company X has a defined benefit pension plan for its 100 employees. On 1/1/19X1, pension plan assets have a fair value of $230,000, accumulated benefit obligation is $285,000, and the projected benefit obligation is $420,000. Ten employees are expected to resign each year for the next 10 years. They will be eligible to receive benefits. Service cost for 19X1 is $40,000. On 12/31/19X1, the projected benefit obligation is $490,000, fair value of plan assets is $265,000, and accumulated benefit obligation is $340,000. The expected return on plan assets and the interest rate are both 8%. No actuarial gains or losses occurred during the year. Cash funded for the year is $75,000.

Pension expense equals:

Service cost	$40,000
Interest on projected benefit obligation 8% × $420,000	33,600
Expected return on plan assets 8% × $230,000	(18,400)
Amortization of actuarial gains and losses	—
Amortization of unrecognized transition amount	34,545[a]
Pension expense	$89,745

[a] Projected benefit obligation	$420,000
Fair value of pension plan assets	230,000
Initial net obligation	$190,000

$$\text{Amortization } \frac{\$190,000}{5.5 \text{ years}^b} = \$34,545$$

$$^b \frac{n(n+1)}{2} \times P = \frac{10(10+1)}{2} \times 10 = 550$$

$$\frac{550}{100} = 5.5 \text{ years (average remaining service period)}$$

The journal entries at 12/31/19X1 follow:

Pension Expense	89,745	
Cash		75,000
Deferred Pension Liability		14,745
Intangible Asset—Pension Plan	60,255	
Additional Pension Liability		60,255

Computation follows:

Accumulated benefit obligation— 12/31/19X1	$340,000
Fair value of plan assets—12/31/19X1	265,000
Minimum liability	$ 75,000
Deferred pension liability	14,745
Additional pension liability	$ 60,255

Disclosures—footnote disclosure for a pension plan follow:

• Describing the plan, including benefit formula, funding policy, employee groups covered, and retirement age

• Components of pension expense

• Pension assumptions (e.g., interest rate, mortality rate, employee turnover)

• Reconciling funded status of plan with employer amounts recognized on the balance sheet, including fair value of plan assets, projected benefit obligation, and unrecognized prior service cost

• Present value of vested and nonvested benefits

• Weighted-average assumed discount rate involved in measuring the projected benefit obligation

• Weighted-average expected return rate on pension plan assets

• Amounts and types of securities included in pension plan assets

• Amount of approximate annuity benefits to employees

Settlement in a Pension Plan

As per FASB 88, a settlement is discharging some or all of the employer's pension benefit obligation. Excess plan assets can revert to the employer. A settlement must satisfy *all* of the following criteria:

• Irrevocable

• Relieves pension benefit responsibility

• Materially curtails risk related to the pension obligation

The amount of gain or loss recognized in the income statement when a pension obligation is settled is limited to the unrecognized net gain or loss from realized or unrealized changes in either the pension benefit obligation or plan assets caused from actual experiences being different from original assumptions. All or a pro rata share of the unrecognized gain or loss is recognized when a plan is settled. If full settlement occurs, all unrecognized gains or losses are recognized. If only a part of the plan is settled, a pro rata share of the unrecognized net gain or loss is recognized.

An example of a settlement is when the employer furnishes employees with a lump-sum amount to give up pension rights. The gain or loss resulting is included in the current year's income statement.

Curtailment in a Pension Plan

As per FASB 88, a curtailment occurs when an event significantly reduces future service years of present employees or eliminates for most employees the accumulation of defined benefits for future services. An example is a plant closing that ends employee services prior to pension plan expectations. The gain or loss is recognized in the current year's income statement and contains the following elements:

• Unamortized prior service cost attributable to employee services no longer needed

• Change in pension benefit obligation due to the curtailment

Termination in a Pension Plan

When termination benefits are offered by the employer, accepted by employees, and the amount can reasonably be determined, an expense and liability are recognized. The amount of the accrual equals the down payment plus the present value of future payments to be made by the employer. The entry is to debit loss and credit cash (down payment) and liability (future payments). Footnote disclosure of the arrangement should be given.

Trustee Reporting for a Defined Benefit Pension Plan

FASB 35 deals with the reporting and disclosures of the trustee of a defined benefit pension plan. Generally accepted accounting principles must be followed. Financial statements are *not* required to be issued by the plan. If they are issued, reporting guidelines have to be followed. The prime objective is to assess the plan's capability to meet retirement benefits.

The balance sheet presents pension assets and liabilities as an offset. Operating assets are at book value. In determining net assets available, accrual accounting is followed. An example is accruing for interest earned but not received. Investments are shown at fair market value. An asset shown is "contributions receivable due from employer." In computing pension plan liability, participants' accumulated benefits are *excluded*. In effect, plan participants are equity holders rather than creditors of the plan.

Disclosure is required of:

• Net assets available for benefits.

• Changes in net assets available for benefits, including net appreciation in fair value of each major class of investments.

• Actuarial present value of accumulated plan benefits. Accumulated plan benefits include benefits anticipated to be paid to retired employees, beneficiaries, and present employees.

• Changes in actuarial present value of accumulated plan benefits.

• Description of the plan, including amendments.

• Accounting and funding policies.

There may exist an annuity contract in which an insurance company agrees to give specified pension benefits in return for receiving a premium.

PERMANENT DIFFERENCE A permanent difference is an item that affects either book income or taxable income but never both.

It does *not* reverse itself. Interperiod tax allocation is *not* applicable to permanent differences. Examples of permanent differences are

• Amortization expense on goodwill is not tax deductible.

• Premium on life insurance for executives is not tax deductible.

• Interest income on municipal securities is not taxable.

• Difference between percentage depletion and cost depletion.

• Special deductions under the tax law for domestic dividends received.

• Depreciation for book and tax differ due to different bases of carrying the related asset. The different bases arise from a business combination treated as a purchase for book purposes and a tax-free exchange for tax purposes.

See also Income Tax Accounting.

PERSONAL FINANCIAL PLANNING This is a process for arriving at comprehensive solutions to an individual's personal, business, and financial problems and concerns. It therefore involves the development and implementation of total coordinated plans for the achievement of his or her overall financial objectives. Each individual will have different financial objectives, depending on the circumstances, goals, attitudes, and needs. But the total objectives of most people can be classified as follows:

1. Protection against personal risks such as death, disability, or unemployment
2. Capital accumulation for family purposes in case of emergency
3. Provision for retirement income
4. Reduction of tax burden
5. Estate planning
6. Investment and property management

Personal financial planning covers a wide variety of financial services and products:

1. Tax planning and management
2. Investments

3. Insurance
4. Retirement planning
5. Estate planning

Our economic growth, the tax structure, and the changes that have taken place in our social framework have created complexity in financial planning. The following events should be noted:

- Increasingly complex tax laws.
- A complex economy and proliferation of available financial products.
- The difficulty of saving for retirement.
- Middle-class individuals are now in higher income tax brackets.
- Inflationary pressures create artificial increases in income and losses in purchasing power.

Most people are not trained to deal with these complex factors. Financial planning has emerged as an important new profession in recent years. Personal financial planning can address money matters and help find ways to ensure a client's secure financial future.

PERSONAL FINANCIAL PLANNING SOFTWARE

Computer software in personal financial planning enables the individual to accumulate and evaluate sources of income and expenses. An analysis of the deviation between actual and budget figures may be made. Personal assets and liabilities are determined and valued in order to derive net worth. The person's objectives may be quantified and appraised over time. Some packages keep track of the investment portfolio and analyze it. Financial planning may be done, including that for tax, retirement, insurance, and estate. In essence, personal financial planning enables the strategic management of a person's financial affairs. A good planning package is Andrew Tobias's *Managing Your Money*™. Additionally, templates exist that may be used along with a spreadsheet program.

Financial management programs enable basic functions such as budgeting, checkbook management, analysis of cash flow, and financial calculations. With regard to checkbook management, the program will combine check writing, allocations, and recording. The program will write and print out the check, update the check balance, and post expenditures to the appropriate budget category.

Financial calculation software aids in capital needs analysis and in determining effects of compounding and inflation. The person inputs the beginning amount, growth rate, and period, and then the computer performs the calculations. By using a growth formula, one can see the impact of different growth assumptions on varying beginning amounts. If there is a goal-seeking formula, one can work backward to see what kind of growth or how much capital is needed to start with to accomplish a desired sum of money at a particular date.

Financial calculations can also be involved with life expectancy analysis. Life expectancy calculations take personal data—such as age, sex, height, weight, and behavioral information (e.g., eating habits, fitness)—and translate them into a life expectancy estimate.

PERSONAL FINANCIAL STATEMENTS

These may be prepared for an individual or family to show financial status. The accrual basis is followed. Some uses include computation of net worth, obtaining credit, retirement planning, estate planning, tax planning, and to meet disclosure requirements (e.g., public figures). AICPA's Statement of Position No. 82–1 titled "Accounting and Financial Reporting for Personal Financial Statements" presents the accounting and disclosure requirements, including valuation approaches in arriving at current value amounts. Further guidance on accounting and reporting are offered in Statements on Standards for Accounting and Review Services 1 and 6 as well as the AICPA's "Personal Financial Statements Guide."

In the Statement of Financial Condition, assets are reflected at the estimated current value and are listed in the order of liquidity (maturity). Current value may be determined based on recent transactions of similar items, appraisals, present value of future cash flows from the asset, adjusting historical cost for inflation, and so on. In determining current value of assets, a deduction should be made for relevant selling costs. Historical cost may be provided as supplementary information. There is no breakdown between current and noncurrent classifications in the balance sheet.

Investments should be shown by major category, such as real estate. Significant investments in a sole proprietorship or partnership should be segregated. For instance, a material interest in a closely held company should be shown separately from the equity investment in other companies. Ownership of property (e.g., community property) should be ascertained under the applicable state law. If assets are jointly owned, only the individual's beneficial interest should be reported.

Asset valuation guidelines exist. Receivables should be reported at the discounted value of future cash receipts. The discount rate is the interest rate the debtor would typically incur for financing. Marketable securities, including stocks and bonds, are recorded at current quoted market prices. In the event a stock is not traded on the financial statement date, the bid price should preferably be used. When valuation difficulty exists with a particular security, a reputable brokerage firm may be consulted. Precious metals should be shown at current value. Life insurance should be reported at cash surrender value after deducting any loans against it. Documentation exists in the form of insurance company reports. With regard to retirement accounts, the current balance in IRA and Keogh plans should be listed. Also included are the current value of vested benefits in company profit-sharing and pension plans. The amounts shown are the proceeds to be received today. The investment in a closely held business can be valued by a qualified appraiser, such as one affiliated with the Institute of Business Appraisers. The practitioner should refrain from valuing the business, since an appearance of lack of independence (and even knowledge) may present a legal problem. Real estate should be at anticipated selling price using a licensed appraiser's report. Personal property should be valued at appraised value derived from a specialist's opinion or reference to a guide indicating valuation of personal items (e.g., blue book for auto values). Wholesale value rather than retail value should be used because the former would be received upon sale of the item by the individual. Intangible assets should be at appraisal value. If not possible, value can be based on anticipated sale proceeds or discounted value of future receipts from the asset. However, historical cost can be used if current value is not objectively determinable. Do not spend much time estimating the value of household items, since an approximation is usually sufficient. A listing of assets may take the following form:

Asset	Description	Current Value	Percentage of Total Assets

The accountant must be assured that current value figures are accurate. Legal liability problems may arise if unreasonable amounts are used. It is best to retain independent appraisers to derive current values. The practitioner must also insist on adequate documentation to support the figures, especially if possible litigation may arise.

Liabilities are reported at current value by payment date, without distinction between current and noncurrent. Guidelines exist in the valuation of liabilities. Payables should be at the discounted value of future payments, utilizing the interest rate implicit in the transaction. In the event debt may be settled at

an amount less than the discounted value of the payments, the lower amount should be used. Usually, the liability equals the principal and accrued interest due. A noncancelable commitment should be reflected at the present value of future payments, such as alimony payments. Separately listed should be personal, investment, and business liabilities. Excluded from liabilities is nonrecourse debt that was subtracted in the determination of investment values. The current balance of the mortgage should be listed. Include loans for business or investment purposes, including margin accounts. Debt should not be included if it was considered in the valuation of a closely held firm. Include obligations with respect to limited partnership investments if a personal liability exists for those debts.

Income taxes are estimated on the difference between assets and liabilities and their tax bases. Taxes are based *as if* assets have been sold. Disclosure should be given of the methods and assumptions employed in the computation of income taxes. In making tax estimates, the effect of previous year's unpaid tax obligations and the current year's estimates should be taken into account. Also considered are withholding tax payments.

■ Example

An individual owns ABC stock that was bought 5 years ago for $8,000. The stock is currently worth $17,000. The individual is in the 38% tax bracket. If the individual sold the stock today, there would be a $9,000 gain, which would result in $3,420 in taxes. The $3,420 should be included in the "provision for estimated taxes on the difference between carrying amounts and tax bases of assets and liabilities." Since the $3,420 constitutes an amount of taxes that would be payable upon sale of the stock, it should be presented as a credit in the Statement of Financial Condition reducing the individual's net worth.

An illustrative Statement of Financial Condition follows:

Mr. and Mrs. J. Smith
Statement of Financial Condition
December 31, 19X2

Assets	
Cash	$ 5,000
Interest and dividends receivable	200
Marketable securities	10,000
Interest in closely held company	6,000
Cash surrender value of life insurance	1,000
Real estate	100,000
Personal property	30,000
Total	$152,200

Liabilities	
Credit cards	$ 6,000
Income taxes payable	3,000
Loans payable	10,000
Mortgage payable	60,000
	$ 79,000
Estimated taxes on the differences between the estimated current values of assets, the current amounts of liabilities, and their tax bases	40,000
Net worth	33,200
Total	$152,200

As an option, a Statement of Changes in Net Worth may be prepared. It is useful in showing the mix of business and personal items in personal financial statements. The statement should be broken down into realized and unrealized portions. Increases and decreases in net worth are shown. Examples of items increasing net worth are income, increases in current value of assets, decreases in the current amounts of liabilities, and decreases in estimated taxes on the difference between estimated current asset values and liability amounts and their tax bases. Items decreasing net worth are expenses, decreases in current values of assets, increases in current amounts of liabilities, and increases in estimated taxes.

Also optional are comparative financial statements.

An income statement is *not* prepared.

Disclosures are recommended to better appraise an individual's or family's financial health. Disclosures include

• Individuals covered by the statement

• Methods used in determining current values

• Change in method or assumption from a prior year

• Nature of joint ownership of property

• Identification of specific industries and companies where a material percentage of total assets are invested

• Percentage of ownership in an identified closely held business, including the nature of business activities consummated, basis of accounting, and summarized financial data

• Identification of intangibles, including estimated lives

• Face value of life insurance

• Vested rights in pension and stock ownership plans

• Methods and estimates employed in computing income taxes

• Particulars of receivables and payables such as interest rates, pledged items, and maturities

• Noncapitalized commitments such as rental agreements

If you see a client's assets are concentrated in one category, you should recommend a move toward diversification. If there is a high concentration of illiquid assets but yet significant impending debt exists, you should point out this precarious financial situation to the client. An evaluation should be made of which assets are being financed by debt and the reasonableness of the interest rate. Is debt being incurred for personal assets or investment assets? Is the repayment schedule of debt comfortable for the client? What are the sources of repaying that debt? Do client goals match actual results? Projections should be made to determine whether the client is going in the direction of meeting obligations. If not, corrective action should be taken.

PHILLIPS CURVE   Economic history indicates that the twin objectives of price stability and full employment (such as 4% unemployment rate) have been extremely difficult to achieve. Many economists believe that there is an apparent conflict between maintaining stable prices and achieving low employment throughout the economy due to the strong tendency for the general price level to begin to rise before full employment is reached. The relationship between inflation and the unemployment rate is described by a Phillip's curve—named after A. W. Phillips, a British economist who proposed it in the late 1950s. Figure 1 illustrates a conventional Phillips curve and indicates the nature of the trade-off between lower unemployment and high rates of inflation. Every point on the curve denotes a different combination of unemployment and inflation. A movement along the curve reflects the reduction in one at the expense of a gain in the other. The dilemma posed by the curve is that the economy must accept inflation in order to achieve full employment or to accept a high unemployment rate to control inflation. To the extent that a Phillips curve phenomenon actually exists, economic policy makers are confronted with a difficult choice of finding a fiscal-monetary mix. Figure 2 shows statistical evidence on the trade-off. Ideally, policy makers wish

Figure 1 The Phillips Curve

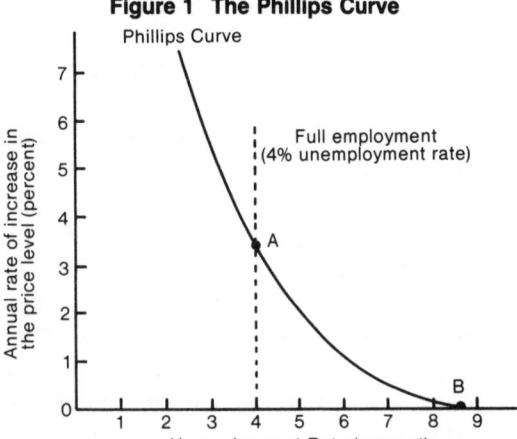

Figure 2 U.S. Unemployment and Inflation Rates 1963–1984

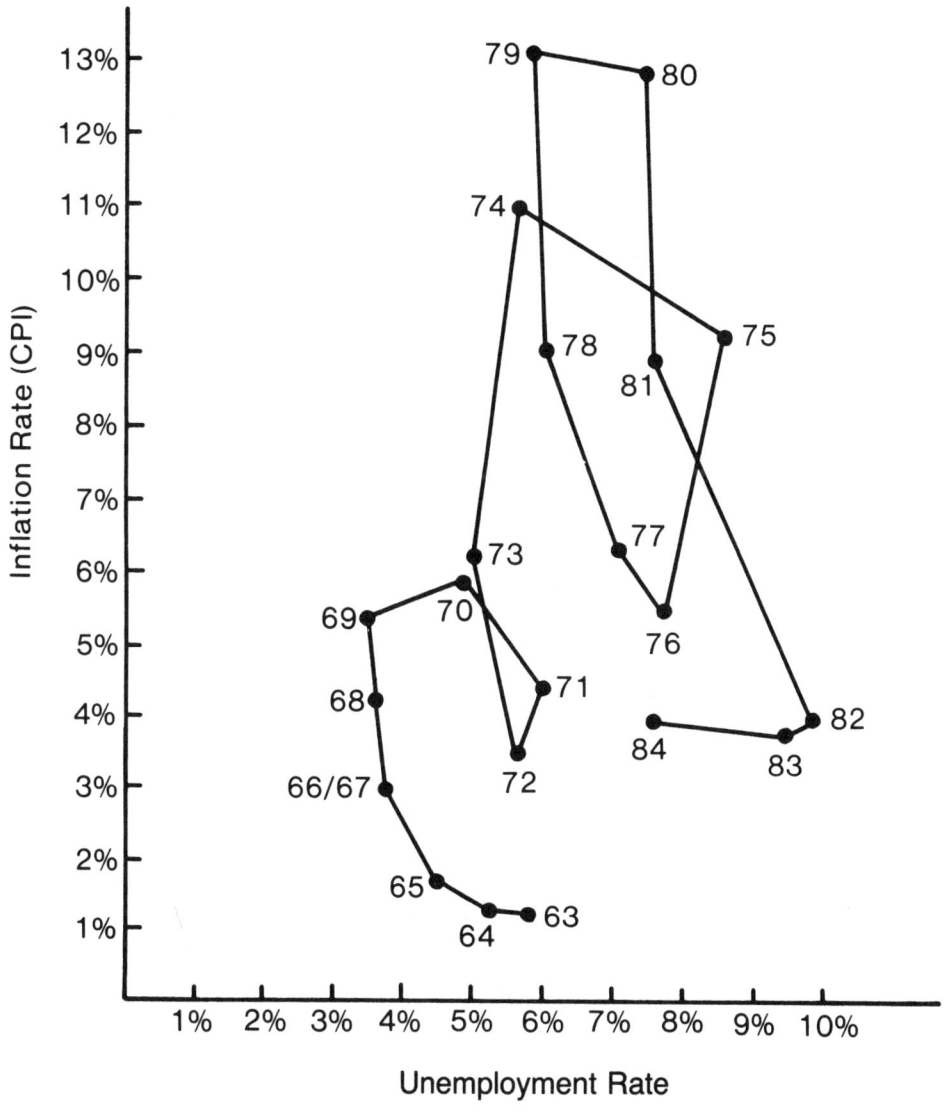

to find a policy mix that would shift the Phillips curve downward and to the left, thus making price stability and full employment more compatible and bearable. Unfortunately, in the recent past, experiencing "stagflation" shows the curve shifting outward to the right.

POOLING-OF-INTERESTS METHOD The pooling method is used to account for the acquisition of another company when the acquiring company exchanges its voting common stock for the voting common stock of the acquired company and all of twelve criteria are met. *See also* Business Combinations.

PORTFOLIO THEORY AND CAPITAL ASSET PRICING MODEL (CAPM)

Most financial assets are not held in isolation; rather, they are held as parts of portfolios. Therefore, risk-return analysis should not be confined to single assets only. It is important to look at portfolios and the gains from diversification. What is important is the return on the portfolio, not just the return on one asset, and the portfolio's risk.

Portfolio Return

The expected return on a portfolio (r_p) is simply the weighted average return of the individual sets in the portfolio, the weights being the fraction of the total funds invested in each asset:

$$r_p = w_1 r_1 + w_2 r_2 + \cdots + w_n r_n = \sum_{j=1}^{n} w_j r_j$$

where $r_j =$ expected return on each individual asset,

$w_j =$ fraction for each respective asset investment,

$n =$ number of assets in the portfolio.

$$\sum_{j=1}^{n} w_j = 1.0$$

■ Example 1

A portfolio consists of assets A and B. Asset A makes up one third of the portfolio and has an expected return of 18%. Asset B makes up the other two thirds of the portfolio and is expected to earn 9%. What is the expected return on the portfolio?

Asset	Return(r_j)	Fraction (w_j)	$w_j r_j$	
A	18%	⅓	⅓ × 18% =	6%
B	9%	⅔	⅔ × 9% =	6%
			$r_p =$	12%

Portfolio Risk

Unlike returns, the risk of a portfolio (σ_p) is not simply the weighted average of the standard deviations of the individual as-

sets in the contribution, for a portfolio's risk is also dependent on the correlation coefficients of its assets. The correlation coefficient is a measure of the degree to which two variables "move" together. It has a numerical value that ranges from -1.0 to 1.0. In a two-asset (A and B) portfolio, the portfolio risk is defined as:

$$\sigma_p = \sqrt{w_A^2 \sigma_A^2 + w_B^2 \sigma_B^2 + 2 w_A w_B \cdot \rho_{AB} \sigma_A \sigma_B}$$

where $\sigma - A$ and $\sigma - B =$ standard deviations of assets A and B, respectively.

w_A and $w_B =$ weights, or fractions, of total funds invested in assets A and B

$\rho_{AB} =$ the correlation coefficient between assets A and B.

Incidentally, the correlation coefficient is the measurement of joint movement between two securities.

Diversification

As can be seen in the previous formula, the portfolio risk, measured in terms of σ_p is not the weighted average of the individual asset risks in the portfolio. We have in the formula of the third term (ρ), which makes a significant contribution to the overall portfolio risk. What the formula basically shows is that portfolio risk can be minimized or completely eliminated by *diversification*. The degree of reduction in portfolio risk depends upon the correlation between the assets being combined. Generally speaking, by combining two perfectly negatively correlated assets ($P = -1.0$), we are able to eliminate the risk completely. In the real world, however, most securities are negatively but not perfectly correlated. In fact, most assets are positively correlated. We could still reduce the portfolio risk by combining even positively correlated assets. An example of the latter might be ownership of two automobile stocks or two housing stocks.

■ Example 2

Assume the following:

Asset	σ	w
A	20%	1/3
B	10%	2/3

The portfolio risk then is

$$\sigma_p = \sqrt{w_A^2\sigma_A^2 + w_B^2\sigma_B^2 + 2\,w_Aw_B \cdot \rho_{AB}\sigma_A\sigma_B}$$
$$= \sqrt{(1/3)^2(0.2)^2 + (2/3)^2(0.1)^2 + 2\rho_{AB}(1/3)(2/3)(0.2)(0.1)}$$
$$= \sqrt{0.0089 + 0.0089\rho_{AB}}$$

(a) Now assume that the correlation coefficient between A and B is +1 (a perfectly positive correlation). This means that when the value of asset A increases in response to market conditions, so does the value of asset B, and it does so at exactly the same rate as A. The portfolio risk when $\rho = +1$ then becomes:

$$\sigma_p = \sqrt{0.0089 + 0.0089\rho_{AB}} = \sqrt{0.0089 + 0.0089(1)}$$
$$= \sqrt{0.0178} = 0.1334 = 13.34\%$$

(b) If $\rho = 0$, the assets lack correlation and the portfolio risk is simply the risk of the expected returns on the assets, that is, the weighted average of the standard deviations of the individual assets in the portfolio. Therefore, when $\rho_{AB} = 0$, the portfolio risk for this example is:

$$\sigma_p = \sqrt{0.0089 + 0.0089\rho_{AB}}$$
$$= \sqrt{0.0089 + 0.0089(0)}$$
$$= \sqrt{0.0089} = 0.0943 = 9.43\%$$

(c) If $\rho = -1$ (a perfectly negative correlation coefficient), then as the price of A rises, the price of B declines at the very same rate. In such a case, risk would be completely eliminated. Therefore, when $\rho_{AB} = -1$, the portfolio risk is

$$\sigma_p = \sqrt{0.0089 + 0.0089\rho_{AB}}$$
$$= \sqrt{0.0089 + 0.0089(-1)}$$
$$= \sqrt{0.0089 - 0.0089} = 0 = 0$$

When we compare the results of (a), (b), and (c), we see that a positive correlation between assets increases a portfolio's risk above the level found at zero correlation, whereas a perfectly negative correlation eliminates that risk.

■ Example 3

To illustrate the point of diversification, assume data on the following three securities are as follows:

Year	Security X (%)	Security Y (%)	Security Z (%)
19X1	10	50	10
19X2	20	40	20
19X3	30	30	30
19X4	40	20	40
19X5	50	10	50
r_j	30	30	30
σ_p	14.14	14.14	14.14

Note here that securities X and Y have a perfectly negative correlation, and securities X and Z have a perfectly positive correlation. Notice what happens to the portfolio risk when X and Y, and X and Z are combined. Assume that funds are split equally between the two securities in each portfolio.

Year	Portfolio XY (50% − 50%)	Portfolio XZ (50% − 50%)
19X1	30	10
19X2	30	20
19X3	30	30
19X4	30	40
19X5	30	50
r_p	30	30
σ_p	0	14.14

Again, see that the two perfectly negative correlated securities (XY) result in a zero overall risk.

Markowitz's Efficient Portfolio

Dr. Harry Markowitz, in the early 1950s, provided a theoretical framework for the systematic composition of optimum portfolios. Using a technique called "quadratic programming," he attempted to select from

Figure 1 Efficient Frontier

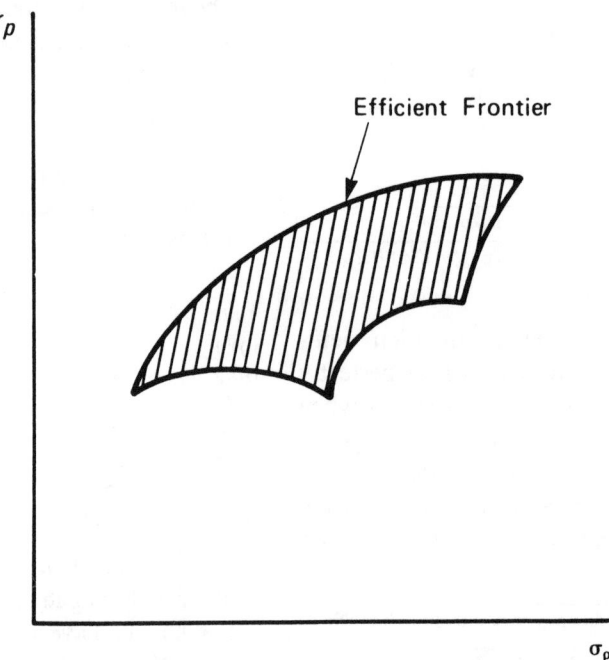

among hundreds of individual securities, given certain basic information supplied by portfolio managers and security analysts. He also weighted these selections in composing portfolios.

The central theme of Markowitz's work is that rational investors behave in a way that reflects their aversion to taking increased risk without being compensated by an adequate increase in expected return. Also, for any given expected return, most investors will prefer a lower risk and for any given level of risk, prefer a higher return to a lower return. Markowitz showed how quadratic programming could be used to calculate a set of "efficient" portfolios such as illustrated by the curve in Figure 1. In Figure 2, an efficient set of portfolios that lie along the ABC line, called "efficient frontier" is noted. Along this frontier, the investor can receive a maximum return for a given level of risk or a minimum risk for a given level of return. Specifically, comparing three port-

folios—A, B, and D—portfolios A and B are clearly more efficient than D because portfolio A could produce the same expected return but at a lower risk level, whereas portfolio B would have the same degree of risk as D but would afford a higher return.

Figure 2 Efficient Portfolio

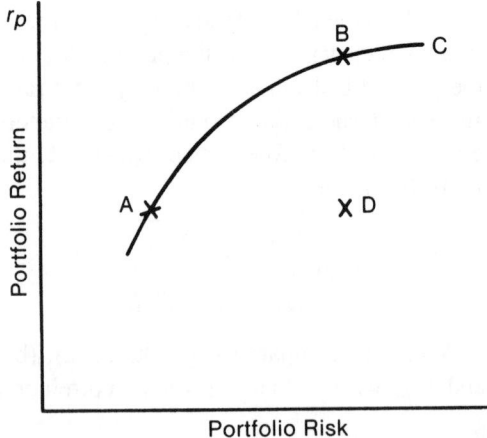

Figure 3 Risk-Return Indifference Curves

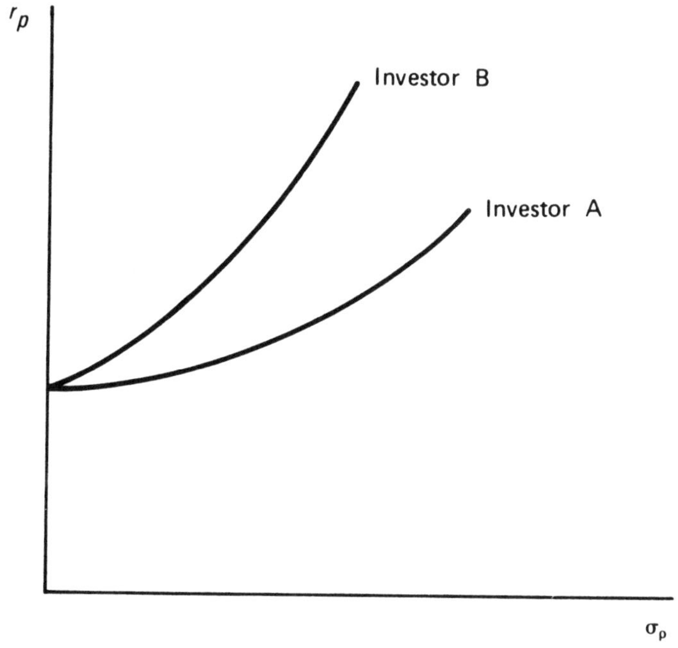

To see how the investor tries to find the optimum portfolio, we first introduce the *indifference curve*, which shows the investor's trade-off between risk and return. Figure 3 shows the two different indifference curves for two investors. The steeper the slope of the curve, the more risk averse the investor is. For example, investor B's curve has a steeper slope than investor A's. This means that investor B will want more incremental return for each additional unit of risk. Figure 4 depicts a family of indifference curves for investor A. The objective is to maximize his or her satisfaction by attaining the highest curve possible.

By matching the indifference curve showing the risk-return trade-off with the best investments available in the market as represented by points on the efficient frontier, investors are able to find an optimum portfolio. According to Markowitz, investor A will achieve the highest possible curve at point B along the efficient frontier. Point B is thus the optimum portfolio for this investor.

Portfolio Selection as a Quadratic Programming Problem

A portfolio selection problem was formulated by Markowitz as a quadratic programming model as follows:

$$\text{Min } E(r_p) - \lambda V(r_p)$$

subject to

$$\Sigma x_i = 1$$
$$x_i \geqq 0$$

where $E(r_p)$ = the expected return,
$V(r_p)$ = the variance or covariance of any given portfolio,
x_i = proportion of the investor's total investment in security i,
n = number of securities.

Especially, λ(Lambda) is called the coefficient of risk aversion. It represents the rate at which a particular investor is just willing to exchange expected rate of return for risk. $\lambda = 0$ indicates the investor is a risk lover, whereas $\lambda = 1$ means he or she is a risk averter.

Figure 4 Matching the Efficient Frontier and Indifference Curves

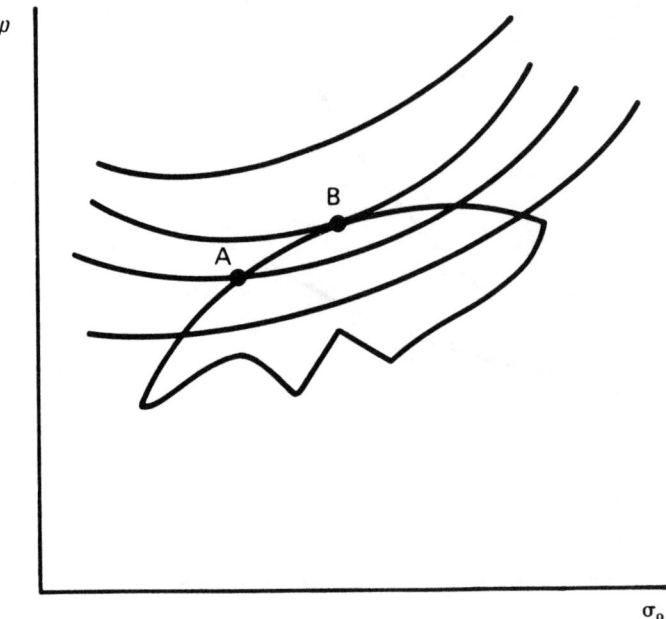

The resulting solution to the problem would identify a portfolio that lies on the *efficient* portfolio. If one knows the coefficient of risk aversion, λ, for a particular investor, the model will be able to find the *optimal* portfolio for that investor.

The Market Index Model

For even a moderately sized portfolio, the formulas for portfolio return and risk require estimation of a large number of input data. Concerned with the computational burden in deriving these estimates led to the development of the following *market index model:*

$$r_j = a + b\, r_m$$

where r_j = return on security j.

r_m = return on the market portfolio,

b = the beta, or systematic risk, of a security.

What this model attempts to do is measure the systematic or uncontrollable risk of a security. The beta is measured as follows:

$$b = \text{Cov}\,(r_j, r_m)/\sigma^2_m$$

where $\text{Cov}(r_j, r_m)$ = the covariance of the returns of the securities with the market return.

σ^2_m = the variance (standard deviation squared) of the market return.

The market return is the return on the Standard & Poor's 500 or Dow Jones 30 Industrials.

An easier way to compute beta is to determine the slope of the least-squares linear regression line $(r_j - r_f)$, where the excess return of the security $(r_j - r_f)$ is regressed against the excess return of the market portfolio $(r_m - r_f)$. The formula for beta is

$$b = \Sigma MK - n\,\bar{M}\bar{K}/(\Sigma M^2 - n\,\bar{M}^2)$$

where $M = (r_m - r_f)$,

$K = (r_j - r_f)$,

n = the number of periods,

$\bar{M}$ = the average of M,

$\bar{K}$ = the average of K.

The market index model was initially proposed to reduce the number of inputs required in portfolio analysis. It can also be justified in the context of the *capital asset pricing model*.

The Capital Asset Pricing Model (CAPM)

The CAPM takes off where the efficient frontier concluded with an assumption that there exists a risk-free security with a single rate at which investors can borrow and lend. By combining the risk-free asset and the efficient frontier, we create a whole new set of investment opportunities that will allow us to reach higher indifference curves than would be possible simply along the efficient frontier. The $r_f mx$ line in Figure 5 shows this possibility. This line is called the capital market line (CML) and the formula for this line is

$$r_p = r_f + (r_m - r_f / \sigma_m - 0)\sigma_p$$

$$\left(r_p = r_f + \left(\frac{r_m - r_f}{\sigma_m - 0} \right) \sigma_p \right)$$

which indicates the expected return on any portfolio (r_p) is equal to the risk-free return (r_f) plus the slope of the line times a value along the horizontal axis (σ_p) indicating the amount of risk undertaken.

The Security Market Line

We can establish the trade-off between risk and return for an *individual security* through the security market line (SML) in Figure 6. SML is a general relationship to show the risk-return trade-off for an *individual security*, whereas CML achieves the same objective for a *portfolio*.

The formula for SML is

$$r_j = r_f + b (r_m - r_f)$$

where $r_j =$ the expected (or required) return on security j,

$r_f =$ the risk-free security (such as a T-bill),

$r_m =$ the expected return on the market portfolio (such as Standard & Poor's 500 Stock Composite Index or Dow Jones 30 Industrials),

$b =$ beta, an index of nondiversifiable (noncontrollable, systematic) risk.

Figure 5 Graph of CAPM

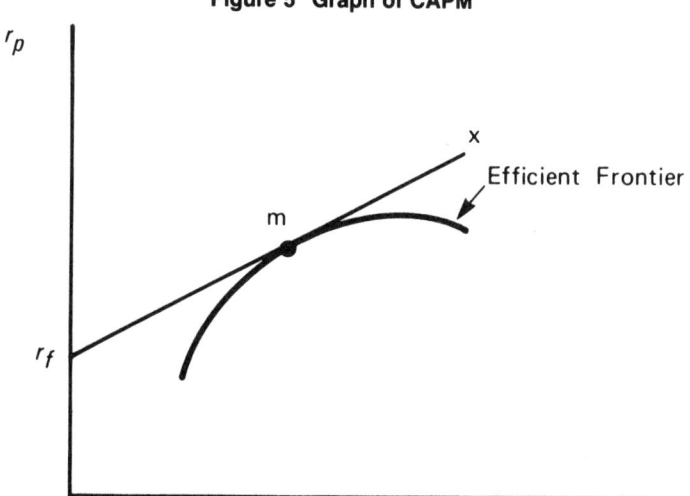

Figure 6 The Security Market Line (SML)

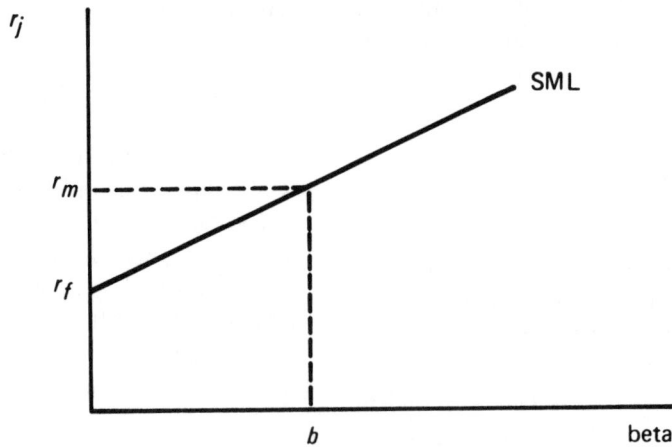

This formula is called the *Capital Asset Pricing Model (CAPM)*. The model shows that investors in individual securities are only assumed to be rewarded for systematic, uncontrollable, market-related risk, known as the beta (*b*) risk. All other risk is assumed to be diversified away and thus is not rewarded.

The key component in the CAPM, beta (*b*), is a measure of the security's volatility relative to that of an average security. For example: $b = 0.5$ means the security is only half as volatile, or risky, as the average security; $b = 1.0$ means the security is of average risk; and $b = 2.0$ means the security is twice as risky as the average risk.

The whole term $b(r_m - r_f)$ represents the risk premium, the additional return required to compensate investors for assuming a given level of risk.

Thus, in words, the CAPM or (SML) equation shows that the required (expected) rate of return on a given security (r_j) is equal to the return required for securities that have no risk (r_f) plus a risk premium required by investors for assuming a given level of risk. The higher the degree of systematic risk (*b*), the higher the return on a given security demanded by investors.

■ **Example 4**

Assuming that the risk-free rate (r_f) is 8% and the expected return for the market (r_m) is 12%, then if

$b = 0$ (risk-free security) $r_j = 8\% + 0(12\% - 8\%)$ $= 8\%$

$b = 0.5$ $r_j = 8\% + 0.5(12\% - 8\%) = 10\%$

$b = 1.0$ (market portfolio) $r_j = 8\% + 1.0(12\% - 8\%) = 12\%$

$b = 2.0$ $r_j = 8\% + 2.0(12\% - 8\%) = 16\%$

See also Beta Coefficient.

POST AUDIT A post audit occurs subsequent to the time a transaction took place. For example, the independent auditor examines the validity of the record keeping of an item by looking at documentation after the occurrence of the event.

PRECIOUS METALS These include gold and silver. Advantages of precious metals are liquidity, international markets, and hedge against inflation. But instability in price exists. The prices usually rise in difficult times and decline in stable periods. There is no periodic tax, such as with real estate.

Gold

Gold is a valuable commodity constituting a private store of value. The measurement is in troy ounces. It is an attractive investment in times of depreciating paper currency and when low interest rates exist. Low interest rates encourage gold investment since other types of investment provide low returns. Gold investment may be in the form of bullion, coins, shares of a mining company, certificates, jewelry, and futures.

Gold typically performs contrary to common stock. As common stock decreases in price, gold increases in price. Thus, gold can be used to diversify an investment portfolio. Transaction costs change depending upon the kind of gold involved. However, the percentage commission drops as the quantity bought increases.

Gold coins can be bought from post offices, banks, and gold dealers. Gold coins vary in price based on quality and content. Commissions usually vary from 2% to 4%. Coins are easily marketable and movable.

Gold bullion may be purchased from banks and dealers. Dealer markups and commissions range from 3% to 10%, depending upon the quantity transacted. *Tip*: Assaying to test for gold content may be needed. A gold certificate may also be bought, showing ownership in a specified number of gold ounces stored at the bank. Advantages of gold certificates are that they may not be subject to state sales tax applicable to bullion and there is no need to be concerned with loss from theft since they are held in a bank vault.

Indirect ownership may be gotten by acquiring shares in a gold mine. But market price of the stock may not always go in the same direction as the physical gold. Gold mining companies are listed on the major exchanges and in the over-the-counter market. Most gold mines are located in South Africa.

Mutual funds solely investing in gold stocks and gold bullion also exist (e.g., Fidelity Select Gold and Lexington Gold). Diversification is achieved through mutual fund ownership. Gold futures may be gotten on some commodities exchanges. A down payment as little as 10% of the contract's value can be made to buy the contract. The low margin requirement furnishes a leveraging opportunity. Commissions are usually below 1% of the value of the contract. Gold futures are traded in some U.S. and foreign exchanges.

Disadvantages With Physical Gold Ownership

• High transaction and storage costs.
• Price variability resulting in high risk. Volatility in price partly arises from changes in the international market caused usually from speculation.
• No dividends are received.
• Bearer form for some types of gold investment (e.g., bullion and coins). If lost or stolen, there is no protection from registration.

Silver

Silver may be in the form of bars, coins, jewelry, or flatware. There are also futures contracts traded on some commodities exchanges. Return is in the form of appreciation in the value of the silver. Silver is substantially less in price relative to gold. Carrying costs are quite high.

Market prices of silver mining companies depend both on the price of physical silver and the financial position of the firms themselves.

PREFERRED STOCK Although participating preferred stock rarely exists, if it does, it may be partially or fully participating. In the case of partially participating, preferred

stockholders participate in excess dividends over the preferred dividend rate proportionately with common stockholders, but there is a maximum additional rate. For example, an 8% preferred stock issue may permit participating up to 12%, so that an extra 4% dividend may be tacked on. In the case of fully participating preferred stock, there is a distribution for the current year at the preference rate plus any cumulative preference. Further, the preferred stockholders share in dividend distributions in excess of the preferred stock rate on a proportionate basis, using the total par value of the preferred stock and common stock. For instance, a 10% fully participating preferred stock will get the 10% preference rate plus a proportionate share based on the total par value of the common and preferred stock of excess dividends once common stockholders have obtained their matching 10% of par of the common stock.

■ Example

Assume 5% preferred stock, $20 par, 5,000 shares. The preferred stock is partially participating up to an additional 2%. Common stock is $10 par, 30,000 shares. A $40,000 dividend is declared. Dividends are distributed as follows:

	Preferred	Common
Preferred stock, current year ($100,000 × 5%)	$5,000	
Common stock, current year ($300,000 × 5%)		$15,000
Preferred stock, partial ($100,000 × 2%)	2,000	
Common stock, matching ($300,000 × 2%)		6,000
Balance to common stock		12,000
Total	$7,000	$33,000

Cumulative preferred stock means that if no dividends are paid in a given year, the dividends accumulate and must be paid before any dividends can be paid to noncumulative stock.

The liquidation value of preferred stock means that in corporate liquidation, preferred stockholders will receive the liquidation value (sometimes stated as par value) before any funds may be distributed to common stockholders.

Disclosure for preferred stock includes liquidation preferences, call prices, and cumulative dividends in arrears.

When preferred stock is converted to common stock, the preferred stock and paid-in-capital account are eliminated and the common stock and paid-in-capital account are credited. If a deficit results, retained earnings would be charged.

■ Example

Preferred stock shares having a par value of $300,000 and paid-in-capital (preferred stock) of $20,000 are converted into common stock. There are 30,000 preferred shares having a $10 par value per share. Common stock shares issued are 10,000 shares having a par value of $25.

The journal entry is

Preferred stock	300,000	
Paid-in-Capital (preferred stock)	20,000	
Common Stock (10,000 × $25)		250,000
Paid-in-Capital (common stock)		70,000

PRELIMINARY AUDIT

1. An initial engagement requiring an appraisal of the entire business and accounting system of the client. The adequacy of internal control is a prime consideration so that a proper auditing plan may be formulated.
2. Audit work conducted before year-end so that less audit testing is required at the close of the year. A preliminary audit tests transactions and accounting records to assure that the accounts are properly stated.

PRICE/BOOK VALUE RATIO

The price/book value ratio equals:

$$\frac{\text{Market price per share}}{\text{Book value per share}}$$

Market price per share should generally be higher than book value per share due to infla-

tion and good corporate performance over the years. Market price is based on current prices, whereas book value is based on historical prices. The higher the ratio, the more desirable, since it shows the stock market places a higher value on the company. It should be noted that in some cases, the book value per share may in fact be higher than the market price per share. This is the case for many banks, for example.

■ **Example**

A company's market price per share is $20 and its book value per share is $25. The price/book value ratio equals:

$$\frac{\$20}{\$25} = 0.8$$

The analytical implication may be that the company has not been performing well since market price is below book value. Perhaps the company has financial and operating problems.

It should be noted, however, that some analysts view a buying situation to exist when book value is above market price because the stock may be undervalued. *See also* Book Value per Share.

PRICE-EARNINGS RATIO (P/E RATIO) The

price-earnings ratio equals market price of stock divided by earnings per share. It is used by potential investors in deciding whether to invest in the company. A high P/E ratio is desirable because it indicates that investors highly value a company's earnings by applying to it a higher multiple. The P/E ratio of a company is dependent upon several factors, including quality of earnings, stability of earnings, risk trend in earnings, cash flow, liquidity position, solvency status, and growth potential, among others. Financial analysts who are of the opinion that the firm will generate future profit at higher levels than present may value the stock higher than its current earnings may justify.

■ **Example**

A company's earnings per share is $5 and the market price per share is $50. The P/E multiple is 10.

PRICE INDICES   There are various price indices that are used to measure living costs, price-level changes, and inflation. They are

1. *Consumer Price Index (CPI)*—measures the cost of buying a fixed bundle of goods (some 400 consumer goods and services), representative of the purchases of the typical working-class urban family. The fixed basket is divided into the following categories: food and beverages, housing, apparel, transportation, medical care, entertainment, and other. Generally referred to as a "cost-of-living index," it is published by the Bureau of Labor Statistics of the U.S. Department of Labor. The CPI is widely used for *escalation clauses*. The base year for the CPI index was 1967, at which time it was assigned 100.

2. *Producer Price Index (PPI)*—like the CPI, the PPI is a measure of the cost of a given basket of goods priced in wholesale markets, including raw materials, semifinished goods, and finished goods. The PPI is published monthly by the Bureau of Labor Statistics of the Department of Commerce. The PPI signals changes in the general price level, or the CPI, some time before they actually materialize. (Since the PPI does not include services, caution should be exercised when the principal cause of inflation is service prices.) For this reason, the PPI and especially some of its subindexes, such as the *index of sensitive materials*, serve as one of the *leading indicators* that are closely watched by policy makers.

3. *GNP Deflator (Implicit Price Index)*—a weighted average of the price indexes used to deflate the components of GNP. Thus, it reflects price changes for goods and services bought by consumers, businesses, and gov-

ernments. The GNP deflator is found by dividing current GNP in a given year by constant (real) GNP. Because it covers a broader group of goods and services than the CPI and PPI, the GNP Deflator is a very widely used price index that is frequently used to measure inflation. The GNP deflator, unlike the CPI and PPI, is available only *quarterly*, not monthly. It too is published by the U.S. Department of Commerce.

See also Economic Indicators; Indexation; Index of Leading Economic Indicators.

PRICE-LEVEL ACCOUNTING
Price-level information is *optional* by a company. At one time, disclosure was required. If presented, certain guidelines exist.

Historical cost is first stated in terms of current cost. Current cost is then adjusted to constant purchasing power using the average consumer price index (CPI) for the current year as follows:

$$\text{Replacement cost} \times \frac{\text{Average CPI for current year}}{\text{CPI at time of transaction}}$$

In terms of general inflation, the following two types of accounts exist:

• *Monetary accounts.* 1. Monetary assets include cash and claims to cash (e.g., receivables). Monetary assets remain intact in the price-level balance sheet because they are stated in current dollars. During a period of inflation, holding monetary assets results in a purchasing power loss shown in the price-level income statement. 2. Monetary liabilities are obligations payable in dollars (e.g., accounts payable, notes payable, bonds payable, and advances to unconsolidated subsidiaries). Monetary liabilities remain intact in the price-level balance sheet. During a period of inflation, owing money results in a purchasing power gain shown in the price-level income statement.

• *Nonmonetary accounts.* 1. Nonmonetary assets are in older dollars and require adjustment to current dollars in the price-level balance sheet. Examples are land, equipment, machinery, and goodwill. 2. Nonmonetary

liabilities are those payable in *services*, not dollars. An example is warranty payable.
3. Stockholders' equity representing equity securities that were issued in older dollars.

Purchasing power gain or loss on monetary items has to be considered.

■ Example

On 1/1/19X1, monetary assets were $70,000 and monetary liabilities were $20,000. During the year, net monetary assets (monetary assets less monetary liabilities) increased by $40,000. The CPI indices for 19X1 were

1/1/19X1	200
Average for 19X1	215
12/31/19X1	220

	Historical Cost		Conversion Factor	Average CPI Dollars
1/1/19X1 Net monetary assets	$50000	×	215/200	$53750
Increase in net monetary assets	40000	×	215/215	40000
				$93750
12/31/19X1 Net monetary assets	$90000	×	220/215	92093
Purchasing power loss				$ 1657

Inflationary disclosures include the following items in terms of their inflation adjusted amounts: sales, income from continuing operations, net income, cash dividends, market price of stock, inventory, fixed assets, intangible assets, cost of sales, depreciation, amortization, and purchasing power gain or loss. *See also* Inflation.

PRICING A SPECIAL ORDER
Pricing of a special order is a short-term and nonroutine decision such as whether to accept a production order at an offered price that is below the normal selling price or what price to charge for a product that could be produced with otherwise idle facilities.

■ Example

Assume product X normally sells for $20 per unit. The unit variable cost is $12. Total fixed costs are $100,000 for the currently

produced 20,000 units. Thus, fixed cost per unit is currently $5. Idle capacity is assumed to exist. A prospective customer offers to buy 100 units at $15. The $15 offered price is of course less than the current selling price of $20. However, in this special order decision, the company should sell at the $15 price because profitability results, as indicated following:

Sales	100 × $15	$1,500
Less: Variable costs	100 × $12	1,200
Contribution margin		$ 300
Less: Fixed costs		0*
Net income		$ 300

* At idle capacity, total fixed cost does not increase with an additional order.

See also Contribution Approach to Pricing.

PRIOR PERIOD ADJUSTMENT The two types of prior period adjustments are (1) correction of an error that was made in a prior year and (2) recognition of a tax loss carry forward benefit arising from a purchased subsidiary (curtailed by the 1986 Tax Reform Act).

When a single year is presented, prior period adjustments adjust the beginning balance of retained earnings. The presentation follows:
- Retained earnings—1/1 unadjusted
- Prior period adjustments (net of tax)
- Retained earnings—1/1 adjusted
- Add: Net income
- Less: Dividends
- Retained earnings—12/31

Errors may be due to mathematical mistakes, incorrect application of accounting principles, or misuse of the facts existing when the financial statements were prepared. Further, a change in principle from one that is not GAAP to one that is GAAP is an error correction. Disclosure should be made of the nature of the error and the effect of correction on earnings.

When comparative statements are prepared, a retroactive adjustment for the error is made as it effects the prior years. The retroactive adjustment is disclosed by showing the effects of the adjustment on previous years' earnings and component items of net income.

■ **Example**

In 19X1, a company incorrectly charged furniture for promotion expense amounting to $30,000. The error was discovered in 19X2. The correcting journal entry is

Retained Earnings	30,000	
Furniture		30,000

■ **Example**

X Company acquired Y Company on 1/1/19X3 recording goodwill of $60,000. Goodwill was not amortized. The correcting entry on 12/31/19X5 follows:

Amortization Expense (1500 × 1 for 19X5)	1,500	
Retained Earnings (1500 × 2 for 19X3 and 19X4)	3,000	
Goodwill		4,500

■ **Example**

At the end of 19X2, a company failed to accrue telephone expense that was paid at the beginning of 19X3. The correcting entry on 12/31/19X3 is

Retained Earnings	16,000	
Telephone Expense		16,000

■ **Example**

On 1/1/19X2, an advance retainer fee of $50,000 was received covering a 5-year period. In error, revenue was credited for the full amount. The error was discovered on 12/31/19X4 before closing the books. The correcting entry is

12/31/19X4 Retained Earnings	30,000	
Revenue		10,000
Deferred Revenue		20,000

■ Example

A company bought a machine on January 1, 19X4, for $32,000 with a $2,000 salvage value and a 5-year life. By mistake repairs expense was charged. The error was discovered on December 31, 19X7, before closing the books. The correcting entry follows:

Depreciation Expense	6,000	
Machine	32,000	
Accumulated Depreciation		24,000
Retained Earnings		14,000

Accumulated depreciation of $24,000 is calculated following:

$$\frac{\$32,000 - \$2,000}{5} = \$6,000 \text{ per year} \times 4 \text{ years}$$
$$= \$24,000$$

The credit to retained earnings reflects the difference between the erroneous repairs expense of $32,000 in 19X4 versus showing depreciation expense of $18,000 for 3 years (19X4–19X6).

■ Example

At the beginning of 19X5, a company bought equipment for $300,000 with a salvage value of $20,000 and an expected life of 10 years. Straight-line depreciation is used. In error, salvage value was not deducted in computing depreciation. The correcting journal entries on 12/31/19X7 follow:

	19X5 and 19X6
Depreciation taken $300,000/10 × 2 years	$60,000
Depreciation correctly stated $280,000/10 × 2 years	56,000
	$ 4,000

Depreciation	28,000	
Accumulated Depreciation		28,000
Depreciation for current year		
Accumulated Depreciation	4,000	
Retained Earnings		4,000
Correct prior year depreciation misstatement		

PRIOR SERVICE COST This is the retroactive cost for employee services performed before the date of adoption or amendment to the pension plan. As a result, the projected benefit obligation will increase. *See also* Pension Plans.

PRIVATE PLACEMENT In a private placement, a company issues equity and debt securities directly to either one or a few large investors. The large investors are financial institutions such as insurance companies, pension plans, and commercial banks.

Advantages of Private Placement Versus Public Issuance

• The flotation cost is less. Flotation cost is the expense of registering and selling the stock issue. Examples are brokerage commissions and underwriting fees. The flotation cost for common stock exceeds that for preferred stock. Flotation cost expressed as a percentage of gross proceeds is higher for smaller issues than for larger ones.

• It avoids SEC filing requirements.

• It avoids the disclosure of information to the public at large.

• There is less time involved to obtain funds.

• It may not be practical to issue securities in the public market when a company is so small that an investment banker would not find it profitable.

• The company's credit rating may be low and as a consequence, investors may not be interested in buying securities when the money supply is limited.

Disadvantages of Private Placement Versus Public Issuance

• It is more difficult to obtain significant amounts of money privately.

• Large investors usually employ stringent credit standards requiring the company to be in a strong financial position.

• Large institutional investors may watch more closely the company's activities.

• Large institutional investors are more ca-

pable of obtaining voting control of the company.

PRIVILEGED COMMUNICATION This is a confidential relationship between parties for which the recipient of the information is legally allowed to withhold disclosure of it. An example is the relationship between client and lawyer. There is *no* such common law relationship between client and CPA. However, some states have passed statutes recognizing this relationship.

PROBABILITY PROPORTIONAL TO SIZE (PPS) SAMPLING PPS sampling estimates the maximum amount of dollar value error that probably exists in an account. PPS sampling involves defining the sampling unit, selecting the sample, computing sample size, and appraising sample results (no sample errors, occurrence of sample errors, and significance thereof).

In PPS sampling, the sampling unit is the individual dollar. Thus, the population is the total dollars involved. Each individual dollar in the population has the same probability of being chosen. However, the auditor does *not* select and audit individual dollars in the population. Instead, the CPA will examine the customer accounts or transactions (referred to as logical units) associated with the specific dollars that are selected for sampling.

■ **Example**

The auditor wishes to test the reasonableness of a client's recorded accounts receivable. Confirmations are mailed to a random sample of customers. Each customer's account is a logical unit. The total of all logical units subject to audit is the sample.

The more dollars associated with a logical unit, the greater is the chance for selection. A drawback, however, is the PPS is not best suitable to test an account for understatement.

■ **Example**

A client's accounts receivable is $1,000,000. A required sample size of 2,000 is computed. The sampling interval is computed to be $500 ($1,000,000/2,000). The auditor selects a random start that has to be a number between one and the sampling interval ($500). This is necessary so the auditor may select the first logical unit from the first interval. The first logical unit is the one containing the dollar amount corresponding to the random start. After selecting the logical unit containing the random start dollar, the auditor then proceeds to select each logical unit associated with every xth dollar thereafter (x being the sampling interval size). Assume the auditor chooses a random start derived from a random number table of $26. The auditor would then select the logical unit associated with the 26th dollar as the first sample item and would proceed to choose the logical units associated with the 526th dollar ($26 and $500), the 1,026th dollar ($26 and $500 and $500), the 1,526th dollar ($26 and $500 and $500 and $500), and so on until all 2,000 logical units are chosen. In effect, the auditor has segregated the $1,000,000 of accounts receivable into 2,000 intervals of $500 each.

Because of the selection of logical units associated with every xth dollar (x equals the computed sampling interval), all logical units with dollar amounts equal to or in excess of the sampling interval will be selected for the sample with 100% certainty. This assures that customer accounts of greater magnitude (amounts equal to or greater than the sampling interval) will be included in the sample for testing.

PPS is appropriate when the auditor's purpose is to ascertain the existence of overstatement errors. Therefore, it is a good approach for examining asset balances, such as receivables, securities, and inventory.

PPS is best appropriate when the population contains debit balances. If the auditor finds zero or credit balances in the population,

special design considerations are required. Also, design modification is needed in the event the audited amount of the sampling unit exceeds the recorded amount (causing the book value to be understated) or less than zero (making the overstatement error to be greater than the recorded book value).

PPS sampling should be employed only if a few errors of overstatement are anticipated. If there are many overstatement errors that are uncovered, there is a higher probability that the auditor will reject an acceptable recorded amount. *Recommendation*: If many overstatement or understatement errors are expected, a sampling method other than PPS should be used, such as classical variables sampling. *See also* Classical Variables Sampling; Sampling.

PROCESS COSTING   This is a cost accumulation system that aggregates manufacturing costs by departments or by production processes. Total manufacturing costs are accumulated by two major categories—direct materials and conversion costs (the sum of direct labor and factory overhead applied). Unit cost is determined by dividing the total costs charged to a cost center by the output of that cost center. Process costing is appropriate for companies that produce a continuous mass of like units through a series of operations or processes. Process costing is generally used in such industries as petroleum, chemicals, oil refinery, textiles, and food processing.

The process-costing method uses what is called the *cost of production report,* which summarizes the total cost charged to a department and the allocation between the ending work-in-process inventory and the units completed and transferred to the next department or finished goods inventory. The output of a processing department during a given period is measured in terms of *equivalent units* of production, which is the expression of the physical units of output in terms of doses or amount of work applied thereto.

The cost of production report generally consists of four sections:

1. *Physical flow* accounts for the physical flow of units in and out of a department.

2. *Equivalent production* is the sum of (a) units in process, restated in completed units and (b) total units actually produced. The computation of equivalent units of production depends on the flow of cost method-*weighted average* or *FIFO*.

3. *Costs to account for* accounts for the incurrence of costs that were (a) in process at the beginning of the period; (b) transferred in from previous departments; and (c) added by the department during the current period.

4. *Costs accounted for* accounts for the disposition of costs charged to the department that were (a) transferred out to the next department or finished goods inventory; (b) completed and on hand; and (c) in process at the end of the period. The total of the *Costs to account for* must equal the total of the *Costs accounted for*.

In computing the unit cost for a processing center, when a beginning inventory of work-in-process exists, two specific assumptions about the flow of costs are used—*weighted average* and *FIFO*. Under weighted average, the costs in the beginning inventory are averaged with the current period's costs to determine one average unit cost for all units passing through the cost center in a given month. Under FIFO, costs in the beginning inventory are not mingled with the current period's costs but transferred out as a separate batch of goods at a different unit cost from units started and completed during the period.

■ **Example**

The Portland Cement Manufacturing Company, Inc., manufactures cement. Its processing operations involve quarrying, grinding, blending, packing, and sacking. For cost accounting and control purposes, there are four processing centers: Raw Material No. 1, Raw Material No. 2, Clinker, and Cement. Separate cost of production reports are pre-

pared in detail with respect to the foregoing cost centers. The following information pertains to the operation of Raw Material No. 2 Department for July 19A:

	Materials	Conversion
Units in process July 1		
800 bags	complete	60% complete
Costs	$12,000	$56,000
Units transferred out		
40,000 bags		
Current costs	$41,500	$521,500
Units in process, July 31		
5,000 bags	complete	30% complete

1. Using the weighted average method of costing, we can determine
   a. Equivalent production units and unit costs by elements
   b. Cost of work-in-process for July
   c. Cost of units completed and transferred
2. We can do the same thing, using the FIFO method of costing.

1 and 2 (a)

Computation of Output in Equivalent Units

	Physical Flow	Materials	Conversion
WIP, beginning	800(60%)		
Units transferred in	44,200		
Units to account for	45,000		
Units completed and transferred out	40,000	40,000	40,000
WIP, end	5,000(30%)	5,000	1,500
Units accounted for	45,000		
Equivalent units used for weighted average		45,000	41,500
Less: Old equivalent units for work done on beginning inventory in prior period		800	480
Equivalent units used for FIFO		44,200	41,020

1 (b) (c)

Cost of Production Report—Weighted Average Raw Material No. 2 Department
for the Month Ended July 31, 19A

	WIP Beginning	Current Costs	Total Costs	Equivalent Units	Average Unit Cost
Materials	$12,000	$ 41,500	$ 53,500	45,000	$ 1.1889
Conversion costs	56,000	521,500	577,500	41,500	13.9156
	$68,000	563,000	631,000		$15.1045

Cost of goods completed 40,000 × $15.1045		$604,180
WIP, end:		
Materials 5,000 × $1.1889	$ 5,944.50	
Conversion 1,500 × 13.9156	20,873.40	$ 26,817.90
Total costs accounted		$631,000(rounded)

2 (b) (c)

Cost of Production Report—FIFO Raw Material No. 2 Department for the Month Ended July 31, 19A

	Total Costs	Equivalent Units	Unit Costs
WIP, beginning	$ 68,000		
Current costs:			
Materials	41,500	44,200	$ 0.9389
Conversion costs	521,500	41,020	12.7133
Total costs to account for	$631,000		$13.6522
WIP, end:			
Materials			
5,000 × $0.9389	$ 4,694.50		
Conversion			
1,500 × $12.7133	19,069.95	23,764.45	
Cost of goods completed, 40,000 units:			
• WIP, beginning to be transferred out first	68,000		
• Additional costs to complete 800 × (1 − 0.6) × $12.7133	4,068.26		
• Cost of goods started and completed this month 39,200 × $13.6522			
	535,166.24	$607,234.50	
Total costs accounted for		$631,000(rounded)	

Answers are summarized as follows:

1 and 2.

	Weighted Average		FIFO	
	Materials	Conversion	Materials	Conversion
a. Equivalent units	45,000	41,500	44,200	41,020
Unit costs	$1.1889	$13.9156	$0.9389	$12.7133
b. Cost of WIP	$26,817.90		$23,764.45	
c. Cost of units completed and transferred	$604,180		$607,234.50	

PRODUCT-FINANCING ARRANGEMENTS

As per FASB 49, the arrangement involving the sale and repurchase of inventory is in substance a financing arrangement. It mandates that the product-financing arrangement be accounted for as a borrowing instead of a sale. In many cases, the product is stored on the company's (sponsor's) premises. Further, often the sponsor will guarantee the debt of the other entity.

Types of product-financing arrangements include:

• Sponsor sells a product to another business and agrees to reacquire the product or one basically identical to it. The established price to be paid by the sponsor typically includes financing and holding costs.

• Sponsor has another company buy the product for it and agrees to repurchase the product from the other entity.

• Sponsor controls the distribution of the product that has been bought by another company in accord with the aforementioned terms.

In all situations, the company (sponsor) either agrees to repurchase the product at given prices over specified time periods or guarantees resale prices to third parties.

When the sponsor sells the product to the other firm and in a related transaction agrees

to repurchase it, the sponsor should record a liability when the proceeds are received to the degree the product applies to the financing arrangement. A sale should *not* be recorded and the product should be retained as inventory on the sponsor's books.

In the case where another firm buys the product for the sponsor, inventory is debited and liability credited at the time of purchase.

Costs of the product, except for processing costs, in excess of sponsor's original production cost or acquisition cost or the other company's purchase cost constitute finance and holding costs. The sponsor accounts for these costs according to its typical accounting policies. Interest costs will also be incurred in connection with the financing arrangement. These should be separately shown and may be deferred.

■ **Example**

On 1/1/19X1, a sponsor borrows $100,000 from another company and gives the inventory as collateral for the loan. The entry is

Cash	100,000	
Liability		100,000

Note that a sale is *not* recorded and the inventory remains on the books of the sponsor. In effect, inventory serves as collateral for a loan.

On 12/31/19X1, the sponsor pays back the other company. The collateralized inventory item is returned. The interest rate on the loan was 8%. Storage costs were $2,000. The entry is

Liability	100,000	
Deferred Interest	8,000	
Storage Expense	2,000	
Cash		110,000

Typically, most of the product in the financing arrangement is eventually used or sold by the sponsor. However, in some cases, small amounts of the product may be sold by the financing entity to other parties.

The entity that gives financing to the sponsor is usually an existing creditor, nonbusiness entity, or trust. It is also possible that the financier may have been established for the *only* purpose of providing financing for the sponsor.

Footnote disclosure should be made of the particulars of the product-financing arrangement. *See also* Revenue Recognition Methods.

PRODUCTION MIX VARIANCE This is a cost variance that arises if the actual production mix deviates from the standard or budgeted mix. In a multiproduct, multiinput situation, the mix variances explain the portion of the *quantity (usage, or efficiency) variance* caused by using inputs (direct materials and direct labor) in ratios different from standard proportions, thus helping determine how efficiently mixing operations are performed. The *material mix variance* indicates the impact on material costs of the deviation from the budgeted mix. The *labor mix variance* measures the impact of changes in the labor mix on labor costs.

$$\begin{matrix} \text{Material} \\ \text{mix} \\ \text{variance} \end{matrix} = \begin{pmatrix} \text{Actual units} & \text{Actual units} \\ \text{used at} & - \text{used at} \\ \text{standard mix} & \text{actual mix} \end{pmatrix} \begin{matrix} \text{Standard} \\ \times \text{unit} \\ \text{price} \end{matrix}$$

$$\begin{matrix} \text{Labor} \\ \text{mix} \\ \text{variance} \end{matrix} = \begin{pmatrix} \text{Actual hours} & \text{Actual hours} \\ \text{used at} & - \text{used at} \\ \text{standard mix} & \text{actual mix} \end{pmatrix} \begin{matrix} \text{Standard} \\ \times \text{hourly} \\ \text{rate} \end{matrix}$$

Probable causes of unfavorable production mix variances are as follows: (1) capacity restraints force substitution; (1) poor production scheduling; (3) lack of certain types of labor; and (4) certain materials are in short supply.

■ **Example**

J Company produces a compound composed of Materials Alpha and Beta that is marketed in 20-pound bags. Material Alpha can be substituted for Material Beta. Standard cost and mix data have been determined as follows:

	Unit Price	Standard Unit	Standard Mix Proportions
Material Alpha	$3	5 lbs	25%
Material Beta	4	15	75
		20 lbs	100%

Processing each 20 pounds of material requires 10 hours of labor. The company employs two types of labor—skilled and unskilled—working on two processes, assembly and finishing. The following standard labor cost has been set for a 20-pound bag.

	Standard Hours	Standard Wage Rate	Total	Standard Mix Proportions
Unskilled	4 hrs	$2	$ 8	40%
Skilled	6	3	18	60
	10 hrs	$2.60	$26	100%

At standard cost, labor averages $2.60 per unit. During the month of December, 100 twenty-pound bags were completed with the following labor costs:

	Actual Hours	Actual Rate	Actual Wages
Unskilled	380 hrs	$2.50	$ 950
Skilled	600	3.25	1,950
	980 hrs	$2.96	$2,900

Material records show

Material Alpha actually used, 700 lbs @ $3.10
Material Beta actually used, 1,400 lbs @ 3.90

Using the previous formulas, the material mix variance and labor mix variance are computed as shown at bottom of page.

PRODUCTION YIELD VARIANCE Production yield variance is a difference between the actual yield and the standard yield. *Yield* is a measure of productivity. In other words, it is a measure of output from a given amount of input. For example, in the production of potato chips, we might expect a certain yield; such as 40% yield, or 40 pounds of chips for 100 pounds of potatoes. If the actual yield is less than the expected or standard yield for a given level of input, the yield variance is unfavorable. A yield variance is computed for labor as well as for materials. A *labor yield variance* is considered the result of the quantity and/or the quality of labor used. The yield variance explains the remaining portion of the *quantity variance* and is caused by a yield of finished product that does not correspond with the quantity that actual inputs should have produced. When there is no mix variance, the yield variance equals the quantity variance.

Material Mix Variance

	Actual Units Used at Standard Mix*	Actual Units at Actual Mix	Difference	Standard Unit Price	Variance (U or F)
Material Alpha	525 lbs	700 lbs	175U	$3	$525U
Material Beta	1,575	1,400	175F	4	700F
	2,100 lbs	2,100 lbs			$175F

* This is the standard mix proportions of 25% and 75% applied to the actual material units used of 2,100 pounds.

Labor Mix Variance

	Actual Hours Used at Standard Mix*	Actual Hours Used at Actual Mix	Difference	Standard Hourly Rate	Variance (U or F)
Unskilled	392 hrs	380 hrs	12F	$2	$24F
Skilled	588	600	12U	3	36U
	980 hrs	980 hrs			$12U

* This is the standard mix proportions of 40% and 60% applied to the actual total labor hours used of 980.

$$\begin{matrix} \text{Material} \\ \text{yield} \\ \text{variance} \end{matrix} = \begin{pmatrix} \text{Actual units} & \text{Actual output} \\ \text{used at} & - \text{used at} \\ \text{standard mix} & \text{standard mix} \end{pmatrix} \times \begin{matrix} \text{Standard} \\ \text{unit} \\ \text{price} \end{matrix}$$

$$\begin{matrix} \text{Labor} \\ \text{yield} \\ \text{variance} \end{matrix} = \begin{pmatrix} \text{Actual hours} & \text{Actual output} \\ \text{used at} & - \text{hours used at} \\ \text{standard mix} & \text{standard mix} \end{pmatrix} \times \begin{matrix} \text{Standard} \\ \text{hourly} \\ \text{rate} \end{matrix}$$

Probable causes of unfavorable production yield variances are (1) low-quality materials and/or labor; (2) faulty equipment; (3) improper production methods; and (4) an improper or costly mix of materials and/or labor.

■ **Example**

A company uses a standard cost system for its production of a chemical product. This chemical is produced by mixing three major raw materials, A, B, and C. The company has the following standards:

36 lbs of material A	@ 1.00	= $ 36.00
48 lbs of material B	@ 2.00	= 96.00
36 lbs of material C	@ 1.75	= $ 63.00
120 lbs of standard mix	@ 1.625	= $195.00

The company should produce 100 pounds of finished product at a standard cost of $1.625 per pound ($195/120 lbs). To convert 120 pounds of materials into 100 pounds of finished chemical requires 400 direct labor hours at $3.50 per hour, or $14 per pound. During the month of December, the company completed 4,250 pounds of output with the following labor: direct labor 15,250 hours @ $3.50. Material records show

Material A	1,160 lbs used
Material B	1,820
Material C	1,480

Material yield variance can be calculated as follows:

With a standard yield of 83⅓% (100/120), 4,250 pounds of completed output should have required 17,000 hours of direct labor (4,250 lbs × 400 direct labor hrs/100). Comparing the hours allowed for the actual input, 14,866.67 hours, with the hours allowed for actual output, 17,000 hours, we find a favorable labor yield variance of $7,466.66, as shown following:

Labor Yield Variance:

Actual hours at expected output	$52,033.34
Actual output (4,250 lbs × 400/100	
= 17,000 hrs @ $3.50 or 4,250 lbs	
@ $14.00)	59,500
	$ 7,466.66F

PROFIT CENTER This is a responsibility center of an organization. It is the unit in an organization that is responsible for revenues earned and costs incurred. A manager of a profit center has control over both revenues and costs and attempts to maximize profit. Examples include a college book division of a publishing company, a houseware department in a retail store, and a product division. A profit center has the following characteristics: (1) its goal is to earn a profit; (2) its management is evaluated by means of contribution income statements, in terms of meeting sales and cost objectives; and (3) its management has the authority to make decisions regarding factors that determine the amount of profit, which may include selection of sales outlets, advertising policy, and selection of sources of supply. *See also* Responsibility Accounting; Segmental Reporting.

PROFIT VARIANCE Profit variance is a difference between actual profit and budgeted

	Actual Input Units at Standard Mix	Actual Output Units at Standard Mix*	Difference	Standard Unit Price	Variance (U or F)
Material A	1,338 lbs	1,275 lbs	63U	$1.00	$ 63U
Material B	1,784	1,700	84F	2.00	168U
Material C	1,338	1,275	63U	1.75	110.25U
	4,460	4,250			$341.25U

*This is the standard mix proportions of 30%, 40%, and 30% applied to the actual *output* units used of 4,250 lbs.

profit. Profit is affected by three basic items: sales price, sales volume, and costs. In a multiproduct firm, if all products are not equally profitable, profit is also affected by the mix of products sold. *See also* Contribution Margin; Profit Variance Analysis.

PROFIT VARIANCE ANALYSIS This, often called *gross profit analysis*, deals with how to analyze the profit variance which constitutes the departure between actual profit and the previous year's income or the budgeted figure. The primary goal of profit variance analysis is to improve performance and profitability in the future.

Profit, whether it is *gross profit* in *absorption costing* or *contribution margin* in *direct costing*, is affected by at least three basic items: sales price, sales volume, and costs. In addition, in a multiproduct firm, if not all products are equally profitable, profit is affected by the mix of products sold.

The difference between budgeted and actual profits are due to one or more of the following:

1. Changes in unit sales price and cost, called *sales price* and *cost price variances*, respectively. The difference between sales price variance and cost price variance is often called a *contribution-margin-per-unit variance* or a *gross-profit-per-unit variance*, depending upon the type of costing system, that is, absorption costing or direct costing. Contribution margin is considered a better measure of product profitability because it deducts from sales revenue only the variable costs that are controllable in terms of fixing responsibility. Gross profit does not reflect cost-volume-profit relationships. Nor does it consider directly traceable marketing costs.

2. Changes in the volume of products sold summarized as the *sales volume variance* and the *cost volume variance*. The difference between the two is called the *total volume variance*.

3. Changes in the volume of the more profitable or less profitable items, referred to as the *sales mix variance*.

Detailed analysis is critical to management when multiproducts exist. The volume variances may be used to measure a change in volume (while holding the mix constant) and the mix may be employed to evaluate the effect of a change in sales mix (while holding the quantity constant). This type of variance analysis is useful when the products are substituted for each other or when products that are not necessarily substitutes for each other are marketed through the same channel.

Types of Standards in Profit Variance Analysis

To determine the various causes for a favorable variance (an increase) or an unfavorable variance (a decrease) in profit we need some kind of yardstick to compare against the actual results. The yardstick may be based on the prices and costs of the previous year or any year selected as the base period. Some companies are summarizing profit variance analysis data in their annual report by showing departures from the previous year's reported income. However, one can establish a more effective control and budgetary method rather than the previous year's data. Standard or budgeted mix can be determined using such sophisticated techniques as *linear* and *goal programming*.

Single-Product Firms

Profit variance analysis is simplest in a single-product firm, for there is only one sales price, one set of costs (or cost price), and a unitary sales volume. An unfavorable profit variance can be broken down into four components: sales price variance, cost price variance, sales volume variance, and cost volume variance.

The *sales price variance* measures the impact on the firm's contribution margin (or

gross profit) of changes in the unit selling price. It is computed as:

Sales price variance
   = (Actual price − Budget price) × Actual sales

If the actual price is lower than the budgeted, for example, this variance is unfavorable; it tends to reduce profit. The *cost price variance*, on the other hand, is simply the summary of price variances for materials, labor, and overhead. (This is the sum of material price, labor rate, and factory overhead spending variances.) It is computed as:

Cost price variance
   = (Actual cost − Budget cost) × Actual sales

If the actual unit cost is lower than budgeted, for example, this variance is favorable; it tends to increase profit. We simplify the computation of price variances by taking the sales price variance less the cost price variance and call it the *gross-profit-per-unit variance* or *contribution-margin-per-unit variance*.

The *sale volume variance* indicates the impact on the firm's profit of changes in the unit sales volume. This is the amount by which sales would have varied from the budget if nothing but sales volume had changed. It is computed as:

Sales volume variance
   = (Actual sales − Budget sales) × Budget price

If actual sales volume is greater than budgeted, this is favorable; it tends to increase profit. The *cost volume variance* has the same interpretation. It is

(Actual sales − Budget sales) × Budget cost per unit

The difference between the sales volume variance and the cost volume variance is called the *total volume variance*.

■ **Example**

The controller of the Royalla Publishing Company prepared the following comparative statement of operations for 19A and 19B.

	19A	19B
Sales in units	97,500	110,000
Selling price	$ 9.00	$ 8.80
Sales revenue	$877,500	$968,000
Cost of goods sold	$585,000	$704,000
Gross profit	$292,500	$264,000

The controller was very pleased with the performance of the company in 19A. Analyze the decline in gross profit between 19A and 19B by calculating:
(a) Sales price variance
(b) Cost price variance
(c) Sales volume variance
(d) Cost volume variance
(e) Total volume variance (sales volume variance − cost volume variance) or (sales mix variance + sales quantity variance)
(f) Sales mix variance
(g) Sales quantity variance

19A gross profit	$292,500
19B gross profit	264,000
Decrease in gross profit to be accounted for	$ 28,500

(a) *Sales price variance*:

19B actual sales revenue	$968,000
19B actual sales revenue at 19A price (110,000 @ $9)	990,000
	$ 22,000U

(b) *Cost price variance*:

19B actual	$704,000
19B actual at 19A cost per unit (110,000 @ $6*)	660,000
	$ 44,000U

*19A cost per unit = $585,000/97,500 = $6

(c) *Sales volume variance*:

19B actual volume at 19A price	$990,000 (110,000 × $9)
19A actual volume at 19A price	877,500
(19B actual − 19A actual) × 19A price	$112,500F

(d) *Cost volume variance:*

19B actual volume at 19A cost	$660,000 (110,000 × $6)
19A actual volume at 19A cost	585,000
(19B actual − 19A actual) × 19A cost	$ 75,000U

(e) *Total volume variance*

= Sales volume variance − Cost volume variance
= $112,500F − $75,000U = $37,500F

which is broken down into the sales mix variance and the sales quantity variance as follows:

(f) *Sales mix variance* = *0* since we have only one product in this problem.

(g) *Sales quantity variance*

19B Actual Volume	19A Budgeted Volume	Difference	19A Gross Profit per Unit*	Variance ($)
110,000	97,500	12,500F	$3	$37,500F

* 19A gross profit per unit = 19A selling price − 19A cost of goods sold = $9 − $6 = $3

The decline in gross profit of $28,500 can be explained as follows:

	Gains	Losses
Gain due to *favorable* sales volume variance	$112,500F	
Losses due to:		
Unfavorable sales price variance		$22,000U
Unfavorable cost price variance		44,000U
Unfavorable cost volume variance		75,000U
	$112,500F	$141,000U

The decrease in gross profit is thus accounted for:

$$\$141,000U - \$112,500F = \$28,500U$$

Multiproduct Firms

When a firm produces more than one product, there is a fourth component of the profit variance. This is the *sales mix variance*—the effect on profit of selling a different proportionate mix of products than that which has been budgeted. This variance arises when different products have different contribution margins. In a multiproduct firm, actual sales volume can differ from that budgeted in two ways. The total number of units sold could differ from the target aggregate sales. In addition, the mix of the products actually sold may not be proportionate to the target mix. Each of these two different types of changes in volume is reflected in a separate variance.

The total volume variance is divided into the two: the *sales mix variance* and the *sales quantity variance*. These two variances should be used to evaluate the marketing department of the firm. The sales mix variance shows how well the department has done in terms of selling the more profitable products, whereas the sales quantity variance measures how well the firm has done in terms of its overall sales volume. They are computed as:

Sales mix variance = (Actual sales at budget mix
− Budget sales at budget mix)
× Budget CM (or gross profit)/unit

Sales quantity variance = (Actual sales at budget mix
− Actual sales at budget mix)
× Budget CM (or gross profit)/unit

Total volume variance = (Actual sales at actual mix
− Budget sales at budget mix)
× Budget CM (or gross profit)/unit

■ Example

The Lake Tahoe ski store sells two ski models—model X and model Y. For the years 19X1 and 19X2, the store realized a gross profit of $246,640 and only $211,650, respectively. The owner of the store was astounded since the total sales volume in dollars and in units was higher for 19X2 than for 19X1, yet the gross profit achieved actually declined. Following are the store's unaudited operating results for 19X1 and 19X2. No fixed costs were included in the cost of goods sold per unit.

		Model X				Model Y		
Year	Selling Price	Cost of Goods Sold per Unit	Sales (in units)	Sales Revenue	Selling Price	Cost of Goods Sold per Unit	Sales (in Units)	Sales Revenue
1	$150	$110	2,800	$420,000	$172	$121	2,640	$454,080
2	160	125	2,650	424,000	176	135	2,900	510,400

Explain why the gross profit declined by $34,990. Include a detailed variance analysis of price changes and changes in volume both for sales and cost. Also subdivide the total volume variance into changes in price and changes in quantity.

Sales price and sales volume variances measure the impact on the firm's *CM* (or gross profit) of changes in the unit selling price and sales volume. In computing these variances, all costs are held constant in order to stress changes in price and volume. Cost price and cost volume variances are computed in the same manner, holding price and volume constant. All these variances for the Lake Tahoe ski store are computed following.

Sales Price Variance

Actual sales for 19X2:
Model X 2,650 × $160 = $424,000
Model Y 2,900 × 176 =   510,400 $934,400
Actual 19X2 sales at 19X1 prices:
Model X 2,650 × $150 = $397,500
Model Y 2,900 × 172 =   498,800   896,300
                                 $ 38,100F

Sales Volume Variance

Actual 19X2 sales at 19X1 prices: $896,300
Actual 19X1 sales (at 19X1 prices):
Model X 2,800 × $150 = $420,000
Model Y 2,640 × 172 =   454,080   874,080
                                 $ 22,220F

Cost Price Variance

Actual cost of goods sold for 19X2:
Model X 2,650 × $125 = $331,250
Model Y 2,900 × 135 =   391,500 $722,750
Actual 19X2 sales at 19X1 costs:
Model X 2,650 × $110 = $291,500
Model Y 2,900 × 121 =   350,900   642,400
                                 $ 80,350U

Cost Volume Variance

Actual 19X2 sales at 19X1 costs: $642,400
Actual 19X1 sales (at 19X1 costs):
Model X 2,800 × $110 = $308,000
Model Y 2,640 × 121 =   319,440   627,440
                                 $ 14,960U

Total volume variance = sales volume variance − cost volume variance = $22,220F − $14,960U = $7,260F

The total volume variance is computed as the sum of a sales mix variance and a sales quantity variance as follows:

	Sales Mix Variance				
	19X2 Actual Sales at 19X1 Mix*	19X2 Actual Sales at 19X2 Mix	Difference	19X1 Gross Profit per Unit	Variance ($)
Model X	2,857	2,650	207U	$40	$ 8,280U
Model Y	2,693	2,900	207F	51	10,557F
	5,550	5,550			$ 2,277F

* This is the 19X1 mix (used as standard or budget) proportions of 51.47% (or 2,800/5,440 = 51.47%) and 48.53% (or 2,640/5,440 = 48.53%) applied to the actual 19X2 sales figure of 5,550 units.

	Sales Quantity Variance				
	19X2 Actual Sales at 19X1 Mix*	19X1 Actual Sales at 19X1 Mix	Difference	19X1 Gross Profit per Unit	Variance ($)
Model X	2,857	2,800	57F	$40	$2,280F
Model Y	2,693	2,640	53F	51	2,703F
	5,550	5,440			$4,983F

* A favorable total volume variance is due to a favorable shift in the sales mix (that is, from Model X to Model Y) and also to a favorable increase in sales volume (by 110 units), which is shown as follows.

Sales mix variance	$2,277F
Sales quantity variance	4,983F
	$7,260F

However, there remains the decrease in gross profit. The decrease in gross profit of $34,990 can be explained as follows:

	Gains	Losses
Gain due to increased sales price	$38,100F	
Loss due to increased cost		80,350U
Gain due to increase in units sold	4,983F	
Gain due to shift in sales mix	2,277F	
	$45,360F	$80,350U

Hence, net decrease in gross profit = $80,350 − $45,360 = $34,990U.

Despite the increase in sales price and volume and the favorable shift in sales mix, the Lake Tahoe ski store ended up losing $34,990 compared to 19X1. The major reason for this comparative loss was the tremendous increase in cost of goods sold, as indicated by an unfavorable cost price variance of $80,350. The costs for both Model X and Model Y went up quite significantly over 19X1. The store has to take a close look at

the cost picture. Even though only variable costs were included in cost of goods sold per unit, both variable and fixed costs should be analyzed in an effort to cut down on controllable costs. In doing that, it is essential that responsibility be clearly fixed to given individuals. In a retail business like the Lake Tahoe ski store, operating expenses such as advertising and payroll of store employees must also be closely scrutinized.

Sales Mix Analysis

Many product lines often include a lower margin price leader model and a high-margin deluxe model. For example, the automobile industry includes in its product line low-margin energy-efficient small cars and higher margin deluxe models. In an attempt to increase overall profitability, management would wish to emphasize the higher margin expensive items, but salespeople might find it easier to sell lower margin cheaper models. Thus, a salesperson might meet the unit sales quota with each item at its budgeted price but because of mix shifts could be far short of contributing his or her share of budgeted profit. Management should realize that (1) greater proportions of more profitable products mean higher profits and (2) higher proportions of lower margin sales reduce overall profit despite the increase in overall sales volume. That is to say that an unfavorable mix may easily offset a favorable increase in volume, and vice versa.

Performance Reports

Profit variance analysis aids in fixing responsibility by separating the causes of the change in profit into price, volume, and mix factors. With responsibility resting in different places, the segregation of the total profit variance is essential. The performance reports based on the analysis of profit variances must be prepared for each responsibility center, indicating the following:

1. Is it controllable?
2. Is it favorable or unfavorable?
3. If it is unfavorable, is it significant enough for further investigation?
4. Who is responsible for what portion of the total profit variance?
5. What are the causes for an unfavorable variance?
6. What is the remedial action to take?

The performance report must address these types of questions. The report is useful in two ways: (1) in focusing attention on situations in need of management action and (2) in increasing the precision of planning and control of sales and costs. The report should be produced as part of the overall standard costing and *responsibility accounting* system. *See also* Responsibility Accounting; Sales Mix Variance; Variance Analysis.

PROFITABILITY INDEX This, also called *excess present value index* or *cost-benefit ratio*, is the ratio of the total present value (PV) of future cash inflows to the initial investment (I). That is, PV/I. This index is primarily used as a means of ranking projects in *capital rationing* situations. In a single-project case, if the index is greater than 1, then you should accept the project. *See also* Capital Rationing.

PRO FORMA This refers to a financial statement or account that contains hypothetical (assumed) figures. The assumptions supporting the estimates are disclosed. In a sense, it is a what-if situation. The purpose is to show a proposed future financial condition.

PROGRAM EVALUATION AND REVIEW TECHNIQUE (PERT) PERT is a useful management tool for planning, scheduling, costing, coordinating, and controlling complex projects such as
- Formulation of a master budget
- Construction of buildings

• Installation of computers
• Scheduling the closing of books
• Assembly of a machine
• Research and development activities

Questions to be answered by PERT include

• When will the project be finished?
• What is the probability that the project will be completed by any given time?

The PERT technique involves the diagrammatic representation of the sequence of activities comprising a project by means of a *network*. The network (1) visualizes all of the individual tasks (activities) to complete a given job or program; (2) points out interrelationships; and (3) consists of activities (represented by arrows) and events (represented by circles), as shown following.

1. *Arrows*—represent tasks or activities that are distinct segments of the project requiring time and resources.

2. *Nodes* (*circles*)—symbolize events or milestone points in the project representing the completion of one or more activities and/or the initiation of one or more subsequent activities. An event is a point in time and does not consume any time in itself, as does an activity.

In a real-world situation, the estimates of completion times of activities will seldom be certain. To cope with the uncertainty in activity time estimates, the PERT proceeds by estimating *three* possible duration times for each activity. As shown in Figure 1, the numbers appearing on the arrows represent these three time estimates which are needed to complete the various events. These time estimates are (1) the most optimistic time, labeled a; (2) the most likely time, m; and (3) the most pessimistic time, b.

For example, the optimistic time for completing activity B is 1 day, the most likely time is 2 days, but the pessimistic time is 3 days. The next step is to calculate an expected time, which is determined as follows:

$$t_e \text{ (expected time)} = (a + 4m + b)/6$$

For example, for activity B, the expected time is

$$(1 + 4(2) + 3)/6 = 12/6 = 2 \text{ days}$$

As a measure of variation (uncertainty) about the expected time, the standard deviation is calculated as follows:

$$\sigma = (b - a)/6$$

For example, the standard deviation of completion time for activity B is

$$(3 - 1)/6 = 2/6 = 0.33 \text{ days}$$

Expected activity times and their standard deviations are computed in this manner for all the activities of the network and arranged in the tabular format, as shown on top of page 360.

Figure 1 Network Diagram

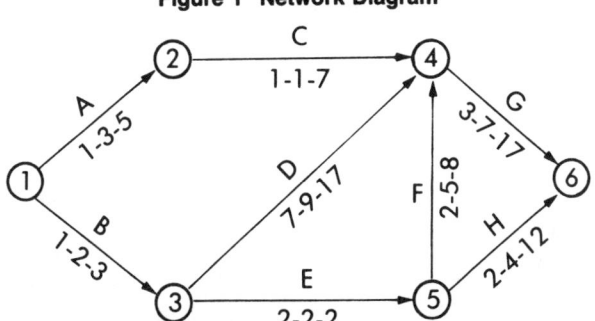

Activity	Predecessors	a	m	b	t_e	σ
A	None	1	3	5	3.0	0.67
B	None	1	2	3	2.0	0.33
C	A	1	1	7	2.0	1.00
D	B	7	9	17	10.0	1.67
E	B	2	2	2	2.0	0.00
F	E	2	5	8	5.0	0.67
G	C,D,F	3	7	17	8.0	2.33
H	E	2	4	12	5.0	1.67

To answer the first question, we need to determine the network's *critical path*. A path is a sequence of connected activities. In Figure 1, 1-2-4-6 would be an example of a path. The critical path for a project is the path that takes the longest amount of time. The sum of the estimated activity times for all activities on the critical path is the total time required to complete the project. These activities are "critical" because any delay in their completion will cause a delay in the project. The critical path is the minimum amount of time needed for the completion of the project. Thus, the activities along this path must be shortened in order to speed up the project. Activities not on the critical path are not critical, since they will be worked on simultaneously with critical path activities and their completion could be delayed up to a point without delaying the project as a whole.

An easy way to find the critical path involves the following two steps: (1) identify all possible paths of a project and calculate their completion times and (2) pick the one with the longest amount of completion time, which is the critical path. (When the network is large and complex, we need a more systematic and efficient approach, which is reserved for an advanced management science text.)

In the example, we have:

Path	Completion Time
A-C-G	13 days (3 + 2 + 8)
B-D-G	20 days (2 + 10 + 8)
B-E-F-G	17 days (2 + 2 + 5 + 8)
B-E-H	9 days (2 + 2 + 5)

The critical path is B-D-G, which means it takes 20 days to complete the project.

The next important information we want to obtain is, What is the chance that the project will be completed within a contract time, say, 21 days? To answer the question, we introduce the standard deviation of total project time around the expected time, which is determined as follows:

Standard deviation (project)
$$= \sqrt{\frac{\text{Sum of the squares of the standard}}{\text{deviations of all critical path activities}}}$$

Using the standard deviation and table of areas under the normal distribution curve (see Appendix, Table 5), the probability of completing the project within any given time period can be determined.

Using the formula just given, the standard deviation of completion time (the path B-D-G) for the project is as follows:

$$\sqrt{\frac{(0.33)^2 + (1.67)^2 + (2.33)^2}{= \sqrt{0.1089 + 2.7889 + 5.4289}}}$$

$$= \sqrt{8.3267} = 2.885 \text{ days}$$

Assume the expected delivery time is, say, 21 days. The first step is to compute z, which is the number of standard deviations from the mean represented by our given time of 21 days. The formula for z is

$z = $ (Delivery time − Expected time)/ Standard deviation

Therefore, $z = $ (21 days − 20 days)/2.885 days = 0.35. The next step is to find the probability associated with the calculated value of z by referring to a table of areas under a normal curve (see Appendix, Table 5).

From Table 5 we see the probability is 0.63683, which means that there is close to a 64% chance that the project will be completed in less than 21 days.

Summary and Remarks

1. The expected completion time of the project is 20 days.
2. There is a better than 60% chance of fin-

ishing before 21 days. We can also obtain the chances of meeting any other deadline if we wish.

3. Activities B-D-G are on the critical path. They must be watched more closely than the others; for if they fall behind, the whole project falls behind.

4. If extra effort is needed to finish the project on time or before the deadline, we have to borrow resources (such as money and labor) from any activity *not* on the critical path.

5. It is possible to reduce the completion time of one or more activities, which will require an extra expenditure of cost. The benefit from reducing the total completion time of a project by accelerated efforts on certain activities must be balanced against the extra cost of doing so. A related problem is to determine which activities must be accelerated to reduce the total project completion time. Critical Path Method (CPM), also known as PERT/COST, is widely used to deal with this subject.

PERT is a technique for project management and control. It is *not* an optimizing decision model since the decision to undertake a project is initially assumed. It will not evaluate an investment project according to its attractiveness or the time specifications we observe.

PROGRAM-PLANNING-BUDGETING SYSTEM
(PPBS) PPBS is a planning-oriented approach to developing a program budget. A program budget is a budget in which expenditures are based primarily on programs of work and secondarily on character and object. It is a transitional type of budget, between the traditional character and object budget on the one hand and the performance budget on the other. The major contribution of PPBS lies in the planning process, that is, the process of making program policy decisions that lead to a specific budget and specific multiyear plans.

PROGRAM TRADING This is a blanket term for strategies used by investors attempting to profit or *hedge* by trading stocks on New York exchanges against stock index futures in the Chicago future exchanges.

PROJECTED BENEFIT OBLIGATION This is the actuarial discounted amount of future employee benefits to be paid using *future* salary levels for services rendered up to the current year. *See also* Pension Plans.

PROJECT SELECTION AND ZERO–ONE PROGRAMMING
A more general approach to solving *capital rationing* problems is the use of *zero–one* integer programming. Here the objective is to select the mix of projects that maximizes the net present value (NPV) subject to a budget constraint.

■ Example

A company with a fixed budget of $250,000 needs to select a mix of acceptable projects from the following:

Projects	I($)	PV($)	NPV($)
1	70,000	112,000	42,000
2	100,000	145,000	45,000
3	110,000	126,500	16,500
4	60,000	79,000	19,000
5	40,000	38,000	−2,000
6	80,000	95,000	15,000

Using the data just given, we can set up the problem as a zero–one integer programming problem such that

$$x_j = \begin{cases} 1 \text{ if project } j \text{ is selected} \\ 0 \text{ if project } j \text{ is not selected } (j = 1,2,3,4,5,6) \end{cases}$$

The problem then can be formulated as follows:
Maximize

$$\text{NPV} = \$42,000x_1 + \$45,000x_2 + \$16,500x_3 \\ + \$19,000x_4 - \$2,000x_5 + \$15,000x_6$$

subject to

$70,000x_1 + \$100,000x_2 + \$110,000x_3 + \$60,000x_4$
$+ \$40,000x_5 + \$80,000x_6 \leqq \$250,000$

$$x_j = 0,1 \ (j = 1,2, \ldots ,6)$$

Using the zero–one programming solution routine, the solution to the problem is

$$x_1 = 1, \ x_2 = 1, \ x_4 = 1$$

and the NPV is \$106,000. Thus, projects 1, 2, and 4 should be accepted.

The strength of the use of zero–one programming is its ability to handle mutually exclusive and interdependent projects.

■ **Example**

Suppose that exactly one project can be selected from the set of projects 1, 3, and 5. Since either 1, 3, or 5 must be selected and only one can be selected, exactly one of the three variables x_1, x_3, or x_5 must be equal to 1 and the rest must be equal to 0. The constraint to be added is

$$x_1 + x_3 + x_5 = 1$$

Note that, for example, if $x_3 = 1$, then $x_1 = 0$ and $x_5 = 0$ in order for the constraint to hold.

■ **Example**

Suppose that projects 2 and 4 are mutually exclusive, which means neither, or either one of both (not both) should be selected. The constraint to be added:

$$x_2 + x_4 \leqq 1$$

Note that the following three pairs satisfy this constraint:

$$x_2 = 0 \text{ and } x_4 = 0$$
$$x_2 = 1 \text{ and } x_4 = 0$$
$$x_2 = 0 \text{ and } x_4 = 1$$

But $x_2 = 1$ and $x_4 = 1$ violates this constraint, since $1 + 1 = 2 > 1$.

■ **Example**

Suppose if project 3 is selected then project 4 must be selected. In other words, a mutual dependence exists between projects 3 and 4. An example might be a project such as building a second floor, which requires the first floor to precede it. Then the constraint to be added is

$$x_3 \leqq x_4$$

Note that if $x_3 = 1$, then x_4 must be equal to 1. However, x_4 can be equal to 1 and x_3 can be equal to either 1 or 0. That is, the selection of project 4 does not imply that project 3 must be selected. *See also* Capital Rationing; Integer Programming; Mutually Exclusive Investments; Zero–One Programming.

PROSPECTUS A prospectus is prepared by an entity that wishes to issue securities to investors. In the case of an issuance to the public, filing requirements of the Securities and Exchange Commission must be met. Included in the prospectus are financial statements, disclosures (e.g., lawsuit), business plans, overview of corporate operations, and information regarding officers.

A "red herring" is a preliminary prospectus that has not been finalized. Later, a statutory prospectus is prepared, which is the final version.

Prospectuses are also prepared by mutual funds and limited partnerships.

PROXY A proxy is the authorization given by a stockholder of a company to another to vote for him at an election (e.g., board of directors) or for a corporate resolution. The transfer is restricted in duration and usually is only for a specific occasion.

PURCHASE METHOD A business combination is accounted for under the purchase method when the acquiring company pays cash or incurs liabilities to buy the acquired company. *See also* Business Combinations.

QUADRATIC PROGRAMMING (QP) QP is a special class of mathematical programming problems having a *quadratic* objective function and a *linear* constraint set. From the standpoint of solution methods, QP problems are relatively simple compared with other nonlinear programming forms. This is because the form of the QP problem is not too different from the standard linear programming (LP) problem. In fact, the strong similarity with the LP model has led to computational procedures that, with some modifications, utilize the simplex method to derive optimal solutions to QP problems. A classical example of a QP problem is the portfolio selection model as formulated by Harry Markowitz. The objective in the Markowitz model is to minimize some measure of risk associated with the portfolio (variance) while maximizing return on the total investment. The object is to determine the amount of funds to commit to each security from among a set of specified securities. In the area of cost accounting, the GP formulation was extended to the joint cost problem in order to determine optimal price and output policies. *See also* Mathematical Programming; Portfolio Theory and Capital Asset Pricing Model (CAPM).

QUALITATIVE ANALYSIS Accountants and financial managers must not forget the *qualitative* factors in decision making, in addition to the quantitative or financial factors highlighted by *incremental analysis* or otherwise. They are the factors relevant to a decision that are difficult to measure in terms of money. Qualitative factors may include (1) effect on employee morale, schedules, and other internal elements; (2) relationships with and commitments to suppliers; (3) effect on present and future customers; and (4) long-term future effect on profitability.

In some decision-making situations, qualitative aspects are more important than immediate financial benefit from a decision.

■ Example

In selecting a laboratory site for a high-tech company, the proximity to leading academic institutions may be far more critical from a long-term standpoint than a short-term tax benefit offered by a particular state trying to obtain the laboratory.

QUALITY OF EARNINGS These are the accounting and financial characteristics that have an impact on the earning power of a firm, as shown in its net income figure. These charac-

teristics are complex and interrelated, and are subject to wide varieties of interpretation by analysts, depending upon their own analytical objectives. Furthermore, measurements of some of the characteristics may be extremely difficult, elusive, and perhaps impossible. Nevertheless analysts cannot avoid sorting through the characteristics to determine which of them are favorable in terms of earnings quality and which are unfavorable, and to determine the degree to which they exist. They are then in a position to rank the relative quality of earnings of companies in an industry as well as to restate the companies' net incomes.

Favorable Characteristics in Earnings

• The degree to which the accounting policies employed reflect the economic reality of a company's transactions.

• The degree of realism used to develop estimates of current and future conditions; referring here to the degree of risk attached to estimates or assumptions that may ultimately prove overoptimistic or unwarranted.

• The degree to which sufficient provision has been made for the maintenance of assets and for the maintenance and enhancement of present and future earning power.

• The degree of earnings stability associated with a firm. This refers also to the degree to which income statement components are recurring in nature.

• The stability and growth trend of earnings as well as the predictability of factors that may affect their future levels.

Unfavorable Characteristics of Earnings

• The degree to which accounting changes that are inconsistent with economic reality have been made.

• The degree to which income manipulation exists.

• The degree to which unrealistic deferrals of costs exist.

• The degree to which a company has underaccrued or overaccrued its expenses.

• The degree to which a company has recognized revenue prematurely or belatedly.

• The degree to which unjustified reductions in discretionary costs have been made. Such reductions may deprive the business of expenditures needed for future growth.

• The degree to which highly subjective and uncertain accounting estimates are associated with the recognition of revenue and expense items. In general, the further revenue and expense recognition is removed from the point of cash receipt and payment, the less objective the transaction and the more subjective the interpretations involved.

• The degree to which assets are overstated and liabilities are understated.

• The degree of risk attached to the probability of future realization of different types of assets.

• The degree of operating leverage associated with the firm.

• The degree to which a firm is susceptible to the business cycle.

• The degree to which inflationary profits are included in net income.

The quality of the earnings figure of any given company for any particular time period is a matter of the degree to which favorable and unfavorable characteristics exist, and that the significance of the characteristics depends upon their relevance to and the point of view of the individual financial analyst.

QUANTITY DISCOUNT MODEL The *economic order quantity* (EOQ) model does not take into account quantity discounts, which is not realistic in many real-world cases. Usually, the more you order, the lower the unit price you pay. Quantity discounts are price reductions for large orders offered to buyers to

induce them to buy in large quantities. If quantity discounts are offered, the buyer must weigh the potential benefits of reduced purchase price and fewer orders that will result from buying in large quantities against the increase in carrying costs caused by higher average inventories. Hence, the buyer's goal in this case is to select the order quantity that will minimize total costs, where total cost is the sum of carrying cost, ordering cost, *and* purchase cost:

Total cost = Carrying cost + Ordering cost + Purchase cost

$$= C \times (Q/2) + O(D/Q) + PD$$

where C = carrying cost per unit,
O = ordering cost per order,
D = annual demand,
P = unit price,
Q = order quantity.

A step-by-step approach to finding the economic order quanity *with* quantity discounts is summarized following.

1. Compute the *economic order quantity* (*EOQ*) when price discounts are ignored and the corresponding costs using the new cost formula just given. Note EOQ = $\sqrt{2OD/C}$.

2. Compute the costs for those quantities greater than the EOQ at which price reductions occur.

3. Select the value of Q that will result in the lowest total cost.

■ Example

Assume ABC store buys sets of steel at $40 per set from an outside vendor. ABC will sell 6,400 sets evenly throughout the year. ABC desires a 16% return on investment (cost of borrowed money) on its inventory investment. In addition, rent, taxes, and so on for each set in inventory is $1.60. The ordering cost is $100 per order.

Assume further that ABC was offered the following price discount schedule:

Order quantity(Q)	Unit price (P)
1 to 499	$40.00
500 to 999	39.90
1000 or more	39.80

First, the EOQ with no discounts is computed as follows:

$$\text{EOQ} = \sqrt{2(6,400)(100)/8.00}$$
$$= \sqrt{160,000} = 400 \text{ sets.}$$

Total cost = $8.00(400/2) + $100(6,400/400)
+ $40.00(6,400)

$$= \$1,600 + 1,600 + 256,000 = \$259,200$$

We see that the value that minimized the sum of the carrying cost and the ordering cost but not the purchase cost was EOQ = 400 sets. As can be seen in Figure 1, the further we move from the point 400, the greater will be the sum of the carrying and ordering costs. Thus, 400 is obviously the only candidate for the minimum total cost value within the first price range. $Q = 500$ is the only candidate within the $39.90 price range, and $Q = 1,000$ is the only candidate within the $39.80 price bracket. These three quantities are evaluated in Table 1 and illustrated in Figure 1. We find that the EOQ *with* price discounts is 500 sets. Hence, ABC store is justified in going to the first price break, but the extra carrying cost of going to the second price break more than out-

Figure 1 Inventory Cost and Quantity

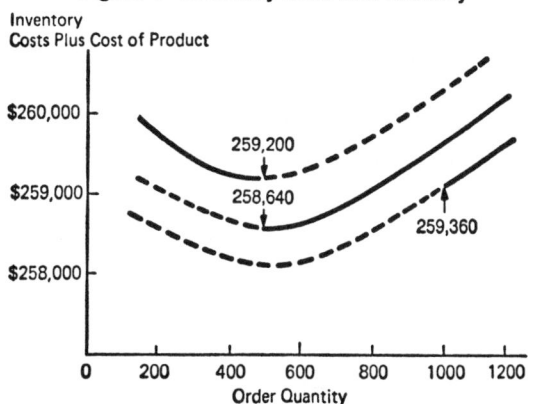

weighs the savings in ordering and in the cost of the product itself.

Table 1 Annual Costs With Varying Order Quantities

Order Quantity	400	500	1,000
Ordering cost			
$100 × (6,400/order quantity)	$ 1,600	$ 1,280	$ 640
Carrying cost			
$8 × (order quantity/2)	1,600	2,000	4,000
Purchase cost			
Unit price × 6,400	256,000	255,360	254,720
Total cost	$259,200	$258,640	$259,360

Advantages and Disadvantages of Quantity Discounts

Buying in large quantities has some favorable and some unfavorable features for a firm. The advantages are lower unit costs, lower ordering costs, fewer stockouts, and lower transportation costs. On the other hand, there are disadvantages, such as higher inventory carrying costs, greater capital requirement, and higher probability of obsolescence and deterioration.

QUANTITY THEORY OF MONEY This is the classical theory of the relationship between the money supply and the price level. The theory states that the level of prices in the economy is directly proportional to the quantity of money in circulation. That is, a given percentage change in the quantity of money will cause an equal percentage in the price level in the same direction. *See also* Equation of Exchange.

QUASI-REORGANIZATION A quasi-reorganization occurs when a company decides to eliminate a deficit in retained earnings

through the restatement of assets to market value, liabilities, and stockholders' equity accounts. A company is provided with a fresh start when management believes that the business can become profitable. It allows for the business to continue in essence on the same basis as if legal reorganization had occurred, without the problem and cost typically associated with a legal reorganization. There must be approval from stockholders and creditors. The steps involved follow: (1) there is a write-down of assets to reflect their fair market value; (2) there is a restatement in the capital stock, resulting in additional paid-in-capital by lowering par value; and (3) there results a zero balance in retained earnings after the deficit is eliminated through the transfer of part of capital to the retained earnings account. Retained earnings will bear the quasi-reorganization date.

■ Example

A business having a $3,500,000 deficit undertakes a quasi-reorganization. There is an overstatement in assets of $800,000 compared to fair market value. The balances in capital stock and paid-in-capital are $5,000,000 and $1,500,000, respectively. The following entry is made to effect the quasi-reorganization:

Paid-in-Capital	1,500,000	
Capital Stock	2,800,000	
Assets		800,000
Retained Earnings		3,500,000

Note that the paid-in-capital account has been fully wiped out, so the remaining debit goes to capital stock.

R

RANDOM SAMPLE In random sampling there is an equal probability of each sampling unit being chosen. Further, every possible combination of sampling units has the same chance of being in the sample. The auditor has to be sure that the sample selected is representative of the population from which it is drawn.

A random sample typically involves the following steps:

• Relating identifying numbers (or letters) to sampling units in the population

• Deriving a random sample from the population with the aid of a random number table or a random number generator computer program

The sampling unit may be in physical or monetary terms. Examples of physical identifiers are check number, invoice number, page number, and warehouse row and bin number. Monetary units are in terms of cumulative dollar values in the population. In other words, whatever the order of physical units containing the dollars,their values are cumulative in dollar increments and the aggregate value at any point represents the last dollar included. The probability of choosing a physical unit increases in direct proportion to its dollar value. Thus, the sampling probabilities are proportional to size. *Note*: It is possible that one sampling unit may have more than one randomly selected dollar.

Random sampling may be used for nonstatistical and statistical applications. *See also* Sampling.

RANDOM WALK THEORY According to this theory, stock prices move in an unpredictable and random way due to stock market efficiency. A company's market price of stock goes randomly around real (intrinsic value). But there is a periodic change in the intrinsic value arising from new information. Present security prices are independent of previous ones. Hence, historical prices are not an accurate barometer of future prices.

According to random walk theory, financial information material enough to impact future value is available to knowledgeable investors. Thus, new data affecting stock price are immediately reflected in market value. At a particular point in time, market price is the optimum estimate of stock value, including all available information.

Random walk theorists do not reject the prediction of stock prices based on accurate forecasting of company earnings and dividends. But they do reject employing

prior market price analysis in forecasting future market price. *See also* Efficient Market.

REAL ESTATE Generally, returns on real estate outperform those on stocks. Further, the standard deviation of real estate returns is typically less than the standard deviation of stock returns.

Types of real estate that the client may invest in include undeveloped land, residential rental property (e.g., single-family houses for rental, multi-unit apartments), and commercial property (e.g., office buildings, shopping centers, industrial property).

Besides location, the factors to be considered in making a particular real estate investment include method of financing the purchase of property, before-tax cash flow, after-tax cash flow, vacancy rate for rental property, gain or loss for tax purposes, and management problems.

Investing in Land

In real estate investing, land is in the forefront. While in 1989, real estate syndicates are down considerably, land investing is substantially up. Particular growth is in private pre-development land. The major reason for the interest in pre-development land was the Tax Reform Act of 1986 which eliminated many of the tax benefits of investing in commercial and residential property.

While some land investments are speculative, there are many land partnerships tied into specialized research and strong business planning. In analyzing the client's proposed land investment, the accounting practitioner should determine if the land arrangement is structured to eliminate serious risks, managerial ability, and marketing effectiveness.

Since land is not income-producing, there should be provision to retire the debt even if there is no salability of the property. Thus, there should be a lengthy period for the debt reduction (e.g., 8 years rather than 2 years).

If the debt schedule period is too short, foreclosures or requests for additional financing may ensue.

One type of land investment is undeveloped or underdeveloped lots already zoned for commercial development located by urban centers. Advantages of the urban strategy are that the urban centers will likely have future demand, rental income should be at competitive and consistent rates, and prime location exists. Disadvantages with the urban approach are the restricted choice of available undeveloped lots, metropolitan situated land is competitive, significant dependence upon the "downtown" development cycle, and metropolitan cities are more prone to crime and deterioration.

Determining the Cash Flow from Real Estate

A necessary task in analyzing an income-producing property is determining the before-tax cash flow. When the cash flow is known, we can figure the return on the investment, calculate the tax shelter, and evaluate the investment.

■ Example

Your client wanted to calculate the cash flow of a property offered to him for investment. We will go through this analysis, step by step, as an example of the process and format which the practitioner should follow. The client is considering a duplex apartment. The property is located in an attractive suburb. The cost of the building is $219,000 and a $175,000, 30-year mortgage at a 12% fixed rate is anticipated. The projected figures are based on the first full year of operation.

Step 1. Figuring Gross Income

The building has two three-bedroom apartments. To judge how much the apartments could rent for, your client compared his building to ones in the area which were similar in quality of location and construction.

He studied advertisements and questioned area real estate brokers. After weighing this information, he decided the three-bedroom could rent for $950. Thus, the total maximum yearly rental income was $22,800.

$$2 \times \$950 = \$1,900$$
$$\$1,900 \times 12 = \$22,800$$

Additional income of $800 from laundry fees would make the possible total gross income $23,600.

Step 2. Vacancy and Credit Losses

To estimate the reduction in gross income caused by vacancies and bad debts, your client looked at the result of the survey conducted by the local realtors and apartment associations. He estimated that the vacancy and bad debt rate would be 2% of possible gross income or $472 (2% of $23,600). See Table 1.

Step 3. Operating Expenses

For estimates of operating expenses, your client carefully examined the record of previous costs by category. He came up with the cost figures as shown in the chart, which are basically the previous costs plus adjustments for inflation.

Step 4. Net Operating Income

The projected operating expenses totaled $4,510 or 19.50% of gross operating income ($23,128). This left a net operating income (NOI) of $18,618 ($23,128 − $4,510). Now we proceed to calculating before-tax cash flow.

Step 5. Debt Service (Principal and interest payments)

Payments at 12% on a $175,000, 30-year fixed-rate mortgage would be $1800.08 per month or $21,601 annually (principal amount is $635).

Step 6. Before-Tax Cash Flow

The estimated before-tax cash flow was ($2,983) on an investment of $44,000 ($219,000 − $175,000). In order to compute after-tax cash flow, we have to add principal payments and deduct annual depreciation as follows:

Before-Tax Cash Flow	($2,983)
Add: Principal	635
Less: Depreciation	5,575
Taxable Income (loss)	$(7,923)
Client's Income Tax Rate	x .35
Value of Taxable Loss	$ 2,773

* Assumption: The depreciable base of the building is 70% of $219,000 = $153,300. Annual depreciation is therefore $5,575 ($153,300/27.5 years by straight line).

Table 1 Annual Property Operating Data
(12 months—projected)

Gross Scheduled Income		22,800
+ Other Income		800
Total Gross Income		23,600
− Vacancy/Credit Losses (2%)		472
Gross Operating Income (GOI)		23,128
Operating Expenses (with percent of GOI)		
Property insurance	1.93%	446
Real Estate Taxes	13.22%	3,058
Repairs and Maintenance	1.45%	335
Sewer and Water	2.90%	671
Total Operating Expenses (19.50%)		4,510
Net Operating Income (80.50%)		18,618
− Debt Service (Principal and Interest)		21,601
Before-Tax Cash Flow		(2,983)

Then after-tax cash flow is:

Before-Tax Cash Flow	$(2,983)
Add: Value of Taxable Loss	2,773
After-Tax Cash Flow	$(210)

Note: Due to the deductibility of interest payments and annual depreciation for income tax purposes, after-tax cash flow is reduced by a substantial amount. (In this example, after-tax was only −$210 as compared to before-tax of −$2,983. *Don't forget*: We did not even take into account the potential appreciation of the property. The return on the investment in this building should be calculated on the basis of both annual after-tax cash flows and the selling price of the property at the end of the holding period.

Determining the Value of Income-Producing Property

There are several rule-of-thumb methods to arrive at the estimated value of an income-producing property. They include:

• *Gross Income Multiplier*. Gross income multiplier is calculated as: Purchase price/gross rental income.

■ Example

In your client's example, the gross income multiplier is:

$$\$219,000/\$23,600 = 9.28.$$

A duplex in the similar neighborhood may be valued at "8 times annual gross." Thus, if its annual gross rental income amounts to $23,600, the value would be taken as $188,800 (8 x $23,600). *Warning*: This approach should be used with caution. Different properties have different operating expenses that must be taken into account in determining the value of a property.

• *Net Income Multiplier*. Net income multiplier is calculated as:

Purchase price/net operating income (NOI)

In your client's example, the net income multiplier is:

$$\$219,000/\$18,618 = 11.76$$

• *Capitalization rate*. Capitalization rate is almost the same as the net income multiplier, only used more often. It is the reciprocal of the net income multiplier. That is:

Net operating income (NOI)/purchase price

■ Example

The duplex's capitalization rate is $18,618/$219,000 = 8.5%. Whether it is over-priced or not depends on the rate of the similar type property derived from the market place. Suppose the market rate is 10%. That means the fair market value of the similar duplex is $18,618/10% = $186,180. Your client may be overpaying for this property.

How Much Can the Client Afford To Spend For Housing?

An accurate way to determine what kind of house the client can afford is to make two basic calculations: How much can the client pay each month for the long-term expenses of owning a home (e.g., mortgage payments, maintenance and operating expenses, insurance and property taxes)? And, how much cash does the client have to spend for the initial costs of the purchase (e.g., the down payment, points and closing cost)?

Many lenders use various rules of thumb to determine a borrower's housing affordability. They include:

• *35-Percent Rule of Thumb*. A borrower can afford no more than 35 percent of monthly take-home pay.

• *Multiple of Gross Earnings Rule*. The price should not exceed roughly 2 to 2½ times the family's gross annual income.

• *Percent of Monthly Gross Income Rule*. The monthly mortgage payment, property taxes and insurance should not exceed 25% to 28% of the family's monthly gross income, or about 35% for a Federal Housing Administration (FHA) or Veterans Administration (VA) mortgage.

See also Real Estate Investment Trust (REIT); Real Estate Syndicate.

REAL ESTATE INVESTMENT TRUSTS (REITs)

REITs are corporations that operate much like closed-end mutual funds, investing shareholders' money in diversified real estate

or mortgage portfolios instead of stocks or bonds. Their shares trade on the major stock exchanges or over the counter.

By law, REITs must distribute 95% of their net earnings to shareholders, and in turn they are exempt from corporate taxes on income or gains. Since REIT earnings are not taxed before they are distributed, you get a larger percentage of the profits than with stocks. REIT yields are high, ranging between 5½ to 10½%.

Types of REITs

There are three types of REITs: (1) equity REITs invest primarily in income-producing properties; (2) mortgage REITs lend funds to developers or builders; and (3) hybrid REITs do both. Experts feel that equity REITs are the safest.

Basics About REITs

Where to buy	• Stockbrokers
Pluses	• Dividend income with competitive yields
	• Potential appreciation in price
	• A liquid investment in an illiquid area
	• Means of portfolio diversification and participation in a variety of real estate with minimal cash outlay
Minuses	• Possible glut in real estate or weakening demand
	• Market risk: possible decline in share price
Safety	• Low
Liquidity	• Very high: shares traded on major exchanges or over the counter and therefore sold at any time
Taxes	• Income subject to tax upon sale

How to Select a REIT

Before buying any REIT be sure to read the latest annual report, *The Value Line Investment Survey* or *Audit Investment's* Newsletter, *Realty Stock Review*. Check the following points.

• *Track record*—how long in business as well as solid dividend record.

• *Debt level*—make sure that the unsecured debt level is low.

• *Cash flow*—make sure that operating cash flow covers the dividend.

• *Adequate diversification*—beware of REITs investing in only one type of property.

• *Property location*—beware of geographically depressed areas.

• *Type of property*—nursing homes, some apartment buildings, shopping centers presently favored; ''seasoned'' properties preferred.

• *Aggressive management*—avoid REITs that do not upgrade properties.

• *Earnings*—monitor earnings regularly; be prepared to sell when the market of property location weakens.

See also Real Estate.

REAL ESTATE SALES FASB No. 66 deals with the accounting for sales of real estate. In the case of real estate sales (other than retail land sales), the accrual basis of accounting is generally used to recognize profit provided:

• Sale is complete (e.g., parties are bound and the risks of ownership have been transferred).

• Collectibility of the selling price is assured or can be estimated.

If these conditions are not met, revenue is deferred until they are satisfied.

Retail land sales should be recognized under accrual accounting provided all of the following criteria are satisfied:

• The refund period has expired.

• Cumulative payments of principal and interest equal or exceed 10% of the contract sales price.

• Collectibility of the receivables exists.

• There is nonsubordination of receivables.

• Development has been completed.

REAL ESTATE SYNDICATE A real estate syndicate (limited partnership) is an investment having potential for substantial gain. The *general partner* makes property investment and management decisions but has the entire liability. The general partner may be one or more individuals or a corporation. This partner sells participation units to *limited partners* whose obligations are typically limited to their investments. Ownership may be in unnamed properties (a blind pool) or in specific existing properties. *Caution*: Investors should know that often general partners make a lot of money by purchasing property themselves and selling them to other partners. In addition to cash investments, debt is often used as well in property acquisition.

A public limited partnership exists where the minimum investment is substantially less than the minimum investment necessary in a private offering. A public offering requires SEC registration.

The distribution to partners is decided upon by the general partner. A manager is typically retained to handle the affairs of the real estate holding.

Tax benefit is in the form of deductible depreciation and interest expense. Profits of partnership arrangements pass directly to the partners. Thus, no double taxation exists. *Note*: Losses on real estate investments that the taxpayer does not manage cannot exceed the amount for which he is at risk. "At risk" means the taxpayer cannot deduct a loss in excess of the adjusted cost basis. However, there is a phase-in period for the rules related to real estate in that the taxpayer can deduct 20% of the losses from passive rental properties in 1989, and 10% in 1990 provided the investment was made before enactment of the Tax Reform Act of 1986. Losses from investments made after enactment of the act are disallowed in the current year completely to the extent that they exceed passive income.

A limited partnership permits the investor to have diversification in real estate holdings compared to individual ownership.

Disadvantages of Limited Partnership

- Limited partners have little control.
- High fees charged by the general partner often range between 5% to 25%.
- The debt funds if not repaid will force foreclosure.
- There is a lack of marketability in limited partnership shares since they are not traded.

The investor should take into account the following when looking at real estate arrangements:

- Possible litigation against the partnership.
- Prior success or failure.
- Delays in payout to limited partners.
- Whether funds are invested in unspecified future projects or in identifiable ones.
- Whether limited partnership investment is publicly or privately received. A private offering is typically local and has a restricted number of investors.

See also Real Estate Investment Trusts (REITs); Limited Partnership; Basic Forms of Business Organization.

RECESSION This represents a lower phase of a business cycle, in which the economy's output (GNP), income, and employment is declining, coupled with a declining rate of business investment and consumer spending. Two to three successive quarterly declines in GNP is usually the sign of recession. Economists, however, have never made the distinction between recession and depression clear. It is the old rule of thumb that if your neighbor loses his or her job, it is a recession, and if you lose yours, it is a depression. *See also* Business Cycle; Depression.

RECONCILIATION This is a determination of the items necessary to bring the balances of two or more related accounts or statements into agreement.

A reconciliation statement shows the details of the differences between any two accounts. This type of statement may be used, for example, for the reconciliation of an account on the home office books containing transactions with a branch office. It would involve a showing of the balance of the branch office account and the corresponding home office account on the branch office books, as well as a listing of the details making up the differences.

A bank reconciliation can also be prepared. The purpose is to uncover any mistakes or irregularities in either the company's or the bank's records. The bank reconciliation should be prepared by one who does not have physical custody of the cash or who does not record cash transactions in the books of account.

A special four-column bank reconciliation (proof of cash) reconciles the book and bank balances at the start and end of the accounting period as well as cash receipts and cash payments for the period.

When preparing the bank reconciliation, the adjusted bank balance has to agree with the adjusted book balance. Journal entries are made to update the cash account so that it ties into the ending balance in the bank statement. Reconciling differences apply to (1) items shown on the company's books but not on the bank statement and (2) items presented on the bank statement but not on the depositor's books.

The bank balance is adjusted for items reflected on the company's books that are not on the bank statement. They include

Outstanding checks—the total of the outstanding checks is subtracted from the bank balance. The exception is an uncleared certified check, which is not deemed outstanding because both the company and bank know about it.

Deposits in transit—the deposits are added to the bank balance.

Errors in recording checks—mistakes,

such as transposition errors, can be made in entering checks. For example, an item should be added to the bank balance when it was previously overstated on the books.

Bank errors in charging or crediting the company's account—if a company's account is charged by mistake for another firm's cleared check, the company's bank balance is understated. Thus, the company should add the amount of the check to its bank balance. On the other hand, if a deposit made by a firm is incorrectly credited to the account of another company, the latter should reduce its bank balance.

The book balance (cash account) is adjusted for items shown on the bank statement that are not reflected on the books. They include

Bank charges—fees for bank services reduce the book balance.

NSF checks—these are checks that have bounced due to inadequate funds in the customer's checking account. (NSF means Not Sufficient Funds.) The book balance is reduced for them.

Collections—notes and other items are collected by the bank for a fee. The proceeds received less the charge is credited to the firm's account. The net amount increases the book balance.

Interest earned—interest income credited by the bank on the checking account increases the book balance.

Errors on the books—various kinds of mistakes can be made on the books. Two examples of them and explanations of how they would be corrected follow (assume that the amount of the check is correct):

1. A check is written ($70) for more than the amount entered as a cash disbursement ($64). In this case, cash disbursements are understated by $6 and thus the book balance should be reduced by that amount.

2. A check is written ($110) for less than the amount shown as a cash disbursement ($118). Here, cash disbursements are over-

stated. Thus, the balance per books should be increased by $8 to correct for the error.

■ Example

Smith Corporation provides the following information at December 31, 19X1:
• Balance per bank statement—December 31, 19X1, $101,240
• Balance per books—November 30, 19X1, $87,000
• Cash receipts for December, $40,000
• Cash payments for December, $38,000
• Outstanding checks—December 31, 19X1:
>   #108 for $12,000
>   #112 certified check for $7,000
>   #114 for $5,000
• Received cash—December 31, 19X1, $4,000; deposited on January 2, 19X2
• Return of $300 check, made out to Lakeside Corporation, by the bank on December 26, 19X1, due to absence of countersignature
• Incorrect entry on bank statement for December 16, 19X1, deposit, $2,010; actual deposit, $2,100
• Erroneous charge of $200 against Smith Corporation account for check issued by Stone Corporation
• December 20, 19X1: collection on a note receivable by bank for Smith Corporation, $1,100, including $100 in interest; collection charge, $20
• Bank service charge for December 19X1 per debit memorandum, $50
• Erroneous debit memorandum of December 21, 19X1 to charge the firm's Account for settlement of a bank loan in which check #82 was issued on December 20, 19X1, $2,000
• Incorrect credit to Smith Corporation account for December 14, 19X1, Smart Corporation deposit, $800

Balance per books—12/31/19X1		$ 89,000*
Add: Collection on note receivable		
Principal	$ 1,000	
Interest	100	1,100
		$ 90,100
Deduct: Charge back of Lakeside check	$ 300	
Service charge	50	
Collection charge	20	370
Adjusted book balance		$ 89,730
Balance per bank—12/31/19X1		$101,240
Add: Deposit in transit	$ 4,000	
Error in deposit	90	
Check of Stone Corp. incorrectly charged to our account	200	
Debit memorandum of December 21	2,000	6,290
		$107,530
Deduct: Outstanding checks		
#108	$12,000	
#114	5,000	
	$17,000	
Deposit of Smith Corp. credited to our account in error	800	17,800
Adjusted bank balance		$ 89,730

* To determine the December book balance, the calculations are 87,000 + 40,000 − 38,000 = $89,000.

Appropriate journal entries are

Cash	1,100	
Notes Receivable		1,000
Interest Income		100
Accounts Receivable	300	
Bank Charges	70	
Cash		370

REFINANCING OF SHORT-TERM DEBT TO LONG-TERM DEBT
A short-term obligation shall be reclassified as a long-term obligation in the following cases:

1. After the year-end of the financial statements but before the audit report is issued, the short-term debt is rolled over into a long-term obligation or an equity security is issued in substitution.

or

2. Prior to the audit report date, the company enters into a contract for refinancing of the current obligation on a long-term basis and *all* of the following are met:

• Agreement does not expire within one year.

• No violation of the agreement exists.

• The parties are financially capable of meeting the requirements of the agreement.

The proper classification of the refinanced item is under long-term debt and *not* stockholders' equity even if equity securities were issued in substitution of the debt. When short-term debt is excluded from current liabilities, a footnote should describe the financing agreement and the terms of any new obligation to be incurred.

If the amounts under the agreement for refinancing vary, the amount of short-term debt excluded from current liabilities will be the *minimum* amount expected to be refinanced based on conservatism. The exclusion from current liabilities cannot be greater than the net proceeds of debt or security issuances, or amounts available under the refinancing agreement.

Once cash is paid for the short-term debt even though the next day long-term debt of a similar amount is issued, the short-term debt shall be shown under current liabilities since cash was disbursed.

REGISTRATION STATEMENT
The registration statement is the disclosure document that must be filed with the SEC in order to issue securities to the public. The first part of the registration statement is a prospectus, and the second part contains supplemental data about the company of particular interest to the SEC. Management is legally liable for material misstatements or omissions in the registration statement. *See also* Prospectus.

REGRESSION ANALYSIS
This is a very popular statistical method used to project sales, cash flows, and earnings. It is also widely used to estimate the *cost-volume formula* (also called the *flexible budget formula*), which takes the following functional form:

$$y = a + bx$$

where $y =$ the semivariable (mixed) costs to be broken up,

$x =$ any given measure of activity such as production volume, machine hours, or direct labor hours,

$a =$ the fixed cost component,

$b =$ the variable rate per unit of x.

The regression method is a statistical procedure for estimating mathematically the average relationship between the dependent variable y and the independent variable x. *Simple regression* involves one independent variable, for example, direct labor hours (DLH) or machine hours alone, whereas *multiple regression* involves two or more activity variables. (We will assume simple *linear* regression throughout this discussion, which means that we will use the $y = a + bx$ relationship.)

In estimating the values of a and b, the regression method attempts to find a line of *best fit*. To find the line of best fit, a technique called the *method of least squares* is used.

Figure 1 Actual (y) Versus Estimated (y′)

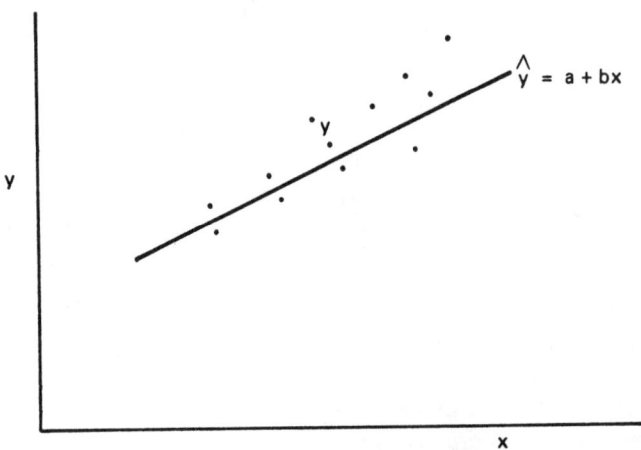

The Method of Least Squares

To explain the least-squares method, we define the error as the difference between the observed value and the estimated value of some semivariable cost and denote it with u. Symbolically:

$$u = y - y'$$

where y = observed value of a semivariable expense,

y' = estimated value based on $y' = a + bx$.

The least-squares criterion requires that the line of best fit be such that the sum of the squares of the errors (or the vertical distance in Figure 1 from the observed data points to the line) is a minimum, that is,

$$\text{Min } \Sigma u^2 = \Sigma(y - y')^2$$

Using differential calculus we obtain the following equations, called *normal equations*:

$$\Sigma y = n \cdot a + b \cdot \Sigma x$$
$$\Sigma xy = a \cdot \Sigma x + b \cdot \Sigma x^2$$

Solving the equations for b and a yields:

$$b = \frac{n \Sigma xy - (\Sigma x)(\Sigma y)}{n \Sigma x^2 - (\Sigma x)^2}$$

$$a = \bar{y} - b \bar{x} \text{ where } \bar{y} = \Sigma y/n \text{ and } \bar{x} = \Sigma x/n$$

The formula for a is a shortcut formula, which requires the computation of b first. This will save a considerable amount of time.

■ Example

To illustrate the computations of b and a, we will use the data following. All the sums required are computed and shown following.

DLH(X)	Factory Overhead (y)	xy	x^2
9 hours	$ 15	135	81
19	20	380	361
11	14	154	121
14	16	224	196
23	25	575	529
12	20	240	144
12	20	240	144
22	23	506	484
7	14	98	49
13	22	286	169
15	18	270	225
17	18	306	289
174 hours	$225	3,414	2,792

From the previous table:

$$\Sigma x = 174 \quad \Sigma y = 225 \quad \Sigma xy = 3,414 \quad \Sigma x^2 = 2,792$$
$$\bar{x} = \Sigma x/n = 174/12 = 14.5$$
$$\bar{y} = \Sigma y/n = 225/12 = 18.75$$

Substituting these values into the formula for b first:

$$b = \frac{n\Sigma xy - (\Sigma x)(\Sigma y)}{n\Sigma x^2 - (\Sigma x)^2}$$

$$= \frac{(12)(3,414) - (174)(225)}{(12)(2,792) - (174)^2} = \frac{1,818}{3,228} = 0.5632$$

$$a = \bar{y} - b\bar{x}$$
$$= (18.75) - (0.5632)(14.5) = 18.75 - 8.1664$$
$$= 10.5836$$

Our final regression equation is

$$y' = \$10.5836 + \$0.5632x$$

where y' = estimated factory overhead,
x = DLH.

RELATED PARTY TRANSACTIONS As per FASB 57, related party information should be disclosed in the financial statements. As per SAS 47, the auditor should know that the substance of a given transaction may be materially at variance with its legal form. If a client transacts business with another entity at more favorable terms than normal, a related party relationship may exist. The auditor should conduct substantive tests in such a way as to identify the existence and terms of related party transactions.

To identify transactions with related parties, the auditor should

• Review minutes of the board of directors

• Review transactions with major customers, suppliers, borrowers, and lenders

• Review large, unusual, and nonrecurring transactions

Once related party transactions have been identified, they should be examined so that the auditor can gain satisfaction as to the purpose, extent, and nature of the transactions. Further, the practitioner must satisfy himself or herself with the related party disclosures in the financial statements.

RELEVANT COSTING When analyzing the manufacturing and selling functions, account-ants are constantly faced with the problem of choosing alternate courses of action. Typical questions to be answered include

1. What to make?
2. How to make it?
3. Where to sell the product or service?
4. What price should be charged?

In the short run, the accountant is typically confronted with the following nonroutine, nonrecurring types of decisions:

1. Accept or reject a special order.
2. Make or buy.
3. Add or drop a certain product line.
4. Utilize scarce resources.
5. Sell or process further.

In each of these situations, the ultimate decision rests upon cost data analysis. Cost data is important in many decisions, since they are the basis for profit calculations. However, not all costs are of equal importance in decision making, and accountants must identify the costs that are relevant to a decision. Such costs are called *relevant costs*. The relevant costs are the expected future costs, which differ between the decision alternatives. Therefore, the *sunk costs* are *not* relevant to the decision at hand because they are past and historical costs. The *incremental* or *differential* costs are *relevant* since they are the ones that differ between the alternatives. For example, in a decision on whether to sell an existing business for a new one, the cost to be paid for the new venture is relevant. However, the initial cost of the old business is not relevant to the decision because it is a sunk cost.

REORGANIZATION This is a major change in a company's financial structure as a result of an alteration in the rights and interests of stockholders. In effect, the failed business is reorganized so it can continue to operate as per Chapter 11 of the Bankruptcy Reform Act of 1978. A Chapter 11 reorganization may be initiated voluntarily by the debtor

or involuntarily by creditors. *See also* Business Failure.

RESEARCH AND DEVELOPMENT COSTS

Research is the testing done in search for a new product, service, process, or technique. Research can also be aimed at deriving a material improvement to an existing product or process. Development is the translation of the research into a design for the new product or process. Development may also result in material improvement in an existing product or process. As per FASB 2, research and development costs are expensed as incurred. However, R&D costs incurred under contract for others that are reimbursable are charged to a receivable account rather than expensed. Further, materials, equipment, and intangibles purchased from others that have alternative future benefit in R&D activities are capitalized. The depreciation or amortization on such assets is classified as R&D expense. If no alternative future use exists, the costs should be expensed.

R&D costs include the salaries of personnel involved as R&D activities. R&D costs also include a rational allocation of indirect (general and administrative) costs. If a group of assets are acquired, allocation should be made to those that relate to R&D efforts. When a business combination is accounted for as a purchase, R&D costs are assigned their fair market value.

Expenditures paid to others to conduct R&D activities are expensed.

Examples of R&D activities include
• Formulation and design of product alternatives and testing thereof
 • Laboratory research
 • Engineering functions until the point the product satisfies operational requirements for manufacture
 • Design of tools, molds, and dies involving new technology
 • Preproduction prototypes and models

• Pilot plant costs

Examples of activities that are not for R&D include:
 • Quality control
 • Seasonal design changes
 • Legal costs of obtaining a patent
 • Market research
 • Identifying breakdowns during commercial production
 • Engineering follow-up in the initial stages of commercial production
 • Rearrangement and start-up activities, including design and construction engineering
 • Recurring and continuous efforts to improve the product
 • Commercial use of the product

FASB 2 does not apply to regulated industries and to the extractive industries (e.g., mining).

According to FASB 86, costs incurred for computer software to be sold, leased, or otherwise marketed are expensed as R&D costs until technological feasibility exists, as indicated by the development of a detailed program or working model. After technological feasibility exists, software production costs should be deferred and recorded at the lower of unamortized cost or net realizable value. Examples of such costs include debugging the software, improvements to subroutines, and adaptions for other uses. Amortization begins when the product is available for customer release. The amortization expense should be based on the higher of (1) the percent of current revenue to total revenue from the product and (2) the straight-line amortization amount.

As per FASB 68, if a business enters into an arrangement with other parties to fund the R&D efforts, the nature of the obligation must be determined. In the case where the entity has an obligation to repay the funds irrespective of the R&D results, a liability has to be recognized with the related R&D expense. The journal entries are

Cash
  Liability
  Research and Development Expense
    Cash

A liability does not exist when the transfer of financial risk involved to the other party is substantive and genuine. If the financial risk applicable with R&D is transferred because repayment depends only on the R&D possessing future economic benefit, the company accounts for its obligation as a contract to conduct R&D for others. In this case R&D costs are capitalized and revenue is recognized as earned and becomes billable under the contract. Footnote disclosure is made of the terms of the R&D agreement, the amount of compensation earned, and the costs incurred under the contract.

When repayment of loans or advances to the company depends only on R&D results, such amounts are deemed R&D costs incurred by the company and charged to expense.

If warrants or other financial instruments are issued in an R&D arrangement, the company records part of the proceeds to be provided by the other parties as paid-in-capital based on their fair market value on the arrangement date.

RESIDUAL INCOME (RI) RI is the operating income that an *investment center* is able to earn above some minimum return on its assets. It is a popular alternative performance measure to *return on investment (ROI)*.

RI is computed as:

RI = Net operating income
  − (Minimum rate of return on investment
                  × Operating assets)

Residual income, unlike ROI, is an absolute amount of income rather than a rate of return. When RI is used to evaluate divisional performance, the objective is to maximize the total amount of residual income, not to maximize the overall ROI percentage figure.

■ **Example**

Assume that operating assets are $100,000, net operating income is $18,000, and the minimum return on assets is 13%. Residual income is $18,000 − (13% × $100,000) = $18,000 − $13,000 = $5,000.

RI is sometimes preferred over ROI as a performance measure because it encourages managers to accept investment opportunities that have rates of return greater than the charge for invested capital. Managers being evaluated using ROI may be reluctant to accept new investments that lower their current ROI even though the investments would be desirable for the entire company. Advantages of using residual income in evaluating divisional performance include (1) it is an economic income taking into account the opportunity cost of tying up assets in the division; (2) the minimum rate of return can vary depending on the riskiness of the division; (3) different assets can be required to earn different returns depending on their risk; (4) the same asset may be required to earn the same return regardless of the division it is in; and (5) maximizing dollars rather than a percentage leads to goal congruence. *See also* Divisional Performance Evaluation.

RESPONSIBILITY ACCOUNTING This is the system for collecting and reporting revenue and cost information by areas of responsibility. It operates on the premise that managers should be held responsible for their performance, the performance of their subordinates, and for all activities within their responsibility center. Responsibility accounting, also called *profitability accounting* and *activity accounting*, has the following advantages:

1. It facilitates delegation of decision making.

2. It helps management promote the concept of management by objective, in which managers agree on a set of goals. The manager's

performance is then evaluated based on his or her attainment of these goals.

3. It provides a guide to the evaluation of performance and helps to establish standards of performance that are then used for comparison purposes.

4. It permits effective use of the concept of *management by exception*, which means that the manager's attention is concentrated on the important deviations from standards and budgets.

Types of Responsibility Centers

A well-designed responsibility accounting system establishes responsibility centers within the organization. *A responsibility center* is defined as a unit in the organization that has control over costs, revenues, and/ or investment funds. Responsibility centers can be one of the following types:

Cost center—the unit within the organization that is responsible only for costs. Examples include the production and maintenance departments of a manufacturing company, and the admissions department of a university. *Variance analysis* based on *standard costs* and *flexible budgets* would be a typical performance measure of a cost center.

Profit center—the unit that is held responsible for the revenues earned and costs incurred in that center. Examples might include a sales office of a publishing company, an appliance department in a retail store, and an auto repair center in a department store. *The contribution approach to cost allocation* is widely used to measure the performance of a profit center.

Investment center—the unit within the organization that is held responsible for the costs, revenues, and related investments made in that center. The corporate headquarters or division in a large decentralized organization would be an example of an investment center. *Return on investment* and *residual income* are two key performance measures of an investment center.

Figure 1 (p. 381) illustrates the manner in which responsibility accounting can be used within an organization and highlights profit and cost centers.

Cost Center Performance and Standard Costs

One of the most important phases of responsibility accounting is establishing standard costs and evaluating performance by comparing actual costs with the standard costs. The difference between the actual costs and the standard costs, called the *variance*, is calculated for individual *cost centers*. Variance analysis is a key tool for measuring performance of a cost center.

The standard cost is based on physical and dollar measures; it is determined by multiplying the standard quantity of an input by its standard price. Two general types of variances can be calculated for most cost items: (1) *a price variance* and (2) *a quantity variance*. The price variance is calculated as follows:

$$\begin{array}{l} \dfrac{\text{Price}}{\text{variance}} = \dfrac{\text{Actual}}{\text{quantity}} \times \left(\dfrac{\text{Actual}}{\text{price}} - \dfrac{\text{Standard}}{\text{price}}\right) \\[2mm] = AQ \times (AP - SP) \\[2mm] = \underset{(1)}{(AQ \times AP)} - \underset{(2)}{(AQ \times SP)} \end{array}$$

The quantity variance is calculated as follows:

$$\begin{array}{l} \dfrac{\text{Quantity}}{\text{variance}} = \left(\dfrac{\text{Actual}}{\text{quantity}} - \dfrac{\text{Standard}}{\text{quantity}}\right) \times \dfrac{\text{Standard}}{\text{price}} \\[2mm] = (AQ - SQ) \times SP \\[2mm] = \underset{(2)}{(AQ \times SP)} - \underset{(3)}{(SQ \times SP)} \end{array}$$

Figure 2 (page 382) shows a general model (3-column model) for variance analysis that incorporates the items (1), (2), and (3) from the previous equations.

Figure 1 Organization Chart

Company XYZ

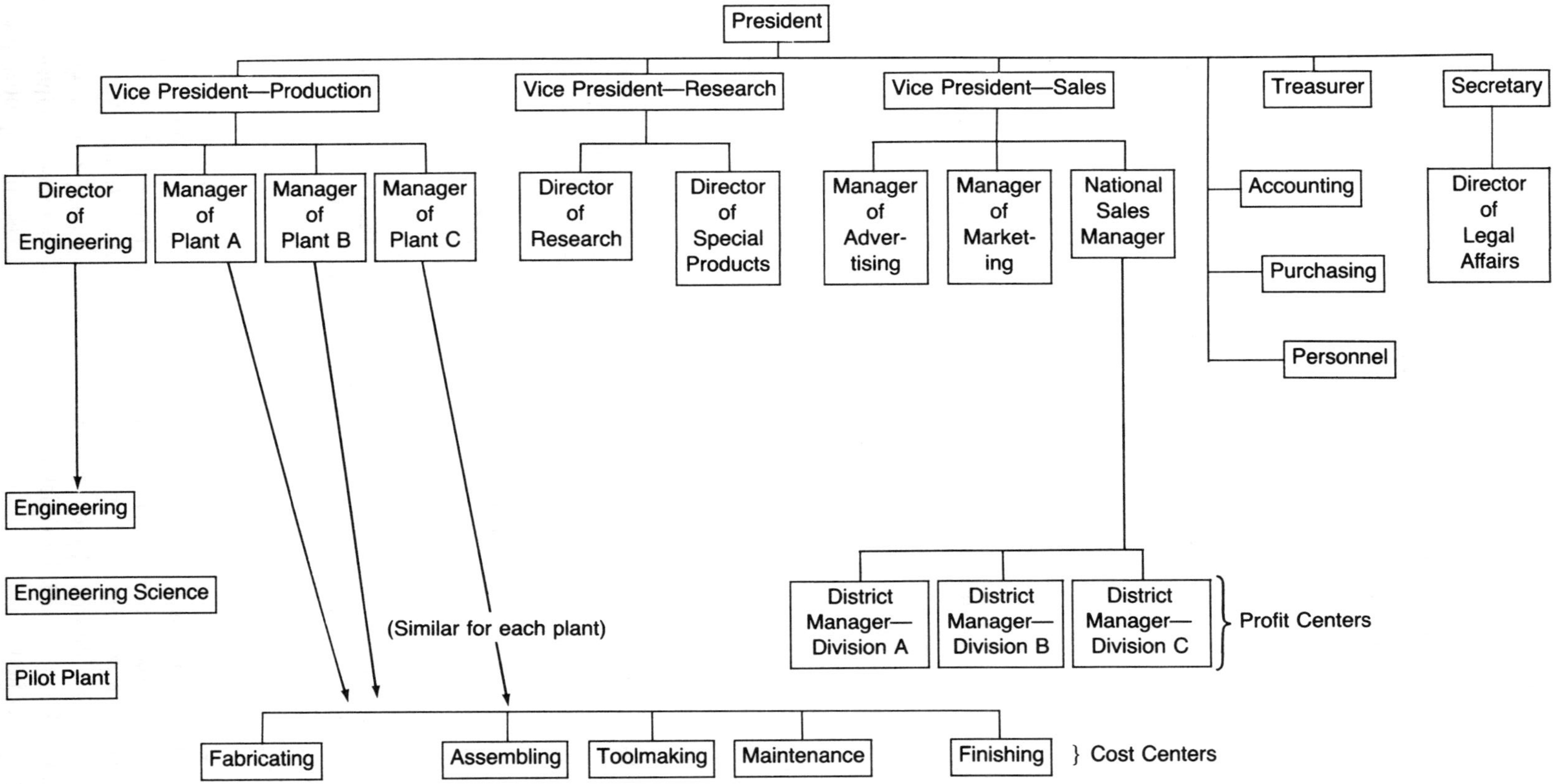

```
                                    President
   ┌──────────────┬───────────────┬───────────────┬──────────────────────┐
   │              │               │               │                      │
Vice President  Vice President  Vice President   Treasurer          Secretary
 Production      Research          Sales
   │              │               │               │                      │
   │         ┌────┴────┐     ┌─────┼─────┐    Accounting            Director
   │         │         │     │     │     │                            of
Director  Director  Director Manager Manager National  Purchasing   Legal Affairs
  of        of       of       of      of     Sales
Engineering Research Special Adver-  Market-  Manager  Personnel
                    Products tising   ing
```

Manager of Plant A   Manager of Plant B   Manager of Plant C

Engineering

Engineering Science

Pilot Plant

(Similar for each plant)

District Manager—Division A   District Manager—Division B   District Manager—Division C   } Profit Centers

Fabricating   Assembling   Toolmaking   Maintenance   Finishing   } Cost Centers

Figure 2 A General Model for Variance Analysis for Variable Manufacturing Costs

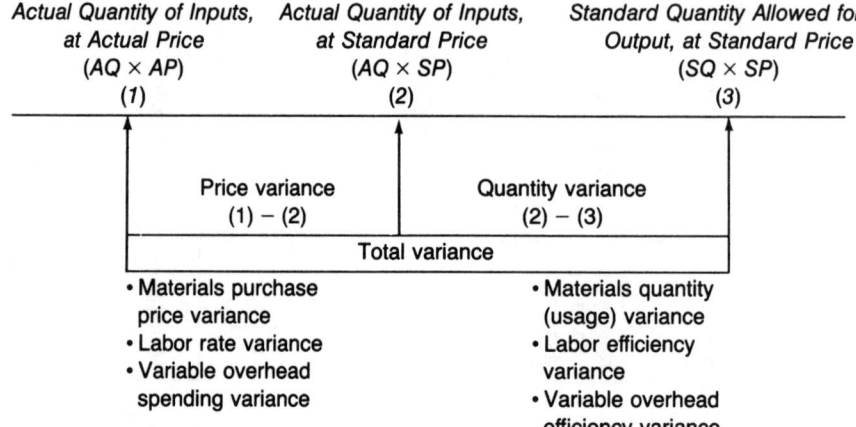

Advantages and Disadvantages of Standard Costing

Standard costing has many advantages, including

1. Aiding in cost control and performance evaluation.
2. "Red flagging" current and future problems through the "management by exception" principle.
3. Improving performance by recommending paths for corrective action in cost reduction.
4. Fixing responsibility.
5. Being a vehicle of communication between top management and supervisors.
6. Establishing selling prices and transfer prices.
7. Determining bid prices on contracts.
8. Setting business goals.
9. Aiding in the planning and decision-making processes.
10. Simplifying bookkeeping procedures and saving clerical costs. Standard costing is not without some drawbacks, however, such as the possible biases involved in deriving standards and the disfunctional effects of setting improper norms and standards.

We will now illustrate by example variance analysis for each of the variable manufacturing cost items.

Materials Variances

A materials price variance is isolated at the time of purchase of the material. Therefore, it is normally computed based on the actual quantity purchased. The purchasing department is responsible for any materials price variance that might occur. The materials quantity (usage) variance is computed based on the actual quantity used. Note that the production department is responsible for any materials quantity variance that might occur. The possible causes for *unfavorable* materials variances are given following.

Possible Causes for Unfavorable Materials Variances

1. *Materials price variance*
   a. Inaccurate standard prices
   b. Failure to take a discount on quantity purchases
   c. Failure to shop for bargains
   d. Inflationary cost increases
   e. Scarcity in raw material supplies resulting in higher prices
   f. Purchasing department inefficiencies
2. *Materials quantity (usage) variance*
   a. Poorly trained workers
   b. Improperly adjusted machines
   c. Use of improper production method

d. Outright waste on the production line
e. Use of a lower grade material purchased in order to economize on price

■ Example 1

ABC Corporation uses a standard cost system. The standard variable costs for Product J are as follows:

Materials: 2 lbs at $3 per lb
Labor: 1 hr at $5 per hr
Variable overhead: 1 hr at $3 per hr

During March, 25,000 pounds of material were purchased for $74,750 and 20,750 pounds of material were used in producing 10,000 units of finished product. Direct labor costs incurred were $49,896 (10,080 direct labor hours) and variable overhead costs incurred were $34,776. Using the general model (3-column model), the materials variances are presented below.

It is important to note that the amount of materials purchased (25,000 pounds) differs from the amount of materials used in production (20,750 pounds). The materials purchase price variance was computed using 25,000 pounds purchased, whereas the material quantity (usage) variance was computed using the 20,750 pounds used in production. A total variance cannot be computed because

of the difference. Alternatively, we can compute the materials variances as follows:

Materials purchase price variance
$= AQ \times (AP - SP) = (AQ \times AP) - (AQ \times SP)$
$= 25,000$ lbs ($2.99 - $3)
$= \$74,750 - \$75,000 = \$250F$

Materials quantity (usage) variance
$= (AQ - SQ) \times SP$
$= (20,750$ lbs $- 20,000$ lbs$) \times \$3$
$= \$62,250 - \$60,000 = \$2,250U$

Labor Variances

Labor variances are both isolated when labor is used for production. They are computed in a manner similar to the materials variances, except that in the 3-column model the terms "hours" and "rate" are used in place of the terms "quantity" and "price." The production department is responsible for both the prices paid for labor services and the quantity of labor services used. Therefore, the production department must explain why any labor variances occur (see following).

Possible Causes for Unfavorable Labor Variances

1. *Labor price (rate) variance*
   a. Increase in wages
   b. Poor scheduling of production resulting in overtime work

Materials Variances

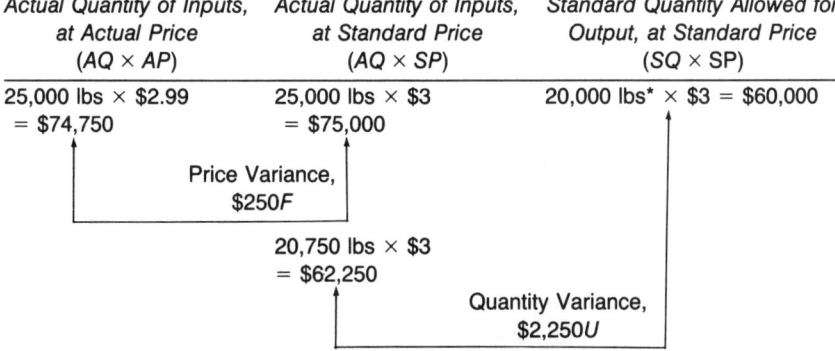

Actual Quantity of Inputs, at Actual Price (AQ × AP)	Actual Quantity of Inputs, at Standard Price (AQ × SP)	Standard Quantity Allowed for Output, at Standard Price (SQ × SP)
25,000 lbs × $2.99 = $74,750	25,000 lbs × $3 = $75,000	20,000 lbs* × $3 = $60,000

Price Variance, $250F

20,750 lbs × $3 = $62,250

Quantity Variance, $2,250U

* 10,000 units actually produced × 2 lbs allowed per unit = 20,000 lbs

c. Use of workers commanding higher hourly rates than contemplated in the standards

2. *Labor efficiency variance*
   a. Poor supervision
   b. Use of unskilled workers paid lower rates or the wrong mixture of labor for a given job
   c. Use of poor quality machinery
   d. Improperly trained workers
   e. Poor quality of materials requiring more labor time in processing
   f. Machine breakdowns
   g. Employee unrest
   h. Production delays due to power failure

■ Example 2

Using the same data given in Example 1, the labor variances can be calculated as shown below.

Variable Overhead Variances

The variable overhead variances are computed in a way very similar to the labor variances. The production department is usually responsible for any variable overhead variance that might occur. Some of the possible causes for any overhead variance are given following. Variances for fixed overhead are of questionable usefulness for control purposes since these variances are usually beyond the control of the production department.

Possible Causes for Unfavorable Variable Overhead Variances

1. *Variable overhead spending variance*
   a. Increase in supplier prices
   b. Increase in labor rates
   c. Inaccurate standards
   d. Waste
   e. Theft of supplies
2. *Variable overhead efficiency variance*
   a. Poorly trained workers
   b. Use of poor quality materials
   c. Use of faulty equipment
   d. Poor supervision
   e. Employee unrest
   f. Work interruptions
   g. Poor production scheduling
   h. A lack of automation and computerization in processing

Labor Variances

Actual Hours of Input, at the Actual Rate ($AH \times AR$)	Actual Hours of Input, at the Standard Rate ($AH \times SR$)	Standard Hours Allowed for Output, at the Standard Rate ($SH \times SR$)
10,080 hrs × $4.95 = $49,896	10,080 hrs × $5 = $50,400	10,000 hrs* × $5 = $50,000

Rate Variance, $504F	Efficiency Variance, $400U

Total Variance, $104F

* 10,000 units actually produced × 1 hr allowed per unit = 10,000 hrs. Note that the symbols (AQ, SQ, AP, and SP) have been changed to (AH, SH, AR, and SR) to reflect the terms "hour" and "rate." Alternatively, we can calculate the labor variances as follows:

Labor rate variance $= AH \times (AR - SR) = (AH \times AR) - (AH \times SR)$
$= 10,080 \text{ hrs } (\$4.95 - \$5) = \$49,896 - \$50,400 = \$504F$

Labor efficiency variance $= (AH - SH) \times SR$
$= (10,080 \text{ hrs } - 10,000 \text{ hrs}) \times \$5 = \$50,400 - \$50,000$
$= \$400U$

■ Example 3

Using the same data given in Example 1, the variable overhead variances can be computed as shown below.

Mix and Yield Variances

The material quantity variance is divided into a material mix variance and a material yield variance. The material mix variance measures the impact of the deviation from the standard mix on material costs, while the material yield variance reflects the impact on material costs of the deviation from the standard input material allowed for actual production. The material mix variance is computed by holding the total input units constant at their actual amount. On the other hand, the material yield variance is computed by holding the mix constant at the standard amount.

The computations for labor mix and yield variances are the same as those for materials. If there is no mix, the yield variance is the same as the quantity (or usage) variance.

Probable Causes of Unfavorable Mix Variances

1. When capacity restraints force substitution
2. Poor production scheduling
3. Lack of certain types of labor
4. Certain materials are in short supply

Probable Causes of Unfavorable Yield Variances

1. The use of low-quality materials and/or labor
2. The existence of faulty equipment
3. The use of improper production methods
4. An improper or costly mix of materials and/or labor

See also Production Mix Variance; Production Yield Variance.

RETAIL INVENTORY METHOD The retail inventory method is used by retail stores to determine the valuation of ending inventory. A cost to retail ratio is determined which is then applied to the final inventory stated at selling price. *See also* Inventory Valuation.

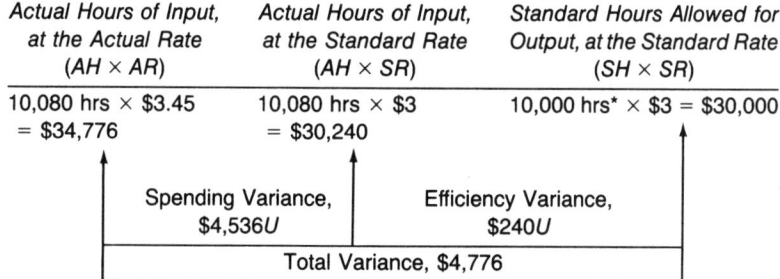

Variable Overhead Variances

Actual Hours of Input, at the Actual Rate (AH × AR)	Actual Hours of Input, at the Standard Rate (AH × SR)	Standard Hours Allowed for Output, at the Standard Rate (SH × SR)
10,080 hrs × $3.45 = $34,776	10,080 hrs × $3 = $30,240	10,000 hrs* × $3 = $30,000
	Spending Variance, $4,536U	Efficiency Variance, $240U
	Total Variance, $4,776	

* 10,000 units actually produced × 1 hr allowed per unit = 10,000 hrs. Alternatively, we can compute the variable overhead variances as follows:

Variable overhead spending

$$\text{variance} = AH \times (AR - SR)$$
$$= (AH \times AR) - (AH \times SR) = 10,080 \text{ hrs}$$
$$(\$3.45 - \$3) = \$34,776 - \$30,240 = \$4,536U$$

$$\text{Variable overhead efficiency variance} = (AH - SH) \times SR$$
$$= (10,080 \text{ hrs} - 10,000 \text{ hrs}) \times \$3$$
$$= \$30,240 - \$30,000 = \$240U$$

RETIREMENT AND PENSION PLANNING

Many people do not prepare for retirement even though it is a major event in their lives. Retirement planning involves an explicit consideration of present versus future needs and an examination of how present resources may be allocated to serve future needs. A financial advisor such as a financial planner, a CPA, or a life insurance agent may be called upon to advise clients on the type of retirement plan necessary to meet their particular needs.

The first step in retirement planning is to develop retirement goals. Once they have been set, specific savings plans aimed at achieving them should be developed. It is essential to economic security in old age to provide some income to accomplish retirement goals. Means of saving for retirement are social security, employer retirement and pension plans, annuities, and individual retirement and savings plans. An easy way to plan for retirement is to state retirement income objectives as a percentage of present earnings. For example, if one desires a retirement income of 70% of his or her final take-home pay, the amount necessary to fund this need can be determined.

Types of Pension and Retirement Plans

Two major sources of retirement income are company-sponsored pension plans and individual retirement plans. They are summarized following:

Company-sponsored pension plans
- Qualified company retirement plans
- Profit-sharing plans
- 401(k) salary reduction plans
- Tax-sheltered annuities (TSA)
- Employee stock ownership plans (ESOP)
- Simplified employee pension plan (SEP)

Individual retirement plans
- Individual retirement accounts (IRAs)
- Keoghs
- Annuities

Company-Sponsored Pension Plans

Qualified company retirement plans—the IRS permits a corporate employer to make contributions to a retirement plan that is qualified. *Qualified* means that it meets a number of specific criteria in order to deduct from taxable income contributions to the plan. The investment income of the plan is allowed to accumulate untaxed.

Profit-sharing plans—a type of defined contribution plan. Unlike other qualified plans, employees may not have to wait until retirement to receive distributions. Since the company must contribute only when it earns a profit, the amount of benefit at retirement is highly uncertain.

401(k) salary reduction plans—in addition to, or in place of, a qualified pension plan or profit-sharing plan, one may set up a 401(k) salary reduction plan, which defers a portion of the salary for retirement. This is like building a nest egg for the future by taking a *cut* in pay. Tax savings more than offset a paper cut (on paper) since employees end up with more take-home pay and more retirement income.

■ Example

A client saves 10% of his $40,000-a-year salary in a 401(k) plan. He is married with two children, is the only wage earner in the family, and does not itemize deductions. How will the client fare with a 401(k) plan and without one?

Take-Home Pay

	With 401(k) Plan	Without 401(k) Plan
Base pay	$40,000	$40,000
Salary reduction	4,000	None
Taxable income	$36,000	$40,000
Federal and FICA taxes	8,159	9,279
Savings after taxes	None	4,000
Take-home pay	$27,841	$26,721
Extra take-home pay under 401(k) $1,120		

Retirement income will grow faster inside a tax-sheltered plan, such as 401(k), than outside one. This is because the interest earned will go untaxed and keep compounding.

Tax-sheltered annuities (TSA)—if one is an employee of a nonprofit institution, he or she is eligible for a TSA. A TSA is similar to the 401(k), but one may withdraw the funds at any age for any reason without tax penalty. He or she must pay ordinary taxes on all withdrawals.

Employee stock ownership plans (ESOP)—a stock bonus plan. The contributions made by the employer are tax deductible.

Simplified employee pension (SEP)—a plan whereby an employer makes annual contributions on the employee's behalf to an individual retirement account set up by the employee.

Individual Retirement Plans

Individual Retirement Accounts (IRAs)—if one does not have a company retirement plan or would like to supplement a company plan through additional private savings, the benefits of tax deferral can also be attained through individual-oriented investments, such IRAs, Keoghs, and annuities.

The IRA is a retirement savings plan that individuals set up themselves. The IRA is a qualified individual retirement plan whereby contributions not only grow tax free but are also either tax deductible or not included in their income. Under the Tax Reform Act of 1986, however, a person who is covered by an employer's retirement plan or who files a joint return with a spouse who is covered by such a plan may be entitled to only a partial deduction or no deduction at all, depending on the adjusted gross income (AGI). The deduction begins to decrease when the taxpayer's income rises above a certain level and is eliminated altogether when it reaches a higher level. The deduction

is reduced or eliminated entirely depending on filing status and income, as follows:

If Filing Status Is	Deduction Is Reduced if AGI Is Within Range of	Deduction Is Eliminated if AGI Is
Single or Head of Household	$25,000—$35,000	$35,000 or more
Married—joint return, or Qualifying widow(er)	$40,000—$50,000	$50,000 or more
Married—separated return	$ 0—$10,000	$10,000 or more

A person *not* covered by an employee retirement plan can still take a full IRA deduction of up to $2,000 or 100% of compensation, whichever is less.

Keoghs—a person who is self-employed may set up a Keogh plan. Keogh contributions are tax sheltered and their earnings are tax deferred. The overall federal limit on annual contributions is 25% of annual compensation or $30,000, whichever is less.

Annuities—a savings account with an insurance company or other investment company. A person makes either a lump-sum deposit or periodic payments to the company and at retirement is "annuitized"—receives regular payments for a specified time period (usually a certain number of years or for the rest of life). All of the payments build up tax free and are taxed only when withdrawn at retirement, a time when an individual is usually in a lower tax bracket. Annuities pay off at retirement; life insurance pays off at death.

Annuities come in two basic varieties: fixed and variable.

Fixed rate annuities—the insurance company guarantees principal plus a minimum rate of interest. If one has little tolerance for risk, the fixed annuity is an ideal investment. In buying a fixed annuity, be aware of two interest rates. One is the minimum guaranteed rate, which applies for the duration of the contract. The other is the "current" rate of interest, which reflects market conditions.

Variable annuities—the company does not provide the same guarantee as fixed annu-

ities. The company invests in common stocks, corporate bonds, or money market instruments, and the investment value fluctuates with the performance of these investments. Note that with a variable annuity, a policyholder bears the risk of the investment options. The good thing is that most companies allow switching to another fund within the variable variety. Note that annuities can be for everybody. For young people, the vehicles are an excellent forced savings plan. For older people, they are tax-favored investments that can guarantee an income for life.

Pitfalls of Annuities

• Penalties for early withdrawals of money imposed by the IRS and insurance company.

• Surrender charges if a policyholder decides to cash in the contract early.

• The so-called nonqualified annuities, which are annuities with the tax-deferral feature but which are paid for with after-tax dollars. Qualified annuities, on the other hand, are used to fund such vehicles as Individual Retirement Accounts (IRAs) and pension plans. In a qualified annuity, the contributions not only grow tax free but are also either tax deductible or not included in one's income.

Unlike pension plans and IRAs, there are no limitations on the amunt to be contributed to an annuity.

RETURN This is a key consideration in the investment decision. It is the reward for investing. The investor must compare the expected return for a given investment with the risk involved. The return on an investment consists of the following sources of income: (1) periodic cash payments, called *current income*, and (2) appreciation (or depreciation) in market value, called *capital gains* (or *losses*).

Current income, which is received on a periodic basis, may take the form of interest, dividend, rent, and the like. Capital gains or losses represent changes in market value.

A capital gain is the amount by which the proceeds from the sale of an investment exceeds its original purchase price. If the investment is sold for less than its purchase price, then the difference is a capital loss.

The way we measure the return on a given investment depends primarily on how we define the relevant period over which we hold our investment, called the holding period. We use the term *holding period return* (HPR), which is the total return earned from holding an investment for that period of time. It is computed as follows:

$$HPR = \frac{\text{Current income} + \text{Capital gain (or loss)}}{\text{Purchase price}}$$

In the case of stock, we use the following symbols:

$$r = \frac{D_1 + (P_1 - P_0)}{P_0}$$

where r = expected return for a single period,

D_1 = dividend at the end of the period,

P_1 = price per share at the end of the period,

P_0 = price per share at the beginning of the period.

In words,

$$r = \frac{\text{Dividends} + \text{Capital gain}}{\text{Beginning price}}$$

$$= \text{Dividend yield} + \text{Capital gain yield}$$

■ Example

Consider the investment in stock A and B over a one-year period of ownership:

	Stock	
	A	B
Purchase price (begininng of year)	$100	$100
Cash dividend received (during the year)	13	18
Sales price (end of year)	107	97

The current income from the investment in stocks A and B over the one-year period

are $13 and $18, respectively. For stock A, a capital gain of $7 ($107 sales price − $100 purchase price) is realized over the period. In the case of stock B, a $3 capital loss ($97 sales price − $100 purchase price) results.

Combining the capital gain return (or loss) with the current income, the total return on each investment is summarized following.

	Stock	
Return	A	B
Current income	$13	$18
Capital gain (loss)	7	(3)
Total return	$20	$15

Thus, the holding period return on investments A and B are

$$\text{HPR (stock A)} = \frac{\$13 + (\$107 - \$100)}{\$100} = \frac{\$13 + \$7}{\$100}$$

$$= \frac{\$20}{\$100} = 20\%$$

$$\text{HPR (stock B)} = \frac{\$18 + (\$97 - \$100)}{\$100} = \frac{\$18 - \$3}{\$100}$$

$$= \frac{\$15}{\$100} = 15\%$$

See also Annual Percentage Rate (APR); Arithmetic Average Return Versus Geometric Average Return; Bond Yield Mean—Effective Rate of Return on a Bond; Yield Spread.

RETURN ON PENSION PLAN ASSETS The return (interest and dividends) on the fair market value of pension plan assets acts to decrease the pension expense provision for the year. *See also* Pension Plans.

REVENUE EXPENDITURE A revenue expenditure is an expenditure that only benefits less than a year and is therefore immediately expensed. An example is a repair to a fixed asset (e.g., tuneup). *See also* Capital Expenditure.

REVENUE RECOGNITION METHODS Revenue may be recognized under different methods

depending on the particular circumstances. Revenue is associated with a gross increase in assets or a decrease in liabilities. The methods that may be used include realization, completion of production, during production, and cash basis.

Realization—revenue is recognized when goods are sold or services are performed. It results in an increase in net assets. This method is used almost all of the time. At realization, the earnings process is complete. Further, realization is consistent with the accrual basis, meaning that revenue is recognized when earned rather than when received. Realization should be used when the selling price is determinable, future costs can be estimated, and an exchange has taken place that can be objectively measured. There must exist a reasonable basis to determine anticipated bad debts. There are exceptional situations in which another method of revenue recognition should be used. These are now discussed.

At the completion of production—revenue is recognized prior to sale or exchange. There must exist a stable selling price, absence of material marketing costs to complete the final transfer, and interchangeability in units. This approach is used with agricultural products, byproducts, and precious metals when the aforementioned criteria are met. It is also used in accounting for construction contracts under the completed contract method.

During production—revenue recognition is made in the case of long-term production situations where an assured price for the completed item exists by contractual agreement and a reliable measure of the degree of completion at various stages of the production process is possible. An example is the percentage of completion method used in accounting for long-term construction contracts.

Construction contracts—under the completed contract method, revenue should not be recognized until completion of a contract. The method should be used only when the

use of the percentage of completion method is inappropriate.

Under the percentage of completion method, revenue is recognized as production activity is occurring. The gradual recognition of revenue levels out earnings over the years and is more realistic since revenue is recognized as performance takes place. This method is preferred over the completed contract method and should be used when reliable estimates of the extent of completion of each period is possible. If not, the completed contract method should be used. Percentage of completion results in a matching of revenue against related expenses in the benefit period.

Using the cost-to-cost method, revenue recognized for the period equals:

$$\frac{\text{Actual costs to date}}{\text{Total estimated costs}} \times \text{Contract price}$$
$$= \text{Cumulative revenue}$$

Revenue recognized in prior years is deducted from the cumulative revenue to determine the revenue in the current period. An example follows:

- Cumulative Revenue (1–4 years)
- *Revenue Recognized* (1–3 years)
- Revenue (Year 4–current year)
- Revenue less expenses equals profit

■ Example

In year 4 of a contract, the actual costs to date were $50,000. Total estimated costs are

$200,000. The contract price is $1,000,000. Revenue recognized in the prior years (years 1–3) were $185,000.

$$\frac{\$50,000}{\$200,000} \times \$1,000,000$$
$$= \$250,000 \text{ Cumulative revenue}$$

Cumulative revenue	$250,000
Prior year revenue	185,000
Current year revenue	$ 65,000

Regardless of whether the percentage of completion method or the completed contract method is used, conservatism dictates that an obvious loss on a contract should immediately be recognized even before contract completion.

Journal entries under the construction methods using assumed figures are presented below.

In the last year when the construction project is completed, the following additional entry is made to record the profit in the final year:

	Percentage of Completion	Completed Contract
Progress Billings on Construction-in-Progress	Total billings	Total billings
Construction-in-Progress	Cost + Profit	Cost
Profit	Incremental profit for last year	Profit for all the years

Construction-in-progress less Progress billings is shown net. Usually, a debit figure results, which is shown as a current asset.

	Percentage of Completion		Completed Contract	
Construction-in-Progress	100,000		100,000	
Cash		100,000		100,000
Construction costs				
Progress Billings Receivable	80,000		80,000	
Progress Billings on Construction-in-Progress		80,000		80,000
Periodic bililngs				
Construction-in-Progress	25,000		No entry	
Profit		25,000		
Yearly profit recognition based on percentage of completion during the year				

Construction-in-progress is an inventory account for a construction company. If a credit balance occurs, the net amount is shown as a current liability.

Cash basis—in the case of a company selling inventory, the accrual basis is used. However, when certain circumstances exist, the cash basis of revenue recognition is used. Namely, revenue is recognized upon collection of the account. The cash basis instead of the accrual basis must be used when one or more of the following exist:

• Selling price is not objectively determinable at the time of sale.
• Inability to estimate expenses at the time of sale.
• Risk exists as to collections from customers.
• Uncertain collection period.

Revenue recognition under the installment method equals the cash collected times the gross profit percentage. Any gross profit not collected is deferred on the balance sheet until collection occurs. When collections are received, realized gross profit is recognized by debiting the deferred gross profit account. The balance sheet presentation is

> Accounts receivable (Cost + Profit)
> Less: Deferred gross profit
> Net accounts receivable (Cost)

It is important to note that a service business that does not deal in inventory (e.g., accountant, doctor, lawyer) has the option of either using the accrual basis or cash basis. *See also* Franchise Fee Revenue; Product-Financing Arrangements; Revenue Recognition When A Right of Return Exists.

REVENUE RECOGNITION WHEN A RIGHT OF RETURN EXISTS

In the situation when a buyer has a right of returning the merchandise bought, the seller can recognize revenue only at the time of sale, in accordance with FASB 48, provided that *all* of the following conditions are satisfied:

• Selling price is known.
• Buyer has to pay for the goods even if the buyer is unable to resell them. An example is a sale of a good from a manufacturer to a wholesaler. No provision must exist that the wholesaler has to be able to sell the item to the retailer.
• If the buyer loses the item or it is damaged in some way, the buyer still has to pay for it.
• Purchase by the buyer of the item has economic feasibility.
• Seller does not have to render future performance in order that the buyer will be able to resell the goods.
• Returns may be reasonably estimated.

In case any one of the previous criteria are not met, revenue must be deferred along with deferral of related expenses until the criteria have been satisfied or the right-of-return provision has expired. An alternative to deferring the revenue would be to record a memo entry as to the sale.

The ability of a company to predict future returns involves consideration of the following:

• Predictability is detracted from when there is technological obsolescence risk of the product, uncertain product demand changes, or other material external factors.
• Predictability is lessened when there is a long time period involved for returns.
• Predictability is enhanced when there exists a large volume of similar transactions.
• Seller has previous experience in estimating returns for similar products.
• Nature of customer relationship and types of product involved.

FASB 48 does not apply to dealer leases or real estate transactions, nor to service industries. *See also* Revenue Recognition Methods.

REVIEW A review is the next step above a compilation. There is some assurance expressed on the financial statements. A review is mostly composed of inquiry and analytical procedures applied to financial information so that the accountant has a reasonable basis to express limited assurance that no material adjustments have to be made to the financial statements in order for them to be in conformity with GAAP (or another comprehensive basis of accounting).

Review procedures do *not* involve a study and appraisal of internal control or the gathering of competent evidential matter. Thus, an opinion cannot be expressed. Although the accountant may look to areas that materially affect the financial statements, the review engagement may not be relied upon to disclose all significant matters that may be revealed if an audit engagement was involved.

In a review engagement, the practitioner should

• Obtain a letter of engagement.

• Obtain familiarity with the accounting policies employed in the industry.

• Obtain an understanding of the organization and operations of the client, including operating locations.

• Become familiar with the nature of the client's balance sheet and income statement accounts.

• Look at the client's production, distribution, and compensation methods.

• Understand the product line or services performed by the client.

• Note related-party transactions.

• Conduct inquiry and analytical procedures, including

Client independence.

Basis of accounting followed.

Procedures to record, classify, and summarize transactions.

Adequacy of disclosures.

Comparing current year financial information to prior year financial data.

Comparing actual figures to budgeted figures.

Identifying abnormal changes.

Comparing financial information with nonfinancial data (e.g., sales to employees).

Looking at the minutes of stockholders' and board of directors' meetings.

• Read the financial statements and related footnotes.

• Obtain a report from another accountant who is involved with reviewing a material component of the entity.

• Inquire about changes in business activities, accounting methods, and practices.

• Resolve incomplete, inaccurate, or questionable matters.

• Obtain a client representation letter, if desired.

• Document review procedures in the workpapers.

• Prepare the review report.

The following should be contained in the review report:

• Identification of the financial statements.

• Statement that the review was performed in accord with standards established by the AICPA.

• Statement that all information included in the financial statements is the representation of management (owners).

• Definition of a review in that it consists mostly of inquiries of company personnel and analytical procedures to financial data.

• Statement that a review is significantly less in scope than an audit. There is no expression of an opinion on the financial statements taken as a whole.

• If warranted, the issuance of limited assurance. The accountant may state that he or she is not aware of any needed material modifications to the financial statements to make them into conformity with GAAP (or another comprehensive basis of accounting).

• Disclosure of any material modifications that are needed to the financial statements.

• Completion date of the review.

• Accountant's signature.

Each page of the reviewed financial statements should be labeled "See Accountant's Review Report." The practitioner may also want to expand the label to include "and the Notes to the Financial Statements." Further, each page of the financial statements may be labeled "unaudited."

When the accountant is prevented from conducting necessary review procedures, a review report may *not* be issued. Instead, a compilation report may be called for. *Caution*: Professional judgment has to be exercised considering the reasons for the preclusion of the audit report.

In case independence is impaired, a review report may not be issued.

The accountant may issue a review report on only *part* of the financial statements (e.g., balance sheet).

An accountant who was originally retained to perform an audit may be asked to step down to a lower level of service (audit to a review or compilation). The accountant must consider the following before agreeing to such a move:

• Client reasons for the change, including scope limitations

• Degree of additional audit procedures to finalize the audit engagement

• Client cost of performing the additional auditing procedures

Special Note: If the accountant is not permitted by the client to inquire with the client's legal counsel regarding litigation claims or the client refuses to provide a representation letter, a scope limitation exists which prevents the issuance of an opinion. This type of scope limitation is such that it would prevent an accountant from issuing a compilation or review report. However, if proper justification exists for the step-down, the account-

ant's report should *not* make reference to the change in engagement or to the application of any audit procedures performed. The compilation or review report may be rendered. *See also* Compilation.

RISK Risk refers to the variability of cash flow (or earnings) around the expected value (return). Risk can be measured in either absolute or relative terms. Statistics such as *standard deviation* and *coefficient of deviation* are used to measure risk.

First, the expected value, A, is

$$\bar{A} = \sum_{i=1}^{n} A_i P_i$$

where A_i = the value of the ith possible outcome,

P_i = the probability that the ith outcome will occur,

n = the number of possible outcomes.

Then, the absolute risk is measured by the standard deviation:

$$\sigma = \sum_{i=1}^{n} (A_i - \bar{A})^2 P_i$$

The relative risk is measured by the coefficient of variation, which is $\sigma/\bar{A}$

■ Example

The ABC Corporation is considering investing in one of two mutually exclusive projects. Depending on the state of the economy, the projects would provide the following cash inflows in each of the next 5 years:

State	Probability	Proposal A	Proposal B
Recession	0.3	$1,000	$ 500
Normal	0.4	2,000	2,000
Boom	0.3	3,000	5,000

To compute the expected value (A), the standard deviation (σ), and the coefficient of variation, it is convenient to set up the following tables:

For proposal A:

A_i($)	P_i	A_iP_i ($)	$(A_i - \bar{A})$ ($)	$(A_i - \bar{A})^2$ ($)
1,000	0.3	300	−1,000	1,000,000
2,000	0.4	800	0	0
3,000	0.3	900	1,000	1,000,000
		$\bar{A} = 2{,}000$		$\sigma^2 = 2{,}000{,}000$

Since $\sigma^2 = 2{,}000{,}000$, $\sigma = 1{,}414$. Thus:

$$\frac{\sigma}{\bar{A}} = \frac{\$1{,}414}{\$2{,}000} = 0.71$$

For proposal B:

A_i ($)	P_i	A_ip_i ($)	$(A_i - \bar{A})$ ($)	$(A_i - \bar{A}^2)$ ($)
500	0.3	150	−1,950	3,802,500
2,000	0.4	800	−450	202,500
5,000	0.3	1,500	2,550	6,502,500
		$\bar{A} = 2{,}450$		$\sigma^2 = 10{,}507{,}500$

Since $\sigma^2 = 10{,}507{,}500$, $\sigma = \$3{,}242$. Thus:

$$\frac{\sigma}{\bar{A}} = \frac{\$3{,}242}{\$2{,}450} = 1.32$$

Therefore, proposal A is relatively less risky than proposal B, as indicated by the lower coefficient of variation.

Sources of Risk

There are the following different sources of risk involved in investment and financial decisions. Investors and decision makers must take into account the type of risk underlying an asset.

1. *Business risk*—caused by fluctuations of earnings before interest and taxes (operating income). Business risk depends on variability in demand, sales price, input prices, and amount of operating leverage.

2. *Liquidity risk*—represents the possibility that an asset may not be sold on short notice for its market value. If an investment must be sold at a high discount, then it is said to have a substantial amount of liquidity risk.

3. *Default risk*—the risk that a borrower will be unable to make interest payments or principal repayments on debt. For example, there is a great amount of default risk inherent in

the bonds of a company experiencing financial difficulty.

4. *Market risk*—Prices of all stocks are correlated to some degree with broad swings in the stock market. Market risk refers to changes in a stock's price that result from changes in the stock market as a whole, regardless of the fundamental change in a firm's earning power.

5. *Interest rate risk*—refers to the fluctuations in the value of an asset as the interest rates and conditions of the money and capital markets change. Interest rate risk relates to fixed income securities such as bonds. For example, if interest rates rise (fall), bond prices fall (rise).

6. *Purchasing power risk*—relates to the possibility that an investor will receive a lesser amount of purchasing power than was originally invested. Bonds are most affected by this risk since the issuer will be paying back in cheaper dollars during an inflationary period.

7. *Systematic and unsystematic risk*—Many investors hold more than one financial asset. The portion of a security's risk, called unsystematic risk, can be controlled through diversification. This type of risk is unique to a given security. Business, liquidity, and default risks fall in this category. Nondiversifiable risk, more commonly referred to as systematic risk, results from forces outside the firm's control and are therefore not unique to the given security. Purchasing power, interest rate, and market risks fall into this category. This type of risk is measured by the *beta* coefficient.

Risk Analysis

Risk analysis is the process of measuring and analyzing the risks associated with financial and investment decisions. It is important especially in making capital investment decisions because of the large amount of capital involved and the long-term nature of the investment being considered. The higher the

risk associated with a proposed project, the greater the return that must be earned to compensate for that risk. There are several methods for the analysis of risk, including *risk-adjusted discount rate*, *certainty equivalent*, *Monte Carlo simulation*, sensitivity analysis, and *decision trees. See also* Beta Coefficient; Capital Asset Pricing Model (CAPM); Return; Risk Analysis in Capital Budgeting; Risk-Return Trade-off.

RISK ANALYSIS IN CAPITAL BUDGETING   Risk

analysis is important in making capital investment decisions because of the large amount of capital involved and the long-term nature of the investments being considered. The higher the risk associated with a proposed project, the greater the rate of return that must be earned on the project to compensate for that risk.

Since different investment projects involve different risks, it is important to incorporate risk into the analysis of capital budgeting. There are several methods for incorporating risk, including
1. Probability distributions
2. Risk-adjusted discount rate
3. Certainty equivalent
4. Simulation
5. Sensitivity analysis
6. Decision trees (or probability trees)

Probability Distributions

Expected values of a probability distribution may be computed. Before any capital budgeting method is applied, compute the expected cash inflows or, in some cases, the expected life of the asset.

■ Example 1

A firm is considering a $30,000 investment in equipment that will generate cash savings from operating costs. The following estimates regarding cash savings and useful life, along with their respective probabilities of occurrence, have been made:

Annual Cash Savings		Useful Life	
$ 6,000	0.2	4 years	0.2
8,000	0.5	5 years	0.6
10,000	0.3	6 years	0.2

Then, the expected annual saving is

$$\begin{array}{r} \$\ 6,000\ (0.2) = \$1,200 \\ 8,000\ (0.5) = \ \ 4,000 \\ 10,000\ (0.3) = \underline{\ \ 3,000} \\ \$8,200 \end{array}$$

The expected useful life is

$$\begin{array}{r} 4\ (0.2) = 0.8 \\ 5\ (0.6) = 3.0 \\ 6\ (0.2) = \underline{1.2} \\ 5\ \text{years} \end{array}$$

The expected NPV is computed as follows (assuming a 10% cost of capital):

$$NPV = PV - I = \$8,200\ (PVIFA_{10\%,5}) - \$30,000$$
$$= \$8,200\ (3.791) - \$30,000$$
$$= \$31,086 - \$30,000 = \$1,086$$

The expected IRR is computed as follows: by definition, at IRR,

$$I = PV$$
$$\$30,000 = \$8,200\ (PVIFA_{i,5})$$
$$PVIFA_{i,5} = \frac{\$30,000}{\$8,200} = 3.659$$

which is about halfway between 10% and 12% in Table 4 in the Appendix, so that we can estimate the rate to be 11%. Therefore, the equipment should be purchased, since (1) NPV = $1,086, which is positive, and/or (2) IRR = 11%, which is greater than the cost of capital of 10%.

Risk-Adjusted Discount Rate

This method of risk analysis adjusts the cost of capital (or discount rate) upward as projects become riskier. Therefore, by increasing the discount rate from 10% to 15%, the expected cash flow from the investment must be relatively larger or the increased discount rate will generate a negative NPV and the proposed acquisition/investment would be turned down.

The use of the risk-adjusted discount rate is based on the assumption that investors demand higher returns for riskier projects. The expected cash flows are discounted at the risk-adjusted discount rate and then the usual capital budgeting criteria such as NPV and IRR are applied.

■ Example 2

A firm is considering an investment project with an expected life of 3 years. It requires an initial investment of $35,000. The firm estimates the following data in each of the next 3 years:

After-Tax Cash Inflow	Probability
−$5,000	0.2
$10,000	0.3
30,000	0.3
50,000	0.2

Assuming that a risk-adjusted required rate of return (after taxes) of 20% is appropriate for the investment projects of this level of risk, compute the risk-adjusted NPV.

First:

$$\bar{A} = -\$5,000(0.2) + \$10,000(0.3) + \$30,000(0.3)$$
$$+ \$50,000(0.2) = \$21,000$$

The expected NPV = $21,000 $(PVIFA_{20\%,3})$ − $35,000 = 21,000 (2.106) − $35,000 = $44,226 − $35,000 = $9,226.

Certainty Equivalent

The certainty equivalent approach to risk analysis is drawn directly from the concept of utility theory. This method forces the decision maker to specify at what point the firm is indifferent to the choice between a certain sum of money and the expected value of a risky sum.

Once certainty equivalent coefficients are obtained, they are multiplied by the original cash flow to obtain the *equivalent certain* cash flow. Then, the accept-or-reject decision is made, using the normal capital budgeting criteria. The risk-free rate of return is used as the discount rate under the NPV method and as the cutoff rate under the IRR method.

■ Example 3

XYZ, Inc., with a 14% cost of capital after taxes, is considering a project with an expected life of 4 years. The project requires an initial certain cash outlay of $50,000. The expected cash inflows and certainty equivalent coefficients are as follows:

Year	After-Tax Cash Flow ($)	Certainty Equivalent Coefficient
1	10,000	0.95
2	15,000	0.80
3	20,000	0.70
4	25,000	0.60

The risk-free rate of return is 5%; compute the NPV and IRR. The equivalent certain cash inflows are obtained as follows:

Year	After-Tax Cash Inflow ($)	Certainty Equivalent Coefficient	Equivalent Certain Cash Inflow ($)	PV at 5%	PV ($)
1	10,000	0.95	9,500	0.9520	9,044
2	15,000	0.80	12,000	0.9074	10,884
3	20,000	0.70	14,000	0.8630	12,096
4	25,000	0.60	15,000	0.8223	12,345
					44,369

NPV = $44,369 − $50,000 = −$5,639

By trial and error, we obtain 4% as the IRR. Therefore, the project should be rejected, since (1) NPV = −$5,639, which is negative and/or (2) IRR = 4% is less than the risk-free rate of 5%.

Simulation

This risk analysis method is frequently called Monte Carlo simulation. It requires that a probability distribution be constructed for each of the important variables affecting the project's cash flows. Since a computer is used to generate many results using random numbers, project simulation is expensive.

Sensitivity Analysis

Forecasts of many calculated NPVs under various alternative functions are compared to see how sensitive NPV is to changing

conditions. It may be found that a certain variable or group of variables, once their assumptions are changed or relaxed, drastically alters the NPV. This results in a much riskier asset than was originally forecast.

Decision Trees

Some firms use decision trees (probability trees) to evaluate the risk of capital budgeting proposals. A decision tree is a graphical method of showing the sequence of possible outcomes. A capital budgeting tree would show the cash flows and NPV of the project under different possible circumstances. The decision tree method has the following advantages: (1) it visually lays out all the possible outcomes of the proposed project and makes management aware of the adverse possibilities and (2) the conditional nature of successive years' cash flows can be expressly depicted. The primary disadvantage is that most problems are too complex to permit year-by-year depiction. For example, for a 3-year project with three possible outcomes following each year, there are 27 paths. For a 10-year project (again with three possible outcomes following each year) there will be about 60,000 paths.

▪ Example 4

A firm has an opportunity to invest in a machine that will last 2 years, initially cost $125,000, and has the following estimated possible after-tax cash inflow pattern: In year 1, there is a 40% chance that the after-tax cash inflow will be $45,000, a 25% chance that it will be $65,000, and a 35% chance that it will be $90,000. In year 2, the after-tax cash inflow possibilities depend on the cash inflow that occurs in year 1; that is, the year 2 after-tax cash inflows are conditional probabilities. Assume that the firm's after-tax cost of capital is 12%. The estimated conditional after-tax cash inflows (ATCI) and probabilities are given following.

If ATCI1 = $45,000		If ATCI1 = $65,000		If ATCI1 = $90,000	
ATCI2($)	Probability	ATCI2($)	Probability	ATCI2($)	Probability
30,000	0.3	80,000	0.2	90,000	0.1
60,000	0.4	90,000	0.6	100,000	0.8
90,000	0.3	100,000	0.2	110,000	0.2

Then the decision tree—which shows the possible after-tax cash inflow in each year, including the conditional nature of the year 2 cash inflow and its probabilities—can be depicted as follows:

Time 0	Time 1	Time 2	NPV at 12%	Joint Probability	Expected NPV
		$ 30,000	−$60,905[a]	0.120[b]	−$7,309
	$45,000	60,000	−36,995	0.160	−5,919
		90,000	−13,085	0.120	−1,570
		80,000	−3,195	0.050	−160
−$125,000	65,000	90,000	4,775	0.150	716
		100,000	12,745	0.050	637
		90,000	27,100	0.035	949
	90,000	100,000	35,070	0.280	9,820
		110,000	43,040	0.035	1,506
				1.000	−$1,330

[a] $NPV = PV - I = \dfrac{\$45,000}{(1 + 0.12)} + \dfrac{\$30,000}{(1 + 0.12)^2} - \$125,000$

$= \$45,000\,(PVIF_{12\%,1}) + \$30,000\,(PVIF_{12\%,2}) - \$125,000$

$= \$45,000\,(0.893) + \$30,000\,(0.797) - \$125,000$

$= \$40,185 + \$23,910 - \$125,000 = -\$60,905$

[b] Joint probability = (0.4)(0.3) = 0.120

The last column shows the calculation of expected NPV, which is the weighted average of the individual path NPVs where the weights are the path probabilities. In this example, the expected NPV of the project is −$1,330, and the project should be rejected.

Correlation of Cash Flows Over Time

When cash inflows are independent from period to period, it is fairly easy to measure the overall risk of an investment proposal. In some cases, however, especially with the introduction of a new product, the cash flows experienced in early years affect the size of the cash flows in later years. This is called the time dependence of cash flows, and it has the effect of increasing the risk of the project over time.

■ Example 5

Janday Corporation's after-tax cash inflows (ATCI) are time-dependent, so that year 1 results (ATCI1) affect the flows in year 2 (ATCI2), as follows:

If ATCI1 is $8,000 with a 40% probability, the distribution for ATCI2 is

0.3	$ 5,000
0.5	10,000
0.2	15,000

If ATCI1 is $15,000 with a 50% probability, the distribution for ATCI2 is

0.3	$10,000
0.6	20,000
0.1	30,000

If ATCI1 is $20,000 with a 10% chance, the distribution for ATCI2 is

0.1	$15,000
0.8	40,000
0.1	15,000

The project requires an initial investment of $20,000 and the risk-free rate of capital is 10%.

The company uses the expected NPV from decision tree analysis to determine whether the project should be accepted. The analysis is below.

Since the NPV is positive ($5,306), Janday Corporation should accept the project.

Normal Distribution and NPV Analysis

With the assumption of independence of cash flows over time, the expected NPV would be

$$NPV = PV - I = \sum_{t=1}^{n} \frac{\bar{A}_t}{(1 + r)^t} - I$$

The standard deviation of NPVs is

Time 0	Time 1	Time 2	NPV at 10%	Joint Probability	Expected NPV
		$ 5,000	−$8,598[a]	0.12[b]	−$1,031
	$ 8,000	10,000	−4,463	0.20	−893
		15,000	−331	0.08	−26
		10,000	1,901	0.15	285
−20,000	15,000	20,000	10,165	0.30	3,050
		30,000	18,429	0.05	921
		15,000	10,576	0.01	106
	20,000	40,000	31,238	0.08	2,499
		50,000	39,502	0.01	395
				1.00	$5,306

[a] NPV = PV − I = $8,000 PVIF$_{10,1}$ + $5,000 PVIF$_{10,2}$ −$20,000
   = $8,000 (0.9091) + $5,000 (0.8264) − $20,000 = $8,598
[b] Joint probability of the first path = (0.4) (0.3) = 0.12

$$\sigma = \sqrt{\sum_{t=1}^{n} \frac{\sigma_t^2}{(1+r)^{2t}}}$$

The expected value ($\bar{A}$) and the standard deviation (σ) give a considerable amount of information by which to assess the risk of an investment project. If the probability distribution is normal, some probability statement regarding the project's NPV can be made. For example, the probability of a project's providing NPV of less or greater than zero can be computed by standardizing the normal variate x as follows:

$$z = \frac{x - NPV}{\sigma}$$

where x = the outcome to be found,
NPV = the expected NPV,
z = the standardized normal variate whose probability value can be found in Table 5 in the Appendix.

■ Example 6

Assume an investment with the following data:

	Period 1	Period 2	Period 3
Expected cash inflow ($\bar{A}$)	$5,000	$4,000	$3,000
Standard deviation (σ)	1,140	1,140	1,140

Assume that the firm's cost of capital is 8% and the initial investment is $9,000. Then the expected NPV is

$NPV = PV - I$

$= \dfrac{\$5,000}{(1+0.08)} + \dfrac{\$4,000}{(1+0.08)^2} + \dfrac{\$3,000}{(1+0.08)^3}$
$\qquad\qquad\qquad\qquad\qquad - \$9,000$

$= \$5,000(PVIF_{8,1}) + \$4,000(PVIF_{8,2})$
$\qquad\qquad\qquad + \$3,000(PVIF_{8,3}) - \$9,000$

$= \$5,000(0.926) + \$4,000(0.857)$
$\qquad\qquad\qquad + \$3,000(0.794) - \$9,000$

$= \$4,620 + \$3,428 + \$2,421 - \$9,000$
$\qquad\qquad\qquad\qquad\qquad = \$1,430$

The standard deviation about the expected NPV is

$$\sigma = \sqrt{\sum_{t=1}^{n} \frac{\sigma_t^2}{(1+r)^{2t}}}$$

$$= \sqrt{\frac{\$1,430^2}{(1+0.08)^2} + \frac{\$1,430^2}{(1+0.08)^4} + \frac{\$1,430^2}{(1+0.08)^6}}$$

$$= \sqrt{\$2,788,411} = \$1,670$$

The probability that the PV is less than zero is then:

$$z = \frac{x - NPV}{\sigma}$$

$$= \frac{0 - \$1,430}{\$1,670} = -0.863$$

The area of normal distribution that is z standard deviations to the left or right of the mean may be found in Table 5 in the Appendix. A value of z equal to -0.863 falls in the area between 0.1949 and 0.1922 in Table 5. Therefore, there is approximately a 19% chance that the project's NPV will be zero or less. Putting it another way, there is a 19% chance that the IRR of the project will be less than the risk-free rate.

CAPM in Capital Budgeting

Portfolio considerations play an important role in the overall capital budgeting process. Through diversification, a firm can stabilize earnings, reduce risk, and thereby increase the market price of the firm's stock. The *beta* coefficient can be used for this purpose.

The capital asset pricing model (CAPM) can be used to determine the appropriate cost of capital. The NPV method uses the cost of capital as the rate to discount future cash flows. The IRR method uses the cost of capital as the cutoff rate. The required rate of return, or cost of capital according to the CAPM, or security market line (SML), is equal to the risk-free rate of return (r_f) plus a risk premium equal to the firm's beta coefficient (b) times the market risk premium ($r_m - r_f$):

$$r_j = r_f + b(r_m - r_f)$$

■ Example 7

A project has the following projected cash flows:

Year 0	Year 1	Year 2	Year 3
$(400)	$300	$200	$100

The estimated beta for the project is 1.5. The market return is 12%, and the risk-free rate is 6%. Then the firm's cost of capital, or required rate of return is

$$r_j = r_f + b(r_m - r_f) = 6\% + 1.5(12\% - 6\%) = 15\%$$

The project's NPV can be computed using 15% as the discount rate:

Year	Cash Flow ($)	PV at 15%	PV ($)
0	(400)	1.000	(400)
1	300	0.870	261
2	200	0.756	151
3	100	0.658	66
			78[a]

[a] NPV

The project should be accepted since its NPV is positive, that is, $78. Also, the project's IRR can be computed by trial and error. It is almost 30%, which exceeds the cost of capital of 15%. Therefore, by that standard also the project should be accepted. *See also* Beta Coefficient; Capital Asset Pricing Model (CAPM); Risk.

RISK PREMIUM   This is the amount by which the required return on an asset or security exceeds the *risk-free rate*, r_f. In terms of the *capital asset pricing model* (CAPM), it can be expressed as $b\ (r_m - r_f)$, where b is the security's *beta* coefficient, a measure of *systematic risk*, and r_m is the required return on the market portfolio. The risk premium is the additional return required to compensate investors for assuming a given level of risk. The higher this premium, the more risky the security, and vice versa. *See also* Beta Coefficient; Capital Asset Pricing Model (CAPM).

RISK-RETURN TRADE-OFF   Integral to the theory of finance and investment is the concept of a risk-return trade-off. All financial decisions involve some sort of risk-return trade-off. The greater the risk associated with any financial decision, the greater the return expected from it. For example, in the case of working capital management, the less inventory a firm keeps, the higher the expected return (since less of the firm's current assets is tied up), but also the greater the risk of running out of stock and thus losing potential revenue.

Risk, along with the return, is a major consideration in investment decisions. The investor must compare the expected return from a given investment with the risk associated with it. Generally speaking, the higher the risk undertaken, the more ample the return, and conversely, the lower the risk, the more modest the return. (See Figure 1, page 401.) In the case of investment stock, the investor would demand higher return from a speculative stock to compensate for the higher level of risk.

Proper assessment and balance of the various risk-return trade-offs is part of creating a sound financial and investment plan.

ROUND LOT   A round-lot transaction involves units of 100 shares each. *See also* Odd-Lot; Stock Orders.

RULE OF 78   The Rule of 78, sometimes called the *Sum of the Digits*, is a method that banks use to develop a loan amortization schedule. It results in a borrower paying more interest in the beginning of a loan when he or she has the use of more of the money and less and less interest as the debt is reduced. Therefore, it is important to know how much interest can be saved by prepaying after a certain month and how much of the loan is still owed.

Figure 1 Return Versus Risk

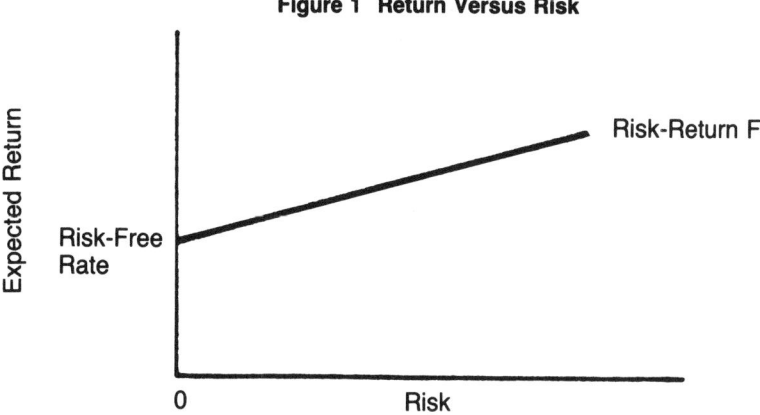

■ Example

Assume you borrow $3,180 ($3,000 principal and $180 interest) for 12 months, so your equal monthly payment is $265 ($3,180/12). You want to know how much interest you save by prepaying after six payments. You might guess $90 ($180 × 6/12), reasoning that interest is charged uniformly each month. Good guess but wrong. Here is how the Rule of 78 works.

1. First, add up all the digits for the number of payments scheduled to be made, in this case the sum of the digits 1 through 12.

$$(1 + 2 + 3 \ldots + 12 = 78)$$

Generally, you can find the sum of the digits (SD) using the following formula:

$$SD = n(n + 1)/2 = 12(12 + 1)/2$$
$$= (12)(13)/2 = 156/2 = 78$$

where n = the number of months.
(The sum of the digits for a 4-year (48 months) loan is 1,176 [(48)(48 + 1)/2 = (48)(49)/2 = 1,176]. See Table 1, page 402 (Loan Amortization Schedule).

2. In the first month, before making any payments, you have the use of the entire amount borrowed. You thus pay 12/78ths (or 15.39%) of the total interest in the first payment. In the second month, you pay 11/78ths (14.10%); in the third, 10/78ths (12.82%); and so on down to the last pay-ment, 1/78ths (1.28%). Thus, the first month's total payment of $265 contains $27.69 (15.39% × $180) in interest and $237.31 ($265 − $27.69) in principal. The twelfth and last payment of $265 contains $2.30 (1.28% × $180) in interest and $262.70 in principal.

3. In order to find out how much interest is saved by prepaying after the sixth payment, you merely add up the digits for the remaining six payments. Thus, using the previous formula, 6(6 + 1)/2 = 21. This means that 21/78ths of the interest, or $48.46 (21/78 × $180), will be saved.

4. To calculate the amount of principal still owed, subtract the total amount of interest already paid, $131.54 ($180 − $48.46), from the total amount of payments made, $1,590 (6 × $265), giving $1,458.46. Then subtract this from the original $3,000 principal, giving $1,541.54 still owed.

5. Does it pay to pay off after the sixth pay-ment? It depends on how much return you can get from investing elsewhere. In this example, you needed $1,541.54 to pay off the loan to save $48.46 in interest. For loans of longer maturities, the same rules apply, though the actual sum of the digits will be different. Thus, for a 48-month loan, you would pay in the first month 48/1176ths of the total interest, in the second month, 47/1176ths, and so on.

Table 1   Loan Amortization Schedule
(Based on a loan of $3,180 [$3,000 principal and $180 interest])

Payment Number	Fraction (Percent) Earned by Lender	Monthly Payment	Interest	Principal
1	12/78 (15.39%)	$ 265	$ 27.69[a]	$ 237.31[b]
2	11/78 (14.10%)	265	25.39	239.61
3	10/78 (12.82%)	265	23.08	241.92
4	9/78 (11.54%)	265	20.77	244.23
5	8/78 (10.26%)	265	18.46	246.54
6	7/78 (8.97%)	265	16.15	248.85
7	6/78 (7.69%)	265	13.85	251.15
8	5/78 (6.41%)	265	11.54	253.46
9	4/78 (5.13%)	265	9.23	255.77
10	3/78 (3.85%)	265	6.92	258.08
11	2/78 (2.56%)	265	4.62	260.38
12	1/78 (1.28%)	265	2.30	262.70
78	78/78 (100%)	$3,180	$180.00	$3,000.00

[a] $27.69 = $180.00 × 12/78 (15.39%)
[b] $237.31 = $265 − $27.69

RULE OF 72 AND RULE OF 69   To determine how many years it takes to *double* investment money, the *rule of 72* is used. Under it, dividing the number 72 by the fixed rate of return equals the number of years it takes for annual earnings from the investment to double. That is,

$$72/r \text{ (in percent)}$$

■ Example

Assume you bought a piece of property yielding an annual return of 25%. Then the investment will double in less than 3 years.

$$72/25 = 2.88 \text{ years}$$

The *rule of 69*, which is very similar to the rule of 72, states that an amount of money invested at r percent per period will double in

$$69/r \text{ (in percent)} + 0.35 \text{ periods}$$

■ Example

Using the same data from the previous example,

$$69/25 + 0.35 = 2.76 + 0.35 = 3.11 \text{ years}$$

S

SAFE HARBOR RULE This rule by the SEC protects a registrant and independent CPA from lawsuits for a subsequently proved inaccurate projection as long as it was made in ''good faith'' and the assessment was reasonably based. The plaintiff has the burden of proof to establish that the forecasts and projections did *not* have a reasonable basis or were *not* disclosed in good faith.

SAFETY STOCK This is extra units of inventory a firm must carry as protection against possible stockouts. The safety stock must be carried when the firm is not certain about either the demand of the product or lead time or both. *See also* Inventory Planning and Control; Optimal Reorder Point.

SALES-LEASEBACK ARRANGEMENT The lessor sells property and then leases it back for use. One reason for this transaction may be that the lessor was in need of funds. *See also* Leases.

SALES MIX VARIANCE This is the effect on profit of selling a different proportionate mix of products than had been budgeted. This variance arises when different products have different contribution margins. The sales mix variance shows how well the department has done in terms of selling the more profitable products, while the *sales volume variance* measures how well the firm has done in terms of its sales volume.

Sales mix variance = (Actual sales at budgeted mix
　　　− Actual sales at actual mix)
　　　　× Budgeted contribution margin per unit

■ Example

Assume that the XYZ Company has the following expected contribution margin (CM) for 19A:

Product A	30 units at $2.00 per unit of CM	$ 60.00
Product B	70 units at $1.00 per unit of CM	70.00
		$130.00

Assume actual CMs for the year are

Product A	45 units at $1.75	$ 78.75
Product B	50 units at $1.25	62.50
		$141.25

Then the sales mix variance is computed as follows:

	Actual Sales at Budgeted Mix*	Actual Sales at Actual Mix	Difference	Budgeted CM	Variance ($)
Product A	28.5 units	45	16.5 units	$2.00	$33.00F
Product B	66.5	50	16.5	1.00	16.50U
	95.0	95			$16.50F

* This is the budgeted sales mix proportions of 30% and 70% applied to 95 units actually sold.

See also Profit Variance Analysis; Sales Volume Variance.

SALES PRICE VARIANCE   This is the difference between actual selling price per unit and the budgeted selling price per unit multiplied by the actual number of units sold.

Sales price variance
    = (Actual price − Budgeted price) × Actual sales

If the actual price is greater than the budgeted price, a variance is favorable; otherwise, it is unfavorable. *See also* Profit Variance Analysis.

SALES-TYPE LEASE   The lessor is a manufacturer or dealer in the rental property. The lessor records profit on the assumed sale of the item in the year of lease and interest revenue over the life of the lease. *See also* Leases.

SALES VOLUME VARIANCE   Sales volume (quantity) variance is the difference between the actual number of units sold and the budgeted number multiplied by the budgeted selling price per unit.

Sales price variance
    = (Actual sales − Budgeted sales) × Budgeted price

If the actual sales is greater than the budgeted sales, a variance is favorable; otherwise, it is unfavorable. Responsibility for the sales volume variance usually rests with the marketing department. *See also* Profit Variance Analysis.

SAMPLING   In their examinations of financial statements, auditors often encounter balances resulting from many small repetitive transactions. Clearly, it is not cost effective to in-spect every transaction or document for a particular characteristic. Auditors typically select a *sample* of transactions and examine those items for desired characteristics. Then, on the basis of the findings in the sample, they make inferences about the true (but unknown) occurrence of the characteristics in the audit *population*. There are two basic methods of selecting samples from populations: nonstatistical (judgment or nonrandom) sampling and statistical (random or probability) sampling.

Nonstatistical Sampling

In nonstatistical sampling, personal knowledge and opinion are used to identify those items from the population that are to be included in the sample. Nonstatistical sampling therefore relies on the auditor's seasoned experience in drawing an appropriate sample. This technique is used primarily when the audit population consists of either a small number of high-dollar-value items or items with an immaterial aggregate amount. The auditor uses professional judgment to decide how many and which items should be included in the sample. For example, this method typically would be used in selecting 20 additions to property and equipment, worth $200,000, for vouching when total additions consist of 40 items aggregating $250,000.

Statistical Sampling

In statistical sampling, all the items in the population have a chance of being chosen in the sample. It relies on the laws of probability in selecting the sample data. In auditing, this method of sampling is used primarily when making judgments about an audit popu-

lation consisting of a large number of homogeneous items. For example, an auditor may use this technique to estimate the percentage of deviation from an established internal control procedure relating to sales when 85,000 sales transactions have been processed during the year.

Statistical Selection

Random selection of the sample is an indispensable part of any statistical sampling plan. The underlying basic concepts of a simple random sample are (1) every item in the population has an equal chance of being chosen for inclusion in the sample and (2) the auditor selecting the sample will not influence or bias the selection in any way. The most common ways to select random samples are

1. *Simple* (*unrestricted*) *random sampling*—selects samples by methods that allow each possible sample to have an equal probability of being picked and each item in the entire population to have an equal chance of being included in the sample. The methods of selection are typically either by reference to a table of random numbers or to a computer program that generates random numbers.

2. *Systematic sampling*—elements are selected from the population at a uniform interval that is measured in time, order, or space. This method differs from simple random sampling in that each item has an equal chance of being selected but each sample does not have an equal chance of being selected. Compared to random sampling, systematic sampling is a more efficient, faster sampling methodology since it consists of basically counting out the sampling units using a uniform interval. In simple random sampling, a one-to-one relationship must be set up between the sampling units and a table of random numbers (which may be generated through computer programs). In addition, a systematic sample is considered less random than the simple random sample because the former may introduce a bias into the sampling

process if there is a cyclical pattern in the population being tested that may coincide with the interval being used to select the sample.

3. *Stratified sampling*—the population is divided into relatively homogeneous groups, called *strata*, according to a common characteristic (such as the stratification of total credit sales into open account sales and credit card sales). For this purpose, one of two approaches can be used. Either we select at random from each stratum a specified number of items corresponding to the proportion of that stratum in the population as a whole or we draw an equal number of items from each stratum and give weight to the results according to the stratum's proportion of total population. With either approach, stratified sampling guarantees that every item in the population has a chance of being selected.

4. *Cluster* (*block*) *sampling*—the population is divided into groups, called *clusters*. A random sample is then selected from the clusters. A cluster consists of contiguous transactions. For example, a cluster selected from a population of all vouchers processed for the year 19X1 might be all vouchers processed on March 3, June 20, and September 10, 19X1. This sample includes only three sampling units out of 250 business days since the sampling unit in this example is a period of time rather than the individual transaction. This method is not widely used in auditing.

See also Audit.

SCATTERGRAPH METHOD The scattergraph method is a graphical procedure used to separate a mixed (semivariable) cost into the fixed and the variable cost portion. In this method, a semivariable expense is plotted on the vertical axis (or y-axis) and activity measure is plotted on the horizontal axis (or x-axis). Then a *regression* line is fitted by visual inspection of the plotted x-y data, as shown in the figure on page 406. The scattergraph method is relatively easy to use and simple

to understand. However, it should be used with extreme caution, because it does not provide an objective test for assuring that the regression line drawn is the most accurate fit for the underlying observations. *See also* Cost Behavior Analysis; Cost Behavior Patterns.

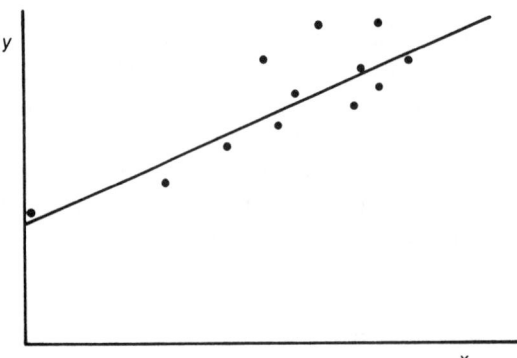

SECURITY VALUATION   The process of determining security valuation involves finding the present value of an asset's expected future cash flows using the investor's required rate of return. Thus, the basic security valuation model can be defined mathematically as follows:

$$V = \sum_{t=1}^{n} \frac{C_t}{(1 + r)^t}$$

where V = intrinsic value or present value of an asset,

C_t = expected future cash flows in period $t = 1, \ldots , n,$

r = investor's required rate of return.

See also Bond Valuation; Common Stock Valuation.

SEGMENTAL REPORTING   Financial reporting for business segments is useful in evaluating segmental performance, earning potential, and risk. Segmental reporting may be by industry, foreign geographic area, export sales, major customers, and governmental contracts. The financial statement presentation for segments may appear in the body, footnotes, or separate schedule to the financial statements. Segmental information is not required for nonpublic companies or in interim reports. An industry segment sells merchandise or renders services to outside customers. Segmental information assists financial statement users in analyzing financial statements by allowing improved assessment of an enterprise's past performance and future prospects.

Segmental data occurs when a company prepares a full set of financial statements (balance sheet, income statement, statement of cash flows, and related footnotes). Segmental data is shown for each year presented. Information reported is a disaggregation of consolidated financial information.

Accounting principles employed in preparing financial statements should be used for segmental information, except that numerous intercompany transactions eliminated in consolidation are included in segmental reporting on a gross basis.

Reporting Requirements

A segment must be reported if one or more of the following criteria are met:

• Revenue is 10% or more of total revenue.

• Operating income or loss is 10% or more of the combined operating profit.

• Identifiable assets are 10% or more of the total identifiable assets.

Factors to be considered when determining industry segments are

• Nature of the product. Related products or services have similar purposes or end uses (e.g., similarity in profit margins, risk, and growth).

• Nature of the production process. Homogeneity may be indicated when there is interchangeable production or sales facilities, equipment, service groups, or labor force.

• Nature of the market. Similarity exists in geographic markets serviced or types of customers serviced.

Reportable segments are determined by

• Identifying specific products and services

• Grouping those products and services by industry line into segments

• Selecting material segments to the company as a whole

A grouping of products and services by industry lines should take place. A number of approaches are possible. However, not one method is appropriate in determining industry segments in every case. In many cases, management judgment is necessary to determine the industry segment. A starting point in deriving an industry segment is by *profit center*. A profit center is a component that sells mostly to outsiders for a profit.

When the profit center goes across industry lines, it should be broken down into smaller groups. A company in many industries not accumulating financial information on a segregated basis must disaggregate its operations by industry line.

Although worldwide industry segmentation is recommended, it may not be practical to gather. If foreign operations cannot be disaggregated, the firm should disaggregate domestic activities. Foreign operations should be disaggregated where possible and the remaining foreign operations treated as a single segment.

As per FASB 14, a segment that was significant in the past, even though not meeting the 10% test in the current year, should still be reported upon if it is expected that the segment will be significant in the future.

Segments should constitute a substantial portion, meaning 75% or more of the company's total revenue to outside customers. The 75% test is applied separately each year. However, in order to derive 75%, as a matter of practicality, not more than 10 segments should be shown. If more than 10 are identified, it is possible to combine similar segments.

Note that even though intersegmental transfers are eliminated in the preparation of consolidated financial statements, they are includable for segmental disclosure in determining the 10% and 75% rules.

In applying the 10% criteria, the accountant should note the following:

• *Revenue*—a separation should exist between revenue to unaffiliated customers and revenue to other business segments. Transfer prices are used for intersegmental transfers. Accounting bases followed should be disclosed.

• *Operating profit or loss*—operating earnings of a segment excludes general corporate revenue and expenses that are not allocable, interest expense (unless the segment is a financial type, such as one involved in banking), domestic and foreign income taxes, income from unconsolidated subsidiaries or investees, income from discontinued operations, extraordinary items, cumulative effect of a change in accounting principles, and minority interest. Note that directly traceable and allocable costs should be charged to segments when applicable thereto.

• *Identifiable assets*—assets of a segment include those directly in it and general corporate assets that can rationally be allocated to it. Allocation methods should be consistently applied. Identifiable assets include those consisting of a part of the company's investment in the segment (e.g., goodwill). Identifiable assets do not include advances or loans to other segments except for income therefrom that is used to compute the results of operations (e.g., a segment of a financial nature).

▪ Example

A company provides the following data regarding its business segments and overall operations:

	Segment A	Segment B	Company*
Revenue	$2,000	$1,000	$12,000
Direct costs	500	300	5,000
Company-wide costs (allocable)			800
General company costs (not allocable)			1,700

* Excludes segment amounts

Company-wide costs are allocable based on the ratios of direct costs. The tax rate is 34%.

The profits to be reported by segment and for the company as a whole are as follows:

	Segment A	Segment B	Company
Revenues	$2,000	$1,000	$15,000
Less:			
Direct costs	(500)	300	5,800
Indirect costs (allocated)			
$800 × $500/$5,800	(69)		
$800 × $300/$5,800		(41)	
			(800)
Segment margin	$1,431	$ 659	
General company costs			(1,700)
Income before tax			$ 6,700
Income tax (34%)			2,278
Net income			$ 4,422

Disclosures

Disclosures are not required for 90% enterprises (e.g., a company that derives 90% or more of its revenue, operating profit, and total assets from one segment). In effect, that segment is the business. The dominant industry segment should be identified.

Disclosures to be made by segments include

• Aggregate depreciation, depletion, and amortization expense.

• Capital expenditures.

• Company's equity in vertically integrated unconsolidated subsidiaries and equity method investees. Note the geographic location of equity method investees.

• Effect of an accounting principle change on the operating profit of the reportable segment. Also include its effect on the company.

• Material segmental accounting policies not already disclosed in the regular financial statements.

• Transfer price used.

• Allocation method for costs.

• Unusual items affecting segmental profit.

• Type of products.

Consolidation Aspects

If a segment includes a *purchase method* consolidated subsidiary, the required segmental information is based upon the consolidated value of the subsidiary (e.g., fair market value and goodwill recognized) and *not* on the values recorded in the subsidiary's own financial statements. However, transactions between the segment and other segments, which are eliminated in consolidation, are included in reportable segmental information.

Segmental data is *not* required for *unconsolidated subsidiaries* or other *unconsolidated investees*. Note that each subsidiary or investee is subject to the rules of FASB 14 that segment information be reported.

Some types of typical consolidation eliminations are *not* eliminated when reporting for segments. For instance, revenue of a segment includes intersegmental sales and sales to unrelated customers.

A full set of financial statements for a foreign investee that is *not* a subsidiary does not have to disclose segmental information when presented in the same financial report of a primary reporting entity except if the foreign investee's separately issued statements already disclose the required segmental data.

Other Requirements

Segmental disclosure is also required when

• 10% or more of revenue or assets is associated with a foreign area. Presentation must be made of revenue, operating profit or loss, and assets for foreign operations in the aggregate or by geographic locality. A foreign geographic area is a foreign country or group of homogeneous countries. Factors considered in deriving this grouping decision are proximity, economic affinity, and similar business environments.

• 10% or more of sales is to one customer. A group of customers under common control is construed as one customer.

• 10% or more of revenue is obtained from domestic government contracts or a foreign government.

In the previous cases, the source of the

segmental revenue should be disclosed along with the percentage so derived.

In some instances, restatement of prior period information is required for comparative reasons. The nature and effect of restatement should be disclosed. Restatement is needed when financial statements of the company as a whole have been restated. Also, restatement occurs when there is a pooling of interests. Restatement is also needed when a change has occurred in grouping products or services for segment determination or change in grouping of foreign activities into geographic segments.

As per FASB 24, segmental data are not required in financial statements that are presented in another company's financial report if those statements are

• Combined in a complete set of statements and both sets are presented in the same report

• Presented for a foreign investee (not a subsidiary of the primary enterprise) unless the financial statements disclose segment information (e.g., those foreign investees for which such information is already required by the SEC)

• Presented in the report of a nonpublic company

If an investee uses the cost or equity method and is not exempted by one of the previous provisions, its full set of financial statements presented in another enterprise's report must present segmental information if such data are significant to statements of the primary enterprise. Significance is determined by applying the percentage tests of FASB 14 (i.e., 10% tests) in relation to financial statements of the primary enterprise without adjustment for the investee's revenue, operating results, or identifiable assets.

SELL-OR-PROCESS-FURTHER DECISION When two or more products are produced simultaneously from the same input by a joint process, these products are called *joint products*.

The term *joint costs* is used to describe all the manufacturing costs incurred prior to the point where the joint products are identified as individual products, referred to as the *split-off point*. At the split-off point, some of the joint products are in final form and salable to the consumer, whereas others require additional processing. In many cases, the company might have the option: It can sell the products at the split-off point or process them further for increased revenue. In connection with this type of decision, joint costs are considered irrelevant, since the joint costs have already been incurred at the time of the decision and therefore are *sunk* costs. The decision will rely exclusively on additional revenue compared to the additional costs incurred due to further processing.

■ Example

Assume a company produces three products, A, B, and C, from a joint process. Joint production costs for the year were $120,000. Product A may be sold at the split-off point or processed further. The additional processing requires no special facilities and all additional processing costs are variable. Sales values and cost needed to evaluate the company's production policy regarding product A follow:

Units Produced	Sales Value at Split-off	Additional Cost and Sales Value After Further Processing	
		Sales	Cost
3,000	$60,000	$90,000	$25,000

Should product A be sold at the split-off point or processed further? To answer this question all we need to do is compare incremental revenue with the incremental costs as follows:

Incremental sales revenue	$30,000 ($90,000 − $60,000)
Incremental costs, additional processing	25,000
Incremental gain	$ 5,000

Therefore, product A should be processed further. Keep in mind that the joint production cost of $120,000 is not included in the analysis since it is a sunk cost and therefore irrelevant to the decision.

SENSITIVITY ANALYSIS   Sensitivity analysis, or post-optimality analysis, is a technique for determining how the optimal solution to a *linear programming* problem changes if the problem data such as objective function coefficients or right-hand side values change. To an alert accountant and financial analyst, the optimal solution not only provides answers—given assumptions about resources, capacities, and prices in the problem formulation—but should raise questions about what would happen *if* conditions should change. Some of these changes might be imposed by the environment, such as changes in resource costs and financial and product market conditions. Some, however, represent questions raised by the decision maker because they are changes that he or she can initiate, such as enlarging capacities or adding new activities. Sensitivity analysis is essentially a *what-if* (*simulation*) technique that is most effective in attacking the uncertainty or risk

about the future. *See also* Linear Programming (LP); Simulation.

SERIAL BOND   A serial bond is a bond issue that matures in installments. The time intervals for the maturity dates are usually equally spaced. Each installment may have a different interest rate associated with it. The portion due within the year is classified as a current liability, with the balance being presented as a noncurrent liability.

Serial bonds are widely used by school districts and other taxing authorities that borrow money to finance public projects, for example, a new public school, public water/sewage treatment facilities, and the like. The money is borrowed based upon agreement that a specific tax will be levied to pay off the obligation. As the taxes are collected, the cash is used to pay off the indebtedness.

■ **Example**

Serial bonds carrying 7% interest payable (3½% semiannually) are sold to yield 5% per annum with the following maturity dates: $10,000 at the end of 12 months; $20,000 at the end of 18 months; and $30,000 at the end of 24 months. The calculations are

	Price	Premium
Serial No. 1 (due in 12 months = 2 interest periods)		
Principal: $10,000 × 0.95181	$ 9,518	
Interest: $10,000 × 1.92742	675	
	10,193	$ 193
Serial No. 2 (due in 18 months = 3 interest periods)		
Principal: $20,000 × 0.92861	18,572	
Interest: $20,000 × 2.85602	1,999	
	20,571	571
Serial No. 3 (due in 24 months = 4 interest periods)		
Principal: $30,000 × 0.90595	27,179	
Interest: $30,000 × 3.76197	3,950	
	31,129	1,129
Total All Serials	$61,893	
Total Premium* on All Serials		$1,893

   * This issue is sold at a premium since its interest rate (7%) is greater than the yield rate (5%).

The corresponding entry to record the sale of the bonds would be

Cash	61,893	
Serial Bonds Payable		60,000
Premium on Bonds Payable		1,893

SETTLEMENT IN PENSION PLAN A settlement occurs when there is a complete or partial discharge of the employer's obligation under the plan. *See also* Pension Plans.

SHADOW PRICE Shadow price in *linear programming* (LP) is imputed value, not an actual value; that is, maximum price that management is willing to pay for an extra unit of a given scarce resource. For example, an accountant and financial manager who have solved an LP problem might wish to know whether it pays to add capacity in hours in a particular department. The manager would be interested in the monetary value to the firm of adding, say, an hour per week of assembly time. This monetary value is usually the additional profit that could be earned. This amount is the shadow price. A shadow price is, in a way, an *opportunity cost*—the profit that would be lost by not adding an additional hour of capacity. To justify a decision in favor of a short-term capacity decision, the manager must be sure that the shadow price exceeds the actual price of that expansion.

■ **Example**

Suppose that the shadow price of an hour of the assembly capacity is $6.50, whereas the actual market price is $8. That means it does not pay to obtain an additional hour of the assembly capacity. *See also* Linear Programming (LP).

SHARPE SINGLE-INDEX MODEL The number of data inputs for even a moderate-sized portfolio using the Markowitz portfolio selection model (*quadratic programming* model) can be quite staggering. William Sharpe developed a model that drastically reduced the data requirements necessary to perform portfolio analysis. The Sharpe model is called the single-index or market index model. Sharpe suggests that all securities are linearly related to a market index. This relationship can be expressed through the equation:

$$r_j = a + b_{r_m} + u_j$$

where a = alpha and b = beta, the index of systematic risk, which represents the individual securities' relationship with the market. The random error u_j represents the unsystematic or nonmarket-related return of an individual asset. Securities are assumed to be related to one another through their relationship with the market. Rather than computing the covariances of all combinations of securities in a portfolio, the Sharpe model assumes that all securities are related to one another through their relationship with a market index such as the Standard & Poor's 500 Index. *See also* Beta Coefficient; Portfolio Theory and Capital Asset Pricing Model (CAPM).

SHORT SELLING Selling short a stock is an approach used by an investor to gain when the price of a stock drops. The investor attempts to sell high and buy low. To undertake a short sale the broker borrows the security from someone else and then sells it for the investor to another. Proceeds from the sale are kept in the brokerage account. Later on, the investor buys the shares back. The investor can "sell short against the box" when he or she sells short shares actually owned (not borrowed shares). The investor loses money if the repurchase price is higher than the original selling price.

To undertake a short sale, the short seller must have a margin account. The Federal Reserve mandates that a short seller must have in a margin account cash or securities worth at least 50% of the market value of

the stock he or she wants to sell short. Stock can only be sold short on an "up tick." However, over-the-counter stocks may be sold short at any time. Short sellers typically pay no interest charge but will pay brokerage commissions on the selling price and repurchase price.

Situations Where Short Selling May Be Advisable

• Expectation of a price decline in the stock.

• Desire to postpone showing a gain and paying taxes on it from one year to the next. For instance, 100 shares of XYZ Company bought at $20 now have a market price of $32. If the investor sells now, a tax must be paid on the gain. If it is desired to postpone the gain to next year, the investor can short XYZ Company stock against the box. The broker will retain the certificate in a vault and sell it short. Since the investor owns the stock and has sold it short, he or she has a hedge against increases or decreases in stock price. If the stock goes to $45 per share by the time it is sold in the next year, an additional gain of $13 per share is made but there is a $13 loss on the stock sold short.

• Desire to protect oneself when for some reason the investor cannot currently sell the stock. For example, an investor may purchase stock through a payroll purchase plan at the end of the quarter but may not obtain the certificate until a number of weeks later. It may be advisable for the investor to sell the shares short to lock in the gain.

■ Example

An investor sells short 100 shares of ABC Company stock having a market price of $60. Thus, the selling price is $6,000. The broker holds onto the proceeds of the short sale in "street name." If the investor buys the stock back at $50, a $10 per share profit is earned, or a total of $1,000.

SIMPLE RATE OF RETURN Simple (accounting, or unadjusted) rate of return is a measure of profitability obtained by dividing the expected future annual net income by the required investment. Sometimes the *average* investment rather than the original initial investment is used as the required investment, which is called *average rate of return*.

■ Example

Consider the following investment:

Initial investment	$8,000
Estimated life	20 years
Expected annual net income	$700

Then, the simple rate of return is $700/$8,000 = 8.75%. Using the average investment, which is usually assumed to be one half of the original investment, the average rate of return will be doubled, as follows:

$$\$700/1/2(\$8,000) = \$700/\$4,000 = 17.5\%$$

SIMPLE REGRESSION This involves one independent (explanatory) variable in regression analysis. For example, total factory overhead is explained by only one activity variable (such as either direct labor hours or machine hours). Also, an asset's return is a function of the return on a market portfolio (such as Standard & Poor's 500). It takes the following form:

$$y = a + bx$$

where y = dependent variable,
  x = independent variable,
  a = constant,
  b = slope.

See also Multiple Regression; Regression Analysis.

SIMPLEX METHOD OF LP The simplex method is a computational method of solving a *linear programming (LP)* problem. It is an algorithm, which is a reiterative computational procedure, such that successively larger (smaller) values of the objective function in a maximization (minimization) problem are

obtained at each step. The procedure is guaranteed to yield the optimal solution in a finite number of steps. The simplex method is capable of solving large-scale problems, whereas the *graphical method* can typically solve a two-variable problem. In practical applications of LP, computer software packages that employ the simplex method are available for obtaining optimal solutions. *See also* Linear Programming (LP); Graphical Method of LP.

SIMULATION This is an attempt to represent a real-life system via a model to determine how a change in one or more variables will affect the rest of the system. Simulation will not provide an optimal solution to a problem except by trial and error. It will provide comparisons of alternative systems or how a particular system works under specified conditions. It is a technique used for *what-if* scenarios. The advantages of simulation are (1) when a model has been constructed, it may be used over and over to analyze different types of situations; (2) it allows modeling of systems whose solutions are too complex to describe by one or several mathematical relationships; (3) it requires a lower level of mathematical skill than do optimization models; and (4) it is usually cheaper than building the actual system and testing it in operation. Financial models that are used to generate budgets and help answer a variety of what-if questions are examples of simulation. *See also* Budgeting Models; Corporate Planning Models; Financial Models; Monte Carlo Simulation; Optimization Models; Sensitivity Analysis; Simulation Models.

SIMULATION MODELS These are basically *what-if* models that attempt to simulate the effects of alternative policies and assumptions about the firm's external environment. They are basically a tool for management's laboratory. They are detailed representations of the real world. Most *financial and budgeting models* are simulation models that are

designed primarily for generating projected financial statements, budgets, and special reports, and for performing a variety of what-if analyses in an effort to find the best course of action for the company. Thanks to computer software such as spreadsheets and financial modeling languages, more and more companies are building and using modeling for their planning and decision-making efforts. Another type of simulation is *Monte Carlo simulation*, which is used when a system has a random, or chance, component. *See also* Budgeting Models; Corporate Planning Models; Financial Models.

SINGLE-PREMIUM WHOLE LIFE (SPWL) INSURANCE SPWL insurance is a policy with a low-risk investment flavor. For a minimum amount of $5,000, paid once, a policyholder gets a paid-up insurance policy. The money is invested at a guaranteed rate of interest, for one year or longer. SPWL has the following features:

1. Cash value earns interest immediately at competitive rates.
2. May borrow interest earned annually after first year.
3. May take out a loan for up to 90% of principal at lower rates.
4. Receive permanent life insurance coverage.
5. Withdrawals and loans before age 59½ are subject to a nondeductible 10 percent tax penalty. They used to be 100 percent tax-free.
6. Tax-deferred accumulation of cash values.
7. Tax-free death benefits to named beneficiaries.

Minuses of SPWL include:
1. There are usually surrender charges if the money is taken out.
2. Interest rate is generally guaranteed for only one year and could drop.

When shopping for SPWL, it is advisable to get answers to the following questions:

1. What is the net interest rate at which the cash value will grow? The net interest rate is the yield after subtracting costs of the insurance and administrative expenses.

2. What is the surrender charge?

3. Are there any loan-processing fees? What is the loan interest rate?

4. Is there a bailout plan, which enables one to cash in the policy without penalty if interest rates drop below the initial rate?

SINKING FUND A sinking fund represents cash or assets placed into a fund periodically and the return earned thereon (e.g., interest income, dividend income) which is accumulated for a specific purpose, such as to pay off debt at maturity, retire stock, or for capital expansion. Some bond issues require that the company establish a sinking fund to redeem the bonds at maturity. The cash and securities comprising the sinking fund are usually shown as a single amount under long-term investments.

SOCIAL ACCOUNTING, DISCLOSURE, AND AUDIT Social accounting is a branch of accounting that aids a business in determining whether society benefits from the goals and programs of the business. It therefore provides information on the social and environmental impacts of doing business. It discloses the social costs and benefits of business activities. It also involves an audit in connection with the performance of its public interest, nonprofit, social activities. These audits usually are performed primarily for internal benefit and typically are not released to the public. The social audit may be performed routinely by internal or external consulting groups, as part of regular internal audits. These evaluations consider social and environmental impacts of corporate activities.

SOLVENCY MEASURES Solvency is the ability of a company to meet its long-term debt payments (principal and interest). Long-term creditors (e.g., suppliers, loan officers) are interested in whether the company will have adequate funds to satisfy obligations when they mature. Consideration is given to the long-term financial and operating structure of the business. An analysis is made of the magnitude of noncurrent liabilities and the realization risk in noncurrent assets. Corporate solvency also depends on earning power since a company will not be able to satisfy its obligations unless it is profitable.

When it is practical for the financial analyst to do so, he or she should use market value of assets instead of book value in ratio computations since it is more representative than true worth.

Measures of long-term debt paying ability include:

• *Long-term debt to stockholders' equity*—high leverage indicates risk because it may be difficult for the company to meet interest and principal payments as well as obtain further reasonable financing. The problem is particularly acute when a company has cash problems. Excessive debt means less financial flexibility because the entity will have more of a problem in obtaining funds during a tight money market.

• *Cash flow to long-term debt*—evaluates the adequacy of available funds to satisfy noncurrent obligations.

• *Net income before taxes and interest to interest* (*interest coverage ratio*)—indicates the number of times interest expense is covered. It is a safety margin indicator because it shows the degree of decline in income that a company can tolerate.

• *Cash flow generated from operations plus interest to interest*—indicates available cash to meet interest charges. Cash not profit pays interest.

• *Net income before taxes and fixed charges to fixed charges*—helps in appraising a firm's ability to meet fixed costs. A low ratio points to risk because when corporate activity falls, the company is unable to meet its fixed charges.

• *Cash flow from operations plus fixed charges to fixed charges*—a high ratio indicates the ability of the company to meet its fixed charges. Further, a company with stability in operations is better able to meet fixed costs.

• *Noncurrent assets to noncurrent liabilities*—Long-term debt is ultimately paid from long-term assets. Thus, a high ratio affords more protection for long-term creditors.

• *Retained earnings to total assets*—the trend in this ratio reflects the firm's profitability over the years.

■ Example

The following partial balance sheet and income statement data are provided for Company D:

Long-term assets	$700,000
Long-term liabilities	500,000
Stockholders' equity	300,000
Net income before tax	80,000
Cash flow provided from operations	100,000
Interest expense	20,000
Average norms taken from competitors:	
Long-term assets to long-term liabilities	2.0
Long-term debt to stockholders' equity	0.8
Cash flow to long-term liabilities	0.3
Net income before tax plus interest to interest	7.0

Company D's ratios are

Long-term assets to long-term liabilities	1.4
Long-term debt to stockholders' equity	1.67
Cash flow to long-term liabilities	0.2
Net income before tax plus interest to interest	5.0

After comparing the company's ratios with the industry norms, it is evident that the firm's solvency is worse than its competitors' due to the greater degree of long-term liabilities in the capital structure and lower interest coverage.

SPECIAL-PURPOSE FINANCIAL STATEMENT

A special-purpose financial statement is one useful just to *limited* users. In certain instances, a company may prepare such statements to accompany certified general-purpose financial statements. Usually, specialized statements are prepared when firms file specified data useful in governmental and trade statistics.

SPECIAL REPORTS The independent CPA may be asked to conduct necessary procedures in order to issue a special report. As per SAS 14, the major categories of special reports are

• Reports on financial statements not prepared in accordance with GAAP but rather with another comprehensive basis

• Reports on specific items, elements, or accounts of a financial statement

• Reports on compliance with a contract related to audited financial statements

• Reports on data includable in prescribed forms or schedules

SPECIAL TERMINATION BENEFITS TO EMPLOYEES An expense should be accrued when an employer offers special termination benefits to an employee, he accepts the offer, and the amount is subject to reasonable estimation. The amount equals the current payment plus the discounted value of future payments.

When it can be objectively measured, the effect of changes on the employer's previously accrued expenses applicable to other employee benefits directly associated with employee termination should be included in measuring termination expense.

■ Example

On 1/1/19X1, as an incentive for early retirement, the employee receives a lump sum payment today of $50,000 plus payments of $10,000 for each of the next 10 years. The discount rate is 10%. The journal entry is

Expense	111,450	
Estimated Liability		111,450
Present value $10,000 × 6.145* =	61,450	
Current payment	50,000	
Total	$111,450	

* Present value factor for $n = 10$, $i = 10\%$ is 6.145.

See also Pension Plans.

SPEECH RECOGNITION SOFTWARE Speech recognition products allow the accountant and financial executive to verbally command the microcomputer to perform such tasks as spreadsheet, data base management, and word processing. Software and hardware (boards) exist so one can input data by talking to the computer, move the cursor, and fill in information on a spreadsheet. For example, Super Soft's Scratch Pad with Voice Drive™ is a voice-driven spreadsheet that gives the PC the ability to recognize speech and translate it into commands that the system's spreadsheet comprehends. Computer-voice Corporation's board permits the user to insert voice messages into a Symphony worksheet or document. IBM's Personal Computer Voice Communications Option™, which is an adapter card, supports voice recognition, voice storage, voice synthesis, and telephone management. It allows the IBM PC to read aloud answers to data base questions. Dragon Systems™ has a program allowing IBM PC-AT users to recognize thousands of words spoken by the same individual.

SPOILAGE This refers to *unacceptable* production units that are disposed of at salvage value. Financial management should know the nature and cause of the spoilage so corrective action can be taken, if possible. The spoilage may apply to completed or partially completed goods. Net spoilage cost equals:

Total manufacturing cost to the rejection point
+ Disposal costs (or − Net disposal value)

The two types of spoilage are *normal* and *abnormal*.

Normal spoilage occurs even when manufacturing is running efficiently. It is expected in the production process and is not controllable by management in the short term. Costs of normal spoilage are deemed an element of the cost of making *good* units and are therefore inventoriable product costs. The costs should be accumulated separately and allocated to work-in-process or finished goods, depending on the point in the production process at which the spoilage occurred. *Recommendation:* When normal spoilage occurs at a specific point in the manufacturing process, the cost should be allocated over all units that have passed this point. For example, if spoilage took place upon completion of the goods, no cost of normal spoilage would be allocated to ending work-in-process.

Abnormal spoilage is spoilage that is not anticipated to take place under efficient manufacturing conditions. It is *not* an inherent element in the production process. Abnormal spoilage is typically considered controllable by the factory foreman and results from an unfavorable condition. Examples are abnormal spoilage due to breakdown in equipment and inferior materials. Costs of abnormal spoilage should be charged off as a loss for the current period. It is recommended that the loss account be shown as a separate item when a detailed income statement is prepared to highlight the problem.

■ **Example**

A job order calls for 1,200 shirts. Product costs are materials $1.75, labor $5, and overhead $3. One hundred shirts are spoiled and have to be sold as seconds for $5 each. Assume spoilage occurred as a result of a specific job order. The entries are

Work-in-Process	11,700	
Materials Inventory		2,100
Salaries Payable		6,000
Applied Overhead		3,600
Spoiled Goods Inventory	500	
Work-in-Process		500
Finished Goods	11,200	
Work-in-Process		11,200

As a result, the recorded cost of manufacturing the shirts is $11,200 and the unit cost per shirt is $10.18 ($11,200/1,100 good shirts).

SPREAD   A spread is buying a call option (long position) and the writing of a call option (short position) in the same stock. A sophisticated investor may write numerous spreads to profit from differences in option premiums. There is significant return potential with high risk. The kinds of spreads include:

• *Vertical*—the purchase and writing of two contracts at different exercise prices with the same expiration date.

• *Horizontal*—the purchase and writing of two options with the same exercise price but for different periods.

• *Diagonal*—combination of horizontal and vertical spread.

A spread requires the investor to both purchase and sell a call. The gain or loss from a spread position depends on the change between two option prices as the price of the stock rises or falls. The price spread is the difference between two option prices.

A speculator using a vertical bull spread expects a rise in stock price, but the strategy lowers risk. A ceiling on gain or loss exists.

A speculator employing a vertical spread anticipates a declining stock price. The investor sells short the call with the lower strike price and puts a cap on upside risk by purchasing a call with a higher strike price.

A spread may be bought to maximize return or to lower risk. They are *not* traded on listed exchanges but instead have to be acquired through brokerage firms that are members of the Put and Call Brokers and Dealers Association.

Computer analysis helps with this type of investment.

SPREADSHEETS   These permit values (numeric data or formulas) and text (words, labels) to be entered at any location on an electronic columnar pad. They are entered in cells identified by row and column locations. They resemble a grid. Mathematical relationships can be expressed between different areas on the sheet. *Remember*: When one number is altered, every other number related to it is similarly changed. For example, you can study how earnings change as sales change, which is helpful for forecasting and modeling purposes. What-if answers come forth easily. The accuracy of a spreadsheet depends on the reliability of the formulas governing the relationship between various figures. In formulating a spreadsheet, you should follow a standardized sequential operation that is logical and consistent.

In moving data into a consolidation worksheet, beware that data will not go into a "protected cell."

Tip: Spreadsheets allow for applications in audit, tax, financial planning, and management service.

Evaluation of Spreadsheets

In evaluating spreadsheets, you must take into account the availability of the following features:

• Maximum number of columns and rows.

• Ease of use and flexibility, such as the ability to maneuver within the spreadsheet.

• Availability of template programs.

• Formulas involved and functions to be performed.

• Existence of minimum, maximum, and random functions.

• Mathematical functions, including cross-footing, extensions, absolute value, average value, logarithms, square root, trigonometric, and statistics. The spreadsheet program should allow for your own mathematical formulations.

• Recalculation order, such as row versus column.

• Existence of data base commands within the spreadsheet. This eliminates the need to find a program that can import data from another data base program.

• Alpha and numeric functions, which permit the entry of labels and mathematical calculations.

• Logic functions, so the accountant can utilize conditional values.

• Transposition ability to interchange the presence of cells, columns, or rows.

• Ability of what-if calculations. Formulas are the means by which mathematical and what-if calculations are performed. What-if analysis shows the effect of changes on another specific variable or on the whole picture (financial statements, budget, and financial analysis).

• Sorting and searching capabilities, such as the ability to arrange and access data in alphabetical and numerical sequence.

• Iteration, referring to changing a variable what-if situation. In changing a variable dependent upon another variable, which in turn is dependent on a third variable, it becomes apparent that an exact recalculation is often impossible. Iteration eliminates this problem by overcoming the circular reference structure.

• Inserting, editing, deleting, copying, retaining, and outputting functions. Included are column and row functions such as copying, moving, adding, or deleting multiple columns or rows.

• Spreadsheet consolidation (linking) where columns from one spreadsheet can be moved to another.

• Locking (protecting) and unlocking (unprotecting) cells. This capability refers to the protection of cells so contents in rows and columns will not be accidentally destroyed by the operator entering data over them.

• The number of different worksheets that can be displayed in the different windows.

• Ability to link parts of files created by one module with those created by another (i.e., a change in the value in the spreadsheet will automatically update the information in a letter produced by a word processing program).

Spreadsheet Applications

The applications of spreadsheets to the accounting practitioner are unlimited.

• Any imaginable type of what-if analysis involving alternative situations (e.g., what the client's tax liability will be, assuming different tax options are taken; what is the effect on the accounts if taxes are increased by 4%?).

• Preparing working papers (e.g., trial balances).

• Preparing financial statements.

• Planning budgets and forecasts.

• Preparing and analyzing payroll.

• Analyzing revenue by volume, price, and product-service mix.

• Analyzing expenses.

• Specifying costs in terms of volume, price, and category.

• Converting from cash to accrual basis and vice versa.

• Aging accounts receivable.

• Managing inventory.
  • Inventory extensions and footings.
  • Determining inventory management figures, including estimated sales and carrying costs per unit.
  • Production forecasts.
  • Economic order quantity.

- Liability valuation (such as aging accounts payable) and liability classification (such as breaking down notes payable into current and noncurrent portions).
- Expense calculations and reports such as for depreciation.
- Breakdown of expenses by category (e.g., selling expenses into promotion and entertainment, commissions, and travel).
- Analyzing cash flow (e.g., debt levels, interest rates) and balancing the checkbook.
- Performing integrated business plans in which income statements, balance sheets, statements of cash flow, and other related schedules can be integrated into one model.
  - Analyzing financial statements.
    - Ratio computations.
    - Earnings per share.
    - Rate of return (i.e., assets, equity).
    - Cost-revenue relationship (i.e., advertising to sales).
    - Input-output relationship, such as effect of volume on costs.
    - Horizontal and vertical analysis.
  - Financial aspects of the business.
    - Capital expenditure analysis.
    - Capital budgeting analysis.
    - Future value analysis.
    - Break-even analysis.
    - Managing assets.
    - Lease versus buy.
    - Productivity measures.
    - Loan amortization tables.
    - Acquisitions analysis of other companies.
    - Investment selection.
    - Preparing portfolio investment transactions and balances.
    - Optimal financing mix (i.e., debt-equity).
  - Cost and managerial accounting.
    - Divisional and departmental performance evaluation (i.e., cost center).
    - Product line measures.

- Overhead calculations.
- Variance determination (standard to actual, budget to actual) in dollars and percentage terms.
- Job costing.
- Tax preparation and planning.
- CPA firm practice management.
  - Time sheets by employee for control and billing purposes.
  - Client statistics for evaluation and reporting purposes.
  - Arriving at answers in seconds when meeting with the client without having to redo calculations manually.
- Generate data files compatible with certain statistical packages for conducting regression analysis and other statistical procedures. (Here, a single data file may be used for multiple applications.)
- Marketing aspects, such as product line appraisal by market share, revenue and costs by geographic area, and sales by customer.

Linking spreadsheets together enables you to carry labels, numbers, and formulas from one spreadsheet to another automatically. For example, a spreadsheet may use the input from several hundred numbers that result in ten final numbers. These ten numbers may then be transferred to another spreadsheet without having to input the hundred numbers again. Also, you can place formulas and labels of columns and rows from one spreadsheet to another.

Turner Hall Publishing's Note™ lets you embed comments within the 1–2–3 spreadsheet with ease. Comments can either be highlighted or concealed. The software allows you to attach notes to specific cells to document the details of the worksheet. You can note the assumptions for a formula or the source of an input value. Pad is a 1–2–3 file that has to be used to link Note It and 1–2–3. The notepad should be placed in an empty area of the spreadsheet. If it is put in a place that will be

manipulated, it will be erased with new data.

Avoiding Errors

Spreadsheet errors and disasters can be avoided if certain controls are practiced and work is documented. The Spreadsheet Auditor™ utility package by Consumers Software can be used to verify formulas in a spreadsheet by printing them in the same gridlike format as a spreadsheet. It tells the accountant which formulas have problems. It shows in a two-dimensional grid the formulas that conform to the spreadsheet format. The software also assists in documenting the spreadsheet by preparing a permanent record. The Spreadsheet Auditor provides the derivation of each cell. Spreadsheet Auditor has cross- and circular referencing, capability for macro extension, and side printing of the spreadsheet. It lets the user avoid spreadsheet disasters. The program becomes more essential with the greater sophistication of a spreadsheet. There is a sideprint feature that permits the accountant or financial manager to print wide spreadsheets or audit reports sideways.

Cambridge Software's Spreadsheet Analyst™ for Lotus 1–2–3 has an automatic scan to assist in finding errors, cross-referencing, a circular reference locator, and probing. Thus, it lets you ascertain the logic behind the worksheet and trace formulas and values flowing into certain cells. It allows for documenting the worksheet and identifying specific problems. *See also* Template.

STANDARD DEVIATION This is a statistic that measures the tendency of data to be spread out. Accountants and financial managers can make important inferences from past data with this measure. The standard deviation, denoted with and read as *sigma*, is defined as follows:

$$\sigma = \sqrt{\frac{(x - \bar{x})^2}{n - 1}}$$

where $\bar{x}$ is the mean.

▪ Example

One and one-half years of quarterly returns are listed below for Amko Motors stock.

Time Period	x	$(x - \bar{x})$	$(x - \bar{x})^2$
1	10%	0	0
2	15	5	25
3	20	10	100
4	5	−5	25
5	−10	−20	400
6	20	10	100
	60		650

From the previous table, note that

$$\bar{x} = 60/6 = 10\%$$
$$\sigma = \sqrt{(x - \bar{x})/n - 1} = \sqrt{650/(6 - 1)}$$
$$= 130 = 11.40\%$$

The Amko Motors stock has returned on the average 10% over the last six quarters, and the variability about its average return was 11.40%. The high standard deviation (11.40%) relative to the average return of 10% indicates that the stock is very risky.

Standard deviation is also a measure of the dispersion of a probability distribution. It is the square root of the mean of the squared deviations from the *expected value* $E(x)$.

$$\sigma = \sqrt{\Sigma \, (x_i - E(x))^2 \, p_i}$$

It is commonly used as an absolute measure of risk. The higher the standard deviation, the higher the risk. *See also* Decision Making Under Uncertainty.

STATEMENT OF AFFAIRS This shows a company's assets at anticipated liquidation values. Liabilities are shown at the estimated amounts that would be received by creditors upon corporate liquidation. Forced liquidation values will typically be less than historical cost. Emphasis is placed on the legal status or resources and claims against them.

The financial statement is appropriate in cases of actual or pending bankruptcy. Creditors and owners use the statement to estimate amounts realizable upon asset disposition and the priority of claims. Another possible use is by a creditor who desires to look at pessimistic figures for the firm in the event severe financial difficulties arise. In this case, a worst case scenario is presented.

A typical Statement of Affairs presents the following information:

Assets
Assets pledged with fully secured creditors
Assets pledged with partially secured creditors
Free assets
Liabilities
Liabilities having priorities
Fully secured liabilities
Partially secured liabilities
Unsecured creditors

A trustee often prepares a realization and liquidation report showing financial activities for the accounting period. The following information is usually given:

Assets realized
Assets not realized
Assets acquired
Liabilities liquidated
Liabilities not liquidated
Liabilities incurred
Expenses
Revenues

■ **Example**

Company XYZ is bankrupt. The historical cost of assets and liabilities is $800,000 and $300,000, respectively. If not for forced-liquidation, the market value of the net assets would be slightly higher than historical cost. However, the liquidation value of the assets and liabilities is $700,000 and $300,000, respectively. The Statement of Affairs follows.

Company XYZ
Statement of Affairs
December 31, 19X1

Assets		Liabilities	
	$700,000	Liabilities	$300,000
		Stockholders' equity	400,000
Total assets	$700,000	Total liabilities and equity	$700,000

As a result of liquidation, the company suffers a loss of $100,000 representing the difference between net assets on a historical cost basis ($500,000) and liquidation value basis ($400,000).

STATEMENT OF CASH FLOWS As per FASB 95, a Statement of Cash Flows is required in the annual report. In addition, separate reporting is mandated for certain information applicable to noncash investments and financing transactions. The objective of the statement is to furnish useful data regarding a company's cash receipts and cash payments for a period. There should exist a reconciliation between net income and net cash flow from operations. Further, the net effects of operating transactions that impact earnings and operating cash flow in different periods should be disclosed.

The Statement of Cash Flows explains the change in *cash and cash equivalents* for the period. A cash equivalent is a short-term very liquid investment satisfying the following criteria:

• Easily convertible into cash.
• Very near the maturity date so there is hardly any chance of change in market value due to interest rate changes. Typically, this criterion is solely applicable to investments having original maturities of 3 months or less.

Some examples of cash equivalents are commercial paper, money market fund, and Treasury bills. Disclosure should be made of the company's policy for determining

which items represent cash equivalents. A change in such policy is accounted for as a change in accounting principle, which requires the restatement of previous year's financial statements for comparative purposes.

The Statement of Cash Flows classifies cash receipts and cash payments as arising from investing, financing, or operating activities.

Investing activities include making and collecting loans, buying and selling fixed assets, and purchasing debt and equity securities in other entities. Cash inflows from investing are comprised of

• Collections or sales of loans made by a company and of another firm's debt instruments that were purchased by the company
• Receipts from sales of equity securities of other companies
• Amount received from disposing of fixed assets

Cash outflows for investing activities include

• Disbursements for loans made by the company and payments to buy debt securities of other entities
• Disbursements to buy equity securities of other companies
• Payments to buy fixed assets

Included in financing activities are receiving equity funds and furnishing owners with a return on their investment. Also included is debt financing and repayment or settlement of debt. Another element is obtaining and paying for other resources derived from creditors on noncurrent credit.

Cash inflows from financing activities are comprised of

• Funds received from the sale of stock
• Funds obtained from the incurrence of debt

Cash outflows for financing activities include

• Dividend payments
• Repurchase of stock
• Paying off debt
• Other principal payments to long-term creditors

Operating activities relate to manufacturing and selling goods or the rendering of services. They do not apply to investing or financing functions. Cash flow derived from operating activities typically apply to the cash effects of transactions entering into profit computation.

Cash inflows from operating activities include

• Cash sales or collections on receivables arising from the initial sale of merchandise or rendering of service.
• Cash receipts from returns on loans, debt securities, or equity securities of other entities. Included are interest and dividends received.
• Receipt of a litigation settlement.
• Reimbursement under an insurance policy.

Cash outflows for operating activities include

• Cash paid for raw material or merchandise for resale
• Principal payments on accounts payable arising from the initial purchase of goods
• Cash payments to suppliers
• Employee payroll expenditures
• Payments to governmental agencies (e.g., taxes, penalties, fees)
• Payments to lenders and other creditors for interest
• Lawsuit payment
• Charitable contributions
• Cash refund to customers for defective merchandise

If a cash receipt or cash payment applies to more than one classification (investing, financing, operating), classification is made as to the activity that is the main source of that cash flow. For instance, the purchase and sale of equipment to be used by the company is typically construed as an investing activity.

In the case of foreign currency cash flows, use the exchange rate at the time of the cash flow in reporting the currency equivalent of foreign currency cash flows. The impact of changes in the exchange rate on cash balances held in foreign currencies shall be shown as a separate element of the reconciliation of the change in cash and cash equivalents for the period.

The Statement of Cash Flows presents the net source or application of cash by operating, investing, and financing activities. The net effect of these flows on cash and cash equivalents for the period shall be reported so that the beginning and ending balances of cash and cash equivalents may be reconciled.

The *direct method* is preferred in that companies should report cash flows from operating activities by major classes of gross cash receipts and gross cash payments and the resulting net amount. A company using the direct method should separately present the following types of operating cash receipts and cash payments:
• Cash received from customers, licensees, and lessees
• Receipts from dividend and interest
• Other operating cash receipts
• Cash paid to employees and suppliers for goods or services
• Cash paid to advertising agencies and insurance companies
• Payment of interest
• Tax payments
• Other operating cash payments

Additional breakdowns of operating cash receipts and disbursements may be made to enhance financial reporting. For example, a manufacturing company may divide cash paid to suppliers into payments applicable to inventory acquisition and payments for selling expenses.

Although the direct method is preferred, a company has the option of using the indirect (reconciliation) method. Under the indirect method, the company reports net cash flow from operating activities indirectly by adjusting profit to reconcile it to net cash from operating activities. This is shown in the operating section within the body of the statement or in a separate schedule. If presented in a separate schedule, the net cash flow from operating activities is presented as a single line item. The adjustment to reported earnings involves
• Effects of deferrals of past operating cash receipts and cash payments (e.g., changes in inventory and deferred revenue), and accumulations of anticipated future operating cash receipts and cash payments (e.g., changes in receivables and payables)
• Effects of items whose cash impact relates to investing or financing cash flows (e.g., depreciation expense, amortization expense, gain and loss on the sale of fixed assets, and gain or loss on the retirement of debt)

From the above discussion, we can see that there is basically one difference in statement presentation between the direct and indirect methods. It solely relates to the operating section. Under the direct method, the operating section presents gross cash receipts and gross cash payments from operating activities with a reconciliation of net income to cash flow from operations in a separate schedule. Under the indirect method, gross cash receipts and gross cash payments from operating activities are *not* shown. Instead, there is only presented the reconciliation of net income to cash flow from operations in the operating section *or* in a separate schedule with the final figure of cash flow from operations presented as a single line item in the operating section.

Within the Statement of Cash Flows, there should be separate presentation of cash inflows and cash outflows from investing and financing activities. For example, the purchase of fixed assets is an application of cash, whereas the sale of a fixed asset is a source of cash. Both are shown separately to aid readers in analyzing the financial statements.

Debt incurrence would be a source of cash, whereas debt payment would be an application of cash. Thus, $800,000 cash received from debt incurrence would be shown as a source, whereas the payment of debt of $250,000 would be presented as an application. The net effect is $550,000.

Separate disclosure shall be made of investing and financing activities impacting upon assets or liabilities that do *not* affect cash flow. This disclosure may be footnoted or shown in a schedule. Further, a transaction having cash and noncash elements should be discussed but only the cash aspect should be shown in the Statement of Cash Flows. Examples of noncash activities of an investing and financing nature are bond conversion, purchase of a fixed asset by the incurrence of a mortgage payable, capital lease, and nonmonetary exchange of assets.

Cash flow per share shall *not* be shown in the financial statements since it will detract from the importance of the earnings per share statistic.

An analysis of the Statement of Cash Flows assists creditors and investors in

• Evaluating the entity's ability to obtain positive future net cash flows

• Appraising the company's ability to satisfy debt

• Analyzing the firm's dividend-paying ability

• Establishing an opinion regarding the company's capability to derive outside financing

• Formulating when a difference exists between net income and cash flow

• Evaluating the impact on the firm's financial position of cash and noncash investing and financing transactions

■ Example

Summarized following is financial information for the current year for Company M, which provides the basis for the statements of cash flows:

Company M
Consolidated Statement of Financial Position

	1/1/X1	12/31/X1	Change
Assets:			
Cash and cash equivalents	$ 600	$ 1,665	$1,065
Accounts receivable (net of allowance for losses of $600 and $450)	1,770	1,940	170
Notes receivable	400	150	(250)
Inventory	1,230	1,375	145
Prepaid expenses	110	135	25
Investments	250	275	25
Property, plant, and equipment, at cost	6,460	8,460	2,000
Accumulated depreciation	(2,100)	(2,300)	(200)
Property, plant, and equipment, net	4,360	6,160	1,800
Intangible assets	40	175	135
Total assets	$8,760	$11,875	$3,115
Liabilities:			
Accounts payable and accrued expenses	$1,085	$ 1,090	$ 5
Interest payable	30	45	15
Income taxes payable	50	85	35
Short-term debt	450	750	300
Lease obligation	—	725	725
Long-term debt	2,150	2,425	275
Deferred taxes	375	525	150
Other liabilities	225	275	50
Total liabilities	4,365	5,920	1,555
Stockholders' equity:			
Capital stock	2,000	3,000	1,000
Retained earnings	2,395	2,955	560
Total stockholders' equity	4,395	5,955	1,560
Total liabilities and stockholders' equity	$8,760	$11,875	$3,115

Source: Statement of Financial Accounting Standards No. 95, *Statement of Cash Flows*, 1987, Appendix C, Example 1, pp. 44–51. Reprinted with permission of the Financial Accounting Standards Board.

Company M
Consolidated Statement of Income
for the Year Ended December 31, 19X1

Sales	$13,965
Cost of sales	(10,290)
Depreciation and amortization	(445)
Selling, general, and administrative expenses	(1,890)
Interest expense	(235)
Equity in earnings of affiliate	45
Gain on sale of facility	80
Interest income	55
Insurance proceeds	15
Loss from patent infringement lawsuit	(30)
Income before income taxes	1,270
Provision for income taxes	(510)
Net income	$ 760

The following transactions were entered into by Company M during 19X1 and are reflected in the previous financial statements:

a. Company M wrote off $350 of accounts receivable when a customer filed for bankruptcy. A provision for losses on accounts receivable of $200 was included in Company M's selling, general, and administrative expenses.

b. Company M collected the third and final annual installment payment of $100 on a note receivable for the sale of inventory and collected the third of four annual installment payments of $150 each on a note receivable for the sale of a plant. Interest on these notes through December 31 totaling $55 was also collected.

c. Company M received a dividend of $20 from an affiliate accounted for under the equity method of accounting.

d. Company M sold a facility with a book value of $520 and an original cost of $750 for $600 cash.

e. Company M constructed a new facility for its own use and placed it in service. Accumulated expenditures during the year of $1,000 included capitalized interest of $10.

f. Company M entered into a capital lease for new equipment with a fair value of $850. Principal payments under the lease obligation totaled $125.

g. Company M purchased all of the capital stock of Company S for $950. The acquisition was recorded under the purchase method of accounting. The fair values of Company S's assets and liabilities at the date of acquisition are presented below:

Cash	$ 25
Accounts receivable	155
Inventory	350
Property, plant, and equipment	900
Patents	80
Goodwill	70
Accounts payable and accrued expenses	(255)
Long-term note payable	(375)
Net assets acquired	$950

h. Company M borrowed and repaid various amounts under a line-of-credit agreement in which borrowings are payable 30 days after demand. The net increase during the year in the amount borrowed against the line-of-credit totaled $300.

i. Company M issued $400 of long-term debt securities.

j. Company M's provision for income taxes included a deferred provision of $150.

k. Company M's depreciation totaled $430, and amortization of intangible assets totaled $15.

l. Company M's selling, general, and administrative expenses included an accrual for incentive compensation of $50 that has been deferred by executives until their retirement. The related obligation was included in other liabilities.

m. Company M collected insurance proceeds of $15 from a business interruption claim that resulted when a storm precluded shipment of inventory for one week.

n. Company M paid $30 to settle a lawsuit for patent infringement.

o. Company M issued $1,000 of additional common stock of which $500 was issued for cash and $500 was issued upon conversion of long-term debt.

p. Company M paid dividends of $200.

Based on the financial data from the preceding example, the following computations illustrate a method of indirectly determining cash received from customers and cash paid to suppliers and employees for use in a statement of cash flows under the direct method:

Cash received from customers during the year:

Customer sales		$13,965
Collection of installment payment for sale of inventory		100
Gross accounts receivable at beginning of year	$2,370	
Accounts receivable acquired in purchase of Company S	155	
Accounts receivable written off	(350)	
Gross accounts receivable at end of year	(2,390)	
Excess of new accounts receivable over collections from customers		(215)
Cash received from customers during the year		$13,850

Cash paid to suppliers and employees during the year:

Cost of sales		$10,290
General and administrative expenses	$1,890	
Expenses not requiring cash outlay (provision for uncollectable accounts receivable)	(200)	
Net expenses requiring cash payments		1,690
Inventory at beginning of year	(1,230)	
Inventory acquired in purchase of Company S	(350)	
Inventory at end of year	1,375	
Net decrease in inventory from Company M's operations		(205)
Adjustments for changes in related accruals:		
Account balances at beginning of year		

Accounts payable and accrued expenses	$1,085		
Other liabilities	225		
Prepaid expenses	(110)		
Total		1,200	
Accounts payable and accrued expenses acquired in purchase of Company S		255	
Account balances at end of year			
Accounts payable and accrued expenses	1,090		
Other liabilities	275		
Prepaid expenses	(135)		
Total		(1,230)	
Additional cash payments not included in expense			225
Cash paid to suppliers and employees during the year			$12,000

Presented on page 427 is a statement of cash flows for the year ended December 31, 19X1, for Company M. This statement of cash flows illustrates the direct method of presenting cash flows from operating activities.

Company M
Consolidated Statement of Cash Flows
for the Year Ended December 31, 19X1
Increase (Decrease) in Cash and Cash Equivalents

Cash flows from operating activities:		
Cash received from customers	$13,850	
Cash paid to suppliers and employees	(12,000)	
Dividend received from affiliate	20	
Interest received	55	
Interest paid (net of amount capitalized)	(220)	
Income taxes paid	(325)	
Insurance proceeds received	15	
Cash paid to settle lawsuit for patent infringement	(30)	
Net cash provided by operating activities		$1,365
Cash flows from investing activities:		
Proceeds from sale of facility	600	
Payment received on note for sale of plant	150	
Capital expenditures	(1,000)	
Payment for purchase of Company S, net of cash acquired	(925)	
Net cash used in investing activities		(1,175)
Cash flows from financing activities:		
Net borrowings under line-of-credit agreement	300	
Principal payments under capital lease obligation	(125)	
Proceeds from issuance of long-term debt	400	
Proceeds from issuance of common stock	500	
Dividends paid	(200)	
Net cash provided by financing activities		875
Net increase in cash and cash equivalents		1,065
Cash and cash equivalents at beginning of year		600
Cash and cash equivalents at end of year		$1,665

Reconciliation of net income to net cash provided by operating activities:

Net income		$ 760
Adjustments to reconcile net income to net cash provided by operating activities:		
Depreciation and amortization	$ 445	
Provision for losses on accounts receivable	200	
Gain on sale of facility	(80)	
Undistributed earnings of affiliate	(25)	
Payment received on installment note receivable for sale of inventory	100	
Change in assets and liabilities net of effects from purchase of Company S:		
Increase in accounts receivable	(215)	
Decrease in inventory	205	
Increase in prepaid expenses	(25)	
Decrease in accounts payable and accrued expenses	(250)	
Increase in interest and income taxes payable	50	
Increase in deferred taxes	150	
Increase in other liabilities	50	
Total adjustments		605
Net cash provided by operating activities		$1,365

Supplemental Schedule of Noncash Investing and Financing Activities

The company purchased all of the capital stock of Company S for $950. In conjunction with the acquisition, liabilities were assumed as follows:

Fair value of assets acquired	$1,580
Cash paid for the capital stock	(950)
Liabilities assumed	$ 630

A capital lease obligation of $850 was incurred when the company entered into a lease for new equipment.

Additional common stock was issued upon the conversion of $500 of long-term debt.

Disclosure of Accounting Policy

For purposes of the statement of cash flows, the company considers all highly liquid debt instruments purchased with a maturity of three months or less to be cash equivalents.

Presented below is Company M's statement of cash flows for the year ended December 31, 19X1, prepared using the indirect method.

Company M
Consolidated Statement of Cash Flows
for the Year Ended December 31, 19X1
Increase (Decrease) in Cash and Cash Equivalents

Cash flows from operating activities:		
Net income		$ 760
Adjustments to reconcile net income to net cash provided by operating activities:		
Depreciation and amortization	$ 445	
Provision for losses on accounts receivable	200	
Gain on sale of facility	(80)	
Undistributed earnings of affiliate	(25)	
Payment received on installment note receivable for sale of inventory	100	
Change in assets and liabilities net of effects from purchase of Company S:		
Increase in accounts receivable	(215)	
Decrease in inventory	205	
Increase in prepaid expenses	(25)	
Decrease in accounts payable and accrued expenses	(250)	
Increase in interest and income taxes payable	50	
Increase in deferred taxes	150	
Increase in other liabilities	50	
Total adjustments		605
Net cash provided by operating activities		1,365

Cash flows from investing activities:
Proceeds from sale of facility	600	
Payment received on note for sale of plant	150	
Capital expenditures	(1,000)	
Payment for purchase of Company S, net of cash acquired	(925)	
Net cash used in investing activities		(1,175)
Cash flows from financing activities:		
Net borrowings under line-of-credit agreement	300	
Principal payments under capital lease obligation	(125)	
Proceeds from issuance of long-term debt	400	
Proceeds from issuance of common stock	500	
Dividends paid	(200)	
Net cash provided by financing activities		875
Net increase in cash and cash equivalents		1,065
Cash and cash equivalents at beginning of year		600
Cash and cash equivalents at end of year		$1,665

Supplemental Disclosures of Cash Flow Information

Cash paid during the year for:
Interest (net of amount capitalized)	$220
Income taxes	325

Supplemental Schedule of Noncash Investing and Financing Activities

The company purchased all of the capital stock of Company S for $950. In conjunction with the acquisition, liabilities were assumed as follows:

Fair value of assets acquired	$1,580
Cash paid for the capital stock	(950)
Liabilities assumed	$ 630

A capital lease obligation of $850 was incurred when the company entered into a lease for new equipment.

Additional common stock was issued upon the conversion of $500 of long-term debt.

Disclosure of Accounting Policy

For purposes of the statement of cash flows, the company considers all highly liquid debt instruments purchased with a maturity of 3 months or less to be cash equivalents.

STATISTICAL SOFTWARE Software packages for models have statistical functions, including standard deviation, multiple regression, correlation, univariate and multivariate analysis, frequency distributions, cross tabulations, log-linear modeling, cluster analysis, variance analysis, factor analysis, time series analysis, matrix, and data graphing of statistical information.

A model base management system generates mathematical models and can change and store components. There is also an interrelationship between the models and the data base. A hierarchical set of alternatives can be selected by a decision maker to reach an objective.

■ Example

SPSS Incorporated's SPSS/PC™ statistical package greatly assists the financial manager in performing extensive statistical analysis. The executive can use up to 200 variables per record, inclusive of factors obtained directly from the data file and those obtained from the analysis.

STATUTORY AUDIT A statutory audit is one performed to comply with particular requirements set forth by a regulatory agency.

STOCK-INDEX FUTURES A stock-index futures contract is an agreement to purchase or sell a broad stock market index, including the New York Stock Exchange Composite Stock Index, S&P 500 Stock Index, and the Value Line Composite Stock Index. For an investor with limited funds, an S&P 100 futures contract may be entered into because of the lower margin deposit required. With a stock index futures contract, the investor is able to "play" the general change in the overall stock market. Rather than a particular stock, the "market as a whole" is bought and sold. If one expects a bull market but cannot predict an increase in price of a specific company, the purchase (long position) of a stock-index future is advantageous. On the other hand, if an investor wants to protect the portfolio from a drop in value due to a bear market, he or she can sell a stock-index future. *See also* Futures Contract.

STOCK OPTION PLAN A contractual privilege provided to a company's officers and other employees giving them the right to buy a given number of shares of the company's stock, at a stated price, within a specified time period. Usually, such rights are given to corporate employees as compensation for services or as incentives.

Noncompensatory plans are *not* primarily designed to provide employees compensation for services rendered. No compensation expense is recognized. A noncompensatory plan has *all* of the following characteristics:
1. All employees are offered stock on some basis (e.g., equally, percent of salary).
2. Most full-time employees may participate.
3. A reasonable period of time exists to exercise the options.
4. The price discount for employees on the stock is not better than that afforded to corporate stockholders if there was an additional issuance to the stockholders.

The purpose of a noncompensatory plan is to obtain funds and to induce greater widespread ownership in the company among employees.

Accounting for a noncompensatory stock plan is one of simple sale. The option price is the same as the issue price.

A compensatory plan exists if any one of the four criteria are *not* met. Consideration received by the firm for the stock equals the cash, assets, or employee services obtained.

In a compensatory stock option plan for executives, compensation expense should be recognized in the year in which the services are performed. The deferred compensation is determined at the measurement date as the difference between the market price of the stock at that date and the option price. When there exists more than one option plan, compensation cost should be computed separately for each. If treasury stock is used in the stock option plan, its market value and not cost is to be used in measuring the compensation.

The measurement date is the date upon which the number of shares to be issued and the option price are known. The measurement date cannot be changed by provisions that reduce the number of shares under option in the case of employee termination. A new measurement date occurs when an option renewal takes place. The measurement date is not altered when stock is transferred to a trustee or agent. In the case of convertible stock being awarded to employees, the measurement date is the one upon which the conversion rate is known. Compensation is measured by the higher of the market price of the convertible stock or the market price of the securities to which the convertible stock is to be converted.

There may be a postponement in the measurement date to the end of the reporting year if all of the following conditions exist:
• A formal plan exists for the award.

• The factors determining the total dollar award is designated.

• The award relates to services performed by employees in the current year.

■ Example

On 1/1/19X1, 1,000 shares are granted under a stock option plan. At the measurement date, the market price of the stock is $10 and the option price is $6. The amount of the deferred compensation is

Market price	$10
Option price	6
Deferred compensation	$ 4
Deferred compensation equals:	
1,000 shares × $4 = $4,000	

Assume the employees must perform services for 4 years before they can exercise the option.

On 1/1/19X1, the journal entry to record total deferred compensation cost is

Deferred Compensation Cost	4,000	
Paid-in-Capital—Stock Options		4,000

Deferred compensation is a contra account against stock options to derive the net amount under the capital stock section of the balance sheet.

On 12/31/19X1, the entry to record the expense is

Compensation Expense	1,000	
Deferred Compensation		1,000
$4,000/4 years = $1,000		

The capital stock section on 12/31/19X1 would show stock options as follows:

Stock options	$4,000
Less: Deferred compensation	1,000
Balance	$3,000

Compensation expense of $1,000 would be reflected for each of the next 3 years as well.

At the time the options are exercised when the market price of the stock at the exercise date exceeds the option price, an entry must be made for stock issuance.

Assuming a par value of $5 and a market price of $22, the journal entry for the exercise is

Cash ($6 × 1,000)	6,000	
Paid-in-Capital—Stock Options	4,000	
Common Stock ($5 × 1,000)		5,000
Paid-in-Capital		5,000

If the market price of the stock was below the option price, the options would lapse, requiring the following entry:

Paid-in-Capital—Stock Options	4,000	
Paid-in Capital		4,000

Note: In the case where an employee leaves after finishing the required service years, no effect is given to recorded compensation and the nonexercised options are transferred to paid-in-capital. In the situation where the employee leaves before the exercise period, previously recognized compensation is adjusted currently.

If the grant date is prior to the measurement date, we have to estimate the deferred compensation costs until the measurement date so that compensation expense is recognized when services are performed. The difference between the actual figures and estimates are treated as a change in estimate during the year in which the actual cost is determined.

When the measurement date comes after the grant date, compensation expense for each period from the date of award to the measurement date should be based on the market price of the stock at the close of the accounting period.

In a variable plan granted for previous services, compensation should be expensed in the period the award is granted.

When the employee performs services for several years prior to the stock being issued,

an accrual should be made during these periods for compensation expense applicable to the stock issuance related thereto.

When employees receive cash in settlement of a previous option, the cash paid is used to measure the compensation. If the ultimate compensation differs from the amount initially recorded, an adjustment should be made to the original compensation. It is accounted for as a change in estimate.

The accrual of compensation expense may necessitate estimates that have to be revised later. An example is when an employee resigns from the company and hence does not exercise his stock option. Compensation expense should be reduced when employee termination occurs. The adjustment is accounted for as a change in estimate.

Footnote disclosure for a stock option plan includes the status of the plan, number of shares under option, option price, number of shares exercisable, and the number of shares issued under the option during the year.

Compensation expense is deductible for tax purposes when paid, but deducted for book purposes when accrued. This results in interperiod income tax allocation involving a deferred income tax credit. If for some reason reversal of the temporary difference will not occur, a permanent difference exists that does not affect profit. The difference should adjust paid-in-capital in the period the accrual takes place.

STOCK ORDERS   Various stock orders may be placed by the investor through the broker, including:

• *Market order*—the purchase or sale of stock is at the current market price.

• *Limit order*—a purchase of stock is at no more than a given price or a sale is at no less than a stated price. The broker retains the order until a stipulated date or until terminated by the investor.

■ **Example**

A limit order is placed to buy at $30 or less a stock now selling at $32. If the stock goes up to $40, the broker will not purchase it; if it declines to $30, the broker buys it immediately.

• *Stop-loss order*—an order to buy or sell a stock when it increases to or declines below a stipulated price. Assume 100 shares of ABC Company are owned having a current price per share of $25. A stop-loss order is given to sell the stock if it declines to $20. By selling the stock at a predetermined price, the investor is insulated from further declines in stock price.

• *Time order*—an order is placed for the broker to sell at a given price during a specified time period or until the order is canceled. Assume the investor desires to sell 100 shares of XYZ Company at $60 per share. The investor believes the stock price will go up to $60 in one month. It is currently $55. The investor places a time order with the broker to sell the shares at $60, specifying a limit of one month.

STOCK RIGHT   In a stock rights offering, existing common stock owners have a *preemptive right* allowing them to maintain their percentage interest in the company. They can buy new shares before they are issued to the public.

■ **Example**

An investor owns 5% of ABC Company. The company decides to issue 6,000 additional shares. The investor has the right to purchase 300 shares of the new issue.

The right permits the investor to buy new common stock at an exercise (subscription) price for a short time, typically no more than several weeks. The exercise price is less than the current market price of the stock.

■ Example

A company has 4,000,000 shares outstanding and desires to issue another 100,000 shares. Each current stockholder will receive one right per share owned. Hence, a stockholder needs 40 rights to purchase one new share.

Advantages to investors of the stock rights option are to lower the exercise price and to avoid paying a brokerage commission.

If a stockholder does not desire to purchase additional shares, he can sell the rights in the secondary market. Obviously, if a right is not used prior to the expiration date, its value is lost.

A right's value is dependent upon whether a stock is traded *rights-on* or *rights-off* (ex-rights). In a *rights-on* situation, the stock is traded with rights attached so the investor who buys a share receives the attached stock right. In a *rights-off* situation, the stock and rights are separable and are traded in different markets. Regardless of the form of the rights, the value of a right equals:

$$\frac{\text{Market price of current stock} - \text{Exercise price of new stock}}{\text{Number of rights to purchase one share}}$$

■ Example

The current market price of stock is $40. The new share has an exercise price of $32. An investor desires four rights to buy one new share. The right equals

$$\frac{\$40 - \$32}{4} = \frac{\$8}{4} = \$2$$

If the stock continues around a $40 price, the value of the right is $2.

STOCK TYPES

• *Blue chip stocks* are securities of high-quality companies with a long earnings and dividend record. They are considered long-term investments. There is dependable return with little risk. Investors who want to avoid risk are attracted to them. An example is General Electric.

• *Growth stocks* are those having a long-term record of above-average earnings and appreciation in price. However, they may fluctuate in price. There is low or no dividends because profits are retained for future expansion. Growth stocks typically grow faster than the economy and the industry they are in. Younger people find growth stocks attractive for retirement planning. An example is a high-tech company, such as one in robotics.

• *Income stocks* have higher average and dividend payout ratios. They are attractive to investors desiring high current income with minimal risk. There is less emphasis on appreciation in market price. Older people relying on fixed income find them particularly suitable. Income stocks may also be advisable when uncertainty exists in the economy. Income stocks are typically of companies in stable industries, such as utilities.

• *Cyclical stocks* are securities having market price and profits change with the business cycle. Examples are airlines and steel companies.

• *Defensive stocks* are least impacted by economic downturns. They are consistent and safe securities. However, a lower return is earned. They are recommended for an older individual who wishes to avoid downside risk in the economy. Recession-resistant companies include pharmaceuticals and utilities.

• *Speculative stocks* do not have a long-term track record of high profits and dividends. Uncertainty exists as to future market price of the stock. Although significant risk exists for loss, there is the potential for high return. An example is a penny stock of a new company.

STOCK WARRANT   A stock warrant is the option to buy a specified number of shares at a given price for a stated time period. The subscription price *exceeds* the current market

price. A warrant may or may not be on a one-to-one basis with the common stock held. Warrants are much longer in life than stock options. They typically have an exercise period of several years. Some do not have a maturity date.

Usually, warrants are issued as sweeteners for a debt or equity issue. The company may be able to float a bond at a lower interest rate. Most warrants are detachable from the bond and have their own market price. Thus, warrants may be exercised while the bond continues to exist. Warrants are traded on organized exchanges, including the American Stock Exchange (where most are traded) and the New York Stock Exchange.

Warrants are not often issued and are not available for all securities. There are no dividends or voting rights associated with them. The warrant holder indirectly participates in the appreciation in market price of the related common stock. The price of a warrant is typically listed along with that of the common stock.

If the market price of the common stock increases, the warrant holder may either sell it in the secondary market (since the warrant will also go up in value) or exercise the warrant to obtain the stock. Trading in warrants is speculative due to the potential fluctuation in return, since the value of the warrant depends on the related common stock.

■ **Example**

A warrant of ABC company stock enables the holder to buy one share for $30. If the stock rises above $30, the warrant increases in value. If the stock falls below $30, the warrant's value is lost.

Typically, the exercise price of a warrant is constant over the warrant's life. However, the price of some warrants may increase as the expiration date approaches. Exercise price is adjusted for stock dividends and stock splits.

The return on a warrant for a holding period not exceeding one year is

$$\frac{\text{Selling price} - \text{Purchase price}}{\text{Purchase price}}$$

■ **Example**

A warrant costing $15 is sold for $18. The return is

$$\frac{\$18 - \$15}{\$15} = \frac{\$3}{\$15} = 20\%$$

If the holding period exceeds one year, the return equals

$$\frac{\dfrac{\text{Selling price} - \text{Purchase price}}{\text{Years}}}{\text{Average investment}}$$

■ **Example**

Assume a warrant costing $10 is sold for $15 after 4 years. The return is

$$\frac{\dfrac{\$15 - \$10}{5}}{\dfrac{\$15 + \$10}{2}} = \frac{\$1.00}{\$12.50} = 8\%$$

The value of the warrant is greatest when the market price of the related stock equals or exceeds the warrant's exercise price. The value of a warrant equals:

(Market price of common stock − Exercise price of warrant) × Number of common stock shares bought for one warrant

■ **Example**

A warrant has an exercise price of $40. Two warrants equal one share. The market price of the stock is $50. The value of the warrant is

$$(\$50 - \$40) \times 0.5 = \$5$$

Generally, the market value of a warrant exceeds its intrinsic value, or *premium*, because of the speculative nature of warrants. As the value of a warrant increases, the premium usually goes down. Premium equals:

Value of premium = Market price of warrant
                                     − Intrinsic value

■ Example

The warrant in the prior example has a market price of $7. Thus, the premium is $2 ($7 − $5).

■ Example

A company issues 400 bonds worth $400,000. One bond has 6 warrants attached. Each warrant allows the investor to buy one share of stock at $14. The warrant will have no value at the issue date if the stock has a price below $14. If the stock rises to $22, the warrant will be worth $8. Thus, 6 warrants are worth $48 (6 × $8).

■ Example

A company's common stock has a market price of $50 per share. One warrant can be used to buy one share at $42 in the next 2 years. The intrinsic (minimum) value per warrant is $8 [($50 − $42) × 1]. Since the warrant has 2 years remaining and can be used for speculative purposes, it may be traded at an amount in excess of $8. If the warrant is selling at $11, it has a premium of $3.

Even if the stock is selling below $42 per share, there may be a market value to the warrant because speculators may want to buy it if they anticipate future appreciation in market price of the stock. For example, if the common stock was at $40, there is a negative intrinsic value of $2, but the warrant may have a dollar value of $1 arising from positive expectations of an increase in market price of the stock.

Leveraging may be done to maximize return.

■ Example

An investor has $10,000 of available funds. If common stock is bought at $50 per share, then 200 shares could be purchased. If market price goes to $55, there is a gain of $1,000. However, if the $10,000 was invested in warrants having a price of $5 per share, then 2,000 warrants could have been bought (assuming 1 warrant = 1 share). If the price of the warrant increases by $5, the gain is $10,000. The return on the warrant is 100%, while the return on the common stock is only 10%. *Warning*: If the market price of the stock dropped by $5, the investor would lose $1,000. But if he or she invested in the warrants, the entire $10,000 would be lost, assuming that no warrant premium exists.

If an investor is to achieve maximum price potential from a warrant, the market price of the common stock must equal or exceed the warrant's exercise price. Further, lower priced issues provide greater leverage opportunity. *Recommendation*: A warrant with a low unit price causes higher price volatility and less downside risk, and thus is preferred to a warrant with a high unit price.

The investor may use warrants to protect a speculative transaction. For instance, an investor sells a stock short and the price increases. The speculator cannot keep the short position continually open; it may be too costly to wait until a drop in market price. The investor may protect the short sale by buying a warrant, fixing the purchase price and limiting the potential loss on the trade.

■ Example

An investor sells short 100 shares at $12 each. He then buys warrants for 100 shares at $10 each. The cost of the option is $3 per share, or a total of $300. In essence, the investor is buying the stock at $13 per share. If the stock increases above $12, the loss is limited to $1 per share.

Advantages of Warrants

• The price of the warrant is tied into the related common stock.

• The low unit cost permits the investor to obtain leverage from a smaller investment thus enhancing return. The low unit cost also involves less downside risk.

Disadvantages of Warrants

• No dividends are received.
• The entire investment in the warrant may be lost if market price of the stock declines.

Accounting by the Issuer of Stock Warrants

For the issuing company, warrants are common stock equivalents and as such dilute earnings per share.

If bonds are issued along with *detachable* stock warrants, the portion of the proceeds applicable to the warrants is credited to paid-in-capital. The basis for allocation is the relative values of the securities at the time of issuance. In the event that the warrants are *not detachable*, the bonds are accounted for solely as convertible debt. There is *no* allocation of the proceeds to the conversion feature.

■ Example

A $20,000 convertible bond is issued at $21,000 with $1,000 applicable to stock warrants. If the warrants are not detachable, the entry is

Cash	21,000	
Bonds Payable		20,000
Premium on Bonds Payable		1,000

If the warrants are detachable, the entry is

Cash	21,000	
Bonds Payable		20,000
Paid-in-Capital—Stock Warrants		1,000

In the event that the proceeds of the bond issue were only $20,000 instead of $21,000 and $1,000 could be attributable to the warrants, the entry is

Cash	20,000	
Discount	1,000	
Bonds Payable		20,000
Paid-in-Capital—Stock Warrants		1,000

See also Options: Calls and Puts; Stock Right.

STOP-LOSS ORDER *See* Stock Orders.

STRADDLE This is an integration of a call and put on the identical stock with the same strike price and exercise date. A speculator trading on both sides of the market uses it. The speculator is looking for a material change in stock price in either direction to obtain a gain in excess of the cost of both options. A loss equal to the cost of the options will occur if a significant price movement does not take place. Thus, there is high risk with this investment strategy. The straddle holder may increase profit potential but also has risk by closing one option prior to closing the other.

■ Example

A call and put are bought on a March option for $6 each when the stock price is $50. The total investment is $1,200 ($600 × 2). At expiration, the stock rises to $75. There is a profit on the call of $19 ($25 − $6) and a loss on the put of $6. The net gain is $13, or $1,300 in total.

STRATIFIED SAMPLING When using stratified sampling, the auditor segregates the population into homogeneous subgroups (strata). The auditor then samples each strata. The sample results should be separately appraised and combined to provide an estimate of the population characteristics. Homogeneity is enhanced when very high or low value items are segregated into individual strata. Homogeneity in population improves the efficiency of the sample. Thus, usually fewer items have to be examined to appraise several strata separately than to evaluate the whole population. Stratification benefits the sampling proc-

ess and enhances auditor ability to relate sample selection to the materiality and turnover of items. The type of audit procedures applied to each stratum may vary based on individual circumstances and the nature of the environment. An application of stratified sampling is when total accounts receivable (population) is broken down into groups based on dollar balances for confirmation purposes. An illustration follows:

Stratum	Method of Selection Used	Type of Confirmation
All accounts of $50,000 or more	100% confirmed	Positive
All other accounts under $50,000	Random number table selection	Positive

Stratification can also be applied to type of transaction and by transaction frequency. Stratification is recommended in the case where a variable under scrutiny changes substantially within different parts of the population. This approach is usually used in classical variables sampling and often in attributes sampling. *See also* Sampling.

SUBSEQUENT EVENT   A subsequent event is an important occurrence between the date of the financial statements and the audit report date. It requires footnote disclosure because of its significance to financial readers of the statements. It may have an influence upon their decisions. Usually, the subsequent event has a material effect upon financial position or operating performance. Examples are when the company is accused of an illegal act by the government, extraordinary loss, lawsuit, and a permanent decline in the market price of stock investments.

SUBSTANTIVE TEST   A substantive test substantiates the validity of account balances. There exist the following three types of substantive tests: (1) transaction tests; (2) tests of balances; and (3) analytical review. The

purpose of testing transactions and balances is to obtain evidence of the correctness of recording transactions and deriving account balances. Attention is given to identifying irregularities. To ascertain the validity of financial statement numbers, statistical sampling may be employed. Transaction tests occur periodically throughout the year or at year-end. A transaction test is when, for instance, the auditor traces a cash payment from the cash disbursements journal to the cash account in the general ledger for agreement. A test of balances is when the auditor compares the book balance of cash to the bank balance. This test is performed about year-end. Another substantive test is computing dividend revenue on stocks owned and substantiating the amount recorded. In an analytical review, the CPA looks to the reasonableness of financial statement items by examining relationships. Discrepancies are noted. For example, if promotion and entertainment expense to sales went from 2% last year to 30% this year, a "red flag" exists. Analytical review procedures may be applied to overall corporate financial data, information for business segments, and to individual items. When reasonable relationships exist, there is corroborating evidence to the account balance. *See also* Analytical Procedures; Transaction Test.

SUPPLY-SIDE ECONOMICS VERSUS DEMAND-SIDE ECONOMICS   Supply-side economics aims at achieving efficiency through economic policies and measures designed to stimulate production. On the other hand, *demand-side economics* focuses on regulating aggregate demand. *Keynesian economics*, since it tends to focus on fiscal and monetary policies to control aggregate demand, has been characterized as demand-side economics. Supply-side economics relies heavily on the direct use of *incentives*. For example, reductions in marginal tax rates—the taxes paid on the last dollar of taxable income—

provide direct incentives to work, save, and invest, thereby stimulating aggregate supply rather than aggregate demand. Tight monetary control to curb inflation is another principal prescription of supply-side economics. *See also* Keynesian Economics.

SYSTEMATIC SAMPLING This consists of sequencing all items of the population. Sampling units are put in order (e.g., numerical). Audit software that has routines for systematic sampling is available. The auditor then divides the population into *n* intervals of equal size based on the number of sampling units that must be chosen for the sample (*n*). He or she then chooses a sampling unit from each of the derived intervals. The selection interval can be determined by dividing the population size (*N*) by the required sample size (*n*).

■ **Example**

The auditor is examining 1,000 sales invoices from a population of 20,000 invoices. One random starting point is employed. Each 20th invoice is chosen. In order that 1,000 invoices are selected, the auditor moves up or down from the random starting point. If a random starting point of invoice number 100 is selected, invoice number 80 (100 − 20) and 60 (100 − 40) are included in the sample, as well as every twentieth invoice number after 100 (i.e., 120, 140, 160, and so on). If the auditor selected 10 random starting points, 100 invoices (1,000/10) would be selected for audit. Thus, the auditor would select every two hundredth invoice number (20,000/100) before and after each random beginning point.

■ **Example**

The population is 10,000 units and the sample size is 1,000 units. The auditor selects a random starting point between 1 and the sampling interval of 10 (10,000/1,000). This forces the auditor to choose the first sampling

unit from the first interval. After including the random start unit as part of the sample, the accountant then sequentially selects every tenth item of the population. Typically, this approach results in a true random sample. Note that if a cyclical pattern in the population exists that coincides with the selection interval, a bias may result; that is, if every tenth sampling unit or multiple of 10 happens to be a departmental manager, then based on the random start, the sample derived may yield either all departmental managers or none. However, the possibility of introducing a bias into the sample as a result of a cyclical pattern in the population would be minimized by picking multiple starting points in the selection process. But if multiple starting points are chosen, then the sampling interval that was previously selected must be multiplied by the number of random starts so that the required sample size is unchanged.

When there is no numerical sequence to a population, the auditor will find it easier to use a systematic random sample rather than a pure random sample. If documents, records, or transactions are unnumbered, there is no need with systematic sampling to number them physically. If random number table selection was involved, the drawback would be to require numbering. With systematic sampling, the auditor uses the sampling interval as the basis to select the document to examine.

Systematic sampling may be employed for both statistical and nonstatistical sampling. *See also* Sampling.

SYSTEMS SOFTWARE This usually is for a particular micro to facilitate use. It is a buffer (communication) between the accountant or application programs (e.g., spreadsheet) and the hardware (including operating peripherals). It includes operating systems and programming languages (e.g., BASIC). Systems software reconciles the differences between different models of micros and permits the

accountant to work with whatever model is involved.

The operating system is a collection of general-purpose programs. The operating system is executed when the computer is turned on. It acts as an interface among the operator, the computer, and the applications software. *Key point*: The operating system supports the input, output, processing, storage, and control activities of the micro. It contains the instructions to the hardware for allowing access to the computer memory.

Functions of the operating system include loading and executing programs, keeping track of information within memory and/or external storage sources, transferring information between hardware elements of the micro system, and directing computer operations.

Important: The operating system includes utilities (common functions) such as changing files, backup of file data, and printing information. It has a minimum main storage, thus reducing the storage that can be used for applications.

IBM batch programs enable the carrying out of a series of DOS commands at one time. *Save Valuable Time*: A batch file conducts the DOS commands sequentially as if they were manually typed. A batch file is identified with the .BAT file name extension. For example, AUTO-EXEC.BAT™ provides start-up commands to configure the system as needed. There can also be more than one batch program run, referred to as a chain of two or more programs. IBM batch programs allow for program looping, conditional tests, and program branching. Two or more batch programs can be chained, passing information between them.

Computers of different manufacturers may be able to use the same application programs if they run on the same operating system (e.g., MS-DOS). They are referred to as clones or compatibles.

What You Need to Know: Multitasking operating systems permit several application programs to share the processor and other operating facilities. The advantage is that you can go from task to task quickly or do more than one task at the same time. Multitasking, multiuser operating systems include Microsoft's Xenix™ and AT&T's Unix™.

Window operating systems represent an alternative operating environment to MS-DOS (called DOS shells). These operating systems in effect surround DOS with a shell, turning the display into a menu-oriented "desktop" for selecting and running PC applications. Each window operating system is slightly different from the others but has the basic ultimate objective of loading alternative DOS and taking control of the machine. Examples are Microsoft Windows,™ IBM's Topview,™ Digital Research GEM Desktop™, and Quarterback Office System's DesqView™. They enable the user to present the display into a menu-oriented desktop with features such as concurrency, multiple windowing, cutting and pasting, and file switching for dedicated applications. They are in a sense an alternative operating environment substitute for integrated software. The windowing operating systems provide the convenience of integrated software without being limited to one package and requiring the replacement of the installed applications base.

The windows allow for *mundane* multitasking (not real multitasking) where you can switch quickly from one program to another program so they seem to be running simultaneously. For example, you can move from a data base to a spreadsheet very fast. The ability to change the nature of the window presents significant power.

T

TAX PLANNING Tax planning is done by a tax practitioner to minimize the income tax liability of a client. To do so, it is essential to analyze the tax consequences of alternative client decisions. Is the client missing any tax-saving opportunities? A long-term tax-planning strategy should be developed that takes into account the client's age, income, liquidity needs, family status, estate-planning preferences, and so on. There are many comprehensive tax publications to refer to, such as those published by Prentice Hall Information Services.

Reasons to Postpone Taxes

• Client will be in a lower tax bracket in a future year.

• Client lacks the funds to meet the present tax requirement.

• Client can earn a return on the funds that he or she would have had to pay the federal and local taxing authorities.

• Client, by deferring payment of taxes, will be paying in cheaper dollars because of the inflationary effect.

• Client may possibly avoid the tax payment.

Recommendation: Have the client properly time the receipt of income and the payment of expenses to minimize the tax payment, particularly if the client's income is on the borderline between two tax brackets. A good tax strategy is to receive income in a year in which it will be taxed at a lower rate and to pay tax-deductible expenses in a year in which it will receive the most benefit.

■ Example

Your client is in a high tax bracket this year but expects to be in a lower one next year. The client should increase tax-deductible expenses in the high tax year (e.g., making a thirteenth mortgage payment). The client should delay receiving income in the high tax year (e.g., have the employer pay a bonus next year for the services rendered in the prior year).

It may be advantageous for your client to defer the receipt of salaries, bonuses, commissions, and professional fees to the following year so that the tax may be postponed until the filing of next year's tax return. (This assumes that tax rates will be the same or decline the following year.) Also, money has a time value since it could be invested with the expectation of a return.

Your client may take advantage of a de-

ferred-compensation agreement, representing a contract for payments of current services to be made in the future. As a result, there are tax savings in the current year.

Tax-Exempt Income

Sources of tax-exempt income should be searched out. There is a tax-free buildup for certain types of life insurance and deferred annuity policies. Taxes may be postponed on the interest earned until the policy matures.

Funds received from a life insurance contract paid to beneficiaries when the insured dies is generally not taxable. Also, disability benefits and health insurance benefits are excludable when attributable to premiums paid by the holders. Casualty insurance proceeds not exceeding the basis of assets are also tax exempt.

The client should try to obtain tax-exempt income whenever possible. The client receives the full benefit of that income because taxes are not paid on it. Thus, tax-free income is worth much more than taxable income. You can determine the equivalent taxable income as follows:

$$\text{Equivalent taxable income} = \frac{\text{Tax-free income}}{1 - \text{Marginal tax rate}}$$

Interest earned on municipal bonds used for traditional governmental purposes and qualified private activity bonds is not subject to federal tax and is exempt from tax of the state in which the bond was issued.

Interest on U.S. government bonds are fully taxed by the federal government but exempt from state and local taxes.

You must disclose on the client's tax return the amount of tax-exempt income received.

Delaying Paying Tax on Interest

The client can defer reporting interest as income if he or she keeps U.S. savings bonds after their maturity date or has a tax-free exchange of the U.S. bonds for another non-transferable U.S. obligation.

The client can postpone taxes by buying a U.S. Series EE savings bond. The bonds are issued on a discount basis with interest represented by yearly increases in the redemption value. Tax on the interest may be postponed until the maturity date of the bond or when redeemed. Further, taxes may still be postponed by converting the Series EE bond to a Series HH bond at maturity.

Defer interest income by purchasing financial instruments (e.g., certificates of deposit, Treasury bills, U.S. savings bonds) maturing in a later year. Taxes are not due on the interest until the investment matures and the interest income is made available.

Be careful: Interest on zero-coupon bonds is taxable even before the interest is received.

Stock Transactions

A technique for postponing the tax on the gain from a disposition of stock while simultaneously protecting that gain is to sell short. If the client owns appreciated stock, he or she may sell short near the end of the year and then deliver the stock to the dealer and realize the gain after the new year.

Tax Strategies If the Client Has Children

The client can engage in several income-shifting strategies to shift income to his or her children. The client can give the child money to buy U.S. savings bonds or to purchase an annuity from an insurance company. Parents can give appreciating assets (e.g., growth stocks) to their young children. Caution must be exercised since there may be a gift tax consequence if the value of the gift is in excess of $10,000 ($20,000 where the taxpayer and spouse make a joint election). There may be no tax until the asset is sold or the annuity payments start. If the sale takes place after the child is 14, the

capital gain is taxed at the child's *lower* tax rate.

Net unearned income is taxed at the parent's rate if the child is under age 14. However, in general, the first $1,000 of net unearned income is taxed at the child's lower rate. *Recommendation*: The client should structure the child's investments so the child recognizes only $1,000 of net unearned income in a particular year, with the excess deferred until the child is 14.

It pays to shift income to children over 14, such as through a savings account in the child's name, say for a college education.

Interest Deduction

Mortgage interest is deductible only on the client's first and second homes (e.g., vacation home). He or she cannot deduct interest on that portion of a mortgage loan that exceeds the cost of the property including improvements. However, the client can deduct the interest on loan proceeds in excess of the cost (plus improvements) of the property but limited to its fair market value if the funds are used to pay educational or medical expenses. Excess mortgage proceeds not used for medical or education expenses will be treated in a manner similar to personal interest. Points paid to obtain a *new* mortgage are tax deductible. *Beware*: Points incurred on the refinancing of a mortgage are only deductible over the life of the loan unless the proceeds of the refinanced mortgage are used for home improvements.

■ Example

The client paid $100,000 for a home and made capital improvements of $10,000. He or she can borrow up to $110,000 and the interest will be entirely deductible. The client may use the available funds to meet payments on credit card balances and auto loans.

Interest on personal loans (e.g., auto loans, credit cards, and interest on tax deficiencies) is being phased out. Allowable interest deductions for personal loans are

| 1989 | 20% of interest incurred |
| 1990 | 10% of interest incurred |

Tax Strategy: Have the client take out a mortgage loan and use the proceeds to buy personal items (e.g., an auto) so that he or she may get a tax deduction for the interest.

If the client uses credit cards for expenses just prior to year-end, he or she can still claim a current year deduction even though the bill is not paid until next year.

Interest on debt incurred for investment purposes may be partially or totally deductible. However, interest is disallowed on debt used to acquire securities that generate tax-free income.

Self-Employed Client

A home office deduction is limited to the net income arising from the trade or business. The home office deduction in excess of net income may be carried forward to future years.

In general, the client can immediately expense up to $10,000 of equipment acquired in a particular year. The amount that may be expensed must be reduced, dollar for dollar, to the extent that the cost of the equipment exceeds $200,000.

Pension Plan Considerations

There are various types of pension plans. One may set up an Individual Retirement Account (IRA) and/or Keogh plan. There are also employer-sponsored pension and profit-sharing plans. The client is not usually taxed on pension monies until he or she begins to make withdrawals from the plans. If the client withdraws money from a pension plan, he or she can avoid taxes by rolling it over into another qualified pension plan

within 60 days. The client is not taxed until he or she later takes those funds out.

Individual Retirement Account

If an individual is working and not covered by (i.e., not an active participant in) another retirement plan, he or she may deduct an annual IRA contribution of up to $2,000 ($4,000 if both husband and wife are working). The deduction is treated as an adjustment to gross income in arriving at adjusted gross income. If the client is working and is an active participant in another retirement plan, he or she may deduct IRA contributions (up to $2,000) if the adjusted gross income is below $25,000 a year ($40,000 for a married couple filing a joint return). However, if the client is an active participant in another retirement plan, he or she may not make deductible IRA contributions if the adjusted gross income is in excess of $35,000 a year ($50,000 for a joint return). The deduction will be disallowed proportionately as adjusted gross income increases within the phase-out range (i.e., $25,000–$35,000 for single taxpayers and $40,000–$50,000 for married taxpayers filing a joint return). *Warning*: If one spouse is an active participant in another retirement plan, then both spouses will be subject to the phase-out rules.

Even if the IRA contribution is not deductible, the client does not have to pay tax now on the return earned from the IRA investment. The interest earned on the account is tax-deferred until withdrawn. Hopefully, at retirement, the taxable income will be lower and will result in less tax. Even if the lower retirement tax rate is not expected, the tax-deferred aspect is desirable so as to spread taxable income over several years or to lower taxable income in any one particular year.

Keogh Plan

Keogh pension plans are for self-employed individuals who may contribute up to 20% of the net self-employed income (before considering the deduction), up to a maximum of $30,000 per year. The monies earn interest without being currently taxed. A client may have a Keogh even though he or she has an IRA. A client may also have a Keogh plan for his or her self-employed income even though the client belongs to an employer's retirement plan. A client cannot withdraw Keogh funds without penalty until age 59½, and withdrawals must commence by age 70½. Under certain circumstances, one can, with stringent limitations, borrow against the funds in the Keogh.

A distribution from a retirement plan that equals 50% or more of the balance in the plan may be rolled over into an IRA or Keogh without being taxed as current income.

401(k) Plans

The employer may offer a contributory employee pension plan, allowing the employee to voluntarily put in some of his or her current income together with the employer's contribution. The employee's money is deducted from current income.

The 401(k) Plans are salary-reduction plans, permitting the employee to deposit into a retirement account, through the company, part of his or her income. The plan enables the employee to defer taxes on part of his or her salary. The limitation on compensation that can be deferred was $7,000 in 1987. This amount was indexed for inflation using the Consumer Price Index starting in 1988. Money may be withdrawn with minimal or no penalty in the event of financial hardship. Loans are allowed from 401(k) plans but not from IRAs. FICA tax is not deducted on contributions to salary reduction plans.

Real Estate Transactions

The client can avoid *current* tax on a sale of a home if the adjusted sales price of the former residence is used to purchase a new

home. Further, if a homeowner is 55 or older, there is available a one-time exclusion on the first $125,000 of the profit on the sale of the home.

Gifts

Gifts are not included in the taxable income of the recipient. They may be taxed to the donor. Nonliquid holiday gifts or bonuses received from the employer are also tax free. The client can make a gift to another person which is exempt up to $10,000 per year ($20,000 if the gift is from a taxpayer and his or her spouse). *See also* Tax Software.

TAX SHELTER A tax shelter is a tax-favored investment engaged in usually by a partnership or joint venture. Typically, the investment requires a sizable sum of money and high risk.

The tax shelter investment typically results in losses, generally noncash in nature (e.g., depreciation) or arising from accelerated payments that go to the benefit of the individual taxpayer and may be used to offset other income. The result is the lowering of taxable income. Although the Tax Reform Act of 1986 has eliminated mostly all tax shelters, there are some that still exist. An example is a working interest in oil and gas properties. Tax shelters in real estate have been virtually eliminated. It should be noted that deductible real estate losses are capped at $25,000 but are reduced for taxpayers with adjusted gross incomes between $100,000 and $150,000. Losses are not deductible within the $25,000 cap unless the client actively participates in managing the property and owns at least 10% of the property for the entire year. The $25,000 cap is to be reduced by 50% of the amount by which the taxpayer's adjusted gross income is in excess of $100,000. Active participation mandates that the client be involved in the operations on a regular, continuous, and substantial basis. Losses over $25,000 may only be applied against gains

from other passive investments. *Recommendation*: If the client has tax-sheltered losses, he or she should invest in a profitable general partnership or an "S" corporation.

Losses on real estate investments (e.g., Real Estate Investment Trusts) that the client does not manage cannot exceed the amount for which he or she is at risk. "At risk" means that the client cannot deduct a loss that exceeds the adjusted cost basis (cost and improvements) of the property. However, there is a phase in period for the rules related to real estate in that the client can deduct 20% of the losses from passive rental properties in 1989 and 10% in 1990, provided the investment was made before the enactment of the Tax Reform Act of 1986 (10/22/86). Losses from investments made subsequent to enactment are disallowed in the current year completely to the extent that they exceed passive income.

Since the maximum tax rate is 28%, there is much less of an incentive to invest in real estate tax shelters. Income from the sale of tax shelter assets is subject to the ordinary income tax rates.

TAX SOFTWARE In choosing tax software, it is imperative that your microcomputer system and the nature of your practice be considered. Tax packages have to be compatible with the user's hardware and its components. Also, tax software should be acquired that integrates with the present accounting software used in keeping your client's books. Time and cost savings will ensue. Consideration should always be given to the vendor's ability to update the tax packages for recent changes in the tax laws. It is also preferred that the software being tested be analyzed by independent consultants before distribution, such as by a national CPA firm. The practitioner should also thoroughly test the software prior to use to assure that it will do what it is supposed to, given the nature of the tax issue and your practice. For exam-

ple, it must be able to generate accurate forms and schedules as well as minimizing the taxpayer's liability. It should not only prepare the appropriate returns but also provide itemized listings to support the numbers such as 1099s.

Input of data may either be through preprinted forms, interview schedules, or client-prepared information. Obviously, tax software must have good documentation. The manuals should be clear, understandable, and user-friendly. Client data of a recurring nature should be retained in the form of diskette so that it will not have to be input each period. Also, output forms have to meet Internal Revenue Service and local tax agency requirements, and at the same time meet client and practitioner requirements (i.e., compatibility with the practitioner's standard policies).

Amps Tax ™ by Amps Software has many input items along with HELP commands. It generates reports detailing carry backs and carry forwards. It contains, for example, the order that carry overs should be applied and contains the complex logic for minimum tax calculations.

Volts Tax Software Pack™ by Hanover Software is a tax preparation package enabling the user to immediately input data when interviewing the client. If desired, information sheets can also be filled out by clients and then entered.

Micro-Tax™ by Microcomputer Tax Systems has different modules to satisfy different needs (i.e., individual returns, corporate returns, partnership returns).

Tax-planning and compliance software, in general, furnishes the minimum tax that will result under alternative tax options (what-if analysis). There should also be a software feature to override the least tax in the event of extenuating circumstances (i.e., the client is in a new business expecting significantly more profit in future years). The tax-planning result should be clear and under-standable to the client. Typically, it should indicate for each tax strategy recommendation the tax liability that would result along with all major supporting calculations by category.

To meet tax-planning needs, the software must be flexible to derive a fairly accurate predictable conclusion. It should have sufficient integrative ability in terms of prospectively determining the different tax liabilities depending on alternative scenarios, potential tax consequences, ability to change one variable and see its effect on others, and ability to use alternative tax rate schedules depending on changing circumstances. However, excessive variables should be avoided since too much complexity may occur.

Ernst and Whinney's Tax-Plan™ handles planning for carry backs and carry forwards. Tax Plan can handle the calculations of tax liability, refunds, carry backs, and so on.

A-plus Tax™ of Arthur Andersen can accommodate many what-if situations. It can consolidate multiple work and trial balances. It provides many forms and supporting schedules. The Professional Tax Plan Program enables one to project and plan tax alternatives and investments.

The Tax Planning Template™ by Permar and Associates can be used with Lotus 1–2–3 or Symphony.

Of course, the tax practitioner may also develop his or her own tax-planning program with the aid of an electronic spreadsheet (e.g., Lotus 1–2–3).

Tax research assistance may be obtained by accessing on-line data bases like the AICPA's Lexis System™. To use, a keyword or group of words is entered (e.g., accelerated cost recovery system) and relevant literature references are generated. *See also* Tax Planning.

TECHNICAL ANALYSIS In the opinion of technical analysts, market direction and magnitude can be predicted. The stock market is

analyzed via numerous indicators, such as studying economic variables. Companies' stock prices usually move with the market since they react to a host of demand and supply forces. Technical analysts attempt to forecast short-term price changes and then recommend when to buy and sell. A consistent pattern in prices or a relationship between stock price and other market data is searched out. Technical analysts also prepare charts and graphs of market data over time, including prices and volume.

A sample company's stock chart follows:

Figure 1 Sample Company Stock Chart

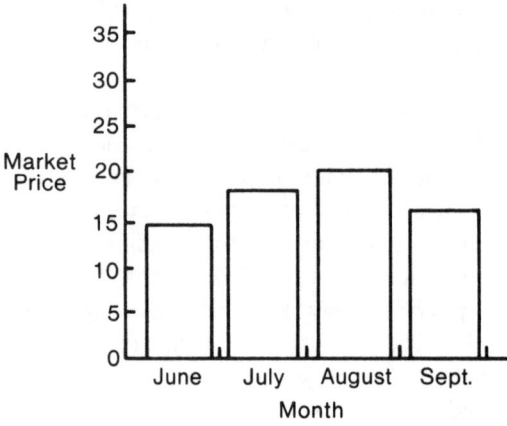

Some terms used in technical analysis follow:

• *Momentum*—the degree of change in stock price or a market index over a specified time period.

• *Accumulation*—an increase in stock price with significant volume that is going from "weak hands" to "strong hands."

• *Distribution*—a decrease in stock price on significant volume that is going from "strong hands" to "weak hands."

• *Resistance phase*—the time interval in which stock prices move with difficulty.

• *Consolidation phase*—the time period when prices move within a narrow band.

• *Bellwether stock*—a stock that typifies market condition (e.g., IBM).

The two major tools used are key indicators and charting.

Key Indicators

There are several indicators reflective of market and stock performance, including trading volume, market breadth, Barron's Confidence Index, mutual fund cash position, short selling, odd-lot theory, and the Index of Bearish Sentiment.

Trading volume—indicative of the health of the market. Price follows volume. For instance, a higher price may be anticipated with increased volume.

Market volume depends on supply/demand and reflects strength or weakness in the market. There is a strong market when volume increases as prices rise. A weak market is indicated when volume increases as prices drop.

When supply exceeds demand, prices decline and vice versa. An examination of demand/supply concentrates on the short run rather than the long run.

Volume is closely tied into the change in stock price. A bullish market occurs if a new high occurs on heavy trading volume. But a new high on light volume is construed as a temporary occurrence. A new low with light volume is deemed significantly better than one with high volume since fewer investors are involved. A high volume with a new low price is a particularly bearish sign.

In the case where prices reach a new high on increased volume, there may exist a potential reversal when current volume is less than the previous rally's volume. A rally with declining volume is questionable and may foreshadow a price reversal. There is a bullish sign when prices rise after a long decline and then reach a level equal to or greater than the prior trough. A bullish sign exists when volume on the secondary trough is less than the first one. It is a bearish sign when price declines on heavy volume; it is indicative of a reversal in trend.

A *selling climax* occurs when there is a price decline for a long time period at an increasing rate coupled with increased volume. Subsequent to the selling climax, it is anticipated that prices will increase, and the low at the climax point is not expected to be violated for a long time. At the culmination of a bear market, a selling climax often takes place.

If prices have been increasing for several months, a low price increase together with high volume is a bearish indicator.

An *upside/downside index* reveals the difference between stock volume advancing and declining. It is typically based on a 10-day or 30-day moving average. Changes in market direction may be reviewed by examining the index. The sustenance of a bull market depends on strong buying.

The *final stage* in a major increase in stock price is referred to as the *exhaustion move*. It takes place when price and volume decline quickly. A trend reversal is indicated.

Muller and Company has a "net volume" service for major listed securities. *Accumulation* occurs when net volume increases. *Distribution* occurs when net volume decreases. When net volume is constant or rises when prices are dropping, there is accumulation under weakness and an expected reversal exists. However, constant or declining net volume with a price increase points to distribution under strength and an expected reversal.

Market breadth—refers to the dispersion of a general price increase or decrease. It may aid as an advance indicator of a major decline or increase in stock prices. It may be useful in evaluating the prime turning points in the market based on stock market cycles. In a bull market, there is a long time period in which particular securities reach their peak slowly, with the number of individual peaks increasing as market averages move to a turning point. In a bear market, the prices of numerous securities decline materially in a short time period. In determining market weakness, the investment analyst examines whether many stocks are declining in price while the averages increase. In predicting the culmination of a bear market, consideration is given to the extent of selling pressure.

With a market breadth indicator, there is a measurement of the activity of a broader group of securities than that contained in a restricted market average (e.g., Dow Jones Industrial Average). The Dow Jones Industrial Average may not be representative of the entire market since emphasis is given to large companies in the weighting process. Market breadth may relate to advances and declines in all securities on an exchange.

A sign that the bull market may be ending is when the Dow Jones Industrial Average is increasing but the number of declining issues continually outnumber the advancing ones. This indicates that conservative investors are purchasing blue chips but do not have confidence in the overall market. An upturn in the market is pointed to when the Dow Jones Industrial Average is declining but advances recurringly exceed declines.

An assumption of breadth analysis is that numerous stocks decline in price for a short period in a bear market. An examination of the change in market breadth may aid in forecasting a sell-off in stock. In the final phase of a bear market, the net advance-decline line decreases by several thousand, Dow Jones Industrials decline several percentage points, and trading volume materially rises.

Market breadth can also be used to evaluate specific stocks. Net advances or declines may be appraised.

■ Example

ABC Company trades 200,000 shares for the day, with 120,000 rising in price, 70,000 decreasing in price, and 10,000 having no change. The net volume difference is therefore 50,000 traded on upticks. An examination should be made of any divergence be-

tween the price trend and the net volume of the company. If there is a divergence, the security analyst may anticipate a reversal in the price trend. Accumulation is evident when there exists declining price and increasing net volume.

Barron's Confidence Index—if the security analyst looks at what bond traders are doing now, he can predict what stock traders will be doing later. A lead time of several months is typically assumed. *Barron's* publishes the index each week. It equals:

$$\frac{\text{Yield on Barron's 10 top-grade corporate bonds}}{\text{Yield on Dow Jones 40 bond average}}$$

■ Example

The Dow Jones yield is 14%, while the Barron's yield is 13%. The Confidence Index equals:

$$\frac{13\%}{14\%} = 92.9\%$$

There is a lower yield in the numerator since it is comprised of higher quality bonds. Less risk generates a lower return. Because top-grade bonds have lower yields than lower grade ones, the index will be less than 100%. Typically, the trading range goes between 80% to 95%. If bond investors are bullish, there is a small difference between the yields on high-grade and low-grade bonds.

In bearish times, bond investors desire to hold top-quality issues. Investors who continually place funds in average or lower quality bonds will demand a higher yield for greater risk. In this case, the index will drop due to a larger denominator. When much confidence exists, investors will be inclined toward lower grade bonds, causing the yield on high-grade bonds to decline while the yield on low-grade bonds will increase.

Mutual fund cash position—by looking at the pattern of mutual funds, the security analyst may formulate the purchasing potential of large institutional investors. The In-

vestment Company Institute publishes the following useful ratio:

$$\frac{\text{Mutual fund cash and cash equivalents}}{\text{Total assets}}$$

A change in the statistic reveals the thinking of institutional portfolio management. The ratio is typically between 5% to 25%. If the cash position is 15% or more of assets, there is a material amount of purchasing power, which may point to a stock market increase. The higher the cash position, the more bullish the sign. When cash is invested, stock prices will rise. A low cash position is a bearish indicator.

Short selling—takes place when investors are of the opinion that stock prices will decline. Technical analysts are interested in the number of shares sold short. They also appraise for the month the ratio of:

$$\frac{\text{Reported short interest position}}{\text{Daily average value}}$$

Short interest refers to the number of stocks sold short at a particular time. A bullish sign is a high ratio, while a bearish sign is a low ratio. Typically, the ratio for all stocks on the New York Stock Exchange is between 1.0 and 1.75. A sign of a market low is when the short-interest ratio is 2.0 or more.

The following of short sales by the security analyst is referred to as a *contrary opinion rule*. Some analysts are of the opinion that an increase in the number of short sellers is a bullish indication. It is believed that short sellers become emotional and overreact. Further, the short seller will subsequently buy the short-sold stock. An increase in short sales and volume will result in additional market supply. Then when there is a drop in the market, short sellers will reacquire their shares, generating increased market demand.

There are some security analysts, however, that are of the opinion that increased

short selling points to a downward and technically weak market that is caused by pessimism. The short seller is anticipating a drop in stock prices.

The Wall Street Journal, for example, publishes the amount of short interest on the New York Stock Exchange and the American Stock Exchange. Through an examination of short interest, the security analyst can predict future market demand and ascertain if the current market is pessimistic or optimistic. A significant short interest in a stock may raise the question of its being overvalued.

Limitations of Short-Interest Information

• Short interest may follow a similar pattern to market price changes.

• Data may not be available for some time after the short sales take place (e.g., 2 weeks).

Odd-lot theory—holds that knowledgeable investors should sell when small traders are buying and buy when they are selling. Statistics on odd-lot volume activity can be found in *The Wall Street Journal* and *Barron's*. *Note*: In the SEC Statistical Bulletin, volume is expressed in dollars.

The odd-lot index is the ratio of odd-lot buys to odd-lot sells. The ratio typically falls between 0.40 and 1.60. Some technical analysts evaluate the ratio of total odd-lot volume to round-lot volume, and the ratio of odd-lot short sales to total odd-lot sales. These statistics may verify conclusions formed through the evaluation of the ratio of odd-lot selling volume to odd-lot buying volume.

As per the theory, the small trader is correct most of the time but does not recognize key market turns. For instance, odd-lot traders properly begin selling some of their stocks in an up market; but as the market continues to improve, the small traders attempt to make a killing by initiating a significant buy position. This will occur just prior to a market drop (e.g., stock market crash on October

19, 1987). Similarly, odd-lotters will initiate selling significantly just before the end of a bear market. The technical analyst concludes that a market turn is eminent in case odd-lot volume rises in an increasing stock market.

Index of Bearish Sentiment—prepared by Investors Intelligence and based on the opposite of investment advisory service recommendations. The index is based on contrary opinion, in that you should do the opposite of that recommended in the reports of investment advisory firms. According to Investors Intelligence, when 42% or more of advisory services are bearish, the market will rise. When 17% or less of the services are bearish, the market will drop.

The index equals:

$$\frac{\text{Number of services that are bearish}}{\text{Total number of services providing an opinion}}$$

A movement approaching 10% indicates the Dow Jones Industrial Average is shortly going to go from bullish to bearish. When the index nears 60%, the Dow Jones Industrial Average is shortly going to move from bearish to bullish. It is expected that the advisory services are trend followers instead of anticipators. Hence, the services' least bearish reports mean the market will decline, and the most bearish reports mean the market will rise.

Option trading activity in calls and puts—by examining the trading activity in options, the investment analyst can forecast market trends. The put-call ratio equals:

$$\frac{\text{Put Volume}}{\text{Call Volume}}$$

The ratio rises when there is greater put activity due to investor pessimism around market bottom. The ratio decreases because of greater call activity arising from optimism around the market peak.

The option buy (initial option transaction reflecting a long position) call percentage equals:

$$\frac{\text{Open buy call transactions}}{\text{Total call volume}}$$

A high ratio indicates investor optimism, while a low ratio infers caution.

Charting

Three basic kinds of charts are line, bar, and point-and-figure. With a line or bar chart, the vertical line indicates price while the horizontal one reflects time. On a line chart, closing prices are connected using a straight line. With a bar chart, vertical lines are at each time period. The high and low prices are indicated at the top and bottom of each bar. There is a horizontal line across the bar indicating the ending price.

Figure 2   Line Chart

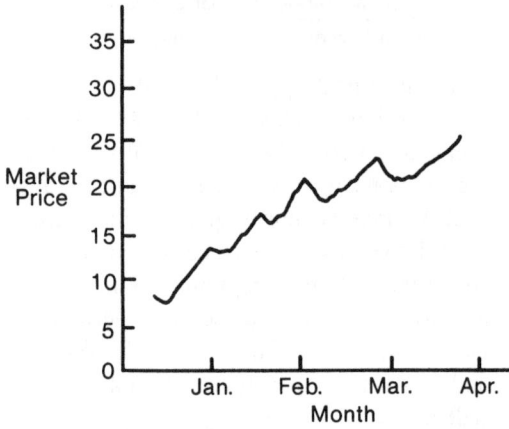

Figure 3   Bar Chart

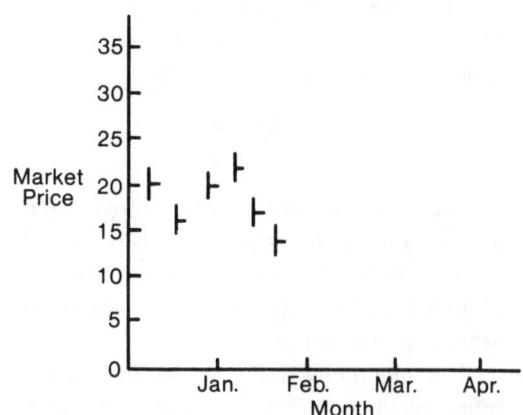

Point-and-figure charts reveal emerging price patterns in the overall market and for particular stocks. Typically, the closing price is only charted. X connotes a price increase while 0 signifies a decrease. The time horizon covered may be one year or less for active securities and more than one year for those that are inactive.

Point-and-figure charts reveal a vertical price scale. Plots on the chart are made when there is a price change by a predetermined amount. There is a depiction of substantial changes and their reversal. Significance of movement depends on the investment analyst's perspective. Closing prices or interday prices may be used in evaluation depending on time constraints. Typically, predetermined figures are 1 or 2 points for medium-priced stocks, 3 or 5 points for high-priced stocks, and ½ point for low-priced stocks. Usually, charts have specific volume information.

Figure 4   Point-and-Figure Chart

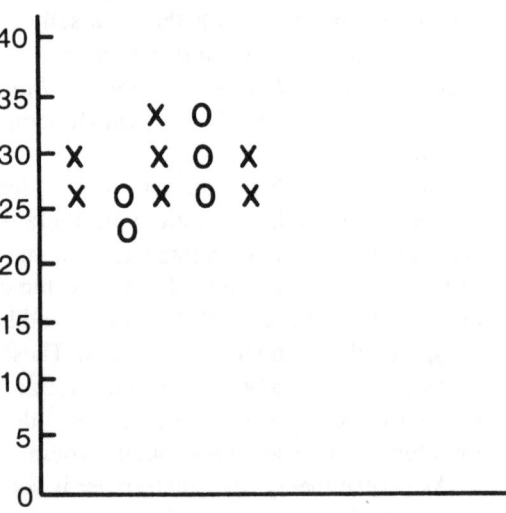

The technical analyst plots prices depicting a trend in a single column, moving to the next column only if a trend in reversal occurs. The price is typically rounded to the nearest dollar and the beginning rounded price is plotted first. No entry is made if

the rounded price remains the same. A different rounded price is plotted. If new prices are in the same direction, they are shown in the same column. A reversal starts a new column.

Information is provided about resistance levels (points). Market direction is indicated by a breakout from the resistance level. The longer the sideways movement prior to a break, the more the stock can rise in price.

The charts help to identify if the market is in a major upturn or downturn and if a reversal in trend is likely. The price that may be accomplished by a particular stock or market average is also revealed. The degree of price swing possible may also be evident.

Moving average—can be looked at to appraise intermediate and long-term stock movements. By comparing the change in current prices to the long-term moving average of prices, a reversal in a major uptrend in price of a specific stock or general market may be revealed. A moving average reveals the direction and degree of change of highly volatile numbers.

It is computed by averaging a portion of the series and then adding the next number to the numbers already averaged, omitting the first number and deriving a new average.

Typically, a 200-day moving average of daily closing prices is used. The average price is usually graphed on stock charts to uncover direction. A "buy" signal exists when the 200-day average line is constant or increases after a decline and when the daily stock price moves up above the average line.

Table 1   Moving Average

Day	Index	Three-Day Moving Total	Three-Day Moving Average
1	115		
2	122		
3	108	345 (Days 1–3)	115 (345/3)
4	111	341 (Days 2–4)	113.7 (341/3)

A "buy" recommendation is indicated when stock price increases above the 200-day line, then proceeds down toward it but not through it, and then goes up again. A "sell" recommendation occurs when the average line is constant or moves down after a rise and when the daily stock price goes down through the average line. A sell is also indicated when stock price is below the average line, then rises toward it, but rather than going through it the price drops down again.

Relative strength analysis—a stock price may be predicted by appraising *relative strength* equal to

$$\frac{\text{Monthly average stock price}}{\text{Monthly average market index (or industry group index)}}$$

Another approach is to determine the ratio of specific industry group price indexes to the total market index.

If a stock or industry group shows better performance than the overall market, the stock is viewed favorably because strong stocks and groups typically become stronger. There may be a differentiation made between relative strength in an upward versus declining market. If a stock does better than the market average in an advance, it may shortly turn around. However, if the stock does better than the rest of the market in a decline, that stock will typically remain strong.

Support and resistance levels—the lower end of a trading range is the support level, whereas the upper end is the resistance level. Support exists when a stock goes to the lower level of trading since new investors may now want to acquire it. In that case, new demand takes place in the market. Resistance occurs when a security approaches the high side of the normal trading range. Investors who bought on a prior high may deem this as an opportunity to sell the stock at a gain. If market price exceeds the resistance point or is below the support point (in a breakout, investors assume the stock is trading in a

new range and that higher or lower trading values may occur.

Figure 5 Support and Resistance

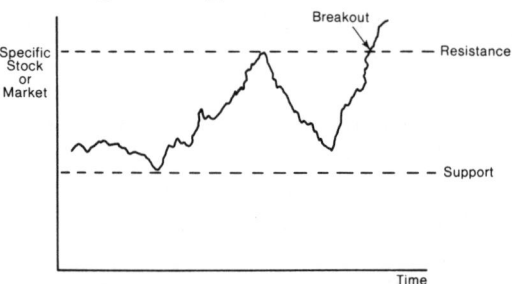

Figure 6 Dow Theory Chart

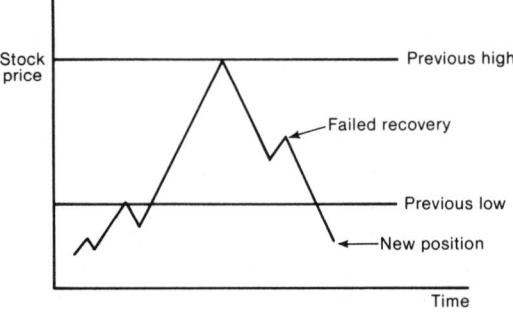

Dow Theory—looks at the movement in the Dow Jones Industrial Average and the Dow Jones Transportation Average. According to the theory, the trend in the overall market is essential because it indicates the end of both bull and bear markets. It is an after-measure with no prediction ability. It does not forecast the timing of a reversal but only confirms that a reversal has taken place.

There are three movements going on simultaneously:

• *Primary trend* is bullish or bearish and typically lasts 28 to 33 months.

• *Secondary trend* runs counter to the primary movement and typically lasts 3 weeks to 3 months.

• Daily fluctuation comprises the first two movements of the market.

Secondary movements and daily variability are important since they show a long-term primary market trend.

A major primary increase in market averages coexists with intermediate secondary downward reactions, eliminating a significant amount of the prior rise. At the end of each reaction, a price recovery takes place falling short of the previous high. If subsequent to an unsuccessful recovery, a downward reaction goes below the low point of the last previous reaction, the market is in a primary downturn.

The rationale for the Dow Theory is that the market is increasing when the cyclical movements of the market averages increase over time and the successive market lows get higher; the market is down when the successive highs and successive lows in the stock market are lower than the prior highs and lows. Some technical analysts believe the movement of the Dow Jones Transportation Average must confirm the action of the Dow Jones Industrial Average to indicate that there is a bull or bear market occurring. Other technical analysts are of the opinion that employing the Dow Jones Industrial Average in this way has lost substantial reliability because these two averages do not typically move in a similar pattern.

TELECOMMUNICATIONS This applies to communications between computers in different locations—usually some distance apart. To communicate properly, the computers must use the same standard transmission procedure (protocols). A good communications program will have several protocol options, permitting communication with different types of equipment. Although it usually occurs over telephone lines, radio waves and satellite are possible.

A protocol translates signals so it is comprehendible by the computer. Popular examples are ASCII, XModem, and Kermit. ANSI is a protocol allowing for the transfer of graphics. Telink is a protocol enabling batch

file transfer. A computer with a communications board (RS–232C Serial Port), telecommunications software, and a modem are necessary for asynchronous communication (a terminal may also be used, preferably a smart terminal). The software is required to communicate between computers within the company, in time-sharing situations, and to access on-line data bases.

Communications packages typically reserve part of the computer memory as a buffer. Financial data can be downloaded from a mainframe, mini, or micro. Information is put in the capture buffer awaiting later disposition (e.g., saving to disk or printing the information out with a printer). Alternatively, one can load financial data from a disk into the buffer for telecommunication transmission (uploading) to another computer in ASCII if asynchronous communication is used (as opposed to synchronous communication). The information-handling functions are the core of the telecommunications program. The software aids the manipulation of information coming over the modem. Some communications packages have the ability for error checking of information received. Examples of popular communications software are Microstuf's Crosstalk™ and Hayes Smartcom II™. Lattice's Side-Talk™ transfers files or receives mail while the computer is being used for other things.

Desirable Features in Telecommunications Programs

- Menus including help
- Selected baud rates
- Telephone directory storage
- Automatic log-on procedures
- Automatic redial
- Selection of file transfer protocols
- Capture function enabling the writing to disk of the contents on the screen

Communications software allows accountants in multiple offices in different geographic areas to communicate with each other, such as by electronic mail, or to transfer files and documents between offices. For example, a report draft might be sent to another practice office to obtain a concurring review and/or further instructions may be sent to participating offices. Information may be transferred from a distant data base to do spreadsheet analysis. Bulletin boards can enable the CPA to share current accounting and auditing information with clients. An example is Deloitte, Haskins and Sells' PC Forum™.

A serial interface hooks up the computer to other remote computers with the use of a modem. Baud refers to the serial information transfer speed. The rate equals the number of bits-per-second (BPS) transmitted. The 300-, 1,200-, and 2,400-BAUD modems are usually used. *Recommendation*: Use a faster modem when typing is at a minimum and uploading or downloading is at a maximum. A good modem is Hayes Smartcom 2400™. Drawbacks to faster modems are poorer transmission on-line quality and increased cost. Typically, higher speed modems are compatible with lower speed modems. *Warning*: Do not purchase one without this downward capability.

Tip: If the typical usage is to access an on-line service where the major purpose is reading information and typing replies or messages, a 300-BPS modem is adequate.

Security modems exist, such as IT&T's Security Modem™. They allow only authorized users to access confidential information. The IT&T modem has three graduated levels of security and stores security codes for users. On receiving the correct password, the modem sends instructions to hang up and makes the call-back on a second line to prevent any risk of interception. With the Cermetek Microelectronics' Security Modem™, there are built-in audit trail capabilities to monitor who is accessing private files.

Most telecommunications to Information Services is asynchronous. However, it is pos-

sible to use an application for synchronous communication between a PC and mainframe. This will allow micros to communicate with corporate mainframes that are synchronous. Hayes Synchronous Interface™ makes synchronous communications software independent of hardware. Note that synchronous is faster and more error free than asynchronous. Synchronous communication permits greater use of micros as a communication to mainframes.

TEMPLATE Many spreadsheet programs have templates, or overlay programs, to go with the specific spreadsheet program used, to enhance productivity. Templates, or overlays, are guides in preparing the spreadsheet and are predetermined files, including formulas and row and column labels for specific applications. In essence, they are worksheet models to solve particular kinds of problems. Templates (models) permit the referencing of cells and formulations of interrelated formulas and functions. They are reused for similar situations. Templates are ideal for worksheets whose structure and formulas are flexible to encompass numerous types of tasks.

After the accountant or financial manager loads in the spreadsheet, the template file comes next. All that remains is to put in the numbers. The variables and formulas are placed in the template. The template in effect has the model in it. Data is input and the outcome obtained. Templates may be "canned" or specially prepared by the practitioner. When templates are canned, template designs are included in the documentation. Templates may be modified to achieve the client's particular requirements.

Remember: Templates can come as separate programs or be part of a sophisticated spreadsheet package. A good supplier of canned templates is 4–5–6 World of California. When internally prepared, the template must be well documented so it is comprehend-

ible by later users, who may have to make desired changes to it. *Note*: Multiple templates can be linked together to formulate more complex applications. They are good for standardized operations. One spreadsheet template may be used to begin or add to another template. For instance, predefined templates are a routine set of calculations that may be copied into other worksheets to derive a broader template.

Take full advantage: Templates may be used for all kinds of accounting and financial applications. For example, templates exist for inventory counts, computing inventory values, depreciation schedules, analyzing revenue and expenses, and financial analysis. CPA+™ is a comprehensive set of accounting templates to perform functions of general ledger, financial statements, accounts payable, accounts receivable, and payroll. As mentioned earlier, 4–5–6 offers a host of templates and add-on utilities. The practitioner may also download templates from numerous sources, such as the Lotus Forum on CompuServe.

In consolidating spreadsheet templates, the practitioner may add rows and columns where each cell must match. *See also* Spreadsheet.

10-K This is the annual filing that public companies have to make with the Securities and Exchange Commission. Included are financial statements and supplementary data. Detailed schedules in support of financial statement figures are given. Some types of disclosures provided are revenue, operating earnings, segmental sales and profit, and general business data. The 10-K is more inclusive than the annual report. *See also* 10-Q.

10-Q This is the quarterly filing of public companies with the Securities and Exchange Commission. Interim financial statements with related footnotes are provided. The statements may or may not be audited. Data

may be for one quarter and/or cumulative from the beginning of the year. Comparisons are provided to prior similar periods. *See also* 10-K.

TERM STRUCTURE OF INTEREST RATES

The term structure of interest rates, also known as a *yield curve*, shows the relationship between length of time to maturity and yields of debt instruments. Other factors such as default risk and tax treatment are held constant. An understanding of this relationship is important to corporate treasurers who must decide whether to borrow by issuing long- or short-term debt. It is also important to investors who must decide whether to buy long- or short-term bonds. Fixed income security analysts should investigate the yield curve carefully in order to make judgments about the direction of interest rates. A yield curve is simply a graphical presentation of the term structure of interest rates. A yield curve may take any number of shapes, that is, a flat (vertical) yield curve (Figure 1-A), a positive (ascending) yield curve (Figure 1-B), an inverted (descending) yield curve (Figure 1-C), and a humped (ascending and then descending) yield curve (Figure 1-D). As to the shape of the yield curve that changes over time, there are three major explanations, or theories, of yield curve patterns. They are the (1) expectation theory; (2) liquidity preference theory; and (3) market segmentation, or "preferred habitat," theory.

Expectation Theory

The expectation theory postulates that the shape of the yield curve reflects investors' expectations of future short-term rates. Given the estimated set of future short-term interest rates, the long-term rate is then established as the geometric average of future interest rates.

■ Example

At the beginning of the first quarter of the year, suppose a 91-day T-bill yields a 6% annualized yield and the expected yield for a 91-day T-bill at the beginning of the second quarter is 6.4%. Under the expectation theory, a 182-day T-bill is equivalent to having successive 91-day T-bills and thus should offer investors the same annualized yield. Therefore, a 182-day T-bill issued at the beginning of the first quarter of the year should yield 6.2%, which is an arithmetic mean (average) of successive 91-day T-bills.

$$1/2\ (6.00 + 6.40) = 1/2\ (12.40) = 6.20\%$$

Mathematically, a current long-term yield is a geometric average of current and successive short-term yields, or

$$(1 + {}_tR_n)^n = (1 + {}_tR_1)(1 + {}_{t+1}r_1)\ .\ .\ .\ (1 + {}_{t+n-1}r_1)$$

where the subscripts to the left of the variable, $t, t + 1, \ldots$, signify the period, and the subscripts to the right, $1, 2, \ldots , n$ signify the maturity of the debt instrument. R is the

Figure 1 Alternative Term-Structure Patterns

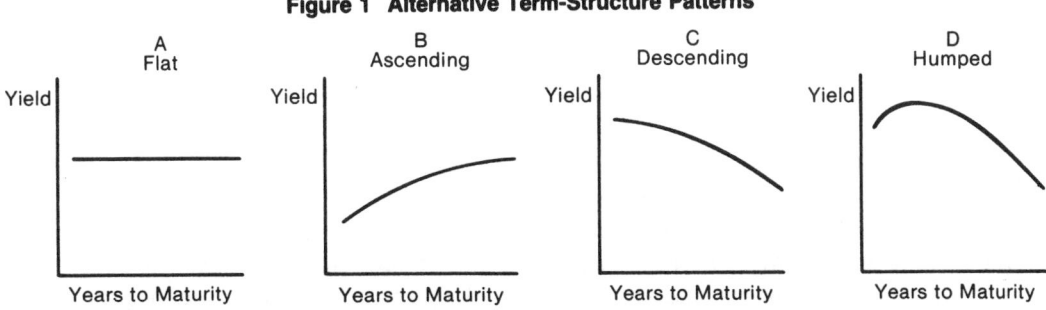

current yield, and r is a future (expected) yield.

A positive (ascending) yield curve (Figure 1-B) implies that investors expect short-term rates to rise, whereas a descending (inverted) yield curve (Figure 1-C) implies that they expect short-term rates to fall.

■ Example

Suppose a current 2-year yield is 9%, or $_tR_2 = 0.09$, and a current 1-year yield is 7%, or $_1R_t = 0.07$.
Then the expected 1-year future yield $_{t+1}r_1$ is 0.11037, or 11.04%:

$$(1 + {_tR_2})^2 = (1 + {_tR_1})(1 + {_{t+1}r_1})$$
$$(1.09)^2 = (1.07)(1 + {_{t+1}r_1})$$
$$1.1881 = (1.07)(1 + {_{t+1}r_1})$$
$$(1 + {_{t+1}r_1}) = 1.1881/1.07$$
$$_{t+1}r_1 = 1.11037 - 1 = 0.11037 = 11.04\%$$

Liquidity Preference Theory

The liquidity preference theory contends that risk-averse investors prefer short-term bonds to long-term bonds because long-term bonds have a greater chance of price variation, that is, carry greater interest rate risk. Accordingly, the theory states that rates on long-term bonds will generally be above the level called for by the expectation theory. Current long-term bonds should include a liquidity premium as additional compensation for assuming *interest rate risk*. This theory is nothing but a modification of the expectation theory.

Mathematically, a current 2-year rate is a geometric average of a current and a future 1-year rate *plus* a liquidity risk premium L:

$$(1 + {_tR_2})^2 = (1 + {_tR_1})(1 + {_{t+1}r_1}) + L$$

Because of a liquidity premium, a yield curve would be upward sloping rather than vertical when future short-term rates are expected to be the same as the current short-term rate.

Market Segmentation (Preferred Habitat) Theory

The market segmentation theory does not recognize expectations and emphasizes the rigidity in loan allocation patterns by lenders. Some lenders (such as banks) are required by law to lend primarily on a short-term basis. Other lenders (such as life insurance companies and pension funds) prefer to operate in the long-term market. Similarly, some borrowers need short-term money (e.g., to build up inventories), while others need long-term money (e.g., to purchase homes). Thus, under this theory, interest rates are determined by supply and demand for loanable funds in each maturity market spectrum.

THEORY OF CAPITAL STRUCTURE The theory of capital structure is closely related to the firm's *cost of capital*. Capital structure is the mix of the long-term sources of funds used by the firm. The primary objective of capital structure decisions is to maximize the market value of the firm through an appropriate mix of long-term sources of funds. This mix, called the optimal capital structure, will minimize the firm's overall cost of capital. However, there are arguments about whether an optimal capital structure actually exists. The arguments center on whether a firm can, in reality, affect its valuation and its cost of capital by varying the mixture of the funds used. There are four different approaches to the theory of capital structure:
1. Net operating income (NOI) approach
2. Net income (NI) approach
3. Traditional approach
4. Modigliani-Miller (MM) approach
All four use the following simplifying assumptions:
1. No income taxes are included.
2. The company's dividend payout is 100%.
3. No transaction costs are incurred.

4. The company has constant earnings before interest and taxes (EBIT).

5. There is a constant operating risk.

Given these assumptions, the company is concerned with the following three rates:

1.
$$k_i = \frac{I}{B}$$

where k_i = yield on the firm's debt (assuming a perpetuity),

   I = annual interest charges,

   B = market value of debt outstanding.

2.
$$k_e = \frac{EAC}{S}$$

where k_e = the firm's required rate of return on equity or cost of common equity (assuming no earnings growth and a 100% dividend payout ratio),

   EAC = earnings available to common stockholders,

   X = market value of stock outstanding.

3.
$$k_o = \frac{EBIT}{V}$$

where k_o = the firm's overall cost of capital (or capitalization rate),

   EBIT = earnings before interest and taxes (or operating earnings),

   $V = B + S$ and is the market value of the firm.

In each of the four approaches to determining capital structure, the concern is with what happens to k_i, k_e, and k_o when the degree of leverage, as denoted by the debt/equity (B/S) ratio, increases.

The Net Operating Income (NOI) Approach

The net operating income approach suggests that the firm's overall cost of capital, k_o, and the value of the firm's market value of

debt and stock outstanding, V, are both independent of the degree to which the company uses leverage. The key assumption with this approach is that k_o, is constant regardless of the degree of leverage.

■ Example 1

Assume that a firm has $6,000 in debt at 5% interest; that the expected level of EBIT is $2,000; and that the firm's cost of capital, k_o, is constant at 10%. The market value (V) of the firm is computed as follows:

$$V = \frac{\text{EBIT}}{k_o} = \frac{\$2,000}{0.10} = \$20,000$$

The cost of external equity (k_e) is computed as follows:

EAC = EBIT − I = $2,000 − ($6,000 × 5%)

$\qquad$ = $2,000 − $300 = $1,700

$\qquad$ S = V − B = $20,000 − $6,000 = $14,000

$$k_e = \frac{\text{EAC}}{\text{S}} = \frac{\$1,700}{\$14,000} = 12.14\%$$

The debt/equity ratio is

$$\frac{B}{S} = \frac{\$6,000}{\$14,000} = 42.86\%$$

Assume now that the firm increases its debt from $6,000 to $10,000 and uses the proceeds to retire $10,000 worth of stock and also that the interest rate on debt remains at 5%.

The value of the firm now is

$$V = \frac{\text{EBIT}}{k_o} = \frac{\$2,000}{0.10} = \$20,000$$

The cost of external equity is

$EAC = EBIT − I$ = $2,000 − ($10,000 × 5%)

$\qquad$ = $2,000 − $500 = $1,500

$\qquad$ S = V − B = $20,000 − $10,000 = $10,000

$$k_o = \frac{\text{EAC}}{\text{S}} = \frac{\$1,500}{\$10,000} = 15\%$$

The debt/equity ratio is now

$$\frac{B}{S} = \frac{\$10,000}{\$10,000} = 100\%$$

Figure 1 Cost of Capital: Net Operating Income Approach

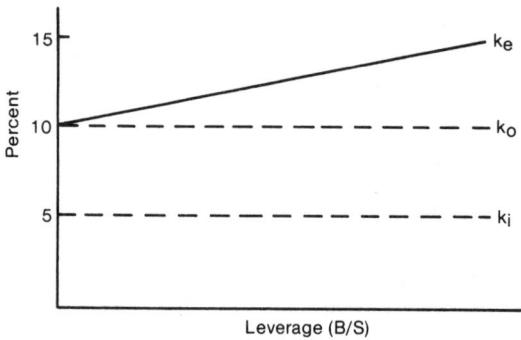

Since the NOI approach assumes that k_o remains constant regardless of changes in leverage, the cost of capital cannot be altered through leverage. Hence, this approach suggests that there is no one optimal capital structure, as evidenced in Figure 1.

The Net Income (NI) Approach

Unlike the net operating income approach, the net income approach suggests that both the overall cost of capital, k_o and the market value of the firm, V, are affected by the firm's use of leverage. The critical assumption with this approach is that k_i and k_e remain unchanged as the debt/equity ratio increases.

■ Example 2

Assume the same data given in Example 1 except that k_e equals 10%. The value of the firm, V, is computed as follows:

$$EAC = EBIT - I = \$2,000$$
$$- (\$6,000 \times 5\%) = \$1,700$$

$$V = S + B = \frac{EAC}{k_e} + B$$

$$= \frac{\$1,700}{0.10} + \$6,000$$

$$= \$17,000 + 6,000 = \$23,000$$

The firm's overall cost of capital is

$$k_o = \frac{EBIT}{V} = \frac{\$2,000}{\$23,000} = 8.7\%$$

The debt/equity ratio in this case is

$$\frac{B}{S} = \frac{\$6,000}{\$17,000} = 35.29\%$$

Now assume as before that the firm increases its debt from \$6,000 to \$10,000, uses the proceeds to retire that amount of stock, and that the interest rate on debt remains at 5%. Then the value of the firm is

$$EAC = EBIT - I = \$2,000$$
$$- (\$10,000 \times 5\%) = \$1,500$$

$$V = S + B = \frac{EAC}{k_e} + B$$

$$= \frac{\$1,500}{0.10} + \$10,000$$

$$= \$15,000 + \$10,000 = \$25,000$$

The overall cost of capital is

$$k_o = \frac{EBIT}{V} = \frac{\$2,000}{\$25,000} = 8\%$$

The debt/equity ratio is now

$$\frac{B}{S} = \frac{\$10,000}{\$15,000} = 66.67\%$$

The NI approach shows that the firm is able to increase its value, V, and lower its cost of capital, k_o, as it increases the degree of leverage. Under this approach, the optimal capital structure is found farthest to the right in Figure 2.

Traditional Approach

The traditional approach to valuation and leverage assumes that there is an optimal capital structure and that the firm can increase its

Figure 2 Cost of Capital: Net Income Approach

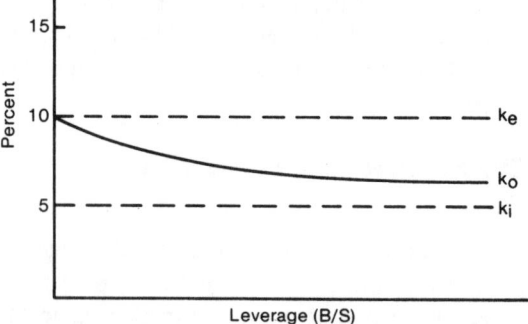

value through leverage. This is a moderate view of the relationship between leverage and valuation that encompasses all the ground between the NOI approach and the NI approach.

■ Example 3

Assume the same data given in Example 1. Assume, however, that k_e is 12%, rather than the 12.14% or 10% with the NOI or NI approaches illustrated previously. The value of the firm is

$$EAC = EBIT - I = \$2,000$$
$$- (\$6,000 \times 5\%) = \$1,700$$

$$V = S + B = \frac{EAC}{k_e} + B$$

$$= \frac{\$1,700}{0.12} + \$6,000$$

$$= \$14,167 + \$6,000 = \$20,167$$

The overall cost of capital is

$$k_o = \frac{EBIT}{V} = \frac{\$2,000}{\$20,167} = 9.9\%$$

The debt/equity ratio is

$$\frac{B}{S} = \frac{\$6,000}{\$14,167} = 42.35\%$$

Assume, as before, that the firm increases its debt from $6,000 to $10,000. Assume further that k_i rises to 6% and k_e at that degree of leverage is 14%. The value of the firm, then, is

$$EAC = EBIT - I$$
$$= \$2,000 - (\$10,000 \times 6\%)$$
$$= \$2,000 - \$600 = \$1,400$$

$$V = S + B = \frac{EAC}{k_e} + B$$

$$= \frac{\$1,400}{0.14} + \$10,000 = \$10,000 + \$10,000$$

$$= \$20,000$$

The overall cost of capital is

$$k_o = \frac{EBIT}{V} = \frac{\$2,000}{\$20,000} = 10.0\%$$

the debt/equity ratio is

$$\frac{B}{S} = \frac{\$10,000}{\$10,000} = 100\%$$

Thus the value of the firm is lower and its cost of capital slightly higher than when the debt is $6,000. This result is due to the increase in k_e and, to a lesser extent, the increase in k_i. These two observations indicate that the optimal capital structure occurs before the debt/equity ratio equals 100%, as shown in Figure 3.

Miller-Modigliani (MM) Position

Miller-Modigliani (MM) advocates that the relationship between leverage and valuation is explained by the NOI approach. More specifically, MM's propositions are summarized following.

1. The market value of the firm and its cost of capital are independent of its capital structure.
2. k_e increases so as to exactly offset the use of cheaper debt money.
3. The cutoff rate for capital budgeting decisions is completely independent of the way in which an investment is financed.

Factors Affecting Capital Structure

Many financial managers believe, in practice, that the following factors influence financial structure:
1. Growth rate of future sales

Figure 3 Capital Structure vs. Cost of Capital

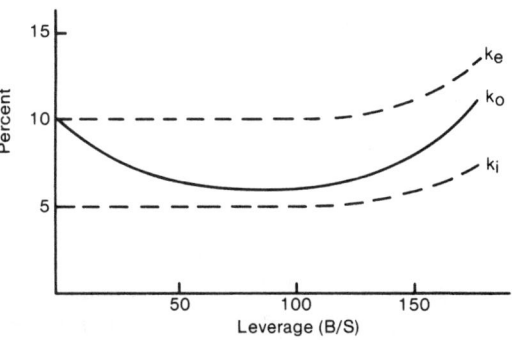

2. Stability of future sales
3. Competitive structures in the industry
4. Asset makeup of the individual firm
5. Attitude of owners and management toward risk
6. Control position of owners and management
7. Lenders' attitude toward the industry and a particular firm

See also Cost of Capital; Leverage.

THINKING PROGRAMS Accountants and financial executives often have to prepare written reports, such as management letters and specialized analyses of operations. Writing skills may be aided with respect to organization, clarity, and communication by using thinking software. "Idea" (outline) programs enable the user to sequence his or her thoughts in proper order. Outline processors allow accountants and financial managers to formulate a logical outline from random ideas entered into the computer. The computer has the information labeled, organized, and structured. A certain set of information can be a major category, while other pieces are identified as subordinates. In effect, we have a "brainstorm" processor for the practitioner to improve the quality of report writing with minimum time and effort.

Living Videotext's "Think Tank"™ breaks a piece of information into component parts by testing them as a headline within the outline. Each headline becomes a separate component. Text material is entered below each headline. The software enables the accountant or financial person to continually check with the main outline to assure the writer is still on the right track. Ashton-Tate's Framework™ idea processor allows for the grouping of several different frames in subsections of an outline.

THREE-WAY ANALYSIS This involves the computation of three variances for factory overhead: *spending*, *efficiency*, and *volume*. The budget variance in the *two-way analysis* is

separated into spending and efficiency variances. When an analysis of historical costs permits the estimation of variable and fixed overhead but the accounting records do not allow the separation of actual overhead costs into their variable and fixed elements, this three-way analysis of overhead variance is used. The three-way analysis provides the following reconciliation between and actual and applied overhead:

Actual	Flexible Budget	Flexible Budget	Applied Costs
Actual factory overhead costs	$(AH \times SR)$ for variable + Budgeted fixed overhead costs	$(SH \times SR)$ for variable + Budgeted fixed overhead costs	$(SH \times SR)$ for variable + Fixed overhead rate × Activity allowed

Three-way	Spending Variance	Efficiency Variance	Volume Variance
Two-way	Budget Variance		Volume Variance

where AH = actual hours used,
SH = standard hours allowed,
SR = standard overhead rate.

See also Responsibility Accounting; Two-Way Analysis; Variance Analysis.

TIME AND BILLING SOFTWARE (T&B) T&B software keeps track of hours incurred—by activity—of different staff for a particular client. Sources of time information are hourly rates, time sheets, practice management reports, and financial reports. At the end of a period, there is a bill prepared based on hours worked and billing rate. In case a flat fee is involved, hourly data aid the accountant or financial consultant in appraising staff productivity. The software also provides for employee expenses chargeable to the client. The hourly rate may be adjusted depending on the client serviced (e.g., higher fees for clients where legal exposure is greater). T&B

programs can give projected fees to current and prospective clients for an engagement.

Software can provide analyses of actual, budget, and variance figures for chargeable and nonchargeable time by type of function performed, and in the aggregate.

Features of Time and Billing Software

- Input controls of the system to appraise reasonableness of data.
- Flexibility in billing and management report format.
- Accommodation of different coding schemes.
- Generation of statements when required for specific clients (e.g., a bill for a particular tax, audit, or management advisory service).
- Ability to update one file while working on another file.
- Recurring billing (e.g., a client is billed monthly for a flat fee).
- Program flexibility such as in allowing itemized transaction billing, automatic billing codes, and free-form billing.
- Past-due reports and statements, including aging.
- Monthly summaries.
- Client past history reports (e.g., billings to client, when payments are made, last time fee was increased).
- Sort capability.
- Productivity report capability such as analyzing the profitability of staff operating at a given pay rate.
- Allowance for multiple-rate billing when the same staff person is charged out at different hourly rates, based on different jobs done or type of client serviced.
- Hours of nonbillable activity by type.
- Percentage of change in time to perform a task compared to the previous year.
- Advance billings.
- Comparison of expected billing rate with actual billing rate.
- Months having the most unbillable time.
- Trend in uncollectible client accounts.

- Evaluation of the reasonableness of the relationship between billable and nonbillable time.
- Extent of time lost in trying to get new business that was not forthcoming.
- Evaluation of overtime. Is it excessive?
- Partial billings and billing adjustments.
- Categorization of clients (e.g., new client, long-term client).
- Classification of fee arrangement (e.g., minimum fee, hourly fee, per-diem rate, flat fee).
- Aged unbilled work-in-process by client.
- Evaluation of client complaint to fee charged.
- Utilization of time percentages. Some packages incorporate a clock/timer that permits you to maintain a running tally of hours spent on a particular work area.
- Output of exception reports, such as jobs that are overdue.

An example of a time and billing package is Systematic Data Marketing Corporation's Time Management and Billing System.™ It prepares invoices and statements, maintains and controls accounts receivable and cash receipts, and generates the following reports and graphs:

- *Client or activity analysis report*—computes the billings of the firm by client or activity.
- *Employee analysis and history report*—measures staff productivity and profitability. It provides employee hours charged, billing, reimbursable expenses, and so on.
- *Billing history graphs*—generates a bar graph comparing billed versus billable amounts for clients.
- *Miscellaneous schedules and reports*—includes aged work-in-process schedules, activity summary, billing worksheet by client, automatic retainer billing, and aged accounts receivable schedules.

UniLink's Professional Time and Billing™ has an unlimited number of clients/ engagements, on-line data verification, work-

in-process aging, finance/late charge capability, progress billing, and user-defined selection fields within the client and engagement files for selective management reporting. It also contains employee, partner, firm service code, and client realization in productivity reports.

TIME VALUE OF MONEY AND ITS APPLICATIONS

The time value of money is a critical consideration in financial and investment decisions. For example, compound interest calculations are needed to determine future sums of money resulting from an investment. Discounting, or the calculation of present value, which is inversely related to compounding, is used to evaluate future cash flow associated with capital budgeting projects. There are plenty of applications of time value of money in accounting and finance. We will discuss the concepts, calculations, and applications of future values and present values.

Future Values—Compounding

A dollar in hand today is worth more than a dollar to be received tomorrow because of the interest it could earn from putting it in a savings account or placing it in an investment account. Compounding interest means that interest earns interest. For the discussion of the concepts of compounding and time value, let us define:

F_n = Future value
  = The amount of money at the end of year n

P = Principal

i = Annual interest rate

n = Number of years

Then:

F_1 = Amount of money at end of year 1
  = Principal and interest = $P + iP = P(1 + i)$

F_2 = Amount of money at end of year 2 = $F_1(1 + i)$
  = $P(1 + i)(1 + i) = P(1 + i)^2$

The future value of an investment compounded annually at rate i for n years is F_n = $P(1 + i)^n$ = $P \cdot FVIF_{i,n}$ where $FVIF_{i,n}$ is the future value interest found in Table 1 in the Appendix.

■ Example 1

Paul Nani places $1,000 in a savings account earning 8% interest compounded annually. How much money will he have in the account at the end of 4 years?

$$F_n = P(1 + i)^n$$
$$F_4 = \$1,000 (1 + 0.08)^4$$

From Table 1 in the Appendix, the $FVIF$ for 4 years at 8% is 1.361. Therefore:

$$F_4 = \$1,000 (1.36) = \$1,361$$

■ Example 2

Steve Hahn invested a large sum of money in the stock of Sigma Corporation. The company paid a $3 dividend per share. The dividend is expected to increase by 20% per year for the next 3 years. He wishes to project the dividends for years 1 through 3.

$$F_n = P(1 + i)^n$$
$$F_1 = \$3(1 + 0.2)^1 = \$3 (1.200) = \$3.60$$
$$F_2 = \$3(1 + 0.2)^2 = \$3 (1.440) = \$4.32$$
$$F_3 = \$3(1 + 0.2)^3 = \$3 (1.728) = \$5.18$$

Intrayear Compounding

Interest is often compounded more frequently than once a year. Banks, for example, compound interest quarterly, daily, and even continuously. If interest is compounded m times a year, then the general formula for solving for the future value becomes

$$F_n = P \left(1 + \frac{i}{m}\right)^{n \cdot m} = P \cdot FVIF_{i/m, n \cdot m}$$

The formula reflects more frequent compounding $(n \cdot m)$ at a smaller interest rate per period (i/m). For example, in the case of semiannual compounding $(m = 2)$, the previous formula becomes

$$F_n = P \left(1 + \frac{i}{2}\right)^{n \cdot 2} = P \cdot FVIF_{i/2, n \cdot 2}$$

As m approaches infinity, the term $(1 + i/m)^{n \cdot m}$ approaches $e^{i \cdot n}$ where e is approximately 2.71828, and F_n becomes

$$F_n = P \cdot e^{i \cdot n}$$

The future value increases as m increases. Thus, continuous compounding results in the maximum possible future value at the end of n periods for a given rate of interest.

■ Example 3

Assume that $P = \$100$, $i = 12\%$, and $n = 3$ years. Then:

Annual compounding ($m = 1$):
$$F_3 = \$100(1 + 0.12)^3 = \$100(1.404)^3 = \$140.49$$

Semiannual compounding ($m = 2$):
$$F_3 = \$100\left(1 + \frac{0.12}{2}\right)^{3.2} = \$100(1 + 0.06)^6$$
$$= \$100(1.419) = \$141.90$$

Quarterly compounding ($m = 4$):
$$F_3 = \$100\left(1 + \frac{0.12}{4}\right)^{3.4} = \$100(1 + 0.3)^{12}$$
$$= \$100(1.426) = \$142.60$$

Monthly compounding ($m = 12$):
$$F_3 = \$100\left(1 + \frac{0.12}{12}\right)^{3.12}$$
$$= \$100(1 + 0.01)^{36} = \$100(1.431)$$
$$= \$143.10$$

Continuous compounding ($e^{i \cdot n}$):
$$F_3 = \$100 \cdot e^{(0.12 \cdot 3)}$$
$$= \$100(2.71828)^{0.36}$$
$$= \$100(1.433) = \$143.30$$

Future Value of an Annuity

An annuity is defined as a series of payments (or receipts) of a fixed amount for a specified number of periods. Each payment is assumed to occur at the end of the period. The future value of an annuity is a compound annuity that involves depositing or investing an equal sum of money at the end of each year for a certain number of years and allowing it to grow.

Let: S_n = the future value on an n-year annuity
     A = the amount of an annuity

Then we can write:

$$S_n = A(1 + i)^{n-1} + A(1 + i)^{n-2} + \ldots + A(1 + i)^0$$
$$= A[(i + i)^{n-1} + (1 + i)^{n-2} + \ldots + (1 + i)^0]$$
$$= A \cdot \sum_{t=0}^{n-1} (1 + i)^t$$
$$= A \frac{[(1 + i)^n - 1]}{i} = A \cdot FVIFA_{i,n}$$

where $FVIFA_{i,n}$ represents the future value interest factor for an n-year annuity compounded at i percent and can be found in Table 2 in the Appendix.

■ Example 4

Lisa Clarke wishes to determine the sum of money she will have in her savings account at the end of 6 years by depositing \$1,000 at the end of each year for the next 6 years. The annual interest rate is 8%. The $FVIFA_{8\%, 6 \text{ years}}$ is given in Table 2 in the Appendix as 7.336. Therefore:

$$S6 = \$1,000 \, (FVIFA_{8,6}) = \$1,000 \, (7.336) = \$7,336$$

Present Value—Discounting

Present value is the present worth of future sums of money. The process of calculating present values, or discounting, is actually the opposite of finding the compounded future value. In connection with present value calculations, the interest rate i is called the discount rate. Recall that

$$F_n = P(1 + i)^n$$

Therefore:

$$P = \frac{F_n}{(1 + i)^n} = F_n \left[\frac{1}{(1 + i)^n}\right] = F_n \cdot PVIF_{i,n}$$

where $PVIF_{i,n}$ represents the present value interest factor for \$1 and is given in Table 3 in the Appendix.

■ Example 5

John Jaffe has been given an opportunity to receive \$20,000 6 years from now. If he can earn 10% on his investments, what is the most he should pay for this opportunity?

To answer this question, one must compute the present value of $20,000 to be received 6 years from now at a 10% rate of discount. F_6 is $20,000, i is 10%, which equals 0.1, and n is 6 years. $PVIF_{10,6}$ from Table 3 is 0.565.

$$P = \$2,000 \left[\frac{1}{(1 + 0.1)^6} \right]$$
$$= \$20,000(PVIF_{10,6})$$
$$= \$20,000(0.565) = \$11,300$$

This means that John Jaffe, who can earn 10% on his investment, could be indifferent to the choice between receiving $11,300 now or $20,000 6 years from now since the amounts are time equivalent. In other words, he could invest $11,300 today at 10% and have $20,000 in 6 years.

Present Value of Mixed Streams of Cash Flows

The present value of a series of mixed payments (or receipts) is the sum of the present value of each individual payment. We know that the present value of each individual payment is the payment times the appropriate $PVIF$.

■ Example 6

Bonnie Brown has been offered an opportunity to receive the following mixed stream of revenue over the next 3 years:

Year	Revenue
1	$1,000
2	2,000
3	500

If she must earn a minimum of 6% on her investment, what is the most she should pay today? The present value of this series of mixed streams of revenue follows:

Year	Revenue ($)	× PVIF	= Present Value
1	1,000	0.943	$ 943
2	2,000	0.890	1,780
3	500	0.840	420
			$3,143

Present Value of an Annuity

Interest received from bonds, pension funds, and insurance obligations all involve annuities. To compare these financial instruments, we need to know the present value of each. The present value of an annuity (p_n) can be found by using the following equation:

$$P_n = A \cdot \frac{1}{(1 + i)^1} + A \cdot \frac{1}{(1 + i)^2} + \ldots + A \cdot \frac{1}{(1 + i)^n}$$
$$= A \left[\frac{1}{(1 + i)^1} + \frac{1}{(1 + i)^2} + \ldots + \frac{1}{(1 + i)^n} \right]$$
$$= A \cdot \sum_{t=1}^{n} \frac{1}{(1 + i)^t}$$
$$= A \cdot \frac{\left[1 - \frac{1}{(1 + i)^n} \right]}{i} = A \cdot PVIFA_{i,n}$$

where $PVIFA_{i,n}$ represents the appropriate value for the present value interest factor for a $1 annuity discounted at i percent for n years, which is found in Table 4 in the Appendix.

■ Example 7

Assume that the revenues in Example 6 form an annuity of $1,000 for 3 years. Then the present value is

$$P_n = A \cdot PVIFA_{i,n}$$
$$P_3 = \$1,000 \ (PVIFA_{6,3}) = \$1,000 \ (2.673) = \$2,673$$

Perpetuities

Some annuities go on forever. Such annuities are called perpetuities. An example of a perpetuity is preferred stock, which yields a constant dollar dividend indefinitely. The present value of a perpetuity is found as follows:

$$\text{Present value of a perpetuity} = \frac{\text{Receipt}}{\text{Discount rate}} = \frac{A}{i}$$

■ Example 8

Assume that a perpetual bond has an $80-per-year interest payment and that the discount rate is 10%. The present value of this perpetuity is

$$P = \frac{A}{i} = \frac{\$80}{0.10} = \$800$$

Applications of Future Values and Present Values

Future and present values have numerous applications in accounting, finance, and investments, which will be discussed throughout the Encyclopedia. Five of these applications follow.

Deposits to Accumulate a Future Sum (or Sinking Fund)

An individual might wish to find the annual deposit (or payment) that is necessary to accumulate a future sum. To find this future amount (or sinking fund) we can use the formula for finding the future value of an annuity.

$$S_n = A \cdot FVIFA_{i,n}$$

Solving for A, we obtain:

$$\text{Sinking fund amount} = A = \frac{S_n}{FVIFA_{i,n}}$$

■ Example 9

Karen Black wishes to determine the equal annual end-of-year deposits required to accumulate $5,000 at the end of 5 years, when her son enters college. The interest rate is 10%. The annual deposit is

$$S_5 = \$5,000$$
$$FVIFA_{10,5} = 6.105 \quad \text{(from Table 2)}$$
$$A = \frac{5,000}{6.105} = \$819$$

In other words, if she deposits $819 at the end of each year for 5 years at 10% interest, she will have accumulated $5,000 at the end of the fifth year.

Amortized Loans

If a loan is to be repaid in equal periodic amounts, it is said to be an amortized loan. Examples include auto loans, mortgage

loans, and most commercial loans. The periodic payment can easily be computed as follows:

$$P_n = A \cdot PVIFA_{i,n}$$

Solving for A, we obtain:

$$\text{Amount of loan} = A = \frac{P_n}{PVIFA_{i,n}}$$

■ Example 10

Kim Naomi has a 40-month auto loan of $5,000 at a 12% annual interest rate. He wants to find out the monthly loan payment amount.

$$i = 12\%/12 \text{ months} = 1\%$$
$$P_{40} = \$5,000$$
$$PVIFA_{1,40} = 32.835 \quad \text{(from Table 4)}$$

Therefore:

$$A = \frac{\$5,000}{32.835} = \$152.28$$

So, to repay the principal and interest on a $5,000, 12%, 40-month loan, Kim Naomi has to pay $152.28 a month for the next 40 months.

■ Example 11

Assume that a firm borrows $2,000 to be repaid in three equal installments at the end of each of the next 3 years. The bank wants 12% interest. The amount of each payment is

$$P_3 = \$2,000$$
$$PVIFA_{12,3} = 2.402$$

Therefore:

$$A = \frac{\$2,000}{2.402} = \$832.64$$

Each loan payment consists partly of interest and partly of principal. The breakdown is often displayed in a loan amortization schedule. The interest component is larger in the first period and subsequently declines, whereas the principal portion is smallest in

the first period and increases thereafter, as shown in the following example.

■ Example 12

Using the same data as in Example 11, we set up the following amortization schedule:

Year	Payment	Interest	Repayment of Principal	Remaining Balance
1	$832.64	$240.00[a]	$592.64	$1,407.36
2	832.64	168.88	663.76	743.60
3	832.83[b]	89.23	743.60[c]	

[a] Interest is computed by multiplying the loan balance at the beginning of the year by the interest rate. Therefore, interest in year 1 is $2,000(0.12) = $240; in year 2 interest is $1,407.36(0.12) = $168.88; and in year 3 interest is $743.60(0.12) = $89.23. All figures are rounded.

[b] Last payment is adjusted upward

[c] Not exact because of accumulated rounding errors

Rates of Growth

In finance, it is necessary to calculate the compound annual interest rate, or rate of growth, associated with a stream of earnings.

■ Example 13

Assume that the Geico Company has earnings per share of $2.50 in 19X1, and 10 years later the earnings per share has increased to $3.70. The compound annual rate of growth of the earnings per share can be computed as follows:

$$F_n = P \cdot FVIF_{i,n}$$

Solving this for FVIF, we obtain

$$FVIF_{i,n} = \frac{F_n}{P}$$

$$FVIF_{i,10} = \frac{\$3.70}{\$2.50} = \$1.48$$

From Table 3 an *FVIF* of 1.48 at 10 years is at $i = 4\%$. The compound annual rate of growth is therefore 4%.

Bond Values

Bonds call for the payment of a specific amount of interest for a stated number of years and the repayment of the face value

at the bond's maturity. Thus a bond represents an annuity plus a lump sum. Its value is found as the present value of this payment stream. The interest is usually paid semiannually.

$$V = \sum_{t=1}^{n} \frac{I}{(1 + r)^t} + \frac{M}{(1 + r)^n}$$

$$= I(PVIFA_{r,n}) + M(PVIF_{r,n})$$

where $I =$ interest payment per period,

$M =$ par value, or maturity value, usually $1,000,

$r =$ investor's required rate of return,

$n =$ number of periods.

■ Example 14

Assume there is a 10-year bond with a 10% coupon, paying interest semiannually and having a face value of $1,000. Since interest is paid semiannually, the number of periods involved is 20 and the semiannual cash inflow is $100/2 = $50.

Assume that investors have a required rate of return of 12% for this type of bond. Then the present value (V) of this bond is

$$V = \$50(PVIFA_{6,20}) + \$1,000 (PVIF_{6,20})$$
$$= \$50(11.470) = \$1,000(0.312)$$
$$= \$573.50 + \$312.00 = \$885.50$$

Note that the required rate of return (12%) is higher than the coupon rate of interest (10%), and so the bond value (or the price investors are willing to pay for this particular bond) is less than its $1,000 face value.

TOTAL PROJECT APPROACH Total project approach (or comparative statement approach) is an approach that looks at all the items of revenue and cost data under two alternatives and compares the net income or contribution margin results. Other approaches are the *incremental analysis* and the *opportunity cost approach*.

■ Example

Assume the SBC Company is planning to expand its productive capacity. The plans

consist of purchasing a new machine for $50,000 and disposing of the old machine without receiving anything. The new machine has a 5-year life. The old machine has a 5-year remaining life and a book value of $12,500. The new machine will reduce variable operating costs from $35,000 per year to $20,000 per year. Annual sales and other operating costs are shown below.

	Present Machine	New Machine
Sales	$80,000	$80,000
Variable costs	35,000	20,000
Fixed costs:		
Depreciation		
(straight-line)	2,500*	10,000
Insurance, taxes,		
etc.	4,000	4,000

* Note that the depreciation expense of $2,500 of the old machine is irrelevant because it is a *sunk* cost.

The total project approach results in the following:

	Present Machine	New Machine	Increment (or difference)
Sales	$80,000	$80,000	—
Less: Variable costs	35,000	20,000	$(15,000)
Contribution margin	$45,000	$60,000	$ 15,000
Less: Fixed costs			
Depreciation	—	10,000	10,000
Other	4,000	4,000	—
Net income	$41,000	$46,000	$ 5,000

The schedule for the total project approach shows an increase in profit of $5,000 with the purchase of the new machine. *See also* Incremental Analysis; Opportunity Cost Approach.

TRADING ON EQUITY This, also known as *financial leverage*, means the use of borrowed funds in the capital structure of a firm. Trading *profitably* on the equity, also known as *positive* (*favorable*) *financial leverage*, means that the borrowed funds generate a higher rate of return than the interest rate paid for the use of the funds. The excess accrues to the benefit of the owners because it magnifies, or increases, their earnings. *See also* Financial Leverage; Leverage.

TRANSACTION TEST A transaction test is an audit procedure involving the examination of specific transactions and related documentation. It is an element of the testing process to determine the degree to which the CPA may rely on internal controls to uncover errors. Evidence is obtained to assist in rendering an audit opinion with respect to the fairness of financial statement presentation. Test of transactions include the substantiation of dollar amounts such as through recalculations, and tracing transactions from initiation to culmination in the financial statements. But it should be noted that transaction tests are of significantly less scope than analytical review. The procedure involved is to select a specified number of specific transactions for testing in order to ascertain whether proper controls exist. The ensuing error rate is computed. If there is an acceptable error rate, reliance can be placed on the client's recording and posting of transactions. Transaction tests provide the auditor with guidance in deriving the scope of the audit needed. Test of transactions is significantly used in substantive testing as well as in the area of internal control. *See also* Compliance Test; Substantive Test.

TRANSFER PRICING Goods and services are often exchanged between various divisions of a decentralized organization. A major goal of transfer pricing is to enable divisions that exchange goods or services to act as independent businesses. The question then is, What monetary values should be assigned to these exchanges or transfers? Market price? Some kind of cost? Some version of either? Unfortunately, there is no single transfer price that will please everybody—that is, top management, the selling division, and the buying division. Various transfer pricing schemes are available, such as *market price*, *cost-based price*, or *negotiated price*.

The choice of a transfer pricing policy (i.e., which type of transfer price to use) is normally decided by top management. The

decision will typically include consideration of the following:

• *Goal congruence*—Will the transfer price promote the goals of the company as a whole? Will it harmonize the divisional goals with organizational goals?

• *Performance evaluation*—Will the selling division receive enough credit for its transfer of goods and services to the buying division? Will the transfer price hurt the performance of the selling division?

• *Autonomy*—Will the transfer price preserve autonomy, the freedom of the selling and buying division managers to operate their divisions as decentralized entities?

• Other factors such as minimization of tariffs and income taxes and observance of legal restrictions.

Transfer prices can be based on
• Market price
• Cost-based price—variable or full cost
• Negotiated price
• General formula, which is usually the sum of variable costs per unit and opportunity costs for the company as a whole (lost revenue per unit on outside sales)

Market Price

Market price is the best transfer price, in the sense that it will maximize the profits of the company as a whole if it meets the following two conditions: (1) there exists a competitive market price and (2) divisions are independent of each other. If either one of these conditions is violated, market price will not lead to an optimal economic decision for the company.

Cost-Based Price—Variable or Full Cost

Cost-based transfer price, another alternative transfer pricing scheme, is easy to understand and convenient to use. But there are some disadvantages, including
• Inefficiencies of selling divisions are passed on to the buying divisions with little

incentive to control costs. The use of standard costs is recommended in such cases.

• The cost-based method treats the divisions as cost centers rather than profit or investment centers. Therefore, measures such as ROI and RI cannot be used for evaluation purposes.

The variable cost-based transfer price has an advantage over the full cost method because in the short run it may tend to ensure the best utilization of the overall company's resources. The reason is that, in the short run, fixed costs do not change. Any use of facilities, without incurrence of additional fixed costs, will increase the company's overall profits.

Negotiated Price

A negotiated price is generally used when there is no clear outside market. A negotiated price is a price agreed upon between the buying and selling divisions that reflects unusual or mitigating circumstances. This method is widely used when no intermediate market price exists for the product transferred and the selling division is assured of a normal profit.

■ Example 1

Company X just purchased a small company that specializes in the manufacture of part No. 323. Company X is a decentralized organization and will treat the newly acquired company as an autonomous division called Division B with full profit responsibility. Division B's fixed costs total $30,000 per month, and variable costs per unit are $18. Division B's operating capacity is 5,000 units. The selling price per unit is $30. Division A of Company X is currently purchasing 2,500 units of Part No. 323 per month from an outside supplier at $29 per unit, which represents the normal $30 price less a quantity discount. Top management of the company must decide what transfer price should be used.

Top management may consider the following alternative prices:

(a) $30 market price
(b) $29—the price that Division A is currently paying to the outside supplier
(c) $23.50 negotiated price, which is $18 variable cost plus ½ of the benefits of an internal transfer [($29 − $18) × ½]
(d) $24 full cost, which is $18 variable cost plus $6 ($30,000/5,000 units) fixed cost per unit
(e) $18 variable cost

We will discuss each of these prices:

(a) $30 would not be an appropriate transfer price. Division B cannot charge a price more than the price Division A is paying now ($29).
(b) $29 would be an appropriate transfer price if top management wants to treat the divisions as autonomous investment centers. This price would cause all of the benefits of internal transfers to accrue to the selling division, with the buying division's position remaining unchanged.
(c) $23.50 would be an appropriate transfer price if top management wants to treat the divisions as investment centers but wants to share the benefits of an internal transfer equally between them, as follows.

Variable costs of Division B	$18.00
½ of the difference between the variable costs of Division B and the price Division A is paying ($29 − $18) × ½	5.50
Transfer price	$23.50

Note that $23.50 is just one example of a negotiated transfer price. The exact price depends on how the benefits are divided.

(d) $24 [$24 = $18 + ($30,000/5,000 units)] would be an appropriate transfer price if top management treats divisions like cost centers with no profit responsibility.

All benefits from both divisions will accrue to the buying division. This will maximize the profits of the company as a whole but affect adversely the performance of the selling division. Another disadvantage of this cost-based approach is that inefficiencies (if any) of the selling division are being passed on to the buying division.

(e) $18 would be an appropriate transfer price for guiding top management in deciding whether transfers between the two divisions should take place. Since $18 is less than the outside purchase price of the buying division and the selling division has excess capacity, the transfer should take place because it will maximize the profits of the company as a whole. However, if $18 is used as a transfer price, then all of the benefits of the internal transfer accrue to the buying division and it will hurt the performance of the selling division.

General Formula

It is not easy to find a cure-all answer to the transfer pricing problem, since the three problems of goal congruence, performance evaluation, and autonomy must all be considered simultaneously. It is generally agreed, however, that some form of competitive market price is the best approach to the transfer pricing problem. The following formula would be helpful in this effort:

Transfer price = Variable costs per unit
+ Opportunity costs per unit
for the company as a whole

Opportunity costs are defined here as net revenue foregone by the company as a whole if the goods and services are transferred internally. The reasoning behind this formula is that the selling division should be allowed to recover its variable costs plus opportunity cost (i.e., revenue that it could have made

Figure 1

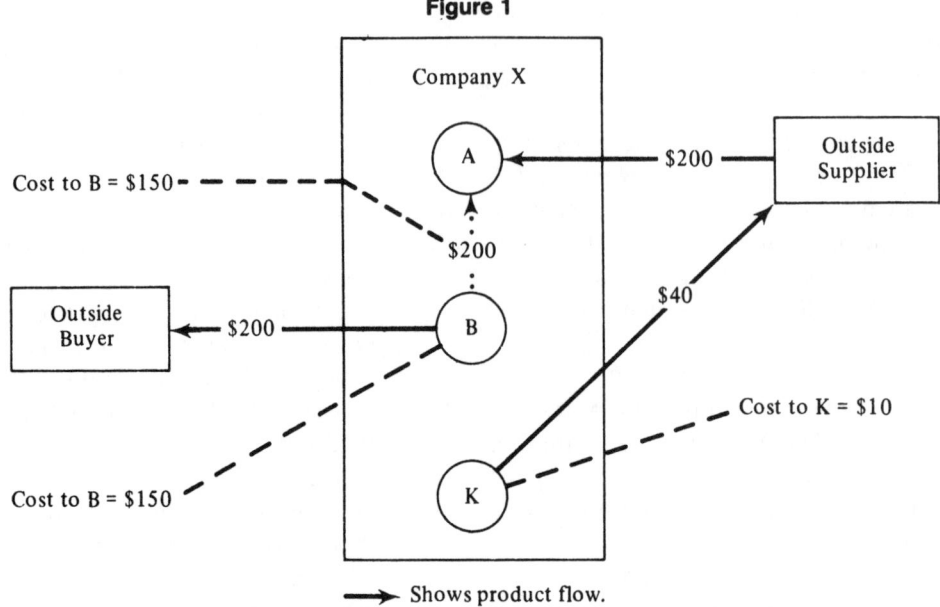

Company X

Cost to B = $150

A

$200

Outside
Supplier

$200

Outside
Buyer

$200

B

$40

Cost to K = $10

Cost to B = $150

K

→ Shows product flow.

by selling to an outsider) of the transfer. The selling department should not have to suffer lost income by selling within the company.

■ Example 2

Company X has more than 50 divisions, including A, B, and K. Division A, the buying division, wants to buy a component for its final product and has an option to buy from Division B or from an outside supplier at the market price of $200. If Division A buys from the outside supplier, it will in turn buy selected raw materials from Division K for $40. This will increase its contribution to overall company profits by $30 ($40 revenue minus $10 variable costs). Division B, on the other hand, can sell its component to Division A or to an outside buyer at the same price. Division B, working at full capacity, incurs variable costs of $150. Will the use of $200 as a transfer price lead to optimal decisions for the company as a whole? Figure 1 depicts the situation.

The optimal decision from the viewpoint of Company X as a whole can be looked at in terms of its net cash outflow, as follows:

	Division A's Action	
	Buy From B	Buy From Outsider
Outflow to the company as a whole	$(150)	$(200)
Cash inflows	—	to B: $50($200 − $150)
		to K: $30($ 40 − $ 10)
Net cash outflow to the company as a whole	$(150)	$(120)

To maximize the profits of Company X, Division A should buy from an outside supplier. The transfer price that would force Division A to buy outside should be the sum of variable costs and opportunity costs, that is,

$$150 + $50 + $30 = $230 \text{ per unit}$$

In other words, if Division B charges $230 to Division A, Division A will definitely buy from the outside source for $200.

TRANSFER OF RECEIVABLES AND RECOURSE

According to FASB 77, a sale is recorded for the transfer of receivables with recourse

if *all* of the following criteria are satisfied:

1. The transferor gives up control of the future economic benefits applicable to the receivables (e.g., repurchase right).

2. The liability of the transferor under the recourse provisions is estimable.

3. The transferee cannot require the transferor to repurchase the receivables unless there is a recourse provision in the contract.

When the transfer is treated as a sale, gain or loss is recognized for the difference between the selling price and the net receivables. The selling price includes normal servicing fees of the transferor and appropriate probable adjustments (e.g., debtor's failure to pay on time, effects of prepayment, and defects in the transferred receivable). Net receivables equal gross receivables plus finance and service charges minus unearned finance and service charges.

In case the selling price varies during the term of the receivables due to a variable interest rate provision, the selling price is estimated with the use of an appropriate "going market interest rate" at the transfer date. Later changes in the rate cause a change in estimated selling price, not in interest income or interest expense.

If one of the aforementioned criteria is not satisfied, a liability is recognized for the proceeds received.

Footnote disclosures include

• Amount received by transferor

• Balance of the receivables at the balance sheet date

TREASURY STOCK Treasury stock is issued shares that have been bought back by the company. The two methods to account for treasury stock are

1. *Cost method*—Treasury stock is recorded at the cost to purchase it. If treasury stock is later sold above cost, the entry is

> Cash
> > Treasury Stock
> > Paid-in-Capital

If treasury stock was sold instead at below cost, the entry is

Cash
Paid-in-Capital—Treasury Stock (up to amount available)
Retained Earnings (if paid-in-capital is unavailable)
> Treasury Stock

If treasury stock is donated, only a memo entry is needed. When the treasury shares are later sold, the entry based on the market price at that time is

> Cash
> > Paid-in-Capital—Donation

An appropriation of retained earnings equal to the cost of treasury stock on hand is required.

Treasury stock is shown as a reduction from total stockholders' equity.

2. *Par value method*—Treasury stock is recorded at its par value when bought. If treasury stock is purchased at more than par value, the entry is

> Treasury Stock—Par Value
> Paid-in-Capital—original premium per share
> Retained Earnings—if necessary
> > Cash

If treasury stock is purchased at less than par value, the entry is

> Treasury Stock—Par Value
> > Cash
> > Paid-in-Capital

Upon sale of the treasury stock above par value, the entry is

> Cash
> > Treasury Stock
> > Paid-in-Capital

Upon sale of the treasury stock at less than par value, the entry is

Cash
Paid-in-Capital (amount available)
Retained Earnings (if paid-in-capital is insufficient)
Treasury Stock

An appropriation of retained earnings equal to the cost of the treasury stock on hand is required. Treasury stock is shown as a contra account to the common stock it applies to under the capital stock section of stockholders' equity.

TREASURY STOCK METHOD This method is used to compute the common stock equivalency of options and warrants in the earnings per share statistic. *See also* Earnings per Share.

TREND ANALYSIS A common method for forecasting sales or earnings is the use of trend analysis, which is a special case of regression analysis. This method involves a regression whereby a trend line is fitted to a time series of data. The trend line equation can be shown as

$$y = a + bx$$

The formulas for the coefficients a and b are essentially the same as the ones for simple regression. However, for regression purposes, a time period can be given a number so that $\Sigma x = 0$. When there is an odd number of periods, the period in the middle is assigned a zero value. If there is an even number, then -1 and $+1$ are assigned the two periods in the middle, so that again $\Sigma x = 0$.

With $\Sigma x = 0$, the formula for b and a reduces to the following:

$$b = \frac{n\Sigma xy}{n\Sigma x^2}$$

$$a = \Sigma y/n$$

■ **Example**

Case 1 (odd number)
19X1 19X2 19X3 19X4 19X5
$x = $ -2 -1 0 $+1$ $+2$

Case 2 (even number)
19X1 19X2 19X3 19X4 19X5 19X6
$x = $ -3 -2 -1 $+1$ $+2$ $+3$

In each case, $\Sigma t = 0$.

■ **Example**

Consider TDK Company whose historical earnings per share (EPS) follow:

Year	EPS
19X1	$1.00
19X2	1.20
19X3	1.30
19X4	1.60
19X5	1.70

Since the company has f years' data, which is an odd number, the year in the middle is assigned a zero value.

Year	x	EPS(y)	xy	x²
19X1	-2	$1.00	-2.00	4
19X2	-1	1.20	-1.20	1
19X3	0	1.30	0	0
19X4	$+1$	1.60	1.60	1
19X5	$+2$	1.70	3.40	4
	0	$6.80	1.80	10

$$b = \frac{(5)(1.80)}{(5)(10)} = \frac{9}{50} = \$0.18$$

$$a = \frac{\$6.80}{5} = \$1.36$$

Therefore, the estimated trend equation is

$$\hat{y} = \$1.36 + \$0.18x$$

where $\hat{y} = $ estimated EPS,
    $x = $ year index value.

To project 19X6 sales, we assign $+3$ to the x value for the year 19X6. Thus:

$$\hat{y} = \$1.36 + \$0.18(+3)$$
$$= \$1.36 + \$0.54$$
$$= \$1.90$$

See also Regression Analysis.

TREND (HORIZONTAL) ANALYSIS This looks at the trend in accounts over the years and aids in identifying areas of wide divergence

mandating further attention. Horizontal analysis may also be presented by showing trends relative to a base year.

■ Example

X Company's revenue in 19X1 was $200,000 and in 19X2 was $250,000. The percentage increase equals

$$\frac{\text{Change}}{\text{Prior year}} = \frac{\$50,000}{\$200,000} = 25\%$$

See also Vertical Analysis.

TROUBLED DEBT RESTRUCTURING

In a troubled debt restructuring, the debtor has financial problems and is relieved of part or the full amount of the obligation by the creditor. The concession is from debtor-creditor agreement, imposed by law, or relates to foreclosure and repossession. Troubled debt restructurings may include

• Debtor gives creditor receivables from third parties or other assets in satisfaction of the obligation.

• Debtor transfers stock to creditor to satisfy the debt.

• Modification of the terms of obligation, including reducing the interest rate, extending the maturity date, or downwardly adjusting the face amount of the debt.

The debtor recognizes an extraordinary gain (net of tax) on the restructuring but the creditor recognizes a loss. The loss may be ordinary or extraordinary depending on whether the creditor's arrangement is unusual and infrequent. Generally, the loss is deemed ordinary.

Debtor

The gain to the debtor equals the difference between the fair value of the assets exchanged and the book value of the obligation including accrued interest. Additionally, there may be a gain on disposal of assets exchanged in the transaction equal to the difference between the fair market value and the book value of the transferred assets. The latter gain or loss is *not* a gain or loss on restructuring but instead an ordinary gain or loss relating to asset disposal.

■ Example

A debtor transfers assets having a fair market value of $70 and a book value of $50 to settle a payable having a carrying value of $85. The gain on restructuring is $15 ($85 − $70). The ordinary gain is $20 ($70 − $50).

A debtor may provide the creditor with an equity interest. The debtor records the equity securities issued based on fair market value and not the recorded value of the debt extinguished. The excess of the recorded payable satisfied over the fair value of the issued securities represents an extraordinary item.

A modification in terms of an initial debt contract is accounted for prospectively. A new interest rate may be determined based on the new terms. This interest rate is then used to allocate future payments to lower principal and interest. When the new terms of the agreement result in the sum of all the future payments to be *less* than the carrying value of the payable, the payable is reduced and a restructuring gain recorded for the difference. Future payments are deemed a reduction of principal only. Interest expense is not recorded.

A troubled debt restructuring may result in a *combination* of concessions to the debtor. This may take place when assets or an equity interest are given in *partial* satisfaction of the obligation and the balance is subject to a modification of terms. Two steps are involved: (1) the payable is reduced by the fair value of the assets or equity transferred and (2) the balance of the debt is accounted for as a "modification of terms" type restructuring.

Direct costs, such as legal fees, incurred by the debtor in an equity transfer reduce the fair value of the equity interest. All other

costs reduce the gain on restructuring. If there is no gain involved, they are expensed.

■ Example

The debtor owes the creditor $200,000 and has expressed that due to financial problems there may be difficulty in making future payments. Footnote disclosure of the problem should be made by both debtor and creditor.

■ Example

The debtor owes the creditor $80,000. The creditor relieves the debtor of $10,000. The balance of the debt will be paid at a subsequent time.

The journal entry for the debtor is

Accounts Payable	10,000	
Extraordinary Gain		10,000

The journal entry for the creditor is

Ordinary Loss	10,000	
Accounts Receivable		10,000

■ Example

The debtor owes the creditor $90,000. The creditor agrees to accept $70,000 in full satisfaction of the obligation.

The journal entry for the debtor is

Accounts Payable	20,000	
Extraordinary Gain		20,000

The journal entry for the creditor is

Ordinary Loss	20,000	
Accounts Receivable		20,000

The debtor should disclose the following in the footnotes:

• Particulars of the restructuring agreement

• The aggregate and per share amounts of the gain on restructuring

• Amounts that are contingently payable, including the contingency terms

Creditor

The creditor's loss is the difference between the fair value of assets received and the book value of the investment. When terms are modified, the creditor recognizes interest income to the degree that total future payments are greater than the carrying value of the investment. Interest income is recognized using the effective interest method. Assets received are reflected at fair market value. When the book value of the receivable is in excess of the aggregate payments, an ordinary loss is recognized for the difference. All cash received in the future is accounted for as a recovery of the investment. Direct costs of the creditor are expensed.

The creditor does not recognize contingent interest until the contingency is removed and interest has been earned. Further, future changes in the interest rate are accounted for as a change in estimate.

The creditor discloses the following in the footnotes:

• Loan commitments of additional funds to financially troubled companies

• Loans and/or receivables by major type

• Debt agreements in which the interest rate has been downwardly adjusted, including an explanation of the circumstances

• Description of the restructuring terms

TRUST   A trust is a fiduciary relationship in which a trustee holds property for the benefit of a beneficiary. The grantor creates the trust. There is a distinction between the corpus (property) and income generated from it. The trust agreement stipulates the manner of distribution of principal and income. A trust is typically created by the owner of property who transfers property to the trustee. The administration of a trust typically is done without any court interference. The administration is usually in the form of managing funds to provide money to an income beneficiary and then to a remainderman.

A trust is a special form of ownership that provides sound management of assets and insulates them from tax and creditors. Trusts transfer property ownership to a third party, the trust, while permitting the real

owner to keep control by appointing himself, another person, or a financial institution to act as trustee. The trustee assures that the beneficiaries receive proper benefit.

Advantages of Having a Trust

• Avoiding the costs applicable to outright ownership of property
• Improves administrative convenience
• Shelters owner from lawsuits and creditors
• Enables faster inheritance
• May reduce the tax burden
• Tailored to meet obligations
• Management may be done by a trusted third party
• Property is transferred to minors without the need for a guardian
• Protects inheritor's principal against unwise spending

Flexibility: One can empower the trustee with as much or as little power to make decisions as desired.

An irrevocable trust transfers trust assets outside the grantor's ownership and is immune from lawsuits and creditors' claims against the grantor. Irrevocable trusts established prior to death are not included in the deceased probatable estate, reducing access to the decedent's property from creditors' claims. However, this does not guard against estate taxation.

Irrevocable and revocable living trusts are not includable in the probate of the decedent's estate and thus result in faster inheritance. Because trusts are not included in the probatable estate, probate costs are lower since they depend on the estate's size.

To enable the trust's income to be taxed at the lower marginal tax rate of the beneficiary instead of the higher marginal tax rate of the grantor, the following conditions have to exist:

• The grantor relinquishes his or her reversionary interest in both the principal and income of the trust for at least more than 10 years or the beneficiary's lifetime.
• The grantor relinquishes control over the income payable to persons other than himself or herself during the trust period.
• The grantor gives up certain administrative powers (e.g., grantor cannot reacquire the trust capital).
• The grantor cannot revoke the trust.
• The trust's income cannot be distributed or accumulated for future disposition to the grantor or his or her spouse, nor can it be used to meet the grantor's support obligations (e.g., payment of college tuition for children).

Warning: Revocable trusts provide no tax advantages to the grantor and thus should be considered for nontax reasons.

Recommendation: Use an irrevocable trust when the grantor's main concern is to transfer part of his or her assets prior to death so as to lower estate taxes. The appreciation in value of the trust is not subject to gift or estate taxes.

T-STATISTICS   T-statistics (or t-value) is a measure of the statistical significance of an independent variable, x, in explaining the dependent variable y. It is determined by dividing the estimated regression coefficient, b, by its standard error, s_b. It is then compared with the table t-value. (See Table 6 in the Appendix). Thus, the t-statistic measures how many standard errors the coefficient is away from zero. Generally, any t-value greater than $+2$ or less than -2 is acceptable. The higher the t-value, the greater the confidence we have in the coefficient as a predictor. Low t-values are indications of low reliability of the predictive power of that coefficient. *See also* Cost Behavior Analysis; Regression Analysis.

TURNOVER   This refers to the number of times an asset (e.g., inventory, accounts receivable) is replaced during an accounting period, typically one year. Usually, turnover is the

ratio of sales to a balance sheet item, such as sales to fixed assets. A high turnover rate is favorable because it indicates the efficient utilization of assets.

■ Example

Beginning and ending inventory are $30,000 and $40,000, respectively. Cost of sales is $300,000. Inventory turnover equals

$$\text{Inventory turnover} = \frac{\text{Cost of sales}}{\text{Average inventory}}$$
$$= \frac{\$300,000}{\$35,000} = 8.6 \text{ times}$$

See also Balance Sheet Analysis.

TWO-WAY ANALYSIS Two-way analysis of variance is the computation of two variances—*price* and *quantity* variances for direct materials and direct labor, and *budget* and *volume* variances for factory overhead. The budget variance is the difference between actual overhead costs and the budget overhead based on standard hours allowed. The volume variance (denominator variance) is the difference between denominator volume and actual volume multiplied by a predetermined fixed overhead rate. The two-way analysis for factory overhead stops here; it does not break up the budget variance into *spending* and *efficiency* variances. See the general model that provides the two-way and three-way analyses for factory overhead that follows.

See also Three-Way Analysis; Variance Analysis.

	Actual Costs Incurred	Budget Based on Actual Inputs	Budget: Based on Standard Inputs Allowed for Actual Output	Applied: Standard Inputs Allowed for Actual Output
Total overhead Three-way analysis	xxx	xxx Spending variance	xxx Efficiency variance	xxx Volume variance
Two-way analysis		Budget variance		Volume variance

U

UTILIZATION OF SCARCE RESOURCES   In general, the emphasis on products with higher contribution margin maximizes a firm's total net income, even though total sales may decrease. This is not true, however, where there are constraining factors and scarce resources. The constraining factor is the factor that restricts or limits the production or sale of a given product. The constraining factor may be machine hours, labor hours, or cubic feet of warehouse space. *Special Note*: In the presence of these constraining factors, maximizing total profits depends on getting the highest contribution margin *per unit* of the factor (rather than the highest contribution margin per unit of product output).

■ Example

Assume that a company produces two products, A and B, with the following contribution margins (CM) per unit.

	A	B
Sales	$8	$24
Variable costs	6	20
CM/unit	$2	$ 4
Annual fixed costs	$42,000	

As is indicated by CM per unit, B is more profitable than A since it contributes more to the company's total profits than A ($4 vs. $2). But let us assume that the firm has a limited capacity of 10,000 labor hours. Further, assume that A requires 2 labor hours to produce and B requires 5 labor hours. One way to express this limited capacity is to determine the contribution margin per labor hour.

	A	B
CM/unit	$2.00	$4.00
Labor hours required per unit	2	5
CM per labor hour	$1.00	$ .80

Since A returns the higher CM per labor hour, it should be produced and B should be dropped.

V

VALIDITY TEST A validity test is an audit technique to determine whether a recorded financial statement item has been properly stated. When performing validity tests, the auditor attempts to satisfy himself of the accuracy, appropriateness, relevance, and authorization of recorded transactions by the entity. The approach utilized in testing activity is dependent upon the nature and dollar magnitude of the transactions involved. When transactions are tested, the auditor may employ a number of techniques to choose a reliable sample and undertake various tests on the transactions.

VARIANCE ANALYSIS A standard cost is a predetermined cost of manufacturing, servicing, or marketing an item during a given future period. It is based on current and projected future conditions. The norm is also dependent upon quantitative and qualitative measurements. Standards are set at the beginning of the period. Examples are sales quotas, standard costs (e.g., material price, wage rate), and standard volume.

Variance analysis compares standard to actual performance. Variances may be as detailed as necessary, considering the cost-benefit relationship. Evaluation of variances may be done yearly, quarterly, monthly, daily, or hourly, depending on the importance of identifying a problem quickly. Since the managerial accountant does not know actual figures (e.g., hours spent) until the end of the period, variances can only be arrived at then. A material variance requires highlighting who is responsible and taking corrective action. Insignificant variances need not be looked into further unless they recur repeatedly and/or reflect potential difficulty.

One measure of materiality is to divide the variance by the standard cost. A variance of less than 5% may be deemed immaterial. In some cases, materiality is looked at in terms of dollar amount or volume level. For example, the cost accountant may set a policy looking into any variance that exceeds $10,000 or 20,000 units, whichever is less. Guidelines for materiality also depend upon the nature of the particular element as it affects corporate performance and decision making. For example, where the item is critical to the future functioning of the business (i.e., critical part, promotion, repairs), limits for materiality should be such that reporting is encouraged. Further, statistical techniques can be used to ascertain the significance of cost and revenue variances.

Often the reason for the variance is out-of-date standards or a poor budgetary process. Thus, it may not be due to actual performance.

Standards and variance analyses resulting therefrom are essential in financial analysis and decision making.

Advantages of Standards and Variances

- Assist in decision making.
- Formulate selling price.
- Set and evaluate corporate objectives.
- Cost control.
- Highlight problem areas through the "management by exception" principle.
- Pinpoint responsibility for undesirable performance so that corrective action may be taken. Variances in product activity (cost, quantity, quality) are typically the foreman's responsibility. Variances in sales are often the responsibility of the marketing manager. Variances in profit usually relate to overall operations. It should be noted that if variances indicate strengths, they should be further taken advantage of.
- Facilitate communication within the organization.
- Assist in planning by forecasting needs (e.g., cash requirements).
- Establish bid prices on contracts.

Setting Standards

Standards are based on the particular situation being appraised. Some examples follow.

Situation	Standard
Cost reduction	Tight
Pricing policy	Realistic
High-quality goods	Perfection

Types of Standards

- *Basic*—not changed from period to period. They form the basis to which later period performance is compared. What is unrealistic about it is that no consideration is given to a change in the environment.

- *Maximum efficiency*—perfect standards assuming ideal, optimal conditions. Realistically, certain inefficiencies will occur.
- *Currently attainable*—based on efficient activity. They are possible but difficult to achieve. Considered are normal occurrences, such as anticipated machinery failure.
- *Expected*—figures that come very close to actual figures.

Sales Variances

Sales variances are computed to gauge the performance of the marketing function.

▪ Example

Western Corporation's budgeted sales for 19X1 were

Product A: 10,000 units at $6 per unit	$ 60,000
Product B: 30,000 units at $8 per unit	240,000
Expected sales revenue	$300,000

Actual sales for the year were

Product A: 8,000 units at $6.20 per unit	$ 49,600
Product B: 33,000 units at $7.70 per unit	254,100
Actual sales revenue	$303,700

There is a favorable sales variance of $3,700, consisting of the sales price variance and the sales volume variance.

The sales price variance equals

Actual selling price vs. Budgeted selling price
× Actual units sold

Product A ($6.20 vs. $6 × 8,000)	$1,600 Favorable
Product B ($7.70 vs. $8 × 33,000)	9,900 Unfavorable
Sales price variance	$8,300 Unfavorable

The sales volume variance equals

Actual quantity vs. Budgeted quantity
× Budgeted selling price

Product A (8,000 vs. 10,000 × $6)	$12,000 Unfavorable
Product B (33,000 vs. 30,000 × $8)	24,000 Favorable
Sales volume variance	$12,000 Favorable

Cost Variances

When a product is made or a service is performed, the managerial accountant has to compute these three measures:

1. Actual cost equals actual price times actual quantity, where actual quantity equals actual quantity per unit of work times actual units of work produced.

2. Standard cost equals standard price times standard quantity, where standard quantity equals standard quantity per unit of work times actual units of work produced.

3. Control variance equals actual cost less standard cost.

Control variance has the following elements:

• Price (rate, cost) variance (Standard price vs. Actual price × Actual quantity)

• Quantity (usage, efficiency) variance (Standard quantity vs. Actual quantity × Standard price)

These are computed for both material and labor.

A variance is unfavorable when actual cost is higher than standard cost.

Material Variances

The cost accountant can use the material price variance to evaluate the activity of the purchasing department and to see the impact of raw material cost changes on profitability. The material quantity variance is the responsibility of the production supervisor.

■ Example

The standard cost of one unit of output (product or service) was $15: three pieces at $5 per piece. During the period, 8,000 units were made. Actual cost was $14 per unit; two pieces at $7 per piece.

Material Control Variance	
Standard quantity × Standard price (24,000 × $5)	$120,000
Actual quantity × Actual price (16,000 × $7)	112,000
	$ 8,000F

Material Price Variance	
Standard price vs. Actual price × Actual quantity ($5 vs. $7 × 16,000)	$ 32,000U

Material Quantity Variance	
Standard quantity vs. Actual quantity × Standard price (24,000 vs. 16,000 × $5)	$ 40,000F

The manager may not be able to control material price variances when higher prices are due to inflation or shortage situations.

The reason as well as the responsible party for an unfavorable material variance follow:

Reason	Responsible Party
Overstated price paid	Purchasing
Failure to detect defective goods	Receiving
Inefficient labor or poor supervision	Foreman
Poor mix in material	Production manager
Rush delivery of materials	Traffic
Unfavorable quantity variance	Foreman
Unexpected change in production volume	Sales manager

To correct for an unfavorable material price variance, the manager can increase selling price, substitute cheaper materials, change a production method or specification, or engage in a cost-reduction program.

Labor Variances

The standard labor rate should be based on the contracted hourly wage rate. Where salary rates are set by union contract, the labor rate variance will usually be minimal. Labor efficiency standards are typically estimated by engineers on the basis of an analysis of the production operation.

Labor variances are determined in a manner similar to that in which material variances are determined.

■ Example

The standard cost of labor is 4 hours times $9 per hour, or $36 per unit. During the period, 7,000 units were produced. The actual cost is 6 hours times $8 per hour, or $48 per unit.

Labor Control Variance

Standard quantity × Standard price (28,000 × $9)	$252,000
Actual quantity × Actual price (42,000 × $8)	336,000
	$ 84,000U

Labor Price Variance

Standard price vs. Actual price × Actual quantity ($9 vs. $8 × 42,000)	$ 42,000F

Labor Quantity Variance

Standard quantity vs. Actual quantity × Standard price (28,000 vs. 42,000 × $9)	$126,000U

Possible reasons for a labor price variance and the one responsible follow.

Reason	Responsible Party
Use of overpaid or excessive number of workers	Production manager or union contract
Poor job descriptions	Personnel
Overtime	Production planning

In the case of a shortage of skilled workers, it may be impossible to avoid an unfavorable labor price variance.

The cause and responsible entity for an unfavorable labor efficiency variance follow.

Cause	Responsible Entity
Inadequate supervision	Foreman
Improper functioning of equipment	Maintenance
Insufficient material supply or poor quality	Purchasing

Overhead Variances

The overhead variance comprises the controllable and volume variances. Relevant computations follow.

• Overhead control variance equals actual overhead versus standard overhead (standard hours times standard overhead rate).

• Controllable variance equals actual overhead versus budget adjusted to standard hours. *Note*: Budget adjusted to standard hours equals fixed overhead plus variable overhead (standard hours times standard variable overhead rate).

• Volume variance equals standard overhead versus budget adjusted to standard hours.

■ Example

The following data are provided:

Budgeted overhead (includes fixed overhead of $7,500 and variable overhead of $10,000)		$17,500
Budgeted hours		10,000
Actual overhead		$ 8,000
Actual units produced		800
Standard hours per unit of production		5
Preliminary calculations:		
Budgeted fixed overhead ($7,500/10,000 hrs)		$ 0.75
Budgeted variable overhead ($10,000/10,000 hrs)		1.00
Total budgeted overhead ($17,500/10,000 hrs)		$ 1.75
Standard hours (800 units × 5 hrs per unit)		4,000

Overhead Control Variance

Actual overhead		$ 8,000
Standard overhead		
Standard hours	4,000 hrs	
Standard overhead rate	× $1.75	7,000
		$ 1,000U

Controllable Variance

Actual overhead		$ 8,000
Budget adjusted to standard hours		
Fixed overhead	$7,500	
Variable overhead (Standard hours × Standard variable overhead rate 4,000 × $1)	4,000	11,500
		$ 3,500F

Volume Variance

Standard overhead	$ 7,000
Budget adjusted to standard hours	11,500
	$ 4,500U

The controllable variance is the responsibility of the foreman, since he influences actual overhead incurred. The volume variance is the responsibility of management executives and production managers, since they are involved with plant utilization.

Variable overhead variance information is helpful in arriving at the output level and output mix decisions. It also assists in appraising decisions regarding variable inputs. Fixed overhead variance data provide information regarding decision-making astuteness when buying some combination of fixed plant size and variable production inputs.

Possible Reasons for a Recurring Unfavorable Overhead Volume Variance

- Buying the wrong size plant
- Improper scheduling
- Insufficient orders
- Shortages in material
- Machinery failure
- Long operating time
- Inadequately trained workers

When idle capacity exists, this may indicate long-term operating planning problems.

Variances to Evaluate Marketing Effort

Prior to setting a marketing standard in a given trade territory, the manager should examine prior, current, and forecasted conditions for the company itself and the given geographical area. Standards will vary depending upon geographical location. In formulating standard costs for the transportation function, minimum cost traffic routes should be selected on the basis of the given distribution pattern.

Standards for advertising costs in particular territories will vary depending upon the types of advertising media needed, which are in turn based on the type of customers the advertising is intended to reach as well as the nature of the competition.

Some direct-selling costs can be standardized, such as product presentations for which a standard time per sales call can be established. Direct-selling expenses should be related to distance traveled, frequency of calls made, and so on. If sales commissions are based on sales generated, standards can be based on a percentage of net sales.

Time and motion studies are usually a better way of establishing standards than prior performance, since the past may include inefficiencies.

Cost variances for the selling function may pertain to the territory, product, or personnel.

Salesperson Variances

The manager should appraise salesforce effectiveness within a territory, including time spent and expenses incurred.

■ Example

Sales data for a company follow.

Standard cost	$240,000
Standard salesperson days	2,000
Standard rate per salesperson day	$ 120
Actual cost	$238,000
Actual salesperson days	1,700
Actual rate per salesperson day	$ 140

Total Cost Variance	
Actual cost	$238,000
Standard cost	240,000
	$ 2,000*F*

The control variance is broken down into salesperson days and salesperson costs.

Variance in Salesperson Days	
Actual days vs. Standard days × Standard rate per day (1,700 vs. 2,000 × $120)	$ 36,000*F*

The variance is favorable because the territory was handled in fewer days than expected.

Variance in Salesperson Costs	
Actual rate vs. Standard rate × Actual days ($140 vs. $120 × 1,700)	$ 34,000*U*

An unfavorable variance results because the actual rate per day is greater than the expected rate per day.

■ Example

A salesperson called on 55 customers and sold each an average of $2,800 worth of merchandise. The standard number of calls is 50, and the standard sale is $2,400. Variance analysis looking at calls and sales follows.

Total Variance	
Actual calls × Actual sale 55 × $2,800	$154,000
Standard calls × Standard sale 50 × $2,400	120,000
	$ 34,000

The elements of the $34,000 variance are

Variance in Calls	
Actual calls vs. Standard calls × Standard sale (55 vs. 50 × $2,400)	$ 12,000

Variance in Sales	
Actual sale vs. Standard sale × Standard calls ($2,800 vs. $2,400 × 50)	$ 20,000

Joint Variance	
(Actual calls vs. Standard calls) × (Actual sale vs. Standard sale) (55 vs. 50) × ($2,800 vs. $2,400)	$ 2,000

Warehousing Costs Variances

Variances in warehousing costs can be calculated by looking at the cost per unit to store the merchandise and the number of orders anticipated.

■ Example

The following information applies to a product:

Standard cost	$12,100
Standard orders	5,500
Standard unit cost	$ 2.20
Actual cost	$14,030
Actual orders	6,100
Actual unit cost	$ 2.30

Total Warehousing Cost Variance	
Actual cost	$14,030
Standard cost	12,100
	$ 1,930*U*

The total variance is segregated into the variance in orders and variance in cost.

Variance in Orders	
Actual orders vs. Standard orders × Standard unit cost 6,100 vs. 5,500 × $2.20	$1,320*U*

Variance in Cost	
Actual cost per unit vs. Standard cost per unit × Actual orders $2.30 vs. $2.20 × 6,100	$ 610*U*

Conclusion

Variance analysis is essential to the organization for the appraisal of all aspects of the business, including manufacturing, marketing, and service. Unfavorable variances must be examined to ascertain whether they are controllable by management or uncontrollable because they relate solely to external factors. When controllable, immediate corrective action must be undertaken to handle the problem. If a variance is favorable, an examination of the reasons for it should be made so that corporate policy may include the positive aspects found. Further, the responsible entity for a favorable variance should be recognized and rewarded.

VERTICAL ANALYSIS   In vertical analysis, a significant item on a financial statement is used as a base value and all other items on the financial statement are compared to it. In performing vertical analysis for the balance sheet, total assets is assigned 100%. Each asset is expressed as a percentage of total assets. Total liabilities and stockholders' equity are also assigned 100%. Each liability and stockholders' equity account is then expressed as a percentage of total liabilities and stockholders' equity. In the income statement, net sales is given the value of 100% and all other accounts are appraised in comparison to net sales. The resulting figures are then given in a common size statement.

Vertical analysis points to possible prob-

lem areas to be evaluated by the financial analyst.

■ Example

X Company
Common Size Income Statement
for the Year Ended 12/31/19X5

Sales	$40,000	100%
Less: Cost of sales	10,000	25%
Gross profit	$30,000	75%
Less: Expenses	4,000	10%
Net income	$26,000	65%

Vertical analysis is helpful in disclosing the internal structure of the business. It shows the relationship between each income statement account and revenue. It indicates the mix of assets that produces the income and the mix of the sources of capital, whether by current or long-term liabilities or by equity funding. Besides making internal evaluation possible, the results of vertical analysis are also employed to appraise the company's relative position in the industry. *See also* Trend (Horizontal) Analysis.

W

WEIGHTED AVERAGE This is an average of observations having different degrees of importance or frequency. The formula for a weighted average is

$$\text{Weighted average} = \Sigma wz$$

where x = the data values and w = relative weight assigned to each observation, expressed as a percentage or relative frequency. *See also* Mean.

WEIGHTED-AVERAGE COSTING VERSUS FIRST-IN, FIRST-OUT
In process costing, two typical assumptions are made regarding the flow of costs of the beginning work-in-process inventory. They are weighted-average costing and first in, first out (FIFO) costing.

Weighted-average costing is a procedure for computing the unit cost of a process by which the beginning work-in-process inventory costs are added to the costs of the current period, and a weighted average is obtained by dividing the combined costs by equivalent units. Thus, there is only one average cost for goods completed. *Equivalent units* under weighted-average costing may be computed as follows:

Units completed + (Ending work-in-process
$\qquad\qquad$ × Degree of completion [%])

On the other hand, under *FIFO*, beginning work-in-process inventory costs are separated from added costs applied in the current period. Thus, there are two unit costs for the period: (1) beginning work-in-process units completed and (2) units started and completed in the same period. Under FIFO, the beginning work-in-process is assumed to be completed and transferred first. Equivalent units under FIFO costing may be computed as follows:

Units completed + (Ending work-in-process
$\qquad\qquad$ × Degree of completion [%])
− (Beginning work-in-process
$\qquad\qquad$ × Degree of completion [%])

■ Example

To illustrate, the following data relate to the activities of Department A during the month of January:

	Units
Beginning work-in-process (100% complete as to materials; ⅔ complete as to conversion)	1,500
Started this period	5,000
Completed and transferred	5,500
Ending work-in-process (100% complete as to materials; ⁶⁄₁₀ complete as to conversion)	1,000

485

Equivalent production in Department A for the month is computed using *weighted-average costing*, as follows:

	Materials	Conversion Costs
Units completed and transferred	5,500	5,500
Ending work-in-process		
Materials (100%)	1,000	
Conversion costs (60%)		600
Equivalent production	6,500	6,100

Equivalent production in Department A for the month is computed using *FIFO costing*, as follows:

	Materials	Conversion Costs
Units completed and transferred	5,500	5,500
Ending work-in-process		
Materials (100%)	1,000	
Conversion costs (60%)		600
Equivalent production	6,500	6,100
Minus: Beginning work-in-process		
Materials (100%)	1,500	
Conversion costs (⅔)		1,000
	5,000	5,100

See also Process Costing.

WORKING CAPITAL MANAGEMENT Net working capital equals current assets less current liabilities. Management of working capital entails considering two related problems: (1) managing the firm's investment in current assets and (2) managing the firm's use of short-term or current liabilities. Involved are decisions on how assets should be financed (e.g., short-term debt, long-term debt, or equity). Managing working capital involves a trade-off between return and risk. If funds go from fixed assets to current assets, there is a reduction in liquidity risk, greater ability to obtain short-term financing, and enhanced flexibility because the entity can more readily adjust current assets to changes in sales volume. But less of a return is earned because the yield on fixed assets is more than that of current assets. Financing with noncurrent debt has less liquidity risk than financing with current debt. However, long-term debt often has a higher cost than short-term debt because of the greater uncertainty, which detracts from overall return.

Rule of Thumb: The longer the time period involved to buy or produce goods, the more working capital is required. Working capital also applies to the volume of purchases and the cost per unit. For example, if you can receive a raw material in 2 weeks, you need less of an inventory level than if 2 months lead time is involved. *Tip*: Purchase material early if significantly lower prices are available and if the material's cost savings exceed inventory carrying costs. *See also* Accounts Receivable Management; Cash Management; Inventory Planning and Control.

WORKING PAPERS As per Statement on Auditing Standards No. 41, working papers are required on an audit engagement. They assist in performing and reviewing audit work. The form and content of the working papers may vary depending on the nature of the particular engagement. Further, the auditor may supplement working papers by other means. Working papers should show that the fieldwork standards have been met. In this regard, there should be documentation that a study and analysis of the internal control structure has been undertaken. Further, the work performed and by whom should be spelled out along with audit findings. *See also* Audit.

Y

YIELD The cost of a corporate bond is expressed in terms of yield. Two types of yield calculations are

1. *Simple Yield*

$$\frac{\text{Nominal interest}}{\text{Present value of bond}}$$

It is not as accurate as yield to maturity.

2. *Yield to Maturity* (effective interest rate)

$$\frac{\text{Nominal interest} + \dfrac{\text{Discount}}{\text{Years}} - \dfrac{\text{Premium}}{\text{Years}}}{\dfrac{\text{Present value} + \text{Maturity value}}{2}}$$

■ Example

A $100,000, 10%, 5-year bond is issued at 96. The simple yield is

$$\frac{\text{Nominal interest}}{\text{Present value of bond}} = \frac{\$10,000}{\$96,000} = 10.42\%$$

The yield to maturity is

$$\frac{\text{Nominal interest} + \dfrac{\text{Discount}}{\text{Years}}}{\dfrac{\text{Present value} + \text{Maturity value}}{2}} = \frac{\$10,000 + \dfrac{\$4,000}{5}}{\dfrac{\$96,000 + \$100,000}{2}}$$

$$\frac{\$10,800}{\$98,000} = 11.02\%$$

When a bond is issued at a discount, the yield (effective interest rate) is greater than the nominal (face, coupon) interest rate.

When a bond is issued at a premium, the yield is less than the nominal interest rate. *See also* Bond Accounting; Bond Yield.

YIELD SPREAD This is the difference between the yields received on two different types of bonds with different ratings. In times of economic uncertainty, the yield spread increases because investors demand higher premiums on risky issues to compensate for the increased chance of default. *See also* Bond Ratings.

Z

ZERO-BASE BUDGETING (ZBB)

ZERO-BASE BUDGETING (ZBB) ZBB is budgeting from scratch as if the budget was being started for the first time. The steps involved in ZBB are

• Ascertain objectives and activities required

• Evaluate alternative ways of accomplishing each activity

• Appraise alternative budget figures for different activity levels

• Formulate performance measures

• Rank activities in the order of their importance

ZBB usually begins with the decision units that are at the lowest levels in the firm for which a budget is formulated. *Decision packages* are prepared for each unit. The packages describe alternative means of accomplishing a task, including the manager's recommended way. The cost and time associated with the recommended and alternative means of carrying out the task are specified. Top management may decide not to fund the project, fund it as recommended by the manager, or proceed with the project according to one of the alternative approaches (e.g., less costly).

An illustrative decision package follows:

Decision Package
Task A

Alternative
$43,000, 800 hours

Recommendation $50,000, 1,000 hours

Alternative
$30,000, 500 hours

The problem with ZBB is cost versus benefit. The significant cost involved to prepare a ZBB may outweigh the benefits to be derived. *See also* Budgeting for Profit Planning.

ZERO-COUPON BOND

ZERO-COUPON BOND This is a bond sold at a deep discount. The interest, instead of being paid out directly, is added to the principal semiannually, and both the principal and the accumulated interest are paid at maturity. Although a fixed rate is implicit in the discount and the specific maturity, they are not fixed income securities in the traditional sense because they provide for no periodic income. Although the interest on the bond is paid at maturity, accrued interest, though not received, is taxable yearly as ordinary income. Zero-coupon bonds have two basic advan-

tages over regular coupon-bearing bonds: (1) a relatively small investment is required to buy these bonds and (2) a specific yield is assured throughout the term of the investment.

ZERO–ONE PROGRAMMING

This is a special case of *integer programming* where integer variables are restricted to values of either zero or one. In a *capital rationing* problem, the decision variables are restricted to either zero or one, implying total investment (inclusion in a portfolio) or no investment (exclusion from the portfolio). *See also* Capital Rationing; Integer Programming; Project Selection and Zero–One Programming.

Z SCORES: FORECASTING BUSINESS FAILURES

The recent past has witnessed an increasing trend in bankruptcies. Will your client go bankrupt? Is the company you are working for on the verge of bankruptcy? Who will go bankrupt—your major customer, your important supplier, your borrower? If you can predict with reasonable accuracy that the company you are interested in is developing financial distress, you could better protect yourself and recommend means for corrective action.

In 1968, using a blend of the traditional financial ratios and a statistical method known as multiple discriminant analysis (MDA), Edward Altman developed a bankruptcy prediction model that produces a Z score as follows:

$$Z = 1.2*X_1 + 1.4*X_2 + 3.3*X_3 + 0.6*X_4 + 0.999*X_5$$

where:
X_1 = Working capital/Total assets,
X_2 = Retained earnings/Total assets,
X_3 = Earnings before interest and taxes (EBIT)/Total assets,
X_4 = Market value of equity/Book value of debt,
X_5 = Sales/Total assets.

Altman also established the following guidelines for classifying firms:

Z score	Probability of Failure
1.8 or less	Very high
1.81–2.99	Not sure
3.0 or higher	Unlikely

The Z score is known to be about 90% accurate in forecasting business failure one year in the future and about 80% accurate in forecasting it two years in the future. For a more detailed discussion of Z Score, see Edward I. Altman, "Financial Ratios, Discriminant Analysis, and the Prediction of Corporate Bankruptcy," *Journal of Finance*, September 1968.

Now we will illustrate the computation by setting up a Z score spreadsheet using a computer program like Lotus 1-2-3. Table 1 (page 490) shows the 7-year financial history and the Z scores of Navistar International (formerly, International Harvestor).

After creating the data worksheet and calculating the Z scores, it is a good idea to develop a graph for these values, as shown in Figure 1 (page 491).

The graph shows that Navistar International performed at the edge of the ignorance zone ("unsure area") for the years 1975 through 1979. Since 1980, though, the company started signaling a sign of failure. However, by selling stock and assets, the firm managed to survive. Since 1982, the company showed an improvement in its Z scores, but it still has a long way to go.

More Applications of the Z Score

Accountants and financial managers apply Z score in numerous ways. For example,
1. *Financial management analysis*—The score can indicate whether capital expansion and dividends should be curtailed to keep needed funds within the business.

Table 1 Navistar International Z Score Data and Score

| | Balance Sheet | | | | | | | Income Statement | | Stock Data | Calculations | | | | | | Miscellaneous Graph Values | | |
| | Current Year Assets | Total Assets | Current Liabilities | Total Liabilities | Retained Earnings | Net Worth | Working Capital | Sales | EBIT | Market Value | WC/TA | RE/TA | EBIT/TA | MKT/TL | SALES/TA | Z Score | TOP GRAY | BOTTOM GRAY | GRAY | Year |
	CA	TA	CL	TL	RE	NW	WC	SALES	EBIT	MKT						A	B	C	X
1979	3266	5247	1873	3048	1505	2199	1393	8426	719	1122	0.2655	0.2868	0.1370	0.3681	1.6059	3.00	2.99	1.81	1979
1980	3427	5843	2433	3947	1024	1896	994	6000	−402	1147	0.1701	0.1753	−0.0688	0.2906	1.0269	1.42	2.99	1.81	1980
1981	2672	5346	1808	3864	600	1482	864	7018	−16	376	0.1616	0.1122	−0.0030	0.0973	1.3128	1.71	2.99	1.81	1981
1982	1656	3699	1135	3665	−1078	34	521	4322	−1274	151	0.1408	−0.2914	−0.3444	0.0412	1.1684	−0.18	2.99	1.81	1982
1983	1388	3362	1367	3119	−1487	243	22	3600	−231	835	0.0065	−0.4423	−0.0687	0.2677	1.0708	0.39	2.99	1.81	1983
1984	1412	3249	1257	2947	−1537	302	155	4861	120	575	0.0477	−0.4731	0.0369	0.1951	1.4962	1.13	2.99	1.81	1984
1985	1101	2406	988	2364	−1894	42	113	3508	−242	570	0.0470	−0.7872	−0.1006	0.2411	1.4580	0.22	2.99	1.81	1985

Figure 1 Altman's Z Score Graph

Navistar International

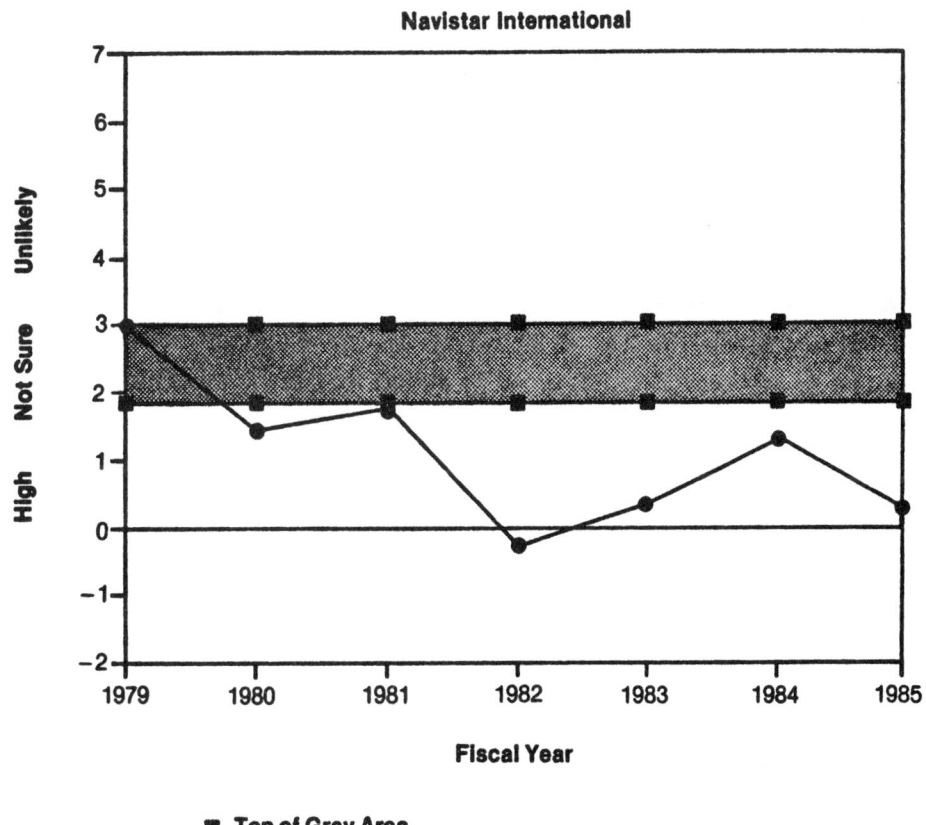

Fiscal Year

■ **Top of Gray Area**

● **Bottom of Gray Area**

2. *Merger analysis*—The Z score can help identify potential problems with a merger candidate.

3. *Loan credit analysis*—Bankers and lenders can use it to determine if they should extend a loan. Other creditors such as vendors have used it to determine whether to extend credit.

4. *Investment analysis*—The Z score model can help an investor in selecting stocks of potentially troubled companies.

5. *Auditing analysis*—External CPA auditors are able to use this technique to assess whether the client will continue as a going concern. If not, disclosure is required in the audit report.

6. *Legal analysis*—Those who manage other people's investments tend to get sued if the investment goes sour. The Z score can help either side of the argument.

Appendix

Table 1 Future Value of $1
$$F_n(1 + i)^n = FVIF_{i,n}$$

Periods	4%	6%	8%	10%	12%	14%	20%
1	1.040	1.060	1.080	1.100	1.120	1.140	1.200
2	1.082	1.124	1.166	1.210	1.254	1.300	1.440
3	1.125	1.191	1.260	1.331	1.405	1.482	1.728
4	1.170	1.263	1.361	1.464	1.574	1.689	2.074
5	1.217	1.338	1.469	1.611	1.762	1.925	2.488
6	1.265	1.419	1.587	1.772	1.974	2.195	2.986
7	1.316	1.504	1.714	1.949	2.211	2.502	3.583
8	1.369	1.594	1.851	2.144	2.476	2.853	4.300
9	1.423	1.690	1.999	2.359	2.773	3.252	5.160
10	1.480	1.791	2.159	2.594	3.106	3.707	6.192
11	1.540	1.898	2.332	2.853	3.479	4.226	7.430
12	1.601	2.012	2.518	3.139	3.896	4.818	8.916
13	1.665	2.133	2.720	3.452	4.364	5.492	10.699
14	1.732	2.261	2.937	3.798	4.887	6.261	12.839
15	1.801	2.397	3.172	4.177	5.474	7.138	15.407
20	2.191	3.207	4.661	6.728	9.646	13.743	38.338
30	3.243	5.744	10.063	17.450	29.960	50.950	237.380
40	4.801	10.286	21.725	45.260	93.051	188.880	1469.800

Table 2   Future Value of an Annuity of $1

$$S_n = \frac{(1 + i)^n - 1}{i} = FVIFA_{i,n}$$

Periods	4%	6%	8%	10%	12%	14%	20%
1	1.000	1.000	1.000	1.000	1.000	1.000	1.000
2	2.040	2.060	2.080	2.100	2.120	2.140	2.220
3	3.122	3.184	3.246	3.310	3.374	3.440	3.640
4	4.247	4.375	4.506	4.641	4.779	4.921	5.368
5	5.416	5.637	5.867	6.105	6.353	6.610	7.442
6	6.633	6.975	7.336	7.716	8.115	8.536	9.930
7	7.898	8.394	8.923	9.487	10.089	10.730	12.916
8	9.214	9.898	10.637	11.436	12.300	13.233	16.499
9	10.583	11.491	12.488	13.580	14.776	16.085	20.799
10	12.006	13.181	14.487	15.938	17.549	19.337	25.959
11	13.486	14.972	16.646	18.531	20.655	23.045	32.150
12	15.026	16.870	18.977	21.395	24.133	27.271	39.580
13	16.627	18.882	21.495	24.523	28.029	32.089	48.497
14	18.292	21.015	24.215	27.976	32.393	37.581	59.196
15	20.024	23.276	27.152	31.773	37.280	43.842	72.035
20	29.778	36.778	45.762	57.276	75.052	91.025	186.690
30	56.085	79.058	113.283	164.496	241.330	356.790	1181.900
40	95.026	154.762	259.057	442.597	767.090	1342.000	7343.900

Table 3 Present Value of $1

$$P = \frac{1}{(1 + i)^n} = PVIF_{i,n}$$

Periods	4%	5%	6%	8%	10%	12%	14%	16%	18%	20%	22%	24%	26%	28%	30%	40%
1	0.962	0.952	0.943	0.926	0.909	0.893	0.877	0.862	0.847	0.833	0.820	0.806	0.794	0.781	0.769	0.714
2	0.925	0.907	0.890	0.857	0.826	0.797	0.769	0.743	0.718	0.694	0.672	0.650	0.630	0.610	0.592	0.510
3	0.889	0.864	0.840	0.794	0.751	0.712	0.675	0.641	0.609	0.579	0.551	0.524	0.500	0.477	0.455	0.364
4	0.855	0.823	0.792	0.735	0.683	0.636	0.592	0.552	0.516	0.482	0.451	0.423	0.397	0.373	0.350	0.260
5	0.822	0.784	0.747	0.681	0.621	0.567	0.519	0.476	0.437	0.402	0.370	0.341	0.315	0.291	0.269	0.186
6	0.790	0.746	0.705	0.630	0.564	0.507	0.456	0.410	0.370	0.335	0.303	0.275	0.250	0.227	0.207	0.133
7	0.760	0.711	0.665	0.583	0.513	0.452	0.400	0.354	0.314	0.279	0.249	0.222	0.198	0.178	0.159	0.095
8	0.731	0.677	0.627	0.540	0.467	0.404	0.351	0.305	0.266	0.233	0.204	0.179	0.157	0.139	0.123	0.068
9	0.703	0.645	0.592	0.500	0.424	0.361	0.308	0.263	0.225	0.194	0.167	0.144	0.125	0.108	0.094	0.048
10	0.676	0.614	0.558	0.463	0.386	0.322	0.270	0.227	0.191	0.162	0.137	0.116	0.099	0.085	0.073	0.035
11	0.650	0.585	0.527	0.429	0.350	0.287	0.237	0.195	0.162	0.135	0.112	0.094	0.079	0.066	0.056	0.025
12	0.625	0.557	0.497	0.397	0.319	0.257	0.208	0.168	0.137	0.112	0.092	0.076	0.062	0.052	0.043	0.018
13	0.601	0.530	0.469	0.368	0.290	0.229	0.182	0.145	0.116	0.093	0.075	0.061	0.050	0.040	0.033	0.013
14	0.577	0.505	0.442	0.340	0.263	0.205	0.160	0.125	0.099	0.078	0.062	0.049	0.039	0.032	0.025	0.009
15	0.555	0.481	0.417	0.315	0.239	0.183	0.140	0.108	0.084	0.065	0.051	0.040	0.031	0.025	0.020	0.006
16	0.534	0.458	0.394	0.292	0.218	0.163	0.123	0.093	0.071	0.054	0.042	0.032	0.025	0.019	0.015	0.005
17	0.513	0.436	0.371	0.270	0.198	0.146	0.108	0.080	0.060	0.045	0.034	0.026	0.020	0.015	0.012	0.003
18	0.494	0.416	0.350	0.250	0.180	0.130	0.095	0.069	0.051	0.038	0.028	0.021	0.016	0.012	0.009	0.002
19	0.475	0.396	0.331	0.232	0.164	0.116	0.083	0.060	0.043	0.031	0.023	0.017	0.012	0.009	0.007	0.002
20	0.456	0.377	0.312	0.215	0.149	0.104	0.073	0.051	0.037	0.026	0.019	0.014	0.010	0.007	0.005	0.001
21	0.439	0.359	0.294	0.199	0.135	0.093	0.064	0.044	0.031	0.022	0.015	0.011	0.008	0.006	0.004	0.001
22	0.422	0.342	0.278	0.184	0.123	0.083	0.056	0.038	0.026	0.018	0.013	0.009	0.006	0.004	0.003	0.001
23	0.406	0.326	0.262	0.170	0.112	0.074	0.049	0.033	0.022	0.015	0.010	0.007	0.005	0.003	0.002	
24	0.390	0.310	0.247	0.158	0.102	0.066	0.043	0.028	0.019	0.013	0.008	0.006	0.004	0.003	0.002	
25	0.375	0.295	0.233	0.146	0.092	0.059	0.038	0.024	0.016	0.010	0.007	0.005	0.003	0.002	0.001	
26	0.361	0.281	0.220	0.135	0.084	0.053	0.033	0.021	0.014	0.009	0.006	0.004	0.002	0.002	0.001	
27	0.347	0.268	0.207	0.125	0.076	0.047	0.029	0.018	0.011	0.007	0.005	0.003	0.002	0.001	0.001	
28	0.333	0.255	0.196	0.116	0.069	0.042	0.026	0.016	0.010	0.006	0.004	0.002	0.002	0.001	0.001	
29	0.321	0.243	0.185	0.107	0.063	0.037	0.022	0.014	0.008	0.005	0.003	0.002	0.001	0.001	0.001	
30	0.308	0.231	0.174	0.099	0.057	0.033	0.020	0.012	0.007	0.004	0.003	0.002	0.001	0.001	0.001	
40	0.208	0.142	0.097	0.046	0.022	0.011	0.005	0.003	0.001	0.001						

Table 4 Present Value of an Annuity of $1

$$P_n = \left[\frac{1 - \dfrac{1}{(1+i)^n}}{i}\right] = PVIFA_{i,n}$$

Periods	4%	5%	6%	8%	10%	12%	14%	16%	18%	20%	22%	24%	26%	28%	30%	40%
1	0.962	0.952	0.943	0.926	0.909	0.893	0.877	0.862	0.847	0.833	0.820	0.806	0.794	0.781	0.769	0.714
2	1.886	1.859	1.833	1.783	1.736	1.690	1.647	1.605	1.566	1.528	1.492	1.457	1.424	1.392	1.361	1.224
3	2.775	2.723	2.673	2.577	2.487	2.402	2.322	2.246	2.174	2.106	2.042	1.981	1.923	1.868	1.816	1.589
4	3.630	3.546	3.465	3.312	3.170	3.037	2.914	2.798	2.690	2.589	2.494	2.404	2.320	2.241	2.166	1.849
5	4.452	4.330	4.212	3.993	3.791	3.605	3.433	3.274	3.127	2.991	2.864	2.745	2.635	2.532	2.436	2.035
6	5.242	5.076	4.917	4.623	4.355	4.111	3.889	3.685	3.498	3.326	3.167	3.020	2.885	2.759	2.643	2.168
7	6.002	5.786	5.582	5.206	4.868	4.564	4.288	4.039	3.812	3.605	3.416	3.242	3.083	2.937	2.802	2.263
8	6.733	6.463	6.210	5.747	5.335	4.968	4.639	4.344	4.078	3.837	3.619	3.421	3.241	3.076	2.925	2.331
9	7.435	7.108	6.802	6.247	5.759	5.328	4.946	4.607	4.303	4.031	3.786	3.566	3.366	3.184	3.019	2.379
10	8.111	7.722	7.360	6.710	6.145	5.650	5.216	4.833	4.494	4.192	3.923	3.682	3.465	3.269	3.092	2.414
11	8.760	8.306	7.887	7.139	6.495	5.988	5.453	5.029	4.656	4.327	4.035	3.776	3.544	3.335	3.147	2.438
12	9.385	8.863	8.384	7.536	6.814	6.194	5.660	5.197	4.793	4.439	4.127	3.851	3.606	3.387	3.190	2.456
13	9.986	9.394	8.853	7.904	7.103	6.424	5.842	5.342	4.910	4.533	4.203	3.912	3.656	3.427	3.223	2.468
14	10.563	9.899	9.295	8.244	7.367	6.628	6.002	5.468	5.008	4.611	4.265	3.962	3.695	3.459	3.249	2.477
15	11.118	10.380	9.712	8.559	7.606	6.811	6.142	5.575	5.092	4.675	4.315	4.001	3.726	3.483	3.268	2.484
16	11.652	10.838	10.106	8.851	7.824	6.974	6.265	5.669	5.162	4.730	4.357	4.033	3.751	3.503	3.283	2.489
17	12.166	11.274	10.477	9.122	8.022	7.120	6.373	5.749	5.222	4.775	4.391	4.059	3.771	3.518	3.295	2.492
18	12.659	11.690	10.828	9.372	8.201	7.250	6.467	5.818	5.273	4.812	4.419	4.080	3.786	3.529	3.304	2.494
19	13.134	12.085	11.158	9.604	8.365	7.366	6.550	5.877	5.316	4.844	4.442	4.097	3.799	3.539	3.311	2.496
20	13.590	12.462	11.470	9.818	8.514	7.469	6.623	5.929	5.353	4.870	4.460	4.110	3.808	3.546	3.316	2.497
21	14.029	12.821	11.764	10.017	8.649	7.562	6.687	5.973	5.384	4.891	4.476	4.121	3.816	3.551	3.320	2.498
22	14.451	13.163	12.042	10.201	8.772	7.645	6.743	6.011	5.410	4.909	4.488	4.130	3.822	3.556	3.323	2.498
23	14.857	13.489	12.303	10.371	8.883	7.718	6.792	6.044	5.432	4.925	4.499	4.137	3.827	3.559	3.325	2.499
24	15.247	13.799	12.550	10.529	8.985	7.784	6.835	6.073	5.451	4.937	4.507	4.143	3.831	3.562	3.327	2.499
25	15.622	14.094	12.783	10.675	9.077	7.843	6.873	6.097	5.467	4.948	4.514	4.147	3.834	3.564	3.329	2.499
26	15.983	14.375	13.003	10.810	9.161	7.896	6.906	6.118	5.480	4.956	4.520	4.151	3.837	3.566	3.330	2.500
27	16.330	14.643	13.211	10.935	9.237	7.943	6.935	6.136	5.492	4.964	4.525	4.154	3.839	3.567	3.331	2.500
28	16.663	14.898	13.406	11.051	9.307	7.984	6.961	6.152	5.502	4.970	4.528	4.157	3.840	3.568	3.331	2.500
29	16.984	15.141	13.591	11.158	9.370	8.022	6.983	6.166	5.510	4.975	4.531	4.159	3.841	3.569	3.332	2.500
30	17.292	15.373	13.765	11.258	9.427	8.055	7.003	6.177	5.517	4.979	4.534	4.160	3.842	3.569	3.332	2.500
40	19.793	17.159	15.046	11.925	9.779	8.244	7.105	6.234	5.548	4.997	4.544	4.166	3.846	3.571	3.333	2.500

Table 5   Normal Distribution Table

Areas Under the Normal Curve

Mean 1.81

.9648

Z	0	1	2	3	4	5	6	7	8	9
0.0	0.5000	0.5040	0.5080	0.5120	0.5160	0.5199	0.5239	0.5279	0.5319	0.5359
0.1	0.5398	0.5438	0.5478	0.5517	0.5557	0.5596	0.5636	0.5675	0.5714	0.5753
0.2	0.5793	0.5832	0.5871	0.5910	0.5948	0.5987	0.6026	0.6064	0.6103	0.6141
0.3	0.6179	0.6217	0.6255	0.6293	0.6331	0.6368	0.6406	0.6443	0.6480	0.6517
0.4	0.6554	0.6591	0.6628	0.6664	0.6700	0.6736	0.6772	0.6808	0.6844	0.6879
0.5	0.6915	0.6950	0.6985	0.7019	0.7054	0.7088	0.7123	0.7157	0.7190	0.7224
0.6	0.7257	0.7291	0.7324	0.7357	0.7389	0.7422	0.7454	0.7486	0.7517	0.7549
0.7	0.7580	0.7611	0.7642	0.7673	0.7703	0.7734	0.7764	0.7794	0.7823	0.7852
0.8	0.7881	0.7910	0.7939	0.7967	0.7995	0.8023	0.8051	0.8078	0.8106	0.8133
0.9	0.8159	0.8186	0.8212	0.8238	0.8264	0.8289	0.8315	0.8340	0.8365	0.8389
1.0	0.8413	0.8438	0.8461	0.8485	0.8508	0.8531	0.8554	0.8577	0.8599	0.8621
1.1	0.8643	0.8665	0.8686	0.8708	0.8729	0.8749	0.8770	0.8790	0.8810	0.8830
1.2	0.8849	0.8869	0.8888	0.8907	0.8925	0.8944	0.8962	0.8980	0.8997	0.9015
1.3	0.9032	0.9049	0.9066	0.9082	0.9099	0.9115	0.9131	0.9147	0.9162	0.9177
1.4	0.9192	0.9207	0.9222	0.9236	0.9251	0.9265	0.9278	0.9292	0.9306	0.9319
1.5	0.9332	0.9345	0.9357	0.9370	0.9382	0.9394	0.9406	0.9418	0.9430	0.9441
1.6	0.9452	0.9463	0.9474	0.9484	0.9495	0.9505	0.9515	0.9525	0.9535	0.9545
1.7	0.9554	0.9564	0.9573	0.9582	0.9591	0.9599	0.9608	0.9616	0.9625	0.9633
1.8	0.9641	0.9648	0.9656	0.9664	0.9671	0.9678	0.9686	0.9693	0.9700	0.9706
1.9	0.9713	0.9719	0.9726	0.9732	0.9738	0.9744	0.9750	0.9756	0.9762	0.9767
2.0	0.9772	0.9778	0.9783	0.9788	0.9793	0.9798	0.9803	0.9808	0.9812	0.9817
2.1	0.9821	0.9826	0.9830	0.9834	0.9838	0.9842	0.9846	0.9850	0.9854	0.9857
2.2	0.9861	0.9864	0.9868	0.9871	0.9874	0.9878	0.9881	0.9884	0.9887	0.9890
2.3	0.9893	0.9896	0.9898	0.9901	0.9904	0.9906	0.9909	0.9911	0.9913	0.9916
2.4	0.9918	0.9920	0.9922	0.9925	0.9927	0.9929	0.9931	0.9932	0.9934	0.9936
2.5	0.9938	0.9940	0.9941	0.9943	0.9945	0.9946	0.9948	0.9949	0.9951	0.9952
2.6	0.9953	0.9955	0.9956	0.9957	0.9959	0.9960	0.9961	0.9962	0.9963	0.9964
2.7	0.9965	0.9966	0.9967	0.9968	0.9969	0.9970	0.9971	0.9972	0.9973	0.9974
2.8	0.9974	0.9975	0.9976	0.9977	0.9977	0.9978	0.9979	0.9979	0.9980	0.9981
2.9	0.9981	0.9982	0.9982	0.9983	0.9984	0.9984	0.9985	0.9985	0.9986	0.9986
3.0	0.9987	0.9990	0.9993	0.9995	0.9997	0.9998	0.9998	0.9999	0.9999	1.0000

Table 6   T-Table (Values of t)

d.f.	$t_{.100}$	$t_{.050}$	$t_{.025}$	$t_{.010}$	$t_{.005}$	d.f.
1	3.078	6.314	12.706	31.821	63.657	1
2	1.886	2.920	4.303	6.965	9.925	2
3	1.638	2.353	3.182	4.541	5.841	3
4	1.533	2.132	2.776	3.747	4.604	4
5	1.476	2.015	2.571	3.365	4.032	5
6	1.440	1.943	2.447	3.143	3.707	6
7	1.415	1.895	2.365	2.998	3.499	7
8	1.397	1.860	2.306	2.896	3.355	8
9	1.383	1.833	2.262	2.821	3.250	9
10	1.372	1.812	2.228	2.764	3.169	10
11	1.363	1.796	2.201	2.718	3.106	11
12	1.356	1.782	2.179	2.681	3.055	12
13	1.350	1.771	2.160	2.650	3.012	13
14	1.345	1.761	2.145	2.624	2.977	14
15	1.341	1.753	2.131	2.602	2.947	15
16	1.337	1.746	2.120	2.583	2.921	16
17	1.333	1.740	2.110	2.567	2.898	17
18	1.330	1.734	2.101	2.552	2.878	18
19	1.328	1.729	2.093	2.539	2.861	19
20	1.325	1.725	2.086	2.528	2.845	20
21	1.323	1.721	2.080	2.518	2.831	21
22	1.321	1.717	2.074	2.508	2.819	22
23	1.319	1.714	2.069	2.500	2.807	23
24	1.318	1.711	2.064	2.492	2.797	24
25	1.316	1.708	2.060	2.485	2.787	25
26	1.315	1.706	2.056	2.479	2.779	26
27	1.314	1.703	2.052	2.473	2.771	27
28	1.313	1.701	2.048	2.467	2.763	28
29	1.311	1.699	2.045	2.462	2.756	29
inf.	1.282	1.645	1.960	2.326	2.576	inf.

The t-value describes the sampling distribution of a deviation from a population value divided by the standard error.

Degrees of freedom (d.f.) are in the first column. The probabilities indicated as subvalues of t in the heading refer to the sum of a one-tailed area under the curve that lies outside the point t.

For example, in the distribution of the means of samples of size $n = 10$, d.f. $= n - 2 = 8$; then 0.025 of the area under the curve falls in one tail outside the interval $t \pm 2.306$.

INDEX OF ENTRIES

Foundations of

Physics

Tom Hsu, Ph.D

First Edition
CPO Science
Peabody, Massachusetts 01960

cpo
science

About the Author

Dr. Thomas C. Hsu is a nationally recognized innovator in science and math education and the founder of CPO Science (formerly Cambridge Physics Outlet). He holds a Ph.D. in Applied Plasma Physics from the Massachusetts Institute of Technology (MIT), and has taught students from elementary, secondary and college levels across the nation. He was nominated for MIT's Goodwin medal for excellence in teaching and has received numerous awards from various state agencies for his work to improve science education. Tom has personally worked with more than 12,000 K-12 teachers and administrators and is well known as a consultant, workshop leader and developer of curriculum and equipment for inquiry-based learning in science and math. With CPO Science, Tom has published textbooks in physical science, integrated science, Earth and space science, and also written fifteen curriculum Investigation guides that accompany CPO Science equipment. Along with the CPO Science team, Tom is always active, developing innovative new tools for teaching and learning science, including an inquiry-based chemistry text.

Foundations of Physics, First Edition
Copyright © 2004 CPO Science
ISBN 1-58892-057-7
1 2 3 4 5 6 7 8 9 - QWE - 07 06 05 04

CPO Science
26 Howley Street
Peabody, MA 01960
(978) 532-7070
http://www.cposcience.com

Printed and bound in the United States of America

CPO Science Development Team

Lynda Pennell – Educational Products, Executive Vice President

B.A., English, M.Ed., Administration, Reading Disabilities, Northeastern University; CAGS Media, University of Massachusetts, Boston

Nationally known in high school restructuring and for integrating academic and career education. Served as the director of an urban school with 17 years teaching/administrative experience.

Thomas Narro – Product Design, Senior Vice President

B.S., Mechanical engineering, Rensselaer Polytechnic Institute

Accomplished design and manufacturing engineer; experienced consultant in corporate reengineering and industrial-environmental acoustics.

Scott Eddleman – Curriculum Manager

B.S., Biology, Southern Illinois University; M.Ed., Harvard University

Taught for 13 years in urban and rural settings; nationally known as trainer of inquiry-based science and mathematics project-based instruction; curriculum development consultant.

Michael Grady – Technical/Service Coordinator

Oversees all customer and technical service issues and assures customer satisfaction.

Laine Ives – Curriculum Writer

B.A., English, Gordon College; graduate work, biology, Cornell University, Wheelock College

Experience teaching middle and high school, here and abroad; expertise in developing middle school curriculum and hands-on activities.

Mary Beth Abel Hughes – Curriculum Writer

B.S., Marine biology, College of Charleston; M.S., Biological sciences, University of Rhode Island

Taught science and math at an innovative high school; expertise in scientific research and inquiry-based teaching methods and curiculum development.

Sonja Taylor – Curriculum Writer

B.S.,Chemistry, Stephen F. Austin State University

Taught chemistry and biology for four years. Exptertise in teaching with inquiry and technology.

Bruce Holloway – Senior Creative Designer

Pratt Institute, N.Y.; Boston Museum School of Fine Arts

Expertise in product design, advertising, and three-dimensional exhibit design. Commissioned for the New Hampshire Duck Stamp for 1999 and 2003.

Michelle Permatteo – Staff and Development Service Coordinator

Oversees all the details necessary to keep the professional development team working smoothly.

Polly Crisman – Graphic Designer and Illustrator

B.F.A., University of New Hampshire

Graphic artist with expertise in advertising and marketing design, freelance illustrating, and caricature art.

Patsy DeCoster – Staff Development and Service Director

B.S., Biology/Secondary education, Grove City College; M.Ed., Tufts University

Curriculum and professional development specialist. Taught science for 12 years. National inquiry-based science presenter.

Erik Benton – Professional Development Specialist

B.F.A., University of Massachusetts

Taught for 8 years in public and private schools, focusing on inquiry and experiential learning environments.

Matt Lombard – Photographing and Marketing

B.S., Salem State College

Oversees all marketing activities for CPO Science. Expertise in equipment photography and catalog design.

Susan Gioia– Education Office Administrator

Oversees all the details necessary to keep the education product team working smoothly.

CPO Science Equipment and Instrumentation

Greg Krekorian – Production manager

Roger Barous – Machinist

John Erickson – Electrical engineer

Nick Loy – Electrical engineer

George Silva – Electrical engineer/software

Dr. Darren Garnier – Physicist/software

Jim Hall – Electrical engineer

Shawn Greene – Electronics specialist

Kathryn Gavin – Quality specialist

David Zucker – Industrial engineer

Science Content Consultants

Stacy Kissel – Physics Teacher, Brookline High School, Brookline, Massachusetts

Eight years teaching experience physics, math and integrated science.

Kristy Beauvais – Physics Teacher, Concord-Carlisle Regional High School, Concord, Massachusetts

Six years teaching experience in physics and chemistry.

Dr. Darren Garnier – Research Physicist, Columbia University/MIT

Extensive experience with experiment design. Developed software and applications for the CPO Data Collector.

Dr. David Guerra – Associate Professor, Department Chair Physics, St. Anselm College, Manchester, New Hampshire

Fourteen years college teaching experience. Research laser development and applications.

David Bliss – Physics Teacher, Mohawk Central High School, New York, New York

Thirty-two years teaching experience.

Dr. Jeffrey Williams – Bridgewater State College, Bridgewater, Massachusetts

Physics department chairman.

Thomas C. Altman – Physics Teacher, Oswego High School, New York, New York

Twenty-one years teaching experience, NSTA Award winner, and inventor of Altman Holography Method.

Dr. Mitch Crosswait – Nuclear Engineer/Physicist, United States Government , Alexandria, VA.

Research scientist and technology analyst. Evaluates programs for their technical merit and advises government on science and technology.

Technical Consultants

Tracy Morrow – Framework expert, technical editing programs, and training of staff.

Julie Dalton – Senior Copy Editor, Journalist, sports writer and former English teacher.

James Travers – Graphic design and animation.

Mary Ann Erickson – Indexing/Glossary, Technical Writing and Engineering.

Science Content Reviewers

Dr. Jeff Schachter

Physicist
Boston, Massachusetts

Dr. Willa Ramsay

Science Education Consultant
San Diego, California

Beverly T. Cannon

Physics Teacher
Highland Park High School
Dallas, Texas

Betsy Nahas

Physics Teacher
Chelmsford High School
Westford, Massachusetts

Bruce Ward

Nuclear Medical Technician
Boston, Massachusetts

Dr. Michael Saulnier

Physicist
Boston, Massachusetts

Lebee Meehan

Physicist
National Aeronautics and Space Administration
Houston, Texas

Dr. Manos Chaniotakis

Physicist
Massachusetts Institute of Technology
Cambridge, Massachusetts

David Binette

Engineering Student
Cornell University
Ithaca, New York

Hetta Englehardt

Student
Brookline High School
Brookline, Massachusetts

Ziliang Lin

Student
Brookline High School
Brookline, Massachusetts

Science Through Discovery

The whole of science is nothing more than a refinement of everyday thinking.
Albert Einstein

In many learning situations, you are expected to study prescribed materials and come up with correct answers by yourself. In science, you usually read the information and then experiment in a laboratory to visualize what you read. With the *Foundations of Physics Program* you will find that science is experienced through carrying out investigations and solving problems.

What you learn in school should be connected to what you see in the world. These connections will contribute to your success in learning physics. You will learn to observe how and why something happens by observing an action and then connecting your observations to the natural laws of science. In your life, you will need to ask insightful questions, plan, organize your work, look for and analyze information, try out an idea and if it doesn't work, try again. Physics teaches you how to problem solve, analyze observed actions, and test their ideas.

The *Foundations of Physics* program provides you the opportunity to analyze ideas, formulate questions, find your own ways to solve problems, and work with other students.

About the Physics Student Text

Foundations of Physics is an inquiry-centered program that combines the best attributes of "conceptual" and mathematical approaches to learning physics. Direct observation comes first; you will discover firsthand what happens. Each new concept is introduced through connections to real world applications, either in the lab or though the reading in the text. Theoretical information through the readings is provided to give you the "how" and "why." What you learn from the investigations and reading will show how fundamental concepts explain a wide range of phenomena. An application at the end of each chapter pulls concepts together to connect topics in the chapter to the real world.

The text emphasizes conceptual understanding and is written in a clear, informal and reader-friendly style. Margin notes provide an outline to aid you in finding the main ideas and concepts. Because we learn in different ways, nearly every concept is presented in words and through graphs, charts and tables. Conceptual knowledge is supported by basic mathematical techniques found in math topics such as algebra. You learn to use important equations as a means to analyze data and solve quantitative problems. Many example problems are provided through a problem solving technique to help you to learn how to approach a word problem and solve it.

Foundations of Physics contains Nine Units and has Thirty One Chapters. Each Chapter is divided into three Sections. You will notice that many of the important concepts are repeated in different ways, equations are highlighted with an explanation for each symbol and example problems are solved for you. Applications that follow each Chapter (with the exception of the first and last Chapters) explain how physics is used in practical ways.

Student Text Main Components

Main text: In addition to reading about science concepts and skills, you will discover brief stories about important inventions, real world connections, environmental issues, and interesting facts.

Chapter pages: Each chapter starts with two pages that outline what you will learn in the chapter. These pages provide you with a brief summary, the key questions for each Investigation, vocabulary, and learning goals.

Review questions: After each section, there are review questions that evaluate what you have learned and support you and your teacher in choosing what needs to be reviewed and which concepts to discuss further.

Glossary: The glossary is where you will find the meaning of words that describe important science concepts and essential vocabulary. You can also find references to important people who are discussed in your reading.

Index: This section helps you find more specific topic information by giving page numbers that refer to the topic. You can use the index while studying to find information.

Reference tables: The inside back cover of the book is a quick reference for physical constants, variable names, and scientific notation.

Student Text Pages

Sidenotes (idea headers): In the left margin of each page you will find phrases, short sentences, and questions to guide you in understanding the most important ideas. These sidenotes will also help you skim the text and quickly find information when you are reviewing and studying for tests.

Illustrations: Use the illustrations, graphs, charts, and data tables to help you understand the reading. These reading tools help most students improve their understanding of the key concepts.

Vocabulary words: The vocabulary words are highlighted in blue. You need to understand their meanings to be successful in science and will find the same vocabulary used in many contexts and repeated throughout the text. The definitions can be found in the glossary.

Data tables: These tables will help you understand complex information, organize numerical data, and provide examples of how to collect and present data.

Figure number/captions: As you are reading, notice the references to the word *Figure* followed by a number. These figures are found on the right side of the page in the form of an illustration, picture, or chart. The figure number indicates which figure goes with the text you are reading and gives you another way to understand the information in the reading.

STUDENT TEXT PAGES

Icon representing unit topic

Main text including highlighted vocabulary words

Introduction to section content

Section number and title

Illustrations that support content

Side note highlighting new ideas in reading

Table organizing important concepts and data

Figure number is referenced from the text

Left page (20)

3.1 Speed

Nothing in the universe stays still. The book on the table might appear to be sitting still, but the Earth is moving through space in its orbit around the sun at a speed of 66,000 miles per hour. You and the book move with the Earth. This section is about speed, which is the first part of a describing motion. Just saying that something is fast is not enough description to truly compare speeds. You can easily walk faster than a turtle, yet you would not say walking speed was fast compared with the speed of driving a car. The first step to understanding motion is to define speed very precisely.

What do we mean by speed?

An example of speed — Consider a bicycle that is moving along the road. The graphs below show the position of the bicycle at different times. The speed of the bicycle is the answer to the following questions.

- How many meters does the bicycle move for each second?
- Does the bicycle move the same number of meters every second?

Moving at a speed of **1** meter per second

Time (seconds)

Distance (meters)

Moving at a speed of **3** meters per second

Time (seconds)

Distance (meters)

The precise meaning of speed — The speed of the bicycle is the distance it moves divided by the time it takes. A bicycle moving at 3 m/sec covers three meters every second. In five seconds the bicycle has moved 15 meters. The bicycle in the diagram is moving at constant speed. Constant speed means it covers the same distance in meters every second.

prevent matter from traveling faster than the speed of light.

20

Right page (21)

Chapter 3

Calculating speed

Speed is distance divided by time — Speed is a measure of the *distance* traveled in a given amount of *time*. Therefore, to calculate the speed of an object, you need to know two things:

- The distance traveled by the object.
- The time it took to travel the given distance.

Speed is calculated by dividing the distance traveled by the time taken. For example, if you drive 90 miles in 1.5 hours (Figure 3.1), then the speed of the car is 90 miles divided by 1.5 hours, which is equal to 60 miles per hour.

What does "per" mean? — The word "per" means "for every" or "for each." The speed of 60 miles per hour is short for saying 60 miles *for each* hour. You can also think of the word "per" as meaning "divided by." The quantity before the word per is divided by the quantity after it. For example, 90 miles ÷ 1.5 hours equals 60 miles per hour.

Units for speed — Since speed is a ratio of distance over time, the units for speed are a ratio of distance units over time units. If distance is in miles and time in hours, then speed is expressed in miles per hour (miles/hours). In the metric system, distance is measured in centimeters, meters, or kilometers. Metric units for speed are centimeters per second (cm/sec), meters per second (m/sec), or kilometers per hour (km/h). Table 3.1 shows many different units commonly used for speed.

Figure 3.1: *A driving trip with an average speed of 60 miles per hour.*

$$\frac{90\ miles}{1.5\ hours} = 60\ miles\ per\ hour\ (mph)$$

Table 3.1: Some Common Units for Speed

Distance	Time	Speed	Abbreviation
meters	seconds	meters per second	m/sec
kilometers	hours	kilometers per hour	km/h
centimeters	seconds	centimeters per second	cm/sec
miles	hours	miles per hour	mph
inches	seconds	inches per second	in/sec, ips
feet	minutes	feet per minute	ft/min, fpm

Calculate speed in meters per second

A bird is observed to fly 50 meters in 7.5 seconds. Calculate the speed of the bird in meters per second

1) You are asked to find speed in m/sec.
2) You are given the distance in m and time in sec.
3) v = d ÷ t
4) v = 50 m ÷ 7.5 sec
   = 6.67 m/sec

3.1 Speed

21

Topics and degree of difficulty

A high school physics course covers many different topics. The philosophy of how we chose topics is described below.

- The topics in this book cover the complete content for a standards-based introductory course in physics, with an emphasis on practical application of physics to real technology.
- Topics start with practical concepts developed through hands-on investigation, then proceed to theory. For example, we start with circuits that can be built with wires and batteries. Only after you have completed a thorough investigation and discussed of circuits do we proceed to the more difficult and abstract treatment of electric charges and fields.
- We excluded historical information in the text that was not necessary for the understanding of the concepts. While the history of physics is important, it is not necessary to learn and apply physics to real world problems. History is covered in our ancillary materials.
- Practical physics such as music, heat transfer, electronics, and the strength of materials is presented as well as more traditional theoretical material such as forces and fields.

The text contains far more material than we expect anyone to teach in a one year course. This provides a variety of choices of topics for your teacher to cover. Some of the topics selected are more advanced than others and may be skipped without affecting the overall flow of a course. The advanced topics are indicated with the ⟨Advanced topic⟩ icon on the header of the page. Advanced topics include calculations that are more difficult or outside the normal scope of an introductory course.

When the force and lever arm are not perpendicular ⟨Advanced topic⟩

Force and lever arm are not always perpendicular

Torque is easiest to calculate when the lever arm and force are at right angles to each other. In this situation the lever arm is the same as the distance between the point where the force is applied and the center of rotation. When the force and lever arm are *not* perpendicular, an extra step is required to calculate the length of the lever arm.

Torque in English units

In the English system of units, torque is measured in inch-pounds or foot-pounds. A torque of one foot-pound is created by a force of one pound applied with a lever arm of one foot. One foot-pound is equal to 12 inch-pounds.

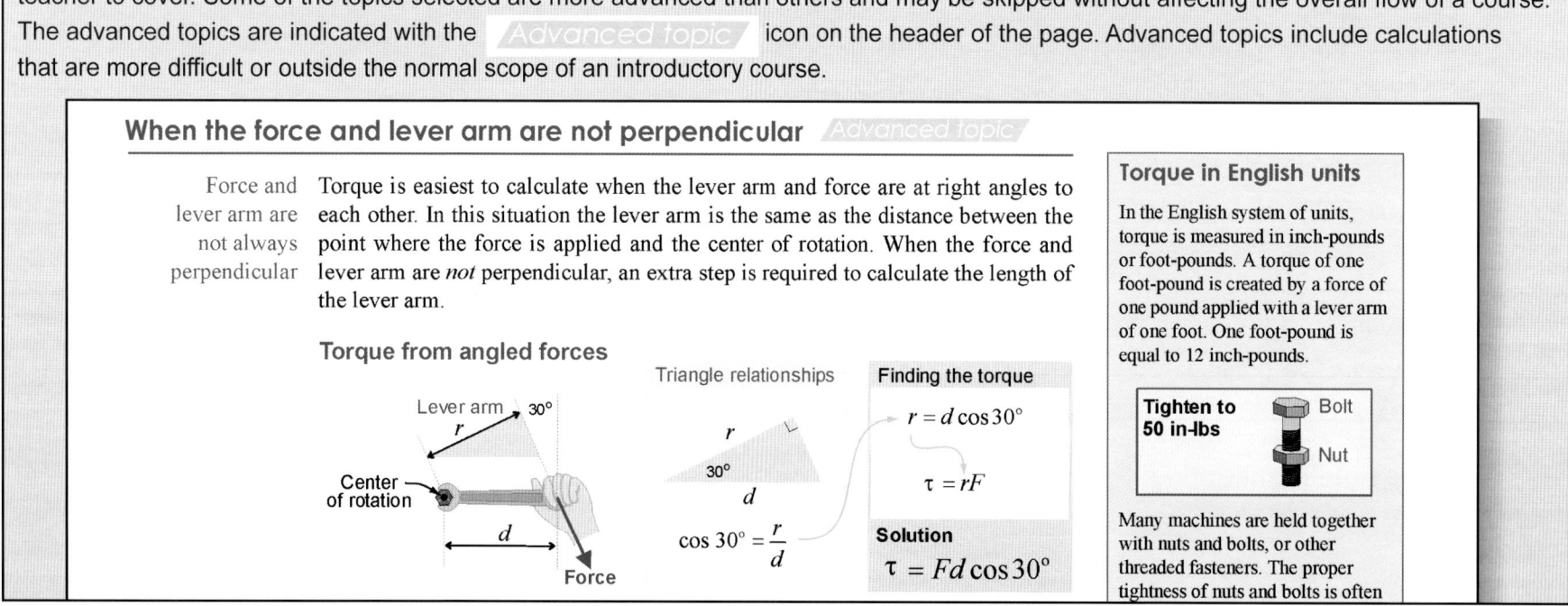

Torque from angled forces

Triangle relationships

Finding the torque

$r = d\cos 30°$

$\cos 30° = \dfrac{r}{d}$

$\tau = rF$

Solution

$\tau = Fd\cos 30°$

Tighten to 50 in-lbs — Bolt / Nut

Many machines are held together with nuts and bolts, or other threaded fasteners. The proper tightness of nuts and bolts is often

Investigation Text

The Investigations lab manual provides a series of 87 hands-on investigations, one for each of the 87 content sections of the text ((excluding the introduction and conclusion). This is a true inquiry-based approach to teaching physics: most of the investigations are performed before you read the corresponding section in the student text. Concepts are discovered and explored rather than proven or demonstrated. The equipment, lab manual and text were designed together to seamlessly reinforce your learning. Graphics in the text and lab manual precisely match what you use and see in the lab. Content development in the text is structured around lab experiences. In this way, you see and explore natural laws of science while you read about how they work.

Familiar things happen, and mankind does not bother about them. It requires a very unusual mind to undertake the analysis of the obvious.
Alfred North Whitehead

Features of the Investigation

Key question: Each Investigation starts with a key question that conveys the focus of the lesson. This question tells you what information you need to collect in order to answer the questions at the end of the Investigation.

Data tables: Data tables help you collect and organize your data in a systematic manner.

Learning objectives (goals): At the top of each investigation are the learning goals. These statements will explain what you will have learned and what you be able to do after completing the Investigation.

Brief introduction: This information helps you understand why the exercise is important to complete and, in most cases, how it connects to other sections of your reading.

Icons and section title: The icon is a reminder of the unit that you are studying. The section title corresponds to the reading in your student text.

Numbered steps: The Investigation sequence numbers point out the sequence of steps you will need to follow to successfully complete the Investigation. These steps highlight specific stages of the scientific method such as: following directions, completing hands-on experiments, collecting and analyzing data and presenting the results. The *Applying your Knowledge* step asks you to reflect on what you have learned and to explain your findings.

Illustrations: The illustrations support your understanding of the Investigation procedures.

Fill-in answer sheets: Your teacher will provide you with answer sheets to fill in the data tables and written responses. At times your teacher may collect this data to compile class results. You can also use the sheets to reinforce your reading in your student text.

INVESTIGATION PAGES

Section number referenced from the student text

Section title reference from the student text

Key question

Major learning objective for the Investigation

Icon representing unit topic

Investigation sequence numbers

Illustrations and charts that support content

Explanation of Investigation content

Example space for data*

Detailed explanations of Investigation procedures, equipment setup, and data collection

Thought-provoking question

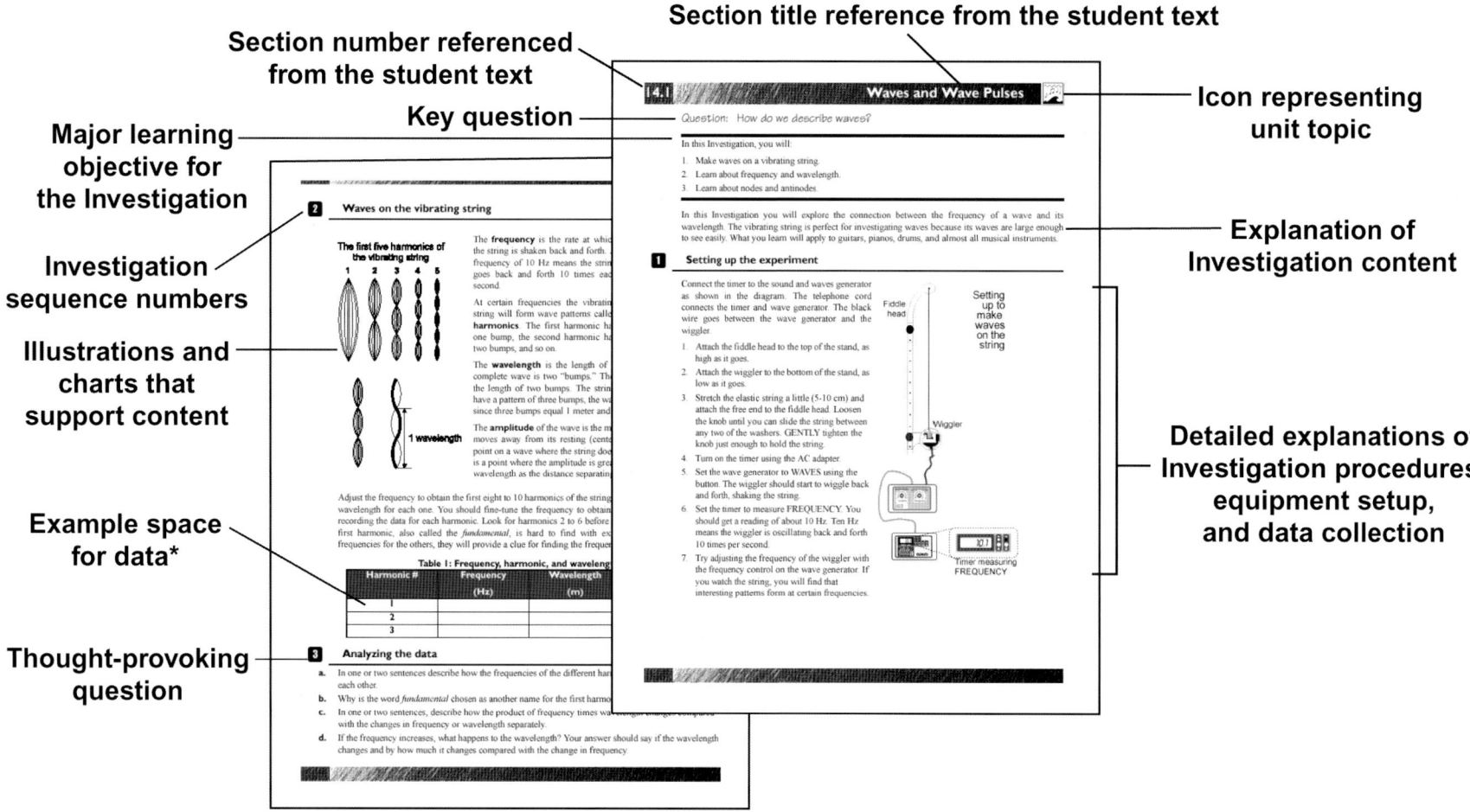

* Note: All data and answers to questions will be written on a separate, fill-in answer sheet

Student Text Chapter Pages

Each *Unit* is comprised of three *Chapters* and one application. Each chapter has a front page called a Chapter page. This page outlines the objectives or major topics that will be covered and the most important vocabulary. It is important to refer back to these pages to check to see if you have understood information about each topic. Features of the Chapter Pages include:

Learning objectives: These goals are the major ideas that you will explore throughout the chapter. You should check this list by going back and re-reading to make sure you can explain each of these concepts in writing or to another person.

Vocabulary: The list of vocabulary words at the beginning of the chapter will familiarize you with the words in the chapter. Understanding the science vocabulary will help you learn the concepts in the readings. Reviewing the vocabulary list to identify terms that you are familiar with is a good way to begin each chapter.

Unit Icons Guide

Unit icons are used to identify what unit topic you are studying. You will see these icons with the chapter number on the right-hand chapter page and on the Investigation right hand corners.

	Unit One: Measurement and Motion		Unit Six: Light and Optics
	Unit Two: Motion and Force in One Dimension		Unit Seven: Electricity and Magnetism
	Unit Three: Motion and Force in 2 and 3 Dimensions		Unit Eight: Matter and Energy
	Unit Four: Energy and Momentum		Unit Nine: The Atom
	Unit Five: Waves and Sound		Chapter 31: The Edge of Physics

CHAPTER PAGES

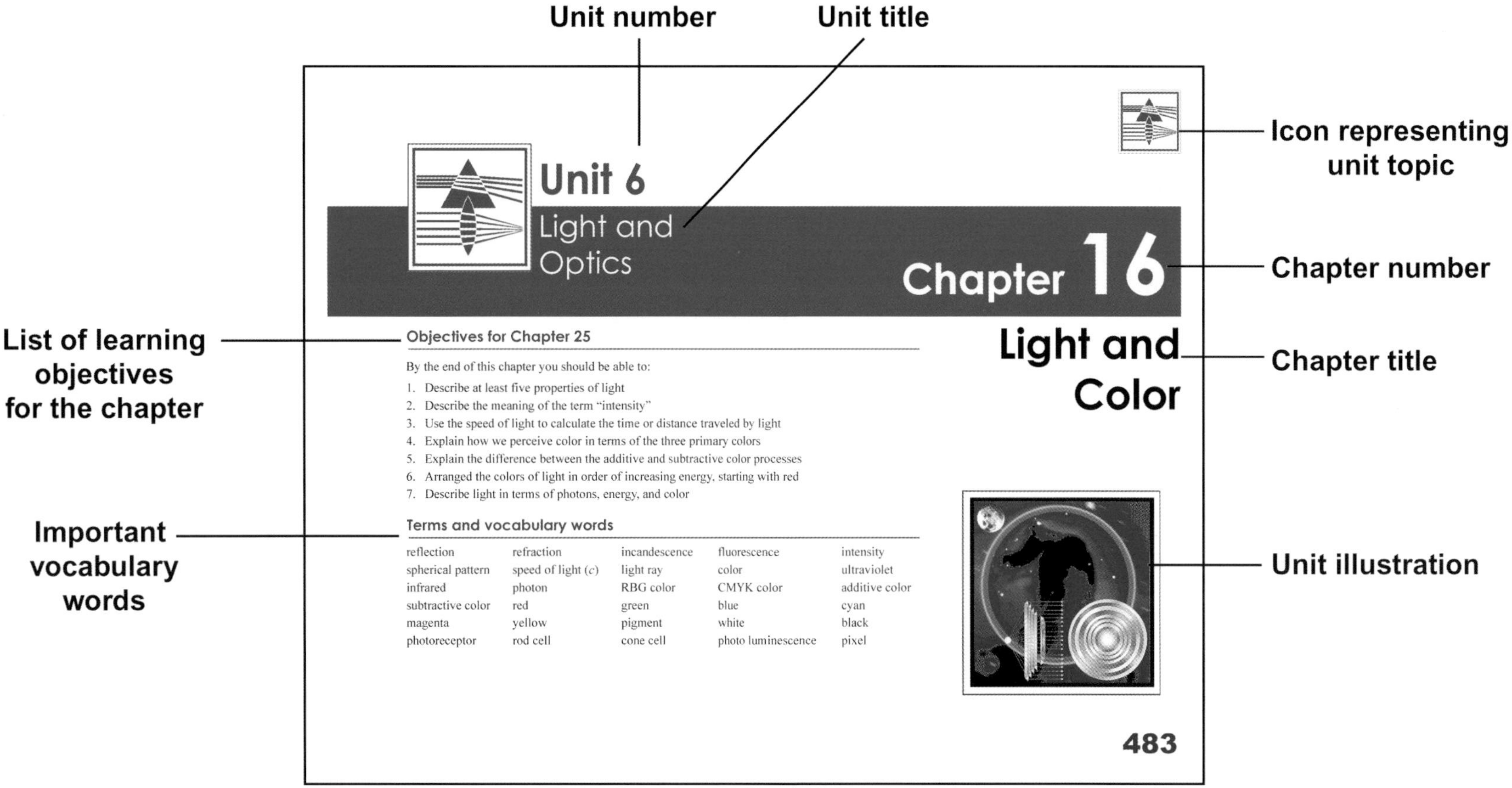

Unit number

Unit title

Icon representing unit topic

Unit 6
Light and Optics

Chapter number

Chapter 16

Chapter title

Objectives for Chapter 25

By the end of this chapter you should be able to:

1. Describe at least five properties of light
2. Describe the meaning of the term "intensity"
3. Use the speed of light to calculate the time or distance traveled by light
4. Explain how we perceive color in terms of the three primary colors
5. Explain the difference between the additive and subtractive color processes
6. Arranged the colors of light in order of increasing energy, starting with red
7. Describe light in terms of photons, energy, and color

List of learning objectives for the chapter

Light and Color

Terms and vocabulary words

reflection	refraction	incandescence	fluorescence	intensity
spherical pattern	speed of light (*c*)	light ray	color	ultraviolet
infrared	photon	RBG color	CMYK color	additive color
subtractive color	red	green	blue	cyan
magenta	yellow	pigment	white	black
photoreceptor	rod cell	cone cell	photo luminescence	pixel

Important vocabulary words

Unit illustration

483

Introduction

Unit 1: Measurement and Motion

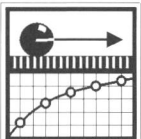

Unit 2: Motion and Force in One Dimension

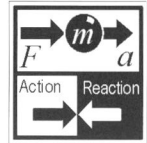

Unit 3: Motion and Force in 2 and 3 Dimensions

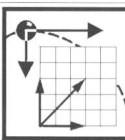

CONTENTS

Table of Contents

CONTENTS

Unit 7: Electricity and Magnetism

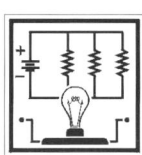

CONTENTS

Table of Contents

xi

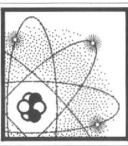
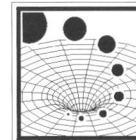

Introduction

The Science of Physics

Objectives for Chapter 1

By the end of this chapter you should be able to:

1. Describe what physics is about
2. Describe the process of inquiry and the relationship between inquiry and learning physics.
3. Describe the difference between matter and energy.
4. Explain the relationship between a theory, a hypothesis, a natural law and an experiment.
5. Describe at least three examples of how physics knowledge is used in a career or occupation outside of physics.

Terms and vocabulary words

natural law	process	analysis	inquiry	hypothesis
experiment	theory	energy	matter	scientific evidence
objectivity	repeatability			

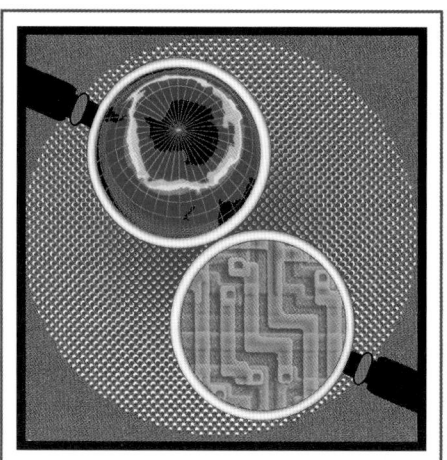

1.1 The Science of Physics

What is physics and why study it? Many students think physics is a complicated set of rules, equations to memorize, and confusing laws. Although this is sometimes the way physics is *taught*, it is not a fair description of the science. In fact, physics is about finding the simplest and *least complicated* explanation for things. It is about observing how things work and finding the fundamental connections between *cause* and *effect* that explain why nature does what it does.

Three fundamental aspects of physics are:

- **Describing the organization of the universe**. The *universe* is defined as everything that exists. Everything in the universe is believed to be either matter or energy (Figure 1.1). Matter is "stuff" that has mass. You are made of matter, and so is a rock and the air around you. Energy is the ability to make things change. Energy is exchanged any time anything gets hotter, colder, faster, slower, or changes in any other observable way. A new idea in physics adds a third component to the universe: *information*. Information describes how matter and energy are arranged. For example, information describes how the matter in this book is organized into pages, printed words, etc. The physics of describing information is relatively new and not yet well defined.

- **Understanding the natural laws that govern the universe.** We believe all events that happen in nature obey a set of *natural laws* that do not change. The natural laws are the rules that govern the fundamental workings of the universe. A second aspect of physics is understanding the natural laws that relate cause and effect in the universe to matter and energy. For example, one such law governs motion. If a ball rolls down a ramp, it will have a certain speed at the bottom. If the same ball rolls down the same ramp again, it will have the same speed. Nature is reliable in that it *always* obeys the same natural laws.

- **Deducing and applying natural laws.** The third key aspect of physics is the process of deducing the natural laws and applying them to real situations. This part of physics includes experiment and analysis. Analysis is the process of breaking down a complex situation or problem into smaller parts that can be understood in terms of the natural laws. Real-life situations are rarely simple and must be analyzed before knowledge of physics can be applied. For example, the motion of an airplane depends on more than just the force from the engines. The motion of the air (wind) and the resistance of the air are important factors. To apply the laws of motion to an airplane in a meaningful way, you need to analyze its motion in order to identify all the important factors.

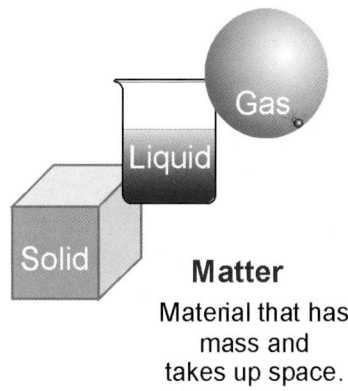

Matter
Material that has mass and takes up space.

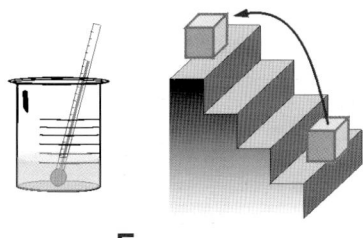

Energy
The ability to make things change, such as temperature, height, or speed.

Figure 1.1: *The universe contains only matter and energy.*

Learning physics through inquiry

Physics is learned by observing what happens and thinking clearly about cause and effect. For example, when you drop a ball, gravity pulls it down (Figure 1.2). Dropping a ball is a specific event that happens. *Things fall under the influence of gravity* is an observation that connects an effect (things falling) to a cause (gravity). Over centuries, we have discovered the natural laws by looking for consistent patterns in observations of events. When we learn the natural laws, we gain understanding of *why* something happens. More importantly, we can predict when it will happen again or even how to *make* it happen (or prevent it from happening).

Observation

Objects fall under the influence of gravity when they are dropped.

Figure 1.2: *A observation about how things behave when they are dropped.*

We do not know all the laws of nature. We are still learning physics by observing how the universe works and trying to deduce the laws (the causes) from what we can observe (the effects). In physics as in other areas of science, the process of learning through observing is called inquiry. The process of inquiry is similar to the process of solving a mystery. Inquiry starts with questions (Figure 1.3). For example:

1. Why does it take more force to move heavier objects?

2. Does it take twice as much force if the object weighs twice as much?

3. How can we measure force?

4. How can we measure motion in a way that we can relate it to force?

Observation

It takes more force to move a heavy cart than it does to move a light cart.

Inquiry

What is the relationship between force and motion?

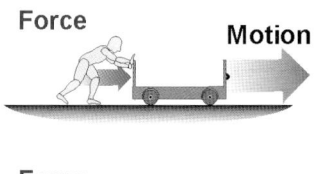

Inquiry is a skill you use every day. You continually test your ideas against your observations and over time, you develop *common sense*. Common sense is actually the physics of everyday life, to a large degree. For example, consider pushing a cart of groceries. You *know* more force is required to push heavier carts and less force to push lighter carts. Common sense says that heavier carts take more force to push. However, you were not born with this knowledge! The knowledge that makes up common sense came from trying it yourself (inquiry) and drawing conclusions from what you experienced. The common-sense understanding of force is part of a fundamental natural law of physics.

This book will help you deepen and broaden the understanding of physics you already have from your own common sense. Your knowledge will be increased by doing Investigations that strip away unnecessary complications, allowing you to focus on the essence of each natural law. Much of the physics you learn will come from thinking about what you observe during an Investigation, talking over your ideas with friends and with your instructor, and also reading this book.

Figure 1.3: *Observation leads to inquiry and inquiry is how we learn.*

Inquiry is an excellent way to learn physics

As you do the investigations that accompany this book, you will try to deduce the natural laws of physics using your own process of inquiry. Each of the important natural laws is introduced by investigating one or more real systems. The systems are chosen to show how the law under investigation causes observable changes that can be used to deduce the law itself. For example, you will apply force to moving objects and measure how fast they move. Through this experience, you discover a natural law that connects force and motion (Figure 1.4). This is an extremely powerful law because it applies to ALL forces and ALL motions, whether the moving object is a golf ball or a planet.

There are other ways to learn the natural laws. One way is to have them recited to you. Another way is to read them. Reading and listening are necessary, but often are not enough to allow you to *understand* and *use* the knowledge. For example in soccer there is a rule that says a team gets a penalty if a defensive player is 'off sides'. This rule is difficult to understand unless you know a lot more about soccer, including the definition of 'off sides' and who counts as a defensive player. Just reading the rule in a book will not help you use the rule. You need to see how the rule is applied to the game, how it affects the scoring of the game and under what circumstances it is used.

Three valuable things are learned by discovering the natural laws through inquiry:

1. You will learn the basic natural laws that describe how the universe and everything in it works. This includes scientific concepts such as atoms, mass, and force. It also includes very practical things such as bicycles, antilock brakes, televisions, and the digital recording of music.

2. Someday, maybe tomorrow, you will be stumped by something that does not work in your life outside the classroom. It is very unlikely this book or any other book will have taught you to fix the exact thing that has you stumped. Inquiry teaches you how to systematically observe almost *any* system to find out how it generally works. Once you know how something generally works, you can often figure out how to make it work for *you*. This is an extraordinarily useful skill.

3. Learning the natural laws by observing them in real systems will help you use what you learn to solve real-life problems. Like most knowledge, the value in knowing physics really comes from understanding how to *apply* what you know to situations *different* from the one in which you first learned the knowledge.

Natural law

The change in motion of an object is proportional to the force applied and inversely proportional to the mass of the object.

Application of the law

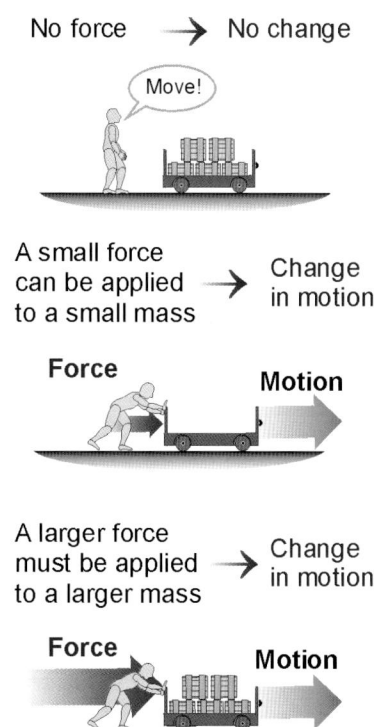

Figure 1.4: *An example of a natural law and its application.*

Problem-solving techniques

Learning physics helps you become a better problem-solver. Problem solving means using what you know to figure out something you don't know. Analysis and problem solving go together. You cannot solve a problem until you analyze it to find out which laws apply and what you know already about the problem. This book presents and demonstrate some useful techniques that help you apply your knowledge of physics to solving problems. Solved *example problems* appear in every section. You can recognize example problems by the icon and the blue box around them.

Example problem icon

The technique for problem solving has four steps:

1. Determine what the problem asks you to find out.
   Be very specific. For example, when a problem asks how fast something is moving, the answer is the *speed*. Do not get sidetracked looking for things you do not need.

2. Identify information you are given.
   Information may be measurements, such as mass or length. Information may also be descriptive. For example, "at rest" means something is not moving and has a speed of zero.

3. Identify laws or relationships
   Identify relationships that involve what you need to know and/or information you are given. For example, if you want to know speed and are given distance and time, you would write down the formula for speed that includes distance and time. Some problems require more than one relationship.

4. Apply the given information and the relationships
   Once you have collected the information and the relationships, you will be able to see how to use what you know to get the solution. The solution may take more than one step. For example, you may need to use one relationship to find something that is needed for a second relationship.

These problem-solving steps are a useful technique for finding solutions in many subjects and situations, not just physics!

Calculate time from speed and distance

How long to take to travel 2,000 kilometers at a speed of 100 kilometers per second?

1) You are asked to find time.
2) You are given the distance in km and speed in km/h.
3) Time is distance ÷ speed
4) Time = 2,000 km ÷ 100 km/h
   = 20 hours

The organization of this book

Two themes are emphasized throughout *Foundations of Physics*. These themes are *energy* and *atoms* and they connect all areas of physics. They also connect physics to chemistry, biology, and other areas of science and technology. For example, the connection between the speed of a ball and the temperature of the air is not obvious. But once you understand energy and atoms, you can use one to explain the other. Energy describes the ability of a system to make things change. The "things" that change are usually made of matter. Most matter is composed of atoms. The same basic laws that explain the motion of a ball also apply to the motion of atoms and are the foundation for understanding temperature, sound, and even electricity.

Figure 1.5 shows the major topics and units in the book. Each icon identifies a particular unit.

The concept of energy is introduced through the study of motion and force in Units 1-4. These four units build a foundation of concepts and principles that apply to all of physics. The first four units also give you practice in analytical thinking and problem solving using familiar systems such as rolling balls and ramps. Later units develop concepts that are more abstract.

Units 5 and 6 introduce waves, sound, light, and optics. The unit starts by exploring motion that repeats, like a pendulum. Waves are repeating motions that travel, carrying energy and information. For example, cell phones use microwaves to carry voices. A study of light, mirrors, and lenses concludes this unit, including a discussion of time travel and Einstein's theory of special relativity.

Energy and atoms are found again in Unit 7 with the study of electricity and magnetism. The unit starts with the exploration of circuits and electric power. Then we look inside the atom for the fundamental nature of electricity itself. From electricity we move to magnetism and show how electric motors and generators work. The unit concludes with an introduction to semiconductors and electronics.

The last two units (8 and 9) focus on the interactions of matter and energy, building on the conceptual foundation of energy and atoms. The meaning of temperature and the flow of heat are explained in terms of energy and atoms. Properties of solids, liquids, and gases are investigated, and used. For example, to design something strong enough to resist breaking. Unit 9 delves inside the atom and into the fundamental forces that make the universe work. Chapters on chemistry and nuclear reactions show how our understanding of atoms connects to the real world.

Chapter 31 is somewhat special, and takes a short look at some advanced ideas near the cutting edge of what we understand.

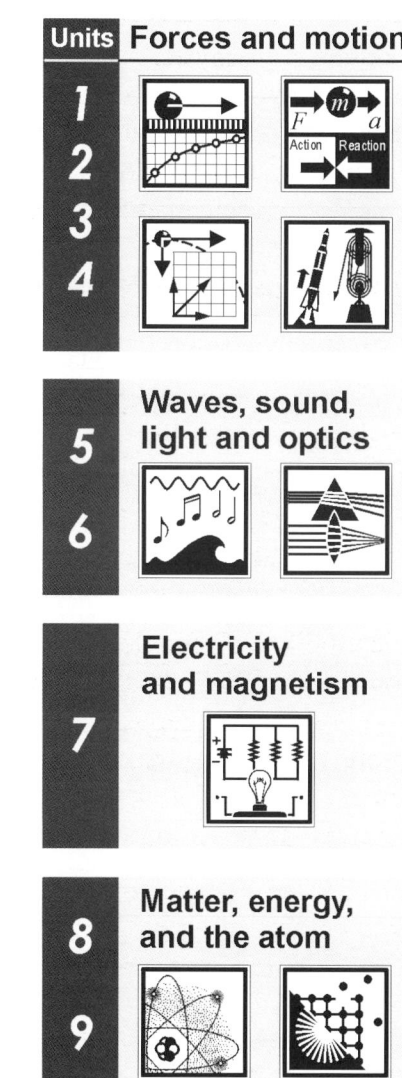

Figure 1.5: *Organization of the nine units in the book. Chapter 31 is special (last chapter).*

1.2 The Development of Scientific Knowledge

Like solving a mystery, the goal of inquiry is to uncover truth. In science, the truth is an explanation that correctly predicts what happens all the time in every situation. For example, light approaching a mirror at a certain angle reflects off the mirror at the same angle. This statement is called the *law of reflection*. The law of reflection is true because it correctly predicts how light reflects off a mirror every time. How do scientists uncover the truth?

Models and explanations

People are naturally curious and learn by watching and trying out their ideas. For example, watch a small child learn to open a jar (Figure 1.6). The child tries everything she knows, including biting the jar, dropping it, pulling on it, shaking it. By chance, she tries twisting the lid—and it comes off. She tries it again—and the lid comes off again. The child learns to open a jar by *trying everything and remembering what works*. A child who has learned how to open a jar by twisting the top quickly tries the same tactic on every jar. Once a rule is learned through experience, we naturally generalize and try to apply the rule to other, similar situations.

Scientific knowledge develops the same way a child learns to open a jar. Of course, as adults we are more systematic in what we try and how we interpret what we observe. However, we still try things, and observe what happens. We then create a mental model called an *explanation* to connect what was observed with what we know. For example, a simple explanation for why rivers and streams flow is that water flows downhill. If you need water to flow to a specific location, you arrange the land so the place you want the water to flow is downhill from the water source.

Scientific knowledge grows by systematically extending simple explanations to include more complex situations. For example, water in a pipe normally flows downhill. But you can easily make water in a straw flow uphill by sucking on the straw. The model for flowing water must be revised to include the possibility of suction forcing water to flow uphill. To describe "suction", we introduce the concept of pressure. Water can be sucked up a straw because water flows from higher pressure to lower pressure (Figure 1.7). This is a new explanation that both explains the old observations (water flows downhill) and the new observations (sucking water uphill in a straw). It is important to remember that *we were not born with this knowledge*. We developed scientific knowledge through the observations, thoughts, and experiments of many people over many centuries.

Figure 1.6: *We learn new things by trying everything and remembering what works!*

Simple model
Water flows downhill

Improved model
Water flows from high pressure to low pressure

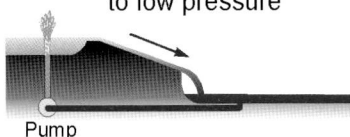

Pump

Figure 1.7: *Models usually start simple and are improved to explain new observations.*

The importance of experiments

The search for scientific knowledge begins with someone thinking about something they saw. This thinking eventually takes the form of a hunch, or **hypothesis** about how one thing affects another. For example, how the steepness of a ramp affects the time it takes a ball to roll down.

Observations in physics are usually described by variables. Variables are things that you can measure. For example, speed is a familiar variable that describes how fast a ball is moving. An **experiment** is a situation set up specifically to test what happens under controlled conditions (Figure 1.8). An experiment allows you to change one variable at a time so you can determine precisely how other variables respond to specific changes.

A good hypothesis successfully describes the results of an observation or experiment. For example, a hypothesis might be that the speed of a ball rolling down a ramp follows a certain formula. A graph of real data can be used to confirm the hypothesis. Or, the data might show that the hypothesis is wrong! Even the smartest people rarely get the correct hypothesis without doing many experiments. The validity of a hypothesis improves as more experiments are completed and analyzed.

A **theory** is a comprehensive explanation of how and why a process in nature works the way it does. Theories are formulated from many well tested hypotheses. Like hypotheses, theories are rarely correct at first. For example, it was once believed that heat is a fluid that moves from hot to cold. Hot objects have more of this fluid than cold objects. People tested this theory and eventually found it to be incorrect. But the process of testing the theory led to a better theory of heat that we still believe today. New scientific theories are discovered gradually, by many people working and thinking together.

A theory that correctly explains 1,000 experiments but fails to explain the 1,001st cannot be completely correct. However, an unexplained experiment does not usually mean a theory is totally wrong. More likely, the theory is *incomplete*. In fact, the purpose of scientific research (or, to some people, the motivation for it) is to find experiments where existing theories do NOT give the right prediction. A theory that makes the wrong prediction is a clue that there is something new to be discovered!

Experiments are vital because they are the only true test of whether a theory is correct or not. A natural law is a theory that has reliably described the outcome of every single experiment over a long period of time. Few theories make it to this level of confidence because it is a very rigorous test. In the dark ages people believed scientific truth could be determined purely by thinking. Today we believe otherwise. The truth is what actually happens in experiments. To unravel the mysteries of nature, our thinking must continually be guided by what nature actually does in experiments.

Variables   force
angle
time
weight
speed
distance

Experiment

Distance (cm)	Speed (cm/sec)
10	100
20	140
30	171
40	198
50	221
60	242
80	280
90	297

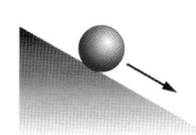

Model   Speed vs. distance

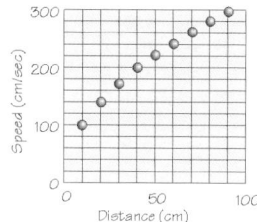

Prediction

At 55 centimeters, the speed of the ball will be 231 cm/sec.

Figure 1.8: *We use experiments to test and evaluate theories. A natural law is "discovered" when a theory successfully explains the results of every single experiment over a long period of time.*

Scientific evidence

The goal of an experiment is to produce **scientific evidence**. Scientific evidence may be in the form of measurements, data tables, graphs, observations, or any other information that describes what happens in the experiment (Figure 1.9). Two important characteristics of scientific evidence are that it be objective and repeatable. "Objective" means the evidence should describe only what actually happened as exactly as possible. The personal opinions of the person doing the experiment do not count as scientific evidence. "Repeatable" means that others who repeat the same experiment observe the same results. Good scientific evidence must pass the tests of both objectivity and repeatability.

Scientific evidence may also be produced by observing nature without actually doing an experiment. However, the same rules of objectivity and repeatability apply. For example, Galileo used his telescope to observe the moon and recorded his observations by sketching what he saw (Figure 1.9). His sketches describe in detail what he actually saw through the telescope, therefore they pass the test of objectivity. Others who looked through his telescope saw the same thing, therefore the sketches pass the test of repeatability. The scientific evidence of Gallileo's sketches convinced people that the Moon was actually a world like the Earth with mountains and valleys. This was not what people believed prior to Galileo's time.

It is important that scientific evidence be communicated clearly, with no room for misunderstanding. This means we must attach careful meanings to concepts like "force" and "work." Many "everyday" words will be defined very precisely in physics. Usually, the physics definition is similar to the way you already use the word, but more exact. For example, a quantity of "work" in physics means using a certain strength of force to move an object a certain distance. This definition allows a quantity of work to be defined with a precise measurement that tells someone else exactly how much combined force and distance were involved. Words like "a lot" or "easy" leave too much room for misunderstanding. Scientific evidence requires careful definition of words and measurements so others know exactly what you mean.

The way scientific evidence is gathered is usually important to understanding what the evidence means. Any presentation of scientific evidence always includes a description of how the evidence was collected. For example, an experiment includes a procedure, which describes how the experiment was done. The procedure includes important details, such as what instruments were used to make any measurements. The procedure must include enough details that someone else familiar with physics can repeat the same experiment to verify the repeatability of the evidence.

Examples of scientific evidence

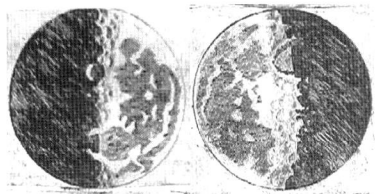

Pictures or sketches that show actual observations

time (sec)	speed (m/sec)	position (m)
0.0	0.00	0.00
0.2	0.83	0.08
0.4	1.66	0.33
0.6	2.50	0.75
0.8	3.33	1.33
1.0	4.16	2.08

Measurements and data

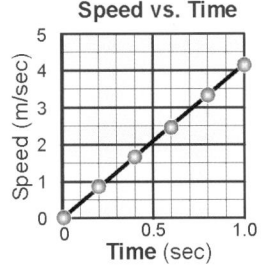

Graphs and charts made from measurements

Figure 1.9: *Some examples of scientific evidence.*

A good theory that started out wrong

All the natural laws we know today started as theories that were often wrong! The discovery of oxygen and its importance to fire and life is a good example. When a candle is burned in a closed container, the flame burns for a moment then quickly goes out. If a living organism such as a mouse is placed in a closed container, it will eventually suffocate. These observations led early scientists to inquire about the nature of fire and life.

An early theory of fire proposed that all materials contained a substance called *phlogiston* (pronounced FLO-jis-tuhn). When wood burned, it released its phlogiston (Figure 1.10). The ash of the burned wood was the true material, without its phlogiston. When substances burned in a closed container, the air became saturated with phlogiston and extinguished the flames. Too much phlogiston was thought to be toxic to life. A mouse eventually died in a closed container because phlogiston was given off during breathing and suffocated the mouse. In fact, when Joseph Priestly discovered oxygen in 1774, he declared the substance "dephlogisticated air." Today we know that oxygen makes up about one-fifth of the air in Earth's atmosphere.

The phlogiston theory received wide support by most scientists throughout much of the 18th century. Eventually however, accurate scientific evidence from experiments revealed problems with the theory. For example, when a metal burned, it was supposed to lose phlogiston. However, the metal ash left over after burning weighed *more* than the metal did before it had supposedly lost phlogiston. This implied that the removed phlogiston must have weighed less than zero. The work of Antoine Lavoisier (1743-94) finally disproved the phlogiston theory. Through careful experiments, Lavoisier concluded that as a metal burns, it increases in weight because it gains oxygen. Lavoisier made a symbolic break from the phlogiston theory by burning all his books that supported the theory. His theory of oxidation soon replaced the phlogiston theory and remains a part of modern chemistry.

While the phlogiston theory was not correct, it led to an important discovery. Oxygen was discovered partly because people were looking for phlogiston. In this book and other science books, you find a collection of natural laws and explanations for how things work. What is often left out is that the laws and explanations were nearly always incorrect at first. We learn new things by putting forth an idea and then testing it to see if it is right. *We cannot learn without starting from an idea, even the wrong idea.* As you learn physics, never be afraid to suggest an explanation for what you see. It does not matter if it is the right explanation, especially if you are just starting to understand what is happening. The scientific evidence you gather in experiments will eventually lead you to the correct explanation.

Wood = ashes + phlogiston

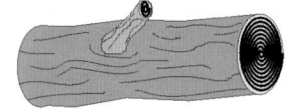

Fire is phlogiston leaving the wood

Ashes are *dephlogisticated* wood (pure wood)

Figure 1.10: *The phlogiston theory was an early attempt to explain fire.*

Scientific knowledge and the Solar System

The way people gradually understood the relationship between Earth, the sun, and the planets is a good example of how scientific knowledge develops. When you look at the sky, you see the sun rise in the east and set in the west. The sun seems to circle around the Earth. The planets, the moon, and the stars have similar apparent motion. Early theories of astronomy assumed that everything actually did move around the Earth. Ptolemy, a second-century Greco-Egyptian astronomer and geographer, is credited with creating a model for astronomy in which the Earth is at the center. In Ptolemy's theory, the stars, sun, and planets are affixed to the celestial spheres which rotate around the flat disk of the Earth. The sketch at the top of Figure 1.11 shows an explorer who reaches the edge of the Earth peering out from under the first, and lowest, celestial sphere, which contains the sky, clouds and air.

To most people, Ptolemy's model explained what they saw. To others, his model had problems, even before Galileo turned his telescope skyward. One of the biggest problems was that the planets sometimes reverse direction as they move through the night sky! This is because the apparent motion of the planets depends on the relative positions of the planets and the Earth in their respective orbits around the sun. For example, Mars sometimes appears to move backward in sky. Nicolaus Copernicus (1473-1543) correctly deduced that the planets revolve around the sun and not the other way around. However, Copernicus was not widely believed at any time during his life.

A more convincing argument for a sun-centered solar system was made almost 70 years later by Galileo. With his telescope, Galileo observed that Jupiter had four moons that moved around it. He correctly reasoned that if moons could move around Jupiter, why couldn't the Earth also move around the sun? Convinced of the truth of Copernicus's theory, Galileo spent much of his life trying to convince people to believe the evidence of their own observations. Then, as now, people often prefer to keep on believing what they already think they know, even when the evidence clearly shows such beliefs to be wrong! Scientists like Galileo showed great courage by insisting people face the evidence of their own eyes and learn about nature by observing what nature actually does.

Many historians believe the scientific revolution began with the acceptance of the Copernican model of the solar system. The importance of this event is not that Copernicus had the right answer. The importance is that, for the first time, scientific evidence was used to decide the difference between the right explanation and the wrong one. Remember, scientific evidence comes from direct observation, *what is actually measured or seen to happen*. Before the scientific revolution, people believed more in tradition than in what they observed with their own senses.

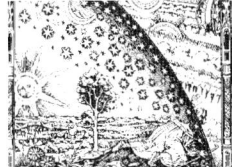

Early civilizations believed the Earth was covered by a dome on which the sun, stars and planets moved.

In the Middle Ages people thought the sun, stars, and planets circled the Earth which sat in the center.

Today we know the Earth and planets orbit around the sun and the stars are very far away.

Figure 1.11: *Three different models for the Solar System that were believed at different times in history.*

1.3 Physics Is Useful

Physics plays a role in nearly everything you do. You will see how physics applies to your life by doing the Investigations and reading how physics is used in everyday situations. There are many careers that use the concepts learned through a study of physics. This section describes a few examples.

Engineering

Engineering is the practice of using scientific knowledge to develop technology. *Technology* includes all the inventions and techniques humans have developed, such as cars, microwave ovens, computers, and even the horse-drawn plow. Engineering and technology are based on the fundamental laws of physics. For example engineers apply the laws of forces (Chapters 5 and 6) and strength of materials (Chapter 27) to design a bridge that can carry traffic safely across a river (Figure 1.12).

Cell phones are designed by *electrical engineers* using the physics of electricity (Chapters 19-24) and light waves (Chapter 18). A cell phone uses microwaves to carry your voice from the phone to a relay station (Figure 1.13). The relay station sends the information to a switch, where it is routed to the closest switch to the person you are calling. Your voice then passes from that switch to another relay station, then to the destination telephone. Other engineers design the mechanical parts of the cell phone so it will work properly.

Automobiles are also developed by engineers using physics. For example, engines are designed by *mechanical engineers* using concepts of force, motion, energy, and power (Chapters 10-12). The engine's fuel—gasoline, is developed by *chemical engineers* also applying concepts from physics including temperature, heat (Chapters 25-26) and how different chemicals react with each other (Chapter 29).

Even the manufacture of a simple plastic toy requires understanding physics. A machine (called a molding machine) takes hot, liquid plastic and squirts it into a mold that has the shape of the toy. When the plastic cools, it hardens and the mold is opened so the toy can be removed. Physics is used all the way from the design of the molding machine, the plastic, its melting and the filling of the mold, to the machine that opens the mold and removes the finished toy.

Figure 1.12: *Engineers work together to design complex technology—like bridges. A great deal of physics knowledge goes into the design of a bridge.*

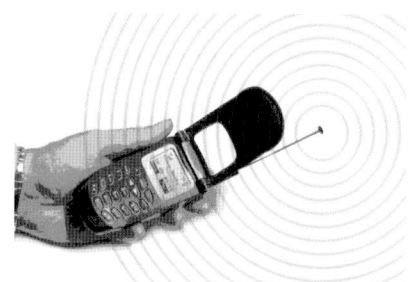

Figure 1.13: *A cell phone is an example of technology that uses many principles of physics.*

Medicine and health professions

Physics is important to physicians, athletes, and other people in careers that focus on the human body. The body obeys the laws of physics just like everything else in the universe. One area where physics knowledge is necessary is the instrumentation used in sports and medicine, such as an x-ray machine. A second area is the working of the body itself, such as the flow of blood or the action of muscles.

Medicine today depends intensively on technology that is based on the laws of physics. For example, you expect to go to a hospital and get an x-ray if you think your finger is broken (Figure 1.14). An x-ray can show what lies beneath the skin, which otherwise could not be seen. X-rays are produced by machines based on the physics of the atom (Chapters 28 and 30) and the properties of light (Chapter 18). X-rays are a high-energy form of light, just like light from the sun. For another example, ultrasound equipment can take moving pictures of a baby before it is born using the properties of waves and sound (Chapters 14 and 15).

Physics also applies to the internal working of the body itself. For example, *arteriosclerosis* is a disease of the arteries that makes them smaller inside. Smaller arteries restrict the flow of blood and increase blood pressure, increasing the risk of heart disease. The relationship between the flow of a fluid (blood), pressure, and the size of an artery is part of physics (Chapter 27). Most living animals need to stay warm to live. The relationship between temperature, heat, and energy is also part of physics (Chapter 25).

Athletes and coaches make very direct use of physics. Almost all forms of sports involve forces and motion, both of which are described by physics (Chapters 5 and 6). An athlete's body uses energy to perform activities such as swimming, running, or jumping. For example, the energy required to jump over a high bar is described by physics (Figure 1.15 and Chapter 10). A bicycle is the most efficient machine ever invented to transform forces from the human body into energy of motion. Bicycles work on the principles of torque and rotating motion—again, all part of physics (Chapters 9 and 11).

Many trainers and coaches use *biomechanics* to help athletes reach their maximum performance. Biomechanics is the science of forces and their interaction with the human body and its muscles. For example, slow-motion video may be used to analyze the technique of a high jumper. The timing of the jump and the forces applied by each leg can be determined by analyzing the video using the principles of physics. High-jumpers can often improve by changing their technique to make more effective use of those forces.

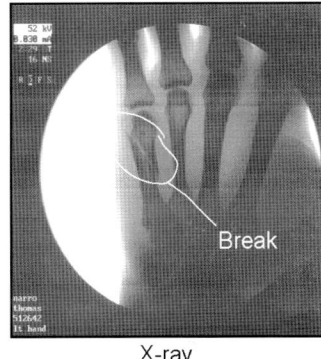

X-ray

Figure 1.14: *This x-ray shows a broken bone in the little finger.*

Figure 1.15: *Physics is used to analyze athletic performance and help athletes improve their technique.*

Business and finance

A successful business makes good decisions on what products to make, what products to sell, and how its products compare to other products. A basic understanding of physics is useful for anyone who must make decisions based on technology. For example, a company that produces cars needs to create cars that use the latest technology, and are competitive with technology offered by other car manufacturers (Figure 1.16). Like all technology, new technology in cars is based on physics. For example, the introduction of air bags (Chapter 12) and antilock brakes (Chapter 4) both made cars safer to drive by changing the forces acting on a car, on the road and on passengers in the car. These new technologies were expensive to develop and many different designs were proposed. Car companies needed physics to decide which designs offered the best combination of performance and cost.

Physics is also useful in business for its approach to analysis and problem solving. A person who learns physics also learns many very effective ways to analyze data and draw conclusions about what is happening. Good business decisions almost always consider data that describes the various options a company can take. For example, business data might include the cost of buying paint and paying the employees who paint cars. In order to decide whether to use two colors or one to paint a new car, all of the data should be analyzed, so the company knows the cost of the decision and the potential benefits. A real-life business is described by many thousands of bits of data exactly like this. Physics is one of the very best ways to learn how to analyze data and draw conclusions (Figure 1.17).

Businesses rely on technology, such as computers, heating systems, lighting systems, and electricity. Each of these technologies includes many choices and each choice has different benefits and limitations. For example, a company might decide to use incandescent light bulbs because the people making the decision like the warmer light of an incandescent bulb. Fluorescent light bulbs often have a colder, bluish light. However, incandescent light bulbs use much more energy than fluorescent light bulbs and so may increase the use of air conditioning in order to remove the heat they generate. Electricity, light, and heat are all described by physics (Chapters 16, 19, and 26). A wise business leader makes decisions that assess the trade-offs between different choices of technology. These trade-offs almost always require a basic understanding of physics to interpret correctly.

Figure 1.16: *Companies that make cars have seen dramatic changes in technology, all influenced by the application of physics.*

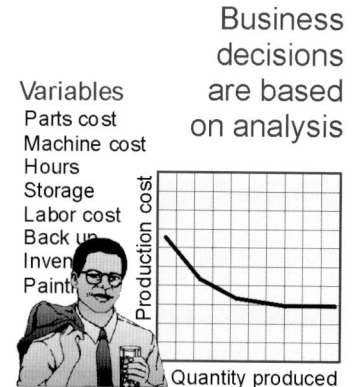

Figure 1.17: *Good business decisions are based on analysis of data, similar to physics.*

Art, music, and food

The creation and perception of light and color is important to anyone who paints, takes pictures, makes movies, or works with any type of image. The human eye sees three basic colors: red, green, and blue. Other colors are made by combining different proportions of red, green, and blue. Physics describes how light is made and how color is created (Chapter 16).

Today, we are accustomed to sharing images through such media as photographs, videos, books, and magazines. The reproduction of an image is another area where physics is used. The images you see in photographs or magazines are printed in four special colors of ink: cyan, magenta, yellow, and black. A printer can create almost any color by using a combination of just these four colors (Figure 1.18). The exact colors of the four inks are determined by the physics of light (chapter 16).

All types of video cameras, digital cameras, or film cameras use *optics*. Optics is the physics and technology of working with light (Chapter 17). Everyone who produces video uses physics knowledge every time they adjust the lights on a set or change the color balance of a camera. In addition, many special effects are created with devices such as mirrors, lenses, and prisms. People who do special effects need to understand the physics behind how these devices work in order to use them effectively.

Almost everyone enjoys listening to musical sound. Sound is a traveling vibration in the air that is created by vibrating strings, speakers, or other devices. The creation of sound and the movement of sound are part of physics (Chapter 15). The physics of sound is used by people who set up concerts, design musical instruments, play music on every variety of instrument, and even by people who design buildings where musicians will perform. The technology of electronic amplification and recording of music is also based on physics (Figure 1.19 and Chapter 24).

Even everyday activities such as cooking use physics. You are using physics when you set the temperature of an oven hotter because you want to cook something faster. Food cooks when its temperature rises. Temperature rises because heat energy flows from the hotter oven into the cooler food. Increasing the temperature of the oven causes heat energy to flow from the oven into the food faster, which is why it cooks faster. Temperature and the process of heat flowing are described by physics (Chapters 25 and 26).

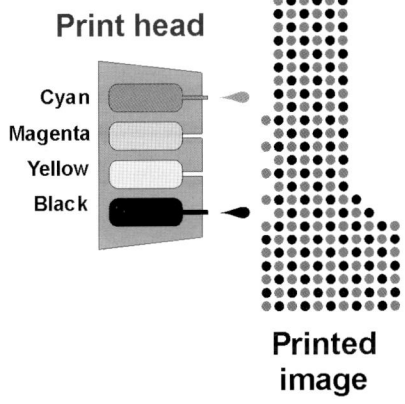

Figure 1.18: *Ink jet printers use the physics of color to reproduce full-color images.*

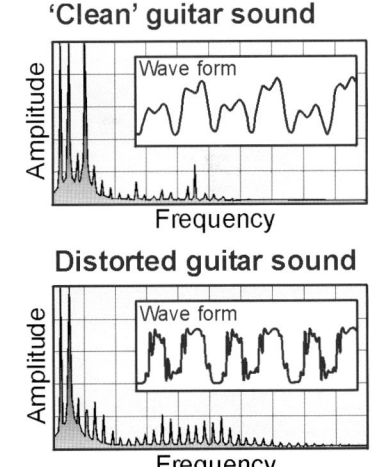

Figure 1.19: *Physics is used to shape the sound of an electric guitar.*

The relationship between physics and other fields of science

You probably recognize science as being divided into different fields. For example, biology is the study of living things. Chemistry is the study of how atoms and elements create the world we experience. Astronomy is the study of stars, galaxies, and the vast universe of which the Earth is a part. The division of science into separate fields was done to help people organize scientific knowledge. However, the concepts in all of the divisions of science are interrelated.

Physics is sometimes called the fundamental science because it provides the conceptual framework that underlies all of science. Physics breaks down nature into its simplest processes such as the force between two objects. In contrast, chemistry, biology, and astronomy study complex interactions, such as the growth of an animal, the formation of a star, or the combustion of gasoline in air. The complexity of the universe is why it is important to understand the basic principles across different fields of science. Biology can tell you how things living grow. Physics tells you that all the processes that occur during living and growing obey the laws of physics *even though we may not know the details of how those processes actually work*.

Any natural process or technology must obey the laws of physics. There is no exception. In many cases, physics can tell you whether an explanation might be right or has no chance of being right. If the explanation violates one of the laws of physics, it cannot be right, no matter whether it is biology, chemistry, astronomy, ecology, or any other science. Still, knowing that everything depends on physics, and proceeding from physics to understanding biology are two very different things. Physics can tell us how two atoms interact with each other. But there are so many atoms in an animal that physics is nearly useless for understanding large-scale behavior, such as how animals grow, or how they reproduce.

Physics is often considered the least complex of the basic sciences because it describes how a few particles and four forces create the elements and fundamental interactions in the universe. Chemistry is concerned with more complex systems than physics. Our world contains millions of chemicals made from the basic elements and even more interactions between the chemicals. Biology is the most complex of the sciences because it describes the physical processes that occur in life. Even a small living creature such as a bacteria, is an organization of thousands of chemicals and interactions between chemicals. This book is designed to help you make connections between physics, chemistry, and biology (Figure 1.20).

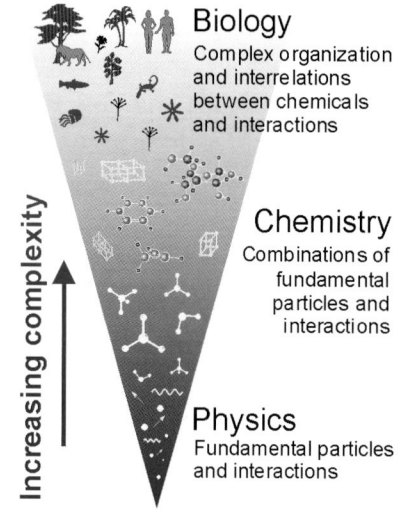

Figure 1.20: *The relationship between physics and other basic sciences.*

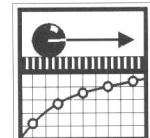

Unit 1

Measurement and Motion

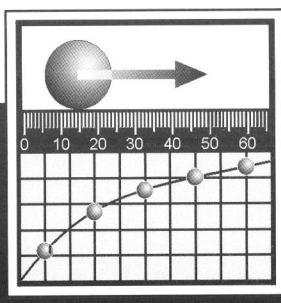

Chapter 2

Measurement and Units

Objectives for Chapter 2

By the end of this chapter you should be able to:

1. Express lengths in metric and English units.
2. Convert distances between different units.
3. Calculate the surface area of simple shapes such as rectangles, triangles, and circles.
4. Calculate the surface area and volume of simple solids such as cubes and spheres.
5. Describe time intervals in hours, minutes, and seconds.
6. Convert time in mixed units to time in seconds.
7. Describe two effects you feel every day that are created by mass.
8. Describe the mass of objects in grams and kilograms.
9. Use scientific notation to represent large and small numbers.

Terms and vocabulary words

meter	centimeter	millimeter	kilometer	inch
foot	mile	surface area	volume	weight
metric system	conversion factor	time interval	precision	accuracy
kilogram	gram	mass	English system	atom
inertia	molecule	mixture	element	base
power of ten	exponent	scientific notation	distance	length

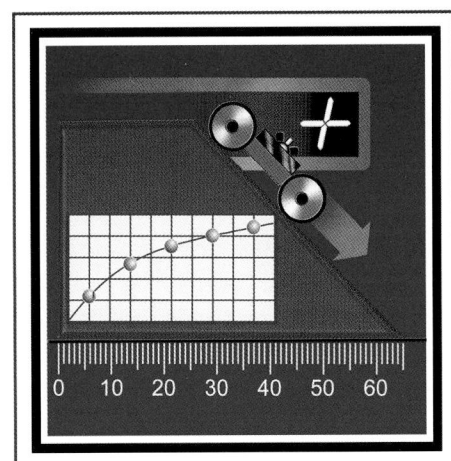

17

2.1 Distance and Length

To do science you need a precise way to describe the natural world. In physics, many things are described with measurements. For example, 2 meters is a measurement of length. Two meters is a little more than the height of an average person. Measurements such as length, mass, speed, and temperature are important in science because they are a language that allows us to communicate information so everyone understands exactly what we mean. This section is about length, one of the most important measurable quantities in physics. For example, you could not communicate how far away something is without having a way to measure length.

Thinking about distance

Measurements A measurement is a precise value that tells how much. How much what, you ask? That depends on what you are measuring. The important concept in measurement is that it communicates the amount in a way that can be understood by others. For example, 2 meters is a measurement because it has a quantity (2) and gives a unit (meters, Figure 2.1).

Units All measurements need units. Without a unit, a measurement cannot be understood. For example, if you told someone to walk 10, she would not know what to do: 10 feet, 10 meters, 10 miles, 10 kilometers are all 10—but the units are different and therefore the distances are also different. Units allow people to communicate amounts. For communication to be successful, physics uses a set of units that have been agreed upon around the world.

Distance and length Distance is the amount of space between two points (Figure 2.2). You can also think of distance as how far apart two objects are. You probably have a good understanding of distance from everyday experiences, like the distance from one house to another, or the distance between California and Massachusetts. The concept of distance in physics is the same, but the actual distances may be much larger and much smaller than anything you normally think of as a distance.

Distance is measured in units of length Distance is measured in units of **length**. You are already familiar with some units of length, like inches and miles. Others you may not have used before, like kilometers and millimeters.

Measurement
A measurement is a quantity and a unit.

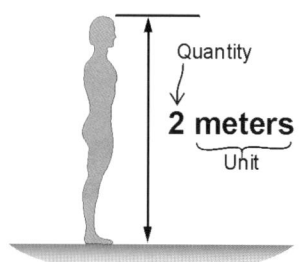

Figure 2.1: *Measurements always include both a quantity and a unit. The unit is how you know what the quantity means.*

Distance
Distance is the amount of space between two points.

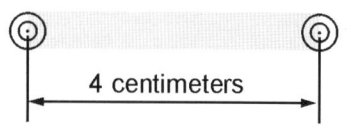

Figure 2.2: *The definition of distance.*

Two common systems of length units

There are two common systems
There are two common systems of standardized (or agreed upon) units that are used for measuring distances, the English system and the metric system. The English system uses inches (in), feet, yards (yd.), and miles (mi) for length. The metric system uses millimeters (mm) centimeters (cm), meters (m), and kilometers (km). You probably have contact with both systems of units every day. For example, driving distances are often expressed in miles (Figure 2.3), but races in track and field are usually expressed in meters (Figure 2.4).

Scientists use metric units
Almost all fields of science use metric units because they are so much easier to work with. In the English system, there are 12 inches in a foot, 3 feet in a yard, and 5,280 feet in a mile. In the metric system, there are 10 millimeters in a centimeter, 100 centimeters in a meter, and 1,000 meters in a kilometer. Factors of 10 are easier to remember than 12, 3, and 5,280. The diagram below will help you get a sense for the metric units of distance.

Figure 2.3: *Some distances are measured using units in the English system, such as miles.*

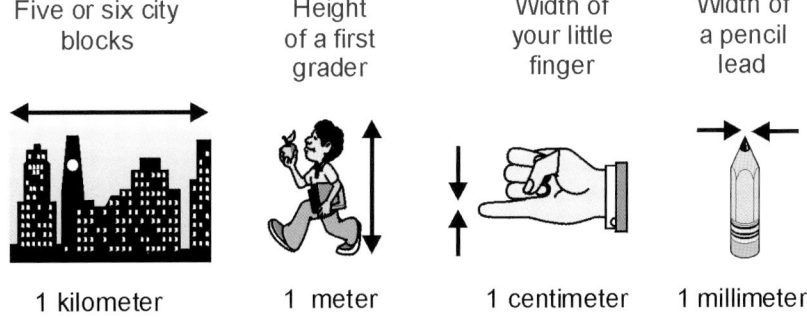

Five or six city blocks	Height of a first grader	Width of your little finger	Width of a pencil lead
1 kilometer	1 meter	1 centimeter	1 millimeter

Figure 2.4: *Some distances are measured using units in the metric system, such as meters.*

You will use both systems of measurement
To solve problems by applying science in the real world, you will need to know both sets of units, English and metric. For example, a doctor will measure your height and weight in English units. The same doctor will prescribe medicine in milliliters (mL) and grams (g), which are metric units. Plywood is sold in 4-foot-by-8-foot sheets—but the thickness of many types of plywood is given in millimeters. Some of the bolts on a car have English dimensions, such as 1/2 inch. Others have metric dimensions, such as 13 millimeters. Because both units are used, it is a good idea to know both metric and English units.

Measuring length

Scientists use the metric system

The metric system is officially named the Systeme International d'Unites (SI in all languages, abbreviated from the French). As you probably learned in other courses, there are four length units related to the meter (Table 2.1). We will use all four at different times because each is convenient for describing a different range of lengths.

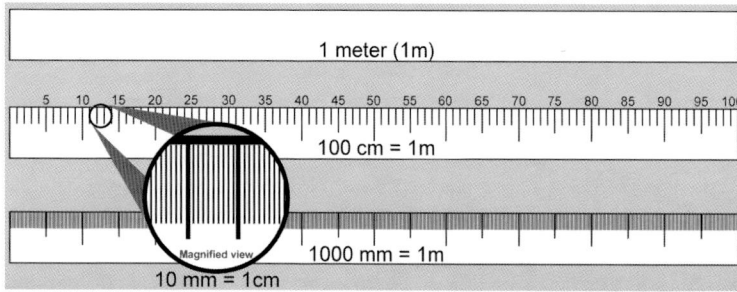

Inches, feet, yards and miles

The common units of measurement in the English system are inches, feet, yards, and miles. An inch is about the width of your thumb. Things smaller than an inch are measured in fractions of inches, like one-fourth or one-eighth of an inch (1/4, 1/8). Notice these fractions are multiples of one-half, not of one-tenth, like in the metric system. Table 2.2 shows the relationships between inches, feet, yards, and miles. Remembering these ratios is not as easy as remembering powers of ten.

Converting from one unit to another

It is often necessary to take a measurement in one unit and translate it into a different unit. This is called *converting* and it is done with relationships between units called **conversion factors**. (see the inside back cover.) To do a conversion, you arrange the conversion factors as ratios and multiply them so the units cancel out. The example shows how to convert 100 kilometers to miles.

Converting units

Cancel units in pairs

$$100 \ \cancel{km} \times \frac{1,000 \ \cancel{m}}{1 \ \cancel{km}} \times \frac{1 \ mile}{1,609 \ \cancel{m}} = \frac{100 \times 1,000 \ miles}{1,609} = 62.1 \ miles$$

Multiply and divide numbers

Answer

Conversion factors

Table 2.1: Metric length units

Length	Equivalent length
1 m	100 cm
1 m	1,000 mm
1 cm	10 mm
1 km	1,000 m

Table 2.2: English length units

Length	Equivalent length
1 inch	0.0833 foot
1 foot	12 inches
1 yard	3 feet
1 mile	5,280 feet

Convert length in yards to meters

A football field is 100 yards long. What is this distance expressed in meters?

1) You are given distance in yards.
2) You are asked to find distance in meters.
3) 1 yard = 3 feet,
   1 foot = 0.3048 meters
4)

$$100 \ \cancel{yds} \times \frac{3 \ \cancel{ft}}{1 \ \cancel{yd}} \times \frac{.3048 \ m}{1 \ \cancel{ft}} = 91.4 \ m$$

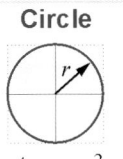

Surface and volume

Surface area | Many processes in nature require you to describe how much surface or volume an object has. The units of surface and volume are based on the unit of length. For example, a surface that measures 2 meters by 2 meters has a surface area of 4 square meters (m^2). That means four 1-meter squares completely cover the surface. If the measurements of the sides are in inches, then the area will be in square inches. Figure 2.5 shows the surface area of some simple shapes.

Volume | The volume of an object is equal to the number of unit cubes that completely fill the object. For rectangular objects, volume is length × width × height. For example, the volume of a 2-meter cube is 8 cubic meters ($2m \times 2m \times 2m = 8\ m^3$). Eight 1-meter cubes completely fill the space inside. The volume for some simple solid shapes is shown in the diagram (Figure 2.6).

Surface area of solid objects | A solid object has surface area as well as volume. For example, the 2-meter cube has a surface area of 24 square meters ($24\ m^2$). There are six faces on a cube and each face is 4 square meters, making a total of 24 m^2.

Converting area and volume | You need to apply the conversion factor *twice* when converting areas from one unit to another. This is because the units of area are length × length. For example, the 2-meter square has a surface area of 40,000 square centimeters (cm^2). For a volume conversion you need to apply the conversion factor *three* times because the units of volume are length × length × length.

Area of simple shapes	Circle

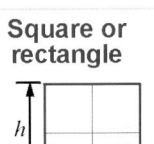

$A = \pi r^2$

Square or rectangle	Triangle

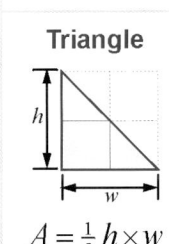

$A = h \times w$ $A = \frac{1}{2} h \times w$

Figure 2.5: *The surface area of some simple shapes.*

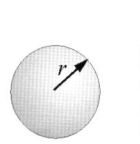 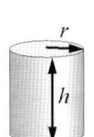 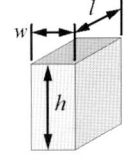

Sphere   Cylinder   Rectangular solid

°	Surface area
Sphere	$S = 4\pi r^2$
Cylinder	$S = 2\pi r^2 + 2\pi rh$
Rectangular solid	$S = 2hw + 2hl + 2wl$

	Volume
Sphere	$V = \frac{4}{3}\pi r^3$
Cylinder	$V = \pi r^2 h$
Rectangular solid	$V = lwh$

Figure 2.6: *Surface area and volume.*

Calculate surface and volume

A basketball has a radius of 12.5 centimeters. Calculate the surface area and volume of the ball.

1) You are asked to find surface area and volume.
2) A ball is shaped like a sphere and you are given the radius.
3) Surface area: $A = 4\pi r^2$; volume: $V = (4/3)\pi r^3$
4) Solve:

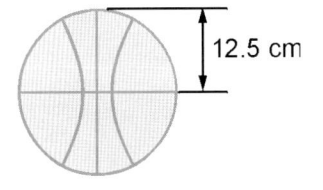

12.5 cm

Surface area

$A = 4(3.14)(12.5)^2 = 1,963\ cm^2$

Volume

$V = \frac{4}{3}(3.14)(12.5)^3 = 8,181\ cm^3$

2.2 Time

Time is a fundamental property of the universe. Though time itself is difficult to define, changes in time are easy to understand. Our bodies change with time (Figure 2.7). Our planet and our universe change with time. The steady movement of time creates a past, present, and future. Learning about how things change with time motivates much of our study of nature. Many key physics concepts are based on how certain quantities change with time, such as your location. This section reviews some of the properties and techniques for working with time and measurements of time.

Figure 2.7: *The flow of time is an important part of our experience of life. In order to understand nature, we need to investigate how things change with time.*

Two ways to think about time

Two ways to think about time	In physics, just as in your everyday life, there are two ways to think about time (Figure 2.8). One way is to identify a particular moment in time. The other way is to describe a quantity of time. The same word—time—means two things that are very different in science.
What time is it?	If you ask, "What time is it?" you usually want to identify a moment in time relative to the rest of the universe and everyone in it. To answer this question, you would look at a clock or at your watch at one particular moment. For example, 3 P.M. Eastern Time on April 21, 2004, tells the time at a certain place on Earth.
How much time?	If you ask, "How much time?" (did something take to occur, for instance), you are looking for a quantity of time. To answer, you need to measure an interval of time with both a beginning and an end. For example, you might measure how much time has passed between the start of a race and when the first runner crosses the finish line. A quantity of time is often called a time interval. Whenever you see the word *time* in physics, it usually (but not always) means a time interval. Time intervals in physics are almost always in seconds, and are represented by a lower case letter *t*.

What time is it?

How much time?

Figure 2.8: *There are two different ways to understand time: "What time is it?" and "How much time passed?"*

How is time measured?

Units for measuring time
You are probably familiar with the common units for measuring time: seconds, hours, minutes, days, and years. But you may not know how they relate to each other. Table 2.1 gives some useful relationships between units of time

Table 2.1: Some units for time

Time unit	... in seconds...	... and in days
1 second	1	0.0001157
1 minute	60	0.00694
1 hour	3,600	0.0417
1 day	86,400	1
1 year	31,557,600	365.25
1 century	3,155,760,000	36,525

Figure 2.9: *Electronic timers have displays that show mixed units. Colons (:) separate the units.*

Choosing the right unit is important
Imagine that somebody you just met asks you how old you are. You would probably not give your age in seconds. The number would be too big and would change too fast. A year is a better unit for describing a person's age. Choosing the unit most suited to the time you want to measure is an important skill.

Physics requires time in seconds
In physics, calculations often require that time be expressed in seconds. However, seconds are very short. Minutes and hours are more convenient for everyday time measurement. As a result, time intervals are often given in mixed units, such as 2 minutes and 15 seconds. If you have a time interval that is in mixed units, you will have to convert it to seconds before doing physics calculations.

Convert mixed units to seconds
To convert a time into seconds, you first separate the total into the amount of time in each unit. Then you convert the amount of time in each unit to seconds. Finally, you add up the number of seconds in each amount to get the total time in seconds.

Reading a digital timer
Most timing equipment displays time in hours, minutes, and seconds with colons separating each unit. The seconds number may also have a decimal that shows fractions of a second (Figure 2.9). To read a timer, you need to recognize and separate the different units.

Convert a mixed time to seconds

How many seconds are in 1 hour, 26 minutes, and 31.25 seconds (Figure 2.9)?

1) You are asked for time in seconds.
2) You are given a time interval in mixed units.
3) 1 hour = 3,600 sec
   1 minute = 60 sec
4) Do the conversion:
   1 hour = 3,600 seconds
   26 minutes = 26 × 60
            = 1,560 seconds

Add all the seconds:
t = 3,600 + 1,560 + 31.25
  = 5,191.25 seconds

Time scales in physics

One second
The second is the basic unit of time in both the English and metric systems. One second is about the time it takes to say "one thousand." There are 60 seconds in a minute and 3,600 seconds in an hour. The second was originally defined in terms of one day: There are 86,400 seconds in an average day of 24 hours (86,400 = 3,600 × 24).

Time in physics
Things in the universe happen over a huge range of time intervals. Figure 2.10 gives a few examples of time scales that are considered in physics as well as other sciences. The average life of a human being is 2.2 billion seconds. The time it takes a mosquito to flap its wings once is 0.0005 seconds. The time it takes light to get from this page to your eyes is 0.000000002 seconds.

Time in experiments
In many experiments, you will be observing how things change with time. For example, when you drop a ball, it falls to the ground. You can make a graph of the height of the ball versus the time since it was released. The *time* is the time interval measured from when the ball was released. This graph shows how the height of the ball changes with time. The graph shows that it takes the ball about 0.45 seconds to fall a distance of 1 meter. Many of the experiments you will do in the lab will involve measuring times between 0.0001 seconds and a few seconds. When making graphs of results from experiments, the time almost always goes on the horizontal (or x) axis.

An experiment involving time

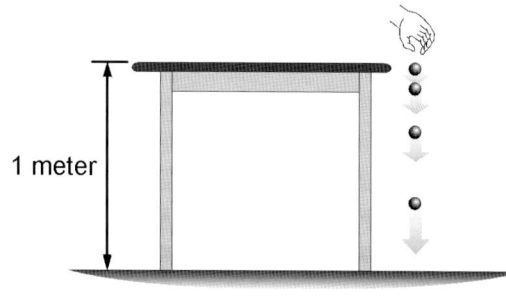

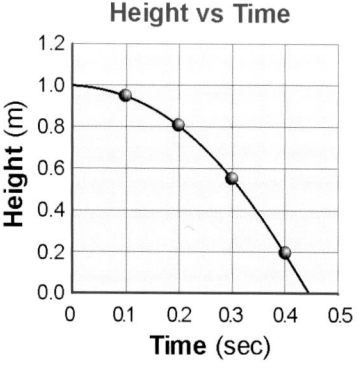

Height vs Time

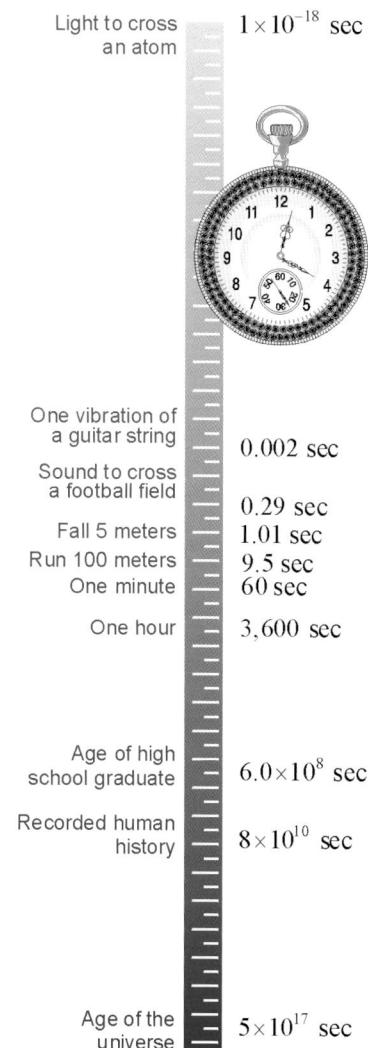

Light to cross an atom	1×10^{-18} sec
One vibration of a guitar string	0.002 sec
Sound to cross a football field	0.29 sec
Fall 5 meters	1.01 sec
Run 100 meters	9.5 sec
One minute	60 sec
One hour	3,600 sec
Age of high school graduate	6.0×10^{8} sec
Recorded human history	8×10^{10} sec
Age of the universe	5×10^{17} sec

Figure 2.10: *Some time intervals in physics.*

Accuracy and precision

Measurements are never "perfect"

Measurements of time in experiments are never exact. For example, you cannot determine that something takes *exactly* 10 seconds. Why not? This is because all measurements of time are made with clocks, and all clocks have a limit to how small a time they can measure. For example, suppose you have a very good clock that can measure time to 0.01 seconds. You claim the time is exactly 10 seconds because your clock shows 10.00. However, suppose the time was in fact 10.002 seconds. Your clock rounded the measurement off to 10.00. So the best way to describe your time measurement is 10.00 +/- 0.005 seconds. The actual time could have been different from 10.00 seconds by up to 0.005 seconds in either direction, and your measurement would not show it.

Precision

The word precision means how small a difference a measurement can show. A clock that can read to 0.01 seconds has a precision of 0.01 seconds. Many of your lab experiments will be done with clocks that are precise to one ten-thousandth of a second (0.0001 sec).

Accuracy

The word accuracy in physics means how close a measurement is to the true value. For example, a meter stick that has been stretched can make a measurement of length that is precise to one millimeter. But the measurement will not be accurate because the meter stick is no longer a meter long! Figure 2.11 illustrates the meaning of accuracy and precision.

Why accuracy and precision are important

Accuracy and precision are important because experiments are done to see whether they agree or disagree with what you believe will happen. A measurement that is not accurate may give you the wrong conclusion. A measurement that is not precise may not be able to tell the difference between agreement or disagreement.

Comparing measurements

In physics, and in life, whether two things are the same depends on how closely you need to look. For many of your lab experiments, two time measurements of 0.0233 sec and 0.0234 sec can be considered the same because they differ by only 0.0001 seconds. This time interval is the precision limit of the clock (Figure 2.12). A similar limit (0.001 m) exists for measuring length with a meter stick. When analyzing the observations you make in the lab, you must consider both the accuracy and the precision of your measurements before making a conclusion.

Accurate

Accurate and precise

Precise but not accurate

Not accurate and not precise

Figure 2.11: *The difference between accuracy and precision.*

Clock

Smallest measureable time interval = 0.0001 sec

Meter stick

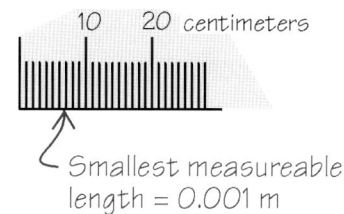

Smallest measureable length = 0.001 m

Figure 2.12: *The precision limits of a clock and meter stick.*

2.3 Mass, Matter and the Atom

Mass is the third of three basic quantities that are the foundation of physics, along with length and time. Once you can describe mass, length, and time, you have a framework for understanding how and why things move. This section is about mass and also about atoms. Virtually all of the mass in things around you is in the form of atoms. A block of steel looks smooth because the atoms of which it is made are so small. The air is transparent because the atoms in air are far apart and light goes right between them.

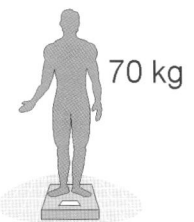

Two ways to think about mass

Mass is a measure of matter Very simply, mass is the amount of "stuff" an object contains. Matter is anything that has mass and takes up space. *You* are matter, and so is the air you breathe and the paper in this book. Mass is a measure of how much matter there is. A grain of salt has very little mass and a planet has a great amount of mass.

The two effects of mass The amount of mass an object contains has two important effects:

1. The more mass an object has, the more **weight** it has. Weight is the force of the Earth's gravity pulling down (Figure 2.13). Gravity acts on an object's mass.

2. The more mass an object has, the harder it is to start moving or stop from moving. The tendency of an object to resist changes in motion is called inertia. Inertia comes from mass.

Weight The most common way to measure mass is to measure the force of gravity acting on it. When you stand on a bathroom scale, you are measuring the force of gravity acting on your mass. Gravity pulls with a force of 2.2 pounds for every kilogram of mass. As shown in Figure 2.13, a person with a mass of 70 kilograms would have a weight of 154 pounds (154 lbs = 70 kg × 2.2 lbs/kg).

Inertia It is easy to pick up a tennis ball and throw it. A tennis ball has a mass of less than 0.1 kilogram. It is much more difficult to pick up a 5 kilogram bowling ball and throw it (Figure 2.14). Throwing a ball involves a large change in speed. Throwing a bowling ball is harder because a bowling ball has 50 times as much mass as a tennis ball and therefore has 50 times as much inertia to overcome.

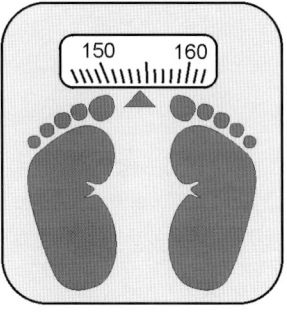

Figure 2.13: *Weight is a measure of the force of gravity pulling on mass.*

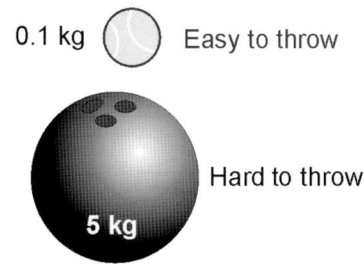

Figure 2.14: *Objects with more mass are harder to move compared with objects with less mass.*

Measuring mass

The kilogram — Mass is measured in **kilograms**. One kilogram was originally defined as the mass of 1 liter of water. A liter is a volume of 1,000 cubic centimeters (Figure 2.15). The 1 liter bottle of soda you buy in the grocery store is mostly water and has a mass of about 1 kilogram.

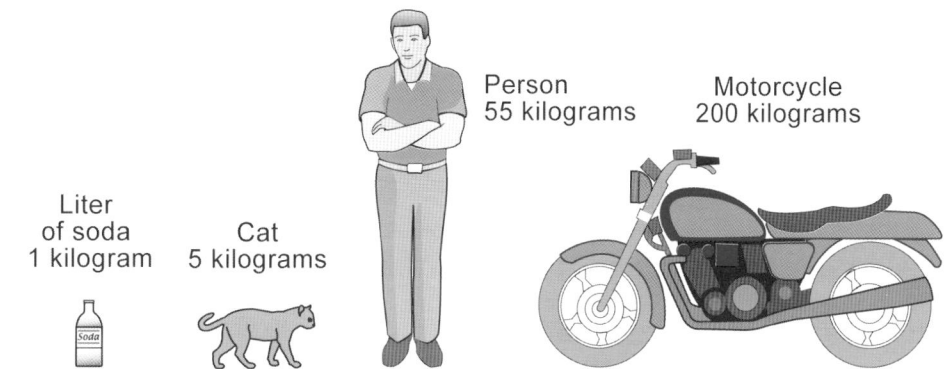

Person
55 kilograms

Motorcycle
200 kilograms

Liter
of soda
1 kilogram

Cat
5 kilograms

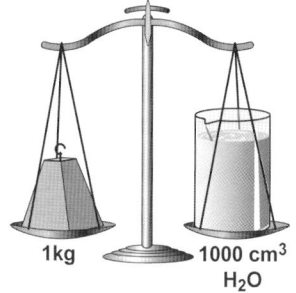

1kg   1000 cm³
H₂O

Figure 2.15: *The kilogram is defined as the mass of 1000 cubic centimeters of water.*

Equal masses mean equal amounts of matter — When we say an object has a mass of exactly one kilogram, we are saying that the object has the same amount of matter as one kilogram of water. Even if we do not know what the object is made of, we can measure how much matter it has. Air is very light, but air still has mass. One cubic meter of air has a mass of about 1 kilogram. If you put your hand out of the window in a moving car you can feel the mass of the air.

Grams — For small amounts of matter, like medicines, the kilogram is too large a unit of mass to be convenient. One gram is one-thousandth of a kilogram. Equivalently, 1 kilogram is 1,000 grams. One grain of rice is about a gram.

The range of masses — Like distance and time, you will encounter a very wide range of masses in physics. A single bacteria has a mass of 0.000000001 kilogram. Later in this book we will do calculations with atoms, which have masses a *thousand billion* times smaller than a bacteria. We will also analyze the motion of the planet Earth and the moon. The mass of the Earth is about 6 trillion, trillion kilograms. That is a six with 24 zeroes after it. Figure 2.16 shows a range of masses of objects in the universe that have been studied in physics.

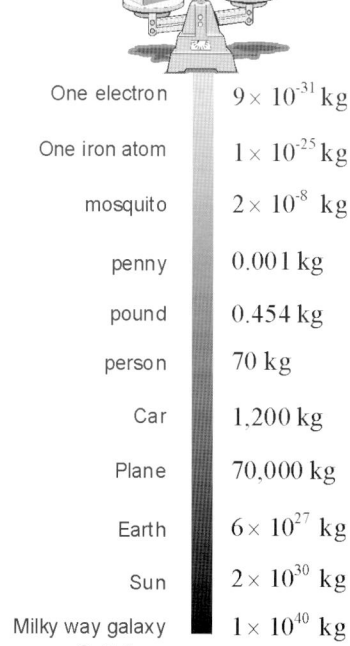

One electron	9×10^{-31} kg
One iron atom	1×10^{-25} kg
mosquito	2×10^{-8} kg
penny	0.001 kg
pound	0.454 kg
person	70 kg
Car	1,200 kg
Plane	70,000 kg
Earth	6×10^{27} kg
Sun	2×10^{30} kg
Milky way galaxy	1×10^{40} kg

Figure 2.16: *The scale of masses of things in the universe.*

Very large and very small numbers

Describing large and small quantities

It is hard to imagine doing math with a number like 6 trillion, trillion. Don't worry if you cannot get your mind around this huge number—no one can without a reference. Fortunately, there is a shorthand method to deal with numbers this large. The method is called scientific notation and it also works for extremely small numbers, like the mass of an atom. You will need to learn this method of working with large and small numbers because physics covers such a wide range of length, time, and mass.

Scientific notation for large numbers

Scientific notation works by expressing very small or very large numbers as the product of two numbers that are individually much easier to deal with. The first number is called the base. The second number is a power of ten. Any number of any size can be represented as a base times a power of ten. For example, consider the number 2,500: It is equal to 25×100. The number 25 is the base. The number 100 is a power of ten (10 squared) and is usually written 10^2. The small numeral 2 in 10^2 is called the exponent. In scientific notation, the number 2,500 can be rewritten as 25×10^2. For the number 2,500, this is more trouble than it is worth. But 6 trillion trillion in scientific notation is 6×10^{24}. The scientific notation number is much easier to write than 6,000,000,000,000,000,000,000,000.

Writing the base

The base is usually written with only one digit in front of the decimal point. For example, 2,500 would be written 2.5×10^3 because 10^3 is 1,000. One way to figure out what power of ten you need is to count the number of times you have to move the decimal point to the left. To make 2,500 into 2.5 you have to move the decimal three places; the correct multiplier is ten multiplied by ten three times, or 10^3.

Scientific notation for small numbers

Scientific notation also works for numbers less than one. Powers of ten that are negative mean numbers smaller than one. The number 0.0025 can be written as 2.5×0.001. The number 0.001 is $1 \div 1000 = 1 \div 10^3 = 10^{-3}$. Written in scientific notation, the number 0.0025 becomes 2.5×10^{-3}. It is important to remember that a negative sign on the exponent of 10 does not mean the whole number is negative! Negative exponents mean a value that is less than one. Figure 2.17 shows some helpful powers of ten for both small and large numbers. The tables in Figure 2.17 can also be found inside the back cover of this book.

Numbers larger than 1

$10^1 = 10$
$10^2 = 100$
$10^3 = 1,000$
$10^4 = 10,000$
$10^5 = 100,000$
$10^6 = 1,000,000$
$10^7 = 10,000,000$
$10^8 = 100,000,000$
$10^9 = 1,000,000,000$

Numbers smaller than 1

$10^{-9} = 0.000\,000\,001$
$10^{-8} = 0.000\,000\,01$
$10^{-7} = 0.000\,000\,1$
$10^{-6} = 0.000\,001$
$10^{-5} = 0.000\,01$
$10^{-4} = 0.000\,1$
$10^{-3} = 0.001$
$10^{-2} = 0.01$
$10^{-1} = 0.1$

Words for large and small numbers

1×10^9	1 billion
1×10^6	1 million
1×10^3	1 thousand
1×10^{-3}	1 thousandth
1×10^{-6}	1 millionth

Figure 2.17: *Some examples of scientific notation. Larger tables can be found inside the cover of this book.*

Matter and atoms

Atoms All the matter you are familiar with is made of atoms. You do not experience atoms directly because they are so small. The head of a pin contains 10^{20} atoms (Figure 2.18). Aluminum foil is thin but still more than 200,000 atoms thick (Figure 2.19). A single atom is about 10^{-10} meters in diameter. That means you might lay 10,000,000,000 (10^{10}) atoms side by side in a 1-meter long space.

The mass of an atom There are 92 different types of atoms in ordinary matter. Each of the types is called an element. Each element has is own properties, such as density and the ability to combine with other elements. The atoms with the smallest mass are those of the element hydrogen. The mass of a single hydrogen atom is 1.67×10^{-27} kilograms. Most of the hydrogen on the Earth is found in water. The atoms with the largest mass are those of the element uranium. Uranium occurs naturally in certain kinds of rock, combined with oxygen and other elements. The element iron is in between hydrogen and uranium. An atom of iron has about 56 times the mass of a hydrogen atom, at 9.3×10^{-26} kilograms. This is still an incredibly small mass.

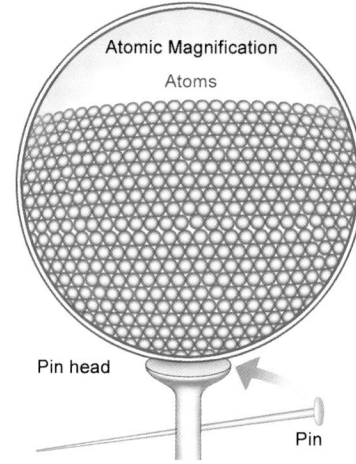

Figure 2.18: *Atoms are so small that the head of a pin contains 10^{20} atoms.*

Molecules and mixtures A molecule is a group of two or more atoms that are joined together. If you could look at water with a powerful microscope you would find each molecule of water is made from one oxygen atom and two hydrogen atoms. Glucose is a sugar in food. A molecule of glucose is made of carbon, oxygen, and hydrogen atoms.

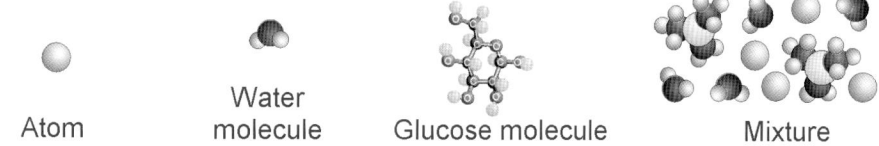

Atom · Water molecule · Glucose molecule · Mixture

The matter you normally experience is made of mixtures of molecules. Wood is a mixture that contains water and more than 100 other types of molecules. Air is also a mixture that contains oxygen, nitrogen, water, and other molecules.

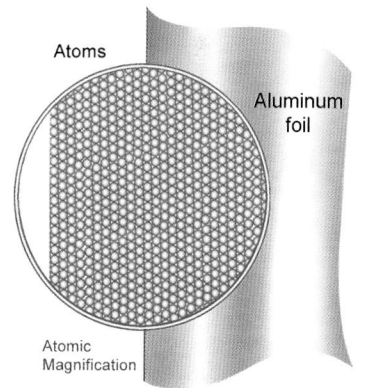

Figure 2.19: *A sheet of aluminum foil is 200,000 atoms thick.*

Solids, liquids and gases

Solid, liquid, and gas
The three most common forms of matter are called solid, liquid, and gas. Solid matter holds its shape and does not flow. Ice is a good example of a solid. Liquid matter keeps its volume constant but can flow and change its shape. Water is a good example of a liquid. Gaseous matter flows like liquid, but also can expand or contract to fill any size container. Air is a good example of a gas.

Solid
Matter at low temperatures is often solid. Atoms in a solid stay together because the energy per atom is too low to break the bonds between atoms (Figure 2.20). Imagine a marching band marching in place with *everyone holding hands*. People move but they stay in the same spot relative to others. When the marching band moves, everyone moves together, like the atoms in a solid.

Liquid
The liquid form of matter occurs at a higher temperature than the solid form. Liquids flow because atoms have enough energy to move around by temporarily breaking and reforming bonds with neighboring atoms (Figure 2.21). Imagine a room full of people dancing. The crowd generally stays together, *but people have enough energy to move around and switch partners*, like the atoms in a liquid.

Gas
The gas form of matter occurs at an even higher temperature than the liquid form. Gas atoms have enough energy to completely break bonds with each other (Figure 2.22). Gas can expand because atoms are free to move independently. Imagine many people running fast in different directions. Every person is moving independently with a lot of space between people, like the atoms in a gas.

Plasma
At temperatures greater than 11,000 °C the atoms in a gas start to break apart. In the plasma form, matter becomes ionized as electrons are broken loose from atoms. Because the electrons are free to move independently, plasma can conduct electricity. Lightning is a good example of plasma. The sun is another example.

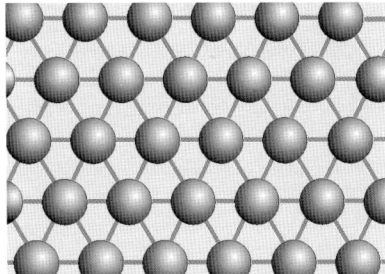

Figure 2.20: *Atoms in a solid stay bonded together.*

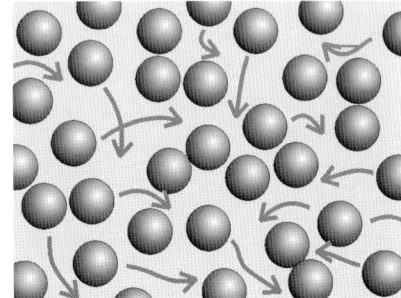

Figure 2.21: *Atoms in a liquid stay close together but can move around and exchange places.*

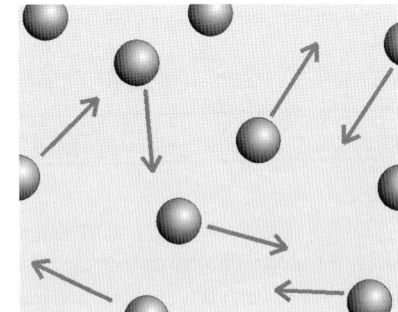

Figure 2.22: *Atoms in a gas move fast and are separated by relatively large spaces.*

Application: Nanotechnology

The prefix "nano" means extremely small. A *nanometer* is 10^{-9} meters, which is a thousand times smaller than a bacterium. Nanotechnology is the technology of creating devices the size of bacteria—or smaller. Nanotechnology is a relatively new area of science and engineering. Only in the past decade have scientists been able to manipulate atoms and matter on a small enough scale to make nanotechnology possible. Future applications for nanotechnology include robots that can enter your arteries and clean out blood clots and miniature satellites that could explore the planets. The nanotechnology of today is mostly in computers and sensors that are based on the techniques for making computer chips.

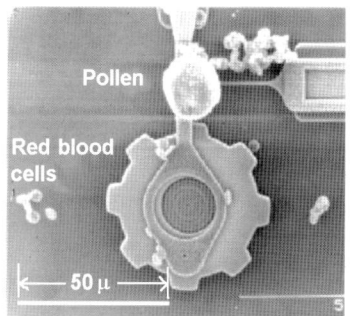

Figure 2.23: *This tiny gear is part of an experimental pump for moving cells. (Courtesy Sandia National Laboratory)*

The size of nanotechnology
The length unit used for nanotechnology is the *micron* (μ). One micron is one-millionth of a meter (1×10^{-6} m). The width of a single strand of your hair is about 50 μ. Figure 2.23 shows a tiny blood pump with a gear that is about the width of a hair. Single cells are between 1 μ and 10 μ; several red blood cells can be seen in the microphotograph of the blood pump. With a width of 0.18 μ, the wires inside computer chips are about the smallest structures regularly produced by human technology. These wires are 300 times smaller than a hair and 10 times smaller than a cell.

Figure 2.24: *This tiny MEMS turbine has blades that are 300 microns high. It could be used to make an electric generator to power other small machines. (Courtesy MIT)*

MEMS
One category of nanotechnology is MEMS (MicroElectronic Mechanical Systems). MEMS are tiny machines with micron-sized moving parts. There is a MEMS sensor in the air bag in your car. This sensor has a tiny arm with a small mass at the end. If the car comes to a sudden stop, the mass tries to keep moving because of its inertia. An electronic circuit detects the movement and triggers the air bag. The entire sensor is so small that a dozen would fit inside the "0" in the 2003 on a penny. An experimental MEMS turbine (Figure 2.24) might allow the creation of electrical generators smaller than the point of your pencil.

Micron-sized mirrors
Another successful MEMS device is the micro-mirror. A high-definition video projector uses an array of 1280-by-720 of these tiny mirrors that measure 14 μ on a side (Figure 2.25). A TV display consists of thousands of points that can change color and brightness. The micro-mirror array has a single mirror for each point (or pixel) of the display. Each mirror can flip up and down to turn a pixel on or off.

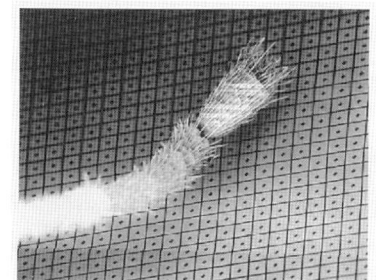

Figure 2.25: *These micro-mirrors are so small they are dwarfed by the leg of a bug. (Courtesy Texas Instruments)*

Chapter 2 Review

Vocabulary review

Match the following terms with the correct definition. There is one extra definition in the list that will not match any of the terms.

Set One

1. English system
2. metric system
3. conversion factor
4. kilogram

  a. Uses millimeters, centimeters, meters, and kilometers to measure distance
  b. Used when changing the units of a measurement
  c. Uses inches, feet, yards, and miles to measure distance
  d. A unit used to measure weight
  e. A unit used to measure mass

Set Two

1. volume
2. surface area
3. precision
4. accuracy

  a. Measured in square meters (m^2)
  b. How close a measurement is to the true value
  c. How small a difference a measurement can show
  d. The average of several measurements
  e. Measured in cubic meters (m^3)

Set Three

1. mass
2. weight
3. scientific notation
4. element
5. molecule

  a. The amount of matter an object contains
  b. Only contains one type of atom
  c. The amount of space an object occupies
  d. Two or more atoms joined together
  e. The force with which gravity pulls on an object
  f. used to express very large and very small numbers more compactly

Concept review

1. Why are units important when measuring quantities?

2. What are the two common systems of units?

3. Why is it important to understand both English and metric systems of units?

4. Give an example of a quantity that is often measured in metric units and a quantity that is often measured in English units.

5. A student expresses the volume of a fish tank in cm^2. Explain her mistake.

6. What are the two different meanings of the word time?

7. When making a graph, is time usually plotted on the x-axis or the y-axis?

8. Explain the difference between the terms precision and accuracy.

9. Heather uses a balance to measure the mass of her kitten. She repeats the measurement three times and finds the mass to be 1.25 kg each time. The actual mass of the kitten is 0.80 kg. Were Heather's measurements accurate? Were they precise?

10. Give an example of an element, a molecule, and a mixture.

11. Do atoms move more freely in solids or in gases?

12. Many measurements are so common that units are not usually used. See if you know the units for these measurements.

    a. A big car race called the Indianapolis 500. 500 what?

    b. If you go to Canada, the speed limit is 100. 100 what?

    c. A famous basketball player is 7-2. 7 what? 2 what?

    d. The speed limit on a road in the US is 65. 65 what?

    e. You buy a pair of men's pants that are 29/32. 29 what? 32 what?

13. Wood is a _____ that contains water and more than 100 other types of __.

14. State whether you would measure each quantity in kilometers, meters, centimeters, or millimeters.

    a. The width of a room

    b. The length of an ant

    c. The height of a soda bottle

    d. The distance from your house to school

15. List two units commonly used for measuring mass.

16. How is the kilogram defined?

17. Which two types of numbers are often expressed in scientific notation?

Problems

1. Order the following lengths from shortest to longest.
   a. 17.4 millimeters
   b. 24 kilometers
   c. 31 feet
   d. 8.1 centimeters

2. Convert:
   a. 25 kilometers = ___ miles
   b. 3 miles = ___ feet
   c. 400 centimeters = ___ meters
   d. 7 inches = ___ millimeters

3. A box is 0.8 m long, 1 m wide, and 0.5 m tall.
   a. Calculate its surface area in m^2.
   b. Calculate its surface area in cm^2.
   c. Calculate its volume in m^3.

4. A cylindrical can is 15 cm tall and has a radius of 3 cm.
   a. Calculate the can's surface area in cm^2.
   b. Calculate the can's volume in cm^3.

5. How many minutes are in one year?

6. Express each number in scientific notation:
   a. 10,000
   c. 300,000,000
   e. 0.000023
   b. 520
   d. 0.000001
   f. 0.00444

7. Express each number in regular decimal notation:
   a. 2.33×10^6
   c. 9.13×10^2
   e. 5.2×10^{-7}
   b. 9.9999×10^4
   d. 1.3×10^{-1}
   f. 8.01×0^{-3}

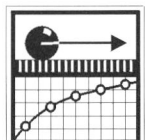

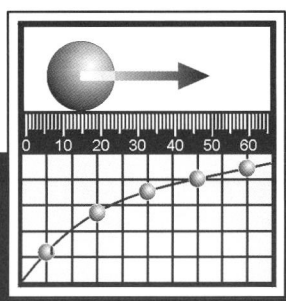

Unit 1
Measurement and Motion

Chapter 3

Objectives for Chapter 3

By the end of this chapter you should be able to:

1. Calculate time, distance, or speed when given two of the three values.
2. Identify the variables in an experiment.
3. Design an experiment where all the variables but one are controlled.
4. Draw and interpret graphs of experimental data including speed versus position, speed versus time, and position versus time.
5. Use a graphical model to make predictions that can be tested by experiments.
6. Determine speed from the slope of a position versus time graph.
7. Determine distance from the area under a speed versus time graph.

Terms and vocabulary words

speed	distance	time	variables	independent variable
graph	*x*-axis	*y*-axis	data	experimental variable
slope	model	angle	origin	constant
initial speed	procedure	trial	at rest	dependent variable
constant speed	rate	position		control variable

Models of Motion

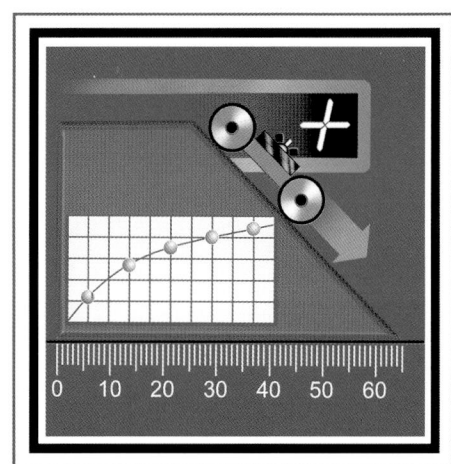

3.1 Speed

This section is about speed, which is the first part of describing motion. Nothing in the universe stays still. A book on a table might appear to be sitting still, but the Earth is moving through space in its orbit around the sun at a speed of 66,000 miles per hour. You and the book move with the Earth. In physics, just saying that something is fast is not enough description to truly understand its speed. You can easily walk faster than a turtle, yet you would not say walking speed was fast compared with the speed of driving a car. The first step to understanding motion is to define speed very precisely.

What do we mean by speed?

An example of speed

Consider a bicycle that is moving along the road. The graphs below show the position of two bicycles at different times. To understand the concept of speed, think about the following two questions regarding the motion of each bicycle.

- How many meters does the bicycle move during each second?
- Does the bicycle move the same number of meters every second?

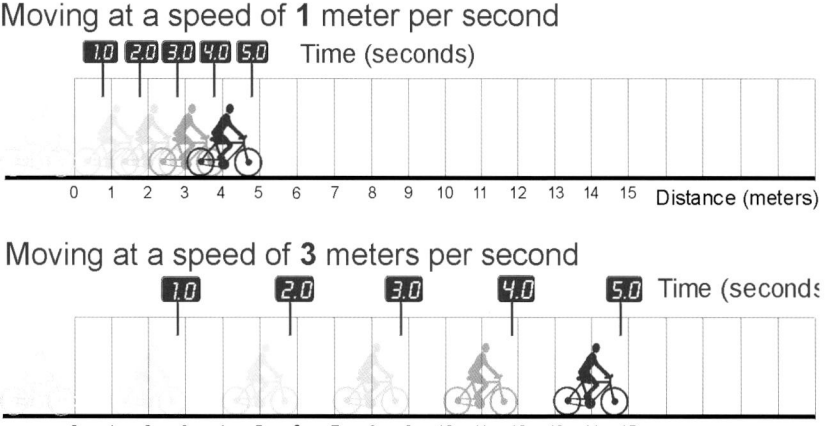

The precise meaning of speed

The speed of a bicycle is the distance it travels divided by the time it takes. At 1 m/sec, a bicycle travels 1 meter each second. At 3 m/sec, a bicycle travels 3 meters each second. Both bicycles in the diagram are moving at constant speed. Constant speed means the same distance is traveled every second.

Everyday speed and the fastest speed in the universe

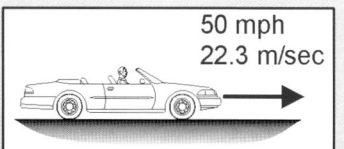

50 mph
22.3 m/sec

Meters per second are good units to use for describing everyday motion. Consider traveling in a car at 50 miles per hour. In the car, this may not seem that fast. However, 50 mph is a little more than 22 meters per second. Twenty-two meters is the height of a five-story building. Twenty-two meters per second means traveling this distance every second.

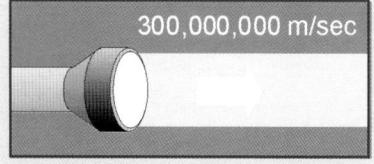

300,000,000 m/sec

The fastest speed in the universe is the speed of light. Light moves at 300 million meters per second (3×10^8 m/sec). If you could make light travel in a circle, it would go around the Earth 7 1/2 times in one second. We believe the speed of light is the ultimate speed limit in the universe. The laws of physics prevent matter from traveling faster than the speed of light.

Calculating speed

Speed is distance divided by time

Speed is a measure of the *distance* traveled in a given amount of *time*. Therefore, to calculate the speed of an object, you need to know two things:

- The distance traveled by the object.
- The time it took to travel the distance.

Speed is calculated by dividing the distance traveled by the time taken. For example, if you drive 90 miles in 1.5 hours (Figure 3.1), then the speed of the car is 90 miles divided by 1.5 hours, which is equal to 60 miles per hour.

What does "per" mean?

The word "per" means "for every" or "for each." The speed of 60 miles per hour is short for saying 60 miles *for each* hour. You can also think of the word "per" as meaning "divided by." The quantity before the word per is divided by the quantity after it. For example, 90 miles ÷ 1.5 hours equals 60 miles per hour.

Units for speed

Since speed is a ratio of distance over time, the units for speed are a ratio of distance units over time units. If distance is in miles and time in hours, then speed is expressed in miles per hour (miles/hours). In the metric system, distance is measured in centimeters, meters, or kilometers. Metric units for speed are centimeters per second (cm/sec), meters per second (m/sec), or kilometers per hour (km/h). Table 3.1 shows many different units commonly used for speed.

$$\frac{90 \text{ miles}}{1.5 \text{ hours}} = 60 \text{ miles per hour (mph)}$$

Figure 3.1: *A driving trip with an average speed of 60 miles per hour.*

Table 3.1: **Some Common Units for Speed**

Distance	Time	Speed	Abbreviation
meters	seconds	meters per second	m/sec
kilometers	hours	kilometers per hour	km/h
centimeters	seconds	centimeters per second	cm/sec
miles	hours	miles per hour	mph
inches	seconds	inches per second	in/sec, ips
feet	minutes	feet per minute	ft/min, fpm

Calculate speed in meters per second

A bird is observed to fly 50 meters in 7.5 seconds. Calculate the speed of the bird in meters per second

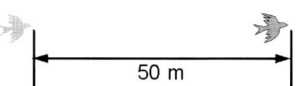

50 m

1) You are asked to find speed in m/sec.
2) You are given the distance in m and time in sec.
3) v = d÷t
4) v = 50 m ÷ 7.5 sec
   = 6.67 m/sec

Relationships between distance, speed, and time

How far do you go if you drive for 2 hours at a speed of 100 km/h?

Mixing up distance, time, and speed

This is a common form of question in physics. You know how to get speed from time and distance. How do you get distance from speed and time? The answer is the reason mathematics is the language of physics. A mathematical description of speed in terms of distance and time can easily be rearranged while preserving the original connections between variables.

Let the letter v stand for "speed," the letter d stand for "distance traveled," and the letter t stand for "time taken." If we remember that the letters stand for those words, we can now write a mathematically precise definition of speed.

Speed

Speed (m/sec) $\qquad v = \dfrac{d}{t}$ $\qquad$ Distance traveled (meters)

Time taken (seconds)

Three forms of the speed formula

There are three ways to arrange the three variables that relate distance, time, and speed. You should be able to work out how to get any of the three variables if you know the other two.

The equation . . .	. . . gives you . . .	. . . if you know . . .
$v = d \div t$	speed	time and distance
$d = vt$	distance	speed and time
$t = d \div v$	time	distance and speed

Using formulas

Remember that the words or letters stand for the values that the variables have. For example, the letter t will be replaced by the actual time when we plug in numbers for the letters. You can think about each letter as a box that will eventually hold a number. Maybe you do not know yet what the number is. Once we get everything arranged according to the rules, we can fill the boxes with the numbers that belong in each one. The last box left will be our answer. The letters (or variables) are the labels that tell us which numbers belong in which boxes.

Calculate time from speed and distance

How far do you go if you drive for 2 hours at a speed of 100 kilometers per hour?
1) You are asked for distance.
2) You are given time in hours and speed in km/h.
3) $d = vt$
4) $d = 2$ hrs $\times$ 100 km/h
   $= 200$ kilometers

Why the letter v is used for speed

In physics, we use the letter v to represent speed in a formula. If this seems confusing, remember that v stands for velocity. Speed and velocity are related. Speed is a single measurement that tells how fast you are going, like 100 km/h. Velocity means you know both your speed and your direction. An example of a velocity is saying you are going 100 kmh traveling straight north. In physics, direction is shown with a new kind of variable called a vector. We will cover vectors in Chapter 7. When you see a v with an arrow over it ($\vec{v}$) it means speed and direction (the vector). A v without the arrow just means speed.

How to solve physics problems

Physics problems   Physics problems usually give you some information and ask you to figure out something else that is related to the information you are given. Solving physics problems is excellent practice because they teach you to analyze information and think logically about how to get an answer. This skill is important in all careers. For example, financial analysts are expected to look at information about businesses and determine which companies are succeeding. Doctors collect information about patients and must figure out what is causing pain or an illness. Mechanics gather information about a car and have to figure out what is causing a malfunction and how to fix it. All these examples use problem-solving skills.

A four-step   The technique for solving problems has four steps. Follow these steps and you will
technique   be able to see a way to the answer most of the time and will at least get partial credit almost every time.

Step 1	Step 2	Step 3	Step 4
What do you want to find?	What do you know?	Identify useful relationships	**Solve the problem**

Step	What to do
1	Identify clearly what the problem is asking for. If you can, figure out exactly what variables or quantities need to be in the answer.
2	Identify the information you are given. Sometimes this includes numbers or values. Other times it includes descriptive information you must interpret. Look for words like **constant** or **at rest**. In a physics problem, saying something is constant means it does not change. That is useful information. The words "at rest" in physics mean the speed is zero. You may need conversion factors to change units.
3	Identify any relationships that involve the information you are asked to find and also the information you are given. For example, suppose you are given a speed and time and asked to find a distance. The relationship $v = d \div t$ relates what you are asked for to what you are given.
4	Combine the relationships with what you know to find what you are asked for. Once you complete steps 1-3, you will be able to see how to solve most problems. If not, start working with the relationships you have and see where they lead.

Calculate distance from time and speed

A space shuttle is traveling at a speed of 7,700 meters per second. How far does the shuttle travel in kilometers in one hour? At an altitude of 300 kilometers, the circumference of the shuttle's orbit is 42 million meters. How long does it take the shuttle to go around the Earth one time?

1) This is a two-part problem asking for distance in kilometers and time in hours.
2) You are given a speed and time for the first part, and a speed and distance for the second.
3) $d = vt$, and $t = d \div v$
   1 hour = 3,600 seconds
   1 km = 1,000 m
4) Part 1:
   $d = (7,700 \text{ m/sec})(3,600 \text{ sec})$
     = 27,720,000 m
   Convert to kilometers:
     = 27,720,000 ÷ 1,000
     = 27,720 km
   Part 2:
   $t = 42 \times 10^6 \text{ m} \div 7,700 \text{ m/sec}$
     = 5,455 seconds
   Convert to minutes:
     = 5,455 ÷ 60
     = 90.9 minutes

3.2 Observations of Motion

Knowing how quantities like speed are affected by other variables is an important part of physics. For example, the speed of a ball rolling downhill is different at different positions along the hill. The relationship between the position and speed of the ball is described by a model. In physics, a model is a description of the relationship between variables. This section describes a graphical model (graph). A graph describes the relationship between two variables. If you have a graph and you know the value of one variable you can use the graph to predict the value of the other variable. Making models is an important part of science and engineering. If we have a model, we can predict what will happen because we know how changes in one variable affect the others.

Variables

Speed
Time
Position

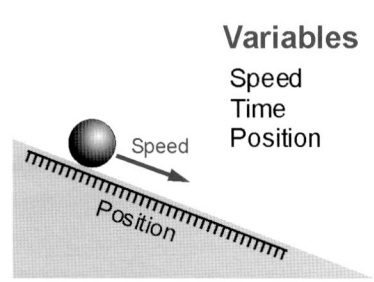

Figure 3.2: *Three of the variables that describe a ball rolling down a ramp.*

Variables and models

Variables
: Factors that affect the results of an experiment are called variables. For example, consider a ball rolling down a ramp (Figure 3.2). Speed is a variable. Time is another variable. The position on the hill is another variable. The first step in building a model is to decide which of the variables are important and should be included in the model.

Making a good model
: A useful model is one that matches what actually happens. For this reason, models are created by measuring what actually happens, then basing the model on the data from the measurements. For example, to make a model of speed on a ramp, you would do an experiment to measure the speed at different positions along the ramp (Figure 3.3). The data are the speeds and positions you measure. The model works when you can substitute positions and the model predicts speeds that match the ones you measure. Once your model matches the results of your experiment, you can use the model to predict the speed on different ramps without having to do a new experiment.

Change one thing at a time
: Often, more than one variable can affect the results of an experiment, so it is best to change *only one variable at a time*. For example, if you change both the mass of the ball and the angle of the ramp, you will not be able to figure out which of the two variables caused the speed to change. To test the effect of changing the angle, the values of the other variables must be kept the same.

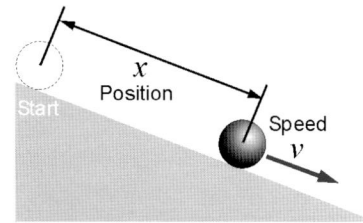

Position (m)	Speed (m/sec)
0.0	0.00
0.1	0.91
0.2	1.29
0.3	1.58
0.4	1.82
0.5	2.04
0.6	2.23
0.7	2.41
0.8	2.58
0.9	2.74
1.0	2.88

Figure 3.3: *Collected data from an experiment observing the motion of a ball rolling down a ramp.*

Motion on a ramp

The speed of a ball on a ramp

When a ball is set on a ramp, it rolls down. The farther down the ramp the ball rolls, the faster it goes. Many of the important relationships in the physics of motion were discovered by observing balls rolling down ramps. For example, both Galileo and Isaac Newton conducted experiments with balls on ramps. The laws of motion you will learn in Chapter 5 are physical models that were deduced by observing balls rolling up and down ramps. Of course, the laws apply to much more than just balls on ramps! However, a ball on a ramp is a simple system to observe accurately and therefore makes the laws clear to see.

The initial speed

Consider an experiment that measures the speed of a ball at different positions as it rolls down a straight ramp. The speed depends on a number of variables. The most important ones are shown in Figure 3.4. One variable is the speed (if any) the ball has when it is released. The initial speed is the speed an object has at the start of the experiment. The initial speed often depends on the starting point of the motion. The starting point is another variable.

The angle

The angle of the ramp is another important variable. Downhill motion is caused by gravity. On a level surface, gravity pulls directly against the surface and no motion results. The steeper the angle, the larger the force of gravity directed along the ramp. As we will see, larger forces create more rapid increases in speed.

Friction

Friction is another variable. All motion creates friction. Friction acts to reduce motion, or slow things down. A certain fraction of the force of gravity is taken up by overcoming friction. If there were no friction, a ball would have even greater speed at the bottom of a ramp.

Size, mass, and shape are also important variables

The mass and size of the ball are also variables that affect its motion. It may surprise you but mass does not have as big an effect on the speed of the ball as you might think. The way the ball is made also matters. Solid balls and hollow balls increase speed at different rates even when the ramp is at the same angle. The different performance of solid and hollow balls comes from their *rolling* motion as they move down. Rolling motion can be complicated and is discussed later, in Chapters 8 and 9.

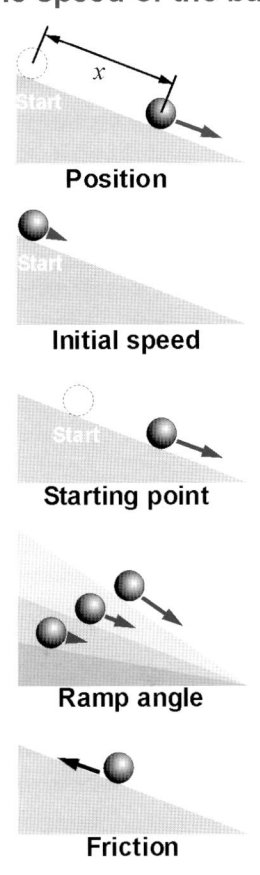

Variables that affect the speed of the ball

Position

Initial speed

Starting point

Ramp angle

Friction

Size, mass, shape

Figure 3.4: *The most important variables that affect the speed of a ball rolling down a ramp.*

Experimental techniques

Control and experimental variables

We do experiments to find out what happens when we change a variable such as the angle of a ramp. The variable that is changed is called the experimental variable. The variables that are kept the same are called the control variables (Figure 3.5). When you change one variable and control all of the others, we call it a *controlled experiment*. Controlled experiments are the best way to get reliable data. If you observe that something happens (the ball goes faster, for example), you know *why* it happened (because the ramp was steeper). There is no confusion over which variable caused the change.

Experiments often have several trials

Many experiments are repeated many times. For example, you might roll a ball down a ramp 10 times. Each repetition of the experiment is called a trial. To be sure of your results, each trial must be as close to identical as possible to all the other trials. In an ideal experiment, the only allowed change from trial to trial is in the one variable you are testing (the experimental variable).

Experimental technique

Your experimental technique is how you actually do the experiment. For example, you might release the ball using one finger. If this is your technique, you want to do it the same way every time. By developing a good technique, you make sure your results accurately show the effects of changing your experimental variable. If your technique is sloppy, you may not be able to tell if any differences you observe are due to sloppy technique or to changes in your experimental variable.

Procedures

The procedure is a collection of all the techniques you use to do an experiment. Your procedure for testing the ramp angle might have several steps. Good scientists keep careful track of their procedures so that they can come back another time and repeat their experiments. Writing the procedures down in a lab notebook is a good way to keep track of them (Figure 3.6).

Scientific results must always be repeatable

What good would a new discovery be if nobody believed you? Having good techniques and procedures is the best way to be sure your results are *repeatable*. Discoveries must always be able to be repeated by someone other than you. If other people can follow your procedure and get the same results, then most scientists would accept your results as being true. Writing good procedures is the best way to ensure that others can repeat and verify your experiments.

Experimental question
How does the angle of a ramp change in the speed of the ball?

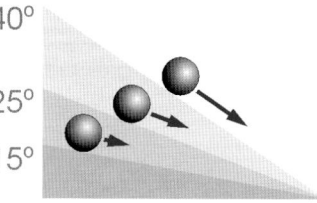

Experimental variable	Control variables
Angle	Initial speed position mass size shape starting point

Figure 3.5: *Experimental variables and control variables depend on what the purpose of the experiment is.*

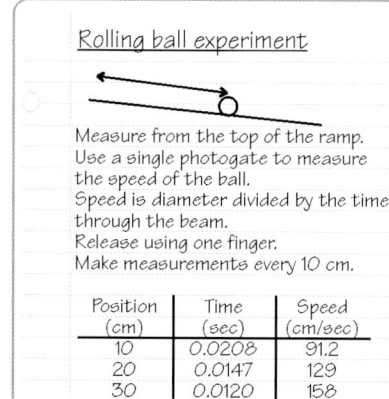

Rolling ball experiment

Measure from the top of the ramp.
Use a single photogate to measure the speed of the ball.
Speed is diameter divided by the time through the beam.
Release using one finger.
Make measurements every 10 cm.

Position (cm)	Time (sec)	Speed (cm/sec)
10	0.0208	91.2
20	0.0147	129
30	0.0120	158

Figure 3.6: *An example of a procedure with some data written in a lab notebook.*

Graphical data

Graphs   A graph shows how two variables are related with a picture that is easy to understand. Graphs are a way of representing data. The example graph below shows that the speed of a ball changes as it rolls downhill. You can see from the graph that the farther the ball goes, the higher its speed gets. The information in the graph is the same as the information in the table to the right. We make graphs because they are easier to read than tables of numbers.

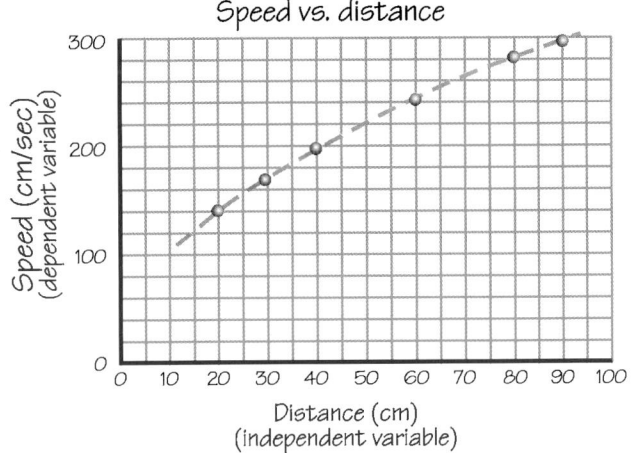

Speed vs. distance

Distance (cm)	Speed (cm/sec)
20	140
30	171
40	198
60	242
80	280
90	297

The dependent variable   To a scientist, a graph is a language that shows the relationship between two variables. By convention, graphs are drawn a certain way just like words are spelled certain ways. The dependent variable goes on the y-axis which is vertical. In the example, speed is the dependent variable because we believe the speed *depends* on how far down the ramp the ball gets.

The independent variable   The independent variable goes on the horizontal or x-axis. In the example, distance is the independent variable. We say it is *independent* because we are free to make the distance anything we want by choosing where on the ramp to measure. The variable *time* is sometimes an exception to this rule. Time usually goes on the x-axis, even though we do not have direct control over the time variable.

How to make a graph

Each box = 1	Each box = 10	Each box = 20
15	150	300
10	100	200
5	50	100
0	0	0

Letting each box = 20 fits the biggest data point (297 cm/sec)

1   Decide what to put on the *x* and *y* axes.

2   Make a scale for each axis by counting boxes to fit your largest value. Count by multiples of 1, 2, 5, or 10 to make plot points. Make the graph big and include units on your graph. Use as much area on the graph paper as you can.

3   Plot your points by finding the *x*-value and drawing a line upward until you get to the right *y*-value. Put a dot for each point.

4   Draw a smooth curve that shows the pattern of the points. Do not simply connect the dots.

5   Create a title for your graph.

Graphical models

A graph is also a model

A graphical model uses a graph to make predictions based on the relationship between the variables on the *x*- and *y*-axes. A graph is a form of a mathematical model because it shows the connection between two variables (Figure 3.7).

Using a graphical model to make a prediction

Suppose you want to find out what the speed of the ball would be 50 centimeters from the start. You did not measure the speed there. Yet the graph can give you a very accurate answer.

1 To predict the speed, start by finding 50 centimeters on the *x*-axis.

2 Draw a line vertically upward from 50 centimeters until it hits the curve you drew from your data.

3 Draw a line horizontally over until it reaches the *y*-axis.

4 Use the scale on the *y*-axis to read the predicted speed.

5 For this example, the model graph predicts the speed to be 220 cm/sec.

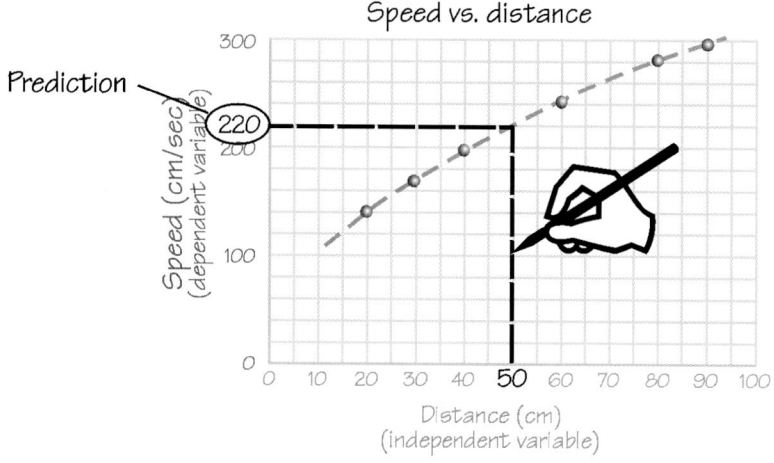

Checking the accuracy of a model

If the graph is created from accurate data, the prediction will also be accurate. You could check by doing another experiment and measuring the speed of the ball at 50 centimeters. You should find it to be very close to the prediction from your graph. Although useful, graphical models are limited because a graph does not show *why* the connection exists or *how* one variable affects the other.

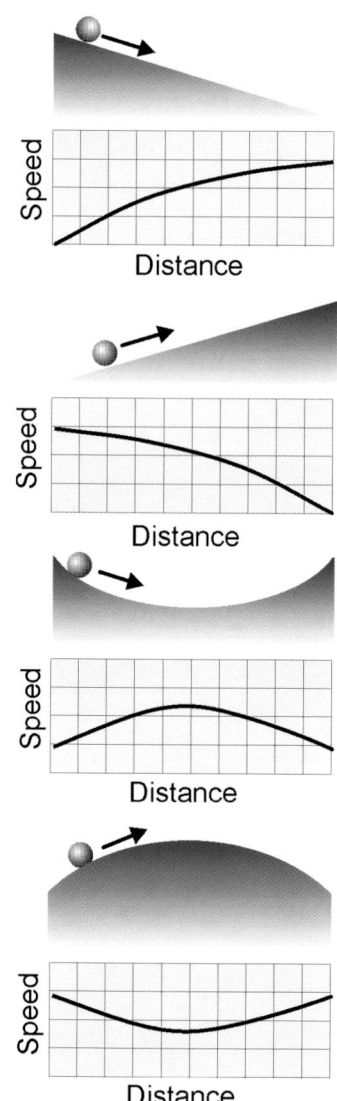

Figure 3.7: *Some different shapes for ramps and their corresponding speed versus distance graphs.*

Recognizing relationships in data

Cause and effect relationships
In many experiments you are looking for a cause and effect relationship. How does changing one variable affect another? Graphs are a simple way to see whether there is a connection between two variables or not. You cannot always tell from looking at tables of data. With a graph, the connection is easier to see.

Patterns indicate relationships
When there is a relationship between the variables, a graph shows a clear pattern. For example, the speed and distance variables show a strong relationship. When there is no relationship, the graph looks like a collection of dots. No pattern appears. The number of rock bands a student can name in one minute and the last two digits of his or her phone number are two variables that are not related.

Strong relationship

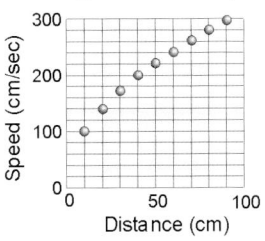

Weak relationship

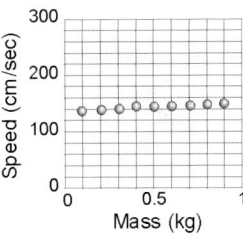

Strong relationship between variables

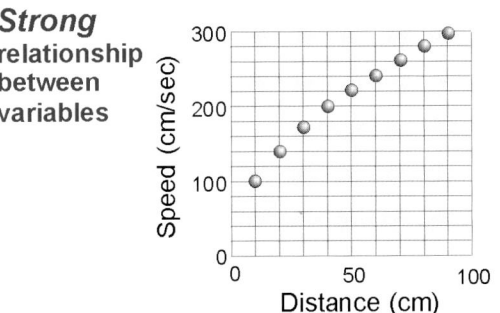

No relationship between variables

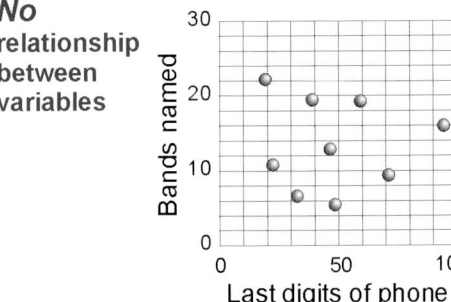

Figure 3.8: *In a strong relationship (top graph), a big change in distance creates a big change in speed. In a weak relationship (above graph), a big change in mass causes almost no change in speed.*

Strong and weak relationships
You can tell how strong the relationship is from the pattern. If the relationship is strong, a small change in one variable makes a big change in another. If the relationship is weak, even a big change in one variable has little effect on the other. In weak relationships, the points may follow a pattern but there is not much change in one variable compared with big changes in the other (Figure 3.8).

Inverse relationships
Some relationships are inverse. When one variable increases, the other decreases. If you graph how much money you spend against how much you have left, you see an inverse relationship. The more you spend, the less you have. Graphs of inverse relationships often slope down to the right (Figure 3.9).

Inverse relationship

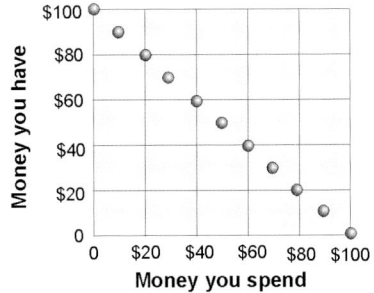

Figure 3.9: *A typical graph for an inverse relationship.*

3.3 Analyzing Motion with Graphs

There are three graphs you can get from speed, distance, and time measurements of a ball rolling down a ramp. The speed versus distance graph was a convenient model for making predictions. The second of the three graphs is position versus time, and the third is speed versus time. Each of the graphs is useful and teaches something new about motion. This section explores the meaning of the position versus time and speed versus time graphs.

Position and distance

Position | In physics, the word position refers to the location of an object at one instant. For example, suppose you stretch out a measuring tape and stand at the 2-meter mark. Relative to the edge of the tape, your position would be 2 meters. If you move to the 3-meter mark, your new position would be 3 meters (Figure 3.10).

The origin | A position is always specified relative to an origin. The origin is a reference point that stays fixed. In the previous example of a measuring tape, the origin would be the start of the tape. In straight-line laboratory experiments, position is usually given in meters away from a starting point. When navigating on the surface of the Earth, position is specified in longitude and latitude (Figure 3.11). The reference for zero latitude is the Earth's equator. The reference for zero longitude is the Royal Observatory in Greenwich, England.

Speed is the rate of change in position | Position gives us a new way to think about speed. Speed is the *rate* at which the position of an object changes. In physics, the word rate means the ratio of how much something changes divided by how long the change takes. A high rate means a large change in a short time. A low rate means either a small change or a long time for the change to happen. Speed is the rate of change of position with time.

Position and distance | Distance is related to, but different from position. You have already learned that distance is a measure of length *without* regard to direction. To understand the difference, suppose you walk 10 meters in one direction, and turn around and walk 10 meters back. The distance you walked is 20 meters. But your position is zero meters—because you walked right back to where you started from.

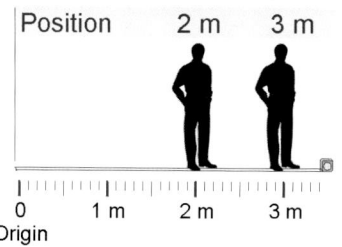

Figure 3.10: *In physics, your position describes where you are relative to the origin at one instant of time.*

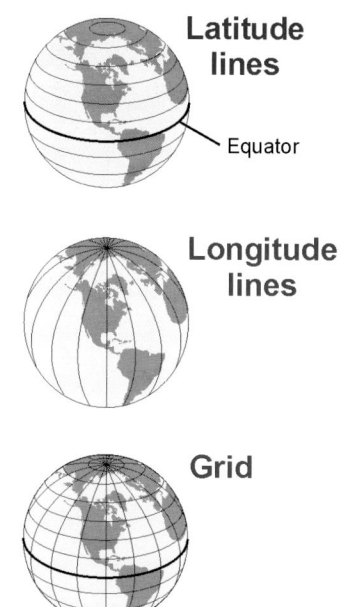

Figure 3.11: *Position on the surface of the Earth is specified in terms of longitude and latitude lines that make a grid around the globe.*

The position vs. time graph

An example trip   Suppose you travel between two cities that are 90 miles apart. You drive at 60 mph for 1 hour, take a half-hour rest, then drive for another 1/2 hour at the same speed (60 mph). At the end, you meet a friend who calculates your speed to be only 45 mph (90 mi ÷ 2 hrs). Is your friend's calculation accurate?

Average and instantaneous speed   The calculation is accurate, except that it is a calculation of your **average speed**. Average speed is equal to the total distance traveled divided by the total time taken. During the trip itself, the speed could have been very different. In fact, during most trips the speed changes quite a bit. The speedometer in your car shows **instantaneous speed**. Instantaneous speed is the speed you are going at any moment.

The position versus time graph   A position versus time graph shows a more detailed history of the drive, including when the car was moving, and when it was stopped. The graph shows that during the first hour, your position gradually increased from your initial position (0 miles) to a point 60 miles away. It then shows that you were stopped between 1 hour and 1.5 hours because your position didn't change. Finally, the graph shows that you started driving again at 1.5 hours and changed your position until you reached a point 90 miles away from your starting point. The graph contains much more information because it shows the instantaneous speed all through the trip.

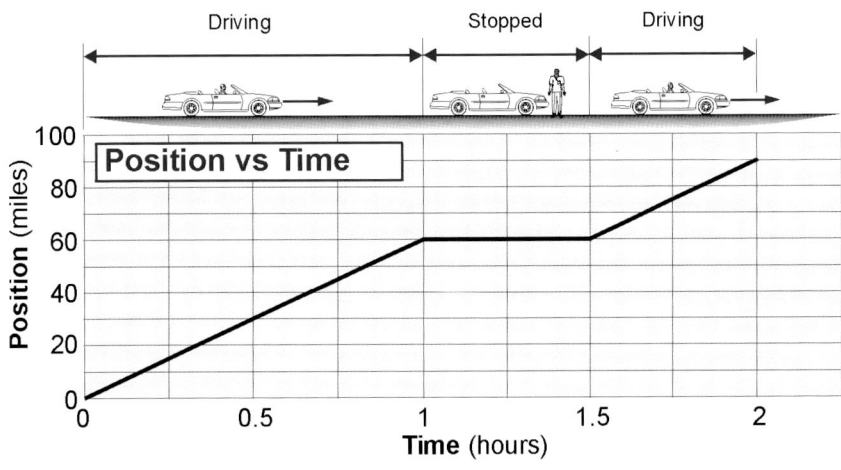

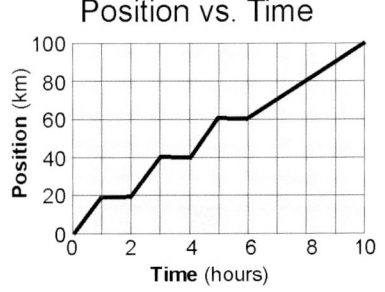

Interpret a position vs. time graph

The position versus time graph below shows a boat traveling through a long canal. The boat has to stop at locks for changes in water level.

a) How many stops does the boat make?

b) What is the boat's average speed for the whole trip?

c) What is the highest speed the boat reaches?

a) The boat makes three stops because there are three horizontal sections on the graph.

b) The average speed is 10 km/h (100 km ÷ 10 hr).

c) The highest speed is 20 km/h. You can tell because of the position changes by 20 km in one hour for the first, third, and fifth hours of the trip.

Determining speed from the slope of a position vs. time graph

Position versus time
The graph below shows the position versus time for a ball rolling along a level floor. The ball rolled a distance of 10 meters in 10 seconds. The average speed is 1 m/sec. If the graph is a complete description of the motion, you should be able to figure out the speed of the ball from the graph, and you can.

The definition of slope
The slope of a line is the ratio of the "rise" (vertical change) to the "run" (horizontal change) of the line. The rise is determined by finding the height of the triangle shown. The run is determined by finding the length along the base of the triangle. Here, the *x*-values represent time and the *y*-values represent position.

The slope is the speed
Remember that speed is defined as the distance traveled divided by the time taken. As long as you travel in a straight line, distance is just the difference in position between where you finished and where you started. This is equal to the rise (vertical change) on the graph. The run (horizontal change) on the graph is the time taken for the trip. The slope is "rise" divided by "run," which is the distance traveled divided by the time taken, which is the speed. *This is an important result!* The slope of a position versus time graph is the speed.

The slope of a graph

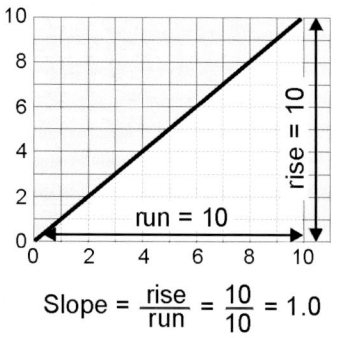

$$\text{Slope} = \frac{\text{rise}}{\text{run}} = \frac{10}{10} = 1.0$$

The slope of position vs. time is the speed

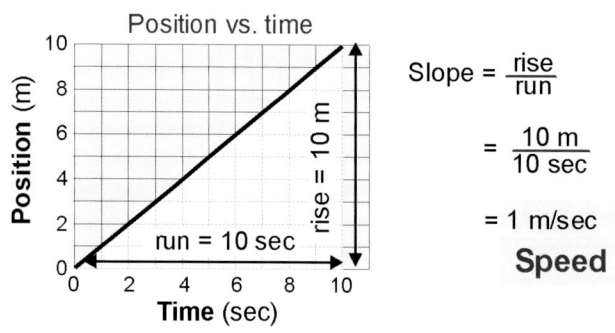

$$\text{Slope} = \frac{\text{rise}}{\text{run}}$$

$$= \frac{10 \text{ m}}{10 \text{ sec}}$$

$$= 1 \text{ m/sec}$$

Speed

Straight lines mean constant speed
A straight line has a constant slope. If the slope changed, the line would curve, like the example in Figure 3.12. The straight line in the graph of position versus time for the rolling ball shows that the speed is constant over the entire motion. This is another important result: A straight line on a position versus time graph tells you that the motion is at a constant speed.

Constant speed *away* from the origin

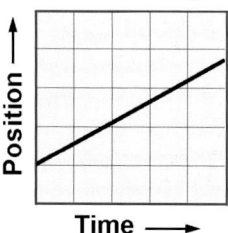

Constant speed *toward* the origin

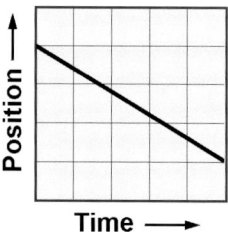

Speed that is *not* constant

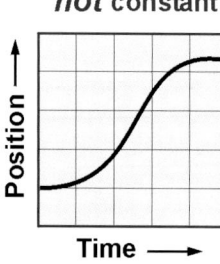

Figure 3.12: *Three examples of position versus time graphs showing different types of motion.*

The speed vs. time graph

The speed versus time graph

The speed versus time graph has speed on the *y*-axis and time on the *x*-axis. This graph tells a very accurate history of how the speed of a moving object changes with time. The speed versus time graph is useful even if the speed is not changing. For example, the graph in Figure 3.13 shows the speed versus time for a ball rolling at constant speed on a level floor. On this graph, a constant speed is a straight horizontal line. If you follow the line over to where it intersects the *y*-axis, you can see that the speed of the ball is one meter per second. The graph also shows that the speed stays constant at 1 m/sec for 10 seconds.

Distance equals area on the speed versus time graph

The information about an object's position is also present in the speed versus time graph, but you need to know how to find it. Remember, the distance traveled is equal to the speed of the ball multiplied by the time it moves. Suppose we draw a rectangle on the speed versus time graph between the line that shows the speed and the *x*-axis. The area of a rectangle is equal to its length times its height. On this graph, length is equal to time and height is equal to speed. Therefore, area on the graph is speed multiplied by time, which is the distance traveled. *This is an important result.* The area on a speed versus time graph is equal to the distance traveled. This rule is true as long as the *x*-axis represents a speed of zero.

Constant speed

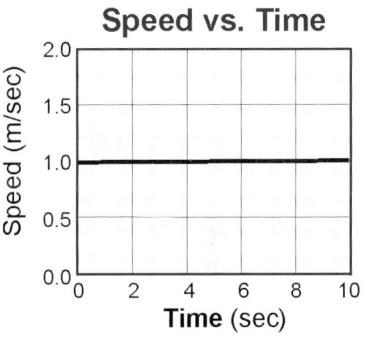

Figure 3.13: *The speed versus time graph of a ball moving on a level floor at a constant speed of 1 meter per second.*

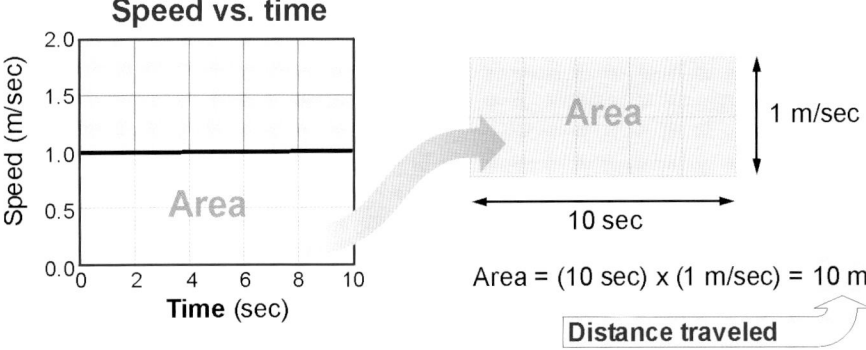

The speed vs. time graph for downhill motion

A ball rolling down hill Consider an experiment with a ball rolling downhill. The speed of the ball increases as it rolls downward. The speed versus time graph looks like Figure 3.14. This graph shows a speed that starts at zero. Two seconds later, the speed is two meters per second. A speed versus time graph that shows any slope (like this one does) indicates that the speed is changing.

The distance traveled when speed is changing The speed versus time graph gives us a way to calculate the distance an object moves even when its speed is changing. The distance is equal to the area on the graph, but this time the area is a triangle instead of a rectangle. The area of a triangle is one-half the base times the height. The base is equal to the time just as before. The height is equal to the speed of the ball at the end of two seconds. For the graph in the example, the ball moves two meters between the time $t = 0$ and the time $t = 2$ seconds.

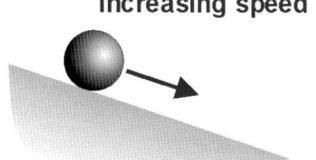

Increasing speed

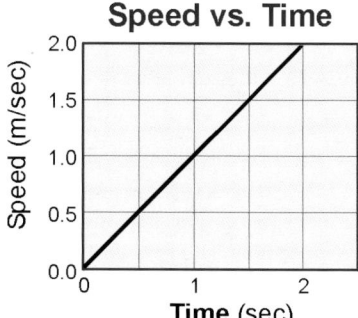

Figure 3.14: *The speed versus time graph for a ball rolling downhill shows a speed that increases with time.*

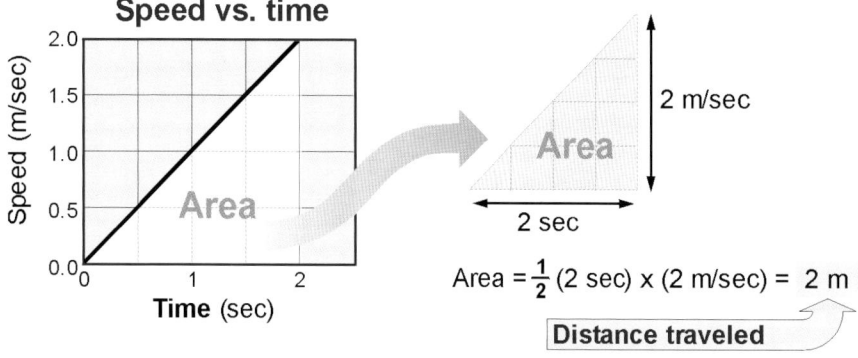

Speed vs. time

Area $= \frac{1}{2}$ (2 sec) x (2 m/sec) = **2 m**

Distance traveled

Motion with decreasing speed The speed versus time graph does not always slope up and to the right. Figure 3.15 shows a graph that slopes down as time goes on. A graph like this shows the speed is *decreasing*. The area under the graph is still equal to the distance traveled. The example is from a car putting on its brakes. This car started with the speed of 30 meters per second, and its speed decreased to zero in six seconds. A quick calculation shows that the stopping distance for the car is equal to 90 meters.

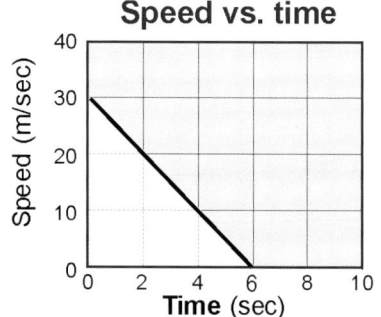

Speed vs. time

distance $= \frac{1}{2}(30 \text{ m/sec}) \times (6 \text{ sec})$
$= 90 \text{ m}$

Figure 3.15: *A speed versus time graph for a car during braking.*

50

Application: Slow-motion Photography

You have probably seen slow-motion photography if you watch sports on television. It looks as if everything takes much longer than it does in real time. Slow-motion photography is also very useful in science. Many things in nature move so quickly it is hard to see enough detail to figure out what is happening. For example, a slow-motion camera can allow you to see the motion of a hummingbird's wings or the turning of an engine. At their normal speeds these motions are far too rapid to see clearly.

Creating the illusion of motion   A video camera does not photograph moving images. It takes a sequence of still images called *frames*, and changes them fast enough that your brain perceives a moving image. The standard for video is to change frames 30 times per second. At this rate, a sequence of still images is perceived as smooth motion.

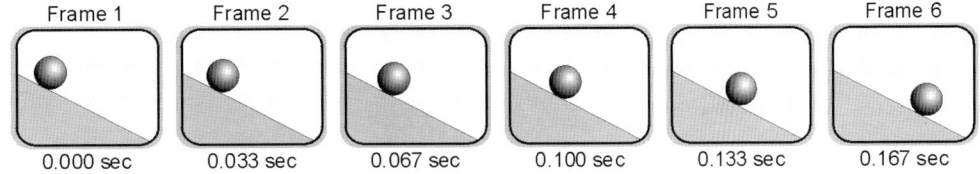

Making a slow-motion movie   To take a slow-motion movie, the camera captures more frames per second. Instead of taking 30 per second, it may take 120 frames per second. The slow-motion effect comes from playing the movie back at the standard rate of 30 frames per second. The motion appears four times slower because the playback rate is four times slower than the rate at which the pictures were actually taken.

Using video to analyze motion   You can use an ordinary video camera to analyze motion in laboratory experiments. Many professional quality VCRs allow you to advance a video one frame, at a time. Each frame represents one-thirtieth of a second. The speed of an object can be determined by comparing the object's position in two consecutive frames. The speed of the object is equal to the distance it moved between frames divided by 1/30 of a second. Figure 3.16 shows a sequence of frames taken from video of a ball rolling over the top of a hill. The ball slows down near the top of the hill. You can tell because the distance the ball moves between frames gets less and less as the ball gets near the top of the hill.

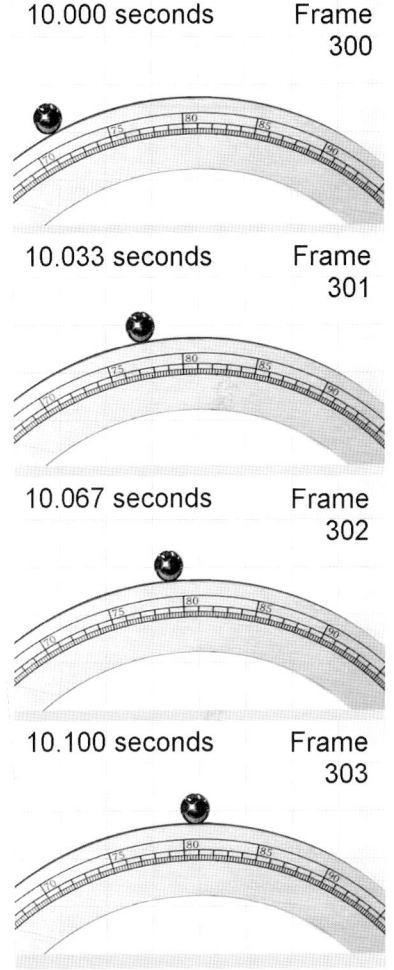

Figure 3.16: *A sequence of video images showing the motion of a ball rolling over the top of a hill. You can see that the ball slows down as it goes over the hill.*

Strobe photography

Stopping motion with photography

There is a second way to do stop-motion photography. In this method, a special light called a *strobe* light is used. A strobe light repeatedly flashes very bright pulses of light. Suppose the flashes are one-tenth of a second apart. A regular still-film camera sees the moving object only every tenth of a second, when the strobe flashes. If the camera is left with a long exposure time, all of the flashes from the strobe appear on the same image on film. As a result the film looks like Figure 3.17. There are multiple images of the moving object separated by the time between flashes of the strobe. For this image, you can see the head of the golf club gets faster toward the bottom of the swing. You can tell because it moves a greater distance between flashes of the strobe near the bottom of the swing.

Figure 3.17: *This strobe photograph shows a golf swing. Each separate image is one flash of the strobe light. From the separation between images, you can see that the speed of the club head increases as it is swung down toward the ball. (Photo courtesy of Palm Press, Inc. ©2003 Harold & Esther Foundation.)*

Ordinary cameras

When a normal (still frame) camera photographs a moving object, the image can be blurry. The blur occurs because it takes a certain minimum amount of light to expose the film. An image becomes blurry if the object moves while the film is still collecting light. Still frame cameras can open and close the shutter that lets in light in one-thousandth of a second. This seems fast, but it takes only a few millimeters of motion to create a blurry image.

Strobe lights

A strobe light can be used to take a sharp image of a rapidly moving object. To do this, the strobe is flashed only once with a very bright but very short pulse of light. The flash is so short that the object does not move during the light pulse. A strobe light can flash a pulse many times faster than the mechanical shutter on a camera can move. The single rapid flash provides enough light to capture an image on film without blurring.

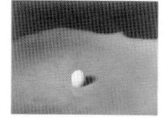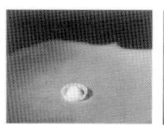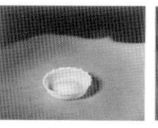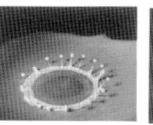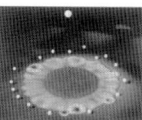

Figure 3.18: *(At left) Sequence of strobe photographs showing a drop of milk splashing into a cup. (Photo courtesy of Palm Press, Inc. ©2003 Harold & Esther Foundation.)*

The famous sequence of photographs above show a drop of milk splashing into a cup (Figure 3.18). Each image was caught by a single pulse of a strobe light. Dr. Harold Edgerton is famous for perfecting strobe photography. Many discoveries have been made using Edgerton's strobe technique to photograph moving objects.

Chapter 3 Review

Vocabulary Review

Match the following terms with the correct definition. There is one extra definition in the list that will not match any of the terms.

Set One

1. speed
2. per
3. variable
4. model
5. scale

a. On the axis of a graph, the number of units represented by a line
b. Measurable quantity that can change
c. Ratio of the distance traveled by an object divided by the time taken
d. Shows how variables in a physical system are related to each other
e. Product of the distance an object travels and the time required
f. Term meaning "for each"

Set Two

1. instantaneous speed
2. dependent
3. graphical model
4. independent
5. average speed

a. Variable generally plotted on the x-axis
b. Shows a relationship between variables
c. Slope of a position vs. time graph at any point
d. Variable generally plotted on the y-axis
e. Total distance divided by total time for a trip
f. Time required to move a certain distance

Set Three

1. position
2. distance
3. data
4. slope
5. strong relationship

a. Information collected
b. A large change in one variable always results in a predictable, large change in a second variable
c. Sum of the length of movement and the time required for the movement
d. Location of an object at some instant
e. Measure of length between one point to another
f. Ratio of rise to run on a graph

53

Concept review

1. Which two quantities are needed to determine the speed of an object?

2. Fill in the missing information in the table showing common units for speed below:

Distance	Time	Speed	Abbreviation
meters	seconds		
			km/h
		centimeters per second	
miles			mph
		inches per second	
			ft/min

3. Write the three meaningful formula arrangements of the variables speed, distance and time. Let v = speed, t = time and d = distance.

4. Summarize the four-step problem solving process by listing the four steps mentioned in the text.

5. Why is it important to only change one variable at a time in an experiment?

6. You wish to do an experiment to determine how a ball's size affects its speed as it rolls down a ramp. List the experimental and control variables in this experiment.

7. Explain the difference between an independent variable and a dependent variable.

8. Why are graphs often more useful than tables of data?

9. Summarize how to make a graph by listing the steps you would follow.

10. You wish to make a graph of the angular position of the moon above the horizon every 15 minutes between 9:00 p.m. and 3:00 a.m. one night.

    a. What is the independent variable?

    b. What is the dependent variable?

    c. On which axis should you graph each variable?

11. Give your own example of a pair of variables that would show:

    a. a strong relationship.

    b. a weak relationship.

    c. no relationship.

    d. an inverse relationship.

12. What is the difference between the terms *position* and *distance*?

13. How is the slope of a straight, best-fit line determined?

14. What does the slope of a position vs. time graph represent?

15. Sam rolls down his driveway on a skateboard while Beth keeps track of his position every second for 15 seconds. When they make a graph of the data, the best-fit line for the position vs. time graph is a curved line. What does this indicate about Sam's speed?

16. Sketch the shape of the position vs. time graph for each situation:

    a. An automobile stopped at a traffic light

    b. A cyclist traveling at a constant speed on a highway.

    c. An airplane gradually rolling to a stop on its runway.

17. What is the importance of the area under a speed vs. time graph?

18. Sketch the shape of the speed vs. time graph for each situation in question 16.

Problems

1. The sound from an underwater explosion is recorded by sailors on a submarine 4.80×10^3 meters away 3.2 seconds after the explosion occurs. According to their data, what is the speed of sound in water?

2. If it takes 500 seconds for the light from the sun to reach the Earth, what is the distance to the sun in meters? (The speed of light is 3.00×10^8 m/s).

3. If Lexi bikes at an average speed of 22 mph, how many hours will it take for her to cover a 110 mile course?

4. You travel on the highway at a rate of 65 mph for 1 hour and at 55 mph for 1.5 hours and 47 mph for 3 hours.

   a. What is the total distance you have traveled?

   b. What is your average speed during the trip?

5. On July 2, 1988, Steve Cram of England ran a mile in 3.81 minutes. Calculate his speed in miles per hour.

6. The uniform motion of a cart is represented on the graph below. What is the speed of the cart?

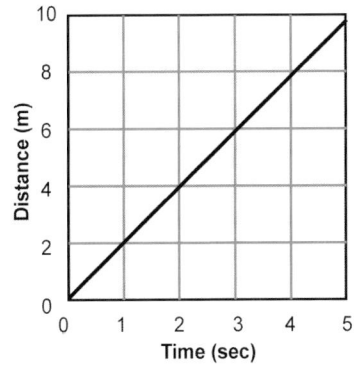

7. The graph below represents the relationship between the position (distance) and time for the motion of an object.

   a. During which time period is the object's speed changing?

   b. What is the speed of the object at time, t = 5 seconds?

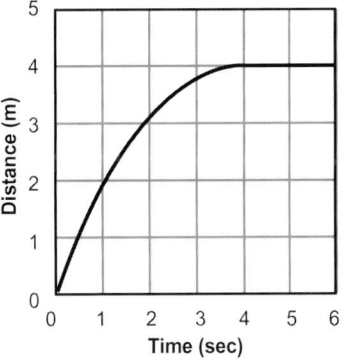

8. The graph below represents the relationship between the position (displacement) and time for a car.

   a. During which time interval is the car at rest?

   b. During which time interval is the car moving at a constant speed?

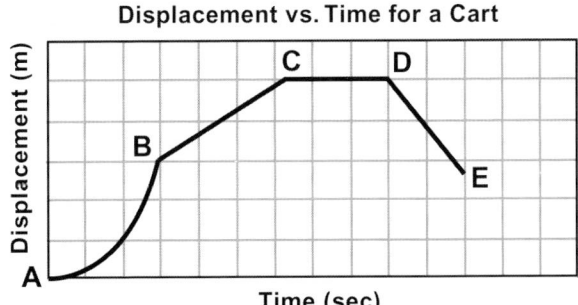

Displacement vs. Time for a Cart

9. A Global Positioning Satellite (GPS) receiver uses communications with orbiting satellites to determine position anywhere on the surface of the Earth. Many people have GPS receivers in their cars to help them with directions.

John drives his car to a friend's house which is 3.2 kilometers away on the same straight road as John's house. John uses a GPS receiver to measure his position every 0.40 kilometers. He records his position and also the speed from his speedometer in the data table shown below. Construct a graph of speed vs. position to describe John's trip.

| Speed (m/s) | 0 | 10 | 15 | 20 | 23 | 23 | 21 | 17 | 0 |
| Position (km) | 0 | 0.4 | 0.8 | 1.2 | 1.6 | 2.0 | 2.4 | 2.8 | 3.2 |

10. Examine the graphs below and write brief description of the motion represented by each.

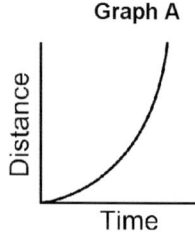

Graph A

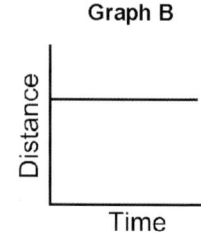

Graph B

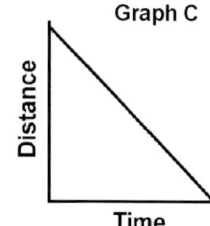

Graph C

11. Look at the graphs below. Indicate the strength of the relationship between variables by labeling the relationships shown as strong, weak or none.

a.

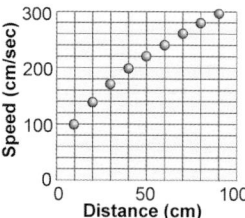

b.

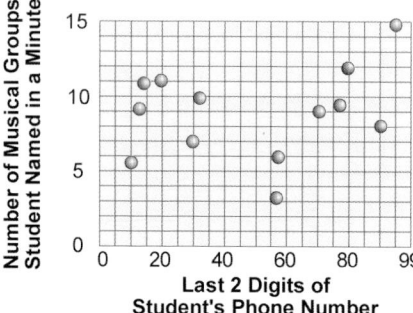

c.

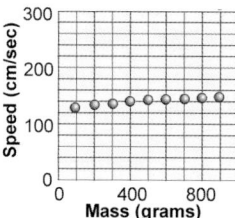

56

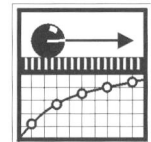

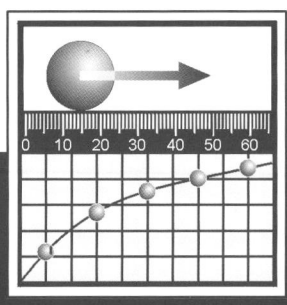

Unit 1
Measurement and Motion

Chapter 4

Accelerated Motion in a Straight Line

Objectives for Chapter 4

By the end of this chapter you should be able to:

1. Calculate acceleration from the change in speed and the change in time.
2. Give an example of motion with constant acceleration.
3. Determine acceleration from the slope of the speed versus time graph.
4. Calculate time, distance, acceleration, or speed when given three of the four values.
5. Solve two-step accelerated motion problems.
6. Calculate height, speed, or time of flight in free fall problems.
7. Explain how air resistance makes objects of different masses fall with different accelerations.

Terms and vocabulary words

acceleration	delta (Δ)	m/sec^2	initial speed	constant acceleration
uniform acceleration	slope	free fall	term	acceleration due to gravity (g)
air resistance	time of flight	friction	terminal speed	

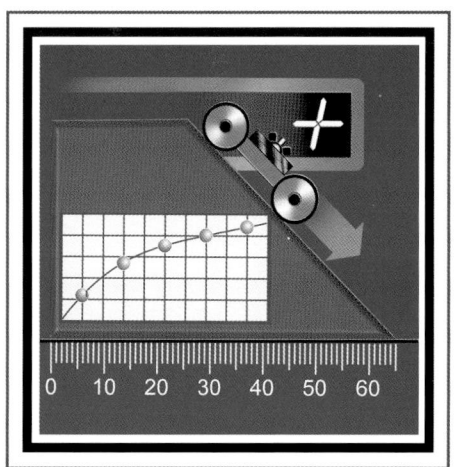

4.1 Acceleration

The speed of moving objects rarely stays the same for long. Acceleration is the way we describe change in speed and this chapter is about acceleration. You experience acceleration every day. You speed up and slow down as you walk, and you probably ride in a car or bus that also speeds up and slows down. Any time your speed changes, you experience acceleration.

Acceleration of a car

Acceleration   Acceleration is the rate of change in the speed of an object. Rate of change means the ratio of the amount of change divided by how much time the change takes.

An example of acceleration   Suppose you are driving and your speed goes from 20 to 60 miles per hour in four seconds (Figure 4.1). The change is 40 miles per hour, 60 mph - 20 mph. The time it takes to change speeds is 4 seconds. The acceleration is 40 mph divided by 4 seconds, or 10 mph/sec. Your car accelerated 10 mph per second. That means your speed increased by 10 miles per hour each second. Table 4.1 shows how your speed changed during those four seconds of acceleration.

Acceleration is the rate at which speed changes

Change in time is 4 seconds

Change in speed = 40 mph (60 mph - 20 mph)
= 18.1 m/sec (27 m/sec - 8.9 m/sec)

Common units $\text{Acceleration} = \dfrac{40 \text{ mph}}{4 \text{ seconds}} = 10 \text{ mph/sec}$

Metric units $\text{Acceleration} = \dfrac{18.1 \text{ m/sec}}{4 \text{ seconds}} = 4.5 \text{ m/sec/sec}$

Acceleration in metric units   In metric units, the car's speed increases from 8.9 m/sec to 27 m/sec. The acceleration in metric units is 4.5 meters per second per second (18.1 m/sec ÷ 4 sec). The interpretation is that the speed increases by 4.5 meters per second every second. The unit of meters per second per second is usually written as meters per second squared (m/sec^2).

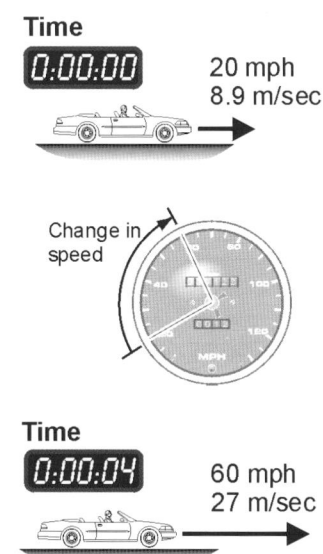

Figure 4.1: *A car accelerating from 20 miles per hour to 60 miles per hour in four seconds.*

Table 4.1:
Speedometer readings every second during acceleration

Time	Speed
0 (start)	20 mph
1 second	30 mph
2 seconds	40 mph
3 seconds	50 mph
4 seconds	60 mph

The difference between speed and acceleration

Comparing speed and acceleration

Speed and acceleration both describe motion but they are not the same thing. Speed is the rate at which an object's position changes. Speed is measured in meters per second. Acceleration is the rate at which an object's *speed* changes. Acceleration is measured in meters per second per second, or meters per second squared (m/sec^2). If an object has an acceleration of 1 m/sec^2, its speed increases by 1 m/sec every second.

$$\text{Acceleration} = \frac{\text{Change in speed}}{\text{Change in time}} = \frac{\frac{\text{meters}}{\text{second}}}{\text{second}} = \frac{\text{meters}}{\text{second} \times \text{second}} = \frac{\text{m}}{\text{sec}^2}$$

Acceleration and speed in the same direction

The acceleration of an object can be in the same direction as its speed or in the opposite direction. Speed increases when acceleration is in the same direction as speed. For example, a ball rolling down a ramp has an acceleration in the same direction as its speed. The data table in Figure 4.2 shows a speed that increases by 1 m/sec^2 every second.

Acceleration and speed in opposite directions

A ball rolling *up* a ramp has an acceleration in the opposite direction to its speed. As the ball goes up, its speed *decreases*. When the acceleration is -1 m/sec^2, the speed decreases by 1 m/sec every second. The data in Figure 4.3 show the decreasing speed of a ball as it rolls up a ramp.

Using positive and negative signs

Because speed and acceleration can have opposite directions, it is useful to assign positive and negative signs. A common choice is to make positive to the right, and negative to the left. A positive speed means the object is moving to the right. A negative speed describes an object moving to the left.

Positive and negative acceleration

When speed and acceleration are the *same* sign, the speed increases. When acceleration and speed have the *opposite* sign the speed decreases. If *both* speed and acceleration are negative, it can be a little tricky to interpret. For example, suppose a ball is rolling down a ramp sloped to the left. If you make motion to the left negative, the speed and acceleration are both negative. The speed of the ball gets larger in the negative direction, which means the ball gets faster as it moves to the left.

Positive speed and acceleration moving down hill

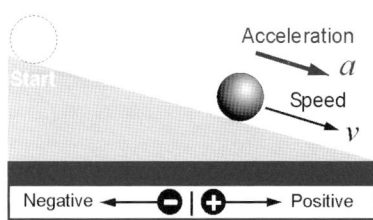

Time (sec)	Speed (m/sec)
0.0	0.0
1.0	1.0
2.0	2.0
3.0	3.0

Figure 4.2: *Acceleration of a ball rolling down a ramp.*

Positive speed and negative acceleration moving up hill

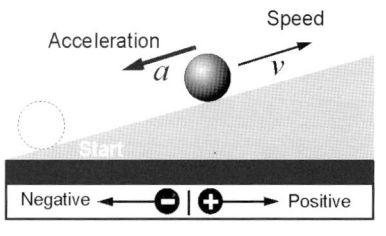

Time (sec)	Speed (m/sec)
0.0	5.0
1.0	4.0
2.0	3.0
3.0	2.0

Figure 4.3: *Acceleration of a ball rolling up a ramp.*

Calculating acceleration

You accelerate coasting downhill
Acceleration is the change in speed divided by the change in time. In this type of logic it is convenient to use the Greek letter delta (Δ), which translates to "the change in." When you see the Δ symbol, replace it in your mind with the phrase "the change in." The acceleration can then be written as $\Delta v / \Delta t$, which translates to "the change in speed (v for velocity) divided by the change in time."

Acceleration
(definition)

$$a = \frac{\Delta v}{\Delta t}$$

Acceleration (m/sec^2)   Change in speed (m/sec)

Change in time (sec)

Acceleration from experiments
The formula for acceleration can also be written in a form that is convenient for experiments. In experiments you typically measure a sequence of speeds at different times. For example, v_1 is the speed at one time, t_1, and v_2 is the speed at a later time, t_2. The change in speed is $v_2 - v_1$. The corresponding change in time is $t_2 - t_1$. The acceleration can be calculated using the formula below. This is actually the same formula as the previous one except the quantity Δv has been replaced by $v_2 - v_1$ and Δt has been replaced by $t_2 - t_1$.

Acceleration
(from experimental data)

Change in speed (m/sec)

$$a = \frac{v_2 - v_1}{t_2 - t_1}$$

Acceleration (m/sec^2)

Change in time (sec)

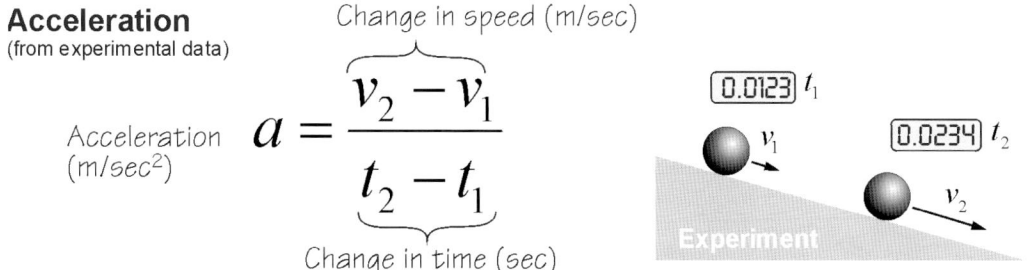

What do units of seconds squared mean?
Many physics problems will use acceleration in m/sec^2. Writing acceleration in units of meters per *second squared* is really just a mathematical shorthand. The units of square seconds do not have physical meaning in the same way that square inches mean surface area. It is better to think about acceleration in units of speed change per second. If you encounter an acceleration of 10 m/sec^2, this number means the speed is increasing by 10 m/sec every second.

Constant speed and constant acceleration

Zero acceleration
An object has zero acceleration if it is traveling at constant speed in one direction. You might think of zero acceleration as "cruise control." If the speed of your car stays the same at 60 miles per hour, your acceleration is zero. A ball rolling along a level floor with no friction also has zero acceleration and moves at constant speed. Motion with zero acceleration appears as a straight horizontal line on a speed versus time graph.

Constant acceleration
Constant acceleration is different from constant speed. An object moving with **constant acceleration** has a speed that changes by the same amount every second. Motion with constant acceleration appears as a sloped straight line on a speed versus time graph. Constant acceleration is sometimes called **uniform acceleration** in physics problems. A ball rolling down a straight ramp has constant acceleration. A dropped object in free fall also has constant acceleration.

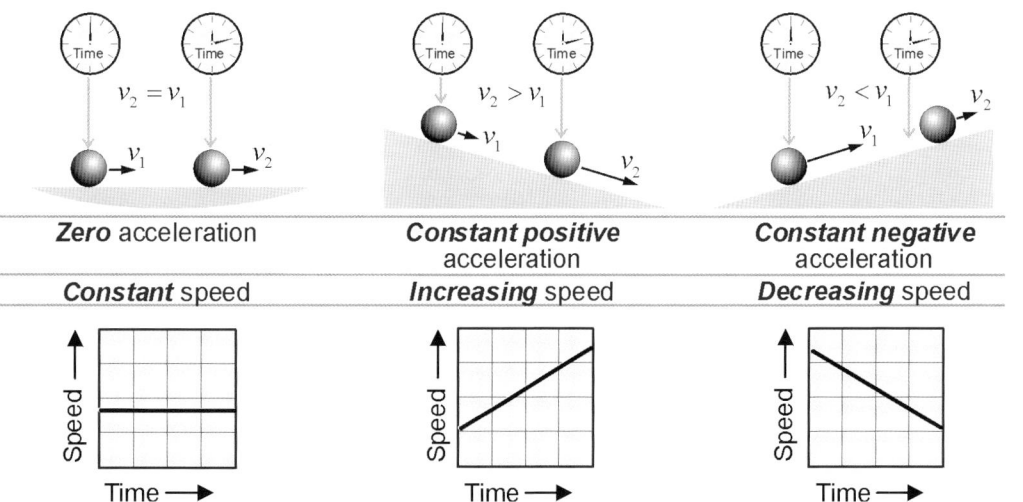

| **Zero** acceleration | **Constant positive** acceleration | **Constant negative** acceleration |
| **Constant** speed | **Increasing** speed | **Decreasing** speed |

Acceleration with zero speed
An object can have acceleration but no speed. Consider a ball rolling up a ramp. As the ball slows down, eventually its speed becomes zero and at that moment the ball is at rest. However, the ball is still accelerating down because its speed continues to change. The moment after it stops, the ball is moving down. An object can also have speed and no acceleration (constant speed).

Acceleration from changing direction

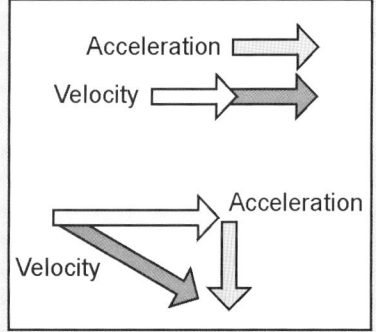

A more general definition of acceleration is the rate of change of velocity. The velocity includes information about an object's speed and direction. Acceleration can cause a change in speed or a change in direction, or both.

In Chapter 7, you will see that it is possible to have acceleration and have the speed stay constant; an object moving at constant speed in a circle is an example of this kind of motion. The speed stays the same but the direction constantly changes.

In fact, *any* change in an object's state of motion—either direction or speed—is due to acceleration. In the next chapter, you will see that any acceleration also implies the presence of forces.

The speed vs. time graph for accelerated motion

The speed versus time graph
The graph below shows an example from an experiment with a ball rolling down a ramp. The time is measured between when the ball is released and when its speed is measured somewhere along the ramp. You can see the speed of the ball increases the longer it rolls down.

Experiment

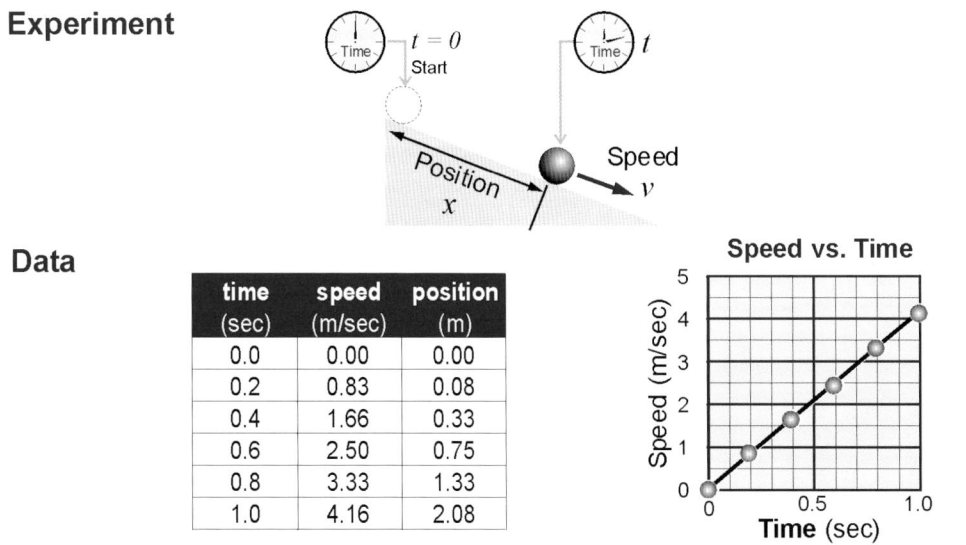

Data

time (sec)	speed (m/sec)	position (m)
0.0	0.00	0.00
0.2	0.83	0.08
0.4	1.66	0.33
0.6	2.50	0.75
0.8	3.33	1.33
1.0	4.16	2.08

The graph shows a straight line
The graph shows a straight line. This means the speed of the ball increases by the same amount every second. The graph (and data) also show that the speed of the ball increases by 0.83 m/sec every two-tenths (0.2) of a second. This graph shows *constant acceleration* because the speed changes by the same amount every second. The speed versus time graph of any motion with constant acceleration always looks like a straight line with a non-zero slope.

Acceleration
The graph in the diagram above shows an acceleration of 4.16 m/sec^2. This is calculated by dividing the total change in speed (4.16 m/sec) by the total change in time (1 second). You could do the calculation using any two points on the graph and find the same acceleration. For example, if you looked between 0.4 and 0.6 seconds, you would also calculate an acceleration of 4.16 m/sec^2.

The acceleration of cars

The advertisement for a powerful sports car claims the car can go from zero to 60 miles per hour in four seconds. This claim is all about acceleration. A speed of 60 mph is equal to 26.8 m/sec. The car's average acceleration is 6.7 m/sec^2 (26.8 m/sec ÷ 4 sec).

An average car accelerates from rest to 60 mph in 12 to 20 seconds. At 12 seconds, the acceleration is 2.23 m/sec^2. At 20 seconds, the acceleration is 1.34 m/sec^2. The practical limit for cars is 9.8 m/sec^2. Greater acceleration than this would take a force greater than the force of gravity holding the car down to the road.

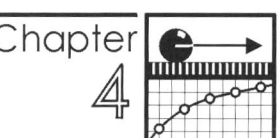

Acceleration from the speed vs. time graph

Slope From the last section, you know that the slope of a graph is equal to the ratio of *rise* to *run*. On the speed versus time graph, the rise and run have special meanings, as they did for the distance versus time graph. The *rise* is the amount the speed changes. The *run* is the amount the time changes.

Acceleration and slope Remember, acceleration is the change in speed over the change in time. This is exactly the same as the ratio of rise over run on a speed versus time graph. *This is an important result!* The slope of the speed versus time graph is the acceleration.

The slope of a graph

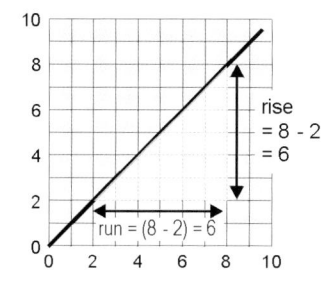

$$\text{Slope} = \frac{\text{rise}}{\text{run}} = \frac{6}{6} = 1.0$$

Acceleration from the slope of the speed vs. time graph

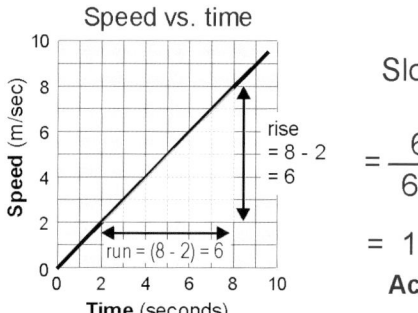

$$\text{Slope} = \frac{\text{rise}}{\text{run}}$$

$$= \frac{6\ \text{m/sec}}{6\ \text{seconds}}$$

$$= 1\ \text{m/sec}^2$$

Acceleration

Make a triangle to get the slope To determine the slope of the speed versus time graph, take the rise or change in speed and divide by the run or change in time. It is helpful to draw the triangle shown above to help figure out the rise and run. The rise is the height of the triangle. The run is the length of the base of the triangle.

Complex speed versus time graphs You can use slope to recognize when there is acceleration in complicated speed versus time graphs. The highest acceleration is at the steepest slope (B) on the graph. Level sections on the graph (A) show an acceleration of zero. Sections that slope down (C) show negative acceleration (slowing down).

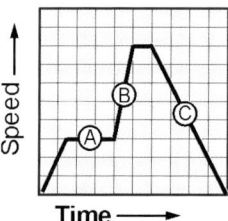

Calculate acceleration from a speed versus time graph

The following graph shows the speed of a bicyclist going over a hill. Calculate the maximum acceleration of the cyclist and say when in the trip it occurred.

Speed vs. Time

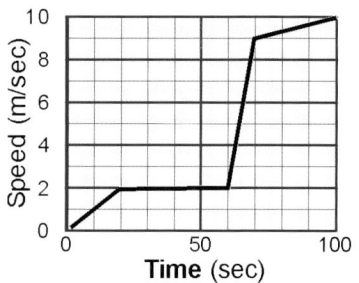

1) You are asked for the acceleration.
2) You are given a graph of speed versus time.
3) a = slope of graph
4) The steepest slope is between 60 and 70 seconds, when the speed goes from 2 to 9 m/sec.
   a = (9 m/sec - 2 m/sec)
       ÷ (10 sec)
     = 0.7 m/sec²

4.2 A Model for Accelerated Motion

The speed, distance, and time for a moving object are related by a formula: $v = d \div t$. This formula is a model that tells you the speed if you know the distance traveled and time taken. This section introduces a similar model for accelerated motion. The model includes the variables of distance, time, speed, and acceleration. Because there are more variables, the model includes two formulas. One formula relates speed, acceleration, and time. A second formula gives the distance traveled.

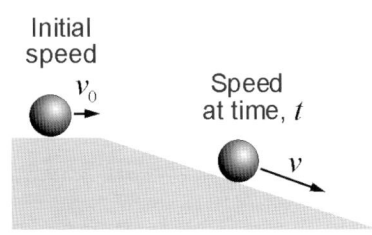

Figure 4.4: *A ball begins with an initial speed, and its speed increases as it accelerates down the ramp.*

The speed of an object that is accelerating

Begin with the acceleration formula
To get a formula for the speed of an accelerating object, we can rearrange the experimental formula we had for acceleration. Consider a ball that starts with an initial speed, v_0 (Figure 4.4). At time, $t = 0$, the ball encounters a ramp and starts to accelerate. A time t later, the speed of the ball is v. The acceleration (a) of the ball is the change in speed divided by the change in time, or $a = (v - v_0) \div t$.

Acceleration
(from experimental data)

Acceleration (m/sec^2)
$$a = \frac{v - v_0}{t}$$
Change in speed (m/sec)
Change in time (sec)

Solve for the speed
If we rearrange this formula, we can get the speed, v, of the ball at any time, t, after it starts moving.

Speed
(constant acceleration)

Initial speed (m/sec)
Acceleration (m/sec^2)
Speed (m/sec) $v = v_0 + at$ ← Time (sec)

First term
Initial speed

Second term
Increase or decrease
from acceleration

How to interpret the formula
You can think of this formula in two pieces. In physics, a piece of an equation is called a term. The first term of the formula is the speed the object starts with, or its initial speed. The second term is the amount the speed changes due to acceleration.

Calculate speed in accelerated motion

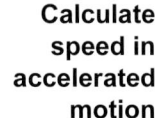

A ball rolls at 2 m/sec onto a ramp. The angle of the ramp creates an acceleration of 0.75 m/sec^2. Calculate the speed of the ball 10 seconds after it reaches the ramp.

2 m/sec

1) You are asked for the speed.
2) You are given an initial speed acceleration, and time.
3) $v = v_0 + at$
4) $v = 2$ m/sec
   $+ (.75$ m/sec$^2)(10$ sec$)$
   $= 9.5$ m/sec

64

Distance traveled in accelerated motion

An example experiment The distance traveled by an accelerating object can be found by looking at the speed versus time graph. The graph below shows a ball that started with an initial speed of 1 m/sec (Figure 4.5). The ball starts accelerating and after 1 second its speed has increased to 5.16 m/sec. How far does the ball move down the ramp?

Distance from the speed versus time graph When the speed versus time graph is made so that the *y*-axis starts at zero, the distance traveled is equal to the area under the line representing the motion. This area has two pieces. The first piece is a rectangle that represents the distance the ball would have gone had its speed stayed constant. The second piece is a triangle. The triangle represents the additional distance the ball moves because its speed is increasing.

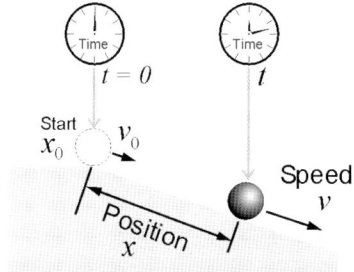

Time (sec)	Speed (m/sec)	Position (m)
0.0	1.00	0.00
0.2	1.83	0.28
0.4	2.66	0.73
0.6	3.50	1.35
0.8	4.33	2.13
1.0	5.16	3.08

Figure 4.5: *Data from an accelerated motion experiment using a ball rolling down a ramp. The ball starts down the ramp with an initial speed of 1 m/sec.*

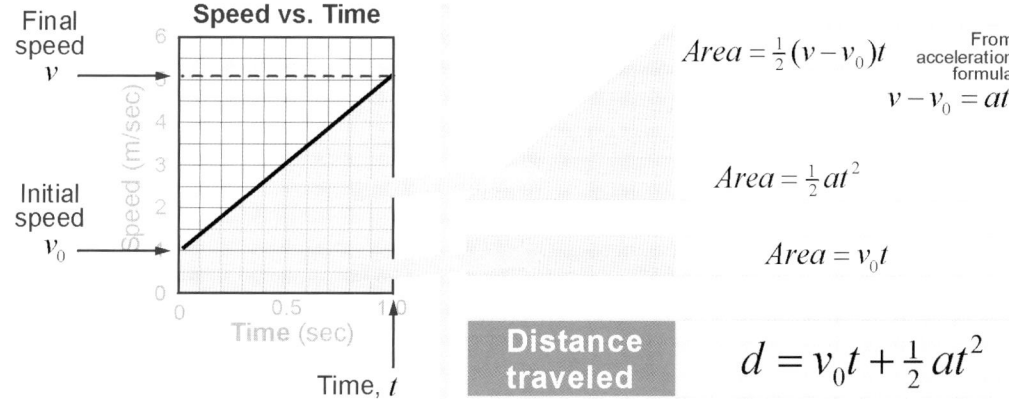

$$Area = \frac{1}{2}(v - v_0)t \quad \text{From acceleration formula}$$

$$v - v_0 = at$$

$$Area = \frac{1}{2}at^2$$

$$Area = v_0 t$$

Distance traveled $\quad d = v_0 t + \frac{1}{2}at^2$

Calculating areas on the graph The area of the gray-shaded rectangle is the initial speed × time (*area* = $v_0 t$). The area of the triangle is 1/2 the change in speed (*v* - v_0) × time. However, according to the formula for speed, the change in speed is equal to acceleration × time. Using this result, the area of the triangle is one-half the acceleration × time squared (*area* = $\frac{1}{2}at^2$). The total distance, *d*, the ball moves is the sum of the areas of the triangle and the rectangle (*d* = $v_0 t + \frac{1}{2}at^2$).

Calculating the distance traveled This formula allows us to calculate how far the ball moves. The calculation is shown in Figure 4.6. You can see that the calculated distance of 3.08 meters agrees with the position of the ball one second after being released (Figure 4.5).

Calculating the distance the ball travels

$$d = v_0 t + \frac{1}{2}at^2$$

$$= (1 \text{ m/sec})(1 \text{ sec})$$
$$+ (0.5)(4.16 \text{ m/sec}^2)(1 \text{ sec})^2$$

$$= 1 \text{ m} + 2.08 \text{ m}$$

$$= 3.08 \text{ meters}$$

Figure 4.6: *Calculating the distance.*

A model for accelerated motion

Including initial position in the model

We need to add one more detail to complete the model for motion with constant acceleration. It is possible that a moving object may not start at the origin. Let x_0 be the starting position. The distance an object moves is equal to its change in position $(x - x_0)$. We can replace the distance traveled, d, with the change in position. The final formula describes the position of an object moving with constant acceleration.

Position of a moving object
(constant acceleration)

Initial position   Distance moved at *constant* initial speed

$$x = x_0 + v_0 t + \tfrac{1}{2}at^2$$

Add or subtract distance depending on acceleration

First term   Second term   Third term

What the formula means

The formula for the position has three terms. The first term is the starting position. The second term is the distance the object would have moved if its speed had stayed constant. The third term adds or subtracts distance depending on the acceleration. If the acceleration is negative, this term will *decrease* the total distance traveled because the object moves slower for part of its motion. If the acceleration is positive, this term will *increase* the total distance traveled because the object moves faster than its initial speed for part of its motion.

The model has two formulas

We now have both formulas for a model of motion with constant acceleration. The first formula describes speed. The second formula describes position. In many physics problems both formulas will be used. When using the formulas outside of textbook physics problems, be aware that constant acceleration is usually only an approximation.

Accelerated motion formulas
(constant acceleration)

$$v = v_0 + at$$
$$x = x_0 + v_0 t + \tfrac{1}{2}at^2$$

v	Speed (m/sec)	x	Position (m)
v_o	Initial speed (m/sec)	x_o	Initial position (m)
a	Acceleration (m/sec²)	t	Time (sec)

Calculate position from speed and acceleration

A ball traveling at 2 m/sec rolls onto a ramp that tilts upward. The angle of the ramp creates an acceleration of -0.5 m/sec². How far up the ramp does the ball get at its highest point? (HINT: The ball keeps rolling upward until its speed is zero.)

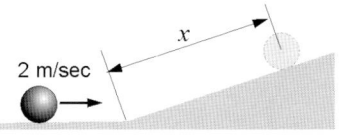

1) You are asked for distance.
2) You are given an initial speed and acceleration. You may assume an initial position of 0.
3) $v = v_0 + at$
   $x = x_0 + v_0 t + \tfrac{1}{2}at^2$
4) At the highest point the speed of the ball must be zero.
   $0 = 2$ m/sec $- 0.5t$
   $t = 4$ seconds
   Now use the time to calculate how far the ball went.
   $x = (2$ m/sec$)(4$ sec$)$
   $\quad - (0.5)(.5$ m/sec²$)(4$ sec$)^2$
   $\quad = 4$ meters
   At its highest point, the ball has moved 4 meters up the ramp.

Solving motion problems with acceleration

Many practical problems involving accelerated motion have more than one step. That means you cannot use just one formula and plug in the numbers to find the answer. You need a strategy for working a way to the answer. The following questions will help you solve multiple-step problems.

List variables 1. Make a list of all the variables that might appear and assign values to those you know. This list usually includes: x, x_0, v, v_0, a, and t.

Cancel terms that are zero 2. Are any of the variables equal to zero? If a variable is zero, any terms including that variable are also zero and may be canceled out. In many problems, the initial position, x_0, and initial speed, v_0, are zero. If no initial position is given, you may assume it is zero.

When does speed become zero? 3. If an object is moving upward, its speed becomes zero when it reaches its highest point.

Use both formulas 4. When you look at one of the formulas, could you get an answer if only you knew one more piece of information? This "extra information" is often the acceleration or the time. For these problems you can usually use the other formula to find the missing piece of information.

Calculate time from distance and acceleration

A car at rest accelerates at 6 m/sec². How long does it take to travel 440 meters (about a quarter-mile) and how fast is the car going at the end?

6.0 m/sec²

1) You are asked for time and speed.
2) You are given $v_0 = 0$, $x = 440$m, and $a = 6$ m/sec²
   assume $x_0 = 0$
3) $v = v_0 + at$
   $x = x_0 + v_0t + \frac{1}{2}at^2$
4) Since $x_0 = v_0 = 0$, the position equation reduces to:
   $x = \frac{1}{2}at^2$
   440 m $= -(0.5)(6$ m/sec²$)t^2$
   $t^2 = 440 \div 3 = 146.7$
   $t = 12.1$ seconds

Now use the time to calculate the speed.
   $v = (6$ m/sec²$)(12.1$ sec$)$
   $= 72.6$ m/sec

This is 162 miles per hour.

Calculate position from time and speed

A ball starts to roll down a ramp with zero initial speed. After one second, the speed of the ball is 2 m/sec. How long does the ramp need to be so that the ball can roll for 3 seconds before reaching the end?

1) You are asked to find position (length of the ramp).
2) You are given $v_0 = 0$, $v = 2$m/sec at $t = 1$ sec, $t = 3$ sec at the bottom of the ramp, and you may assume $x_0 = 0$.
3) After canceling terms with zeros, $v = at$ and $x = \frac{1}{2}at^2$
4) This is a two-step problem. First, you need the acceleration, then you can use the position formula to find the length of the ramp.
   $a = v \div t = (2$ m/sec$) \div (1$ sec$)$
   $= 2$ m/sec²

   $x = \frac{1}{2}at^2 = (0.5)(2$ m/sec²$)(3$ sec$)^2$
   $= 9$ meters

4.2 A Model for Accelerated Motion

67

4.3 Free Fall and the Acceleration due to Gravity

From experience, we know that objects tend to fall to the ground. Whether released from rest, tossed up into the air, or thrown down forcefully, objects tend to eventually return to the surface of the Earth. This section is about gravity. Gravity causes objects to accelerate as they fall down. In fact, a definition of *down* is "the direction objects fall."

The acceleration due to gravity

Free fall · An object is in free fall if it is moving under the influence of gravity only. For example, if you drop a ball, it is in free fall from the instant it leaves your hand until it hits the ground. A ball thrown upward is also in free fall, because once it leaves your hand its motion is determined by the influence of gravity.

Gravity accelerates objects at 9.8 m/sec² · You know from experience that free falling objects speed up, or accelerate, as they fall. When objects accelerate due to gravity, they always accelerate at the *same* rate. Gravity causes all free falling objects to accelerate at 9.8 m/sec² toward the center of the Earth (Figure 4.7). The acceleration of 9.8 m/sec² is so important, it is given its own name (acceleration due to gravity) and its own symbol (g). When you see a lowercase italic *g* in a physics equation, it usually stands for an acceleration of 9.8 m/sec².

The sign of *g* · Whether the acceleration is positive or negative depends on how you choose to set up a problem. For some problems it is convenient to assign the direction away from the Earth's surface (up) to be the positive direction. This choice makes down the negative direction. For this choice, the acceleration is -9.8 m/sec². For problems that involve only downward motion, it is often more convenient to make down the positive direction. If down is positive, the acceleration is +9.8 m/sec².

g decreases with altitude · The value of *g* depends on the distance from the center of the Earth. The acceleration of gravity is equal to 9.8 m/sec² only at the Earth's surface. At high altitude, the acceleration is smaller. The radius of the Earth is 6,380 kilometers. The acceleration due to gravity becomes appreciably less than 9.8 m/sec² when the altitude becomes significant compared to the radius of the Earth.

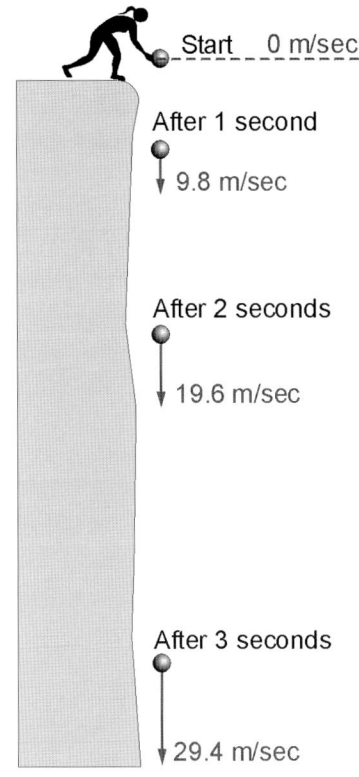

The speed of a falling object increases by 9.8 m/sec every second

Start   0 m/sec

After 1 second
↓ 9.8 m/sec

After 2 seconds
↓ 19.6 m/sec

After 3 seconds
↓ 29.4 m/sec

Figure 4.7: *The speed of a ball dropped off a cliff increases by 9.8 m/sec every second.*

Free fall with initial velocity

Motion formulas for free fall The motion of an object in free fall is described by the equations for speed and position with constant acceleration. The acceleration, a, is replaced by the acceleration due to gravity, g. The variable, x has also been replaced with y since height is usually shown on the y-axis of a graph. Care must be taken when setting up a problem to determine the correct sign of the acceleration. The formulas assume up is positive, therefore the acceleration due to gravity is $-g$. If down is positive, then the negative signs in both formulas must be changed to positive.

Free fall motion formulas

(Choosing **up** as **positive**)

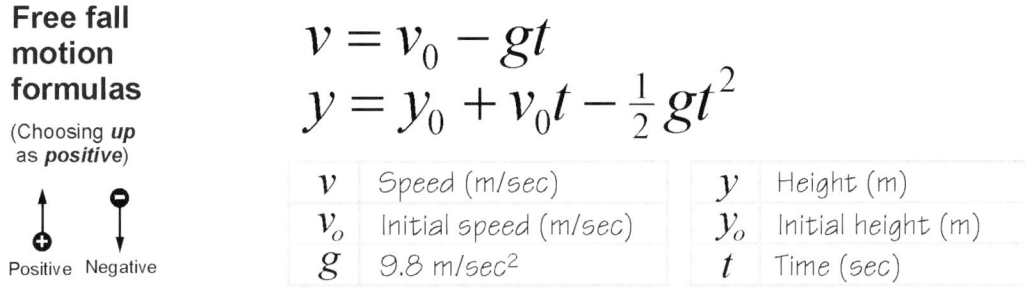

$$v = v_0 - gt$$
$$y = y_0 + v_0 t - \tfrac{1}{2} gt^2$$

v	Speed (m/sec)		y	Height (m)
v_o	Initial speed (m/sec)		y_o	Initial height (m)
g	9.8 m/sec²		t	Time (sec)

Upward and downward motion When an object's initial speed is downward, the acceleration due to gravity increases the speed until the object hits the ground. When the initial speed is upward, at first the acceleration due to gravity causes the speed to decrease. For example, a ball thrown straight up slows as it rises. At the highest point, the speed is zero. After reaching the highest point, an object in free fall starts back down and its speed increases exactly as if it were dropped from the highest point with zero initial speed.

An example of free fall with upward motion Figure 4.8 shows the motion of a ball thrown upward with an initial speed of 19.6 m/sec. The acceleration due to gravity reduces the speed of the ball by 9.8 m/sec every second. After one second, the ball is still traveling upward with a speed of 9.8 m/sec. After two seconds, the ball has a speed of zero and has reached its maximum height. After three seconds, the speed of the ball is -9.8 m/sec. The negative sign indicates the ball is moving down. After four seconds, the ball has a speed of -19.6 m/sec and has returned to the height at which it was first thrown upward. Note: air resistance has been ignored in this example (see page 71)!

The speed changes by -9.8 m/sec every second

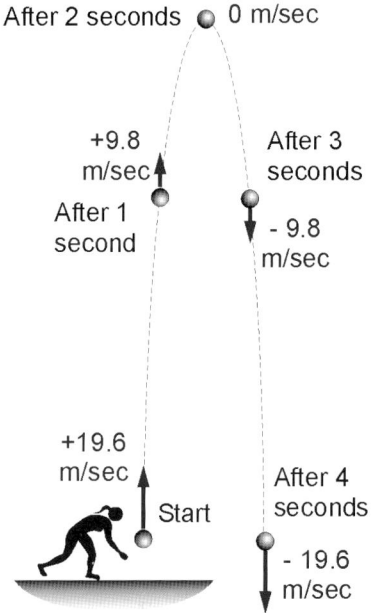

Time (sec)	Speed (m/sec)	Height (m)
0.0	19.60	0.00
1.0	9.80	14.70
2.0	0.00	19.60
3.0	-9.80	14.70
4.0	-19.60	0.00

Figure 4.8: *The motion of a ball launched upward with the speed of 19.6 m/sec.*

Solving problems with free fall

Acceleration is 9.8 m/sec² in free fall Free fall problems are like other problems with constant acceleration. The chief difference is that you know the acceleration is 9.8 m/sec² downward, even if it is not given in the problem.

Types of free fall problems Most free fall problems ask you to find either the height or the speed. Height problems often make use of the knowledge that the speed becomes zero at the highest point of an object's motion. In many situations, this knowledge allows you to calculate the time of flight and use that to find the height.

A problem with upward initial speed For example, consider a ball tossed upward with an initial speed of 5 m/sec. What is the maximum height reached by the ball? At the maximum height, the final speed is zero. We can use the formula for speed to find the time it takes the ball to reach its maximum height.

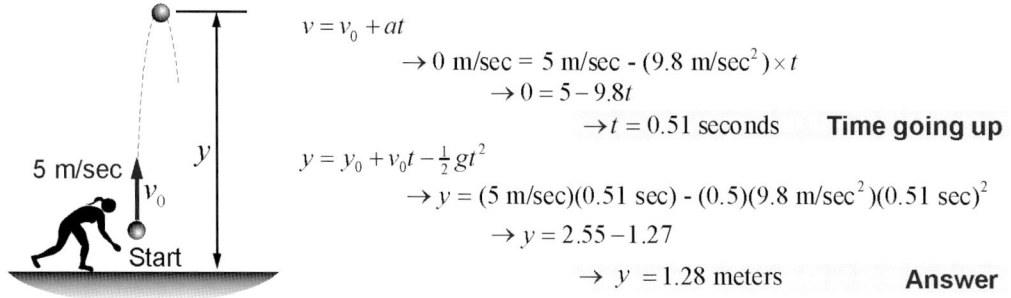

$$v = v_0 + at$$
$$\rightarrow 0 \text{ m/sec} = 5 \text{ m/sec} - (9.8 \text{ m/sec}^2) \times t$$
$$\rightarrow 0 = 5 - 9.8t$$
$$\rightarrow t = 0.51 \text{ seconds} \qquad \textbf{Time going up}$$

$$y = y_0 + v_0 t - \tfrac{1}{2}gt^2$$
$$\rightarrow y = (5 \text{ m/sec})(0.51 \text{ sec}) - (0.5)(9.8 \text{ m/sec}^2)(0.51 \text{ sec})^2$$
$$\rightarrow y = 2.55 - 1.27$$
$$\rightarrow y = 1.28 \text{ meters} \qquad \textbf{Answer}$$

Finding the height You find the height by using the position formula and the time of flight. The ball rises to a maximum height of 1.28 meters. This is not very high; to reach the height of a three-story building (12 meters), a ball would have to be thrown upward with a speed of 15 m/sec (34 miles per hour).

Finding the time If a problem asks for the time of flight, remember that an object takes the same time going up as it takes coming down. For example, for the ball that was tossed upward, it took 0.51 seconds to reach its highest point. It takes another 0.51 seconds for the ball to get back down to the height at which it started, so the total time of flight is 1.02 seconds.

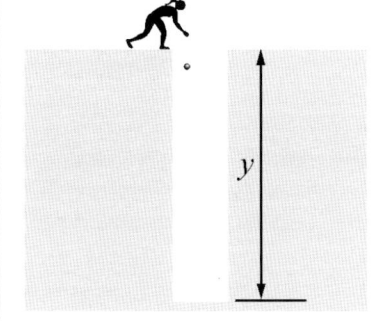
70

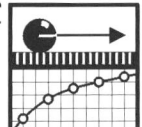
Air resistance and mass

The acceleration of gravity does not depend on mass

The acceleration due to gravity does not depend on the mass of the object which is falling. This seems like a statement that cannot possibly be true. A feather and a brick do not fall at the same rate when they are dropped. However, the reason they do not fall at the same rate is because gravity is not the only influence on the motion. Objects that are dropped in air are not truly in free fall. Air creates friction that resists the motion of objects moving through it. Air friction can be substantial; if you put your hand out the window of a moving car, you feel a significant force pushing back against your hand. The feather falls slower because the resistance of the air is proportionately greater on the feather than on the brick. If one were to repeat the experiment in a chamber from which the air had been pumped out, the brick and feather fall at exactly the same rate. (See sidebar.)

When air friction can be ignored

All of the formulas and examples discussed in this section are exact only in a vacuum (no air). Fortunately, for small, dense objects at low speeds, friction from air resistance is so small it may be neglected. You may safely assume that $a = g = 9.8$ m/sec^2 for speeds of up to several meters per second.

Air resistance and surface area

Air resistance may not be ignored for objects that have a large surface area and a low weight. A flat piece of paper is a good example of this sort of object. The more surface area an object has, the more air it has to push through when moving. The more air it has to push, the more the air will reduce the acceleration. Crumpling a piece of paper into a small ball greatly reduces its surface area. The air friction on a crumpled ball of paper is so small that the ball falls at the same rate as a brick.

Terminal speed

The faster something falls, the more air it must plow through each second. As a result, the resistance from air friction increases as a falling object's speed increases. Eventually, the rate of acceleration is reduced to zero and the object falls with constant speed. Unless the object changes shape, it can never travel any faster than this. The maximum speed at which an object falls when limited by air friction is called the **terminal speed**. The terminal speed depends on the shape, size, and weight of the object. Thin, streamlined objects such as an arrow have a higher terminal speed than light, wide objects such as a sheet of paper.

Parachutes and air resistance

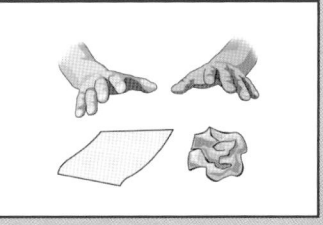

Take two identical sheets of paper. Crumple one of the pieces into a tight ball. Drop both at the same time from the same height. Which hits the ground first? Try to explain your observations using the concept of air resistance.

Parachutes use air resistance in order to reduce the terminal speed of a skydiver. Alone, the skydiver has a small amount of surface area and a terminal speed over 100 mph. The parachute increases the surface area dramatically, creating much greater air resistance. The skydiver reaches a slower terminal speed—one that allows for a safe landing.

Application: Antilock Brakes

Brakes are often considered the most important devices on a vehicle. Antilock braking systems (or ABS) are standard on most new cars and trucks today. With the help of constant computer monitoring, these systems give the driver more control when stopping quickly. ABS prevents a car from skidding by ensuring that the wheels of the vehicle do not lock up during heavy braking. If the wheels keep turning the driver is better able to steer and keep the vehicle under control.

Friction and traction

Traction Friction between the tires and the road, called *traction*, is what allows a car to grab the road for steering, acceleration, and braking (Figure 4.9). Without traction, a moving vehicle tends to continue moving in the direction it is going because of its inertia. Anything that gets between the tires and the road results in a loss of traction and can cause dangerous slips and slides. Ice, sand, and water are common hazards that can lead to loss of traction.

Braking Friction is also used inside the braking system to slow or stop a vehicle. When you step on the brake pedal, a force is transferred to brake pads that squeeze against a disk attached to the wheel (Figure 4.10). The rubbing brake pads create friction that resists the motion of the car, and the car decelerates.

Locking the brakes If brakes are applied too hard or too fast, a rolling wheel *locks up*, which means it stops turning and the car skids. This usually results in the tires screeching against the road and the car eventually skidding to a stop. Wheel lockup happens because the car has much more inertia than its wheel. Once a wheel is skidding instead of rolling, it is no longer possible to steer.

Before ABS, drivers were taught to "pump" the brakes repeatedly in emergency braking situations. Pumping the brakes means to repeatedly brake hard and then take your foot off the brakes to let the wheels roll briefly for steering. This technique is difficult and requires practice to be used effectively. It takes a skilled driver to sense the changing balance between friction from the brakes and traction with the road, allowing for maximum braking and steering at the same time.

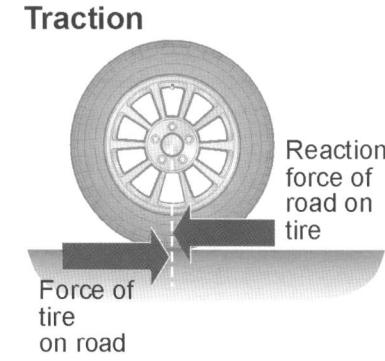

Traction

Figure 4.9: *Traction comes from an action-reaction pair of forces acting between the tire and the road.*

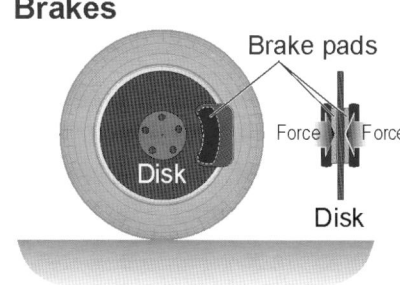

Brakes

Figure 4.10: *When brakes are applied, the brake pads push against the disk, creating friction that slows the rotation of the wheel.*

Antilock braking systems

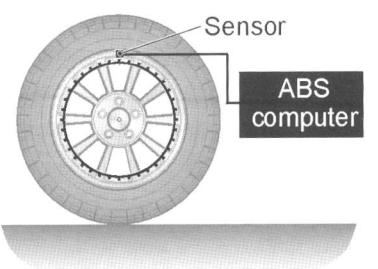

Using what is there	Antilock brakes (ABS) essentially pump the brakes automatically, much faster than any human could. An ABS system prevents wheel lockup under a wide range of traction conditions including water, ice, snow and sand. ABS uses the same basic braking system but adds a control computer that constantly monitors the vehicle's wheel speed (the rate at which the vehicle's wheels are spinning). The computer is able to rapidly cycle the brakes on and off.

Figure 4.11: *The wheel-speed sensor sends information about each wheel's rotation to the ABS computer.*

Wheel-speed sensors	With four-wheel ABS, the computer monitors input from four *wheel-speed sensors*, one on each wheel (Figure 4.11). As the wheel spins, each sensor constantly monitors the speed of the wheel and reports the information to the control computer. The computer compares the rate at which the speed of each wheel is changing (acceleration) with the maximum rate at which a wheel can decelerate without losing traction. The computer bases its decision on average traction measurements taken from different tires in many driving conditions.

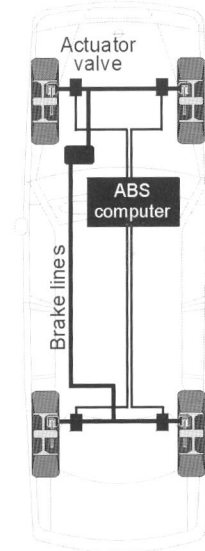

What the control computer does	When the control computer decides the deceleration in a wheel is too rapid, the computer opens a small valve called an actuator valve (Figure 4.12). The actuator valve releases pressure in the brake line which lets up on the brakes. This happens very quickly, before a wheel has come to a complete stop and starts to skid. Once the brakes have been released, traction with the road quickly spins the wheel back up to normal speed. When the wheel reaches normal speed, the ABS computer starts the cycle over by closing the actuator valve and allowing braking to resume.

How to know when ABS is working	The automatic pumping of the brakes continues until the computer no longer senses a skid is about to occur. Some systems can apply and release the brakes up to 15 times a second. When the ABS computer is actively pumping the brakes, the driver hears a "gr-r-r-r" sound that comes from the rapid on-off cycling of the braking system. It may sound bad but this is a normal noise and the sign of a correctly functioning ABS. Some cars employ a similar system to prevent wheels from spinning while accelerating or turning corners. This system is often called "traction control." Traction control can be very useful on roads covered with snow.

Figure 4.12: *The ABS computer can open and close the actuator valves on brakes for all four wheels.*

Chapter 4 Review

Vocabulary review

Match the following terms with the correct definition. There is one extra definition in the list that will not match any of the terms.

Set One

1. acceleration

2. uniform acceleration

3. slope

4. m/sec^2

a. Total distance divided by time
b. Change in speed over time
c. Unit for measuring acceleration
d. Occurs when an object's speed changes by the same amount each second
e. Change in y-values divided by the change in x-values on a graph

Set Two

1. distance

2. initial speed

3. change of velocity

4. zero acceleration

5. free fall

a. Slope of the graph of acceleration vs. time
b. Area under the graph of speed vs. time
c. Area under the graph of acceleration vs. time
d. Horizontal line on a speed vs. time graph
e. Starting speed of an object
f. The movement of objects that are affected by gravity only

Concept review

1. Distinguish between average speed and instantaneous speed.

2. How can the instantaneous speed of an object be determined from a graph of position vs. time?

3. Name the three things that must be known about an object to calculate its acceleration and then arrange them in an equation for calculating acceleration.

4. A bicycle racer may experience positive, negative, or zero acceleration at various times during a race.

   a. Identify when each of these accelerations would occur.

   b. Explain what happens to the biker's speed when she is moving in a straight line with positive, negative, and then zero acceleration.

5. A toy car starts from rest at the top of a hill and rolls down the hill with a constant acceleration.

   a. Sketch the shape of the speed vs. time graph that describes its motion.

   b. Explain how you could use the graph to determine the car's acceleration.

6. A graph is made of the speed vs. time of a plane as it flies from San Francisco to the Kahului Airport on Maui. How could the distance traveled by the plane be determined from the graph?

7. Sketch the shape of the speed vs. time graph for:

   a. a car coming to a stop at a red light.

   b. a cue ball on a pool table rolled at constant speed from one end to the other.

8. A coin is tossed into the air. Compare the direction of its velocity to the direction of its acceleration while it is moving upward, at its peak, and moving downward.

9. What is the meaning of a negative sign when discussing motion compared to the Earth?

10. A mouse races a rhinoceros from the roof of a tall building to the ground. Both jump from the roof at the same time. Who hits the ground first? Explain your answer. (Assume that air resistance has no effect on either one.)

11. Referring to the rhinoceros and the mouse from question #10, on which animal is the force applied by the air greater?

12. While watching a skydiver from the ground, you see that when opening a parachute he slows down but continues to fall toward the ground. Later you are watching a movie about skydivers. The jumpers appear to move upward after opening their parachutes. Explain the difference between your observations in the two cases.

Problems

1. A pilot flies his plane north 600 kilometers in 2 hours and then turns west and flies 800 kilometers in 5 hours.

   a. Calculate the average speed of the plane during the first 2 hours of the trip.

   b. Calculate the average speed of the plane during the last 5 hours of the trip.

   c. Calculate the average speed of the plane for the entire trip.

2. Base your answers to the following questions on the graph below which represents the motion of two cars (A and B) on a straight road. Car A is initially at rest some distance down the road. Car A starts moving at the same instant that car B passes. The time is measured from the moment car A starts moving, when both cars are at the same position along the road.

   a. What is the instantaneous speed of each car at $t = 50$ sec?

   b. Compare the distance traveled by car A and car B from $t = 0$ to $t = 60$ sec.

   c. Over what time interval are the speeds of car A and car B constant?

   d. Calculate the acceleration of car A and car B from $t = 0$ to $t = 60$ sec.

   e. During the time intervals given below, which car traveled the greatest distance?

      1. car A from $t = 0$ to $t = 30$ sec

      2. car A from $t = 30$ to $t = 60$ sec

      3. car B from $t = 0$ to $t = 30$ sec

      4. car B from $t = 30$ to $t = 60$ sec

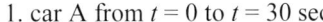

3. Seth starts from rest at the end of his driveway and accelerates down the road on his skateboard at 0.40 m/s^2 for 12 seconds. What is his speed at the end of the 12 seconds?

4. Blair fires a paintball from his gun. The paintball travels the 30-centimeter length of the barrel in 0.066 seconds. Assuming the paintball accelerates uniformly, use this information to answer the following questions:

   a. What is the average speed of the paintball?

   b. What is the instantaneous speed of the paintball when it leaves the barrel?

   c. What is the acceleration of the paintball in the barrel?

5. The escape speed is the minimum speed an object needs to completely break free from the gravity of a planet. The escape speed for the Earth is approximately 2.88×10^4 km/hr or 8,000 m/sec. If an object starts from rest and accelerates at 20 m/sec^2, how many seconds will it take to reach escape speed? What distance will it travel during this time?

6. A skydiver jumps from an airplane. Data is collected to determine her speed as she descends. The graph shown is prepared from this data. Using this graph, answer the questions that follow:

   a. What is the acceleration of the skydiver from $t = 0$ to $t = 6$ sec?

   b. How far does the skydiver fall between the fourth and eighth second?

   c. What is the acceleration of the skydiver from $t = 9$ to $t = 15$ sec?

75

7. Tom rides his bicycle from home to his friend Tony's house in 25 minutes. He spends 35 minutes there and returns home in 30 minutes. Use the graph to find the distance from Tom's house to Tony's house.

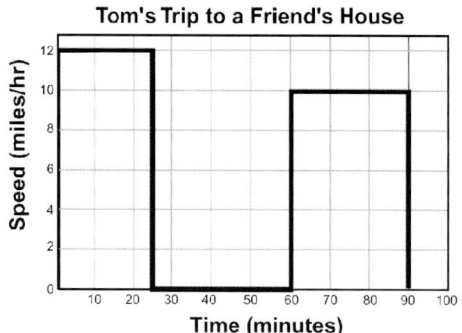

8. The graph to the right represents the motion of Amy's radio controlled go-cart as she operates the cart in her driveway. The cart begins at the garage door and moves in a straight line. Briefly describe the motion of the cart for each interval on the graph (A-B, B-C, C-D, D-E, E-F, F-G, and G-H).

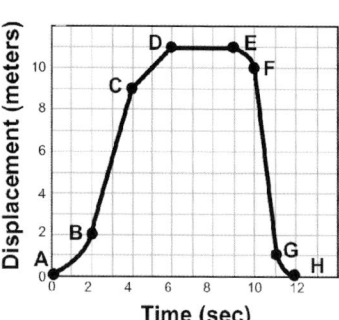

9. A ball is dropped out of a window. Which graph of speed vs. time shown below best represents the motion of the ball as it moves toward the ground?

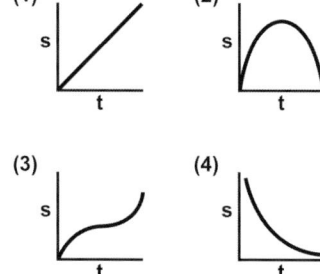

10. The graph below represents the relationship between speed and time for a cart that travels in a straight line.

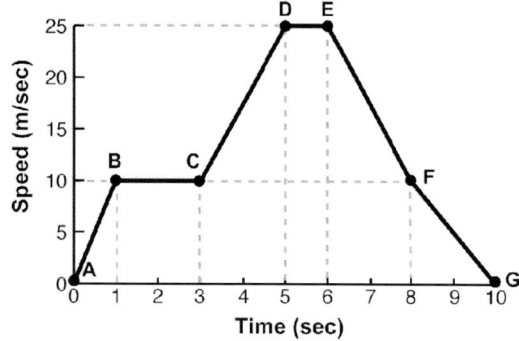

a. What is the total distance traveled by the cart during the first three seconds?

b. During which intervals does the cart have a positive acceleration?

c. What is the acceleration of the cart during interval C-D?

11. A ball is thrown straight up in the air at a speed of 114 m/s. What is the speed and direction of the ball after 8 seconds?

12. A ball is thrown straight up at a speed of 58.8 m/s. Calculate its position after 7.2 seconds.

76

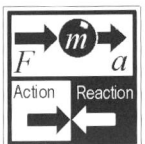

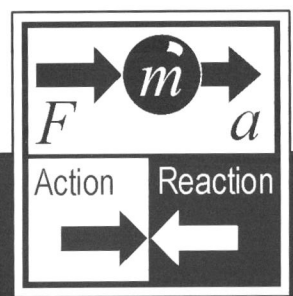

Unit 2

Motion and Force in One Dimension

Chapter 5

Newton's Laws: Force and Motion

Objectives for Chapter 5

By the end of this chapter you should be able to:

1. Describe how the law of inertia affects the motion of an object.
2. Give an example of a system or invention designed to overcome inertia.
3. Measure and describe force in newtons (N) and pounds (lbs).
4. Calculate the net force for two or more forces acting along the same line.
5. Calculate the acceleration of an object from the net force acting on it.
6. Determine whether an object is in equilibrium by analyzing the forces acting on it.
7. Draw a diagram showing an action-reaction pair of forces.
8. Determine the reaction force when given an action force.

Terms and vocabulary words

force	inertia	law of inertia	Newton's first law	net force
dynamic	equilibrium	static	Newton's second law	locomotion
newton (N)	action	reaction	Newton's third law	

5.1 The First Law: Force and Inertia

Sir Isaac Newton (1642-1727), an English physicist and mathematician, was one of the most brilliant scientists ever. Before the age of 30, he had made several important discoveries in physics and had invented a whole new kind of mathematics, calculus. The three laws of motion discovered by Newton are probably the most widely-used natural laws in all of science. Newton's laws are the model which connects the forces acting on an object, its mass, and its resulting motion. This chapter is about Newton's laws and the first section is about the first law, the law of inertia.

Force

Changing an object's motion

Suppose you want to move a box from one side of the room to the other. What would you do? Would you yell at it until it moved? "Hey, box, get going! Move to the other side of the room!" Of course not! You would *push* it across the room (or maybe pull it). In physics terms, you would apply a *force* to the box.

Force is an action that can change motion

A force is what we call a *push or a pull*, or *any action that has the ability to change an object's motion*. Forces can be used to increase the speed of an object, decrease the speed of an object, or change the direction in which an object is moving. For something to be considered a force, it does not necessarily have to change the motion, but it must have the ability to do so. For example, if you push down on a table, it probably will not move. But if the legs were to break, the table *could* move. Therefore, your push qualifies as a force.

Creating force

Forces can be created by many different processes. For example, gravity creates force. Muscles can create force. The movement of air or other matter can create force. Electricity and magnetism can create force. Even light can create force. No matter how force is created, its effect on motion is described by Newton's three laws.

Changes in motion only occur through force

Forces create changes in motion, and *there can be no change in motion without also having a force* (Figure 5.1). Anytime there is a change in motion a force must exist, even if you cannot immediately recognize the force. For example, when a rolling ball stops by hitting a wall, its motion changes rapidly. That change in motion is caused by the wall exerting a force that stops the ball.

This will not work

Only **force** has the ability to change motion

Figure 5.1: *Force is the action which has the ability to change motion. Without force, the motion of an object cannot be started or changed.*

Inertia

Objects tend to keep doing what they are doing

Consider that box you wish to move across the room. The box will not move unless you apply a force to it. What if the box had been moving and you wanted to stop it? Again, yelling a command will not make it stop. The only way to stop the box is to apply enough force in a direction opposite to its motion. In general, objects tend to continue doing what they are already doing. If they are moving, they tend to keep moving, in the same direction, at the same speed. If they are at rest, they tend to stay at rest. This idea is known as Newton's first law of motion.

Newton's first law

Newton's first law states that all objects want to keep doing what they are doing—in other words, they tend to resist changes in motion. But some objects are better at resisting changes than others. Inertia is a term used to measure the ability of an object to resist a change in its state of motion. An object with a lot of inertia takes a lot of force to start or stop; an object with a small amount of inertia requires a small amount of force to start or stop. Because inertia is a key idea in Newton's first law, the first law is sometimes referred to as the law of inertia.

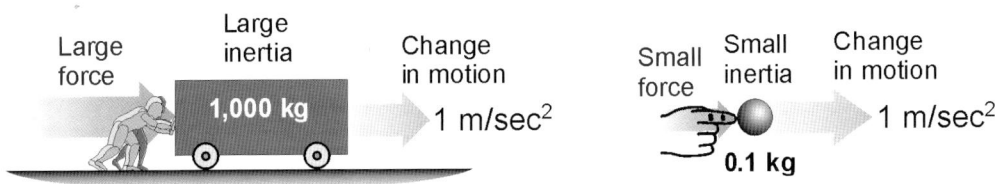

Large force · Large inertia · **1,000 kg** · Change in motion · 1 m/sec²

Small force · Small inertia · **0.1 kg** · Change in motion · 1 m/sec²

Inertia is a property of mass

The amount of inertia an object has depends on its mass. More massive objects have more inertia than less massive objects. Recall that mass is a measure of the amount of matter in an object. Big trucks are made of more matter than small cars; thus, they have greater mass and a greater amount of inertia. It takes more force to stop a moving truck because it has more inertia than a small car. This is a common-sense application of the first law.

Origin of the word "inertia"

The word "inertia" comes from the Latin word *inertus*, which can be translated to mean "lazy." It can be helpful to think of things that have a lot of inertia as being very lazy when it comes to change. In other words, they want to maintain the status quo and keep doing whatever they are currently doing.

Which systems in a car overcome the law of inertia?

The engine supplies force that allows you to change motion (accelerate) by pressing the gas pedal.

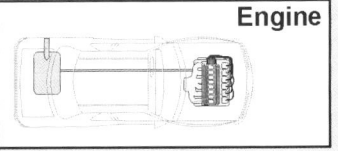

Engine

The brake system is designed to help you change your motion by slowing down.

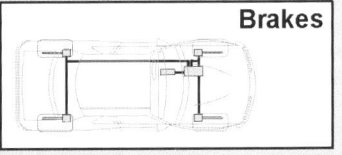

Brakes

The steering wheel and steering system is designed to help you change your motion by changing your direction

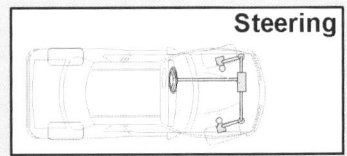

Steering

Can you think of three parts of a bicycle that are designed to overcome the law of inertia?

5.1 The First Law: Force and Inertia

Applications of Newton's first law

Seat belts and air bags | Two very important safety features of automobiles are designed with Newton's first law in mind: seat belts and air bags. Suppose you are driving down the highway in your car at 55 miles per hour when the driver in front of you slams on the brakes. You also slam on your brakes to avoid an accident. Your car slows down but the inertia of your body resists the change in motion (slowing down). Your body tries to continue doing what it was doing—traveling at 55 miles per hour. Luckily, your seat belt (and air bag, in an extreme case) is designed to counteract your inertia and slow your body down with the car (Figure 5.2).

Cup holders | A cup holder does almost the same thing for a cup. Consider what happens if you have a can of soda on the dashboard. What happens to the soda can when you turn sharply to the left? Remember, the soda can was not at rest to begin with. It was moving at the same speed as the car. When your car goes left, the soda can's inertia causes it to keep moving forward (Figure 5.3). The result is quite a mess. Automobile cup holders are designed to keep the first law from making messes.

The tablecloth trick | Have you ever wondered how a magician is able to pull a tablecloth out from underneath dishes set on a table? It's not a trick of magic at all, but just physics. The dishes have inertia and therefore tend to resist changes in motion. Before the magician pulls on the cloth, the dishes are at rest. So when the tablecloth is whisked away, the inertia of the dishes keeps them at rest. This trick works best when the tablecloth is pulled very rapidly and the table is small. It would be quite difficult to perform this trick with the long table in the diagram below. Can you think why the long table would make the trick hard to do?

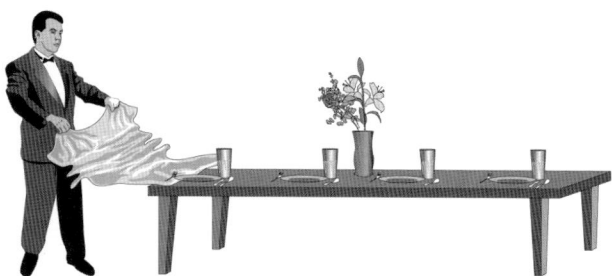

Traveling at constant speed

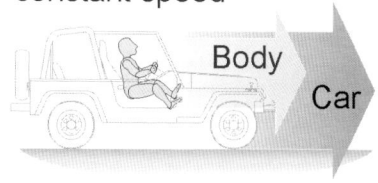

Sudden stop

Figure 5.2: *Because of its inertia, your body tends to keep moving when your car stops suddenly. This can cause serious injury if you are not wearing a seat belt.*

Figure 5.3: *Because of its inertia, a soda can on the dashboard will tend to keep moving forward when the car turns left.*

5.2 The Second Law: Force, Mass, and Acceleration

Newton's discovery of the connection between force, mass, and acceleration was a milestone in our understanding of science. The second law is the most widely used equation in physics because it is so practical. This section shows you how to apply Newton's second law to practical situations.

Newton's second law of motion

Force is related to acceleration
The acceleration of an object is equal to the force you apply divided by the mass of the object. This is Newton's second law, and it states precisely what you already know intuitively. If you apply more force to an object, it accelerates at a higher rate. If an object has more mass it accelerates at a lower rate because mass has inertia. The rate of acceleration is the ratio of force divided by mass.

Newton's second law

$$a = \frac{F}{m}$$

Acceleration
(m/sec²)

Force (N)

Mass (kg)

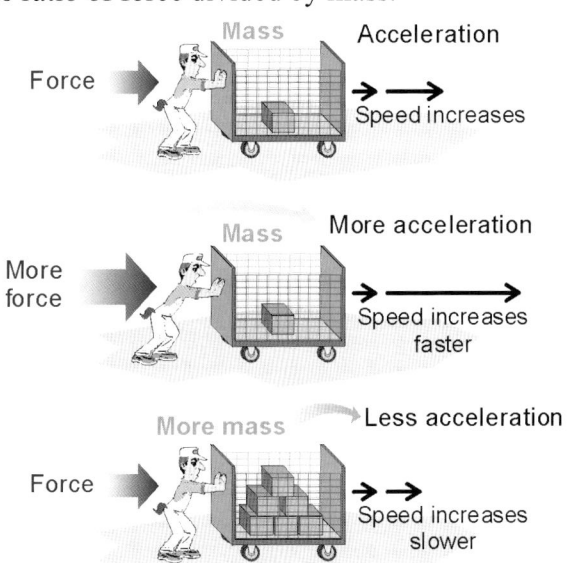

Force — Mass — Acceleration
Speed increases

More force — Mass — More acceleration
Speed increases faster

Force — More mass — Less acceleration
Speed increases slower

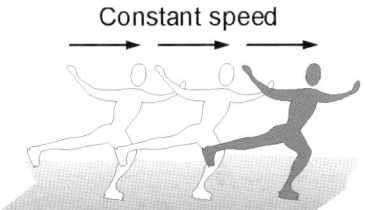

Constant speed

Coasting at constant speed requires no force.
(if there is no friction)

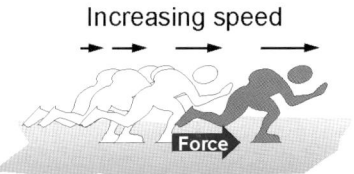

Increasing speed

Force

Speeding up or slowing down DOES require force.

Figure 5.4: *An ice-skater can coast for quite a long time because motion at constant speed does not require force. If there were no friction, a skater could coast at constant speed forever. Force is required only to speed up, turn, or stop.*

Motion at constant speed
Force is not necessary to keep an object in motion at constant speed. An ice-skater will coast for a long time without any outside force (Figure 5.4). However, the ice-skater does need force to speed up, slow down, turn, or stop. Recall that changes in speed or direction always involve acceleration. Force *causes* acceleration, and mass *resists* acceleration.

The definition of force

Pounds: In the English system, the unit of force (pound) was originally defined by gravity. One pound is the force of gravity pulling on a mass of 0.454 kilograms. When you measure your weight in pounds on a bathroom scale, you are measuring the force of gravity acting on your mass.

One pound (lb) is the force exerted by gravity on a mass of 0.454 kg.

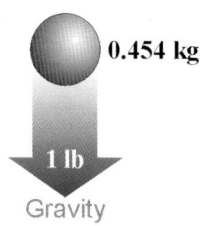

One newton (N) is the force it takes to accelerate 1 kg at 1 m/sec² .

Newtons: The metric definition of force depends on the acceleration per unit of mass. A force of one newton is exactly the amount of force needed to cause a mass of one kilogram to accelerate at one m/sec². We call the unit of force the **newton** because force in the metric system is defined by Newton's second law. The newton is a useful way to measure force because it connects force directly to its effect on matter and motion. A net force of one newton will always accelerate a 1-kilogram mass at 1 m/sec² no matter where you are in the universe.

Converting newtons and pounds: The newton is a smaller unit of force than the pound. A force of one pound is equal to 4.448 newtons. This means a pound of force can accelerate a 1-kilogram mass at 4.448 m/sec². Pounds are fine for everyday use here on Earth but inconvenient for physics because of the conversion factor of 4.448.

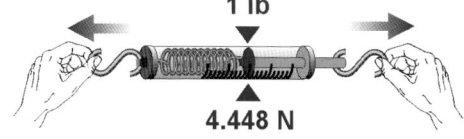

1 pound = 4.448 newtons

What is force?

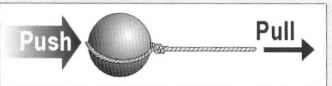

The simplest concept of force is a push or a pull.

On a deeper level, force is the *action* that has the ability to create or change motion. Pushes or pulls do not always change motion. But they *could*.

The unit of force is derived from fundamental quantities of length, mass, and time. Using the second law, the units of force work out to be kg-m/sec². A force of 1 N causes a 1 kg mass to accelerate at 1 m/sec². We could always write forces in terms of kg-m/sec². This would remind us what force is. But, writing kg-m/sec² everywhere would be a nuisance. Instead we use newtons. One newton (1 N) is one kg-m/sec².

Using the second law of motion

Net force The force (*F*) that appears in the second law is called the net force. When used this way, the word "net" means *total*. There are often many forces acting on the same object. Acceleration results from the combined action of all the forces that act on an object. To solve problems with multiple forces, you have to add up all the forces to get a single net force before you can calculate the acceleration.

Multiple forces 10 N + 30 N = 20 N **Net force**

Three forms of the second law The second law can be rearranged three ways. Choose the form that is most convenient for calculating what you want to know. The three ways to write the law are summarized below.

Three forms of the second law

Use . . .	if you want to find . . .	and you know . . .
$a = \dfrac{F}{m}$	The acceleration (*a*)	The net force (*F*) and the mass (*m*)
$F = ma$	The net force (*F*)	The acceleration (*a*) and the mass (*m*)
$m = \dfrac{F}{a}$	The mass (*m*)	The acceleration (*a*) and the net force (*F*)

Units for the second law To use Newton's second law in physics calculations, you must be sure to have units of m/sec^2 for acceleration, newtons for force, and kilograms for mass. Many problems will require you to convert forces from pounds to newtons. Other problems may require you to convert weight in pounds to mass in kilograms. Remember also that *m* stands for *mass* in the formula for the second law. Do not confuse the variable *m* in the second law with the abbreviation "m" that stands for *meters*.

Calculate the acceleration of a cart on a ramp

 m = 0.5 kg

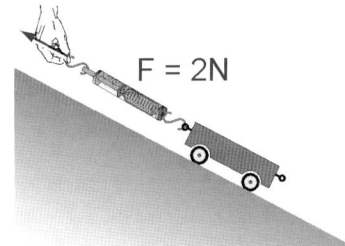

F = 2N

A cart rolls down a ramp. Using a spring scale, you measure a net force of 2 newtons pulling the car down. The cart has a mass of 500 grams (0.5 kg). Calculate the acceleration of the cart.

1) You are asked for acceleration (a).
2) You are given mass (m) and force (F).
3) Newton's second law applies.
   a = F/m
4) Plug in numbers. Remember that 1 N = 1 kg·m/sec^2.
   a = (2 N) / (0.5 kg)
   = (2 kg·m/sec^2) / (0.5 kg)
   = 4 m/sec^2

Finding the acceleration of moving objects

Dynamics The word dynamic refers to problems involving motion. In dynamics problems, the second law is often used to calculate the acceleration of an object when you know the force and mass. For example, the second law is used to calculate the acceleration of a rocket from the force of the engines and the mass of the rocket.

Direction of acceleration The acceleration is in the same direction as the net force. Common sense tells you this is true, and so does Newton's second law. Speed *increases* when the net force is in the same direction as the motion. Speed *decreases* when the net force is in the opposite direction as the motion.

Positive and negative We often use positive and negative numbers to show the direction of force and acceleration. A common choice is to make speed, force, and acceleration positive when they point to the right. Speed, force, and acceleration are negative when they point to the left. You can choose which direction is to be positive, but once you choose, be consistent in assigning values to forces and accelerations.

Speed **decreases** when the net force is opposite to the direction of motion

Speed **increases** when the net force is in the same direction as the motion

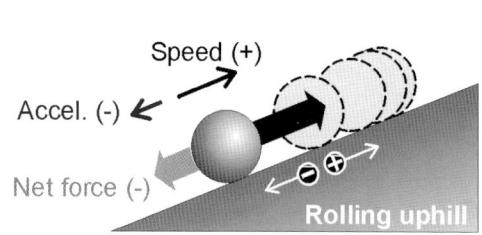

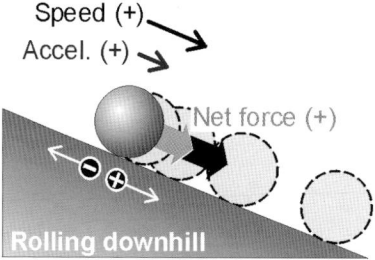

The sign of acceleration When solving problems, the acceleration always has the same sign as the net force. If the net force is negative, the acceleration is also negative. When both speed and acceleration have the same sign, the speed increases with time. When speed and acceleration have opposite signs, speed decreases with time. Careful use of positive and negative values helps keep track of the direction of forces and accelerations.

Acceleration from multiple forces

Three people are pulling on a wagon applying forces of 100 N, 150 N, and 200 N. Determine the acceleration and the direction the wagon moves. The wagon has a mass of 25 kilograms.

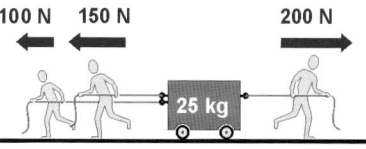

1) You are asked for the acceleration (a) and direction.

2) You are given the forces (F) and mass (m).

3) The second law relates acceleration to force and mass (a = F÷m).

4) First, assign positive and negative directions. Next, calculate net force. Finally, use the second law to determine the acceleration from the net force and the mass.

5) F = -100N - 150 N + 200N
   = -50N

   a = (-50 N)÷(25 kg)
   = -2 m/sec^2.

   The wagon accelerates 2 m/sec^2 to the left.

Finding force from acceleration

Amount of force needed   Newton's second law allows us to determine how much force is needed to cause a given acceleration. Engineers apply the second law to match the force developed by different engines to the acceleration required for different vehicles. For example, an airplane taking off from a runway needs to reach a certain minimum speed to be able to fly. If you know the mass of the plane, Newton's second law can be used to calculate how much force the engine must supply to accelerate the plane to take-off speed.

Forces that must have been   The second law also allows us to determine how much force *must have been* present to cause an observed acceleration. Wherever there is acceleration there must also be force. Any change in the motion of an object results from acceleration. Therefore, any change in motion must be caused by force. When a tennis ball hits a racquet, it experiences high acceleration because its speed goes rapidly to zero then reverses direction. The high acceleration is evidence of tremendous forces between the racquet and the ball, causing the ball to flatten and the racquet strings to stretch. Newton's second law can be used to determine the forces acting on the ball from observations of its acceleration.

Force to accelerate a plane taking off

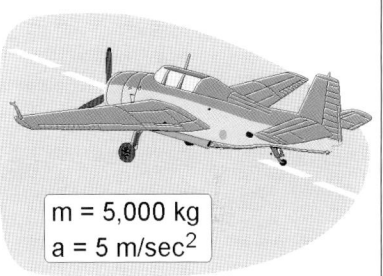

m = 5,000 kg
a = 5 m/sec²

An airplane needs to accelerate at 5 m/sec² to reach take-off speed before reaching the end of the runway. The mass of the airplane is 5,000 kilograms. How much force is needed from the engine?

1) You asked for the force (F).

2) You are given the mass (m) and acceleration (a).

3) The second law applies.
   F = ma

4) Plug in numbers.
   Remember that
   1 N = 1 kg·m/sec².
   F = (5,000 kg) × (5 m/sec²)
   = 25,000 N

Force on a tennis ball striking a racquet

A tennis ball contacts the racquet for much less than one second. High-speed photographs show that the speed of the ball changes from -30 to +30 m/sec in 0.006 seconds. If the mass of the ball is 0.2 kg, how much force is applied by the racquet?

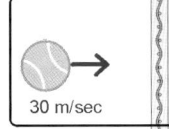 30 m/sec

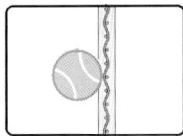

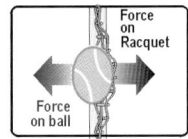 Force on Racquet / Force on ball

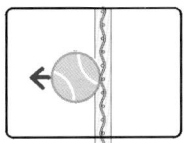

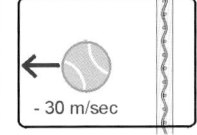 - 30 m/sec

1)   You are asked for force (F).

2)   You are given the mass (m), the change in speed ($V_2 - V_1$), and the time interval (t).

3)   Newton's second law (F = ma) relates force to acceleration. Acceleration is the change in speed divided by the time interval over which the speed changed ($a = (V_2 - V_1)/t$).

4)   Use the change in speed to calculate the acceleration. Use the acceleration and mass to calculate the force.

5) $a = (60 \text{ m/sec}) \div (0.006 \text{ sec}) = 10,000 \text{ m/sec}^2$
        $F = (0.2 \text{ kg}) \times (10,000 \text{ m/sec}^2) = 2,000 \text{ N}$. This force is equal to three times the weight of the tennis player and 1,000 times the weight of the tennis ball.

Finding forces when acceleration is zero

Zero acceleration means zero net force
When acceleration is zero, the second law allows us to calculate unknown forces in order to balance other forces we know. Think about a gymnast hanging motionless from two rings (Figure 5.5). The force of gravity pulls down on the gymnast. The acceleration must be zero if the he is not moving. The net force must also be zero because of the second law. The only way the net force can be zero is if the ropes pull upward with a force exactly equal and opposite the force of gravity pulling downward. If the downward force (or weight) of the gymnast is -700 newtons, then each rope carries an upward force of +350 newtons.

Equilibrium
The condition of zero acceleration is called equilibrium. In equilibrium, all forces cancel out leaving zero net force. Objects that are standing still are in equilibrium because their acceleration is zero. Objects that are moving at constant speed and direction are also in equilibrium.

Static problems
A static problem usually means there is no motion. Most static problems involve using the requirement of zero net force (equilibrium) to determine unknown forces. Engineers who design bridges and buildings solve static problems to calculate how much force must be carried by cables and beams. The cables and beams can then be designed so that they safely carry the forces that are required. The net force is also zero for motion at constant speed! Constant speed problems are treated like static problems as far as forces are concerned.

Figure 5.5: *This gymnast is not moving so the net force must be zero. If the weight of the gymnast is 700 N, then each rope must pull upward with a force of 350 N in order to make the net force zero.*

A static force problem

A woman is holding two dogs on a leash. If each dog pulls with a force of 80 newtons, how much force does the woman have to exert to keep the dogs from moving?

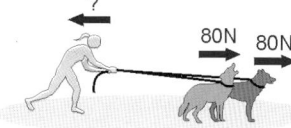

1) You are asked for force (F).
2) You are given two 80 N forces and the fact that the dogs are not moving (a = 0).
3) Newton's second law says the net force must be zero if the acceleration is zero.
4) The woman must exert a force equal and opposite to the sum of the forces from the two dogs. Two times 80 N is 160 N, so the woman must hold the leash with an equal and opposite force of 160 N.

5.3 The Third Law: Action and Reaction

This section is about the often-repeated phrase "For every action there is an equal and opposite reaction." This statement is known as Newton's third law of motion. Newton's first and second laws of motion discuss single objects and the forces that act on them. Newton's third law discusses pairs of objects and the interactions between them. Forces in nature always occur in pairs, like the top and bottom of a sheet of paper. You cannot have one without the other.

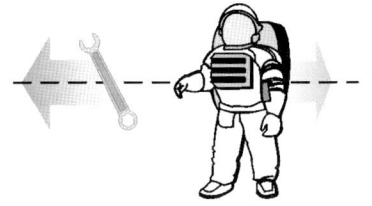

Figure 5.6: *An astronaut can move in space by throwing an object in the direction opposite where the astronaut wants to go.*

Forces always occur in action-reaction pairs

Moving in space is a problem
The astronauts working on the space station have a serious problem when they need to move around in space. There is nothing to push on. How do you move around if you have nothing to push against?

Forces always come in pairs
The solution is to throw something opposite the direction you want to move. This works because *all forces always come in pairs*. If this seems like a strange idea, think through the following example. Suppose an astronaut throws a wrench. A force must be applied to the wrench to accelerate it into motion. The inertia of the wrench resists its acceleration. Because of its inertia, the wrench pushes back against the gloved hand of the astronaut. The wrench pushing on the astronaut provides a force that moves the astronaut in the opposite direction (Figure 5.6).

Forces on objects at rest
Forces also come in pairs when objects are not moving. For example, consider this book. It is probably lying open on a table. The weight of the book exerts a force on the table, the same as it would exert on your hands if the book were resting on your hands. The table pushes back upward on the book with a force equal and opposite the book's weight. A chain of force pairs keeps going because the table pushes down on the floor and the floor pushes back up on the table (Figure 5.7). The floor pushes down on the walls and the Earth pushes back up on the walls to hold up the floor.

Action-reaction pairs
The two forces in a pair are called **action** and **reaction**. Anytime you have one, you also have the other. If you know the strength of one you also know the strength of the other since both forces are always equal. The two forces in an action-reaction pair always point in exactly opposite directions and act on different objects.

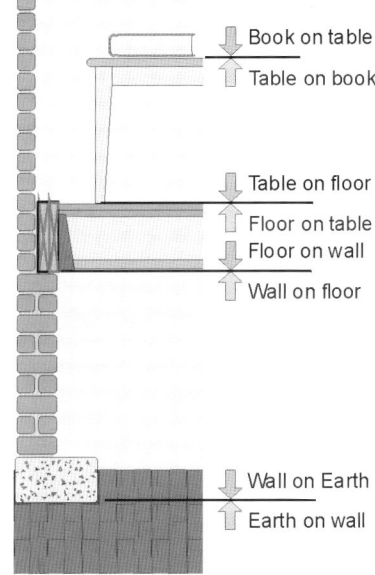

Figure 5.7: *Forces always come in action-reaction pairs. The two forces in a pair are equal in strength and opposite in direction.*

Newton's third law of motion

The first and second laws
The first and second laws apply to single objects. The first law states that an object will remain at rest or in motion at constant speed and direction until acted upon by an external force. The second law states that net force causes acceleration and mass resists acceleration.

The third law operates on pairs of objects
In contrast to the first two laws, the third law of motion applies to pairs of objects because *forces always come in pairs*. Newton's third law states that for every action force there has to be a reaction force that is equal in strength and opposite in direction. For example, to move on a skateboard you push your foot against the ground (Figure 5.8). The reaction force is the ground pushing back against your foot. The reaction force is what pushes you forward, because it is the force that acts on *you*. Your force against the ground pushes the Earth; however, the planet is so large that there is no perceptible motion resulting from your force.

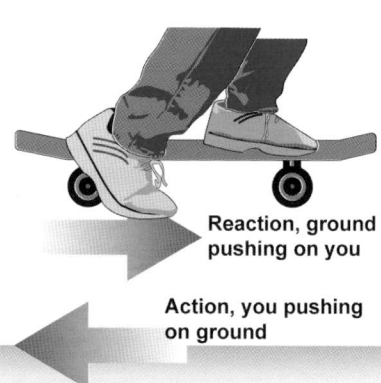

Reaction, ground pushing on you

Action, you pushing on ground

Action/reaction forces act on different objects
The action/reaction forces act on separate objects, *not* on the same object. For example, the action-reaction pair that is required to move a skateboard in the traditional way includes your foot and the Earth. Your foot pushing against the ground is the action force. The ground pushing back on your foot is the reaction force. The reaction force makes you move because it acts on *you* (Figure 5.8). Why doesn't your foot make the ground move? Simply because the force is too small to accelerate the huge mass of the Earth. Even though the reaction force that acts on you is the same size, you are much less massive than Earth. The same size reaction force *is* big enough to accelerate you.

Figure 5.8: *All forces come in pairs. When you push on the ground (action), the reaction of the ground pushing back on your foot is what makes you move.*

Stopping action and reaction confusion
It is easy to get confused about action and reaction forces. People often ask, "Why don't they cancel each other out?" The reason is that the action and reaction forces act on *different* objects. The action force of your foot acts on the Earth; the Earth's reaction force acts on you. The forces do not cancel; they act on different objects.

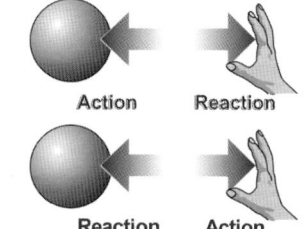

Action   Reaction

Reaction   Action

Action and reaction
It does not matter which is the action force and which is the reaction. Whichever force you call the action makes its counterpart the reaction. The important thing is to recognize which force acts on which object (Figure 5.9). To apply the second law properly, you need to identify the forces acting on the object for which you are trying to find the acceleration.

Figure 5.9: *It does not matter which force you call the action and which the reaction. The action and reaction forces are interchangeable.*

Solving problems with action-reaction forces

Thinking about which force is acting on which object

In many physics problems you are asked to determine the acceleration of a moving object from the forces acting on it. In the last section, you learned that the net force is the total of all forces acting *on* an object. Very often one of the forces will be a reaction force to a force created *by* the object. For example, consider a small cart attached to a spring (Figure 5.10). When you push the spring against a wall, a force is created. When you let the cart go, the force from the spring accelerates the cart away from the wall. But the force from the spring is pushing on the wall, so what force accelerates the cart? The answer is the *reaction force* of the wall pushing back on the spring. Since action-reaction forces always act on different objects, any force created by an object cannot accelerate the object itself.

A cart attached to a spring

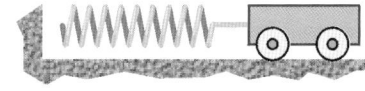

The spring is compressed against the wall

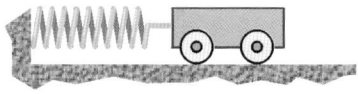

Force of spring against wall (*action*)

Force of wall against spring (*reaction*)

Figure 5.10: *Analyzing the action and reaction forces for a cart launched off a wall by a spring.*

Determine the reaction forces from people pushing a cart

Three people are each applying 250 newtons of force to try to move a heavy cart. The people are standing on a rug. Someone nearby notices that the rug is slipping. How much force must be applied to the rug to keep it from slipping? Sketch the action and reaction forces acting between the people and the cart and between the people and the rug.

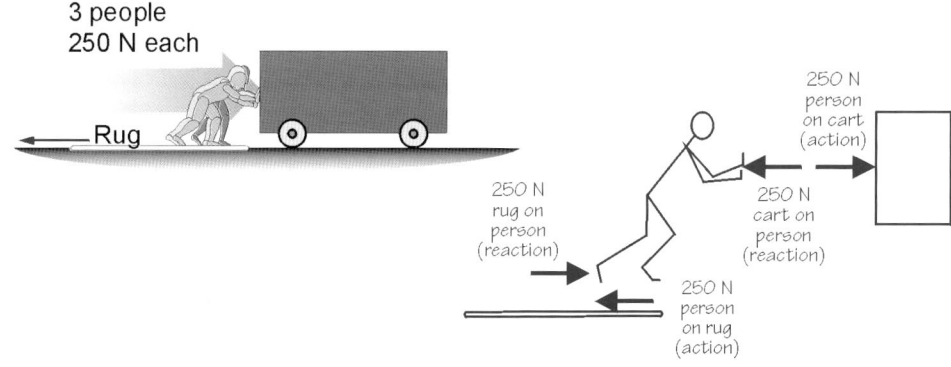

1)   You are asked for how much force (F) it takes to keep the rug from slipping.
2)   You are given that three forces of 250 N are being applied.
3)   The third law says that each of the forces applied creates a reaction force.
4)   Each person applies a force to the cart and the cart applies an equal and opposite force to the person. The force on the rug is the sum of the reaction forces acting on each person. The total force that must be applied to the rug is 750 N in order to equal the reaction forces from all three people.

Locomotion	The act of moving or the ability to move from one place to another is called locomotion. Any animal or machine that moves depends on Newton's third law to get around. When we walk, we push off the ground and move forward because of the ground pushing back on us in the opposite direction.
In the water	When something swims, it pushes on water and the water pushes back in the opposite direction. As a result, the animal, submarine, or even microscopic organism moves one way, and a corresponding amount of water moves in the opposite direction. The movement of a boat through water results from a similar application of Newton's third law. When a lone paddler in a kayak exerts an action force pushing the water backwards, the reaction force acts on the paddle, pushing the paddle and thus the kayak forward (Figure 5.11).
In the air	Whether insect, bat, bird, or machine, any object that flies under its own power moves by pushing the air. Living creatures flap their wings to push air, and the air pushes back, propelling them in the opposite direction. Jets, planes, and helicopters push air, too. In the specific example of a helicopter, the blades of the propeller are angled such that when they spin, they push the air molecules down (Figure 5.12). The air molecules, according to Newton's third law, push back up on the spinning blades and lift the helicopter.
The natural jet engine in a squid	Squid can use jet propulsion to move very quickly. A squid can fill a large chamber in its body with water. The chamber has a valve the squid can open and close. When the squid needs to move, it squeezes the water inside its body with powerful muscles, then opens its valve and shoots out a jet of water. The squid moves in the opposite direction from the reaction force of the jet pushing back on the squid's body.

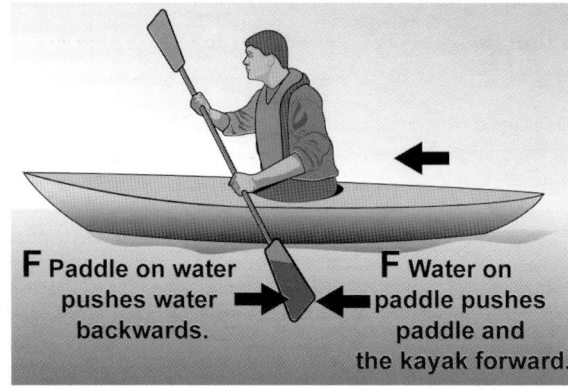

Figure 5.11: *Action and reaction forces for a kayak moving through the water.*

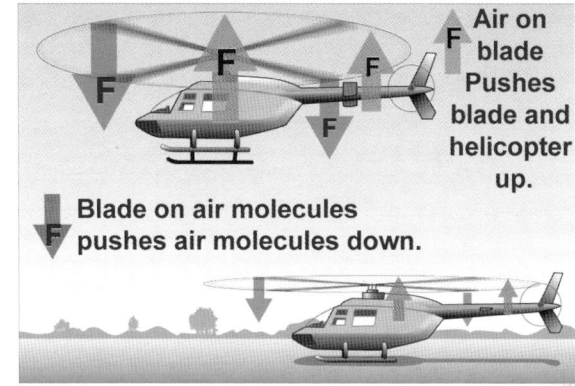

Figure 5.12: *Action and reaction forces on a helicopter.*

Application: Biomechanics

Biomechanics is the science of how physics is applied to muscles and motion. Many athletes use principles of biomechanics to improve their performance. People who design sports equipment use biomechanics to achieve the best performance by matching the equipment design to the athlete's body. Physicians, carpenters, people who build furniture, and many others also use biomechanics in their work. Any machine that relies on forces from the human body also relies on biomechanics.

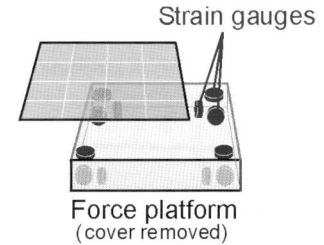

The force platform — A force platform can be thought of as a very sophisticated scale. Instead of containing springs, as your bathroom scale might, a force platform contains *strain gauges* (Figure 5.13). When a person steps or jumps on the platform, each strain gauge produces a reaction force and also a signal proportional to the strength of the reaction force. The force readings given off by the platform are referred to as ground reaction forces or GRF's.

Figure 5.13: *A force platform has 12 strain gauges arranged to measure forces in the x, y, and z directions at each of the corners.*

Measuring force in three directions — There are usually 12 strain gauges, three in each corner of a force platform oriented along the *x*-, *y*-, and *z*-axes. When force is applied to the platform, electrical signals from all 12 strain gauges are sent to a computer. The computer converts the signals to 12 separate force readings. From these readings, data is generated regarding the magnitude, direction, and sequence of GRF's being produced. Based on the relative magnitude of forces on each gauge, the center of pressure, or location of the force, can also be calculated.

Who uses force platforms? — Force platforms are used in many different fields including medicine and athletics. Physicians, technicians, and therapists use force platforms in clinical settings to help in the diagnosis and rehabilitation of walking disorders. *Biomechanists*, including athletic trainers, use force platforms for research and to help athletes improve their technique. Equipment designers and manufacturers use information from force platforms in the design of sports equipment such as running shoes.

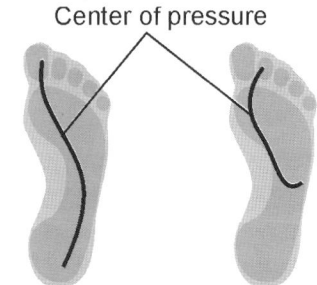

The center of pressure — The center of pressure is the place on your foot at which the average force is exerted against the ground. The center of pressure moves as your foot changes its contact point with the ground during walking or running. Force platform analysis is often used to evaluate the differences caused by various types of shoes, different track surfaces, walking versus running, and changes in gait patterns before and after surgery (Figure 5.14).

Figure 5.14: *The center of pressure for two runners with different running styles.*

Force from a vertical jump

Jumping is a common sports skill

The vertical jump is a common sport skill. Vertical jumps are seen in many different sports including basketball, volleyball, soccer, football, baseball, tennis, etc. A force platform makes an excellent tool to analyze the forces between the jumper's foot and the floor.

Measuring the forces from a vertical jump

To start the experiment, the athlete stands motionless in the middle of the platform (Figure 5.15). The "standing still" data is used to measure the weight of the athlete. That weight is converted to mass, using the second law ($m = F \div g$). The mass data is stored for later use. When given the command by the researcher, the athlete bends and jumps as high as possible. The force platform measures the force from each strain gauge at a rate of 250 to 1,000 measurements per second.

The force versus time curve

The biomechanist uses the data to generate a force-time curve. The total force recorded is the combination of the athlete's weight and the force produced during the jump. A typical force-time curve for a vertical jump is shown at the bottom of Figure 5.15. In this case, the athlete weighs 550 newtons. The peak GRF recorded is approximately 1,340 newtons. The time from the start of the jump until the athlete leaves the platform is just about one second. Once the athlete takes off and no longer touches the force table, the force readings drop to zero until the athlete lands back on the platform. The total time that the force is zero corresponds to the time in the air, a piece of information that allows other calculations to be made later.

Other characteristics of jumping motion

The force table data can be used to calculate many characteristics of the jumping motion. The total energy used can be calculated, as well as the maximum height reached. The force generated by the athlete's legs can also be determined along with maximum acceleration, and the balance of force between right and left leg.

Other biomechanical techniques

The technique of *electromyography* monitors the nerve signals to muscles and can determine the relative strength and sequence of contractions in the muscles being used in the jumping activity. When combined with video equipment, position and time data can give a complete cinematic and kinetic analysis of the activity.

Force platform

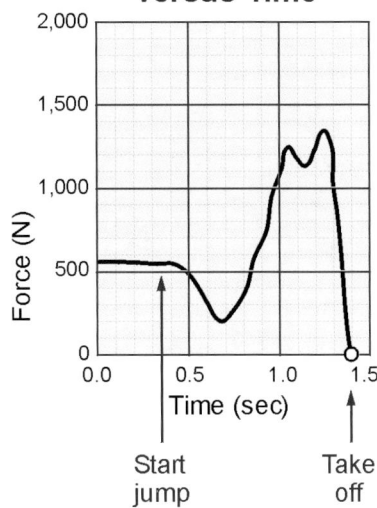

Force in z-direction versus Time

Figure 5.15: *A force platform can be used to measure the vertical force exerted during a vertical jump.*

Chapter 5 Review

Vocabulary Review

Match the following terms with the correct definition. There is one extra definition in the list that will not match any of the terms.

Set One	
1. force	a. Force that accelerates 1 kg at a rate of 1 m/s^2
2. inertia	b. Action with the ability to change an object's motion
	c. A problem with zero net force and/or no motion
3. newton	d. Volume of an object
	e. Force needed to accelerate 1 kg at a rate of 4.448 m/s^2
4. pound	f. The ability of an object to resist acceleration
5. static	

Set Two	
1. net force	a. Forces always occur in pairs
	b. Motion of an object tends to be maintained by its inertia
2. Newton's first law	
	c. Condition of zero acceleration
3. Newton's second law	d. Total force acting on an object
	e. An object's acceleration is caused by force and
4. Newton's third law	resisted by mass
	f. The acceleration of an object is inversely
5. equilibrium	proportional to the net force

Concept review

1. Name two units commonly used to measure force. How are they related?

2. Are the following statements true or false? Explain your answers using an example.

   a. Applying a force to an object will make it move.

   b. To keep an object moving, a force must be applied.

   c. A force must be applied to change the direction of a moving object.

3. To tighten the head of a hammer on its handle, it is banged against a surface as shown to the right. Explain how Newton's first law is involved.

4. How can rolling a bowling ball help you to determine the amount of matter in the ball?

5. List at least three parts of an automobile that are designed to overcome the effects of Newton's first law. Briefly explain the function of each.

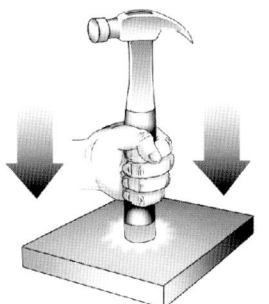

6. State Newton's second law in words. Write an equation expressing the law.

7. Explain how the unit of force used by scientists, the newton, is defined.

8. In Skylab, where objects are said to be weightless, an equal arm balance could not be used to measure the mass of an object. How could you measure the mass of an object in this situation?

9. Explain the difference between mass and weight. State common units for each.

10 What is the difference between the terms "force" and "net force"?

11. In physics problems, velocities, accelerations, and forces often appear with + (positive) or - (negative) signs. What do those signs indicate?

12. How does the sign of the force applied to an object compare with the sign of the acceleration?

13. What do motionless objects have in common with objects that are moving in a straight line with constant speed?

14. What is the difference between dynamic problems and static problems? Give an example of each.

15. You and your little 6 year old cousin are wearing ice skates. You push off each other and move in opposite directions. How does the force you feel during the push compare to the force your cousin feels? How do your accelerations compare? Explain.

16. You jump up. The Earth does not move a measurable amount. Explain this scenario using all three of Newton's laws of motion.

17. Explain the motion of swimming in terms of Newton's third law.

Problems

1. Calculate:
   a. the weight of a 16-newton object in pounds
   b. the weight of a 7-pound object in newtons
   c. the weight of a 3-kilogram object on Earth in newtons
   d. the mass in kilograms of an object that weighs 12 newtons on Earth

2. How does the inertia of a 200-kg object compare to the inertia of a 400-kg object?

3. A constant force is applied to a cart, causing it to accelerate. If the mass of the cart is tripled, what change occurs in the acceleration of the cart?

4. If the net force acting on an object is tripled, what happens to its acceleration?

5. On the planet of Venus, the acceleration due to gravity is 8.86 m/s^2. What is the mass of a man weighing 800 N on the surface of that planet?

6. A 60-kilogram boy rolls downhill on a bicycle with a mass of 12 kilograms. What net force is acting on the boy and his bicycle if he accelerates at a rate of 3.25 m/s^2?

7. A young girl whose mass is 30 kilograms is standing motionless on a 2-kg skateboard holding a 7-kg bowling ball. She throws the ball with an average force of 75 N.
   a. What is the magnitude of her acceleration?
   b. What is the magnitude of the acceleration of the bowling ball?

8. On the planet Mercury, a person with a mass of 75 kg weighs 280 N. What is the acceleration due to gravity on Mercury?

9. As a baseball player strikes the ball with his bat, the 1-kg bat applies an average force of 500 N on the 0.15-kg baseball for 0.20 seconds.
   a. What is the force applied by the baseball on the bat?
   b. What is the acceleration of the baseball?
   c. What is the speed of the baseball at the end of the 0.2 seconds?

10. The graph represents the motion of a 1500-kg car over a 20-second interval. During which interval(s) is the net force on the car zero?

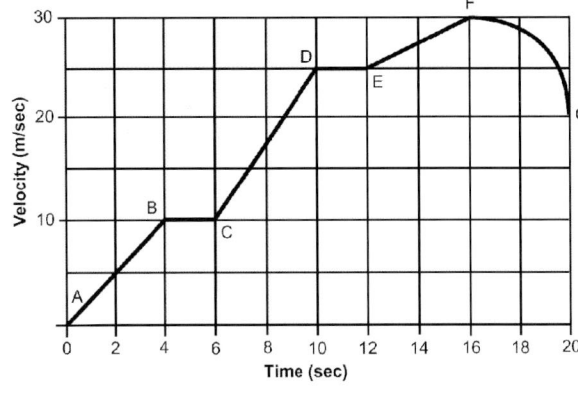

11. Referring to the graph, what force is being applied to the car during interval C-D?

12. Two forces are applied to a 2-kilogram block on a frictionless horizontal surface as shown in the diagram. Calculate the acceleration of the block.

Frictionless surface

13. The graph to the right represents the acceleration of an object as a function of the force applied to the object. What is the mass of the object?

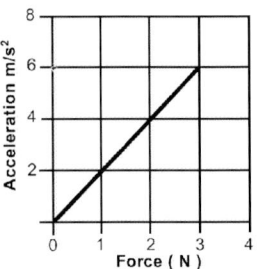

14. A 50-kg woman wearing a seat belt is traveling in a car that is moving with a velocity of 10 m/s. In an emergency, the car is brought to rest in 0.50 seconds. What force does the seat belt exert on the woman so that she remains in her seat?

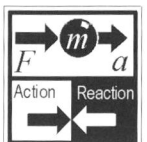

Unit 2
Motion and Force in One Dimension

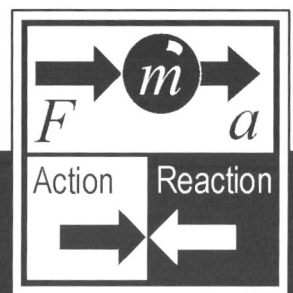

Chapter 6

Forces and Equilibrium

Objectives for Chapter 6

By the end of this chapter you should be able to:

1. Calculate the weight of an object using the strength of gravity (*g*) and mass.
2. Describe the difference between mass and weight.
3. Describe at least three processes that cause friction.
4. Calculate the force of friction on an object when given the coefficient of friction and normal force.
5. Calculate the acceleration of an object including the effect of friction.
6. Draw a free-body diagram and solve one-dimensional equilibrium force problems.
7. Calculate the force or deformation of a spring when given the spring constant and either of the other two variables.

Terms and vocabulary words

mass	weight	weightless	g-force	friction
static friction	sliding friction	rolling friction	viscous friction	air friction
normal force	extension	net force	free-body diagram	lubricant
equilibrium	ball bearing	dimension	spring	Hooke's law
compression	spring constant	deformation	restoring force	coefficient of friction
engineering	design cycle	subscript	prototype	coefficient of static friction

6.1 Mass, Weight and Gravity

People often use the words "mass" and "weight" interchangeably. However, in physics they are not the same. Mass is not weight. Mass is not volume (size) either. Mass is a fundamental property describing the amount of matter in an object that does not change. Weight is *not* a fundamental property of an object. Weight is a *force* created by gravity. Since the strength of gravity is different in different places in the universe, the weight of the same object will be different in different places, such as on the Moon. In this section, you will learn about how mass, weight, and gravity are related.

Mass and weight

Mass is a measure of matter   In Chapter 1, you learned that the term mass is used in science to describe the amount of matter an object contains. You are made out of much more matter than a paper clip, so your mass is much greater than the mass of a paper clip.

Mass is a constant   The mass of an object is the same anywhere in the universe. Consider a suitcase full of clothes. The mass of the packed suitcase is a measure of the amount of matter it contains. The amount of matter does not change with location, so a 10-kilogram suitcase is always 10 kilograms, even on Mars (Figure 6.1). The only way to change the mass would be to physically remove something, such as some clothes. Actually, this is not quite true *exactly*. Mass *does* change when objects move at speeds close to the speed of light (Chapter 18). However, the speed of light is so great that the difference is far too small to worry about even at the very highest speeds you are likely to encounter.

Weight is a force   The word weight is used to describe the force of gravity acting on an object. If somebody asks you, "How much do you weigh?" what they are technically asking is, "With how much *force* does gravity pull on you?"

Weight is not constant   The strength of gravity is not constant throughout the universe (Chapter 8). For example, the strength of gravity on the surface of the Earth is 2.6 times stronger than on the surface of Mars. Since an object's weight depends on the strength of gravity, weight is not constant. The same 10-kilogram suitcase weighs 98 newtons on Earth but only 38 newtons on Mars. Gravity is even weaker on the moon, where the weight of a 10 kg suitcase would be only 16 newtons.

Earth

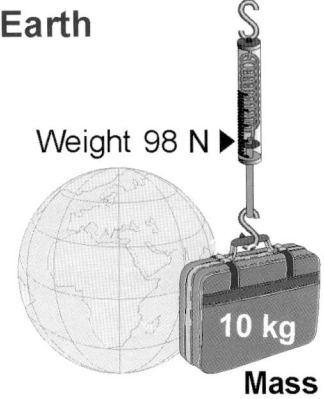

Weight 98 N ▶

Mass

Mars

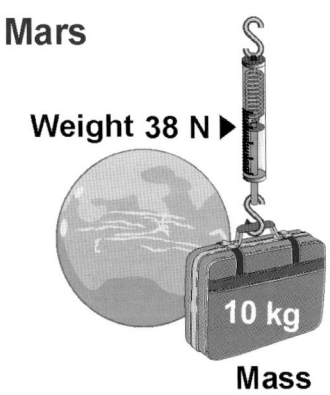

Weight 38 N ▶

Mass

Figure 6.1: *The weight of an object depends on the strength of gravity wherever the object is. The mass always stays the same.*

Calculating weight with mass and gravity

Weight varies since strength of gravity varies — The weight of an object depends on two things: its mass and the strength of gravity. Remember, the mass of an object is constant no matter where it is being measured. But the strength of gravity is different at different locations in the universe. The weight of an object depends on both its mass and the strength of gravity at the location where the weight is being calculated or measured.

Weight
(g at the Earth's surface)

Weight force (N) $\quad F_w = mg \quad\longleftarrow$ mass (kg)

Strength of gravity (9.8 N/kg)

F_w is the symbol for weight — Since weight is a force, we use the letter F to represent it. The little w next to the F stands for weight and reminds us which force is being considered. The w (or any letter or number written below another character) is called a subscript; we would say "F sub w" if we were telling someone what we were writing. The F and w always stay together since they function as one symbol for the force of gravity or the weight of the object.

The strength of gravity on Earth — In the equation for weight, the strength of gravity near the surface of the Earth is represented by the letter g. Within +/- 60 km of sea level, the value of g is approximately 9.8 N/kg. That means that gravity pulls on each kilogram of mass with a force of 9.8 newtons. A 1-kilogram object weighs 9.8 newtons. A 2-kilogram object weighs 19.6 N. A 10-kilogram object weighs 98 N.

The strength of gravity on Jupiter — What if you wanted to know the weight of an object somewhere else in the Solar System? The strength of gravity is different on or near different planets. For example, the strength of gravity on Jupiter is much stronger than it is on Earth. At the top of Jupiter's atmosphere, the value of g is approximately 23 N/kg. That means the weight of a 1-kilogram object on Jupiter would be 23 newtons, about 2 1/3 times what it would weigh on Earth. The strength of gravity also decreases with altitude above a planet's surface (Chapter 8).

Two meanings for g

g	g
Strength of gravity (9.8 N/kg)	Acceleration of gravity (9.8 m/sec²)

In Chapter 4, you learned that the symbol "g" stands for the acceleration of gravity in free fall, which is 9.8 m/sec². In this chapter, you are being introduced to another meaning for g, and that is the strength of gravity, which is 9.8 N/kg.

In Chapter 4, we discussed objects that were in free fall being accelerated by the force of gravity. Here, we are discussing the force of gravity acting on all objects, whether they are accelerating or not.

When calculating weight, it is more natural to discuss gravity in N/kg instead of m/sec². This is because objects may not be in motion but they still have weight. The two meanings for g are equivalent since a force of 9.8 N acting on a mass of 1 kg produces an acceleration of 9.8 m/sec².

Gravity, acceleration, and weightlessness

Weightlessness

An object is weightless when it feels no net force from gravity. There are two ways to become weightless. The one easiest to understand is to get away from any source of gravity, such as planets, stars, or similar objects of large mass. The space between the planets has so little gravity that an object is essentially weightless.

Weight and acceleration

A second way to become weightless is to be in *free fall*. To understand how falling can make you weightless, think about being in an elevator. Riding in an elevator that is accelerating upward makes you feel *heavier*. When the elevator is accelerating upward, the floor pushes against your feet to accelerate your body along upward with the rest of the elevator. If you are standing on a scale in the elevator, the scale reads your weight *plus* the additional force applied to accelerate you. If the elevator accelerates upward at 9.8 m/sec^2, the scale reads twice your normal weight. You feel twice as heavy because the elevator pushes on your feet with an additional force (*ma*) equal to your weight (*mg*).

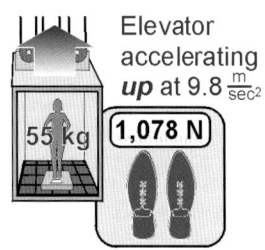

Elevator at **rest** or moving with **constant speed**

55 kg | 539 N

Elevator accelerating **up** at 9.8 $\frac{m}{sec^2}$

55 kg | 1,078 N

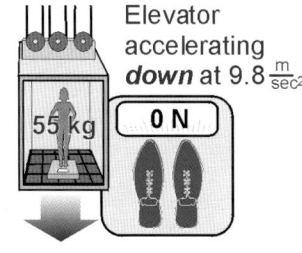

Elevator accelerating **down** at 9.8 $\frac{m}{sec^2}$

55 kg | 0 N

Free fall and weightlessness

Now consider an elevator in free fall. The elevator is accelerating downward at 9.8 m/sec^2. The scale feels *no force* because it is falling away from your feet at the same rate you are falling. As a result, you are weightless. A body in free fall is weightless because every particle of mass is accelerating downward.

g forces

Airplane pilots and race car drivers often describe forces they feel from acceleration as **g** forces (Figure 6.2). These *g* forces are not really forces at all, but are created by inertia. Remember, inertia is resistance to being accelerated. A body that is forced to accelerate upward at 1 *g* "feels" 9.8 extra newtons on every kilogram. A very fit human can withstand 6 or 7 *g*'s of acceleration before the *g* forces prevent blood from flowing properly and cause loss of consciousness.

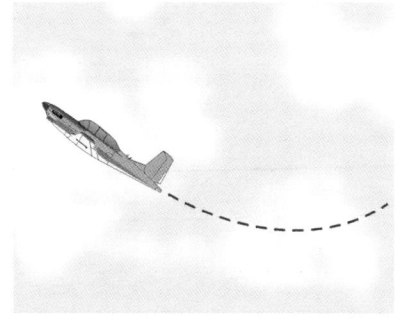

Figure 6.2: *An aircraft in a tight turn subjects the pilot to high g forces.*

Using weight in physics problems

Do not substitute mass for force

Many problems in physics give you the mass of an object yet ask for forces to be used or calculated. In these kinds of problems you must often calculate the weight of the object. Weight is a force, measured in newtons or pounds. Mass is *not* a force, mass is measured in kilograms. If you use a quantity in kilograms in a formula that asks for a force, you will get the wrong answer.

Weight in equilibrium problems

Very often, weight problems involve equilibrium where forces are balanced. For example, how much force does it take to lift a 2-kilogram book from a table? If the book is lifted very slowly, there is almost no acceleration. Therefore, the minimum force it takes is just equal to the weight of the book. If you apply a force equal to the book's weight, the book is in equilibrium and there is no force holding it down to the table. Theoretically, the tiniest additional force causes the book to rise. Although the problem asked how much force would lift the book, you may assume that the required answer is the force needed to counteract the book's weight, which is 19.6 newtons (19.6 N = 2 kg × 9.8 N/kg). You may assume problems like this are always looking for the minimum force required, with no acceleration.

Weight on other planets or high altitudes

The other common type of weight problem involves other planets (or high altitudes) where the strength of gravity (g) is not the same as on the surface of the Earth. Even though the mass of an object is the same, the weight varies depending on the strength of gravity. For these kinds of problems use the value for g that is given in the problem.

Calculate weight on Jupiter

How much would a person who weighs 490 N (110 lbs) on Earth weigh on Jupiter? Since Jupiter may not actually have a surface, "on" means at the top of the atmosphere. The value of g at the top of Jupiter's atmosphere is 23 N/kg.

Jupiter

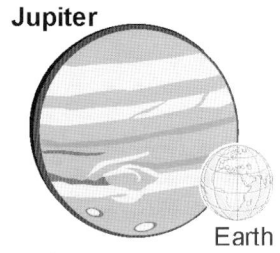

Earth

1) You are asked for the weight.
2) You are given the weight on Earth and the strength of gravity on Jupiter.
3) $F_W = mg$.
4) First, find the person's mass from the weight and strength of gravity on Earth:
   m = (490 N) ÷ (9.8 N/kg)
   = 50 kg
   Next, find the weight on Jupiter:
   Fw = (50 kg) × (23 N/kg)
   = 1,150 N (259 lbs)

Calculate force required to hold up an object

A 10-kilogram ball is supported at the end of a rope. How much force (tension) is in the rope?
1) You are asked to find force.
2) You are given a mass of 10 kilograms.
3) The force of the weight is: $F_W = mg$ and g = 9.8 N/kg.
4) The word "supported" means the ball is hanging motionless at the end of the rope. That means the tension force in the rope is equal and opposite to the weight of the ball.
   F_W = (10 kg) × (9.8 N/kg) = 98 N.
   The tension force in the rope is 98 newtons.

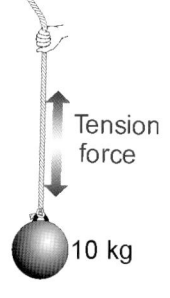

Tension force

10 kg

6.2 Friction

Frictional forces are forces that resist or oppose motion. Everyone has experienced frictional forces. Friction is what slows you down when coasting in a car or on a bicycle. You may not realize that friction is also necessary to speed up. Friction between the tires and the road is what allows forces to be transmitted from the road to the tires, accelerating the car or bicycle. This section is about frictional forces, what causes them and what different types of frictional forces exist. You will also learn how to estimate frictional forces, and how to calculate how frictional forces affect the motion of objects.

The force of friction

What causes friction?
Friction results from relative motion between objects, such as the bottom of a cardboard box and the floor it is sliding across. If you looked through a powerful microscope, you would see that all surfaces have microscopic hills and valleys, even surfaces that appear smooth and shiny. As the surfaces slide (or try to slide) across each other, the hills and valleys interfere. This interference is what causes friction. Surfaces with lots of hills and valleys interfere a lot, so we say that a lot of friction exists. A good example of high friction would be two pieces of sandpaper rubbed together. Surfaces with liquid in between them interfere with each other less. An ice cube sliding across a wet floor has very little friction.

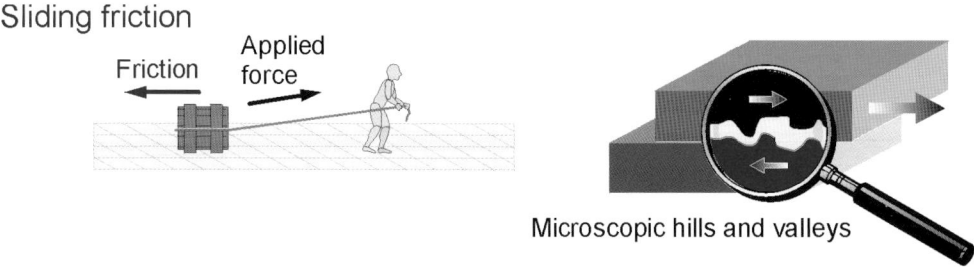

Sliding friction

Friction — Applied force

Microscopic hills and valleys

Friction resists motion
Friction is a resistive force. Describing friction as resistive means that it *always works against the motion that produces it.* For example, as you push a box across a floor, the forward motion creates frictional forces that essentially push back on the box. The frictional forces make the box harder to move because they act opposite the direction of motion.

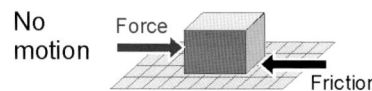

No motion — Force / Friction

Static friction: exists when two surfaces try to move across each other but not enough force is applied to cause motion.

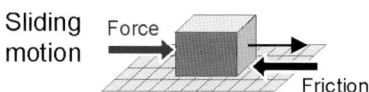

Sliding motion — Force / Friction

Sliding friction: exists when two surfaces slide across each other.

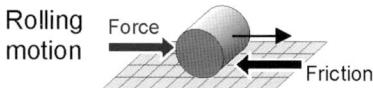

Rolling motion — Force / Friction

Rolling friction: exists when one object rolls over another object.

Motion through air — Friction

Air friction: (air resistance) exists when air moves around an object.

Motion through water — Friction

Viscous friction: exists when objects move through water or other fluids.

A model for friction

Friction depends on many factors
The amount of friction that exists when a box is pushed across a smooth floor is very different from the amount of friction that exists when the same box is pushed across a carpeted floor. Every combination of surfaces produces a unique amount of friction depending on the types of materials, the degrees of roughness, the presence of dirt or oil, and other factors. Even the friction between two identical surfaces changes as the surfaces are polished by sliding across each other. No one model or formula can accurately describe the many processes that create friction. Even so, some simple approximations are useful.

Friction is proportional to the force holding surfaces together
The force of friction is approximately proportional to the force squeezing two sliding surfaces together. For example, consider pulling a piece of paper across the table. If you pull the paper at constant speed, the force you must apply is equal in strength to the force of friction. It is easy to pull the paper alone, because the force holding it to the table is only its own weight. The force of friction is less than the weight of the paper. However, the weight of a brick placed on top of the paper creates much more force holding the paper against the surface of the table. The increased force between the paper and table creates more friction. As a result, it takes more force to pull the paper because the force of friction is larger.

The coefficient of friction
The **coefficient of friction** is a measure of the strength of sliding friction between two surfaces. A coefficient of *one* means the force of friction is equal to the force holding the surfaces together. A coefficient of *zero* means there is no friction no matter how much force is applied to squeeze the surfaces together. The coefficient of friction is most often a number between zero and one. The symbol used for coefficient of friction is the Greek letter μ, which is pronounced "myou." The force between the two surfaces is called the normal force (F_n). The model is called dry sliding friction because it is most accurate when the surfaces are dry.

Friction
(dry sliding friction)

Friction force (N) $\quad F_f = \mu \, F_n \longleftarrow$ Normal force (N)

$\overset{\text{Coefficient of friction}}{}$

Calculate the force of friction

A 10 N force pushes down on a box that weighs 100 N. As the box is pushed horizontally, the coefficient of sliding friction is 0.25. Determine the force of friction resisting the motion.

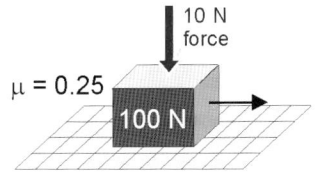

$\mu = 0.25$
10 N force
100 N

1) You are asked for the force of friction (F_f).
2) You are given the weight (F_w), the applied force (F) and the coefficient of sliding friction (μ)
3) The normal force is the sum of forces pushing down on the floor ($F_f = \mu F_n$).
4) First, find the normal force:
   $F_n = 100\ N + 10\ N$
   $\quad = 110\ N$
   Use $F_f = \mu F_n$ to find the force of friction:
   $F_f = (0.25) \times (110\ N)$
   $\quad = 27.5\ N$

Calculating the force of friction

The normal force The normal force is the force perpendicular to both surfaces which are moving relative to each other. In many problems, the normal force is the *reaction* in an action-reaction pair. The action force of the pair is the force created by an object's weight pressing down on the supporting surface. The reaction force is the surface pushing back up to support the object. If additional forces are applied perpendicular to a sliding surface, the normal force is equal to the weight of the object *plus* the extra applied force.

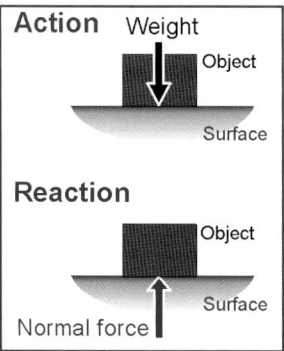

Surfaces	μ_{static}	$\mu_{sliding}$
rubber on concrete	0.80	0.65
wood on wood	0.50	0.20
ice on ice	0.10	0.03
glass on glass	0.94	0.40
steel on steel	0.74	0.57

Static and sliding friction It takes a certain minimum amount of force to make an object start sliding. The maximum net force that can be applied *before* an object starts sliding is called the force of **static friction**. Static friction is not created by motion, but results from the same interlocking hills and valleys that create sliding friction. Static friction can be described by a similar model to sliding friction. The **coefficient of static friction** (μ_s) relates the maximum force of static friction to the normal force.

Static friction

Friction force (N)   Coefficient of static friction

$$F_f = \mu_s F_n$$

Normal force (N)

Static friction is greater than sliding friction The coefficient of static friction is nearly always greater than the coefficient of sliding friction. This is because it takes more force to break two surfaces loose than it does to keep them sliding once they are already moving. Table 6.1 gives some representative values for static and sliding friction.

Low μ values indicate slippery surfaces There are coefficients of friction for each type of friction (static, sliding, rolling, air, and viscous). Notice that the sliding friction coefficient for ice on ice is 0.03, a value very close to zero. The low value of μ tells you that ice cubes rubbed across one another experience very little friction. The coefficient of sliding friction for rubber on concrete is 0.80, a value very close to one. Tires are made of rubber because rubber and concrete do not slide across each other very easily.

Calculate the force of static friction

A steel pot with a weight of 50 N sits on a steel countertop. How much force does it take to start the pot sliding.

1) You are asked for the force to overcome static friction (F_f).
2) You are given the weight (F_w) and both surfaces are steel.
3) $F_f = \mu_s F_n$.
4) $F_f = (0.74) \times (50 \text{ N})$
   $= 37 \text{ N}$

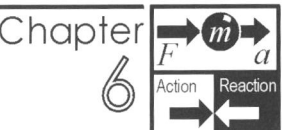

Friction and motion

How does friction affect acceleration? When calculating the acceleration of an object, the F that appears in Newton's second law ($a = F \div m$) stands for the net force. Remember, the net force is the total of all of the forces acting on an object that could cause acceleration. The net force *includes the force of friction*. In most cases, the net force is equal to the force applied minus the force of friction. As a result, friction tends to reduce the amount of acceleration produced by forces applied to an object.

The force of static friction An applied force *less* than the force of static friction will produce *no* acceleration because it is not enough to start an object moving. The force of static friction is equal and opposite to any applied force, up to the maximum allowed by the formula on the previous page ($F_f = \mu_s F_n$). For example, suppose you calculate a force of static friction of 10 newtons. No motion occurs if a 5-newton force is applied because 5 N is less than the maximum (10 N) force of static friction. In this case, the *actual force of static friction is 5 newtons*, not the maximum of 10 newtons calculated by the formula. If you think about it, friction cannot *cause* an object to move, so the force of static friction cannot exceed the force applied to an object.

Friction reduces acceleration Since frictional forces reduce the net applied force, the acceleration we observe will always be less than it would have been if there were no friction. If you know the applied force acting on an object, the weight of the object, and the coefficient of friction between the interacting surfaces, you can determine the acceleration of the object from the net force (applied forces - friction forces).

Calculate the acceleration of a car including friction

The engine applies a forward force of 1,000 newtons to a 500-kilogram car. Find the acceleration of the car if the coefficient of rolling friction is 0.07.

1) You are asked for the acceleration (a).

2) You are given the applied force (F), the mass (m), and the coefficient of rolling friction (μ).

3) Relationships that apply: $a = F \div m$, $F_f = \mu F_n$, ($F_w = mg$ and $g = 9.8$ N/kg).

4) The normal force equals the weight of the car: $F_n = mg = (500 \text{ kg})(9.8 \text{ N/kg}) = 4,900$ N.

The friction force is: $F_f = (0.07)(4,900 \text{ N}) = 343$ N.

The acceleration is the net force divided by the mass:

$a = (1,000 \text{ N} - 343 \text{ N}) \div (500 \text{ kg}) = (657 \text{ N}) \div (500 \text{ kg}) = 1.31 \text{ m/sec}^2$

Perpetual motion

Throughout history, many people have claimed to have invented a machine that will run forever with no outside force. We call these fanciful inventions perpetual motion machines and none have ever worked.

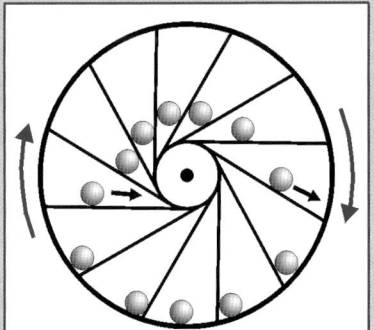

A design for a (claimed) perpetual motion machine. The balls rolling down the right side are supposed to turn the wheel.

Perpetual motion machines do not work because there is always some friction. Friction always opposes motion, which sooner or later slows everything down.

If someone shows you a device that seems to go without stopping, be suspicious. There is no escape from friction. So somewhere you will find a hidden plug or a battery supplying force.

Reducing the force of friction

All surfaces experience some friction

Frictional forces are unavoidable. Any motion where surfaces move across each other or through air or water always creates some friction. Unless a force is continually applied, friction eventually slows all motion to a stop. For example, bicycles have very low friction, but even the best bicycle slows down if you coast on a level road. Friction cannot be completely eliminated but it can be reduced. Many clever inventions have been created to reduce the force of friction.

Lubricants reduce friction in machines

Keeping a fluid such as oil between sliding services keeps the surfaces from actually touching each other. Instead of wearing away each other's bumps and depressions, surfaces separated by oil stir up the oil instead. The force of friction is greatly reduced, and surfaces do not wear out as fast. A fluid used to reduce friction is called a lubricant. You add oil to a car engine so the pistons can slide back and forth with less friction. Even water can be used as a lubricant under conditions where there is not too much heat. A common use of powdered graphite, another lubricant, is to spray it into locks so that a key slides more easily.

Ball bearings

In systems where there are axles, pulleys, and rotating objects, ball bearings are used to reduce friction. Ball bearings change sliding motion into rolling motion. Rolling motion creates much less friction than sliding motion. For example, a metal shaft rotating in a hole rubs and generates a great amount of friction. Ball bearings are small balls of steel that go between the shaft and the inside surface of the hole. The shaft rolls on the bearings instead of rubbing against the walls of the hole. Well-oiled bearings rotate easily and greatly reduce friction (Figure 6.3).

Magnetic levitation

Another method of reducing friction is to separate two surfaces with a cushion of air. A hovercraft floats on a cushion of air created by a large fan. Electromagnetic forces can also be used to separate surfaces. Working prototypes of a magnetically levitated (or maglev) train have been built from several designs. A maglev train floats on a cushion of force created by strong electromagnets (Figure 6.4). Once it gets going, the train does not touch the rails. Because there is no contact, there is far less friction than with a train on tracks. The ride is smoother, allowing for much faster speeds.

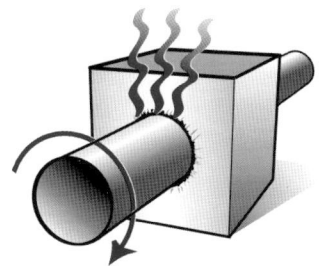

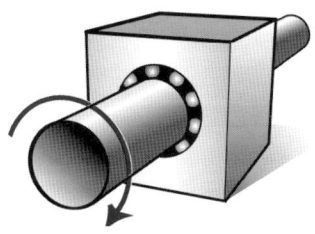

Figure 6.3: *The friction between a shaft (the long pole in the picture) and an outer part of a machine produces a lot of heat. Friction can be reduced by placing ball bearings between the shaft and the outer part.*

Figure 6.4: *In a maglev train, there is no contact between the moving train and the rail. This means that there is very little friction.*

Using friction

Friction is useful for brakes and tires

There are many applications where friction is both useful and necessary. For example, the brakes on a bicycle create friction between two rubber *brake pads* and the rim of the wheel. Friction between the brake pads and the rim slows down the bicycle. Friction is also necessary to make a bicycle go. Without friction the bicycle's tires would not grip the road. Designing tires that *maximize* friction is a multibillion dollar industry.

Weather condition tires

Rain and snow can act like lubricants to separate tires from the road. As a tire rolls over a wet road, the rubber squeezes the water out of the way so that there can be good contact between rubber and road surface. Tire treads have grooves that allow space for water to be channeled away from the road-tire contact point (Figure 6.5). A smooth rubber tire tread without grooves slides easily on a wet road. Special irregular groove patterns, along with tiny slits on the contact surface have been employed on "snow tires" to provide increased traction in snow. These tires increase friction by keeping snow from getting packed into the treads and by allowing the contact surface of the tire to change shape in order to grip the uneven surface of a snow covered road.

Nails

Friction is the force that keeps nails and screws in place (Figure 6.6). A nail is actually a form of a wedge. The material into which a nail is driven, such as wood, pushes against the nail from all sides with compression forces. Each blow from the hammer drives the nail deeper into the material, increasing the contact surface and the total force keeping the nail in place. The large compression force creates a proportionally large static friction force. Removing a nail can often seem more difficult than hammering it in.

Cleated shoes

In many cases, it is desirable to increase the friction between the soles of shoes and the ground. For example, football players and soccer players wear special shoes with *cleats*. Cleats are like teeth that stick out from the bottom of the shoe and dig into the ground. Cleats greatly increase the friction between the shoe and the ground. The increased friction means players can exert much greater forces against the ground to accelerate. Cleats also help players keep from slipping on the field.

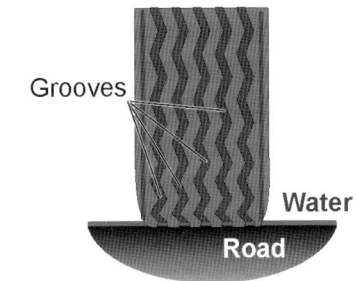

Figure 6.5: *Grooved tire treads allow space for water to be channeled away from the road-tire contact point, allowing for more friction in wet conditions.*

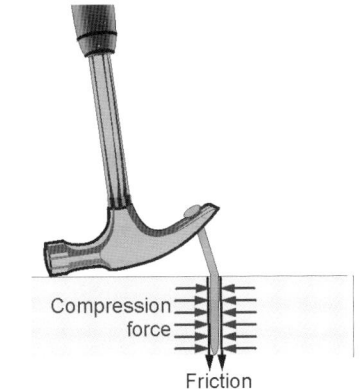

Figure 6.6: *Friction is what makes nails hard to pull out and gives them the strength to hold wood together.*

6.3 Equilibrium of Forces and Hooke's Law

In Chapter 5, you learned that the motion of an object depends on the net force acting on it. You also learned that when the net force acting on an object is zero, the object experiences no acceleration. This situation is called equilibrium. This section is about equilibrium and the important role equilibrium plays in the world in and outside of the physics classroom. You will also learn about Hooke's Law, which describes the forces created by springs, rubber bands, and other objects that stretch. The natural spring-like behavior of all materials is what creates forces between inanimate objects that "know" how to be exactly equal and opposite.

Equilibrium

Definition of equilibrium — When the net force acting on an object is zero, the forces on the object are balanced. We call this condition equilibrium. Because of Newton's second law ($a = F \div m$), objects in equilibrium experience no change in motion (no acceleration). When in equilibrium, an object at rest stays at rest, and a moving object continues to move with the same speed and direction.

Equilibrium does not mean no force — Physics students sometimes *wrongly* believe that if an object is in equilibrium, it must mean that there are no forces acting on the object. This is not correct. Newton's second law simply requires that for an object to be in equilibrium, the net force, or the sum of the forces, has to be zero. This *could* mean that there are no forces acting on it. But it is more probable that there *are* forces acting, and that the forces balance each other out by adding up to zero.

Equilibrium		Net force	Non-equilibrium	
No motion	50 N 50 N	+ 50 N - 50 N ———— 0	Acceleration from net forces	Free fall
Motion at constant speed and direction	50 N Force 5 m/sec 50 N Friction	+ 50 N - 50 N ———— 0	50 N 35 N **Net force** + 50 N - 35 N = +15 N	9.8 m/sec² **Net force** = weight

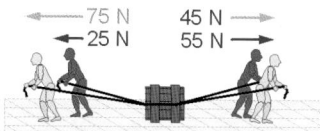

Free-body diagrams

Forces on a free-body diagram
Many problems have more than one force applied to an object in more than one place. To keep track of the number and direction of all the forces, it is useful to draw a free-body diagram. A free-body diagram contains only the object under consideration. All connections or supports are removed and replaced by the forces they exert on the object.

An accurate free-body diagram includes every force acting on an object. All forces that are included must *act on the object*, not on other objects. This means many forces may be reaction forces.

An example situation
As an example of a free-body diagram, consider a 30-newton book resting on a table that weighs 200 newtons. The book is on one corner of the table so that its entire weight is supported by one leg. Figure 6.7 shows a free-body diagram of the forces acting on the table.

The free-body diagram for the table
Because the table is in equilibrium, the net force acting on it must be zero. The weight of the book acts *on the table*. The weight of the table acts *on the floor*. The force acting *on the table* is the reaction to its weight acting on the floor. The correct free-body diagram shows six forces. Equilibrium requires that the upward reaction at each leg be one-quarter the weight of the table (50 newtons). The leg beneath the book also supports the weight of the book (80 N = 50 N + 30 N).

The purpose of a free-body diagram
By separating an object from its physical connections, a free-body diagram makes it possible to identify all forces and where they act. A reaction force is usually present at any point an object is in contact with another object or the floor. Forces due to weight or acceleration may be assumed to act directly on an object, often at its center.

Representing positive and negative forces
There are two ways to handle positive and negative directions in a free-body diagram. One way is to make all upward forces positive and all downward forces negative. The second way is to draw all the forces in the direction you believe they act on the object. When you solve the problem, if you have chosen correctly, all the values for each force are positive. If one comes out negative, it means the force points in the opposite direction from what you guessed.

Real-life situation

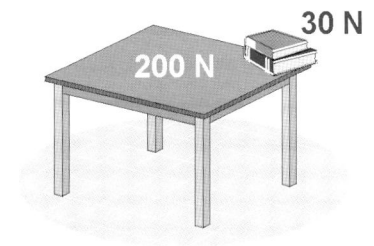

Free-body diagram

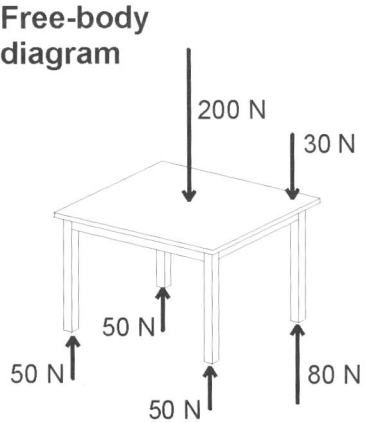

Equilibrium condition

	+50 N
	+ 50 N
-200 N	+ 50 N
-30 N	+ 80 N
-230 N	+ 230 N

Figure 6.7: *A free-body diagram showing forces acting on a table. The table is in equilibrium, so the total upward force is equal to the total downward force.*

Applications of equilibrium

Equilibrium helps identify forces

Equilibrium and the second law are also used to prove the existence of forces that are otherwise difficult to see. Consider a book at rest on a table. If we see that an object is at rest, we know its acceleration is zero. That means the net force must also be zero. If we know one force (such as weight), we know there is another force in the opposite direction to make the net force zero (the normal force).

Finding forces by using equilibrium

One of the most common applications of equilibrium is to find an unknown force. If an object is not moving, then you know it is in equilibrium and the net force must be zero. This condition allows you to find an unknown force, if you know the other forces acting on the object, such as its weight. For example, suppose two cables are used to support a sign. The force in each cable must be half the weight of the sign (Figure 6.8). You know the total upward force from the cables must equal the downward force of the sign's weight because the sign is in equilibrium.

Equilibrium in three directions

Objects are free to move in three directions: up-down, right-left, and front-back. The three directions are called three dimensions (3-D). These dimensions are usually given the names x, y, and z (Figure 6.9). When an object is in equilibrium, forces must balance *separately* in each of the x, y, and z dimensions. For example, the block in the diagram in figure 6.9 will move upward (+z). The net force is zero in the x and y directions, so there will be no acceleration in the x or y direction. However, forces are not balanced in the up-down direction. Chapter 7 will discuss equilibrium of forces in three dimensions in more detail.

Figure 6.8: *Two cables must each exert an upward force of 50 N to support a sign with a weight of 100 N.*

The three dimensions x, y, and z

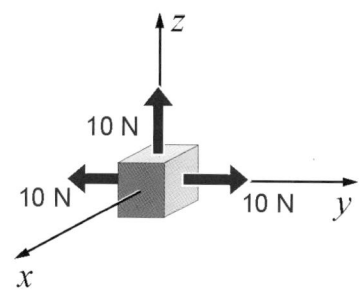

Figure 6.9: *Objects are free to move in three dimensions, and therefore equilibrium implies balance of forces in all three dimensions. This box is not in equilibrium because there is a net force in the z-direction.*

Use equilibrium to find an unknown force

Two chains are used to lift a small boat. One of the chains has a force of 600 newtons. Find the force in the other chain if the mass of the boat is 150 kilograms.

1) You are asked for the force.

2) You are given one of two forces and the mass.

3) Relationships that apply: net force = zero, $F_w = mg$ and $g = 9.8$ N/kg.

4) The weight of the boat is $F_w = mg = (150$ kg$)(9.8$ N/kg$) = 1,470$ N.

   Let F be the force in the other chain, The condition of equilibrium requires that:

   $F + (600$ N$) = 1,470$ N, therefore F = 870 N.

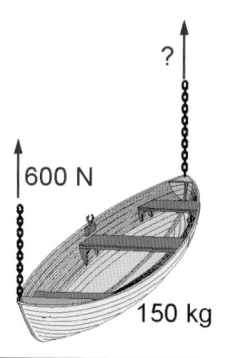

The force from a spring

Springs exert forces A jack-in-the-box is a children's toy that uses a spring. When the top comes off, the clown pops out of the box and into the air (Figure 6.10). Since the weight of the clown pulls down, the force from the spring is bigger than the weight. The difference in force accelerates the clown out of the box. Springs are used in many devices to create force. There are springs holding up the wheels in a car, springs to close doors, and a spring in a toaster that pops up the toast .

Characteristics of springs The most common type of spring is a coil of metal or plastic that creates a force when it is extended (stretched) or compressed (squeezed). The force from a spring has two important characteristics.

1. The force always acts in a direction that tries to return the spring to its unstretched shape. For example, when you extend a spring it pulls back. If you compress a spring it pushes back against your applied force.

2. The strength of the force is proportional to the amount of extension or compression in the spring. For example, suppose you extend a certain spring by 10 centimeters and it makes a force of 5 newtons (Figure 6.11). If you extend the same spring by 20 centimeters, it will make a force of 10 newtons.

Forces created by a spring

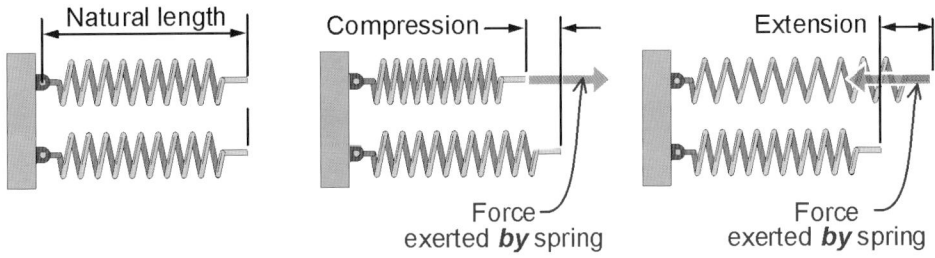

Restoring force When a spring is extended or compressed, the spring tries to "restore" itself to its original length. The force created by an extended or compressed spring is called a "restoring force" because it always acts in a direction to restore the spring to its natural length.

Figure 6.10: *A jack-in-the-box is a children's toy that relies on a spring.*

Force is proportional to change in length

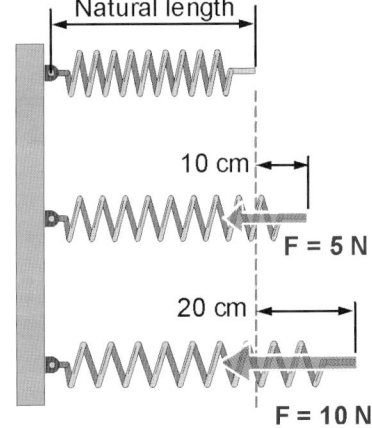

Figure 6.11: *The force exerted by a spring is proportional to the amount the spring is extended or compressed.*

Restoring force and Hooke's law

Deformation Every spring has a natural (unstretched) length. The change in length from extension or compression is called deformation. The deformation of a spring is measured relative to its natural length (Figure 6.12). For example, suppose a spring with a natural length of 10 centimeters is compressed to 8 centimeters. The spring has a deformation (-x) of -2 centimeters because 2 centimeters is the difference between the natural and compressed lengths. Extension creates positive deformation (+x) and compression creates negative deformation (-x).

Strength of the restoring force For a given amount of deformation, the strength of the restoring force depends on how a spring is made and out of what material. Springs made from thick metal wire exert strong forces, even from small deformations. Springs made from thin wire or plastic exert only small forces even when deformed a large amount.

The spring constant, k The relationship between strength and deformation is described by the spring constant (k). A high value of k means the spring deforms very little even under relatively large forces. The springs in automobile shock absorbers are very *stiff* because they have a large spring constant. A loose spring, such as a Slinky™ has a low value of k.

The unit for k is N/m The spring constant is measured in units of newtons per meter, which is abbreviated N/m. Looking at the units of k gives insight into what the spring constant means. The spring constant represents how many newtons of restoring force the spring exerts per meter that it is extended or compressed. For example, a spring with a spring constant of 10 N/m exerts 10 newtons of force for every meter that it is extended or compressed from its natural length.

Hooke's law
(springs)

$$F = -kx$$

Force (N) —— $F = -kx$ —— Spring constant (N/m), Deformation (m)

Hooke's law The relationship between force, spring constant, and deformation is called Hooke's law. The negative sign indicates that positive deformation (extension) creates a restoring force in the negative (opposite) direction. Negative deformation (compression) creates a restoring force in the positive direction.

Deformation of a spring

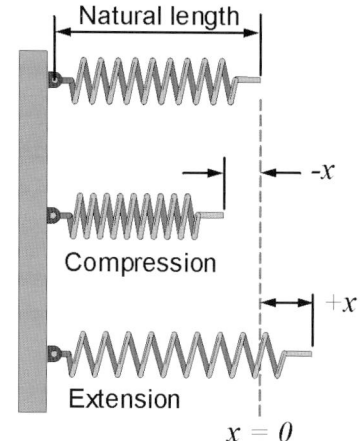

Figure 6.12: *The deformation (x) of a spring is measured relative to its natural unstretched length.*

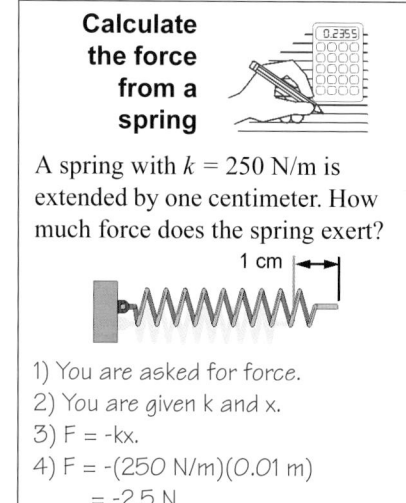

Calculate the force from a spring

A spring with $k = 250$ N/m is extended by one centimeter. How much force does the spring exert?

1) You are asked for force.
2) You are given k and x.
3) F = -kx.
4) F = -(250 N/m)(0.01 m)
    = -2.5 N

110

More about action-reaction and normal forces

Reaction forces   Now that you understand equilibrium and Hooke's law, we can revisit the normal force and answer the following question: How does a wall know exactly how much reaction force to push back with when you apply an action force? A wall cannot think for itself or calculate a physics formula.

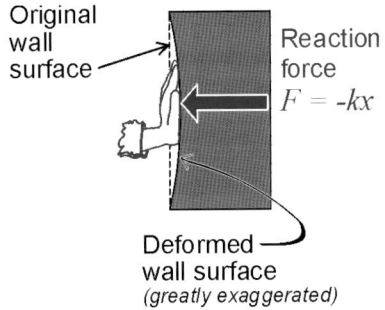

Figure 6.13: *The reaction force is created by deformation of the wall, acting in accordance with Hooke's law.*

A force applied to a wall, creates an equal and opposite reaction force.

Action force (acts on wall)

Reaction force (acts on you)

Solid materials act like springs   To better understand what creates a reaction force, we must look more closely at the point of contact between your hand and the wall. If we could look at it very closely, on a microscopic level, we would see that the wall is deformed a very small amount by the force from your hand. All solid materials act like springs because they deform when forces are applied. Soft materials like rubber deform more than hard materials like wood and steel.

Solid materials also exert restoring forces   When you push against the wall, it deforms proportionately to the strength of your push. Like a spring, the wall exerts a restoring force back on your hand proportional to the amount it has deformed (Figure 6.13). If you push with a larger force, the wall deforms a larger amount. The larger deformation results in a larger restoring force. The restoring force from the wall is always exactly equal and opposite to the force you apply, because it is *caused by the deformation resulting from the force you apply.*

The what, the how, and the why   The conditions of equilibrium allow us to verify that reaction forces exist. These reaction forces are the source of the normal force in certain situations, such as a table supporting a book. Equilibrium and Newton's second law allow us to calculate the strength of the reaction force or normal force. Finally, Hooke's law allows us to explain how the normal force is created, why its strength is always equal to the applied force, and why its direction is opposite to the applied force. A wall does not exert the correct force by being "smart"; it simply deforms in response to the applied force, based on Hooke's law.

Calculate the restoring force from a solid

The spring constant for a piece of solid wood is 1×10^8 N/m. Use Hooke's law to calculate the deformation when a force of 500 N (112 lbs) is applied.

1) You are asked for the deformation (x).
2) You are given the force and spring constant (F and k).
3) $F = -kx$. therefore $x = -F \div k$.
4) $x = -(500 \text{ N}) \div (1 \times 10^8 \text{ N/m})$
     $= -5 \times 10^{-6}$ m,
or five-millionths of a meter, much smaller than the thickness of a hair. This is why you do not notice deflections of solid materials except under very large forces.

Application: The Design of Structures

A structure is anything designed to withstand forces without breaking and without excessive deformation. We are surrounded by structures. A house is a structure, and so is a bridge, a building, a car, and almost every other object around you, even a tree. To design a structure, you first need to know what forces act and how, and where the forces are applied. The forces on a structure are found by applying the conditions of equilibrium. Most structures are designed to act in equilibrium, which means the structures are not accelerating. At least, they are not accelerating by coming apart!

A bridge is a simple structure

Consider the very simple structure of a bridge with two supports. To work, the bridge must bear weight—people, vehicles, animals—without breaking. The supports for the bridge must in turn be able to bear the weight of the bridge, to hold it up. Suppose there are 40 people on a bridge. Each person weighs 600 N and the bridge itself weighs 6,000 N. How strong must the bridge supports be?

Analysis of the forces

By drawing a free-body diagram, we can identify the forces which must be acting if the bridge is not moving (Figure 6.14). The downward force is 30,000 newtons, the weight of the people and bridge (40×600 N + 6,000 N). The upward force must be equal and opposite to the downward force in order to make the net force on the bridge zero. Each support must therefore be able to withstand a force of 15,000 newtons (3,370 pounds).

Engineering and technology

The analysis of forces in order to design structures is part of *mechanical engineering*. In a broad sense, engineering is the application of science to solving real-life problems, such as designing a bridge. A bridge and other inventions created by engineers are part of *technology*. From the invention of the plow to the computer, all technologies arise from someone's application of science to the solution of a practical problem.

Bridge

Free-body diagram

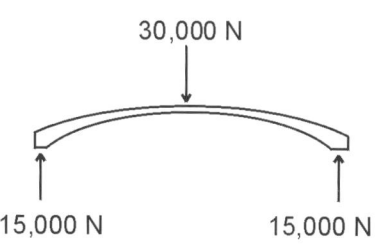

Figure 6.14: *A basic force analysis of a bridge. A more accurate analysis would allow for distributing the weight of the people unevenly all along the bridge instead of in the center.*

Science
Physics
Chemistry
Biology
Astronomy
Earth Science

Engineering
Mechanical engineer
Chemical engineer
Electrical engineer
Aerospace engineer
Civil engineer
Nuclear engineer

Technology
Automobile
Plastics
Telephone
Airplane
Suspension bridge
MRI scanner

The engineering design cycle

Design, prototype, test, then evaluate

The design of a bridge has many steps. The design starts with a concept that is an idea for how the bridge will be made. A prototype is constructed to test the bridge design. The prototype is tested to see if it works as designed. The test results are evaluated and used to correct any problems or improve the performance. The process of design-prototype-test-evaluate is called the engineering cycle (Figure 6.15). The most reliable technology goes through the cycle many times and each cycle leads to more improvements.

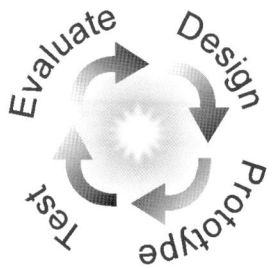

Figure 6.15: *The engineering design cycle is how an invention gets from concept to reality.*

A sample engineering problem

A small-scale project is a good illustration of the design cycle. Suppose you are given a box of toothpicks and some glue, and are assigned to build a bridge that will hold a 25-newton brick. After doing research, you come up with an idea for how to make the bridge. Your idea is to make the bridge from four structures connected together. Your structure is a truss because you have seen bridges that use trusses. Your idea is called a *conceptual design*.

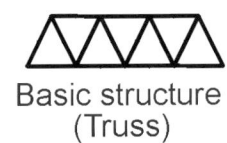

Basic structure (Truss)

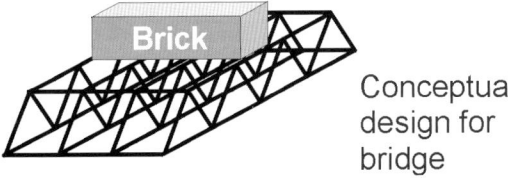

Conceptual design for bridge

The importance of a prototype

Your next step is to build a prototype and test it. If you can determine how much force it takes to break *one* structure, you would know if four structures will hold the brick. Your prototype should be close enough to the real-life bridge so that what you learn from testing can be applied to the final structure. For example, if your final bridge is to be made with round toothpicks, your prototype also has to be made with round toothpicks.

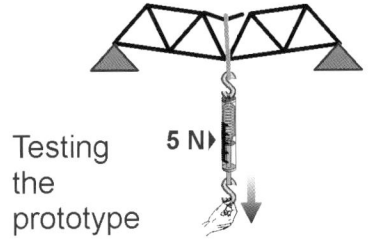

Testing the prototype

Testing the prototype

You test the prototype truss by applying more and more force until it breaks. You learn that your truss breaks at a force of 5 newtons. Since the brick weighs 25 newtons, four trusses are not enough. Based on the test results, your bridge design may be revised to use seven trusses instead of four (Figure 6.16). The *evaluation* of test results is a necessary part of any successful design. Testing identifies potential problems in the design in time to correct them.

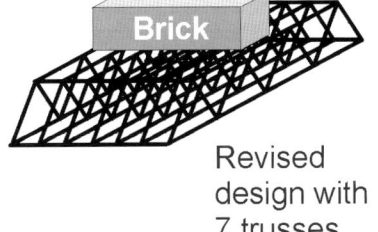

Revised design with 7 trusses

Figure 6.16: *Testing the prototype tells you if it is strong enough. Testing often leads to a revised design; above, for example, using more trusses.*

Chapter 6 Review

Vocabulary Review

Match the following terms with the correct definition. There is one extra definition in the list that will not match any of the terms.

Set One

1. air friction
2. normal force
3. weight
4. friction
5. viscous friction

a. A force created by the motion of objects through water or other fluids
b. A measure of how hard two surfaces are pushing against each other
c. A force that always acts in the direction in which an object is moving
d. A force created by air flowing around a moving object
e. A force caused by motion that always opposes the motion that caused it
f. The force with which gravity pulls on an object

Set Two

1. sliding friction
2. coefficient of friction
3. net force
4. gravity
5. rolling friction
6. static friction

a. The force that exists when one object rolls over another object
b. The force that exists when two surfaces try to move across each other but not enough force is applied to actually cause motion
c. The total of all the forces acting on an object
d. The ratio of friction force divided by normal force
e. The acceleration of an object on Earth
f. A force that is created between two surfaces sliding across each other
g. A force that pulls every mass toward every other mass

Set Three

1. spring constant
2. g force
3. free-body diagram
4. lubricant
5. deformation
6. dimension

a. A change in length due to extension or compression
b. Shows all of the forces acting on an object
c. Reduces friction
d. The force between compressed objects
e. The ratio of force to deformation for a spring
f. Perceived "force" felt by an accelerating object due to the object's own inertia
g. A direction

Concept review

1. Explain how an object's weight is related to its mass.

2. If you were to travel to the moon, where gravity is weaker than on Earth, would your weight be the same, or more, or less? Would your mass be the same, or more, or less?

3. What are the two ways a person could feel weightless?

4. A backpack has a weight of 85 N and is sitting on the floor. Describe what happens to the backpack in each case:

   a. You pull up on the backpack with a force of 50 N.

   b. You pull up on the backpack with a force of 85 N.

   c. You pull up on the backpack with a force of 86 N.

5. What is the cause of sliding friction?

6. If you are pulling a sled carrying your little brother to the right, in which direction is the force of friction on him? Which type of friction is involved?

7. How is static friction different from the other types of friction? How is it similar?

8. List the type of friction involved in each of the following cases:

   a. A soccer ball slows as it rolls on the grass.

   b. You drag a heavy backpack across a desk.

   c. A skydiver's parachute slows her descent.

   d. A piano stays at rest as you attempt to push it.

   e. A diver hits the surface of the water and comes to a stop before reaching the bottom of the pool.

9. The coefficient of friction is usually a number between ____ and ____.

10. Which is usually greater for a pair of surfaces, the coefficient of static friction or the coefficient of sliding friction? Why?

11. You push a heavy box with a force of 250 N, and it does not move. What is the force of static friction between the box and the floor?

12. List three ways to reduce friction between objects.

13. Give some examples of how friction is useful in our daily lives.

14. Read each statement and decide whether it is true or false:

    a. If an object is in equilibrium, then there can't be any forces acting on it.

    b. If an object is in equilibrium, then it must be at rest.

    c. If the net force on an object is zero, then it is in equilibrium.

15. You stretch a spring to the right. What is the direction of the force the spring exerts on your hand?

16. How is the force of a spring related to the distance it is extended or compressed?

17. What is the meaning of the negative sign in Hooke's law?

18. Which spring would be easier to stretch, one with a spring constant of 10 N/m or one with a spring constant of 30 N/m?

115

Problems

1. Calculate the weight of each of the following:

   a. A 60-kg person on Earth.

   b. A 4-kg cat on Earth.

   c. A 30-kg dog on Jupiter.

2. Calculate the mass of each of the following:

   a. A car that weighs 15,000 N on Earth.

   b. A frog that weighs 12 N on Jupiter.

3. Chris has a mass of 75 kg. He stands on a scale in an elevator that is accelerating downward at 4.9 m/sec^2. What force does the scale display in newtons?

4. Calculate the static friction between your sneakers (rubber) and the sidewalk (concrete) if your mass is 55 kg.

5. While vacuuming, you pull the sofa away from the wall. The sofa weighs 500 N, and the force of sliding friction between the sofa and the carpet is 200 N. Calculate the coefficient of sliding friction between the sofa and the carpet.

6. While ice skating, you push off of a wall with a force of 100 N. Calculate your acceleration if you have a mass of 50 kg and the coefficient of sliding friction between your skates and the ice is 0.10.

7. Draw the free-body diagram for each object:

   a. A 1-kg rock sitting on a table.

   b. A 500-N box at rest that you are pushing on with a force of 100 N.

   c. A 20-kg monkey hanging from a tree limb by both arms.

8. Two children are fighting over a toy. While holding onto the toy, Toni applies a force of 15 N to the right. Marie applies a force of 20 N to the left. The mass of the toy is 2.5 kg. Calculate the acceleration of the toy.

9. Calculate the size of the restoring force in each scenario:

   a. A spring with a spring constant of 20 N/m is stretched 0.5 m.

   b. A spring with a spring constant of 3 N/m is compressed 0.1 m.

   c. A wall with a spring constant of 5 x 10^7 N/m is compressed 1 × 10^{-5} m.

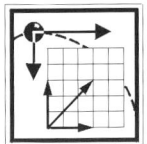

Unit 3

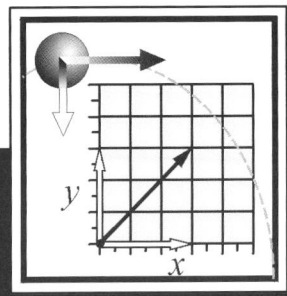

Motion and Force in 2 and 3 Dimensions

Chapter 7

Using Vectors: Motion and Force

Objectives for Chapter 7

By the end of this chapter you should be able to:

1. Add and subtract displacement vectors to describe changes in position.
2. Calculate the x and y components of a displacement, velocity, and force vector.
3. Write a velocity vector in polar and x-y coordinates.
4. Calculate the range of a projectile given the initial velocity vector.
5. Use force vectors to solve two-dimensional equilibrium problems with up to three forces.
6. Calculate the acceleration on an inclined plane when given the angle of incline.

Terms and vocabulary words

vector	scalar	magnitude	x-component	y-component
cosine	parabola	Pythagorean theorem	displacement	resultant
position	resolution	right triangle	sine	dynamics
tangent	normal force	projectile	trajectory	Cartesian coordinates
range	velocity vector	equilibrium	inclined plane	polar coordinates
scale	component			

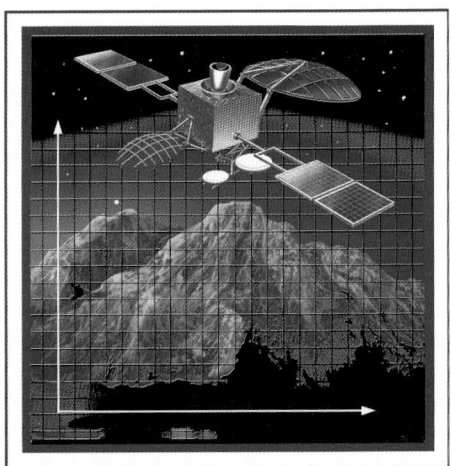

7.1 Vectors and Direction

When describing motion, direction is often important. A plane, boat, or car cannot get to its destination unless the driver has information about the direction she must travel. A vector is a quantity that includes information about direction. After reading this section, you will be able to draw and calculate the components of vectors and use vectors to solve problems involving motion and forces. You should also recognize the difference between vectors and scalars.

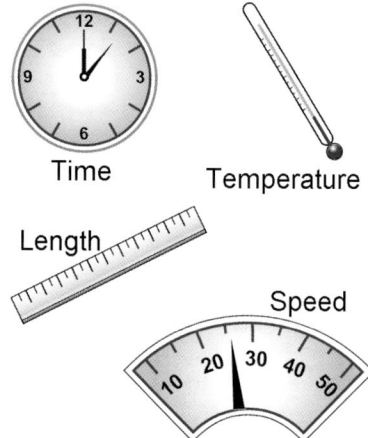

Figure 7.1: *Some examples of scalar quantities.*

Scalars and Vectors

Scalars have magnitude   A scalar is a quantity that can be completely described by one value: the magnitude. You can think of magnitude as size or amount, including units. Temperature is a good example of a scalar quantity (Figure 7.1). If you are sick and use a thermometer to measure your temperature, it might show 101°F. The magnitude of your temperature is 101, and degrees Fahrenheit is the unit of measurement. The value of 101°F is a complete description of the temperature because you do not need any more information.

Examples of scalars   Many other measurements are expressed as scalar quantities. If you compete in a race at a track meet, you use a scalar to express the length of the race. If you run 100 meters, the magnitude of the length of the race is 100, measured in the unit of meters. Afterward, you would also use a scalar to express your time for the race. A time of 11 seconds has a magnitude of 11 measured in the units of seconds. You might also use a scalar to express your average speed during the race.

Vectors have direction   Sometimes a single number does not include enough information to describe a measurement. The location of a place is an example where a single value, such as distance, is not enough to completely describe where the place is. For example, knowing a new pizza place is 1 kilometer away is not enough information to locate the place. You also need to know the direction. You *would* have enough information if you were told the place was 1 kilometer in a direction 40 degrees east of north (Figure 7.2). The information "1 kilometer 40 degrees east of north" is an example of a vector. A vector is a quantity that includes both magnitude and direction. Vectors require more than one number, which is one reason they are different from scalars.

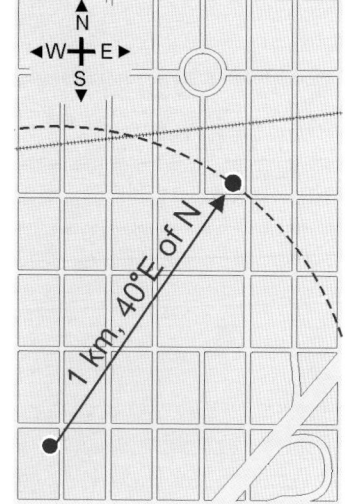

Figure 7.2: *A vector includes information about magnitude (distance) and direction.*

118

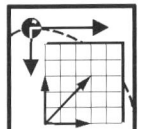
Drawing the displacement vector

Using a scale A vector can be represented with an arrow. The length of the arrow shows the magnitude of the vector, and the arrow points in the direction of the vector. When drawing a vector as an arrow you must choose a scale. For a walk in a field, an appropriate scale would be to let 1 centimeter represent 1 meter.

The displacement vector If you walk five meters east, your displacement can be represented by a 5 centimeter arrow pointing to the east (Figure 7.3). The displacement vector describes a change in position. Displacement vectors have units of distance.

Measuring displacement Suppose you walk 5 meters east, turn, go 8 meters north, then turn and go 3 meters west. Where are you relative to your starting point? You can represent each leg of the walk by a displacement vector. One vector starts at the end of the previous one, just like each leg of the walk starts at the end of the previous leg. The diagram below shows the trip as a sequence of three displacement vectors.

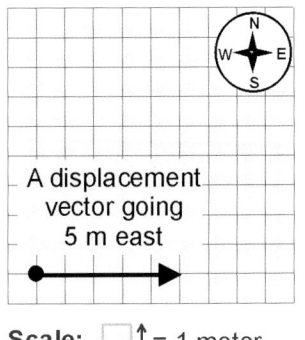

A displacement vector going 5 m east

Scale: ▯ ↕ = 1 meter

Figure 7.3: *A displacement vector that goes 5 meters east.*

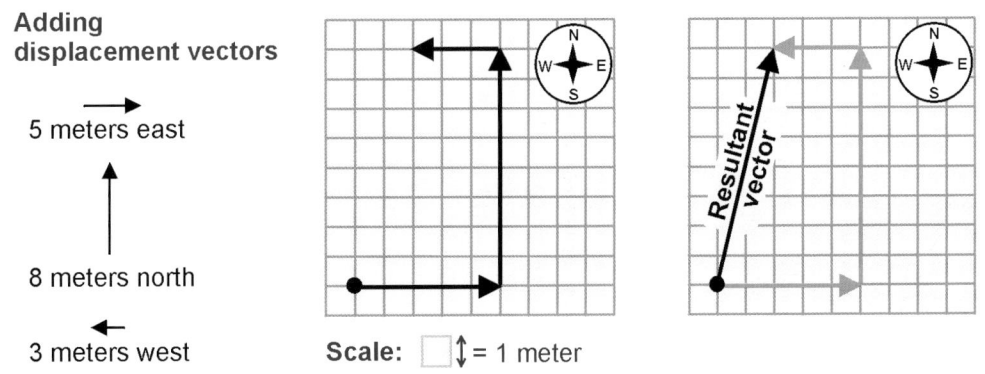

Adding displacement vectors

5 meters east

8 meters north

3 meters west

Scale: ▯ ↕ = 1 meter

Be careful adding vectors

You cannot usually add vectors like regular numbers. For example, if you simply added 5 m + 8 m + 3 m, the result is 16 m. This IS the distance you walked, but it is NOT your final position. When adding vectors, you must be careful to understand what you are trying to calculate. If the answer is position, you need to add displacement vectors, using a graph or by components. If the answer is the distance traveled, you can add the magnitudes of the displacement vectors and not worry about direction.

Drawing a resultant At the end of the trip, your position is 8 meters north and 2 meters east of where you started. In physics the position is where you are. The diagonal vector that connects the starting position with the final position is called the resultant. The resultant is the sum of two or more vectors added as shown in the diagram above. You could have walked a shorter distance by going 2 meters east and 8 meters north, and still ended up in the same place. The resultant shows the most direct line between the starting position and the final position.

Representing vectors with components

Adding vectors Drawing carefully scaled arrows to add vectors can be time-consuming. There is an easier way to add vectors mathematically. For example, suppose you walk 5 meters northeast, as shown in Figure 7.4. Notice that you end up in the exact same place as if you had walked 4 meters east then 3 meters north. In fact, every displacement vector in two dimensions can be represented by two vectors: a north-south vector, and an east-west vector. The process of describing a vector in terms of two perpendicular directions is called **resolution**.

Components of a vector The displacement vector can be written (4,3) m. The first number in the parentheses is a vector in the east-west direction and the second number is a vector in the north-south direction. The two perpendicular vectors are called **components** of the original vector. You actually walked the diagonal line but your displacement can be written as if you did the walk in two perpendicular segments.

Cartesian, or *x-y* coordinates To understand what component vectors mean, you have to know what *coordinate system* the components are referenced to. The example displacement of (4,3) m is in **Cartesian** coordinates. Cartesian coordinates are also known as *x-y* coordinates. Adding vectors is easiest in Cartesian coordinates.

x and y components The vector in the east-west direction is called the **x-component** because the *x*-axis on a graph represents the east-west direction. The *x*-component in Figure 7.4 is 4 m. The vector in the north-south direction is called the **y-component** because the *y*-axis on a graph usually represents the north-south direction. The *y*-component of the example is 3 m. The *x* and *y* components are also sometimes called horizontal and vertical components.

Polar coordinates The degrees on a compass are an example of a **polar** coordinate system. Polar coordinates use a length and an angle; for example, the same vector (4,3) m can be expressed as (5 m, 37°) which is 5 m at 37 degrees north of east (Figure 7.5). The angles in standard polar coordinates are given relative to the positive *x*-axis. Displacements on a map used for navigation are usually given in polar coordinates because they are the natural coordinate system for use with a compass. Vectors in polar coordinates are difficult to add and subtract, and are usually converted first to Cartesian coordinates.

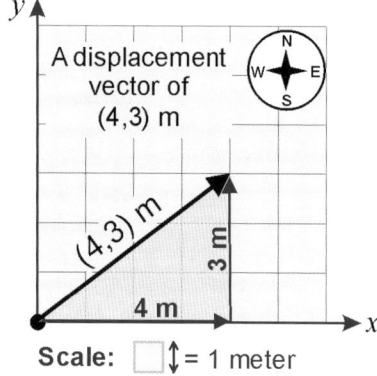

Figure 7.4: *The 5 m northeast vector has an east-west component of 3 m east and a north-south component of 4 m north.*

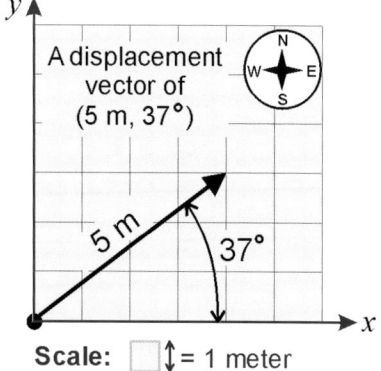

Figure 7.5: *A polar coordinate version of the same vector as above, in Figure 7.4.*

Adding and subtracting vectors

Symbols for vectors Vectors are indicated with arrows over the symbol for the variable. For example, the displacement vector is written as $\vec{x}$. The variable x without an arrow is the distance, and is *not* a vector. In this chapter, we will introduce vectors for several familiar variables, including displacement ($\vec{x}$), velocity ($\vec{v}$), and force ($\vec{F}$).

Adding vectors Writing vectors in components makes it much easier to add them. Suppose we take the example of page 119 (left). The first vector is 5 meters east. This can be written $\vec{x}_1 = (5,0)$ m. The 5 meters is the distance east and the 0 means there was no distance north. The next vector is $\vec{x}_2 = (0,8)$ m representing a distance of 8 meters north. The third vector is $\vec{x}_3 = (-3,0)$ m and the negative 3 meters indicates that the direction is west (not east). To get the resultant you just add the x components and y components separately: $\vec{x}_1 + \vec{x}_2 + \vec{x}_3 = (2,8)$ m. Adding numbers is easier and more accurate than drawing arrows on graph paper.

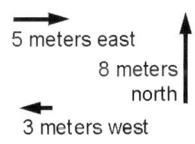
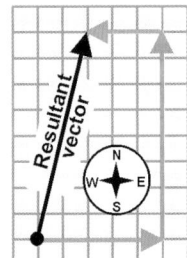

Adding component vectors $\vec{x} = \vec{x}_1 + \vec{x}_2 + \vec{x}_3$

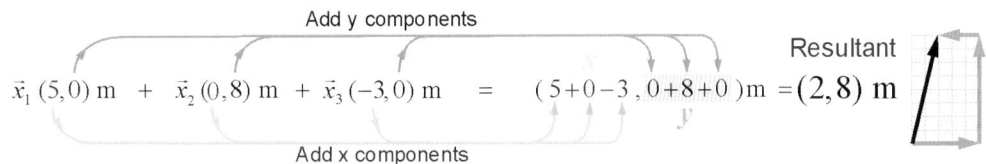

Subtracting vectors To subtract one vector from another vector, you subtract the components. To see how this works, consider the two vectors, $\vec{x}_1 = (4,3)$ m, and $\vec{x}_2 = (0,1)$ m. When the vectors are subtracted, $\vec{x}_1 - \vec{x}_2 = (4,2)$ m. Subtracting vectors is equivalent to going backward for the vector being subtracted.

Subtracting component vectors $\vec{x} = \vec{x}_1 - \vec{x}_2$

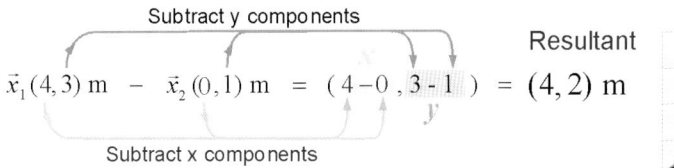

Calculate a resultant vector by adding components

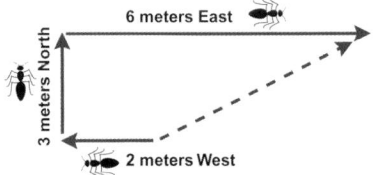

Example: An ant walks 2 meters west, 3 meters north, and 6 meters east. What is the displacement of the ant?

1) You are asked for the resultant vector.
2) You are given three displacement vectors.
3) Make a sketch of the ant's path, and add the displacement vectors by components.
4) Solve:

$\vec{x}_1 = (-2,0)$ m
$\vec{x}_2 = (0,3)$ m
$\vec{x}_3 = (6,0)$ m

$\vec{x}_1 + \vec{x}_2 + \vec{x}_3 = (-2+6,3)$ m
$= (4,3)$ m

The final displacement is 4 meters east and 3 meters north from where the ant started.

Calculating vector components

Adding vectors Finding the components of a vector is easy when the vector points in one of the four compass directions (along the x- or y-axis). Finding the components of a vector at an angle requires using the properties of triangles. Any displacement vector can be represented on a graph by a triangle with two sides parallel to the x- and y-axes, as shown in Figure 7.6.

Finding components graphically To find components graphically, draw a displacement vector as an arrow of appropriate length at the specified angle. For example, Figure 7.6 shows how to draw a displacement vector $\vec{x} = (5\ \text{m}, 37°)$. A protractor is used to mark the angle and a ruler to draw the arrow. The x-component of the vector is the projection of the arrow along the x-axis. The y-component is the projection along the y-axis.

Finding components mathematically Finding components using trigonometry is quicker and more accurate than the graphical method. The variable r is used to represent the length of the vector. The angle is represented with the symbol θ. The triangle is a right triangle since the sides are parallel to the x- and y-axes. The ratios of the sides of a right triangle are determined by the angle. These ratios are called sine and cosine. The sine of the angle is the ratio y/r where y is the y-component of the vector. The cosine of the angle is the ratio x/r where x is the x-component of the vector. Both the sine and cosine are between 0 and 1 and are built into scientific calculators (see sidebar).

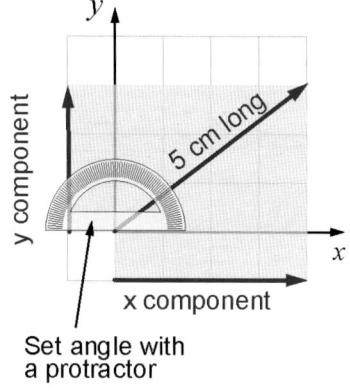

Figure 7.6: *The triangle formed by the displacement vector (4,3) m.*

Sine and cosine on a calculator

Scientific calculators have buttons that calculate the sine and cosine of angles. For example, to calculate the sine of 37 degrees on most calculators, you use the following sequence:

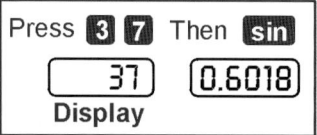

The sine of 37 degrees is 0.6018. On most calculators you do not have to press the equals (=) button to calculate the trigonometric functions.

Finding the components of a vector

Vector	Triangle	Relationships	Components
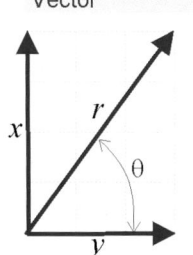	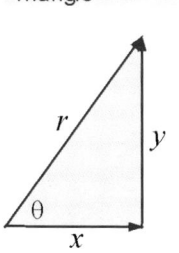	$\sin\theta = \dfrac{y}{r}$	$y = r\sin\theta$
		$\cos\theta = \dfrac{x}{r}$	$x = r\cos\theta$
		$\tan\theta = \dfrac{y}{x}$	

122

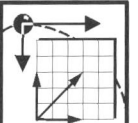
Finding the magnitude of a vector

$a^2 + b^2 = c^2$ When you know the *x*- and *y*- components of a vector, you can find the magnitude using the Pythagorean theorem. This useful theorem states that $a^2 + b^2 = c^2$, where *a, b,* and *c* are the lengths of the sides of any right triangle. For example, suppose you need to know the distance represented by the displacement vector (4,3). If you walked east 4 meters then north 3 meters, you would walk a total of seven meters. This is a distance, but it is not the distance specified by the vector, or the shortest way to go. The vector (4,3) m describes a single straight line. The length of the line is 5 meters because $4^2 + 3^2 = 5^2$.

The Pythagorean theorem

$$a^2 + b^2 = c^2$$

a and *b* are the lengths of the short sides of a right triangle.

c is the length of the side opposite the right angle.

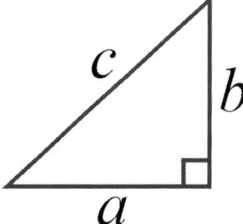

Finding the angle of a vector

In some problems, you know the sides of the triangle but want to find the angle. The inverse sine is a function that gives you the angle if you know the ratio y/r. The inverse tangent gives the angle if you know the ratio y/x.
A calculator can also do the inverse of the sine, cosine, or tangent. For example, suppose you have a vector where *y* = 3 and *x* = 4. That makes the tangent 0.75 (3/4).

What is the angle?

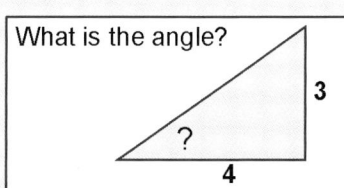

Calculators either have an INV (inverse) key or a tan⁻¹ key. Depending on your calculator, one of the following sequences of buttons should work.

Find two vectors that have a certain resultant

Robots are programmed to move with vectors. A robot must be told exactly how far to go and in which direction for every step of a trip. A trip of many steps is communicated to the robot as a series of vectors. A mail-delivery robot needs to get from where it is to the mail bin on the map. Find a sequence of two displacement vectors that will allow the robot to avoid hitting the desk in the middle.

1) You are asked to find two displacement vectors.
2) You are given the starting and final positions.
3) The resultant vector must go from the start to the final position.
4) Solve:
    The robot starts at (1,1) m and the mail bin is at (5,5) m. The displacement required is (5,5) m - (1,1) m = (4,4) m. First go up 4 meters, then over 4 meters.
    $\vec{x}_1 = (0,4)$ m, $\vec{x}_2 = (4,0)$ m
    Check the resultant: (4,0) m + (0,4) m = (4,4) m

Distances in meters

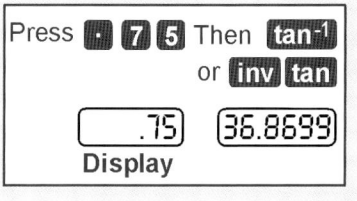

Press `.` `7` `5` Then `tan⁻¹` or `inv` `tan`

7.2 Projectile Motion and the Velocity Vector

Imagine that you are watching a game of basketball. A player must decide how fast and at what angle to throw the ball in order to score. The ball starts moving upward at an angle. Then it moves downward at an angle toward the basket. As the ball moves, its velocity changes direction, first pointing upward, then downward. This section is about the velocity vector, which describes both the speed of the ball and its direction of motion. The velocity vector of a thrown ball follows a very predictable curve under the influence of gravity. This section will explain why a ball follows a curved path and how you can determine exactly where it will land.

Projectiles and trajectories

Definition of projectile
Any object that is moving through the air affected only by gravity is called a **projectile**. Examples of projectiles include a basketball thrown toward the basket, a car driven off a cliff by a stunt person, and a skier going off a jump. Flying objects such as airplanes and birds are not projectiles because they are affected by forces from their own power, and not just the force of gravity.

Trajectories
The path a projectile follows is called its **trajectory**. The trajectory of a thrown basketball follows a special type of arch-shaped curve called a **parabola** (Figure 7.7). A projectile launched at a steep angle will result in a tall and narrow parabola. A wide and low parabola results from a launch at an angle close to the horizontal. The distance a projectile travels horizontally is called its **range**. The range of a projectile depends on its initial angle, speed and height of the ground.

The velocity vector
The **velocity vector** is the speed and direction of the motion at a point along the trajectory (Figure 7.8). The velocity vector changes as the ball moves and both the speed and direction are different at different places along the trajectory. To calculate the motion of a projectile, we first must develop a way to work with the velocity vector.

Friction
An object's trajectory is not always a perfect parabola. Air resistance and other forms of friction add additional forces. To keep things clear, this section will assume air resistance and other forms of friction are minimal and can be ignored.

Figure 7.7: *When you throw a ball, it follows a curved path called a parabola.*

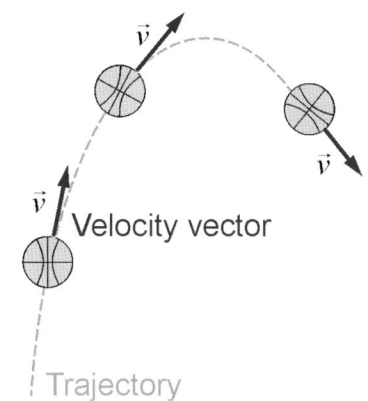

Figure 7.8: *The velocity vector usually changes its direction and its magnitude all along the trajectory of a projectile.*

124

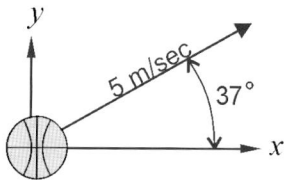
The velocity vector

What the velocity vector means

The velocity vector ($\vec{v}$) is a way to precisely describe the speed and direction of motion. For example, suppose a ball is launched at 5 meters per second at an angle of 37 degrees (Figure 7.9). At the moment after launch the velocity vector for the ball in polar coordinates is written: $\vec{v} = (5 \text{ m/sec}, 37°)$. In x-y components, the same velocity vector is written as $\vec{v} = (4, 3)$ m/sec. Both representations tell you exactly how fast and in what direction the ball is moving at that moment.

Speed is the magnitude of the velocity vector

The *magnitude* of the velocity vector is the *speed* of the object, which is 5 m/sec in the example. The speed is represented by a lower case *v* *without* the arrow. When a velocity vector is represented graphically, the lengths are proportional to speed, not distance. For example, the graph in Figure 7.10 shows the velocity vector $\vec{v} = (4, 3)$ m/sec as an arrow on a graph.

Interpreting the x-y components of velocity

If there were no gravity, the ball would continue with the same initial velocity. For every 5 meters the ball moves along the 37 degree direction, it also moves 4 meters along x and 3 meters along y. The ball moves on the 5 m/sec arrow in Figure 7.10, but it is useful to *think* about the motion as being separated into a speed along x and a different speed along y. When written as $\vec{v} = (4, 3)$ m/sec, the components are really just a mathematical way to separate the velocity into individual speeds in the x and y directions.

Two ways to write a velocity vector

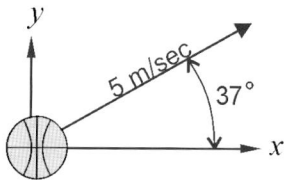

$\vec{v} = (5 \text{ m/sec}, 37°)$

$\vec{v} = (4, 3) \text{ m/sec}$

Figure 7.9: *Different ways to write a velocity vector.*

Draw a velocity vector and calculate its magnitude (speed)

Draw the velocity vector $\vec{v} = (5, 5)$ m/sec and calculate the magnitude of the velocity (the speed), using the Pythagorean theorem.

1) You are asked to sketch a velocity vector and calculate its magnitude (speed).
2) You are given the x-y component form of the velocity.
3) Set a scale of 1 cm = 1 m/sec to draw the sketch.
   The Pythagorean theorem says $a^2 + b^2 = c^2$.
4) Solve:

$$v^2 = (5 \text{ m/sec})^2 + (5 \text{ m/sec})^2 = 50 \text{ m}^2/\text{sec}^2$$

$$v = \sqrt{50 \text{ m}^2/\text{sec}^2} = 7.07 \text{ m/sec}$$

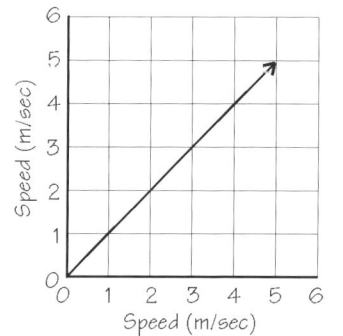

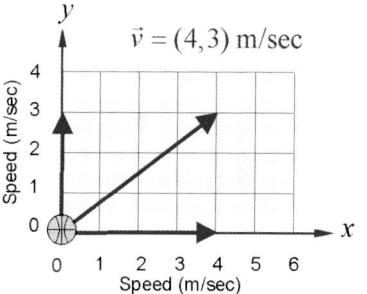

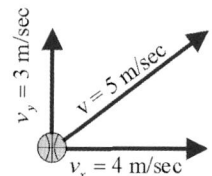

Figure 7.10: *Drawing and interpreting a velocity vector.*

The components of the velocity vector

Writing a velocity vector Velocity vectors are broken into components just like displacement vectors. For example, suppose a car is driving 20 meters per second in a direction as shown on the map in Figure 7.11. The direction of the vector is 127 degrees. The polar representation of the velocity is $\vec{v} = (20$ m/sec, $127°)$.

Calculating x and y components In x-y form, a velocity vector is written $\vec{v} = (v_x, v_y)$ where v_x and v_y are the x and y components. The magnitude of the vector is the speed, v, without the arrow. You can take any velocity vector and make a triangle for which the legs of the triangle are the components (v_x and v_y) and the long side (hypotenuse) of the triangle is the speed (v). For drawing the triangle, the angle is $180°-127°$, or $53°$. The sine, cosine, and tangent of the angle are ratios of v_x, v_y, and v as shown below. The ratios can be rearranged to solve for the components.

$\vec{v} = (20$ m/sec, $127°)$

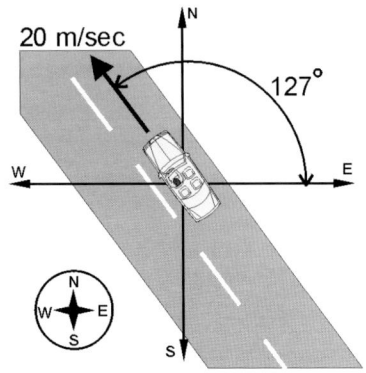

Figure 7.11: *A car driving with a velocity of 20 m/sec at 127 degrees.*

Finding the components of a velocity vector

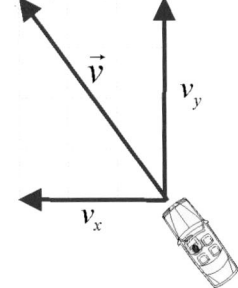

Analysis	Relationships	Application

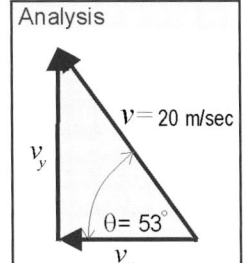

$\sin\theta = \dfrac{v_y}{v}$ → $v_y = v\sin\theta$

$\cos\theta = \dfrac{v_x}{v}$ → $v_x = -v\cos\theta$

$\tan\theta = \dfrac{v_y}{v_x}$

$$v_y = (20 \text{ m/sec})\sin 53° = 16 \text{ m/sec}$$
$$v_x = -(20 \text{ m/sec})\cos 53° = -12 \text{ m/sec}$$

$$\vec{v} = (-12, 16) \text{ m/sec}$$

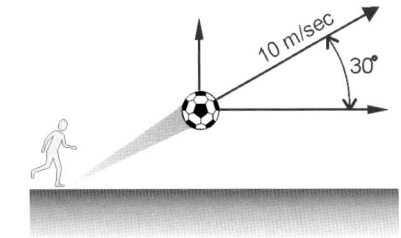

Figure 7.12: *The velocity of a soccer ball kicked at an angle.*

Calculate the components of a velocity vector

A soccer ball is kicked at a speed of 10 m/s and an angle of 30 degrees (Figure 7.12). Find the horizontal and vertical components of the ball's initial velocity.

1) You are asked to calculate the components of the velocity vector.
2) You are given the initial speed and angle.
3) Draw a diagram and use $v_x = v\cos\theta$ and $v_y = v\sin\theta$.
4) Solve: $v_x = (10$ m/s$)(\cos 30°) = (10$ m/s$)(0.87) = 8.7$ m/s
   $v_y = (10$ m/s$)(\sin 30°) = (10$ m/s$)(0.5) = 5$ m/s

Adding velocity vectors *Advanced topic*

Why you might add velocity vectors There are circumstances where the total velocity of an object is a combination of velocities. One example is the motion of a boat on a river. The boat moves with a certain velocity relative to the water. The water is also moving with another velocity relative to the land. The velocity of the boat *relative to the land* is the sum of the boat's velocity relative to the water plus the water's velocity relative to the land. A similar situation applies to aircraft flying in a wind.

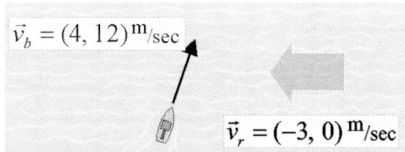

To calculate the resultant velocity ...

Add components

$v_x = 4 - 3 = 1$ m/sec
$v_y = 12 + 0 = 12$ m/sec

$\vec{v} = (1,\ 12)$ m/sec

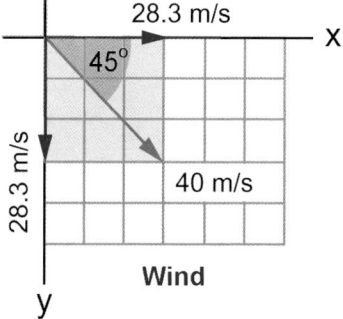

Figure 7.13: *Finding components of the engine's velocity*

An example of adding velocity vectors Velocity vectors are added by components, just like displacement vectors. To calculate a resultant velocity, add the *x* components separately and the *y* components separately. For example, suppose a boat is moving with a velocity of $\vec{v}_b = (4,12)$ m/sec. The river is moving with a velocity of $\vec{v}_r = (-3,0)$ m/sec. The resultant velocity of the boat is $\vec{v} = (1,12)$ m/sec. Any boat traveling across a current must steer slightly upstream to compensate for the velocity of the water.

Calculate the components of a velocity vector

An airplane is moving at a velocity of 100 m/s in a direction 30 degrees NE relative to the air. The wind is blowing 40 m/s in a direction 45 degrees SE relative to the ground. Find the resultant velocity of the airplane relative to the ground.
1) You are asked to calculate the resultant velocity vector.
2) You are given the plane's velocity and the wind velocity.
3) Draw diagrams and add the components to get the resultant velocity.
4) Figure 7.13 shows the plane velocity vector.
$v_x = 100 \cos 30^\circ = 86.6$ m/sec, $\quad v_y = 100 \sin 30^\circ = 50$ m/sec
Figure 7.14 shows the wind velocity vector.
$v_x = 40 \cos 45^\circ = 28.3$ m/sec, $\quad v_y = -40 \sin 45^\circ = -28.3$ m/sec

The resultant $\vec{v} = (86.6 + 28.3, 50 - 28.3) = (114.9, 21.7)$ m/sec.

Figure 7.14: *Finding components of the wind's velocity*

Gravity only accelerates vertical motion	At the start of the chapter, we set out to understand projectile motion. For a projectile, the force of gravity makes one direction of motion different from another. Motion that is up or down is changed by the acceleration of gravity. Motion that is sideways is not similarly affected. Because gravity acts differently on vertical and horizontal motion, it is useful to separate motion into components that are vertical and horizontal.
Independence of horizontal and vertical motion	Once a velocity vector has been separated, the horizontal and vertical components can be analyzed independent of each other. This means that the horizontal velocity has no effect on the vertical velocity and vice-versa. What was a complicated, curved problem in x and y becomes two separate, straight-line problems, one in x and the other in y. These separate problems may be solved by the methods of Chapters 3 and 4. The way to analyze projectile motion is to *consider vertical and horizontal directions separately.*
Horizontal motion	Consider a ball that rolls off a table with a velocity of 5 meters per second. Once it leaves the table, the ball is a projectile because it feels only the influence of gravity. The horizontal velocity of a projectile remains constant during the entire time it is in the air because no horizontal force acts on it (ignoring air friction). Since there is no force, the horizontal acceleration is zero ($a_x = 0$). That means the ball will keep moving to the right at 5 meters per second (Figure 7.15). The horizontal distance a projectile moves can be calculated according to the formula:

Horizontal distance
projectile motion

x component of initial velocity (m/sec)

distance in x (m) $x = v_{ox}t$ ← Time in flight (sec)

Keeping track of variable names	To keep track of things, the velocity components are labeled with subscripts for x and y, and also for initial values. For example, the variable v_{ox} is the x component of the initial velocity vector $\vec{v}_0 = (v_{ox}, v_{oy})$. When solving projectile motion problems, there get to be many letters to keep track of. The key is to be very organized about writing down what each variable means, and *always write the subscripts* or you will lose track of what is what and quickly become confused.

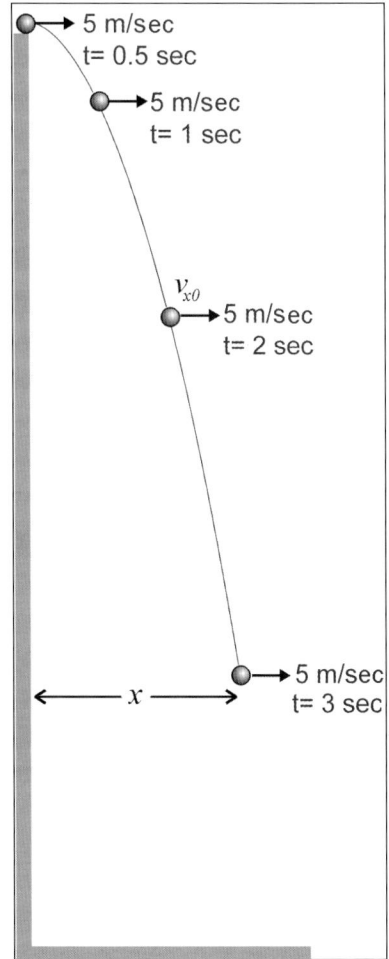

Figure 7.15: *The ball's horizontal velocity remains constant while it falls because gravity does not exert any horizontal force.*

Vertical motion *Advanced Topic*

Vertical motion Analyzing the vertical motion of a projectile is more complicated because gravity accelerates objects in the vertical direction. This motion is the same as that of an object in free fall. The ball's vertical speed changes by 9.8 m/sec each second.

Vertical velocity
projectile motion

$$v_y = v_{oy} - gt$$

Vertical distance
projectile motion

$$y = v_{oy}t - \frac{1}{2}gt^2$$

y	Distance in y (m)
v_y	y component of velocity (m/sec)
v_{oy}	y component of <u>initial</u> velocity (m/sec)
g	Acceleration of gravity (9.8 m/sec²)
t	Time in flight (sec)

$v_{oy} = 0$

$t = 1$ sec

v_y

9.8 m/sec

$t = 2$ sec

v_y

19.6 m/sec

y

$t = 3$ sec

v_y

29.4 m/sec

These are the same as the free fall equations If you look back to Chapter 4, you will recognize that these are the exact same equations we derived for free fall. We can use them again for the vertical motion of a projectile because the horizontal and vertical components of the motion can be separated.

When the initial vertical velocity is zero The simplest type of projectile motion involves an object launched horizontally, like a stunt car driving off a cliff. When the car leaves the edge of the cliff, its initial velocity is entirely horizontal. Therefore, the initial vertical velocity component is zero.

Analyze a horizontally launched projectile

A stunt driver steers a car off a cliff at a speed of 20 meters per second. He lands in the lake below two seconds later. Find the height of the cliff and the horizontal distance the car travels.

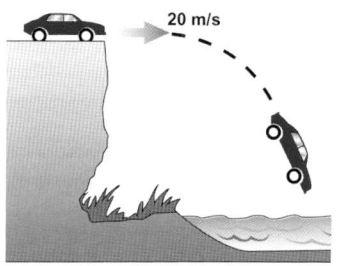

20 m/s

1) You are asked for the vertical and horizontal distances.
2) You know the initial speed and the time.
3) Relationships that apply:
   $y = v_{oy}t - 1/2\ gt^2$, $x = v_{ox}t$
4) The car goes off the cliff horizontally, so $v_{oy} = 0$
   $y = -(1/2)(9.8m/s^2)(2\ s)^2$
   $= -19.6$ meters.
   The negative sign shows the car is below its starting height.
   Use $x = v_{ox}t$, to find the horizontal distance.
   $x = (20\ m/s)(2\ s)$
   $= 40$ meters

Vertical velocity depends on launch speed and angle

A soccer ball kicked off the ground is also a projectile, but it starts with an initial velocity that has vertical and horizontal components. The launch angle determines how the initial velocity divides between vertical (y) and horizontal (x) directions. A projectile launched at a steep angle will have a large vertical velocity component and a small horizontal velocity. One launched at a low angle will have a large horizontal velocity component and a small vertical one (Figure 7.16).

Calculating velocity components

The initial velocity components of an object launched at a velocity $\vec{v}_0$ and angle θ are found by breaking the velocity into x and y components.

Components of initial velocity

$$v_{ox} = v_o \cos\theta \qquad v_{oy} = v_o \sin\theta$$

v_o	Magnitude of initial velocity (m/sec)
v_{ox}	x component of initial velocity (m/sec)
v_{oy}	y component of initial velocity (m/sec)
θ	Launch angle (degrees)

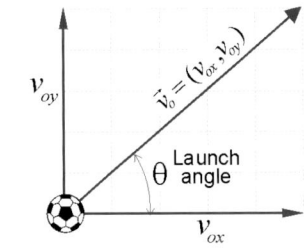

Vertical velocity is zero at the top

The vertical velocity of an upwardly launched projectile decreases by 9.8 meters per second each second as the object moves upward. Eventually, the vertical velocity reaches zero, and the object starts to move downward. At the top of the trajectory, the vertical velocity is zero. This does not mean the projectile has stopped moving at this point. It is still moving horizontally at the same speed it was initially.

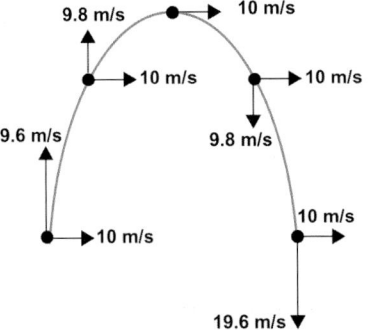

Vertical velocity along the trajectory

As the object begins to fall, its vertical velocity increases at the same rate with which it decreased. The trajectory is symmetric, and the time the projectile takes to move upward is the same as the time it takes to move downward. When it falls to its launch height, the projectile is moving at the same speed as when it was launched, but it is moving in a different direction.

Components of initial velocity

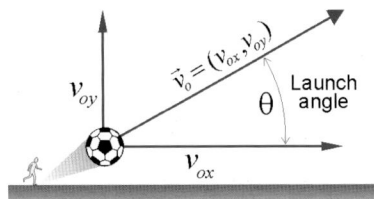

Steep angle

v_{oy} much *larger* than v_{ox} makes a high trajectory

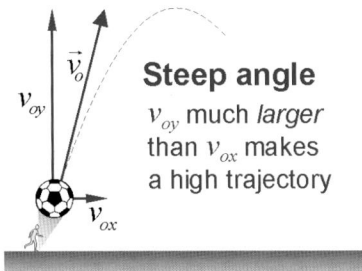

Shallow angle

v_{oy} much *smaller* than v_{ox} makes a low trajectory

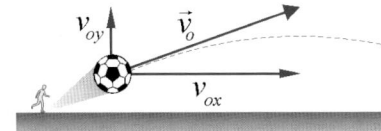

Figure 7.16: *The trajectory depends on the balance of vertical and horizontal velocity components. This balance is determined by the launch angle.*

130

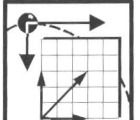

Range of projectiles *Advanced Topic*

Range increases as velocity squared

The range, or horizontal distance, traveled by a projectile depends on the launch speed and the launch angle. The greater the launch speed, the greater the range a projectile will have at a specific angle. The launch range is proportional to the square of the velocity. Doubling the launch speed quadruples the range of the projectile. This means a football kicked at 10 meters per second will travel four times as far as one kicked at the same angle at 5 meters per second.

Calculating the range

The range of a projectile is calculated from the horizontal velocity and the time of flight. The vertical velocity is responsible for giving the projectile its air time. The time of flight is twice the time it takes the projectile to reach the top of its trajectory, where $v_y = 0$. A projectile travels farthest when launched at 45 degrees. At this angle, its velocity is evenly divided between horizontal and vertical.

Range of a projectile

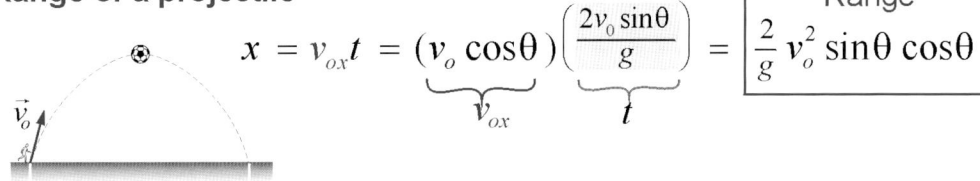

$$x = v_{ox}t = (v_o \cos\theta)\left(\frac{2v_0 \sin\theta}{g}\right) = \frac{2}{g}v_o^2 \sin\theta \cos\theta$$

Different launch angles can have the same range

The more the launch angle varies from 45 degrees, the smaller the range. A projectile launched at 30 degrees will have the same range as one launched at 60 degrees, because both angles are 15 degrees from 45. A projectile launched at 30 degrees has a fast horizontal velocity but a short air time. The projectile launched at 60 degrees has a long air time but a slow horizontal velocity. As a result, they have the same range. This holds true for any pair of angles adding to 90.

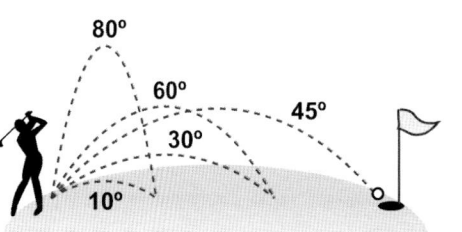

Hang time

If you have ever watched a skilled basketball player take a leap toward the basket, you have probably thought he or she seemed almost to float through the air for a period of time. That time spent in the air is called hang time.

You can easily calculate your own hang time. Run toward a doorway and jump as high as you can, touching the wall or door frame. Have someone watch to see exactly how high you reach. Measure this distance with a meter stick.

The vertical distance formula can be rearranged to solve for time:

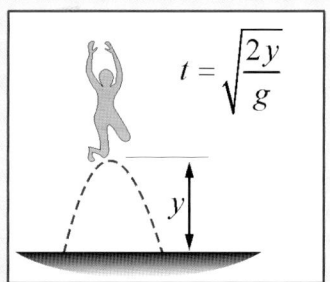

$$t = \sqrt{\frac{2y}{g}}$$

Plug in your jump height in meters for y and solve for the time. This represents the time you move upward; double it to find your hang time.

7.3 Forces in Two Dimensions *Advanced topic*

A block at rest on a level, flat table will remain motionless. A block on a frictionless slope will begin to slide immediately as you let it go. In both cases gravity is pulling on the block with a force equal to its weight. But the *effect* of gravity is different in the two scenarios. The effect is different because force is a vector, and the relationship between force and motion is a relationship between vectors. This section first explores the force vector and then describes an example of how the force vector is used to solve the problem of motion down a ramp.

The force vector

What the force vector means

The force vector ($\vec{F}$) is a way to precisely describe the strength and direction of a force. For example, suppose you push against a block with a force of 35 newtons at an angle of 30 degrees from the horizontal (Figure 7.17). Some of your force accelerates the block, and some of your force pushes the block into the table. The force is most accurately described as a vector. Like other vectors, $\vec{F}$ can be written in polar coordinates: $\vec{F} = (35$ N, $-30°)$. The force can also be written in x-y components: $\vec{F} = (30.3, -17.5)$ N. Both representations tell you exactly how strong the force is and in what direction it is pushing.

The magnitude of the force vector

The magnitude of the force vector is the *strength* of the force. In the example, the magnitude is 35 newtons. Like other vectors, the magnitude is related to the x and y components by the Pythagorean theorem: $a^2 + b^2 = c^2$. For the example force in Figure 7.18, the calculation is: $35^2 = 30.3^2 + 17.5^2$. The magnitude of the force is represented by a capital letter F, but *without* the arrow. When a force vector is represented graphically, the length is proportional to the magnitude of the force.

Interpreting the x-y components of force

The x and y components of a force vector can be thought of as actual forces. In fact, if the x and y component forces were applied along their appropriate axes, their effect would be *exactly the same as the single force* (Figure 7.18). You can think of the single force as the *resultant* of adding the component forces together. In many problems, the solution can be found by breaking forces up into components and analyzing each direction separately, just as with projectile motion.

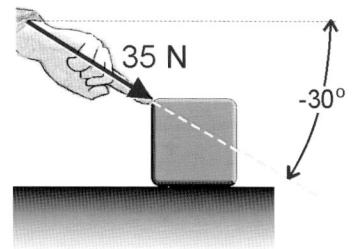

Force vector
(polar coordinates)

$$\vec{F} = (35 \text{ N}, -30°)$$

Figure 7.17: *Like other vectors, force can be represented in polar coordinates.*

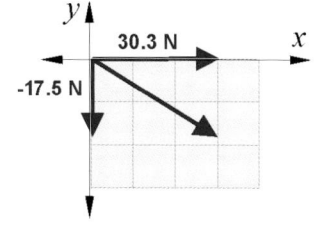

Force vector
(x-y components)

$$\vec{F} = (30.3, -17.5)\text{ N}$$

Figure 7.18: *Force can also be represented in x-y components.*

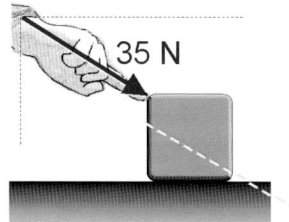

Equilibrium of forces *Advanced topic*

Balanced forces If an object is in equilibrium, all of the forces acting on it are balanced and the net force is zero. If the forces act in two dimensions, then all of the forces in the x-direction and y-direction balance *separately*. As you may have guessed, the word *separately* means the forces in the x direction must total to zero *and* the forces in the y direction must total to zero.

Example of equilibrium To do a force balance, all forces must be represented in x-y components. For example, imagine a gymnast with a weight of 700 newtons who is supporting himself on two rings with his arms straight below his shoulders. If he is at rest, and therefore in equilibrium, the net force on his body is zero. Gravity pulls down with a force of 700 N, so the ropes must pull up on his arms with a total force of 700 N. Each arm holds half of his weight, or 350 N (Figure 7.19).

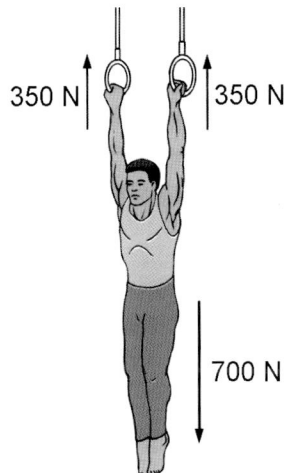

Forces applied at an angle It is much more difficult for a gymnast to hold his arms out at a 45-degree angle. To see why, consider that each arm must still support 350 newtons vertically to balance the force of gravity. When the gymnast's arms are at an angle, only part of the force from each arm is vertical. The total force must be larger because the vertical *component* of force in each arm must still equal half his weight.

Calculating the total force The total force in each arm is the magnitude (F) of the force vector ($\vec{F}$). The vertical component (F_y) at 45 degrees must be 350 N. The diagram below shows how to use the y-component to find the total force in the gymnast's left arm.

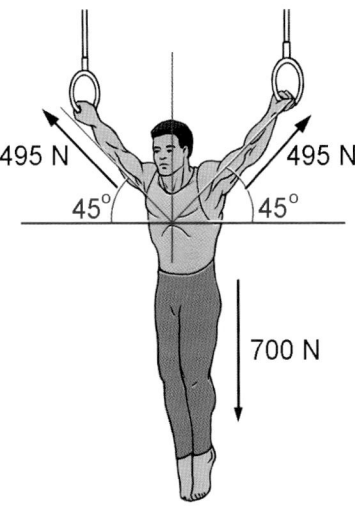

Components of a force vector

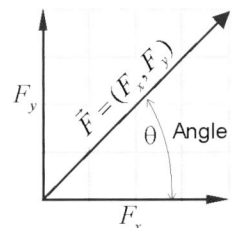

$F_x = F\cos\theta$

$F_y = F\sin\theta$

Equilibrium in y-direction (vertical)

$350\ N = F_y$

$= F\sin\theta$

$F = \dfrac{350N}{\sin 45°} = 495\ N$

The force in the right arm must also be 495 newtons because it also has a vertical component of 350 N (Figure 7.19). Although it is not shown, the horizontal components of force from right and left arms cancel each other because they have equal magnitude and are in opposite directions.

Figure 7.19: *A gymnast holding himself in equilibrium must use greater force to keep his arms at 45 degrees than is needed in keeping them vertical.*

The inclined plane

Definition of inclined plane An inclined plane is a straight surface, usually with a slope. A wood ramp is a good example of an inclined plane. The angle of the incline is the angle relative to the horizontal direction (Figure 7.20). When objects move along an incline they move parallel to the surface.

Forces on an inclined plane Consider a block sliding down a ramp. There are three forces that act on the block. These three forces are always present with any inclined plane. The three forces are: gravity (weight), the reaction force from the surface acting on the block, and friction. Motion along the ramp depends on the sum of these three forces. Because the ramp is usually at an angle, the three forces must be treated as vectors.

Choosing coordinates along the ramp The best coordinates to use for an inclined plane are aligned with the surface, and not with gravity (Figure 7.21). This is because any motion must occur parallel to the surface. By lining up the coordinates with the incline, motion in the x direction is along the surface. There is usually no motion in the y direction, because it would mean lifting off or going through the ramp.

Resolving the weight vector in ramp coordinates The force of gravity on an object always acts in a direction toward the center of the Earth. When the surface is a ramp, the direction of gravity is still straight toward the ground but is *not* perpendicular to the surface of the ramp. To treat the force of gravity, it must be resolved into components parallel (x) and perpendicular (y) to the ramp. If the angle of incline is theta (θ), then the weight of the block is represented by the vector $\vec{F}_w = (mg \sin\theta, mg \cos\theta)$.

An inclined plane

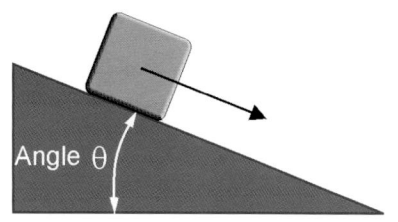

Figure 7.20: *A ramp is an example of an inclined plane.*

Coordinates for an inclined plane

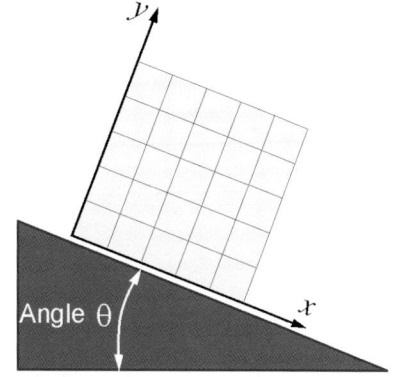

Figure 7.21: *Choosing coordinates along the incline.*

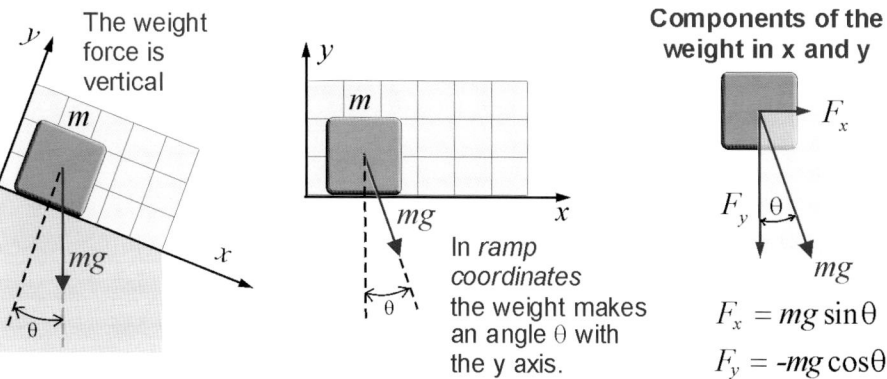

The weight force is vertical

In *ramp coordinates* the weight makes an angle θ with the y axis.

Components of the weight in x and y

$F_x = mg \sin\theta$

$F_y = -mg \cos\theta$

134

Resolution of forces on an inclined plane *Advanced topic*

Force along the incline — A block accelerates down a ramp because its weight creates a force parallel to the incline. If the ramp is analyzed as shown in Figure 7.22, the force parallel to the surface (F_x) is given by $F_x = mg \sin\theta$.

Normal force — When discussing forces, the word "normal" means "perpendicular to." For a block on a ramp, equilibrium of forces perpendicular to the ramp surface is what prevents the block from going through the ramp or lifting off it. The normal force acting on the block is the reaction force from the weight of the block pressing against the ramp. To make equilibrium in the y-direction, the normal force on the block is equal and opposite to the component of the block's weight perpendicular to the ramp (F_y). The diagram below shows that the normal force acting on the block (F_N) is equal to $+mg\cos\theta$.

Force parallel to ramp

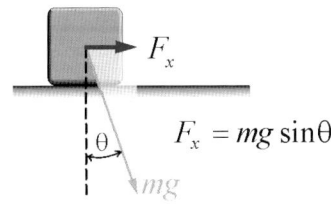

$F_x = mg \sin\theta$

Figure 7.22: *The force parallel to the ramp (F_x).*

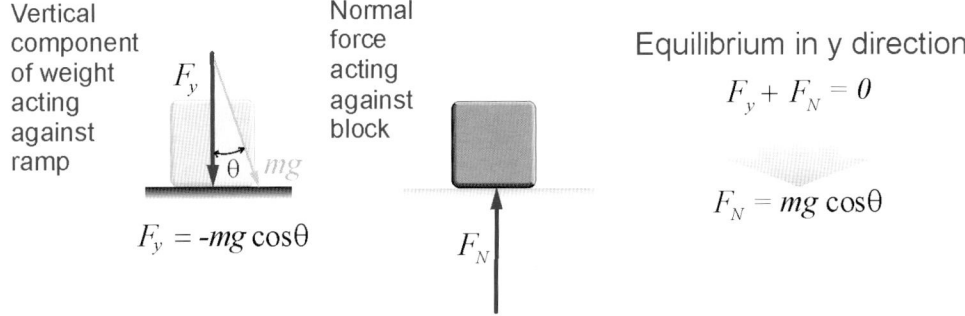

Vertical component of weight acting against ramp

$F_y = -mg\cos\theta$

Normal force acting against block

F_N

Equilibrium in y direction

$$F_y + F_N = 0$$

$$F_N = mg\cos\theta$$

Friction — If an object is moving, the force of friction acts opposite the direction of motion. On a ramp for which the coordinates are like Figure 7.23, the friction force is in the negative x direction, acting opposite to the motion. If the block is at rest on the ramp, then the direction of the friction force is opposite the way the block *would* move if there were no friction.

Magnitude of the friction force on a ramp — The magnitude of the friction force between two sliding surfaces is roughly proportional to the force holding the surfaces together. For a ramp, that means the friction force is proportional to the normal force. In Chapter 6, you learned that the friction force for sliding friction is μF_N, where μ is the coefficient of friction. For a ramp, the friction force is therefore $-\mu mg\cos\theta$ (Figure 7.23).

Friction force

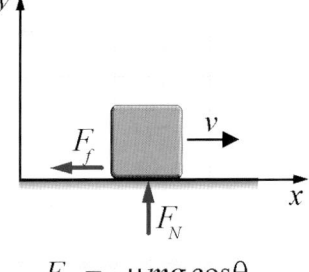

$F_f = -\mu mg\cos\theta$

Figure 7.23: *The friction force is opposite to the velocity.*

Motion on an inclined plane *Advanced topic*

Slope and acceleration A block on a ramp accelerates downward if the force (F_x) acting parallel to the ramp exceeds the force of static friction. The greater the angle of the ramp, the greater the downward acceleration. The acceleration increases because greater angles direct more of the block's weight in the direction parallel to the ramp rather than perpendicular to it.

Calculating the acceleration Newton's second law can be used to calculate the acceleration once you know the components of all the forces on an incline. According to the second law, $a = F \div m$, where a is the acceleration and m is the mass. Since the block can only accelerate along the ramp, the force that matters is the net force in the x direction, parallel to the ramp. With no friction, the net force is $F_x = mg \sin\theta$. The acceleration is therefore: $a = g \sin\theta$. The net force in the y direction is always zero. This must be true because an object on an inclined plane does not accelerate off the surface or sink through it.

Acceleration on a ramp
(no friction)

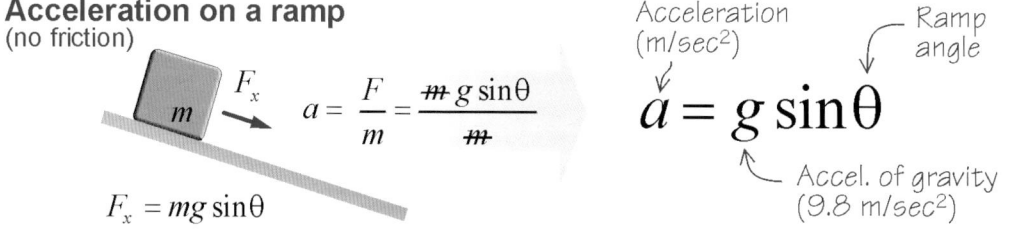

$$F_x = mg \sin\theta$$

$$a = \frac{F}{m} = \frac{\cancel{m} g \sin\theta}{\cancel{m}}$$

$$a = g \sin\theta$$

Acceleration (m/sec²)

Ramp angle

Accel. of gravity (9.8 m/sec²)

Accounting for friction If friction is included, the acceleration is reduced from gsinθ. Including friction, The net force acting along a ramp is $F_x = mg\sin\theta - \mu mg\cos\theta$. The resulting acceleration is $a = g(\sin\theta - \mu\cos\theta)$. For a smooth surface, the coefficient of friction (μ) is usually in the range 0.1 - 0.3.

Acceleration on a ramp
(including friction)

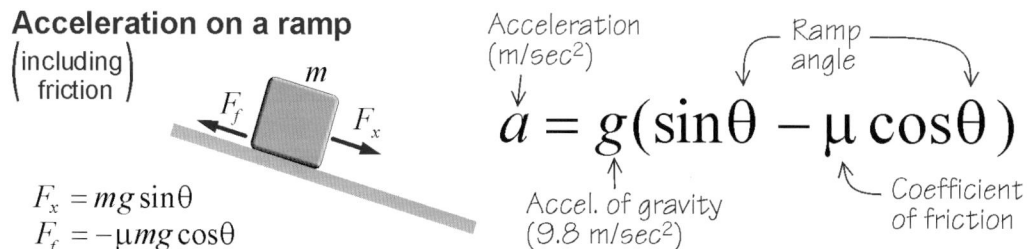

$$F_x = mg \sin\theta$$
$$F_f = -\mu mg \cos\theta$$

$$a = g(\sin\theta - \mu \cos\theta)$$

Acceleration (m/sec²)

Ramp angle

Accel. of gravity (9.8 m/sec²)

Coefficient of friction

Calculate the acceleration of a skier on a slope

A skier with a mass of 50 kg is on a hill making an angle of 20 degrees. The friction force is 30 N. What is the skier's acceleration?

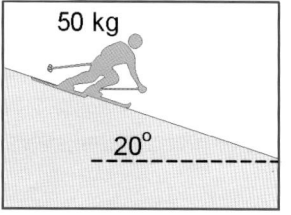

50 kg

20°

1) You are asked to find the acceleration.

2) You know the mass, friction force, and angle.

3) The relationships that apply are: $a = F \div m$, $F_x = mg\sin\theta$

4) Calculate the x component of the skier's weight:
$F_x = (50$ kg$)(9.8$ m/sec²$) \times (\sin 20°)$
$= 167.6$ N

Calculate the force:
$F = 167.6$ N - 30 N = 137.6 N

Calculate the acceleration:
$a = 137.6$ N $\div 50$ kg
$= 2.75$ m/sec²

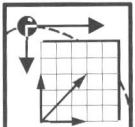

The vector form of Newton's second law *Advanced Topic*

The acceleration vector When we introduced Newton's second law in Chapter 5, we said the acceleration caused by a force was also in the direction of the force. Although we did not say it at the time, this statement implies that acceleration is a vector since it has direction. In fact, an object moving in three dimensions can be accelerated in the *x*, *y*, and *z* directions. In component form, the acceleration vector can be written in a similar way to the velocity vector: $\vec{a} = (a_x, a_y, a_z)$ m/sec^2.

The vector equation is three component equations The most general form of Newton's second law is a relationship between two vectors (force and acceleration) and one scalar (mass).

Newtons second law (vector form)

$$\underset{\substack{Force\ (N)\\(vector)}}{\vec{F}} = m\underset{\substack{Acceleration\ (m/sec^2)\\(vector)}}{\vec{a}}\ \ \overset{mass\ (kg)}{}$$

x components $\quad F_x = ma_x$

y components $\quad F_y = ma_y$

z components $\quad F_z = ma_z$

Now that we have worked with vectors and components, it is more useful to think of the second law as three separate equations. There is one equation for each of the coordinate directions. Forces in the *x* direction cause acceleration in the *x* direction. Forces in the *y* direction cause acceleration in the *y* direction and likewise for z.

Dynamics If you know the forces acting on an object, you can predict its motion in three dimensions. For example, this is how the computers that control space missions determine when and for how long to run the rocket engines. The computers determine the magnitude and direction of the required acceleration and use the engines to get exactly the right force. The process of calculating three-dimensional motion from forces and accelerations is called **dynamics**.

Calculate the acceleration from 3-D forces

A 100 kg satellite has many small rocket engines pointed in different directions that allow it to maneuver in three dimensions. If the engines make the following forces, what is the acceleration of the satellite?
$\vec{F}_1 = (0, 0, 50)$N
$\vec{F}_2 = (25, 0, -50)$N
$\vec{F}_3 = (25, 0, 0)$N

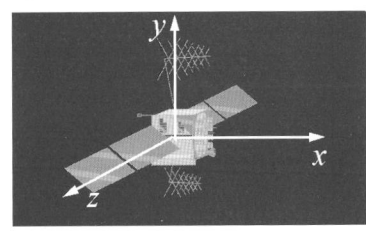

1) You are asked to find the acceleration.
2) You know the mass and forces.
3) The relationships that apply are: $\vec{a} = \vec{F} \div m$, $\vec{F}$ = net force
4) Calculate the net force by adding components.
net $\vec{F} = (50, 0, 0)$ N
Calculate the acceleration:
$a_y = a_z = 0$
$a_x = 50N \div 100$ kg
$= 0.5$ m/sec^2
$\vec{a} = (0.5, 0, 0)$ m/sec^2

Application: Robot Navigation

Imagine you wanted to make a map of the sea floor around a shipwreck deep in the ocean. Instead of swimming down to the bottom yourself, you could send a robot in your place. Robots use vectors to keep track of where they have gone and where they want to go. Another example of robots using vectors is a self-driving car. In the future you may be able to buy a car that does not require a human driver. Imagine getting in to your car and saying, "To the museum, please!" Prototype cars that drive themselves have been built and tested.

Controlling robots
Robots are machines, usually controlled by computer, intended to perform one or more tasks. They are often used to perform tasks that humans cannot do, like making a map of the ocean floor, or that humans do not want to do, like driving to the same place over and over. A driving robot uses maps stored in its memory and signals from satellites to plot a course from its current position to its destination.

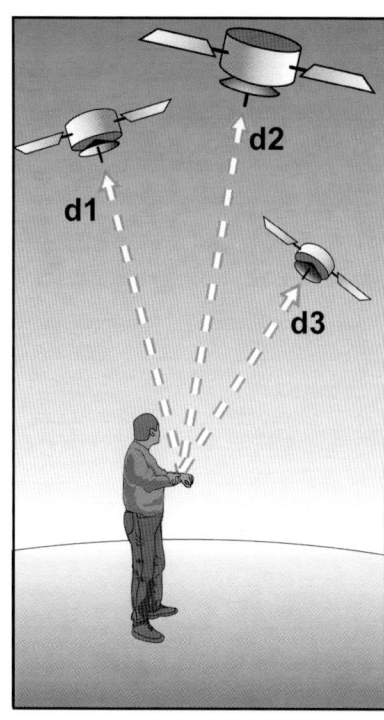

Figure 7.24: *A Global Positioning System (GPS) receiver determines its position to within a few meters anywhere on the surface of the Earth. The receiver works by comparing signals from three different GPS satellites.*

1. The robot's computer looks up the coordinates of the destination.

2. Using the GPS to find its current position, the robot determines the vector displacement to the destination

3. With information stored about streets, the robot creates a path made of many vectors. The sum of these is the displacement.

Destination	Latitude	Longitude
Office	76.30	76.00
Home	75.27	75.30
School	65.11	65.15
Museum	72.43	72.61
Beach	85.20	82.15
Cinema	73.03	73.01
Store	73.20	73.15

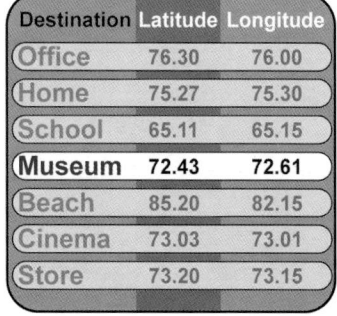 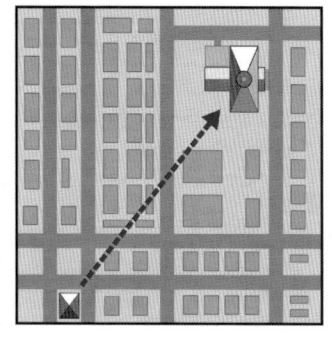 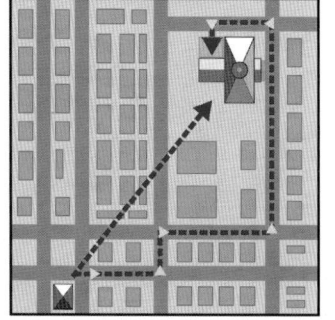

Global Positioning System (GPS)
In orbit around Earth are 24 satellites that transmit radio signals as part of a positioning or navigation system. At any one time, up to 12 of those satellites are in the sky, all transmitting their own unique code and location. A GPS receiver reads the codes, and uses vectors to find its position relative to the satellites (Figure 7.24).

138

Knowing your position

Triangulation | Using the location of other objects to find your position is called *triangulation*. On the planet's surface, knowing your distance to one object reduces your possible locations to a circle; two objects eliminates everything but two points; and with three objects, you can figure out your location exactly. GPS receivers use triangulation to calculate a position from the signals from three satellites.

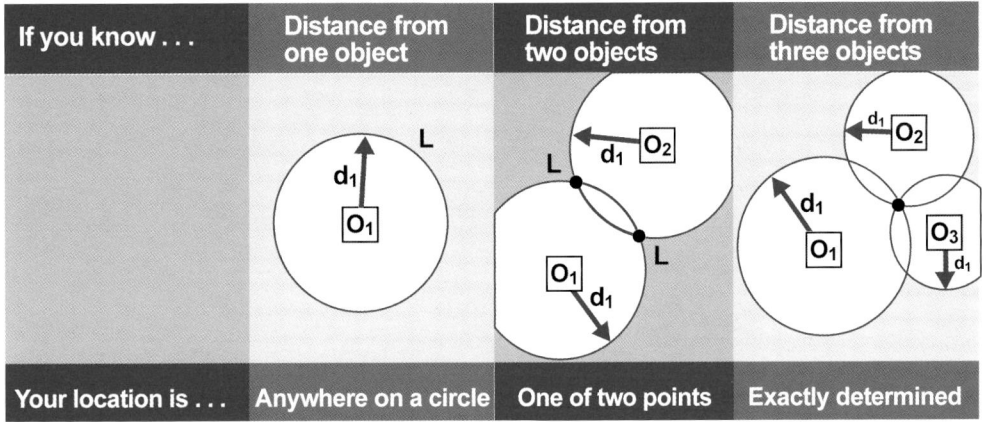

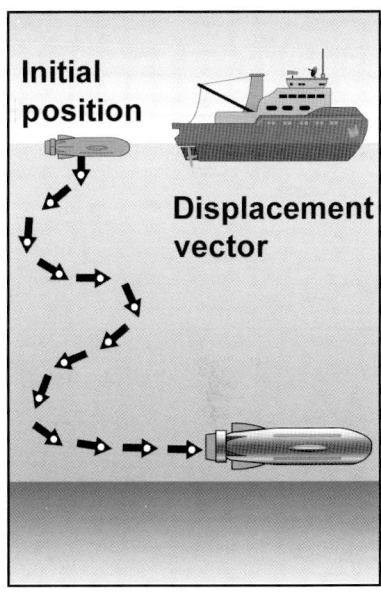

Figure 7.25: *The inertial navigation system (INS) on a robot submarine is used to calculate the submarine's motion in many small displacement vectors by sensing its acceleration.*

Inertial navigation system (INS) | Sometimes, robots cannot use the GPS. Radio waves do not travel through water, so underwater robots use a different navigation system. If you have ever ridden on a bus with your eyes closed, you can sense which direction the bus is turning because your body can sense acceleration. Electronics and gyroscopes give a robot a very accurate sense of acceleration in all three dimensions. The inertial navigation system (INS) used by robot submarines uses acceleration to constantly update its displacement vector (Figure 7.25). For each small amount of time, the INS "feels" which direction it is traveling, and represents the distance it has traveled in that time as a vector. By recording its starting position and adding all the vectors together, the INS provides the control computer with a current position vector.

If the robot is underwater for too long, it can start to get confused. Small errors add up over time to produce significant errors in the position calculated by the INS. In order for a robot submarine to navigate long distances, it must come to the surface every so often to reorient itself with GPS information.

Chapter 7 Review

Vocabulary Review

Match the following terms with the correct definition. There is one extra definition in the list that will not match any of the terms.

Set One

1. velocity
2. projectile
3. displacement
4. components
5. trajectory

  a. A scalar quantity
  b. The path a projectile follows
  c. The distance and direction an object is from its starting point
  d. Vectors at right angles that combine to make another vector
  e. Speed with direction
  f. An object moving through the air that is only affected by the force of gravity

Set Two

1. scalar
2. vector
3. parabola
4. inclined plane
5. magnitude

  a. A straight, sloped surface
  b. The horizontal distance a projectile travels
  c. A quantity that has direction
  d. The mathematical name for the shape of a projectile's path
  e. A quantity that can be completely described by a single number and unit
  f. The scalar length of a vector

Set Three

1. resultant
2. vertical
3. horizontal
4. range

  a. The component of a projectile's velocity that is affected by gravity
  b. The component of a projectile's velocity that is not affected by gravity
  c. The sum of two or more vectors
  d. The horizontal distance a projectile travels
  e. The maximum height of a projectile

Concept review

1. Explain the difference between scalar and vector quantities.

2. Classify each of the following as a scalar or vector:

   a. height

   b. displacement

   c. velocity

   d. area

3. Draw a vector to show a displacement of 100 meters at an angle of 30 degrees. Use a scale for your drawing.

4. You walk 1 kilometer north to the store, turn around, and return home. What is your displacement?

5. What is the maximum resultant of a 1 centimeter vector and a 4 centimeter vector? What is the minimum resultant?

6. Vectors can be expressed using Cartesian coordinates and polar coordinates. What type of quantity is each coordinate when a vector is expressed using Cartesian coordinates? What type of quantity is each coordinate when a vector is expressed using polar coordinates?

7. If a vector is at 45 degrees, what do you know about the magnitude of its components?

8. List three advantages of using components rather than a scale drawing to add a set of vectors.

9. What is the only force that affects the motion of a projectile?

10. Which component of a projectile's velocity changes as it moves through the air, the horizontal component or the vertical component?

11. A ball rolls off the edge of a horizontal table. What is the initial vertical velocity component?

12. A soccer ball is kicked off the ground at an angle of 45 degrees.

    a. At the top of its path, is its velocity entirely horizontal, entirely vertical, or a combination of both? Explain your reasoning.

    b. At the top of its path, is its acceleration entirely horizontal, entirely vertical, or a combination of both? Explain your answer.

13. At what angle should a ball be thrown for it to travel a maximum distance?

14. A ball kicked at an angle of 25 degrees will have the same range as a ball kicked at the same speed at ___ degrees.

15. What does it mean for an object to be in equilibrium?

16. Give three examples of objects moving along an inclined plane.

17. A sled is sliding down an icy hill.

    a. List the three forces that act on the sled as it moves down the hill.

    b. Draw a diagram to show the direction of each of the forces on the sled.

18. Which force acting on an object on an inclined plane causes it to accelerate?

19. Which force acting on an object on an inclined plane decreases its acceleration?

20. If an object is in equilibrium, what is the net force in the *x*-direction? In the *y*-direction?

Problems

1. Add the following sets of vectors. N = north, W = west, and S = south.

   a. 2 cm N + 7 cm W

   b. 5 m S + 8 cm N

   c. 30 m/s W + 50 m/s S

   d. 5 cm N + 7 cm W + 9 cm S

2. Resolve the vector (6 cm, 25 degrees) into *x-y* components.

3. Calculate the components of the vector representing a velocity of 40 meters per second at an angle of 55 degrees.

4. A pilot wants to fly directly to the west. The engine pushes the plane at 100 m/s, and there is a crosswind blowing to the south at 30 m/s. Determine the exact angle at which the pilot should head.

141

5. You and a friend are rowing a boat. You aim it toward a dock directly across the 100 meter-wide river and paddle at a speed of 1 m/s. You both are concentrating on rowing, so you do not notice that there is a 2 m/s current pushing you downstream. How far from the dock will you be when you reach the shore? Will the time it takes to cross the river be affected by the current?

6. You take a running jump off the end of a diving platform at a speed of 7 m/s and splash into the water 1.5 seconds later.
   a. How far horizontally do you land from your takeoff point?
   b. How high is the diving platform?

7. A model rocket is launched into the air so that its initial horizontal speed is 20 m/s and its initial vertical speed is 39.2 m/s. Complete the chart by finding the horizontal and vertical components of the velocity each second.

Time (s)	Horizontal speed (m/s)	Vertical speed (m/s)
0	20.0	39.2
1		
2		
3		
4		
5		
6		
7		
8		

8. A circus performer wants to land in a net 5 meters to the right of where she will let go of the trapeze. If she is 10 meters above the net, how fast must she be moving horizontally when she lets go?

9. You hit a baseball at a speed of 35 m/s and an angle of 40 degrees. A player catches the ball at the same height off the ground as the hit.
   a. Find the horizontal and vertical components of the ball's initial velocity.
   b. How many seconds will the ball take to get to the top of its path?
   c. How much time will the ball spend in the air?
   d. How far off the ground will the ball be at its highest point?
   e. How far horizontally will the ball travel?

10. A swing is designed so the ropes hang at an angle of 10 degrees from the vertical. A child with a weight of 200 newtons sits on the swing.
    a. How much tension is in each rope?
    b. How does the tension compare with the tension in a swing with ropes that are completely vertical?

11. Chris rides a sled down a hill with a slope of 22 degrees. The combined weight of Chris and his sled is 500 newtons.
    a. What is the normal force of the ground on the sled?
    b. Calculate the component of the weight that is parallel to the ground.
    c. Assuming the ground is frictionless, what is Chris's acceleration?
    d. If Chris's little sister also rides on the sled, their combined weight is 700 newtons. What is the new acceleration?
    e. Compare your answers to parts c and d. Can you explain this?

12. A 2 kilogram object slides down a frictionless slope.
    a. Calculate its acceleration if the slope is angled at 30 degrees.
    b. Calculate its acceleration if the slope is angled at 60 degrees.
    c. Compare your answers to parts a and b. Can you explain this?

13. A heavy cardboard box full of books slides down a wooden inclined plane with a certain acceleration. Identify whether each suggested change would result in an increased acceleration, decreased acceleration, or no change in the acceleration.
    a. greasing the inclined plane to lower the coefficient of sliding friction
    b. adding more books to the box
    c. decreasing the angle of the inclined plane

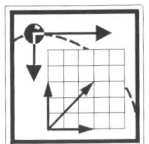

Unit 3

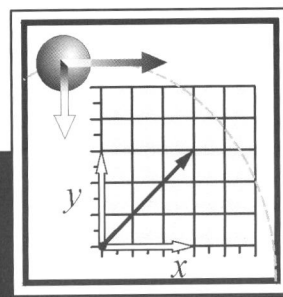

Motion and Force in 2 and 3 Dimensions

Chapter 8

Motion in Circles

Objectives for Chapter 8

By the end of this chapter you should be able to:

1. Calculate angular speed in radians per second.
2. Calculate linear speed from angular speed and vice-versa.
3. Describe and calculate centripetal forces and accelerations.
4. Describe the relationship between the force of gravity and the masses and distance between objects.
5. Calculate the force of gravity when given masses and distance between two objects.
6. Describe why satellites remain in orbit around a planet.

Terms and vocabulary words

rotate	revolve	axis	law of universal gravitation
circumference	linear speed	angular speed	centrifugal force
radian	orbit	centripetal force	centripetal acceleration
ellipse	satellite	angular displacement	gravitational constant

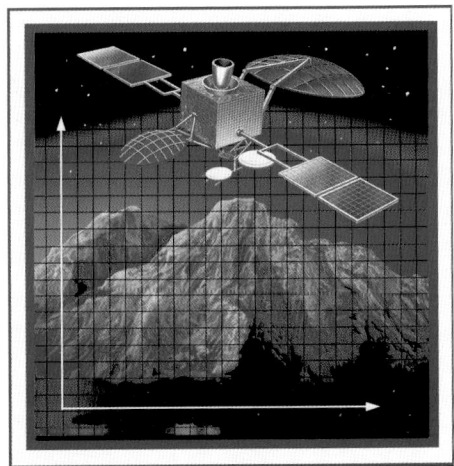

8.1 Motion in Circles

The motion that we have studied so far in this book is what physicists call *linear motion*. Linear motion is well described by position, velocity, and acceleration. But that is not the only kind of motion. Planets orbiting the sun, a child on a merry-go-round, and a basketball spinning on a fingertip are all examples of *circular motion*. Circular motion repeats itself in circles. This chapter introduces several ideas that are important to understanding circular motion. In the first section, you will encounter the circular versions for the familiar variables of position, velocity, and acceleration.

Describing objects moving in a circle

Rotating and revolving | A basketball spinning on your fingertip and a child on a merry-go-round both experience circular motion. Each moves around an imaginary line called an **axis**. The basketball's axis runs from your finger up through the center of the ball (Figure 8.1). The child's axis is a vertical line in the center of the merry-go-round (Figure 8.2). While their motions are similar, there is a fundamental difference. The ball's axis is internal. We say an object **rotates** about its axis when the axis is inside the object. The child's axis is external. The child **revolves** around the outside axis. Objects can rotate and revolve at the same time. The Earth revolves around the sun once every year while it rotates on its own axis once each day (Figure 8.3). What are other examples of objects that revolve or rotate?

Angular speed | When describing the motion of objects moving in a circle, we usually want to know the speed at which an object is spinning. **Angular speed** is the rate at which an object rotates or revolves. It is sometimes called rotational speed. Angular speed describes the amount an object turns in a specific time period. To calculate angular speed you divide the angle an object has rotated by the time it takes to rotate. For example, if a basketball turns 15 times in three seconds, its angular speed is 3 rotations per second (15 rotations ÷ 3 sec).

Units of angular speed | There are two ways in which angular speed is measured. One is by the number of complete turns per unit of time. The RPM—rotation per minute—is a unit commonly used to measure angular speed. The second way to measure angular speed is by the change in angle per unit of time, expressed in degrees per second or radians per second.

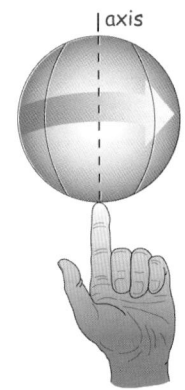

Figure 8.1: *A basketball rotates around an internal axis.*

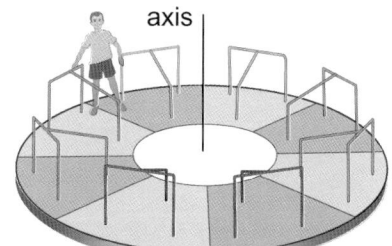

Figure 8.2: *The child revolves around an external axis.*

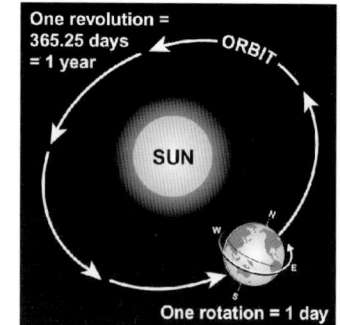

Figure 8.3: *The Earth both rotates on its own axis and revolves around the sun.*

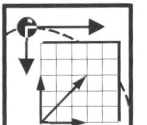
Angular speed in radians per second

1 radian equals 57.3 degrees

You used degrees when you first learned how to measure angles. However, the degree is not the most convenient unit for using angles to calculate angular speed. For the purpose of angular speed, the radian is a better unit of angle. One radian equals 57.3 degrees (approximately). Radians are better for angular speed because a radian is a ratio of two lengths, and it does not have any units in the sense that *meters* or *seconds* are units.

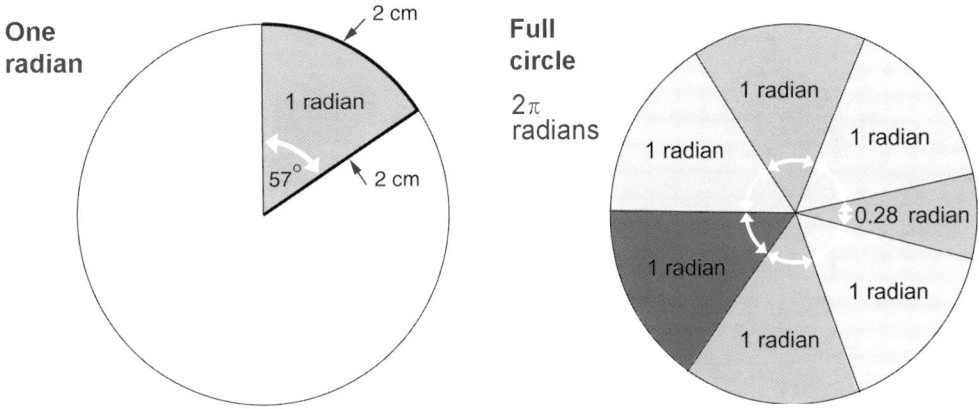

Angular speed

$$\omega = \frac{\theta}{t}$$

Angular speed (rad/sec)

Angle turned (rad)

Time taken (sec)

Radius and arc length

One radian is the angle that has an arc length equal to the radius of the circle. The circle in the diagram has a radius of 2 centimeters. An angle with a measure of 57.3 degrees, or 1 radian, encloses an arc length, or portion of the circumference, of 2 centimeters. If you could pick up the radius and bend it around the circle, it would enclose an angle equal to 1 radian. Remember, a full circle has a circumference of 2π multiplied by the radius. A radian encloses an arc length of one radius, so there are 2π or 6.28 radians in a full circle.

Angular speed in radians per second

The angular speed in radians per second (rad/sec) is equal to the change in angle divided by the change in time. Angular speed is represented with a lower case Greek omega (ω). The calculation of angular speed is similar to the calculation of linear speed, except angle replaces distance. The units of angular speed are *1/sec* because the radian is not a true unit. When we write *rad/sec* the "rad" is there to remind us that the angle is in radians. When canceling units in a problem, you may ignore radians.

Calculate angular speed in rad/sec

A bicycle wheel makes six turns in 2 seconds. What is its angular speed in radians per second?

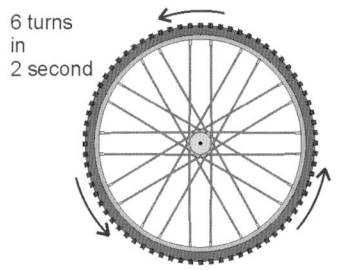

6 turns in 2 second

1) You are asked for the angular speed.
2) You are given turns and time.
3) There are 2π radians in one full turn. $\omega = \theta/t$
4) Solve: $\omega = (6 \times 2\pi) \div (2\ sec)$
$= 18.8\ rad/sec$

The relationship between linear and angular speed

Circumference of a circle

A wheel rolling along the ground has both a linear speed and an angular speed. If the wheel is not slipping, the two speeds are related by the circumference of the wheel. As you might recall from geometry, the circumference is the distance around a circle. The circumference depends on the radius of the circle.

Circumference of a circle

Circumference (m) $C = 2\pi r$ — Radius (m)

Calculating linear speed

A point at the edge of a wheel moves one circumference in each turn of the circle. The linear speed (v) is therefore the circumference divided by the time it takes to make one turn. You can see that the factor $2\pi \div t$ is the angular speed, ω. If the angular speed is in units of rad/sec, the relationship between linear and angular speed is given by the formula below. Automobile speedometers use this formula to calculate the linear speed of a car based on the angular speed and radius of the tires.

Circumference
$$v = \frac{2\pi r}{t}$$
Time for 1 turn

$$= \left(\frac{2\pi}{t}\right) \times r$$

$$= \omega r$$

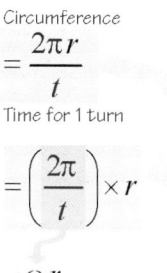

Linear and angular speed

Linear speed (m/sec) $v = \omega r$ — Radius (m)

Angular speed (rad/sec)

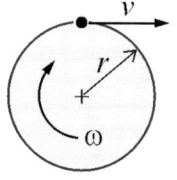

Linear speed varies with radius

The angular speed of a wheel is the same for all points on the wheel. However, the linear speed of a point on a wheel depends on how far the point is from the center of rotation. Consider a wheel that is spinning in place. Points at the outer edge of a wheel move faster than points nearer to the center. The point at the very center of the wheel ($r = 0$) is not moving at all.

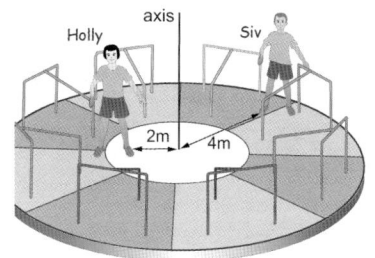
146

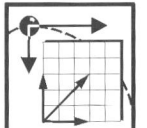

Relating angular speed, linear speed, and displacement

The speed of a rolling wheel

For a rolling object like a wheel, the forward speed is equal to the linear speed of a point at the edge of the wheel. As a wheel rotates, the point touching the ground passes around its circumference. When the wheel has turned one full rotation, it has moved forward a distance equal to its circumference. Therefore, the linear speed of a wheel is its angular speed multiplied by its radius, or $v = \omega r$.

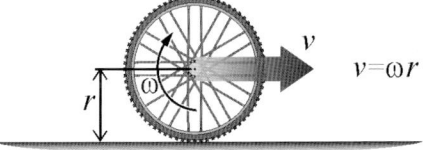

The linear speed of a rolling wheel

$v = \omega r$

A wheel moves forward one circumference in one rotation

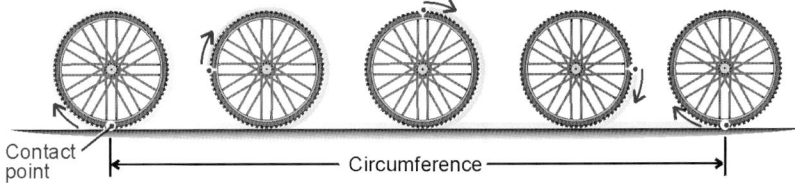

Contact point | Circumference

Speedometers and odometers

The speedometer and odometer on an automobile measure the speed and distance traveled by translating the circular motion of the wheels into linear motion. They take into account the size of tires used on cars for which they are designed. If tires of the wrong radius are used, the speed and distance will be inaccurate. If the tires are replaced with larger ones, the speedometer will display a slower speed than what the car is actually traveling. As a result, the driver might exceed the speed limit without knowing it.

Angular displacement

Linear displacement is measured in units of distance. Angular displacement (angle) is represented by the Greek letter theta (θ) and is measured in units of angles, such as radians. The total angular displacement can be many revolutions. For example, a displacement of 12π radians is equal to six rotations, because one rotation is 2π radians. An angular displacement of 540 degrees is one-and-one-half turns, since 360 degrees is a full turn.

Calculate angular speed from linear speed

A bicycle has wheels that are 70 cm in diameter (35 cm radius). The bicycle is moving forward with a linear speed of 11 m/sec. Assume the bicycle wheels are not slipping and calculate the angular speed of the wheels in RPM.

11 m/sec

1) You are asked for the angular speed in RPM.
2) You are given the linear speed and radius of the wheel.
3) $v = \omega r$, 1 rotation = 2π radians
4) Solve: $\omega = v \div r$
$ = (11 \text{ m/sec}) \div (.35 \text{ m})$
$ = 31.4 \text{ rad/sec}.$
Convert to RPM:

$$\omega = \frac{31.4 \text{ rad}}{sec} \times \frac{60 \text{ sec}}{min} \times \frac{rotation}{2\pi \text{ rad}}$$

$$= 300 \text{ rpm}$$

8.2 Centripetal Force

Imagine whirling a potato around your head on a string (Figure 8.4). If the string breaks, the potato flies off and no longer moves in a circle. To keep the potato moving in a circle, the string supplies a force that always points toward the center of the circle. A similar force is required for any object in circular motion. A planet in orbit, a race car going around a track, and a child riding on a merry-go-round all depend on forces to keep them in circular motion. In this section, you will learn about forces acting on objects moving in circles.

Centripetal force

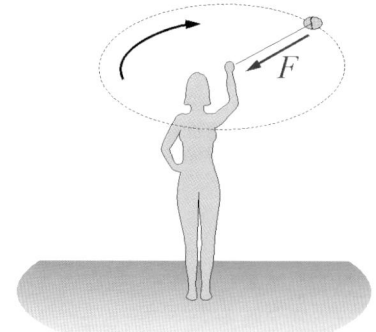

Figure 8.4: *An object on a string is kept moving in a circle by the inward force of the string.*

Acceleration	We usually think of acceleration as a change in speed. But because velocity includes both speed and direction, acceleration can also be a change in the direction of motion.
Centripetal force causes circular motion	Any force that causes an object to move in a circle is called a centripetal force. Even though it is given its own name, centripetal force is not a new type of physical force. Any type of force can be a centripetal force if its action causes an object to move in a circle. The friction between a car's tires and the road is the centripetal force that allows the car to turn through a bend in the road (Figure 8.5). The lack of friction on an icy road is what makes it difficult for a car to turn.
Direction of centripetal force	Whether a force makes an object accelerate by changing its speed or by changing its direction depends on the direction of the force. A force in the direction of motion causes the object to speed up or slow down. A force applied perpendicular to the motion causes the object to change its path from a line to a circle, without changing speed. A centripetal force is always perpendicular to an object's motion, toward the center of the circle.

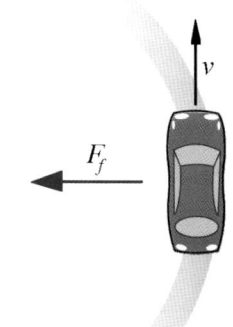

Figure 8.5: *Friction between the road and tires allows the car to turn the bend. The centripetal force (friction) is toward the center of the circle, perpendicular to the velocity.*

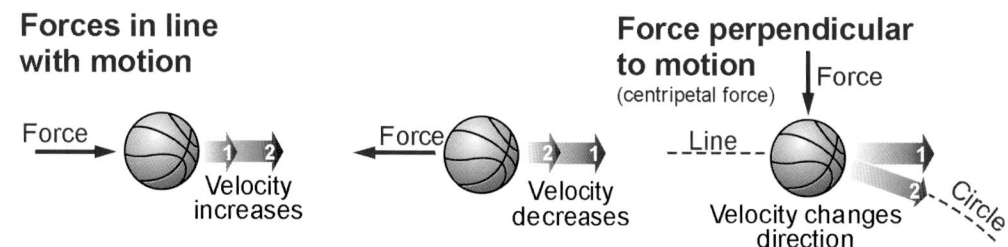

148

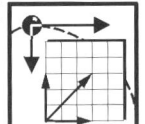
Calculating centripetal force

Mass, speed, and radius
The magnitude of the centripetal force needed to move an object in a circle depends on the object's mass and speed, and on the radius of the circle.

1. Newton's second law says force is proportional to mass. The greater the mass of an object, the greater the centripetal force needed to change its motion.

2. As speed increases, a greater centripetal force is required to keep bending an object's path into a circle. The strength of centripetal force is proportional to the square of the speed.

3. The larger the radius of the circle, the more gradually an object's direction of motion changes. A smaller centripetal force results in a path making a larger circle. Therefore, radius and centripetal force are inversely related.

Centripetal force

$$\underset{\text{Centripetal force (N)}}{F_c} = \frac{\underset{\substack{\text{Mass} \\ \text{(kg)}}}{m} \overset{\substack{\text{Linear speed} \\ \text{(m/sec)}}}{v^2}}{\underset{\text{Radius of path (m)}}{r}}$$

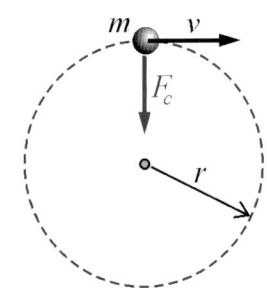

Centripetal force at the amusement park

A popular amusement park ride consists of a spinning cylindrical room in which riders stand with their backs against the wall. The room spins faster and faster, and then the floor suddenly drops out from beneath the riders' feet. The passengers seem to magically stick to the wall, suspended above the floor.

Calculate centripetal force

Example: A 50-kilogram passenger on an amusement park ride stands with his back against the wall of a cylindrical room with radius of 3 meters (see sidebar). What is the centripetal force of the wall pressing into his back when the room spins and he is moving at 6 meters per second?

1) You are asked to find the centripetal force.
2) You are given the radius, mass, and linear speed.
3) The formula that applies is $F_c = mv^2 \div r$.
4) Solve:
   $F_c = (50 \text{ kg})(6 \text{ m/sec})^2 \div (3 \text{ m}) = 600 \text{ N}$

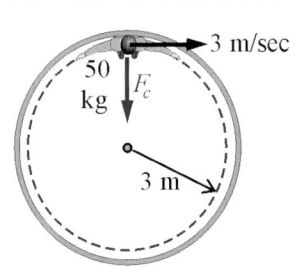

What seems to be magic can be explained easily with physics. The force of the wall pushing against a rider's back provides the centripetal force to move the rider in a circle. Friction between the rider's back and the wall prevents the person from sliding down to the floor.

Centripetal acceleration

Centripetal force causes centripetal acceleration Acceleration is the rate at which an object's velocity changes as the result of a force. Centripetal acceleration is the acceleration of an object moving in a circle due to the centripetal force. A race car driving down a straight track has no centripetal acceleration. A race car making a sharp turn has a large centripetal acceleration. Centripetal acceleration is a measure of the rate at which the direction of an object's velocity changes.

The formula for centripetal acceleration The easiest way to find a formula for centripetal acceleration is by comparing Newton's second law and the formula for centripetal force. According to the second law, force equals mass times acceleration. Centripetal force must also equal mass times centripetal acceleration. You can see by comparing the two formulas that centripetal acceleration must be speed squared divided by the radius of the circular motion

Centripetal acceleration

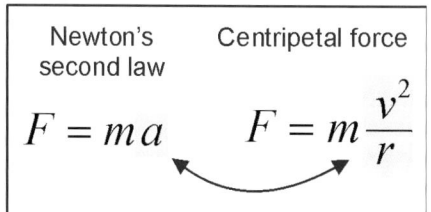

Centripetal acceleration (m/sec²)
$$a_c = \frac{v^2}{r}$$
Speed (m/sec)
Radius (m)

Newton's second law	Centripetal force
$F = ma$	$F = m\dfrac{v^2}{r}$

Direction of centripetal acceleration The direction of an object's acceleration is always in the direction of the net force. Therefore, the centripetal acceleration is in the same direction as the centripetal force, toward the center of the circle. Like the direction of the centripetal force, the direction of the centripetal acceleration constantly changes as an object moves in a circle.

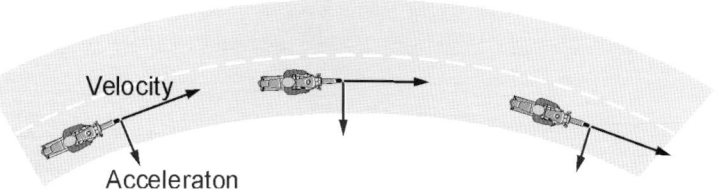

Velocity

Acceleraton

Calculate centripetal acceleration

A motorcycle drives around a bend with a 50-meter radius at 10 m/sec. Find the motor cycle's centripetal acceleration and compare it with g, the acceleration of gravity.

1) You are asked for centripetal acceleration and a comparison with g (9.8 m/sec²).
2) You are given the linear speed and radius of the motion.
3) $a_c = v^2 \div r$
4) Solve:
   $a_c = (10 \text{ m/sec})^2 \div (50 \text{ m})$
   $= 2 \text{ m/sec}^2$
   The centripetal acceleration is about 20% or 1/5 that of gravity.

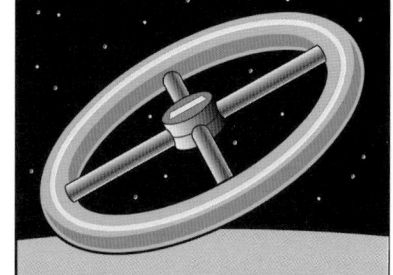

Figure 8.6: *The rotation of a wheel-shaped space station creates centripetal acceleration that simulates the feeling of gravity.*

150

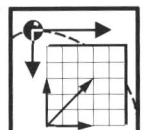
Centrifugal force

Inertia As Newton's first law states, an object in motion tends to stay in motion at a constant speed in a straight line if there is no net force acting on it. We call an object's tendency to resist a change in its motion its *inertia*. An object moving in a circle is constantly changing its direction of motion. A centripetal force is required to cause this change in direction.

Riding in a turning car You can feel your inertia when you are riding in a car that is driving around a bend. Imagine yourself sitting in the center of a smooth back seat. What happens to you if the car is moving at a fast speed and suddenly turns to the left? Your body slides to the right until it is stopped by the seat belt or the door of the car. Why does this occur? Your body, like any body, will keep moving in a straight line unless an opposing force prevents the motion. When forces between the car's tires and the ground cause the car to turn, you continue to move straight ahead because the smooth seats do not provide a frictional force large enough to oppose your motion. While it may feel as though you are thrown to the right, you are not. *The car turns to the left below you* making it seem like your body moves to the right. The force between the seat belt or the door of the car then provides the centripetal force to move you around the bend.

Centrifugal force Although the centripetal force pushes you toward the center of the circular path, it seems as if there also is a force pushing you to the outside. This apparent outward force is called **centrifugal force**. While it feels like an actual force acting on you, centrifugal force is *not a true force* exerted on your body. It is simply your tendency to move in a straight line due to inertia. This is easy to observe by twirling a small object at the end of a string. When the string is released, the object flies off in a straight line tangent to the circle. No outward force pushes it away from the center of the circle, but the lack of a centripetal force keeps it from continuing to move in its circular path.

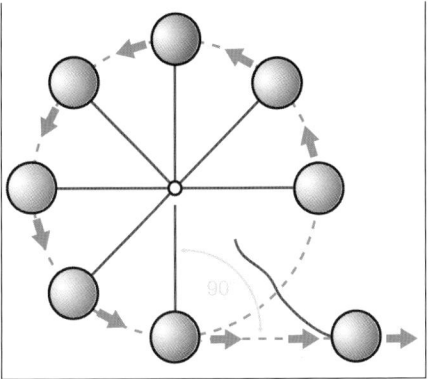

Banked turns

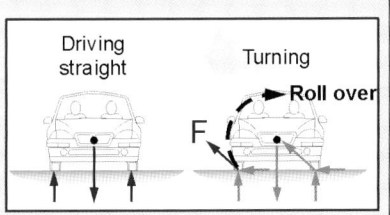

In a turn, the road exerts a sideways centripetal force on the wheels of a car, as well as the upward force reaction to the car's weight. At high speed, the resultant force on the inside wheel can lift the car and flip it to the outside of the curve.

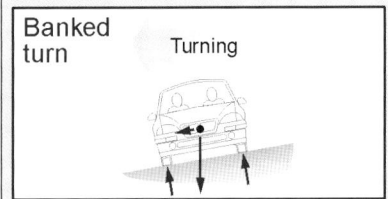

To allow safe travel at highway speeds, most roads bank the curves. In a banked curve the road slopes up, away from the center of the curve. The road acts like a ramp and the centripetal force is partly supplied by the parallel component of the car's own weight.

8.3 Universal Gravitation and Orbital Motion

One of the most important sources of centripetal force is gravity. The sun's gravity keeps the planets moving in nearly circular orbits. This section is about gravity, orbits, and the motion of planets and satellites.

Newton's law of universal gravitation

The law of universal gravitation
Sir Isaac Newton first deduced that the force responsible for making objects fall on Earth is the same force that keeps the moon in orbit. This idea is known as the law of universal gravitation. Gravitational force exists between all objects that have mass. The strength of the gravitational force depends on the mass of the objects and the distance between them.

You do not feel the attraction between ordinary masses
All objects that have mass attract each other. You do not notice the attractive force between ordinary objects because gravity is a relatively weak force. It takes a great deal of mass to create enough gravity so that the force can be felt. For example, an attractive force exists between the person and the apple in Figure 8.7. The force is too small to feel because the masses are small. A force also exists between the person and Earth; we call this force *weight*. The weight force is strong enough to feel because the Earth has a huge mass. Gravity forces tend to be important only when one of the objects has a mass the size of a planet.

Direction of the gravity force
The force of gravity between two objects always lies along the line connecting their centers. As objects move, the force of gravity changes its direction to stay pointed along the line of those centers. For example, the force between Earth and your body points from your center of mass to the center of mass of the planet itself. The direction of Earth's gravity is what we use to define "down." Down is the direction of the gravitational force between any object and Earth.

The force of gravity between two masses points along a line joining their centers

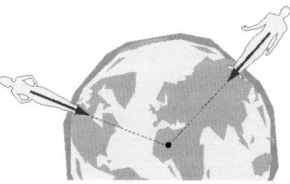

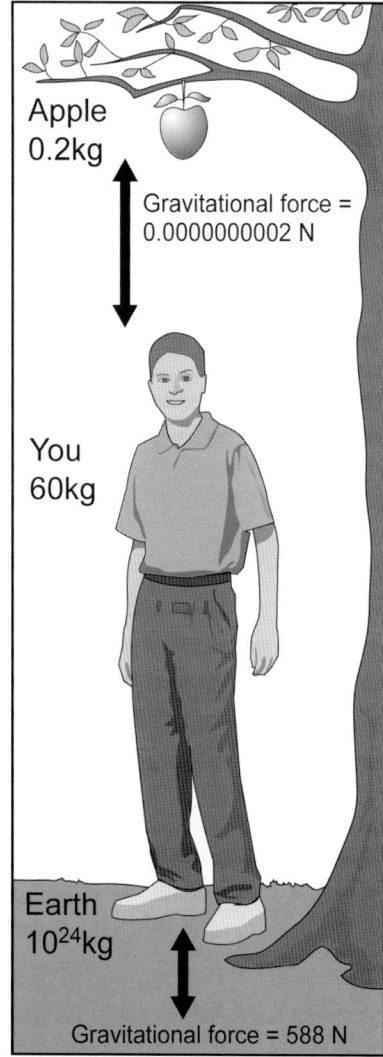

Apple
0.2kg

Gravitational force = 0.0000000002 N

You
60kg

Earth
10^{24}kg

Gravitational force = 588 N

Figure 8.7: *The gravitational force between you and the Earth is much stronger than the force between you and the apple because the Earth is much more massive.*

Calculating the gravitational force between objects

Mass and gravity The attractive force of gravity between two objects is proportional to the mass of both objects multiplied together. If one object doubles in mass, then the force between the objects doubles. If both objects double in mass, then the force of gravity between them is multiplied by four.

Distance and gravity Distance is also important when calculating gravitational force. The closer objects are to each other, the greater the force between them; the farther apart, the weaker the force. The gravitational force is inversely related to the square of the distance, so doubling the distance reduces the force to one-fourth its original value. Tripling the distance reduces the force to one-ninth its original value.

Determining distance The distance is measured from the center of one object to the center of the other. To find the force between you and Earth, you must use the distance to the planet's center. If you climb a hill, this distance increases, so the force decreases. However, this change in distance is insignificant when compared with Earth's radius, so the difference in the force is not noticeable.

The law of universal gravitation The law of universal gravitation allows you to calculate the gravitational force between two objects from their masses and the distance between them. The law includes a value called the **gravitational constant**, or "G." This value is the same everywhere in the universe. The universal law of gravitation can be used to find the force between small objects like apples and to find the force between huge objects like planets, moons, and stars.

Law of universal gravitation

Mass 1, Mass 2 (kg)

$$Force (N) \quad F = G\frac{m_1 m_2}{r^2}$$

Gravitational Constant (6.67×10^{-11} $N \cdot m^2/kg^2$)

Distance between masses (m)

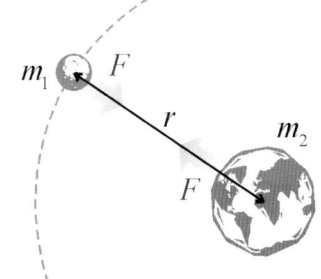

m_1 F

r

m_2

F

Calculate the weight of a person on the moon

The mass of the moon is 7.36×10^{22} kg. The radius of the moon is 1.74×10^6 m. Use the equation of universal gravitation to calculate the weight of a 90 kg astronaut on the surface of the moon.

90 kg

1) You are asked to find a person's weight on the moon.
2) You are given the radius and the masses.
3) The formula that applies is $F_g = Gm_1m_2 \div r^2$.
4) Solve:

$$F_g = \left(6.67 \times 10^{-11} \atop N \cdot m^2/kg^2\right)$$

$$\times \frac{(90 \, kg)(7.36 \times 10^{22} \, kg)}{(1.74 \times 10^6 \, m)^2}$$

$$= 146 \, N$$

By comparison, on Earth the astronaut's weight would be 90 kg x 9.8 m/s² or 882 N. The force of gravity on the moon is approximately one-sixth what it is on Earth.

Orbital motion

Satellites   A **satellite** is an object that is bound by gravity to another object such as a planet or star. The moon, Earth, and the other planets are examples of natural satellites. Artificial satellites that move around the Earth include the Hubble Space Telescope, the International Space Station, the space shuttles, and satellites used for communication. The first artificial satellite, Sputnik I (which translates "traveling companion") was launched by the former Soviet Union on October 4, 1957. Many hundreds of satellites have been sent into space since then.

Orbits and gravitational force   An **orbit** is the path followed by a satellite. The orbits of many natural and human-made satellites are circular, or nearly circular. The centripetal force that bends the motion of a satellite into an orbit comes from the gravitational attraction between the satellite and the planet it orbits.

Launching a satellite   The motion of a satellite is closely related to projectile motion. If an object is launched above the Earth's surface at a slow speed, it will follow a parabolic path and fall back to Earth (Figure 8.8). The faster it is launched, the farther it travels before reaching the ground. At a launch speed of about 8 kilometers per second, the curve of a projectile's path matches the curvature of the planet. At this speed, an object goes into orbit instead of falling back to Earth. You can think about the motion of a satellite in orbit as *falling around the Earth*. A satellite in orbit is actually in free fall but as it falls the Earth curves away beneath it.

Elliptical orbits   Not all orbits are perfectly circular. If an object is launched above Earth at more than 8 kilometers per second, the orbit will be a noncircular **ellipse**. An object in an elliptical orbit does not move at a constant speed. It moves fastest when it is closest to the object it is orbiting because the force of gravity is strongest there.

The orbits of planets and comets   The planets in our solar system have nearly circular orbits, but they are not perfect circles. All the planet's orbits are slightly elliptical. The orbit of the Earth around the sun is only 2 percent different from a perfect circle. Comets, however, orbit the sun in very long elliptical paths (Figure 8.9). Their paths bring them very close to the sun and then out into space, often beyond Pluto. Some comets take only a few years to orbit the sun once, while others travel so far out that a solar orbit takes thousands of years.

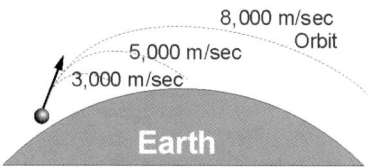

Figure 8.8: *The faster an object is launched, the farther it travels before landing. If an object is launched fast enough, it falls into orbit around the Earth.*

Orbits and the inner Solar System

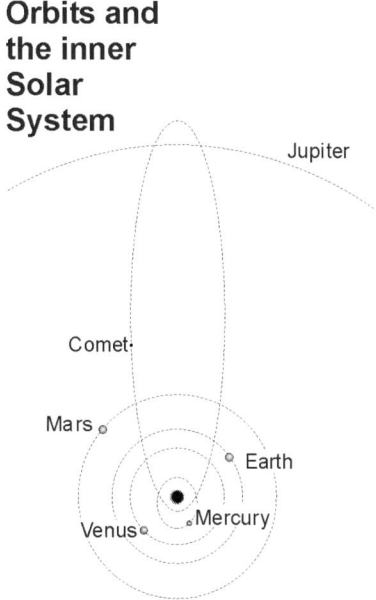

Figure 8.9: *The orbits of the inner planets (except for Mercury's) are nearly circular. Comets have highly elliptical orbits.*

154

Application: Satellite Motion

In 1957, the first artificial, human-made Earth satellite was launched by the Soviets. Called Sputnik, it created a sensation and sparked the space race between the United States and the Soviet Union. This competition culminated in 1969, when US astronauts Neil Armstrong and Buzz Aldrin landed on the surface of the moon. Firsthand human exploration of the moon ended in the 1970s, though development of artificial satellites continued. Today the satellite industry is a multibillion dollar business involving hundreds of companies in dozens of countries. Nearly every person on Earth is affected day-to-day in some way by satellites orbiting far overhead, in the vacuum of space.

The orbit equation For a satellite in a circular orbit, the force of Earth's gravity pulling on the satellite equals the centripetal force required to keep it in its orbit. If this were not so, the satellite would either get closer to, or farther away from, Earth and the orbit would not remain circular. We can apply the knowledge from this chapter to determine the relationship between a satellite's orbital radius, r, and its orbital velocity, v (Figure 8.10).

Geostationary satellites Most people in the United States—and many millions more around the world—are familiar with weather satellites. These satellites stay above the same point on Earth so that their pictures are of that place 24 hours a day. This "hovering" over the same spot is possible because the satellites are in a special kind of orbit called geostationary. A satellite in geostationary orbit completes one orbit in exactly one day, so that its motion follows the motion of the ground underneath it (Figure 8.11). Many communications and TV broadcast satellites are also in geostationary orbits. This is why a satellite dish antenna can receive a signal 24 hours a day but stay in a fixed position. If the TV satellite were not in a geostationary orbit, the dish antenna would have to move around to track the satellite.

The altitude of geostationary orbit To keep up with the Earth's rotation, a geostationary satellite must travel the entire circumference of its orbit ($2\pi r$) in 24 hours (86,400 seconds). To stay in orbit, the satellite's radius and velocity must also satisfy the orbit equation in Figure 8.10. The combination of these two conditions determines the radius of geostationary orbit, which is 42,300 kilometers from the center of the Earth (Figure 8.11). The altitude of the orbit is 35,920 kilometers above the planet's surface, after subtracting 6,380 kilometers for the radius of Earth itself.

Centripetal force		Gravitational force

$$\frac{m_s v^2}{r} = G\frac{m_s m_E}{r^2}$$

Orbit equation

$$r = \frac{Gm_E}{v^2}$$

r	Orbit radius
G	Gravitational constant
m_E	Mass of the Earth
v	Satellite linear velocity

Figure 8.10: *The relationship between orbital speed (v) and the radius (r) of a satellite's orbit.*

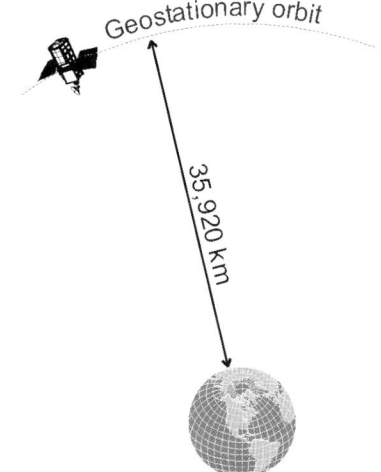

Figure 8.11: *A satellite in geostationary orbit stays above the same place on the Earth as it moves around in its orbit.*

Use of HEO and geostationary orbits

There are many satellites in geostationary orbit

All geostationary satellites must orbit directly above the equator. This means that the geostationary "belt" is the prime real estate of the satellite world. Currently, more than 300 satellites occupy "slots" in geostationary orbit, and their number continues to grow. There have been international disputes over the right to the prime geostationary slots, and there have even been cases where satellites in adjacent slots have interfered with each other. To avert cluttering up the geostationary belt with dead satellites, all geostationary satellites reaching the end of their lifetimes are now designed to conduct a "graveyard burn" which propels them into a higher, non-geostationary orbit, away from the congestion.

Polar regions cannot "see" geostationary orbit

Geostationary satellites provide excellent images and TV coverage for most regions of the Earth, but they do not cover the polar regions. To a ground observer at latitudes above 70 degrees, a geostationary satellite appears less than 10 degrees above the horizon. At this low angle, even small hills interfere with reception of signals from the satellite.

Highly elliptical orbit (HEO)

There is no way to place a satellite directly over the Earth's north or south pole permanently. However, there is a way to maximize the time a satellite spends over a polar region. Such satellites are placed in a highly elliptical orbit (or HEO), which means the orbit is highly elongated (Figure 8.12). The orbital ellipse is arranged such that one side of the ellipse is far away from the Earth, while the other side is quite close.

Perigee and apogee

The closest approach of an elliptical orbit is called the perigee. The farthest point in the orbit is called the apogee. If you solve the equations for the trajectory of an elliptical orbit, the velocity at apogee is slower than the velocity at perigee by the ratio of r_p/r_a, the orbital radii at perigee and apogee. This means a satellite will slow down as it approaches apogee, and speed back up at it moves toward perigee. If apogee is above the north or south pole, then the satellite will spend most of its time above the pole where it is moving slowest. A communications satellite in a HEO with its apogee above the north pole is in line-of-sight of the northern hemisphere of the Earth for most of its orbital period. A pair of satellites in north polar HEO can provide continuous coverage for northern regions.

HEO orbit

Figure 8.12: *A north polar HEO is an exaggeratedly elliptical orbit that allows a satellite to spend most of its time being visible from the northernmost latitudes.*

Chapter 8 Review

Vocabulary Review

Match the following terms with the correct definition. There is one extra definition in the list that will not match any of the terms.

Set One

1. centripetal force
2. law of universal gravitation
3. rotate
4. radian
5. revolve
6. centripetal acceleration

a. It states that all objects attract each other with a force that depends on mass and distance
b. An angle measure equal to about 57.3 degrees
c. The force that keeps an object moving in a circle; it is directed toward the center of the circle
d. There are 360 of these in a circle
e. To spin about an internal axis
f. To move in a circle about an external axis
g. The rate at which the velocity vector changes direction for an object moving in a circle

Set Two

1. centrifugal force
2. axis
3. circumference
4. G
5. angular speed
6. ellipse

a. A constant equal to $6.67 \times 10^{-11} \ \text{N} \cdot \text{m}^2/\text{kg}^2$
b. The distance around a circle
c. The imaginary line about which an object spins
d. The acceleration due to gravity
e. The shape of the orbital path of planets in our solar system
f. A so-called force that seems to pull a revolving object outward; not a true physical force
g. The rate at which an object spins

Concept review

1. State whether each of these objects rotates or revolves:

   a. a globe

   b. a satellite orbiting Earth

   c. a toy train traveling around a circular track

   d. a fan blade

2. State whether each of the following units is appropriate to express angular speed:

   a. rotations per second

   b. meters per second

   c. RPM

3. How many radians are in a full circle?

4. Two ants are sitting on a spinning record. The ant at point A is closer to the center of the record than the ant at point B. How do their angular speeds compare? How do their linear speeds compare?

5. A cyclist rides clockwise around a circular track at a constant speed. What is the direction of her velocity at points A, B, and C? What is the direction of the centripetal force on her at these points? What is the direction of the centripetal acceleration at each point?

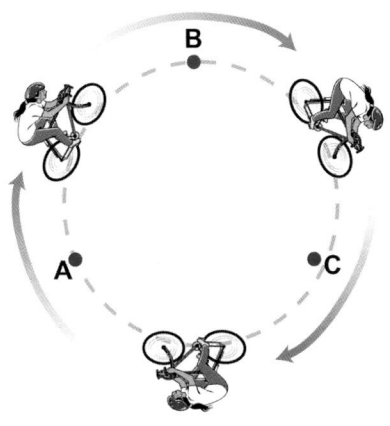

6. If the cyclist in the preceding question rides her bike at a faster speed, but in the same path, explain what happens to:
   a. the centripetal force
   b. the centripetal acceleration

7. Give three examples of forces that can act as the centripetal force keeping an object in circular motion.

8. If centrifugal force is not a true force, explain why it is called a force at all.

9. Explain what happens to the gravitational force between two objects as they are moved closer together.

10. What happens to the gravitational force between two objects if the mass of one is doubled? What if the mass of both objects is doubled?

11. Why do you weigh slightly less in a high-flying airplane?

12. How is projectile motion similar to orbital motion?

Problems

1. Marion rides her racing bicycle at a speed of 8 m/sec. The bicycle wheels have a radius of 34 cm.
   a. What is the angular speed of the wheels?
   b. How many times does each wheel go around during a 10-minute ride?

2. Chris runs around a circular track with a radius of 30 m. He makes 5 trips around the track in 220 seconds.
   a. What is the circumference of the track?
   b. How many meters does he run?
   c. What is his angular speed?
   d. What is his linear speed?

3. Convert the following:
   a. 30 degrees to radians
   b. 220 degrees to radians
   c. 2 radians to degrees
   d. 4.25 radians to degrees
   e. 2 revolutions to radians

4. The wheel of an in-line skate has a radius of 3 cm. What is the linear speed of the skater if the wheel turns at 25 rad/sec?

5. A car tire has a radius of 33 cm. The tire turns a total of 10,250 radians during a trip to the store. How many meters did the car travel?

6. A 50-kg ice skater turns a bend at 7 m/sec. If the radius of the curve is 5 m, what is the centripetal force provided by the friction between the blade of the skate and the ice?

7. A piece of clay with a mass of 0.30 kg is tied to the end of a string 6.5 meters in length, and then is whirled around in a horizontal circle at a speed of 6 m/sec.
   a. What is the centripetal acceleration of the clay?
   b. What is the tension in the string?

8. Calculate the gravitational force of attraction between two 55-kilogram people standing 0.25 m apart.

9. Pluto has a mass of 1.5×10^{22} kg and a radius of 1.15×10^{6} m.
   a. What is the acceleration due to gravity on Pluto?
   b. How much would a 70-kilogram person weigh on Pluto? Compare the value of that weight on Pluto with the person's weight on Earth.

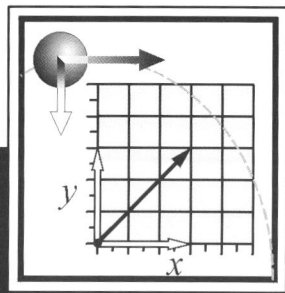

Unit 3

Motion and Force in 2 and 3 Dimensions

Chapter 9

Torque and Rotation

Objectives for Chapter 9

By the end of this chapter you should be able to:

1. Calculate the torque created by a force.
2. Solve problems by balancing two torques in rotational equilibrium.
3. Define the center of mass of an object.
4. Describe a technique for finding the center of mass of an irregularly shaped object.
5. Calculate the moment of inertia for a mass rotating on the end of a rod.
6. Describe the relationship between torque, angular acceleration, and rotational inertia.

Terms and vocabulary words

torque	center of mass	angular acceleration	rotational inertia
rotation	translation	center of rotation	rotational equilibrium
lever arm	center of gravity	moment of inertia	line of action

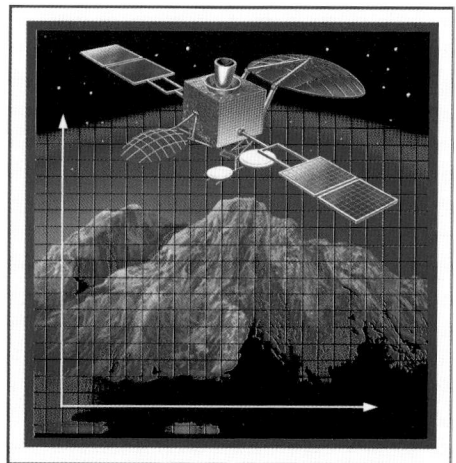

9.1 Torque

Force is the action that creates changes in linear motion. For rotational motion, the same force can cause very different results. For example, think about pushing against a door at its hinges and pushing against a door at its handle with the same force. For rotational motion, the *torque* is what is most directly related to the motion, not the force. Whether you are creating rotational motion by opening a jar, screwing in a light bulb, using a wrench, or opening a door, you are using torque. This section is about torque and the relationship between torque and rotational motion.

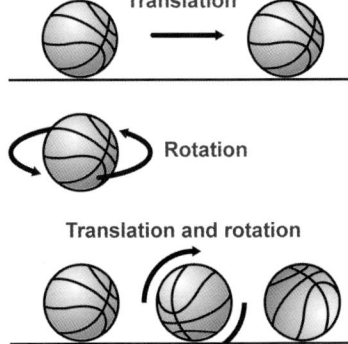

Figure 9.1: *Translation occurs when a ball moves in a line. Rotation occurs when it spins. Both can also occur at the same time.*

What is torque?

Torque and force   A torque is an action that causes objects to rotate. A torque is required to rotate an object, just as a force is required to move an object in a line (Figure 9.1). Torque is the rotational equivalent of force: if force is a *push* or *pull*, then torque is a *twist*.

How torque and force differ   Torque is *not* the same thing as force. Torque is created by force, but it also depends on where the force is applied and the point about which the object rotates. For example, a door pushed at its handle will easily turn and open, but a door pushed near its hinges will not move as easily (Figure 9.2). The force may be the same but the torque is quite different.

The center of rotation   The point or line about which an object turns is its **center of rotation**. For example, a door's center of rotation is at its hinges. A force applied far from the center of rotation produces a greater torque than a force applied close to the center of rotation. Doorknobs are positioned far from the hinges to provide the greatest amount of torque for a given force. If you have ever accidentally tried to open a door by pushing on the hinged side, you know that even a large force did not cause the door to open. Forces applied near the hinges create very little torque *because* they are applied close to the center of rotation.

Translation and rotation   Forces may cause an object to move and/or spin (Figure 9.1). Motion in which an entire object moves is called **translation**. Motion in which an object spins is called **rotation**. The type of motion that results from an applied force depends on the location and direction of the force, whether torque is created by the force, and whether any part of the object is fixed in place.

Figure 9.2: *A door rotates around its hinges and a force creates the greatest torque when applied far from the hinges.*

160

The torque created by a force

The line of action Torque is created when the line of action of a force does not pass through the center of rotation. The line of action is an imaginary line that follows the direction of a force and passes though its point of application. For example, when you pull on a wrench, the line of action of your force passes at a distance from the center of rotation (the bolt). The force creates torque because it acts to rotate the wrench (Figure 9.3). Forces applied in this way act to cause rotation.

A force that makes no torque No torque is created when the line of action goes *through* the center of rotation. For example, pushing on a wrench in its long direction is useless for tightening a bolt. Pushing in the long direction creates no torque because the line of action of the force passes through the center of rotation. The application of the force does *not* act in a way to cause the wrench to rotate.

The lever arm The direction in which the force is applied is also important. To open a door, you apply a force to the knob perpendicular to the door. If you push parallel to the door, toward the hinges, it will not open. To get the maximum torque, the force should be applied in a direction that creates the greatest *lever arm*. The lever arm is the perpendicular distance between the line of action of the force and the center of rotation (Figure 9.4).

Calculating torque The torque (τ) created by a force is equal to the lever arm (r) times the magnitude of the force (F). Torque is usually represented by the lower case Greek letter "tau" (τ). In sketches, a torque is represented by an arc with an arrow indicating the direction of rotation the torque would cause. When calculating torque, be careful determining the length of the lever arm. If the line of action passes through the center of rotation, the lever arm is zero, and so is the torque, no matter how large a force is applied.

The line of action of a force

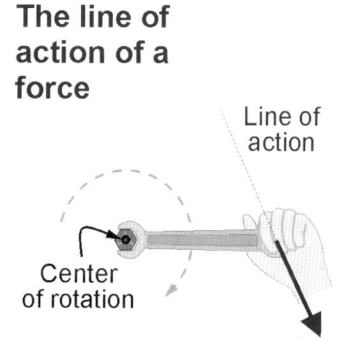

Figure 9.3: *The line of action is an imaginary line that follows the direction of a force and passes though its point of application.*

The lever arm of a force

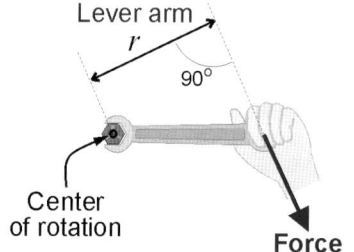

Figure 9.4: *The lever arm is the perpendicular distance between the line of action of the force and the center of rotation.*

Torque

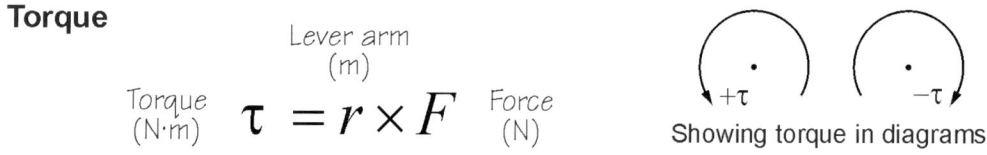

$$\underset{\substack{\text{Torque} \\ \text{(N·m)}}}{\tau} = \underset{\substack{\text{Lever arm} \\ \text{(m)}}}{r} \times \underset{\substack{\text{Force} \\ \text{(N)}}}{F}$$

Showing torque in diagrams

Calculating torque

Torques can be added and subtracted
If more than one torque acts on an object, the torques are combined to determine the net torque. If the torques tend to make an object spin in the same direction (clockwise or counterclockwise), they are added together (Figures 9.5). If the torques tend to make the object spin in opposite directions, the torques are subtracted. To keep the addition and subtraction straight, torques that tend to cause counterclockwise rotation are usually assigned positive values. Torques that tend to cause clockwise rotation are therefore negative. The total torque is calculated by adding up each individual torque, keeping track of the positive and negative signs.

Units of torque
The units of torque are force times distance, or newton-meters. A torque of 1 N-m is created by a force of 1 newton acting with a lever arm of 1 meter. Because torque is a product of two variables, it is possible to create the same torque with different forces. For example, a 10-newton force applied with a lever arm of 0.1 meter also produces a torque of 1 N-m.

Torque about different centers
Torque is always calculated around a *particular center of rotation*. For this reason, the same force may cause different torques when an object is allowed to rotate around different points. For example, a force of 1 newton applied to a 1-meter board creates a torque of 0.5 N-m when the board rotates about its center (Figure 9.6). The same force creates a torque of 1 N-m, or twice as great, when the board rotates about its end.

Positive and negative torque

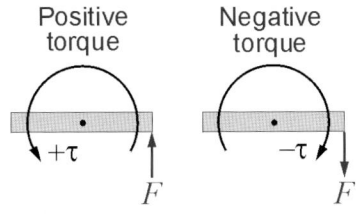

Positive torque   Negative torque

Adding torques

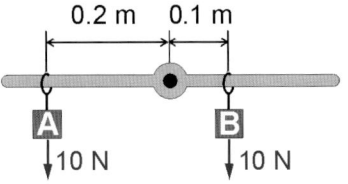

0.2 m   0.1 m

A   B

10 N   10 N

$$\tau_A = +2\ \text{N} \cdot \text{m}$$
$$\tau_B = -1\ \text{N} \cdot \text{m}$$
$$\tau_A + \tau_B = +1\ \text{N} \cdot \text{m}$$

Figure 9.5: *The terms clockwise and counterclockwise are used to describe the direction of torques.*

Calculate a torque

A force of 50 newtons is applied to a wrench that is 30 centimeters long. Calculate the torque if the force is applied perpendicular to the wrench so the lever arm is 30 cm.

1) You are asked to find the torque.
2) You are given the force and lever arm.
3) The formula that applies is $\tau = rF$.
4) Solve:

$$\tau = (-50\ \text{N})(0.3\ \text{m}) = -15\ \text{N·m}$$

30 cm

50 N

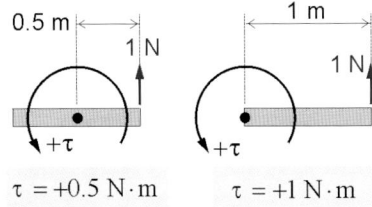

0.5 m   1 m

1 N   1 N

$+\tau$ $+\tau$

$\tau = +0.5\ \text{N} \cdot \text{m}$ $\tau = +1\ \text{N} \cdot \text{m}$

Figure 9.6: *The torque created by a force depends on the location of the center of rotation.*

Rotational equilibrium

Net torque is zero | When an object is in rotational equilibrium, the net torque applied to it is zero. For example, if an object such as a see-saw is not rotating, you know the torque on each side is balanced. An object in rotational equilibrium can also be rotating at constant speed, like a wheel.

Using rotational equilibrium | Rotational equilibrium is often used to determine unknown forces. Any object that is not moving is in rotational equilibrium *and* in translational equilibrium. Both kinds of equilibrium are often needed to find unknown forces. For example, consider a 10-meter bridge that weighs 500 newtons supported at both ends. A person who weighs 750 newtons is standing 2 meters from one end of the bridge. What are the forces (F_A, F_B) holding the bridge up at either end?

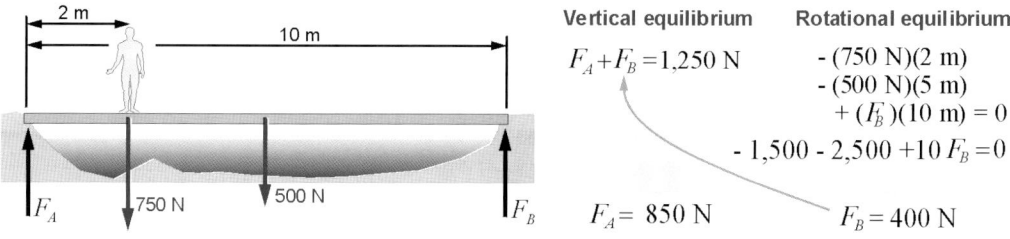

Vertical equilibrium

$$F_A + F_B = 1{,}250 \text{ N}$$

$$F_A = 850 \text{ N}$$

Rotational equilibrium

$$-(750 \text{ N})(2 \text{ m})$$
$$-(500 \text{ N})(5 \text{ m})$$
$$+(F_B)(10 \text{ m}) = 0$$
$$-1{,}500 - 2{,}500 + 10 F_B = 0$$

$$F_B = 400 \text{ N}$$

Vertical equilibrium | For the bridge not to move up or down, the total upward force must equal the total downward force. This means $F_A + F_B = 1{,}250$ N. Unfortunately, balanced force in the vertical direction does not tell you how the force is divided between the two ends, F_A and F_B.

Solving for the unknown forces | For the bridge to be in rotational equilibrium, the total torque *around any point* must be zero. If we choose the left end of the bridge, the torque created by force F_A is zero because its line of action passes through the center of rotation. By setting the total of the remaining torques to zero, the force on the right support (F_B) is calculated to be 400 newtons. Since the total of both forces must be 1,250 N, that means the force on the left (F_A) must be 850 N. This kind of analysis is used to solve many problems in physics and engineering, including how strong to make bridges, floors, ladders, and other structures that must support forces.

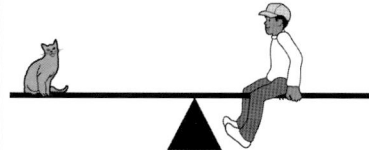

When the force and lever arm are not perpendicular *Advanced topic*

Force and lever arm are not always perpendicular

Torque is easiest to calculate when the lever arm and force are at right angles to each other. In this situation the lever arm is the same as the distance between the point where the force is applied and the center of rotation. When the force and lever arm are *not* perpendicular, an extra step is required to calculate the length of the lever arm.

Torque from angled forces

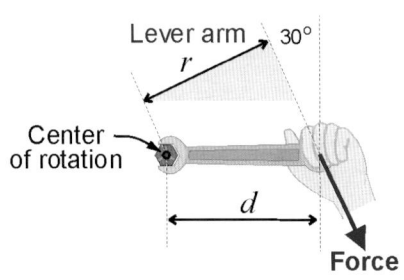

Triangle relationships

Finding the torque

$$r = d \cos 30°$$

$$\cos 30° = \frac{r}{d}$$

$$\tau = rF$$

Solution

$$\tau = Fd \cos 30°$$

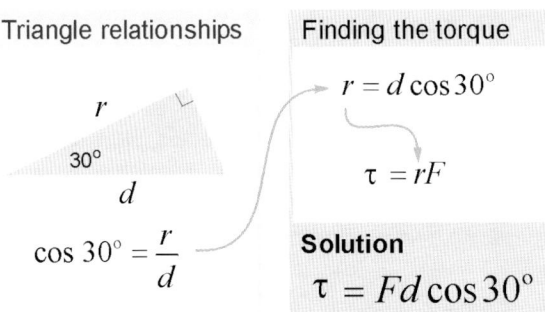

Torque in English units

In the English system of units, torque is measured in inch-pounds or foot-pounds. A torque of one foot-pound is created by a force of one pound applied with a lever arm of one foot. One foot-pound is equal to 12 inch-pounds.

Tighten to 50 in-lbs

Bolt

Nut

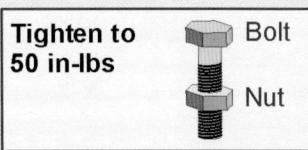

Many machines are held together with nuts and bolts, or other threaded fasteners. The proper tightness of nuts and bolts is often specified in foot-pounds of torque. If a nut is too tight, it may strip the threads or snap the bolt. If a nut is too loose, it may vibrate off the bolt. Each size nut has a proper tightening torque.

Calculate a torque from an angled force

A 20-centimeter wrench is used to loosen a bolt. The force is applied 0.20 m from the bolt. It takes 50 newtons to loosen the bolt when the force is applied perpendicular to the wrench. How much force would it take if the force was applied at a 30-degree angle from perpendicular?

1) You are asked to find the force.
2) You are given the force and lever arm for one condition.
3) The formula that applies is τ = rF.
4) Solve: The torque required to loosen the bolt
  τ = (50 N)(0.2 m) = 10 N·m
  To get the same torque with a force applied at 30 degrees:
  10 N·m = F × (0.2 m)cos30° = 0.173 F
  F = 10 N·m ÷ 0.173 = 58 N. It takes a larger force.

Bolt — 20 cm

Force

9.2 Center of Mass

The shape of an object and the way its mass is distributed affect the way the object moves and balances. For example, it is much easier to tip over a tall, thin vase than a short, wide tea kettle. This section talks about the center of mass, which is the point around which an object balances. The location of the center of mass explains why some objects are stable and others easily topple over.

Finding the center of mass

The motion of a tossed object In Chapter 7 you learned that a ball thrown into the air at an angle moves in a parabola. But what if an irregularly shaped object is thrown? If you throw a soda bottle so it spins during its flight, the general shape of its path will also be a parabola. If you watch the bottle closely, one specific point moves in a perfect parabola. This point is located on the axis about which the bottle spins.

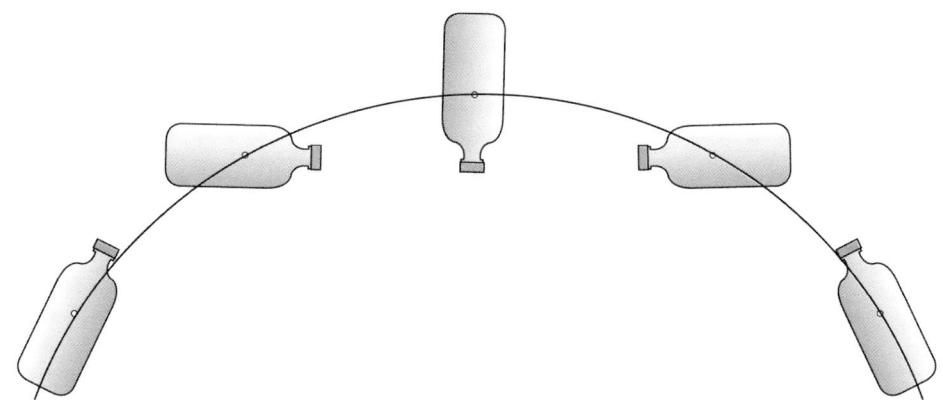

Defining center of mass There are three different axes about which an object will naturally spin. The point at which the three axes intersect is called the center of mass (Figure 9.7). The center of mass is defined as the average position of all the particles that make up the object's mass. It is easy to find the center of mass for a symmetrically shaped object made of a uniform material such as a solid rubber ball or a wooden cube. The center of mass is located at the geometric center of the object. If an object is irregularly shaped, the center of mass can be found by spinning the object and finding the intersection of the three spin axes.

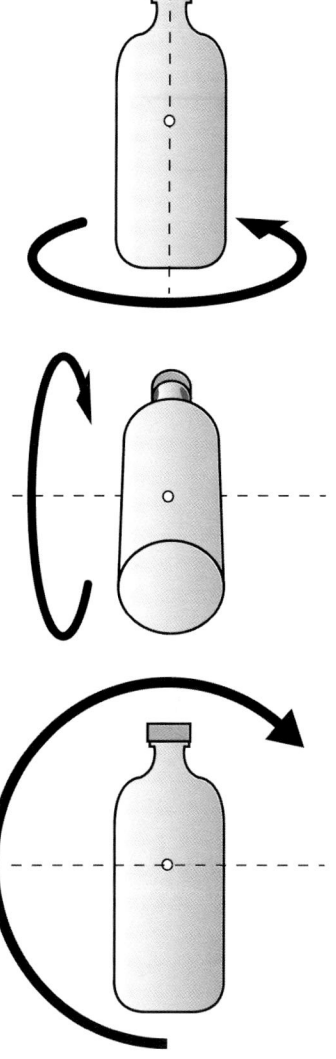

Figure 9.7: *An object naturally spins about three different axes. Their intersection is the center of mass.*

Finding the center of mass

The center of mass may not be "in" an object

There is not always material at an object's center of mass. The center of mass of a donut is at its very center—where there is only empty space. The same is true for a coffee mug, boomerang, and an empty box.

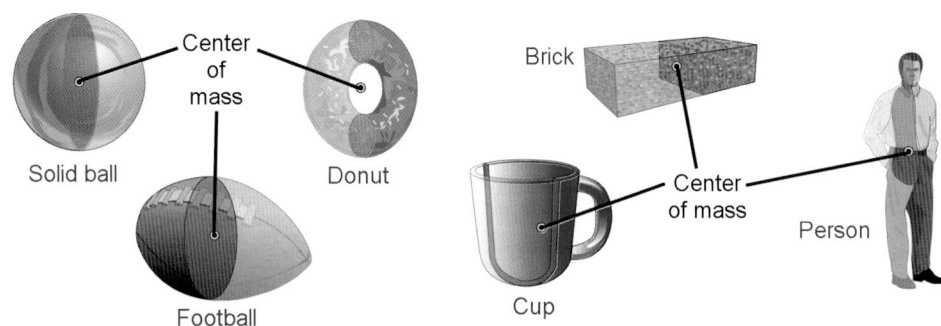

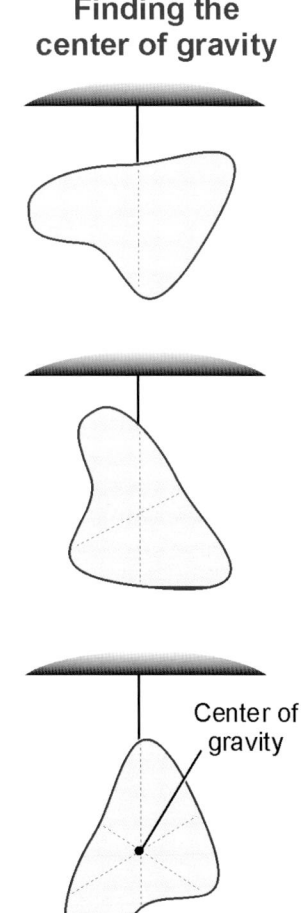

The center of gravity

Closely related to the center of mass is the center of gravity. The center of gravity is the average position of an object's weight. It is also the point at which we consider the force of gravity to act on an object. If the acceleration due to gravity is the same at every point in an object, the center of mass and center of gravity are at the same location. This is the case for most everyday objects, so the two terms are often used interchangeably.

Finding the center of gravity

An object's center of gravity can easily be found experimentally. If an object is suspended from a point at its edge, the center of gravity will always fall in the line directly below the point of suspension. If the object is suspended from two or more points, the center of gravity can be found by tracing the line below each point and finding the intersection of the lines (Figure 9.8).

Centers of mass and gravity may differ

For very tall objects, such as skyscrapers, the acceleration due to gravity may be slightly different at points throughout the object. Gravity is stronger closer to the surface of the earth, so the pull of gravity at the bottom of a tall building is slightly stronger than the pull at the top. The top half therefore weighs less than the bottom half, even when both halves have the same mass. While the center of mass will be halfway up the building, the center of gravity will be slightly below the center.

Figure 9.8: *The center of gravity of an irregularly shaped object can be found by suspending it from two or more points.*

166

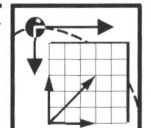
Balance and the center of mass

Balancing an object — To balance an object such as a book or a pencil on your finger, you must place your finger directly under the object's center of gravity. The object balances because the torque caused by the force of the object's weight is equal on each side.

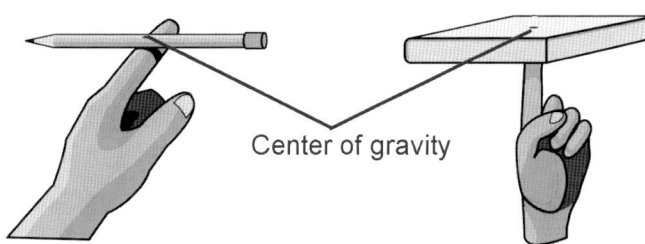

Center of gravity

The area of support — For an object to remain upright, its center of gravity must be above its area of support. The area of support includes the entire region surrounded by the actual supports. For example, a table's area of support is the region bounded by its four legs. Your body's support area is not only where your feet touch the ground, but also the region between your feet. The larger the area of support, the less likely an object is to topple over.

When an object will topple over — An object will topple over if its center of mass is not above its area of support. For example, a block will topple over if it is tipped far enough. Imagine a straight line drawn from the center of gravity toward the center of the Earth. If this line passes through the area of support, the object will not topple. If the line passes outside the area of support, the object will topple over if it is not held upright.

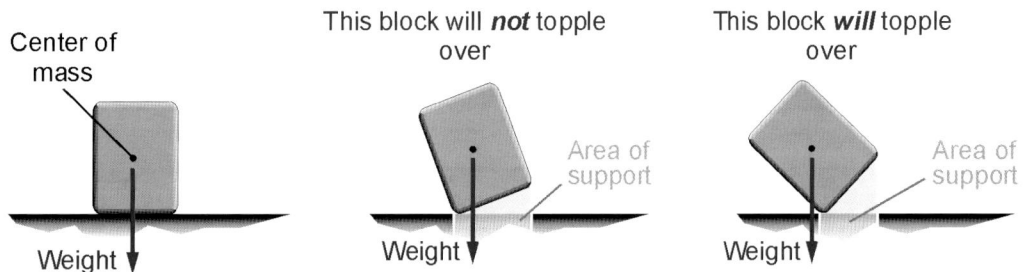

Center of mass

This block will **not** topple over

This block **will** topple over

Area of support

Area of support

Weight

Weight

Weight

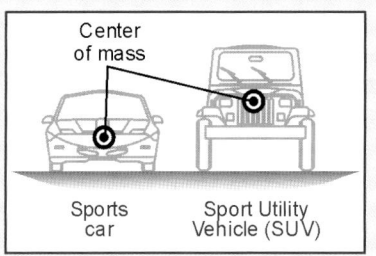

SUV rollovers

Center of mass

Sports car

Sport Utility Vehicle (SUV)

Many injuries and fatalities from auto accidents involve rollovers. Sports cars are designed with a wide wheelbase and a low center of mass to reduce the risk of rolling over at high speed. Sport utility vehicles (SUVs), however, have a relatively high center of mass compared with their wheelbase. Because of that high center of mass, an SUV is more likely to roll over in an accident. According to government statistics, 62 percent of fatal accidents in SUVs involve rollovers, while only 22 percent of those in passenger cars involve rollovers.*

*National Highway Traffic Safety Administration

9.3 Rotational Inertia

Imagine that you lift the front wheel of your bicycle off the ground. A friend applies a force to the tire and makes the wheel spin. It keeps spinning until the torque provided by friction eventually slows it to a stop. Just as objects moving in a line have inertia, spinning objects have rotational inertia.

Rotation and Newton's first law

Spinning objects tend to keep spinning

Recall Newton's first law of motion: An object at rest will remain at rest and an object in motion will remain in motion at a constant velocity unless acted on by a net force. Until now we have applied this law to objects in linear motion. Newton's first law also applies to objects in rotational motion. A spinning object will keep spinning at a constant angular speed unless acted on by a net torque. Just as a force is needed to change the motion of an object moving in a line, a torque is needed to change the angular speed or axis of a rotating object.

Rotational inertia

Inertia is the name for an object's resistance to a change in its motion (or lack of motion). Rotational inertia is the term used to describe an object's resistance to a change in its rotational motion. The more mass an object has, the greater its linear inertia and the harder it is to change its motion. The same is true for rotational inertia. Objects with greater mass usually have greater rotational inertia than objects with less mass. For example, bicycle wheels are designed with spokes rather than solid disks in order to reduce the wheels' mass and make them easier to spin. However, it is also possible to make a less massive object have *more* rotational inertia than a more massive object.

Mass distribution affects rotational inertia

An object's rotational inertia depends not only on the total mass, but also on the way mass is distributed. When the mass is concentrated near the object's axis of rotation, it is easy to spin (Figure 9.9). When the mass is far from the axis of rotation, it is difficult to spin. You can feel the difference by attaching two masses to a meter stick. First place the masses close to the center of the meter stick, and rotate it with one hand. Then move the masses to the ends of the meter stick and compare its resistance to spinning. It is much harder to spin when the masses are at the ends. The reason is that the farther the masses are from the center, the greater distance they must move with each rotation.

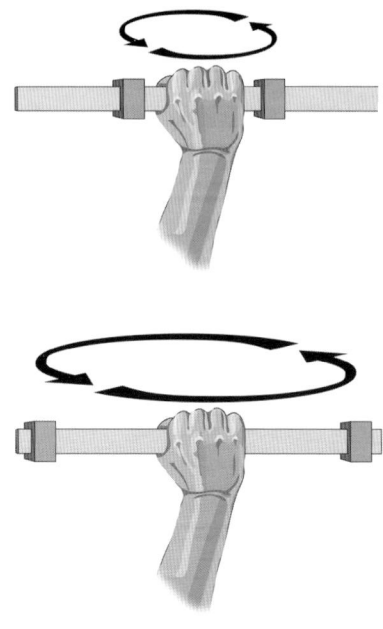

Figure 9.9: *The meter stick is easier to spin when the masses are closer to the center.*

Rotational inertia

The meaning of rotational inertia

Inertia is a measure of resistance to acceleration. To understand rotational inertia, we need to find a form of Newton's second law that applies to rotating motion. According to Newton's second law ($a = F \div m$), the linear acceleration is equal to force divided by the mass. Because inertia is created by mass, in most circumstances an object's *linear* inertia is equal to its mass. For rotating motion, we need an equation that relates torque, and *angular acceleration* in a similar way as force and linear acceleration are related by $a = F \div m$.

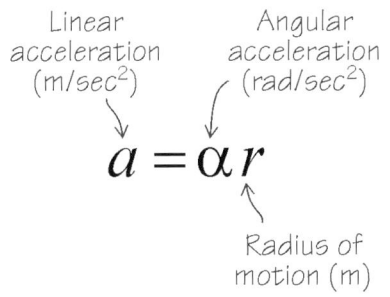

$$a = \alpha r$$

Figure 9.10: *The relationship between linear and angular acceleration.*

Angular acceleration

The rate at which angular speed changes is called angular acceleration. The angular acceleration is the change in angular speed divided by the change in time. For example, suppose a wheel starts at rest. Five seconds later the wheel is rotating with an angular speed of 100 rad/sec. The angular acceleration of the wheel is 20 rad/sec^2, meaning the angular speed increases by 20 rad/sec each second.

Linear and angular acceleration

In Chapter 8, you learned that the linear speed (v) is equal to the angular speed (ω) times the radius of the motion (r). A similar relationship exists between the linear acceleration (a) and angular acceleration (α) (Figure 9.10). The units of angular acceleration are rad/sec^2, although the radian is not a true unit (Chapter 8).

The form of rotational inertia

To find what rotational inertia is, consider the force it takes to start moving a mass fixed to the end of rod that is free to rotate (Figure 9.11). The acceleration of the mass is given by $a = F \div m$. To put the equation into rotational motion variables, the force is replaced by the torque about the center of rotation ($F = \tau \div r$). The linear acceleration is replaced by the angular acceleration ($a = \alpha r$). The resulting formula has a quantity mr^2 that connects the torque and angular acceleration in the exact same way that mass connects force and linear acceleration. This quantity (mr^2) is therefore the rotational inertia.

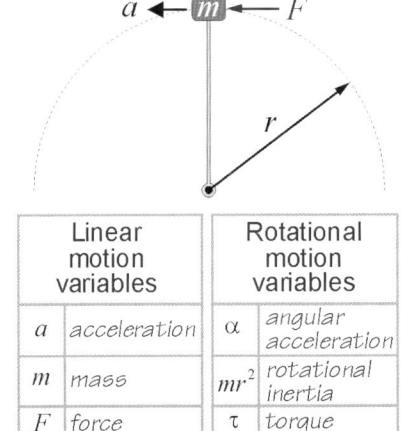

Linear motion variables		Rotational motion variables	
a	acceleration	α	angular acceleration
m	mass	mr^2	rotational inertia
F	force	τ	torque

Figure 9.11: *A rotating mass on a rod can be described with variables from linear or rotational motion.*

Newton's second law
(linear motion variables)

$$a = \frac{F}{m}$$

Mass (kg)

Newton's second law
(rotating point mass)

$$\alpha = \frac{\tau}{mr^2}$$

Rotational inertia (kg·m²)

The moment of inertia

Rotational inertia of solid objects   The product of mass × radius squared (mr^2) is the rotational inertia for a point mass where r is measured from the axis of rotation. Because of the r in mr^2, mass that is farther from the axis of rotation has much more rotational inertia than mass close to the axis. For example, a 1-kilogram mass on a 2-meter rod has *four times* the rotational inertia of the same mass on a 1-meter rod. That means it takes four times as much torque to produce the same angular acceleration.

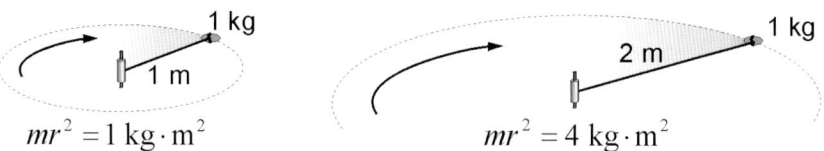

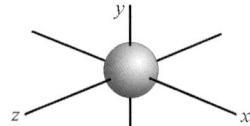

Sphere of mass, m, radius, R

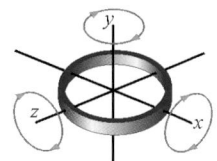

Hoop of mass, m, radius, R

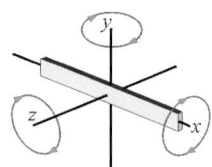

Bar of mass, m, length, l

The moment of inertia   A solid object contains mass distributed at different distances from the center of rotation. Because rotational inertia depends on the *square* of the radius, the distribution of mass makes a big difference for solid objects, such as steel balls. The sum of mr^2 for all the particles of mass in a solid is called the moment of inertia (I). Figure 9.12 shows the moment of inertia for some simple solid shapes when rotated about an axis passing through the center. Notice the moment of inertia of the same shape is different depending on which rotation axis is chosen. In Chapters 11 and 12, you will see the moment of inertia used instead of mass in many calculations involving rotational motion, including kinetic energy and angular momentum.

Comparing solid and hollow objects   A hoop has a greater moment of inertia than a solid disk of the same mass. This is because all the mass of a hoop is at a large radius. Some of the mass of a solid disk is at smaller radii and therefore contributes less rotational inertia. In fact, the mass at the center contributes no rotational inertia since its radius is zero. In general, a solid object has a lower moment of inertia than a hollow object *of the same mass*.

Rotational inertia depends on the axis   The axis about which an object rotates affects its moment of inertia. If an object rotates about an axis that does not pass through its center of mass, it usually has a greater moment of inertia. You can feel this for yourself using the meter stick with the masses on it. No matter where you place the masses, it will always be easier to spin the meter stick when your hand is between the masses.

Moment of Inertia			
	Axis of rotation		
	x	y	z
Sphere	$\frac{2}{5}mR^2$	$\frac{2}{5}mR^2$	$\frac{2}{5}mR^2$
Hoop	$\frac{1}{2}mR^2$	mR^2	$\frac{1}{2}mR^2$
Bar		$\frac{1}{12}ml^2$	$\frac{1}{12}ml^2$

Figure 9.12: *The moment of inertia of some simple shapes rotated around axes that pass through their centers.*

Rotation and Newton's second law

Angular
acceleration
of a wheel

When a torque is applied to an object, it spins in the direction of the applied torque (Figure 9.13). Its angular speed increases at a rate directly proportional to the net torque and inversely proportional to the object's moment of inertia. For example, the moment of inertia of a bicycle wheel is about 0.1 kg-m². When the brakes are applied, a force of 100 newtons is applied at the rim of the wheel, at a radius of 0.35 m. The torque produced by this force is 35 N-m. The angular acceleration is the torque divided by the moment of inertia, or 350 rad/sec² (35 N-m ÷ 0.1 kg-m²). The angular speed of the wheel increases by 350 radians per second each second the torque is applied.

Newton's second law
*(rotational motion
variables)*

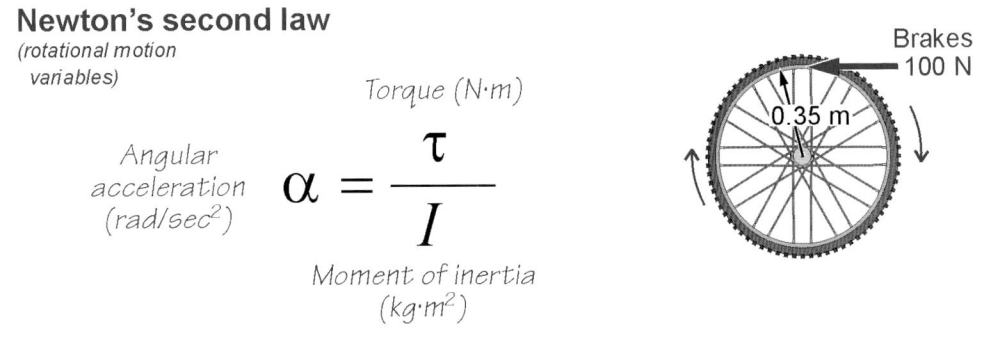

$$\underset{\substack{\text{Angular}\\ \text{acceleration}\\ (rad/sec^2)}}{\alpha} = \frac{\overset{Torque\ (N \cdot m)}{\tau}}{\underset{\substack{Moment\ of\ inertia\\ (kg \cdot m^2)}}{I}}$$

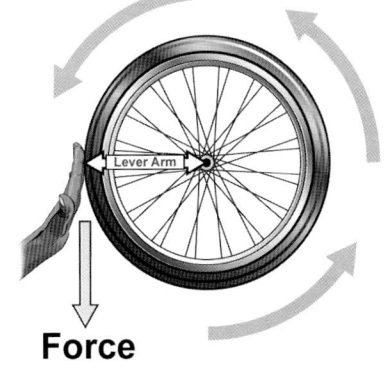

Force

Figure 9.13: *If you apply a torque to a wheel, it will spin in the direction of the torque. The greater the torque, the greater the angular acceleration.*

New variables
in familiar
relationships

Although rotational motion has a completely new set of variables, the relationships are similar. Force causes linear acceleration, torque causes angular acceleration. Mass is a measure of linear inertia. The moment of inertia (I) is a measure of rotational inertia.

Force causes linear acceleration.   Torque causes angular acceleration.

Application: Bicycle Physics

A modern bicycle is the most efficient machine ever invented for turning human muscle power into motion. Bicycles work by a series of transformations from forces to torques and back. By changing the radius of a bicycle's gears, the rider can choose different ratios between the force applied to the pedals and the force applied to the road.

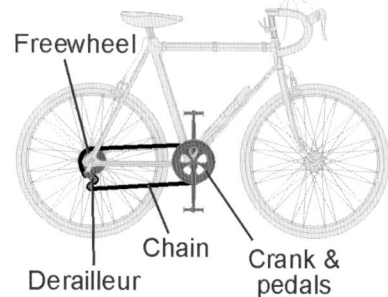

Figure 9.14: *The components of a bicycle drive system.*

Parts of the drive system

The drive system of a multispeed bicycle has four major parts (Figure 9.14).

1. The crank and pedals are where force is applied

2. The chain transmits the force to the rear wheel.

3. A set of gears called a freewheel transfers the force from the chain to the back wheel of the bicycle. The back wheel transmits the force to the road.

4. A derailleur allows the chain to switch gears and change the force ratio between the pedals and the road.

Force and torque on the crank

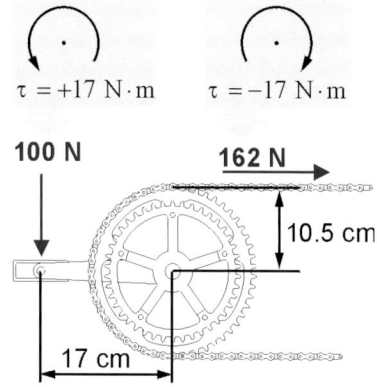

A force applied to the pedals creates a torque on the crank. A crank is 17 centimeters long and a 100-newton force on the pedal creates a torque of 17 N-m. The crank on a road bicycle usually has two gears called chainwheels. The larger chainwheel has 52 teeth and a diameter of 10.5 cm. When the crank is in rotational equilibrium, the force on the chain is 162 N. The force is multiplied because the chainwheel has a smaller radius and it takes a larger force to balance the torque from the 100 N force applied to the pedals.

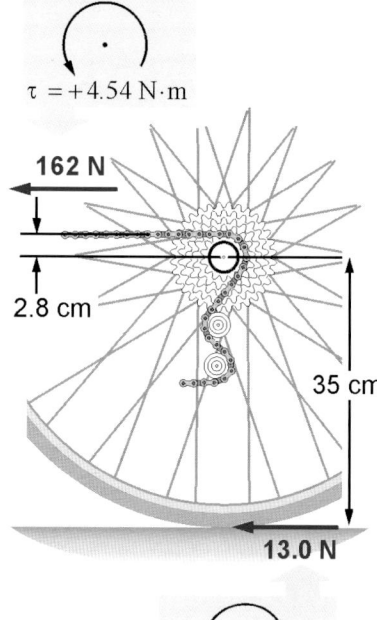

Figure 9.15: *Torques and forces on the rear wheel.*

Force and torque on the rear wheel

The 162-newton force creates a torque on the rear wheel that depends on the gear the chain is on. The small gear on a freewheel has 14 teeth and a radius of 2.8 cm. The torque applied to the rear wheel is then 4.54 N-m, which is 162 N × 0.028 m. The torque applied by the chain is balanced by the torque created by the force of the road pushing back on the bicycle. The radius of the wheel is 35 centimeters. The force applied by the road is therefore 4.5 N-m ÷ 0.35 m = 13.0 N. This is the force that moves the bicycle forward (Figure 9.15).

172

Changing gears

Force and torque with the small chainwheel

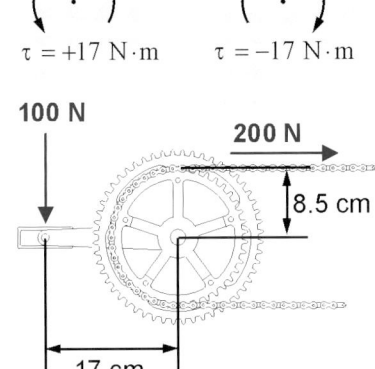

$\tau = +17$ N·m $\qquad \tau = -17$ N·m

100 N

200 N

8.5 cm

17 cm

The derailleurs (front and rear) make it easy to move the chain onto different gears. The different gears change the ratio of forces and torques on the crank and the rear wheel. For example, the rider can select the smaller chainwheel, which has a radius of 8.5 cm. When 100 N is applied to the pedals, the force on the chain is now 200 N, compared with 162 N with the chain on the larger chainwheel. The force is greater because the torque applied by the chain on the crank must still balance the torque from the pedals (17 N-m), but at a smaller radius.

Force and torque on the rear wheel   Suppose the rider uses the derailleur to select the largest gear in the freewheel. This gear typically has 32 teeth and a radius of 6.5 cm. The 200 N force from the chain creates a torque of 13 N-m on the rear wheel (Figure 9.16). This results in a force on the ground of 37.1 N, almost three times larger than the force of 13 N obtained with the other combination of gears.

High gear   With the combination of the large chainwheel and small freewheel gear, a 100 N force applied to the pedals creates a 13 N force on the road. This is a relatively small force compared with the input force of 100 N. The advantage is that the rear wheel turns four times (52 teeth ÷ 13 teeth) for every turn of the pedals. This combination is called high gear. High gear is used for high speeds on level ground or going down hill because each turn of the pedals moves the bicycle forward four times the circumference of the wheel.

Low gear   The combination of the small (42-tooth) chainwheel and large (32-tooth) freewheel gear is called *low gear*. In low gear, the 100 N force on the pedals creates a 37.1 N force on the ground. The trade-off is in speed. One turn of the pedals in low gear turns the rear wheel only 1.3 times (42 teeth ÷ 32 teeth). Low gear is used for high-force, low-speed riding, such as climbing hills or starting from a stop.

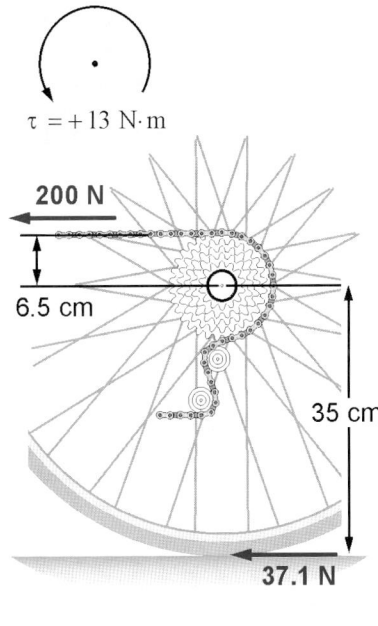

$\tau = +13$ N·m

200 N

6.5 cm

35 cm

37.1 N

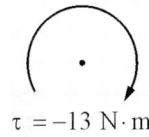

$\tau = -13$ N·m

Figure 9.16: *Forces and torques on the rear wheel when the chain is on the 32-tooth gear of the freewheel.*

Chapter 9 Review

Vocabulary Review

Match the following terms with the correct definition. There is one extra definition in the list that will not match any of the terms

Set One

1. rotational inertia

2. angular acceleration

3. torque

4. lever arm

5. axis of rotation

a. The rotational equivalent of force
b. An object's resistance to a change in its rotational motion
c. The line about which an object spins
d. The distance between the fulcrum and the place where a force is applied to an object
e. The time required for one rotation
f. A change in an object's rotational speed

Set Two

1. translation

2. center of gravity

3. moment of inertia

4. rotational equilibrium

5. center of mass

a. Occurs when an object's center of mass moves from one point to another
b. The average position of all the particles that make up an object's mass
c. When the net force on an object is zero
d. The average position of an object's weight
e. When the net torque on an object is zero
f. The average value of mr^2 for all particles that make up an object's mass

Concept review

1. How are torque and force similar? How are they different?

2. What is the difference between translation and rotation? What determines which type of motion an object will experience?

3. Why does a long-handled wrench make it easier to loosen a bolt?

4. You use torque to move when you pedal a bike. How does the torque provided by your feet when they are in a vertical line compare to the torque when one foot is in front of the other? Explain.

5. Which force will create the greatest amount of torque on the shovel?

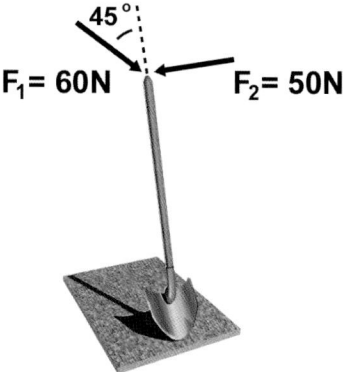

45°

$F_1 = 60N$ $F_2 = 50N$

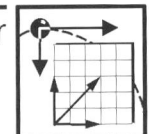
6. If the see-saw is balanced, which person has the greater weight? How do you know this?

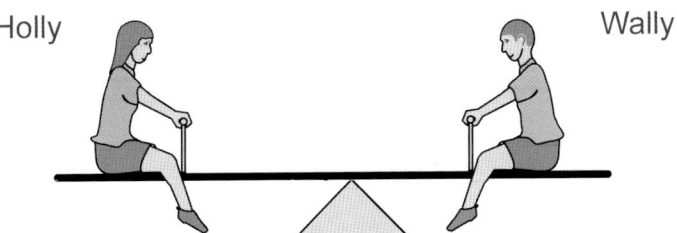

Holly   Wally

7. What does it mean to say an object is in rotational equilibrium?

8. When is it okay to use the terms center of gravity and center of mass interchangeably?

9. Choose the letter of the point that is the center of mass of each object.

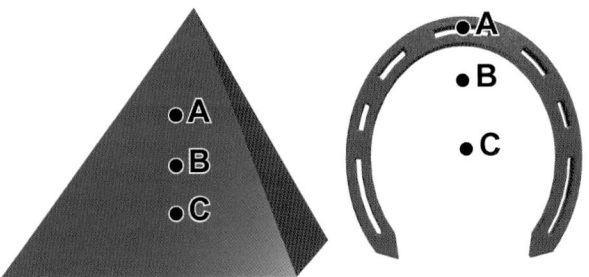

10. Tightrope walkers often use long poles to help them balance. Explain why this makes sense.

11. If you spin an egg in its shell, stop it for an instant, and then release it, it will start spinning again. Explain why this happens. Will the same thing happen if the egg is hard boiled? Why or why not?

12. Explain how you can experimentally locate an object's center of gravity.

13. Which object(s) will topple? Each object's center of gravity is marked.

14. Which two factors determine an object's rotational inertia?

15. Which would be easier to spin, a 3 kg bowling ball or a 3 kg barbell? Why?

16. How are torque, rotational inertia, and angular acceleration related?

175

Problems

1. You use a wrench to loosen a bolt. It finally turns when you apply 250 N of force perpendicular to the wrench at a distance 0.3 m from the bolt. Calculate the torque.

2. A torque of 60 N-m can be created by a 30 N force acting perpendicularly to a 2 m lever arm. How can a 15 N force be used to create the same torque? How far from the center of the see-saw should Helena sit if she wants to balance Lindsey's torque?

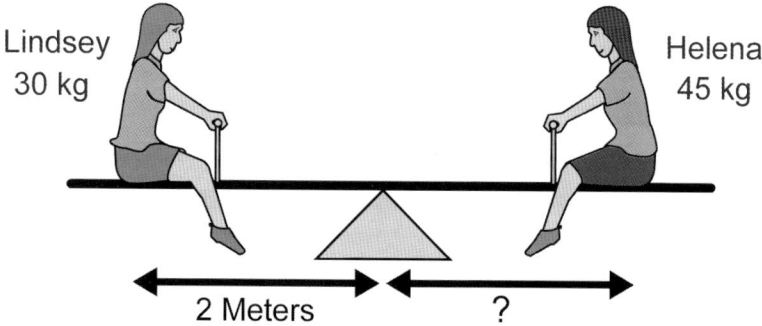

3. What is the unknown mass if the rod is balanced? Assume the rod's mass is negligible when compared with the mass of the blocks.

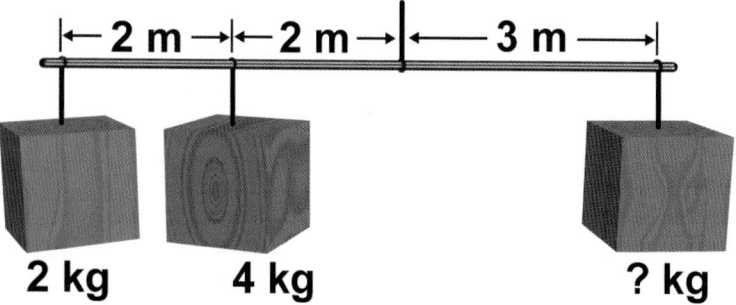

4. Calculate the moment of inertia of each of the following objects rotated about an axis through its center of mass:

   a. a solid rubber ball with a radius of 0.10 m and a mass of 2 kg

   b. a hollow rubber ball with a radius of 0.15 m and a mass of 1 kg

   c. a meter stick with a mass of 0.3 kg

   d. a ring with a radius of 0.25 m and a mass of 4 kg

5. What torque is required to spin a wheel with a moment of inertia of 2.5 kg-m^2 at an angular acceleration of 5 rad/s^2?

6. Ed wants to determine the moment of inertia of the propeller on his helicopter. He applies a torque of 3,000 N-m and measures the propeller's angular acceleration to be 10 rad/s^2. What is the propeller's moment of inertia?

7. A carousel at an amusement park has a total moment of inertia of 60,000 kg-m^2 when children are sitting on all of its horses. When it starts spinning, the motor supplies a torque of 15,000 N-m. What is the resulting angular acceleration?

Unit 4
Energy and Momentum

Chapter 10

Work and Energy

Objectives for Chapter 10

By the end of this chapter you should be able to:

1. Analyze a simple machine in terms of input force, output force, and mechanical advantage.
2. Calculate the mechanical advantage for a lever or rope and pulleys.
3. Calculate the work done in joules for situations involving force and distance.
4. Give examples of energy and transformation of energy from one form to another.
5. Calculate potential and kinetic energy.
6. Apply the law of energy conservation to systems involving potential and kinetic energy.

Terms and vocabulary words

machine	energy	input force	output force	thermal energy
ramp	gear	screw	rope and pulleys	closed system
work	lever	friction	mechanical system	simple machine
potential energy	kinetic energy	radiant energy	nuclear energy	mechanical advantage
chemical energy	mechanical energy	joule	pressure energy	conservation of energy
electrical energy	input	output	input arm	output arm
fulcrum				

177

10.1 Machines and Mechanical Advantage

The human body is capable of exerting forces up to a few times its own weight. How did ancient people move huge stones to build monuments like the Great Pyramid of Giza long before the invention of trucks and engines? The answer is that people are ingenious and the ancient builders developed simple machines that allowed then to multiply by many times the force from their muscles. In this section, you will learn how simple machines manipulate forces to accomplish useful tasks.

Machines

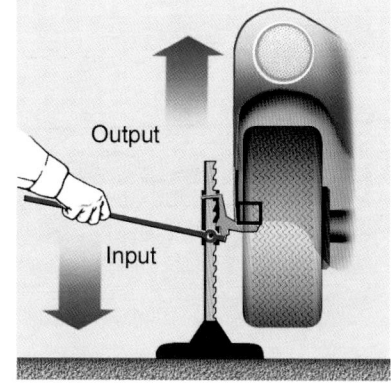

Figure 10.1: *A jack is a simple machine that allows a single person to lift a car with only the force from their muscles.*

Machines and mechanical systems

The ability of humans to build buildings and move mountains began with our invention of machines. A machine is a device that is created by humans to do something. A screwdriver is a very simple example of a machine created to turn screws. A bicycle is a more complex machine. All the parts of a bicycle work together to transform forces from your muscles into speed and motion. In fact, the bicycle is one of the most efficient machines ever invented.

A simple machine you should know how to use

Suppose you must lift a 2,000 kilogram automobile so you can change a tire. The road is deserted and there is no one to help you. Fortunately you know some practical physics and you remember that inside the trunk of the car is a *jack*. A jack is an example of a simple machine. In physics the term "simple machine" means a machine that uses only the forces directly applied and accomplishes its task with a single motion. You attach the jack under the car and are easily able to lift the car yourself, and with only one hand (Figure 10.1). The jack multiplies the force from your arm by many times. The force from your arm is transformed into a much larger force, one capable of lifting a car.

The bicycle as a machine

The output is forward motion

The input is force applied to pedals

Figure 10.2: *Applying the ideas of input and output to a bicycle. The bicycle is a very efficient machine.*

The concepts of input and output

Machines are designed to do something useful. The best way to analyze what a machine does is to think about the machine in terms of input and output. The *input* includes everything you do to make a machine work. For a bicycle, one input is force applied to the pedals. Another input is force applied to the handlebar to steer. The *output* is what the machine does for you. The output of a bicycle is force applied to the road that makes the bicycle accelerate or overcome friction (Figure 10.2). All machines can be described in terms of input and output.

178

Mechanical advantage

Input and output forces A simple machine is analyzed in terms of forces applied *to* the machine and forces applied *by* the machine. A lever is a good example of a simple machine. The jack described on the preceding page is an example of a lever. In order to lift the car you apply a force to the arm of the jack (Figure 10.3). The force you apply is called the input force. The arm of the jack rotates around a pin and pushes a hook that lifts the car. The output force of the lever is the force that pushes on the hook.

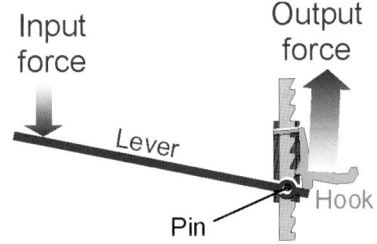

Figure 10.3: *A jack is an example of a lever. The input force is applied to the lever. The output force is applied by the lever to lift the car.*

Mechanical advantage Mechanical advantage is the ratio of output force to input force. If the mechanical advantage is bigger than one, the output force is bigger than the input force (Figure 10.3). A mechanical advantage smaller than one means the output force is smaller than the input force. For a typical automotive jack the mechanical advantage is 30 or more. For a mechanical advantage of 30, a force of 100 newtons (22.5 pounds) applied to the input arm of the jack produces an output force of 3,000 newtons (675 pounds)—enough to lift one corner of an automobile.

Mechanical Advantage

Mechanical advantage $$MA = \frac{F_o}{F_i}$$ Output force (N)

Input force (N)

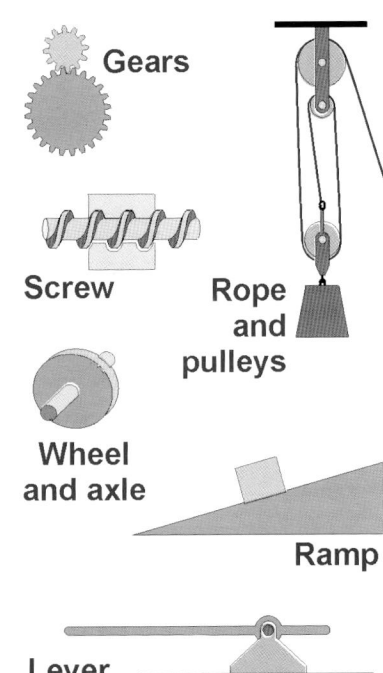

Gears

Screw

Rope and pulleys

Wheel and axle

Ramp

Lever

Figure 10.4: *The basic types of simple machines.*

How mechanical advantage is created If you use a jack to lift a car you will notice that you have to move the arm of the jack a lot to raise the car only a little. Machines create mechanical advantage by trading off between force and distance. On the input of the jack, a small force has to move a large distance. On the output of the jack, a much larger force moves only a small distance. Later in the chapter you will see that the inverse relationship between force and distance is characteristic of all simple machines, and is due to a powerful natural law in physics (conservation of energy).

Types of simple machines There are a few basic kinds of simple machines that create mechanical advantage. The lever, wheel and axle, rope and pulleys, screw, ramp, and gears are the most common types (Figure 10.4). Complex machines such as a bicycle combine many simple machines into mechanical systems. A mechanical system is an assembly of simple machines that work together to accomplish a task.

The mechanical advantage of a lever

Example of a lever: A simple lever is a board balanced on a log (Figure 10.5). The board can rotate around the log. Pushing down on one end of the board creates an upward force on the other end. If the board is used to lift a rock, the force you apply is the input force. The force that lifts the rock is the output force.

Analyzing a lever: The essential features of a lever are the input arm, output arm, and fulcrum. The fulcrum is the point about which the lever rotates. The input arm is the distance between the input force and the fulcrum. The output arm is the distance between the output force and the fulcrum. The lower diagram in Figure 10.5 shows how to find the input and output arms and the fulcrum for the board-and-log lever.

The mechanical advantage of a lever: When the input arm is longer than the output arm, the output force is greater than the input force. If the input arm is 10 times longer than the output arm, then the output force will be 10 times greater than the input force. The mechanical advantage of a lever is the ratio of length of the input arm divided by the length of the output arm.

Mechanical Advantage of a lever

Mechanical advantage

$$MA_{lever} = \frac{L_i}{L_o}$$

← Length of input arm (m)

← Length of output arm (m)

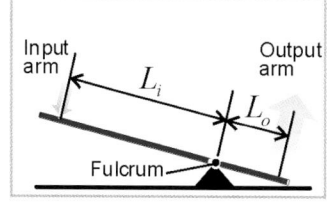

The three types of levers: There are three basic types of levers, as shown in Figure 10.6. They are classified by the location of the input and output forces relative to the fulcrum. All three types are used in many machines and follow the same basic rules. The mechanical advantage is the ratio of the lengths of the input arm over the output arm.

The output force can be *less* than the input force: You can make a lever where the output force is *less* than the input force. The input arm is shorter than the output arm on this kind of lever. The human arm is a good example. Compare where the bicep connects to the arm (input arm) with the location of the weight (output arm) in Figure 10.6 on third-class levers.

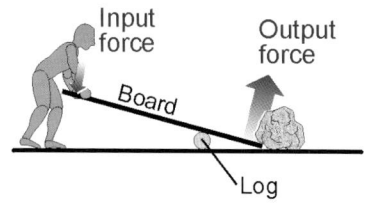

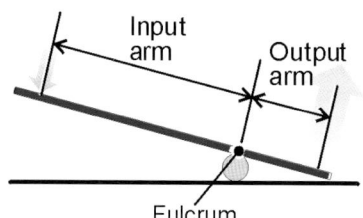

Figure 10.5: *A board and log used as a lever to move a rock.*

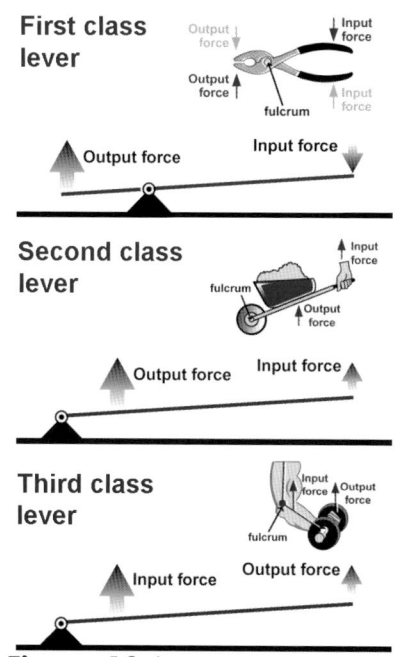

Figure 10.6: *The three classes of levers.*

180

How a lever works

Trading force for distance   When the mechanical advantage is larger than one, the input arm of a lever moves a much larger distance than the output arm. In fact, if the mechanical advantage is three, the input arm moves three times more than the output arm (Figure 10.7). In return, the output force is three times greater than the input force. The ratio of output motion to input motion is the *inverse* of the ratio of output force to input force. This principle is true for all simple machines. Force is multiplied by trading larger motions for smaller motions.

Torque and the mechanical advantage of a lever   A lever works by rotating about its fulcrum. The mechanical advantage can be deduced by calculating the *torques* created by the input and output forces. The input force creates a (positive) counterclockwise torque. The output force on the rock creates a reaction force on the lever. The torque created by the reaction force is clockwise (negative). When the lever is in equilibrium the net torque must be zero. The mechanical advantage of a lever follows directly from setting the net torque to zero (Figure 10.8).

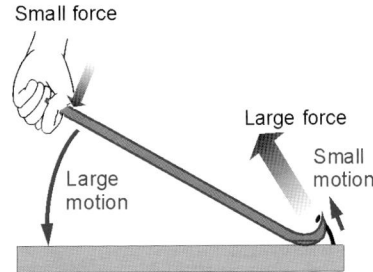

Figure 10.7: *A crowbar pulling a nail is an example of a lever. A small input force acts over a large motion to create a large output force acting over a small motion.*

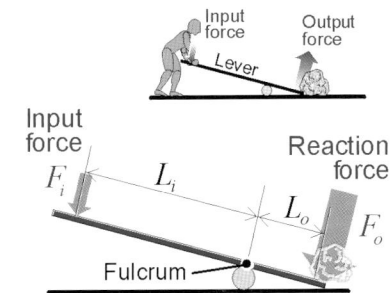

Calculate torques

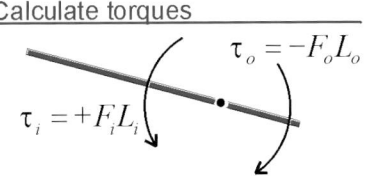

$$\tau_i = +F_i L_i \qquad \tau_o = -F_o L_o$$

Set net torque = 0

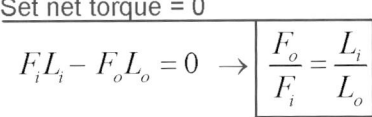

$$F_i L_i - F_o L_o = 0 \quad \rightarrow \quad \boxed{\dfrac{F_o}{F_i} = \dfrac{L_i}{L_o}}$$

Figure 10.8: *Balancing the torques acting around the fulcrum of a lever.*

Calculate the position of the fulcrum for a lever

Where should the fulcrum of a lever be placed so one person weighing 700 newtons can lift the edge of a stone block with a mass of 500 kilograms? The lever is a steel bar three meters long. Assume a person can produce an input force equal to their own weight. Assume that the output force of the lever must equal half the weight of the block to lift one edge.

1) You are asked to figure out the location of the fulcrum.
2) You are given the input force, length of the lever, and the mass to be lifted.
3) The weight of an object is equal to its mass times 9.8 N/kg. The mechanical advantage of a lever is the ratio of length of the input arm divided by length of the output arm.
4) Solve the problem:
   Output force = F_o = (1/2)(500 kg)(9.8 N/kg) = 2,450 N
   The required mechanical advantage is: MA = F_o/F_i = (2,450 N)/(700 N) = 3.5.
   The mechanical advantage of a lever is the ratio of lengths: MA = L_i/L_o = 3.5.
   From this equation you know that $L_i = 3.5\,L_o$.
   The total length of the lever is 3 meters; that means $L_i + L_o = 3$ m.
   Substitute for the length of the input arm to solve for the length of the output arm.
   $(3.5\,L_o) + L_o = 3$ m
   $4.5\,L_o = 3$ m
   $L_o = 0.67$ m, the fulcrum should be placed 0.67 meters from the edge of the block.

Mechanical advantage of ropes and pulleys

The forces in ropes and strings

A tension force is a pulling force acting along the direction of the rope. Ropes and strings carry tension forces along their length. If friction is small, the force in a rope is the same everywhere. This means that if you were to cut the rope and insert a force scale, the scale would measure the same tension force at any point.

The forces in ropes and pulleys

Figure 10.9 shows three different arrangements of a rope and pulleys. Each arrangement uses a different number of pulleys and has a different number of strands of rope supporting the load. An input force applied to the rope is felt at every point along the rope. As a result, in case (A) the load feels two upward forces equal to the input force. In case (B) the load feels three times the input force, and in case (C) the load feels four times the input force.

Mechanical advantage of ropes and pulleys

If there are four strands of rope directly supporting the load, each newton of force you apply produces four newtons of output force. Therefore, arrangement (C) has a mechanical advantage of 4. The output force is four times greater than the input force. Because the mechanical advantage is 4, the input force for machine (C) is one-fourth the output force. If you need an output force of 20 N, you only need an input force of 5 N.

Trading force for motion

If a rope and pulley machine has a mechanical advantage of four, then the input rope must be pulled four meters for every meter the load is lifted. Four strands of rope support the load to get a mechanical advantage of four. When the load rises by one meter, each strand must be shortened by a meter, resulting in a total pull of four meters. Like all simple machines, ropes and pulleys obey the rule by trading off advantage in force for reduction in motion.

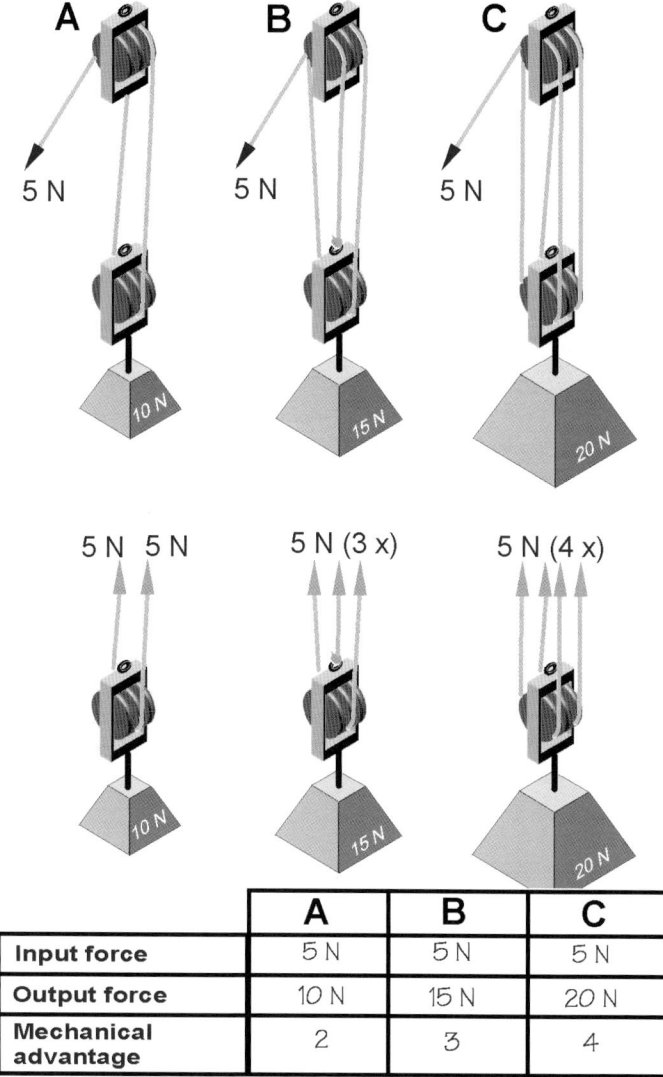

	A	**B**	**C**
Input force	5 N	5 N	5 N
Output force	10 N	15 N	20 N
Mechanical advantage	2	3	4

Figure 10.9: *The block and tackle machine is a simple machine using one rope and multiple pulleys. The rope and pulleys can be arranged to create different amounts of mechanical advantage depending on how many strands of rope support the load being lifted.*

182

Wheels, gears, and rotating machines

The wheel and axle

To understand how a wheel works, consider dragging a sled that holds a heavy weight. You must overcome the entire force of friction to pull the sled. If the sled is on wheels, the friction force occurs between the wheel and axle (Figure 10.10). The radius of the axle is much smaller than the radius of the wheel. As a result, the force required to pull the load is reduced by the ratio of the axle radius to the wheel radius. If the axle is 10 times smaller than the wheel, this results in a reduction of 10 times in force.

Other advantages of the wheel and axle

There are other ways a wheel and axle provide advantages. Friction occurs mostly where the wheel and axle touch. This area can be sealed against contamination from dirt and lubricated with grease to reduce friction. A second advantage is that rolling friction creates less resistance than sliding friction. Rolling motion creates less wearing away of material compared with two surfaces sliding over each other.

Gears change torque and rotating speed

Some machinery, such as small drills, require low torque at high rotating speeds. Other machinery, such as mill wheels, require high torque at low rotating speeds. Since they act like rotating levers, **gears** also allow the torque carried by different axles to be changed with the speed. Gears are better than wheels because they have teeth and don't slip as they turn together. Two gears with their teeth engaged act like two touching wheels that cannot slip relative to each other (Figure 10.11).

The gear ratio

The *input gear* is the one you turn, or apply forces to. The *output gear* is connected to the output of the machine. The *gear ratio* is the ratio of output turns to input turns. Because gear teeth don't slip, moving 36 teeth on one gear means that 36 teeth have to move on any connected gear. If one gear has 36 teeth it turns once to move 36 teeth. If the connected gear has only 12 teeth, it has to turn three times to move 36 teeth ($3 \times 12 = 36$). Smaller gears turn faster because they have fewer teeth.

Mechanical advantage of gears

For a rotating machine, the mechanical advantage is the ratio of output torque to input torque. With gears the trade-off is made between torque and rotation speed. An output gear will turn with *more* torque when it rotates slower than the input gear. The mechanical advantage of a pair of gears is therefore the *inverse* of the gear ratio (Figure 10.11).

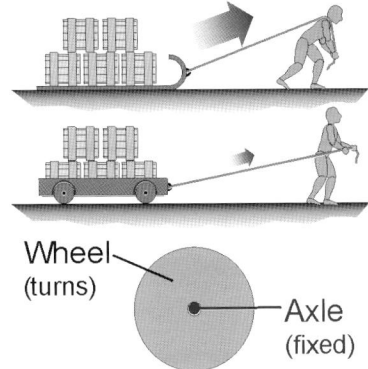

Figure 10.10: *It takes more force to drag a sled than to pull a cart with wheels and axles.*

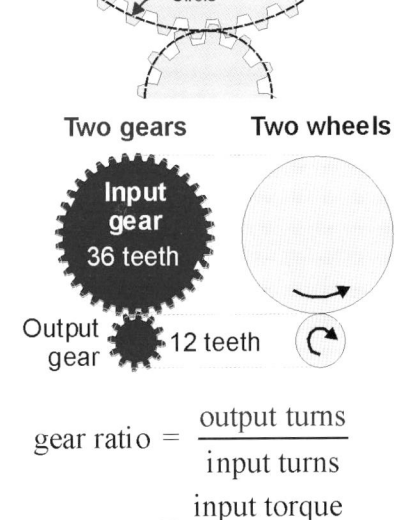

$$\text{gear ratio} = \frac{\text{output turns}}{\text{input turns}}$$

$$= \frac{\text{input torque}}{\text{output torque}}$$

Figure 10.11: *Gears act like touching wheels, but with teeth to keep them from slipping as they turn together.*

Ramps and screws

Ramps   It is easier to push a heavy cart up a ramp than it is to lift the same weight straight up. Ramps reduce input force by increasing the distance over which the input force needs to act. For example, suppose a 10 meter ramp is used to elevate a cart one meter. If the weight of the cart is 1,000 newtons, then the force required to push it up the ramp is one-tenth that weight, or 100 newtons (Figure 10.12).

Mechanical advantage of a ramp   When friction is negligible, the mechanical advantage of a ramp is equal to the distance along the ramp divided by the height of the ramp. In theory, the ramp in Figure 10.12 has a mechanical advantage of 10. Of course, with practical ramps there is always friction. And because of friction, the practical mechanical advantage is always less that the theoretical value. Friction also places limits on how a mechanical advantage can be achieved. A ramp with a mechanical advantage of 100 would probably not work as expected because the force expended to overcome friction would be greater than the force saved by making a ramp with such a small angle. The design of a ramp is a balance between mechanical advantage and friction.

Screws   A **screw** is a simple machine that turns rotating motion into linear motion. A thread wraps around a screw at an angle, like the angle of a ramp (Figure 10.13). In fact, the analysis of how a screw works treats a screw thread just like a rotating ramp. Imagine unwrapping one turn of a thread to make a ramp. Each turn of the screw advances the nut the same distance it would have gone sliding up a ramp. The lead of a screw is the distance it advances in one turn. A screw with a lead of one mm would advance one millimeter for each turn.

Mechanical advantage of a screw   Screws are used to hold things together because the combination of a screw and a lever (wrench) have tremendous mechanical advantage. By itself, the mechanical advantage of a screw is similar to the mechanical advantage of a ramp. The vertical distance is the lead of the screw. The distance along the ramp is measured along the average circumference of the thread. A quarter-inch screw you find in a hardware store has a lead of 1.2 millimeters and a circumference of 17 millimeters along the thread. In theory, the mechanical advantage is 14. In real machines the mechanical advantage is less because of friction.

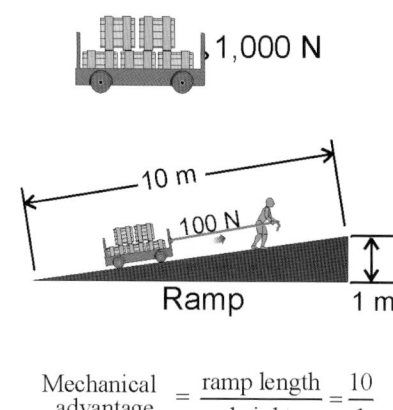

$$\text{Mechanical advantage} = \frac{\text{ramp length}}{\text{height}} = \frac{10}{1}$$

Figure 10.12: *The mechanical advantage of a ramp.*

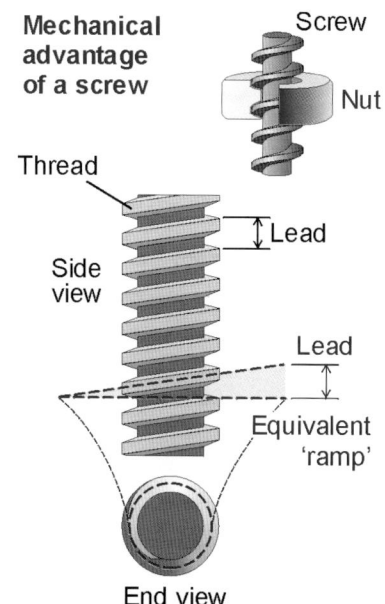

Figure 10.13: *A screw works like a rotating ramp.*

10.2 Work

All simple machines obey a rule that says any advantage in force must be compensated by applying the force over a proportionally longer distance. This rule is an example of one of the most powerful laws in all of physics. The law involves the physics meaning of *work*, which is the subject of this section.

"Work" in physics

A pushing force does **no** work if the wall does **not** move.

A pushing force **does** work if the wall moves even a little.

Figure 10.14: *Work is done (in the physics sense) only if a force causes movement.*

The meaning of "work"   The word "work" is used in many different ways.

- You *work* on science problems.
- You go to *work*.
- Your toaster doesn't *work*.
- Taking out the trash is too much *work*.

What *work* means in physics   In physics, work has a very specific meaning that is *different* from any of the meanings listed above. In physics, work is done by forces. The amount of work done is equal to the force times the distance over which the force acts. When you see the word *work* in a physics problem, it means the quantity you get by multiplying force and distance.

Work involves change   In physics, work represents a measurable change in a system, caused by a force. If you push on a wall and it does not move, when you are done pushing, the system is exactly the same as it was. Your force created no change and therefore did no work (Figure 10.14). In reality, the wall moves a little as you push. But, when you release your push, the wall moves back, doing work on you! Over the whole process, the *net* (total) work done is zero. If a system finishes in exactly the same state it started, then the work exchanged is zero.

Work and energy   The definition of work will make more sense when you see how work fits into the big picture of energy and systems. Work is one way systems change the amount of energy they have. When work is *done on* a system, its energy increases. For example, if you stretch a rubber band by pulling on it (doing work) you *increase* the energy of the rubber band. When a system *does* work, the energy of the system decreases. For example, if the stretched rubber band is used to launch a paper airplane, its energy is spent by doing work on the plane (Figure 10.15).

Work done stretching a rubber band increases its energy.

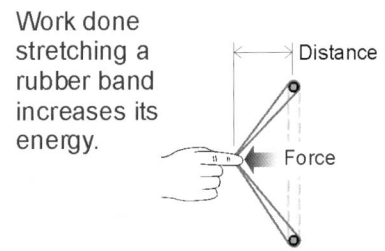

Distance

Force

Distance

Force

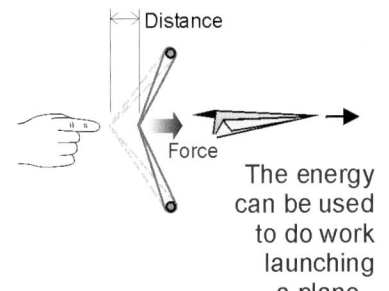

The energy can be used to do work launching a plane.

Figure 10.15: *The relationship between work and energy.*

The work done by a force

Work is done *by* forces *on* objects   In physics, work is done by forces. When thinking about work you should always be clear about which force is doing the work. Work is done on objects. If you push a block one meter with a force of one newton, you have done one joule of work *on the block*. It is necessary to keep careful track of where the work goes because later you will see that it may be possible to get some or all of the work back.

Units of work   The unit of measurement for work is the joule. One joule of work is done by a force of one newton acting over a distance of one meter. If you push a box with a force of one newton for a distance of one meter, you have done exactly one joule of work (Figure 10.16).

Force parallel to the distance   In general, the work done by a force is equal to the force times the distance moved *in the direction of the force*. When the force and distance are in the same direction (parallel), you can calculate the work in joules by multiplying the force in newtons by the distance in meters.

Force at an angle to the distance   When the force and distance are at an angle, only part of the force does work. For example, suppose a force was directed along an angle making a triangle with sides whose lengths were 3, 4, and 5. The fraction of the force that does work is four-fifths of the total force, because the distance is aligned with the "4" side of the triangle and the force is aligned with the "5" side. The work done by the force is only 4/5 of what it would have been if the force and distance were parallel.

Problem	Analysis	Solution
		$W = Fd \times \left(\dfrac{4}{5}\right)$
		$= Fd \cos 37°$

Work and vectors   From Chapter 7 you might recognize the ratio 4/5 is the same as the cosine of the angle between the force and the distance (37°). In general, both force and distance are vectors. To calculate the work done, you multiply the magnitudes of the force and distance vectors, then multiply again by the cosine of the angle between them.

186

1 joule is the amount of work done by a force of 1 newton acting over a distance of 1 meter.

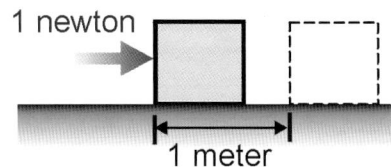

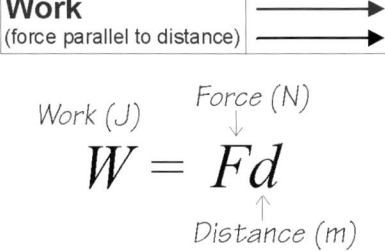

Work (force parallel to distance)

$$W = Fd$$

Work (J)   Force (N)   Distance (m)

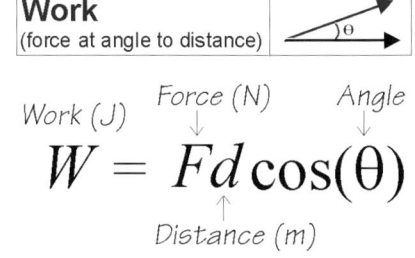

Work (force at angle to distance)

$$W = Fd \cos(\theta)$$

Work (J)   Force (N)   Angle   Distance (m)

Figure 10.16: *The definition of work and how to calculate work if you know the force and distance.*

Work done against gravity

Work against gravity depends only on height Many situations involve work done by or against the force of gravity. When you lift something off the floor, you are doing work against gravity. Because gravity always pulls straight down, the work done is easy to calculate because it does not matter *what path you take*. The work done by or against gravity is equal to the weight of the object (force) times the change in height (distance). Whether you take a zig-zag stairway or an elevator, the work done is the same.

Why the path does not matter This remarkable fact results from another way of looking at work for motion at an angle to a force. The work done is the force times the *distance moved in the direction of the force*. This is mathematically the same as our previous definition. To understand what it means, consider climbing up a zig-zag stair. The distance moved is always along the stair. The force of gravity is always down. The distance moved *along the force of gravity* is just the height of each leg of the stair. The work done against gravity on each section of the stair is the height of that section times your weight. The total for the zig-zag path adds up to the same amount of work you would have done by jumping straight up (if you could!).

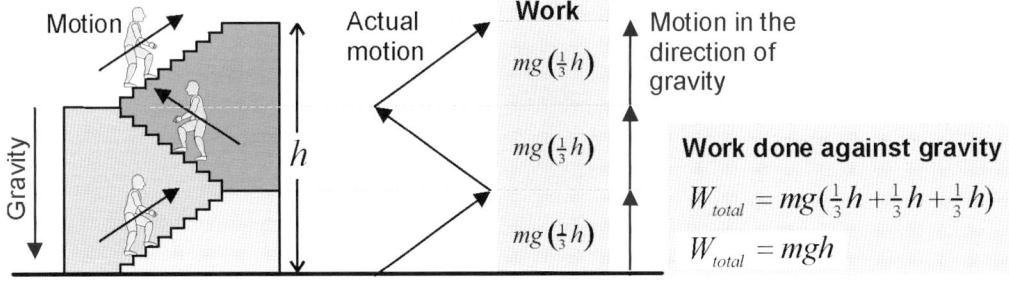

The difference between force and work Going up a stair or ramp is certainly easier than climbing straight up. Stairs and ramps are easier because you need less force. But you do have to apply the force for a much longer distance. In the end, the amount of work done is the same. Of course if there is friction, *you* might have to do more work on a stair or ramp because you have to overcome friction. Work done *against* friction, however, is not the same as work done on *you*. Remember what we said on the last page about keeping track of work done by which force on which object.

A crane lifts a steel beam with a mass of 1,500 kg. Calculate how much work is done against gravity if the beam is lifted 50 meters in the air. How much time does it take to lift the beam if the motor of the crane can do 10,000 joules of work per second?

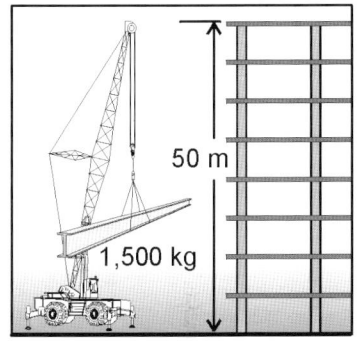

50 m

1,500 kg

1) You are asked for the work and the time it takes to do the work.

2) You are given mass, height, and the work done per second.

3) Use the formula for work done against gravity, W = mgh.

4) Solve:
W = (1,500 kg)(9.8 N/kg)(50 m)
= 735,000 J

At a rate of 10,000 J/sec, it takes: 735,000 ÷ 10,000 = 73.5 seconds to lift the beam.

Work done by a machine

Work and machines   Work is usually done when a force is applied to a simple machine. For example, when a block and tackle machine lifts a heavy load, force is applied by pulling on the rope. As a result of the force, the load moves a distance upward. Work has been done by the machine because force was exerted over a distance.

Input work and output work   All machines can be described in terms of input work and output work. As an example, consider using the block and tackle machine to lift a load weighing 10 newtons. The load moves a distance of one-half meter. The machine has done five joules of work on the load (Figure 10.17), so the work output is five joules.

Calculating input work   What about the work input? The force on the rope is only five newtons because the machine has a mechanical advantage of two. But the rope must be pulled one meter in order to raise the load one-half meter. The input work is the force applied to the rope times the distance the rope was moved. This is five newtons times one meter, or five joules. The work input is the same as the work output.

Output work can never exceed input work   The example illustrates a rule that is *true for all machines*. You can never get more work out of a machine than you put into it. Nature does not give something for nothing. When you design a machine that multiplies force, you pay by having to apply the force over a greater distance. The force and distance are related by the amount of work. In a perfect (theoretical) machine, the output work is exactly equal to the input work.

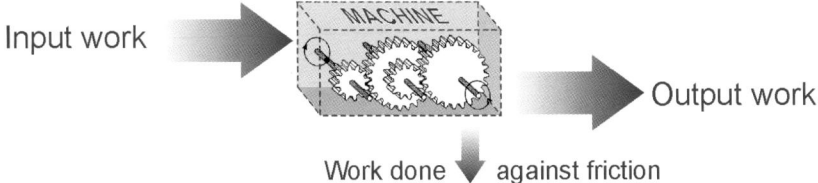

Friction reduces output work   In a practical machine, there is always friction. When friction comes from motion and creates force, friction removes energy from the machine. In any machine some of the input work goes to overcoming friction. The output work is always less than the input work because of the energy lost to friction.

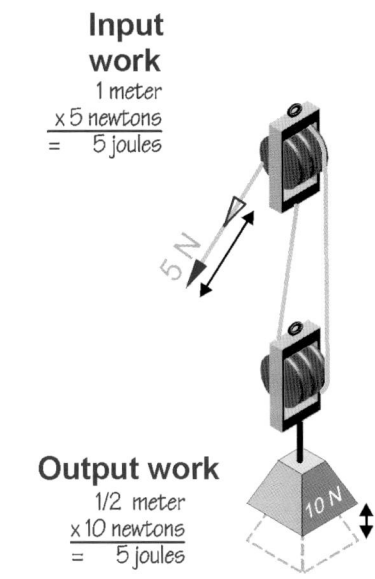

Input work
1 meter
x 5 newtons
= 5 joules

Output work
1/2 meter
x 10 newtons
= 5 joules

Figure 10.17: *For a frictionless rope and pulley machine the work output equals the work input even though the output and input forces are different.*

Perpetual motion

A perpetual motion machine is a machine for which the work output equals or exceeds the work input. Many inventors have claimed to make one, and none has ever worked because the laws of physics make it impossible. The U.S. Patent and Trademark Office is always looking out for inventions claiming to be perpetual motion machines.

10.3 Energy and Conservation of Energy

Our universe is made of *matter* and *energy*. Matter is something that has mass and takes up space—you might call it "stuff." Energy describes the ability of a physical system to make things change. Energy appears in different forms, such as motion and heat. Energy can travel in different ways, such as light, sound, or electricity. The workings of the universe (including all of our technology) can be viewed as energy flowing from one place to another and changing back and forth from one form to another.

What is energy?

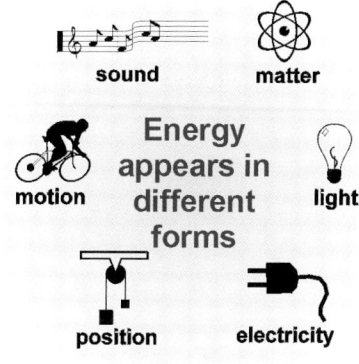

Figure 10.18: *Energy appears in many different forms.*

The definition of energy — Energy describes a system's ability to cause change. A system that has energy has the ability to do work. That means anything with energy can produce a force that is capable of acting over a distance. The force can be any force, and it can come from any source, such as your hand, the wind, or a spring (Figure 10.18).

1. A moving ball has energy because it can create force on whatever tries to stop it or slow it down.

2. A sled at the top of a hill has energy because it can move a distance down the hill and produce forces as it goes.

3. The wind has energy because it can create forces on any object in its path.

4. Electricity has energy because it can turn a motor to make forces.

5. Gasoline has energy because it can be burned to make force in an engine.

6. You have energy because you can create forces.

Work and energy — Energy is measured in joules, the same units as work because work is the transfer of energy. Energy is the *ability* to make things change. Work is the *action* of making things change. Energy moves through the action of work. When you push a cart up a ramp some of the energy is transferred to the cart by doing work (Figure 10.19). Your energy decreases by the amount of work done. The energy of the cart increases by the same amount of work (if there is no friction). Whenever work is done, energy moves from the system *doing* the work to the system on which the work is *being done*.

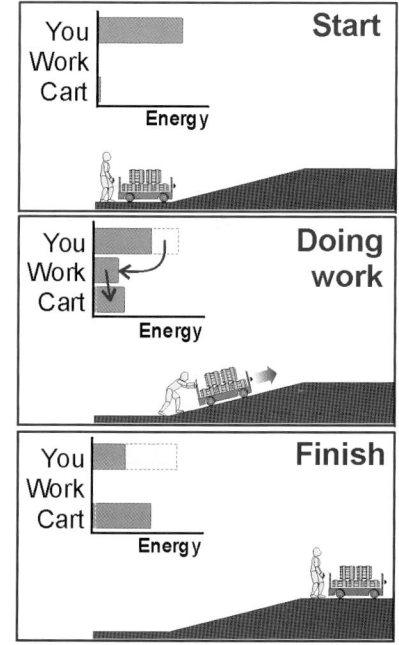

Figure 10.19: *Energy moves when work is done.*

Different forms of energy

How energy is used   One way to understand energy is to think of it as nature's money. Energy can be spent and saved in a number of different ways any time you want to do something. You can use energy to buy speed, height, temperature, mass, and other things. But you need energy to start with, and what you spend diminishes what you have left.

Mechanical energy   Mechanical energy is the energy possessed by an object due to its motion or its position. Mechanical energy can be either *kinetic* (energy of motion) or *potential* (energy of position).

Light energy   Radiant energy includes light, microwaves, radio waves, x-rays, and other forms of electromagnetic waves (Chapters 18 and 26).

Nuclear energy   Nuclear energy is energy contained in matter itself. Nuclear energy can be released when heavy atoms in matter are split up or light atoms are put together. Radioactivity also releases nuclear energy (Chapter 30).

Electrical energy   Electrical energy is something we take for granted whenever we plug an appliance into an outlet (Chapter 20). The electrical energy we use is derived from other sources of energy. For example, the energy may start as chemical energy in gas. The gas is burned, releasing heat energy. The heat energy makes hot steam. The steam turns a turbine, making mechanical energy. Finally, the turbine turns an electric generator, producing electrical energy (Figure 10.20).

Chemical energy   Chemical energy is energy stored in molecules. The chemical energy stored in batteries changes to electrical energy when you connect wires and a light bulb. Your body also uses chemical energy when it converts food into energy so that you can walk or think. Chemical reactions release chemical energy (Chapter 29).

Thermal energy   Heat is an example of thermal energy. Thermal energy is energy that can be measured by differences in temperature. Hot objects have more thermal energy than cold objects (Chapter 25).

Pressure energy   You may not have heard the term pressure energy. Pressure in gases and liquids is a form of energy (Chapter 27). It takes work to blow up a balloon. Some of the work is stored as energy in the form of higher-pressure air inside the balloon.

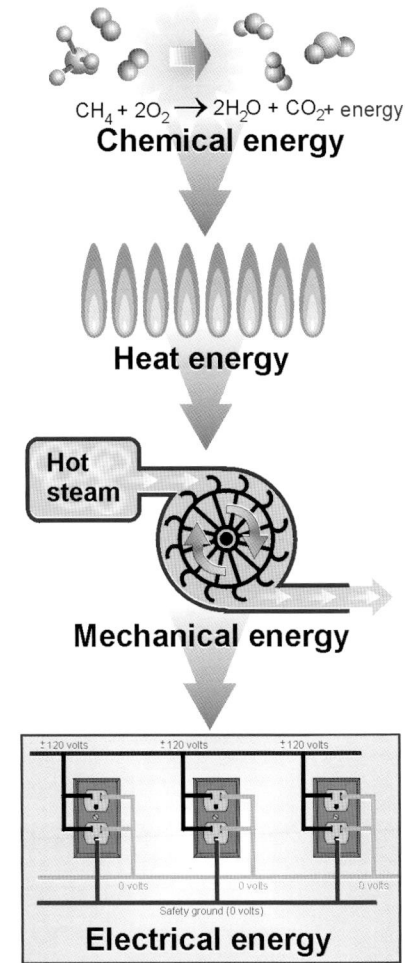

$CH_4 + 2O_2 \rightarrow 2H_2O + CO_2 +$ energy
Chemical energy

Heat energy

Hot steam

Mechanical energy

Electrical energy

Figure 10.20: *Some of the forms energy takes on its way to your house or apartment.*

Potential energy

Potential energy	When something is lifted off the ground, it can fall back down and exert force as it falls. Exerting force while falling means doing work. When you lift an object higher, you increase its **potential energy** because the higher an object is, the more ability it has to do work when it falls.
	Objects that have potential energy do not use the energy until they move. That is why it is called *potential* energy. Potential means that something is capable of becoming active. Any object that can move to a lower place has potential energy.
Potential energy comes from gravity	An object's potential energy comes from the gravity of the Earth. Consider a marble that is lifted off the table. Since the Earth's gravity pulls the marble down, you must apply a force to lift it up. Applying a force over a distance requires doing work, which gets stored as the potential energy of the marble. Technically, energy from height is called *gravitational potential energy*. Other forms of potential energy also exist, such as energy stored in springs.
Calculating potential energy	The potential energy an object has represents the amount of work the object can do by changing its height. In our discussion of work and machines, you may remember that the work you get out of a machine can never exceed the work you put in. The same is true of potential energy. In fact, the potential energy an object can release coming down is exactly the same as the work you must put in to move the object upward in the first place. For an object of mass (*m*) raised a height (*h*), the work done against gravity equals *mgh*. This is also the formula for calculating the potential energy!

Potential Energy

$$\text{Potential energy (joules)} \quad E_p = mgh$$

— Mass (kilograms)
← Height (meters)
Strength of gravity (9.8 N/kg)

Energy from work	There is a symmetry between work and energy that appears throughout physics. You can only do as much work as you have energy for. And the energy you have is equal to the work done to create the energy in the first place.

Calculating the potential energy of a cart

A cart with a mass of 102 kg is pushed up a ramp. The top of the ramp is 4 meters higher than the bottom. How much potential energy is gained by the cart? If an average student can do 50 joules of work each second, how much time does it take to get up the ramp?

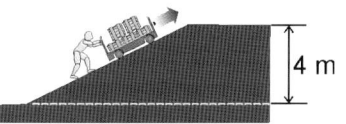 102 kg

4 m

1) You are asked for the potential energy and time.

2) You are given mass, height, and the work done per second.

3) Use the formula for potential energy Ep = mgh.

4) Solve:
Ep = (102 kg)(9.8 N/kg)(4 m)
= 3,998 J

At a rate of 50 J/sec, it takes:
3,998 ÷ 50 = 80 seconds to push the cart up the ramp.

Kinetic energy

Kinetic energy is energy of motion

An object in motion has energy because it is moving. A moving mass can exert forces, as you would quickly observe if someone ran into you in the hall. Energy of motion is called kinetic energy. The kinetic energy of a moving object depends on two things: mass and speed.

Kinetic energy and mass

The kinetic energy of a moving object is proportional to the object's mass. If you double the mass, you also double the kinetic energy. For example, consider a two kilogram rabbit moving at a speed of one meter per second; it has one joule of kinetic energy (Figure 10.21). A larger rabbit moving at the same speed has more energy. This follows from the fact that it takes more work to *stop* a heavier rabbit. A four kilogram rabbit moving at 1 m/sec has two joules of kinetic energy.

Kinetic energy increases as speed squared

The kinetic energy of a moving object also depends on the speed of the object. Consider the two kilogram rabbit moving at 1 m/sec. It has one joule of kinetic energy. If the rabbit ran at 2 m/sec, it would have four joules of kinetic energy. If the speed of an object doubles, its kinetic energy increases four times (Figure 10.22). Mathematically, kinetic energy increases as the square of speed. If the speed increases by three, the kinetic energy increases by nine because $3^2 = 9$.

The formula for kinetic energy

The kinetic energy of a moving object is equal to one-half the object's mass times the square of its speed.

Kinetic Energy

Kinetic energy (J) $\quad E_k = \dfrac{1}{2}mv^2 \quad$ Mass (kg) ... Speed (m/sec)

Kinetic energy and driving

When a car stops, its kinetic energy of motion ($1/2\ mv^2$) is completely converted into work done by the brakes (Fd). Since brakes supply nearly constant force, the stopping distance (d) is proportional to the initial kinetic energy. Going 60 miles per hour, a car has four times as much kinetic energy as it does at 30 miles per hour. That means it takes four times the distance to stop at 60 mph compared with 30 mph (Figure 10.23). At 90 mph a car has nine times as much energy as it does at 30 mph, and it requires *nine times* farther to stop.

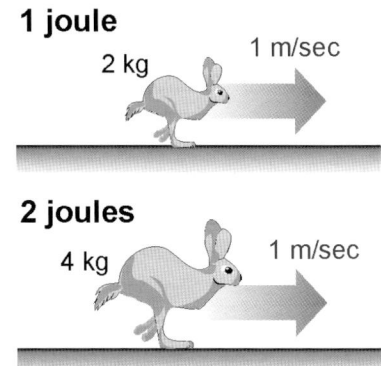

Figure 10.21: *Kinetic energy is proportional to mass.*

Figure 10.22: *Doubling the speed multiplies the kinetic energy by four.*

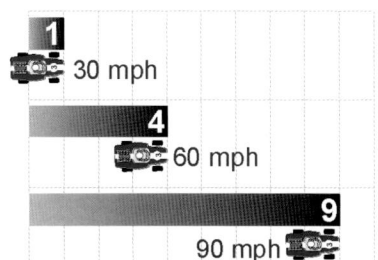

Figure 10.23: *Kinetic energy and braking distances.*

The formula for kinetic energy

Deriving the equation for kinetic energy

The kinetic energy of a moving object is exactly equal to the amount of work required to get the object from at rest to its final speed. The calculation is similar to the analysis used for potential energy, except the math has more steps. To start, suppose a ball of mass (m) is at rest. A force (F) is applied and creates acceleration (a). After a distance (d), the ball has reached speed (v).

Step 1 Work is force times distance, but force is mass times acceleration. The work done on the ball is therefore its mass × acceleration × distance.

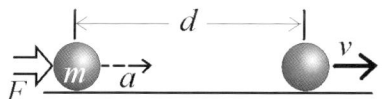

$$W = Fd = (ma) \times d = mad$$

Step 2 The kinetic energy formula involves only mass and speed. Is there a way to get speed from acceleration and distance? In Chapter 4 you found a relationship between distance traveled, acceleration, and time.

$$d = \tfrac{1}{2}at^2$$

Step 3 Replacing distance in the equation for work and combining similar terms creates:

$$W = ma(\tfrac{1}{2}at^2) = \tfrac{1}{2}ma^2t^2$$

Step 4 When an object starts from at rest with constant acceleration, its speed is equal to its acceleration multiplied by the time it has been accelerating. Mathematically, $v = at$, therefore $v^2 = a^2t^2$. This is the result that is needed. Replace the a^2t^2 with v^2 and the resulting work (W) is exactly the formula for kinetic energy.

$$v = at \;\rightarrow\; v^2 = a^2t^2 \qquad W = \tfrac{1}{2}m(a^2t^2) \qquad W = \tfrac{1}{2}mv^2$$

Why it works Remember, this calculation is the work done on the ball to bring it from at rest up to a final speed (v). As with potential energy, the kinetic energy of a moving object is equal to the work done to create the energy.

Calculating the kinetic energy of a moving car

A car with a mass of 1,300 kg is going straight ahead at a speed of 30 m/sec (67 mph). The brakes can supply a force of 9,500 N. Calculate:
a) The kinetic energy of the car.
b) The distance it takes to stop.

1,300 kg   30 m/sec

1) You are asked for the kinetic energy and stopping distance.

2) You are given mass, speed, and the force from the brakes.

3) Kinetic energy $E_k = 1/2\ mv^2$
   Work, $W = Fd$

4) Solve:
$E_k = (1/2)(1,300\ kg)(30\ m/sec)^2$
   $= 585,000\ J$

To stop the car, the kinetic energy must be reduced to zero by work done by the brakes.
$585,000\ J = (9,500\ N) \times d$
$d = 62\ meters$

Conservation of energy

Energy
transformations

Energy is always moving and changing. If you skate uphill you do work to get to the top. Going down hill, your speed increases because potential energy is converted into kinetic energy. When you apply the brakes they get very hot and wear away. The kinetic energy partly becomes heat energy and partly goes to breaking away particles from the brakes. From the energy perspective, first, work was done to gain potential energy (top of hill), which was then converted to kinetic energy (bottom), and then heat and friction (Figure 10.24).

The law of
conservation of
energy

The concept of energy is important because of the following fact: The total energy in the universe remains constant. As energy takes different forms and changes things by doing work, nature keeps perfect track of the total. No new energy is created and no existing energy is destroyed. This concept is called the law of conservation of energy. The rule you met earlier concerning the input and output work of a machine is an example of the law of conservation of energy.

The law of conservation of energy

Energy can never be created or destroyed, only changed
from one form to another.

An example of
energy
conservation

What happens when you throw a ball straight up in the air? The ball leaves your hand with kinetic energy due to the speed you give it as you let go. As the ball goes higher, it gains potential energy (Figure 10.25). The potential energy gained equals the kinetic energy lost and the ball slows down as it goes higher.

Eventually, all initial kinetic energy is gone. The ball is as high as it will go and its upward speed is zero. The original kinetic energy has been completely exchanged for an equal amount of potential energy. The ball falls back down again and accelerates as it falls. The gain in speed comes from potential energy being converted back to kinetic energy. If there were no friction, the ball would return to your hand with the same speed it started with—except in the opposite direction.

The flow of energy

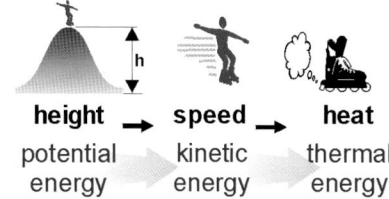

height → speed → heat
potential   kinetic   thermal
energy   energy   energy

Figure 10.24: *Some energy transformations on a skating trip.*

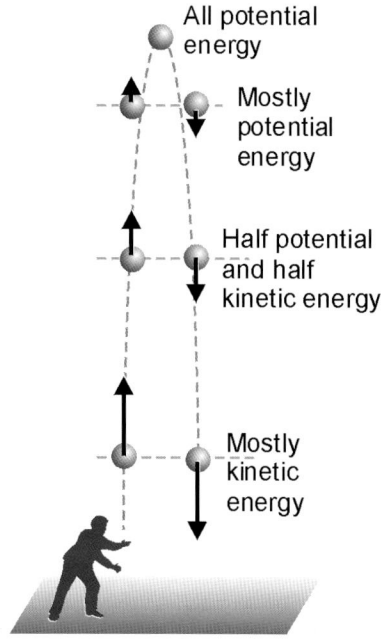

All potential energy

Mostly potential energy

Half potential and half kinetic energy

Mostly kinetic energy

Figure 10.25: *When you throw a ball up in the air, its energy transforms from kinetic to potential and back to kinetic.*

Energy in a closed system

Energy and systems The conservation of energy is most useful when it is applied to a closed system. Remember, you choose a system to include the things you are interested in. A closed system means you do not allow any matter or energy to cross the boundaries of the system you choose. Because of the conservation of energy, the total amount of matter and energy in your system stays the same forever.

Applying conservation of energy For example, suppose your system is a ball rolling along a track with a hill and a valley (Figure 10.26). The ball is released from rest at the highest point (h_0). The total energy in the system is the potential energy of the ball at the start. Later, the ball is at a lower height (h) moving with speed (v). At this time the ball has both potential and kinetic energy.

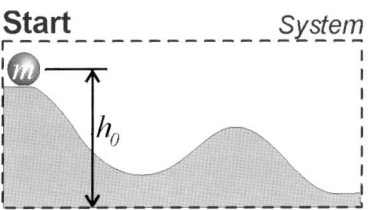

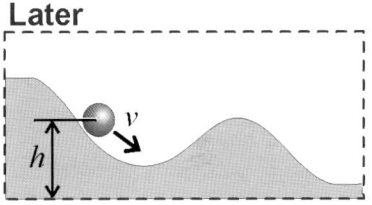

Figure 10.26: *A ball rolling on a hilly track is a good system for investigating the conservation of energy.*

Energy at start 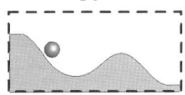 $E = mgh_0$

Energy later $E = mgh + \frac{1}{2}mv^2$

Because of conservation of energy, we can write an equation that describes the total energy of the ball anywhere on the track.

Energy at start = energy later $\qquad mgh_0 = mgh + \frac{1}{2}mv^2$

Since mass (m) appears in every term, we can cancel it out. When the equation is rearranged some interesting things can be deduced about the motion of the ball.

$$mgh_0 = mgh + \frac{1}{2}mv^2 \qquad v = \sqrt{2g(h_0 - h)}$$

1. The mass of the ball does not matter since mass does not appear.

2. The speed of the ball depends only on the change in height ($h_0 - h$).

Friction can divert some energy The law of conservation of energy holds true even when there is friction. Some of the energy is converted to heat or to the wearing away of material. The energy converted to heat or wear is no longer available to be potential energy or kinetic energy, but it was not destroyed.

Application: Hydroelectric Power

Every day in the United States the average person uses about 90 *million* joules of electrical energy. This energy comes from many sources, including burning coal, gas and oil, nuclear power, and hydroelectric power. In hydroelectric power the potential energy of falling water is converted to electricity. No air pollution is produced, nor hazardous wastes created. If you are lucky enough to live near a source of falling water, hydroelectric power is, in many ways, an ideal method for producing energy. Approximately 7 percent of the electricity used in this country comes from hydroelectric power.

What is a hydroelectic power system?

A typical hydroelectric power system starts with a dam placed across a river. The water builds up behind the dam and creates a large difference in potential energy from the top to the bottom (Figure 10.27). Water flows down through giant tubes cast in the concrete of the dam.

Energy transformation

At the bottom of the dam, the water turns a turbine. A turbine is a spinning wheel specially designed to extract as much kinetic energy as possible from moving water. The turbine turns an electric generator which produces electricity. In a hydroelectric power plant the energy is transformed from potential energy of water to kinetic energy of water, then to kinetic energy of the turbine, and finally to electrical energy.

Hoover Dam and Lake Mead

Hoover Dam near Las Vegas, Nevada is a famous hydroelectric power plant. It was built in 1935 to control flooding by the Colorado River and to make hydroelectric power. The dam is 221 meters high and 379 meters wide. To withstand the enormous pressure of the water, it is 203 meters thick at the base, narrowing to 13 meters at the top, which is not much wider than your classroom. Figure 10.28 shows an aerial view of Hoover Dam and Lake Mead, the reservoir behind it.

Energy produced depends on height difference and flow rate

The energy available depends on two factors: the height difference between the inlet and outlet of the dam, and the flow rate of water. At Hoover Dam, the peak flow rate is 700 cubic meters of water per second. The water drops about 200 meters from the inlet to the turbine. The water from the dam is divided among seventeen turbines and generators.

Schematic of a hydroelectric dam

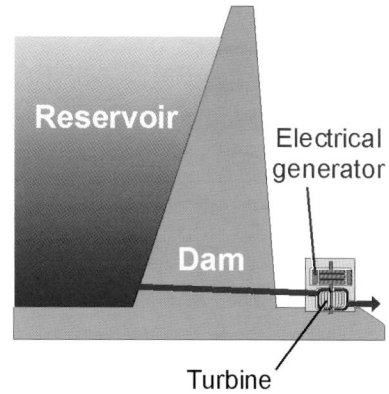

Figure 10.27: *The working parts of a hydroelectric power plant.*

Figure 10.28: *Hoover Dam, near Las Vegas, Nevada, and its reservoir, Lake Mead.*

Applying energy conservation to Hoover Dam

Conservation of energy You can use the conservation of energy to calculate just how much energy the Hoover Dam gets from the waters of the Colorado River. Start by calculating the potential energy of one kilogram of water 200 meters above the turbine. The potential energy works out to 1,960 joules for each kilogram of water passing through the dam.

The flow rate of Hoover Dam The flow rate of the Colorado is 700 m³/sec—a lot of water. The average classroom has a volume of 150 m³ (Figure 10.29). The flow through the Hoover Dam is equivalent to almost 4 2/3 classrooms full of water every second. Another way of putting it is that one cubic meter of water has a mass of 1,000 kilograms. The water flow through Hoover Dam is 700,000 kilograms per second.

Energy efficiency The turbine and generator are about 80 percent efficient. That means 80 percent of the 1,960 joules in each kilogram of water is turned into electricity, or that Hoover Dam produces 1,100 million joules of electrical energy every second.

Hoover Dam supplies energy for a large city There are 86,400 seconds in a day, which makes the daily energy output of Hoover Dam approximately 95×10^{12} (trillion) joules. It takes 90 million joules per day to support an average person, so Hoover Dam can supply all the electricity for about 1 million people, the population of a large city.

Examples of other hydroelectic power plants Ninety-five trillion seems like—and is—a huge number, but people use a lot of energy. Hoover Dam is only the ninth largest hydroelectric power plant in the United States. The Grand Coulee Dam on the Columbia River in Washington state produces five times as much electricity as Hoover Dam. When it is completed, the James Bay hydropower project in northern Quebec, Canada, will supply more than 20 times as much electricity as Hoover Dam.

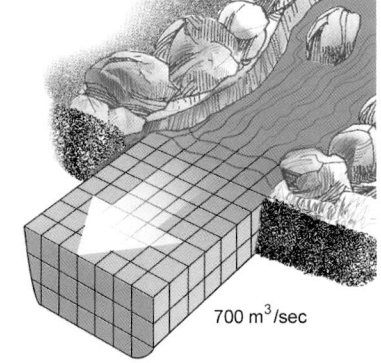

700 m³/sec

Figure 10.29: *The flow rate of the Colorado River is 700 m³/sec.*

Chapter 10 Review

Vocabulary Review

Match the following terms with the correct definition. There is one extra definition in the list that will not match any of the terms.

Set One

1. work
2. mechanical advantage
3. input force
4. output force
5. energy

a. The force applied by a machine to do work
b. The ability to cause change; appears in different forms such as heat and motion
c. Ratio of output force to input force
d. The action of making things change; equal to force times distance
e. Energy possessed by an object due to its position
f. The force you apply to operate a machine

Set Two

1. friction
2. closed system
3. input work
4. output work
5. joule

a. Always less than the input work
b. Equal to one newton-meter of work
c. Calculated by multiplying mass by velocity.
d. Created when you don't allow any matter or energy to cross chosen boundaries
e. For a rope and pulley system, equal to input force times length of rope that is pulled
f. Force that all real machines must work against

Set Three

1. pressure energy
2. nuclear energy
3. radiant energy
4. chemical energy
5. mechanical energy

a. Energy stored in bonds between atoms in molecules
b. Energy used when you plug an appliance into an outlet
c. Energy possessed by an object due to its motion or position
d. Energy contained in the internal structure of atoms
e. Energy of electromagnetic waves
f. Energy that exists inside an air-filled balloon relative to the air outside the balloon

Set Four

1. thermal energy
2. conservation of energy
3. potential energy
4. kinetic energy
5. simple machine

a. A device that uses electrical energy to do work.
b. Energy can never be created or destroyed, only changed from one form to another
c. Energy of motion
d. Energy that can be measured by differences in temperature
e. A mechanical device that uses only forces applied to it and does its task in one motion
f. Energy of position

Concept review

1. Describe the measurements you would need to take, if any, and the calculations you must do to find the mechanical advantage of each of the following simple machines:

   a. lever

   b. rope and pulleys

   c. wheel and axle

   d. ramp

2. What is the unit used to represent mechanical advantage?

3. What is the major difference between 1st, 2nd, and 3rd class levers?

4. "Force is multiplied by trading larger motions for smaller motions." This principle is true for all simple machines. Explain how this principle is true for a rope and pulley system.

5. The word *work* has a very specific meaning in physics. Why is it that no work is done, in the physics sense, if a force of 1,000 N is applied to a brick wall that does not move?

6. Why is the joule a unit of energy *AND* a unit of work?

7. Many inventors have attempted to make a perpetual motion machine, but none have succeeded. Will a perpetual motion machine ever be invented? Why or why not?

8. Stacy eats a bowl of cornflakes for breakfast and then rides her bicycle to school. When Stacy pedals the bicycle, a mechanical device transforms the mechanical energy from the turning wheel into electrical energy to run a small flashing taillight for highway safety. Describe each energy transformation that must occur to eventually allow the taillight to work. Use the following terms in your description: mechanical energy, light energy, nuclear energy, electrical energy, chemical energy, and thermal energy. Hint: start your description all the way back with the sun and follow the transformations to the end.

9. A car going twice as fast requires four times as much stopping distance. What is it about the kinetic energy formula that accounts for this fact?

10. Harold bounces on a trampoline. At what point in his motion does he have the highest potential gravitational energy, and at what point does he have the highest kinetic energy? Explain.

11. In general, the work done by a force is equal to the force times the distance moved in the direction of the force. Thus, when the force is applied parallel to the distance moved, the work is equal to force times distance. What if the force and distance are at an angle? Explain how to find the work done by a force when it is exerted at an angle to the motion of an object. Give a daily life example to support your explanation.

Problems

1. A weight of 200 newtons is placed 4 meters from the fulcrum of a first class lever. An input force of 80 newtons is used to lift the weight.

   a. Draw a diagram of this lever, with forces and distances labeled.

   b. How far from the fulcrum must the input force be applied to lift the weight?

2. Michelle pulls on the input rope of a block and tackle system to raise an 400 N canoe. There are 4 supporting ropes in the block and tackle system.

   a. What is the tension in each supporting rope?

   b. How much input rope must Michelle pull to lift the canoe 3 meters off the ground?

   c. What is the mechanical advantage of the block and tackle system?

3. Shawn wants to set up a lever to lift the edge of his refrigerator so he can clean the floor underneath. Shawn weighs 450 N, and the refrigerator weighs 1000 N. Shawn can produce an input force equal to his weight, and the output force of the lever must equal half the weight of the refrigerator to lift one edge. Shawn has a 2.5 m steel bar to use for the lever. Where should he place the fulcrum of the lever? Show all work and draw a labeled diagram of the lever, showing input and output forces and distances.

1000 N

4. Martha must carry a 50 N package up three flights of stairs. Each flight of stairs has a height of 2 m, and the actual distance of the diagonal path she walks up the stairs is 10 m. What is the total work done on the package?

5. In one 8-hour workday, a forklift operator at a particular distribution warehouse lifts a total of 100,000 N of boxes. Each box must be lifted to a height of 1.5 m and carried an average of 10 m to the shipping dock. What is the net work done against gravity?

6. An interesting and potentially dangerous phenomenon that can occur in a large city is an exploding manhole. When underground cables become frayed, the cable insulation can smolder and catch fire, and the build-up of gases released can explode, sending the manhole cover as much as 50 feet in the air! Manhole covers can weigh as much as 300 lbs, (a mass of 136 kg). Suppose a 136 kg manhole cover is launched 50 feet in the air. Find the following:

   a. What is the potential energy of the manhole cover when it reaches 50 feet above the ground? (Don't forget to convert feet to meters!)

   b. What is the speed of the manhole cover when it hits the ground on its descent, in m/s and mph?

Unit 4

Energy and Momentum

Chapter 11

Energy Flow and Power

Objectives for Chapter 11

By the end of this chapter you should be able to:

1. Give an example of a process and the efficiency of a process.
2. Calculate the efficiency of a mechanical system from energy and work.
3. Give examples applying the concept of efficiency to technological, natural and biological systems.
4. Calculate power in technological, natural, and biological systems.
5. Evaluate power requirements from considerations of force, mass, speed, and energy.
6. Sketch an energy flow diagram of a technological, natural, or biological system.

Terms and vocabulary words

efficiency	process	input	output	food calorie
reversible	irreversible	power	horsepower	producer
energy flow	watt	cycle	food chain	power transmission
herbivore	carnivore	decomposer	food web	energy conversion
steady state	ecosystem			

11.1 Efficiency

We all know by now that people are not perfect. Machines are not perfect either. This section is about one of the most important "imperfections" in a machine, or in any process that involves energy. That imperfection involves the *efficiency* with which energy changes or moves. Since nearly everything that happens in the universe involves energy, the concept of efficiency applies to much more than just machines made by humans. Scientists believe that less-than-perfect efficiency is a characteristic of *all* natural processes and is also the reason time goes forward, and not backward.

What efficiency means

The definition of efficiency The efficiency of a process is the ratio of output to input. A process that is 100 percent efficient means that 100 percent of what you start with ends up being what you want at the end of the process. For example, suppose you use an elevator to move people (Figure 11.1). The output of the elevator is potential energy; people are moved up. The input is electrical energy to a motor. A typical elevator has an efficiency of about 10 percent. That means 100 joules of electrical energy are used for every 10 joules of potential energy gained by the people inside.

Processes Efficiency is defined for a process. A **process** is any activity that changes things and can be described in terms of input and output. The elevator in Figure 11.1 can be seen as a process for converting electrical energy (input) to potential energy (output). The growth of a tree is also a process. For a tree, the input is energy from the sun, carbon from the air, and nutrients from the soil. The output is growth and reproduction of more trees. All processes can be characterized by an efficiency, including an elevator, a tree growing, and any other process you can think of.

Energy efficiency and other kinds of efficiency In this chapter, efficiency means the ratio of *energy* output divided by *energy* input (Figure 11.2), and also you may assume that "efficiency" means *energy efficiency*. However, efficiency can be defined for any kind of input and output. For example, if the process is investing money, the input and output would be measured in dollars. The efficiency would be the ratio of money you have after investing divided by the money you put in. The way efficiency is calculated depends on the type of process you have and what you choose to be the inputs and outputs.

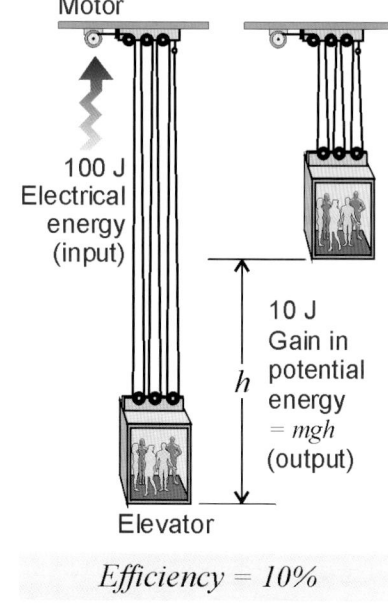

Figure 11.1: *An elevator can be viewed as a process that converts electrical energy to potential energy with an efficiency of 10 percent.*

Efficiency
(energy efficiency)

$$\varepsilon = \frac{E_o}{E_i}$$

Energy output (J)

Efficiency

Energy input (J)

Figure 11.2: *The definition of energy efficiency.*

Efficiency in mechanical systems

The ideal machine   Efficiency is usually expressed in percent. An ideal machine would be 100 percent efficient. However, real machines are never 100 percent efficient. Some work is always done against friction. A machine that is 75 percent efficient produces 3 joules of output work for every 4 joules of input work. At 75 percent efficiency, one joule out of every four (25 percent) is lost to friction.

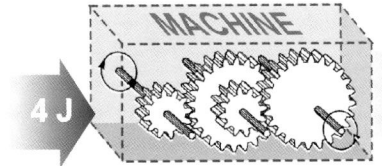

A machine with 75% efficiency

Input energy 4 J

3 J Output work

1 J Energy lost to friction

How friction affects machines   Because of friction, work output is always less than work input. For example, a wheel turning on an axle gets hot. When the wheel gets hot, it means some of the input work is being converted to heat by the action of friction. The work output is reduced by the work that is converted to heat, resulting in lower efficiency.

Where does the energy go?   According to the law of conservation of energy, energy cannot ever be lost, so the *total* efficiency of any process is 100 percent. When we say a machine is 75 percent efficient, we mean 75 percent of the energy ends up being used in the way we want. For example, a car's useful output energy is kinetic energy of motion and potential energy for climbing hills. All other forms of energy are considered "losses," such as heat from the radiator and exhaust gasses. When calculating the car's efficiency, only the usable energy is counted as output.

Automobiles   In general, cars are not very efficient users of energy; 13 percent is typical. This means only 13 percent of the energy released by burning gasoline is converted to work done moving the car. The rest of the energy becomes heat, wears away engine parts, moves air around the car, and is spent in other ways that do not result in work done by the wheels.

Energy use in a typical car

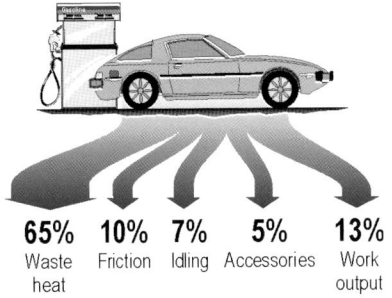

65%	10%	7%	5%	13%
Waste heat	Friction	Idling	Accessories	Work output

Calculate the efficiency of a rubber band

A 12-gram paper airplane is launched at a speed of 6.5 m/sec with a rubber band. The rubber band is stretched with a force of 10 N for a distance of 15 cm. Calculate the efficiency of the process of launching the plane.

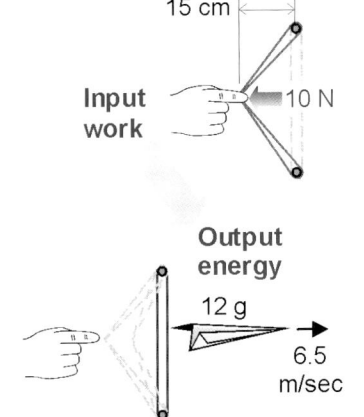

15 cm

Input work   10 N

Output energy

12 g

6.5 m/sec

1) You are asked for the efficiency.
2) You are given the input force and distance and the output mass and speed.
3) Efficiency is output energy divided by input energy.
The input energy is work = F x d.
The output energy E_k = 1/2 mv².
4) Solve:
$\varepsilon = (0.5)(0.012 \text{ kg})(6.5 \text{ m/sec})^2$
$/ (10 \text{ N})(0.15 \text{ m})$
$= 0.26 \text{ or } 26\%$

11.1 Efficiency

203

Efficiency in natural systems

The meaning of efficiency

Energy drives all the processes in nature, from winds in the atmosphere to nuclear reactions occurring in the cores of stars. In the environment, efficiency is interpreted as the fraction of energy that goes into a particular process. For example, the Earth receives energy from the sun. Some of the energy is absorbed and some is reflected back into space. The Earth absorbs sunlight with an average efficiency of 78 percent.

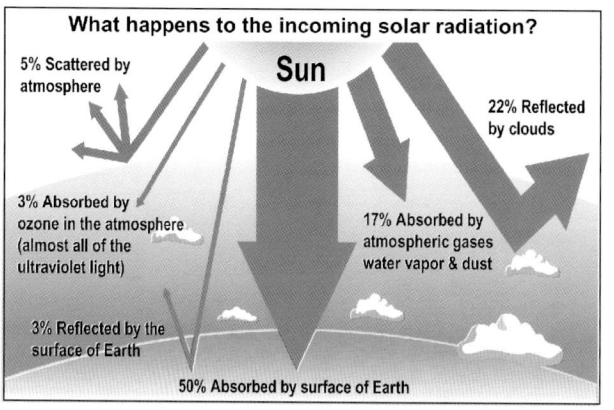

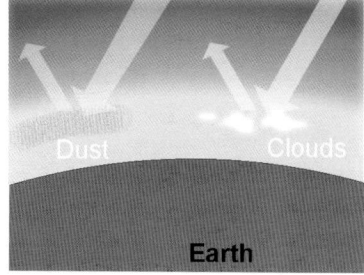

Figure 11.3: *Dust and clouds reflect light back into space, decreasing the efficiency with which the Earth absorbs energy from the sun.*

The importance of solar efficiency

The efficiency of the Earth at absorbing solar energy is critical to living things. If the efficiency *decreased* by a few percent, the Earth's surface would become too cold for life. Some scientists believe that many volcanic eruptions or a nuclear war would decrease the absorption efficiency by spreading dust in the atmosphere. Dust reflects solar energy (Figure 11.3). On the other hand, if the efficiency *increased* by a few percent, it would get too hot to sustain life. Too much carbon dioxide in the atmosphere might increase the absorption efficiency (Figure 11.4). Scientists are concerned that the Earth has already warmed a few degrees as a result of carbon dioxide released by human technology.

Figure 11.4: *Carbon dioxide and other greenhouse gases in the atmosphere absorb some energy that otherwise would have been radiated back into space. This increases the efficiency with which the Earth absorbs energy from the sun.*

Efficiencies always add up to 100%

It is important to remember that, in any system, all of the energy goes somewhere. For example, rivers flow downhill. Most of the potential energy lost by water moving downhill becomes kinetic energy in motion of the water. Erosion takes some of the energy and slowly changes the land by wearing away rocks and dirt. Friction takes some of the energy and heats up the water. If you could add up the efficiencies for every single process, that total would be 100 percent.

Efficiency in biological systems

Calories in food

People and animals constantly take in food for the energy needed to sustain life. Because living things typically use a lot a energy, the energy in what you eat is measured in food calories. A single food calorie is equal to 4,187 joules. Next time you eat a pint of ice cream, consider that it represents 800,000 joules of energy (Figure 11.5). By comparison, one joule is the work equivalent of lifting one pint of ice cream 21 centimeters.

Efficiency is low for living things

In terms of output work, the energy efficiency of living things is typically very low. Almost all of the energy in the food you eat becomes heat and waste products; very little becomes physical work. Of course, living creatures do much more than physical work. For example, you are reading this book.

Estimating the efficiency of a human

To estimate the efficiency of a person doing physical work, consider climbing a mountain 1,000 meters high. For the average person with a mass of 70 kilograms, the increase in potential energy is 686,000 joules. The potential energy comes from work done by muscles. A human body doing strenuous exercise uses about 660 food calories per hour. It takes about three hours to climb the mountain, during which time the body uses 1,980 calories (8,300,000 J). The energy efficiency is about 8 percent (Figure 11.6).

Baseline metabolic rate

The overall energy efficiency for a person is actually lower than 8 percent. An average person uses 55-75 calories per hour when sitting completely still. The rate at which your body uses energy while at rest is called your baseline metabolic rate (or BMR). During a 24-hour period, a person with a BMR of 65 cal/hr uses 1,536 calories, or 6,430,000 joules. Even if you did the equivalent work of climbing a 1,000- meter mountain every day, your average efficiency is only 4.6 percent.

Efficiency of plants

The efficiency of plants is similar. Photosynthesis in plants takes input energy from sunlight and creates sugar, a form of chemical energy. To an animal, the output of a plant is the energy stored in sugar, which can be eaten. The efficiency of pure photosynthesis is 26 percent, meaning 26 percent of the sunlight absorbed by a leaf is stored as chemical energy. As a whole system however, plants are only 1 to 3 percent efficient. The system efficiency is lower than 26 percent because leaves absorb only a third of the energy in sunlight, some energy goes into reproducing, and some energy goes into growth and other plant functions.

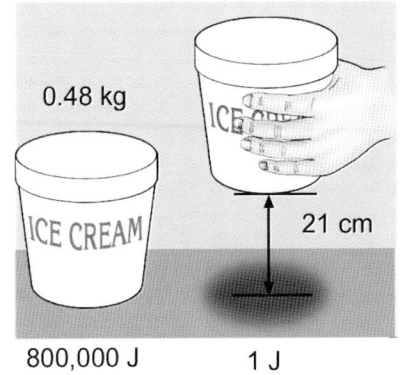

Figure 11.5: *Food contains a huge amount of energy compared with typical work output.*

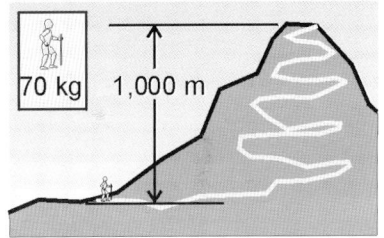

$E_p = mgh$

$= (70 \text{ kg})(9.8 \text{ N/kg})(1,000 \text{ m})$

$= 686,000 \text{ J}$

Figure 11.6: *A 70-kilogram hiker gains 686,000 joules of potential energy climbing a 1,000-meter mountain.*

Efficiency and the arrow of time

A connection between efficiency and time The efficiency is less than 100 percent for virtually all processes that convert energy from one form to any other form except heat. After 2,000 years of thinking about it, we believe that the inevitable "loss" of energy into heat is connected to why time flows forward and not backward. The connection between efficiency and time is not at all obvious, but read along and see if it makes sense to you.

The arrow of time Think of time as an arrow pointing from the past into the future. All processes move in the direction of the arrow, and never go backward (Figure 11.7).

Reversible processes Suppose a process were 100 percent efficient. As an example, think about connecting two marbles of equal mass by a string passing over an ideal pulley that has no mass and no friction (Figure 11.8). One marble can go down, transferring its potential energy to the other marble, which goes up. This ideally efficient process can go forward and backward as many times as you want. In fact, if you watched a movie of the marbles moving, you could not tell if the movie were playing forward or backward. To a physicist, this process is reversible, meaning it can run forward or backward in time.

Friction and the arrow of time Now suppose there is a tiny amount of friction. The efficiency of transferring potential energy is reduced to 99 percent. Because some potential energy is lost to friction, one marble does not go all the way down, and the other does not go all the way up. Every time the marbles exchange energy, some is lost and the marbles don't rise quite as high as they did the last time. And if you made a movie of the motion, you could tell whether the movie was running forward or backward. Because of the energy lost to friction, any process with an efficiency less than 100 percent runs only one way, *forward with the arrow of time.*

Irreversible processes Friction turns energy of motion into heat. Once energy is transformed into heat, the energy cannot ever completely get back into its original form. Because energy that becomes heat cannot get back to potential or kinetic energy, any process for which the efficiency is less than 100 percent is irreversible. Irreversible processes can only go forward in time. Since processes in the universe almost always lose a little energy to friction, time cannot run backward. If you study physics further, this idea connecting energy and time has many other implications.

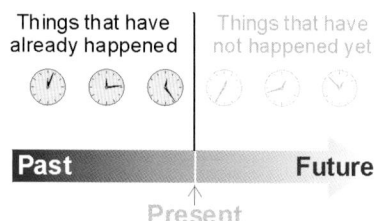

The arrow of time

Figure 11.7: *Time can be thought of as an arrow pointing from the past into the future.*

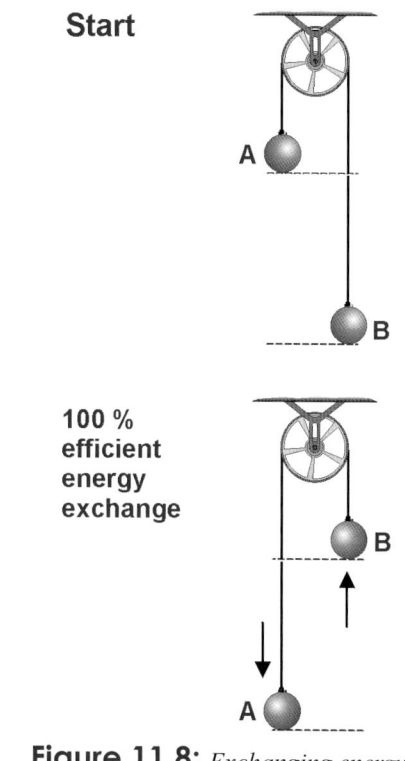

Figure 11.8: *Exchanging energy with a perfect frictionless, massless pulley.*

206

11.2 Energy and Power

In science the words energy and power have specific meanings and they do not mean the same thing. Energy is the ability to cause change and is measured in joules. But change can happen slowly or quickly. If you run up the stairs or walk up the stairs your increase in potential energy is the same. What is different is the *rate* at which your energy changes. The change in energy happens quickly when you run up the stairs. The change is slower when you walk. The rate at which energy flows or changes is called *power.* Power is measured in joules per second and is the subject of this section.

Doing work fast or doing it slowly

How fast work is done It makes a difference how fast you do work. Suppose you drag a box with a force of 100 newtons for 10 meters in 10 seconds. You do 1,000 joules of work. Your friend drags a similar box and takes 60 seconds. You both do the same amount of work because the force and distance are the same. But something is different. You did the work in 10 seconds and your friend took six times longer.

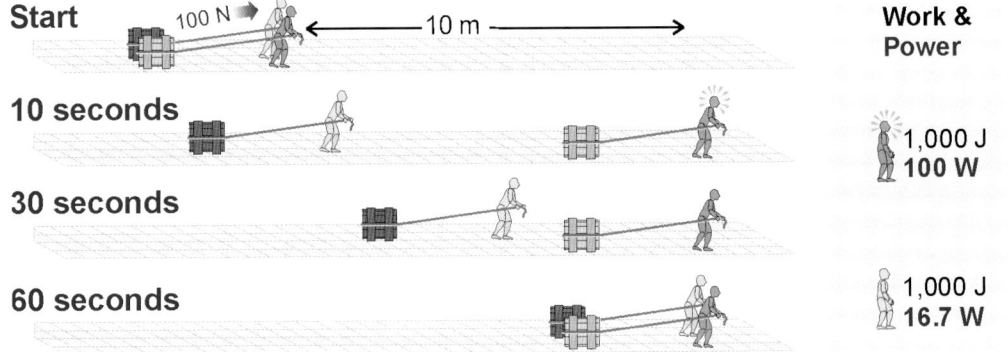

Power is the rate of doing work or using energy Power is equal to the amount of work done divided by the time it takes to do the work. In physics, when you see the word "power" you should think "energy used divided by time taken." This is similar to thinking about speed as "distance traveled divided by time taken." For example, doing 1,000 joules of work in 10 seconds equals power of 100 joules per second (1,000 J ÷ 10 sec). Doing the same amount of work in 60 seconds equals power of only 16.7 joules per second (1,000 J ÷ 60 sec).

Calculate power in climbing stairs

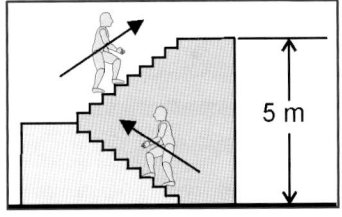

A 70 kg person goes up stairs 5 m high in 30 seconds.
a) How much power does the person need to use?
b) Compare the power used with a 100-watt light bulb.

(1) You are asked for power.

(2) You are given mass, distance, and time.

(3) Relationships that apply:

$$E_p = mgh \quad P = E/t$$

(4) Solve:

$$E_p = (70 \text{ kg})(9.8 \text{ N/kg})(5 \text{ m})$$
$$= 3430 \text{ J}$$
$$P = (3{,}430 \text{ J})/(30 \text{ sec})$$
$$= 114 \text{ watts}$$

(a)   114 W

(b) This is a little more power than a 100-watt light bulb. Many human activities use power comparable to a light bulb.

Power

Units of power — The unit of power in physics is the **watt**, named after James Watt (1736-1819), the Scottish engineer and inventor of the steam engine. One watt (1 W) is equal to one joule of work done in one second. Another unit of power commonly used is the **horsepower**. One horsepower is equal to 746 watts. As you may have guessed, one horsepower was originally the average power output of a horse (Figure 11.9).

Two interpretations of power — Power is used to describe two similar situations. The first situation is work being done by a force. Power is the rate at which the work is done. The second situation is energy flowing from one place to another, such as electrical energy flowing through wires. The power is the amount of energy that flows divided by the time it takes. In both situations the units of power are joules per second, or watts.

Calculating power — To calculate power, you take the quantity of work or energy and divide by the time it takes for the work to be done or the energy to move.

Power

Power (W) $\quad P = \dfrac{E}{t}$ $\qquad$ Change in work or energy (J)

$\qquad\qquad\qquad\qquad\qquad\qquad$ Change in time (sec)

As an example, 100 kilograms of water per second fall down 10 meters to turn a turbine. The change in energy is *mgh* or (100 kg)×(9.8 N/kg)×(10 m) = 9,800 J. If the energy change happens in one second, the power is 9,800 watts (Figure 11.10).

A second way to calculate power — There is a second useful formula for power. Work is force times distance. Power is work divided by time. Combining these two relationships gives another way to calculate power: power is force times speed. If you apply a constant force of 100 newtons to drag a sled at a constant speed of 2 meters per second, you use 200 watts of power. Since both force and velocity are vectors, you may multiply them to calculate power if they are in the same direction. When the force and velocity are at an angle to each other, you must also multiply by the cosine of the angle.

Power
(alternate formula) $\quad$ Power (W) $\quad P = \vec{F} \cdot \vec{v}$

$\qquad\qquad\qquad\qquad\qquad$ Force (N) $\qquad$ Velocity (m/sec)

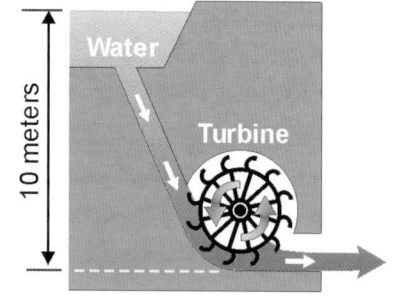

1 horsepower (1 hp)	1 watt (1 W)

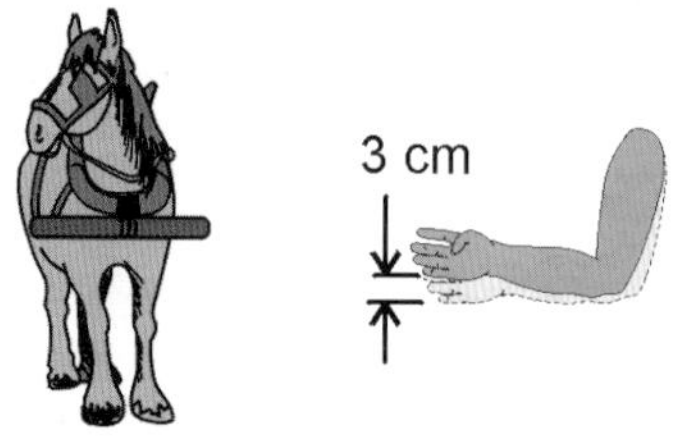

The power output of a farm horse $\qquad$ 3 cm

The power it takes to raise your arm 3 cm in 1 second

1 watt = 1 joule per second

1 horsepower = 746 watts

Figure 11.9: *Units of power.*

Water

10 meters

Turbine

100 kg

Figure 11.10: *A flow of 100 kilograms of water per second dropping 10 meters represents an energy flow (power) of 9,800 watts.*

Power in human technology

Ranges of power You probably use technology with a wide range of power every day. On the high end of the power scale are cars and trucks. A typical car engine makes 150 horsepower (hp), which is 112,000 watts (W). This power is delivered in the form of work done by the wheels. Moderate power devices include appliances such as washing machines, fans, and blenders. Many household machines have electric motors that do work. Common motors found around the house range from 1 horsepower (746 watts) down to 1/20th of a horsepower (37 watts). Many appliances have "power ratings" that indicate their power. For example, a blender might say it uses 1/3 hp, indicating a power of about 250 watts. Table 11.1 below lists the power used by some everyday machines.

Table 11.1: Power used by some common devices

Machine	Power used (W)	Machine	Power used (W)
Lawn mower	2,500	Electric drill	200
Refrigerator	700	Television	100
Washing machine	400	Desk lamp	100
Computer	200	Small fan	50

Estimating power requirements Machines are designed to use the appropriate amount of power to create enough force to do work they are designed to do. You can calculate the power required if you know the force you need and the rate at which things must move. For example, suppose your job is to choose a motor for an elevator. The elevator must lift 10 people, each with a mass of 70 kilograms. The specification for the elevator says it must move between each floor (3 meters) in 3 seconds.

The energy required is given by $E_p = mgh$. Substituting the numbers results in a value of = (10×70 kg)×(9.8 N/kg)×(3 m) = 20,580 J. This amount of energy is used in 3 seconds, so the power required is 20,580 J ÷ 3 seconds = 6,860 W. Motors are usually sold by horsepower, so divide again by 746 W/hp to get 9.2 hp. A more accurate calculation would add weight of the elevator car as well as the people, and some extra power for rapid acceleration.

Estimate power required by a fan

A fan uses a rotating blade to move air. How much power is used by a fan that moves 2 cubic meters of air each second at a speed of 3 m/sec. Assume air is initially at rest and has a density of 1 kg/m³. Fans are inefficient; assume an efficiency of 10 percent.

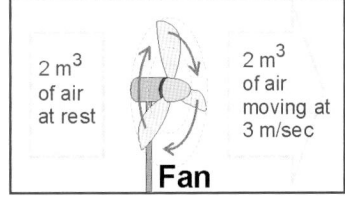

2 m³ of air at rest

2 m³ of air moving at 3 m/sec

Fan

(1) You are asked for power.

(2) You are given volume, density, speed, and time.

(3) Relationships that apply:
$\rho = m/V$, $E_k = 1/2\ mv^2$, $P = E/t$

(4) Solve:
$m = \rho V = (1\ kg/m^3)(2\ m^3) = 2\ kg$
$E_k = (0.5)(2\ kg)(3\ m/sec)^2$
$= 9\ J$

At an efficiency of 10 percent, it takes 90 joules of input power to make 9J of output energy.

$P = (90\ J)/(1\ sec)$
$= 90\ watts$

Power in natural systems

Stars and supernovae

Natural systems exhibit a much greater range of power than human technology. At the top of the power scale are stars. The sun has a total power output of 3.8×10^{26} watts. This is tremendous power, especially considering the sun has been shining continuously for more than 4 billion years. A supernova is the explosion of an old star at the end of its normal life. These explosions are among the most powerful events in the known universe, releasing 10 billion times the power of the sun. Fortunately, supernovae (or supernovas) are rare, occurring about once every 75 years in the Milky Way galaxy (Figure 11.11).

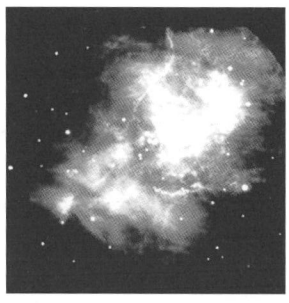

Figure 11.11: *The Crab Nebula is the remains of a supernova explosion that was seen from Earth in 1054 AD. The supernova was so bright it could be seen during the day, according to the records of Chinese astronomers of the time.*

Energy from the sun

Almost all of the sun's power comes to the Earth as radiant energy, including light. The top of the Earth's atmosphere receives an average of 1,373 watts of solar power per square meter. In the summer at northern latitudes in the United States, about half that power (660 W/m²) makes it to the surface of the Earth. The rest is absorbed by the atmosphere or reflected back into space. In the winter, the solar power reaching the surface drops to 350 W/m². About half of the power reaching the Earth's surface is in the form of visible light. The remaining power is mostly infrared and ultraviolet light.

Estimating the power in wind

The power received from the sun is what drives the weather on Earth. To get an idea of the power involved in weather, suppose we estimate the power in a gust of wind. A moderate wind pattern covers 1 square kilometer and involves air up to 200 meters high. This represents a volume of 200 million cubic meters (2×10^8 m³). The density of air is close to 1 kg/m³, so the mass of this volume of air is 200 million kilograms.

Figure 11.12: *A powerful storm system moves a great amount of air.*

Assume the wind is moving at 10 m/sec (22 mph) and it takes 3 minutes to get going. The power required to start the wind blowing is the kinetic energy of the moving air divided by 180 seconds (3 minutes). The result is 56 million watts, nearly the power to light all the lights in a town of 60,000 people. Compared with what people use, 56 million watts is a lot of power. But 1 square kilometer receives 1.3 *billion* watts of solar power. A 10 m/sec wind gust represents only 4 percent of the available solar power. An average storm delivers much more power than 56 million watts because much more air is moving (Figure 11.12).

Power in biological systems

Power output of people and animals

A physically fit human can sustain peak power of about 300 watts for a short time and a steady 100 watts for hours. A good size horse has an average work output of one horsepower, or 746 watts. Only 200 years ago, a person's own muscles and those of their animals were all anyone had for power. Compare that to what is easily accessible today. The average lawn mower has a power of 2,500 watts—the equivalent power of three horses *plus* three people.

Range of animal power

The power output of animals varies with the size of the animal. Big animals need more power to get up and move. For example, a blue whale can sustain a power output of 500 hp (373,000 W), about the same as a large truck. Insects use very little power. For example, the power output of a flying insect is 0.0001 watts. Actually, since insects outnumber people on Earth by more than 100,000 to 1, the total power output of insects is greater than the power output of people.

6,000 W

300 W

373,000 watts

0.0001 W

Most of the power output of animals takes the form of heat. An average person produces 100 watts of heat continuously. A crowd of people can give off so much heat that buildings need air conditioning to remove the heat, even in the winter.

Power used by plants

The solar power used by plants is typically one-third of the power in visible light falling on their leaves. By this estimate, a large tree uses 6,000 watts of solar power in full sun, about the same power as a motor scooter. The power used by plants goes mostly into growth of new plant material and moving water from the roots out to the leaves. The output power from plants is input power for animals. Even though less than 1 percent of the input power from the sun becomes food for animals, it is enough to support the entire food chain on Earth.

Estimate the average input power of a person

An average diet includes 2,500 food calories per day. Calculate the average power this represents in watts over a 24-hour period. One food calorie equals 4,187 joules.

Breakfast

Dinner

Lunch

(1) You are asked for power.

(2) You are given the energy input in food calories and the time.

(3) Relationships that apply:
1 food calorie = 4,187 J, P = E/t

(4) Solve:
E = (2,500 cal)(4,187 J/cal)
= 10,467,500 J

There are 60 x 60 x 24 = 86,400 seconds in a day.

P = (10,467,500 J)
/ (86,400 sec)
= 121 watts

This is a bit more than the power used by a 100-watt light bulb.

11.3 Energy Flow in Systems

Looking at the big picture, our universe is matter and energy organized in *systems*. There are large systems, like our solar system composed of the sun, planets, asteroids, comets, smaller bits of matter, and lots of energy. There are smaller systems within the solar system, such as the ecology of the Earth. In fact, there are systems within systems ranging in scale from the solar system, to the Earth, to a single animal on the Earth, to a single cell in the animal, right down to the scale of a single atom. In every single system energy flows, creating change. This section presents a few brief examples of how energy flows in systems.

Following an energy flow

The energy flow in a pendulum
A pendulum is a system in which a mass swings back and forth on a string. At its highest point, a pendulum has only potential energy, because it is not moving. At its lowest point, a pendulum has kinetic energy. Kinetic energy and potential energy are the two chief forms the energy of a pendulum can take. As the pendulum swings back and forth, the energy flows back and forth between potential and kinetic, with a little lost to friction. An energy diagram might look like Figure 11.13.

Energy conversion
Energy flows almost always involve energy conversions. In a pendulum, the chief conversion is between potential and kinetic energy. A smaller conversion is between kinetic energy and other forms of energy created by friction, such as heat, air motion, and wearing away the string.

Making an energy flow diagram
One of the first steps to understanding an energy flow is to write down the forms that energy takes. If you choose the system to be a pendulum, there are three chief forms of energy: potential energy, kinetic energy, and losses from friction.

The next step is to diagram the flow of energy from start to finish for all the important processes that take place in the system.

The last step is to try to estimate how much energy is involved and what are the efficiencies of each energy conversion. Almost every conversion will involve some loss of energy to heat, wear, or another source of friction.

Pendulum

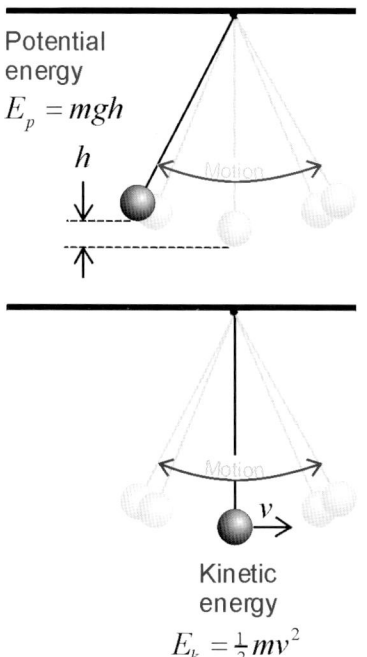

Potential energy
$E_p = mgh$

h

Kinetic energy
$E_k = \frac{1}{2}mv^2$

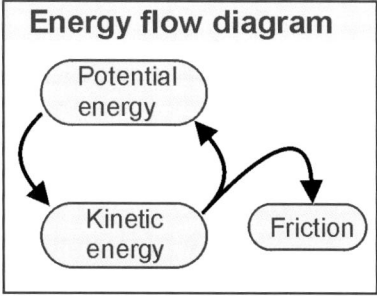

Energy flow diagram

Figure 11.13: *In a pendulum, the energy mostly flows back and forth between potential energy and kinetic energy. Some energy is lost to friction on every swing.*

Energy flows in human technology

Processes   The energy flow in technology can usually be broken down into four types of processes. Complex machines often include two, three, or even all four processes. A very complex machine such as a car includes multiple types of each process.

Storage   1. **Energy storage:** Examples of energy storage technologies are batteries (chemical energy,) springs (elastic potential energy), pressure (fluid energy), height (gravitational potential energy), gasoline (chemical energy), and motion (kinetic energy).

Conversion   2. **Energy conversion:** Many machines convert one type of energy to another. For example, an electric motor converts electrical energy to mechanical energy. A pump converts mechanical energy to fluid energy.

Transmission   3. **Power transmission:** Power is the rate of energy flow through a system. Some examples of different methods of power transmission are: through wires (electrical), through tubes (fluid power), through mechanisms such as cables, gears or levers (mechanical power), or through light (radiant power).

Output   4. **Output use:** This is the form the energy needs to be in to accomplish the purpose of the technology. A bulldozer does mechanical work as its output. An electric stove has heat as its output. A light bulb makes light.

Energy flow in a rechargeable drill   A rechargeable electric drill is a good example of a device that uses all four processes. Energy is stored in a battery (storage). Power from the battery gets to the motor by wires (electrical transmission). The motor converts electrical energy to mechanical energy (energy conversion). The rotation of the motor is transferred to the drill bit by gears (mechanical transmission). The spinning drill bit cuts wood (output work). An energy flow diagram for the drill is shown in Figure 11.14.

Efficiency   Every process in an energy flow has an efficiency. For example, batteries are typically 45 percent efficient. If you put 100 joules into a battery, you only get 45 joules out. Mechanical transmissions can be 95 percent efficient. Electric motors are moderately efficient; 65 percent is a good average. The overall efficiency of the drill is calculated by multiplying the efficiencies for each process. For the rechargeable drill, the overall efficiency is only 28 percent ($0.45 \times .65 \times .95$).

Rechargeable electric drill

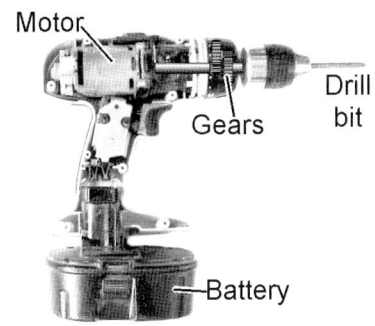

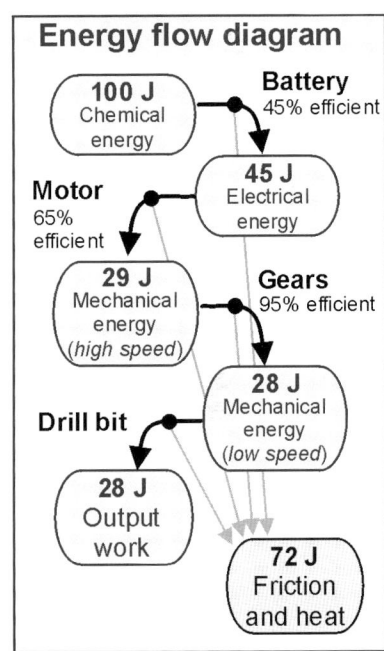

Figure 11.14: *The energy flow in a rechargeable electric drill. Each step in the energy flow has losses to heat or friction.*

Energy flows in natural systems

Steady state energy balance

The energy flow in technology tends to start and stop. For example, you turn your car's motor on, drive somewhere, and turn it off. The energy flows in natural systems tend to be **steady state**. Steady state means there is a balance between energy in and energy out so that the total energy remains the same. A good example of a system in steady state is the Earth as a planet. Energy from the sun represents energy input. But the Earth is warm compared with the chill of empty space. Consequently, the Earth radiates thermal energy back into space. The average energy of the Earth stays about the same because the energy input from the sun is balanced by the power radiated back into space (Figure 11.15).

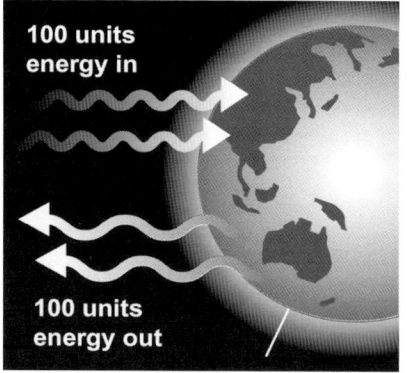

Figure 11.15: *The total energy of the Earth stays relatively steady because the energy input from the sun equals the energy radiated back into space.*

Natural systems work in cycles

Many of the energy flows in nature occur in **cycles**. The water cycle is a good example. Radiant energy from the sun is absorbed by water, mostly the oceans, and also lakes. Some water evaporates into the air, carrying energy from the warm water into the atmosphere. The water vapor goes up into the atmosphere and cools, releasing its energy to the air. The cooled water condenses into droplets as rain, which falls back to the ground. Eventually, the rainwater makes its way back to the ocean through rivers and groundwater and the cycle begins again. The water cycle moves energy from the oceans into the atmosphere (Figure 11.16).

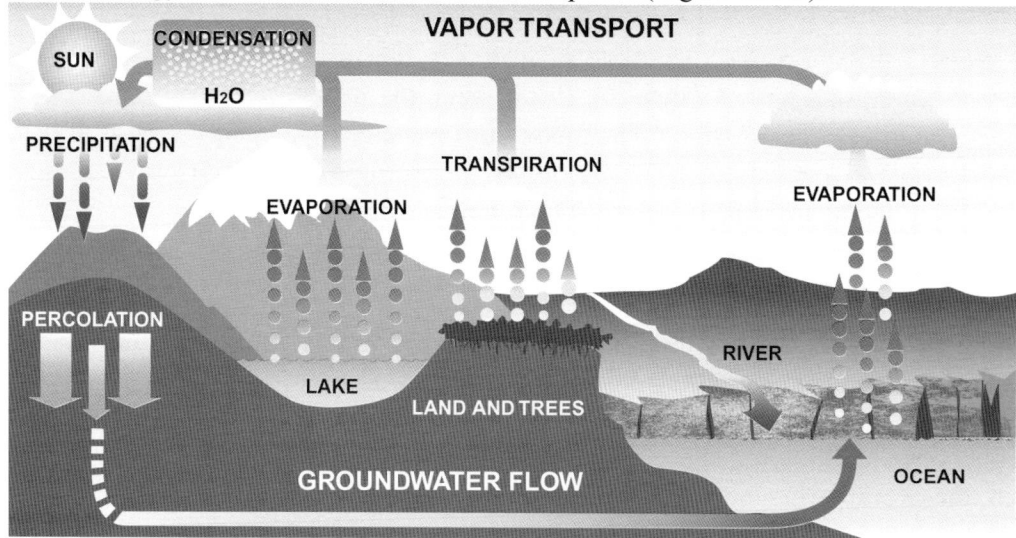

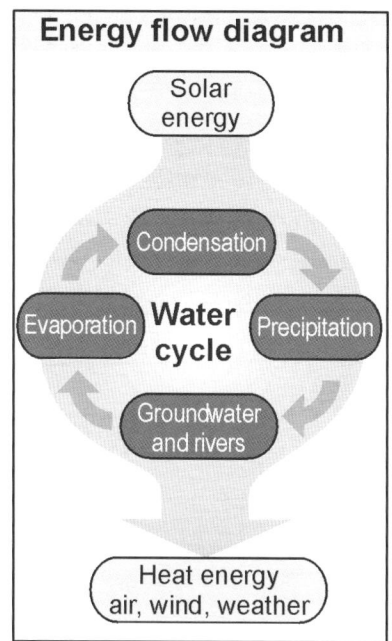

Figure 11.16: *An energy flow diagram for the water cycle.*

Energy flows in biological systems

Producers and food chains

A food chain is a series of processes through which energy and nutrients are transferred between living things. At the bottom of the food chain are producers. Producers are plants and one-celled organisms that use energy from the sun. Producers create biological molecules such as carbohydrates, fats, and proteins, which store energy from the sun in forms that can be passed on to animals higher in the food chain. Most producers are very small. The most numerous producers are phytoplankton, small organisms that live near the surface of the oceans.

Herbivores

The next step up the food chain are called herbivores. A herbivore is an organism that eats plants. Herbivores include rabbits, snails, most insects, some fish, deer, and many other land and sea animals. Herbivores concentrate the energy output from plants into proteins, fats, and animal tissue. It takes many producers to support one herbivore. Think of how many blades of grass a rabbit can eat.

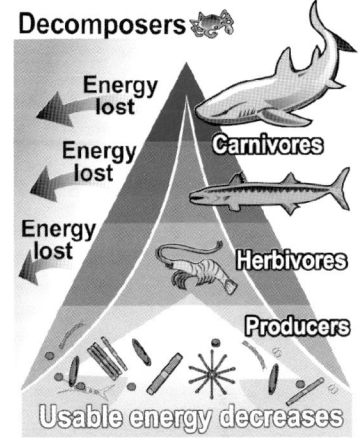

Figure 11.17: *The energy pyramid is a good way to show how energy moves through an ecosystem.*

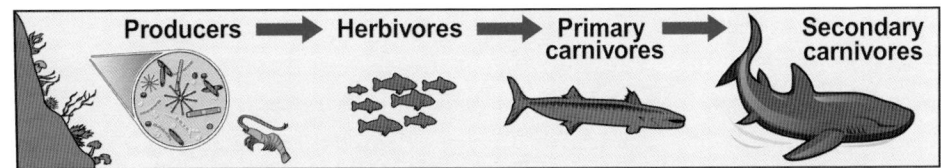

Carnivores and decomposers

Carnivores eat concentrated energy and proteins, fats, and carbohydrates in the bodies of herbivores. A *primary* carnivore eats herbivores. A hawk is an example of a primary carnivore. Hawks eat mice and other small animals that eat plants. *Secondary* carnivores eat other carnivores as well as herbivores. A shark is an example of a secondary carnivore. Sharks eat fish that eat other fish, as well as fish that eat plants. Another important group in the food chain are decomposers. Decomposers break down waste and bodies of other animals into nutrients that can be used by plants. Earthworms and many bacteria are examples of decomposers.

Food webs and ecosystems

An ecosystem is an interdependent collection of plants and animals that support each other. A food chain is like one strand in a food web. A food web connects all the producers and consumers of energy in an ecosystem. A good way to look at the energy flow in a food web is in the form of a pyramid (Figure 11.17). Figure 11.18 shows an energy flow diagram for an ecosystem.

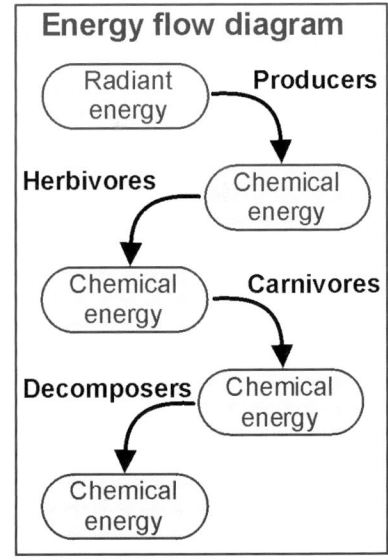

Figure 11.18: *Energy flow in an ecosystem.*

Application: Energy from Ocean Tides

Tides are enormous flows of water created by gravity in the Earth-moon system. Tides occur because the force of gravity falls off with distance (the inverse square law). The gravity of the moon acting on the Earth is stronger on the side of the Earth that faces the moon than on the opposite side. If the Earth could change its shape, lunar gravity would make the Earth slightly egg-shaped. The long axis of the "egg" would always be along a line between the Earth and moon. The Earth, however, is sturdy rock and cannot change its shape in response to the position of the moon. But the oceans are liquid and *can* change their shape. Figure 11.19 shows an exaggerated diagram of how the surface of the ocean responds to lunar gravity. Because the Earth rotates once per day, a person standing in many locations on the Earth sees the oceans go up and down twice per day.

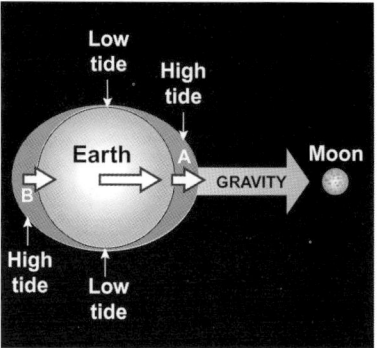

Figure 11.19: *The gravity of the moon causes the tides on Earth.*

Power in tides

Estimating the energy in tides | The energy and power in tides is enormous. A simple estimate can be made using what you know about energy. The surface area of the Earth is 511 billion square kilometers, 71% of which is covered by water. Suppose half the water in the oceans is lifted 1/2 meter higher than average (Figure 11.20). That means lifting 180,000 trillion (1.8×10^{17}) kilograms of water, and creating a potential energy difference of 1.8 million trillion joules (1.8×10^{18} J). Since tides go up and down in some places twice per day, this flow of energy occurs over 12 hours, representing a power of 41 trillion watts (4.1×10^{13} W). This simple estimate is five times the total power used by the 6 billion people living on the planet today.

The source of tidal energy | The power that sloshes the oceans around and creates tides comes from the total potential and kinetic energy of the Earth-moon system. Tides represent a frictional force on the motion of the Earth and moon. Every day the tides take a bit of energy away from the system. Friction from tides slows down the rotation of the Earth, making the day longer by 0.0016 seconds every 100 years. The moon also takes longer in its orbit by a tiny fraction of a second. Fifty billion years from now the slow energy transfer of tides will cause the rotation of the Earth to become synchronized with the orbit of the moon, making a day and a month both equal to 47 hours. Fortunately, 50 billion years is so far into the future that we need not worry much about days and months getting longer.

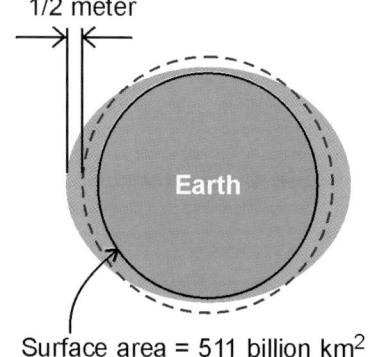

Figure 11.20: *Estimating the energy and power available in the tides.*

216

Extracting tidal power

Advantages of tidal power
Many experimental projects have been built to harness the power of tides. Like hydroelectric power, energy from tides creates no pollution, nor does it use up fossil fuels such as petroleum or coal. Three promising techniques are being evaluated.

Tidal basin power
The simplest approach is to create a basin that fills up at high tide, when the ocean is at its highest. At low tide, the basin empties out through a turbine (Figure 11.21). The potential energy of the water is converted to electricity by a turbine and generator, just like other forms of hydroelectric power (see Chapter 10). The tidal power stations in the Bay of Fundy in eastern Canada produce 20 million watts of electric power when the tide goes out, twice a day. The St. Malo tidal power station in France generates a peak power of 240 million watts.

The underwater propeller approach
The second approach uses underwater propellers that act like windmills (Figure 11.22). The propeller blades can swivel so that they generate power when the tide is going out or when it is coming in. This is an advantage over the basin approach, which can only generate power when the tide goes out.

The float and weight approach
A third approach makes small amounts of power for signal lights, radio beacons, and other instruments that need to operate continuously and are relatively close to shore. A tether anchors a cable to the ocean floor. A sliding weight on the cable is attached to a float that goes up and down with the tides. The falling weight operates a tiny generator to provide electric power to instruments.

Tide power is active research
Developing tidal power is an active area of engineering research around the world. A practical tidal power plant must be extremely rugged. Because equipment is out in the ocean, it must withstand hurricanes, ice storms, and other violent weather. Many clever ideas are being tried and there is plenty of room for invention. Maybe one day you will think of a new and clever way to use the energy from tides.

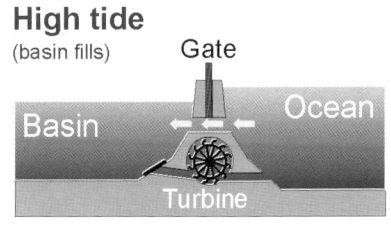

High tide
(basin fills)

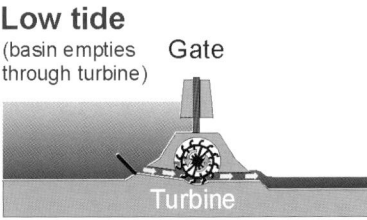

Low tide
(basin empties through turbine)

Figure 11.21: *How a tidal-basin power plant works. The turbine only makes power when the tide is low. The basin fills when the tide is high.*

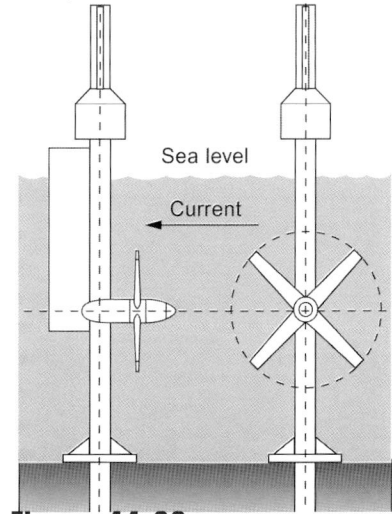

Figure 11.22: *The underwater-propeller approach to tide power.*

Chapter 11 Review

Vocabulary Review

Match the following terms with the correct definition. There is one extra definition in the list that will not match any of the terms.

Set One

1. efficiency
2. input
3. output
4. food calorie
5. process

  a. A unit that represents the energy in what you eat; equal to 4,187 J
  b. Ratio of output to input; usually expressed as a percent
  c. In real machines, this is always less than the input
  d. Any activity that changes things
  e. In the plant growth process - represented by the sun, carbon from the air, and nutrients from the soil
  f. Another term for useful output energy

Set Two

1. reversible
2. irreversible
3. power
4. watt
5. horsepower

  a. Energy used divided by the time taken
  b. A process that can run forwards or backwards in time
  c. A unit of power, named after the inventor of the steam engine
  d. A unit of energy
  e. A unit of power equal to 746 watts
  f. Process that only goes forward in time

Set Three

1. energy conversion
2. energy flow
3. food chain
4. producer
5. herbivore

  a. A series of processes through which energy and nutrients are transferred between living things
  b. Connects all producers and consumers of energy in an ecosystem; sometimes illustrated in the form of a pyramid
  c. Often represented by a diagram that shows different energy conversions taking place
  d. Usually an animal that eats plants
  e. Plants and one-celled organisms that use energy from the sun
  f. Takes place when energy flows back and forth between kinetic and potential energy, as in a pendulum

Set Four

1. carnivore
2. decomposer
3. food web
4. steady state
5. ecosystem

  a. Connects all producers and consumers of an ecosystem; sometimes illustrated as a pyramid
  b. An inter-dependent collection of plants and animals that support each other
  c. A condition in which there is a balance between power in and power out
  d. An animal that eats only plants
  e. Organisms that obtain concentrated energy from eating herbivores and/or carnivores
  f. Organisms, such as bacteria and earthworms, that break down organic material

Concept review

1. What is the difference between an ideal machine and a real machine, in terms of efficiency?

2. A consumer foundation states that buying energy efficient products is one of the smartest ways you can reduce energy usage and help prevent air pollution.

   a. What, in general terms, is an "energy efficient" product?

   b. How will using an energy efficient product reduce energy usage and prevent air pollution?

3. If the efficiency of pure photosynthesis is 26%, why is the whole system of a plant only 1 to 3% efficient?

4. Bicycles can have efficiencies as high as 85%. Is the remaining 15% of the input energy lost? Does this contradict the law of conservation of energy?

5. Would the efficiency of a motorcycle be higher or lower than the efficiency of a bicycle? Explain your reasoning.

6. Why is the energy efficiency of biological systems typically very low?

7. In everyday language, the words energy and power are often used interchangeably, but they actually do NOT mean the same thing. What is the difference between energy and power in the physics sense?

8. Describe the two interpretations of power and the two ways to calculate power.

9. Why do you suppose that we still use the unit called horsepower to describe the power delivered by a machine?

10. Two students are working out in the weight room. Erik lifts a 50-pound barbell over his head 10 times in one minute. Patsy lifts a 50-pound barbell over her head 10 times in 10 seconds. Who does the most work? Who delivers the most power?

11. Two mountain lions run up a steep hillside. One animal is twice as massive as the other, yet the smaller animal got to the top in half the time. Which animal did the most work? Which delivered the most power?

12. List two examples of technology you use each day that have a high power rating, and two examples of technology that have a relatively low power rating. Explain why these particular examples have high and low power ratings.

13. Steve lifts a toolbox 0.5 meters off the ground in one second. If he does the same thing on the moon, does he have to use more power, less power, or the same amount of power? Explain.

14. At each level of the food web pyramid, about 90% of the usable energy is lost in the form of heat.

    a. Which level requires the most overall input of energy to meet its energy needs?

    b. Use the diagram information to explain why a pound of beefsteak costs more than a pound of corn.

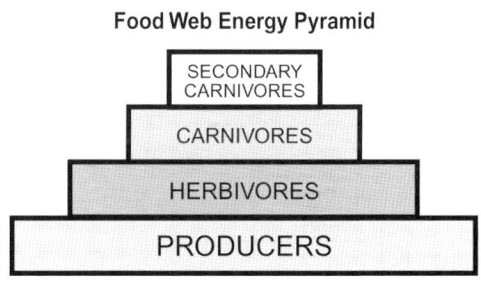

Food Web Energy Pyramid

SECONDARY CARNIVORES

CARNIVORES

HERBIVORES

PRODUCERS

15. Use the diagram below to answer questions a through d.

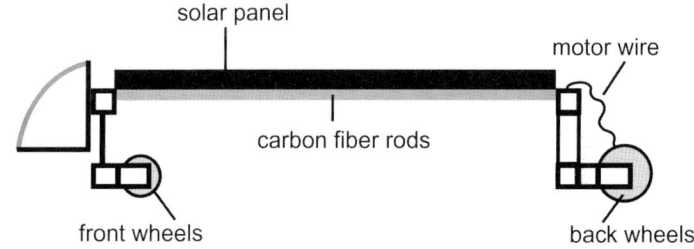

solar panel

motor wire

carbon fiber rods

front wheels

back wheels

    a. What component of the model solar car represents the energy storage process?

    b. What specific energy conversions take place?

    c. What sort of power transmission take place?

    d. What is the output use?

Problems

1. What is the efficiency of an escalator that uses 200 joules of electrical energy for every 20 joules of energy gained by the riders?

2. Michelle, a basketball star, takes her 75-kg body up a 3.0-meter staircase in 3.0 seconds.

   a. What is her power rating in watts?

   b. What is her power rating in horsepower?

   c. How many joules of work does Michelle do?

   d. If Michelle uses 10 food calories to do the work, what is her energy efficiency?

3. Robert's blue car has a 40-horsepower engine that can accelerate from 0 mi/hr to 60 mi/hr in 16 seconds. Matt's 1970 Dodge Challenger has a 375-horsepower engine. You can assume that the cars have the same mass, both have uniform acceleration, and you can neglect friction. How many seconds will it take Matt to go from 0 mi/hr to 60 mi/hr?

4. A 2.0-horsepower engine runs a water pump for 24 hours.

   a. Calculate the work done by the engine.

   b. What would happen if a 1.0-horsepower engine was used to pump the same amount of water?

5. Carmine uses 800 joules of energy on a jack that is 85% efficient to raise her car to change a flat tire.

   a. How much energy is available to raise the car?

   b. If the car weighs 13,600 newtons, how high off the ground can she raise the car?

6. Suppose you exert 200-newtons of force to push a heavy box across the floor at a constant speed of 2.0 m/sec.

   a. What is your power rating, in watts?

   b. What would happen to your power rating if you used the same force to push the box at 1.0 m/sec?

7. Suppose your job is to choose a motor for an escalator. The escalator must be able to lift 20 people at a time, each with a mass of 70 kg. The escalator must move between the two floors, which are 5 meters apart, in 5 seconds.

   a. What energy is required to do this work?

   b. What is the power rating of the required motor, in horsepower?

8. Leroy takes in about 3,000 food calories per day. Calculate the average power this represents in watts over a 24 hour period.

9. Fill in the joules of energy for each box below. Compute the output work and total wasted energy. What is the overall efficiency of the model solar car?

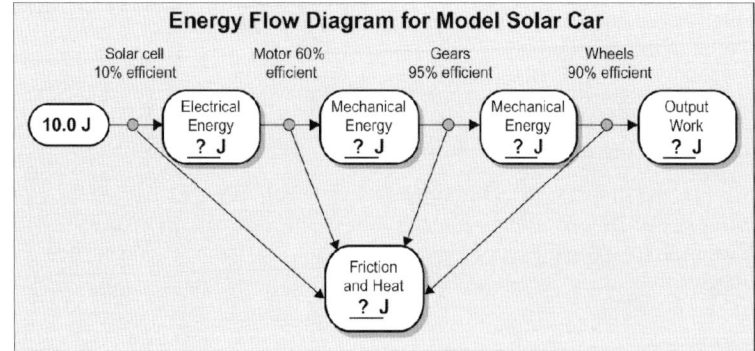

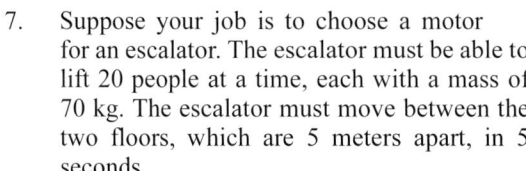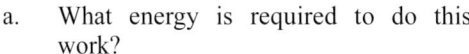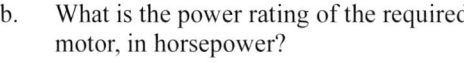

Unit 4

Energy and Momentum

Chapter 12

Momentum

Objectives for Chapter 12

By the end of this chapter you should be able to:

1. Calculate the linear momentum of a moving object given the mass and velocity.
2. Describe the relationship between linear momentum and force.
3. Solve a one-dimensional elastic collision problem using momentum conservation.
4. Describe the properties of angular momentum in a system—for instance, a bicycle.
5. Calculate the angular momentum of a rotating object with a simple shape.

Terms and vocabulary words

| momentum | linear momentum | angular momentum | conservation of momentum | elastic |
| inelastic | collision | gyroscope | moment of inertia | impulse |

12.1 Momentum

According to Newton's first law, objects tend to continue in the motion they already have with the same speed and the same direction. You already know it takes force to change the speed of a moving object, because you must do work to change the object's kinetic energy. But it also takes force to change an object's direction of motion, even if the speed remains the same. The more mass an object has, the more force it takes to deflect its motion. Why is this true? This section is about *momentum*, which is a property of moving matter. Momentum describes the tendency of objects to keep going in the same direction with the same speed. Changes in momentum result from forces or create forces.

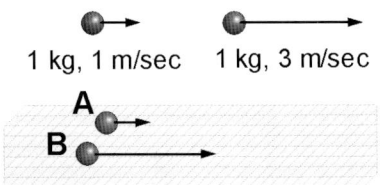

Figure 12.1: *The momentum of each ball depends on its mass and velocity. Ball B has more momentum than ball A.*

Momentum comes from mass in motion

An example Consider two balls of the same mass moving in the same direction with different velocities (Figure 12.1). The same 1 N force is applied to deflect the motion of each ball. What happens? Does the force deflect both balls equally?

Momentum You probably guessed that the slower ball is deflected more than the faster ball (Figure 12.2). The difference in deflection is due to the difference in momentum. Momentum is a property of moving mass that resists changes in a moving object's velocity vector (speed *or direction*). The faster ball has more momentum therefore its direction requires more force to change compared to the slower ball.

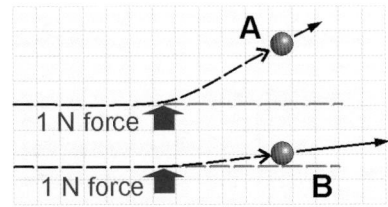

Figure 12.2: *Ball B deflects much less than ball A when the same force is applied because ball B has greater momentum.*

Momentum and inertia Inertia is another property of mass that resists changes in velocity. However, inertia depends only on mass. Momentum depends on both mass and velocity. The momentum of a moving object increases as its mass or its speed increases. Momentum is also a vector, and depends on direction. Inertia is a scalar.

Kinetic energy and momentum are different Kinetic energy and momentum are different quantities, even though both depend on mass and speed. Kinetic energy is a scalar, meaning it does not depend on direction. Two balls with the same mass and speed will always have the same kinetic energy. Momentum is a vector, so it *always* depends on direction. Two balls with the same mass and speed have opposite momentum if they are moving in opposite directions (Figure 12.3).

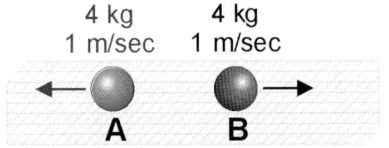

	Kinetic energy	Momentum
A	2 J	− 4 kg·m/sec
B	2 J	+ 4 kg·m/sec

Figure 12.3: *Two balls with the same mass and speed can have the same kinetic energy but opposite momentum.*

Calculating momentum

Momentum is mass times velocity   The momentum of a moving object is its mass multiplied by its velocity. That means momentum increases with both mass and velocity. For example, if a car and a truck are moving at the same velocity, the truck will have more momentum because it has greater mass. If two trucks of equal mass are moving, the one with the greater velocity has more momentum. Momentum is measured in units of kilogram-meters per second, or kg-m/s.

Momentum

$$\text{Momentum (kg·m/sec)} \quad \vec{p} = m\vec{v} \quad \overset{\text{Mass (kg)}}{\underset{\text{Velocity (m/sec)}}{}}$$

Momentum is a vector   When talking about momentum, it is important to include the direction of motion. For many problems, it is convenient to choose positive and negative signs to indicate direction. Generally, momentum to the right is positive, and momentum to the left is negative (Figure 12.4). Because momentum has both magnitude and direction, momentum is always a vector. The symbol for momentum is a lower case "p" with an arrow above it ($\vec{p}$) to show that it is a vector.

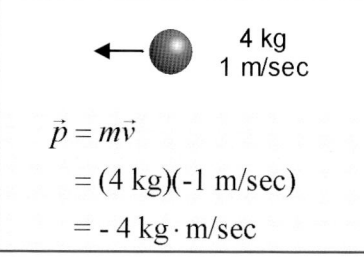

$$\vec{p} = m\vec{v}$$
$$= (4 \text{ kg})(-1 \text{ m/sec})$$
$$= -4 \text{ kg·m/sec}$$

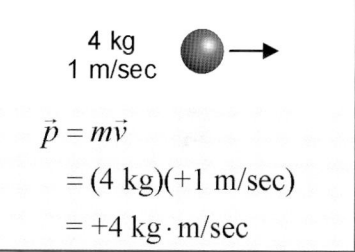

$$\vec{p} = m\vec{v}$$
$$= (4 \text{ kg})(+1 \text{ m/sec})$$
$$= +4 \text{ kg·m/sec}$$

Figure 12.4: *Velocity often is defined to be positive to the right and negative to the left. That means momentum is also positive to the right and negative to the left.*

Compare the momentum of a moving car and a motorcycle

A car is traveling at a velocity of 13.5 m/sec (30 mph) north on a straight road. The mass of the car is 1,300 kg. A motorcycle passes the car at a speed of 30 m/sec (67 mph). The motorcycle (with rider) has a mass of 350 kg. Calculate and compare the momentum of the car and motorcycle.

1) You are asked to calculate momentum.
2) You are given the masses and velocities.
3) Momentum is $\vec{p} = m\vec{v}$
4) Solve: For the car,

$$\vec{p} = (1,300 \text{ kg})(13.5 \text{ m/sec}) = 17,550 \text{ kg·m/sec}$$

for the motorcycle and rider,

$$\vec{p} = (350 \text{ kg})(30 \text{ m/sec}) = 10,500 \text{ kg·m/sec}$$

The car has more momentum even though it is going much slower.

Momentum without mass

We have defined momentum for objects with mass. But momentum is a fundamental property of matter and energy. Light also carries momentum even though it is pure energy with no mass. The momentum of light depends on the energy of the light.

Conservation of momentum and Newton's third law

The law of conservation of momentum

If you are on a skateboard and throw a heavy rock forward, you will find that you move backward (Figure 12.5). The faster you throw, the faster you move backward. This effect is due to the law of conservation of momentum. When a system of interacting objects is not influenced by outside forces (like friction), this law says the total momentum of the system cannot change. When you throw a rock forward, the rock gets forward (positive) momentum. Because the total momentum cannot change, you move with backward (negative) momentum. The positive, forward momentum gained by the rock is exactly canceled by your gain of negative, backward momentum. As a result, the total momentum of the system (you and the rock) is the same before and after you throw the rock (Figure 12.6).

Momentum and the third law

The law of conservation of momentum is a consequence of Newton's third law, the law of action and reaction. To see the relationship, consider two balls connected by a spring. The balls are motionless and therefore have no momentum. When you compress the spring, the third law says the balls exert equal forces (through the springs) in opposite directions on one another, $-F_1 = F_2$.

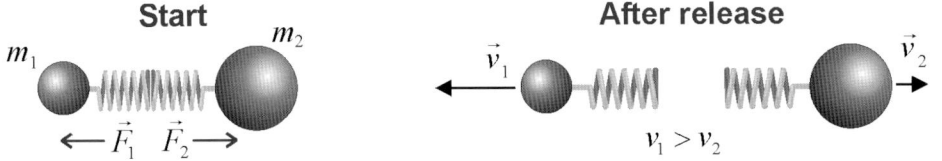

Proving the law of conservation of momentum

Remember from Newton's second law that the equal and opposite forces create opposite accelerations, which create opposite velocities. The accelerations are inversely proportional to the masses, so the velocities are also inversely proportional to the masses. Heavy objects end up with less velocity and light objects with more velocity. The velocities caused by the original equal and opposite forces are exactly as predicted by the law of momentum conservation.

Momentum conservation

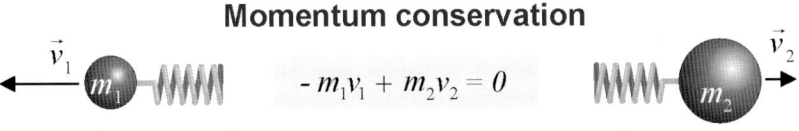

v_1 is greater than v_2 because m_2 is greater than m_1,

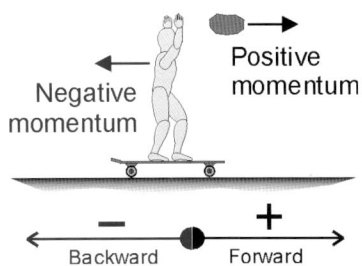

Figure 12.5: *If you throw a rock forward from a skateboard, you will move backward in response.*

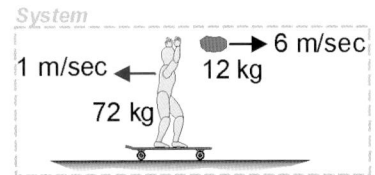

Forward momentum

$$\vec{p} = (12 \text{ kg})(6 \text{ m/sec})$$
$$= 72 \text{ kg} \cdot \text{m/sec}$$

Backward momentum

$$\vec{p} = (72 \text{ kg})(-1 \text{ m/sec})$$
$$= -72 \text{ kg} \cdot \text{m/sec}$$

Total change of momentum

$$+ 72 \text{ kg} \cdot \text{m/sec}$$
$$- 72 \text{ kg} \cdot \text{m/sec}$$
$$\vec{p} = \quad 0$$

Figure 12.6: *The forward (positive) momentum of the rock exactly cancels the backward (negative) momentum from your own motion. The total change in momentum for the system (that being you and the rock) is zero.*

224

Collisions in one dimension

Momentum transfer in collisions A collision occurs when two or more objects hit each other. During a collision, momentum is transferred from one object to another. According to the law of momentum conservation, the total momentum before the collision is equal to the total momentum after the collision. The velocities of objects after a collision depend on their masses, initial velocities, and the type of collision.

Elastic and inelastic collisions In an **elastic collision**, the objects bounce off each other with no loss in the total kinetic energy. The collision of two hardened steel balls is very close to a perfectly elastic collision (Figure 12.7). In an **inelastic collision**, objects change shape or stick together, and "lose" some kinetic energy to heat, sound, or friction. A clay ball hitting another clay ball is an example of an inelastic collision. So are two vehicles colliding (Figure 12.8). In both cases, some of the kinetic energy is used to permanently change an object's shape.

Momentum is conserved in all collisions Momentum is conserved in both elastic and inelastic collisions, even when kinetic energy is not conserved. Conservation of momentum makes it possible to determine the speeds and directions of objects after a collision. If you observe objects after a collision, momentum conservation also allows you to determine how they were moving *before* the collision.

Elastic collisions

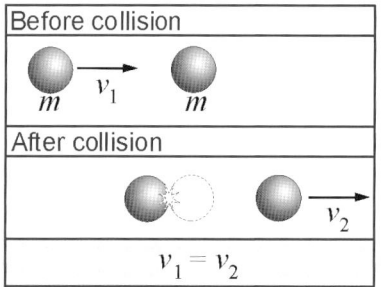

Figure 12.7: *Examples of elastic collisions.*

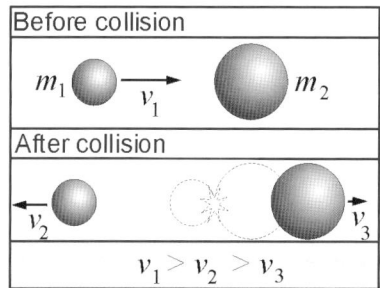

Collision type	Before collision	After collision
Elastic or inelastic: objects bounce off each other in the collision.	m_1 →$\vec{v}_1$ ←$\vec{v}_2$ m_2	m_1 ←$\vec{v}_3$ m_2 →$\vec{v}_4$
	$m_1\vec{v}_1 + m_2\vec{v}_2 = m_1\vec{v}_3 + m_2\vec{v}_4$	
Elastic or inelastic: objects stick to each other after the collision.	m_1 →$\vec{v}_1$ ←$\vec{v}_2$ m_2	$m_1 + m_2$ →$\vec{v}_3$
	$m_1\vec{v}_1 + m_2\vec{v}_2 = (m_1 + m_2)\vec{v}_3$	

Remember that velocity can be positive or negative. The table above shows how to apply conservation of momentum to collisions in a straight line.

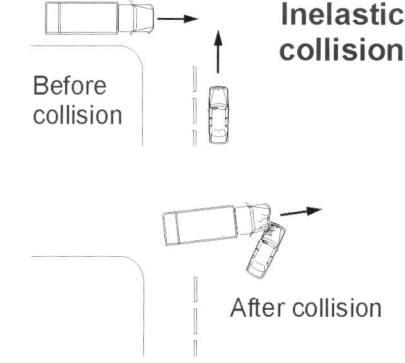

Inelastic collision

Figure 12.8: *Example of an inelastic collision.*

Solving momentum problems

Applying conservation of momentum to physical situations — Using momentum to analyze problems takes practice. The first step is usually to draw a diagram and label positive and negative directions. Decide whether the collision is elastic or inelastic. Determine if the objects bounce apart or stick together. Finally, assign different variable names to all the masses and velocities before and after the collision.

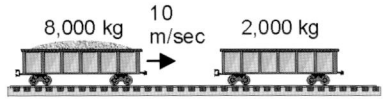

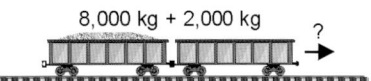

Figure 12.9: *What is the velocity of the two train cars together after one has collided with the other?*

Inelastic collision of train cars

A train car moving to the right at 10 m/s collides with a parked train car (Figure 12.9). They stick together and roll along the track. If the moving car has a mass of 8,000 kg and the parked car has a mass of 2,000 kg, what is their combined velocity after the collision?

1) You are asked for the velocity.
2) You are given the masses and the initial velocity of the moving car. You know the collision is inelastic because the cars stick together.
3) Apply the law of conservation of momentum. Because the cars stick together, consider the two cars to be one object after the collision.
   $m_1v_1 + m_2v_2 = (m_1 + m_2)v_3$ (from second row of table on previous page)
4) Solve:
   $(8,000 kg)(10 m/s) + (2,000 kg)(0 m/s) = (8,000 + 2,000 kg)v_3$
   $v_3 = 8$ m/s. The train cars move to the right together at 8 m/s.

Elastic collision of billiard balls

Two 0.165 kg billiard balls roll toward each other and collide head-on (Figure 12.10). Initially, the 3-ball has a velocity of 0.5 m/s. The 7-ball has an initial velocity of -0.7 m/s. The collision is elastic and the 7-ball rebounds with a velocity of 0.4 m/s, reversing its direction. What is the velocity of the 3-ball after the collision?

1) You are asked to find the 3-ball's velocity after the collision.
2) You are given mass, initial velocities, and the 7-ball's final velocity. You can treat the collision as elastic since it involves billiard balls.
3) Make a diagram (Figure 12.10). Apply conservation of momentum to find the 3-ball's final velocity. $m_1v_1 + m_2v_2 = m_1v_3 + m_2v_4$
4) Solve:
   $(.165 kg)(.5 m/s) + (.165 kg)(-.7 ms) = (.165 kg) v_3 + (.165 kg)(.4 m/s)$
   $-.033 kgm/s = (.165 kg) v_3 + 0.066 kgm/s$
   $v_3 = -0.6$ m/s. The 3-ball travels at -0.6 m/s, the negative value indicating its movement in the opposite direction as the arrow in the diagram.

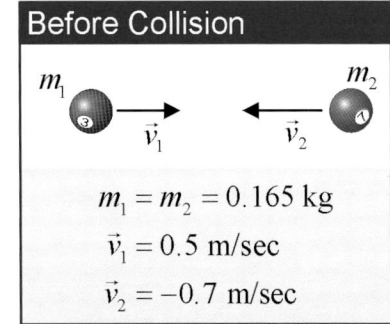

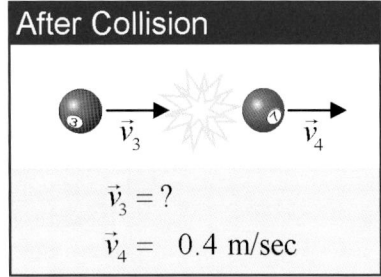

Figure 12.10: *Analyzing a collision between two billiard balls.*

Collisions in two and three dimensions *Advanced topic*

Two-dimensional collisions

Most real-life collisions do not occur in one dimension. In a two- or three-dimensional collision, objects move at angles to each other before or after they collide. For example, two billiard balls might have a two-dimensional collision as shown in the diagram below. Momentum conservation still applies and can be used to determine the directions and velocities before or after the collision. Because angles are involved, the math is more complicated. There are also more variables, so both energy and momentum equations need to be used.

Using momentum conservation

In order to analyze two-dimensional collisions you need to look at each dimension separately. Momentum is conserved *separately* in the x and y directions. The first step is to choose the best coordinates. Usually you will want to make the x-axis align with one of the initial velocities. Next, each velocity vector is resolved into its components along x and y. Momentum is calculated separately in the x and y directions both before and after the collision. The total x-momentum must be the same before and after the collision. The same goes for the total y-momentum.

Before collision

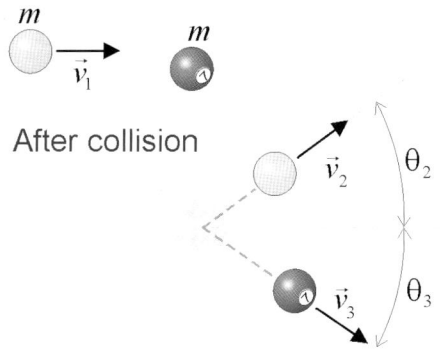

After collision

Applying the conservation laws

Before	=	After

Momentum in the x-direction

$$m\vec{v}_1 = m\vec{v}_2 \cos\theta_2 + m\vec{v}_3 \cos\theta_3$$

Momentum in the y-direction

$$0 = m\vec{v}_2 \sin\theta_2 - m\vec{v}_3 \sin\theta_3$$

Kinetic energy *(elastic collision only)*

$$\tfrac{1}{2}mv_1^2 = \tfrac{1}{2}mv_2^2 + \tfrac{1}{2}mv_3^2$$

Energy conservation

For elastic collisions, kinetic energy is also conserved. That means the total kinetic energy before the collision equals the total kinetic energy after the collision. Many two-dimensional problems require a separate equation for energy conservation.

Accident reconstruction

Police forensics specialists use conservation of momentum and other physics knowledge to analyze traffic accidents. Skid marks, debris such as broken glass, and other clues allow investigators to reconstruct the events of an accident scene with surprising accuracy.

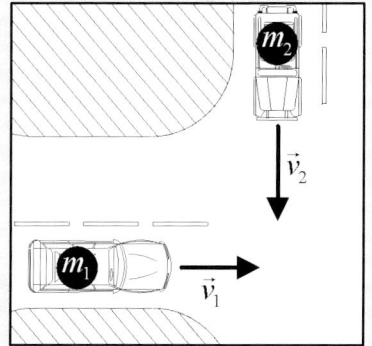

Skid marks are used to determine the directions of the vehicles before and after the crash. Skid marks can also be used to estimate velocities. With information on friction, skid distances, and directions, the forensics specialists use momentum conservation to determine the vehicles' velocities before and after the crash.

12.2 Force is the Rate of Change of Momentum

Momentum changes when a net force is applied. The converse is also true: If momentum changes, forces are created. If momentum changes quickly, large forces are involved. In fact, the second law is really a prescription for relating force to the change in momentum. As a practical application, all cars sold today are equipped with safety devices designed to slow down any change in momentum from a crash. The real purpose of seat belts and air bags is to reduce the force on your body by spreading out the change in momentum from a crash over a longer period of time (Figure 12.11). This section discusses the relationship between forces and momentum.

Car crash safety

Figure 12.11: *Seat belts and air bags work together to safely stop passengers in the event of a crash.*

Force results from changes in momentum

In the last section, you learned the momentum of an object is its mass times its velocity. When the velocity of an object changes, then its momentum also changes. From Newton's second law you know that the force on an object is related to acceleration. When the acceleration is high, the force is also high. Rapid changes in momentum imply large accelerations, and therefore result in large forces (Figure 12.12). In a car crash your momentum might change very fast—fast enough to create forces that could injure you severely.

Crashes and seat belts

When a car crashes to a stop, the momentum of the car drops to zero as the body of the car crumples. Car bodies are designed to absorb the momentum of a crash by crumpling as slowly as possible. A passenger without a seat belt, however, can fly forward and change momentum very fast by hitting the windshield, steering wheel or dashboard. Seat belts are made of very strong fabric that stretches slightly when a force is applied. By holding you in the seat, a seat belt keeps *your* momentum from changing any faster than the momentum of the whole car.

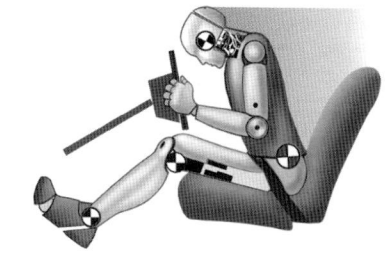

Figure 12.12: *Crash-test dummies are used in car safety tests. Sensors mounted in many places on the dummy record the forces experienced during a crash.*

Air bags

Air bags work together with seat belts to bring passengers to a stop as gradually as possible. An air bag inflates when the force applied to the front of a car reaches a dangerous level. The air bag deflates slowly as the passenger's body applies a force to the bag upon impact. The force of impact pushes the air out of small holes in the air bag, and the force of rapid momentum change is dissipated over time. Many cars now contain both front and side air bags.

Force and momentum change

Force is rate of change of momentum

The relationship between force and motion follows directly from the second law. Acceleration is the change in speed divided by the change in time. In this type of logic it is convenient to use as a symbol the Greek letter *delta* (Δ) which translates to "the change in." When you see the Δ symbol, replace it in your mind with the phrase "the change in." The acceleration can then be written as $\Delta v/\Delta t$, which translates to "the change in speed divided by the change in time."

Newton's second law $\vec{F} = m\dfrac{\Delta \vec{v}}{\Delta t}$ **Translation** $\text{Force} = \text{mass} \times \dfrac{\text{change in velocity}}{\text{change in time}}$

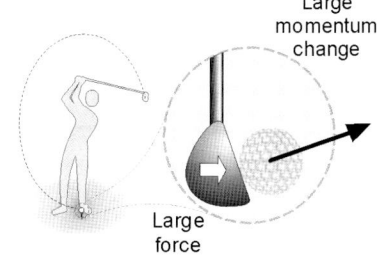

Figure 12.13: *Large forces produce a large change in momentum, such as when you hit a golf ball.*

Momentum form of the second law

Mass multiplied by the change in velocity ($m\Delta \vec{v}$) is the same as the change in momentum ($\Delta \vec{p}$). We can rewrite the second law in a form that shows force is equal to the rate of change in momentum. Large forces produce a proportionally large change in momentum (Figure 12.13).

Newton's second law *(momentum form)*   Force (N) $\vec{F} = \dfrac{\Delta \vec{p}}{\Delta t}$ ← *Change in momentum (kg·m/sec)* ← *Change in time (sec)*

The momentum form of Newton's second law is sometimes more useful than the acceleration form ($F = ma$). For example, pure energy can have momentum, but not mass. The momentum form of the second law is used to do calculations with light and atoms because light is pure energy that has momentum without mass.

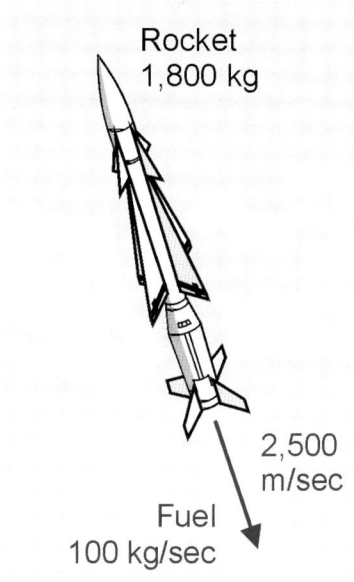

Rocket
1,800 kg

2,500 m/sec

Fuel
100 kg/sec

Figure 12.14: *Momentum change from the fuel creates the force that drives a rocket forward.*

Calculate force on a rocket from the change in momentum

Starting at rest, an 1,800 kg rocket takes off, ejecting 100 kg of fuel per second out of its nozzle at a speed of 2,500 m/sec. Figure 12.14 shows a diagram of the motion. Calculate the force on the rocket from the change in momentum of the fuel.

1) You are asked for the force exerted on the rocket.
2) You are given that the rocket ejects fuel at 100 kg/sec at a speed of 2,500 m/sec.
3) Use the equation F = Δp/Δt.
4) Solve: Δp = (100 kg)(-2,500 m/sec) = -25,000 kg-m/sec
            F = Δp / Δt = (-25,000 kg-m/sec) ÷ (1 sec) = -25,000 N
   The rocket exerts the -25,000 N force on the fuel. The fuel exerts an equal and opposite force on the rocket of +25,000 N which makes the rocket go forward.

Impulse

Force from elastic and inelastic collisions

A rubber ball and a clay ball are dropped on the hard floor of a gym (Figure 12.15). The rubber ball has an elastic collision and bounces back upward. The clay ball hits the floor with a thud and stays there (inelastic collision). Both balls have the same mass and are dropped from the same height. They have the same speed as they hit the floor. Which ball exerts a greater force on the floor?

Bounces have greater momentum change

The best way to determine the greater force is to compare the change in momentum. For example, suppose both balls are 1 kg, moving at 2 m/sec when they hit the floor (Figure 12.16). The momentum of the rubber ball goes from -2 kg-m/sec to +2 kg-m/sec, a net change of +4 kg-m/sec. The momentum of the clay ball goes from -2 kg-m/sec to zero, for a net change of +2 kg-m/sec. The rubber ball (elastic collision) has twice the change in momentum. The momentum change is always greater when objects bounce compared with when they do not bounce.

What can be learned from a change in momentum

The rubber ball exerts twice as much force as the clay ball since it has twice the change in momentum. This is approximately right however, there is a detail left to solve. A change in momentum tells you how the *product* of force and time changes, but not force or time individually. A change of 4 kg-m/sec could result from a force of 4 N for 1 second or a force of 1 N for four seconds. In fact, the change in momentum could result from any combination of force and time with a product of 4 N-sec when multiplied together.

Impulse

The product of a force and the time the force acts is called the impulse. To find the impulse, you rearrange the momentum form of the second law. Because collisions happen fast, it is not always possible to calculate the force and time individually.

Impulse

$$\text{Impulse (N·sec)} \longleftarrow \boxed{\vec{F}\Delta t} = \Delta \vec{p} \leftarrow \begin{array}{l}\text{Change in momentum} \\ (kg\cdot m/sec)\end{array}$$

Units of impulse

Notice that the force side of the equation has units of N-sec, while the momentum side has units of momentum, kg-m/sec. However different they look, these are the same units, since 1 N is 1 kg-m/s^2. Impulse can be expressed in kg-m/sec (momentum units) or in N-sec.

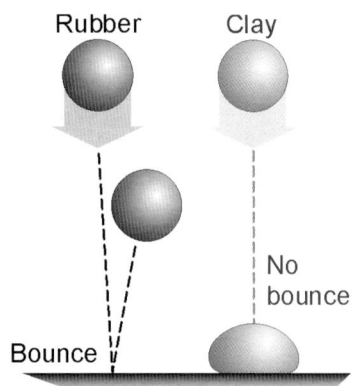

Figure 12.15: *A rubber ball bounces because it has an elastic collision with the floor. A clay ball has an inelastic collision and does not bounce.*

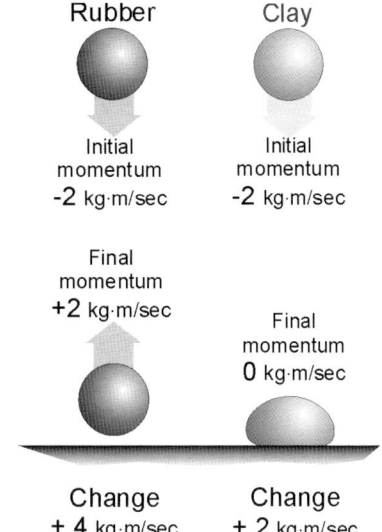

Figure 12.16: *Calculating the momentum change for the rubber ball versus the clay ball.*

12.3 Angular Momentum

An object that is spinning tends to keep spinning because of angular momentum. Angular momentum is a lot like linear momentum except that it applies to rotating motion. The conservation of angular momentum is why an ice skater spins faster when she pulls her arms in and why a cat can twist in midair to land on its feet. Angular momentum is also why the moon orbits the Earth instead of being drawn straight in by Earth's gravity. This section introduces angular momentum and describes a few examples of systems where angular momentum plays an important role.

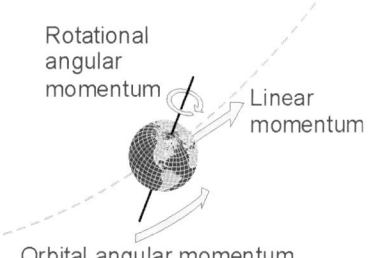

Figure 12.17: *The Earth has both linear and angular momentum in its rotation and its revolution around the sun.*

What is angular momentum?

Two types of momentum We distinguish between two types of momentum. Momentum resulting from an object moving in linear motion is called linear momentum. Linear momentum was the subject of the first two sections of this chapter. Momentum resulting from the rotation (or spin) of an object is called angular momentum.

Objects can have both types of momentum An object may have both types of momentum. For example, the Earth has linear momentum and angular momentum. It has linear momentum because the entire Earth moves as it travels around the sun. It also has angular momentum because the Earth is rotating as it is moving, and because the Earth orbits around the Sun (Figure 12.17). The motion of the Earth is determined by the conservation of both linear and angular momentum.

Understanding angular momentum To get a sense for why objects have angular momentum, think about a wheel that is spinning (Figure 12.18). The wheel has mass and every part of the wheel is moving (except the exact center). That means each particle of mass in the wheel has linear momentum. Particles far from the center are moving fastest and have more linear momentum. The angular momentum of the wheel comes from the organized motion of the *entire wheel* around a center of rotation. Angular momentum is a separate quantity from linear momentum and is always defined about a specific center of rotation.

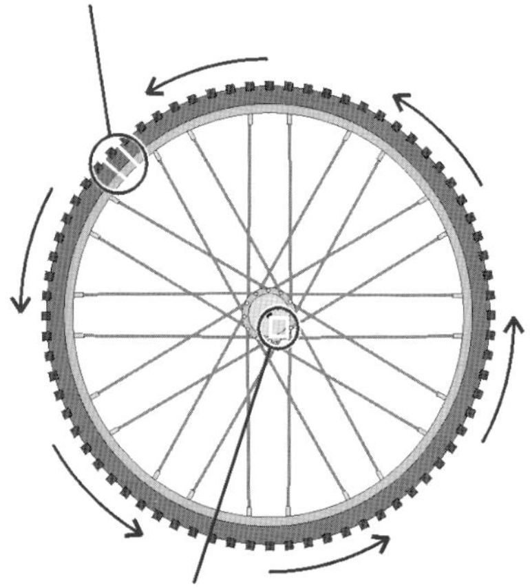

This piece is moving fast and has high linear momentum

This piece near the center of rotation is moving slowly and has low linear momentum

Figure 12.18: *Mass that is close to the center of rotation has less momentum because it is moving more slowly.*

The importance of angular momentum Angular momentum is important because it obeys a conservation law separate from linear momentum. Angular momentum is also a fundamental property of elementary particles in the atom, like electrons and protons (Chapter 28).

Conservation of angular momentum

Why angular momentum is important
Angular momentum is important because it obeys a conservation law, as does linear momentum. The total angular momentum of a closed system stays the same. The only way to change a system's angular momentum is to apply a torque.

Mass and speed
Like linear momentum, angular momentum is proportional to mass and speed. The faster an object rotates, the more angular momentum it has. *Unlike* linear momentum, however, the shape of an object makes a big difference in the angular momentum. This is very different from linear momentum, which depends only on the total mass of an object.

The distribution of mass
With angular momentum, the *moment of inertia* around the center of rotation is important instead of the mass. Mass that is far from the center has a larger moment of inertia and contributes more angular momentum. Mass close in to the center has a smaller moment of inertia and contributes less angular momentum. Mass at the exact center of rotation has zero moment of inertia and zero angular momentum.

The spinning skater and the diver
A spinning figure skater provides a good example of how angular momentum affects motion. When the skater is spinning with her arms out, the mass in her arms is relatively far from her center of rotation. She has a large moment of inertia and is spinning relatively slowly. When she pulls her arms in her moment of inertia decreases because the mass of her arms has moved nearer to the center of rotation. As her arms come in, she starts spinning much faster! She spins faster because her total angular momentum must stay the same, even though the moment of inertia has decreased (Figure 12.19). The opposite effect happens when a spinning diver comes out of a tuck. Straightening out puts more of the diver's body mass farther from the center of rotation. And this slows the diver's rotational speed.

Angular momentum changes through torque
Angular momentum can change through the application of torque. Similar to linear momentum, the net torque on a rotating object equals the rate of change of its angular momentum. Since friction can exert torque, a spinning figure skater eventually slows down and loses her angular momentum. To get a spin going, the skater pushes against the ice with her skates, creating a reaction torque on her body that increases her angular momentum.

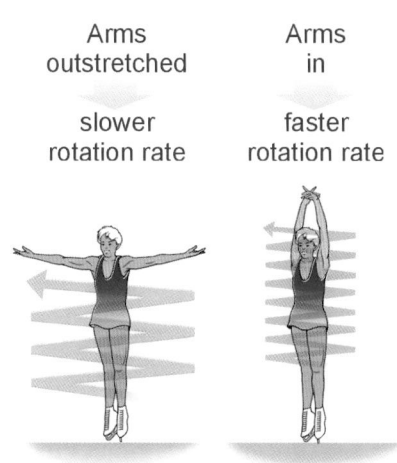

Arms outstretched — slower rotation rate

Arms in — faster rotation rate

Figure 12.19: *The skater's angular velocity increases when she decreases her moment of inertia.*

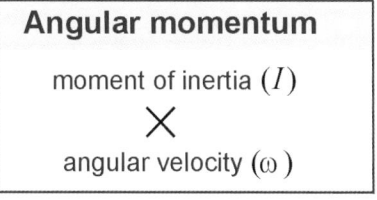

Angular momentum

moment of inertia (I)

$\times$

angular velocity (ω)

Conservation of angular momentum

$\uparrow I \omega \downarrow$ $\downarrow I \omega \uparrow$

Calculating angular momentum

Formula for angular momentum

Angular momentum is calculated in a similar way to linear momentum, except the mass and velocity are replaced by the moment of inertia and angular velocity. The angular momentum is the moment of inertia of an object times its angular velocity. The capital letter "*L*" is used for angular momentum, with a vector symbol above it. (For review, check Sections 9.3 for moment of inertia and 8.1 for angular velocity.) The SI units of angular momentum are kg-m²/s.

Angular momentum

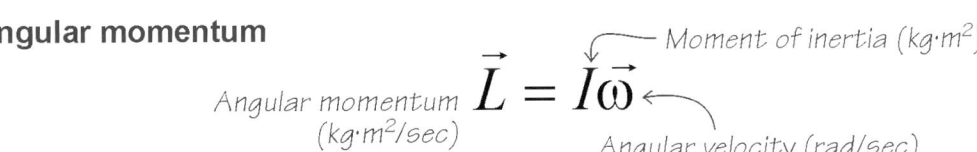

Angular momentum
(kg·m²/sec)
$$\vec{L} = I\vec{\omega}$$
Moment of inertia (kg·m²)
Angular velocity (rad/sec)

Calculating angular momentum

To calculate the angular momentum, you need to know the angular velocity and the moment of inertia. Angular velocity should be in radians per second (rad/sec). The moment of inertia is in units of kg-m².

Moment of inertia

Remember from Chapter 9 that the moment of inertia of an object is the average of mass × radius² for the whole object. Since the radius is measured from the axis of rotation, the moment of inertia depends on the axis of rotation. Figure 12.20 gives the moment of inertia for simple geometric shapes rotated around axes that pass through their centers.

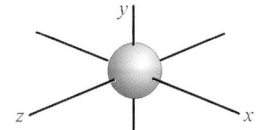

Sphere of mass, *m*, radius, *R*

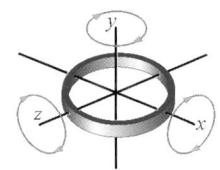

Hoop of mass, *m*, radius, *R*

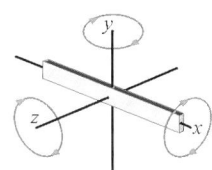

Bar of mass, *m*, length, *l*

Calculate angular momentum for two objects of equal mass and different shapes

An artist is making a moving metal sculpture. She takes two identical 1 kg metal bars and bends one into a hoop with a radius of 0.16 m. The hoop spins like a wheel. The other bar is left straight with a length of 1 meter. The straight bar spins around its center, like the *y*-axis in Figure 12.20. Both have an angular velocity of 1 rad/sec. Calculate the angular momentum of each and decide which would be harder to stop.

1) You are asked for the angular momentum.
2) You are given the angular velocity, shape, and mass.
3) Use the equation L=Iω.
4) Hoop: I = (1 kg)(0.16 m)² = .026 kg-m²; L = (1 rad/sec)(0.026 kg-m²) = 0.026 kg-m²/sec
   Bar: I = (1/12)(1 kg)(1 m)²· = .083 kg-m²; L = (1 rad/sec)(0.083 kg-m²) = 0.083 kg-m²/sec
   The bar has more than three times as much angular momentum as the hoop, and is therefore harder to stop.

	Moment of Inertia		
	Axis of rotation		
	x	**y**	**z**
Sphere	$\frac{2}{5}mR^2$	$\frac{2}{5}mR^2$	$\frac{2}{5}mR^2$
Hoop	$\frac{1}{2}mR^2$	mR^2	$\frac{1}{2}mR^2$
Bar		$\frac{1}{12}ml^2$	$\frac{1}{12}ml^2$

Figure 12.20: *Moment of inertia for some simple shapes.*

Gyroscopes and angular momentum

The angular momentum vector

Angular momentum has a direction and behaves almost like any other vector. The direction of the angular momentum vector is along the axis of rotation (Figure 12.21). Counterclockwise rotation is usually chosen to have positive angular momentum. Clockwise rotation therefore has negative angular momentum.

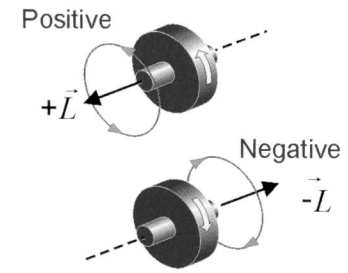

Figure 12.21: *The direction of the angular momentum vector.*

Torque resists change in angular momentum

Similar to linear momentum, changing the direction of the angular momentum vector creates a torque that resists the change. This is often demonstrated by holding a spinning bicycle wheel. The wheel resists being turned sideways because the turn shifts the direction of the angular momentum vector. This principle explains why bicycles stay vertical when their wheels are spinning, but fall over easily when standing still.

Gyroscopes

A gyroscope is a device that contains a spinning object with a lot of angular momentum. Gyroscopes can do amazing tricks because they conserve angular momentum. For example, a *spinning* gyroscope can easily balance on a pencil point. The gyroscope falls right off when it is not spinning.

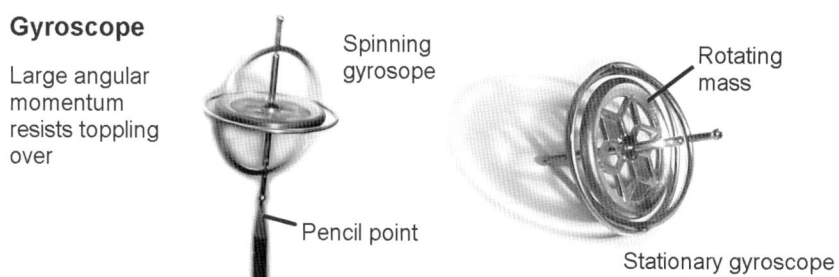

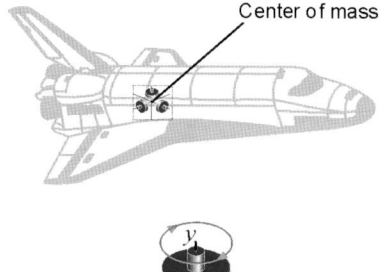

Gyroscopes on the Space Shuttle

Figure 12.22: *The gyroscope on the space shuttle is mounted at the center of mass, allowing a computer to measure rotation of the spacecraft in three dimensions.*

Turning the space shuttle

The space shuttle (and other spacecraft) use gyroscopes for control. The shuttle's gyroscope works like three spinning wheels aligned along each of the coordinate axes (Figure 12.22). When the shuttle makes a small rotation, the movement is resisted by the angular momentum of the gyroscope wheels. Sensors on each wheel detect the small torques created in the x, y, and z directions. By analyzing the torques from the gyroscope, an on-board computer is able to accurately measure the rotation of the shuttle and maintain its orientation in space.

234

Application: Jet Engines

Almost all modern airplanes use jet propulsion to fly. Jet engines (and rockets) work because of conservation of momentum (Figure 12.23). Air enters the front of the jet engine. The air is compressed and mixed with fuel in the middle. The fuels burns and heats the air, causing it to expand to many times its original volume. The expanding air leaves the engine's exhaust in a very fast stream, called a jet, which is where the jet engine gets its name. The fast-moving exhaust jet has negative momentum. To conserve momentum, the airplane gains positive momentum, and goes forward. A jet engine creates thrust force on an airplane by changing the momentum of air passing through the engine.

Figure 12.23: *Momentum transfer in a jet airplane.*

The turbojet — The diagram below shows a cutaway view of a turbojet engine. The main component of the engine is a high-speed rotating shaft with a series of fans. Air entering the engine passes first through a series of fans in the compressor. The angle of the blades on the compressor fans changes from the inlet to the combustion chamber. Because of that change in blade angle, air passing through the compressor is squeezed and the pressure increases (Figure 12.24).

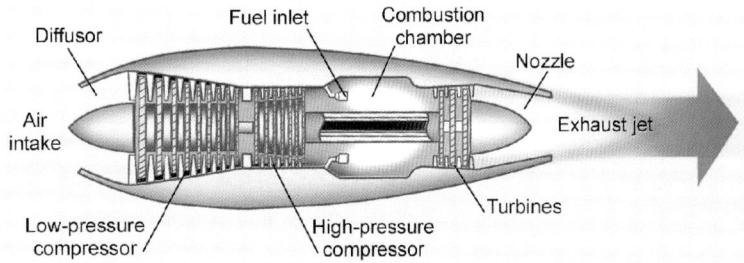

How a turbojet works — As the pressure of the air increases, the temperature also rises. Fuel is injected into the hot air in the combustion chamber. The fuel burns, heating and expanding the air. The expanding hot air exits the engine in a fast jet. The exhaust speed of modern passenger jet engines is greater than 300 m/sec (670 mph). The tremendous noise from the engines comes from the exhaust jet colliding with the still air around the plane.

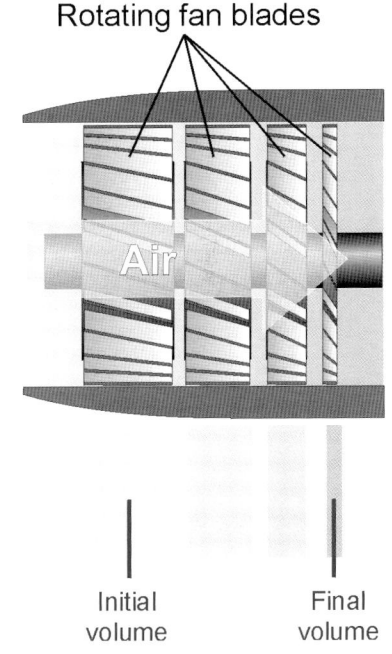

Figure 12.24: *The compressor in a turbojet engine.*

The "turbo" in a turbojet — The exhaust jet passes through a second set of fans called the turbine. The motion of the exhaust jet spins the turbine. The turbine extracts a small fraction of the power of the exhaust jet to turn the compressor fans. It is possible to make a turbojet engine with only one moving part!

Turbofan engines

Turbofan engines The diagram below shows a cutaway view of a turbofan jet engine. The Boeing 757-200 passenger jet uses two of these engines and can fly 3,500 miles carrying 186 people at a cruising speed of 270 m/sec (600 mph).

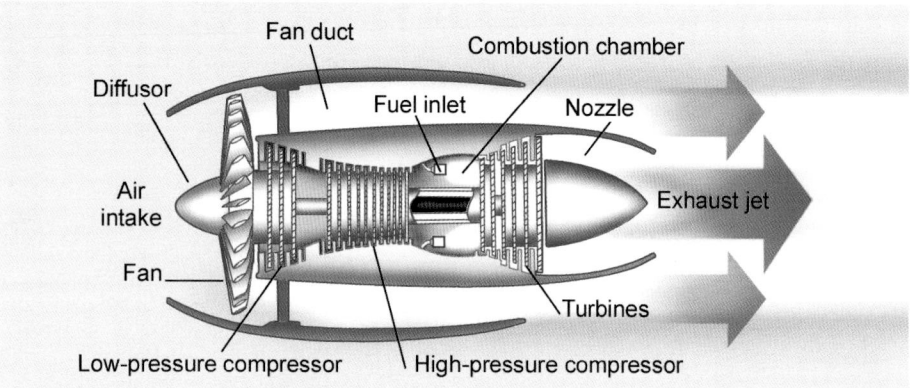

Turbofan engines are more fuel efficient The turbofan engine has a bypass fan driven by the main jet engine. The fan acts like a propeller to push some of the air around the main jet. The bypass air still generates thrust because it is pushed by the fan. The turbofan engine is much more fuel efficient than a plain turbojet. For example, the Pratt and Whitney PW-2037 turbofan engine used on Boeing 757s generates a takeoff thrust of 170,000 N (38,000 lbs) and uses 48 percent less fuel than a turbojet engine of equal size.

Momentum conservation At takeoff, the PW-2037 engine moves 550 kg of air and fuel per second. By analyzing the change in momentum (Figure 12.25), you can calculate the speed of the exhaust jet. To create a thrust force of 170,000 N, the average exhaust speed of the jet is 310 m/sec. The engine thrust force is equal to the change in momentum per second.

Rocket engines A rocket engine uses the same principles as a jet, except that in space, there is no oxygen. A jet engine on Earth burns fuel using oxygen from the air. A rocket has to carry the oxygen along with the fuel. Most rockets have to carry so much oxygen and fuel that the payload (people or satellites) is usually less than 5 percent of the total mass of the rocket at launch. The other 95 percent is fuel.

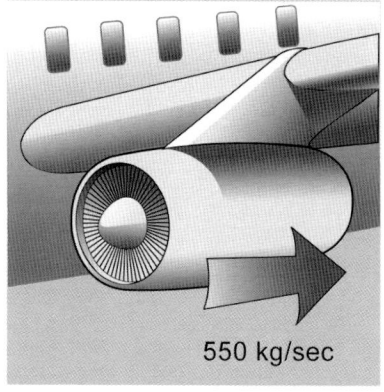

550 kg/sec

Figure 12.25: *Calculating the thrust of the turbofan jet engine by applying the conservation of linear momentum. This large jet engine has a mass flow rate of 550 kg of air per second.*

Chapter 12 Review

Vocabulary Review

Match the following terms with the correct definition. There is one extra definition in the list that will not match any of the terms.

Set One

1. linear momentum
2. angular momentum
3. conservation of momentum
4. impulse

a. When a system of interacting objects is not influenced by outside forces, the total momentum of the system cannot change
b. Momentum due to the rotation or spin of an object
c. Momentum due to an object moving in a straight line
d. The average of mass times radius squared for an object
e. Product of force multiplied by time the force acts

Set Two

1. elastic
2. inelastic
3. collision
4. gyroscope
5. moment of inertia

a. Occurs when two or more objects hit each other
b. Collision in which objects bounce off each other with no loss in total kinetic energy
c. Collision in which objects change shape or stick together
d. Device that contains a spinning object with high angular momentum
e. Average of mass times radius squared for an object
f. Device that inflates when the force applied to the front of a car reaches a dangerous level

Concept review

1. Compare and contrast kinetic energy and momentum. How are they similar? How are they different?
2. Why is momentum considered a vector quantity?
3. Decide which of the following statements are correct about momentum. If a statement is correct, simply answer "correct." If a statement is incorrect, re-write the statement to make it correct.

   a. The momentum of any object is conserved and therefore remains constant.
   b. Objects with mass have momentum.
   c. All moving objects have momentum.
   d. Momentum is measured in joules.
   e. An object moving at a constant speed has no momentum.
   f. The momentum of two objects with equal mass will be equal.

   g. If two objects of different mass move at the same speed, they will have the same momentum.
   h. When an object's velocity changes, its momentum changes.
   i. The momentum of an accelerating object increases.
   j. The momentum of a faster object will always be greater than the momentum of a slower object.
   k. If an object has zero momentum, then it has zero kinetic energy.

4. Consider a bulldozer at rest and a hockey player moving across the ice.

   a. Which has greater mass?

   b. Which has greater velocity?

   c. Which has greater momentum? Explain.

5. A bicycle rider doubles her speed. What happens to her momentum?

6. The law of conservation of momentum is a consequence of which one of Newton's laws of motion?

7. Howard tries to jump from a rowboat to a nearby dock. Why is this probably a bad idea, even if the distance from the rowboat to the dock seems short enough to jump?

8. How does the momentum of a jet engine's backward exhaust compare to the momentum of the jet going forward? Are the velocities of the backward exhaust and the forward jet the same? Explain.

9. When playing a game of billiards, you use a long stick to hit a white ball (the "cue ball") that then collides with numbered balls to send them into pockets or holes around the edge of the table. Sometimes, you want the cue ball to come to a sudden stop after it knocks into a numbered ball so that the cue ball doesn't follow the numbered ball into a pocket. Suppose you manage to collide the cue ball head-on with a numbered ball and the cue ball stops.

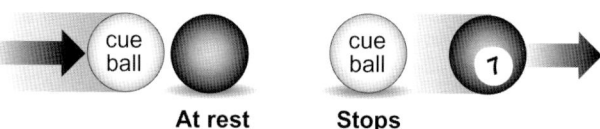

At rest   **Stops**

   a. What is true about the total momentum of the colliding billiard balls before and after the collision?

   b. Is this collision more like an elastic or more like an inelastic collision? Explain.

   c. What is true about the kinetic energy of the cue ball before and after the collision?

   d. How does the velocity of the cue ball before the collision compare to the velocity of the numbered ball after the collision? (Assume a perfectly elastic collision.)

   e. What do you predict would happen to the balls if the cue ball were to hit the numbered ball at an angle rather than head-on?

10. What is the difference between impact and impulse?

11. Is the unit used to represent impulse equivalent to the momentum unit? Explain.

12. Is it true that in a collision, the net impulse experienced by an object is equal to its momentum change? Explain.

13. Padding is used in baseball gloves, goalie mitts, motorcycle helmets, and gymnastic mats. Explain the physics reason behind the use of padding in these cases.

14. What is the secret to catching a water balloon without breaking it? Explain using physics.

15. Contrary to popular belief, cars that crumple in a collision are safer than cars that rebound when they collide. Explain why this is so.

16. What is the difference between linear and angular momentum? Can an object have both types of momentum at the same time? Explain.

17. Suppose a solid cylinder and a hollow cylinder of the same mass and radius are released on an incline. Which rolls with greater acceleration? Explain.

18. Suppose two solid cylinders of the same radius but very different masses are released on an incline. How do their accelerations compare? Explain.

19. A physics teacher stands on a small rotating platform and holds a 10-pound weight in each hand with her arms outstretched. A student helps by starting the teacher in a slow rotation. The teacher then pulls her arms in and holds the weights close to her body.

   a. How does the teacher's angular momentum compare before and after pulling her arms in?

   b. How does the teacher's moment of inertia compare before and after pulling her arms in?

   c. How does the teacher's angular velocity compare before and after pulling her arms in?

Problems

1. Could a 1000-kg elephant moving very slowly (0.5 m/sec) ever have less momentum than a 0.15-kg baseball pitched by a major-leaguer? Justify your answer.

2. Which has more momentum: a boat with a mass of 1200 kg moving at 50 m/sec, or a truck with a mass of 6000 kg moving at 10 m/sec? Show your work.

3. A 0.040-kg golf ball leaves the head of a golf club with a speed of 50 m/s.

   a. What is the momentum of the golf ball in kg-m/sec?

   b. How fast would a 0.15-kg baseball have to be thrown to have the same momentum? Find your answer in m/sec and then convert it to mph.

4. A demolition derby is a car-crashing contest. Suppose a 1200-kg car moving at 12 m/sec crashes head-on and sticks to a 1000-kg car moving at 16 m/sec in the opposite direction.

   a. Is this collision elastic or inelastic? Why?

   b. What is the velocity of the cars after the collision?

5. Two baseball players accidentally run into each other when trying to catch a fly ball. Player #1 is 75 kg and is moving east at 3 m/sec. Player #2 is 70 kg and is moving west at 2 m/sec. How fast are they moving together after the collision? (Find the speed and specify the direction of motion).

239

6. Jessie rolls a 45-kg bowling ball down a long hallway at 5 m/sec. Sue rolls a 50-kg bowling ball down the same hallway in the opposite direction at a velocity of -7 m/sec. The balls collide, and the 45-kg ball moves away at - 8.5 m/sec after the collision. Find the final velocity of the 50-kg ball.

7. An average force of 20 N is exerted on an object for 2 sec.

   a. What is the impulse?

   b. What is the change in momentum?

8. Tracy has a mass of 65 kg and is driving her sports car at 30 m/sec when she must suddenly slam on her brakes to avoid hitting a moose in the road. The air bag brings her body to rest in 0.40 sec.

   a. What average force does the airbag exert on Tracy?

   b. If Tracy's car had no air bag, the windshield and structure of the car would have stopped her body in 0.001 sec. What average force would the windshield have exerted?

9. A solid ball has a mass of 0.5 kg and a radius of 0.1 m. It rolls along the ground at 3 m/s.

   a. Calculate its moment of inertia.

   b. Calculate its angular momentum.

   c. Calculate its linear momentum.

10. An ice skater spins at an angular speed of 10 rad/sec with her arms down at her sides. Her moment of inertia is 1.5 kg-m^2.

    a. What is her angular momentum?

    b. If she lifts her arms out, her moment of inertia increases to 3 kg-m^2. What is her new angular speed?

Unit 5
Waves and Sound

Chapter 13

Harmonic Motion

Objectives for Chapter 13

By the end of this chapter you should be able to:

1. Identify characteristics of harmonic motion, such as cycles, frequency, and amplitude.
2. Determine period, frequency, and amplitude from a graph of harmonic motion.
3. Use the concept of phase to compare the motion of two oscillators.
4. Describe the characteristics of a system that lead to harmonic motion.
5. Describe the meaning of natural frequency.
6. Identify ways to change the natural frequency of a system.
7. Explain harmonic motion in terms of potential and kinetic energy.
8. Describe the meaning of periodic force.
9. Explain the concept of resonance and give examples of resonance.

Terms and vocabulary words

harmonic motion	cycle	period	frequency	amplitude
hertz (Hz)	damping	periodic motion	periodic force	resonance
phase	phase difference	equilibrium	restoring force	stable equilibrium
unstable equilibrium	oscillator	natural frequency	steady state	piezoelectric effect

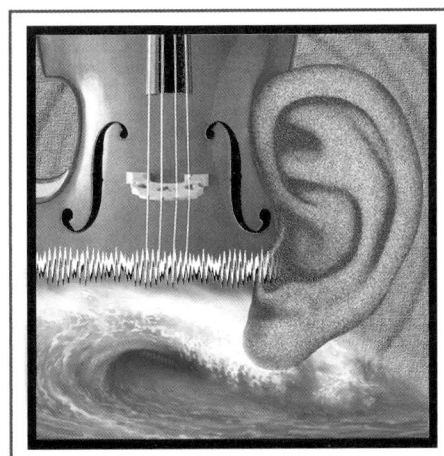

13.1 Harmonic motion

As you watch moving things, you see two different kinds of motion. One kind of motion goes from place to place without repeating. This is called *linear motion*. The concepts of distance, time, speed, and acceleration come from thinking about linear motion.

The second kind of motion repeats itself over and over. This is called harmonic motion and is the subject of this section. The word "harmonic" comes from *harmony* which means "multiples of." Harmonic motion has multiple cycles, repeated over and over. A pendulum swinging back and forth is a good example of harmonic motion (Figure 13.1).

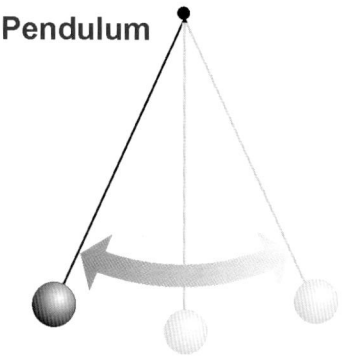

Pendulum

Figure 13.1: *A pendulum swings back and forth in harmonic motion.*

Cycles, systems, and oscillators

What is a cycle? The cycle is the building block of harmonic motion. A cycle is a unit of motion that repeats over and over. All harmonic motion is a repeated sequence of cycles. The cycle of the pendulum is shown below.

The cycle of the pendulum

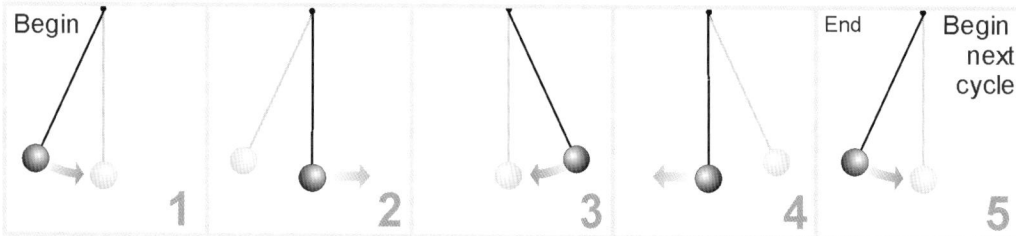

Finding the cycle When investigating harmonic motion we start by identifying the basic cycle. A cycle has a beginning and an end. Between the beginning and end, the cycle has to include all the motion that repeats. The cycle of the pendulum is defined by where we choose the beginning. If we start the cycle when the pendulum is all the way to the left, the cycle ends when the pendulum has returned all the way to the left. The motion of the pendulum is one cycle after the other with no gaps between cycles.

Definition of an oscillator A system in harmonic motion is called an **oscillator**. A pendulum is one example of an oscillator, a vibrating bead on a rubber band is another (Figure 13.2).

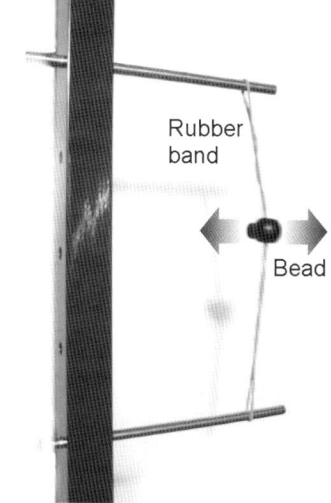

Rubber band

Bead

Figure 13.2: *A bead going back and forth on a stretched rubber band is a good example of an oscillator in harmonic motion.*

Harmonic motion is very common

Music comes from oscillations

Sound is an oscillation of the air. Musical instruments and speakers are oscillators that we design to create sounds. If you gently touch a speaker making sound, you can feel the rapid in-out cycles. The oscillation travels through the air to where it hits your eardrum. There is harmonic motion at every step, from the original musical instrument to the speaker to the detection of sound in your ear.

Pendulum clock

Pendulum

Oscillators are used in communications

Almost all modern communication technology relies on fast electronic oscillators. Cellphones use oscillators that make more than 100 million cycles each second. FM radio uses oscillators between 95 million and 107 million cycles per second. When you tune a radio you are selecting the frequency of the oscillator you want to listen to. Each station sets up an oscillator at a different frequency. Sometimes you can receive two stations at once when you are traveling between two radio towers with nearly the same frequency.

Figure 13.3: *A pendulum clock uses the period of a pendulum to count time.*

Oscillators are used to measure time

The cycles of many oscillators always repeat in the same amount of time. This makes harmonic motion a good way to keep time. If you have a pendulum that has a cycle one second long, you can count time in seconds by counting cycles of the pendulum. Grandfather clocks and mechanical watches count cycles of oscillators to keep time (Figure 13.3). Even today, the world's most accurate clocks keep time by counting cycles of light from a cesium atom oscillator. Modern atomic clocks are accurate to within one second in 1,400,000 years!

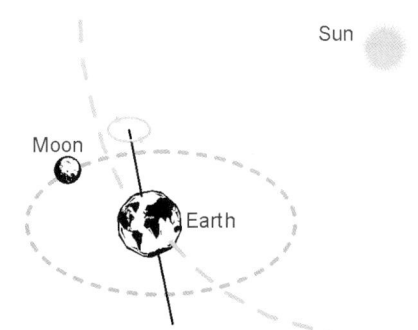

Sun

Moon

Earth

Natural cycles involving the Earth

Earth is a part of several oscillating systems. An *orbit* is a type of cycle because it is repeating motion. The Earth-sun system has an orbital cycle of one year, which means Earth completes one orbit around the sun in a year. The Earth-moon system has a orbital cycle of approximately one month. Earth itself has several different cycles (Figure 13.4). The Earth rotates on its axis once a day, creating the 24-hour cycle of day and night. There is also a wobble of the Earth's axis that completes a full cycle every 22,000 years, moving the orientation of the north and south poles around by hundreds of miles. There are cycles in weather, such as El Niño and La Niña oscillations in ocean currents that produce fierce storms every decade or so. Much of our planet's ecology depends on cycles.

Figure 13.4: *The Earth, moon, and sun form a system with many cycles.*

Describing harmonic motion

Choosing a system
In science we often refer to "a system." A system is a group we choose that includes all the things we are interested in. Choosing the system helps us concentrate on what is important and exclude what is not important. For the pendulum, the system is the hanger, string, and weight. We do not need to include the floor or the table, since these are not directly important to the motion.

We choose a system depending on what we want to investigate. If we wanted to see how gravity affected the pendulum, then we would have to include Earth's gravity as part of the system.

Period is the time for one cycle
What makes harmonic motion useful for clocks is that each cycle takes the same amount of time. The time for one cycle is called the period. Some clocks have a pendulum with a period of two seconds. The clock's gears cause the minute hand to move one-sixtieth of a turn for every 30 swings of the pendulum. The period is one of the important characteristics of all harmonic motion (Figure 13.5).

Frequency is the number of cycles per second
Frequency is closely related to period. The frequency of an oscillator is the number of cycles it makes per second. Every day we experience a wide range of frequencies. Your heartbeat probably has a frequency between one-half and two cycles per second. A plucked rubber band might have a frequency of 100 cycles per second (Figure 13.6). The sound of the musical note "A" has a frequency of 440 cycles per second. The human voice contains frequencies mainly between 100 and 2,000 cycles per second. Frequency and period are inversely related. The period is the time per cycle. The frequency is the number of cycles per time.

Frequency is measured in hertz
The unit of one cycle per second is called a hertz. A frequency of 440 cycles per second is usually written as 440 hertz, or abbreviated 440 Hz. The hertz is a unit that is the same in English and metric measurement systems. When you tune into a station at 101 on the FM dial, you are setting the oscillator in your radio to a frequency of 101 megahertz (abbreviated MHz, which is 1 million hertz) or 101,000,000 Hz. You hear music when the oscillator in your radio is exactly matched to the frequency of the oscillator in the transmission tower connected to the radio station.

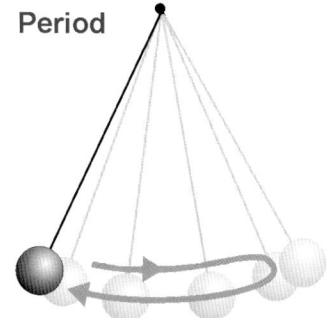

Period

The period is the time to complete one cycle.

Figure 13.5: *The period is the time it takes to complete one cycle.*

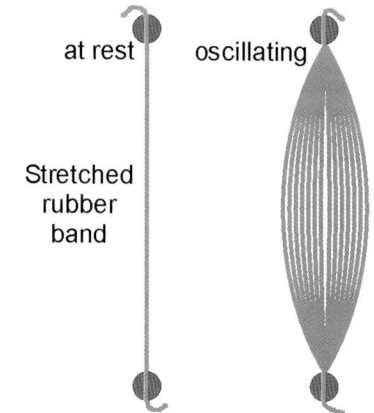

at rest   oscillating

Stretched rubber band

A ***frequency*** of 100 Hz means the oscillating rubber band completes 100 cycles each second.

Figure 13.6: *The definition of frequency.*

Amplitude

Amplitude describes the size of a cycle
Another important characteristic of a cycle is its size. The period tells how long the cycle lasts. The amplitude describes how big the cycle is. With mechanical systems (such as a pendulum), the amplitude is often a distance or angle. With other kinds of oscillators, the amplitude might be voltage or pressure. The amplitude is measured in units that match the oscillation you are describing.

Measuring amplitude
The amplitude is the maximum amount the system moves away from equilibrium. For a pendulum, the equilibrium is at the center. The amplitude is the amount the pendulum swings away from center (Figure 13.7). The amplitude is also half the total motion from one extreme to the other because a pendulum spends as much time to the right of center as it does to the left. It is often easiest to determine amplitude by measuring the total side-to-side motion and dividing by two.

Amplitude and energy
The motion of an oscillator has energy. Sometimes the energy is kinetic, as when the pendulum is swinging through the lowest point in its cycle and has its highest speed. At other times in the cycle the energy is potential, such as when the pendulum reaches the farthest point in the cycle and is raised above its equilibrium point. As you might suspect, the energy of an oscillator is proportional to the amplitude of the motion. Large-amplitude motions have higher energy than small-amplitude motions (Figure 13.8).

Damping
Friction drains energy away from motion and slows a pendulum down. Just as with linear motion, harmonic motion is reduced by friction. The effect of friction is to slowly reduce the amplitude of the system. If you start a pendulum swinging you will observe that the amplitude slowly decreases until the pendulum is hanging motionless. We use the word damping to describe the gradual loss of amplitude of an oscillator. Damping is due to friction acting to reduce motion.

Damping is a gradual loss of amplitude due to friction

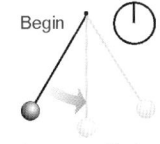  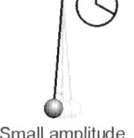

Begin — Large amplitude — Small amplitude

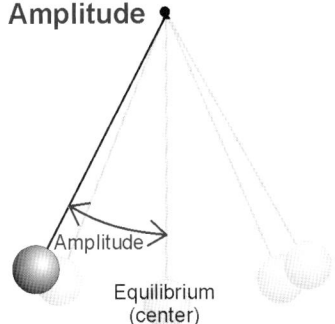

The **amplitude** is the maximum amount the system moves away from equilibrium

Figure 13.7: *The definition of amplitude.*

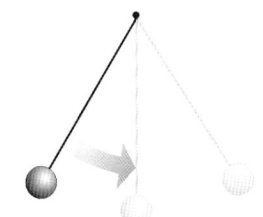

High energy = large amplitude

Low energy = small amplitude

Figure 13.8: *The energy of an oscillator is proportional to its amplitude.*

Harmonic motion graphs

Cycles and time   Harmonic motion graphs are easy to recognize because they show oscillation and cycles (Figure 13.9). Most graphs of harmonic motion show how things change with time. For example, the diagram below shows a graph of position versus time for a pendulum. The graph shows repeating cycles just like the motion. Seeing a pattern of cycles on a graph is an indication that harmonic motion is present.

Using positive and negative numbers   Harmonic motion graphs often use positive and negative values to represent motion on either side of center. We usually choose zero to be at the equilibrium point of the motion. The example graph below shows a pendulum swinging from plus-20 centimeters to minus-20 centimeters and back. The amplitude is the maximum distance away from center, or 20 centimeters.

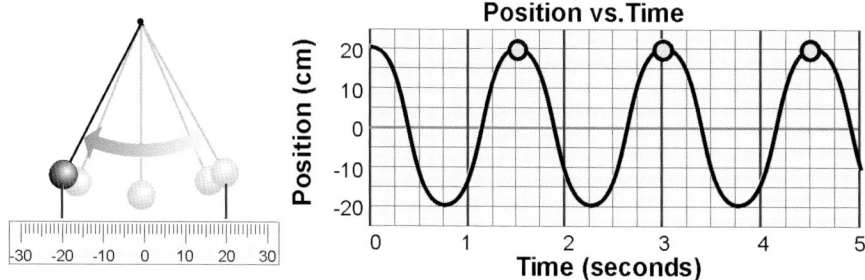

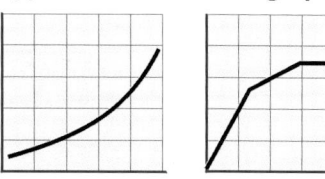

Typical harmonic motion graphs

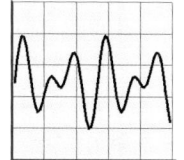 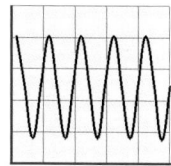

Figure 13.9: *Graphs of linear motion do not show cycles. Harmonic motion graphs show oscillation and cycles.*

Harmonic graphs repeat every period   Notice that the graph above returns to the same place every 1.5 seconds. No matter where you start, you come back to the same value 1.5 seconds later. Graphs of harmonic motion repeat every period, just as the motion repeats every cycle. Harmonic motion is sometimes called periodic motion for this reason.

Amplitude and period on a graph   To get the period from a graph, start by identifying one complete cycle. The cycle must begin and end in the same place on the graph (Figure 13.10). Once you have identified a cycle, you use the time axis of the graph to determine the period. The period is the time difference between the beginning of the cycle and the end. The amplitude is half the distance between the highest and lowest points on the graph. For the example in Figure 13.10, the amplitude is 20 centimeters.

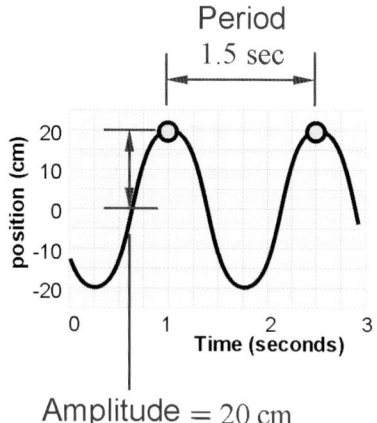

Figure 13.10: *Reading amplitude and period from a graph.*

246

Circles and the phase of harmonic motion

Circular motion   Circular motion is very similar to harmonic motion. For example, a turning wheel returns to the same position every 360 degrees. Rotation is a cycle, just like harmonic motion. One key difference is that cycles of circular motion *always* have a length of 360 degrees (Figure 13.11).

The phase of an oscillator   Degrees are also convenient to describe where an oscillator is in its cycle. For example, how would you identify the moment when a pendulum was one-tenth of the way through its cycle? If we let one cycle be 360 degrees, then one-tenth of that cycle is 36 degrees. Thirty-six degrees is a measure of the phase of the oscillator. The word "phase" means where the oscillator is in the cycle.

What we mean by "in phase"   The concept of phase is important when comparing one oscillator with another. Suppose you observe two identical pendulums, with exactly the same periods. If you start them together, their graphs would look like the diagram below left. You would describe the two pendulums as being *in phase* because their cycles are aligned and each one is always at the same place at the same time.

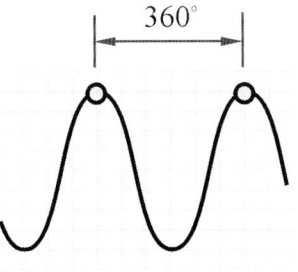

Figure 13.11: *A full turn of a circle is 360 degrees. One full cycle of harmonic motion is also 360 degrees.*

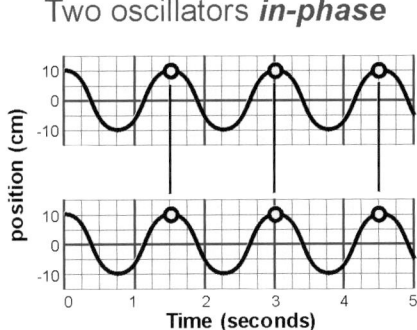

Two oscillators *in-phase*

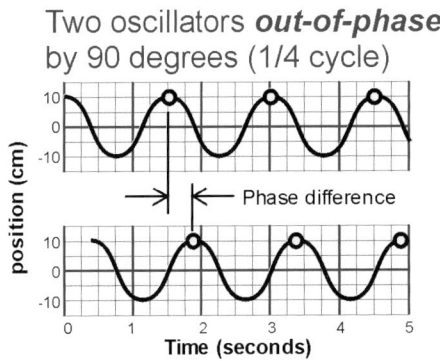

Two oscillators *out-of-phase* by 90 degrees (1/4 cycle)

Out of phase   If you start the first pendulum swinging a little before the second one, the graphs look like the diagram above right. Although, they have the same cycle, the first pendulum is always a little ahead of the second. The graph shows the lead of the first pendulum as a phase difference. Notice that the top graph reaches its maximum 90 degrees *before* the bottom graph. We say the two pendulums are *out of phase* by 90 degrees, or one-fourth of a cycle.

13.2 Why Things Oscillate

Harmonic motion occurs throughout nature. This section explains why some systems tend to have harmonic motion and other systems do not. Harmonic motion occurs when a system is *stable*, has *restoring forces*, and has some property that provides *inertia*. Once you know what to look for, you can predict when harmonic motion is probable. The opposite is also true. By observing harmonic motion, you can learn much about the stability, forces, and inertia of a system.

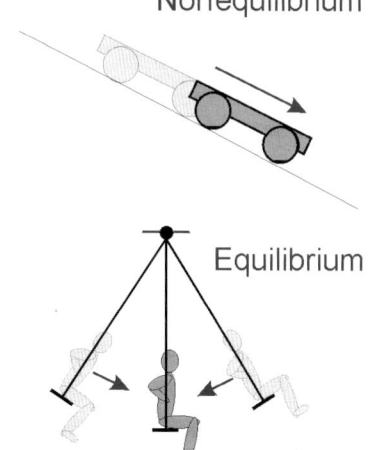

Nonequilibrium

Equilibrium

Restoring force and equilibrium

Different kinds of systems
If you set a wagon on a hill and let it go, the wagon rolls down and does not come back (Figure 13.12). If you push a child on a swing, the child goes away from you at first, but then comes back. The child on the swing shows harmonic motion while the wagon on the hill does not. What is the fundamental difference between the two situations? Are there ways to predict when harmonic motion will occur?

Figure 13.12: *Examples of equilibrium and nonequilibrium situations.*

Equilibrium
Systems that have harmonic motion move back and forth around a central or equilibrium position. You can think of equilibrium as the system at rest, undisturbed, with zero net force acting. A wagon on a hill is *not* in equilibrium, because the force of gravity pulls the wagon down the moment you let it go. A child sitting motionless on a swing *is* in equilibrium because the swing stays put until you apply a force.

Restoring forces
Equilibrium is maintained by restoring forces. A restoring force is any force that always acts to pull the system back toward equilibrium. For example, if the child on the swing is moved forward, gravity pulls her back, toward equilibrium. If she moves backward, gravity pulls her forward, back to equilibrium again (Figure 13.13).

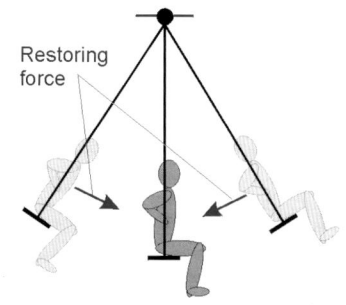

Restoring force

When harmonic motion happens
Any system with both equilibrium and restoring forces is a good candidate for harmonic motion. A disturbance in the system can start harmonic motion. For example, a pendulum at rest hangs straight down, in equilibrium. Pulling back the weight disturbs the equilibrium. The pendulum oscillates back and forth around its equilibrium position under the action of the restoring forces. Eventually, friction slows it down and the system returns to equilibrium.

Figure 13.13: *Equilibrium is maintained by restoring forces in a system.*

248

Inertia

Inertia causes an oscillator to go past equilibrium	Newton's first law explains why harmonic motion happens for moving objects. According to the first law, an object in motion stays in motion unless acted upon by a force. Think about a pendulum swinging. At the bottom of the swing the net force on the pendulum is zero because that is the equilibrium position. But the pendulum has inertia that carries it through the bottom of the swing. Inertia causes the pendulum to overshoot its equilibrium position every time. The result is harmonic motion. You can analyze the motion in steps.

The cycle of the pendulum

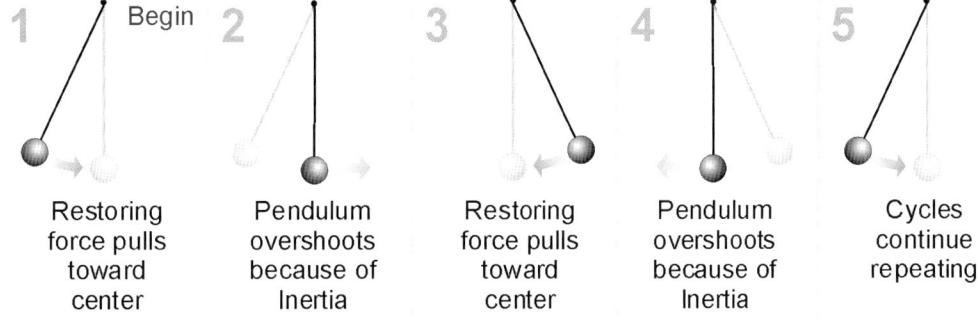

1. Begin — Restoring force pulls toward center
2. Pendulum overshoots because of Inertia
3. Restoring force pulls toward center
4. Pendulum overshoots because of Inertia
5. Cycles continue repeating

1. The restoring force pulls the pendulum toward the center (equilibrium).

2. The pendulum overshoots the center because of its inertia.

3. The restoring force pulls back toward the center, slowing and reversing the pendulum's direction.

4. The pendulum overshoots the center again, because of inertia.

5. The cycle repeats, creating harmonic motion.

Inertia is common to all oscillators	All systems that oscillate on their own have some property that acts like inertia, and some type of restoring force. Oscillation results from the interaction of the two effects: inertia and restoring force.

Harmonic motion in machines

So far we have been discussing systems that move with harmonic motion on their own. Many machines create harmonic motion by actively pushing or rotating parts. In these machines the motion is not caused by the interaction of restoring forces and inertia.

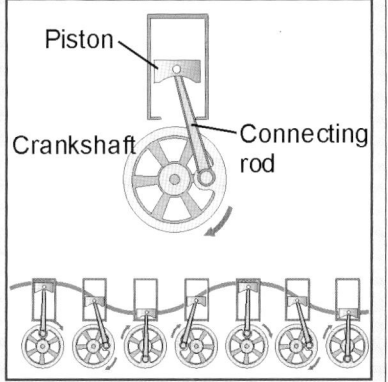

Piston

Crankshaft — Connecting rod

For example, the piston of a car engine goes up and down as the crank turns. The piston is in harmonic motion, but the motion is caused by the rotation of the crankshaft and the attachment of the connecting rod. The up-and-down motion of the needle on a sewing machine is another example of harmonic motion created by machinery.

Stable and unstable

Unstable equilibrium Not all systems in equilibrium show harmonic motion when disturbed. A marble at the top of a hill is an example. The marble may be perfectly balanced and in equilibrium. If we disturb it with a little push, it rolls away—but it does not come back to the top of the hill. That marble on the hill is an good example of unstable equilibrium. In unstable systems there are forces that act to pull the system *away* from equilibrium when disturbed. Unstable systems do not usually result in harmonic motion.

Unstable equilibrium

If the system moves away from equilibrium, forces tend to move it farther away.

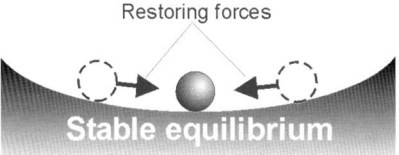

Restoring forces

Stable equilibrium

If the system moves away from equilibrium, forces tend to pull it back toward equilibrium again.

Stable equilibrium The bottom of a valley is an example of stable equilibrium. Stable is the opposite of unstable. If we move the marble from that hill to a valley and let it go down one side, we see it in harmonic motion. The marble oscillates back and forth around its equilibrium position. In the valley, when we push the marble away from the bottom, it always feels a force pulling it back. If we push it to the left, the force pulls the marble back to the right. If we push it to the right, the force pulls back to the left. The force always acts to return the marble to its equilibrium position.

Restoring forces create stability The valley is a stable equilibrium because its shape creates restoring forces that tend to return the system to equilibrium. Stable systems almost always create harmonic motion when disturbed. The pendulum is another example of a stable equilibrium because gravity always acts to pull the pendulum back to center

Why airplanes have tails

Airplanes have tails to make them stable while flying. In Chapter 9, you learned that objects tend to rotate about the center of mass. Consider the rotation of an airplane around its center of mass. No matter which way the airplane rotates (nose up or nose down), wind blowing against the tail fins creates a force that tends to straighten the plane out again.

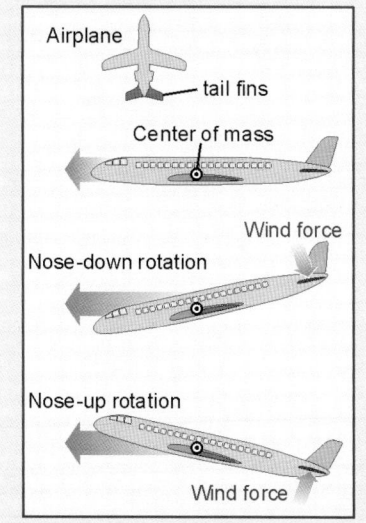

Airplane
tail fins
Center of mass
Wind force
Nose-down rotation
Nose-up rotation
Wind force

The tail is located as far as possible from the center of mass, usually at the very end of the plane. The farther back the tail is, the more effective is the restoring force at resisting the rotation of the plane.

The natural frequency

Systems tend to have a preferred frequency

If you watch a pendulum, or a swing, or any other oscillator, you will observe a curious fact. Once it starts moving, the system tends to oscillate with a particular frequency. For example, a certain pendulum swings with a frequency of two cycles per second (2 Hz). Every time you set the pendulum swinging, it always swings with the same frequency and no other.

Natural frequency

The natural frequency is the frequency at which systems tend to oscillate when disturbed. Everything that can oscillate has a natural frequency, and most systems have more than one. The natural frequency is useful to know because many inventions are designed to work at a specific frequency. For example, a pendulum clock might have a pendulum with a natural frequency of exactly one cycle per second (1 Hz). The second hand moves one-sixtieth of a turn for each swing of the pendulum. The accuracy of the clock depends on the natural frequency of the pendulum. Watches, computers, and many devices rely on the precise natural frequency of quartz crystals.

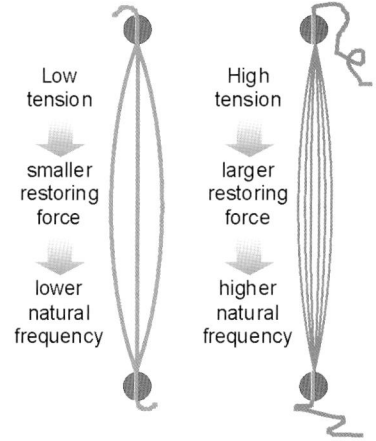

Figure 13.14: *Stretching a rubber band tighter (right) increases the restoring force and raises the natural frequency.*

Stronger restoring forces raise the natural frequency

The natural frequency comes from the interaction of force and inertia. If the restoring forces are very strong, a system tends to respond quickly and have a high natural frequency. If you pluck a stretched rubber band, it oscillates at its natural frequency. If you stretch the rubber band (Figure 13.14) and make it tighter, it oscillates at a higher natural frequency. The natural frequency goes up because the restoring forces are larger in the tight rubber band. If you pluck the steel string of a guitar it oscillates much faster than a rubber band, at more than 200 hertz. The steel is very strong and creates large restoring forces.

Adding inertia decreases the natural frequency

Adding inertia (that is, increasing mass) has the opposite effect on the natural frequency. A system with more inertia is harder to accelerate and responds slowly, lowering the natural frequency. The bass strings on a guitar are wound with extra wire to make them heavier. The increased mass creates more inertia and the strings oscillate slower because the natural frequency is lower. Tying a steel nut on the rubber band will show the same effect. The added inertia of the steel nut greatly lowers the natural frequency of the system (Figure 13.15).

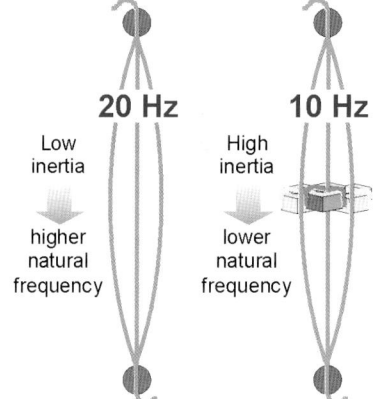

Figure 13.15: *Adding a steel nut greatly increases the inertia of a stretched rubber band. As a result, the natural frequency decreases.*

Changing the natural frequency

Acceleration and natural frequency
The natural frequency is proportional to the acceleration of a system. Systems with high acceleration have a high natural frequency. Systems with low accelerations have lower natural frequencies.

Newton's second law
Newton's second law can be applied to see the relationship between acceleration and natural frequency. The acceleration is proportional to the force divided by the mass. The force is the restoring force. The mass is the inertia. If the ratio of force divided by mass *increases*, the natural frequency *increases*. If the ratio of force divided by mass *decreases*, the natural frequency *decreases*. Figure 13.16 shows how to change the natural frequency of several common oscillators.

Newton's second law and natural frequency

$$\underset{\textit{Acceleration}}{a} = \frac{\overset{\textit{Force}}{F}}{\underset{\textit{mass}}{m}} \qquad \underset{\textit{frequency}}{\overset{\textit{Natural}}{f_n}} \propto \frac{\overset{\textit{Restoring force}}{F}}{\underset{\textit{Inertia (mass)}}{m}}$$

Natural frequency and the response time of a system
A system with a high natural frequency can respond to changes faster than a system with a low natural frequency. This is because of the relationship between acceleration and natural frequency. This principle is applied directly to the design of cars. Cars have springs in the shock absorbers on each wheel that allow the wheel to independently follow bumps in the road. The body of the car stays relatively level as the wheels move up and down. The system of a car and shock absorbers is a mass on a spring oscillator with a natural frequency. The natural frequency is proportional to the ratio of the spring force to the mass of the car. Sports cars have low mass and stiff springs, creating a high natural frequency. The high natural frequency means the car can respond quickly to changes in direction. It also means the car responds to bumps in the road which is why sports cars tend to have a stiff, bumpy ride. A touring car has a larger mass, softer springs, and a lower natural frequency. The low natural frequency means the car does not respond to high-frequency bumps in the road, and therefore rides smoother. However, a big touring car does not steer quickly.

To *decrease* the natural frequency

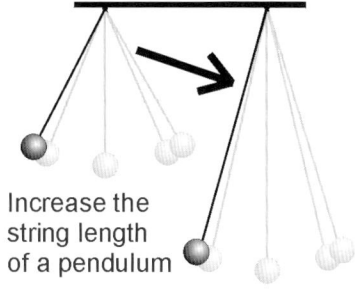

Increase the string length of a pendulum

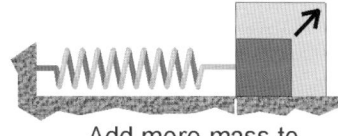

Add more mass to a mass on a spring

To *increase* the natural frequency

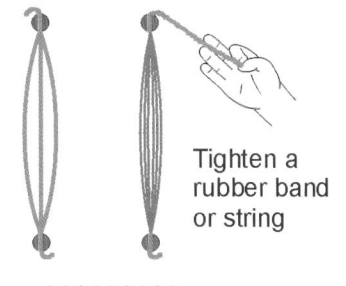

Tighten a rubber band or string

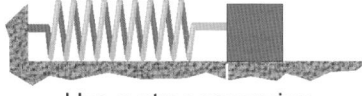

Use a stronger spring with a mass on a spring

Figure 13.16: *Changing the natural frequencies of some common oscillators.*

13.3 Resonance and Energy

It takes force to get a system moving and continued application of force increases the energy of the system. With linear motion, we learned how to relate applied force to motion and energy (see Chapters 5 through 10). With harmonic motion, the connection between force, motion, and energy is more complex. Newton's laws still apply, but the *frequency* of the force also matters. Even a small force applied with a rhythm matching the natural frequency can produce surprisingly large motion and energy. Resonance, the subject of this section, explores the connection between the frequency of a force and the effect of oscillating forces on motion and energy.

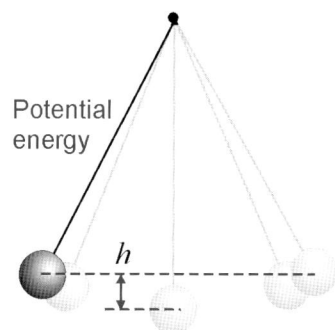

Figure 13.17: *A pendulum has potential energy at the top of its swing because it has lifted a height (h) above its lowest point.*

Energy in harmonic motion

Potential energy — Harmonic motion involves both potential energy and kinetic energy. As an example, consider the motion of a pendulum. At the highest point of the cycle the pendulum is momentarily stopped (Figure 13.17). It has no kinetic energy because its speed is zero. The pendulum *does* have potential energy though, because it is raised above its equilibrium position.

Kinetic energy — At the low point of the cycle all the potential energy has been converted to kinetic energy. The pendulum has its highest speed at the lowest point in the cycle (Figure 13.18). As the pendulum swings through the low point it climbs up again, converting its kinetic energy back into potential energy.

Energy "sloshes" back and forth — Oscillators like a pendulum, or a mass on a spring, continually exchange energy back and forth between potential and kinetic. The total energy is a combination of potential and kinetic energy. A graph of energy versus time shows the exchange. The potential energy is low when the kinetic energy is high and vice-versa.

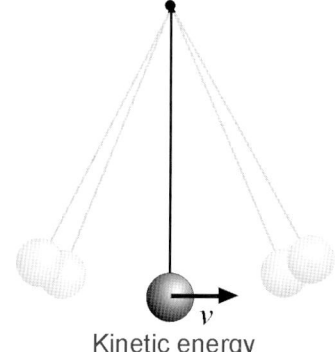

Figure 13.18: *At the bottom of the swing, a pendulum has kinetic energy because it is moving with speed (v).*

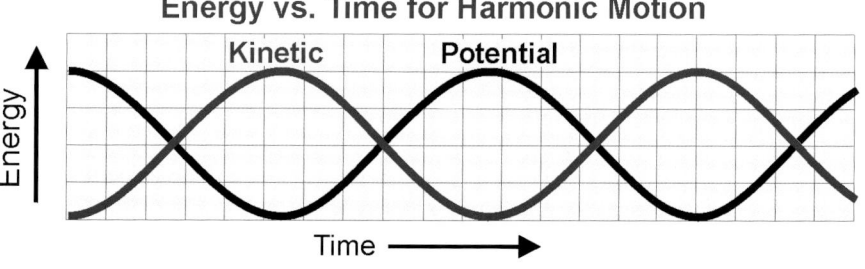

Energy vs. Time for Harmonic Motion

Periodic forces and the natural frequency

Definition of periodic force   In linear motion, the application of steady force creates constant acceleration. Speed and position both increase. In harmonic motion, we are mostly concerned with forces that go back and forth because these types tend to be associated with back-and-forth motion. A force that oscillates in strength or direction is called a *periodic force*. Periodic forces create harmonic motion. Harmonic motion also creates periodic forces. The vibration of a motorcycle engine is caused by periodic forces created by the harmonic up-and-down motion of the pistons in the engine.

Periodic force and natural frequency   The effect of a periodic force on a system depends both on the frequency of the force and the frequency of the system. Consider a child being pushed on a swing. The swing is like a pendulum and it has a natural frequency of back-and-forth motion. To get a big swinging motion going, you push every time the swing reaches the end of its motion (Figure 13.19). Each push is given at the same time in each cycle of motion. In physics language, you apply a *periodic force* at the *natural frequency* of the swing. In time, your repetition of small pushes builds up a large amplitude of motion.

Forces that are not at the natural frequency   Consider what would happen if you pushed a child on a swing at random times. Sometimes your pushes *add* to the motion and sometimes they act *against* the motion. Random pushes do not smoothly increase the amplitude of the motion. In fact, even a periodic force applied at the wrong frequency does not work. Figure 13.20 shows a periodic force applied at twice the natural frequency of the swing. One push helps the motion and the next is against the motion.

Resonance   The amplitude of harmonic motion increases *dramatically* when periodic forces are applied to a system at its natural frequency. When the frequencies of the force and the system are matched, each push adds in phase to the last. Even small repetitive pushes add up over time to build large motions. This behavior is called **resonance**. Resonance occurs when the frequency of a periodic force matches the natural frequency of a system. As a result of this matching, even small forces can build very large amplitudes because systems in resonance often accumulate large amounts of energy. Although the physical laws are the same as for linear motion, resonance is a unique property of harmonic motion.

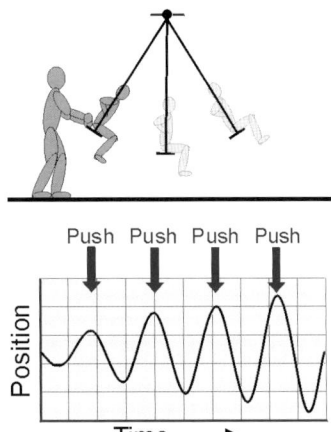

Figure 13.19: *A pushing applied once per cycle is a periodic force. The amplitude of the swing grows with each push.*

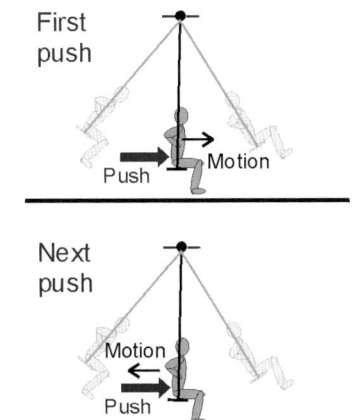

Figure 13.20: *Pushing in the same direction twice per cycle means every other push is in the wrong direction.*

Resonance

A system view of resonance A good way to understand resonance is to think about three distinct parts of any interaction between a system and a force. The first part is the periodic force itself that is applied to the system. The second part is the system itself. The third part is the response of the system to the periodic force. If the force matches the natural frequency of the system, the response is to build up a large amplitude motion, or resonance. If the force is *not* matched to the natural frequency of the system, the response is much smaller, and there is no resonance.

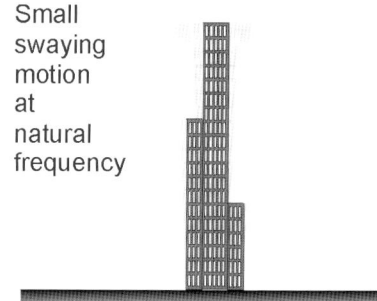

Small swaying motion at natural frequency

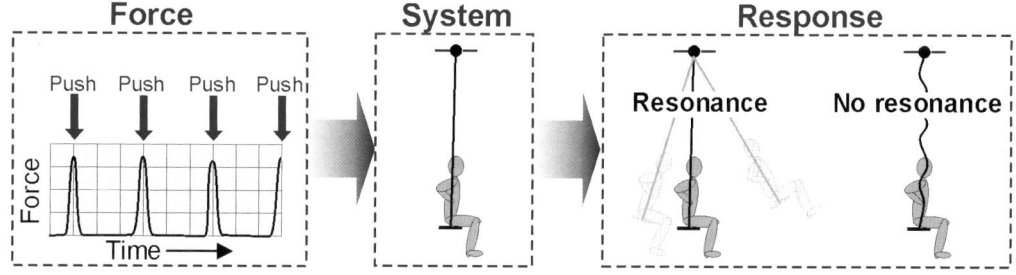

When resonance occurs Resonance occurs when the frequency of a periodic force matches the natural frequency of a system in harmonic motion. Every system that can oscillate has a natural frequency and most systems have more than one. That means resonance occurs all around you, because every system with a natural frequency also can have resonance. For example, buildings can sway back and forth, have a natural frequency, and have resonance. In areas where there are earthquakes, it is very important that the natural frequency of a building definitely not be in the range of frequencies at which the ground shakes during a quake. If the natural frequency of a building matches the frequency of an earthquake, resonance occurs and the building is destroyed by its own shaking (Figure 13.21).

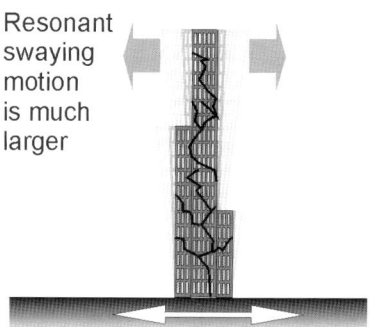

Resonant swaying motion is much larger

Periodic force from earthquake

Figure 13.21: *Tall buildings sway when the wind blows and when the ground shakes during an earthquake. If the natural frequency of the building matches that of the earthquake, resonance occurs. In resonance, the Earth's motion "pumps" the motion of the building and the amplitude of swaying grows until the building is destroyed.*

Energy flow is very efficient at resonance Energy flows through the applied force into the system in motion. The energy flow is very efficient when the system and the applied force are in resonance. You can think of the system in resonance as storing up each small input of energy from every cycle of the applied force. Many technological systems make use of resonance to create energy at a particular frequency; for example, a cellphone transmitter is based on resonance at 2.4×10^9 Hz (2.4 GHz).

Energy, resonance, and damping

Resonant systems accumulate energy

A system in resonance acts like an accumulator of energy. The energy comes from the applied force. The energy is stored as potential and kinetic energy of the motion or oscillation. Resonant systems are found in many technologies because they are so effective at building up energy from the repetition of small forces at the right frequency (Figure 13.22).

Limits to amplitude at resonance

Suppose you apply a small periodic force at the natural frequency of a pendulum. You might think the amplitude of motion would just keep growing and growing. In reality, that is not what happens. Two factors tend to limit how large a resonant motion can get. The first factor is the system itself. In most systems, the natural frequency changes a little as the amplitude gets larger. The small frequency shift means a periodic force no longer matches the exact natural frequency. Even a small mismatch in frequency greatly reduces the efficiency at which the force pumps energy into the system.

Friction and steady state

The second factor that limits the amplitude is friction. The energy lost to friction goes up as the amplitude increases. As the amplitude increases, at some level the energy lost to friction balances the energy input from the applied force. Once the balance point is reached, the amplitude stops increasing and the system is in **steady state**. In steady state the amplitude remains constant.

The balance between damping and energy input

Steady state is a balance between damping from friction and the strength of the applied force. If you have ever dribbled a basketball in place, then you have experienced a resonant system in steady state (Figure 13.23). The ball bounces in a steady rhythm as long as you keep supplying a constant push with your hand on every bounce. Remove your hand and damping takes over. The bounces get shorter and shorter until the ball is at rest on the floor. Start to push harder and the amplitude of the bounces increases. The steady-state amplitude is a balance between energy lost by damping and energy supplied by the applied force.

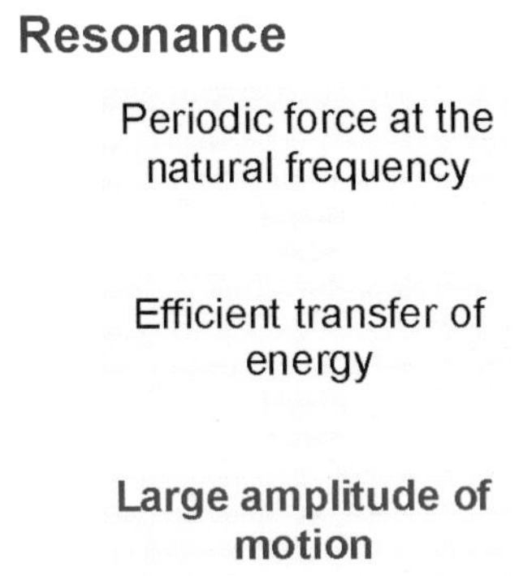

Resonance

Periodic force at the natural frequency

Efficient transfer of energy

Large amplitude of motion

Figure 13.22: *Resonance allows small input forces to accumulate large amounts of energy in a system.*

Figure 13.23: *Dribbling a basketball on a floor is a good example of resonance with steady-state balance between energy loss from damping and energy input from your hand.*

Application: Quartz Crystals

You may not realize how much of modern technology relies on precise timekeeping. For example, computers do not work unless each circuit in the computer is synchronized with the other circuits to better than a few billionths of a second. When you see a fast computer advertised at "2 GHz," what the manufacturer is telling you is that the clock inside the computer ticks 2 billion times per second. Each tick of the clock means the computer can do something like add part of a number or write a character to the screen. Faster clocks mean computers can do more things each second.

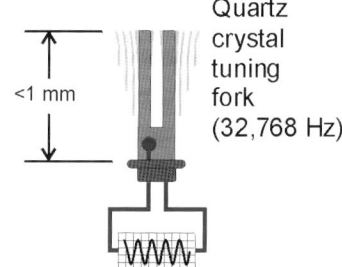

Electrical signal at 32,768 Hz

Quartz crystals are used in electronics The precise heartbeat of nearly all modern electronics is a tiny quartz crystal oscillating at its natural frequency. The resonance of a quartz crystal is so accurate that even the least expensive varieties vary by less than one in a million seconds. A $5 watch and a $10,000 computer both use the same quartz crystal technology.

Figure 13.24: *Inside a quartz crystal watch is a tiny tuning fork made from a piezoelectric quartz crystal. The natural frequency of the tuning fork is 32,768 hertz.*

The piezoelectric effect In 1880, Pierre Curie and his brother Jacques discovered that crystals could be made to oscillate by applying electricity to them. This is known as the piezoelectric effect. A piezoelectric crystal works two ways. If the crystal oscillates mechanically, it produces an electric oscillation of the same frequency. The reverse is also true: If an oscillating electrical signal is applied, the crystal will vibrate mechanically.

Piezoelectric effect

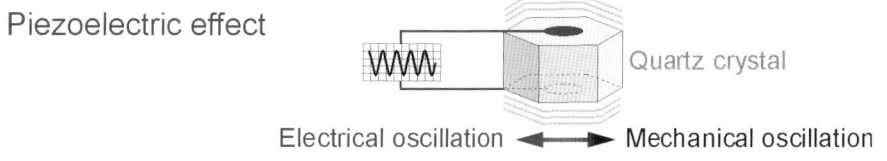

Electrical oscillation ←→ Mechanical oscillation

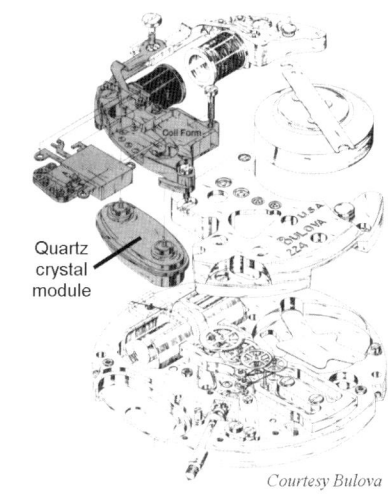

Courtesy Bulova

Quartz crystals in watches Quartz is an ideal piezoelectric crystal because it is easy to get and very stiff. By cutting crystals of quartz in different ways, they can be made to vibrate at almost any frequency. The quartz crystal in most watches is cut like a tiny tuning fork (Figure 13.24) and has a natural frequency of 32,768 Hz. An electric circuit applies a small electrical signal at natural frequency and the quartz crystal resonates and produces a very stable time signal. The high-quality pocket watch in Figure 13.25 keeps time using a quartz crystal of this type.

Figure 13.25: *The inside of a watch uses a quartz crystal to keep time. The crystal regulates a tiny electric motor that turns gears to move the hands of the watch.*

Chapter 13 Review

Vocabulary review

Match the following terms with the correct definition. There is one extra definition in the list that will not match any of the terms.

Set One

1. cycle
2. period
3. amplitude
4. hertz
5. damping
6. natural frequency

a. One cycle per second
b. A system that has harmonic motion
c. The gradual loss of amplitude of an oscillator
d. The time for one cycle to occur
e. Preferred rate of oscillation for a system in harmonic motion
f. One unit of periodic motion
g. The maximum amount of motion away from equilibrium

Set Two

1. resonance
2. phase
3. equilibrium
4. harmonic motion
5. restoring force
6. oscillator

a. Tends to move a system away from equilibrium
b. Motion that repeats itself over and over
c. The location of an oscillator in its cycle
d. Occurs when the natural frequency matches the frequency of an applied periodic force
e. A system that undergoes harmonic motion
f. Condition of a body in harmonic motion at the central point
g. Tends to return a system to equilibrium

Concept review

1. Identify the following as examples of harmonic or linear motion.
   a. A child moving down a playground slide
   b. The vibration of a tuning fork
   c. The spinning of the Earth on its axis
   d. A driver making a right hand turn at an intersection
   e. A bouncing ball
2. Describe the difference between appearance of a graph of linear motion and harmonic motion.
3. Two players are dribbling basketballs at the same time. How would the motion of the basketballs compare if they were in phase?
4. A young child asks you to push him on a swing. Explain how the term resonance is related to the motion of the child on the swing.
5. Using a swing as an example of harmonic motion, identify the:
   a. period
   b. frequency
   c. cycle
   d. amplitude

6. A long spring is stretched between two friends and vibrated. The vibration causes harmonic motion so that, at one instant in time, the spring looks like the diagram at the right. Sketch the diagram on your paper and label the following: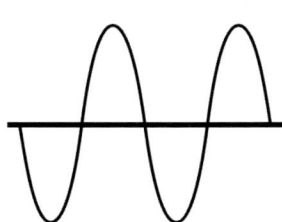
   a. equilibrium position
   b. amplitude
   c. length of one cycle
7. Your favorite radio station is 106.7. What are the units on this number and what do they mean in terms of harmonic motion?
8. How can the natural frequency of a vibrating string be changed? Cite two examples of changes that will create a different natural frequency.
9. A system with harmonic motion is called an oscillator. Name at least two common oscillators.
10. Describe the difference between a damping and a restoring force.
11. What causes oscillation of a system?

12. What is the difference between stable and unstable equilibrium? State an example of each type of equilibrium.

13. Astronauts are unable to use a conventional equal arm balance to measure mass while in orbit because of the "weightless" condition of all objects in Skylab. How might mass be determined using an oscillator?

14. A mass attached to a spring is oscillating with harmonic motion. Describe the changes in its acceleration in one cycle of oscillation.

15. Describe the transformations of energy that take place in an oscillating pendulum.

16. If you rub a moistened finger on the top of a thin glass goblet it can be made to "ring". Explain this using terms such as natural frequency, periodic force, and resonance.

17. Resonant systems accumulate energy which increases the amplitude of oscillation. There is a limit to the magnitude of the amplitude. What is the name for the point at which this limit is reached? Under what condition is this limit reached?

Problems

1. The diagram to the right shows the position vs. time for a harmonic oscillator.

   a. Name 4 pairs of points that are in phase.

   b. Name 4 pairs of points that are 180° out of phase.

2. The diagram below shows the position vs. time graphs for four swinging pendulums.

   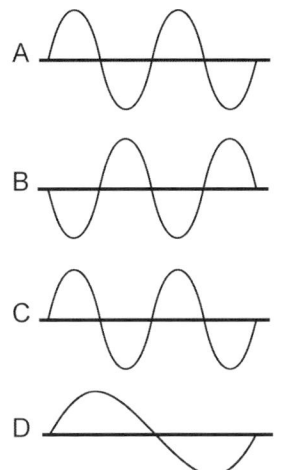

   a. Which pendulums are in phase?

   b. Which pendulums are 180° out of phase?

3. The wings of a ruby-throated hummingbird move at a frequency of 70 hertz. How long does it take for a complete wing-beat cycle?

4. The Earth is part of several oscillating systems. Listed are the frequencies of several common cycles. For each cycle, find the period in seconds, then convert the period so that it is reported using the unit in which it is normally measured, then identify the cycle by common name.

   a. Frequency = 3.1668×10^{-8} Hz

   b. Frequency = 1.16×10^{-5} Hz

   c. Frequency = 4.21×10^{-7} Hz

5. Referring to the diagram below, rank the numbered positions in order from the highest to the lowest amount of kinetic energy.

   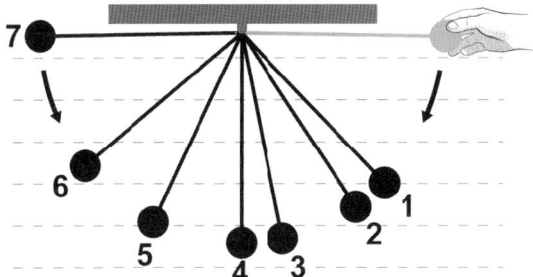

6. Referring to the diagram above, rank the numbered positions in order from the highest to the lowest amount of potential energy.

7. The diagram below represents a graph of velocity vs. time for the harmonic motion of the pendulum shown. Match the lettered points on the graph which best represent the numbered positions of the pendulum.

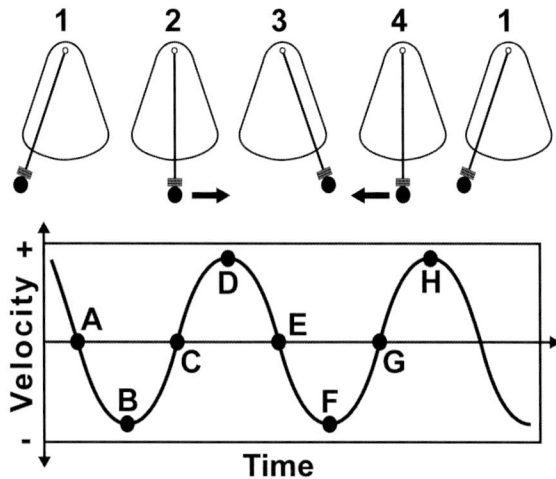

8. Use the graph of the position vs. time of a vibrating mass on a spring to answer the questions below:

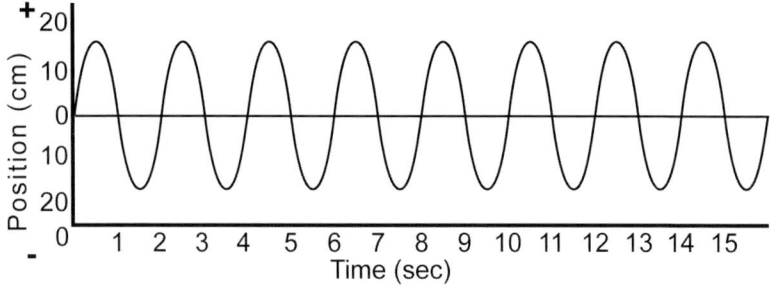

a. What is the amplitude of the vibrating mass?
b. What is the period of oscillation of the mass?
c. What is the frequency of vibration of the mass?
d. How many cycles are represented by the diagram?

9. A simple pendulum hangs vertically at rest. The bottom of the bob is at a height of 1.0 m. The 1.5 kg bob is then moved away from its equilibrium position so that it is at a height of 1.25 m. Find the speed of the bob as it passes through the equilibrium position once released. (Assume no energy loss.)

10. Penny, a 392- newton girl, "pumps" her 5.0-kg swing until she is traveling at a speed of 7.5 m/s as she passes closest to the ground at a height of 0.42 m. How high above the ground will the swing travel if there is no damping?

11. Objects of known mass are attached to a spring. When the spring is stretched and released, the period of the spring is recorded. A graph of the results is displayed below. Using the graph, determine the mass of an object that oscillates with a frequency of 0.286 Hz.

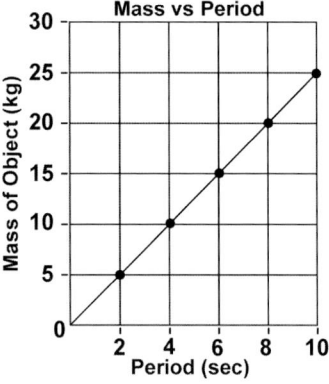

12. A spring oscillates with a frequency of 23 Hz when a mass 1.4 kg is suspended from it. What is the frequency of oscillation if the mass is increased to 6.4 kg?

13. The wings of a mosquito make one complete cycle every 1.67×10^{-3} seconds. To what frequency of sound does this correspond?

Unit 5
Waves and Sound

Waves

Objectives for Chapter 14

By the end of this chapter you should be able to:

1. Recognize a wave in nature or technology.
2. Measure or calculate the wavelength, frequency, amplitude, and speed of a wave.
3. Give examples of transverse and longitudinal waves.
4. Sketch and describe how to create plane waves and circular waves.
5. Give at least one example of reflection, refraction, absorption, interference, and diffraction.
6. Describe how boundaries create resonance in waves.
7. Describe the relationship between the natural frequency, fundamental mode, and harmonics.

Terms and vocabulary words

wave	propagation	amplitude	frequency	wavelength
hertz (Hz)	wave pulse	transverse wave	longitudinal wave	oscillation
crest	trough	wave front	circular wave	plane wave
continuous	fixed boundary	open boundary	reflection	refraction
absorption	boundary condition	incident wave	reflected wave	refracted wave
standing wave	superposition principle	natural frequency	resonance	mode
node	constructive interference	fundamental	harmonic	boundary
interference	destructive interference	diffraction	absorption	antinode

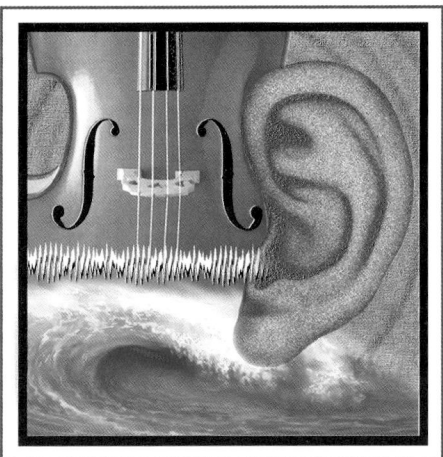

14.1 Waves and Wave Pulses

A ball floating on water can oscillate up and down in harmonic motion. But something else happens to the water as the ball oscillates. The surface of the water oscillates in response and the oscillation spreads outward from where it started. An oscillation that travels is a **wave** and waves are the subject of this section.

A wave is an oscillation that travels.

  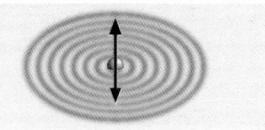

What you learn will apply to water waves, sound waves, and light waves you see around you all the time. You watch a great musician on a stage. The voice or instrument creates waves that carry the sound to your ears. You dial a cell phone to call a friend. A microwave comes from the phone's antenna and carries a signal to your friend. Even gravity has waves that astronomers believe are created when black holes crash into each other.

Why learn about waves?

Waves carry information and energy

We use waves to carry information and energy over great distances. In music, the sound wave that travels through the air carries information about the vibration of a guitar string from the instrument to your ear. Your ear receives the vibration of the sound wave and your brain perceives music. In a similar way, a radio wave carries sounds from a transmitter to your stereo. Another kind of radio wave carries television signals. A microwave carries cell phone conversations. Waves carry energy and information from one place to another. The information could be sound, color, pictures, commands, or many other useful things.

Waves are all around us

Waves are part of everyday experience. We might not recognize all the waves we see, but they are there. Consider standing on almost any road and looking around. How are you affected by waves? Figure 14.1 gives some examples of waves that are so common that you have experienced all of them even though you may not have known they were waves.

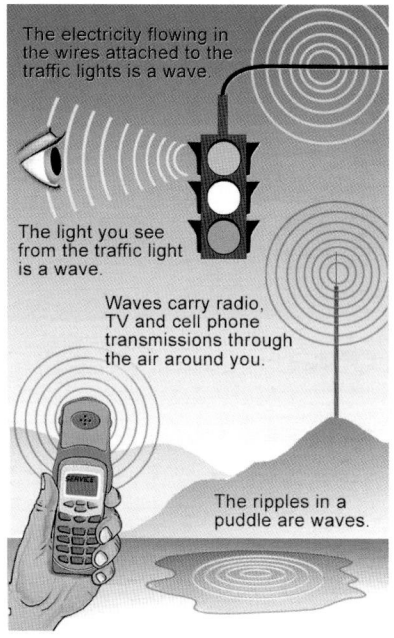

Figure 14.1: *This scene contains many examples of waves.*

→ *The light from the stoplight that you see with your eyes is a wave.*

→ *The ripples in a puddle of water are waves.*

→ *The electricity flowing in the wires attached to the street lights is a wave.*

→ *Waves carry radio and television and cell phone transmissions through the air all around you.*

262

Recognizing waves around you

How do you recognize a wave? All waves have certain things in common. All waves are traveling oscillations that move energy from one place to another. The energy might be in actual motion, or it might be sound, light, or another form of energy that can support oscillations. When you see the things in this list, you should suspect that there is some kind of wave involved.

Evidence for suspecting there are waves:

- Anytime you see a vibration that moves, there is a wave.
- Anything that makes or responds to sound uses waves.
- Anything that makes or responds to light uses waves.
- Anything that transmits information through the air (or space) without wires uses waves. This includes cell phones, radio, and television.
- Anything that allows you to "see through" objects uses waves. This includes ultrasound, computerized axial tomography (CAT) scans, magnetic resonance imaging (MRI) scans, and x-rays.

An example of a wave carrying information You will find waves whenever information, energy, or motion is transmitted over a distance without anything obviously moving. The remote control on a TV is an example. To change the channel you can use the remote or get up and push the buttons with your finger. Both actions carry information (the channel selected) to the TV. One uses physical motion and the other uses a wave that goes from the remote control to the television (Figure 14.2). Your knowledge of physics and waves tells you there must be some kind of wave because information traveled from one place to another, and nothing appeared to move. The wave is actually an infrared light wave, which is invisible to the eye.

Waves are a form of traveling energy A wave moving across the surface of water is different from water moving, as in a stream. As the wave moves by, an individual particle of water oscillates up and down with the wave but remains in the same place. Watch a floating stick as a wave passes and you will see the stick bob up and down in about the same place as the wave moves under it (Figure 14.3). What is moving is the energy of the wave. The energy moves through the water causing the surface to oscillate up and down as the wave energy passes through. A wave is a traveling form of energy.

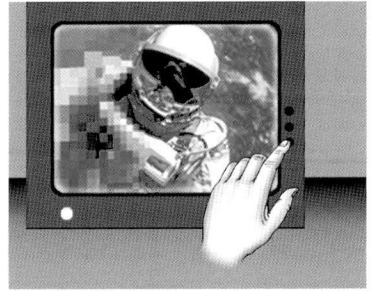

Using physical force

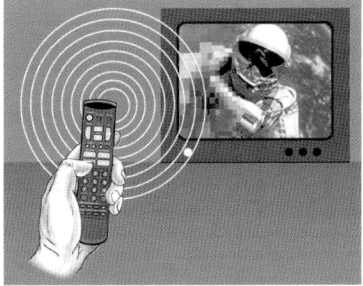

Using a wave

Figure 14.2: *Two ways to change the channel. One way is with a physical force from your finger. The second way is with a wave from the remote control.*

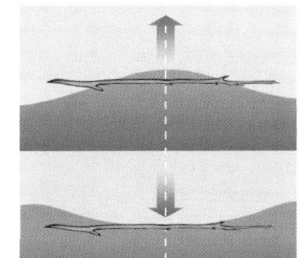

Figure 14.3: *A stick bobs up and down as a wave passes, but the stick and the water beneath it stay, on average, in the same place.*

Characteristics of waves

Basic properties   Waves have cycles, frequency, and amplitude, just like oscillations. Because waves spread out and move, they have new properties of wavelength and speed. Also, because waves are spread out, we have to be careful how we define and measure frequency and amplitude.

Frequency   The frequency of a wave is a measure of how often it oscillates at any given point. (Figure 14.4). To measure the frequency, we look at one place as the wave passes by. The frequency of the oscillating motion of one point is the frequency of the wave. The wave also causes distant points to oscillate up and down *with the same frequency*. A wave carries its frequency to every area it reaches.

Frequency is measured in Hz   Wave frequency is measured in hertz (Hz), just like any oscillation. A frequency of one hertz (1 Hz) describes a wave that makes everything it touches go through a complete cycle once every second. Laboratory-size water waves typically have low frequencies, between 0.1 and 10 hertz. Sound waves have higher frequencies, from 20 hertz to 20,000 hertz. Light waves have even higher frequencies, in the 10^{12} Hz range.

Amplitude   The amplitude of a wave is the largest amount that it moves above or below the equilibrium level (Figure 14.5). The equilibrium level for a water wave is the surface of the water when it is completely still (dotted line in Figure 14.5). You can also think of the amplitude as one-half of the distance between the highest and lowest places.

Wavelength   Wavelength is the length of one complete cycle of a wave (Figure 14.6). For a water wave, this would be the distance from a point on one wave to the same point on the next wave. You can measure the wavelength from high point to high point (crest-to-crest), low point to low point (trough-to-trough), or as the length of a cycle relative to the equilibrium level. Physicists use the Greek letter lambda (λ) to represent wavelength. You write a lambda like an upside down "y."

The ***frequency*** of a wave is the frequency at which each point oscillates.

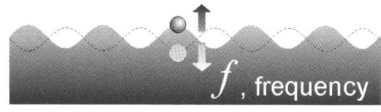

Figure 14.4: *The frequency of a wave.*

The ***amplitude*** of a wave is the maximum movement away from equilibrium.

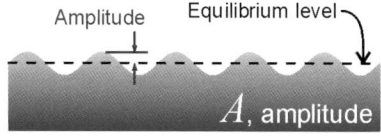

Figure 14.5: *The amplitude of a wave.*

The ***wavelength*** of a wave is the length of one complete cycle.

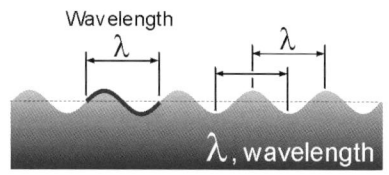

Figure 14.6: *The wavelength is the length of one complete cycle. The wavelength can be measured from any point on a cycle to the same point on the next cycle.*

Wave pulses and the speed of a wave

Speed The speed of a wave describes how fast the wave can transmit an oscillation from one place to another. Waves can have a wide range of speeds. Most water waves are slow; a few miles per hour is typical. Light waves are extremely fast—186,000 miles per *second*. Sound waves travel at about 660 miles per hour, faster than water waves but much slower than light waves.

The speed of a wave pulse A **wave pulse** is a short length of wave, often just a single oscillation. Imagine stretching an elastic string over the back of a chair, as in the diagram below. To make a wave pulse, pull down a short length of the string behind the chair and let go. This creates a "bump" in the string that races away from the chair. The moving "bump" is a wave pulse. The wave pulse moves *on* the string, but each section of string returns to the same place after the wave moves past. The speed of the wave pulse is what we mean by the speed of a wave.

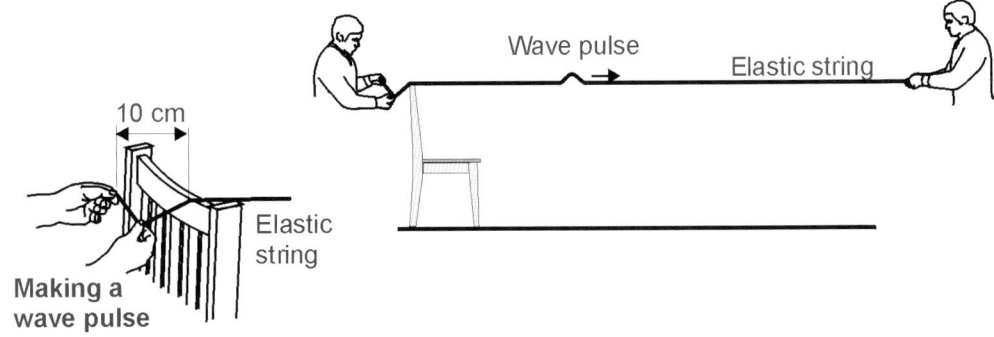

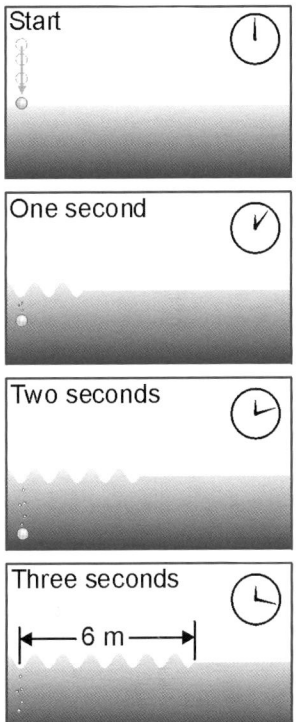

Calculating the speed of the wave

$$v = \frac{6 \text{ m}}{3 \text{ sec}} = 2 \text{ m/sec}$$

Figure 14.7: *The speed of a wave is the speed at which oscillations spread outward from where the wave started.*

What is the speed of a wave? The speed of a wave is different from the speed of whatever the wave is causing to move. In the wave pulse example, the string moves up and down as the pulse passes. But the up-down speed of the string is not the speed of the wave. The speed of the wave describes how quickly a movement of one part of the string is transmitted to another place on the string. To measure the speed of the wave, you would start a pulse in one place and measure how long it takes the pulse to affect a place some distance away. A similar technique works for measuring the speed of water waves. A stone dropped in a pond starts a ripple (wave). The speed of the wave is the speed at which the ripple spreads (Figure 14.7).

The relationship between speed, frequency, and wavelength

Speed is frequency times wavelength
The cycles of a wave move. The speed of the wave is the speed at which a cycle moves. In one complete cycle, a wave moves forward one wavelength (Figure 14.8). Remember, speed is distance traveled divided by time taken. For a wave the distance traveled is one wavelength and the time it takes is one period. The speed of a wave is therefore its wavelength divided by the period of its cycle. Since frequency is the inverse of period, it is usually easier to calculate the speed of a wave by multiplying wavelength and frequency. The result is true for sound waves, light waves, and even gravity waves. Frequency multiplied by wavelength is the speed of the wave.

Speed of a wave

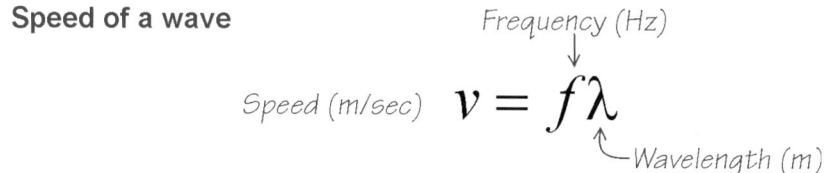

A student does an experiment with waves in water. The student measures the wavelength of a wave to be 5 centimeters. By using a stopwatch and observing the oscillations of a floating ball, the student measures a frequency of 4 Hz. If the student starts a wave in one part of a tank of water, how long will it take the wave to reach the opposite side of the tank 2 meters away?

Calculate how long it takes a wave to move from one place to another

1) You are asked for the time it takes to move a distance of 2 meters.
2) You are given the frequency, wavelength, and distance.
3) The relationship between frequency, wavelength, and speed is v = fλ. The relationship between time, speed, and distance is v = d ÷ t.
4) Rearrange the speed formula to solve for the time: t = d ÷ v.
   The speed of the wave is the frequency times the wavelength.
   v = fλ = (4 Hz)(5 cm) = 20 cm/sec = 0.2 m/sec.
   Use this value to calculate the time:
   t = (2 m) ÷ (0.2 m/sec) = 10 seconds

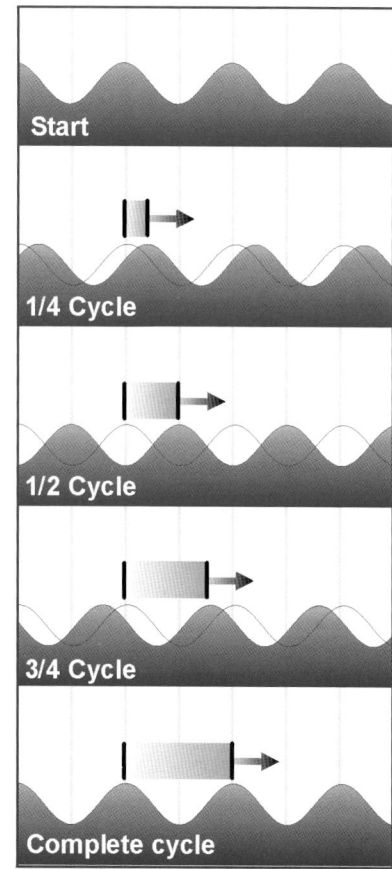

$$v = \frac{\text{distance}}{\text{time}} = \frac{\text{wavelength}}{\text{period}}$$

$$= \frac{\lambda}{T} = \left(\frac{1}{T}\right)\lambda = f\lambda$$

Figure 14.8: *The speed of a wave equals the frequency times the wavelength.*

Transverse and longitudinal waves

Waves spread through connections   A wave moves along a string because the string is continuous. By continuous we mean it is connected to itself. Waves spread through connections. If we were to break the string in the middle, the wave would not spread across the break. Whenever you have an extended body that is all connected to itself, you get waves. A lake is an example: Waves can travel all the way across a lake because the water is continuous from one shore to another.

Transverse waves   A transverse wave has its oscillations perpendicular to the direction the wave moves (Figure 14.9). The wave moves from left to right. The oscillation is up and down. Water waves are also transverse waves because the up and down oscillation is perpendicular to the motion of the wave.

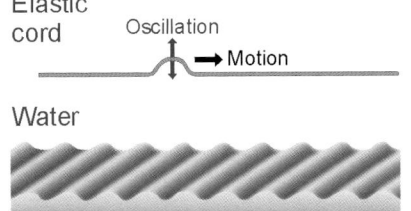

Figure 14.9: *A wave pulse on an elastic cord and ripples on water are two examples of transverse waves.*

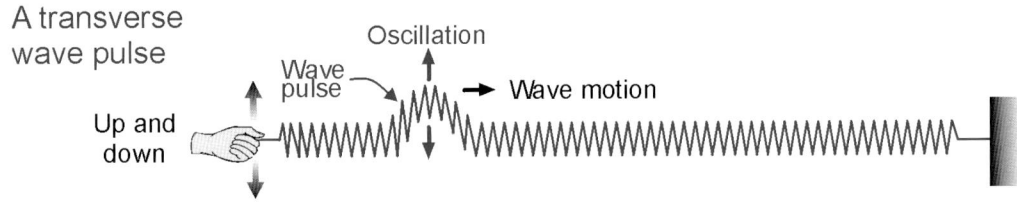

Longitudinal waves   A longitudinal wave has oscillations in the same direction as the wave moves. Stretch a Slinky® with one end fastened to the wall. Give the free end a sharp push toward the wall and pull it back again. You see a compression wave of the Slinky® that moves toward the wall. The compression wave on the Slinky® is a longitudinal wave because the compression is in the direction the wave moves (Figure 14.10).

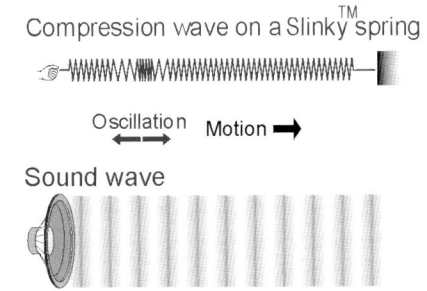

Figure 14.10: *A compression wave on a Slinky® and a sound wave are two examples of longitudinal waves.*

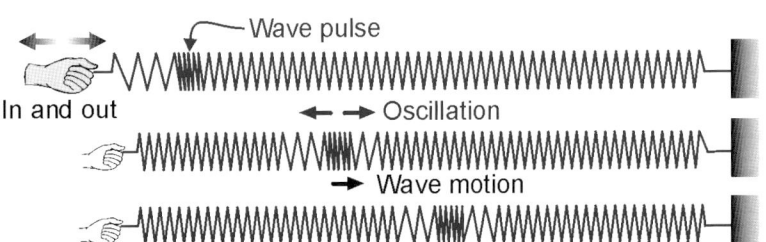

14.2 Motion and Interaction of Waves

What happens when two waves hit each other, or hit a wall? This section discusses how waves interact with each other and with objects they encounter. This section uses water waves as a familiar example to introduce concepts that apply to all waves. Water waves make good examples because they are big and slow, so you can see the details of what happens. Light and sound waves are harder to study directly because light waves are small and fast, and sound waves are invisible. Almost every process we observe with water waves also occurs with sound and light waves.

The **crest** of a wave is the high point

The **trough** of a wave is the low point.

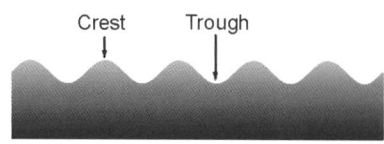

Figure 14.11: *Crests and troughs are the maximum and minimum points in a wave.*

Wave shapes

Crests, troughs, and wave fronts

You can think of a wave as a moving pattern of high points and low points. A **crest** represents all the high points of one cycle of a wave. A **trough** represents all the low points (Figure 14.11). When describing the shape and motion of waves, it is useful to think in terms of the crests. As the wave moves, the crests move. The crests are sometimes called **wave fronts**. A wave front describes the shape of the crest of a wave.

One- and two-dimensional waves

Waves on a string are one-dimensional because they can move along only one axis. Waves on the surface of water are two-dimensional since they can move along two axes (*x* and *y*). The shape of the wave fronts of two-dimensional waves affects how the waves spread out and move. The shape of the wave front is determined by how the wave is created and what the wave encounters as it moves. The shape of the wave front can change, as you will see later in the Chapter. Waves also can be three-dimensional, moving along three axes (*x*, *y*, and *z*). Light and sound waves are three-dimensional waves.

Plane waves and circular waves

You can make wave fronts in all shapes but **plane waves** and **circular waves** are easiest to create and study (Figure 14.12). The crests of a plane wave form straight lines so the wave fronts are also straight lines. A plane wave can be created by disturbing the surface of water in a line. The crests of a circular wave form circles and the wave fronts of circular waves are expanding circles. A circular wave is started by disturbing the water at a single point. A fingertip touched to the surface will start a circular wave.

Plane waves

Circular waves

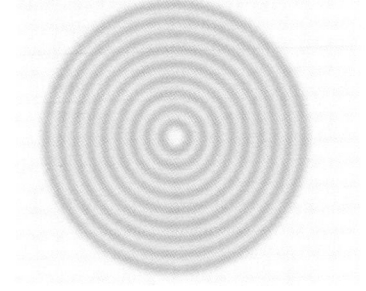

Figure 14.12: *Plane waves and circular waves are types of two-dimensional waves.*

268

Propagation of waves

Why waves move   The word propagation means "to spread out and grow." Propagation is a good word for describing the motion of waves because it describes what happens. To see why a wave propagates, consider a water wave. When you drop a stone into water, some of the water is pushed aside and raised up by the stone (A). The higher water pushes the water next to it out of the way as it tries to get back down to equilibrium (B). The water that has been pushed then pushes on the water in front of *it*, and so on. The wave spreads through the interaction of each bit of water with the water immediately next to it (C).

Propagation of a water wave

Equilibrium surface

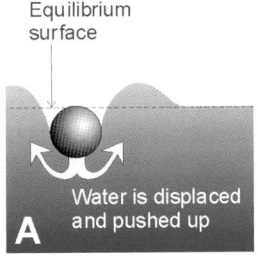 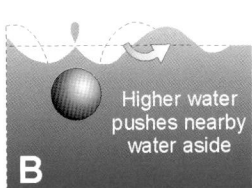 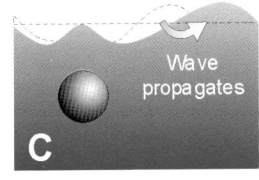

A — Water is displaced and pushed up

B — Higher water pushes nearby water aside

C — Wave propagates

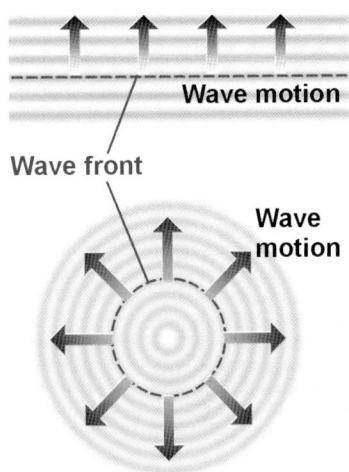

Wave motion

Wave front

Wave motion

Figure 14.13: *The shape of a wave front determines the direction the wave moves. Waves move perpendicular to their wave fronts.*

Determining the direction the wave moves   The shape of the wave front determines the direction in which the wave moves. Circular waves have circular wave fronts that move outward from the center (Figure 14.13). Plane waves have straight wave fronts that move in a line perpendicular to the wave fronts. To change the direction the wave is moving, you have to change the shape of the wave front. In later chapters, we will see that this is exactly how lenses work.

Continuous surface

Discontinuous surface

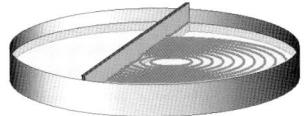

Figure 14.14: *A pan of water has a continuous surface. A wall across the pan makes the surface discontinuous. A wave does not spread across a discontinuous surface.*

Waves propagate through continuous materials   Water waves propagate along surfaces that are continuous. In discussing waves, the word "continuous" means that any part of the surface connects to any other part without having to leave the surface. If the connections are broken (becoming discontinuous), the wave may not be able to propagate across the break. For example, a single pan of water has a continuous surface and waves can spread to every part of the surface. If you put a ruler across the pan the surface becomes discontinuous because the surface on one side of the wall cannot be influenced by the surface on the other side. A wave on one side will not propagate across the wall (Figure 14.14)

Waves and boundaries

Boundaries — A boundary is a place where conditions change. For example, the surface of a wall is a boundary. The end of a string is also a boundary for the string. Waves are affected by boundaries and we use boundaries to shape and control waves. What a wave does at a boundary depends on the **boundary conditions**. The surface of a wall is a **fixed boundary** for water waves because the boundary does not move. A free end of a string is an **open boundary** for string waves because the end can move in response to the wave.

The four wave interactions — Waves can interact with boundaries in four different ways (Figure 14.15). The first three interactions (reflection, refraction, diffraction) occur at the boundary. Diffraction occurs when waves go around boundaries or through openings in boundaries. Absorption can occur at a boundary, but usually happens within the body of a material after a wave crosses a boundary.

Reflection	The wave can bounce off the boundary and go in a new direction.
Refraction	The wave can pass straight into and through the boundary.
Diffraction	The wave can bend around or through holes in the boundary.
Absorption	The wave can lose amplitude and/or disappear after crossing the boundary.

Combinations of the four interactions — Sometimes, the wave can do all four things at once, partly bouncing off, partly passing through, partly being absorbed, and partly going around. You may have noticed the radio in a car sometimes loses the station as you enter a tunnel. Part of the wave that carries the signal bends around the entrance to the tunnel and follows you in. Part is absorbed by the ground. The deeper you go in the tunnel, the weaker the wave gets until the radio cannot pick up the signal at all and you hear static. Simple things like mirrors and complex things like ultrasound or x-rays all depend on how waves act when they encounter boundaries.

Reflection

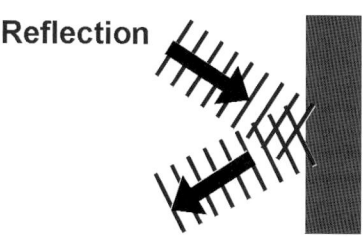

Refraction

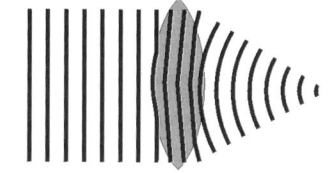

Diffraction

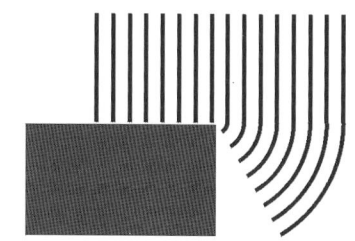

Absorption

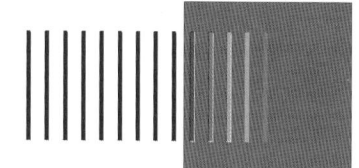

Figure 14.15: *The four basic interactions between waves and boundaries.*

270

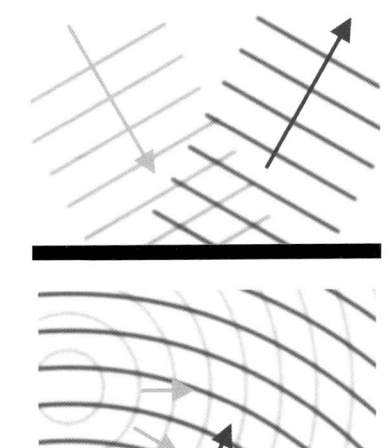
Reflection and refraction

Reflection When a wave bounces off a boundary we call it reflection. Any boundary where there is a sudden change in material almost always causes reflection. For example, if you make water waves travel toward a wall they will be reflected. If the boundary is straight, the wave that reflects is like the original wave but moving in a new direction. A plane wave reflecting from a straight boundary will also be a plane wave. A circular wave reflecting from a straight boundary will also be a circular wave (Figure 14.16). The wavelength and frequency of a wave are usually unchanged by reflection.

Refraction Waves can cross boundaries and pass into or through some materials. For example, placing a thin plate on the bottom of a shallow tray of water creates a boundary where the depth of the water changes. If you look carefully, you see that waves are bent as they cross the boundary where the depth of water changes (Figure 14.17). The wave starts in one direction and changes direction as it crosses. We call it refraction when a wave changes direction as it crosses a boundary and say the wave is *refracted* in the process of changing direction.

Curved boundaries Boundaries that are not straight can be used to change the shape of the wave fronts and therefore change the direction of a wave. For example, a curved boundary can turn a plane wave into a circular wave. Curved boundaries are used with both reflecting and refracting surfaces.

Figure 14.16: *Reflection of plane waves and circular waves from a boundary.*

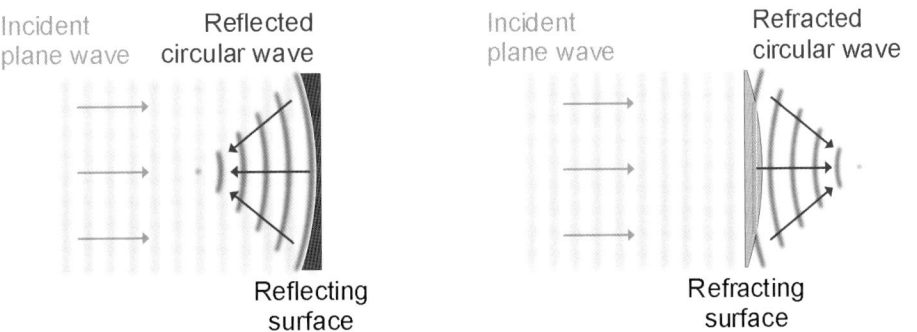

Incident, reflected, and refracted waves The wave approaching a boundary is called the incident wave. A wave reflected from a boundary is a reflected wave. A wave that is bent passing through a boundary is called a refracted wave.

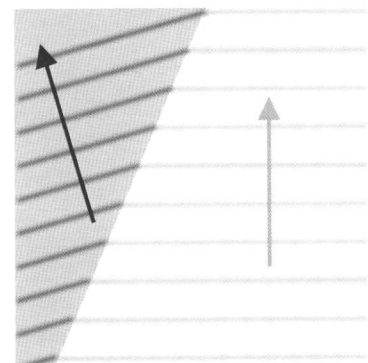

Figure 14.17: *Refraction of water waves crossing a boundary where the water's depth changes.*

Diffraction and absorption

Absorption Waves can be absorbed as they pass through objects. Absorption is what happens when the amplitude of a wave gets smaller and smaller as it passes through a material. Some objects and materials have properties that absorb certain kinds of waves (Figure 14.18). A sponge can absorb a water wave while letting the water pass. A heavy curtain absorbs sound waves. Theaters often use heavy curtains so the audience cannot hear backstage noise. Dark glass absorbs light waves, which is how some kinds of sunglasses work.

Absorption transfers energy The energy of a wave is transferred to the material the wave is absorbed by. This is dramatically illustrated by the destructive power of hurricanes. Wind blowing over water waves exerts force on the wave. The force of the wind transfers energy from the wind to the wave causing the amplitude of the waves to grow large. When a large wave hits the shore all of its energy is released quickly as the wave is absorbed by everything in its path.

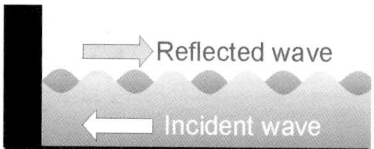

A sharp boundary creates strong reflections.

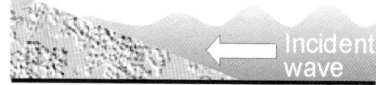

A soft boundary absorbs wave energy and may not produce much reflection.

Figure 14.18: *A hard wall reflects a water wave. A sloped sponge absorbs the wave.*

Water waves absorb energy from the wind, increasing their amplitude

Diffraction Waves can bend around obstacles and go through openings. The process of bending around corners or passing through openings is called diffraction. We say a wave is *diffracted* when it is changed by passing through a hole or around an edge. Diffraction usually changes the direction and shape of the wave. For example, diffraction turns a plane wave into a circular wave when the wave passes through a narrow opening (Figure 14.19). Diffraction explains why you can hear someone in another room even if the door is open only a crack. Diffraction causes a sound wave to spread out from the crack.

Diffraction through a small opening turns plane waves into circular waves.

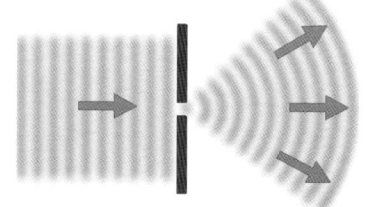

Figure 14.19: *Diffraction allows waves to bend around corners and spread out through small openings.*

Interference and the superposition principle

The superposition principle

It is common for there to be many waves in the same system at the same time. For example, if you watch the ocean you can see small waves on the surface of large waves. When more than one wave is present, the total oscillation of any point is the sum of the oscillations from each individual wave. This is called the superposition principle. According to the superposition principle, if there are two waves present (A and B), the total oscillation at any point in time (C) is the sum of the oscillations from wave (A) and wave (B). In reality, single waves are quite rare. The sound waves and light waves you experience are the superposition of thousands of waves with different frequencies and amplitudes. Your eyes, ears, and brain separate the waves in order to recognize individual sounds and colors.

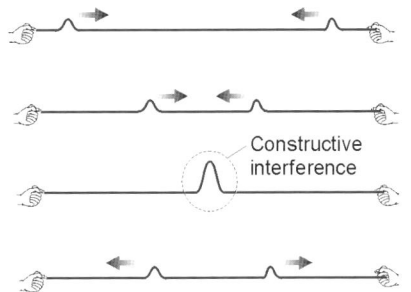

Figure 14.20: *Two wave pulses on the same side add up to make a single, bigger pulse when they meet. This is an example of constructive interference.*

The superposition principle

A + B = C

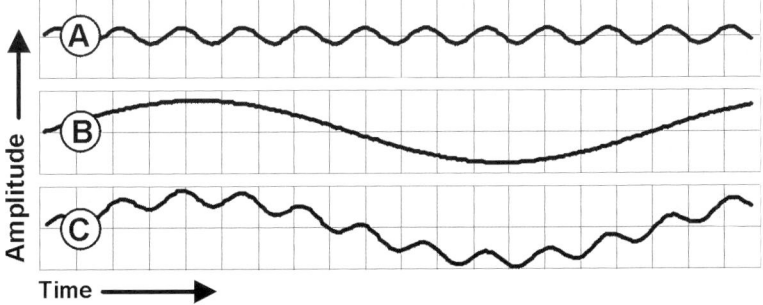

Constructive interference

If two waves add up to create a larger amplitude, constructive interference has occurred. Figure 14.20 shows how the constructive interference of two wave pulses makes a single larger pulse at the moment they pass each other. Sometimes on the ocean two big waves add up to make a gigantic wave that may only last a short time but is taller than ships, and can have a terrible impact.

Destructive interference

If two wave pulses are started on opposite sides of an elastic cord, something different happens. When the pulses meet in the middle, they cancel each other out. One wave wants to pull the string up and the other wave wants to pull it down. The result is that the string is flat and both pulses vanish for a moment. This is called destructive interference. In destructive interference, waves add up to make a smaller amplitude (Figure 14.21).

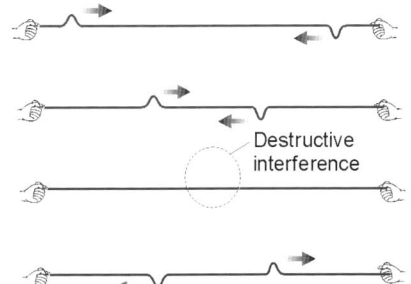

Figure 14.21: *Two equal wave pulses on opposite sides subtract when they meet. The upward movement of one pulse exactly cancels with the downward movement of the other. For a moment there is no pulse at all. This is an example of destructive interference.*

14.3 Natural Frequency and Resonance

Waves can show natural frequency and resonance, just like oscillators. The natural frequency of a wave depends on the wave and also on the system that contains the wave. In this section you will learn that resonance in waves comes from the interaction of a wave with reflections from the boundaries of its system. The concepts of resonance and natural frequency apply to a huge range of natural and human-made systems that include waves. The tides of the oceans, the way our ears separate sound, and even a microwave oven are examples of systems that can be explained by waves and resonance.

Boundary conditions and reflections

Resonance and reflections
Resonance in waves is caused by reflections from the boundaries of a system. To understand resonance in a wave, consider a stretched elastic string that is fixed to a wall at one end. If you start a wave pulse on the free end of the string, the wave travels to the string's other end and reflects off the wall (top of Figure 14.22).

How wave pulses reflect
If you watch carefully, you will observe that a wave pulse launched on the top reflects back on the bottom of the string. When the pulse gets back to where it started, it reflects again, and is back on top of the string. Every reflection from a boundary inverts the wave pulse. After the second reflection, the pulse is traveling in the original direction again (Figure 14.22).

How resonance is created
To make resonance, you apply a periodic force by shaking the end of the string up and down at regular intervals. Each up and down shake makes a new wave pulse. The timing of the shaking must be just right. To build up a large wave, you wait until a reflected pulse has returned to your hand before launching a new pulse. The new pulse adds to the reflected pulse to make a bigger pulse (constructive interference). The bigger pulse moves away and reflects again. You wait until the reflection gets back to your hand and then shake the string to add a third pulse. The total wave pulse is now three times as large as at the start. Resonance is created when you keep adding pulses so that each new pulse is launched at the exact time a reflected pulse arrives from the far end of the string. After a dozen shakes the string develops a single large wave motion, and you have created resonance (Figure 14.23). The resonance is created by the addition of new wave pulses with reflections from the boundary at the fixed end of the string.

Reflection of a wave pulse

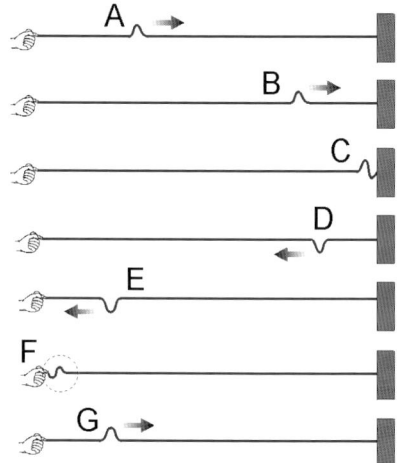

Growing a wave pulse

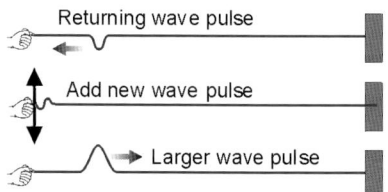

Figure 14.22: *Reflections of a wave pulse on an elastic string.*

Resonance

Elastic string

Figure 14.23: *A vibrating string in resonance has a single large wave pattern such as this.*

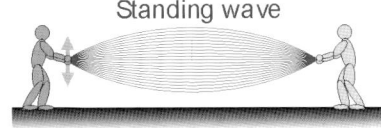
Standing waves and natural frequency

Standing waves   A wave that is confined between boundaries is called a standing wave. In a standing wave the boundaries reflect the wave back on itself and the wave is trapped or confined in one place. Standing waves can become large if resonance occurs. For example, a jump rope can make a large standing wave if you shake one end up and down at the natural frequency of the rope (Figure 14.24).

Figure 14.24: *You can make a standing wave by shaking one end of a jump rope up and down with the right frequency.*

The vibrating string   A vibrating string is a good experiment for investigating standing waves and resonance. A vibrating string oscillates at its natural frequency when it is plucked in the middle and let go. The oscillation looks like the standing wave in Figure 14.24. A jump rope is a large example of a vibrating string. For a lab experiment, an elastic string about a meter long is more appropriate. The top end of the string is fixed by a clamp (Figure 14.25). A periodic force is applied to the bottom end of the string with a small-amplitude shaking motion. Each back-and-forth cycle of the applied force sends a wave pulse up the string.

Matching the natural frequency   The experiment consists of watching what happens to the string as the frequency of the periodic force is changed. For most frequencies the string wiggles around a small amount but nothing much happens. But when the frequency of the applied force gets close to the natural frequency of the string, a large-amplitude standing wave develops. The standing wave forms when the string is in resonance.

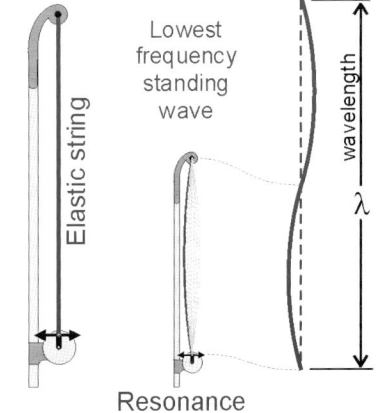

Why resonance happens   You can think of a standing wave in terms of wave pulses created by the oscillation of the applied force. Resonance happens when the period between oscillations of the force is the same as the up-and-back travel time for a wave pulse on the string. Because the wave pulses move quickly, you do not see them. The string develops a standing wave in a second or less. The standing wave has a wavelength of twice the length of the string (Figure 14.25).

Boundaries and natural frequency   By itself, a wave does not have a natural frequency. If you had an elastic string that was infinitely long, there would be no natural frequency because a wave you launched from one end would never come back. With all waves, resonance and natural frequency are dependent on reflections from boundaries of the system containing the wave.

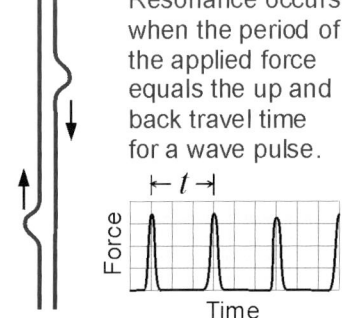

Resonance occurs when the period of the applied force equals the up and back travel time for a wave pulse.

Figure 14.25: *The string is half a wavelength of the standing wave.*

Harmonics

Harmonics | As the frequency of the applied force changes, different standing wave patterns appear on the string (Figure 14.26). The standing wave with the longest wavelength is called the fundamental. The fundamental has the lowest frequency in a series of standing waves called harmonics. The second harmonic occurs at twice the frequency of the fundamental. The third harmonic occurs at three times the frequency of the fundamental. For example, suppose a vibrating string has a fundamental frequency of 10 hertz. The second harmonic will be at a frequency of 20 hertz and the third harmonic will be at 30 hertz. In the laboratory you may be able to observe 10 or more harmonics of the same string.

The cause of harmonics | The second harmonic occurs when pulses are launched so each new wave pulse adds up to every *second* reflected pulse. There are two pulses on the string at a time to make the second harmonic (Figure 14.27). The frequency of the second harmonic is twice the fundamental frequency because there are twice as many reflected wave pulses on the string. For the third harmonic, each new pulse adds up to every *third* reflected pulse and there are three pulses on the string at a time. The shapes of the waves patterns correspond to the number of waves pulses on the string.

Increasing the resonant frequency | If the elastic string is made tighter, the restoring forces get stronger and the fundamental (natural) frequency increases. The frequency of each harmonic also increases since harmonics occur at multiples of the fundamental. For example, if the frequency of the fundamental is raised to 20 hertz (Hz), the second harmonic will occur at a frequency of 40 hertz and the third at 60 hertz.

Almost all systems have harmonics | Almost all systems which have a natural frequency also have harmonics. Each harmonic behaves like another natural frequency. That means the same system can show resonance at the fundamental frequency or any harmonic. In the next chapter we will see that harmonics are very important to the quality of sound from musical instruments. For another example, car engines have oscillating parts (pistons) that move rapidly up and down creating vibrating forces. To avoid resonant vibrations, the whole car must be designed so none of its parts have natural frequencies that match harmonics of the frequencies generated by moving parts in the engine.

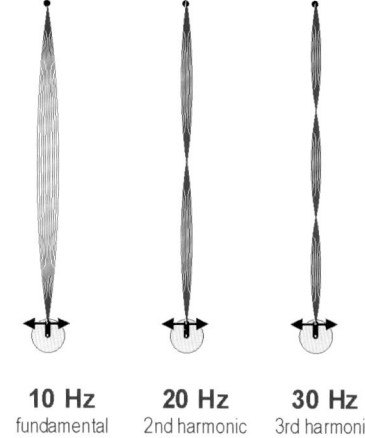

10 Hz — fundamental   20 Hz — 2nd harmonic   30 Hz — 3rd harmonic

Figure 14.26: *The first three standing wave patterns of a vibrating string. The patterns occur at multiples of the fundamental frequency.*

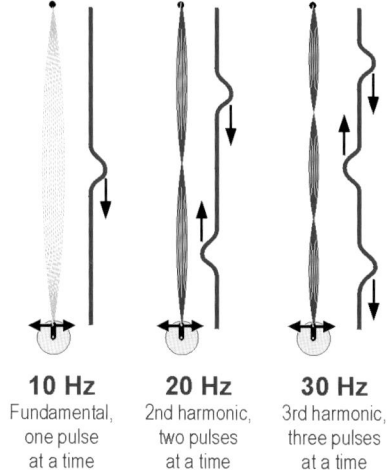

10 Hz — Fundamental, one pulse at a time   20 Hz — 2nd harmonic, two pulses at a time   30 Hz — 3rd harmonic, three pulses at a time

Figure 14.27: *The harmonic number is also the number of wave pulses on the string at one time.*

Energy and waves

Energy of a wave   The energy in a wave alternates between two forms, like the energy in an oscillator. For example, with a vibrating string the energy is potential energy at the maximum amplitude of each cycle. The potential energy comes from stretching the string. The wave has the most potential energy when the string is stretched the most, at maximum amplitude. The kinetic energy comes from the motion of the string. The wave has its maximum kinetic energy as the string swings through its equilibrium straight-line shape (Figure 14.28). The energy transformations in a water wave are also between potential (height) and kinetic (moving mass) energy. All waves propagate by exchanging energy between two forms. For water and elastic strings, the exchange is between potential and kinetic energy. For sound waves, the energy oscillates between pressure and kinetic energy. In light waves, energy oscillates between electric and magnetic fields.

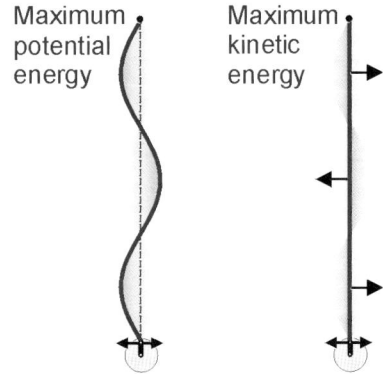

Figure 14.28: *The wave has the maximum potential energy at its most stretched position. The maximum kinetic energy occurs when the string swings through equilibrium (resting).*

Frequency and energy   The energy of a standing wave is proportional to the frequency. Figure 14.29 shows three standing waves with the same amplitude and different frequencies. The wave with the higher frequency has more energy. For a standing wave on a string, the energy increases because the string must move faster to complete more cycles per second at higher frequencies. The result is true for almost all waves. The energy of a wave is proportional to its frequency.

Amplitude and energy   The energy of a wave is also proportional to amplitude. Given two standing waves of the same frequency, the wave with the larger amplitude has more energy. With a vibrating string, the potential energy of the wave comes from the stretching of the string. Larger amplitude means the string has to stretch more and therefore stores more energy.

Why are standing waves useful?   Standing waves can be used to store energy at specific frequencies. With the wave on the string you observed how a small input of energy at the natural frequency accumulated over time to build a wave with much more energy. Musical instruments use standing waves to create sound energy of exactly the right frequency. Radio transmitters and cell phones also use standing waves to create power at specific frequencies. The standing waves are electrical in these applications.

Lowest frequency, lowest energy

Double frequency, double energy

Triple frequency, triple energy

Figure 14.29: *The energy of a wave is proportional to its frequency.*

Describing waves

Wavelength

A vibrating string can move so fast that your eye averages out the motion and you see a wave-shaped blur (Figure 14.30). At any one moment the string is really in only one place within the blur. The wavelength is the length of one complete "S" shape on the string.

Nodes and antinodes

Standing waves have nodes and antinodes. A node is a point where the string stays at its equilibrium position (Figure 14.31). An antinode is a point where the wave is as far as it gets from equilibrium. A fixed boundary forces the string to always have a node at the boundary. It is also possible to make standing waves with an open boundary (loose end) that have an antinode at the end of the string.

Frequency and wavelength relationship

High frequency waves have short wavelength compared with low frequency waves. This is generally true of all waves, and comes from the relationship between the speed of a wave, its frequency, and its wavelength. The speed of a wave is not usually affected much by changes in frequency or wavelength. Since speed is frequency times wavelength, for speed to stay the same, the wavelength must go down if the frequency goes up. In fact, if the frequency doubles, the wavelength must be reduced by exactly one-half to compensate. If the frequency is increased by a factor of 10, the wavelength decreases to one-tenth what it was.

Modes

A vibrating string has two distinct modes. A *mode* is a category of types of wave behavior. One mode of the vibrating string is a rotating wave and the other mode is a transverse wave (Figure 14.32). In the rotating mode, the string spins around in a circular motion. Because the string moves in circles, the wave looks the same from the front and from the side. In the transverse mode, the string moves back and forth in a flat motion. The wave looks different from the front and side.

Modes and natural frequency

Most systems that can support waves have different modes. In many systems the different modes have different natural frequencies. The two modes of the vibrating string both stretch the string the same amount and have the same natural frequency. The transverse mode usually occurs when the oscillating force is directly under the fixed end of the string. If the oscillating force is offset from the string, a slight twist develops and the rotating mode results.

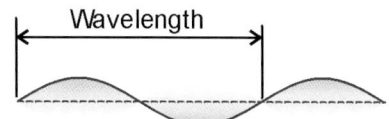

Figure 14.30: *The wavelength of a standing wave is the length of one complete cycle.*

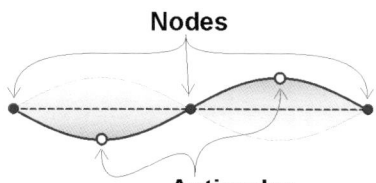

Figure 14.31: *A standing wave may have several nodes and antinodes.*

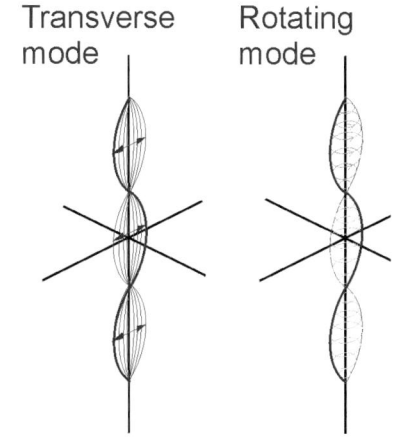

Figure 14.32: *A vibrating string has two possible modes.*

278

Standing waves in two and three dimensions

Many modes of vibration
Most vibrating objects have more complex shapes than a string. Complex shapes create more ways an object can vibrate. Two- and three-dimensional objects tend to have two or three *families* of modes. Often, each family of modes has its own natural frequency including a fundamental and harmonics. The vibrations of real objects can be complex because more than one mode can be active at one time. For example, when a musician strikes a cymbal, the brass plate vibrates. A careful analysis would show more than 10 different modes of vibration in the motion of the cymbal. Each mode contributes to the sound of the cymbal and the richness of the sound comes from the complexity of the vibrations.

Vibrations of a circular disc
The diagram Figure 14.33 shows two families of modes for a vibrating circular disc, like the head of a drum. Two of the different modes in each family are shown. A skillful drummer knows how and where to hit the drum to make mixtures of the different modes and get particular sounds. The radial modes have nodes and antinodes that are circles. The angular modes have nodes and antinodes that are radial lines from the center of the circle. A circular disc has two dimensions because you can identify any point on the surface with two coordinates (radius, angle). Two-dimensional systems usually have two distinct families of vibrating modes. One family of modes has nodes and antinodes along the radius coordinate. The second family of modes has nodes and antinodes along the angle coordinate.

Waves in a water glass
You can also see the two modes of a circular surface with a glass full of water. If you run a moistened finger around the rim of the glass, you can see circular modes. The nodes and antinodes are circles. If you rock the glass side to side, you get a sloshing wave that is the longest wavelength of the angular modes. It is possible to get resonance with both modes.

Vibration of a guitar top
The top of a guitar has a very complex structure of vibrating modes (Figure 14.34). The bands of light and dark are contours of motion away from equilibrium. The lowest frequency mode (upper left) has the fewest nodes and the simplest pattern. As the frequency increases, the number of nodes increases and the patterns become more complex. Some patterns are harmonics within the same family of modes and others belong to different families of modes.

Radial modes

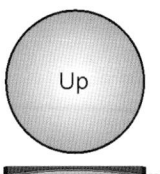 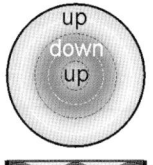

Angular modes

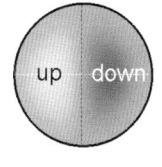 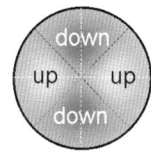

Figure 14.33: *The two different families of modes for standing waves on a circular disk, like the top of a drum.*

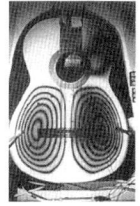 

268 Hz   980 Hz

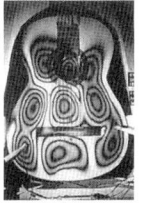 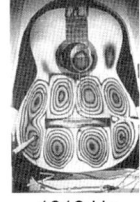

873 Hz   1010 Hz

Figure 14.34: *Vibrating modes of an acoustic guitar top.*

Application: Microwave Ovens

You have probably used a microwave oven to heat food. Consider the following experiment. Two identical ceramic cups are placed in a microwave oven. One cup is half full of water and the other cup is empty and dry. The power is turned on for 90 seconds. When the microwave turns off, the two cups are removed. The cup with the water is hot but the empty cup is still cold; the microwaves selectively heated the cup with the water and not the empty cup (Figure 14.35). If both cups had been placed in a gas or an electric oven, both would have gotten hot.

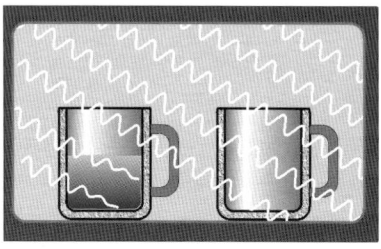

Figure 14.35: *Microwaves are absorbed by liquid water but pass through other materials, such as the ceramic in the cup.*

Resonance of water molecules | Microwave ovens use resonance to heat liquid water molecules. A water molecule is two atoms of hydrogen bonded to one atom of oxygen. The molecule is slightly more positive on one side and more negative on the opposite side. When electricity is present, the negative end of each water molecule tries to line itself up toward the positive direction of the electricity. If the electricity reverses, the water molecule tends to swing back again through interaction with neighboring water molecules. Each molecule acts like it is connected with springs to other molecules. Because molecules have mass, each water molecule acts like a tiny oscillator with a natural frequency of 2.45 billion hertz (2.45 gigahertz) (Figure 14.36).

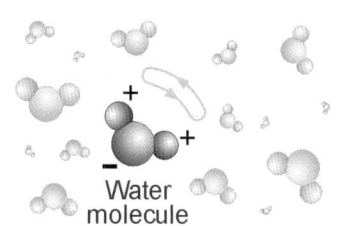

Figure 14.36: *A water molecule oscillates back and forth with a natural frequency of 2.45 GHz.*

Microwaves and resonance | The microwaves in a microwave oven are waves of electricity that oscillate 2.45 billion times per second (2.45 GHz). This frequency precisely matches the natural frequency at which water molecules rotate back and forth. Therefore, microwaves create resonance with water molecules and energy transfers very efficiently between the microwaves and the water molecules. The resulting transfer of wave energy is what heats up the water (Figure 14.37).

Other molecules are not resonant at 2.45 GHz | A dry cup has no water molecules in it. There are no molecules in ceramic that have natural frequencies near 2.45 GHz so the microwaves pass right through and are not absorbed. In fact, only liquid water molecules have a natural frequency of 2.45 GHz. Water molecules frozen as ice do not move as easily and have a different natural frequency. When heating frozen food in a microwave, the energy is absorbed by tiny amounts of liquid water. The liquid heats up nearby ice and melts more liquid. The defrost cycle on a microwave oven turns the microwaves on and off to allow time for the tiny pockets of liquid water to melt nearby ice and create more liquid.

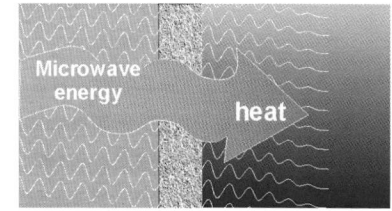

Figure 14.37: *Energy from microwaves is strongly absorbed by water molecules because of the 2.45 GHz resonance.*

Making microwaves

Making microwaves
For a microwave oven to work, the microwaves need to be created with a frequency of 2.45 GHz. This is done using a standing wave, similar to the standing wave you observed with the vibrating string. For microwaves, however, the boundary is metal since metal reflects microwaves. The wavelength of 2.45 GHz microwaves is 12.2 centimeters. To make a standing wave on the vibrating string, the length of the string was one half of a wavelength. The same is true for microwaves. The distance between the metal reflectors must be half a wavelength, or about 6.1 centimeters.

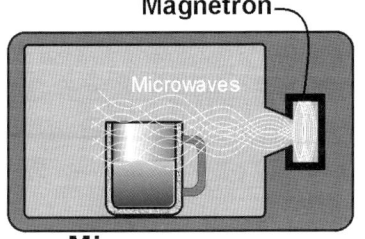

Microwave oven

The magnetron
The microwaves in an oven are created inside a device called a *magnetron*. The magnetron is a small metal chamber with inside dimensions that create a standing microwave with a resonant frequency of 2.45 GHz. The standing wave is driven by oscillations of electricity in a similar way as the standing wave on the string was driven by the oscillating force applied to the end of the string. Figure 14.38 shows a schematic of a magnetron and the standing wave inside. A real magnetron is not square inside but curved. Microwaves are three-dimensional waves and the inside of the magnetron is shaped to create a three-dimensional standing wave.

Getting microwaves out of the magnetron
A hole in the magnetron lets some of the wave's energy out to cook food. The inside of the microwave oven is lined with metal which reflects microwaves and keeps them inside the oven. The microwaves that come out of the magnetron bounce around the inside of the oven until they are absorbed by water molecules in the food you are trying to cook. You should never turn on an empty microwave oven. With nothing to absorb the energy, the microwaves can feed energy back into the magnetron. Feedback can cause the standing wave to reach amplitudes large enough to melt parts of the magnetron.

Figure 14.38: *A magnetron works like a metal box with a length of 6.1 centimeters, half the wavelength of a microwave. Inside the magnetron is a standing microwave with a frequency of 2.45 GHz.*

14.3 Natural Frequency and Resonance

281

Chapter 14 Review

Vocabulary Review

Match the following terms with the correct definition. There is one extra definition in the list that will not match any of the terms.

Set One

1. amplitude
2. frequency
3. wavelength
4. longitudinal wave
5. transverse wave
6. diffraction

a. Number of times a wave oscillates in a unit of time
b. Causes oscillations perpendicular to the direction of motion of the wave
c. Product of frequency and velocity
d. Greatest amount of movement from the equilibrium position
e. Causes oscillations parallel to the direction of motion of the wave
f. The spreading out of a wave when it passes through an opening
g. Distance from crest to crest on a wave

Set Two

1. harmonic
2. superposition
3. destructive
4. reflection
5. refraction
6. node

a. Waves bouncing off a boundary
b. Interference that results in a smaller amplitude
c. A standing wave pattern that occurs at multiples of the fundamental frequency
d. The absorption of a wave
e. Occurs when two waves are in the same system at the same time
f. Point on a standing wave that does not move
g. Change of direction by a wave as it crosses a boundary

Concept review

1. What is relationship between the frequency, wavelength and speed of a wave?

2. Explain the difference between a pulse and a wave.

3. The wave characteristics amplitude and wavelength are both measured in meters. How are they different?

4. The frequency of a wave is the number of vibrations or cycles per second. How is this related to the period of a wave?

5. Write a formula relating the speed of a wave to its period and wavelength.

6. Draw a transverse wave with an amplitude of 2 cm and a wavelength of 4 cm. Label a crest and a trough on the wave.

7. As a wave front strikes a boundary, four interactions may occur. Name and briefly describe each interaction.

8. Read the descriptions below and indicate which type of wave interaction has most likely occurred.

   a. Your friend yells to you from across the park but you are not able to hear him.

   b. As you drive on a hot summer day, you look off in the distance and see what appears to be water on the road.

   c. At sunset on a clear day the sun appears to be oval instead of round.

   d. People are talking in the next room and, with the door only slightly opened, you are able to hear their conversation.

9. How are standing waves created? What determines their amplitude?

10. A wave is propagated on a string by the exchange of potential and kinetic energy. Describe the points of maximum potential and kinetic energy for a vibrating string.

Problems

1. In glass, the speed of light is reduced. Calculate the speed of red light with a frequency of 4.33×10^{14} Hz if its wavelength is 4.17×10^{-7} m.

2. A sound wave travels at 340 m/s and has a frequency of 256 Hz. What is its wavelength?

3. A sound wave with a frequency of 512 Hz and a wavelength of 2.99 m is directed toward the bottom of a lake to measure its depth. If the echo of the sound from the bottom is heard 0.25 seconds later, how deep is the lake?

4. A honeybee moves its wings at a frequency of 225 hertz. How much time does it take the honeybee's wings to make one complete vibration?

5. Use the diagram of a spring below to answer the questions which follow:

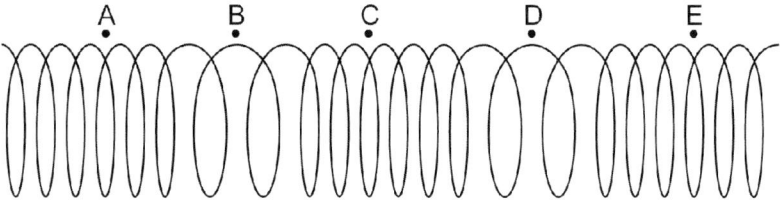

   a. Which type of wave is represented on the spring?

   b. Use the letters to represent an interval of one wavelength.

   c. Compressions are made horizontally. In what direction does the energy travel?

6. Below are diagrams representing interactions between waves and boundaries. Identify each interaction by name.

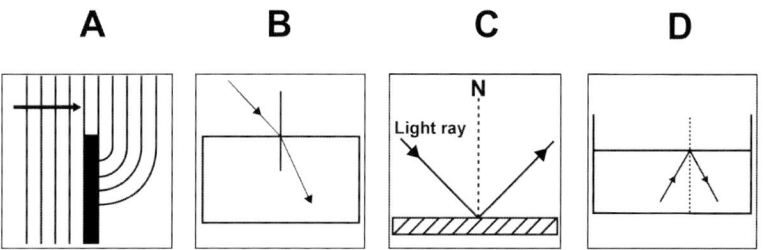

7. Two waves are superimposed in each diagram.

   a. Which pair of waves will completely cancel each other?

   b. Which pair of waves will result in a wave with the largest amplitude?

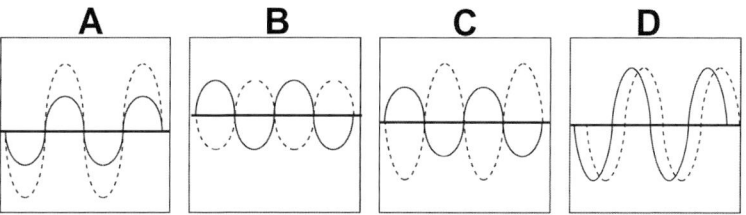

8. Using the diagram of four standing waves in the same medium, answer the questions below.

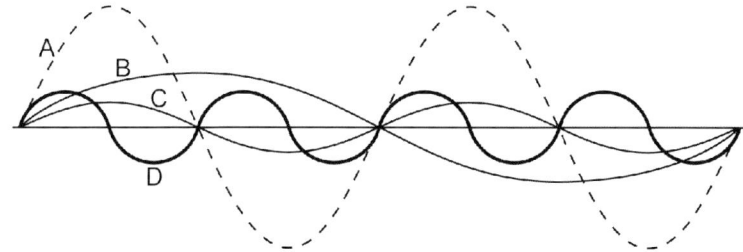

   a. Which two waves have the same wavelength?

   b. Which wave has the lowest frequency?

   c. Which wave has the smallest amplitude?

283

9. Two waves, A and B, travel in the same direction in the same medium at the same time. Graphs representing their motion are shown below. Answer the questions that follow based on the graphs.

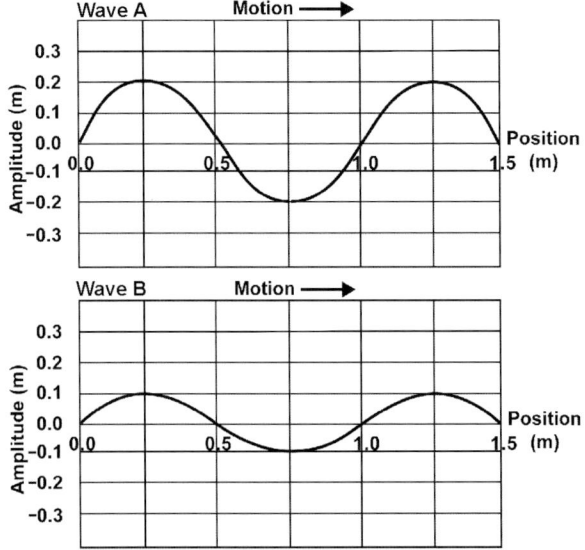

a. Use a sheet of graph paper to draw the wave that would be produced by the superposition of waves A and B.

b. What is the amplitude of the resultant wave?

c. What is the wavelength of the resultant wave?

10. The diagram represents a cork floating at point P on a transverse water wave. At the instant shown, in what direction is the cork moving?

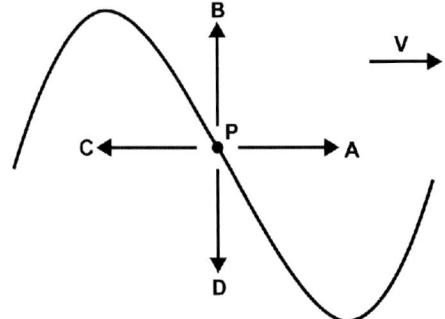

11. The diagram represents plane wave fronts being produced in a shallow water tank, referred to as a ripple tank. The frequency of the generator is 20 Hz. Answer the questions which follow based on this information and the diagram.

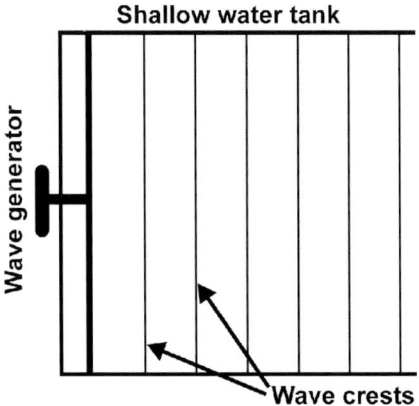

a. What is the period of the wave?

b. Use a ruler to determine the wavelength of the waves.

c. Determine the speed of the wave.

284

Unit 5

Waves and Sound

Chapter 15

Sound

Objectives for Chapter 15

By the end of this chapter you should be able to:

1. Explain how the pitch, loudness, and speed of sound are related to properties of waves.
2. Describe how sound is created and recorded.
3. Give examples of refraction, diffraction, absorption, and reflection of sound waves.
4. Explain the Doppler effect.
5. Give a practical example of resonance with sound waves.
6. Explain the relationship between the superposition principle and Fourier's theorem.
7. Describe how the meaning of sound is related to frequency and time.
8. Describe the musical scale, consonance, dissonance, and beats in terms of sound waves.

Terms and vocabulary words

pressure	frequency	pitch	superposition principle	decibel
speaker	acoustics	microphone	fundamental	wavelength
stereo	Doppler effect	supersonic	frequency spectrum	shock wave
resonance	node	antinode	dissonance	harmonic
reverberation	note	sonogram	Fourier's theorem	rhythm
musical scale	cochlea	consonance	longitudinal wave	beats
octave				

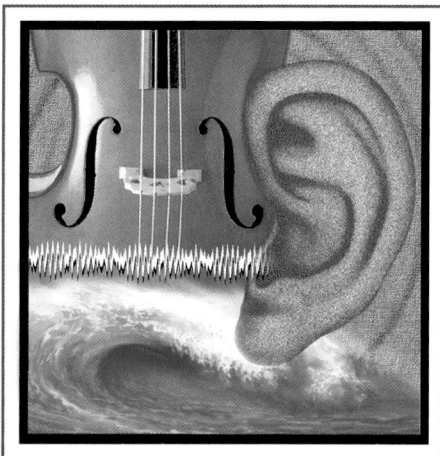

15.1 Properties of Sound

Like other waves, sound has the fundamental properties of frequency, wavelength, amplitude, and speed. Because sound is such a part of human experience, you probably already know its properties, but you know them by different names. For example, you almost never hear someone complain about the high amplitude of sound. What you hear instead is that the sound is too *loud*.

What is sound?

Sound is a wave that carries vibrations
Touch the moving cone of a speaker and you can feel it vibrating. Because the speaker is in air, its vibration spreads out through the air as sound. Sound is a vibration that travels as a wave through solids, liquids, or gases. Figure 15.1 shows an illustration of a speaker, a sound wave, and the oscillation of the air. The forward and backward movement of the speaker cone creates the wave that carries the sound through the air from the speaker to your ear.

Sound comes from vibrations too fast to see
Anything that vibrates makes sound. You can't directly see that sound is a wave because the frequency is too high to see the individual vibrations. The slowest vibration we can hear is 20 Hz, or 20 vibrations per second. Anything moving back and forth 20 times per second is just a blur. Your ear is most sensitive to sounds that vibrate between 100 Hz and 2,000 Hz. The sounds in a human voice are within this range.

Loudness and pitch
Sound has properties of loudness and pitch. The loudness of a sound depends on the amplitude of vibration. A speaker making a loud sound moves back and forth more than a speaker making a soft sound. The pitch of a sound depends on the frequency of vibration. A speaker making a high pitched sound like a siren vibrates with a higher frequency than the same speaker making a low pitched sound like thunder.

Sound moves through matter
Sound waves travel faster in liquids and solids than they do in air. You can hear voices through a solid wall because the sound wave in the air pushes on the wall and makes a sound wave in the wall. That sound wave travels through the solid wall and generates a new sound wave in the air on the other side. Sound *cannot* travel through the vacuum of space. Sound waves can only move through matter.

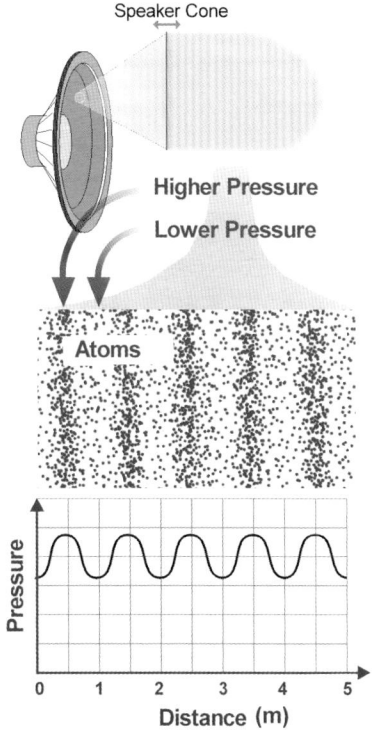

Figure 15.1: *What a sound wave might look like if you could see the atoms. The effect is greatly exaggerated to show the variation. In an actual sound wave, the difference in pressure between the highest and lowest is much smaller, less than one part in a million. From the graph you can see the wavelength of this sound is about one meter.*

The frequency of sound

Frequency and pressure change
The frequency of sound tells you how fast the pressure oscillates. The low humming noise from an electrical transformer has a frequency of 60 hertz (Hz). This means the oscillating pressure of the air goes back and forth 60 times per second. The scream of a fire truck siren may have a frequency of 3,000 Hz. This corresponds to 3,000 oscillations per second in the pressure of the air.

Frequency and pitch
We hear the different frequencies of sound as having different pitch. A low-frequency sound has a low pitch, like the rumble of a big truck. A high-frequency sound has a high pitch, like a whistle or siren. The range of frequencies that humans can hear varies from about 20 Hz to 20,000 Hz. Animals can hear different ranges of sound. For example, bats can hear sound up to frequencies of 200,000 Hz or more.

Most sound has more than one frequency
Most sound that we hear contains not just one but many frequencies. For example, three frequencies can be added to create a complex sound. Remember, we discussed the superposition principle in the last chapter. Complex sound is created by the superposition of many frequencies. In fact, the sound of the human voice contains thousand of different frequencies—all at once. (Figure 15.2).

Complex sound is made from many frequencies

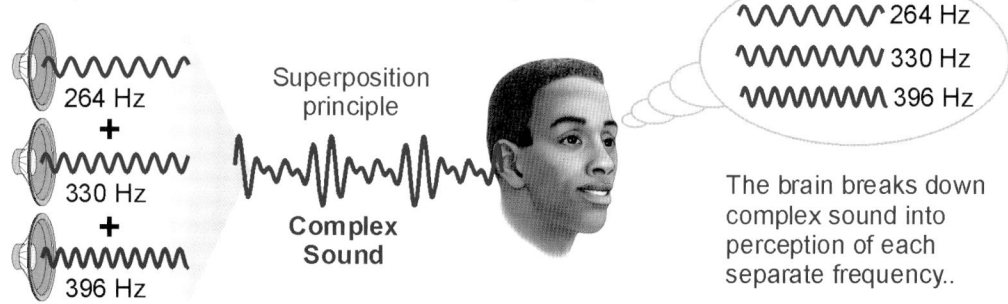

How we hear complex sound
When we hear complex sounds, the nerves in the ear respond separately to each different frequency. The brain interprets the signals from the ear and creates a "sonic image" from the frequencies. The meaning in different sounds is derived from the patterns in how the different frequencies get louder and softer.

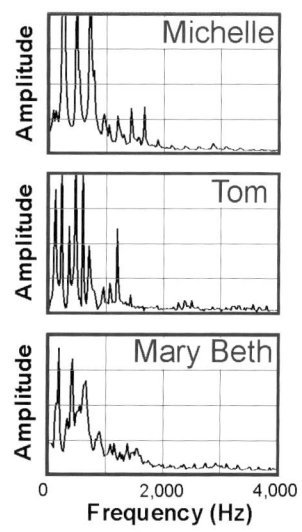

Figure 15.2: *The frequencies in three people's voices as they say the word "hello." The highest amplitudes are between 100 and 1,000 Hz. The peaks come from harmonics of each person's fundamental frequency. Women have higher fundamental frequencies than men, the peaks for the two women's voices are farther apart than for the male voice.*

The loudness of sound

The decibel scale   The loudness of sound is measured in decibels (dB). As you might expect, loudness is determined mostly by the amplitude of a sound wave. The amplitude of a sound wave is one-half of the difference between the highest pressure and the lowest pressure in the wave. Because the pressure change in a sound wave is very small, almost no one uses pressure to measure loudness. Instead we use the decibel scale. Most sounds fall between 0 and 100 on the decibel scale, making it a very convenient number to understand and use.

Table 15.1: Some common sounds and their loudness in decibels

10-15 dB	A quiet whisper 3 feet away
30 dB	Background sound level at a house in the country
40 dB	Background sound level at a house in the city
45-55 dB	The noise level in an average restaurant
65 dB	Ordinary conversation 3 feet away
70 dB	City traffic
90 dB	A jackhammer cutting up the street 10 feet away
110 dB	A hammer striking a steel plate 2 feet away (very loud)
120 dB	The threshold of physical pain from loudness

The sensitivity of the ear   How we hear the loudness of sound is affected by the frequency of the sound as well as by the amplitude. The Equal Loudness Curve on the right shows how sounds of different frequencies compare. Sounds near 2,000 Hz seem louder than sounds of other frequencies, even at the same decibel level. For example, the Equal Loudness Curve shows that a 40 dB sound at 2,000 Hz sounds just as loud as an 80 dB sound at 50 Hz. The human ear is most sensitive to sounds between 300 and 3,000 Hz. The ear is less sensitive to sounds outside this range. Most of the frequencies that make up speech are between 300 and 3,000 Hz.

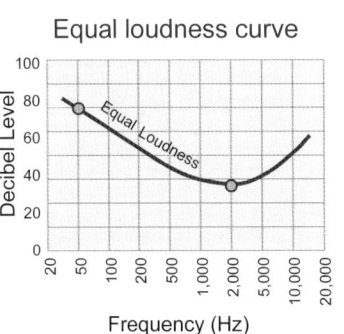

Equal loudness curve

The decibel scale

The decibel scale is a *logarithmic* measure of the amplitude of sound waves. This is different from linear measures you are familiar with. In a logarithmic scale, equal intervals correspond to multiplying by 10 instead of adding equal amounts. For example, every increase of 20 decibels (dB) means the pressure wave has 10 times greater amplitude.

Logarithmic scale	Linear scale
Decibels (dB)	Amplitude
0	1
20	10
40	100
60	1,000
80	10,000
100	100,000
120	1,000,000

We use the decibel scale because our ears can hear such a wide range of amplitudes. Our ears also hear changes in loudness proportional to decibels and not to amplitude. Thus, every 20 dB increase sounds about twice as loud.

How sound is created

Vibrations create sound
Anything that vibrates with a frequency between 20 and 20,000 Hz will make a sound that people can hear. The air around you is probably full of overlapping sound waves because so many objects in nature and technology vibrate. When a motor spins, it vibrates and the vibration creates a sound wave that you hear as a low hum. When your heart beats it also makes a vibration that doctors use a stethoscope to hear. Since sound travels through any material, solid, liquid, or gas, sound waves created in one place spread easily.

Voices
The human voice is a complex sound that starts in the larynx, a small structure at the top of your windpipe. The term *vocal cords* is somewhat misleading because the sound-producing structures are not really cords but are folds of expandable tissue that extend across a hollow chamber known as the voice box. The sound that starts in the larynx is changed by passing through openings in the throat and mouth (Figure 15.3). Different sounds are made by changing both the vibrations in the larynx and the shape of the openings.

Speakers
A **speaker** is a device that is specially designed to reproduce sounds accurately. The working parts of a typical speaker include a magnet, a coil of wire, and a cone. When electricity is flowing through it, a coil of wire acts like a magnet. When the electricity flows one way, the magnetism created by the coil is attracted to the central magnet and the speaker cone moves outward (Figure 15.4). When the electricity in the coil is reversed, the coil is repelled by the central magnet and the speaker cone moves inward. To create sound, electricity in the coil oscillates. The coil moves back and forth with the same frequency, and sound of that frequency is created by the movement of the cone attached to the coil.

Acoustics
Reducing the loudness of sound is important in many applications. For example, a library might want to absorb all sound to maintain quiet. A recording studio might want to block sound from the outside from mixing with sound from the inside. **Acoustics** is the science and technology of sound. Knowledge of acoustics is important to many careers, from the people who design stereo speakers to the architects who designed your school.

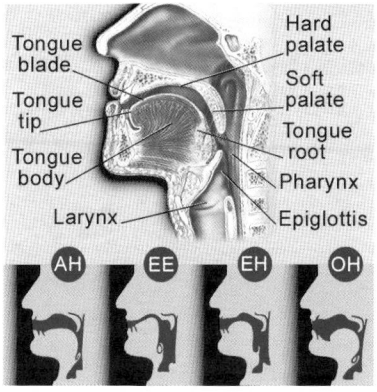

Figure 15.3: *The human voice is created by a combination of vibrating folds of skin in the larynx and the resonant shapes of the throat and mouth.*

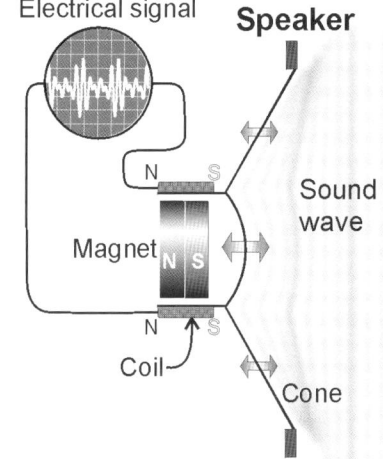

Figure 15.4: *How a speaker produces sound.*

Recording sound

Music was rare 100 years ago

We often take for granted that we can listen to our favorite music anytime we wish. This was not true 100 years ago, when the only way to hear music was to be close to the musicians while they were playing. Very few people were able to listen to a variety of musicians so as to even *have* a favorite. The recording of sound was a technological breakthrough that transformed human experience.

The microphone

To record a sound you must store the pattern of vibrations in a way that can be replayed and be true to the original sound. A common way to record sound starts with a microphone. A microphone transforms a sound wave into an electrical signal with the same pattern of oscillation (top of Figure 15.5).

Analog to digital conversion

In modern digital recording, a sensitive circuit called an *analog to digital converter* measures the electrical signal 44,100 times per second. Each measurement consists of a number between 0 and 65,536 corresponding to the amplitude of the signal. One second of compact-disk-quality sound is a list of 44,100 numbers. The numbers are recorded as data on a CD.

Playback of recorded sound

To play the sound back, the string of numbers is read by a laser and converted into electrical signals again by a second circuit. The second circuit is a *digital to analog converter*, and it reverses the process of the previous circuit. The playback circuit converts the string of numbers back into an electrical signal. The electrical signal is amplified until it is powerful enough to move the coil in a speaker and reproduce the sound (bottom of Figure 15.5).

Stereo sound

Most of the music you hear has been recorded in stereo. A stereo recording is actually two recordings, one to be played from the right speaker and the other from the left speaker. Stereo sound feels more "live" because it creates slight differences in phase between sound reaching your left and right ears. When you listen to a live concert you can hear that a singer is on the left and a guitar player is on the right. This is because the sound from the singer reaching your left ear is slightly out of phase (ahead) of the sound reaching your right ear. Your brain interprets the difference in phase to provide a sense of depth. A stereo recording can do the same thing. If you close your eyes and listen to a good stereo recording, you can hear different instruments coming from different places.

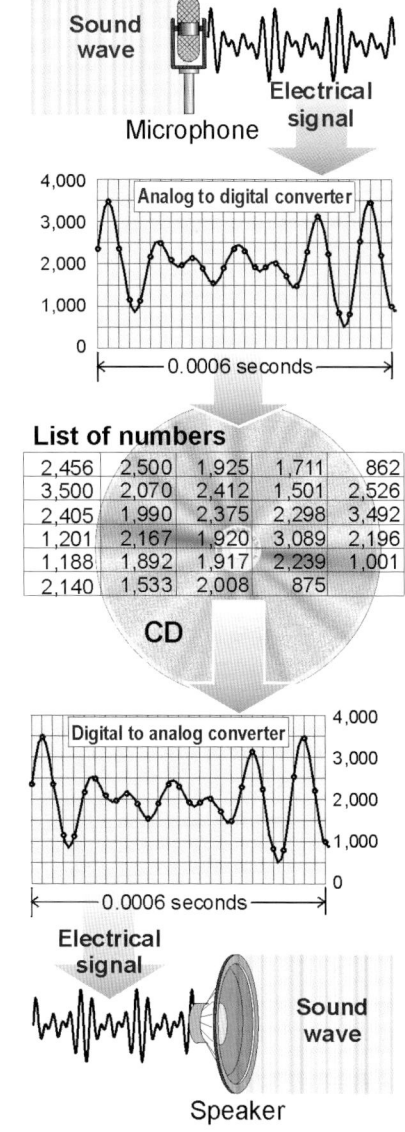

Figure 15.5: *The process of digital sound reproduction.*

15.2 Sound Waves

Scientifically, sound is one of the simplest and most common kinds of waves—but what a huge influence it has on our everyday experience of life. We know sound is a wave because:

1. Sound has both frequency (that we hear directly) and wavelength (demonstrated by simple experiments).

2. The speed of sound is frequency times wavelength.

3. Resonance happens with sound.

4. Sound can be reflected, refracted, and absorbed and also shows evidence of interference and diffraction.

A close look at a sound wave

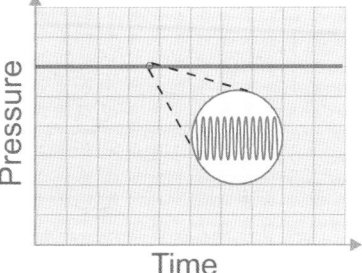

Figure 15.6: *The amplitude of a sound wave is very small. Even an 80 dB noise (quite loud) creates a pressure variation of only a few millionths of an atmosphere.*

Close-up of a sound wave
A sound wave is a wave of alternating high-pressure and low-pressure regions of air. Anything that vibrates in air creates a sound wave. The wave travels away from the source and eventually reaches our ear, where it vibrates the eardrum and we hear the sound.

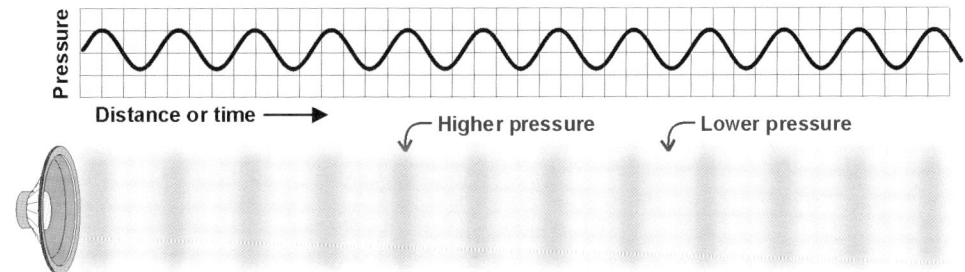

The pressure waves are small
The actual oscillations in pressure from a sound wave are very small (Figure 15.6). Table 15.1 gives some examples of the amplitude for different decibel levels. As you can see, the human ear is remarkably sensitive. For instance, if you were looking at a pile of a million coins, you could not notice one missing. But the human ear can easily hear a pressure wave that is only two parts different out of 100 million. This exquisite sensitivity is why hearing can be damaged by listening to loud sounds for a long time.

Table 15.1:
Loudness and amplitude of sound waves in air

Loudness in decibels	Amplitude of pressure wave (fraction of 1 atmosphere)
20 dB	2 / 1,000,000,000
40 dB	2 / 100,000,000
80 dB	2 / 1,000,000
120 dB	2 / 10,000

The wavelength of sound

Sound is a longitudinal wave

Sound waves are longitudinal waves because the air is compressed in the direction of travel. You can think of a sound wave like the compression wave on a Slinky™. Anything that vibrates creates sound waves as long as there is air or some other matter. Sound does *not* travel in space (a vacuum). Science fiction movies always add sound to scenes of spaceship battles. Were the scenes accurate, there would be silence because there is no air in space to carry the sound waves.

Range of wavelengths of sound

The wavelength of sound in air is comparable to the size of everyday objects. The chart below gives some typical frequencies and wavelengths for sound in air. As with other waves, the wavelength of a sound is inversely related to its frequency (Figure 15.7). A low-frequency 20 hertz sound has a wavelength the size of a large classroom. At the upper range of hearing, a 20,000 hertz sound has a wavelength about the width of your finger.

Table 15.2: Frequency and wavelength for some typical sounds

Frequency (Hz)	Wavelength	Typical source
20	17 meters	rumble of thunder
100	3.4 meters	bass guitar
500	70 cm (27")	average male voice
1,000	34 cm (13")	female soprano singer
2,000	17 cm (6.7")	fire truck siren
5,000	7 cm (2.7")	highest note on a piano
10,000	3.4 cm (1.3")	whine of a jet turbine
20,000	1.7 cm (2/3")	highest pitched sound you can hear

Why the wavelength of sound is important

Although we usually think about different sounds in terms of frequency, the wavelength can also be important. If you want to make sound of a certain wavelength, you often need to have a vibrating object that is similar in size to the wavelength (Figure 15.8). This is the reason pipes for organs are made in all different sizes. Each pipe is designed for a specific wavelength of sound.

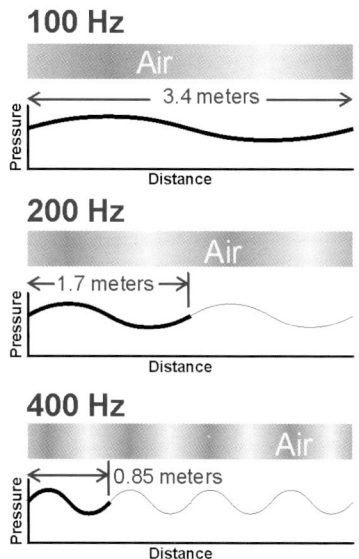

Figure 15.7: *The frequency and wavelength of sound are inversely related. When the frequency goes up, the wavelength goes down proportionally.*

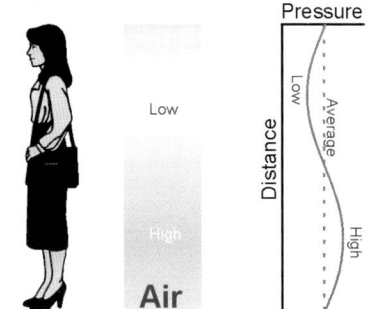

Figure 15.8: *A 200 Hz sound has a wavelength about equal to the height of a person.*

The Doppler effect

Definition of the Doppler effect If an object is stationary, observers on all sides will hear the same frequency. When an object is moving, the sound it makes will *not* be the same to all observers. People moving with the object or to the side of it hear the sound as if the object were stationary. People in front of the object hear sound of higher frequency. People behind the object hear sound of lower frequency. The shift in frequency caused by motion is called the Doppler effect and it occurs when a sound source is moving at speeds less than the speed of sound.

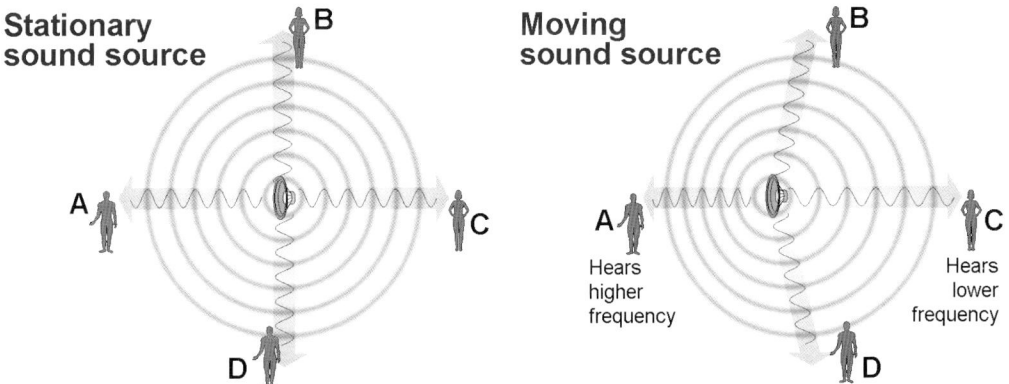

Stationary sound source B A C D

Moving sound source B A Hears higher frequency C Hears lower frequency D

The cause of the Doppler effect The Doppler effect occurs because an observer hears the frequency at which wave fronts arrive. Wave fronts are closer together in front of a moving object because the object moves forward between wave crests. Observer (A) in front hears a higher frequency because the wave fronts are closer together. The opposite is true for an observer behind. The motion of the object makes more space between successive waves. According to observer (C), the wave fronts get farther apart and the frequency goes down. The greater the relative speed, the larger the shift in frequency.

Demonstrating the Doppler effect You can observe the Doppler effect with a small battery-powered beeper. When the beeper is standing still, it makes a steady sound of a certain frequency. Have a friend whirl the beeper around their head on a string. The sound will no longer have a steady frequency. The frequency shifts up and down with each rotation according to whether the beeper is moving toward you or away from you.

Doppler radar

The Doppler effect also happens with reflected waves, including light waves. With Doppler radar, an electromagnetic wave is sent out from a transmitter. The wave reflects from moving objects, such as a car. The frequency of the reflected wave is increased if the car is moving toward the source and decreases if the car is moving away.

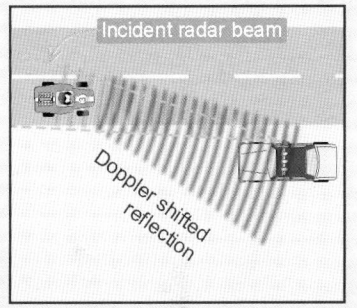

Incident radar beam

Doppler shifted reflection

The amount of the Doppler shift is proportional to the speed of the car. The speed of the car can be accurately measured by comparing the original frequency with the frequency of the reflected wave. Doppler radar is used to enforce speed limits, to measure the speed of wind in storms, and in many other applications where speed needs to be measured from a distance.

The speed of sound

Sound is fast, about 340 meters per second
: The speed of sound in air is 343 meters per second (660 miles per hour) at one atmosphere of pressure and room temperature (21°C). The speed increases with temperature and also with pressure. Passenger jets fly slower than sound, usually around 400 to 500 miles per hour. An object is subsonic when it is moving slower than sound.

Sonic booms
: We use the term supersonic to describe motion at speeds faster than the speed of sound. Many military jets are capable of supersonic flight however, only one kind of passenger jet, the Concorde, is supersonic (Figure 15.9). If you were on the ground watching the Concorde fly toward you, there would be silence. The sound would be *behind* the plane, racing to catch up. A shock wave forms where the wave fronts pile up (diagram below). The pressure change across the shock wave is what causes a very loud sound known as a *sonic boom*.

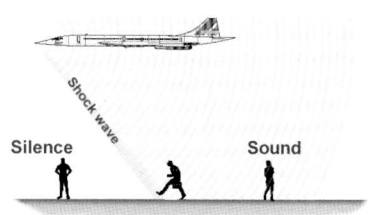

Figure 15.9: *The Concorde is a supersonic jet. If one flew overhead, you would not hear the sound until the plane was far beyond you. The boundary between sound and silence is called a shock wave. It is almost as if all the sound were compressed into a thin layer of air. The person in the middle hears a sonic boom as the shock wave passes over him. Because the sonic boom can shatter windows, planes are not allowed to fly over cities at supersonic speeds.*

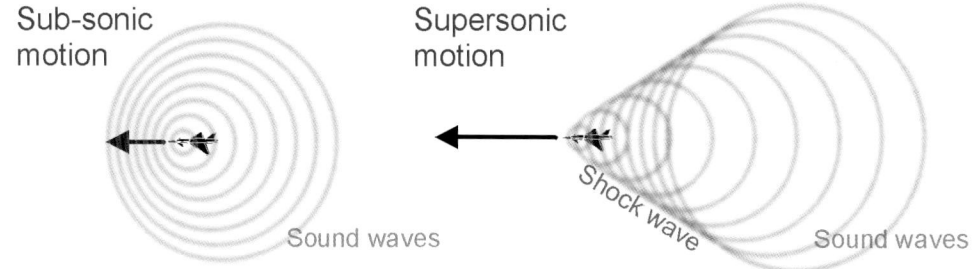

The speed depends on pressure and temperature
: The speed of a sound wave in air depends on how fast air molecules are moving. If the molecules are moving slowly (cold), sound does not travel as quickly as when they are moving fast (hot). The kind of molecules also affects the speed of sound. Air is made up of mostly of oxygen (O_2) and nitrogen (N_2) molecules. Lighter molecules, like hydrogen (H_2), move faster for a given temperature. Because of the speed difference, sound travels faster in hydrogen than in air.

Sound in liquids and solids
: The speed of sound in materials is often faster than in air (Figure 15.10). The restoring forces in solid steel, for example, are much stronger than in a gas. Stronger restoring forces tend to raise the speed of sound. People used to listen for an approaching train by putting an ear to the rails. The sound of an approaching train travels much faster through steel rails than through air.

Material	Sound speed (m/sec)
Air	330
Helium	965
Water	1530
Wood (average)	2000
Gold	3240
Steel	5940

Figure 15.10: *The speed of sound in various materials (helium and air at 0°C and 1 atmospheric pressure).*

294

Standing waves and resonance

Resonance of sound Spaces enclosed by boundaries can create resonance with sound waves. Almost all musical instruments use resonance to make musical sounds. A pan pipe is a good example of resonance in an instrument. A pan pipe is made of many tubes of different lengths (Figure 15.11); one end of each tube is closed and the other end is open. Blowing across the open end of a tube creates a standing wave inside the tube. The frequency of the standing wave is the frequency of sound given off by the pipe. Longer pipes create longer wavelength standing waves and make lower frequencies of sound. Shorter pipes create shorter wavelength standing waves and therefore make higher frequencies of sound.

Standing wave patterns The closed end of a pipe is a closed boundary. Remember from the previous chapter that a closed boundary makes a node in the standing wave. The open end of a pipe is an open boundary to a standing wave in the pipe. An open boundary makes an antinode in the standing wave. Figure 15.11 shows different standing waves that have a node at the closed end and an antinode at the open end. Notice that the wavelength of the fundamental mode is four times the length of the pipe. It follows that a pipe will be resonant to a certain sound when its length is one-fourth the wavelength of the sound.

Designing a musical instrument Suppose you wish to make a pipe that makes a sound with a frequency of 660 hertz (the note E). Using the relationship between frequency and wavelength, you calculate the required wavelength is (343 m/sec) ÷ (660 Hz) = 0.52 meters. The length of pipe needs to be one-fourth of the wavelength to make a resonance in the fundamental mode. One quarter of 52 centimeters is 13 centimeters. If you make a pipe that is 13 centimeters long with one closed end, it will have a natural frequency of 660 hertz. This is the principle on which musical instruments are designed. Sounds of different frequencies are made by standing waves. A particular sound is selected by designing the length of a vibrating system to be resonant at the desired frequency.

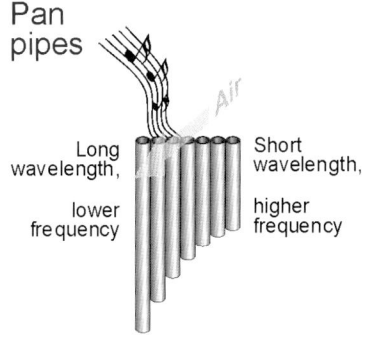

Pan pipes

Long wavelength, lower frequency

Short wavelength, higher frequency

Standing waves in a pan pipe

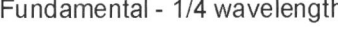

Closed end   Open end

Node   Antinode

wavelength

Fundamental - 1/4 wavelength

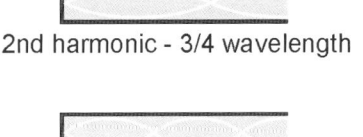

2nd harmonic - 3/4 wavelength

3rd harmonic - 1 1/4 wavelength

Figure 15.11: *A pan pipe is made from tubes of different length. The diagrams show the fundamental and harmonics for standing waves of sound in a pan pipe.*

Interaction between sound waves and boundaries

Interactions of sound and materials

Like other waves, sound waves can be reflected by surfaces and refracted as they pass from one material to another. Diffraction causes sound waves to spread out through small openings. Carpet and soft materials can absorb sound waves. Figure 15.12 shows examples of sound and materials.

Reverberation

Sound waves reflect from hard surfaces. In a good concert hall, the reflected sound adds to the direct sound. You hear a multiple echo called reverberation. The right amount of reverberation makes the sound seem livelier and richer. Too much reverberation and the sound gets muddy from too many reflections. Concert hall designers work hard on the shape and surface of the walls and ceiling to provide the best reverberation. Some concert halls even have movable panels that can be raised or lowered from the ceiling to help shape the sound.

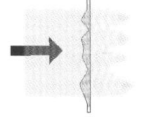 **Refraction**  **Reflection**

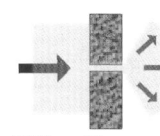 **Diffraction**  **Absorption**

Figure 15.12: *Sound displays all the properties of waves in its interactions with materials and boundaries.*

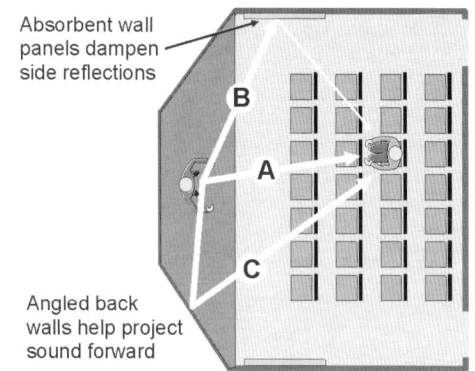

Absorbent wall panels dampen side reflections

Angled back walls help project sound forward

Making a good concert hall

Direct sound (**A**) reaches the listener along with reflected sound (**B, C**) from the walls. The shape of the room and the surfaces of the walls must be designed so that there is some reflected sound, but not too much.

Interference can also affect sound quality

Reverberation also causes interference of sound waves. When two waves interfere, the total can be louder or softer than either wave alone. The diagram above shows a musician and an audience of one person. The sound reflected from the walls interferes as it reaches the listener. If the distances are just right, one reflected wave might be out of phase with the other. The result is that the sound is quieter at that spot. An acoustic engineer would call it a *dead spot* in the hall. Dead spots are areas where destructive interference causes some of the sound to cancel with its own reflections. It is also possible to make very loud spots where sound interferes constructively. The best concert halls are designed to minimize both dead spots and loud spots.

Ultrasound

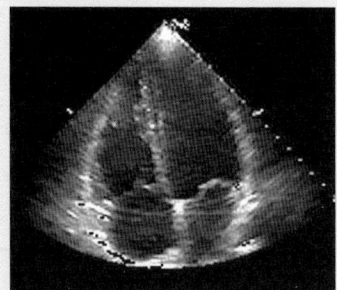

Ultrasound is sound that has very high frequency, often 100,000 Hz or more. We cannot hear ultrasound, but it can pass through the human body easily. Medical ultrasound instruments use the refraction and reflection of sound waves inside the body to create images. Doctors often take ultrasound pictures of the human body. The ultrasound image pictured above is a heart.

The frequency spectrum and Fourier's theorem

Adding waves — Imagine holding a microphone in a noisy room with music playing and people talking. The microphone records a single "wave form" that describes the variation of pressure with time. The recorded wave form is usually complex (Figure 15.13). Yet you could easily distinguish the music from individual voices if you were in the room. The complex wave form recorded by the microphone is the same thing your ears hear. Somehow, this single complex wave form must contain all the sound from the music and voices.

Fourier's theorem — Fourier's theorem says that any wave form can be represented as a sum of single frequency waves. Remember that the superposition principle stated that many single waves add up to one complex wave. Fourier's theorem says the opposite is also true: Any complex wave can be made from a sum of single frequency waves. In fact, complex waves are best thought of in terms of *component frequencies*. A complex wave is really a sum of component frequencies, each with its own amplitude and phase. Figure 15.14 shows how a square wave can be built up from component frequencies.

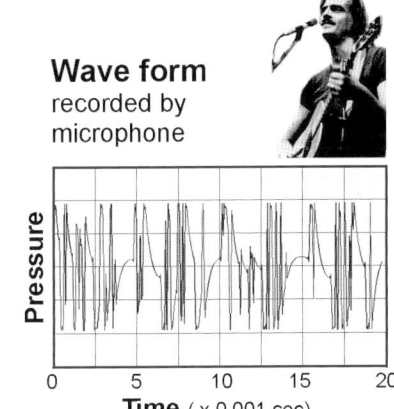

Wave form recorded by microphone

Figure 15.13: *The recorded wave form from 0.02 seconds of music.*

The **spectrum** shows the frequencies that make up a complex wave form.

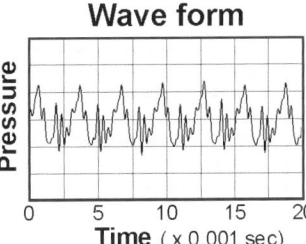

Wave form

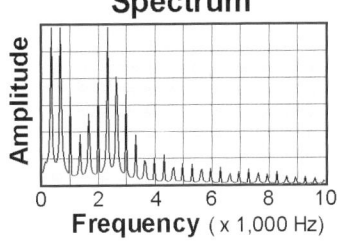

Spectrum

Frequency spectrum — A **frequency spectrum** is a graph that shows the amplitude of each component frequency in a complex wave. For example, the wave form in the diagram above is from an acoustic guitar playing the note E. The frequency spectrum shows that the complex sound of the guitar is made from many frequencies; in fact, from the evenly spaced peaks you can identify many harmonics in the sound.

Wave form and spectrum change with time — Both the wave form and the spectrum change as the sound changes. The wave form and spectrum in the diagram represent a sample of only 0.02 seconds from the sound. The meaning in sound comes from the changing pattern of frequencies.

Original wave

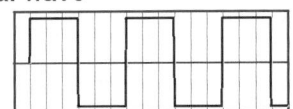

First five components

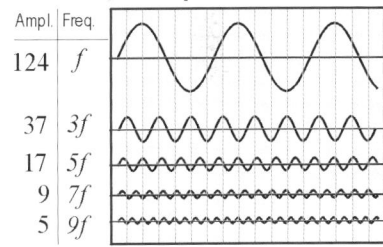

Ampl.	Freq.
124	f
37	$3f$
17	$5f$
9	$7f$
5	$9f$

Sum of first five components

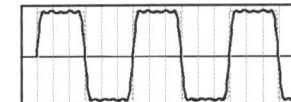

Figure 15.14: *Building a square wave from components with different frequencies and amplitudes.*

15.3 Sound, Perception, and Music

Sound is everywhere in our daily environment. Hearing is one of the most important of our senses and the ear and brain are constantly perceiving and processing sound. We actively use sound to communicate and we listen to sound for information about what is going on around us. In this section you will learn about how we hear a sound wave and how the ear and brain construct meaning from sound. This section will also introduce some of the science behind musical sound. Musical sound is a rich language of rhythm and frequency, developed over thousands of years of human culture.

Patterns of frequency

Constructing meaning from sound | Think about reading one single word from a story. You recognize the word, but it does not tell you much about the story. When you read the whole story you put all the words together to get the meaning. The brain does a similar thing with different frequencies of sound. A single frequency by itself does not have much meaning. The meaning comes from patterns in many frequencies together.

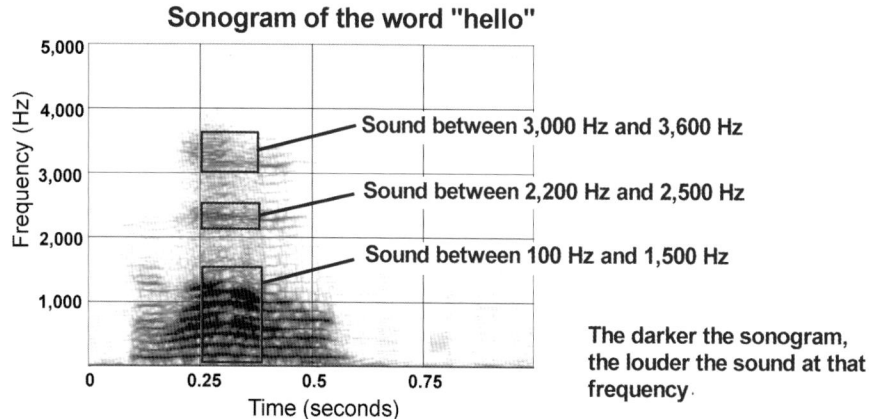

Sonograms | A **sonogram** is a special kind of graph that shows how loud sound is at different frequencies (Figure 15.15). The sonogram above is for a male voice saying "hello." The word lasts from 0.1 seconds to about 0.6 seconds. You can see lots of sound below 1,500 hertz and two bands of sound near 2,350 and 3,300 hertz. Every person's sonogram is different, even when saying the same word.

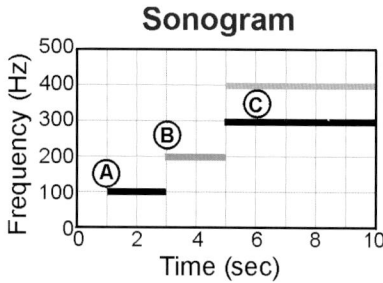

Figure 15.15: *A sonogram shows how the loudness of different frequencies of sound changes with time.*

Reading a sonogram

A sonogram includes information about frequency, loudness, and time. The vertical axis represents frequency. The example in Figure 15.15 shows frequencies from 0 to 500 Hz. The horizontal axis represents time. Darker areas represent louder sounds.

The example sonogram shows four frequencies of sound over a period of 10 seconds.

A) A loud sound at 100 Hz that lasts from 1 to 3 seconds.

B) A softer sound at 200 Hz that lasts from 3 to 5 seconds.

C) A soft sound at 400 Hz and a louder sound at 300 Hz, both starting at 5 seconds.

298

How we hear sound

Hearing sound

We get our sense of hearing from the cochlea, a tiny fluid-filled organ in the inner ear (Figure 15.16). The inner ear actually has two important functions: providing our sense of hearing and our sense of balance. The three semicircular canals near the cochlea are also filled with fluid. Fluid moving in each of the three canals tells the brain whether the body is moving left-right, up-down, or forward-backward.

How the cochlea works

The perception of sound starts with the eardrum. The eardrum vibrates in response to sound waves in the ear canal. The three delicate bones of the inner ear transmit the vibration of the eardrum to the side of the cochlea. The fluid in the spiral of the cochlea vibrates and creates waves that travel up the spiral. The spiral channel of the cochlea starts out large and gets narrower near the end. The nerves near the beginning see a relatively large channel and respond to longer-wavelength, lower-frequency sound. The nerves at the small end of the channel respond to shorter-wavelength, higher-frequency sound.

The range of human hearing

The range of human hearing is between 20 hertz and 20,000 hertz (or 20 kilohertz, abbreviated kHz). The combination of the eardrum, bones, and the cochlea all contribute to the limited range of hearing. You could not hear a sound at 50,000 Hz (50 kHz), even at 100 decibels (loud). Animals such as cats and dogs can hear much higher frequencies because of more sensitive structures in their inner ears.

Hearing ability changes with time

Hearing varies greatly with people and changes with age. Some people can hear very high frequency sounds and other people cannot. People gradually lose high frequency hearing with age. Most adults cannot hear frequencies above 15,000 Hz, while children can often hear to 20,000 Hz.

Hearing can be damaged by loud noise

Hearing is affected by exposure to loud or high-frequency noise. The nerve signals that carry sensation of sound to the brain are created by tiny hairs that shake when the fluid in the cochlea is vibrated. Listening to loud sounds for a long time can cause the hairs to weaken or break off. Before there were safety rules about noise, people who worked in mines or other noisy places often became partly deaf by the time they retired. It is smart to protect your ears by keeping the volume reasonable and wearing ear protection if you have to stay in a loud place. Many musicians wear earplugs to protect their hearing when playing concerts.

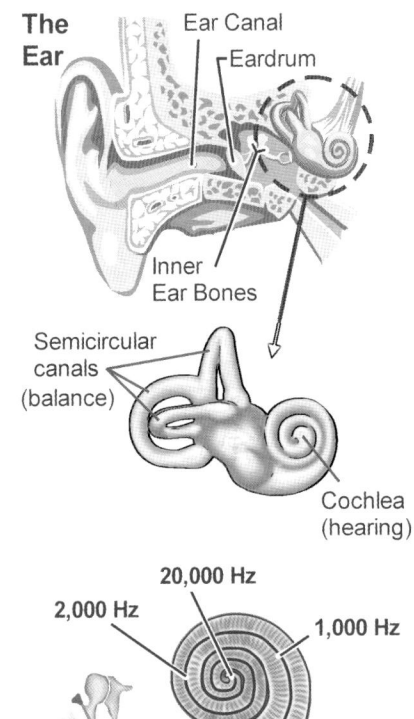

Figure 15.16: *The structure of the inner ear. When the eardrum vibrates, three small bones transmit the vibration to the cochlea. The vibrations make waves inside the cochlea, which vibrates nerves in the spiral. Each part of the spiral is sensitive to a different frequency.*

Music

Pitch — The pitch of a sound is how high or low we hear its frequency. Pitch and frequency usually mean the same thing. However, because pitch depends on the human ear and brain, sometimes pitch and frequency can be different. The way we hear a pitch can be affected by the sounds we heard before and after.

Rhythm — **Rhythm** is a regular time pattern in a sound. Rhythm can be loud and soft, tap-tap-TAP-tap-tap-TAP-tap-tap-TAP. Rhythm can be made with sound and silence or with different pitches. People respond naturally to rhythm. Cultures are distinguished by their music and the special rhythms used in the music.

The musical scale — Music is a combination of sound and rhythm that we find pleasant. Styles of music can be very different however, all music is created from carefully chosen frequencies of sound. Most of the music you listen to is created from a pattern of frequencies called a **musical scale**. Each frequency in the scale is called a **note**. The range between any frequency and twice that frequency is called an **octave** (see sidebar). Notes that are an octave apart in frequency share the same name. Within the octave there are 8 primary notes in the Western musical scale. Each of the eight notes is related to the first note in the scale by a ratio of frequencies (see sidebar). The scale that starts on the note C (264 Hz) is show in the diagram below.

C major scale								
Note	C	D	E	F	G	A	B	C
Frequency (Hz)	264	297	330	352	396	440	495	528
Ratio to C-264	$\frac{1}{1}$ $\left(\frac{264}{264}\right)$	$\frac{9}{8}$ $\left(\frac{297}{264}\right)$	$\frac{5}{4}$ $\left(\frac{330}{264}\right)$	$\frac{4}{3}$ $\left(\frac{352}{264}\right)$	$\frac{3}{2}$ $\left(\frac{396}{264}\right)$	$\frac{5}{3}$ $\left(\frac{440}{264}\right)$	$\frac{15}{8}$ $\left(\frac{495}{264}\right)$	$\frac{2}{1}$ $\left(\frac{528}{264}\right)$

Choosing the notes

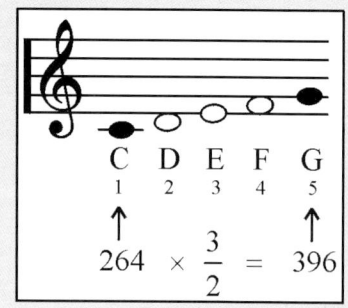

C D E F G
1 2 3 4 5

$$264 \times \frac{3}{2} = 396$$

The notes on a musical scale are related to the first note by ratios of frequency. For example, the fifth note has a frequency 3/2 times the frequency of the first note. If the first note is C-264 Hz, then the fifth note has a frequency of 1.5 times 264, or G-396 Hz.

Octaves

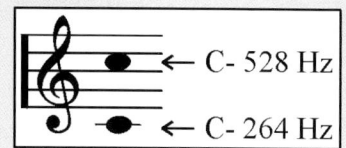

← C- 528 Hz

← C- 264 Hz

Two notes are an octave apart when the frequency of one note is double the frequency of the other. Notes that are an octave apart are given the same name because they sound similar to the ear. For example, the note C has a frequency of 264 Hz. Frequencies of 132 Hz and 528 Hz are also named "C" because they are an octave apart from C-264 Hz.

Consonance, dissonance, and beats

Harmony Music can have a profound effect on people's moods. The tense, dramatic sound-track of a horror movie is a vital part of the audience's experience. Harmony is the study of how sounds work together to create effects desired by the composer. Harmony is based on the frequency relationships of the musical scale.

Beats An interesting thing happens when two frequencies of sound are close, but not exactly the same. The phase of the two waves changes in a way that makes the loudness of the sound seem to oscillate or beat. Sometimes the two waves are in phase, and the total is louder than either wave separately. Other times the waves are out of phase and they cancel each other out, making the sound quieter. The rapid alternation in amplitude is what we hear as beats. Most people find beats very unpleasant to listen to. Out-of-tune instruments make beats. The frequencies in the musical scale are specifically chosen to reduce the occurrence of beats.

Beats come from adding two waves that are slightly different in frequency

Why we hear beats

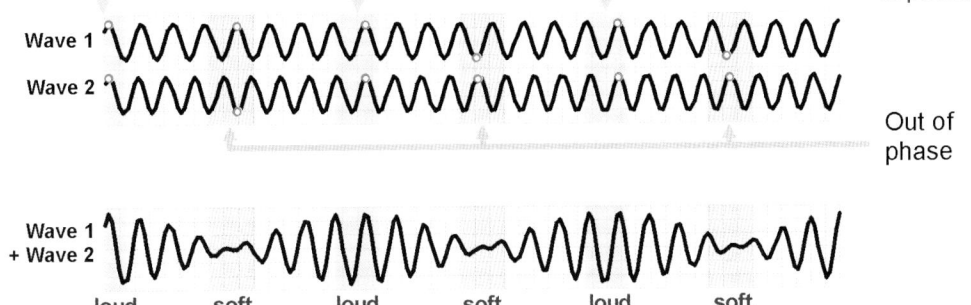

Consonance and dissonance When we hear more than one frequency of sound and the combination sounds good, we call it consonance. When the combination sounds bad or unsettling, we call it dissonance. Consonance and dissonance are related to beats. When frequencies are far enough apart that there are no beats, we get consonance. When frequencies are too close together, we hear beats that are the cause of dissonance. Dissonance is often used to create tension or drama. Consonance can be used to create feelings of balance and comfort.

Echolocation and beats

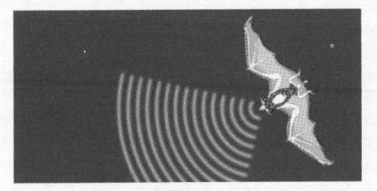

Bats navigate at night using ultrasound waves instead of light waves. A bat's voice is like a "sonic flashlight" shining a beam of sound. A bat emits bursts of sound that rise in frequency, called "chirps." When the sound reflects off an insect, the bat's ears receive the echo. Since the frequency of the chirp is always changing, the echo comes back with a slightly different frequency. The difference between the echo and the chirp makes *beats* that the bat can hear. The beat frequency is proportional to how far the insect is from the bat. A bat can triangulate the insect's position by comparing the echo from the left ear with that from the right ear.

Harmonics and the sound of instruments

The same note can sound different

The same note sounds different when played on different instruments. As an example, suppose you listen to the note C-264 Hz played on a guitar and the same C-264 Hz played on a piano. A musician would recognize both notes as being C because they have the same frequency and pitch. But the guitar sounds like a guitar and the piano sounds like a piano. If the frequency of the note is the same, what gives each instrument its characteristic sound?

Instruments make mixtures of frequencies

The answer is that the sound from an instrument is not a single pure frequency. The most important frequency is still the fundamental note (C-264 Hz, for example). The variation comes from the harmonics. Remember, harmonics are frequencies that are multiples of the fundamental note. We have already learned that a string can vibrate at many harmonics. The same is true for all instruments. A single C from a grand piano might include 20 or more different harmonics.

Recipes for sound

A good analogy is that each instrument has its own *recipe* for the frequency content of its sound. The guitar sound shown in Figure 15.17 has a mix of many harmonics. For this guitar, the fundamental is twice as big as the 2nd harmonic. There are strong 3rd, 4th and 5th harmonics. The piano recipe has a different mix.

Rise and fall times

The rate at which loudness builds and falls off also influences how we hear a sound. The *rise* time is the time it takes to reach maximum loudness. The *fall* time is the time over which the sound dies away (Figure 15.18). Rise time and fall time are related to resonance and damping in an instrument, and are different for each instrument. Rise and fall times are also different for each harmonic, even from the same instrument. Higher harmonics have faster rise times and shorter fall times.

Synthesized instruments

Today, it is easy to purchase electronic keyboards or computer programs that *synthesize* many different instrument sounds. For example, a keyboard may have buttons that allow you to choose "drums," "flute," "piano," "trumpet," or other sounds. The word "synthesize" means "to put together" and that is exactly how electronic instruments work. The sound of each instrument is synthesized by programming a recipe of harmonics and specifying the rise and fall time for each frequency. A good synthesizer may use 64 different frequencies *for each note* to simulate an instrument sound, each with separate rise and fall times.

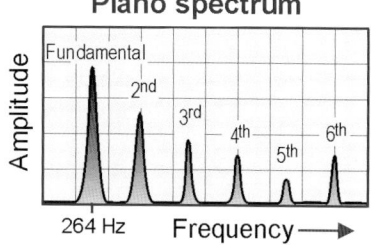

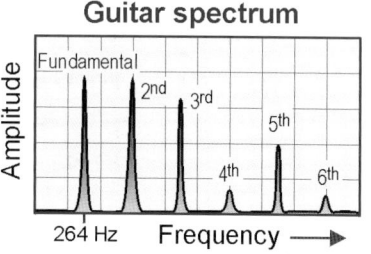

Figure 15.17: *The sound of the note C played on a piano and on a guitar. Notice that the fundamental frequencies are the same but the harmonics have different amplitudes and widths.*

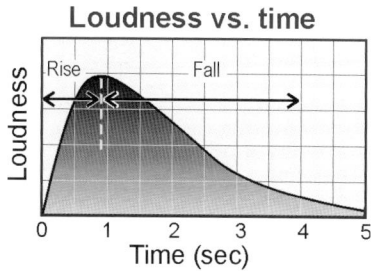

Figure 15.18: *The rise and fall times determine the rate at which loudness build up and falls off for a given frequency of sound.*

Application: Sound from a Guitar

The guitar has become a central instrument in popular music. Guitars come in many types but share the common feature of making sound from vibrating strings. Before 1900 guitars came in two basic varieties. Classical guitars use soft strings, made of nylon today. Folk guitars use steel strings, which are harder on the fingers but much louder. The invention of the electric guitar around 1930 and its cousin, the electric bass, made the voice of the guitar loud enough to be a melody or lead instrument.

Design of the guitar   A standard guitar has six strings that are stretched along the neck. The strings have different weights and therefore different natural frequencies. The heaviest string has a natural frequency of 82 Hz and the lightest a frequency of 330 Hz. Each string is stretched by a tension force of about 125 newtons (28 pounds). The combined force from six strings on a folk guitar is more than the weight of a person (750 N or 170 lbs). The guitar is tuned by changing the tension in each string. Tightening a string raises its natural frequency and loosening lowers it.

Each string can make many notes   A typical guitar string is 63 centimeters long. To make different notes, the vibrating length of each string can be shortened by holding it down against one of many metal bars across the neck called frets (Figure 15.19). The frequency goes up as the vibrating length of the string gets shorter. A guitar with 20 frets and six strings can play 126 different notes, some of which are duplicates.

Amplification   A vibrating string by itself does not make a loud sound. To make a practical instrument, the vibration from the string needs to amplified. An acoustic guitar amplifies the vibration by coupling the string to the top of the guitar. The guitar top is a large surface that can push much more air around than a thin string. A similar amplification effect can be heard by holding a tuning fork against a hard surface that can vibrate, such as a window pane (Figure 15.20).

Resonance   Acoustic guitar sound is also shaped by sound waves bouncing around inside the guitar. Because the shape of the guitar is irregular, there are many resonances. In general, large-bodied guitars have stronger long wavelength, low-frequency sounds, and are louder. Small-bodied acoustic guitars often lack low frequencies in their balance of sound. As with all instruments, guitar sounds have many harmonics. The highest-quality guitars are prized for both the richness of their sound (many harmonics) and their even balance across high and low frequencies.

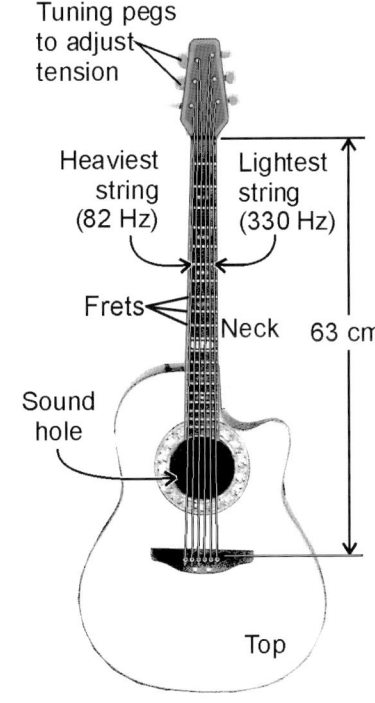

Figure 15.19: *A six-string acoustic guitar.*

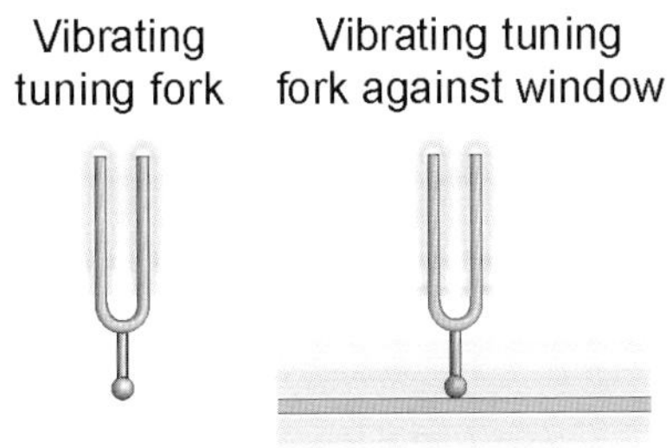

Vibrating tuning fork   Vibrating tuning fork against window

Figure 15.20: *The sound of a tuning fork becomes much louder when the vibrations are amplified by a surface, such as a glass window.*

Electric guitars and basses

How electric guitars work

The electric guitar uses electronics to amplify sound from the vibrating strings. Electric guitar *pickups* are made of a coil of wire wound around a set of strong magnets (Figure 15.21). The steel strings are slightly magnetized by being near the magnets in the pickups. As the magnetized strings vibrate up and down, an oscillating electric current is created in the coil by induction (see Chapter 23). The electric current is amplified and sent to a speaker to make sound.

Modifying sound electronically

Sound from an electric guitar is not an exact reproduction of the vibrations of the strings. The vibrating signals from the pickups change as they pass through the circuits of the amplifier. Electronic effects chosen by the musician add harmonics, echoes, or emphasize higher or lower frequencies before the electrical signal is turned into sound by the speakers. A common effect is called "distortion" and it adds the "growl" or "fuzz" to a guitar sound. Figure 15.22 shows wave forms from a "clean" sound and a "distorted" sound.

Guitar pickup

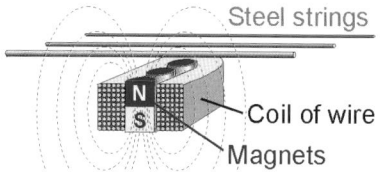

Figure 15.21: *A schematic of a guitar pickup showing the magnets, coil, and strings.*

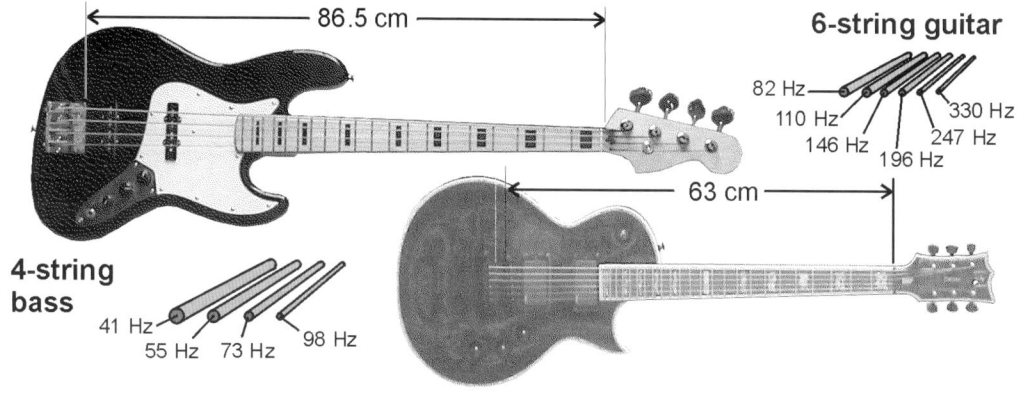

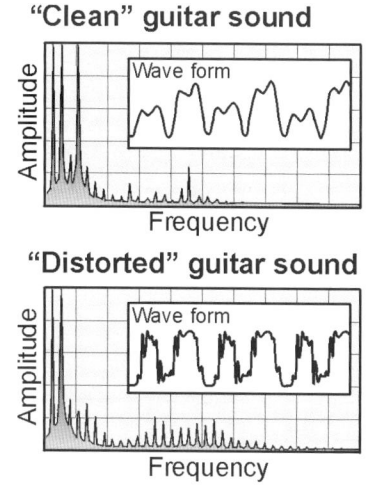

Figure 15.22: *Wave forms from "clean" and "distorted" guitar sounds. Notice that both sounds have the same fundamental frequency but the distorted sound has more high-frequency harmonic content.*

The bass guitar

The thump-thump rhythm you hear in the background of many songs comes from an electric bass, which is a guitar designed to play very low frequencies. The strings on a bass guitar are much heavier and longer than on a standard guitar. The extra mass and length both contribute to lower frequencies. The four strings on a traditional bass guitar have natural frequencies from 41 to 98 hertz. Like the guitar, bass players can make different notes on each string by holding the strings against frets to change the vibrating length.

Chapter 15 Review

Vocabulary review

Match the following terms with the correct definition. There is one extra definition in the list that will not match any of the terms.

Set One

1. pitch
2. pressure
3. decibels
4. acoustics
5. microphone

  a. Unit for measuring the loudness of sound
  b. Device used to change sound energy to an electrical signal
  c. Characteristic we hear as proportional to frequency
  d. The science and technology of sound
  e. Oscillation of this quantity in the air is what carries a sound wave
  f. Device used to change an electric signal to sound energy

Set Two

1. Doppler effect
2. longitudinal
3. spectrum
4. reverberation
5. Fourier's theorem

  a. Complex waves are the sum of single frequency waves
  b. Graph showing amplitude versus frequency
  c. Causes the sonic "boom" of high speed airplanes
  d. Sound is a wave of this type
  e. Shift in the frequency of sound caused by motion of the source of sound
  f. Sound made from multiple echoes

Set Three

1. sonogram
2. octave
3. musical scale
4. consonance

  a. Separation between two notes where the frequency of one is twice the frequency of the other
  b. Unpleasant combination of sounds
  c. Graph showing the frequency and loudness of a sound versus time
  d. Set of notes related to one another by specific frequency ratios
  e. Combination of sounds considered pleasant

305

Concept review

1. Sound travels faster in a liquid or a solid than in a gas. Why?

2. If a small piece of space debris were to strike a space station, workers on the inside might hear the sound made by the collision, but workers outside the station would not. Explain.

3. How are pitch and frequency of a sound related?

4. Your parents complain that the "rap" you are listening to is not music. Based upon the information in this section, what thoughts can you offer to support your choice of music?

5. As you tune your clarinet, you hear an oscillating sound your instructor calls beats. What causes them and how can you use them to tune your instrument?

6. Why does an "A" played on a piano not sound exactly like an "A" produced by a guitar?

7. A steel string does not produce a loud sound by itself. Explain how an acoustic guitar produces a loud sound when a string is "plucked."

8. How does an electric guitar pickup produce an amplified sound?

9. The decibel scale is used to measure the "loudness" of a sound. How is loudness (the decibel scale) of a sound related to the amplitude of the sound wave?

10. Most people know that sound is a wave. List at least three pieces of evidence to support the idea that sound is a wave.

11. How is the wavelength of sound produced by a musical wind instrument related to the size of the instrument?

12. A patron at a concert claims that she cannot hear clearly certain notes being played unless she moves her head slightly to one side or the other. Explain how this could happen.

13. Parents are concerned for the hearing of their children who wear stereo headsets adjusted to high volume settings. Using Table 15.1, explain why their concerns are justified.

14. When an astronomer observes the sun, she notices that the light from one edge is slightly shifted toward the red end of the visible spectrum while the opposite edge is slightly shifted toward violet. What causes this shift?

15. While scuba diving, Roy and his partner become separated. Roy taps on his scuba tank to help his partner locate him. Why is this technique not as useful underwater as it might be at the surface?

16. As the temperature increases, the fundamental frequency produced by a flute changes slightly. Does it increase or decrease? Give an explanation for your answer.

17. What causes consonance and dissonance?

Problems

1. Students in a physics class prepare "musical instruments" to play in lab. They cut tubes of ½-inch PVC pipe to various lengths. When students blow across the open end and cover the bottom with a thumb, fundamentals of the scale are produced. Approximately what length of tube will produce the fundamental frequency of 264 hertz, "middle C"? (Assume the speed of sound is 340 m/s.)

2. On a day when the speed of sound is 344 m/s, Tom hollers and hears an echo 2.4 seconds later. How far away is the object that caused the echo?

3. A pipe closed on one end is 2.46 m long. On a day when the speed of sound 345m/s, what is the fundamental frequency of this pipe?

4. Human hearing depends upon both the frequency and the intensity of the sound. Answer the questions below based upon the graph of Decibel Level as a function of Frequency.

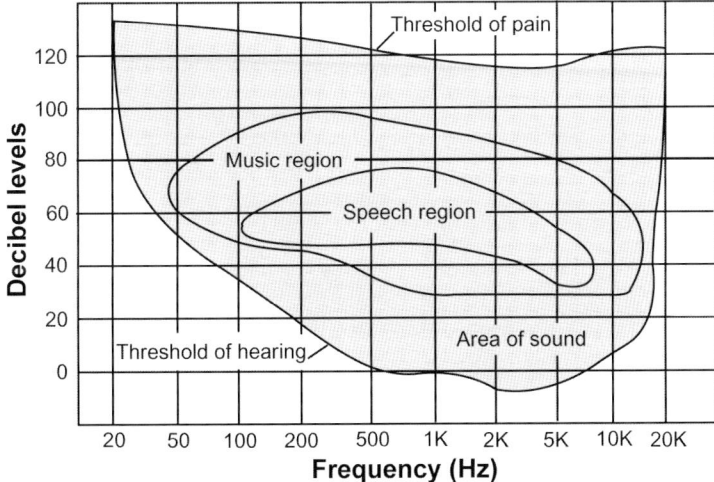

a. At which frequency is the threshold of pain lowest?

b. What is the approximate range of frequencies for speech?

c. What is the decibel range for most speech?

d. At what frequency are our ears most receptive?

5. The diagram represents wave fronts produced by a source moving at constant velocity through air. Answer the following questions based upon the diagram and your knowledge of the Doppler Effect.

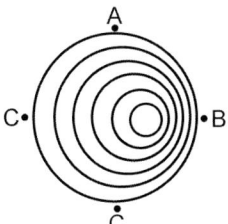

a. In which direction is the source moving?

b. If this were a sound source, at which point would the pitch be highest?

c. If the source were to accelerate, what would happen to the wavelength immediately behind the source?

6. A sonar signal requires 1.31 seconds to travel to the bottom of the ocean and back to the ship's depth finder in water 1,000 meters deep. What is the speed of the sound signal?

7. The speed of sound in air at 20°C is about 343 m/s. A 1.2 m tube closed on one end has a fundamental frequency measured to be 80 hz. Is the temperature higher or lower than 20°C? Justify your answer with an explanation/calculation.

8. Which pair of component waves would most likely produce the complex wave pattern shown below? Assume the times axis is horizontal and the same for all graphs.

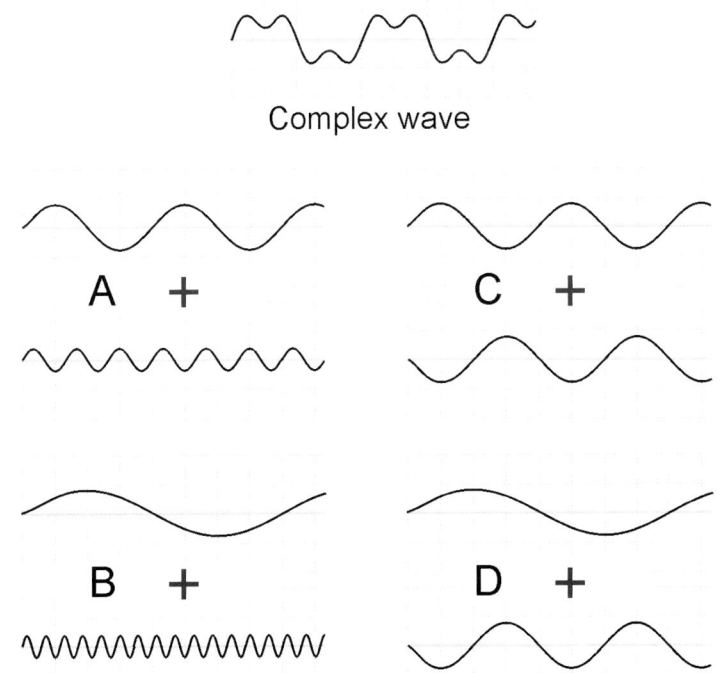

Complex wave

307

9. Examine the diagram which illustrates two waves of different frequencies (50 hz and 55 hz) and the sum of these two waves.

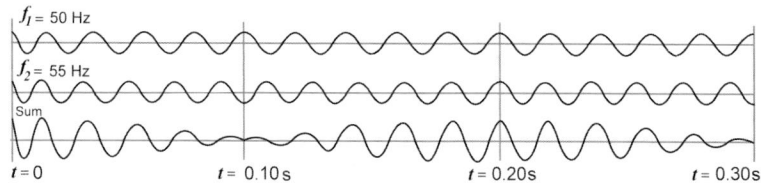

$f_1 = 50$ Hz

$f_2 = 55$ Hz

Sum

$t = 0$ 　　$t = 0.10$s 　　$t = 0.20$s 　　$t = 0.30$s

a. What is represented at $t = 0.00$ sec, $t = 0.10$ sec, $t = 0.20$ sec and $t = 0.30$ sec on the diagram representing the sum of the two waves?

b. What is the period between beats? (Hint: The time between two louder or "softer" sounds)

c. What is the beat frequency? (Hint: The reciprocal of the period)

10. Examine the diagrams of 4 objects whose velocities differ with respect to the sound they emit.

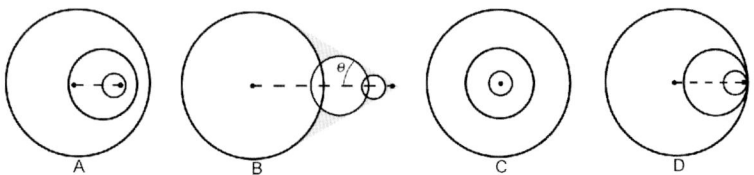

A 　　 B 　　 C 　　 D

a. Indicate the speed of each object relative to the speed of sound.

b. Indicate for which objects the Doppler effect occurs and for which a shock wave occurs.

11. The graph below on the left shows the wave amplitude of the fundamental harmonic produced by a tuning fork with a frequency of 264 hz. The graph on the right shows the spectrum of wave amplitudes produced by a musical instrument playing the same fundamental note.

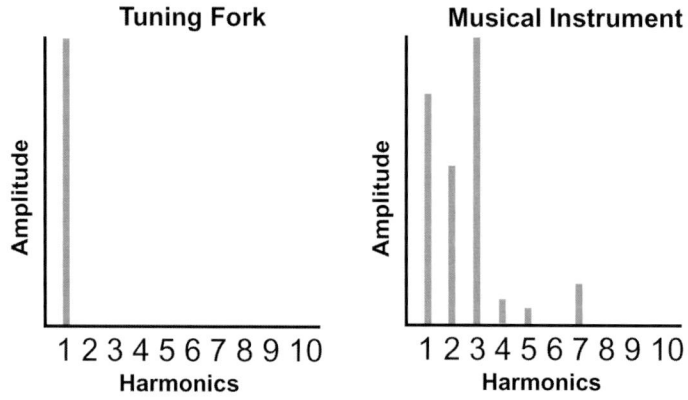

Tuning Fork 　　 **Musical Instrument**

Amplitude

1 2 3 4 5 6 7 8 9 10 　　 1 2 3 4 5 6 7 8 9 10

Harmonics 　　 **Harmonics**

a. What frequencies does the instrument produce?

b. List the frequencies produced in order of intensity from greatest to least.

Unit 6
Light and Optics

Chapter 16

Light and Color

Objectives for Chapter 16

By the end of this chapter you should be able to:

1. Describe at least five properties of light.
2. Describe the meaning of the term "intensity."
3. Use the speed of light to calculate the time or distance traveled by light.
4. Explain how we perceive color in terms of the three primary colors.
5. Explain the difference between the additive and subtractive color processes.
6. Arrange the colors of light in order of increasing energy, starting with red.
7. Describe light in terms of photons, energy, and color.

Terms and vocabulary words

reflection	refraction	black	fluorescence	intensity
color	blue	light ray	CMYK color	ultraviolet
infrared	photon	RBG color	photoluminescence	additive color
white	red	green	spherical pattern	cyan
magenta	yellow	pigment	speed of light (*c*)	incandescence
pixel	rod cell	cone cell	subtractive color	photoreceptor

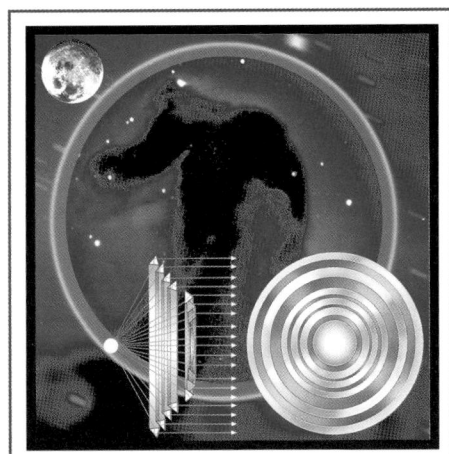

309

16.1 Properties and Sources of Light

Every time we look at something, light is involved. Whether we are looking at a light bulb or a car or this book, it is light that brings the information to our eyes. People have wondered how the eye sees for thousands of years. In the past, philosophers suggested light was a fluid that flowed from a candle flame or a beam that comes from the eye. We now know that we see objects by their reflected light. This chapter will discuss the properties of light, how we sense these properties, and how light is created.

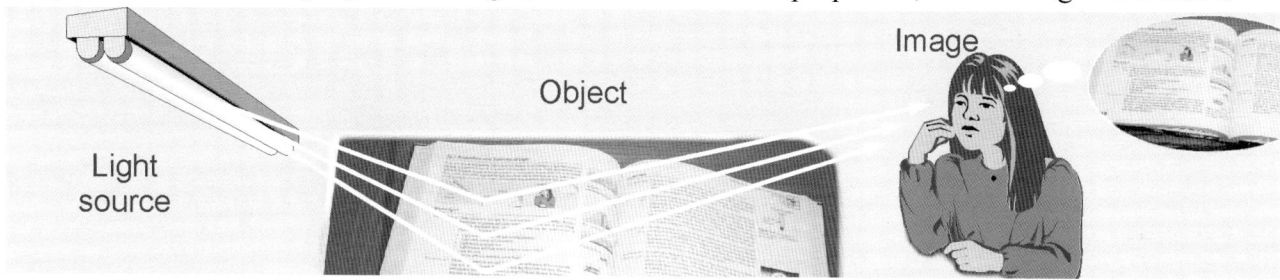

What is light?

Light is a form of energy

Today we believe that light, like sound and heat, is a form of energy. We have learned how to generate and control light energy to do all sorts of useful things. We have discovered much about light by observing the world around us (Figure 16.1). We know that:

- Light travels extremely fast and over long distances.
- Light carries energy and information.
- Light travels in straight lines.
- Light bounces and bends when it comes in contact with objects.
- Light has color.
- Light has different intensities, can be bright or dim.

How do we see?

What physically occurs as you see this page? Light from the lights in your classroom reflects off the page and into your eyes. The reflected light carries information about the page that allows your brain to construct an image of the page. You see because light in the room *reflects* from the page into your eyes. If you turn out the lights in the room you cannot see the page because the page does not give off its own light. We see most of the world by reflected light.

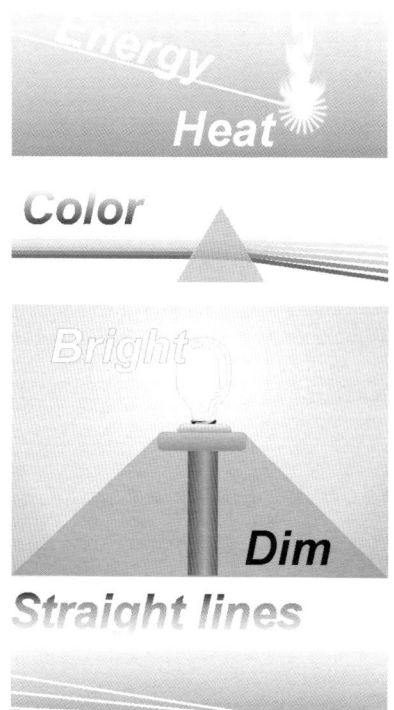

Refraction

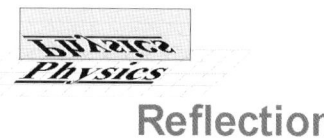

Reflection

Figure 16.1: *Some words and properties that are associated with light. What words do you use to describe light?*

Electric light

| The electric light | To see, there must be a source of light that can reflect from objects. For most of human history people relied on the sun, moon, and fire to provide the light they needed. Thomas Edison's electric light bulb (1879) is one of the most important inventions in the progress of human development. Chances are that the light you are using to read these words is coming from an electric light. |

Incandescent Light

Hot, glowing filament emits light

Figure 16.2: *An incandescent light bulb generates light by heating a piece of metal.*

| Incandescent light bulbs | The process of making light with heat is called incandescence. Incandescent bulbs generate light when electricity passes through a thin piece of metal wire called a filament. The filament heats up and gives off light (Figure 16.2). The atoms inside the filament, convert electrical energy to heat and then to light. Unfortunately, incandescent bulbs are not very efficient. Only a small fraction of the energy of electricity is converted into light. Most of the energy becomes heat. In fact, the primary function of some incandescent bulbs is to make heat. For example, incandescent heat lamps are used to help chicken's eggs hatch or keep a restaurant's french fries warm. |

| Fluorescent light bulbs | The other common kind of electric light is the fluorescent bulb (Figure 16.3). We see many fluorescent bulbs in schools and businesses and even in homes, because they are much more efficient than incandescent bulbs. Compared with a standard incandescent bulb, you get four times as much light from a fluorescent bulb for the same amount of electricity. This is possible because fluorescent bulbs convert electricity directly to light without generating a lot of heat. |

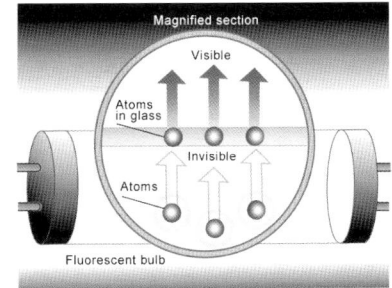

Figure 16.3: *Fluorescent lights generate light by exciting atoms with electricity.*

| How fluorescent bulbs make light | To make light, fluorescent bulbs use high-voltage electricity to energize atoms of gas that fill the bulb. These atoms release the electrical energy as light, in a process known as fluorescence. We cannot directly see the light given off by the atoms in the fluorescent bulbs, because it is high-energy ultraviolet, the same kind of light that gives you a sunburn. Another step is needed to get useful light. The ultraviolet light is absorbed by other atoms in a white coating on the inside surface of the bulb. This coating re-emits the energy as white light that we see. Even with the two-step process, fluorescent bulbs are still four times more efficient than incandescent bulbs. |

Light carries energy and power

The intensity of light

Light is a form of energy that travels. This is obvious if you stand outside on a hot day. The energy from the sun is what makes you warm. This energy comes to the Earth as light. The intensity of light is the amount of energy per second falling on a surface. For example, on a bright sunny day, 500 joules of light energy may fall on a single square meter of surface (Figure 16.4). The intensity of this light is 500 watts per meter squared (500 W/m²). Remember from Chapter 11 that a watt is an energy flow of one joule per second.

Spherical pattern

Although we say that light travels in straight lines, most light sources distribute their light equally in all directions, making a spherical pattern. If you stuck a bunch of toothpicks into an orange, the toothpicks would point outward in all directions just like light radiates outwards in all directions from the sun (Figure 16.5). You can see a bare light bulb from anywhere in a room because the bulb emits light in all directions.

Light intensity follows an inverse square law

Because light spreads out in a sphere, the intensity decreases the farther you get from the source. For example, suppose a light bulb gives off 10 watts of light. The light is spread around a sphere in all directions. The area of a sphere is $4\pi r^2$, where r is the radius. If the radius is 1 meter, the area is 12.6 m². The light intensity is 0.8 W/m² (10 W ÷ 12.6 m²). If the radius is 2 meters (twice as far), the intensity is four times less because the same amount of light is spread out over 4 m² instead of 1 m². The intensity of light from a small source follows an inverse square law because its intensity diminishes as the square of the distance.

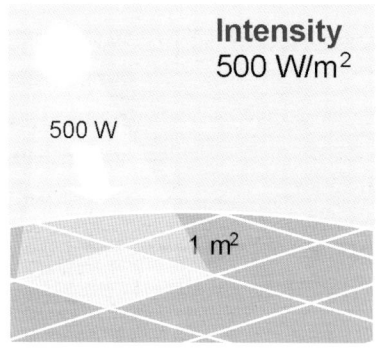

Figure 16.4: *Intensity is the power of light per unit area. In the summer, the intensity of sunlight reaches 500 watts per square meter.*

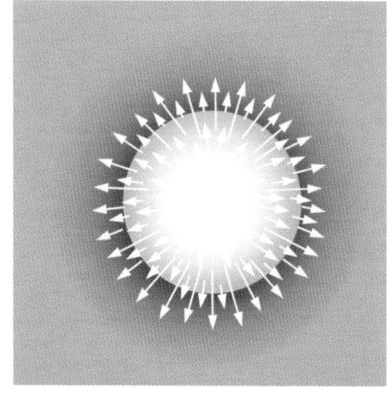

Figure 16.5: *Light emitted from the sun or from a light bulb travels in a spherical distribution of straight lines.*

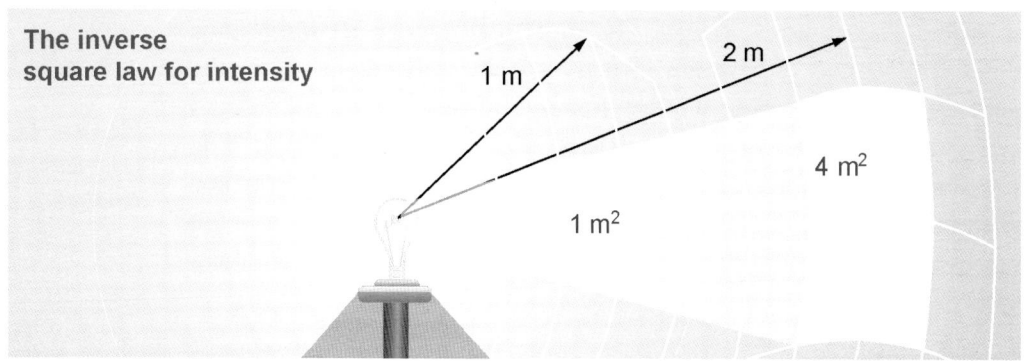

The inverse square law for intensity

1 m

2 m

4 m²

1 m²

Light carries information

Information in images

We rely on light to bring us *information* about the world around us. To see the connection between light and information, consider that a video camera captures a picture as a series of colored dots. At the time this book was printed, a high quality video picture was 720 dots wide by 480 dots high (Figure 16.6). The amount of information in a video picture is roughly the same as the number of dots—346,000 for a video image (720 × 480). The human eye is a very sophisticated light detector, much better than a video camera. The human eye can see more than 100 million dots. Every time you look around, your brain is receiving more than a million dots of information each second and processing the information to give you a picture of what is around you.

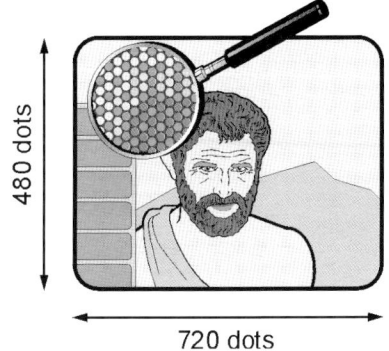

Figure 16.6: *The best quality standard TV picture is 346,000 dots, 720 dots wide by 480 dots high.*

Information in sound

Today, most voice information is also carried by light. In Chapter 15, you read about how music is converted to a string of numbers that can be recorded on a computer. The same string of numbers can be sent on a laser beam by turning the beam on and off very fast. More than 1 billion numbers per second can be sent on a single laser beam. The fiber-optic networks you read about are pipelines for information carried by light (Figure 16.7).

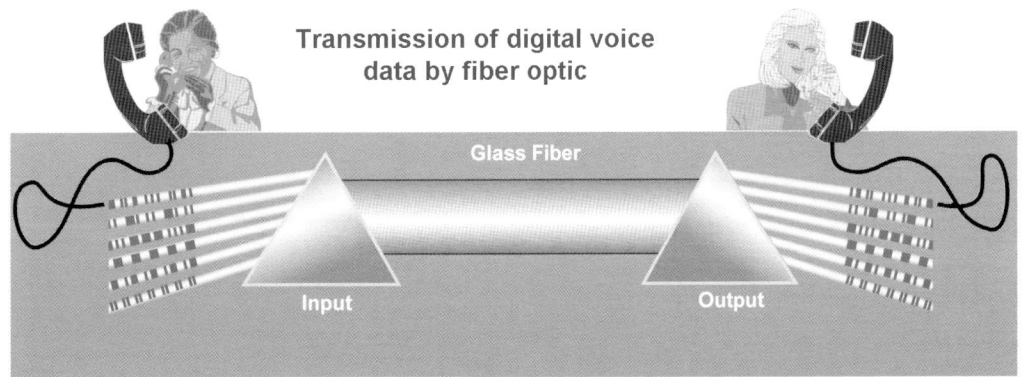

Transmission of digital voice data by fiber optic

Glass Fiber

Input

Output

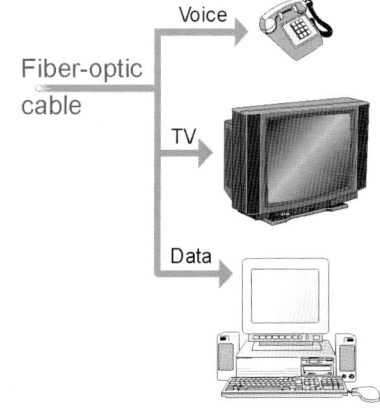

Figure 16.7: *A single fiber-optic cable can carry more than enough information to support television, telephone, and computer data.*

Information in computer data

Most of the data transmitted across the Internet is also carried by light. A network of fiber-optic cables crisscrosses the country carrying data from one computer to another. In some cities, a fiber-optic cable comes directly into homes and apartments carrying telephone, television, and Internet signals.

16.1 Properties and Sources of Light

313

The speed of light

Comparing the speeds of sound and light

Consider what happens when you shine a flashlight on a distant object. You do not see the light leave your flashlight, travel to the object, bounce off, and come back to your eyes. But that is exactly what happens. You do not see it because it happens so fast. For example, suppose you shine a flashlight on a mirror 170 m away. The light travels to the mirror and back in about one-millionth of a second (0.000001 sec). Sound travels much slower than light. If you shout, you will hear an echo one second later from the sound bouncing off a wall 170 m away and back to your ears. Light travels almost a million times faster than sound.

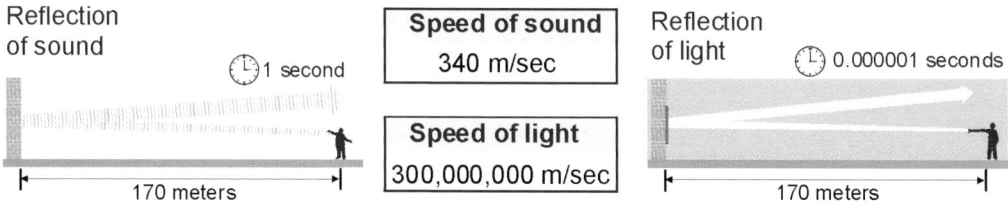

Reflection of sound		Speed of sound	Reflection of light	
1 second		340 m/sec	0.000001 seconds	
170 meters		Speed of light 300,000,000 m/sec	170 meters	

The speed of light, $c = 3 \times 10^8$ m/sec

The speed at which light travels through air is approximately 300 million meters per second. This is such a high speed that it is difficult to comprehend. Light is so fast it can travel around the entire Earth 7 1/2 times in 1 second. The **speed of light** is so important in physics that it is given its own symbol, a lower case c. When you see this symbol in a formula, remember that $c = 3 \times 10^8$ m/sec.

The sound of thunder lags the flash of lightning

The speed of light is so fast that when lightning strikes a few miles away, we hear the thunder several seconds after we see the lightning. At the point of the lightning strike, the thunder and lightning are simultaneous. But just a mile away from the lightning strike, the sound of the thunder is already about 5 seconds behind the flash of the lightning.

Accurate measurement of c

Using very fast electronics we are able to measure the speed of light accurately in lab experiments. One technique used to measure the speed of light is to record the time a pulse of light leaves a laser and the time the pulse returns to its starting position after making a round trip. The best accepted experimental measurement for the speed of light in air is 299,792,500 m/sec. For most purposes, we do not need to be this accurate and may use a value for c of 3×10^8 m/sec.

Calculating the time it takes for light and sound to go a mile

Calculate the time it takes light and sound to travel the distance of one mile, which is 1,609 meters.

1) You are asked for time.

2) You are given distance and you may find the speed of sound and light.

3) $t = d \div v$

4) For sound:
$t = (1,609 \text{ m}) \div (340 \text{ m/sec})$
$= 4.73 \text{ seconds}$

For light:
$t = (1,609 \text{ m}) \div (3 \times 10^8 \text{ m/sec})$
$= 0.0000054 \text{ seconds}$
$(5.4 \times 10^{-6} \text{ sec})$

Light can bounce (reflection) and bend (refraction)

Light rays, reflection, and refraction

When light moves through a material it travels in straight lines. But when light rays travel from one material to another, the rays may reflect (Figure 16.8) or refract (Figure 16.9). When describing reflection or refraction, it is useful to represent light by one or more imaginary lines traveling in the direction of the light. These imaginary lines are called light rays. The light that appears to bounce off the surface of an object is shown by a *reflected ray*. The light that bends as it crosses a surface into a material is shown as a *refracted ray* (diagram below). Reflection and refraction cause many interesting changes in the images we see.

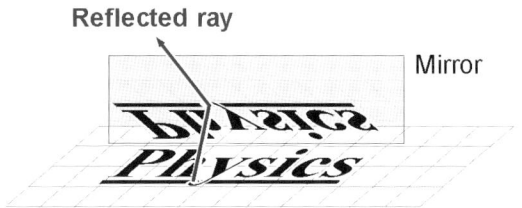 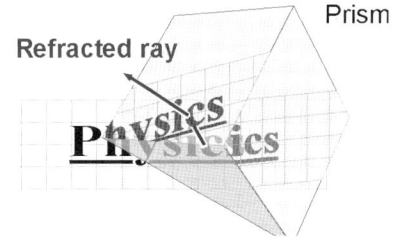

Figure 16.8: *Light rays are reflected in a mirror, causing us to see an inverted image.*

Figure 16.9: *Light rays are refracted (or bent) by a prism, causing the image to be distorted.*

Mirrors

When you look in a mirror, objects that are in front of the mirror appear as if they are behind the mirror. This is because light rays are reflected by the mirror. Your brain perceives the light as if it always traveled in a straight line. You see a reflected image *behind* a mirror because the reflected *light rays* reaching your eye are the same as if the object really were behind the mirror.

A glass of water

When light rays travel from air to water they refract. This is why the images we see looking through a glass full of water are different from the images we see when we move the glass away from our eyes. Try looking at some objects through a glass of water; move the glass closer and farther away from the objects. Does it remind you of anything your have ever used, such as a magnifying glass?

Twinkling of stars

Another example of refraction of light is the twinkling of a star in the night sky (Figure 16.10). As starlight travels from space into the Earth's atmosphere, the rays are refracted. Since the atmosphere is constantly changing, the amount of refraction also changes. The image of a star appears to "twinkle" because the light coming to your eye is constantly making small changes in its path.

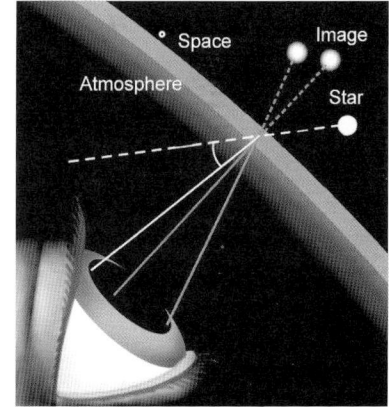

Figure 16.10: *The twinkle of a star is due to the changes in the bending of light as the light moves through the atmosphere.*

16.2 Color and Vision

The rainbow of colors our eyes can see ranges from deep red, through the yellows, greens, and blues, to deep purples like violet. The order of colors is always the same when white light is separated with a prism: red, orange, yellow, green, blue, and violet. This order of the colors can be remembered by their initials ROY-G-BV, which is pronounced "roy-gee-biv." In this section, we will discuss how light makes different colors and how we perceive color. The discussion may surprise you.

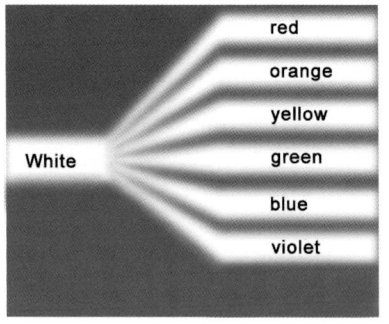

Figure 16.11: *White light is the combination of all the colors.*

White light, color, and energy

White light | When all the colors of the rainbow are combined, we do not see any particular color. We see light without any color. We call this combination of all the colors of light white light (Figure 16.11). White light is a good description of the ordinary light that is all around us most of the time. The light from the sun and the light from most electric lights is white light.

Where does color come from? | So why does some light appear as a particular color? Near the turn of the 20th century, Albert Einstein proposed a new way of thinking about light. He theorized that color had something to do with the energy of light. All of the colors in the rainbow are simply light of different energies. Red light has the lowest energy we can see, and violet light the highest energy. As we move through the rainbow from red to yellow to blue to violet, the energy of the light increases.

Energy and light from a flame | What do we mean when we talk about the energy of light? Think about the flames coming from a gas stove, a blow torch, or a gas grill. These are very hot flames and they are *blue*. The atoms of gas in the flame have high energy so they give off blue light. The flame from a match or from a burning log in the fireplace is reddish orange. These flames are not nearly as hot as those from gas, so the atoms have a lower energy. The low energy light from a match flame appears red or yellow.

A way to think about light energy | You can think of the energy of light being like the kinetic energy of a ball thrown upward: too little energy and we cannot see the light at all. The lowest energy of light we can see appears red (Figure 16.12). Light of intermediate energy appears green, and higher energy light appears blue. The energy of ultraviolet light is even higher than blue, but we cannot see ultraviolet or higher energy light.

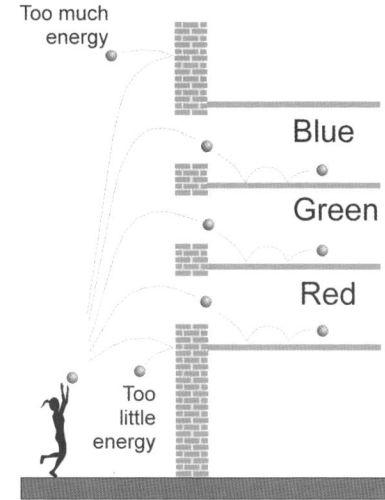

Figure 16.12: *We can think of different colors of light like balls with different kinetic energies. Blue light has a higher energy than green light, like the balls that make it into the top window. Red light has the lowest energy, like the balls that can only make it to the lowest window.*

316

How the human eye sees color

How we see color Scientists have discovered cells in the retina (back) of the eye that contain **photoreceptors**. Light from an image passes through the lens of the eye and falls on the photoreceptors in the back of the eye (Figure 16.13). When light hits a photoreceptor cell, the cell releases a chemical signal that travels down the optic nerve to the brain. In the brain, the signal is translated into a perception of color.

Rods and cones Our eyes have two types of photoreceptors, called rod cells and cone cells. **Cones** (cone cells) respond to color. There are three types of cone cells. One kind gives off its strongest signal for red light. Another kind works best with green light and the last kind works best for blue light. Each kind of cone is tuned to respond best at a certain energy range of light. Because there are only three kinds of cones, it is accurate to say we see only three colors of light. We see white light when all three types of cone cells (red, green, blue) are equally stimulated (Figure 16.14).

Rod cells see black and white The rod cells respond only to differences in intensity, and not to color. **Rods** (rod cells) essentially see in black, white, and shades of gray. However, rod cells are much more sensitive than cone cells and work at very low light levels. At night, colors seem washed out because there is not enough light for your cones to work. When the overall light level is very dim, you are actually seeing "black and white" images from your rod cells.

Black and white vision is sharper than color vision An average human eye contains about 130 million rod cells and only 7 million cone cells. You can think of each photoreceptor cell as being one dot in a total image. The brain assembles all the dots to create the image. Because there are more rod cells, finer details appear sharpest when there is high contrast between light and dark areas. In bright light, each cone cell applies color to many rod cells. The cone cells are concentrated near the center of the retina, making color vision best at the center of the eye's field of view.

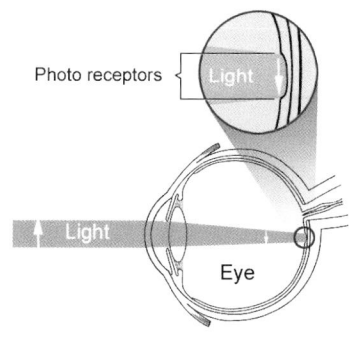

Figure 16.13: *The photoreceptors that send color signals to the brain are in the back of the eye.*

Photoreceptors in the eye

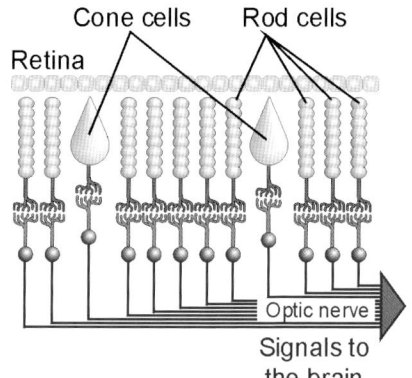

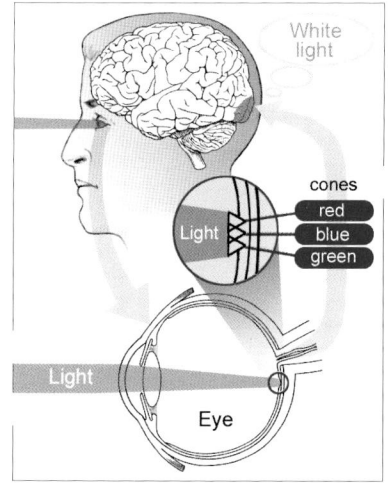

Figure 16.14: *Because white light is the mixture of all the colors, all three types of cones (red, blue, and green) are stimulated.*

How we see colors other than red, green, and blue

How we perceive color

The three color receptors in the eye allow us to see millions of different colors. When the brain receives a signal only from the red cone cells, it thinks red. If there is a signal from the green cone cells but neither the blue nor red, the brain thinks green (Figure 16.15). This seems simple enough.

The additive color process

Now consider what happens if the brain gets a strong signal from both the red and the green cone cells at the same time. The sensation created is different from either red or green. It is what we have learned to call *yellow*. Whether the light is actually yellow, or a combination of red and green, the cones respond the same way and we perceive yellow. If all three cones are sending a signal to the brain at once, we think white. The brain makes color by an additive process because new colors are formed by the addition of more than one signal from the cone cells.

The additive primary colors

The additive primary colors are red, green, and blue. In reality, our brains are receiving all three color signals just about all of the time. We don't see everything white because the strength of the signal matters. It is too simple to say that red and green make yellow. If there is a lot of red and only a little green the color is *orange* instead of yellow (Figure 16.16). Orange is more toward red. All the different shades of color we can see are made by changing the proportions of red, green, and blue.

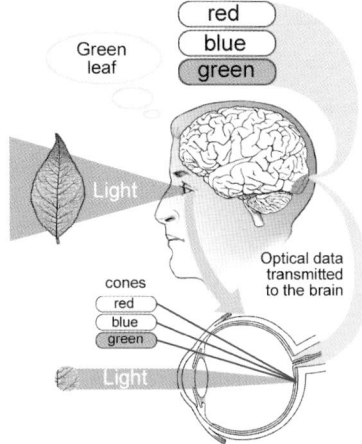

Figure 16.15: *If the brain gets a signal from only the green cone, we see green.*

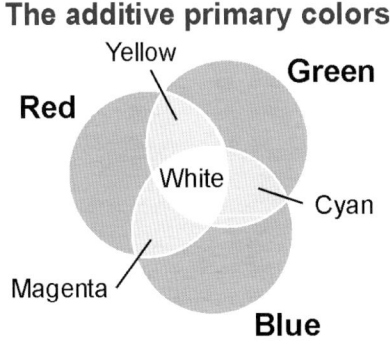

The additive primary colors

White = red + green + blue
Yellow = red + green
Magenta = red + blue
Cyan = blue + green

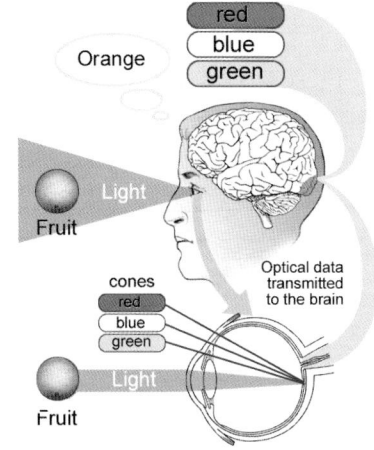

Figure 16.16: *If there is a strong red signal and a weak green signal, we see orange.*

Not all animals see the same colors

To the best of our knowledge, only humans and other primates (such as chimpanzees and gorillas) have all three kinds of red, green, and blue color sensors. Dogs and cats lack any color sensors; they have only rod cells that sense black, white, and shades of gray. Other animals have color sensors that are neither red, blue, nor green but respond to different colors altogether.

How we see the colors of things

We see mostly reflected light

When we see an object, the light that reaches our eyes can come from two different processes.

1. The light can be emitted directly from the object, like a light bulb or glow stick.

2. The light can come from somewhere else, like the sun, and we see the objects by reflected light.

Most of what we see is from reflected light because most objects around us don't produce their own visible light. When you look around, you are seeing light originally from the sun (or electric lights) that is reflected from objects.

What gives objects their color?

When we look at a blue piece of cloth, we believe that the quality of blue is in the cloth, which is not true. The reason the cloth looks blue is because the chemicals in the cloth have absorbed all the colors of light *other than blue*. Since blue light is reflected, it is the color that reaches our eyes (Figure 16.17). The blue was never in the cloth. The blue was hidden or mixed in with the other colors in white light even before it reached the cloth. The cloth unmasked the blue by taking away all the other colors and sending only the blue to our eyes.

The subtractive color process

Colored fabrics and paints get color from a subtractive process. Chemicals, known as pigments, in the dyes and paints absorb some colors and allow the color you actually see to be reflected. Pigments work by taking away specific colors from white light, which is a mixture of all the colors.

The subtractive primary colors

To make all colors by subtraction we also need three primary pigments. We need one that absorbs blue, and reflects red and green. This pigment is called yellow. We need another pigment that absorbs only green, and reflects red and blue. This is a pink-purple called magenta. The third pigment is cyan, which absorbs red and reflects green and blue. Cyan is a slightly greenish shade of light blue. Magenta, yellow, and cyan are the three subtractive primary colors (Figure 16.18). By using different proportions of the three pigments, a paint can appear almost any color by varying the amount of reflected red, green, and blue light. For example, to make black, add all three and all light is absorbed, reflecting none.

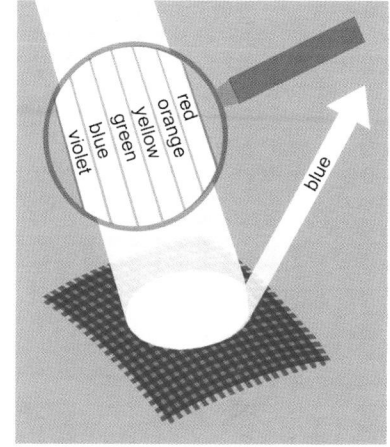

Figure 16.17: *You see a blue cloth because pigments in the fabric absorb all colors except blue. Blue light gets reflected to your eyes.*

The subtractive primary colors (in white light)

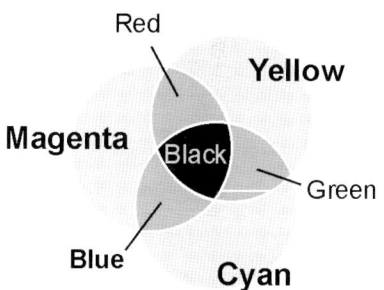

Magenta + yellow = red
Yellow + cyan = green
Cyan + magenta = blue
Magenta + yellow + cyan = black

Figure 16.18: *The three subtractive primary colors.*

Why are plants green?

Light is necessary for photosynthesis

Plants are green because of how they use visible light. In a very unique way, plants absorb physical energy in the form of light and convert it to chemical energy in the form of sugar. The process is called *photosynthesis*. The graph in Figure 16.19 shows the colors of visible light that plants absorb. The *x*-axis on the graph represents the colors of visible light. The *y*-axis represents the amount of light absorbed by plant pigments for photosynthesis.

Chlorophyll

The green pigment, chlorophyll **a**, is the most important light-absorbing pigment. You can see on the graph that chlorophyll **a** absorbs light at each end of the spectrum. In other words, chlorophyll **a** reflects most of the green light and absorbs blue and red light. Plants are green because they reflect green light from the sun and absorb the red and blue. In fact, plants will not grow well if they are placed under pure green light.

Why leaves change color

Notice that chlorophyll **b** and carotenoids (orange pigments) absorb light where chlorophyll **a** does not. These extra pigments help plants catch more light. Leaves change color when chlorophyll **a** breaks down and these pigments become visible. They are the cause of the beautiful bright reds and oranges that you see when leaves change color in the fall.

Plants reflect some light to keep cool

Why don't plant pigments absorb all colors of light? The reason is the same reason you wear light colored clothes when it is hot outside. Like you, plants must reflect some light to avoid absorbing too much energy and overheating.

Visible light has just the right energy for life

The colors in visible light (red-violet) represent only a tiny fraction of the possible energy light can have. For example, ultraviolet light has energy higher than blue or violet light. Infrared light has energy lower than red light. Our eyes cannot see either of these "colors." Almost all living things on Earth see visible light because this range of colors has just the right amount of energy for living things to use. Ultraviolet light, for example, has too much energy. It can break apart important molecules. Infrared radiation is mostly absorbed by water vapor and carbon dioxide in the atmosphere.

Absorption of light by plants

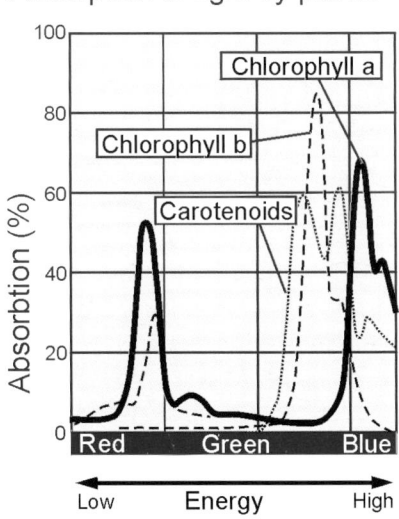

Figure 16.19: *The lines in the graph show which colors of light are absorbed by plant pigments. Chlorophyll a and b absorb blue light and red light, leaving green light to be reflected. This is why plants look green most of the time.*

How does a color TV work?

TV makes its own light   Televisions give off light. They do not rely on reflected light to make color. You can prove this by watching a TV in a dark room. You can see light from the TV even if there are no other sources of light in the room. Computer monitors and movie projectors are similar. All these devices make their own light.

The RGB color process   To make color with a TV, you can use red, green, and blue (RGB) directly (Figure 16.20). You do not need to use the subtractive colors. Turn your TV to a channel that doesn't come in. Use a magnifying glass to look closely at the static on the screen. You will notice something interesting. The screen is made of tiny red, green, and blue dots. The dots are called pixels and each pixel gives off its own light. The pixels are separated by very thin black lines. The black lines help give intensity to the colors and help make the darker colors darker. From far away, you cannot see the individual pixels. What you see is a nice, smooth, color picture.

Mixing primary colors   By turning on the different color pixels at different intensities, TV sets can mix the three colors to get millions of different colors. For example, a light brown tone is 88 percent red, 85 percent green, and 70 percent blue. A television makes this color by lighting the red, green, and blue pixels to these percentages.

Video cameras   A video camera does the opposite of a television. A video camera has red, green, and blue sensors, similar to the cones in your eye (Figure 16.21). The camera records an image by measuring the percentages of red, green, and blue in the light coming through the camera lens. The device inside that actually captures the light is called a CCD sensor. The CCDs in most video cameras are quite small, typically 1 centimeter square or less.

Two complementary color processes   All devices that make their own light use the RGB (red, green, blue) color model. They create millions of colors by varying the strengths of each of the three primaries. Anything that relies on reflected light to make color uses the CMYK color process (cyan, magenta, yellow, black; the letter K stands for black). The CMYK process is used for printing inks, fabric dyes, and even the color of your skin. In both cases, the colors that you *see* are the colors of light that are *not absorbed* by pigments. The RGB process generates the light you see and the CMYK process subtracts all *except* the light you see.

Figure 16.20: *A television makes colors using tiny glowing dots of red, green, and blue.*

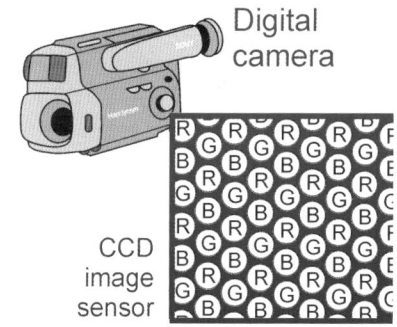

Figure 16.21: *Digital cameras have an array of tiny light sensors, that are sensitive to red, green, and blue light.*

16.3 Photons and Atoms

You could name many things that create light; the sun, lightning, fire, and fluorescent bulbs are a few examples. The thing that is common to all these different sources of light is that they are made of atoms. Virtually all of the light you see is created by atoms. In fact, atoms can both create and absorb light. This section is about how atoms create light and how light is describes on the tiny scale of atoms.

The photon theory of light

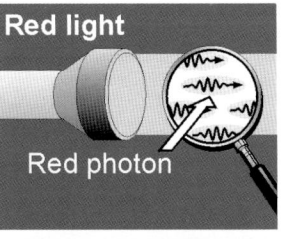

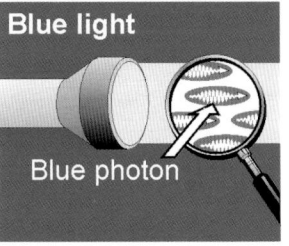

Figure 16.22: *Blue photons have a higher energy than red photons.*

Photons — Just like matter is made of tiny particles called atoms, light energy comes in tiny bundles called photons. In some ways photons act like jellybeans of different colors. Each photon has its own color, no matter how you mix them up.

Color and photons — The lowest-energy photons we can see are the ones that appear a dull red in color (Figure 16.22). The highest-energy photons we can see are the color of blue tending to deep violet. Low-energy atoms make low-energy photons and high-energy atoms make high-energy photons. As atoms gain energy, the color of the light they produce changes from red to yellow to blue and violet.

White light — White light is a mixture of photons with a wide range of colors (energies). This is a clue that white light is created by atoms that also have a wide range of energy. You can see how this works by watching the filament of a light bulb on a dimmer switch. When the switch is set very low, the filament is relatively cool (low energy) and the light is very red. As you turn up the dimmer switch, the filament gets hotter and hotter. The hotter it gets, the more green and blue light is created. At full power the bulb appears a brilliant white—which means it is creating a uniform spread of photons of all colors.

Temperature and energy — For a given temperature, the atoms in a material have a range of energy that goes from zero up to a maximum that depends on the temperature. Figure 16.23 shows how the energy is distributed between the atoms in a material for several temperatures. At a temperature of 600°C, you can see that some atoms have just enough energy to make red light (electric stove). At 2,600°C, there are atoms that can make all colors of light, which is why the hot filament of a light bulb appears white. At room temperature (20°C) a rock gives off no visible light at all.

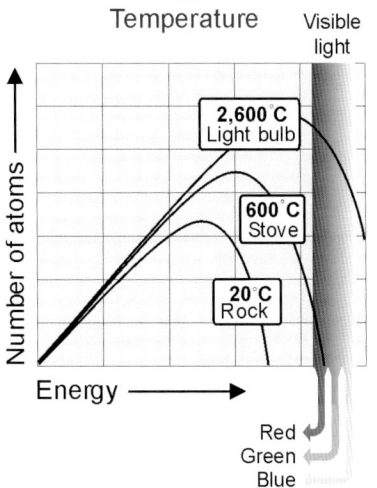

Figure 16.23: *The number of atoms with a given amount of energy depends on the temperature.*

Photons and the intensity of light

Energy, color, and intensity | Intensity measures power per unit area. There are two ways to make light of high intensity. One way is to have high- energy photons. A second way is to have a lot of photons even if they are low-energy (Figure 16.24). In practical terms, to make a red light with an intensity of 100 W/m² takes a lot more photons then it does to make the same intensity with blue light. The color of light depends on the energy of each photon. The intensity of light is a combination of both the number of photons and the energy per photon.

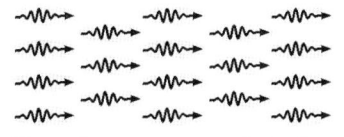

Many low-energy red photons

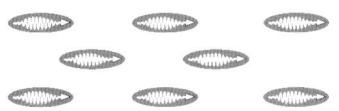

Fewer high-energy blue photons

Figure 16.24: *The number and energy of photons determine the intensity of the light.*

Glow-in-the-dark plastic | Consider an amazing but very common material: glow-in-the-dark plastic. If this material is exposed to light, it stores some energy and later is able to release the energy by giving off its own light. The plastic can only make light if it is "charged up" by absorbing energy from other sources of light. You can test this theory by holding your hand on some "uncharged" plastic and then exposing it to bright light. If you then bring the plastic into a dark area and remove your hand, you can see that the areas that were covered by your hand are dark while the rest of the plastic glows (Figure 16.25).

Photo luminescence | The glow-in-the-dark effect comes from atoms of the element phosphorus that are in the plastic. When photons of light collide with phosphorus atoms, the energy from the photons is stored in the atoms. Slowly, these atoms release the stored energy as pale green light. The process of releasing stored energy as light is called photo luminescence.

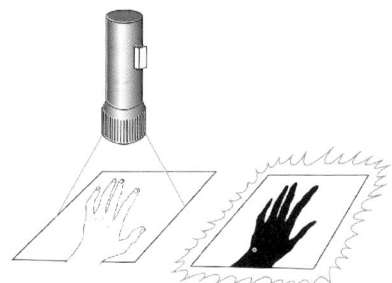

Figure 16.25: *The light from the flashlight cannot energize the phosphorus atoms that your hand blocks. These atoms will not glow because they did not receive any energy from photons from the flashlight.*

An experiment with photon energy | You can use glow-in-the-dark plastic to show that a *single atom interacts with a single photon at a time*. A simple experiment shows that red light does not activate glow-in-the-dark plastic. For a phosphorus atom to give off a green photon, it must absorb equal or greater energy. If one red photon is absorbed the atom does not get enough energy to make a green photon. If a single atom could absorb two or more red photons it could get enough energy to emit a green photon. However, the material stays dark and does not glow no matter how intense a red light is used. But even a dim blue light will cause the plastic to glow because one blue photon has *more* energy than a green photon. The explanation is that each phosphorus atom absorbs (or emits) only one photon at a time.

Light and atoms

The process of how light is reflected

The light you see that is carrying the image of this page is reflected from the light source by which you are reading. But how exactly does reflection occur? The atoms on the surface of the paper in the white areas of the page absorb the light from the room and immediately emit almost all of the light back in all directions. You see a white page because the atoms on the surface of the paper absorb and re-emit light of all colors equally (Figure 16.26). The black letters are visible because light falling on black ink is almost completely absorbed and no light is re-emitted. Where there is no light coming from the page, you see black.

Most atoms absorb and emit light

It turns out that almost all atoms absorb and emit light. What is different about the phosphorus atoms in glow-in-the-dark plastic is the *time* between the absorption and the emission of the light. For most atoms, the absorption and emission of light happens in less than one-millionth of a second. This is so fast that only the most sensitive instruments can detect the time delay. Phosphorus atoms have a special ability to delay the emission of a photon for a relatively long time.

When thinking about photons and atoms is necessary

Think about photons and atoms the next time you turn on the light in a dark room. The light that you see coming off the wall started at the light bulb. It was absorbed by the atoms in the paint, and its energy was re-emitted as photons of the color that you see. This all happens thousands of times faster than a blink of your eye. It all happens so fast that we may accurately describe the light as reflecting off the surfaces, as we will in the next chapter. When we are interested in the overall path that light travels, we need not worry about the microscopic details. Only when studying the behavior of very small systems such as individual atoms do we need to explicitly consider the detailed interaction of atoms and photons.

Light from chemical reactions

Another source of energy that allows atoms to emit light is from chemical changes in materials. Many chemical changes release energy. Some of the energy is absorbed within atoms and subsequently emitted as light. For example, the warm flickering glow from a candle comes from trillions of atoms in the wick giving up photons as they combine with oxygen atoms in the air (Figure 16.27). The light that comes from a glow stick is also made through chemical changes.

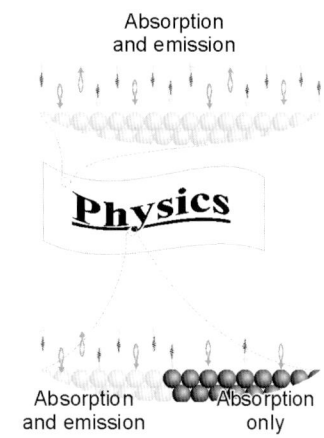

Figure 16.26: *White paper absorbs and immediately re-emits photons of all colors in all directions. Black ink absorbs photons of all colors and emits none, which is why it looks black.*

Figure 16.27: *The light from a candle flame comes from energy released by chemical changes.*

324

Application: Color printing

Printing is an ancient art, almost as old as written history. Fragments of whole printed pages have been found in China that are more than 1,400 years old. Early printers carved blocks of wood and pressed them in ink to print a page. To make a printing block, the printer carefully carved out the wood around any areas that were to be inked, such as letters. A new block had to be created for each different page. A new block also had to be created for each different color.

High-quality color printing Today, printing is so common we hardly think about it. Pick up almost any catalog and you will see beautifully reproduced color. Modern printing presses use the four-color process (CMYK) to produce rich, vivid colors from only four inks.

Color separations To print a color photograph, the image is first converted into four separate images in cyan, magenta, yellow, and black (color separations). Each color separation represents what will be printed with its matching CMYK color. For example, the cyan separation is printed with cyan ink, the magenta separation with magenta ink, and so on. Figure 16.28 shows the four color separations from an image of the author's daughter. Of course, were this book printed with the four-color process, the image would be in full color.

Halftone screens make a picture into dots Each color separation turned into a *halftone screen*. A halftone turns the image into a series of small dots. The size of the dots is proportional to the darkness of the color. The example on the right has 50 dots per inch. A magazine printer might use 150-180 dots per inch. The dots are necessary to allow space for all four colors. The final image will contain cyan, magenta, yellow, and black dots all close together. The dots in the final print are so close they are perceived as a continuous color.

Halftone screen

The printing press On the printing press, each of the four separations is printed on the same paper by a separate printing station. Careful alignment of the printing stations ensures that the dots line up and do not overlap each other. If the dots do not line up, the printed image is blurry. You may have seen a color newspaper photo that is blurry because the dots were not lined up. Newspapers print with coarse halftone screens; with a magnifying glass, you can see the dots easily.

Separating an image into the four process colors

Full color image

Cyan   Magenta

Yellow   Black

Figure 16.28: *To be printed by a full-color press, an image is separated into separate cyan, magenta, yellow, and black images.*

The four-color printing process

Making all colors from just four

The CMYK process allows all colors to be made with just four colors of ink. For example, suppose you want the color green. To see green, you need to remove the red and blue from white light. If you look at Table 16.1 below, to absorb red and blue, you need a mixture of cyan and yellow ink. If you were mixing paint, this is exactly what to do. You get green paint by mixing equal quantities of cyan and yellow paint.

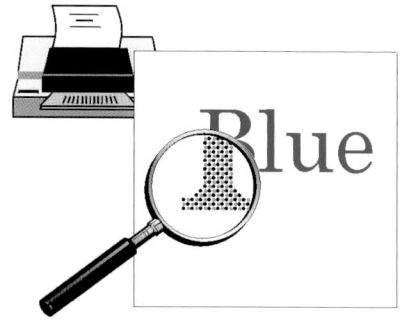

Table 16.1: The three subtractive primary colors

The color . . .	. . . absorbs . . .	. . . and reflects . . .
Cyan	Red	Blue and green
Magenta	Green	Red and blue
Yellow	Blue	Red and green

Figure 16.29: *Printed color images actually consist of tiny dots spaced very closely together.*

Printing presses do not mix ink

On a printing press, mixing inks to make each color is impossible because there are so many colors to print. Instead, dots of each of the four colors are printed very close together. If you take a powerful magnifying glass you can see the individual cyan, magenta, yellow, and black dots in a printed picture (Figure 16.29).

Black

You see black when no light is reflected. In theory, if you add magenta, cyan, and yellow, you have a mixture that absorbs all light so it looks black. Some electronic printers actually make black by printing cyan, magenta, and yellow together. Because the dyes are not perfect, you rarely get a good black this way. Better printers use a black ink to make black separately.

Color laser and ink-jet printers

Color computer printers also work by putting tiny dots on paper. The dots use the same four colors, cyan, magenta, yellow, and black. With an ink-jet printer, tiny drops of ink are squirted by a print head that moves back and forth across the paper. The image is built up from thousands of tiny dots printed in rows across the paper (Figure 16.30). With a laser printer the dots are formed by tiny particles of colored plastic which are melted onto the paper. High-resolution color printers print as many as 1,200 dots per inch.

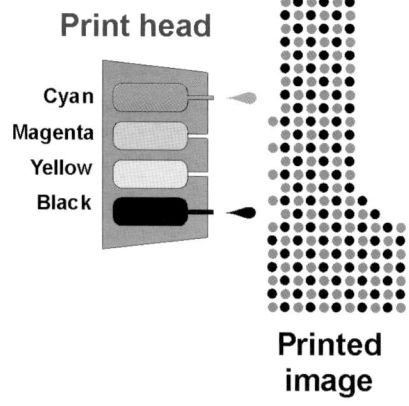

Figure 16.30: *To print a colored image, an ink-jet printer scans its print head back and forth, laying down lines of colored dots by squirting tiny droplets of each of the four colors of ink.*

Chapter 16 Review

Vocabulary Review

Match the following terms with the correct definition. There is one extra definition in the list that will not match any of the terms.

Set One

1. fluorescent
2. incandescence
3. inverse square law
4. speed of light

a. 340 m/s
b. 300,000,000 m/s
c. Making light with heat
d. A type of bulb that creates light by passing electricity through a gas.
e. The mathematical relationship describing how the intensity of light diminishes with distance.

Set Two

1. cones
2. photoreceptors
3. rods
4. pigments
5. photon

a. Photoreceptors that respond to color
b. Photoreceptors that respond to black and white
c. The shimmering of star light traveling through air
d. Bundle of light energy
e. Cells in the back of the eye that create the sense of vision
f. Chemicals that absorb specific colors of light

Set Three

1. white light
2. intensity
3. additive primary colors
4. subtractive primary colors

a. Red, blue, green
b. Yellow, magenta, cyan
c. Orange, violet, green
d. Measure of the amount of energy falling on a surface each second
e. A combination of all the colors of light

Set Four

1. blue light
2. CMYK
3. photo luminescence
4. red light

a. How a candle gives off light
b. Made up of low energy visible photons
c. Made up of high energy visible photons
d. The process of releasing stored energy as light
e. The four-color process used by modern printing presses

327

Concept review

1. How is an incandescent bulb different from a fluorescent bulb?

2. In what units is light intensity measured?

3. You wish to read a book in your bedroom. There is enough light for you to read if you use either ar 100 W ceiling light or a 15 W desk lamp. Both use the same type of bulb. Explain why you can read with the less powerful desk lamp.

4. List three ways light can be used for communication.

5. Why do we see lightning before we hear thunder?

6. Compare reflection and refraction.

7. What is white light?

8. How could a blacksmith tell the temperature of a fire long before thermometers were invented?

9. Why is it difficult to distinguish among different colors in a dimly lit room?

10. How can we see many different colors if our eyes only contain three types of cones?

11. Add the colors of light:

    a. red + blue =

    b. blue + green =

    c. red + green =

    d. red + blue + green =

12. Why is mixing pigments called color subtraction?

13. What color results when cyan, magenta, and yellow pigments are mixed?

14. Answer true or false for each:

    a. A green object reflects green light.

    b. A blue object absorbs red light.

    c. A yellow object reflects green light

    d. A white object absorbs red light.

15. Why is it a good idea to wear a white shirt rather than a black shirt on a hot sunny day?

16. Why will a plant grow more quickly if it is grown in white light rather than green light?

17. Explain how a television makes pictures of many colors using only three types of pixels.

18. Use the photon theory of light to describe two ways to create high intensity with both high energy and low energy photons?

19. Explain how glow-in-the-dark materials work.

Unit 6
Light and Optics

Chapter 17

Optics

Objectives for Chapter 17

By the end of this chapter you should be able to:

1. Describe the functions of convex and concave lenses, a prism, and a flat mirror.
2. Describe how light rays form an image.
3. Calculate the angles of reflection and refraction for a single light ray.
4. Draw the ray diagram for a lens and a mirror showing the object and image.
5. Explain how a fiber-optic circuit acts like a pipe for light.
6. Describe the difference between a real image and a virtual image and give an example of each.

Terms and vocabulary words

lens	mirror	prism	optics	geometric optics
specular reflection	diffuse	converging	diverging	law of reflection
normal line	ray diagram	magnification	object	index of refraction
focal point	focal length	optical axis	light ray	magnification
critical angle	Snell's law	real image	virtual image	chromatic aberration
refraction	fiber optics	dispersion	magnifying glass	spherical aberration
reflection	diffraction	telescope	focus	total internal reflection
resolution	pixel	image	focal plane	thin lens formula

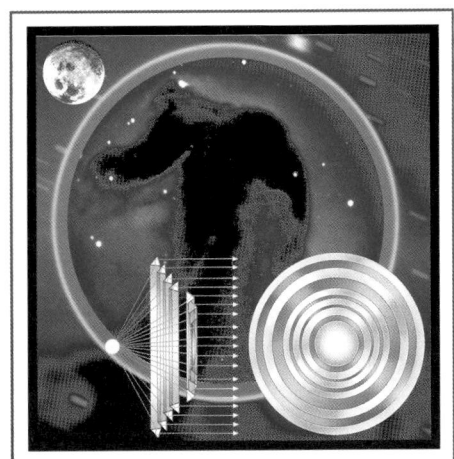

17.1 Reflection and Refraction

Look at your thumb through a strong magnifying glass. It looks huge. Of course, your hand is the same size it always was, even though what you see is a giant thumb (Figure 17.1). The explanation for why and how magnification occurs is part of the science of optics. Optics is a branch of physics that deals with the way light behaves. Optical devices you have probably used include mirrors, telescopes, eyeglasses, contact lenses, and magnifying glasses. This section introduces the fundamental ideas behind optics and the formation of images. It is truly amazing how much can be accomplished by clever application of the basic laws for reflection and refraction.

Figure 17.1: *When you look through a magnifying glass, your thumb appears huge.*

What is optics?

Definition of optics
The overall study of how light behaves is called optics. The branch of optics that focuses on the creation of images is called geometric optics, because it is based on relationships between angles and lines that describe light rays. With a few rules from geometry we can explain how images are formed by devices like lenses, mirrors, cameras, telescopes, and microscopes. Optics also includes the study of the eye itself because the human eye forms an image with a lens.

Light rays
As described in Chapter 16, light is energy that is always in motion. As light moves through a material, such as air, the light travels in straight lines. If three people in a room see the same vase, it is because light rays travel straight from the vase to their eyes (Figure 17.2). We draw lines called light rays on diagrams showing how light travels through space. Think of a light ray as an imaginary arrow following a thin beam of light. Drawing 2 or 3 rays is usually enough to determine if an image will be created, and the location and size of the image.

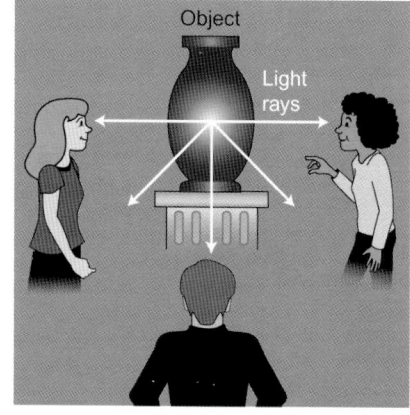

Figure 17.2: *Light rays travel in straight lines from the objects we see to our eyes.*

Basic geometry
Light rays may bend when they cross a boundary between materials. For example, a magnifying glass bends light rays when the rays cross from air into glass and back from glass into air again. When light rays bend, images may appear smaller or larger than the actual objects being viewed. A magnifying glass works because the curved surface of a glass lens bends light in a particular way. In geometric optics we use the laws of reflection and refraction to trace how light rays travel through materials such as air and glass. Models deduced from geometric optics are used to design cameras, telescopes, and other optical instruments.

Basic optical devices

Optical devices are common	Almost everyone has experience with optical devices and their effects. For example, trying on new glasses, checking your appearance in a mirror, or admiring the sparkle from a diamond ring all involve optics. Through experiences like these, most of us have seen optical effects created by three basic optical devices: the lens, the mirror, and the prism.

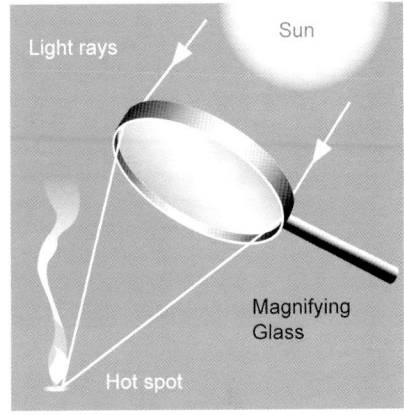

Figure 17.3: *Light rays passing through a magnifying glass converge to a point.*

Lenses	A lens is an optical device that is used to bend light in a specific way. A converging lens bends light so that the light rays come together to a point. This is why a magnifying glass makes a hot spot of concentrated light (Figure 17.3). The human eye contains a single converging lens. A diverging lens bends light so it spreads light apart instead of coming together. An object viewed through a diverging lens appears smaller than it would when viewed without the lens.
Mirrors	A mirror is a familiar optical device—you probably used one this morning. Mirrors reflect light and allow us to see ourselves (Figure 17.4). Flat mirrors show a true-size image. Curved mirrors distort images by causing the light rays to come together or spread apart. A fun house at the circus uses curved mirrors to make you look thin, wide, or upside down. The curved side-view mirrors on a car make any cars behind you look farther away than they really are.
Prisms	A prism is another optical device that can cause light to change directions. A prism is a solid piece of glass with flat polished surfaces. A common triangular prism is shown in the diagram below. Prisms are used to bend and/or reflect light. Many optical devices such as telescopes, cameras, and supermarket laser scanners use prisms of different shapes to bend and reflect light in precise ways

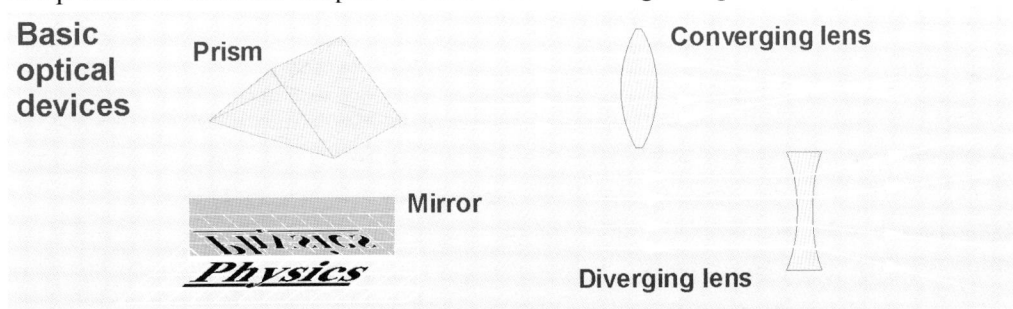

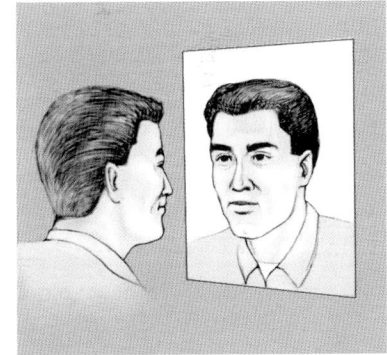

Figure 17.4: *The image you see in a flat mirror is life-size and oriented as if you were standing in front of yourself but reversed left-to-right.*

Reflection

The image in a mirror

When you look at yourself in a mirror, you see your own image as if your exact twin were standing in front of you, but reversed right-to-left. The image appears as far into the mirror as you are in front of the mirror (Figure 17.5). If you step back, so does your image.

Incident and reflected rays

Images appear in mirrors because of how light is reflected by mirrors. In the last chapter, we learned that light is reflected from all surfaces, not just mirrors. But not all surfaces form images. The reason is that there are two types of reflection. Consider a ray of light coming from a light bulb. The incident ray follows the light falling onto the mirror. The reflected ray follows the light bouncing off the mirror.

Specular reflection

A ray of light that strikes a shiny surface generates a single reflected ray. This type of reflection is called specular reflection. In specular reflection each incident ray bounces off in a single direction (Figure 17.6). Images are produced in polished surfaces that create specular reflection, such as on the surface of a mirror. If you look closely at a mirror illuminated by a light bulb, somewhere the reflected light forms an image of the light bulb itself. In fact, a surface which has perfect specular reflection is invisible. If you look at that surface, you see reflections of other things, *but you do not see the surface itself.*

Diffuse reflection

A surface that is not shiny creates diffuse reflection. In diffuse reflection, a single ray of light scatters into many directions (Figure 17.6). Diffuse reflection is caused by the roughness of a surface. Even if a surface feels smooth to the touch, on a microscopic level it may be rough. For example, the surface of a wooden board creates a diffuse reflection. In a lighted room, you see the board by reflected light, but you cannot see an image of a light bulb in the board. When you look at a diffuse reflecting surface *you see the surface itself.*

Diffuse and specular reflection together

Many surfaces are in between rough and smooth. These kinds of surfaces create both kinds of reflection. For example, a polished wood tabletop can reflect some light in specular reflection, and the rest of the light in diffuse reflection. The specular reflection creates a faint reflected image on the table surface. You also see the table surface itself by light from diffuse reflection.

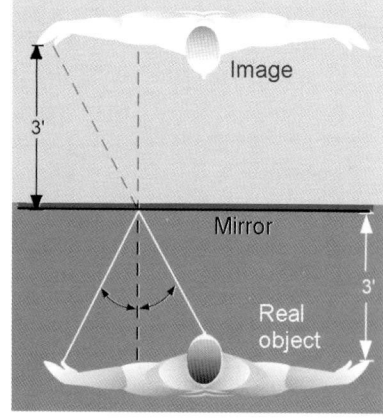

Figure 17.5: *The image you see in a flat mirror is the same distance behind the mirror as you are in front of it.*

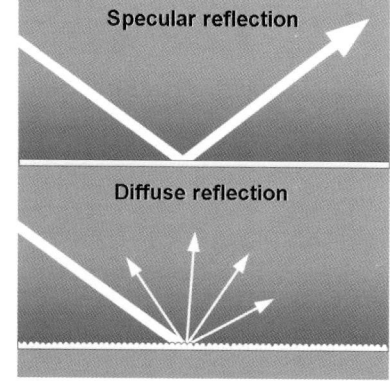

Figure 17.6: *Specular and diffuse reflections.*

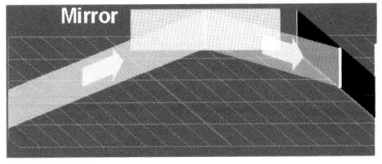

The law of reflection

The law of reflection
The law of reflection relates the direction of a reflected ray to the direction of the incident ray in specular reflection. The law of reflection is easy to remember: Light rays reflect from a mirror at the same angle which they arrive.

The normal line
The tricky part of using the law of reflection is defining the angles of the incident and reflected rays. To be consistent, angles are always measured relative to the normal line. The normal line is an imaginary line perpendicular to the surface of a mirror from the point where the incident ray touches the mirror. You draw the normal line by starting where the incident ray strikes the mirror and drawing a line perpendicular to the mirror's surface (Figure 17.7).

Drawing a ray diagram
A ray diagram is the clearest way to show how light rays interact with mirrors, lenses, and other optical devices. A ray diagram is an accurately drawn sketch showing the path of one or more light rays. Incident and reflected rays are drawn as arrows on a ray diagram. A mirror is drawn as a solid line. The normal line is drawn as a dotted line perpendicular to the mirror surface.

Measuring the angle of incidence and reflection
The angles of incidence and reflection are measured as shown in the ray diagram in Figure 17.7. Both angles are always measured between the light rays and the normal line. The law of reflection also applies to light reflected by curved mirrors (Figure 17.8). With curved mirrors, however, the direction of the normal line changes.

Actual experiment

Ray diagram

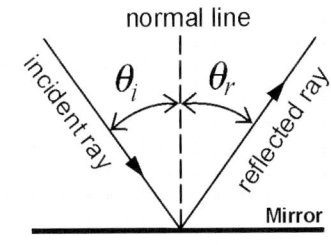

θ_i = angle of incidence
θ_r = angle of reflection

Figure 17.7: *The angle of incidence, θ_i, is equal to the angle of reflection, θ_r.*

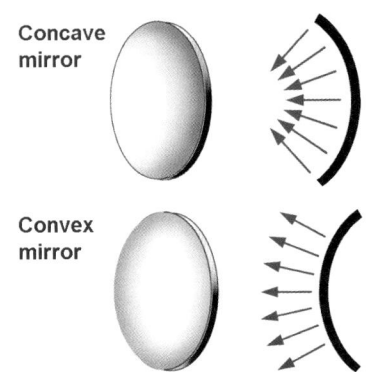

Figure 17.8: *Two common curved mirrors are convex and concave.*

Law of reflection

A light ray is incident on a plane mirror with a 30-degree angle of incidence. Sketch the incident and reflected rays and determine the angle of reflection.
1) You are asked for a ray diagram and the angle of reflection.
2) You are given the angle of incidence.
3) The law of reflection states the angle of reflection equals the angle of incidence.
4) The angle of reflection is 30°.

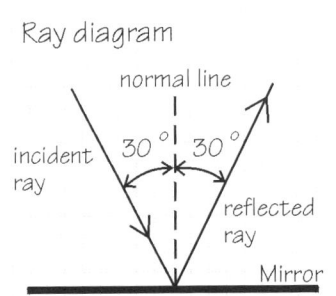

Ray diagram

Refraction

Refraction is the bending of light rays

Light rays may bend as they cross a boundary from one material to another, like from air to water. This bending of light rays is known as refraction. You can see a good example of refraction by looking at a straw in a glass of water (Figure 17.9). The straw appears to break where it crosses the surface of the water. It is obvious that the straw has not actually broken, but that visual effect is caused by refracted light rays. The light rays from the straw are refracted (or bent) when they cross from water back into air before reaching your eyes. Refraction causes the *image* of the straw in the water to appear out of place, not the straw itself.

The index of refraction

The ability of a material to bend rays of light is described by the index of refraction (n). The index of refraction is represented by a lowercase letter n. The index of refraction for air is approximately 1.00. Water has an index of refraction of 1.33. A diamond has an index of refraction of 2.42. The high index of refraction is what creates the sparkling quality that makes diamonds so attractive. Table 17.1 lists the index of refraction for some common materials.

The difference in index of refraction

When a ray of light crosses from one material to another, the amount it bends depends on the difference in index of refraction between the two materials. If the difference is large, the light ray bends a lot. For example, a light ray crossing from air into a diamond at 45 degrees is bent by 28 degrees. The difference in index of refraction between air and diamond is 1.42. The same light ray going from air into water bends by just 13 degrees. The light ray bends less because the difference in index of refraction between air and water is only 0.33.

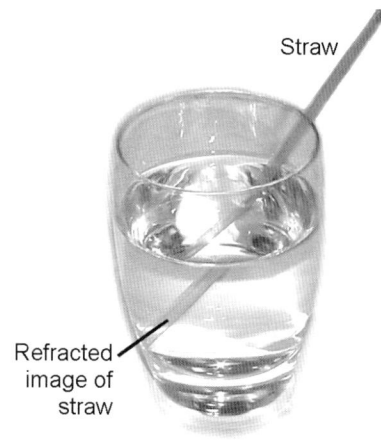

Figure 17.9: *A straw seems to separate at the point it enters the water in the glass. This illusion is created because light is refracted as it travels from water to air.*

Table 17.1:
The index of refraction for some common materials

Material	Index of refraction
Vacuum	1.0
Air	1.0001
Water	1.33
Ice	1.31
Glass	1.5
Diamond	2.42

Refraction from air into diamond

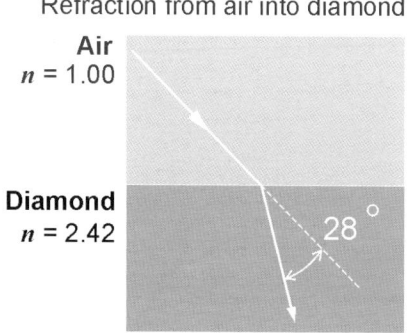

Refraction from air into water

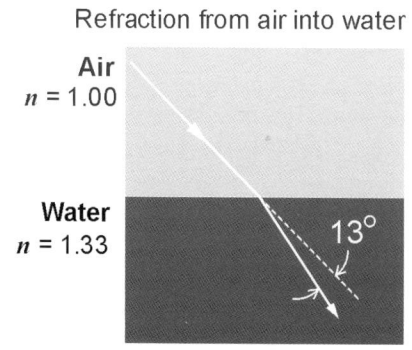

Snell's law of refraction ~~Advanced Topic~~

The angles of incidence and refraction To analyze refraction, the angles of light rays are described relative to a normal line. The angle of incidence (θ_i) is the angle between the incident ray and the normal, the same as for a mirror. The angle of refraction (θ_r) is the angle between the refracted ray and the normal (diagram below).

The direction a light ray bends The direction in which a light ray bends depends on whether it is moving from a high index of refraction to a lower index or vice versa. A light ray going from a low index of refraction into a higher index bends *toward the normal*. A light ray going from a high index of refraction to a low index bends *away from the normal*.

The index of refraction in both materials Refraction occurs when light crosses a boundary between materials with a different index of refraction. The amount that light is refracted depends on the index of refraction in both materials. The *incident* material is the material containing the incident light ray. The index of refraction in the incident material is given the symbol "n-sub-i" (n_i). The *refractive material* contains the refracted ray and its refractive index is "n-sub-r" (n_r).

Snell's law Snell's law is the relationship between the angles of incidence and refraction and the index of refraction of both materials. When light passes completely through a refractive material, Snell's law must be used twice to calculate the path of a ray: the first time going into the material and the second time coming back out again.

Snell's law

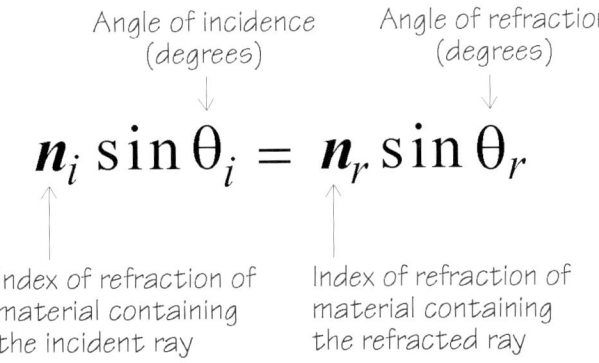

$$n_i \sin\theta_i = n_r \sin\theta_r$$

Angle of incidence (degrees)
Angle of refraction (degrees)
Index of refraction of material containing the incident ray
Index of refraction of material containing the refracted ray

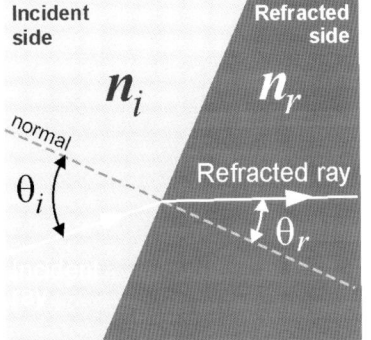

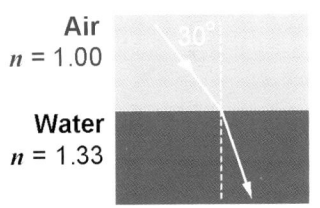

Reflection and the critical angle

Total internal reflection

When light goes from a high-index material such as glass back into air, it bends away from the normal. Mathematically, it means the angle of refraction is always greater than the angle of incidence. For example, in water ($n = 1.33$) when the angle of incidence is 48 degrees, the angle of refraction is 81 degrees (diagram below). When the angle of refraction reaches 90 degrees, the refracted ray is traveling straight along the surface of the water. For water, this happens when the angle of incidence is 49 degrees. At angles greater than 49 degrees, *there is no refracted ray.* All of the light is reflected back into the water. This is called total internal reflection. Total internal reflection occurs when the angle of refraction becomes greater than 90 degrees.

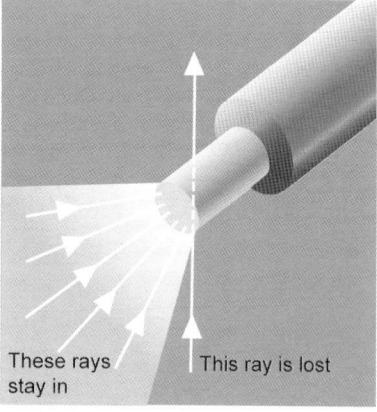

Figure 17.10: *Light entering a glass rod at greater than the critical angle is trapped inside the glass.*

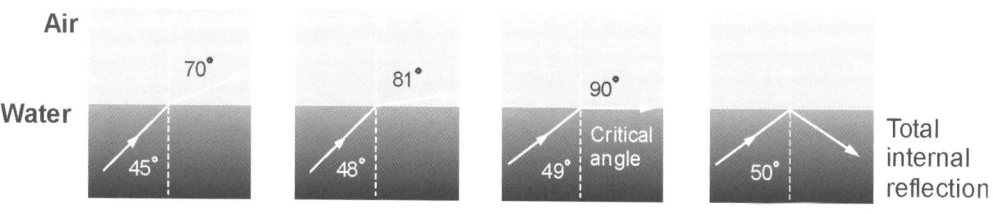

The critical angle

The angle at which light begins reflecting back *into* a refractive material is called the critical angle, and it depends on the index of refraction. The critical angle for glass is about 42 degrees. The critical angle for water is about 49 degrees.

Fiber optics are pipes for light

Suppose you have a rod of solid glass and you send light into the end at an angle of incidence greater than the critical angle (Figure 17.10). The light reflects off the wall and bounces back into the glass. It then reflects off the opposite wall as well. In fact, the light always approaches the wall at greater than the critical angle so it always bounces back into the glass. You have constructed a *light pipe,* so to speak: Light goes in one end and comes out the other. If the glass rod is made very thin, it becomes flexible, but still traps light by total internal reflection. **Fiber optics** are made of thin glass fibers and use total internal reflection to carry light, even around bends and corners (Figure 17.11). A bundle of fiber optics can make an *image pipe,* where each fiber transmits one dot of an image from one end of the bundle to the other end. Image pipes are used for inspections in surgery, for example. Fiber optics are also used for communications and data signals.

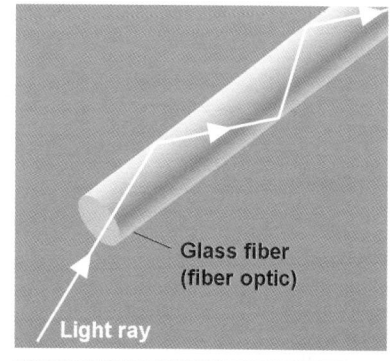

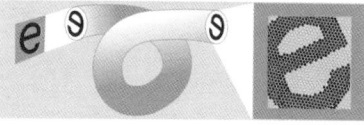

Fiber optic image pipe

Figure 17.11: *Fiber optics are thin glass fibers that trap light by total internal reflection.*

Dispersion and prisms

Observing the spectrum with a prism

The index of refraction for most materials varies by a small amount depending on the color of the incident light. For example, glass has an index of refraction slightly greater for blue light than for red light. When white light passes through a glass prism, blue is bent more than red (Figure 17.12). Colors between blue and red are bent proportional to their position in the spectrum. Remember, ROYGBV is the order of colors in the spectrum of visible light: Red, orange, yellow, green, blue, violet. Yellow is in the middle of the spectrum so yellow rays are bent about halfway between red rays and blue rays. If white light from a brightly illuminated slit passes through a prism and falls on a screen, the spectrum of colors in white light forms a rainbow on the screen.

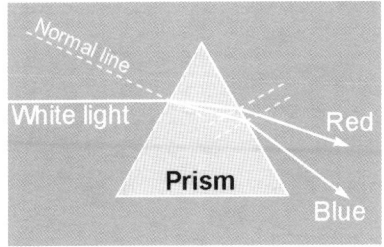

Figure 17.12: *A prism separates the colors of white light by dispersion.*

Dispersion

The variation in refractive index with color is called dispersion. The indices of refraction listed in Table 17.1 were measured by observing the bending of a specific color of yellow light. This color was chosen because it is the center of the visible spectrum.

Rainbow

A rainbow is an example of dispersion in nature. Tiny rain droplets act as prisms separating the colors in the white light rays from the sun. The different colors of light that reach your eye come from rain droplets at different levels in the sky (Figure 17.13). Next time you see a rainbow, notice that the colors follow ROYGBV (roy-gee-biv) from top to bottom.

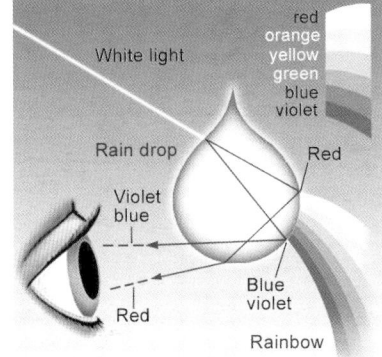

Figure 17.13: *Dispersion in drops of water separates the colors of sunlight in a rainbow.*

Chromatic aberration

Dispersion causes a multicolored image formed by single lens to be slightly blurry. A lens forms an image by focusing light. Since the index of refraction is higher for blue light, a lens focuses blue light to a point nearer to the lens than red light. For example, if the film in a camera is placed where red light is in sharp focus, then any blue light in the image will be slightly out of focus, or blurry. This error is known as chromatic aberration. Expensive camera lenses minimize chromatic aberration by using multiple single lenses made from different kinds of glass (Figure 17.14). If at least one of the lenses is a diverging lens, it is possible to make red and blue light focus to the same point. Of course, the colors between red and blue are still slightly blurred but the amount of blur is greatly reduced.

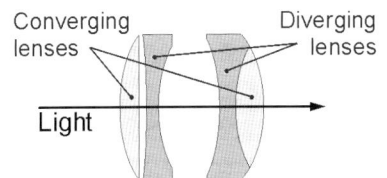

Figure 17.14: *This camera lens design uses four single lenses and corrects for chromatic aberration.*

17.2 Mirrors, Lenses, and Images

We receive most of our information through images carried by light. In this sense, "image" is hard to define exactly. You can think of an image as a picture that organizes light in a way that duplicates the way light is organized somewhere else. For example, the image of a tree duplicates the pattern of light from the tree itself. In fact, the world we see is a world of images created on the retina of the eye by the lens in the front of the eye (Figure 17.15). This section is about images and how images are created by mirrors and lenses. You will learn how to use lenses and mirrors to make images larger or smaller, upright or upside down, near or far away.

Images

Objects and images
It is helpful to think about optics in terms of objects and images. Objects are real physical things that give off or reflect light rays. Images are "pictures" of objects that are formed in space where light rays meet. Images are formed by mirrors lenses, prisms, and other optical devices (Figure 17.16). Images are fundamentally a way of organizing light and have no physical substance like matter does. In fact, clever optics can create images that would be impossible to make with matter.

Rays come together in an image
Each point on an object gives off light rays in all directions. That is why you can see an object from different directions. Suppose you could collect many rays from one point on an object and bring them back together again. You would have created an *image* of that point. An image is a place where many rays that originated from the same point on an object meet together again. A camera works by collecting the rays from an object so they form an image on the film.

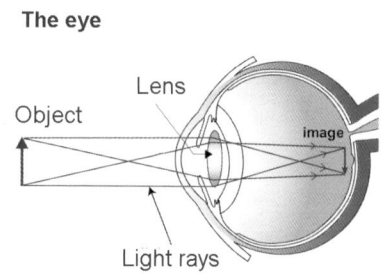

The eye

Figure 17.15: *We see because the eye forms images on the retina at the back of the eyeball.*

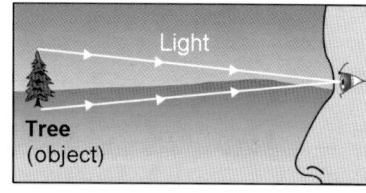
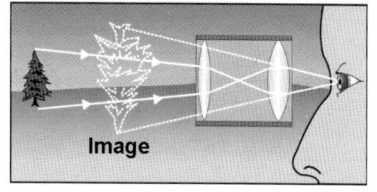

Figure 17.16: *You see the tree because light from the tree reaches your eye. The image of the tree in a telescope is not the real tree, but instead is a different way of organizing light from the tree. A telescope organizes the light so that the tree appears bigger.*

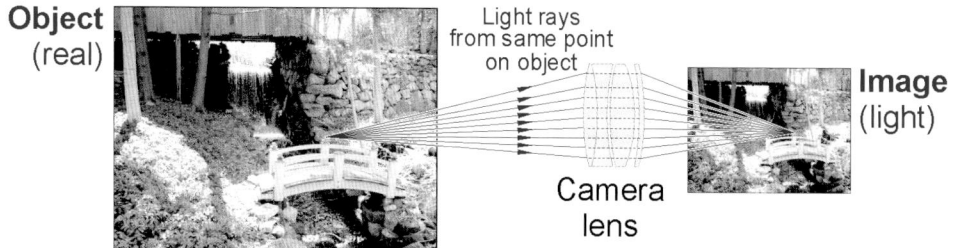

Object (real) Light rays from same point on object **Image** (light) Camera lens

338

The image in a mirror

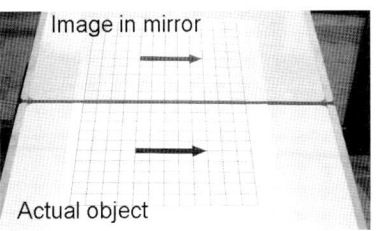

Figure 17.17: *The image in a flat mirror is not left-right reversed.*

Image from a flat mirror The most common image we see every day is our own reflection in a mirror. If we stand in front of a flat mirror, our image appears the same distance in the mirror as we are in front of the mirror. If we move back the image seems to move back into the mirror. If we raise our left hand, the hand on the left side of the image is raised.

The image of an arrow in a mirror The photograph in Figure 17.17 shows a mirror in front of a piece of graph paper that has an arrow drawn on it. The arrow on the graph paper is an *object* because it is a physical source of (reflected) light. The image of the arrow appears in the mirror. Look carefully and you see that the image of the arrow appears the same number of squares *into* the mirror as the paper arrow is in front of the mirror.

Ray diagram

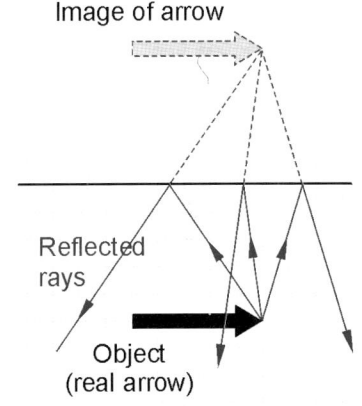

Figure 17.18: *A ray diagram of the arrow in the mirror, showing the location of the virtual image.*

Finding the image in a ray diagram Figure 17.18 shows a ray diagram of the arrow and mirror. The head of the arrow is a source of light rays. The ray diagram traces three light rays that leave the tip of the arrow and reflect from the mirror. These rays obey the law of reflection. *The reflected rays appear to come from a point behind the mirror.* You can tell by extending back the line of the reflected rays (indicated by dotted lines). The image of the tip of the arrow is formed at the point where the extensions of the reflected rays meet. Remember, we said an image forms when many rays from the same point on an object come together again. You can see from the diagram that the image appears exactly the same distance behind the mirror as the arrow is in front of the mirror.

Mirrors form virtual images The image in a mirror is called a virtual image because the light rays do not *actually* come together. They only *appear* to have come from a place where they were together. If you put a piece of paper behind the mirror, you do not see an image of the arrow on the paper. The virtual image in a flat mirror is created by the eye and brain. If light rays appear to come from a point, we see them as if they *did* come from that point. The brain does not say, "Aha, this is a mirror! I will see the arrow where it really is, over there!" Even after you learn physics, your brain will not work that way. Your brain sees the arrow where the light rays *appear* to come from had they always traveled in a straight line from the object.

Lenses

A lens and its optical axis

A lens is made of transparent material with an index of refraction different from air. The surfaces of a lens are curved to refract light in a specific way. The exact shape of a lens's surface depends on how strongly and in what way the lens needs to bend light that passes through it. Nearly all lenses are designed with an optical axis. The optical axis usually goes through the center of the lens. Light traveling along the optical axis is not bent at all by the lens.

Focal point and focal length

Light rays that enter a converging lens parallel to its axis bend to meet at a point called the focal point (Figure 17.19). Light can go through a lens in either direction so there are always two focal points, one on either side. The distance from the center of the lens to the focal point is called the focal length. The focal length is usually the same for both focal points of a lens.

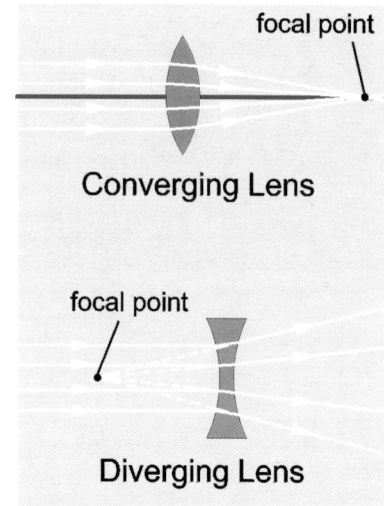

Figure 17.19: *Converging and diverging lenses.*

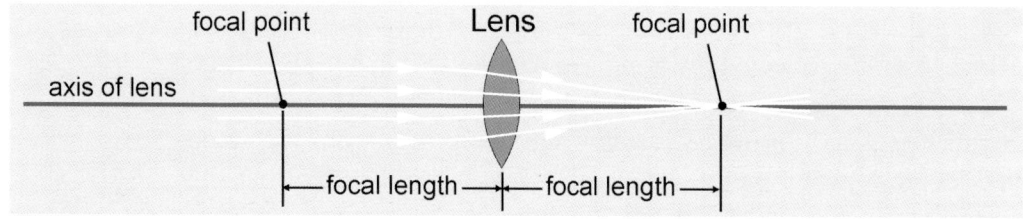

Converging and diverging lenses

As mentioned above, a converging lens bends an incident light ray parallel to the optical axis toward the focal point. A diverging lens bends an incident light ray parallel to the axis outward, away from the focal point (Figure 17.19).

Lenses follow Snell's law of refraction

Most lenses have surfaces that are parts of a sphere. The normal to a spherical surface is always a radius from the center. When light rays fall on a spherical surface from air, they bend *toward* the normal (Figure 17.20). For a convex lens, the first surface (air to glass) bends light rays toward the focal point. At the second surface (glass to air), the rays bend *away* from the normal. Because the second surface "tilts" the other way, it also bends light rays toward the focal point. Although it is not shown, both surfaces of a diverging lens bend light away from the optical axis. For either type of lens, refraction follows Snell's law.

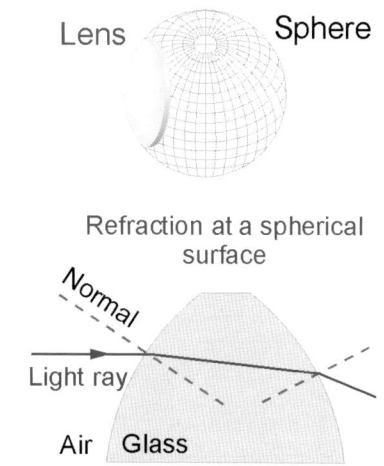

Figure 17.20: *Most lenses have spherical shaped surfaces.*

The image formed by a lens

The focus and focal plane of the lens
The images formed by a lens are created in the same way the image was formed by the mirror. Many rays from the same point on an object are collected and brought to a focus. The focus is where the rays from a point on the object come back together to form the equivalent point on the image. The surface where the image forms is called the focal plane of the lens.

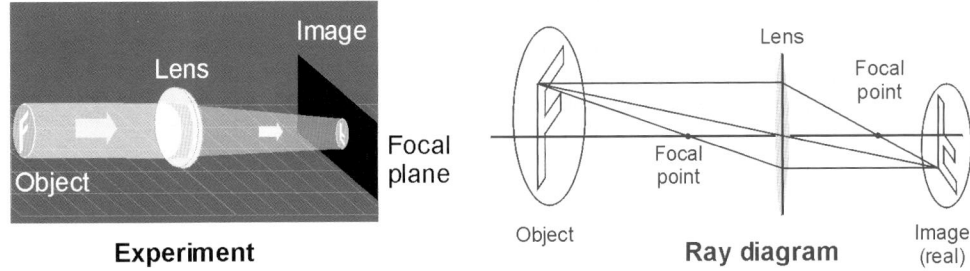

Experiment **Ray diagram**

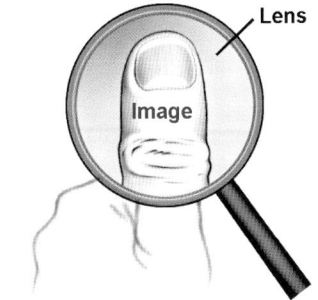

Image in a magnifying glass

Virtual images in a lens
A lens can form a virtual image just as a mirror does. For example, a convex lens used as a magnifying glass creates a virtual image. Rays from the same point on an object are bent by the lens so that they appear to come from a much larger object (Figure 17.21). Virtual images are also created by diverging lenses.

Ray diagram

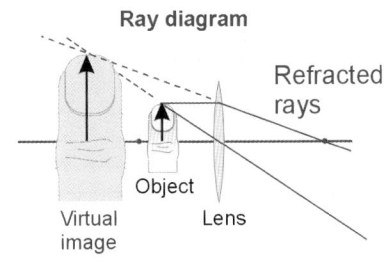

Real images in a lens
A converging lens can also form a real image. In a real image, light rays from the object *actually* come back together on the focal plane. If you put a piece of paper on the focal plane, you see an image formed where the light rays come together. When the object is very far away from a convex lens, the focal plane is at the focal length. If the object is closer, the image forms farther from the lens.

Figure 17.21: *A magnifying glass is a lens that forms a virtual image that is larger-than-life and appears behind the lens.*

Magnification
The images from a lens may be smaller than life size, or equal to or larger than life size. The magnification of a lens is the ratio of the size of the image divided by the size of the object. For example, a lens with a magnification of 4.5 creates an image that appears 4 1/2 times larger than the real-life object (Figure 17.22).

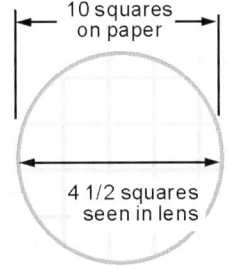

Magnification of 4.5

The orientation of images
Images from a lens may be right side up or inverted. The image of a distant object made with a single convex lens is always inverted. The lenses in movie projectors also invert images. The film is put in upside down so that it appears right side up on the screen.

Figure 17.22: *A lens showing an image magnified by 4.5.*

Drawing ray diagrams of lenses

What a ray diagram tells you
A ray diagram is the best way to understand what type of image is formed by a lens, and whether the image is magnified or inverted. To draw a ray diagram for a lens, you need to know the focal length and the distance of the object from the lens. An upward arrow is used to represent the object.

The three principal rays
To find the location of the image, there are three rays that are the easiest to draw (Figure 17.23). These three rays follow the rules for how light rays are bent by the lens. The three rules are:

1. A light ray passing through the center of the lens is not deflected at all (A).

2. A light ray parallel to the axis passes through the far focal point (B).

3. A light ray passing through the near focal point emerges parallel to the axis (C).

Ray diagrams
The first step in making an accurate ray diagram is to set up a sheet of graph paper by drawing a straight horizontal line to be the optical axis. The lens itself is drawn as a vertical line crossing the axis. The last step in setting up is to draw the two focal points, f, on the axis. The focal points should be the same distance on either side of the lens. It is important that the ray diagram be drawn to *scale*. For example, a scale often used with graph paper is one box equals 1 centimeter.

Drawing the object
Draw an arrow on the left side of the lens to represent the object. The distance from the arrow to the lens must be correctly scaled. For example, an object 20 centimeters away from a lens is drawn 20 boxes to the left of the lens in the ray diagram.

Finding the image
To find the image, draw three rays from the tip of the arrow. The first ray goes straight through the center of the lens. The second ray goes parallel to the axis and bends through the far focal point. The third ray goes through the near focal point and bends to become parallel to the axis. The point where the three rays intersect is where the image of the tip of the arrow will be. Remember, an image forms where many rays from the same point on an object come together again. This is a *real image* because the rays *actually* come together. The image is also smaller than life size and is inverted.

342

Setting up

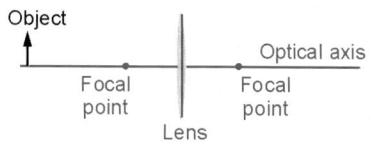

(A) Drawing the first ray

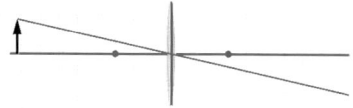

(B) Drawing the second ray

(C) Drawing the third ray

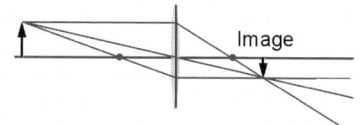

Figure 17.23: *The process of drawing a ray diagram.*

Characteristics of images formed by a lens

Ray diagram for a converging lens
If an object is placed to the left of a converging lens at a distance greater than the focal length, an inverted image is formed on the right-hand side of the lens. This is a *real* image, because it is formed by the actual intersection of light rays from the object. Real images can be projected on a surface. For example, the image from an overhead projector can be shown on a screen.

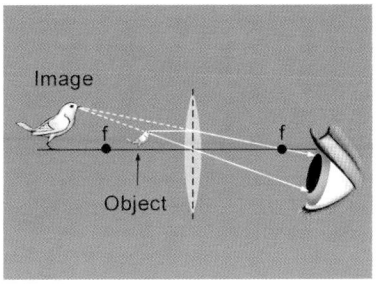

Figure 17.24: *A converging lens becomes a magnifying glass when an object is located inside the lens's focal length.*

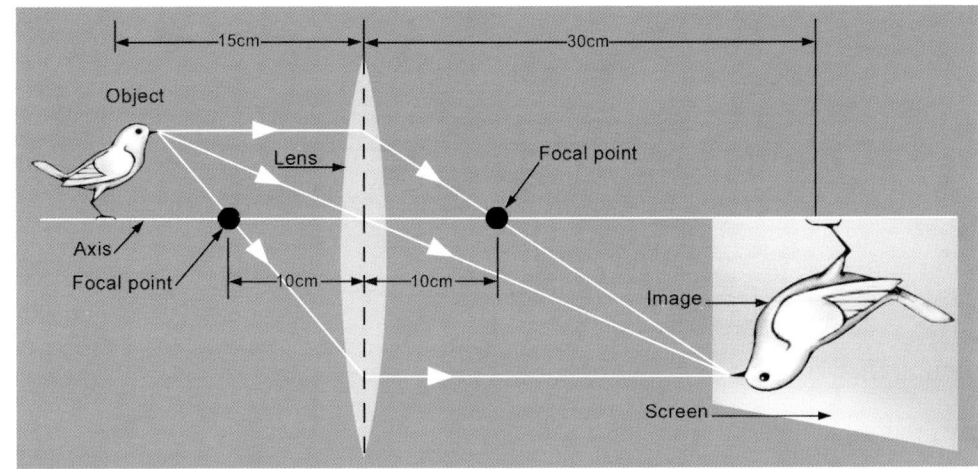

Magnifying glass
A converging lens acts as a magnifying glass when the object is closer to the lens than one focal length. The image formed by a magnifying glass is virtual and appears behind the lens (Figure 17.24).

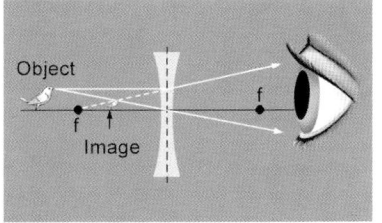

Figure 17.25: *A diverging lens always has the same ray diagram, which shows a smaller image.*

Diverging lens
A diverging lens is thicker around the edges and thinner in the center. The image formed by a diverging lens is virtual and right side up. The image is always smaller and appears on the same side of the lens as the object (Figure 17.25). A ray diagram for a diverging lens follows similar rules, except that a parallel incident ray emerges from the lens at an angle away from the axis. A light ray traveling through the center of the lens continues undeflected.

Image summary table
The different types of images formed by a single lens are listed in Table 17.2. The magnification varies depending on the distance of the object from the lens. To find the magnification, you would have to draw a ray diagram.

Table 17.2:
Images formed by a lens

Lens	Object	Image
Converging	Beyond focal length	Real
Converging	Inside focal length	Virtual
Diverging	Any	Virtual

17.3 Optical Systems

Most of the optical technology we use is not as simple as a single lens or mirror. For example, a camera may contain several lenses, a prism, and a mirror. The telephoto function in a camera is created by a pair of lenses. When you zoom in and out, the camera changes the separation between the lenses. As the separation changes, the magnification also changes. This section is about optical systems. Optical systems are built from lenses, mirrors, and prisms. An optical system collects light and may use refraction and reflection to form an image, or may process light in other ways.

Describing an optical system

The functions of an optical system
An optical system is a collection of mirrors, lenses, prisms, or other optical elements that performs a useful function with light. Optical systems can be described by a number of characteristics. The first characteristic, forming an image, was discussed in the last section. Other characteristics are:

1. The location, type, and magnification of the image.

2. The amount of light that is collected.

3. The accuracy of the image in terms of sharpness, color, and distortion.

4. The ability to change the image, like a telephoto lens on a camera.

5. The ability to record an image (or images) on film or electronically.

The image from a pinhole camera
The more light an optical system collects, the brighter the image it can form. A simple optical system can be made with a pinhole in a box (Figure 17.26). No image forms on the front of the box because rays from many points of the image can reach the same point on the box. An image *does* form inside the box. That image forms because light rays that reach a spot on the surface are restricted by the pinhole to come from only one spot on the object.

A lens makes a brighter image than a pinhole
The image formed by a pinhole is very dim because the pinhole is small and does not allow much light to come through. The image formed by a lens is brighter because a lens is larger and collects more light. Each point on the image is formed by a cone of light collected by the lens. With a pinhole, the cone is much smaller and therefore the image has a much lower light intensity.

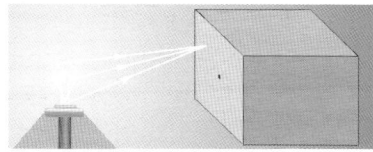

No image forms on the face of the box because light from many points on the object falls on the same place.

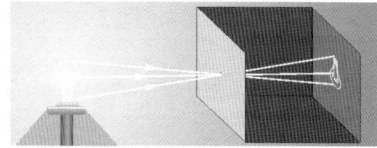

A pinhole forms a dim image by restricting light from each spot on the object to a single spot on the back of the box.

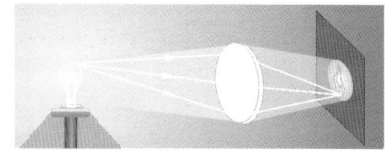

A lens forms a bright image by focusing more light from each point on the object to the equivalent point on the image.

Figure 17.26: *The images formed by a pinhole camera and a lens are different in brightness because different amounts of light are collected to form each point of the image.*

The sharpness of an image

Aberrations are imperfect focusing of light

In a perfect image, light from a single point on an object is focused to a perfect point on an image. Real optical systems are never perfect. Light from a point on an object focuses to a small *area* on the image, but not a sharp point. Defects in the image are called aberrations and can come from several sources.

Chromatic aberration

Chromatic aberration is caused by dispersion. Remember, dispersion causes light of different colors to bend by different amounts. With a single glass lens, for example, an image in red light focuses slightly farther away than an image in blue light (Figure 17.27). A multicolored image is slightly blurry because each color focuses at a different distance from the lens. Chromatic aberration can be reduced by using multiple lenses with different refractive indices. A combination of a converging and a diverging lens can bring both red and blue light into focus at the same point. Of course, other colors are still slightly out of focus, but not by much.

Spherical aberration

Spherical aberration causes a blurry image because light rays farther from the axis focus to a different point than rays near the axis (Figure 17.28). This error is minimized by blocking all but the center of a lens. For example, a camera lens is restricted by an adjustable hole called the f-stop; a larger f-number (smaller opening) reduces spherical aberration but also reduces the amount of light reaching the film. A better way to reduce spherical aberration is to make the lens a different shape. A lens with a parabolic surface does not have spherical aberration. The best camera and telescope lenses use parabolic surfaces.

The diffraction spot size

A third image defect comes from diffraction. Diffraction causes a point on an object to focus as a series of concentric rings around a bright spot (diagram below). It occurs because a lens collects only a limited amount of light from a point on an object. A larger lens collects more light and the spot size formed by diffraction gets smaller. For this reason, larger lenses produce sharper images.

Chromatic aberration

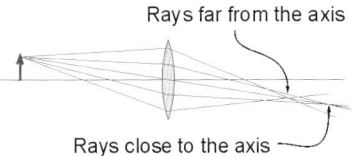

Red rays focus here

Blue rays focus here   Blur

Figure 17.27: *Chromatic aberration occurs when different colors focus at different distances from the lens.*

Spherical aberration

Rays far from the axis

Rays close to the axis

Reducing spherical aberration

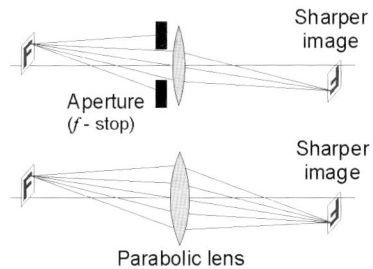

Sharper image

Aperture (*f* - stop)

Sharper image

Parabolic lens

Figure 17.28: *Spherical aberration causes a point to focus to a blur. This error can be reduced by using only the center of the lens, or using a lens with a parabolic surface.*

Diffraction

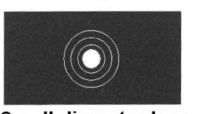

Large diameter lens
Smaller spot size
Sharper image

Small diameter lens
Larger spot size
Fuzzier image

Thin lens formula

Calculating image and object distances

Drawing ray diagrams is useful for learning how lenses work, but it is inaccurate and takes time. The thin lens formula is a mathematical way to do ray diagrams with algebra instead of drawing lines on graph paper. Like ray diagrams, the thin lens formula can be used to predict the location, size, and orientation of an image produced by a lens. For optical systems made of several lenses, it is much easier to predict the resulting image with the thin lens formula instead of using ray diagrams.

How to use the thin lens formula

The thin lens formula relates the focal length (f) to the distance between the object and the lens (d_o) and the distance from the lens to where an image forms (d_i).

Thin lens formula

$$\frac{1}{d_o} + \frac{1}{d_i} = \frac{1}{f}$$

Object distance (cm) — Image distance (cm) — Focal length (cm)

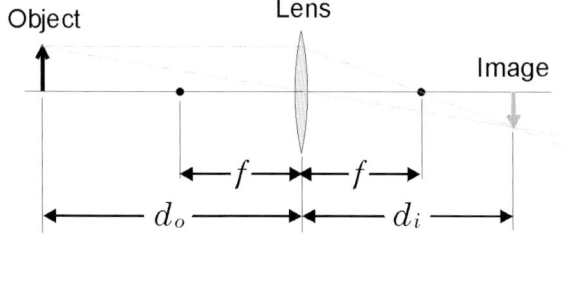

Positive and negative signs

To keep track of whether objects or images are to the right or left of lenses, the thin lens formula uses a *sign convention*. The sign convention assumes light goes from left to right. When the object and image appear like the diagram above, all quantities are positive.

1. Object distances are *positive* to the left of the lens and *negative* to the right of the lens.

2. Image distances are *positive* to the right of the lens and *negative* to the left of the lens.

3. Negative image distances (or object distances) mean *virtual* images (or objects). Positive image distances indicate *real* images.

4. Focal length is *positive* for a converging lens and *negative* for a diverging lens.

Location of an image from the thin lens formula

Calculate the location of the image if the object is 6 cm in front of a converging lens with a focal length of 4 cm.

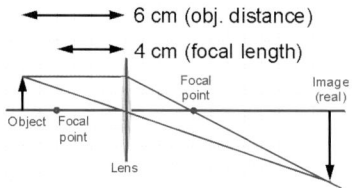

1) You are asked for image distance.

2) You are given the focal length and object distance.

3) The thin lens formula applies:
   $1/d_i = 1/f - 1/d_o$

4) Solve for d_i
   $1/d_i = 1/4 - 1/6$
   $1/d_i = 3/12 - 2/12 = 1/12$
   $d_i = 12$ cm
   The image forms 12 cm to the right of the lens.

Approximations

The thin lens formula assumes the lenses have no thickness. This is a good assumption when objects and images are far away compared with the thickness of a lens.

346

Changing the size of an image

Image relay   A technique known as image relay is used to analyze an optical system made of two or more lenses. The main idea behind image relay is that the image produced by the first lens (1) becomes the object for the second lens (2), and so on. The magnified image you see when you look through a telescope or microscope is produced this way. The ray diagram below shows the image relay analysis for a telescope made with two convex lenses. The first lens (1) forms an image (image 1) between the lenses. This intermediate image is the object for the second lens (2) which forms the final image (image 2). Notice that the intermediate image is inverted while the final image is right-side-up.

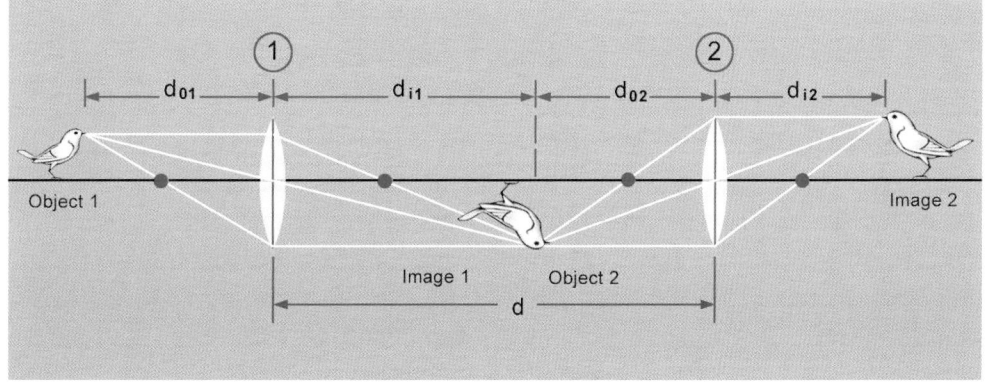

The compound microscope

The microscope that you use in biology class is probably a compound microscope. The optical system of a compound microscope uses two converging lenses. The lens closest to the object, the objective, makes a real, larger, inverted image of the object.

This real image is inside the focal length of the eyepiece lens you look through. Since the image is inside its focal length, the eyepiece lens produces a magnified virtual image of the image from the objective lens. The overall magnification is the magnification of the objective multiplied by the magnification of the eyepiece. For example, a 5× eyepiece lens with a 100× objective lens produces an overall magnification of 500 (5 × 100).

Why multiple lenses are useful   Multiple lenses are useful because they allow an optical system to change the size of an image. Remember, the size of the image from a single lens depends on the distance between the object and the lens. If you are looking at a bird through a camera lens, you cannot easily change the distance between you and the bird. It is much easier to change the optical system. A *telephoto lens* is made from several lenses separated by a certain distance. The magnification depends on the distance between the lenses. By adjusting that distance, the image can be made to appear larger or smaller. The same principle applies to the zoom lens on a video camera.

Recording images

The technology of recording images

Before the invention of the camera, the only way to store an image was to draw it or paint it. Since both drawing and painting take skill and time, few images survive from early history. Today, images are so easy to save that you have seen many thousands of them in photographs, on TV, in magazines, and elsewhere.

Recording images on film

There are two basic techniques for recording images. One uses film. Film records an image by using special inks that respond to light. For a black and white photograph, the ink darkens in response to the intensity of light. Where light on the image is intense, the ink becomes dark. Where the image is dark, the ink remains light. Because dark and light are inverted, this image is known as a *negative* (Figure 17.29). A positive image is created by shining light through the negative onto photographic paper, also coated with light-sensitive ink. Light areas on the negative allow light through and darken corresponding areas on the photograph. A color photograph uses three different colors of light-sensitive ink.

Recording images electronically

The second technique for recording an image is electronic. A digital camera uses a tiny sensor called a CCD, which is located at the focal plane of the camera lens. On the surface of the CCD are thousands of tiny light sensors. There are separate light sensors for red light, blue light, and green light (Figure 17.30). For each sensor, the amount of light is recorded as a number from 0 to 255. For example, if the red sensor records 255, it is seeing the most red light it can handle. A recording of 0 means the sensor sees no light. A color image is recorded as a table of numbers. Each point on the image has three numbers corresponding to the amount of red light, blue light, and green light. The resolution of a digital camera is the number of points, called pixels, that can be recorded by the CCD. A *2 megapixel* camera stores 2 million pixels per image. Since each pixel is three numbers, a 2 megapixel image actually requires 6 million numbers to be stored.

Recording moving images

A video camera records a sequence of images one after another, 30 times per second. Because each image requires so many numbers, a single video image typically includes less than 300,000 pixels. The lower resolution is why single images from video cameras look grainy or blurry when they are printed.

Actual scene

Film (negative image)

Photograph (positive image)

Figure 17.29: *Recording an image on film is a two-step process.*

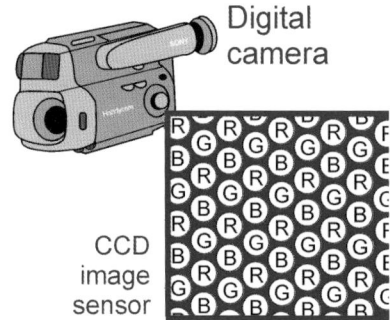

Digital camera

CCD image sensor

Figure 17.30: *A digital camera records an image as intensity of red, green, and blue light.*

348

Application: The Telescope

A telescope is an example of an optical system that has played an important part in human history. When people think of a telescope, most of them think of a refracting telescope. A refracting telescope is usually built like a tube with lenses at each end. Galileo was the first person to use a refracting telescope to learn about the moon and planets.

The refracting telescope   An astronomical refracting telescope is constructed of two converging lenses with different focal lengths. The lens with the longest focal length is called the objective and the shorter focal length lens is the eyepiece.

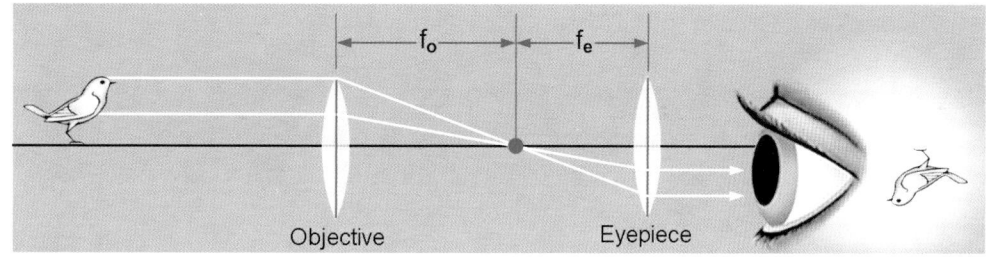

As you can see from the diagram, the ray from the top of the object ends up below the axis as it enters the eye of the observer. This shows that the image from this refracting telescope is inverted. Inverted images are usually fine for looking at objects in space. It does not matter if the image of a star is upside down. But, looking at distant birds or animals upside down is annoying.

A telescope with right-side-up images   To rectify this problem, the converging eyepiece is replaced by a diverging lens in a terrestrial refracting telescope. This arrangement of lenses produces an image that is right-side-up. The design of the terrestrial telescope also sets the lenses a distance apart equal to the sum of their focal lengths.

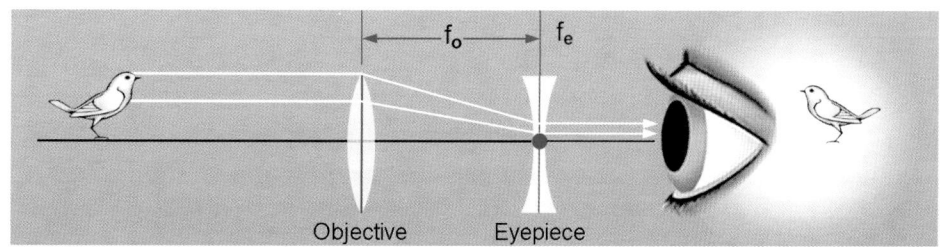

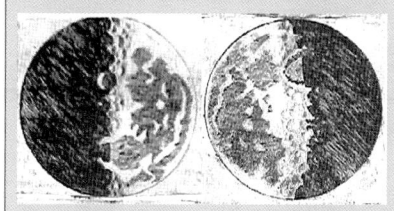

Newtonian reflecting telescope

Larger telescopes can see more distant objects

The larger the diameter of the objective of a telescope, the more light it can gather to form an image. Consequently, a large-diameter telescope can see faint images in the night sky. Objects appear faint for two reasons. One is that they may actually give off very little light, like a planet that gives off only reflected light from the sun. The other reason is that the object is far away. A huge galaxy that is far away appears dimmer than a single star that is close (remember the inverse square law). A refracting telescope is limited by the size of the lens that can be made. Large glass lenses are heavy and difficult to make.

Newtonian reflecting telescope

All large modern telescopes use a concave mirror instead of an objective lens. The most successful design of *reflecting* telescope is called a Newtonian telescope, after Sir Isaac Newton, who designed and built the first one. Although we think of the three laws of motion when we think of Newton, he also made many important contributions to optics, and was the first to prove white light is made of many colors.

Mirror arrangement

In the Newtonian telescope, light falls on a curved mirror that focuses the light in a similar way as the objective lens in a refracting telescope. A small secondary mirror directs the light rays that are reflected off the mirror so that they move toward an eyepiece lens (Figure 17.31). The eyepiece is located so that the distance between it and the mirror is equal to the sum of their focal lengths. This combination of mirrors and lenses collects more light than your eye could do alone. Newtonian telescopes have been built with mirrors as large as 8 meters in diameter, and they can see objects that are so faint they are near the edge of the observable universe.

The Hubble Space Telescope is a reflector

The Hubble Space Telescope orbiting the Earth is a reflecting telescope (Figure 17.32). The Hubble's main mirror has a diameter of 2.4 meters (about 8 feet). Although there are telescopes on Earth with larger mirrors, the Hubble telescope is uniquely valuable because it is above the Earth's atmosphere. Distant objects are much clearer through the Hubble because there is no distortion from the atmosphere refracting light rays from distant galaxies before they get to the telescope.

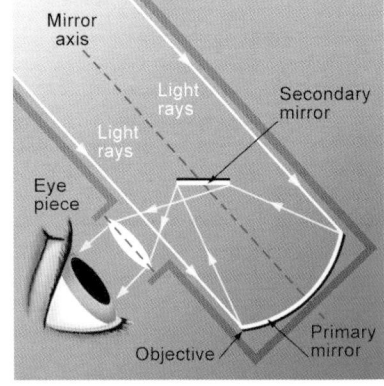

Figure 17.31: *A Newtonian reflecting telescope uses a curved mirror to collect light.*

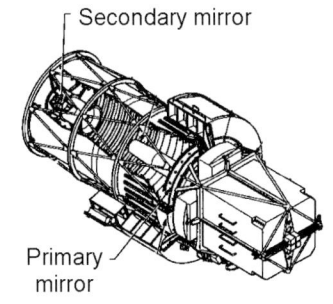

Figure 17.32: *The Hubble Space Telescope is a reflecting design with a 2.4-meter diameter primary mirror. (NASA)*

Chapter 17 Review

Vocabulary review

Match the following terms with the correct definition. There is one extra definition in the list that will not match any of the terms.

Set One

1. diffuse reflection
2. lens
3. normal
4. optics
5. specular reflection

a. Law of reflection
b. Reflection from a rough surface
c. Reflection from a shiny surface
d. The overall study of how light behaves
e. A line drawn perpendicular to a surface
f. Optical device used to bend light in a specific way

Set Two

1. angle of incidence
2. angle of reflection
3. incident ray
4. ray diagram
5. refraction

a. The bending of light
b. A light ray that comes off an object and strikes a surface
c. A light ray that bounces off a surface
d. The angle between the normal and the incident ray
e. The angle between the normal and the reflected ray
f. An accurately drawn sketch showing the path of light rays

Set Three

1. angle of refraction
2. index of refraction
3. medium
4. Snell's Law

a. The equation that predicts refraction
b. The equation that converts light to mass
c. The angle between the normal and the refracted ray
d. A material or substance that a wave can travel through
e. A property of a material that describes the material's ability to bend light

Set Four

1. chromatic aberration
2. dispersion
3. real image
4. total internal reflection
5. virtual image

a. The result of light rays meeting in space
b. A fuzzy image as a result of dispersion
c. Spreading of different colors of light by a prism
d. A fuzzy image as a result of the size of the lens
e. The result of an angle of refraction greater than 90°
f. The result of light rays spreading out but appearing to come from a point

Concept review

1. State the law of reflection. Does this law hold true for specular reflection? Does it hold true for diffuse reflection?

2. Refer to the diagram below. State the correct term for each item listed:

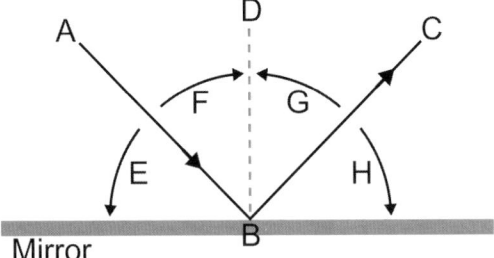

a. Line A-B

b. Line D-B

c. Line B-C

d. Angle F

e. Angle G

3. Use the diagram to answer the following questions:

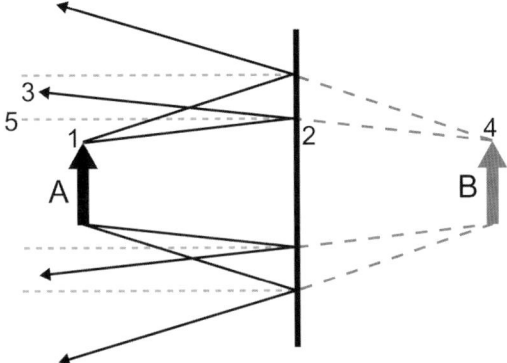

a. If A is a real object in front of a mirror, is B a real image or a virtual image?

b. Line 1-2 is the incident ray from the object to the mirror. Identify the corresponding reflected ray.

c. Line 1-2 is the incident ray from the object to the mirror. Identify the ray that our eye "creates" to allow us to see the virtual image.

d. Object A is 8 cm in front of the mirror. How far away is the image from the object?

4. Refer to Table 17.1 in the text. Which material has a greater ability to bend light, ice or glass? How do you know?

5. Consider the diagram shown. Ray A-B represents the incident ray. Identify the refracted ray in each case:

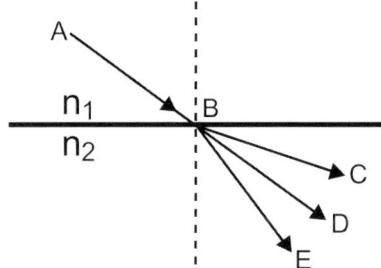

a. n_1 is greater than n_2

b. n_1 is equal to n_2

c. n_1 is less than n_2

6. Explain how fiber optic cables utilize the properties of reflection and refraction.

7. When white light passes through a prism, which color refracts more, yellow or green?

8. According to the sign conventions used with the thin lens formula, object distances to the left of the lens are _____ but image distances to the left of the lens are _____.

9. According to the sign conventions used with the thin lens formula, negative image distances imply _____ images while positive image distances imply _____ images.

10. The diagram below shows an object to the left of a converging (+) lens and the real image produced to the right of the lens. Use the diagram to identify the following rays.

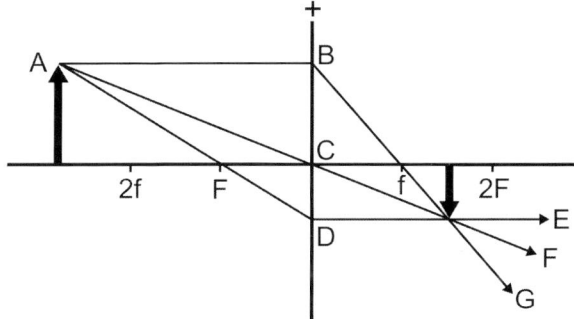

a. The ray of light that travels from the object to the lens along a line parallel to the optical axis.

b. The ray of light that travels from the object to the center of the lens.

c. The ray of light that travels from the object through the focal point to the lens

353

Problems

1. The diagram below shows an object in front of a plane mirror and three rays of light traveling from the object to the mirror. For each ray, draw the corresponding reflected ray, and the virtual ray that we would see coming from the image.

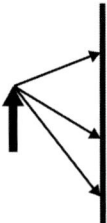

2. The angle between the incident ray striking a mirror and the reflected ray leaving a mirror is 60 degrees. What is the angle of incidence?

3. The phrase "MY MOM" is held in front of a mirror. When you read it in the mirror what do you read? Try it and find out. Make sure you use capital letters.

Use the diagram below to answer questions 4 through 6.

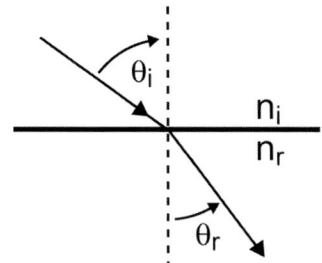

4. An incident ray of light strikes a piece of flint glass (n=1.66) at an angle of incidence of 40 degrees. What is the angle of refraction for this ray inside the glass?

5. Light travels from air into ethyl alcohol. The sine of the incident angle is 0.6427 and the sine of the refracted angle is 0.4726. What is the index of refraction for ethyl alcohol?

6. What angle of incidence would result in an angle of refraction of 30 degrees for light going from air into fused quartz (n=1.46)?

7. An object is placed 10 cm in front of a thin converging lens that has a focal length of 6 cm. Where will the image be located?

Unit 6

Light and Optics

Chapter 18

Wave Properties of Light

Objectives for Chapter 18

By the end of this chapter you should be able to:

1. Calculate the frequency or wavelength of light when given one of the two.
2. Describe the relationship between frequency, energy, color, and wavelength.
3. Identify at least three different waves of the electromagnetic spectrum and an application of each.
4. Interpret the interference pattern from a diffraction grating.
5. Use the concept of polarization to explain what happens as light passes through two polarizers.
6. Describe at least two implications of special relativity with regards to energy, time, mass, or distance.

Terms and vocabulary words

x-ray	spectrum	microwave	index of refraction	electromagnetic wave
spectrometer	gamma ray	radio wave	transmission axis	diffraction grating
special relativity	polarization	polarizer	rest energy	destructive interference
ultraviolet	time dilation	infrared	speed of light	constructive interference
visible light	wavelength			

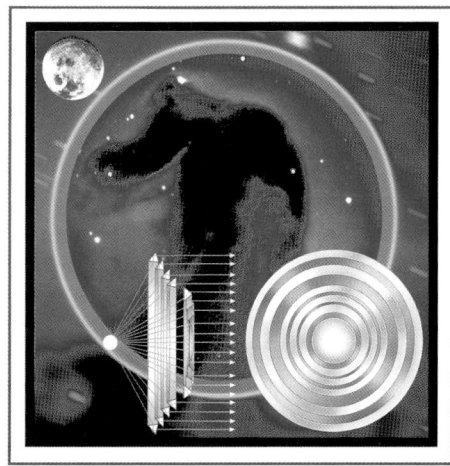

18.1 The Electromagnetic Spectrum

Today, we believe a photon of light also has the properties of a wave, like sound does. Like all waves, light can be described by frequency, wavelength, amplitude, and speed. In the case of light, we use our eyes instead of our ears to sense the wave. Although we cannot see the wave motion of light, its existence is confirmed by the results of many experiments. Light is a small part of a whole series of waves called the *electromagnetic spectrum*. This series of waves includes radio waves, microwaves, and x-rays. This chapter explores the broader picture of light as part of the electromagnetic spectrum.

Traveling oscillations of electricity and magnetism

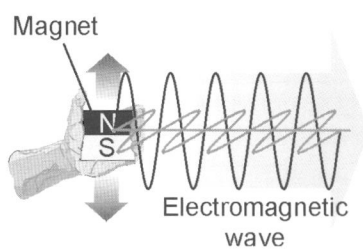

Figure 18.1: *If you could shake a magnet up and down 450 trillion times per second, you could make an electromagnetic wave that you would see as red light.*

Energy fields — When we say that light is a wave, what exactly is waving? This is a difficult question to answer. When you push the north poles of two magnets together, they repel each other while still some distance apart. The magnets feel force without touching each other because magnets create an *energy field* in the space around them. The energy field is what creates forces on other magnets. Electricity also creates an energy field. You may have sensed the effects of this energy field in the air during a thunderstorm, or from static electricity on a dry day.

Electromagnetic waves are oscillations of an energy field — The energy field created by electricity and magnetism can *oscillate* and it supports waves that move, just as water supports water waves. These waves are called electromagnetic waves, and light is one of them. Anything that creates an oscillation of electricity or magnetism also creates electromagnetic waves. When you move a magnet up and down, you are creating an electromagnetic wave (Figure 18.1). If you could shake the magnet up and down 450 trillion times per second, you would make waves of red light.

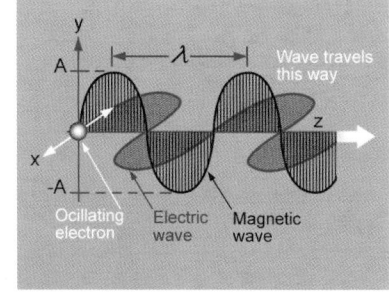

Figure 18.2: *A 3-D view of an electromagnetic wave showing the electric and magnetic portions of the wave. The wavelength and amplitude of the waves are labeled λ and A, respectively.*

Electricity and electromagnetic waves — You can also make electromagnetic waves with electricity. For example, if you could switch the electricity on and off repeatedly in a wire, the oscillating electricity would make an electromagnetic wave. In fact, this is exactly how radio towers make radio waves. Electric currents oscillate up and down the metal towers and create electromagnetic waves of the right frequency to carry radio signals. Electromagnetic waves have both an electric part and a magnetic part (Figure 18.2), and the two parts exchange energy back and forth like a pendulum exchanges potential and kinetic energy back and forth.

Frequency and wavelength of light

Frequency	4.6×10^{14} to 7.5×10^{14} Hz
Wavelength	4×10^{-7} to 6.5×10^{-7} meters wavelength

The frequency of light The frequency of light waves is incredibly high: 10^{14} is a 1 with 14 zeros after it. Red light has a frequency of 460 trillion, or 460,000,000,000,000 cycles per second. Light wave frequencies are so high, we use units of terahertz (THz) to measure them. One THz is a trillion hertz (10^{12} Hz), or a million megahertz.

The wavelength of light Because the frequencies are so high, the wavelengths are tiny. Waves of red light have a length of only 0.00000065 meter (6.5×10^{-7}m). Figure 18.3 shows the size of a light wave relative to other small things. Because of the high frequency and small wavelength, we do not normally see the true wavelike nature of light. Instead, we see reflection, refraction, and color.

Frequency and color With other waves, we found that energy was proportional to frequency. Higher-frequency waves have more energy than lower-frequency waves. The same is true of light. The higher the frequency of the light, the higher the energy of the wave. Since color is related to energy, there is also a direct relation between color, frequency, and wavelength. Table 18.1 shows the color, frequency, and wavelength of visible light. One nanometer is 10^{-9} meters.

Table 18.1: Frequencies and wavelengths of light

Energy (relative)	Color	1×10^{-6} m	Wavelength (nanometers)	Frequency (THz)
Low	Red		650	462
↕	Yellow		580	517
	Green		530	566
	Blue		470	638
High	Violet		400	750

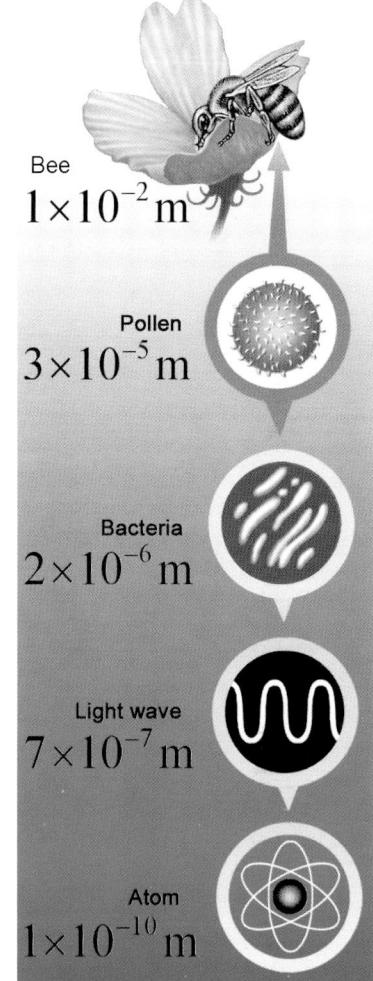

Figure 18.3: *A bee is about a centimeter long; a grain of pollen is about 0.03 mm wide; a bacterium is about 2.0×10^{-6} m long; the wavelength of the longest wave we can see is 7×10^{-7} m = 700 nm; and an atom is about 0.1 nm in diameter.*

The speed of light waves

The speed of light is frequency times wavelength

In the previous chapter we talked about the speed of light as being incredibly fast (3×10^8 m/sec) and being represented by its own symbol, c. Not only light, but all electromagnetic waves travel at that speed in a vacuum. Like other waves, the speed of light is equal to the product of frequency and wavelength.

The speed of light
(relationship between frequency and wavelength)

$$\underset{\substack{\text{Speed of light} \\ (3 \times 10^8 \text{ m/sec})}}{\underbrace{}}\ c = f\lambda\ \overset{\text{Wavelength (m)}}{}$$

Frequency (Hz)

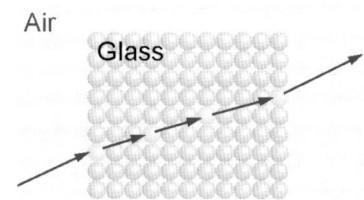

Air   **Glass**

Figure 18.4: *The passage of light through a material takes more time because the light must continuously be absorbed and re-emitted to pass through neighboring atoms.*

To calculate the wavelength of light or any electromagnetic waves, we use the speed of light formula. For example, to calculate the wavelength from the frequency, the formula is rearranged to solve for wavelength, $\lambda = c \div f$. Red light with a frequency of 462×10^{12} Hz, has a wavelength of 649×10^{-9} m:
649×10^{-9} m = $(3 \times 10^8$ m/s$) \div (462 \times 10^{12}$ Hz$)$.

Light travels slower through materials where $n > 1$

The index of refraction (n) from the last chapter, is actually the ratio of the speed of light in a material to the speed of light in vacuum. When passing through a material like glass, light is continuously absorbed and re-emitted by neighboring atoms (Figure 18.4). In between atoms, light moves at its normal speed. But the process of absorption and emission adds a delay moving "through" each atom. As a result, light travels more slowly through materials than it does in a vacuum. The speed of light in a material is equal to the speed of light in a vacuum divided by the refractive index of the material. For example, water has a refractive index of 1.33. The speed of light in water is 2.2×10^8 m/sec ($3 \times 10^8 \div 1.33$).

Wavelengths are shorter in refractive materials

When moving through a material, the frequency of light stays the same. If 462×10^{12} waves go in per second, then 462×10^{12} waves must come out per second. Otherwise waves would pile up at the boundary between materials. Because the frequency stays the same, the wavelength of light is also reduced by the index of refraction. For example, the wavelength of light in water is equal to its wavelength in air divided by 1.33, the index of refraction for water.

Calculate the wavelength of light

Calculate the wavelength in air of blue-green light that has a frequency of 600×10^{12} Hz.

1) You are asked for the wavelength.
2) You are given the frequency.
3) The speed of light is $c = f\lambda$.
4) $\lambda = c \div f$
   $= (3 \times 10^8$ m/sec$)$
   $\div (600 \times 10^{12}$ Hz$)$
   $= 5 \times 10^{-7}$ m

Waves of the electromagnetic spectrum

Visible light is a small part of the energy range of electromagnetic waves. The whole range is called the electromagnetic spectrum and visible light is in the middle of it. On the low-energy end of the spectrum are radio waves with wavelengths billions of times longer than those of visible light. Gamma rays, on the high-energy end, have wavelengths millions of times smaller than those of visible light.

Figure 18.5: *A 100-megahertz radio wave (FM) has a wavelength of 3 meters, about the height of a classroom.*

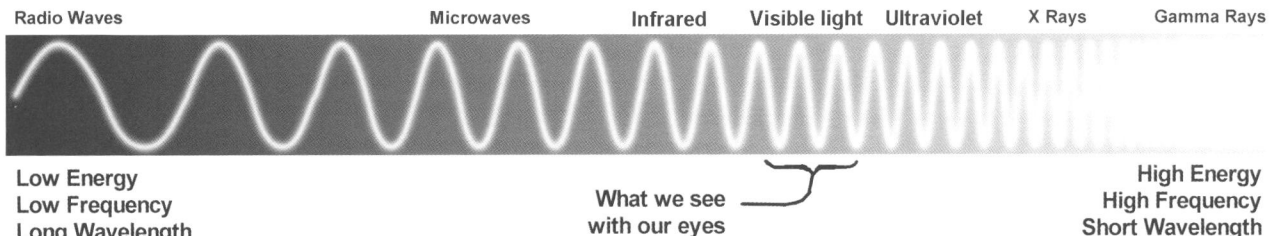

| Radio Waves | Microwaves | Infrared | Visible light | Ultraviolet | X Rays | Gamma Rays |

Low Energy
Low Frequency
Long Wavelength

What we see with our eyes

High Energy
High Frequency
Short Wavelength

Radio waves | Radio waves are on the low-frequency end of the spectrum. They have wavelengths that range from hundreds of meters down to less than a centimeter (Figure 18.5). Radio broadcast towers are so tall because they have to be at least one-quarter of a wavelength long.

Microwaves | Microwaves range in length from approximately 30 cm (about 12 inches) to about 1 mm (the thickness of a pencil lead). Cell phones and microwave ovens use microwaves (Figure 18.6). The waves in a microwave oven are tuned to the natural frequency of liquid water molecules. The high intensity of microwaves inside an oven rapidly transfers energy to water molecules in food. The absorption of microwave energy (heating) occurs through some depth since microwaves can penetrate many centimeters. The statement "microwaves cook from the inside out" is not exactly true. However, microwaves do heat food at more than just the surface, unlike conventional ovens which heat food only at the surface.

Figure 18.6: *Cell phone transmissions are made with microwaves.*

Infrared waves | The infrared (or IR) region of the electromagnetic spectrum lies between microwaves and visible light. Infrared includes wavelengths from 1 millimeter to about 700 nanometers. Infrared waves are often referred to as radiant heat (Figure 18.7). Although we cannot see infrared waves with our eyes, we can feel them with our skin. Heat from the sun comes from IR waves in sunlight. Objects that are warmer than their surroundings also radiate energy as IR waves. This is how infrared security cameras can see people in the dark.

Figure 18.7: *Infrared radiation is known as heat.*

Medium- to high-energy electromagnetic waves

Visible light   The rainbow of colors of visible light is in the medium-energy range of the electromagnetic spectrum with wavelengths between 700 and 400 nanometers. When most people talk about "light," they are usually referring to this part of the spectrum. However, when scientists talk about "light," they may be referring to any part of the electromagnetic spectrum from radio waves to gamma rays.

Ultraviolet waves   Ultraviolet radiation has a range of wavelengths from 400 down to about 10 nanometers. Sunlight contains ultraviolet waves. A small amount of ultraviolet radiation is beneficial to humans, but larger amounts cause sunburn, skin cancer, and cataracts. Most ultraviolet light is blocked by ozone in the Earth's upper atmosphere (Figure 18.8). A hole in the Earth's ozone layer is of concern because it allows more ultraviolet light to reach the surface of the planet, creating problems for humans, plants, and animals.

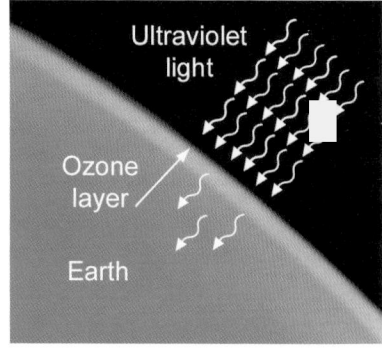

Figure 18.8: *Most of the ultraviolet light from the sun is absorbed by the Earth's ozone layer.*

X-rays   X-rays are high-frequency waves that have great penetrating power and are used extensively in medical and manufacturing applications (Figure 18.9). Their wavelength range is from about 10 nanometers to about 0.001 nm (or 10-trillionths of a meter). X-rays are strongly absorbed by calcium and other heavy elements. When you get a medical x-ray, the film darkens where bones are because the intensity of the x-rays has been absorbed before reaching the film. X-rays allow doctors to quickly determine the extent of an injury such as a broken bone. The x-ray on the right shows a clear break in the little finger.

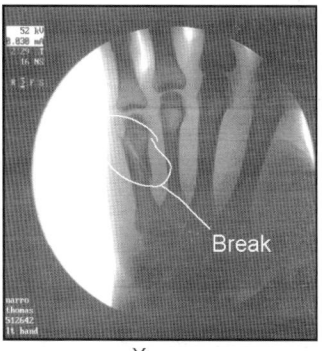

X-ray

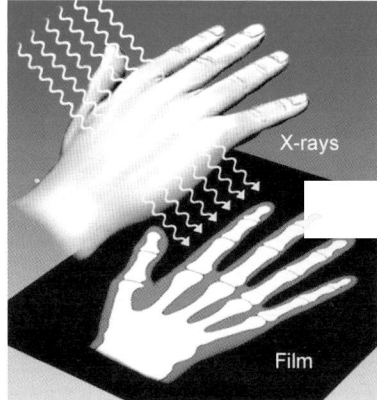

Figure 18.9: *X-rays have a high enough energy to go through your soft tissue but not through your bones.*

Gamma rays   Gamma rays have wavelengths of less than about 10-trillionths of a meter. Gamma rays are generated in nuclear reactions, and are used in many medical applications. Gamma rays can push electrons right out of an atom and break chemical bonds, including the chemical bonds holding the molecules in your body together. You do not want to be around strong gamma rays without a heavy shield.

360

18.2 Interference, Diffraction, and Polarization

In science, we recognize the correct explanation by comparing what we believe with what nature actually does. Saying light is a wave does not mean much unless light actually does the things that waves do. The experimental proof of the wave nature of light is the topic of this section. We know light is a wave because it shows interference, diffraction, resonance, frequency, wavelength, and light has the same relationship between speed, frequency, and wavelength as other waves.

The interference of light waves

Young's double-slit experiment

In 1807, Thomas Young (1773-1829) did the most convincing experiment demonstrating that light is a wave. In the experiment, a beam of light falls on a pair of parallel, very thin slits in a piece of metal. After passing through the slits, the light falls on a screen. You might expect to see two bright stripes on the screen where the light came through the slits, with the rest of the screen in shadow. However, when Young looked at the screen, he saw a pattern of alternating bright and dark bands, called an interference pattern.

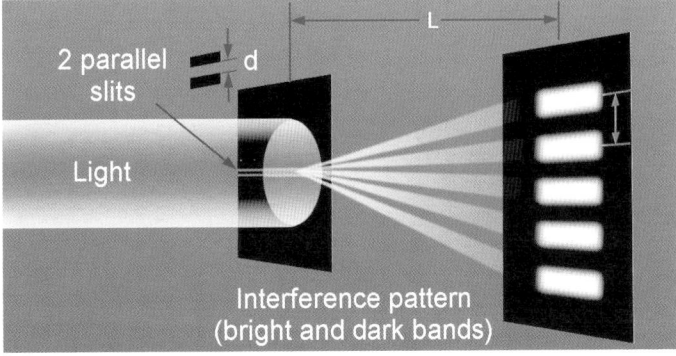

Interference of light waves

An interference pattern is created by the addition of two waves. The bright bands are at locations where the light waves from both slits meet at the screen in phase. When two waves meet in phase, they add up to make a bigger (brighter) wave. In Chapter 14, we called this type of addition constructive interference (Figure 18.10). The dark bands appear when the light waves from both slits meet out of phase and subtract from each other. The light intensity is lower because of destructive interference (Figure 18.10).

Constructive interference

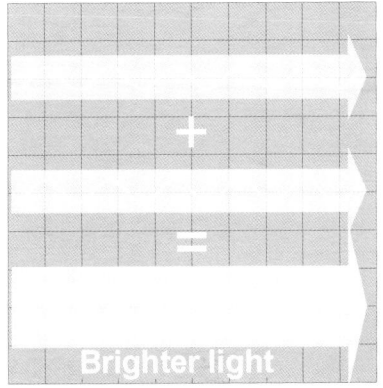

Destructive interference

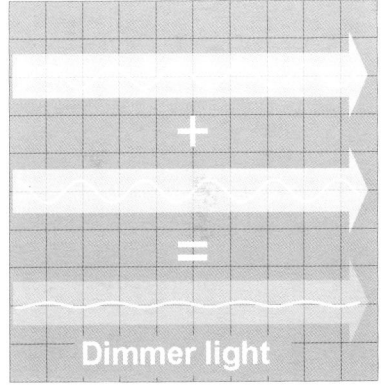

Figure 18.10: *Constructive interference creates brighter light (top). Destructive interference creates dimmer light (bottom).*

Diffraction gratings and spectrometers

Diffraction grating A diffraction grating creates an interference pattern of light similar to the pattern for the double slit. A grating acts like *many* parallel slits and the interference effect is much more dramatic. A grating is actually a series of thin parallel grooves on a piece of glass or plastic. When light falls on (or through) a diffraction grating, each groove acts like a separate source of light. You can think of a grating as a series of long thin slits.

The central spot Consider light that passes through a diffraction grating and falls on a screen (Figure 18.11). A bright spot called the *central spot* appears directly in front of the grating where the light passes straight through.

The first-order bright spot Another bright spot appears on either side of the central spot. These additional bright spots are called the *first order* because they come from waves that are one whole wavelength different in phase. The condition for forming a first order bright spot is that the path difference for light rays from two adjacent grooves is equal to 1 wavelength. This condition is satisfied when $\lambda = d\sin\theta$, where d is the spacing between the grooves on the grating (Figure 18.11). Bright spots will also be seen when the path difference for rays from adjacent grooves equals two wavelengths, three wavelengths, or any integer number of wavelengths. These extra spots appear farther from the central spot than the first order, and are labeled second-order, third-order, and so on.

The diffraction pattern of laser light When laser light is used, a diffraction pattern shows well-defined spots. A laser makes a single wavelength of light. Common red lasers make light with a wavelength of 650 nanometers.

The spectrometer A diffraction grating spreads out multicolored light into a spectrum. This happens because each point on the screen is a point of constructive interference for a *different wavelength of light*. A spectrometer is a device that measures the wavelength of light. A diffraction grating can be used to make a spectrometer because the wavelength of the light at the first-order bright spot is $\lambda = d\sin\theta$. Many spectrometers have a scale printed that allows you to read the wavelength directly from the pattern of light made by the grating (Figure 18.12).

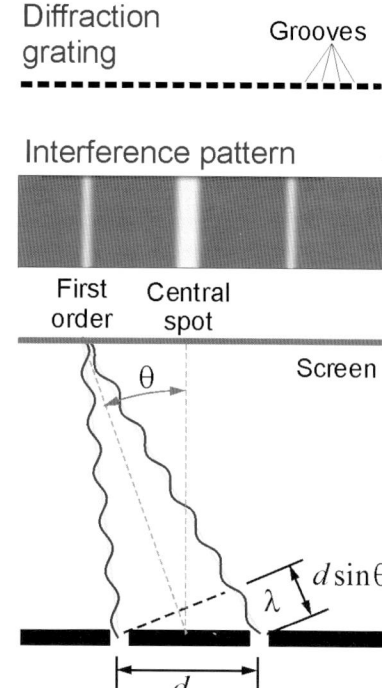

Figure 18.11: *The interference pattern from a diffraction grating.*

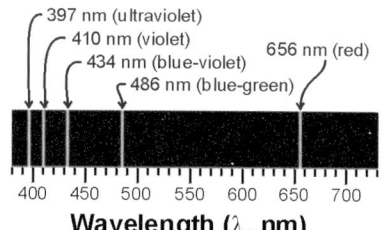

Figure 18.12: *The spectrum of hydrogen seen in a spectrometer.*

362

Polarization

Polarization of a wave on a spring

An easy way to think about polarization is to think about shaking a spring back and forth. If the spring is shaken up and down it makes vertical polarization. If the spring is shaken back and forth it makes horizontal polarization. Waves move *along* the spring in its long direction. The oscillation of the wave (and its polarization) is *transverse* or perpendicular to the direction the wave travels.

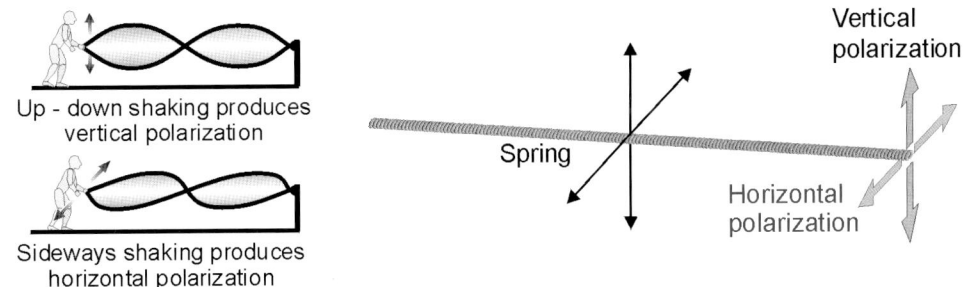

Polarization vector

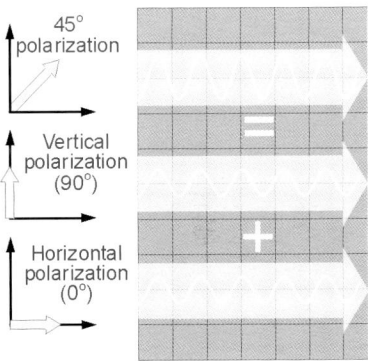

Figure 18.13: *Polarization is a vector. A wave with polarization at 45 degrees can be represented as the sum of two waves. Each of the component waves has smaller amplitude.*

The direction of polarization is a vector

Polarization can be intermediate between horizontal and vertical. For example, a spring that is shaken at a 45-degree angle to the vertical will create a polarization that is also at 45 degrees. In Chapter 7, we learned that a vector can be resolved into components in two directions. The direction of polarization is also a vector and can be resolved into components in two directions. You can think of a wave that has 45-degree polarization as the addition of two (smaller amplitude) component waves with horizontal and vertical polarizations (Figure 18.13).

Polarization of light waves

Polarization is another wave property of light. The fact that light shows polarization tells us that light is a *transverse wave*. This means the oscillation of energy in a light wave is perpendicular to the direction the wave moves. For light, we measure polarization by the orientation of the electrical part of the wave (Figure 18.14). Like a spring, the polarization of a light wave may be resolved into two perpendicular directions we usually call *horizontal* and *vertical*.

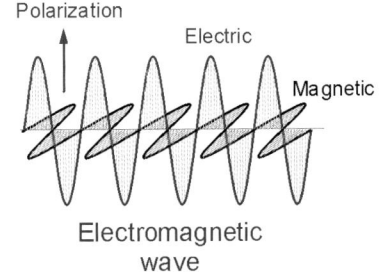

Figure 18.14: *The polarization of a light wave is the direction of the electric part of the wave.*

Unpolarized light

Most of the light that you see is *unpolarized*. That does not mean the light has no polarization. Unpolarized light is actually an equal mixture of all polarizations. We call ordinary light unpolarized because no single polarization dominates the mixture.

Polarizers

Making polarized light

A polarizer is a material that selectively absorbs light depending on polarization. Microscopically, polarizers divide incident light into two polarizations parallel and perpendicular to the transmission axis of the polarizer. Light with perpendicular polarization is absorbed by the polarizer. Light with parallel polarization is re-emitted and appears to "pass through" the polarizer. *Light that comes through a polarizer has only one polarization, in the direction of the transmission axis of the polarizer.* After passing through a polarizer, light is polarized because it contains only a single polarization.

Polarizing unpolarized light

On average, unpolarized light divides equally between parallel and perpendicular polarizations. Therefore, 50 percent of the intensity of unpolarized light will be transmitted through a "perfect" polarizer (Figure 18.15 A). Real polarizers are not perfect, and always transmit less light than a perfect polarizer would.

Transmission varies with the angle of polarization

A single polarizer re-emits a fraction of incident light polarized at an angle to the transmission axis. The fraction depends on the angle between the polarization of the incident light and the transmission axis of the polarizer. For example, suppose the incident polarization is 30 degrees (to horizontal). A vertical polarizer transmits 25% of the incident light and a horizontal polarizer transmits 75%.

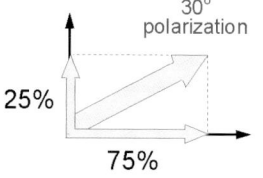 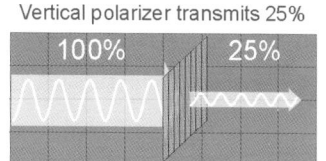 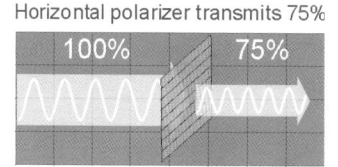

Transmission of light through two polarizers

Two polarizers in succession transmit a variable fraction of the incident light. The first polarizer transmits 50 percent and polarizes the light. If the transmission axis of the second polarizer is perpendicular to the first, the light is completely absorbed and no light is emitted (Figure 18.15 B). If the axis of the second polarizer is at 45 degrees to the axis of the first one then half the light reaching the second polarizer is transmitted (Figure 18.15 C), which is 25% of the incident light. This occurs because the light from the first polarizer is polarized at 45 degrees relative to the transmission axis of the second polarizer.

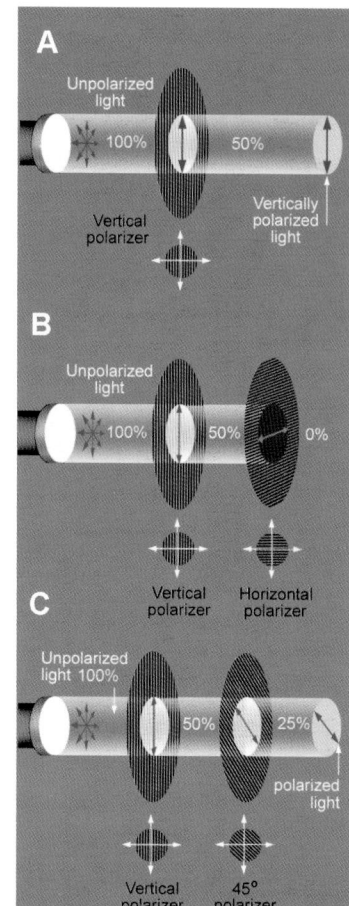

Figure 18.15: *The percentage of light transmitted through two polarizers depends on the angle between the transmission axes of the two polarizers.*

Applications of polarization

Polarized sunglasses

Polarizing sunglasses are used to reduce the glare of reflected light (Figure 18.16). Light that reflects at low angles from horizontal surfaces is polarized mostly horizontally. Thus, polarized sunglasses are made to block light waves with horizontal polarization. Because glare is horizontally polarized, it gets blocked by polarized sunglasses much more than other light that is unpolarized. Using these glasses, you can still see the light reflected from other objects, but the glare off a surface such as water is blocked.

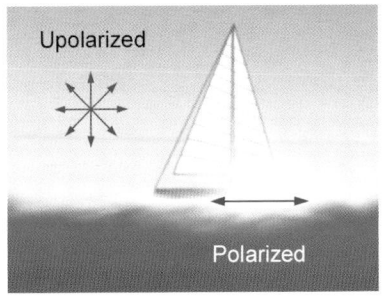

LCD computer screens

The LCD (liquid crystal diode) screen on a laptop computer uses polarized light to make pictures. The light you see starts with a lamp that makes unpolarized light. A polarizer then polarizes all the light. The polarized light passes through thousands of tiny pixels of liquid crystal that act like windows. Each liquid crystal window can be electronically controlled to act like a polarizer, or not. When a pixel is *not* a polarizer, the light comes through, like an open window, and you see a bright dot.

Dark dots are made by crossing polarizers

The transmission axis of the liquid crystal is at right angles to the polarization direction of the light leaving the first polarizer. When a pixel becomes a polarizer, the light is blocked and you see a dark dot. The picture is made of light and dark dots. To make a color picture there are separate polarizing windows for each red, blue, and green pixel.

Limits to LCD technology

Because the first polarizer blocks half the light, LCD displays are not very efficient, and are the biggest drain on a computer's batteries. LCD displays also suffer from low contrast between light areas and dark areas.

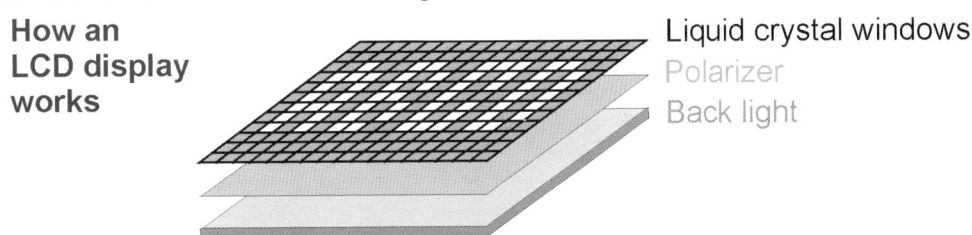

Figure 18.16: *Unpolarized light from the sun is polarized horizontally when it reflects off the water. Polarized sunglasses block out this light; regular sunglasses do not.*

Try looking at an LCD screen through polarizing sunglasses. Explain what you see when you rotate the sunglasses to change the angle of the transmission axis of the polarizing lenses relative to the LCD screen.

18.3 Special Relativity

Science fiction writers are fond of creating interesting effects such as time travel. It may surprise you, but time travel into the future is actually possible. It just takes a lot of energy, much more energy than we know how to get or control. Albert Einstein's theory of special relativity makes a connection between time and space that depends on how fast you are moving. This section is a brief exploration of the theory of special relativity, which is a fascinating area of physics still being developed.

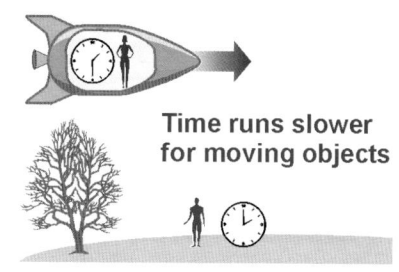

Time runs slower for moving objects

What special relativity is about

The relationship between matter, energy, time, and space
The theory of special relativity describes what happens to matter, energy, time, and space at speeds close to the speed of light. The fact that light *always* travels at the same speed forces other things about the universe to change in surprising ways. Special relativity does not affect ordinary experience because objects need to be moving faster than 100 million m/sec before the effects of special relativity become obvious. However, these effects are observed every day in physics labs.

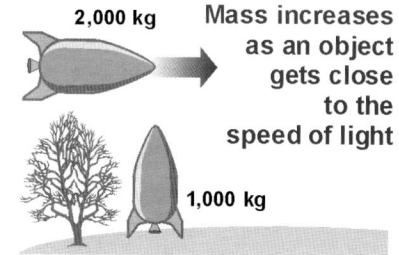

2,000 kg

Mass increases as an object gets close to the speed of light

1,000 kg

Time may move slower
1. Time moves more slowly for an object in motion than it does for objects that are not in motion. In practical terms, clocks run slower on moving spaceships compared with clocks on the ground. By moving very fast, it is possible for one year to pass on a spaceship while 100 years have passed on the ground. This effect is known as time dilation.

Mass may increase
2. As objects move faster, their *mass increases*. The closer the speed of an object gets to the speed of light, the more of its kinetic energy becomes mass instead of motion. Matter can never exceed the speed of light because adding energy creates more mass instead of increasing an object's speed.

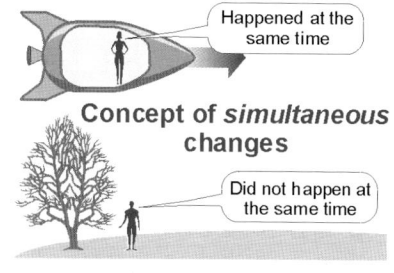

Happened at the same time

Concept of *simultaneous* changes

Did not happen at the same time

The meaning of simultaneous
3. The definition of the word "*simultaneous*" changes. Two events that are simultaneous to one observer may not be simultaneous to another who is moving.

Distances may contract
4. The length of an object measured by one person at rest will not be the same as the length measured by another person who is moving close to the speed of light. The object does not get smaller or larger, *space itself* gets smaller for an observer moving near the speed of light.

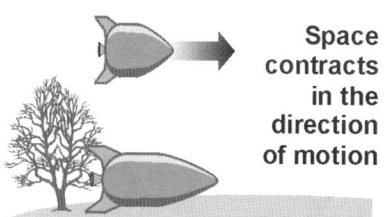

Space contracts in the direction of motion

The speed of light paradox

How you can be moving and appear at rest

The theory of special relativity comes from thinking about light. Einstein thought about what light would look like if you could see it when it wasn't moving. Instead of making the light stop, Einstein thought about traveling beside it—going the same speed as light itself. Imagine you could move as fast as light and were traveling right next to the beam from a flashlight. If you looked over, you should see the light standing still, *relative to you*. A similar situation occurs when two people are driving on a road side-by-side at the same speed. The two people look at each other and appear (to each other) not to be moving relative to each other, because both are traveling at the same speed.

The way speed normally adds

Consider a person on a railroad train moving a constant speed of 10 m/sec. If you are standing on the track, that person gets 10 meters closer to you every second. Now consider what happens if that person on the train throws a ball at you at 10 m/sec. In one second, the ball moves forward on the train 10 meters. The train also moves toward you by 10 meters. Therefore, the ball moves toward you 20 meters in one second. The ball approaches you with a speed of *20 m/sec* as far as you are concerned (Figure 18.17).

How you expect light to behave

Einstein considered the same trick using light instead of a ball. If the person on the train were to shine a flashlight toward you, you would expect the light to approach you faster. In fact, the light should come toward you at 3×10^8 m/sec plus the speed of the train.

The speed of light does not behave this way

That is not what happens (Figure 18.18). The light comes toward you at a speed of 3×10^8 m/sec *no matter how fast the train approaches you!* This experiment was done in 1887 by Albert A. Michelson and Edward W. Morley. They used the Earth itself as the "train". The Earth moves with an orbital speed of 29,800 m/sec. Michelson and Morley measured the speed of light parallel and perpendicular to the orbital motion of the Earth. They found the speed to be exactly the same! This result is not what they expected, and was confusing to everyone. Like all unexpected results, it forced people to rethink what they thought they already knew. Einstein's theory of special relativity was the result and it totally changed the way we understand space and time.

A girl throws a ball at 10 m/sec relative to her frame of reference

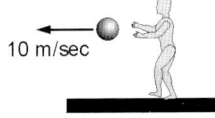

Her frame of reference is moving at 10 m/sec

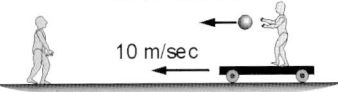

An observer at rest sees the ball approach at 20 m/sec.

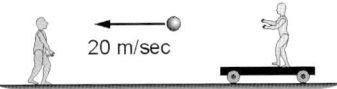

Figure 18.17: *A ball thrown from a moving train approaches you at the speed of the ball relative to the train plus the speed of the train relative to you.*

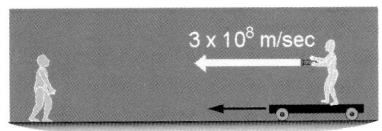

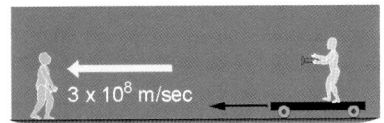

Figure 18.18: *The speed of light appears the same to all observers independent of their relative motion.*

Speed, time, and clocks

Einstein's thinking

With this new idea that the speed of light is constant to all observers, Einstein thought about what this meant for everything else in physics. One of the strangest results that came out of special relativity is that time is dilated, or stretched out, by the motion of an observer. His conclusion about the flow of time is as revolutionary as it is inescapable.

A light clock on a spaceship

Einstein considered a clock that measures time by counting the trips made by a beam of light going back and forth between two mirrors (Figure 18.19). The clock is on a moving spaceship. A person standing next to the clock sees the light go back and forth straight up and down. The time it takes to make one trip is the distance between the mirrors divided by the speed of light.

How the light clock appears on the ground

To someone who is not moving, the path of the light is not straight up and down. The light appears to make a zigzag because the mirrors move with the spaceship (Figure 18.20). The observer on the ground sees the light travel a longer path. This would not be a problem, *except that the speed of light must be the same to all observers, regardless of their motion.*

The paradox

Suppose it takes light one second to go between the mirrors. The speed of light must be the same for both people, yet the person on the ground sees the light move a longer distance! How can this be?

Time itself must be different for a moving object

The only way out is that *one second on the ground is not the same as one second on the spaceship.* The speed of light is the distance traveled divided by the time taken. If one second of "ship time" was longer than one second of "ground time," then the problem is resolved. Both people measure the same speed for light of 3×10^8 m/sec. The difference is that one second of "ship time" is *longer* than one second of "ground time."

Time slows down close to the speed of light

The consequence of the speed of light being constant is that *time slows down for objects in motion, including people.* If you move fast enough, the change in the flow of time is enormous. For a spaceship traveling at 99.9 percent of the speed of light, 22 years pass on Earth for every year that passes on the ship. The closer the spaceship's speed is to the speed of light, the slower time flows.

A light clock counts trips of light between two mirrors

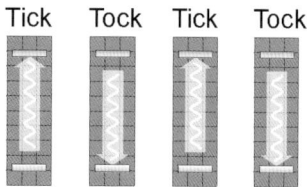

Figure 18.19: *A light clock measures time by measuring the how long it takes a pulse of light to move between two parallel mirrors.*

In the ship the light goes straight up and down

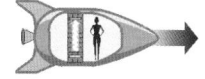

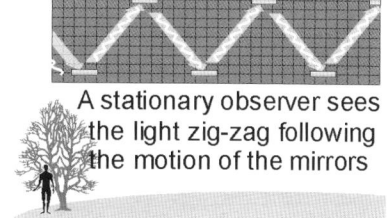

A stationary observer sees the light zig-zag following the motion of the mirrors

Figure 18.20: *A clock that counts ticks of light going back and forth in a spaceship. The light pulse of a light clock that is moving relative to an observe traces out a triangular path.*

Consequences of time dilation

Proof of time dilation
The idea that moving clocks run slower is difficult to believe. Before Einstein's theory of special relativity, time was always considered a universal constant. One second was one second, no matter where you were or what you were doing. After Einstein, we realized this was not true. The rate of time passing for two people depends on their relative motion.

Atomic clocks
One of the most direct measurements of this effect was done in the early 1970s by synchronizing two precise atomic clocks. One was put on a plane and flown around the world, the other was left on the ground. When the flying clock returned home, the clocks were compared. The clock on the plane measured less time than the clock on the ground. The difference agreed precisely with special relativity.

The frequency of light depends on relative motion
Because light is a wave, it has a frequency. Anything that has a frequency acts like a clock because you can count cycles. With this in mind, let's go back to the flashlight on the railroad track. The person moving on the train has a red flashlight making 462×10^{12} waves per second. You see the same 462×10^{12} waves of light in a shorter amount of time because your "second" is shorter than the second of the flashlight. If the train is moving at 70 percent of the speed of light, the waves arrive at your eye at a rate of 630×10^{12} waves per second. This is not red light, it is *blue light*. The effect is similar to, but more dramatic than the Doppler shift for sound waves. The frequency of light becomes more blue if an object is approaching you and more red if the object is moving away from you.

Discovery of the expanding universe
The technological advances of the last 75 years have allowed astronomers to build larger and larger telescopes. Since larger telescopes can see fainter objects, astronomers were able to see objects much farther away than anything seen in the thousands of years humans have been observing the night sky. They discovered that the farther away they looked, the more red the light became. The only possible explanation is that distant galaxies are all moving away from each other. If galaxies are moving away from each other, they must have been closer together in the past. In fact, we now believe the entire universe was once quite small, possibly smaller than a single atom. About 13 billion years ago the universe literally exploded, and it has been expanding and cooling ever since.

The twin paradox

2004, one twin leaves and one stays. Both are 23 years old.

2024, Traveling twin returns and is 30 years old. Twin who stayed is 43 years old.

A well-known thought experiment regarding time dilation is known as the twin paradox. The story goes like this: Two twins are born on Earth. They grow up to young adults and one of the twins becomes an astronaut.
The astronaut twin goes on a mission into space. The space ship in which the twin travels moves at a velocity near the speed of light. Because of traveling at this high speed, the clocks on the ship, including the twin's biological clock, run much slower than the clocks on Earth. Upon returning from a trip that was only a few years by the ship clocks, the traveling twin learns that the twin that stayed behind is much older.

The equivalence of energy and mass

Relationship between mass and energy

The equation E = mc^2 is probably the most recognized symbol of physics. This equation tells us that matter and energy are really two forms of the same thing. If you put enough energy in one place, you get matter. If you dissolve matter, you get energy. The law of energy conservation becomes a law of mass/energy conservation. The amount of energy it takes to create a kilogram of matter is calculated using Einstein's formula.

Einstein's mass - energy formula

Energy (J) $\quad E = mc^2$

Mass (kg)

Speed of light (3 x 10^8 m/sec)

Why matter cannot travel as fast as light

If a particle of matter is as rest, it has a total amount of energy equal to its rest energy. The rest energy is the rest mass (m_0) of the particle multiplied by the speed of light squared ($E_{rest} = m_0c^2$). If work is done to a particle by applying force, the energy of the particle increases. At speeds that are far from the speed of light, all the work done increases the kinetic energy of the particle. As the speed approaches the speed of light, however, the work does two things. Some of the work goes to increasing the speed of the particle. *Some of the work goes to increasing the particle's mass.* The closer the speed gets to the speed of light, the larger the proportion of work that goes to increasing mass. It would take an infinite amount of work to accelerate a particle to the speed of light, because at the speed of light the mass of a particle also becomes infinite. In physics, *infinity* has a well defined meaning, it means *larger than anything possible*.

Einstein's thinking

Although Einstein's argument is beyond the scope of this book, he was able to deduce the equivalent of mass and energy by thinking about the momentum of two particles moving near the speed of light. Remember from Chapter 12, momentum involves mass and speed. Kinetic energy also involves mass and speed. The speed of light must be the same for all observers regardless of their relative motion. Energy and momentum must be conserved. The only way to resolve these two constraints is for mass to increase as the speed of an object gets near the speed of light. The increase in mass comes from energy.

Calculate the equivalents of mass and energy

A nuclear reactor converts 0.7% of the mass of uranium to energy. If the reactor used 100 kg of uranium in a year, how much energy is released? One gallon of gasoline releases 1.3 × 10^8 joules. How many gallons of gasoline does it take to release the same energy as the uranium?

1) You are asked for energy in joules and gallons of gas
2) You are given the mass, a percent converted to energy, and J/gallon for gasoline.
3) Einstein's formula: E = mc^2
4) The amount of mass converted to energy is:
   m = 0.007 × 100 kg = 0.7 kg
   Energy released is:
   E = (0.7 kg)(3 × 10^8 m/sec)^2
     = 6.3 × 10^{16} J
   To calculate the equivalent in gasoline divide by the energy per gallon:
   N = 6.3 × 10^{16} J ÷ 1.3 × 10^8 J/g
     = 4.8 × 10^8 gallons
   This is 480 million gallons of gasoline.

Simultaneity

The meaning of "simultaneous"

When we say that two events are simultaneous, we mean they happen at the same time. Since time is not constant for all observers, whether two events are simultaneous depends on the relative motion of the observer. In special relativity, simultaneity is defined by the time it takes light to get from one place to another.

Two events that appear simultaneous

The example that Einstein gave to help explain this concept starts with two lightning strikes hitting the front and back of a moving train. Imagine you are watching the train from a distance. You are the same distance from the front and back of the train when the lightning strikes (Figure 18.21). You see the two bolts of lightning hit the train at the same time. To you, the two events (lightning strikes) are *simultaneous* because it takes the same amount of time for light from either event to reach you.

The events are *not* simultaneous to a moving observer

For a person sitting on the train however, it is a different situation. Suppose the person is in the center of the train. If the train were at rest, the person would also observe two simultaneous lightning strikes. But, the train *is* moving and as a result, the two lightning strikes are *not* simultaneous to the person on the train. The person on the train sees the light hit the front of the train first, and then the back of the train afterward. Because the velocity of the train has no effect on the speed of light, the light from both lightning strikes travels at the same speed. But the person is moving *toward* the point where lightning struck the front of the train. Light from the front of the train has a shorter distance to travel before reaching the person. The person is moving *away* from the point where lightning struck the rear of the train. Light from the rear has a longer distance to go to reach the person.

The definition of *simultaneous* in special relativity

No information can travel faster than the speed of light. This means the *definition of simultaneous is when light from two events reaches the observer at the same time*. Whether the events "really" happened at the "same time" is only a meaningful question in this interpretation. Einstein's example shows that two events that are simultaneous to one observer may not be simultaneous to another observer moving relative to the first. This effect is real and not just a trick of language. In collisions between subatomic particles, whether or not two events are simultaneous often affects the outcome of experiments.

Simultaneity depends on the relative motion of your frame of reference

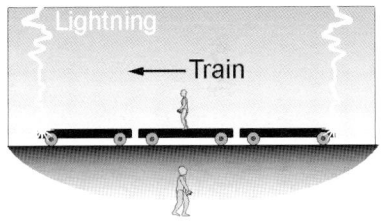

Observer on the ground
The two lightning strikes are simultaneous.

Observer on the train
The lightning strikes the front of the train first, then the rear..

Figure 18.21: *The two lightning strikes are simultaneous to the observer at rest, but the observer moving with the train sees the lightning strike the front of the train first.*

Application: Holography

The stunning 3D images that are produced by a hologram captivate people. A normal picture looks the same from any angle. A hologram looks different from different angles, just like a real scene does. A well made hologram appears to have depth and perspective as if the actual three dimensional scene were embedded in the picture. In many ways, the three dimensional scene *is* embedded in the hologram, except it is done with the *phase* of light and not with solid objects. As amazing as holograms are however, they are not quite up to what science fiction special effects make them! There are limits to what a hologram can do.

Figure 18.22: *The brightness, level of detail, front-to-back order, and size give you cues that your brain interprets placing the rock formation in front of the mountain range. (Photo courtesy James I. Sammons, Sammon's INK, Ltd.)*

How do we see 3D?

Shading and vanishing point
: An artist can create the sensation of depth in a picture. Things further away can be drawn smaller and light can be shaded differently on different sides of objects. By making things change size as they get 'further away' in the picture, and by using color and shading a good artist can make a flat picture look like a three dimensional scene as viewed from one place. A photograph creates the illusion of depth in a similar way. Differences in size, shape, and shading capture the sensation of depth (Figure 18.22).

Two views
: A true 3-D scene looks different when seen from different angles. There have been several inventions that recreate aspects of 3D images. Most are based on the fact that we have two eyes and we see things simultaneously from two different angles. Your left eye has a view of the world, and your right eye has the same view, but from a slightly different angle. Your brain combines the two slightly different images from each eye to see 3D. Your earliest experience with 3D images may have come from a *stereo-viewer* where you put flat round disks into the top and looked through the two eyepieces (figure 18.23). As you clicked through the images on the disk you saw pictures with amazing depth. The stereo-viewer is derived from a technique of taking two pictures of the same scene with two cameras spaced the same distance apart as our eyes. The illusion of 3D from a stereo-viewer is limited however, because it only shows a scene from a single perspective. You cannot move "around" the image to see objects from different sides, like you can in a real 3D scene such as a model.

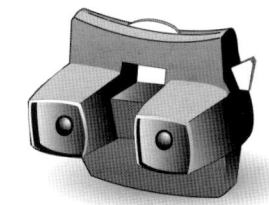

Figure 18.23: *An early 3-D stereo-viewer showed different images to each eye, simulating the effect of stereo vision.*

372

A real object is different than a picture

Wave fronts A flat object gives off a flat wave front and you see the same image from every angle. A real object gives off light in a 'wave front' that is shaped like the actual object. For example, the wave front of light reflecting from a vase is similar in shape to the vase itself (figure 18.24). Depending on the angle, you see different parts of this wave front. The light from the left side of the vase travels out towards the left. People on the left side of the room can see the left side of the vase. People on the right can't see the left side because they don't get that part of the wave front.

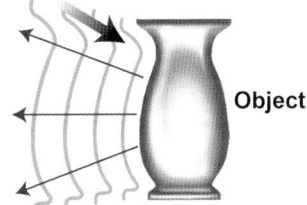

Figure 18.24: *The shape of the wave from a 3-D object (vase) is similar to the shape of the object.*

How a hologram works A hologram duplicates the three dimensional shape of the wave front that was coming from the real object. A hologram is made by using interference of waves to create constructive and destructive interference that makes the wave look different from different angles, similar to a diffraction grating. Even though a hologram itself is flat, when light strikes a hologram it bounces off with the same wave front as would be coming from a real object (figure 18.25). When you see the wave front your brain thinks that it is looking at a real object. You can change your angle and see the image that you would see if you were looking at the real object. You can move over to the left side of the wave front and see what only the people standing on the left would have seen.

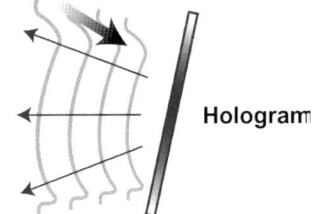

Figure 18.25: *A hologram looks three dimensional because it recreates the original shape of the wave front from the original object.*

Making a hologram To make a hologram you need to use the interference from a beam of light that has been divided into two beams. One half the beam bounces off the object that will be in the hologram. This is the *image beam*. The other half of the beam goes right to the film. This is the *reference beam.* The interference of the image beam and the reference beam creates an interference pattern on the film (figure 18.26). When the film is developed it looks nothing like the original object. That is because the film recorded the interference of the two beams, not the image itself. To recreate the image, you must shine light on the hologram from the same direction as the original reference beam. The light that bounces off the hologram recreates the original image beam, including the depth and three-dimensional sensation. The hologram looks different from different angles because you see a different interference pattern at different angles, just as you did with a diffraction grating.

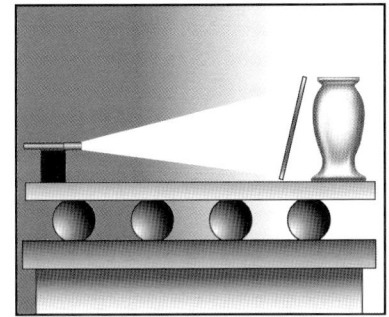

Figure 18.26: *Making a hologram.*

Chapter 18 Review

Vocabulary Review

Match the following terms with the correct definition. There is one extra definition in the list that will not match any of the terms.

Set One

1. electromagnetic waves
2. gamma rays
3. diffraction grating
4. rest energy
5. spectrometer

a. Generated in nuclear reactions
b. Creates interference patterns when light is passed through
c. Instrument used to measure the wavelength of light
d. Used to measure the mass of a photon
e. Equal to $m_0 c^2$
f. Include radio waves, x-rays, gamma rays, ultraviolet, infrared, and visible light

Set Two

1. c
2. infrared
3. n
4. ultraviolet

a. Type of electromagnetic wave that can cause sunburn
b. The variable used to represent the speed of light
c. Electromagnetic wave that has the highest frequency
d. The variable used to represent the index of refraction
e. Type of electromagnetic wave we feel as heat

Set Three

1. electromagnetic spectrum
2. mass
3. polarization
4. special relativity
5. time

a. The characteristic "plane" on which a wave is vibrating
b. This quantity increases as you travel faster
c. This quantity decreases for a moving observer relative to a stationary observer
d. Range of longitudinal waves
e. The range of electromagnetic waves
f. A theory that describes the behavior of matter, energy, time and space

Concept review

1. Give an example of an energy field.

2. Describe an electromagnetic wave.

3. List the different types of electromagnetic energy from highest energy to lowest energy.

4. Which color of visible light has the highest frequency? Which has the lowest frequency?

5. True or False: All electromagnetic waves travel at the same speed in a vacuum.

6. Use the formula $c = f\lambda$ and write an equation to solve for f and for λ.

7. Explain how microwaves cook food.

8. We often say that light slows down when it goes through glass but speeds up again when it leaves the glass. Explain how the light 'speeds back up'.

9. Why must the frequency of light be the same regardless of the material it is traveling through?

10. Explain how Thomas Young demonstrated the wave nature of light.

11. What causes the first order bright spot when light goes through a diffraction grating?

12. Why can you see a rainbow when white light goes through a diffraction grating?

13. What does it mean to say a wave is polarized?

14. Explain what a polarizer does to uppolarized light.

15. Why does a LCD display use so much energy?

16. How was time dilation proven?

17. Describe the "twin paradox."

Problems

1. A red key chain laser has a wavelength of 650 nm (6.50×10^{-7} m). Calculate the frequency of the laser.

2. Calculate the frequency of a radio wave with a wavelength of 1.5 m.

3. In the movie *Predator 2*, the alien was able to tune his visor so that he could see infrared waves ($\lambda = 1 \times 10^{-5}$ m) and ultraviolet waves ($\lambda = 1 \times 10^{-8}$ m). What were the frequency settings for this device?

4. Blue light has a frequency of 6.40×10^{14} Hz. When it is traveling through Lucite, its velocity is 2.00×10^{8} m/s. What is its wavelength?

5. The index of refraction (n) is found by dividing the speed of light in a vacuum (c) by the speed of light in a material (v). If light travels at a velocity of 1.239×10^{8} m/s in a diamond, calculate the index of refraction of diamond.

6. Zircon has an index of refraction of 1.92. What is the speed of light when it is traveling through zircon?

7. A fiber optic cable is made of flint glass with an index of refraction of 1.66. If this cable is 10,000 m long, how much time would be required for light to pass through its length?

8. When light passes through two slits in a diffraction grating that are separated by a measured distance (d) a bright spot will form on a screen located a measured distance from the grating (L). The first order bright spot will form a distance (x) from the central bright spot. This distance is a function of the wavelength (λ) of the light. The ratio is $\lambda/d = x/L$. Algebra changes this to $\lambda = dx/L$. Light shines through a diffraction grating with $d = 2.5 \times 10^{-4}$ m. Dots appear on a screen $L = 2.0$ m away and the distance to the first order bright spot (x) is 0.25 m. What is the wavelength of the light?

376

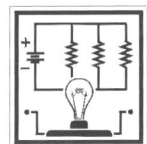

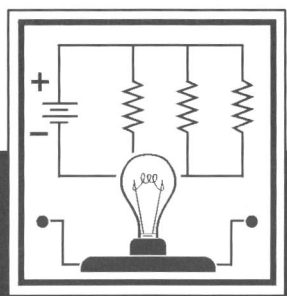

Unit 7

Electricity and Magnetism

Chapter 19

Electricity

Objectives for Chapter 19

By the end of this chapter you should be able to:

1. Describe the difference between current and voltage.
2. Describe the connection between voltage, current, energy, and power.
3. Describe the function of a battery in a circuit.
4. Calculate the current in a circuit using Ohm's law.
5. Draw and interpret a circuit diagram with wires, battery, bulb, and switch.
6. Measure current, voltage, and resistance with a multimeter.
7. Give examples and applications of conductors, insulators, and semiconductors.

Terms and vocabulary words

electricity	electric current	voltage	resistance	Ohm's law
battery	open circuit	closed circuit	short circuit	switch
circuit diagram	electrical conductivity	potentiometer	wire	volt
electrical symbols	amperes (amps)	multimeter	ohm	resistor
ammeter	electrical insulator	semiconductor	conductor	electric circuit

377

19.1 Electric Circuits

Imagine your life *without* electricity. There would be no TVs, computers, refrigerators, or light bulbs. All of the products that are made by machines, from clothes to newspapers, would have to be made by hand. The use of electricity has become so routine that many of us never stop to think about what happens when we switch on a light or turn on a motor. This section is about electricity and electrical circuits. Circuits are usually made of wires to carry electricity and devices that use electricity.

Electricity

Figure 19.1: *A waterwheel uses a current of water to turn a wheel and do useful work.*

What is electricity? | Electricity refers to the presence of electric current in wires, motors, light bulbs, and other devices. Electricity is usually invisible and is a form of energy that comes from the motion of tiny particles inside and in between atoms. This chapter and the next will introduce the practical use of electricity. The exact identity of the moving particles that create electric current will be discussed in Chapter 21.

Electric current | Electric current is similar to a current of water, but electric current flows in solid metal wires so it is not visible. A good way to think about electric current is in terms of its ability to carry energy and power as it flows. An electric current can do work just as a current of water can. For example, a waterwheel turns when a current of water exerts a force on it (Figure 19.1). A waterwheel can be connected to a machine such as a loom for making cloth, or to a millstone for grinding wheat into flour. Before electricity was available, waterwheels were used for many machines. Today, the same tasks are done using energy from electric current. Look around right now and you can probably see wires carrying electric current into a house and a building.

Figure 19.2: *Electricity uses an electric current to power light bulbs and electric motors.*

Electricity can be powerful and dangerous | Electric current can carry a lot of power. For example, an electric saw can cut wood much faster than a hand saw (Figure 19.2). An electric motor the size of a basketball can do as much work as five big horses or fifteen strong people. Electric current can also be dangerous. Touching a live electric wire can inflict a very serious injury. The more you know about electricity, the easier it is to use it safely.

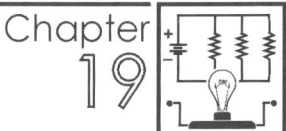

Electric circuits

Electricity travels in circuits

An electric circuit is something that provides a complete path through which electricity travels. A good example of a circuit is the one in an electric toaster. Bread is toasted by heaters that convert electrical energy to heat. The circuit has a switch that turns on when the lever on the side of the toaster is pulled down. When the switch is on, electric current flows in one side of the plug from the socket in the wall, through the toaster, and back out the other side of the plug.

A circuit of pipes distributes water through a house.

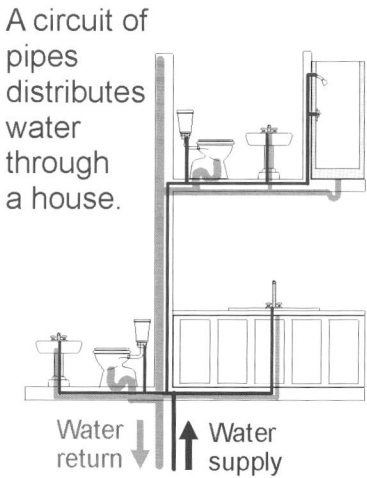

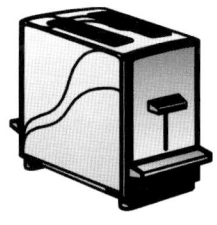

Electric toaster

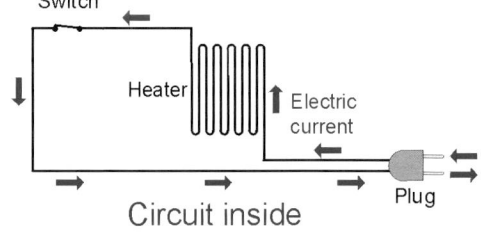

Circuit inside

Wires are like pipes for electricity

Wires in electric circuits are similar in some ways to pipes and hoses that carry water (Figure 19.3). Wires act like pipes for electric current. Current flows into the house on the supply wire and out on the return wire. The big difference between wires and water pipes is that you cannot get electricity to leave a wire the way water leaves a pipe. If you cut a water pipe, the water comes out. If you cut a wire, the electricity immediately stops flowing.

A circuit of wires distributes electric current through a house.

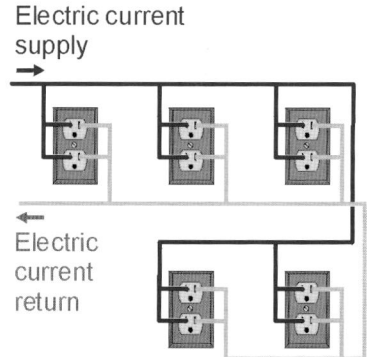

Examples of circuits in nature

Circuits are not confined to appliances, wires, and devices built by people. People's first experience with electricity was in the natural world. Some examples of natural circuits are:

- The nerves in your body are an electrical circuit connecting muscles to messages from the brain.
- The tail of an electric eel makes an electric circuit when it stuns a fish with a jolt of electricity.
- The Earth makes a giant circuit when lightning carries electric current between the clouds and the ground.

Figure 19.3: *In a house or other building, we use pipes to carry the flow of water and wires to carry the electric current.*

Circuit diagrams and electrical symbols

Circuit diagrams   Circuits are made up of wires and electrical components such as *batteries*, *light bulbs*, *motors*, and *switches*. When designing a circuit, it is often necessary to draw the arrangement of the electrical components. This is most easily done with a circuit diagram. When drawing a circuit diagram, symbols are used to represent each part of the circuit. These electrical symbols are quicker and easier to draw than realistic pictures of the components.

Electrical symbols   A circuit diagram is a shorthand method of describing a real circuit. The electric symbols used in circuit diagrams are standard, so anyone familiar with electricity can interpret a circuit diagram. Figure 19.4 shows some common electric components and their electrical symbols. The picture below shows an actual circuit and its circuit diagram. See if you can match the symbols in the circuit diagram with each part of the simple circuit.

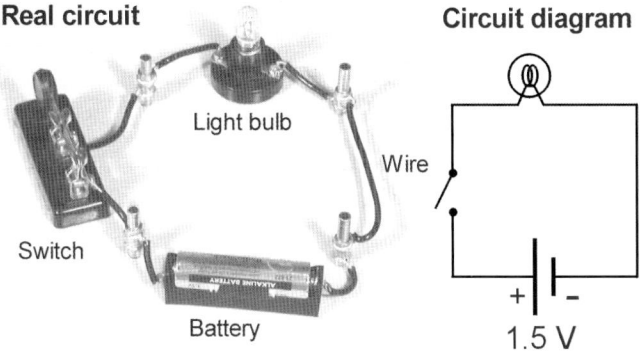

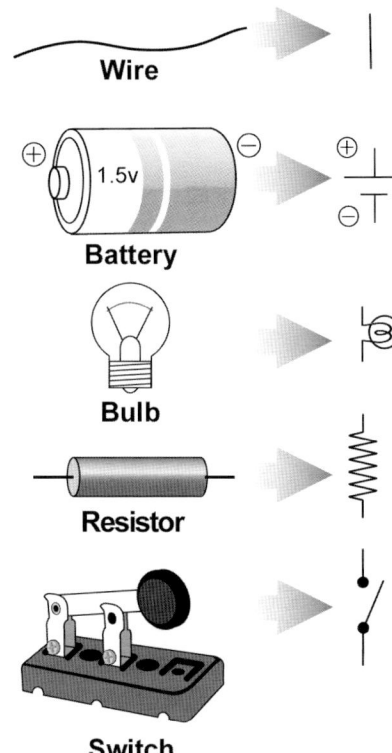

Figure 19.4: *These electrical symbols are used when drawing circuit diagrams.*

Resistors   A resistor is an electrical component that uses the energy carried by electric current in a specific way. In many circuit diagrams any electrical device that uses energy is shown with a resistor symbol. A light bulb, heating element, speaker, or motor can be represented with a resistor symbol. When you analyze a circuit, many electrical devices may be treated as resistors for the purpose of figuring out the electrical current flowing in the circuit.

Open and closed circuits

Batteries
The positive end of a battery is a source of electric current. The negative end of the battery is a return of electric current. When a battery is connected to an electric circuit, current flows out of the positive end, through the circuit, and back to the negative end.

Open and closed circuits
Unlike water, electric current only flows through a **closed** circuit. A closed circuit is a circuit with a complete and unbroken path between the source of the current and the return of the current to the source. A circuit with a switch turned to the off position or a circuit with any break in it is called an **open** circuit. Electricity cannot travel through an open circuit.

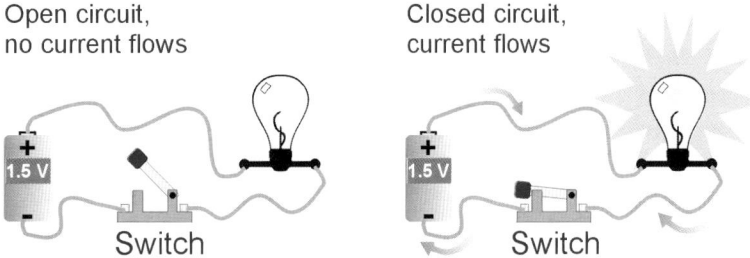

Open circuit,
no current flows

Closed circuit,
current flows

Switch   Switch

Switches
Switches are used to turn electricity on and off. Turning the switch off creates an open circuit by making a break in the wire. The break stops the flow of current because electricity cannot normally travel through air.

Breaks in circuits
A common problem found in circuits is that an unintentional break occurs. If there are any breaks, the circuit is open and electric current cannot travel through the circuit. If you look inside a light bulb that has burned out, you will see that the thin wire that glows inside the bulb, called the filament, is broken. This creates an open circuit and the bulb will not light.

Short circuits
A **short circuit** is not the same as either an open or closed circuit. A short circuit is usually an accidental extra path for current to flow in. A short circuit is an easy (but dangerous) shortcut that current can travel through to avoid one or more of the electrical components in the circuit. Short circuits are covered in more detail in a later section when we talk about *parallel* and *series* circuits.

Why electricity does not leak from open circuits

Electric current is usually the flow of electrons around atoms in a metal, like copper. Atoms are mostly empty space and there is plenty of room for the electrons to flow around the copper atoms.

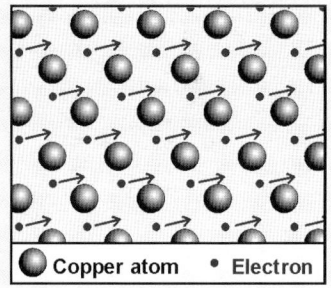

⬤ **Copper atom**   • **Electron**

Electric current does not leak from a wire because very strong forces maintain an exact balance between the density of electrons and the density of copper atoms. One electron can move away from its atom only if another electron comes in to keep the balance. If any did leak out, there would be more atoms than electrons. The forces between atoms and electrons are so great that this does not happen except in extreme circumstances.

19.2 Current and Voltage

Current and voltage are the two *most important* concepts to understanding electricity. Current is what actually flows through wires, carries energy, and does work. Like water, electric current only flows when there is a difference in energy. Water current flows downhill from high to low energy. The difference in energy that makes water flow is measured in height. Electric current also flows because of a difference in energy. *Voltage* measures the difference in energy between two places in a circuit. Current flows in response to differences in voltage just like water flows in response to differences in height. Current is what flows and does work. Voltage differences are what make current flow.

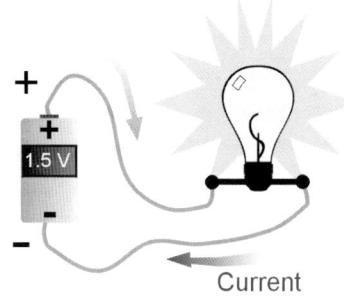

Figure 19.5: *The direction of current is from the positive to the negative end of a battery. This definition of current is called conventional current and was proposed by Ben Franklin in the 1700's. Scientists later discovered that the particles that carry electricity in a wire actually travel from negative to positive. However we still use Franklin's definition today. You will learn more about the particles that make current later in this unit.*

Current

Measuring electric current

As you learned in the previous section, electric current is the flow of electricity. The flow of water in a hose might be measured in gallons per minute. Electric current is measured in units called amperes, or amps (A) for short. One amp is a flow of a certain quantity of electricity in one second. The unit is named in honor of Andre-Marie Ampere (1775-1836), a French physicist who studied electricity and magnetism.

Current flows from positive to negative

The direction of electric current is from positive to negative (Figure 19.5). If you examine a battery you will find one end marked with a plus side, typically the end with the raised metal dimple. The other end of a battery is marked negative.

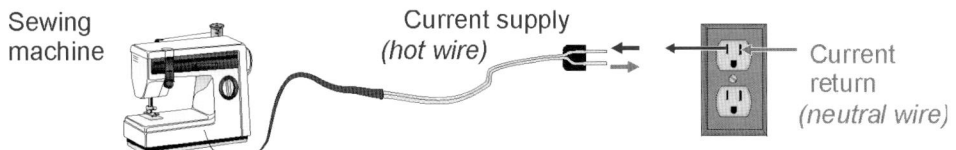

Current in equals current out

The amount of electric current entering a circuit always equals the amount exiting the circuit. When you plug an appliance into the wall, there are two wires that carry current. The current source is on one (the hot wire) and the return is on the other (neutral wire). You can think about this rule conceptually like steel balls flowing through a tube. When you push one in, one comes out. The rate at which balls flow in equals the rate at which balls flow out (Figure 19.6).

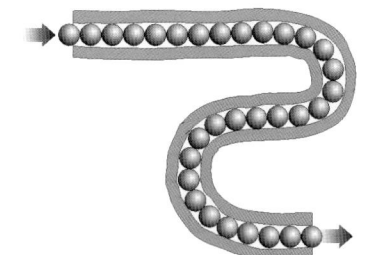

Figure 19.6: *Balls can flow through a tube even though the number of balls in the tube stays the same. When one ball goes in, another comes out.*

Voltage

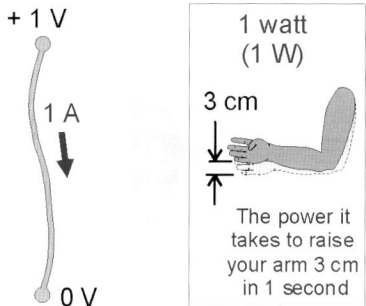

Energy and voltage Voltage is a measure of electric *potential energy,* just like height is a measure of gravitational potential energy. When one point in a circuit has a higher voltage, that point is at a higher potential energy than another point at lower voltage. Voltage is measured in volts (V). Like other forms of potential energy, voltage *differences* represent energy that can be used to do work. For electricity, the way to extract the energy is to let the voltage cause current to flow through a circuit.

Figure 19.7: *The power equivalent of one amp at one volt.*

What voltage means A voltage difference of 1 volt means 1 amp of current does 1 joule of work in 1 second. Since 1 joule per second is a watt (power) you can interpret voltage as measuring the available electrical power per amp of current that flows (Figure 19.7). The voltage in your home electrical system is 120 volts, which means each amp of current carries 120 watts of power. The higher the voltage, the more power is carried by each amp of electric current.

Making higher voltage by stacking batteries

Using a meter to measure voltage Humans cannot see or feel voltage, therefore an electric meter is necessary to find the voltage in a circuit. The most common type of meter is a multimeter, which can measure voltage or current. To measure voltage, the probes attached to the meter are touched to two places in a circuit. The meter reads positive voltage when the red (positive) probe is at a higher voltage than the black (negative) probe.

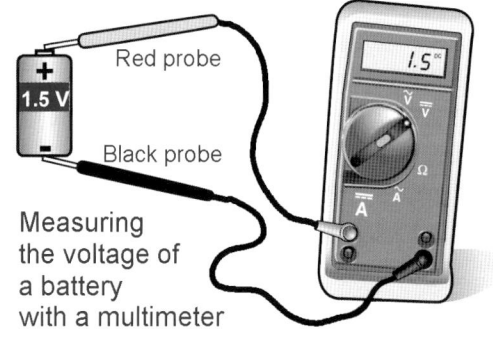

Measuring the voltage of a battery with a multimeter

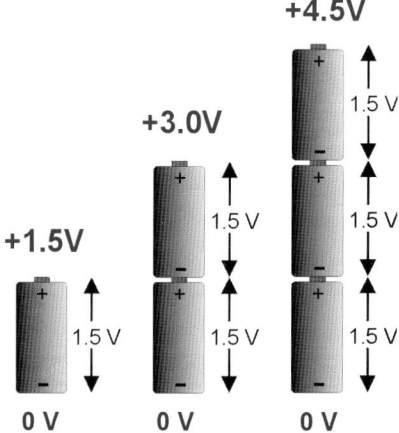

Meters measure voltage difference A multimeter measures the *difference* in voltage between two places in a circuit. If the meter is connected across a battery, it will read the voltage difference between the positive and negative terminals of the battery. *All measurements of voltage are actually measurements of voltage difference.* For example, a reading of +1.5 volts means the red probe is touching a point in the circuit that is 1.5 volts higher in potential energy than the point the black probe is touching. In fact, you can make larger voltage differences by stacking batteries (Figure 19.8).

Figure 19.8: *The positive end of a 1.5 volt battery is 1.5 volts higher than the negative end. If you connect batteries positive-to-negative, each battery adds 1.5 volts to the total. Three batteries make 4.5 volts. Each unit of current coming out of the positive end of the three-battery stack has 4.5 joules of energy.*

Batteries

Batteries   A battery uses chemical energy to create a voltage difference between its two terminals. When the current leaves a battery, it carries energy. If the battery has a voltage of 1.5 volts, then 1 amp of current carries an energy of 1.5 joules per second, or 1.5 watts. The current can give up its energy when it passes through an electrical device such as a light bulb. When a bulb is lit, the energy is taken from the current and is transformed into light and heat energy. The current returns to the battery where it gets more energy.

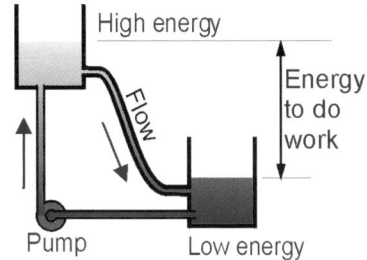

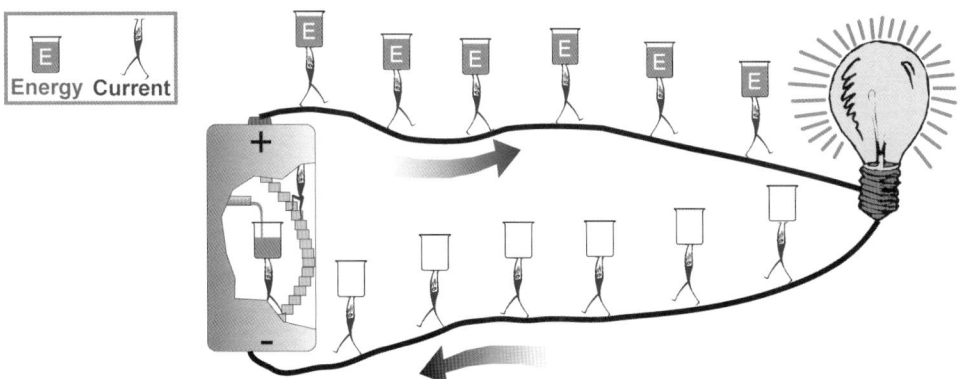

Figure 19.9: *A battery raises electric current back up to higher voltage (energy) similarly to how a pump pushes water back up to high energy so it can flow and do work again.*

Batteries are like pumps   Two water tanks connected with a pump make a good analogy for a battery in a circuit (Figure 19.9). The pump gives potential energy to the water as it lifts it up to the higher tank. As the water flows down, its potential energy is converted into kinetic energy. In a battery, chemical reactions provide the energy to pump the current from low voltage to high voltage. The current can then flow back to low voltage through a circuit and use its energy to turn motors and light bulbs.

Battery voltage   A fully charged battery adds energy proportional to its voltage. The positive end of a 1.5 volt battery is 1.5 joules higher in energy than the negative end. That means every amp of current that leaves the positive end has 1.5 joules more energy than it has after traveling through the circuit. The voltage of a battery depends on how the battery is constructed and what chemicals it uses. Nickel Cadmium (NiCd) batteries are 1.2 volts each. Lead acid batteries, like the one in a car, are usually 12 volts. Different voltages can also be made by combining multiple batteries.

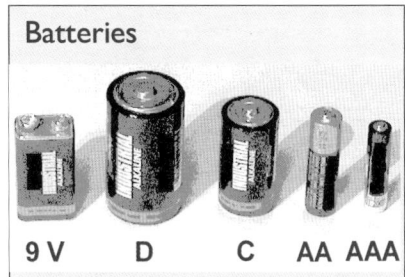

Batteries

9 V   D   C   AA AAA

Batteries come in different sizes as well as different voltages. A D-size battery stores more energy than a AAA-size battery, even though the voltage is the same. That means a D battery can keep 1 amp of current flowing for much longer than a AAA battery can.

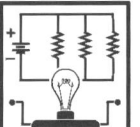

Measuring current in a circuit

Measuring current with a meter   Electric current can be measured with a multimeter. To measure current, the circuit must be set up differently than for measuring voltage. If you want to measure current in a circuit, you must make it flow *through* the meter. That usually means you must break your circuit somewhere and rearrange wires so the current passes through the meter. For example, the diagram below shows a circuit with a battery and bulb. The meter has been inserted into the circuit to measure current. If you trace the wires, the current comes out of the positive end of the battery, through the light bulb, *through the meter*, and back to the battery. The meter in the diagram measures 0.37 A of current. Some electric meters, called ammeters, are designed specifically to measure only current.

Measuring Current

Setting up the meter   If you use a multimeter, you must set its dial to measure current. Multimeters can measure two different types of electric current, called alternating current (AC) and direct current (DC). You will learn about the difference between alternating and direct current in a later section. For circuits with light bulbs and batteries, you must set your meter to the direct current setting.

Be careful measuring current   The last important thing about measuring current is that the meter itself can be damaged if too much current passes through it. Your meter may contain a *circuit breaker* or *fuse*. Circuit breakers and fuses are two kinds of devices that protect circuits from too much current by creating a break in the circuit and stopping the current. If your meter does not work, the circuit breaker or fuse may have created an open circuit. A circuit breaker can be reset but a fuse must be replaced.

Circuit breakers

Circuit breaker

Wires can get dangerously hot if they carry more current than they are designed for. Electric circuits in your house contain *circuit breakers* that prevent more than the allowable 15 or 20 amps of current from flowing through the wires. A circuit breaker uses temperature-sensitive metal that expands with heat. When the current gets too high, the metal bends and breaks the circuit.

Most overloads are caused by using too many electric appliances on the same circuit at one time. If the total current draw from all of the appliances exceeds the rated current on the breaker, the circuit breaker trips and breaks the circuit before the wires get hot enough to cause a fire. If this happens to you, you must unplug some appliances before you reset the circuit breaker.

19.3 Electrical Resistance and Ohm's Law

You can apply the same voltage to different circuits and different amounts of current will flow. For example, when you plug in a desk lamp about 1 amp of current flows. If a hair dryer is plugged into the same outlet (with the same voltage) *10 amps* of current will flow. The amount of current that flows in a circuit is determined by the resistance of the circuit. Resistance is the subject of this section.

Electrical resistance

Current and resistance
The resistance is a measure of how easily electric current moves through an object or electrical device. A device with low resistance, such as a copper wire, allows current to easily move through it. An object with high resistance, such as a rubber band, does not allow current to pass through it easily.

A water analogy
The relationship between electric current and resistance can be compared to water flowing out of a bottle through an opening (Figure 19.10). If the opening is large, the resistance is low and lots of water flows out quickly. If the opening of the bottle is small, there is a lot of resistance and the water flow is slow.

Circuits
The total amount of electrical resistance in a circuit determines the amount of current that in the circuit for a given voltage. Every device that uses electrical energy adds resistance to a circuit. The more resistance the circuit has, the less current that flows. For example, if you string several light bulbs together, the resistance in the circuit increases and the current decreases, making each bulb dimmer than a single bulb would be.

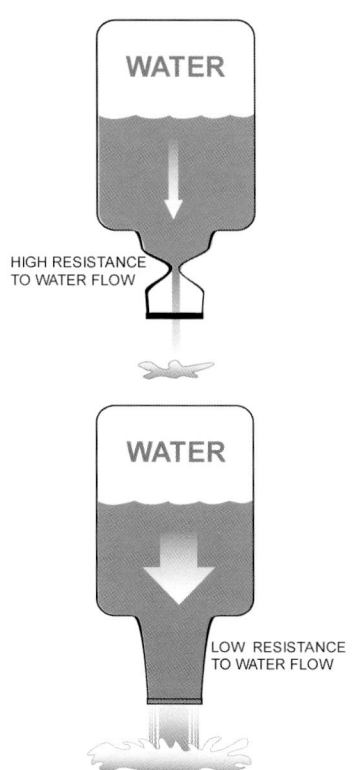

Figure 19.10: *Just as with water, only a small amount of electric current passes through the opening when resistance is high. A large amount of current passes through the opening when resistance is low.*

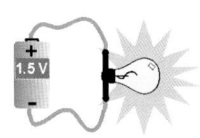

One bulb
Single resistance
Full current

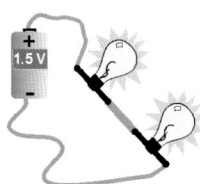

Two bulbs
Twice the resistance
Half the current

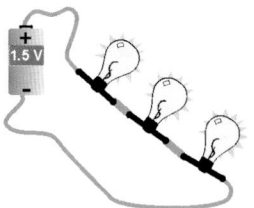

Three bulbs
Three times the resistance
One-third the current

386

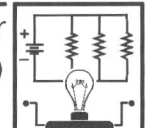

Measuring resistance

The ohm   Electrical resistance is measured in units called ohms. This unit is abbreviated with the Greek letter *omega* (Ω). When you see Ω in a sentence, think or read "ohms." For a given voltage, the greater the resistance, the less the current. If a circuit has a resistance of 1 ohm, then a current of 1 ampere flows when a voltage of 1 volt is applied. As an example, a 100-watt light bulb has a resistance of 145 Ω. When the light bulb is attached to the 120-volt circuit in your house, a current of 0.83 amps flows.

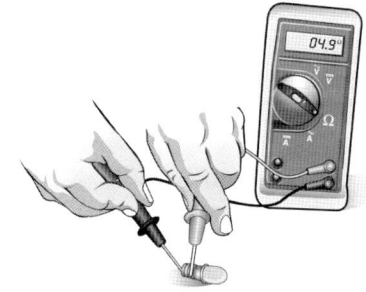

Figure 19.11: *You can measure the resistance of a light bulb with an electric meter.*

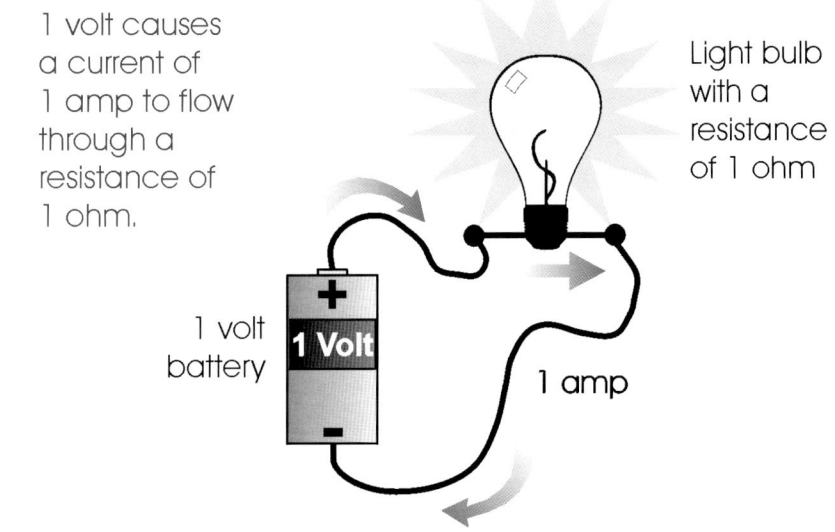

1 volt causes a current of 1 amp to flow through a resistance of 1 ohm.

Light bulb with a resistance of 1 ohm

1 volt battery

1 Volt

1 amp

How resistance is measured

A multimeter measures resistance by passing a precise amount of current through an electrical device. The meter then measures the voltage it takes to cause the current to flow. The resistance is calculated from the voltage and current. The currents used to measure resistance are typically very small, 0.001 amps or less.

Resistance of wires   The wires used to connect circuits are made of metals such as copper or aluminum and have very low resistance. The resistance of wires is usually so low compared with other devices in a circuit that you can ignore resistance from the wires when measuring or calculating the total resistance. The exception is when there are large currents. If the current is large the resistance of wires may be important.

Current, voltage, and resistance   You can use a multimeter to measure the resistance of wires, light bulbs, and other devices (Figure 19.11). Set the dial on the meter to the resistance setting and touch the meter leads to each end of the device. The meter will display the resistance in ohms (Ω), kilo-ohms (×1,000 Ω), or mega-ohms (×1,000,000 Ω).

Ohm's law

Ohm's law
The mathematical relationship that relates current, voltage, and resistance in a circuit is called Ohm's law. Current is directly proportional to voltage and is inversely proportional to resistance. If you know the voltage and resistance in a circuit, you can calculate the current by dividing the voltage by the resistance.

Ohm's Law

$$\text{Current (amps, A)} \quad I = \frac{V}{R} \quad \begin{array}{l}\text{Voltage (volts, V)} \\ \\ \text{Resistance (ohms, }\Omega\text{)}\end{array}$$

Equation	Gives you...	If you know...
$I = V \div R$	current (I)	voltage and resistance
$V = I \times R$	voltage (V)	current and resistance
$R = V \div I$	resistance (R)	voltage and current

The connection between current and voltage
Ohm's law makes the connection between the voltage applied to a circuit and the amount of current that flows. Devices such as motors are designed with a specific resistance that allows them to draw the proper current when connected to the proper voltage. For example, a particular 1.5 V electric motor requires 0.75 amps. The motor is designed with a resistance of 2 Ω When connected in a circuit with a 1.5-volt battery, the motor draws the right current (0.75 A = 1.5 V ÷ 2 Ω).

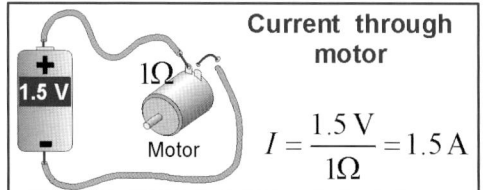

Current through motor

$$I = \frac{1.5\,\text{V}}{1\Omega} = 1.5\,\text{A}$$

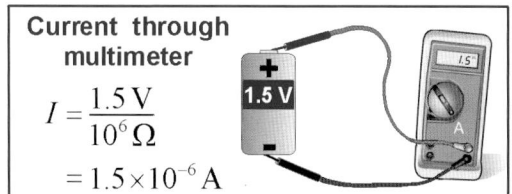

Current through multimeter

$$I = \frac{1.5\,\text{V}}{10^6\,\Omega}$$
$$= 1.5 \times 10^{-6}\,\text{A}$$

High resistance means low current
When measuring voltage in a circuit, you do *not* want current to pass through the multimeter itself. Multimeters are designed to have high resistance for voltage measurement, typically 1 million ohms (1 MΩ) or more. According to Ohm's law, the current into the multimeter when measuring 1.5 volts is only 1.5×10^{-6} amps ($1.5\,\text{V} \div 1 \times 10^6\,\Omega$). This small extra current is not likely to affect your circuit.

Calculate the current flowing in a circuit

A light bulb with a resistance of 2 ohms is connected in a circuit that has a single 1.5-volt battery. Calculate the current that flows in the circuit. Assume the wires have zero resistance.

Circuit

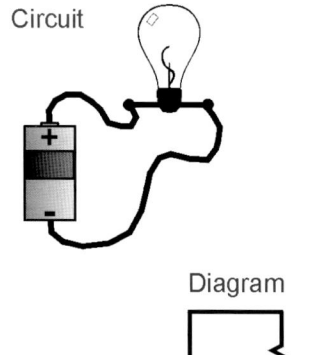

Diagram

$1.5V$ ⎓ 2Ω

1) You are asked for the current.
2) You are given the voltage and resistance.
3) Ohm's law relates current, voltage, and resistance
4) Solve:
   I = (1.5 V) ÷ (2 Ω)
   = 0.75 A

The light bulb draws 0.75 amps of electric current.

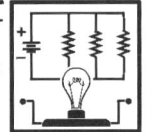

The resistance of electrical devices

Resistance of common devices

The resistance of electrical devices ranges from very small (0.001 Ω) to very large (10×10⁶ Ω). Each device is designed with a resistance that allows the right amount of current to flow when connected to the voltage the device was designed for. For example, a 100-watt light bulb has a resistance of 145 ohms. When connected to 120 volts from a wall socket, 0.83 amps flows and the bulb lights (Figure 19.12).

Resistances match operating voltage

If you connect a 1.5 V battery to an ordinary 100-watt bulb, you will get no light at all. The reason is that there is not enough current. According to Ohm's law, 1.5 volts can push only 0.01 amps through 145 ohms of resistance. This amount of current is much too small to make the bulb light. A 100-watt bulb is designed with the appropriate resistance to draw the right amount of current at 120 volts. Most electrical devices are similarly designed to operate correctly at a certain voltage.

The resistance of skin

Your skin has a fairly large resistance. A typical resistance of dry skin is 100,000 ohms or more. You can safely handle a 9-volt battery because the resistance of your skin is high. According to Ohm's law, 9V ÷ 100,000Ω is only 0.00009 amps. This is not enough current to be harmful. On average, nerves in the skin can feel a current of around 0.0005 amps. You can get a dangerous shock from 120 volts from a wall socket because that is enough to push 0.0012 amps (120V÷100,000Ω) through your skin, more than twice the amount you can feel.

Water lowers skin resistance

Wet skin has much lower resistance than dry skin. Because of the lower resistance, the same voltage will cause more current to pass through your body when your skin is wet. The combination of water and 120-volt electricity is especially dangerous because the high voltage and lower resistance make it possible for large (possibly fatal) currents to flow.

Changing resistance

The resistance of many electrical devices varies with temperature and current. For example, a light bulb's resistance increases when there is more current through the bulb. This change occurs because the bulb gets hotter when more current passes through it. The resistance of many materials, including those in light bulbs, increases as temperature increases. A graph of current versus voltage for a light bulb shows a curve (Figure 19.13). A device with constant resistance would show a straight line on this graph.

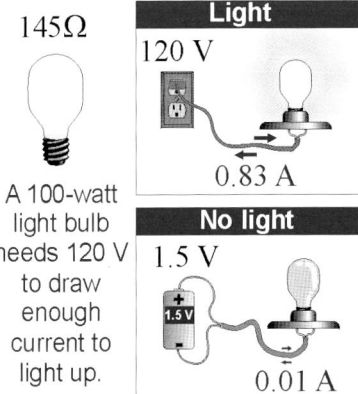

145Ω

A 100-watt light bulb needs 120 V to draw enough current to light up.

Figure 19.12: *The resistance of a light bulb is chosen so the bulb draws the correct current when connected to 120 volts from a wall socket. The bulb will not light connected to a battery because there is not enough current.*

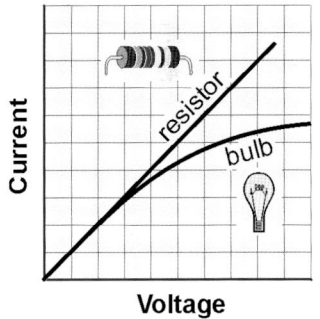

Figure 19.13: *The current versus voltage graph for a resistor is a straight line with a constant slope. The graph for a light bulb is curved with a decreasing slope because resistance increases with current.*

Conductors and insulators

Conductors   Current passes very easily through some kinds of materials, such as copper. A material such as copper is called a conductor because it can *conduct*, or carry, electric current. The electrical resistance of wires made from conductors is very low. Most metals are good conductors.

Insulators   Other materials, such as glass and plastic, do not allow current to flow easily through them. These materials are classified as electrical insulators because they insulate against (or block) the flow of current. Things made from insulators usually have very high resistance.

Semiconductors   Some materials are neither conductors nor insulators. These materials are named semiconductors because their ability to carry current falls between that of conductors and insulators. Computer chips, LEDs, and some types of lasers are made with semiconductors.

Electrical conductivity   No material is a perfect conductor or insulator. Some amount of current will flow through all materials if a voltage is applied. The electrical conductivity describes a material's ability to pass electric current. Materials with high conductivity (like metals) allow current to flow easily and are good conductors. Materials with low conductivity block current from flowing and are insulators

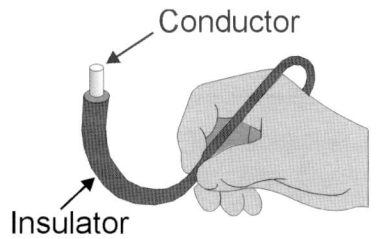

Figure 19.14: *A wire uses both conductors and insulators. The conductor carries the current through the center. The insulator keeps the current from reaching you when you touch the wire.*

Electrical properties	Category	Example materials	
High conductivity **Low resistance**	Conductors	silver gold copper	aluminum tungsten iron
	Semiconductors	carbon germanium	silicon
Low conductivity **High resistance**	Insulators	air paper ice	glass rubber plastic (most)

Applications of conductors and insulators   Both conductors and insulators are necessary materials in human technology. For example, a wire has one or more conductors on the inside and an insulator on the outside (Figure 19.14). An electrical cable may have twenty or more conductors, each separated from the others by a thin layer of insulator.

Breakdown voltage

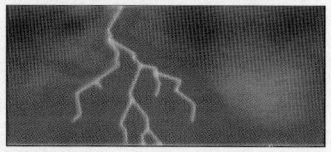

Even the best insulators will become conductors when the voltage gets high enough. For example, air is normally a good insulator. One centimeter of air will remain an insulator up to about 10,000 volts. When the voltage exceeds 10,000 V/cm (the breakdown voltage), atoms in the air split apart and release electrons that can carry current. Air becomes a conductor, as it does in a lightning strike.

390

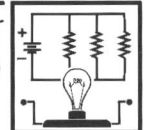
Resistors

Resistors are used to control current	Resistors are electrical components that are designed to have a well-defined resistance that remains the same over a wide range of currents. Resistors are used to control the amount of current in circuits. They are found in many common electronic devices such as computers, televisions, telephones, and stereos.
Fixed resistors	There are two main types of resistors, fixed and variable. Fixed resistors have a resistance that cannot be changed. If you have ever looked at a circuit board inside a computer or other electrical device, you have seen fixed resistors. They are small skinny cylinders or rectangles with colored stripes on them. Because resistors are so tiny it is impossible to label each one with the value of its resistance in numbers. Instead, the colored stripes are a code that tells you the resistance.
Variable resistors	Variable resistors, also called potentiometers, can be adjusted to have a range of resistance. If you have ever turned a dimmer switch or volume control, you have used a potentiometer. When the resistance of a dimmer switch is increased, the current decreases, and the bulb is dimmed. Inside a potentiometer is a circular resistor and a little sliding contact called a wiper, as shown below. The wiper moves when you turn the knob and is connected to a wire (B). The resistance between the wires at A and C always stays the same. As you turn the knob the resistance between A and B changes. The resistance between B and C also changes, but in the opposite direction. A potentiometer like the one in the diagram below can have a resistance between zero and 10 ohms, depending on the position of the wiper and which terminals are connected to the circuit.

The resistor color code

Color	Number
black	0
brown	1
red	2
orange	3
yellow	4
green	5
blue	6
violet	7
grey	8
white	9

1st digit
2nd digit
multiplier
accuracy

Color	Accuracy
silver	+/- 10%
gold	+/- 5%
brown	+/- 1%

Reading the code

Red
Green
Orange
Silver

$25 \times 10^3 = 25,000\Omega$

The first two stripes on a resistor tell the first two digits of its resistance. The third stripe tells you the power of 10 by which the first digits must be multiplied. The fourth stripe indicates the accuracy tolerance of the resistor.

The red and green stripes on the example resistor indicate that the first two digits are 2 and 5. The orange stripe means the 25 must be multiplied by 10 three times, for a total of 25,000 Ω. The silver fourth stripe shows that the tolerance is +/- 10%.

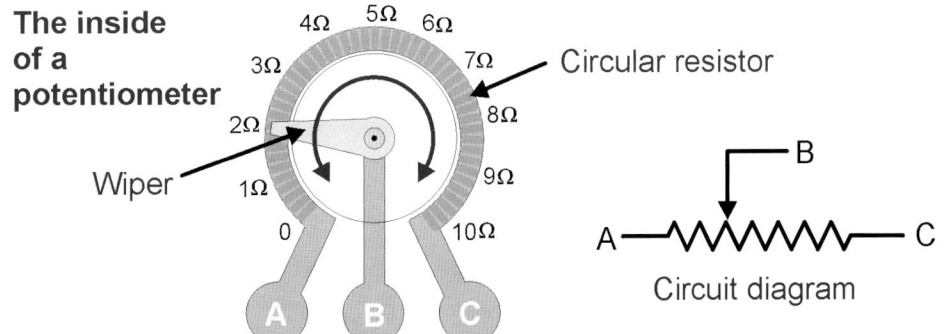

The inside of a potentiometer

Wiper

Circular resistor

4Ω 5Ω 6Ω 3Ω 7Ω 2Ω 8Ω 1Ω 9Ω 0 10Ω

A B C

B

A —ᴧᴧᴧᴧᴧ— C

Circuit diagram

Application: Hybrid Gas/Electric Cars

According to most specialists on the subject, world oil supplies are decreasing and the environmental impact of automobile pollution is increasing. The most promising near-term technology for reducing both problems is the hybrid gas/electric car. Hybrid cars and vehicles use a gasoline-powered engine and an electric motor (Figures 19.15 and 19.16). Several models now on the road get gas mileage close to 60 miles per gallon, twice the fuel economy of ordinary cars.

Automotive technology

Electric cars — Electric motors can generate high forces very fast, are quiet, and produce no pollution. Despite these advantages, electric cars have not been widely accepted. The biggest problem is that one kilogram of gasoline yields more than 30 times the energy stored in one kilogram of batteries. To store enough energy to be practical, electric cars are heavy and have a range of only 50 to 100 miles before the batteries need to be recharged. Recharging is slow, and takes many hours.

Conventional gas-powered cars — The gasoline engine in a car is ideal for transportation in many ways. Gasoline is a compact fuel in that it contains a lot of energy in a relatively small and light form that is easy to store and transport. Some disadvantages are the pollution and decreasing supply of oil.

Hybrid cars — Hybrid cars combine the advantages of gasoline as a fuel, with many of the advantages of electric power. In the most promising hybrids on the market today, a small, efficient gasoline engine is combined with a battery-powered electric motor. These two power sources work together to achieve good performance and excellent fuel efficiency.

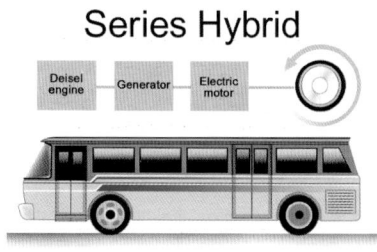

Series Hybrid

Figure 19.15: *A series hybrid like this bus has a gasoline engine that powers a generator directly, which produces electricity to power an electric motor that moves the bus.*

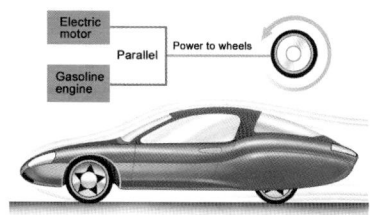

Parallel Hybrid

Figure 19.16: *A parallel hybrid can be powered by either the gasoline engine or the electric motor, or by both. Today's hybrid cars are parallel hybrids and use advanced aerodynamics to increase efficiency.*

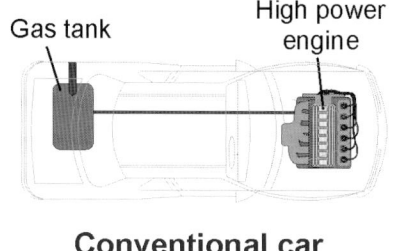

Gas tank   High power engine

Conventional car

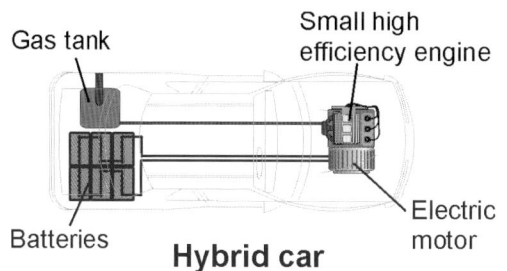

Gas tank   Small high efficiency engine

Batteries   Electric motor

Hybrid car

Hybrid car technology

Conventional car engines
Ordinary car engines are built with extra power capacity to provide rapid acceleration when passing or starting. Cruising at constant speed requires less than 15 percent of a typical engine's maximum power. Fuel efficiency suffers because large engines are inefficient at the low power levels used for 95 percent of driving. Conventional engine designs are a compromise between high power needed for acceleration and low power needed for normal driving.

Gas-engine use in a hybrid car
In a hybrid car, the small, high-performance gasoline engine is used for normal driving. The electric motor supplies extra power for fast starts and for rapid acceleration. The gas engine can be relatively powerful while producing ultra-low levels of emissions. One hybrid model has an engine that weighs a mere 124 pounds yet produces 67 horsepower.

Hybrid cars do not need to be "plugged in" overnight to be recharged like pure electric cars. The gasoline engine includes an electric generator that continuously recharges the batteries while you are driving.

Electric-motor use in a hybrid car
The high-efficiency electric motors in hybrids can be up to 90 percent efficient. At low speed and when idle, the gas engine shuts off and the electric motor takes over. Drivers have been surprised—and pleased—by the hybrid car's quietness when operating in full-electric mode.

Regenerative braking
One of the most innovative developments in hybrid technology is *regenerative braking*. Conventional braking systems dissipate a car's kinetic energy through friction, resulting in heat. In a hybrid car however, the electric motor also works as a generator. Regenerative braking uses some of the car's kinetic energy to turn the motor (generator) and charge the batteries during slowing or stopping. This process recycles kinetic energy that would otherwise have been lost as heat.

Battery technology
The first hybrid cars used heavy lead-acid batteries similar to the ones used in conventional cars to start the engine. New battery technologies such as lithium-ion batteries are lighter and smaller than lead-acid batteries. Hybrid cars will continue to improve and replace conventional cars as battery technology gets better.

Current and voltage in hybrid cars

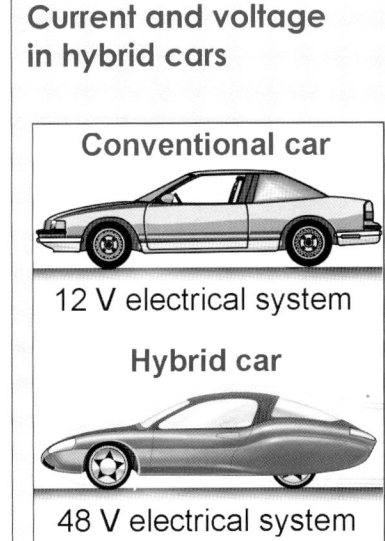

Conventional car

12 V electrical system

Hybrid car

48 V electrical system

The electrical systems in conventional cars use 12 volts. The battery is only used to start the engine, and is designed to supply high current (50 amps or more) for a short time.

Hybrid cars use 96-volt electrical systems (or higher). At 96 V, each amp of current carries 96 watts of power instead of 12, as in a conventional (12 V) car. Hybrids typically use multiple banks of specialized batteries to make the higher voltage. Unlike ordinary car batteries, hybrid car batteries are designed to supply steady current for long periods of time.

Chapter 19 Review

Vocabulary Review

Match the following terms with the correct definition. There is one extra definition in the list that will not match any of the terms.

Set One

1. ampere
2. electrical resistance
3. electric current
4. potentiometer
5. electric circuit

a. A complete path for electric current to flow
b. Used to measure current
c. The unit in which electric current is measured
d. A measure of how easily current flows through an electrical device
e. The flow of electricity
f. A variable resistor

Set Two

1. voltage
2. ohm
3. electrical symbol
4. ammeter
5. switch

a. A simple diagram used to represent a wire, battery, bulb or other component in a circuit
b. An electric meter used to measure voltage
c. Used to turn electricity on and off
d. The unit in which electrical resistance is measured
e. An electric meter used to measure current
f. Describes the power in watts carried by each amp of current

Set Three

1. voltmeter
2. open circuit
3. circuit breaker
4. short circuit
5. volt

a. An accidental low-resistance path in circuit that allows high currents to flow
b. A device that stops current in a circuit if the current gets too high
c. The unit in which voltage is measured
d. A circuit with a break in it
e. The unit in which electric potential energy is measured
f. An electrical device used to measure voltage

Set Four

1. Ohm's law
2. insulator
3. conductor
4. resistor

a. A material that does not allow current to flow through it easily
b. A device used to control the amount of current in a circuit
c. A device that increases current in a circuit
d. Relates current, voltage, and resistance in a circuit
e. A material that allows current to flow through it easily

Concept review

1. Explain the similarities and differences between electric current and water current.

2. Why are electrical symbols used when making circuit diagrams?

3. Draw the electrical symbols for each of the following:

   a. resistor

   b. bulb

   c. battery

   d. switch

   e. wire

4. A circuit contains a battery, switch, and resistor. Draw its circuit diagram.

5. Explain the difference between an open circuit and a closed circuit.

6. Explain the function of a circuit breaker or fuse.

7. What provides the push to current in a circuit?

8. How is a battery's voltage related to the amount of energy it supplies to current in a circuit?

9. You install two batteries in a flashlight such that their positive ends are facing each other. Will the flashlight work? Explain your answer.

10. Where does the energy supplied by a battery come from?

11. Give an example of a material with high electrical resistance and one with low resistance.

12. Which three quantities in a circuit can be measured with a multimeter?

13. You are doing an investigation with circuits in class. Your lab partner gathers the supplies for the investigation and you notice the multimeter contains only one probe. Can you use this meter to measure current? Can you use it to measure voltage? Explain your answers.

14. A battery is connected to a light bulb, creating a simple circuit. What happens to the current in the circuit if

   a. the bulb is replaced with a bulb having a higher resistance?

   b. the bulb is replaced with a bulb having a lower resistance?

   c. the battery is replaced with a battery having a higher voltage?

15. List the unit in which each of the following is measured:

   a. current

   b. voltage

   c. resistance

16. According to Ohm's law, how is current related to the resistance in a circuit? How is current related to the voltage?

17. Why is it important to make sure your hands are dry before you plug wires into electrical outlets?

18. Explain why the current versus voltage graph is a straight line for a resistor but is curved for a light bulb.

19. What is the difference between a conductor and an insulator?

20. State whether each material is a conductor, semiconductor, or an insulator:

   a. carbon

   b. gold

   c. glass

   d. copper

   e. air

21. If a material has a low resistance, does it have a high or low electrical conductivity?

22. Explain why electrical wires in homes are covered with a layer of plastic.

23. How is a potentiometer different from a fixed resistor?

24. List two uses for a potentiometer.

25. Why do fixed resistors often contain colored stripes?

395

Problems

1. A hair dryer draws a current of 10 A when it is plugged into a 120-volt circuit. What is the resistance of the hair dryer?

2. A light bulb with a resistance of 2 Ω is connected to a 1.5 V battery. What is the current in the circuit?

3. A battery supplies 0.25 amps of current to a motor with a resistance of 48 ohms. What is the voltage of the battery?

4. A portable CD player has a resistance of 15 Ω and requires 0.3 A of current to function properly. How many 1.5 V batteries must be used in the CD player?

5. A flashlight bulb has a resistance of approximately 6 ohms. It works in a flashlight with two AA alkaline batteries. How much current does the bulb draw?

6. Household circuits in the United States commonly run on 120 volts of electricity. Circuit breakers are frequently installed to open a circuit if it draws more than 15 amps of current. What is the minimum amount of resistance that must be present in the circuit to prevent the circuit breaker from activating?

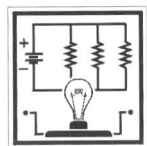

Unit 7

Electricity and Magnetism

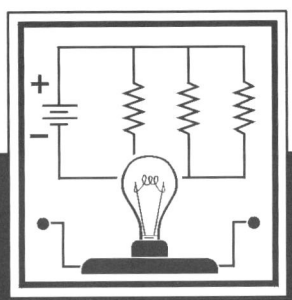

Chapter 20

Electric Circuits and Power

Objectives for Chapter 20

By the end of this chapter you should be able to:

1. Recognize and sketch examples of series and parallel circuits.
2. Describe a short circuit and why a short circuit may be a dangerous hazard.
3. Calculate the current in a series or parallel circuit containing up to three resistances.
4. Calculate the total resistance of a circuit by combining series or parallel resistances.
5. Describe the differences between AC and DC electricity.
6. Calculate the power used in an AC or DC circuit from the current and voltage.

Terms and vocabulary words

series circuit	parallel circuit	short circuit	network circuit	circuit analysis
power	Kirchhoff's voltage law	voltage drop	direct current (DC)	alternating current (AC)
kilowatt	Kirchhoff's current law	horsepower	power factor	circuit breaker
watt	kilowatt-hour			

20.1 Series and Parallel Circuits

A simple electric circuit contains one electrical device, a battery, and a switch. Flashlights use this type of circuit. However, most electrical systems, such as a stereo, contain many electrical devices connected together in multiple circuits. This section talks about the two fundamental ways to connect multiple devices in a circuit. Series circuits have only one path for current to flow. Parallel circuits have branches and multiple paths for current to flow. A complex system like a stereo has networks of both series and parallel circuits.

Series circuits

Series circuits contain one path

A series circuit contains only one path for current to flow. The amount of current is the same at all points in a series circuit. For example, the circuit below has three bulbs connected in series. Since there is only one path for the current, the same current goes through each bulb, making each one equally bright.

Series circuit

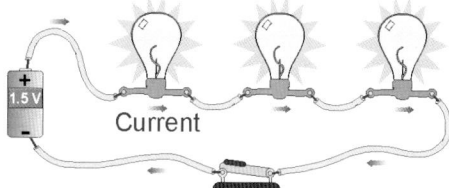

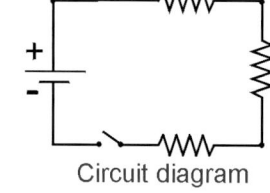

Stopping current

If there is a break at any point in a series circuit, the current will stop everywhere in the circuit. Inexpensive strings of holiday lights are wired with the bulbs in series. When one bulb burns out, the current stops and none of the bulbs will light (Figure 20.1). Connecting bulbs in series uses the least amount of wire, so strings of lights connected in series are less expensive to manufacture.

Using series circuits

There are times when devices are connected in series for specific purposes. On-off switches are placed in series with the other components in most electrical devices (Figure 20.2). When a switch is turned to the off position, it breaks the circuit and stops current from reaching all of the components in series with the switch. Dimmer switches placed in series with light bulbs adjust the brightness by changing the amount of current in the circuit.

Series circuit

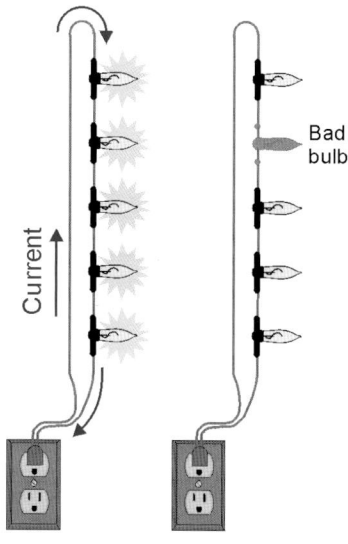

Figure 20.1: *Inexpensive holiday lights are wired in series. When one bulb burns out, the whole circuit is broken and all the lights go out.*

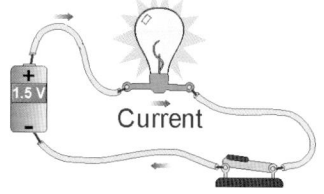

A switch "in series"

Figure 20.2: *Switches are usually placed "in series" with other elements in a circuit so that they can stop the flow of current in the whole circuit.*

398

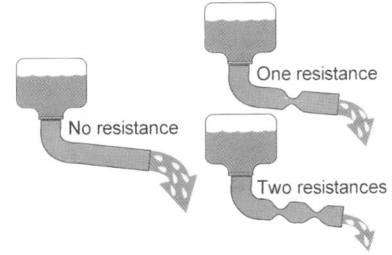

Current and resistance in a series circuit

Adding resistance in series   Each resistance in a series circuit adds to the total resistance of the circuit. Think about adding pinches to a hose (Figure 20.3). Each pinch adds more resistance and reduces the current of water flowing in the hose. The total resistance of a hose is also the sum of the resistances from each pinch.

Adding resistances in series

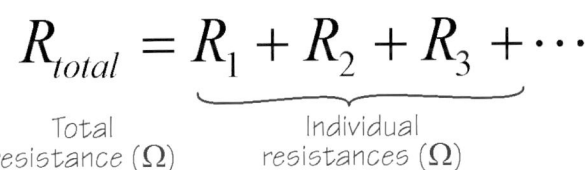

$$R_{total} = R_1 + R_2 + R_3 + \cdots$$

Total resistance (Ω)   Individual resistances (Ω)

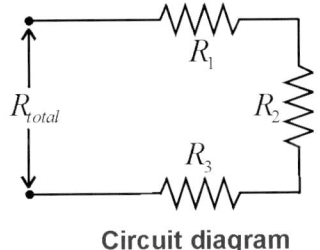

Circuit diagram

One resistance

No resistance

Two resistances

Figure 20.3: *Resistances in series add up like pinches in a hose. Each one reduces the current in the whole circuit.*

Calculating current   If you know the voltage and the total resistance in a circuit, you can calculate the current using Ohm's law. To calculate the total resistance for a series circuit you can simply add up all the individual resistances. Since the current is the same everywhere in a series circuit, use Ohm's law to calculate the current by dividing the voltage applied to the circuit by the total resistance of the circuit.

Resistance in wires and batteries   Every part in a circuit has some resistance, even the wires and batteries. However, light bulbs, resistors, motors, and heaters usually have much greater resistance than wires and batteries. Therefore, when adding resistances, we can almost always leave out the resistance of wires and batteries.

Series circuit of three 1 Ω bulbs

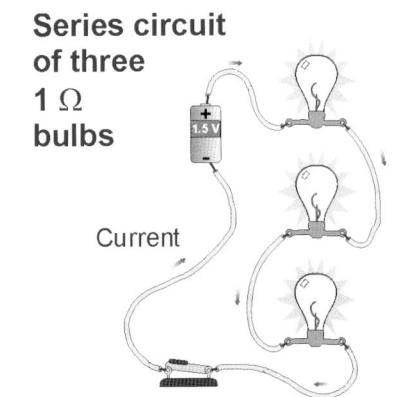

Current

Circuit diagram

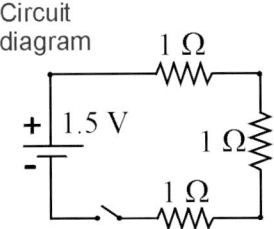

Total resistance = 3Ω

Figure 20.4: *Adding resistances in a series circuit of three 1Ω bulbs. The total resistance is 3Ω*

Calculate the current in a series circuit

How much current flows in a circuit with a 1.5-volt battery and three 1 ohm resistances (bulbs) in series? (Figure 20.4)

1) You are asked to calculate current.

2) You are given the voltage and resistances.

3) Use Ohm's law, I = V÷R, and add the resistance in series.

4) Solve:
   Resistance = $R_1 + R_2 + R_3$ = 1Ω + 1Ω + 1Ω = 3Ω
   Current, I = (1.5 V)÷(3Ω)=0.5 A

Voltage in a series circuit

Energy
You have learned that energy is not created or destroyed, but can be transformed from one form to another. As current flows along a series circuit, each bulb, motor, or other type of resistor transforms some of the electrical energy into another form of energy. As a result, the *voltage gets lower after each resistance.*

The voltage drop
We often say each separate resistance creates a voltage drop as the current passes through. Ohm's law is used to calculate the voltage drop across each resistor. For example, in the three-bulb series circuit below, the voltage drop across each bulb (1V) is found by multiplying the current (1A) by the resistance (1Ω). The diagram below shows how the power carried by the current is used. The current leaves the battery at a potential of 3V therefore each amp carries 3 watts of electrical power. The first bulb uses 1 watt and the voltage drops by one volt ($V = IR = 1\,A \times 1\,\Omega$). The next bulb uses the same power and the voltage drops by one volt again.

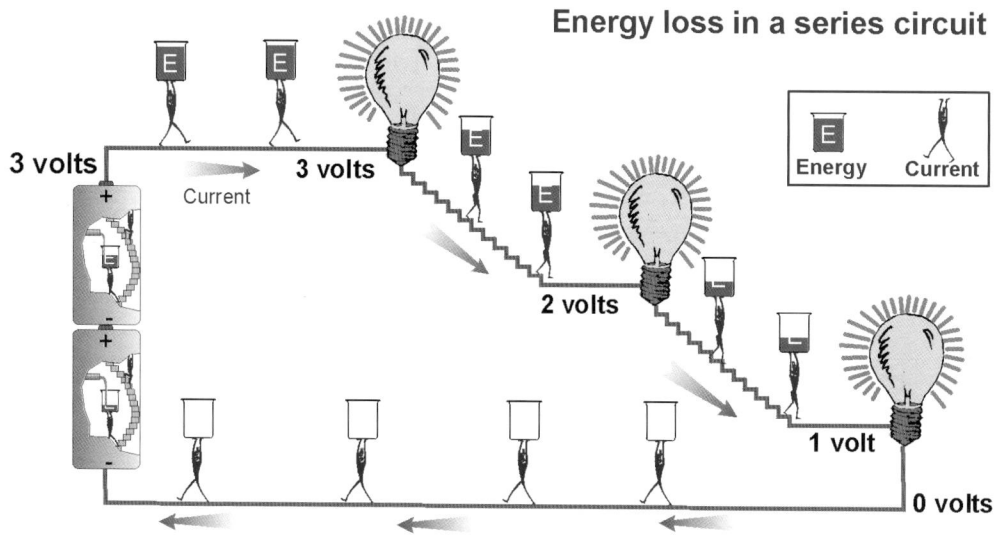

Energy loss in a series circuit

Kirchhoff's voltage law
Over the entire circuit, the power used by all of the resistors must equal the power supplied by the battery. This means the total of all the voltage drops must add up to the total voltage supplied by the battery. This is known as Kirchhoff's voltage law, after German physicist Gustav Robert Kirchhoff (1824-87):

Although the terms "battery" and "cell" are often used interchangeably, cells are the building blocks of batteries. AA, C, and D batteries each contain a single 1.5V cell. A chemical reaction inside a cell supplies electric current.

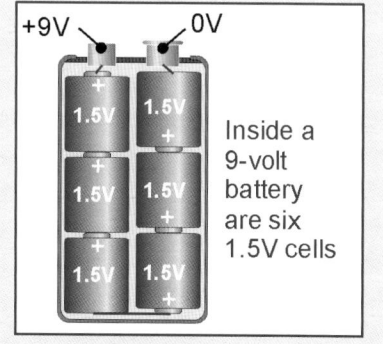

Inside a 9-volt battery are six 1.5V cells

If a battery contains multiple cells, they may be connected in series or parallel. If a higher voltage is needed, the cells are connected in series. Six 1.5-volt cells in series make up the 9-volt battery shown above.

If a battery must supply a large current, a larger cell may be used or multiple cells may be connected in parallel. Parallel cells make a battery with the voltage of one cell but with a greater current capacity.

Parallel circuits

Multiple paths for current
Unlike series circuits, parallel circuits contain more than one path for current to flow through. A parallel circuit contains at least one point where the circuit divides, providing multiple paths for the current. Sometimes these paths are called *branches*. The current through a branch is also called the *branch current*.

Kirchhoff's current law
Because there are multiple branches, the current is not the same at all points in a parallel circuit. When analyzing a parallel circuit, remember that the current always has to go somewhere. The total current in the circuit is the sum of the currents in all the branches. At every branch point the current flowing out must equal the current flowing in. This rule is known as Kirchhoff's current law.

Three bulbs in parallel
For example, suppose you have three 3Ω light bulbs connected in parallel. Because each bulb has a direct wire to the battery with no voltage drops, each bulb sees 3 volts of potential difference. That means that each 3Ω bulb draws a current of 1 amp. If there are three bulbs drawing 1 amp each, then the battery must supply a total of 3 amps. At the first branch point, 1 amp splits off to the first bulb and 2 amps continue to the next two bulbs. After passing through the bulbs, the current combines again and 3 amps flows back to the battery. *Note: This example uses 3Ω bulbs instead of 1Ω bulbs used in the previous example.*

Parallel circuit

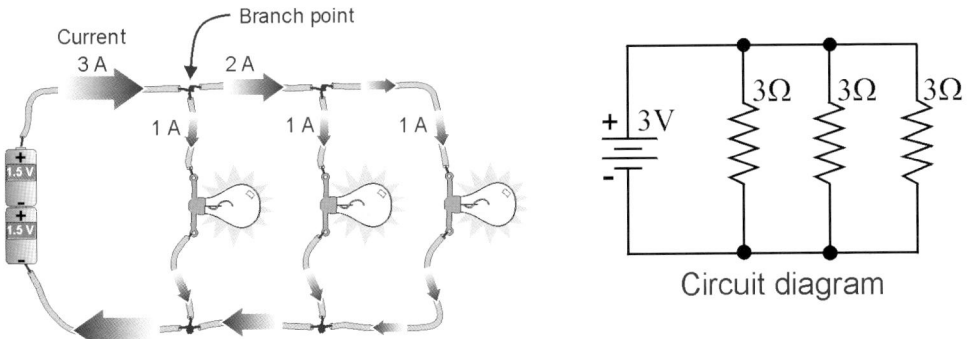 

Circuit diagram

Kirchhoff's current law
All the current flowing into a branch point in a circuit has to flow out.

Why aren't birds electrocuted?

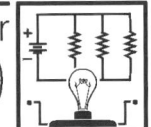

16,000 volts

If high-voltage wires are so dangerous, how do birds sit on them without being instantly electrocuted? First, the bird's body has a higher resistance than the electrical wire. The current tends to stay in the wire because the wire is an easier path.

The most important reason, however, is that the bird has both feet on the same wire. That means the voltage is the same on both feet and no current flows through the bird.

If a bird had one foot on the wire and the other foot touching the electric pole, then there would be a voltage difference across the bird's feet, a lot of electricity would pass through the bird, and it would not survive.

20.1 Series and Parallel Circuits **401**

Voltage and current in a parallel circuit

Voltage In a parallel circuit the *voltage* is the same across each branch because each branch has a low resistance path back to the battery. The amount of current in each branch in a parallel circuit is *not* necessarily the same. The resistance in each branch determines the current in that branch. Branches with less resistance have larger amounts of current than branches with more resistance.

Advantages of parallel circuits Parallel circuits have two big advantages over series circuits.

1. Each device in the circuit sees the full battery voltage.

2. Each device in the circuit may be turned off independently without stopping the current flowing to other devices in the circuit.

Remember, in a series circuit each additional resistance reduces the current in the whole circuit. And, opening a break anywhere in a series circuit stops the current to all devices on the circuit. Parallel circuits use more wires but are used for most of the wiring in homes and businesses because of the two advantages above.

Short circuits A **short circuit** is a parallel path in a circuit with zero or very low resistance. Short circuits can be made accidentally by connecting a wire between two other wires at different voltages. Short circuits are dangerous because they can draw huge amounts of current. For example, suppose you connect a length of wire across a circuit, creating a second current path as shown below.

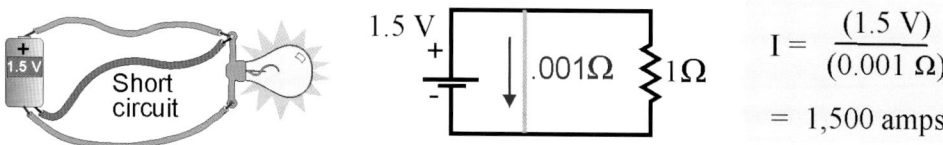

$$I = \frac{(1.5\ V)}{(0.001\ \Omega)}$$

$$= 1,500\ \text{amps}$$

The grey wire in the diagram makes a short circuit because it makes a very low resistance (0.001 Ω) between 1.5 and zero volts. According to Ohm's law, the current through the offending wire could be as high as 1,500 amps! This much current would melt the wire in an instant and probably burn you as well. Short circuits are always a concern when working around electricity. Fuses or circuit breakers are protection from the high current of a short circuit.

402

Calculate the current in a parallel circuit

Two bulbs with different resistances are connected in parallel to batteries with a total voltage of 3 volts. Calculate the total current supplied by the battery.

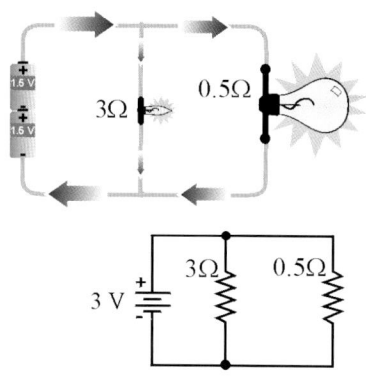

1) You are asked for the current.
2) You are given the voltage and resistance.
3) Use Ohm's law: I = V ÷ R.
4) For the 3Ω bulb:
   I = (3 V) ÷ (3 Ω) = 1 A.
   For the 0.5 Ω bulb:
   I = (3 V) ÷ (0.5 Ω) = 6 A.

   The battery must supply the current for both bulbs, which adds up to 7 amps.

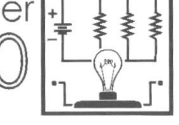
Resistance in parallel circuits

More branches means more current In series circuits, adding an extra resistance increases the total resistance of the whole circuit. The opposite is true in parallel circuits. Adding resistance in parallel provides another path for current, and more current flows. When more current flows for the same voltage, the total resistance of the circuit decreases.

Similarity to checkout lines A similar result occurs in the check-out area of a grocery store. If only one register is open, every person must pass through the same lane, and the rate of people leaving the store is slow. If a second register opens, half of the people will pass through each lane. The average amount of time each person has to spend waiting in line will be cut in half, and the total flow of people through the store is higher.

Example of a parallel circuit Figure 20.5 shows the parallel circuit of three 3Ω bulbs used in a previous example. The total current in this circuit is 3 amps. The voltage is 3 volts. According to Ohm's law, the circuit acts like it has a resistance of 1Ω ($R=V\div I$). Three 3Ω resistors add up to a total resistance of 1Ω. This happens because every new path in a parallel circuit allows more current to flow for the same voltage. The resistance of the whole circuit (as seen by the battery) decreases.

The formula for adding parallel resistances If you work backward from current and voltage, you can derive a formula for the total resistance of a parallel circuit. The formula allows you to calculate the total current that flows in the circuit using Ohm's law and the total resistance. At the end of the chapter, you will see that all the outlets in your house or apartment are connected in parallel. Every device you plug in adds a parallel resistance and draws more current.

Adding resistances in parallel

$$\frac{1}{R_{total}} = \underbrace{\frac{1}{R_1} + \frac{1}{R_2} + \frac{1}{R_3} + \cdots}$$

Total resistance (Ω) Individual resistances (Ω)

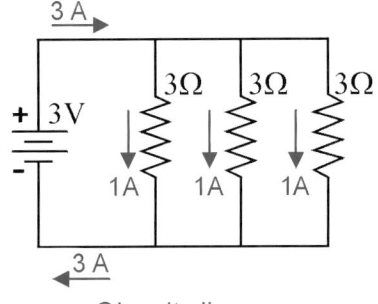

3 A

+ 3V

3Ω 3Ω 3Ω

1A 1A 1A

3 A

Circuit diagram

Figure 20.5: *A parallel circuit with three equal resistances divides the current three ways.*

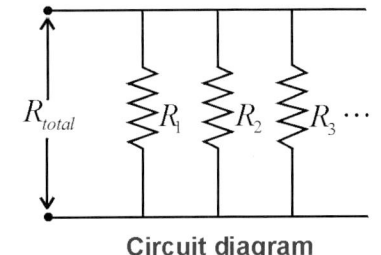

R_{total} R_1 R_2 $R_3 \cdots$

Circuit diagram

Calculate the resistance of a parallel circuit

A circuit contains a 2 ohm resistor and a 4 ohm resistor in parallel. Calculate the total resistance of the circuit.

1) You are asked for the resistance.

2) You are given the circuit diagram and resistances.

3) Use the rule for parallel resistances.

4) Solve:

$$\frac{1}{R_{total}} = \frac{1}{2\Omega} + \frac{1}{4\Omega} = \frac{3}{4\Omega}$$

$$R_{total} = \frac{4}{3}\Omega \,(1.33\Omega)$$

20.2 Analysis of Circuits

Electric circuits perform so many useful tasks that it is impossible to give examples of every type of circuit. There are circuits in computers, refrigerators, cars, televisions, cell phones, and every device that uses electricity. Electrical engineers are people who design circuits. Designing a good circuit is like a puzzle: You need to get a certain current and voltage output, and there may be a current and voltage input. This section is a brief introduction to designing and analyzing circuits that contain only resistors. In later chapters you will be introduced to some other kinds of electrical devices that appear in circuits, such as capacitors, transistors, and diodes. Even though they are presented for resistor circuits, the three rules of this section apply to all circuits, even the most complex ones.

The three circuit laws

Why circuit analysis is useful
Before you can design a circuit, you need to know how to figure out what a circuit does. All circuits work by manipulating currents and voltages. The process of circuit analysis means figuring out what the currents and voltages in a circuit are, and also how they are affected by each other. There are three basic laws that are the foundation of circuit analysis. Together with the formulas for combining resistors, these three laws are the framework for solving any circuit problem.

Ohm's law
Ohm's law, $I = V/R$, relates current, voltage, and resistance in a circuit. It can be used to find one quantity when the other two are known (Figure 20.6, top).

Kirchhoff's current law
Kirchhoff's current law says the total current flowing into any junction in a circuit equals the total current flowing out of the junction (Figure 20.6, middle).

Kirchhoff's voltage law
Kirchhoff's voltage law says the total of all voltage drops and voltage gains around any loop of a circuit must be zero (Figure 20.6, bottom). The voltage law is the trickiest to use because you have to choose a direction you believe the current will flow around the loop. You do not have to choose the right direction; the current comes out negative if you guess wrong. You do, however, have to choose and stick with your choice until the whole problem is solved. A voltage *increase* in the direction of the assumed current flow is counted as *positive*. A voltage *decrease* in the direction of current flow is counted as *negative*. The signs reverse if the voltage change is opposite to the assumed direction of current.

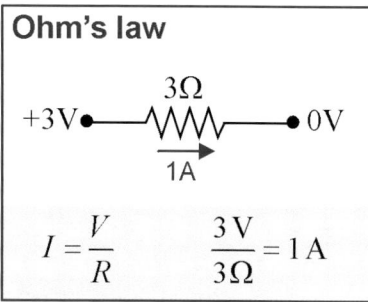

Ohm's law

$$I = \frac{V}{R} \qquad \frac{3\,V}{3\,\Omega} = 1\,A$$

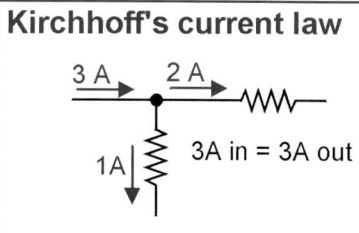

Kirchhoff's current law

The total current into a junction equals the total current out of the junction.

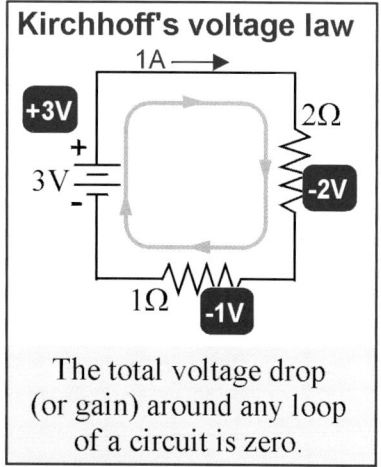

Kirchhoff's voltage law

The total voltage drop (or gain) around any loop of a circuit is zero.

Figure 20.6: *The three circuit laws.*

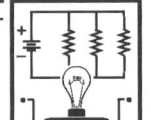

A voltage divider circuit

Changing voltage in a circuit Nearly all electronic devices use a voltage divider somewhere in the circuit. This is because electrical devices work within a certain range of voltage. For example, the input circuit for a microphone is designed for a voltage up to 0.1 volts. The circuit for a speaker operates at 48 volts (Figure 20.7). If you want to record a speaker output directly into a microphone input, you need to divide the voltage by 480 (48 ÷ 0.1). This can be done with two resistors in a voltage divider circuit.

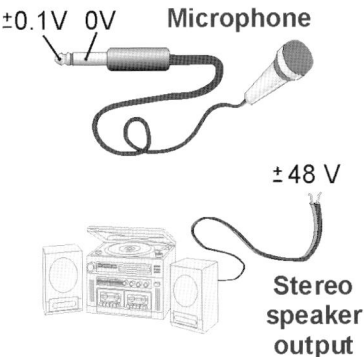

Figure 20.7: *Voltages from typical music electronics.*

A simple voltage divider Consider the series circuit with two resistors shown in Figure 20.8. The total resistance of this circuit is 10 ohms (9Ω + 1Ω). The total current is 1 amp from Ohm's law (10V ÷ 10Ω). What is the voltage at point (A)?

Analyzing the circuit We can use Kirchhoff's voltage law to find the answer. Assume the current flows according to the light blue loop. The battery starts at +10V. Resistor R_1 drops the voltage by 9V. This voltage drop is calculated from Ohm's law and the resistance, V = 1A × 9Ω. Resistor R_2 drops the voltage by 1V (1A × 1Ω). Around the whole loop the sum of the voltage gains and drops is zero (+10 - 9 - 1 = 0).

The circuit divides by 10 The voltage at point (A) is 1 volt because it is the battery voltage (10V) minus the voltage drop across R_1 (9V). The circuit is a voltage divider. The voltage at point (A) is the battery voltage divided by 10. If the battery had been 20V, the voltage at point (A) would be 2 volts. No matter what the battery voltage, the voltage at point (A) will always be one-tenth as great.

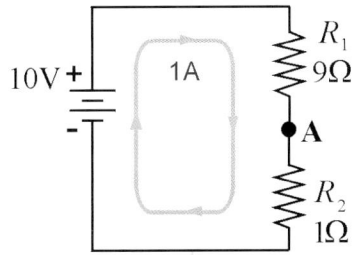

Voltage divider circuit

Input and output voltage Think of the battery voltage as the *input voltage*, and the voltage at point (A) as the *output voltage* (Figure 20.8, bottom). The output voltage (V_o) is always lower than the input voltage (V_i) by the ratio $R_2 ÷ (R_1 + R_2)$. For the example circuit, the dividing ratio was 1/10, but it could be any number depending on which resistors you choose. For example, if R_2 was 10Ω and R_1 was 4,790Ω, the output voltage would be the input voltage divided by 480.

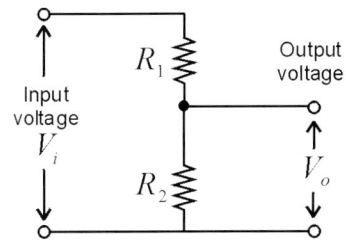

Voltage divider circuit

$$\text{Output voltage (V)} \quad V_o = \left(\frac{R_2}{R_1 + R_2}\right) V_i \quad \text{Input voltage (V)}$$

Resistor ratio

Figure 20.8: *The top diagram shows a circuit that divides the battery voltage by 10. The same circuit divides any voltage by a ratio of R_1 and R_2 (bottom diagram).*

Solving circuit problems

Using a systematic approach It is best to take a systematic approach when analyzing circuits. The following steps are a general guide that will help you solve circuit problems.

1) Identify what the problem is asking you to find. Assign variables to the unknown quantities.

2) Make a large clear diagram of the circuit. Label all of the known resistances, currents, and voltages. Use the variables you defined to label the unknowns.

3) You may need to combine resistances to find the total circuit resistance. Use multiple steps to combine series and parallel resistors. Table 20.1 is a good guide.

4) If you know the total resistance and current, use Ohm's law as $V = IR$ to calculate voltages or voltage drops. If you know the resistance and voltage, use Ohm's law as $I = V \div R$ to calculate the current.

5) An unknown resistance can be found using Ohm's law as $R = V \div I$, if you know the current through the resistor and the voltage drop across it.

6) Use Kirchhoff's current and voltage laws as necessary.

There is often more than one way to solve circuit problems. Finding solutions to complex circuits requires creativity, logical thinking, and practice.

Calculate the resistor needed to limit current in a series circuit

A bulb with a resistance of 1Ω is to be used in a circuit with a 6-volt battery. The bulb requires 1 amp of current. If the bulb were connected directly to the battery, it would draw 6 amps and burn out instantly. To limit the current, a resistor is added in series with the bulb. What size resistor is needed to make the current 1 amp?

1) You are asked to calculate the resistance.
2) You are told it is a series circuit and given the voltage, total current, and one resistance.
3) Use Ohm's law, R = V ÷ I, and add the resistance in series.
4) Solve:
   Total resistance = 6V ÷ 1A = 6Ω.
   Since the bulb is 1Ω, the additional resistor must be 5Ω to get a total 6Ω of resistance.

Table 20.1:
Comparing series and parallel circuits

Series	Parallel
One path for current	**Multiple** paths for current
Same current at every point	**Current may be different** in each branch
Voltage drops across each resistance	**Same voltage** across each resistance
Break anywhere stops current in **entire** circuit	Break might only stop current in **one branch** of circuit
Total resistance $R_{total} = R_1 + R_2 + \cdots$	**Total resistance** $\dfrac{1}{R_{total}} = \dfrac{1}{R_1} + \dfrac{1}{R_2} + \cdots$
Adding series resistances **decreases** the total current	Adding parallel resistances **increases** the total current

 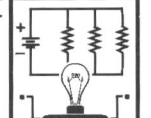

Network circuits

Resistors in both series and parallel In many circuits, resistors are connected both in series and in parallel. Such a circuit is called a network circuit. A network circuit contains more than one path for current to flow along, but also contains resistors in both series and parallel in one or more of the paths (Figure 20.9).

Solving a network circuit There is no single formula for adding resistors in a network circuit. Often, you must simplify the circuit step by step, using either the series or parallel resistor formula to combine two or more resistors. Keep combining resistors until you are left with one resistor having a resistance equivalent to the original combination.

Calculating currents and voltages From the total resistance and voltage you can use Ohm's law to calculate the total current. You can then work back through the circuit, calculating voltage drops at intermediate points if necessary. For very complex circuits, electrical engineers use computer programs that can rapidly solve equations for the circuit using Kirchhoff's laws.

Network circuit of three 3 Ω bulbs

Circuit diagram

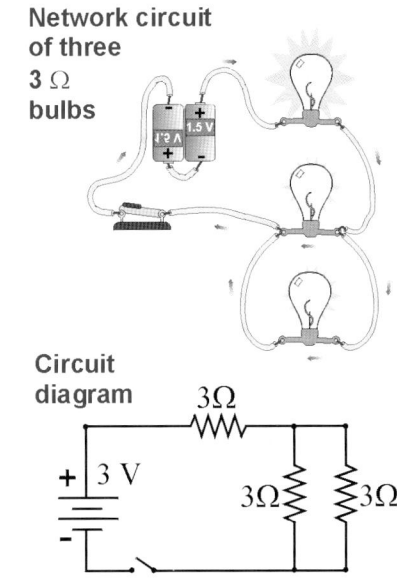

Figure 20.9: *An example network circuit with three bulbs.*

Calculate the currents and voltages in a three-resistor network circuit

Three bulbs, each with a resistance of 3Ω, are combined in the circuit shown in Figure 20.9. Three volts are applied to the circuit. Calculate the currents in each of the bulbs. From your calculations, do you think all three bulbs will be equally bright?

1) You are asked to calculate the currents.
2) You are given the circuit diagram, voltages, and resistances.
3) Use Ohm's law, R = V ÷ I, and the series and parallel resistance formulas.
4) First, reduce the circuit by combining the two parallel resistances.

$$\frac{1}{R_{total}} = \frac{1}{3\Omega} + \frac{1}{3\Omega} = \frac{2}{3\Omega} \longrightarrow R_{total} = \frac{3}{2}\Omega = 1.5\Omega$$

Calculate the total resistance of 4.5Ω by adding up the remaining series resistances.
Calculate the total current using Ohm's law: I = 3V ÷ 4.5Ω = 0.67A.
The two bulbs in parallel have the same resistance, so they divide the current equally; each one gets 0.33 amps.
The single bulb in series gets the full current of 0.67 amps, but the other two bulbs get only 0.33 amps each. That means the bulbs in parallel will be much dimmer since they only get half the current.

20.3 Electric Power, AC, and DC Electricity

In the last chapter, the volt was defined by the amount of energy carried by each amp of current in one second. A current of 1 amp flowing through a voltage difference of 1 volt does 1 joule work of work per 1 second. Since one joule per second is one watt, this definition really links voltage, current, and *power*. If you look carefully at a stereo, hair dryer, or other household appliance, you find that most devices list a "power rating" that tells how many watts the appliance uses (Figure 20.10). In this section you will learn what these power ratings mean, and how to calculate electricity costs of using various appliances.

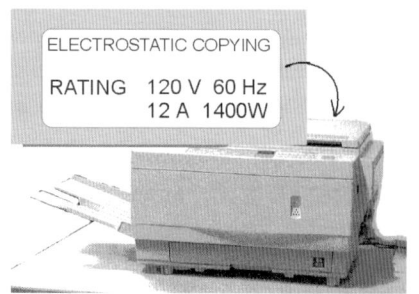

Figure 20.10: *The back of an electrical device often tells you how many watts it uses.*

Electric power

The three electrical quantities

You have learned about three important electrical quantities:

Current	Current is the flow of electricity. Current is measured in amperes.
Voltage	Voltage measures the potential energy difference between two places in a circuit. Voltage differences produce current. Voltage is measured in volts.
Resistance	Resistance measures the ability to resist current. Resistance is measured in ohms.

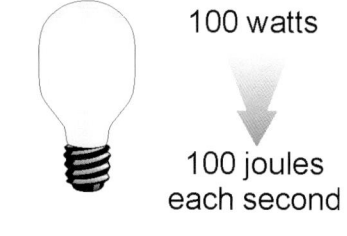

100 watts

100 joules each second

Paying for electricity

Electric bills sent out by utility companies do not charge by the volt, the amp, or the ohm. And you may have noticed that electric appliances in your home usually include another unit – the *watt*. Almost every appliance has a label that lists the number of watts it uses. You may have purchased 60-watt light bulbs, a 1,000-watt hair dryer, or a 1,500-watt toaster oven.

Measuring power

The watt (W) is a unit of power. Remember from Chapter 11 that power is the rate at which energy moves or is used. Since energy is measured in joules, power is measured in joules per second. One joule per second is equal to one watt (Figure 20.11). A 100-watt light bulb uses 100 joules of energy *every second*. This means the bulb transform 100 joules of electrical energy into heat and light every second. The longer the bulb is turned on, the more electrical energy it uses, and the higher your monthly electricity bill.

300 watts

300 joules each second

Figure 20.11: *One watt is an energy flow of one joule per second. A 100-watt light bulb uses 100 joules every second. A person running uses about 300 watts, or 300 joules every second.*

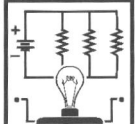

Power in electric circuits

Power in a circuit | A voltage of one volt means one amp of current can do one joule of work each second. Since one joule per second is one watt, this definition of a volt is really a formula for calculating power from current and voltage. If the voltage and current in a circuit are multiplied together, the result is the power used by the circuit.

Electrical power

Voltage (V)

$$\text{Power (W)} \quad P = VI \quad \leftarrow \text{Current (A)}$$

Voltage × Current = Power

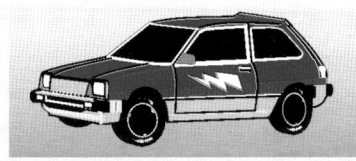

$$\frac{joules}{amp \times sec} \times \frac{amp}{} = \frac{joules}{sec}$$

Watts and kilowatts | One watt is a pretty small amount of power. In everyday use, larger units are more convenient to use. For example, a 1,500-watt toaster oven may be labeled "1.5 kW" instead of "1,500 W." A kilowatt (kW) is equal to 1,000 watts.

Horsepower | The other common unit of power often seen on electric motors is the horsepower. One horsepower is 746 watts. Electric motors you find around the house range in size from 1/25th of a horsepower (30 watts) for a small electric fan to 2 horsepower (1,492 watts) for an electric saw.

Voltage and current | Power depends on both current and voltage. You can get 1,000 watts of power from 1,000 amps at 1 volt, or from 10 amps at 100 volts. It would take a very large wire to carry 1,000 amps. Most electrical systems that use a lot of power also operate at high voltages, typically over 100 volts.

Calculate the power used by a small light bulb

A light bulb with a resistance of 1.5Ω is connected to a 1.5-volt battery in the circuit shown at right. Calculate the power used by the light bulb.
1) You are asked to find the power used by the light bulb.
2) You are given the voltage of the battery and the bulb's resistance.
3) Use Ohm's law, I = V/R, to calculate the current; then use the power equation, P=VI, to calculate the power.
4) Solve: I = 1.5V ÷ 1.5Ω = 1A
    P = 1.5V × 1A = 1.5 W; the bulb uses 1.5 watts of electric power.

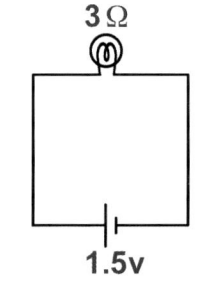

3 Ω

1.5v

Electric cars

Many people believe that eventually all cars will be electric because they give off little or no pollution. Electric cars are challenging to build because of the power required by a car. An average automobile gas engine makes 100 horse-power, or about 75,000 watts.

Suppose in your electric car you wanted to use 12-volt batteries, like the ones used to *start* cars today. To make 75 kilowatts of power at 12 volts, you need a current of 6,250 amps. By comparison, most people's entire homes use less than 100 amps.

The solution is to use more efficient motors and higher voltages. The higher the voltage, the more power can be carried by each amp of current. For example, some electric buses use 96-volt systems.

Paying for electricity

Your electric bill   What do you buy from the electric utility company? If you look at your electric bill, you will see that the utility company charges you for the number of kilowatt-hours of electricity you use. One kilowatt-hour (kWh) means that a kilowatt of power has been used for one hour. Since power multiplied by time is energy, a kilowatt-hour is a unit of *energy*. One kilowatt-hour is 3.6×10^6 joules.

Kilowatt-hours   Electric companies charge for the number of kilowatt-hours used during a set period of time, often a month (Figure 20.12). Your home is connected to a meter that counts kilowatt-hours used; regularly, a person comes to read the meter's total so that the electric company knows how much to charge you.

Estimating the cost   If you know the cost per kilowatt-hour your utility company charges, you can estimate the cost of running an appliance for a period of time.

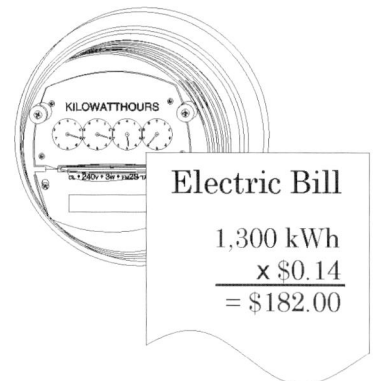

Figure 20.12: *Most people pay an electric bill monthly that charges for the kilowatt-hours of energy used.*

Calculate the currents and voltages in a three-resistor network circuit

Your electric company charges 14 cents per kilowatt-hour. Your coffee maker has a power rating of 1,050 watts. How much does it cost to use the coffee maker one hour per day for a month?

Coffeemaker
AC 120 V   8.75 A
1050 W Heating Element

1) You are asked to find the cost of using the coffee maker.
2) You are given the power in watts and the time.
3) Use the power formula $P = VI$ and the fact that 1 kWh = 1kW x 1h.
4) Solve: Find the number of kilowatts of power that the coffee maker uses.
　　1,050 W × 1 kW/1,000 W = 1.05 kW
　　Find the kilowatt-hours used by the coffee maker each month.
　　1.05 kW × 1 hr/day x 30 days/month = 31.5 kWh per month
　　Find the cost of using the coffee maker.
　　31.5 kWh/month × $0.14/kWh = $4.41 per month

Table 20.2:
Typical power ratings

Appliance	Power (watts)
Electric stove	5,000
Electric heater	1,500
Hair dryer	1,000
Iron	800
Washing machine	750
Light	100
Small fan	50
Clock radio	10

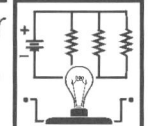

Alternating (AC) and direct (DC) current

DC current   The current from a battery is always in the same direction. One end of the battery is positive and the other end is negative. The direction of current flows from positive to negative. This is called direct current, or DC. Most of the experiments you do in the lab use DC current.

AC current   Imagine putting a battery on a rotating wheel. You could touch wires against the wheel so the voltage applied to the circuit alternated back and forth between positive and negative (Figure 20.13). If the voltage alternates, so does the current. When the voltage is positive the current in the circuit is clockwise (see graph). When the voltage is negative the current is the opposite direction. As you might have guessed, this type of current is called alternating current, or AC.

AC is used for most electric power   AC current is used for almost all high-power applications because it is easier to generate and to transmit over long distances. For example, all the power lines you see overhead carry AC current. The plugs in the walls of your apartment or house or classroom also carry AC.

The frequency of AC electricity   With DC electricity, the voltage and current tell the whole story. AC electricity is more complicated. The frequency at which the voltage alternates is an important characteristic of AC electricity. In the United States, most AC power alternates at a frequency of 60 Hz. This means the voltage on the same wire switches back and forth between positive and negative 60 times each second.

The waveform of AC electricity   The second important characteristic is the shape of the voltage versus time graph. Since it looks like a wave, this shape is normally called the waveform. Figure 20.14 shows the waveform of common household AC electricity. This waveform is called a sine wave because it is related to the sine function from trigonometry.

Peak and average voltages   The 120 volt AC (VAC) electricity used in homes and businesses alternates between peak values of +170 V and -170 V at a frequency of 60 Hz. This kind of electricity is called 120 VAC because +120V is the *average* positive voltage and -120V is the average negative voltage. AC electricity is usually identified by the average voltage, not the peak voltage.

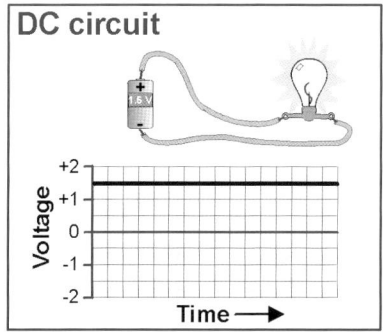

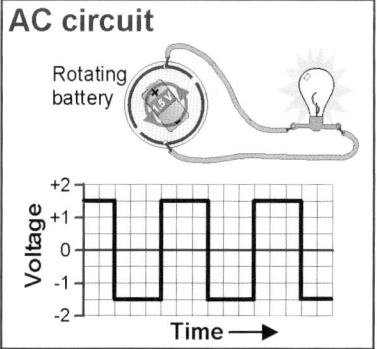

Figure 20.13: *You could make an AC circuit by rotating a battery and connecting the circuit to a disc with sliding electrical contacts.*

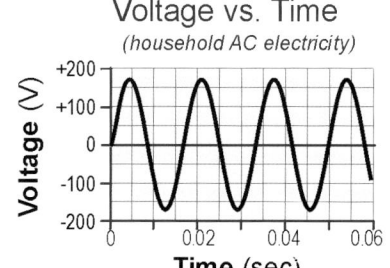

Figure 20.14: *The voltage versus time graph for common household AC electricity.*

Voltage, current, and power for AC circuits

Power in resistive circuits
The power in an AC circuit with only resistances is calculated in the same way as the power in a DC circuit. The difference is that *average* values are used for voltage and current. For example, a 100-watt light bulb uses a power of 100 watts. The average AC voltage from the wall socket is 120V. That means the average current through the bulb is 0.82 amps (100W ÷120V). Devices such as light bulbs and heaters are pure resistances, but motors and transformers are not.

Peak current and average current
The peak current through a bulb or any other AC device is much higher than the average current. From Ohm's law, you can easily calculate the resistance of a 100-watt bulb to be 145Ω (120V÷0.83A). The peak current is the peak voltage divided by the resistance, or 1.17 A (170V÷145Ω). The peak current is 41 percent higher than the average current.

Motors and devices that are not pure resistances
For a circuit containing a motor, the power calculation is a little different from that for a simple resistance like a light bulb. Because motors store energy and act like generators (Chapter 23), the current and voltage are not in phase with each other. For example, when the voltage reverses to a motor, the current cannot respond immediately. This means the current is always a little behind the voltage (Figure 20.15). Because the current is not synchronized with the voltage, the average power in a motor is *less* than the average current times the average voltage.

The power factor
Electrical engineers use a **power factor** (*pf*) to calculate power for AC circuits. For a circuit with only resistors, the power factor is 100 percent and the power is equal to the average current times the average voltage. For a motor or transformer, the power factor is typically 80 percent or less, depending on the design of the device. The power in an AC circuit is given by the formula below, which is similar to the power formula we had before except that it includes the power factor.

Electrical power
(AC circuits)

Average voltage (V) ↘   Average current (A) ↙

Power (W) $P = VI \times pf$ ← Power factor (0 - 100%)

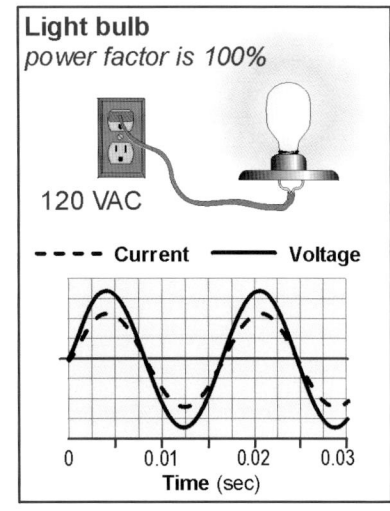

Light bulb
power factor is 100%

120 VAC

- - - - Current ——— Voltage

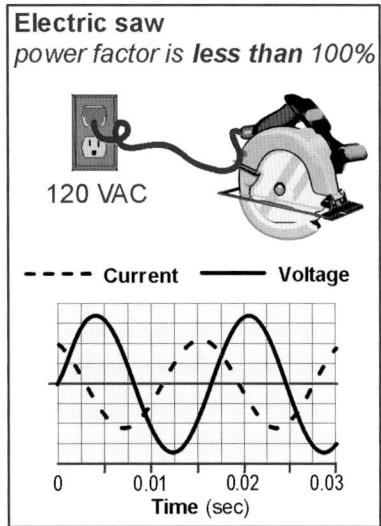

Electric saw
*power factor is **less than** 100%*

120 VAC

- - - - Current ——— Voltage

Figure 20.15: *Power in an AC circuit may be less than current times voltage because the current and voltage may be out of phase, as with an electric saw.*

Application: Wiring in Homes and Buildings

You use electric current in your house every day. When you plug in an electric appliance, you connect it to a circuit created by wires in the walls. The wires eventually connect to power lines outside your house that bring the current from a power station.

Wire sizes and circuit breakers
The 120 VAC electricity comes into a typical home or building through a circuit breaker panel. The circuit breakers protect against wires overheating and causing fires. The wires in a house are different sizes to carry different amounts of current safely (Figure 20.16). For example, a circuit made with 12-gauge wire can carry 20 amps. This circuit is protected with a circuit breaker rated for 20 amps that opens the circuit automatically if more than 20 amps of current flows.

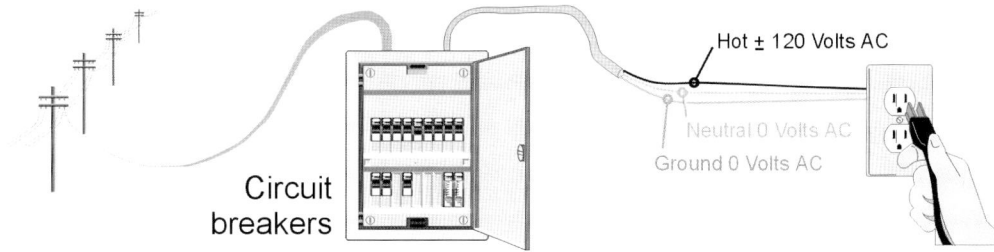

Hot ± 120 Volts AC

Neutral 0 Volts AC
Ground 0 Volts AC

Circuit breakers

Wire gauge	Current (amps)
12	20
14	15
16	10
18	7

Figure 20.16: *Different gauges of wire can carry different amounts of current safely.*

Hot, neutral, and ground wires
Each wall socket has three wires feeding it. The hot wire carries 120 volts AC. The neutral wire stays at zero volts. When you plug something in, current flows in and out of the hot wire, through your appliance (doing work) and back through the neutral wire. The ground wire is for safety and is connected to the ground (0 V) near your house. If there is a short circuit in your appliance, the current flows through the ground wire rather than through you.

G4round fault interrupt (GFI) outlets
Electrical outlets in bathrooms, kitchens, or outdoors are now required to have ground fault interrupt (GFI) outlets installed (Figure 20.17). A GFI outlet contains a circuit that compares the current flowing out on the hot wire and back on the neutral wire. If everything is working properly, the two currents should be exactly the same. If they are different, some current must be flowing to ground through another path, such as through your hand. The ground fault interrupter detects any difference in current and immediately breaks the circuit. GFI outlets are excellent protection against electric shocks, especially in wet locations.

Ground fault interrupt (GFI) outlet

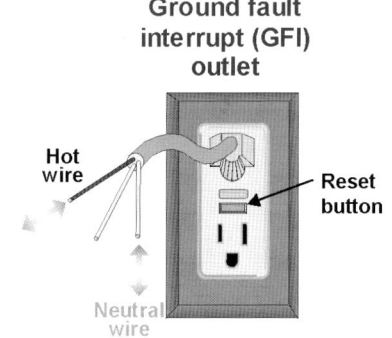

Hot wire

Reset button

Neutral wire

Figure 20.17: *A ground fault interrupt outlet might be found in bathrooms and kitchens where water may be near electricity.*

Why parallel circuits are used The electric circuits in homes and buildings are parallel circuits. Two properties of parallel circuits make them a better choice than series circuits.

1. Each outlet has its own current path. This means one outlet can have something connected and turned on (with current flowing), while another outlet has nothing connected or something turned off (no current flowing).

2. Every outlet has the same voltage because the hot side of every outlet is connected to the same wire that goes to the main circuit breaker panel.

Why series circuits are not If outlets and lights were wired in series, turning off anything electrical in the circuits would break the whole circuit. This is not practical; you would have to keep everything on all the time just to keep the refrigerator running. Also, in a series circuit, everything you plugged in would use some energy and would lower the voltage available to the next outlet.

Parallel wiring of electrical outlets

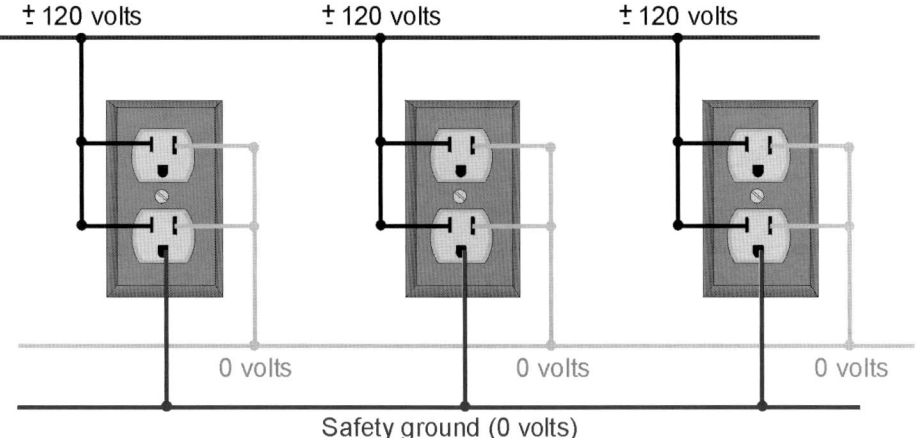

Multiple parallel circuits Each room in a house typically has its own parallel circuit, protected by the appropriate sized circuit breaker. For example, all the outlets in one bedroom might be on one circuit and the outlets in the living room might be on a separate circuit. By dividing the circuits up, many electrical devices can be connected without drawing too much current through any one wire (see sidebar).

What happens if you plug too many things into a socket?

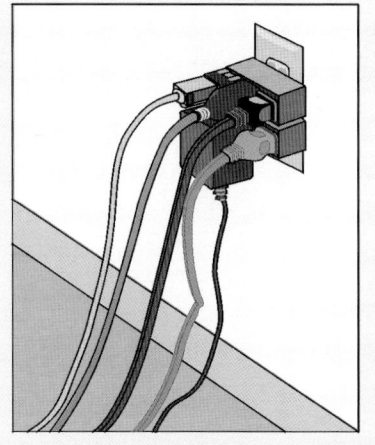

In a parallel circuit, each connection uses as much current as it needs. If you plug in a coffee maker that uses 10 amps and a toaster oven that uses 10 amps, a total of 20 amps needs to come through the wire.

If you plug too many appliances into the same circuit or outlet, you will eventually use more current than the wires can carry without overheating. Your circuit breaker will click open and stop the current. You should unplug things to reduce the current in the circuit before resetting the circuit breaker.

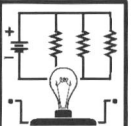

Chapter 20 Review

Vocabulary Review

Match the following terms with the correct definition. There is one extra definition in the list that will not match any of the terms.

Set One

1. kilowatt
2. series circuit
3. parallel circuit
4. network circuit
5. power

a. A circuit that is always open
b. A circuit that contains two or more paths for current to flow
c. A circuit that contains components in both series and parallel
d. The rate at which energy flows
e. A circuit that contains only one path for current to flow
f. Equal to 1,000 watts

Set Two

1. watt
2. Kirchhoff's voltage law
3. Kirchhoff's current law
4. direct current
5. alternating current

a. States that all current flowing into a branch point in a circuit must flow out
b. Current that periodically reverses direction
c. The unit in which power is measured
d. Says the sum of the voltage drops around a loop circuit equals the battery voltage
e. Current that only flows in one direction
f. Says that current is directly proportional to voltage and is inversely proportional to resistance

Concept review

1. Explain what a series circuit is and when one might be used.

2. A circuit contains a battery and two bulbs connected in series. What happens if one of the bulb burns out?

3. What happens to the total circuit resistance as more bulbs are added to a series circuit? Why?

4. A circuit contains a battery and two bulbs connected in parallel. What happens if one of the bulbs burns out?

5. The current in a _____ circuit is the same at every point. The current in a _____ circuit can be different at different points.

6. What happens to the total circuit resistance as more branches are added in a parallel circuit? Why?

7. Sketch a network circuit containing resistors. Identify the parallel branches and the series connections.

8. What is a short circuit? How is a short circuit created?

9. Identify and explain the three circuit laws.

10. In a voltage divider circuit, the output voltage is always _____ than the input voltage.

11. A 100 watt light bulb converts 100 ____ of electrical energy into heat and light energy each _____.

12. List three units in which power can be measured.

13. Explain what happens to the electrical energy used by a fan.

14. The unit kilowatt-hour is used to measure _____, not power.

15. Explain how the electric company determines how much to bill each home every month.

16. What is the difference between AC and DC current?

17. The _____ is always between 0 and 100% in an AC circuit since the power in a motor is always _____ than the average current times the average voltage.

415

Problems

1. Calculate the total resistance of each combination of resistors:

   a. Three 4 Ω resistors in series

   b. A 5 Ω resistor and a 2 Ω resistor in series

   c. Two 4 Ω resistors in parallel

   d. A 6 Ω resistor and a 9 Ω resistor in parallel

2. Calculate the total resistance and the current for the circuit shown below.

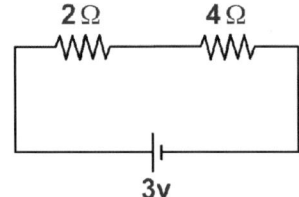

3. Calculate the unknown resistance in the circuit shown below.

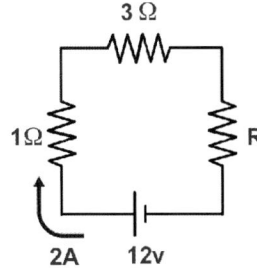

4. Calculate the total resistance, total current, and current in each branch for each circuit shown below.

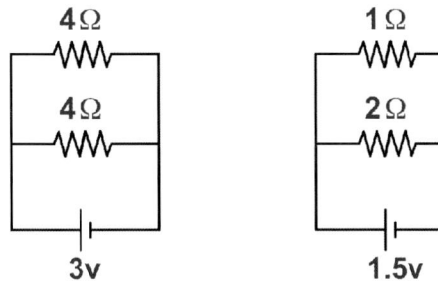

5. Calculate the output voltage for a voltage divider circuit that contains a 12 Ω resistor and a 6Ω resistor if the input voltage is 24 V.

6. Calculate the total resistance and total current in the network circuit shown below.

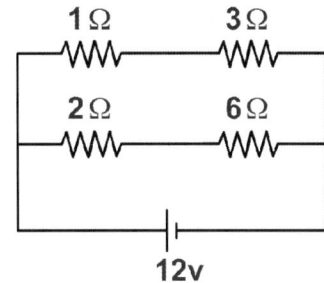

7. A hair dryer has a power rating of 1000 W when connected to a 120 V outlet. How much current does it draw?

8. A television draws 0.8 A of current when connected to a 120 V outlet. Calculate its power.

9. A digital alarm clock has a power rating of 10 W.

   a. Calculate the number of kilowatt-hours of energy used by the alarm clock in one day.

   b. Calculate the cost of using the alarm clock for one year if one kilowatt-hour of energy costs $0.15.

416

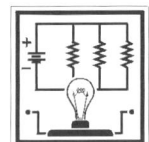

Unit 7
Electricity and Magnetism

Chapter 21

Electric Charges and Forces

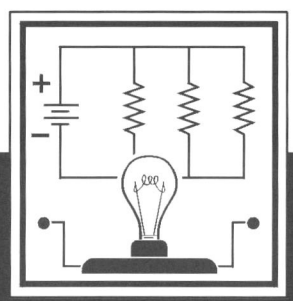

Objectives for Chapter 21

By the end of this chapter you should be able to:

1. Describe and calculate the forces between like and unlike electric charges.
2. Identify the parts of the atom that carry electric charge.
3. Apply the concept of an electric field to describe how charges exert force on other charges.
4. Sketch the electric field around a positive or negative point charge.
5. Describe how a conductor shields electric fields from its interior.
6. Describe the voltage and current in a circuit with a battery, switch, resistor, and capacitor.
7. Calculate the charge stored in a capacitor.

Terms and vocabulary words

charge	electrically neutral	static electricity	positive charge	negative charge
electric forces	charge by friction	electroscope	protons	neutrons
electrons	gravitational field	charged	induction	Coulomb's law
capacitor	parallel plate capacitor	microfarad	coulomb	electric field
capacitance	charge polarization	shielding	test charge	farad
field	inverse square law	discharged	field lines	

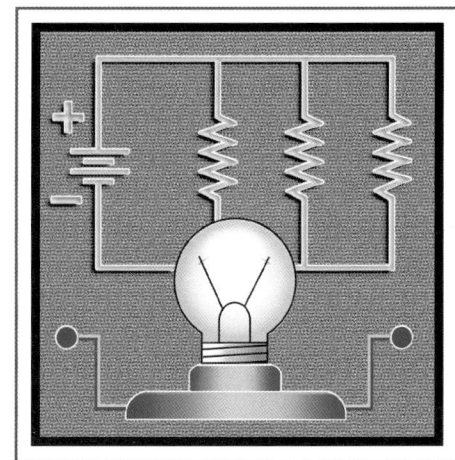

21.1 Electric Charge

The last two chapters have developed the uses and properties of electricity without digging into what electricity is on a fundamental level. This chapter will fill in the missing foundation by exploring the properties of electric charge. Electric charge is a fundamental property of matter. The forces between positive and negative electric charge are what hold atoms together and also are what make electric current flow. In fact, in this section you will see that electric current is the motion of electric charge. This section will also discuss electric forces, fields, and static electricity.

Positive and negative charge

Two types of charge — If you have ever felt a shock when touching a doorknob or removing clothes from the dryer, you have experienced the effect of electric charge (Figure 21.1). Electric charge, like mass, is a fundamental property of matter. An important difference between mass and charge is that there are two types of charge, called positive and negative.

Neutral objects — All ordinary matter contains both positive and negative charge. You do not usually notice the charge because most matter contains the exact same number of positive and negative charges. When the number of positive charges equals the number of negative charges, the total charge is zero. An object is electrically neutral when it has equal amounts of both types of charge. Your pencil, textbook, and even your body are all electrically neutral, as is almost all matter.

Net charge — Objects can lose or gain electric charges. If an object has more negative charges than positive charges, the net (or total) charge is negative (Figure 21.2). If it has more positive charges than negative charges, it has a positive net charge. The net charge is also sometimes called *excess* charge because a charged object has an excess of either positive or negative charges.

Transferring charge — A tiny imbalance in either positive or negative charge on an object is the cause of static electricity. If two neutral objects are rubbed together, charges may be rubbed off one object and onto the other. This is what happens to clothes in the dryer and to your socks when you walk on a carpet. The shock you feel is the excess charge moving between you and the charged object to restore neutral charge balance.

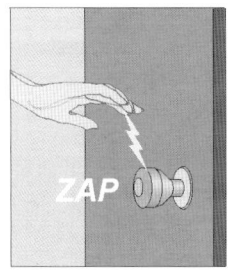

Static electricity

Figure 21.1: *Touching a metal object on a dry day can give you a shock from static electricity.*

This object is neutral

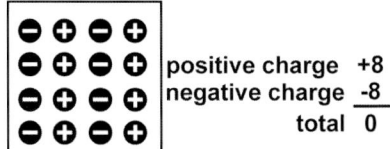

positive charge +8
negative charge -8
total 0

This object is charged

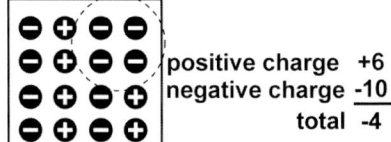

positive charge +6
negative charge -10
total -4

Figure 21.2: *If an object has an unequal number of positive and negative charges, it has a net charge.*

The source of electric charge

Charge is a property of the particles that make up the atom

Electric charge is a property of the particles inside an atom. The nucleus at the center of the atom contains positive charges called protons and neutral particles called neutrons (diagram below). Outside the nucleus are negative charges called electrons. The charge on the proton and electron are exactly equal and opposite. Since a complete atom has equal numbers of protons and electrons, atoms have zero net electric charge. Chapter 28 has a detailed discussion of the atom. For now, it is important only to know that electric charge is a property of exceedingly tiny particles in atoms. Electrons are the smallest and lightest particles and have negative charge. Protons have positive charge and are much larger than electrons, though still only a hundred-thousandth the size of an atom!

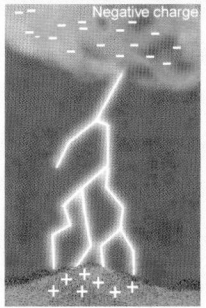

Lightning is caused by a huge buildup of charge. As particles in a cloud collide, charges are transferred between them. Positive charges build up on smaller particles and negative charges on bigger ones. Gravity and wind push positively charged particles toward the top of the cloud and negatively charged particles to the bottom.

Structure of an atom

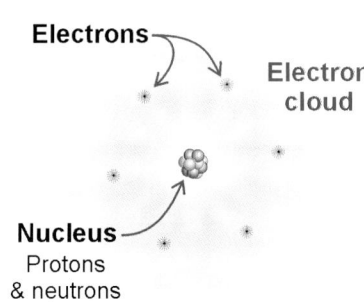

Electrons

Electron cloud

Nucleus
Protons & neutrons

	Mass (kg)	Charge (coulombs)
Electron	9.109×10^{-31}	-1.602×10^{-19}
Proton	1.673×10^{-27}	$+1.602 \times 10^{-19}$
Neutron	1.675×10^{-27}	0

Negative charge on the bottom of a cloud causes the ground to become positive. When enough charges have been separated by the storm, the cloud, air, and ground act like a giant circuit. All the accumulated negative charges flow from the cloud to the ground, heating the air along the path (to as hot as 20,000°C) so that it glows like a bright streak of light.

The coulomb is the unit of charge

The unit of electric charge is the coulomb (C). The name is chosen in honor of Charles-Augustin de Coulomb (1736-1806), the French physicist who succeeded in making the first accurate measurements of the force between charges. One coulomb is a *very* large amount of charge. One coulomb of charge is equal to the charge of 6×10^{18} protons or electrons. The static electricity discussed in the previous two pages typically results from an excess charge of less than one-millionth of a coulomb.

Label charge with a plus or minus

A quantity of charge should always be identified with a positive or a negative sign. The units of coulombs apply to both positive and negative charge. For example, -2×10^{-6} C describes a negative charge of two-millionths of a coulomb.

Electric forces

Attraction and repulsion

Electric forces are created between all electric charges. Because there are two kinds of charge (positive and negative) the electrical force between charges can be attractive or repulsive. Electrical forces are different from gravity. Because there is only one kind of mass gravity only causes attractive forces between masses.

Like charges repel and unlike charges attract

Whether two charges attract or repel each other depends on whether they are the same or different. A positive and a negative charge will attract each other. Two positive charges will repel each other. Two negative charges will also repel each other. The force between charges is illustrated by the diagram below.

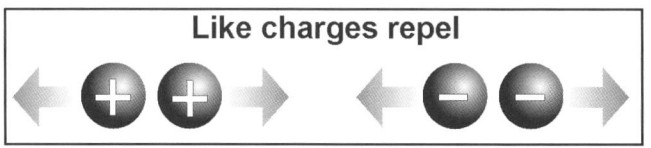 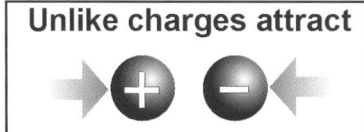

Parts of an electroscope

The forces between the two kinds of charge can be observed with an electroscope. An electroscope contains two very thin *leaves* of metal that can swing from a central rod (Figure 21.3) connected to a metal ball. Charges can flow freely between the ball and the leaves. An insulator holds the rod in place and keeps charges from getting to the outside of the electroscope.

Charging an electroscope

Suppose a positively charged rod touches the metal ball of an electroscope. Some negative electrons are attracted to the rod. The metal ball and leaves of the electroscope are left with a net positive charge. Since both leaves have the same positive charge, the leaves repel each other and spread apart.

Testing an unknown charge with an electroscope

Once an electroscope is charged, it can be used to test other charged objects. The leaves spread farther apart if another positively charged rod is brought near the metal ball. This happens because the positive rod attracts some negative electrons from the leaves toward the ball, increasing the positive charge on the leaves. If a negatively charged rod is brought near the ball, the opposite effect occurs. A negatively charged rod repels negative electrons from the ball into the leaves where they neutralize some of the positive charge. The positive charge on the leaves is reduced and the leaves get closer together.

The electroscope

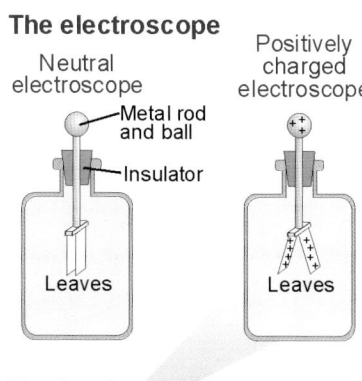

Testing for positive or negative

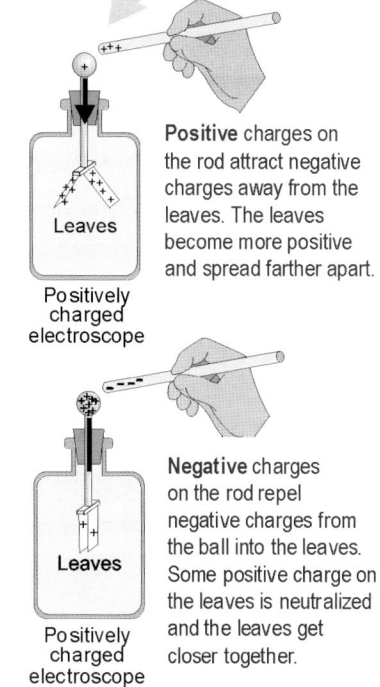

Positive charges on the rod attract negative charges away from the leaves. The leaves become more positive and spread farther apart.

Negative charges on the rod repel negative charges from the ball into the leaves. Some positive charge on the leaves is neutralized and the leaves get closer together.

Figure 21.3: *An electroscope can be used to directly observe the forces between positive and negative charges.*

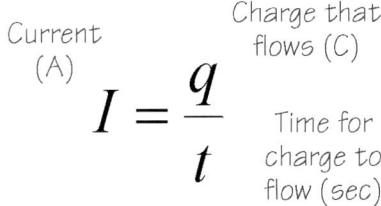

Current and charge

Current is the flow of charge	The previous chapters identified current as the flow of electricity. We can now be more specific and say current is the movement of electric charge through a circuit. You can think of electric current much as you would think of a current of water. If a faucet is on, you can measure the rate of water flow by finding out how much water comes out in one minute. You might find that the current (or flow) is 10 gallons per minute. In a circuit, you can measure the current by counting the amount of electric charge that flows through a wire in one second. *One ampere is a flow of one coulomb per second.* Higher current means more charge flows per second. For example, a current of 10 amperes means that 10 coulombs of charge flow through the wire every second.

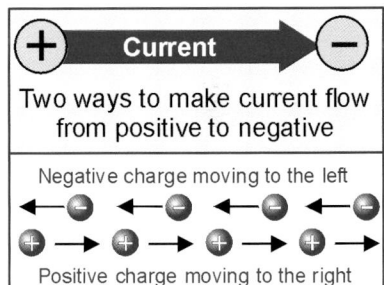

Current and the motion of charges	The direction of current was historically defined as the direction that positive charges move. However, both positive and negative charges can carry current. In conductive liquids (salt water) both positive and negative charges carry current. In solid metal conductors, only the electrons can move, so current is carried by the flow of negative electrons. No matter what the sign of the charge carrier, positive current is always defined to flow from positive to negative (Figure 21.4).

Figure 21.4: *Electron flow and the direction of current.*

Electron flow and the drift velocity	Electrons in a wire bounce around at high speed colliding with fixed atoms. When a voltage is applied, electrons are attracted to the positive voltage. However, the random bouncing speed is so high, even high voltages only deflect the electrons slightly. An applied voltage causes a slow *drift velocity* to be added to the random bouncing. The electron drift velocity is what creates electrical current.

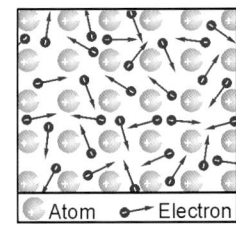

The source of current carrying electrons	Batteries do not provide most of the electrons that flow in a circuit. Current flows because the voltage from a battery makes electrons that are *already in the wire* move. This is why a light bulb goes on as soon as you connect a circuit. A copper wire contains many electrons bouncing randomly around between atoms. Without an applied voltage, as many electrons bounce one way as the other. There is no net flow of electrons and no electrical current. The electrons only acquire an average drift velocity (and carry current) when a voltage is applied.

Electric current
(current is the rate of flow of charge)

$$I = \frac{q}{t}$$

Current (A) — Charge that flows (C) — Time for charge to flow (sec)

Calculate the current from the flow of charge

Two coulombs of charge pass through a wire in five seconds. Calculate the current in the wire.
1) You are asked to find the current.
2) You are given the charge and the time.
3) Use the equation I = q/t.
4) Solve: I = (2 C) ÷ (5 sec)
　　　= 0.4 C/sec or 0.4 A

Conductors and insulators

Electrons are too small to be seen

When you look at a wire, you cannot see the current passing through it. Of course, neither can you see the atoms. Both the electrons that carry current and atoms are far too small to be visible. If you *could* see atoms, however, you would find that a metal like copper is a three dimensional matrix of atoms that are fixed in place. Flowing around the fixed atoms is a sea of moving electrons. The electrons are what carry the current in a conductor. When current flows, the electrons are moving in response to the forces created by a difference in voltage. But since electrons have negative charge, they move *opposite* the direction of current flow.

Electrons in insulators are trapped

All materials contain electrons. The electrons in insulators, however, are not free to move—they are tightly bound inside atoms. Since the atoms are fixed in place, the electrons in insulators are also fixed in place. Current cannot flow through an insulator because there are no movable charges with which to make the current.

Electrons in semiconductors

A semiconductor has a few free electrons, though not as many as a conductor has. The diagram below illustrates the internal structures of conductors, insulators, and semiconductors.

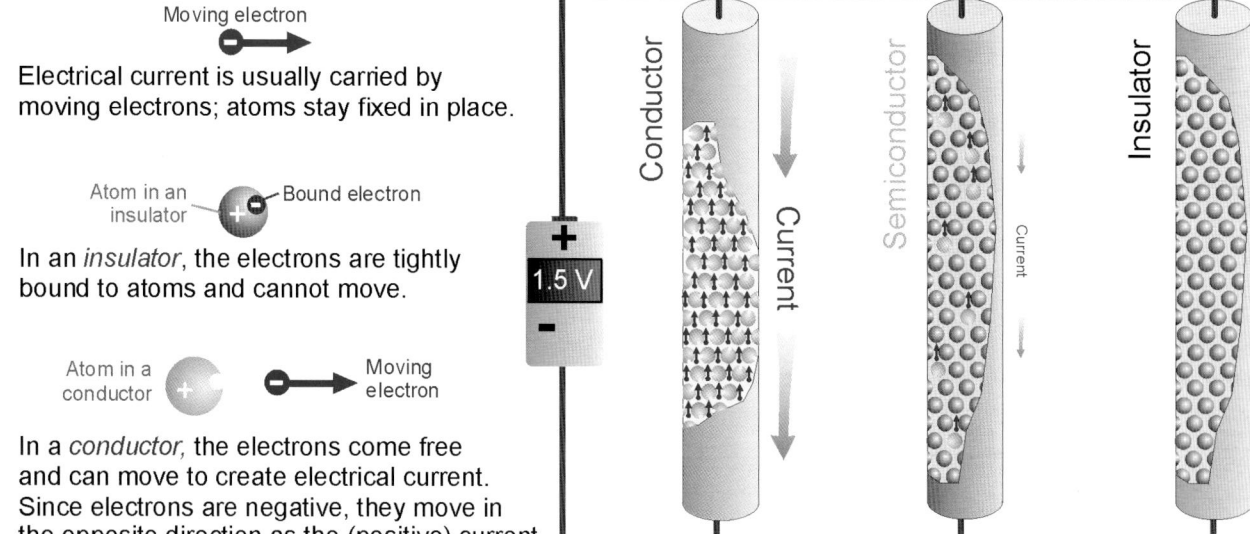

Moving electron

Electrical current is usually carried by moving electrons; atoms stay fixed in place.

Atom in an insulator — Bound electron

In an *insulator*, the electrons are tightly bound to atoms and cannot move.

Atom in a conductor — Moving electron

In a *conductor,* the electrons come free and can move to create electrical current. Since electrons are negative, they move in the opposite direction as the (positive) current.

Static electricity, charge polarization, and induction

Charging by friction When two neutral objects are rubbed together, charge is transferred from one to the other and the objects become oppositely charged. This is called charging by friction. Objects charged by this method will attract each other. For example, a balloon will become negatively charged if rubbed on hair or fur. After losing a few electrons, the hair will have a net positive charge and will then be attracted to the balloon. This tends to work best with fine, straight hair on a dry day.

Polarization A charged balloon will stick to a (neutral) wall or other insulating surface. When a negatively charged balloon is near a wall, electrons inside atoms in the wall are repelled. Since the wall is made of insulating material, the repelled electrons are not free to travel between atoms. The electrons *can* move within each atom, so they spend more time on the side of the atom that is farthest from the balloon. The atoms become polarized; one end is positive and the other is negative (Figure 21.5). The balloon is both attracted to the positive side of each atom and repelled by the negative side. The force of attraction is stronger because the positive side of each atom is closer to the balloon than the negative side.

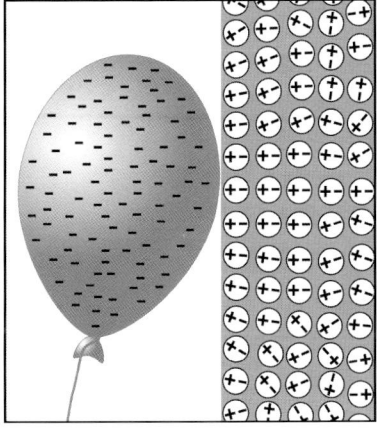

Figure 21.5: *When a charged balloon is brought near a wall, the atoms in the wall become polarized. The balloon is then attracted to the wall and will stick to it.*

Conductors Atoms in a material only become polarized if the material is an insulator. In a conductor, electrons are free to move from atom to atom so the entire object becomes polarized. A negatively charged balloon brought near a conducting object polarizes the object, and an attractive force results. However, as soon as the balloon touches the conducting object, some of the balloon's excess electrons move onto the object. Balloon and object become negatively charged and repel each other. This is why a balloon sticks to a wood door but not a metal doorknob.

Charging by induction Because charges can flow, a charged object like a rubbed balloon may be used to charge an electroscope by induction. To charge by induction, the electroscope is first connected by a wire to a large neutral object. When the balloon comes near, the charge on the balloon induces an opposite charge to flow through the wire onto the electroscope. The wire is then removed so the charge on the electroscope cannot flow back where it came from. The electroscope stays charged after the balloon is removed (Figure 21.6) The leaves spread apart because the added charge repels *itself* and spreads out through the electroscope.

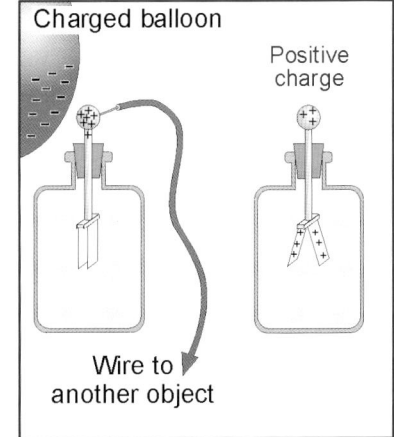

Figure 21.6: *Charging an electroscope by induction.*

21.2 Coulomb's Law

Unlike charges attract, and like charges repel. In this section you will learn about Coulomb's law, which describes the strength of the force between two charges. Coulomb's law is one of the fundamental relationships in the universe because atoms are held together by the electrical attraction between protons (positive) and electrons (negative). The strength of the force determines how close the electrons and protons get, and therefore determines the size of atoms. Since we are made of atoms, Coulomb's law indirectly determines our size as well.

Coulomb's law relates charge, distance, and force

The strength of electric forces   The force between two charges gets stronger if the charges are closer together. The force also gets stronger if the amount of charge is larger. Coulomb's law relates the force between two single charges (q_1, q_2) separated by a distance (r).

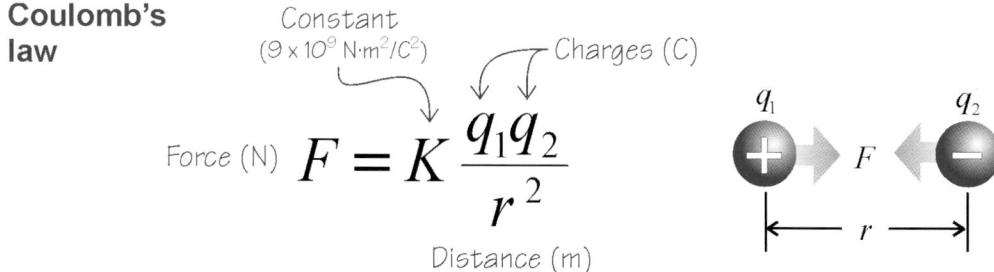

Coulomb's law

Constant $(9 \times 10^9 \ N \cdot m^2/C^2)$

Charges (C)

Force (N) $F = K \dfrac{q_1 q_2}{r^2}$

Distance (m)

Force and charge   The force between charges is directly proportional to the magnitude, or amount, of each charge (Figure 21.7). Doubling one charge doubles the force. Doubling both charges quadruples the force.

Force and distance   The force between charges is inversely proportional to the square of the distance between them. Doubling the distance reduces the force by a factor of 2^2, decreasing the force to one-fourth its original value. Tripling the distance reduces the force to one-ninth its original value. This relationship is called an **inverse square law** because force and distance follow an inverse square relationship. The force between charges decreases very quickly as charges are moved apart.

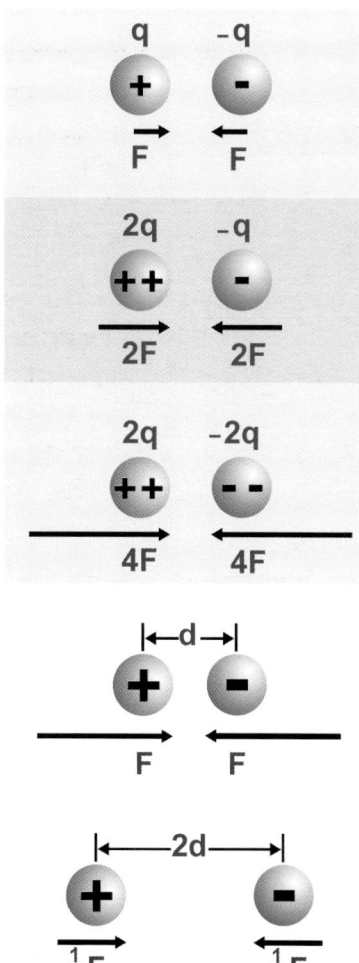

Figure 21.7: *The force between charges depends on the magnitude of the charges and the distance between them.*

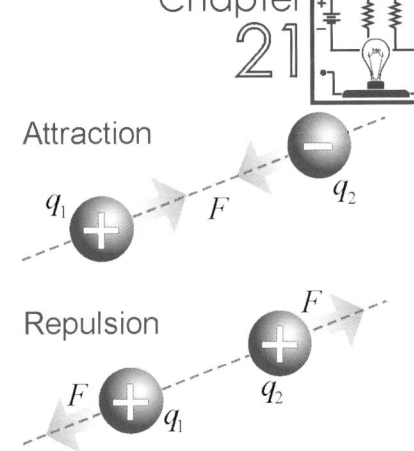

The force between charges

Point charges Coulomb's law can be used to calculate the force between two point charges. Charges are considered "point-like" if they are physically much smaller than the distance between them. For example, two marbles a meter apart may be treated as points because the diameter of a marble is much smaller than 1 meter. Two baseballs 10 centimeters apart would NOT be considered as points, because the baseballs' sizes are not that different from their 10-centimeter separation.

The direction of the force The direction of the force between two charges lies on the line between them. Figure 21.8 illustrates this concept for both attractive and repulsive forces. Electric forces always occur in pairs according to Newton's third law, like all forces. If the charges are both positive or both negative, the direction of the forces will be away from each other. If one is positive and the other is negative, the direction of the forces will be toward each other.

Figure 21.8: *The force between two charges is directed along the line connecting their centers.*

The magnitude of force between charges Forces between charges are so strong it is hard to imagine. For example, a cubic millimeter of carbon the size of your pencil point contains about 77 coulombs of positive charge in its protons and exactly then same amount of negative charge. If you could separate the positive and negative charge by one meter, the attractive force between the charges would be 50 thousand, *billion* newtons. This is about the same force as the weight of a billion trucks (Figure 21.9) — all from one cubic *millimeter* of pure charge.

Calculate the force between two static charges

Two balls are each given a static electric charge of one ten-thousandth (0.0001) of a coulomb. Calculate the force between the charges when they are separated by one-tenth (0.1) of a meter. Compare the force with the weight of an average 70 kg person.

1) You are asked to calculate the force and compare it to a person's weight.
2) You are given the charges and separation, and the mass of the person.
3) Use Coulomb's law, $F = -Kq_1q_2/R^2$, for the electric force and $F=mg$ for the weight.
4) Solve:
  $F = (9\times10^9 \text{N}\bullet\text{m}^2/\text{C}^2)(0.0001\text{C})(.0001\text{C}) \div (0.1 \text{ m})^2$
  $= 9,000 \text{ N}$
The weight of a 70 kg person:
  $F = mg = (70 \text{ kg})(9.8 \text{ N/kg}) = 686 \text{ N}$
The force between the charges is 13.1 times the weight of an average person ($9,000 \div 686$).

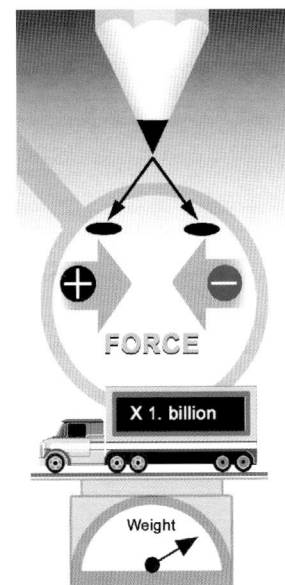

Figure 21.9: *If you could separate the positive and negative charge in a pencil point, the force pulling the charge back together exceeds the weight of a billion trucks.*

Fields and forces

Fields   The concept of a field is used to describe any quantity that has a value for all points in space. For example, there is a temperature field in your classroom because the temperature has a value at every point in the room. The Earth creates a gravitational field in the space around it. The moon is held in orbit around the Earth by its interaction with the Earth's gravitational field.

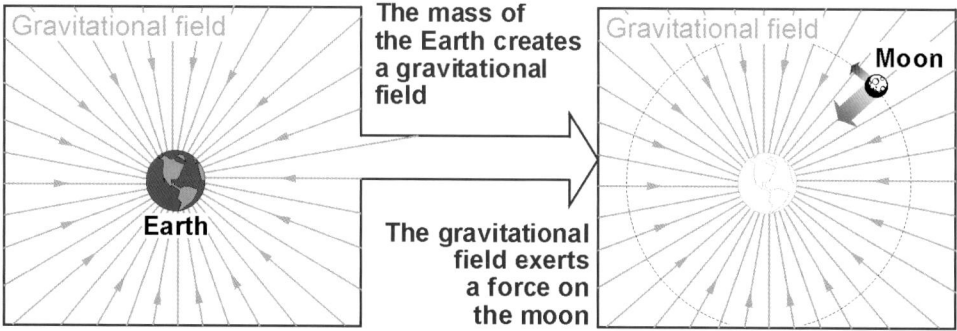

Force fields   Scientists believe forces between two objects do not act directly from one object to another. Instead, one object creates a force field. The force field then creates the force on the second object. *This applies to all forces.* You can sometimes (like with gravity) calculate the force between objects directly, skipping the force field. In reality, however, forces between objects are always exchanged through fields. Mass creates a gravitational field that exerts forces on other masses. Charge creates an electric field that creates forces on other charges. You can think of the field as the *way* forces are transmitted between objects.

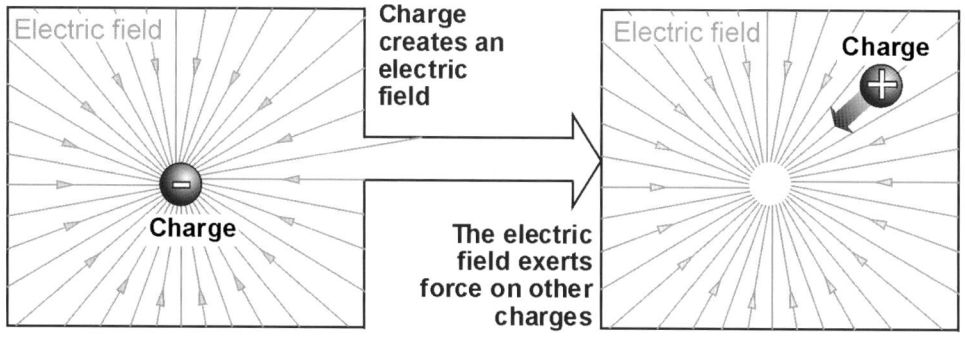

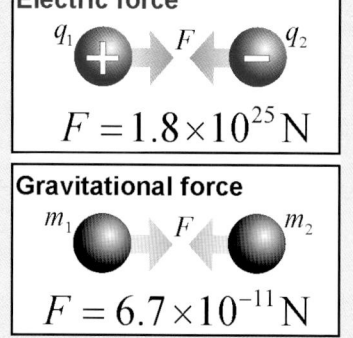

Drawing the electric field

An electric field exists around a charge
The force between charges is always transmitted through the electric field. First, a charge (called the *source* charge) creates an electric field in the space around it. Second, the electric field makes forces on other charges.

Strength of an electric field
The strength and direction of the electric field created by a charge depends on charge and distance. A larger source charge makes a stronger electric field. The electric field gets weaker with increasing distance from the source charge.

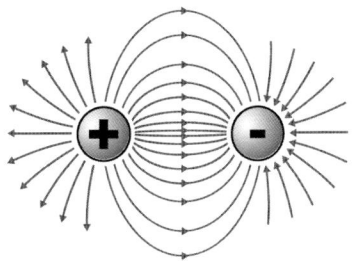

Direction of an electric field
The direction of the electric field depends on the sign of the source charge. To determine the direction, imagine placing an imaginary positive test charge in the region of the field. Because it is imaginary, the test charge itself does not change the electric field. The electric field points in the direction of the force felt by the positive test charge. Electric field lines therefore point *toward* negative charges and *away* from positive charges (Figure 21.10). Because of this convention, a positive charge placed in an electric field will feel a force in the direction of the field, and a negative charge will feel a force opposite the direction of the field.

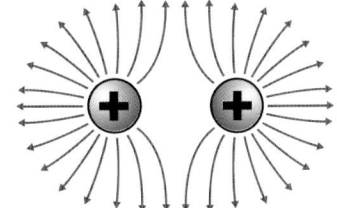

Field lines
It is sometimes convenient to diagram the field in a particular region. Vectors called field lines are used to indicate the direction of a field. The direction of a field line indicates the direction of the force exerted on a positive charge placed in the field. The strength of the field is indicated by the spacing between the field lines. The field is strong in the region where the field lines are close together and is weak where the lines are far apart.

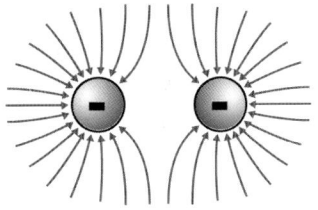

The field lines show the force on a positive test charge.

Field lines always point away from positive charge and toward negative charge.

The spacing of the lines indicates the strength of the electric field.

 Strong field  Weak field

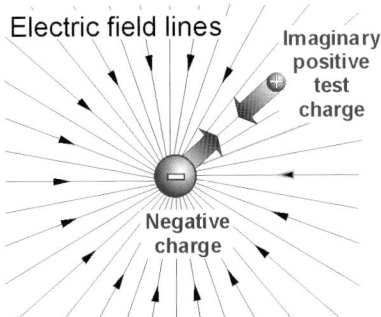

Electric field lines

Imaginary positive test charge

Negative charge

Figure 21.10: *The electric field around two or more charges can be found be imagining the force on an imaginary positive test charge at various points in the region.*

Electric fields and electric force

Measuring electric fields How is an electric field measured? And how does it relate to electric force? The comparison between gravitational and electric fields helps answer this question.

Gravitational field strength The strength of the gravitational field determines the strength and direction of gravitational force on an object. We call this force the object's *weight*. On the Earth's surface, the gravitational field creates 9.8 N of force on each kilogram of mass. The equation relating force (F) and mass (m) is written $F = mg$ where g is the strength of the gravitational field (9.8 N/kg).

Electric field strength The strength of the electric field determines the amount of force a charged object feels near another charged object. The object that creates the field is often called the *source* charge. The charge you place to test the force is the *test* charge. The force (F) on the test charge is equal to the amount of charge (q) multiplied by the electric field (E), or $F = qE$.

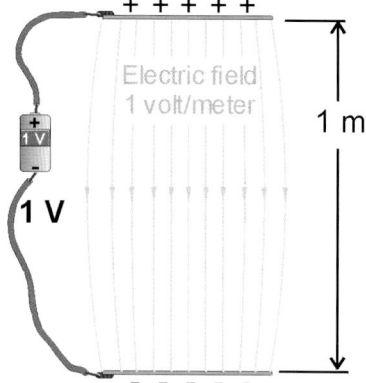

Figure 21.11: *A potential difference of 1 volt across a distance of 1 meter makes an electric field of 1 volt per meter (V/m).*

Field	Units	Equation	Interpretation
Gravity	$\vec{g} = \frac{\text{newtons}}{\text{kilogram}}\left(\frac{N}{kg}\right)$	$\vec{F} = m\vec{g}$	The force ($\vec{F}$) on an object is the mass (m) × field strength ($\vec{g}$)
Electricity	$\vec{E} = \frac{\text{newtons}}{\text{coulomb}}\left(\frac{N}{C}\right)$	$\vec{F} = q\vec{E}$	The force ($\vec{F}$) on an object is the charge (q) × field strength ($\vec{E}$)

Units of electric field With gravity, the strength of the field is in newtons per kilogram (N/kg) because the field describes the amount of force per kilogram of mass. With the electric field, the strength is in *newtons per coulomb* (N/C) for a similar reason. The electric field describes the amount of force per *coulomb of charge*. For example, a 10 C test charge feels 10 times as much force as a 1 C test charge in the same field.

Alternate units for the electric field The electric field can be expressed in more practical units. Remember, one volt is one joule per coulomb. A joule is equal to a newton-meter. By combining the relationships between units you can prove that one newton per coulomb is the same as one *volt per meter*. This is a prescription for how to make an electric field in the lab. A voltage difference of one volt over a space of one meter makes an electric field of 1 V/m (Figure 21.11). That same field exerts a force of one newton on a one-coulomb test charge (Figure 21.12).

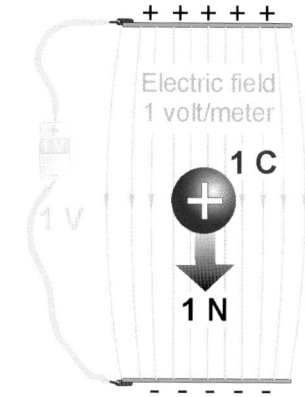

Figure 21.12: *An electric field of 1 volt per meter (V/m) creates a force of 1 newton on a 1-coulomb test charge.*

428

Accelerators and electric shielding

How to make an electron beam accelerator

An electric field can be produced by maintaining a voltage difference across any insulating space, such as air or a vacuum. Many electrical devices use electric fields created in this way. For example, suppose a flat plate is given a negative voltage and a metal screen is given a positive voltage (Figure 21.13). Electrons are repelled from the plate and attracted to the screen. Because the screen has holes, many of the electrons pass right through. Because the electrons feel a force between the plates, this device is an accelerator for electrons. It is easily possible to make a beam of electrons move at a speed of 1 million m/sec with such a device. Electron beams generated this way are used in x-ray machines, televisions, computer displays, and many other technologies.

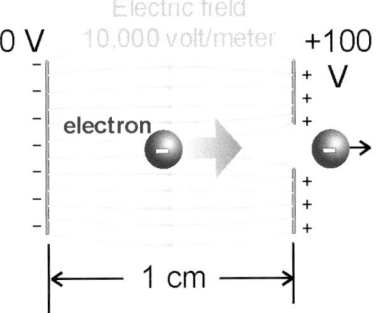

Figure 21.13: *Electric fields are used to create beams of high-speed electrons.*

Conductors can block electric fields

In a conductor, charges are free to move under the influence of any electric field. When a conductor is placed in an electric field, a very interesting thing happens. If the field is positive, negative charges move toward it until the field is neutralized. If the field is negative, electrons move away leaving enough positive charge behind to neutralize the field. On the inside of the conductor, the field is zero!

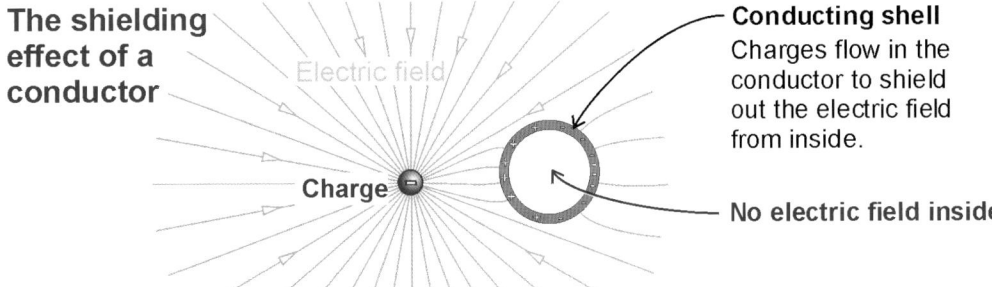

Shielding out electrical interference

Electric fields are created all around us by electric appliances, lightning, and even static electricity. These stray electric fields can interfere with the operation of computers and other sensitive electronics. Many electrical devices and wires that connect them are enclosed in conducting metal shells to take advantage of the shielding effect. For example, if you unwrap a computer network wire, you will find eight smaller wires wrapped by aluminum foil. The aluminum foil is a conductor and shields the wires inside from electrical interference (Figure 21.14).

Computer network cable

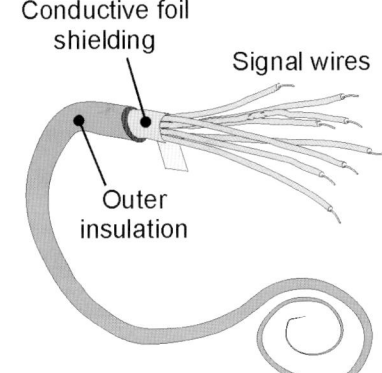

Figure 21.14: *A shielded computer network cable using conductive foil to block electrical interference.*

21.3 Capacitors

The circuits introduced in the last two chapters contained only resistances. In resistor circuits the current stops flowing immediately when the voltage is removed. The subject of this section is a device called a *capacitor* which holds charge, like a bucket holds water. If the voltage is removed from a circuit containing a capacitor, the current keeps going for a while, until the capacitor is empty of charge. Almost all electric appliances, including televisions, cameras, and computers, use capacitors in their circuits. Capacitors are also a useful tool for investigating the relationship between electric charge, voltage, and current.

A capacitor is a storage device for electric charge

A capacitor stores charge

A capacitor is a device that stores charge. You can think of a capacitor like a capped bottle with a hose attached. Current flowing into a capacitor fills the bottle with electric charge until it is full. Once a capacitor is full of charge, current stops flowing until some charge is emptied out again. Current flowing out of a capacitor empties charge out of the bottle. Current can keep flowing out until the charge has been completely emptied from the capacitor.

The comparison to a bottle of water is not totally accurate because current cannot flow *through* a capacitor. Also, capacitors fill equally with positive and negative charge. When you see how a capacitor is made (in a few pages), this distinction will become clearer.

Charging a capacitor

A capacitor can be charged by connecting it to a battery or any other source of current. As the capacitor fills up, the voltage across its terminals increases. When the capacitor is full, its voltage is equal to the battery voltage. Current stops flowing into a full capacitor because there is no longer any voltage difference between the capacitor and the battery (Figure 21.15).

Discharging a capacitor

A capacitor can be discharged by connecting it to any closed circuit that allows current to flow. A low-resistance circuit will discharge the capacitor quickly because high current carries away charge faster. A high-resistance circuit will discharge a capacitor more slowly because high resistance limits the current, therefore limits the rate at which charge flows out of the capacitor.

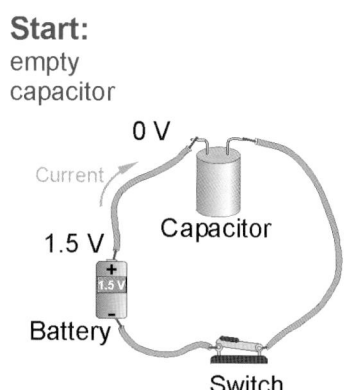

Start: empty capacitor

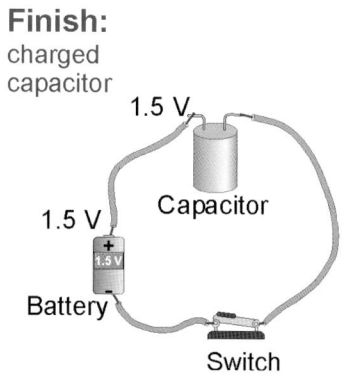

Finish: charged capacitor

Figure 21.15: *When the switch is first closed, current flows and carries charge into the capacitor.*

As the capacitor charges, it builds up its own voltage that opposes the flow of current.

When the capacitor is fully charged, it has the same voltage as the battery and no more current flows.

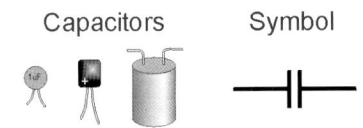

Current and voltage in capacitor circuits

Capacitors in circuits
The symbol for a capacitor in a circuit is shown in Figure 21.16 along with diagrams of actual capacitors. Capacitors can be connected in series or parallel in circuits, just like resistors. Unlike resistors, the current and voltage for a capacitor have a more complex relationship.

Current
The current flowing into or out of a particular capacitor depends on four things:

1. The amount of charge already in the capacitor.
2. The voltage applied to the capacitor by the circuit.
3. Any circuit resistance that limits the current flowing in the circuit.
4. The capacitance of the capacitor

A simple capacitor circuit
Consider the circuit with an empty capacitor, switch, resistor, and battery shown in Figure 21.17. When the switch is closed, the current in the circuit is greatest because the capacitor is empty. In fact, the current is exactly what it would have been if the capacitor were not there. If the voltage is 1.5 V and the resistance is 15 Ω, the current initially in the circuit is 0.1 amps.

Current and voltage while charging a capacitor
The current in the circuit starts high and gets lower over time. The current gets lower because the battery voltage attracts negative charge to one side of the capacitor. The negative charge attracts an equal amount of positive charge to the other side. As charge fills up the capacitor, it creates a voltage difference between the two terminals of the capacitor. Charge continues to fill up the capacitor until the capacitor voltage is equal and opposite to the battery voltage.

Current and voltage change with time
As the capacitor charges, the current in the circuit decreases. This is because the current flow is proportional to the voltage difference between the battery and the capacitor. As the voltage on the capacitor increases, the voltage difference gets lower and the current flow gets lower in response. The graphs in Figure 21.18 show how the current and voltage change in the circuit.

Voltage of a charged capacitor
A fully charged capacitor contains equal amounts of positive and negative charge. Because both kinds of charge are present but separated, a capacitor develops a voltage across its two terminals, like a battery. The voltage across a fully charged capacitor is equal and opposite to the voltage applied to the circuit.

Capacitors　　Symbol

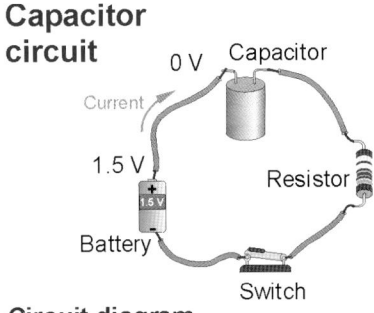

Figure 21.16: *Capacitors and the circuit symbol for a capacitor.*

Capacitor circuit

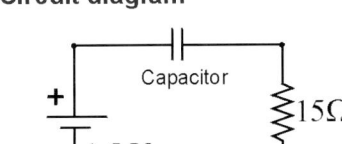

Circuit diagram

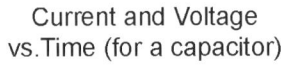

Figure 21.17: *A simple capacitor circuit with a resistor, capacitor, switch, and battery.*

Current and Voltage vs. Time (for a capacitor)

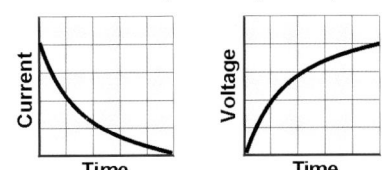

Figure 21.18: *Current and voltage graphs for a circuit charging a capacitor (after the switch is closed).*

How a capacitor works inside

Parallel plate capacitors

The simplest type of capacitor is called a parallel plate capacitor (Figure 21.19). It is made of two conductive metal plates that are close together. When a parallel plate capacitor is charged, one plate is negative and the other is positive. To keep the positive and negative charge from coming together, a sheet of plastic or other insulating material is placed between the charged plates.

Making a simple capacitor

A cardboard milk container and aluminum foil can be used to make a capacitor. The cardboard is an effective insulator. The aluminum can be shaped so that it covers the inside and outside surfaces (Figure 21.20). Wires can be connected to the aluminum to conduct the charge into and out of the capacitor.

The amount of charge in a capacitor

The amount of charge a capacitor can store depends on several factors:

1. The voltage applied to the capacitor.
2. The insulating ability of the material between the positive and negative plates.
3. The area of the two plates (larger areas can hold more charge).
4. The separation distance between the plates.

The limit to a capacitor

Unlike a bottle full of water which has a fixed volume, the amount of charge stored in a capacitor increases when more voltage is applied. For example, the same capacitor charged to 10 volts has twice as much charge as when it is charged to 5 volts. The ultimate limit to how much charge may be stored in a capacitor is the strength of the insulating material between the conducting plates. As the voltage increases, eventually the electric field in the insulator gets so large that the insulator breaks down and becomes a conductor itself. A miniature version of lightning happens inside the capacitor and the positive and negative charges flow through and neutralize each other.

Cylindrical capacitors

Parallel plate capacitors are not very practical to use in most devices because they must be very large to store enough charge to be useful. If a parallel plate capacitor has a dielectric between its plates and is made of a flexible material, it can be rolled into the shape of a cylinder. This allows each plate to have a large area while the capacitor fits into a small space. Some other types of capacitors use chemical reactions to store charge, like tiny batteries.

Parallel plate capacitor

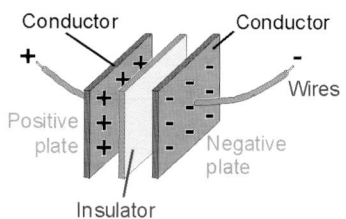

Figure 21.19: *The symbol for a capacitor in a circuit diagram is two parallel lines.*

A milk carton capacitor

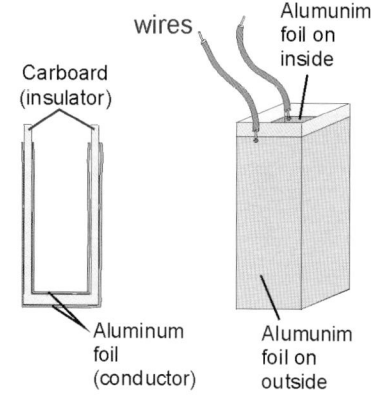

Figure 21.20: *Using a milk carton and aluminum foil to make a capacitor. BE CAREFUL with this project because you can get quite a shock by charging it against a carpet on a dry day.*

Capacitance

The ability to store charge The ability of a capacitor to store charge is called capacitance (*C*). Capacitance is measured in farads (F). A one-farad capacitor can store one coulomb of charge when the voltage across its plates is one volt. One farad is a large amount of capacitance, so the microfarad (μF) is frequently used in place of the farad. There are 10^6 microfarads in one farad. Most capacitors in electronic devices are measured in microfarads or even smaller units. The equation for capacitance tells how much charge a capacitor stores per volt.

Capacitance

$$\underset{\text{Charge (C)}}{q} = \overset{\overset{\text{Capacitance}}{(C/V)}}{C} \underset{\text{Voltage (V)}}{V}$$

Capacitor

More capacitance means more charge A capacitor with a large capacitance can hold more charge at the same voltage compared with a capacitor with a small capacitance. For example, if a one-farad capacitor is connected to a 1.5-volt battery, it will store a charge of 1.5 coulombs when fully charged. If a two-farad capacitor is connected to a 1.5-volt battery, it will hold three coulombs of charge.

Factors affecting capacitance There are three factors that affect a capacitor's ability to store charge. The size of the capacitor is the most obvious factor. The greater the area of a capacitor's plates, the more space for storing charge, and the greater the capacitance. The distance between the plates also affects the capacitance. The closer together the plates are, the greater the capacitance. The third factor is the type of insulator placed between the plates. The capacitance is the least when there is nothing between the plates, and can be many times greater when the right insulator is used.

Using a capacitor Batteries are used to supply energy for use over a long period of time, while capacitors are used for quick bursts of energy. Cameras use capacitors to supply energy to flash bulbs. When you turn on a camera, it takes a few seconds for the capacitor to become charged. Pressing the shutter button completes the circuit connecting the capacitor to the bulb. A large current flows through the bulb for a short time producing a very bright flash, until the capacitor's charge is gone.

Calculate capacitance and voltage for a capacitor

A capacitor holds 0.02 coulombs of charge when fully charged by a 12-volt battery. Calculate its capacitance and the voltage that would be required for it to hold one coulomb of charge.

1) You are asked to find the capacitance and the voltage needed to hold 1 C of charge.
2) You are given the voltage and corresponding charge.
3) Use *C = q/V* to calculate the capacitance.
4) Solve:
   C=(0.02 C)÷(12 V)
   =0.001667 F or 1667 μF

Rearrange *C = q/V* to get *V = q/C* and calculate the voltage required to store a charge of 1 C on the capacitor.

V = (1 C) ÷ (0.001667 F)
= 600 V

The capacitor would hold one coulomb of charge at a voltage of 600 volts. Most capacitors would be destroyed by a voltage this high.

Application: How a Television Works

Television has completely changed our ability to see and experience things without actually being there. Moving color pictures with sound are so powerful that little imagination is needed to understand what is being shown. Today's special effects are so realistic that a person of 100 years ago could probably be convinced that a TV was actually a window into a world of live dinosaurs. How is this done? How does a television create moving color pictures?

Red, green, and blue phosphors If you look at the screen of a TV with a magnifying glass, you see an array of colored dots called phosphors (Figure 21.21). There are red, green, and blue phosphors to make each of the primary colors. The dots are so small that your eye blurs them together to make continuous color. In Chapter 16 you learned that all colors can be made from combinations of red, green, and blue. To make any color, the red, green, and blue phosphors are made to glow with different intensities. In the NTSC television standard, the visible picture is about 480 lines high and each line contains 640 phosphors of each color.

The picture tube and electron guns The working part of a television is the picture tube (Figure 21.22). At the back of the picture tube are three electron guns which make three beams of energetic electrons. An electron gun (Figure 21.23) has three key components: an emitter of electrons, a control grid, and an accelerator that uses electric fields to get the electrons moving at high speed. The emitter is heated up to a high temperature and electrons come off its surface. The small delay between turning on a television and the picture appearing is due mostly to the time it takes to heat up the emitter plate.

Acceleration by electric fields in the electron gun The accelerator plate is kept at a positive voltage thousands of volts higher than the emitter. The accelerator voltage is maintained by a high-voltage capacitor between the emitter and accelerator. The voltage difference creates a strong electric field between the plates. The electric field accelerates the electrons from the emitter towards the accelerator. The beam is created by the electrons that pass through a small hole in the accelerator plate. Of course, some of the electrons also hit the accelerator plate itself and go back through the circuit. In a true electron gun, the shape of the electric field steers most of the electrons through the hole and not into the plate.

Figure 21.21: *A television picture is made from thousands of glowing dots called phosphors.*

Television picture tube

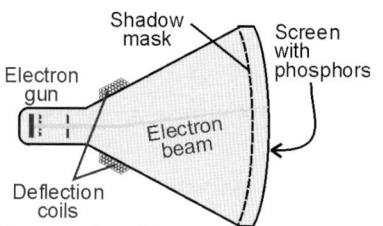

Figure 21.22: *The picture tube inside a television set.*

Parts of an electron gun

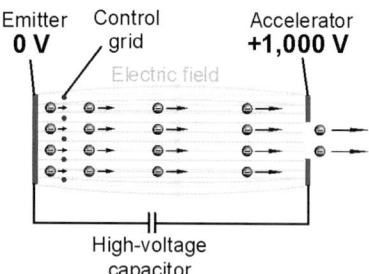

Figure 21.23: *Schematic of an electron gun inside a picture tube.*

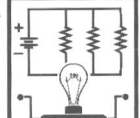

Drawing the picture

Drawing the picture with an electron beam The phosphors are at the front of the picture tube, which is the part you watch. When an electron beam hits a phosphor, the kinetic energy of the electrons is converted into light and the phosphor glows for a short time. The electron beam essentially "draws" the picture on the back of the TV screen and redraws it 30 times each second. At this rate the human eye sees continuous smooth motion.

The shadow mask In between the electron guns and the screen is a very precise metal screen called a shadow mask. The shadow mask contains one hole for each one of the phosphors on the screen. The shadow mask is aligned with both the screen phosphors and the electron guns so that each beam can only hit phosphors of one color (Figure 21.24). Since there are three beams, a TV can simultaneously light up three phosphors next to one another, one for each of the three primary colors.

The control grid sets the brightness of each phosphor You can think of a moving TV image as a series of still images called frames. To draw each frame, the electron beams scan from left to right across the screen in horizontal lines. As each beam goes across, the voltage on the control grid is changed by the TV signal carrying the picture. When the control grid is negative, it repels electrons back to the emitter and the beam is too weak to reach the phosphors and make them glow. When the control grid is positive, many electrons are attracted from the emitter, the beam has lots of energy, and the phosphor glows very brightly. By varying the voltage on the control grid, the beam energy can be adjusted to make each phosphor as bright as it needs to be.

CRTs and other display technologies Television picture tubes and computer screens are sometimes called cathode ray tubes (CRTs). A cathode is a source of electrons, like the emitter of the electron gun. The beams of energy that came from cathodes were called cathode rays before they were identified as electrons. A cathode ray tube is a device that creates an image from an electron beam from a cathode. CRTs are large because of the distance needed to steer the electron beam to the far corners of the screen. CRTs have been used since television was invented in the 1930s, but are finally giving way to newer and more compact technologies. For example, liquid crystal display (LCD) and plasma screen displays use completely different approaches to making television images.

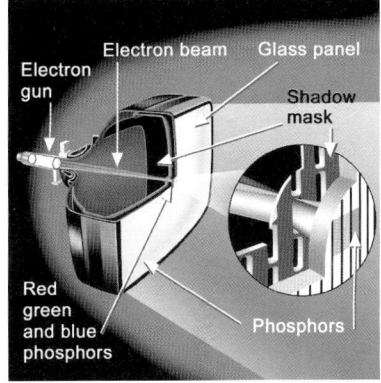

Figure 21.24: *How the shadow mask in a picture tube works.*

Steering the electron beam

The electron beam is steered back and forth across the screen by electromagnets. Magnets and electromagnets are the subject of the next two chapters. You will find that electricity and magnetism are closely related. Changing magnetism can cause electric current to flow. The reverse is also true because electric current creates magnetism.

Chapter 21 Review

Vocabulary Review

Match the following terms with the correct definition. There is one extra definition in the list that will not match any of the terms.

Set One

1. Coulomb's law
2. electric charge
3. farad
4. neutral
5. electroscope

a. Having equal amounts of positive and negative charge
b. An instrument used to determine whether an object is charged
c. Used to calculate the force between two charges
d. The unit in which capacitance is measured
e. A fundamental property of matter; can be positive or negative
f. The unit in which charge is measured

Set Two

1. proton
2. coulomb
3. polarization
4. electron
5. static electricity

a. The unit in which charge is measured
b. When one side of an atom or object has a net negative charge and the other side has a net positive charge
c. A subatomic particle with negative charge
d. A subatomic particle with no charge
e. A subatomic particle with positive charge
f. The buildup of electric charge on an object

Set Three

1. capacitor
2. capacitance
3. ampere
4. electric field
5. drift speed

a. A flow of one coulomb of charge per second
b. The ability of a capacitor to store charge
c. Exists in the space around a charge
d. The average speed of all the current carrying electrons in a wire
e. One joule per coulomb
f. A device that stores charge

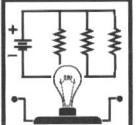

Concept review

1. Why don't we usually notice the electric charge in everyday objects?

2. What does it mean to say an object is electrically neutral?

3. If a neutral object loses negative charges, what will its net charge be?

4. Two negative charges will _____ each other. Two positive charges will _____ each other. A positive charge and a negative charge will _____ each other.

5. Draw a model of an atom, showing all three types of particles.

6. A negatively charged balloon is held near the top of a neutral electroscope but doesn't touch it. What is the charge on the electroscopes leaves?

7. A circuit has a current of 2 A. How many coulombs of charge will pass by a point in the circuit in:

   a. 1 second

   b. 5 seconds

   c. 1 minute

8. Which type of charges are free to move in a metal?

9. Electric current is defined as the direction in which _____ charges move, or opposite the direction in which _____ charges move.

10. Explain how electrons move through a wire.

11. Explain what happens when a positively charged balloon is used to charge a neutral electroscope by induction. What charge does the electroscope obtain?

12. Coulomb's Law is an inverse square law because the _____ and the _____ follow an inverse square relationship.

13. Two protons are 1 m apart. What happens to the force between them if they are moved to a distance of 2 m apart?

14. What happens to the strength of an electric field as you get farther away from a charge that creates the field?

15. An electric field shows the direction of the force a _____ charge would feel if placed in the field.

16. List two units that can be used to measure electric fields.

17. How is a gravitational field similar to an electric field? How are the two types of fields different?

18. Which forces are stronger, electric or gravitational?

19. Explain why the electric field inside a conductor is zero.

20. What is a parallel plate capacitor?

21. A battery is attached to a parallel plate capacitor as shown below.

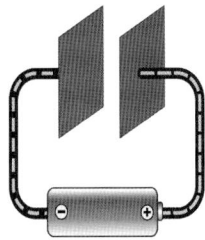

   a. Which plate will become positive and which will become negative?

   b. Will the positive plate gain electrons, gain protons, lose electrons, or lose protons?

   c. Will the negative plate gain electrons, gain protons, lose electrons, or lose protons?

22. What happens to the current in a circuit as a capacitor is discharging? Why?

23. How much charge can a 3 F capacitor store if it is connected to a 1 volt battery?

24. What three factors affect a capacitor's ability to store charge?

437

Problems

1. Twenty coulombs of charge pass by a point in a circuit in 30 seconds. What is the current?

2. Calculate the force between a pair of one coulomb charges that are 0.01 m apart.

3. Calculate the force between a 2 C positive charge and a 3 C negative charge separated by a distance of 0.5 m.

4. The repulsive force between two identical charges is measured to be 0.1 N when the charges are 0.2 m apart. Calculate the magnitude of each charge.

5. A capacitor in a camera flash is charged by four 1.5 V batteries. It holds a maximum of 0.015 C of charge. What is its capacitance?

6. A capacitor holds 0.06 coulombs of charge when fully charged by a 9-volt battery.

   a. Calculate its capacitance.

   b. How much voltage would be required for it to hold 2 coulombs of charge?

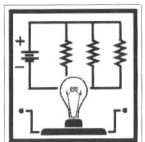

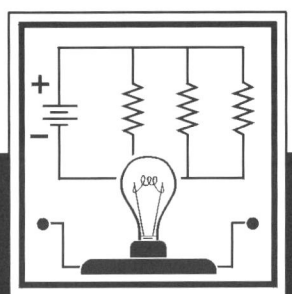

Unit 7

Electricity and Magnetism

Chapter 22

Magnetism

Objectives for Chapter 22

By the end of this chapter you should be able to:

1. Describe the forces between two permanent magnets.
2. Sketch the magnetic field of a single permanent magnet.
3. Predict the direction of the force on a magnet placed in a given magnetic field.
4. Explain why ferromagnetic materials always attract magnets of either pole.
5. Describe the theory behind why a compass works.
6. Use a compass to find the direction of true north.

Terms and vocabulary words

magnet	north pole	south pole	magnetization	demagnetization
magnetic field	compass	magnetic field lines	diamagnetic	paramagnetic
ferromagnetic	gauss	soft magnet	magnetic declination	
magnetic domain	hard magnet	permanent magnet		

22.1 Properties of Magnets

Magnetism has fascinated people since earliest times. Until the period of the Renaissance, many people thought magnetism was a form of life because it could make rocks move. We know that magnets stick to refrigerators and pick up paper clips or pins. They are also part of electric motors, computer disk drives, burglar alarm systems, and many other common devices. This chapter develops some of the properties of magnets and magnetic materials.

What is a magnet?

Magnets and magnetic materials
If a material is magnetic, it has the ability to exert forces on magnets or other magnetic materials. Some materials are actively magnetic, and we call them magnets. Other materials are attracted to nearby magnets but do not show magnetism otherwise. Iron and steel are in the second category because they are attracted by magnets but are not themselves always magnets. A magnet on a refrigerator is attracted to the magnetic material (steel) that makes up the refrigerator's door.

Permanent magnets
A permanent magnet is a material that keeps its magnetic properties, even when it is not close to other magnets. Bar magnets, refrigerator magnets, and horseshoe magnets are good examples of permanent magnets.

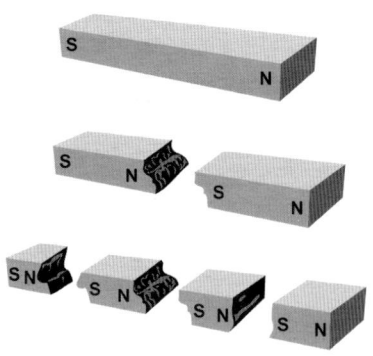

Figure 22.1: *If a magnet is cut in half, each half will have both a north pole and a south pole.*

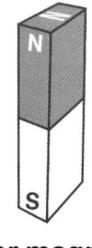  

Bar magnet   **Horseshoe magnet**   **Magnetic materials**

Poles
All magnets have two opposite poles, called the north pole and south pole. If a magnet is cut in half, each half will have its own north and south pole (Figure 22.1). It is impossible to have just a north or a south pole by itself. The north and south poles are comparable to the two sides of a coin. Every coin has two sides, just as every magnet has a north and a south pole.

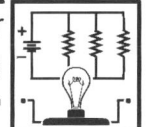

The magnetic force

Attraction and repulsion

When near each other, magnets exert magnetic forces on each other. Magnets can both attract and repel each other. Whether the magnetic force between two magnets is one of attraction or repulsion depends on the alignment of the poles (Figure 22.2). If two opposite poles are facing each other, the magnets will attract each other. If two like poles face each other, the magnets repel each other.

Most materials are transparent to magnetic forces

Magnetic forces can pass through many materials with no apparent decrease in strength. For example, one magnet can drag another magnet though a solid piece of wood or through your hand! Plastics, wood, and most insulating materials are virtually transparent to magnetic forces. Conducting metals, like aluminum, also allow magnetic forces to pass through, but may change the forces. Iron and a few metals near iron on the periodic table have strong magnetic properties. Iron and iron-like metals block magnetic forces and are discussed later in this chapter.

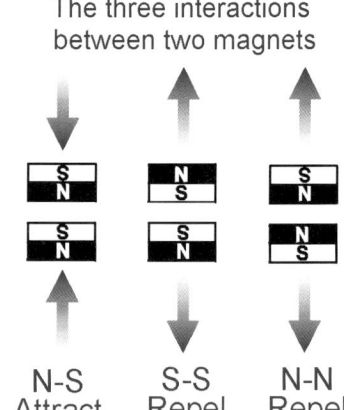

The three interactions between two magnets

N-S Attract   S-S Repel   N-N Repel

Figure 22.2: *The force between two magnets depends on how the poles are aligned.*

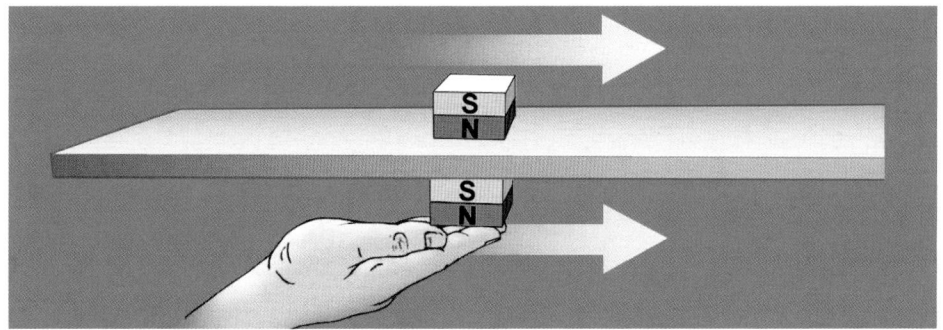

Comparing magnetic and electric forces

Magnetic forces are used in many applications because they are relatively easy to create and can be very strong. There are many ways to make magnets with forces that are strong enough to lift a car or even a moving train (Figure 22.3). Small magnets are everywhere; for example, some doors are sealed with magnetic weatherstripping that blocks out drafts. There are several patents for magnetic zippers and many handbags, briefcases, and cabinet doors close with magnetic latches. Although electric forces are stronger than magnetic forces, they are harder to create and control. It is much more difficult to keep electric charge separated than it is to make a magnet.

Figure 22.3: *Powerful magnets are used to lift discarded cars in a junkyard.*

The force between two magnets

Distance and the magnetic force

The strength of the force between magnets depends on the distance between them. When magnets are close together, the force between them is strong. As magnets are moved farther apart, the attractive or repulsive force gets weaker. Because every magnet has two poles, the force between two magnets decreases with distance much faster than the force between two electric charges.

Why magnetic force decreases rapidly with distance

Consider two magnets attracting each other. The total force between the magnets is the sum of the forces between *all four* magnetic poles. When two magnets are separated by a distance that is large compared with their size, both pairs of north and south poles are about the same distance away (diagram below). As a result, the attractive and repulsive forces nearly cancel each other out.

Forces between all 4 poles of 2 magnets

When magnets are close together the two closest poles have the largest contribution to the total force.

When magnets are separated by more than a few times their size, the attract and repel forces tend to cancel each other. The total force decreases rapidly as the separation increases.

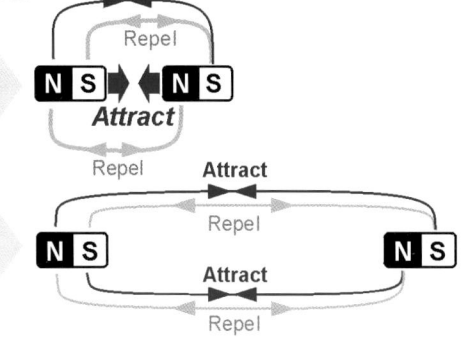

Magnetic force does not obey an inverse square law

Mathematically, the force between two magnets decreases with distance much more rapidly than an inverse square law (Figure 22.4). If you try to squeeze two repelling magnets together, you can easily feel how quickly the force gets strong as the magnets get very close together. Separate a pair of small magnets by a few centimeters and you can hardly feel a force at all.

Torque between two magnets

Two magnets near each other often feel a twisting force, or *torque*. This is also a result of having two poles. One pole is attracted and the other is repelled. The combination of attractive and repulsive forces on the same magnet creates a torque. Figure 22.5 shows how the torque on a test magnet changes, depending on its position relative to a fixed source magnet.

Comparing force vs. distance

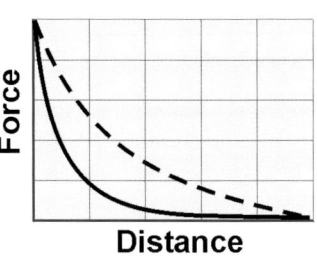

– – – Electrical force and gravity
(inverse square law)

—— Force between two magnets

Figure 22.4: *The magnetic force decreases with distance much faster than does either gravity or the electric force. Gravity and the electric force between point charges both obey an inverse square law. The force between two magnets does not.*

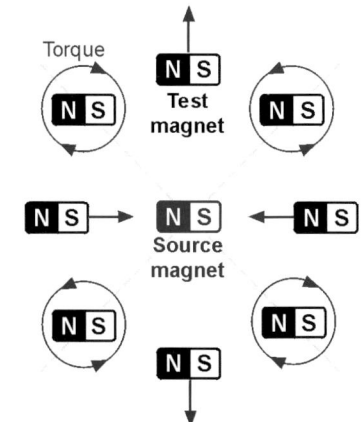

Figure 22.5: *The torques or forces on a test magnet at different positions around a fixed-source magnet.*

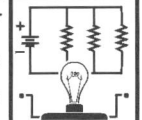

The magnetic field

Describing magnetic force

People investigating magnetism needed a way to describe the forces between two magnets. They knew that the force depended on the direction and orientation of the two magnets and also on the distance between them. The force between two magnets is transmitted through a magnetic field. Remember, from the last chapter, the word "field" in physics means that there is a quantity (such as force) that is associated with every point in space. There are many other kinds of fields. For example, the "odor field" near a sewer would be strongest nearest the sewer and get weaker farther away.

Using a test magnet to trace magnetic field lines

All magnets create a magnetic field in the space around them, and the magnetic field creates forces on other magnets. Imagine you have a small *test magnet* (Figure 22.6) that you are moving around another magnet (the *source magnet*). The north pole of your test magnet feels a force everywhere in the space around the source magnet. To keep track of the force, imagine drawing an arrow in the direction in which the north pole of your test magnet is pulled or pushed as you move it around. The arrows that you draw show you the magnetic field. If you connect all the arrows, you get lines called magnetic field lines.

Understanding magnetic field lines

How do you interpret a drawing of a magnetic field? The number of field lines in a certain area indicates the relative strength of the magnetic field in that area. The closer the lines are together, the stronger the field. The arrows on the field lines indicate the direction of the force on the *north pole* of a test magnet (Figure 22.7). Magnetic field lines always point away from a magnet's north pole and toward its south pole.

The interaction of fields

Magnetic fields are necessary to precisely describe how magnets exert forces on each other. Every magnet creates a magnetic field. If two magnets are close, their magnetic fields interact and exert forces on each magnet. Calculations with magnetic fields are complicated and there is no simple formula like Coulomb's law. However, experienced engineers and physicists are able to calculate magnetic fields and forces so precisely that it is possible to predict magnetic effects inside a single atom. For example, the medical technique of magnetic resonance imaging (MRI) is based on magnetic stimulation of atoms in your body.

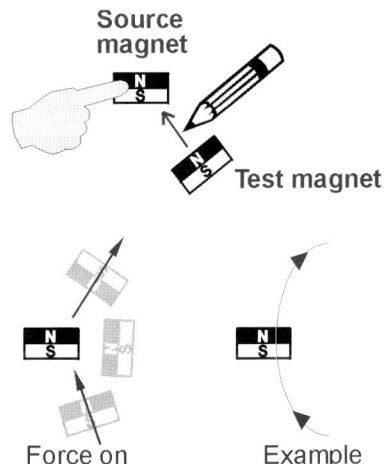

Figure 22.6: *Drawing a field line with a test magnet.*

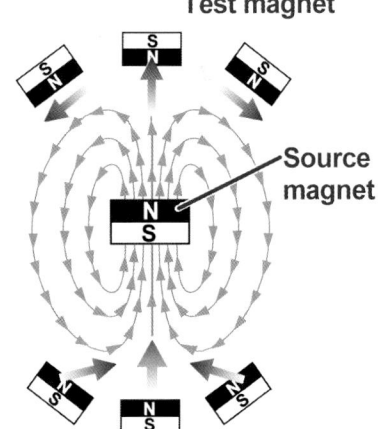

Figure 22.7: *The magnetic field is defined in terms of the force exerted on the north pole of another magnet.*

22.2 Magnetic Properties of Materials

It seems unusual that magnets can attract and repel other magnets but can only *attract* objects such as steel paper clips and nails. The reason this is true and the explanation for magnetism itself lie inside the atoms that make up matter. This section takes a microscopic look inside materials to explain their magnetic properties. Magnetism, like charge and mass, is a fundamental property of the particles that make up all atoms of matter. Whether or not we observe magnetism in a material depends on how the atoms in the material are arranged.

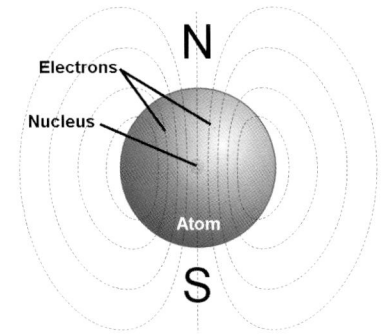

Figure 22.8: *Some atoms have magnetic fields that derive mainly from the motion of electrons surrounding the nucleus.*

The source of magnetism

Electrons and magnetism The sources of nearly all magnetic effects in matter are the electrons in atoms. There are two ways in which electrons create magnetism. First, the electrons move around the nucleus and their motion makes the entire atom a small magnet (Figure 22.8). Second, electrons themselves act as though they were magnets.

Why magnetic properties vary in materials All atoms have electrons, so you might think that all materials should be magnetic. In fact, there is great variability in the magnetic properties of materials. The variability comes from the arrangement of electrons within atoms of different elements. The electrons in some atoms align to cancel out one another's magnetic influence. In other atoms, the electrons may align themselves in a way that strengthens the overall magnetic field.

Diamagnetic materials While all materials show some kind of magnetic effect, the magnetism in most materials is too weak to detect without highly sensitive instruments. In diamagnetic materials, the electrons are oriented so their individual magnetic fields cancel each other out. The net magnetic field of each atom is zero. When placed in a region with a magnetic field, the motion of the electrons is disturbed, and diamagnetic materials become very slightly magnetic.

Paramagnetic materials Individual atoms in paramagnetic materials *are* magnetic because the magnetism of individual electrons does not completely cancel. However, the atoms themselves are randomly arranged so the overall magnetism of a sample with many atoms is zero (Figure 22.9). An external magnetic field causes the atoms to become partially aligned, and a paramagnetic material becomes weakly magnetic.

Paramagnetic material

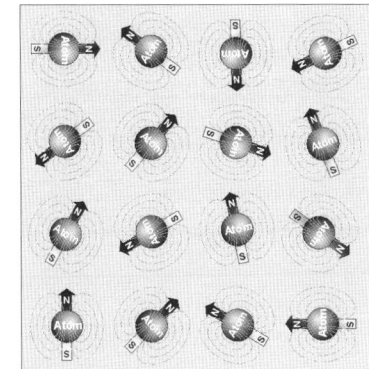

Figure 22.9: *Atoms in a paramagnetic material act like magnets. However, the atoms are randomly arranged so that the net magnetic effect is zero. If placed in a magnetic field however, the atoms align so that the material is weakly magnetic.*

444

Ferromagnetism

Ferromagnetic materials

A small group of metals have very strong magnetic properties, including iron, nickel, and cobalt. These metals are the best known examples of ferromagnetic materials. The electrons in each atom of a ferromagnetic material (like iron) align so their magnetic fields do not cancel each other. Individual atoms of ferromagnetic materials do not act independently like they do in paramagnetic materials. Instead, atoms with similar magnetic orientations line up with neighboring atoms in groups called magnetic domains. By combining atoms, the magnetic strength of a domain is greatly multiplied compared with a single atom.

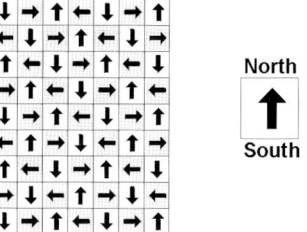

Unmagnetized magnetic domains

North

South

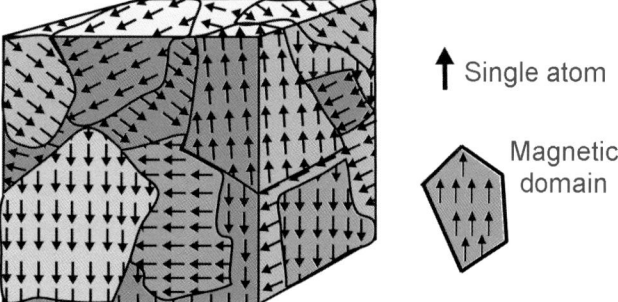

↑ Single atom

Magnetic domain

The alignment of domains to a north magnetic pole

Magnetic domains can grow or shrink in response to magnetic fields. For example, if you bring the north pole of a magnet near iron, the south pole of each atom in the iron is attracted to the magnet's north pole (Figure 22.10). All south-pointing magnetic domains quickly grow larger as atoms are attracted by the external magnet. Other magnetic domains shrink if they have magnetic poles pointed the wrong way. The iron becomes magnetized because it develops a south pole in response to the external north pole. For example, a paper clip sticks to a magnet because the magnetic domains in the steel that are attracted to the magnet have grown and the domains that are repelled by the magnet have shrunk.

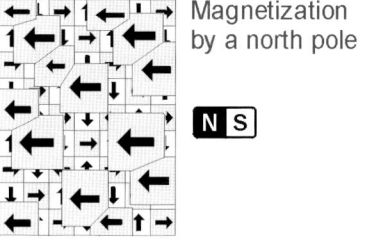

Magnetization by a north pole

N **S**

Domains realign to attract any pole

If you bring the magnet's south pole near the paper clip, the opposite happens. Domains grow that have north poles facing the external magnet's south pole. This is why a magnet will always attract ferromagnetic materials, regardless of whether the magnet's north or south pole approaches the object. Domains in a ferromagnetic material can easily realign themselves to be attracted to either pole.

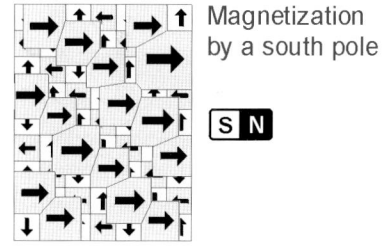

Magnetization by a south pole

S **N**

Figure 22.10: *Magnetic domains in a ferromagnetic material will always orient themselves to attract a permanent magnet. If a north pole approaches, domains grow that have south poles facing out. If a south pole approaches, domains grow that have north poles facing out.*

Properties of ferromagnetic materials

Creating permanent magnets

If a magnet near a ferromagnetic material is removed, the domains in the material tend to go back to their random orientation. However, if an object made of a magnetic material is repeatedly stroked with a magnet or is placed in a very strong magnetic field, the domains become so well aligned that they stay aligned even after the external magnet is removed. This is how permanent magnets are made.

Hard magnets

Ferromagnetic materials differ in their ability to become and remain magnetized. Materials that make good permanent magnets are called hard magnets. The domains in these materials tend to remain aligned and are useful in devices that require permanent magnets. Because it is difficult to change the orientation of magnetic domains in hard magnets, creating permanent magnets out of these materials requires the application of a strong external magnetic field.

Materials for permanent magnets

Steel, which contains iron and carbon, is a common and inexpensive material used to create hard magnets. Typical bar and horseshoe magnets are made of steel. Most magnets however, are no longer made of steel. Stronger magnets are made from ceramics containing nickel and cobalt, or the rare earth metal neodymium. Using these materials, it is possible to manufacture magnets that are very small but also very strong and harder to demagnetize than steel magnets.

Soft magnets

Materials that lose their magnetism quickly are called soft magnets. Soft magnets are easy to magnetize with even a weak bar magnet. You can see both the magnetization and demagnetization of small iron nails or paper clips using a magnet (Figure 22.11). If you use the north end of a bar magnet to pick up a nail, the nail becomes magnetized with its south pole toward the magnet. Because the nail itself becomes a magnet, it can be used to pick up other nails. If you separate that first nail from the bar magnet, the entire chain demagnetizes and falls apart.

Demagnetization

Even hard magnets can be demagnetized. If a magnet is vibrated or repeatedly struck, the domains can become unaligned and the magnetism will weaken. Forcing two south poles (or two north poles) together is enough to demagnetize some steel magnets. High temperatures can also demagnetize magnets, because the energy of high-temperature atoms can exceed the energy that keeps the atoms aligned in magnetic domains.

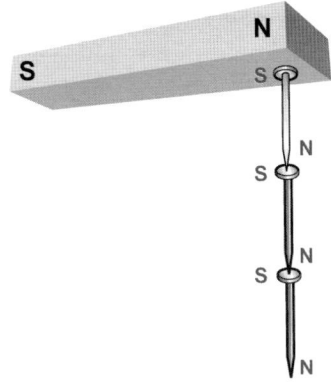

Figure 22.11: *Iron nails become temporarily magnetized when placed near a magnet.*

There are no liquid magnets

The atoms in a liquid are free to move around. That means they cannot be fixed into place with their magnetic poles aligned. There are no liquid permanent magnets for this reason. Permanent magnetism is a property only of solids. In fact, if you heat a magnetic solid up, it loses its magnetism. The temperature at which this happens is called the Curie temperature. This temperature varies between materials and is approximately 360°C for nickel, 770°C for iron, and 1100°C for cobalt.

22.3 The Magnetic Field of the Earth

The biggest magnet on Earth is the planet itself. The Earth has a magnetic field that has been useful to travelers for thousands of years. Compasses, which contain small magnets, interact with the Earth's magnetic field to tell direction. Certain animals, including migratory birds, can feel the magnetic field of the Earth and use their magnetic sense to tell which direction is north or south. This section is about the magnetic field of the Earth.

Discovering and using magnetism

Lodestone

As early as 500 B.C. people discovered that some naturally occurring materials—such as *lodestone* and *magnetite*—have magnetic properties. The Greeks observed that one end of a suspended piece of lodestone pointed north and the other end pointed south, helping sailors and travelers to find their way. This discovery lead to the first important application of magnetism—the *compass* (Figure 22.12).

The Chinese "south pointer"

The invention of the compass is also recorded in China, in 220 B.C. Writings from the Zheng dynasty tell stories of how people would use a "south pointer" when they went out to search for jade, so that they wouldn't lose their way home. The pointer was made of lodestone. It looked like a large spoon with a short, skinny handle. When balanced on a plate, the "handle" was aligned with magnetic south.

The first iron needle compass

By 1088 A.D., iron refining had developed to the point where the Chinese were making a small needle-like compass. Shen Kua recorded that a needle-shaped magnet was placed on a reed floating in a bowl of water. Chinese inventors also suspended a long, thin magnet in the air, realizing in both cases that the magnet ends were aligned with geographic north and south. Explorers from the Sung dynasty sailed their trading ships all the way to Saudi Arabia using compasses among their navigational tools. About 100 years later a similar design appeared in Europe and soon spread through the region.

Compasses and exploration

By 1200, explorers from Italy were using a compass to guide ocean voyages beyond the sight of land. The Chinese also continued exploring with compasses, and by the 1400s, they were traveling to the east coast of Africa. The compass, and the voyages that it made possible, led to many interactions among cultures.

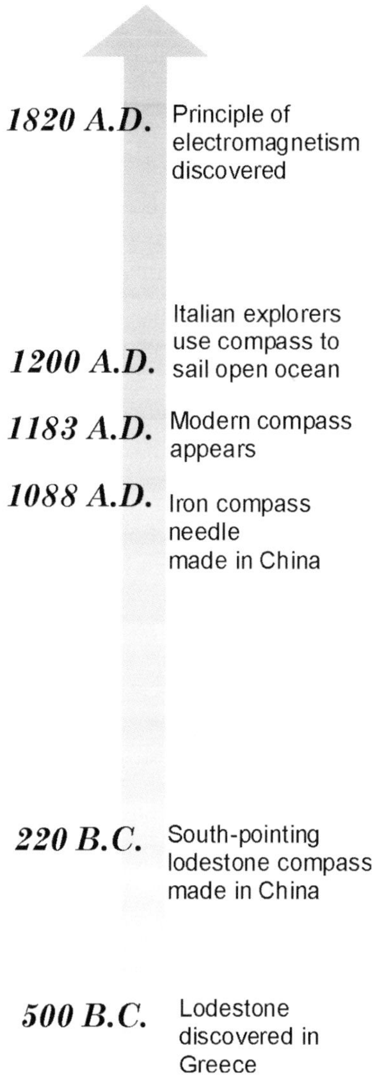

1820 A.D. Principle of electromagnetism discovered

1200 A.D. Italian explorers use compass to sail open ocean

1183 A.D. Modern compass appears

1088 A.D. Iron compass needle made in China

220 B.C. South-pointing lodestone compass made in China

500 B.C. Lodestone discovered in Greece

Figure 22.12: *Time line of the discovery of lodestone and the development of the modern compass.*

How does a compass work?

A compass is a magnet	A compass needle is a magnet that is free to spin. The needle spins until it lines up with any magnetic field that may be present. (Figure 22.13). Because the north pole of a magnet is attracted to the south pole of another magnet, the north pole of a compass needle always points toward the south pole of a permanent magnet. This is in the direction of the field lines.
North and south poles	The origin of the terms "north pole" and "south pole" of a magnet come from the direction that a magnetized compass needle points. The end of the magnet that pointed towards geographic north was called the north pole of the magnet and opposite pole was called south. The names were decided long before people truly understood why a compass needle worked.

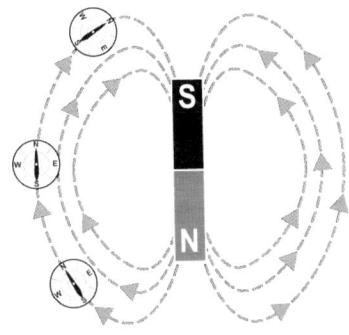

Figure 22.13: *A compass needle aligns itself with the magnetic field lines. The north pole of the compass needle points toward the south pole of the bar magnet.*

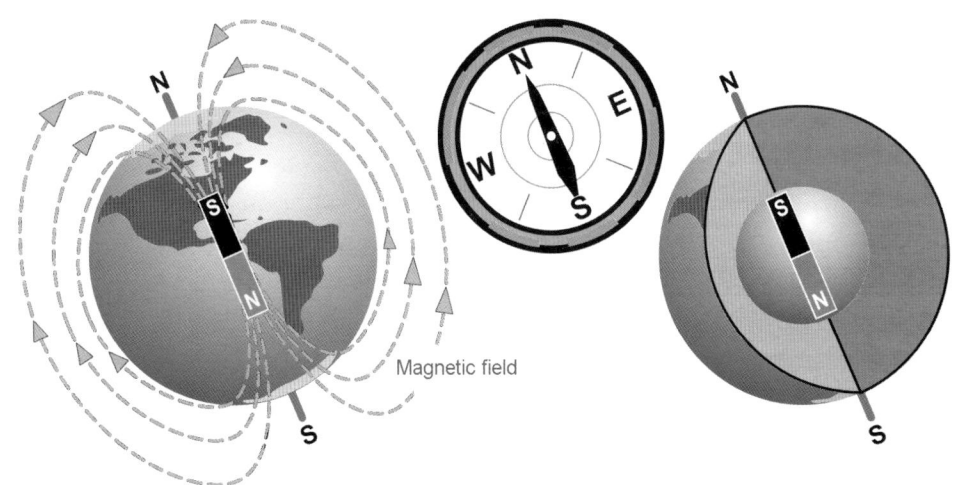

Magnetic field

The Earth is a magnet	The *geographic* north and south poles of the Earth are the points at which the Earth's axis of rotation intersects the planet surface. When you use a compass, the north-pointing end of the needle points toward a spot near (but not exactly at) the Earth's geographic north pole. The Earth's *magnetic* poles are defined by the planet's magnetic field. That means the *south magnetic pole* of the planet is near the north geographic pole. The Earth has a planetary magnetic field that acts as if the core of the planet contained a giant magnet oriented like the diagram above.

Some animals have biological compasses

Many animals, including species of birds, frogs, fish, turtles, and bacteria, can sense the magnetic field of the Earth. Migratory birds are the best known examples. Scientists have found magnetite, a magnetic mineral, in bacteria and in the brains of birds. Tiny crystals of magnetite may act like compasses and allow the animals to sense the small magnetic field of the Earth.

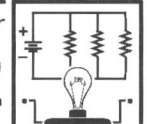

The source of the Earth's magnetism

The strength of the Earth's magnetic field
The magnetic field of the Earth is very weak compared with the strength of the field on the surface of the ceramic magnets you probably have in your classroom. For this reason you cannot trust a compass to point north if any magnets are close by. The gauss is a unit used to measure the strength of a magnetic field. A small ceramic permanent magnet has a field of a few hundred up to 1,000 gauss at its surface. By contrast, the magnetic field averages about 0.5 gauss at Earth's surface. Of course, the field is much stronger nearer to the core of the planet.

The Earth's magnetic core
While the core of the Earth is magnetic, we know it is not a permanent magnet. Studies of earthquake waves reveal that the Earth's core is made of hot, dense molten iron, nickel, and possibly other metals that slowly circulate around a solid inner core (Figure 22.14). The motion of the molten iron creates electric currents, which produce a magnetic field like that made by an *electromagnet* (Chapter 23).

Reversing poles
Historical data shows that both the strength of the Earth's magnetic field and the location of the north and south magnetic poles can switch places. Studies of magnetized rocks in the Earth's oceanic crust provide evidence that the poles have reversed many times over the last tens of millions of years (Figure 22.15). The reversal has happened every 500,000 years on average. The last field reversal occurred roughly 750,000 years ago so the Earth is overdue for another change of magnetic polarity.

The next reversal
Today, the Earth's magnetic field is losing approximately 7 percent of its strength every 100 years. We do not know whether this trend will continue, but if it does, the magnetic poles could reverse in the next 2,000 years. During a reversal, the Earth's magnetic field would not completely disappear. However, the main magnetic field that we use for navigation would be replaced by several smaller fields with poles in different locations.

Movements of the magnetic poles
The location of the Earth's magnetic poles is always changing—slowly—even between full reversals. Currently, the magnetic south pole (to which the north end of a compass points) is located about 1,000 kilometers (600 miles) from the geographic north pole. When navigating with a compass, it is necessary to take this difference into account.

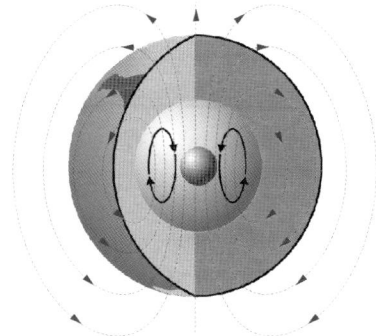

Figure 22.14: *Scientists believe motion of molten metals in the Earth's outer core create its magnetic field.*

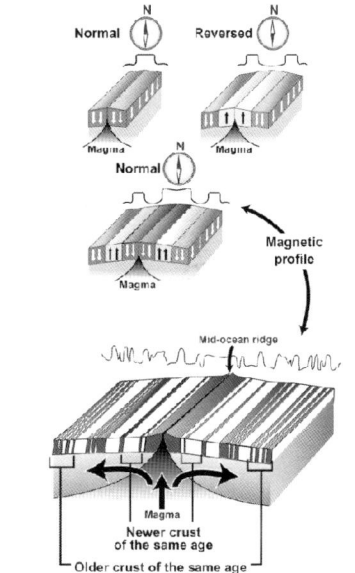

Figure 22.15: *When oceanic crust is made on the seafloor at mid-ocean ridges, the crustal rock records Earth's polarity.*

Magnetic declination

Compensating for pole differences

Because the Earth's geographic north pole (true north) and magnetic south pole are not located at the exact same place, a compass will not point *directly* to the geographic north pole. Depending on where you are, a compass will point slightly east or west of true north. The difference between the direction a compass points and the direction of true north is called magnetic declination. Magnetic declination is measured in degrees and is indicated on topographical maps.

Finding true north with a compass

Most good compasses contain an adjustable ring with a degree scale and an arrow that can be turned to point toward the destination on a map (Figure 22.16). The ring is turned the appropriate number of degrees to compensate for the declination. If you were using the map shown below, you would have to adjust your compass by 16 degrees to find true north.

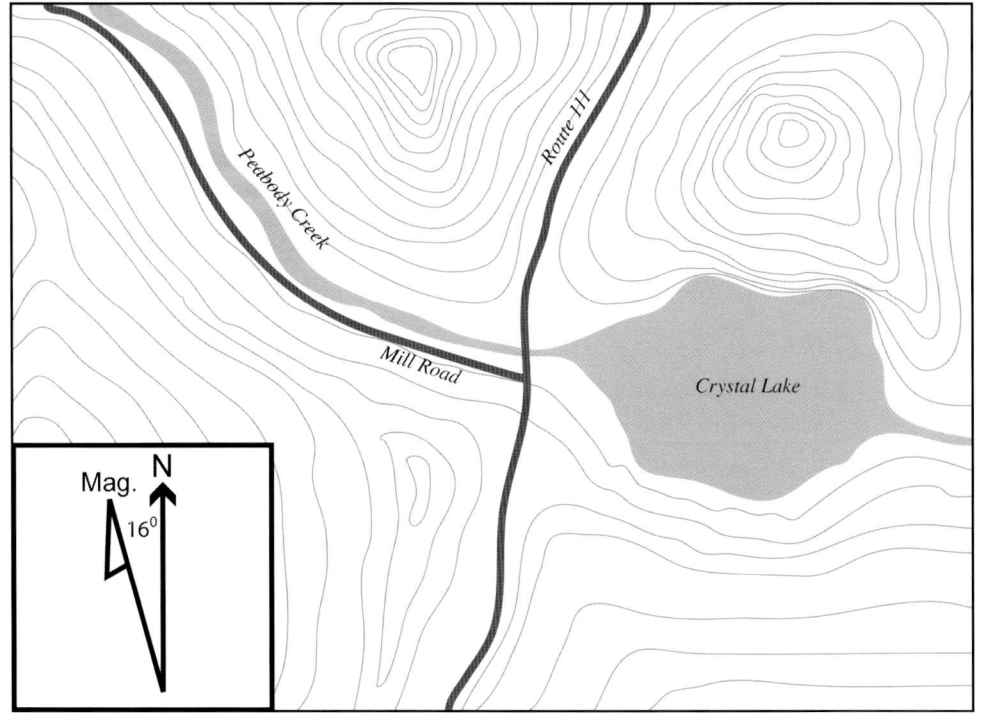

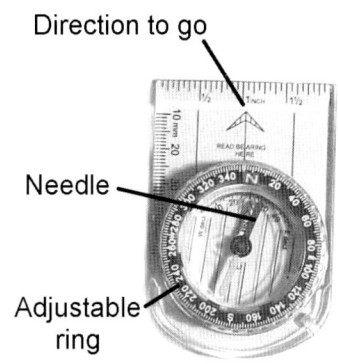

Figure 22.16: *This compass has an adjustable ring that is rotated to set the direction you want to go. After correcting for the declination, you rotate the whole compass until the north-pointing end of the needle lines up with zero degrees on the ring. The large arrow points in the direction you want to go.*

Orienteering

What was once a necessary survival skill is today a challenging competition. Competitors in orienteering are given a compass, a destination, and map. They must find their way to the destination using wilderness navigation skills to get around many obstacles, such as rivers or mountains.

Application: Magnetic Resonance Imaging

Imagine how medical diagnosis worked before x-rays, ultrasound, or magnetic resonance imaging (MRI). A doctor of 100 years ago might have had to perform surgery just to find out what was wrong. Today we enjoy the benefits of advanced medical technologies that allow doctors to see inside the body without having to perform surgery that might be more dangerous than the illness.

What an MRI scanner does   MRI is a powerful diagnostic technology. An MRI scanner makes a three-dimensional map of the *inside* of the body. As the name implies, MRI technology uses magnets and resonance to create images (Figure 22.17).

Magnetic field of the nucleus   The nucleus of every atom has a magnetic field (Figure 22.18). The nuclear magnetic field has a different strength for different elements. For example, a hydrogen nucleus has a different magnetic field than a carbon nucleus. The nuclear magnetic field is very small, however, it is important in MRI.

Energy and magnetic orientation   Consider what happens to a magnet in a strong magnetic field. The magnet wants to align itself so that its own north pole points in the direction of the magnetic field. If you want to turn the magnet opposite to the field, you have to apply a force, and thus do work. Applying force and doing work means exchanging energy. As a result, a magnet that *opposes* the field has higher energy than a magnet that is aligned *with* the field. Left alone, magnets tend to settle into the lowest energy position and align themselves with the magnetic field around them.

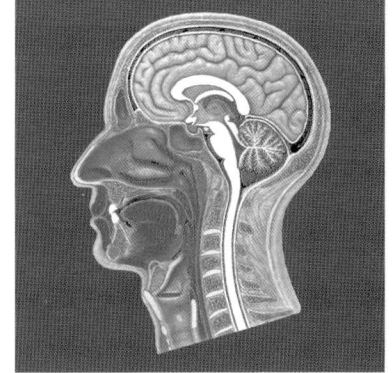

Figure 22.17: *An MRI image.*

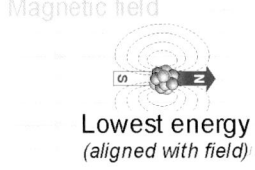

Magnetic field

Lowest energy
(aligned with field)

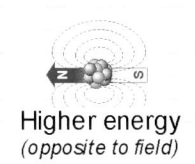

Higher energy
(opposite to field)

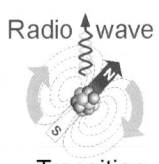

Radio wave

Transition

Energy exchange by a nucleus in a magnetic field   As you learned in the last unit, atoms exchange energy through electromagnetic radiation, including light. Because the nucleus of an atom acts like a small magnet, there is an energy difference depending on whether the nucleus is aligned with, or opposed to, an applied magnetic field. If a nucleus absorbs the right amount of energy, it will flip its magnetic orientation from aligned to opposed. If the same nucleus is left in the opposed (high energy) position, it quickly flips back to being aligned with the field and gives off the change in energy as radio waves.

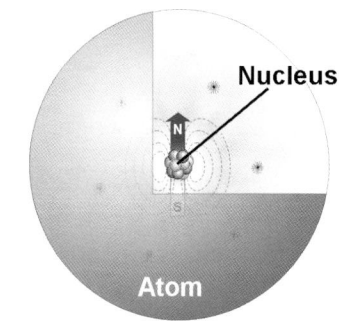

Nucleus

Atom

Figure 22.18: *The nucleus of an atom has a magnetic field of its own.*

The MRI scanning machine

What an MRI scanner does

An MRI scanner uses the magnetism of the nucleus to map out the locations of different elements in the body. The large cylinder you slide into is a powerful magnet (Figure 22.19). The magnet creates a strong and very uniform magnetic field. The magnetic field creates a preferred orientation for the nuclei of atoms in the body. When a body is inside an MRI scanner, the nuclei of every atom tends to line up with the magnetic field.

Each nucleus is a small resonant oscillator

A nucleus is in equilibrium with the magnetic field when its own magnetic poles are aligned with the field. The interaction between the magnetism of the nucleus and the external field creates a restoring force. Remember, from Chapter 13, restoring forces tend always to push systems back toward equilibrium. Because the nucleus has mass it also has inertia. The combination of a restoring force and inertia makes each nucleus into a tiny oscillator that can rotate back and forth around the magnetic field (Figure 22.20). The resonant frequency of the nuclear oscillator depends on the ratio of the mass of the nucleus to its magnetic strength. Since each element has a different mass and field strength, each element also has a different resonant frequency.

MRI uses radio waves at the natural frequency of the nucleus

The MRI scanner measures the absorption and emission of radio waves that are tuned to the natural frequency of different nuclei. For example, one set of frequencies might be used to map the density of hydrogen atoms in a body. Since hydrogen is in water, the body has a lot of hydrogen. A different frequency is used to map calcium atoms, which are found in bones. A third frequency is used for carbon atoms, and so on. Because the radio waves can pass right through the body, the MRI scan is able to make three dimensional images of the body's interior. These images are so detailed that doctors can see tiny veins and arteries clearly. Best of all, the procedure is virtually risk-free to the patient—and painless in the bargain.

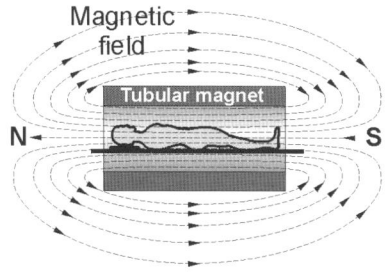

Figure 22.19: *For an MRI scan, the patient lies down in the center of a tubular magnet. The magnetic field inside the magnet is very uniform. MRI scanners use electromagnets instead of permanent magnets.*

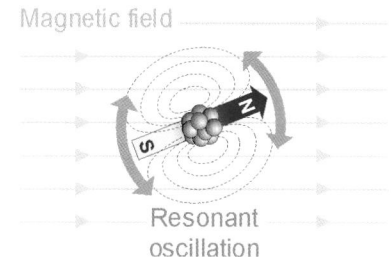

Figure 22.20: *The magnetic field creates a restoring force that makes an atom's nucleus into a resonant oscillator.*

Chapter 22 Review

Vocabulary Review

Match the following terms with the correct definition. There is one extra definition in the list that will not match any of the terms.

Set One

1. magnetic declination
2. poles
3. magnetic domain
4. permanent magnet

a. A material that keeps its magnetic properties, even when not close to other magnets
b. The two opposite ends of a magnet
c. The difference between the direction in which a compass points and the direction of the geographic north pole
d. A group of magnetic atoms that line up to create a net magnetic field in a ferromagnetic material
e. An area of a magnet that is nonmagnetic

Set Two

1. paramagnetic
2. magnetic field
3. diamagnetic
4. ferromagnetic
5. compass

a. Weakly magnetic material; each atom is magnetic but atoms are randomly arranged
b. A material that contains no moving charges
c. The least magnetic of all materials; equal numbers of electrons spin in each direction in this material's atoms
d. A magnetic device used for navigation
e. The most magnetic type of material; atoms line up with neighboring atoms to form domains
f. Exists in the region around a magnet

Concept review

1. List three objects made of magnetic materials.

2. A north pole of a magnet will _____ the north pole of a second magnet. A south pole will _____ another south pole. A north pole will _____ a south pole.

3. Explain how the force between two magnetic poles depends on the distance between them.

4. What does the spacing of magnetic field lines tell you?

5. Magnetic fields have direction. How is the direction determined?

6. How are magnetic poles and electric charges similar? How are they different?

7. What is the source of magnetism in materials?

8. Compare diamagnetic, paramagnetic, and ferromagnetic materials.

9. If all materials contain moving electrons, why is the magnetism in most materials too weak to measure?

10. What are magnetic domains?

11. Compare hard magnets and soft magnets.

12. How can a permanent magnet be created?

13. Name two ways a magnet can become demagnetized.

14. Where is the magnetic north pole located with respect to the Earth's geographic poles?

15. How is a compass used to determine direction?

16. What do scientists believe to be the source of the Earth's magnetic field?

17. What evidence do scientists have to support the theory that the poles of the Earth are constantly changing?

18. What is magnetic declination?

Problems

1. The magnet shown in the picture on the left is dropped and breaks into three pieces. Recopy the diagram of the pieces and label the north and south poles on each piece.

2. A compass is located at point X near a bar magnet as shown below. Which diagram shows the proper direction of the compass needle?

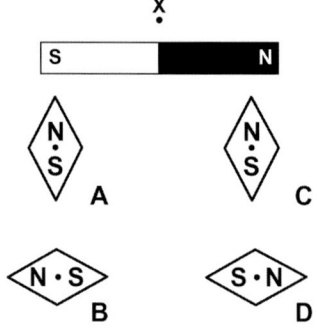

3. Which diagram below best represents the magnetic field near a bar magnet?

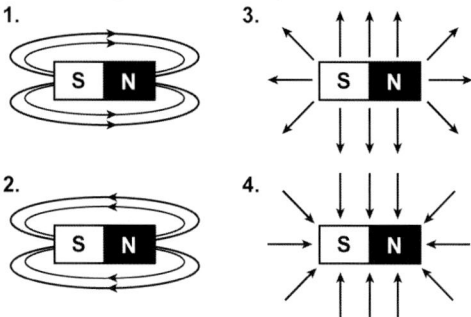

4. Which magnet(s) pictured below experience a clockwise torque?

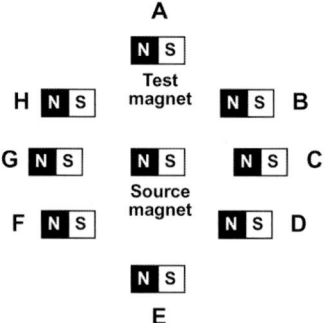

5. Which pair of objects will NOT experience an attractive magnetic force?

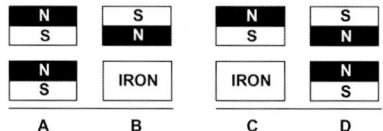

6. Two cross-country skiers refer to a topographic map and note that the magnetic declination is 16 degrees east in the area where they are skiing. If they were to ski 10 km north according to their compasses, how far would they be from a point that is 10 km true north of their position?

7. The diagram below shows magnetic field lines that result when a piece of soft iron is placed between unlike magnetic poles. At which point is the strength of the magnetic field greatest?

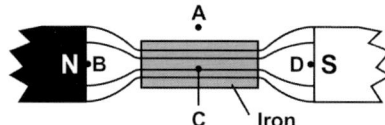

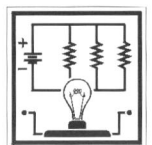

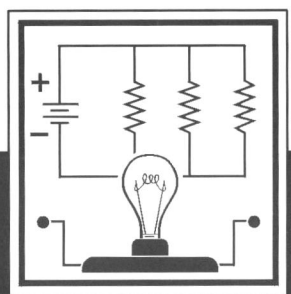

Unit 7
Electricity and Magnetism

Chapter 23

Electricity and Magnetism

Objectives for Chapter 23

By the end of this chapter you should be able to:

1. Predict the direction of the force on a moving charge or current carrying wire in a magnetic field by using the right-hand rule.
2. Explain the relationship between electric current and magnetism.
3. Describe and construct a simple electromagnet.
4. Explain the concept of commutation as it relates to an electric motor.
5. Explain how the concept of magnetic flux applies to generating electric current using Faraday's law of induction.
6. Describe three ways to increase the current from an electric generator.

Terms and vocabulary words

gauss	right-hand rule	coil	solenoid	magnetic field
tesla	Faraday's law	induction	induced current	magnetic flux
	commutator	generator	electromagnet	polarity

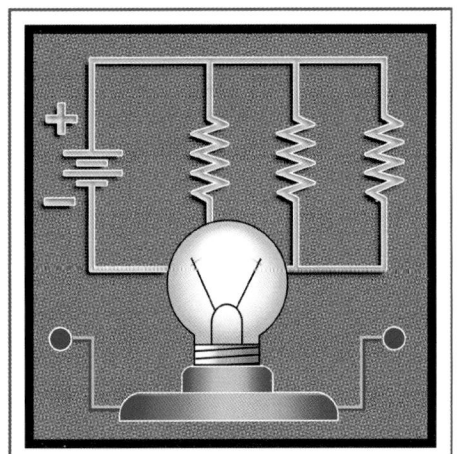

23.1 Electric Current and Magnetism

For a long time, people thought electricity and magnetism were unrelated. As scientists began to understand electricity better, they searched for relationships between electricity and magnetism. The breakthrough discovery was made in front of a class of students. In 1819, Hans Christian Oersted, a Danish physicist and chemist, and a professor, placed a compass needle near a wire through which he could make electric current flow. When the switch was closed, the compass needle moved just as if the wire were a magnet. We now know that magnetism is created by the motion of electric charge and that electricity and magnetism are really two forms of the same basic force.

The magnetic field of a wire carrying current

An experiment with a wire and compasses

Wires carrying electric current create magnetic fields. Consider the following experiment. A long straight wire is connected to a battery with a switch. The wire passes through a board with a hole in it. Around the hole are many compasses which can detect any magnetic field (Figure 23.1).

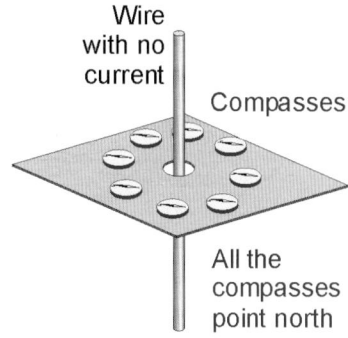

Figure 23.1: *An apparatus for investigating the magnetic field around a straight wire.*

The response of the compasses to electric current

When the switch is off, the compasses all point north (Figure 23.2). As soon as the switch is closed, the compasses point in a circle. The compasses stay pointing in a circle as long as electric current is flowing in the wire. If the current stops, the compasses return to pointing north again. If the current is reversed in the wire, the compasses again point in a circle, but in the opposite direction.

The magnetic field of a wire

The experiment with the compasses shows that a wire carrying electric current makes a magnetic field around it. The magnetic field lines are concentric circles with the wire at the center. As you may have guessed, the direction of the field depends on the direction of the current in the wire. The right-hand rule can be used to tell how the magnetic field lines point. When your thumb is in the direction of the current, the fingers of your right hand wrap in the direction of the magnetic field.

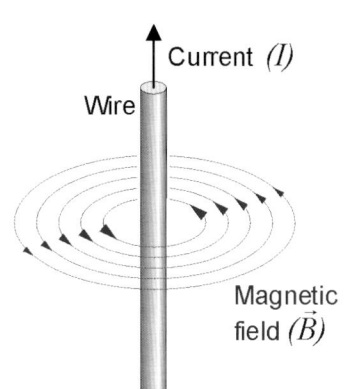

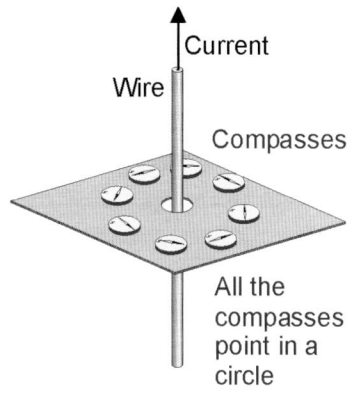

Figure 23.2: *The compass needles all form a circle when the current is switched on in the wire.*

Magnetic forces and electric currents

The force between two wires Two wires carrying electric current exert force on each other, just like two magnets. The forces can be attractive or repulsive depending on the direction of current in both wires.

Observing the force between wires As an example, consider two parallel wires. When the current flows in the same direction in both wires, the wires attract each other. If the currents go in opposite directions, the wires repel each other. For the amount of current in most electric circuits the forces are small, but can be seen with careful experiments. For example, if the wires are 1 meter long and each carries 100 amps of current (a lot), the force between them is 0.1 newton when the wires are 1 centimeter apart.

Current in the **same** direction

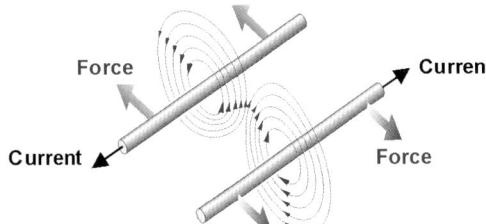
Current in **opposite** directions

Wires are **attracted** to each other Wires **repel** each other

Force on a current in a magnetic field The force between wires comes from the interaction of the magnetic field with moving current in the wire. A similar effect can be seen with a wire in any magnetic field. For example, Figure 23.3 shows a wire between two magnets. The wire feels a force when current is flowing. *The force is perpendicular to both the current and the magnetic field.* This is a new kind of behavior for a force. Magnetic forces between currents require you to work in all three dimensions because force, current, and magnetic field are all at right angles to one another.

The right-hand rule The direction of the force can be deduced from the right-hand rule. If you bend the fingers of your right hand as shown in Figure 23.4, your thumb, index, and middle finger indicate the directions of the force, current and magnetic field. It does not matter which finger (or thumb) is assigned to which of the three quantities. The rule works correctly as long as you use your *right* hand (not your left).

Force on a current in a magnetic field

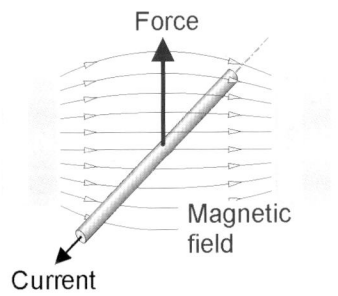

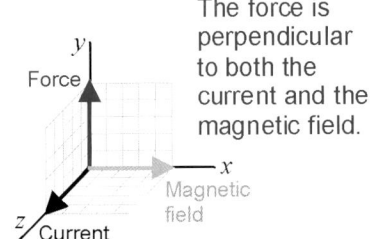
The force is perpendicular to both the current and the magnetic field.

Figure 23.3: *Forces on a current-carrying wire in a magnetic field.*

The right-hand rule
(for force, current, and field)

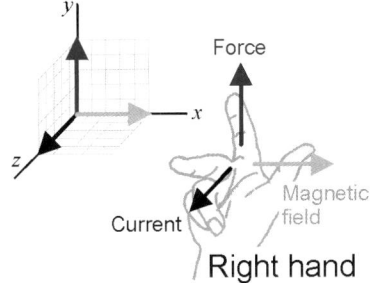
Right hand

Figure 23.4: *The right-hand rule for the direction of the force between a current and a magnetic field.*

The magnetic field of loops and coils

Making a strong magnetic field from current The magnetic field around a single wire is too small to be of much use. There are two techniques to make strong magnetic fields from current flowing in wires.

1. Many wires are bundled together, allowing the same current to create many times the magnetic field of a single wire.

2. Bundled wires are made into coils which concentrate the magnetic field in their center.

Bundling wires When wires are bundled, the total magnetic field is the sum of the fields created by the current in each individual wire. By wrapping the same wire around into a coil, current can be "reused" as many times as there are turns in the coil (Figure 23.5). This works because the current that creates the magnetic field is the *total current* crossing a surface perpendicular to the wire. It does not matter if the current is in one wire or 50 wires. For example, suppose a wire carries one amp of electric current. A coil with fifty turns of this wire creates the same magnetic field as a single wire with 50 amps of current. A coil with 50 turns is preferable since it is easier and safer to work with one amp than it is to work with 50 amps.

Coils and solenoids A coil concentrates the magnetic field at its center. When a wire is bent into a circular loop, field lines on the inside of the loop squeeze together. Field lines that are closer together indicate a higher magnetic field. Field lines on the outside of the coil spread apart, making the average field lower outside the coil than inside. The most common form of electromagnetic device is a coil with many turns (Figure 23.6) that is sometimes called a solenoid.

Where coils are used A coil takes advantage of these two techniques (bundling wires and making bundled wires into coils) for increasing field strength. Coils are used in electromagnets, speakers, electric motors, electric guitars, and almost every kind of electric appliance that has moving parts. As you will read in the next section, magnetic forces are the simplest way to make electric currents do mechanical work. Coils are the most efficient way to make a strong magnetic field with the least amount of current, which is why coils are found in so many electric appliances.

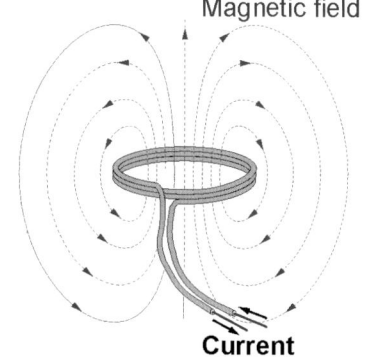

Figure 23.5: *The magnetic field of a coil of wire carrying a current.*

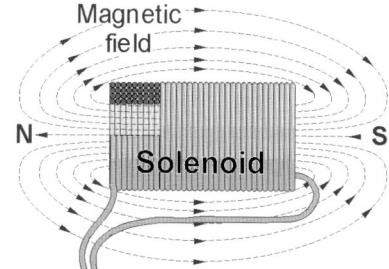

Figure 23.6: *A solenoid is a tubular coil of wire with many turns. The upper left corner of the solenoid in the diagram has been cut away to show the arrangement of wires.*

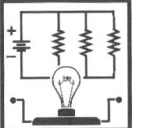

The true nature of magnetism

Coils and permanent magnets

The magnetic field of a coil and the magnetic field of a cylindrical magnet are identical (Figure 23.7). Both have a north and south pole and both have the same shape of field lines. In fact, if all you could measure was the magnetic field itself, you could not tell whether it was made by current flowing in a coil or by a permanent magnet.

Permanent magnets and atomic currents

Permanent magnets and electromagnets create the same magnetic field because *magnetism is fundamentally an effect created by electric current.* Remember, from the last chapter, that the magnetism of individual atoms creates the magnetic field of a permanent magnet. Now we can see why atoms themselves are magnetic. The electrons moving around the nucleus carry electric charge. Moving charge makes electric current so the electrons around the nucleus create currents within an atom. These currents create the magnetic fields that determine the magnetic properties of atoms.

How atomic currents add up

When the current from many atoms is all in the same direction (Figure 23.8), the atoms act like a single large loop of current. The magnetic fields from each atom add up to make a single, larger magnetic field, as if the atoms were replaced by a coil carrying the loop current. The magnetic field of a permanent magnet is the sum of individual fields from trillions and trillions of individual atoms.

Not all atoms are magnetic

All matter is not normally magnetic for several reasons. First, atoms heavier than hydrogen contain many electrons. The current from each electron in the same atom is *not* usually in the same direction. In fact, in most atoms the currents created by individual electrons almost completely cancel each other out. For every electron making clockwise current, there is one making counterclockwise current. As a result, the majority of atoms contain zero net current, and therefore do not have a magnetic field.

Why only some materials are magnetic

The second reason most matter is not magnetic is that the currents in neighboring atoms do not line up. One single atom might be magnetic, but it is neutralized by the magnetic atom next to it—which is pointing in the opposite direction. Only the ferromagnetic elements (iron, nickel, cobalt, etc.) have both magnetic atoms and a tendency for neighboring atoms to align their magnetic poles.

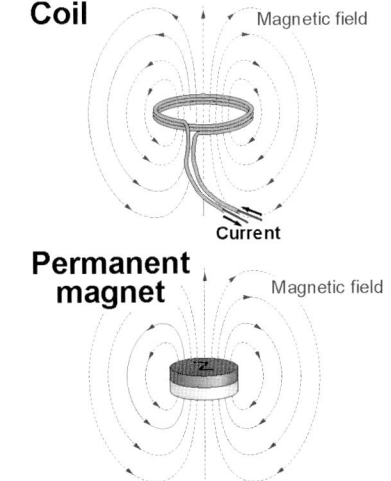

Figure 23.7: *The magnetic field of a coil is identical to the field of a disk-shaped permanent magnet.*

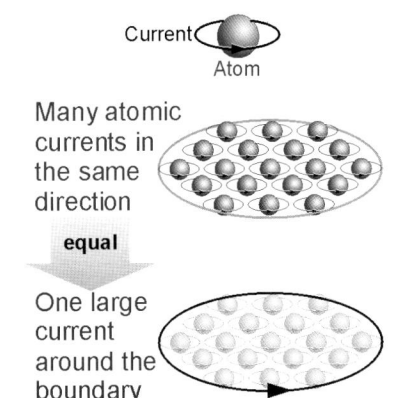

Figure 23.8: *Atoms with their currents oriented the same way act like one large coil of wire carrying current in the same direction of rotation.*

The magnetic force on a moving charge

Magnetic force on a moving charge The magnetic force on a wire is really due to force acting on moving charges in the wire. A charge moving in a magnetic field feels a force perpendicular to both the magnetic field and to the direction of motion of the charge.

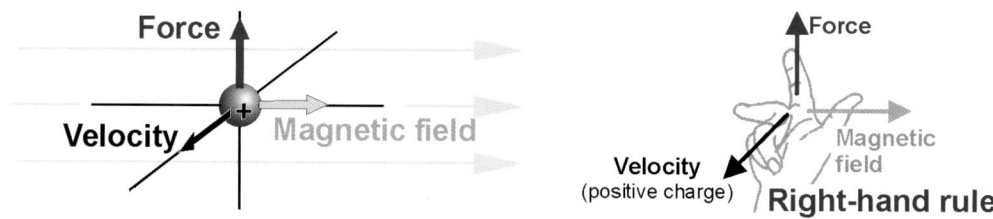

The tesla, a unit of magnetic field The strength of the force depends on the strength of the field, the charge, and the speed at which the charge is moving. A magnetic field that has a strength of 1 tesla (1 T) creates a force of 1 newton (1 N) on a charge of 1 coulomb (1 C) moving at 1 meter per second. This relationship is how the unit of magnetic field is defined. Since one coulomb per second is the same as one amp, the relationship is usually written in terms of amps and meters instead of coulombs and m/sec. In this form, the equation says a 1 T magnetic field exerts 1 N of force on a current of 1 A flowing for 1 meter perpendicular to the magnetic field.

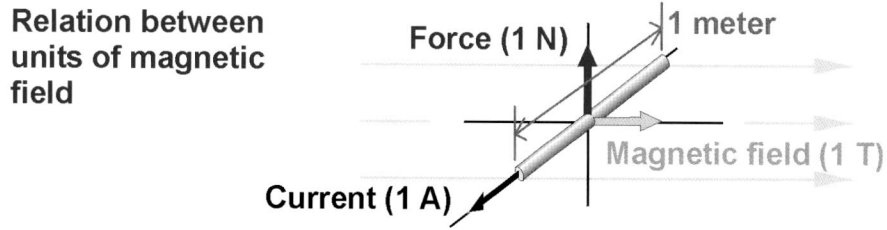

Tesla, gauss, and typical field strengths One tesla is a *very* strong magnetic field. The **gauss**, another common unit for magnetic field is much smaller; 10,000 gauss equal one tesla. The magnetic field of the Earth is about one-half gauss, or 5×10^{-5} T. The field near a strong permanent magnet can be as high as 0.3 T. The strongest electromagnets ever created have reached fields of 100 teslas for a fraction of a second.

Making charges orbit

In Chapter 8, you learned that forces perpendicular to velocity create circular motion. This is also true for charges in magnetic fields. A charge moving perpendicular to a magnetic field moves in a circular orbit.

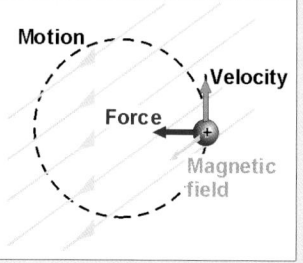

A charge moving at an angle to a magnetic field moves in a spiral.

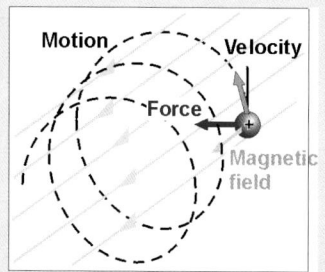

Magnetic forces are used to deflect the electron beam in a television (Chapter 22) and in other applications that use moving electric charge.

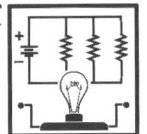

Calculating magnetic fields and forces

Magnetic fields and forces are complex calculations

Magnetic fields are three-dimensional and are created by magnetic domains or currents distributed in three-dimensional objects. Except for a few simple cases, the calculations are difficult and beyond the scope of this book. The calculation of magnetic forces is even harder because forces come from interactions between the field and magnetic domains or currents throughout the volume of a object. These types of calculations are usually done by computer programs.

The field of a straight wire

The field of a straight wire is proportional to the current in the wire and inversely proportional to the radius from the wire. The field lines make concentric circles with a direction given by the right-hand rule.

Magnetic field near a wire

$$\underset{\text{field (T)}}{\overset{\text{Magnetic}}{}} \vec{B} = 2 \times 10^{-7} \, \frac{\overset{\text{Current (A)}}{I}}{\underset{\text{Radius (m)}}{R}}$$

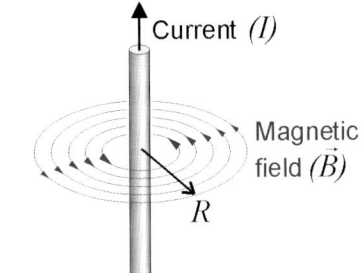

Current *(I)*

Magnetic field *(B̄)*

R

The field at the center of a coil

The magnetic field at the center of a coil comes from the whole circumference of the coil. As a result, the field is a factor of π times larger (π ≈ 3.14) than the field of a straight wire. If the coil has N turns, the magnetic field at the center is multiplied by N. For example, a coil of 25 turns will have a magnetic field 25 times stronger than a coil of one turn.

Magnetic field at the center of a coil

$$\underset{\text{field (T)}}{\overset{\text{Magnetic}}{}} \vec{B} = 2\pi \times 10^{-7} \, \frac{\overset{\text{Turns (#)}\quad\text{Current (A)}}{NI}}{\underset{\text{Radius of coil (m)}}{R}}$$

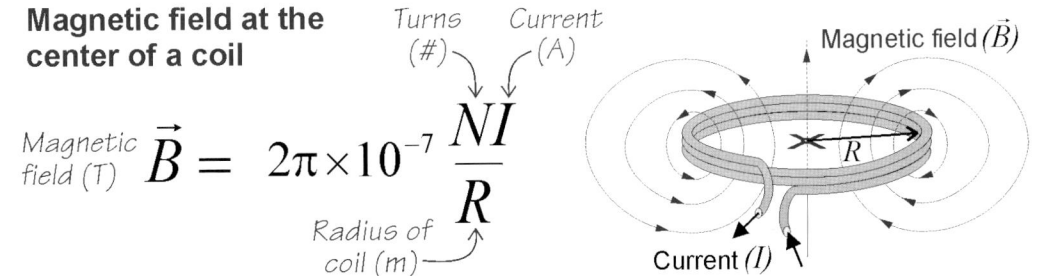

Magnetic field *(B̄)*

R

Current *(I)*

Calculate the magnetic field at the center of a coil

A current of 2 amps flows in a coil made from 400 turns of very thin wire. The radius of the coil is 1 centimeter. Calculate the strength of magnetic field (in tesla) at the center of the coil.

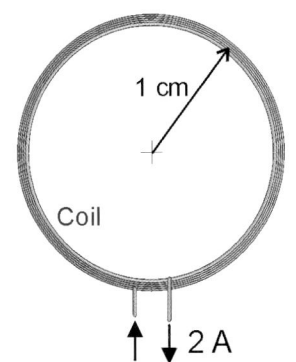

1 cm

Coil

2 A

1) You are asked for the magnetic field in tesla.
2) You are given the current, radius, and number of turns.
3) Use the formula for the field of a coil: B = 2π × 10⁻⁷ NI ÷ R
4) Solve:

B = (2π × 10⁻⁷)(400)(2A) ÷ (.01m)
  = 0.05 T

23.2 Electromagnets and the Electric Motor

Magnets made with electric current are called electromagnets, and they are the subject of this section. Electromagnets are very useful in many technologies because they can be made much stronger than permanent magnets, and can be switched on and off. The magnetic poles of an electromagnet can even be reversed. This section will also show you how electromagnets work in electric motors, generators, and many familiar devices.

Electromagnets

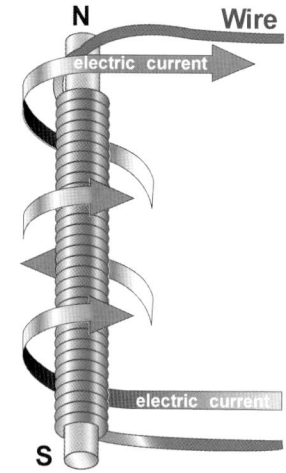

Figure 23.9: *A simple electromagnet is a coil of wire wrapped around a rod of iron or steel.*

A coil of wire   Electromagnets are magnets that are created when electric current flows in a coil of wire. The simplest electromagnet uses a coil of wire, often wrapped around an iron core (Figure 23.9). Because iron is magnetic, it concentrates and amplifies the magnetic field created by the current in the coil.

The poles of an electromagnet   The north and south poles of an electromagnet are located at each end of the coil (Figure 23.9). Which end is the north pole depends on the direction of the electric current. When your fingers curl in the direction of current, your thumb points toward the magnet's north pole. This method of finding the magnetic poles is another example of the *right-hand rule* (Figure 23.10*)*. You can switch the north and south poles of an electromagnet by reversing the direction of the current in the coil. This is a great advantage over permanent magnets.

Current and the strength of an electromagnet   Electromagnets have advantages over permanent magnets and are more useful in many applications. By changing the amount of current in an electromagnet, you can easily change its strength or even turn its magnetism on and off. Electromagnets can also be designed to be much stronger than permanent magnets by using a large amount of electric current.

The electromagnet in a toaster   Toasters use electromagnets. The sliding switch on a toaster both turns on the heating circuit and sends current to an electromagnet. The electromagnet attracts a spring-loaded metal tray to the bottom of the toaster. When a timing device signals that the bread has been toasting long enough, current to the electromagnet is cut off. This releases the spring-loaded tray, which then pushes up on the bread so that it pops out of the toaster.

The right-hand rule

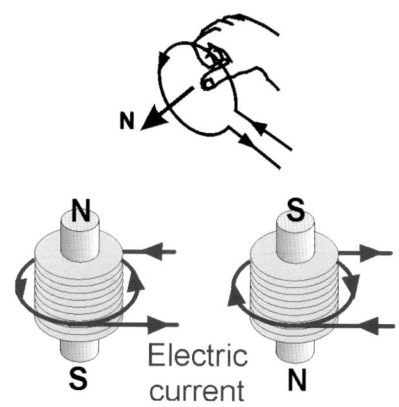

Figure 23.10: *The right-hand rule: When your fingers curl in the direction of current, your thumb points toward the magnet's north pole.*

Building an electromagnet

Wire and a nail You can easily build an electromagnet from wire and a piece of iron, such as a nail. Wrap the wire snugly around the nail many times and connect a battery as shown in Figure 23.11. When current flows in the wire, the nail becomes a magnet. Use the right-hand rule to figure out which end of the nail is the north pole and which is the south pole. To reverse north and south, reverse the connection to the battery, making the current flow the opposite way.

Increase the electromagnet's strength You might expect that more current would make an electromagnet stronger. This is correct, and it can be achieved in two ways:

1   You can apply more voltage by adding a second battery.

2   You can add more turns of wire around the nail, while using only one battery.

Why adding turns works The second method works because the magnetism in your electromagnet comes from the *total* amount of current flowing *around* the nail (Figure 23.12). If there is 1 ampere of current in the wire, each loop of wire adds 1 ampere to the total amount that flows around the nail. Ten loops of 1 ampere each make 10 total amperes flowing around. By adding more turns, you use the same current over and over to get stronger magnetism.

Resistance Of course, nothing comes for free. By adding more turns you also increase the resistance of your coil. Increasing the resistance makes the current a little lower and generates more heat. A good electromagnet strikes a balance between having enough turns to make the magnet strong and not having so many turns that the resistance is too high.

Factors affecting the field The magnetic field created by a simple electromagnet depends on three factors:

*   The amount of electric current in the wire.
*   The amount and type of material in the electromagnet's core.
*   The number of turns in the coil.

In more sophisticated electromagnets, the shape, size, material in the core, and winding pattern of the coil each can be changed to control the strength of the magnetic field produced.

A simple electromagnet

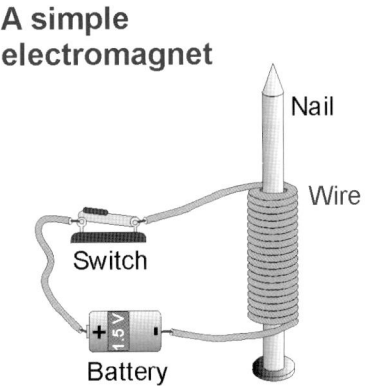

Figure 23.11: *Making an electromagnet from a nail, wire, and a battery.*

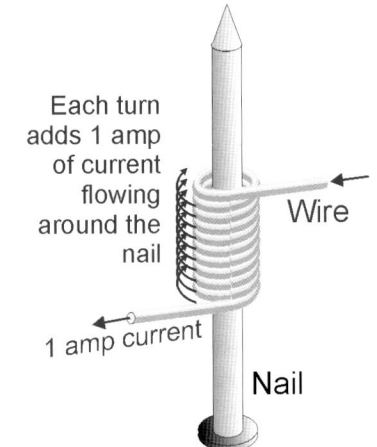

Figure 23.12: *Adding turns of wire increases the total current flowing around the electromagnet. The total current in all the turns is what determines the strength of the electromagnet.*

The principle of the electric motor

| Imagine a spinning disk with magnets | An electric motor uses electromagnets to convert electrical energy into mechanical energy. One set of magnets rotates around the axis of the motor and turns the shaft. The other set of magnets is stationary and does not rotate. The stationary set of magnets pushes and pulls on the rotating magnets to turn the motor. |

To see how this works, imagine a disk that is free to spin. Around the edge of the disk are permanent magnets arranged so their north and south poles alternate facing outward. Figure 23.13 is a diagram of this rotating disk.

| How to make the disk spin | The south pole of another magnet is now brought near the disk. The new magnet attracts the north pole of magnet (B) and repels the south pole of magnet (A). These forces make the disk spin a small distance counterclockwise. |

| Reversing the magnet is the key | To keep the disk spinning, the external magnet must be reversed as soon as magnet (B) passes by. Once the magnet has been reversed, magnet (B) will now be repelled and magnet (C) will be attracted. As a result of the push-pull, the disk continues to rotate counterclockwise. |

| The principle of an electric motor | The disk will keep spinning as long as the external magnet is reversed every time the next magnet in the disk passes by. This is the operating principle of the electric motor. One or more stationary magnets reverse their poles to push and pull on a rotating assembly of magnets. In the example, permanent magnets are used. In an actual electric motor, one or both sets of magnets (rotating and stationary) are electromagnets. |

| Knowing when to reverse the magnet | The disk is called the *rotor* because it can rotate. The key to making the rotor spin smoothly is to reverse the polarity of the stationary magnet when the disk is in the right position. The reversal should occur just as a rotor magnet passes by. If the reversal comes too early, the rotor magnet is repelled before it reaches the stationary magnet. If the reversal is too late, the stationary magnet attracts the rotor magnet backwards after it has passed. For the highest efficiency, the switching of the stationary magnet must be synchronized with the passage of each magnet in the rotor. |

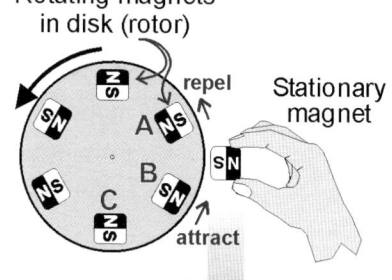

Reverse the polarity of the stationary magnet.

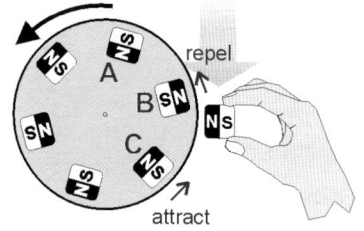

Figure 23.13: *Using a single magnet to spin a disk of magnets. Reversing the magnet in your fingers attracts and repels the magnets in the rotor, making it spin.*

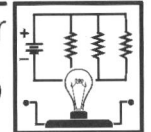
Commutation

How electromagnets are used in electric motors

In some electric motors, an electromagnet replaces the permanent magnet that was reversed by flipping it around. The switch from north to south is done by reversing the electric current in the coil. The sketch below shows how the electromagnet keeps the rotor spinning.

First the electromagnet repels magnet A and attracts magnet B

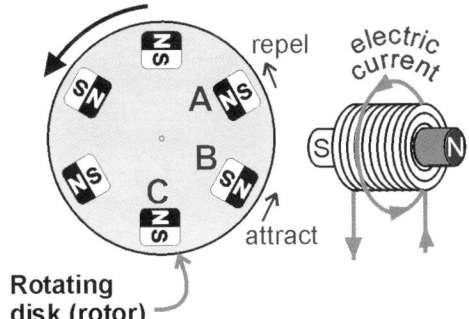

Rotating disk (rotor)

Then the electromagnet switches so it repels magnet B and attracts magnet C.

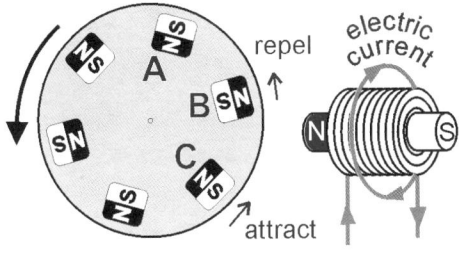

Blender

Laptop computer

The commutator is a kind of switch

The electromagnet must switch from north to south as each magnet in the rotor passes by. The process of reversing the current in the electromagnet is called commutation and the switch that makes it happen is called a *commutator*. As the rotor spins, the commutator switches the direction of current in the electromagnet. This makes the side of the electromagnet facing the rotor change polarity from north to south and back again. The electromagnet alternately attracts and repels the magnets in the rotor, and the motor turns.

The three things you need to make a motor

Electric motors are very common (Figure 23.14). All types of electric motors have three key components. The components are:

1 A rotating element (rotor) with magnets.

2 A stationary magnet that surrounds the rotor.

3 A commutator that switches the electromagnets from north to south at the right place to keep the rotor spinning.

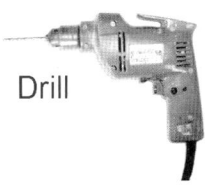

Drill

Figure 23.14: *There are electric motors all around you, even where you do not see them. These three common devices all use electric motors. Question: where are the electric motors in a laptop computer? All laptops have at least one and some have several.*

How a battery-powered electric motor works

Inside a small electric motor

If you take apart an electric motor that runs on batteries, it does not look like the motor you built in the lab. The same three mechanisms are there; the difference is in the arrangement of the electromagnets and permanent magnets. The picture below shows a small battery-powered electric motor and what it looks like inside with one end of the motor case removed. The permanent magnets are on the outside, and they stay fixed in place.

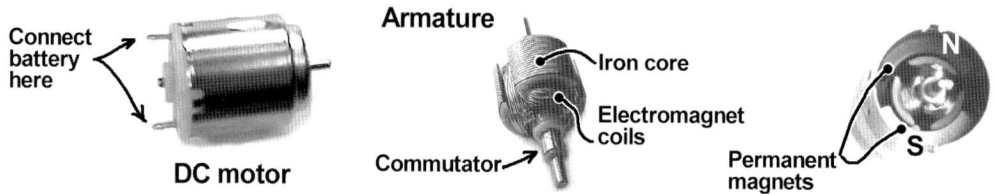

Electromagnets and the armature

The electromagnets are in the rotor, and they turn. The rotating part of the motor, including the electromagnets, is called the *armature*. The armature in the picture above has three electromagnets, corresponding to the three coils (A, B, and C) in the sketch below.

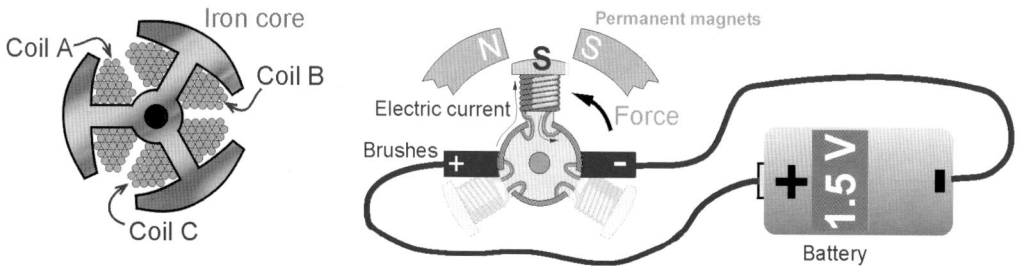

How the switching happens

The wires from each of the three coils are attached to three metal plates (commutator) at the end of the armature. As the rotor spins, the three plates come into contact with the positive and negative *brushes*. Electric current flows through the brushes into the coils. As the motor turns, the plates rotate past the brushes, switching the electromagnets from north to south by reversing the positive and negative connections to the coils. The turning electromagnets are attracted and repelled by the permanent magnets and the motor turns.

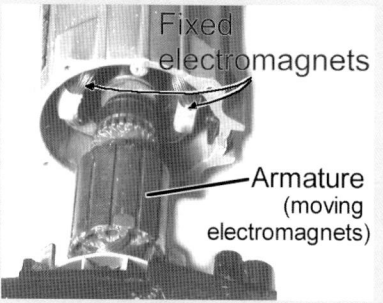

23.3 Induction and the Electric Generator

Motors transform electrical energy into mechanical energy. Electric generators do the opposite. They transform mechanical energy into electrical energy. In this section you will learn how generators produce electricity. You will learn an example of the important principle of *symmetry* in physics.

Electromagnetic induction

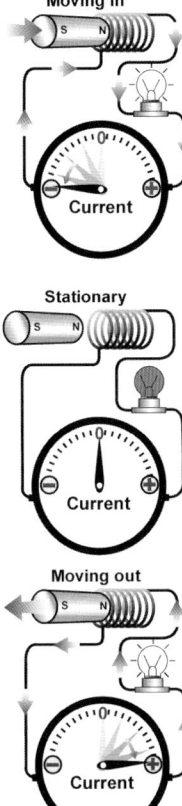

Moving in

Stationary

Moving out

Figure 23.15: *A moving magnet produces a current in a coil of wire.*

Magnetism and electricity
A current flowing through a wire creates a magnetic field. The reverse is also true. If you move a magnet near a coil of wire, a current will be produced. This process is called electromagnetic induction, because a moving magnet *induces* electric current to flow.

Symmetry in physics
Many laws in physics display *symmetry.* When a physical law is symmetric, a process described by the law works in both directions. Earlier in this chapter you learned that moving electric charge creates magnetism. The symmetry is that changing magnetic fields also cause electric charge to move. Nearly all physical laws display symmetry of one form or another.

Current flows as the magnet moves into the coil
Figure 23.15 shows an example of an experiment demonstrating electromagnetic induction. In the experiment, a magnet can move in and out of a coil of wire. The coil is attached to an ammeter that measures the electric current produced. When the magnet moves into the coil of wire, *as it is moving,* electric current is induced in the coil and the ammeter swings to the left. The current stops if the magnet stops moving.

Current reverses as the magnet moves out
When the magnet is pulled back out again, *as it is moving,* current is induced in the opposite direction. The ammeter swings to the right as the magnet is moving out. Again, if the magnet stops moving, the current also stops.

Current is induced only by changing magnetic fields
Current is only produced if the magnet is moving because a *changing* magnetic field is what creates current. Moving magnets induce current because they create changing magnetic fields. If the magnetic field does not change, such as when the magnet is stationary, the current is zero. If the magnetic field is *increasing,* the induced current is in one direction. If the field is *decreasing,* the induced current is in the opposite direction.

Magnetic flux

Not all moving magnets induce current
Suppose an inventor overhears the story about moving magnets making electricity. The inventor gets a magnet and sets up a coil of wire and an ammeter. The inventor shakes the magnet up and down, throws it around the room, moves it every which way (Figure 23.16). But, the experiment does not work. No current is measured by the ammeter.

Magnetic field lines
A moving magnet induces current in a coil *only if* the magnetic field of the magnet passes through the coil. If a magnet is far away, its field does not pass through the coil and no amount of motion will cause current to flow. The closer the magnet is, the more of its magnetic field is linked through the coil, and the stronger the induced current.

Magnetic flux
Recall that magnetic field lines point outward from the north pole of a bar magnet and loop around to the south pole. If a coil of wire is placed near the north pole of a bar magnet, many of the magnet's field lines pass through the coil. The magnetic flux *through* the coil is a measure of the amount of the magnetic field lines encircled by the coil (Figure 23.17). The magnetic flux depends on the size of the coil, its orientation, and the strength of the magnetic field. A coil can enclose more flux if it is larger, has more turns, or if the magnetic field is stronger. Note, the flux has to go *through* the coil, not past it. A coil that is parallel to the field does *not* capture any flux because the field lines are not enclosed by the coil.

Changing flux causes current to flow
It is the change in *magnetic flux* through a coil that induces current to flow. You can think of magnetic flux as the amount of magnetic field *linking* the magnet and the coil. If the magnetic flux increases, current flows in one direction. If the flux decreases, current flows in the opposite direction.

Faraday's law of induction
The amount of current depends on the rate at which the magnetic flux changes. The greater the rate of change of flux, the greater the current. This relationship is known as Faraday's law of induction. When you move a magnet into or out of a loop of wire during the process of electromagnetic induction, you create a current by changing the magnetic flux through the loop. The faster you move the magnet, the greater the rate of change of the flux, and the greater the current.

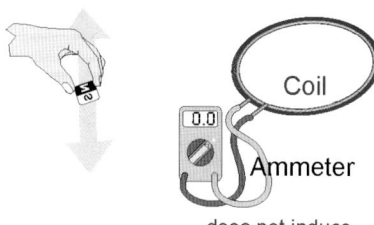

Moving a magnet up and down here ...

... does not induce current to flow in a coil that is far away.

Figure 23.16: *Moving a magnet far from a coil does not create much (if any) induced current in the coil.*

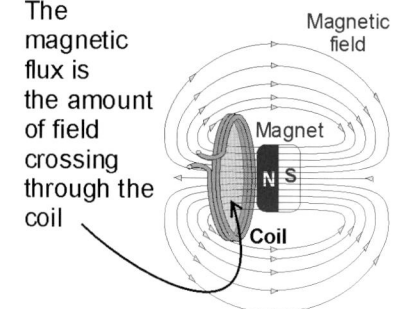

The magnetic flux is the amount of field crossing through the coil

Magnetic field

Magnet

Coil

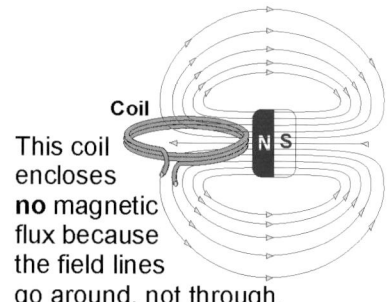

Coil

This coil encloses **no** magnetic flux because the field lines go around, not through.

Figure 23.17: *The magnetic flux through a loop of wire depends on the size of the loop and the strength of the magnetic field.*

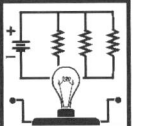

Faraday's law of induction

Faraday's law

Faraday's law says the current in a coil is proportional to the rate at which the magnetic field passing through the coil (the flux) changes. To make sense of this law, consider a coil of wire rotating between two magnets (Figure 23.18).

The induced current in a coil rotating through a magnetic field

When the coil is in position (A), the magnetic flux points from left to right. As the coil rotates (B), the number of field lines that go through the coil decreases. As a result, the flux starts to decrease and current flows in a negative direction.

At position (C), the largest negative current flows because the *rate of change* in flux is greatest. The graph of flux versus time has the steepest slope at position (C), and that is why the current is largest. Remember, current is proportional to the rate of change of flux, not flux itself. In fact, at position (C), no magnetic field lines are passing through the coil at all and therefore the flux through it is *zero*.

As the coil continues to rotate (D), flux is still decreasing by getting more negative. Current flows in the same direction, but decreases proportionally to the decreasing rate of change (the slope of flux versus time levels out). At position (E), the flux through the coil reaches its most negative value. The slope of the flux versus time graph is zero and the current is zero. As the coil rotates through (F), the flux starts increasing and current flows in the opposite direction.

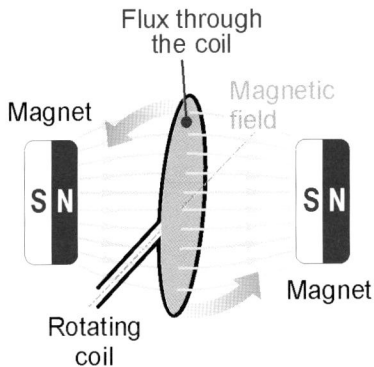

Figure 23.18: *A rotating coil in a magnetic field provides a demonstration of Faraday's law. The flux through the coil is the amount of magnetic field passing through the area enclosed by the coil.*

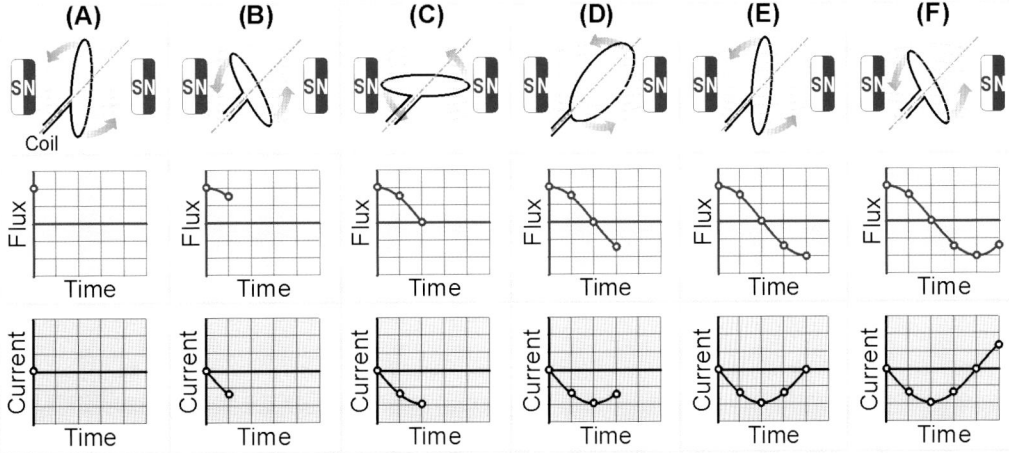

Energy conservation and Faraday's law

The electric current produced by induction does not create electrical energy from nothing. The induced current makes its own magnetic field that opposes the rotation of the coil. Because of the coil's own field, it takes force to make the coil rotate. The electrical energy created by a rotating coil can never exceed the work done to make the coil turn.

Generating electricity by induction

How a generator makes electricity A generator is a device that uses induction to convert mechanical energy into electrical energy. An effective laboratory generator can be made from a spinning disk with magnets in it. As the disk rotates, first a north pole and then a south pole pass the coil. When a north pole is approaching, the current flows one way. When the north pole passes and a south pole approaches, the current flows the other way. As long as the disk is spinning, there is a changing magnetic flux through the coil and electric current is induced to flow.

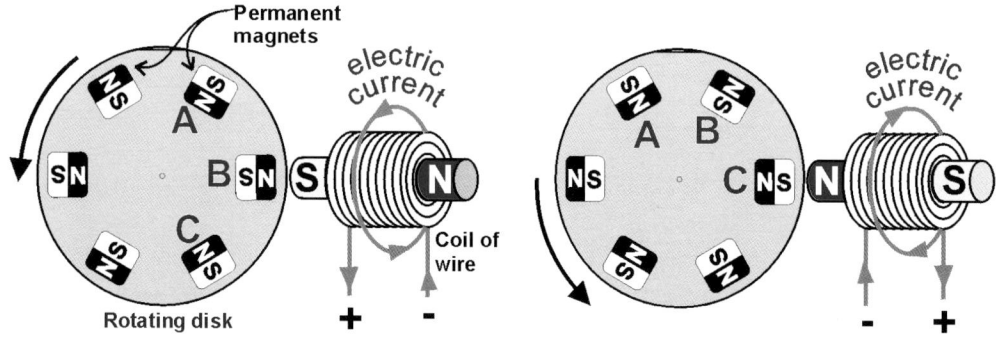

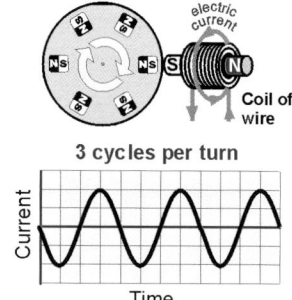

6 magnets in rotating disk

3 cycles per turn

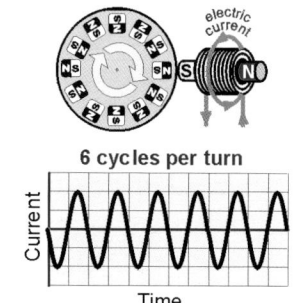

12 magnets in rotating disk

6 cycles per turn

Figure 23.19: *The frequency of the AC current depends on how many times per second the field reverses.*

Alternating current Because the magnet near the coil alternates from north to south as the disk spins, the direction of the current reverses every time a magnet passes the coil. *This creates an alternating current.* The frequency of the alternating current is the frequency at which magnets pass the coil (Figure 23.19). Generators are the source of alternating current that is supplied to your home.

Energy for generators The electrical energy created by a generator is not created from nothing. Work must be done to move the magnets that produce the current. Power plants contain a rotating machine called a *turbine* (Figure 23.20). The turbine is kept turning by a flow of expanding air or steam heated by gas, oil, coal, or nuclear energy. The energy stored in the gas, oil, coal, or nuclear fuel is transformed into the kinetic energy of the turning turbine, which is then transformed into electrical energy by the generator. Windmills and hydroelectric dams use energy from wind and water to turn the turbines that turn the generators and produce electricity.

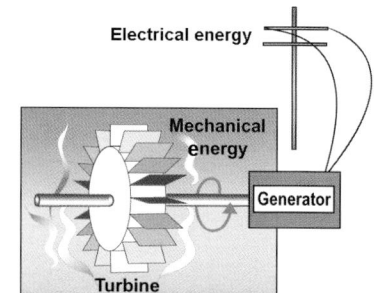

Figure 23.20: *A power plant generator contains a turbine that turns magnets inside loops of wire, generating electricity.*

Transformers

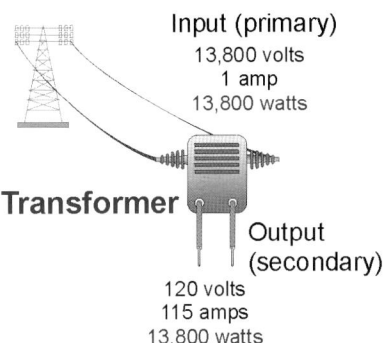

Electricity is transmitted at high-voltage

From the perspective of physics, it makes sense to distribute electricity from a generator to homes using very high voltage. For example, high-voltage power lines carry current at 13,800 volts. Since power is current × voltage, that means each amp of current carries 13,800 watts of power. The problem is, you would not want 13,800 volts coming to your wall outlet. With a voltage this high, you probably would not *survive* plugging in an appliance!

Figure 23.21: *A high power transformer can reduce the voltage keeping the power constant.*

Electric power transformers

The voltage that appears in the outlet in your wall is 120 V AC. The device that steps down the voltage from the power line to 120 volts is called a transformer. Transformers are extremely useful because they efficiently change voltage and current, while providing the same total power. for example, a transformer can take one amp at 13,800 volts and convert it to 115 amps at 120 volts (Figure 23.21).

Transformers operate on electromagnetic induction

The transformer uses electromagnetic induction, similar to a generator. Figure 23.22 shows what a transformer looks like inside its case. You may have seen one inside a doorbell or an AC adapter. The two coils are called the *primary* and *secondary* coils. The input to the transformer is connected to the primary coil. The output of the transformer is connected to the secondary coil. The two coils are wound around a steel core. The steel acts to channel and amplify the magnetic flux, which couples the two coils.

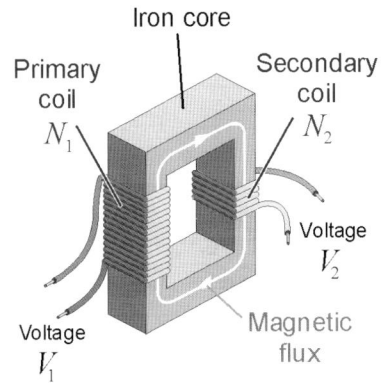

How the two coils work

Consider what happens when current is increasing in the primary coil. This creates an increasing magnetic flux through the secondary coil. The increasing flux in the secondary induces current to flow through any circuit connected to the output of the transformer. The useful characteristic of transformers is that *the two coils can have a different number of turns*. For example, suppose the primary coil has 100 turns and the secondary coil has 10 turns. Because the secondary has fewer turns, each amp of current that flows in the primary induces 10 times the current to flow in the secondary! The ratio of voltage is inverse to the ratio of current. If 100 V is applied to the primary, only 10 V appears on the secondary.

Voltage relationship

$$\frac{V_2}{V_1} = \frac{N_2}{N_1}$$

Turns of secondary

Turns of primary

Transformers only work with AC

Transformers only work with AC current. Remember, the rate of change of magnetic flux is what induces current to flow. The current must go up and down in the primary coil in order to keep the magnetic flux changing in the secondary coil.

Figure 23.22: *The relationship between voltages and turns for a transformer.*

Application: Trains That Float by Magnetic Levitation

Friction and wear take an expensive toll on vehicles. The cost is both in fuel efficiency and in maintenance. Mass transit vehicles such as trains operate seven days a week. If you drove an ordinary car 500 miles per day, every day, you would reach the 100,000 mile life of a typical car in seven months! Magnetic levitation (abbreviated maglev) trains float many centimeters above the track. Wear is almost eliminated because there are few moving parts that carry heavy loads. Friction is greatly reduced, thereby increasing fuel economy. Many engineers believe maglev technology will become the standard for mass transit systems over the next 100 years.

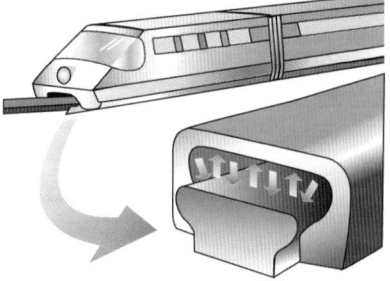

Figure 23.23: *A maglev train track has electromagnets in it that both lift the train and pull it forward.*

Magnetically levitated trains Maglev train technology uses electromagnetic force to lift the train 10-20 cm above the track (Figure 23.23). Depending on the design, magnets are used in the train, track, or both train and track. The track and train repel each other through powerful magnetic fields. The train "floats" on a nearly frictionless cushion of magnetic force. Although air friction is still present, friction between wheel and rail is eliminated. Because of reduced friction, maglev trains reach high speeds using less power than a normal train. In 1999, in Japan, a prototype five-car maglev carrying 15 passengers reached a record speed of 552 kilometers (343 miles) per hour. Maglev trains are now being developed and tested in Germany and the United States as well.

Electromagnet-based maglev Two different approaches are being used to develop maglev technology. One approach uses electromagnets on either the train or the track, or both. Powered magnets are necessary to get the high lift needed for the fastest speeds. This type of maglev is being tested for long-distance runs between cities or across continents. Unfortunately, powered tracks are very expensive to construct and use a great deal of electricity.

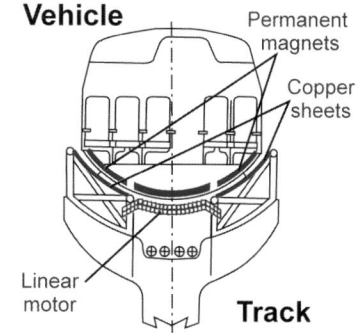

Figure 23.24: *The Magplane uses permanent magnets to levitate the vehicle.*

Permanent-magnet maglev A second approach uses permanent magnets in the train and relies on the *eddy current* effect in the track to create lift. This approach is simpler, more reliable, and better suited for urban areas where extreme high speed is not necessary. The best developed example of the permanent magnet approach is the Magplane (Figure 23.24). Developed by Dr. D. Bruce Montgomery at Massachusetts Institute of Technology, the Magplane borrows from aircraft technology as it banks and rolls into turns using spoilers and wing surfaces for control.

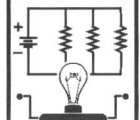

How the Magplane levitates

Eddy currents To understand the eddy current effect, consider the following experiment. A magnet is dropped down a copper tube and a cardboard tube of the same size. The magnet in the copper tube falls slower than the magnet in the cardboard tube. As the magnet falls, a ring of copper tube ahead of the magnet sees an increasing magnetic field. In accordance with Faraday's law, an induced current flows around the copper, making a temporary electromagnet. The magnetic field of the induced current pushes on the falling magnet, slowing it down (Figure 23.25). The currents induced in the copper tube are called *eddy currents*. An eddy current is a circular current flowing in a solid conductor in a changing magnetic field.

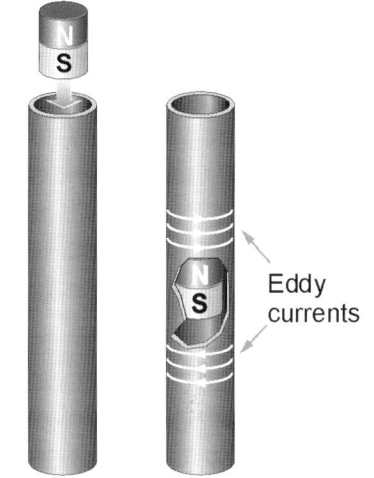

Figure 23.25: *An experiment to demonstrate eddy currents. The falling magnet is slowed by the magnetic field it creates by inducing eddy currents in the pipe.*

How eddy currents lift the Magplane The underside of a Magplane contains powerful permanent magnets. The surface of the Magplane track is made from curved copper sheets (Figure 23.26). As the Magplane moves forward, eddy currents are induced to flow in the copper sheets on the track. The eddy currents create a magnetic field that pushes against the field of the permanent magnets and lifts the train off the track. The faster the train moves, the more powerful the induced eddy currents become, and the higher the train floats off the track. The Magplane is a very elegant technology because it requires no moving parts and no power supplies for either the train or the track.

The drive system of Magplane Of course, the train has to be kept moving or the eddy currents will not flow. In the center of the track are a set of electromagnet coils arranged as a linear motor. The coils push and pull on a set of permanent magnets along a line running down the center of the Magplane's underside. As with an ordinary electric motor, the polarity of the electromagnets in the track switches in a controlled rhythm which drives the Magplane forward and can accelerate or decelerate the vehicle.

Stopping and starting When picking up or discharging passengers, the Magplane rides on wheels, like a bus. The wheels are also used at very slow speeds during starting and stopping. Once the Magplane gets going above a speed of 10 miles per hour, the eddy current forces from the track become strong enough to gently lift the train off its wheels. During most of its operation, the Magplane is truly flying over the track with a much smoother and quieter ride than any aircraft.

Figure 23.26: *The Magplane: vehicle and track.*

Chapter 23 Review

Vocabulary Review

Match the following terms with the correct definition. There is one extra definition in the list that will not match any of the terms.

Set One

1. commutator
2. electromagnetic induction
3. electromagnet
4. armature

a. The process by which a changing magnetic field causes electric current to flow
b. A rotating part of an electric motor that contains electromagnets
c. A switch that makes an electromagnet's poles reverse
d. The part of an electric motor that holds the armature
e. A magnet created by electric current flowing in a coil of wire

Set Two

1. magnetic flux
2. generator
3. electric motor
4. right hand rule

a. Used to determine the location of an electromagnet's north pole if the direction of current is known
b. A device that uses electromagnetic induction to change mechanical energy into electrical energy
c. A device that changes electrical energy into mechanical energy
d. A device that switches alternating current to direct current
e. The amount of magnetic field crossing a certain surface area.

Set Three

1. magnetic field
2. Faraday's law
3. transformer
4. solenoid
5. gauss

a. Exists in the region around a magnet
b. A unit in which the strength of a magnetic field is measured
c. A unit for measuring voltage in a coil
d. A cylindrical coil of wire with many turns
e. The current induced in a coil depends on the rate of change of magnetic flux through the coil
f. Steps down AC voltage from the power lines to your house

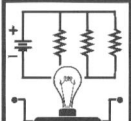
Concept review

1. What is created by a moving electric charge?

2. When the right hand rule is used to find the direction of the magnetic field near a current carrying wire, your thumb points in the direction of the _____ and your fingers wrap in the direction of the _____.

3. Two parallel wires carry current. When the currents run in the same direction, the wires _____ each other; when the currents run in opposite directions, the wires _____ each other.

4. Where does a coil concentrate its magnetic field?

5. When a charge moves through a magnetic field, it experiences a force. On what three things does the size of the force depend?

6. When a charge moves through a magnetic field, how can the direction of the force be determined?

7. A charge that enters perpendicular to a magnetic field will move in a _____; a charge that enters at an angle to a magnetic field will move in a _____.

8. Name two units used for measuring the strength of a magnetic field. Which unit represents a stronger field?

9. What is an electromagnet?

10. Why are electromagnets frequently used instead of permanent magnets?

11. List three devices that contain electromagnets.

12. How can you determine where an electromagnet's north pole is located?

13. Make a diagram of an electromagnet. Indicate the direction of the current and the location of the north and south poles.

14. How can you make an electromagnet stronger?

15. An electric motor uses electromagnets to convert _____ energy into _____ energy.

16. List three main components of an electric motor.

17. What happens to the poles of the electromagnet in a motor as the rotor spins? Why must this happen?

18. What is electromagnetic induction?

19. What happens if the strength of a magnetic field in the region around a wire changes?

20. If a magnet is held still near a coil of wire, will it cause current to flow? Why or why not?

21. A permanent magnet is held near a loop of wire, creating a magnetic flux through the loop. List two ways the flux through the wire can be changed.

22. A generator converts _____ energy into _____ energy.

23. Explain the function of a transformer.

Problems

1. A wire is oriented vertically in a region of space. Current flows from the top of the wire toward the bottom. Imagine looking down on the wire. Use the right hand rule to determine whether the magnetic field is directed clockwise or counterclockwise around the wire.

2. Imagine that a magnetic field exists on the page of your textbook, directed from right to left. A positive charge moves from the top of the page toward the bottom of the page. Use the right hand rule to determine the direction of the force exerted on the moving charge.

3. Calculate the size of the magnetic field that exists at a distance of 5 cm from a straight wire carrying 1 A of current.

4. A coil of wire has 25 turns, each with a radius of 2 cm. If the coil carries 3 A of current, what is the strength of the magnetic field at its center?

5. The electromagnet in a motor has its north pole facing the rotor at the instant shown in the diagram. In which direction is the rotor spinning?

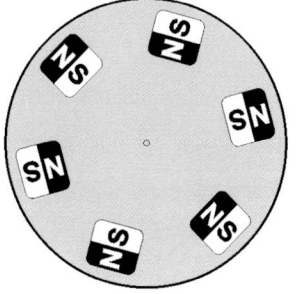
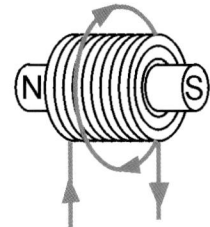

6. Some electric toothbrushes contain rechargeable batteries that are charged by placing the toothbrush on a plastic charging base. Because both the bottom of the toothbrush and the base are made of an insulating material, current does not flow from the base to the toothbrush. How do you think the toothbrush battery gets recharged?

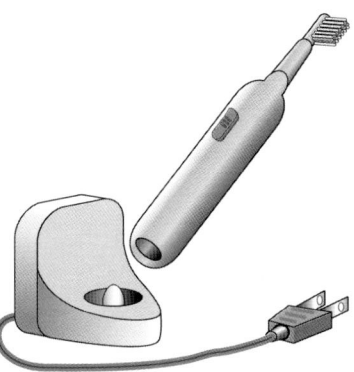

7. A transformer contains 9000 turns in its primary coil and 30 turns in its secondary coil. If the voltage of the secondary coil is 120 V, what is the voltage of the primary coil?

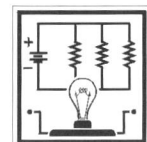

Unit 7
Electricity and Magnetism

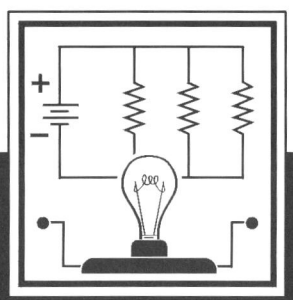

Chapter 24

Electronics

Objectives for Chapter 24

By the end of this chapter you should be able to:

1. Describe how a diode and transistor work in terms of current and voltage.
2. Explain the difference between a p-type and an n-type semiconductor.
3. Construct a half-wave rectifier circuit with a diode.
4. Construct a transistor switch.
5. Describe the relationship between inputs and outputs of the four basic logic gates.
6. Construct an adding circuit with logic gates.

Terms and vocabulary words

forward bias	reverse bias	bias voltage	*p*-type	*n*-type
depletion region	hole	collector	emitter	base
conductivity	*p-n* junction	logic gate	rectifier	diode
transistor	amplifier	gain	analog	digital
AND	OR	NAND	NOR	binary
CPU	program	memory	bit	integrated circuit

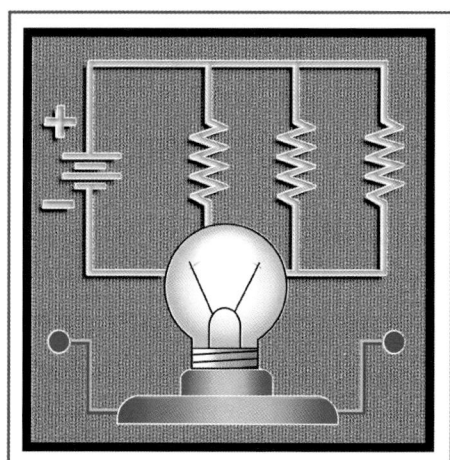

24.1 Semiconductors

It is almost impossible to do anything today without being affected by electronics. Electronic devices are in telephones, computers, video games, cars, watches—a virtually endless list. Contemporary explorers on land and sea carry electronic global positioning system (GPS) receivers to keep from getting lost. Electronic devices use semiconductors to precisely control current and voltage in circuits. This chapter introduces some of the more important semiconductor components used in all electronic devices, including diodes, transistors, and integrated circuits.

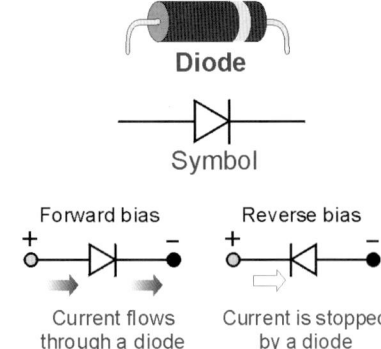

Figure 24.1: *A diode and its circuit symbol. The stripe indicates the negative side when the diode is forward biased.*

Diodes

What a diode does　A diode is a one-way valve for electric current. Current can only flow one way through a diode and not the other way. Diodes are a basic building block of all electronics and are used to control the direction of current flowing in circuits. A common diode looks like a small cylinder with a stripe on one end (Figure 24.1).

Forward and reverse bias　When a diode is connected in a circuit so current flows through it, we say the diode is forward biased. When the diode is reversed so it blocks the flow of current, the diode is reverse biased. If you plot the current through the diode versus the voltage across the diode, the graph will looks like Figure 24.2.

The bias voltage　In a forward-biased diode the current stays at zero until the voltage reaches the bias voltage (V_b), which is 0.6 V for common silicon diodes. You can think of the bias voltage as the amount of energy difference it takes to open the diode. Once the voltage gets higher than the bias voltage, diodes have low resistance.

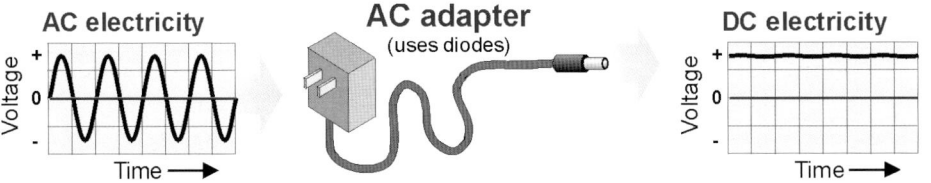

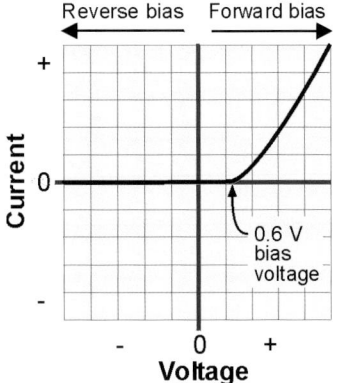

Figure 24.2: *The current versus voltage graph for a common silicon diode.*

Diodes and AC adapters　An important application for diodes is in AC to DC adapters. Most electronic devices need DC electricity, including stereos, laptop computers, and battery chargers. The adapter uses a circuit of diodes to turn AC into DC. Diodes are ideal for this type of circuit because they only allow current flow in one direction.

Transistors

A transistor is a flow control valve for current	A transistor allows you to *control* the current, not just block it in one direction. A transistor is like a variable flow valve for current. A good analogy for a transistor is a pipe with an adjustable gate. When the gate is closed, the pipe has very high resistance and not much water flows. When the gate is open, the pipe has low resistance and water flows easily. The adjustable gate is a control for the flow through the pipe.

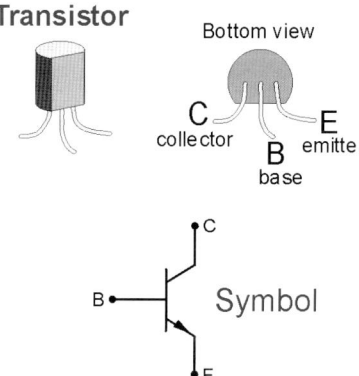

Transistor

Figure 24.3: *What a transistor looks like along with its connections and circuit symbol.*

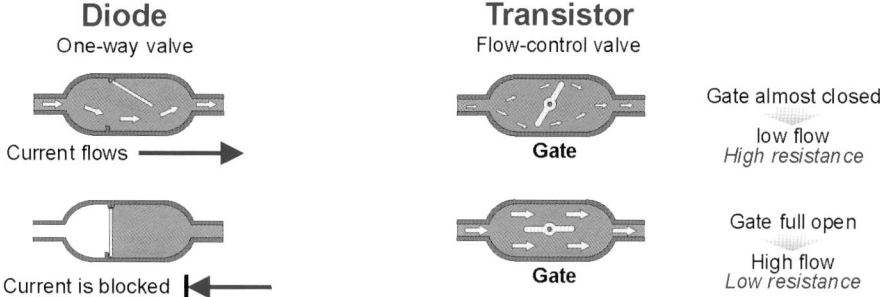

Connections and resistance of a transistor	A transistor has three terminals (Figure 24.3). The main path for current is between the collector and emitter. The base controls how much current flows, just like the gate controlled the flow of water in the pipe. You can think about a transistor like a potentiometer that can be electrically controlled. Remember, the resistance of a potentiometer was changed by turning a knob. The resistance of a transistor is changed by changing the current flowing into the base.
The current versus voltage graph	The current versus voltage graph for a transistor is more complicated than for a simple resistor because there are three variables. The resistance depends on current flowing into the base (I_b). A transistor is very sensitive; ten-millionths of an amp makes a big difference in the resistance between the collector and emitter. For a given value of I_b, the relationship between the voltage (V_{ce}) and current (I_{ce}), between collector and emitter, is similar to the relationship for a resistor. The exception is that the collector-emitter voltage must still exceed a 0.6 V bias voltage for the transistor to become fully active. Figure 24.4 shows a typical current versus voltage graph for a transistor.

Current vs. Voltage for a Transistor
(base current, $1\,\mu A = 1 \times 10^{-6}\,A$)

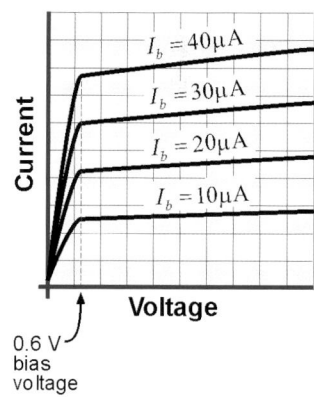

Figure 24.4: *Current versus voltage graphs for a transistor at four different base-emitter voltages.*

Conductivity and semiconductors

Conductivity | The relative ease at which electric current flows through a material is known as conductivity. Conductors (like copper) have very high conductivity. Insulators (like rubber) have very low conductivity.

Semiconductors can change their conductivity | Semiconductors are materials that do not fit into either of these categories. The conductivity of a semiconductor depends on its conditions. For example, at low temperatures and low voltages a semiconductor acts like an insulator. When the temperature and/or the voltage is increased, the conductivity increases and the material acts more like a conductor. The ability to pass current in one direction and block current in the opposite direction comes from the ability of semiconductors to change their electrical conductivity in response to a change in voltage.

Why metals are conductors | Metals are good conductors because a small percentage of electrons are free to separate from atoms and move independently. With only a small push from a battery, electrons in a conductor move from atom to atom throughout the material. In an insulator, the electrons are tightly bonded to atoms and cannot move. Since the electrons cannot move, they cannot carry current, and that explains why an insulator *is* an insulator.

Electrons in a semiconductor | The electrons in a semiconductor are also bound to atoms, but the bonds are relatively weak. The energy from a battery or heat is enough to free a few electrons, which can then move and carry current. The density of free electrons is what determines the conductivity of a semiconductor. If there are many free electrons to carry current, the semiconductor acts more like a conductor. If there are few electrons, the semiconductor acts like an insulator.

Silicon is the most common semiconductor | Silicon is the most commonly used semiconductor. Atoms of silicon have 16 electrons. Twelve of the electrons are bound tightly inside the atom. Four electrons are near the outside of the atom and only loosely bound. In pure silicon, the atoms are arranged so that each of the four outer electrons is paired with another electron from each of four neighboring atoms (Figure 24.5). At room temperature a fraction of the electrons in silicon have enough energy to break free from their pairs and carry current. The small population of free electrons is what makes silicon a semiconductor.

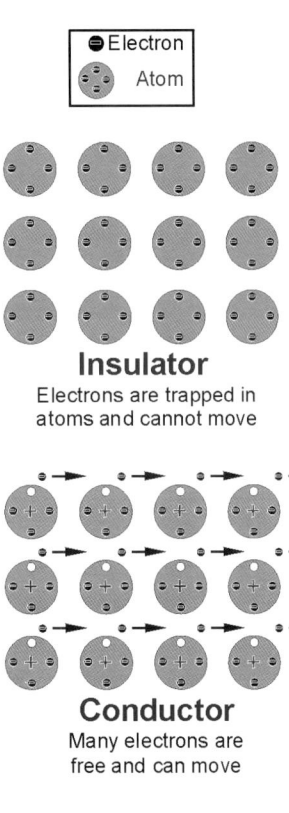

Insulator
Electrons are trapped in atoms and cannot move

Conductor
Many electrons are free and can move

Semiconductor
A few electrons are free and can move, but most are weakly bonded to atoms

Figure 24.5: *Electrons in insulators, conductors, and semiconductors.*

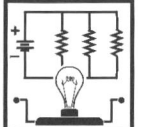

Changing the conductivity of semiconductors

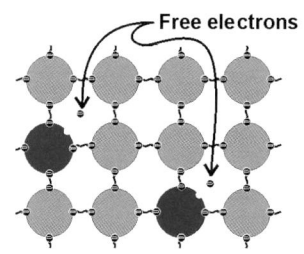

Adding impurities to a semiconductor Anything that changes the number of free electrons has a huge effect on conductivity in a semiconductor. For example, adding an impurity of 1 boron atom per 10 million silicon atoms increases the conductivity by 20,000 times. Useful semiconductors are created by adding impurities to adjust conductivity.

n-type semiconductors Phosphorus atoms have five outer electrons compared with silicon's four. When a phosphorus atom tries to fit in with four silicon atoms, four of its five outer electrons pair up with the neighboring silicon atoms. The extra electron does not pair up and is free to carry current. Adding a phosphorus impurity to silicon *increases* the number of electrons that can carry current. Silicon with a phosphorus impurity makes an n-type semiconductor. Current in an n-type semiconductor is carried by electrons with *negative* charge (Figure 24.6).

***n*-type** semiconductor
When phosphorus bonds with silicon, one electron is left free

Figure 24.6: *An* n-*type semiconductor.*

p-type semiconductors When a small amount of *boron* is mixed into silicon the opposite effect happens. A boron atom has three outer electrons, one less than silicon. When a boron atom tries to fit into silicon it needs another electron so it can pair up with its four neighbors. The boron atom captures an electron from a neighboring silicon atom.

When an electron is taken by a boron atom, the silicon atom is left with a positive charge. The silicon atom with the missing electron is called a *hole* because it needs to be filled with another electron. The positive silicon atom attracts an electron from one of *its* neighbors, and the *hole moves.* The new hole takes an electron from *its* neighbor and *the hole moves again.* In fact, as electrons jump from atom to atom, the positive hole moves in the opposite direction and can carry current. Silicon with a boron impurity is a p-type semiconductor. The current in a *p*-type semiconductor is carried by holes with *positive* charge (Figure 24.7).

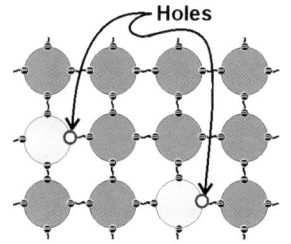

***p*-type** semiconductor
When boron mixes with silicon, an extra electron is needed to bond with silicon's 4 electrons

Figure 24.7: *A* p-*type semiconductor. Each boron atom creates a "hole" where an electron is needed to match pairs with silicon.*

***p*-type** semiconductor

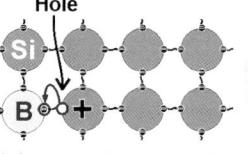

A boron atom creates a hole by taking an electron from a silicon atom

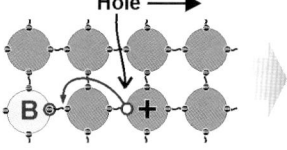

The hole acts like a moving positive charge as electrons jump from atom to atom

The p-n junction

The *p-n* junction A p-n junction forms where *p*-type and *n*-type semiconductor materials meet. Initially the *n* side has free electrons and the *p* side has holes. Some negative electrons from the *n* side flow over to the *p* side and combine with the positive holes. As the electrons move, the *n* side becomes positively charged and the *p* side becomes negatively charged. The charge difference grows until it is large enough to keep any more electrons from crossing over. For silicon, equilibrium is reached when the *n* side is 0.6 volts more positive than the *p* side.

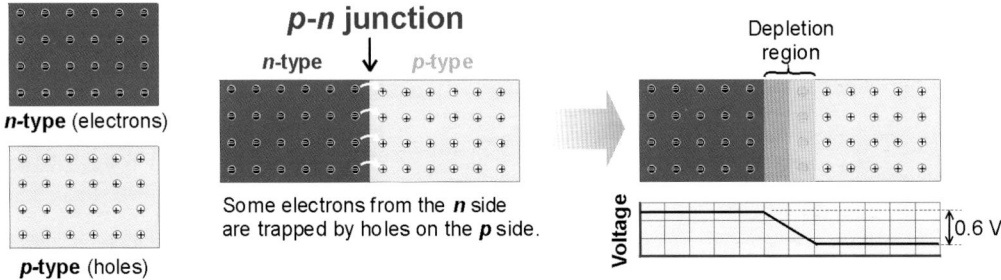

n-type (electrons)

p-type (holes)

p-n junction

n-type → *p*-type

Some electrons from the *n* side are trapped by holes on the *p* side.

Depletion region

0.6 V

The depletion region When an electron fills a hole, a neutral silicon atom is left. As a result, the material right near the p-n junction has neither electrons nor holes. This area is called the depletion region. The depletion region has no movable charges that can carry current because the electrons and holes have combined to make neutral silicon atoms. As a result, *the depletion region becomes an insulating barrier to the flow of current*.

The depletion region can be changed The depletion region is affected by external voltages. It can grow and become a stronger insulator, or disappear and allow current to flow. The depletion region can change quickly because it is thin (0.5 millionths of a meter) and electrons are small and fast. Computer chips are made from semiconductors with *p-n* junctions. The fundamental limit to how fast computers work is the speed at which the depletion region can change from an insulator to a conductor.

Semiconductors and crystals

A crystal is a solid in which all the atoms are perfectly organized in neat rows and columns. Semiconductors are made from perfect crystals of silicon, or at least as perfect as human technology can achieve.

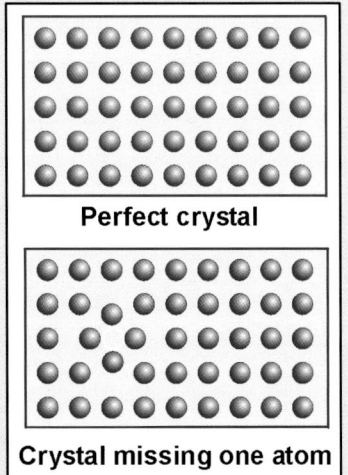

Perfect crystal

Crystal missing one atom

When an atom of silicon is out of place, it acts like an impurity, because the electrons in neighboring atoms cannot pair up one-to-one. If too many atoms are out of place, the precise effects of the added impurities are changed and the *p-n* junction may not work the way it is supposed to.

The physics of diodes

Reverse biased
p-n junction The depletion region of a *p-n* junction is what gives diodes, transistors, and all other semiconductors their useful properties. Suppose an external voltage is applied in a direction that attracts electrons on the *n* side. The same voltage also attracts holes on the *p* side. Both electrons and holes are drawn away from the junction and the depletion region gets larger. Even as the voltage increases, no current can flow because it is blocked by a larger (insulating) depletion region.

A reverse biased
p-n junction

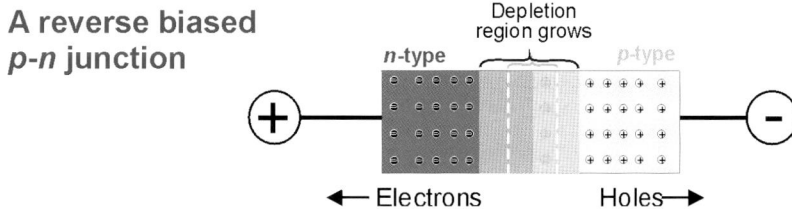

Forward biased
p-n junction Now suppose the opposite voltage is applied. Both electrons and holes are repelled *toward* the depletion region. As a result, the depletion region gets smaller. The larger the opposing voltage gets, the smaller the depletion region becomes. When the applied voltage becomes greater than 0.6 V, the depletion region *goes away completely*. Once the depletion region is gone, electrons are free to carry current across the junction and the semiconductor becomes a conductor.

A forward biased
p-n junction

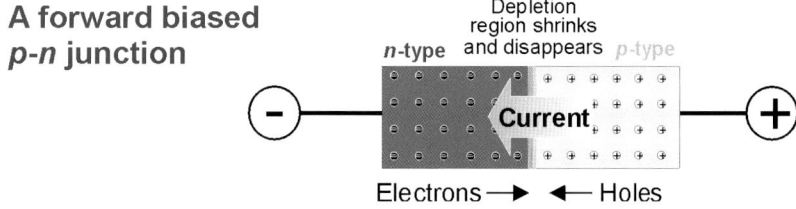

A p-n junction
is a diode To summarize the last two paragraphs:

1. The *p-n* junction *blocks* the flow of current from the *n* side to the *p* side.

2. The *p-n* junction *allows* current to flow from the *p* side to the *n* side if the voltage difference is more than 0.6 volts.

In short, a *p-n* junction is a *diode*. Current is only allowed to flow in one direction across the junction. Transistors (see sidebar) have two *p-n* junctions.

Transistors

A transistor is made from two *p-n* junctions back to back. The three terminals are connected to the three regions as shown in the diagram below. The layer of *p*-type semiconductor in an actual transistor is much thinner than the *n*-type layers on either side.

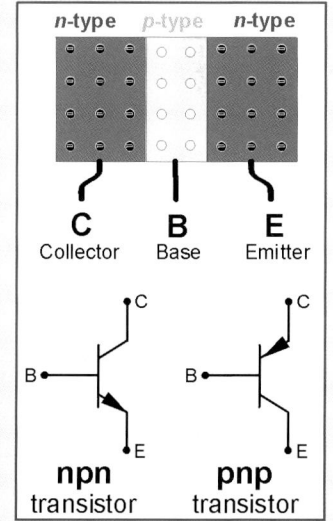

With a transistor, a small current flowing into the base can control a large current from the collector to emitter by changing the conductivity of the depletion region. An *npn* transistor (shown) has a *p*-type layer sandwiched between two *n*-type layers. A *pnp* transistor is the inverse. an *n*-type semiconductor is between two layers of *p*-type.

24.2 Circuits with Diodes and Transistors

Electric circuits made with diodes and transistors can do much more than circuits with only resistors and capacitors. For example, your stereo uses a transistor circuit to amplify the tiny electrical signal from a CD until it carries enough current to drive speakers. This section presents a few examples of important and useful types of circuits made with transistors and diodes.

A rectifier circuit turns AC electricity into DC

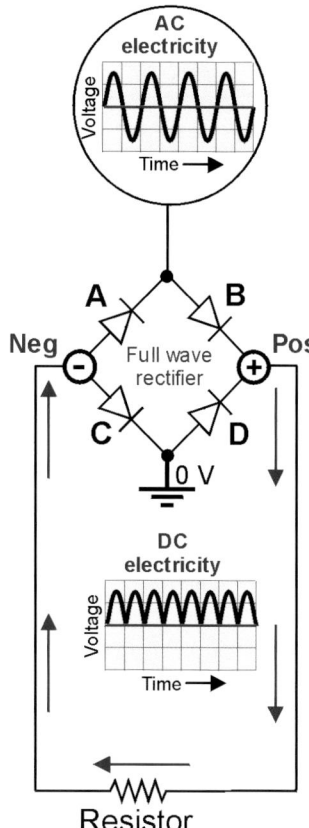

Figure 24.8: *A bridge-rectifier circuit uses the entire AC cycle by inverting the negative portions.*

A single diode AC-DC converter
: A diode can convert alternating current electricity to direct current. Consider what happens when an AC voltage is applied to a diode. The diode only conducts current in one direction. When the AC cycle is positive, the voltage passes through the diode because the diode is conducting and has low resistance. When the AC cycle is negative, the voltage is blocked by the diode because the diode has a very large resistance to current in the reverse direction. A single diode is called a *half-wave rectifier* since it converts half the AC cycle to DC.

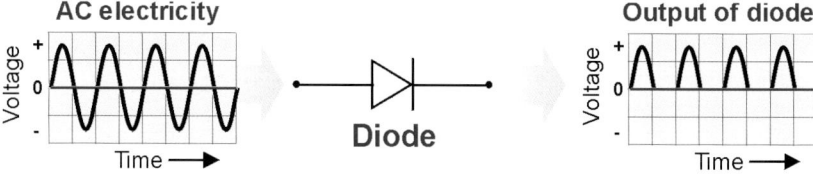

A 4-diode AC-DC converter
: There is a way to convert the whole AC cycle to DC with 4 diodes arranged in the circuit shown in Figure 24.8. This circuit is called a *full-wave rectifier*. A version of the full-wave rectifier circuit is in nearly every AC adapter you have ever used.

How the 4-diode circuit works
: When the AC cycle is positive, current flows through diode (B) through the resistor and back through diode (C). The current flows out of the positive terminal of the bridge rectifier and back to the negative terminal. When the AC cycle is negative, current flows through diode (D) through the resistor and back through diode (A). On either part of the AC cycle, the resistor always sees current coming out of the positive terminal and going back into the negative terminal. The result is a (bumpy) DC current. The bumps can be smoothed out with a capacitor.

A transistor switch

Transistors as electronic switches   In many electronic circuits a small voltage or current is used to switch a much larger voltage or current. Transistors work very well for this application because they behave like switches that can be turned on and off *electronically* instead of using manual or mechanical action.

Turning a transistor on and off   Consider an *npn* transistor. Because there are two *p-n* junctions, the transistor normally blocks current in both directions. The current in the *p* layer is carried by positive holes. When positive current flows into the base, electrons are drawn in from the *n*-type regions and the whole *p* layer becomes a conductor. It typically takes only a tiny amount of base current (10 millionths of an amp) to turn a transistor from an insulator (off) into a conductor (on).

The resistance of a switch   You can think of a regular mechanical switch as a device that goes from very high resistance to very low resistance. When the switch is open, the resistance is greater than a million ohms (Ω). When the switch is closed, the resistance drops to 0.001 ohms or less. Transistor switches work because very small currents to the base change the resistance of the transistor by almost as great an amount. For example, when the current into the base is zero, a transistor has a resistance of 100,000 ohms or more. When a tiny current flows into the base, the resistance drops to 10 ohms or less. The resistance difference between "on" and "off" for a transistor switch is not as great as for a mechanical switch, but it is good enough for many useful circuits.

A transistor switch

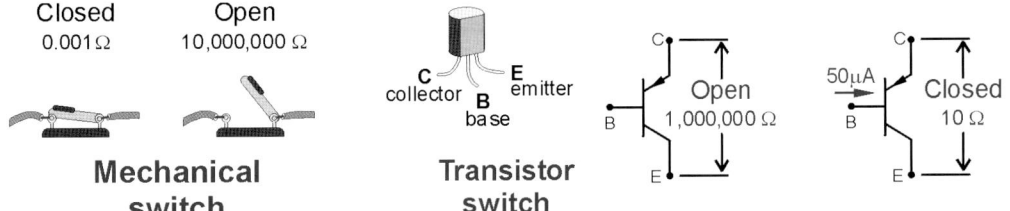

Figure 24.9: *A transistor used as a switch to turn on a light bulb.*

A transistor switch circuit   An example transistor switch circuit is shown in Figure 24.9. Closing the switch causes a small current to flow into the base of the transistor. This turns the transistor "on" and current flows through lighting the bulb.

A transistor amplifier

Gain and amplifiers
One of the most important uses of a transistor is to amplify a signal. In electronics, the word "amplify" means to make the voltage or current of the input signal larger without changing the shape of the signal. For example, an amplifier with a gain of five would change a 1-volt signal into a 5-volt signal, leaving the shape of the voltage versus time graph the same. The output voltage of an amplifier is equal to the input voltage multiplied by the gain.

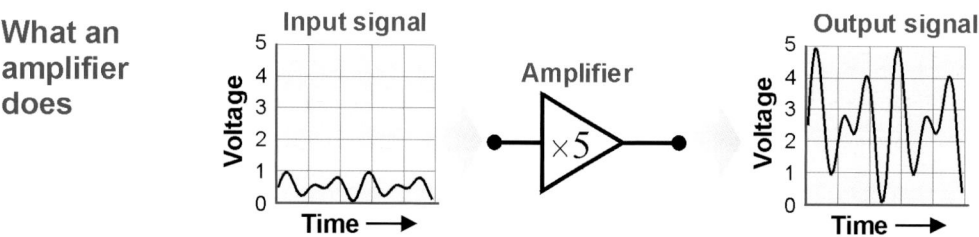

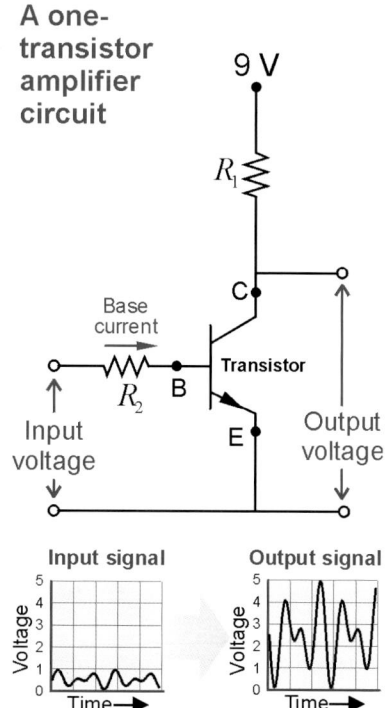

A one-transistor amplifier circuit
Transistor voltage amplifiers work because the resistance between the collector and emitter is proportional to the base current. Figure 24.10 shows a basic amplifier made with a single transistor and one resistor. In an amplifier circuit, the transistor is not switched fully "on" like it is in a switching circuit. Instead, the transistor operates partially on and its resistance varies between a few hundred ohms and about 10,000 ohms, depending on the specific transistor.

How the circuit works
The combination of the transistor and R_1 is a voltage divider. If the transistor's resistance is equal to R_1, the output is half the supply voltage, or 4.5 V. When the transistor's resistance drops, the output voltage also drops. The base resistor is chosen so that the transistor operates with its resistance near R_1 at the average value of the input voltage.

Figure 24.10: *An amplifier circuit using one transistor.*

Relationship between input and output voltage
The base current is proportional to the input voltage divided by R_2. If the input voltage rises, the base current rises and the resistance of the transistor drops. When the input voltage falls, the base current falls and the transistor resistance increases. In the example, an input voltage between 0 and 1 V, produces an output between 0 and 5 V, or five times larger than the input. The output is also *inverted* from the input. When the input voltage goes up, the output voltage goes down. When the input voltage goes down, the output voltage goes up.

Electronic logic

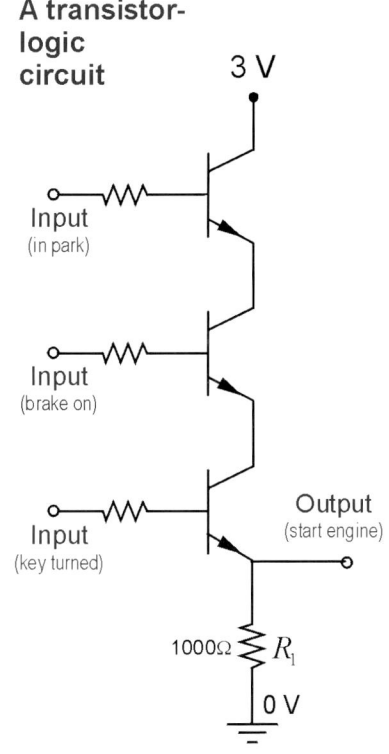

A transistor-logic circuit

Circuits that make decisions — Many electronic circuits are designed to perform certain functions only if a number of input conditions are met. For example, the circuit that starts your car only works when a) the car is in park, b) the brake is on, and c) the key is turned. The circuit that applies power to start the engine must evaluate three conditions before it turns itself on. How do electronic circuits make decisions like this?

Electronic logic — Logic circuits are designed to compare inputs and produce specific output when all the input conditions are met. Logic circuits assign voltages to the two logical conditions of TRUE (T) and FALSE (F). For example, for 3-volt circuits, 3 V is considered TRUE and 0 V is considered FALSE. Using this "electronic logic," the problem of the car starter circuit is summarized by the table below. There are three inputs corresponding to the three conditions that must be satisfied. There is one output which starts the car if TRUE and does not start the car if FALSE.

INPUT Car in park	INPUT Brake on	INPUT Key turned		OUTPUT Start engine
0 V	0 V	0 V		0 V
3 V	0 V	0 V		0 V
3 V	3 V	0 V		0 V
3 V	0 V	3 V		0 V
0 V	3 V	3 V		0 V
3 V	3 V	3 V		3 V

Figure 24.11: *A circuit with three transistors that solves a three-input AND logical decision.*

A circuit that solves the three input logic problem — The circuit with three transistor switches shown in Figure 24.11 does exactly what the table prescribes. This circuit operates like a big voltage divider. The three transistors in series act like one resistor and R_1 is the other. If *any* of the three transistors has a high resistance compared with R_1, then the output is close to zero volts. If all three transistors are "on," their total resistance is much less than R_1 and the output voltage is close to 3 volts. The only way for the output to be 3 V is when all three transistors are on, which only happens if all three inputs are TRUE. The circuit of Figure 24.11 is an example of an AND logic circuit. An AND circuit compares its inputs and makes the output TRUE only if the first input is TRUE *and* the second is TRUE *and* the third is TRUE, etc.

Voltages between 0 V and 3 V

Logic circuits treat a range of voltages as TRUE or FALSE. For example, in 3V logic, any voltage less than 1 V is FALSE and any voltage greater than 1.5 V is TRUE.

24.3 Digital Electronics

We seem to live in a so-called "digital age" where everything is better if it is "digital." Supposedly, CDs have better sound because they are digital. Commercials claim digital TV has better picture quality. As with most advertising, the truth is not quite so clear cut. You do not directly hear digital signals or see digital signals. You hear and see analog signals. This section will help you understand the important difference between the digital world of computer-based electronics and the analog world of our senses.

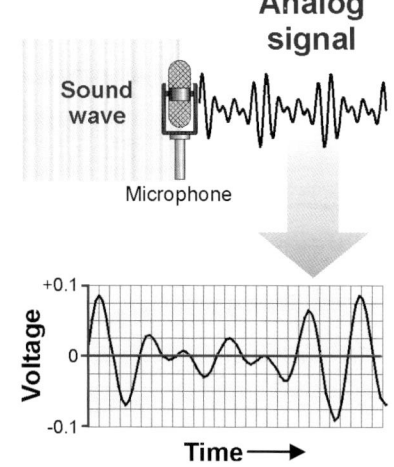

Figure 24.12: *A microphone creates an analog signal, shown by the voltage versus time graph.*

Analog and digital signals

Signals and information

A signal is anything that carries information. Today the word signal usually means a voltage, current, or light wave that carries information. In electronics, signals are usually voltages and the information is contained in the way the voltages vary with time. For example, a voice is a sound wave. A microphone converts the variations in air pressure from the sound wave into variations in voltage in an electrical signal (Figure 24.12).

Analog signals

The voltage versus time graph from a microphone is an example of an analog signal. The voltage in an analog signal can have continuous values. For example, a particular microphone might produce a voltage from -0.1 V to + 0.1 V. The signal from the microphone is a continuous voltage between - 0.1 V and + 0.1 V (Figure 24.12). The information in an analog signal is contained in both the value of the signal and the way the signal changes with time.

Digital signals

A digital signal can only be on or off. For the digital signals in many computers, on is 3 volts, off is zero volts. A 3-volt digital signal has only two values: 0 V or 3 V. A digital signal is very different from an analog signal. The information in a digital signal is coded in the sequence of changes between 0 V and 3 V. Figure 24.13 shows an example of a digital signal, like the one from a CD player.

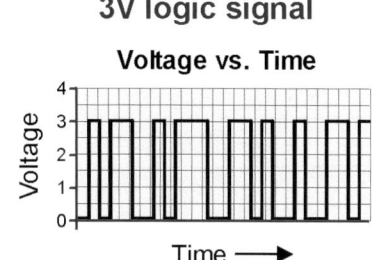

Figure 24.13: *A digital signal is a sequence of transitions between HIGH and LOW logic voltages. The voltage versus time graph shown is a 3V logic signal.*

Comparing analog and digital signals

At first glance, the claim that digital signals are better seems impossible. How can a signal that can only be on or off tell you as much as a signal that can have all the values in between? The answer is that digital signals can send billions of ones and zeros per second, carrying more information than analog signals. Digital signals are also easier to store, process, and reproduce than analog signals.

Digital information

Information in analog signals
All circuits use real voltages and currents that are analog variables. The difference is in how the *information* in a signal is used by a circuit. In an analog circuit the voltage or current *is* the information. For example, an electronic thermometer makes a voltage proportional to temperature. The higher the temperature, the higher the voltage.

Information in digital signals
In a digital circuit, the information is not in the voltages or currents directly, but instead is coded in the patterns of change between high and low voltages. For example, the temperature could be represented by a number between 0 and 99. The digital temperature signal assigns a code to each digit.

Table 24.1: Binary Coded Decimal (BCD) for the digits 0-9

#	Code	#	Code	#	Code	#	Code
0	0000	3	0011	6	0110	9	1001
1	0001	4	0100	7	0111		
2	0010	5	0101	8	1000		

Digital representation of a number
To represent a temperature of 25°C as a digital signal requires the code for "2" followed by the code for "5." If the electronics uses 3V logic, then 3 V is a "1" and zero volts is a "0." The number 25 is represented by a sequence of 8 voltages in the order shown in Figure 24.14.

Bits and representation of letters
In a digital signal, a bit is a place in the signal that can be either a 0 or a 1. All 10 numbers can be represented by four bits in Binary Coded Decimal. The letters in the alphabet also have codes. Since there are more letters, it takes more bits to have a unique code for each letter (including the lower case letters). A few of the codes for the alphabet are shown in Table 24.2. A digital signal for the word "face" is shown in Figure 24.15.

Table 24.2: The American Standard Code for Information Interchange (ASCII)

	Code		Code		Code		Code
A	0100 0001	D	0100 0100	a	0110 0001	d	0110 0100
B	0100 0010	E	0100 0101	b	0110 0010	e	0110 0101
C	0100 0011	F	0100 0110	c	0110 0011	f	0110 0110

Digital coding for the number 25

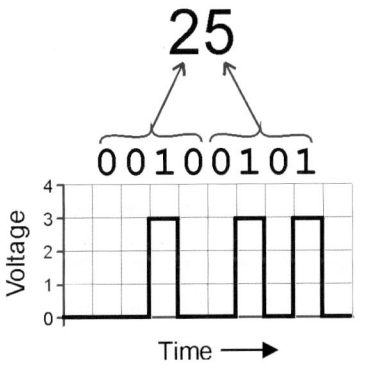

Figure 24.14: *Digital code for the number 25.*

Digital coding for the word "*face*"

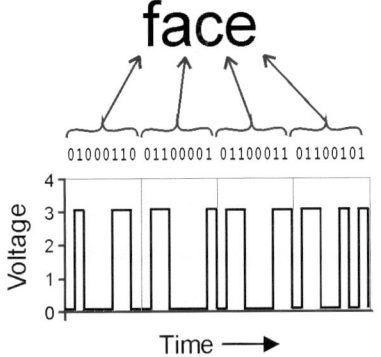

Figure 24.15: *Digital code for the word "face."*

Computers

Circuits as information processors   You can think about a circuit as a processor of analog information. Currents and voltages applied to the input of the circuit result in other currents and voltages at the output. The amplifier or the AC-DC rectifier are examples of circuits that process an input to create a specific kind of output.

Circuits are task-specific   Analog circuits are designed to do a particular task, such as amplifying a signal. To make a circuit do something different, you have to build a different circuit. This is often inconvenient. For example, you can make an analog circuit start the car if three conditions are met. It would take a completely different circuit to start if only two out of the three conditions were met.

Why computers are useful   A computer is an electronic device for processing digital information. Computers have **programs** that tell them how to process the information. To make a computer do something different, you just need a different program. *The electronic circuits stay the same*. This is a tremendous advantage, and is the reason digital electronics have become a foundation of human technology.

The memory system   All computers have three key systems (Figure 24.16). The **memory** stores digital information. The information might be words, numbers, pictures, or programs that tell the computer what to do with the letters, numbers, or pictures. The average classroom computer can store about 800 billion bits of information. For comparison, this chapter has about 6,000 words averaging seven letters each plus a space. It takes 380,000 bits to store the words in the chapter as ASCII codes. The average computer memory can hold the words in 2 million chapters of this length.

The CPU   Information from memory is processed by the **central processing unit**, or CPU. The CPU of a computer is a huge circuit using more than a billion transistors. The program tells the CPU what to do with each string of digital data that comes in from memory.

The input/output system   The last key part of a computer is the input-output system, or I/O. The I/O system includes the keyboard, display, sound interface, network interface, and other subsystems that allow the CPU and memory to interact with you or other electronic devices (such as other computers).

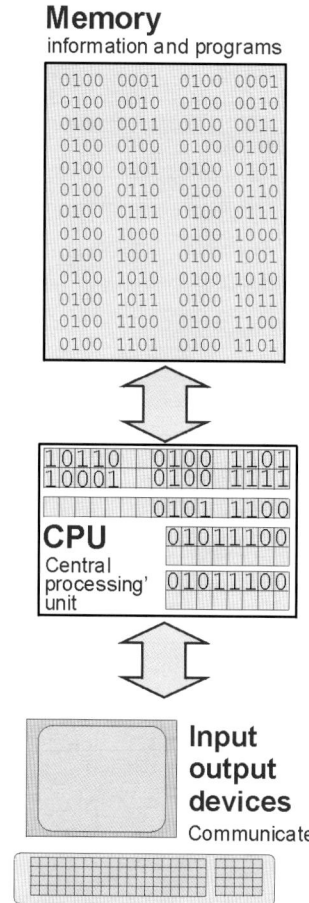

Figure 24.16: *The key systems of a computer.*

490

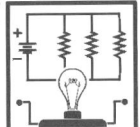

Logic circuits

Computers use logic circuits
Inside a computer are circuits that take a signal of ones and zeros and do something to create a different signal of ones and zeros. Since the ones and zeros are represented by voltages, the electronics also work with voltages. You have already met your first digital circuit: the AND circuit used to solve the car starter problem.

The four basic logic gates
Circuits called logic gates are the basic building blocks of computers and almost all digital systems. The fundamental logic gates are called AND, OR, NAND, and NOR. As their names imply, these gates compare two input voltages and produce an output voltage based on the inputs. The diagram below shows the output of each of the four logic gates for every combination of inputs.

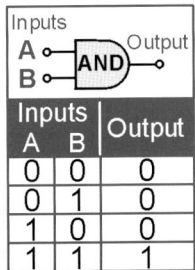

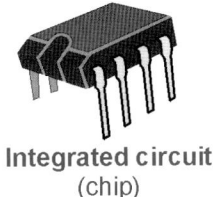

Integrated circuit
(chip)

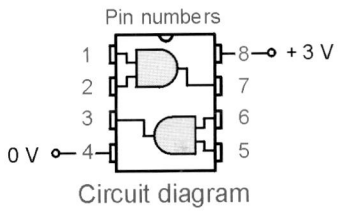

Figure 24.17: *An integrated circuit with two AND gates.*

Chips and integrated circuits
Logic gates are built from many transistors in integrated circuits, commonly known as "chips." Figure 24.17 shows a picture of a chip that has two AND circuits. This chip operates with 3V signals and must be supplied with 3 volts to pin 8 and zero volts to pin 4. The inputs and outputs are connected to pins 2-7.

An example logic circuit
As an example of how logic is constructed, suppose a computer wants to "recognize" a four-bit number. The computer memory stores the number 3, which has a code of 0011. The keyboard also types the number 3. An AND gate returns a one only if both signals are one. A NOR gate returns a one only if both signals are zero. A second OR compares the output of the first two and returns a one if either of its inputs is one. The output of this circuit will be four ones (3V on each) only if the number entered by the keyboard exactly matches the number in the computer's memory. The CPU of a computer contains millions of such circuits.

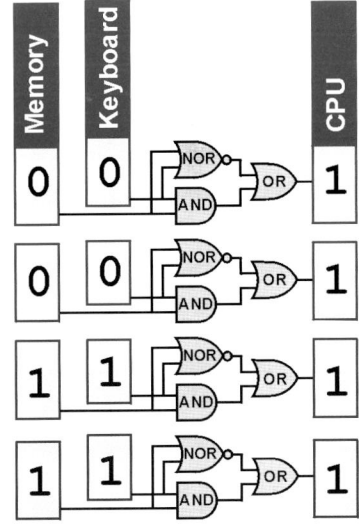

Figure 24.18: *A logic circuit to compare two four-bit electronic numbers.*

Application: Electronic Addition of Two Numbers

Computers in science are useful for many reasons. One reason is to do complicated calculations such as calculating the magnetic field from a coil at places other than its center. To do calculations, computers represent all numbers in zeros and ones using the binary number system. Once numbers are in binary, electronic logic circuits can be used to add, subtract, multiply and divide them.

The decimal numbering system   In an ordinary number, each digit represents a power of 10. The digit farthest to the right equals the number of tens to the zeroth power ($10^0 = 1$). The digit to the immediate left is the number of tens to the first power ($10^1 = 10$). The next digit is the number of tens to the second power and so on. The quantity represented by the number is calculated by summing the digits multiplied by the appropriate power of ten. For example, the number 115 equals $1 \times 10^2 + 1 \times 10^1 + 5 \times 10^0$.

The binary number system   It would take 10 different voltages to represent 10 digits. Making circuits work on 10 voltages is difficult, so all numbers in computers are represented in binary. Binary numbers work the same as decimal numbers except each digit represents a power of two instead of a power of 10. The diagram below shows how the number 115 is represented in binary.

Decimal number

Power of 10	10^2	10^1	10^0
Value	100	10	1

1	1	5

$100 + 10 + 5 = 115$

Binary number

Power of 2	2^6	2^5	2^4	2^3	2^2	2^1	2^0
Value	64	32	16	8	4	2	1

1	1	1	0	0	1	1

$64+32+16+0+0+2+1 = 115$

Adding binary numbers   To add two numbers, each digit is lined up just as you would with decimal numbers (Figure 24.19). A zero plus one equals one. One plus one equals 10, with the one being carried to the next digit to the left. The usual rules of arithmetic hold for binary numbers. For example, with decimal numbers one plus one equals two. The same is true in binary numbers, except the calculation is written $1 + 1 = 10$. In binary, the number 10 is really *two* in the decimal system.

Binary addition

0	1	1
+0	+0	+1
0	1	10

10	10	100
+1	+10	+10
11	100	110

Figure 24.19: *Adding two numbers in binary.*

Floating point numbers

Integer numbers have no decimal point. In computer technology, non integer numbers are stored in a form of scientific notation called *floating point*. A floating point number has two parts: the first is the multiplier and the second is the power of two.

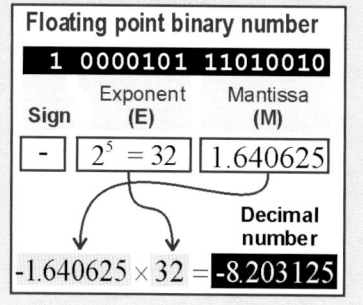

Floating point binary number

1	0000101	11010010
Sign	Exponent (E)	Mantissa (M)
-	$2^5 = 32$	1.640625

Decimal number

$-1.640625 \times 32 = -8.203125$

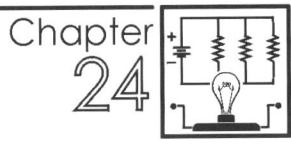
An electronic adding circuit

A circuit to add two one-bit binary numbers

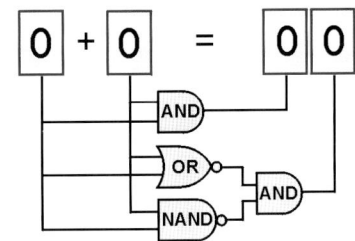

Components of an adding circuit

Two one-bit binary numbers can be added with four logic gates: two AND gates, a NOR gate, and a NAND gate, as shown in Figure 24.20. To see how this circuit works, consider the process of addition. Two single digit numbers can have four different sums, as shown below. The sum has at most two digits.

Result

First number	0	1	0	1	
Second number	+0	+0	+1	+1	1 0
Result of addition	0 0	0 1	0 1	1 0	

Two's place ↗   ↖ One's place

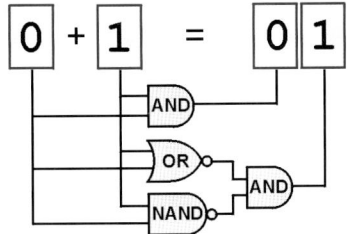

The logic for the two's place

To see how the circuit is designed, consider the logical relationship between the two input numbers and each of two digits of the result. The two's place should be a one only if the first number is one and the second number is one. This is done electronically with an AND gate.

The logic for the one's place

The one's place of the result is a little harder to figure out. The one's place should be a zero if both inputs are zero, *or* if both inputs are one. The one's place should be a one if either input number is one, but not both. This cannot be done with a single AND, NAND, OR, or NOR gate. It can be done with the combination of three gates shown in Figure 24.20. The diagram below shows how the logic in the circuit works. This type of diagram is called a truth table by the electrical engineers who design digital circuits. If you experiment with digital electronics, you will find other ways to make an adding circuit, with other gates (for example, XOR). The other circuits are left for your future exploration.

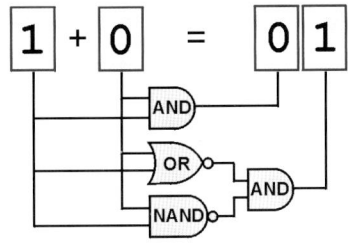

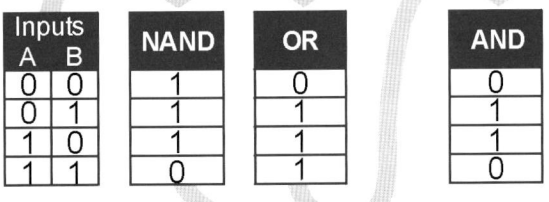

Inputs A B	NAND	OR	AND
0 0	1	0	0
0 1	1	1	1
1 0	1	1	1
1 1	0	1	0

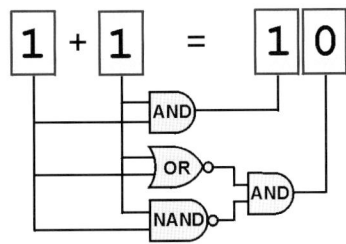

Figure 24.20: *A one-bit binary adder circuit.*

Chapter 24 Review

Vocabulary Review

Match the following terms with the correct definition. There is one extra definition in the list that will not match any of the terms.

Set One

1. diode
2. reverse biased
3. base
4. forward biased
5. conductivity

a. When a diode is connected so current will flow through it
b. Small currents flowing into this terminal of a transistor control larger currents between the other terminals
c. When a diode is connected so current will not flow through it
d. A one-way valve for electric current
e. Reverses the direction of current in a circuit
f. A measure of how easily current flows through a material

Set Two

1. transistor
2. collector
3. p-n junction
4. bias voltage
5. semiconductor

a. Device with very high conductivity
b. Minimum needed for current to flow through a forward-biased diode
c. Terminal where current enters a transistor before exiting through the emitter
d. Location where p-type and n-type semiconductor materials are joined together
e. A variable flow valve for current
f. Material that can act like either a conductor or an insulator, depending on the conditions

Set Three

1. n-type
2. p-type
3. rectifier
4. depletion region
5. amplify

a. Semiconductor containing holes that move from atom to atom
b. A negatively charged material
c. Semiconductor containing free electrons that move from atom to atom
d. To increase the voltage or current of the input signal
e. Contains no free electrons or holes; stops current from flowing
f. Converts AC current to DC current

Set Four

1. analog
2. digital
3. bit
4. logic gates
5. integrated circuit

a. A place in a signal that can be either a 0 or a 1
b. Compare digital input signals to generate a digital output signal
c. Made of many transistors; often called a chip
d. A program that tells a computer how to process information
e. A signal that can have continuous values
f. A signal that can only be on or off

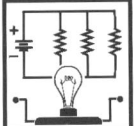
Concept review

1. Distinguish between the two ways in which a diode can be connected in a circuit.

2. Why is it important to know a diode's bias voltage?

3. How does the graph of current vs. voltage for a diode compare to the current vs. voltage graph for a resistor?

4. Explain the function of the base connection on a transistor.

5. Under what conditions does a semiconductor act like an insulator?

6. How is the number of free electrons in a semiconductor related to its conductivity?

7. What effect do impurities have on semiconductors? Why?

8. What is the difference between an n-type semiconductor and a p-type semiconductor?

9. Why does the n side of a p-n junction become positively charged?

10. Why does the depletion region of a semiconductor act like an insulator?

11. How can the size of the depletion region be changed?

12. What is the difference between a half-wave rectifier and a full-wave rectifier?

13. How is a transistor switch similar to a mechanical switch? How is it different?

14. Give an example of a device that uses a logic circuit.

15. Which type of signal can only be on or off?

16. Explain how different numbers and letters can be represented using only zeroes and ones.

17. Describe the main components of a computer.

18. List the four main types of logic gates.

Problems

1. The diagram below shows the input voltage for an AC circuit.

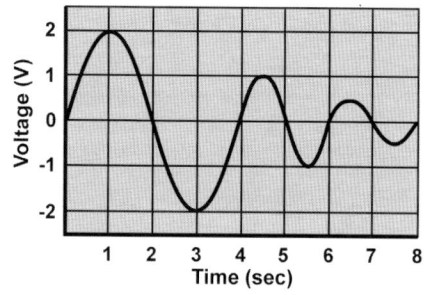

   a. A half-wave rectifier (single diode) is added to the circuit. Sketch the output voltage vs. time graph for the diode.

   b. A full-wave rectifier is added to the circuit. Sketch the output voltage vs. time graph.

2. An amplifier has a gain of 3. The input signal (voltage vs. time) is shown below. Sketch a graph of the output signal.

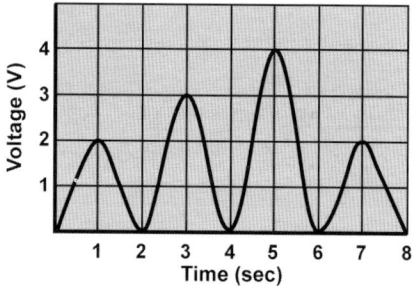

3. List the decimal number that corresponds to each binary number:

   a. 0001

   b. 0010

   c. 0111

4. The circuit is used on your locker at school. What conditions will allow for the locker to be opened?

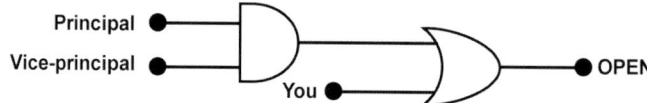

   a. You and the principal must open it together, but not alone

   b. You and the vice-principal must open it together, but not alone

   c. You can open it, or the principal and vice-principal must open it together.

   d. The principal or the vice-principal can open it, but not together

5. Which input conditions must be met for the output to be true?

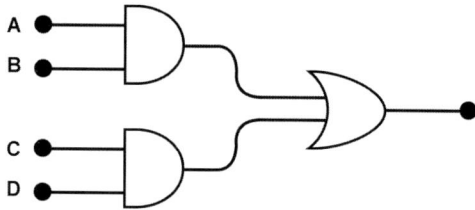

   a. A and B, but not C and D

   b. A or B, and C or D

   c. A and B and C and D

   d. A and B or C and D

Unit 8
Matter and Energy

Chapter 25

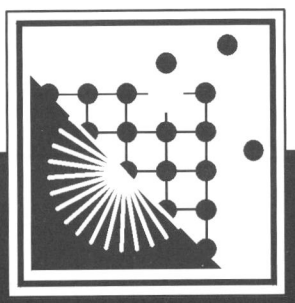

Energy, Matter, and Atoms

Objectives for Chapter 25

By the end of this chapter you should be able to:

1. Describe the relationship between atoms and matter.
2. Find an element in the periodic table.
3. Identify the differences between elements, compounds, and mixtures.
4. Convert temperatures between Fahrenheit, Celsius, and Kelvin scales.
5. Understand the concept of absolute zero temperature.
6. Describe the phases of matter and explain solid, liquid, and gas in terms of energy and atoms.
7. Describe the concepts of heat and thermal energy and apply them to real-life systems.
8. Perform basic calculations with specific heat.

Terms and vocabulary words

atom	compound	element	mixture	molecule
periodic table	Kelvin	Celsius	thermometer	Fahrenheit
specific heat	temperature	calorie	absolute zero	random
melting point	heat of vaporization	boiling point	evaporation	ionized
condensation	thermal energy	relative humidity	British thermal unit (BTU)	heat
solid	plasma	liquid	heat of fusion	gas

497

25.1 Matter and Atoms

We experience a tremendous variety of matter. You can easily list several hundred different examples of matter in your home. Your list might include wood, many kinds of plastic, concrete, plaster, glass, copper wires, steel pots, paint, water, leaves, and even the air you breathe. Humans have wondered about the diversity of matter since early in recorded history. A growing tree creates wood from water, air, and soil. The observation that wood is created from other forms of matter suggests that wood is not a fundamental substance but is made from simpler things. Is it possible that all the different forms of matter are made from a few ingredients? If so, what are the basic ingredients of matter?

Three big questions

Question #1   Think about cutting matter into pieces. When you cut a piece of wood, you have two smaller pieces of wood. It seems logical that there should be a "smallest" piece of wood that is still "wood". Large pieces of wood must be made of smaller pieces of wood. More generally ...

What is the smallest piece of matter?

Question #2   Matter does not always stay the same. If you freeze water it becomes ice. Water is liquid and flows. Ice is hard and solid. Water and ice act like very different materials. But when you heat ice, it becomes water again. It is natural to assume that ice and water are two forms of the same substance (Figure 25.1).

Why can the same kind of matter assume different forms, like solid or liquid?

Question #3   Think about what happens when you heat wood in a candle flame. The wood turns into black, powdery ashes. If you take the ashes out of the flame they do not turn back into wood as they cool down. Ashes appear to be a completely different substance from wood (Figure 25.2).

How can one kind of matter (like wood) turn into another kind of matter with very different properties (like ashes)?

Physics and chemistry   The search for answers to the first question is part of physics. The science of chemistry is the search for answers to the second and third questions. We don't have complete answers to any of the three questions for all types of matter.

Figure 25.1: *Steam, water, and ice are three forms of the same substance that can easily be converted into each other.*

Figure 25.2: *Wood and ashes are different substances. The conversion from wood into ashes does not reverse when the ashes cool down.*

498

Matter is made of tiny particles

Brownian motion — A speck of dust dropped into a glass of water swirls around as it floats on the water surface. If the dust speck is *very* small and you look at it with a powerful microscope, its motion is *not* what you might imagine. The dust speck moves in a jerky irregular way. It looks like a bumper car where the dust speck is being bounced around by impacts from smaller, invisible but fast moving objects. The jerky movement of a dust speck in water is an example of Brownian motion and provides a clue to identifying the smallest particle of matter.

The idea of atoms — In 430 BC, the Greek philosopher Democritus and his teacher Leucippus proposed that matter must be made of small particles they called atoms. They had no proof that such matter particles existed, but it made sense that there should be a smallest particle of matter. Few believed them, and for the next 2,300 years atoms were just an idea. In 1803, the English scientist John Dalton revived the idea of atoms, but he also lacked proof. In 1905, Albert Einstein finally proved that matter was made of tiny particles by explaining Brownian motion.

Why Brownian motion occurs — A large speck of dust moves smoothly as it floats around. This is because a large speck of dust, though small by definition, is so much larger than a particle of water, and is hit by so many thousands of those particles, that a single collision is not noticeable (Figure 25.3).

If the dust speck is *very* small, collisions with single particles of water are visible because the speck is hit by only a few particles at a time and its mass is not so much larger than a single particle of water. Moving water particles bump into the dust speck and cause Brownian motion (Figure 25.4).

A human-sized example — To get an idea of the scale of things, imagine throwing marbles at a tire inner tube floating in the water. If you keep throwing marbles, the inner tube will slowly move. The motion of the inner tube will be smooth because each marble weighs a lot less than the tube. Next think about throwing marbles at a paper cup floating on the water. The cup visibly moves under the impact of each marble. This is because the weight of the cup is not that much greater than the weight of a single marble. Brownian motion proves that matter exists in microscopic particles, smaller than a tiny dust speck. We call the particles atoms and molecules.

Smooth motion

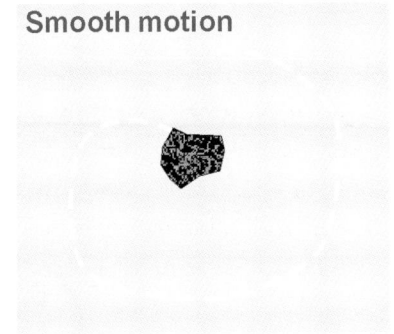

Figure 25.3: *A large floating dust speck moves smoothly because it is much larger than a particle of water.*

Brownian motion

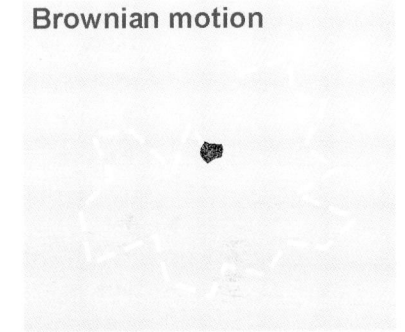

Figure 25.4: *A tiny dust speck shows Brownian motion because of collisions with particles of water. Question: Why does the dust speck move around? Why doesn't it stay still? The answer is in this chapter and involves temperature.*

Atoms and molecules

The smallest piece of matter

Suppose you want to make the smallest possible piece of gold. You can keep cutting a piece of gold into smaller and smaller pieces until you cannot cut it any more. That smallest piece is one atom. A single atom is the smallest amount of gold you can have.

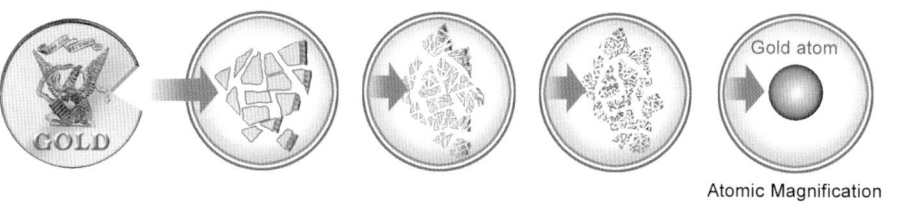

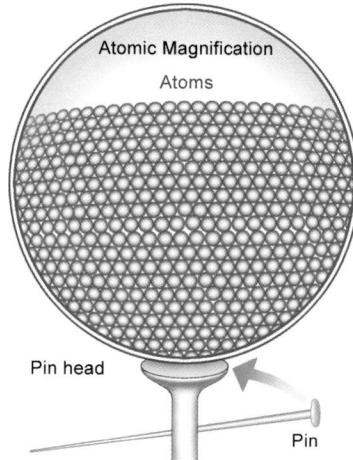

Figure 25.5: *The head of a pin contains more than 10^{20} atoms.*

Atoms

We now know that all the matter you are familiar with is made of atoms. Atoms make up everything that we see, hear, feel, smell, and touch. We don't experience atoms directly because they are so small. The head of a pin contains 10^{20} atoms (Figure 25.5). Aluminum foil is thin but is still more than 200,000 atoms thick (Figure 25.6). A single atom is about 10^{-10} meters in diameter. That means you can lay 10,000,000,000 (10^{10}) atoms side by side in a one meter length.

Molecules

A molecule is a group of two or more atoms that are joined together. If you could look at water with a powerful microscope you would find each particle of water is made from one oxygen atom and two hydrogen atoms.

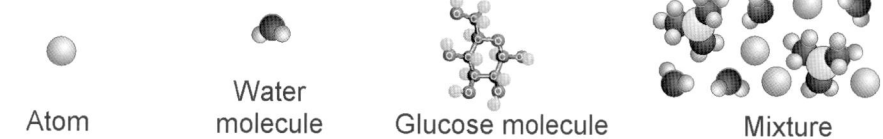

Atom   Water molecule   Glucose molecule   Mixture

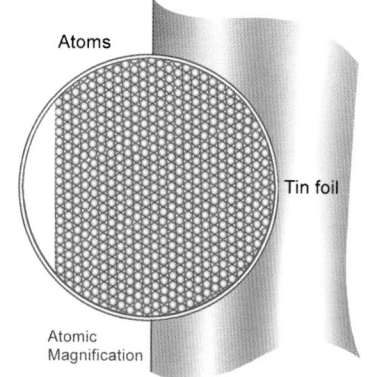

Figure 25.6: *A sheet of thin aluminum foil is 200,000 atoms thick.*

Matter is mostly molecules and mixtures

Most matter you encounter is made of molecules, or mixtures of molecules. For example, glucose is a common sugar found in food. Each molecule of glucose has six carbon atoms, six oxygen atoms and 12 hydrogen atoms. Grape soda is a mixture that contains water molecules, sugar molecules, molecules that make the purple color, and other molecules that create grape flavor and make the soda fizzy.

Elements

Explaining the diversity of matter
You can make millions of colors by mixing different amounts of red, green, and blue. Is it possible that millions of different kinds of matter are really mixtures of a few simpler things? The ancient Greeks thought so. Their theory proposed that all matter was made of four fundamental elements: *air*, *fire*, *water*, and *earth*. According to the Greek theory of matter, everything could be made by combining different amounts of the four elements. For example, wood contained certain proportions of water, earth, air, and fire. When wood was burned, the smoke was the fire and air. The ash left over was earth. Gold was a different mixture with more earth and less water. The theory was based on simple observations.

The early Greek theory of the elements

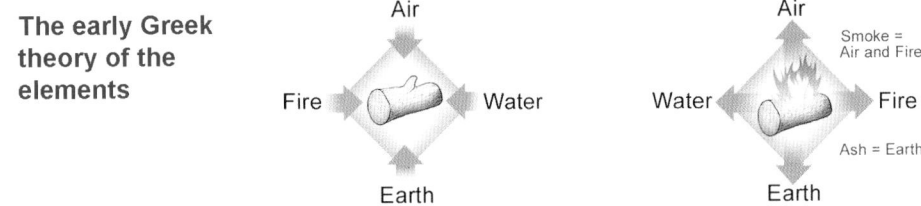

Elements
The Greeks had the right idea, but not the right elements. Today we know that nearly all the matter in the world is made from 92 different elements. Water is made from the elements hydrogen and oxygen. Air contains mostly nitrogen and oxygen. Steel is mostly iron and carbon, with a few exotic elements mixed in, like vanadium and chromium. Rocks are mostly silicon and oxygen. We get different kinds of matter from different combinations of the naturally occurring elements.

Atoms and elements
Each of the 92 elements has a unique type of atom. All atoms of a given element are similar to each other. If you could examine a million atoms of carbon you would find them all to be similar. But carbon atoms are different from iron atoms, or oxygen atoms. The atoms of an element are similar to atoms of the same element but different from atoms of other elements. You will find much more detail about atoms in Chapter 28.

One atom
One single atom is the smallest particle of an element that retains the identity of the element. Since all atoms of the same element are similar, every atom of carbon is identifiable as carbon. Similarly, every atom of gold is identifiable as gold.

The search for the elements

The search for the true elements has been a goal of people for thousands of years. Fortunes and medicine were among many historical reasons people were interested. If the difference between gold and lead was just a change in recipe, then it might be possible to make lead into gold! The person who found the right recipe would be rich. The search for the secret of turning lead into gold developed into the "false science" of alchemy during the Middle Ages. Other early experimenters believed sickness was an imbalance in the elements of the body. Various treatments were devised to adjust the amount of "ill-humours" present in a sick body. The experiments and observations of the alchemists and healers led directly to our modern understanding of chemistry. Chemistry is the science of how substances interact with each other, like wood burning in air. The foundation of chemistry is the study and description of the properties and interactions between the elements.

The periodic table of elements

The periodic table   The periodic table (graphic below) shows the elements in order from atomic number 1 (hydrogen) to number 92 (uranium). Elements with atomic numbers greater than 92 can be made in a laboratory but are not normally found in nature. The periodic table also groups the elements by their chemical properties. All the elements in the same column have similar chemical properties. For, example all the elements in column 18 are noble gases that do not form molecules with other atoms. The elements in the middle columns are all metals.

Mass and atomic number   The mass of an atom is proportional to its atomic number. The lightest atom is hydrogen at the top left. The heaviest atom shown is uranium (bottom right).

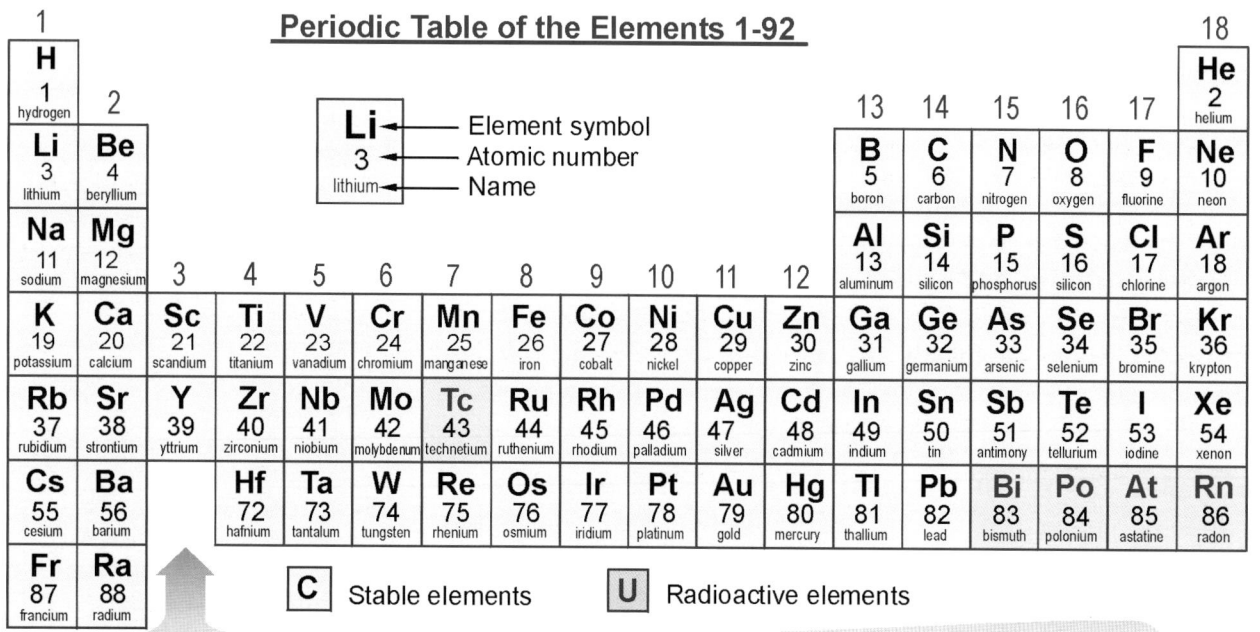

Periodic Table of the Elements 1-92

502

The diversity of matter

Compounds Salt is a solid crystal that dissolves in water and is commonly used to flavor foods. Sodium as a pure element is a soft, silvery metal. Chlorine as a pure element is a yellow-green, toxic gas. Salt is actually a chemical combination of the elements sodium and chlorine even though the properties of salt are very different from the properties of sodium or chlorine (Figure 25.7). The incredible diversity of matter we experience is created by combinations of the 92 basic elements into compounds, like salt. A compound is made of more than one element. Water is also a compound since it is made of molecules containing hydrogen and oxygen. Pure elements are rare. Most matter exists in the form of compounds.

Salt Crystal

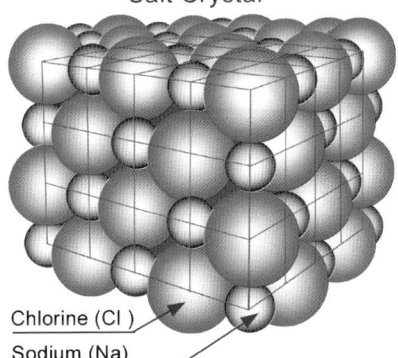

Chlorine (Cl)
Sodium (Na)

Figure 25.7: *Salt is a combination of sodium atoms and chlorine atomss.*

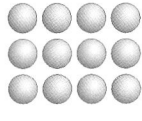

Element
One single
kind of atom

Compound
Molecules containing more
than one kind of atom

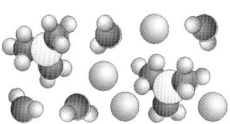

Mixture
Combination of different
compounds and/or elements

● Carbon atom   ○ Hydrogen atom

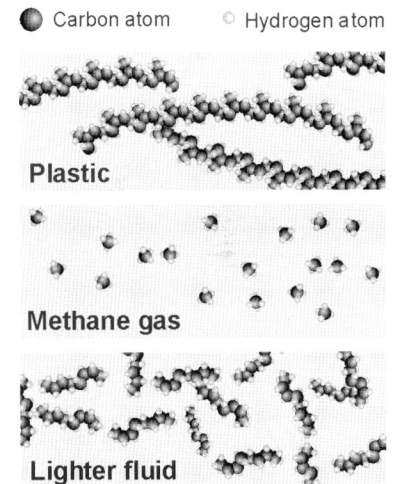

Plastic

Methane gas

Lighter fluid

Figure 25.8: *Material properties depend more on molecules than on atoms. Carbon and hydrogen atoms can make methane gas, lighter fluid, wax, or plastic depending on how they are arranged into molecules.*

Molecules and properties of materials The properties of matter depend on how the atoms are arranged into molecules and mixtures. For example, one carbon atom with four hydrogen atoms makes a methane molecule. Methane is a flammable gas used to heat houses. Ten carbon atoms and 22 hydrogen atoms make a decane molecule. Decane is an oily liquid which you may have used as charcoal lighter fluid. Other combinations of carbon and hydrogen make wax and plastic. You would be surprised how many different substances can be made from just carbon and hydrogen!

How one material changes into another You can rearrange the same atoms into different molecules and get completely different materials (Figure 25.8). Wood and ashes are made from the same elements, just arranged in different molecules. The heat that turns wood into ashes is actually providing energy to break bonds between atoms, combine some with oxygen from the air, and rearrange the atoms into different molecules. That is how one substance can turn into something else.

25.2 Temperature and the Phases of Matter

The concepts of warm and cold are familiar to everyone. What causes ice to feel cold and fresh coffee to feel hot? The simple answer is temperature. Ice feels cold because its temperature is less than the temperature of your skin. Coffee feels hot because its temperature is greater than your skin temperature. Temperature is related to energy and determines whether matter takes the form of solid, liquid, or gas.

Temperature scales

Fahrenheit — There are two commonly used temperature scales. In the Fahrenheit scale, water freezes at 32 degrees and boils at 212 degrees (Figure 25.9). There are 180 Fahrenheit degrees between the freezing point and the boiling point of water. Temperature in the United States is commonly measured in Fahrenheit. For example, 72°F is a comfortable room temperature.

Celsius — The Celsius scale divides the difference between the freezing and boiling points of water into 100 degrees (instead of 180). Water freezes at 0°C and boils at 100°C. Most science and engineering temperature measurement is in Celsius because 0 and 100 are easier to remember than 32 and 212. Most other countries use the Celsius scale for all descriptions of temperature, including daily weather reports.

Converting between Fahrenheit and Celsius

$$T_{\text{Fahrenheit}} = \frac{9}{5}T_{\text{Celsius}} + 32 \qquad T_{\text{Celsius}} = \frac{5}{9}(T_{\text{Fahrenheit}} - 32)$$

Fahrenheit to Celsius — To convert from Fahrenheit to Celsius, subtract 32 then multiply by five-ninths. Subtracting 32 is necessary because water freezes at 32°F and 0°C. The factor of 5/9 is applied because the Celsius degree is larger than the Fahrenheit degree.

Celsius to Fahrenheit — To convert from Celsius to Fahrenheit, multiply by 9/5 then add 32. If you travel to other countries, you will want to learn the difference between the two temperature scales. A weather report that says 21°C in London, England, predicts a pleasant day, suitable for shorts and T-shirt. A weather report predicting 21°F in Minneapolis, Minnesota, means a heavy winter coat, gloves, and a hat. The United States is one of the few countries still using the Fahrenheit scale.

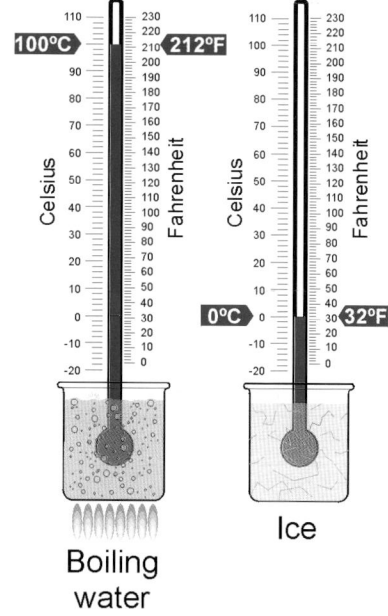

Water boils at 100°C (212°F) and freezes at 0°C (32°F)

Figure 25.9: *The Celsius and Fahrenheit temperature scales.*

Measuring temperature

Human temperature sense

Our sense of temperature is not very accurate. Humans can sense when something is warm or cold, but cannot sense exact temperature. If you walk into a 65°F room from being outside on a winter day, the room feels warm. The same room will feel cool if you come in from outside on a hot summer day.

Thermometers

A thermometer is an instrument that measures temperature. The common alcohol thermometer (Figure 25.10) uses the expansion of liquid alcohol. As the temperature increases, the alcohol expands and rises up a long, thin tube. The temperature is measured by the height the alcohol rises. The thermometer can read small changes in temperature because the bulb at the bottom has a much larger volume than the tube.

How thermometers work

There are many ways to make a thermometer. All thermometers are based on some physical property (such as color or volume) that changes with temperature. A thermistor is a device that changes its electrical resistance as the temperature changes. Some electronic thermometers sense temperature by measuring the resistance of a thermistor. A thermocouple is another electrical sensor that measures temperature. A thermocouple is made by joining two metals of different elements. A small electrical voltage is created where the metals touch. The voltage depends on the temperature. An electronic thermometer that uses a thermocouple measures the voltage and converts it to temperature. Some kinds of chemicals change color at different temperatures. One brand of baby bathtub has a thermometer strip that changes color when the water is too hot or cold.

Writing temperatures
Temperatures in Fahrenheit and Celsius are measured in degrees indicated with a little circle and the capital letters F or C. The temperature 72°F reads "72 degrees Fahrenheit." Likewise, 21°C reads "21 degrees Celsius."

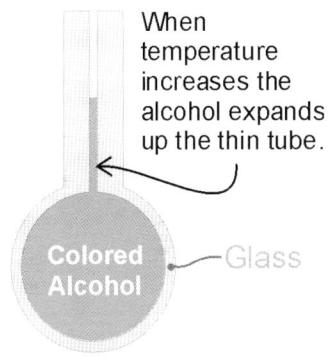

When temperature increases the alcohol expands up the thin tube.

Colored Alcohol — Glass

Figure 25.10: *How an alcohol thermometer works. The alcohol is often colored red to make it easier to see. Older thermometers used mercury, a silver liquid metal, instead of colored alcohol. Mercury is no longer used because it is toxic.*

Converting from Celsius to Fahrenheit

A friend in Paris sends you a recipe for a cake. The French recipe says to bake the cake at a temperature of 200°C for 45 minutes. At what temperature should you set your oven, which reads temperature in Fahrenheit?

1) You are asked for the temperature in Fahrenheit.
2) You are given the temperature in Celsius.
3) Use the conversion formula $T_F = (9/5)T_C + 32$.
4) $T_F = (9/5)(200) + 32 = 392$ degrees

What temperature is

Temperature and energy
Temperature is a measure of the kinetic energy of individual atoms. Imagine you had a microscope powerful enough to see individual atoms in a solid at room temperature. You would see that the atoms are in constant motion. The atoms in a solid material act like they are connected by springs (Figure 25.11). Each atom is free to move a small amount. When the temperature goes up, the energy of motion increases and the atoms jostle more vigorously.

Average motion
We already know the relationship between motion and kinetic energy for a single object (or atom). For a *collection* of atoms, the situation is different. The kinetic energy of the collection has two distinct parts. The kinetic energy you already know comes from the motion of the whole collection. If all the atoms were moving identically, the velocity of each individual atom would be the same as the velocity of the whole collection. However, this is not what really occurs.

Random motion
Each atom in a collection can also have random motion. Random motion is motion that is scattered equally in all directions. In pure random motion the average change in position for the whole collection is zero. The average is zero because there are as many atoms moving one way as there are moving the opposite way. The collection as a whole stays in the same place.

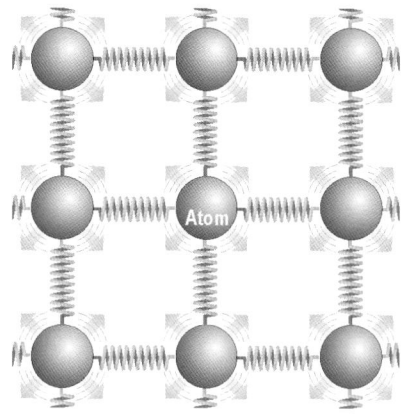

Figure 25.11: *Atoms in a solid are connected by bonds that act like springs. The atoms vibrate and the temperature measures their average energy of vibration.*

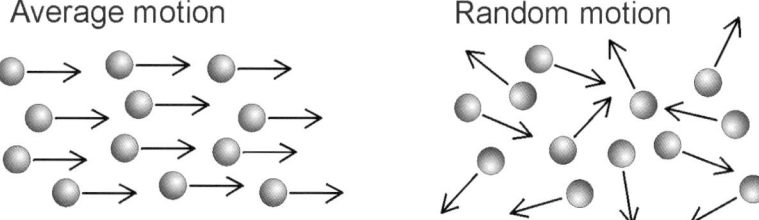

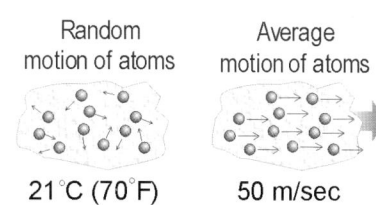

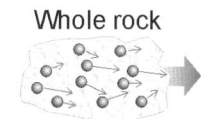

Temperature and random motion
Temperature measures the kinetic energy per atom due to random motion. Temperature is not affected by any kinetic energy associated with average motion. That is why throwing a rock does not make it hotter (Figure 25.12). When you throw a rock you give each atom in the rock the same average motion because all the atoms move together. *Temperature affects only the random motion of atoms.* When you heat a rock with a torch, each atom moves around more, but the whole rock stays in the same place because temperature does not affect average motion.

Figure 25.12: *A collection of atoms can have both average motion and random motion. That is why a thrown rock has both a velocity and a temperature.*

Absolute zero and the limits of temperature

Absolute zero   There is a limit to how cold matter can get. As the temperature is reduced atoms move more and more slowly. When the temperature gets down to absolute zero, the atoms have the lowest energy they can have and the temperature cannot get any lower. You can think of absolute zero as the temperature where atoms are completely frozen, like ice, with no motion. Technically, atoms can never become absolutely motionless, but the distinction does not matter for most situations. Absolute zero occurs at minus 273°C (-459°F). It is not possible to have a temperature lower than absolute zero.

Quantum effects   Technically, we believe atoms can never stop moving completely. Even at absolute zero some tiny amount of energy is left. For our purposes this "zero point" energy might as well be truly zero because the rules of quantum physics prevent the energy from ever going any lower. Figuring out what happens when atoms are cooled to absolute zero is an area of active research.

The Kelvin scale   The Kelvin temperature scale is useful for many scientific calculations because it starts at absolute zero. For example, the pressure in a gas depends on how fast the atoms are moving. The Kelvin scale is used because it measures the actual energy of atoms. A temperature in Celsius measures only the *relative* energy, relative to zero Celsius.

Converting to Kelvin   The Kelvin (K) unit of temperature is the same size as the Celsius unit. Add 273 to the temperature in Celsius to get the temperature in Kelvins. For example, a temperature of 21°C is equal to 294 K (21 + 273).

Converting Celsius to Kelvin $$T_{\text{Kelvin}} = T_{\text{Celsius}} + 273$$

High temperatures   Temperature can be raised almost indefinitely. As the temperature increases, exotic forms of matter appear. For example, at 100,000K atoms start to come apart and become a plasma. In a plasma the atoms themselves are broken apart into separate positive ions and negative electrons. Plasma conducts electricity and is formed in lightning and inside stars. Figure 25.13 may help you get a sense for the temperatures at which different things happen.

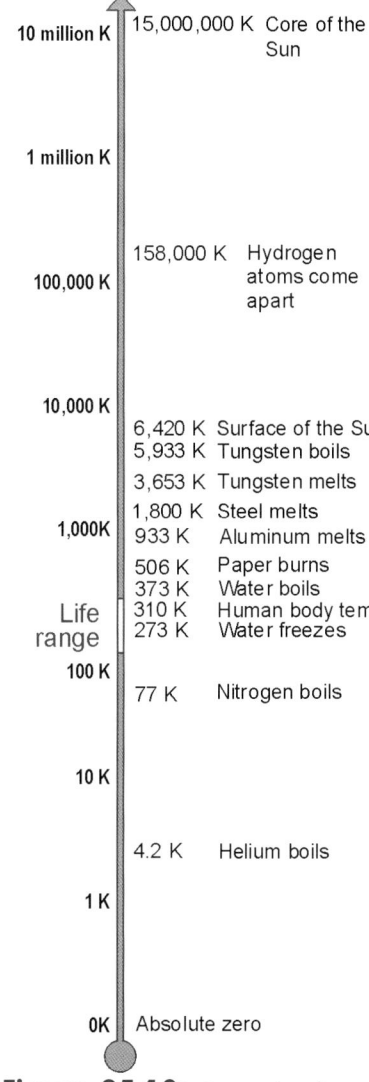

Figure 25.13: *A sample of temperatures in the universe. Most of our lives occur in a narrow 100°C range around the freezing point of water (223 K - 323 K).*

The phases of matter

Solid, liquid, and gas   The three most common phases of matter are called solid, liquid, and gas. Matter in the solid phase holds its shape and does not flow. Ice is a good example of a solid. Matter in the liquid phase keeps its volume constant but can flow and change its shape. Water is a good example of a liquid. Matter in the gas phase flows like liquid, but also can expand or contract to fill any size container. Air is a good example of a gas.

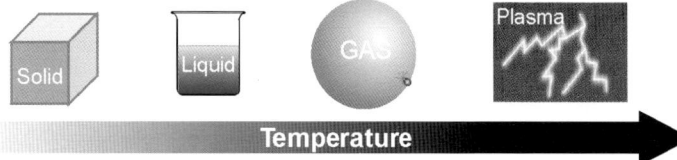

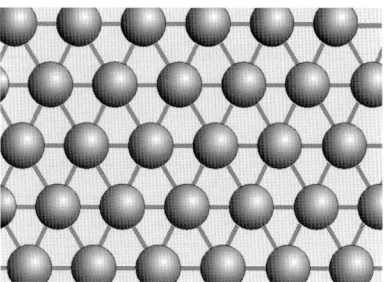

Figure 25.14: *Atoms or molecules in a solid stay bonded together.*

Solid   Matter at low temperatures is often solid. Atoms or molecules in a solid stay together because their thermal energy is too low to break the bonds between them (Figure 25.14). Imagine a marching band marching in place *with every one holding hands.* People move but each stays in the same place relative to others. Everyone in a marching band moves together, like the atoms in a solid.

Liquid   The liquid phase occurs at a higher temperature than the solid phase. Liquids flow because the atoms have enough energy to move around by temporarily breaking and reforming bonds with neighboring atoms (Figure 25.15). Imagine a room full of people dancing. The crowd generally stays together, *but people have enough energy to move around and switch partners,* like the atoms in a liquid.

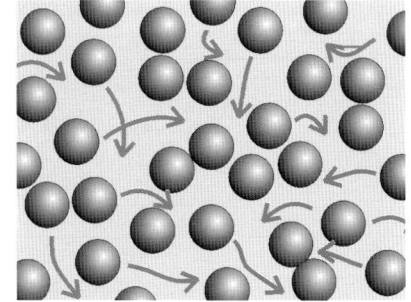

Figure 25.15: *Atoms in a liquid stay close together but can move around and exchange places.*

Gas   The gas phase occurs at a higher temperature than the liquid phase. Gas atoms have enough energy that bonds between neighbors are completely broken (Figure 25.16). Gas expands because atoms can move independently. Imagine many people running fast in different directions. Every person is moving independently with a lot of space between people, like the atoms in a gas.

Plasma   At temperatures greater than 10,000 K the atoms in a gas start to break apart. In the plasma state, matter becomes ionized as electrons are broken loose from atoms. Because the electrons are free to move independently, plasma can conduct electricity. Lightning is a good example of plasma. The sun is another example.

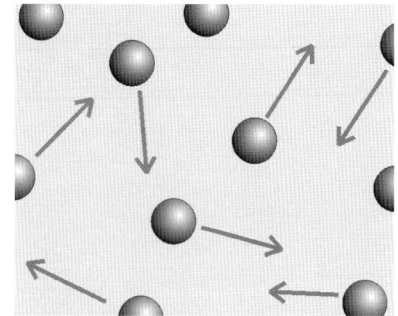

Figure 25.16: *Atoms in a gas move fast and are separated by relatively large spaces.*

Changing from solid to liquid

Melting The melting point is the temperature at which a material changes phase from solid to liquid. Melting occurs when the kinetic energy of individual atoms equals the attractive force between atoms. Different materials have different melting points because the bonds between atoms have different strengths. Water melts at 0°C (32°F). Iron melts at a much higher temperature, about 1,500°C (2,800°F). The difference in melting points tells us the attractive force between iron atoms is much greater than the attractive force between water molecules.

Heat of fusion The heat of fusion is the amount of energy it takes to change one kilogram of material from solid to liquid or vice versa. The energy goes to make or break bonds between atoms. Table 25.1 gives some representative values of the heat of fusion (h_f) for common materials. Note how large the values are. It takes 335,000 joules of energy to turn one kilogram of ice into liquid water.

Phase changes take energy When thermal energy is added or subtracted from a material, either the temperature changes, or the phase changes, but usually not both at the same time. Think about heating a block of ice that has a temperature of -20°C. As you add heat energy, the temperature increases. Once it reaches 0°C, *the temperature stops increasing* as ice starts to melt and form liquid water. As you add more heat, more ice becomes water but the temperature stays the same. The energy (heat) goes to changing the phase from solid to liquid. Once all the ice has become liquid water, the temperature starts to rise again as more heat is added. This can easily be observed with an ordinary thermometer in a *well-stirred* experiment.

Table 25.1:
Heat of fusion for common materials

Material	Heat of fusion (J/kg)
Water	335,000
Wax	175,00
Aluminum	321,000
Iron	267,000
Silver	88,000

Calculating the energy for changing from solid to liquid

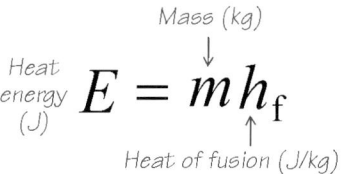

$$E = m\,h_f$$

Heat energy (J) — Mass (kg) — Heat of fusion (J/kg)

Calculate the energy to melt ice

How many joules does it take to melt a 30 gram ice cube at 0°C?

1) You are asked for heat energy (E) in joules.

2) You are given mass (m) and that the material is ice.

3) Use the phase change equation $E = mh_f$

4) E = (0.03 kg)(335,000 J/kg) = 10,050 J

Start with ice at -20°C

Add heat energy at a constant rate.

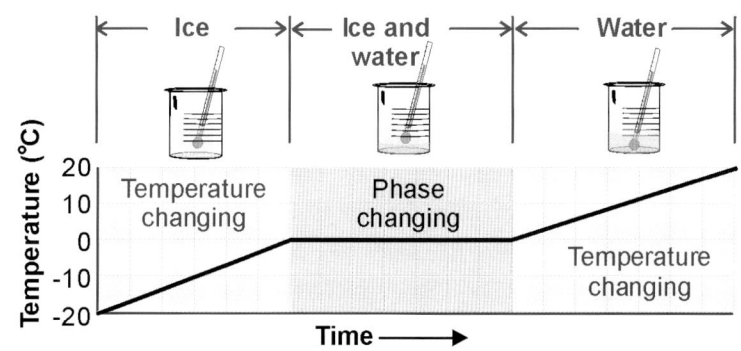

Changing from liquid to gas

Boiling The boiling point is the temperature at which the phase changes from liquid to gas. Water boils at 100°C (212°F) at one atmosphere of pressure. The steam rising from a pot of boiling water is water molecules in the gas phase. Even metals such as iron can become a gas, although it takes a much higher temperature. Iron boils above 2,900°C (5,200°F).

Heat of vaporization Just as with melting, it takes energy for an atom to go from liquid to gas. The heat of vaporization is the amount of energy it takes to convert one kilogram of liquid to one kilogram of gas. In a gas, all the bonds between one atom and its neighbors are completely broken. Some representative values for the heat of vaporization are given in Table 25.2. It takes 2,256,000 joules to turn a kilogram of water into a kilogram of steam! That is why stoves and steam irons require so much electricity. The heat of vaporization is much greater than the heat of fusion because breaking bonds between atoms or molecules takes much more energy than exchanging bonds. In a liquid, molecules move around by *exchanging* bonds with neighboring molecules. The energy needed to break one bond is recovered when the molecule forms a new bond with its neighbor.

Energy and phase change If you add heat to a pot of boiling water at 100°C, the temperature of the water stays right at the boiling point. The heat you add goes to changing water atoms from the liquid phase to the gas phase. The temperature of the boiling water will stay at 100°C until all the liquid has been converted to steam (Figure 25.17). Heat can change a material's temperature or its phase, but not both at the same time.

Table 25.2:
Heat of vaporization for common materials

Material	Heat of vaporization (J/kg)
Water	2,256,000
Alcohol	854,000
Liquid nitrogen	201,000
Lead	871,000
Silver	2,336,000

Calculating the energy for changing from liquid to gas

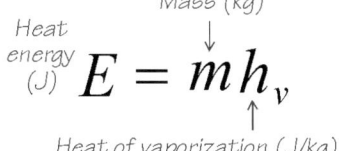

$$E = m h_v$$

Heat energy (J) — Mass (kg) — Heat of vaporization (J/kg)

Figure 25.17: *It takes 2,256,000 joules to turn one kilogram of liquid water at 100°C into steam.*

Calculating the heat needed to boil water into steam

A steam iron is used to remove the wrinkles from clothes. The iron boils water in a small chamber and vents steam out the bottom. How much energy does it require to change one-half gram (0.0005 kg, or about half a teaspoon) of water into steam?

1) You are asked for the heat energy required (E) in joules.
2) You are given that the material is water, and the mass (m) is 0.0005 kg.
3) The heat of vaporization equation applies: E = mh$_v$
4) E = (0.0005 kg) (2,256,000 J/kg)

= 1,128 joules.

A typical steam iron takes about 5 seconds to boil this amount of water.

Evaporation and condensation

Evaporation Evaporation occurs when molecules go from liquid to gas at temperatures *below* the boiling point. Evaporation happens because temperature measures the *average* random kinetic energy of molecules. Some have energy above the average and some below the average. Some of the highest energy molecules have enough energy to break bonds with their neighbors and become a gas if they are near the surface. Molecules with higher than average energy are the source of evaporation.

Evaporation cools liquids Evaporation takes energy away from a liquid. The molecules that escape are the ones with the most energy. The average energy of the molecules left behind is lowered. Evaporation cools the surface of a liquid because the fastest molecules escape and carry energy away. That is why we sweat on a hot day. The evaporation of sweat from your skin cools your body (Figure 25.18).

Figure 25.18: *Evaporation is how we sweat. When water evaporates from the skin it carries away energy and cools the body.*

Condensation Condensation occurs when molecules go from gas to liquid at temperatures below the boiling point (Figure 25.19). Water vapor in the air often condenses on cool surfaces. Water molecules with less than the average energy may stick to a cool surface forming drops of liquid water. Condensation raises the temperature of a gas because atoms in a gas have more energy than atoms in a liquid. Low energy gas atoms condense into liquid leaving higher energy (warmer) atoms in the gas.

Air contains water vapor Ordinary air contains some water vapor. Evaporation adds water vapor to the air. Condensation removes water vapor. The percentage of water vapor in the air is a balance between evaporation and condensation. When air is saturated, it means the processes of evaporation and condensation are exactly balanced. If you try to add more water vapor to saturated air, it condenses into liquid water again.

Relative humidity The relative humidity tells how close the air is to saturation. When the relative humidity is 100 percent, the air is completely saturated. That means any water vapor that evaporates from your skin is condensed right back again, which is why you feel hot and sticky when the humidity is high. The body's natural cooling mechanism cannot work effectively because the air is already saturated with water vapor. The opposite is true in the dry air of desert climates. Hot desert air has a very low relative humidity, allowing water to evaporate rapidly. This is why dry heat feels more bearable than humid heat.

Figure 25.19: *Dew is formed by condensation. Water vapor in the air condenses to form liquid droplets. Condensation warms the air since the heat of vaporization is given up when the water goes from gas to liquid.*

25.3 Heat and Thermal Energy

To change the temperature of matter you need to add or subtract energy in the form of heat. When you want to get your house warm in the winter you add heat. If you want to cool your house in summer you remove heat. This section makes the connection between temperature, heat, and energy. By the end of the section you should be able to figure out how much heat to add or subtract when you want to change the temperature by a certain number of degrees.

The relationship between heat, energy, and temperature

What causes hot and cold?
You can warm your cold hands by holding them against a hot cup of coffee (Figure 25.20). What property of the hot coffee cup flows into your hands to make them warm? For a long time people thought a fluid called *caloric* was responsible. Think of *caloric* as "liquid heat." According to this theory, hot coffee was hot because it had more *caloric* than cold coffee. Your hands warm up because caloric flows from the hot cup to your colder hands. It seemed like a good explanation, *except it was wrong*. If you carefully measure the mass of an object when it is hot and when it is cold, you find the mass is exactly the same. If the caloric theory were correct, the hot object (with more caloric) should have more mass than the cold object.

Figure 25.20: *You can warm your hands around a cup of hot coffee because heat flows from hot to cold, carrying energy to your hands.*

Thermal energy
Today we know that *energy* is what flows from hot to cold and warms up your hands. Thermal energy is energy stored in materials because of differences in temperature. Remember, temperature measures the random kinetic energy of *each* atom. The thermal energy of an object is the total amount of random kinetic energy for *all* the atoms in the object.

Temperature and thermal energy
Temperature is not the same as thermal energy. Imagine heating a cup of coffee to a temperature of 100°C. Next think about heating up 1,000 cups of coffee to 100°C (Figure 25.21). The final temperature is the same in both cases but the amount of energy needed is very different. It takes more energy to heat up 1,000 cups than to heat up a single cup. The amount of thermal energy depends on the temperature and also on the amount of matter you have.

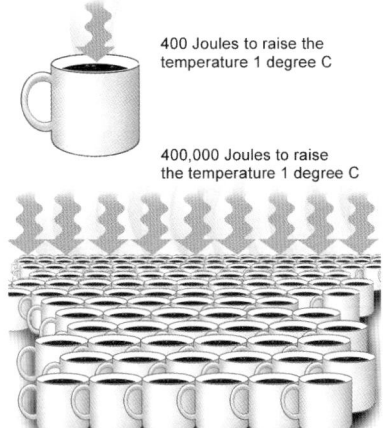

400 Joules to raise the temperature 1 degree C

400,000 Joules to raise the temperature 1 degree C

Figure 25.21: *It takes 400 joules to raise the temperature of one cup of coffee one degree. It takes 400,000 joules to raise the temperature of 1,000 cups of coffee the same one degree.*

512

Heat and thermal energy

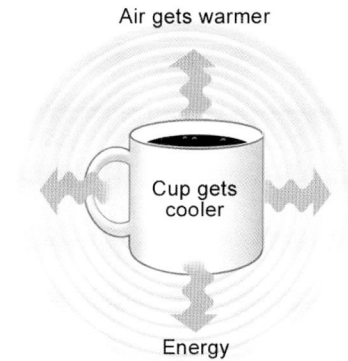

Figure 25.22: *Heat carries thermal energy from hot to cold. The cup gets cooler and the air in the room gets warmer.*

Heat   Heat is what we call thermal energy that is moving. Heat naturally flows from hot to cold and moves thermal energy from higher temperatures to lower ones. When you leave a cup of hot coffee on the table, it cools down. Heat flows from the hot coffee to the cooler air in the room. The thermal energy of the hot coffee is decreased by the heat that flows. The thermal energy of the air is increased by the heat that flows. Everything balances; the increase in thermal energy of the air is exactly the same as the decrease in thermal energy of the coffee (Figure 25.22).

Joules   The joule (J) is the unit of heat (or thermal energy) used for physics and engineering. Heat is a form of energy and the joule is the same unit used for all other forms of energy. There are also other commonly used units to measure heat. Each unit was developed to measure heat in a different application. For physics calculations, you may have to convert from the other units to joules.

Calories   The calorie is a unit of heat often used in chemistry. One calorie is the amount of heat required to raise the temperature of one gram of water by one degree Celsius. The calorie is larger than the joule. There are 4.18 joules in one calorie.

British thermal units (Btu)   The air conditioner or furnace in your house is rated in British thermal units (Btu). One Btu is the amount of heat required to raise the temperature of one pound of water by one degree Fahrenheit. A typical home-heating furnace can produce 10,000 to 100,000 Btu per hour. One Btu equals 1,055 joules.

Units of heat and thermal energy	Practical application
1 joule = energy to push with a force of 1 newton for 1 m.	Heat added
1 BTU = 1055 joules	1 kg of water at 10°C (50°F) + 41,840 J / 10,000 cal / 39.7 BTU = 1 kg of water at 20°C (68°F)
1 calorie = 4.184 joules	

Specific heat

Differences in materials The same amount of heat causes a different change in temperature in different materials. For example, if you add four joules of heat to one gram of water, the temperature goes up by about one degree Celsius. If you add the same four joules of heat to one gram of gold, the temperature goes up by 31°C! The different temperature rise happens because different materials have different abilities to store thermal energy (Figure 25.23).

Specific heat The **specific heat** is the quantity of heat it takes to raise the temperature of one kilogram of material by one degree Celsius. Water is an important example; the specific heat of water is 4,184 J/kg°C. It takes 4,184 joules to raise the temperature of one kilogram of water by one degree Celsius. The specific heat of gold is 129 J/kg°C. The temperature of gold rises quickly compared with water because its specific heat is much less than the specific heat of water (129 compared with 4,184). Table 25.3 gives the specific heat of some common materials.

The heat equation The heat equation is used to calculate how much heat (E) it takes to make a temperature change ($T_2 - T_1$) in a mass (m) of material with specific heat (c_p).

Heat equation

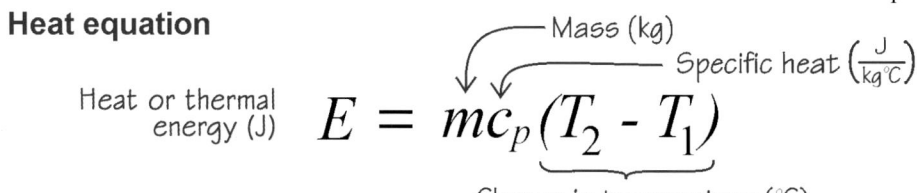

$$E = mc_p(T_2 - T_1)$$

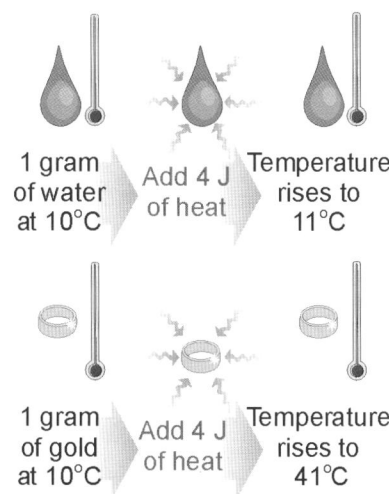

Figure 25.23: *The same amount of heat causes the temperature of silver to rise much more than the temperature of water.*

Table 25.3: Specific heat of common materials

Material	Specific heat (J/kg°C)
Air at 1 atm	1,006
Water	4,184
Aluminum	900
Steel	470
Silver	235
Oil	1,900
Concrete	880
Glass	800
Gold	129
Wood	2,500

NOTE: Specific heat often changes with temperature and pressure.

Calculate the heat required to reach a temperature.

One kilogram of water is heated in a microwave oven that delivers 500 watts of heat to the water. One watt is a flow of energy of one joule per second. If the water starts at 10°C, how much time does it take to heat up to 100°C?

1) You are asked for the time (t) to reach a given temperature (T_2).
2) You are given the mass (m) of water, power (P), and initial temperature (T_1). The specific heat of water is 4,184 j/kg°C.
3) The heat equation, $E = mc_p(T_2-T_1)$, gives the heat required. Power is energy over time: P = E/t.
4) First, calculate the heat required: E = (1 kg) (4,184 J/kg°C) (100°C - 10°C) = 376,560 joules. Next, recall that 500 watts is 500 joules per second. At 500 J/sec, it takes 376,560÷500 = 753 seconds, or about 12.6 minutes.

Why the specific heat is different for different materials

Why specific heat varies

Materials with heavy atoms or molecules have low specific heat compared with materials with lighter atoms. This is because temperature measures the energy per atom. Heavy atoms mean fewer atoms per kilogram. Energy that is divided between fewer atoms means more energy per atom, and therefore more temperature change.

An example: silver and aluminum

Suppose you add four joules of heat to a gram of silver and four joules to a gram of aluminum. Silver's specific heat is 235 J/kg°C and four joules is enough to raise the temperature of the silver by 19°C. Aluminum's specific heat is 900 J/kg°C, and four joules only raises the temperature of the aluminum by 5°C. The silver has fewer atoms than the aluminum because silver atoms are heavier than aluminum atoms. When heat is added, each atom of silver gets more energy than each atom of aluminum because there are fewer silver atoms in a gram. Because the energy per atom is greater, the temperature increase in the silver is also greater.

Why is the specific heat of aluminum almost 4 times greater than the specific heat of silver?

 Silver
Specific heat: **235** J/kg°C

1 gram
Heavier atoms, mean **fewer** atoms per gram.

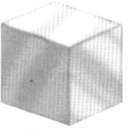 **Aluminum**
Specific heat: **900** J/kg°C

1 gram
Lighter atoms, mean **more** atoms per gram.

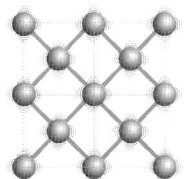

Energy is spread over **fewer** atoms

More energy per atom

Higher temperature gain per joule (lower specific heat)

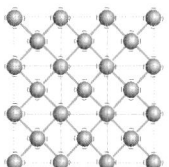

Energy is spread over **more** atoms

Less energy per atom

Lower temperature gain per joule (higher specific heat)

Elements with heavier atoms have lower specific heat because ...

Temperature depends on the energy *per atom*

cold   warm   hot

Thermodynamics

The first law of thermodynamics

The total amount of energy in any closed system is constant.

Work

Heat   **Mechanical energy**

Chemical energy

Thermodynamics is a branch of physics that deals with the relationship between thermal energy and other forms of energy. The first law of thermodynamics is a restatement of the law of conservation of energy, including thermal energy.

The second law of thermodynamics

In a closed system energy flows from hot to cold

High temperature

Heat Work Mechanical energy   Chemical energy

Low temperature

Many machines (including your car engine) get useful work as energy flows from higher temperature to lower temperature. The second law says there must be a temperature difference for a machine to extract useful work from thermal energy.

Application: The Refrigerator

What would we do without refrigeration? Many foods are produced far away from where you buy them. The fact that you can buy fruits, vegetables, dairy products, eggs, and meat almost everywhere all year round is due mainly to the invention of the refrigerator. A refrigerator moves thermal energy out of the inside of the appliance, making things inside it colder. The thermal energy is pumped to the outside of the refrigerator, making the room warmer (Figure 25.24). If you think about how heat usually flows, a refrigerator should not work! Heat usually flows from hot to cold, not the other way around. However, if you turn off the power to the refrigerator, the situation reverts to normal. Heat flows from the room (warm) to the inside of the refrigerator and things will not stay frozen. It takes power (electricity) to make heat flow opposite to its normal direction.

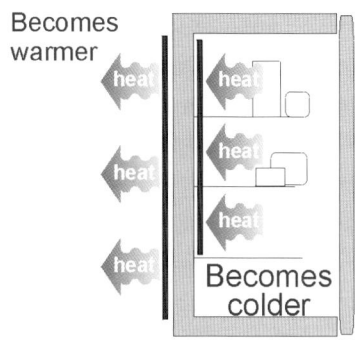

Figure 25.24: *A refrigerator moves heat from the colder inside to the warmer outside.*

Gas cools when it expands
When you pop open a can of soda, you may notice that the escaping gas feels cold. When a gas at high pressure expands to low pressure, the gas cools. The cooling effect happens because energy of vibration is transformed into energy of motion as the molecules rapidly expand away from each other. The cooling effect of an expanding gas is what makes a refrigerator work.

The principle of a refrigerator
In a refrigerator, the cooling effect is created by pumping a high-pressure liquid through a tiny hole, called an expansion valve. The liquid becomes a gas because the pressure is very low on the cold side of the valve. The gas used in refrigerators typically drops from 40°C to -20°C between the highest and lowest pressure. A refrigerator moves heat by circulating a fluid that changes from a warm, high-pressure liquid to a cold, low-pressure gas/liquid mixture.

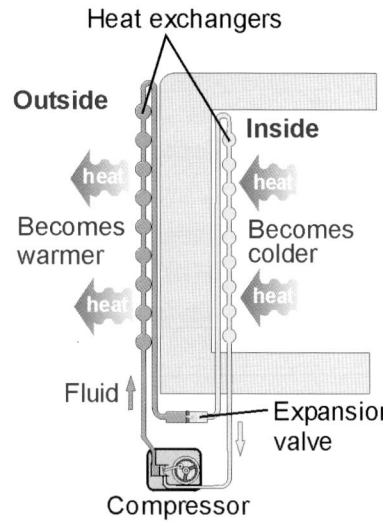

Figure 25.25: *The working parts of a refrigerator. A fluid flows through the tubes and changes from liquid to gas at different places.*

How an expansion valve works

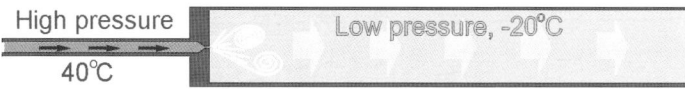

The compressor and heat exchangers
A refrigerator has two *heat exchangers* and a special pump called a compressor (Figure 25.25). One heat exchanger is colder than the inside of the refrigerator and absorbs heat from inside. The other heat exchanger is hotter than room-temperature air and rejects the heat into the room. The compressor creates the pressure difference and is what makes the burbling noise when the refrigerator is on. The best way to learn how a refrigerator works is to follow some fluid through the cycle from the compressor through the heat exchangers and back.

The refrigeration cycle

Expansion and cooling — The cooling effect begins with expansion of high-pressure liquid through the expansion valve. The liquid becomes very cold gas as it passes through the hole and enters the low-pressure part of the cycle. The gas is so cold that it condenses partly into cold liquid. Heat flows into the cold gas/liquid mixture through the inside heat exchanger because the mixture is colder than the air in the refrigerator.

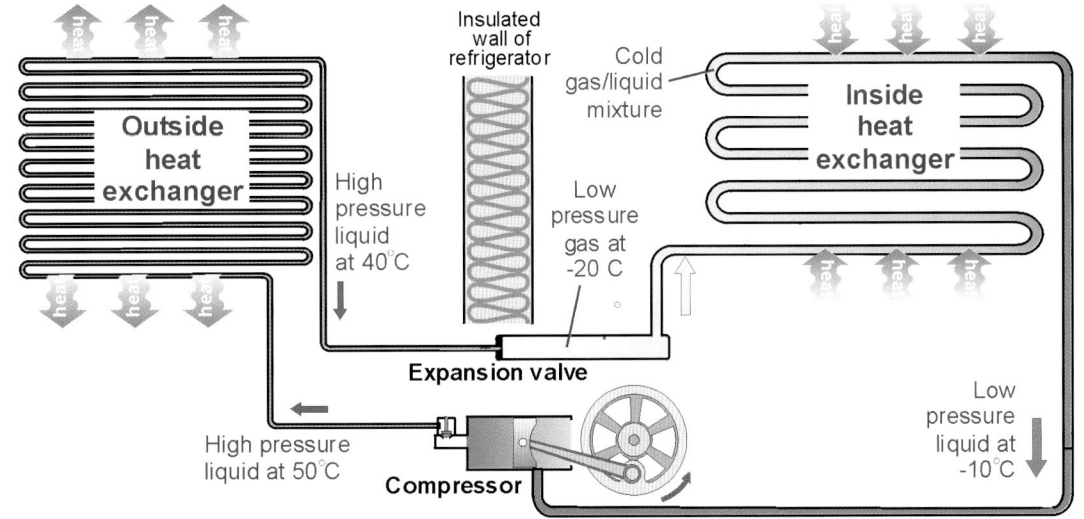

Rejecting heat to the room — The cold, low-pressure mixture is raised back to high pressure by the compressor. Raising the pressure makes the temperature go up and the high-pressure liquid is warmer than room-temperature air. The high-pressure liquid loses heat to the room and cools down as it flows through the outside heat exchanger. The high-pressure liquid flows back to the expansion valve, where it expands back into cold, low-pressure gas again. The fluid in the refrigerator continuously cycles from low pressure (cold) to high pressure (hot), carrying thermal energy with its flow.

Conservation of energy — As clever as it is, a refrigerator still obeys the law of conservation of energy. The heat energy absorbed by the room equals the heat energy taken out of the refrigerator plus the electrical energy you have to supply to make the compressor work. If you leave a refrigerator door open, the room actually gets warmer overall.

Air conditioners

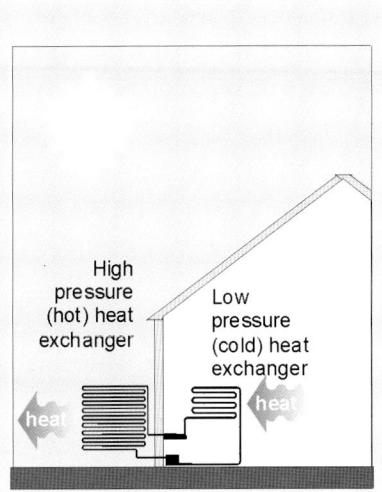

An air conditioner is just like a refrigerator, except that the whole house becomes the inside of the refrigerator. The cold, low-pressure heat exchanger is inside the house. The hot, high-pressure heat exchanger is outside the house. An air conditioner moves thermal energy from inside to outside, making the air in the house cooler and the air outside warmer.

Chapter 25 Review

Vocabulary Review

Match the following terms with the correct definition. There is one extra definition in the list that will not match any of the terms.

Set One

1. atom
2. compound
3. element
4. mixture
5. molecule

a. Combination of different compounds and/or elements
b. Smallest particle of a compound
c. Made from two or more elements
d. Air, water, fire and earth
e. 92 are used to make all kinds of matter
f. The smallest particle of an element

Set Two

1. gas
2. liquid
3. plasma
4. solid

a. Temporarily broken bonds allow some movement
b. State in which matter is ionized; electrons are separated from atoms
c. State in which matter has the lowest thermal energy
d. Matter with a temperature below 0 K
e. Atoms are free to move independently

Set Three

1. absolute zero
2. joule
3. Celsius scale
4. Kelvin scale
5. thermal energy

a. Energy stored in materials due to temperature difference
b. Water freezes at 0° and boils at 100°
c. Unit used to represent thermal energy
d. Water freezes at 32° and boils at 212°
e. Temperature scale that starts at -273 °C
f. Theoretical temperature where molecules are virtually motionless with the lowest possible thermal energy

Set Four

1. melting point
2. specific heat
3. evaporation
4. heat of fusion
5. saturated

a. Measure of the energy to cause 1 kg of material to melt
b. Heat to raise the temperature of 1 kg of material 1 degree
c. Air in which condensation and evaporation are balanced
d. Change of phase from liquid to gas below the boiling point
e. Heat to raise the temperature of 1 pound of water 1 degree
f. Temperature at which materials change phase from solid to liquid

Concept review

1. As you observe the movement of a smoke particle under a microscope you see irregular, "jerky" motion called Brownian movement. What is the cause of this motion?

2. Compare and contrast the terms *compound* and *molecule*.

3. Compare and contrast the terms *atom* and *element*.

4. A student from Germany flies to visit a family in Oswego, New York. He hears the captain report the weather on arrival as "clear and sunny with temperatures in the low 20's." He changes on the plane into shorts and a T-shirt. Explain his behavior.

5. The operation of all thermometers is based on some physical property that changes with temperature. Describe the operation of **two** different thermometers based upon these physical properties.

6. Fahrenheit and Celsius degrees are most commonly used to indicate temperature on household thermometers. Which degree is larger? How can this be determined?

7. Temperature is a measure of the kinetic energy or the motion of the molecules of an object. What type of molecular motion is responsible for temperature differences?

8. Compare and contrast the Celsius and Kelvin scales of temperature.

9. What causes compounds such as water to change phase from solid to liquid or gas to plasma?

10. Heat is added to ice at its melting point and to the same amount of water at its boiling point. Describe the difference in the amount of heat needed to change the phase of water in each case.

11. Explain why evaporation causes the temperature of an evaporating liquid to decrease.

12. The following graphs represent "temperature vs. time" graphs for 1-kilogram masses of various materials under various heating or cooling circumstances. Match each graph with a statement that could correctly represent the circumstances.

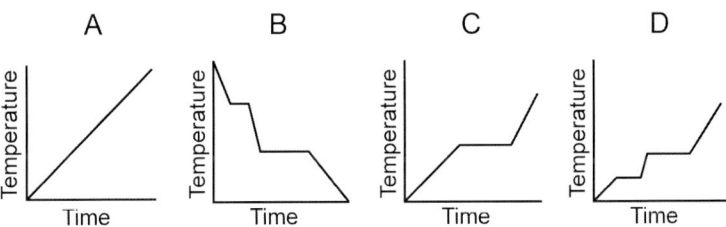

a. A material changing from solid to liquid to gas.

b. A material whose heat of fusion is greater than its heat of vaporization.

c. A material whose specific heat is greatest in the liquid phase.

d. A material which is present in only one phase.

13. Below are three diagrams of ionic compounds in their phases. Label each diagram as solid, liquid or gas. Summarize the characteristics of each phase.

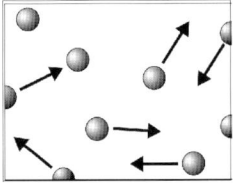 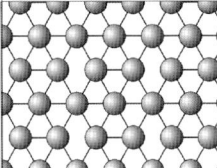 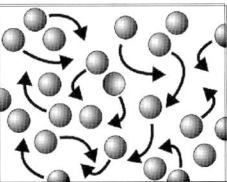

14. Which would cause a more severe burn to your skin: exposure to 1 kilogram of steam at 100° Celsius or 1 kilogram of liquid water at 100° Celsius? Explain your answer.

15. Why is it more comfortable to exercise on a day when the relative humidity is low?

16. Which contains more heat, a 100 milliliter beaker of water at 98°C or a bathtub full of water at 0°C? Explain your answer.

17. The specific heat of gold is less than the specific heat of aluminum. Explain why this is so.

18. Explain why using a bicycle pump to inflate a tire will cause the tire to feel warmer.

19. Ed thinks that he can cool his kitchen by leaving the refrigerator door open. What is wrong with this thinking?

20. Which graph below best represents the relationship between the Celsius temperature of an ideal gas and the average kinetic energy of its molecules? What is the approximate temperature represented at the point where the slope line crosses the x-axis?

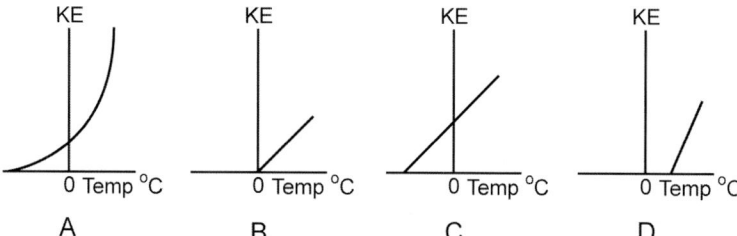

Problems

1. How much heat is required to change the temperature of 0.5 kilogram of aluminum from 25°C to 37°C?

2. 0.25 kilograms of an unknown material absorbs 322.5 joules of energy as its temperature rises from 20°C to 30°C. What is the material?

3. A 0.15-kg piece of glass is dropped into 100 milliliters of water whose temperature is 20°C. The temperature of the water rises 4°C. What was the original temperature of the glass? (Assume no loss of heat to the air or the container)

4. Answer questions a through h based upon the diagram below which represents a cooling curve for 10 kilograms of a substance as it cools from a vapor at 160°C to a solid at 20°C. Energy is removed from the material at a rate of 200.0 kilojoules per minute.

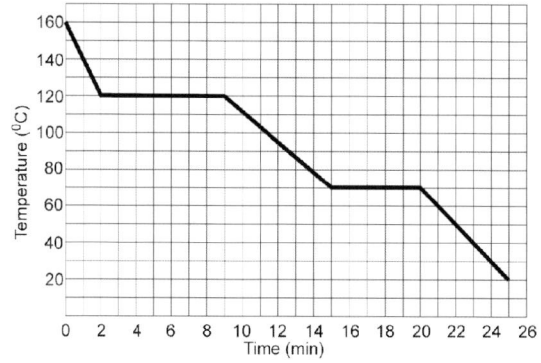

a. Calculate the heat of fusion of the substance.

b. Calculate the specific heat of the substance as a liquid.

c. What is the melting point of the substance in Kelvin?

d. What is the boiling point of the substance in degrees Celsius?

e. What is the freezing point of the substance in degrees Fahrenheit?

f. Calculate the number of BTUs of heat energy removed as the substance changes from the gas phase to the liquid phase.

g. What is the difference in temperature, measured in degrees Celsius, between the boiling point and the freezing point of this substance?

h. What is the difference in temperature, measured in Kelvin, between the boiling and freezing points of the substance?

Unit 8
Matter and Energy

Chapter 26

Heat Transfer

Objectives for Chapter 26

By the end of this chapter you should be able to:

1. Explain the relationship between temperature and thermal equilibrium.
2. Explain how heat flows in physical systems in terms of conduction, convection, and radiation.
3. Apply the concepts of thermal insulators and conductors to practical systems.
4. Describe free and forced convection and recognize these processes in real-life applications.
5. Identify the relationship between wavelength, color, infrared light, and thermal radiation.
6. Calculate the heat transfer in watts for conduction, convection, and radiation in simple systems.
7. Explain how the three heat-transfer processes are applied to evaluating the energy efficiency of a house or building.

Terms and vocabulary words

infrared	windchill factor	thermal insulator	thermal equilibrium	forced convection
R-value	convection	blackbody spectrum	thermal conductivity	thermal conductor
blackbody	heat transfer	thermal radiation	free convection	heat transfer coefficient
conduction				

26.1 Heat Conduction

Almost everyone has accidentally picked up a hot pot from the stove and *quickly* realized it was too hot to hold. A pot feels hot because heat flows from the pot into your skin, causing your skin temperature to rise uncomfortably fast. The science of how heat flows is called heat transfer. There are three ways heat transfer works: conduction, convection, and radiation. This section is about conduction, which is the transfer of heat by direct contact of particles of matter.

Heat flow and thermal equilibrium

The cause of heat transfer
The rate of heat transfer is proportional to the difference in temperature. Consider standing outside when the air temperature is 68°F (20°C). You probably will not feel extremely cold because the temperature difference between your skin (75°F) and the air is only seven degrees. Your body loses heat relatively slowly. If the air temperature were to drop to 40°F (4°C), you would quickly feel cold. You get cold because five times more heat flows out of your body each second when there is a 35-degree difference compared with a 7-degree difference.

Heat transfer in living things
Heat flow is necessary for life. Biological processes release energy. Your body regulates its temperature through the constant flow of heat. The inside of your body averages 98.6°F. Humans are most comfortable when the air is around 75°F because the rate of heat flow out of the body matches the rate at which the body generates heat internally. If the air is 50°F, you get cold because heat flows too rapidly from your skin to the air. If the air is 100°F, you feel hot partly because heat flows from the air to your body and partly because your body cannot get rid of its internal heat fast enough (Figure 26.1).

Thermal equilibrium
Two bodies are in thermal equilibrium with each other when they have the same temperature. In thermal equilibrium, no heat flows because the temperatures are the same (Figure 26.2). In nature, heat *always* flows from hot to cold until thermal equilibrium is reached. For example, if you leave a cup of hot coffee on the table, heat flows from the cup to the room until everything is the same temperature. Putting the hot coffee in an insulated cup only slows the process down. Heat still flows, only slower. Hot coffee in an insulated cup takes *longer* to reach thermal equilibrium with the room, but the end result is the same.

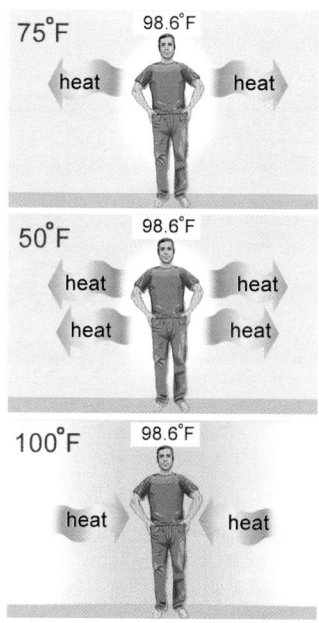

Figure 26.1: *Heat flow depends on the temperature difference.*

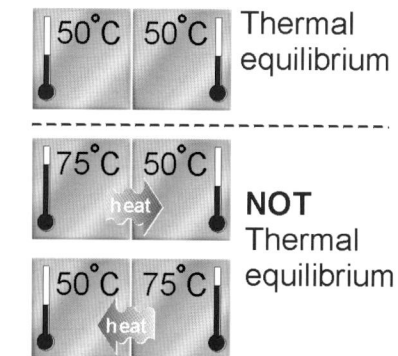

Figure 26.2: *No heat flows when objects are at the same temperature.*

522

Heat conduction

Conduction   Conduction is the transfer of heat *through* materials by the direct contact of matter. Imagine two blocks of metal at different temperatures. What happens if you bring the blocks together so that they touch? The warmer block will cool down and the colder block will warm up. Heat flows from the warmer block to the colder block by conduction (Figure 26.3). The heat keeps flowing until both blocks are at the same temperature.

Thermal conductors   Dense metals like copper and aluminum are very good thermal conductors. Think about holding one end of a copper pipe while the other end is in a hot flame. Copper is a good thermal conductor so heat flows rapidly from one end of the pipe to the other. You cannot hold on for long because the pipe gets hot so quickly.

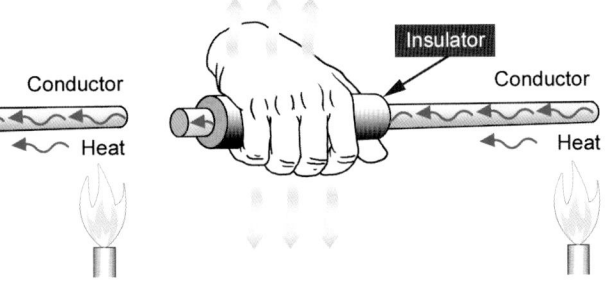

Thermal insulators   A thermal insulator is a material that conducts heat poorly. Styrofoam is a good example. You can comfortably hold a hot copper pipe surrounded by a centimeter of Styrofoam. Heat flows very slowly through the plastic so that the temperature of your hand does not rise very much. Styrofoam gets its insulating ability by trapping spaces of air in bubbles (Figure 26.4). We use thermal insulators to maintain temperature differences without allowing much heat to flow.

The ability to conduct heat depends on many factors   All materials conduct heat at some rate. Solids usually are better heat conductors than liquids, and liquids are better conductors than gases. The ability to conduct heat often depends more on the structure of a material than on the material itself. For example, solid glass is a thermal conductor when it is made into windows. When glass is spun into fine fibers and made into insulation (fiberglass), the combination of glass fibers and trapped air makes a thermal insulator.

Heat flow by conduction

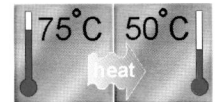

Figure 26.3: *Conduction is the flow of heat through direct contact of matter.*

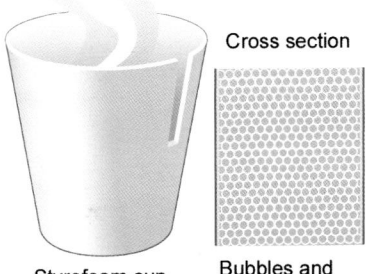

Figure 26.4: *Fiberglass insulation and Styrofoam derive their insulating ability from trapping air between fibers or in bubbles.*

Thermal conductivity

Thermal conductivity

The thermal conductivity of a material describes how well the material conducts heat. Materials with high thermal conductivity are good thermal conductors, such as copper, aluminum, and other metals. Materials with low thermal conductivity are insulators, such as fiberglass and Styrofoam. Table 26.1 gives the thermal conductivity of some common materials.

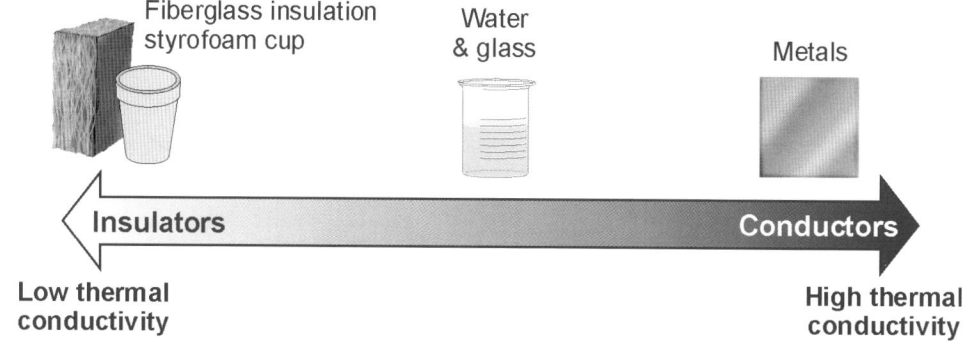

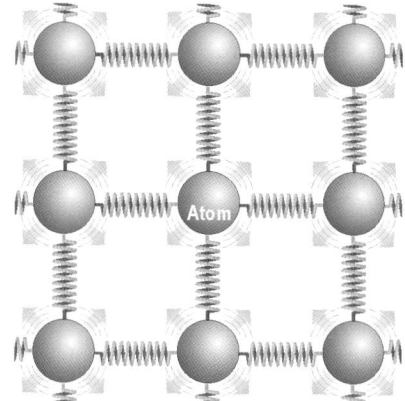

Figure 26.5: *The bonds between atoms act like springs that allow atoms to vibrate and transmit the vibration to neighboring atoms.*

Conduction in solids and liquids

Heat conduction in solids and liquids works by transferring energy through bonds between atoms or molecules. The bonds between neighboring atoms or molecules act like springs (Figure 26.5). If you shake one end of a spring, eventually the motion is transferred to the other end. Thermal motion is transferred along bonds in a similar way. The result is that energy flows from hotter atoms to cooler atoms. Solid materials are the best conductors because solids have a high density of atoms connected by strong bonds.

Conduction in a gas

Heat conduction in a gas works through collisions between atoms. Hotter atoms in a gas move faster. A fast atom slows down a little when it collides with a slower atom. A slow atom speeds up a bit when it collides with a faster atom. Some of the kinetic energy of hotter gas atoms is transferred, one collision at a time, to cooler atoms. Gases are thermal insulators because atoms are much farther apart and collisions are less effective at transferring energy than bonds between atoms.

Conduction in liquids

Liquids conduct heat better than gases but not as well as solids. The atoms in a liquid are close together, like in a solid. But, the bonds between atoms are not very strong, more like a gas.

Table 26.1:
Thermal conductivity of common materials

Material	Thermal cond. (W/m°C)
IIa diamond	2,650
Copper	401
Aluminum	226
Steel	43
Rock	3
Glass	2.2
Ice	2.2
Liquid water	0.58
Wood	0.11
Wool fabric	0.038
Fiberglass insulation	0.038
Styrofoam	0.025
Air	0.026

The heat conduction equation

A metal bar connects two beakers of water at different temperatures. Heat flows through the bar.

Predicting heat flow In many cases we want to know how much heat per second flows. For example, to keep your house at the same temperature, any heat that flows out the windows must be replaced by energy you pay for. In physics, power is the flow of energy per second. Power is measured in watts; a watt is a joule per second. We will use the symbol P_H for the power transferred by heat. The power transferred by heat conduction (P_H) depends on four factors (Figure 26.6):

*   The area through which the heat flows (A).

*   The length the heat has to travel (L).

*   The temperature difference ($T_1 - T_2$).

*   The thermal conductivity of the material (κ).

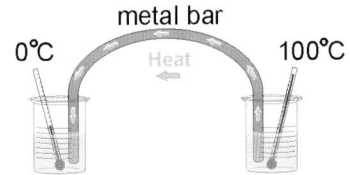

Heat conduction equation

$$P_H = \kappa \frac{A}{L}\left(T_2 - T_1\right)$$

Heat flow (watts) — Area cross section (m²) — Temperature difference (C) — Thermal conductivity (w/m°C) — Length (m)

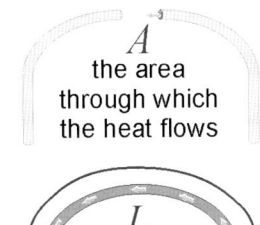

A
the area through which the heat flows

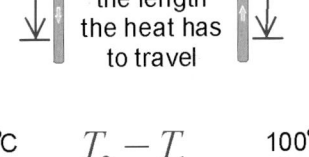

L
the length the heat has to travel

Calculate heat transfer through a metal bar

A copper bar connects two beakers of water at different temperatures (Figure 26.6). One beaker is at 100°C and the other is at 0°C. The bar has a cross section area of 0.0004 m² and is one-half meter (0.5 m) long. How many watts of heat are conducted through the bar from the hot beaker to the cold beaker? The thermal conductivity of copper is 401 w/m°C.

1) You are asked for the power transferred as heat.
2) You are given the area, length, temperature difference, and thermal conductivity.
3) The heat conduction equation is $P_H = kA(T_2-T_1)/L$.
4) Solve the problem:

$P_H = (401 \text{ w/m}^0\text{C})(0.0004 \text{ m}^2)(100\ ^0\text{C})/(.5 \text{ m}) = 32 \text{ watts}$

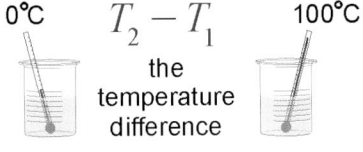

$T_2 - T_1$
the temperature difference

κ
the thermal conductivity of the metal

Figure 26.6: *The variables that appear in the heat conduction equation.*

26.2 Convection

Convection is the transfer of heat by the motion of liquids and gases. A candle flame provides a good example of convection. If you hold your hand a half meter directly above a candle flame, you will quickly feel heat (Figure 26.7). Hold your hand the same distance to the side and you feel no heat at all. You feel heat directly above the flame because hot air rises after being heated by the flame. The heat carried by the motion of the air is an example of convection.

The causes of convection

Why convection occurs

Convection in a gas occurs because gas expands when heated. When a gas expands, the mass is spread out over a larger volume so the density decreases. Hot gas with lower density is lighter than surrounding cooler gas and floats upward. Convection occurs because currents flow when hot gas rises and cool gas sinks.

Convection in liquids

Convection in liquids also occurs because of differences in density. Hot liquid is less dense than cold liquid. If you watch the surface of a pot of boiling water, you can see the convection currents. The hottest water rises from the bottom of the pot. Cooler water near the surface sinks. The circulating flow of water is very effective at transferring heat from the bottom of the pot to the surface.

Free convection

When the flow of gas or liquid comes from differences in density and temperature, it is called free convection. The heat rising above a candle flame is an example of free convection. The water circulating in a boiling pot of water is also an example of free convection.

Forced convection

When the flow of gas or liquid is circulated by pumps or fans it is called forced convection. Many homes and buildings are heated by forced convection. A furnace heats water in a boiler. Pumps circulate water through the boiler to get it hot then circulate the hot water to rooms where the heat is needed.

Convection systems

Many heat transfer systems use a combination of free and forced convection. For example, a common home-heating system uses copper tubes and pumps to circulate hot water. Forced convection carries the heat from the boiler to finned copper tubes in each room. Free convection transfers the heat from the finned tubes to the air in the room. (Figure 26.8)

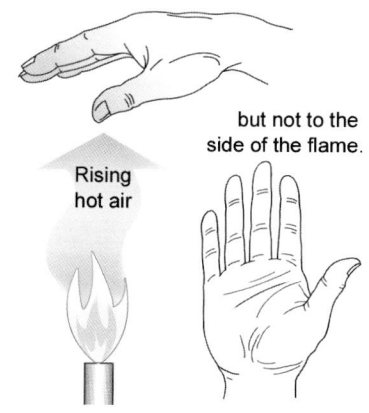

Your hand gets hot above the flame...

but not to the side of the flame.

Rising hot air

Figure 26.7: *The rising column of hot air over a candle flame is an example of convection.*

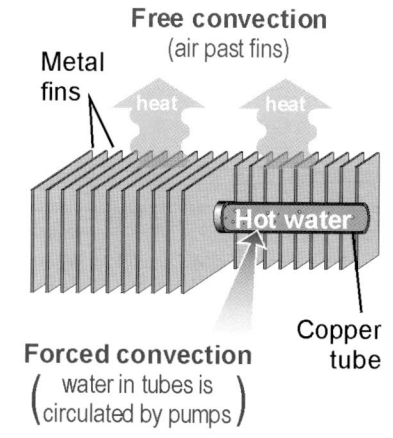

Free convection (air past fins)

Metal fins

heat   heat

Hot water

Copper tube

Forced convection (water in tubes is circulated by pumps)

Figure 26.8: *Homes heated with hot-water boilers use both free convection and forced convection.*

Convection depends on speed and surface area

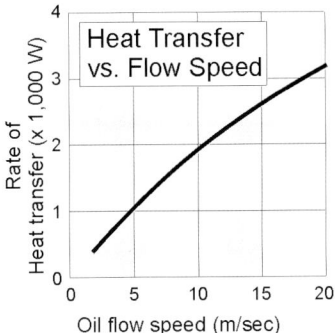

Faster flow increases heat transfer   Think about standing outside on a cold day. You get cold much faster when the wind is blowing. The faster the wind blows, the more effectively heat is carried away from your body. Motion increases heat transfer by convection in all fluids. Figure 26.9 shows the heat transferred by oil flowing in a tube in the engine of a car. The amount of heat transferred to the oil depends on the flow speed.

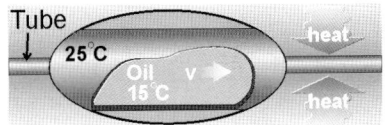

The windchill factor   The Antarctic explorers who invented the windchill factor did a very simple experiment in convection. They measured how long it took for a gallon of water to freeze in air at different temperatures and wind speeds. They found a temperature of 0°F with a 30-mile-per-hour wind froze the water in the same time as a lower temperature (-26°F) with no wind. A windchill of -26°F means your skin loses heat at the same rate as if the air temperature were actually -26°F with no wind. The chart below shows the windchill for different temperatures and wind speeds.

Figure 26.9: *The rate of heat transfer changes dramatically with the speed of flow.*

1 gallon of water freezes solid in equal time

Air temperature of -26°F (-32°C) with no wind.   -26°F ▶

Air temperature of 0°F (-18°C) with 30 mph wind.   0°F ▶   wind

Wind Chill Equivalent Temperatures (F)	Air temperature (°F)						
	-20	**-10**	**0**	**10**	**20**	**30**	**40**
10	-41	-28	- 16	-4	9	21	34
Wind **20**	-48	-35	-22	-9	4	17	30
speed **30**	-53	-39	-26	-12	1	15	28
(mph) **40**	-57	-43	-29	-15	-1	13	27

Fins increase heat transfer   Almost all devices made for convection have fins (Figure 26.10). Convection transfers heat between a surface and a moving fluid. If the surface contacting the fluid is increased, the rate of heat transfer also increases. Fins provide a tremendous increase in surface area and greatly increase the rate of heat transfer. Motorcycle engines, car radiators, and home-heating elements are examples of devices that use fins to enhance heat transfer by convection.

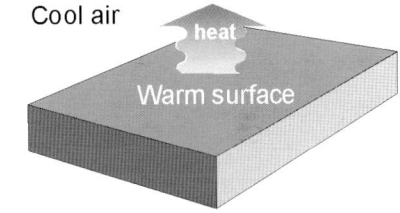

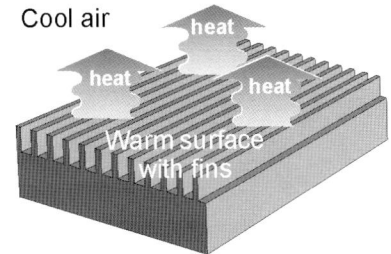

Figure 26.10: *Fins dramatically increase the surface area, improving heat transfer by convection.*

Convection in the environment

Convection and weather
Currents caused by convection are responsible for much of our weather. Warm air rises off the surface of the Earth. As the warm air rises higher it cools. The cooler air sinks back down, creating a circulation pattern.

Sea breezes
The sea breezes that form near coastlines are a good example of circulation patterns created by convection. During the day, the land is warmed by the sun more than water because rocks and earth have a lower specific heat than water. Warm air over land rises because of convection and is replaced by cooler air from the ocean. A daytime sea breeze blows from the ocean inward (Figure 26.11). In the evening the circulation pattern reverses. At night the ground cools rapidly but the ocean remains warm because water has a high specific heat. Warm air rises over the water and is replaced with cooler air from over the land. The nighttime breeze blows from the land out to the sea (Figure 26.12).

Convection in the ocean
Much of the Earth's climate is regulated by giant convection currents in the oceans. Dense, cold water from melting ice near the poles sinks to the ocean floor and flows toward the equator. Warmer water from the equator circulates back toward the poles near the ocean surface. The weather pattern known as El Niño causes heavy storms in some years. El Niño is caused by an oscillation in the flow of convection currents in the Pacific Ocean.

Figure 26.11: *During the day, a sea breeze is created when hot air over the land rises because of convection and is replaced by cooler air from the ocean.*

Figure 26.12: *At night, temperatures reverse and a land breeze occurs. This happens because the land cools more rapidly than the ocean.*

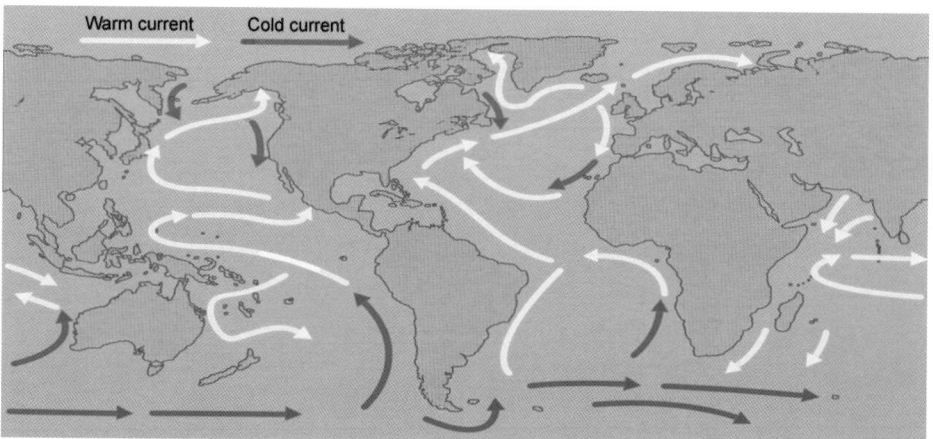

528

A model for convection

Temperature difference   The rate of heat transfer is proportional to the temperature difference. For example, a 0°C (32°F) wind blowing on bare skin will carry away much more heat than a 20°C (68°F) wind because the colder wind creates a larger temperature difference between the air and skin.

The heat transfer coefficient, h   A simple model for convection includes the contact area (A) and the temperature difference ($T_2 - T_1$). The complicated effects of flow speed and surface conditions are grouped together in the heat transfer coefficient, h. A value of $h = 1$ W/m^2°C means that one watt of heat is transferred from each square meter of area when the temperature difference is one degree Celsius. Most practical heat transfer systems have a value of h between 10 and 10,000 W/m^2°C (Table 26.2). The convection equation shows how to calculate the power of heat transferred (P_H).

Heat flow (watts) —   — Area contacting fluid (m^2)

$$P_H = hA\left(T_2 - T_1\right)$$

Heat transfer coefficient (W/m^2·°C)   Temperature difference (C)

Condition	Range of heat transfer coefficients (W/m^2-C)
Free convection	
Gases	5 - 25
Oil	10 - 60
Water	100 - 1,000
Forced convection	
Gases	10 - 300
Oil	50 - 2,000
Water	100 - 20,000

Calculate the heat lost through a glass window

The surface of a window is a temperature of 18°C (64°F). A wind at 5°C (41°F) is blowing on the window fast enough to make the heat transfer coefficient 100 W/m^2·°C. How much heat is transferred between the window and the air if the area of the window is 0.5 square meters? (Figure 26.13)

1) You are asked for the rate of heat transfer.

2) You are given the temperature difference, area, and heat transfer coefficient.

3) Use the convection equation $P_H = hA(T_2-T_1)$.

4) Solve: $P_H = (100)(0.5)(13) = 650$ watts.

This is a lot of heat to lose out your window! Storm windows and double-pane glass help reduce convection by preventing the outside air from contacting the inner window.

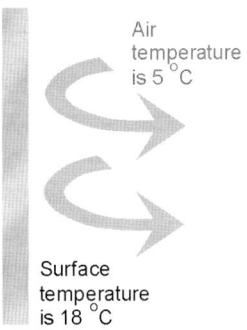

Air temperature is 5°C

Surface temperature is 18°C

Figure 26.13: *Cold air absorbs heat by convection when it blows on the outside surface of a window.*

26.3 Radiant Heat

If you stand in the sun you can feel warm even on a cold day. The heat you feel from the sun comes from the energy of light waves soaking into your skin. Radiation is heat transfer by electromagnetic waves. Virtually all of the energy that makes the Earth warm comes from the sun as radiation. Radiation plays an important role in heat transfer here on Earth, too, as you will discover in this section.

Properties of thermal radiation

Definition of thermal radiation

Thermal radiation is electromagnetic waves (including light) produced by objects because of their temperature. All objects with a temperature above absolute zero give off thermal radiation. Thermal radiation comes from the thermal energy of atoms. The power in thermal radiation increases with higher temperatures because the thermal energy of atoms increases with temperature (Figure 26.14).

Objects emit and absorb radiation

Thermal radiation is also absorbed by objects. An object constantly receives thermal radiation from everything else in its environment. Otherwise all objects would eventually cool down to absolute zero by radiating their energy away. The temperature of an object rises if more radiation is absorbed. The temperature falls if more radiation is given off. The temperature adjusts until there is a balance between radiation absorbed and radiation emitted.

Some surfaces absorb more energy than others

The amount of thermal radiation absorbed depends on the surface of a material. Black surfaces absorb almost all the thermal radiation that falls on them. For example, black asphalt pavement gets very hot in the summer sun because it effectively absorbs thermal radiation. A silver mirror surface reflects most thermal radiation, absorbing very little. A mirrored screen reflects the sun's heat back out your car window, helping your car stay cooler on a hot day (Figure 26.15).

Radiation can travel through space

Thermal radiation can travel through the vacuum of space. Conduction and convection cannot carry heat through space because both processes require matter to transfer heat. Radiation is different. Because the energy is carried by electromagnetic waves, radiation does not require matter to provide a path for the heat to flow. Radiant energy also travels very fast — at the speed of light.

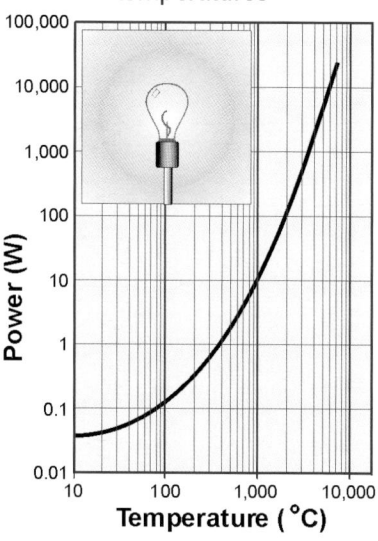

Thermal radiation power emitted per cm^2 at different temperatures

Figure 26.14: *The higher the temperature of an object, the more thermal radiation it gives off.*

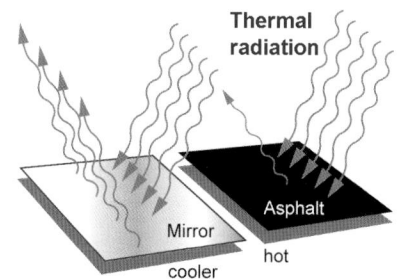

Figure 26.15: *Black or dark colored surfaces absorb most of the thermal radiation they receive. Silver or mirrored surfaces reflect most of the thermal radiation they receive.*

Thermal radiation and infrared light

Thermal radiation is mostly invisible infrared light

At room temperature, we do not see objects by their thermal radiation. We see objects by the light they reflect from other sources. We do not see the thermal radiation because it occurs at infrared wavelengths invisible to the human eye. The power versus wavelength graph shows how light from thermal radiation is spread over a range of wavelengths. A rock at room temperature does not "glow" the curve for 20°C does not extend into visible wavelengths. All of the thermal radiation at 20°C is in invisible infrared light. Up to a few thousand degrees Celsius most of the energy in thermal radiation is in infrared light.

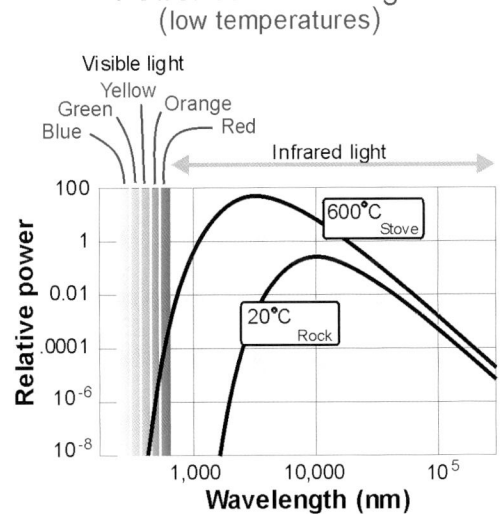

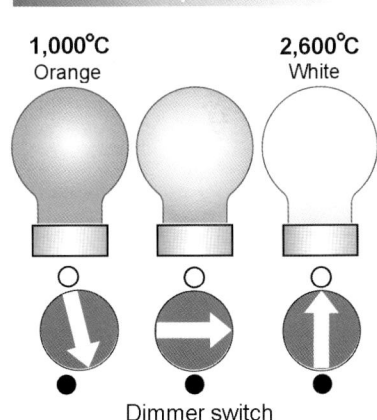

Figure 26.16: *Objects glow different colors at different temperatures. The glow comes from the visible part of the blackbody spectrum.*

Why hot objects glow

As objects heat up they start to give off visible light, or glow. At 600°C objects glow dull red, like the burner on an electric stove. The curve for 600°C on the power versus wavelength graph shows some radiation emitted in red and orange visible light, though most of the energy is still radiated as invisible infrared. More than 99.9% of the radiant heat from a hot stove element is in infrared light.

Temperature and color

As the temperature rises, thermal radiation produces shorter-wavelength, higher-energy light. At 1,000°C the color is yellow-orange, turning to white at 1,500°C (Figure 26.16). If you carefully watch a bulb on a dimmer switch, you see its color change as the filament gets hotter. The bright white light from a bulb is thermal radiation from an extremely hot filament, near 2,600°C (Figure 26.17).

Infrared thermometers

Between room temperature and 600°C the power of thermal radiation increases more than a hundred times. You may have had a doctor look in your ear with a thermometer that measured your temperature. Ear thermometers work by measuring the power of infrared thermal radiation.

Figure 26.17: *A dimmer switch and an incandescent bulb provide a good way to see the effect of temperature on the color of thermal radiation.*

The blackbody spectrum

Perfect absorption of light

To a physicist, an object is perfectly *black* when it absorbs all radiation that falls on its surface. If all radiation is absorbed, than any radiation coming off the surface can only be thermal radiation. A perfect **blackbody** is a surface that reflects nothing and emits pure thermal radiation. Most objects reflect some radiation and therefore emit less thermal radiation than a perfect blackbody. To a physicist, the white-hot filament of a bulb is a good blackbody. All light from the filament is thermal radiation, almost none of it is reflected from other sources.

The blackbody spectrum

The graph of power versus wavelength for a perfect blackbody is called the **blackbody spectrum**. The curve for 2,600°C shows that radiation is emitted over the whole range of visible light. White light is a mixture of colors and incandescent light bulbs need the high temperature to make a balanced white light. The sun has a surface temperature of 5,500°C. From the blackbody spectrum for 5,500°C you can see the sun produces visible light, infrared light, and quite a lot of harmful, high-energy, ultraviolet light as well.

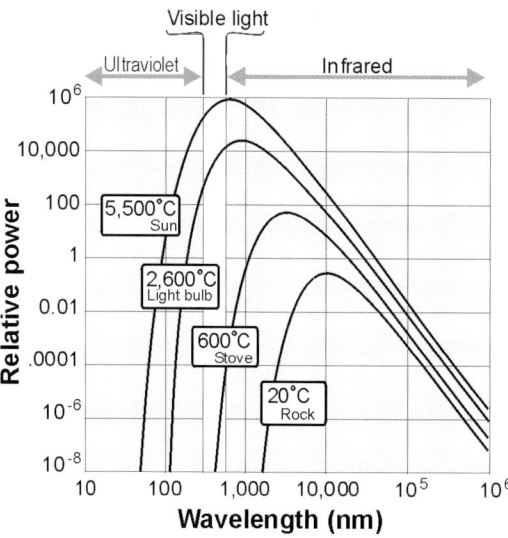

The blackbody spectrum
(Power vs. Wavelength)

Figure 26.18: *Sirius is a hot blue star in the constellation Canis Major. Sirius is one of the brightest stars in the night sky.*

Stars and the blackbody spectrum

A star is a near-perfect blackbody. According to the blackbody spectrum the distribution of energy between different wavelengths (colors) depends strongly on the temperature. Therefore, a star's color tells us the temperature of the star. The temperature and brightness tell us the size of the star. From the temperature and size, astronomers can calculate the mass of the star, how old it is, and how long it is likely to keep shining. For example, we know the sun is around 4 billion years old and we can expect sunshine for another 4 billion years.

The temperature and color of stars

Stars have different temperatures. Stars bigger than the sun burn hotter and radiate more blue-white light. Sirius in the constellation of Canis Major is a hot, young star about twice as big as the sun (Figure 26.18) and 22 times as bright. Because its temperature is hotter, Sirius appears bluer than the sun. Older stars called red giants are huge and cooler than the sun. The star Betelgeuse is a red giant. Light from these stars is redder than light from the sun because the temperature is lower.

A model for radiation

The total power emitted as thermal radiation by a blackbody depends on temperature (T) and surface area (A). The Stefan-Boltzmann formula allows us to calculate the power. Real surfaces usually emit less than the blackbody power, typically 10 to 90 percent. The power emitted as thermal radiation power increases as T^4 (Figure 26.19). At temperatures over 500°C, radiation almost always transfers more heat than convection or conduction (Figure 26.20).

The Kelvin temperature scale is used in the Stefan-Boltzmann formula because thermal radiation depends on the temperature *above absolute zero*. When you are given a problem, remember to add 273 if the temperatures are in Celsius.

Stefan - Boltzmann formula

Power (watts) — Surface area (m²)
$$P = \sigma A T^4$$
Stefan-Boltzmann constant (5.67 x 10⁻⁸ W/m²K) — Absolute temperature (K)

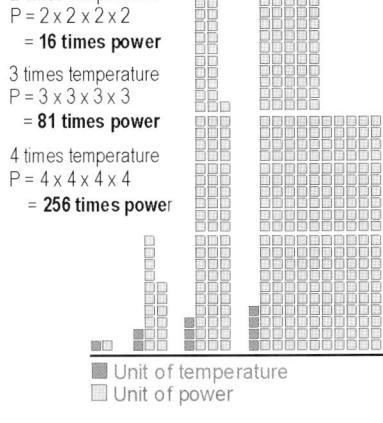

2 times temperature
$P = 2 \times 2 \times 2 \times 2$
= **16 times power**

3 times temperature
$P = 3 \times 3 \times 3 \times 3$
= **81 times power**

4 times temperature
$P = 4 \times 4 \times 4 \times 4$
= **256 times power**

■ Unit of temperature
□ Unit of power

Figure 26.19: *Thermal radiation increases like the fourth power of the temperature. This means every time the temperature doubles, the power of radiation increases by 16 (16 = 2⁴).*

Calculate the radiation power from a small light bulb filament

The filament in a light bulb has a diameter of 0.5 millimeters and a length of 50 millimeters. The surface area of the filament is 4×10^{-8} m². If the temperature is 3,000 K, how much power does the filament radiate?

1) You are asked for the power radiated.

2) You are given the size, surface area, and temperature in Kelvins.

3) Use the Stefan-Boltzmann formula: $P = \sigma A T^4$.

4) Solve: $P = (5.7 \times 10^{-8} \text{ W/m}^2\text{K}^4)(4 \times 10^{-8} \text{ m}^2)(3000 \text{ K})^4$

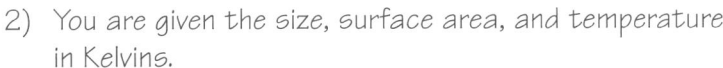

$= 0.2$ watts

This is not much light! Incandescent bulbs are not very efficient at converting electrical energy to light.

Heat transfer between a heating element and a pot 10 cm above the stove

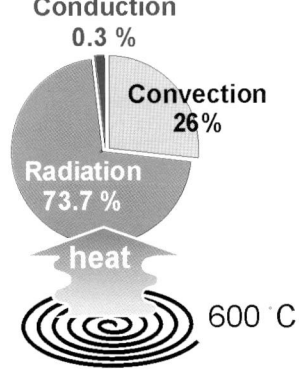

Conduction
0.3 %

Convection
26%

Radiation
73.7 %

heat

600 °C

Figure 26.20: *Comparing heat transfer by convection and radiation at different temperatures.*

Application: Energy-efficient Buildings

Heat transfer is very important to the design of homes and buildings. In winter, the temperature inside is greater than the temperature outside. Heat flows out and any that is lost must be replaced with heat we pay for, produced by electricity, oil, wood, or gas. In summer the situation is reversed. We want to keep the heat outside. Heat that leaks in must be pumped back out with air conditioning, using expensive electricity. An efficient house does not lose too much heat in winter nor gain too much heat in summer.

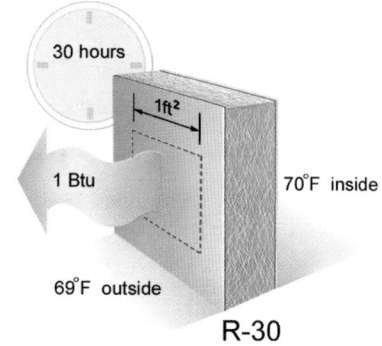

Figure 26.21: *What R-30 means in terms of heat flow.*

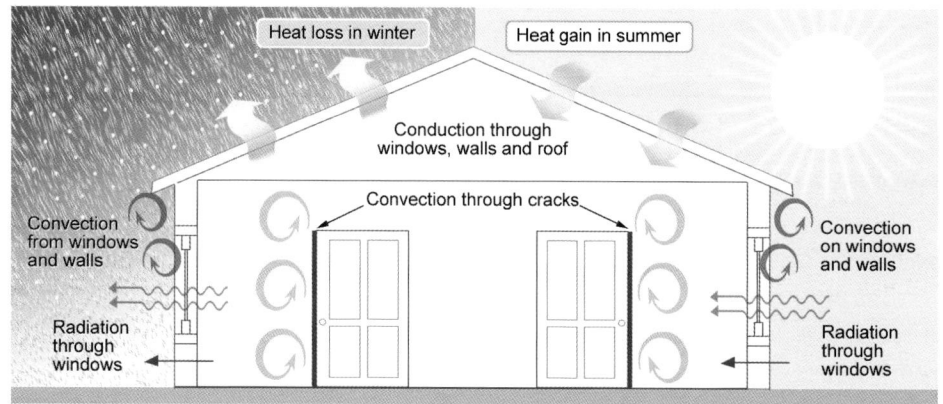

R-value   The R-value is a measure of resistance to heat flow by conduction. A low R-value means heat flows quickly. A high R-value means heat flows slowly. A wall rated at R-1 means it takes one hour for one Btu (1,054 J) of heat to pass through one square foot when the temperature difference is 1°F. One Btu is not much heat; it takes about 25 Btu to heat a cup of coffee. A typical (cold-climate) home-heating system produces more than 50,000 Btu per hour. In Northern climates, houses require R-30 in the roof, which means it takes 30 hours for one Btu of heat to pass through each square foot when the temperature difference is 1°F (Figure 26.21).

The R-value of a wall or roof   The walls and roofs of houses built today are insulated with materials such as fiberglass or foam. Table 26.3 lists the R-value for some common building materials. The total R-value of a wall is equal to the sum of the R-values for each layer. For example, a roof with one-half inch of plywood, nine inches of fiberglass insulation, and one-half inch of plaster board would have a total R-value a bit greater than R-31.

Table 26.3:
R-values for common building materials

Material	R-value
1/2-inch plywood	0.62
1/2" plaster board	0.45
8" concrete	1
4" wood (pine)	4
1" foam board	7
3.5" fiberglass ins.	13
6" fiberglass ins.	19
9" fiberglass ins.	30

Reducing heat loss

Heat loss through windows

Convection is the chief cause of heat loss through thin materials, such as glass windows. To reduce convection, modern windows have double or triple panes of glass (Figure 26.22). The outer pane of glass stops the wind from reaching the inner pane of glass. By separating the inner and outer panes of glass, heat must travel through the insulating air space between them. This greatly reduces heat transfer. Older homes without double-pane windows may use *storm windows*. A storm window also provides a second pane of glass closer to the outside.

Other sources of convection

Cracks around doors and siding are also a large source of heat loss by convection. Weatherstripping is an effective way to seal openings around doors and windows and reduce air exchange between inside and outside. To slow down air flowing through siding, many homes are now built with a wind barrier, or house wrap.

Radiation

In Southern climates, preventing heat transfer by radiation is an important design goal. Radiation passes through glass windows easily and the energy is absorbed by interior surfaces. One strategy for reducing radiation heat gain is to use low emissivity (low-E) windows. A low-E window has two (or three) panes of glass. The inside surface is treated with a special coating that reflects infrared light but allows most visible light to pass through (Figure 26.23). You can still see through the windows but much of the heat is blocked.

Energy use for heating and cooling

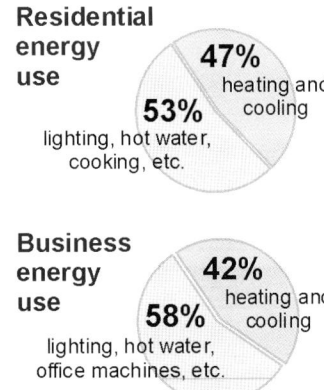

Heating and air conditioning use a lot of energy. These two uses are responsible for 47 percent of all the energy used by homes and 42 percent of that used by businesses. By many estimates, as much as half of this energy could be saved by designing buildings to be better at controlling heat transfer. Every state has a *building code* which includes rules for constructing homes and commercial buildings to meet higher standards of energy efficiency. Insulation, double-pane windows, low-E glass, and weatherstripping are part of all modern building-code requirements.

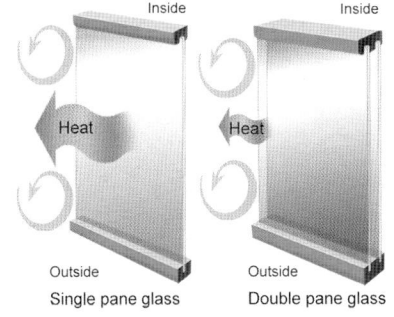

Figure 26.22: *Double-pane glass windows greatly reduce heat loss by convection because the outside air does not contact the inner window pane.*

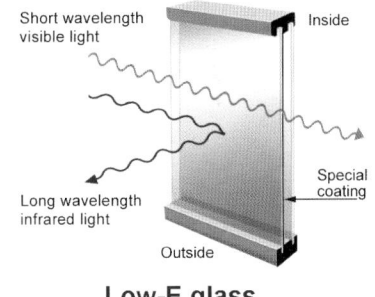

Figure 26.23: *A special coating on the glass of a low-E window transmits most visible light but reflects infrared light.*

Chapter 26 Review

Vocabulary Review

Match the following terms with the correct definition. There is one extra definition in the list that will not match any of the terms.

Set One

1. conduction
2. wind chill factor
3. blackbody
4. forced convection
5. free convection

a. Heat flow between a surface and a fluid being circulated by fans and pumps
b. Heat flow between a surface and a fluid with circulation driven by buoyancy forces
c. A value representing a quantity of heat absorbed by mass
d. Describes of the effect of air flow on heat loss
e. Transfer of heat through materials by direct contact
f. Emits pure thermal radiation

Set Two

1. thermal equilibrium
2. R-value
3. thermal radiation
4. thermal conductivity
5. thermal insulator

a. Transfer of heat at the speed of light
b. Characteristic of two bodies at the same temperature
c. Measure of resistance to heat flow
d. Measure of ability to reflect heat
e. Ability of heat to pass through a material
f. A material that conducts heat poorly

Set Three

1. heat transfer
2. infrared
3. blackbody spectrum
4. heat transfer coefficient
5. convection

a. Represents effects of flow speed and surface conditions
b. Caused by expansion of heated gases; causes sea breezes
c. Part of the spectrum near purple visible light
d. Wavelength of light which transfers thermal energy
e. The science of how heat flows
f. Graph of power vs. wavelength for perfect black bodies

Concept review

1. Answer the following:

   a. Name a factor affecting the rate of heat transfer.

   b. Describe the direction of heat transfer between two objects.

   c. Explain how thermal equilibrium affects heat transfer.

2. Two objects, A and B, are in contact with one another. Initially the temperature of A is 300 K, and temperature of B is 400 K. Which diagram correctly indicates the direction heat flow?

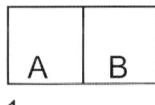 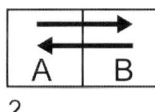 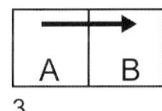 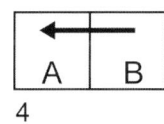

1   2   3   4

3. When you step out of the shower the tile floor feels cold but the bath mat feels warm even though they are both at room temperature. Why?

4. Wood is a poorer conductor than glass but wooden buildings are insulated using glass fibers. Why?

5. Compare the ability of solids, liquids and gases to conduct heat.

6. A copper rod conducts heat from one area of higher temperature to one of lower temperature at a certain rate. If the diameter of the rod is doubled, how would this affect the rate of heat conduction?

7. All objects at a temperature above absolute zero constantly emit thermal radiation. Why do objects not cool to absolute zero by emitting all their thermal energy?

8. Ammonia boils at -33°C. Referring to the chart of wind chill equivalent temperatures, estimate the highest temperature and accompanying wind speed that could be used to prevent ammonia from boiling.

Wind chill equivalent
Temperatures (F)

Air temperature (°F)

Wind speed (mph)	-20	-10	0	10	20	30	40
10	-41	-28	-16	-4	9	21	34
20	-48	-35	-22	-9	4	17	30
30	-53	-39	-26	-12	1	15	28
40	-57	-43	-29	-15	-1	13	27

9. Explain why it might be easier to sail toward the shore in a sailboat during the day rather than at night.

10. At room temperature, wood feels warmer than metal. At what temperature will both seem to be the same temperature? Explain.

11. You are asked to shovel the snow from the driveway on a sunny winter day. You have plans for the afternoon. Your brother suggests that you scatter the black ashes from the woodstove on the driveway. Is this a good idea or is your brother causing trouble?

12. Astronauts in an orbiting space station are trying to celebrate a fellow astronaut's birthday with burning candles on a birthday cake. The candles will not stay lit. Why?

13. Examine the diagram below. Both sunlight and light from a light bulb contain harmful ultraviolet radiation. Why are you more likely to get sunburn from the sun than from a light bulb?

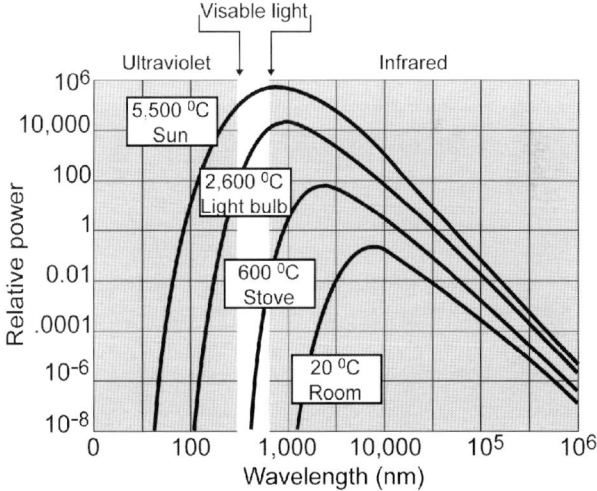

The Blackbody Spectrum
(Power vs. Wavelength)

Problems

1. As a dimmer switch is turned, the temperature of the filament in an incandescent bulb increases from 100°C to 1,592°C. By how many times is the thermal radiation increased?

2. The filament of a 100-watt bulb is 5.0 centimeters long. What must be the diameter of the filament if the bulb has an operating temperature of 2800 K?

3. A bar of copper and a bar of aluminum of the same area and thickness are in thermal contact. The temperature at the outer surface of the copper is 80°C while the temperature of the aluminum is maintained at 20°C at its outer surface. When heat conduction through the bimetal object reaches a steady state, what is the temperature at the interface?

4. When the equation for heat flow by conduction, $P_H = k(A/L)(T_2-T_1)$, is used by engineers, the ratio L/k is called the R-value. Rearrange the equation to include the R-value. Using your solution, determine the effect a four-fold increase in R-value of the insulation would have on the heat loss in a home.

5. Two insulated containers, A and B, containing identical amounts of water are connected by a copper rod. The initial temperature of A is 100°C and B's temperature is 20°C. Assuming all heat lost by A is transferred to B through the copper rod, as A's temperature decreases to 80°C, what change occurs in the heat flow?

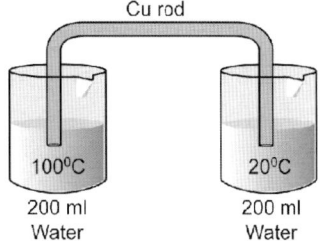

Cu rod

100ºC
200 ml
Water

20ºC
200 ml
Water

6. If an aluminum bar 0.25 meters long and 0.0075 meters in diameter is substituted for the copper bar in problem #5, calculate the initial rate of energy flow. The thermal conductivity for aluminum is 226 W/m°C.

7. If you place your hand in a beaker of water at room temperature (20°C), what is the rate of heat flow? Assume your hand has a surface area of 0.08m² and the heat transfer coefficient of the water is 200 W/m²-°C

8. The temperature inside a room is maintained at 20°C while the outside temperature is -20°C. What is the rate at which heat is transferred to a window pane by convection? The window dimensions are as follows: length = 0.67 m., width = 0.50 m, thickness = 0.25 cm. The heat transfer coefficient is 5.0 W/m²-°C. Assume the window temperature to be the average of the inside and outside air temperature.

9. In the previous problem it was estimated that the temperature of the glass was the average of the inside and outside temperatures. Find the actual temperature of the inside and the outside of the glass window from the previous problem. K for glass = 0.82 W/m²-°C.

10. In spring, some skiers like to "show a little skin" while skiing. Suppose some brazen individual were to ski in nothing but a bathing suit when the temperature was 5°C. How much net heat energy would be lost due to radiation from the skin of the skier in an hour of skiing? Assume the area of the exposed skin is 1.5 m² and typical body temperature is 37°C.

Unit 8
Matter and Energy

Chapter 27

The Physical Properties of Matter

Objectives for Chapter 27

By the end of this chapter you should be able to:

1. Perform calculations involving the density of solids, gases, and liquids.
2. Apply the concepts of force, stress, strain, and tensile strength to simple structures.
3. Describe the cause and some consequences of thermal expansion in solids, liquids, and gases.
4. Explain the concept of pressure and calculate pressure caused by the weight of fluids.
5. Explain how pressure is created on a molecular level.
6. Understand and apply Bernoulli's equation to flow along a streamline.
7. Apply the gas laws to simple problems involving pressure, temperature, mass, and volume.

Terms and vocabulary words

stress	density	strain	tensile strength	cross section area
pressure	volume	tension	compression	elastic, elasticity
fluid	brittle	ductile	safety factor	modulus of elasticity
alloy	airfoil	buoyancy	fluid mechanics	ideal gas law
Boyle's law	streamline	laminar flow	turbulent flow	Bernoulli's equation
pascal (Pa)	Charles' law	gas constant (R)	composite material	thermal expansion

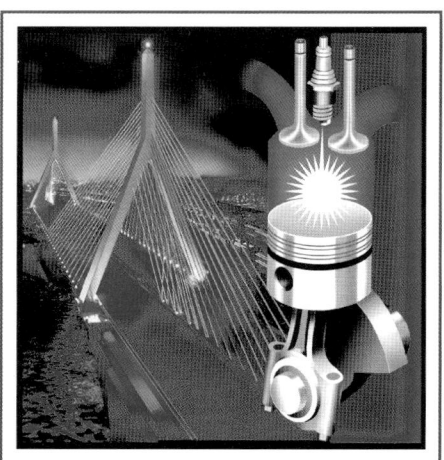

27.1 Properties of Solids

Solid materials normally hold their shape and do not flow like liquids. Solids have a wide range of properties that make them useful to us. Some solids are strong and heavy, like steel. Some solids are light and bouncy, like rubber. Other solids are hard and brittle, like glass. This section will explore some of the properties of solids.

Density of solid materials

Materials have a wide range of density
Solid materials have a wide range of densities (Table 27.1). One of the densest metals is platinum with a density of 21,450 kg/m³. Platinum is twice as dense as lead and almost three times as dense as steel. A ring made of platinum has three times as much mass as a ring of the exact same size made of steel. Rocks have lower density than metals, between 2,200 and 2,700 kg/m³. As you might expect, the density of wood is less than rock, ranging from 400 to 600 kg/m³.

The definition of density
The density of a material is the ratio of mass to volume. Density is a physical property of the material and stays the same no matter how much material you have. For example, a steel cube one meter on a side has a mass of 7,800 kilograms. A steel nail has a volume of 1.6 millionths of a cubic meter, 1.6×10^{-6} m³, and a mass of 12.7 grams (0.0127 kg). The density of the nail and cube is the same (Figure 27.1).

The density formula
The formula for density is mass divided by volume. Most engineers and scientists use the greek letter rho (ρ) to represent density. The density is often used to calculate the mass of material from the volume of an object.

Density

$$\rho = \frac{m}{V}$$

Density (kg/m³)   Mass (kg) / Volume (m³)

Use	if you know	and want to find
$\rho = m \div V$	mass and volume	density
$m = \rho \times V$	volume and density	mass
$V = m \div \rho$	mass and density	volume

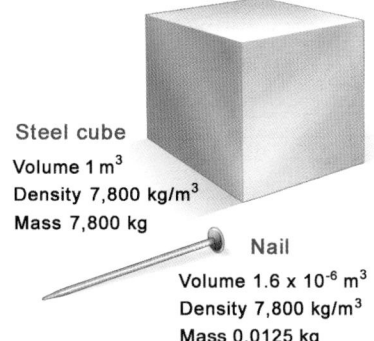

Steel cube
Volume 1 m³
Density 7,800 kg/m³
Mass 7,800 kg

Nail
Volume 1.6×10^{-6} m³
Density 7,800 kg/m³
Mass 0.0125 kg

Figure 27.1: *The density of a steel nail is the same as the density of a solid steel cube*

Table 27.1: Densities of common materials

Material	Density (kg/m³)
Platinum	21,450
Lead	11,340
Steel	7,800
Titanium	4,500
Aluminum	2,700
Glass	2,700
Granite	2,640
Concrete	2,300
Sandstone	2,200
Plastic	2,000
Brick	1,600
Rubber	1,200
Liquid water	1,000
Ice	920
Oak (wood)	600
Pine (wood)	440
Cork	120

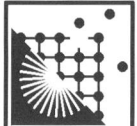

The strength of materials

Force

How much does the object bend or deform under an applied force?

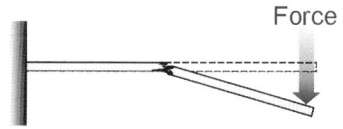

Force

How much force can the object take before it breaks?

The meaning of "strength" The concept of physical "strength" means the ability of an object to hold its form even when force is applied. We use solid materials for many applications because of their strength. It would be foolish to build a bridge from gas or liquid because these forms of matter have no strength! However, solid materials vary widely in strength. You would not build a bridge from wax, even though wax is a solid. The strength of an object (like a bridge) depends on the answers to two questions:

1. How much does the object bend or deform under applied force? (Figure 27.2)

2. How much force can the object take before it breaks?

Figure 27.2: *Two questions that we use to define the physical strength of an object.*

Separating design from material properties The strength of an object can be further broken down into *design* and *materials*. As an example, think about breaking two sticks of a strong wood, like oak. A small force can break a thin stick. A thicker stick takes more force to break even though the wood itself is the same (Figure 27.3). To evaluate the properties of oak *as a material* it is necessary to separate out the effects of design, such as shape and size. The strength of a material is described in terms of *stress*, instead of force.

Force and stress The stress in a material is the ratio of the force acting through the material divided by the cross section area through which the force is carried. The cross section area is the area perpendicular to the direction of the force. Dividing force by cross section area (mostly) separates out the effects of size and shape from the strength properties of the material itself. The Greek letter sigma (σ) is used for stress. Stress (σ) is force (*F*) divided by cross section area (*A*).

Stress

$$\sigma = \frac{F}{A}$$

Stress (N/m²)   Force (N)   Area (m²)

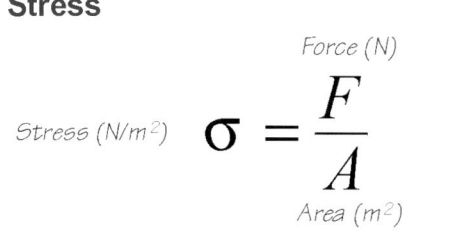

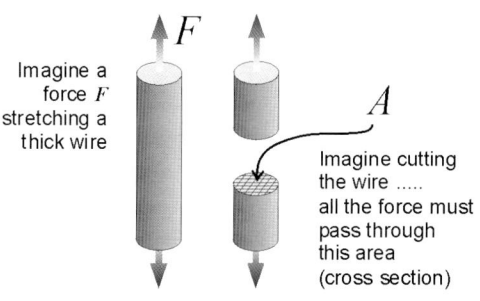

Imagine a force *F* stretching a thick wire

A

Imagine cutting the wire ..... all the force must pass through this area (cross section)

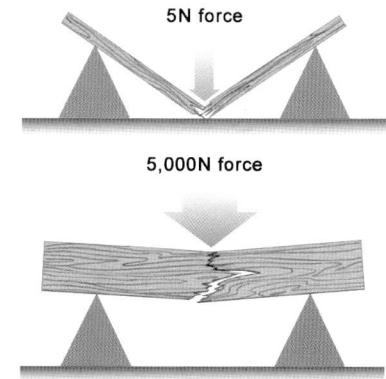

5N force

5,000N force

Figure 27.3: *It takes a much larger force to break a beam of oak than to break a thin stick.*

The breaking strength

Stress and breaking
Materials break when the stress within them reaches the limit the material can take. Soft solids like wax break at a low value of stress. Materials like steel break at a much higher stress level. The breaking strength of a material is best understood in terms of the maximum stress the material can withstand. A wire with a large diameter can support more force than a smaller-diameter wire at an equal stress level (Figure 27.4)

Tensile strength
The tensile strength is the stress at which a material breaks under a tension force. Tension forces are "stretching" forces, like the diagram below. Strong materials like steel have high tensile strength. Weak materials like wax and rubber have low tensile strength. Materials like wood and plastic have tensile strength between rubber and steel. Table 27.2 lists the tensile strength of some common materials.

Tension force

Strength in bending
The tensile strength also describes how materials break in bending. Imagine you have a rubber bar. When you bend the bar, it stretches in tension in on one side and squeezes together in compression on the other side. The bar breaks when the stress on the tension side reaches the tensile strength of the material. The same idea applies to bars, or beams, made of wood or steel.

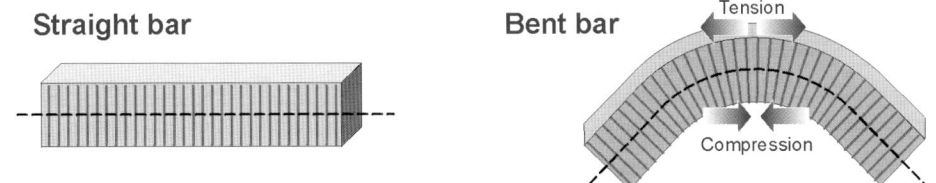

Units for stress
The metric unit of stress is the pascal (Pa). One pascal is equal to one newton of force per square meter of area (1 N/m²). Most stresses are much larger than one pascal. Strong materials like steel and aluminum can take stresses of 100 million pascals. The English unit for stress is pounds per square inch (psi). A stress of one psi is equivalent to one pound of force for each square inch of area (1 lb/in²).

542

Table 27.2:
Tensile strength of common materials

Material	Tensile strength (MPa)
1 MPa = 1 million Pa	
Titanium	900
Steel (alloy)	825
Steel (type 1010)	400
Aluminum (alloy)	290
Aluminum (pure)	110
Oak (wood)	95
Pine (wood)	60
Nylon plastic	55
Rubber	14

Breaking wires of different size

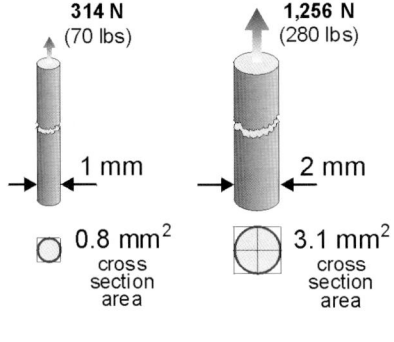

$$\sigma = \frac{314\ N}{0.8\ mm^2} \qquad \sigma = \frac{1,256\ N}{3.1\ mm^2}$$

$$= 400\ \frac{N}{mm^2} \qquad = 400\ \frac{N}{mm^2}$$

Figure 27.4: *A thicker wire can support more force at the same stress as a thinner wire because the cross section area is increased.*

Designing things to be strong enough

Designing for success
Engineers use the properties of materials to evaluate their designs. You can design something strong enough *not* to break only when you understand the forces and conditions that *will* make it break. Analysis of failure is a *very* important part of the process of design.

Safety factors
The safety factor is the ratio of how strong something *is* compared with how strong it has to be. For example, suppose you need to choose a steel wire to support a weight of 1,000 newtons. A safety factor of 10 means you choose the wire to have a breaking strength of 10,000 newtons, 10 times stronger than it has to be. The safety factor allows for things that might weaken the wire (like rust) or things you did not consider in the design (like heavier loads).

Some kinds of failure give warning
The *way* something fails is also important to consider. Wooden ladders are not as strong as aluminum ladders of the same weight. But wooden ladders break slowly, making splintering and cracking noises that warn you to get down fast. Aluminum ladders break quickly with no warning. Aluminum ladders are designed with a higher safety factor because they can fail quickly without warning.

Evaluate three designs for a bridge

Three designs (Figure 27.5) have been proposed for supporting a section of road. Each design uses three supports spaced at intervals along the road. Evaluate the strength of each design. The factor of safety must be 5 or higher even when the road is bumper-to-bumper on all 4 lanes with the heaviest possible trucks.

Design #1:
The stress is 1,500,000 N ÷ 0.015 m² = 100 MPa. The tensile strength of the steel is six times greater (600 MPa) than the stress in the tube, so the safety factor is 6.
Design #1 is acceptable for strength.

Design #2:
The stress is 1,500,000 N ÷ 0.015 m² = 100 MPa. The tensile strength of the aluminum alloy is only 2.9 times greater (290 MPa) than the stress in the tube, so the safety factor is only 2.9.
Design #2 is NOT acceptable because the safety factor is too low.

Design #3:
The stress is 1,500,000 N ÷ 0.03 m² = 50 MPa. The tensile strength of the steel in the cables is 8 times greater (400 MPa) than the stress in the cable, so the safety factor is 8.
Design #3 is acceptable for strength.

Example problem

The road must be held from above by 3 supports.

A total of 4.5 million N of force is required to hold up the road.

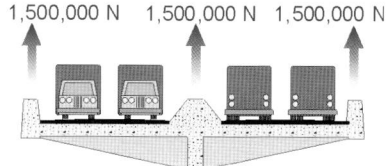

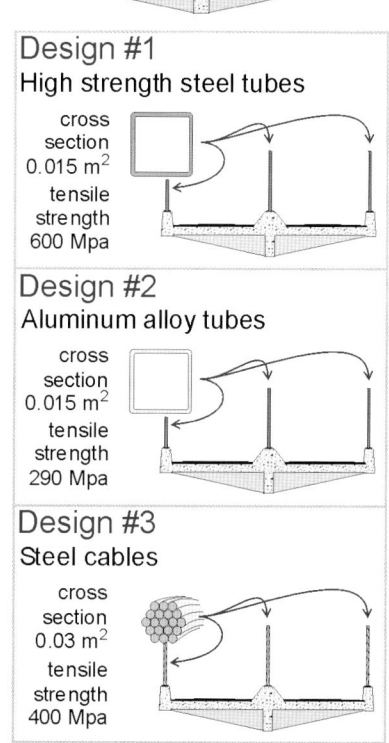

Figure 27.5: *Three designs to support a road from above.*

Elastic properties of solids

Table 27.3: Modulus of elasticity of common materials

Material	Modulus of elasticity (MPa)
1 MPa = 1 million Pa	
Steel	200,000
Titanium	180,000
Aluminum	70,000
Oak (wood)	14,000
Pine (wood)	9,000
Nylon plastic	2,000
Rubber	100

Elasticity of materials

Elasticity measures the ability of a material to stretch. In Chapter 6 you studied Hooke's law which states that the distance a spring stretches is proportional to the applied force. A more general form of Hooke's law applies to three-dimensional solid materials. In the general form of Hooke's law, *stress* and *strain* take the place of force and distance.

Strain is the amount a material deforms

The strain is the amount a material has been deformed, divided by its original size. For example, imagine stretching a rubber rod by one centimeter (0.01 m). If the rod started with a length of one meter, the strain is 0.01, or 1 percent. The Greek letter epsilon (ε) is usually used to represent strain.

Strain

Change in length (m)

$$\text{Strain} \quad \varepsilon = \frac{\Delta l}{l}$$

Original length (m)

Hooke's Law for solids
(F = -kx for springs)

Modulus of elasticity (Pa)

Stress (Pa) $\sigma = -E\varepsilon$ *Strain*

Stress — Stressed length — Original length

Δl — l

Hooke's law for solids

Hooke's law for solids states that the strain in a material is proportional to the applied stress. The modulus of elasticity plays the role of the spring constant for solids. Rubber has a very low modulus of elasticity. A small stress in rubber creates a relatively large strain. Steel has a very high modulus of elasticity. Steel is often used for structures because a lot of stress produces very little strain. Table 27.3 gives the modulus of elasticity for some common materials.

Elastic and brittle materials

A material is elastic when it can take a large amount of strain before breaking. Rubber is a good example of an elastic material. You can easily stretch rubber tubing to three times its original length, a strain of 200 percent. A brittle material breaks at a very low value of strain. Glass is a good example of a brittle material (Figure 27.6). You cannot stretch glass even one-tenth of a percent (0.001) before it breaks. Concrete, rock, and some plastics are also brittle.

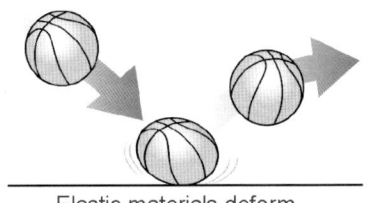

Elastic materials deform without breaking

Brittle materials break instead of deforming (much)

Figure 27.6: *Elastic materials deform when they are stressed. Brittle materials break.*

Thermal expansion

Atoms and thermal expansion   Almost all solid materials expand as the temperature increases. As the temperature increases, the vibration energy of atoms also increases. The increased vibration makes each atom take up a little more space, causing thermal expansion.

The coefficient of thermal expansion   The coefficient of thermal expansion describes how much a material expands for each change in temperature. A thermal expansion coefficient of 10^{-4} per °C means each one degree Celsius rise in temperature causes an object to expand by .0001 times its original length. Table 27.4 gives the thermal expansion coefficient for common materials.

Thermal Expansion

Change in length (m)   Coefficient of thermal expansion

$$\frac{\Delta l}{l} = \alpha (T_2 - T_1)$$

Original length (m)   Change in temperature (C)

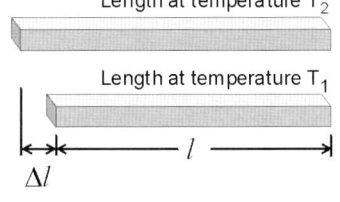

Length at temperature T_2

Length at temperature T_1

Materials contract as well as expand   The thermal expansion coefficient works both ways. If the temperature *decreases*, objects *contract*. The amount of contraction or expansion is equal to the temperature change times the coefficient of thermal expansion. Many structures (Figure 27.7) include design features that allow for thermal expansion or contraction.

Thermal stress   Thermal stress is stress caused by differences in temperature. Thermal expansion is a type of strain caused by temperature changes. Thermal stress occurs when materials are not allowed to expand or contract when the temperature changes. For example, pouring boiling water into a heavy glass often causes the glass to crack. The surface of the glass touching the hot water heats up quickly and tries to expand. The rest of the glass does not heat up as quickly and expands at a lower rate. The difference in expansion causes stress which cracks the glass if the stress is greater than the tensile strength of glass. Hooke's law can be used to calculate the stress produced by thermal expansion or contraction.

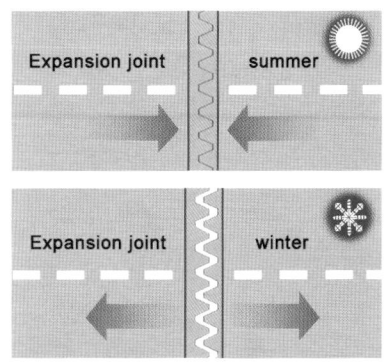

Figure 27.7: *Concrete bridges always have expansion joints to allow the concrete to expand and contract with changes in the temperature.*

Table 27.4:
Coefficient of thermal expansion for common materials

Material	Coefficient of thermal expansion ($\times 10^{-5}$ per C)
Steel	1.2
Brass	1.8
Aluminum	2.4
Glass	2.0
Copper	1.7
Concrete	1
Nylon plastic	8
Rock	7
Rubber	16
Wood	3

Types of solid materials

Plastics   Plastics are solids formed from long chain molecules (Figure 27.8). Different plastics can have a wide range of physical properties including strength, elasticity, thermal expansion, and density. Many common plastics melt and can be formed easily when they are liquid. Other plastics are liquid at room temperature and harden when heated.

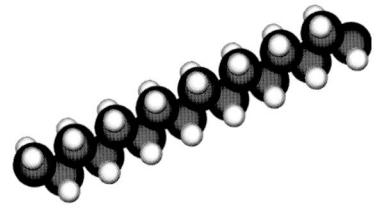

Figure 27.8: *Plastics are made of long-chain molecules.*

Ductile metals   Metals are strong and relatively easy to form. Metals that bend and stretch easily without cracking are called ductile. Copper and some kinds of steel are considered ductile metals. Other metals are hard and brittle, like cast iron. Some metals are very soft, like lead. Some metals are light, like aluminum or magnesium.

Alloys   The properties of metals can be changed by mixing elements. An alloy is a metal that is a mixture of more than one element. For example, brass is an alloy made from copper and tin. Steel is an alloy typically made from 99 percent iron and 1 percent carbon. The strength of steel can be improved further by adding other elements, such as vanadium, chromium, and molybdenum. More than 100 different alloys of steel are in common use. Virtually all common objects made from metal are made from alloys rather than pure elements.

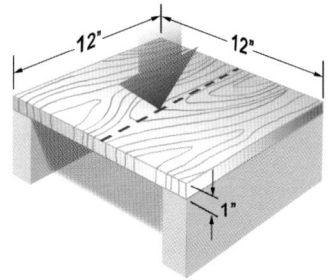

A karate chop easily breaks the wood along the grain, but not across he grain.

Figure 27.9: *The properties of wood vary with the direction of the grain.*

Material properties can change with direction   Many materials have different properties in different directions. Wood is a good example of this kind of material. Wood has a *grain* that is created by the way trees grow. Wood is very difficult to break against the grain, but easy to break along the grain (Figure 27.9). Plywood is strong in two directions because it is made from layers. The grain of the wood grain alternates direction in each layer.

Composite materials   Composite materials are made from strong fibers supported by much weaker plastic. Like wood, composite materials tend to be strongest in a preferred direction. Fiberglass and carbon fiber are two examples of useful composite materials (Figure 27.10). Individual fibers can be stronger than steel but are too flexible to be useful. To make useful materials, fibers are bundled or woven and then embedded in plastic. Modern composite materials can be lighter and stronger than steel. However, composite materials are only strong in the direction of the fibers and are weak in the direction across the fibers.

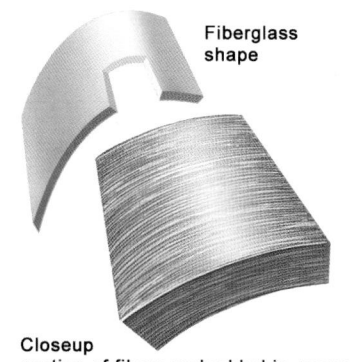

Fiberglass shape

Closeup section of fibers embedded in epoxy

Figure 27.10: *Fiberglass and carbon fiber are composite materials.*

27.2 Properties of Liquids and Fluids

Liquids are a type of fluid. Fluids can change shape and flow when forces are applied to them. Gas is also a fluid because gas can change shape and flow. Liquids can be thin like water or thick like syrup. Liquids can be light like alcohol, or dense like mercury. This section introduces some of the properties of fluids. The concepts apply to liquids and gases.

Density and buoyancy

Table 27.5:
Densities of common liquids

Material	Density (kg/m³)
Mercury	13,560
Glycerin	1,264
Water	1,000
Oil	888
Alcohol	789

Density — The density of a liquid is the ratio of mass to volume, just like the density of a solid. Because the atoms have more energy in a liquid, they tend to be slightly farther apart. Because the atoms are farther apart, the density of a liquid is almost always less than the density of the same material in the solid phase. Table 27.5 gives the density of some common liquids.

Why objects sink — Because liquid can flow, objects of higher density sink through a liquid of lower density. Liquids of higher density also sink in liquids of lower density. Water has a higher density than oil. If you pour water into oil, the water sinks to the bottom.

Why objects float — Objects of lower density float on liquids of higher density. Wood floats on water because wood has a lower density than water. A steel boat floats because the boat is mostly full of air. The *average* density of the boat is less than the density of water. Fill a steel boat with water and it sinks because the average density rises.

Ice is less dense than water — Water is an exception to the rule about the density of solid and liquid phases of a substance. Ice floats because it is *less* dense than water. If ice were denser than water, it would sink. When water molecules freeze into ice crystals, they form a hexagonal pattern that has an unusually large amount of empty space (Figure 27.11). That empty space explains why ice is less dense than liquid water.

Buoyancy — An object submerged in liquid feels an upward force called buoyancy (Figure 27.12). The buoyancy force is exactly equal to the *weight of liquid displaced* by the object. Objects float if the buoyancy force is greater than their own weight. Objects sink if the buoyancy force is less than their own weight. If you think carefully about weight and volume, you will recognize that buoyancy derives from differences in the density of things.

Ice crystals and snowflakes

Figure 27.11: *Water molecules form crystals with a lot of empty space.*

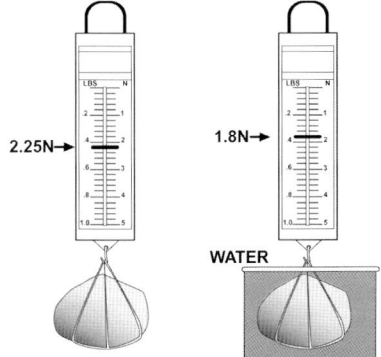

Figure 27.12: *Submerged objects feel lighter because of buoyancy forces.*

Pressure

Force and fluids   Think about what happens when you push down on a balloon. The downward force you apply creates forces that act in other directions as well as down. For example, sideways forces push the sides of the balloon out. This is very different from what happens when you push down on a bowling ball. The solid ball transmits the force directly down. Because fluids can easily change shape, forces applied to fluids create more complex effects than forces applied to solids.

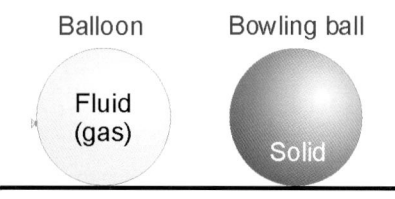

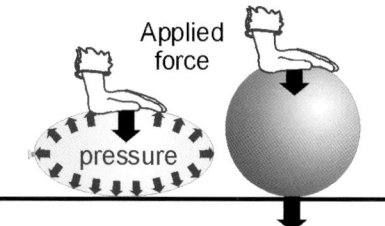

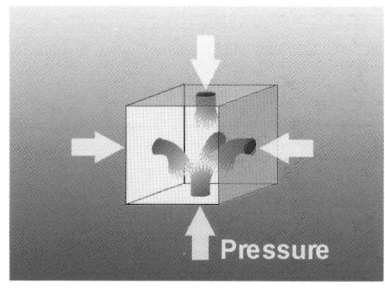

Figure 27.13: *Pressure exerts equal force in all directions in liquids that are not moving. If you put a box with holes underwater, pressure makes water flow in from all sides.*

Pressure   Forces applied to fluids create pressure instead of stress. Like stress, pressure is a ratio of force per unit area. Unlike stress however, pressure acts in all directions, not just the direction of the applied force (Figure 27.13). Pressure is caused by forces acting on and within fluids. For example, gravity creates pressure in a pool of water. The air flowing around a wing creates pressure that lifts an airplane.

Pressure is an important concept   The concept of pressure is central to understanding how fluids behave within themselves and also how fluids interact with surfaces, such as containers. The motion of fluids depends on pressure and density in a similar way as the motion of solids depends on force and mass. In agreement with the third law (action-reaction), pressure exerts forces on all surfaces that come in contact with a fluid.

Units of pressure   Pressure is force per unit area, like stress. A pressure of 1 N/m^2 means a force of one newton acts on each square meter. The metric unit of pressure is the N/m^2, named the pascal (Pa). One pascal is equal to a pressure of one newton of force per square meter of area (N/m^2). The English unit of pressure is pounds per square inch (psi). One psi describes a pressure of one pound of force per square inch of area (lb/in^2). One pascal is a much smaller amount of pressure than one psi (Figure 27.14).

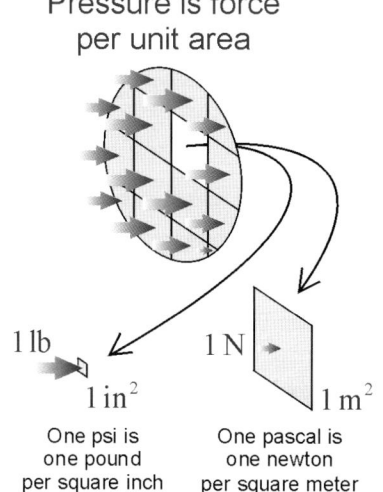

Figure 27.14: *Two common units for pressure are Pa (N/m^2) and psi (lbs/in^2).*

548

Pressure caused by gravity

Pressure from the weight of a liquid

Gravity is one cause of pressure because fluids have weight. The pressure increases the deeper you go beneath the surface of a fluid because the weight of fluid above you increases with depth. The rate at which pressure increases depends on the density of the fluid. Heavy fluids (water) create more pressure than light fluids (air) at the same depth.

The atmosphere

Air is a fluid and the atmosphere of the Earth has a pressure. At ground level, a column of air one meter square has a mass exceeding 10,000 kilograms and a pressure of 101,000 N/m². The density of air is very low, but the atmosphere is more than 80,000 meters deep (Figure 27.15). We are not crushed because the pressure of air inside our lungs is the same as the pressure outside.

The ocean

Water is much denser than air and pressure under the ocean surface increases rapidly with depth (Figure 27.16). At a depth of 1,000 meters the pressure is nearly 10 million N/m², or almost 100 times the pressure of the atmosphere. Submarines must be engineered and built to withstand these deep ocean pressures.

Pressure is equal at equal depth

The pressure at the same depth is the same everywhere in any liquid that is not moving. It does not matter what the shape of the container is. The formula below gives the pressure in a fluid that is not moving.

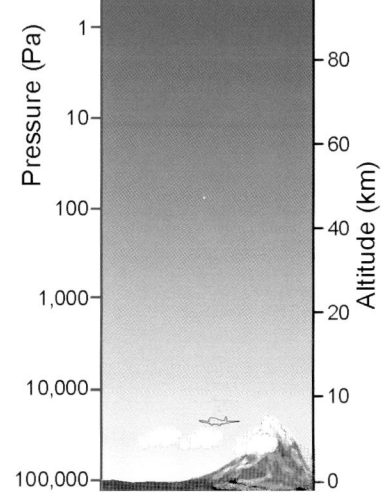

Figure 27.15: *The pressure of the atmosphere decreases with altitude. Atmospheric pressure comes from the weight of air.*

Pressure in a liquid

Liquid of density, ρ

$$\underset{\substack{\text{Pressure}\\(Pa, N/m^2)}}{} P = \underset{\substack{\uparrow\\ \text{Strength of gravity (9.8 N/kg)}}}{\rho} \overset{\substack{\text{Density (kg/m}^3)\\\downarrow}}{g} d \leftarrow \text{Depth (m)}$$

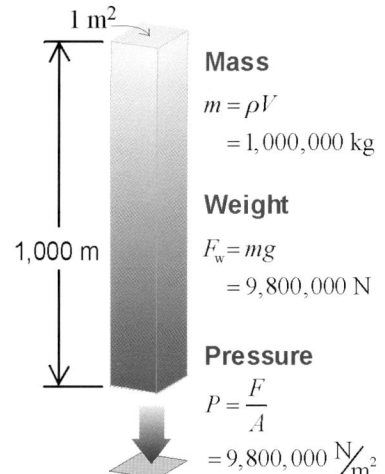

Figure 27.16: *The pressure at any point in a liquid is created by the weight of liquid above that point.*

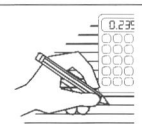

Pressure below the surface of the ocean

Calculate the pressure 1,000 meters below the surface of the ocean. The density of water is 1,000 kg/m³. The pressure of the atmosphere is 101,000 Pa. Compare the pressure 1,000 meters deep with the pressure of the atmosphere.

1) You are asked for the pressure and to compare it to one atmosphere.
2) You are given the density and depth.
3) Use the pressure formula P= ρgd and add the atmospheric pressure to water pressure.
4) P = (1,000 kg/m³)(9.8 N/kg)(1,000 m) + 101,000 Pa
   = 9,800,000 Pa + 101,000 Pa = 9,901,000 Pa, or 99 times atmospheric pressure.

Pressure, molecules, and force

The molecular explanation On the microscopic level, pressure comes from collisions between atoms or molecules. The molecules in fluids (gases and liquids) are not bonded tightly to each other as they are in solids. Molecules move around and collide with each other and with the solid walls of a container.

Pressure and the third law Think about water in a jar. The water exerts pressure against the inside of the jar. On a microscopic level, water molecules are moving around and they bounce off the jar. It takes force to make a molecule reverse its direction and bounce the other way. The bouncing force is applied *to* the molecule *by* the inside surface of the jar. According to the third law, an equal and opposite reaction force is exerted *by* the molecule *on* the jar. The reaction force is what creates the pressure acting on the inside surface of the jar. Trillions of molecules per second are constantly bouncing against every square millimeter of the inner surface of the jar. Pressure comes from the collisions of those many, many atoms.

Pressure and force

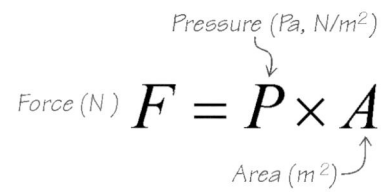

$$F = P \times A$$

Force (N), Pressure (Pa, N/m²), Area (m²)

Figure 27.17: *Pressure creates a force on any surface immersed in a liquid. The force is equal to the pressure times the area that contacts the liquid.*

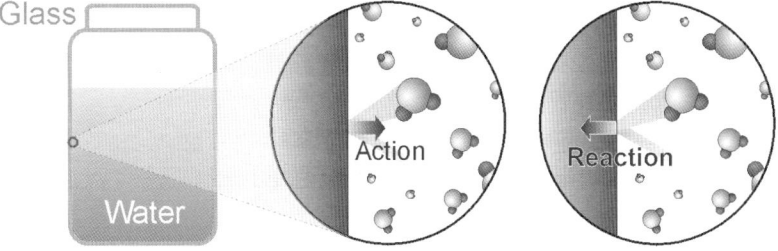

Pressure creates forces on surfaces Pressure creates a force on any surface immersed in liquid. The force is equal to the pressure times the area that contacts the liquid (Figure 27.17). Dams and submarines are built to withstand the tremendous pressure forces deep underwater.

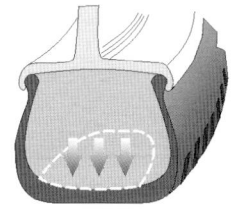

Figure 27.18: *The pressure inside your tire is what holds your car up. When your tire pressure is too low, your tire squashes down because more area is needed to get enough force to hold up the car.*

Pressure in car tires

(English units)

A car tire is at a pressure of 35 psi. Four tires support a car that weighs 4,000 pounds. Each tire supports 1,000 pounds How much surface area of the tire is holding up the car? (Figure 27.18)
1) You are asked for area.
2) You are given force and pressure.
3) Force is pressure times area, so area is force divided by pressure.
4) A = F÷P = (1,000 lbs)÷(35 psi) = 28.5 in².
This is about equal to a patch of tire measuring 5-by-5.7 inches.

Motion of fluids

Applying the laws of motion to fluids

The study of motion of fluids is called fluid mechanics. Fluid mechanics is a complex subject because fluids can change shape. To understand fluid motion we cannot think of the whole fluid at once because different parts might be moving differently (Figure 27.19). Instead, we focus our attention on a small sample — so small that we can assume all the fluid in the sample is moving together, like a solid block. The principles of fluid motion can be discovered by applying the physical laws we already know to the motion of the small sample of fluid. Fluids move according to the same fundamental laws of motion as solid objects.

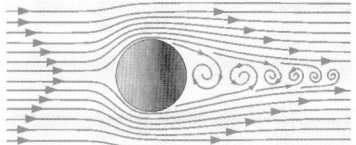

Figure 27.19: *Water flowing around a pole. The water reverses direction immediately behind the pole and forms swirls called eddies.*

The speed of fluids

Moving fluids usually do not have a single speed. The speed is often different at different places in a fluid. For example, think about thick syrup flowing down a plate held at an angle. The syrup near the plate sticks to the surface and moves very slowly. The syrup near the surface moves much faster (Figure 27.20).

Fluids flow because of pressure differences

Fluids flow because of differences in pressure. Think about water flowing in a garden hose. The pressure is high where the hose is connected to the faucet. The pressure decreases along the hose and is zero at the outlet.

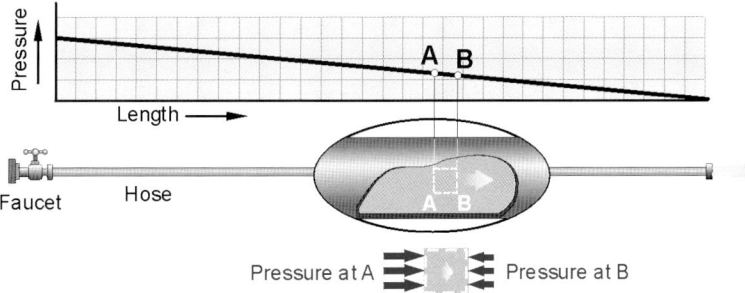

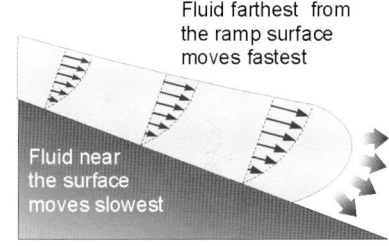

Figure 27.20: *A flow of syrup down a plate. Arrows represent the speed of the fluid at every point. Friction slows the syrup touching the plate. The top of the syrup moves fastest because the drag from friction decreases away from the plate surface.*

Consider a cube-shaped sample of water within the hose. The pressure is higher at point A than at point B. The pressure difference makes a net force pushing the cube of water onward. The water flows because the pressure at one end of the hose is higher than the pressure at the other end. Fluids flow because of unequal pressures just like solids move because of unequal forces.

Energy in fluids

Pressure and energy

Pressure and energy are related. Remember, our definition of energy was the stored ability to exert force and do work. Fluid in a container has energy because any pressure created by the fluid pushes on the sides of the container with forces that can do work. One joule of work is done when a pressure of one pascal pushes a surface of one square meter a distance of one meter. The volume swept out by the expanding fluid is one cubic meter (Figure 27.21). One joule per cubic meter is a *potential energy density* just like one kilogram per cubic meter is a *mass density*.

Pressure is potential energy

Differences in pressure create potential energy in fluids just like differences in height create potential energy from gravity. A pressure difference of one N/m² is equivalent to a potential energy density of one joule per m³ (Figure 27.22). The potential energy is equal to volume times pressure.

Pressure and potential energy

$$\underset{\substack{\text{Potential} \\ \text{energy (J)}}}{} E = \underset{\substack{\uparrow \\ \text{Volume (m}^3)}}{\overset{\overset{\text{Pressure (Pa, N/m}^2)}{\downarrow}}{P}} V$$

Total energy in a fluid

The law of conservation of energy applies to fluids as it does to anything else. Imagine a tank of water with a hole in the side. A stream of water squirts out of the hole. The pressure energy of the water inside the tank is converted to the kinetic energy of water squirting out of the hole. The total energy of a small mass of fluid is equal to its potential energy from gravity (height) plus its potential energy from pressure plus its kinetic energy. The formula below gives the total energy.

Energy of a small mass of fluid

$$E_{total} = \underset{\substack{\text{Potential} \\ \text{energy from} \\ \text{gravity}}}{mgh} + \underset{\substack{\text{Potential} \\ \text{energy from} \\ \text{pressure}}}{PV} + \underset{\substack{\text{Kinetic} \\ \text{energy}}}{\frac{1}{2}mv^2}$$

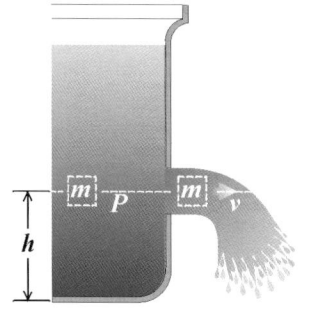

Pressure and work

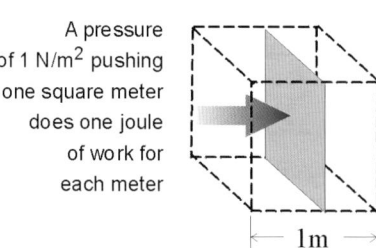

A pressure of 1 N/m² pushing one square meter does one joule of work for each meter

Figure 27.21: *Pressure does work as fluids expand. A pressure of one pascal does one joule of work pushing one square meter a distance of one meter.*

Pressure and energy density

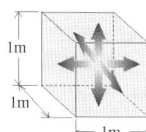

A pressure difference of one newton per square meter (inside to outside)

is equivalent to

One joule of potential energy per cubic meter

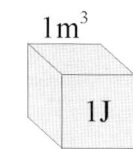

Figure 27.22: *Pressure is a form of potential energy because work can be done.*

552

Energy conservation and Bernoulli's equation

Deriving Bernoulli's equation The law of conservation of energy is called Bernoulli's equation when applied to a fluid. To get Bernoulli's equation, we set the energy inside and outside the container to be equal (step 1). We then notice that mass and volume can be combined as density (step 2).

Step 1: Set energy equal inside and outside

$$\underset{\text{the container}}{\text{Energy inside}} = \underset{\text{the container}}{\text{Energy outside}}$$

$$mgh_1 + P_1 V + \tfrac{1}{2}mv_1^2 = mgh_2 + P_2 V + \tfrac{1}{2}mv_2^2$$

Step 2: Replace mass (m) and volume (V) by density (ρ).

$$\rho gh_1 + P_1 + \tfrac{1}{2}\rho v_1^2 = \rho gh_2 + P_2 + \tfrac{1}{2}\rho v_2^2$$
$$= \text{constant}$$

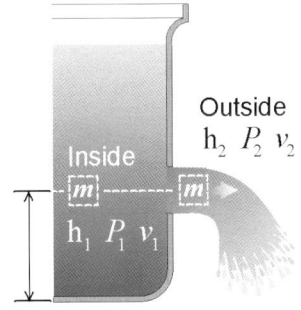

Outside
h_2 P_2 v_2

Inside

h_1 P_1 v_1

Figure 27.23: *These streamlines show the flow of air around a car. Fluid flows along streamlines. Fluid does not flow across streamlines.*

The three variables Bernoulli's equation says the three variables of height, pressure, and speed are related by energy conservation. If one variable increases, at least one of the other two must decrease. For example, if speed goes up, pressure goes down.

Bernoulli's equation

$$\rho gh + P + \tfrac{1}{2}\rho v^2 = \text{constant}$$

Along any
streamline
in a fluid

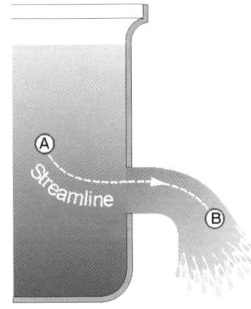

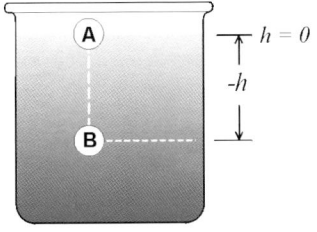

Liquid of density, ρ

$h = 0$

$-h$

At point A
$\rho gh + P = 0$

At point B
$\rho g(-h) + P = 0$
$P = \rho gh$

Streamlines Streamlines are imaginary lines drawn to show the flow of fluid. We draw streamlines so that they are always parallel to the direction of flow (Figure 27.23). Bernoulli's equation tells us that the quantity $\rho gh + P + \tfrac{1}{2}\rho v^2$ is the same *anywhere along a streamline*. If the fluid is not moving ($v = 0$), then Bernoulli's equation gives us the relation between pressure and depth, remembering that depth is negative height (Figure 27.24).

Figure 27.24: *In an unmoving fluid we choose h = 0 at the surface where the pressure (P) is also zero. The value of $\rho gh + P$ at point A is zero. Bernoulli's equation says that at point B the value of $\rho gh + P$ must also be zero.*

Applying Bernoulli's equation

Airfoils The wings of airplanes are made in the shape of an airfoil. Air flowing along the top of the airfoil (B) moves faster than air flowing along the bottom of the airfoil (C). The speed is different because the shape of the airfoil forces the air on the top of the wing to take a longer path than the air under the wing.

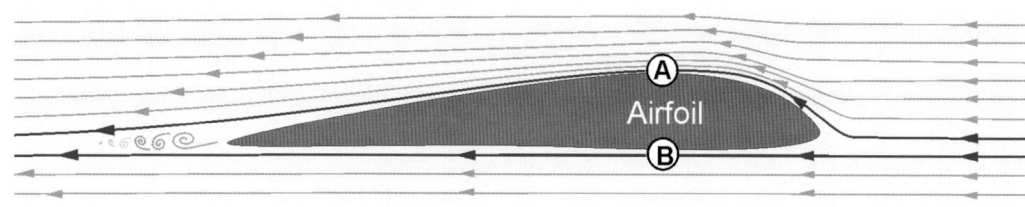

Lift forces According to Bernoulli's equation, if the speed goes up, the pressure goes down. When a plane is moving, the pressure on the top surface of the wings is lower than the pressure beneath the wings. The difference in pressure is what creates the lift force that supports the plane in the air.

Choosing streamlines By picking the right streamlines we can use Bernoulli's equation to calculate the lift force on the wing. Streamline A goes over the top surface of the wing. Streamline B goes under the wing. The quantity in Bernoulli's equation ($\rho gh + P + \rho v^2/2$) must be the same at points (A) and (B) because both streamlines start very close to the same place in front of the wing.

At point Ⓐ
$$\rho gh + P + \tfrac{1}{2}\rho v^2$$

At point Ⓑ
$$= \rho gh + P + \tfrac{1}{2}\rho v^2$$

Solve for the pressure difference ▷

$$P_B - P_A = 3{,}781 \, \text{N}/\text{m}^2$$

Calculating lift force When air above the wing is moving 150 meters per second and air below the wing is moving 125 m/sec, the difference in pressure is 3,781 N/m². An airplane with 20 square meters of wing surface would experience a lift force of 75,600 newtons, almost 17,000 pounds.

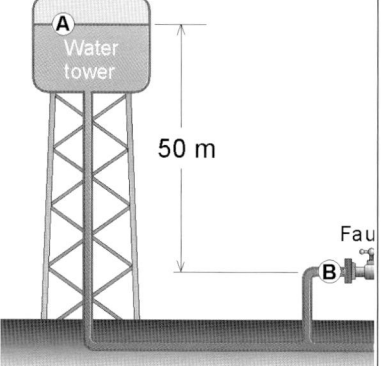

Fluids and friction

Viscosity
Viscosity measures a fluid's resistance to flow. Thick fluids like syrup have a high viscosity. It takes a large pressure difference to make syrup flow fast. Thin liquids like water have a low viscosity. Even a small pressure difference can produce a large flow of water because the viscosity of water is so low.

The cause of viscosity
Viscosity is caused by forces that act between atoms and molecules in a liquid. Corn oil has a high viscosity because corn oil is made of large molecules that interfere as they slip over each other. Water has a low viscosity because water molecules are small and move around each other easily (Figure 27.25).

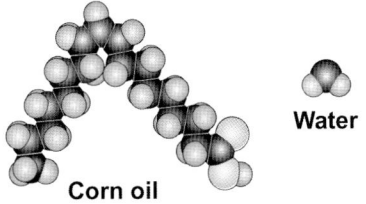

Figure 27.25: *Molecules of different sizes are one of the reasons liquids have different viscosities*

The effect of temperature
The viscosity of liquids decreases with temperature increase. Thick fluids like corn oil flow much easier when they are hot because the viscosity is greatly reduced. The reduction in viscosity with raised temperatures comes from the increase in molecular motion. Warmer molecules in rapid motion have enough energy to jostle around each other more easily. Oil for a car engine is specially made to have the right viscosity at different temperatures.

Laminar flow
Friction in fluids also depends on the type of flow. In laminar flow the streamlines are smooth and parallel. Fluid in laminar flow does not mix across streamlines. A faucet running water at a very low rate produces laminar flow (Figure 27.26). The water runs out in a clear, smooth stream. Laminar flow usually creates the lowest amount of friction.

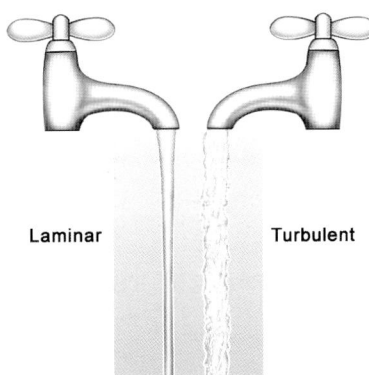

Figure 27.26: *Water running from a faucet can be either laminar or turbulent depending on the rate of flow.*

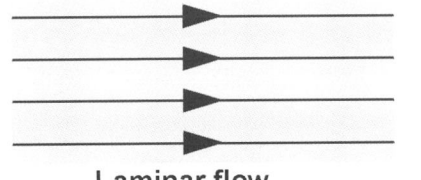

Laminar flow

Turbulent flow

Turbulent flow
When fluid moves fast, the flow often becomes turbulent. In turbulent flow the streamlines are broken up into very disorganized patterns. There is constant churning and mixing of fluid in turbulent flow. A faucet at high volume produces turbulent flow (Figure 27.26). The stream of water appears foamy from the rapid mixing. Turbulent flow creates much higher friction than laminar flow.

27.3 Properties of Gases

Gases are fluids because gases can change shape and flow when forces are applied. Gases are different from liquids because they can expand and contract, greatly changing their density. The density of liquids and solids remains nearly constant. This section introduces some of the properties of gases.

Density and buoyancy in air and other gases

Density   Gases have much lower densities than liquids because the atoms in a gas are much farther apart than in a liquid. The density of air is about one kilogram per cubic meter. Air feels "light" because air is 1,000 times less dense than water.

Air is not "nothing"   Air may seem like "nothing" but all the oxygen our bodies need and the carbon needed by plants comes from air. As a tree grows, the soil does not sink down to supply mass for the tree. All of the carbon atoms in wood come from carbon dioxide (CO_2) in the air.

Air is a mixture of gases   Air is the most important gas to living things on the Earth. The atmosphere of the Earth is a mixture of nitrogen, oxygen, water vapor, argon, and a few trace gases (Figure 27.27). Molecules of nitrogen (N_2) and oxygen (O_2) account for 97.2 percent of the mass of air. The amount of water vapor depends on the temperature and relative humidity.

Sinking in a gas   Because gas can flow and has a very low density, objects of higher density sink quickly. For example, if you drop a penny, it falls through the air easily because the density of the penny is 9,000 times greater than the density of air.

Floating in a gas   Objects of lower density can float on gas of higher density. A helium balloon floats because the average density of the balloon (and helium inside) is less than the density of air (Table 27.6).

Buoyancy   An object submerged in gas feels an upward buoyancy force. You do not notice buoyancy forces from air because the density of ordinary objects is so much greater than the density of air. Just as with liquids, the buoyancy force is exactly equal to the weight of gas displaced by an object. Whether an object sinks or floats depends on whether the buoyancy force is greater or less than the object's weight.

Composition of the Earth's Atmosphere
(by weight @ 70% relative humidity)

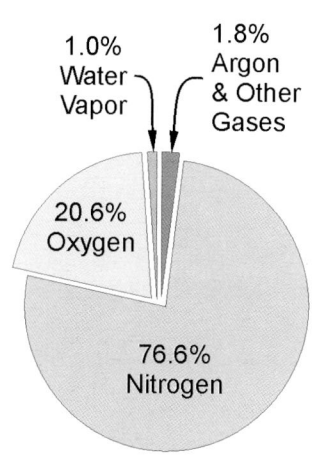

Figure 27.27: *Air is a mixture of gases.*

Table 27.6: Densities of common gases at 1 atm and 27°C.

Gas	Density (kg/m³)
Carbon dioxide	1.8
Argon	1.6
Oxygen	1.3
Air	1.2
Nitrogen	1.1
Helium	0.16

Pressure and Boyle's Law

Pressure and temperature affect density

The density of a gas depends on pressure and temperature. If the pressure increases, the density may also increase. If the pressure decreases, the density may also decrease. This is very different from liquids or solids. The density of a liquid or solid stays almost the same when the pressure is changed. Depending on the pressure and temperature, the density of a gas can vary from near zero (in outer space) to densities greater than solids.

Boyle's law

The pressure goes up if you squeeze gas into a smaller volume while keeping temperature constant. This rule is known as Boyle's law. Pressure increases because the same number of molecules are squeezed into a smaller space. The molecules hit the walls more often because there are more molecules per cubic meter. The pressure increases because there are more collisions. The formula for Boyle's law relates the pressure and volume of gas. If the mass and temperature are kept constant, the product of pressure times volume stays the same. The subscripts 1 and 2 in the formula indicate the pressure and volume at two different conditions.

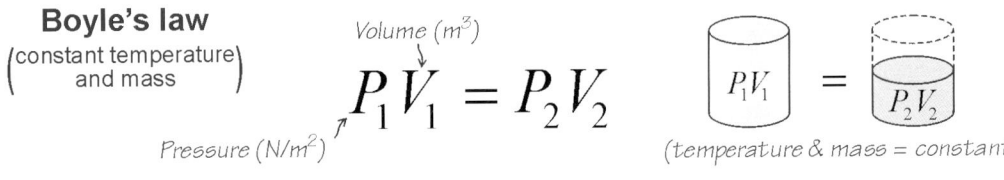

Boyle's law
$\left(\begin{array}{c}\text{constant temperature}\\\text{and mass}\end{array}\right)$

$Volume\ (m^3)$

$$P_1 V_1 = P_2 V_2$$

$Pressure\ (N/m^2)$

$P_1 V_1 = P_2 V_2$

(temperature & mass = constant

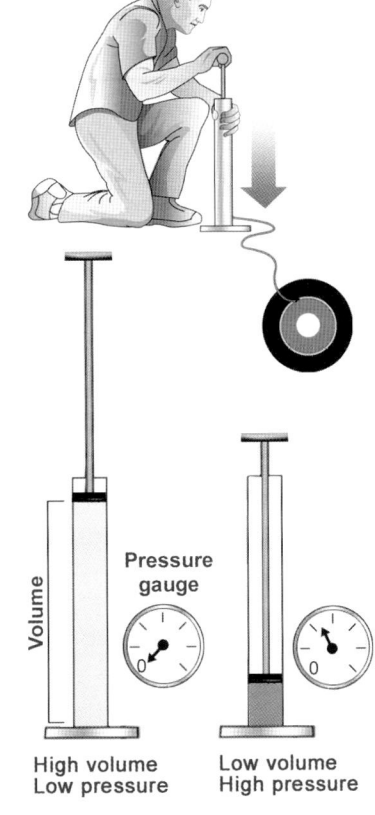

Volume

Pressure gauge

High volume
Low pressure

Low volume
High pressure

Figure 27.28: *A bicycle pump changes the volume of air to increase the pressure.*

Calculate the pressure increase from a change in volume

(English units)

A bicycle pump creates high pressure by squeezing air into a smaller volume (Figure 27.28). If air at atmospheric pressure (14.7 psi) is compressed from an initial volume of 30 cubic inches to a final volume of three cubic inches, what is the final pressure?

1) You are asked for pressure.
2) You are given initial and final volume.
3) Apply Boyle's law: $P_1 V_1 = P_2 V_2$
4) $P_2 = (V_1/V_2) \times P_1 = (30 \div 3) \times 14.7 = 147$ psi.
NOTE: Your tire pressure gauge will read 132.3 psi (147 - 14.7) because most pressure gauges measure the pressure DIFFERENCE between inside the gauge and the atmosphere outside.
Boyle's law and the other gas laws use "absolute pressure," which is pressure relative to zero. Gauges read "gauge pressure," which is pressure above the pressure of the atmosphere.

Temperature and pressure

Charles' law   The pressure of a gas is affected by temperature. If the mass and volume are kept constant, the pressure goes up when the temperature goes up. The pressure goes down when the temperature goes down. There is also a formula known as Charles' law that relates volume and temperature (Figure 27.30).

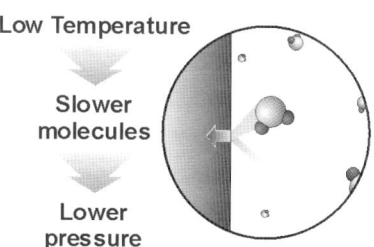

Low Temperature

Slower molecules

Lower pressure

Pressure - temperature relationship
(constant volume and mass)

$$\text{Pressure } (N/m^2) \quad \frac{P_1}{T_1} = \frac{P_2}{T_2}$$

$$\text{Temperature } (K)$$

$$\frac{P_1}{T_1} = \frac{P_2}{T_2}$$

(volume & mass = constant)

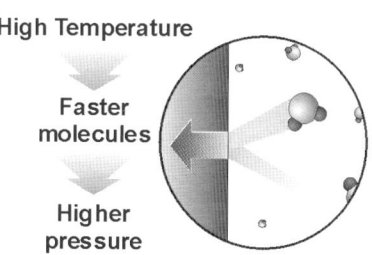

High Temperature

Faster molecules

Higher pressure

Figure 27.29: *Faster molecules create higher pressure because they exert larger forces as they bounce.*

Pressure and temperature   Pressure increases with temperature because hot molecules move faster than cold molecules. The temperature of a gas is a measure of the kinetic energy of moving molecules. The higher the temperature, the faster the molecules are moving. A faster molecule creates more force when it bounces off a surface. The increase in force creates a corresponding increase in pressure (Figure 27.29).

Use temperature in Kelvins   The temperature that appears in the formula above *must be in Kelvins*. The speed of gas molecules depends on their energy compared with the energy they have when the temperature is absolute zero. At absolute zero, molecules are essentially standing still. Because the Kelvin scale starts at absolute zero, it measures the total kinetic energy of gas molecules relative to zero energy.

Converting Celsius to Kelvin

$$T_{\text{Kelvin}} = T_{\text{Celsius}} + 273$$

Calculate the pressure increase at high temperature

(English units)

A can of hair spray has a pressure of 300 psi at room temperature (21°C or 294 K). The can is accidentally moved too close to a fire and its temperature increases to 800°C (1,073 K). What is the final pressure in the can?

1)   You are asked for pressure.
2)   You are given initial and final temperatures.
3)   Apply the pressure - temperature relation $P_1 \div T_1 = P_2 \div T_2$.
4) $P_2 = (T_2 \div T_1) \times P_1 = (1,073 \div 294) \times 300 = 1,095$ psi. ...!

This is why you should NEVER put spray cans near heat. The pressure can increase so much that the can explodes.

Charle's law
(constant pressure & mass)

$$\frac{V_1}{T_1} = \frac{V_2}{T_2}$$

$$\text{Volume } (m^3)$$

$$\text{Temperature } (K)$$

Figure 27.30: *Charles' law shows the relationship between the temperature and volume of a gas.*

The ideal gas law

Table 27.7:
Gas constants for common gases

The ideal gas law   The ideal gas law combines the pressure, volume, and temperature relations for a gas into one equation which also includes the mass of the gas. In physics and engineering, mass (m) is used for the quantity of gas. In chemistry, the ideal gas law is usually written in terms of the number of moles of gas (n) instead of the mass (m).

Ideal gas law

Pressure (N/m^2)

Temperature (K)

$$PV = mRT$$

Volume (m^3)   Mass (kg)   Gas constant ($J/kg \cdot K$)

Gas	Gas constant (R, J/kg-K)
Air	287
Argon	208
Nitrogen (N_2)	297
Oxygen (O_2)	260
Carbon dioxide	189
Helium	2078
Water vapor	462
Methane	518
Propane	189

The gas constant   Each different kind of gas has its own value of the gas constant (R). You need to select the appropriate value for R when using the ideal gas law. Table 27.7 lists the gas constant for several common gases. The gas constants are different because the size and mass of gas molecules are different. The gas constant for air is an average based on the proportions of oxygen and nitrogen in air.

Using the combined gas law   The values for the gas constant in Table 27.7 are in metric units. To use these values with the ideal gas law, pressure is in pascals, volume in meters cubed, mass in kilograms, and temperature in Kelvins. Since the law applies to the total amount of gas, pressure needs to be absolute pressure, not gauge pressure. Absolute pressure is gauge pressure plus the pressure of the atmosphere (101,000 pascals).

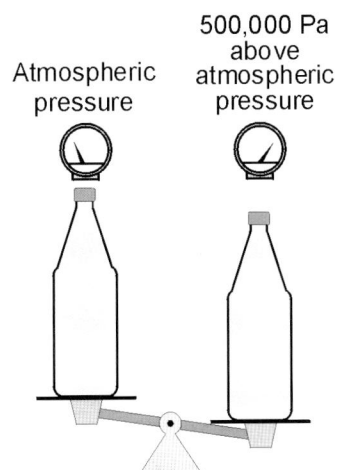

500,000 Pa above atmospheric pressure

Atmospheric pressure

Mass difference of 12.1 grams

Figure 27.31: *Two bottles of air at different pressures have different masses. The bottle at higher pressure has more mass because there are more air molecules in it.*

Calculate the mass of air from the ideal gas law

(metric units)

Two soda bottles contain the same volume of air at different pressures (Figure 27.31). Each bottle has a volume of 0.002 m³ (two liters). The temperature is 21°C (294 K). One bottle is at a gauge pressure of 500,000 pascals (73 psi). The other bottle is at a gauge pressure of zero. Calculate the mass difference between the two bottles.

1) You are asked for a mass difference.
2) You are given the volume, temperature, gauge pressure, and the gas is air.
3) Use the ideal gas law, PV = mRT with R = 287 J/kg-K.
   Convert gauge pressure to absolute pressure by adding 101,000 Pa.
4) First bottle: m = PV/RT = (601,000 x.002)÷(287 x 294) = 0.0143 kg
   Second bottle: m = PV/RT = (101,000 x .002)÷(287 x 294) = 0.0024 kg
   The difference is .0121 kg, or 12.1 grams.

Application: The Deep Water Submarine Alvin

Most of the Earth's surface lies under the oceans. Deep beneath the ocean surface are undersea mountains and volcanoes, strange forms of life, and many clues to the past and present condition of our planet. Exploring the deep ocean requires courage and very sophisticated engineering. The exploration submarine Alvin is famous for research done during deep dives (Figure 27.32). Scientists aboard Alvin have made many remarkable discoveries, including forms of life that live near deep hot spots where there is no light and pressures are 400 times greater than on the Earth's surface.

Figure 27.32: *The Alvin deep water sub can dive to depths of 4,500 meters below the ocean surface.*

Pressure force   At 4,500 meters, the water pressure is 44 million N/m^2. This extreme pressure is equivalent to the weight of a car supported on an area the size of your big toe! The Alvin is 7.1 meters long and 3.7 meters tall, but the spherical pressure hull inside (where scientists work) is only two meters in diameter. The force acting on the two-meter sphere is equal to the pressure times the area. For Alvin, the force on one side of the pressure hull is 31 million pounds (138 million N)!

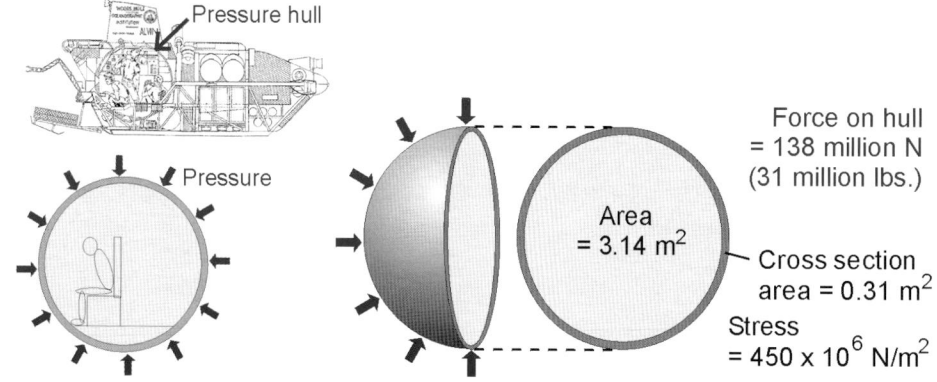

Stress in the hull   The pressure hull is spherical because a sphere is the strongest shape that can withstand compression. To withstand the pressure, the hull is made from titanium alloy 4.9 centimeters thick (almost two inches). The tensile strength of the titanium alloy is greater than 900×10^6 N/m^2. The cross section area of the hull is 0.31 m^2. The stress in the hull is 450×10^6 N/m^2. The titanium alloy used in Alvin's hull is one of the strongest materials ever developed. A hull of ordinary steel or aluminum would be crushed flat by the forces exerted by the ocean's enormous pressure. This is why only robot probes are used to explore deeper parts of the ocean (Figure 27.33).

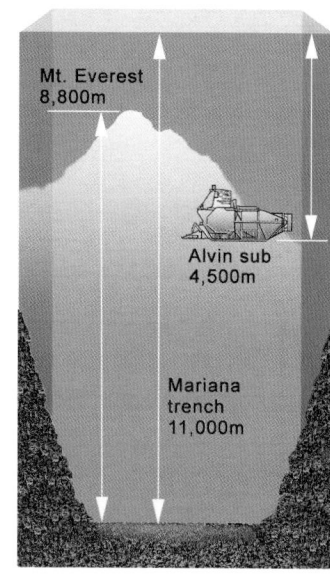

Figure 27.33: *The deepest part of the ocean floor lies more than 8,000 meters below the surface. Even the Alvin cannot reach this depth. The deepest places have only been seen with robot probes.*

560

Air for life support and buoyancy control

Staying level   Alvin and other submarines control their depth by changing their buoyancy. Aboard the submarine is a chamber that can be filled with air or water. The amount of air and water is adjusted with pumps until the average density for the whole submarine is the same as the density of water. When the average densities are matched (neutral buoyancy), the submarine neither rises nor sinks. To rise, some water is pumped out of the tank and replaced with air. The average density decreases and the submarine rises because of the positive buoyancy force. To dive, water is pumped into the tank and air is released. The average density becomes greater than the density of water and the submarine sinks (negative buoyancy).

Submarine
Mass: 10,000 kg
Volume: 10.00 m³

Average density
1,000 kg/m³

(Buoyancy tank 1/2 full)

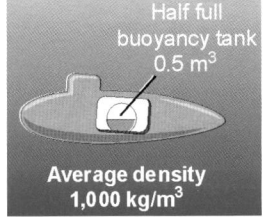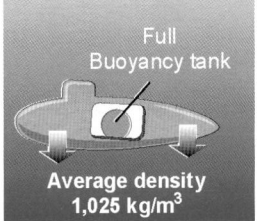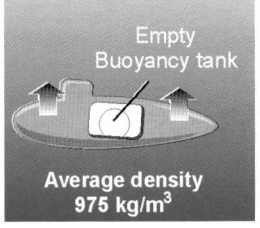

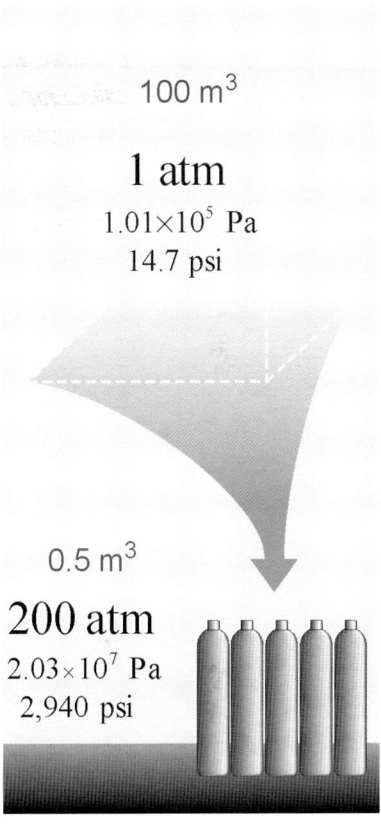

Figure 27.34: *Air can be compressed to high pressures and stored in small volumes.*

Life support   Air for breathing is kept in tanks at very high pressure. At 20 breaths per minute, an average adult inhales 0.08 m³ of air each minute. The interior volume of Alvin's hull has a volume of just over 2 m³. The normal three person crew would breath all the air in the hull in just eight minutes. A seven-hour mission with a crew of three requires at least 100 m³ of air. This volume can be stored in a tank with a volume of 0.5 m³ by raising the pressure (Boyle's law) to 200 times atmospheric pressure. Air tanks for diving typically store air at pressures near or exceeding 200 atmospheres. (Figure 27.34)

The Alvin   The Alvin has made more than 3,500 dives, and is considered the most productive research submarine in the world. Exploring undersea volcanoes and discovering strange new life forms are part of Alvin's long and successful career. In addition to research, Alvin has participated in several exciting recovery missions. In 1966, Alvin located and recovered a nuclear weapon when the plane carrying it crashed into the ocean off the coast of Spain. In 1986, Alvin made a dozen dives to the Titanic, which in 1912 had sunk in 3,789 meters of water.

Chapter 27 Review

Vocabulary Review

Match the following terms with the correct definition. There is one extra definition in the list that will not match any of the terms.

Set One

1. density
2. stress
3. strain
4. tensile strength
5. elasticity

a. Ratio of force acting on a substance to the cross-sectional area through which it acts
b. Measure of the ability of a material to stretch before breaking
c. Ratio of actual strength compared to nominal strength
d. Ratio of the mass of a substance to its volume
e. The amount a material is deformed divided by its original size
f. The stress at which a material breaks under tension force

Set Two

1. ductile
2. alloy
3. buoyancy
4. pressure
5. brittle

a. Upward force applied by a fluid on an immersed object
b. Force per unit area in a fluid, acts in all directions
c. Describes metals made from a mixture of more than one element
d. Downward force acting only perpendicular to an object
e. Describes metals that bend and stretch easily without cracking
f. Describes materials that break at a very low value of strain

Set Three

1. airfoil
2. laminar flow
3. Bernoulli's equation
4. Boyle's law
5. absolute zero

a. Law relating pressure and area at constant volume
b. Fluids move in parallel and smooth lines
c. Law relating pressure and volume at constant temperature
d. Fluids move with different speeds on top and bottom
e. Law of conservation of energy applied to fluids
f. Temperature at which molecules would be essentially standing still

Concept review

1. Which has greater density, a sewing needle made of steel or a heavy bar of steel from which the needle is made?

2. Liquid mercury has a density of approximately 13,600 kg/m^3. Use Table 27.1 on page 540 to decide which of the listed materials will float in mercury.

3. When inquiries are made about the strength of a material, what two questions must be answered to best describe a material's physical strength?

4. Both stress and pressure may be calculated as the ratio of force to area. How do the definitions for *stress* and *pressure* differ?

5. Explain why road beds and other structures experiencing high stress are often made of concrete containing steel rods or cables.

6. The load capacity of a bridge is often stated on a sign at the bridge. How is it possible for vehicles weighing 2 or 3 times the stated capacity to travel across the bridge with no apparent effect at one time and yet fail at a later time?

7. Golf balls are commonly constructed by covering a rubber core with a rubber-cord winding and a durable cover. Why does it make no sense to make the core (or the rest of the golf ball, for that matter) of glass?

8. Rubber and steel are both elastic, yet rubber is not used in making automobile springs or as structural members in bridges and buildings. Explain why rubber is not used.

9. Glass marbles can be fractured by heating them in a frying pan for several minutes and then dropping them into cold water. Explain.

10. Concrete sidewalks, bridges and roadways are built in sections. Give an explanation for this.

11. To which board would a karate expert apply her "chop" to most easily break the board? Explain.

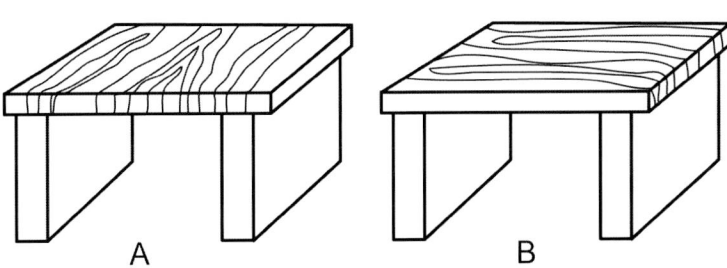

A   B

12. Steel is more dense than water but steel ships float in water. Explain.

13. With regard to motion, force is to the mass of a solid as _____ is to _____ of a fluid.

14. A diver swims down in a pool and lies on the bottom. Compared to the average pressure exerted on the diver in this position, would he experience more, less, or the same average pressure if he were standing on the bottom of the pool? Explain.

15. People who drive on the loose sand of the beaches in the Outer Banks of North Carolina are advised to lower the pressure of their tires to 20 lb/in^2 or less. Explain why this is done.

16. In the diagram of the airfoil, is the internal pressure greater at location A or B? Explain.

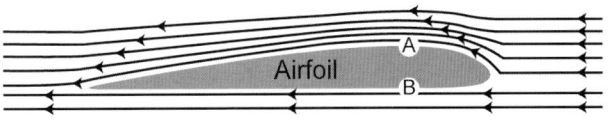

Airfoil

17. The Goodyear blimp carries TV cameras and people aloft in a gondola suspended under the inflated part of the blimp and yet a single person is not able to float in air. Explain why.

18. Two identical, rigid, air-tight containers are filled with air at 20°C. Container A is filled at a pressure of 2 atmospheres while container B is filled at 4 atmospheres of pressure. The containers are placed on a balance as shown. On which side is container A?

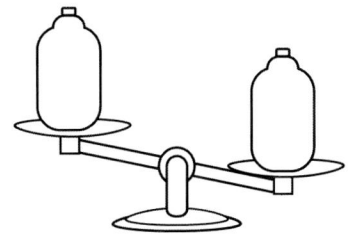

563

Problems

1. A 355 milliliter can of diet cola has a mass of 0.349 kilograms. Will it float in water? Show calculations to support your answer.

2. The winners of a bridge building contest find that their model bridge will hold 2.45 kg of mass before breaking. The cross-sectional area of the supporting members of the bridge is 2 cm^2. How much stress was applied to the supporting members of the bridge?

3. A bridge built with a safety factor of 5 bears a sign declaring the safe load limit to be 7 tons. How much weight can the bridge hold before collapsing?

4. The steel alloy string on a certain musical instrument is 0.75 mm in diameter. A musician, tightening the string to tune the instrument, stretches the steel string until it breaks. How much force was applied to the string?

5. The main steel span of the Golden Gate Bridge in San Francisco is 1,280 meters long. If the temperature changes from 10°C to 20°C during the day, how much longer is this span at the end of the day?

6. A lead object weighing 45.2 newtons in air is placed in a container of oil. Calculate its weight in oil.

7. As you breathe, air is forced into your lungs by a pressure difference between atmospheric pressure often stated as "760 mm of Hg" and an internal lung pressure of "759 mm of Hg." These pressure designations refer to the pressure present at the bottom of columns of mercury 760 or 759 mm in depth. What is the equivalent pressure given in pascals that pushes air into your lungs?

8. If you drive on a beach of soft sand, you must reduce the pressure in your tires from approximately 35 lbs/in^2 to 20 lbs/in^2 to increase the effective area of your tires and reduce your chances of becoming stuck. By what percentage is the "footprint" of your tires increased?

9. Water is sprayed from a fire hose into a burning building 20 meters above the ground.

    a. With what speed does the water leave the fire hydrant on the ground?

    b. What is the pressure of the water at the hydrant?

10. As a scuba diver begins her ascent to the surface in a lake from a depth of 30 meters she exhales a bubble with a volume of 1 liter. Just before the bubble breaks at the surface, what is its volume? (Assume the temperature of the water is constant at all depths.)

11. On a warm summer day (temperature 25°C, 1 atm pressure) you buy your young cousin a helium filled balloon. It has a volume of 0.25 m^3. Your cousin accidentally releases the balloon. To what volume does the balloon expand if it rises to a height at which the temperature is -40°C and the pressure is 1.01×10^4 Pa?

12. If 15.0 grams of water are placed in a 1.50 liter pressure cooker and heated to a temperature of 400°C, what is the pressure inside the container?

13. Lines which attach to the foil (the kite) in a relatively new sport of kiteboarding will support a weight of 2,200 newtons. If the lines that support 2,200 newtons are 2 mm in diameter, how much weight would be supported by a line of the same material with a diameter of 1.5 mm?

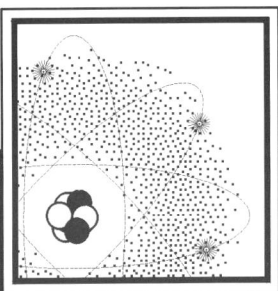

Unit 9
The Atom

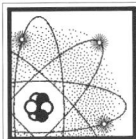

Chapter 28

Inside the Atom

Objectives for Chapter 28

By the end of this chapter you should be able to:

1. Describe the structure of an atom.
2. Describe the four forces acting inside an atom.
3. Use the periodic table to obtain information about the atomic number, mass number, atomic mass, and isotopes of different elements.
4. Predict whether a certain nucleus is stable or unstable and explain why.
5. Distinguish between and provide examples of chemical reactions and nuclear reactions.
6. Describe how atomic spectral lines can be explained by energy levels and quantum states.
7. Explain quantum theory as it relates to light and electrons.
8. Describe the major developments in quantum theory and identify the scientists associated with each.

Terms and vocabulary words

nucleus	electron	proton	neutron	atomic mass
atomic mass unit	electromagnetic force	strong nuclear force	weak force	element
atomic number	mass number	isotope	radioactive	nuclear reaction
quantum	spectral line	spectrum	quantum state	energy level
quantum numbers	Pauli exclusion principle	Planck's constant	wave function	probability
orbital	uncertainty principle	photoelectric effect	photon	chemical reaction
spectrometer	quantum physics			

565

28.1 The Nucleus and Structure of the Atom

This section introduces the structure of the atom. The atom was first thought to be the smallest particle of matter that could exist. Today we understand that atoms themselves are made from even smaller particles. Knowing the structure of the atom makes it possible to explain many properties of matter, just as knowing the structure of DNA makes it possible to explain many processes in biology.

Three particles make up the atom

Charge of the three particles
Atoms are made of three kinds of particles: electrons, protons, and neutrons (Table 28.1). Protons are particles with positive electric charge. Electrons are particles with negative electric charge. Neutrons are neutral and have zero charge. The charge on the electron and proton are exactly equal and opposite. If you put a proton and an electron together, the total charge is zero.

Particles in the atom		Relative Charge	Relative Mass
Electron		-1	1
Proton		+1	1,835
Neutron		0	1,837

Mass of the three particles
Electrons are tiny and light. Protons and neutrons are much larger and more massive. The mass of the proton is 1,835 times the mass of the electron. Neutrons have a bit more mass than protons, but the two masses are so close that we usually assume they are the same. Because the mass of a proton is tiny by normal standards, scientists use atomic mass units (amu). One amu is 1.661×10^{-27} kg, slightly less than the mass of a proton. One electron has a mass of 0.0005 amu.

Atoms are neutral
The positive charge in neutral atom equals the negative charge. A *neutral* atom has a total charge of zero (Figure 28.1). Because the number of electrons equals the number of protons in a complete atom they tend to stay neutral because electric forces are very strong. Any atom with excess protons usually attracts electrons until it becomes neutral again.

Table 28.1:
Charge and mass of particles in the atom (metric units)

Mass (kg)	Charge (coulombs)
Electron	
9.109×10^{-31}	-1.602×10^{-19}
Proton	
1.673×10^{-27}	$+1.602 \times 10^{-19}$
Neutron	
1.675×10^{-27}	0

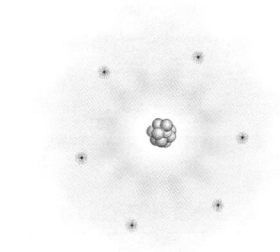

Carbon atom	Charge
6 electrons	-6
6 protons	+6
6 neutrons	0
Total charge	0

Figure 28.1: *The total positive and negative charge of a neutral atom equals zero.*

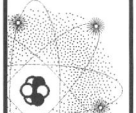
Structure of the atom

The nucleus The neutrons and protons are grouped together in the nucleus, which is at the center of the atom (Figure 28.2). There are no electrons in the nucleus, only protons and neutrons. The nucleus is extremely small, even compared with a single atom. If the atom were the size of your classroom, the nucleus would be the size of a single grain of sand in the center of the room.

The electron cloud The electrons are found outside the nucleus. Because electrons are so fast and light, physicists tend to speak of the electron "cloud" rather than talk about the exact location of each electron. Think about a swarm of bees buzzing in a "cloud" around a beehive. It is not easy to precisely locate any one bee, but you can easily see that, on average, the bees are confined to a cloud of a certain size around the hive. On average, electrons are confined to a similar cloud around the nucleus.

Structure of an atom

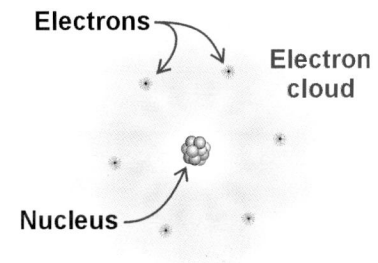

Figure 28.2: *Protons and neutrons are found in the nucleus of an atom. Electrons are outside the nucleus in the "electron cloud." NOTE: To make the diagram clear, the nucleus is shown immensely larger than it would be if the diagram were drawn to scale.*

Mass and the nucleus

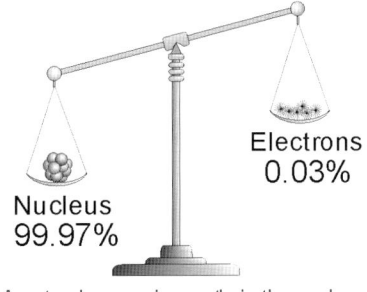

An atom's mass is mostly in the nucleus.

Most of an atom's mass is concentrated in the nucleus. The number of electrons and protons is the same but electrons are so light they contribute very little mass. For example, a carbon atom has six protons, six electrons, and six neutrons. The mass of the nucleus is 12 amu. The mass of the electrons is only 0.003 amu. So 99.97 percent of the carbon atom's mass is in the nucleus and only 0.03 percent is in the electron cloud.

Electrons and the size of atoms

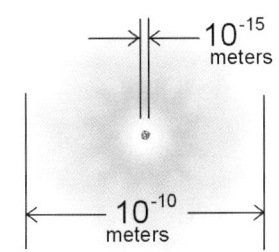

An atom is the size of its electron cloud. The nucleus is tiny by comparison.

The size of an atom depends on how far the electrons spread out. When we talk about the "size" of an atom, what we really mean is how close atoms get to each other. Unless the atoms are chemically bonded together, the electron cloud of one atom does not normally overlap the electron cloud of another. For this reason, the size of an atom is more accurately the size of the electron cloud. The electron cloud is 10,000 times larger than the incredibly tiny nucleus.

Forces in the atom

Electromagnetic forces

Electrons are bound to the nucleus by electromagnetic force. The force is the attraction between protons (positive) and electrons (negative). A good analogy is our planet Earth orbiting the sun. The gravity of the sun creates a force that pulls the Earth toward the center. The Earth's momentum causes it to orbit rather than fall straight in. In a similar manner, an electron in the outer part of an atom is attracted to protons in the nucleus. The momentum of the electron causes it to move around the nucleus rather than falling straight in (Figure 28.3).

Strong nuclear force

Neutrons are the "glue" that holds the protons in the nucleus together. We already know that electric force is large. That means the positively charged protons in the nucleus of an atom repel each other with a great force. What holds the nucleus together? There is another force even stronger than the electric force. We call it the strong nuclear force. The strong nuclear force attracts neutrons and protons to each other. If there are enough neutrons, the attraction from the strong force overcomes repulsion from the electric force and the nucleus stays together. For every atom heavier than helium there is at least one neutron for every proton in the nucleus.

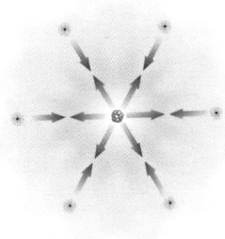

Figure 28.3: *The negative electrons are attracted to the positive protons in the center, or nucleus, of the atom.*

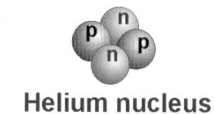

Helium nucleus

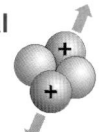

Electrical force

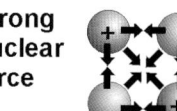

Strong nuclear force

Weak force

There is another nuclear force called the weak force. The weak force is weaker than both the electric force and the strong nuclear force. If you leave a solitary neutron outside the nucleus, the weak force eventually causes it to break up into a proton and an electron. The weak force does not play an important role in a stable atom, but comes into action in certain special cases when atoms break apart.

Gravity

The force of gravity inside the atom is much weaker even than the weak force. It takes a relatively large mass to create enough gravity to make a significant force. We know particles inside an atom do not have enough mass for gravity to be an important force on the scale of atoms. But there are many unanswered questions. Understanding how gravity works inside atoms is an unsolved mystery in physics.

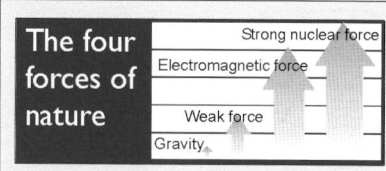

The four forces of nature

Strong nuclear force
Electromagnetic force
Weak force
Gravity

Every process in the universe that we *understand* can be explained in terms of the four fundamental forces (strong, electromagnetic, weak, and gravity). But there are many things that we do not yet understand. A physics book written in the year 2100 might well list other forces. Maybe you will discover one of them!

Elements and atoms

Elements The variety of matter we find in nature (here on Earth) is made from 92 different types of atoms called elements. Water is made from the elements hydrogen and oxygen. Rocks are mostly silicon and oxygen. The atoms of all the 92 elements are created from the same three basic particles: electrons, protons, and neutrons.

Atomic number All atoms of the same element have the same number of protons in the nucleus. For example, every atom of helium has two protons in its nucleus. Every atom of iron has 26 protons in its nucleus (Figure 28.4). The atomic number of each element is the number of protons in its nucleus. The periodic table arranges the elements in increasing atomic number. Atomic number one is hydrogen with one proton. Atomic number 92 is uranium with 92 protons.

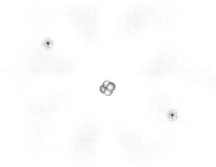

Helium atom

- · · 2 electrons
- ○ ○ 2 protons
- ○ ○ 2 neutrons

Periodic Table of the Elements

Stable and found in nature

Radioactive and found in nature

Radioactive and made only in the laboratory

| Li ← | Atomic symbol (Li = lithium) |
| 3 ← | Atomic number (3 = 3 protons / 3 electrons) |

H 1																	He 2
Li 3	Be 4											B 5	C 6	N 7	O 8	F 9	Ne 10
Na 11	Mg 12											Al 13	Si 14	P 15	S 16	Cl 17	Ar 18
K 19	Ca 20	Sc 21	Ti 22	V 23	Cr 24	Mn 25	Fe 26	Co 27	Ni 28	Cu 29	Zn 30	Ga 31	Ge 32	As 33	Se 34	Br 35	Kr 36
Rb 37	Sr 38	Y 39	Zr 40	Nb 41	Mo 42	Tc 43	Ru 44	Rh 45	Pd 46	Ag 47	Cd 48	In 49	Sn 50	Sb 51	Te 52	I 53	Xe 54
Cs 55	Ba 56		Hf 72	Ta 73	W 74	Re 75	Os 76	Ir 77	Pt 78	Au 79	Hg 80	Tl 81	Pb 82	Bi 83	Po 84	At 85	Rn 86
Fr 87	Ra 88		Rf 104	Db 105	Sg 106	Bh 107	Hs 108	Mt 109									

| La 57 | Ce 58 | Pr 59 | Nd 60 | Pm 61 | Sm 62 | Eu 63 | Gd 64 | Tb 65 | Dy 66 | Ho 67 | Er 68 | Tm 69 | Yb 70 | Lu 71 |
| Ac 89 | Th 90 | Pa 91 | U 92 | Np 93 | Pu 94 | Am 95 | Cm 96 | Bk 97 | Cf 98 | Es 99 | Fm 100 | Md 101 | No 102 | Lr 103 |

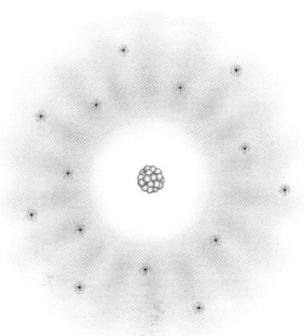

Iron atom

- · 26 electrons
- ○ 26 protons
- ○ 30 neutrons

Figure 28.4: *A helium atom has 2 electrons, 2 protons, and 2 neutrons. An iron atom has 26 electrons, 26 protons, and 30 neutrons.*

Determining the number of protons in the nucleus

How many protons are in the nucleus of an atom of vanadium (V)?

1) You are asked for the number of protons.

2) You are given that the element is vanadium.

3) The number of protons is the atomic number.

4) Vanadium is atomic number 23 so there are 23 protons in the nucleus of a vanadium atom.

Isotopes

Isotopes   There are different ways to form the nucleus of a lithium atom. Each form is called an isotope. All the isotopes of lithium have three protons but they have different numbers of neutrons. Different isotopes exist for atoms of each element. Some isotopes occur naturally. For example, lithium has two naturally occurring isotopes (Li^6 and Li^7). Other isotopes may be created in a laboratory for research.

Mass number   The mass number is the total number of particles (protons and neutrons) in the nucleus. Different isotopes of the same element have different mass numbers. For example, there are 2 natural isotopes of lithium. Lithium six (Li^6) has a mass number of 6 with 3 protons and 3 neutrons in the nucleus. Lithium seven (Li^7) has a mass number of 7 with 3 protons and 4 neutrons in the nucleus (Figure 28.5).

Stable and unstable   Not all isotopes are stable. If an isotope has too many (or too few) neutrons, the nucleus eventually breaks up and we say the atom is radioactive. In a *stable* isotope the nucleus stays together. In an *unstable* isotope the nucleus is radioactive and eventually breaks up. Radioactivity is discussed more in Chapter 30.

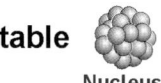 **Stable**   Nucleus   **Radioactive (unstable)**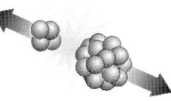

Naming isotopes   Mass numbers are written above the element symbol in the periodic table. They are also written to the upper right of the symbol as shown in Figure 28.5. When a physicist says "lithium seven" (Li^7), they are talking about atoms of lithium with seven particles in the nucleus (3 protons and 4 neutrons).

Chemical properties   Different isotopes of the same element have the same chemical properties. The chemical properties are the same because electrons determine how atoms combine with other atoms (see Chapter 29). Changing the number of neutrons affects only the nucleus, and not the electrons. The chemical identity makes some radioactive isotopes very useful for research and medicine. For example, suppose some of the phosphorus in a DNA molecule were replaced with a radioactive isotope of phosphorus. By looking for the radioactive phosphorus, it is possible to follow exactly how specific DNA molecules are used in a living body.

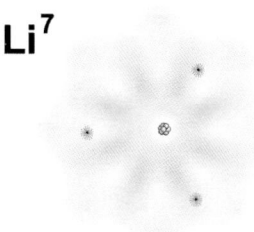

Li^7

Lithium^7 atom

✳ ✳ ✳	3 electrons
◉ ◉ ◉	3 protons
◎ ◎ ◎ ◎	4 neutrons

Figure 28.5: *The mass number is equal to the total number of protons plus neutrons in the nucleus. A lithium 7 atom has three protons and four neutrons in its nucleus.*

Radioactive isotopes

Most of the matter you see is not radioactive. Almost all the naturally produced radioactive isotopes broke apart long ago in the Earth's history. Uranium is one of the rare few radioactive isotopes still found in nature. We can still find U^{238} because it takes a very long time to break down.

People often create radioactive isotopes in the laboratory for use in medicine. For example iodine^{131} (I^{131}) is used to track how well blood is flowing in the body.

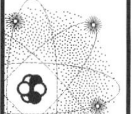

Atomic mass

Atomic mass Elements in nature usually have a mixture of isotopes. For example, the periodic table lists an atomic mass of 6.94 for lithium. That does NOT mean there are 3 protons and 3.94 neutrons in a lithium atom! On average, 94 percent of lithium atoms are Li[7] and 6 percent are Li[6] (Figure 28.6). The *average* atomic mass of lithium is 6.94 because of the mixture of isotopes. The table below gives the mass numbers and average atomic masses for the stable isotopes of elements 1 - 26.

Units of atomic mass The atomic mass of an atom is usually given in atomic mass units (amu). One amu is 1.66×10^{-27} kg, and is defined as one-twelfth (1/12) the mass of a carbon-12 atom. To determine the mass of a single atom, you multiply the atomic mass in amu by 1.66×10^{-27} kg/amu. For example, an "average" lithium atom has a mass of 1.15×10^{-26} kg ($6.94 \times 1.66 \times 10^{-27}$ kg/amu). This is a very small mass!

1.01 H 1		Average atomic mass (amu)
6.94 Li 3	9.01 Be 4	
22.99 Na 11	24.31 Mg 12	
39.10 K 19	40.08 Ca 20	44.96 Sc 21
85.47 Rb 37	87.62 Sr 38	88.91 Y 39

94% of lithium atoms are Li[7]
6% of lithium atoms are Li[6]

Figure 28.6: *The common periodic table lists the average atomic mass for each element. For most elements the average includes several different isotopes.*

⚛	Atomic Number	Element Symbol	Element Name	Mass Numbers of Stable Isotopes	Average Atomic Mass (amu)
Atomic Mass for Stable Isotopes of Elements 1 - 26	1	H	Hydrogen	1, 2	1.008
	2	He	Helium	3, 4	4.003
	3	Li	Lithium	6, 7	6.941
	4	Be	Beryllium	9	9.012
	5	B	Boron	10, 11	10.81
	6	C	Carbon	12, 13	12.01
	7	N	Nitrogen	14, 15	14.07
	8	O	Oxygen	16, 17, 18	16.00
	9	F	Fluorine	19	19.00
	10	Ne	Neon	20, 21, 22	20.18
	11	Na	Sodium	23	22.99
	12	Mg	Magnesium	24, 25, 26	24.31
	13	Al	Aluminum	27	26.98
	14	Si	Silicon	28, 29, 30	28.09
	15	P	Phosphorus	31	30.97
	16	S	Sulfur	32, 33, 34, 36	32.06
	17	Cl	Chlorine	35, 37	35.45
	18	Ar	Argon	36, 38, 40	39.95
	19	K	Potassium	39, 41	39.10
	20	Ca	Calcium	40, 42, 43, 44, 46, 48	40.08
	21	Sc	Scandium	45	44.96
	22	Ti	Titanium	46, 47, 48, 49, 50	47.88
	23	V	Vanadium	51	50.94
	24	Cr	Chromium	50, 52, 53, 54	52.00
	25	Mn	Manganese	55	54.94
	26	Fe	Iron	54, 56, 57, 58	55.85

A graph of protons versus neutrons

Making a stable nucleus
A nucleus is unstable if there are too few or too many neutrons. If there are too few neutrons, the electrical repulsion between protons tears the nucleus apart. If there are too many neutrons, the nucleus tends to eject one or more of them.

The ratio of protons to neutrons
The chart of stable isotopes shows a graph of protons versus neutrons. Each dark blue square represents a stable nucleus. For carbon (six protons) you can see two blue squares representing six and seven neutrons. The chart tells you that carbon has two stable isotopes, C^{12} and C^{13}. For light elements, the number of neutrons and protons is about equal. As the elements get heavier, more neutrons than protons are required to keep the nucleus stable. Only two stable isotopes have fewer neutrons than protons — can you find them?

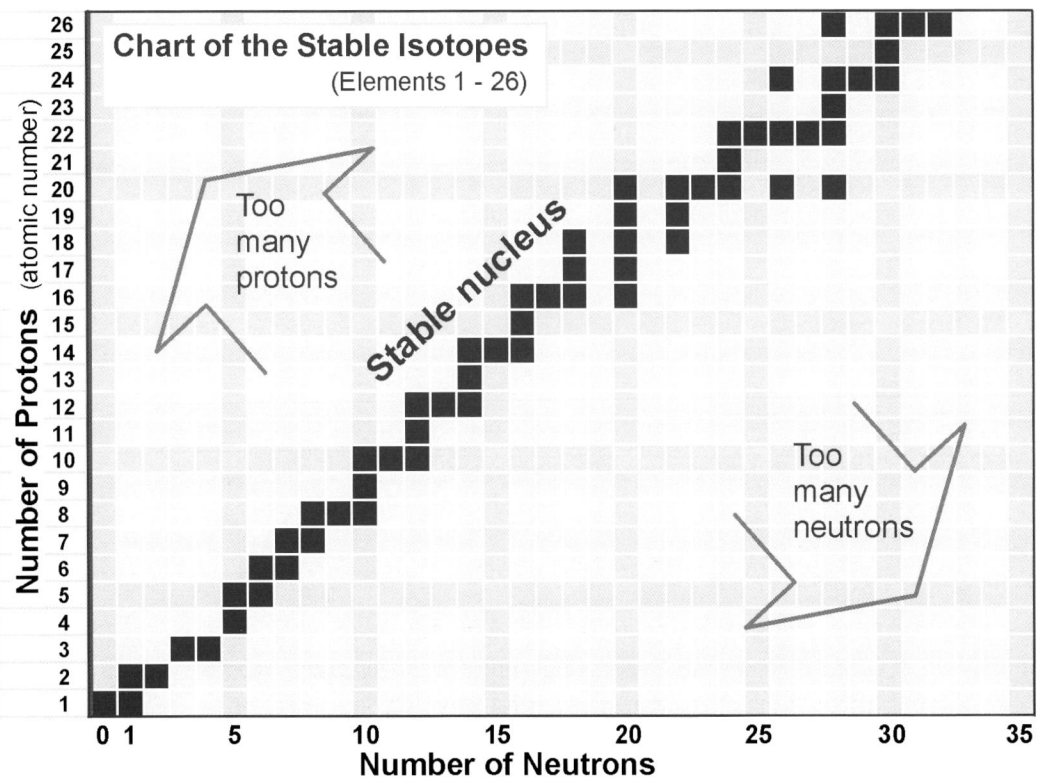

Fe	Iron
Mn	Manganese
Cr	Chromium
V	Vanadium
Ti	Titanium
Sc	Scandium
Ca	Calcium
K	Potassium
Ar	Argon
Cl	Chlorine
S	Sulfur
P	Phosphorus
Si	Silicon
Al	Aluminum
Mg	Magnesium
Na	Sodium
Ne	Neon
F	Fluorine
O	Oxygen
N	Nitrogen
C	Carbon
B	Boron
Be	Beryllium
Li	Lithium
He	Helium
H	Hydrogen

Chart of the Stable Isotopes
(Elements 1 - 26)

Too many protons

Stable nucleus

Too many neutrons

Number of Protons (atomic number)

Number of Neutrons

Determine the number of neutrons in a nucleus

How many neutrons are in the nucleus of an atom of titanium 49 (Ti^{49})?

1) You are asked for the number of neutrons.

2) You are given that the isotope is titanium 49.

3) The number of neutrons is the mass number minus the atomic number.

4) Titanium is atomic number 22. If 22 of the 49 particles in the Ti^{49} nucleus are protons, then there must be 27 neutrons (49 - 22).

Reactions inside and between atoms

Molecules   Most atoms in nature are found combined with other atoms into molecules. A molecule is a group of atoms that are chemically bonded together. For example, H_2O (water) is a molecule formed by two hydrogen atoms and one oxygen atom.

Chemical reaction

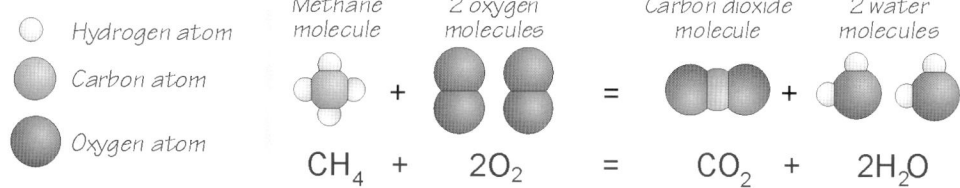

$$CH_4 + 2O_2 = CO_2 + 2H_2O$$

Chemical reactions   A chemical reaction rearranges the same atoms into different molecules. For example, the chemical reaction between methane (natural gas) and oxygen rearranges one carbon atom, four hydrogen atoms, and four oxygen atoms. The same nine atoms that make up the methane and oxygen molecules are rearranged to become carbon dioxide and water molecules. Chemical reactions rearrange atoms into new molecules but do not change atoms into other kinds of atoms.

Nuclear reaction

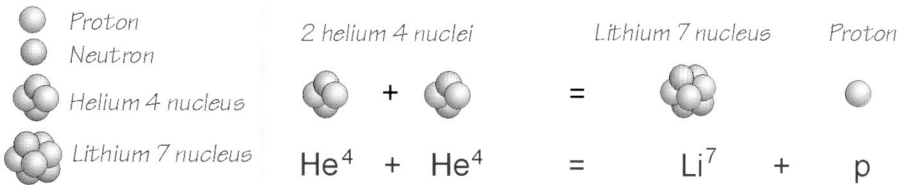

$$He^4 + He^4 = Li^7 + p$$

Nuclear reactions   A nuclear reaction is any process that changes the nucleus of an atom. Because the nucleus is affected, a nuclear reaction can change atoms of one element into atoms of a different element. For example, two helium nuclei can be combined to create one lithium nucleus and an extra proton. There is even a nuclear reaction that turns lead into gold! The ability to change one element into another is one important way nuclear reactions are different from chemical reactions.

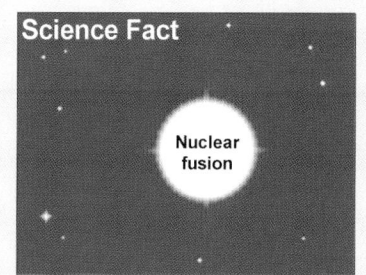

Science Fact

Nuclear fusion

Fusion is a type of nuclear reaction that combines small atoms to make larger atoms. The energy produced in stars like the sun comes from fusion reactions. The interior of the sun is about 15 million degrees Celsius. At this high temperature, nuclei are moving fast enough they can almost touch despite the electric force pushing them apart. If two nuclei get close enough for the strong force to reach, a fusion reaction can occur.

On Earth, we would need to generate about 100 million degrees Celsius to create fusion of hydrogen for producing energy. The higher temperature is necessary because reactors on Earth do not have the sun's immense gravity helping to force atoms together. Many countries are working together on fusion research. Someday we may get our energy from clean power plants using nuclear fusion.

28.2 Electrons and Quantum States

Nearly every property of matter we experience is determined by the behavior of electrons in atoms. The color of paints comes from how electrons absorb light. Oxygen is vital to life because of how it makes chemical bonds with other elements. Chemical bonds are formed between electrons of different atoms. The size of atoms is determined by how far electrons range from the nucleus. The exception is mass; mass derives from the nucleus. Just about everything else is determined by electrons.

The birth of quantum physics

The discovery of quantum physics
The electrons in an atom obey a very strange set of rules. The Danish physicist Niels Bohr (1885-1962) was the first person to put the clues together correctly and in 1913 proposed a theory that described the electrons in an atom. A brilliant scientist, Bohr is often called the father of quantum physics. Quantum physics is the branch of science that deals with extremely small systems such as an atom.

The spectrum
An unusual feature of light was the clue that lead to the discovery of quantum physics. When a substance is made into a gas and electricity is passed through the gas, light is given off, like in a neon sign. When people examined the light carefully, they observed that the light did not include all colors. Instead they saw a few very specific colors, and the colors were different for different substances (Figure 28.7). The characteristic pattern of colors is called a spectrum. The colors of clothes, paint, and everything else around you come from this unusual property of substances to emit or *absorb* light of only certain colors (Figure 28.8). Since the energy of light depends on the color, the lines in a spectrum meant that substances could only emit light of certain energies.

Spectrometers and spectral lines
Each individual color is called a spectral line because each color appears as a line in a spectrometer. A spectrometer is a device that spreads light into its different wavelengths, or colors. The diagram below shows a spectrometer made with a prism. The spectral lines appear on the screen on the right.

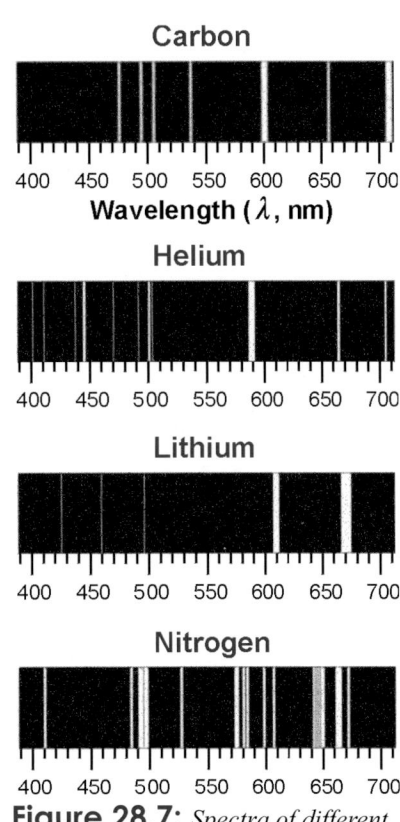

Figure 28.7: *Spectra of different elements.*

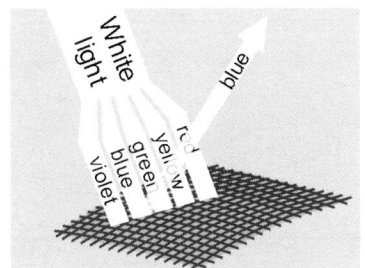

Figure 28.8: *Cloth looks blue because molecules in the dye absorb all colors of light except blue.*

Simple prism spectrometer

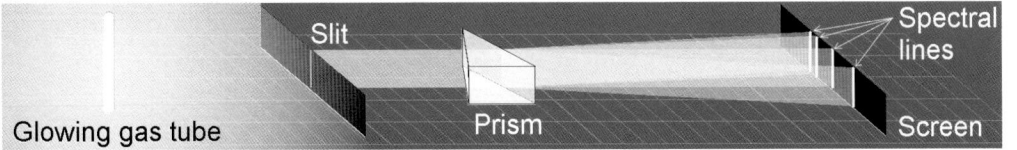

574

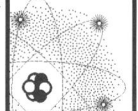

The hydrogen spectrum

Johann Balmer's discovery

The spectrum shown below is from hydrogen. When hydrogen gas is heated, it gives off this unique pattern of colors. The first serious clue to an explanation of the spectrum was discovered in 1885 by Johann Balmer, a Swiss high school teacher. He showed that the wavelengths of the light given off by hydrogen atoms could be predicted by a mathematical formula (Balmer's formula).

The visible spectrum of hydrogen

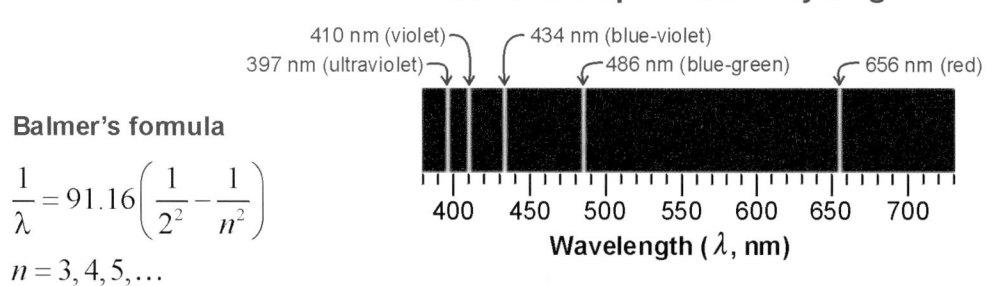

410 nm (violet) — 434 nm (blue-violet)
397 nm (ultraviolet) — 486 nm (blue-green) — 656 nm (red)

Wavelength (λ, nm)

Balmer's formula

$$\frac{1}{\lambda} = 91.16\left(\frac{1}{2^2} - \frac{1}{n^2}\right)$$

$$n = 3, 4, 5, \ldots$$

n	λ (nm)	Color
3	656	Red
4	486	Blue-green
5	434	Blue-violet
6	410	Violet
7	397	Ultraviolet

Using the Balmer formula

In Balmer's formula, n is an integer greater than two. For example, if we chose $n = 4$, then the formula predicted a wavelength of 486 nm. This exactly matches the blue-green line in the hydrogen spectrum. Choosing $n = 3, 4, 5, 6, 7$ correctly gives the wavelengths of other spectral lines of hydrogen. Balmer had found the pattern but still could not explain what caused it.

What the formula implied

Something inside a hydrogen atom corresponds to the numbers ($n = 3, 4, 5 \ldots$) from the Balmer's formula. The mechanism in hydrogen that creates light acts like the numbers are click stops on a switch. The switch can be set to any integer, such as 2 or 3, but not to any number in between, such as 2.5. Of course, there is not a switch inside each atom, but you may find the true explanation even stranger.

The Discovery of helium

Atoms can absorb light at the same wavelengths that they emit light. When a bright light containing all wavelengths is passed through a gas, dark spectral lines indicate which wavelengths of light are absorbed. The spectra of the sun shows many dark spectral lines.

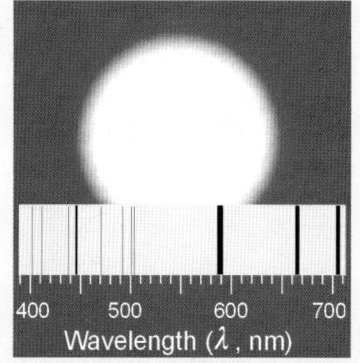

Wavelength (λ, nm)

The element helium is a light gas that is very rare on Earth. In fact, helium was not discovered on this planet. It was discovered in the sun, hence the name. In Greek, *helios* means "sun." Astronomers saw a series of spectral lines in the sun that did not match any known element on Earth. Helium was first identified from its spectrum of light from the sun. Researchers were then able to find it on Earth because they knew what to look for.

Quantum states

The quantum meaning of the word "state"

Neils Bohr proposed that electrons in the atom were limited to certain quantum states. In quantum physics the word "state" means the *complete* description of a system. If you know the quantum state of an electron, you know *everything* you can know about that electron: its energy, how it is moving, where it is, and its spin. If you could know the *state* of a used car, in the quantum sense, you would know much more than its every scratch or speck of dirt. You would know the location, motion, and energy of every single atom in the car — enough information to *exactly* duplicate the car, at the same temperature, with every detail the same. This is too much to know, which is why "transporter beams" exist only in science fiction.

Quantum states in the atom

The quantum states in an atom have certain allowed values of energy, momentum, position, and spin. A graph showing the energy of an electron within an atom looks like a hilly surface with peaks and valleys. Each quantum state represents a valley on the energy graph big enough to hold a single electron. An electron can be found in one valley or another, but never in between.

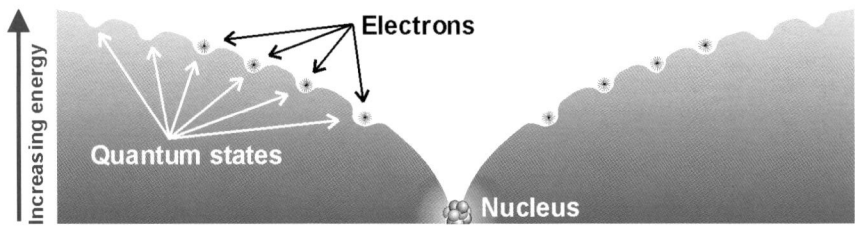

Quantum numbers

The number (n) in the Balmer formula is one of four quantum numbers that describe which quantum state an electron is in. To understand quantum numbers, think of an atom like a parking garage for electrons. Each parking space in the garage is a quantum state that can hold one electron. Quantum numbers are the code describing each space where an electron can be parked. To locate an electron you need to know the numbers of its code. The code has four numbers (n, l, m, s) and each number can only have values corresponding to actual parking spaces (quantum states). Every quantum state in the atom is identified by a unique combination of the four quantum numbers (see sidebar).

---

n, l, m, s

The four quantum numbers of an electron

Every electron in an atom can be completely described by the values of its four quantum numbers: n, l, m, and s.

The first quantum number (n) can be any integer bigger than zero.

The second quantum number (l) must be a positive integer from zero to n-1. For example, if $n = 1$, the only possibility is $l = 0$. If $n = 2$, then l can be 0 or 1.

The third quantum number (m) is an integer that can go from -l to +l. For example, if $l = 3$, m can have any of seven values between -3 and +3 (m = -3, -2, -1, 0, 1, 2, 3).

The fourth quantum number (s) can only be either +1/2 or -1/2.

Each possible combination of values for the four quantum numbers represents one quantum state. For example, one of the two quantum states in the first energy level has quantum numbers: $n = 0$, $l = 0$, $m = 0$, and $s = +1/2$. The other state in the first level has $n = 0$, $l = 0$, $m = 0$, $s = -1/2$.

From the four quantum numbers it is possible to calculate everything about the electron, including its energy, angular momentum, average position, and spin.

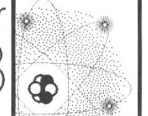

Energy levels and spectra

Energy and quantum states The energy of an electron depends on which quantum state it is in. Quantum states that keep the electron far from the nucleus have more energy than states that allow the electron to fall closer in. If an electron moves to a quantum state closer to the nucleus, the difference in energy is released (often converted to light).

Energy levels The quantum states in an atom are grouped into energy levels. All the quantum states in each level have approximately the same energy. A good analogy is a multilevel parking garage. Each floor of the garage has a limited number of parking spaces for cars. Each parking space can hold one car. Each energy level is like one floor of the garage. Each quantum state in an energy level is like a parking space for one electron. The diagram in Figure 28.9 shows how the quantum states are arranged in the first five energy levels. The first level has two states, and can therefore hold two electrons. The second and third levels have eight quantum states. The fourth and fifth levels have 18 states.

Energy levels explain spectral lines Bohr explained that spectral lines are produced by electrons moving between different energy levels. An electron in a hydrogen atom dropping from the third level to the second level gives off an amount of energy exactly equal to the red line in the hydrogen spectrum. An electron falling from the fourth level to the second level gives off more energy, creating the blue-green line in the spectrum. All of the spectral lines described by the Balmer formula correspond to electrons falling from higher levels to the second energy level. Bohr's model developed into the quantum theory of the atom.

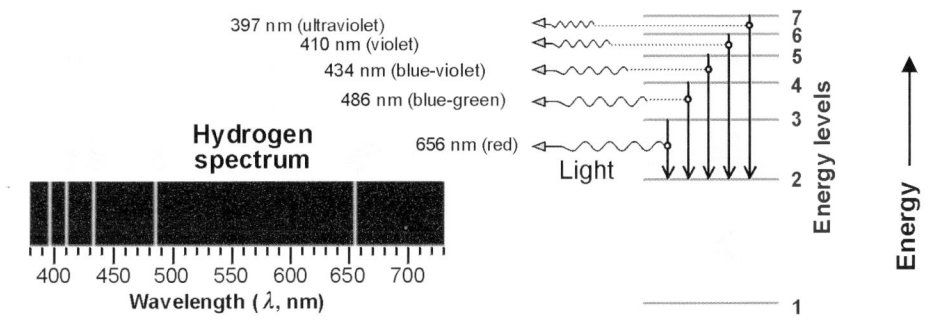

The first five energy levels

5th

n	l	m	s	electrons
5	0	0	+1/2, -1/2	
5	1	-1	+1/2, -1/2	
5	1	0	+1/2, -1/2	
5	1	1	+1/2, -1/2	
4	2	-2	+1/2, -1/2	
4	2	-1	+1/2, -1/2	
4	2	0	+1/2, -1/2	
4	2	1	+1/2, -1/2	
4	2	2	+1/2, -1/2	

total = 18

4th

n	l	m	s
4	0	0	+1/2, -1/2
4	1	-1	+1/2, -1/2
4	1	0	+1/2, -1/2
4	1	1	+1/2, -1/2
3	2	-2	+1/2, -1/2
3	2	-1	+1/2, -1/2
3	2	0	+1/2, -1/2
3	2	1	+1/2, -1/2
3	2	2	+1/2, -1/2

total = 18

3rd

n	l	m	s
3	0	0	+1/2, -1/2
3	1	-1	+1/2, -1/2
3	1	0	+1/2, -1/2
3	1	1	+1/2, -1/2

total = 8

2nd

n	l	m	s
2	0	0	+1/2, -1/2
2	1	-1	+1/2, -1/2
2	1	0	+1/2, -1/2
2	1	1	+1/2, -1/2

total = 8

1st

n	l	m	s
1	0	0	+1/2, -1/2

total = 2

Figure 28.9: *The quantum numbers for electrons in the first five energy levels.*

The Pauli exclusion principle & the periodic table

A quantum state can hold one electron

According to the quantum theory, two electrons in an atom can never be in the same quantum state at the same time. This rule is known as the Pauli exclusion principle after Wolfgang Pauli, the physicist who discovered it. The exclusion principle prevents all the electrons in an atom from falling immediately to the lowest energy level. Once all the quantum states in the first level are occupied by electrons, the next electron has to go into a higher energy level.

The periodic table

The rows of the periodic table correspond to the number of quantum states in each energy level. The first energy level has two quantum states. Hydrogen (H) has one electron and helium (He) has two electrons. These two elements are the only ones in the top row of the periodic table because there are only two quantum states in the first energy level. The next element, lithium (Li), has three electrons. Lithium begins the second row because the third electron goes into the second energy level. The second energy level has eight quantum states and there are eight elements in the second row of the periodic table, ending with neon. Neon (Ne) has 10 electrons, which exactly fill all the quantum states in the first and second levels. Potassium (K) has 11 electrons, and starts the third row because the eleventh electron goes into the third energy level.

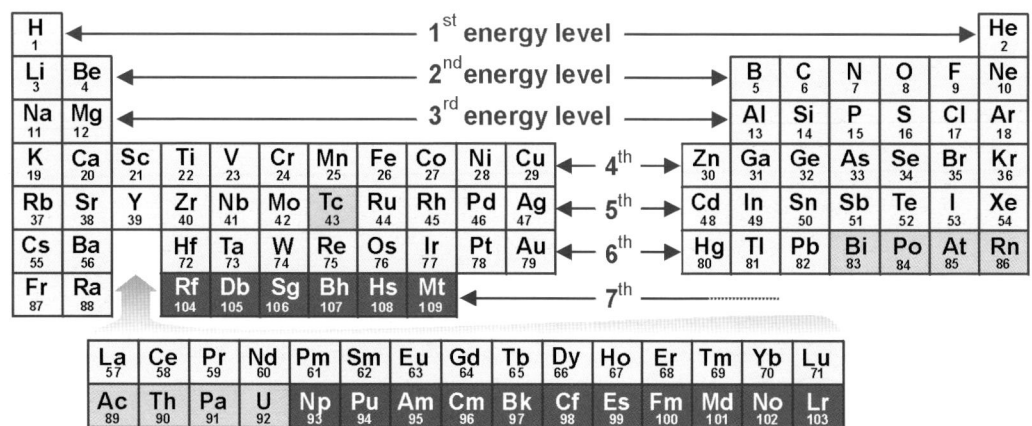

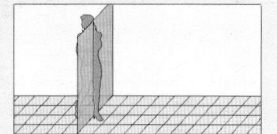

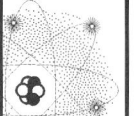

The "shape" of quantum states

Orbitals In chemistry, the quantum states for electrons in an atom are called orbitals. The name comes from an older idea that electrons moved in orbits around the nucleus, like planets around the sun. Today, we know quantum states are *not* similar to orbits (Figure 28.10), but the name *orbital* is still commonly used.

Molecules have a shape The shape of a molecule is important to what the molecule does. For example, the two hydrogen atoms in a water molecule make an angle of 104 degrees. The 104-degree angle is created by the shape of the quantum states of the oxygen atom in the middle of the molecule. Many substances dissolve in water because the 104-degree angle puts both hydrogen atoms on one side. Many medicines work because the shape of a molecule fits precisely with another molecule found in the body, like pieces in a puzzle.

The shape of orbitals Each "orbital" shape shows the most likely locations for a pair of electrons with matching quantum numbers n, l, and m. The $l = 0$ shapes are spherical. The $l = 1$ shapes fall along the three coordinate axes x, y, and z. The $l = 2$ shapes are more complex (Figure 28.10). The orbital shapes overlap in an atom with many electrons. The shape of the electron cloud of an atom comes from the shapes of all the orbitals that contain electrons.

Outer orbitals form the shape of molecules The structure of molecules comes from the shapes of the orbitals of each atom making up the molecule. When atoms bond, they tend to align along the orbitals that hold the outermost electrons. For example, carbon has six electrons. The first two go in the inner (n = 1) quantum states. The last four electrons occupy quantum states with n = 2, and are available for bonding with other atoms. Carbon combines with four hydrogen atoms to make *methane*. The four hydrogen atoms in a methane molecule line up with the corners of a tetrahedron. The shape comes from the orbitals occupied by the four electrons in the n = 2 states.

Orbital shapes for n = 1, 2, 3

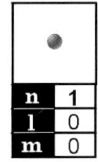
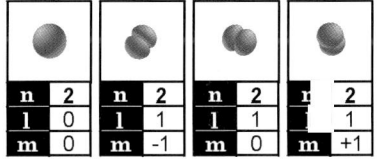
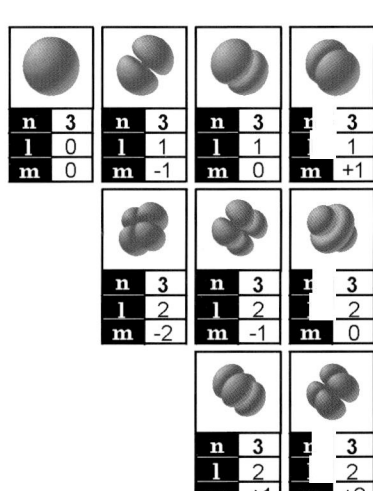

Figure 28.10: *The shapes and relative sizes of the orbitals for quantum numbers n = 1, 2, and 3. Each shape is two quantum states corresponding to s = +1/2 and -1/2.*

28.3 The Quantum Theory

In the microscopic world of atoms and particles, familiar rules such as Newton's laws of motion do not tell the correct story. The quantum theory describes what happens to matter and energy when things get very small, on the scale of single atoms. The structure of the atom and the behavior of electrons are described by the quantum theory. This section will describe some of the basic ideas. As you read, keep in mind that quantum theory is far from complete. Quantum physics is a relatively young field of science and many discoveries are yet to be made.

Classical physics	Quantum physics
Matter is particles	Matter is both a particle & a wave
Newton's laws of motion	Quantum mechanics
Coulomb's law and wave theory of light	Photon theory of light

Figure 28.11: *Classical versus quantum physics.*

The discovery of "new" physics

Discovering new knowledge   Nature always behaves the "right" way. The clash between an unexpected observation and our imperfect knowledge leads us to say, "That was not supposed to happen!" In science, "pushing the limits" means trying to understand the *unexpected* result. Starting with Newton's laws (1685), "classical physics" was very successful at explaining things (Figure 28.11). The quantum theory started when classical physics disagreed with results of new experiments.

Two outstanding puzzles   The quantum theory began between 1899 and 1905 with Max Planck and Albert Einstein. Planck was trying to understand why light given off by hot materials follows the blackbody spectrum (see Chapter 26). Einstein was thinking about the photoelectric effect. Neither phenomenon could be explained by classical physics.

The photoelectric effect   When light falls on the surface of a metal, sometimes electrons are emitted from the surface. This is called the photoelectric effect. If the light is made brighter, the metal absorbs more energy. Classical physics predicts that electrons coming off the metal should have more kinetic energy when the light is made brighter. But that is NOT what happens. Classical physics gives the wrong answer.

Results of experiments   Experiments on the photoelectric effect showed that the *frequency* of the light is the most important variable. With low frequency (long wavelength) red light, no electrons come off at all, even if the light is very bright. As the frequency increases (more blue), electrons start to be emitted. The kinetic energy of the emitted electrons also depends on the frequency of the light. The higher the frequency, the more energy the emitted electrons have (Figure 28.12).

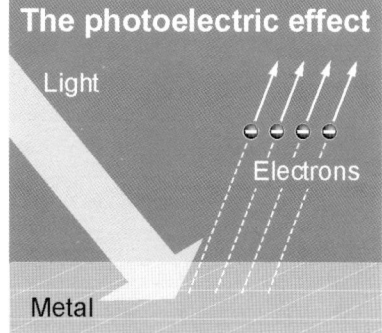

Observations

Light below a threshold frequency produces *no* electrons, *no matter how intense*.

The *energy* of emitted electrons is proportional to the *frequency* of light, not the intensity.

The *number* of emitted electrons is proportional to the *intensity* of the light.

Figure 28.12: *The photoelectric effect.*

The quantum theory of light

The photon   In 1899 Max Planck proposed that light existed in small bundles of energy called photons. The smallest amount of light you could have is a single photon. Bright light consists of billions of photons per second while dim light has very few photons per second. Planck's idea was very different from the wave theory of light. You can make a wave as small as you want by reducing the amplitude. You could not split a photon. You could make light of one photon, 10 photons, or 10 trillion photons, but you could never make half a photon.

Classical concept:
Light is a continuous wave carrying energy

The energy of a photon   According to Planck, the energy of a single photon is related to its frequency by the formula $E = hf$, where h is Planck's constant (Figure 28.13). Higher frequency means higher photon energy. Planck's constant is very small, $h = 6.626 \times 10^{-34}$ J-sec. The energy of a single photon is also small. A typical flashlight produces 10^{20} photons per second! Like atoms, photons are such small quantities of energy that light appears as a continuous flow of energy under normal circumstances.

Quantum concept:
Light is quantum bundles of energy called photons that have wave-like properties

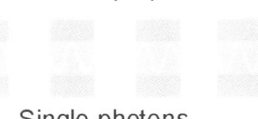

Single photons

Einstein explains the photoelectric effect   The truth of the quantum theory was confirmed in 1905 when Albert Einstein published his explanation of the photoelectric effect. Einstein proposed that an atom can absorb only one photon at a time. An electron needs a minimum amount of energy to break free from an atom. If the energy of the photon is too low there is not enough energy to free an electron and no photoelectric effect is observed. Making brighter light does not help. Brighter light has more photons, but none with enough energy to free an electron.

If the frequency of light gets higher, at a particular frequency one photon has just enough energy to free an electron. Even if the light is made very dim, you get exactly one electron for each photon of light.

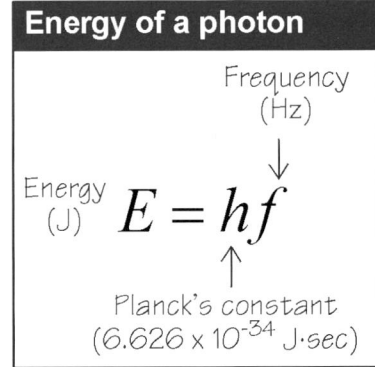

Wavelength and kinetic energy   If light of even higher frequency is used, there is more than enough energy in each photon to free an electron. Part of the photon energy goes to freeing the electron and the rest becomes kinetic energy of the electron. Making the frequency still higher (more blue) increases the amount of "leftover" energy available to become kinetic energy. Einstein's explanation matched perfectly with the data collected in experiments. His explanation of the photoelectric effect was strong evidence that the quantum theory of light was correct.

Figure 28.13: *You can think of a photon as a bundle of energy with a frequency. The photon energy is given by Planck's formula.*

Quantum theory

What "quantum" means

Planck's theory became a quantum description of light. To a physicist, if something is *quantized,* it can only exist in whole units, not fractions of units. For example, the number of students assigned to a class is quantized. There can be 25 students, or 26 or 32 or any other whole number, but there cannot be 25.3 students. Light is quantized and one photon is the smallest unit, or *quantum* of light. A quantum of something is the smallest amount that can exist.

Waves and particles

In the quantum theory, all matter and energy have both wavelike and particle-like properties. Light acts like a wave from far away. But up close, light acts "particle-like" because the wave is made of individual photons. An electron acts like a particle when it is both free to move and far from other electrons. However, if an electron is confined in a small space (an atom), it behaves like a wave.

The wavelength of a particle

The wavelength of a particle (λ) depends on its mass (m) and speed (v), according to the DeBroglie formula (Figure 28.14). The wavelengths of particles tend to be extremely small. An electron moving at a million meters per second has a wavelength of only 7×10^{-10} meters. The short wavelength is why an electron looks like a particle most of the time. The wave properties only become apparent when the electron is confined to a space near the size of its wavelength, such as an atom.

Properties of wave/particles

You might think quantities like position and velocity can be applied to an electron as if it were a tiny baseball. For example, the electron could be at exactly one meter moving at exactly 100 m/sec. Quantum theory gives a completely different picture. When you try to look at extremely small details, quantum theory tells us that the electron is really spread out into a wave. You cannot say where on the wave the electron "is." The electron has no exact value of position (Figure 28.14).

We do not usually see particles act like waves

The wavelike properties of matter are not normally seen unless you look at very fine details. If the smallest important detail of a system you are trying to study is much larger than the quantum wavelength ($\lambda=h/mv$), then you can use Newton's laws or the wave theory of light and you will get the right answer. If important details are within a factor of 10 (or smaller) compared with the quantum wavelength, then you must use quantum theory to get an accurate answer.

Classical concept:
Electron is a particle described by mass (m) and speed (v)

Quantum concept:
Electron 'particle' is spread out into a wave

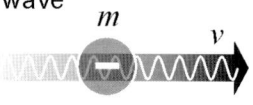

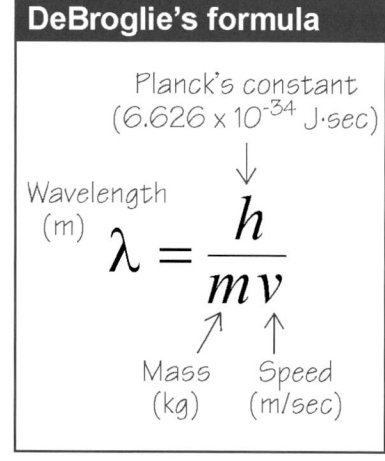

Figure 28.14: *The DeBroglie formula gives the wavelength of a moving particle. The wavelength of an electron is close to the size of an atom.*

582

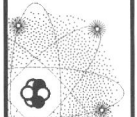

The uncertainty principle

The uncertainty principle

Quantum theory puts limits on how precisely we can know the value of quantities such as position, momentum, energy, and time. In ordinary (classical) physics you could say an electron is exactly at a certain place, at a certain time, with a certain speed and energy. In the quantum world this is not true. The uncertainty principle places a limit on how precisely these four parameters can be measured. Planck's constant (h) shows up again, as it often does in quantum theory.

Understanding the uncertainty principle

The uncertainty principle arises because the quantum world is so small. When you see a car, your eye collects trillions of photons that bounce off the car. Photons are so small compared with a car that the car is not affected by your looking at it. To "see" an electron you also have to bounce a photon off it, or interact with the electron in some way. Because the electron is so small, even a single photon moves it and changes its motion. That means the moment you use a photon to locate an electron, you push it so you no longer know precisely how fast it is going. In fact, any process of observing in the quantum world changes the very system you are trying to observe. The uncertainty principle works on pairs of variables because measuring one always disturbs the other in an unpredictable way (Figure 28.15).

The meaning of the uncertainty principle

The uncertainty principle has some very strange implications. In the quantum world, anything that *can* happen, *does* happen. Put more strongly, unless something is specifically *forbidden* from happening, it *must* happen. For example, suppose you could create a particle out of nothing, then make it disappear again. Suppose you could do this so fast that it was within the energy and time limit of the uncertainty principle. You could break the law of conservation of energy if you did it quickly enough and in a very small space. *We believe this actually happens.* Physicists believe the so-called "vacuum" is not truly empty when we consider details so small the uncertainty principle prevents us from seeing them. There is considerable experimental evidence that supports the belief that particles of matter and antimatter are continually popping into existence and disappearing again, out of pure nothing. This implies that empty space (vacuum) may have energy of its own, even when there is absolutely no ordinary matter or energy present.

Uncertainty principle

The uncertainty in position (Δx) multiplied by the uncertainty in momentum (Δp) can never be less than $h/_{2\pi}$

$$\Delta x \Delta p \geq \frac{h}{2\pi}$$

The uncertainty in energy (ΔE) multiplied by the uncertainty in time (Δt) can never be less than $h/_{2\pi}$

$$\Delta E \Delta t \geq \frac{h}{2\pi}$$

Figure 28.15: *The two pairs of variables related by the uncertainty principle.*

Quantum Computers

The uncertainty principle does not normally affect us because we can't see details as small as Planck's constant. However, the uncertainty principle does put a limit on how small we can make computer circuits, magnetic disk drives, and other devices that rely on extremely small details.

Probability and the quantum theory

Quantum theory and probability

Calculations in quantum physics do not result in knowing what *will* happen, but instead give the probability of what is likely to happen. This is a very strange concept. For example, take the motion of a ball tossed in the air. According to Newton's laws, you can calculate exactly where the ball will be at every moment of its motion. If the ball were an electron, this calculation would not be possible. You could calculate that there is a 98 percent *chance* the electron is at a particular place and time. But there is a 2 percent chance it is somewhere else! The result of any calculation in quantum physics is the *probability* of something occurring.

The meaning of probability

To understand probability, consider tossing a penny. There are two ways for the penny to land: heads up or tails up. The term "probability" describes the chance for getting each possible outcome of a system. A physicist would say there is equal probability that the penny lands heads or tails. With a single penny, there is a 50 percent probability of getting heads, and a 50 percent probability of getting tails. Suppose you flip 100 pennies and record the number of 'heads'. You repeat the same experiment 100 times to see how consistent your results are. The graph of your results looks like figure 28.16. The graph tells you that there is a 5.5% chance that you will get exactly 50 heads out of 100 coin tosses. If you repeated the experiment 1,000 times you would expect 55 experiments to come up with exactly 50 heads and 50 tails. While you can never accurately predict the outcome of one toss of the penny, you *can* make accurate predictions about a collection of many tosses.

The wave function

Quantum theory uses probability to predict the behavior of large numbers of particles. In quantum physics, each quantum of matter or energy is described by its **wave function**. The wave function mathematically describes how the probability for finding a quantum of matter or energy is spread out in space (Figure 28.17). For example, quantum physics allows you to calculate the probability of one electron being in a certain place. If you observe a trillion identical electrons, you can say with great precision how many will be found at that place. But quantum theory still cannot tell you where *any* single electron is. Because of its basis in probability, quantum theory can only make accurate predictions of the behavior of large systems with many particles.

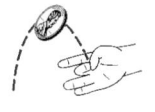

Heads   Tails

Outcome of 100 coin tosses

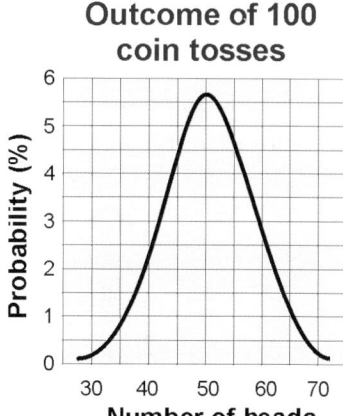

Figure 28.16: *The probability for the outcome of 100 tosses of a penny.*

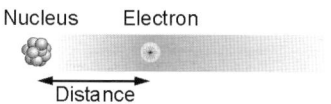

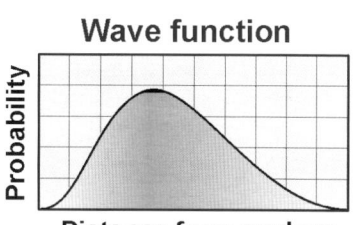

Figure 28.17: *The wave function describes how the probability of a quantum of matter or energy is spread out in space.*

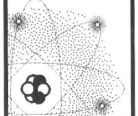

Application: The Laser

The word *laser* is an acronym for Light Amplification by Stimulated Emission of Radiation. A laser is a device that depends on both quantum mechanics and optics. The light from lasers has special properties that make possible such technologies as compact disks, laser surgery, and fiber-optic communications. Since the development of the first laser in 1960, laser-based products and services have grown to a multibillion dollar industry.

One photon

Ordinary light (not coherent)
Many photons with random phase

Coherent light
All photons are organized in phase

Coherence of laser light   The special characteristics of laser light are that it is coherent and monochromatic. The word *coherent* means that all the photons of light are lined up in such a way that they have the same phase. To understand coherence, consider light as a wave that is broken up into many small pieces (Figure 28.18). Each piece is a single photon. In ordinary light, the photons are scrambled so that each is independent of the others. Each photon carries the wave pattern but many photons do not add up to a single wave. In coherent light, the photons are aligned in phase so that they create a single, continuous wave pattern.

Figure 28.18: *The difference between coherent light and ordinary light (which is not coherent).*

Lasers are monochromatic   Normal light (white light) contains a mixture of many colors. Monochromatic light contains only one single frequency. Because all the photons have the same frequency, they also all have the same wavelength. For example, a common red laser has a wavelength of 650 nanometers.

The three components of a laser   Although there are many different types of lasers, they all have three main parts: a pump, laser material, and a laser cavity. The pump is the source of energy that starts the laser process. The energy of the pump can come from many different sources. The pump in a compact disk player's laser uses a continuous low-voltage electric current. The helium neon lasers used in grocery store scanners use high-voltage electric current. Some very high-power lasers use a chemical process to pump energy into the laser.

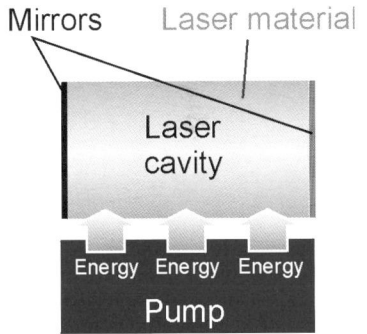

Figure 28.19: *The three main components of a laser are the laser cavity, the laser material, and the pump. The laser cavity is made by sandwiching the laser material between two mirrors.*

Laser materials   Many materials, such as crystals of ruby, nitrogen gas, and even colored gelatin, have the properties needed to be a laser material. The special atomic configuration of a laser material gives it the ability to store energy for release as light. The laser cavity is a space between two mirrors where light can bounce back and forth (Figure 28.19). The release of stored energy in the laser material makes the light stronger with each bounce.

How lasers make light

Emission and absorption of photons
As energy is absorbed by an atom in a laser material, one electron moves to a higher energy level. The energy is released as a photon when the electron falls back down to its normal (lower) energy level. In normal materials, this absorption and release happen almost simultaneously. In laser materials, there is a time delay between the absorption of the energy and the subsequent release of a photon.

Stimulated emission
The atoms and molecules used in a laser have an internal structure that traps an electron in a higher level. The electron remains trapped in the higher level until it is liberated by a photon with just the right energy. When a *stimulating photon* with the right energy does come along, the atom emits a photon with the exact same energy and phase as the stimulating photon (Figure 28.20). It is this property of atoms to emit photons that match other photons that makes the laser possible. The process of light emission triggered by a photon is called *stimulated* emission.

A standing wave forms in the laser cavity
A laser material has many photons in many atoms in its system. The *laser cavity* ensures that the emission from each atom is synchronized with a resonant light wave in the laser. The simplest laser cavity is made of two parallel mirrors (Figure 28.21). Light traveling between the mirrors forms a standing wave. Every photon in the standing wave is in phase with every other photon. To get light out of the laser, one of the mirrors is made with a reflectivity less than 100 percent. A fraction of the photons bouncing back and forth pass through the partially reflected mirror and create the laser light that you see.

Amplification of photons
To see how *amplification* works, consider one photon starting out across the cavity. This photon hits an energized atom, which releases a second photon matching the first (Figure 28.22). Now two photons hit two other energized atoms, releasing two more matching photons, for a total of four. As long as there are atoms with electrons in higher energy levels, any photon moving in the cavity triggers a chain reaction releasing many photons, all with identical phase and energy. The process of multiplying photons through stimulated emission is called light amplification by stimulated emission of radiation, or simply, *laser*.

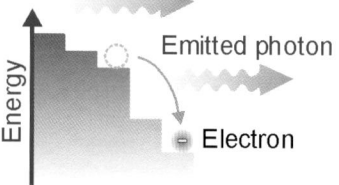

Stimulated emission

Electrons in high energy levels emit photons that match the stimulating photon.

Figure 28.20: *The process of stimulated emission.*

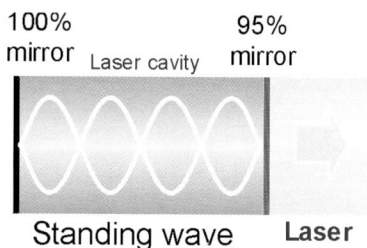

Standing wave **Laser light**

Figure 28.21: *The standing wave in the laser cavity.*

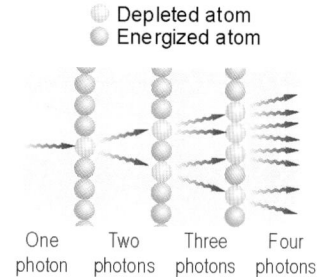

Light amplification by stimulated emission

Figure 28.22: *The process of light amplification.*

586

Chapter 28 Review

Vocabulary review

Match the following terms with the correct definition. There is one extra definition in the list that will not match any of the terms.

Set One

1. nucleus
2. proton
3. atomic mass unit
4. atomic number
5. electron

a. Negatively charged particle in an atom
b. Defined as $1/12^{th}$ the mass of a single atom of the isotope C^{12}
c. Number of protons in the nucleus
d. Particle with positive charge and a mass slightly less than 1 amu
e. Neutral particle in an atom
f. Center of an atom; contains most of the mass of an atom

Set Two

1. mass number
2. isotopes
3. strong force
4. radioactive
5. nuclear reaction

a. Attracts protons to neutrons
b. Atoms with the same atomic number, but different atomic mass
c. A nucleus with too many neutrons to be stable causes an atom to be described this way
d. Total number of protons and neutrons in the nucleus
e. Rearrangement of atoms to form a different molecule
f. May result in the formation of an atom of a different element

Set Three

1. spectral lines
2. photoelectric effect
3. energy levels
4. exclusion principle
5. quantum

a. The smallest possible unit of certain measured quantities such as charge or light energy
b. The quantum states in an atom are grouped into these
c. Electrons that fall into the nucleus
d. Light produced by electrons moving between energy levels creates these
e. Electrons are emitted when light falls on a surface
f. No two electrons can occupy the same quantum state at the same time.

Concept review

1. Summarize the properties of the major atomic particles by completing the chart below:

Particle Name	Relative Charge	Relative Mass	Mass (kg)	Charge (C)
Electron				
Proton				
Neutron				

2. If electrons are in constant motion, explain why atoms tend to remain neutral rather than lose electrons.

3. The electric forces between protons of the nucleus are large, positive and mutually repulsive. Why does this force not cause the positively charged protons to fly apart?

4. List the four forces of nature in order from strongest to weakest, name the particles involved in their action, and describe how they might affect an atom structurally.

5. Using the terms mass number and atomic number, describe the difference between the various isotopes of carbon.

6. If the mass number of an atom is the sum of protons and neutrons in the atom, why is the atomic mass of an atom of magnesium given as 24.31?

7. Using the "Chart of Stable Isotopes" in this chapter, state whether or not C^{14} is stable and offer an explanation for your statement.

8. Hydrogen reacts with oxygen to form water. Helium reacts to form lithium. One is a nuclear reaction, the other a chemical reaction. Identify each and state a major difference between chemical and nuclear reactions.

9. Which particle in the atom is responsible for most characteristics of matter?

10. How is the color of your clothing related to the electronic structure of the atom?

11. What does a physicist mean by the term quantum state?

12. To locate an electron in an atom, you need to know the four _____ of its address: n, l, m, and s.

13. When an electron in one quantum state moves to a state closer to the nucleus, does it gain or lose energy?

14. Use the analogy of a multi-level parking garage to explain the terms quantum state and energy level.

15. When heated, an unknown gas emits light with wavelengths of 589 nm and 704 nm, creating colored lines at these frequencies in a bright-line spectrum as observed in a spectrometer. The spectra of four gases are shown below. Which of the four is the unknown gas?

Carbon

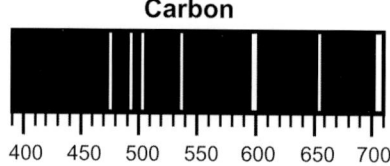

400 450 500 550 600 650 700

Helium

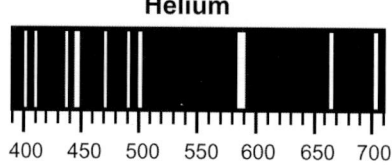

400 450 500 550 600 650 700

Lithium

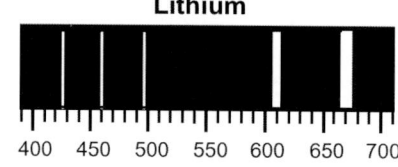

400 450 500 550 600 650 700

Nitrogen

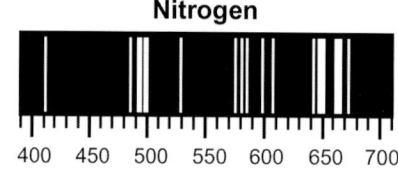

400 450 500 550 600 650 700

Wavelength (nm)

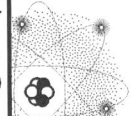
16. What is the most important variable in photoelectric effect experiments?

17. How are the wavelength and energy of a photon related?

18. When do electrons exhibit particle-like properties? When do they exhibit wave-like properties?

19. State the "l" quantum number for each orbital shape.

A   **B**   **C**

20. Explain how the uncertainty principle relates to the notion that the exact position of an electron can never be determined precisely.

21. What does the wave function of a quantum of matter describe?

22. Summarize the contributions of the following scientists to the quantum theory:

    a.   Johann Balmer

    b.   Neils Bohr

    c.   Wolfgang Pauli

    d.   Max Planck

    e.   Albert Einstein

    f.   Louis DeBroglie

Problems

1. List the element that contains each number of protons:

    a.   22

    b.   36

    c.   79

2. Calculate the mass of a C^{12} atom in kilograms.

3. Calculate the number of neutrons in the isotope of uranium identified as U^{235}.

4. A fictitious element, pennium (symbol: Pe) has two isotopes, Pe^{25} and Pe^{31}. In an average sample of pennium, 8 of 10 atoms are Pe^{31}. What is the atomic mass for pennium?

5. Refer to the "Chart of the Stable Isotopes" to answer the following questions. Use appropriate symbolism in your answers.

    a.   Which two isotopes have fewer neutrons than protons?

    b.   Which number(s) of neutrons is not found in a stable isotope?

    c.   Which element on the chart has the most stable isotopes? How many stable isotopes does it have?

    d.   What is the only element whose stable isotope contains no neutrons?

    e.   Name the stable isotopes of argon.

6. Sulfur's common isotopes are stable. Using this information and the chart "Atomic Mass for Stable Isotopes of Elements 1-26", solve the following problems:

    a.   Assuming that sulfur's most common isotope occurs with far greater regularity than others, what is the most common isotope of sulfur?

    b.   How many protons and neutrons does this isotope have?

7. Johann Balmer predicted that other spectral lines in the ultraviolet frequency would be found if n in his formula represented numbers larger than 7. Use Balmer's formula: $(\lambda = 91.16/(1/2^2 - 1/n^2))$ to predict the wavelength of light that might be emitted if $n = 8$.

8. Johann Balmer predicted that other wavelength of spectral lines in the infrared region would be identified if the 2 in the fraction $1/2$ were replaced by the number 3. Use the Balmer's formula, substituting $1/3$ for $1/2$, to predict the wavelength of light produced by a hydrogen atom when $n = 4$. Was his prediction correct?

9. A photon of ultraviolet light with wavelength 5.0×10^{-7} meters is directed at a zinc metal surface. It causes an emission of electrons from the surface of the zinc.

    a. Calculate the energy of the incident photon.

    b. Assuming it takes 1.0×10^{-19} joules to remove the electron from the surface of the metal, how much kinetic energy does the emitted electron have?

10. Find the wavelength of an electron traveling at 1.23×10^{6} m/sec.

11. Find the wavelength of a 2000 kg car traveling at 100 km/hr.

12. A tetrahedral (a pyramid with four triangular faces) is painted with 1 face black, 1 face orange and 2 faces white. If it is tossed into the air, what is the probability of:

    a. An orange face landing down (as the base)?

    b. An orange face appearing as one of the exposed (non-base) sides?

    c. An orange or black side landing as the base?

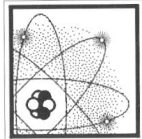

Unit 9
The Atom

Chapter 29

Chemical Reactions

Objectives for Chapter 29

By the end of this chapter you should be able to:

1. Classify matter as substances, homogeneous or heterogeneous mixtures, or solutions.
2. Tell the difference between chemical change and physical change.
3. Describe the types of chemical bonds and the role of electrons in forming bonds between atoms.
4. Write and balance the chemical equation for a simple reaction.
5. Explain how the terms *acid*, *base*, *organic*, and *solution* relate to living systems.
6. Describe the role of photosynthesis in maintaining life on Earth.

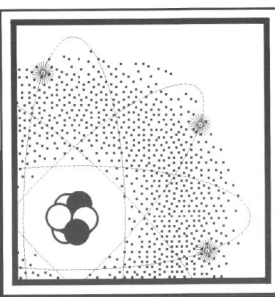

Terms and vocabulary words

substance	mixture	physical change	compound	heterogeneous mixture
solute	double bond	solubility	solvent	homogeneous mixture
dissolve	solution	polar molecule	chemical bond	alkali metal
noble gas	element	valence electrons	transition metal	balanced equation
pH	covalent bond	amino acid	acid	organic chemistry
ion	ionic bond	hydrocarbon	protein	activation energy
products	reactants	carbohydrate	reaction	exothermic reaction
refine	octane	halogen	photosynthesis	endothermic reaction
base	chemical change	cracking	petroleum	Lewis dot diagram
fat				

29.1 Chemistry

Chemistry is the science of how atoms and elements create the world we experience. Relatively speaking, physics is the least complex of the basic sciences. A few particles and four forces create the elements and fundamental interactions in the universe. Chemistry is the next level up in complexity. Our world contains millions of chemicals made from the basic elements and even more interactions between chemicals. Biology is the highest level of complexity. Even a small living creature, a bacterium, is an organization of thousands of chemicals and interactions between chemicals. This chapter connects physics to chemistry and biology (Figure 29.1).

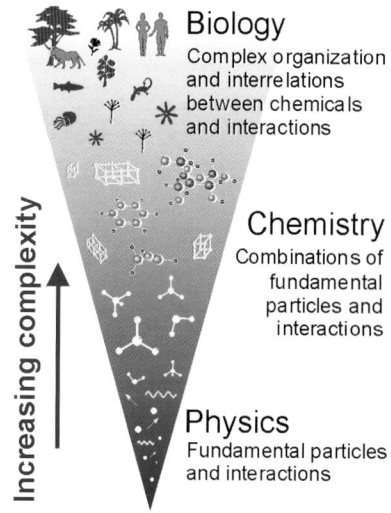

Figure 29.1: *The relationship between the sciences of physics, chemistry, and biology.*

Substances and mixtures

Substances and mixtures | Matter can be divided into two categories: mixtures and substances. A pure substance is the same throughout and cannot be separated into different substances. Pure water is an example of a substance. Every particle of water is exactly the same as every other particle. Mixtures contain more than one kind of substance and can be separated. For example, cola is a mixture that can be separated into carbonated water, corn syrup, caramel color, phosphoric acid, and flavors. Figure 29.2 shows the categories of matter.

Elements and compounds | Substances are divided into elements and compounds. Elements contain only one type of atom. Gold and silver and iron are examples of elements. Compounds contain more than one type of atom. The different atoms in compounds are often bonded together into molecules. Water is an example of a compound because water contains the elements oxygen and hydrogen.

Homogeneous and heterogeneous | There are two types of mixtures. A homogeneous mixture is the same throughout. Brass is an example of a homogeneous mixture. Brass is made of 70 percent copper and 30 percent zinc. If you cut a brass candlestick into ten pieces, each piece would contain the same percentage of copper and zinc. A heterogeneous mixture is one in which different parts are not necessarily the same. Chicken noodle soup is a common heterogeneous mixture. One spoonful might contain broth, noodles, and chicken, while another spoonful contains only broth. Concrete is another heterogeneous mixture.

Substances

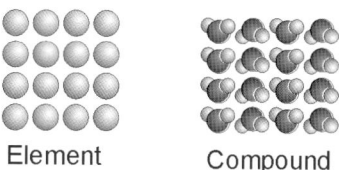

Element   Compound

Mixtures

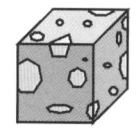 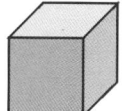

Heterogeneous   Homogeneous
mixture   mixture

Figure 29.2: *Matter can be classified into elements, compounds, and mixtures.*

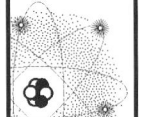

Physical change and chemical change

Physical change   The concept of temperature and changes of phase between solid, liquid, and gas (see Chapter 25) are traditionally considered part of chemistry, as are the gas laws (see Chapter 27). These kinds of changes in matter are called physical changes, because matter changes physical form but one substance does not change into a completely different substance.

Chemical change   A chemical change turns one type of substance into a different substance which may have very different properties. An example of chemical change is burning wood into carbon dioxide, water, and ashes.

Properties of materials   Many properties of materials are affected by chemical changes. Properties such as strength, elasticity, hardness, viscosity, taste, density, stickiness, and specific heat are all affected by chemical change. We use chemical changes to create materials with properties that are useful. For example, Teflon® is a plastic that is slippery and resists chemical attack by many materials. The properties of Teflon® come from chemistry, both in making it and understanding how it interacts with other substances. The rubber in car tires is another example of a material that has been modified by chemical changes. A process called *vulcanization* inserts pairs of sulfur atoms into the long chain molecules of natural rubber. The sulfur ties adjacent molecules together like rungs on a ladder and makes vulcanized rubber much harder and more durable.

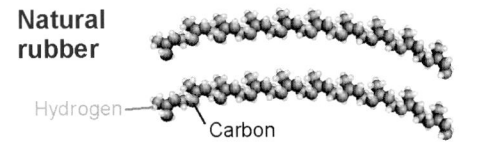

Natural rubber

Hydrogen

Carbon

Vulcanized rubber

Sulfur

Recognizing chemical change   Chemical changes rearrange atoms into new molecules which usually have different properties from the original molecules. For example, a chemical change occurs when you mix baking soda (solid) with vinegar (liquid mixture). The baking soda changes to carbon dioxide gas (making bubbles) and a new solid which settles to the bottom of the vinegar. The mixture gets colder and the vinegar loses some of its acid tartness. Bubbling, new substances, temperature changes and color changes (Figure 29.3) are all evidence of chemical change.

Bubbling

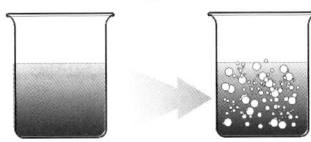

A new gas is forming?

Turns cloudy

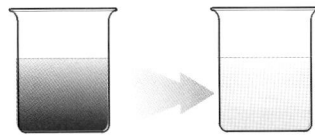

A new solid is forming?

Temperature change

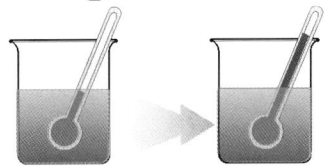

Chemical bonds are changing?

Color change

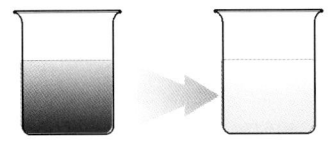

A new substance is forming?

Figure 29.3: *Evidence for chemical change.*

Water and solutions

Definition of a solution

A solution is a special kind of mixture. In a solution, molecules of solute are free to move around among molecules of solvent. A solution of salt in water is a good example. Salt is a solid at room temperature. When salt is dissolved in water, the molecules are separated and become free to move. The solvent (water) acts to separate (dissolve) the molecules of salt (Figure 29.4).

Life depends on solutions

Solutions make life possible. Chemical activity within living things can only occur if atoms and molecules are able to meet and have reactions. The human body is mostly water because water is needed to dissolve the many chemicals that interact inside the body. All the forms of life that we know are chemically based on solutions in which water is the solvent.

Solubility

Solubility describes the amount of solute that will dissolve in a given amount of solvent. Table 29.1 gives some representative solubilities in kilogram of solute per kilogram of water. For example, 0.36 kg of salt will dissolve in one kilogram of water at 25°C. If you add any more than that, the excess salt remains solid and does not dissolve. Water is called the *universal solvent* because so many chemicals have high solubility in water, though "universal" is not completely accurate. From the table, you can see that chalk does not dissolve in water.

Solubility and temperature

The solubility of solids in liquids usually rises with temperature. For example, heating up a kilogram of water allows more than 0.36 kilogram of salt to dissolve. The increase in solubility occurs because molecules in warm liquids are moving faster. Faster (hotter) water molecules can break molecules away from a solid more readily than slower (colder) molecules.

Powders dissolve faster

Substances that are meant to dissolve are often made in powders, like salt and sugar. Powders dissolve quickly because they have a tremendous amount of surface area exposed to the solvent.

Solubility of gases

Gases and other liquids can also be part of a solution. Fish can breath in water because oxygen is soluble in water. The gills in fish extract dissolved oxygen from water in a similar way as our lungs extract oxygen from the air. The fizz in soda comes from dissolved carbon dioxide gas.

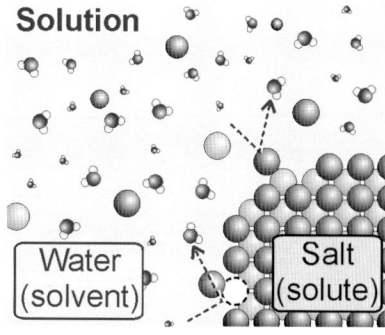

Figure 29.4: *A solution is a mixture of separated molecules of solute moving around in the solvent. The process of dissolving occurs when molecules of solvent hit molecules of solute and knock them into solution.*

Table 29.1:
The solubility of common substances in water at 25°C

Substance	Solubility (kg/kg H_2O)
Chalk	0
Nitrogen	1.8×10^{-5}
Oxygen	4.1×10^{-5}
Carbon dioxide	0.0015
Salt	0.36
Sugar	1.1

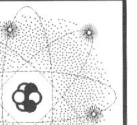

29.2 Chemical Bonds

Almost every atom in the matter you experience is bonded to at least one other atom. For example, the oxygen in the air is not in the form of single atoms, but molecules made from two oxygen atoms bonded together. Glass is a combination of silicon and oxygen atoms. Salt is made from sodium and chlorine atoms. However, salt dissolves in water and glass does not. The chemical bond between the silicon and oxygen atoms in glass is different from the bond between sodium and chlorine atoms in salt. This section introduces the different types of chemical bonds that form between atoms.

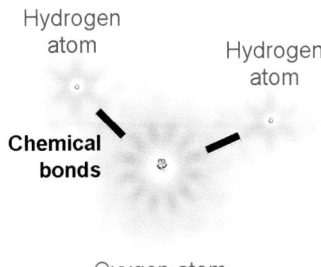

The importance of chemical bonds

Electrons form chemical bonds A chemical bond forms when atoms exchange or share electrons. Two atoms that are sharing one or more electrons are chemically bonded together and move together. A water molecule is an example of three atoms connected by two chemical bonds. Each hydrogen atom shares its single electron with the oxygen atom at the center (Figure 29.5). Almost all the elements form chemical bonds easily. This is why most of the matter you experience is made of atoms bonded together as molecules.

Water molecule (H₂O)

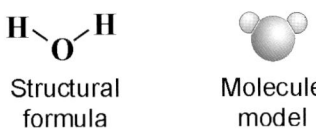

Figure 29.5: *Three ways to show the chemical bonds in a water molecule.*

Chemical bonds determine properties Most of the properties of substances come from how they form chemical bonds with other substances. For example, the nonstick coating on cooking pans is "nonstick" because it does *not* form chemical bonds with substances in food. The active ingredient in aspirin works because it bonds with chemicals in the body called *prostaglandins* and prevents them from creating swelling that causes pain.

The importance of the molecule The properties of substances are properties of the *molecule*, not of the elements that are in the molecule. Aspirin is made from carbon, hydrogen, and oxygen. By themselves, these elements do not have the property of reducing pain. Even other molecules formed from the same elements have extremely different properties. For example, polyethylene plastic wrap and formaldehyde (a toxic preservative) are also made from just carbon, oxygen, and hydrogen. The beneficial properties of aspirin come from the precise way the atoms are arranged in the molecule (Figure 29.6). Chemical bonds are important because they control how molecules are formed and how they interact with other molecules.

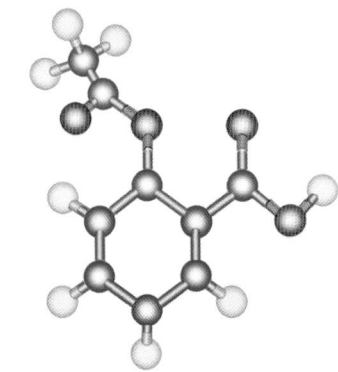

Figure 29.6: *This molecule is acetylsalicylic acid, the active ingredient in aspirin.*

Valence, electrons, and chemical bonds

Valence electrons   Not all electrons in an atom participate in making chemical bonds. Only the electrons in the highest *unfilled* energy level make bonds. Electrons that make bonds are called **valence electrons**. For example, carbon has six electrons. Two are in the first energy level, which is completely filled. The remaining four electrons are in the second energy level, which is unfilled since it can hold eight electrons. Carbon has four valence electrons because there are four electrons in the unfilled second level (Figure 29.7).

Each valence electron can make one bond   An atom can make one chemical bond for each valence electron. Since carbon has four valence electrons, one carbon atom can bond with up to four other atoms. The methane molecule is an example of carbon with four bonds. Bonds can also involve two or more valence electrons. Molecules of the chemical *benzene* have six carbon atoms and six hydrogen atoms shaped in a ring (Figure 29.8). There are **double bonds** between every other carbon atom in the ring. A double bond uses two valence electrons from each atom. Triple bonds with three valence electrons are also common.

Chemically similar elements   Elements with the same number of valence electrons are *chemically similar*, meaning the same number of chemical bonds are made with the same elements. For example, the elements lithium (Li), sodium (Na), and potassium (K) each have one valence electron. Two atoms of each of these elements form a molecule with one atom of oxygen (Figure 29.9). Three atoms bond per nitrogen atom, and one per fluorine atom. The elements lithium, sodium, and potassium, along with rubidium (Rb), cesium (Cs) and francium (Fr) are called the **alkali metals**. All are soft, silvery metals with similar chemical properties, and all are very reactive.

Noble gases   Elements in which the last energy level is completely full have no valence electrons. Helium (He), neon (Ne), and argon (Ar) are the first three elements in the group of **noble gases**. These elements cannot form chemical bonds because their atoms have no available valence electrons. The noble gases also include krypton (Kr), xenon (Xe), and radon (Rn). The six noble gases are the only elements that do not form chemical bonds with other elements. Argon makes up about 1 percent of the atmosphere; the other five gases are relatively rare on Earth.

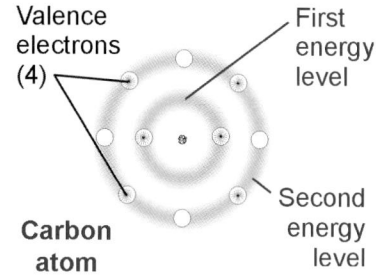

Figure 29.7: *A carbon atom has four valence electrons in the second energy level.*

Figure 29.8: *The benzene molecule is a ring of six carbon atoms and six hydrogen atoms.*

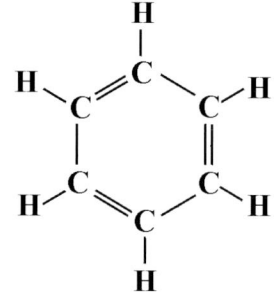

Lithium oxide	Li_2O	Li–O–Li
Sodium oxide	Na_2O	Na–O–Na
Potassium oxide	K_2O	K–O–K

Figure 29.9: *All the alkali metals form oxides with two atoms per oxygen atom.*

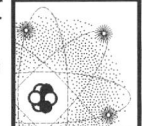

Why chemical bonds form

Atoms form bonds to reach lower energy

Chemical bonds are a form of potential energy. Imagine pulling adhesive tape off a surface. It takes energy to separate atoms that are bonded together just like it takes energy to pull tape off a surface. If it takes energy to separate bonded atoms, then the same energy must be released when the bond is formed. This is a direct consequence of the law of conservation of energy. Energy is released when atoms come together into molecules. The atoms in matter are usually found in molecules because molecules have lower energy than free atoms. Like a ball rolling downhill, systems in nature tend to settle into the configuration of lowest energy.

Atoms bond to get eight valence electrons

Atoms are most stable when they have either 2 or 8 valence electrons. The noble gases already have eight, so they are stable and do not form bonds with other atoms. Other atoms form chemical bonds so that they can share electrons to reach that stable number of eight. The Lewis dot diagram (Figure 29.10) shows the element symbol surrounded by one to eight dots representing the valence electrons. Carbon has four dots, hydrogen one. One carbon atom bonds with four hydrogen atoms because this molecule (methane) allows the carbon atom to have eight valence electrons—four of its own and four shared with hydrogen atoms.

Molecules with oxygen

Oxygen has six valence electrons. That means oxygen needs two more electrons to get to eight. One oxygen atom bonded with two hydrogen atoms (water) is one way to make eight. One oxygen atom can also bond with one beryllium atom. Beryllium has two valence electrons. Oxygen can also share electrons with another oxygen atom. The oxygen molecule (O_2) has one double bond connecting two oxygen atoms. Almost all the oxygen in the atmosphere exists in the form of oxygen molecules. Complex molecules are formed by multiple atoms sharing valence electrons so that each one can achieve the required number of eight.

Some elements prefer to lose electrons

Some elements can achieve the stable eight electrons more easily by losing an electron than by gaining one. Sodium (Na) is a good example of this type of element. It has a full eight electrons in the second level, and one valence electron in the third level. If the single valence electron is given away, sodium is left with a stable eight electrons in the (full) second level. For this reason, sodium tends to form bonds that allow it to give up its single valence electron.

Lewis dot diagrams

Neon
8 valence electrons

$:\ddot{Ne}:$

Fluorine
7 valence electrons

$:\ddot{F}\cdot$

Oxygen
6 valence electrons

$:\ddot{O}\cdot$

Nitrogen
5 valence electrons

$:\dot{N}\cdot$

Carbon
4 valence electrons

$\cdot\dot{C}\cdot$

Boron
3 valence electrons

$\cdot\dot{B}\cdot$

Beryllium
2 valence electrons

$\ddot{Be}$

Lithium
1 valence electron

$\dot{Li}$

Hydrogen
1 valence electron

$\dot{H}$

$$\begin{matrix} & H & \\ H : & \ddot{C} & : H \\ & \ddot{H} & \end{matrix}$$
Methane molecule (CH_4)

Figure 29.10: *Lewis dot diagrams show valence electrons as dots around the element symbol. Atoms form bonds to get eight valence electrons by sharing with other atoms.*

The periodic table

Valence and the periodic table

The periodic table arranges elements from left to right by the number of valence electrons. The alkali metals (group 1) have one valence electron. Group 2 elements have two valence electrons. Group 17 elements have seven valence electrons. These elements are called halogens. The halogens are very reactive since they only need to gain one electron to get to eight valence electrons. The noble gases (group 18) have no valence electrons and do not form chemical bonds with other atoms.

Transition metals

The elements in groups 3 to 12 are called the transition metals. These elements have electrons in the fourth and fifth energy levels. The bonding patterns for transition metals are more complex because of the large number of electrons in the highest unfilled level.

Number of valence electrons

Periodic table of the elements

1	2	*varies*										3	4	5	6	7	8
Alkali metals **1**	**2**															Halogens	Noble gases **18**
H 1	**2**											**13**	**14**	**15**	**16**	**17**	He 2
Li 3	Be 4				Transition metals							B 5	C 6	N 7	O 8	F 9	Ne 10
Na 11	Mg 12	**3**	**4**	**5**	**6**	**7**	**8**	**9**	**10**	**11**	**12**	Al 13	Si 14	P 15	S 16	Cl 17	Ar 18
K 19	Ca 20	Sc 21	Ti 22	V 23	Cr 24	Mn 25	Fe 26	Co 27	Ni 28	Cu 29	Zn 30	Ga 31	Ge 32	As 33	Se 34	Br 35	Kr 36
Rb 37	Sr 38	Y 39	Zr 40	Nb 41	Mo 42	Tc 43	Ru 44	Rh 45	Pd 46	Ag 47	Cd 48	In 49	Sn 50	Sb 51	Te 52	I 53	Xe 54
Cs 55	Ba 56		Hf 72	Ta 73	W 74	Re 75	Os 76	Ir 77	Pt 78	Au 79	Hg 80	Tl 81	Pb 82	Bi 83	Po 84	At 85	Rn 86
Fr 87	Ra 88		Rf 104	Db 105	Sg 106	Bh 107	Hs 108	Mt 109									

La 57	Ce 58	Pr 59	Nd 60	Pm 61	Sm 62	Eu 63	Gd 64	Tb 65	Dy 66	Ho 67	Er 68	Tm 69	Yb 70	Lu 71
Ac 89	Th 90	Pa 91	U 92	Np 93	Pu 94	Am 95	Cm 96	Bk 97	Cf 98	Es 99	Fm 100	Md 101	No 102	Lr 103

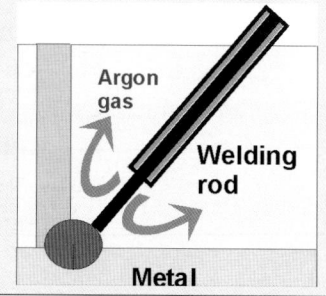

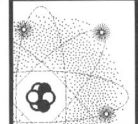

Ionic and covalent bonds

Ionic bonds Most chemical bonds fall into two categories, depending on whether the valence electrons are transferred or shared. Electrons in an ionic bond are effectively transferred from one atom to another. Atoms that either gain or lose an electron become ions. Ions may have either positive or negative electric charge. The atom which takes the electron acquires an overall negative charge. The positive and negative ions are attracted to each other, creating the bond. Ionic bonds tend to form between more than one pair of atoms at a time. The bond between sodium (Na) and chlorine (Cl) in sodium chloride (salt) is a good example of an ionic bond. In a crystal of salt each sodium ion is attracted to all the neighboring chlorine ions (Figure 29.11).

Covalent bonds In a covalent bond the electrons are shared between atoms. The bonds between hydrogen and carbon in a methane molecule are covalent bonds. The electrons in a covalent bond act like ties between the two atoms. An important difference between covalent and ionic bonds is that covalent bonds act only between the atoms in a single molecule, while ionic bonds act between all adjacent atoms (ions). Molecules joined by covalent bonds also tend to be much harder to separate into their individual atoms.

Alkali metals tend to form ionic bonds Whether a covalent or ionic bond is formed depends on how close each atom is to the stable number of eight valence electrons. The alkali metals with one valence electron have a high tendency to give up an electron. The halogen elements with seven valence electrons have a high tendency to take an electron. If you put an alkali (Na) with a halogen (Cl), you get an ionic bond because one atom *strongly* wants to lose an electron and the other *strongly* wants to gain one.

Examples of covalent bonds Elements that have two to six valence electrons tend to form covalent bonds with each other since the tendency to take or receive electrons is more matched. For example, all the bonds in silicon dioxide (glass) are covalent bonds between silicon and oxygen atoms. Diamonds are the hardest substance known. A diamond is a pure carbon crystal in which every carbon atom is joined to four other carbon atoms by a covalent bond (Figure 29.12). The hardness of diamonds is due to the fact that four covalent bonds must be broken to move each carbon atom.

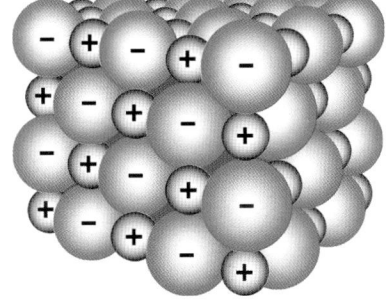

Figure 29.11: *The ionic bonds in a salt crystal (NaCl) come from electrical attraction between negative chlorine ions and positive sodium ions.*

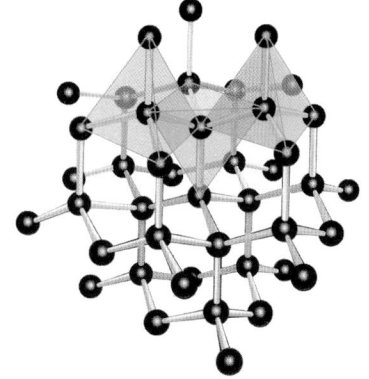

Figure 29.12: *A diamond crystal is made of pure carbon connected by a strong network of covalent bonds.*

Acids and bases   When substances are dissolved in water they divide into two categories called *acids* and *bases*. An acid creates a sour taste and can dissolve reactive metals like zinc. Vinegar and lemon juice are examples of acids. A base creates a bitter taste and tends to feel slippery. Ammonia is an example of a base.

What makes an acid   Acid molecules include ionic bonds. When an acid dissolves in water, the ionic bond breaks to create two ions. For example, hydrochloric acid (HCl) separates into a hydrogen ion (H^+) that has lost an electron and a chlorine ion (Cl^-) with an extra electron. Water molecules are polar, which means they have a positive and a negative side. The H^+ ion attaches to the negative side of a water molecule to form a *hydronium ion* (H_3O^+). The strong chemical reactivity of the hydronium ion is what results in the properties of acids.

| Chlorine / Hydrogen | Oxygen | | Cl⁻ | H₃O⁺ |
| HCl molecule | + | H₂O molecule | Chlorine ion | + Hydronium ion |

Bases are the opposite of acids   The opposite of an acid is a base. Instead of *adding* a hydrogen ion to water molecules, bases have a strong *attraction* for hydrogen ions. When a base such as ammonia (NH_3) is dissolved in water, the molecules of ammonia take a hydrogen ion (proton) from water molecules and become ammonium ions (NH_4^+). The missing hydrogen makes water molecules into hydroxide (OH^-) ions.

When an acid and a base are mixed together, the OH^- and H_3O^+ ions combine readily to form plain *neutral* water again. Antacid medicines are made from bases that combine with and neutralize acids in the stomach.

The pH scale   The pH is a measure of the concentration of H_3O^+ (acid) ions in a solution. The pH scale goes from 0 to 14. A solution with pH less than 7 is an acid. The lower the pH, the higher the concentration of H_3O^+ ions and the stronger the acid. A pH of 7 is neutral. Neutral water has a small concentration (10^{-7}) of H_3O^+ ions. A pH above 7 is a base because the OH^- ion decreases the concentration of H_3O^+ ions. The higher the pH, the stronger the base. The pH scale is shown in Figure 29.13.

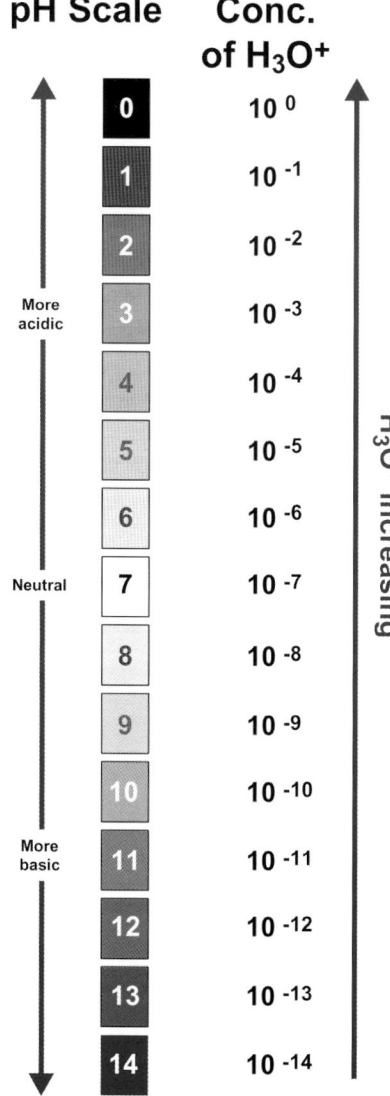

pH Scale   **Conc. of H₃O⁺**

	pH	Conc. of H₃O⁺
	0	10^0
	1	10^{-1}
	2	10^{-2}
More acidic	3	10^{-3}
	4	10^{-4}
	5	10^{-5}
	6	10^{-6}
Neutral	7	10^{-7}
	8	10^{-8}
	9	10^{-9}
	10	10^{-10}
More basic	11	10^{-11}
	12	10^{-12}
	13	10^{-13}
	14	10^{-14}

H_3O^+ increasing

Figure 29.13: *The pH scale.*

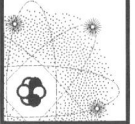

Organic chemistry

Organic chemistry is the chemistry of carbon
Organic chemistry is the chemistry of carbon and its compounds. Carbon can make a tremendous variety of molecules because each carbon atom can make up to four bonds. Carbon chemistry is called *organic* because all life on Earth is based on carbon. Twenty three percent of your body mass is carbon atoms. The rest is mostly water (oxygen and hydrogen, Figure 29.14).

Proteins
Proteins are complex molecules that are the building blocks of living things. The cartilage in your joints is made from proteins. A protein called hemoglobin carries oxygen in your blood. The enzymes that break down food in your stomach are proteins. Figure 29.15 shows a typical protein molecule. Proteins may have thousands of atoms in a single molecule.

Amino acids
Proteins are built from simpler molecules called amino acids. There are 20 amino acids that make up nearly all the proteins in the human body. The three simplest amino acids are shown below (glycine, alanine, and serine).

Glycine   Alanine   Serine

Fats and carbohydrates
Fats and carbohydrates are two other types of carbon molecules found in the body. Fats are typically long chain molecules, such as lauric acid (below) found in coconuts. Carbohydrates include sugars and starches, such as glucose (below). Thousands of different fat or carbohydrate molecules are used by plants and animals.

Lauric acid

Glucose

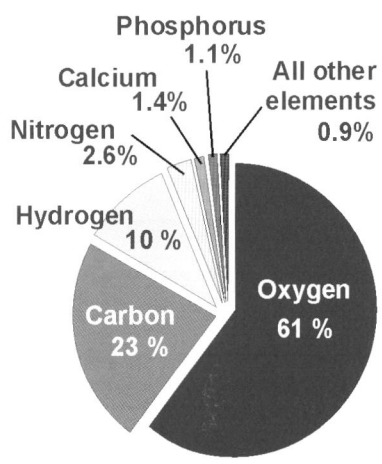

Figure 29.14: *The mass of your body is mostly oxygen, carbon, and hydrogen.*

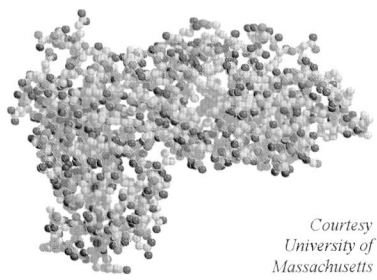

Courtesy University of Massachusetts

Figure 29.15: *A single protein molecule often includes thousands of atoms. This protein is called kinase, and is involved in chemical messages between cells.*

29.3 Chemical Reactions

Chemical reactions rearrange atoms into different molecules. If you leave a steel nail out in the rain, the shiny silver surface soon turns brown with rust. Rust forms through a chemical reaction between iron in the nail and oxygen in the water (Figure 29.16). Chemical reactions are the process through which chemical changes happen, like iron turning to rust.

Products and reactants

Products and reactants in chemistry

In cooking you start with *ingredients* that are combined into different *foods*. In chemical reactions you start with reactants that are combined into products. The reactants and products may include atoms, molecules, and energy. An example of a reaction is the combination of two hydrogen molecules with one oxygen molecule to make two water molecules. Hydrogen and oxygen are the reactants. Water and energy are the products.

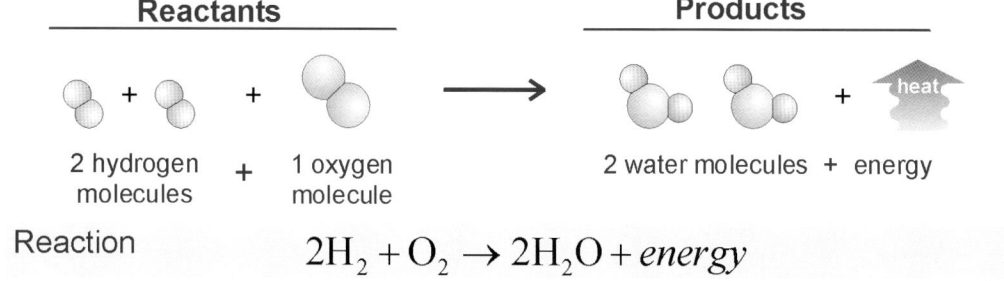

Reactants	**Products**
2 hydrogen molecules + 1 oxygen molecule	2 water molecules + energy

Reaction $2H_2 + O_2 \rightarrow 2H_2O + energy$

Writing chemical reactions

Chemical reactions are often written like equations with the reactants on the left and the products on the right. In the equation above, H_2 represents a hydrogen molecule. The symbol O_2 represents an oxygen molecule and H_2O is a water molecule. The subscripts tell how many atoms there are in one molecule. For example, the subscript 2 in H_2O means there are two hydrogen atoms in a water molecule.

Hydrogen as a fuel

Many researchers believe that hydrogen will eventually replace gasoline as a fuel. The chemical reaction between hydrogen and oxygen releases almost three times more energy per kilogram than does gasoline. Because the only products of the reaction are water and heat, burning hydrogen produces no pollutants.

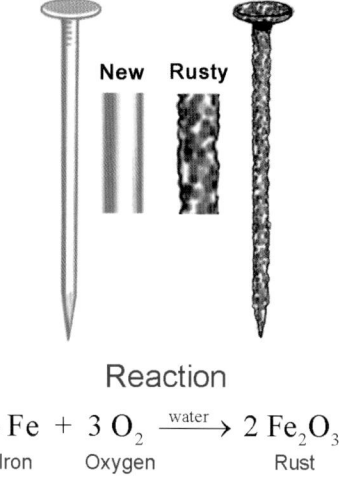

New   Rusty

Reaction

$4\,Fe + 3\,O_2 \xrightarrow{\text{water}} 2\,Fe_2O_3$

Iron   Oxygen   Rust

Figure 29.16: *The formation of rust from oxygen and iron is an example of a common chemical reaction.*

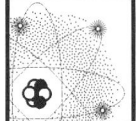
Chemical reactions and energy

Starting a reaction   If you put pure hydrogen and oxygen together nothing happens until you make a spark. Then a rapid chemical reaction occurs (burning), releasing much energy. The hydrogen and oxygen combine to make water and heat (Figure 29.17). It takes energy to start a reaction (the spark) and energy is released by the reaction (heat).

Activation energy   Chemical reactions proceed in two stages. First, the chemical bonds must be broken between the atoms in the reactants. The energy needed to break chemical bonds in the reactants is called the activation energy of the reaction. The spark supplies the activation energy to start the reaction between hydrogen and oxygen. The reaction starts with a few molecules near the spark.

$$\text{Reaction:} \quad 2H_2 + O_2 \rightarrow 2H_2O + energy$$

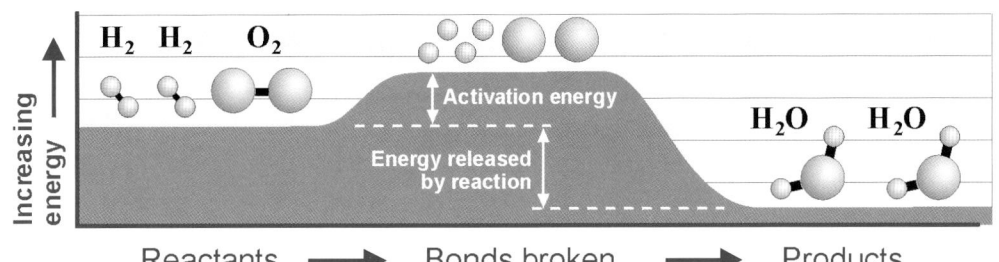

Exothermic reactions   In the second stage, new bonds form between atoms to make the products of the reaction. Forming bonds *gives off* energy. The reaction releases energy (exothermic) if forming new bonds gives off more energy than it took to break the old bonds. The hydrogen and oxygen reaction is exothermic. Once they are started, exothermic reactions tend to keep going because each reaction releases enough activation energy to start the reaction in neighboring molecules.

Endothermic reactions   A reaction *uses* energy (endothermic) if new bonds formed in the products release *less* energy than it took to break the original bonds in the reactants. Endothermic reactions do not usually keep going unless energy is supplied. For example, if you make a spark in water, a few molecules might react but reactions do not occur in the rest of the water. However, energy supplied by an electric current can turn water molecules back into hydrogen and oxygen molecules.

Start

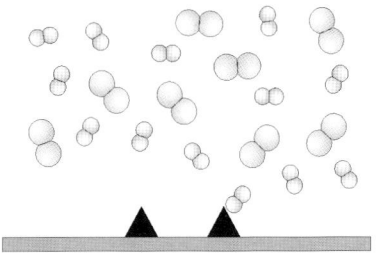

Spark splits nearby molecules

Energy released splits more molecules and reaction grows

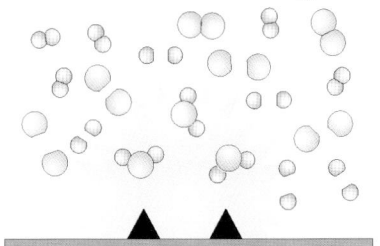

Figure 29.17: *The reaction between hydrogen and oxygen releases a great deal of energy.*

Working with chemical equations

Balanced chemical equations   Chemical reactions rearrange atoms, but do not create new atoms. That means the equation for a chemical reaction must have the same number and type of atoms on the reactant side as on the product side. A chemical equation is **balanced** when the number of each type of atom is the same in reactants and products.

An example of a balanced equation   Acid rain damages buildings and statues through reactions between acid in rainwater and calcium carbonate in limestone. For example, hydrochloric acid (HCl) reacts with calcium carbonate ($CaCO_3$) to form carbon dioxide gas (CO_2), water (H_2O), and calcium chloride ($CaCl_2$). If the reaction is written with one of each molecule (lower left), there is one more hydrogen and chlorine atom in the products than in the reactants. These extra atoms must come from somewhere! The *balanced* reaction adds another HCl molecule to the reactants (lower right).

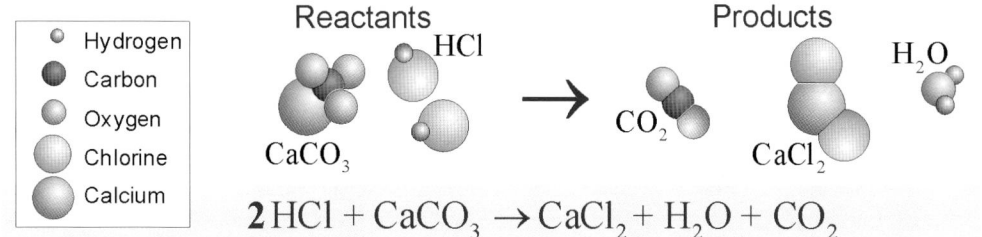

$$2\,HCl + CaCO_3 \rightarrow CaCl_2 + H_2O + CO_2$$

Unbalanced reaction	**Balanced reaction**
$HCl + CaCO_3 \rightarrow CaCl_2 + H_2O + CO_2$	$2\,HCl + CaCO_3 \rightarrow CaCl_2 + H_2O + CO_2$

Atom count

	Reactants	Products	
Hydrogen	○	○ ○	✗
Carbon	●	●	✓
Oxygen	○○○	○○○	✓
Chlorine	○	○○	✗
Calcium	○	○	✓

Atom count

	Reactants	Products	
Hydrogen	○ ○	○ ○	✓
Carbon	●	●	✓
Oxygen	○○○	○○○	✓
Chlorine	○○	○○	✓
Calcium	○	○	✓

Balancing a chemical equation

$$\boxed{1 \rightarrow 2 \rightarrow 3 \rightarrow 4}$$

Step 1:
Make sure you have the correct chemical formula for each molecule in the products or reactants.

Step 2:
Write the equation for the reaction down using one molecule of each type.

Step 3:
Count the number of atoms of each type in the products. Also, count the number of atoms of each type in the reactants.

Step 4
Adjust the number of molecules of product or reactant until the total number of each type of atom is the same on both sides of the equation. This usually takes some trial and error.

You cannot change the subscripts within a molecule. For example the molecule $CaCl_2$ has two chlorine atoms. You cannot change the subscript 2 to 3 and make $CaCl_3$ to get an extra chlorine atom. $CaCl_3$ is a different molecule from $CaCl_2$.

604

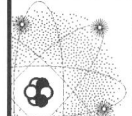
Mass in chemical reactions

Table 29.2:
Atomic mass of
the first 20 elements

Using balanced equations
A balanced chemical equation is like a recipe. It tells you how many of each molecule the reaction uses and produces. Counting molecules is not practical so we usually need the *mass* of reactants and products of a chemical reaction.

Calculating mass of products and reactants
The first step is to determine the mass of each atom or molecule that appears in the equation. This is done by adding up the masses of each atom from Table 29.2 (or a periodic table). The second step is to use the balanced equation to determine how many molecules of each type are needed. In the example, there are two hydrochloric acid molecules, so the reaction uses twice the mass of a single molecule. The masses are often listed in atomic mass units (amu), but for use with a chemical equation, the masses may be assumed to be in kilograms.

Element		Mass (amu)
1 - H	hydrogen	1.01
2 - He	helium	4.00
3 - Li	lithium	6.94
4 - Be	beryllium	9.01
5 - B	boron	10.8
6 - C	carbon	12.0
7 - N	nitrogen	14.0
8 - O	oxygen	16.0
9 - F	fluorine	19.0
10 - Ne	neon	20.2
11 - Na	sodium	23.0
12 - Mg	magnesium	24.3
13 - B	aluminum	27.0
14 - Si	silicon	28.1
15 - P	phosphorus	31.0
16 - S	sulfur	32.1
17 - Cl	chlorine	35.5
18 - Ar	argon	40.0
19 - K	potassium	39.1
20 - Ca	calcium	40.1

Step 1:
Calculate the mass of each molecule or atom.

	HCl	$CaCO_3$	$CaCl_2$	H_2O	CO_2
Hydrogen	1.01			2 x 1.01	
Carbon		12.0			12.0
Oxygen		3 x 16.0		16.0	2 x 16.0
Chlorine	35.5		2 x 35.5		
Calcium		40.1	40.1		
Total (kg)	**36.5**	**100.1**	**111.1**	**18.0**	**44.0**

Step 2:
Use the balanced equation to calculate the masses of reactants and products.

Balanced equation

$$2\,HCl + CaCO_3 \rightarrow CaCl_2 + H_2O + CO_2$$

NOTE: *This reaction uses two molecules of HCl, so the mass of one molecule is doubled.*

hydrochloric acid (HCl)	73.0 kg	calcium chloride ($CaCl_2$)	111.1kg
calcium carbonate ($CaCO_3$)	100.1 kg	water (H_2O)	18 kg
		carbon dioxide (CO_2)	44 kg
Total reactants	173.1 kg	Total products	173.1 kg

Mass conservation in chemical reactions
Note that the total mass of reactants and products is the same. This is an example of a rule that *chemical reactions conserve mass.* Conservation of mass follows directly from the fact that the same atoms appear in both products and reactants.

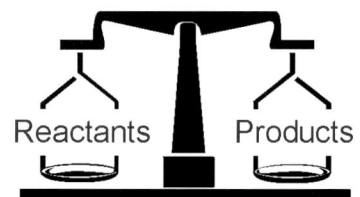

Reactants   Products

Figure 29.18: *The mass of the products must equal the mass of the reactants.*

Photosynthesis

The importance of photosynthesis

The energy that supports life on Earth starts with a reaction that takes energy from sunlight and stores it as chemical bonds in molecules of glucose. This reaction is called photosynthesis. Photosynthesis occurs mostly in plants; however, a few bacteria are also capable of photosynthesis. Animals (including ourselves) also get energy from photosynthesis, by eating plants or other animals that eat plants. Nearly all energy in living things can be traced to this important reaction.

The photosynthesis reaction

$$6\,CO_2 \;+\; 6\,H_2O \;\xrightarrow{\text{light}}\; C_6H_{12}O_6 \;+\; 6\,O_2$$

Carbon dioxide   Water   Glucose   Oxygen

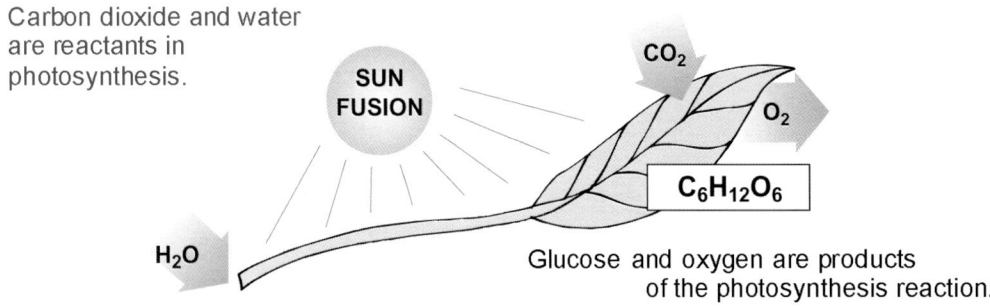

Carbon dioxide and water are reactants in photosynthesis.

Glucose and oxygen are products of the photosynthesis reaction.

Photosynthesis releases oxygen

A second useful product of photosynthesis besides energy is oxygen. Without plants, the Earth's atmosphere would have no oxygen, and could not support life. Although oxygen is a very common element, it is usually trapped by rocks and minerals in molecules like calcium carbonate ($CaCO_3$).

Photosynthesis removes CO_2

A third crucial function of photosynthesis is to remove carbon dioxide from the atmosphere. For every glucose molecule produced, six molecules of carbon dioxide are removed from the air, and six molecules of oxygen are produced. Carbon dioxide absorbs infrared radiation and therefore traps heat in the atmosphere. If too much carbon dioxide is present, the Earth cannot cool itself by radiating energy into space. Higher levels of carbon dioxide may be responsible for the warming of our planet by several degrees over the past 200 years.

Respiration

$$C_6H_{12}O_6 \;+\; 6\,O_2 \;\longrightarrow\; 6\,CO_2 \;+\; 6\,H_2O$$

Animals who eat plants get energy by breaking up glucose molecules. This process is called respiration. The reactions of respiration proceed in many steps, but the end result is that glucose and oxygen are used up and carbon dioxide and water are produced.

The oxygen required by living animals is used for respiration, as you can see from the chemical reaction above. In the history of life on Earth, plants evolved first and the oxygen in the planet's atmosphere was created by photosynthesis. Animals evolved later, once the atmosphere had accumulated sufficient oxygen.

606

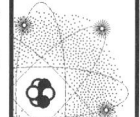

Application: Energy from Gasoline

Almost 40 percent of all the energy we use comes from petroleum (oil). Two thirds of the petroleum used is for cars and trucks in the form of gasoline and diesel fuel. Petroleum is created over millions of years by the decay of plants and animals through chemical reactions deep in the Earth. Petroleum is not a single substance but a complex mixture of many substances, most of them compounds of hydrogen and carbon, with smaller amounts of oxygen, nitrogen, and sulfur.

Refining   A process called refining separates petroleum into molecules with different numbers of carbon atoms. The smaller molecules are used in gasoline. Heavier molecules become kerosene and heating oil. The heaviest molecules become tar and asphalt used for road building (Figure 29.19).

Range of molecule sizes	End use
$C_1 - C_{12}$	Gasoline and light fuels, such as aviation fuel
$C_{12} - C_{18}$	Kerosene and heating oil
$C_{19} - C_{30}$	Grease, motor oil, wax
$C_{31} - C_{36+}$	Tar and asphalt

The reactions of burning gasoline   When one kilogram of gasoline is burned in oxygen, about 40 million joules of energy are released. In a perfect reaction, all the hydrocarbon molecules are completely burned to yield carbon dioxide and water. Unfortunately, in an engine not all the fuel burns completely and pollutants such as carbon monoxide are also formed. Impurities in fuel, such as sulfur and nitrogen in the air, also have reactions that form pollutants such as oxides of nitrogen and sulfuric acid.

Perfect combustion reaction

$$2\,C_8H_{18} + 25\,O_2 \xrightarrow{\text{spark}} 16\,CO_2 + 18\,H_2O + energy$$

Iso-octane   Oxygen   Carbon   Water
dioxide

Actual combustion reaction

$$2\,C_8H_{18} + 27\,O_2 + N_2 + S \xrightarrow{\text{spark}} 15\,CO_2 + CO + 17\,H_2O + 2\,NO + H_2SO_4 + energy$$

Iso-octane Oxygen Nitrogen Sulfur   Carbon   Carbon   Water   Nitrogen   Sulfuric
                            dioxide monoxide   oxides   acid

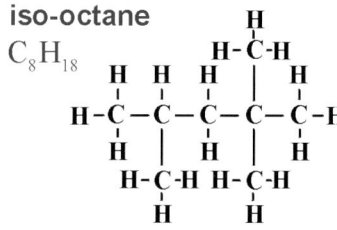

Figure 29.19: *Some of the many molecules found in gasoline. These are examples of hydrocarbons, molecules made with only hydrogen and carbon.*

Gasoline engines and fuels

How engines work
Car engines use the expansion of hot gas from burning gasoline to make power. As shown in Figure 29.20, the spark plug makes a spark to start the reaction. The hot gas expands and pushes against the piston to turn the engine. The engine works most efficiently if the expansion creates a smooth strong push against the piston. If the gasoline burns too fast, the piston gets a single hard slam instead of a smooth push. Excessive force on the piston causes a knocking or pinging sound and can damage the engine.

What octane rating of gasoline means
Car engines work best with gasoline that burns relatively slowly and smoothly. The octane rating of a gasoline is a measure of how fast it burns. The higher the octane number, the *slower* and more evenly the gasoline burns. The molecule *iso-octane* burns slowly and smoothly and has an octane value of 100. The molecule *n-heptane* (Figure 29.19) burns extremely fast and is assigned an octane rating of 0. A gasoline with an octane rating of 87 burns at the same rate as a mixture of 87 percent *iso-octane* and 13 percent *n-heptane*. New car engines are designed to work with 86 or 87 octane gasoline. An older engine designed for 89 octane gasoline may not run well on 87 octane because the burn rate is too fast.

How high-octane gasoline is produced
Most of the molecules in refined petroleum are straight-chain hydrocarbons, with good examples being *n-heptane* and *butane* (Figure 29.19). Molecules that have straight chain structures like *n-heptane* are fast burning. Molecules that have branches like *iso-octane* are slower burning. To raise the octane number, refined gasoline is processed by a slow heating process in the presence of the minerals silicon dioxide (SiO_2) and aluminum oxide (Al_2O_3). This extra heating process is called cracking and is why high-octane gasoline is more expensive. Cracking splits up long chain molecules into shorter molecules with more branching.

Gasohol
Many other fuels are being researched as replacements for gasoline. Ethyl and methyl alcohol (Figure 29.21) burn cleaner than straight gasoline because the molecules already contain some oxygen. To reduce smog pollution, some areas sell a blend of gasoline and 10 percent alcohol called *gasohol*. Because alcohol burns slower than gasoline, adding 10 percent alcohol raises the octane rating by 2.5 to 3 points.

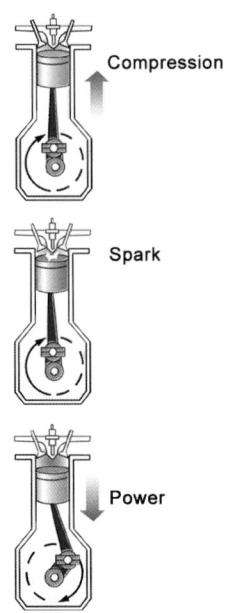

Figure 29.20: *Hot gas expanding against a piston pushes the piston down to turn the engine.*

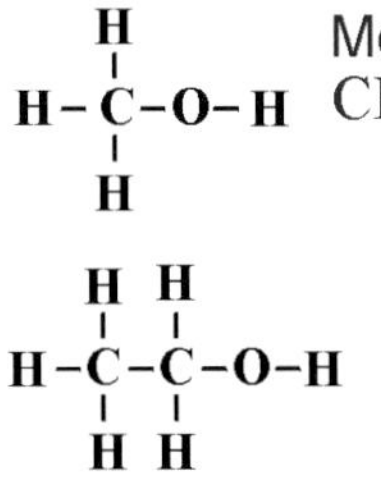

Figure 29.21: *Ethyl and methyl alcohol are blended with gasoline to reduce pollution.*

Chapter 29 Review

Vocabulary Review

Match the following terms with the correct definition. There is one extra definition in the list that will not match any of the terms.

Set One

1. element
2. compound
3. mixture
4. solvent
5. heterogeneous

a. Mixture that is the same throughout
b. Component parts can be separated
c. Substance which contains more than one type of atom
d. Substance which contains only one type of atom
e. Substance in which dissolved materials move and separate
f. Mixture which does not appear the same throughout

Set Two

1. valence
2. covalent bond
3. Lewis dot diagram
4. alkali metals
5. ionic bond

a. Formed as electrons are shared between atoms
b. Chemically similar, active elements with one valence electron
c. Formed as electrons are transferred from one atom to another
d. Formed when atoms exchange or share electrons
e. Electrons that make chemical bonds
f. Used to represent electrons available for bonding

Set Three

1. pH
2. amino acids
3. products
4. activation energy
5. endothermic

a. Substances produced by a chemical reaction
b. Measure of H_3O^+ ions in a solution
c. Reactions that absorb more energy than they give off
d. Molecules from which proteins are built
e. Required to break bonds so a chemical reaction can occur
f. Heating process that produces shorter molecules with branches

609

Concept review

1. Strawberry Jello® is a homogeneous mixture, but strawberry Jello® containing mixed fruit is a heterogeneous mixture. Explain the basis for the distinction made between the two types of Jello® mixtures.

2. Emily and Kayla are mixing chemicals according to their instructor's directions. They are asked to indicate whether or not a chemical reaction takes place in each instance. List at least four indicators they might look for as evidence that a chemical reaction is taking place.

3. "Fish swim in a solution, moving through the solvent and breathing one of the solutes." Explain this statement using the terms *solution, solvent,* and *solute.*

4. "Properties of substances are the properties of the *molecules*, not of the *elements* in the molecule." Use an example of a compound produced that illustrates the statement above.

5. All alkali metals have similar chemical characteristics. Noble gases behave like one another. Alkali metals do not behave like noble gases. Explain what makes elements similar to those in their group but uniquely different from elements not in their group.

6. Diagrams of two fictitious elements, dimeum (Di) and gummium (Gu) are shown below represented by Lewis dot diagrams. Compare the chemical activity of these two elements.

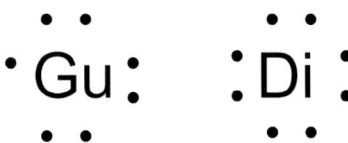

7. Why are atoms more often found combined as molecules rather than as single atoms in nature?

8. What factor determines whether ionic or covalent bonds will form between two elements?

9. In your grandfather's younger years, children sometimes "had their mouths washed out with soap" for using foul language. On good days, granddad might have been rewarded with the taste of lemonade made from freshly squeezed lemons. When comparing soap and lemonade, one is an acid, the other a base.

   a. How can you tell the difference?

   b. What is the approximate pH of each?

10. Carbon is an extremely important element because all life on Earth is based upon its presence in thousands of different molecules. What is the basis for carbon's inclusion in such a wide variety of molecules?

11. List the products and reactants in the chemical reaction shown as an equation below.
$$CH_4 + 2O_2 \rightarrow CO_2 + 2H_2O$$

12. As a cake bakes in the oven, baking soda decomposes to form the following three things: sodium carbonate, water and carbon dioxide. ($2NaHCO_3 \rightarrow Na_2CO_3 + H_2O + CO_2$) The carbon dioxide produced causes the cake to rise. If the oven is turned off, the baking stops. What type of reaction does the baking of a cake represent?

13. What conditions must be met for a chemical equation to be considered balanced?

14. Write the steps to find the mass required or produced for each reactant or product.

15. List three functions crucial to the survival of life on Earth which are performed by the chemical reaction known as photosynthesis. Explain the importance of each function.

16. If pure iso-octane gasoline is burned, it produces carbon dioxide and water and yields energy. Why is there such concern over the products of gasoline combustion engines?

17. The powerful, explosive force of dynamite comes from a decomposition reaction. Heat, electricity or light is usually added to start the reaction. What name would be given to these forms of energy when referring to this reaction?

18. Examine the diagrams of iso-octane and n-heptane. Iso-octane is rated at a higher octane than n-heptane. What gives iso-octane a higher octane rating than n-heptane?

Problems

1. Write a balanced equation for the each of the following reactions:

    a. $Al + H_2SO_4 \rightarrow Al_2(SO_4)_3 + H_2$

    b. $Zn + AgNO_3 \rightarrow Zn(NO_3)_2 + Ag$

    c. $Ag_2SO_4 + AlCl_3 \rightarrow AgCl + Al_2(SO_4)_3$

    d. $C_2H_6 + O_2 \rightarrow CO_2 + H_2O$

2. Find the mass of each molecule in atomic mass units (amu). Use Table 29.2 on page 605.

    a. C_2H_6

    b. PCl_3

    c. N_2O_5

3. For the reaction $MgCO_3 \rightarrow MgO + CO_2$ calculate the amount of MgO produced if 84.3 kilograms of $MgCO_3$ is used. Use Table 29.2 on page 605.

4. For the reaction $2C_3H_6 + 9O_2 \rightarrow 6CO_2 + 6H_2O$, how much C_3H_6 is required to produce 792 kilograms of CO_2? Use Table 29.2 on page 605.

5. Label each of the following using one (or more) of the following to classify it: *pure substance, solution, heterogeneous mixture,* or *homogeneous mixture.*

    a. salt in a shaker

    b. salt and pepper in one shaker

    c. tossed salad

    d. air

    e. petroleum

    f. n-Heptane

    g. powdered drink

    h. gravel in a bucket of water

    i. salt water

6. For each of the following decide the type of change indicated and label the event as a physical *(P)* or chemical *(C)* change.

    a. Hot, molten lead for making black-powder shot hardens in the mold

    b. As the cap is removed from a bottle of soda, bubbles rise

    c. Lead nitrate solution added to sodium iodide solution produces a yellow solid.

    d. As ammonium nitrate is added to water in a beaker, the beaker becomes cold.

    e. When calcium carbonate is added to hydrochloric acid, bubbles of gas form

    f. When you blow in a straw in your glass of milk, bubbles rise to the surface.

    g. When water is heated on a stove, the temperature rises.

    h. Refining separates petroleum into molecules with different numbers of carbon atoms.

    i. Cracking splits long chain molecules into shorter branched molecules.

7. Examine the Lewis dot diagrams for the atoms pictured. Redraw the fluorine and lithium atoms combined as a molecule. Also redraw the nitrogen and three hydrogen atoms combined as a molecule. For each, state whether the bonding is covalent or ionic.

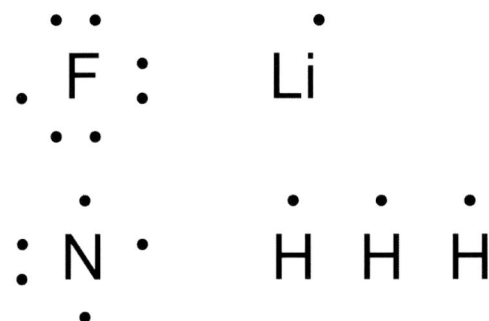

8. Label the molecules listed as organic *(O)* or inorganic *(I)*.

   a. CH_3COOH

   b. H_2O

   c. CH_4

   d. $C_6H_{12}O_6$

9. Show by calculation that the mass of the chemical reactants shown in the equation below is the same as the mass of the products. What law of nature is demonstrated? Use Table 29.2 on page 605.
$$Ca(OH)_2 + CO_2 \rightarrow CaCO_3 + H_2O$$

10. State whether each of the following bonds is ionic or covalent:

    a. C - C

    b. Na - Cl

    c. C - N

    d. C - O

    e. Ca - Cl

11. Identify the correct group or groups of elements described in each of the following statements. Use the "Periodic Table of the Elements" to help you answer these questions.

    a. All members of the halogen group are very active and contain 7 valence electrons.

    b. Called the transition metals, the group has complex bonding patterns.

    c. The noble gases are inert and do not commonly react with any other elements.

    d. The alkali metals have one valence electron and are very active.

    e. Containing the "element of life" on Earth, they are able to form four bonds.

12. Balance the equation below and use it to answer the questions that follow.
$$NH_3 + O_2 \rightarrow NO + H_2O$$

    a. How many atoms of each kind are present in the reactants?

    b. How many atoms of each kind are present in the products?

    c. How many molecules are present on the reactant side of the equation?

    d. How many molecules are present on the product side of the equation?

    e. To be considered balanced, what must be the same on both sides of the chemical equation?

612

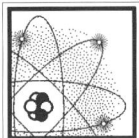

Unit 9
The Atom

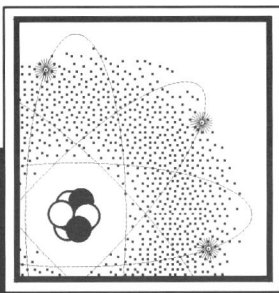

Chapter 30

Nuclear Reactions and Radiation

Objectives for Chapter 30

By the end of this chapter you should be able to:

1. Describe the cause and types of radioactivity.
2. Explain why radioactivity occurs in terms of energy.
3. Use the concept of half-life to predict the decay of a radioactive isotope.
4. Write the equation for a simple nuclear reaction.
5. Describe the processes of fission and fusion.
6. Describe the difference between ionizing and nonionizing radiation.
7. Use the graph of energy versus atomic number to determine whether a nuclear reaction uses or releases energy.

Terms and vocabulary words

radioactive	alpha decay	beta decay	gamma decay	radiation
isotope	radioactive decay	energy barrier	intensity	inverse square law
shielding	fission reaction	CAT scan	ionizing	nonionizing
ultraviolet	fusion reaction	Geiger counter	rem	nuclear waste
neutron	antimatter	x-ray	neutrino	background radiation
dose	fallout	detector	half-life	

30.1 Radioactivity

You would be very surprised if you saw a bus turn itself into two cars and a van. A radioactive atom does something almost as strange. If left alone, a radioactive atom spontaneously turns into other kinds of atoms. The process releases energy and can produce elements that would not otherwise be found in nature, like radon gas. Although radioactivity is a natural process, it can also be created by human technology. This section talks about radioactivity.

The discovery of radioactivity

The discovery of radioactivity
The word radioactivity was first used by Marie Curie in 1898. A brilliant and tenacious experimenter, Curie noticed that minerals containing uranium gave off some kind of invisible energy that could expose photographic film. She invented the word radioactivity to describe the property of certain substances to give off invisible "radiations" that could be detected by films.

Three kinds of radioactivity
Many scientists pursued the mystery of radioactivity. They quickly learned that there were three different kinds of radiation given off by radioactive materials. The scientists called them "rays" because the radiation carried energy and moved in straight lines, like light rays. Alpha rays came from uranium and could be stopped easily by a thin sheet of material such as paper. Beta rays had more penetrating power. Gamma rays were hardest of all to stop. Many centimeters of a dense material (like lead) were needed to stop gamma rays (Figure 30.1).

Radioactive decay
We now know that radioactivity comes from the nucleus of the atom. If the nucleus has too many neutrons, or is unstable for any other reason, the atom undergoes radioactive decay. The word *decay* means to *break down* and in radioactive decay, the nucleus breaks down and forms a different nucleus. Almost all elements have some isotopes that are radioactive and other isotopes that are not radioactive. For example, three isotopes of carbon occur naturally: C^{12}, C^{13}, and C^{14}. Both C^{12} and C^{13} have stable nuclei and are not radioactive. C^{14} has one too many neutrons and is radioactive because the unstable nucleus of C^{14} decays into stable nitrogen-14 (N^{14}), giving off beta radiation in the process (Figure 30.2). Alpha and beta radiations are particles emitted by the decay of a nucleus.

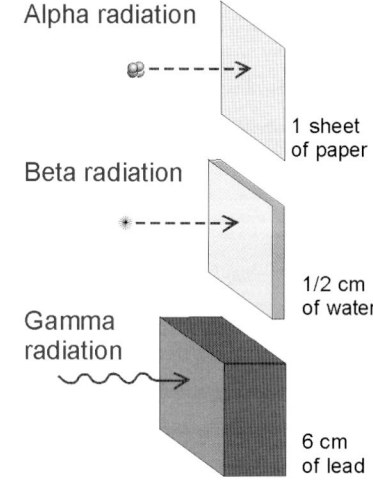

Figure 30.1: *What it takes to stop alpha, beta, and gamma radiation of equal energy.*

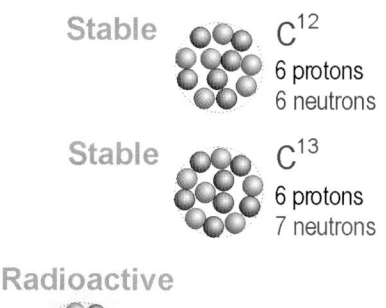

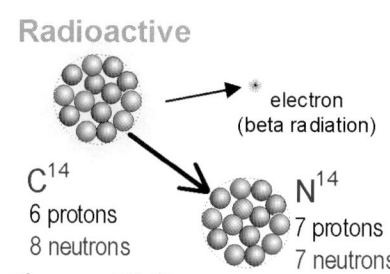

Figure 30.2: *Three isotopes of carbon, one of which is radioactive carbon-14 (C14).*

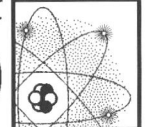
The three types of radioactivity

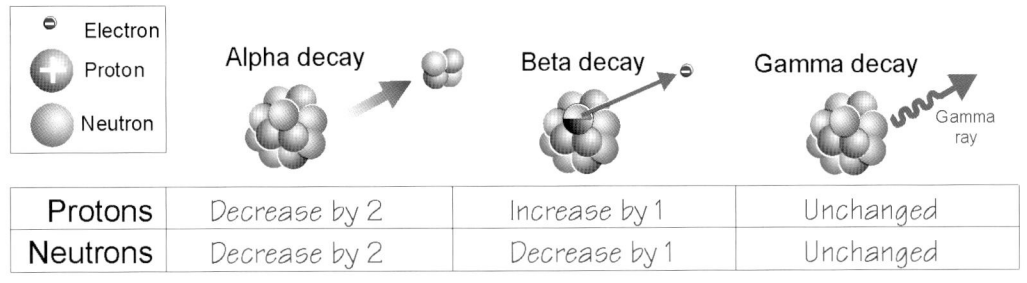

	Alpha decay	Beta decay	Gamma decay
Protons	Decrease by 2	Increase by 1	Unchanged
Neutrons	Decrease by 2	Decrease by 1	Unchanged

Alpha radiation   In alpha decay, the nucleus ejects two protons and two neutrons. Check the periodic table and you can quickly show that two protons and two neutrons are the nucleus of a helium-4 (He^4) atom. Alpha radiation is actually fast-moving He^4 nuclei. When alpha decay occurs, the atomic number is reduced by two because two protons are removed. The atomic mass is reduced by four because two neutrons go along with the two protons. For example, uranium-238 undergoes alpha decay to become thorium-234.

Beta radiation   Beta decay occurs when a neutron in the nucleus splits into a proton and an electron. The proton stays behind in the nucleus, but the high energy electron is ejected from the nucleus and is the source of beta radiation. This fast electron is still called a beta particle because it is the source of the beta rays observed by Henri Bequerel in 1895. During beta decay the atomic number increases by one because one new proton is created. The atomic mass stays about the same because neutrons and protons have nearly identical mass.

Gamma radiation   Gamma decay is how the nucleus gets rid of excess energy. Gamma decay is not truly a decay reaction in the sense that the nucleus becomes something different. In gamma decay the nucleus emits a high-energy photon (electromagnetic radiation), but the number of protons and neutrons stays the same. The nucleus decays from a state of high energy to a state of lower energy. Gamma ray photons are energetic enough to break apart other atoms, making them dangerous to living things. Gamma rays require heavy shielding to stop. Alpha and beta decay are often accompanied by gamma radiation from the same nucleus.

How a smoke detector works

Smoke detectors contain a tiny amount of americium-241 (Am^{241}), a radioactive isotope that emits alpha radiation. When an alpha particle hits a molecule of air, it knocks off an electron, making the air ionized. The positive ion and negative electron are collected by positive- and negative-charged metal plates attached to the battery in the smoke detector. The flow of ions and electrons creates a tiny electric current that is measured by the electronics of the smoke detector.

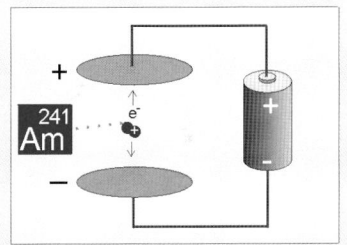

When smoke is in the air, particles of smoke interrupt the flow of ions and electrons. The electric current collected by the metal plates drops. The circuit in the smoke detector senses the drop in current and sounds the alarm.

Radioactive decay releases energy

Energy and radioactivity

Radioactive decay gives off energy. The energy comes from the conversion of mass into energy. If you started with one kilogram of C^{14} it would decay into 0.999988 kg of N^{14}. The difference of 0.012 grams is converted directly into energy via Einstein's formula $E = mc^2$. Because the speed of light (c) is such a large number, a tiny bit of mass generates a huge amount of energy. In fact, the energy released by the decay of one kilogram of C^{14} is equivalent to that released by 27,000 kilograms of gasoline! Fortunately, the decay of C^{14} takes a long time and the energy is released slowly, over thousands of years.

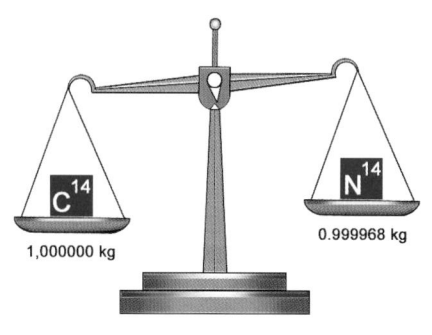

1,000,000 kg   0.999968 kg

Mass difference

$$\begin{array}{r} 1.000000 \text{ kg} \\ - 0.999988 \text{ kg} \\ \hline 0.000012 \text{ kg} \end{array}$$

Energy released

$$E = mc^2$$
$$= (0.000012 \text{ kg})(3 \times 10^8 \text{ m/sec})^2$$
$$= 1.1 \times 10^{12} \text{ joules}$$

Activation energy

The radioactive decay of C^{14} does not happen immediately because it takes a small input of energy to start the transformation from C^{14} to N^{14}. The energy needed to start the reaction is called an **energy barrier** (Figure 30.3). The decay of C^{14} is slow because the energy barrier is high compared with the energy of the reaction. The decay of radioactive O^{14} is much faster because the energy barrier is lower compared with the energy of the reaction.

Why radioactivity occurs

Radioactivity occurs because everything in nature tends to move toward lower energy. A ball rolls downhill to the lowest point. A hot cup of coffee cools down. Both are examples of systems that move from higher energy to lower energy over time. The same is true of the nucleus. A radioactive nucleus decays because the neutrons and protons have lower overall energy in the final nucleus than they had in the original one (Figure 30.4).

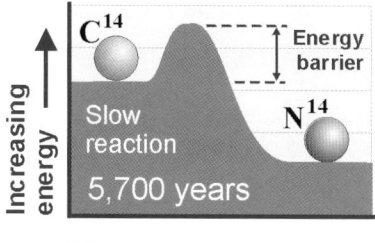

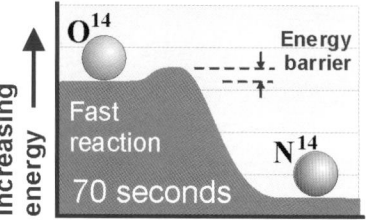

Figure 30.3: *The lower the energy barrier, the more likely the atom is to decay quickly.*

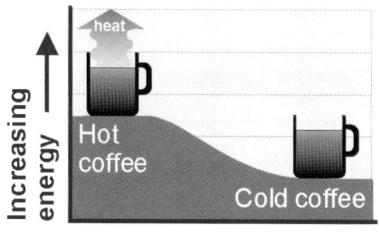

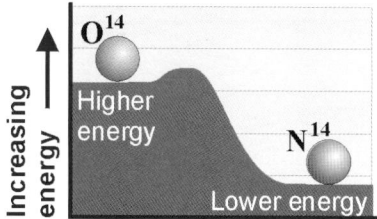

Figure 30.4: *Systems in nature tend to move toward lower energy. Radioactive decay allows the nucleus to rearrange itself to lower its energy.*

616

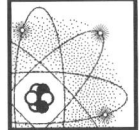

The half-life

Chance and radioactivity

Radioactive decay depends on chance. It is possible to predict the average behavior of lots of atoms, but impossible to predict when any one atom will decay. Flipping a coin is a good analogy. You cannot predict whether a specific toss will come up heads or tails. But, you can make a good prediction of the average outcome of 10,000 tosses. Since the chances are 50/50, out of 10,000 coin tosses you expect about 5,000 to be heads and about 5,000 to be tails. Since even small samples of ordinary materials contain many more then 10,000 atoms, it is possible to accurately predict the average rate of decay.

The half-life

One very useful prediction we can make is the half-life. The half-life is the time it takes for one half of the atoms in any sample to decay. For example, the half-life of carbon-14 is about 5,700 years. If you start out with 200 grams of C^{14}, 5,700 years later only 100 grams will still be C^{14}. The rest will have decayed to nitrogen-14 (Figure 30.5). If you wait another 5,700 years, half of your 100 remaining grams of C^{14} will decay, leaving 50 grams of C^{14} and 150 grams of N^{14}. Wait a third interval of 5,700 years, and you will be down to 25 grams of C^{14}. *One half of the atoms decay during every time interval of one half-life.*

The half-life of different isotopes varies greatly

The half-life of radioactive materials varies greatly. Uranium-238 (U^{238}) has a half-life of 4.5 billion years. It was created in the nuclear reactions of exploding stars, the remains of which condensed to form the solar system. We can still find uranium-238 on Earth because the half-life is so long. The isotope fluorine-18 (F^{18}) has a half-life of 1 hour, 50 minutes. This isotope is used in medicine. Hospitals have to make it when they need it because it decays so quickly. Any natural F^{18} decayed billions of years ago. Carbon-15 has a half-life of 2.3 seconds. Scientists who make C^{15} in a laboratory have to use it immediately.

Radioactive decay series

Most radioactive materials decay in a series of reactions. For example, radon gas comes from the decay of uranium in the soil (Figure 30.6). Radon itself decays into lead in a chain of three alpha decays and two beta decays. Radon is a source of indoor air pollution in some houses that do not have adequate ventilation. Many people test for radon before buying a house.

Radioactive decay of C^{14}

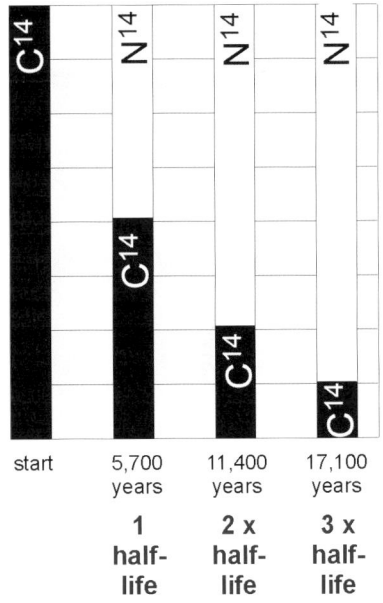

Figure 30.5: *After 5,700 years (one half-life), half of a 200-gram sample of C^{14} has decayed to N^{14}.*

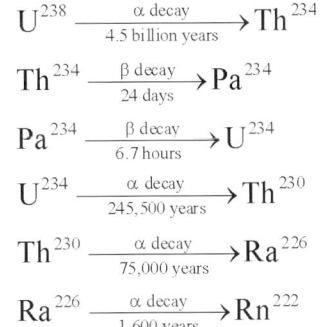

Figure 30.6: *The series of decay reactions that produces radon-222 (Ra^{222}) from uranium (U^{238}).*

Applications of radioactivity

Power from radioactivity
The power released by radioactive decay depends on the energy released by the reaction and on the half-life. Isotopes with a short half-life give off lots of energy in a short time and can be extremely dangerous. Isotopes with a long half-life (like carbon-14) give off only tiny amounts of power, and usually are much less dangerous. For example, spreading out the decay energy of one kilogram of C^{14} over its 5,700-year half-life yields an average power of about six watts. This is one-tenth the power of a 60-watt light bulb. Many satellites use radioactive decay for power because energy can be produced for a long time without refueling.

Carbon dating
Living things contain a large amount of carbon. The isotope carbon-14 is used by archeologists to determine age. C^{14} has a half-life of 5,700 years. We find C^{14} in the environment because it is constantly being produced in the upper atmosphere by cosmic rays—high energy particles from the sun and elsewhere in the universe. The ratio of carbon-14 to carbon-12 in the environment is a constant, determined by the balance between production and decay of C^{14}. As long as an organism is alive, it constantly exchanges carbon with the environment. The ratio of C^{14} to C^{12} in the organism stays the same ratio as in the environment.

How carbon dating works

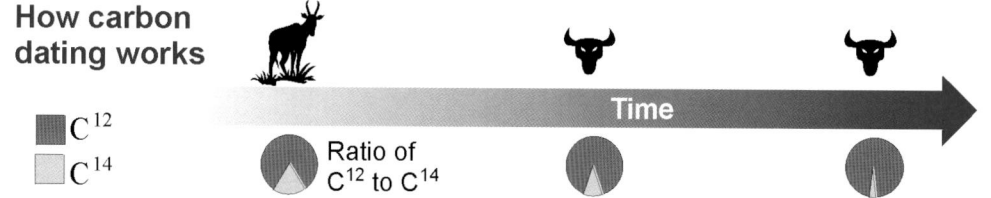

■ C^{12}
□ C^{14}

Ratio of C^{12} to C^{14}

Time

Why carbon dating works
When a living organism dies it stops exchanging carbon with the environment. All the carbon-12 in the organism remains because C^{12} is a stable isotope. Almost no new carbon-14 is created because most cosmic rays do not reach the ground. As the carbon-14 decays, the ratio of C^{14} to C^{12} slowly gets smaller with age. By measuring this ratio, an archeologist can tell how long it has been since the material was alive. Carbon dating works reliably up to about 10 times the half-life, or 57,000 years. After 10 half-lives there is not enough carbon-14 left to measure accurately. Carbon dating only works on material that has once been living, such as bone or wood.

Determine how much Carbon^{14} is left after 5 half-lives

A sample of 1,000 grams of the isotope C^{14} is created. The half-life of C^{14} is 5,700 years. How much C^{14} remains after 28,500 years?

1) You are asked for the amount of C^{14} left after 28,500 years.

2) You are given the half-life is 5,700 years.

3) One half the C^{14} decays every half-life.

4) 28,500 years is 5 times the half-life. The amount of C^{14} is reduced by half every 5,700 years.

Start: 1,000 grams

5,700 years: 500 grams

11,400 years: 250 grams

17,100 years: 125 grams

22,800 years, 62.5 grams

28,500 years, 31.2 grams

Answer = 31.2 grams

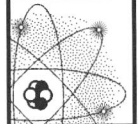

30.2 Radiation

The word radiation means the flow of energy through space. There are many forms of radiation. Light, radio waves, microwaves, and x-rays are forms of electromagnetic radiation. The energy in alpha and beta radiation comes from moving particles. Ultrasound is radiation of sound energy through the air. Many people mistakenly think of radiation as only associated with nuclear reactions. This section will explore the topic of radiation and how radiation affects matter.

Intensity

$$\text{Intensity} \atop (W/m^2) \quad I = \frac{P}{A} \quad {Power\ (W) \atop Area\ (m^2)}$$

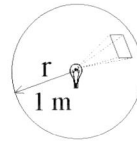

$$\text{Area}, \quad A = 4\pi r^2 = 12.6\ \text{m}^2$$

$$\text{Intensity}, \quad I = \frac{100\ \text{W}}{12.6\ \text{m}^2}$$
$$= 7.96\ \text{W/m}^2$$

Intensity

Definition of intensity — The intensity of radiation measures how much power flows per unit of area. On a clear day, the intensity of sunlight on the surface of the Earth is about 1,000 watts per square meter (W/m²). A good flashlight produces an intensity of about 100 W/m² in the brightest part of the beam at a distance of a half- meter.

The inverse square law — When radiation comes from a single point, the intensity decreases inversely as the square of the distance. This is called the inverse square law and it applies to all forms of radiation. If you get two times farther away from a radiation source, the intensity is reduced to one-fourth what it was (1/4 = 1/2²). If you get 10 times farther away, the intensity is reduced to one hundredth of what it was because 1 divided by 10² = 0.01. Figure 30.7 shows how the inverse square law works.

Radiation spreads out as it travels, lowering the intensity.

The inverse square law comes from geometry — The inverse square law is a property of geometry. Think of a 100-watt light bulb at the center of a sphere. The intensity at the surface of the sphere is 100 watts divided by the area of the sphere (4πr²). At twice the distance, the area of the sphere is four times greater. Since the same amount of power is spread over a larger area, the intensity goes down. Mathematically, the area goes up like the square of the radius, so the intensity goes down like the inverse square of the radius. This is the inverse square law.

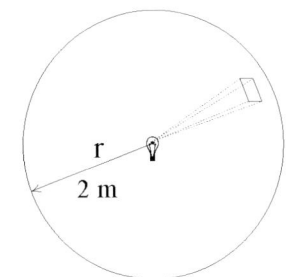

$$\text{Area}, \quad A = 4\pi r^2 = 50.4\ \text{m}^2$$

$$\text{Intensity}, \quad I = \frac{100\ \text{W}}{50.4\ \text{m}^2}$$
$$= 1.99\ \text{W/m}^2$$

Figure 30.7: *The inverse square law comes from the fact that the power in radiation is spread out over a sphere of radius (r).*

When is radiation harmful?

When radiation is harmful

Radiation becomes harmful when it has enough energy to remove electrons from atoms. The process of removing an electron from an atom is called ionization. Visible light is not harmful because each photon does not have enough energy to ionize an atom. Visible light is an example of nonionizing radiation. Ultraviolet (UV) light is harmful because an ultraviolet photon has enough energy to eject an electron from an atom. UV light is an example of ionizing radiation. Figure 30.8 shows the difference between the two categories of radiation.

Why ionizing radiation is dangerous

Ionizing radiation can be harmful because it can break chemical bonds in DNA and other important biological molecules. The human body constantly repairs itself from microscopic damage caused by naturally occurring, low intensity radiation. However, too much radiation overwhelms the body's ability to heal itself. For example, too much UV light from the sun causes sunburn and can damage your eyes. Exposure to prolonged high levels of ionizing radiation has been linked to cancer and other serious diseases.

Limit your exposure to ionizing radiation

It is wise to limit your exposure to ionizing radiation whenever possible. Limit your exposure to the sun's ultraviolet rays to avoid a higher risk of skin cancer. If you ever work with radioactive materials, keep your distance, use shielding materials, and do your work efficiently and quickly. Shielding materials, such as lead, block radiation. Distance also reduces exposure. Moving three times farther away reduces your exposure by 89 percent (inverse square law).

Measuring radiation absorbed by people

Ionizing radiation absorbed by people is measured in a unit called the rem. The total amount of radiation received by a person is called a dose, just like a dose of medicine. Radiation doses in people are measured in rems instead of watts because different kinds of radiation are absorbed differently by body tissues. For example, gamma rays are more dangerous than alpha particles because the skin stops alpha particles. Gamma rays can penetrate to internal organs. One watt of gamma radiation results in a dose of one rem. It takes 20 watts of alpha radiation to produce a dose of one rem. The safe limit for people who work with radiation is five rem per year. The average person absorbs about 0.3 rem per year from radiation sources in the environment.

Non-ionizing radiation
Energy is absorbed by electrons.

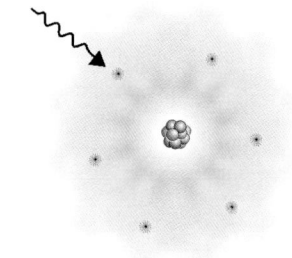

Ionizing radiation
Energy is enough to knock electrons out of the atom.

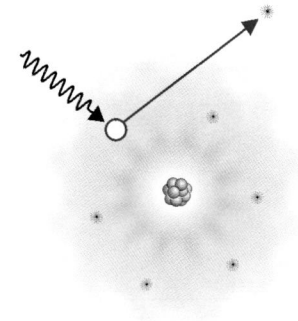

Figure 30.8: *The difference between ionizing and nonionizing radiation.*

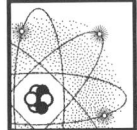

Sources of radiation

Background radiation Ionizing radiation is a natural part of our environment. There are two chief sources of radiation you will probably be exposed to: background radiation and radiation from medical procedures such as x-rays. Background radiation comes from the environment. Background radiation results in an average dose of 0.3 rem per year for someone living in the United States. Background radiation levels can vary widely from place to place. They can also vary based on the types of activities you do.

Sources of background radiation The chart in Figure 30.9 shows the average breakdown of background radiation in the United States. Uranium and other radioactive elements are part of the Earth. The decay of radioactive materials in rocks and soil is a source of natural radiation. Radioactive radon gas is present in the atmosphere, in very small quantities. Cosmic rays are another source of radiation. Cosmic rays are high-energy particles that come from outside our solar system. More than 10,000 cosmic ray particles pass through your body every second. Flying in a commercial plane increases your exposure to ionizing cosmic radiation because you are above much of the atmosphere. The atmosphere acts as a shield for this radiation. Human technology also contributes to radiation in the environment. The testing of nuclear weapons since 1945 has distributed a small amount of radioactive material all over the Earth. Radioactive material from nuclear weapons is called fallout, and contributes about 2% of the background radiation.

Radiation from the sun The sun is a source of radiation, both beneficial (light) and harmful (ultraviolet). Many scientists are concerned that thinning of the Earth's ozone layer will allow more harmful UV radiation to reach the planet's surface. Sunbathing increases your exposure to UV radiation.

Radiation from medical procedures Medical x-rays generate low doses of radiation. A typical chest x-ray produces a dose of 0.02 rem. A single x-ray produces less than 10 percent of the dose you get every year from environmental sources of radiation. That does not mean there is no risk from x-rays. It is just that the potential health benefit of an x-ray is usually worth whatever small increased risk there might be.

Environmental sources of α, β, γ radiation

(alpha, beta, and gamma only)

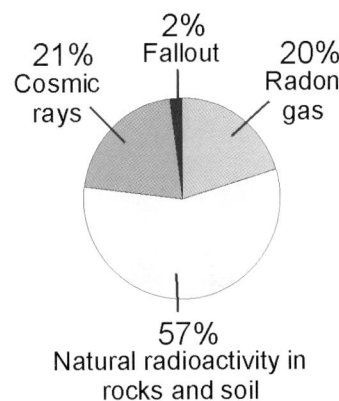

Figure 30.9: *The sources of background radiation from the environment.*

X-ray machines

X-rays and medical applications

X-rays are photons, like visible light photons only with much more energy. A typical medical x-ray photon has almost 100,000 times more energy than a photon of red light, and more that 10,000 times more than an ultraviolet photon from the sun. Unlike UV radiation, which does not have enough energy to get past human skin, x-rays have enough energy to penetrate deeply into the human body. There are two important medical uses for x-rays: to make images of the body (diagnostic x-rays) and to destroy unhealthy cells, such as cancer (therapeutic x-rays).

Diagnostic x-rays

Diagnostic x-rays are used to produce images of bones and teeth on x-ray film. X-ray film turns black when exposed to x-rays. Images on x-ray film are made by passing x-rays through the body and onto the film. Bones and teeth contain elements of higher atomic number, such as calcium. The inner electrons of heavier atoms such as calcium are in energy levels comparable to the energy of an x-ray photon. Electrons in calcium atoms are strong absorbers of x-rays because their energy levels match the x-ray photons. By comparison, the soft tissues of the body contain mostly light elements such as carbon, hydrogen, and oxygen. The energy levels of the lighter elements are much lower, so most x-rays pass right through. Bones appear white on x-ray film because the calcium atoms in bones absorb more of the x-ray photons than does the surrounding tissue (Figure 30.10). Modern diagnostic x-ray machines use highly sensitive film, so only very low doses of x-rays are needed to produce images.

Therapeutic x-rays

Therapeutic x-rays are used to destroy diseased tissue, such as cancer cells. Low levels of x-rays do not destroy cells, but high levels do. A typical therapeutic x-ray procedure uses many beams of x-rays. Each beam by itself is too weak to destroy cells. The beams are made to overlap at the place where the doctor wants to destroy diseased cells. The energy in the region of overlap is much higher because all the beams add up. This process can destroy diseased cells without killing healthy tissue. Figure 30.11 shows an illustration of how the multiple-beam treatment works.

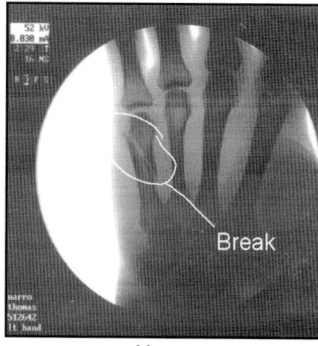

X-ray

Figure 30.10: *This x-ray shows a broken bone in one finger. Bones show white in x-ray film because they absorb x-rays more than surrounding tissue.*

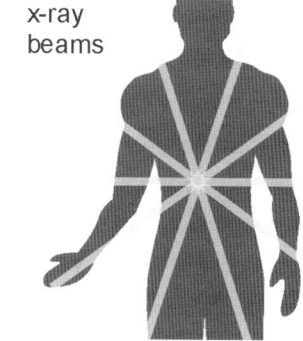

x-ray beams

Figure 30.11: *Multiple beams of x-rays are used in therapeutic treatments for cancer.*

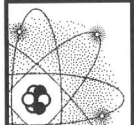

CAT scans

CAT scans use x-rays

The advent of powerful computers has made it possible to use diagnostic x-rays not only to produce pictures on x-ray film, but also to produce three-dimensional images of bones and other structures within the body. The process of creating such three-dimensional images is called computerized axial tomography, or CAT scan.

How a CAT scan is made

To produce a CAT scan, a computer controls an x-ray machine as it takes pictures of the body from different angles. Each single picture is like an ordinary x-ray. The three-dimensional image is constructed by the computer from combining pictures of the same place taken from different angles.

Three-dimensional images from multiple views

To see how this process works, imagine you are controlling a robot rover mapping an unknown part of another planet. Your only way to see the planet is with a TV camera mounted on the rover. You stop the rover and take a picture that shows two rocks in the distance. From your camera position the rocks appear separated by four meters (Figure 30.12). But one view is not enough information to reconstruct a map showing where the rocks are. A second view from a different angle solves the problem. From the second position, the rocks appear seven meters apart. There is only one way the rocks can be arranged so they appear 4 m apart in one view and 7 m apart in a second view taken from a known position relative to the first. Two views allow you to uniquely determine the positions of the two rocks.

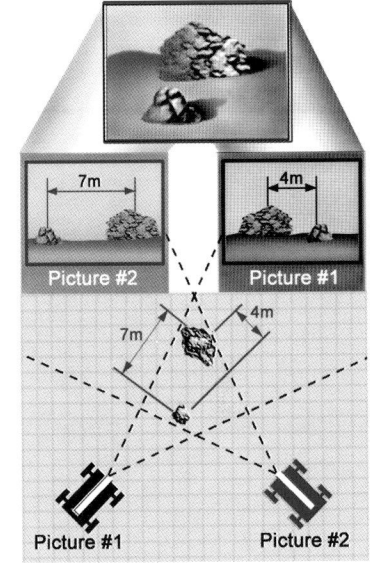

Figure 30.12: *How three-dimensional information can be determined by combining two views of the same objects.*

CAT scans compared with x-rays

CAT scans use a similar multi-image principle to the one described for the rover. A single x-ray exposure is like a single TV picture. It shows how far apart the bones and other body parts are, but not how deep in the body they are. By taking multiple x-ray images from multiple angles and combining the image information in a computer, incredibly detailed, three-dimensional renderings of the body can be produced. X-ray imaging by computer is far more sensitive than x-ray film, so images of virtually all parts of the body can be obtained. For example, CAT scans can show detailed, three-dimensional images of blood vessels in the heart or tumors in the brain, all without any surgery (Figure 30.13).

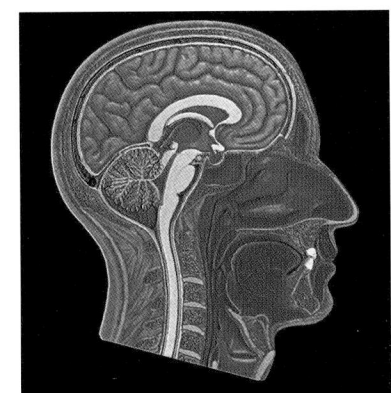

Figure 30.13: *The three-dimensional image from a CAT scan.*

Measuring radiation

Observing what you cannot see

People who work with radiation use radiation detectors to tell when radiation is present and to measure its intensity. You are already familiar with one radiation detector, your own eyes. Unfortunately, ionizing radiation is invisible to the eye. For example, the ultraviolet light that tans your skin on a sunny day is invisible ionizing radiation. You may think the bright light you see is what gives you the tan—or burn. But in fact what you see is only the visible portion of sunlight. The ultraviolet portion of sunlight is invisible. Fortunately, UV radiation from the sun is always accompanied by bright visible light as well. The presence of bright visible light from the sun tells you the harmful UV radiation is there as well.

Invisibility adds to the danger of radiation

Other types of ionizing radiation cannot be so easily detected by the human body, directly or indirectly. High temperatures are dangerous but people work with hot things all the time because you can feel heat in time to pull away before getting burned. In the experimental development of x-rays, researchers were badly hurt because you cannot feel harmful levels of ionizing radiation. Radiation damage to cells does not become evident for hours or days after the exposure. Thus the extent of a sunburn is often not known until the day after. One of the great dangers of ionizing radiation is that you cannot tell you are being hurt until it is too late and the damage has been done. People who work around ionizing radiation use many types of detectors to warn them of unsafe conditions.

The Geiger counter

The Geiger counter is a type of radiation detector invented to measure x-rays and other ionizing radiation. A Geiger counter is a gas-filled tube with electrodes on either end (Figure 30.14). The electrodes are connected to a power source that creates a voltage of several hundred volts between the electrodes. Normally, the gas in the tube is neutral and no electric current flows. However, if the tube is exposed to ionizing radiation, positive and negative ions are created in the gas by the radiation. These ions carry electric current, which can be measured. The more radiation that is present, the larger the current becomes. The amount of current in the Geiger counter is a measure of how much radiation is present. Geiger counters are routinely used to measure all types of ionizing radiation.

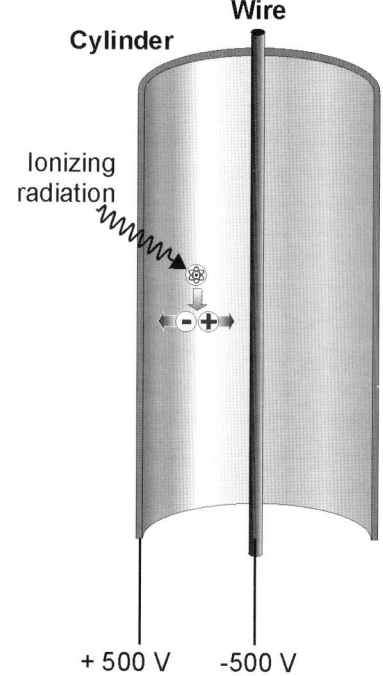

Figure 30.14: *A Geiger counter detects radiation by electrically collecting ions of gas. The cylinder is positive and the wire in the center is negative. Ionizing radiation knocks electrons from molecules of gas in the cylinder. The ions and electrons make an electric current that is proportional to the intensity of the radiation.*

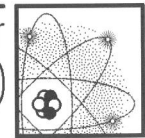

30.3 Nuclear Reactions and Energy

A nuclear reaction is any process that changes the nucleus of an atom. Radioactive decay is one form of nuclear reaction. Because the nucleus is affected, a nuclear reaction can change one element into another. You can even create a nuclear reaction that turns lead into gold. The ability to change elements is one important way nuclear reactions are different from chemical reactions. Remember, a chemical reaction can rearrange atoms into different molecules but cannot change atoms of one element into atoms of another element.

Nuclear reactions

Equations for nuclear reactions   Nuclear reactions are written in a similar way as chemical reactions. The mass number of each isotope is written by the element symbol. Individual particles such as electrons (e-) protons (p) and neutrons (n) may also appear in a reaction. The example below is a reaction that combines helium and carbon to make oxygen.

A nuclear reaction

$$He^4 + C^{12} \rightarrow O^{16} + \text{energy}$$

Mass is not conserved in nuclear reactions   If you could take apart a nucleus and separate all of its protons and neutrons, the separated protons and neutrons would have more mass than the nucleus did. This bizarre fact is explained by Einstein's formula ($E = mc^2$), which tells us that mass can be converted to energy, and vice versa. The mass of a nucleus is reduced by the energy that is released when the nucleus comes together. Nuclear reactions can convert mass into energy.

Energy is higher in nuclear reactions   Nuclear reactions involve much more energy than chemical reactions. The energy in a nuclear reaction is much greater because nuclear reactions involve the strong nuclear force. Chemical reactions only involve electrical forces between electrons distant from the nucleus. The electrical force acting on an electron far from the nucleus is much smaller than the strong force acting on a proton or neutron in the nucleus itself. The difference in strength between the forces involved is the reason chemical reactions are much less energetic than nuclear reactions.

Turning lead into gold

For almost 2,000 years people have sought a way to turn lead and other metals into gold. The many clever schemes people invented were always unsuccessful.

With today's understanding of nuclear physics, it is now possible to make lead into gold. We don't do it because the process is much more expensive than gold itself.

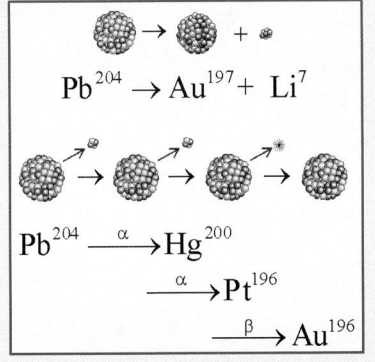

$$Pb^{204} \rightarrow Au^{197} + Li^7$$

$$Pb^{204} \xrightarrow{\alpha} Hg^{200}$$
$$\xrightarrow{\alpha} Pt^{196}$$
$$\xrightarrow{\beta} Au^{196}$$

Gold (Au^{197}) has 79 protons and 118 neutrons. The closest stable isotope of lead is lead-204 (Pb^{204}), with 82 protons and 122 neutrons. One possible reaction to turn lead into gold would be to split away a lithium-7 (Li^7) nucleus (three protons and four neutrons). A second possibility would be to make the lead undergo two alpha decays and a beta decay to the isotope Au^{196}. Neither of these occurs in nature because lead is stable!

The source of energy in nuclear reactions

Energy of the nucleus   When separate protons and neutrons come together in a nucleus, energy is released. Think about many balls rolling downhill (Figure 30.15). The balls roll down under the force of gravity and potential energy is released. Protons and neutrons are attracted by the strong nuclear force and also release energy as they come together. The more energy that is released, the lower the energy of the final nucleus. The energy of the nucleus depends on the mass and atomic number. The nucleus with the lowest energy is iron-56 with 26 protons and 30 neutrons (the low point on the graph below). Protons and neutrons assembled into nuclei of carbon or uranium have higher energy (and are higher on the graph).

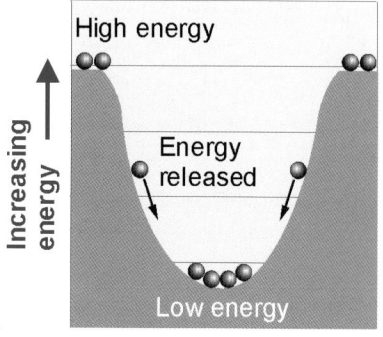

Figure 30.15: *The force of gravity pulls balls down to the lowest point in a valley. Energy is released as the balls roll down and they have the lowest energy at the bottom of the valley.*

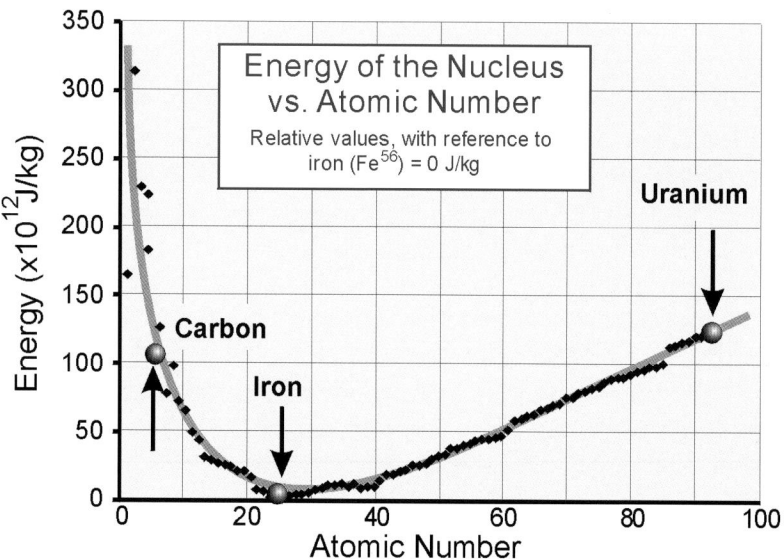

Nuclear energies are very large   The graph above compares the energy of the nucleus in one kilogram of matter for elements 2 (helium) through 92 (uranium). Note that the units of energy are hundreds of trillions (10^{12}) of joules per kilogram of material! Nuclear reactions often involve huge amounts of energy as protons and neutrons are rearranged to form different nuclei. A nuclear reaction releases energy when it produces a nucleus that is lower down on the graph. A nuclear reaction uses energy when it creates a nucleus that is higher up on the graph.

Different nuclei have different energies

Two opposing forces are at work in the nucleus. The electromagnetic force causes protons to repel each other. The strong nuclear force causes protons and neutrons to attract each other. The iron-56 nucleus has the best balance between the two effects. Lighter nuclei are less tightly bound (more energy) because there are too few neutrons and protons contributing to the strong attractive force. Heavy nuclei are less tightly bound (higher energy) because the repulsion from the protons competes with the attraction from the strong force.

Fusion reactions

Fusion reactions | A fusion reaction is a nuclear reaction that combines, or fuses, two smaller nuclei into a larger nucleus. Fusion reactions can release energy if the final nucleus is lower on the energy of the nucleus graph (Figure 30.16). For example, a kilogram of carbon (atomic number 6) contains 104 trillion joules (TJ) of nuclear energy according on the graph. Two carbon atoms have a total of 12 protons and 12 neutrons. These same particles can combine to make one nucleus of magnesium-24 (Mg^{24}). According to the graph, a kilogram of Mg^{24} has 48 TJ of nuclear energy. If the protons and neutrons in a kilogram of carbon are rearranged to form magnesium, about 56 trillion joules of energy is released.

Fusion reactions need very high temperatures | It is difficult to make fusion reactions occur because positively charged nuclei repel each other. The attraction from the strong nuclear force has a very short reach. Two nuclei must get very close for the attractive strong nuclear force to overcome the repulsive electric force. One way to make two nuclei get close is to make the temperature very high. The temperature must be high enough to strip all the electrons from around the nucleus. If temperature is raised even higher, nuclei slam together with enough energy to almost touch, allowing the strong force to take over and initiate a fusion reaction. The hydrogen fusion reactions in the core of the sun occur at temperature of about 15 million degrees Celsius.

Density and fusion power | It takes high density as well as high temperature to make significant energy from fusion reactions. A single fusion reaction makes a lot of energy for a single atom. But a single atom is tiny. To produce enough power to light a single 100-watt bulb requires 10^{14} fusion reactions per second. The density of atoms must be large enough to get a high rate of fusion reactions.

Fusion in the sun | The Sun and other stars make energy from fusion reactions. The temperature at the core of the sun is about 15 million Celsius. The density is so high that a tablespoon of material weighs more than a ton. The primary fusion reaction that happens in the sun combines hydrogen nuclei to make helium, converting two protons and two electrons into two neutrons along the way. All of the energy reaching the Earth from the sun comes ultimately from fusion reactions in the sun's core.

Energy release by a fusion reaction

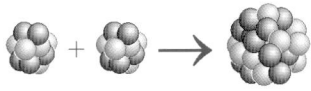

$$C^{12} + C^{12} \rightarrow Mg^{24} + energy$$

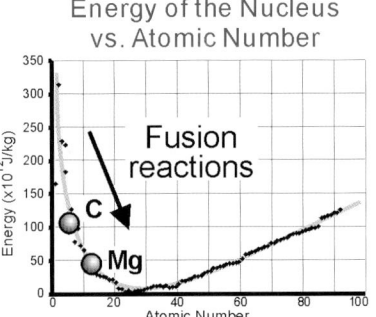

Energy of the Nucleus vs. Atomic Number

+104 TJ   Energy of carbon (C) nucleus

-48 TJ   Energy of magnesium (Mg) nucleus

+56 TJ   Energy released by fusion of carbon into magnesium.

Figure 30.16: *An example of a fusion reaction.*

Fission reactions

Fission reactions A fission reaction splits up a large nucleus into smaller pieces. For elements heavier than iron, breaking the nucleus up into smaller pieces releases nuclear energy (Figure 30.17). For example, a kilogram of uranium (atomic number 92) has about 123 trillion joules (TJ) of nuclear energy. A fission reaction splits the uranium nucleus into two pieces. Both pieces have a lower atomic number, and are lower on the energy of the nucleus graph. The average energy of the nucleus for a combination of molybdenum-99 (Mo^{99}) and tin-135 (Sn^{135}) is 25 TJ/kg. The fission of a kilogram of uranium into Mo^{99} and Sn^{135} releases the difference in energies, or 98 trillion joules. This amount of energy from a golf-ball-sized piece of uranium is enough to drive an average car 19 million miles!

Fission is triggered by neutrons A fission reaction typically happens when a neutron hits a nucleus with enough energy to make the nucleus unstable. Fission breaks the nucleus into two smaller pieces and often releases one or more extra neutrons. Some of the energy released by the reaction appears as gamma rays and some as kinetic energy of the smaller nuclei and the extra neutrons. For example, a possible fission reaction for uranium-235 (U^{235}) is shown in the diagram in Figure 30.17.

Chain reactions A chain reaction occurs when the fission of one nucleus triggers fission of many other nuclei. In a chain reaction, the first fission reaction releases two (or more) neutrons. The two neutrons hit two other nuclei and cause fission reactions that release four neutrons. The four neutrons hit four new nuclei and cause fission reactions that release eight neutrons. The number of neutrons increases rapidly. The increasing number of neutrons causes more nuclei to have fission reactions and enormous energy is released.

Fission products are radioactive The small nuclei produced by fission are called *fission products*. Fission products usually have too many neutrons to be stable. For example, Mo^{99} is radioactive and has two radioactive decays before it reaches a stable nucleus of ruthenium-99 (Ru^{99}). First, molybdenum-99 (Mo^{99}) decays to technetium-99 (Tc^{99}), which then decays to ruthenium-99. The decay from Tc^{99} to Ru^{99} has a half-life of 211,000 years. The term **nuclear waste** includes used fuel from nuclear reactors that contain radioactive isotopes such as Mo^{99} that have long half-lives.

Energy release by a fission reaction

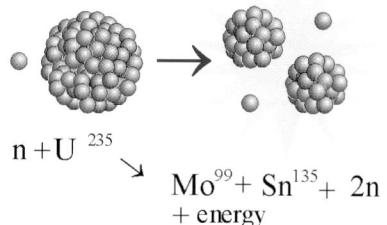

$n + U^{235}$

$Mo^{99} + Sn^{135} + 2n$
+ energy

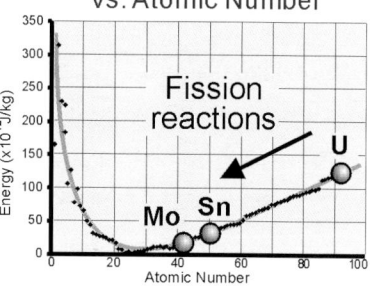

+123 TJ	Energy of uranium (U) nucleus.
−25 TJ	Average energy of nuclei of molybdenum (Mo) and Tin (Sn)
+98 TJ	Energy released by fission of uranium into Mo and Sn.

Figure 30.17: *Fission of uranium releases some nuclear binding energy because elements of lower atomic number are lower on the graph of energy versus atomic number.*

Rules for nuclear reactions

Conservation of energy and momentum
Nuclear reactions obey rules called conservation laws. You have already met two of the conservation laws. The law of conservation of energy applies to nuclear reactions just as it does to any other process in physics. The total amount of energy before the reaction has to equal the total amount of energy after the reaction. The law of conservation of momentum also applies. The total momentum (linear and angular) before the reaction must equal the total after the reaction.

Energy stored as mass
Energy stored as mass must be included in order to apply the law of conservation of energy to a nuclear reaction. The energy of a particle's mass is added to the usual potential and kinetic energy. The energy from mass is given by Einstein's formula $E = mc^2$ where m is the mass of the particle. Even small amounts of mass contain tremendous energy because c^2 is such a large number.

Conservation of charge
Nuclear reactions must conserve electric charge. The total amount of electric charge before the reaction must equal the total electric charge after the reaction.

Conservation of baryons and leptons
There are conservation laws that apply to the type of particles before and after a nuclear reaction. Protons and neutrons belong to a family of particles called *baryons*. Both protons and neutrons have a *baryon number* of one. The total baryon number before and after the reaction must be the same. For the reactions in this book, that means the total number of protons plus neutrons must stay the same before and after the reaction. Electrons come from a family of particles called *leptons*. An electron has a *lepton number* of one. Another conservation law states that the total lepton number must stay the same before and after the reaction.

Conservation Laws

Reactants → Products
$$He^4 + C^{12} \rightarrow O^{16} + energy$$

Conservation Laws	
Mass/energy	The total mass + energy of reactants equals total mass + energy of products
Linear momentum	Total linear momentum of reactants equals total linear momentum of products
Angular momenum	Total angular momentom of reactants equals total angular momentum of products
Electric charge	Total electric charge of reactants equals total electric charge of products
Baryons	Total baryon number of reactants equals total baryon number of products
Leptons	Total lepton number of reactants equals total lepton number of products

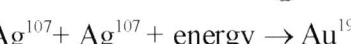

Antimatter, neutrinos, and other particles

Other particles of matter

The matter you meet in the world ordinarily contains protons, neutrons, and electrons. But, there are other particles of matter besides these three. Cosmic rays contain particles called *muons* and *pions*. Thousands of particles called *neutrinos* from the sun pass through you every second and you cannot feel them.

Matter and antimatter

Every particle of matter has an antimatter twin. Antimatter is the same as regular matter except properties like electric charge are reversed. An antiproton is just like a normal proton except it has a negative charge. An antielectron (also called a *positron*) is like an ordinary electron except that it has positive charge. Some nuclear reactions create antimatter.

Antimatter reactions

When antimatter meets an equal amount of normal matter, both the matter and antimatter are converted to pure energy. For example, if an antiproton meets a normal proton, the two particles are immediately converted to pure energy. Antimatter reactions release thousands of times more energy than ordinary nuclear reactions. If a grain of sand weighing 0.002 kilogram made of ordinary matter were to collide and react with a grain of sand made from 0.002 kg of antimatter, the resulting explosion would release 400 trillion joules of energy, enough to power a large city for almost a week (Figure 30.18). From a single grain of sand!

Neutrinos

In Section 30.1 you read about beta decay, where a neutron disintegrates into a proton and an electron. When beta decay was first discovered, physicists were greatly disturbed to find that the energy of the resulting proton and electron was less than the energy of the disintegrating neutron. Where was the missing energy going? The famous Austrian physicist Wolfgang Pauli proposed that there must be a very light, previously undetected neutral particle that was carrying away the missing energy. We now know the missing particle is a type of neutrino. In beta decay, a neutron becomes a proton, an electron, and an *antineutrino* (Figure 30.19). Neutrinos and antineutrinos react only weakly with matter and are therefore extremely difficult to detect. A neutrino can easily pass through the entire Earth without any measurable interaction with any other particle. Despite the difficulty of detection, several carefully constructed neutrino experiments have detected neutrinos coming from nuclear reactions in the sun.

Figure 30.18: *A bit of antimatter the size of a grain of sand would release enough energy to power a small city if it combined with an equal amount of normal matter.*

Beta decay of a neutron

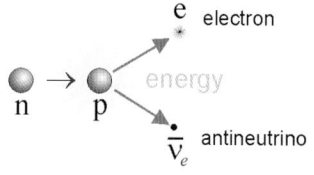

$$n \rightarrow p + e + \overline{\nu}_e + \text{energy}$$

Figure 30.19: *The particles given off in beta decay. The neutrino is represents by the Greek letter Nu (ν). The subscript "e" means it is an electron neutrino (there are three types). The bar on top means it is an antineutrino.*

630

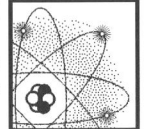

Application: Nuclear Power

Schematic of a nuclear power plant

In a conventional nuclear power plant, the U^{235} fission reaction is used to generate electricity (Figure 30.20). The process of getting electricity from nuclear reactions takes many steps. First, nuclear reactions in uranium produce heat in the reactor core. The heat is carried through high pressure hot water into the steam generator. Heat in the steam generator boils water and makes steam. The steam turns a turbine. In the last step, the turbine is connected to an electric generator that makes electricity. The steam is condensed and pumped back to the steam generator.

The fission chain reaction

one neutron one fission → Two neutrons two fissions → Four neutrons four fissions

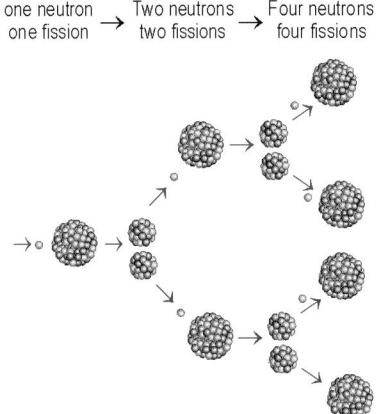

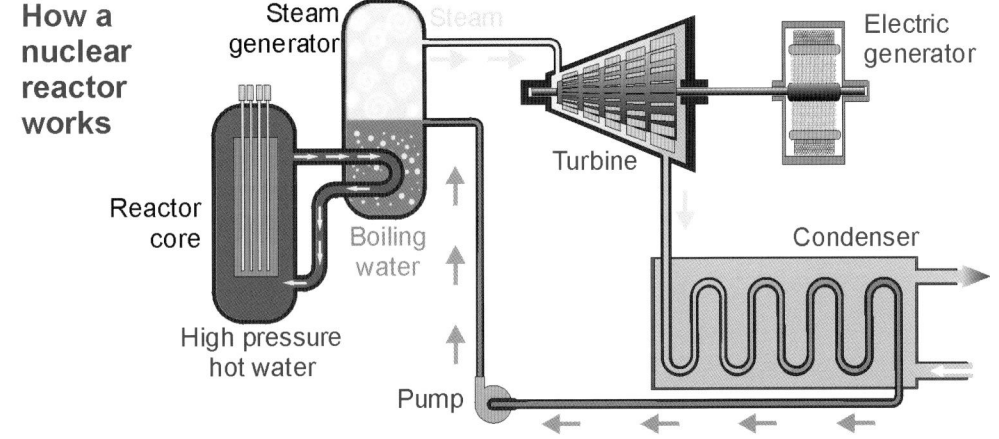

Figure 30.20: *The U^{235} fission chain reaction. Each fission reaction releases extra neutrons that make more fission reactions.*

Producing uranium fuel

To get enough U^{235} to power a nuclear reactor, uranium-bearing ore must first be mined from the Earth. Most natural uranium is the isotope U^{238}, which is less reactive than U^{235}. Uranium must be processed to increase the fraction of U^{235} before it can be used as fuel in a reactor. That process is called enrichment.

The reactor core

The reactor core contains long fuel rods of enriched uranium in a heavy pressure vessel filled with water. Between the fuel rods are *control rods*, made from cadmium, an element which absorbs neutrons (Figure 30.21). Neutrons absorbed by the control rods cannot create more fission reactions. The deeper the control rods are placed in the reactor core, the fewer neutrons are available and the slower the chain reaction proceeds. In an emergency, the control rods are released and drop into the reactor, shutting down the chain reaction completely.

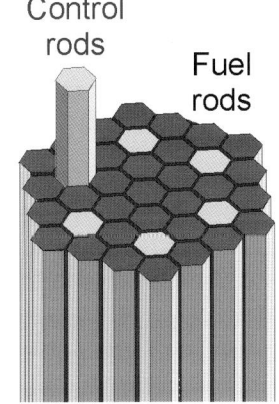

Figure 30.21: *The reactor core contains fuel rods and control rods. The control rods absorb neutrons and slow down the chain reaction.*

Fusion and the future of nuclear energy

The use of nuclear energy Today, 20 percent of US electric power comes from nuclear fission plants like the one described. Other countries, such as France, use fission power for as much as 70 percent of their electricity. Nuclear fission reactors do not burn fossil fuels such as oil, or natural gas. This means no carbon dioxide or other air pollutants are produced. Unfortunately nuclear fission *does* produce dangerous nuclear waste (see sidebar) and uses technology that can be used to make nuclear weapons. As with many technologies, there is a trade-off between risk and benefit.

Fusion power In the future, nuclear energy is likely to come from *fusion* power instead of fission. Fusion reactions have all the benefits of fission, but generate little or no nuclear waste. The easiest fusion reaction to produce on Earth is the fusion of deuterium and tritium (reaction below). Deuterium (H^2) is an isotope of hydrogen with one neutron. Tritium (H^3) is an isotope of hydrogen with two neutrons.

$$H^2 + H^3 \rightarrow He^4 + n + \text{ energy}$$

Fusion fuel comes from seawater The only by-products of this reaction are helium and a neutron. No radioactive nuclei are produced, so there is no dangerous spent nuclear fuel that needs to be isolated from the environment. Fusion fuel is abundant and relatively inexpensive. Deuterium is found naturally in seawater. Tritium does not occur naturally. However, tritium can be produced by combining the neutron from the deuterium-tritium reaction with lithium (reaction below). Lithium is a very common element in the Earth's crust. This secondary reaction allows a fusion power plant to generate part of its own fuel.

$$Li^6 + n \rightarrow H^3 + He^4 + \text{ energy}$$

Fusion power is technically difficult Nuclear fusion is in many ways an ideal energy source since it uses inexpensive, abundant fuel and it generates little harmful waste. However, it has proven very difficult to build a fusion reactor capable of generating electricity. One difficulty is heating the deuterium and tritium fuel to more than 50 million degrees Celsius. Fusion fuel, in the form of a hot plasma, must be contained in a magnetic force field and kept isolated from solid materials. The tokamak reactor (Figure 30.22) is the most successful experimental fusion reactor yet constructed.

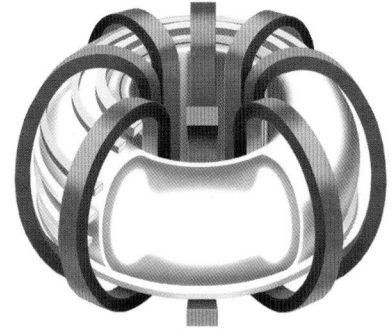

Figure 30.22: *A tokamak fusion reactor confines the hot plasma in a doughnut-shaped chamber. Temperatures in fusion experiments typically reach 80 million °C, five times hotter than the core of the sun.*

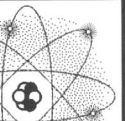

Chapter 30 Review

Vocabulary Review

Match the following terms with the correct definition. There is one extra definition in the list that will not match any of the terms.

Set One

1. alpha decay
2. gamma decay
3. radioactive decay
4. energy barrier
5. half-life

a. Emission of high energy electromagnetic radiation from the nucleus
b. Energy needed to start radioactive decay
c. time required for 50% of a remaining isotope to decay
d. Spontaneous nuclear reaction in which one nucleus becomes a different nucleus
e. Shield to protect scientists from high energy particles
f. Nuclear reaction resulting in the loss of 4 atomic mass units

Set Two

1. CAT scan
2. ionizing
3. rem
4. Geiger counter
5. x-ray

a. High energy photons which can penetrate the human body
b. Radical electromagnetic mammography detector
c. Three dimensional x-ray image; computerized axial tomography
d. In general, radiation capable of removing electrons from atoms
e. Unit for measuring the dose of radiation received
f. Radiation detector of x-rays and other ionizing radiation

Set Three

1. fusion
2. antimatter
3. neutrino
4. fallout
5. chain reaction

a. Low level radiation due mostly to natural causes
b. Occurs as the fission of one nucleus causes the fission of others
c. Combination of smaller nuclei to produce larger ones
d. Converts both to pure energy when combined with matter
e. Particle created in beta decay along with an electron
f. Created by nuclear weapons testing; responsible for 2% of background radiation

633

Concept review

1. Marie Curie referred to radioactivity as an invisible radiation that exposed photographic plates. What causes materials to be radioactive and what part of the atom is affected?

2. Summarize the three kinds of radioactive decay by completing the chart below.

Decay	Proton #change	Neutron #change	Ejected particle	Penetrating ability
Alpha				
Beta				
Gamma				

3. In what ways are energy changes which occur in chemical reactions similar to those which occur in radioactivity? How are they different?

4. Scientists cannot predict when an individual nucleus will decay but can predict when half of the nuclei present will have decayed. Explain how.

5. Carbon-14 can be used to estimate the age of once-living organisms to an age of about 57,000 years. Why is there a limit to the age which can be determined?

6. Light is projected on a screen. As the distance to the screen is increased, describe what happens to the intensity of the light and the area covered by the light.

7. Radiation can take many forms. Why are some forms harmful? Give two examples which are harmful.

8. X-rays are highly energetic photons. They can be used to destroy unhealthy cancer cells. How is this done without killing healthy cells?

9. A CAT scan can yield 3-D pictures of the internal structure of the human body. Explain how this is done.

10. Infrared radiation (heat) can be harmful but damage can be avoided by simply moving away from the source. What makes the damage from UV light, x-rays and other forms of ionizing radiation more difficult to avoid?

11. In a chemical reaction, balanced equations are written using the law of conservation of mass. Can this same law be applied to nuclear reactions? Explain your answer.

12. Why is the energy released from a nuclear reaction so much greater than the energy from a chemical reaction?

13. Fission and fusion are both sources of tremendous amounts of energy. Neither is without drawbacks. Compare "positives" and "negatives" of the two nuclear reactions, fusion and fission, as a means of supplying energy for mankind by naming at least one positive and one negative for each method.

Reaction	Positive	Negative
Fission		
Fusion		

14. Use the graph shown below and the "Periodic Table of Elements" to number the elements in order of increasing energy of their nuclei.

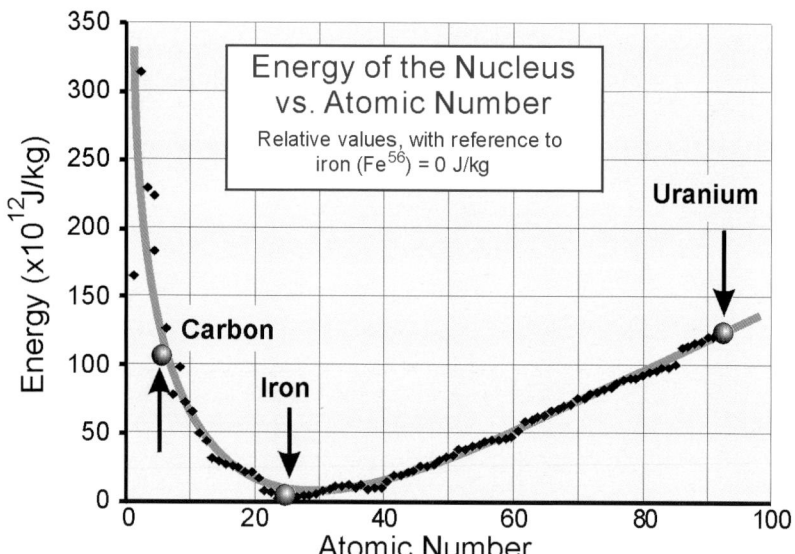

a. carbon

b. iron

c. magnesium

d. lithium

e. lead

f. krypton

15. Describe what occurs if a proton were to contact an anti-proton.

16. It is proposed to make S^{34} by combining He^3 and P^{31}. If the nuclei named are the only particles involved, explain why this reaction will not take place.

17. Two types of nuclear reactions that produce energy, fusion and fission, differ in the manner in which the energy is released. In what way do they differ?

18. How was the law of conservation of energy responsible for the discovery of the neutrino?

Problems

1. A 1,000-kilogram bomb made of TNT releases about 4.2×10^9 joules of energy when exploded. How much mass is converted to energy by this explosion?

2. A proton and an anti-proton collide head-on. How much energy is released from this collision? (Remember the mass of a proton is 1.673×10^{-27} kg.)

3. 0.25 kilograms of a substance undergo radioactive decay. What mass of the original isotope will remain after 5 half-lives?

4. Radon has a half-life of 3.8 days. How long does it take for 16 grams of radon to be reduced to 2 grams of radon?

5. Chris holds a light bulb one meter from the wall illuminating a circle 25 centimeters in diameter. He moves the bulb to a distance of 3 meters from the wall. Answer the following questions:

   a. What is the diameter of the new circle of illumination?

   b. How does the new intensity of illumination compare to the original intensity?

6. A miner is unaware that he is exposed to a 0.005 watt gamma radiation source 0.25 meters from his work station one day. Upon its discovery, his station is closed down.

   a. What is the intensity of radiation received by this miner?

   b. What is the intensity for a miner 2 meters away?

7. In one year, an individual working at a nuclear power plant receives 35 watts of alpha radiation and 2 watts of gamma radiation in one year.

   a. What is her dose of radiation for the year?

   b. Should she be permitted to return to work?

8. Using the graph of "Energy of the Nucleus vs. Atomic Number" on the previous page and your knowledge of nuclear reactions, indicate which pairs of nuclei would be most likely to release energy by fission and which would release energy by fusion:

   a. He^4 and C^{12}

   b. U^{235} and Sn^{135}

   c. C^{12} and C^{12}

9. Identify the type of each reaction:

a. $^{66}_{29}Cu \rightarrow {}^{66}_{30}Zn + {}^{0}_{-1}e$

b. $^{204}_{82}Pb \rightarrow {}^{200}_{80}Hg + {}^{4}_{2}He$

c. $^{1}_{0}n \rightarrow {}^{1}_{1}H + {}^{0}_{-1}e$

d. $^{59}_{28}Ni + {}^{0}_{-1}e \rightarrow {}^{59}_{27}Co$

e. $^{15}_{8}O \rightarrow {}^{15}_{7}N + {}^{0}_{+1}e$

10. Use the graph below showing the radioactive decay of nitrogen-13 to answer the following questions:

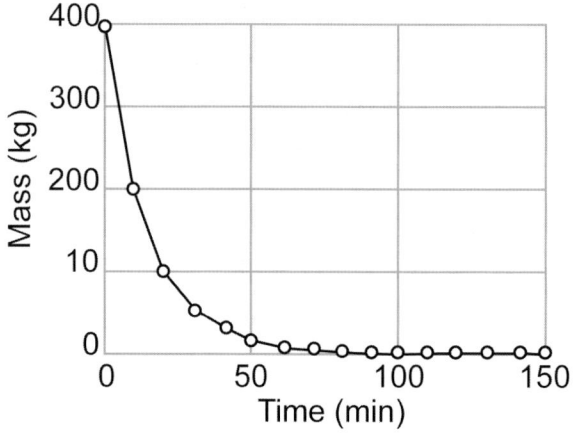

a. How much nitrogen-13 remains after 40 minutes?

b. How long is one half-life for nitrogen-13?

636

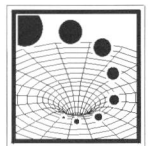

Frontiers in Physics

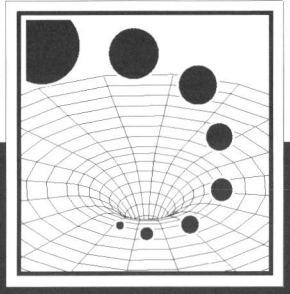

Chapter 31

The Edge of What We Know

Objectives for Chapter 31

The universe is a wonderful and complex place. We are far from understanding how nature works in all of its detail. This chapter talks about far-out ideas in physics that are areas of active research. The discussion is a broad overview only, touching on a few interesting points. Many entire books have been written on *each* of the ideas discussed on *each page* of this chapter. Scientists and all sorts of people are doing experiments and debating with each other whether these ideas are the right ones to describe nature, or not. Only continued experiments will tell. As you read this chapter, do not worry about understanding all of what you read. The smartest people in the world do not completely understand all of these ideas. The purpose of the chapter is to give you a flavor of how truly interesting and surprising the universe is, and also to encourage you to explore further some of the concepts discussed here.

Terms and vocabulary words

antimatter	equivalence principle	meson	baryon	dark matter
event horizon	elementary particles	red shift	big bang	quark
inertial mass	gravitational mass	lepton	escape velocity	boson
reference frame	general relativity	black hole	curved space	

31.1 The Origin of the Universe

The universe is, well, everything. All of matter and all of energy are part of the universe. It seems very strange to think the universe *had* a beginning, partly because it is such a huge stretch of the mind to imagine the entire universe itself. Like the rest of this chapter, a book written 50 years from now may present a different story from the ideas in the next few pages. But today that seems improbable. The evidence for the origin of the universe is very strong.

The expanding universe

Milky Way Galaxy
When we look out into space with powerful telescopes, we see stars of our own Milky Way Galaxy. The Milky Way contains about 200 billion stars in a spiral form (Figure 31.1). Some of the stars are like the sun. Some are hotter, some are cooler, some older, some younger. Just recently we have discovered that many stars have planets like the planets in our solar system.

The universe contains billions of galaxies
Beyond our galaxy with its 200 billion stars are other galaxies. We can see billions of galaxies, many of them as full of stars as our own. This is the universe on its largest scale.

The laws of physics seem to be the same
In Chapter 28, you learned that each element has a characteristic pattern of light called a *spectrum*. When we look at the light from distant galaxies, we see the spectra of familiar elements. That tells us that other galaxies also have hydrogen, helium, lithium, oxygen and the same elements as our own galaxy. Because the lines have the same pattern, it also tells us that the laws of physics are the same.

Red shift
The spectra of each element observed in a distant galaxy has the same pattern as here on Earth, but appears shifted toward longer wavelengths (red). The appearance of spectral-line patterns at longer wavelength is called red shift. For example, the spectrum of helium from one distant galaxy appears at 30 nanometers longer wavelength than from the sun (Figure 31.2). The spectra are red shifted *because galaxies are moving away from each other*. The Doppler effect and special relativity cause light to be red shifted if the source of light and the observer are moving away from each other. Galaxies that are farther away have a larger red shift so they are moving away even faster. The universe is expanding.

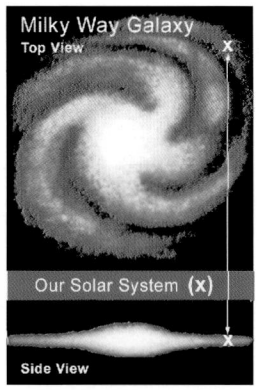

Figure 31.1: *The Milky Way Galaxy is a typical spiral galaxy, like many others.*

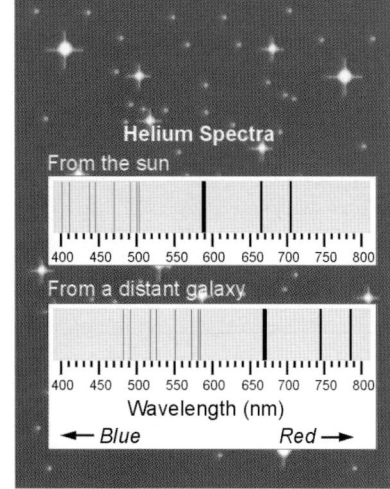

Figure 31.2: *Light from distant galaxies show spectra that are red-shifted. Notice the same pattern of spectral lines from helium is at a longer wavelength in light from a distant galaxy.*

The big bang

An expanding universe implies a beginning

If the universe is expanding, then it must have been smaller in the past. It seems reasonable to ask how small was the early universe? And how long has it been since the universe was small? The best evidence indicates that the age of the universe is 13 billion years, plus or minus a few billion years. This is roughly four times older than the age of the sun. This range of ages for the universe agrees with other estimates, such as the oldest stars we can see.

The big bang

It also appears that the universe was once very small, possibly smaller than a single atom. Sixteen billion years ago a cataclysmic explosion occurred and the universe started growing from a tiny point into the incredible vastness we now observe. In jest, someone called this beginning the "big bang" and the name stuck. We have no idea why the universe came into existence or what came before the big bang. It is not clear these questions can even be answered by science.

Evidence for the big bang

We do see evidence for the big bang itself. The fact that galaxies are expanding away from each other is a strong argument for the big bang. As far as we can look into the universe, we find galaxies are expanding away from each other (Figure 31.3). We do not see galaxies coming toward each other.

The cosmic background radiation

When you light a match, the flame bursts rapidly from the first spark and then cools as it expands. When the big bang exploded, it also created hot radiation. This radiation has been expanding and cooling for 16 billion years. The radiation is now at a temperature only 2.7 K above absolute zero and it fills the universe. The *cosmic background radiation* is the "smoke" from the big bang that fills the room (that is, the universe), even 16 billion years later (Figure 31.4).

Ratios of the elements

We have other evidence that supports the big bang theory. The proportion of hydrogen to helium is consistent with the physics of the big bang (Figure 31.5). Elements heavier than hydrogen and helium are formed in stars. When stars reach the end of their life cycle, they spread heavy elements such as carbon, oxygen, and iron out into the universe. If the universe were significantly older, there would be more heavy elements present compared with hydrogen and helium.

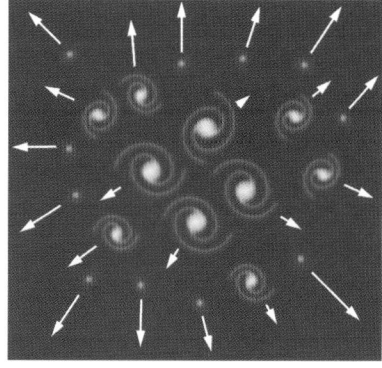

Figure 31.3: *The observed expansion of the universe is strong evidence for the big bang theory.*

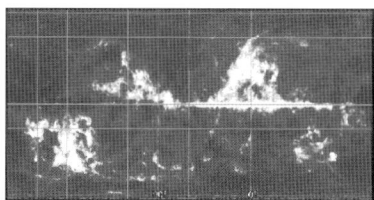

Figure 31.4: *The COBE satellite measured this image of the cosmic background radiation. (NASA)*

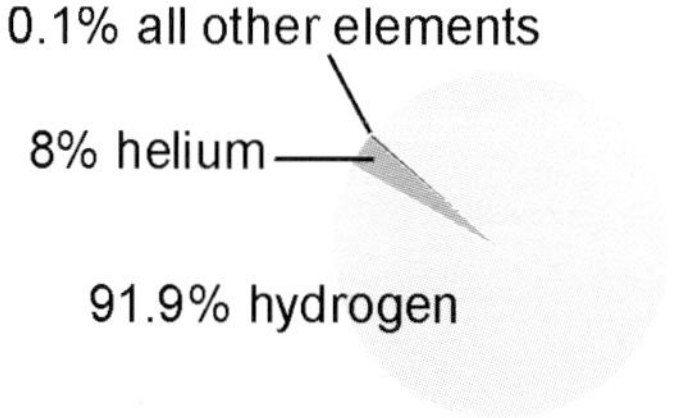

0.1% all other elements

8% helium

91.9% hydrogen

Elements in the universe

Figure 31.5: *The universe is mostly hydrogen with a small amount of helium and tiny amounts of other elements.*

A one-page history of the universe

The first second
Immediately after the big bang the universe was a hot, dense fireball of expanding energy (Figure 31.6). At an age of 0.01 seconds, the estimated temperature of the fireball was 100 billion degrees (10^{11} K). This temperature is so high that protons could not stay together. The universe consisted of exotic particles and photons.

Protons and neutrons form at 4 minutes
As the universe expanded, it cooled down as its energy spread out over a larger volume. About four minutes after the big bang, the universe had expanded and cooled enough that protons and neutrons could stick together to form the nuclei of atoms. Because atoms were still flying around with high energy, heavy nuclei got smashed apart immediately. In fact, only one helium atom survives for every 12 hydrogen atoms. Almost no elements heavier than helium were created. When we look at the matter in the universe today, we see this ratio of hydrogen to helium left by the big bang, with the exception of elements formed much later in stars.

Matter and light decouple in 700,000 years
For the next 700,000 years the expanding universe was like the inside of a star: hot ionized hydrogen and helium. At the age of 700,000 years, the universe had expanded enough to become transparent to light. At this point, the light from the fireball was freed from constant interaction with hot matter. The light continued to expand separately from matter and became the cosmic background radiation we see today.

Stars and galaxies form
When the universe was about 1 billion years old, it had expanded and cooled enough that galaxies and stars could form. At this point the universe probably began to look similar to how it looks today. The sun and solar system formed about 4 billion years ago, by which time the universe was 12 billion years old.

Unresolved questions
While scientists feel relatively confident about the overall "universal" picture, they are not confident about the details. There are many puzzling observations yet to be fully explained. One problem is that today matter is clumped in stars and galaxies. Yet the cosmic background radiation is smooth and uniform to better than one part in 10,000. There are also recent observations that suggest the expansion of the universe is accelerating. This is a puzzle because, if anything, the expansion should be decelerating as the combined effect of gravity from the matter in the universe slows down the expansion.

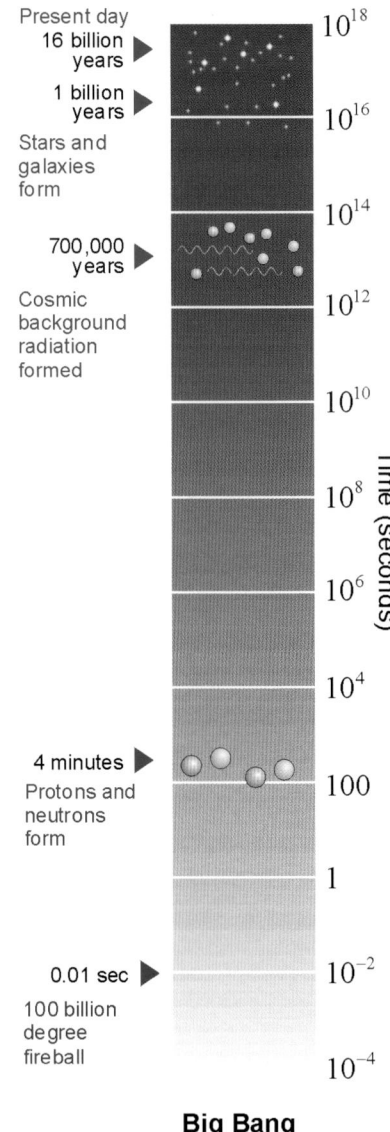

Figure 31.6: *A brief time line of the universe.*

The far future of the universe

Two different futures

Our current theories suggest two very different options for the far future of the universe (Figure 31.7). We do not know which one is the correct description. It is possible the correct answer is neither of the options we are considering today. This is an area of active research in physics and astronomy.

Continued expansion and cooling

The universe could continue to expand and cool. This option is called the *open universe*. Our sun will continue to shine pretty much as it is for another 4 billion years. Eventually it will become a white dwarf, which is a small hot ball of electrons, protons, and neutrons. Over time, the white dwarf will cool off by radiation and become cold. After 100 billion years, a similar scenario will happen to all of the stars in the universe. The universe becomes a cold stellar graveyard filled with dwarf stars, black holes, and low-energy radiation. Eventually even the black holes and dwarf stars evaporate, leaving only radiation

Reversal followed by Big Crunch

If there is enough matter in the universe, the combined effect of gravity will eventually slow the expansion down and reverse it. This option is called the *closed universe*. When the expansion stops, the universe would then start falling inward on itself. Over many billion years the universe would slowly heat up as it came together. Eventually the universe might come back to a small point again in a big crunch. Some theorists believe that the universe is a repeating cycle of big bang and big crunch.

Density and dark matter

Which of the two options lies in the future depends on how much mass there is in the universe. This is something we are trying hard to find out. The amount of matter in stars and galaxies is what we can see because this matter gives off light. The "light" matter is less than 5 percent of the matter needed to "close" the universe. We can also deduce that dark matter exists from its gravitational effects on matter we can see. For example, you could calculate the mass of Earth by observing the orbit of the moon. From the motion of galaxies we know there is much more dark matter than matter in stars. The total mass of dark matter appears to exceed that of light matter, but is still not enough to close the universe. New research however, has discovered mass for the neutrinos, and the possibility of forms of "dark energy". Whether the universe is open or closed is not known.

Open universe

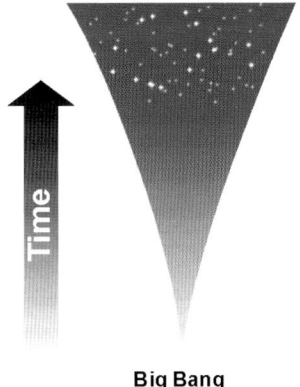

Big Bang

Closed universe

Big Crunch

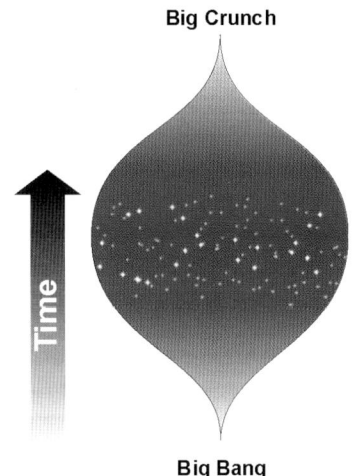

Big Bang

Figure 31.7: *Two quite different scenarios for the evolution of the universe.*

31.2 Gravity and General Relativity

Einstein's theory of general relativity describes gravity in a fundamentally different way than does Newton's law of universal gravitation. According to Einstein, the presence of mass changes the shape of space-time itself. In general relativity, an object in orbit is moving in a straight line through curved space. The curvature of space itself causes a planet to move in an orbit. The force we call gravity is an effect created by the curvature of space and time.

Inertial mass and gravitational mass

The two interpretations for g In Chapter 6, we discussed two interpretations for g. One interpretation is that g represents the strength of the gravitational field, or 9.8 newtons per kilogram of mass. The second interpretation is that an object in free fall experiences an acceleration of 9.8 m/sec². We argued that both interpretations were identical because the mass (m) that appears in Newton's second law is the same mass (m) that appears in Newton's law of universal gravitation (Figure 31.8).

Inertial mass The mass that appears in the second law is a measure of an object's inertia. Inertia means resistance to acceleration. This mass is often called inertial mass because an object with more mass has more inertia and requires more force to accelerate.

Gravitational mass The mass that appears in the law of gravitation is a measure of an object's ability to act *through*, and be *acted on* by gravity. The gravitational mass is a measure of an object's susceptibility to force of gravity. Two masses attract each other with a force that is proportional to the product of their masses. The force law is identical to the situation where two electric charges attract each other with a force proportional to the product of the two charges.

The paradox and the solution What is the problem, you say? Is it not the same "*m*" in both formulas? The problem is that, at first glance, *inertia has nothing to do with gravity*. Why should an object's resistance to acceleration be the exact same property that determines an object's interaction with gravity? Why should it be the same "*m*" in both formulas? The results of every experiment *tell us that the "m" is the same*. But why? The coincidence seemed too perfect for Einstein. His brilliant theory of general relativity showed how inertia and gravity are intimately connected.

Newton's law of gravitation

Gravitational mass (kg)
↓
$$F = G\frac{m_1 m_2}{r^2}$$

Newton's second law

$$a = \frac{F}{m}$$
↑
Inertial mass (kg)

The paradox
Why does the same property of matter determine both the effect of gravity and the resistance to acceleration?

Figure 31.8: *The difference between gravitational mass and inertial mass.*

The equivalence principle

Different perspectives on the same motion

Consider the example of a boy and girl who jump into a bottomless canyon, where there is no air friction. On the way down, they play catch and throw a ball back and forth. If the girl looks at the boy, she sees the ball go straight to him. If the boy looks at the girl, he sees the ball go straight to her. However, an observer at rest watching them fall sees the ball follow a curved zigzag path back and forth (Figure 31.9). Who is correct? What is the real path of the ball?

The boy and girl perceive no gravity

Both are correct. Imagine enclosing the boy and girl in a windowless box falling with them. From inside their box, they see the ball go straight back and forth. To the boy and girl in the box, the ball follows the exact same path it would *if there were no gravity*. Remember, gravity would cause the ball to follow a curved path.

The reverse situation

Next, imagine the boy and girl are in the same box throwing the ball back and forth in deep space, *where there is no gravity*. This time the box is accelerating upwards. When the boy throws the ball to the girl, the ball does not go straight to her, but drops in a parabola toward the floor. This happens because the floor is accelerating upward and pushing the girl with it. The girl moves up while the ball is moving toward her. But, from her perspective she sees the ball go down. If the girl calculates the path of the ball, she finds it to be a parabola *exactly like what it would follow if there was a force of gravity pulling it downward.*

Reference frames and the equivalence principle

In physics, the box containing the boy and girl is called a reference frame. Everything they can do, measure, or see is inside their reference frame. The equivalence principle says that *no experiment the boy or girl do can distinguish whether they are feeling the force of gravity or they are in a reference frame that is accelerating*. The only way to tell is to look outside the box.

The meaning of the equivalence principle

A experiment done in a reference frame at rest on the surface of the Earth finds a gravitational force of 9.8 N/kg. Suppose a person does the same experiment in a spaceship in deep space that is accelerating at 9.8 m/sec^2. The experiment *also finds a gravitational force of 9.8 N/kg, even though there is no gravity*. According to the equivalence principle, *any* result from *any* experiment is exactly the same whether the experiment is done in a place with a gravitational force of 9.8 N/kg or in a reference frame that is accelerating at 9.8 m/sec^2.

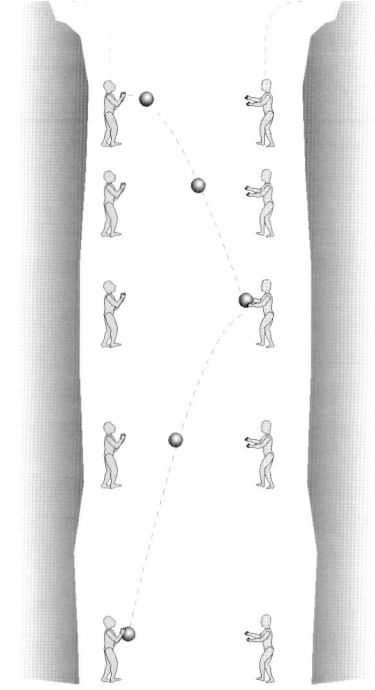

How it appears to a stationary observer

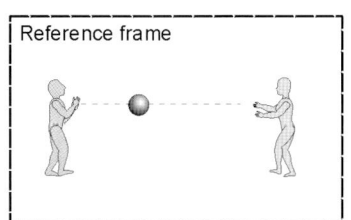

How it appears to them in their reference frame

Figure 31.9: *How the path of the ball appears to an outside observer and in the accelerating reference frame of the boy and girl.*

Curved space-time

Light and the equivalence principle

The equivalence principle applies to any experiment, even an experiment that measures the path taken by light. In Chapter 18, we discussed the theory of special relativity, which says the speed of light is the same for all observers whether they are moving or not. In order to make the equivalence principal true for experiments that measure the speed of light, two things must be true.

1. Space itself must be curved.

2. The path of light must be deflected by gravity, even though light has no mass.

Flat space

To understand what we mean by curved space, consider rolling a ball along a sheet of graph paper. If the graph paper is flat the ball rolls along a straight line. A flat sheet of graph paper is like "flat space." In flat space, parallel lines never meet, all three angles of the triangle add up to 180 degrees, etc. Flat space is what you would consider "normal."

Curved space

The presence of a large mass such as a star creates curved space in the region close to the star. Figure 31.10 shows an example of a graph paper made of rubber which has been stretched down in one point. If you roll a ball along this graph paper, it bends as it rolls near the "well" created by the stretch. From directly overhead, the graph paper still looks square. If you look straight down on the graph paper, the path of the ball appears to be deflected by a force pulling it toward the center. You might say the ball felt a force of gravity which deflected its motion. And, you would be right. The effect of curved space is identical to the force of gravity.

Orbits and curved space

In fact, close to a source of gravity, straight lines become circles. A planet moving in an orbit is actually moving in a straight line through curved space. This is a strange way to think, but all of the experimental evidence we have gathered tells us it is the right way to think.

Proving general relativity

The event that made Einstein famous was his prediction that light from distant stars should be bent by the curvature of space near the sun. People were skeptical because, according to Newton's law of gravitation, light is not affected by gravity. In 1919 an expedition was launched to see if Einstein was right by observing a star near the sun during a solar eclipse. Einstein was right.

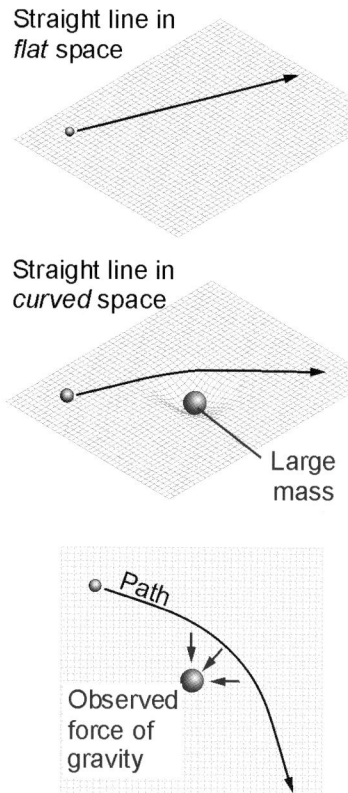

Straight line in *flat* space

Straight line in *curved* space

Large mass

Path

Observed force of gravity

Figure 31.10: *Large amounts of mass cause space to become curved. An object following a straight path in curved space bends the same way as if it were acted on by a force we call gravity.*

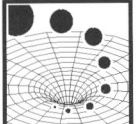

Black holes

General relativity predicts black holes

One of the strangest predictions of general relativity is the existence of black holes. To understand a black hole, consider a rocket trying to leave the Earth. If the rocket does not go fast enough, the Earth's gravity eventually pulls it back. The minimum speed a rocket must go to escape the planet's gravity is called its escape velocity. The stronger gravity becomes, the higher the escape velocity.

The escape velocity of a black hole

If gravity becomes strong enough, the escape velocity can reach the speed of light. A *black hole* is an object with such strong gravity that its escape velocity equals or exceeds the speed of light. When the escape velocity equals the speed of light, nothing can get out because nothing can go faster than light. In fact, even light cannot get out, because in general relativity, light is affected by gravity. The name *black hole* comes from the fact that anything that falls in never comes out. Since no light can get out, the object is "black" (Figure 31.12).

Figure 31.11: *On Earth, light travels in nearly straight lines because the Earth's escape velocity is much less than the speed of light.*

Black holes are extremely compact matter

To make a black hole, a very large mass must be squeezed into a very tiny space. For example, to make the Earth into a black hole, you would have to squeeze the mass of the entire planet down to the size of a marble as wide as your thumb. For a long time, nobody took black holes seriously because they seemed so extreme that they could never actually be real.

We see black holes by what is around them

But then astronomers started finding them. You might think it would be impossible to see a black hole—and it is. But, you *can see* what happens *around* a black hole. In Chapter 10, you learned that an object loses potential energy as it falls. When an object falls into a black hole, it loses so much energy that a significant fraction of its mass turns into energy. Any matter that falls into a black hole gives off so much energy it creates incredibly bright radiation as it spirals its way down. Astronomers believe the core of our own Milky Way Galaxy contains a black hole with a mass more than 1 million times the mass of the sun.

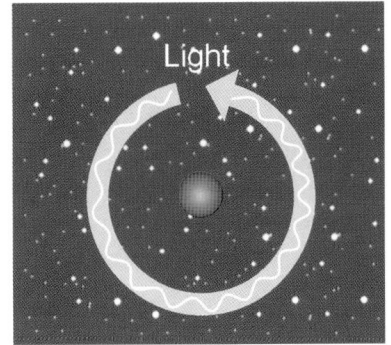

Figure 31.12: *Light from a black hole cannot escape because the escape velocity is higher than the speed of light.*

The event horizon

Black holes have very strange properties. The event horizon is the sphere around a black hole at which the escape velocity just equals the speed of light. Once something crosses the event horizon, it is lost to our universe forever. Special relativity (Chapter 18) made a connection between time and the speed of light. Because of this connection, *time slows down to a stop at the event horizon.*

31.3 The Standard Model

The three-particle atomic model (protons, electrons, neutrons) was very successful. However, just as scientists were getting confident, a particle was discovered with negative charge but 200 times the mass of a electron. More particles were discovered, and then more, and soon there were a more than a hundred elementary particles. A common goal of science is to explain complexity with a few basic principles. The proton, electron, and neutron were able to explain all 92 elements. Physicists started looking for a similar way to simplify what they called the *particle zoo*.

A walk through the particle zoo

Sorting particles into categories   When you walk through a zoo, many animals are sorted by shared characteristics. Mammals tend to have two or four legs, birds have feathers, and snakes have no legs at all. Particles also fall into categories, although the properties we use to sort them are not as familiar as legs, fur, or feathers. Table 31.1 shows a partial list of elementary particles sorted into the four basic types. Notice that some come in three varieties with positive, negative, and zero electric charge. The sigma particle (Σ^+, Σ^-, Σ^0) is an example.

Baryons and mesons   Protons and neutrons are examples of baryons. Baryons are relatively heavy particles, with the mass of a proton or heavier. Each baryon is made of three even smaller objects called *quarks*. The pion (π) particle is a meson. Mesons are made of two quarks. Both baryons and mesons feel the strong nuclear force. Remember, the strong nuclear force holds the nucleus of an atom together by creating attraction between neutrons and protons.

Leptons   The electron is a lepton. Leptons are particles that have no internal structure. That means leptons are not made from anything else and are truly elementary by themselves. The lightest leptons are called neutrinos. There are three kinds of neutrinos, one for each of the other types of leptons. Like the electron, the more massive leptons (μ, τ) have negative charge.

Bosons   The last type of particles are called bosons. Bosons are particles that carry *forces*. The particle of light we met in Chapter 16, the photon, is a boson. The first two bosons have zero mass. The next two have a relatively large mass.

Table 31.1:
A partial list of elementary particles

Name	Symbol	Mass (amu)
Baryons		
Neutron	n	1.009
Proton	p	1.007
Lambda	Λ	1.20
Sigma	Σ^+ Σ^- Σ^0	1.28
Omega	Ω^-	1.80
Mesons		
Pion	π^+ π^- π^0	0.15
Kaon	$K^+ K^- K^0$	0.53
D	$D^+ D^- D^0$	2.0
J/Psi	J/ψ	3.3
B	$B^+ B^- B^0$	5.7
Leptons		
Neutrino	ν_e ν_τ ν_μ	$<5 \times 10^{-11}$
Electron	e	5.5×10^{-4}
Muon	μ	0.11
Tau	τ	1.9
Bosons		
Photon	γ	0.0
Gluon	g	0.0
W	W^+ W^-	86
Z	Z	98

Note: masses are average for families of particles.

Matter and antimatter

The quantum equations include antimatter

An ordinary proton has a positive charge, and a mass of 1 atomic mass unit (amu). An ordinary electron has a negative charge equal and opposite to the charge of the proton. In 1928, Paul Dirac (1902-84), an English physicist, published a paper that incorporated Einstein's theory of special relativity into quantum mechanics. When you solve any equation with a square root, there are two solutions, one positive and one negative. for example, $\sqrt{4} = \pm 2$. Dirac found two similar solutions to the quantum equation for the electron. The negative solutions correspond to antimatter. Antimatter is matter that has all the same properties as regular matter except the electric charge is reversed, along with other "charge-like" properties.

Antimatter has the opposite charge

The *positron* (anti-electron) has the same mass as a normal electron but a positive charge. An *antiproton* has the mass of an ordinary proton, but a negative charge. As each new particle was discovered, each also turned out to have an antiparticle. For example the antiparticle of the positive pion (π^+) is the negative pion (π^-). The pion with zero charge (π^0) is its own antiparticle because it has no electric charge.

Reactions between matter and antimatter

When ordinary matter and antimatter meet, both particles are turned into pure energy. The amount of energy is given by Einstein's formula ($E = mc^2$) where m is the combined mass of both particles.

Charge-like properties

The discussion of antiparticles gets a little more complex because *particles have other "charge-like" properties besides electric charge.* An example of a property of particles that behaves like charge is the *baryon number*. A proton has a baryon number of +1 and an antiproton has a baryon number of -1. These other charge-like properties obey conservation laws, like electric charge. For example, the total baryon number before a reaction must equal the total baryon number after the reaction. Particles and antiparticles created from pure energy are usually created together to conserve charge-like properties.

Symbols for antimatter

Sometimes an antiparticle is represented with a bar over the symbol. For example, an electron neutrino has the symbol v_e. The anti-electron neutrino has the symbol $\overline{v}_e$. Similarly, a proton is represented by p and an antiproton by $\overline{p}$. The exception to this rule is when the charge of the particle is already included in the symbol, such as with the pions (π^+, π^-).

Energy from antimatter

Matter-antimatter reactions are the most energetic reaction in the known universe. For example, if you could take one barrel of water and add it to one barrel of anti-water, the energy released would be enough to power the entire United States for a year. That means every light bulb, every car, every factory, every furnace, and every type of energy used for any purpose.

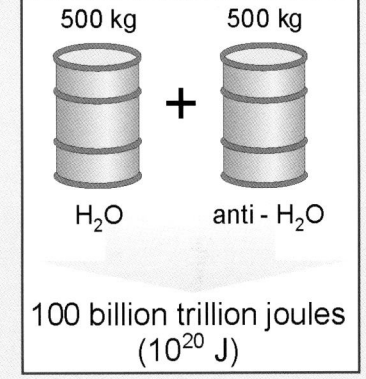

500 kg   500 kg

H_2O anti - H_2O

100 billion trillion joules
(10^{20} J)

Of course, you could never contain the antimatter enough to be let it react in a controlled fashion. Today scientists work with antimatter in the most minute quantities, not much more than particles at a time. There is no permanent antimatter occurring in the natural universe as far as we know. Any antimatter used in a laboratory must be created from pure energy.

The standard model of particles

Protons and neutrons are made of quarks

At first, people believed atoms were the smallest particle of matter. Then it was discovered that atoms had internal *structure* and were themselves made of protons, neutrons, and electrons. As physicists conducted more sophisticated experiments, they discovered that the *proton* and *neutron* also have internal structure. Today we believe only leptons (electron, etc.) and bosons (photon, etc.) are truly elementary particles. Baryons and mesons are made of simpler particles called quarks.

6 quarks and 6 antiquarks

There are six quarks (Figure 31.13) and each has an antiquark, making a total of 12 types of quark. The up, charm, and top quarks have a charge of + 2/3. The down, strange, and bottom quarks have a charge of - 1/3. A proton is made of two up quarks and a down quark, written "uud". The charge of the proton is plus one (+2/3 + 2/3 - 1/3). A neutron is made of one up quark and two down quarks (udd) and has a charge of zero (+ 2/3 - 1/3 -1/3). All the baryon-type particles are made of three quarks. All the mesons are made of quark-antiquark pairs (Figure 31.14). For example, the positive pion (π^+) is made from an up quark and an anti-down quark. Antiquarks are written with a bar over the letter name.

The three families

The quarks and leptons are grouped into three families. The four lightest particles are in the first family, including the electron, electron neutrino, up quark, and down quark. Almost all of the matter we see is made from the first family because these are the lightest particles and therefore have the lowest energy. We only see the second and third families in very high-energy situations. Such situations include particle accelerator experiments, cosmic rays, the environment of black holes and exotic forms of matter found in stellar remnants like neutron stars.

We do not see isolated quarks

Quarks are never found by themselves. The force that binds quarks to each other is extremely strong. If you try to pull the two quarks in a meson apart, you have to do work and add energy. It takes so much energy to pull the quarks apart that there is enough energy to create *two new quarks*. Remember, according to Einstein's formula, you can create matter from energy ($m = E \div c^2$). The new quarks pair up with the ones you are trying to pull apart, creating two new mesons where there was only one. As a result, you still do not have a quark by itself.

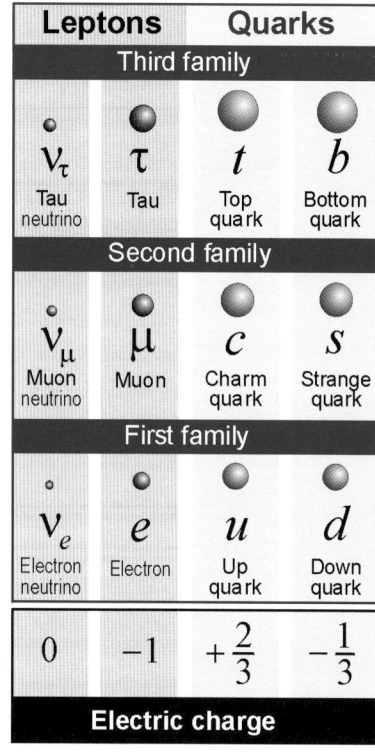

Figure 31.13: *The standard model for particles of matter.*

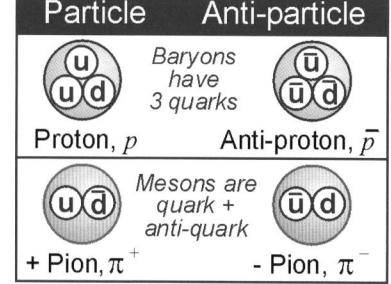

Figure 31.14: *The quark structure for examples of a baryon and meson.*

648

The standard model of forces

The four forces in nature We see four forces in nature. The interactions of matter and energy occur through the four forces. In order from strongest to weakest, the four forces are:

1. The strong nuclear force, relative strength = 10.

2. The electromagnetic force, relative strength = 0.0073.

3. The weak nuclear force, relative strength = 10^{-7}.

4. The gravitational force, relative strength = 10^{-45}.

In Chapter 21, we learned about fields and forces. A field is an area of space that contains energy that can exert forces on particles. The quantum theory of fields requires that energy be quantized. You can think of a quantum of energy as a *particle*. We have already discussed the first field quantum, the photon.

Every field has an associated particle All of the four forces in nature are transmitted through fields. Each of the fields has a particle associated with it. The particle that transmits the electric and magnetic field is the photon.

How a particle transmits force To see how particles transmit force, consider two people on skates (Figure 31.15). One person throws a bowling ball to the other (A). The ball carries momentum away from the thrower (B) and gives the momentum to the receiver (C). The thrower moves to the left and the receiver moves to the right. If the ball were invisible, you might think a force of repulsion existed between the two people (D). Particles carry forces between other particles in a similar way.

The strong and weak nuclear forces The strong nuclear force is transmitted by *gluons,* which also carry the force between quarks. The weak nuclear force is transmitted by the W and Z bosons. Figure 31.16 shows the particles that carry the four forces in the standard model.

Gravity is an unsolved mystery The standard model includes a *graviton* to carry the gravitational force. However, no one has ever observed a graviton and the incomplete understanding of how gravitons interact with other particles is one of the biggest unresolved problems with the standard model. We know the standard model is an incomplete theory partly because it does not include gravity.

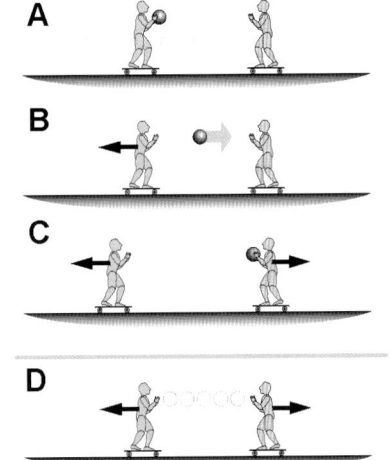

Figure 31.15: *Two people on skateboards throwing a ball back and forth. The motions of the people make it appear as if they are exerting a repulsive force on each other.*

Force carrying particles		
Gluons	Strong nuclear force *Short range*	
γ Photon	Electromagnetic force *Long range*	
$W^+ \quad W^- \quad Z^0$ Bosons	Weak nuclear force *Short range*	
Graviton	Gravitational force *Long range*	

Figure 31.16: *The force-carrying particles and their forces and ranges.*

650

A

aberration – a distortion in an optical image when compared to the original object.

absolute zero – the theoretical temperature at which there is zero thermal energy and atoms completely stop moving; 0 K on the Kelvin temperature scale.

absorption – occurs when the amplitude of a wave decreases and/or disappears as it passes through a material due to the material taking up some or all of the wave's energy.

acceleration – the rate of change of velocity over time; acceleration is a vector quantity with a magnitude and a direction.

acceleration due to gravity (g) – the acceleration of an object due to Earth's gravitational field strength; equal to 9.8 m/sec^2 on Earth.

accuracy – the quality of being exact and free from error.

acid – a compound that contributes hydrogen ions, H^+, to a solution.

acoustics – the science and technology of how sound behaves.

action – one of the two equal and opposite forces in an action-reaction pair, according to Newton's third law of motion.

activation energy – the threshold energy that must be reached for a chemical reaction to break the chemical bonds in the reactants and initiate the reaction.

additive color process (RGB) – the process through which new colors are formed by the addition of multiple colors; the additive primary colors of light are red, green, and blue.

air friction – the force that resists the motion of objects moving through air.

air resistance – the resisting effect on a moving object due to friction of air.

airfoil – a body with a shape that generates a large force normal to the direction of the surrounding fluid's motion.

alkali metal – any of the elements of group 1 (lithium, sodium, potassium, rubidium, cesium and francium) in the periodic table of elements.

alloy – a metal that is a mixture of more than one element.

alpha decay – a radioactive transformation in which a nucleus emits an alpha particle, decreasing the atomic number by two; an alpha particle consisting of two protons and two neutrons and signified by the Greek letter alpha (α).

alternating current (AC) – electric current that reverses its direction at regularly recurring intervals, usually many times per second.

amino acid – an organic acid containing the amino group (NH_2); a constituent of proteins.

ammeter – an instrument for measuring electric current flow in amperes.

ampere (amp or A) – the unit of measure for electric current.

amplify – to increase the magnitude of a signal by increasing its amplitude.

amplitude – the maximum value of a quantity that varies periodically from its base or equilibrium value to either extreme.

analog signal – a continuous electrical signal that varies in magnitude.

analysis – the detailed examination of experimental results to determine whether they support the hypothesis.

AND – a type of logic gate whose output is "1" only when both of its inputs are "1."

angle – the geometric figure formed by two lines extending from the same point.

angle of refraction – the angle formed between a refracted ray and the normal to the surface at the point of refraction.

angular acceleration – the change of angular velocity per unit of time.

angular displacement (θ) – the displacement of an object spinning on its axis, measured in radians or degrees.

angular momentum – the momentum due to an object's rotation or spin; it is the product of the object's moment of inertia multiplied by its angular velocity.

antimatter – material made of antiparticles of matter (positrons, antiprotons and antineutrons); when antimatter and matter meet, annihilation occurs, and both the matter and antimatter are converted to pure energy.

antinode – a point in a standing wave where the amplitude of the wave is at its maximum.

astronomical refracting telescope – an optical telescope arrangement consisting of a converging objective and eyepiece that produces a real inverted image.

at rest – a condition in which the speed of an object is zero.

atom – the smallest particle of an element that can exist alone or in combination with other atoms.

atomic mass – the average mass of all the known isotopes of an element, weighted for their relative natural abundance; usually given in atomic mass units (amu).

atomic mass unit (amu) – a unit of measure for expressing the mass of atoms, molecules, or nuclear particles equal to 1.661×10^{-27} kg; the atomic mass unit is defined as the mass of 1/12 of a carbon-12 atom.

atomic number – the number of protons that an atom contains.

average speed – the distance an object travels divided by the time elapsed regardless of variations in speed during the trip.

axis – (1) the line about which an object rotates; (2) one of the reference lines of a coordinate system.

B

background radiation – the radiation in the natural environment including cosmic rays and the radiation from naturally-occurring radioactive elements.

balanced equation – a chemical reaction in which the number and type of atoms on the reactant side and product side are equal.

baryon – a group of heavy elementary particles that includes protons and neutrons.

base – (1) a compound that contributes hydroxyl ions, OH⁻, to a solution.

base – (2) in scientific notation, the number between 1 and 10 that is multiplied by a power of ten.

base – (3) one of the three terminals of a transistor; the bias voltage between the base and emitter controls the current in the emitter and the collector.

battery – a device that uses chemical energy to generate electric energy.

beat – the pulsations of sound produced when two similar frequencies interfere with each other.

Bernoulli's equation – relates fluid pressure to its speed, density, and potential energy; the law of conservation of energy as applied to a steady flow of fluids.

beta decay – a radioactive transformation in which a neutron splits into a proton and an electron; the electron is emitted as a beta particle and the proton stays in the nucleus, increasing the atomic number by one.

bias voltage – a voltage across a semiconductor junction that is used to control current flow in the junction.

big bang – a theory of the origin and evolution of the universe.

binary – a system of numbers with two as its base and only using the digits "0" and "1."

bit – a single state of a digital signal, signified by a "0" or a "1."

black – the condition created by the absorption of all visible wavelengths of light; black objects reflect little or no light.

black hole – a theoretical region of time-space with such strong gravity that its escape velocity is equal to the speed of light.

blackbody – an ideal surface that reflects nothing, completely absorbs all radiant energy falling on it, and emits pure thermal radiation.

blackbody spectrum – the characteristic form of the graphic distribution of power vs. wavelength for a perfect blackbody.

blue – one of the primary colors of the additive color process; one kind of the three types of the primary color photoreceptor cone cells in the eye; the color of light that has wavelengths of approximately 455 to 492 nanometers.

boiling point – the characteristic temperature of a material at which the phase changes from liquid to gas; water boils at 100°C (212°F).

boson – an elementary particle that obeys Bose-Einstein statistics.

boundary – the interface or common surface between two adjacent materials that a wave travels through.

boundary condition – a set of requirements to be met at a specific place (the boundary) that provides a solution to the system's equations.

Boyle's law – a rule stating that the pressure of a gas is inversely proportional to its volume at constant temperature.

British Thermal Unit (Btu) – a unit of energy equal to the quantity of heat required to increase the temperature of one pound of water at standard pressure by 1°F; the abbreviation is Btu; equal to 1.055×10^3 J.

brittleness – the property of a material that describes its ability to fracture without being deformed; a brittle material breaks under a low strain with little deformation.

Brownian motion – the random, irregular motion of small particles in a fluid due to collisions with atoms and molecules.

buoyancy – an upward force a fluid exerts on a submerged object; the buoyancy force is equal to the weight of liquid displaced by the object.

C

calorie (c) – a unit of heat energy often used in chemistry; equal to the quantity of heat required to raise one gram of water by 1°C; a food calorie, or Calorie, is equal to 1,000 calories, or 4,200 J; equal to 4.2 J.

capacitance (C) – a measure of the ability of conductors and insulators to store electric charge; the unit of capacitance is the farad (F).

capacitor – a device consisting of two parallel conductors separated by insulating material that is used for storing electric charge.

carbohydrate – any of a group of organic compounds derived from carbon, hydrogen, and oxygen that are an energy component of foods, including sugars, starches, and celluloses.

carnivore – an organism that eats the flesh of animals, including decomposers, herbivores, and/or other carnivores.

Cartesian coordinate – a set of numbers (x, y) used to locate a point, where x is the distance to the point along the x-axis and y is the distance to the point along the y-axis; also known as a rectangular coordinate.

CAT scan – an x-ray process that produces a three-dimensional image; multiple x-rays are taken in different cross sections at different angles and combined into the final image.

Celsius scale – a temperature scale on which zero equals the temperature that water freezes (0°C) and 100 is the temperature that water boils (100°C) at standard temperature and pressure.

center of gravity – a fixed point at which the force of gravity acts on an object.

center of mass – the point about which an object moves as if the entire object's mass is at that point and all external forces were applied at that point; the point at which the object's three axes of spin intersect.

center of rotation – the point or line around which an object rotates.

centimeter (cm) – a metric unit of length equal to 0.01 meter.

central processing unit (CPU) – the digital circuits in a computer that interpret and execute the instructions of a computer program.

centrifugal force – the effect of inertia on an object moving in a curve; centrifugal force is not a true force.

centripetal acceleration – the acceleration of an object moving in a circular path; the centripetal acceleration is in the same direction as the centripetal force, toward the center of the circle.

centripetal force – a force that causes an object to move in a circular path, rather than continuing in a straight line; a centripetal force is directed toward the center of the circle.

charge – (1) another term for electric charge; (2) to load a capacitor with electrical energy by putting current through the capacitor.

charge by friction – the mechanical transfer of electric charge between two different objects by rubbing them together.

charge polarization – the separation of the positive and negative charge in an object's atoms due to the effect of an electric field.

Charles' law – a rule stating that the volume of a gas is directly proportional to its temperature at constant pressure.

chemical bond – the strong attractive force that holds together atoms in molecules and crystalline salts.

chemical change – a change in a substance that involves the breaking and reforming of chemical bonds to make one or more new substances.

chemical energy – the energy stored in chemical bonds.

chemical reaction – a process in which a substance is changed into one or more new substances; atoms are rearranged into new molecules, but atoms are not changed into other types of elements.

chromatic aberration – the distortion of an image by a lens caused by variations in the angle of refraction of different wavelengths of light resulting in color fringes.

circuit – see *electric circuit*.

circuit analysis – the process of calculating currents and voltages in a circuit.

circuit breaker – a safety device that interrupts the flow of current in a circuit when the current exceeds a predetermined limit; circuit breakers can be reset.

circuit diagram – a drawing using standard symbols that illustrates the arrangement of an electric circuit's components; also known as a schematic circuit diagram.

circular waves – waves that originate from a single point of disturbance and travel out in all directions; waves with concentric circular crests.

circumference – the distance of the enclosing boundary around a circle; for a sphere, the length of any great circle on the sphere.

closed circuit – an electric circuit through which current flows.

closed system – a system that is isolated so it cannot exchange energy or matter with its surroundings.

CMYK color process – see *subtractive color process (CMYK)*.

cochlea – a tiny, fluid-filled bone structure in the inner ear that contains the essential organs of hearing.

coefficient of friction – the ratio of the frictional force between two objects in contact (parallel to the surface of contact) to the normal force with which the objects press together.

coefficient of static friction – the ratio of the frictional force preventing two objects in contact with each other from sliding or rolling against each other to the normal force with which the objects press against each other.

coefficient of thermal expansion – a factor by which a material expands under temperature changes; units are 1/°C.

coil – a current-carrying wire made into loops; the magnetic field through the center of the coil is intensified as more loops are included, and the field strength is proportional to the current times the number of loops.

collector – one of the three terminals of a transistor where the current flows into the transistor and the magnitude of the current depends on the base bias voltage.

collision – occurs when two or more objects hit each other, transforming or converting the kinetic energy while conserving momentum.

color – the visual appearance of light corresponding to wavelength.

commutation – the process of reversing the current in an electric motor's electromagnet.

components – two or more vectors with the same effect as the given vector.

composite material – an engineered material made up of two or more materials with different characteristics; the resulting material has improved characteristics over its component materials.

compound – a substance containing more than one type of atom or elements that cannot be separated by physical means.

compressed – squeezed or shrunk.

compression – a reduction in the volume of a substance due to pressure.

condensation – the gradual transformation of matter from the gas to the liquid phase when the temperature is above the melting point.

conduction – (1) the transfer of thermal energy through materials by the direct contact of particles of matter; this energy transfer does not involve movement of the materials themselves; (2) the transfer of electricity by a material.

conductivity – see *electrical conductivity*.

conductor – see *thermal conductor and electrical conductor*.

cones – photoreceptor cells in the eye that respond to color.

consonance – a harmonious or agreeable combination of frequencies heard when sounds are played simultaneously.

constant – a quantity that remains at the same value when others quantities are changing.

constant acceleration – an acceleration that does not change; it is due to a velocity that changes at a constant rate.

constant speed – a maintained speed that does not vary.

constructive interference – occurs when two or more waves in the same phase are added together to create a wave of larger amplitude than the original waves.

continuous – connected or unbroken.

control variable – a variable in an experiment that is kept the same throughout the experiment.

controlled experiment – experiment in which when one variable is changed and all the others are controlled or stay the same throughout the experiment.

convection – the transfer of thermal energy by the flow of liquids or gases in currents.

converging – the coming together of light rays.

converging lens – a type of lens that bends light so that parallel rays entering the lens are bent toward the focal point as they exit the lens.

conversion factor – the number by which you multiply or divide a quantity in one unit to express the quantity in a different unit.

convex – having a curved form that bulges out in the middle.

cosine – to determine the x-component of a vector, the cosine of the included angle is the ratio of the x-component to the vector.

coulomb (C) – the unit for electric charge.

Coulomb's law – the attraction or repulsion between two electric charges is inversely proportional to the square of the distance between them.

covalent bond – a type of chemical bond formed when two atoms share electrons.

cracking – a process using heat and catalytic methods to break down heavier hydrocarbons into smaller molecules.

crest – the top or highest point of a wave.

critical angle – the angle at which light is totally reflected back into a material.

cross section area – the area of an imaginary or real cut made through an object.

current – see *electric current.*

cyan – a greenish light blue that is created when red light is absorbed from white light and blue and green light are reflected or when blue and green light are projected onto a common surface.

cycle – (1) in natural systems, a process of energy flows that maintains a system in steady state, (2) in oscillating systems, a unit of motion that recurs regularly.

D

damping – the gradual decrease of amplitude of an oscillation or wave

dark matter – a type of matter that theoretically exists to explain the motion of galaxies.

data – (1) measurements used as a basis for calculation; (2) information in numerical form that can be digitally transferred, transmitted, or processed.

decibel (db) – the dimensionless unit of a logarithmic scale for expressing the relative intensity of sounds.

decomposer – an organism that causes organic matter to decay; decomposers process organic matter back into the form of inorganic nutrients and energy.

deformation – for a spring, a deformation is the alteration in length due to extension or compression.

delta (Δ) – the symbol that indicates the difference or change between two quantities.

density – the characteristic ratio of a material's mass to its volume.

dependent variable – the variable in an experiment that changes in response to changes made to the independent variable; this variable is plotted on the y-axis of a graph.

depletion region – under reverse bias conditions, it is the region of a p-n junction where there are no available charge carriers.

destructive interference – when two or more out-of-phase waves are combined to create a wave of smaller amplitude than the original waves.

detector (radiation) – a device used to indicate the presence of radiation.

diamagnetic material – a material whose atoms have equal numbers of electrons spinning in each direction, giving the material a net magnetic field of zero; these materials are weakly repulsed by external magnetic fields.

diffraction – when waves change shape and direction as they pass through openings, around obstacles, or through boundaries.

diffraction grating – an optical device consisting of an assembly of parallel narrow slits or grooves that interfere with incident radiation to produce areas of maxima and minima that can result in spectra.

diffuse reflection – the random scattering of light rays at different angles when a beam of light is reflected off a rough surface.

digital signal – a "continuous" electrical signal that varies between two arbitrary states such as "0" and "1."

dimension – any of the three directions of movement.

diode – a semiconductor device with a p-n junction that allows current flow in one direction and blocks current in the other direction.

direct current (DC) – electric current that flows in one direction only.

discharge – to remove charge from a capacitor or other electrical energy storage device.

dispersion – the variation in the amount of refraction that occurs when different wavelengths of light cross a boundary from one transparent medium to another, resulting in the breakdown of constituent wavelengths seen as spectrum.

displacement – the difference between an object's initial and final positions; it is a vector quantity.

dissolved – the state in which solute particles are evenly distributed throughout a solvent.

dissonance – an unpleasant combination of frequencies heard when sounds are played simultaneously.

distance – the measure of space between two separate points; distance is a scalar value and does not depend upon direction.

diverge – the spreading apart of light rays.

diverging lens – a type of lens that bends light so that parallel rays are bent away from the focal point as they exit the lens.

Doppler effect – the change in the observed frequency of a wave due to the relative motion of the source and observer.

dose – the total amount of radiation received by a person, measured in rems.

double bond – a type of molecular bond between atoms in which two pairs of electrons are shared equally.

ductility – property of a material which describes its capability to be deformed without fracturing; a ductile material is not brittle.

dynamic – relating to motion of an object or system under the influence of forces.

dynamics – the process of calculating three-dimensional motion from forces and acceleration.

E

ecosystem – a functional system that includes the organisms of a natural community and their environment.

efficiency – the ratio of a machine's useful energy output to the energy input; the ratio of the work done by a system or machine to the energy input.

elastic collision – occurs when objects bounce off each other without breaking, changing shape, or losing energy due to heat or sound.

elasticity – the property of a material that describes its ability to regain its original size and shape after a deforming force has been removed.

electric charge – a fundamental property of matter; the unit of charge is the coulomb (C).

electric circuit – an arrangement of interconnected paths capable of carrying electric currents.

electric current – a flow of electric charge; current is measured in amperes (A); also known as current.

electric field – a region of electric force surrounded by electrically charged objects.

electric force – a fundamental force that charged materials or objects exert on each other.

electrical conductivity – the ability of a material to conduct or carry electric current; the inverse of resistance.

electrical conductor – a material with very low resistance that is used to efficiently carry electric current.

electrical energy – the type of energy resulting from the position of an electrical charge in an electrical field.

electrical insulator – a material that is a poor conductor of electric current.

electrical symbol – a simple symbol used to represent a component of a circuit in circuit diagrams.

electrically neutral – (1) an object that has a balanced amount of positive and negative charge, possessing no net charge; (2) an object (such as a neutron) with no electrical charge.

electricity – a physical phenomenon involving electrical charges and their effects when at rest and in motion.

electromagnet – a magnet made by inserting a magnetic core into a current-carrying wire coil; the core is magnetized while the current is switched on and demagnetized when the current is switched off.

electromagnetic induction – the process of producing current by the relative motion between a conductor and a magnetic field.

electromagnetic spectrum – the range of electromagnetic wave frequencies from very low frequencies like radio waves up through higher frequencies like infrared, visible light, x-rays, and gamma rays.

electromagnetic wave – a type of wave propagated by an oscillating or vibrating electric charge; consists of oscillating electric and magnetic fields that move at the speed of light.

electron – a negatively charged particle that comprises the outer layers of the atom; its mass is 9.11×10^{-3} kg; it carries a negative charge of 1.6×10^{-19} coulombs.

electroscope – an instrument used to detect charged objects.

elementary particles – an indivisible particle that is one of the fundamental constituents of matter.

ellipse – an oval shape, formed by the path of a point that moves so that the sum of the distances from a pair of fixed points, called foci, is a constant; an ellipse is the shape of the orbital path of planets in our solar system.

emitter – one of the three terminals of a transistor, where all the current from the collector and base exits the transistor.

endothermic reaction – a reaction in which more energy is required to break the bonds in reactants than is released from the formation of new bonds in the products; a reaction that requires energy to continue.

energy – the ability to make things change; energy is required to make a force do work, change motion, raise temperature, create new matter, break chemical bonds, or push electric current through a wire.

energy barrier – the input energy required to start radioactive decay; it consists of the strong nuclear force and the electromagnetic force within the nucleus.

energy conversion – the process of changing energy from one form to another.

energy flow – the conversion and/or transmission of one form of energy to another.

energy levels – a set of quantum states, all at approximately the same value of energy; electrons must absorb or emit energy to change levels.

engineering – the application of science to solve technical problems.

engineering cycle – a process used to build devices that solve technical problems; the four steps this cycle are creating a design, building a prototype, testing the prototype, and evaluating test results.

English system – a standardized system of measurement that uses distance units of inches, yards, and miles and weight measurements of pounds and tons.

equilibrium – (1) in physics, occurs when the forces on an object are balanced; (2) in chemistry, the state in which the solute in a solution is both dissolving and coming out of solution at the same rate.

equivalence principle – in general relativity, the principle that to an observer, the local effects of a gravitational field are indistinguishable from the effects from acceleration of the observer's frame of reference.

evaporation – the gradual conversion of matter from the liquid to the gas phase when the temperature is below the boiling point.

event horizon – the sphere around a black hole at which the escape velocity equals the speed of light.

exothermic reaction – a reaction that occurs when less energy is needed to break reactant bonds than is released when new products form; a reaction that produces enough energy to continue.

experiment – a test done under controlled conditions to make a discovery, test a hypothesis, or demonstrate a known fact.

experimental technique – the methods used to do an experiment.

experimental variable – a variable in an experiment that is changed by the experimenter; the experimental variable is plotted as an independent variable on the x-axis of a graph.

exponent – the small numeral shown to the upper right of a quantity that tells you how many times to multiply the quantity by itself.

extend – to stretch or elongate.

eyepiece – the lens or combination of lenses nearest the eye in an optical instrument; used to produce a final virtual magnified image of the previous image in the system.

F

Fahrenheit scale – a temperature scale on which 32 is the temperature at which water freezes (32°F) and 212 is the temperature at which water boils (212°F).

fallout – the radioactive material that descends to Earth from a nuclear explosion.

farad (F) – the metric, or SI, unit of capacitance.

Faraday's law of induction – states that a current is induced through a coil when there is a change in the magnetic field around it; the current flow is proportional to the rate of the field's change.

fat – nutrient molecule that is a glyceride of fatty acid.

ferromagnetic material – a material that exhibits a strong attraction to an external magnetic field due to the internal magnetic moments of the material's atoms spontaneously organizing into a common direction.

fiber optics – the use of thin, transparent fibers to transmit light; optical fibers are used in bundles to transmit information.

field – a mathematical description of how forces are distributed between particles in space.

field lines – vectors used to indicate the direction of force in a field.

fission – a nuclear reaction in which an atomic nucleus is split, resulting in the release of large amounts of energy.

fixed boundary – a boundary that is stationary and does not move in response to a wave.

fluid – a substance that can change shape and flow; both gases and liquids are fluids.

fluid mechanics – the study of the motion of fluids.

fluorescence – occurs when energy supplied by electromagnetic radiation causes atoms to excite and emit light energy.

focal length – the distance from the center of a lens to the focal point.

focal plane – a plane passing through the focal point that is perpendicular to the optical axis of a lens or mirror.

focal point – the point at which light rays either meet or diverge after passing through a lens parallel to the principal axis.

focus – (1) another term for the focal point; (2) to adjust the eyepiece or objective of a telescope so that the image can be clearly seen.

food chain – a hierarchy of feeding relationships between the organisms of a biological community; each level of organisms feeds on the level below.

food web – interrelated food chains within a biological community.

foot (ft) – the unit of length in the English system of measurement; equal to 0.3048 meters.

force – any action on a body that causes it to change motion; force is a vector and always has a magnitude and direction.

force field – a field that exerts a force on objects in its vicinity; examples include magnetic fields, gravitational fields, and electric fields.

forced convection – occurs when the flow of gas or liquid results from being circulated by fans or pumps.

forward bias – a voltage required by a diode (semiconductor junction) in the direction that produces current.

Fourier's theorem – states that nearly every wave can be expressed by superimposing single frequency waves.

free convection – occurs when the flow of gas or liquid results from differences in density and temperature.

free fall – movement that is due only to the force of gravity.

free-body diagram – a diagram showing all the force vectors that are acting on an object.

frequency – (1) in harmonics, the number of repetitions or cycles made in a unit of time; (2) in waves, the number of wavelengths that pass a given point in a specific unit of time.

frequency spectrum – a graphic representation showing the relative contribution to an overall sound made by each component frequency.

friction – the force that opposes the relative motion of bodies.

fulcrum – the point about which a lever rotates.

fundamental – the standing wave that has the lowest frequency and longest wavelength in a series of standing waves.

fusion – a nuclear reaction in which two atomic nuclei join together to form a larger nucleus.

G

g – the acceleration due to gravity equal to 9.8 m/sec^2.

g force – a force a body would feel as the acceleration of gravity; used as a unit of measurement for bodies undergoing the stress of acceleration.

gain – increase in signal power that is produced by an amplifier.

gamma decay – a quantum transition between two energy levels of a nucleus, in which a gamma ray is emitted; a gamma ray consists of a high energy photon.

gas – a phase of matter that flows and can expand or contract to fit any container; the atoms or molecules of a gas have free, random motion.

gas constant (R) – a physical constant in the equation for the ideal gas law; equal to 8.3 joules per Kelvin per mole.

gauss (G) – a unit of magnetic flux density; equal to 10^{-4} tesla; Earth's average magnetic field strength is approximately 0.3-0.5 G.

gear – wheel with teeth; two or more gears can be connected to transfer motion from one place to another; gears are used to change the speed and/or direction of rotational motion.

Geiger counter – a device used for detecting and counting ionizing radiation particles.

general relativity – Einstein's theory that relates the theory of special relativity to noninertial frames of reference and incorporates gravity; and in which events take place in a curved space.

generator – a device that uses induction to convert mechanical energy into electrical energy.

geometric optics – the branch of optics that describes the behavior of light in terms of light rays; geometric optics is concerned with the use of lenses and mirrors and how light is reflected and refracted.

gram (g or gm) – a metric unit of mass equal to 0.001 kilogram.

graph – a diagram that represents the change of a variable in comparison with one or more other variables.

graphical model – a model that shows the relationship between two variables on a graph so that the relationship is easily seen and understood.

gravitational constant (G) – the constant in the equation of Newton's law of universal gravitation; equal to 6.67×10^{-11} Nm^{2}kg^{-2}, and is the same throughout the universe.

gravitational field – a region of space in which one body attracts other bodies as a result of their mass.

gravitational mass – the mass of an object as measured by the force of attraction between masses; inertial and gravitational masses are equal in a uniform gravitational field.

green – one of the primary colors of the additive color process; one of the primary photoreceptor cone cells in the eye; the color of light that has wavelengths of approximately 492 to 577 nanometers.

gyroscope – a spinning object that tends to maintain a fixed orientation in space due to its angular momentum.

H

half-life – the average time required for one half of the atoms in a radioactive material to decay.

hard magnet – a material that is difficult to magnetize or demagnetize.

harmonic – a frequency that is a multiple of the fundamental note; a standing wave that has a frequency that is a multiple of the fundamental frequency; a multiple of the natural frequency.

harmonic motion – motion that repeats itself as in the case of a pendulum, rotating wheel, or other oscillator.

heat – the form of energy that results from the random motion of molecules; thermal energy that flows or is moving.

heat of fusion – the amount of energy it takes to change one kg of solid to one kg of liquid; the amount of energy it takes to change the phase of the material without changing the temperature.

heat of vaporization – the amount of energy it takes to change one kg of liquid to 1 kg of gas; the amount of energy it takes to change the phase without changing temperature.

heat transfer – the flow of thermal energy from one object to another due to a temperature difference.

heat transfer coefficient (h) – a constant used in calculating heat transfers in the convection equation; the heat transfer coefficient takes into account the fluids, flow speed, and surface conditions.

herbivore – an organism that eats only producers or vegetation.

hertz (Hz) – the unit of one cycle per second used to measure frequency.

heterogeneous mixture – a mixture composed of nonuniform constituents.

homogeneous mixture – a mixture having uniform composition throughout.

Hooke's law – states that the force applied to a spring is directly proportional to the deformation of the spring.

horsepower (hp) – a unit of power equal to 746 watts.

hydrocarbon – one of a group of chemical compounds composed of only carbon and hydrogen; the largest source of hydrocarbons is petroleum crude oil.

hypothesis – a prediction or an unproven model that can be tested by experimentation; a hypothesis is the starting point for future investigation.

I

ideal gas law – an equation expressing the relationship between pressure, volume, mass and temperature of a gas.

image – a picture of an object that is formed when light rays given off or reflected from the object meet.

image relay – a technique for an optical system made up of multiple lenses and/or mirrors; the image produced by the first lens becomes the object for the second lens, and so on through the system.

impulse – the single application of an outside force that causes a change in momentum; it equals the product of the force and the time applied.

incandescence – occurs when visible light is produced by an object's high temperature.

inch – a unit of length commonly used in the United States; equal to 1/12 foot or 2.54 centimeters.

incident ray – a light ray from an object that strikes a surface.

incident wave – a wave coming into contact with a surface or boundary.

inclined plane – a flat, smooth surface at an angle to a force.

independent variable – the variable in an experiment that is manipulated by the experimenter and that causes changes in the dependent variable in the experiment; this variable is plotted on the *x*-axis of a graph.

index of refraction (*n*) – a ratio that expresses how much a ray of light bends when it passes from one kind of material to another.

induced current – the flow of electric current due to a changing magnetic field around the conductor.

induction (electrostatic) – the process of electrically charging an object by bringing it physically near another charged object.

inelastic collision – a type of collision where the objects stick together or change shape and lose kinetic energy; in any type of collision, momentum is always conserved.

inertia – the resistance of a body to a change in motion.

infrared – the section of the electromagnetic spectrum below the red end of visible light and above microwaves; infrared waves are invisible to the human eye and are usually in the form of radiant heat.

initial speed – the speed an object has at the beginning of an experiment.

input – the work or energy put into a machine; the resources used by a machine.

input arm – the distance on a lever between the fulcrum and the point where the input force is applied.

input force – the force applied to a machine.

inquiry – to explore and investigate through observation.

instantaneous speed – an object's speed measured at a precise moment in time.

insulator – see *thermal insulator and electrical insulator*.

integrated circuit – a circuit that incorporates many components into one functional unit.

intensity – a measure of the brightness of light that is related to the total number of photons per second.

interference pattern – the pattern of pressure, brightness, and darkness, or other wave characteristic resulting from the superposition of waves of the same kind and frequency.

inverse square law – any law in which a physical quantity varies with the distance from a source inversely as the square of the distance.

ion – an atom, which by the gain or loss of one or more electrons, has an electrical charge.

ionic bond – a type of chemical bond in which electrons are transferred between atoms, converting the atoms into ions.

ionization – a process by which a neutral atom or molecule loses or gains electrons, acquiring a net charge and becoming an ion.

ionize – a process by which electrons are added to or removed from electrically neutral atoms.

ionizing radiation – electromagnetic radiation with enough energy to remove an electron from, or ionize, an atom.

irreversible process – a process that cannot run forward and backward using the same series of steps; a process for which the efficiency is less than 100%.

isotope – A different form of the same element with different numbers of neutrons and different mass numbers, but the same number of protons and the same atomic number.

J

joule (J) – a unit for measuring energy and work; it is equal to one newton of force multiplied by one meter of distance.

K

Kelvin scale – temperature scale starting at absolute zero and measuring the actual energy of atoms; on this scale water freezes at 273 K and boils at 373 K.

kilogram (kg) – the unit of mass in the SI system; equal to the mass of the international prototype kilogram stored at Sevres, France.

kilowatt (kW) – a unit of power equal to 1,000 watts or 1,000 joules per second.

kilowatt-hour (kWh) – power companies' convenient measure of energy equal to the energy transferred by one kilowatt of power in one hour; equal to 3.6×10^6 joules.

kinetic energy – the energy a body or system possesses due to motion.

Kirchhoff's current law – states that the sum of the currents flowing into any point in a circuit equals the current flowing out of that point in the circuit.

Kirchhoff's voltage law – states that the sum of the voltages of all the voltage-generating components equals the sum of the voltages of all the voltage-consuming components.

L

laminar flow – a streamlined flow where the adjacent layers of a fluid flow smoothly together.

law of conservation of energy – energy cannot be created or destroyed although it can be changed from one form to another.

law of conservation of momentum – the principle that, in the absence of outside forces, the total momentum of a system is constant although momentum may be transferred within the system.

law of inertia – another term for Newton's first law of motion.

law of reflection – states that when a light ray reflects off a surface, the angle of incidence is equal to the angle of reflection.

law of universal gravitation – the force of attraction between two objects is directly related to their masses and indirectly related to the square of the distance between them; also known as Newton's law of universal gravitation.

length (l) – a measured distance.

lens – a specially-shaped optical device made of transparent material like glass that is used to bend light rays.

lepton – a type of elementary particle having a mass smaller than the proton mass and interacting with electromagnetic and gravitational fields.

lever – a type of simple machine consisting of a rigid bar able to turn around a fixed point called a fulcrum; it is used to move or lift a load.

lever arm – the distance between the line of action of the force and the center of rotation at the fulcrum.

Lewis dot diagram – a structural formula in which electrons are represented by dots; two dots between atoms represents a covalent bond.

lift force – the net force on an airfoil acting perpendicular to the fluid flow.

light ray – a beam of light that travels in a straight line and has a very small cross section.

line of action – an imaginary line that follows the direction of a force and passes through its point of application.

linear momentum – the momentum due to an object's linear movement; it is the product of the object's mass multiplied by its velocity.

liquid – a phase of matter that keeps a constant volume but can flow and change its shape; a liquid's atoms or molecules move about, and intermolecular forces are strong enough to keep a constant volume.

locomotion – progressive movement as of an animal or a vehicle.

logic circuit – a circuit that processes digital signals; its output depends upon the states of its inputs and the logic functions of its gates.

logic gate – a type of simple logic circuit with a single logic function.

longitudinal wave – a wave whose oscillations are in the same direction as the wave travels; an example is a sound wave.

lubricant – a substance used to reduce friction between parts or objects moving against each other.

M

m/sec – a metric unit of measure for velocity.

machine – a type of mechanical system capable of performing work.

magenta – a pink-purple color created when green light is absorbed and red and blue light are reflected or when blue and red light are projected onto a common surface.

magnetic – a property of materials describing their ability to exert forces on magnets or other magnetic materials.

magnetic declination – the angle that indicates the difference between magnetic south from true north.

magnetic domain – a region of a material in which atoms with similar magnetic orientations align in the same direction, increasing their magnetic field strength rather than cancelling each other out as they do when randomly aligned.

magnetic field – a region of magnetic force surrounding magnetic objects.

magnetic field lines – the vector arrows used to indicate the direction of magnetic force within a magnetic field.

magnetic flux – a measure of a magnetic field's strength through an area based on the number of the magnetic force's lines passing through the area; its unit is the weber (Wb).

magnetic force – a force exerted on a particle or object in a magnetic field; the magnetic force can be either attractive or repulsive depending upon the object's alignment to the magnetic poles, and its material properties.

magnetic north pole – one of the two regions of a magnetic field where the field forces are the strongest; magnetic poles have only been found in opposite pairs and have not been singly isolated.

magnetic south pole – one of the two regions of a magnetic field where the field forces are the strongest; magnetic poles have only been found in opposite pairs and have not been singly isolated.

magnetize – to develop or strengthen a magnetic field in an object in response to an external magnetic field.

magnification – the amount that an optical system changes the apparent size of an object; the magnification of a telescope is the ratio of the focal lengths of the objective to the eyepiece.

magnifying glass – a simple converging lens that produces an enlarged right-side-up image of the object being viewed.

magnitude – a quantity's size or amount without regard to its direction.

mass – a measure an object's inertia; the amount of matter an object has.

mass number – the total number of protons and neutrons in the nucleus of an atom.

matter – anything that has mass and occupies space.

mechanical advantage – the ratio of output force to input force.

mechanical energy – the energy possessed by an object due to its motion or its position.

mechanical system – a series of interrelated, moving parts that work together to accomplish a specific task.

melting point – the characteristic temperature of a material at which its phase changes from solid to liquid; the kinetic energy of the atoms overcomes the attractive force between the atoms.

memory – the digital circuit in a computer in which digital information can be stored and then retrieved.

meson – a type of elementary particle with strong nuclear interactions and baryon number equal to zero.

meter (m) – the international standard unit of length; equal to the length of the path traveled by light in 1/299,792,458 of a second.

metric system – a standardized system of measuring based on the meter and the kilogram and using multiples of 10.

microfarad (μF) – a unit of capacitance equal to 10^{-6} farads.

microphone – a device that transforms sound waves into electrical signals for the purpose of transmitting or recording sound.

mile (mi) – a unit of length commonly used in the United States; equal to 5,280 feet or 1,609.344 meters.

millimeter (mm) – a metric unit of length equal to 0.001 meter.

mirror – an optical device that reflects light.

mixture – a substance that contains a combination of different compounds and/or elements and be separated by physical means.

mode – a pattern of wave motion or vibration.

model – a mathematical or physical representation of an actual system.

modulus of elasticity – the ratio of the stress on a material to the amount of strain produced.

molecule – a neutral group of atoms that are chemically bonded together; it is the smallest particle of a compound that can exist by itself and retain the properties of the compound.

moment of inertia – a vector quantity that describes the distribution of mass in an object; the rotational equivalent of mass.

momentum – a vector quantity that is the product of an object's mass and its velocity.

multimeter – a test instrument used for measuring voltage, current, and resistance.

musical scale – a series of musical notes arranged from low to high in a special pattern.

N

NAND – a type of logic gate whose output is "0" only when each of its inputs is "1."

natural frequency – the frequency at which a system tends to oscillate when disturbed.

natural law – the set of rules that governs the fundamental workings of the universe.

negative charge – one of two types of electric charge; electrons carry a negative charge.

net force – the amount of force that overcomes an opposing force to cause motion; the net force can be zero if the opposing forces are equal.

network circuit – a complex circuit containing multiple paths and resistors that are connected both in series and in parallel.

neutrino – a neutral elementary particle having zero rest mass and spin of ½.

neutron – an uncharged particle found with protons in the nucleus of atoms; it is approximately the same size as a proton with a mass of 1.67×10^{-27} kg.

newton (N) – the SI, or metric, unit of force.

Newton's first law of motion – states that an object at rest remains at rest until acted on by an unbalanced force; an object in motion continues with constant speed and direction in a straight line unless acted on by an unbalanced force.

Newton's second law of motion – states that the acceleration of an object is directly proportional to the force acting on it and inversely proportional to its mass.

Newton's third law of motion – states that whenever one object exerts a force on another, the second object exerts an equal and opposite force on the first.

noble gas – any of the gases in group 18 of the periodic table of elements; they do not form chemical bonds with other elements and are usually chemically inert.

node – a stationary point with zero amplitude in a standing wave.

nonionizing radiation – electromagnetic radiation that is absorbed by atoms without ionizing them.

NOR – a type of logic gate whose output is "1" only if both inputs are "0."

normal – a line that is perpendicular to an object's surface.

note – a frequency in a musical scale.

n-type semiconductor – a semiconductor with an added impurity where the conduction electron density exceeds the hole density; the opposite of a p-type.

nuclear chain reaction – occurs when the neutrons from a fission reaction cause the fission of more atoms, starting a succession of self-sustaining nuclear fissions, resulting in the continuous release of nuclear energy.

nuclear energy – the type of energy derived from nuclear reactions.

nuclear reaction – a process involving changes in an atom's nucleus; atoms of one element can be changed into atoms of different elements.

nuclear waste – the unwanted radioactive by-products from the nuclear industry and from materials used in research, industry, and medicine.

nucleus – the central, positively-charged, dense core of an atom that contains protons and neutrons.

O

object – the source of light rays, either given off or reflected, in an optical system.

objective – the lens or combination of lenses nearest the object in an optical instrument.

objectivity – a characteristic of scientific evidence. Scientific evidence is considered objective if it describes only what actually happens and is observed, free from any personal opinions or bias the experimenter may have.

octane – a rating that indicates how fast a gasoline burns after ignition; the rating scale is defined between 0 (n-hepatine) and 100 (isooctane); indicates the antiknocking tendencies of a gasoline.

octave – a frequency difference that is double or half the starting frequency.

ohm (Ω) – the unit of measurement for electrical resistance.

Ohm's law – the mathematical relationship in which current in an electric circuit is directly proportional to the voltage applied and inversely proportional to the resistance.

open boundary – a boundary that is free to move in response to a wave.

open circuit – an electric circuit with a broken pathway and no current.

optical axis – the line joining the centers of curvature of lenses and/or mirrors in an optical system.

optics – the study of the behavior of light.

OR – a type of logic gate whose output is "1" when any of its inputs are "1."

orbit – a regular, repeating, curved path that an object in space follows around another object due to the effects of gravity between the objects.

orbital – the region of space occupied by an electron in an atom; a term used by chemists for quantum state.

organic chemistry – the chemistry of the structure, preparation, properties, and reactions of carbon compounds.

origin – the point where something begins; a fixed reference point; the point of a coordinate system where all the coordinate axes meet.

oscillation – a motion that varies periodically back and forth between two values.

oscillator – a system that periodically varies between two values, positions, or states; a system that has harmonic motion.

output – the work or energy produced by a machine; the product of a system or machine.

output arm – the distance on a lever between the fulcrum and where the output force is exerted.

output force – the force produced by a machine.

P

parabola – the distinctive, arched shape of a projectile's trajectory.

parallel circuit – a circuit in which components are connected so the current can take more than one path.

parallel plate capacitor – a capacitor consisting of two parallel metal plates with an insulator filling the space between them.

paramagnetic material – a material that can be magnetized when placed in an external magnetic field; its properties are due to the unpaired electron spins of the material's atoms.

pascal (Pa) – the metric, or SI, unit of pressure; one pascal is equal to one newton of force acting on one square meter of surface.

Pauli exclusion principle – the rule, according to quantum theory, stating that no two electrons in an atom can simultaneously occupy the same quantum state.

period – the amount of time it takes for one repetition of a cycle.

periodic force – a force that oscillates in strength or direction.

periodic motion – cycles of motion that repeat for every period of time; an example is harmonic motion.

periodic table of elements – a table that visually organizes all known elements; elements are grouped in the table in order of atomic number, and columns are grouped by the elements' properties.

permanent magnet – a magnetic object that retains its magnetism when an external magnetic field is removed.

petroleum – a naturally-occurring liquid hydrocarbon that is a mixture of various organic chemicals; it is refined for use as fuel, petrochemicals, and lubricants; also known as crude oil.

pH – the measure of the concentration of H_3O^+ (hydronium) ions in a solution.

phase – the point where an oscillator is in its cycle in relation to its starting point.

phase difference – the difference between two cycles with the same frequency; it is measured either as an angle or a time.

photoelectric effect – effect observed when light incident to certain metal surfaces causes electrons to be emitted.

photoluminescence – the emission of light from a substance that has absorbed light energy.

photon – according to quantum theory and the particle concept of light, a photon is the smallest discrete packet of energy that makes up light; the quantum of electromagnetic radiation.

photoreceptors – highly specialized, light-sensitive cells in the retina of the eye.

photosynthesis – a chemical reaction performed by plants in which energy from the sun is converted to chemical energy; carbon dioxide and water are converted to sugar and oxygen in this reaction.

physical change – a change in a substance's physical properties.

piezoelectric effect – the effect shown by certain types of crystals that produce voltage across their surfaces when they are compressed or distorted.

pigment – a solid that reflects color of a certain wavelength and absorbs colors of other wavelengths, allowing your eyes to perceive the reflected color.

pitch – the property of a sound determined by the frequency of the waves producing it; the highness or lowness of a sound.

pixel – the smallest part of an electronic picture image.

Planck's constant (h) – a fundamental constant that is the ratio of a photon's quantum energy to its frequency; equal to 6.63×10^{-34} J-sec.

plane wave – waves that originate from a straight line disturbance and move in a straight line direction.

plasma – an ionized gas phase of matter; the atoms or molecules of plasma are broken down into a mixture of free electrons and ions; examples of plasma include stars, lightning, and neon-type lights.

p-n junction – the interface between a p-type semiconductor and an n-type semiconductor; it allows current to flow in only one direction.

point charges – charges whose dimensions are small compared with their distance apart from one another.

polar coordinate – a group of numbers, or coordinate, ($r, I,$) used to locate a point, where r is the distance from the origin and I is the angle between the positive x-axis and a ray from the origin to the point.

polar molecule – a molecule with a positive and a negative pole.

polarity – the property of a system that has two directions or signs with opposite characteristics; examples include electrical polarity with opposite charges or potentials or magnetic polarity with opposite magnetic poles.

polarization – limiting the orientation of a transverse wave, especially of light.

polarizer – a device or material that polarizes light.

position – an object's location in space compared to where it started.

positive charge – one of two types of electric charge; protons carry a positive charge.

potential energy – the work a body or system can do because of its position or state.

potentiometer – a mechanical, continuously-adjustable resistor.

power – the amount of work done per unit of time; work done divided by the time it takes to do the work; the rate of energy transfer or work done; the unit of power is the watt (W).

power factor – the loss of power in an alternating current circuit due to the phase difference between the voltage and the current.

power of ten – the result when ten is multiplied by itself; 1,000 is the third power of ten ($10 \times 10 \times 10$ or 10^3); powers of ten are positive for values greater than 1 and negative for values less than 1.

precision – the degree of mutual agreement among a series of individual measurements, values, or results.

pressure – the force exerted per unit area; fluid pressure acts in all directions.

pressure energy – the energy stored in a pressure differential.

prism – an optical device used to separate white light into its component colors by dispersion.

probability – mathematical rules governing the relative possibility of an event occurring.

procedure – all the experimental techniques used to run an experiment; procedures must be repeatable to ensure the results are accurate and true.

process – (1) a set of actions or steps performed to achieve a given purpose; (2) any activity that changes things and can be described in terms of input and output.

producer – an organism that manufactures organic nutrients directly from simple inorganic raw materials.

product – a substance formed as a result of a chemical reaction.

program – the set of instructions that tells a computer how to process data.

projectile – an object that is launched by an applied external force and whose motion ideally is only affected by gravity.

propagation – to spread out or travel through a medium; wave motion.

protein – a complex molecule composed of amino acids joined by peptide links that are the building blocks of living things.

proton – a positively charged particle found with neutrons in an atom's nucleus; its mass is 1.67×10^{-27} kg; it carries a positive charge of 1.60×10^{-19} coulombs.

prototype – a working model of a design that can be tested to see if it works.

p-type semiconductor – a semiconductor with an added impurity where the hole density exceeds the conduction electron density; the opposite of an n-type.

Pythagorean theorem – in a right triangle, the square of the length of the hypotenuse equals the sum of the squares of the lengths of the other two sides.

Q

quantum – the smallest discrete quantity of energy released or absorbed in a process; the photon is the quantum of an electromagnetic wave.

quantum number – one of the quantities that specifies the value of a quantum state; the value is an integer or half integer.

quantum physics – the branch of science that explains the behavior of matter and energy on the atomic and subatomic scale.

quantum state – the set of characteristics completely describing the state of electrons in an atom.

quark – a hypothetical basic particle that is theoretically a constituent of elementary particles.

R

radian (rad) – a type of angle measurement; one radian is defined as the central angle of a circle where the two radii and the arc joining them are all equal in length; one radian equals 57.3 degrees.

radiant energy – another term for electromagnetic energy.

radiation – (1) the process of emitting radiant energy; (2) the particles and energy that are emitted from radioactive substances.

radio wave – a form of electromagnetic waves with a wavelength greater than a few millimeters (bordering with microwaves); its main application is carrying information for radios and televisions.

radioactive – an unstable atomic state in which the nucleus emits radiation in the form of particles and energy until it becomes more stable or disintegrates.

radioactive decay – the spontaneous disintegration of a material with the release of radiation.

ramp – a type of simple machine consisting of a uniformly sloping surface.

random motion – motion that is scattered equally in all directions.

range – the distance a projectile travels horizontally.

rate – the amount of change of a quantity per unit of time.

ray diagram – a diagram that shows how light rays behave as they go through an optical system.

reactant – a substance that enters into and is altered in the course of a chemical reaction.

reaction – one of the two equal and opposite forces in an action-reaction pair according to Newton's third law of motion.

real image – the reproduction of an object produced by light rays that converge through the image; it forms on the side of the lens opposite the object; for example, a slide projector produces a real image on a screen.

red – one of the primary colors along with blue and green of the additive color process; one of the primary photoreceptor cone cells; the color of light that has wavelengths of approximately 622 to 770 nanometers.

red shift – a Doppler shift of light towards longer wavelengths.

reference frame – a coordinate system assigning positions and times to events.

refine – a process used to remove impurities; to separate petroleum into its component parts.

reflected wave – a wave that is bounced off a boundary.

reflection – the process by which waves or light return or bounce off a surface or a boundary between two materials.

refracted wave – the part of a wave that travels into and through a boundary; also known as a transmitted wave.

refraction – the process by which waves change direction while traveling into and through a surface or a boundary between two materials.

relative humidity – the ratio of the amount of water vapor in the air to the equilibrium amount at a given temperature; shows how close the air is to maximum saturation.

rem – a unit for measuring ionizing radiation which takes into account the damage to humans.

resistance – the opposition that a device or material offers to the flow of electric current.

resistor – an electrical device that regulates current in circuits.

resolution – (1) the ability of a lens system to reproduce the details of an object as details in the image; (2) the procedure of separating a vector into its components.

resonance – a large oscillation created when the frequency of a driving force matches the system's natural frequency.

rest energy – the energy equivalent to the rest mass of a particle or body; the quantity of mc^2 where c is the speed of light.

restoring force – a force that always acts to pull an oscillating system back toward equilibrium.

resultant – the single vector that represents the sum of a number of vectors and connects the starting position with the final position.

reverberation – multiple reflections of sound building up and blending together.

reverse bias – a voltage across a diode with polarity such that little or no current is produced; the opposite of forward bias.

reversible process – an ideal process that can be returned to its original starting condition through the same series of steps; a process that can run forward or backward.

revolve – to move around, or orbit, an external axis.

RGB color process – see *additive color process (RGB)*.

rhythm – the organization of a sound into regular time patterns.

right triangle – a triangle, one of whose angles is $90°$.

right-hand-rule – the rule used to determine a magnetic field's direction in the presence of a current; when the thumb of your right hand points in the direction of conventional current, your fingers wrap in the magnetic field's direction.

rods – photoreceptor cells in the eye that respond to differences in brightness.

rolling friction – the force that resists the motion of any body rolling over the surface of another.

rope and pulleys – a type of simple machine; a pulley is a wheel with a rim that rotates on a shaft and carries a rope, transmitting motion and force.

rotate – to spin around an internal axis.

rotational equilibrium – occurs when the torques on an object are balanced.

rotational inertia – see *moment of inertia*.

R-value – a measure of resistance to the flow of heat by conduction; a higher number indicates better insulating property.

S

safety factor – the ratio between the breaking load on something and the safe permissible load on it.

satellite – an object in orbit that is bound by gravity to another object.

saturation – when a solution contains as much of a dissolved solid, liquid, or gas as will dissolve into the solution at a given temperature and pressure; when the processes of evaporation and condensation are in equilibrium.

scalar – a quantity having magnitude only, and no direction; examples are mass, distance, and time.

scale – a ratio or constant factor used to change the size or magnitude of a quantity in a uniform way.

scientific evidence – information from experiments that is in a form such as data and graphs.

scientific notation – a mathematical abbreviation for writing very large or very small numbers; numbers are expressed as products consisting of a base between 1 and 10 multiplied by an appropriate power of 10.

screw – a type of simple machine consisting of a threaded body and grooved head that turns rotational motion into linear motion; it is used to fasten things together when its body is twisted into a material.

semiconductor – a solid crystalline material whose electrical resistance is temperature dependent and can be controlled or changed.

series circuit – a circuit where the components are connected one after the other so the same current moves through each component with only one possible path.

shielding – (1) radiation, reducing or blocking ionizing radiation by using a shield or other device; (2) electrical, a conductive metal casing used to shield electrical devices from stray electric fields.

shock wave – the compressed wave fronts that form in front of a supersonic object; the wavefronts form a boundary between sound and silence.

short circuit – a electric circuit where the resistance is very low, causing currents much higher than the circuit was designed to handle.

simple machine – an unpowered mechanical device that uses only one motion to change the size or direction of a force.

sine – to determine the y-component of a vector, the sine of the opposite angle is the ratio of the vector's y-component to itself.

sliding friction – resistance created when two surfaces move against each other in continuous contact.

slope – a line's vertical change divided by its horizontal change.

Snell's Law – a mathematical relationship that can be used to calculate the angle at which a light ray will bend as it moves from one material into another.

soft magnet – a magnetic material that is relatively easily magnetized or demagnetized; an example is iron.

solenoid – a device consisting of a current-carrying coil of wire with a movable central magnetic core; when the wire is energized, a magnetic field is produced within the coil, pulling the core into position.

solid – a phase of matter that has a definite volume and shape and does not flow; the atoms or molecules of a solid occupy fixed positions, and intermolecular forces are strong.

solubility – the ability of a substance to form a solution with another substance; the amount of solute that can be dissolved in a certain volume of solvent under certain conditions.

solute – the substance dissolved in a solution; the solute is dissolved by the solvent.

solution – a mixture that is homogeneous at the molecular level and the components are uniformly distributed throughout.

solvent – the component of a solution that dissolves the solute.

sonogram – a graphic representation of sound showing frequency, time, and intensity.

speaker – a device that converts electrical signals into sound; used to reproduce sound accurately.

specific heat – a characteristic property of a substance equal to the amount of heat energy, measured in calories, required to raise the temperature of one gram of the substance 1°C.

spectral line – each specific wavelength of light emitted or absorbed by an element as it appears in a spectrometer.

spectrometer – an optical instrument used for producing, examining, and measuring the different wavelengths of the electromagnetic spectrum; also known as a spectroscope.

spectrum – the characteristic wavelengths of light emitted or absorbed by elements; the pattern of characteristic wavelengths of electromagnetic radiation emitted from a source such as sunlight dispersed by a prism.

specular reflection – reflection that occurs off smooth surfaces; the light ray is not scattered, and the reflected image is undistorted.

speed – the measure of distance traveled in a given amount of time without regard to direction; the magnitude of the velocity vector; distance divided by time.

speed of light (c) – the speed of light is a constant equal to 299,792,458 m/s in a vacuum.

spherical aberration – the distortion of an image from a spherical mirror or lens caused by the rays from a point object failing to converge to a point image.

spherical pattern – the distribution of light rays emitted from a source of light that travel in straight lines going in every direction from the source.

spring – an elastic device that can be compressed or extended, and that when released, returns to its former shape.

spring constant (k) – a constant that represents how much a specific spring deforms under a force.

stable equilibrium – a state of equilibrium in which a system tends to return to its original state when disturbed.

standing wave – a wave trapped in one spot that is formed when two identical waves travel in opposite directions between two boundaries.

static – without motion or change.

static electricity – a buildup of either positive or negative charge on an insulated object's surface.

static friction – the force that resists the initiation of sliding motion between two surfaces in contact with each other; no motion results.

steady state – occurs in a system when the total energy of that system remains the same over time.

stereo – a method of sound reproduction involving multiple speakers to approximate the spatial distribution of the original sound.

strain – the ratio of the change of an object's length to its original size.

streamline – a line indicating the direction of fluid flow in a laminar flow.

stress (σ) – force divided by the area on which it acts; its unit of measure is the pascal (Pa)

strong nuclear force – the strongest fundamental force in the atom that attracts neutrons and protons to each other, holding the atomic nucleus together.

subscript – a letter, symbol, or number written below and to the right of another symbol; used to indicate the number of atoms of a kind in a molecule for chemical reactions.

subsonic – motion that is slower than the speed of sound in air.

substance – a mixture that cannot be separated using physical means.

subtractive color process (CMYK) – the process through which colors are created by the removal of colors by absorption, allowing the reflection of the desired color; the subtractive primary colors of pigment are magenta, cyan, and yellow.

superconductivity – a condition of zero electrical resistance that exists for certain materials at very low temperatures.

superposition principle – states that when two or more waves overlap, the amplitude of the resulting wave is the sum of the amplitudes of the individual waves.

supersonic – motion that is faster than the speed of sound in air.

surface area – the measurement of the extent of an object's surface or area without including its thickness.

switch – a device for opening, closing, or changing the connections in an electric circuit.

T

tangent – the ratio of an angle's sine to its cosine.

temperature – the measurement used to quantify the sensations of hot and cold; a measurement of the average kinetic energy of molecules in a substance.

tensile strength – the measure of how much pulling, or tension, a material can withstand before breaking or deforming permanently.

tension – a force that stretches or pulls a material.

term – a component of an equation.

terminal speed – the maximum speed reached by an object in free fall; the speed at which forces of gravity and air resistance are equal.

terrestrial refracting telescope – a refracting telescope arrangement using an inverting lens between the objective lens and the eyepiece to form a right-side-up image.

tesla – a metric, or SI, unit of magnetic flux density equal to one weber per square meter.

test charge – a charge used for measuring electric fields.

theory – an explanation or hypothesis that has been well tested but is not yet proven.

theory of special relativity – a theory by Albert Einstein that natural laws are the same in all frames of reference and that the speed of light in a vacuum is constant for all observers, regardless of the motion of the source or observer.

thermal conductivity – a measure of a material's ability to conduct thermal energy.

thermal conductor – a material through which heat can easily flow.

thermal energy – the total kinetic energy contained in a material's atoms and molecules.

thermal equilibrium – occurs when two bodies have the same temperature; no heat flows because the temperatures are the same.

thermal insulator – a material that conducts heat poorly.

thermal radiation – the energy emitted by objects in the form of electromagnetic waves as a result of the thermal motion of their molecules.

thermal stress – mechanical stress induced by a change in temperature when part of a body is not free to contract or expand.

thermistor – an electrical component that changes its electrical resistance as the temperature changes.

thermocouple – an electrical sensor that measures temperature.

thermometer – an instrument that measures temperature.

thin lens formula – states that the sum of the inverse of the object and image distances equals the inverse of the focal length of the lens.

time (t) – a measurement of duration between events; all or part of the past, present, and future.

time dilation – according to Einstein's theory of special relativity, a clock appears to run slower to an observer moving relative to the clock than to an observer who is at rest with respect to the clock.

time interval – the time separating two events.

time of flight – the elapsed time an object or projectile spends in the air.

torque (τ) – a measure of how much a force acting on an object causes the object to rotate.

Glossary

total internal reflection – occurs when light traveling from a more optically dense to a less optically dense medium approaches the boundary greater than the critical angle and reflects back.

trajectory – the curved path a projectile follows; its curve is due to a constant horizontal velocity and an accelerating vertical velocity.

transistor – a semiconductor device with three terminals used to control current.

transition metal – any of the elements in groups 3-12 in the periodic table of elements; they are distinguished by having valence electrons present in more than one shell.

translation – linear motion involving change of position without rotation.

transmission axis – the orientation of a polarizer filter.

transverse wave – a wave whose oscillations move perpendicular to the direction the wave travels.

trial – each time an experiment is run.

trough – the lowest or bottom point of a wave.

turbulent flow – an irregular and random motion of fluid flow.

U

uncertainty principle – according to quantum theory, the laws of physics can only control the probability of certain events; the act of observing at the quantum level changes the outcome of the event.

uniform acceleration – see *constant acceleration*.

unstable equilibrium – a state of equilibrium in which a disturbance or force acts to pull the system away from equilibrium.

V

valence electron – the electrons in an atom that are involved in the formation of chemical bonds.

variable – a symbol used to represent an undetermined component in an experiment or a function.

vector – a quantity that has both magnitude and direction; examples are weight, velocity, and magnetic field strength.

velocity – the measure of distance traveled in a given amount of time including direction.

velocity vector – the speed and direction of motion at a point along a trajectory; the velocity vector changes direction and magnitude throughout the path of the projectile's trajectory.

virtual image – an optical image formed when rays of light appear to be coming from a place other than where the actual object exists; a virtual image cannot be projected on a screen.

viscous friction – the force that resists the movement of objects in fluids.

visible light – a form of electromagnetic waves with wavelengths capable of being detected by the human eye, ranging in wavelength from approximately 400 nm (bordering on ultraviolet) to 700 nm (bordering on infrared).

volt (V) – the unit of measurement for electrical potential energy.

voltage – the amount of potential energy that each unit of electric charge has.

voltage drop – the loss of voltage potential across a component in a series circuit.

volume – a measure of the space occupied by a object.

W

watt (W) – the SI, or metric, unit of power defined as one joule per second; equals the voltage multiplied by the current of the circuit.

wave – an oscillation that propagates through a medium, transferring energy from one point to another.

wave front – another term for the crests of a wave.

wave function – a complex-valued function containing all the information that can be known about a quantum of matter or energy.

wave pulse – a single occurence of a wave; not a continuous wave.

weak force – one of the fundamental forces in the atom that governs certain processes of radioactive decay.

weight – a force created by gravity; the gravitational force with which bodies attract each other.

weightless – having no net force from gravity; a body can be weightless because it is in free fall or because it is away from any source of gravity.

white light – the appearance of light that is the combination of all the colors of light.

wind chill factor – the loss of body heat due to a given combination of wind speed and temperature.

wire – the conductor for electric current in a circuit; it is usually made of metal and may have an insulating sheath surrounding it.

work – the quantity of force multiplied by distance; the energy used to move something.

X

x-axis – the horizontal axis of a graph.

x-component – a vector component in the east-west, or horizontal, direction.

x-rays – a penetrating electromagnetic radiation of photons with high energy.

Y

y-axis – the vertical axis of a graph.

y-component – a vector component in the north-south, or vertical, direction.

yellow – a color created when blue light is absorbed and red and green are reflected or when green and red light are projected onto a common surface.

Index

669

A
B
C

Index

Index

671

Index

679

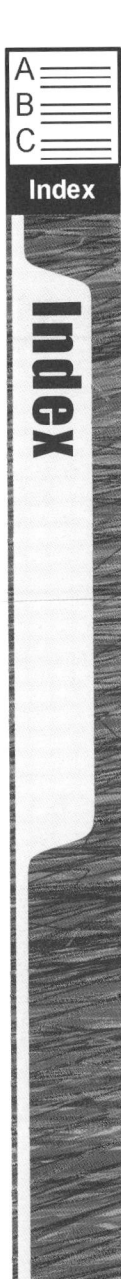

A B C

Index

Index

683

Index

BRITANNIA
100
DOCUMENTS
THAT SHAPED
A NATION

GRAHAM STEWART

Atlantic Books
London

First published in hardback in Great Britain in 2010 by Atlantic Books and Callisto,
imprints of Atlantic Books Ltd.

Copyright © Graham Stewart, 2010

10 9 8 7 6 5 4 3 2 1

A CIP catalogue record for this book is available from the British Library.

Callisto ISBN: 978 0 85740 022 2
Atlantic Export ISBN: 978 1 84887 945 4

Design and layout by www.carrstudio.co.uk
Printed in Great Britain

Callisto and Atlantic Books
Imprints of Atlantic Books Ltd
Ormond House
26–27 Boswell Street
London
WC1N 3JZ

www.atlantic-books.co.uk

For my young nephew,

Rufus Stewart

CONTENTS

I THE DARK AGES

II THE MEDIEVAL AGE

LIST OF ILLUSTRATIONS

Integrated Illustrations

First Picture Section

Page from the *Lindisfarne Gospels*. © The British Library Board/HIP/TopFoto.

Bayeux Tapestry. akg-images/Erich Lessing.

Magna Carta. © The British Library Board/HIP/TopFoto.

Map of Great Britain from *Abbreviatio Chronicorum Angliae*. © The British Library Board.

Declaration of Arbroath. SCOTLANDSIMAGES.COM/Crown Copyright 2007. The National Archives of Scotland.

Second Picture Section

Founder's Charter upon Act of Parliament. The Master and Fellows of King's College, Cambridge.

Mary Rose from the Anthony Roll. The Art Archive/Magdalene College Cambridge/Eileen Tweedy.

Monteagle Letter and Guy Fawkes's Confession. The National Archives, London. SP14/216 (11a).

Union Flag design. © National Library of Scotland.

Scottish National Covenant. © National Library of Scotland.

Third Picture Section

Death Warrant of Charles I. Houses of Parliament, Westminster, London, UK/The Bridgeman Art Library.

Act of Union. SCOTLANDSIMAGES.COM/Crown Copyright 2007/The National Archives of Scotland.

The Plum-Pudding in Danger. Library of Congress Prints and Photographs Division, LC-USZC4-8791.

Poverty map of London. Atlantic Books Collection.

Fourth Picture Section

War recruitment poster. The Granger Collection/Topfoto.

British Empire map. The Art Archive/Lords Gallery/Eileen Tweedy.

London Blitz damage map. The City of London, London Metropolitan Archives.

Sgt. Pepper album cover. © Apple Corps Ltd.

The Dodi and Diana condolence book at Harrods. Courtesy of Harrods.

INTRODUCTION

In the summer of 1647, Britain was slipping towards anarchy. Five years of civil war had left the Royalist forces broken and scattered. Although King Charles I was held captive, his enemies remained hesitant and unsure. Parliament was in disarray, its politicians reduced to making self-serving gestures having long since lost control of the revolution they had helped set in motion. Only one power in the land seemed capable of restoring order, but even the New Model Army, for all its battle-hardened prowess in war, was riven with dissent in the moment of its apparent victory. Belligerent and unpaid, it marched on the capital. On arrival, its commander-in-chief, Sir Thomas Fairfax, was appointed Constable of the Tower of London. As he was given a tour around the mighty fortified keep, a selection of its treasures was presented for his inspection. Eventually he was shown a fragile document that was already over 400 years old and not even written in English. Nonetheless, it was what the general had specifically requested to see. 'This is that,' he declared, gazing reverentially at the Magna Carta, 'which we have fought for, and by God's help we must maintain.'

Was the Civil War really a contest over an aged scrap of manuscript? Could the English, so often derided for their indifference to grand ideas, have made such a big issue out of a thirteenth-century set of dictates? In the search to find meaning out of the internecine conflict that gripped the British Isles in the 1640s, historians have identified many strands of discord – social, national, political, economic and religious. There is, however, no reason to assume that those who accompanied Sir Thomas Fairfax on his tour of the Tower looked at him strangely when he pronounced on the importance of Magna Carta. In assembling their case against the Crown, Parliamentarians had spent much of the previous twenty years searching out old documents that they believed provided the legal proof that their case was just and that arbitrary rule was alien to the ancient constitution.

At the beginning of the twenty-first century, Magna Carta still receives an occasional mention in the press and in Parliament, and most Britons are aware of its importance, even if they cannot exactly recall why. Actually, most of it was repealed in the nineteenth century and the provisions that remain tend to make the news only because they are perceived to be under threat. The Act of Union of 1707 is another national treasure that crops up in modern debate, principally because of a Scottish nationalist movement whose nationalist aim is to have it consigned to the dustbin of history. For all the opinions expressed about the Act of Union, how many people have seen it, or even have a mental picture of what it looks like? Much the same may be said of the Bill of Rights, whose 300th anniversary in 1989 was greeted with nationwide indifference.

The contrast with the United States of America could not be sharper. Daily, queues shuffle slowly and reverentially through the neoclassical portico of the National Archives in Washington, DC, for a glimpse of the documents that founded the nation. A high proportion of Americans not only know what their Declaration of Independence and Bill of Rights look like, they even have a pretty good recollection of what they say. In fact, America's Founding Fathers did not hit upon all their deep philosophical ideas, albeit neatly wrapped up in a few choice expressions, in one blinding flash of original genius. For, like Sir Thomas Fairfax, they had an almost mystical reverence for the eloquent defence of rights, freedoms and equality before the law that had been scratched upon the historic parchments of the country they had left behind.

The Founding Fathers of the United States borrowed liberally from Britain's archival heritage, even as they were trying to set themselves apart from Britain. Crucially, however, a fundamental difference divided the two English-speaking nations. The Americans – thereafter copied by most of the world – opted for a written constitution while the British persevered with their uncodified system of laws and precedents. Perhaps an absence of what are generally perceived as 'founding documents' has made modern Britons believe that their country's venerable statutes and charters are not especially relevant and that their only real appeal lies in their charming calligraphy.

Certainly, many of the documents collated in this book are a visual delight, but that is not why they are here. They cover a wide range of national endeavours, from law and politics, literature and science, inventions and city planning to sport, economics and religion. The principle guiding their selection is that they definitively shaped their age, and most of them still resonate today. For while we may not be

governed by a single constitutional document, we are governed by many, drawn from the better part of two millennia of history – and a representative sample of the greatest of them are collected and contextualized here.

What is more, the term 'governed' is meant not only in a narrow administrative sense. Our expressions have been shaped by the great translations of the Bible, by the works of Shakespeare and by the extraordinary compilation of words and meanings made by Dr Samuel Johnson. The influence of Adam Smith's treatise guides the way in which we do business. We may no longer travel on trains designed by George and Robert Stephenson, nor do we toil over one of Richard Arkwright's water frames, but we must make a trip (not by rail) to some exceptionally remote parts of Britain to avoid evidence of their influence in industrializing, moulding and uniting the country. All, once, had to be imagined and developed, using ink and paper and, as such, deserve recognition here.

Restricting the number of documents presented to one hundred is, intentionally, a tight discipline. No matter how carefully considered, the choice is ultimately based on personal opinion and therefore open to debate. One could easily fill the entire book with Acts of Parliament and still lament the lack of space available to include many more with a sound claim to fame. To do so, though, would be at the expense of presenting a reasonable spread of documents from across a wider range of national activity. Providing this range necessarily involves selecting some documents as representative of their theme. In this way, the 1832 Reform Act represents legislative measures towards greater democracy. The absence here of subsequent reform acts is not intended to diminish their importance, merely to recognize that they carried on a process that the 1832 Act started. Nor is this book just a compendium of 'firsts' – the *Rocket* was not the original steam train, nor the Spitfire the pioneer fighter plane, nor were the MCC's Laws the first rule book on cricket. Sometimes it is the document that best expresses an idea, rather than the one that takes the earliest crack at it, that makes the more persuasive case for inclusion. Ultimately, this is a book about documents that have made Britain what it is today, a national focus that must automatically shut out concepts that, while conceived by Britons, are not primarily or exclusively rooted in British society. British inventions that have shaped the world really need a book of their own. An attempt to do them all justice here would only blur the purpose of the compilation.

This is an attempt to tell the history of Britain through its seminal documents. It is not, of course, the whole story, any more than the history of a nation can be told purely through the lives of its monarchs, or the tales of its writers, or the

body-counts from its battlefields. There are, therefore, limits to this approach. For instance, serfdom withered and died during the Middle Ages. It was not abolished by any single statute. Sometimes it is the absence of a document that changed the course of British history. The freedom of the press was not created by the stroke of a legislative diktat. Rather, it began to take shape after Parliament's failure to renew the Licensing Act in 1694. Thereafter, press censorship was primarily regulated by the libel laws (although, famously, in the theatre, the Lord Chamberlain endeavoured to keep a lid on smut and sedition between 1737 and 1968). Nonetheless, for a nation that prides itself on its empiricism and 'muddling through' attitude, it is striking how elemental some statues have proved.

Finally, it is important to recognize that, despite centuries' worth of destructive wars, fires, deliberate desecration, ignorance and absent-mindedness, we are still in possession of so much of our archival inheritance. Not all nations are equally blessed. Britain's good fortune in this respect owes much to the actions of a few individuals. For instance, many of the most important manuscripts to have survived from Anglo-Saxon England might have been lost following the dissolution of the monasteries and the political traumas of the early seventeenth century, had they not been collected and preserved by two men. One of them was Matthew Parker (1504–75), archbishop of Canterbury, who bequeathed his manuscript library to Corpus Christi College, Cambridge. The other was the seventeenth-century MP, Sir Robert Cotton (1571–1631).

Having failed to interest the state in establishing an academy 'for the study of antiquity and history', Cotton began buying as many historic documents as he could afford for the library that he built for Cotton House, his four-storey home adjoining the House of Commons. Politicians as well as antiquarians were given free rein to examine his collection, finding numerous historical precedents with which to challenge the increasingly arbitrary rule of King Charles I. Cognizant of the danger contained in the manuscripts, the king had the library impounded and Cotton briefly imprisoned. Upon his release, he was denied access to his own collection and was still petitioning for readmission when he died, in May 1631, apparently of grief at his library's fate. Seemingly, Charles I – as much as Sir Thomas Fairfax – was fully aware of the potency of old documents.

Yet Cotton's irreplaceable collection – which included not just Magna Carta but also the Lindisfarne Gospels, *Beowulf* and the *Anglo-Saxon Chronicle* – remained intact. In 1701 his grandson, fearful of what might happen when his 'two illiterate' grandchildren inherited it, sold it to the nation. It was the first time that an Act of

Parliament secured books and manuscripts for the benefit of the public. Cotton's collection is now in the safe care of the British Library. Truly, we owe a profound debt of gratitude not just to Cotton and Parker but to all those men and women in private houses, churches, libraries, universities and museums who across the centuries dedicated themselves to preserving manuscripts for posterity, often when others struggled to see the point. It is thanks to their efforts that we can examine the documents that shaped a nation.

I

THE DARK AGES

1ST CENTURY A.D.
THE VINDOLANDA TABLETS

ROMAN EXPERIENCES OF LIFE IN BRITANNIA

Britannia was a province of the Roman Empire from the first to the fifth century AD, as long a period as separates the English Civil War from the present day. Yet what do we really know about this long period of Roman rule? Thankfully, accounts such as that by the great historian Tacitus (c. AD 55–120) have survived. For all their contemporary propaganda and rhetorical passages coloured with artistic licence, they tell us much about how Britain was conquered. However, what happened there during the following 300 years has been more a matter for archaeologists.

It is primarily from the remains of its desecrated monuments and hidden treasure that a picture of Roman Britain has emerged. This is because after the Roman legions departed in AD 410, a 'Dark Age' descended during which neglect, adaptation and outright destruction did so much to erase testimonies from the land that Romans thought of as the end of the known world.

Intricate floor mosaics and indoor plumbing provide evidence of domestic comfort in the villas of the wealthy and the influential (by comparison, such plumbing was beyond the grasp of even an eighteenth-century British aristocrat). The remains of forts and cities offer a sense of Rome's ambitious military and civic planning. The network of roads provided an infrastructure so valuable that, resurfaced, parts of it still connect the country nineteen centuries later.

Following Julius Caesar's abortive expeditions in 55 and 54 BC, in AD 43 the emperor Claudius launched an invasion of the province that the Romans had named Britannia. Although their grip was briefly imperilled during the rebellion of Queen Boudicca of the Iceni tribe in AD 60–61, the invaders clung on and proceeded to consolidate their hold, either by pitting their military might against the hostile British tribes or by bribing the biddable ones into collaboration. Leaving Ireland well alone, the legionaries moved into southern Wales and pushed up into northern Scotland, where their general, Agricola, defeated the Caledonian tribes in

AD 84. Thereafter, the Romans fell back to a tighter west–east defensive line roughly between the River Clyde and the Firth of Forth. However, after the emperor Hadrian visited Britain in AD 122, that boundary was redrawn to the south by the construction of his great seventy-three-mile wall running from the Solway Firth to the Tyne. This northern perimeter of Roman rule has furnished some of the most important insights into the lives of the conquerors.

Ironically, the really poignant narratives are not the testaments intended to endure but rather those consciously dumped in the rubbish pit. During the 1970s, discarded writing tablets began to be unearthed from the site of the Roman fort of Vindolanda, west of Hexham. These were, for the most part, ink inscriptions written on the smooth surfaces of thin leaves of wood, between one and three millimetres thick and postcard-sized. Although they are charred or broken fragments the damp environment has, remarkably, helped preserve them over the better part of two millennia. The earliest appear to date from around AD 90, when Vindolanda was already a fort but before Hadrian's defensive wall system was built nearby.

Many of the writing tablets, now held in the British Museum, are examples of Roman army bureaucracy: receipts for provisions and other commercial transactions, inventories, work assignments, requests for leave and appeals for clemency. From one report, we learn that the fort was garrisoned by soldiers of the First Cohort of Tungrians. The nominal strength was 752 men, but many of them were in fact posted elsewhere. At other times, it was garrisoned by the Ninth Cohort of Batavians. The Tungrians came from the area

THE ROMANS IN BRITAIN

55 BC Julius Caesar launches the first Roman expedition to Britain, landing near Deal.

54 BC Julius Caesar's second expedition to Britain.

AD 43 The emperor Claudius orders a full-scale invasion of Britain.

AD 47–50 Londinium (London) founded.

AD 51 Revolt by the British chieftain Caratacus is crushed and Caratacus is paraded through Rome.

AD 61 Boudicca, Queen of the Iceni, revolts and sacks Colchester, London and St Albans before being defeated.

AD 84 The Battle of Mons Graupius during the invasion of Caledonia (Scotland) by Agricola, governor of Britannia.

AD 122 Work begins on the construction of Hadrian's Wall.

AD 142 The Antonine Wall is constructed between the Forth and the Clyde. It is abandoned by AD 164.

AD 216 Roman Britain is administratively divided into two: Britannia Superior (the South) and Britannia Inferior (the North).

AD c.270 Construction begins of the 'Saxon Shore' of coastal forts to repel Germanic pirates.

AD 306 Constantine is proclaimed Roman emperor at York.

AD 369 Mounting numbers of attacks by Picts and Irish-Scots are repelled by the Roman general Theodosius.

AD 396 The Roman general Stilicho assumes authority in Britain and organizes a defence against attacks by Picts, Irish and Saxons.

AD 402 The Sixth Victrix Legion is withdrawn from Britain.

AD 407 The remaining legion, the Second Augusta, is withdrawn from Britain.

AD 410 The emperor Honorius confirms the Roman departure from Britain.

around the River Meuse and the Batavians from the mouth of the Rhine and the Scheldt, which makes these Roman soldiers, in modern-day terms, Germans and Dutch.

Such documents provide a sense of where Vindolanda's troops came from, how they were organized and even what they were eating. However, they also provide many more personal details. The extent of literacy is evident from the fact that some of the letters are written by – rather than about – slaves. There are the familiar gripes and expressions of lofty condescension voiced by occupying forces down the centuries. Their relations are either being tapped for useful presents or badgered to send money to cover accrued debts. They are also chided for not writing more often. There is the grim reality of being posted far from home. One soldier refers

The writing on this tablet from Vindolanda, dating from c. AD 97–103, reads in translation: 'the Britons are unprotected by armour. There are very many cavalry. The cavalry do not use swords nor do the wretched Brits mount in order to throw javelins.'

to the natives, the Brittones, by a derisory nickname, Brittunculi, which, roughly translated, means 'Wretched Brits'.

It was not just at javelin distance that Roman soldiers could expect interaction with the natives. Even after Hadrian's Wall was constructed as a heavily fortified barrier, it was also a customs post for cross-border trade, suggesting continuing dealings with those who lived on the far side. Nonetheless, any attempt by Hadrian's successor, Antoninus Pius, to re-establish the Clyde–Forth frontier along the turf ramparts of his Antonine Wall had been abandoned by AD 164, not much more than twenty years after its construction.

Thereafter, while Roman civilization appeared entrenched in the English South and the Midlands, the evidence suggests there were recurring revolts in the North. This necessitated the maintenance of a Roman army in Britain so powerful that it became a destabilizing force in imperial politics, nominating its own – often rival – claimants as rulers. It was, for instance, at York that Constantine was proclaimed emperor in AD 306.

The breakdown of direct authority from Rome was matched by the deteriorating situation elsewhere along the fringes of imperial territories. Troops that ought to have remained in Britain were transferred to the continent, both as part of the internecine struggle for political supremacy between rival power-brokers and in increasingly desperate efforts to hold back the Barbarian onslaught along the empire's contracting Germanic frontiers.

In Britain, Rome's enemies seized their chance. Picts attacked from the north while the defences of the southern English coast were probed by Saxon pirates. Nevertheless, Britannia was still essentially an imperial province when, in AD 410, the Visigoths sacked Rome. In that year an appeal was sent from Britannia to the emperor Honorius requesting help. From Ravenna, where his court had removed itself, Honorius replied that he no longer had any soldiers to spare and that, consequently, Britannia would have to fend for herself. Although he may have meant it as a temporary expedient, the decision ensured the collapse of Roman Britain.

c.710
THE LINDISFARNE GOSPELS

AN ILLUMINATED MASTERPIECE FROM THE DARK AGES

A page from the Lindisfarne Gospels is depicted in the first plate section.

During the fourth century, Christianity spread throughout Britain. Tolerated by the Roman occupiers from AD 313, following the emperor Constantine's Edict of Milan, it was the state religion by 382. The test, however, was whether it could survive the legions' departure in 410.

It fell to the new generation of Romano-British chiefs – among them perhaps a leader later mythologized as King Arthur – to defend the faith against pagan invaders: the Germanic tribes that poured into the country from the mid-fifth century onwards. In the sixth century, as the Britons largely lost the fight, the tenets of Christianity were rubbed out in the wake of the incomers.

In the lands they now occupied, the Germanic immigrants established regional kingdoms. Tribes of Angles settled in the Midlands and the North, giving their name to a new geographical expression – England. Their intermingling with Saxon settlers first led Europeans in the seventh century to coin the term 'Anglo-Saxon' to distinguish them not only from Britain's Celtic inhabitants but from the Saxon tribes remaining on the continent. In turn, Anglo-Saxons described the Celtic Britons they displaced as *wealas*, the Old English word for 'stranger' from which the modern English word 'Welsh' is derived.

During this bleakest period of the 'Dark Ages', Christianity survived only where it lay out of the Anglo-Saxons' reach. St Patrick (c.385–461), a Romano-Briton by birth, took the Christian message across to Ireland. In turn, the Irish missionary St Columba established his monastery on the southern Hebridean island of Iona in 563. From such outposts, the faith was spread throughout the Irish kingdom of Dalriada in western Scotland and to the native Picts beyond.

Christianity returned to England by two routes, one Celtic, the other Roman. In 597, Pope Gregory the Great sent (St) Augustine on a mission from Rome to Canterbury where he baptized the Anglo-Saxon king of Kent, Æthelbert. Converting royalty proved a shrewd 'top-down' means of securing powerful protectors for the

Roman Church. Æthelbert's daughter, Æthelburga, married Edwin, king of the Deiran dynasty in Northumbria. At Easter 627, this most powerful of northern rulers followed his wife's example and converted to Christianity along with his court. After Edwin's death, the Northumbrian throne passed to Oswald, a member of the rival Bernician dynasty. Oswald had previously been exiled on Iona and he encouraged its missionaries to settle in Northumbria.

Among Oswald's gifts to them was Lindisfarne. This small island, which twice daily is both connected to and cut off from the Northumbrian coast by the tide, became one of the focal points for the Columban mission spreading out from Ireland and Scotland. While the Church in northern England was staffed largely by Celtic monks, the doctrine became more identifiably Roman during the later years of the seventh century and, in particular, after 664 when the Synod of Whitby pronounced against the Celtic calendar for Easter. Like the other monastic settlements, the monastery at Lindisfarne acclimatized itself to the universal claims of the Roman Church. Over a period of years, a specifically Celtic Christian tradition in the British Isles began to wane.

Lindisfarne was particularly fortunate in enjoying the strong patronage of Northumbria's monarchs. When the relics of St Cuthbert, its former bishop, were brought there in 698, it became a place of pilgrimage. It was probably with the intention of their being set on the high altar next to St Cuthbert's shrine that the Lindisfarne Gospels were written.

Bound together after completion in a metal-framed cover (subsequently lost), the book contains the gospels of the four evangelists. It is written

EARLY CHRISTIANITY IN BRITAIN

AD 63 According to the twelfth-century chronicler William of Malmesbury, Jesus' disciple, Joseph of Arimathea, reaches Glastonbury.

c.209–304 St Alban becomes Britain's first Christian martyr, although the exact date is disputed.

313 The emperor Constantine legalizes Christianity throughout the Roman Empire.

314 The bishops of London, York and Lincoln attend the Council of Arles.

382 Christianity becomes the state religion throughout the Roman Empire.

5th century Christianity in Britain is in decline following the withdrawal of Rome and the invasion of pagan Germanic tribes.

563 The Irish missionary St Columba establishes his monastery on Iona. The conversion of Scotland follows.

589 St David, a Welsh preacher who founded monastic settlements in Wales and Cornwall, dies.

597 Pope Gregory the Great sends Augustine on a mission to England. Augustine becomes the first archbishop of Canterbury and converts the Kentish king, Æthelbert.

627 The Northumbrian king, Edwin, is converted to Christianity.

635 Aidan of Iona founds the Lindisfarne monastery.

664 The Synod of Whitby accepts the Roman rather than the Celtic calendar for Easter.

735 Bede translates the Gospel of St John into Old English.

793 Vikings sack Lindisfarne monastery.

c.990 Alfric, an English abbot, translates part of the Old Testament into Old English.

in Latin, the source for which was an edition, probably Italian in origin, of the Vulgate. In this respect it was far from unique, but what made it one of the highest manifestations of Anglo-Saxon culture was the rich artistry with which it was illustrated.

Remarkably, it appears to be the work of one hand. If we are to believe the assurance of Aldred – a monk who, in the mid-tenth century, inserted between its Latin lines a word-for-word translation into Old English – we even know the identity of this gifted and extraordinarily patient artist-scribe. He was Eadfrith, Lindisfarne's bishop from 698 to 721.

Although we cannot be certain that Aldred's attribution is accurate, subsequent scholarship generally supports the book's likely provenance as Lindisfarne in the period of Eadfrith's bishopric. Certainly, the monastic community there was sufficient to support him in his undertaking. An extensive library of books, gathered from across Europe, was also available for consultation in the nearby monasteries of Monkwearmouth and Jarrow. Familiarity with such sources may also help explain the Lindisfarne Gospels' eclectic borrowing from different artistic styles. The result was a work that developed a new English art form, which harmonized influences from Celtic, Germanic, Anglo-Saxon, Roman, Byzantine, Middle Eastern and even Coptic art.

Each of the four gospels is introduced with a portrait of the evangelist and his symbol (a man for Matthew; a lion for Mark; a calf for Luke; an eagle for John). A 'carpet page' follows in which the symbol of the cross is contained within a pattern. This form of decoration was common to the Coptic art of the Egyptian Christians, but is augmented in the Lindisfarne Gospels by especially elaborate interwoven rhythmic patterns, with geometrical knots and depictions of birds and animals in the Celtic style. Next comes the 'incipit page'. Here the opening capital letter and the first words of each gospel are surrounded by rich ornamentation, with the first words transcribed in runic fashion. The attention to detail is astounding. For instance, in the incipit page (folio 139r) of the Gospel of Luke, there are 10,600 individually painted red dots in the adornment surrounding the initial.

This level of laboriously executed intricacy is all the more remarkable given that much of it would have been done with relatively primitive implements, without means of magnification and by candlelight. The personal cost of creating such a visual masterpiece must surely have been considerable eye-strain for its lone artist-scribe. Given Eadfrith's other burdensome monastic duties, it represented an extraordinary dedication to art and devotion to faith.

Costs of a different kind were incurred in the luxurious nature of the materials. The Lindisfarne Gospels were written on 259 folio sheets of vellum, whose quality of calfskin far exceeds that generally found in other important documents of the period. Nor were the pigments exclusively derived from local sources. Among the colours used appears to be lapis lazuli, which was quarried in Afghanistan.

The fact that a monk, working on a tiny windswept Northumbrian island, could draw on the resources of much of the known world demonstrates the extent to which this corner of Anglo-Saxon England not only connected itself with the visual remnants of Celtic faith but also fully acknowledged its place within the Roman orthodoxy of European Christendom.

Just as it was not cut off from that greater community, so neither was it spared from its assailants. In 793, Vikings launched a surprise attack on Lindisfarne, sacking the monastery. Further assaults followed, forcing the bishop and most of his monks to flee to the greater safety of the mainland. With them, they took St Cuthbert's remains and the Lindisfarne Gospels, first to Chester-le-Street and later to Durham. It was probably at Chester-le-Street that Aldred added his between-line textual translation into Old English. In doing so, he gave the work an additional importance as the oldest surviving example of the gospels in the English language.

The Lindisfarne Gospels eventually became part of the Cottonian Library after its removal from Durham during the Reformation, and at length found their way, first to the British Museum, and later to the British Library, where they remain to this day.

731

BEDE'S *HISTORIA ECCLESIASTICA GENTIS ANGLORUM*

THE FIRST GREAT HISTORY
OF THE ENGLISH CHURCH AND PEOPLE

While the gospels were being adorned on the island of Lindisfarne, a mere six miles away on the mainland another monk was writing one of the most important English documents of the first millennium. His name was Bede and the masterpiece on which he was working was his *Historia Ecclesiastica Gentis Anglorum* ('Ecclesiastical History of the English Nation').

Born around 673 in the nearby environs of what is now Tyneside, Bede was entrusted at the age of seven to the local monastery, which had two closely affiliated endowments, six miles apart, at Monkwearmouth and Jarrow. This twin monastery had been newly founded by Benedict Biscop, an abbot who had amassed a wealth of manuscripts from a life spent travelling through Europe.

By contrast – and despite living to the age of about sixty-two – Bede may never have ventured further than York. His window on the world was the scholarly treasure-trove at his disposal in Biscop's library. It was there that, having learned Latin, Greek and even some Hebrew, he was able to immerse himself not only in the works of Pope Gregory the Great but even in such non-Christian writers as Vergil.

Bede's interest was not merely in obtaining knowledge but in adding to it. He wrote poems, songs, biblical commentaries and biographies of St Cuthbert as well as of his local abbots. His enquiring mind ranged over subjects as diverse as the calendar and chronology, grammar and natural science. Yet it was in his devotion to the history of England that he made his greatest contribution.

Written in Latin, the *Historia Ecclesiastica* is Bede's attempt to relate England's story from the invasion of Julius Caesar to the year 731. Although primarily the

account of how Christianity – and, in particular, the Roman Church – came to establish itself in England, Bede remains our principal source for early Anglo-Saxon England's political and military history.

It is through Bede that the most coherent attribution of early Germanic settlement has been handed down. He was insistent that the Angles colonized the North and the Midlands, the Saxons the South-West and South-East, and the Jutes Kent. He was also a detailed chronicler of the early Church in his native Northumbria, providing a lengthy account of the Synod of Whitby's debate over when to hold Easter and the reign of his hero, King Edwin. One of Bede's most celebrated passages relates Edwin's analogy of the acceptance of Christian teaching, using the image of the flight of a sparrow, passing briefly from the dark and cold of a winter's night through the warmth of a lighted hall and back into the unknown: 'Somewhat like this appears the life of man, but of what follows or what went before, we are utterly ignorant.'

From Chapter 14: The Conversion of King Edwin

So King Edwin with all the nobles of his nation and very many of the people received the faith and the laver of holy regeneration in the eleventh year of his reign, which was the year of our Lord's incarnation 627, and about 180 years from the coming of the English into Britain. He was baptised at York on the holy day of Easter, 12 April, in the church of the Apostle Peter which he himself had hastily built there in wood, while he was a catechumen [one undergoing conversion] receiving instruction for his baptism. In that city also he gave an episcopal see to his teacher and bishop, Paulinus. But as soon as he was baptised, he was eager by Paulinus's direction to construct in that place a larger and more majestic church of stone, in the middle of which might be enclosed the oratory which he had made before. When the foundations had been laid around the former oratory, he began to build the church foursquare. But before the walls reached their full height the king himself was wickedly killed, and left the work to be completed by his successor, Oswald. However, for six years on end from that time, that is, until the end of the reign of the king, Paulinus by his consent and favour preached the word of God in that province; and as many as were foreordained to eternal life believed and were baptised, among whom were the sons of King Edwin, Osfrith and Eadfrith, who had both been born to him in his exile by Cwenburh, daughter of Ceorl, king of the Mercians.

How reliable is Bede's scholarship? As he put it in a brief autobiographical note, he drew his narrative 'either from ancient documents, or from the tradition of the elders, or from my own knowledge'. For the period of the Roman conquest, he relied upon classical authors and, for the coming of the Anglo-Saxons, on the sixth-century Welsh monk Gildas, whose [*Liber Querulus*] *De Excidio Britanniae* ('On the Ruin of Britain') was a diatribe against the sins of his fellow Britons. Inevitably, Bede's chronology was patchy for this Dark Age, until he was able to build into a flowing narrative with the re-emergence of English Christianity in the seventh century. He was firmly on the side of buttressing religious faith in England and, in particular, was determined to inculcate in English a sense of being part of a greater Roman Christendom. Holding strong beliefs in papal authority, he intended his readers to draw the appropriate conclusions from his chronicle of a young nation stumbling from pagan superstition to religious certainty. Despite these pedagogic aims, Bede's scholarship lifted him beyond the narrow channels of propaganda and patronage. He made every effort to ensure that his research was based on the most reliable information rather than simple regurgitation. Furthermore, his writing style showed a very human sensibility as well as a gift for storytelling.

Perhaps inevitably, Bede was particularly conscious of events in his native Northumbria. However, far from being parochial in intent, his bias is, if anything, weighted towards an over-emphasis on the extent of English unity. Reviving echoes of Roman Britain, he believed that several of the Anglo-Saxon rulers, including the Northumbrian monarchs Edwin and Oswald, should be recognized not just as the leaders of their own regional kingdoms but as effective emperors of all England. To such rulers the *Anglo-Saxon Chronicle* would later designate the title of 'Bretwalda' ('Britain ruler'). In depicting history in this way, Bede helped create the perception of a common English identity and destiny. Indeed, it was his usage that did much to popularize the use of the terms 'England' and 'English'.

In 735, four years after he had completed his great history, Bede lay dying. Despite his physical decline, he endeavoured to keep his mind active by translating the Gospel of St John into Old English and composing a five-line 'death song' musing on the thought that

BEDE'S LIST OF 'BRETWALDAS'

Ælle of Sussex, reigned 488–c.514

Ceawlin of Wessex, reigned 560–92

Æthelbert of Kent, reigned 590–616

Raedwald of East Anglia, reigned c.600–24

Edwin of Northumbria, reigned 616–33

Oswald of Northumbria, reigned 633–42

Oswiu of Northumbria, reigned 642–70

To which list the *Anglo-Saxon Chronicle* added:

Egbert of Wessex, reigned 802–39

mortals can never know how a man's soul will be judged in the afterlife. What most endured of Bede's own reputation rested with his *Historia Ecclesiastica*. Copies were made soon after his death and were translated into Old English in the ninth century. Other editions in the original Latin were exported across a European continent that was at last able to enjoy the fruits of Anglo-Saxon scholarship where previously the literary traffic had flowed only in the other direction. As the first historian to systematically use the *anno domini* dating chronology, he eventually influenced its adoption across Europe.

Meanwhile, in the small corner of England where Bede had spent his entire life, the culture that had nurtured him was under renewed assault. The Viking raids that harassed Lindisfarne also forced the monasteries of Monkwearmouth and Jarrow to be evacuated by the beginning of the ninth century. However, in the eleventh century Bede's presumed grave was discovered and his remains were re-interred in Durham Cathedral. The tradition of describing him as 'Venerable' survived long after the custom for so entitling other monks had withered. The other title that has stuck to him over the centuries, which no amount of subsequent discovery and research has diminished, is 'the Father of English History'.

8TH–10TH CENTURY
BEOWULF

THE GREATEST SURVIVING WORK
OF ANGLO-SAXON LITERATURE

Ｗe do not know who wrote the epic poem *Beowulf*, nor whether its eponymous hero sprang from the creator's imagination or was at least distantly based on a long-dead and subsequently mythologized figure whose deeds grew more extraordinary with repeated telling. An inter-generational debate among historians has failed to determine the century from which the story dates or even the English kingdom in which it was written. However, there is no disputing that *Beowulf* is the greatest surviving poem written in the Old English language.

The story is set in sixth-century Scandinavia, yet draws on aspects of old Germanic legends. Some of the words used suggest it may have been produced in one of the kingdoms settled by the Angles. Although the central characters belong to a pagan world, there are biblical references. For instance, it is stated that the monstrous Grendel is Cain's descendant. The work is assumed not to pre-date the eighth century nor to be later than the tenth century.

Beowulf is 3,182 lines in length and is written in the alliterative metre typical of most Old English poetry. It is about a hero governed only by duty, honour and bravery, who finds all too often that his supposed companions either fight among themselves or run away at the first sign of danger. As might be expected of a story set in a warrior society, it is suffused with strong and masculine descriptions; but far from merely being a blood-curdling tale of gore and brutality, its tone is frequently philosophical and reflective.

Grendel, a terrifying semi-human monster, makes repeated attacks on the great hall of Heorot, a Danish kingdom, dragging off and killing one unsuspecting victim after another. Wracked by fear, the community faces disintegration. Hope arrives in the shape of Beowulf, who travels from the land of the Geats in southern Sweden with fourteen warriors bent on freeing the people of Heorot from Grendel's terror.

The opening page of Beowulf, written in Old English on vellum:

Ay, we the Gar-Danes', in days of yore, the great kings', renown have heard of: how those princes valour display'd. Oft Scyld Scef's son from bands of robbers, from many tribes, their mead-benches drag'd away: inspired earls with fear, after he first was found destitute: he thence look'd for comfort, flourished under the clouds, in dignities throve, until him every one of those sitting around over the whale-road must obey, tribute pay: that was a good king! To him a son was afterwards born, a young one in his courts, whom God sent for comfort to the people: he the dire need felt that they ere had suffered while princeless, for a long while. To him therefore the Lord of life, Prince of glory, gave worldly honour. Beowulf was renown'd, the glory widely sprang of Scyld's offspring In the Scanian lands: So shall a warlike chief Work with good, with bounteous money-gifts, in his paternal home . . .

When Grendel arrives for another raid on the hall, Beowulf wrestles with him, tears off his arm and inflicts a mortal injury. Grendel's mother, more terrible still, seeks revenge and carries off one of the king of Heorot's closest henchmen. Beowulf, having volunteered to track down Grendel's mother, finds her in her lair at the bottom of a lake. A great underwater fight ensues in which Beowulf succeeds in killing the monstrous matriarch.

Beowulf returns to Sweden a hero and is eventually elevated to the throne. He rules long and wisely over his people until a dragon, which has guarded treasure for 300 years, is disturbed and goes on the rampage, burning Beowulf's hall to cinders. Despite his now advanced age, Beowulf summons up his courage and pledges to slay the dragon. However, so fearsome is the beast that Beowulf's followers flee in terror, leaving him to his fate. Only a young kinsman, Wiglaf, stands by him. Beowulf gets the upper hand in the fight but, just as he is about to slay the dragon, his sword shatters and the creature inflicts a poisonous wound. Wiglaf helps him kill the beast but the venom takes its effect and Beowulf's life ebbs away.

By his fidelity, Wiglaf has shown himself Beowulf's worthy successor and becomes king. He berates those who left the fallen hero to his nemesis, bringing dishonour on themselves and giving hope to the kingdom's enemies. The poem concludes with Beowulf's interment in a great barrow with the dragon's treasure. Around him, his people lament 'that of all the kings upon the earth he was the one most gracious and fair-minded, kindest to his people and keenest to win fame'.

With themes that embrace the hero as saviour, the testing of bravery, the nobility of the quest and the pitting of man against monster, *Beowulf* contains many staples of Western storytelling. J. R. R. Tolkien's *The Hobbit* and his *Lord of the Rings* trilogy are perhaps the greatest of the twentieth-century works for which it has been an inspiration. While Professor of Anglo-Saxon at the University of Oxford in the 1930s, Tolkien did much to popularize *Beowulf* as a great work of poetry rather than merely as a document of historical importance. Indeed, for many centuries it was scarcely known and it was not until 1815 that the first published edition appeared. It had survived in the meantime in only one manuscript – whose whereabouts prior to the sixteenth century are not recorded – and was acquired by the British Museum in the eighteenth century. Fortunately, the museum had two copies made, a decision that proved indispensable to future generations of scholars who would otherwise have been unable to decipher passages in the original manuscript after it was damaged in a fire not long afterwards.

878–890
THE TREATY OF
ALFRED AND GUTHRUM

ESTABLISHING THE BOUNDARY BETWEEN ANGLO-SAXON
AND VIKING-OCCUPIED ENGLAND

The survival of Christian Britain was as fragile as the parchments upon which the monks of Jarrow and Lindisfarne chronicled and commemorated it. During the eighth century, fresh waves of invasion by a new pagan foe, the Vikings, threatened to drive it back to the periphery.

Sailing from Scandinavia, the Norsemen and Danish warriors reached far-flung corners of the island. Wales suffered least, beyond some incursions along the coast. In Scotland, however, the Vikings seized the northern and western isles, sacking the monastery at Iona in the process. England came under intense attack, with the looting of Lindisfarne just a foretaste. In 867 the previously dominant kingdom of Northumbria fell to the invader. The Midlands kingdom of Mercia capitulated the following year. By 871 every kingdom had been overwhelmed – with the exception of Wessex. If it fell, Anglo-Saxon England was lost.

The fate of Wessex rested with its new king, the twenty-two-year-old Alfred. He had become battle-hardened the previous year, helping his brother to see off one Viking assault at Ashdown in Berkshire, only to lose successive encounters thereafter. Further battles and parleys followed, with the Vikings penetrating deep into Wessex. They held Reading; then even Exeter fell to them. In January 878 their warlord, Guthrum, launched a surprise onslaught, seizing Chippenham and almost capturing Alfred.

Slipping from his pursuers' grasp, Alfred became a fugitive, seeking sanctuary in the reed beds and bogs around Athelney in Somerset. Despite the reality that much of his kingdom was overrun, he refused to give up, instead sending word that his followers should meet at the stone of his grandfather, King Egbert. Gathering them around him, he marched to meet Guthrum's army. At Edington in Wiltshire

This silver penny was minted during the rule of King Alfred over Wessex (871–99). It depicts Alfred on the obverse while on the reverse a cross and a monogram of Londonia acknowledge the absorption of London into his realm.

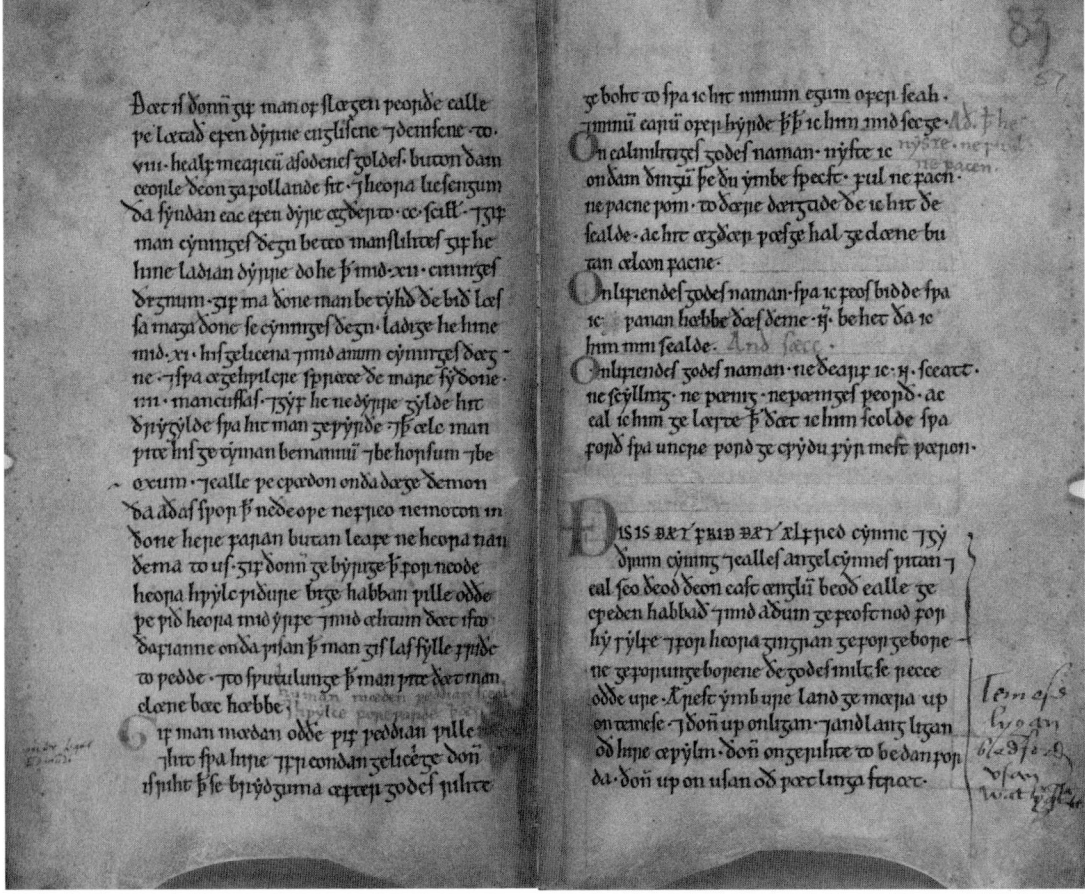

The Treaty of Alfred and Guthrum. The words describing the Saxon–Viking boundary line appear, in Old English, in the last paragraph on the right-hand side of the document (a translation appears on the facing page).

in May 878 the two sides fought one of the decisive battles of English history. Alfred was victorious. The Vikings were routed.

Stunned and impressed, Guthrum came to see Alfred at Aller in Somerset and in the church there a remarkable ceremony took place. Guthrum converted to Christianity. Alfred became his godfather, even raising him from the baptismal font. The two Christian leaders then spent a fortnight together at Wedmore where they drew up a peace treaty. The Vikings would hold on to their conquests in Northumbria and East Anglia (where Guthrum would rule), while agreeing to leave Wessex alone.

Although the peace did not hold, the treaty brought Alfred sufficient breathing space to strengthen both his army and his personal authority. Thus when fresh Viking attacks were made on Kent in 885, Alfred was able to see them off and

From the Treaty of Alfred and Guthrum

This is the peace which King Alfred and King Guthrum and the councillors of all the English race and all the people which is in East Anglia have all agreed on and confirmed with oaths, for themselves and for their subjects, both for the living and those yet unborn, who care to have God's grace upon ours.

First concerning our boundaries: up the Thames, and then up the Lea, and along the Lea to its source, then in a straight line to Bedford, then up the Ouse to the Watling Street. . . .

enter London. He rebuilt the city on the largely abandoned site of the Roman Londinium. Sometime shortly thereafter, he renewed the treaty with Guthrum. This is the version of the treaty that survives, with London in Alfred's domain, demarcating Anglo-Saxon from Viking-occupied England. (It can be found today at Corpus Christi College, Cambridge.) As the first clause makes clear, the new boundary line ran along the Thames estuary, up the Lea, thence to Bedford, then up the Ouse and along Watling Street.

This agreement represented only a partial victory for the Anglo-Saxons. It accepted rather than challenged Viking authority over eastern and northern England, the territory that became known as the Danelaw. However, such acknowledgement was the prerequisite of containment, the real achievement of the treaty. And in containing the Viking threat behind this line, it not only gave Alfred time to build forts, construct a navy and reform his army, it also helped solidify the political unity of the non-Danelaw areas of England under the rule of the royal house of Wessex. Some of the coins minted during the remainder of Alfred's reign proclaimed him *rex Anglorum*. Even if he could not really claim to be king of England, he was at least ruler of the free English. It would be for his tenth-century successors – Edward the Elder and, in particular, Athelstan – to defeat the Danelaw and unify all England under one rule.

c.890–1116

THE *ANGLO-SAXON CHRONICLE*

SHINING LIGHT UPON THE DARK AGES

T he *Anglo-Saxon Chronicle* is the most comprehensive record of English history in the first millennium. It is also the most immediate account extant from the reign of King Alfred through to the middle of the twelfth century. Furthermore, it is the oldest surviving significant set of annals of any European people written in their native language.

The fact that it is in Old English is important in itself. Following the example of Bede's *Historia Ecclesiastica*, we might expect works compiled in places of learning to be in Latin. However, during the ninth century the reach of Latin as a common spoken language was diminishing even among some of the country's cultured elite. English had become the usual language in which laws, wills and even many charters were expressed, an assertion of national identity that King Alfred actively encouraged. Not only did he personally work on translating into English such Latin works as Pope Gregory's *Liber Regulae Pastoralis* ('Pastoral Cares'), he also sponsored a programme of scholarship to make available in English what he believed were those 'books which may be most necessary for all men to know'.

Whether Alfred directly commissioned the *Anglo-Saxon Chronicle* cannot be confirmed, for the oldest such written claim dates from after the Norman Conquest. Nevertheless, its composition began in Wessex during his reign. It may have been driven by the desire to collect and preserve what was known of earlier events, as well as to relate them to the contemporary achievements of Alfred's victories over the Danes and the growing sense of Wessex's role in holding together Anglo-Saxon England.

The *Chronicle* is not one document but several, for it was copied and updated in a number of locations. It is not known how many copies may once have existed, but nine have survived, either complete or in fragment. The earliest version is no

land gedælde þ͛ gende wæron ⁊ hupa algende wæron.

Her wicingþ here to exancestre fram þam peþþ ham ⁊ da mette hie
micel myst on þæ ⁊ þær for þ͛ead· cxx· scypa æt sƿanewic·
⁊ þ͛ cing ælfred æfter þam gehorsodan here mid fyrd e þ͛ ad
oþ exancester· ⁊ hi hindan ofridan ne mihte ⁊ hi him gislas
sealdon ⁊ þ͛ a fela ⁊ þ͛ ahte habban wolde· ⁊ micle aþas sƿoron
⁊ da godne frið heoldon· ⁊ þa onhærfest gefor se here on
myrcena land ⁊ hit gedældon sum ⁊ sume ceolƿulfe sealdon·

Her hine bestæl se here on midne ƿinter ofer· xii· niht
to cyppanhamme ⁊ geridon ƿessexna land ⁊ þ͛ ar gesæton
⁊ micel þæs folces ofer sæ adræfdon· ⁊ þæs oþres þone mæstan
dæl hi geridon ⁊ þ͛ folc hym to gebigde buton þam cininge
ælfrede ⁊ he lytle werede uneþelice æfter wudum for ⁊ on
mor fæstenum· ⁊ þæs ilcan ƿintres wæs inƿereis broðor
⁊ heaþdenes on ƿessexna wice mid· xxiii· scypa ⁊ hine man
þær ofsloh ⁊ dccc· manna mid him ⁊ lx· manna hiƿ þeres·
⁊ dær wæs se guðfana genumen þe hie hræfn heton·

And þæs on eastron worhte ælfred cing lytle werede geworc
æt æþelinga igge ⁊ of þam geworce wæs winnende ƿið
þone here ⁊ sum up fætena sedæl· se dæl ne hit wæs· þa on
þære· sƿii· ƿucan ofer eastron he gerad to ecgbrihtes stane
be eastan sealwuda ⁊ him coman þær ongen sum up fæce
ealle· ⁊ wilsæte ⁊ hamtunscir sedæl þe hi re behronan wæs·
⁊ his gefægne wæron· ⁊ he for þæs embe ane niht of þam wicu
to iglea ⁊ dæs eft embe ane niht to eðandune· ⁊ þær gefeaht
ƿið ealne þone here ⁊ hine gefly mde ⁊ him æfter rad

From the *Anglo-Saxon Chronicle*, 1016

[King Edmund overtook the Danes] at Ashingdon, and there a fierce battle was fought. The ealdorman Eadric did as he had often done before: he and the men from Herefordshire and south Shropshire were the first to set the example of flight, and thus he betrayed his royal lord and the whole nation. Cnut was victorious, and won all England by his victory. Among the slain were Bishop Eadnoth, Abbot Wulfsige . . . and all the flower of England.

longer extant, but, once copied and distributed, it provided the common source material upon which the succeeding versions drew, especially in their coverage of the period between the first and ninth centuries. Thereafter, these copies were separately updated from their various locations by a succession of scribes, with all the varying emphases and detail that such a process entailed.

The 'Parker Chronicle', now kept at Corpus Christi College, Cambridge, appears to have been started around 891 in Winchester and covers the years from 60 BC to AD 1070. The Bodleian Library in Oxford holds the 'Laud Chronicle', written in Peterborough from a copy probably originating in Canterbury. Updated regularly until 1154, it continued the annals furthest, beyond the Anglo-Saxon age and into the troubled reign of King Stephen. The other versions are in the British Library. These were written in Canterbury, Abingdon and Worcester (the latter containing much material gleaned from northern English sources). With no collective cut-off point, they finish their accounts at various dates in the tenth and eleventh centuries. So arbitrary are some endings that one of the Abingdon scribes stopped abruptly halfway through a report on the Battle of Stamford Bridge in 1066. The paragraph was eventually finished by a much later twelfth-century hand.

That these chronicles remain far and away the most important and reliable source for Anglo-Saxon history does not mean that they are without bias or devoid of propaganda. There is, for instance, a presumption in favour of Wessex, the rights of the Church and of the Anglo-Saxons over the Vikings. Yet by its nature, the *Chronicle* – unlike Bede's history – ranges beyond the work of a single historian imposing his personal interpretation upon events. Thus, despite the elements that the different versions have in common, it is often their points of factual variation and differing regional emphasis that undermine the notion of the *Chronicle* as merely an exercise in composing an 'official' version of events.

II

THE MEDIEVAL AGE

LATE 11TH CENTURY
THE BAYEUX TAPESTRY

THE STORY OF THE NORMAN CONQUEST

Part of the Bayeux Tapestry is depicted in the first plate section.

Can the Bayeux Tapestry be considered a document, let alone a British one? Technically, it is not even a tapestry, for that would mean it was woven by a shuttle and loom. It is in fact an embroidery, created by needles threading dyed wool through linen cloth. Although only fifty centimetres high, its nine sections were sewn together so that it stretches over seventy metres in length.

That it is an artwork should not detract from its primary importance: it was made to document and justify events perhaps as little as a decade after they occurred. Like a newsreel delivered in the format of a comic strip, it tells in sequential words and images the story of the Norman Conquest of England. In doing so, it represents the opening salvo of 900 years of Anglo-French rivalry. Celebrating a French achievement and displayed in the French city from which it takes its name, it would later enthral Napoleon Bonaparte who declared that it 'records one of the most memorable deeds of the French nation and preserves the memory of the pride and courage of our ancestors'.

Given that he hoped to launch a cross-Channel invasion of his own, Napoleon's boast was understandable, but he was actually admiring what is almost certainly an English work of art, most probably made in Kent by English embroiderers. The superiority of English needlework during the period was widely acknowledged. Furthermore, although the inscriptions are in Latin, there is a familiarity with the way English names are spelled. Some of the more standardized images appear to have been copied from the Canterbury scriptoria of St Augustine's Abbey and Christ Church.

The version of events related by the Bayeux Tapestry is central to our understanding of one of the most important events in British history. Its narrative commences in 1064, with the Anglo-Saxon king Edward the Confessor dispatching his brother-in-law, Harold Godwinson, earl of Wessex, on a trip to

Normandy. The son of Æthelred the Unready, King Edward was childless and, at different times, seems to have made various (not legally binding) promises as to his preferred heir. One recipient of his approval was William, duke of Normandy. Although William was only Edward's second cousin at one remove, he was looked on favourably by Edward, who had spent much of his youth in Normandy as a refugee when the Danish king Canute and his sons occupied the English throne.

It is not clear from other sources what spurred Harold to make his fateful crossing of the English Channel to visit William's court. It may have been an accidental shipwreck. The Bayeux Tapestry implies that it was an official mission that went wrong, forcing William to rescue the young English prince from the clutches of Normandy's enemy, Guy of Ponthieu. In return, Harold is depicted, his hands placed on religious reliquaries, under the caption 'UBI HAROLD SACRAMENTUM FECIT WILLELMO DUCI' ('Where Harold made an oath to Duke William'). The assumption is that he made a solemn vow to support William's claim to the English throne on Edward the Confessor's death.

Subsequently, the tapestry shows Edward on his deathbed, affirming Harold as his chosen heir. Backed by the high council, the Witan, Harold is crowned king, but a comet in the sky portends ill fortune (Halley's Comet passed over England in April 1066). In the lower margin, the ghostly image of ships is thinly picked out. Taking his horses with him, William duly sails to England to stake his claim to the throne. The last third of the tapestry narrates the course of the Battle of Hastings. Its most famous sequence depicts Harold's death. Tantalizingly, there is more than one way to read this section. The words 'HAROLD REX INTERFECTUS EST' ('Here King Harold was killed') appear to connect not one but two Anglo-Saxon warriors. 'HAROLD REX' is above a soldier who appears to have been struck in the eye by an arrow, but the rest of the description seems to relate to a soldier being felled by Norman cavalry.

THE END OF ANGLO-SAXON ENGLAND

5 January 1066 King Edward the Confessor dies.

6 January Harold II is crowned king, probably in Westminster Abbey.

20 September At the Battle of Fulford, the invading force of Earl Tostig and Harald Hardrada, king of Norway, defeats the forces of the earls of Mercia and Northumberland.

25 September At the Battle of Stamford Bridge, Harold defeats the invaders; Tostig and Hardrada are killed.

28 September William, duke of Normandy, lands with his army at Pevensey.

14 October At the Battle of Hastings (Senlac Hill) Harold is killed.

November William takes London.

25 December William is crowned king of England in Westminster Abbey.

1069–70 During the 'Harrying of the North', William crushes dissent by laying waste to northern England.

1071 Hereward the Wake's revolt in the Fens is suppressed.

1086 The Domesday Book is collected.

1087 William is fatally injured while laying siege to Mantes in France.

The seal of William the Conqueror.

The most plausible explanation is that both men are Harold, struck first by an arrow and then felled by the horseman's sword. Holes in the linen suggest the felled warrior may originally also have had an arrow in his eye.

William was the illegitimate son of Duke Robert of Normandy and a tanner's daughter, who was officially the duke's mistress. The tapestry aimed to legitimize his seizure of England. Accordingly, it shows how Harold paid the consequence for breaking a solemn oath that William should be given the throne, even if as a captive he had given it only under duress. Yet as a work of propaganda, the tapestry is surprisingly sympathetic to the vanquished foe. Harold is depicted as a heroic and noble figure. Indeed, the first half of the tapestry seems to be far more about him than about William. During his stay in France, Harold is shown personally rescuing men from dangerous quicksand. In contrast, after they land in England Norman troops are depicted burning down the homes of innocent women and children. Far from being a divinely ordained walkover, the Battle of Hastings is accurately

depicted as a close encounter, full of twists and turns. Nor are inconvenient details excluded, such as Edward's dying affirmation of Harold as his successor. Perhaps the most substantive omission is Harold's startling victory against an invading force led by the king of Norway at Stamford Bridge, outside York. The battle was fought only eighteen days before the exhausted English army, force-marched to the south coast, found itself facing the Norman cavalry at Hastings.

Who might have commissioned such a work? It was long assumed that the patron was William's diminutive wife, Queen Matilda. However, given the sympathetic rendering of Edward the Confessor and Harold, an intriguing alternative has been suggested in the personality of another queen depicted in the work: Edith. Despite being both Edward's widow and Harold's sister, Queen Edith played a politically skilful hand after the Norman Conquest, thereby ensuring – unusually – that she was not stripped of her estates. It is possible that the tapestry was her way of threading a path between honouring her Anglo-Saxon past and collaborating with a Norman future. If so, it must have been commissioned before her death in 1075.

Odo, bishop of Bayeux, remains another strong possibility. Odo was William's half-brother and he was created earl of Kent, where the Bayeux Tapestry was most likely made. However, having been appointed regent of England during William's absences in Normandy, he overreached himself by attempting to become pope too and fell out with William in 1082. The tapestry may have been a futile attempt to flatter his half-brother. It certainly flatters Odo, whose own prominence in the success of the events is highlighted.

The final section of the tapestry – which may have depicted William's coronation – is lost, but it is more astonishing that the rest has been preserved. The property of Bayeux Cathedral since at least the fifteenth century (it is first mentioned in an inventory of 1476), it was lucky to survive both the destructive zeal of Calvinist despoilers, who ransacked the cathedral in 1562, and the order for it to be torn up and used as canvas covers by French revolutionaries in 1792. In 1944, Heinrich Himmler – who decided it was 'important for our glorious and cultured Germanic history' – made a last-minute attempt to cart it off via Paris to Berlin and was prevented only by the speedy advance of the Allied armies following D-Day. It was a timely rescue, not least since it might not have survived in the ruins of the Third Reich. Bayeux itself was the first city to be liberated by British troops in the Normandy landings. A monument to their casualties subsequently placed there reads 'NOS A GULIELMO VICIT VICTORIS PATRIAM LIBERAVIMUS' – 'We, once conquered by William, have now set free the Conqueror's native land.'

1086
THE DOMESDAY BOOK

WILLIAM THE CONQUEROR'S SURVEY OF THE NATION
AND THE CENTRALIZATION OF STATE POWER

In the twentieth year of his English rule, William the Conqueror ordered a comprehensive assessment of his kingdom, in terms of who owned what, how much each holding was worth, what it might yield in taxes, and the services that tenants owed. The result was the Domesday Book. It listed not only the names of the landowners and the extent of their property, but also the use to which their land was put, right down to its ploughing capacity and the presence of fishponds. As such, the Domesday Book was unparalleled in scope and purpose, for nowhere else in Europe had so detailed a record been attempted. It is central to our understanding of the feudal state created by the Norman Conquest.

It was at Christmas 1085, while William was with his court at Gloucester, that he directed the work to commence. The contemporary account in the *Anglo-Saxon Chronicle* struggled to conceal its sense of awe when describing the extent of the ambition: 'So very thoroughly did he have the inquiry carried out that there was not a single "hide", nor one virgate of land, not even – it is shameful to record it, but it did not seem shameful for him to do – not even one ox, nor one cow, nor one pig which escaped notice in his survey.'

The principal omissions were Cumbria, Northumberland and County Durham, the northern territories not fully under Norman control and hotly disputed with the Scottish king, Malcolm Canmore. Although no record survives for Winchester and London, this may be because the relevant manuscripts are lost rather than because the two great cities were deliberately excluded. However, full surveys were made of all the counties of England south of the River Tees as well as the Welsh border areas. In all, the Domesday Book makes reference to 13,418 places. For many villages, this is their first recorded mention in history.

Remarkably, the information was gathered within seven months. The well-organized system that delivered these results subdivided England into multi-county regions and designated a panel of commissioners to each. These teams travelled to every village and borough, taking down evidence testified to under oath in the local provincial courts. Careful note was made of the leading landowners, the manors and estates, their extent and the features of the holdings, subtenures, slaves and value, both in 1086 and at the end of Edward the Confessor's reign in 1066. The information was then sent for analysis and revision to Winchester.

At Winchester, the vast quantity of material was summarized so that it could be made available in a readily accessible format. This version is known as 'Great Domesday' and is written in a single hand (with some insertions and corrections in a second hand). However, it excludes Essex, Suffolk and Norfolk. Perhaps because they filed late, no summary was created for these counties. Instead, for them we have the full and unabridged circuit returns, bound together in a second volume known as 'Little Domesday'. In addition, the circuit returns for Cornwall, Devon, Dorset and Wiltshire have been preserved at Exeter Cathedral. This 'Exon Domesday' allows historians to compare the raw data directly with the overview provided in 'Great Domesday'.

It is hardly surprising that so thorough an exercise acquired the epithet Domesday. To all those brought forth to testify under oath, its result must indeed have seemed as final as the Day of Judgment. The entire process was clearly an assertion of the intrusive powers of the Norman state, an authority far more centralized than Anglo-Saxon forms of government, even if it was partly dependent upon the latter's old tax records. Yet although it showed that the king owned a fifth of the country (with a further quarter owned by the Church), Domesday's instigation was in some ways the consequence of Norman insecurity.

Much of William's reign was devoted to building strong castles and suppressing revolts, both in England and back in Normandy, where he died after injuring himself sacking Mantes the year after Domesday's completion. The need to suppress repeated insurrections stretched the capacity of the Norman war-machine. Furthermore, in 1085 a costly army had to be garrisoned in readiness for an expected – but ultimately aborted – invasion by the allied armies of the Danish king and the count of Flanders (the last Scandinavian invasion attempt in English history). It is in this light that the Domesday project must be seen: as an attempt to update the tax assessments as well as to assert the feudal dues upon which the survival of this security-conscious Norman state depended.

Epheh̅ ten̅ de rege in̅ eccla de Cantetone .ii. uirg̅ t̅re 7 dimid̅. t̅ra .e̅. ii. car̅. In d̅nio .e̅. dimid̅ car̅. cu̅ .ii. uillis 7 .vi. bord̅. Ibi .ii. ac̅ siluę minute. Valer .xx. sol̅.

Stefan capellan ten̅ ecclam de Milvertone cu̅ una uirg̅ 7 uno ferding̅. t̅ra .e̅. i. car̅. Ibi .x. ac̅ silue.

Aluieu p̅br ten̅ de rege .i. hidā in Sudpertone. t̅ra .e̅. i. car̅. q̅ ibi .e̅. cu̅ .i. bord̅ 7 uno seruo. Ibi .viii. ac̅ t̅re. Valer .xx. solid̅.

In eccla Carentone iacer .i. hida 7 dim̅. Ibi .e̅. in d̅nio .i. car̅ 7 dimid̅ cu̅ p̅bro 7 .i. uillo 7 uno bord̅. Ibi .xl. ac̅ pasturę 7 .xx. ac̅ siluę. Valer .xx. solid̅.

In eccla de Perettne iacent .iii. uirg̅ t̅re. t̅ra .e̅. i. car̅ q̅ ibi .e̅. Valer .xx. solid̅.

Has .ii. ecclas tenuit Peritel ep̅s. Modo s̅t in manu regis.

Leofus ten̅ Stra q̅ tenuit de rege .E. 7 geldb̅ p una uirg̅ t̅ra. t̅ra .e̅. i. car̅ q̅ ibi .e̅ cu̅ i. seruo 7 .ii. bord̅. Ibi molin redd̅ .vi. den̅ 7 .vi. ac̅ t̅re. Valer .x. solid̅.

Turstin ten̅ Lega p̅t ei tenuit .T.R.E. 7 geldb̅ p .i. hida. t̅ra .e̅. i. car̅. Ibi s̅t .ii. bord̅. Valer .x. solid̅.

Goduin ten̅ dimid̅ hid̅ in q̅ uocat Ragiol de rege in elemosina. Valer .iii. sol̅. Valer .xii. sol̅.

In eccla de Cura .e̅ dimid̅ hida. Ibi t̅r p̅br .i. car̅.

Eddida monialis ten̅ in elemosina de rege .xii. den̅ t̅re. Ibi s̅t .ii. b̅ .xx. ac̅ silue 7 pasture. Val̅ .v. solid̅.

Due nonne ten̅ de rege in elemosina .ii. u̅ uirg̅ 7 dimid̅ in Henstoke. t̅ra .e̅. i. car̅. Ibi .e̅. i. car̅. 7 .v. ac̅ t̅re. Valer .v. solid̅.

In Chenemeresdone .e̅ dimid̅ hida t̅ra. Val̅ .x. sol̅. Petrus ep̅s tenuit. Modo .e̅ in manu regis.

TERRA COMITIS EVSTACHII.

Comes Eustachius tenuit de rege Dunestone. Aleuuin̅ tenuit .T.R.E. 7 geldb̅ p una hida 7 una u̅ uirg̅. t̅ra .e̅. iiii. car̅. De ea in d̅nio .ii. uirg̅ t̅re 7 dim̅. ibi .i. car̅. 7 ii. serui 7 .vii. uilli 7 .viii. bord̅ cu̅ .iii. car̅. Ibi molin redd̅ .xv. den̅ 7 .iii. ac̅ t̅re. 7 .xxx. ac̅ pasturę 7 .xii. ac̅ siluę. Valuit 7 ual̅ .iiii. lib̅. Aluied ten̅ de comite.

Ipse Aluied ten̅ de co. Cenua. Leuuin̅ tenuit .T.R.E. 7 geldb̅ p .i. hida 7 dim̅. t̅ra .e̅. iiii. car̅. In d̅nio .e̅. i. car̅ 7 ii. serui 7 .i. uilli 7 i. bord̅ cu̅ .ii. car̅. Ibi .xxvi. ac̅ t̅re 7 .x. ac̅ pasturę 7 .ii. ac̅ siluę. Valuit .l. sol̅. Modo .xl. solid̅.

Eurard ten̅ de co. Lechesuude. Aluuard tenuit .T.R.E. 7 geldb̅ p una u̅ uirg̅. t̅ra .e̅. iii. car̅. In d̅nio .e̅ dimid̅. 7 .iii. serui 7 iii. uilli 7 .iii. bord̅ cu̅ i. car̅ 7 dimid̅. Ibi .ii. molini redd̅ .ii. plubis ferri 7 .ii. ac̅ t̅re 7 .xx. ac̅ siluę. Valuit 7 ual̅ .xxx. solid̅.

Ipse comes ten̅ Lachestone. Uiuieu tenuit .T.R.E. 7 geldb̅ p .v. hid̅. t̅ra .e̅. vii. car̅. De ea s̅t in d̅nio .iiii. hidę 7 ibi .ii. car̅ 7 ii. serui 7 .v. uilli 7 .vii. bord̅ cu̅ .iii. car̅. Ibi molin redd̅ .vi. den̅ 7 l. ac̅ t̅re 7 .ix. ac̅ pasturę 7 .ii. ac̅ siluę minutę. Valuit 7 ual̅ .c. solid̅.

Aluied ten̅ de co. Celesuorde. Thur tenuit .T.R.E. 7 geldb̅ p .ii. hid̅. t̅ra .e̅. iii. car̅. De ea s̅t in d̅nio .ii. hidę 7 dim̅. 7 .ii. uilli 7 .ii. bord̅ cu̅ i. car̅. 7 in d̅nio alia. Ibi .v. ac̅ t̅re. Silua .c. ę̅ lg̅. 7 una ę̅ lat̅. Valer .lx. sol̅.

Aluied ten̅ de co. Belestone. Toui tenuit .T.R.E. 7 geldb̅ p .iiii. hid̅. t̅ra .e̅. vi. car̅. In d̅nio .e̅. i. car̅ 7 dim̅. cu̅ .i. seruo. 7 .v. uilli 7 .ii. bord̅ cu̅ .ii. car̅. Ibi molin redd̅ .xv. solid̅ 7 .xxii. ac̅ t̅re 7 .xx. ac̅ pasturę. Silua .iii. ę̅ lg̅ 7 .ii. ę̅ lat̅. Valuit .iii. lib̅ modo .iiii. lib̅.

Comitissa iba̅ ten̅ de rege Chimeresdene. Uiuieu tenuit .T.R.E. 7 geldb̅ p .v. hid̅. t̅ra .e̅. viii. car̅. De ea s̅t in d̅nio .ii. hidę 7 .iii. uirg̅ 7 ibi .ii. car̅ 7 .vi. serui 7 .viii. uilli 7 .vii. bord̅ cu̅ car̅ Ibi .xxv. ac̅ t̅re 7 .xii. ac̅ pasturę. Silua .iii. ę̅ lg̅ 7 una ę̅ lat̅. Valuit 7 ual̅ .vi. lib̅.

Morulfus ten̅ de co. Sumerdone. Wlnod tenuit .T.R.E. 7 geldb̅ p .v. hid̅. t̅ra .e̅. v. car̅. De ea s̅t in d̅nio .iii. hidę 7 ibi .ii. car̅ 7 .iii. serui. 7 .v. uilli 7 .x. bord̅ cu̅ .iii. car̅. Ibi molin redd̅ .iii. den̅. 7 .v. ac̅ t̅re. pastura .iii. ę̅ lg̅. 7 .ii. ę̅ lat̅. Valer .c. solid̅.

TERRA HVGONIS COMITIS.

Comes Hugo ten̅ de rege Tedintone. 7 Will̅ de eo. Ednod tenuit .T.R.E. 7 geldb̅ p una hida. t̅ra .e̅. iii. car̅. In d̅nio .e̅ una car̅. 7 .iii. serui. 7 .v. uilli 7 .ii. bord̅ cu̅ .ii. car̅. Ibi .v. ac̅ t̅re 7 .c. ac̅ pasturę. 7 .xl. ac̅ siluę. Valuit 7 ual̅ .xl. solid̅.

Will̅ ten̅ de co. Santuде. T.R.E. geldb̅ p .ii. hid̅. t̅ra .e̅. v. car̅. In d̅nio .e̅. i. car̅ cu̅ .i. seruo. 7 .viii. uilli cu̅ .i. car̅. Ibi .xx. ac̅ t̅re 7 .l. ac̅ siluę 7 molin. Valuit 7 ual̅ .iii. lib̅.

Will̅ ten̅ de co. Alet. Ednod tenuit .T.R.E. 7 geldb̅ p dim̅ hid̅. t̅ra .e̅. ii. car̅ cu̅ .i. seruo. 7 .ii. bord̅ 7 i. uillo 7 .ii. ac̅ t̅re 7 .xxxvi. ac̅ pasturę. 7 .vi. ac̅ siluę. Valuit .xx. sol̅. modo .xv. sol̅.

Eccla s̅ Severi ten̅ de co. Henestrich. Ednod tenuit .T.R.E. 7 geldb̅ p .iiii. hid̅. t̅ra .e̅. iii. car̅. De ea s̅t in d̅nio .iii. hidę 7 dim̅ 7 ibi .ii. car̅. 7 .iiii. serui 7 .vi. bord̅ cu̅ .i. car̅. Ibi .xxx. ac̅ t̅re 7 .xx. ac̅ pasturę. 7 silua .iii. ę̅ lg̅. 7 .i. ę̅ lat̅. Valer .iiii. lib̅ 7 .x. sol̅.

TERRA COMITIS MORITONIENS.

Comes Moriton ten̅ de rege Candel. 7 Turstin de co. Syuuard tenuit .T.R.E. 7 geldb̅ p .vi. hid̅. t̅ra .e̅. v. car̅. De ea s̅t in d̅nio .iii. hidę 7 ibi .iii. car̅. 7 .ii. serui 7 .ii. uilli 7 .ii. bord̅ cu̅ .i. car̅. Ibi molin redd̅ .xviii. den̅ 7 una ac̅ t̅re 7 dimid̅. Silua .vii. ę̅ lg̅. 7 .ii. ę̅ lat̅. Valuit .iii. lib̅. modo .c. solid̅.

Malger ten̅ de co. Seuenehantone. Aluuard tenuit .T.R.E. 7 geldb̅ p .vii. hid̅. t̅ra .e̅. vii. car̅. De ea s̅t in d̅nio .v. hidę 7 dim̅. 7 ibi .iii. car̅. 7 .ii. serui 7 .vii. uilli 7 .vii. bord̅ cu̅ .iii. car̅. Ibi molin redd̅ .v. solid̅. 7 .xl. ac̅ t̅re. Valuit .viii. lib̅. modo .c. solid̅.

De hoc s̅t ablatę .xx. ac̅ siluę 7 .xxv. ac̅ mortę 7 pa. 7 s̅t in Sudpere q̅ regis.

Malger ten̅ de co. Contune. Godric tenuit .T.R.E. 7 geldb̅ p .m. hid̅. t̅ra .e̅. iii. car̅. In d̅nio .e̅. i. car̅. 7 .ii. uilli cu̅ .vi. bord̅ h̅nt .i. car̅.

Ansger ten̅ Sterttune de co. Aluuard tenuit. Valer .lx. sol̅. T.R.E. 7 geldb̅ p .iii. hid̅. t̅ra .e̅. vii. car̅. In d̅nio .e̅. i. car̅. dim̅. 7 .ii. serui 7 .xxiii. uilli 7 .iiii. bord̅ cu̅ .iii. car̅ dim̅. Ibi molin sine censu. 7 .ii. ec̅ ac̅ siluę. 7 .l. ac̅ pasturę redd̅ .iiii. blomal ferr̅. Val̅ .iii. lib̅.

Ipse comes ten̅ Sceptone. Algar tenuit .T.R.E. 7 geldb̅ p .vi. hid̅. t̅ra .e̅. vii. car̅. De ea s̅t in d̅nio .iiii. hidę dim̅ 7 ibi iii. mi̅. 7 ibi .ii. car̅. 7 dim̅. 7 iii. serui 7 .x. uilli 7 .iii. bord̅ 7 .xv. ac̅ t̅re. Valuit .c. solid̅. modo .iiii. lib̅.

Gerard ten̅ de co. Lopene. Aluuard tenuit .T.R.E. 7 geldb̅ p .i. hid̅. t̅ra .e̅. i. car̅. Ibi .i. bord̅ 7 .i. seruo. 7 .x. ac̅ t̅re. Valer .x. solid̅.

Rotbert ten̅ de co. Cruuetere. Eccla s̅ Suuithun Wincon̅ tenuit .T.R.E. Ibi s̅t .x. hide. sed n̅ geldb̅ nisi p̅ .iii. hid̅. t̅ra .e̅. xii. car̅. De ea .e̅ in d̅nio .i. hida 7 ibi .iii. car̅. 7 .vii. serui 7 .vii. uilli 7 .x. bord̅ cu̅ .x. car̅. Ibi .vi. ac̅ t̅re 7 .xx. ac̅ siluę. pasturę .i. leuu̅ 7 dimid̅ lat̅. Valuit 7 ual̅ .iiii. lib̅.

Ansger ten̅ de co. Iete. Ulnos tenuit .T.R.E. 7 geldb̅ p .v. hid̅. t̅ra .e̅. v. car̅. In d̅nio s̅t .ii. car̅. 7 .v. serui 7 .v. uilli 7 .iiii. bord̅ cu̅ .ii. car̅. Ibi molin redd̅ .xiiii. solid̅. 7 .xviii. ac̅ t̅re. Silua .iii. u̅ 7 dimid̅ lg̅ 7 .ii. u̅ lat̅. Valer .c. solid̅.

Ipse com̅ ten̅ Tintehalle. Eccla s̅ Glastingie tenuit .T.R.E. Ibi s̅t .viii. hide 7 una u̅ uirg̅. sed q̅ v. hid̅ geldb̅. t̅ra .e̅. x. car̅. De ea s̅t in d̅nio .iiii. hide 7 ibi .iii. car̅. 7 .v. serui 7 .xx. uilli 7 .vii. bord̅ cu̅ .vii. car̅. Ibi molin redd̅ .xx. denar̅ 7 .x. ac̅ t̅re 7 .cc. ac̅ pasturę 7 .iiii. ac̅ siluę. Valer .xvi. lib̅. Hugo ten̅ de co. unu̅ ic de ipsa t̅ra. iud̅ .c. marc̅ 2f5a

From the Domesday Book's survey of Somerset, 1086

XVII The Land of Count Eustace

COUNT EUSTACE held of the King (North or West) NEWTON. Leofwine held in TRE [tempora regis Eduardis (in the time of King Edward the Confessor)] and it paid geld for 1 hide and 1 virgate of land. There is land for 4 ploughs. Of this 2½ virgates of land are in demesne, and there is 1 plough and 2 slaves; and 7 villans and 6 bordars with 3 ploughs. There is a mill rendering 15d. and 7 acres of meadow, and 33 acres of pasture and 17 acres of woodland. It was and is worth £4. Alvred of Marlborough holds it of the count.

The recording scribe provides plenty of grim evidence of William's brutality. The Conqueror quelled dissent by laying waste large swathes of northern England and killing, disinheriting or forcing into exile the old Anglo-Saxon nobility. So comprehensive was the Norman land-grab that Domesday's statistics suggest that, by 1086, only 8 per cent of England was still in the hands of its pre-1066 native English owners. What did survive, however, was the traditional unit of local administration, the county or 'shire'.

The fraught circumstances of its production should not distract from the scale of the Domesday Book's achievement. Not only did it surpass anything of its kind attempted previously, but nothing as comprehensive would again be attempted in Britain until the introduction of national censuses in the nineteenth century. More than 900 years after its completion, Domesday remains a legally admissible source of evidence for property entitlement.

The Domesday Book itself, in addition to the 'Domesday chest' in which it was formerly kept, can be seen at The National Archives in Kew. A version is now available online, with an English translation of the original Latin.

OPPOSITE: A page of the Domesday Book for the county of Somerset. A translation of one of the entries in the first column, for land held by Count Eustace, can be seen above. A 'hide' was a measure of land (between 60 and 120 acres) used to assess liability for land tax, while a 'virgate' was equivalent to one-quarter of a hide.

1166
THE ASSIZE OF CLARENDON

THE DEVELOPMENT OF CRIMINAL COURTS, THE
COMMON LAW AND TRIAL BY JURY

Villiam the Conqueror may have imposed the feudal social order upon England, but because neither he nor his successors passed much fresh legislation, Norman England's legal customs changed little from Anglo-Saxon practices. Furthermore, while the task of presiding over county courts was assumed by the senior Norman baron in the area – acting in his role as sheriff – it was the Anglo-Saxon administrative and legal jurisdiction of the shire that defined the limit of his authority.

It was during the reign of Henry II (1154–89) that the barons' judicial powers began to be weakened. Henry set in motion reforms that shaped the English legal system for the next 800 years. In addition to his judges sitting as the King's Bench at Westminster, royal judges were instructed to tour the country administering justice. This 'assize system' continued until it was replaced by crown courts in 1971. Thus it was that serious crimes came to be treated less as localized disputes, affecting chiefly those they concerned, but rather as breaches of the 'King's peace', to be dealt with by representatives of the royal court adhering to and extending a single body of precedent, the common law.

Initially, these reforms did little to change the lot of the lowest ranks of the peasantry. Tied to a baronial estate, they could still expect judgment from their lord and master. 'Freemen', on the other hand, with the money and inclination to pursue justice further, gained the opportunity to have their cases heard before royal justices, sitting with a jury.

Trial by jury is the most famous clause of the Assize of Clarendon, a set of royal instructions for justices dating from 1166. It mandates twelve 'of the more lawful' men from each 'hundred' (the shire subdivision) and four from every town to declare on oath before the county sheriff, or district justices, the

The Assize of Clarendon, 1166

Here begins the assize of Clarendon made by King Henry II with the assent of the archbishops, bishops, abbots, earls and barons of all England.

1. In the first place the aforesaid King Henry, on the advice of all his barons, for the preservation of peace, and for the maintenance of justice, has decreed that inquiry shall be made throughout the several counties and throughout the several hundreds through twelve of the more lawful men of the hundred and through four of the more lawful men of each vill upon oath that they will speak the truth, whether there be in their hundred of vill any man accused or notoriously suspect of being a robber or murderer or thief, or any who is a receiver of robbers or murderers or thieves, since the lord king has been king. And let the justices inquire into this among themselves and the sheriffs among themselves.

2. And let anyone, who shall be found, on the oath of the aforesaid, accused or notoriously suspect of having been a robber or murderer or thief, or a receiver of them, since the lord king has been king, be taken and put to the ordeal of water, and let him swear that he has not been a robber or murderer or thief, or receiver of them, since the lord king has been king, to the value of 5 shillings, as far as he knows.

3. And if the lord of the man, who has been arrested, or his steward or his vassals shall claim him by pledge within the third day following his capture, let him be released on bail with his chattels until he himself shall stand his trial.

4. And when a robber or murderer or thief or receiver of them has been arrested through the aforesaid oath, if the justices are not about to come speedily enough into the county where they have been taken, let the sheriffs send word to the nearest justice by some well-informed person that they have arrested such men, and the justices shall send back word to the sheriffs informing them where they desire the men to be brought before them; and let the sheriffs bring them before the justices. And together with them let the sheriffs bring from the hundred and the vill, where they have been arrested, two lawful men to bear the record of the county and of the hundred as to why they have been taken, and there before the justice let them stand trial.

5. And in the case of those who have been arrested through the aforesaid oath of this assize, let no man have court or justice or chattels save the lord king in his court in the presence of his justices; and the lord king shall have all their chattels. But in the case of those who have been arrested otherwise than by this oath let it be as is customary and due.

6. And let the sheriffs, who have arrested them, bring them before the justice without any other summons than that they have from him. And when robbers or murderers or thieves, or receivers of them, who have been arrested through the oath or otherwise, are handed over to the sheriffs, let them receive them immediately and without delay.

7. And in the several counties where there are no gaols, let such be made in a borough or some castle of the king at the king's expense and from his wood, if one shall be near, or from some neighbouring wood at the oversight of the king's servants, to the end that in them the sheriffs may be able to guard those who shall be arrested by the officials accustomed to do this, or by their servants.

8. Moreover, the lord king wills that all shall come to the county courts to take this oath, so that none shall remain behind on account of any franchise which he has, or any court or soke, which he may have, but that they shall come to take this oath.

9. And let there be no one within his castle or without, nor even in the honour of Wallingford [a large estate in Oxfordshire], who shall forbid the sheriffs to enter into his court or his land to take the view of frankpledge [a collective guarantee of good conduct made by a group of householders in early medieval England] and to see that all are under pledges; and let them be sent before the sheriffs under free pledge.

10. And in cities or boroughs let no one hold men or receive them into his house or on his land or in his soke, whom he will not take in hand to produce before the justice, should they be required; or else let them be in frankpledge.

11. And let there be none in a city or a borough or a castle or without it, nor even in the honour of Wallingford, who shall forbid the sheriffs to enter into their land or their soke to arrest those who have been accused or are notoriously suspect of being robbers or murderers or thieves or receivers

of them, or outlaws, or persons charged concerning the forest; but the king commands that they shall aid the sheriffs to capture them.

12. And if anyone shall be taken in possession of the spoils or robbery or theft, if he be of evil repute and bears an evil testimony from the public and has no warrant, let him have no law. And if he has not been notoriously suspect on account of the goods in his possession, let him go to the ordeal of water.

13. And if anyone shall confess to robbery or murder or theft, or the harbouring those who have committed them, in the presence of the lawful men or in the hundred court, and afterwards he wish to deny it, let him not have his law.

14. Moreover the lord king wills that those who shall be tried by the law and absolved by the law, if they have been of ill repute and openly and disgracefully spoken of by the testimony of many and that of the lawful men, shall abjure the kings lands, so that within eight days they shall cross the sea, unless the wind detains them; and with the first wind they shall have afterwards they shall cross the sea, and they shall not return to England again except by the mercy of the lord king; and both now, and if they return, let them be outlawed; and on their return let them be seized as outlaws.

15. And if the lord king forbids that any vagabond, that is, a wanderer or unknown person, shall be given shelter anywhere except in a borough, and even there he shall not be given shelter longer than one night, unless he become sick there, or his horse, so that he can show an evident excuse.

16. And if he shall remain there longer than one night, let him be arrested and held until his lord shall come to give surety for him, or until he himself shall procure safe pledges; and let him likewise be arrested who gave him shelter.

17. And if any sheriff shall send word to another sheriff that men have fled from his county into another county, on account of robbery or murder or theft or the harbouring of them, or on account of outlawry or of a charge concerning the kings forest, let him (the second sheriff) arrest them; and even if he knows of himself or through others that such men have fled into his county, let him arrest them and guard them until he has taken safe pledges for them.

18. And let all the sheriffs cause a record to be made of all fugitives who have fled from their counties; and let them do this before the county courts and carry the names of those written therein before the justices, when next they come to them, so that these men may be sought throughout England, and their chattels may be seized for the needs of the king.

19. And the lord king wills that from the time the sheriffs shall receive the summons of the itinerant justices to present themselves before them, together with the men of the county, they shall assemble them and make inquiry for all who have newly come into their counties since this assize; and they shall send them away under pledge to attend before the justices, or they shall keep them in custody until the justices come to them, and then they shall present them before the justices.

20. Moreover the lord king forbids monks or canons or any religious house to receive any men of the lower orders as a monk or a canon or a brother, until it be known of what reputation he is, unless he shall be sick unto death.

21. Moreover the lord king forbids anyone in all England to receive in his land or his soke or in a house under him any one of that sect of renegades who were branded and excommunicated at Oxford. And if anyone shall so receive them, he himself shall be at the mercy of the lord king, and the house in which they have dwelt shall be carried outside the village and burnt. And each sheriff shall swear an oath that he will observe this, and shall cause all his officers to swear this, and also the stewards of the barons and all knights and freeholders of the counties.

And the lord king wills that this assize shall be kept in his realm so long as it shall please him.

identity of the criminal suspect. This is not the first mention of a jury, which was an Anglo-Saxon concept. Indeed, King Æthelred the Unready issued a decree requiring 'that they will not accuse any innocent man or shield any guilty one'. However, the Assize of Clarendon makes more explicit a jury's role. Initially, its function was closer to that of a grand jury, determining whether there was sufficient evidence to justify a trial rather than to determine the subsequent outcome in court.

The Assize of Clarendon concerned charges relating to murder, robbery and theft, its provisions being revised in 1176 by the Assize of Northampton. The latter encouraged more severe penalties, identified forgery and arson as indictable crimes and transferred further power from the baronial sheriffs to the royal justices. Neither document abolished such ancient practices as trial by ordeal in the establishing of guilt. Specifically endorsed by both documents is the 'trial by water' (the throwing of the bound suspect into a pool, innocence being determined by an inability to float). Nonetheless, the increasing recourse to – and evolution in the role of – juries shifted procedures towards the presentation of evidence. The Church abolished trial by ordeal in 1215. Seven years later, the practice was established of calling petty juries of twelve men from the neighbourhood to determine the guilt or innocence of the accused. From 1367, a unanimous verdict from all twelve jurors was necessary, a requirement that endured until the majority verdict was deemed acceptable in 1967.

1215
MAGNA CARTA

THE 'GREAT CHARTER' LIMITS ARBITRARY POWER
AND ESTABLISHES AN ENGLISHMAN'S RIGHT
TO HABEAS CORPUS

Magna Carta is depicted in the first plate section.

In a country without a written constitution, no article of law has achieved more hallowed status than 'the Great Charter'. The document agreed between King John and his barons in the meadows of Runnymede, on the Surrey banks of the Thames in June 1215, is far more than merely a statement of the restraints placed on arbitrary power in medieval England. From the seventeenth century onwards, and throughout the expanding English-speaking world, its provisions were recalled, inspiring and fortifying those who cherished their British inheritance as well as those who sought to break away from it. The seventeenth-century radical politician John Wilkes pronounced it 'the distinguishing characteristic of all Englishmen'. For the Founding Fathers of the United States it was also a seminal text, an early draft for expressions to be extended and given new life in the US Constitution. Indeed, Magna Carta has perhaps shaped the modern world as much as any document in this book. Between a quarter and a third of mankind is governed according to the legal principles it enshrines.

It is therefore important to remember that its terms were almost immediately breached and that, despite its subsequent renewal, the claim that it represented the pivotal declaration of liberties was vigorously reasserted only in the reign of Queen Elizabeth I, when printed editions of the country's statutes opened with it. Most of its provisions were abolished by the Statute Law Revision Act of 1863. The original document contained sixty-three chapters. Today, only four of them remain on the British statute book. (These are chapters 1, 13, 39 and 40 of the document drawn up in 1215, corresponding to chapters 1, 9 and 29 in the revised version of 1225.)

So, why the fuss? First, because Magna Carta enshrines a legal philosophy that became the defining statement of the curtailment of power – that the ruler is not

above the law. A sovereign may be head of state, but the state itself is a greater legal entity to which he, or she, is subject. Thus a ruler is not entitled to be a despot. Second, the chapters that have endured on the British statute books are highly significant. Although chapter 1, affirming the freedom of the English Church, was effectively made redundant by the Reformation, and chapter 13 guarantees – without specifying – the ancient freedoms of the City of London and other towns, it is chapters 39 and 40 that remain, however chipped away, a cornerstone of due process. Chapter 39 articulates what later became the cherished principle of habeas corpus ('you have the body') – that nobody can be detained without being subject to a fair trial. The state cannot simply lock up whomever it pleases:

> [39] No free man shall be taken or imprisoned or disseised [deprived or dispossessed of property] or outlawed or exiled or in any way ruined, nor will we go or send against him, except by the lawful judgment of his peers or by the law of the land.

> [40] To no one will we sell, to no one will we deny or delay right or justice.

Chapter 39 provided the framework for the seventh article of the US Bill of Rights (the Fifth Amendment of the US Constitution) that no person shall 'be deprived of life, liberty, or property, without due process'. In Britain, this freedom from arbitrary arrest and imprisonment was given closer legal definition by the Habeas Corpus Act of 1679. It has been temporarily suspended only during war and national emergency, although the length of time that a suspect can be held without charge was extended under the anti-terrorism legislation of the first decade of the twenty-first century.

Magna Carta was born out of acute political crisis. The barons resented the taxes and impositions forced upon them by King John, whose rule (1199–1216) was marked by hardship and cruelty at home and defeat abroad. The loss to France of Normandy (save for the Channel Islands) in 1204 speeded up the process whereby the barons were forced to decide whether they considered themselves as English or Norman landowners; but at the time they considered the loss a disaster. John had compounded the situation in 1207 by refusing to confirm Pope Innocent III's choice of Stephen Langton as archbishop of Canterbury. The pope responded by placing England under an interdict that suspended the administering of religious

rites, initially preventing even the conducting of marriage services or burials in consecrated ground. Having been excommunicated, John was forced in 1211 to abase himself by surrendering his kingdoms (both England and Ireland – which had been invaded by Henry II) to the pope who, in turn, leased them back to John in return for 1,000 marks a year and bonds of fealty and homage.

The feudal dues that John expected were no longer being freely given, with many barons refusing to assist in his ongoing struggle against the French king, Philip (II) Augustus. When the latter crushed John's forces at the Battle of Bouvines in Flanders in 1214, John faced outright insurrection. Whilst the dissenting barons were essentially self-interested, they were also assisted by Stephen Langton in drawing up their demands in a more moderate, inclusive language. The result was Magna Carta. It drew on the pledges to rule within constraints that Henry I had made in his Coronation Charter of 1100. However, the document framed by Langton and the barons was different. It was not a monarch's personal statement of good intent, but a hard-won declaration to which subsequent rulers found themselves legally bound.

Such an outcome was not clear when John appended his seal in 1215. Having returned to Innocent III's good graces, he wasted no time in getting the pope to annul Magna Carta. Civil war recommenced, abetted by the landing of French troops at Thanet; the future French monarch, Louis VIII, even joined forces with the barons in London. However, the crisis soon passed with John's timely demise from dysentery in 1216, to be succeeded by Henry III, aged only nine. Those around him, including Langton, ensured that Magna Carta was redrafted and reissued in 1216, 1217 and again, with further small revisions, in 1225. It was this last version that became law in 1295 and from which those articles still operable derive their statutory authority.

Of the original document of 1215, four copies survive: one at Lincoln Cathedral, one at Salisbury Cathedral and two at the British Library. Of the latter, one was damaged in a fire in 1731; the other, still complete, was allegedly found in a London tailor's shop in the seventeenth century. The remaining extant copies were made for the subsequent reissues in Henry III's reign. Among these versions, one is owned by the Australian government and displayed in the Parliament building in Canberra. Another, privately owned, is on permanent loan to the National Archives in Washington, DC, where it hangs alongside the Declaration of Independence, the Bill of Rights and the US Constitution.

c.1250
THE CHRONICLES OF MATTHEW PARIS

A DISTINGUISHED EXAMPLE OF MEDIEVAL CARTOGRAPHY AND ILLUSTRATION

I t was not until the sixteenth century, with the invention of triangulation, that maps conveyed with at least some relative accuracy the shape and scale of the British Isles. Earlier generations of travellers were largely forced to rely on local knowledge or to keep to the major tracks. Indeed, before the mid-thirteenth century, the few Britons familiar with cartography had to make do with representations that were more schematic than geographical.

Matthew Paris's map of Britain is depicted in the first plate section.

Around 1250, an English monk named Matthew Paris (*c.*1200–59) drew a series of maps that are far more accomplished than anything that survives prior to that time. Although to the modern eye his depiction of Britain is greatly removed from reality, his draughtsmanship nonetheless aimed at rendering the country in an essentially accurate rather than schematic fashion.

At first glance, the claim to accuracy hardly rings true. The coastlines of Wales and Scotland (which Paris thought was almost totally dissected from the mainland by the Firths of Clyde and Forth) are not recognizable. Indeed, only the basic shape of Cornwall can be easily discerned. However, the picture becomes clearer once it is understood that the map's central artery is the road from Dover to Berwick. Thus Kent does not stick out to the south-east of London but lies due south, roughly where the Isle of Wight ought to be. Once this is comprehended, suddenly the rump of East Anglia, for instance, can be made out.

It is not just the importance of the Dover–Berwick road that should be noted but also the emphasis given to those other sources of navigation, rivers. London is clearly marked as the most important city among the over 250 places and features named. 'Snaudun' marks the mountains of Snowdonia. More surprisingly, both Hadrian's Wall and the Antonine Wall are depicted, despite having tumbled

into ruin over 800 years previously. This suggests that Paris may have had access to Roman manuscripts that have since been lost. The eastern slant of Scotland replicates the cartography of the second-century Greek astronomer, Ptolemy.

On the frontispiece of his Historia Anglorum, *the monk kneeling beneath the Virgin and Child is, in fact, a self-portrait of the author, Matthew Paris.*

Paris's significance was not confined to cartography. As a chronicler of his times, he wrote over a million words and his most important work was the *Chronica Majora*. In it, he updated the *Flores Historiarum* ('Flowers of History') of Roger of Wendover, one of his predecessors at the Benedictine abbey at St Albans. To Roger's history, from the Creation to 1234, Paris added his contemporary analysis of the years 1235 to 1259. It is a remarkable narrative, suffused with news and gossip. Paris was not a detached and cocooned scholar but a man familiar with some of the greatest figures in the realm. When away from St Albans, he appears to have spent much time attending ceremonial events and court occasions, where he hobnobbed with some exceptionally well-placed sources for his testimony. A trip to Bergen even led to a meeting with Hákon IV of Norway.

Paris was a confidant of both King Henry III and his younger brother, Richard of Cornwall, who, as 'King of the Romans' and an aspirant to the throne of the Holy Roman Empire, was active in the politics of the German lands. Frequently critical of the pope, Paris was also a staunch defender of English rights, lacing his chronicles with his own opinions and prejudices. Thus, while they cannot be regarded as either impartial or, in places, strictly accurate, they do provide telling and often first-hand knowledge of English politics. Furthermore, they were written from the standpoint of someone whose independent spirit was such that he could accept King Henry's patronage and admire his piety, yet comment critically on his political skills and indecisiveness. 'The lot of historians,' Paris sighed, 'is hard indeed, for, if they speak the truth, they provoke man, and if they record falsehoods, they offend God.'

Paris decorated his chronicles with illustrations, often in the margins. Although his artistry was naive by some contemporary standards, his efforts to observe from life, as well as merely copying stylized reproduction, earn him a significant place in the development of British art. He drew some of the earliest known depictions of London and his picture of an elephant is justly famous. His *Historica Anglorum* is prefaced with tinted line-drawings of the English kings. Since he knew Henry III personally, his representation of him there may even be relatively accurate.

Matthew Paris's *Chronica Majora* is kept at Corpus Christi College, Cambridge.

ANGEVINS AND PLANTAGENETS

Angevins

Henry II 1154–89

Richard I 'the Lionheart' 1189–99

John 1199–1216

Plantagenets

Henry III 1216–72

Edward I 1272–1307

Edward II 1307–27

Edward III 1327–77

Richard II 1377–99

(House of Lancaster)

Henry IV 1399–1413

Henry V 1413–22

Henry VI 1422–61 and 1470–71

(House of York)

Edward IV 1461–70 and 1471–83

Edward V 1483

Richard III 1483–5

1265
SIMON DE MONTFORT'S
SUMMONS FOR A PARLIAMENT

THE ROOTS OF A REPRESENTATIVE PARLIAMENT

It was in 1236 that the council of the king, busy discussing legal issues and matters of state at Westminster, was first described as a 'parliament'. While the term may then have been only recently coined, the institution was already ancient. Its antecedence stretched back not only to the council of barons and clergy that had periodically advised the Norman rulers but to the traditional Anglo-Saxon convocation of nobles, the Witan ('the knowing ones'), which had surrounded Alfred the Great.

During the fourteenth century, this assembly became more recognizably the House of Lords. In contrast, Parliament's representative element – which later evolved into the House of Commons – had its roots in a power struggle between King Henry III and his opponents, led by a seemingly unlikely champion of English national consciousness, Simon de Montfort.

The circumstances of Henry III's extreme youth – his 'minority' – on assuming the throne were propitious for those who wanted to exercise power on his behalf. The re-enforcement of the previously revoked Magna Carta was one example of this; the more assertive line taken by his council of barons and clerics on appointments and expenses another. With the passing of years, his need to compensate for shortfalls in revenue from the lost French territories – and the cost of holding on to mutinous Gascony – pushed Henry into demanding significant tax rises. And, in post-Magna Carta England, he found himself having to seek Parliament's permission to do so. In 1254 two knights from each county were asked to attend Parliament in order to approve a grant of taxation.

Henry also had to deal with a particularly strong challenge from his charismatic lieutenant in Gascony, Simon de Montfort. Following a childhood spent in southern France where his father had ruthlessly suppressed Christian heretics,

de Montfort inherited the earldom of Leicester. His marriage to Eleanor, the king's widowed teenage sister, in 1238, had made him Henry's brother-in-law. However, it was his removal from Gascony following claims of heavy-handedness, subjection to a show trial and his subsequent failure to be properly remunerated that helped turn this tough, driven and deeply devout natural leader into the king's critic and influential enemy.

Forgetting his own Gallic origins, de Montfort discovered the language of English patriotism, leading the campaign to rid Henry of his foreign relations and advisers. Henry's expensive attempts to secure the Sicilian throne for his second son, Edmund, particularly riled the barons. In June 1258, Parliament met in Oxford and, with de Montfort among the guiding hands, agreed a revolutionary statement known as the Provisions of Oxford. The original document is lost, but its contents are known. The king's power was to be severely curtailed by a new council of fifteen men, acting with executive authority. The concept that the monarch would henceforth cease to control his own appointments, as well as the money raised to enact his policies, was, in the context of medieval Europe, an extraordinary repudiation of the rights of crowned heads. Nor was this merely a case of a few self-serving barons muscling in upon the throne to exploit their sovereign's weakness. The work of the council was to be debated by Parliament, which should meet at least three times a year. The king's distrusted foreign relations and advisers were to be expelled. Every county would elect four knights to examine and express to the king's chief legal officer, the justiciar, local discontents with the sheriffs. When the final form of the declaration was inscribed in Latin and French the following year, it was also written – most tellingly – in English.

Financial and political necessity forced Henry to agree, temporarily, to the provisions, but in 1261 he felt strong enough, backed with the authority of a papal bull, to repudiate them. Having made their revolutionary declarations, de Montfort and the barons were in no mood to tamely acquiesce. England, once again, was plunged into civil war. De Montfort, however, had a broad following, enjoying strong popularity in the Midlands, London and the South East as well as among the bishops. At Lewes in Sussex, his army, donning the crosses of crusaders, crushed the royal forces, taking both King Henry and his son, Prince Edward, prisoner.

In the midst of this emergency (a French invasion was also expected), executive power was effectively in the hands of de Montfort, the bishop of Chichester and the earl of Gloucester who – nominally in the king's name – formed a triumvirate to

rule England at the head of a council of nine. De Montfort issued writs requesting that each county elect four 'prudent and law-worthy' knights to attend Parliament. They were joined at Westminster in January 1265 by two burgesses elected from a list of major towns. For the first time, commoners were elected to sit in Parliament.

These representatives of town and county sat with the barons and clergy in Westminster Hall. They were not yet a separate House of Commons. Their manner of election varied in the towns, but may have been open to all freeholders in the counties. Nonetheless, in the range of policy areas that it presumed to debate, in the stipulation that members must be elected and in the breadth of its composition, the 'de Montfort Parliament' denotes a significant moment in the early development of democracy. As the historian Simon Schama has put it, 'It inaugurated the union between patriotism and insubordination.'

Almost immediately, the advance seemed undone. Prince Edward escaped custody and in August 1265 his forces routed de Montfort's army at Evesham. Surrounded by the bodies of his fallen son and his supporters, de Montfort himself was cut down – characteristically – fighting on foot in the thick of the action. Although in the years after his death parliaments were convened without

his knights and burgesses in attendance, the increasing cost of government ensured that the innovation had to be returned to, and the precedent more firmly set. This was partly because after 1265 the assent of the knights and burgesses in Parliament was deemed legally necessary for the raising of taxes.

Indeed, it was to raise money for his Scottish wars that de Montfort's nemesis, now King Edward I, summoned his 'Model' Parliament of 1295. It consisted of over 500 members, including not only the lords temporal and spiritual but also knights from every shire plus two burgesses from 110 boroughs. After 1325, these representatives were a permanent feature of parliamentary government and soon after were sitting in their own chamber, distinct from the unelected barons. One nod to popular will that came in consequence was that from 1363, English – not French – was enshrined as the official language spoken at Westminster. Furthermore, by then Parliament's hearing of petitions ensured that it, rather than the monarch, drove through new laws. This legislative right was the prerogative of the nascent House of Lords until a judicial decision of 1489 stated that laws could be enacted only with the support of both houses, and by then the commoners alone could veto the king's taxes.

The writ and return from Bedfordshire and Buckinghamshire, issued in 1274 and depicted above, is the oldest surviving example of a royal writ. The practice of sending such writs, ordering the election of members to Parliament, began with de Montfort in 1265 and continues to this day.

1284
THE STATUTE OF RHUDDLAN

EDWARD I'S ANGLICIZATION OF THE
PRINCIPALITY OF WALES

Opposite: Section of the six-foot-long roll comprising the Statute of Rhuddlan. The text is in Latin.

Three sources of authority contested Wales at the commencement of the thirteenth century. The first was the English Crown. Periodic military campaigns had scoured England's neighbour, making inroads and building strongholds without establishing total domination. The second was the Marcher lords, the descendants of Norman barons whose estates ran not only along the Welsh borderlands but also deep into southern Wales. While nominally within the English realm, these territories were essentially the fiefdoms of their barons. Marcher law, not English law, governed their inhabitants.

The third source of authority was indigenous and was exercised in the domains of the Welsh princes. There was no law of primogeniture guaranteeing the succession to the eldest son. By the end of the twelfth century, the royal houses of Powys and Deheubarth, principalities respectively of central and south-west Wales, had been weakened by internecine rivalry. However, in the north, the mountainous princely state of Gwynedd endured and became dominant. By 1257, the authority of Gwynedd's prince, Llewelyn ap Gruffudd, stretched south from Snowdonia to embrace two-thirds of the country. A decade later, via the Treaty of Montgomery, a trade was made of token diplomatic gestures, with Henry III recognizing Llewelyn's claim to be 'Prince of Wales' in return for his acknowledging the English monarch as his feudal overlord.

The ambiguous question of whose will had seniority started to resolve itself with the succession of Edward I. One of the most determined and ruthless men ever to sit on the English throne, Edward had no intention of flattering Llewelyn, who had, after all, previously sought to interfere in English politics on the side of Simon de Montfort (to whose daughter Llewelyn was betrothed). Aware of his heightening personal danger, Llewelyn refused repeated summons to do homage to Edward either at, or following, his coronation in 1274. This snub provided the

MEDIEVAL WALES

*c.*1200–1240 Llywelyn ab Iorwerth (Llywelyn the Great) is Prince of Gwynedd and effective ruler of most of Wales.

1241 With the Treaty of Gwerneigron. Dafydd ap Llywelyn, Prince of Gwynedd, pledges loyalty to Henry III, cedes much of Flintshire to him and effectively relinquishes his right to the other Welsh lands claimed by his father, Llywelyn ap Iorwerth.

1246–82 Dafydd's nephew, Llywelyn ap Gruffudd (Llywelyn the Last), is Prince of Gwynedd.

1267 In the Treaty of Montgomery, Henry III acknowledges Llywelyn ap Gruffudd as Prince of Wales.

1277 Edward I invades Gwynedd, forcing Llywelyn to agree to the Treaty of Aberconwy, curtailing his authority and acknowledging Edward as his overlord.

1282–3 In the Second War of Welsh Independence, Llywelyn's brother Dafydd rebels against Edward I.

1283 Edward I begins construction of Caernarfon, Conwy and Harlech castles.

1284 The Treaty of Rhuddlan is made.

1294–5 Madog ap Llywelyn proclaims himself Prince of Wales and leads a fresh revolt, capturing Caernarfon before suffering defeat at the Battle of Maes Moydog.

1301 Edward I revives the title of 'Prince of Wales' and bestows it on his son, the future Edward II.

1400–1412 Owain Glyndwr rebels.

1472 Edward IV's Council of Wales and the Marches is convened at Ludlow.

1485 The Anglo-Welsh Henry Tudor becomes King Henry VII of England.

perfect pretext for Edward. In 1277, he invaded Gwynedd with a mighty army swelled not only with English knights but with Llewelyn's Welsh enemies. Losing his fertile lands in Anglesey and facing a bleak winter in the mountains, Llewelyn surrendered and finally did Edward homage at a ceremony in Worcester. His reward was to be allowed to continue in a much-reduced Gwynedd that retained Anglesey but was shorn of most of its other Welsh acquisitions. Meanwhile the English refortified their castles and administered English law in a high-handed manner guaranteed to upset Welsh sensitivities.

Welsh resentment reached breaking point in 1282, when Llewelyn's brother Dafydd started a rebellion. Llewelyn felt compelled to come to his brother's aid, but early successes were quickly undone. Marching into Powys, Llewelyn was killed in a skirmish while Dafydd was betrayed and handed over to the English. He was duly hanged, drawn and quartered, his head being taken and mounted on a pike next to that of his brother at the Tower of London. Rather than complete the collection, other Welsh leaders scrambled to abase themselves before Edward.

The king responded by embarking on an even more expensive castle-building programme of such grandeur that the mighty walls of Caernarfon, for instance, were modelled on those that protected Constantinople. The framework for the new political settlement was set out in the Statute of Rhuddlan in 1284. Also known as the 'Statute of Wales', the document dismembered Gwynedd, with Snowdonia and Anglesey passing to the English Crown. Anglesey was one of the new, English-style counties created in the north, along with Flint, Caernarfon and Merioneth. Privileged boroughs were established for the benefit of English settlers. Crimes were henceforth to be judged in the courts of English law.

Yet the Statute of Rhuddlan also established limits to anglicization in North Wales that became the template for the rest of the country. Much Welsh custom was retained. In most civil law cases, Welsh practice was tolerated alongside English common law. Only the more antiquated aspects of the native customary law were abolished.

These measures were followed, in 1301, by an imaginative act of political and symbolic appropriation. Having dispensed with the royal house of Gwynedd, Edward proclaimed his own son, the future Edward II, as Prince of Wales in a ceremony at the place of his birth, Caernarfon Castle.

1320

THE DECLARATION
OF ARBROATH

A STATEMENT OF SCOTTISH INDEPENDENCE

In 1290, Scotland was set to share the same monarch as England. In northern Scotland, the Celtic traditions and Gaelic tongue seemed remote from the culture and language of its southern neighbour. It was only as recently as the 1260s that the Western Isles and the Hebrides had finally been wrestled from Norway. Nonetheless, the Scottish court was highly anglicized in its customs and outlook. Many of the great barons – such as the Balliol and Bruce families – were of Norman stock, owning land in England as well as in Scotland. Even Scottish kings had periodically done homage to the English Crown in return for holding on to their southern property, although the Scottish monarchs never accepted that these acts of abasement infringed their sovereignty over their own realm. The major source of conflict had always been where the border lay, with repeated harrying by both sides between the rivers Tyne and Tweed. However, there had been no significant conflict between the Scots and the English for over seventy years, both sides apparently accepting the previsions of the Treaty of York of 1237, which had drawn the border from Berwick-upon-Tweed to the Solway Firth. Alexander III, who had proved a wise king of Scots since 1249, was both the nephew and the son-in-law of England's Henry III.

In 1286, Alexander was thrown from his horse over a cliff at Kinghorn in Fife, plunging his realm into crisis. The heir to the Scottish throne was his three-year-old granddaughter Margaret ('the Maid of Norway'), whose father was Eric II of Norway. A period of acute instability beckoned, in which others with lesser claims but stronger wills were poised to assert themselves. A solution, of sorts, was offered by the English king, Edward I. He suggested that his son, the future Edward II, should marry Margaret of Norway. Their descendants would ensure a union of the crowns (if not, explicitly, a union of the kingdoms). The scheme was dashed by

The Declaration of Arbroath is depicted in the first plate section.

SCOTTISH WARS OF INDEPENDENCE

First War of Independence

1296 Edward I sacks Berwick and defeats the Scottish army at Dunbar. John Balliol abdicates and Scottish nobles give homage to Edward.

1297 William Wallace leads the resistance movement.

1304 The last major Scottish stronghold, Stirling Castle, falls to the English. John Comyn, joint 'Guardian of Scotland', negotiates the terms of Scottish submission.

1305 William Wallace is executed in London.

1306 Robert the Bruce murders John Comyn and is crowned king of Scots at Scone.

1307 Edward I dies and is succeeded by his son, Edward II.

1314 Robert the Bruce wins the Battle of Bannockburn.

1320 The Declaration of Arbroath asserts Scottish independence.

1327 Edward II is deposed and murdered, and succeeded by Edward III.

1328 Robert the Bruce invades northern England and signs the Treaty of Northampton–Edinburgh in which England acknowledges Scottish independence, and Bruce's son and heir, David, marries Edward III's sister.

1329 Robert the Bruce dies and is succeeded by his infant son, David II.

Second War of Independence

1332 Bruce's Scottish enemies and Edward III unite to support Edward Balliol's claim to the Scottish throne over David II and win the Battle of Dupplin Moor. Edward Balliol is crowned king but is soon forced to flee to England.

1333 Balliol invades Scotland with the support of the English, who win a devastating victory at the Battle of Halidon Hill.

1334 Unable to sustain support among the Scottish nobles, Balliol returns to England.

1335 Edward III invades Scotland and reaches Perth.

1337 The outbreak of the Hundred Years War diverts Edward III's attention to fighting the French, and Sir Andrew Murray regains strongholds in the name of David II.

1346 David II invades England and is captured at the Battle of Neville's Cross, thereafter spending eleven years in captivity.

1357 The Treaty of Berwick frees David II. Although much of the Scottish borders remain in English hands, English efforts to dictate the nation's succession are effectively ended.

an unexpected tragedy – in 1290, on her way to Scotland from Norway, Margaret died. There was no other direct claimant to the Scottish throne.

The constitutional crisis provided Edward I with his opportunity to push himself forward as Scotland's overlord. It was clear that he was the effective power-broker when the fourteen different claimants to the throne all pledged their fealty to him and the 'Guardians' overseeing this Scottish succession contest asked Edward to arbitrate. John Balliol, a direct descendant via the maternal line of the twelfth-century Scottish king David I, seemed a likely stooge, so Edward chose him.

Such was Edward's avarice and arrogance that even this arrangement fell short of his expectations. He proceeded to act in such a high-handed manner that Scotland allied with France, England's ancient enemy. Edward responded by invading Scotland in 1296, dethroning and imprisoning Balliol and ruling the kingdom as if it were his own. To drive home that this was now a takeover, not a partnership, the Great Seal was smashed and the Stone of Destiny, upon which Scottish kings had been crowned, together with the national archives and the crown regalia, were all carted off to England.

A process by which the English and Scottish courts might harmoniously have come together was replaced by a new master–servant relationship that inflamed Scotland's sense of its separate identity. A resistance movement led by William Wallace had initial success, notably at Stirling Bridge in 1297, before being crushed at Falkirk in 1298. Captured, Wallace was hanged, drawn, burned and quartered in 1305. His place was quickly taken by a new leader who had a distant claim to the throne. Robert the Bruce (1274–1329) decided he had not much to lose by staking his right to rule. Having gained little from pledging fealty to Edward, he was under censure for murdering his political rival and Balliol's nephew, John Comyn, in – of all places – a church.

In 1306, Bruce was crowned king of Scots. The following year Edward died. The inscription etched upon his tomb in Westminster Abbey lauded him as *Scottorum Malleus* ('the Hammer of the Scots'). His successor, Edward II, was an altogether weaker character and distracted by English resistance to his taking of favourites. Here was the opportunity for Robert the Bruce to seize his chance to strengthen his shaky authority, defeat his own Scottish opponents and unite the country against English domination.

After years of guerrilla warfare, the critical events took place in 1314. Edinburgh Castle was retaken from the English. Edward II dispatched an army to relieve his garrison at the other great strategic fortress at Stirling, but his forces were

comprehensively routed nearby, at Bannockburn. Although sent homewards to think again, Edward still refused to recognize Robert the Bruce as Scotland's legitimate ruler and campaigns along the border continued.

It was not just the English monarch who remained hostile to the Scots king. The papacy had excommunicated Bruce. Seeking to have this revoked – as well as to secure recognition of Scottish independence and, indeed, to explain why English hostility had diverted Scots from active involvement in the crusade against Islam – eight Scottish earls and thirty-eight barons attached their seals to an appeal sent to Pope John XXII in Avignon. Although this original document was subsequently lost, a copy was kept and is now in the care of the National Archives of Scotland in Edinburgh.

Written in Latin and probably drafted by Bernard, the abbot of Arbroath Abbey and chancellor of Scotland, the Declaration of Arbroath is one of the earliest surviving, all-encompassing statements of Scottish self-determination. It also promulgated an extraordinary constitutional notion, implying that Scotland's monarch was chosen by the people (albeit, in reality, the nobles), rather than by God. Hence, if ever Bruce surrendered to England, the Scots would replace him with another king. One statement in particular expressed the strength of national feeling: '...for, as long as but a hundred of us remain alive, never will we on any conditions be brought under English rule. It is in truth not for glory, nor riches, nor honours that we are fighting, but for freedom – for that alone, which no honest man gives up but with life itself.'

This became the ringing declaration of Scotland's independent identity. It succeeded with the pope, who recognized Bruce's claim and, with it, Scottish independence, in 1324. English acceptance followed grudgingly in 1328, although the Anglo-Scottish peace lasted only four years. Dissident Scottish nobles disinherited by Bruce allied with England and won victories at Dupplin Moor in 1332 and at Halidon Hill the following year. A renewed struggle for power ensued between the followers of John Balliol's son, Edward, and Bruce's infant successor, David II.

Despite subsequent, if temporary, English occupations of southern Scotland and the Scots' 'auld alliance' with the French, a decisive reconquest did not follow, not least because of England's increasing preoccupation with fighting in France during the Hundred Years War. The spirit of cross-border hostility remained nonetheless, and it was not until the Treaty of Edinburgh in 1560 that lasting peace between Scotland and England was agreed. Its claim to nationhood acknowledged, Scotland ended up in union with, rather than conquered by, its more powerful southern neighbour.

1382–95
WYCLIF'S BIBLE

THE TRANSLATION OF THE BIBLE INTO ENGLISH

Before the Reformation in the sixteenth century, the greatest intellectual challenge to the theology and prerogatives of the Catholic Church in England was posed by a lecturer at Oxford University, John Wyclif.

Having ceased to honour paying the feudal dues to the pope agreed by King John, the government's relations with the papacy had become increasingly fractious, while the papacy itself stood on the verge of the grave schism between 1378 and 1417: rival popes based in Rome and Avignon vied for the allegiance of Christendom. But whatever grumbles existed about the Church's aggrandizement of temporal power and all the related consequences of worldliness and corruption, there remained no path to salvation other than through its good graces.

Although there had, of course, been whinges about Church abuses before, John Wyclif's erudition carried a weight that added a previously absent *gravitas* to the attacks. A Yorkshireman, born around 1328, he was a student at Oxford by 1350, returning there to lecture in theology and philosophy. During the 1370s, his ideas became increasingly unorthodox. To describe his thinking as Protestant would be anachronistic, but his arguments did foreshadow many of those put forward by the shapers of the Reformation.

Wyclif was concerned by the scale of the Church's vast – and self-serving – wealth, not to mention the distraction this created from its vocation to aid the poor. He questioned the papacy's presumptions to intervene within the sphere of national governments. He attacked the claims made for transubstantiation, disputing that, in the administering of the Eucharist, bread and wine became the body and blood of Christ.

John Wyclif (c.1328–84).

Wyclif's translation of 1 Corinthians 13

If I speke with tungis of men and of aungels and I haue not charite, I am maad
as bras sownynge, or a cymbal tynklynge. and if I haue profecie and knowe alle
mysteries and al kynnyng. and if I haue al feith, so that I moue hills fro her
place, and I haue not charite I am nought. and if I departe alle my goodis into
the metis of pore men, and if I bitake my bodi so that I brenne and if I haue
not charite it profitith to me no thing. charite enuyeth not, it doith not wickidli,
it is not blowun, it is not coueitous, it sekith not tho thingis that ben his owne.
it is not stired to wraththe, it thenkith not yuel, it ioieth not on wickidnesse,
but it ioieth togidre to treuthe, it suffrith alle thingis, it bileueth all thingis, it
hopith alle thingis, it sustained alle thingis. charite fallith neuere doun. whethir
profecies schulen be voidid, eithir langagis schulen ceese, eithir science schal be
distried. for aparti we knowen, and aparti we profecien. but whanne that schal
come that is parfyt, that thing that is of parti schal be auoidid. whanne I was a
litil child I spak as a litil child, I thoughte as a litil child; but whanne I was
made a man I voidide tho thingis that weren of a litl child. and we seen now
bi a myrour in derknesse, but thanne face to face. now I knowe of parti, but
thanne I schal knowe as I am knowun. and now dwellen feith, hope and charite
these thre, but the moost of these is charite.

1 Corinthians 13 in the Authorized Version (1611)

Though I speak with the tongues of men and of angels, and have not charity, I
am become as sounding brass, or a tinkling cymbal. And though I have the gift
of prophecy, and understand all mysteries, and all knowledge; and though I have
all faith, so that I could remove mountains, and have not charity, I am nothing.
And though I bestow all my goods to feed the poor, and though I give my
body to be burned, and have not charity, it profiteth me nothing.
Charity suffereth long, and is kind; charity envieth not; charity vaunteth not
itself, is not puffed up, Doth not behave itself unseemly, seeketh not her own,
is not easily provoked, thinketh no evil; Rejoiceth not in iniquity, but rejoiceth
in the truth; Beareth all things, believeth all things, hopeth all things, endureth
all things.

Charity never faileth: but whether there be prophecies, they shall fail; whether there be tongues, they shall cease; whether there be knowledge, it shall vanish away. For we know in part, and we prophesy in part. But when that which is perfect is come, then that which is in part shall be done away. When I was a child, I spake as a child, I understood as a child, I thought as a child: but when I became a man, I put away childish things. For now we see through a glass, darkly; but then face to face: now I know in part; but then shall I know even as also I am known. And now abideth faith, hope, charity, these three; but the greatest of these is charity.

Wyclif's most important claim was that the Bible, not the Church, was the only source of divine authority. Thus, adherence to the scriptures, rather than obedience to the requirements of the Church, was the path to reaching a state of grace. This was a precursor to the central tenet of Martin Luther's Protestantism – justification by faith.

Wyclif was not a natural rabble-rouser; rather, he was a distinguished scholar with influential allies, receiving protection from one of the most powerful men in the country, Edward III's third son, John of Gaunt. His message, however, was essentially egalitarian: that the poor and those of no rank should have the means to understand God's word without the intercession of an official clergy.

He recieved his first serious rebuke in 1377 when Gregory XI issued papal bulls condemning Wyclif's teaching on nineteen grounds and summoning him to face the charges. Instead, the errant academic escaped with a light admonition to keep quiet. When the Peasants' Revolt broke out in 1381, his enemies were quick to link his teaching to this violent and anarchic disorder. After the authorities at Oxford ordered him to desist from publicly disputing transubstantiation, he left the university for Lutterworth in Leicestershire where he had been rector since 1374. The archbishop of Canterbury summoned a council that condemned Wyclif's teaching (without naming him) as heretical, while for good measure Parliament made the profession of such heresies a prisonable offence. Nonetheless, Wyclif managed to avoid prosecution, continuing to write from his obscurity in Lutterworth, where he died in 1384.

Before his passing, he had begun work on a revolutionary document – the Bible in English. This was in itself a challenge to the pope, as the Church prescribed only

SPREADING GOD'S WORD IN ENGLISH

1384 John Wyclif's Bible is the first complete translation in English.

1395 John Purvey produces his amended version of Wyclif's Bible.

1408 The Synod of Oxford prohibits any unauthorized Bible translation.

1526 William Tyndale's translation is the first printed New Testament in English.

1535 Miles Coverdale's translation is the first printed complete Bible.

1537 The Matthew Bible is published by John Rodgers.

1538 The Great Bible is the first English Bible to be authorized for public use.

1539 A revised version of the Matthew Bible is produced by Richard Taverner.

1560 The Geneva Bible is the first to number the verses of every chapter.

1568 The Bishops' Bible is authorized for public use.

1609–10 The Douai–Rheims Bible is the first complete English-language Catholic Bible.

1611 The 'Authorized King James' Bible is published.

one translation of the Bible: the Vulgate, compiled – in Latin – by St Jerome at the beginning of the fifth century. Yet a Bible in the vernacular tongue was the logical conclusion of Wyclif's teaching, since the common people searching for salvation through the word of scripture had little chance of finding it if they could not understand the Latin in which it was written. An English-language Bible would mean they no longer had to rely on the clergy's potentially self-serving interpretation. At last, the unmediated scripture could be read by – or read to – the laity in their own language.

How much of the translation was personally undertaken by Wyclif remains a matter of academic debate. The chronicler Henry Knighton, writing shortly after Wyclif's death, stated that he 'translated from Latin into the language not of angels but of Englishmen, so that he made that common and open to the laity, and to women who were able to read, which used to be for literate and perceptive clerks'. This, according to Knighton, was an abhorrent development, for 'the jewel of the church is turned into the common sport of the people'. In fact, sections of the Bible had been translated into English before, but never in a comprehensive or widely available format. It was Wyclif's followers who finished the task. Nicholas Hereford completed the first attempt, generating a literal translation from the Vulgate. Then, around 1395, a smoother, more idiomatic, version came from the pen of John Purvey.

In the absence of printing, which was still to be invented, the number of copies produced was limited by the speed of scribes. To overcome this, Wyclif's followers, who became known as Lollards, travelled around the country, disseminating their Bible's contents. Although an exact number cannot be ascertained, it is clear that a great many copies came into circulation, of which 170 have survived into the modern day. To the authorities of Church and state, this was a direct challenge that had to be suppressed. In 1401, Henry IV issued a statute, *De heretico comburendo* ('On the Burning of the Heretic') which Parliament passed, making clear the justice that would be meted out to owners of Wyclif's Bible. In 1408, the Synod of Oxford prohibited all

future translation of the Bible into English without official licence. In 1427, on the order of Pope Martin V, Wyclif's bones were dug up from the Lutterworth churchyard, burned and dumped in the River Swift.

In the short term, the repression was effective. Lollardy continued but only as an underground movement, although its central tenets were picked up on the continent, finding an especially receptive audience in Bohemia. Even when the most influential adherent there, John Hus, was duly burned at the stake in 1415, Wyclif's ideas could not be unthought. What was needed was a fresh crisis in the Church and a new invention – printing – that would truly put the word of scripture in the people's hands. It was in this respect that John Wyclif was 'the morning star of the Reformation'.

1440–6
HENRY VI'S CHARTERS FOR ETON COLLEGE AND KING'S COLLEGE, CAMBRIDGE

EDUCATING THE ELITE

The Charter of King's College, Cambridge is depicted in the second plate section.

Where schooling was available in the fifteenth century, it was mostly offered informally through the local parish church. There, children might gain a basic acquaintance with the alphabet as well as religious instruction. At a more structured level, there were schools attached to cathedrals, of which Canterbury, Rochester and Ely pre-dated the Norman Conquest. Collegiate churches, monasteries and hospitals also founded schools. Grammar schools, offering the grounding in Latin that was deemed useful for boys (but not girls) wanting to make the study of law or theology their future profession, or to trade in Europe, were also beginning to emerge during this period.

These various forms of schooling catered primarily for local children. Less common were 'public schools', which were endowed foundations, open to boys drawn from all over the country. For much of the medieval period, the nobility had sent their heirs neither to school nor to university, preferring to see them develop chivalric, rather than scholastic, values within aristocratic households. From the fifteenth century onwards it was to public schools that the social elite increasingly sent their sons. Consequently, public schools came to play the foremost role in moulding and shaping the experiences of most of Britain's political leaders, as well as a high proportion of those distinguishing themselves in many other fields of activity as well. Although not the oldest, it was Eton College, near Windsor Castle, that emerged as the greatest of these institutions. Indeed, it would be hard to think of any other school in the Western world with a comparable predominance in national life.

Despite being an independent school, Eton was founded by a monarch and its provost was originally a state appointment. Still a nine-month-old baby when he became king in 1422, the pious and ineffective Henry VI inherited the thrones

of both England and France. He had effectively lost the latter by the time he was old enough to rule in his own right and would lose the former in the civil wars known as the Wars of the Roses. Mentally unstable, he was deposed and imprisoned in the Tower of London where, in 1471, he was murdered. Nonetheless, two of Britain's most famous foundations owe their existence to him.

Henry VI was only eighteen when he founded Eton, to provide lodging and a schooling for the sons of the wealthy and influential; but it was also endowed to educate seventy poor boys. Despite the expanding proportion of fee-paying 'Oppidans' in the succeeding centuries, these seventy scholars or 'collegers' – selected by competitive examination – remained at the core of the school with initially free and later subsidized fees.

In his designs for Eton, Henry was especially influenced by the example of the leading public school, Winchester College, which had been founded in 1382 by William of Wykeham as a 'feeder' for his university foundation, New College, Oxford. To provide the same continuity of learning, Henry duly founded King's College, an institution at Cambridge to rival New College at Oxford. Like Eton, it too was to have a provost and seventy scholars, all of whom had to have attended Eton beforehand. Henry's vision for King's College was grandiose and in 1446 he laid the foundation stone for its chapel. It proved to be one of the wonders of late perpendicular architecture, but neither Henry nor his next four successors saw it completed. The Wars of the Roses so badly disrupted construction that it was not finished until the sixteenth century.

THE GROWTH OF UNIVERSITIES

1096 Teaching begins at Oxford.

1209 Cambridge University is founded.

1261 A university is founded at Northampton. It is shut by royal writ in 1265.

1413 St Andrews University is founded.

1451 Glasgow University is founded.

1495 King's College, Aberdeen, is established with university status. It merges with Marischal College (est. 1593) to formally become Aberdeen University in 1860.

1582 Edinburgh University is founded.

1592 Trinity College, Dublin, is founded.

1595 The Scottish Parliament donates a grant to erect a university at Fraserburgh. It is abandoned in 1605.

1822 Wales's oldest degree-awarding body, St David's College, is established at Lampeter. It becomes a constituent member of the University of Wales in 1971.

1826 University College London (UCL) is established as the first to admit students regardless of faith. It gains legal status in 1836.

1829 King's College, London, is established for Anglican students. It becomes, with UCL, the first constituent college of the University of London in 1836.

1832 Durham University is founded. It gains its royal charter in 1837.

1845 Queen's University, Belfast, receives its royal charter.

1880 Victoria University is established as a federal body in Manchester. Colleges in Liverpool and Leeds join it before subsequently breaking away.

1893 The University of Wales is established.

1900 Birmingham University is established and is soon followed by other 'red-brick' or 'civic' universities at Liverpool (1903), Leeds (1904), Sheffield (1905) and Bristol (1909).

Although it anomalously enjoyed (until 1853) its own degree-awarding powers, King's was a college of Cambridge University. England's second oldest university dated from the early thirteenth century when scholars seeking to escape the violence of Oxford townsfolk decamped there. By 1400, Oxford was still the dominant institution of higher education, with perhaps 1,200 students to Cambridge's 400. Henry VI, however, feared that Oxford was tainted with the Lollard 'heresy' of John Wyclif's teaching and his decision to endow Cambridge helped redress the balance, so that by the century's end the two universities were of roughly equal size and prestige.

Teaching was in Latin (although Greek was also taught in Oxford from the 1460s onwards) and the curriculum focused on theology, philosophy and the arts. Sixty of King's seventy scholars studied theology, four studied canon law, two studied medicine, two astronomy and two civil law. The collegiate

The chapel of King's College from an engraving by David Loggan, c.1660.

structure strengthened the sense of an inter-generational community, with undergraduates – who might be as young as fifteen in the sixteenth century – often living in the same buildings as their fellows. Yet despite the preponderance of students destined for holy orders, the colleges of Oxford and Cambridge were not comparable to monasteries. When the new humanist learning, with its reliance on classical Greek philosophers, took hold in the sixteenth century, the Dutch scholar Erasmus became one of those who studied at Queens' College, Cambridge. The wealth of both universities was massively increased as a result of Henry VIII stripping the monasteries of their assets. Henry refounded what became each institution's two grandest colleges, Christ Church at Oxford and Trinity College, Cambridge.

Throughout its first 400 years, Eton's curriculum was geared towards providing a classical education. Given that Latin was the language of the Church and the

law, this focus was not surprising in the fifteenth and sixteenth centuries. By the eighteenth century however, the justification for persevering with Greek and Latin had less to do with their vocational applicability than that they offered a sufficiently difficult test of intellectual ability. Whether the classical emphasis provided sufficient training for the Cambridge Mathematics 'tripos' was more questionable. Despite producing Kingsmen ranging from John Harington, the Elizabethan inventor of the flushing water closet, to Robert Walpole, the first prime minister, the dependence on Eton's gene pool certainly ossified King's. It finally admitted its first non-Etonians in 1865 and thereafter developed a reputation for liberal, progressive and left-wing thinking.

While retaining their social exclusivity, both Oxford and Cambridge lost some of their academic rigour in the eighteenth and early nineteenth centuries, contentedly enjoying the independence they had secured by spiralling endowment income and a virtual monopoly in producing Anglican clergymen. During this period, not only was the education offered at Edinburgh and Glasgow universities generally superior, but from 1826 competition emerged from new English foundations like University College London. However, Oxford and Cambridge restored their intellectual primacy by reforms in the mid-nineteenth century, and made their degrees available to non-Anglicans. Eton likewise reformed and broadened its curriculum, although it maintained its enduring and remarkable prominence in educating the leaders of Church and state over the succeeding 150 years. By 2010, there had been nineteen Old Etonian prime ministers, while Oxford and Cambridge had, between them, educated forty-one of Britain's fifty-five prime ministers. Other universities had educated only three.

Their predominance might have been readily understandable if Oxford and Cambridge were merely finishing schools for those seeking bureaucratic accreditation or parochial and worldly attainment, but they also enhanced their credentials as leading research institutions. As such, they attracted many of the world's finest minds, supplanting in this respect the previously dominant universities of Germany and Central Europe. By the twenty-first century, some exceptionally wealthy American universities like Harvard and Yale could claim a competitive edge, while others achieved parity. Nonetheless, it was principally Cambridge academics who achieved two of the most seismic breakthroughs of the twentieth century: splitting the atom in 1932 and unravelling the structure of DNA in 1953. One Cambridge college alone – Trinity – has produced more Nobel Prize winners than the whole of France.

1485

WILLIAM CAXTON'S PUBLICATION OF MALORY'S *MORTE D'ARTHUR*

THE SPREAD OF PRINTED BOOKS AND THE ENDURING APPEAL OF THE ARTHURIAN LEGEND

By the fifteenth century, literacy in English was spreading but it still faced two significant barriers. The first was the time-consuming production, scarcity and great cost of manuscript books. The second was the assumption that Latin should remain the language for expressing abstract or high ideas. The printing revolution, which Johann Gutenberg began at Mainz around 1454 and William Caxton brought to England, did much to remove these restraints.

Born in Kent between 1415 and 1424, Caxton was possibly the son of a merchant. Whilst he received some schooling, he was not educated with the intention of pursuing a career either in the Church or in the legal profession. Rather, he became an apprentice in the Mercers' Company in London. The Mercers dealt in haberdashery, cloth and silks, for which Britain's most important business was with the Low Countries. In order to be at the heart of this trade, Caxton moved to Bruges and there, in 1465, he became governor of the prosperous Flemish city's English community. Indeed, his evident ability was such that he found himself negotiating England's trade deals with both Flanders and the Hanseatic League.

Movable-type printing already existed in the Rhine valley and when in 1471 Caxton moved to Cologne he acquired a press. Although he did not give up his career as a textiles merchant, he realized that he was well placed to corner the market in translating fashionable texts from French into English for sale in England. Initially, he personally undertook some of the translation work, covering himself against charges that he lacked the requisite scholarly credentials by securing the unimpeachable patronage of Edward IV's sister, Margaret, duchess of Burgundy. Having completed its translation from the original French, he published the

IN SEARCH OF ARTHUR

*c.*540 Gildas in his *De Excidio Britanniae* ('On the Ruin of Britain') mentions the Battle of Mount Badon but omits any mention of Arthur.

*c.*600 The Welsh poem *Y Gododdin* refers to a heroic fighter being 'not Arthur'. The oldest surviving copy of *Y Gododdin*, however, dates from the thirteenth century.

*c.*830 The *Historia Brittonum* lists twelve battles fought by Arthur.

1125 Arthur's great deeds are lauded by William of Malmesbury in his *Gesta Regum Anglorum* ('Deeds of the Kings of England').

1136 Geoffrey of Monmouth completes his *Historia Regum Britanniae* ('History of the Kings of Britain'), which provides a full – if highly elaborated – account of Arthur's career.

1155 The Round Table is mentioned in a French version of Geoffrey's *Historia* by Robert Wace.

*c.*1160–90 The French writer, Chrétien de Troyes, introduces the Grail and the knights Lancelot, Gawain and Perceval in his cycle of Arthurian romances.

1190 A grave at Glastonbury Abbey is 'identified' as Arthur's resting place.

*c.*1198 In his *Historia Rerum Anglicarum*, William of Newburgh casts doubt on the authenticity of Geoffrey of Monmouth's claims.

*c.*1210 Robert de Boron transforms Chrétien's 'grail' into the 'Holy Grail'.

*c.*1250 (date disputed) Arthur is a character in the Welsh folk tales of the *Mabinogion*.

1278 Arthur's supposed remains are reinterred at Glastonbury in the presence of Edward I.

c. late 14th century *Morte Arthure*, a 4,346-line alliterative poem, is written in Middle English.

*c.*1370–90 The Arthurian legend is referenced in Geoffrey Chaucer's *Canterbury Tales*.

1469–70 Sir Thomas Malory writes *Morte d'Arthur*.

1485 *Morte d'Arthur* is printed by William Caxton.

1599 Edmund Spenser dies while writing *The Faerie Queene*, a poem based upon Arthurian virtues.

1691 Henry Purcell's semi-opera *King Arthur* is performed, with a libretto by John Dryden.

Recuyell of the Historyes of Troye, the world's first printed book in English, in 1474. He quickly followed it with another translation, the *Game and Playe of the Chesse*.

By 1476, Caxton had returned to England, setting up his printing press by Westminster Abbey. His first offering was a further translation, the *Dictes or Sayengis of the Philosophres*, but his emphasis soon switched from publishing translated French-language texts to the works of native authors. Of these, the first was his *editio princeps* of Geoffrey Chaucer's *Canterbury Tales*. In all, he published over one hundred works, some in Latin, but the overwhelming majority in English.

Malory's account of Arthur, Sir Bedevere and Excalibur

Therfore, sayd Arthur vnto Syr Bedwere, take thou Excalybur, my good swerde, and goo with it to yonder watersyde. And whan thou comest there I charge the throwe my swerde in that water, and come ageyn and telle me what thou seest. My lord, said Bedwere, your commaundement shal be doon and lyghtly brynge you worde ageyn. So Syr Bedwere departed, and by waye he beheld that noble swerde, that the pomel and the hafte was al of precyous stones. And thenne he sayd to hymself, yf I throwe this ryche swerde in the water, therof shal neuer come good, but harme and losse. And thenne Syr Bedwere hydde Excalybur vnder a tree. And so as sone as he myght, he came ageyn vnto the kyng and sayd he had ben at the water. What sawe thou there? sayd the kyng. Syr, he sayd, I sawe nothynge but wawes and wyndes. That is vntrewly sayd of the, sayd the kynge. Therfore goo thou lyghtelye ageyn and do my commaundemente; as thou arte to me leef and dere, spare not, but throwe it in.

Than Syr Bedwere retorned ageyn and took the swerde in hys hande, and than hym thought synne and shame to throwe awaye that nobyl swerde. And so efte he hydde the swerde and returned ageyn, and tolde the kyng that he had ben at the water and done his commaundemente. What sawe thou there? sayd the kyng. Syr, he sayd, I sawe nothynge but the waters wappe and wawes wanne. A, traytour vntrewe, sayd Kyng Arthur, now hast thou betrayed me twyse. Who wold haue went that thou, that hast been to me so leef and dere, and thou arte named a noble knyghte, and wold betraye me the richesse of the swerde? But now goo ageyn lyghtly, for thy longe taryeng putteth me in grete ieopardye of my lyf, for I haue taken colde. And but yf thou do now as I byd the, yf euer I may see the I shal slee the myn owne hands, for thou woldest for my ryche swerde see me dede,

Then Syr Bedwere departed and wente to the swerde, and lyghtly took hit vp and wente to the watersyde. And there he bounde the gyrdyl aboute the hyltes, and thenne he threwe the swerde as farre as the water as he myght. And there cam an arme and an hande about the water, and mette it and caught it, and shoke it thryse and braundysshed, and then vanysshed awaye the hande wyth the swerde in the water. So Syr Bedwere came ageyn to the kyng and tolde hym what he sawe. Alas, sayd the kyng, helpe me hens, for I drede me I haue taryed ouer longe.

The consequence of this breakthrough for English literacy and literature can hardly be overstated. Caxton, however, was no intellectual concerned with shaping academic debate, but rather an industrious businessman who recognized a gap in the market, especially for popular romantic fiction. It was not until printing presses fell into the hands of political and religious dissidents that books were to become not just a profitable industry but an effective challenge to the authority of the unreformed Church and state.

Caxton, who died in 1491 or 1492, either failed to grasp, or chose not to pioneer, this development. He did not print the works of the humanist 'new learning' let alone the arguments of identified heretics. Indeed, it was telling that perhaps his most successful publication looked not forward to the Renaissance but backwards to the myths underpinning medieval chivalry. This was the *Morte d'Arthur*.

The title resulted from a misunderstanding by Caxton. Its author, Sir Thomas Malory (c.1415–71), had actually intended it to be called *The Whole Book of King Arthur and his Noble Knights of the Round Table*. Malory had adapted a mixture of sources, such as Geoffrey of Monmouth, Layamon and Chrétien de Troyes. Many of them were French, but they also included the fourteenth-century *Morte Arthure*, an alliterative poem written in Middle English. Malory wrote in rhythmic, accessible English prose, which Caxton divided up into twenty-one books. It was not until 1934 that a manuscript was discovered in the Winchester College Library without Caxton's divisions, revealing far more clearly the eight tales of Arthurian legend upon which Malory's work was structured. It was published as a new standard edition by Eugene Vinaver in 1947.

Beyond his knighthood there was little in the recorded facts of Malory's own life that tallied with the chivalric quests of Sir Galahad. Most of *Morte d'Arthur* was written while Malory was incarcerated in the Tower of London during a period of nearly eighteen years spent in one prison or another on a variety of charges (for which he was never tried), which ranged from the attempted murder of the duke of Buckingham to cattle rustling, theft, rape, jail-breaking and robbery at his local abbey. Nevertheless, *Morte d'Arthur* was responsible for perpetuating the fame of the Arthurian legend far beyond the fifteenth century. It not only inspired the Victorian painters of the Pre-Raphaelite Brotherhood and the poet Alfred, Lord Tennyson, but helped ensure that throughout the twentieth and early twenty-first century, Arthur and the Knights of the Round Table, Guinevere, Merlin and Morgan le Fay remained familiar characters in popular culture, and Camelot and Avalon enchanting destinations for the imagination.

III

RELIGION AND
THE RENAISSANCE

1525–6
TYNDALE'S NEW TESTAMENT

THE LANGUAGE OF PROTESTANT SCRIPTURE

On the eve of the Reformation, the ban on English-language versions of the Bible was still in force. The persecution of John Wyclif's Lollard followers in the early fifteenth century stood as a warning to anyone minded to risk fresh accusations of heresy. Nevertheless, a clear opportunity to challenge authority was presented by the rising support for religious reform in Germany that followed the denunciation of Martin Luther by the imperial Diet of Worms in 1521, and the success of printing presses in disseminating dissident opinion. None were more active in mounting this challenge than those inspired and emboldened by Martin Luther's stand against papal supremacy.

The man who decided to take the risk of producing a new, and widely available, translation of the Bible was William Tyndale. Born around 1494 in Gloucestershire, he had studied at Oxford University and was ordained into the priesthood. Significantly for his later work as a translator, he also learned Greek, possibly either under Erasmus at Cambridge or by reading Erasmus's New Testament translation in Latin with the Greek original alongside. Given the politics of the time, Tyndale failed in his attempt to get his English-language translation printed legally in England, so he left London bound for Hamburg. While there, he may also have spent time in Wittenberg, possibly meeting Luther who had published a German-language version of the New Testament in 1522. Tyndale's New Testament in English was finished in 1525, but an injunction disrupted its publication in Cologne. Tyndale duly moved to Worms, a centre of Lutheran activity, where the completed work was published by Peter Schoeffer.

The next stage was getting it to England and Scotland, a feat achieved by smuggling the books concealed in bales of cloth. Henry VIII's lord chancellor, Cardinal Wolsey, led the campaign to seize and destroy the several thousand copies that reached England, in which he was largely successful. Of Schoeffer's first print run, only one complete copy is still in existence and it was discovered in Stuttgart

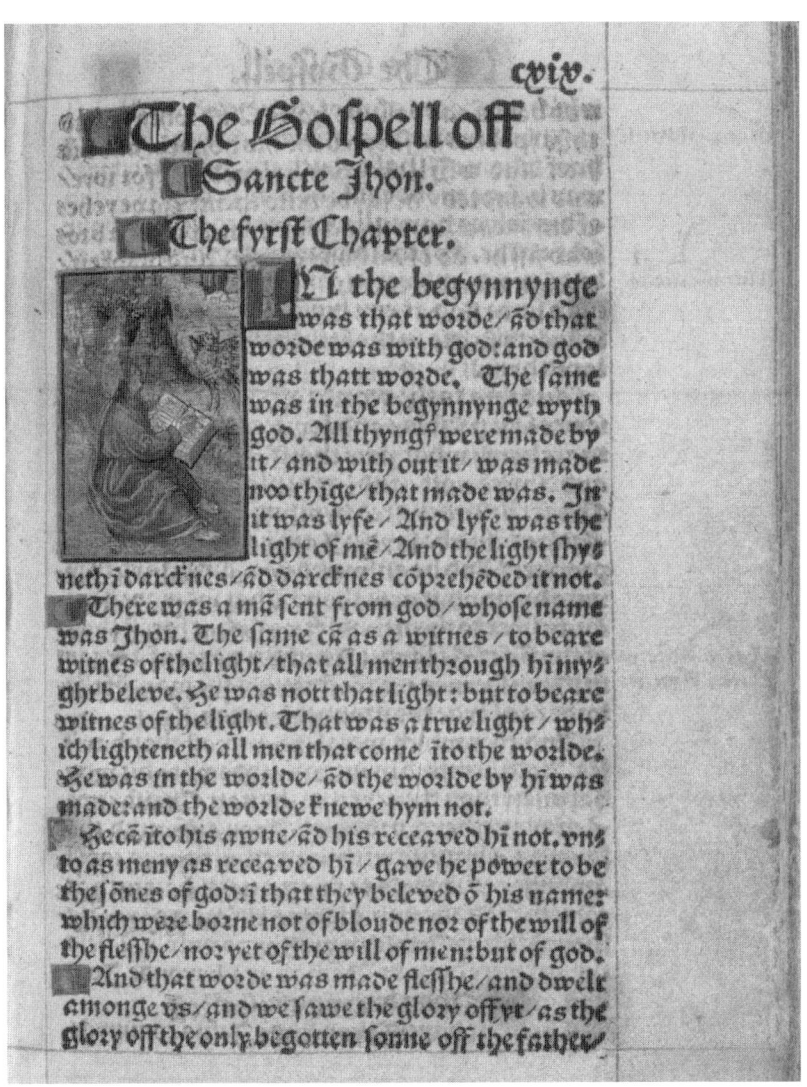

¶ The Gospell off Sancte Jhon.

¶ The fyrst Chapter.

In the begynnynge was that worde/ so that worde was with god: and god was thatt worde. The same was in the begynnynge wyth god. All thyngs were made by it/ and with out it/ was made noo thige/ that made was. In it was lyfe/ And lyfe was the light of me/ And the light shyneth i darcknes/ so darcknes coprehedeo it not.

There was a ma sent from god/ whose name was Jhon. The same cã as a witnes/ to beare witnes of the light/ that all men through hi myght beleve. He was nott that light: but to beare witnes of the light. That was a true light / whi ich lighteneth all men that come ito the worlde. He was in the worlde/ so the worlde by hi was made: and the worlde knewe hym not.

He cã ito his awne/ so his receaveo hi not. vnto as meny as receaveo hi / gave he power to be the sones of god: i that they beleved o his name: which were borne not of blonde nor of the will of the flesshe/ nor yet of the will of men: but of god.

And that worde was made flesshe/ and dwelt amonge vs/ and we sawe the glory off yt/ as the glory off the only begotten sonne off the father/

Opening page of St John's Gospel from the first edition of Tyndale's New Testament.

as recently as 1996. Two other largely complete copies also remain: one, in the British Library, is denuded solely of its title page, while the copy in the library of St Paul's Cathedral is less comprehensive, missing seventy leaves.

Tyndale's New Testament differed significantly from the Wyclif Bible of the Lollards. Whereas the latter had been translated from the Latin Vulgate, Tyndale achieved greater authenticity by translating from the original Greek. Being printed, rather than handwritten, it could be produced and circulated in far larger numbers. Rough copies were soon being churned out by an enterprising printer in Antwerp. This emphasis on popularizing the word of scripture and placing it at the heart of belief was central to Protestant theology, as well as making a distinct departure

from the Church of Rome's approach. 'I defy the Pope and all his laws,' Tyndale proclaimed, 'and if God spare my life, I will cause the boy that drives the plough in England to know more of the Scriptures than the Pope himself.'

Hunted by the agents of both Henry VIII and the Holy Roman Empire, Tyndale had to live and work in Worms and Antwerp undercover. Despite these conditions, his output remained formidable, turning out a succession of Protestant theological tracts while also antagonizing his powerful enemies further by condemning Henry VIII's divorce from Catherine of Aragon. Nonetheless, his main task remained translating the rest of the Bible. He was hard at work on this, translating from the Hebrew Old Testament and had reached the end of Chronicles, when an Englishman named Henry Philips inveigled him out of his Antwerp safe house and betrayed him for money. Dragged off to Vilvoorde Castle outside Brussels, Tyndale was imprisoned for sixteen months, put on trial and found guilty of heresy, for which the punishment was death. A chain was fastened around his neck with which he was first strangled before being burned at the stake on 6 October 1536. His last words were recorded as, 'Lord, open the king of England's eyes.'

Although Henry VIII never adopted Lutheran beliefs, in one sense he was persuaded to permit Tyndale a posthumous victory. Only months after the translator's death, the king licensed the first official Bible in English. Also drawing on the 1535 translation of the Lutheran Miles Coverdale, it was in reality two-thirds the work of the 'heretic' Tyndale. Such was both its literary and scholarly quality that Tyndale's version shaped all subsequent translations. In particular, the committee that produced the King James Bible – the Authorized Version – in 1611 retained much of Tyndale's language.

It would have been foolish to attempt anything else. Tyndale's style was poetic, yet simple, giving preference to words that were Anglo-Saxon rather than French or Latin in derivation, which undoubtedly made his work more accessible to those with minimal education – the ploughboys of whom he spoke. He produced phrases that remain familiar to us almost half a millennium later: 'fight the good fight,' 'the spirit is willing,' 'take up thy bed and walk,' 'no man can serve two masters,' 'the powers that be'. It was a style that influenced the writers of the sixteenth century, being especially influential in the work of William Shakespeare. Indeed, Tyndale's place in the history of English literature lies not only beside his fellow theologians but alongside that of the Bard. Centuries after he met his violent fate, Tyndale is still shaping not just the way the English-speaking world praises God, but also the way that it expresses itself in day-to-day conversation.

1530

PARLIAMENT'S PETITION TO THE POPE TO ANNUL HENRY VIII'S MARRIAGE

THE ENGLISH CHURCH SPLITS FROM ROME

On 11 June 1509, the new king, Henry VIII, married his late brother's widow, the Spanish princess Catherine of Aragon. In the course of the following twenty-four years, she became pregnant six times but only a daughter, Mary, survived infancy. With his wife soon to reach her fortieth year, Henry gave up hope that she would provide him with the male heir upon which he believed the security of the Tudor dynasty depended. After all, the family had come to power only as the consequence of the thirty years of dynastic struggle known as the Wars of the Roses, and the sole precedent for an English queen attempting to rule in her own right was hardly encouraging: the Empress Matilda's failed effort in 1141.

Unfortunately for Catherine of Aragon, by 1526 Henry had fallen for one of his wife's ladies-in-waiting. Much younger than Catherine, Anne Boleyn seemed far more likely to bear him a son, but to marry her Henry needed first to receive from the pope an annulment of his first marriage. This became known, euphemistically, as the 'King's Great Matter'. Pondering his failure to produce an heir, Henry had alighted on a text in Leviticus, warning that a sexual relationship with a brother's wife would be cursed with childlessness. The case rested on the suggestion that the original papal dispensation, authorizing Henry to marry his brother's widow, should not have given because it had been based upon the belief that Catherine's first marriage had not been consummated. It was a presumption suddenly convenient to dispute. However, Pope Clement VII procrastinated, refusing to meekly do the English king's bidding. His decision was not based on doctrine alone: Rome had been sacked and Clement was the virtual prisoner

From parliament's petition to the pope, 1530

To the most holy father and Lord in Christ, Lord Clement, by divine providence seventh pope of that name, we kiss your feet in all humility and pray for your happiness which we desire to be eternal, in our Lord Jesus Christ.

Most blessed father, in the case of the marriage of our unconquered and most serene prince, our Lord, defender of the faith of England and France and Lord of Scotland, many relevant arguments on the matter have been used to entreat and petition your Holiness for help, so that a conclusion can be reached as quickly as possible – a conclusion which we have long desired with all our hearts and, so far, have awaited from your Holiness in anticipation, but without result. Consequently, because this dispute has been so long protracted that it is now critical, our kingdom finds itself in a situation where we cannot be altogether silent. Our Royal Majesty, our head and to that extent the soul of us all, and we in his words – like limbs in harmony with the head, a soundly unified body – have prayed with much anxiety to your Holiness. We have, however, prayed in vain. So we are now impelled by the weight of our grief, separately and individually, to write and make this demand.

of the Holy Roman Emperor, Charles V, who was also Catherine's nephew.

Never one to be kept waiting, Henry tried to speed up the process with a succession of diplomatic overtures to Clement. On 13 July 1530, the most elaborate of these took the form of a parliamentary petition to which the archbishops of Canterbury and York attached their seals, together with those of four bishops and the leading peers of the realm. Presumptively taking the likelihood of an annulment for granted, it urged the pope to hurry up with granting it.

His Holiness was not to be so easily swayed, with the momentous consequence that it was Henry who divorced England from Rome. Thomas Cranmer, once installed as the new archbishop of Canterbury, dutifully set to his task. In May 1533 he pronounced that Henry's marriage to Catherine was annulled and that the private marriage ceremony the king had contracted with Anne was legal. If Anne were to give birth, any child of hers would therefore be legitimate. In the same year, Parliament bowed to Henry's will and asserted Rome's jurisdiction over England to be illegal. The 1534 Act of Supremacy declared Henry to be 'the only supreme head of the Church'.

The king's personal problems led to the creation of a state Church, independent of Rome, but they did not make the country Protestant. Indeed, for the laity, the change made only superficial differences to their daily worship. The Church of England remained essentially Catholic. The 1539 Act of Six Articles not only demonstrated that Henry was still opposed to Protestant 'heresies' but reaffirmed Catholic doctrine on clerical celibacy and transubstantiation (the presence of Christ's body and blood in the bread and wine of the sacrament). The traditional liturgy was kept in place as was the power of Church courts. That the bishops were appointed by the Crown was only a formal acknowledgement that it was the monarch who had, in reality, mostly been nominating them in previous centuries.

This painting, attributed to Joos van Cleve, shows Henry VIII in c.1535 while he was married to Anne Boleyn. His scroll quotes the gospel of Mark 16:15, 'Go ye into all the world, and preach the Gospel to every creature.'

Yet while life in the parish and the cathedral continued with merely minor modifications, monastic houses fared very differently. In the wake of revelations of corruption and scandal, the minor monasteries were dissolved in 1536. This was followed in 1539 by legislation to dissolve the major monasteries. By 1540, the Crown had taken over 800 monastic houses. The primary rationale was financial. The state needed money, in particular to engage in war with France. Indeed, by 1547, two-thirds of the revenue raised from monastic dissolution had been wasted on this martial enterprise. From 1545 the wealth of the private or institutional chapels known as chantries was also appropriated by the state. This represented not just an extraordinary transferral of resources, but a frontal assault on the traditional spiritual institutions of the nation.

Alas, the woman for whom Henry deemed it worth breaking with Rome soon disappointed him. After several attempts, she produced a mere daughter, Elizabeth. Henry had Anne beheaded in 1536 on (spurious) charges of adultery, incest and treason, and proceeded to marry the third of his six wives, Jane Seymour. She died giving birth to the male heir for whom he had been prepared to go to such lengths. As Edward VI, he was to succeed his father in 1547, transforming the state religion during his brief reign to the Protestant faith. The greater irony, however, was that for all his desire for a son, it was Henry's daughter, Elizabeth, who ultimately proved the most capable and celebrated ruler of the age.

1536

THE ANGLO-WELSH
ACT OF UNION

WALES ENTERS INTO FORMAL UNION WITH ENGLAND

The victory of Henry Tudor over Richard III at the Battle of Bosworth Field in 1485 had ended the thirty-year-long Wars of the Roses and put on the English throne a family whose blood was part Welsh.

What this meant for Wales was initially unclear. Indeed, during the preceding 200 years, the constitutional relationship between Wales and England had been complicated. Conquered by Edward I, the principality of Wales in the west and north-west was carved into English-style shires. By contrast, the extension of the English Crown's authority in eastern and southern Wales was far more evolutionary. These lands were the semi-autonomous domains of earls of Anglo-Norman descent, the 'Marcher' lords.

During the reign of Henry VII (as Henry Tudor became), Wales enjoyed a form of dominion status within the English realm and was administered by a prerogative council, meeting mostly in Ludlow in Shropshire. At first, this system continued after the accession of Henry VIII, but it was not to endure. Two Acts of Parliament, in 1536 and 1543, which later became known as the Acts of Union, were passed with the explicit intention of ensuring that Wales was 'incorporated, united and annexed' by England.

Of the two acts, that of 1536 was the more important. The Marcher territories were divided into shires and administered on the same county-government model as in England. This created the shires of Denbigh, Montgomery, Radnor, Brecon, Pembroke, Glamorgan and Monmouth. Together with the shires created in the north and west by Edward I, they would be represented in Parliament by twenty-seven MPs.

The legislation struck at the heart of the old Marcher legal autonomy, by establishing that the English common law had supremacy and was to be applied

c.715 – THE LINDISFARNE GOSPELS

The opening page, known as the incipit page, of the Gospel of St Matthew. Stylistically, the decorative details share many common characteristics with Anglo-Saxon jewellery design.

LATE 11TH CENTURY – THE BAYEUX TAPESTRY

'Here King Harold was killed', states the Bayeux Tapestry. Harold is popularly assumed to be both the warrior with the arrow in his eye and the figure being felled by the Norman cavalryman.

1215 – MAGNA CARTA

Only four of the first copies issued of Magna Carta survive. This is the best-preserved of the two versions held at the British Library.

c.1250 – THE CHRONICLES OF MATTHEW PARIS

Matthew Paris's mid-thirteenth-century map of Britain is the oldest surviving example of a map that attempts – however imperfectly – to portray geographical accuracy rather than merely to present a schematic representation of the island. Over 250 places are marked as well as long-defunct features like the Hadrian and Antonine Walls.

1320 – THE DECLARATION OF ARBROATH

Eight Scottish earls and thirty-eight barons attached their seals to the Latin plea to Pope John XXII to recognize Scotland as an independent nation.

From the Act of Union, 1536

Albeit the Domynyon Principalitie and Countrey of Wales justly and rightuouslye is and ever hath ben incorporated annexed united and subjecte to & under the Imperiall Crowne of this Realme, as a verrye membre and joynte of the same, Wherfore the Kinges moost Roiall Magestie of mere droite and verye right is verie hedde King Lorde and Ruler, yet notwithstanding by cause that in the same Countrey Principalitie and Dominion dyvers rightes usagis lawes and customes be farre discrepant frome the Lawes and Customes of this Realme, And also by cause that the people of the same Dominion have and do daily use a speche nothing like ne consonaunt to the naturall mother tonge used within this Realme, somme rude and ignorant people have made distinccion and diversitie betwene the Kinges Subjectes of this Realme and hys Subjectes of the said Dominion and Principalitie of Wales, wherby greate discorde variaunce debate dyvysion murmur and sedicion hath growen betwene his said subjectes; His Highnes therfor of a singuler zele love and favour that he beareth towardes his Subjectes of his said Dominion of Wales, mynding and entending to reduce them to the perfecte order notice & knowlege of his lawes of this his Realme, and utterly to extirpe all and singuler the senister usages and customes differinge frome the same, and to bringe his said Subjectes of this his Realme and of his said Dominion of Wales to an amicable concorde and unitie, Hath by the deliberate advise consent and agreament of the Lordes spirituall and temporall and the Commons in this present assembled and by the auctoritie of the same, ordeyned enacted and establisshed that his said Countrey or Dominion of Wales shalbe stonde and contynue for ever incorporated united and annexed to and with this his Realme of Englande; And that all and singuler personne and personnes borne and to be borne in the said Principalitie Countrey or Dominion of Wales, shall have enjoye and inherite all and singuler fredomes liberties rightes privileges and lawes within this Realme and other the Kynges Dominions as other the Kinges Subjectes naturally borne within the same, have enjoye and enherite: And that all and singular personne and personnes inheritable to any Manours Landes Tenements Rentes Revercions services or other Hereditaments, which shall discende within the set Principalitie, Countrey or Dominion of Wales, or within any particuler Lordshippe parte or parcell of the said Countrey or Dominion of Wales, shall forever inherite and be inheritable to the same Manours Landes Tenementes Rentes Revercions and Hereditamentes after the Englisshe tenure, without division or particion, and after the forme of the Lawes of this Realme of Englande, and not after any tenure ne after the fourme of any Welshe Lawes

or Customes; And that the Lawes Ordynaunces and Statutes of this Realme of Englande for ever, and none other Lawes Ordenaunces ne Statutes, shalbe had used practised & executed in the said Countrey or Dominion of Wales and every parte therof, in like manner and forme and order as they ben and shalbe had used practised and executed in this Realme, and in such like manner and forme as hereafter by this acte shalbe further establisshed and ordeyned; any acte statute usage custome president libertie privilege or other thing, had made used graunted or suffred to the contrary, in any wise notwithstanding.

throughout Wales. However, distinctive chancery and exchequer courts were established, while four Courts of Great Sessions, equipped with their own circuit and permanent judges, presided over twelve of the Welsh shires. Monmouth's exclusion from this arrangement (it was attached to the Oxford circuit) left ambiguous its status as to whether it was in England or Wales. Across Wales, law enforcement was to be overseen by justices of the peace, chosen by the local gentry.

The growth of this powerful squirearchy class was stimulated by the abolition of Welsh inheritance law, which was replaced by England's tradition of primogeniture, solidifying landownership as the prerogative of eldest sons. The social gulf between them and other freeholders widened in a society that still had a very small merchant class. Besides wealth, the most obvious demonstration of this gulf was language. The fact that the 1536 act established English as the language of official business did much to separate the increasingly English-speaking squirearchy from the rest of the native-speaking community.

However, although the Welsh language ceased to be used in legal and administrative matters, it was not actively suppressed. Indeed, a statute of 1563 ordered the Bible and the Book of Common Prayer to be translated into Welsh, which did much to preserve and develop the language. Nor was the imposition of Anglicanism initially met with the same level of resentment as in Ireland. Whereas the overwhelming majority of Irish remained implacably Catholic, in Wales by contrast, Protestantism successfully took root across most of the country. In this respect, Welsh society was not divided by the sort of penal laws that reduced Ireland's majority religionists to second-class status under the law. Only in the nineteenth century, with the Nonconformist revival, did the division between church and chapel become one of the most contentious issues in Welsh life, forcing, belatedly, the disestablishment of the Anglican Church there in 1920.

1546

THE ANTHONY ROLL

THE INVENTORY AND DEPICTION OF
KING HENRY VIII'S ROYAL NAVY

The Royal Navy made possible Britain's emergence as the world's fore-most commercial and imperial power, yet until the beginning of the sixteenth century neither the English nor the Scottish governments owned particularly impressive navies. This began to change with the investment made by Henry VIII in building a great fleet. No document better illustrates the results of that decision than the Anthony Roll.

It is a visual depiction of the fifty-eight ships in Henry VIII's navy, accompanied by an inventory of each vessel's munitions. The roll takes its name from its compiler, Anthony Anthony, an official of the ordnance, who presented his work to the king in 1546. The fleet is depicted on three vellum rolls, each about five and a half yards long. Both the descriptions and the artwork appear to be in Anthony's hand. The result doubtless pleased Henry, who generally delighted in viewing manifestations of his own power. After the king's death, Anthony stayed at his post, serving successively Edward VI, Mary I and Elizabeth. His Dutch father had come to England to supply beer to Henry's army and, when not attending to his formal duties, Anthony found time to part-own the appropriately named Ship brewhouse by the docks of East Smithfield just beyond the Tower of London. He died in 1563.

Although the birth of the Royal Navy is traditionally ascribed to Alfred the Great, and ships sailed in successive monarchs' service in the centuries thereafter, Henry VIII is usually considered the founder of the modern navy. Not only did he order mighty warships to be constructed, he also created a naval administrative bureaucracy as well as the capacity needed to maintain and develop the 'senior service' thereafter.

It is thanks to the Anthony Roll that a contemporary depiction of what Henry's fleet looked like has survived. It starts with the grandest of them all, the *Henry*

The Mary Rose from the Anthony Roll is depicted in the second plate section.

85

THE GROWTH AND DECLINE OF THE ROYAL NAVY

1547 At his death, Henry VIII's navy comprises fifty-eight vessels.

1707 The 227 ships of the Royal Navy are supplemented by the three ships of the Royal Scots Navy when the two fleets are merged.

1793 At the outset of renewed war with France, the Royal Navy comprises about 500 ships.

1805 In the year of Nelson's great victory at Trafalgar, the Royal Navy has grown to about 950 ships.

1840 The first screw-propeller-powered steamship, HMS *Rattler*, is launched.

1849 The first steam-powered battleship, HMS *Agamemnon*, is ordered.

1860 The launch of HMS *Warrior*, the first all iron-hulled and armoured warship, heralds the coming of the 'ironclads' and the decline of wooden ships.

1901 The first Royal Navy submarine, HMS *Holland 1*, is launched.

1905 With ten big guns and a speed of 21 knots, HMS *Dreadnought* is both the world's best-armed and fastest battleship. She makes previous designs effectively obsolete.

1914 The Royal Navy enters the First World War as by far the globe's most powerful fleet, led by 18 dreadnoughts, 29 non-dreadnought battleships, 20 town-class cruisers, 15 scout cruisers, 200 destroyers and 150 cruisers. Almost 35,000 sailors are killed during the conflict.

1918 The first aircraft carrier, HMS *Argus*, comes into commission.

1922 The age of Royal Navy global dominance ends with the Washington Treaty, which establishes equality between the Royal Navy and the US Fleet in battleships, battlecruisers and aircraft carriers.

1939 The Royal Navy enters the Second World War with 15 battleships and battlecruisers, 7 aircraft carriers, 66 cruisers, 184 destroyers, 60 submarines and 45 escort and patrol vessels.

1945 By the end of the Second World War, there are 885 ships in Royal Naval service. During the war 278 ships have been sunk and over 50,000 sailors killed.

1960 There are 202 ships in the fleet.

1963 Britain's first nuclear-powered submarine, HMS *Dreadnought*, comes into commission.

1980 There are 162 ships in the fleet.

1982 Falklands War. Six ships are sunk and ten more damaged.

2000 There are 98 ships in the fleet.

2010 There are 88 ships in the fleet.

Grace à Dieu. Launched in 1514 and alternatively known as the *Great Harry*, she was 165 feet (50 metres) long and carried 43 cannons besides 141 smaller guns. Manned by up to 1,000 crew, she was, of her type, without comparison anywhere in Europe. Her end, nonetheless, was unheroic. During Mary's reign she burned out while in dry dock, due, it was stated to 'neckclygens and lake of over-syth'.

The fact that Henry's fleet included fourteen oar-powered galleasses (larger and taller than regular galleys) and row-barges is among the Roll's many surprises. Such craft were customary in the Baltic and the Mediterranean but had long since ceased to be native to the seas around the British Isles. Yet it is Antony's illustration of the *Mary Rose* – the only surviving contemporary depiction – that attracts the most attention. He may well have painted her just as she was about to go down. The finished rolls were presented to Henry some months after he had watched, horrified, from the shore, as his beloved warship keeled over and sank while about to engage the French fleet on 19 July 1545. Initially it was hoped she might be raised from the Solent, which may still have been the case when Henry took possession of the roll. In reality, efforts to salvage her proved fruitless. It took until 1982 for the remains of her hull and starboard side to be lifted from the Solent's protecting silt and put on display in Portsmouth, the haven she was trying to defend. The archaeological evidence suggests that Anthony's depiction was inaccurate in the siting of the gunports and contained some artistic licence, but was certainly based on her actual design rather than merely being symbolic.

In 1680, Charles II made a present of the first and third of the Anthony Rolls to Samuel Pepys, who had been temporarily forced to resign his secretaryship of the Admiralty. Cut up and pasted into two volumes, they are now in the safe keeping of the great diarist's alma mater, Magdalene College, Cambridge. The second roll remained intact and is in the British Library. It had particularly fascinated the future 'Sailor King', William IV (1765–1837), who used to bore guests by indulging in lengthy readings from its ships' inventories. He gifted it to his illegitimate daughter Mary, who married Charles Fox, a successor of Anthony as surveyor of the ordnance.

1549

THE BOOK OF COMMON PRAYER

THE LITURGY OF THE CHURCH OF ENGLAND

T he Book of Common Prayer established the liturgy of the Church of England, replacing the traditional Catholic service, which had been conducted in Latin, with a simpler, uniform service said in English. Over the succeeding centuries, its evocative language accompanied generations of men and women through the most important and poignant ceremonies of their lives, from baptism, through marriage and on, ultimately, to the grave.

Opposite: Title page of the first edition of the Book of Common Prayer. Without the Book of Common Prayer there would be no 'dearly beloved'; a bride and groom would not be joined together 'in holy Matrimony which is an honourable estate' and one that 'is not by any to be enterprised, nor taken in hand, unadvisedly, lightly, or wantonly'. At the graveside, there would be no 'In the midst of life we are in death' nor 'Earth to earth, ashes to ashes, dust to dust'.

Before the break with Rome, parishes had used the Latin rite, which was universally applied across Europe, albeit in a language that only the well-educated could understand. Nor was Latin the only bar to comprehension. The rite was assembled in a confused manner and was contained not in a single book but spread across several. Throughout Britain, there was no agreement over which of the different formats to favour, although the 'uses' of Sarum (Salisbury) had become the most popular.

Such variation ended abruptly in 1549 when the Act of Uniformity imposed the Book of Common Prayer as the sole liturgy to be used in every parish of the Established Church in England, Wales and Ireland. It is of significant constitutional importance that Parliament took it upon itself to legislate in this manner. From the break with Rome until that moment, approving the doctrine and liturgy of the Church of England had been a royal prerogative. Thereafter, it was a parliamentary one.

THE

booke of the common
prayer and admi-
nistration of
the
Sacramentes, and other
rites and ceremonies of
the Churche: after the
vse of the Churche
of England.

LONDINI IN OFFICINA
Edouardi Whitchurche.

Cum priuilegio ad imprimendum solum.

ANNO. DO. 1549. Mense
Iunii.

The principal author of the Book of Common Prayer was Thomas Cranmer (1489–1556), the first Protestant – and married man – to be archbishop of Canterbury. A Cambridge don who was attracted to Martin Luther's ideas, Cranmer appeared destined for a career of minor scholarship in the Fens until Henry VIII got to hear of his supportive suggestions for effecting divorce from Catherine of Aragon. Suddenly, Cranmer found himself conducting diplomatic business and, in 1533, was appointed to the see of Canterbury. Yet Henry was no Protestant, nor was he greatly excited by the prospect of his Church's liturgy being performed in the vernacular tongue. As a result, Cranmer had proceeded no further than an English-language processional litany when Henry died.

Thereafter, Cranmer got his chance. Surrounding the boy-king Edward VI were Protestant-leaning politicians who were determined to drive forward a liturgy in English. It was essentially a happy accident that Cranmer, to whom the task was entrusted, happened to possess an outstanding literary sensibility for the resonance of words. Eschewing contemporary humanist learning's sometimes mannered predilection for Greek and Latin vocabulary, Cranmer – like Tyndale – preferred words of English derivation. Indeed, he consciously used a slightly old-fashioned idiom and, in doing so, helped preserve this linguistic style for future generations. Besides Tyndale and Shakespeare, Cranmer must be rated among the most important shapers of the rhythm of English expression.

The first version of the Book of Common Prayer was introduced in 1547. The Church of England's task, as the state Church, was to hold a compromise position to which those of the old Catholic and new reformed faiths could equally adhere. Two areas of particular debate concerned transubstantiation and purgatory. Reformers disputed Rome's insistence that the sacramental wafer and wine truly became Christ's body and blood, nor could they find any scriptural justification for purgatory. They adjudged the latter to be a convenient invention, designed to maximize devotions and donations to the Church in return for speeding the path of the dead from purgatory to heaven. In both these matters, the wording of the 1547 version left sufficient scope to appease those who clung to Catholic interpretations.

Whatever their intention, such concessions failed to cool the anger of traditionalists outraged by Cranmer's liturgical innovations. An anti-Prayer Book rebellion broke out in the South-West. Exeter was subjected to a thirty-five-day siege and several thousand people died before order was restored. There were also revolts in Oxfordshire, Buckinghamshire and – heightened by social and economic distress – in East Anglia. With the dissent suppressed, by 1552 the reformers felt

sufficiently secure to bring out a revised version of the Prayer Book. This edition, also mostly by Cranmer, was far more overtly Protestant in tone. Even mention of the word 'Mass' had been replaced by 'Holy Communion' (the 1547 version had produced the wordy catch-all, 'Supper of the Lord and the Holy Communion, commonly called the Mass'). Indeed, one of Cranmer's great innovations was to make the laity's access to communion a regular feature of their worship. Previously they might have been called to take it as little as once a year.

Within months of this new version's introduction, Edward VI died of pneumonia and was followed on the throne by his devoutly Catholic half-sister, Mary. She immediately restored the Church to Rome, abolished the Book of Common Prayer and reintroduced the Latin rite. Accused of treason and heresy, Cranmer was burned at the stake.

The turning back of the theological tide lasted only as long as Mary survived. In 1558, the Protestant Elizabeth I succeeded her and the following year a new Act of Uniformity brought back a slightly modified version of the 1552 Book of Common Prayer. This remained in use after the royal house of Tudor gave way to the Stuarts. Indeed, it was Charles I's overzealous attempts to force the Prayer Book upon his Presbyterian-minded Scottish subjects in 1637 that prompted the signing of the Covenant, the defeat of the king's forces and a succession of events that resulted in the English Civil War. Gaining the upper hand in that conflict, English Puritans and their Scottish Presbyterian allies secured the Prayer Book's abolition in 1645.

Their victory, too, was short-lived. Along with the monarchy, it was duly reinstated in an updated version (still substantially in Cranmer's language) authorized in 1662. Despite the nineteenth-century battles between High and Low Church Anglicans over the use of ritual, this 1662 version continued to dictate the Established Church's liturgy into the twentieth century. An effort to produce a new version was voted down in the House of Commons in 1928 and during the century its uniform application varied across Anglican parishes. Finally, in 1980, a new version was approved. This, the not very self-confidently entitled *Alternative Service Book*, aimed at being more accessible for modern tastes. To those who preferred a less prosaic turn of phrase, it succeeded only in highlighting the sonorous superiority and commanding authority of Cranmer's original.

1555

THE ROYAL CHARTER OF THE MUSCOVY COMPANY

THE FIRST JOINT-STOCK COMPANY, FUNDING EXPLORATION AND THE EXPANSION OF TRADE

In 1555, a money-making venture was incorporated by royal charter with the title, 'The Merchants Adventurers of England for the discovery of Lands, Territories, Isles, Dominions and Seigniories Unknown'. It heralded a financial revolution. As the country's first major joint-stock company, it pointed the way to the stock market capitalism that shaped Britain's economic development in the nineteenth and twentieth centuries.

Its birth demonstrated that necessity can be the parent of invention. The textiles industries of the Low Countries had long been the most lucrative focus for English merchants. In the sixteenth century this trade faltered, forcing a search for alternative markets. The news that Portuguese ships were returning from the East Indies laden with highly valuable spices spurred a scramble for eastern riches. Unfortunately, without friendly ports along the route, English ships could scarcely hope to compete against Portugal's strategic advantages. So, in 1553, 240 London merchants pooled their investments to send an expedition with an extraordinarily daring goal: to reach China – then known as Cathay – by discovering a northern passage around the Arctic coasts of Scandinavia and Russia.

It was a trip into the unknown that failed utterly in its stated objectives. Two of the three ships were lost when their crews froze to death. However, one ship, the *Edward Bonaventure*, captained by Richard Chancellor, made it to the mouth of the Dvina and dropped anchor at Archangel. From there, Chancellor was invited to Moscow and was presented to the royal court. He made a favourable impression on Tsar Ivan the Terrible, who promised to open his northern domains to English traders.

Thus a scheme that intended to tap the wealth of the Far East was diverted into doing business with Russia. The royal charter of 1555 entitled the 'Merchant

From the royal charter of the Muscovy Company, 1555

That they by the Name of Merchants Adventurers of England for the discovery of Lands Territories Isles Dominions and Seigniories unknown and not before their late Adventure or Enterprise by Seas or Navigation commonly frequented as aforesaid shall be from henceforth one body and perpetual Fellowship and commonality of themselves both in Deed and in Name and them by the Names of Merchants Adventurers for the discovery of Lands Territories Isles and Seigniories unknown and not by the Seas and Navigations before their said late Adventure or Enterprise by Seas & Navigation commonly frequented. We do encorporate Name and Declare by these presents, And that the same Fellowship and commonalty from henceforth shall be and may have one Governour of the said Fellowship and Commonalty of Merchants Adventurers. And in consideration that the before named Sebastian Cabotto hath been the chiefest Setter forth of this Journey or Voyage therefore we make ordain and constitute him the said Sebastian to be the first and present Governour of the same Fellowship & Commonalty by these presents . . . Know ye therefore that We of our further Royal favour and munificence of our mere motion certain knowledge and especial Grace for as our Heirs and Successors have given and granted and by these presents do Give and Grant unto the same Governour Counsels Assistants Fellowship and Commonalty above named and to their Successors as much as in us is that all the Maynelands Isles Ports Havens Creeks and Rivers of the said Mighty Emperour of all Russia and Great Duke of Musky & c. And all singular other Lands Dominions Territories Isles Ports Havens Creeks Rivers arms of the Sea of all and every other Emperour King Prince Rulers or Governour whatsoever he or they be before the said late Adventure or Enterprise not knowen or by our foresaid Merchants and Subjects by the Seas not commonly frequented nor any part or parcel thereof and lying Northwards North Eastwards or North westwards as is aforesaid by Sea shall not be visited frequented nor haunted by any our Subjects other than of the said Company and Fellowship and their Successors without express License agreement and Consent of the Governour Consulls and assistants of the said Fellowship and Commonalty first above named.

Adventurers' to a trading monopoly with Russia and, as a result, they became commonly known as the Muscovy Company (and later, the Russia Company). The tsar also accorded the company privileges and it was soon exporting English cloth

to Russia, while importing Russian furs, timber (for taller sailing masts), hemp, tar, wax and tallow to England.

In the sixteenth and seventeenth centuries, before the benefits of a competitive free market became accepted doctrine, state monopolies were granted to some expensive commercial enterprises as a means of protecting their initial investment. The monopoly that the English Crown gave to the Muscovy Company for Russian trade lasted until 1587 and was similar in intent to the monopolies granted to the Levant Company in 1581 to trade with the eastern Mediterranean (exporting cloth and bringing back raw silk and Turkish carpets), and to the Hudson Bay Company, which, in 1670, received a monopoly to trade in Canadian furs. The most significant monopoly was granted in 1600, to the East India Company.

The East India Company became the leading example of a joint-stock company, but it was the Muscovy Company that first demonstrated the effectiveness of this form of capitalist organization, effectively starting the tradition of share dealing in the City of London. Previously, investors were sought to sponsor individual ventures, like trade expeditions, receiving their cut of any profit upon the venture's completion. In this way, expeditions were financed one at a time. In contrast, those investing in a joint-stock company were buying share certificates, not in a one-off enterprise, but in an ongoing business concern that might use the money for any number of ventures, paying its shareholders a dividend from annual profits. This was the principle behind what became public limited companies with shares tradable on the stock exchange.

Share issues spread the risk, attracting the large sums of capital necessary for hazardous searches for new markets and subsequent business diversification. The Muscovy Company's investors included some of England's foremost names, including many of the leading politicians, as well as the financier and founder of the Royal Exchange, Thomas Gresham. The most striking name, however, is that of the investor who was appointed the company's governor – Sebastian Cabot.

It was Cabot's father, the Genoa-born John Cabot, who, in sailing out from Bristol in 1497 to the rich fishing shoals off Newfoundland, is often credited with starting England's interest in discovering new worlds. Yet it took more than half a century before the Muscovy Company, with his son at the helm, had the financial backing to mount a sustained campaign of exploration. Between the 1560s and the 1580s, the company sent its agents overland across Russia to meet the shah of Persia, who opened up his realm for the first time to direct trade with England. The company also renewed efforts to sail to China via the icy Siberian waters, battling

the ice and fog to get as far as the Straits of Waigatz in 1556. It was the failure of a venture in 1580 to reach beyond the Kara Sea that suggested ultimate success was still some way off. Meanwhile, others were spurred to look for a route to the Pacific from the opposite direction, with Martin Frobisher and John Davis searching for the North-West Passage between North America and the Arctic.

These impulses to explore and to expand trade manifested themselves in the seventeenth century with the first settlements of what became the British Empire – paid for by joint-stock companies.

The original manuscript of the Muscovy Company's royal charter was destroyed by the Great Fire of London in 1666 but a transcript of it was made, which survives in the London Metropolitan Archives.

1563
FOXE'S *BOOK OF MARTYRS*

CREATING A NARRATIVE OF ENGLISH PROTESTANT
IDENTITY UNDER THREAT FROM CATHOLICISM

No history book did more to establish Queen Mary I's posthumous reputation as 'Bloody Mary', to commemorate the martyrs she burned at the stake, or to entwine national identity with Protestantism, than John Foxe's *Acts and Monuments*, popularly known as 'Foxe's *Book of Martyrs*'.

It made its author Britain's first literary celebrity. The phenomenal sale of his work, which went into four extensively revised editions in his own lifetime and many more thereafter, was surprising for a book whose second edition ran to over 2,300 pages. Yet such was this edition's success that its production was temporarily imperilled because its publisher, John Day, ran out of paper.

Foxe's *Book of Martyrs* was the result of years of diligent – if one-sided – research by Foxe and his team of assistants. Its claims to historic authenticity were reinforced by its extensive recourse to archival material, in particular diocesan registers and the historic manuscripts collected by Matthew Parker, Queen Elizabeth I's first archbishop of Canterbury, many of which it reproduced. What helped to make it a popular sensation was its detailed and lurid woodcut illustrations of the torture and death meted out to Catholicism's opponents.

Most of all, the book's success can be attributed to a simple reality: whilst it was a work of propaganda, presenting only one side of the story, it related events that were at least true in outline, if not always in detail. Upon succeeding her Protestant brother Edward VI in 1553, Mary Tudor wasted little time in restoring the English Church to Rome and stamping out heresy with such vehemence that future generations – with Foxe's help – associated Catholic rule with unrestrained cruelty and despotism.

Edward VI had imprisoned senior prelates who refused to renounce their Catholic doctrine, but they were not put to death. In this respect, Mary's brief

rule represented a return to previous measures against heretics, made worse by the swelling number of her subjects who fell into that category. In the space of three years, she committed 200 men and 60 women to the flames on account of their faith. Given her marriage to the deeply unpopular Philip II of Spain, the precariousness of her situation emboldened her brutality. Even on 17 November 1558, the day she died, she raised herself from a deathbed of considerable pain to confirm the death warrants of two more Protestants.

Some of those burned at the stake during her reign were the leaders of Protestant reform: John Hooper, bishop of Gloucester; Nicholas Ridley, bishop of London; Hugh Latimer, bishop of Worcester; and Thomas Cranmer, the former archbishop of Canterbury. However, most of her victims came from further down the social scale. Some, like the illiterate fisherman Rawlings White and the poor, blind Joan

This woodcut illustration from Foxe's Book of Martyrs shows a group of Protestants being burnt at Smithfield in 1546. Among them was Anne Askew, who was sentenced to death for refusing to name fellow believers. She had been so severely tortured on the rack that she had to be carried to the stake in a chair.

The order and manner of the burning of *Anne Askew,* *Iohn Lacels, Iohn Adams, Nicolas Belenian,* with certaine of the Counsell sitting in Smithfield.

Waist, were reduced to ashes merely for asking others to read the New Testament to them. Supplementing his archival research with potentially less accurate oral evidence, Foxe told all their stories.

Foxe himself had spent Mary's reign in exile. Born around 1516, he had formed his Protestant thinking while a student at Oxford and realized he was in danger when Mary restored the English Church to Rome. It was in 1559, while he was in Basel, Switzerland, that his first work on Protestant martyrs was published. Later that year he returned to England, secure in the knowledge that Elizabeth I's accession made it safe to do so. The first edition of *Acts and Monuments*, in a large folio format of 1,800 pages, was published in 1563. The second edition in 1570 came in two volumes, contained far more illustrations and greatly increased the first edition's scope with extensive coverage of the pre-Reformation Church and the treatment of heretics across Europe.

Despite an outlook made ever more austere by hard work, Foxe was known for his personal acts of charity towards the poor. No advocate of religious toleration, he supported imprisonment and punishment for, most notably, the Anabaptist sect; but because he believed everyone to be capable of personal redemption, he resolutely opposed the death sentence for those whose faiths he so actively denounced.

Revised editions of his *Book of Martyrs* continued to appear after his death in 1587, with contemporary detail added to bring Catholic cruelty up to date. In heightening the atmosphere of fear towards papist and High Church practices, its influence was perhaps greatest during the period of the English Civil War. Thereafter, heavily edited editions became increasingly sensationalist and ghoulish in their focus on the violence meted out to Protestant martyrs. In doing so, they hoped to keep sectarian animosities alive while in fact unintentionally undermining Foxe's reputation as a scholar.

It is arguable that the *Book of Martyrs* may have shaped popular and Low Church suspicion of Catholicism right up to the twentieth century.

1563
THE THIRTY-NINE ARTICLES

THE DOCTRINE OF THE STATE CHURCH

The Thirty-Nine Articles were not just the defining statement on what constituted the doctrine of the Church of England; they became part of the test of who could play an active part in public life. Between 1672 and 1828, anyone wishing to hold civil office in England, Wales or Ireland had to adhere to them. In most cases, a refusal to subscribe excluded from office not just Catholics but also Nonconformists – those Protestants who were not Anglicans.

Like the Book of Common Prayer, the Articles were largely the work of Thomas Cranmer, who served both Henry VIII and Edward VI as archbishop of Canterbury. Under Henry VIII, the Church of England, although separated from Rome, remained Catholic in doctrine. This was made clear by the Six Articles of 1539. It was the succession of Edward VI that allowed Protestant sympathizers to move more firmly into positions where they could change matters. Cranmer was engaged to draw up Forty-Two Articles that would reposition the Church accordingly.

Thomas Cranmer, archbishop of Canterbury, 1533–55.

In 1553, Edward died before the new statement could be enforced. The succession of his Catholic half-sister, Mary, brought the reforms to an abrupt halt. The queen restored Church doctrine to where it had been before her father's break with Rome, and Cranmer, along with many of the other leading reforming theologians, was burned at the stake in Mary's campaign against 'heresy'.

With the accession of Elizabeth I, a Protestant again sat on the throne. The 1559 Act of Supremacy restored the monarch to the position of head of the Church of England, with the title 'supreme governor', but the doctrinal nature of her state Church remained to be determined. For political as well as personal reasons, Elizabeth wanted a compromise solution. She thought it important

99

THE REIGN OF ELIZABETH I

1558 Elizabeth succeeds her half-sister, Mary I.

1560 The Treaty of Edinburgh is signed between Scotland, England and France.

1568 Elizabeth puts her Catholic cousin, Mary, Queen of Scots, under house arrest.

1569 The Rising in the North by Catholics attempts to supplant Elizabeth with Mary.

1577–80 Francis Drake becomes the first Englishman to circumnavigate the globe.

1584 Sir Walter Raleigh establishes the English colony of Virginia in North America.

1586 The Babington plot to supplant Elizabeth with Mary is uncovered.

1587 Mary, Queen of Scots, is executed; Drake destroys a Spanish fleet at Cadiz.

1588 The Spanish Armada is defeated.

1597 A storm scatters the second Spanish Armada attempt.

1597–1601 Rebellion occurs in Ireland.

1601 The Earl of Essex stages an abortive rebellion.

1603 Elizabeth I dies and is succeeded by Mary, Queen of Scots' son, James VI of Scotland.

that the Church's practices should be generally familiar to covert Catholics while making sufficient acknowledgement of Protestant teaching to avoid creating an irretrievable rupture with Puritan adherents of the Geneva theologian John Calvin.

Producing this delicate balancing act was entrusted to Elizabeth's archbishop of Canterbury, Matthew Parker. A great scholar and archivist of historic documents, Parker nonetheless wanted to remain largely faithful to Thomas Cranmer's proposed Forty-Two Articles of 1553. In this he was successful, for the statement of doctrine approved by the Church Convocation in 1563 was little more than a minor revision of Cranmer's work.

The Convocation approved the Thirty-Nine Articles, thus upholding the central Protestant contention of justification by faith rather than merely through good works. Purgatory, the adoration of saints and the use of pardons were dismissed as Rome's inventions. No less contentiously, Article 17 affirmed support for the Calvinist belief in predestination – the premiss that God had secretly predetermined who would receive salvation and who damnation.

The greatest difference between the Thirty-Nine Articles adopted by Elizabeth I and Cranmer's original Forty-Two Articles for Edward VI concerned transubstantiation. The Catholic belief was reaffirmed that the sacrament of Eucharist converted bread and wine into Christ's body and blood. Nonetheless, Elizabeth still remained particularly apprehensive about needlessly offending her Catholic subjects. This fear motivated her rejection of Article 29, thereby reducing the total number of articles to thirty-eight.

Such appeasement proved short-lived, however, because in 1570 Pope Pius V excommunicated Elizabeth and called on English Catholics to rise up and overthrow her. The pope's pronouncement, an incitement to treason in the cause of Roman Catholic orthodoxy, was to have disastrous consequences for England's Catholics. The backlash was not long delayed. In 1571, Article 29 was reinserted, denying in the Eucharist the substance of the body and blood of

Article XXXVII: Of the Civil Magistrates

The Queen's Majesty hath the chief power in this realm of England and other her dominions, unto whom the chief government of all estates of this realm, whether they be ecclesiastical or civil, in all causes doth appertain, and is not nor ought to be subject to any foreign jurisdiction.

Where we attribute to the Queen's Majesty the chief government, by which titles we understand the minds of some slanderous folks to be offended, we give not to our princes the ministering either of God's word or of sacraments, the which thing the Injunctions also lately set forth by Elizabeth our Queen doth most plainly testify: but only that prerogative which we see to have been given always to all godly princes in Holy Scriptures by God himself, that is, that they should rule all estates and degrees committed to their charge by God, whether they be temporal, and restrain with the civil sword the stubborn and evil-doers.

The Bishop of Rome hath no jurisdiction in this realm of England.

The laws of the realm may punish Christian men with death for heinous and grievous offences.

It is lawful for Christian men at the commandment of the Magistrate to wear weapons and serve in the wars.

Christ to 'the wicked and such as be void of lively faith'. All Thirty-Nine Articles were given statutory authority by Parliament in 1571, making adherence from the clergy a legal requirement.

In Scotland, Protestant doctrine was enforced by a different route, being imposed upon a sovereign who remained Catholic. From 1557, Protestant nobles were in armed conflict with their nation's French regent, Mary of Guise (governing on behalf of the young Mary, Queen of Scots, who remained in France). Upon the regent's death in 1560, the Scottish Parliament was convened. It declared void Rome's jurisdiction over Scotland and banned the Catholic Mass. In its place, it drew up an equivalent version of the Thirty-Nine Articles, known as the Confession of Faith. Laying out the new state theology, it was heavily influenced by John Knox, an adherent of John Calvin. Thus the doctrine of the Church of Scotland became Presbyterian rather than Episcopalian.

1566–7
THE CASKET LETTERS

'PROOF' OF MARY, QUEEN OF SCOTS' COMPLICITY IN MURDERING HER HUSBAND

Few documents in British history have caused more speculation than a cache of letters implicating Mary, Queen of Scots, in the murder of her husband. Successive generations have debated their authenticity. What has never been contested, however, is their role in sealing the fate of Scotland's most tragic monarch.

Mary Stuart was just six days old when she inherited the Scottish throne from her father, James V, in 1542. While her French mother acted as regent on her behalf, she was sent at the age of six to the French court in preparation for her marriage to the Dauphin, Francis. They wed in 1558 when Mary was fifteen and Francis fourteen. A year later, they ascended to the throne, the embodiment of the Franco-Scottish 'auld alliance', but the queen of Scots was not to remain the queen of France for long.

Francis died in 1560. Widowed, Mary returned to Scotland the following year to rule the country in her own right, only to discover that it had been politically transformed during her absence. Reformation theology had taken root and Parliament had renounced Scotland's adherence to Rome, abolished the Mass and drawn up an avowedly Protestant 'Confession of Faith'. Young, Catholic, and a woman – making her vulnerable on three counts – Mary thus found herself, precariously, head of state in a country being shaped by hard, unyielding Protestant men of whom the most powerful was her own half-brother, the earl of Moray.

The one concession made to her was that she was permitted Mass in her own chapel at the palace of Holyroodhouse in Edinburgh. This became simultaneously a focal point of irritation to Calvinist hardliners like John Knox as well as a magnet of hope for Scotland's Catholic adherents.

In 1565 she made a disastrous error, marrying her English cousin, Henry, Lord Darnley, a dissolute teenager of ill manners and opportunistic religious views. Too

late, she realized her mistake. In March 1566, a mixture of personal jealousy and political calculation drove Darnley to join a faction that broke into his wife's privy chamber at Holyroodhouse and stabbed to death her unpopular Italian secretary, David Rizzio. Three months later, Mary gave birth to a son and heir, James.

Mary now had an heir, but unfortunately still a husband. Darnley was more than an embarrassment; seemingly deranged, he presented a clear danger. In February 1567, the house outside Edinburgh in which he was recovering (probably from syphilis) was mysteriously blown up with gunpowder. Having escaped from a window, Darnley was strangled in the grounds. Thus began a complicated whodunnit, which, given the number of his enemies, implicated many of Scotland's leading nobles and, some supposed, even Mary herself.

Nonetheless, from the first, the earl of Bothwell was the chief suspect. After the queen formally refused his hand, in April 1567 he abducted her, allegedly raped her and then, the following month, arranged for a marriage service to be conducted over them both. Scottish opinion quickly divided, between those appalled at Bothwell's apparent enslavement of the queen to his will, and those who deduced Mary was complicit and had planned with him both her 'abduction' and the murder of Darnley.

The scandal was too great for the Scottish nobility to bear. They raised forces to confront Bothwell and Mary and, after a brief confrontation at Carberry Hill, Mary was imprisoned in an island fortress on Loch Leven. Still only twenty-four years old, although thoroughly degraded by now, she was forced to abdicate in favour of her infant son, with his Protestant uncle, the earl of Moray, acting as regent.

In May 1568, Mary escaped confinement and raised an army, only to be defeated by Moray's forces. She duly fled to England. Although Queen Elizabeth was her cousin (Mary's great-grandfather was Henry VII), the closeness of their relationship contained as much threat as security. Catholics who had never accepted the validity of Henry VIII's divorce considered Elizabeth illegitimate. To them, Mary was therefore the rightful queen of England. Elizabeth had to decide how her own interests would be best served: by pressurizing the Scots to take back Mary, by keeping her indefinitely as an unwanted guest in England, or by finding a means of hastening her end.

Encouraging Scotland's government to accept Mary as their sovereign once more was seriously considered. To this end, an Anglo-Scots conference was convened at York in 1568, with the intention to discover whether Moray and Mary might

OVERLEAF: A page from the longest of the 'casket letters', in a contemporary copy translated into English from the original French.

for a suirety & mystrustyng die of that that you know, & for his luf
But in the end, after I had spoke twoo or three good word to him
he waxe very mery & glaid. I haue not sene him often sieth I for
ending yo baruet, but I say find no reason for it, It is secretly
herunto, and I feare least it shuld bring you yll happ, or that
it shuld be knowen if you were hurte. Send me word weither you
will haue it, and more morning and mery I shall return, And gaue
farrel I may speik. Now as farr as I percean I may do much to you
Els you percieue I shall not be suspected. As for the rest, I
ne wood when he speake of Edinton, and of that my and brought
of yor brother & suite no thing, but of the Erle of Arguile & elce
I am afraid of him to heare him talk, at the least he assured, he
self that he hate no yll opinion of me. I speaking nothing of these
abrode, neither good nor yll, but avoyding speaking of him. His
falt thynks his gentleman. I haue not sene him. All the Hamiltons be
heire, who accompany me very honestly. All the frend of the els do
com alwaue with me to court him. He hate sent to me a roughtsun
to see him to morrow at his ryssing by him early ryse to morrow in the
morning early. To be short, this bearer shall declare unto
you the rest. And if I shall learne any thing, I will make every
night a memorial thereof. He shall tell you the cause of my stay.
Excuse this letter. for it is to dangerous, wither we say any thing
well sence in it, for I think syppon nothing and syppon greater if you
be at Edinbrough

Now if to plese you my deere lyfe, I spare neither hono confience
nor hazard, nor greatnes, take it in good parte, and not according to th'
interpretacy of yo false brother in lawe, to who I pray you giue no credit
agaynst the most faytefull louer that euer you had or shall haue.
See not also her whose faynid teares you ought not more to regaird then
the true trauails whI indure to deserue her plour, for obtayning of
wch agaynst my owy nature I do betray these that I could let me. God
forgeue me; and giue you my onely frend the good luck & prosperitie that yo
humble & faytefull louer doth wisshe he onto you, who hopith shortly to b
an other thing unto you for the reward of my paynes. I haue not maid one
worde, And it is late, altho I shuld neuer be wery of writing to you yet
will I end, after kissing of yo hand. Excuse my euill writing and reid it
ouer twise. excuse also that I for I had not yester night no pap when
I took these my one memorial remember the frend & wryte unto her
and offten, Loue me allwy

Transcription of the longest of the 'casket letters'

To conclude, for surety, he mistruthith her of that that you know, and for his lyfe. But in the end, after I had spoken two or three good words to him, he was very merry and glad.

I have not seen him this night for ending you braceet, but I can find no clasps for yt; it is ready thereunto, and yet I fear lest it should bring you yll hap, or that shuld be known if you where hurt. Send me word whether you will have it, and more monney, and how farr I may speak. Now so farr as I perceive I may doo much without you; guesse you withir I shall not be suspected. As for the rest, he is mad when he hears of Ledinton, and of you, and my brother. Of your brother he says nothing, but of the Earl of Argile he doth; I am afraid of him to heare him talk, at the last he assurit himself that he hath no yll opinion of him. He speaketh bothing of these abrode, nither good nor yll, but avoid it speaking of him. His father keepith his chambre; I have not seen him.

All the Hamiltons be here who accompany me very honestly. All the friends of the others doo come allwais when I go visit him. He hath sent to me and prayeth me to see him rise in the morning early. To be short, this bearer shall declare unto you the rest; and if I learne anything, I will make every night a memorial thereof. He shall tell you the cause of my stay, Burn this letter, for it is too dangerous, neither is there anything well said in it, for I think upon nothing but upon grief if you be at Edinburgh.

Now if it please you, my deere lyfe, I spare neither hounour, conscience, nor hazard, nor greatness, take it in good part, and not according to the interpretation of your false brother-in-law, to whome I pray you, give no credit against the most faythfull lover that ever you had or shall have.

See not also her whose fayned tears you ought not more to regard than the true travails which I endure to deserve her place, for obtayning of which, against my own nature, I doo betray those that could lett me. God forgive me, and give you, my only friend, the good luck and prosperitie that your humble and fathyfull lover doth wisshe unto you, who hopith shortly to be another thing unto you, for the reward of my paynes.

I have not made one word and it is very late, although I shuld nver be weary in wryting to you, yet will I end, after kissing of your hands. Excuse my eviil wryting, and read it over twise. Excuse also that I scribbled, for I had yesternight no paper when I took the paper of a memorial. Pray remember your friend, and write unto her often; love me allwais as I shall love you.

be reconciled. It quickly turned into a trial in all but name, with Mary's role in Darnley's murder the central issue. The critical evidence was provided by the 'casket letters', which Moray laid before the conference and which had supposedly been found in a silver casket seized from Bothwell's servant, George Dalgliesh. They consisted of eight letters, written in French, and twelve love sonnets from Mary to Bothwell, along with a couple of draft marriage contracts. They dated from the period of Darnley's assassination and appeared to implicate Mary as Bothwell's lover and accessory to murder.

Even at the time there were questions over whether the letters were genuine and the conference broke up without coming to a formal conclusion. Nevertheless, whatever their provenance, the letters cast sufficient doubt to remove any likelihood of England forcing Mary back upon a reluctant Scottish nobility. So Moray returned as regent of Scotland, assisted with English funds, while Mary began eighteen years of imprisonment in England, confined under a house arrest that, although for the most part better than formal incarceration (she had forty servants), was nonetheless irksome. Her chance of reclaiming the Scottish throne through diplomacy had gone.

Still alive, however, was the possibility of her gaining the English Crown. Unfortunately for her, the pro-Catholic Northern Rebellion of 1569, together with the pope's call for Elizabeth's assassination the following year, hardened the hearts of those believing that the Protestant throne would be safer with Mary dead. Fatally, in 1586 Mary encouraged a conspiracy to kill Elizabeth and put herself on the throne with the help of a Spanish invasion. She did not realize that this 'Babington Plot' was being watched (and encouraged) by Elizabeth's spymaster, Sir Francis Walsingham, who had intercepted the damning correspondence. Having been thoroughly incriminated, Mary could finally be convicted of treason.

Reluctantly, Elizabeth was persuaded to bring her cousin to trial. Found guilty, Mary was beheaded at Fotheringhay Castle in Northamptonshire on 8 February 1587, almost exactly twenty years after Darnley's mysterious demise. However, she bequeathed England something that Elizabeth did not – an heir. In 1603, the English throne passed to James VI of Scotland who duly became King James I. He had done little to save his mother while she lived for fear of hampering his chance of this succession. Nonetheless, once established in England, he had her reinterred so that Mary, Queen of Scots, finally lay alongside the rulers of England in Westminster Abbey.

Meanwhile, the casket letters that had done so much to hinder her restoration to her own realm conveniently vanished. What is known is that after the 1568–9 conference they were brought back to Scotland to be placed in the earl of Morton's possession until his execution in 1581, then passing into the hands of the earl of Gowrie until he, too, was executed in 1584. They disappeared thereafter. One plausible theory is that James had them destroyed.

However, translated copies were made of them in Scots, English, Latin and French, from which successive historians drew differing conclusions. Some deductions can now be said to be erroneous. The French translations were wrongly assumed to be the original manuscripts until 1754. The sonnets can be dismissed as inauthentic. At least some of the letters are plausibly in Mary's style but betray signs of having been edited and altered to suit the prosecution's case. In particular, the most important letter, dated January 1567, clearly implies that Mary was preparing to do away with her husband. Supposedly written to Bothwell, certain passages suggest that it was actually intended for someone else entirely.

For 400 years after they were first produced, historians have attempted either to portray the letters as proof of the scheming and wanton nature of Scotland's last Catholic monarch or as evidence of Mary's personal tragedy, helplessly caught up by events and the machinations of devious men. The consensus is now that they are largely the work of forgery and malicious manipulation. Whether the attempt to frame her instead proves her innocence perhaps remains a matter best summarized by a uniquely Scottish verdict – not proven.

1591

MY LADYE NEVELLS BOOKE

WILLIAM BYRD'S WORKS FOR KEYBOARD

When the composer William Byrd died in 1623, the tributes paid to him went far beyond speaking respectfully of the dead. He was described as the 'parent' of British music or, as the records of the Chapel Royal put it, 'a father of musicke'. In life, he had been treated with scarcely less reverence. Despite making no effort to conceal his Roman Catholic faith at a time when it was dangerous to profess it, he escaped serious punishment. Queen Elizabeth I was among those who protected him from her own laws.

In truth, Byrd was not the first British composer to gain a reputation in his own lifetime, nor was he the progenitor of the country's distinct musical traditions, but rather the first Englishman to master the new sounds of Renaissance music. In doing so he produced music that bore comparison with the great continental composers of the period, Palestrina and Victoria, and influenced the sounds of native music-making in the century that followed.

England had already produced a musical genius of the previous generation in Thomas Tallis (*c*.1505–85). Tallis concentrated on liturgical music, most famously his *Lamentations of Jeremiah* for five voices and the forty-voice motet, *Spem in alium*, one of the masterpieces of polyphony, in which separate melodic lines are concurrently sounded by two groups of twenty singers. Born around 1543, Byrd was Tallis's pupil before joining him as joint organist of the Chapel Royal. As with so many subsequent British composers, this appointment within the royal household brought with it not only prestige but state favour. In 1575, Tallis and Byrd went into business together, gaining from Queen Elizabeth a twenty-one-year monopoly to publish all printed music in the realm. In the process, they virtually created the country's music publishing trade.

Nonetheless, it was for a hand-annotated manuscript that Byrd's finest works for keyboard were collated. The anthology, *My Ladye Nevells Booke*, was produced in 1591, probably for Elizabeth, the wife of a Berkshire landowner, Sir Henry

A GOLDEN AGE OF MUSIC

1499 Oxford University awards music degrees.

1560 Thomas Tallis composes the *Lamentations of Jeremiah*.

1568 The first primer for the lute is published.

1570 Tallis composes his forty-part motet, *Spem in alium*.

1575 Tallis and William Byrd jointly publish a motet collection, *Cantiones Sacrae*, and Elizabeth I grants them both a twenty-one-year monopoly on all music printing in England.

1580 The first mention of the ballad 'Greensleeves' appears.

1588 Nicholas Yonge's publication of *Musica Transalpina* popularizes Italian madrigals in Britain.

1588 Byrd publishes *Psalms, Sonnets and Songs of Sadness and Pietie*.

1589 Byrd publishes *Songs of Sundrie Natures*.

1591 Byrd publishes his anthology *My Ladye Nevells Booke*.

1594 Elizabeth I sends a Thomas Dallam organ to the Ottoman sultan.

1597 The publication of John Dowland's *First Book of Songes or Ayres* and Thomas Morley's *A Plaine and Easie Introduction to Practicall Musicke*.

1598 The twenty-one-year monopoly to publish music passes to Thomas Morley.

1600 Thomas Morley's *First Book of Ayres* is published.

*c.*1610 *The Fitzwilliam Virginal Book* is published, a treasure-trove of keyboard music.

1611–12 *Parthenia* is published, with keyboard works by John Bull, William Byrd and Orlando Gibbons.

1612–13 Orlando Gibbons's *First Set of Madrigals and Motets of Five Parts* is published.

1623 Gibbons is appointed organist of Westminster Abbey.

1649 The Welsh-born Thomas Tomkins writes the Royalist lament *Sad Pavan for These Distracted Times*.

Nevill. She may have been one of Byrd's patrons. However, as only two of the compositions are specifically dedicated to her, it is possible that she was one of his pupils and the anthology is a collection of her favourite pieces. Byrd wrote extensively for the virginal, a smaller version of the harpsichord, which was a particularly popular instrument among female players. In all, *My Ladye Nevells Booke* contains forty-two works. These include dances – most of them pavans and galliards – and variations based on such contemporary folk-tunes as 'The Carman's Whistle' and 'Will Yow Walke the Woods soe Wylde'. The manuscript was produced by John Baldwin of St George's Chapel, Windsor. The corrections, however, are believed to be in Byrd's hand.

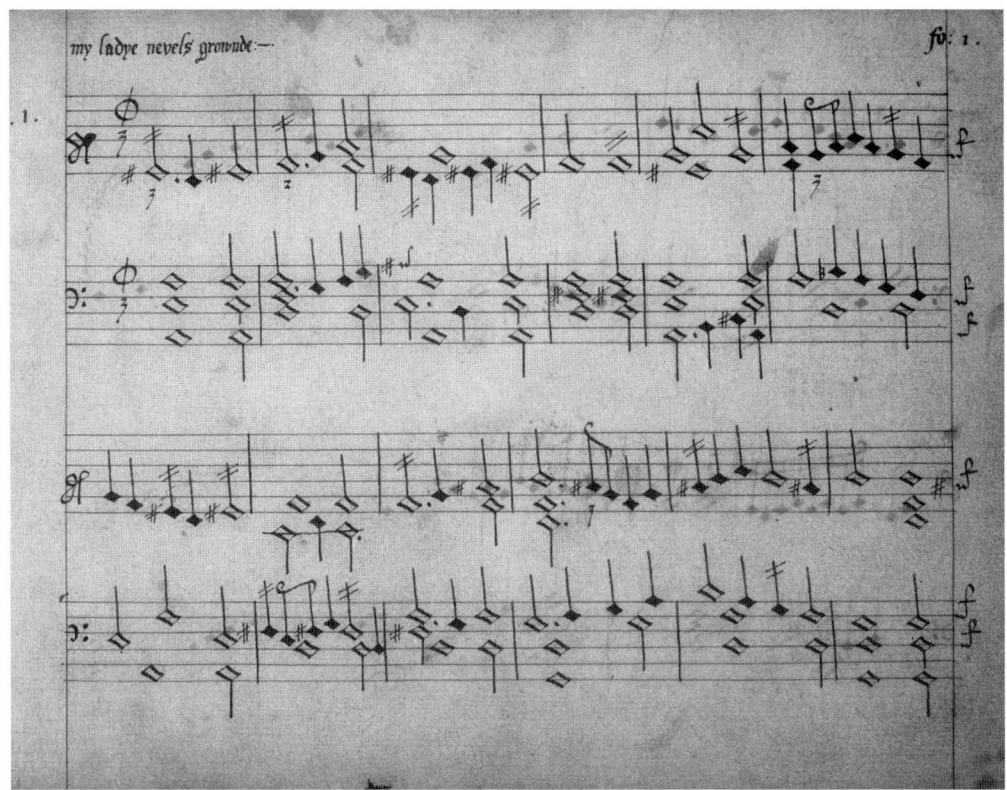

The music of 'My Ladye Nevell's Grownde', the opening piece of William Byrd's keyboard anthology My Ladye Nevells Booke.

Byrd's music stood out not only for its quality but for the versatility of the composer. Over the course of his life, he produced a huge corpus for virtually every major medium apart from the lute. He was as adept at writing popular songs as he was at producing sacred choral music and was an innovator of verse anthems as well as a master of contrapuntal composition. He described his own ability to match music for words: 'There is a certain hidden power in the thoughts underlying the words themselves, so that as one meditates upon the sacred words and constantly and seriously considers them, the right notes, in some inexplicable fashion, suggest themselves quite spontaneously.' He wrote Latin religious music for Catholics as well as English settings for the Prayer Book (despite his Roman beliefs), which proved highly influential, resonating throughout the Anglican liturgy long after his death. Perhaps, though, the most touching epitaph appears at the end of the fourth galliard in *My Ladye Nevells Booke*. There, John Baldwin, unable to contain his excitement appended a simple observation: *mr. w. birde. homo memorabilis.*

1600
THE ROYAL CHARTER OF THE EAST INDIA COMPANY

THE DEVELOPMENT OF BRITISH TRADE AND EMPIRE

The East India Company played the decisive role in establishing Britain's supremacy in India, generating wealth, commerce and industry back home. In doing so, it helped to prove the effectiveness of the joint-stock company as a motor of capitalist activity.

It was not preordained that Britain would be the European country that dominated India. For almost one hundred years after they bombarded Calicut in southern India in 1501, it was the Portuguese who led efforts to control trade, not only with the subcontinent but also with the spice islands of the East Indies (principally modern day-Indonesia and the Malaysian archipelago). By the end of the sixteenth century, however, the Dutch were financing highly lucrative voyages to the East Indies. In 1600, in the rush to grab a slice of this market before the Dutch controlled it all, a group of English merchants and investors founded the East India Company.

They started it with £30,000 raised in capital and a royal charter from Elizabeth I granting a fifteen-year monopoly (subsequently renewed and extended) on all English trading ventures to the East Indies. Given the Dutch competition, there was no time to waste and within months the first five ships were sailing from Torbay for Sumatra. In 1602, a trading base was established at Bantam on Java. Initially, the East India Company funded its voyages one at a time, unlike the rival Dutch East India Company – or Vereenigde Oost-indische Companie (VOC) – which was organized as a joint-stock company, a much more sensible vehicle for attracting long-term investment. By 1657, when Oliver Cromwell renewed the company's charter, it too had become a permanent joint-stock entity.

Copying the Dutch business model was not, of itself, enough to dislodge Holland's grip on the region. The maritime rivalry between the two powers

intensified, three times breaking out into war between 1652 and 1674. It was not until the accession in 1688 of the Dutch *stadtholder*, William of Orange, to the British thrones that the VOC conceded its ascendancy in the East Indies, in return for which the East India Company became the dominant trading organization with India.

This division of spoils proved highly advantageous for the British company. In 1700, India was producing about a quarter of world economic output at a time when Britain was responsible for only around 3 per cent of the total. During the eighteenth and nineteenth centuries, Indian textile exports in calicoes, raw cotton and silk proved much more valuable than the spice-orientated commerce with the East Indies.

The British had gained a foothold on the Indian subcontinent as early as 1613 at Surat and shortly thereafter Sir Thomas Roe established favourable diplomatic relations with India's Mughal emperor, Jahangir. Fortified trading posts were set up at Fort St George and Sutanuti, around which the cities of Madras and Calcutta would develop. The third of the East India Company's great entrepôts was Bombay (Mumbai), which the Portuguese ceded as part of Catherine of Braganza's wedding dowry to Charles II in 1661. During the eighteenth century, as Mughal rule fell apart and power fragmented across India, the East India Company increasingly enforced national security with its own private army, recruited from the Indian population as well as from Europeans. Besides threats from hostile native leaders, the company had to protect itself against the ambitions of India's other trade-settlers, in particular the French. The latter briefly seized Madras before seeing their colonial intentions dealt a shattering blow in the Seven Years War (1756–63).

The defeat of the French and the infighting between native rulers was ably exploited by the East India Company's man on the spot, Robert Clive. The victory of his 3,000 well-drilled soldiers against the Nawab of Bengal's force of 50,000 at Plassey in 1757 created an indelible impression. Following the Treaty of Allahabad in 1765, the Mughal emperor Shah Allam II ceded administrative and fiscal responsibility for Bengal to the East India Company. A private company had, in effect, become the government for 20 million Indians.

For its part, the British government had long supported the East India Company, viewing it as equal to taking the risks, yet whose profits could be creamed off by the Exchequer. Nonetheless, it drew the line at letting the company become a colonial law unto itself. In 1773, Warren Hastings, the Company's governor in Bengal, was given the elevated title of governor-general and, through his four-man council, was

confirmed in his legislative powers there. In return, his appointment was made subject to the British government's approval, and law in Bengal was to be overseen by a judiciary appointed by the British Crown.

This arrangement proved insufficient to stop the East India Company's abuse of its position in India. Its wars of expansion were paid for by high taxation of the Bengalis (even during periods of famine) and much of the province's wealth was repatriated by the company's 'nabobs' to Britain. Eventually, Warren Hastings returned to London, where he was put on trial. After more than six years of legal debate, he was acquitted of the worst charges of malpractice but by then enough had been revealed to prompt drastic curtailment of the East India Company's power. In 1784, the government appointed its own department, the Board of Control for India, with ultimate authority over the East India Company's board of directors. In 1813, the company was stripped of most of its monopoly in India.

Thereafter, its trading activities were increasingly focused upon trafficking Bengali opium to China (sparking war with China and Britain's acquisition of Hong Kong), while using the money it earned there to buy tea, which it then shipped to Britain. Most of all, it had become a tax-raising body, since – through the fortunes of war and the submission of weakened local princes – it was the effective ruler not just of Bengal but of much of eastern

THE ORIGINS OF EMPIRE

1583 Sir Humphrey Gilbert claims Newfoundland for England.

1585 Sir Walter Raleigh's short-lived settlement at Roanoke is set up in modern-day North Carolina.

1600 The East India Company is founded.

1607 The Virginia Colony is established as the first permanent British settlement in the New World, at Jamestown.

1613 The East India Company's first trading settlement in India is established at Surat.

1625 Barbados is claimed for Britain.

1655 Admiral William Penn captures Jamaica from the Spanish.

1661 Bombay (Mumbai) is ceded by Portugal to Britain.

1670 A royal charter is granted to the Hudson Bay Company to exploit the Canadian fur trade.

1713 The Treaty of Utrecht grants Britain the Spanish possessions of Gibraltar and Minorca and the formerly French Canadian domains of Acadia, including Nova Scotia. France effectively gives up its attempt to compete with the Hudson Bay Company.

1757 Robert Clive wins the Battle of Plassey in Bengal.

1765 The Treaty of Allahabad grants the East India Company administrative and fiscal responsibility for Bengal.

1759 James Wolfe captures Quebec from the French.

1763 The Peace of Paris ends the Seven Years War; France cedes its remaining Canadian territories and its claims west of the Mississippi to Britain. Spain cedes Florida to Britain.

1768–71 James Cook undertakes voyages to Australia and New Zealand.

1776 The thirteen American colonies declare independence from the British Crown. The Revolutionary War follows.

1783 Britain acknowledges the independent United States of America.

1784 The British government sets up its Board of Control for India, curtailing the authority of the East India Company.

1788 The first convicts are transported to Botany Bay in Australia.

From the royal charter of the East India Company, 1600

Whereas our most dear and loving Cousin, George, Earl of Cumberland, and our well-beloved Subjects, Sir John Hart of London, Knight, Sir John Spencer of London, Knight, William Starkey, William Smith, John Ellecot, Robert Bailey, and Roger Cotton, have been Petitioners unto us for our Royal Assent and Licence to be granted unto them, that they, at their own Adventures, Costs, and Charges, as well as for the Honour of this our Realm of England, as for the Increase of our Navigation, and advancement of Trade of Merchandise, set forth one or more Voyages, with convenient Number of Ships and pannaces, by way of Traffick and Merchandise to the East-Indies, in the Countries and Parts of Asia and Africa, and to as many of the Islands, Ports and Cities, Towns and Places, thereabouts, as where Trade and Traffic may by all Likelihood be discovered, established or had; divers of which Countries, and many of the Islands, Cities and Ports thereof, have long been discovered by others of our Subjects, albeit not frequented in Trade or Merchandise.

and southern India as well. Despite these taps on Indian wealth, the company had developed a £40 million debt. It tried to raise much needed capital by simply issuing more shares, but in truth, it had over-reached itself. The cost of paying for a 150,000-strong army was prohibitive, a state of affairs that was the direct result of a long period in which the company's directors in Leadenhall Street had enjoyed little effective restraint over what their more ambitious employees were doing in a remote subcontinent where correspondence took months to arrive.

Finally in 1858, after the Indian Mutiny had been suppressed with tremendous barbarity on both sides, the British government assumed control of the East India Company's possessions. Its key assets having been nationalized, the company was wound up in 1874. British rule in India would continue for a further seventy-three years, but the age of informal, privatized empire was officially over.

1601
THE ELIZABETHAN POOR LAW

A NATIONAL SYSTEM OF POOR RELIEF

Throughout the Middle Ages there was no state system of welfare. Rather, providing alms to the poor was regarded as a religious obligation. It was in the reign of Elizabeth I that statutory measures made the treatment of her most needy subjects a matter of national policy.

During the sixteenth century, although the country was getting no poorer, contemporaries nonetheless believed that the problem of vagrancy was becoming more acute. Various reasons for this were put forward: the inflation of the period; the process of land enclosure, which denied the lowest peasants their means of subsistence; a supposed over-reliance on the textiles industry, whose trade went through regular cycles of boom and bust. To make matters worse, the religious upheavals of the Reformation and, in particular, the dissolution of the monasteries, had undermined some of the institutions upon which the destitute had previously relied.

The first laws to be enacted were more concerned with permitting than with enforcing measures of relief. What was to prove a long debate about the supposedly 'deserving' and 'undeserving' poor became a statutory concern when an Act of 1531 sought to draw a distinction between those who were indigent or homeless because of no fault of their own – such as illness or old age – and should thus be permitted to beg in their own parish, and those whose presumed fecklessness made them vagrants, who were therefore denied such rights.

Central government lacked the machinery to do much more than encourage other bodies to take the initiative. It fell to the major cities to innovate. In 1547, the City of London raised a mandatory poor rate from its citizens in order to fund poverty-alleviating schemes.

Implementing such reforms remained a matter for city and town councils until 1572 when parliamentary legislation forced local government throughout England and Wales to introduce compulsory poor rates. While punishments could still be

visited upon those considered idle, the legislation relaxed the criteria by which some of the poor were deemed the agents of their own misfortune. Able-bodied paupers were to be found work to do.

In Scotland, legislation in the 1570s and 1590s firmly placed the onus of providing relief on the Church of Scotland. The 'Kirk' elders assessed those in need and entered their names upon parish lists. This was not quite the model adopted in England and Wales. There, the 1601 Poor Law brought together and codified the various pre-existing acts. As in Scotland, it recognized the parish as the confine of each administrating area, but in addition working alongside churchwardens were to be 'overseers of the poor', unpaid and appointed by justices of the peace. It was their task to assess the need and raise an appropriate poor rate from the community to cover the costs of providing for the old, to supervise work-creation schemes for the unemployed and to initiate apprenticeships for children in desperate circumstances.

Inevitably, some parishes took their statutory obligations more seriously than others. Following the letter of the law was less necessary where there was already considerable private charity or minimal poverty in the neighbourhood; and the disruptions of the Civil War weakened the state's role in ensuring the measures were uniformly applied. There was also an assumption that the levies raised by the parish were for the parish alone and were not freely available to any passing vagrant who happened to turn up in search of benefits. Thus the 1662 Law of Settlement and Removal tried to prevent those likely to become a burden from moving to more prosperous areas (which did not necessarily want to become the destination for large numbers of vagrants) by allowing for their repatriation if they could not demonstrate they had the means for long-term self-support. The extent to which individual parishes made use of this legislation varied according to how much they felt they needed an influx of labour.

Generating work to keep the unemployed occupied proved among the greatest problems. Outdoor relief continued, although some parishes opted to build work-houses, of varying quality and congeniality. Nonetheless, the cost of poor relief spiralled at the end of the eighteenth century. The introduction from 1795 of the Speenhamland system, which sought to guarantee the poor a minimum income, proved ruinously expensive and demonstrated that parishes were often too small in size to bear it. The cost of Poor Law administration in England and Wales rose from £619,000 in 1750 to £8 million in 1818, equivalent to a charge of 13s 3d per head of population.

From the Poor Law, 1601

Be it enacted by the Authority of this present Parliament, That the Churchwardens of every Parish, and four, three or two substantial Housholders there, as shall be thought meet, having respect to the Proportion and Greatness of the Same Parish and Parishes, to be nominated yearly in Easter Week, or within one Month after Easter, under the Hand and Seal of two or more Justices of the Peace in the same County, whereof one to be of the Quorum, dwelling in or near the same Parish or Division where the same Parish doth lie, shall be called Overseers of the Poor of the same Parish : And they, or the greater Part of them, shall take order from Time to Time, by, and with the Consent of two or more such Justices of Peace as is aforesaid, for setting to work the Children of all such whose Parents shall not by the said Churchwardens and Overseers, or the greater Part of them, be thought able to keep and maintain their Children: And also for setting to work all such Persons, married or unmarried, having no Means to maintain them, and use no ordinary and daily Trade of Life to get their Living by : And also to raise weekly or otherwise [by Taxation of every Inhabitant, Parson, Vicar and other, and of every Occupier of Lands, Houses, Tithes impropriate, Propriations of Tithes, Coal-Mines, or saleable Underwoods in the said Parish, in such competent Sum and Sums of Money as they shall think fit] a convenient Stock of Flax, Hemp, Wool, Thread, Iron, and other necessary Ware and Stuff, to set the Poor on Work : And also competent Sums of Money for and towards the necessary Relief of the Lame, Impotent, Old, Blind, and such other among them being Poor, and not able to work, and also for the putting out of such Children to be apprentices, to be gathered out of the same Parish, according to the Ability of the same Parish, and to do and execute all other Things as well for the disposing of the said Stock, as otherwise concerning the Premisses, as to them shall seem convenient.

As a result, the Elizabethan assistances of doles and outdoor relief codified in 1601 were finally replaced by the 1834 Poor Law Amendment Act, legislation motivated by a concern that a generation of urban welfare dependency was being created. Britain was fast becoming an industrial nation and the numbers of those who might opt to become a burden was beyond the means of the parish, with its bucolic notions and limited resources. Indeed, it was assumed that many unskilled people might find the old system far more appealing than working for a living in a factory. To disabuse them of this notion, the workhouse supposedly extended a

Aquatint of the St James's parish workhouse, from the Microcosm of London, *published in 1809. The figures were drawn by the famous caricaturist, Thomas Rowlandson (1756–1827). The background is by Augustus Pugin (1762–1832), father of the celebrated Gothic Revival architect.*

lifeline to them, on the understanding that it was a deliberate stigma, providing its inmates with an existence materially worse than that enjoyed by the struggling, but employed, poor.

These workhouses, to which the pauperized young, old, able-bodied and infirm were brought, were made purposefully disagreeable to an extent that initially went as far as banning inmates bringing – or being given – personal possessions. Although conditions improved in the second half of the nineteenth century, the workhouse remained the last resort for many until the beginning of the twentieth century, when those able to take advantage of the introduction of old-age pensions in 1908 and national insurance sickness and unemployment benefits in 1911 were in a position to avoid them. Further undermined in the 1920s, the last institutions of the Poor Law did not survive the Second World War.

IV

STUART BRITAIN

1605
THE 'MONTEAGLE LETTER'
AND GUY FAWKES'S SIGNED
CONFESSION

THE EXPOSURE OF THE GUNPOWDER PLOT

The 'Monteagle letter' and Guy Fawkes's signed confession are depicted in the second plate section.

On 5 November 1605, King James I of England (James VI of Scotland) and most of his leading politicians, privy councillors, judges and bishops nearly lost their lives in an enormous explosion. The fact that this attempt at mass murder was thwarted can be largely attributed to an anonymous letter written to Lord Monteagle that warned the Catholic peer to stay away from Parliament that day.

The plan to blow up the House of Lords on the occasion of its state opening session was born of desperation. It was conceived by Robert Catesby, a Midlands squire who drew together a small group of fellow Catholic conspirators. Having concluded that Spain would not send another invasion armada and that the new king was not persuadable on the subject of toleration of Catholicism, they decided to dispose of him, together with the country's governing class, in a devastating fireball.

The plotters knew what they wanted but had only a blunt instrument to bring it about. They continued with the plan even after it became clear that the next in line to the throne, Prince Henry, would not be attending the state opening on 5 November. It seems they had, at best, hazy schemes for dealing with the other Protestant claimants to the throne in the aftermath of the carnage at Westminster. Even had they succeeded in taking hostage Princess Elizabeth as a precursor to persuading her to convert to Catholicism, they were hardly men of sufficient rank or influence to hold the country in thrall. Their best hope was perhaps to spark a period of anarchy that would be ended by a foreign invasion. The extraordinary magnitude of their wishful thinking did not make it any less diabolical. Ironically,

their act of treason would be foiled by the patriotism of a fellow Catholic, and the legacy of the 'Gunpowder Plot' was to make life in Britain even more difficult for their co-religionists.

Initially, the plotters rented a house adjacent to the House of Lords and attempted to tunnel towards the chamber. When storage space became available to rent in the vaults under the Lords' chamber, they seized the opportunity, renting it in the name of one of their conspirators, Thomas Percy. Since he was the cousin of the earl of Northumberland, there was no reason for the authorities to be suspicious.

As the date drew near, Catesby was running short of funds to secure his *coup d'état*, so others were brought into the scheme, including Francis Tresham. On 26 October, an anonymous letter was sent to Tresham's brother-in-law, Lord Monteagle, warning him to keep away from the state opening of Parliament, which would receive a 'terrible blow'. Naturally suspicious, Monteagle informed the king's chief secretary, Robert Cecil, earl of Salisbury. Since threats and rumours were not unusual, Salisbury was not minded to take the matter too seriously. Nonetheless, just for good measure, on the afternoon of 4 November, Monteagle and the lord chamberlain, the earl of Suffolk, searched the House of Lords chamber and the vaults underneath. There they stumbled upon a large pile of firewood (concealing thirty-six barrels of gunpowder) and a man who claimed

A contemporary engraving of the gunpowder plotters by the Dutch engraver Crispin van de Passe.

EYGENTLICHE ABBILDVNG WIE ETTLICH ENGLISCHE EDELLEVT EINEN RAHT schließen den König sampt dem gantzen Parlament mit Pulfer zuvertilgen .

to be called (somewhat unimaginatively) John Johnson. When questioned, he said the wood belonged to Thomas Percy.

This seemed to satisfy the inspectors. However, after they had left, Monteagle mentioned to Suffolk that he vaguely knew Percy, a Catholic with no obvious reason to be storing supplies in Westminster. Duly informed, the king insisted that the Palace of Westminster be properly searched again. Late on the night of 4 November, guards returned to the vaults. There, they discovered not only the barrels of gunpowder under the wood but also fire-lighting equipment and the man still purporting to be John Johnson. He was, in fact, the conspirator charged with igniting the fuse, Guy Fawkes.

While Fawkes was carted off for questioning, his colleagues were rounded up. Catesby and Percy died in a shoot-out at their safe house in Staffordshire. At first Fawkes would not yield his secrets until the level of torture was increased. The severity of pain inflicted on him may be gauged by the broken scrawl of his signature. Tried and found guilty, he was hanged, his heart ripped out and his body quartered. The heads of the conspirators eventually adorned the approach to the Palace of Westminster that they had hoped to reduce to rubble. By contrast, Monteagle was rewarded with a generous pension, which he used to invest in land in Virginia.

Bonfires were lit across London to celebrate national deliverance, a tradition that spread across the country, becoming a permanent feature when Parliament promptly responded to the popular clamour and made 5 November a day of annual thanksgiving. As early as the mid-seventeenth century, commemorative fireworks were being let off. The twin themes of anti-Catholicism and loyalty to parliamentary government were reinforced when, on 5 November 1688, William of Orange landed at Torbay and the Glorious Revolution began. Whilst the passage of time has blurred the more overtly sectarian overtones of 'Bonfire Night', it has not dimmed the nationwide desire to celebrate it.

There have been subsequent theories that the plotters were actually the dupes of a government conspiracy to frame Catholics, but they lack supporting evidence. Similarly, the suggestion has been dismissed that the amount of gunpowder used was either too degraded or insufficient to cause serious damage. Modern ballistics tests using comparable gunpowder strength have shown that if 'John Johnson' had detonated his near one ton of explosives, he would, indeed, have succeeded in blowing the king and the political class of his realm sky high.

1606
UNION JACK DESIGNS

THE UNION OF THE SCOTTISH AND ENGLISH CROWNS
AND THE SYMBOL OF A BRITISH IDENTITY

King James VI of Scotland also became James I of England when he succeeded the childless Queen Elizabeth in 1603. He wished, however, to consider himself not just the single head of state of two otherwise separate kingdoms but rather as the ruler of a united entity, as 'King of Great Britain'.

Preliminary designs for the Union flag are depicted in the second plate section.

In October 1607, James assured the Westminster Parliament that 'the benefits which do arise of that union which is made in my blood do redound to the whole island'. In this he was ahead of his time. Although the accompanying union treaty that he envisaged was passed by the Scottish Parliament, it got bogged down in Westminster and was clearly unlikely to be enacted in a form acceptable to His Majesty.

Yet the previous year the two realms had been given a unified emblem. In the succeeding centuries it was unfurled wherever Britons went: circumnavigating the globe with the world's largest navy; flying from barracks, schools, missions and embassies in the four corners of the earth; forming a rallying point for bloodied soldiers upon countless battlefields; rising with each Olympic gold medal won and falling with each colony set free. So far and wide did it journey that it was even the first man-made item to flutter from the world's highest mountain. This was the Union flag – more commonly referred to as the Union Jack – and it became inseparably entwined with the notion of Britishness.

It was brought into being by a royal proclamation of April 1606, 'declaring what Flags South and North Britains shall bear at Sea', which stipulated that all ships henceforth 'shall bear in their maintop the Red Cross, commonly called St George's Cross, and the White Cross, commonly called St Andrew's Cross, joined together, according to a form made by our Heralds and sent by Us to our Admiral to be published to our said Subjects'.

The design of the new flag, intended only for maritime use, was entrusted to the earl of Nottingham. The brief was to combine the crosses of Scotland and England's respective saints, St Andrew and St George. A traditional approach was to halve or quarter the flag between the two devices, but the problem was that whichever cross appeared nearer to the flagstaff, or on the top quarter, would be construed to enjoy a hierarchical precedence. Avoiding giving national offence was as important as coming up with an intelligible design.

Since 1604, Nottingham had toyed with various ideas, none of them satisfactory. These versions have survived although, sadly, not the original successful design, which was probably lost in a fire at Whitehall palace in 1618. Nonetheless, the solution was ingenious: the English cross would lie on top of the Scottish cross, but a section of the Scottish cross alone would appear in the canton – the top, left-hand quarter of the flag, which the laws of heraldry decreed was the most prestigious position.

It immediately became clear that this did not mollify the Scots. On 7 August 1606, the shipmasters of Scotland wrote to the king, protesting at the fact that 'the Scottis Croce, callit Sanctandrois Croce is twyse divydit, and the Inglishe Croce, callit Sanct George, haldin haill and drawne through the Scottis Croce, whiche is thairby obscurit and no takin nor merk to be seene of the Scottish Armes. This will breid some heit and discontentment betwixt your Majesteis subjectis.'

These gripes led to two versions of the Union flag. English ships flew it with the English cross imposed over the Scottish saltire (diagonal cross) while Scottish ships flew it with the Scottish saltire imposed over the English cross. After the 1707 Act of Union, the Scottish version became less evident and was abandoned altogether during the nineteenth century.

In the seventeenth century, officials busied themselves with controlling rather than promoting the Union flag's use. In 1634, instructions were issued that restricted flying the Union flag to ships of the Royal Navy. Henceforth, merchant ships were commanded to fly the St Andrew's cross if they were Scottish and the St George's cross if they were English, the latter being the first to be subsequently incorporated into the top canton of the red ensign. For warships, the Union flag was briefly abandoned with the execution of Charles I. The republican Commonwealth toyed with various versions before the previous design was reinstated for the restoration of the monarchy in 1660.

With the reign of Queen Anne and full legislative union, the Union flag's usage spread. During this period, the blue appears to have been somewhat lighter in hue

than it subsequently became. The current version of the flag was first flown in 1801 to symbolize the Act of Union with Ireland and introduced the Irish diagonal red cross of St Patrick into the design, running it within the St Andrew's cross. In order not to obliterate the Scottish saltire, the Irish saltire was made less thick and was also 'counter-changed' – reversed in each half so that it is lower on the half nearer the flagpole (thereby ceding hierarchical priority to Scotland) but higher on the half more distant from the pole. This was another means of smoothing national sensibilities by ensuring that the precedence given to the Irish saltire – because it lay over the Scottish saltire – was balanced by the Scottish saltire having precedence in the more prestigious half of the design. It also allowed the flag to be flown upside down as a means of signalling distress.

By this time, the flag was ceasing to be purely a device flown by warships and regiments. During Queen Victoria's reign, it became ubiquitous. Occasionally, pedants attempted to assert that civilians had no right to fly it – until officialdom assured them otherwise. There also remained the debate over its name. Technically it was only the 'Union Jack' when flown from the jackstaff of a Royal Navy ship, which explains the origin of the name. The distinction has, however, long been a redundant one, as conceded by an Admiralty circular from 1902. Asked to settle definitively the matter of the flag's name during a House of Lords debate in 1908, the earl of Crewe announced the government's position on the subject, stating that 'the Union Jack should be regarded as the national flag, and may be flown on land by all His Majesty's subjects'.

1611
THE KING JAMES BIBLE

THE AUTHORIZED VERSION OF THE BIBLE IN ENGLISH

An extract from the King James Bible can be found on pages 62 and 63.

The union of the Scottish and English crowns appeared to safeguard the Protestant succession. Less immediately clear was the nature of the Protestantism to be promoted.

Mary, Queen of Scots died adhering to the Catholic faith of her parents, but her son James was brought up from the cradle by others and was, entrusted instead to the care of strict Presbyterians. He emerged into manhood as a serious, scholarly man, greatly interested in theological issues. With a strong sense of his divine right as monarch, he also rejoiced to be free of his Presbyterian schooling. Indeed, while ruling in Edinburgh, he had confronted its Presbyterian Establishment by trying to reintroduce bishops into the Church of Scotland.

Upon his becoming king in London and supreme governor of the Church of England, such episcopalianism more readily fitted in with the religious settlement of his predecessor, Elizabeth. Nonetheless, in the first years of James's reign, different factions looked for signs that he would accommodate their views. Puritans expected greater consideration from a monarch brought up in their culture. Catholics hoped that a king whose wife was widely assumed to have privately converted to their faith, and who had commenced his reign by making peace with Spain, could prove amenable to a restoration of Roman practices.

Instead, James continued a 'broad church' policy intended to ensure that Anglicanism was acceptable to the majority, but in reality displeasing the hardline disciples of both Geneva and Rome for whom compromise represented a retreat from truth. Besides the role of bishops and the issue of predestination, other contentious matters included the more elaborate ceremonies and the vestments worn by Anglican clergy, which were anathema to evangelical Puritans. Imbued with an egalitarian ethos bent on reducing symbols of hierarchy between clergy and laity, they sought simplicity.

It was in the largely vain hope of reaching a lasting settlement on these and other

issues that in 1604 a conference was convened at Hampton Court by the king, his bishops and other prominent theologians. There, whilst making minor changes to the liturgy, they also agreed on something that was to prove a far more significant legacy: the need for a new translation of the Bible. After the failure to prevent Tyndale's translation of the New Testament being smuggled into Britain, a commission had been appointed charged with producing a legal version. Supervised by Miles Coverdale, this became the Great Bible of 1539. Yet neither it nor other versions, such as Archbishop Parker's 'Bishop's Bible', the Calvinist 'Geneva Bible' or – for underground Catholics – the 'Douai Bible', attracted overwhelming devotion. (The exception was in Scotland, where the Geneva Bible had become the standard text.)

Fifty-four revisers were appointed to produce the new version, among whom, at least forty-seven are known to have been actively engaged. Divided into sections, the work was undertaken by groups in Oxford, Cambridge and Westminster. The revisers were expected to follow most closely the Bishop's Bible; but it was Tyndale's style that remained the overwhelming influence. Nevertheless, some of his more controversial translations were reversed; for example, replacing 'congregation' by 'church' and 'love' by 'charity'.

The completed manuscript (subsequently lost) was bought by the king's printer for £3,500. Dedicated to King James I, it was published in 1611 in large bound folio volumes selling for 30 shillings, with the statement 'Appointed to be read in Churches' on its frontispiece. The copyright was held by the Crown, which in turn

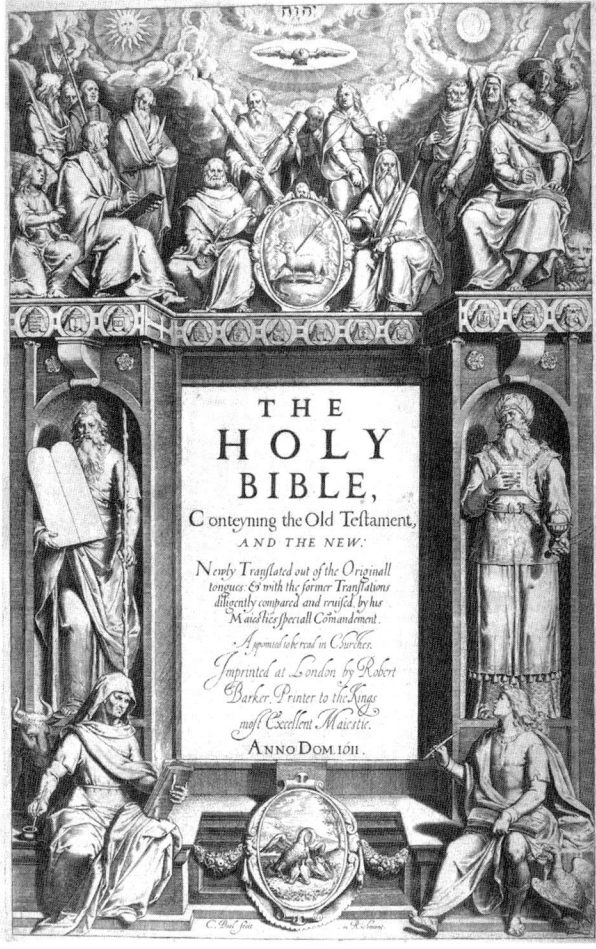

The frontispiece of the first King James Bible features the twelve apostles at the top with Matthew, Mark, Luke and John occupying each of the four corners accompanied by their symbolic animals. In the centre, Moses (left) and Aaron (right) flank the title.

licensed other printers, although, independently, the university presses of Oxford and Cambridge were also given the right to print it. Its official imprimatur ensured its familiar description as the 'Authorized Version'. This is misleading as it never had statutory sanction. However, such was the scale of adoption that the previous versions ceased to be printed, giving it a scriptural monopoly in Protestant worship throughout the British Isles.

In its first year, two versions appeared that became known respectively as the 'He Bible' and the 'She Bible' because of the different gender usage in Ruth 3:15. Subsequent editions decided that the disputed passage should read 'and she went into the citie'. Of the approximately 200 surviving copies of the first edition, about 150 are 'She Bibles'. A far worse discrepancy followed in an edition of 1631, which inadvertently omitted the word 'not' from the seventh commandment, thereby inviting Christians to commit adultery. The edition became known as the 'Wicked Bible'. Other minor infelicities marked out future editions, including one of 1717 that contained the 'parable of the vinegar' instead of 'the vineyard'.

These printers' errors, while beloved of antiquarian book collectors, should not detract from the accomplishment of the King James Bible. More than any other English-language translation, this was the version that endured, perpetuating Tyndale's style and fixing the rhythm of spoken and written English for generations thereafter. It also travelled to the American colonies, helping to wed the New World to similar patterns of speech.

Such was the achievement that in Britain the King James Bible lasted without challenge for over 250 years. Only towards the end of the nineteenth century was there an attempt to tinker with revision. More comprehensive rewrites followed in the twentieth century. Whilst these latest efforts may make greater claims to biblical scholarship and easy accessibility, they have too frequently produced mundane and unmemorable prose, lacking the striking authority of the King James Bible's stirring language and synonym. It is difficult to imagine that they will find the same enduring place in the popular consciousness.

1623
SHAKESPEARE'S FIRST FOLIO

THE PLAYS OF WILLIAM SHAKESPEARE
ARE SAVED FOR POSTERITY

Few of the plays performed on the Elizabethan stage have survived for future generations to enjoy. Most did not make it into print, their scripts never circulating beyond the circle of actors who performed them. From this environment, the name of William Shakespeare could easily have faded to the point where it endured only in a few casual archival references, the titles of his work principally remembered by specialists in theatrical history. Generations of visitors to Holy Trinity church in Stratford-upon-Avon might have walked past his monument, glancing only fleetingly at what they took to be merely one more impressive tribute to a forgotten local worthy.

That Shakespeare is, instead, recalled as one of the transforming geniuses of Western civilization owes much to two of his colleagues in the King's Men, the theatrical company for which he acted, wrote plays and owned shares in its Globe theatre in Southwark. It was John Heminges (allegedly the first actor to play Falstaff) and Henry Condell who decided after Shakespeare's death in 1616 that his plays should be collected in an expensively produced edition in a 'folio' page size. In doing so, they preserved most of his work from the ravages of time and memory.

In the year of Shakespeare's death, a folio of Ben Jonson's dramas was published. This in itself was an innovation and it provided a model that Heminges and Condell determined to follow. No play in Shakespeare's hand still exists, but the compilers of his folio were still in a position to assemble primary material – essential evidence that has subsequently perished. In particular, they gathered documents then still in the King's Men's possession, including the prompt cards from which the actors had first learned their lines.

Access to such original, but sadly ephemeral, records was crucially important, given that much of what had been printed of Shakespeare's work in his own lifetime was of degraded quality. Shakespeare had been commissioned to write

plays specifically for the King's Men and its predecessor, the Lord Chamberlain's Men. Without an effective dramatic copyright law, there had been little incentive to print and circulate his plays because doing so would have enabled rival companies to perform and benefit from his work, despite having not made the original investment in it. In consequence, most of the contemporary editions of his plays were unauthorized versions, badly printed, scarcely proof-read and put together either from notes or from the memories of those who had listened to them or had some hand in their production. Inevitably, they were far from accurate renditions. Errors ranged from garbled lines and serious misquotations to wholly fictitious efforts to fill gaps in lost recollection. Produced in cheap quarto (where the pages are created by twice-folding sheets of paper) paperback format, even

Title page of Shakespeare's First Folio. The note to the reader is by Shakespeare's fellow playwright Ben Jonson, and the engraving is by Martin Droeshout.

To the Reader.

This Figure, that thou here seeft put,
  It was for gentle Shakefpeare cut;
Wherein the Grauer had a ftrife
  with Nature, to out-doo the life :
O, could he but haue drawne his wit
  As well in braffe, as he hath hit
His face ; the Print would then furpaffe
  All, that vvas euer vvrit in braffe.
But, fince he cannot, Reader, looke
  Not on his Picture, but his Booke.

                              B. I.

Mr. WILLIAM
SHAKESPEARES
COMEDIES,
HISTORIES, &
TRAGEDIES.
Published according to the True Originall Copies.

LONDON
Printed by Ifaac Iaggard, and Ed. Blount. 1623.

these versions might not have survived had the production of the folio not ensured Shakespeare's longevity of reputation and, thus, a recognition that even debased and crumbling quarto versions were worth preserving.

It is thanks to the folio compilers' patient scholarship and quest for original sources that we are able to discern the scale of error in these so-called 'bad' quartos. In their opening address 'To the Great Variety of Readers', Heminges and Condell stated that they aimed to reproduce Shakespeare's plays 'as he conceived them' and would not be repeating the quartos' 'divers stolen and surreptitious copies, maimed and deformed by the frauds and stealths of injurious imposters'. It may be argued that a truly authentic reproduction cannot exist because of Shakespeare's understandable tendency to make changes or cuts and to add additional material over the course of successive productions. Nonetheless, the folio's compilers did their best to put together what their own experience and knowledge of Shakespeare's methods taught them were the most polished versions of his art.

The First Folio was published in 1623 and was dedicated to two influential brothers, the earls of Pembroke and Montgomery. Heminges and Condell claimed to be motivated 'without ambition either of self-profit or fame, only to keep the memory of so worthy a friend and fellow alive as was our Shakespeare'. Around 1,000 copies of the First Folio were printed, of which approximately 230 are still in existence, most of the latter incomplete. While five are in the care of the British Library, the largest collection is to be found in

A GOLDEN AGE OF ENGLISH DRAMA

1567 London's first purpose-built playhouse, the Red Lion, opens: it fails within a year.

1576 The Theatre opens in Shoreditch.

1577 The Curtain theatre opens in Shoreditch.

1587 The Rose theatre opens on Bankside, south of the city.

*c.*1588 Christopher Marlowe's *Tamburlaine the Great* is produced.

*c.*1589 Marlowe's *Doctor Faustus* is performed.

*c.*1590 Marlowe's *The Jew of Malta* is performed.

1592 Thomas Kyd's revenge drama *The Spanish Tragedy* is produced, as is Marlowe's *Edward II*.

1593 Marlowe is killed in a brawl.

1594 The Lord Chamberlain's Men is formed.

1597 A 'bad' quarto of Shakespeare's *Romeo and Juliet* is published; a 'good' quarto appears in 1599.

1599 The Globe opens next to The Rose at Bankside.

*c.*1600 Shakespeare's *Hamlet* is first produced.

1603 The Lord Chamberlain's Men become the King's Men.

*c.*1606 Shakespeare's *King Lear* and Ben Jonson's *Volpone* are staged.

1613 John Webster's *The Duchess of Malfi* is performed.

*c.*1613 *The Two Noble Kinsmen* is produced, the last play attributed, at least in part, to Shakespeare.

1614 The fire-damaged Globe is rebuilt.

1616 Shakespeare dies. Ben Jonson's works are published in folio.

1623 Shakespeare's First Folio is published.

Washington, DC, where the Folger Shakespeare Library is the repository of seventy-nine copies. At over 900 pages, copies were initially priced at twenty shillings (£1), a luxurious expense at that time. However, there were buyers, and subsequent editions followed in 1632, 1663, 1664 and 1685.

The First Folio contained thirty-six plays, eighteen of which had never previously been published and might otherwise have vanished for ever. *Twelfth Night, Julius Caesar* and *Macbeth* are among those the Folio saved for posterity. It omitted four plays generally attributed, at least in part, to Shakespeare: *Pericles, The Two Noble Kinsmen, Love's Labour's Won* and *Cardenio*, seemingly on the grounds that they were not purely his own work but rather the result of his collaboration with other playwrights. This is a misfortune since *Love's Labour's Won* and *Cardenio* are now lost to the world.

The title page was illustrated with an engraving of the author by Martin Droeshout, which has proved the source of much debate among those searching for hidden meaning in its slight idiosyncrasies. It is unlikely that the young Droeshout knew Shakespeare at first hand, but that his image should be approved by those who did know him makes it probably a reasonable likeness. It was, however, the tribute published in the Folio by Ben Jonson to 'thou star of poets' and the 'Sweet swan of Avon' that gave the most fitting perspective on the dead playwright's legacy:

> Triumph, my Britain, thou hast one to show
> To whom all scenes of Europe homage owe.
> He was not of an age, but for all time.

1628
THE PETITION OF RIGHT

THE COMMON LAW VERSUS ROYAL ABSOLUTISM

How absolute was the monarch's power? According to the theory of the divine right of kings, their rule was absolute because they were anointed by God to whom, alone, they were answerable. James I of England (and VI of Scotland) was so certain that this was the case that he wrote philosophical discourses on the subject. The issue was no abstract debate, for it went to the heart of whether the constitution offered any effective checks against arbitrary rule.

James had a useful servant in Francis Bacon (1561–1626), successively attorney-general and lord chancellor. Bacon believed that the judiciary's role was to uphold the king's law – that judges were 'lions under the throne', but James also had a determined and equally erudite opponent in Sir Edward Coke (1552–1634). A great advocate of the common law and the independence of the judiciary, Coke argued that the Crown did not enjoy unlimited rights and that it was the judiciary's duty to see that the monarchy exercised its powers only within the law. According to Coke, the king could not issue proclamations that created new laws nor contradict what had already been established by the common law. The son of a Norfolk barrister, Coke had been appointed chief justice of the Court of Common Pleas in 1606 and chief justice of the King's Bench in 1613. Three years later he was dismissed for refusing to do the king's bidding.

Supporters of Coke's views had little reason to cheer when, in 1625, James was succeeded by his son, aged just twenty-four. Charles I, who had inherited his father's belief in the divine right of kings, warned his politicians in 1626 shortly before dissolving the legislature, 'Remember that parliaments are altogether in my power for their calling, sitting, and dissolution; therefore, as I find the fruits good or evil, they are to continue, or not to be.'

The difficulty with this view was that the precedent was well established that taxation could be raised only through parliamentary consent. In pursuing

Overleaf: The Petition of Right. Specifying liberties of the individual that the king may not infringe, the Petition is one of the most significant documents in British constitutional history.

Soit droit fait come est desire.

Humbly shew vnto our Soveraigne Lord the King, The Lords Spirituall, [and]
of the Raigne of King Edward the first comonly called *Statutum de Tallagio non concedendo*
Arch Bishopps, Bishopps, Earles, Barons, Knights, Burgesses, and other the free men of the Como[n]
of King Edward the third, it is declared and enacted, That from thensforth noe person should
of the land. And by other Lawes of this Realme it is provided, That none should be charg[ed]
other then good Lawes and Statute of this Realme, yo[ur] Subiects haue inherited this freedome,
in Parliament. Yet neverthelesse of late divers Comissions directed to sondrie Comission[ers]
to lend certaine somes of money vnto yo[ur] Maiestie. And many of them vppon theire refusall h[ave]
been constreyned to become bound to make apparence, and giue attendance before your P[rivy Councell]
molested and disquieted. And divers other charges haue been layd and levyed vppon y[our people]
others by Commando or direction from your Maiestie or yo[ur] Privy Councell against the [lawes]
of England, It is declared and enacted that noe free man may be taken, or imprisoned,
but by the Lawfull Iudgement of his Peeres, or by the Lawe of the Land. And in the [twenty-eighth year of the reign]
Parliament. That noe man of what estate or condicion that he be, should be put [out of his lands or tenements, nor taken, nor imprisoned, nor disherited, nor put]
to answer by due processe of Lawe. Neverthelesse against the tenor of the said Stat[utes]
imprisoned, without any cause shewed, And when for theire deliveraunce they were brou[ght]
order, and theire keepers comanded to certifie the causes of theire detynor, noe cause was [certified]
yet were returned back to severall prisons without being charged with any thing to w[hich]
Marriners haue been disspersed into divers Counties of the Realme, And the inhabitants a[gainst]
Lawes and customes of this Realme, and to the greate greivaunce and vexation of the peo[ple]
the third, It is declared and enacted, That noe man should be foreiudged of life, or lymbe a[gainst]
Statute of this yo[ur] Realme, noe man ought to be adiudged to death, but by the Lawes estab[lished]
of what time soever is exempted from the proceedings to be vsed, and punishments to be inflicted
Seale haue issued forth, by which certaine persons haue been assigned and appointed Co[missioners]
Souldiers or Marriners, or other dissolute persons ioyning with them, as should comitt any [such]
agreeable to Martiall Lawe, and as is vsed in Armyes in tyme of warr, to proceede to the tria[ll]
By pretext whereof some of yo[ur] Maiesties Subiects haue been by some of the said Comissioners p[ut to death]
Statuts also they might, and by noe other ought to haue been iudged and executed. And all[so]
Lawes and Statute of this your Realme, by reason that divers of yo[ur] officers and ministers o[f Justice]
pretence that the said offenders were punishable onely by Martiall Lawe, and by authority
Lawes and Statuts of this your Realme

They doe therefore humbly pray yo[ur] most excellent maiestie [that no man]
by Act of Parliament. And that none be called to m[ake answer]
for refusall thereof. And that noe freeman in any such manne[r]
Marriners, And that your people may not be soe burthened in [tyme to come]
hereafter noe Comissions of like nature may issue forth to [any person]
or putt to death, contrary to the Lawes and franchise of th[is Realme]
All which they most humbly pray of yo[ur] most excellent M[aiestie]
vouchsafe to declare, that the Awards doeinge and [execution]
And that your Maiestie would be allso gratiously pleased, [for the further comfort and safety of your people, to declare your royall will and pleasure, that in the things aforesaid all your officers]
and Ministers shall serve you according to the Lawes and [Statutes of this Realme]

Kings most Excellent Maiestie

Comons in Parliament assembled. That whereas it is declared and enacted by a Statute made in the tyme
... or Ayde should be layde, or levyed by the King or his heires in this Realme, without the good will and assent of the
realme. And by authoritie of Parliament houlden in the five and twentith yeare of the raigne
... make any Loanes to the King against his will, because such loanes were against reason and the franchise
... or imposicon called a Benevolence, nor by such like charge. By which the Statutes before mencioned, and
... not be compelled to contribute to any Taxe Tallage Ayde or other like charge not sett by comon consent
... Countries haue issued. By meanes whereof your people haue been in divers places assembled, and required
... an oath administred unto them not warrantable by the Lawes or Statutes of this Realme, and haue
... and in other places, and others of them haue been therefore imprisoned, confined, and sondry other wayes
... rall Counties by Lord Lieftenante Deputie Lieftenante, Commissioners for Musters Justice of Peace and
... customes of the Realme. And where also by the Statute called the Greate Charter of the liberties
... of his freehould or liberties, or his free customes, or be outlawed, or exiled, or in any manner destroyed
... entith yeare of the raigne of King Edward the third It was declared and enacted by authoritie of
... or tenements, nor taken nor imprisoned nor disherited, nor putt to death without beinge brought
... he good Lawes and Statute of yo Realme to that end provided, divers of your Subiects haue of late been
... Iustice, by yo Maiesties writte of Habeas corpus there to undergoe and receiue as the Court should
... they were detayned by yo Maiesties speciall comaund signified by the Lords of yo Privy Counsell, and
... make answer according to the Lawe. And whereas of late greate Companyes of Souldiers and
... haue been compelled to receiue them into their houses, and there to suffer them to soiourne against the
... or whereas also by authoritie of Parliament, in the five and twentith yeare of the raigne of King Edward
... of the Great Charter and the Lawe of the land. And by the said Greate Charter and other the Lawes and
Realme, either by the customes of the same Realme, or by Acte of Parliament. And whereas no offender
... Statute of this your Realme. Neverthelesse of late tyme divers Commissions under yo Maiesties Greate
... power, and authoritie to proceede within the land according to the Justice of Martiall Lawe against such
... felony, mutiny, or other outrage or misdemeanor whatsoever, and by such summary course and order as is
... ation of such offenders, and them to cause to be executed and putt to death according to the Lawe Martiall
... in, and where if by the Lawes and Statutes of the land they had deserved death; by the same Lawes and
... no offenders by culler thereof, clayming an exemption haue escaped the punishmente due to them by the
... iustly refused, or forborne to proceede against such offenders according to the same Lawes and Statutes, upon
... as aforesaid. Which Commissions, and all other of like nature are wholly and directly contrary to the said

... eafter be compelled to make or yeild any guiffe, loane, benevolence, tax or such like charge without comon consent
... le such oath, or to giue attendance, or be confined, or otherwise molested, or disquieted concerning the same, or
... noned be imprisoned or detayned. And that yo Maiestie would be pleased to remoue the said Souldiers, and
... And that the aforesaid Commissions for proceeding by Martiall Lawe may be revoked and annulled. And that
... ond whatsoever to be executed as aforesaid, least by culler of them any of yo Maiesties Subiects be destroyed

... ights and liberties according to the Lawes and Statutes of this Realme. And that yo Maiestie would allso
... prejudice of your people in any of the premisses, shall not be drawne hereafter into consequence or example
... fort, and safetie of yo people to declare yo Royall will and pleasure That in the thinge aforesaid all yo officers
... as they tender the honor of yo Maiestie, and the prosperitie of this Kingdome

From the Petition of Right, 1628

To the King's most excellent Majesty: Humbly shew unto our sovereign lord the king, the lords spiritual and temporal, and commons, in parliament assembled, that whereas it is declared and enacted by a statute made in the time of the reign of King Edward the First, commonly called *Statutum de tallagio non concedendo*, that no tallage or aid shall be laid or levied by the King or his heirs in this realm, without the goodwill and assent of the archbishops, bishops, earls, barons, knights, burgesses and other the freemen of the commonalty of this realm; and by the authority of parliament holden in the five and twentieth year of the reign of King Edward the Third, it is declared and enacted, that from thenceforth no person should be compelled to make any loans to the king against his will, because such loans were against reason and the franchise of the land; and by other laws of this realm it is provided, that none should be charged by any charge or imposition called a benevolence, nor by such like charge; by which the statutes before mentioned, and other the good laws and statutes of this realm, your subjects have inherited this freedom, that they should not be compelled to contribute to any tax, tallage, aid or other like charge not set by common consent in parliament. ...

And where also by the statute called *The Great Charter of the Liberties of England*, it is declared and enacted, that no freeman may be taken or imprisoned, or be disseised of his freehold or liberties, or his free customs, or be outlawed or exiled, or in any manner destroyed, but by the lawful judgment of his peers, or by the law of the land.

And in the eight and twentieth year of the reign of King Edward the Third, it was declared and enacted by authority of parliament, that no man of what estate or condition that he be, should be put out of his land or tenements, nor taken, nor imprisoned, nor disherited, nor put to death, without being brought to answer by due process of law.

Nevertheless against the tenor of the said statutes, and other the good laws and statutes of your realm to that end provided, divers of your subjects have of late been imprisoned without any cause shewed ...

They do therefore humbly pray your most excellent majesty, that no man hereafter be compelled to make or yield any gift, loan, benevolence, tax or such like charge, without common consent by act of parliament; and that none be called to make answer, or take such oath, or to give attendance, or be confined, or otherwise molested or disquieted concerning the same, or for refusal

thereof; and that no freeman, in any such manner as is before mentioned, be imprisoned or detained; and that your majesty would be pleased to remove the said soldiers and mariners; and that your people may not be so burthened in time to come; and that the aforesaid Commissions for proceeding by martial law, may be revoked and annulled; and that hereafter no commissions of like nature may issue forth to any person or persons whatsoever to be executed as aforesaid, lest by colour of them any of your majesty's subjects be destroyed, or put to death contrary to the laws and franchise of the land.

an expensive and misbegotten war against Spain, Charles was badly in need of revenue. He therefore dreamed up an alternative means of getting hold of the money by demanding that a loan be forcibly extracted from taxpayers, equal to what he believed Parliament should have guaranteed. Those who refused to pay risked imprisonment. What was unclear was whether this kind of royal demand to pay up or be locked up was legal. Five detainees launched a test case by deploying a writ of habeas corpus, challenging the Crown's right to imprison them without due process, but the courts failed to uphold this most important provision of Magna Carta. Whatever might have been the case previously, it now seemed that Charles I did enjoy the right not only to detain his subjects without due legal process but also to raise revenue from them without the consent of their representatives in Parliament.

The 1628 general election made apparent voters' concerns at this apparent constitutional revolution. A House of Commons was returned that set about challenging untrammelled royal authority. The king's response was to try to bluff it out, claiming that because he observed existing statutes there was no need to have them restated in a new Act of Parliament. Unperturbed, Sir Edward Coke – by now MP for Buckinghamshire and seventy-six years old – proposed that both Houses of Parliament should unite in issuing a Petition of Right. This was an ancient device in which individuals could appeal to the king to reverse a perceived wrongdoing by him or his court. Parliament's petition aimed to make clear that its rights, as well as those of the people, needed defending. It asserted that no one should be forced to pay tax or make a loan without the explicit sanction of Parliament; that habeas corpus and Magna Carta still had legal force, which meant that no one should be detained without due cause having

been demonstrated; that no one should have soldiers or sailors billeted in their property against their will; and that there should be no future commissions for proceeding by martial law.

Charles might have been tempted to ignore the opinion of the House of Commons, but the support lent to its petition by the House of Lords meant indifference was scarcely an option. Reluctantly, he signed his assent across the top of the document with the traditional French phrase used since Norman times, *Soit droit fait come est desire* (in English 'Let right be done as desired'). The petition's drafters, which included Coke, Sir John Eliot and John Pym, argued that they were not seeking new powers, merely clarifying ancient rights – a very English approach to justifying revolt. Charles played them at a similar game, in effect agreeing to the document because it claimed to change nothing. He addressed Parliament prior to proroguing it, in a speech that qualified his assent: 'The profession of both houses, in time of hammering this Petition, was no ways to intrench upon my prerogative, saying, they had neither intention nor power to hurt it. Therefore it must needs be conceived that I have granted no new, but only confirmed the ancient liberties of my subjects.'

Subsequent events soon demonstrated that Charles had no intention of abiding by the Petition of Right, regardless of whether it affirmed old wisdom or heralded new thinking. He prorogued Parliament in 1629 and did not call it again for another eleven years. Sir John Eliot, the leader of the opposition in the Commons, was sent to the Tower of London, where he languished until his death in 1632. Coke died in 1634, shortly after the king's officials had ransacked his home and removed manuscripts, including those he had been writing for his *Institutes of the Laws of England*, a magisterial exposition of the common law.

In the short term, the Petition of Right's only success was in putting an end to the innovation of forced loans. From a longer perspective however, it was a defining document in the history of Britain, drawing a line that monarchs crossed at the risk of being accused of acting unconstitutionally. By heedlessly crossing that line, Charles I proceeded down a path that plunged his kingdoms into civil war and brought about his own execution. When his son, James II, repeated the mistake, a second revolution ensued that dealt a death blow to royal absolutism in Britain.

1638

THE SCOTTISH NATIONAL COVENANT

SCOTLAND'S PLEDGE TO DEFEND PRESBYTERIANISM
AGAINST CHARLES I'S EFFORTS TO ANGLICIZE THE KIRK

D espite being born in Dunfermline, Charles I had little feeling for Scotland. Although he had succeeded to its throne, alongside that of England, in 1625, it took him eight years to venture north to Edinburgh for his coronation as the nation's king. Whilst his casual attitude did not go unnoticed, it was in the matter of his northern kingdom's religious traditions that he demonstrated the most fatal disregard.

The Scottish National Covenant is depicted in the third plate section.

Charles's father had imposed bishops upon the 'Kirk' (as the Church of Scotland was widely known), but had fallen short of forcing total religious uniformity across his politically disunited kingdoms. Charles, who had inherited his father's belief in royal 'divine right' without any of James's canny pragmatism, was determined to ensure that his will would be done throughout Scotland's churches. Moreover, he chose to do so at the very moment that his archbishop of Canterbury, William Laud, was taking Anglicanism along a path of increased 'High Church' ritualism, which to English Puritans and Scottish Presbyterians alike seemed indistinguishable from the Catholic Mass.

In 1637, Charles made a Scottish edition of the Book of Common Prayer mandatory across Scotland, without first securing the approval of the Kirk's General Assembly. It was an incendiary provocation. The new liturgy's introduction was met with a barrage of abuse and hurled stools, which was just the beginning. Charles, rather than beat a retreat, regarded the criticism as evidence of political treason.

The king's determination to press ahead met with one of the most extraordinary documents in Scottish history. Scotland's Calvinists were imbued with the notion that, like the Israelites, they had a bond with God and were his chosen people.

Consequently, a 'National Covenant' was signed on 28 February 1638 in a four-hour ceremony in front of the pulpit of Greyfriars church in Edinburgh. From there, it was taken to the Tailor's Hall in the Cowgate where it was signed by church ministers and town dignitaries. Then it was the turn of the townsfolk to sign, men and women, before copies were made and taken across the country. By the time the process was complete, a majority of the Scottish nobility and a third of the country's clergy had signed the covenant. Some did so in their own blood.

At first reading, the covenant's language appears conservatively worded, asserting its constitutionalism rather than revolutionary demands. This is at least partly misleading. Although it was largely drafted by the clergyman Alexander Hamilton in conjunction with Archibald Johnston of Wariston – a Calvinistic lawyer of the most unbending hue – it was designed to keep united all of the opponents of Charles's anglicizing policy. Given Presbyterianism's love of argument, this could not have been achieved if it had sought to prescribe a tightly defined doctrinal line beyond precedents already set. It nonetheless enshrined the central issue: that the Kirk's doctrine should be determined not by the monarch but by its own General Assembly and the Scottish Parliament.

In November 1638, the Kirk's General Assembly duly gathered in Glasgow without royal sanction. There it renounced both prayer book and bishops, and effectively declared ecclesiastic independence from royal interference. Protestant Scotland stood ready to defend the Calvinist settlement it had established in 1560. Charles would not tolerate such insubordination. 'So long as this Covenant is in force,' he had written five months previously, 'I have no more Power in Scotland than as a Duke of Venice.'

During 1639, the Covenanters raised a sizeable army, funded by two opposing factions – the Scots Kirk and the Scottish nobility – whom it had taken the king's monumental mishandling to finally bring together. In training as well as in morale, it was superior to the 18,000-strong force that Charles sent north to impose his theological will. A military stand-off ensued while Charles conceded the right of both the General Assembly and the Scottish Parliament to convene. The stalemate also granted him time to muster his resources. During the subsequent months, he took decisions that not only helped plunge his kingdoms into civil war but also ultimately sealed his own fate.

Since 1629, Charles had ruled without Parliament at Westminster but in 1640 the need to raise the taxes necessary to prosecute his Scottish campaign forced him to summon it again. When it proved hostile and unwilling to do his business, he

quickly suspended it once more. Defeat soon turned to disaster when the Royalists lost a skirmish at Newburn, allowing the Scots Covenanter army to occupy Newcastle, from where they could block coal supplies. Charles was compelled to offer humiliating terms.

His authority was now crumbling in all three kingdoms. Conflict in Ireland and a second failure to receive parliamentary support at Westminster proved to be the prelude to the outbreak of the Civil War in 1642. The following year, the English Parliamentarians and the Scots Covenanters formed an alliance, called the 'Solemn League and Covenant'. In return for Scottish military assistance, Parliament promised to abolish episcopacy and reform the church in England and Ireland along Presbyterian lines. This assistance proved of great value, particularly at the Battle of Marston Moor in 1644. With Parliament's victory on the battlefield, its pledge to introduce Presbyterian reforms across Britain was honoured.

Although the Covenanters may not have recognized Charles I's right to guide their Church, they were opposed to his execution. With his death, they speedily endorsed his son, Charles II, as king of Scotland, provoking invasion and defeat at the hands of Oliver Cromwell's well-drilled soldiers. Further disappointment ensued. Upon his restoration, Charles II quickly showed himself no friend of Presbyterianism. In 1662, he re-established episcopalianism in Scotland as well as in England, and 300 ministers of the Kirk were removed. Barred from their churches, Covenanter clergy took to meeting clandestinely in outdoor 'Conventicles', risking prosecution and transportation.

In 1679, Greyfriars church again became the Covenanters' meeting ground when 1,200 of them were imprisoned in its kirkyard, pending trial. What ultimately saved their cause was William of Orange's victory in the Glorious Revolution. In 1690, Parliament finally re-established Presbyterianism as the governing theology of Scotland's Established Church.

1647
THE RECORD OF
THE PUTNEY DEBATES

THE NEW MODEL ARMY DEBATES UNIVERSAL
MANHOOD SUFFRAGE

S hould all men by given the vote? Is property theft? These were the issues
that shaped the ideologies of the nineteenth and twentieth centuries, but
they were debated at a senior level long before they became the rallying
calls of Victorian radicals or revolutionary Marxists. In 1647 they were seriously
considered at Putney, when the New Model Army met to decide what to do with
its victory in the Civil War.

The fact that power was by then in the hands of army officers demonstrated
how far five years of warfare had undermined the traditional institutions of Crown
and Parliament. Although civil war between King Charles I and his parliamentary
opponents had broken out in 1642, it was not until the early, indifferent leadership
of the earls of Essex and Manchester gave way to the more skilful generalship of Sir
Thomas Fairfax and Oliver Cromwell that the Parliamentarians gained the upper
hand. The highly trained New Model Army that Fairfax and Cromwell created
proved to be far more than just a disciplined fighting force. Up from its ranks came
a new cadre of men, often from artisan backgrounds, who were literate, sure of
themselves and motivated by religious and political radicalism.

Parliamentarians whose war aims were limited to a mere clipping of royal
excesses began wondering whether they had created a monster they could no
longer control. In April 1645, the Self-Denying Ordinance was passed, preventing any MP or peer from holding command in the New Model Army. Oliver
Cromwell, the MP for Cambridge, was one of the few politicians exempted from
this prohibition on account of his obvious military ability. The stated intention
was to prevent the squabbling of politicians from impairing the performance
of the armed forces, but it also helped to sever the bond between Parliament

and its soldiers. Civil war had transferred power to the barrel of the musket.

In June 1645, the New Model Army proved its effectiveness by crushing the Royalist forces at the Battle of Naseby. Bristol, England's second city, fell in September. Trapped at Oxford, Charles weighed his diminishing options and opted to surrender himself to the Scottish Covenanter forces at Newark in May 1646. In January 1647, the Scots handed him over to Parliament in return for £400,000. It was now up to the politicians to decide how far to take the revolution that the army had won for them. They soon found this prerogative questioned. Suspicious of the politicians' intentions, and angry at the arrears in their pay, the army set up its own General Council, composed of officers and 'agitators' elected from the ranks of common soldiers. Radicals in this General Council believed that they had a better mandate to shape the revolution settlement than those who sat, by grace of a limited franchise, at Westminster.

Frightened, Parliament tried to disband the army only to find it refusing to disperse. Indeed it made clear, ominously, that it was not 'a mere mercenary army, hired to serve an arbitrary power of state'. Seizing custody of the king, it marched on London. With these moves, the army appeared to hold all the cards: it had the weapons, the king, the capital and, with London, the funds. The issue was now what it should do with this power.

The circulation of rival demands indicated the gulf of opinion. The gentry members in the high command had taken up arms to prevent Charles I's destruction of what they viewed as the ancient constitution. They were not interested in the sweeping social and political reforms insisted upon by the more egalitarian-minded agitators, the Levellers. The latter claimed they had fought not merely to free the gentry from the constraints of royal power but for their own rights too. They wanted democracy, demanding that all men (women were not discussed) over the age of twenty-one should be given the vote to elect a new Parliament every two years.

In October and November 1647 the two sides slogged it out – with words rather than swords – when the Army Council met at St Mary's church in Putney, in today's South London. Fortunately, stenographers, led by William Clarke, were engaged to take the minutes and their transcripts (subsequently lost until being found at Worcester College, Oxford, in 1890) provide a detailed account of one of the most fundamental debates in British history.

The Levellers' argument was most eloquently put by Colonel Thomas Rainsborough, who insisted, 'I think that the poorest he that is in England hath a

From the Putney Debates, 1647

John Wildman

Our case is to be considered thus, that we have been under slavery. That's acknowledged by all. Our very laws were made by our conquerors; and whereas it's spoken much of chronicles, I conceive there is no credit to be given to any of them; and the reason is because those that were our lords, and made us their vassals, would suffer nothing else to be chronicled. We are now engaged for our freedom. That's the end of Parliaments: not to constitute what is already [established, but to act] according to the just rules of government. Every person in England hath as clear a right to elect his representative as the greatest person in England. I conceive that's the undeniable maxim of government: that all government is in the free consent of the people. If [so], then upon that account there is no person that is under a just government, or hath justly his own, unless he by his own free consent be put under that government. This he cannot be unless he be consenting to it, and therefore, according to this maxim, there is never a person in England [but ought to have a voice in elections]. If [this], as that gentleman says, be true, there are no laws that in this strictness and rigour of justice [any man is bound to], that are not made by those who[m] he doth consent to. And therefore I should humbly move, that if the question be stated — which would soonest bring things to an issue — it might rather be thus: Whether any person can justly be bound by law, who doth not give his consent that such persons shall make laws for him?

Commissary-General Henry Ireton

Let the question be so: Whether a man can be bound to any law that he doth not consent to? And I shall tell you, that he may and ought to be [bound to a law] that he doth not give a consent to, nor doth not choose any [to consent to]; and I will make it clear. If a foreigner come within this kingdom, if that stranger will have liberty [to dwell here] who hath no local interest here, he, as a man, it's true, hath air, [the passage of highways, the protection of laws, and all] that by nature; we must not expel [him from] our coasts, give him no being amongst us, nor kill him because he comes upon our land, comes up our stream, arrives at our shore. It is a piece of hospitality, of humanity, to receive that man amongst us. But if that man be received to a being amongst us, I think that man may very well be content to submit himself to the law of the land; that is, the law that is made by those people that have a property, a fixed property, in the land. I think, if any man will receive protection from this people though [neither] he nor his ancestors, not any betwixt him and

Adam, did ever give concurrence to this constitution, I think this man ought to be subject to those laws, and to be bound by those laws, so long as he continues amongst them. That is my opinion. A man ought to be subject to a law, that did not give his consent, but with this reservation, that if this man do think himself unsatisfied to be subject to this law he may go into another kingdom. And so the same reason doth extend, in my understanding, [to] that man that hath no permanent interest in the kingdom. If he hath money, his money is as good in another place as here; he hath nothing that doth locally fix him to this kingdom. If that man will live in this kingdom, or trade amongst us, that man ought to subject himself to the law made by the people who have the interest of this kingdom in them. And yet I do acknowledge that which you take to be so general a maxim, that in every kingdom, within every land, the original of power of making laws, of determining what shall be law in the land, does lie in the people – [but by the people is meant those] that are possessed of the permanent interest in the land. But whoever is extraneous to this, that is, as good a man in another land, that man ought to give such a respect to the property of men that live in the land. They do not determine [that I shall live in this land]. Why should I have any interest in determining what shall be the law of this land?

Major William Rainsborough

I think if it can be made to appear that it is a just and reasonable thing, and that it is for the preservation of all the [native] freeborn men, [that they should have an equal voice in election] – I think it ought to be made good unto them. And the reason is: that the chief end of this government is to preserve persons as well as estates, and if any law shall take hold of my person it is more dear than my estate.

Colonel Thomas Rainsborough

I do very well remember that the gentleman in the window [Colonel Rich] [said] that, if it were so, there were no propriety to be had, because five parts of [the nation], the poor people, are now excluded and would then come in. So one on the other side said [that], if [it were] otherwise, then rich men [only] shall be chosen. Then, I say, the one part shall make hewers of wood and drawers of water of the other five, and so the greatest part of the nation be enslaved. Truly I think we are still where we were; and I do not hear any argument given but only that it is the present law of the kingdom. I say still, what shall become of those many [men] that have laid out themselves for the Parliament of England in this present war, that have ruined themselves by fighting, by hazarding all they had? They are Englishmen. They have now nothing to say for themselves.

life to live, as the greatest he; and therefore truly, sir, I think it's clear, that every man that is to live under a government ought first by his own consent to put himself under that government.' The notion was anathema to Cromwell and his son-in-law, General Henry Ireton, who did not see why those without what Ireton called 'an interest or share' (in other words, property and commerce) should frame the laws of those who did have such a stake. Here was the crux of what became – 200 years later – the defining issue of parliamentary reform in the nineteenth century: was the franchise a universal right or a trust placed in those responsible for business and property?

Rainsborough denied Ireton's assertion that he intended anarchy. However, the Utopian, proto-communist statements of some of the Levellers were sufficient to convince moderates that a society of complete equality was their aim. Indeed, an extreme Leveller movement, 'the Diggers', was poised to begin occupying enclosed land and claiming it as the common property of all. It was a fate that Colonel Nathaniel Rich foresaw if Rainsborough's demands for democracy were met, since, he said, in an electorate in which servants greatly outnumbered masters, 'It may happen, that the majority may by law, not in a confusion, destroy property; there may be a law enacted, that there shall be an equality of goods and estates.'

Cromwell tired of a discussion that seemed to be extending the scope for future division rather than solving the immediate concerns – not least what to do with the king, whose brief escape from custody provided a timely reason to bring the conference to a close before it had reached agreement. The Putney Debates were duly postponed and although the Army Council met again in January 1648, the experiment in army democracy was ended – although the arguments raised continued to resonate for centuries to come.

During 1648, the gentry officers remained in control and Rainsborough was killed while besieging Pontefract. In May 1649, an attempted mutiny by army agitators was put down at Burford. However, by then, one of their most arresting demands had been realized: England was a republic.

1649

THE DEATH WARRANT
OF KING CHARLES I

THE EXECUTION OF THE KING

Victorious in the Second Civil War, the Parliamentarian forces took Charles I captive. Whatever hopes may have been entertained that he could be prevailed upon to accept terms for an enduring peace were undermined by his duplicity and efforts to escape. Furthermore, some of his more war-weary opponents were now suspected of being over-ready to compromise. New divisions had opened up because the war had made the army, not Parliament, the greatest power in the land. Influential army officers were concerned that Westminster's politicians might negotiate away the rights that the soldiers believed they had won with their swords. Beheading the king seemed the surest way of avoiding defeat being snatched from the jaws of victory.

Creating the enabling legal process proved difficult, as insufficient support existed for it in Parliament. Thus, to get the necessary numbers, soldiers were posted at Westminster to forcibly exclude those MPs assumed to be hostile. Shorn of the vast majority of its members, the resulting 'Rump Parliament' duly passed an ordinance bringing the king to trial. The opposition of the House of Lords was overcome by ignoring it altogether. In this way, those who had championed the rights of Parliament got their own way by subverting the laws of Parliament.

Trial proceedings began on 20 January 1649 in Westminster Hall. The charges against the king – now ominously described as 'Charles Stuart' – included that he 'hath traitorously and maliciously levied war against the present Parliament, and the people therein represented'. The case was to be heard by 135 commissioners, sitting as a High Court of Justice, although less than half of them had agreed to serve. The verdict was scarcely in doubt. The trial lasted for seven days during which Charles refused to recognize the court's legitimacy and, in turn, was not permitted to address it at length.

Charles I's death warrant is depicted in the third plate section.

THE CIVIL WARS

The First Civil War

1642

22 August Charles I raises his standard at Nottingham, declaring war on Parliament.

23 October The first major battle at Edgehill in Warwickshire ends in a stalemate.

1643

26 July Royalists take England's second city, Bristol.

20 September Parliamentary forces under the earl of Essex win the first Battle of Newbury.

25 September The Solemn League and Covenant creates an alliance between Parliament and the Scots Covenanters.

1644

2 July At Marston Moor, west of York, the Royalist forces are heavily defeated by a combined Scots and Parliamentarian force and Oliver Cromwell demonstrates his ability as a cavalry commander.

22 October The second Battle of Newbury ends in a draw.

1645

6 January Parliament creates a full-time professional force, the New Model Army, under the command of Sir Thomas Fairfax.

14 June The decisive battle of the war is fought at Naseby in Northamptonshire, where Royalist forces are crushed.

11 September Parliamentarian forces retake Bristol.

13 September The marquess of Montrose's Royalist army in Scotland is defeated at the Battle of Philiphaugh.

1646

6 May Charles I hands himself over to the Scots at Newark.

24 June Oxford, the Royalist capital, surrenders.

1647

30 January The Scots hand Charles I over to Parliament. He escapes in November to the Isle of Wight.

The Second Civil War

1648

17 August Cromwell defeats a joint Scots–Royalist invading force at Preston.

19 December Charles I is arrested by the army and returned to London.

1649

30 January Following a swift trial, Charles I is executed.

The Third Civil War

11 September During his Irish campaign, Cromwell's forces massacre the garrison at Drogheda.

1650

3 September Cromwell routs, at Dunbar, the Scottish army loyal to Prince Charles.

1651

3 September Royalist and Scottish forces are defeated by Cromwell at Worcester.

13 October Prince Charles flees to France.

He was sentenced on 27 January. It remains a point of dispute among historians whether the warrant for his execution had been drawn up shortly before or immediately after the sentencing. Certainly, blanks were left for the date and place of execution to be filled in later, and the names of two of the three army officers to whom the warrant was issued had to be changed. It has been speculated that this was because two of the original choices refused to be involved, although authoritative evidence is lacking that the regicides had already begun signing their names even before sentence was passed. Nonetheless, not all the signatures (which were accompanied by individual seals in red wax) were written in a single session. There was a short delay after the first twenty-eight had been added and it was subsequently suggested that some of the second batch of regicides appended their names under duress. It would certainly be convenient for them to later make this claim.

Fifty-nine of the commissioners who had pronounced Charles guilty signed the warrant. The first to sign was John Bradshaw, the presiding judge at the trial. Oliver Cromwell signed third. Other notable Parliamentarian commanders who followed

Contemporary engraving of Charles I's execution outside his Banqueting Hall in Whitehall.

included Henry Ireton (who was Cromwell's son-in-law), John Hutchinson and Thomas Harrison. Noticeable absentees included the army's commander-in-chief, Sir Thomas Fairfax, who had fought to uphold the rights of Parliament, not to kill the king.

On 30 January, Charles duly stepped out through a window of the Banqueting House at Whitehall onto a specially erected scaffold. He was allowed a farewell statement to the public spectators, although his voice did not carry far enough beyond the deep ranks of soldiers encircling the stage. He assured them of his innocence without reneging on the belief in divine right that had got him and his realm into much of the trouble in the first place. 'A subject and a sovereign are clean different things,' he maintained, before announcing that 'I go from a corruptible to an incorruptible Crown.' When the axe severed his head, the crowd responded not with a cheer but a groan. It was an early sign that his enemies had succeeded only in making a martyr out of him.

Within eleven years the republic that replaced Charles's kingship had foundered. At the monarchy's restoration in 1660, the Convention Parliament passed an Act of Indemnity and Oblivion, offering a general pardon to those who had taken up arms against the late king. The exceptions were the regicides. Of the fifty-nine who had signed the death warrant, thirty-nine were still alive. Some sensibly fled, either to the continent or to the American colonies. Those the state could get its hands on were all either executed or imprisoned for life, save for Richard Ingoldsby. Alone of the captured regicides, he escaped punishment when his claim to have signed under duress was accepted.

After execution, Charles I's remains had been interred next to those of Henry VIII in the vault of St George's Chapel at Windsor Castle. With the Restoration, however, the bodies of Cromwell and Ireton were disinterred from Westminster Abbey and, along with the remains of Bradshaw, were publicly hanged and desecrated. Like that of Charles I, Cromwell's head was severed from its body. It was placed on a pike outside Westminster Hall, where it remained for over twenty years, not finding a final resting place until 1960 when it was laid to rest at his old college, Sidney Sussex, Cambridge. Even then, over 300 years after the Civil War, it was deemed safest if the sole identifiable remains of the great regicide should lie in an unmarked grave.

1653

THE INSTRUMENT
OF GOVERNMENT

BRITAIN'S FIRST – AND SHORT-LIVED –
WRITTEN CONSTITUTION

On 4 January 1649, the House of Commons adopted a revolutionary philosophy, voting:

> That the people are, under God, the original of all just power: … that the commons of England, in parliament assembled, being chosen by, and representing, the people, have the supreme power in this nation: … that whatsoever is enacted, or declared for law, by the commons, in parliament assembled, hath the force of law; and all the people of this nation are concluded thereby, although the consent and concurrence of king, or house of peers be not had thereunto.

Within weeks, the king had been executed and the Commons had moved 'that the house of peers in parliament is useless and dangerous, and ought to be abolished'. This assertion was carried into law on 19 March, two days after the legislation was passed formally created a republic.

The reality fell short of what was implied by these highly democratic proclamations. The House of Commons may have gained untrammelled legislative power, but its claim to represent 'the people' was a nonsense. It merely consisted of those MPs whose perceived ideological purity to the revolution meant the army had permitted them to attend. Rather than submit themselves to the popular will, the surviving MPs contrived every means possible to prevent the calling of a general election. Eventually, Oliver Cromwell, tiring of their self-serving ways, marched his troops into the Commons chamber on 20 April 1653 and closed Parliament down.

From the Instrument of Government, 1653

The government of the Commonwealth of England, Scotland, and Ireland, and the dominions thereunto belonging.

I. That the supreme legislative authority of the Commonwealth of England, Scotland, and Ireland, and the dominions thereunto belonging, shall be and reside in one person, and the people assembled in Parliament; the style of which person shall be the Lord Protector of the Commonwealth of England, Scotland, and Ireland.

II. That the exercise of the chief magistracy and the administration of the government over the said countries and dominions, and the people thereof, shall be in the Lord Protector, assisted with a council, the number whereof shall not exceed twenty-one, nor be less than thirteen.

III. That all writs, processes, commissions, patents, grants, and other things, which now run in the name and style of the keepers of the liberty of England by authority of Parliament, shall run in the name and style of the Lord Protector, from whom, for the future, shall be derived all magistracy and honours in these three nations; and have the power of pardons (except in case of murders and treason) and benefit of all forfeitures for the public use; and shall govern the said countries and dominions in all things by the advice of the council, and according to these presents and the laws.

IV. That the Lord Protector, the Parliament sitting, shall dispose and order the militia and forces, both by sea and land, for the peace and good of the three nations, by consent of Parliament; and that the Lord Protector, with the advice and consent of the major part of the council, shall dispose and order the militia for the ends aforesaid in the intervals of Parliament.

V. That the Lord Protector, by the advice aforesaid, shall direct in all things concerning the keeping and holding of a good correspondency with foreign kings, princes, and states; and also, with the consent of the major part of the council, have the power of war and peace.

VI. That the laws shall not be altered, suspended, abrogated, or repealed, nor any new law made, nor any tax, charge, or imposition laid upon the people, but by common consent in Parliament, save only as is expressed in the thirtieth article.

VII. That there shall be a Parliament summoned to meet at Westminster upon the third day of September, 1654, and that successively a Parliament shall be summoned once in every third year, to be accounted from the dissolution of the present Parliament.

VIII. That neither the Parliament to be next summoned, nor any successive Parliaments, shall, during the time of five months, to be accounted from the day of their first meeting, be adjourned, prorogued, or dissolved, without their own consent. . . .

XIII. That the Sheriff, who shall wittingly and willingly make any false return, or neglect his duty, shall incur the penalty of 2000 marks of lawful English money; the one moiety to the Lord Protector, and the other moiety to such person as will sue for the same.

XIV. That all and every person and persons, who have aided, advised, assisted, or abetted in any war against the Parliament, since the first day of January, 1641 (unless they have been since in the service of the Parliament, and given signal testimony of their good affection thereunto) shall be disabled and incapable to be elected, or to give any vote in the election of any members to serve in the next Parliament, or in the three succeeding Triennial Parliaments.

XV. That all such, who have advised, assisted, or abetted the rebellion of Ireland, shall be disabled and incapable for ever to be elected, or give any vote in the election of any member to serve in Parliament; as also all such who do or shall profess the Roman Catholic religion.

XVI. That all votes and elections given or made contrary, or not according to these qualifications, shall be null and void; and if any person, who is hereby made incapable, shall give his vote for election of members to serve in Parliament, such person shall lose and forfeit one full year's value of his real estate, and one full third part of his personal estate; one moiety thereof to the Lord Protector, and the other moiety to him or them who shall sue for the same.

XVII. That the persons who shall be elected to serve in Parliament, shall be such (and no other than such) as are persons of known integrity, fearing God, and of good conversation, and being of the age of twenty-one years.

XVIII. That all and every person and persons seised or possessed to his own use, of any estate, real or personal, to the value of £200, and not within the aforesaid exceptions, shall be capable to elect members to serve in Parliament for counties.

In its place, the army selected 140 persons it deemed sufficiently 'fearing God and of approved fidelity and honesty' to sit as a wholly nominated Parliament. The resulting assembly was a peculiar mixture of religious zealots, unworldly dreamers and traditional landed gentry. A legislature thus contrived was unlikely to hold firm in the turbulent climate of post-Civil War Britain. Nine months later, on 12 December 1653, this Parliament of nominees recognized that it was already out of its very limited depth and resigned.

Four days later, Cromwell endorsed the Instrument of Government, Britain's first written constitution. Drawn up by Major-General John Lambert and a small group of army officers, it vested power in Cromwell as head of state with the title of 'Lord Protector'. He would lead a Council of State, whose first fifteen members were named in the instrument. Both Lord Protector and council were vested with executive authority and also given the power to make legislation, except when Parliament was called. For its part, Parliament should meet for at least five months following general elections, which were to be held every three years. The old suffrage requirements remained in the boroughs but in the counties a new uniform prerequisite was created, with the vote given to persons (men) with property valued at £200 or more. The vote, however, would be denied, for the next four general elections, to those who had fought for the Royalists, and to Catholics eternally. Toleration was shown to all religions 'provided this liberty be not extended to Popery or Prelacy'.

The Instrument of Government created not just a reformed English Parliament but one that for the first time represented the whole British Isles. Sitting with the 400 English and Welsh MPs were to be thirty Irish and thirty Scottish MPs. The (as it transpired, premature) parliamentary union of England, Scotland and Ireland was accompanied by other measures to break down the barriers between the formerly separate nations, including the introduction of free trade between them. Such benefits, however, did not compensate for the grievances felt by Scots towards the new regime being imposed upon them, nor to the native Irish, most of whose land had been confiscated and their Catholic religion proscribed.

The instrument aimed to create rule by a head of state working through a unicameral Parliament or, for those times when the Commons were not sitting, the Council of State. Parliament retained tax-approving powers and the Lord Protector could only briefly delay, not veto, legislation. As part of the intended checks and balances, neither the executive nor the legislature was given total control of the armed forces. However, compared to the democratic and socialist demands heard

at the Putney Debates and from the Levellers, it was a conservative document. The vote was entrusted to gentlemen with sufficient wealth. It was by no means the right of all.

What was more, the state would brook no dissent. In 1655, England and Wales was divided into eleven cantons, each administered by a major-general. In this way, military government was established in peacetime, with the army being used not merely to help maintain civil order and collect taxes but to impose Puritan dictates on private behaviour – shutting down theatres and other places of entertainment and punishing not just lewdness but even minor, harmless, levity among the populace. When in the 1656 general election the country protested by returning MPs opposed to this new order, the Council of State disallowed about one hundred members whom it considered particularly hostile from taking their seats. A further sixty MPs refused to attend in protest at this travesty of democracy.

Like the rule of the major-generals, the Instrument of Government did not last long. It was replaced in May 1657 by the Humble Petition and Advice. This new constitution sought to re-create some of the familiar institutions of the past without reinstalling the Stuarts and their supporters to run them. Most controversially, it proposed reviving the monarchy, offering the Crown to Cromwell. He refused it but accepted the right to choose his eventual successor (who, with kingly assumption, proved to be his son, Richard). The document revived the House of Lords and recast the Council of State as the Privy Council, personnel for which were to be chosen by Cromwell and subject to ratification by MPs. The forty-one men who were sworn into the new House of Lords were largely country gentry and army officers, plus seven members of Cromwell's own family.

These developments simultaneously infuriated genuine revolutionaries while lacking the sort of tradition-conferring legitimacy that appealed to admirers of the pre-Civil War institutions. In reality, the regime was more truly held together by the unique personality of its head of state than had been the case with any previous crowned monarch. Consequently when Cromwell died in September 1658, the republican experiment – or rather experiments – quickly fell apart, succumbing to the restored royal house of Stuart without a fight.

1656

MENASSEH BEN ISRAEL'S HUMBLE PETITION TO THE LORD PROTECTOR

THE READMISSION OF JEWS TO BRITAIN

The Jews were a small but important community in early medieval England. They dominated finance because the Church's stance on usury – charging interest on credit – effectively prohibited Christians from being moneylenders, a position that lasted, with various qualifications and exceptions, until the Reformation. This made Jews both indispensable sources of credit and easy targets for abuse from those struggling to pay their debts. Subject to increasing restrictions and periodic violence, Jews were banned from practising usury by King Edward I in 1275. Worse was to follow. In 1290, having first granted them a compensatory pay-out, the king expelled them from the kingdom.

During the following 350 years, there were officially no Jews in England or Wales. (They were never formally banned from Scotland, although there is scant evidence of them residing there in any numbers.) In truth, a few Sephardic (Spanish and Portuguese) Jews were, unofficially, living and working in seventeenth-century London. The pretence was maintained that they were 'Marrano' Jews, those who had converted to Christianity, but the reality was that in 1657 they opened a secret synagogue in Creechurch Lane. Nonetheless, their numbers were tiny and their status precarious.

This might have remained the situation had not a strand of Puritan thought, British economic self-interest and the theological views of a Dutch rabbi coincided in 1655. With the title 'Lord Protector', the British republic's head of state was Oliver Cromwell. The government executive was the Council of State with John Thurloe as its secretary. Both Cromwell and Thurloe favoured readmitting the Jews, partly as an issue of religious toleration and also as a means of tapping into the financial acumen that Amsterdam's Jews were providing for the Dutch Republic.

Believing it imminent, Puritan millenarians eagerly anticipated the Second Coming which they thought would be prefaced by the conversion of the Jews and their return to Zion. Their arrival, first, in Britain would be a step along this path. Meanwhile, Menasseh Ben Israel (1604–57), an Amsterdam rabbi and publisher, believed that the Messiah would come when Jewish populations could be found in every country of the world. Thus he too wanted them to settle in Britain (he was already under the impression that some American Indians were, in fact, the lost ten tribes of Israel).

THE JEWISH POPULATION IN BRITAIN 1070–1900

1070 William the Conqueror invites Jewish merchants from Rouen to lend money and settle in England.

1144 In Norwich, the first 'blood libel' charge is made against Jews for ritual sacrifice.

1194 Richard the Lionheart orders the Ordinance of the Jewry, a record of all Jewish money transactions.

1218 Pope Innocent III's instruction that all Jews should wear identifying badges is instituted.

1253 Jews are prevented from moving to towns where they are not already established.

1255 The 'Hugh of Lincoln' blood libel gains popular credence.

1264 York's Jewish community is massacred by a mob.

1265 The Crown starts transferring its financial business from Jewish to Italian bankers.

1269 Jews are denied the right to hold property or inherit money.

1275 Edward I's *Statutum de Judaismo* forbids Jews to loan money with interest.

1290 Edward I expels Jews from England in perpetuity. Between 4,000 and 16,000 are forced into exile.

1494 There is evidence of small numbers of Portuguese Jews, nominally converted Christians, privately practising their true faith in England.

1655 The readmission of Jews is debated by the Whitehall Conference.

1657 A synagogue is opened in Creechurch Lane in the City of London.

1664 Charles II promises his protection to English Jews.

1698 The Act of Suppressing Blasphemy confirms that practising the Jewish faith is legal. There are believed to be about 400 Jews in Britain.

1701 Bevis Marks Synagogue is opened in the City of London.

1809 George III's sons, the dukes of Cambridge, Cumberland and Sussex attend a service in the Great Synagogue in Duke's Place, London.

1858 Jews are permitted to take their seats in the Houses of Parliament.

1881 The Jewish population of 48,000 swells to 250,000 by 1914, due largely to Ashkenazi Jews emigrating from Russia and Eastern Europe.

In 1655, Menasseh Ben Israel arrived in London and was granted an audience with Cromwell. Sympathetic to his cause, Cromwell convened the Whitehall Conference, made up of lawyers, theologians and merchants, to discuss Jewish readmittance. In December, the conference broke up without agreement. The theologians were divided and the merchants – fearful of competition – hostile. The legal opinion, however, was favourable. John Glynne, lord chief justice of the Upper Bench, and William Steele, chief baron of the Exchequer, maintained that Edward I's royal edict of expulsion not only had no legislative force but had never been ratified by Parliament. Historians are unclear as to exactly what was agreed. John Evelyn was certain that it meant Jews had legal protection to settle, writing in his diary for 14 December 1655, 'Now were the Jews admitted.'

The following year, Britain went to war with Spain. One of those whose goods were impounded as a result was the Jewish merchant Antonio Rodrigues Robles. Actually of Portuguese descent, he took the matter to court, claiming he was Jewish not Spanish. For some of London's covert Jewish community, the case was a source of unwelcome publicity. There was, however, no further hiding place when, in March 1656, Menasseh headed a list of Jewish signatories in a formal petition, requesting protection and a place to bury their dead. While Cromwell referred the petition to the Council of State, the court delivered an ambiguous verdict that, nevertheless, returned Robles's possessions to him.

The combined effect of these developments was to demonstrate that London's Jewish community openly existed and was not prosecuted for doing so. No formal statement of readmittance was issued and Menasseh returned to Amsterdam, believing that his mission had been a failure (he was so poor that he had to beg Cromwell for the money to travel home with the body of his son who had passed away in London). He was given an annual £100 state pension but died on his way back to Amsterdam. The legality of Jewish settlement in Britain was affirmed by Charles II. Turning down appeals to have them formally banished again, he promised them his protection. They began worshipping openly, in 1701 opening the Bevis Marks synagogue. Nor were they slow in demonstrating their loyalty to their adopted home. During both the American War of Independence and the Napoleonic Wars, London's Jewish community fasted for British victory.

They also assisted Britain in more practical ways, making an incalculable contribution towards establishing the dominance of the City of London as the world's financial centre. In the panic of 1745, London's Jews enlisted for the capital's military defence against the expected Jacobite attack and Samson Gideon provided

valuable funds to shore up Hanoverian rule. Adopting his mother's Christian religion, his son became an MP and in 1789 was rewarded with an Irish peerage.

Despite these services to the state, the path to full acceptance was not a smooth one. In 1754 popular disapproval forced Parliament to scrap new legislation allowing Jews to seek British naturalization. Many Jewish fathers opted to have their children

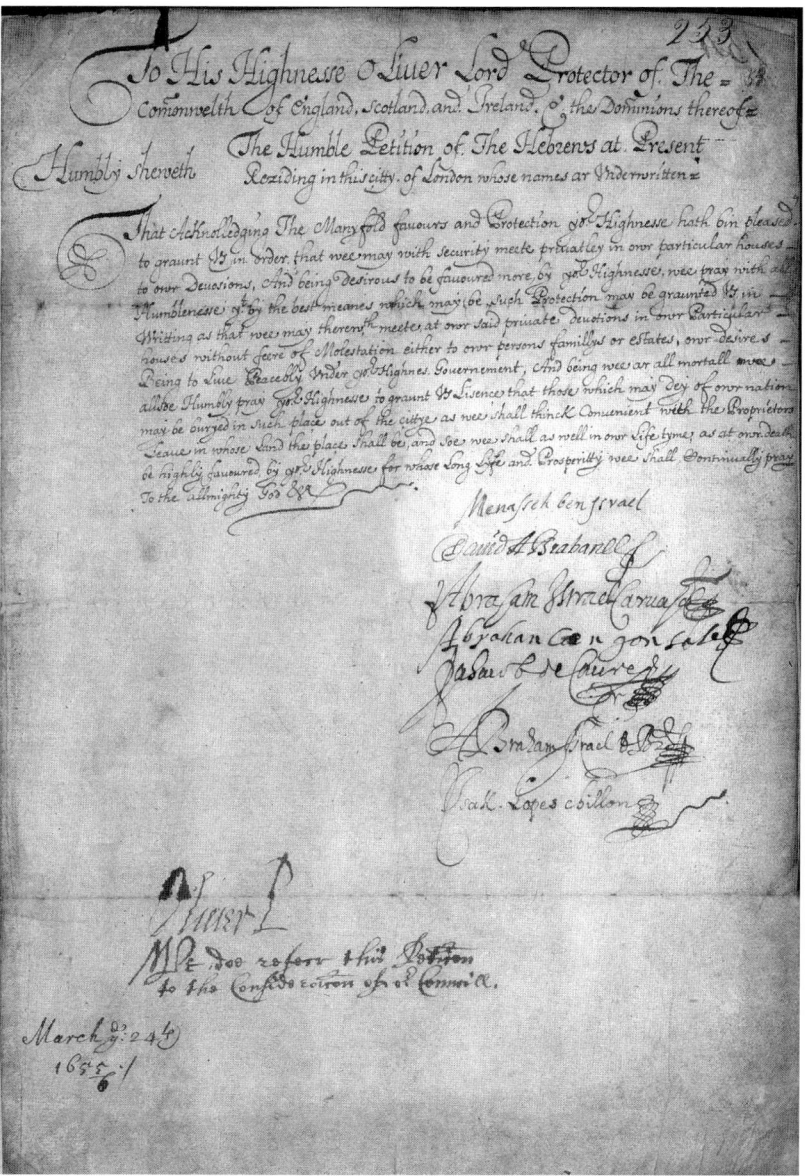

Ben Israel's humble petition on behalf of his fellow Jews. Cromwell has signed it 'Oliver P', the initial standing for his title, 'Protector'.

christened, among them the twelve-year-old Benjamin Disraeli, subsequently leader of the Conservative Party and prime minister in 1868 and 1874–80.

The first practising Jew to be given a baronetcy was the financier and promoter of University College London, Isaac Lyon Goldsmid, in 1841. David Salomons became lord mayor of London in 1855. Despite the election of Lionel Rothschild in 1847 and David Salomons in 1851, the parliamentary oath required members to profess the Christian faith and therefore prevented Jews from taking up their seats in the House of Commons. They were finally allowed to do so in 1858. The first practising Jewish government minister was appointed in 1871 and the first judge in 1873.

By this time, the Jewish population of Britain was around 50,000, heavily concentrated in London. Eight years later there began the wide-scale migration of Ashkenazi Jews, fleeing the poverty and pogroms of Eastern Europe and Russia. Between 1881 and 1914, about 150,000 of them arrived in Britain, soon forming a distinctive community in Stepney in the capital's East End, where a disproportionate number worked as tailors.

This influx quickly became contentious, not only among anti-Semites but also among many settled Jews who looked down upon the far poorer Lithuanian, Polish or Russian new arrivals. Legislation in 1905 barred a right of entry to immigrants with criminal records or a history of destitution, while further measures in 1919 and 1920 prevented them settling if they could not prove they had the means of support. Some who did not want Jewish immigration in large numbers in Britain made common cause with the Zionist movement in hoping Jews would instead settle in Palestine. However, by the end of the 1930s the British government (which held the League of Nations Mandate to administer Palestine) curtailed the flow of settlers there in the face of mounting Arab opposition.

Meanwhile, the Cabinet had responded to Hitler's rise to power in 1933 by a gentle relaxation of the rules governing entry to Britain after the leaders of the Jewish community agreed to shoulder the financial responsibility of those arriving without jobs. About 30,000 came from Central and Eastern Europe over the following five years. Neville Chamberlain's government loosened the criteria again in 1938, to the particular benefit of those aged under seventeen who were allowed to enter the country without visas or parents. Even with these concessions in place, only a further 25,000 Jews (9,000 of them, children) were able to flee to Britain in 1939, before the outbreak of the calamitous war that annihilated around 6 million of those they had left behind.

1660
MEMORANDUM FOR THE ROYAL SOCIETY

THE ADVANCEMENT OF SCIENCE IN THE AGE OF BOYLE, HOOKE AND NEWTON

The Royal Society of London for the Improvement of Natural Knowledge is the oldest scientific society in the world to have enjoyed a continuous existence. Since its foundation in 1660, it has been Britain's premier academy of sciences, promoting research, bringing together leading minds and facilitating the cross-fertilization of ideas that have shaped scientific understanding. It was through the Royal Society that many of Robert Boyle's chemical discoveries and Isaac Newton's universal laws were first disseminated.

Its founding members had met regularly, if informally, in Oxford and London since the 1640s. On 28 November 1660, they gathered at Gresham College to hear a lecture by Christopher Wren, an astronomer as well as a pre-eminent architect. At the meeting's conclusion, twelve of them – including Wren and Boyle, Sir Robert Moray and John Wilkins – decided to found a 'Colledge for the promoting of Phys-ico-Mathematicall Experimentall Learning'. With the patronage of King Charles II, it was incorporated as the Royal Society in 1662. A second charter extended its privileges in 1663 and a third charter of 1669 granted it land. Always independent, it benefited from royal patronage without coming under state control. It essentially started as a forum for thinkers to meet, confer and crystallize ideas at a moment when Britain found itself blessed by a generation of pioneering geniuses whose interests ranged widely across what would subsequently come to be regarded as distinctly separate academic disciplines.

No less important than bringing together Britain's eminent men (women became Fellows only in 1945), the Royal Society also fostered correspondence between the leading scientists in Europe and beyond. This began to be published in March 1665 as *Philosophical Transactions: Giving Some Account of the Present Undertakings,*

THE SCIENTIFIC REVOLUTION

1614 John Napier publishes his work on logarithms for calculation.

1628 William Harvey's *De Moto Cordis* explains the circulation of the blood.

1659 Robert Boyle and Robert Hooke test the properties of air with their 'pneumatical engine' air pump.

1660 The Royal Society is founded in London.

1661 Robert Boyle's *Sceptical Chymist* is published.

1662 Boyle produces his law of ideal gas, showing the inverse proportionality of pressure and volume.

1665 *Philosophical Transactions of the Royal Society*, the world's first 'peer-reviewed' scientific journal, is published.

1665 Robert Hooke's *Micrographia* is published, detailing his observations through microscopy.

1666 Isaac Newton begins work on the development of the Calculus.

1668 Newton builds the first practical reflecting telescope.

1676–8 Hooke elaborates his law of elasticity.

1687 Newton's *Principia Mathematica* explains his laws of motion and universal gravitation.

1704 Newton's *Optiks* is published, popularizing his experiments in colour and light diffraction.

Studies and Labours of the Ingenious in Many Considerable Parts of the World. In the process the Royal Society effectively created modern notions of scientific publishing and peer review, making English rather than Latin the primary language in which science and mathematics were promoted and discussed. The *Philosophical Transactions* remains a publication of international renown to this day, divided since the 1880s into two series, one concerning mathematics, physics and engineering sciences and the other biology.

Many of the Royal Society's early weekly meetings were devoted to performing and discussing experiments. Robert Hooke (1635–1702), the polymath inventor and researcher into optics and gravitation, was appointed 'Curator of Experiments'. At the time, not everyone appreciated the significance of what was being examined. For all King Charles's support of the society, the diarist Samuel Pepys (1633–1703; he was its president from 1684 to 1686) noted that His Majesty 'mightily laughed' at it 'for spending time only in weighing of ayre, and doing nothing else since they sat'. In fact, the investigations being made into atmospheric pressure had considerable value as, in time, the power of steam to transform the world would show.

Besides creating a celebrated library for its members' consultation, the Royal Society published, or paid for the printing of, important contributions to learning. It began by publishing John Evelyn's *Sylva* (a treatise on forest management) and Hooke's *Micrographia*, an extraordinary work of microscopic observations. In 1672, Isaac Newton (1642–1727), Professor of Mathematics at Cambridge, was elected a Fellow and in April 1686 he presented the first part of his *Philosophiae Naturalis Principia Mathematica* to the Royal Society. With its explanation of the basic laws governing physical forces, the *Principia* was immediately recognized as a seminal

From the first journal book of the Royal Society, 1660

Memorandum that Novemb[er] 28 1660. These persons following according to the usuall Custome of most of them, mett together at Gresham Colledge to hear Mr Wrens Lecture, viz The Lord Brouncker, Mr Boyle, Mr Bruce, Sir Robert Moray, Sir Paul Neile, Dr Wilkins, Dr Goddard, Dr Petty, Mr Ball, Mr Rooke, Mr Wren, Mr Hill. And after the Lecture was ended they did according to the usuall Manner, withdrawe for mutuall converse. Where amongst other matters that were discoursed of, Something was offered about a designe of founding a Colledge for the Promoting of Physico-Mathematicall Experimentall Learning.

And because they had these frequent occasions of meeting wth one another, it was proposed that some course might be thought of to improve this meeting to a more regular way of debating things, & according to the Manner in other Countries, where there were voluntary associations of men into Academies for the advancement of various parts of learning, So they might doe something answerable here for the promoting of Experimentall Philosophy.

In order to which it was agreed, that this Company would continue their weekly meetings on wensday at 3 of the clock in the Tearme time at Mr Rookes Chamber at Gresham Colledge. In the vacation at Mr Balls Chamber in the Temple. And towards the defraying of occasionall expenses, every one should at his first admission, pay downe ten shillings, & besides engage to pay one shilling weekly, whether present or absent, whilest he shall please to keep his relation to this company.

contribution and the Society's council declared that 'Mr Newton's work should be printed forthwith.' Embarrassingly, the funds allocated for publishing had already been spent for the year – on a history of fish – so it fell to another Fellow of the Society, the astronomer Edmund Halley (1656–1742), to defray the cost of bringing out one of the greatest opuses in the history of science. Given its author's hesitancy to put his observations into print, this support and encouragement was important. Newton served as the Royal Society's president from 1703 until his death.

1661–70
THE CLARENDON CODE

THE PENALTIES FOR DISSENTING FROM
THE ESTABLISHED CHURCH

The Clarendon Code was a series of statutes passed by Parliament in the immediate aftermath of the monarchy's restoration. The aim was to exclude Puritans from playing an active part in religious and public life.

During the 1650s Anglicanism had suffered a similar fate as befell its supreme governor, Charles I. In alliance with Scottish Presbyterians, Parliament had abolished episcopacy during the Civil War. Meanwhile, toleration of most Protestant sects was introduced. Paradoxically, this widening of religious liberty often had the consequence of emboldening the more intolerant forms of Puritanism. The repression of essentially harmless activities and traditions that were not explicitly condoned in the Bible (including, in some cities, the celebration of Christmas) did much to give the name Puritan its pejorative, killjoy connotations.

During the life of the English republic, about 2,000 of the 9,000 church benefices were held by Puritans. In many cases, they had gained their benefices from traditional Anglican clergy who had been forced into hiding or exile.

With the Crown's restoration in 1660, one of the first tasks was to decide the Church of England's future form. Not all Puritans were necessarily opposed to a state Church so long as it either followed Presbyterian principles or readopted bishops only in a heavily modified role acceptable to moderate Puritan opinion. The talks broke down without agreement, and in consequence episcopacy was revived. With Parliament devising means to restore the displaced Anglican clergy to their former benefices, the incumbent Puritans were faced with a stark choice: accept the readoption of the old Anglican doctrine and liturgy, or get out.

The new king, Charles II, was not personally devout and had no reason to indulge a narrow view of Anglican triumphalism. After all, he owed his life to English Catholic sympathizers and foreign Catholic powers. Like Elizabeth I at her accession just over one hundred years previously, Charles II's instincts were

From the Corporation Act, 1661

III. That all persons who upon the four and twentieth day of December one thousand six hundred sixty and one shall be mayors, aldermen, recorders, bailiffs, town clerks, common council men and other persons then bearing any office or offices of magistracy, or places or trust or other employment relating to or concerning the government of the said respective cities, corporations and boroughs, and cinque ports and their members and other port towns, shall, at any time before the five and twentieth day of March one thousand six hundred and sixty and three, when they shall be thereunto required by the said respective commissioners or any three or more of them, take the oath of allegiance and supremacy and this oath following:

I, A. B., do declare and believe that it is not lawful upon any pretence whatsoever to take arms against the king, and that I do abhor that traitorous position of taking arms by his authority against his person, or against those that are commissioned by him. So help me God.

And also at the same time shall publicly subscribe before the said commissioners or any three of them this following declaration:

I, A. B., do declare that I hold that there lies no obligation upon me or any other person from the oath commonly called the Solemn League and Covenant, and that the same was in itself an unlawful oath, and imposed upon the subjects of this realm against the known laws and liberties of the kingdom. . . .

IX. Provided also, and be it enacted . . . that from and after the expiration of the said commissions no person or persons shall forever hereafter be placed, elected or chosen in or to any the offices or places aforesaid that shall not have within one year next before such election or choice taken the sacrament of the Lord's Supper according to the rites of the Church of England, and that every such person and persons so placed, elected or chosen shall likewise take the aforesaid three oaths and subscribe the said declaration at the same time when the oath for the due execution of the said places and offices respectively shall be administered; and in default hereof every such placing, election and choice is hereby enacted and declared to be void.

*Edward Hyde,
earl of Clarendon
(1609–74).*

for a doctrinally broad-based Established Church. In this, he had the support of his lord chancellor, Edward Hyde, earl of Clarendon. In contrast, Parliament – bent upon punishing past Puritan excesses – was less prepared to be so accommodating and wanted a Church settlement that divided and ruled. Clarendon duly found himself lending his name to laws that went further than either he or his royal master intended.

The 1661 Corporation Act forced town officials to swear an oath of allegiance to the king. This was to be expected, but it also required them to take Anglican communion. What was more, the Act of Uniformity the following year instilled a form of Anglicanism noxious to most Puritans. Having been banned during the republic, the Book of Common Prayer was reintroduced as the only Church liturgy. All clergy had to be ordained by a bishop and subscribe to the Thirty-Nine Articles. Rather than comply, about 2,000 clergymen, mostly Baptists, Presbyterians and independents, resigned their livings. Initially referred to as Dissenters, they were later known as Nonconformists.

Not content to drive them out of the Established Church, the Clarendon Code was also determined to prevent them publicly practising their beliefs at all. Although the Dissenters' faith was acknowledged as lawful, it was to be conducted in private. The 1664 and 1670 Conventicle Acts made it an offence (punishable by a fine or imprisonment) to attend a service of worship that did not use the Book of Common Prayer. The 1665 Five Mile Act prevented dissenting ministers from living within five miles of either their former parish or of any corporate town, unless they first swore an oath of non-resistance. A separate statute, the 1662 Quaker Act, imprisoned more than 1,000 Quakers for their beliefs.

What the Clarendon Code did to Dissenters, the 1673 and 1678 Test Acts did to Roman Catholics. The Test Acts barred Catholics from accepting military or civil office and prevented them from sitting in Parliament. An exception was made for James, duke of York, the heir presumptive to the throne, who had converted to Catholicism. He survived a protracted 'Exclusion Crisis' in which 'Tory' politicians upheld his right and 'Whigs' unsuccessfully tried to block his right to succeed. This

dividing issue is often seen as one of the milestones in the creation of Westminster's two-party system.

Taken together, these measures aimed at ending the strife and upheavals of the Civil War period by creating an Anglican state for an Anglican people. Not only were the official churches only for Anglicans, so were the schools and the two universities. Undoubtedly, the legislation had some success in quelling the scale and visibility of dissent, but it also produced unintended consequences. Unable to enter public life or take part in formal education, the Protestant Dissenters did their own thing and found more profitable avenues to explore. Disproportionate to their numbers, they provided the next generations of bankers, inventors and manufacturers. In any case, far from withering on the vine, by the end of the eighteenth century the number of Nonconformists had swelled thanks to the decision of John Wesley's Methodist followers to break away from the Church of England.

By then, the Clarendon Code had proved less successful than its zealous sponsors hoped and was being largely discarded. The Conventicle Acts were difficult to administer and fell into disuse. Following the Glorious Revolution, Dissenters were allowed, by the 1689 Toleration Act, to form their own congregations. The Five Mile Act had fallen into abeyance long before it was taken off the statute book in 1812. Imprisonment of Quakers ended with the 1672 Declaration of Indulgence. True, measures were passed during the devoutly Anglican Queen Anne's reign to close up the 'occasional conformity' loopholes through which non-Anglicans had come to hold office and to prevent them opening their own schools. However, the crackdown did not long outlast the arrival of the Hanoverian monarchy and was scrapped in 1719. From 1727, annual indemnity acts allowed many non-Anglicans to hold local office.

Finally, in 1828 the Test and Corporation Acts were repealed, making Nonconformists free to hold municipal and state office. Catholics were similarly emancipated the following year. The dismantling of the Restoration's Anglican supremacy was effectively completed between 1868, when mandatory Church rates were abolished, and 1871, with the removal of the last restrictions to non-Anglicans at Oxford and Cambridge universities.

1688

THE IMMORTAL SEVEN'S INVITATION TO WILLIAM OF ORANGE

THE GLORIOUS REVOLUTION

The last successful invasion of England took place not in 1066 but in 1688. In November of that year William of Orange, the hereditary *stadtholder* of the Dutch Republic, landed at Torbay with his 15,000-strong army of Dutch, Swedish, German, Swiss and Huguenot as well as Scottish and English troops. Within seven weeks he was ensconced in London's Whitehall Palace. Yet his actions were widely seen not as those of a hostile occupier and usurper but rather as a welcome liberation from the arbitrary rule of James II. That this was so owed much to the invitation dispatched by the 'Immortal Seven'.

Having survived parliamentary attempts to exclude him from the succession, James II (he was James VII in Scotland) became king upon the death of his brother, Charles II, in 1685. Although he easily defeated a rebellion led by his illegitimate half-brother, the duke of Monmouth (whom he executed), James's position remained a difficult one. He was a devout Roman Catholic ruling three kingdoms of which only Ireland had a majority of his co-religionists. His faith was also at odds with his role as supreme governor of the Church of England.

James had two interlinked objectives: to increase royal authority, and to circumvent the laws that persecuted Catholics. After dispensing with Parliament, he exploited legal loopholes to promote Catholics to key civil and military posts, sacking most of his ministers and preferring to govern with a council of fellow Catholics. The traditions of ancient corporations, the Inns of Court and the college fellowships of Oxford and Cambridge were all overridden as part of James's imposition of religious positive discrimination. Maintaining a standing army in peacetime, he also hoped to dispense with habeas corpus in order to make arbitrary

BRITAIN'S LAST SUCCESSFUL REVOLUTION

1678–81 'The Exclusion Crisis' sees a succession of foiled parliamentary efforts to prevent the Catholic James, duke of York, succeeding his brother, King Charles II.

1685 Charles II dies and is succeeded by James II (James VII in Scotland).

1685 Rebellion by James's illegitimate half-brother and the Protestant pretender to the throne, the duke of Monmouth, ends with Monmouth's execution.

1687 James's Declaration of Indulgence creates religious freedom.

8 June 1688 Seven bishops are imprisoned for refusing to read out James's second Declaration of Indulgence.

10 June James's wife, Mary of Modena, gives birth to a Catholic heir, James Francis Edward.

30 June The seven bishops are acquitted by the courts, and the 'Immortal Seven', powerful figures of church and state, write to William of Orange asking him to invade Britain.

5 November William of Orange lands with his force at Torbay.

21 December James flees London for the continent.

22 January 1689 The Convention Parliament convenes.

13 February William and Mary accept the offer of the English throne as co-regents and accept the Declaration of Rights.

4 April The Scottish Parliament meets in Edinburgh and proceeds to pass the Claim of Right, offering the crown of Scotland to William and Mary.

11 April William and Mary are crowned in Westminster Abbey.

24 May The Toleration Act grants freedom of worship to Protestant Dissenters.

27 July A rising of pro-James Scottish Highlanders loses momentum when its leader, James Graham, Viscount Dundee, is killed at the Battle of Killiecrankie.

1690 James's efforts to hold onto Ireland are crushed at the Battle of the Boyne.

1694 The Triennial Act necessitates the calling of a general election every three years.

1701 The Act of Settlement confirms the Protestant line of succession; James dies in exile.

arrest easier. These initiatives coincided with Louis XIV's persecution of France's Protestant Huguenot minority, a development that James did not condemn. British Protestants began to fear that their monarch was poised to become a second 'Bloody Mary'.

Anglican fears for their Church did not extend as far as protecting the faiths of others. It was in fact James's 1687 Declaration of Indulgence that created religious freedom for all his subjects. He intended to recall Parliament to ratify the declaration but not before he had rigged a general election to make it compliant to his will. When seven bishops – including the archbishop of Canterbury – refused

to read a second Declaration of Indulgence from their pulpits because they believed the king's dispensing authority to be illegal, he had them arrested and committed to the Tower of London. Two days later, on 10 June 1688, James's wife, Mary of Modena, gave birth to a son. Whilst the news delighted James, it sent Protestants into deeper despair – they would have not just one Catholic ruler but a whole succession of them.

On 30 June, the trial of the bishops ended – sensationally – with their acquittal. The courts were openly defying the king. That night, as celebratory bonfires were lit across London and the shires, a group of senior peers of the realm, together with Henry Compton, the bishop of London, wrote to William of Orange asking him to invade. The signatories became known as the 'Immortal Seven'. Besides Compton, they comprised: two leading Whig politicians, Henry Sidney (who drafted the letter) and Edward Russell; the earl of Danby (a Tory who had helped organize William's marriage to James's daughter, Mary, in 1677); the earl of Shrewsbury; the earl of Devonshire; and Lord Lumley, whose troops had been responsible for capturing the fugitive duke of Monmouth during the latter's abortive uprising of 1685.

The letter is truly remarkable. In plain and almost matter-of-fact language, it solicited a war to safeguard the future of Britain. It also perpetuated the widely held but erroneous, allegation that James's infant son was an impostor, smuggled into the royal bedchamber in a bedpan. The signatories risked being beheaded for treason, so, fearing the letter might be intercepted, they signed their names by numbered code. The incriminating epistle was carried to The Hague by Arthur Herbert, an admiral cashiered by James for refusing to serve under Catholic officers. Herbert went disguised as a common sailor and would return to England at the head of the invasion fleet.

For William, the letter from the Immortal Seven was not merely convenient; he had in fact actively solicited it. Plans for assembling his invasion force were already under way, but he needed the letter of invitation from some of Britain's leading figures – Tory, Whig and clergy – before agreeing to proceed. Not only did it grant him a pretext for intervention, it was also evidence that he would enjoy political and Church backing on his arrival. It was, after all, a risky endeavour and William was not only James's son-in-law, as a grandson of Charles I, he was also his nephew. Without the letter, he made clear he would go no further.

William's motivations went beyond restoring political stability to Britain. He wanted British help in containing Louis XIV on the continent. Nonetheless,

From the letter of the Immortal Seven, 1688

These considerations make us of opinion that this is a season in which we may more probably contribute to our own safeties than hereafter (although we must own to your Highness there are some judgments differing from ours in this particular), insomuch that if the circumstances stand so with your Highness that you believe you can get here time enough, in a condition to give assistances this year sufficient for a relief under these circumstances which have been now represented, we who subscribe this will not fail to attend your Highness upon your landing and to do all that lies in our power to prepare others to be in as much readiness as such an action is capable of, where there is so much danger in communicating an affair of such a nature till it be near the time of its being made public. But, as we have already told your Highness, we must also lay our difficulties before your Highness, which are chiefly, that we know not what alarm your preparations for this expedition may give, or what notice it will be necessary for you to give the States beforehand, by either of which means their intelligence or suspicions here may be such as may cause us to be secured before your landing. And we must presume to inform your Highness that your compliment upon the birth of the child (which not one in a thousand here believes to be the queen's) hath done you some injury, the false imposing of that upon the princess and the nation being not only an infinite exasperation of people's minds here, but being certainly one of the chief causes upon which the declaration of your entering the kingdom in a hostile manner must be founded on your part, although many other reasons are to be given on ours.

when issuing his declaration he was careful not to lay his own claim to the throne, preferring to focus on his determination to safeguard the country's liberties by calling a Parliament uncontaminated by James's election rigging.

Dodging James's fleet, William's armada of 49 warships and 2,000 troop transport vessels, borne by 'a Protestant wind', landed at Torbay on 5 November (fittingly, Guy Fawkes Night). A chain of small risings announced popular support. James advanced as far as Salisbury before taking fright. Key commanders, including John Churchill, the future duke of Marlborough, defected to William's camp. Returning to London, James weighed his options and, on 21 December, fled.

In February 1689, William and Mary jointly accepted Parliament's offer of the English throne. On 4 April, the Scottish Convention of Estates renounced its loyalty to James, who had disobeyed 'the fundamental constitution of this Kingdom' and altered it 'from a legal limited monarchy to an arbitrary despotic power'. On the day that they were crowned in Westminster Abbey, William and Mary were also proclaimed Scotland's new king and queen. A Scottish Jacobite rising led by Viscount Dundee was defeated. In Catholic Ireland, however, James found broader loyalty and convened a supportive Parliament there. This Irish power base did not last long. In June 1690, James's forces were decisively defeated by William at the Battle of the Boyne.

From this defeat until his death in 1701, James ran a shadow court in exile from the royal château of Saint-Germain-en-Laye, west of Paris. He still intrigued at reclaiming his throne, turning down Louis XIV's offer to make him king of Poland in case it reduced his chances in Britain. The opportunity never came. After visiting him at St Germain, it was the celebrated novelist, Madame de Lafayette, who delivered the damning verdict: 'As one listens to him, one realises why he is here.'

1689

THE BILL OF RIGHTS

THE CONSTITUTIONAL MONARCHY

The Glorious Revolution did more than replace a Catholic king with his Protestant daughter and son-in-law. It did so on terms, laid out in the Bill of Rights, that fundamentally altered the relationship between the Crown and Parliament. Henceforth, the monarchy's power would be determined by Parliament. If the Bill of Rights did not create a constitutional monarchy, it nonetheless provided the clearest indication that this was the prevailing nature of government in Britain.

Parliament had not sat for three years when James II fled, ahead of William of Orange's entry into London. One of the first actions of the interim authorities was to hold a general election. This returned the 'Convention' Parliament, which met in January 1689. On 13 February 1689 it offered the Crown, jointly, to William and Mary, with conditions attached. The new co-rulers would have to agree to terms drawn up in a document called the Declaration of Rights. Its intent was to limit royal power and enhance the freedom of Parliament. Instead of the occasional summons favoured by past Stuart monarchs, the Declaration stipulated that Parliament should meet regularly, and that the freedom of its members' speech as well as its proceedings must be guaranteed. It would be illegal to levy taxes, or to make or suspend laws, without the explicit endorsement of Parliament.

The Declaration of Rights was passed by the Convention Parliament and put on the statute books as the Bill of Rights. The Scottish Parliament passed it as the Claim of Right. Its primary aim was to deny the Crown the means by which it could descend into despotism. A standing army could not be maintained in peacetime except through parliamentary consent. James II's attempts to disarm his Protestant subjects were thus reversed. The bill specified that Protestants had the right to bear arms for their self-defence. Stripped of its sectarian condition, this clause would form the basis of the Second Amendment of the United States' Constitution over a hundred years later.

Die Martis 12º Februarij 1688

The Declaration of the Lords Spirituall
and Temporall and Comons Assembled att Westm:

Whereas the late King James the second by the
Assistance of diverse evill Councello[r]s Iudges and
Ministers imployed by him did endeavour to
subvert and extirpate the Protestant Religion
and the Lawes and Libertyes of this Kingdome.

By assumeing and excerciseing a Power of dis-
pencing and suspending of Lawes and the execution
of Lawes without consent of Parliament.

By committing and prosecuteing diverse worthy
Prelates for humbly petitioning to be excused from
concurring to the said assumed Power
and causeing to be executed

By issueing a comission under the Great Seale
for erecting a Court called the Court of Comissioners for
Ecclesiasticall Causes.

By levying money for and to the use of the Crown
by pretence of Prerogative for other time and in
other manner then the same was granted by Parliament.

By raiseing and keeping a standing Army within
this Kingdom in time of Peace without consent of
Parliament. and quartering Souldiers contrary to Law.

By causeing severall good subjects being
Protestants to be disarmed at the same time when
papists were both armed

By violateing the free
members to serve in Par[liament]

By causeing
and prosecuted in the
for matters and causes
assent and by divers other
illegall courses By Prosecu
of Kings Bench for matters
cognizable only in Parliament did by div[ers]
other arbitrary & illegall

From the Bill of Rights, 1689

That the pretended power of suspending the laws or the execution of laws by regal authority without consent of Parliament is illegal;

That the pretended power of dispensing with laws or the execution of laws by regal authority, as it hath been assumed and exercised of late, is illegal;

That the commission for erecting the late Court of Commissioners for Ecclesiastical Causes, and all other commissions and courts of like nature, are illegal and pernicious;

That levying money for or to the use of the Crown by pretence of prerogative, without grant of Parliament, for longer time, or in other manner than the same is or shall be granted, is illegal;

That it is the right of the subjects to petition the king, and all commitments and prosecutions for such petitioning are illegal;

That the raising or keeping a standing army within the kingdom in time of peace, unless it be with consent of Parliament, is against law;

That the subjects which are Protestants may have arms for their defence suitable to their conditions and as allowed by law;

That election of members of Parliament ought to be free;

That the freedom of speech and debates or proceedings in Parliament ought not to be impeached or questioned in any court or place out of Parliament;

That excessive bail ought not to be required, nor excessive fines imposed, nor cruel and unusual punishments inflicted;

That jurors ought to be duly impanelled and returned, and jurors which pass upon men in trials for high treason ought to be freeholders;

That all grants and promises of fines and forfeitures of particular persons before conviction are illegal and void;

And that for redress of all grievances, and for the amending, strengthening and preserving of the laws, Parliaments ought to be held frequently.

The bill also dealt with the royal succession. The convenient fiction was perpetrated that James II's flight from his kingdoms meant that he had abdicated. However, the reality was now that the new monarchs owed their power not to the ancient rights of inheritance or to some mystical notion of divine right, but to the say-so of Parliament. The Bill of Rights decreed that the subsequent succession would pass down through Mary's heirs, or, if she had none, those of her sister, Anne. In fact, neither had surviving children, forcing the succession issue to be

OPPOSITE: The Declaration of Rights was presented by the Convention Parliament to William and Mary in February 1689 and put on the statute books as the Bill of Rights ten months later.

readdressed in the 1701 Act of Settlement. Members of the royal family who converted to Catholicism or who married Catholics were debarred from the succession.

The Bill of Rights was only the most important of a series of laws that established the Revolution Settlement. The 1689 Toleration Act lifted the anti-Dissenter penal laws on all Protestant Nonconformists who took the oaths of allegiance and supremacy. The Catholic disabilities remained. The timescale for calling regular parliaments was set by the 1694 Triennial Act, which ensured a general election at least once every three years (this was extended to seven years in 1716 and cut to five years in 1911). William's expensive wars against France entailed extensive debate about taxation at Westminster and the creation of the Bank of England in 1694. The Bill of Rights was modified in 1698 when the maintenance of a standing army was permitted during what proved a temporary period of peace.

The Bill of Rights did not set out with precision which powers belonged to the Crown, which to the legislature and which to the executive. These were shaped by subsequent events, for which the Bill of Rights established part of the constitutional framework, particularly with regard to what the Crown could *not* do. The bill's success could, however, be assessed by one important measure. Arbitrary rule was henceforth consigned to history.

JOHN LOCKE'S *TWO TREATISES OF GOVERNMENT*

THE REFUTATION OF DIVINE RIGHT AND ADVOCACY OF GOVERNMENT BY POPULAR CONSENT

John Locke had more influence upon the world than any other British philosopher. Not only did he provide the Glorious Revolution with its philosophical legitimacy, but his thinking was central to the development of liberalism, influencing the arguments against absolutism in Europe and, more directly, inspiring the Founding Fathers of the United States.

Locke was born in 1632 into a minor Somerset gentry family. His father fought for the Parliamentarians during the Civil War. Locke was educated at Westminster School and Christ Church, Oxford, during the period of the republican Commonwealth. Awarded a college studentship, he demonstrated wide academic curiosity in subjects ranging from theology and philosophy to Greek, medicine, meteorology and chemistry. His breadth of interests brought him into contact with such eminent scientists as Isaac Newton and Robert Boyle.

It was his friendship with Anthony Ashley Cooper, later earl of Shaftesbury, the emerging leader of the Country – or 'Whig' – faction in Parliament, that ensured he was also at the forefront of political controversy. Doubling as the earl's secretary and physician, Locke lodged at his mentor's London mansion, Exeter House. Like Shaftesbury, he suffered recurring ill health and it was partly to escape London's polluted air, as well as to extract himself from an increasingly precarious political situation, that he spent the years between 1675 and 1679 in France. There he made the acquaintance of many of Europe's leading Enlightenment thinkers.

He returned to England but his stay there was soon interrupted. Shaftesbury's attempts to exclude the future James II from the throne collapsed and, fearing incarceration, the earl fled in 1682 to Amsterdam, dying there the following year. Locke departed hurriedly, first to Rotterdam and then to Amsterdam. There, he

dodged English warrants sent to the Dutch to have him arrested by living under the assumed identity of 'Dr Van der Linden'. It was 1688's Glorious Revolution that gave him his chance to go home once more. During his exile he met William of Orange and in February 1689 sailed for England on the ship carrying the future Queen Mary II.

Locke maintained that his *Two Treatises of Government*, finished later that year (but post-dated to 1690 as its year of publication), was his means of defending philosophically the British revolution to the world. In fact, he had begun writing it around 1680–2 and had left the manuscript behind when fleeing to the Dutch Republic. The elapse of time between conception and publication made Locke less the prophet and more the legitimizer of events.

The first treatise kicked away the main prop of the House of Stuart's claim to autocratic power – the divine right of kings. Locke demolished the justification put forward by the political writer Sir Robert Filmer that subjects were to sovereigns as children were to parents because sovereigns, like fathers, were descended from Adam. Giving short shrift to such notions was the easier part of Locke's task. In the second treatise, his implicit target was the view expressed in Thomas Hobbes's 1651 work *Leviathan*, that in order to curb the anarchic rule of Nature that would otherwise make their lives unendurable, the people entered into a contract with the sovereign power. By it, they surrendered their rights in return for being provided with security. In this way the sovereign (whether a monarch or some other form of government) was entitled to exercise absolute power for the greater good of law and order, without which human existence would be 'nasty, brutish, and short'.

Hobbes had done his thinking (in exile) at a time when England had descended into the near anarchy of civil war. His philosophy did not necessarily advocate the despotic wielding of power, but by imagining that the state and society were one and the same he nonetheless provided absolutist regimes with a justification for expecting their subjects' unequivocal submission.

Locke rejected the notion that mankind was faced only with the stark options of anarchy or capitulation to absolute power. On the contrary, he suggested that certain God-given and inalienable rights existed beyond the give or take of the state, among them freedom of action and the ownership of private property. Since these rights were natural, not a retractable gift from government, the latter could remove them only with the consent of those to whom they belonged.

This was the nature of the 'social contract' that Locke believed defined the relationship between government and the governed. The loyalty that the people

1440–6 – HENRY VI'S CHARTERS FOR ETON COLLEGE AND KING'S COLLEGE, CAMBRIDGE

Charter of King's College, Cambridge, 16 March 1446. In the top left-hand corner members of the House of Lords (led by the Lord Chancellor, Archbishop Stafford) with members of the House of Commons below them, are illustrated petitioning King Henry VI, who prays for his foundation. The college's patron saints, St Nicholas and the Virgin Mary, are depicted to the right of the royal coat of arms. The calligraphy is by John Broke, the clerk of the chancery, and the illuminations are by the London artist, William Abell.

1546 – THE ANTHONY ROLL

The Anthony Roll provides the only surviving contemporary depiction of the Mary Rose.

my lord out of the loue i beare to some of youer frendz
i haue a caer of youer preservacion therfor i would
aduyse yowe as yowe tender youer lyf to deuyse some
excuse to shift of youer attendance at this parleament
for god and man hathe concurred to punishe the wickednes
of this tyme and thinke not slightlye of this advertisment
but retyere youre self into youer contri wheare yowe
maye expect the event in safti for thowghe theare be no
apparance of anni stir yet i saye they shall receyue a terrible
blowe this parleament and yet they shall not seie who
hurts them this cowncel is not to be contemned because
it maye do yowe good and can do yowe no harme for the
daungere is passed as soon as yowe haue burnt the letter
and i hope god will giue yowe the grace to mak good
use of it to whose holy proteccion i comend yowe

...towne on the monday night following and Confesseth also that
the said Percy, this Examinate, Robert Catesby, Thomas Wintr
John and xpofer wright mett at the fornamed howse on the
backside of St Clements Jnn on sonday night Last.

He furthr saith that the wednsday before his apprhencon
he went forthe of the Towne to a howse in Enfield
Chase on this side of Theobalds where Wally doth Ly
and thithr Came Robert Catesby Graunt and Thomas
wintr whirn he stayed untill sonday night following.

Hee Confesseth also that ther was speech emongst them to
Drawe Sr walter Rawly to take part with them, being
one that might stand them in good steed; as others in
like sort were named.

Taken before us and subscribed
by the examinate before us

Guido Fawkes
Edward Forsett

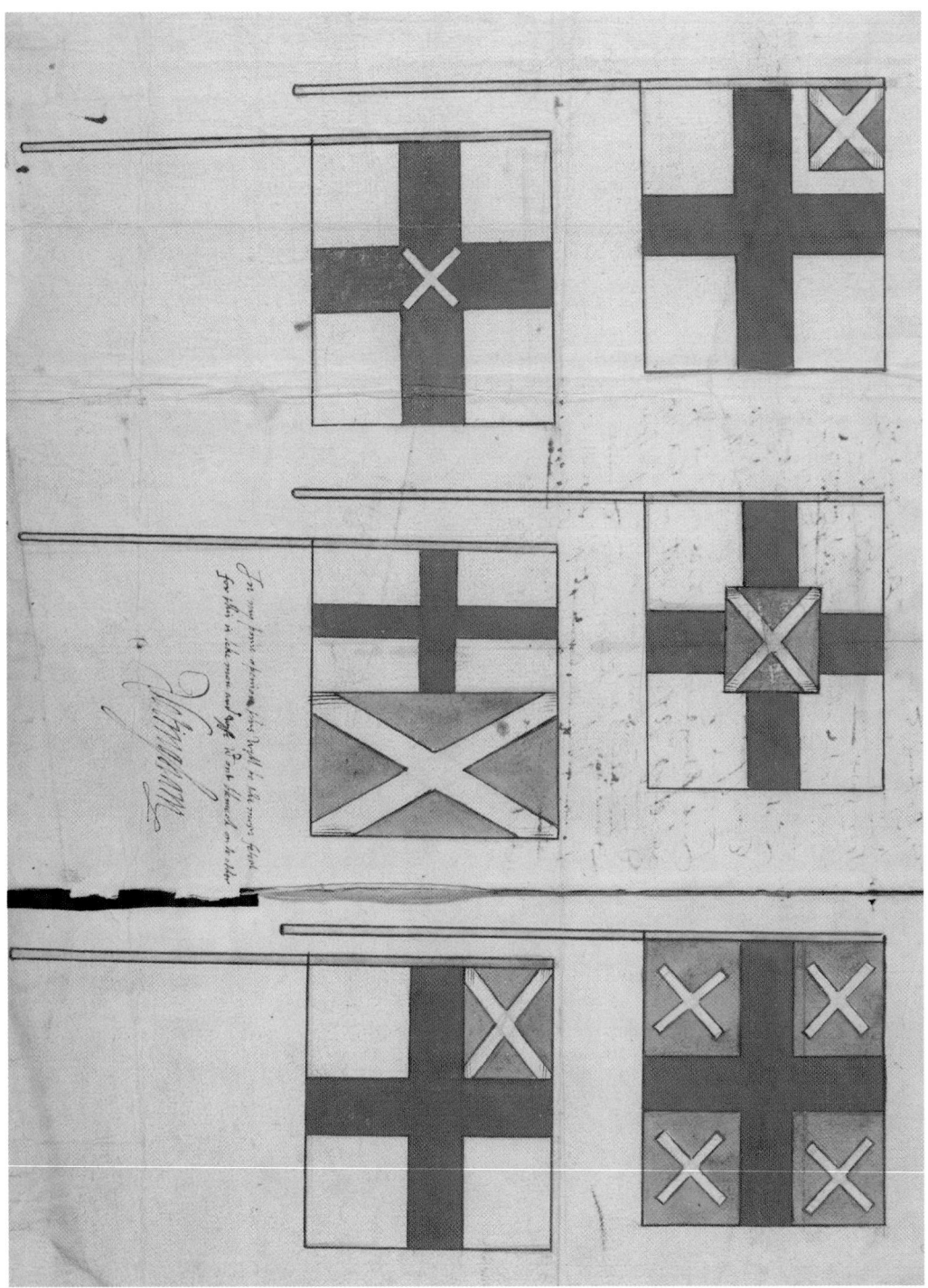

1606 – UNION JACK DESIGNS

Wrestling with the problem of how to give the crosses of St George and St Andrew equal esteem in these preliminary designs for the Union Flag, the Earl of Nottingham inserted his hand-written recommendation below the lower middle design, noting it was 'like man and wife.'

From the Second Treatise, Chapter 18: 'Of Tyranny'

Wherever law ends, tyranny begins, if the law be transgressed to another's harm; and whosoever in authority exceeds the power given him by the law, and makes use of the force he has under his command, to compass that upon the subject, which the law allows not, ceases in that to be a magistrate; and, acting without authority, may be opposed, as any other man, who by force invades the right of another. This is acknowledged in subordinate magistrates. He that hath authority to seize my person in the street, may be opposed as a thief and a robber, if he endeavours to break into my house to execute a writ, notwithstanding that I know he has such a warrant, and such a legal authority, as will impower him to arrest me abroad. And why this should not hold in the highest, as well as in the most inferior magistrate, I would gladly be informed. Is it reasonable, that the eldest brother, because he has the greatest part of his father's estate, should thereby have a right to take away any of his younger brothers portions? or that a rich man, who possessed a whole country, should from thence have a right to seize, when he pleased, the cottage and garden of his poor neighbour? The being rightfully possessed of great power and riches, exceedingly beyond the greatest part of the sons of Adam, is so far from being an excuse, much less a reason, for rapine and oppression, which the endamaging another without authority is, that it is a great aggravation of it: for the exceeding the bounds of authority is no more a right in a great, than in a petty officer; no more justifiable in a king than a constable; but is so much the worse in him, in that he has more trust put in him, has already a much greater share than the rest of his brethren, and is supposed, from the advantages of his education, employment, and counsellors, to be more knowing in the measures of right and wrong.

owed to the state existed on the presumption that the state sought to pursue their best interest. If it wilfully failed to do so, then the people had the right to remove that government.

Ultimate sovereignty thus lay with the people. This was, in effect, an argument for representative democracy. Believing that constitutional restraint made for better government, Locke suggested that government was less likely to tend towards oppression if there was a separation of powers between the legislature and the executive: the former elected, the latter residing in the person of a head of state.

Nor was this the only separation he advocated. Theologically, Locke was a moderate Anglican who set out his attitude in his *Letter on Toleration*. He believed that the state and religion were fundamentally different, the latter being a voluntary matter unrelated to civil promotion or disabilities so long as a Church did not promulgate doctrine at odds with the principles of civil society or force allegiance to a foreign overlord. He also wrote on education and monetary policy (some of his arguments preshadowing the free-trade advocacy of Adam Smith) and, in his *Essay Concerning Human Understanding*, he contradicted Descartes' view that ideas were innate and that universal truths could therefore be deduced by purely rational deduction alone. Rather than such philosophical abstractions, he believed in empirical research, garnered through experience and reflection.

Although the *Two Treatises of Government* was originally published anonymously, it burnished Locke's reputation as an exponent of freedom in the decades after his death in 1704. Locke, the defender of the Glorious Revolution, had created an intelligible theory of limited government as the servant of the people. His thinking infused Whig arguments during the eighteenth century and influenced nineteenth-century liberalism, in particular that of John Stuart Mill. Outside Britain, his legacy was perhaps even more apparent. In 1669 he had helped draft the constitution of the colony of Carolina, and the first American printed edition of his *Two Treatises* was published in Boston in 1773. Its timing was perfect, providing arguments that American colonists would use against what they considered the overweening and unrepresentative authority of George III. No document better conveys Locke's arguments for the separation of powers than the constitution of the United States of America.

1694

THE ROYAL CHARTER OF THE
BANK OF ENGLAND

FINANCE AND THE BANKER OF LAST RESORT

Until the beginning of the seventeenth century, Britain had no major financial sector. There was nothing to compare with the credit revolution taking place in the Dutch Republic, where the Bank of Amsterdam was founded in 1609. The goldsmiths were the nearest London came to a coherent banking community. Providing strongrooms for merchants to deposit their treasure, the goldsmiths brought together the main functions of modern banking, offering deposit and lending facilities and issuing notes redeemable for the valuables in their safe keeping.

However, they were not geared to meet the mounting credit demands of late seventeenth-century government. These became acute following the Glorious Revolution of 1688 because of William III's determination to fight France in a war he could ill afford. Between 1690 and 1697, the state managed to raise around £28 million in revenue but spent £40 million prosecuting the war. Expedients such as the £1 million lottery loan, which offered huge cash prizes, were less a sign of the state's ingenuity than of its failure to develop the institutions necessary to provide long-term security.

The answer to England's financial problems was provided by a Scotsman. William Paterson (1658–1719), an adventurer who had done business in the West Indies and Holland, proposed Britain's first incorporated joint-stock bank, to be called the Bank of England. It would solicit £1.2 million from the public, which would be lent to the government at a rate of 8 per cent interest guaranteed by Parliament. Investors of more than £500 would also get to vote for the bank's board of management.

Investors were attracted not just by the rate of interest but also by the absence of a time limit for repayment. Potentially (and in reality), interest would continue to accrue indefinitely, becoming the National Debt. The state of its finances made

A Short History of British Banking

1546 Henry VIII repeals the usury laws, making lending with interest legal.

1640 Confidence in the Royal Mint is shattered by Charles I's seizure of its gold. Growing use of the private quasi-banking facilities is offered by the goldsmiths – who fund the Parliamentarian war effort.

1659 The first surviving example of a cheque dates from this time.

1690 John Freame and Thomas Gould begin trading as Goldsmith bankers. Their firm eventually becomes Barclays Bank.

1692 Coutts & Co. is founded.

1694 The Bank of England receives its royal charter.

1695 The Bank of Scotland is founded, and the Scottish Parliament grants it a twenty-one year monopoly of public banking in Scotland.

1727 The Royal Bank of Scotland is founded.

1759 The Bank of England issues the first £10 note. The £5 note follows in 1793.

1804–9 The number of 'country banks' outside London increases from 470 to 800.

1811 N. M. Rothschild & Sons established as a bank in London and helps finance the war effort of Britain and her allies during the Napoleonic Wars. For much of the 19th century, Rothschild dominates the international bond market.

1821 The gold standard makes Bank of England notes convertible at a fixed weight of gold. (The gold standard was suspended in 1914 and briefly reintroduced between 1925 and 1931.)

1866 There are 154 joint-stock banks with 850 branches, and 246 private banks with 376 branches.

1870 The Bank of England assumes the right to set interest rates.

1900 There are seventy-seven joint-stock banks and only nineteen private banks left with branches. Consolidation during the Edwardian period creates the domination of the 'Big Five' clearing banks during the 1920s (Barclays, Lloyds, Midland, National Provincial, Westminster).

1946 The Bank of England is nationalized; sterling's exchange rate is fixed relative to the dollar. The system breaks down in 1971, after which sterling's exchange rate floats.

1966 Barclaycard, the first credit card, is introduced in Britain.

1968 The merger of National Provincial and Westminster banks to create 'NatWest' reduces the 'Big Five' to the 'Big Four'.

1971 The coinage is decimalized.

1980s–90s A spate of demutualization of building societies effectively creates a string of new banks.

1986 The 'Big Bang' deregulation of finance markets ushers in a series of mergers and take-overs of British brokerages and merchant banks by foreign banks and restores the City of London's financial supremacy over New York. Banking sector assets increase sevenfold between 1986 and 2006.

1995 Barings Banks – the oldest merchant bank in London – collapses after one of its derivatives traders, Nick Leeson, loses over £800 million in unauthorized speculation.

1997 The Bank of England regains operational independence but loses financial regulatory powers.

2007 £2.15 trillion of capital flows into UK financial institutions.

2008–9 The financial crisis leads to the government nationalizing some banks and taking large shares in others. Lloyds TSB rescues the debt-laden Halifax–Bank of Scotland (HBOS), but then itself needs government support.

the government ill placed to haggle. Among the influential persons won over by Paterson was Charles Montagu, a commissioner of the Treasury. Overcoming the opposition of the goldsmiths and other vested interests, Montagu steered the government towards supporting the legislation and the royal charter that created the Bank of England in 1694.

The bank began in a rented hall in Cheapside with a staff of nineteen. Despite these modest beginnings, its attractiveness to investors was evident from the first. It was launched on 27 July 1694, and eleven days later had successfully raised the required £1.2 million. Initially, there were nearly 1,300 shareholders. Paterson, however, soon fell out with the other directors and quit. Returning to the land of his birth, he conceived and promoted the ill-fated Darien scheme to establish a colony in Central America, which wrecked the Scottish economy and humbled its leaders into seeking full economic, political and monetary union with England. Paterson then helped draw up the terms of the Treaty of Union.

This late-eighteenth-century engraving of Threadneedle Street shows the Bank of England building shortly before its expansion – which resulted in the demolition of its neighbour, the Church of St Christopher-Le-Stocks.

Extract from The Charter of the Corporation of the Governor and Company of the Bank of England, 1694

WILLIAM and MARY, by the Grace of God, King and Queen of England, Scotland, France and Ireland, Defenders of the Faith, &c. To all to whom these Presents shall come, Greeting.

... And all and every Person and Persons, Natives or Foreigners, Bodies Politick and Corporate, who, either as original Subscribers of the said Sum of Twelve Hundred Thousand Pounds so subscribed, and not having parted with their Interests in their Subscriptions, or as Heirs, Successors, or Assignees, or by any other lawful Title derived, or to be derived from, by, or under the said original Subscribers of the said Sum of Twelve Hundred Thousand Pounds so subscribed, or any of them now have, or at any Time or Times hereafter shall have, or be entituled to any Part, Share, or Interest of or in the Principal or Capital Stock of the said Corporation, or the said yearly Fond of One Hundred Thousand Pounds, granted by the said Act of Parliament, or any Part thereof, so long as they respectively shall have any such Part, Share, or Interest therein, shall be, and be called one Body Politick and Corporate, of themselves, in Deed and in Name, by the Name of The Governor and Company of the Bank of England; and them by that Name, one Body Politick and Corporate, in Deed and in Name, We do, for Us, our Heirs, and Successors, make, create, erect, establish, and confirm for ever, by these Presents, and by the same Name, they and their Successors shall have perpetual Succession, and shall and may have and use a Common Seal, for the Use, Business, or Affairs of the said Body Politick and Corporate, and their Successors, with Power to break, alter, and to make anew their Seal from Time to Time, at their Pleasure, and as they shall see Cause. And by the same Name, they and their Successors in all Times coming, shall be able and capable in Law, to have, take, purchase, receive, hold, keep, possess, enjoy, and retain to them and their Successors, any Manors, Messuages, Lands, Rents, Tenements, Liberties, Privileges, Franchises, Hereditaments, and Possessions whatsoever, and of what Kind, Nature, or Quality soever; ... And we do hereby for Us, our Heirs and Successors, declare, limit, direct and appoint, that the aforesaid Sum of Twelve Hundred Thousand Pounds so subscribed as aforesaid, shall be, and be called, accepted, esteemed, reputed and taken, The Common Capital and Principal Stock of the Corporation hereby constituted.

Rivals like the Land Bank were quickly seen off and while small provincial private banks issued their own notes, the Bank of England's notes were subsequently given a monopoly in the London area where their promise to pay the 'bearer' (not just the original depositor) made them easily exchangeable units of currency. By the 1930s the Bank of England had gained a monopoly on producing all England's banknotes (Scottish and Northern Irish banks continued to print notes north of the border and in Ulster). Successive notes bore the image of Britannia. The decision to follow the ancient practice of the coinage and put the monarch's face on the notes began only as late as 1960.

Although the Bank of England was not created as the state's central bank, this is what it became. During the eighteenth century, four-fifths of its business was government-related. It looked after government department accounts and managed a National Debt that increased from £12 million in 1700 to £850 million by 1815. As early as 1781, the prime minister, Lord North, described the bank as 'from long habit and usage of many years . . . a part of the constitution'. The bank's reputation for financial security was acknowledged in a popular catchphrase, 'as safe as the Bank of England', while currency stability created in between the end of the Napoleonic Wars and the onset of the First World War (by a gold standard that valued the pound sterling to a fixed quantity of gold) also helped London emerge as the world's financial centre.

It was as this age was passing, during the inter-war period, that the Bank of England completed its long process of becoming Britain's central bank and lender of last resort. It had been setting the country's interest rates since 1870. How little difference its nationalization in 1946 initially made may be judged by the fact that the same board was retained after the state formally took control. The collapse of an international system of fixed currency exchanges in 1971, and a belief that Treasury interference in interest-rate policy involved more political than economic calculation, led to the bank regaining operational independence in 1997. At the same time, it lost its regulatory role over the City to a new Financial Services Authority. This proved controversial and following the financial crisis of 2008–9, the incoming coalition government in 2010 set about restoring some of the FSA's regulatory powers to the bank.

1701
THE ACT OF SETTLEMENT

ESTABLISHING THE ROYAL SUCCESSION

The Glorious Revolution removed the Catholic James II and replaced him on the throne with William III and Mary II, his Protestant son-in-law and daughter. The Bill of Rights stipulated the subsequent terms of the succession: the children of William and Mary, followed by the children of Mary's sister Anne, followed by any children William might have by a second marriage. Catholics were debarred. Events confounded this careful order. In 1694, Mary died of smallpox, aged only thirty-two and without issue. William continued to rule but as a widower with no interest in remarriage. The next in line, Anne, endured seventeen pregnancies, all of which ended in miscarriage or children who died in infancy. In 1700, her one remaining son died shortly after his eleventh birthday. With his demise passed the last real prospect of the beneficiaries of the Glorious Revolution securing the throne for their descendants.

The monarchy appeared to be heading towards a crisis. The Bill of Rights' prohibition of a Catholic ought to have ruled out any possibility of the Crown being returned to the deposed James II or his son, James Francis Edward Stuart, who were both languishing in French exile as the guests of Louis XIV. However, unless Parliament made clear who the next rightful monarch ought to be after Anne, the scope for dispute and revolt would create a void in which the seizure of power by the exiled Stuarts' supporters could not be discounted.

It was to remove any ambiguity that in 1701 Parliament passed the Act of Settlement. It established that, in the event of Anne dying childless, the throne would pass to the nearest surviving Protestant Stuart relation. This was Sophia, Electress of Hanover, who was James I's granddaughter. Recently widowed from the German state's ruler, the Elector Ernest Augustus, Sophia also had Protestant offspring who could inherit on her death. In the event, she died only weeks before Anne in 1714, whereupon the British throne passed to Sophia's son, George I. A Jacobite rebellion in favour of James Francis Edward was defeated the following year.

ROYAL FAMILY TREE: FROM THE STUARTS TO THE HANOVERIANS

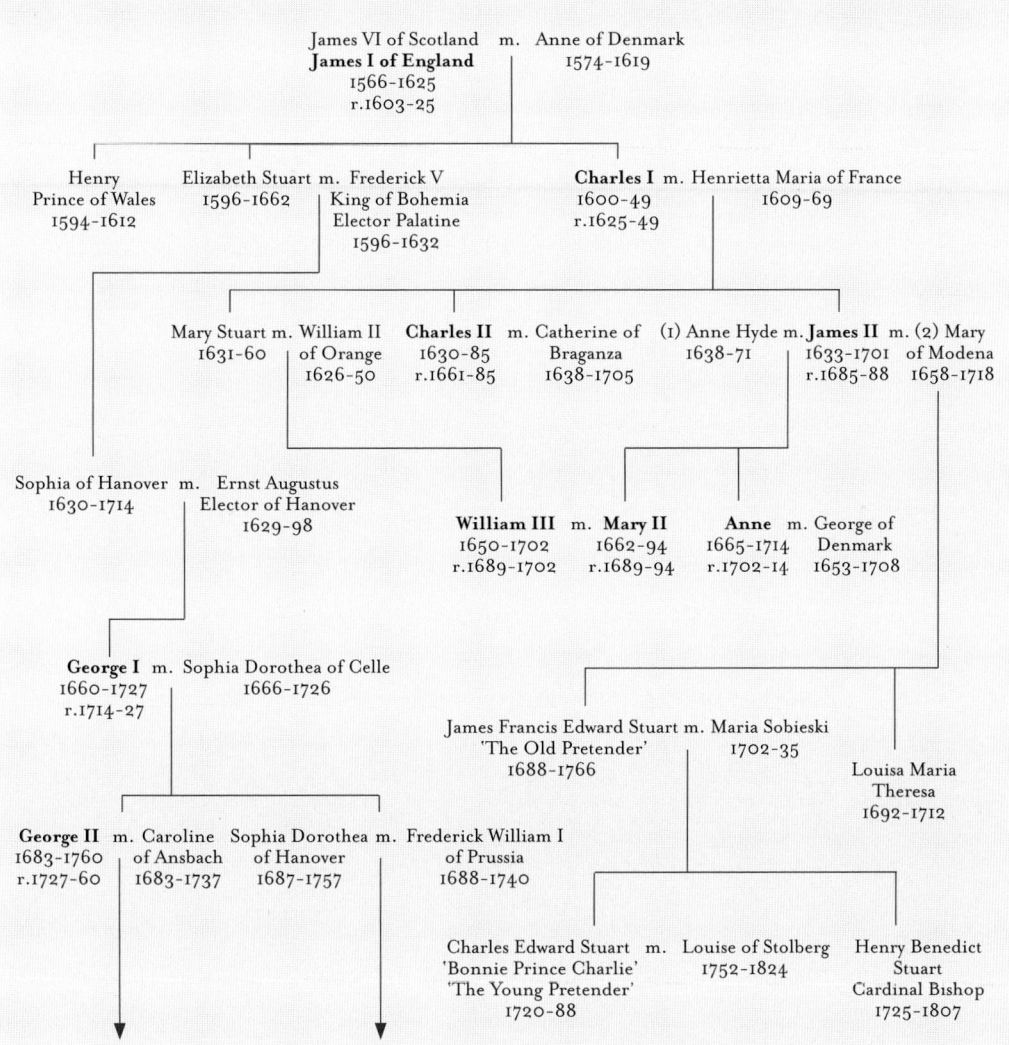

Scotland's response to the passage of the Act of Settlement made clear how real the prospect was of the throne passing on Anne's death to the disinherited Catholic wing of the Stuart family. Rather than endorse Westminster's statute, the Scottish Parliament pointedly refused to follow suit, raising the possibility that on Anne's death, Scotland might declare James Francis Edward the new King of

From the Act of Settlement, 1701

That the most excellent Princess Sophia, Electress and Duchess Dowager of Hanover, daughter of the most excellent Princess Elizabeth, late Queen of Bohemia, daughter of our late sovereign lord King James the First, of happy memory, be and is hereby declared to be the next in succession, in the Protestant line, to the imperial Crown and dignity of the said Realms of England, France, and Ireland, with the dominions and territories thereunto belonging, after His Majesty, and the Princess Anne of Denmark, and in default of issue of the said Princess Anne, and of His Majesty respectively: and that from and after the deceases of His said Majesty, our now sovereign lord, and of Her Royal Highness the Princess Anne of Denmark, and for default of issue of the said Princess Anne, and of His Majesty respectively, the Crown and regal government of the said Kingdoms of England, France, and Ireland, and of the dominions thereunto belonging, with the royal state and dignity of the said Realms, and all honours, styles, titles, regalities, prerogatives, powers, jurisdictions and authorities, to the same belonging and appertaining, shall be, remain, and continue to the said most excellent Princess Sophia, and the heirs of her body, being Protestants: and thereunto the said Lords Spiritual and Temporal, and Commons, shall and will in the name of all the people of this Realm, most humbly and faithfully submit themselves, their heirs and posterities: and do faithfully promise, that after the deceases of His Majesty, and Her Royal Highness, and the failure of the heirs of their respective bodies, to stand to, maintain, and defend the said Princess Sophia, and the heirs of her body, being Protestants, according to the limitation and succession of the Crown in this act specified and contained, to the utmost of their powers, with their lives and estates, against all persons whatsoever that shall attempt anything to the contrary.

Scots. In 1704, the Scottish Parliament passed an Act of Security that asserted its right to choose a different monarch from that chosen by England unless London signed a free-trade agreement. The legislation restricted the choice to Protestant claimants although the likely consequential division clearly created opportunities for Jacobites to exploit. Unwilling to risk the security of the English realm by tolerating a pro-French Scottish king who believed himself entitled to the English throne as well, Westminster quickly began coercing the Scots towards full political

union. The resulting 1707 Act of Union made the Act of Settlement applicable in Scotland.

Thus the Act of Settlement's legacy was profound: it established the succession of all subsequent monarchs of Great Britain and, subsequently, the United Kingdom – entities that it was instrumental in bringing into being. The act also modified the Bill of Rights by stipulating that the monarch had to be not only Protestant but also Anglican. Judicial independence was strengthened by the clause that prevented judges being removed by the monarch. A royal pardon could not block an impeachment by Parliament. However, a measure to prevent Parliament being packed with royal 'placemen', holding government positions or pensions would have separated the legislature from the executive, thereby injuring the development of parliamentary government. It was largely scrapped in 1706 when MPs who accepted office had to fight a by-election to confirm their appointment.

While securing the British monarchy for the house of Hanover, the Act of Settlement sought to bar its sovereigns from putting German considerations before British ones. They could not bestow offices and Crown lands on foreigners, nor could they leave Britain without parliamentary approval. The first of these clauses was later replaced by legislation permitting the naturalization of foreigners, while George I managed to have his travel restrictions lifted within two years of becoming king. Nonetheless, the framers of the 1701 legislation were particularly alive to the potential conflict of national interests with a monarch who was also ruler of Hanover. To prevent Britain being drawn into Hanover's wars, the Act of Settlement established that no fighting on the behalf of foreign countries would be legal without first securing parliamentary assent.

All four Hanoverian Georges as well as William IV combined being king of Britain with ruling Hanover, although only George I spent much time in his German domain. This connection was severed in 1837. Hanover's rules of succession precluded a woman inheriting in her own right, so Queen Victoria ascended the throne in Britain, leaving Hanover to her uncle.

1707
THE ACT OF UNION

THE UNITED KINGDOM OF GREAT BRITAIN

The Act of Union is depicted in the third plate section.

On 11 August 1607, the Scottish Parliament had voted in favour of full political union with England. Less enamoured by the prospect of marriage, Westminster's politicians had jilted the bride at the altar.

One hundred years later, it was England's politicians who came courting. The change of heart was a result of Scotland's determination to choose its own monarch on the death of Queen Anne. It seemed possible that while the house of Hanover would succeed to the English throne, the Scots – despite explicitly legislating for a Protestant succession – might end up restoring the Catholic branch of the Stuart family. The thought of James II's son ruling as James VIII in Edinburgh, perhaps supported by French troops and still claiming to be England's rightful ruler, posed a real threat to the English realm, especially since the country was again engaged in continental warfare against France. Suddenly, the political settlement of the Glorious Revolution looked altogether less secure.

Scotland had not prospered during the century in which its royal family moved to London. In 1700, her widely dispersed population of around 1 million equated to one-fifth of England's size. In terms of prosperity however, the chasm was far greater. At the end of the seventeenth century, famine and emigration conspired to reduce the Scottish population by 15 per cent. It was during these 'Lean Years' that the country gambled much of its remaining wealth in an intrepid scheme to start a colonial trading empire, only to learn a humiliating lesson in the dangers of going it alone.

In 1698, the attempt to establish a Scottish colony at Darien, on the isthmus of Panama, collapsed in ruin. The expedition to colonize a strip of central America that had the potential to become the Atlantic–Pacific trading gateway between Europe and Asia looked strategically shrewd on a map of the world. In reality, establishing 'New Caledonia' in a humid, fever-ridden swamp was ill-conceived from the first. Most of the settlers died in appalling conditions. In the search for

scapegoats, England's callously obstructionist attitude to the scheme made it a target for Scottish blame. Nonetheless, the financial consequences were such that Scotland had to consider going cap in hand to its southern neighbour. Darien had consumed nearly a quarter of the country's liquid capital.

Thus while English supporters of union were guided by security fears, Scottish unionist objectives were primarily economic. After all, Scotland's failure to become a colonial power in a world of protectionist tariffs restricted its access to markets. Threatening to install a rival claimant on its throne was one means of trying to force the English into commercial concessions. The 1704 Act of Security that asserted Scotland's right to choose its own monarch came with the rider that it would not do so if England signed a free-trade agreement.

Westminster was not so easily cajoled. Raising the stakes, it passed an Alien Act that threatened not only to block key Scottish imports but to treat all Scots as foreigners unless the Scottish Parliament either declared for the Hanoverian succession or agreed full political union. Reluctantly, Edinburgh's politicians conceded among themselves that their alternative options were narrowing while each month their financial outlook darkened.

With the blessing of Queen Anne, negotiations began in April 1706. England's lord treasurer, Sidney Godolphin, and the Scottish dukes of Queensberry and Argyll were the driving forces. Commissioners from both nations were appointed to meet in separate rooms and haggle over the details. In July, agreement was reached on the twenty-five articles of the Treaty of Union. These provided the substance of the subsequent Act of Union, which the English Parliament endorsed by 274 votes to 116 and the Scottish Parliament by 110 to 67.

The new nation created would be called the United Kingdom of Great Britain. The house of Hanover would succeed to its throne after Queen Anne's death. The parliament in Edinburgh would be abolished and, instead, forty-five Scottish MPs would join the existing 513 English and Welsh MPs at Westminster, with equal legislative powers. In the upper house, sixteen peers, elected by the far larger old Scottish nobility, would represent the Scots aristocracy in the House of Lords. Although these ratios were less than Scotland was entitled to in terms of comparative population size, they were deemed appropriate to its far smaller fiscal contribution. Scotland would retain its own legal system and the (Presbyterian) Church of Scotland would remain the Established Church north of the border.

In economic matters, the Scots got most of what they wanted. Free trade was established and Scots were given equal access to the colonies of the English – now

British – Empire. Monetary union, as well as common weights and measures were adopted, along with English usage. A financial calculation called The Equivalent compensated Darien shareholders for their losses and offset Scotland's share of the assumption of England's National Debt.

The sum of £20,000 was dispersed among those affected by the changes: financial sweeteners to ensure that the Scottish Parliament voted itself out of existence. While some of the money may have represented legitimate expenses, it looked suspiciously like bribery and encouraged the presumption that the nation had been sold out by those whom the poet Robert Burns later called a 'Parcel of Rogues'. There was widespread protest in Scotland as the prospect of agreement drew near. The public rejoicing in London that marked the Union coming into force on 1 May 1707 found no echo in Edinburgh. There, the bells of St Giles tolled the melody 'Why should I be sad on my wedding day?'

In the short term, the Union delivered neither security for the English nor prosperity to the Scots. Jacobite risings sprang up in Scotland in 1715 and 1745 in an attempt to restore the Catholic house of Stuart on both sides of the border. It was not until Jacobitism was comprehensively crushed at the Battle of Culloden in 1746 that tensions abated. Thereafter, Scotland began to benefit more evidently from the trading opportunities now within its grasp as part of a larger market. Having failed so catastrophically at going it alone in the swamps of Panama, the Scots proceeded to distinguish themselves as fervent colonists under the Union flag. As soldiers, traders, financiers, engineers, politicians and missionaries, Scots were pre-eminent in pushing the perimeters of the British Empire to their furthest extents.

Thus a nation that had been one of Europe's poorest at the beginning of the eighteenth century became one of its richest by the late nineteenth century. The retention of a separate Scottish legal system, as well as the 'Kirk' and long-standing traditions in education acknowledged – and preserved – Scotland's own identity. These separate institutions did not, however, prevent the Scots from also occupying many of the most important offices in London.

For a marriage driven more by contrasting necessities than genuine affection, the Anglo-Scottish union proved remarkably enduring, surviving over 300 years while so many of Europe's other multinational countries fragmented and split. During the nineteenth and twentieth centuries there remained periodic irritation and the natural difficulties created by a union of two nations of vastly different size and power, but no blood was spilled in trying to keep it together. Elsewhere, history during that period offers few comparable examples.

V

HANOVERIAN BRITAIN

1745

THE MUSIC AND LYRICS OF 'GOD SAVE THE KING'

THE ORIGINS OF THE NATIONAL ANTHEM

In July 1745, James II's grandson, Prince Charles Edward Stuart – 'Bonnie Prince Charlie' – landed at Moidart on the west coast of Scotland and the following month raised his standard at Glenfinnan. His intention was to overthrow Hanoverian rule, to revoke the 1701 Act of Settlement and to assert the right of his father, James Francis Edward Stuart, then aged fifty-seven, to the throne for which he had been born.

Many of the Highland Scottish clans were reluctant subjects of the Hanoverian monarchy and quickly pledged allegiance to the Stuart cause. With this swelling band of 'Jacobite' followers, Prince Charles Edward marched into Edinburgh in September, holding court there and defeating government forces outside the city at Prestonpans.

In London there was good reason to panic. With much of the British army engaged on the European continent, fighting in the War of the Austrian Succession, the capital was defended only by a numerically inferior detachment of Guards and a ragbag militia ineffectually blocking the road at Finchley. The capital, it seemed, was on the brink of falling into the hands of a rabble Scottish army, while the country stood in danger of being ruled by a pro-French Roman Catholic with tendencies favourable to absolute monarchy.

It was in this fevered atmosphere that a song was struck up in the theatres at Drury Lane and Covent Garden. Its composer and lyricist remain unclear, the first published form of the tune having appeared, without attribution, the previous year. It may have been a reworking of an earlier tune, bearing some similarities to works by John Bull (1562–1628) and Henry Purcell (1659–95). Whatever its origins, it was perfect for the moment in 1745. It immediately caught on, being sung in the theatres night after night with increasing vehemence and defiance as the crisis

deepened. Indeed, its choruses were echoed across the capital, its popularity fuelled by the publication of the words and music in the *Gentleman's Magazine* and similar newspapers.

The song was 'God Save the King' and it was arranged for performance at Drury Lane by Thomas Arne, who was at that time second only to George Frideric Handel as London's most celebrated composer. Despite being himself a Catholic, Arne was a supporter of the Hanoverian cause. Five years previously, he had composed the song 'Rule Britannia!' (whose lyrics were by the Scottish poet, James Thomson) as the centrepiece of *Alfred: A Masque*, which he performed for the Prince of Wales at Cliveden in Buckinghamshire. 'God Save the King' was intended to rally anti-Jacobite sentiment rather than become a defining declaration of Britishness (there was no concept of a national anthem at that time). Therefore, the lines 'Confound their politics/ Frustrate their knavish tricks' referred to Jacobite sympathizers rather than foreign countries. Various alternative versions soon flourished, one of which included a fourth verse expressing the hope:

> Lord, grant that Marshal Wade
> May by thy mighty aid
> Victory bring
> May he sedition hush
> And like a torrent rush
> Rebellious Scots to crush
> God save the King.

THE JACOBITE RISINGS

1708 Admiral Byng thwarts an attempt by the Old Pretender (James Francis Edward Stuart) to land with French troops in the Firth of Forth.

The 1715 Rising

8 March 1715 The Earl of Mar raises the Scottish clans to the Jacobite cause.

13 November The Jacobite advance is halted at the Battle of Sheriffmuir in Perthshire.

14 November A Jacobite force surrenders at Preston.

23 December The Old Pretender lands at Peterhead with the intention of being crowned King James VIII of Scots at Scone. Instead, he finds the Jacobite forces already demoralized and returns to France on 4 February 1716.

1719 Storms disrupt a pro-Jacobite Spanish invasion fleet. A small landing party surrenders at Glen Shiel.

The 1745 Rising

1744 A storm wrecks a pro-Jacobite French invasion fleet intending to land in Essex.

19 August 1745 Prince Charles Edward Stuart raises his standard at Glenfinnan and claims the Scottish and English thrones for his father.

21 September The Hanoverian camp is overwhelmed at Prestonpans, east of Edinburgh.

4 December Prince Charles's army reaches as far as Derby before retreating to Scotland to raise more support.

17 January 1746 The Jacobites are victorious at the Battle of Falkirk.

16 April The Jacobites are routed at Culloden Moor, near Inverness.

20 September Prince Charles is rescued by a French ship, which takes him back into exile.

1759 A French invasion plan to foment a new Jacobite rebellion is called off.

The words and music for what became the national anthem were published in The Gentleman's Magazine in October 1745.

2.
O Lord our God arife,
Scatter his enemies,
    And make them fall;
Confound their politics,
Fruftrate their knavifh tricks,
On him our hopes we fix,
    O fave us all.

3.
Thy choiceft gifts in ftore
On *George* be pleas'd to pour,
    Long may he reign;
May he defend our laws,
And ever give us caufe,
To fay with heart and voice
    God fave the king.

A SOLILOQUY.

——*From evil ftill educing good.*   Thomfon.

SHALL FREEDOM, now, her care for *Britain* o'er, [fhore!
Spread her white wings, and fpurn her long-lov'd
Our weeping *maids* fhall lawlefs ruffians flain!
To fpare the *babe* our *mothers* kneel in vain?
Infulted, vanquifh'd, in unequal ftrife
Shall the fond hufband ftabb'd refign the wife?
Shall hungry robbers plunder *Englifh* wealth?
And fkulking *Britons* eat their bread by ftealth?
    With thee, O GODDESS! ev'ry *fibil art*,
Peace, plenty, fcience, fhall at once depart;
Incumbent o'er us *Ign'rance* fhall difplay
Her leathern wings, and intercept the day;
Blind Zeal's red torch alone, with hateful light,
Shall juft difclofe the terrors of the night,
While *Superftition*, raving, fhakes the blade,
That fmokes ♄ blood, and glitters thro' ♅ fhade;
What once were men grow brutes at her controul,
Debas'd, enflav'd—in body and in *foul!*
    But whence thefe doubts, and whence the fears
        I feel?
Can rebel outlaws fhake the publick weal?
Slaves— by a beardlefs, hot- brain'd bigot led!——
My indignation burns, my fears are fled;

They come to bid our fleeping virtues rife,
By thefe our Genius fpeaks;—his words are wife:
‘ Hear me, ye fons of *Eafe*, whom *Sloth* difarms,
‘ And *Pleafure* captivates, with tinfel charms,
‘ Yours is the finewy nerve that taught fo late
‘ *France*, conquer'd *France*, to tremble for her fate.
‘ You fmil'd, contemptuous, at the tyrant's nod,
‘ And drew the fword for *Liberty* and GOD;
‘ Each man an hero,—*Glory* all his pay;
‘ And yet you fleep in *Lux'ry*'s lap to day.
‘ The foe's at hand!—there's ruin at the door!
‘ Wake now *for Liberty*, or wake no more!’
Rouz'd at the call, our heroes fhine again,
Old Englifh courage beats in ev'ry vein,
With honeft blufhes ev'ry cheek is dy'd,
And ev'ry hand is to the fword apply'd;
Rome's hoft of fculptur'd faints neglect her pray'r,
And all her curfes are difpers'd in air:
Still, as of old, the cords fhe weaves we break,
Our ftrength returning with the rowzing fhake.
    So *Sampfon*, flumb'ring on an harlot's knee,
With eafe was fetter'd, dreaming he was free;
But —*The Philiftines come!*—he heard and rofe,
Lord of himfelf, the terror of his foes;
Refumes his might, their various arts difdains,
Looks up, and miling breaks the facile chains.
                                        BRITANNICUS.

Field Marshal George Wade was in charge of the army in the north during the Jacobite invasion. This verse was not in Arne's arrangement, did not outlive the crisis and was never a part of the version adopted as the national anthem.

The crisis passed because Prince Charles Edward flunked his chance. Rather than pressing on to take the lightly defended London, he was persuaded at Derby to turn back to gather more support in Scotland. This gave the Hanoverian forces time to muster and, in April 1746, on Culloden Moor near Inverness, the bedraggled and half-starving Jacobite party, wielding swords and uttering ancient battle-cries, was shot to pieces by a modern, well-drilled army commanded by the king's younger son, William, duke of Cumberland. Those who escaped the slaughter were hunted down, often with excessive savagery, and the 'Bonnie Prince' went on the run before escaping to France. This great hope of all those who wanted to restore a Stuart and a Catholic to the British throne died in Rome in 1788, a debauched and broken figure.

By then, 'God Save the King' was becoming recognized as the national anthem, in an innovation that other European countries rushed to follow. Initially, Prussia and Russia copied it to the extent of retaining the same tune, and for most of the nineteenth century it was also the Swedish royal family's anthem. Even the infant United States held on to it, although substituting the loyalist sentiments with new words: 'My country, 'tis of thee'. With the help of the British Empire, it was a tune that travelled the world.

1755
SAMUEL JOHNSON'S
DICTIONARY

THE CELEBRATED ENGLISH-LANGUAGE DICTIONARY

When Samuel Johnson published *A Dictionary of the English Language* in 1755, he was not breaking new ground. There had been Latin–English dictionaries since the fifteenth century, while the first to offer definitions of English words without Latin equivalents was Robert Cawdrey's *A Table Alphabeticall* in 1604. Thus Johnson's work was neither the first nor – despite its 42,773 entries – even the one with the greatest number of words defined. However, it was the one that caught the popular imagination. In its various versions, it remained the most commonly used dictionary until the completion of the *Oxford English Dictionary* in 1928.

Remarkably, it was the product not of a team of lexicographers but of one man's erudition and labour, aided only by five or six copyists working in the garret of his house off Fleet Street. It was not surprising that, denied the support of a patron or an institution, it took Johnson almost nine years to compile. Whilst many of his predecessors had devoted excessive space to Latin and Greek terms, Johnson paid particular attention to everyday language. Furthermore, his compilation was revolutionary in a second respect, because it contained around 114,000 quotations, providing polished literary examples of usage. The result was a dictionary that also strove to be the most significant anthology of English literary quotation then in existence.

Unquestionably, this facet was part of its enduring appeal. Even a critic of Johnson's skills as an etymologist – the writer and politician Thomas Babington Macaulay (1800–59) – readily conceded that it was 'the first dictionary which could be read with pleasure. The definitions show so much acuteness of thought and command of language, and the passages quoted from poets, divines and philosophers are so skilfully selected, that a leisure hour may always be very agreeably spent in turning over the pages.'

Naturally, as the work of one man, it contained some idiosyncrasies, although this was also part of its charm. The famous disdain for Scotland with which he later teased his friend and biographer, James Boswell, was apparent in, for example:

> **Oats** n.s. [*aten*, Saxon] A grain, which in England is generally given to horses, but in Scotland supports the people.

Nor could Johnson resist mockery in matters close to his own experience. His definition of 'Lexicographer' was 'a writer of dictionaries; a harmless drudge', while the entry for 'patron' started, 'One who countenances, supports or protects' before continuing, 'Commonly a wretch who supports with insolence, and is paid with flattery'. He was also honest enough to admit when he did not know the meaning and etymology of some words, whilst also decrying some usages of which he disapproved. He was prepared to include crude terms but drew the line at obscenities.

Samuel Johnson, portrayed at the age of sixty-seven by Sir Joshua Reynolds.

Two thousand copies were printed of the first edition, which appeared in two volumes on 15 April 1755. At £4 10s, the price was far beyond the average means of most and sales were initially sluggish. The following year, Johnson brought out a two-volume abridged version, shorn of quotations, which proved far more popular. He produced a considerably revised edition in 1773, a process that other editors continued, in his name, after his death in 1784, by which time the dictionary was established as a classic work.

He was born the son of a Lichfield bookshop owner in 1709 and was educated at the local grammar school. Little in Samuel Johnson's early years suggested he would become one of the most eminent men of his age. Tall, clumsy, short-sighted and deaf in one ear, as well as subject to involuntary convulsions, he endured poor health throughout his life. Bracing himself for the financial hardship involved, he went up to Pembroke College, Oxford, but dropped out without a degree. (Oxford subsequently conferred upon him an MA in recognition of his dictionary; it is thanks to an honorary doctorate from Trinity College, Dublin, in 1765 that he became known as 'Dr Johnson'.) From 1740 he lived in London,

A SHORT LIST OF ENGLISH DICTIONARIES

1604 Robert Cawdrey's *A Table Alphabeticall* (contains definitions for 2,500 words).

1676 Elisha Coles's *An English Dictionary*.

1702 John Kersey's *New English Dictionary*.

1721 and 1727 Nathan Bailey's *Universal Etymological English Dictionary*.

1730 Nathan Bailey's *Dictionarium Britannicum*.

1755 Samuel Johnson's *Dictionary of the English Language*.

1881 The first volume (A–Ant) of what will be the *Oxford English Dictionary*.

1928 Complete edition of the *Oxford English Dictionary*.

scraping a precarious living as a journalist, a reporter of parliamentary debates and a biographer. He was down on his luck when, in 1746, the offer came from a consortium of publishers to write the dictionary in return for 1,500 guineas, minus expenses.

The work took three times longer than was budgeted for and brought its author no great wealth. However, it did establish his reputation and helped bring him further into the circle of many of the most noted literary and political figures of the age as well as the young James Boswell, with whom he travelled to the Hebrides. The resulting *A Journey to the Western Islands of Scotland* offered a poignant depiction of a pre-Enlightenment world. Always a loyal friend, Boswell's posthumous life of Johnson – detailing his Tory irascibility together with his great compassion and humanity, his struggles with disappointment and physical pain, and recording for posterity his many aphorisms – came to be recognized as one of the foremost examples of the biographical genre.

Johnson also wrote many fine poems, sermons, political essays and produced an edition of Shakespeare's plays, but it was his dictionary that endured. Although the *Oxford English Dictionary* finally and comprehensively superseded his masterpiece, its editors could not escape reproducing over 1,700 of his definitions, duly acknowledged under the letter 'J'.

1766
THE DECLARATORY ACT

WESTMINSTER ASSERTS ITS RIGHT TO TAX AND
LEGISLATE IN THE AMERICAN COLONIES

British politicians did not squander George III's North American colonies in one foolish act, but in several. It is doubtful whether even the most considered understanding of the colonists' desires and aspirations would have prevented an eventual breach, but possibly some loose relationship under the British Crown might have endured, as it did, for instance, in Canada. While the causes of the American War of Independence (known in the United States as the Revolutionary War) were many, they mostly touched upon one overarching question: should a parliament in Westminster enjoy the legal right to tax and order the affairs of distant Americans who had no direct representation in it? This was the substantive issue that the 1766 Declaratory Act sought to settle.

Laws in all thirteen British colonies in America were enacted by their own legislatures. Their lower houses were elected and their rights codified in written constitutions. Nine were classified as 'Crown colonies' where the executive, in the guise of the governor and his council (the upper house of the legislature), were appointed by the king in London. Thus, Britain's principal relationship with these American colonies was via the monarch, not the Westminster Parliament. Some eminent Americans, like Benjamin Franklin, were originally keen to keep this distinction, lamenting how 'Every man in England seems to consider himself as a piece of a sovereign over America; seems to jostle himself into the throne with the king, and talks of our subjects in the Colonies.'

Two problems had emerged by the mid-eighteenth century to trouble this arrangement. The first concerned the constitutional balance in Britain, which had tilted during the previous one hundred years towards viewing the monarch as ruling through, and not over, Parliament. The second issue was that the defence and security of the American colonies imposed costs upon the British taxpayer

From the Declaratory Act, 1766

I. . . . Whereas several of the houses of representatives in his Majesty's colonies and plantations in America, have of late, against law, claimed to themselves, or to the general assemblies of the same, the sole and exclusive right of imposing duties and taxes upon his Majesty's subjects in the said colonies and plantations; and have, in pursuance of such claim, passed certain votes, resolutions, and order, derogatory to the legislative authority of Parliament, and inconsistent with the dependency of the said colonies and plantations upon the Crown of Great Britain: may it therefore please our most excellent Majesty that it may be declared; and be it declared by the King's most excellent Majesty, by and with advice and consent of the Lords Spiritual and Temporal, and Commons, in this present Parliament assembled, and by the authority of the same, that the said colonies and plantations in America have been, are, and of right ought to be, subordinate unto, and dependent upon the imperial Crown and Parliament of Great Britain; and that the King's Majesty, by and with advice and consent of the Lords Spiritual and Temporal, and Commons of Great Britain, in Parliament assembled, had, hath, and of right ought to have, full power and authority to make laws and statutes of sufficient force and validity to bind the colonies and people of America, subjects of the Crown of Great Britain, in all cases whatsoever.

II. . . . And be it further declared and enacted by the authority aforesaid, that all resolutions, votes, orders, and proceedings, in any of the said colonies or plantations, whereby the power and authority of the Parliament of Great Britain, to make laws and statutes as aforesaid, is denied, or drawn into question, are, are hereby declared to be, utterly null and void to all intents and purposes whatsoever.

that the colonists themselves were reluctant to help shoulder. And in Britain, levying taxes was firmly the prerogative of Parliament.

By its end in 1763, the Seven Years War had tilted Anglo-French rivalry, in North America and India, decisively in Britain's favour, but the victory was won at a cost. The National Debt exceeded £129 million with the annual interest charged running at £4.6 million. At a time when the average British male was paying 26 shillings a year in tax, his American cousin was being levied just 1 shilling. His Majesty's subjects in Bristol were not slow to ask why His Majesty's subjects in Boston were let off

THE AMERICAN REVOLUTION

1763 American colonists bristle at George III's proclamation ordering them not to settle Native American land west of the Appalachian Mountains.

1765 The Stamp Act is imposed on all printed matter.

1766 The Stamp Act is abolished, but the right to tax the colonists is asserted by the Declaratory Act.

1767 New 'Townshend duties' are imposed on everyday items including lead, paper and tea.

1770 All Townshend duties repealed except on tea. The Boston 'Massacre' occurs, in which British troops kill five members of a hostile mob.

1773 The 'Boston Tea Party': colonists protest against the East India Company's monopoly of the tea trade.

1774 Coercive Acts are introduced to bring the Boston boycotts to an end. The first Continental Congress meets in Philadelphia with representatives of all thirteen colonies except Georgia to discuss common action.

1775 The first skirmishes of the rebellion take place at Lexington and Concord. The second Continental Congress in Philadelphia puts George Washington in charge of a 'Patriot' army. The indecisive Battle of Bunker Hill is fought near Boston. George III refuses negotiations.

1776 The Continental Congress approves the Declaration of Independence. George Washington proves unable to take New York and abandons Philadelphia.

1777 General Burgoyne's British force surrenders at Saratoga. Washington's army endures a harsh winter at Valley Forge.

1778 France enters the war on the American rebels' side.

1779 Spain declares war on Britain. The British win a victory at Savannah.

1780 The British are victorious at Charleston.

1781 A Franco-American force receives the British General Cornwallis's surrender at Yorktown.

1782 The British Parliament votes to end the war.

1783 Britain acknowledges the independence of the United States at the Treaty of Paris. About 100,000 pro-British loyalists flee the new nation, many going north. George Washington resigns his commission.

so lightly, despite enjoying the personal and commercial protection of the British army and navy. Indeed, it was a costly business to station troops in the colonies to safeguard them against Native American tribes and the French.

Seeking to cover part of the expense, the government in London, led by the prime minister, George Grenville, caused outrage across the Atlantic by imposing upon colonists a Stamp Act that taxed official papers, newspapers and pamphlets, playing cards and dice. The measure was unpopular not just because that is the nature of new taxes but because it was felt to exceed Westminster's remit.

Facing howls of colonial outrage and boycotts of British goods, in July 1765 a new administration was formed under the Marquess of Rockingham that began the process of backing down. The Stamp Act's repeal was accompanied by what, at first, looked merely like a statement designed to save London's face. The Declaratory Act, which passed through both Houses of Parliament with minimal dissent, insisted that Westminster 'had, hath and of right ought to have, full power and authority to make laws and statutes of sufficient force and validity to bind the colonies and people of America'.

What did this mean in practice? Benjamin Franklin at first thought it tolerable only in the sense that it could be considered 'in the same Light with the Claim of the Spanish Monarch to the Title of King of Jerusalem'. Yet it was clear that British politicians – despite lacking an elected mandate from across the Atlantic – were not content to treat Americans with benign neglect. Although nominal, the tax on tea was kept. Also retained was legislation designed to maintain good relations with the Native American tribes by restricting further colonial expansion beyond the Appalachian mountains, which conflicted with the colonists' desire to 'go west'. The escalating disorder and disobedience in radical port cities like Boston all but invited a heavy-handed response, a trap into which the British fell.

There were belated attempts by both sides to stave off outright rebellion. Indeed, the first Continental Congress meeting in Philadelphia in 1774 on the eve of the revolution rejected by just one vote a proposal by the Pennsylvanian politician Joseph Galloway that would have given the thirteen colonies the right to collectively veto Westminster legislation while keeping them within the British Empire. Meanwhile, Lord North's government was reluctant to concede the basis upon which the Declaratory Act rested. It was this that provided the rebel colonists with their most persuasive battle-cry, 'No taxation without representation!'

The result was a bitter conflict that divided the loyalties and sympathies of Britons and colonists alike. The intervention of the French eventually tilted the campaign in the rebel colonists' favour. After British defeat at Yorktown in 1781, London decided to cut its losses. After all, on the eve of war the value of the American colonies' exports to Britain was still worth only a fifth of what was being traded from Jamaica. In 1783 Britain duly recognized the independent United States of America. So ended one phase in Britain's colonial expansion: with the emergence of an English-speaking power that would eventually eclipse the United Kingdom.

1767

JAMES CRAIG'S PLAN FOR EDINBURGH'S NEW TOWN

GEORGIAN URBAN PLANNING AND THE 'SCOTTISH ENLIGHTENMENT'

In the half-century following the monarchy's restoration in 1660, British architecture was transformed by four men of genius: Sir Christopher Wren, Nicholas Hawksmoor, Sir John Vanbrugh and James Gibbs. Their buildings exemplified the dramatic tension and exuberance of the Baroque style that was already so prevalent across Europe. However, after 1715, a new architectural movement in Britain rejected the fussy ornamentation and dramatic artifices of the Baroque. Instead, design was to be more pure, seeking inspiration from a closer study of classical antiquity and the work of the sixteenth-century Italian scholar-architect, Andrea Palladio.

This Classical Revival became the style associated with Whig politics, rationalism and the philosophical principles of the Enlightenment. It found its most sublime expression in the latest 'neo-Palladian' country houses of the Whig aristocracy and the urban planning of a city that was the intellectual capital of Britain's 'Age of Reason' – Edinburgh.

Despite losing its national parliament in 1707, Edinburgh remained the capital of Scotland's separate legal and Church establishments. In addition, while Oxford and Cambridge universities were temporarily descending into intellectual torpor, Edinburgh University was experiencing its golden age. The economist Adam Smith, the philosopher David Hume and the sociologist Adam Ferguson were among the leaders of this Scottish Enlightenment, elevating Edinburgh into a 'Capital of the Mind'.

The city's problem was that it had been built on the volcanic ridge leading from the palace of Holyroodhouse at one end up to the castle at the other. The location of this, the Old Town, and its main artery, the Royal Mile, was a confined site, with

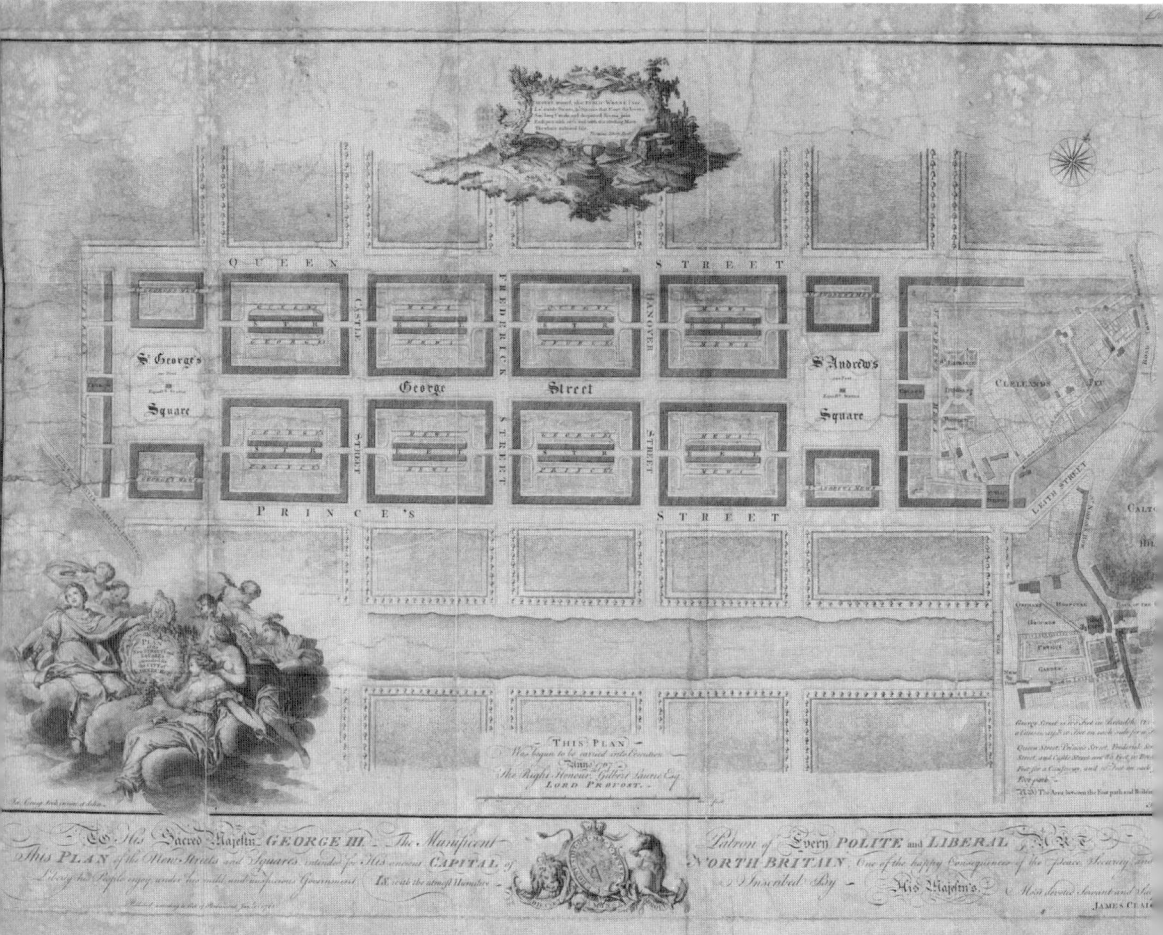

James Craig's winning plan for Edinburgh's New Town, complete with street names exalting both the union of Scotland with England and the Hanoverian succession.

the inevitable consequences that congested and unsanitary buildings were forced precariously upwards rather than outwards. Finally, the city council decided to sponsor the drainage of the land to the north and to build a bridge, beyond which it was proposed to construct an entirely new residential district far more worthy of Edinburgh's moneyed and cultured citizens.

In 1766, a competition to design what became known as the New Town was won by James Craig, a native of the city, aged just twenty-seven, whose uncle was James Thomson, the poet and librettist of 'Rule, Britannia!' Craig envisaged a grid street plan of straight boulevards. After some revisions were made by others, Craig showed his plan to King George III.

The king's approval was never in doubt. He was presented not just with a scheme

of urban planning but with a document that wiped clean the Scottish capital's previous taints of Jacobitism and separatism. Rather, with names like Hanover Street, George Street and Frederick Street, the projected stately avenues boldly proclaimed allegiance to the Hanoverian succession. The west and east ends were to be marked by two grand spaces symbolizing the union of Scotland and England: St George's Square and St Andrew's Square.

Upon completion in 1791, St George's was in fact named Charlotte Square after George III's queen, Charlotte of Mecklenburg. Its buildings were the work of Robert Adam (1728–92). A Scot who had travelled to Rome and worked extensively in London, Robert Adam was among the foremost architects of the period, through his combination of neo-Palladian elegance with exquisite interior decoration inspired by his deep classical knowledge. His work even intruded into the Old Town, where the university quadrangle received his elegant classical treatment.

Craig, however, proved unable to win fresh commissions and died in obscurity in 1795. His debts mounting, he had been forced to pawn his competition winner's gold medal, and he was buried in an unmarked grave. Less than a mile away, his New Town was finally taking shape, however, lined by the stone-fronted townhouses of Adam and others, achieving a harmonious unity by their fashionable emphasis on order and symmetry, the ordered monotony of their layout broken by spacious squares and sweeping crescents.

In England during the 1830s, a reaction set in against classical architecture, manifesting itself in the Gothic Revival. It was this neo-medieval aesthetic that became the most recognizable style of the Victorian age. Yet perhaps because of its connotations of High Church ritualism, Gothic Revival fared less well in Presbyterian Scotland, where classicism's simple austerity continued to marry philosophy with architectural principles. There, study turned from Roman to Hellenic classicism in the work of the architects Thomas Hamilton (1784–1858) and W. H. Playfair (1790–1857), expanding and enhancing the Georgian city with grand Greek Revival buildings. Calton Hill was turned into a Scottish Acropolis and the phrase of the artist Hugh William Williams stuck: Edinburgh was truly the 'Athens of the North'.

1769

ARKWRIGHT'S
WATER FRAME PATENT

TEXTILES AND THE INDUSTRIAL REVOLUTION

In 1760, Britain's textile industry consisted of men and women who sat in their cottages working their own spinning wheels to make thread, which was passed on to weavers. The market for fine muslins was provided by importing quality cloth from India. The smallness of the British enterprise can be measured by how little raw cotton was imported – only around 3 million pounds, which came mostly from South America and the West Indies. By 1789, the situation was transformed. Imports of raw cotton exceeded 32 million pounds, a figure that by 1802 had passed 60 million. The cottage-dweller working away between periodic tendings of the pot over the fire had been replaced by hundreds of employees in huge mills, churning out finished textiles for both the home and export markets at a fraction of the previous price.

Inventions drove this Industrial Revolution, among which Richard Arkwright's water frame heralded the most fundamental change in the scale and organization of manufacturing in Britain.

In 1764, James Hargreaves (c.1720–78), an illiterate carpenter and weaver from Lancashire, was credited with devising the 'spinning jenny'. It represented a significant advance on the traditional tools of the trade because it featured a mobile carriage that allowed multiple spindles to be worked, thereby greatly increasing output. However, it produced brittle thread.

The spinning machine that Richard Arkwright patented in 1769 was different in several respects. It consisted of three sets of rollers that ran parallel to each other and turned the yarn at different speeds, with the fibres twisted and tightened together by a set of spindles. The result was a much stronger thread, which successfully made good-quality cloth from pure cotton.

Other factors were more broadly significant. Hargreaves' jenny was hand-

DRIVING FORCES OF THE INDUSTRIAL REVOLUTION

1700 Total national coal output is estimated at 2,612,000 tons.

1709 Abraham Darby uses coke, rather than wood or charcoal, to smelt iron ore.

1712 Thomas Newcomen's steam engine is used to pump out water from mines.

1733 John Kay patents his flying shuttle.

1742 The publisher, Edward Cave, buys Marvel's Mill in Northamptonshire and converts it into Britain's first water-powered cotton mill. It soon has over a hundred employees.

1761 The Bridgewater Canal opens, the first canal in Britain to be constructed that did not follow an existing watercourse. Originally connecting Worsley to Manchester, it was extended to the Mersey, at Runcorn, in 1766.

1764 James Hargreaves creates the spinning jenny.

1769 Richard Arkwright patents his water frame.

1772 Manchester and Salford have a combined population of about 25,000.

1773 The first factory-produced all-cotton textiles are made.

1775/6 James Watt's steam engine greatly improves upon Newcomen's pump.

1777 The Grand Trunk Canal links the Midlands with the major ports.

1779 Samuel Crompton invents the spinning mule.

1784 Henry Cort patents the puddling process for refining iron ore which, with his steel rolling mill, proves a superior way of producing bar iron from pig iron.

1785 Edmund Cartwright patents his power loom.

1789 The Thames–Severn Canal opens.

1790 The Forth and Clyde Canal opens, allowing vessels to pass through Scotland from the west coast to the east coast.

c.1792 William Murdoch invents gas lighting (but fails to patent it). In 1805 the Philips and Lee cotton mill in Manchester becomes the first to be entirely lit by gaslight.

1800 Manchester and Salford have a combined population of about 95,000.

1815 Sir Humphry Davy invents his safety lamp, permitting deep seams to be mined without igniting flammable gases.

1816 Total national coal output estimated at 15,635,000 tonnes.

powered, which made it compatible with the cottage as the place of work. Arkwright's machine, in contrast, was powered by water and was intended not for the humble home but for large mills yoking the power of rivers. It therefore involved a shift in industrial organization, creating mass-production techniques in factories worked by unskilled labour.

The mill that Arkwright opened at Cromford on the River Derwent in Derbyshire in 1771 emphasised the shift in scale. Within a decade it had 5,000 employees. It exemplified the industrial future and, as such, was a disaster for traditional weavers. Work that had previously been undertaken by skilled labourers could now be done, far more quickly and cheaply, by children as young as six. Unable to compete with this new invention, the response of many whose livelihoods it removed was to try to smash it up. A mob broke into Hargreaves' house and destroyed his working models; in 1779, rioters sacked Arkwright's mill in Chorley in Lancashire. At Cromford, which already resembled a forbidding fortress, he kept a cannon loaded and ready to fire grapeshot against a similar assault. Innovation in working practices came at the price of an abrasive attitude to labour relations.

The long hours, the tough conditions, the dehumanizing nature of the unskilled work and the reality that so many of the employees were children symbolized all that was least attractive about this fresh way of making profits for factory owners.

One of the copies made of Arkwright's water frame patent.

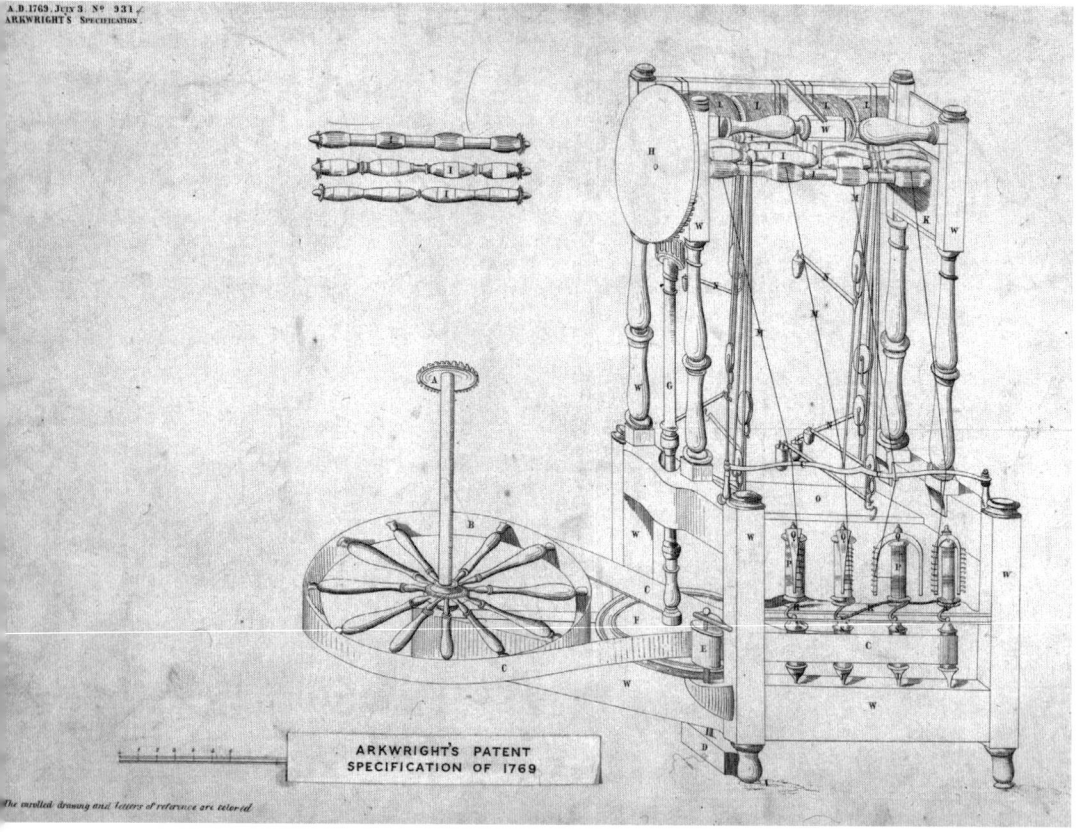

ARKWRIGHT'S PATENT
SPECIFICATION OF 1769

The poet William Blake encapsulated this in his indelible phrase when he wrote of 'dark Satanic Mills'. The description was fair but, on the other hand, factories also brought gains. The wages paid were low, yet sufficiently higher than those often paid to farm labourers, prompting them to leave the fields and make instead for the new northern towns and cities growing up around these novel sources of employment. There were knock-on benefits: the factories produced garments at a fraction of their previous price to the purchaser. The cost of living came down and the mass consumer society was born.

The process also, of course, made the likes of Arkwright extremely rich. His story illustrates the social mobility that the Industrial Revolution brought in its wake. He had been born in Preston in 1732, the youngest of thirteen children. His parents could not afford to send him to school and the only education he received was from a cousin who taught him to read and write. He became a wigmaker before turning his mind from hair to thread, although the water frame with which he made his fortune was not, for the most part, his invention. It has always been disputed exactly how much input he contributed to the design – so much so that he lost the patent for it in 1785. It was probably largely the work of John Kay, a former clockmaker from Warrington whom Arkwright engaged. Kay, in turn, developed a design originally made by Thomas Highs, who has also been credited with the prototype for Hargreaves' jenny.

Whoever came up with the model, it was Arkwright who saw the possibilities for maximizing its potential. He and others like him represented something sufficiently new in England that a French word had to be conscripted: Arkwright was an *entrepreneur*. He died in 1792 in conditions far removed from the circumstances of his birth – having been awarded a knighthood by King George III and having amassed a fortune estimated at £500,000. The machine that had made his success possible was superseded first by Samuel Crompton's 'spinning mule' and thereafter by other developments as water gave way to steam power, an advance that Arkwright had embraced at his factory in Nottingham. He had, nonetheless, lived long enough to see the economy and society of Britain embark on an extraordinary transformation that set the country on course to becoming the workshop of the world.

1772
THE SOMERSET JUDGMENT

SLAVERY IN ENGLAND IS RULED ILLEGAL

S lavery had long been common throughout much of Africa, but it was from the sixteenth century onwards that Britons saw great opportunities for personal gain by joining the trade in human cargo. In this, they were hoping to exploit a market that the Portuguese had already opened up and which other nations, including the French, were also keen to exploit. From ports across Britain, ships sailed out, bound for the West African coast, there to buy slaves from a network of Arab and African traders. During the eighteenth century, when the transatlantic slave trade reached its peak, around 3 million slaves were shipped in horrific conditions across the Atlantic to be worked to death in the British plantations of North America and the sugar-growing islands of the Caribbean. Such were the slaves' importance to the vast profits being generated for their masters that the Westminster Parliament did not think to overrule the colonial legislatures that permitted such exploitation. What, however, was slavery's legal status on the British mainland?

Serfdom, a form of quasi-slavery, had for centuries been part of the feudal structure of medieval England. Tying the lowest class of peasants (and their offspring) to manors, it obliged them to work at least part of the week for their lord in return for shelter, protection and the lease of a plot for personal cultivation. The practice declined rapidly in the fourteenth century when the Black Death created a scarcity of labour, thereby improving the working conditions of those who survived. By the end of the fourteenth century serfdom was all but extinct.

Whether slaves could be legally imported from abroad was disputed. The fact that there was no law on the statute books explicitly endorsing chattel slavery in England did not, of itself, make it illegal. The position of the common law on the subject was not clear-cut, since various judgments had been contradictory. A 1569 judgment on the use of a Russian slave allegedly declared that 'England was too pure an air for slaves to breathe in', although this had not prevented imported slaves

being a continuing presence in Britain nor even the periodic existence of slave markets in cities like Bristol and Liverpool. In 1729 the attorney-general and the solicitor-general both gave their opinions that slaves were not accorded their freedom merely by setting foot on English soil nor through receiving baptism and that, therefore, they could be legally transported from England to plantations.

Modern estimates suggest that in the 1770s there were between 3,000 and 15,000 black people in Britain. Some were free; some were in servitude akin to, or actually involving, slavery. It was during the second half of the eighteenth century that slavery became a far more contentious issue, rousing the Nonconformist conscience and drawing Quakers to the fore in exposing its evils. However, it also disgusted many Anglicans, opening up a division that cut right across the religious and political Establishment.

It was in this changing environment that the campaigner Granville Sharp led a group of abolitionists determined to bring before the courts a new test case on the legality of slaveholding. In James Somerset they found someone they hoped would prove the perfect cause. Somerset was an African-born slave from Virginia who had been brought to England by his master, a Boston customs officer. While in England, Somerset had seized his moment to escape, only to be recaptured. Chained, he was about to be shipped to Jamaica, where he was to be resold, when Sharp's friends managed to serve a writ of habeas corpus that prevented his departure.

BRITAIN AND THE SLAVE TRADE

1562 England's first slave trader, Sir John Hawkins, picks up 500 Africans and sells them to Spanish and Portuguese traders.

1660 The Royal Adventurers into Africa (subsequently the Royal African Company) is granted a monopoly to trade in slaves. Its governor is James, duke of York (later James II).

1698 With the end of the Royal African Company's monopoly, the slave trade is opened up to competition.

1727 The London Meeting of the Society of Friends (the Quakers) condemns the slave trade and prohibits Quakers from trading in or owning slaves.

1729 The Yorke–Talbot ruling by the attorney-general and the solicitor-general states that baptism does not free slaves from their servitude.

1765–69 Sir William Blackstone's *Commentaries on the Laws of England* argues that when a negro arrives in England he 'becomes a freeman'.

1772 Lord Mansfield delivers the Somerset Judgment in *Rex v. Knowles, ex parte Somersett*.

1774 John Wesley's *Thoughts upon Slavery* condemns the practice.

1775 A Royal Commission is established to investigate the slave trade.

1778 *Knight vs Wedderburn* establishes the legal precedent that slavery is illegal in Scotland.

1781 There is popular outrage at the throwing overboard of shackled slaves by the captain of the *Zong*.

1787 The Society for the Abolition of the Slave Trade is launched by Granville Sharp and Thomas Clarkson. By 1792 it has gathered half a million signatures.

1792 The House of Commons passes a bill to abolish the slave trade in four years' time, but it fails to pass in the House of Lords.

1807 The slave trade is abolished.

1833 The Abolition of Slavery Act makes slavery illegal throughout the British Empire (with final anomalies removed by 1843).

Lord Mansfield's judgment: from *Howell's State Trials*, vol. 20

So high an act of dominion must be recognised by the law of the country where it is used. The power of a master over his slave has been extremely different, in different countries. The state of slavery is of such a nature, that it is incapable of being introduced on any reasons, moral or political, but only by positive law, which preserves its force long after the reasons, occasion, and time itself from whence it was created, is erased from memory. It is so odious, that nothing can be suffered to support it, but positive law. Whatever inconveniences, therefore, may follow from the decision, I cannot say this case is allowed or approved by the law of England; and therefore the black must be discharged.

The case was heard by the Court of King's Bench in Westminster Hall. Sitting in judgment was the Scottish jurist, Lord Chief Justice William Murray, earl of Mansfield. Despite his private sympathy, there was little in Mansfield's previous pronouncements to give the abolitionists grounds for excessive optimism. As proceedings unfolded, it was clear that he wanted to keep to the specifics of the case while avoiding making sweeping declarations of general emancipation. Finally, after a lengthy period of deliberation he delivered his judgment on 22 June 1772. No exact record of it exists, only the newspaper reports of what he said. While varying in the exact choice of words, they broadly concurred that what he stated was to the effect that slavery was 'so odious that nothing can be suffered to support it but positive law. Whatever inconveniences, therefore, may follow from the decision, I cannot say this case is allowed or approved by the law of England; and therefore the black must be discharged.' For good measure, he reportedly repeated the dictum he had expressed in a previous case: *Fiat justitia, ruat coelum* ('Let justice be done, though the heavens fall').

In view of Mansfield's reluctance to create a new legal principle, his judgment was specific to the case rather than an absolute statement of emancipation. However, the work of the newspapers in printing and circulating his opinion ensured that the public understood the underlying principle underpinning his ruling – that the holding of slaves was illegal anywhere in England and Wales. In 1777, a judgment by the Court of Session in Edinburgh made explicit that the same applied in Scotland and, indeed, that slavery was incompatible with Scots law.

The Somerset Judgment thus became both a landmark ruling and evidence of the growing power of newspapers in quickly disseminating news and influencing opinion. When the news reached America, it was seen as an ominous sign by some slave-owning colonists, many of whom were soon to fight for independence from Britain. Nevertheless, Mansfield's verdict did not affect the transatlantic trade. It took the untiring work of many campaigners – in particular, by the evangelical Anglicans Thomas Clarkson and William Wilberforce, the latter the Tory MP for Hull – to finally bring the trade's abolition on to the statute book in 1807. As a result the British navy was to be actively deployed thereafter in liberating slaves wherever they were discovered on the seas. In 1833, Westminster finally grasped the nettle and overruled the practices tolerated overseas in its colonies by abolishing slavery throughout the British Empire.

It is not known what became of the freed James Somerset.

1776

ADAM SMITH'S
THE WEALTH OF NATIONS

THE PHILOSOPHY OF FREE-MARKET ECONOMICS

Adam Smith's *An Inquiry into the Nature and Causes of the Wealth of Nations* provided the first truly comprehensive critique of what, until that moment, had been the prevailing economic consensus governing all Western thought. In its place, it promoted a new philosophy: the free market.

The received wisdom that Smith overturned was called mercantilism, which held that trade benefited the seller, who made money from the transaction, rather than the buyer, who had to pay for the purchase. Therefore, the government's role was to encourage exports and discourage imports through various interventions, ranging from prohibition or restriction of certain imports, to the imposition of protective tariffs that made them more expensive and less of a threat to domestic traders. Similarly, guilds and other regulatory bodies protected their members from being undercut. At the core of this mercantilist approach was the belief that trade was a zero-sum game because the wealth of the nation existed in the worth of its commerce and property – which meant that activities diverting that wealth abroad harmed the national wealth.

Published in 1776, when the Industrial Revolution had scarcely begun its transforming role, Smith's *Wealth of Nations* argued that the great assumption upon which mercantilist theory rested was mistaken. Trade was not a one-way transaction that benefited only the seller. His position was that imports could be good for business because they allowed the buyer to purchase what he wanted at a price lower than if he either had to make it himself or rely on an artificially restricted range of suppliers. The resulting saving could be invested more profitably elsewhere. Trade was therefore *mutually* beneficial.

At heart, the argument was expressed by Smith's insistence that 'Consumption is the sole end and purpose of all production.' This observation, at variance with

the traditional favour shown to producers, implied that trade barriers and other protective regulations were, in reality, a means of distorting the true relationship. They stifled competition, creativity and innovation, all of which were in fact motors for increasing the variety and reducing the price of goods. 'People of the same trade seldom meet, even for merriment and diversion,' he claimed, 'but the conversation ends in a conspiracy against the public, or in some contrivance to raise prices.' The role of government was to remove the market-rigging mechanisms whereby producers created cartels or monopolistic restrictive practices.

Adam Smith (1723–90) was a reluctant sitter for portraits, but he did sit for his fellow Scot, James Tassie (1735–99), who made a white enamel medallion of his profile from which this popular engraving was made.

Smith never actually used the term *laissez-faire*, subsequently applied to his views. Whilst he took the view that it was dangerously presumptuous of any government to think it could better direct the use of resources than multitudes of individuals interacting in a free market, he did believe that government was necessary to administer impartial justice, organize national defence, build essential public works and support public provision in areas like schooling where private enterprise could not do the job alone. He supported the notion of an income tax – which, needless to say, was one of the first of his proposals to be taken up by government.

Some of the *Wealth of Nations'* most famous passages deal with its author's attempts to show that self-interest and natural liberty go hand in hand to produce the common good. The virtuous end may not be perceived by the individual searching for the most profitable return for an investment, yet this was the result as if 'led by an invisible hand to promote an end which was no part of his intention'. Indeed, by looking after themselves, those engaged in trade did everyone else a favour too: 'It is not from the benevolence of the butcher, the brewer, or the baker that we expect our dinner, but from their regard of their own interest. We address ourselves not to their humanity, but to their self-love, and never talk to them of our own necessities, but of their advantage.'

The *Wealth of Nations* sold out its first print run within six months, which is somewhat surprising for a two-volume, 900-page work on political economy.

From *The Wealth of Nations*, Book IV, Chapter 2

The general industry of the society never can exceed what the capital of the society can employ. As the number of workmen that can be kept in employment by any particular person must bear a certain proportion to his capital, so the number of those that can be continually employed by all the members of a great society, must bear a certain proportion to the whole capital of that society, and never can exceed that proportion. No regulation of commerce can increase the quantity of industry in any society beyond what its capital can maintain. It can only divert a part of it into a direction into which it might not otherwise have gone; and it is by no means certain that this artificial direction is likely to be more advantageous to the society than that into which it would have gone of its own accord.

Every individual is continually exerting himself to find out the most advantageous employment for whatever capital he can command. It is his own advantage, indeed, and not that of the society, which he has in view. But the study of his own advantage naturally, or rather necessarily leads him to prefer that employment which is most advantageous to the society.

Its author was a shy man, well liked by those who knew him, who was given to wrestling with ideas during long walks, often with such intensity that he found himself miles out of his way. On one occasion he was so distracted from where he was walking that he fell down into a pit of tar.

Smith was born in 1723 in the small Scottish port of Kirkcaldy, where his father was a customs collector. At the age of four he was stolen by gypsies and no more might ever have been heard of him, had he not been quickly rescued. As one of his biographers put it, 'He would have made, I fear, a poor gypsy.' Instead he went at the age of fourteen to study at Glasgow University and then, less profitably, to Balliol College, Oxford, before becoming an academic at Glasgow where his popularly attended lectures provided the basis for his *Theory of Moral Sentiments* in 1759. He began working on the *Wealth of Nations* while travelling through France as the tutor of the young duke of Buccleuch. The tour gave him the opportunity to converse with many of the continent's leading thinkers, including several meetings with Voltaire in Geneva. A slow writer, he completed his masterpiece in London and at his aged mother's house in Kirkcaldy.

Even before Smith's death in 1790, his arguments had found a receptive audience in the government of William Pitt the Younger. However, further progress towards the abolition of tariffs and the adoption of free trade was checked by events at home and abroad: the dislocations of the Napoleonic Wars and the imposition of the Corn Laws in 1815, which increased the price of bread in order to support the profitability of land ownership. Smith's arguments prevailed nevertheless. Many manufacturing tariffs were scrapped during the 1820s, and the age of free trade was explicitly embraced with the repeal of the Corn Laws by Sir Robert Peel in 1846. On the centenary of the *Wealth of Nations'* publication in 1876, the economist and journalist Walter Bagehot proclaimed that its arguments 'have settled down into the common sense of the nation and have become irreversible'.

In fact, Smith's economic theories were about to be threatened by Marxism and the re-emergence of a faith in the positive effects of state intervention. By the 1930s the world had retreated into protectionism, national self-sufficiency planning and rival versions of totalitarianism. With the 1980s and increasing globalization, the *Wealth of Nations'* time appeared to have come again.

> Little else is required to carry a state to the highest degree of opulence from the lowest barbarism, [Smith wrote] but peace, easy taxes, and a tolerable administration of justice: all the rest being brought about by a natural course of things. All governments which thwart the natural course, which force things into another channel, or which endeavour to arrest the progress of society at a particular point, are unnatural, and to support themselves are obliged to be oppressive and tyrannical.

1785
FIRST EDITION OF *THE TIMES*

THE 'THUNDERER' OF THE FREE PRESS

On New Year's Day 1785, a newspaper was launched that established a new benchmark in British journalism. The first edition was called *The Daily Universal Register*, but three years later it changed its name to *The Times*. As such, it achieved extraordinary eminence across the English-speaking world and beyond. This was evident in the decision of so many foreign newspapers to launch with titles that consciously paid it homage: the *New York Times*, the *Irish Times*, the *Times of India*, the *New Straits Times*. Even France's foremost newspaper began in 1861 as *Le Temps* (although following Paris's liberation in 1944, Charles de Gaulle instigated its rebirth as *Le Monde*).

There was nothing to suggest that this newspaper would prove so influential when it started from offices in Printing House Square, an alleyway off Fleet Street to the west of St Paul's Cathedral. The area had been the centre of the printing trade since the time of Caxton and many journals had already been launched there in the eighteenth century, among them Britain's first daily newspaper, the *Daily Courant*, between 1702 and 1735, and the *Morning Post* from 1772. The primary motivation of John Walter, *The Times's* founder, was less about improving the quality of national journalism than using his paper as a vehicle to advertise a new printing technique for which he held the patent. Keen to recoup money lost as a Lloyd's underwriter in the insurance markets, he was inspired by the profit motive and, like many of his newspaper rivals, was amenable to taking government bribes in return for favourable editorial comment.

Success was not instant. Walter found himself sent to Newgate prison, first for libelling the dukes of Clarence and Cumberland, and then for libelling the Prince of Wales as well. Although his 'logographical' printing technique proved a technological dead end, by the beginning of the nineteenth century his newspaper was gaining ground on its rivals. Under the direction of his son, John Walter II, it innovated and became something deemed unusual for the time – independent

and incorruptible. Between 1817 and 1877, it had just two editors, Thomas Barnes and John Thadeus Delane, who between them established its reputation as the most trusted source of information in the country.

Perhaps its greatest merit was its ability to break foreign news before its competitors, a particular benefit to readers whose finances might rest on getting in ahead of other investors. On 22 June 1815, it reproduced the duke of Wellington's dispatch from the battlefield of Waterloo, only four days after it had been written. In 1854, its war correspondent (a post it innovated), William Howard Russell, sent eyewitness reports from the Crimean War so shocking that they ultimately helped bring down the government of the earl of Aberdeen. By the mid-nineteenth century, *The Times* had full-time correspondents posted not just across Europe but in Constantinople and Cairo, and later in Alexandria and Peking. During the Franco-Prussian War of 1870–71, a miniature version of *The Times* was sent by pigeon into the besieged city of Paris. In 1878, during the Congress of Berlin, the German chancellor, Otto von Bismarck, gave a five-hour interview to the *Times* correspondent Henri de Blowitz, who subsequently got a text of the Treaty of Berlin printed in the paper in London even before it was signed in Berlin. For international reputation, it had no rival anywhere in the world.

Although never a radical force in domestic politics, *The Times* championed the cause of parliamentary reform in 1832, gaining a reputation as a paper 'that thundered out' on various subjects. Naturally, it also made enemies. Its attack on Queen Victoria's withdrawal from public life in 1862 spurred even Her Majesty to write to the paper a letter in her defence intended for publication. In 1856, the Whigs' leader,

THE GROWTH OF THE PRESS

1621 *The Courante* is published in London. It contains only foreign news.

1665 The oldest surviving English-language journal, the *Oxford Gazette* (subsequently the *London Gazette*), an official government publication, is launched.

1690 The first edition of *Berrow's Worcester Journal* appears. Along with the *Stamford Mercury*, it claims to be Britain's oldest surviving (non-official) newspaper.

1702 The *Daily Courant* is launched in Fleet Street as the first daily newspaper. It merges with the *Daily Gazetteer* in 1735.

1737 The Belfast *News Letter* is founded. It is the world's oldest surviving English-language daily newspaper.

1748 The *Aberdeen Journal* (subsequently *Press and Journal*) becomes Scotland's first daily newspaper.

1772 The *Morning Post* is founded. It lasts until 1937 when it is subsumed by the *Daily Telegraph*.

1785 John Walter launches the *The Daily Universal Register* which he renames *The Times* in 1788.

1791 The *Observer* becomes the world's first Sunday newspaper.

1821 The *Manchester Guardian* is founded. It becomes the *Guardian* in 1959 and relocates to London in 1964.

1842 The *Illustrated London News* is published, the first weekly to print pictures.

1851 Reuters news agency is established.

1855 The abolition of stamp duties on newspapers reduces their cost and encourages their proliferation.

1855 The *Daily Telegraph* is launched and quickly becomes the market leader.

1896 Lord Northcliffe's *Daily Mail* begins the new age of mass-market journalism.

OVERLEAF: *The front and back pages of the first edition of* The Daily Universal Register, *which was to be renamed* The Times.

THE *Universal* DAILY *Register,*

Printed Logographically — DIEU ET MON DROIT — *By His Majesty's* Patent.

NUMB. 1.] SATURDAY, JANUARY 1, 1785. [Price Two-pence Halfpenny.

The SIXTH NIGHT.
By His MAJESTY's Company

AT the THEATRE ROYAL in DRURY-LANE, this preſent SATURDAY, will be performed

A New COMEDY, called
The NATURAL SON.

The characters by Mr. King, Mr. Parſons, Mr. Benſley, Mr. Moody, Mr. Baddeley, Mr. Wrighten, and Mr. Palmer. Miſs Pope, Miſs Tidſwell, and Miſs Farren.
With new Scenes and Dreſſes.
The Prologue to be ſpoken by Mr. Banniſter, jun.
And the Epilogue by Miſs Farren.
After which will be performed the laſt New Pantomime Entertainment, in two Parts, called
HARLEQUIN JUNIOR;
Or, The MAGIC CESTUS.
The Characters of the Pantomime, by
Mr. Wright, Mr. Williamſon, Mr. Burton, Mr. Staunton, Mr. Williames, Mr. Palmer, Mr. Waldron, Mr. Fawcett, Mr. Chaplin, Mr. Phillimore, Mr. Wilſon, Mr. Alfred, Mr. Spencer, Mr. Chapman, and Mr. Grimaldi. Mrs. Burnet, Miſs Burnett, Miſs Tidſwell, Miſs Barnes, Miſs Cranford, and Miſs Stageldoir.
To conclude with the Repulſe of the Spaniards before
The ROCK of GIBRALTAR.

To-morrow, by particular deſire, (for the 4th time) the revived Comedy of the DOUBLE DEALER, with the favorite Maſque of ARTHUR and EMMELINE.

On Tueſday the Tragedy of VENICE PRESERVED: Jaffier by Mr. Brereton, Pierre by Mr. Benſley, and Belvidera, by Mrs. Siddons: And on Friday the Carmelite. Maſſinger's Play of the MAID of HONOUR, (with alterations and Additions) is in Rehearſal and will ſoon be produced.

NINTH NIGHT. FOR THE AUTHOR.

AT the THEATRE-ROYAL, COVENT-GARDEN, this preſent SATURDAY, January 1, 1785, will be performed, a New Comedy, called
The FOLLIES of a DAY,
Or, The Marriage of Figaro.
With new Dreſſes, Decorations, &c.

The principal characters by Mr. Lewis, Mr. Quick, Mr. Edwin, Mr. Wilſon, Mr. Wewitzer, Mr. Bonnor, Mr. Thompſon, and Mrs. Martyr; Mrs. Bates, Mrs. Webb, Miſs Wewitzer, and Miſs Younge.
With a new Prologue, to be ſpoken by Mr. Davies.
To which will be added, for the the ſixth time,
A new Pantomime, called,
The MAGIC CAVERN,
Or, VIRTUE's TRIUMPH.
With new Scenery, Machinery, Muſic, Dreſſes, and Decorations.

The Scenes chiefly deſigned by Mr. Richards, and executed by him, Mr. Carver, Mr. Hodgins, and Aſſiſtants.

The Overture, Songs, Choruſſes, and the Muſic of the new Pantomime, and compoſed by Mr. Shield.
Nothing under full Price will be taken.
The Words of the Songs, &c. to be had at the Theatre.

MR. WALTER returns his thanks to his Friends and the Public for the great encouragement and generous ſupport he has already received from them to his new improvement in Printing, by the readineſs with which they have ſubſcribed to his intended publication of the works of ſome eminent Authors; and whilſt he ſolicits a continuance of their favours, begs leave to acquaint them that by

The middle of January will be publiſhed,
In One Volume 12mo,
MISCELLANIES IN VERSE AND PROSE,

Intended as a Specimen of his Printing Types at the Logographic Office, Printing-Houſe Square, Blackfriars.—And by the beginning of February, his firſt volume, containing Watts's Improvement of the Mind, with an Introduction written on the occaſion, will be ready to be delivered to the ſubſcribers.

This Day is publiſhed, Price 6d.

PLAN of the CHAMBER of COMMERCE, King's-Arms Buildings, Cornhill, London; which is open every day, for Conſultation, Opinion, and Advice (verbal or in Writing) Mediation, Aſſiſtance, Arbitration, &c. in all *Commercial, Maritime,* and *Inſurance* Affairs, and matters of *Trade* in general; and the *Laws* and *Uſages* relating thereto.—The Addreſs is, To the Director of the Chamber of Commerce, as above.

To be had of Richardſon and Urquhart, Royal Exchange; J. Sewell, Cornhill; T. Whieldon, Fleet-ſtreet; W. Flexney, Holborn; and at the aforeſaid Chamber.

Where may alſo be had, in one Volume Folio,
Mr. Weſkett's COMPLETE DIGEST of the THEORY, LAWS and PRACTICE of INSURANCE; an entire new and comprehenſive work, including all the adjudged Caſes extant, with ſeveral never before printed; Extracts from the Statutes, foreign Ordinances, and marine Treaties; accounts of all the Inſurance Companies the MaritimeCourts, the commercial and maritime Laws, the Law of Nations, &c. the whole forming (alphabetically) a new *Lex Mercatoria.*

☞ "This Work has been compiled with great Care and Induſtry, by one who is evidently a Maſter of the Subject. It abounds with Proofs of extenſive Reading, as well as mature Reflection, and judicious Remarks; and if the completeſt Syſtem of Inſurance that has hitherto been compoſed be entitled to Praiſe, the preſent uſeful Digeſt muſt meet with the Approbation of the commercial World." Crit. Rev. Vol. 52, p. 443.—All the other Literary Journals ſpeak in ſimilar Terms of this Book; which had already been tranſlated abroad.

This Day is publiſhed, in 3 Vols. Price 9s. ſewed.
By the LITERARY SOCIETY,

MODERN TIMES: or The ADVENTURES of GABRIEL OUTCAST. A Novel, in Imitation of Gil Blas.
"Qui capit ille facit."

Printed for the Author, and ſold by J. Walter, Printing-houſe Square, Black-friars; where may be had, gratis, the Plan of this Society, aſſociated for the Encouragement of Literature, who propoſe to print and publiſh at their own Riſk and Expence ſuch original Works as they may approve of, and give their Authors all Profits ariſing from the ſame.

MRS. KING begs leave to acquaint her Friends ſhe opens her SCHOOL at CHIGWELL in ESSEX, on Monday, the 10th of January, for the EDUCATION of YOUNG LADIES: as ſhe has always been accuſtomed to watch and improve the opening mind, hopes to give ſatisfaction to thoſe who truſt her with ſo important a charge.

Till the 10th of January Mrs. King may be ſpoke with at Mr. Kerr's, Bitt-maker to his Majeſty, in the Mews, Charing-croſs.

N. B. Wanted an Apprentice and Half-boarder.

SHIP-  PING
ADVER- TISEMENTS

For NICE, GENOA, and LEGHORN,
(With Liberty to touch at One Port in the Channel,)
The NANCY.
THOMAS WHITE, Commander,

BURTHEN 160 Tons; Guns and Men anſwerable. Lying off the Tower, and will abſolutely depart on Saturday the 8th inſtant.

The ſaid Commander to be ſpoken with every morning at Sam's Coffee-houſe, near the Cuſtom-houſe; at Will's Coffee-houſe, in Cornhill; and at Exchange hours on the French and Italian Walk, or
WILLIAM ELYARD, for the ſaid Commander,
No. 16, Savage-Gardens.

Direct for LISBON,
The NANCY.
JOHN RACKHAM, Commander,

BURTHEN 300 Tons, Men anſwerable. Lying off Horſlydown Chain; Seven-eighths of her Cargo abſolutely engaged, and is obliged by Charter-party to depart on Saturday the 8th inſtant.

The ſaid Commander to be ſpoken with every morning at Sam's Coffee-houſe, near the Cuſtom-houſe; at Will's Coffee-houſe, in Cornhill; and in Exchange hours in the French and Italian Walk; or
WILLIAM ELYARD, for the ſaid Commander,
No. 16, Savage-Gardens.

For NICE, GENOA, and LEGHORN,
(With Liberty to Touch at One Port in the Channel.)
The LIVELY,
ROBERT BRINE, Commander,

BURTHEN 209 Tons, *Guns* and *Men* anſwerable. Lying off Iron Gate.

The ſaid Commander to be ſpoke with every Morning at Sam's Coffee-houſe, near the Cuſtom-houſe; at Will's Coffee-houſe in Cornhill; and in Exchange Hours in the French and Italian Walk; or
WILLIAM ELYARD, for the ſaid Commander,
No. 16, Savage-Gardens.

For CONSTANTINOPLE and SMYRNA, or SMYRNA and CONSTANTINOPLE,
(With Liberty to Touch at One Port in the Channel,)
The BETSEY,
ROBERT LANCASTER, Commander,

BURTHEN 200 Tons, Men anſwerable. Lying at Iron-Gate. Two-thirds of her Cargo engaged, and is obliged to depart by Charterparty, in all the preſent Month of January.

The ſaid Commander to be ſpoke with every Morning at Sam's Coffee-houſe, near the Cuſtom-houſe; at Will's Coffee-houſe in Cornhill; and in Exchange Hours in the French and Italian Walk; or
WILLIAM ELYARD, for the ſaid Commender,
No. 16, Savage-Gardens.

N. B. No Goods to be taken on Board the Veſſel without an Order from the Broker.

NEW NOVELS.
This Day are publiſhed, (in two Volumes, price 5s. ſewed,)

THE YOUNG WIDOW; or, the HISTORY of Mrs. LEDWICH.

The HISTORY of Lord BELFORD and Miſs SOPHIA WOODLEY, 3 vol. 9s. bound.

Printed for the Editor, and ſold by F. Noble, in Holborn;
Where may be had lately publiſhed,
St. Ruthin's Abbey, a Novel, 3 vols. 9s. bound.
The Woman of Letters; or, Hiſtory of Fanny Belton, 2 vol. 7s. bound.
A Leſſon for Lovers; or, Hiſtory of Col. Melville and Lady Richly, 2 vols. 7s. bound.
Literary Amuſements; or, Evening Entertainer, 2 vol. 7s. bound.
Adventures of a Cavalier, by Daniel Defoe, 3 vols. 9s bound.

T. RICKABY, PRINTER,
No. 15, Duke's Court, Drury Lane;

REſpectfully informs his Friends and the Public in general, that the Partnerſhip between him and Mr. Moore being entirely diſſolved, he now intends to carry on every branch of the PRINTING BUSINESS upon his own account;—and having purchaſed a complete aſſortment of the neateſt and beſt materials, is determined to purſue a Mode of Printing which he hopes will meet with the approbation of his employers.

N.B. Cards, Hand-Bills, Circular Letters, and all articles of the kind, accurately printed at a few hours notice, in a manner particularly neat, and at the loweſt prices.
⁂ An Apprentice wanted.

To the Readers of the London Medical Journal.
This day is firſt publiſhed, price 1s.

SYMPATHY DEFENDED; or, the State MEDICAL CRITICISM in London; written to improve the Principles and Manners of the Editor of the London Medical Journal: To which are added the Contents of the Treatiſe on Medical Sympathy, and a Poſtſcript, on account of a premature Review in a late Number of the London Medical Journal.

By a Society of Faculties;
Friends to the Public and Enemies to Impoſition.

"Cum tua non edas, carpis mea carmina, Laeli,
"Carp re vel noli noſtra, ede tua."
MART. Epig.

This pamphlet has been hitherto diſtributed gratuitouſly. The repeated applications for them, particularly from the country, have become ſo numerous, that the Society feel themſelves under the neceſſity of putting them into the hands of a publiſher.
Sold by J. Murray, Bookſeller, Fleet-ſtreet.

Nondum lingua ſilet dextra, peregit opus.
MART.

SHORT-HAND, on the lateſt and moſt approved Principles taught by J. LARKHAM, No 11, Roſe Alley, Biſhopſgate Street.

It would exceed the limits of an advertiſement merely to mention the various errors either in the *plan* or the *execution* of the different ſchemes of Short-hand hitherto made public, or to point out the peculiarities and excellencies of the preſent: Mr. L. therefore only begs leave to obſerve, that the approbation of many gentlemen well known in the literary world, and well verſed in the *Theory* and *Practice* of Short-hand, expreſſed in ſtronger terms than delicacy will permit him to repeat, warrants him in ſaying *his* will be found a ſyſtem of ſhort and ſwift writing, more *eaſy* to acquire and retain, more *expeditiouſly*, more *legible* and more *regular* than any ever yet offered to the Public.

The terms of teaching *one* Guinea, the *uſual* time of learning *ſeven* leſſons.

To the Public.

TO bring out a New Paper at the preſent day; when ſo many others are already eſtabliſhed and confirmed in the public opinion, is certainly an arduous undertaking; and no one can be more fully aware of its difficulties than I am: I, nevertheleſs, entertain very ſanguine hopes, that the nature of the plan on which this paper will be conducted, will enſure it a moderate ſhare at leaſt of public favour; but my pretenſions to encouragement, however ſtrong they may appear in my own eyes, muſt be tried before a tribunal not liable to be blinded by *ſelf-opinion*: to that tribunal I ſhall now, as I am bound to do, ſubmit theſe pretenſions with deference, and the public will judge whether they are well or ill founded.

It is very far from my intention to detract from the acknowledged merit of the Daily Papers now in exiſtence; it is ſufficient that they pleaſe the claſs of readers whoſe approbation their conductors are ambitious to deſerve; nevertheleſs it is certain ſome of the beſt, ſome of the moſt reſpectable, and ſome of the moſt uſeful members of the community, have frequently complained (and the cauſes of their complaints ſtill exiſt) that by radical defects in the plans of the preſent eſtabliſhed papers, they were deprived of many advantages, which ought naturally to reſult from daily publications. Of theſe ſome build their fame on the length and accuracy of parliamentary reports, which unqueſtionably are given with great ability, and with a laudable zeal to pleaſe thoſe, who can ſpare time to read ten or twelve columns of debates. *Others are principally attentive to the politics of* the day, and make it their ſtudy to give ſatisfaction to the numerous claſs of politicians, who, bleſſed with eaſy circumſtances, have nothing better to do, than to amuſe themſelves with watching the motions of miniſters both at home and abroad; and endeavouring to find out the ſecret ſprings that ſet in motion the great machine of government in every ſtate and empire in the world. There is one paper which in no degree interferes with the purſuits of its cotemporaries; it looks upon parliamentary debates as ſacred myſteries, that cannot be ſubmitted to vulgar eyes without profanation; political inveſtigations it apprehends to be little ſhort of treaſon, and therefore *loyally* abſtains from them; it deals almoſt ſolely in advertiſements; and conſequently, though a very uſeful, it is by no means an entertaining paper. Thus it would ſeem that every News-Paper publiſhed in London is calculated for a particular ſet of readers only; ſo that if each ſet were to change its favourite publication for another, the commutation would produce diſguſt, and diſſatisfaction to all; the politician would then find nothing to amuſe him but long accounts of petty ſquabbles about trifles in Parliament, or panegyrics on the men and meaſures that he moſt diſliked; or libels on thoſe whom he moſt revered. The perſon to whom parliamentary debates afford unſpeakable delight, would find himſelf bored with political ſpeculations about the meaſures that the different courts in Europe might probably adopt; or diſguſted with whole pages of advertiſements, in which he felt no concern;—whilſt the plain ſhop-keeper who wanted to find a convenient houſe for his buſineſs, and the ſervant who purchaſed his paper in hopes of ſeeing in it an advertiſement directing where he might find a place to ſuit him, would have their labour for their pains, in peruſing publications, filled with ſenatorial debates, or political eſſays and remarks, which would direct them to nothing leſs than the houſe or place they wanted.—A News-Paper, conducted on the true and natural principles of ſuch a publication, ought to be the Regiſter of the times, and faithful recorder of every ſpecies of intelligence; it ought not to be engroſſed by any particular object; but, like a well covered table, it ſhould contain ſomething ſuited to every palate: obſervations on the diſpoſitions of our own and of foreign courts ſhould be provided for the political reader; debates ſhould be reported for the amuſement or information of thoſe who may be particularly fond of them; and a due attention ſhould be paid to the intereſts of trade, which are ſo greatly promoted by advertiſements.—A paper that ſhould blend all theſe advantages, and by ſteering clear of extremes, hit the happy medium, has long been expected by the public.—Such, it is intended, ſhall be the UNIVERSAL REGISTER, the great objects of which will be to facilitate the *commercial* intercourſe between the different parts of the community, through the channel of *Advertiſements*; to record the principal occurrences of the times; and to abridge the account of debates during the ſitting of Parliament.

It is no leſs the intereſt of the proprietors of News-Papers, than of the public, that every encouragement ſhould be given to advertiſing correſpondents; yet this private intereſt of the proprietors is frequently ſacrificed to the rage for parliamentary debates, to the great injury of trade; for the extreme length of theſe debates ſo greatly retards the publication of the New-Papers which are noted for detailed accounts of them, that the advantages ariſing from this ſpecies of intelligence, though highly acceptable in itſelf, are frequently over-balanced by the inconvienences occaſioned to people in buſineſs by the delay. Theſe inconveniences are great and many; it generally happens, that when either Houſe of Parliament has been engaged in the diſcuſſion of an important queſtion till after midnight, the papers in which the ſpeeches of the Members are reported at large, cannot be publiſhed before noon; nay, they ſometimes are not even ſent to preſs ſo ſoon; conſequently parties intereſted in *ſales* are eſſentially injured, as the advertiſements, inviting the public to attend them at *ten* or *twelve* o'clock, do not appear, on account of a late publication, till ſome hours after.—From the ſame ſource flows another inconvenience; it is ſometimes found neceſſary to *defer* ſales, after they have been advertiſed for a particular day; but the notice of putting them off not appearing early enough, on account of the late hour at which the papers containing it are publiſhed, numbers of people, acting under the impreſſion of former advertiſements, are unneceſſarily put to the trouble of attending.—It will be the object of the *Univerſal Regiſter* to guard againſt theſe great inconveniences, without depriving its readers of the pleaſure of learning what paſſes in Parliament.—It is intended, then, that the debates ſhall be regularly reported in it; but on the other hand, that the publication may not be delayed to the prejudice of people in trade, the ſpeeches will not be given on a large ſcale; the *ſubſtance* ſhall be faithfully preſerved; but all the unintereſting parts will be omitted. I ſhall thus be enabled to publiſh this paper at an early hour; and I propoſe to bring it out *regularly* every morning at *ſix* o'clock. The *Univerſal Regiſter* will therefore have this advantage over the *Daily Advertiſer*, that, though publiſhed as early, it will contain a ſubſtantial account of the proceedings in Parliament the preceding night, which is never to be found in that paper; and compared with the other morning papers it will be found to have the merit of containing in ſubſtance, what they give in long detail (which men in buſineſs cannot well ſpare time to read) and, nevertheleſs, of being publiſhed much ſooner. Theſe circumſtances, it is hoped, will give the *Univerſal Regiſter* at leaſt an *equal* claim to public favour with the parliamentary papers, and the *trading* part of the metropolis, it is preſumed, will find it their advantage to give it the preference.

An eſſential part of the plan of this new paper is, that, for the convenience of advertiſing correſpondents, their favours ſhall, *to a certainty*, be inſerted on the very day that they ſhall direct; provided they deliver them at the office in due time. For the *ſtrict* obſervance of this rule, the credit of the paper ſhall ſtand pledged; and its pretenſions to public countenance will be renounced, if this fundamental principle in its inſtitution ſhall ever be violated, except in caſes of abſolute neceſſity, which human prudence cannot prevent.—And here I beg it may be underſtood that I do not make uſe of the word *neceſſity* as a reſerve, under colour of which, I may, whenever I think fit, be releaſed from my engagements; I mean by that word a neceſſity ariſing from accidents that ſometimes happen in the printing buſineſs, and from which, the moſt careful man cannot, at all times, be ſecure. But ſo far from wiſhing to ſhrink from my engagements, I intend, whenever the length of the Gazette, Parliamentary Debates, &c. ſhall render it impoſſible for me to inſert all the advertiſements promiſed for the day, in *one* ſheet, to print an additional half ſheet, and publiſh it with the ordinary paper without any additional charge to my cuſtomers.—From the difficulty that people experience in procuring the inſertion of their advertiſements even in the *Daily Advertiſer*; and particularly from the impoſſibility of obtaining an *early* inſertion at ſome periods of the year, it may be preſumed that this regulation will greatly recommend the UNIVERSAL REGISTER to public notice, and procure it ſupport.

Theſe, though in my opinion good, are not the *only* grounds on which I build my hopes of ſucceſs. I flatter myſelf, I have ſome claim to public encouragement, on account of a great improvement which I have made in the art of printing. The inconveniences attending the old and tedious mode of compoſing with letters taken up *ſingly*, firſt ſuggeſted the idea of deviſing ſome more expeditious method. The cementing of ſeveral letters together, ſo as that the type of a *whole word* might be taken up in as ſhort a time as that of a *ſingle letter*, was the reſult of much reflection on that ſubject. But the bare idea of cementing was merely the opening, not the accompliſhment or perfection of the improvement. The fount conſiſting of types of words, and not of letters, was to be ſo arranged, as that a compoſitor ſhould be able to find the former with as much facility as he can the latter. This was a work of inconceivable difficulty. I undertook it however, and was fortunate enough, after an infinite number of experiments, and great labour, to bring it to a happy concluſion. The whole Engliſh language is now methodically and ſyſtematically arranged at my fount: ſo that printing can now be performed with greater diſpatch, and at leſs expence, than according to the mode hitherto in uſe.

In bringing this work to perfection, I had not my own advantage ſolely in view; I wiſhed to be uſeful to the community; and it is with pleaſure I ſee that the public will derive conſiderable benefit from my induſtry; for I have reſolved to ſell the REGISTER *One halfpenny* UNDER the price paid for ſeven out of eight of the morning

papers; however I indulge a hope that this sacrifice which I make of the usual profits of printing, will be felt by a generous public; and that they will so far favour me with advertisements, as to enable me to defray the heavy expences attending the literary departments in the paper, and to make a livelihood for myself and my family.—The favour that I now earnestly solicit, I shall diligently labour to preserve, without entertaining a presumptuous wish that I may enjoy it one moment longer, than I shall be found to deserve it.

The *Register*, in its politics, will be of no party: weakened as the country is by a long and expensive war, and rent by intestine divisions, nothing but the union of all parties can save it from destruction. Moderate men, therefore, I trust, will countenance a paper, which has for one of its objects to cool the animosities, stifle the resentments' manage the personal honour, and reconcile the principals of contending parties; while the favours of those will be courted, who support principles, by fair *argument*, and think that a good cause may be injured by personalities, and low invective, the correspondence of such as descend to illiberal abuse, and attack the *man* rather than the *measure*, will always be disregarded. The *Register*, instead of dealing in scurrilities and abusing the great men in power, or the great men out of power; or, instead of deifying the one or the other, will reserve to itself a right of censuring or applauding either, as their conduct may occasionally appear proper or improper.

If censure should be thought necessary, it shall be conveyed in language suited to the respect that is due to the public, before whose tribunal the individual is arraigned; and no provocation shall be deemed an excuse for illiberal abuse, or personality.

Nothing shall ever find a place in the *Universal Register*, that can tend to wound the ear of delicacy, or corrupt the heart: vice shall never be suffered there to wear the garb of virtue: To hold out the former in alluring colours, would strike at the very root of morality; and, concealing the native deformity of vice, might seduce unsuspecting innocence from the paths of virtue.

As a News-Paper ought to be at the service of the Public, by whom it is supported, I shall not hold myself excuseable, through the example of others, in opening the *Register* to one kind of advertisers, and partially shutting it against others: I hold that I have a right to consider only whether the advertisements offered for insertion contain any thing contrary to law or morality; and that, if they do not, I should violate my duty to the public, in refusing to insert them when paid for. A News-Paper in this particular ought to resemble an *Inn*, where the proprietor is *obliged* to give the use of his house to all travellers, who are ready to pay for it, and against whose persons there is no legal or moral objection.

The miscellaneous articles of intelligence will be regularly arranged under the heads of *Theatres, Trials, Ship News, Market Prices, Bills of Entry, Prices Courant, Stocks, Promotions, Marriages, Deaths, &c.* Though it is intended that faithful accounts shall be given of all remarkable trials at law, still those will be more particularly attended to, in which the mercantile world may be most interested. In a word, no pains or expence will be spared, that can render the *Universal Register* of utility to the public.

The miscellaneous articles of intelligence will be regularly arranged under the heads of *Theatres, Trials, Ship News, Market Prices, Bills of Entry, Prices Courant, Stocks, Promotions, Marriages, Deaths, &c.* Though it is intended that faithful accounts shall be given of all remarkable trials at law, still those will be more particularly attended to, in which the mercantile world may be most interested. In a word, no pains or expence will be spared, that can render the UNIVERSAL REGISTER of utility to the public.

Such is the plan that Mr. WALTER has laid down for the conduct of his paper: he now sends it forth into the world, in hopes that it will appear to the public deserving of their encouragement. For his own part, he will no longer expect their countenance and favour, than he shall be found strictly to adhere to the engagements into which he now enters, in this sketch that he humbly begs leave to lay before them.

J. WALTER.

*** Advertisements, Essays, real Articles of Intelligence, &c. to which great attention will be paid, will be taken in at the OFFICE in *Printing-house Square*; and for the greater convenience of the distant parts of the town, at Mr. SEARLE'S, Grocer, No. 55, *Oxford-street*; Mr. THRALE'S, Pastry Cook, *opposite the Admiralty*; M. WILSON'S LIBRARY, No. 45, *Lombard street*; Mr. PRATT'S, Green Grocer, No. 84, *Wapping*; and Mr. STERNEY, No. 156, *opposite St. George's Church, Borough.*

‡§‡ The Ladies and Gentlemen who may be pleased to take in this Paper, may be supplied with it by any of the NEWSMEN.

FOREIGN INTELLIGENCE.

Yesterday arrived the Mails from France *and* Flanders, *which brought the following news.*

Nuremberg, Nov. 25, 1784.

THE agreement concluded between the Emperor's commissaries and those of the Circle of Franconia, with regard to the necessary supply of provisions of every kind for the Imperial troops during their march through the Circle, to the Low Countries, is in substance as follows: 1st, each soldier and non-commissioned officer shall receive at their lodgings, half a pound of flesh, two pounds of bread, roots and a pot of beer, or a bottle of wine, at the rate of 8 kreutzers; 2d, each horse shall have 8 pounds of oats, 10 pounds of hay, and half a truss of straw, at 30 kreutzers; 3d, waggons drawn by four horses or six oxen, may be paid at the rate of 2 florins per head; 4th, nothing more than what is contained in the first article shall be exacted from those who quarter the troops, and whatever surplus they may give shall be paid for in ready money; 5th, officers and all persons following the army, must pay ready money for whatever they contract for.

We are assured that the commissaries of the Circle have requested of those of the Emperor, to insert in this conversation, that, in consequence of the dearth of grain, and particularly of forage, it would be impossible for the Circle, in case of another march through their State, to furnish the troops with supplies; and that they intended addressing his Imperial Majesty on this point.

Francfort, Dec. 16. The military chest is to be established in this city, and to be guarded by the regiment of Priess, which will remain here during the winter. It seems our town will be the rendezvous of a considerable part of the Austrian army, for within these few days we have had 85 commissaries for provisions. Enlisting is carried on with the greatest success in this city and neighbourhood.

On the 7th 300 of Wormser's hussars passed through Hof; 13,019 of the Imperial troops, with 721 horses, were expected in the environs of Landibus, on the 17th current.

The Swiss have refused granting troops to the Dutch.

Cologne, Dec. 21. We learn from Baruth, that on the morning of the 11th instant, the regiment of Coubourg passed through there on their way to Luxembourg.

By letters from Nuremberg of the 13th, we learn, that 25 postilions preceded by an officer, two gentlemen, eight Imperial chasseurs, leading fifty-two saddle horses, belonging to the Emperor, arrived the 6th current at Ratisbonne, and that they are to be followed by two waggons loaded with his Majesty's kitchen furniture.

Orders are given to prepare quarters for the Emperor, at the White Lamb at Nuremberg, and on the 12th and on the 13th at night, the whole of the above mentioned cavalcade entered this city. On the 13th, a large body of Imperial troops passed through Neustadt-An-der-hard, which is to be followed by many other corps, all destined for the Low Countries.

Prince Kaunitz Ritsbourg, Chancellor of State, has disappeared for some days; his place is filled by Vice Chancellor, Count de Cobentzel. On the 3d, dispatches were received from the Imperial Ambassador, at Paris, which employed his Imperial Majesty the whole afternoon; he was the entire evening in his closet, and not at leisure to assist at the opera, as he intended. His Majesty has absolutely rejected the last propositions for a reconciliation from the Court of France, and insists upon the free and unlimited navigation of the Scheld. The declared opposition of France would not change this resolution, as his Majesty's dignity is at stake. The Emperor has often made known these dispositions; he has even been heard to say, that he might forgive an attack from a crowned head, but that he could never forgive the injury done to by the Dutch. According to the declaration of the French Court, although conceived in general, yet friendly terms, it is not imagined that it will openly oppose the Austrians. Who is unacquainted with the powerful influence which the Count de Vergennes and his party have, to inspire the King with other counsels, when fully convinced of his Majesty's invincible resolution? Mean time we see innumerable couriers, and the dispatches are sealed by the Chancellor in person. On the other hand, the King of France's letter, so emphatically mentioned, has existed only in the brains of newsmongers. The truth is, the ministry of Versailles, on the 20th of November, sent a sufficiently energetic memoir to our Cabinet; it was delivered on the 27th of the same month, by the Marquis de Noailles: it is certain no answer was made to it on the 4th current.

Antwerp, Dec. 23. Although the Emperor has accepted the mediation of France, his resolution is, let the result be what it may, to maintain constantly 40,000 men in the Low Countries, to be ready on any emergency. Lodgings are still preparing here for the army; a body of waggoners arrived here, with 100 horses from Luxembourg, for the Emperor's service.

Leige, Dec. 19. His Highness our gracious Prince was this morning consecrated Bishop, by the Marquis of Hoensbroek, Bishop of Ruremonde, assisted by the Abbots of St. Lawrence and St. Giles. This august ceremony was performed in the chapel of the palace, with the usual formalities, and with the most edifying dvotions without any ostentatious preparation. To-morow being theday appointed for inaguration, there will be no illuminations. His Highness wishes they may be suppressed, and in conformity to his paternal views the expences attending them will be converted to objects more useful, and more pleasing to his beneficent heart.

Letters from Sicily inform, that a 24 gun ship, belonging to Chevalier Emo's squadron, sunk in a storm, and that the second in command of her, died in a wound he had received at the bombardment of Suje.

Paris, Dec. 20. We are informed of an answer made by the King of Prussia to the Commandant of Cleves, who wanted to know of his Majesty how he was to act if the Austrian troops should attempt to pass through his territories—The answer was, "That if the Austrian troops marched towards the Dutchy of Cleves, he should tell them they had mistaken the way; if they persisted, he should make prisoners of them; and if they resisted, kill them."

"Signed, *Frederick.*"

L O N D O N.

Yesterday their Majesties came from Windsor, and last night honoured the Theatre with their presence.

This day being New-Year's Day, their Majesties will appear in the drawing room at St. James's, and receive the compliments of the nobility, gentry, and foreign ministers on the occasion of the day. The following Ode, composed by Paul Whitehead, Esq. Poet Laureat, will be sung in the great Council Chamber.

ODE FOR THE NEW YEAR.

Jan. 1st, 1785.

DELUSIVE is the poet's dream,
Or does prophetic truth inspire
The zeal which prompts the glowing theme
And animates th' according Lyre?
Trust the Muse: her eye commands
Distant times, and distant lands
Thro' bursting clouds in opening skies,
Sees from discord union rise,
And friendship bind unwilling foes
In firmer ties than duty knows.
Torn rudely from its parent tree
Yon Scion, rising in the West,
Will soon its genuine glory see,
And court again the fostering breast
Whose pasture gave its powers to spread
And feel their force, and lift an alien head.
The parent tree, when storms impend,
Shall own affection's warmth again,
Again its fostering aid shall lend
Nor hear the suppliant plead in vain,
Shall stretch protecting branches round,
Extend the shelter, and forget the wound,
Two Britons thro' the admiring world,
Shall wing their way with sails unfurl'd;
Each from the other kindred state,
Avert by turns the bolts of fate,
And acts of mutual amity endear
The Tyre and Carthage of a wider sphere.
When Rome's divided eagles flew,
And different thrones her Empire knew,
The varying language soon disjoin'd
The boasted masters of mankind.
But here no ills like those we fear,
No varying language threatens here
Congenial worth, congenial flame,
Their manners and their arts the same;
To the same tongue shall glowing themes afford,
And British heroes act, and British bards restor'd.
Fly swift ye years, ye minutes haste,
And in the future lose the past.
O'er many a thought-afflicting tale,
Oblivion, cast thy friendly veil,
Let not memory breathe a sigh,
Or backward turn th' indignant eye;
Nor the insidious arts of foes
Enlarge the breach that longs to close,
But acts of amity alone inspire
Firm truth, and cordial love, and wake the willing lyre.

The business which brought Mr. Secretary Orde and Mr. Foster, Chancellor of the Exchequer, from Ireland, was finally determined on Tuesday in a cabinet council, held for that purpose. This business was relative to the *Protecting Duties*, so generally called for in Ireland, and an adjustment of several difficulties that occurred in the commercial intercourse between that country and this. The friends of the Irish administration say, that the terms Mr. Orde has obtained from the minister, will give general satisfaction in Ireland: but without fearing the danger of being found false prophets, we do not hesitate to say that these terms, so far from giving general satisfaction, will be received by the Irish as an insult to their understanding, if it be true, as it is reported, that the minister has bound himself to no more than this—"That he "will advise his Majesty to give his royal assent "to a bill or bills sent to him from Ireland, "for imposing certain duties on woollen cloths, "&c. *of an inferior quality*, imported into that "kingdom from Great Britain." Duties, amounting even to a prohibition, on *such* cloths, will never give satisfaction to the Irish, for this reason—very little of such cloths, if any, is imported by them; for the manufacture of lower priced woollens is carried to much greater perfection in Ireland than in England; and even whilst the prohibition to export Irish woollens existed, Ireland, by a smuggled trade, supplied the Americans with coarse cloths, and greatly under-sold the English manufacturer. It is in the making of *superfine* cloths that the English surpass the Irish; it was on *superfine* British woollens that Ireland called for duties, which should operate as a *protection* and encouragement to her own manufacture of *first* cloths; and these duties being refused, nothing in fact is granted.

Three days before Christmas day, a messenger extraordinary from the Court of Petersburgh arrived at the hotel of his Excellency Monsf. Kalitchoff, the Russian Minister at the Hague, with the following memorial, which his Excellency, by order of his Sovereign, immediately delivered to the President of the States General: we are happy to lay before our readers the contents of a memorial, which has for object the preventing of a war, and the preservation of public tranquillity.

"Her Majesty the Empress of all the Russias "never lost sight for a moment since the beginning "of her reign, of the happiness and tranquillity of "Europe in general: it was therefore with the "most lively concern, the received intelligence "that the negociations between the States General and the Emperor, her friend and ally, "had been interrupted by acts of hostility, which "would seem to put it out of the power of "his Imperial Majesty to take any other steps, "than such as the care of his dignity, which "stands committed in the face of Europe, should "suggest. Her Majesty the Empress has given "too many marks of the interest she takes in "the peace and prosperity of the Republic, not "to be confident that their High Mightinesses "will consider the invitation which she new "sends them, to devise means for opening again "the way to accommodation, as the fruits of "the most pure and laudable desire to restore "tranquillity, and prevent hostilities, that might "end in open war, and disturb the peace of all "Europe. Her Majesty then requests their "High Mightinesses will think of the means "that their wisdom may suggest, to bring the dispute to an amicable conclusion, a consummation as salutary as it is useful to both "parties."

This memorial has given an alarm in Amsterdam; for though the Empress seems to breathe nothing but peace; though magnanimity is manifested in it, to a great degree; yet, still it is feared that her connexions with the Emperor may have great influence on her mind, when acting as a mediatrix between the Dutch, and a monarch whom she emphatically calls her *friend* and *ally*.

Lord Grantham arrived in Town on Thursday night: a particular mandate or message from a Great Personage, it is said, was the occasion of his Lordship's haste. A return to official business in Cleveland Row, is supposed to be the object of his Lordship's call from his rural retreat.

GUILDHALL INTELLIGENCE.

The adjourned examination of Mr. Turner, a bankrupt, was resumed yesterday.—The nature of the case was this.—Messrs. Turner and Smith, Linendrapers in Oxford-Road, had failed some time ago, and a commission of bankruptcy issued against them. On their examination, the commissioners were so dissatisfied with their answers, that they committed them both to Newgate. On Thursday they were exemaned again, and Mr. Smith was discharged from his confinement; but his partner, Mr. Turner, not appearing to deserve the same indulgence, was again committed. The commissioners seemed to be of opinion at first, that his examination should be closed; and that he should be made to abide by the answers he had already given: but his creditors wishing that this unhappy man should not perish on this occasion, begged that he might be indulged with another examination, in which he might at last tell the truth, and save his life. The commissioners then gave him three hours more to reflect upon his situation; but the creditors still desirous that he might have time to sleep upon the business, they prolonged the indulgence to yesterday at noon. The creditors had great reason to believe that concealments of property to a considerable ammount, had been made by the bankrupt; and the answers given by him, confirmed them in this opinion, though they were intended by him to remove it. The commissioners met yesterday pursuant to adjournment, and the prisoner having been brought before them, Mr. Morgan, his counsel, opened the business with a written string of interrogatories, which he put to the bankrupt; this mode of proceeding was objected to by Mr. Garrow, counsel for the creditors; he grounded his objection on that, first, such a method would necessarily protract the business of the day to an useless length; second, that it was shewing too great an indulgence to the prisoner, whom he supposed to be previously instructed in his answers, he therefore did not hesitate to prefer a narrative from the prisoner to an interrogatory from his counsel.

Mr. Morgan rose and entered into a short, though interesting detail of the many inconveniences and losses to which people in trade are daily liable to, he did not at all doubt but there were many among the prisoner's creditors, there present, who had some time or other, experienced the truth of his assertion, and who would wish in their misfortunes to have met with indulgence; his argument went to prove that a person in the unhapy circumstances of Mr. Turner, whom poverty with its concomitant disadvantages stared in the face, had the shadow of an excuse to sequester some of his good, to be able thereby in some time, with œconomy and prudent regulation, to satisfy all his creditors; he however by no means approved the conduct of those who concealed their goods to deceive the merchants who trusted them; on the contrary he reprobated it, and thought no punishment too great for the offence; but he contended that the bankrupt then in court was by no means in the predicament alluded to, and consequently was intitled to the indulgence due to innocence, he concluded by mentioning the severity of the laws with respect to bankrupts. Here Mr. Garrow stood up, and was of opinion that poverty or any other wordly inconvenience could not lead an honest man from the paths of probity; if there ever was an example of the kind, the prisoner in question could not plead his right to be excepted; he had given proofs of his dishonest intentions, and he, (Mr. Garrow,) was in possession of a letter which would every way tend to disclose his secret manœuvres; he further asserted that Mr. Turner had been treated with unexampled lenity and favour, he had many advantages allowed him to give him every opportunity of exculpating himself from the crime he was accused of, he feared that his indulgence to the prisoner would draw on him the displeasure of his clients: he owned that the laws were very severe with respect to bankrupts, but he insisted that they were only so for the fair trader, the honest merchant, whose losses were the effects of the capricious deity, rather than those that result from dissipation and extravagance.

The prisoner being asked whether the court was in possession of all the papers notifying all the debts due to him and owing to others, he answered in the affirmative, but being forewarned by his counsel of the fatal consequences of any secret embezzlement, he owned that a Mr. Fairborne, broker, had a bill of his for 18 guineas, that he had given a note of 179l. to Mrs. Wright, (with whom he had lived,) and also seventy odd pounds for having lodged with her. The prisoner answers on the whole were evasive and nugatory. The Commissioners adjourned to a Coffee House, in order to examine him still further in private.

Extract of a letter from Vienna, Dec. 4.

"We are sending off the heavy artillery from this city, which is also to furnish two thousand recruits for the army of the Low Countries. They are raising in Galicia a body of Uhlans, who are to assemble at Brinn."

TO CORRESPONDENTS.

We would with pleasure have inserted gratis *all the Advertisements that were sent to us, had we not received an intimation from the Stamp-Office, that the King's duty must be paid for every advertisement that should appear in our first day's paper; we were therefore obliged to leave out all the favours of our advertising friends, who, unapprised of this circumstance, did not send the stamp-duty with each advertisement.*

TO PARENTS AND GUARDIANS.

A YOUTH properly qualified, may be placed out an Apprentice in a wholesale and retail tea and grocery warehouse in the city, where he will be properly qualified in a genteel lucrative line of business; and at the expiration of his engagement, an opportunity of establishing himself on the spot: a circumstance which seldom happens. As every requisite satisfaction will be given his friends, a liberal premium is expected.——Address a line to Mr. Pugh, at Baker's Coffee-house, Change-Alley,

Lord John Russell, moaned that 'If England is ever to be England again, this vile tyranny of *The Times* must be cut off,' but those at a greater distance saw the value of its independent spirit. '*The Times* is one of the greatest powers in the world,' pronounced Abraham Lincoln, 'in fact, I don't know anything which has more power, except perhaps the Mississippi.' Nonetheless, the quality of its writing and its generally unsensationalist tone were not always matched by the perspicacity of its analysis: it supported the appeasement of Hitler in the 1930s, upheld rapprochement with Stalin in the 1940s and backed the Franco-British occupation of the Suez Canal in 1956. Generally, however, its editorial policy looked favourably on the cause of moderate reform, advocating liberal Conservatism and eschewing campaigning journalism.

Thus *The Times* has always been an influential rather than a popular or profitable paper. It was still selling fewer than 60,000 copies a day when in 1855 the abolition of stamp duty on newspapers created new and competitive domestic rivals like the cheaper *Daily Telegraph*. Even during the twentieth century – until its circulation figures improved in the 1980s – the paper's daily sales were often under a quarter of a million copies, and in the 1950s it even marketed itself with the somewhat exclusive advertising slogan 'Top People Take *The Times*.' Ironically, the paper of choice for the British Establishment had several times to be rescued: first in 1908 by Lord Northcliffe, the innovator of mid-market journalism, before being bought successively by the Anglo-American Astor family, in 1966 by the Canadian Thomson family and, in 1981, by the Australian-born Rupert Murdoch.

The improving authority of rivals, the expanding sources of alternative media information, including radio, television and internet, and a desire to broaden its previously limited readership base all conspired to end *The Times*'s claims to pre-eminence. Despite this, it retained, in at least some aspects, its claim to be Britain's foremost 'newspaper of record'. Its law reports are without equal in the press, its letters page continues to provide a national forum of interaction between the powerful and the general public, and the court and social page is a noticeboard for events and announcements. Its crossword, instigated in 1930, still provides one of the most recognized daily tests of mental dexterity. Most of all, a longevity of over 220 years at the forefront of national and international discourse has earned its central place in the history of Britain's fourth estate.

1788
MARYLEBONE CRICKET CLUB'S CODE OF LAWS

CODIFYING CRICKET

Bat-and-ball games have been played in England since at least the Middle Ages and almost certainly since the Dark Ages. Indeed, cricket's etymology may come from 'cryce', the Old English word for stick. The distance between wickets is still twenty-two yards: the traditional dimension of an Anglo-Saxon farmer's strip-holding.

Surviving early references to cricket proliferate from the seventeenth century and something resembling the modern game dates from that period. The first eleven-a-side match for which there is an authoritative record was played in Sussex in 1697. By 1709, Kent were facing Surrey and the following year undergraduates at Cambridge University began forming teams.

During the eighteenth century, the sport was particularly popular in the southern counties of England, its appeal crossing social divides. In the thirty years after 1767, the acknowledged centre of cricketing talent was, improbably, the small Hampshire village of Hambledon. There, a winning team was marshalled by Richard Nyren, who was the landlord of the Bat & Ball inn. In 1777, the Hambledon Club even humiliated a side drawn up of England's supposed best cricketers by an innings and 168 runs.

Yet despite cricket's rustic roots, its adoption by gentlemen in London facilitated its transformation into the modern game. Matches were played on the commons at Chelsea and Clapham, as well as at the artillery ground in Finsbury. In common with the other leading sports of the day, considerable stakes often awaited the winners, attracting professional promoters, serious betting and even occasional crowd trouble.

As much to regulate the terms for fair gambling as to establish the legality of actions on the field, in 1744 the first cricket rules were drawn up by the London

CRICKET'S EARLY HISTORY

*c.*1550 'Creckett' is played at the Royal Grammar School, Guildford, according to a court testimony of 1598.

1598 Giovanni Florio's English–Italian dictionary mentions 'to play cricket-a-wicket' (there is some debate over whether this is a sport or a sexual act).

1646 The oldest surviving record of a match being played that can be properly authenticated as cricket takes place at Coxheath in Kent.

1697 An eleven-men-a-side game is first mentioned.

1709 Kent v. Surrey is the first recorded county match.

1722 The London Cricket Club is in existence.

1744 The oldest surviving laws are drawn up by the London Cricket Club.

*c.*1767 The Hambledon Club is established in Hampshire and soon fields the most successful side in the country.

1769 John Minshull of the duke of Dorset's XI scores the first recorded century.

1774 The Star and Garter Club of London publishes its Laws of Cricket; the leg before wicket law is established.

1787 Marylebone Cricket Club is founded.

1788 MCC's Code of Laws is laid down.

1794 The oldest recorded interschool match occurs: Charterhouse v. Westminster.

1806 The tradition of the Gentlemen v. Players match begins at Thomas Lord's ground.

1807 Round-arm bowling is first mentioned.

1811 The first women's match at county level, Surrey v. Hampshire, is played.

1814 Thomas Lord selects his third, and final, site for MCC's ground.

1827 The first Oxford v. Cambridge match at Lord's ends in a draw.

Club of which Frederick, Prince of Wales, was president. Other versions followed, with none gaining definitive acceptance.

In 1787 a club was founded that quickly asserted its authority, with its roots in the aristocratic White Conduit Club, whose ground had been swallowed up by urban developers. Two of its luminaries, the earl of Winchelsea and the future duke of Richmond, helped a business-savvy bowler, Thomas Lord, find them a new ground in Marylebone. With this move, Marylebone Cricket Club (MCC) was founded. When the lease expired and the ground was built over to become Dorset Square, Lord found fresh premises in St John's Wood and, taking the original turf with him, he settled on a third – and final – site for the club in 1814. This ground is still called Lord's and remains the headquarters of MCC to this day.

Within a year of its establishment, MCC drew up its own Code of Laws (as the rules were grandly styled). This code quickly gained acceptance throughout the rest of the country while MCC, although no more than a private club, assumed responsibility as the sport's governing body. While other bodies were later set up to administer English Test and county cricket, MCC retained its lead role in setting the guidelines for, and administering, Test cricket throughout the world until 1993, when the International Cricket Council took over. Despite encroachment from the ICC, MCC still owns and retains the right to frame the Laws.

Inevitably, over the past two centuries or more, the Laws have been subject to revision during a period that saw sheep-grazed fields

give way to pitches carefully prepared with a heavy roller and in which the game spread throughout the British Empire. The number of balls bowled in an innings, for instance, was increased from four to five in 1889 and again to six in 1900. The parameters for a Leg Before Wicket (LBW) decision generated considerable debate. Concerned by excessive 'padding away' by batsmen, in 1934 MCC introduced a new law, allowing not just balls pitched in a straight line between the two wickets but even those pitched outside off stump to be capable of producing a LBW verdict. It was on the legality of various bowling actions that the hottest controversy raged. Bowling was delivered underarm during the eighteenth century. However, bowlers increasingly tested the latitude offered by umpires, progressively raising the point at which they released the ball with round-arm deliveries. MCC attempted to end this upward creep by specifically outlawing it in an 1816 law clarification. Unable to make the judgment stick, MCC kept redefining upwards the height at which a delivery could be made, until finally legalizing round-arm in 1835 and overarm in 1864, when the bowler was permitted freedom of delivery so long as he did not throw the ball (i.e. deliver it with a bent arm).

Some of the greatest changes of format have come more recently. Limited-overs competitions were introduced at county level in 1963 and at international level in 1971, the format adopted four years later with the first World Cup. A new limited-overs format, Twenty20 – involving two innings of twenty overs apiece rather than the fifty that had become standard in one-day cricket – was introduced in 2003 and rapidly became popular, especially in India. Despite these innovations, the five-day Test match retains its prestige as the most demanding form of the game, with the 'Ashes' series between England against Australia among the most celebrated contests in world sport.

For all its successful transplantation from Marylebone to Melbourne and its centrality to life in places from Hyderabad to Kingston, Jamaica, cricket has been mythologized as a sport particularly emblematic of the country of its birth. Certainly, the language of cricket has become part of everyday English usage. Whatever the sharper, competitively charged reality on the field, its cultural association with fair play, patience and good sportsmanship remain among qualities that the English fondly imagine are most representative of their own national character traits. Even in spheres far removed from bat and ball, anything resembling sharp practice or underhand behaviour remains decidedly 'just not cricket'. Few other codes of laws have given the world such an ethos without anything stronger than a private members' club to ensure their enforcement.

The Laws Of Cricket, 1788
As revised by The Cricket Club at St Mary-le-bone

THE BALL
Must weigh not less than 5 ounces and a half, nor more than 5 ounces and three-quarters; it cannot be changed during the game but by the consent of both parties.

THE BAT
Must not exceed four inches and one quarter in the widest part.

THE STUMPS
Must be twenty-two inches out of the ground, the bails six inches in length.

THE PARTY
Which goes from home shall have the choice of innings and the pitching of the wickets, which shall be pitched within thirty yards of a centre fixed by the adversaries.

When the parties meet at a third place, the bowlers shall toss for the pitching of the wickets and the choice of going in.

It shall not be lawful for either party during a match, without the consent of the other, to alter the ground by rolling, watering, covering, mowing or beating. This rule is not meant to prevent a striker from beating the ground with his bat near where he stands, during the innings, or to prevent the bowler from filling up holes, watering his ground, or using sawdust, etc., when the ground is wet.

THE BOWLER
Shall deliver the ball with one foot behind the bowling crease, and within the return crease; and shall bowl four balls before he changes wickets, which he shall do but once in the same innings. He may order the striker at his wicket to stand on which side of it he pleases.

THE STRIKER
Is out if the bail is bowled off or the stump bowled out of the ground.

Or, if the ball, from a stroke over or under his bat, or upon his hand (but not his wrists), is held before it touches the ground, although it be hugged to the body of the catcher.

Or, if in striking, or at any time while the ball is in play, both his feet are over the popping-crease, and his wicket is put down, except his bat is grounded within it.

Or, if in striking at the ball, he hits down his wicket.

Or, if under pretence or running a notch or otherwise, either of the strikers prevents a ball from being caught, the striker of the ball is out.

Or, if the ball is struck up and he wilfully strikes it again.

Or, if in running a notch, the wicket is struck down by a throw, or with the ball in hand, before his foot, hand or bat is grounded over the popping-crease; but if the bail is off the stump must be struck out of the ground.

Or, if the striker touches or takes up the ball while in play, unless at the request of the opposite party.

Or, if with his foot or leg he stops the ball, which the bowler, in the opinion of the umpire at the bowler's wicket, shall have pitched in straight line to the wicket and would have hit it.

If the players have crossed each other, he that runs for the wicket which is put down is out; if they are not crossed, he that has left the wicket which is put down, is out.

When a ball is caught, no notch to be reckoned. When a striker is run out, the notch they were running for is not to be reckoned.

When the ball has been in the bowler's or the wicket-keeper's hands, it is considered as no longer in play, and the strikers need not keep within the ground until the umpire has called PLAY; but if the player goes out of ground with an intent to run before the ball is delivered, the bowler may put him out.

If the ball is struck up the striker may guard his wicket either with his bat or his body.

In single wicket matches, if the striker moves out of his ground to strike at the ball, he shall be allowed no notch for such stroke.

THE WICKET-KEEPER
Shall stand at a reasonable distance behind the wicket, and shall not move until the ball is out of the bowler's hand, and shall not by any noise incommode the striker; and if his hands, knees, feet or head, be over or before the wicket, though the ball hit it, it shall not be out.

THE UMPIRES
Are the sole judges of fair and unfair play, and all disputes shall be determined by them; each at his own wicket. But in the case of a catch, which the umpire at the wicket cannot see sufficiently to decide upon, he may apply to the other umpire, whose opinion is conclusive.

They shall allow two minutes for each man to come in, and fifteen minutes between each innings, when the umpire shall call PLAY, the party refusing to play shall lose the match.

When a striker is hurt they are to permit another to come in, and the person hurt shall have his hands in any part of that innings.

They are not to order a player out unless appealed to by the adversaries.

But, if the bowler's foot us not behind the bowling-crease, when he delivers the ball, they must, unasked, call NO BALL.

If the strikers run a short notch the umpire must call NO NOTCH.

That the umpire at the bowler's wicket shall be first applied to, to decide on all catches.

BETS

If the notches of one player are laid against another, the bets depend on the first innings, unless otherwise specified.

If the bets are made on both innings, and one party beats the other in one innings, the notches in the first innings shall determine the bet.

But if the party goes in a second time, then the bet must be determined by the number of the score.

VI

THE YEARS OF REFORM

1792
MARY WOLLSTONECRAFT'S
A VINDICATION OF THE RIGHTS OF WOMAN

THE BIRTH OF FEMINISM

In the period immediately after its publication, *A Vindication of the Rights of Woman* made its author, Mary Wollstonecraft, Europe's most famous female political writer. Although that reputation ebbed in the succeeding decades, her status was restored during the twentieth century with the embrace of much of her feminist philosophy.

Born in 1759, Wollstonecraft was unhappy in her youth. The family wealth was squandered by a bullying and incompetent father, while her mother openly favoured her eldest son. 'What was called spirit and wit in him,' his sister later summarized, 'was cruelly repressed as forwardness in me.' She received only brief schooling, a shortcoming for which she subsequently compensated by vociferous reading and teaching herself several foreign languages.

A propitious marriage – as a recurring theme in Jane Austen's novels emphasized – was the primary means by which middle-class women retained or enhanced their social station. With a minimal dowry, Mary Wollstonecraft's chances were blighted by her father's financial ineptitude. She embarked instead upon a career as a teacher and governess, whose rewards were meagre. Women's education, which had been a feature of Tudor gentry society, had still not fully recovered from the disruptions of the seventeenth century. To make matters worse, Wollstonecraft's efforts were not greatly appreciated by those who employed her.

In two areas, however, women were established in their own right. Since the Restoration, the stage had offered opportunities to women prepared to risk moral compromise. During the eighteenth century, a second, safer market developed in literature written by – and usually for – women. Wollstonecraft determined to

become a writer. In 1787, Joseph Johnson, a sympathetic publisher, brought out her book, *Thoughts on the Education of Daughters.*

The transforming event was the outbreak of the French Revolution. Britons were divided between those like the Whig politician-turned-Tory philosopher Edmund Burke, who preferred the orderly society of the *ancien régime* to the bloody anarchy unleashed by the mob, and radicals like Thomas Paine, the author of *The Rights of Man* (1791), who interpreted events in France as the birth of a new liberty.

Wollstonecraft firmly endorsed the latter view and sought to broaden its message to her own sex. In 1792, Johnson published her *A Vindication of the Rights of Woman.* An instant best-seller, it was soon translated into French and German and was also brought out in

M.ᴿˢ WOLLSTONECRAFT.

Mary Wollstonecraft (1759–97).

an American edition. It argued that a male-ordered society obsessed by rank and position had confined and stunted female development and self-expression. Furthermore, women had connived in their own disadvantage. Upon attaining their goal of marriage they had proceeded to behave as 'weak beings . . . fit only for a seraglio!' Society was constructed so that even 'civilised women of the present century, with a few exceptions are only anxious to inspire love, when they ought to cherish a nobler ambition, and by their abilities and virtues exact respect'.

Her own private life exemplified the struggles of women to gain esteem beyond the parameters of conformity. She fell in love with a bisexual married man, but the relationship was broken off when she suggested to his wife cohabiting with them in a *ménage à trois.* In 1792 she travelled to Paris and there began an affair with an American officer. To protect her from the murderous vengeance of the anti-British French revolutionaries, he registered her at the American Embassy as his wife. However, despite her being pregnant with his child, he largely deserted her to follow his own commercial ventures, and other lovers, before sending her to Scandinavia to conduct his business. Made miserable by his treatment, she twice tried to commit suicide. Rescued once by her maid from an opium overdose and a second time by rowers from drowning under Putney Bridge, she survived, working off some of her pain by using the experience as the basis for an epistolary novel, *A Short Residence in Sweden, Norway and Denmark* (1796). In the radical philosopher

From *A Vindication of the Rights of Woman*, Chapter 2

Women ought to endeavour to purify their heart; but can they do so when their uncultivated understandings make them entirely dependent on their senses for employment and amusement, when no noble pursuits set them above the little vanities of the day, or enables them to curb the wild emotions that agitate a reed, over which every passing breeze has power? To gain the affections of a virtuous man, is affectation necessary? Nature has given woman a weaker frame than man; but, to ensure her husband's affections, must a wife, who, by the exercise of her mind and body whilst she was discharging the duties of a daughter, wife, and mother, has allowed her constitution to retain its natural strength, and her nerves a healthy tone, – is she, I say, to condescend to use art, and feign a sickly delicacy, in order to secure her husband's affection? Weakness may excite tenderness, and gratify the arrogant pride of man; but the lordly caresses of a protector will not gratify a noble mind that pants for and deserves to be respected. Fondness is a poor substitute for friendship!

In a seraglio, I grant, that all these arts are necessary; the epicure must have his palate tickled, or he will sink into apathy; but have women so little ambition as to be satisfied with such a condition? Can they supinely dream life away in the lap of pleasure, or the languor of weariness, rather than assert their claim to pursue reasonable pleasures, and render themselves conspicuous by practising the virtues which dignify mankind? Surely she has not an immortal soul who can loiter life away merely employed to adorn her person, that she may amuse the languid hours, and soften the cares of a fellow-creature who is willing to be enlivened by her smiles and tricks, when the serious business of life is over.

Besides, the woman who strengthens her body and exercises her mind will, by managing her family and practising various virtues, become the friend, and not the humble dependent of her husband; and if she, by possessing such substantial qualities, merit his regard, she will not find it necessary to conceal her affection, nor to pretend to an unnatural coldness of constitution to excite her husband's passions. In fact, if we revert to history, we shall find that the women who have distinguished themselves have neither been the most beautiful nor the most gentle of their sex.

William Godwin she finally met a like-minded man who treated her with respect. Overcoming their mutual opposition to the idea of marriage, they exchanged vows when she discovered she was pregnant by him; but lasting happiness eluded her. In September 1797, aged thirty-eight, she died following complications in giving birth. The child survived and grew up to become the novelist Mary Shelley.

Godwin was heartbroken, but when he published his memoirs he unintentionally severely damaged her posthumous reputation by detailing her bohemian life. As a consequence, she quickly plummeted from her position as the most read and discussed exponent of women's rights, while the personal details Godwin had revealed provided ammunition for her political opponents. It did not help that her deeply sexual and largely unhappy odyssey did not sit easily with the high moral tone adopted by the female Victorian campaigners. Nevertheless, while her writing produced little discernible gain in the short term, she benefited from a reassessment by the women's suffrage movement at the end of the nineteenth century. From then on, her standing continued to recover. The liberal attitudes expressed in *A Vindication of the Rights of Woman* have made the book a central text not only of twentieth-century feminism but of equality itself.

1800

THE ANGLO-IRISH
ACT OF UNION

THE CREATION OF THE UNITED KINGDOM'S PARLIAMENT

Back in 1171, Henry II had launched a full-scale invasion of Ireland. In doing so, he cited papal sanction (Rome was concerned about Ireland's Celtic ecclesiastical traditions); but he was chiefly motivated by greed and the fear that other rivals might establish too strong a foothold there if he did not assert his own authority. Disunited by its competing regional chieftains, the country was taken over piecemeal, with Anglo-Norman barons seizing land predominantly in the south-east. Parliaments were called from 1264. Yet, despite successive campaigns in the fourteenth century, English forces failed to subdue the rest of the island. Indeed, by the fifteenth century, English influence had contracted to the area of the Pale around Dublin. The realization that the whole island could not readily be brought under centralized control ensured its division between the native Gaelic chiefs, the semi-autonomous Anglo-Irish lords and the centre of anglicized leadership in Dublin.

It was Henry VIII who adopted new strategies, seeking to strengthen his own authority while pursuing measures that avoided costly formal colonization. The Dublin Parliament had recognized successive English monarchs as 'Lord of Ireland', but in 1541 this title was upgraded to 'King of Ireland'. In return for acknowledging their royal overlord and English law, the Gaelic chiefs were guaranteed retention of their possessions. Peerages were also conferred upon them in the belief that this would foster their integration and collaboration. However, the adoption of Protestantism and the 'plantation' of (largely Scots Presbyterian) settlers in Ulster succeeded only in widening the divide between the colonists and the colonized. Successive uprisings in the last years of Elizabeth I's reign were put down only at considerable cost.

In the seventeenth century the plight of the Catholic Irish majority worsened significantly. On the eve of the English Civil War, 60 per cent of Ireland was still

in Catholic ownership. Atrocities by both sides in the 1640s were followed in 1649 by Oliver Cromwell's invasion and the ruthless imposition of a new settlement.

Cromwell's experiment in uniting the Irish and English Parliaments, with (Protestant) Irish MPs sitting at Westminster, was undone upon the Restoration. The Anglican Church of Ireland was given statutory authority as the Established Church. Largely left in place was the Protestant land grab, which engulfed 80 per cent of the country. Except in parts of Ulster where Scottish migration created a Presbyterian culture that was both anti-Catholic and anti-Establishment, the imposition of Anglican landowners without a corresponding Anglican yeomanry defined the class division along a clearly delineated religious faultline. Controlled by the all-powerful Anglican landed gentry, the revived Parliament in Dublin proceeded to pass penal laws that stripped Catholics of most of their remaining rights.

Yet Dublin's Protestant 'Ascendancy' politicians also resented interference from the mainland. In 1720, Westminster restated its legal right to legislate on Ireland's behalf, a reality made especially evident when rival economic interests clashed. In Dublin, this battle for ultimate authority found in Henry Grattan a leader gifted with the unusual combination of eloquence and moderation. He appeared victorious when, in 1782–3, Westminster – not wanting a repetition of the American War of Independence closer to home – formally renounced its own legislative powers over Ireland. What Britain retained was executive authority through its appointment of a lord lieutenant based at Dublin Castle.

IRELAND 1169–1800

1169 A Norman army occupies Wexford at the request of Dermot MacMurrough, the ousted king of Leinster.

1171 Henry II of England invades Ireland.

1366 The Statutes of Kilkenny attempt to stop the descendants of English settlers adopting Gaelic Irish customs.

1494 The so-called Poyning's Law asserts that the Irish Parliament is subservient to Westminster.

1541 The Irish Parliament recognizes Henry VIII as king of Ireland.

1560 The Irish Parliament acknowledges the Elizabethan supremacy and Anglicanism as the Established Church.

1592–1603 Rebellion in Ireland is finally suppressed with the surrender of Hugh O'Neill and the assertion of English rule throughout the island.

1608 The plantation of Ulster brings large-scale settlement in the North by Scottish Presbyterians.

1641 A bloody insurrection by Catholics breaks out, in an attempt to regain confiscated lands.

1649 Oliver Cromwell's forces massacre garrisons at Wexford and Drogheda.

1654 The 'Cromwellian Plantation' effectively further curtails Catholic land ownership.

1689 Protestants in Londonderry withstand a 105-day siege by Jacobites loyal to the ousted James II.

1690 At the Battle of the Boyne Protestant forces of William of Orange defeat Catholics loyal to James II.

1695 Penal Laws persecuting Catholics are introduced (by 1714 Catholics own a mere 7 per cent of the land).

1782 The Irish Parliament wins legislative independence from Westminster.

1793 The Catholic Relief Act grants Catholics right to vote on same terms as Protestants.

1798 The United Irishmen's rebellion is crushed.

1800 The Irish Parliament votes itself out of existence by passing the Act of Union, effective from 1801.

From the Act of Union, 1800

Article First. That it be the first Article of the Union of the Kingdoms of Great Britain and Ireland, that the said Kingdoms of Great Britain and Ireland shall, upon the 1st day of January which shall be in the year of our Lord 1801, and for ever after, be united into one Kingdom, by the name The United Kingdom of Great Britain and Ireland; and that the royal style and titles appertaining to the Imperial Crown of the said United Kingdom and its dependencies; and also the ensigns, armorial flags and banners thereof shall be such as H.M., by his royal Proclamation under the Great Seal of the United Kingdom, shall be pleased to appoint.

Article Second. That it be the second Article of Union, that the succession to the Imperial Crown of the said United Kingdom, and of the dominions thereunto belonging, shall continue limited and settled . . . according to the existing laws, and to the terms of union between England and Scotland.

Article Third. That it be the third Article of Union that the said United Kingdom be represented in one and the same Parliament, to be styled The Parliament of the United Kingdom of Great Britain and Ireland.

Article Fourth. That it be the fourth Article of Union that four Lords Spiritual of Ireland by rotation of sessions, and 28 Lords Temporal of Ireland elected for life by the peers of Ireland, shall be the number to sit and vote on the part of Ireland in the House of Lords of the Parliament of the United Kingdom; and 100 commoners (two for each County of Ireland, two for the City of Dublin, two for the City of Cork, one for the University of Trinity College, and one for each of the 31 most considerable Cities, Town and Boroughs) be the number to sit and vote on the part of Ireland in the House of Commons of the Parliament of the United Kingdom.

It was the French Revolution that provoked London into rethinking legislative devolution. The fear was that Ireland might prove susceptible to the republican spirit emanating from Paris or, worse still, become the launching ground for a French invasion of the British mainland. There were also worries that the Dublin Parliament would seek to pass economic policies injurious to Britain. Such fears were well founded. Although a minor French invasion attempt in 1796 ended ignominiously, two years later the 'United Irishmen' launched a major republican uprising. It was defeated. Yet, the scale of the loss of life – perhaps as many as 20,000 lives – underlined the magnitude of the discontent.

How Ireland's greater political liberty and religious toleration might be achieved without threatening the security of the rest of the British Isles now exercised the government of William Pitt the Younger. London nudged the Dublin Parliament into passing the 1793 Catholic Relief Act, permitting Irish Catholics to bear arms, to serve commissions in the army and (for those with 40-shilling freeholds) to vote. There had, in the previous decade, already been some easing in the restrictions on Catholics in terms of property, law, religion and education. The remaining injustices meted out to the Catholic majority – including their inability to sit in Parliament – still needed to be addressed. The problem was that doing so threatened to destroy the Protestant Ascendancy's hold on Irish politics and could expect rough treatment in the Dublin Parliament. William Pitt's solution was to incorporate Irish representation into a United Kingdom-wide Parliament. Thus Catholic emancipation could be granted without those enfranchised becoming more than a small minority at Westminster.

The first attempt was defeated in 1799. But the scheme's advocates persevered. Where argument and persuasion failed, bribery – the tactic that overcame opposition to union in the Scottish Parliament – was successfully deployed in the Irish Parliament. Money and promises of titles proved sufficient inducement to convince waverers and hard bargainers. The Irish Parliament voted itself out of existence by 158 votes to 115.

The Act of Irish Union was passed in August 1800 and came into force on New Year's Day 1801. Dublin's 300-member House of Commons was abolished and in its place, 100 Irish seats were created in the new United Kingdom House of Commons. The Irish peerage also got to vote on which twenty-eight of them would take their seats in the enlarged House of Lords at Westminster. This arrangement resembled that introduced by the 1707 Act of Union for the Scottish peers, except that the Irish representative peers would sit for life. And, unlike the leaders of the

Dublin Castle, from where the lord-lieutenant as viceroy and the chief secretary administered Ireland for the British Crown.

Church of Scotland, four Church of Ireland bishops, serving in rotation, were also admitted to the House of Lords.

Catholic acquiescence in the Anglo-Irish Union had been bought on the pledge of full religious emancipation. Pitt resigned when the intransigence of George III prevented him delivering on his promise. Britain's side of this bargain was thus granted only in 1829 when the Catholic Emancipation Act finally became law. The scarcely tenable situation in which the Established Church in Ireland was Anglican – despite the Presbyterianism of Ulster and overwhelming Catholicism of the rest of the country – endured until its disestablishment finally came in 1869. Although as early as 1832 there were thrity-nine Irish MPs at Westminster opposed to the Act of Union, the long and tortuous path to repeal the legislation of 1800 would take 120 years.

1801
THE GENERAL
ENCLOSURE ACT

LAND RIGHTS AND THE AGRARIAN REVOLUTION

The enclosure of land transformed the English countryside, fundamentally altering the nature of farming and creating a patchwork of hedgerow-bordered fields that became the familiar face of the landscape for most of the nineteenth and twentieth centuries.

Traditionally, the countryside was farmed in open fields in which villagers grew produce in their own, often widely dispersed, strips, which allowed cottagers to engage in subsistence farming. All tenants enjoyed the right to graze whatever livestock they might have on common pasture. In consequence, herds intermingled.

This was an inefficient form of farming. Indeed, the survival of mixed-use land, subject to the rights of so many individuals, undermined any return on investment a landowner might seek to make by improving its quality. Small cultivators were far less likely to have the resources necessary to drain land. Tellingly, much land was left uncultivated. In an effort to extract better value from the soil, enclosure involved withdrawing community rights to common pasture and consolidating strips into single ownership fields that could be hedged or fenced off for private use.

When the first enclosures of common land took place in the thirteenth century, there was still sufficient common pasture to satisfy the needs of the whole village. Indeed, legislation sought to ensure that enclosure did not go so far as to wipe out access to communal grazing. A far greater assault on traditional methods came in the fifteenth century, when manors, keen to meet the growing demand for wool, pushed on with the enclosure of large-scale fields for sheep pasture. Depleting common pasture created unrest and an increasing numbers of dispossessed vagrants. Legislation followed no consistent path during this period, sometimes supporting, at other times hindering, the process according to the perceived

economic circumstances of the moment. Nonetheless, there was a tendency towards trying to limit enclosure and soften the consequences for its victims, especially in areas of traditional mixed husbandry. During the seventeenth century, however, Parliament effectively gave up trying to prevent the process.

Nonetheless, open fields were still prevalent during much of the eighteenth century. It was mostly in the enclosed areas, however, that improvements became viable and where land drainage and strict crop rotation heralded an agrarian revolution. The increasing cultivation of root crops such as turnip provided forage for the hardier and heavier livestock being produced by selective stock-breeding. New breeds of sheep became worth eating, as well as merely shearing.

Across England the pace of enclosure slowed during the first half of the eighteenth century before picking up again after 1750. In seeking to prevent disputes, Parliament was asked to legislate approval for each application for enclosure. This was generally granted when the proposal had the support of three-quarters of the landholders affected. Commissioners duly surveyed and apportioned the land in a manner they deemed equitable, and the dispossessed were compensated. To this approach, there were two major objections – that the process was costly and that the compensation received by those deprived of their common rights was often inadequate.

Opposite: 1801 'inclosure map' of the Northamptonshire parish of Wilby. The area is now on the outskirts of Wellingborough.

By the end of the eighteenth century, the movement for 'improvement' was again in full swing, burdening Parliament with a surge of applications for legislation. Westminster passed almost four thousand enclosure acts between 1750 and 1810, covering about 20 per cent of the land of England and Wales, with the Midlands a particularly intense area of activity. It was to simplify the procedure, reduce costs and speed the process that in 1801 the General Enclosure Act – then known as the 'Inclosure (Consolidation) Act') – was passed. It established a template for the drafting of suitable legislation. In this it was successful, and the transformation was largely complete by the time a further General Enclosure Act in 1845 drew together all the individual grants in an annual act. By comparison, enclosure was still in its relatively early stages in the rest of Western Europe and had scarcely begun in Eastern Europe.

The overall social and economic consequences of enclosure were hotly contested at the time and continue to divide historians now. It would be surprising if such a change, carried out over so long a period and over such varied terrain, produced consistent results. Generally though, it suited the interests of landowners. Yet the nature of land redistribution can be misunderstood. The average farm in the

243

early nineteenth century was still relatively small. Even the effects on the cottager, dispossessed of his common grazing rights, were mixed.

In the short term, though, it was cottagers who appeared to have lost out. They were faced with the choice of either staying on, reduced to the status of hired hands, or turning their backs on the land in search of work in the towns and cities. But these were not invariably unfortunate consequences. Enclosure – married to other agricultural improvements – improved yields. It made food more plentiful and cheaper. In this light, the declining numbers engaged in subsistence farming may be viewed as a positive consequence rather than a sign of harmful effects. The surge in agricultural productivity freed labourers to seek more remunerative work in the towns and cities, providing, in turn, the workforce that made the Industrial Revolution possible and Britain the 'workshop of the world', a status that ultimately raised living standards far beyond what previous generations could have imagined possible.

1805

JAMES GILLRAY'S
THE PLUM-PUDDING IN DANGER

PRESS FREEDOM AND POLITICAL SATIRE

Few men better tested the eighteenth century's limits of the freedom of the press than the caricaturist James Gillray. Viewing his work, foreigners were astonished that his decidedly undeferential lampooning of Britain's royal family and political leaders did not land him in jail. Yet, not only did Gillray remain at liberty, but George III and the Prince of Wales were among those who bought his work.

The Plum-Pudding in Danger is depicted in the third plate section.

In Britain, the freedom of the press was created not by a statute but rather by the failure to renew a statute. In 1695 the Licensing of the Press Act of 1662 – 'for preventing the frequent Abuses in printing seditious treasonable and unlicensed Bookes' – lapsed. The House of Commons refused to extend its life with fresh legislation. Thus a new age of literary liberty began, freed from state censorship. Treason, seditious libel and blasphemy remained on the statute books as the main restraints and, anomalously, between 1737 and 1968 the lord chancellor's department censored the theatre, largely to cut out perceived obscenity, but initially also because of perceived dangers inherent in spectators excited by potentially subversive politics. But compared to anywhere else in Europe, Britain's writers, polemicists and caricaturists enjoyed unparalleled freedom of expression, held in check only by the risk of being sued for libel.

Pamphlets and cheeky, often vulgar, cartoons were churned out lambasting the chicanery and corruption of British politics, particularly between 1721 and 1742 when Sir Robert Walpole was the country's first prime minister. This was the golden age of 'Grub Street', which took its name from the Moorfields neighbourhood of London where many of the hack writers and down-at-heel controversialists eked out their living by chipping away at the pretensions of the rich and powerful.

BRITAIN IN THE AGE OF REVOLUTION

1790 Edmund Burke's *Reflections on the Revolution in France* becomes the classic argument against revolutionary change.

1791 Thomas Paine's *Rights of Man* defends revolutionary change.

1792 The London Corresponding Society is founded to promote radical reform; the Libel Act hands to juries the right to determine libel cases.

1793 Revolutionary France declares war on Britain.

1794–5 The Habeas Corpus Act is suspended.

1795 The size of public meetings is legally restricted to fifty persons.

1796 Edward Jenner injects an eight-year-old boy with his inoculation against smallpox.

1797 A French force lands at Fishguard, Pembrokeshire: the last such incursion on British soil.

1798 Income tax is announced as an emergency measure.

1801 Habeas Corpus is again suspended.

1802 The Treaty of Amiens ends war with France. The Factory Act restricts the working hours of children and improves their conditions. William Cobbett launches his *Political Register*.

1803 Conflict with France is renewed. Lord Ellenborough's Act tightens the common law restrictions on abortion, imposing the death penalty for those performing abortions after a foetus's 'quickening' (about 18–21 weeks).

1805 Nelson's victory at Trafalgar effectively removes the likelihood of Britain being invaded.

1806 Napoleon's imposition of his Continental System tightens economic warfare against Britain.

1808 British troops are dispatched to the (Iberian) Peninsular War: victory is achieved in 1813.

1811 Luddite riots against modern machinery break out. The Regency Act places royal authority in the hands of the Prince Regent during George III's 'madness.'

1812 War breaks out between the United States and Britain and lasts until 1814. Prime Minister Spencer Perceval is assassinated.

1813 Jane Austen's *Pride and Prejudice* is published.

1815 The Battle of Waterloo ends the Napoleonic Wars. Corn Laws introduced to protect domestic agriculture.

1817–18 Habeas Corpus is suspended for the third time.

1819 A radical meeting is violently broken up in Manchester: the so-called Peterloo Massacre. 'Six Acts' are passed to restrict the size of meetings and curtail alleged seditious activities.

1820 The 'Cato Street Conspiracy' to murder the Cabinet is exposed. There is unrest in Scotland.

Among caricaturists, none equalled James Gillray (1756–1815) in fame or skill. His upbringing in the strict Protestant beliefs of the Moravian sect could hardly have provided an early environment less given to levity and vulgarity. It was his apprenticeship with a Holborn letter engraver and his subsequent training at the

Royal Academy School that ensured his skills as a draughtsman were developed and recognized. The market for his subsequent work was already established. William Hogarth (1697–1764) had been the dominant artist-as-satirist from the 1730s to the 1750s. While much of Hogarth's work concerned cautionary tales with moral lessons, Gillray increasingly concerned himself with savaging those in authority. Huge crowds pressed around the shop window of his publisher, Hannah Humphrey (at 18 Old Bond Street until 1798; thereafter at 27 St James's Street), to view his latest lampoons and to buy copies, many of which were colour-tinted by hand.

No man, woman, cause or party was off limits to Gillray. His cynicism was impartial. Furthermore, he supplemented traditional humour with wit, often employing wordplay and providing his characters with speech bubbles – subsequently the standard device of illustrated 'comics' around the world. The carryings-on at court, especially George III's bouts of insanity and the Prince of Wales's debauchery, provided a rich seam of scandal for his satire. He was no less sparing with Westminster politics, which was dominated by two men: the corpulent, easygoing gambler and Whig leader, Charles James Fox; and the lean, boyish and physically fragile Tory prime minister, William Pitt the Younger.

A popular engraving of James Gillray's self-portrait.

After the excitement of the fall of the Bastille had subsided, the increasingly frightening news coming from across the Channel fundamentally recast British politics. While Fox and his fellow radicals continued to applaud what they took to be the victory of liberty, much of Britain recoiled at the accompanying brutality. The outbreak of war with revolutionary France in 1793 made these divisions ever more stark, prompting Gillray to cease being the impartial denigrator of both parties. Never a Francophile (his father had lost an arm fighting the French at the Battle of Fontenoy in 1745), he allied himself – rarely without equivocation – with Pitt's Tories and British patriotism.

It was during this period that Gillray's depiction of John Bull took full shape. The national stereotype had been created by James Arbuthnot in 1712 and, in the hands of later *Punch* cartoonists John Leech and John Tenniel, would appear as a stocky, mostly amiable, figure. Gillray's version was an argumentative and often uncomprehending rustic whom the vicissitudes of life and politics regularly pushed to the verge of fury, but never beyond the point at which he ceased to be a patriot.

Gillray's work also popularized the image of Napoleon Bonaparte – 'Little Boney' – as a scrawny, crazed midget. In *The Plum-Pudding in Danger*, published in February 1805, Gillray anticipated a decisive moment in the Napoleonic Wars. Admiral Horatio Nelson's destruction of the French and Spanish fleets at Trafalgar in October that year removed the threat of invasion. An armed stalemate followed in which Napoleon was master of Europe while the success of the Royal Navy gave Britain mastery of the seas. It is this emerging reality that Gillray depicted, with slices of plum pudding being simultaneously carved by Pitt the Younger (who would die the following year) and Napoleon.

Gillray's powers declined soon thereafter. His eyesight began to fail, then he suffered a breakdown, bouts of madness, and he attempted suicide. He was last seen through his shop window, wandering around disorientated, naked and unshaven, like a grotesque from one of his own cartoons. He died later that day, 1 June 1815, without living to hear of the final defeat of Napoleon at Waterloo seventeen days later. Nonetheless, he left behind a tradition of caricature, satire and lack of deference to those in authority that was continued in the years after his death by his protégé George Cruikshank. The baton has been passed on, through the twentieth century and beyond, by newspaper cartoonists from David Low and Philip Zec to Gerald Scarfe, Steve Bell and Peter Brookes.

1829

STEPHENSON'S DESIGN
FOR *ROCKET*

THE BIRTH OF THE RAILWAY AGE

The success of his *Rocket* at the Rainhill trials in 1829 did more than win £500 prize money for its inventor, George Stephenson: it established that steam locomotives represented the future of travel. As far as covering distances was concerned, it was the single most revolutionary advance since antiquity.

Despite being the child of illiterate parents, George Stephenson's early circumstances were in fact propitious for his subsequent career. He was born in 1781 in the Tyneside mining village of Wylam near a wooden rail track, along which coal wagons were pulled by horse. He spent his childhood not in school, but instead found himself deputed to shoo cows off the track.

It was from mining that the railway age would emerge. Atmospheric steam engines using pistons and cylinders had been invented by Thomas Newcomen to pump water out of mines in 1712. Stephenson's father operated a mine engine until it blinded him. Stationary steam engines were also developed to pull coal wagons along rails, although most of the work was still done by horses.

It was the Cornish engineer, Richard Trevithick, who in 1804 designed the first locomotive that could successfully run a significant distance, pulling both freight and customers on rail track. However, the unreliability of such early locomotives was compounded by their weight. They were too heavy for the rails – whether wooden or iron – to carry them without splitting. Most investors, believing the problem intractable, withdrew finance. At best, it was assumed the engines would never serve more than short lines connecting collieries to canals and ports, with the long-distance travel still done by water.

Having largely taught himself to read and write, Stephenson began designing colliery engines; but his real success came when he was appointed engineer for a line to run the twenty-six miles from Stockton to Darlington. Opened in 1825, it was

the first freight- and passenger-carrying public railway to use steam traction. Leased to whoever wanted to pay to use them, its lines were intended for both horse- and engine-drawn traffic. Championing the latter, Stephenson designed his *Locomotion No. 1*, which caused a stir by pulling thirty-six wagons at an average speed of 4 mph.

Stephenson's success at Darlington led to his being asked to survey a route for a proposed rail track to be operated by the Liverpool and Manchester Railway Company. The company's directors had not decided whether moving locomotives or fixed engines using chains represented the best future for pulling coaches along the line. To test the practicality of the former, they offered a prize to the inventor who could design a locomotive that worked.

Sketch of Rocket's boiler made on 5 October 1829 by John Urpeth Rastrick (1780–1856). Rastrick was one of the three judges who awarded Rocket first prize at the Rainhill Trials.

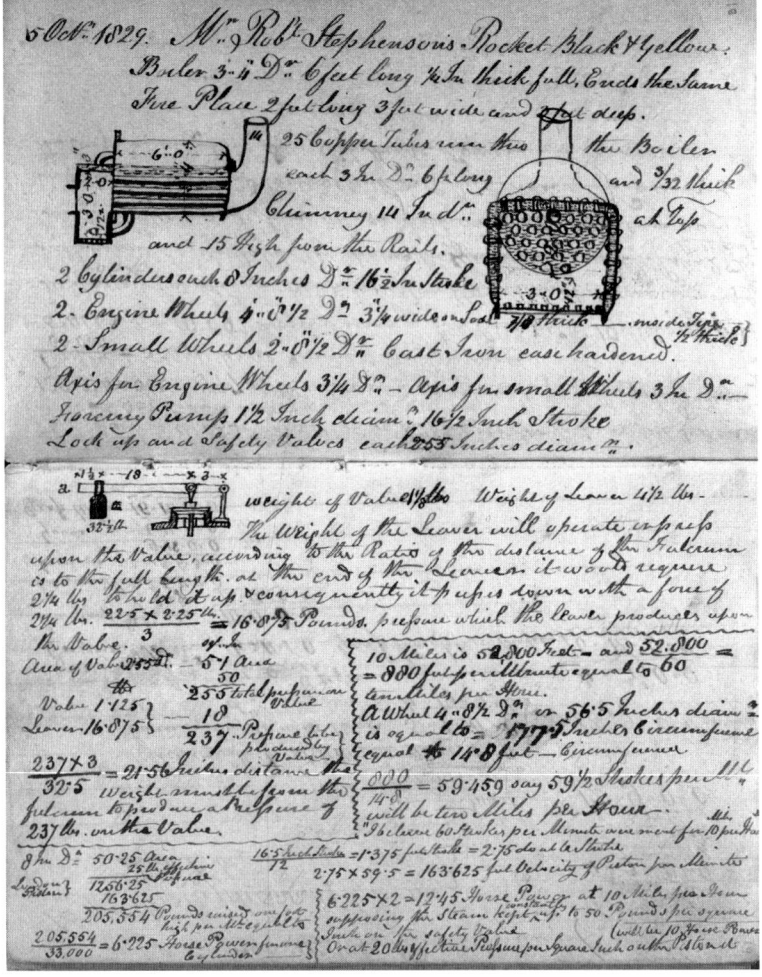

Five entries got as far as the trials, held at Rainhill, east of Liverpool, in October 1829. Such was the curiosity and excitement that crowds in their thousands gathered to watch. At various stages, four of the engines developed teething problems. In the case of one entry, *The Cycloped*, there was a total loss of power when the horse trotting on its drive-belt fell through the locomotive's floor. The clear winner was George Stephenson's *Rocket*. It travelled untroubled for seventy miles, during which it recorded a top speed of 29 mph. The quality of its performance settled the argument. Henceforth, the future of distance travel was by steam locomotive.

The world-changing moment was recognized at the time. Such was the celebration the following year at the official opening of the Liverpool and Manchester Railway that the prime minister, the duke of Wellington, attended. Failing to get out of the way of the fast-approaching *Rocket*, William Huskisson, the duke's parliamentary colleague and a senior Tory politician, fell under its wheels to achieve fame as the first fatality of the railway age.

Much of the credit for *Rocket*'s design actually lay with George Stephenson's son,

THE GROWTH OF THE RAILWAYS

1781 James Watt patents the 'sun and planet gear', which allows a piston to drive a wheel by an off-centre connection.

1783 The invention of the rolling and puddling process creates much stronger iron.

1804 Richard Trevithick's steam locomotive is the first to be able to travel any significant distance by rail.

1825 The Stockton–Darlington Railway opens; George and Robert Stephenson's *Locomotion No. 1* runs on it.

1829 George and Robert Stephenson's *Rocket* sets a world speed record of 29 mph at the Rainhill Trials.

1830 The Liverpool and Manchester Railway opens; there are now ninety-five miles of rail track in Britain.

1837 The first electric locomotive is designed by Robert Davidson.

1840 There are by now 1,500 miles of rail track in Britain.

1841 Isambard Kingdom Brunel's line opens between London and Bristol.

1850 There are 6,000 miles of rail track in Britain.

1857 Steel rails are introduced.

1863 The first section of the London Underground railway is opened, from Paddington to Farringdon Street.

1870 The rail network amounts to 13,400 miles of track.

1900 There are now 18,100 miles of rail track in Britain.

Robert (1803–59). It contained several innovations that, taken together, ensured its superiority. It more effectively transferred heat from the firebox gases into the boiler water because it ran twenty-five copper tubes through the boiler rather than the customary single cylinder. The steam exhaust created a far more powerful air draught thanks to a blast pipe. Connection and stability were improved through direct coupling, with connecting rods and pistons set at a slanting angle rather than vertically. With amendments and improvements, these remained the principles that guided all steam-train design until the technology's replacement in the 1960s.

Thus with *Rocket*, travel by train moved swiftly from impractical novelty to the driving force of the modern world. In the locomotive's first full year of operation,

in 1830, parliamentary approval was given for the construction of 375 miles of public track. A decade later, there were nearly 1,500 miles of track. By 1852, lines connected different parts of both Wales and Scotland to London. By 1870, there were 13,400 miles of track. This expansion made travel practical for Britons who had previously struggled to find the time or money to wander far from their home county. The effect in breaking down parochial attitudes was incalculable. The need for consistent timetabling nationwide led to the abolition of local 'parish time' and its replacement by a uniform Greenwich Mean Time throughout Britain.

Arguments that so important a vehicle for social change should be brought under the auspices of the state were trumped by those who feared the resulting monopoly. For this reason, the construction of competing companies' lines going to the same places was seen not as wasteful but as a sign of healthy competition. The government neither financed nor directed where new lines should go. Parliament merely gave legislative permission to construct lines, to ensure compulsory land purchase and to regulate the terms of use. Nonetheless, an Act of 1844 reserved the future right to take lines into public ownership if necessary and, in the meantime, forced the railway companies to offer at least one daily service for which passengers would be charged no more than a penny a mile.

The speed at which goods – foodstuffs as well as manufactures – could be transported long distances delocalized trade, enhancing markets for producers and driving down costs for consumers. The way in which this rapid expansion was funded had profound consequences, in that joint-stock companies appeared more attractive investment opportunities than government securities. Although subject to spurts of unsustainable boom followed by some inevitable collapses, this transformed capitalism, creating – unusually at that time – a huge sector of the economy in which ownership and control were not one and the same. Nor was the investment confined to Britain. The development of the rail network around the globe was often the work of British companies, underwritten from London.

It was such an outstanding achievement that the growing centrality of rail travel to Britain's economic success in the nineteenth century might be measured by how three successive generations of its innovators ended their days. Richard Trevithick died a pauper in 1833; George Stephenson passed away at his sizeable Derbyshire country house in 1848; his son Robert went on to construct lines and bridges as well as locomotives, became Conservative MP for Whitby, and following his death, in 1859, was buried in Westminster Abbey. It was not just in travel that the railways brought social mobility.

1829

THE CATHOLIC EMANCIPATION ACT

GROWING RELIGIOUS LIBERTY

In the popular consciousness, the link between Roman Catholicism and continental despotism was the single greatest barrier to the acceptance of Rome's adherents in British society. At its most virulent, this animosity lasted for as long as there remained a plausible likelihood of a successful, French-aided, Jacobite invasion bent on undoing the work of the Glorious Revolution. The threat was finally removed by the crushing defeat of Prince Charles Edward's Jacobite forces at Culloden in 1746. In any case, the number of Catholics had by then shrivelled to a tiny proportion, mostly confined to pockets in the countryside where a few aristocrats (presumed eccentric) retained the faith of their forebears. Despite its being the dominant faith in Ireland, perhaps no more than 2 per cent of the population of England and Wales were Catholic.

However, the sense of security of the Hanoverian settlement after 1746 meant that Catholics found themselves increasingly unmolested when opening schools and chapels, even though such activities were still illegal. Their numbers, particularly among the artisan class, began to swell in towns and cities, but they remained a distinct minority, at the mercy of events and sporadic demagoguery. In 1778, following the passage of the Catholic Relief Act, 'No Popery' riots in Edinburgh and Glasgow greeted the readmittance of Catholics to the armed forces and the removal of restrictions on their purchasing property, scaring the government into scrapping plans to make the law applicable in Scotland. London was convulsed in ten days of fighting when, two years later, Parliament refused to bow to the demands of the Protestant Association, led by Lord George Gordon, to repeal the 1778 legislation for the rest of Britain. The houses of Catholics were burned down and Newgate prison and other buildings were ransacked. George III felt compelled to call up 12,000 troops to fire on the mob and restore order. In all,

RELIGIOUS LIBERTY IN BRITAIN

1661 The Corporation Act restricts the holding of government and town office in England and Wales to those taking the Anglican Communion.

1678 The Test Act forces all MPs and peers to deny transubstantiation.

1689 The Toleration Act grants religious liberty to Protestant Dissenters.

1698 The Popery Act gives financial rewards to those who expose clandestine Catholic worship and makes Catholic teachers liable to serve a life prison sentence.

1714 The Schism Act requires all school headmasters in England to be licensed by an Anglican bishop. The Occasional Conformity Act removes a loophole through which Catholics and Dissenters can evade the Test and Corporation Acts. Both acts are repealed in 1718.

1723 State grants are introduced to support Dissenting ministers.

1766 The papacy finally recognizes the house of Hanover as the legitimate monarchy in Britain.

1778 The Catholic Relief Act removes semi-redundant statutes that placed Catholic priests at risk of arrest for felony and restricted Catholics' rights in passing on and acquiring property. Catholics are permitted to join the armed forces.

1780 The Gordon riots in London witness mob violence against extending Catholic rights.

1791 The Catholic Relief Act guarantees Catholic freedom of worship and education, as well as admission to the legal profession. Catholic property owners gain the right to vote.

1813 Unitarians are included in the terms of the Toleration Act.

1821 The Catholic Relief Bill is passed in the Commons but later defeated in the Lords.

1828 The repeal of the Test and Corporation acts opens public office to Dissenters.

1829 The Catholic Emancipation Act removes the remaining legal barriers confronting Catholics, including the right to sit in Parliament.

the anarchy of the Gordon riots caused around 500 casualties. Although acquitted on treason charges, Lord George Gordon was ruined. He later converted to Judaism, was imprisoned for libelling Marie Antoinette and died in Newgate.

Moderate opinion was horrified not just by the anti-Catholic rabble on the streets of London but also by the anti-clericalism of the Terror in France. The sanctuary given to French Catholic royalty, aristocrats and priests fleeing the atheist ideologues of the French Revolution did much to temper previous attitudes. Unusually, Britain found itself in alliance with Bourbon absolutists, by which time native Catholics had made a statement on where their primary loyalties lay. In 1788, the four Catholic 'Vicars Apostolic', together with 240 priests and 1,500 laymen, issued a protestation renouncing the Vatican's temporal authority. The government responded to this overture in 1791 with legislation removing Catholic religious disabilities and making them free to worship without the threat of having their chapels or schools closed down. Catholics owning property with an annual rental of £2 or more were granted the right to vote. However, one major cause of emancipation remained beyond their grasp: the right to sit in Parliament and hold civic or state office.

Seeking to address the discontent of Ireland's Catholic majority, William Pitt the Younger had in 1800 attempted to link the union of the British and Irish Parliaments with full Catholic emancipation. George III, however, remained obstinate, fearful of triggering another Gordon riot and insisting that approving such rights breached his coronation oaths. Without

From the Catholic Emancipation Act, 1829

Whereas by various Acts of Parliament certain restraints and disabilities are imposed on the Roman Catholic subjects of H.M., to which other subjects of H.M. are not liable; and whereas by various Acts certain oaths and declarations, commonly called the declaration against transubstantiation, and the declaration against transubstantiation and the invocation of Saints and the sacrifice of the Mass, as practised in the Church of Rome, are or may be required to be taken, made, and subscribed by the subjects of H.M., as qualifications for sitting and voting in parliament, and for the enjoyment of certain offices, franchise, and civil rights: be it enacted . . . that . . . all such parts of the said Acts as require the said declarations, as a qualification for sitting and voting in Parliament, or for the exercise or enjoyment of any office, franchise or civil right are (save as hereinafter provided and excepted) hereby repealed.

sufficient Cabinet support to face down his monarch, Pitt felt compelled to resign on the matter. Yet the Irish problem would not go away. In 1823, Daniel O'Connell founded the Catholic Association, a pressure group demanding full emancipation. At the County Clare by-election in 1828 he was returned as the MP but was unable to take his seat at Westminster on account of his religious faith.

As the Irish-born scion of a Protestant Ascendancy landowning family, the prime minister, the duke of Wellington, was not naturally sympathetic to O'Connell's cause. Nevertheless, when faced with the possibility of serious disorder in Ireland, he felt compelled to act against his instincts. In pushing through Catholic emancipation he staved off the possibility of civil war in his native land, but at a cost. The issue divided his Tory Party, ensuring that it would be out of office for most of the following decade of reform.

When the act passed into law on 13 April 1829, Catholics were finally allowed to sit in Parliament as well as on lay corporations. Only a small number of restrictions were placed on their admittance to the highest offices of state: they could not become lord chancellor, keeper of the great seal, lord-lieutenant of Ireland or high commissioner of the Church of Scotland. The case for allowing the head of state to become Catholic was not seriously considered. It was unthinkable that the monarch, as supreme governor of the Church of England, would be (or

Field Marshal Arthur Wellesley, 1st duke of Wellington (1769–1852), Anglo-Irish soldier and statesman. As prime minister from 1828 to 1830, the hero of Waterloo was compelled to act against his instincts in pushing through Catholic emancipation. In doing so, however, he staved off the possibility of civil war in Ireland.

would marry) a Catholic; allowing even the possibility would have involved tearing up the whole Glorious Revolution settlement. A nod to Protestant sensibilities also prevented Catholic clergy standing as MPs or wearing their vestments outside church.

The Catholic Emancipation Act had considerable constitutional implications. The rights of the Established Church could be determined by legislation passed by politicians who were not its communicants. The admission to Parliament of Jews in 1858 and atheists in 1886 meant that MPs did not even have to be Christian. The inclusion of the atheists particularly outraged the leaders of Britain's Catholic community. By then, massive Irish emigration had transformed the visibility of the Catholic faith across the mainland's great cities on a scale that few involved in the 1829 legislation could have foreseen.

1832
THE GREAT REFORM ACT

THE SPREAD OF DEMOCRACY

The 'Great' Reform Act of 1832 increased the number of men who could vote in general elections by 50 per cent, from 435,000 to 652,000. In doing so, it brought many middle-class voters within the democratic process. Whilst it meant that about one in five men had the vote, it did little to extend the franchise to the labouring man and did nothing at all for women, regardless of their class. Nevertheless, it signified the first comprehensive attempt to create a more equitably distributed pattern of constituencies across the United Kingdom, initiating a process that within a hundred years would result in universal franchise.

The 1832 legislation created uniform criteria for who was entitled to vote. Prior to its enactment, some constituencies enjoyed something close to universal male suffrage. In other boroughs the vote lay solely in the possession of the members of the town corporation. Those with small electorates often found themselves 'in the pocket' of the local landowner. An 1827 study estimated that of the 658 parliamentary constituencies, the choice in 276 of them was essentially determined by the influence, direct or indirect, of the local grandee. Furthermore, the distribution of seats had ceased to bear much relationship to the shifting population patterns of an industrializing country. Seaside boroughs were massively over-represented, yet northern towns were hugely under-represented. Cornwall and Wiltshire had more borough constituencies than in all eight northern counties. In Scotland, the nature of the franchise was particularly arcane: 4,000 electors returned all the Scottish burgh and county MPs. The member for the capital, Edinburgh, was determined by a mere thirty-three voters.

It was to address the worst anomalies of voting practice and regional distribution that the Whig government of Earl Grey determined to reform the system. The legislation, largely drafted by Lord John Russell (1792–1878), made uniform the

From the Great Reform Act, 1832

Schedule A. [fifty-six boroughs ceasing to return any MPs]

Amersham, Wendover, Bossiney, Callington, Camelford, East Looe, Fowey, Lostwithiel, Newport, St Germans, St Mawes, St Michael (Midshall), Saltash, Tregony, West Looe, Beeralston, Okehampton, Plymouth, Corfe Castle, Stockbridge, Whitchurch, Newtown, Yarmouth, Weobly, Queenborough, New Romney, Newton, Castle Rising, Higham Ferrers, Brackley, Bishop's Castle, Ilchester, Milborne Port, Minehead, Aldeburgh, Dunwich, Orford, Blechingley, Gatton, Haslemere, Bramber, East Grinstead, Seaford, Steyning, Winchelsea, Appleby, Great Bedwin, Dowmton, Heytesbury, Hindon, Ludgershall, Old Sarum, Wootton Bassett, Aldborough, Boroughbridge, Hedon.

Schedule B [Thirty boroughs to return one MP only]

Wallingford, Helston, Launceston, Liskeard, St Ives, Ashburton, Dartmouth, Lyme Regis, Shaftesbury, Wareham, Christchurch, Petersfield, Hythe, Clitheroe, Great Grimsby, Morpeth, Woodstock, Eye, Reigate, Arundel, Horsham, Midhurst, Rye, Calne, Malmesbury, Westbury, Wilton, Droitwich, Northallerton, Thirsk.

Schedule C [Twenty-two new boroughs to return two MPs each]

Macclesfield, Stockport, Devonport, Sunderland, Stroud, Greenwich, Bolton, Blackburn, Manchester, Oldham, Finsbury, Marylebone, Tower Hamlets, Stoke-upon-Trent, Wolverhampton, Lambeth, Brighton, Birmingham, Bradford, Halifax, Leeds, Sheffield.

Schedule D [Twenty new boroughs to return one MP each]

Whitehaven, Gateshead, South Shields, Merthyr Tydvil, Cheltenham, Chatham, Ashton-under-Lyne, Bury, Rochdale, Salford, Warrington, Tynemouth, Frome, Walsall, Kendal, Dudley, Kidderminster, Huddersfield, Wakefield, Whitby.

criteria for voting: in the boroughs, this meant those owning or occupying properties valued above £10 a year and, in the counties, £10 'copyholders' (referring to an archaic, long-term and low-rent tenancy agreement) and £50 leaseholders. Those previously enfranchised because they had 40-shilling freeholds retained their vote. Over-represented parts of the country lost constituencies, while under-represented areas gained new ones.

In March 1831, the proposals passed their second reading in the House of Commons by just one vote. When the bill was defeated at the committee stage a general election was called, which returned a decisive majority for reform. A second attempt was defeated in the House of Lord, provoking anger in many parts of the country at the hereditary chamber's veto. Riots broke out in Bristol. Minor concessions were attached to the third attempt to pass the bill and pressure was put on the king, William IV, to create a dozen pro-reform peerages if the Lords voted it down again. Aware of this threat, the Lords passed the bill on its second reading, only to seek to hold it up on procedural grounds. The government resigned but was reinstalled within the week. It then became known that the king was prepared to go further, creating as many new peerages as were needed to pass the legislation. This time the Lords bowed and, on 4 June 1832, passed the Reform Bill on its third reading. Accompanying reform bills for Scotland and Ireland also became law.

Charles, Earl Grey, prime minister from 1830 to 1834 and one of the architects of the Great Reform Act of 1832.

Although the immediate effect of the Reform Act was to create an extra 217,000 voters, its provisions brought in a further 400,000 electors during the following thirty years. It abolished many of the most flagrantly 'rotten' boroughs, where MPs had been returned by very few voters, yet it changed the social composition of the House of Commons only marginally. In 1833, 217 MPs were the sons of peers or baronets. By 1865, the figure had fallen merely to 180. Constituencies that had been won through blatant corruption became the subject of parliamentary inquiry, with the worst offenders stripped of their victory; but it was not until 1872 that the replacement of open voting with the secret ballot really stamped upon electoral intimidation and vote buying.

THE RIGHT TO VOTE

1832 The Great Reform Act enfranchises about 20 per cent of the adult male population.

1867 The vote is extended to all male urban householders and to lodgers paying more than £10 rent. About 30 per cent of the adult male population is enfranchised. The legislation is extended to Scotland and Ireland in 1868.

1869 Women ratepayers gain the right to vote in local government elections.

1872 The Secret Ballot Act ends 'open' voting in all local and parliamentary elections.

1884 Equal qualification in town and country means that men paying £10 rent or owning property with a £10 value are granted the vote. Over 60 per cent of the adult male population is now enfranchised.

1918 Universal franchise (apart from minor anomalies) applies to all men over twenty-one and all women over thirty.

1928 Men and women have the vote on equal terms at the age of twenty-one.

1948 The abolition of university seats and the end of registration in both home and business constituencies end plural voting.

1969 The voting age is lowered to eighteen.

In one respect the Reform Act's opponents were correct. The Whigs had promised that it represented 'finality'. Indeed, such was Lord Russell's determination in making this claim that he acquired the nickname 'Finality Jack'. Tories like Sir Robert Peel disputed this, arguing that, on the contrary, it created a dangerously precise division of who could vote, based on property and wealth, where previously the criteria had been less overt. Such an explicit class-delineated measure could not endure without further revision. And so it proved, with the numbers enfranchised increased by subsequent Reform Acts in 1867, 1884 and 1918, by which time all men over twenty-one and all women over thirty had the vote. Both sexes got the vote equally at twenty-one in 1928, with the voting age lowered to eighteen in 1969.

1834

THE TAMWORTH MANIFESTO

THE BIRTH OF THE MODERN CONSERVATIVE PARTY

Across Europe in the nineteenth and twentieth centuries, right-wing parties emerged with an uncompromisingly hostile response to the onslaught of liberalism and secularism. By contrast, the forces of Conservatism in Britain adopted a more measured stance, generally seeking to moderate and adapt social change in the hope of reducing destabilizing tendencies rather than to oppose all change outright.

There were many reasons why British Conservatism moved away from the more extreme manifestations of continental 'throne and altar' assertiveness. The first, most obviously, was the relative moderation of British radicalism, which was less determinedly republican or atheist than many European left-wing movements. After the seventeenth century, the British monarchy was rarely threatened by bloody revolution, precisely because it generally kept within its constitutional limits. If British Tories were less extreme than continental 'Ultras', then it was because the institutions they sought to defend drew back from the sort of provocations that caused uprisings and revolutions across Europe in 1848. Security bred moderation. The same was true in religion. For all its defence of its own rights and presumptions, nineteenth-century Anglicanism did not turn its back on the modern world. Unlike the papacy, it did not wholeheartedly denounce the ideals of democracy.

Yet there was no predestined path towards moderation. The Tory Party was born in the 1670s around a group of politicians bent on preserving the constitutional right of the future James II to inherit the throne regardless of his Catholicism. It was their Whig opponents who first taunted them as 'Tories' (an abusive term connotative of Irish Catholic rebels). This taint of Jacobitism was mostly an exaggeration, although Tories did tend to be 'High Church' Anglicans, determined to defend the political supremacy of the Established Church. In the succeeding one

To the Electors of the Borough of Tamworth, 1834

. . . With respect to the Reform Bill itself, I will repeat now the declaration I made when I entered the House of Commons as a member of the Reformed Parliament – that I consider the Reform Bill a final and irrevocable settlement of a great constitutional question – a settlement which no friend to the peace and welfare of this country would attempt to disturb, either by direct or by insidious means.

Then, as to the spirit of the Reform Bill, and the willingness to adopt and enforce it as a rule of government: if, by adopting the spirit of the Reform Bill, it be meant that we are to live in a perpetual vortex of agitation; that public men can only support themselves in public estimation by adopting every popular impression of the day – by promising the instant redress of anything which anybody may call an abuse, by abandoning altogether that great aid of government, more powerful than either law or reason, the respect for ancient rights, and the deference to prescriptive authority – if this be the spirit of the Reform Bill, I will not undertake to adopt it. But if the spirit of the Reform Bill implies merely a careful review of institutions, civil and ecclesiastical, undertaken in a friendly temper combining, with the firm maintenance of established rights, the correction of proved abuses and the redress of real grievances, – in that case, I can for myself and colleagues undertake to act in such a spirit and with such intentions.

hundred years, they fought several general elections on the slogan 'The Church in Danger'.

The social and political discontent that followed the end of the Napoleonic Wars in 1815 brought out the authoritarian side of Tory administrations and it was necessity rather than enthusiasm that prompted the conversion of the prime minister, the duke of Wellington, to the cause of Catholic emancipation. Industrialization and urbanization were transforming the country in ways that traditional Toryism had difficulty comprehending. The party's opposition to the franchise extension of the Great Reform Act placed it decisively on the losing side of the argument. The immediate political price was obvious. In the 1832 general election, only 185 Tory MPs were returned to Parliament. Their opponents numbered 473.

It fell to the new Tory leader, Sir Robert Peel (1788–1850), to decide how Conservatism should respond to its marginalization. A decision to reject the legitimacy of the increasingly democratic temper of the times could either have gifted the future to Whig and Radical administrations or, indeed, begun a process in which normal party politics disintegrated, bringing down the edifice of constitutional parliamentary government. As home secretary, Peel had shown himself a capable administrator who created the Metropolitan Police in 1829. His early political philosophy, however, suggested that he was still, in sentiment, a traditionalist.

More accurately, Peel was a man of contradictions. He inherited a baronetcy, was educated at Eton and Oxford, and became an MP at the age of twenty-one. Far from coming from the landed elite, his father had been one of the pioneering generation of northern industrialists. Peel's background was thus entrepreneurial. He was not only 'new money' but was perceptive enough to recognize when an old nostrum had had its day.

It was this quality that shone through his address to the 586 electors in his Tamworth constituency, in December 1834, at the outset of the 1835 general election campaign. In the narrow sense, his proclamation was scarcely necessary. With no opponent being put up to run against him at Tamworth, Peel's re-election was a foregone conclusion. In reality, his argument was addressed to the wider, national electorate. His manifesto laid out not a specific set of legislative proposals but a new philosophical path for the Tories, realigning the party as one of moderation

FROM TORYISM TO CONSERVATISM

1678–81 The Tories are identified as a parliamentary group loyal to the hereditary right of the Catholic James, duke of York, to succeed to the throne. The term is derived from *Tóraidhe*, the Irish word for 'outlaw'. Their opponents are labelled 'Whigs' from the Scots' word *Whiggamor* or 'cattle drover'.

1715 The flight of the Tory leader, Lord Bolingbroke, to the Old Pretender's court allows the Whigs to taint the Tories with Jacobite treason.

1714–60 During the so-called 'Whig Oligarchy', the Tories are continuously out of government.

1762–3 Lord Bute serves as the first Tory prime minister. The Tories are viewed as the defenders of King George III's royal prerogatives.

1794 The Whig unity fractures over its response to the French Revolution and domestic radicalism. Whig conservatives support the administration of William Pitt the Younger, which is retrospectively categorized as Tory. The realignment ensures that Toryism comes to be associated with patriotism and the philosophy of Edmund Burke.

1783–1806 and 1807–30 The Pittites/Tories are continuously in power.

1812–27 The Tory leader, Lord Liverpool, becomes Britain's longest-serving prime minister.

1829 The Tory Party splits over the decision of its leader, the duke of Wellington, to support Catholic emancipation.

1834 Sir Robert Peel's Tamworth Manifesto realigns Conservatism with moderate reform.

1841 The Conservatives win the general election.

1846 The Conservative Party splits over Peel's repeal of the Corn Laws.

1852 Benjamin Disraeli, the Conservative leader in the Commons, abandons protectionist economics and endorses free trade.

1859 Peel's adherents, including William Ewart Gladstone, join with Whig and Radical factions to found the Liberal Party.

and open-mindedness to reform, rather than as a force of instinctive reaction. Reported and published nationwide, the Tamworth Manifesto became, in effect, the founding charter of the modern Conservative Party.

The manifesto accepted the widened democracy created in 1832 as a settled reality. Instead of opposing change on principle, it pledged the party to a more pragmatic and empirical response, still committed to 'the firm maintenance of established rights' but also wedded to 'the correction of proved abuses and the redress of real grievances'. Even the entitlements of the Church of England were not sacrosanct where there was a case to answer. To some, this looked like an opportunistic sell-out of time-honoured Tory principles.

For Peel, the Tamworth Manifesto was not just about finding a new direction for his party; it was also about asserting his own role as its policy-maker. In aiming to marginalize dissent within its fractious ranks, he helped restore the party to power. One hundred seats were gained in the ensuing general election, enough to demonstrate recovering Tory fortunes.

Peel proceeded to win a working majority in the 1841 election, serving as a reforming prime minister until 1846. It was at that point that he tried to take his supporters further than their adherence to landed interests would allow. Having been converted to the cause of free trade, and conscious of the urgent need to tackle the Irish potato famine, he repealed the agriculture protection measures of the Corn Laws, ushering in an age of cheaper food but also ensuring a division in his own party that forced him from office.

During the succeeding twenty years, the Conservatives were mostly out of power. Some of Peel's followers – including William Ewart Gladstone – drifted towards the Liberal Party. However, the central tenets laid out in the Tamworth Manifesto were eventually revived as the guiding principles of Conservatism. In 1867, a Conservative government passed a second Reform Act that began the enfranchisement of urban working men. Social reform followed in the 1870s. In its attitude to domestic politics, the party spent the twentieth century as a centre-right group, far removed from the sort of right-wing factions that did so much to destabilize liberal Europe between the two world wars.

1838

THE PEOPLE'S CHARTER

DEMANDS FOR POPULAR DEMOCRACY

The 1832 Reform Act scarcely touched the labouring classes. Indeed, the insistence of Whig politicians that their legislation concluded – rather than commenced – the process of widening political representation suggested that the working classes faced permanent exclusion from the political process.

Not satisfied that their interests were taken into account by those in authority, a Co-operative storekeeper, William Lovett (1800–77), and his associates founded the London Working Man's Association in 1836. Run by the working class *for* the working class, it was a pressure group that aimed to secure for labourers the same rights as the middle and upper classes enjoyed.

The association's political objectives were drawn up by Lovett, assisted by the Radical MP Francis Place, in a document entitled the 'People's Charter'. Published in May 1838, it consisted of six demands: universal suffrage for all males (Lovett was dissuaded from including women); annually elected parliaments; voting by secret ballot; abolition of the property qualification for MPs; the payment of MPs; and equally sized constituencies. The common thread uniting these demands was the social broadening and greater accountability of parliamentary government. It could be decided later what policies the resulting democracy might adopt.

The People's Charter became the common ground bringing together otherwise geographically and ideologically disparate radical and working men's organizations. Support was strong and especially vocal in the mill towns of Lancashire, although the waxing and waning of the Chartist campaigns closely followed the trade cycle's consequences for these communities. Many of the leading activists were skilled artisans, literate figures who were well versed in radical publications. Their views on other issues ranged from protectionism to advocacy of free trade and from pro-industrialization to a Luddite desire to return to cottage industries supplying an agrarian-based economy.

The Six Points

OF THE

PEOPLE'S

CHARTER.

1. A VOTE for every man twenty-one years of age, of sound mind, and not undergoing punishment for crime.

2. THE BALLOT.—To protect the elector in the exercise of his vote.

3. No PROPERTY QUALIFICATION for Members of Parliament —thus enabling the constituencies to return the man of their choice, be he rich or poor.

4. PAYMENT OF MEMBERS, thus enabling an honest tradesman, working man, or other person, to serve a constituency, when taken from his business to attend to the interests of the country.

5. EQUAL CONSTITUENCIES, securing the same amount of representation for the same number of electors, instead of allowing small constituencies to swamp the votes of large ones.

6. ANNUAL PARLIAMENTS, thus presenting the most effectual check to bribery and intimidation, since though a constituency might be bought once in seven years (even with the ballot), no purse could buy a constituency (under a system of universal suffrage) in each ensuing twelvemonth; and since members, when elected for a year only, would not be able to defy and betray their constituents as now.

It was Chartism's mixed blessing to attract the energy and attention-grabbing skills of Feargus O'Connor (1794–1855). An Irish MP who had lost his County Cork constituency in 1835, O'Connor began campaigning across the British mainland on the Chartist programme with a mixture of oratorical zeal and scarcely concealed menace, assisted by the newspaper he controlled, the *Northern Star*. For all his passion, his personality was a divisive factor in the movement and helped its opponents characterize it as the dangerous instrument of an aspiring demagogue.

The 'People's Charter' became tied to a parallel innovation in working-class agitation. This was the Convention of the Industrious Classes, a shadow parliament that aimed to set the political agenda. Its delegates met in London in February 1839 and began debating what to do if the real Parliament did not bow to the Charter's demands. Despite the many divisions of opinion, agreement was reached that in this eventuality a general strike would be called to bring the politicians to their senses.

Westminster was not so easily intimidated. When, in July 1839, a copy of the Charter was presented to Parliament with the endorsement of 1,200,000 signatures, the Commons divided, 235 votes to 46, against bothering to discuss its demands. Having moved to Birmingham the Convention was becoming increasingly fractious and broke up in September. With little sign of a nationwide appetite for a general strike, plans for direct action were scaled back. Some hotheads called for a rising, which resulted in November in an ill-conceived skirmish between Chartists and soldiers at Newport, in Wales. The instigators were sentenced to transportation (but pardoned in 1854) while more moderate activists received short jail sentences.

OPPOSITE: The six demands of the People's Charter, published in 1838.

It was during this period that Lovett and O'Connor's paths diverged. Lovett concluded that a movement confined to working-class membership was doomed and that the only hope lay in alliance with the middle classes. The problem with this was that much of the middle class viewed uneducated labourers as the very people with whom they did not wish to share the franchise. Keen to remain the leader of his own movement, O'Connor, by contrast, hoped to lead the National Charter Association, founded in July 1840, on the twin delusions that centralization could be achieved and victory delivered.

A second petition to Parliament in 1842 attracted 3,317,752 signatures. Parliament did not hide its lack of interest, again rejecting considering the Charter by 287 votes to 49. In 1848, while Europe was convulsed by revolutions, a third and final petition was organized. What was intended as a mass rally on Kennington Common proved smaller than anticipated and dispersed in the rain, having been prevented from marching towards Parliament by the police (back-up troops were

on standby). Bathetically, the petition was delivered in three cabs instead. The large number of genuine signatures were discredited by the smaller number of autographs purporting to be those of the duke of Wellington or Mr Punch.

The damp squib of 1848 was a sign of Chartism's terminal decline and it ceased to be a significant force after 1854. O'Connor's reputation was ruined by the collapse of a subscriber-driven scheme that he had devised for small landholders, and in 1852 he became insane, dying three years later. Improving economic conditions did much to quell political unrest. Ex-Chartists increasingly turned to other causes, particularly those that motivated Protestant Nonconformists: educational reform and temperance campaigns against the 'demon drink'.

However, the Great Charter was not a failure, merely a false dawn. A successful working-class political movement did eventually emerge in the guise of the Labour Party, and, ultimately, five of the Charter's six demands were adopted. The MPs' property qualification was scrapped in 1858; the secret ballot was introduced in 1872; legislation in 1876, 1884 and 1918 helped create nearly equal-sized constituencies; in 1911 the payment of MPs came in; universal male suffrage was achieved in 1918. Only the least sensible of the Chartists' demands – annual general elections – has never reached the statute books.

VII

THE VICTORIAN AGE

1839–43
BRUNEL'S DESIGN FOR THE SS *GREAT BRITAIN*

THE WORLD'S FIRST SCREW-PROPELLED, IRON-HULLED OCEAN LINER

Few Victorians better expressed their age's restless energy and the desire to find practical solutions to physical problems than Isambard Kingdom Brunel (1806–59). Almost any of his major engineering triumphs – from the Clifton suspension bridge to the Great Western Railway to the ambitious, if ill-fated SS *Great Eastern* – could be taken as representative of his genius, drive and vision. It was with the SS *Great Britain*, however, that he most demonstrably revolutionized travel and shrank the world.

Steam-powered vessels came into operation at the end of the eighteenth century. The first of these to cross the Atlantic was the American *Savannah*, which in 1819 made the journey from Savannah to Liverpool in twenty-nine days – although it had sufficient steam power for only a small proportion of the trip and relied mostly on its sails. A further fourteen years passed before a British steam-and-sail ship crossed the ocean in the other direction. These were achievements that had uncertain practical application. Sail still remained the only realistic means of transporting large cargos of goods or passengers by sea. It was believed that the amount of fuel necessary to cross the Atlantic purely by steam would take up so much room on board that there would not be space to take sufficient passengers or goods. Therefore, the current wisdom concluded, transatlantic steam travel could never be commercially viable.

Isambard Kingdom Brunel proved otherwise. In 1833, when he was still just twenty-six, he was commissioned by the Great Western Railway to survey, design and engineer their route from London to Bristol. Employing a mixture of impressive bridges, tunnels and viaducts, he proposed taking the London–Bristol line one stop further, crossing the Atlantic by steam to New York. Undaunted by

having no experience as a ship designer, Brunel came up with his solution: the SS *Great Western*, a wooden-hulled paddle steamer which, in the water, displaced 2,300 tons. On her maiden voyage in 1838, she proved that the Atlantic could be crossed by steam power. The rival and smaller *Sirius* beat her into port at New York by a matter of hours (having been forced to burn its own cabin furniture in the effort) but it was the *Great Western* whose design and performance illustrated how the crossing could prove viable.

Temperamentally ill-suited to resting on his laurels, Brunel, when he came to build the *Great Western*'s sister ship, proved himself an even greater driver of innovation. At over 3,000 tons displacement, the SS *Great Britain* was at the time of her launching in 1844 by far the largest vessel in the world. More importantly, she represented a first in two breakthrough technologies: she was not only the world's first large iron craft, with a hull made of wrought-iron plates riveted together, but also the first major screw-propelled ship. Driven by a colossal 1,000-horsepower engine, the single sixteen-foot screw propeller was a late design change, but one

Sectional line drawing with wash of the oscillating paddle engines made by Maudslay Sons & Field for Brunel's SS Great Britain. Following an early modification, the engines achieved 1,663 horsepower (ihp).

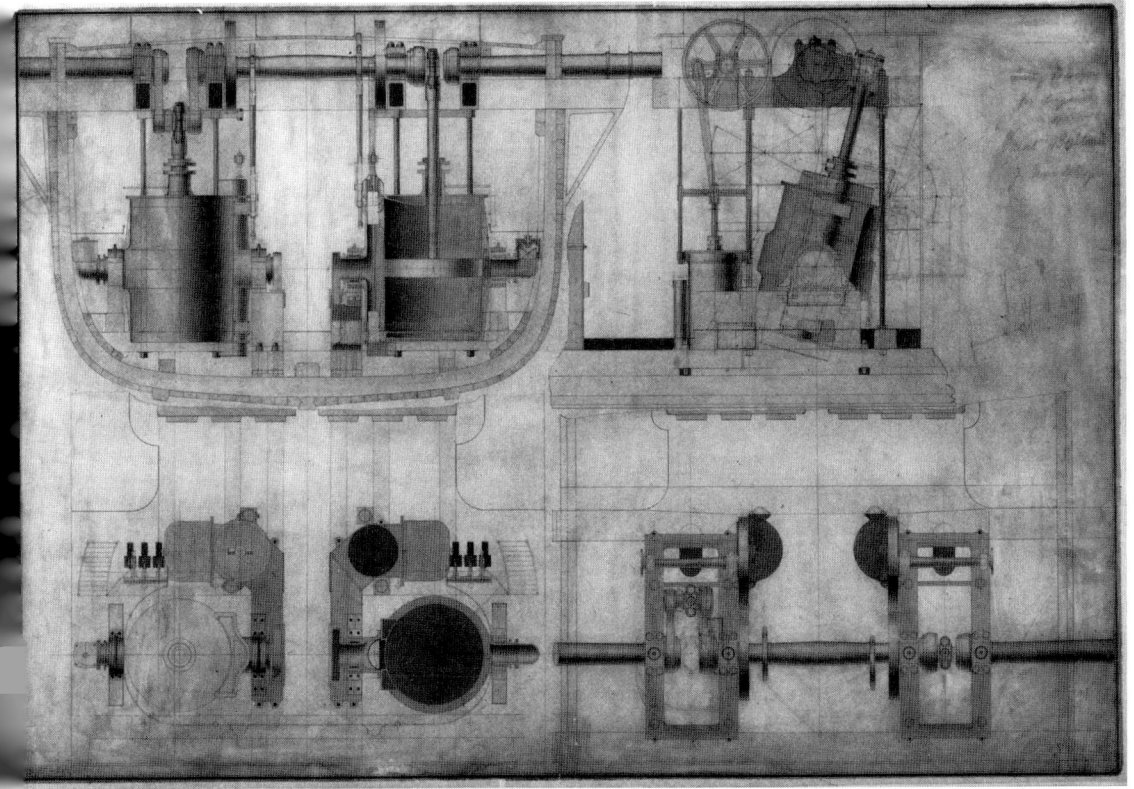

that proved revolutionary. The superiority of her iron hull was demonstrated when in 1846 she ran aground and was stuck off the Irish coast for eleven months before being pulled free, undamaged.

She could carry over 250 passengers (a figure later increased to 750), thereby demonstrating the future possibilities of ocean-going passenger liners. She broke the steam-powered transatlantic speed record on her maiden voyage, reaching America in fourteen days and twenty-one hours. After seeing service as a troopship during the Crimean War and the Indian Mutiny, she switched routes and became an Australia-bound liner, carrying the first 'All England' cricket team to tour in the Antipodes in 1861. By the time her active service ended in 1886, she had travelled nearly 1 million miles. Left as a storage hulk in the Falkland Islands, and subsequently abandoned there in 1937, she was rescued in a state of sad dilapidation in 1970 and brought home to Bristol. Her original iron hull still held together sufficiently for her to float serenely up the River Avon, passing under Brunel's magnificent suspension bridge, before ending her journey back in the same dock from which she had been launched 127 years earlier. There, she was meticulously restored and opened to the public, and can be seen to this day.

1843

CHARLES DICKENS'S
A CHRISTMAS CAROL

POPULAR NOVELS, THE VICTORIAN SOCIAL CONSCIENCE AND THE REVIVAL OF THE CHRISTMAS SPIRIT

Dismissed by some critics as a mere creator of caricatures and mawkish sentimentality, Charles Dickens (1812–70) was, by most popular measures, the greatest novelist in British history and, without question, the most influential.

The fact that the term 'Dickensian' is still used, even by those who have not read his books 150 years after they were written, confirms his centrality to the British psyche. In Dickens's lifetime and thereafter, his audience was never confined to the refined tastes of polite society nor to the ranks of light popular entertainment. Rather, his novels crossed social boundaries, appealing to all classes of reader and both sexes. That was part of their power. Few, if any, politicians, philosophers or artists gained broader acknowledgement or wider appreciation for doing what Dickens did best: holding a mirror up to Victorian Britain and exposing its blemishes.

The social evils were too great and too entrenched to be expunged by any single social reformer, but Dickens influenced movements that attacked some of the most degrading aspects of nineteenth-century life. His novels highlighted the cruelty of the Poor Law of 1834 and, in particular, the workhouse. Many of his works, most memorably *Oliver Twist*, laid bare the brutal treatment of children. His depiction of the Marshalsea prison in *Little Dorrit* helped spur the eventual scrapping of imprisonment for debt in 1869. *Bleak House* painted an uninspiring portrait of the self-serving aspects of the legal system, in particular, Chancery.

A recurring theme in Dickens's work is the fragility of comfort and the sudden reversal of fortune, where wealth may be either won or lost. Of this he had direct

experience. The son of a navy pay-office clerk who fell into debt and was sent to the Marshalsea, at the age of twelve Dickens was wrenched out of a comfortable, middle-class existence and put to work in a warehouse, labelling blacking pots. Eventually, the family fortunes recovered so that he was able to complete his schooling, becoming first a solicitor's clerk and then launching his career in journalism, as a parliamentary reporter. Nevertheless, his truest vocation was to be a novelist and he made his name in 1836 with *The Pickwick Papers*.

In this greatly loved work, Dickens constructed a cosy, snow-bound image of Christmas. Prior to the mid-seventeenth century, the twelve days of Christmas had been a time of nationwide conviviality, charity, gluttony, intoxication and neighbourliness. However, although the prohibitions and censure of Puritans did not outlive the English republic of the 1650s, the festival's spirit of bonhomie had become critically dampened, until by the 1820s it was a shadow of its former self. Disheartened by this, Dickens painted a nostalgic picture of Christmas's old, generous-hearted traditions that very effectively reminded readers what they were missing.

The Pickwick Papers was just the beginning. It was *A Christmas Carol* that forever imprinted itself upon our notions of the festive season. The idea came to him suddenly in October 1843, when he was still only thirty-one. He worked on the manuscript at high speed over a six-week period, adding and crossing out as he went along. *A Christmas Carol* was ready for publication on 19 December in a small bound volume, with four illustrations by the *Punch* cartoonist John Leech. Copies were priced at 5 shillings.

A Christmas Carol tells the story of Ebenezer Scrooge, a cold-hearted miser concerned exclusively with his own business, who regards the good fellowship of Christmas as 'humbug'. As he retires for the night on Christmas Eve he is visited by a succession of ghosts, starting with that of his late business partner, warning him of the consequences if he does not mend his ways. The Ghost of Christmas Past shows Scrooge how his selfishness drove away a former love and contrasts his indifference to Fred, his nephew, with the sympathy that Fred's mother once bestowed on Scrooge during his own unhappy childhood. The Ghost of Christmas Present takes Scrooge on a countrywide tour of the Christmas celebrations staged by even the poorest families, including that of his clerk, Bob Cratchit, whose invalid son, Tiny Tim, will die if Scrooge does not become more charitable. The Ghost of Christmas Yet to Come is a dark, hooded figure who does not speak but whose bony hand points to Scrooge's own depressing demise, robbed on his deathbed

1638 – THE SCOTTISH NATIONAL COVENANT

The declaration of resistance to King Charles I's efforts to enforce High Church Episcopalian practices upon the defiantly Presbyterian Church of Scotland was signed in multiple copies by much of the Scottish nobility and clergy as well as by other Scots. This copy was signed in 1639 by Lord George Gordon who died six years later at the Battle of Alford – fighting for the King.

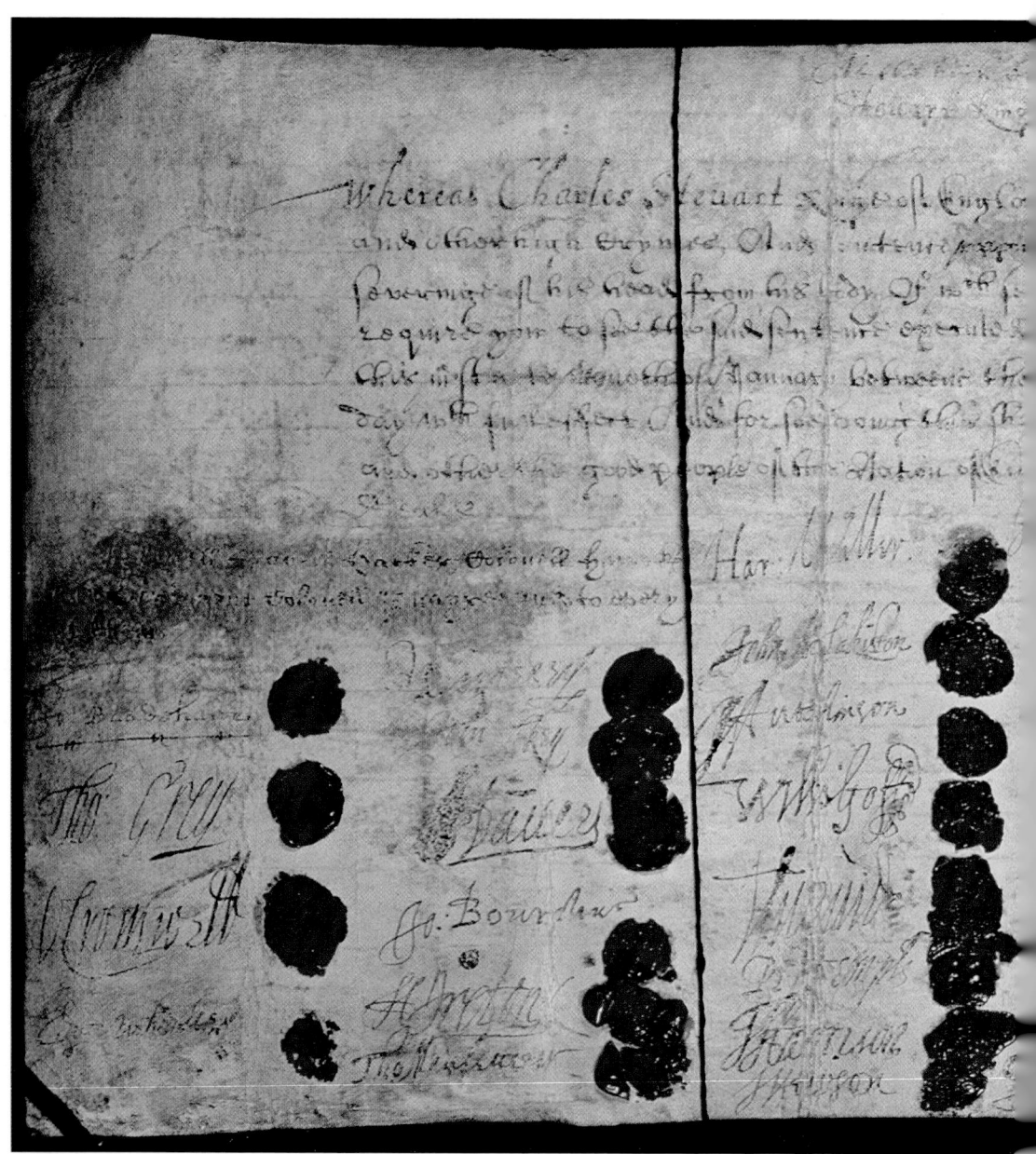

1649 – THE DEATH WARRANT OF CHARLES I
Charles I's death warrant, signed and with the seals of the fifty-nine regicides.
Oliver Cromwell signed third on the left-hand column.

for the hearinge and ordering ... Charles
and Hamden ... Anno ... 1645 ...

standeth ... attaynted and condemned ...
... pronounced against him ... to be ...
... not ... the ... daye ... therefore ...
streete before Whitehall upon ... the ...
... in the morninge ... in the afternoone ...
... And ... require ...
... you in his ... Essex ...

Harland ... Horton

Jo: Mr ...

Henry Marten
... Holles

... Constable
Rich ...
... Cawley
...

... Gree ...

John ...

1707 – THE ACT OF UNION

When the Act of Union passed into law in the Westminster Parliament, Queen Anne had this illuminated 'Exemplification' of the Act presented as a gift to the Scottish Parliament that the legislation abolished. Queen Anne is depicted in the top left-hand corner of the title page. The three holes at the bottom of the parchment were made by the tags attaching the Great Seal.

1805 – JAMES GILLRAY'S THE PLUM-PUDDING IN DANGER

William Pitt the Younger and Napoleon Bonaparte fight for the mastery of sea and land.

and unmourned in his grave. Perturbed and frightened, Scrooge repents and on Christmas morning begins his path to rehabilitation. He joins his nephew Fred's lunch party, joyfully gives money to charity, sends a large turkey anonymously to the Cratchit family for their Christmas feast and decides he should henceforth be like a second father to poor Tiny Tim. Through living all year long in the Christmas spirit, Scrooge finds redemption.

Charles Dickens's original manuscript: the opening page of A Christmas Carol, 1843.

Marley's Ghost. John Leech's etching for the first edition of A Christmas Carol.

A *Christmas Carol* was published at a time when few workers had more than one day's festive holiday and the habit of exchanging presents was not widespread. It reminded readers of the fate of disadvantaged children in the month of the commemoration of Christ's Nativity. Furthermore, it warned the well-off that giving was an obligation as well as a pleasure. They should not close their eyes to the fate of the poor and pretend that the dehumanizing workhouse was all that they deserved.

No other secular work did more to revive the notion of Christmas as the season of goodwill than Dickens's simple morality tale. Coincidentally, it was published at almost exactly the same moment that Henry Cole (subsequently the promoter of the Great Exhibition) commissioned for sale the first printed Christmas card – of a family united at the dinner table celebrating a festive meal. Dickens's offering was an immediate success, although he did not greatly benefit personally. Because of the high production costs that he had chosen to incur, having fallen out with his publisher Chapman and Hall, he made only £130 from the initial sale. When he sued the publishers of an unauthorized edition for piracy, he won the case but had to meet the £700 legal costs himself.

Nonetheless, the speed with which others rushed to make money from the book, not least in the theatrical adaptations that attracted eager audiences, testified to its wide appeal, on the far side of the Atlantic as well as at home. In the United States, Dickens is also celebrated as a founding father of the traditions of the modern Christmas. It was one of President Franklin D. Roosevelt's annual rituals to read Scrooge's story aloud from beginning to end. In Britain, too, the tale seems destined to remain relevant for many a Christmas yet to come.

1851

THE 'CRYSTAL PALACE' DESIGN
FOR THE GREAT EXHIBITION

JOSEPH PAXTON'S INNOVATION IN
ARCHITECTURAL DESIGN

On 1 May 1851, Queen Victoria opened the 'Great Exhibition of Works of Industry of All Nations' in London's Hyde Park, describing the occasion as the greatest day in the country's history. It was the world's first major international exhibition and, over the next six months, 6 million visitors came to see what the industrial and commercial revolution was bequeathing mankind. The single greatest wonder, however, was the 'Crystal Palace' that housed it.

It was the satirical magazine *Punch* that christened the temporary exhibition hall with the name by which it would be forever celebrated. Surprisingly, the revolutionary structure was not the work of any of the great Victorian architects but rather of a garden expert.

Joseph Paxton (1803–65) started his professional life tending the flora of a park in Bedfordshire before becoming head gardener at Chatsworth, the magnificent Derbyshire estate of the dukes of Devonshire. There, he demonstrated his self-taught technical expertise by designing a deceptively delicate conservatory that was, at the time, the largest glass building in the world.

The principles upon which the glasshouses of Chatsworth soared informed Paxton's greatest project. He had observed the strength of a species of giant water lily, the *Victoria amazonica*, by sitting his daughter Annie upon one and floating her across a pond. It inspired Paxton to demonstrate how modern materials and natural forms could unite to produce vast buildings that were structurally strong, yet simple in form and relatively cheap to construct.

Having been drafted in to produce a design for the Great Exhibition's main hall at short notice, Paxton did so on blotting paper with a sketch doodled while attending a board meeting. In this approach, as in its method of execution,

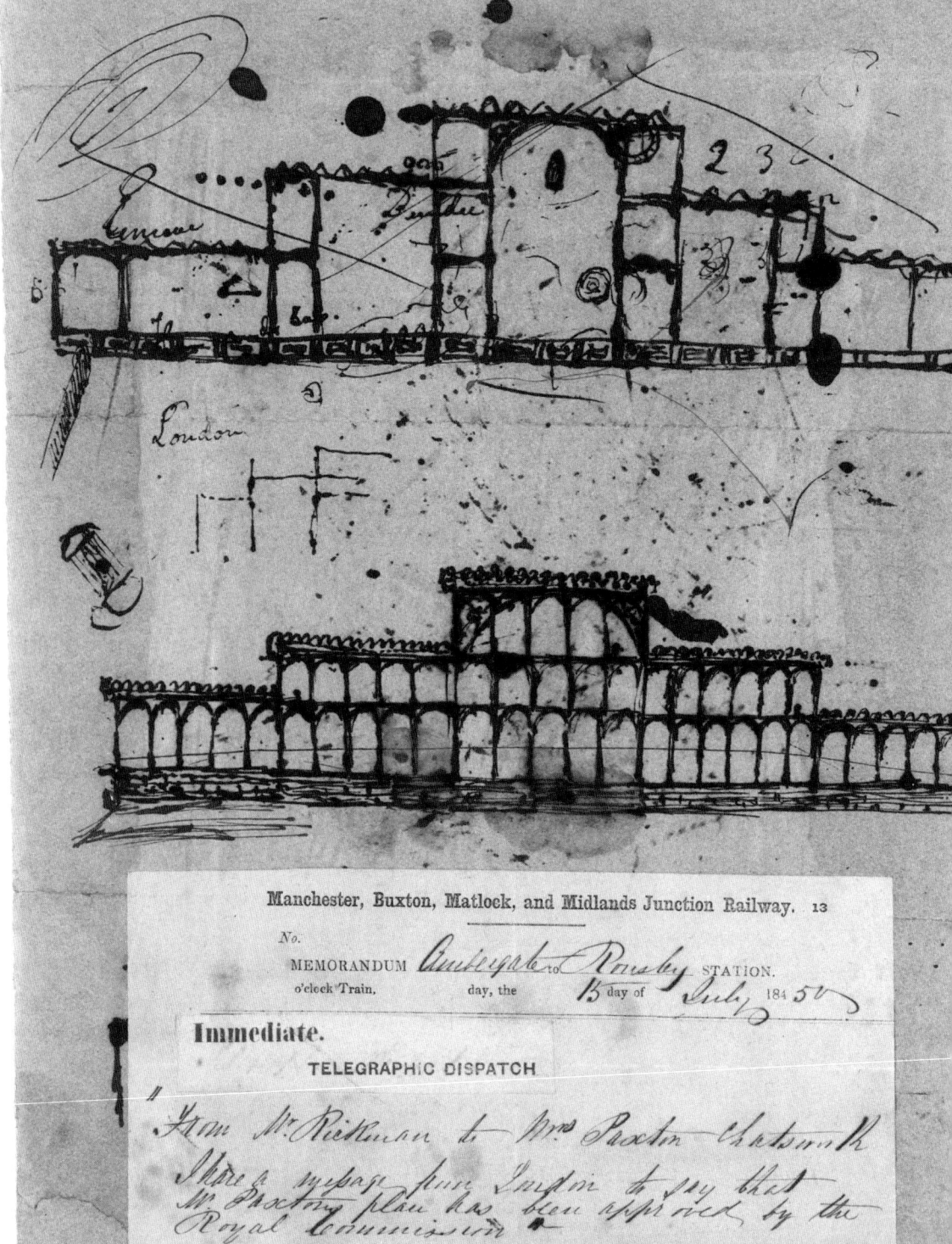

Manchester, Buxton, Matlock, and Midlands Junction Railway. 13

No.

MEMORANDUM *Ambergate* to *Rowsby* STATION.

o'clock Train.   day, the   15 day of   *July*   184 5

Immediate.

TELEGRAPHIC DISPATCH

From Mr Rickman to Mrs Paxton Chatsworth Share a message from London to say that Mr Paxton's plan has been approved by the Royal Commission

Paxton's proposal could not have been more different from the mostly laboured and heavily ornamental schemes offered by the 245 architects who had originally submitted entries. Paxton's solution could be assembled quickly (in itself a major recommendation, given the fast-approaching deadline) by slotting together prefabricated sections. Indeed, the structure was completed within nine months of the submission of his plans. Wrought-iron ribs were raised into position to provide the frame and backbone, supplemented with wood casements and 293,000 panes of glass. Modern construction methods were used. Sliding along a trolley on rails, each glazier could fit over one hundred panes a day. A public outcry at the prospect of felling Hyde Park's ninety-foot-high elm trees meant that the building had to be tall enough to accommodate them inside. When it was finished, it was, at over a third of a mile long, the largest enclosed space in the world. With its nave and transept, it resembled a secular cathedral, one that proclaimed the birth of modern architecture.

The early impetus for the exhibition had been provided by Henry Cole, an Assistant Keeper of Public Records. In 1845, while campaigning for free trade and cheaper bread, the Anti-Corn Law League had successfully run bazaars showcasing British manufactures and raising money through company stalls. Cole proposed an altogether grander venture, which, being international in scope, would provide a forum for British and foreign leaders of industry and commerce to meet, learn and exchange ideas. His scheme attracted the influential support of Queen Victoria's husband, Prince Albert, who chaired the Royal Commission established to investigate its practicality.

THE AGE OF VICTORIA

1837 Queen Victoria succeeds her uncle, William IV. Charles Dickens publishes *Oliver Twist*.

1840 Victoria marries Prince Albert.

1841 Augustus Pugin's *True Principles* sets out the argument for the Gothic Revival in architecture.

1843 The 'Disruption' occurs between the Church of Scotland and the Free Church of Scotland.

1845–9 The Irish suffer the potato famine.

1846 The Corn Laws are repealed.

1847 The 'Ten-Hour' Factory Act is introduced.

1851 The Great Exhibition is mounted in Hyde Park.

1853–6 The Crimean War is fought by Britain, along with France and the Ottoman Empire, against Russia.

1857 The Indian Mutiny challenges British rule.

1858 The first transatlantic telegraph cable is laid: permanent connection is achieved in 1866.

1859 Charles Darwin's *Origin of Species* and J. S. Mill's *On Liberty* are published.

1861 Prince Albert dies, sending Victoria into years of mourning and public withdrawal.

1865 Lewis Carroll publishes *Alice's Adventures in Wonderland*.

1868 The last public execution takes place.

1876 Queen Victoria becomes Empress of India. Alexander Graham Bell patents the telephone.

1878 W. S. Gilbert and Arthur Sullivan's *HMS Pinafore* is performed.

1886 The first Irish Home Rule bill is defeated. The Liberal Party splits.

1895 The National Trust is founded.

1899–1902 The second Anglo-Boer War is fought.

OPPOSITE: Joseph Paxton's inspirational doodle on blotting paper for the 'Crystal Palace'.

Upon opening, the Great Exhibition featured displays from 17,000 exhibitors, which ranged from machinery to fine art. It also attracted visitors from all ranks of society, many of whom availed themselves of another novelty provided for their convenience – public lavatories. Arranging a deal with the Midland Railway, travel promoters like Thomas Cook helped organize the flood of tourists. By the time it closed in October 1851, the Exhibition's profitability was such that the proceeds were used to buy land in South Kensington upon which, in time, the Science, Natural History and Victoria and Albert museums were built: a considerable cultural, scientific and educational legacy.

Paxton was knighted, became MP for Coventry and designed Mentmore Towers in Buckinghamshire for the Rothschild family in a rich, neo-Jacobean style, which, while aesthetically magnificent, was far removed from the masterwork that made him one of the most influential fathers of modern architecture. Conceived at rapid speed as a temporary structure, the Crystal Palace endured for eighty-five years. It was disassembled and put back together again on Sydenham Hill, where it remained as a venue for exhibitions and concerts until destroyed by fire in 1936.

1863

THE RULES OF
ASSOCIATION FOOTBALL

THE 'BEAUTIFUL GAME' TAKES ITS MODERN FORM

Britain's most successful export was cobbled together in a London pub by a group of English public-school boys. Whilst those who gathered at the Freemason's Tavern in Great Queen's Street, Lincoln's Inn Fields, between 26 October and 8 December 1863 may not have actually invented the game of football, it was their codification of it that the rest of the world subsequently accepted as the genuine article.

Football's origins are disputed. By the Middle Ages, rival villages were kicking a ball – and each other – about in various forms, whose common feature may more closely have resembled modern off-pitch hooliganism than on-pitch ball skills. The authorities disapproved of its rowdiness, as well as its tendency to distract young men from militarily useful pursuits like archery, and it became one of the 'idle games' banned by King Edward III in 1363. Not to be outdone, King James I of Scotland also passed a law in 1424 commanding that 'Nae man shall play at fute-ball.'

It was not these ineffectual commands so much as the process of industrialization and urbanization that, by the early nineteenth century, had stifled football as a popular entertainment. That it survived in an organized form was largely thanks to the public schools, where it provided an outlet for adolescent energy and aggression while also offering an opportunity for team-building.

The problem was that each of the schools played it according to their own rules. At Rugby School – and elsewhere – this came to involve the ball-handling techniques that were later codified as rugby football. Other schools also had a variety of traditions in relation to the ethics and the efficacy of tackling, hacking, bundling and drop-kicking. However, when the former public-school boys became undergraduates at Oxford and Cambridge universities, their different experiences of how football was played led to constant argument.

To overcome the mutual incomprehension, in 1848 nine Cambridge under-graduates – old boys of the schools of Eton, Harrow, Marlborough, Rugby, Shrewsbury and Westminster – met to agree a common set of rules. The resulting 'Cambridge Rules' formed the basis for the code adopted in the first meetings of the Football Association (FA) in 1863.

The idea to form the FA as a body that would govern the sport came from a keen rower and footballer for the Barnes Club named Ebenezer Cobb Morley (1831–1924). The clubs that responded to his suggestion to agree the rules were Barnes, Blackheath, Blackheath School and another Blackheath team called Perceval House, together with Forest (the nucleus of the Wanderers, a club based in Battersea), the enigmatic 'N. N. (No Name) Club' of Kilburn, Crusaders, Crystal Palace (unrelated to the current Crystal Palace FC), Kensington School and Surbiton. Charterhouse school also sent a representative before deciding not to affiliate. Similarly, Blackheath opted out when its motion to allow handling and running with the ball was defeated.

The creation of the FA formalized the breach between the ball-handling and non-handling versions, or, in the Oxbridge-lingo of the time, 'rugger' and 'soccer' (that is, 'Association' Football). Those who preferred Blackheath's version formed their own Rugby Football Union in 1871. The rules that the FA agreed were essentially the Cambridge Rules but with minor modifications. It fell to Barnes and Richmond to play the first match under 'Association' auspices. Despite a goal-less draw, *The Field* pronounced it a success, observing: 'Very little difficulty was experienced on either side in playing the new rules, and the game was characterised by great good temper, the rules being so simple and easy of observance that it was difficult for disputes to arise.'

The rules were certainly simple. There were only thirteen of them and authority had not yet been ceded to a single referee. Additions and revisions quickly followed. In 1865, a tape crossbar was added to create a goal height of eight feet and the offside rule came into operation the following year. Football officially became 'a game of two halves' when changing ends after each goal was replaced by swapping at half-time.

The formative influences on the FA came primarily from Cambridge and the public schools rather than from the version of the game played during the 1850s and 1860s in Sheffield. Nevertheless, the FA's success was assured only when working-class clubs from the Midlands and the North sought to affiliate. In this way, the FA rules became the national rules and were also adopted by the

THE RISE OF SPORT IN BRITAIN

1780 'The Derby' is inaugurated at Epsom.

1787 Marylebone Cricket Club (MCC) is founded.

1823 The Rugby schoolboy William Webb Ellis allegedly picks up the ball and runs with it.

1829 The first Oxford v. Cambridge Boat Race takes place: 20,000 spectators watch Oxford win.

1839 The Grand National is inaugurated at Aintree (a similar race had been held there since 1836).

1848 The 'Cambridge Rules' establish a common code for playing football.

1859 George Parr's All-England XI tours Canada and the United States: the first foreign tour of an English cricket team.

1860 At Farnborough, the British champion Tom Sayers fights the American champion John Heenan in the last major bare-knuckle boxing match.

1863 The Football Association (FA) is established, and adopts a code of laws based on the earlier Cambridge rules.

1864 The first county cricket championship.

1867 The 'Queensberry Rules' are established for boxing.

1871 The Rugby Football Union is established, and Scotland beats England in the first rugby international.

1872 The Wanderers beat the Royal Engineers 1–0 in the first FA Cup final; the first football international ends goalless, played between Scotland and England.

1874 At the first Scottish Cup final, Queen's Park beat Clydesdale 2–0 in front of a crowd of 3,000.

1877 The first Wimbledon Lawn Tennis Championship is played. At the first Test match, Australia beats England in Melbourne by 45 runs.

1878 The Bicycle Union (from 1883 National Cyclists' Union) founded to represent exponents of the new cycling craze. Responding to police pressure, in 1890 the union bans racing on roads and restricts competitions to velodromes.

1880 The first cricket Test match in England takes place: England beats Australia by five wickets at the Oval.

1882 Australia defeats England at the Oval by seven runs. A mock obituary notice to English cricket in the *Sporting Times* creates the tradition of 'The Ashes'.

1885 The FA permits professionalism.

1888 The Football League is created on the initiative of a Scottish draper, William MacGregor. The first winner is Preston North End.

1891 The inaugural Scottish Football League is jointly won by Rangers and Dumbarton.

1895 Rugby league splits from rugby union.

1907 Local landowner Hugh Locke King constructs the world's first purpose-built motor racing circuit at Brooklands in Surrey.

1908 The Olympic Games are held at the White City Stadium, London.

Football Association, Laws of the Game, 1863

1. The maximum length of the ground shall be 200 yards, the maximum breadth shall be 100 yards, the length and breadth shall be marked off with flags; and the goal shall be defined by two upright posts, eight yards apart, without any tape or bar across them.

2. A toss for goals shall take place, and the game shall be commenced by a place kick from the centre of the ground by the side losing the toss for goals; the other side shall not approach within 10 yards of the ball until it is kicked off.

3. After a goal is won, the losing side shall be entitled to kick off, and the two sides shall change goals after each goal is won.

4. A goal shall be won when the ball passes between the goal-posts or over the space between the goal-posts (at whatever height), not being thrown, knocked on, or carried.

5. When the ball is in touch, the first player who touches it shall throw it from the point on the boundary line where it left the ground in a direction at right angles with the boundary line, and the ball shall not be in play until it has touched the ground.

6. When a player has kicked the ball, any one of the same side who is nearer to the opponent's goal line is out of play, and may not touch the ball himself, nor in any way whatever prevent any other player from doing so, until he is in play; but no player is out of play when the ball is kicked off from behind the goal line.

7. In case the ball goes behind the goal line, if a player on the side to whom the goal belongs first touches the ball, one of his side shall be entitled to a free kick from the goal line at the point opposite the place where the ball shall be touched. If a player of the opposite side first touches the ball, one of his side shall be entitled to a free kick at the goal only from a point 15 yards outside the goal line, opposite the place where the ball is touched, the opposing side standing within their goal line until he has had his kick.

8. If a player makes a fair catch, he shall be entitled to a free kick, providing he claims it by making a mark with his heel at once; and in order to take such kick he may go back as far as he pleases, and no player on the opposite side shall advance beyond his mark until he has kicked.

9. No player shall run with the ball.

10. Neither tripping nor hacking shall be allowed, and no player shall use his hands to hold or push his adversary.

11. A player shall not be allowed to throw the ball or pass it to another with his hands.

12. No player shall be allowed to take the ball from the ground with his hands under any pretence whatever while it is in play.

13. No player shall be allowed to wear projecting nails, iron plates, or gutta-percha on the soles or heels of his boots.

Scottish Football Association at its foundation in 1873.

Inevitably, this geographical and social spread of FA-affiliated clubs created a clash of cultures between the erstwhile public-school boys, who played for the South's amateur clubs, and the working-class players, who often received expenses and even modest incomes for playing in 'professional' clubs. Initially it was amateur clubs like Wanderers who won the FA Cup, but in the 1883 final Old Etonians were beaten 2–1 by the northern semi-professionals of Blackburn Olympic. After protests, professionalism was formally condoned two years later and the amateurs fell back upon the consolations of contesting their own competitions. The sport's regeneration as the people's game was evident when, in 1888, the Football League began with twelve clubs, all from the Midlands and the North. A second division was added in 1892 and the Scottish League began in 1890. By the beginning of the twentieth century attendances at the biggest matches surpassed 100,000.

By then, football had begun to take root on foreign turf, British expats having exported it to South America, Europe and Russia. When the Fédération Internationale de Football Association (FIFA) was founded as the embryonic international governing body in Paris in 1904, it enforced a single code as the only form of the game it would recognize worldwide. The form chosen was, of course, the rule book of the FA.

1882
THE MARRIED WOMEN'S PROPERTY ACT

WOMEN GAIN THE SAME RIGHTS AS MEN TO OWN PROPERTY AND RUN BUSINESSES

The marriage of Queen Victoria to Prince Albert in 1840 did not diminish the rights of Britain's female head of state. She remained a constitutional monarch, her powers intact, while Albert – for all his advice and influence – was merely her consort.

Other women were not so lucky. At the outset of Victoria's reign, a married woman had no legal identity. As the eighteenth-century jurist Sir William Blackstone put it, 'In law husband and wife are one person, and the husband is that person.' As a result, any property a wife inherited or any income she earned legally belonged to her husband. She could not make contracts or even a will. While there were many instances of a wealthy father employing a lawyer to draft a marriage settlement that safeguarded in trust his daughter's inheritance from a prospective son-in-law, even among the rich these were the exception rather than the rule.

The first changes to matrimonial law were prompted not by a feminist but by a successful poet and novelist who nevertheless wrote to *The Times* in 1838 to insist that 'The natural position of woman is inferiority to man...I never pretended to the wild and ridiculous doctrine of equality.' Yet the legal wrong done to the letter writer, Caroline Norton (1808–77), was so spectacular that it turned the non-rights of wives into a *cause célèbre*.

Her husband, George Norton, was an unfeeling and physically violent man who partly lived off his wife's literary earnings and the useful social connections she made for him. In 1836, he hoped to prepare the way for a divorce by taking her to court on a charge of criminal conversation (adultery) with the prime minister, Lord Melbourne. As a married woman, Caroline Norton was legally disbarred from giving evidence in her own defence. Nonetheless, the – probably groundless –

charge made against her and Melbourne was thrown out for want of evidence. Consequently unable to divorce her, George Norton retaliated by exercising his right as a husband to refuse her access to her children.

Caroline Norton was not so easily crushed and she launched a public campaign to reform the law. Parliament obliged in 1839 with the Infant Custody Act. The legislation provided that wives who had not been found guilty of adultery had the right to custody of their children until they reached the age of seven, with access rights granted to the non-custodial parent thereafter. In itself, it was a modest provision but it represented the first crack in the defence that the husband's rights over his family were absolute.

It did nothing to alter George Norton's right to help himself to his estranged wife's inheritance when her mother died in 1851, an issue that became the next of Caroline Norton's legal battles. She could not divorce him since the law permitted a wife to bring proceedings only on grounds of incest or bigamy (although adultery was sufficient grounds for a husband to divorce his wife). This imbalance, together with the huge cost of bringing proceedings and the necessity of an Act of Parliament to end each marriage, ensured that in England and Wales, between 1800 and 1857, only 186 men and four women obtained divorces.

In 1857 two former lord chancellors, the Tory Lord Lyndhurst and the Whig Lord Brougham, teamed up to steer through the Matrimonial Causes Act, despite the opposition of High Church Anglicans. Henceforth, divorce courts would deal with petitions that had previously lumbered through ecclesiastical courts, criminal courts and Parliament. Over the next thirty years the number of divorces averaged 239 annually (compared to an annual figure of 187,000 marriages being contacted annually). The act gave a wife the right to divorce her husband if his infidelity was compounded by other affronts, like desertion, bigamy or extreme cruelty. For men, however, a wife's adultery was still sufficient grounds alone. This inequality continued in England and Wales until 1923, although Scotland had long regarded adultery by either party to be sufficient grounds.

The campaign to give wives the entitlement to their own inheritance and income was led outside Parliament by a committee of women led by Barbara Leigh Smith and Ursula Mellor Bright. It was also prominently supported by the liberal philosopher and advocate of sexual equality, John Stuart Mill, and had a large measure of cross-party support in the House of Commons. When the Tory MP, Russell Gurney, introduced a bill in 1869, the Liberal government smoothed its passage. Despite qualifying amendments inserted by the House of Lords, the bill

From the Married Women's Property Act, 1882

The fact that any such deposit, annuity, sum forming part of the public stocks or funds, or of any other stocks or funds transferable in the books of the Bank of England or of any other bank, share, stock, debenture, debenture stock, or other interest as aforesaid, is standing in the sole name of a married woman shall be sufficient prima facie evidence that she is beneficially entitled thereto so as to authorise and empower her to receive or transfer the same, and to receive the dividends, interest, and profits thereof, without the concurrence of her husband.

permitted married women to keep their own earnings and investments, as well as to inherit property in their own right. It touched the poor as much as the rich, for, while working-class wives had seldom brought much in the way of property into their marriages, they at last gained the entitlement to keep their own earnings, rather than being legally obliged to surrender their weekly wages to their husband.

Nonetheless, various restrictions still remained and it took the Married Women's Property Act of 1882 to fully banish the notion that a woman's independent legal identity was submerged upon getting married. This removed the legal distinction in property rights between married and single women, while establishing the principle of husbands and wives having separate property rights. That was not all. More than any other legislative statute before or since, it was the 1882 Act that made possible the development of the businesswoman. Until 1882, married women could neither sue nor be sued, which made it hard for them to run a business. By removing sexual inequality with regard to litigation, the Married Women's Property Act opened the way for women to marry and run their own businesses without legal fetter.

1898–9

CHARLES BOOTH'S
'POVERTY MAP' OF LONDON

ANALYZING THE EXTENT AND NATURE
OF LONDON POVERTY

Charles Dickens had used his novels to draw attention to the poverty and distress that disfigured mid-Victorian London. Nearly half a century later, as the Victorian age drew to its close, it was the work of a sociologist, Charles Booth (1840–1916), that most starkly exposed the deprivation still enduring in the world's greatest metropolis.

A part of Charles Booth's 'Poverty Map' of London is depicted in the fourth plate section.

Dickens and Booth came from dissimilar backgrounds, were temperamentally unalike and deployed wholly different methods. Whilst Dickens had known poverty in his childhood, Booth was born into a wealthy Liverpool merchant family and went into the lucrative shipping business with his elder brother. Brought up a Unitarian, he became disillusioned with religion as well as with sentimental attitudes, the effectiveness of traditional charitable giving and organized politics. Concluding that neither greater philanthropy nor better government were enough, he expressed his faith in an altogether less personal force, writing in 1870 that 'Science must lay down afresh the laws of life'.

He used some of the profits from his shipping company to finance a series of sociological surveys that would chart the nature of poverty, industry and religious adherence in late nineteenth-century London. He organized teams of investigators to move from street to street, compiling – through house enquiries, questionnaires and information gathered from school-board visits – the data he deemed essential to explain the reality of life in London. The project took fifteen years and was finally published in 1902, complete in seventeen volumes, as *Life and Labour of the People of London*. Many of his findings had already been released over the preceding years. By 1889, for example, he was able to calculate that 30.7 per cent of Londoners lived in poverty.

Booth recognized that poverty came in different forms and with varying levels of intensity. His work classified the London population into eight categories, ranging at the bottom from Class A (the criminal underclass) and Class B (casual labour) through to Class H (the upper middle class). These divisions were most graphically illustrated in colour-coded street maps, showing which groups lived where in the capital. Other findings suggested that – with the exception of Catholic immigrants – the poorer the families, the less likely they were to attend church or chapel.

However, the primary intention was not just to categorize but to explain the causes of poverty and suggest remedies. While social reformers and the Poor Law had long struggled with the problem of how to differentiate between the 'deserving' and the 'undeserving' poor, Booth concluded that personal fecklessness

and moral shortcomings, although evident, were not the major reasons for widespread poverty. Rather, he pinpointed not the criminal underclass but those who were a little higher up the scale as being the unintentional root of the problem. These were 'Class B' families, dependent on labour that was casual, seasonal, or at the mercy of regular 'boom and bust' trade cycles. The continued existence of this pool of cheap and disposable labour – sometimes immigrant – had the effect of dragging down the incomes of those in more regular employment, for whom poverty was also either a dismal prospect or a hard reality.

Booth wanted the problem of the casual poor to be addressed both by a restructuring of the economy in addition to reform of welfare provision. Industry should be better organized so that it did not both create and rely on this group.

The social researcher and philanthropist Charles Booth (1840–1916).

To help the casual labourers improve their own chances, education and training should be focused on improving their skills. Those who failed to respond should be taken out of the market place and put to work in labour camps. As for the existing Poor Law, it had failed in its intentions. Workhouses were most commonly populated not with the work-shy destitute but with the elderly, whose working lives lay far behind them. Instead of confining them to such degrading institutions, he declared, they should receive old-age pensions.

There were problems with Booth's methodology. As a sociological snapshot of London at the nineteenth century's end, his work had no equal. What it could

not do was provide a historical perspective, and it therefore failed to adequately address questions such as whether conditions were generally improving over time or how the patterns of poverty shifted with social mobility. Nor was it an infallible pointer to the future. No sooner was it completed than the creation of new suburbs changed London's demography and population density.

Nonetheless, while Booth's work may not have enjoyed Dickens' breadth of audience, it was extremely influential with policy-makers. The sociological researcher, social reformer and industrialist Benjamin Seebohm Rowntree adapted Booth's techniques and in 1901 produced a survey of York that suggested that a third of its citizens also lived in poverty. Booth's advocacy of old-age pensions was shared by the Liberal chancellor of the exchequer, David Lloyd George, who in 1908 introduced them for those over seventy. Indeed, during the first half of the twentieth century the remnants of the Victorian Poor Law were dismantled by successive Liberal, Conservative and Labour administrations. Through his cousin-in-law, the social reformer Beatrice Webb (who helped him with his research), Booth's work became a major influence on the 'Fabian' gradualist strand of socialist thinking, with its emphasis on planning and creating social 'efficiency'.

In economic policy, however, Booth rejected free trade, which both the Liberal Party and the early Labour Party supported. Ignoring the effect that cheaper foreign imports had in reducing the cost of living and in encouraging enterprise and diversification, Booth believed they harmed the security of working people's jobs. In 1903, in a supreme irony, he endorsed the protectionist tariff campaign of Joseph Chamberlain, the one-time Liberal radical who had in the end become a Tory imperialist.

VIII

FROM EMPIRE TO
THE WELFARE STATE

1904
THE ANGLO-FRENCH ENTENTE CORDIALE

CROSS-CHANNEL RAPPROCHEMENT

Between the Norman Conquest and Napoleon's defeat at Waterloo in 1815, there had been almost 750 years of suspicion, enmity and conflict between England (and subsequently Britain) and France. However, after the Napoleonic Wars relations between the world's two greatest colonial powers became, by past standards, relatively untroubled. Indeed, during the Crimean War (1854–6) Britain and France even fought on the same side against tsarist Russia.

Nonetheless, their period as allies was a temporary expediency, not a settled policy. No British regiment stirred when the Prussian army invaded France and besieged Paris in 1870. Indeed, successive governments in London pursued a foreign policy of 'splendid isolation' – the avoidance of being drawn into continental entanglements.

Cross-Channel relations slipped back into rancour as the nineteenth century drew to a close. In 1898, during the so-called 'Scramble for Africa' by the European powers, it briefly looked as if shots would be exchanged at Fashoda on the Upper Nile. Instead, cooler heads prevailed and British dominance of Egypt and the Sudan was assured. Yet over the following three years, Britain's international reputation was tarnished by its conduct in South Africa during the Second Anglo-Boer War, notably its internment of Boer (Afrikaner) civilians in 'concentration camps'. At the same time, Joseph Chamberlain, the colonial secretary, investigated the possibilities of an Anglo-German alliance. His endeavours came to nothing, but it was a sign that Britain was preparing to depart from the principles of splendid isolation.

France and Russia had signed a mutual defence pact in 1892 in which each agreed to go to the military aid of the other if attacked by Germany. In contrast, Britain had long been suspicious of Russian intentions towards India and was increasingly perturbed by her encroachments into China, where Britain had

major commercial interests. With this in mind, in 1902 Britain formed an alliance with Japan. This involved supportive neutrality if either country was attacked by a single opponent but guaranteed military assistance if attacked by multiple opponents. Therefore, Britain did not assist Japan during her war with Russia between 1904 and 1905, but Japan did fight on Britain's side in the First World War.

The alliance was a further signal that Britain was ready to pursue a more active diplomatic policy. The French, deciding that this presented an opening that they should not leave to rivals to explore, began a policy of actively courting Britain. It was particularly helpful that although the new king, Edward VII, was the cousin of Germany's Kaiser Wilhelm II, he was a Francophile in his sentiments. When he made a state visit to Paris in April 1903 he was rapturously received. The compliment was returned only two months later when France's President Loubet visited London. The symbolic and psychological adjustments involved in these public and private displays created the conditions for a more formal diplomatic agreement.

The terms of the new understanding were negotiated by the British foreign secretary, Lord Lansdowne (1845–1927), and his counterpart, Théophile Delcassé. The aim was not to agree a formal military pact – which was far beyond what London could be persuaded to commit to – but rather to remove existing sources of rancour: in particular regarding France's growing predominance in Morocco, over which it was trying to establish a protectorate, and British power in Egypt. Agreement was reached and, on

THE ROAD TO THE GREAT WAR

1882 The Triple Alliance, a military pact, is formed between Germany, Austria-Hungary and Italy.

1892 The Franco-Russian alliance agrees terms for mutual assistance in the event of either being attacked.

1902 The Triple Alliance is renewed. The Anglo-Japanese agreement is signed.

1904 The Anglo-French Entente Cordiale is agreed.

1904–5 The Russo-Japanese War is fought, in which Russia is humiliated.

1905 The Schlieffen Plan is devised for a German invasion of France via Belgium. Anglo-French military talks commence.

1906 The Algeciras conference discusses Morocco.

1907 Eyre Crowe's memorandum on Anglo-French alliance warns of German threat.

1908 The 'Young Turks' take power in the Ottoman Empire; Bulgaria declares independence.

1909 Louis Blériot flies across the English Channel, and the spectre of aerial attack is raised.

1911 Germany foments the Agadir crisis.

1912–13 In the First Balkan War Montenegro, Serbia, Greece and Bulgaria fight the Ottoman Empire.

1913 In the Second Balkan War Bulgaria attacks Greece and Serbia.

28 June 1914 A Serb terrorist assassinates the Austrian Archduke Franz Ferdinand and his wife in Sarajevo.

23 July Germany sends an ultimatum to Serbia.

28 July Austria-Hungary declares war on Serbia.

31 July Russia begins general military mobilization.

1 August Germany declares war on Russia and issues an ultimatum to France.

3 August Germany declares war on France.

4 August Germany invades Belgium, and Britain enters the war.

From the Entente Cordiale, 1904

Art. I. His Britannic Majesty's Government declare that they have no intention of altering the political status of Egypt.

The Government of the French Republic, for their part, declare that they will not obstruct the action of Great Britain in that country by asking that a limit of time be fixed for the British occupation . . .

II. The Government of the French Republic declare that they have no intention of altering the political status of Morocco.

His Britannic Majesty's Government, for their part, recognize that it appertains to France, more particularly as a Power whose dominions are conterminous for a great distance with those of Morocco, to preserve order in that country, and to provide assistance for the purpose of all administrative, economic, financial, and military reforms which it may require.

They declare that they will not obstruct the action taken by France for this purpose, provided that such action shall leave intact the rights which Great Britain, in virtue of Treaties, Conventions, and usage, enjoys in Morocco, including the right of coasting trade between the ports of Morocco, enjoyed by British vessels since 1901.

III. His Britannic Majesty's Government, for their part, will respect the right which France, in virtue of Treaties, Conventions, and usage, enjoys in Egypt, including the right of coasting trade between Egyptian ports accorded to French vessels.

IV. The two Governments, being equally attracted to the principle of commercial liberty both in Egypt and Morocco, declare that they will not, in those countries, countenance any inequality either in the imposition of customs duties or other taxes, or of railway transport charges.

8 April 1904 the 'Entente' was signed in London by Lansdowne and the French ambassador to London, Paul Cambon.

The excited talk about this new Entente Cordiale went far beyond the very limited terms of the agreement. Lansdowne did not see it as intrinsically inimical also to reaching a better understanding with Germany. Berlin, however, elected to test the Entente's fibre, hoping to show France how little it could rely on British

words. On 31 March 1905 Kaiser Wilhelm ostentatiously arrived in Tangier, where he delivered speeches that questioned France's intentions in Morocco and demanded that German coaling stations to be set up there, while also posing as the champion of the sultan's freedom of action. Britain, however, stood by France and the resulting conference at Algeciras effectively confirmed France's sphere of interest in Morocco. Germany pulled a second stunt in the region in 1911 (the 'Agadir Crisis'), but again failed to separate Britain and France.

Emboldened by the understanding with Paris, in 1907 the new Liberal foreign secretary, Sir Edward Grey, made an agreement with St Petersburg, clarifying Russian and British spheres of interest in Persia (modern Iran). As with the Anglo-French Entente, this did not commit Britain to a formal military pact. Indeed, there was uncertainty within Whitehall whether Britain had any potentially hazardous obligations even towards France. In 1911, the senior Foreign Office official, Eyre Crowe, advised that Germany *did* present an increasing threat to the security of Europe and to Britain, but went on to add: 'The fundamental fact of course is that the Entente is not an alliance. For purposes of ultimate emergencies it may be found to have no substance at all. For the Entente is nothing more than a

'The generosity of the English!' A contemporary French cartoonist's sceptical view of the Entente of April 1904. Edward VIII tells the French foreign minister, Théophile Delcassé, 'You give me beautiful Egypt and I will allow you to run after Morocco.'

frame of mind, a view of general policy which is shared by the governments of two countries, but which may be, or become, so vague as to lose all content.'

What kept it at the forefront of Britain's consciousness was mounting alarm at Germany's intentions, in particular its accelerated naval-building programme, which appeared to be aimed at confronting the Royal Navy rather than patrolling distant waters. The British army was restructured to include an Expeditionary Force that could, at short notice, be deployed in Europe. Even so, the Cabinet – after deep discussion – declared war on Germany in August 1914 only because Germany had invaded neutral Belgium on its way to attacking France, a violation of the 1839 Treaty of London, which bound Britain to guarantee Belgian neutrality.

Germany tried to dismiss the latter agreement as a 'scrap of paper' in a fatal disregard for the power of old documents. Without the infringement of Belgium's neutrality, Britain might either have stayed out of the conflict altogether or limited its intervention on France's side to naval assistance, without committing troops to a European land war. What we cannot know is whether, if Britain had not got into the habit of thinking of France as an ally because of the 1904 Entente, the British government might have tried to wriggle out of meeting its own obligations in 1914 by claiming that the 1839 Treaty was indeed merely a 'scrap of paper'.

1910–11
THE LIBERAL GOVERNMENT'S LIST OF NOMINEES FOR THE PEERAGE

THE DESTRUCTION OF THE HEREDITARY PEERS' ABILITY TO VETO LEGISLATION

Until 1911, no legislation became law unless it had been approved by the House of Lords. Parliament's upper chamber of hereditary peers did not give up its ancient right lightly. Only the knowledge that resistance would ensure the creation of 500 new pro-reform peers frightened their Lordships into acquiescence. The aristocratic safety valve on popular democracy was finally prised away by the 1911 Parliament Act.

This constitutional revolution was sparked by an extraordinary miscalculation from the upper house. In 1906, the Liberal Party had won a landslide election victory and began implementing a series of major spending commitments, including the creation of old-age pensions and the funding of a naval arms race with Germany. To pay for the rising expenditure, in 1909 the chancellor of the exchequer, David Lloyd George (1863–1945), introduced a budget that proposed a 'supertax' on top of the income tax and the land tax. Although these measures targeted high earners, they also caused particular outrage among country landowners whose wealth had already been eroded by a long agricultural recession. These representatives of 'old money' were the backbone of the Tory-dominated House of Lords and they duly vetoed the so-called 'People's Budget' by 360 votes to 75. In the process they did something far more revolutionary than anything proposed by Lloyd George. The House of Lords had not vetoed a budget for 250 years, during which time a precedent had taken root that the hereditary chamber would not reject finance bills.

The peers claimed they wanted to force a referendum on the sweeping tax changes. Instead the Liberal prime minister, Herbert Asquith, called a snap general election

with the slogan 'Peers versus People'. It proved a hard-fought, eight-week campaign, during which rival politicians traded claims of unconstitutional behaviour. Lloyd George did his best to add insult to injury, telling crowds that the peerage consisted of 500 'ordinary men chosen accidentally from among the unemployed'. The electorate was galvanized: at a time when 70 per cent of men had the vote, the January 1910 general election recorded a turnout of 92 per cent, proportionately the largest in British history. Closing the gap from their humiliating drubbing four years previously, the Tories staged an extraordinary recovery, winning 273 seats, only two fewer than the Liberals.

The result was a hung parliament with Asquith retaining power only with the help of the Irish Nationalists and the infant Labour Party. On 28 April 1910, the House of Lords acknowledged the election result and passed the budget without even a division. Now however, the government was determined to force through legislation that would permanently clip the hereditary chamber's right to veto legislation proposed by the democratic chamber.

The problem was that any such legislation would have to be passed by the hereditary peers for it to become law and the prospect of Tory peers voting to do so was analogous to turkeys voting for Christmas. Looking for leverage, Asquith asked King Edward VII whether he would be prepared to create new peers who would vote for the reform. The problem was that to get a majority would require ennobling over 500 people. All peerages were hereditary and creating this number of them would produce a wholly unwieldy upper chamber, as well as looking like an act of gerrymandering that would drag the monarch into political controversy. A conference was convened between the government and the opposition in the hope of finding a compromise that would make this contingency unnecessary. When it failed to reach agreement, the second general election of the year was called for December 1910. It changed nothing, Tories and Liberals tying on 272 seats each. Asquith remained in power with the support of the minority parties.

The prime minister now introduced the Parliament Bill, which aimed to make illegal any future attempt by the Lords to veto, or even amend, a finance bill. Furthermore, the bill would remove the Lords' veto on all other legislation so long as it had been passed three times in the Commons (with the proviso that two years needed to have elapsed between the initial second reading and the last, third reading). To highlight the Commons' responsiveness to the popular will, the length of time separating general elections was to be cut from seven years to five.

From the list of 500 peerage nominees

Sir George Otto Trevelyan, *Liberal politician and historian.*

Sir Harold Harmsworth, *co-owner of the* Daily Mail *and* Daily Mirror.

Sir Walter Runciman, *Liberal politician.*

Sir Philip Burne-Jones, *painter.*

The Hon. Bertrand Russell, *philosopher.*

General Sir Robert Baden-Powell, *soldier and founder of the Scout Movement.*

Joseph Rowntree, *chocolate maker and social reformer.*

Sir John Gorst, *lawyer and Conservative politician.*

General Sir Ian Hamilton, *soldier who later commanded the ill-fated Dardanelles campaign.*

Gilbert Murray, *classical scholar and Liberal activist.*

J. R. Spender, *editor of the pro-Liberal evening newspaper, the Westminster Gazette.*

Thomas Hardy, *novelist and poet.*

As they prepared to vote on the Parliament Bill, the peers learned that the new king, George V, had agreed that if they rejected the neutering legislation, he would indeed create the requisite number of new peerages to push it through. A paper drawn up by the government's chief whip, Alexander Murray, the Master of Elibank, contained the list of nominees. They ranged from the relatively obscure to the famous, including the historian Sir George Otto Trevelyan, the philosopher Bertrand Russell, the soldier and Boy Scouts founder Robert Baden-Powell, the novelist Thomas Hardy and the creator of *Peter Pan*, J. M. Barrie. What they had in common was that they were expected to do the Liberal government's bidding on parliamentary reform.

Appalled at these prospects, on 10 August 1911 the House of Lords passed the Parliament Bill by the narrow margin of 131 votes to 114. Many 'diehard' Tory peers revolted against their own party's official policy of abstention and the measure was thus passed only because another group of Tory peers, led by Lord Curzon, voted with the government in order to avoid the dilution of aristocratic purity that would otherwise be foisted upon the peerage. Henceforth, the House

of Lords' historic powers were humbled. Its delaying powers were cut from two years to one year in 1947, and life peerages were introduced in 1958. In 1999 the hereditary right to sit in the Lords was abolished, with only ninety-two self-electing hereditary peers remaining – it was stated, temporarily – pending a more comprehensive reform.

However, it was the 1911 Parliament Act – made possible by the threat of 'packing' the House with government nominees – that was the single greatest institutional revolution at Westminster in the twentieth century. It did away with the notion that the upper chamber had the same rights to determine legislation as the lower chamber. Ever after, the House of Lords was reduced to being a chamber that revised, but did not determine, legislation. The power of Britain's aristocracy would never be the same again.

FOURTEEN REASONS FOR SUPPORTING WOMEN'S SUFFRAGE

THE RIGHT OF WOMEN TO VOTE

'Deeds not words' was Mrs Emmeline Pankhurst's exhortation to her Women's Social and Political Union (WSPU). Suffragette militancy might therefore be better represented by a brick and shards of broken glass, or a padlock attached to iron railings, than by a document. Whether direct action helped or hindered the cause of women's enfranchisement is still actively disputed today. Such tactics were denounced at the time by the far more popular National Union of Women's Suffrage Societies (NUWSS), which campaigned tirelessly and, ultimately, successfully to win the moral and intellectual high ground of the debate.

When localized female suffrage groups came together to found the NUWSS in 1896, it seemed likely that at least some women were about to be granted the vote in national elections. The following year, a private members' bill reached as far as the second reading stage at Westminster, where it was approved by 230 votes to 159 before running out of parliamentary time. Rationally, it seemed a logical extension of what had already been enacted for local government, where women ratepayers had won the right to vote in 1869 and had been able to sit on parish and district councils since 1894. With increasing numbers of them paying their own taxes, the old cry of the American colonists was revived: 'No taxation without representation.'

Yet, despite the mildly supportive views of two successive Conservative prime ministers, Lord Salisbury and Arthur Balfour, not a single bill or even a resolution was brought before Parliament between 1897 and 1904. Hope for change was revived when the Liberal Party's landslide election victory of 1906 created a House

NATIONAL UNION OF WOMEN'S SUFFRAGE SOCIETIES,

25, VICTORIA STREET, WESTMINSTER, S.W.

President—Mrs. HENRY FAWCETT, LL.D.

---

14 REASONS

For Supporting Women's Suffrage.

✦✦✦✦✦✦✦✦✦✦✦✦✦✦✦✦✦✦✦✦✦✦✦✦✦✦✦✦✦✦

1.—Because it is the foundation of all political liberty that those who obey the Law should be able to have a voice in choosing those who make the Law.

2.—Because Parliament should be the reflection of the wishes of the people.

3.—Because Parliament cannot fully reflect the wishes of the people when the wishes of women are without any direct representation.

4.—Because most Laws affect women as much as men, and some Laws affect women especially.

5.—Because the Laws which affect women especially are now passed without consulting those persons whom they are intended to benefit.

6.—Because Laws affecting children should be regarded from the woman's point of view as well as the man's.

7.—Because every session questions affecting the home come up for consideration in Parliament.

8.—Because women have experience which should be helpfully brought to bear on domestic legislation.

9.—Because to deprive women of the vote is to lower their positions in common estimation.

10.—Because the possession of the vote would increase the sense of responsibility amongst women towards questions of public importance.

11.—Because public-spirited mothers make public-spirited sons.

12.—Because large numbers of intelligent, thoughtful, hard-working women desire the franchise.

13.—Because the objections raised against their having the franchise are based on sentiment, not on reason.

14.—**Because**—to sum all reasons up in one—**it is for the common good of all.**

of Commons with, at least notionally, a far stronger majority in favour of women's suffrage, although the new government failed to actively promote legislation. Neither the prime minister from 1908, Herbert Asquith (still less Mrs Asquith), nor successive home secretaries supported the cause.

The attitude of the Liberal government was disappointing to the NUWSS, whose president, Millicent Garrett Fawcett (1847–1929) was the widow of a noted Liberal MP. In Manchester, it was as much frustration with the half-hearted attitude of the national Independent Labour Party that stirred the widow of one of its activists, Emmeline Pankhurst (1858–1928), to found the WSPU in 1903.

Initially, Mrs Fawcett's NUWSS and Mrs Pankhurst's WSPU ran rival but essentially complementary campaigns. The former were known as Suffragists and the latter as Suffragettes (a term actually coined by the *Daily Mail*). To begin with, Suffragists neither joined in with nor greatly condemned the more headline-grabbing tactics of Suffragettes, whose efforts to keep the issue at the centre of attention included disrupting public meetings, heckling Liberal politicians and serving prison terms for breaching the peace.

OPPOSITE: The NUWSS's fourteen-point statement of 1912, arguing the case for women's suffrage.

Millicent Fawcett, who did not support fighting for constitutional liberties by unconstitutional means, came to deplore Emmeline Pankhurst's belief that 'the argument of the broken pane, is the most valuable argument in modern politics'. The two groups began to diverge sharply when the Suffragettes turned first to vandalism, smashing windows and slashing Velasquez's *Rokeby Venus* in the National Gallery, then to arson – including an attack on a station and a school – and ultimately to planting bombs, whose failure to kill anyone was as much chance as design.

Efforts in Parliament to pass suffrage legislation were hampered for several reasons. Some MPs no longer wished to be associated with a cause being advocated through intimidation (and it can probably be safely assumed that not many converts at Westminster were won over by the call for 'Votes for Women, Chastity for Men', the new slogan of Mrs Pankhurst's daughter and fellow activist, Christabel). The parliamentary arithmetic also became less promising after 1910 when the eighty-four Irish Nationalist MPs decided to oppose women's suffrage on the grounds that it would take up legislative time that was better spent passing Irish home rule. The prevalence of women activists in the campaign against the 'demon drink' led some politicians to fear that the practical consequence of giving them the vote would be the introduction of Prohibition, while those of an imperialist frame of mind questioned whether the empire could be defended by female voters.

For many MPs, of course, the real root of their objection was naked misogyny.

There was also the question of which women should get the vote. With a third of adult males still unenfranchised, the options were either for all women to gain the suffrage as part of a universal adult franchise bill or for prospective women voters to be subject to the existing property qualifications applicable to men. Whilst the NUWSS were prepared to settle, as an interim measure, for the latter, some Liberals saw it as an unattractive compromise calculating that it would merely add more Tory voters to the electoral register. The best chance of getting legislation onto the statute books came in 1913, when an amendment to include women was attached to legislation extending the male franchise. The opportunity was lost when the Speaker of the House of Commons ruled it out of order on the grounds that it fundamentally altered the nature of the bill.

How Punch *magazine depicted Suffragette militancy in the early 1900s.*

Where the Suffragette campaign did succeed was in inciting the brutality of the state. Imprisoned Suffragettes went on hunger strike and were force-fed through

THE SUFFRAGETTE THAT KNEW JIU-JITSU.
THE ARREST.

methods indistinguishable from torture. In 1913, the home secretary introduced a legal novelty with the 'Cat and Mouse' Act, which released women prisoners on hunger strike only to reimprison them once they had recovered. In that year the cause also gained its martyr when Emily Wilding Davison either threw herself or fell (she took her intentions to the grave) under the king's horse at the Derby. It was a time of desperation. The Pankhursts' Suffragette movement suffered splits and, with the number of new recruits dwindling, stopped publishing details of new members once they fell below 1,000 a year. In contrast, the membership of Millicent Fawcett's non-violent Suffragist NUWSS soared from 21,000 in 1910 to nearly 100,000 by 1914. In choosing to ally itself with the Labour Party, the NUWSS appeared likely to cause the Liberals significant damage, prompting David Lloyd George to open talks with the NUWSS to secure a measure of women's suffrage ahead of the next election. Before anything could be finalized, the First World War broke out.

Winding down their campaign, some Suffragists, including Mrs Fawcett, supported the war, many of them getting involved in nursing and relief work, although some ran pacifist campaigns. Both Emmeline and Christabel Pankhurst loudly backed the war. The common effort against Germany created a new situation in which former domestic foes could be reconciled. With the argument for granting adult male suffrage being enhanced by the patriotic endeavours of the armed forces in France, so the contribution that women were making to the war effort on the home front was cited as a reason for extending the vote to them too. Certainly, the assertion that the empire was not safe in women's hands was shot to pieces. When the conflict ended in 1918, the Representation of the People Act gave the vote to all men over twenty-one and all women over thirty.

Both the WSPU and the NUWSS disbanded, although the latter re-formed in a new guise to campaign for the removal of the remaining sexual discrimination in the age at which the vote was granted. Victory was won in 1928 when Stanley Baldwin's government finally introduced an equal franchise for all men and women over the age of twenty-one. Shortly afterwards, Mrs Pankhurst died, having been selected as the Conservative candidate for Whitechapel. By then, she, no less than British society, had undergone an extraordinary transformation.

1914
WAR RECRUITMENT POSTER

THE FIRST WORLD WAR AND THE PRINCIPLES
OF A VOLUNTEER ARMY

An iconic poster featuring Lord Kitchener is depicted in the fourth plate section.

Britain was the only major European country that went to war in 1914 with its armed forces made up entirely of volunteers. In contrast, the massed ranks fighting for the French republic, the tsar of Russia, the German Kaiser and the emperor of Austria-Hungary, were conscripts.

The differentiation was an important one for it went to the heart of British liberalism. Other states might force their citizens or subjects to serve in the armed forces – even in peacetime – but this was incompatible with British notions of a small state and the rights of the individual. Campaigns during the Edwardian period to introduce mandatory military service along continental lines were resisted by Herbert Asquith's Liberal government.

In the early stages of the war, long queues of volunteers lining the streets outside hastily opened recruitment offices, suggesting Britain had no need to turn to compulsion. The newly appointed secretary of state for war was the much decorated hero of the 1898 Sudanese campaign, Field Marshal Horatio Kitchener, Earl Kitchener of Khartoum (1850–1916), who now called for 100,000 volunteers. Within a month 300,000 had stepped forward. Although many needed no persuading, encouragement took the form of public exhortations to duty, peer pressure, propaganda about German atrocities (some true, some exaggerated, some made up) and poster campaigns.

No poster better caught the popular imagination than the famous Kitchener 'wants you'. The iconic image, dominated by the striking features of the field marshal with his finger outstretched towards the viewer, was the work of a professional illustrator, Alfred Leete (1882–1933). It was originally produced on the cover of *London Opinion*, a weekly magazine, before being reproduced across the nation's billboards. Thus was born one of the most familiar images in

BRITAIN IN ARMS 1914–18

1914

4 August Britain declares war on Germany.

23 April The British Expeditionary Force (BEF) engages the German advance at Mons.

8 October–22 November The First Battle of Ypres; the BEF holds its ground despite heavy losses.

29 October The Ottoman Empire enters the war on the German side.

1915

19 January The first Zeppelin raid hits Yarmouth and King's Lynn. By May 1916, 550 British civilians have been killed by Zeppelins.

22 April The Germans unleash chlorine gas on British troops in the Ypres salient.

25 April–20 December The Gallipoli landings fail to knock Turkey out of the war.

7 May A German U-boat torpedoes and sinks the British-registered cruise liner *Lusitania* off the Irish coast, killing 1,198 passengers, almost one hundred of them children.

17 May A cross-party coalition is formed; Herbert Asquith remains prime minister.

7 December Ottoman troops besiege British and Indian forces at Kut, south-east of Baghdad. After holding out for 147 days, the remaining 13,000-strong Anglo-Indian garrison surrender on 29 April 1916. The majority of them subsequently die in captivity.

1916

27 January Conscription is introduced.

24–30 April The Easter Rising by Irish nationalists in Dublin is suppressed.

31 May The naval battle of Jutland ends inconclusively.

1 July The Somme offensive starts, with 60,000 British casualties on the first day alone.

7 December David Lloyd George replaces Asquith as prime minister.

1917

1 February Germany launches unrestricted submarine warfare, intending to starve Britain into surrender within six months.

11 March Under the command of General Maude, the British Indian army takes Baghdad.

6 April The United States enters the war on the side of Britain and France.

7 June–12 November In the Third Battle of Ypres, British efforts to break out of the Ypres salient stall after 10,000 yards and 70,000 fatalities at Passchendaele.

20 November The first use of British tanks at the Battle of Cambrai briefly breaks through the Hindenburg Line.

9 December General Allenby takes Jerusalem.

1918

3 March Russia signs the Treaty of Brest-Litovsk and withdraws from the war.

21 March The German spring offensive drives the British army back.

11 April Field Marshal Haig issues his desperate 'backs to the wall' order.

8 August A massive British counter-attack takes place at Amiens, resulting in the 'black day of the German army'.

11 November The Armistice is signed.

the history of British advertising. It was also imitated across the Atlantic when the United States entered the war on 6 April 1917, albeit with the gesticulating Kitchener replaced by Uncle Sam.

Kitchener was among the few senior figures who had assumed from the start that the conflict would be a prolonged one. During 1915 it became clear to others that he was right and that, despite the early success of the recruitment campaign, Britain could run out of sufficient volunteers to plug the gaps. Now that the apparent risk of losing the war was rated as more serious than clinging to outmoded and complacent notions of individualism, the campaign became ever louder to match the other combatants' armies with conscription. In tandem came the belief that conscription was more equitable than a system in which public-spirited volunteers were slaughtered in the trenches while 'shirkers' prospered at home.

The Cabinet became increasingly divided on the issue while Asquith sought various compromise solutions. Lord Derby was put in charge of a scheme whereby civilian men of military age 'attested' – without compulsion – that they were willing to serve if called upon. This failed to placate those who argued that it was unfair for married men to make such a commitment when some unmarried men had still failed to do so. In January 1916, Asquith finally conceded that the age of volunteerism was over: the Military Service Act conscripted unmarried men between the ages of eighteen and forty-one. Thirty-four Liberal MPs forlornly voted against the bill and, although it made several Cabinet ministers uneasy, only Sir John Simon, the home secretary, carried his principles as far as to resign on the issue.

To pacify those who felt liberalism's soul had been sold, the status of the conscientious objector was recognized (unlike in most of Europe at the time). Few of those whom the tribunals excused from taking up arms found the alternatives to be soft options, for they included ambulance work or, for those unwilling to carry stretchers, labour camps. However, the greatest handicap to conscription was that many of those who had not volunteered were engaged in essential tasks at home, whether digging coal, in some area of factory activity still deemed unsuitable for the new influx of women workers, or in some other skilled and useful occupation. Hoping to tap the last remaining wells of manpower, in April 1916 the terms of military conscription were widened to make all men under forty-one eligible for call-up. No conscription was imposed upon Ireland, but the threat of its introduction in 1918 led to a huge increase in support for the hardline republicans of Sinn Féin.

By then, the individualist ideals behind the Kitchener poster had gone the way of the great field marshal himself. In June 1916 he was aboard HMS *Hampshire* when it hit a mine off the Orkney Islands, and he went down with the ship. His authority among his political and military colleagues was already waning although he had never lost his national popularity. As the prime minister's wife, Margot Asquith, observed, he remained 'a great poster'.

It is debatable whether the scrapping of volunteering played a role in winning the war. Auckland Geddes, who served as Director of National Service from 1917 to 1919, later concluded that 'the imposition of military conscription added little if anything to the effective sum of our war effort'. Nonetheless, it was reintroduced for the Second World War. The fact that conscription in 1939 was far less politically contentious than it had been in 1916 demonstrated not only how far the prospect of 'total war' had removed the old voluntary distinction between combatant and civilian but also the extent to which the balance between the state and the individual had shifted in the intervening period. More remarkable, conscription – as 'National Service' – was not disbanded until 1960, fifteen years after the Second World War had ended.

1918
CLAUSE IV OF THE LABOUR PARTY CONSTITUTION

THE PHILOSOPHY OF BRITISH SOCIALISM

The Labour Party was founded, as the Labour Representation Committee, in 1900 with the aim of securing parliamentary seats for working-class politicians. Drawn from various pre-existing groups and the trade unions, its members may have adhered to socialist tenets, but the promotion of socialist ideology was not the new organization's stated objective. Indeed, the failure to be explicitly doctrinal quickly ensured the disaffiliation of the Marxist Social Democratic Foundation.

In its first years, the Labour Party (as it became in 1906) drew strength from two developments. In 1903, it negotiated a secret deal with the Liberal Party to avoid running against each other in constituencies where the chances of splitting the progressive vote risked letting in a Conservative. Assisted in this way, Labour won twenty-nine seats in the 1906 general election and began to assume critical mass. The 'Lib-Lab' pact, however, did not survive the First World War. Of greater long-term significance, in terms of members, leverage and funding, was the Labour Party's role as the political wing of the trade union movement. Between 1910 and 1914, the number of trade unionists in Britain rose from 2.5 million to over 4 million. By 1920 it had doubled to more than 8 million.

The First World War provided Labour with both a test and an opportunity. Unable to support the conflict, the pacifist-minded Ramsay MacDonald (1866–1937) resigned as chairman of the Parliamentary Labour Party. However, his pro-war successor, Arthur Henderson (1863–1935), joined the Cabinet. Labour MPs were thus to be found sitting both on the government and on the opposition benches, yet the division in their ranks proved less strategically calamitous than those that tore the Liberal Party apart. The latter took the form of a highly personal fight between Herbert Asquith and David Lloyd George, with the result that in

Clause IV of the Labour Party Constitution, 1918

To secure for the workers by hand or by brain the full fruits of their industry and the most equitable distribution thereof that may be possible upon the basis of the common ownership of the means of production, **distribution and exchange**, and the best obtainable system of popular administration and control of each industry or service.

[words in **bold** added in 1929]

1916 the latter replaced Asquith as prime minister in the coalition government. To this clash of personalities was added the further fracturing of common Liberal purpose over differing notions of how the war should be prosecuted.

Although the war was still not won when Labour convened its party conference at Nottingham in January 1918, it found itself in a far stronger position than previously. The power of the state was being deployed to secure military victory, blowing away many former notions of *laissez-faire* non-interference. A collectivist spirit was allied to calls for ever greater redistribution of wealth. If soldiers were to be conscripted to win the war, so the argument ran, there should be a 'conscription of wealth' to follow. At the same time, the defection from liberalism of pacifist-minded, middle-class intellectuals, who were disgusted by the methods by which Lloyd George sought to win the war, ceased to make Labour merely a party of working-class men and trade unionists.

The author of Clause IV, Sidney Webb.

The consequence was the adoption at Nottingham of Clause IV of the Labour Party's constitution. The clause, which framed the aims and values of the party, was drafted by Sidney Webb (1859–1947), the Fabian Society thinker, a co-founder of the London School of Economics and an advocate of schemes for 'national efficiency'. It committed Labour for the first time to an explicitly socialist ideology – to secure for all workers 'the common ownership of the means of production and the best obtainable system of popular administration and control of each industry and service'.

THE RISE OF THE LABOUR MOVEMENT

1834 The Tolpuddle Martyrs, six agricultural workers in Dorset who covertly form a union, are convicted of making illegal secret oaths and transported to Australia for seven years. Following a public outcry, their sentence is cut to four years.

1868 The Trade Union Congress meets for the first time, in Manchester.

1892 Keir Hardie is elected an independent Labour MP for West Ham South; he loses his seat in 1895.

1893 Hardie co-founds the Independent Labour Party (ILP) in Bradford.

1900 The Labour Representation Committee (LRC) is founded at the Memorial Hall, Farringdon Street, by the ILP, the Fabians, the (Marxist) Social Democratic Federation and trade unions.

1903 One hundred and twenty-seven unions, with 847,000 members, are affiliated to the LRC.

1901 In the Taff Vale verdict the Law Lords rule that the unions may be financially liable for the cost of their strike action.

1906 The LRC wins twenty-nine seats in the general election and is renamed the Labour Party. The Trades Disputes Act reverses the Taff Vale decision and frees the unions from corporate liability for strike action.

1914 The Labour Party supports the war effort. Opposing it, Ramsay MacDonald resigns as chairman of the parliamentary Labour Party. The ILP also opposes the war.

1915 Labour's new leader, Arthur Henderson, enters the war coalition Cabinet.

1924 Ramsay MacDonald becomes the first Labour prime minister, but his minority administration loses power within ten months.

1926 The General Strike is called in defence of miners' demands: it is called off after ten days.

1927 The Trades Disputes Act makes 'sympathetic strikes' illegal.

1929 Labour is the largest party in the general election and forms a minority administration.

1931 The Labour government breaks up over whether to address the financial crisis with budget cuts. Expelled from Labour, MacDonald stays on as prime minister until 1935 in a coalition with the Conservatives.

1932 The ILP disaffiliates from the Labour Party.

1940 Labour joins Winston Churchill's wartime coalition, with Clement Attlee as deputy prime minister.

1945 Labour wins the July general election by a landslide.

1951 Labour loses the general election despite winning more votes: Churchill returns as Conservative prime minister.

1964 Labour wins the general election after thirteen years of Conservative rule: Labour leader Harold Wilson will serve three terms as premier (1964–66, 1966–70 and 1974–76).

1979 Margaret Thatcher defeats Labour prime minister Jim Callaghan in the general election; Labour suffers further election defeats in 1983, 1987 and 1992.

1995 Tony Blair, the architect of 'New Labour', repeals Clause IV.

1997 Labour returns to government after eighteen years in opposition, defeating John Major's Conservatives in a landslide, and remains in office until losing the 2010 general election.

What this phrase meant in practice was open to interpretation. It could involve the state's nationalization of private assets, or it could involve a 'syndicalist' approach in which various affiliations – whether trade unions, guilds or workers' co-operatives – effectively determined productivity, pay and conditions. All that was certain was that it intended to spell bad news for private enterprise. In the event, nationalization proved to be the favoured method, although the unions were appeased and consulted as part of a corporatist approach to economic planning.

Common ownership was not advanced during Labour's first two brief spells in government, in 1924 and 1929–31, under Ramsay MacDonald. There was neither the parliamentary majority nor the will to push forward the principles of Clause IV. This changed with the massive election victory won by Labour in 1945, after which Clement Attlee's government nationalized the 'commanding heights' of industry – including coal, iron and steel, gas, electricity, telecommunications, aviation, road haulage and the railways. This proved to be the apex of the movement for state control.

An attempt to amend Clause IV was defeated in 1959, but the Labour Left's efforts to nationalize Britain's top twenty-five companies in the 1970s were resisted by the party leadership. Thereafter, the most explicitly socialist commitments were made in the 1983 manifesto, and their overwhelming rejection by the electorate began a process of retreat from this form of state control. Its last rites were symbolically read in 1995 when Tony Blair secured the repeal of Clause IV and its substitution with a more anodyne form of words:

> The Labour Party is a democratic socialist party. It believes that by the strength of our common endeavour we achieve more than we achieve alone, so as to create for each of us the means to realise our true potential and for all of us a community in which power, wealth and opportunity are in the hands of the many, not the few, where the rights we enjoy reflect the duties we owe and where we live together freely, in a spirit of solidarity, tolerance and respect.

1921
THE ANGLO-IRISH TREATY

IRISH HOME RULE AND THE CREATION
OF NORTHERN IRELAND

The 'Irish Question' had been the most bitterly contested issue in British politics for nearly thirty years between 1886 and 1914. The decision of William Ewart Gladstone (1809–98) to advocate self-government for Ireland had split his Liberal Party, prompting a wave of defections. Augmented by leading ex-Liberals, the Conservative Party regarded the issue as so central to its purpose that for most of this period it was known as 'the Unionist Party'. This Unionist alliance defeated Gladstone's Irish home rule bills of 1886 and 1893. After 1910, Herbert Asquith's Liberal government became dependent for its parliamentary majority on the Irish Nationalist MPs and could not prevaricate on the matter indefinitely. With the House of Lords' powers of legislative veto removed by the 1911 Parliament Act, it was finally possible to bring Irish home rule onto the statute books despite the strong hostility of the opposition. The act received the royal assent in September 1914.

It was not, however, put into operation. The First World War had broken out the previous month and – with the support of the Irish Nationalist leader, John Redmond – the decision was taken to delay making the legislation effective until the hostilities were over. This was, of course, based on the assumption that the war would last nowhere near as long as its eventual four-year duration. London hoped that the pause would provide a breathing-space to finalize the details of a late amendment that appeared to give those northern Irish counties of Ulster that had Protestant majorities temporary exclusion from rule by the proposed Dublin Parliament.

Determined that the legislation should apply equally to all of Ireland, the Irish Nationalists opposed giving Ulster special treatment. However, any attempt to coerce the predominantly Protestant North into going in with the predominantly Catholic South seemed certain to result in civil war. In 1912, half a million Ulstermen

Irish Nationalism 1886–1938

1886 The first Irish home rule bill is defeated in the Commons.

1890 Charles Stewart Parnell is cited in a divorce case and forced to resign as leader of the Irish Nationalist MPs.

1893 A second Irish home rule bill passes in the Commons but is defeated in the Lords.

1905 Arthur Griffith founds Sinn Féin ('We Ourselves').

1912 A third home rule bill is introduced. In Ulster, half a million sign the Solemn League and Covenant opposing home rule.

1913 Rival paramilitaries, the Ulster Volunteer Force and the Irish Volunteers (later the Irish Republican Army, or IRA), are formed.

1914 The Curragh 'Mutiny'. The Home Rule Act is passed but suspended for the duration of the First World War.

1916 The 'Easter Rising' in Dublin is suppressed and some of its ringleaders are executed.

1918 The threat of wartime conscription boosts Sinn Féin, which wins most Irish seats in the general election.

1919–21 The Anglo-Irish war pits the IRA against the 'Black and Tans'.

1920 The Government of Ireland Act proposes separate home rule assemblies for Northern Ireland in Belfast and Southern Ireland in Dublin.

1921 The Ulster Unionists win 67 per cent in Northern Ireland's first general election, and Sir James Craig becomes prime minister. The Anglo-Irish Treaty ends the conflict between the British government and Irish Nationalists, but Ireland is partitioned.

1922 The Irish Free State endorses the treaty in a general election. The insurrection by elements of the IRA opposed to the Anglo-Irish Treaty starts a civil war. Sectarian riots break out in Northern Ireland.

1923 Pro-treaty forces win the civil war in the Irish Free State.

1924 The anti-treaty leader, Eamon de Valera, founds Fianna Fáil ('Soldiers of Destiny').

1931 The IRA is declared an illegal organization in the Irish Free State.

1932 De Valera forms a Fianna Fáil government and institutes highly protectionist economic policies.

1937 A new constitution is approved in the Irish Free State, which formally lays claim to Northern Ireland.

1938 Britain hands over its naval bases at Berehaven, Queenstown and Lough Swilly to the Irish Free State.

1949 Ireland formally becomes a republic and leaves the British Commonwealth.

and women had signed a 'Solemn League and Covenant', affirming their loyalty to Britain and making clear they would refuse to recognize an Irish government. It was clear that they intended insurrection from the formation of the paramilitary Ulster Volunteer Force in early 1913 to resist forcible integration into a Dublin-based state. It was armed by well-wishers – many of them British Conservatives – and the trouble-stirring German government. After an officers' 'mutiny' at the Curragh

months from the date hereof.

18.   This instrument shall be submitted forthwith by His
Majesty's Government for the approval of Parliament, and by
the Irish signatories to a meeting summoned for the
purpose of the members elected to sit in the House of
Commons of Southern Ireland, and if approved shall be
ratified by the necessary legislation.

Decr 6ᵗʰ 1921

On behalf of the
British Delegation

D Lloyd George

Austen Chamberlain

Birkenhead.

Winston S. Churchill

L. Worthington-Evans

Hamar Greenwood

Gordon Hewart.

On behalf of the Irish
Delegation

Art Ó Gríobhtha (Arthur Griffith)

Mícheál Ó Coileáin

Riobárd Barton

E S D'Ugan

Seoirse Gabhán uí Dhubhthaigh

camp in 1914, it seemed doubtful whether the British army would obey orders to forcibly put down an attempt by Ulster to stay loyal to Britain. To further inflame an already combustible situation, in late 1913 a rival southern paramilitary force, the Irish Volunteers, had been established with the goal of fighting – if it came to that – to ensure that an All-Ireland government was installed. In this state of affairs it was hard to see a way out of bloodshed, whatever course was pursued.

Rather than await a future round of negotiations when the First World War ended, republican militants took events into their own hands. In April 1916 they launched the Easter Rising in Dublin, which at first drew little popular support. However, the heavy-handed manner of its suppression (fifteen of the Rising's leaders were subsequently executed by firing-squad, while Sir Roger Casement, who had conspired with the Germans, was hanged) brought a wave of sympathy and vehement condemnation of British brutality. Belatedly, London tried to bring forward the date of introducing Irish home rule, only to find negotiations breaking down over whether Ulster would be temporarily or indefinitely excluded from it. Mistrust of British intentions, combined with a fear that conscription might be introduced in Ireland, undermined constitutional groups and, in the South, delivered an overwhelming victory in the 1918 general election for the uncompromising republicans of Sinn Féin.

Within weeks, Sinn Féin representatives met in Dublin where they issued a unilateral declaration of independence from the United Kingdom and convened themselves as the parliament of the Irish Republic – the Dáil Éireann. London treated this as a *coup d'état* and refused to recognize the new body. The Dáil claimed sovereignty over the North as well, despite the reality that – having already resolved to stay out of Irish self-government – Ulster's Protestant majority were even less keen to have anything to do with Sinn Féin-led Irish independence. The 1914 legislation was thus, from both sides of the divide, a dead letter.

Coming to terms with this reality, the prime minister, David Lloyd George, tried to wrest back the initiative with a new settlement, the 1920 Government of Ireland Act. Passed by Westminster, the act established two home-rule assemblies – one for Northern Ireland, meeting in Belfast; and one for southern Ireland, meeting in Dublin. The Northern Irish Parliament was successfully instituted at Stormont in the outskirts of Belfast the following year, but few in the South acknowledged the legitimacy of Lloyd George's Dublin Parliament. The Sinn Féin-controlled assembly, the Dáil Éireann, and its president, Eamon de Valera, continued to act as the *de facto* power in the south.

Opposite: The signatories of the Anglo-Irish Treaty. For the British delegation: David Lloyd George (prime minister), Austen Chamberlain (Lord Privy Seal and Conservative Party leader), Lord Birkenhead (lord chancellor), Winston Churchill (colonial secretary), Laming Worthington-Evans (war secretary), Hamar Greenwood (chief secretary for Ireland), Gordon Hewart (attorney general). For the Irish delegation (who signed in Irish): Arthur Griffith (foreign secretary), Michael Collins (finance secretary), Robert Barton (economic affairs secretary), Eamonn Duggan (chief liaison officer) and George Gavan Duffy (Sinn Féin MP).

Rather than concede that the Dáil was an established fact, London continued to treat it as a revolutionary tribunal. Under the charismatic leadership of a former post-office clerk and veteran of the 1916 Rising, Michael Collins (1890–1922), the Irish Volunteers were turned into an effective guerrilla force, the Irish Republican Army (IRA), which, in 1919, began hit-and-run terror attacks on individuals and institutions that remained loyal to the British Crown. The latter responded by meeting terror with terror, its instruments of restoring order – the paramilitary 'Black and Tans' and the Auxiliary Division of the Royal Irish Constabulary – being as indiscriminately violent as the IRA. By 1921, the IRA had killed about 500 police and 200 soldiers, while around 750 real or suspected republicans had died. Ireland was, to all intents and purposes, in a state of war.

When a truce was signed on 8 July 1921, it suited both sides. Michael Collins later told Hamar Greenwood, the chief secretary for Ireland, 'You had us dead beat. We could not have lasted another three weeks.' On the other hand, the British forces were effectively fighting for an unsustainable cause. Formal negotiations began in London in October. The Irish delegation was led by Collins and Arthur Griffith, Sinn Féin's founder, and the British team included Lloyd George, Winston Churchill, Lord Birkenhead and the Conservative Party leader Austen Chamberlain. A deal was struck early on 6 December. Southern Ireland would gain virtual independence as the Irish Free State (this represented far more autonomy than the 1914 Home Rule Act had offered). Nonetheless, it would remain in the British Commonwealth with dominion status similar to that enjoyed by Canada.

This created a debate about whether members of the Dáil should therefore swear an oath of allegiance to the king. In the end it was agreed that they would do so, but only subordinately within the context of the common citizenship that dominion status entailed. Their primary oath would be to uphold the Irish Constitution. The treaty also guaranteed to the Royal Navy the continued use of three deep-water Irish ports. Crucially, the new Irish Free State would not have sovereignty over six counties of Ulster, which retained the right to remain within the United Kingdom.

The Irish delegates may have accepted partition because Lloyd George hinted to them that a future boundary commission might make the northern province effectively unsustainable, forcing it to join the South. In the event, no such alteration took place. The best reason for signing though, was the grimness of the alternative: a resumption of hostilities.

As the delegates' names were added to the treaty, Lord Birkenhead quipped that he might be signing his political death warrant. Michael Collins's riposte

was, 'I may have signed my actual death warrant.' This proved prophetic. The Dáil narrowly approved the treaty by 64 votes to 57 and a general election in the South voted 72 per cent in favour of pro-treaty parties. Having stayed away from the negotiations, de Valera declared them a betrayal and denounced the partition of the island. His wing of the IRA, the 'Irregulars', went to war with the new Irish Free State forces. Collins was ambushed and shot dead by anti-treaty IRA gunmen in his home county of Cork in August 1922.

Michael Collins leaving 10 Downing Street during the peace talks, October 1921.

Eventually, in May 1923, Irish government forces succeeded in suppressing de Valera's insurrection. However, as leader of a new republican party, Fianna Fáil, de Valera would be elected to power in 1932, proceeding to guide his nation's fortunes until 1959, and thereafter, in the more honorific role as president until 1973. Britain returned the 'treaty ports' in 1938, and the Irish Free State, Gaelicized as Éire, was effectively a republic from 1937. It was formally declared as such in 1949 when it left the British Commonwealth. Its constitution continued to lay claim to the 'six counties' of Northern Ireland until 1999.

c.1925

SCHOOL MAP OF
THE BRITISH EMPIRE

IMPERIAL PRIDE, TRADE AND KINSHIP

A map of the British Empire is depicted in the fourth plate section.

Although later generations came to associate the zenith of the British Empire with the reign of Queen Victoria, it actually reached its greatest extent in the 1920s, twenty years before its rapid dissolution began.

During that period, the Union Jack fluttered over a quarter of the world's population and landmass. The First World War had brought about the collapse of the Russian, German, Austro-Hungarian and Ottoman empires, but Britain's had endured. Indeed, Britain found herself taking responsibility for additional colonies that had formerly been ruled by the vanquished. The League of Nations (the predecessor to the United Nations) approved Britain's mandate to run ex-German colonies in Africa, while in the Middle East Britain took over large parts of the disintegrated Ottoman Empire, gaining mandates for Palestine, Transjordan and Iraq.

It would have been impossible for a country the size of the United Kingdom, especially after the financial and material strain of the First World War, to have run all of this vast empire directly. While Britain was the administrative authority in many colonies, by the early decades of the twentieth century the term 'empire' was innappropriate for the majority of the most important countries.

Dominion status conferred home rule to Canada, Newfoundland, South Africa, Australia, New Zealand and the Irish Free State. In most areas of domestic policy these countries ran their own affairs. In foreign policy the relationship was more complicated, not least because it was entwined with the notion of a co-ordinated 'imperial defence'. However, each of the dominions was represented as a separate entity in the League of Nations and could not be forced to declare war on Britain's enemies without the approval of its own government.

India remained, in the well-worn phrase, the 'jewel in the crown'. Nonetheless, even there, British rule was not quite as absolute as the pink colouring on the map

of the world implied. The fact that a mere 500 Britons staffed a civil service responsible for 320 million inhabitants might be considered a testament to bureaucratic efficiency, even if it was as much a sign of light administration. Far from intervening in every aspect of Indian life, no social legislation was imposed on the subcontinent between the revision of the penal code in 1861 and the Age of Consent Act in 1921. Although ultimately what underpinned the Raj was force, this still comprised only 60,000 British soldiers. Indeed, almost half the land area of India was not even run by the British but rather by the maharajahs, nizams and nawabs of its more than 500 princely states. They pledged loyalty to the British Crown as the paramount power and, in return for not making trouble, were mostly left to their own devices.

There was a contradiction at the heart of Britain's relations with her dominions and colonies, in that a country that, until 1932, pursued policies of free trade with foreign countries continued to permit its imperial possessions to slap tariffs on British trade. For instance, by 1931 'British' India's general tariff on importing British goods reached 25 per cent. Dominion governments also protected their home market against the 'mother country' and although negotiated reductions were made in 1932, the Imperialists' goal of Empire Free Trade still remained elusive when the Second World War broke out seven years later.

Yet the worth of the empire – at any rate to Britain – was never more apparent than in 1939 when (apart from the Irish Free State) even those of its members best able to exercise

THE HIGH NOON OF EMPIRE

1899–1902 Britain prevails in the Second Boer War in South Africa.

1901 The Commonwealth of Australia is formed. The protectorate of Nigeria is established.

1904 Empire Day (24 May: Queen Victoria's birthday) is first celebrated.

1906 The Muslim League is founded in Bengal.

1907 New Zealand is granted dominion status.

1910 The Union of South Africa is created, with dominion status.

1911 The 'Coronation Durbar' in New Delhi celebrates the coronation of George V as India's emperor.

1912 The African National Congress (initially the South African Native National Congress) is founded in Bloemfontein to campaign for black rights.

1914 Egypt is formally made a British protectorate. Volunteers from across the empire rally to Britain's war effort.

1919 In India's Amritsar Massacre, troops fire on unarmed protestors killing 379.

1920 Britain is awarded the mandate to administer Palestine. British East Africa becomes the colony of Kenya.

1922 Egypt is given independence. The Palestine Mandate incorporates Transjordan.

1925 Cyprus becomes a British colony.

1930 Mohandas K. Gandhi steps up his civil disobedience campaign in India.

1931 The Statute of Westminster establishes the legislative equality and independence of all six dominions (Australia, Canada, the Irish Free State, New Zealand, South Africa and Newfoundland).

1939–45 The dominions volunteer to fight alongside Britain during the Second World War.

1947 Indian independence from Britain marks the start of Britain's withdrawal from empire.

free will chose to rally to Britain's side. In 1940, with the British Expeditionary Force trapped and awaiting rescue at Dunkirk, the defence of a large sector of southern England was in the hands of Canadian soldiers. By the time the conflict was won, the Canadian government had effectively donated to Britain $4 billion in money and supplies. India supplied the largest volunteer army in history. Even in the darkest days of 1940–1, Britain was never quite 'alone' when she had a vast empire of countries transporting men and resources.

It was the so-called 'white dominions' that were the most popular empire destination for generations of British emigrants. Funds were on offer between the 1920s and 1970s to help populate them (and keep them white). Well-intentioned – if sometimes misguided – philanthropy also dispatched orphans and the underprivileged to what was hoped would be a better life in the sun than in the slums of industrial Britain. Nonetheless, it is telling how little this huge migration was directed by officialdom.

That fact itself is one indicator of the considerable pull that the empire exerted on the imagination despite the criticisms made by some, particularly on the Left, of both its principles and the reality. Popular books and films helped keep alive faith in its moral purpose, whether as a bulwark of democracy (in places where it *was* democratic), as a force for extending law and order, as an environment for promoting missionary work and social improvements, or merely as a means of preventing other countries seizing the same territories and claiming the glory for themselves.

Rudyard Kipling's stories of India enjoyed a wide audience, particularly among children with a sense of adventure. Special events also reinforced the message. Empire Day was launched in 1904 by the Anglo-Irishman Lord Meath, and it continued to be observed, principally by schoolchildren (who got the afternoon off), throughout the inter-war period. With its pavilions and purpose-built Wembley Stadium, the Empire Exhibition of 1924–5 proved even more popular than the Great Exhibition of 1851, drawing a record 27 million visitors. A Canadian track and field manager, Melville Marks 'Bobby' Robinson, organized the first Empire (subsequently Commonwealth) Games in Hamilton, Canada, in 1930.

The most formative influence on young minds, however, must surely have been the map of the world with the imperial possessions coloured in pink. Vast numbers were produced during the period, whether by educational publishers or distributed as special offers to newspaper readers. They were more than an indispensable teaching aid. Almost standard classroom decoration, they were the ever-present focal point on which generations of wandering thoughts must daily have fixed.

1927

THE ROYAL CHARTER
OF THE BBC

BRITAIN'S NATIONAL BROADCASTING CORPORATION

The BBC was the world's first regular television broadcaster and is still the world's largest broadcasting corporation. Even aside from its international reach and reputation, its influence on the knowledge, culture and shared experiences of the British people is beyond calculation.

It started in 1922 as a private enterprise, the British Broadcasting Company Ltd. Its major shareholders were six wireless-set manufacturers, including the business of the pioneer of the technology, Guglielmo Marconi, and British subsidiaries of the American-owned General Electric Company. They hoped to sell more sets, a prospect likely to be achieved only if radio broadcasting was allowed to reach a substantial audience.

Regulating wireless telephony was the responsibility of the Post Office. It wanted to avoid the chaotic race to start up radio stations that had just occurred in the United States, where the result was congestion and interference on the airwaves, low-quality programme-making and bankrupt companies. As favouring the BBC seemed the perfect means of avoiding this outcome, the Post Office granted it the exclusive right to construct transmitters across the country from which to broadcast. It would receive half of the 10-shilling (50p) fee that the Post Office charged listeners for their annual receiving licences.

The BBC's general manager, John Reith (1889–1971), had no background in broadcasting but demonstrated an unremitting determination to use what he described as 'the brute force of monopoly' as a power for moral and cultural enlightenment. He envisaged the BBC as bringing to homes across the country 'all that was best in every department of human knowledge, endeavour and achievement' in its mission to inform, educate and entertain. His first great test came in 1926 when the General Strike brought much of the country to a standstill

From the BBC's Royal Charter, 1927

Whereas it has been made to appear to Us that more than two million persons in Our Kingdom of Great Britain and Northern Ireland have applied for and taken out Licences to instal and work apparatus for . . . the purpose of receiving Broadcast programmes and whereas in view of the widespread interest which is thereby shown to be taken by Our People in the Broadcasting Service and of the great value of the Service as a means of education and entertainment, We deem it desirable that the Service should be developed and exploited to the best advantage and in the national interest . . . [by] a Corporation charged with these duties . . . [and] created by the exercise of Our Royal Prerogative.

and shut down the traditional Fleet Street newspapers. Reith resisted the efforts of some Cabinet ministers to commandeer the BBC for government propaganda, in the process enhancing the company's reputation for independence.

At the same time, Parliament was considering the future of the medium. The Crawford Committee recommended revoking the BBC's licence and transforming the company into a public corporation, guided by the responsibility to be a 'Trustee for the national interest'. Stanley Baldwin's Conservative government endorsed the Crawford Committee's proposals, and on New Year's Day 1927 the BBC was re-established by royal charter as the British Broadcasting Corporation. To avoid commercial advertising, the licence-fee model of funding was retained. There were already over 2 million receiving licences and it was clear millions more were on the way.

The new corporation was the state broadcaster, enjoying a monopoly of all output, with a board of governors nominated by the government. Nevertheless, it had operational and editorial independence. To minimize the risk that it would destroy competition from other forms of media or even peddle an agenda of its own, its news output was at first strictly limited. It was not permitted to broadcast news bulletins until 7 p.m. in order to avoid detracting from the newspaper market, the bulletins being strict summaries of news compiled from the press agencies. The emphasis was on avoiding contentious discussion and any analysis of current affairs.

Gradually, these restrictions were pruned down and lifted, although they shaped an approach that, during the 1930s, tended to shy away from the articulation of

unorthodox views. Winston Churchill was among those who complained that he was not given airtime to voice his opposition to the government's appeasement policy. Critics detected a longer legacy from this period that was evident in the corporation's deferential tone and failure to take risks. It was not until the 1960s that this broke down when the BBC was given a new direction by a modernizing director-general, Hugh Carleton Greene (the brother of the writer Graham Greene). The broadening appeal was not to everyone's taste – the 'Clean-Up TV' campaigner, Mary Whitehouse, concluded that Greene was 'more than anybody else . . . responsible for the moral collapse in this country'.

By then, the BBC was as much a television as a radio broadcaster. The prospect of television was loathed by Reith, a dour Presbyterian Scot who made even his radio announcers read the news in black tie. Nonetheless, it was during his tenure as director-general between 1927 and 1938 that the corporation adopted the medium. At 3 p.m. on 2 November 1936, Leslie Mitchell announced live to camera, 'This is the BBC Television Station at Alexandra Palace,' and Britain's fascination with 'telly' began.

Sir John Reith, who took the BBC from a company to a corporation and served as its first director general from 1927 to 1938.

The first TV programmes were broadcast using two different formats one after the other, John Logie Baird's mechanical electronic system, followed by the wholly electronic Marconi–EMI technology. The latter's better picture quality and scope for future improvement quickly won the day. Because of the cost and limitations of early television sets the audience was small and based in the South-East, where 20,000 sets could receive the BBC's twenty hours a week of programmes in 1939 until the service was shut down for the war. Broadcasting resumed in 1946, and its popularity was hugely boosted by its coverage of Queen Elizabeth II's coronation in 1953.

Since then, the BBC's charter has been renewed and it has remained a public service broadcaster, funded by the licence fee. Despite the best efforts of the welfare state advocate, William Beveridge, its monopoly proved indefensible. In 1954, Winston Churchill's government secured the passage of the Television Act.

SIX DECADES OF HIT TV: THE MOST WATCHED PROGRAMMES

		Channel	Date	Audience (in millions)
1950s				
1	*Wagon Train*	ITV	30/11/1959	13.63
2	*Take Your Pick*	ITV	11/12/1959	13.16
3	*Sunday Night at the London Palladium*	ITV	6/12/1959	13.08
4	*Armchair Theatre: Suspicious Mind*	ITV	22/11/1959	12.74
5	*The Army Game*	ITV	11/12/1959	12.60
1960s				
1	The World Cup Final, 1966	BBC1	30/7/1966	32.30
2	*The Royal Family*	BBC1 & ITV	21/6/1969 (BBC1)/ 28/6/1969 (ITV)	30.69
3	*Royal Variety Performance*, 1965	ITV	14/11/1965	24.20
4	News [John F. Kennedy Assassination]	BBC & ITV	22/11/1963	24.15
5	*Miss World*	BBC1	19/11/1967	23.76
1970s				
1	Apollo 13 splashdown	BBC1 & ITV	17/4/1970	28.60
2	FA Cup final replay: Chelsea v. Leeds United	BBC1 & ITV	29/4/1970	28.49
3	Princess Anne's wedding	BBC1 & ITV	14/11/1973	27.60
4	*To the Manor Born*	BBC1	11/11/1979	23.95
5	*Miss World*	BBC1	20/11/1970	23.76
1980s				
1	*EastEnders*	BBC1	25/12/1986	30.15
2	Royal wedding ceremony	BBC1 & ITV	29/7/1981	28.40
3	*Coronation Street*	ITV	19/3/1989	26.93
4	*Dallas*	BBC1	22/11/1980	21.60
5	*To the Manor Born*	BBC1	9/11/1980	21.55
1990s				
1	Funeral of Princess Diana	BBC1 & ITV	6/9/1997	32.10
2	*Only Fools and Horses*	BBC1	29/12/1996	24.35
3	*EastEnders*	BBC1	2/1/1992	24.30
4	Torvill and Dean: Winter Olympics, 1994	BBC1	21/2/1994	23.95
5	World Cup, 1998: England v. Argentina	ITV	30/6/1998	23.78
2000s				
1	*Only Fools and Horses*	BBC1	25/12/2001	21.34
2	Euro 2004: England v. Portugal	BBC1	24/6/2004	20.66
3	*EastEnders*	BBC1	5/4/2001	20.05
4	*Coronation Street*	ITV	24/2/2003	19.40
5	World Cup, 2006: England v. Sweden	BBC1	20/6/2006	18.50

(Source: BFI)

It permitted commercial television, with various regional companies – operating under fixed-term franchises – producing their own material under the umbrella of Independent Television (ITV) and its regulator, the Independent Television Authority. The development was initially opposed by the Labour Party, which believed greater choice would diminish quality. The viewing preferences of Labour's core voters forced an urgent rethink.

The BBC responded with more channels, launching BBC2 in 1964 (which was the first to broadcast in colour, in 1967) and rearranging its radio output into four (later five) national stations plus various regional stations. Further independent competition came from Channel 4 in 1982 and Sky satellite television in 1989. With the advent of the internet, the 1990s brought a new threat that the corporation decided to embrace, first with its own news website and, in 2007, by streaming its programmes online. Whether its unique funding formula will survive indefinitely remains a matter for debate, although remarkably the BBC's listening and viewing figures have held up surprisingly well, despite the swelling number of competing channels and alternative entertainments on offer. Its modern embrace of popular tastes and periodic vulgarity would have horrified Reith, yet it has still broadly tried to honour his guiding principles – if not his style – to inform, educate and entertain.

1936
EDWARD VIII'S INSTRUMENT
OF ABDICATION

THE ABDICATION CRISIS

There was a widespread fear that the monarchy might not survive the abdication of King Edward VIII. Despite all the dramas of peace and war over the centuries, the prime minister, Stanley Baldwin, thought it appropriate to tell the House of Commons: 'No more grave message has ever been received in Parliament.'

In the seventeenth century Charles I had been executed and his son, James II, had fled into exile. Thereafter, Britain had experienced almost 250 years of constitutional monarchy, its kings and queens having died while still in office. The very idea that Edward VIII (1894–1972) should throw his throne away – within a year of ascending to it – for the love of Mrs Wallis Simpson (1896–1986), a woman who was an acquired taste, dumbfounded many. As Edward's mother, Queen Mary, later told him, it remained 'inconceivable to those who had made such sacrifices during the war that you, as their King, refused a lesser sacrifice'.

Having succeeded his widely respected father, George V, in January 1936, Edward appeared to be an affable, handsome, modern-minded monarch. Yet behind the scenes, his flippant attitude to his duties and his growing attachment to Wallis Simpson caused consternation among those more closely acquainted with him. The general public knew nothing of this until 1 December, when the bishop of Bradford chose the occasion of a diocesan conference to lament the king's failure to recognize that he was in need of God's grace. Reluctant to engage in self-imposed censorship any longer, the press regarded this as the moment to break a story in Britain that was already filling the column inches of the foreign press.

Edward hoped he could marry his twice-married American lover and retain his throne. The Church of England, of which he was supreme governor, forbade

INSTRUMENT OF ABDICATION

I, Edward the Eighth, of Great Britain, Ireland, and the British Dominions beyond the Seas, King, Emperor of India, do hereby declare My irrevocable determination to renounce the Throne for Myself and for My descendants, and My desire that effect should be given to this Instrument of Abdication immediately.

In token whereof I have hereunto set My hand this tenth day of December, nineteen hundred and thirty six, in the presence of the witnesses whose signatures are subscribed.

SIGNED AT
FORT BELVEDERE
IN THE PRESENCE
OF

The Instrument of Abdication signed by Edward VIII and his three brothers – Albert, duke of York (thereafter George VI), Henry, duke of Gloucester and George, duke of Kent.

THE LIFE OF EDWARD VIII

1894 Edward Albert Christian George Andrew Patrick David is born in Richmond, Surrey.

1907 Aged thirteen, Edward is sent to naval college.

1910 Death of Edward VII and accession of George V.

1911 Edward is invested as Prince of Wales.

1912 Edward studies – briefly – at Magdalen College, Oxford.

1919–35 Edward undertakes sixteen tours to various parts of the British Empire.

1933 Edward begins his affair with Wallis Simpson, an American divorcee.

1936 Edward ascends the throne only to abdicate it when the government effectively prevents him from marrying Wallis and remaining king.

1937 Accorded the titles duke and duchess of Windsor, Edward and Wallis marry at the Château de Candé in France. They go on to tour Germany as guests of Hitler.

1940 After undistinguished and potentially compromising war service, the duke (with the duchess) flees France for Lisbon. The duke is made Governor of the Bahamas for the duration of the war, largely to get him out of the way of trouble.

1945 The duke and duchess settle in Paris, supported by a government allowance and an exemption from French income tax.

1951 The duke's largely ghost-written autobiography, *A King's Story*, is published.

1972 The duke of Windsor dies of cancer and is buried with other members of the royal family at Frogmore, Windsor. The duchess becomes increasingly reclusive and bed-ridden.

1986 The duchess of Windsor dies at her home in the Bois de Boulogne, Paris.

a church wedding to divorced persons whose former spouses were still alive. Inconveniently in Mrs Simpson's case, she had *two* living ex-husbands. It was a difficult situation, which, whatever the state of popular opinion, might have been smoothed if only the Church and the political Establishment had wished to do their monarch's bidding. Instead, they saw little in his private demeanour or public posturing to justify conniving in so controversial an action. The possibility that he might contract a morganatic marriage – whereby Wallis Simpson would become his wife but not queen and any children would not succeed to the throne – was effectively ruled out by Baldwin, who assured his king that Parliament would not agree to it.

As prime minister, Baldwin was the decisive figure throughout the crisis. He tightened the screw by insisting that the government would resign if the king persisted with his marriage plans. Baldwin had even taken the precaution of securing the Labour opposition's word that it would refuse to form a government in this eventuality. Alternative politicians lacked either the credibility or a parliamentary majority to carry out the king's wishes. If Edward did not back down, his realm would have no functioning government.

He pleaded for time, but Baldwin insisted on a speedy decision in order to prevent the country becoming divided. His Majesty's own government refused him permission to broadcast directly to his people. Outmanoeuvred, he realized that further prevarication was useless and chose love over duty.

Edward signed the Instrument of Abdication on 10 December. His brothers also appended their signatures to it, including his successor, Prince Albert, duke

of York, who signed under his first name, but who reigned as George VI. An Act of Parliament was rushed through Westminster the following day, giving the abdication document legal effect. Only with the deed done was Edward permitted to broadcast a farewell to his former subjects and to pledge allegiance to his brother, who, as Edward rather pointedly observed, enjoyed the 'matchless blessing enjoyed by so many of you and not bestowed on me – a happy home with his wife and children'.

Indeed, the new king's family, in particular his wife, Queen Elizabeth, and elder daughter, the Princess Elizabeth, were to prove a great support to George VI, a shy, stuttering man who had never wanted his brother's throne but was determined to overcome his limitations in order to do the duty Edward shirked. Created duke of Windsor, Edward married Wallis in June 1937 in a private ceremony, attended by only a few friends, in France, where they were to spend much of the rest of their lives. A perspective on their subsequent level of contentment was eventually offered by Wallis when she confided: 'You have no idea how hard it is to live out a great romance.'

Nothing in Edward's subsequent conduct contradicted the suggestion that the Instrument of Abdication was anything other than a godsend for the monarchy and the British realm.

1936

R. J. MITCHELL'S DESIGN FOR THE SUPERMARINE SPITFIRE, MARK I

A CLASSIC DESIGN THAT HELPED SAVE BRITAIN FROM INVASION IN 1940

No other British airplane, whether civil or military, has remained as deeply in the nation's affection – or gratitude – as the Spitfire. In 1940, it played a crucial role in thwarting the Luftwaffe during the Battle of Britain. Of course, it did not perform this task alone. Aside from the extraordinary bravery of the pilots and the dedication of their ground crews, the honour for winning the Battle of Britain must also be shared with radar and another fighter plane, the Hawker Hurricane. Nonetheless, there was something about the Spitfire that captivated those who flew it as well as catching the imagination of the wider population. It was a delight to fly and a joy to behold.

Even from far off, it was distinctive from the other aircraft circling the skies of southern England during the summer of 1940, particularly in the unusual elliptical shape of its wings. Almost everything about the Spitfire, from its slim nose to its tail, exemplified an aerodynamic appearance. Nor did it merely look good: it had incredible manoeuvrability, with an ability to soar, plunge and make tight turns that often gave it the upper hand in dogfights.

The fact that it ever went into mass production was no small miracle in itself. It had been widely assumed by both the RAF and the Air Ministry in the interwar period that fighters could do little to deter mass attacks by bombers. This attitude, summed up in the oft-repeated statement of ultimate fatalism, 'The bomber will always get through', reinforced the thinking of those who believed that the only means to counter the saturation bombing of Britain was to have the power to threaten comparable retaliation on the enemy. Consequently, priority was given

to the construction of bombers. It was against this orthodoxy that the Supermarine Aviation Works, based in Southampton, persevered with designs for fighter aircraft.

The government had pulled out of funding Supermarine's S 6B flying boat in 1931. It was only because Lady Houston wrote a £100,000 cheque to overcome what she condemned as the parsimony of the prime minister, Ramsay MacDonald, that the S 6B proceeded to win the much-coveted Schneider Trophy later that year and break the world air-speed record. A remarkable monoplane at a time when aircraft were still mostly canvas-covered biplanes, it demonstrated the visionary talent of its designer, R. J. Mitchell. Impressed by Mitchell, in December 1934 the Air Ministry awarded Supermarine £10,000 (almost half the initial cost) towards funding the prototype of a high-powered fighter that retained many of the S 6B's features. The resulting K5054, of which only one was constructed, made its maiden flight in 1936. The Air Ministry promptly ordered 310 of what became the Spitfire Mark I for the RAF.

The Spitfire got its chance because of the fundamental shift in RAF policy. The advocates of change were chief of the air staff, Sir Edward Ellington, and Air Chief Marshal Sir Hugh Dowding. They wanted to see resources switched from bombers to fighters and, crucially, Dowding persuaded the air secretary, Viscount Swinton. Becoming prime minister in 1937, Neville Chamberlain also favoured prioritizing

THE MARKS OF A LEGEND

The dates refer to the first and final placing of orders for production of a particular mark. (PR stands for photo reconnaissance.)

1934	Prototype K5054
June 1936–August 1940	Mk I
April 1939	Mk II; Mk III (order cancelled before production); Mk IV (prototype)
August 1939–October 1941	Mk V
August 1939	Mk VI
August 1940	PR IV
October 1940	Mk VII
January 1942	Mk VIII
April 1942	PR VIII
October 1941–April 1944	Mk IX
August 1941	Mk XI
August 1941	Mk XII
March 1942	F 21
April 1942	F 20 (test flight)
May 1942	Mk X
May 1942	Mk XVI
June 1942	F 22
July 1942–February 1945	Mk XIV
August 1942	Mk XIII
December 1942	Mk XVIII
June 1943	Mk XIX
June 1942–November 1945	F 24
October 1943	F 23

an essentially defensive rather than offensive strategy. With these three influential backers, the newly formed Fighter Command began to take shape, helped by vastly improved financing. In 1935, the air force's £17 million budget had been just half

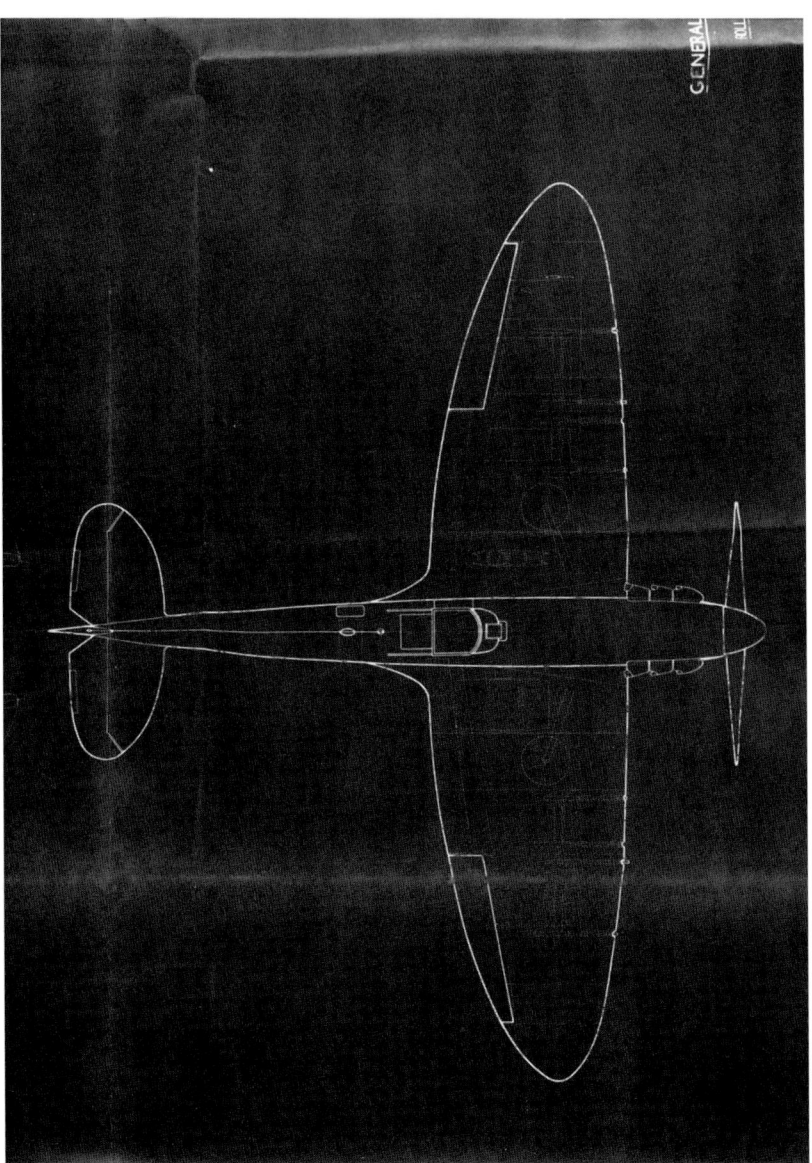

R. J. Mitchell's original chalk drawing for the Spitfire. Even at the prototype stage, the key aspects of the aircraft's aerodynamic elegance and elliptical wing design were well developed.

that spent on the army and a quarter that of the navy. By 1939, prompted largely by the threat of the expanding Luftwaffe, its budget had risen to £133 million, more than either of the other two armed services.

The Spitfire's designer, Reginald Joseph Mitchell, had been born near Stoke-on-Trent in 1895, eight years before the Wright brothers made the world's first powered flight. While working as an apprentice at a local locomotive-building firm, he spent his evenings at night school learning engineering, mechanics and advanced mathematics. In 1917 he joined the Supermarine company, quickly

becoming its chief engineer, and he continued in this position after the company was bought by Vickers. Unlike many aircraft designers, in 1934 he even learned to fly.

Mitchell wanted to call the plane that would become a legend the 'Shrew'. When told that the Air Ministry had instead decided upon 'Spitfire', he grumbled, 'It's the sort of bloody silly name they would give it.' In fact, the brilliantly conceived moniker was the suggestion of Sir Robert McClean, the chairman of Vickers – 'Spitfire' being the affectionate nickname he gave his hot-tempered daughter, Anna. It had an Elizabethan/Jacobean provenance: Shakespeare had used the phrase in *King Lear*, 'Rumble thy bellyful! Spit, fire! spout, rain!' (However, Katharine Hepburn may have helped give the word more contemporary resonance by starring in a Hollywood film entitled *Spitfire* in 1934; it had also been the name of several Royal Navy ships.)

The first of the Mark I Spitfires entered the RAF's service in August 1938. Alas, its creator was not there to see his vision take flight. Mitchell had been fighting his own personal battle since being diagnosed with bowel cancer in 1933 and died on 11 June 1937, aged just forty-two. Despite the pain of his illness, he had stuck to his task until the end and, after his death, his chief draughtsman, Joseph Smith, carried through his design, making a series of small but successful modifications. The major drawback was that the Spitfire, with its hand-fabricated aluminium fuselage, was slower to produce than other contemporary fighters, including the wooden-framed Hawker Hurricane. Supermarine and its subcontractors struggled to make it in sufficient numbers. By the outbreak of war in September 1939, only 187 were in full service with their squadrons.

Fortunately, the feared strike by the Luftwaffe did not come until the summer of 1940, by which time Fighter Command was able to defend the country with nineteen Spitfire and twenty-five Hurricane squadrons. Both aircraft drew their strength from a 12-cylinder piston-powered Rolls-Royce Merlin engine. The Spitfire's armament consisted of eight rapid-firing 0.303 inch Browning machine-guns in its wings. (During the Battle of Britain, the most experienced Spitfire squadron, No. 19, was temporarily fitted with cannon, but they tended to jam.) The Mark I was twenty-nine feet twelve inches long, with a wingspan of thirty-six feet ten inches and could fly at a maximum speed of 362 mph (at 18,500 feet). As one Battle of Britain fighter ace, Adolph 'Sailor' Malan, put it, 'She was a perfect lady. She had no vices. She was beautifully positive. You could dive till your eyes were popping out of your head … she would still answer to a touch.' Pilots of the

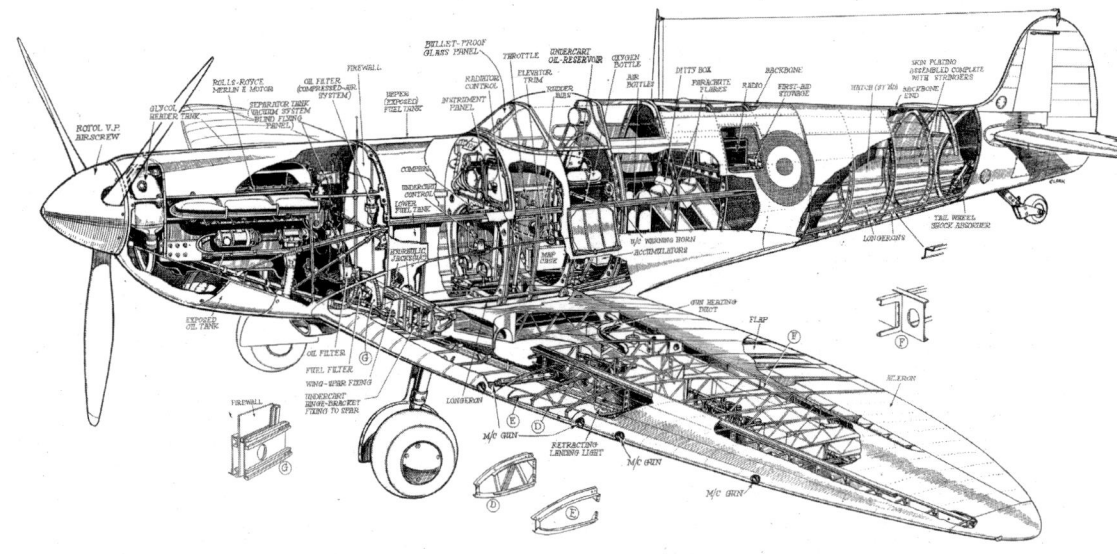

A cutaway drawing of the Spitfire Mk I published in The Aeroplane *on 12 April 1940.*

Luftwaffe's premier fighter, the Messerschmitt Me (or Bf) 109, developed a healthy respect for Mitchell's aircraft.

Of the forty-six different marks and designations produced, the Mark V and Mark IX were the most widely flown. Successive modifications made the Spitfire progressively heavier, faster, and more potently armed, with two 20mm cannons (teething problems now solved) replacing four of the machine guns. By 1943, the Merlin engine had been replaced by the even more powerful Rolls-Royce Griffon, which took the plane to speeds of 454 mph at 26,000 feet. During the course of the conflict, the fighter was deployed in almost every theatre of war. By the time the last Spitfire was completed in 1947, over 20,000 had been built, more than any other RAF fighter plane. Over forty still survive in flying condition.

The last of the Spitfires ceased regular service with the RAF following operational missions in Malaya, in 1954. By that year the Lightning, a supersonic jet fighter, was in development. Yet the passing of the propeller age saw no diminution in the Spitfire's place in the collective consciousness. Even those with no interest in aeronautics recalled her role flown by 'the Few' in her country's 'Finest Hour'. All these years on, who does not still associate the very words 'British freedom' with the soaring image of a lone Spitfire tilting its beautifully crafted wings in acknowledgement?

1938

HITLER AND CHAMBERLAIN'S NOTE: THE MUNICH PACT

THE APPEASEMENT OF NAZI GERMANY

By the early 1930s, Britain's sense of relief at having been on the winning side in the Great War had been swamped by a solemn recognition of the scale of sacrifice involved. Economic depression and the rise of fascism in Europe reinforced the feeling of futility. Amid a growing mood of anti-militarism, many Britons, especially on the Left, looked to the League of Nations (the forerunner to the United Nations) to replace old balance-of-power politics with a 'collective security' approach to problems.

The revulsion at the prospect of rearmament and a dislike of traditional 'sabre-rattling' made the British government's appeasement of Adolf Hitler's regime both possible and, until late in the day, popular. Diplomatic measures to restrict German aggression had been framed by the 1919 Treaty of Versailles, but by the mid-1930s the agreement was widely criticized as one of the causes of Germany's lurch into fascism. Neither Britain nor France chose to uphold the treaty's clauses – not when Hitler remilitarized the Rhineland in March 1936, nor when he annexed Austria two years later. The newsreels showing jubilant crowds welcoming the German army into these areas effectively blunted claims that Hitler's actions lacked the popular support of the very groups they affected.

Hitler's efforts to annex the Sudetenland – the German-speaking region of Czechoslovakia – was far more contentious. Unlike London, Paris had an agreement with Prague to defend the territorial integrity of Czechoslovakia. Although the Sudetenland's German-speaking majority appeared to welcome German annexation, permitting the redrawing of the boundary would effectively make the remaining Czechoslovak state strategically vulnerable should Hitler threaten it at a later date.

Neville Chamberlain (1869–1940), who had been prime minister since May 1937, was determined to take the diplomatic lead in order to permit the transferral

We, the German Führer and Chancellor and the
British Prime Minister, have had a further
meeting today and are agreed in recognising that
the question of Anglo-German relations is of the
first importance for the two countries and for
Europe.

We regard the agreement signed last night
and the Anglo-German Naval Agreement as symbolic
of the desire of our two peoples never to go to
war with one another again.

We are resolved that the method of
consultation shall be the method adopted to deal
with any other questions that may concern our two
countries, and we are determined to continue our
efforts to remove possible sources of difference
and thus to contribute to assure the peace of
Europe.

Neville Chamberlain

September 30, 1938.

of the Sudetenland to Germany in an orderly and peaceful manner that did not provoke Franco-German, and possibly European-wide, war. He flew to Germany to negotiate directly with Hitler, whose stated intention was to invade the Sudetenland regardless of the consequences. Chamberlain thought his efforts had failed, until, on 28 September 1938 – with Hitler's troops poised to cross the Czech border – he was summoned to a conference the following day at Munich. There, he met Hitler, the French prime minister Edouard Daladier, and the Italian fascist leader Benito Mussolini. Together, they agreed that Germany could annex the Sudetenland without fear of retaliation. Deserted by her allies (and not even invited to the conference), the Czechs were forced to acquiesce in the carve-up of their country.

Believing world war had been averted, Chamberlain returned to Britain on 30 September and received a hero's welcome. He believed his great personal achievement during the negotiations had been to come back with a piece of paper (which he held up to the cheering crowds at Heston aerodrome) that he had persuaded Hitler to sign. In this note, the German Führer and the British prime minister renounced war and determined to resolve their future differences purely through diplomacy.

This proved to be the zenith of Britain's appeasement policy. Six months later, and without warning, Hitler invaded the rump Czechoslovakian state that Chamberlain's diplomacy had helped render virtually defenceless. Scrambling to limit further Nazi expansion in Central and Eastern Europe, Britain rushed to offer Poland a guarantee of military support in the event of German invasion. On 3 September 1939, this

OPPOSITE: The Munich 'piece of paper,' signed by Adolf Hitler and Neville Chamberlain, pledging the peaceful resolution of Anglo-German disputes.

'Here is the paper which bears his name upon it as well as mine' – Neville Chamberlain tells the crowds greeting him at Heston aerodrome that Hitler has given him his word at Munich. On the far left of the picture, a tall man is observing intensely. He is the foreign secretary, Lord Halifax.

COUNTDOWN TO WAR: 1939

14 March At Hitler's prompting, Slovakia's provincial assembly declares independence from Czechoslovakia.

15 March Germany invades the remaining rump of the Czech state.

22 March Germany annexes Memel from Lithuania.

28 March–1 April The Spanish Civil War ends in victory for Franco's German- and Italian-backed Nationalists.

31 March Britain announces it will guarantee Poland's sovereignty against attack.

7 April Italy invades Albania.

22 May Germany and Italy agree a 'Pact of Steel'.

24 May The Cabinet agrees to explore terms for a military pact with the Soviet Union.

23 August The Molotov–Ribbentrop non-aggression pact is signed between Germany and the Soviet Union.

24 August Parliament is recalled. The Emergency Powers Act is rushed through.

25 August The British guarantee regarding Poland's security is given legal status.

31 August The Royal Navy is mobilized. The evacuation of children from London begins.

1 September Germany invades Poland.

3 September At 9 a.m. Britain sends Germany a two-hour ultimatum to begin withdrawing from Poland. When no undertaking is received, at 11 a.m. Britain declares war on Germany. At 11.15 a.m. Neville Chamberlain broadcasts to the nation, announcing that it is at war. At 5 p.m. France declares war on Germany.

agreement brought Britain (joined by France) into all-out war with Germany for the second time in twenty-one years.

Chamberlain's agreement at Munich came to be seen as a betrayal of the democratic Czechoslovakian state in a desperate – and ultimately futile – effort by Britain to save herself from war. Indeed, appeasing Hitler at Munich only appeared to give the Führer the wrong impression that he could continue with the forcible annexation of his neighbours with impunity. These 'lessons of Munich' influenced post-war British and American foreign policy, encouraging a more bellicose attitude towards dictatorial regimes, with varying levels of success, including against the Soviet Union in the Cold War, Egypt's President Nasser in the 1956 Suez Crisis and Iraq's Saddam Hussein over his invasion of Kuwait in 1990.

A rival interpretation of Chamberlain's actions at Munich eventually developed in which some historians argued that appeasement saved Britain from fighting a war in 1938 for which she was militarily ill-prepared. This was true, although it also bought Germany eleven months in which to further her own rearmament programme as well. For instance, the Munich agreement delivered into the hands of Hitler's Reich the Skoda armaments factory in the Sudetenland, whose output between October 1938 and September 1939 was almost equal to all British armaments factories put together.

Nevertheless, Chamberlain's aim at Munich was to prevent, rather than defer, war. As his adviser Horace Wilson admitted in 1962: 'Our policy was never designed just to postpone war, or enable us to enter war more united. The aim of appeasement was to avoid war altogether, for all time.' Chamberlain had said as much when he greeted the crowds on his return from Munich with his famously ill-fated comment that he hoped he had brought home 'peace for our time'.

1942
THE BEVERIDGE REPORT

BLUEPRINT FOR THE WELFARE STATE

In December 1942, in the midst of the Second World War, a government white paper became a best-seller. This was Sir William Beveridge's official report, *Social Insurance and Allied Services*, and 635,000 copies of it were snapped up by a British public intrigued and excited by its promise to provide 'freedom from want by securing to each a minimum income sufficient for subsistence'.

It was not just socialists and romantic William Blake-quoting idealists who saw Beveridge as the architect for the New Jerusalem that would rise from the rubble and sub-standard housing of capitalist war-torn Britain. For all sorts of people, his report's proposals became an additional reason for Britain to be fighting, along with self-survival and the defeat of Nazism. Soon after its release, an opinion poll conducted by the British Institute of Public Opinion (BIPO) suggested 86 per cent of respondents supported the report, while only 6 per cent opposed its findings. After the mass unemployment and means tests of the inter-war years, it offered a better tomorrow.

The report identified 'five giants' that needed taming – want, disease, ignorance, squalor and idleness. In the assault on these social ills, the central strategy was to replace the existing varying and non-comprehensive insurance schemes with a standard level of benefit. Beveridge based that level on the assumption of an average household, in which a husband was the breadwinner for a wife and a child. He wanted national insurance to be universal, unlike the scheme established in 1911, which covered only manual workers and those on low incomes. He felt, too, that the scope of old-age pensions should be widened. In place of the remnants of the old Poor Law, taxpayers' money was to be funnelled to the needy and destitute through National Assistance. The taxpayer should also provide a supplementary benefit to families with two or more infants in the form of Child Allowances.

From *Social Insurance and Allied Services*, 1942

In proceeding from this first comprehensive survey of social insurance to the next task – of making recommendations – three guiding principles may be laid down at the outset.

The first principle is that any proposals for the future, while they should use to the full the experience gathered in the past, should not be restricted by consideration of sectional interests established in the obtaining of that experience. Now, when the war is abolishing landmarks of every kind, is the opportunity for using experience in a clear field. A revolutionary moment in the world's history is a time for revolutions, not for patching.

The second principle is that organisation of social insurance should be treated as one part only of a comprehensive policy of social progress. Social insurance fully developed may provide income security; it is an attack upon Want. But Want is one only of five giants on the road of reconstruction and in some ways the easiest to attack. The others are Disease, Ignorance, Squalor and Idleness.

The third principle is that social security must be achieved by co-operation between the State and the individual. The State should offer security for service and contribution. The State in organising security should not stifle incentive, opportunity, responsibility; in establishing a national minimum, it should leave room and encouragement for voluntary action by each individual to provide more than that minimum for himself and his family.

The Plan for Social Security set out in this Report is built upon these principles. It uses experience but is not tied by experience. It is put forward as a limited contribution to a wider social policy, though as something that could be achieved now without waiting for the whole of that policy. It is, first and foremost, a plan of insurance – of giving in return for contributions benefits up to subsistence level, as of right and without means test, so that individuals may build freely upon it.

Some saw the Beveridge Report as merely the completion of a legislative process that had its foundations laid by David Lloyd George, the chancellor of the exchequer in the Liberal government before the First World War, and extended by Winston Churchill and Neville Chamberlain as chancellor and minister of health respectively in the 1924–9 Conservative government. This was not how the report's author saw it. Beveridge made clear that 'My plan is not to develop social insurance:

it is a plan to give freedom from Want by securing to each citizen at all times . . . a minimum income sufficient for his subsistence needs and his responsibilities.' Moreover, his proposals went hand in hand with two important assumptions. The first was that future governments would be able to sustain full, or nearly full, employment in contrast to the high levels of unemployment of the Depression years. The second was that a National Health Service would be established. The report advocated the adoption of both these measures without providing a detailed plan for how they might be made to work.

Ironically, despite a life in social inquiry, it was with reluctance that Sir William Beveridge (1879–1963) accepted the Ministry of Health's request to chair the committee looking into social insurance. As a youthful civil servant in 1908 he had assisted Churchill at the Board of Trade in setting up labour exchanges before becoming director of the London School of Economics from 1919 to 1937 and thereafter Master of University College, Oxford. He wanted to spend the war assisting Ernest Bevin in planning manpower resources at the Ministry of Labour. However, Bevin could not abide Beveridge's conceited attitude and helped ensure his move to social insurance.

Churchill's coalition government accepted the Beveridge Report in principle, while making clear its implementation was a matter for a future, post-war administration. Had the Conservatives won the 1945 general election, much of it would have still been implemented. It was Churchill's Tory 'caretaker' Cabinet in 1945 that introduced the Child Allowance scheme and Beveridge had put on record his opinion that a future Conservative government provided the best chance of his proposals being properly adopted. On the whole, the electorate declined to agree, interpreting some Tories' qualifying statements as a portent that grim post-war economic reality would be cited as the reason for watering down the promised welfare state. After all, something similar had befallen Lloyd George's domestic pledges at the end of the First World War.

The Labour Party, by contrast, was clearly wholeheartedly behind the report and could be trusted not to flinch in the face of financial hardship. This commitment was certainly a factor in Labour's 1945 election triumph, even though creating full employment and nationalizing industries had pride of place in the party's manifesto. Among the casualties of the landslide victory was Beveridge himself, whose fleeting career as a Liberal MP ended in rejection by the voters of Berwick-upon-Tweed. Nonetheless, the influence of this father of the post-war welfare state would outstrip that of all but a few of the politicians elected then, or in subsequent parliaments.

1945
LONDON COUNTY COUNCIL MAP OF LONDON WAR DAMAGE

THE WAR AT HOME AND THE DESTRUCTION AND REBUILDING OF LONDON

One of London County Council's bomb damage maps is depicted in the fourth plate section.

The Second World War was a 'People's War', in which millions of civilians undertook war work. Britain's survival as a free nation was sustained on the farms and down the mines as well as in the munitions factories and on the front line. Merchant ships, bringing in essential resources, ran the same risks of being torpedoed as the Royal Navy. This was 'total war' and nothing better demonstrated the blurring of its distinction between combatants and non-combatants than the bombing of towns and cities.

During the war more than 60,000 British civilians were killed by aerial bombardment while over 2 million homes were destroyed or seriously damaged. In order to cripple the British war effort, the German Luftwaffe targeted cities like Coventry and Birmingham, where military material was rolling off the production lines, as well as ports and shipbuilding centres like Belfast, Clydeside, Portsmouth and Plymouth. The RAF retaliated, beginning what became the ultimately devastating 'strategic' bombing of Germany. Following an RAF attack on the ancient Baltic port city of Lübeck, the Luftwaffe launched attacks on historic British cities such as Bath, Exeter and Canterbury – whose importance was not military but cultural – in what became known as the 'Baedeker Raids' after the famous travel guides. In June 1944, with its diminished air force pulled back to defend its threatened European empire, Germany began launching what it described as its 'vengeance' weapons: V-1 and V-2 missiles targeted at the civilian population where it was most densely concentrated.

The missiles' main target was London, the city that had also borne the brunt of the German assault on Britain in the 'Blitz' of 1940 and 1941. The battering that the

capital received, as well as its citizens' determination to carry on, revealed a defining aspect of the British character, which was summed up as the 'Spirit of the Blitz'. Military planners had incorrectly assumed that the war would start with the saturation bombing of London and other major cities, promoting the mass evacuation of children during September 1939. In reality the attacks over the capital did not begin until the following September, in the closing weeks of the Battle of Britain. They intensified at the end of October 1940 when the Luftwaffe concentrated night-time bombing, pummelling London for seventy-six consecutive nights. Through 1941, the raids became more intermittent but no less severe.

THE WAR AT HOME

Civilians killed in Britain	
1939–1940	23,767
1941	19,918
1942	3,236
1943	2,372
1944	8,475
1945	1,860
Total civilian deaths in Northern Ireland	967
United Kingdom total	60,595

The London Blitz (from the German word *Blitzkrieg*, or 'lightning war') represented a switch in strategy by the Luftwaffe whose original aim had been to knock out the airfields and aircraft of the RAF to ensure German air superiority for a full-scale invasion. It was the RAF's victory in the Battle of Britain, together with the ongoing threat posed by the Royal Navy to a Channel crossing, that forced Hitler to postpone his invasion plans indefinitely. Germany now concentrated instead on trying to obliterate London's docks and intimidate its citizens and politicians into suing for peace. The Luftwaffe dropped high-explosive bombs, which were intended to blast out buildings, as well as incendiary bombs, which were designed to spread fires. The worst attacks were the massive incendiary raids of 29/30 December 1940 and 10/11 May 1941, which, besides causing widespread damage, destroyed many of London's architectural jewels, including Baroque churches in the City and the chamber of the House of Commons. The attacks thereafter subsided while Hitler's attention switched to the invasion of the Soviet Union, on 22 June 1941, until recommencing shortly after D-Day in 1944, with the advent of the missile strikes.

It was in January 1941, while London was still burning, that plans were first devised for post-war reconstruction. To prepare for this, staff of the London County Council's Architect's Department were engaged to plot the damaged areas on 110 ordnance survey maps covering the 117 square miles under the LCC's authority. They continued their work until the last V-2 ballistic missile fell on 27 March 1945, a mere six weeks before Germany's unconditional surrender.

During the course of the war, over 1 million London houses were hit. The highest density of bombs fell in Stepney, the City of London and Holborn, all of which

were struck by more than 600 bombs per 1,000 acres. The LCC maps provide an extraordinarily detailed picture of the extent and concentration of war damage on the capital. The only omissions were a few especially prominent buildings, including railway stations and the Palace of Westminster. Otherwise, the fate of virtually every property – from the giant warehouse to the fine townhouse to the meanest rented apartment – was recorded. Circles marked where the V-1 and V-2 missiles landed. Buildings painted black represented those totally destroyed, and the colour code ranged through the other varying degrees of damage inflicted. Light-blue colouring (which the passage of time has turned greenish-blue) designated areas where the whole area was marked for total clearance and redevelopment.

Although the human cost appalled all, modern architects viewed with excitement the opportunities for redevelopment on so vast a scale, giving them their chance to put right what they saw as London's generations of ill-planned growth. In July 1943, the LCC's architect and chief planner, J. H. Forshaw, and Professor Patrick Abercrombie published the County of London Plan, which went through various changes. There was ambitious talk of creating a modern, integrated city. Comparisons were drawn with Sir Christopher Wren's (unexecuted) plan for rebuilding London after its last great devastating fire, in 1666.

The Wren analogy flattered the talents of those who recast post-war London. While the loss of many pre-war slums was hardly to be regretted on either aesthetic or sanitary grounds, the quality of what replaced them only rarely set spirits soaring. The crude office blocks that rose around St Paul's Cathedral were a particularly offensive insult to their setting. Indeed, it was perhaps fortunate that the more sweeping aspects of the London Plan were never put into practice. Aside from the Royal Festival Hall and a few other modern masterpieces, it was a sorry indictment that, over half a century later, most Britons were thankful not for the new buildings that replaced old favourites, but rather for the instances in which badly damaged buildings were repaired and, in many places, successfully restored.

St Paul's Cathedral survived the destruction of the Blitz and also outlived the post-war modernist blocks that were built on the bomb sites around it.

349

1945
BRIEF ENCOUNTER,
FILM SCRIPT

NOËL COWARD, DAVID LEAN
AND BRITAIN'S STIFF UPPER LIP

OPPOSITE: *A page from the original* Brief Encounter *film script: Laura fears love's consequences.*

Few dramatists better expressed aspects of the British character than Noël Coward. His many artistic gifts embraced playwriting, acting, theatre direction, and the composition of songs that are now synonymous with their period.

Coward's louche persona – redolent of cocktails, cigarette holders and the wearing of silk dressing-gowns – was among his most successful creations. He had actually been born, in 1899, in suburban Teddington into the struggling lower middle class. His father, a failed piano salesman, was driven to drink, but his mother harboured social ambitions for something better. Her son's formal schooling ended when he was nine, at which point his career as a child actor began. From then on, his extraordinary ascent was driven by hard work and voracious reading.

He was only twenty-four when he made his name with his first stage hit, *The Vortex*. The drama, involving a drug-taking son and his nymphomaniac mother, was considered by some to be unseemly. Only slightly less bohemian was the plot of *Private Lives* (1930), which revolves around Amanda and Elyot, a once-married couple, who find themselves in neighbouring honeymoon suites with their new partners.

Coward, however, was at root no political revolutionary. His ambitious 1931 play, *Cavalcade*, celebrated Britain's recent imperial history. In 1933 his review *Words and Music* included his composition 'Mad Dogs and Englishmen', which simultaneously sent up and exalted the colonialists who shouldered Rudyard Kipling's 'white man's burden'. This combination of gentle mockery and affection towards its target was evident in Coward's comic lines and lyrics,

53.

                    DISSOLVE to a shot of the car pulling
                    up near a small bridge over a stream.

LAURA'S VOICE:
          When we were out in the real country - I think it
          was a few miles beyond Brayfield - we stopped the
          car just outside a village and got out. There was
          a little bridge and a stream and the sun was making
          an effort to come out but really not succeeding
          very well. We leaned on the parapet of the bridge
          and looked down into the water. I shivered and
          Alec put his arm around me.

ALEC: Cold ?

LAURA: No - not really.

ALEC: Happy?

LAURA: No - not really.

ALEC: I know what you're going to say - that it isn't
          worth it - that the furtiveness and the necessary
          lying outweigh the happiness we might have together
          - wasn't that it ?

LAURA: Yes, something like that.

ALEC: I want to ask you something - just to reassure
          myself.

LAURA: (her eyes filling with tears) What is it ?

ALEC: It is true for you isn't it? This overwhelming
          feeling that we have for each other - it is as true
          for you as it is for me - isn't it ?

LAURA: Yes - it's true.

                    She bursts into tears and Alec puts his
                    arms closer around her. They stand in
                    silence for a moment and then kiss each
                    other passionately.

                    DISSOLVE to a long shot of Alec and Laura
                    still standing on the bridge.

LAURA'S VOICE:
          I don't remember how long we stayed on that bridge
          or what we said. I only remember feeling that I
          was on the edge of a precipice, terrified yet want-
          ing desperately to throw myself over.

351

a distinctively British form of satire that would later be exemplified by the 1960s double act of Michael Flanders and Donald Swann.

With the outbreak of war, Coward was keen to play his part in stiffening morale, entertaining troops in Burma and the Middle East, and writing the great patriotic song of the Blitz, 'London Pride'. He also starred in a film celebrating the heroism of the Royal Navy, *In Which We Serve*, his first collaboration with the film director David Lean (1908–91). Lean, who went on to direct some of the greatest epics of British cinema, including *Lawrence of Arabia* and *The Bridge On the River Kwai*, also directed film versions of Coward's plays *This Happy Breed*, *Blithe Spirit* and, most memorably of all, *Brief Encounter*.

Brief Encounter's first incarnation was as *Still Life*, one of ten, single-act plays performed in Coward's 1936 dramatic cycle *To-Night at 8.30*. The film version starred Trevor Howard as Alec, a GP, and Celia Johnson as Laura, a conventional, middle-class housewife and mother of twins who is married to a well-meaning but passionless husband. After a chance meeting on a railway platform, they find themselves edging towards an affair. It is a tale of the conflict between surrendering to personal desire and staying true to an ethos of self-denial, honouring social mores and family responsibilities. Ultimately, the latter triumphs and the doomed lovers part. The fact that it was originally staged shortly before Edward VIII did the opposite, abdicating his royal duties for 'the woman I love', gave it an unintended topical piquancy. The film version was released in 1945, at a time when the disruptions of the Second World War had provided plenty of opportunity for extramarital affairs.

Coward juxtaposed the tragic dilemma of his repressed, provincial leads with the uncomplicated, guiltless fun enjoyed by the working-class characters played by Stanley Holloway and Joyce Carey. In this, there were echoes of E. M. Forster's critique of emotionally stultifying suburban values in his Edwardian novels *A Room with a View* and *Howard's End*. Unlike Forster, with his liberal message of emancipation, Coward – whose politics were Conservative despite his off-screen homosexuality – was more sympathetic to bourgeois ethics, appreciating the nobility involved in renunciation.

Brief Encounter was an immediate hit, critically and commercially, at a time when British cinema was at the summit of its popularity. It proved to be the last of Coward's successes for some time. Although they enjoyed frequent revivals from the later 1960s onwards, his carefully crafted dramas were deemed stylized and old-fashioned by the new generation of 'kitchen sink' playwrights of the 1950s and

Celia Johnson and Trevor Howard wrestle with their emotions in Brief Encounter.

early 1960s, many of whom saw the theatre as a place for revealing social reality and a platform for agitating for change. On a different plane, his sophisticated comedies were far removed from the saucy innuendos of the *Carry On* films. Similarly, *Brief Encounter*'s tragic lovers, turning away from personal gratification, seemed hopelessly dated to the 1960s generation of social and sexual liberation. That, however, did not make the national characteristics that Coward depicted any less meaningful, potent or real.

1948

THE BRITISH NATIONALITY ACT

OPENING THE DOOR TO MASS IMMIGRATION
FROM THE COMMONWEALTH

The 1948 British Nationality Act transformed the racial make-up of Britain. At the time that the legislation passed into law, non-white faces were a rare sight in all but a few parts of the country. Even the immigrant communities, new or old, were overwhelmingly European. By holding wide open Britain's door of entry to anyone born anywhere within the borders of her empire and Commonwealth, the 1948 Act forever changed the national composition and set the United Kingdom on a path towards a multiracial, multicultural future.

It may have seemed counter-intuitive for Clement Attlee's government to make so affirmative an expression of faith in the unity of empire only months after India and Pakistan had been granted independence from it. The loss of the 'jewel in the crown' was indeed the beginning of a process of decolonization that would be completed in 1997 with the handover of Hong Kong to China. Nonetheless, in the post-war years there was widespread faith in the future of the British Commonwealth (of which India and Pakistan became members). This was not just a reflexive scramble for a face-saving idea to conceal the reality of a world power in decline. The many peoples of the empire, of all faiths and colours, who had volunteered to fight in the common cause between 1939 and 1945 demanded a retrospective expression of gratitude from – depending on their political viewpoint – their mother country or colonial master.

POST-WAR IMMIGRATION

Year	Total foreign-born population of the UK (in millions)	% of total UK population
1951	2.1	4.2
1961	2.5	4.9
1971	3.2	5.8
1981	3.4	6.2
1991	3.8	6.7
2001	4.9	8.3
2008	6.5	10.7

From the British Nationality Act, 1948

1.—(1) Every person who under this Act is a citizen of the United Kingdom and Colonies or who under any enactment for the time being in force in any country mentioned in subsection (3) of this section is a citizen of that country shall by virtue of that citizenship have the status of a British subject.

(2) Any person having the status aforesaid may be known either as a British subject or as a Commonwealth citizen; and accordingly in this Act and in any other enactment or instrument whatever, whether passed or made before or after the commencement of this Act, the expression "British subject" and the expression "Commonwealth citizen" shall have the same meaning.

(3) The following are the countries hereinbefore referred to, that is to say, Canada, Australia, New Zealand, the Union of South Africa, Newfoundland, India, Pakistan, Southern Rhodesia and Ceylon.

Directly prompted by changes in Canada's citizenship laws, the 1948 Act primarily had in mind the right of entry of those of British descent from the 'white dominions' of Canada, South Africa, Australia and New Zealand. Strictly speaking, it reaffirmed an old policy dating from the start of a previous call to imperial arms. The 1914 British Nationality and Status of Aliens Act gave British citizenship to 'any person born within His Majesty's dominions and allegiances'. As a result, 400 million subjects of the British Empire had effectively been granted the right to settle on a small island off the European continent, but very few of them had done so. Opportunities for migrants usually appeared better for those going to the 'white dominions' than to Britain and the cost of long-distance travel was beyond the means of most Indians, Africans or inhabitants of the Caribbean. Although the history of black settlers in Britain went back at least to the sixteenth century (when Queen Elizabeth I complained there were too many of them) and they had long formed strong communities in port cities like Liverpool and Cardiff by the 1930s, the non-white population of Britain numbered only a few thousand.

The 1948 British Nationality Act came at a time when the cost of travel was falling. The result was immigration from the 'New Commonwealth' (essentially,

The Empire
Windrush's
passenger list, 21
June 1948.

the Indian subcontinent, Africa and the West Indies) on a scale that the framers
of the legislation had never imagined. The influx began when an old troopship,
the *Empire Windrush*, docked at Tilbury on 22 June 1948 with 492 migrants
travelling from Jamaica. Immigrants from the Caribbean had traditionally gone to
the United States, but in 1952 the US government restricted their entry. Britain
became their destination instead. Census returns pointed to a rise in Britain's
'coloured' population from 74,500 in 1951 to 336,000 in 1961. Of these, by far the
largest proportion (171,800) had come from the West Indies, while 81,400 were
from India, 24,900 from Pakistan and 19,800 from West Africa.

The immigrants' contribution became particularly evident in the transport sector
and the health service. Subsequent generations, particularly of Asian descent,

brought an entrepreneurial spirit and entered the professions. Yet the argument raged over whether many of them were doing important, otherwise unfillable, jobs or were changing the nature of the country in a way that left many native-born Britons uncomfortable. During the 1950s, successive Conservative administrations considered plans to reduce the inflow but did not implement them, in part because of a reluctance to be seen to discriminate between black migrants from the New Commonwealth and those of British descent from the 'white dominions', whom they still regarded as 'kith and kin'.

The first restrictions came with the 1962 Commonwealth Immigrants Act, which stemmed the flow by insisting on the possession of employment vouchers. Having opposed restrictions while in opposition, Harold Wilson's Labour government after 1964 tightly controlled the number of vouchers available. However, the government tried to make life more tolerable for those who had already arrived by passing the 1965 Race Relations Act, which made racial discrimination illegal.

The first wave of arrivals were overwhelmingly young males, mostly unskilled or semi-skilled, coming in search of work. Many repatriated some of their earnings back home. Over time, their families came out to join them in Britain, a major factor in the rate of entry remaining above 50,000 a year after the 1962 Act. Faced with an influx from East Africa, in 1968 legislation finally discriminated against those who had not been born in Britain or, failing that, had a parent or grandparent born there.

The heated debate focused on only one aspect of migration policy. In fact, net emigration from Britain exceeded net immigration every year from 1946 to 1979. This was overwhelmingly the result of Britons starting new lives in the sun rather than recent arrivals returning back to the warmer climes they had left behind. Southern Rhodesia (modern Zimbabwe) was a popular destination in the 1950s; during the 1960s, British emigration to Australia and New Zealand ran at between 80,000 and 100,000 a year.

Another aspect of policy that caused a significant migration shift within the British Isles concerned the favourable status accorded the Southern Irish. In 1947, Ireland announced that it was formally becoming a republic and leaving the Commonwealth. Rather than draw the perhaps natural conclusion that the link with Dublin was severed, the 1948 British Nationality Act guaranteed Irish citizens the rights to reside and to vote in Britain. Many took up the offer. In this way, non-members of the Commonwealth ended up enjoying easier entry than Commonwealth members. This process was completed when Britain became part of the free movement of peoples within the European Community.

1949
THE NORTH ATLANTIC TREATY

BRITAIN'S ROLE IN THE COLD WAR

The North Atlantic Treaty was one of the most significant achievements of the post-war Labour government. Through it, the North Atlantic Treaty Organization (NATO) became the cornerstone of British foreign policy for the rest of the century, perpetuating the wartime 'special relationship' between Washington and London, and securing Britain's role as deputy leader of the 'Free World'.

It nonetheless involved the sort of commitment that, after the defeat of Germany in 1945, both Britain and America had hoped to avoid. A year after VE-Day, the number of American troops stationed in Europe had fallen from over 3 million to under 400,000, British troops from 1.3 million to 488,000, and the Canadians from 300,000 to none. In contrast, the Soviet forces remained close to full strength and on a war footing. Despite signing the 1947 Treaty of Dunkirk, an Anglo-French defence pact, Britain's main plan in the event of a Soviet attack on Western Europe was to re-enact the 1940 Dunkirk evacuation and scurry her continental forces back across the English Channel for home defence. In May 1948 the order changed to command them to stand and fight on European soil. It was not until 1950 that the minor comfort of reinforcements was promised in the event of British troops being forced to make a suicidal last stand against the massed divisions of Comrade Stalin. Only the threat of launching an American nuclear strike told in the Western allies' favour.

Even before the Second World War was over, Winston Churchill had begun to fear future Soviet intentions. American public and political opinion was slower to reach the same conclusion but, when it did, it manifested itself forcibly. In March 1947, President Harry Truman addressed Congress on the need to contain the further spread of communism. This 'Truman doctrine' was echoed the following January by Clement Attlee, who warned the British people in a broadcast that 'Soviet Communism pursues a policy of imperialism in a new form – ideological,

The British foreign secretary, Ernest Bevin, signs the North Atlantic Treaty in Washington, DC on 4 April 1949.

economic, and strategic – which threatens the welfare and way of life of the other nations of Europe.'

During 1948, 'Marshall Aid' began, pouring American development money into shattered economies of Britain and Western Europe in the hope of getting them back on their feet and bolstering resistance to the lure of communism. The Soviet Union refused to allow the Eastern European countries that it occupied to join the scheme. Two Moscow-backed moves further confirmed Western suspicions. In February 1948, communists seized power in Czechoslovakia. Four months later, Soviet forces blockaded the Allied sectors of Berlin. Rather than capitulate, the British and Americans responded by a daring airlift of vital supplies into the city and, after eleven months, the siege was lifted. Impressed, German citizens noted that British and American airmen who had previously helped destroy their city now risked their

lives to save it. Ignoring Soviet objections, the Western powers began the process of creating West Germany as a free and independent state.

Britain's foreign secretary was Ernest Bevin (1881–1951), a former general secretary of the Transport and General Workers Union, wartime minister of labour and passionate anti-communist. With Germany disarmed and France's martial traditions needing refounding, Bevin recognized both that Britain was the only European military power of consequence and that she could not hold the continent alone. While he negotiated the Brussels Treaty, a defence pact between Britain, France and the Low Countries in March 1948, his greater aim was to draw this grouping into a wider transtlantic alliance. The result was a ceremony in Washington, DC, in April 1949 in which Bevin joined the representatives of the United States, Canada, France, Italy, Belgium, the Netherlands, Luxembourg, Denmark, Iceland, Norway and Portugal in signing the North Atlantic Treaty. Its core principle was that each signatory state considered a military attack on any one of them to be an attack on all of them. This was the ultimate embodiment of collective security.

During the negotiations, Bevin successfully quashed an American proposal of a presidential guarantee to defend Western Europe rather than a formal alliance. As Bevin well understood, a guarantee was much easier for future presidents, perhaps with hostile Congresses, to water down. Furthermore, in the coming age of nuclear strikes, Britain could hardly hold the line long enough to allow the United States to begin mobilizing troops to send across the Atlantic. What was needed was the forces of a permanent, continent-based alliance and this is what Bevin got.

Even so, the wording of Article 5 still left latitude over whether the response to an attack on one member had to be military rather than merely diplomatic or economic. It was only in 1950, with the Western allies fighting together under UN auspices to repel the communist invasion of South Korea, that the North Atlantic Treaty was transformed from essentially a mutual defence pact into a military organization with an integrated command structure. Its standing body was led by the United States, with General Eisenhower as supreme commander and Britain's Lord Ismay as secretary-general. This replicated the relative importance of the two countries. Britain, as co-instigator and (from 1952) with its own nuclear deterrent, remained the second most important power within NATO even after it had expanded to include Greece and Turkey in 1951, West Germany in 1955, Spain in 1985 and then, with the end of the Cold War, Eastern Europe as well. Beyond its nuclear capacity, the heart of Britain's

From the North Atlantic Treaty, 1949

Article 5: The Parties agree that an armed attack against one or more of them in Europe or North America shall be considered an attack against them all and consequently they agree that, if such an armed attack occurs, each of them, in exercise of the right of individual or collective self-defence recognised by Article 51 of the Charter of the United Nations, will assist the Party or Parties so attacked by taking forthwith, individually and in concert with the other Parties, such action as it deems necessary, including the use of armed force, to restore and maintain the security of the North Atlantic area.

> Any such armed attack and all measures taken as a result thereof shall immediately be reported to the Security Council. Such measures shall be terminated when the Security Council has taken the measures necessary to restore and maintain international peace and security.

Article 6 (1): For the purpose of Article 5, an armed attack on one or more of the Parties is deemed to include an armed attack:

> on the territory of any of the Parties in Europe or North America, on the Algerian Departments of France,[*] on the territory of or on the Islands under the jurisdiction of any of the Parties in the North Atlantic area north of the Tropic of Cancer;

> on the forces, vessels, or aircraft of any of the Parties, when in or over these territories or any other area in Europe in which occupation forces of any of the Parties were stationed on the date when the Treaty entered into force or the Mediterranean Sea or the North Atlantic area north of the Tropic of Cancer.

[* this clause ceased to be applicable after Algeria's independence in 1962.]

NATO contribution was the British Army of the Rhine (BAOR), stationed on the German front line, and the Royal Navy patrolling the North Sea, which from the 1960s could deploy Polaris submarine-launched nuclear missiles. Like France, Britain's position in NATO was supplemented by its permanent seat on the UN Security Council; unlike France, it did not opt out of NATO's integrated command structure (which President Charles de Gaulle regarded as incompatible with French sovereignty).

BRITISH SPENDING ON DEFENCE

Year	Defence budget (£bn)	Budget as % of GDP
1955/56	£1.4	7.1 %
1960/61	£1.6	6.1 %
1965/66	£2.1	5.6 %
1970/71	£2.5	4.7 %
1975/76	£5.3	4.8 %
1980/81	£11.2	4.7 %
1985/86	£17.9	4.9 %
1990/91	£22.3	3.9 %
1995/96	£21.5	2.9 %
2000/01	£23.6	2.4 %
2005/06	£30.6	2.4 %
2008/09	£36.4	2.5 %

The alliance's united stance appeared vindicated by communism's collapse and the disintegration of the Soviet Union between 1989 and 1991. In an extraordinary transformation from putative enmity to fraternity, Eastern European former members of the Warsaw Pact, when freed to pursue their own destiny, rushed to join NATO as a security against any future reassertion of Russian might. In the meantime, NATO sought new purpose as a policeman of what was optimistically termed the 'new world order' – involving itself, for instance, in trying to resolve the conflicts of the former Yugoslavia where a 60,000-strong NATO Implementation Force (IFOR) was dispatched in 1995.

When, three years later, NATO launched air strikes against Serbia in order to persuade President Slobodan Milošević to withdraw his forces from the disputed Serbian territory of Kosovo, where mounting ethnic violence threatened to create a humanitarian catastrophe, it demonstrated how much it had changed its purpose. The Kosovo campaign was the first time in NATO's history that it had attacked a sovereign country whose boundaries were recognized in international law. Despite the humanitarian intentions, the air strikes did not have direct UN sanction and exposed tensions within the alliance.

These tensions grew more significant after 2001 when the United States responded to the al-Qaeda outrages in New York and Washington, DC, by declaring a broad-ranging 'war on terror' and sought partners to assist with operations in Afghanistan and later Iraq. The British government responded fully, but other NATO countries displayed varying degrees of enthusiasm. Some commentators questioned whether the alliance's unity of purpose still existed in the absence of the Soviet threat to mainland Europe. Indeed, many felt that international terrorism and the consequences of 'failed states' around the world called for a thorough debate about NATO's future role. The more it adapted to the new challenges, the more manifest became the uncertainty over where the parameters for action were – or should be – set.

1950

THE EUROPEAN CONVENTION
ON HUMAN RIGHTS

HUMAN RIGHTS, FROM EUROPEAN CONVENTION
TO BRITISH LAW

Jack Straw, the home secretary in Tony Blair's first administration, described the passage of the Human Rights Act in 1998 as the greatest constitutional change since Magna Carta. It incorporated the European Convention on Human Rights into British law. Even in the half-century between the Convention's adoption in 1950 and the Human Rights Act, the former had an effect on British legal developments. In the twenty-first century, it seemed destined to be ever more central to judicial deliberations.

The drafting of the European Convention on Human Rights was undertaken by a committee guided by a leading British politician and lawyer, Sir David Maxwell-Fyfe (1900–67). The son of an impecunious Scottish schoolmaster, Maxwell-Fyfe showed early ambition at George Watson's College in Edinburgh and at Oxford University. At the age of thirty-four he became the youngest King's Counsel (KC) for 250 years and the following year was elected as a Conservative MP in Liverpool. In Churchill's wartime coalition government he was solicitor-general and, in part owing to the work he had undertaken while in that office, he was appointed deputy chief prosecutor in the Nuremberg trial of Nazi leaders. There he succeeded – where others had failed – in cracking the courtroom self-confidence of the most important defendant, Hermann Goering.

The fact that Germany, one of the world's most cultured nations, could have succumbed to the moral degradation of the Third Reich provided a shocking example of what could happen when the rights of the individual were disregarded by an all-powerful totalitarian state answerable only to itself. To Maxwell-Fyfe and his fellow enthusiasts for European integration, it seemed essential that the post-war continent should be rebuilt with stronger legal protection for its citizens. In 1949,

From the European Convention on Human Rights, 1950

ARTICLE 1

The High Contracting Parties shall secure to everyone within their jurisdiction the rights and freedoms defined in Section I of this Convention.

SECTION I

ARTICLE 2

Everyone's right to life shall be protected by law. No one shall be deprived of his life intentionally save in the execution of a sentence of a court following his conviction of a crime for which this penalty is provided by law.

Deprivation of life shall not be regarded as inflicted in contravention of this article when it results from the use of force which is no more than absolutely necessary:

(a) in defence of any person from unlawful violence;

(b) in order to effect a lawful arrest or to prevent escape of a person lawfully detained;

(c) in action lawfully taken for the purpose of quelling a riot or insurrection. . . .

ARTICLE 3

No one shall be subjected to torture or to inhuman or degrading treatment or punishment.

ARTICLE 6

In the determination of his civil rights and obligations or of any criminal charge against him, everyone is entitled to a fair and public hearing within a reasonable time by an independent and impartial tribunal established by law. . . .

Everyone charged with a criminal offence shall be presumed innocent until proved guilty according to law. . . .

ARTICLE 7

No one shall be held guilty of any criminal offence on account of any act or omission which did not constitute a criminal offence under national or international law at the time when it was committed. Nor shall a heavier penalty be imposed than the one that was applicable at the time the criminal offence was committed.

This article shall not prejudice the trial and punishment of any person for any act or omission which, at the time when it was committed, was criminal according the general principles of law recognized by civilized nations.

ARTICLE 8

Everyone has the right to respect for his private and family life, his home and his correspondence.

There shall be no interference by a public authority with the exercise of this right except such as is in accordance with the law and is necessary in a democratic society in the interests of national security, public safety or the economic well-being of the country, for the prevention of disorder or crime, for the protection of health or morals, or for the protection of the rights and freedoms of others.

ARTICLE 9

Everyone has the right to freedom of thought, conscience and religion; this right includes freedom to change his religion or belief, and freedom, either alone or in community with others and in public or private, to manifest his religion or belief, in worship, teaching, practice and observance.

Freedom to manifest one's religion or beliefs shall be subject only to such limitations as are prescribed by law and are necessary in a democratic society in the interests of public safety, for the protection of public order, health or morals, or the protection of the rights and freedoms of others.

ARTICLE 10

Everyone has the right to freedom of expression. This right shall include freedom to hold opinions and to receive and impart information and ideas without interference by public authority and regardless of frontiers. This article shall not prevent States from requiring the licensing of broadcasting, television or cinema enterprises.

The exercise of these freedoms, since it carries with it duties and responsibilities, may be subject to such formalities, conditions, restrictions or penalties as are prescribed by law and are necessary in a democratic society, in the interests of national security, territorial integrity or public safety, for the prevention of disorder or crime, for the protection of health or morals, for the protection of the reputation or the rights of others, for preventing the disclosure of information received in confidence, or for maintaining the authority and impartiality of the judiciary.

ARTICLE 11

Everyone has the right to freedom of peaceful assembly and to freedom of association with others, including the right to form and to join trade unions for the protection of his interests.

No restrictions shall be placed on the exercise of these rights other than such as are prescribed by law and are necessary in a democratic society in the interests of national security or public safety, for the prevention of disorder or crime, for the protection of health or morals or for the protection of the rights and freedoms of others. this article shall not prevent the imposition of lawful restrictions on the exercise of these rights by members of the armed forces, of the police or of the administration of the State.

ARTICLE 12

Men and women of marriageable age have the right to marry and to found a family, according to the national laws governing the exercise of this right.

Britain joined France, Italy, Denmark, Sweden, Norway, Belgium, the Netherlands, Luxembourg and Ireland in signing the Treaty of London, which established the Council of Europe. While political and economic integration became the task of a separate entity, the EEC (later the EU) from 1957, the Council of Europe's main preoccupation was with upholding human rights upon principles laid out by a convention.

As Maxwell-Fyfe was chairman of the Council of Europe's legal and administrative council and *rapporteur* on the drafting committee of the Convention on Human Rights, his considerable energies were brought to the fore. The convention was completed in 1950. However, signatories, including Britain, agreed to abide by it only as part of international treaty law, a legal framework of obligation between nations, rather than between state and citizen. There was initially no European court to hear cases individuals might bring. This changed in 1959 with the establishment of the European Court of Human Rights, with its own judges sitting in Strasbourg and adjudicating on cases brought to them by the citizens of member states. However, Harold Macmillan's government (in which Maxwell-Fyfe, as Lord Kilmuir, was lord chancellor) kept Britain out of this jurisdiction. It was Harold Wilson's Labour government of 1964–70 that gave Britons the belated

right to challenge national judgments at Strasbourg. And following the 1998 Human Rights Act, the trek to Strasbourg became less necessary. Fully operational in 2000, the legislation forced all British courts to act in accordance with the Convention on Human Rights.

These changes were heralded as an advance for equal rights and personal liberty. However, critics of the Human Rights Act have argued that the European convention has ceased to be a basic bulwark against arbitrary rule and has instead become a tool of judicial activism. Certainly, it has led to judges interpreting the broadly phrased wording of the convention in ways that would have horrified Maxwell-Fyfe. For instance, as home secretary between 1951 and 1954, Maxwell-Fyfe supported the death penalty (notoriously refusing clemency in 1953 for Derek Bentley, an illiterate epileptic eighteen-year-old who was hanged for being party to the murder of a policeman) and vigorously opposed the decriminalizing of homosexuality. Yet in 2000 the European Court interpreted the convention's Article 8 ('Everyone has the right to respect for his private and family life') to include group participation in sadomasochist gay sex, effectively overruling the existing British law that had found those who did so guilty of 'gross indecency'.

Following the full implementation of the Human Rights Act, the convention's effects began to be ever more apparent in domestic legal judgments. There were, in particular, profound implications for where the balance was henceforth to be struck between press freedom and the privacy of the individual, and for how terrorist suspects should be treated. A small number of highly controversial judgments threatened to undermine popular support for the supremacy of the convention in British law. At the core was a debate over whether civil society remained workable if the ultimate legal document stressed human rights but not mutual responsibilities. Totalitarian regimes had shown the pitfalls of disregarding the rights of the individual. Maxwell-Fyfe's intentions were not only to prevent a return to Nazism but also to establish the convention as the first trip-wire against the future spread of communism. In 1950, this danger had seemed a real possibility. Yet after sixty years of peace and democracy, judicial interpretation has developed the convention from being an ennobling, if limited, declaration against serious abuses of power into becoming a forum in which even minor day-to-day decision-making by any public body can be legally challenged. The potential costs and restrictions that this imposes upon public bodies are considerable, the consequences for the principles upon which society has long organized itself, transformative.

IX

ELIZABETH II'S BRITAIN

1952
IAN FLEMING'S MANUSCRIPT
FOR *CASINO ROYALE*

CREATING THE BRITON WHO COULD SAVE THE WORLD

Ian Fleming was forty-three years old when he departed from Goldeneye, his Jamaican retreat, bound on his honeymoon. Accompanying him was Anne, his wife, and an attaché case containing the manuscript for his first James Bond novel, *Casino Royale*. Thirteen years later Fleming would be dead, but in that short span he published fourteen Bond adventures and bequeathed to the world the ultimate fictional British hero.

Over 100,000,000 Bond books have been sold. Less verifiably, it has been calculated that more than half the world's population has seen at least one Bond film. As for the character at the centre of it, he has sprung from the written page to evolve into a global cinema phenomenon, outgrowing the original canon of novels but continuing to visit glamorous locations and grapple with international villains and *femmes fatales*. Even today, 007 (Licence to Kill) remains the most famous embodiment of Her Majesty's secret service.

'Everything I write has a precedent in truth,' claimed James Bond's creator. Ian Fleming had been born in 1908 into a privileged background. His Scottish grandfather had founded Fleming's, a merchant bank. His father, an MP, was killed in the First World War when his son was aged only eight. Sent to Eton, Ian Fleming excelled at sport, but his progression to Sandhurst was cut short by illness and his realization that he did not wish to conform. Rejected by the Foreign Office, he worked first for the Reuters news agency (where he honed his ability to write the short, punchy sentences that were to mark his subsequent literary style) and then in stockbroking. It was the outbreak of war in 1939 that generated the experiences that would later inform his novels.

His mother wrote to Winston Churchill to advertise her son's untapped talent and following this and other approaches, Fleming was appointed assistant to

1898–9 – CHARLES BOOTH'S 'POVERTY MAP' OF LONDON

Charles Booth's poverty maps of central London provided a colour-coded guide to the varying prosperity of late-Victorian London. The affluence of Bloomsbury contrasted with the abject poverty endured only a few streets away between Covent Garden and Lincoln's Inn Fields.

■ *Lowest class. Vicious, semi-criminal.*

■ *Very poor, casual. Chronic want.*

■ *Poor. 18 to 21 shillings a week for a moderate family.*

■ *Mixed. Some comfortable, others poor.*

■ *Fairly comfortable. Good ordinary earnings.*

■ *Well-to-do. Middle class.*

■ *Upper-middle and upper classes. Wealthy.*

OPPOSITE: 1945 – LONDON COUNTY COUNCIL MAP OF LONDON WAR DAMAGE

The London County Council's bomb damage maps graphically displayed the extent of both the Blitz and of subsequent rocket attacks on the capital, where one million houses were hit. While much of west London escaped with only sporadic damage, whole swathes of the City of London and the East End were erased – either during the war or in the redevelopment that followed it.

1914 – WAR RECRUITMENT POSTER

Alfred Leete's iconic poster of 1914, featuring Lord Kitchener and his appeal for 100,000 volunteers.

1927 – MAP OF THE BRITISH EMPIRE

Maps showing the extent of the British Empire were often to be found in school rooms and other public places as well as in private homes. This design was produced in 1927 by the Empire Marketing Board, a government-funded body founded the previous year to promote the purchase of goods from the Dominions and Colonies. The Board was wound up in 1933 following the introduction of tariffs against many non-Empire imports.

Total destruction.
Damaged beyond repair.
Seriously damaged, doubtful if repairable.
Seriously damaged, but repairable at cost.
General blast damage, not structural.
Blast damage, minor in nature.
Clearance areas.
Clearance areas.
V1 flying bomb
V2 flying bomb

**1967 – THE BEATLES'
SGT. PEPPER ALBUM
COVER**
*Peter Blake's album cover for
The Beatles' Sgt. Pepper's
Lonely Hearts Club Band
is recognized as a defining
image of Pop Art and an
intriguing expression of the
emerging cult of celebrity.
EMI, the record company,
worried about the cost of
constructing the collage,
though – with the copyright
signed away – Blake made
only about £200.*

**1997 AND AFTER
– CONDOLENCE
BOOKS AND
POPULAR
INSCRIPTIONS TO
DIANA, PRINCESS
OF WALES**
*Upon the death of Diana,
Princess of Wales, condolence
books were opened across
the world to cater for an
extraordinary outpouring of
mass emotion. In Harrod's
department store, in
Knightsbridge, condolence
books were still being signed
on a daily basis in 2010,
more than a decade after
Diana's death. Dodi Fayed,
the son of Mohamed Al-
Fayed, who owned Harrod's
until 2010, died alongside
the princess.*

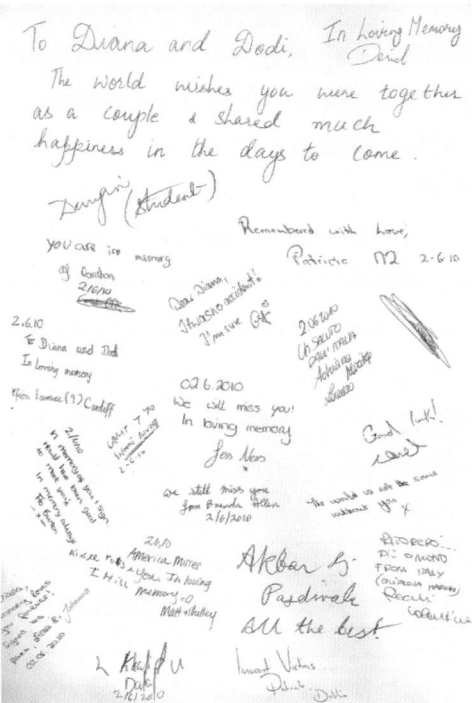

Admiral John Godfrey, the director of naval intelligence. Commander Fleming found himself privy to vital secret operations. He was called upon to devise plans to capture enemy Enigma codebooks and helped organize 30 Assault Unit, a Commando unit charged with seizing important enemy materials before they could be destroyed. He lived life to the full, his work bringing him into contact with extraordinary men. Patrick Dalzel-Job and Wilfred 'Biffy' Dunderdale were among those who provided inspiration for the character of James Bond.

After the war, Fleming was employed as foreign manager of the *Sunday Times* and also wrote travel articles for the paper. In these roles, he dispatched correspondents to report on the emerging Cold War whilst enjoying lavish expenses travelling to exotic places, all of which he drew upon in creating James Bond (whose name he appropriated from the author of a noted book on West Indies ornithology because it sounded 'brief, unromantic, Anglo-Saxon and yet very masculine').

Bond's creator, Ian Fleming (1908–64).

Published by Jonathan Cape in 1953, *Casino Royale* was an instant success. A three-book deal followed. The world in which Bond and his creator moved with its martinis (shaken, not stirred) and fine wines, casinos, fast cars and seductive women appeared extraordinarily glamorous compared to the stark reality of post-war Britain. While Bond sampled beluga caviar, his homeland still endured meat rationing until 1954. This level of escapism was matched by another need that Bond filled. Britain had lost her empire and was humiliated by the Suez Crisis in 1956 (after which disaster Anthony Eden opted to recuperate at Goldeneye). Reassuringly, Bond represented the central role Britain still played in the security of the West in the Cold War. Appropriately, he was periodically extracted from a tight spot by an American CIA operative, Felix Leiter. In 1962, the release of *Dr No*, the first – American-produced – film adaptation, brought Bond's mixture of British cunning and bravery to an ever widening audience. Alongside The Beatles, 007 was quickly established as an internationally recognizable British brand after a long period in which most manifestations of popular culture were either American or Americanized.

Bond's appeal was less agreeable to those who found the character personally and politically repugnant. The left-wing *New Statesman* dismissed the novels as nothing more than 'sex, snobbery and sadism'. Others were no less snooty. Fleming

23

half a measure of Kina Lillet. Shake it very well until its ice-cold
then add a large thin slice of lemon-peel. Got it ? [Certainly, Monsieur.
The barman ~~was clearly~~ *seemed* pleased with the idea ~~of the mixture.~~

Gosh, that's certainly a ~~mants~~ drink, said Leiter.
Bond laughed - when him - er - concentrating, he explained.
I never have more than one drink before dinner, ~~apologised Bond.~~
But I like that, *one* to be large and very strong and very cold and very
well-made. I hate small portions of anything, particularly ~~if its~~ *when they* tasted
bad. This drink's my own invention and I'm going to patent it when I can
think of a good name. [He watched carefully as the deep glass *became* frosted
with the pale golden drink, slightly aerated by the bruising of the
shaker. He ~~lifted his glass to Leiter and~~ *reached for it &* took a long sip. [Excellent,
he said to the barman, but if you can get a vodka made with grain
instead of potatoes, you will find it still better." *mais n'enculons*
pas des mouches" he added ~~in an aside to the barman. The barman~~
grinned. You certainly think things out, said Leiter with amused respect
as they carried their glasses to a corner of the room, ~~and in th~~ *He laughed.*
lowered his voice, you'd better call it the Blue ~~Case Special~~ *Escape* after that
something similar ~~they~~ *someone* threw at ~~you~~ this afternoon. *someone else*
~~and laughed~~ They sat down, Bond laughed. [I see the spot marked
X has been roped off from the public and they're making cars take a
detour over the pavement. I hope it has'nt frightened away any of the

Fleming's original manuscript for Casino Royale: *Bond orders his favourite martini. He subsequently decides to call it a 'Vesper' after the book's femme fatale, Vesper Lynd.*

once returned home unexpectedly to find his wife's literary friends in his drawing room reading out passages and laughing derisively. Even his publisher suggested he tone down the sexual content.

Defending his novels against those who yearned for a return to the clean-living Edwardian heroism of 'Bulldog' Drummond or Richard Hannay, Fleming retorted that 'All history is sex and violence.' Nonetheless, the works of Fleming shared some common factors with those of 'Sapper' (H. C. McNeile) and John Buchan in the streak of chauvinism and the propensity of villains to be foreigners, often with physical deformities. Envisaging how scientific and technological advances made it increasingly possible to hold the world to ransom, Fleming wrote, 'These politicians can't see that the Atomic Age has created the most deadly saboteur in the history of the world, the little man with the heavy suitcase.' Yet while such a villain might spring schemes of dastardly depravity, Bond, like Buchan's heroes before him, exemplified an idea more uplifting: that a sufficiently brave individual could bring about change and even save the world from deadly peril.

1956
THE SÈVRES PROTOCOL

THE SECRET DOCUMENT BEHIND THE SUEZ CRISIS

The Sèvres Protocol was top secret. It engineered the Suez Crisis, one of the most calamitous – and shameful – episodes in British foreign policy. Having destroyed his copy of the incriminating document, Anthony Eden, the prime minister, always denied it had ever existed. Unfortunately for his reputation, the Israeli government kept its copy.

In post-war strategy, successive Labour and Conservative administrations regarded the Middle East as being of vital national importance. The region was host to major British economic investments (especially oil) as well as to British naval and air bases from which to counter the Soviet threat. Clement Attlee's Cabinet considered, before deciding not to use, military action against Iran when it nationalized the Anglo-Iranian Oil (subsequently BP) refinery at Abadan in 1951. However, two years later, the British and United States governments ensured the restoration of their oil concessions by providing backing for a coup in Tehran that overthrew the Iranian leader, Mohammad Mosaddeq.

Meanwhile, in 1952 a military coup in Cairo had removed Britain's client rulers in Egypt and set the path for Gamal Abdel Nasser, an Arab nationalist, to come to power. Although Britain negotiated an orderly withdrawal from its Egyptian bases, it considered as sacrosanct the maintenance of the Suez Canal as an international shipping lane and conduit for Europe's oil supplies. When, on 26 July 1956, Nasser nationalized the Suez Canal, the new British prime minister, Anthony Eden, feared the worst.

Eden's foreign secretary, Selwyn Lloyd, was dispatched to the United Nations in New York to try to broker a settlement. On 14 October, Eden was visited at Chequers, the prime ministerial weekend home, by General Maurice Challe, the deputy chief of staff of the French armed forces, and the French minister for social affairs (deputizing for the foreign minister), Albert Gazier, who put to him an

THE RETREAT FROM EMPIRE: BRITAIN'S FORMER COLONIES GAIN THEIR INDEPENDENCE

1947 India gains independence (and is partitioned, creating also West and East Pakistan).

1948 Ceylon (Sri Lanka) and Burma gain independence.

1949 The Republic of Ireland leaves the Commonwealth.

1954 British troops vacate Egypt and Sudan gains independence.

1957 The Gold Coast (Ghana) gains independence, as does the Federation of Malaya (Malaysia).

1960 Cyprus, British Somaliland and Nigeria gain independence.

1961 Sierra Leone, British Cameroon and Tanganyika gain independence. South Africa, under National Party rule, leaves the Commonwealth.

1962 Jamaica, Trinidad and Tobago, Western Samoa and Uganda gain independence.

1963 Kenya and Zanzibar gain independence, the latter to merge with Tanganyika to form Tanzania.

1964 Northern Rhodesia (Zambia), Nyasaland (Malawi) and Malta gain independence.

1965 Southern Rhodesia makes its unilateral declaration of independence (UDI) from British rule, to avoid black-majority rule. The Gambia gains independence.

1966 Barbados, Lesotho and Botswana gain independence.

1967 Aden (South Yemen) gains independence.

1968 Mauritius and Swaziland gain independence.

1970 Fiji and Tonga gain independence.

1971 Bahrain and Qatar gain independence.

1973 The Bahamas gain independence.

1974 Grenada gains independence.

1976 The Seychelles gain independence.

1978 Dominica gains independence.

1979 The Gilbert Islands (Kiribati) gain independence.

1980 Zimbabwe (formerly Southern Rhodesia) gains independence after a prolonged liberation struggle.

1981 Belize gains independence.

1984 Brunei gains independence.

1996 South Africa under Nelson Mandela rejoins the Commonwealth.

1997 Hong Kong is reunited with China following the expiration of its lease to Britain.

extraordinary proposal. They suggested that if Israel could be persuaded to attack Egypt across the Sinai peninsula this would provide a convenient pretext for the British and French to land peacekeeping forces along the Suez Canal zone. Having secured it, they could from there help bring down Nasser's regime.

Regrettably, Eden thought this was a sound idea. Two days later he travelled with Lloyd to France for talks at the Palais Matignon with Guy Mollet, the French prime minister and his foreign minister, Christian Pineau. Lloyd did not like the plan but lacked the courage to stand up to Eden, whose reputation in foreign policy was high (he had three times been foreign secretary, in 1935–8, 1940–45 and 1951–5). Eden became obsessed with the notion that Nasser was another Hitler whose ambitions it would be calamitous to appease. Fearful of Nasser's support for Algerian nationalists, the French had as much – indeed more – reason than the British to want to see the regional troublemaker toppled. Crucially, Israel had to be brought into the conspiracy too.

The vital negotiations were conducted, in tight secrecy, between 22 and 24 October, at a suitable location – on the Rue Emanuel Girot in the Paris suburb of Sèvres in an elegant villa that had been a hideout for the French Resistance during the war. The talks began with the French delegation, led by Mollet and Pineau, trying to persuade the reluctant Israelis to do their bidding. The Israeli team, led by their prime minister and defence minister, David Ben-Gurion, included Moshe Dayan and Shimon Peres. They were then joined by the British, looking distinctly uncomfortable, in the guise of Selwyn Lloyd and his private secretary, Donald Logan.

Eden preferred not to attend in person and his aloofness was understandable. After all, it was a covert meeting of those conceiving an international conspiracy. Lloyd was ill at ease and it was only after his departure that relations between the French and Israelis improved on the second day. That night, back in London, Lloyd and Eden discussed progress with Pineau. Brushing aside moral and practical complaints, Eden remained enthusiastic. All was set for the third and final day's negotiations at Sèvres. With Lloyd unable to attend, Britain was represented there by Donald Logan and Patrick Dean, an assistant under-secretary of state at the Foreign Office.

The Israelis were finally persuaded, seeing the scheme as a chance to be rid of Nasser, a potentially implacable enemy, whilst cementing better relations with the French and British. It was agreed that Israel would initiate the crisis by invading the Sinai peninsula on 29 October. Feigning shock, the British and French would

3. —

3° – Dans le cas où le Gouvernement EGYPTIEN n'aurait pas dans les délais fixés donné son accord aux clauses de l'appel qui lui a été adressé, les Forces Anglo-Françaises déclancheront le 31 octobre dans les premières heures de la matinée les opérations militaires contre les Forces Egyptiennes.

4° – Le Gouvernement Israélien enverra des Forces afin d'occuper la côte OUEST du Golfe d'AKABA et le groupe des Iles TIRAN et SANAPIR pour assurer la liberté de navigation dans le golfe d'AKABA.

5° – Israël s'engage à ne pas attaquer la JORDANIE pendant la période des opérations contre l'EGYPTE.

Mais, au cas où dans la même période la JORDANIE attaquerait Israël, le Gouvernement Britannique s'engage à ne pas venir en aide à la JORDANIE.

6° – Les dispositions du présent PROTOCOLE doivent demeurer rigoureusement secrètes.

7° – Elles entreront en vigueur après l'accord des Trois Gouvernements.

A surviving copy of the incriminating document that Anthony Eden denied existed. The Sèvres Protocol was hurriedly typed up in French and signed by the French foreign minister, Christian Pineau, the British under-secretary of state, Patrick Dean, and the Israeli prime minister, David Ben-Gurion.

The Sèvres Protocol, 1956

The results of the conversations which took place at Sèvres from 22–24 October 1956 between the representatives of the Governments of the United Kingdom, the State of Israel and of France are the following:

1. The Israeli forces launch in the evening of 29 October 1956 a large scale attack on the Egyptian forces with the aim of reaching the Canal Zone the following day.

2. On being apprised of these events, the British and French Governments during the day of 30 October 1956 respectively and simultaneously make two appeals to the Egyptian Government and the Israeli Government on the following lines:

   A. To the Egyptian Government
      a) halt all acts of war.
      b) withdraw all its troops ten miles from the Canal.
      c) accept temporary occupation of key positions on the Canal by the Anglo-French forces to guarantee freedom of passage through the Canal by vessels of all nations until a final settlement.

   B. To the Israeli Government
      a) halt all acts of war.
      b) withdraw all its troops ten miles to the east of the Canal.

   In addition, the Israeli Government will be notified that the French and British Governments have demanded of the Egyptian Government to accept temporary occupation of key positions along the Canal by Anglo-French forces. It is agreed that if one of the Governments refused, or did not give its consent, within twelve hours the Anglo-French forces would intervene with the means necessary to ensure that their demands are accepted.

   C. The representatives of the three Governments agree that the Israeli Government will not be required to meet the conditions in the appeal addressed to it, in the event that the Egyptian Government does not accept those in the appeal addressed to it for their part.

3. In the event that the Egyptian Government should fail to agree within the stipulated time to the conditions of the appeal addressed to it, the Anglo-French forces will launch military operations against the Egyptian forces in the early hours of the morning of 31 October.

4. The Israeli Government will send forces to occupy the western shore of the Gulf of Aqaba and the group of islands Tirane and Sanafir to ensure freedom of navigation in the Gulf of Aqaba.

5. Israel undertakes not to attack Jordan during the period of operations against Egypt. But in the event that during the same period Jordan should attack Israel, the British Government undertakes not to come to the aid of Jordan.

6. The arrangements of the present protocol must remain strictly secret.

7. They will enter into force after the agreement of the three Governments.

(signed)

CHRISTIAN PINEAU   PATRICK DEAN   DAVID BEN-GURION

issue separate appeals for both sides to disengage and then land their own forces in the canal zone as a buffer between the rivals, supposedly destabilizing Egypt and thereby threatening Nasser's position. Much as the British would have preferred to keep the details off the record, they felt it might look suspicious if they refused Ben-Gurion's request that a summary of what had been agreed should be drawn up and signed.

The resulting protocol was hurriedly typed up in French on a portable typewriter – seemingly without sufficient time to correct minor typing errors and its irregular layout. Three copies were made, one for each of the participating delegations. Pineau signed for the French and Ben-Gurion for the Israelis. Dean initialled each page on behalf of Britain and signed at the end. Stilted congratulations were exchanged over a glass of champagne. The party became more amicable after the British left, when the French and Israelis felt able to toast another consequence – separate and unknown to the British – of their collaboration: namely, French assistance in turning Israel into a nuclear power.

Back in Britain, Eden endorsed Dean's actions whilst being furious that a formal record had been kept. He had the British copy destroyed and tried – in vain – to get the French and Israelis to do likewise (although the French copy was subsequently mislaid).

The Israeli attack went according to plan; British and French troops landed without serious losses, but the plotters had failed to take sufficient account of a crucial factor: the hostility of the United States. Transatlantic relations turned sour. Oil sanctions were threatened. Critically, there was a run on the pound. Lacking the reserves to support the plummeting value of the currency, Harold Macmillan, the chancellor of the exchequer, performed a dramatic

U-turn, arguing in Cabinet for the suspension of the military operation as the only means of securing the vital American financial support that was currently being withheld. Reluctantly, Eden felt compelled to bow to the pressure of the money markets. A ceasefire was arranged for 5 p.m. on 6 November and on 2 December the government formally announced that all British forces were being immediately withdrawn from Egypt.

For Britain it was an unqualified humiliation. The episode appeared to show that this once great power was so economically weak that it could no longer operate a foreign policy independent of American support. The domestic political repercussions were also enormous. The Labour Party found a strong and united voice in opposing the adventure. Middle-class liberals felt alienated by the actions of a Conservative leader they had previously admired. Still suffering from the severe stress that undermined his judgment during the crisis, Eden fell genuinely ill from a bungled gall-bladder operation and resigned in January 1957.

The humbling of Britain's global pretensions was not the least of it. Moscow had previously decided not to intervene against the reformist government in Hungary, but changed its mind when the Suez Crisis provided the necessary distraction. While the world was watching events on the Sinai peninsula, Soviet soldiers and tanks were sent in to crush Budapest's assertion of independence, killing 20,000 Hungarians in the process. The cracks in the Iron Curtain were filled up again with devastating consequences for the world.

Both in Britain and abroad there was widespread suspicion from the first that the Suez Crisis was the consequence of collusion between the British, French and Israelis. Eden had mentioned in a Cabinet meeting of 23 October 'secret conversations which had been held in Paris with representatives of the Israeli Government' about which none of his colleagues chose to challenge him. Only the minister of state at the Foreign Office, Anthony Nutting, resigned. Eden then lied to the House of Commons on 20 December when he stated: 'to say it quite bluntly to the House there was not foreknowledge that Israel would attack Egypt – there was not', a pretence he maintained subsequently.

Nutting was the first official to publicly admit – in his autobiography of 1967 – that there had been collusion at Sèvres. The French and Israeli participants followed suit. It is only because the Israelis refused Eden's request that they burn the secret protocol that we have unanswerable proof of the full extent of the Franco-British conspiracy.

1965

ANTHONY CROSLAND'S DEPARTMENT OF EDUCATION CIRCULAR 10/65

THE ABOLITION OF GRAMMAR SCHOOLS AND THE CREATION OF COMPREHENSIVE SCHOOLS

Before the Second World War, four out of five children never formally acquired a secondary education. They remained at elementary school until the age of fourteen, after which they went into employment. This system was ended by the 1944 Education Act, introduced by the Conservative secretary of state for education in the wartime coalition government, R. A. ('Rab') Butler. Henceforth, all children would leave elementary school at eleven and then have a minimum of four years' secondary schooling. How they performed academically at the age of eleven determined what sort of secondary school they would attend. The majority would be given places in secondary modern schools and from there go straight on to the workplace, while a few went to the small number of technical schools. Around a quarter of the most intelligent, as measured by the 'eleven plus' exam, would proceed to grammar schools, where they could expect a rigorous and challenging curriculum that was intended to prepare them for the prospect of university and a professional career.

The twenty years following the Butler Act witnessed a great breaking down of class barriers and the rise of social mobility, fuelled, in part, by a grammar-school system that provided a free but academically exacting education to those deemed best able to benefit from it regardless of their family's finances or circumstances. It was a motor of the new 'meritocracy', a term first coined in 1958. However, the undoubted excellence of the schooling provided for the gifted contrasted with the quality of what was offered to the majority in secondary moderns, where the bar of aspiration was set lower. To critics, it was inherently unfair to perpetuate a system

that divided children at the age of eleven into two different forms of schooling that usually shaped their subsequent attainments.

In 1965, Anthony Crosland (1918–77) became education secretary in Harold Wilson's Labour government. Educated at Highgate, a highly academic private school, and at Oxford, where he was both a student and a don, Crosland was a convinced modernizer and author of a highly influential book, *The Future of Socialism*. Despite the advantages he had himself derived from it, he detested selective education and declared that he intended 'to destroy every f---ing grammar school' in the country. He wanted them replaced by comprehensive schools, the egalitarian, non-selective model that was already being tested by a number of local education authorities, most notably in Labour-controlled London.

To this effect, he issued Circular 10/65. Although it lacked the statutory power to enforce the comprehensive model, it made clear that this was nonetheless the will of Parliament and that local education authorities were accordingly expected to submit their plans 'for reorganising secondary education in their area on comprehensive lines' to the secretary of state. The circular was actively seized upon by those determined to smash the grammar schools. They argued that the two different models could not continue side by side, for the whole point of comprehensives was that they were mixed-ability institutions. Disingenuously, the claim was made that comprehensives were 'grammar schools for all'. Sceptics countered that better-resourced secondary moderns for all would be the reality.

Whilst comprehensives would have spread even without endorsement by central government, the impetus given to them by Circular 10/65 was palpable. When it was published, there were only 200 comprehensive schools in the country. Five years later, the number had risen to 1,000. In 1975, the returning Labour government carried on the assault on selective institutions by abolishing direct-grant schools, among which were some of the most venerable and high-performing schools in the country. Those that survived did so by becoming private schools – which was hardly what Labour had intended. Overall, the speed at which successful educational establishments, some of which had survived for three or four hundred years, were either closed or transformed beyond all recognition represented nothing short of a cultural revolution. By 1980, 90 per cent of Britain's schools had become comprehensives.

The results were open to interpretation. Social mobility went into decline, although the extent to which this was due to other government policies is debatable. The reputation of comprehensives has suffered because of a tendency

From Department of Education Circular 10/65

It is the Government's declared objective to end selection at eleven plus and to eliminate separatism in secondary education, The Government's policy has been endorsed by the House of Commons in a motion passed on 21st January 1965:

'That this House, conscious of the need to raise educational standards at all levels, and regretting that the realisation of this objective is impeded by the separation of children into different types of secondary schools, notes with approval the efforts of local authorities to reorganise secondary education on comprehensive lines which will preserve all that is valuable in grammar school education for those children who now receive it and make it available to more children; recognises that the method and timing of such reorganisation should vary to meet local needs; and believes that the time is now ripe for a declaration of national policy.'

The Secretary of State accordingly requests local education authorities, if they have not already done so, to prepare and submit to him plans for reorganising secondary education in their areas on comprehensive lines. The purpose of this Circular is to provide some central guidance on the methods by which this can be achieved.

to compare them with the academic grammar schools they replaced rather than the secondary moderns for which comprehensives were often an improvement. Nonetheless, the introduction of comprehensives coincided with new 'child-centred' approaches to teaching, which traditionalists thought lacked rigour. Those wishing to escape this style of teaching either moved to counties like Kent or Buckinghamshire, where many of the 164 residual grammar schools in England survived (as they did in Northern Ireland), or turned to private schools. The fact that the best comprehensives – judged by exam results – tended to be within the catchment areas of some of Britain's most expensive neighbourhoods suggested that Crosland's social experiment unintentionally acted to reinforce social barriers, rather than break them down. In most cases, the best education was still only available to those who could either pay school fees or afford an expensive mortgage.

More than forty years later, Circular 10/65 remained controversial, though the debate had shifted. The Conservative Party gave up attempting to bring back grammar schools, while Labour lost interest in eliminating the few that had survived. Instead, the argument focused on reforming the comprehensives.

1967
THE BEATLES' *SGT. PEPPER* ALBUM COVER

AN ICON OF BRITAIN'S 'SWINGING SIXTIES'

In the 1950s, Britain's youth imported pop music largely from the United States. Home-grown talent either performed cover versions of American hits or adopted an imitative transatlantic style.

By the beginning of the 1960s, rock 'n' roll appeared to be running out of ideas. Without an obvious successor, a variety of rival styles briefly vied for supremacy. It was during this period, in May 1962, that the trad-jazz clarinettist Acker Bilk became the first Briton to reach number one in the American billboard charts with his instrumental number 'Stranger on the Shore'.

Coincidentally, just days later The Beatles signed a contract with Parlophone, a record label owned by EMI, and promptly changed the face of pop music across the world. Within months 'Beatlemania' had conquered Britain and by 1964 had successfully crossed the Atlantic. So began a 'revolution in the head' that placed post-imperial Britain at the heart of a new, vibrant youth culture.

The Beatles were four Liverpudlians: the singer-songwriting duo of John Lennon and Paul McCartney – respectively guitar and bass guitar – with George Harrison also playing guitar and Ringo Starr on drums. They gained valuable professional assistance from their manager, Brian Epstein, and their producer at Parlophone, George Martin. None of this commercial expertise, however, masked the reality that these four working-class lads were the masters of their own destiny. The fact that they wrote their own music was a decisive mark of independence, far removed from the previous notion that pop singers merely performed the work of unseen professional songwriters. Together, Lennon and McCartney proved to be the most successful composers in British history. Despite the break-up of The Beatles in 1970, their popularity endured, as did their critical reputation. By the twenty-first century, they had sold over 1 billion albums worldwide.

The album cover of Sgt. Pepper's Lonely Hearts Club Band is depicted in the fourth plate section.

383

Over successive albums, The Beatles' style developed, as did its complexity. *Please Please Me*, their first album, was recorded in under 600 minutes. More albums followed. In particular, *Revolver* (1966) provided a major staging-post in their progress towards greater musical complexity and the broadening of their audience far beyond the original, if fickle, tastes of teenagers. In 1966 they stopped playing live concerts, choosing to devote more time to exploring new influences and technical advances. Released the following year, *Sgt. Pepper's Lonely Hearts Club Band* took 129 days to complete, devouring 700 hours in London's Abbey Road recording studios. The resulting sound transformed the genre, pointing the way towards the dreamlike 'psychedelic' scene of the late 1960s, with its drugs, freedom from inhibition and student revolt. Indeed, from the singalong – almost Edwardian music-hall – simplicity of 'When I'm Sixty-Four', to the near-heavy-metal instrumental opening of the title track, to the psychedelia of 'Lucy in the Sky with Diamonds', it was a work of extraordinary eclecticism. More than forty years later, it is still regularly cited as the most influential album in the history of popular music.

The *Sgt. Pepper* album cover was the outward sign of the group's ambitions. Breaking away from traditional reliance on the work of commercial designers (who provided a rejected design), a leading British artist was approached. This was Peter Blake, whose work often mixed images from advertising and other popular media. At the time of their first full-length film, *A Hard Day's Night* in 1964, The Beatles were promoted through images of being joyfully pursued across London by screaming and adoring fans. Two years later, the 'Fab Four' were tiring of the mass adulation that had accompanied their rise. For the *Sgt. Pepper* album cover they appeared thinly disguised in fancy dress as bandsmen, surrounded not by their fans, but by a background montage of the people of their choice.

'People We Like' was the artwork's title. The photo shoot took place at Chelsea Manor Studios, Flood Street, London on 20 March 1967, with the characters represented by life-size cut-outs pasted on to hardboard. George Harrison, who was increasingly influenced by Eastern spiritualism, opted for Indian gurus. Ever the controversialist, John Lennon chose Gandhi, Jesus and Hitler, none of whom made the final line-up. Ringo Starr, in contrast, was happy with whatever the rest of the band wanted. In its final form, the background crowd included such eclectic characters as Sir Robert Peel, Karl Marx, Diana Dors and Stuart Sutcliffe, the band's former member, and Lennon's close friend, who had died just before their rise to success. Permission had to be sought to represent people still living.

THE SWINGING SIXTIES

1960 The British paperback publication of D. H. Lawrence's *Lady Chatterley's Lover* is cleared in an obscenity trial. The year's best-selling single is Elvis Presley's 'It's Now or Never'.

1961 The contraceptive pill goes on sale (for married women only until 1970, but the Brook clinic prescribes it to unmarried girls from 1964). Elvis Presley's 'Are You Lonesome Tonight?' is the best-selling single.

1962 The Telstar 1 satellite provides the first live transatlantic television feed. The innovative BBC satire programme *That Was the Week That Was* is broadcast (despite massive popularity, it is scrapped after its second series in 1963). The film version of *Dr No* launches the James Bond films. Frank Ifield's 'I Remember You' is the best-selling single.

1963 The Profumo sex scandal rocks the government. Harold Macmillan resigns as prime minister due to ill-health. 'She Loves You' by The Beatles is the best-selling single.

1964 Labour narrowly wins the general election, ending thirteen years of Conservative government. Barbara Hulanicki opens her first Biba shop and Terence Conran his first Habitat store. Mods and Rockers clash at seaside resorts. Mary Whitehouse holds her first 'Clean Up TV' public meeting. 'Can't Buy Me Love' by The Beatles is the best-selling single.

1965 Sir Winston Churchill dies. Mary Quant's 'miniskirt' design is launched. The death penalty is abolished. 'Tears' by Ken Dodd is the best-selling single.

1966 England wins the football World Cup. Oil is discovered in the North Sea. A slag-heap disaster engulfs a school in Aberfan, killing 144 children. 'Green, Green Grass of Home' by Tom Jones is the best-selling single.

1967 Abortion is legalized in England, Wales and Scotland. The Sexual Offences Act permits homosexual acts for those over twenty-one in private in England and Wales (effective in Scotland in 1980 and Northern Ireland in 1982). 'The Summer of Love' marks the apex of the 'hippie' movement. Engelbert Humperdinck's 'Release Me' is the best-selling single.

1968 The 'I'm Backing Britain' campaign, launched to work an extra half-hour every day without pay to help the economy, is fleetingly popular. *Carry On Up the Khyber* hits the cinemas. 'Hey Jude' by The Beatles is the best-selling single.

1969 The first flight of supersonic airliner Concorde. The first broadcast of colour TV in the UK. The Divorce Reform Act (effective from 1971 in England and Wales) creates 'irretrievable breakdown' as grounds for divorce. *The Italian Job* hits the cinemas. 'Sugar, Sugar' by The Archies is the best-selling single.

Before a personal letter from the band persuaded her, Mae West initially refused, complaining, 'What would I be doing in a lonely hearts club?'

Returning from the Abbey Road studios at dawn to a flat off the King's Road (then a centre of London's 'swinging' fashion scene), the band placed speakers on the window ledge and serenaded the neighbourhood. Their press officer later recollected, 'All the windows around us opened up and people leaned out, wondering. It was obvious who it was on the record. Nobody complained. A lovely spring morning. People were smiling and giving us the thumbs-up.'

1972
THE ACCESSION TREATY TO THE EUROPEAN ECONOMIC COMMUNITY

BRITAIN AND EUROPEAN INTEGRATION

The United Kingdom's decision to sign up to the Treaty of Rome and its successor treaties led – over a thirty-year period – to the biggest transfer of sovereignty in the history of the British state. As far as England was concerned, it was potentially the greatest transferral of authority since 1211, when a temporarily humiliated King John offered his kingdom to the pope.

The rationale for doing so was partly idealistic. The European Economic Community (the European Union after 1993) represented the coming together of countries whose long histories of periodic hostility had been the precursor to two devastating world wars. It was also practical. The period after 1945 witnessed a steady deterioration in Britain's status as a global power. Hopes were raised that becoming a leading member of a new, greater entity could actually increase London's international influence. There was also the reality that in the fifteen years since the EEC's birth, its members' economies and standards of living had improved far more rapidly than had Britain's. In addition, some Conservatives who feared the anti-free-market policies of the left wing of the Labour Party believed that joining the tariff-free 'Common Market' would permanently clip the wings of native socialism, safeguarding the future of capitalism in Britain.

The government's attitude towards European political integration shifted over time. Although Winston Churchill had initially welcomed it, he also summed up Britain's relationship towards it as: 'We are with Europe but not of it. We are linked, but not combined. We are interested and associated, but not absorbed.' In essence, European integration was necessarily a Franco-German project, devised by two Frenchmen, Jean Monnet and Robert Schuman. Britain was not consulted when the Schuman Plan was devised for what became the European Coal and

Steel Community in 1952 and chose not to participate in the talks that led to the signing of the EEC's founding charter, the Treaty of Rome, by France, West Germany, Italy, Belgium, Luxembourg and the Netherlands in 1957. Harold Macmillan's belated attempt to secure British membership was vetoed in 1963 by France's president, Charles de Gaulle, who did so using arguments similar to Churchill's assessment of Britain's continental commitment.

The situation was radically altered by the election of the Conservative leader Edward Heath as prime minister in 1970. He not only saw EEC membership as a means to reverse Britain's relative economic decline but approached the prospect with the zeal of the committed idealist. Whilst the Tory election manifesto had weighed the pros and cons of membership before promising merely 'Our sole commitment is to negotiate; no more, no less', few who knew Heath could have doubted he was determined to get a deal at almost any payable price. It was in this spirit that terms were agreed by June 1971. Divisions on the issue of joining the EEC crossed party boundaries, with opinion polls suggesting widespread scepticism among the electorate. Nevertheless, in October the House of Commons endorsed entry by 356 votes to 244. Upon this mandate, Heath signed the Treaty of Accession in Brussels on 22 January 1972. The treaty was made law by the European Communities Act in October. Membership took effect from 1 January 1973.

The debate was not so easily concluded. At issue was not just what Britain had signed up to, but what she might subsequently find herself committed to in an organization dedicated to 'ever closer union'. Following the Heath government's fall in February 1974, the incoming Labour administration of Harold Wilson tried to paper over its own divisions in 1975 by offering the British electorate a referendum on whether – after a cosmetic renegotiation of the terms – to remain within the EEC. In the midst of an economic crisis, Britain's voters preferred by a ratio of two to one to stay in. The official 'yes' campaign pamphlet sent to every home stated that important decisions in Brussels 'can be taken only if all the members of the Council agree. The minister representing Britain can veto any proposal for a new law or a new tax if he considers it to be against British interests.' In reality, there were already plans to curtail the right to veto. By 1990, European judges were successfully striking down British Acts of Parliament.

European competence over British law received its greatest boost in 1987 when the Single European Act – passed after only a desultory Commons debate – established the Single Market. This process, which was completed by 1992,

Commemorative postage stamps marked Britain's entry into the European Communities in 1973.

1957 The Treaty of Rome creates the European Economic Community (EEC), comprising France, West Germany, Italy, Belgium, Netherlands and Luxembourg. The 'six' also set up Euratom with the aspiration of framing a common nuclear energy policy.

1958 The European Court of Justice is established to interpret the Treaty of Rome's provisions.

1960 The European Free Trade Association (EFTA) is launched to cut tariffs between the UK, Austria, Switzerland, Denmark, Norway, Sweden and Portugal while avoiding creating supranational institutions.

1961 The UK applies to join the EEC (the application is vetoed by France in 1963).

1967 The EEC, Euratom and the European Coal and Steel Community are brought together as the European Community (EC).

1968 The Common Market is completed, removing internal tariffs.

1973 Britain, Denmark and Ireland join the EC.

1975 British membership of the EC is upheld in a national referendum.

1979 The European Monetary System is established. Britain joins but does not commit sterling to the EMS's Exchange Rate Mechanism (ERM). The first direct elections to the European Parliament are held.

1981 Greece joins the EC.

1984 Margaret Thatcher secures a partial budget rebate of UK contributions to the EC.

1986 Spain and Portugal join the EC. The new European flag is unveiled (a circle of twelve gold stars on a blue background).

1987 The Single European Act enters into law, removing national vetoes across the market and instituting regulatory policies in order to create a 'single market'.

1990 Britain pegs sterling within the ERM.

1992 The Maastricht Treaty is signed (it comes into effect in 1993), creating the European Union (EU) and committing members to establishing the single currency, the Euro. Britain retains the right to opt out of the Euro and Social Chapter policies. European citizenship is created.

1992 Sterling is withdrawn from the ERM.

1995 Austria, Sweden and Finland join the EU. A Norwegian referendum rejects membership. The Schengen Pact begins removing border controls between members (though the UK and Ireland do not join).

1997 Britain opts into Maastricht's Social Chapter. The Amsterdam Treaty increases EU legal competence over asylum, immigration, and social and employment policies.

2002 The Euro replaces national currencies. The UK, Sweden and Denmark opt out.

2005 The EU expands to twenty-five members – bringing in Malta, Cyprus, Estonia, Latvia, Lithuania, Poland, Hungary, Slovenia, Slovakia and the Czech Republic. Referenda votes in France and the Netherlands reject an EU constitution.

2007 Romania and Bulgaria join the EU.

2009 The 2007 Lisbon Treaty becomes law, enforcing much of the (supposedly) defeated constitution proposals, further reducing national veto powers, strengthening the EU's common foreign and diplomatic policies, giving legal force to the Charter of Fundamental Rights, and establishing permanent positions for the European president of the Council and the high representative for foreign affairs.

secured the free movement of goods, services, money and people within the European Community (which had by then increased to twelve members) as well as introducing qualified majority voting procedures in related policy areas, thereby ending national vetoes. Generally welcomed by Britain's major exporters, it also brought in its wake a vast extension of new regulation. For its promoter, Margaret Thatcher, it came to represent the high-water mark after which her faith in the European 'project' subsided. Conversely, Labour Party and trade union leaders warmed to its decisive legal influence over working practices and other social issues.

Mrs Thatcher's successor as prime minister, John Major, signed the Maastricht Treaty in 1992, which transferred further areas of law-making to Brussels. In particular, it established monetary union and a single currency, the Euro, for its members – a vast transferral of monetary and economic authority from which Britain and Denmark opted out. In 2007 the Lisbon Treaty was signed with the aim of creating what was effectively a constitution for a European Union that – with the collapse of communism – had spread to twenty-seven members and embraced nearly 500 million people. Measures to coordinate foreign policy were also devised, with an eventual goal that Europe might speak to the world with one voice. The structure of a federal superstate was clearly discernible, if not fully operational.

Supporters of deeper integration maintained that sovereignty was distinct from power and that membership of the European Union enhanced British power. Nevertheless, there remained a democratic deficit at the heart of the project which reduced voters to electing MPs who, over large areas of legislation, were no longer responsible for making the law.

EEC Accession Treaty, 1972

HIS MAJESTY THE KING OF THE BELGIANS,
HER MAJESTY THE QUEEN OF DENMARK,
THE PRESIDENT OF THE FEDERAL REPUBLIC OF GERMANY,
THE PRESIDENT OF THE FRENCH REPUBLIC,
THE PRESIDENT OF IRELAND,
THE PRESIDENT OF THE ITALIAN REPUBLIC,
HIS ROYAL HIGHNESS THE GRAND DUKE OF LUXEMBOURG,
HER MAJESTY THE QUEEN OF THE NETHERLANDS,

THE PRESIDENT OF THE PORTUGUESE REPUBLIC,
HER MAJESTY THE QUEEN OF THE UNITED KINGDOM OF GREAT BRITAIN AND
NORTHERN IRELAND,

UNITED in their desire to pursue the attainment of the objectives of the Treaty
establishing the European Economic Community and the Treaty establishing the
European Atomic Energy Community,

DETERMINED in the spirit of those Treaties to construct an ever closer union among
the peoples of Europe on the foundations already laid,

CONSIDERING that Article 237 of the Treaty establishing the European Economic
Community and Article 205 of the Treaty establishing the European Atomic Energy
Community afford European States the opportunity of becoming members of these
Communities,

CONSIDERING that the Kingdom of Denmark, Ireland and the United Kingdom of
Great Britain and Northern Ireland have applied to become members of these
Communities,

CONSIDERING that the Council of the European Communities, after having
obtained the Opinion of the Commission, has declared itself in favour of the
admission of these States,

HAVE DECIDED to establish by common agreement the conditions of admission and
the adjustments to be made to the Treaties establishing the European Economic
Community and the European Atomic Energy Community and to this end have
designated as their Plenipotentiaries:

The Right Honourable Edward Heath MBE MP,
Prime Minister, First Lord of the Treasury, Minister for the Civil Service;

The Right Honourable Sir Alec Douglas-Home KT MP,
Her Majesty's Principal Secretary of State for Foreign and Commonwealth
Affairs;

The Right Honourable Geoffrey Rippon QC MP,
Chancellor of the Duchy of Lancaster;

Who, having exchanged their Full Powers found in good and due form,
HAVE AGREED as follows:

ARTICLE 1

1. The Kingdom of Denmark, Ireland and the United Kingdom of Great Britain and Northern Ireland hereby become members of the European Economic Community and of the European Atomic Energy Community and parties to the Treaties establishing these Communities as amended or supplemented. . . .

ARTICLE 2

This Treaty will be ratified by the High Contracting Parties in accordance with their respective constitutional requirements. The instruments of ratification will be deposited with the Government of the Italian Republic by 31 December 1972 at the latest.

This Treaty will enter into force on 1 January 1973, provided that all the instruments of ratification have been deposited before that date and that all the instruments of accession to the European Coal and Steel Community are deposited on that date....

ARTICLE 3

This Treaty, drawn up in a single original in the Danish, Dutch, English, French, German, Irish and Italian languages, the Danish, Dutch, English, French, German, Irish and Italian texts all being equally authentic, will be deposited in the archive of the Government of the Italian Republic, which will transmit a certified copy to each of the Governments of the other signatory States.

In witness whereof, the undersigned Plenipotentiaries have affixed their signatures below this Treaty.

Done at Brussels on this twenty-second day of January in the year one thousand nine hundred and seventy-two.

1973

THE COMMUNIQUÉ OF THE SUNNINGDALE AGREEMENT

EFFORTS TO SOLVE NORTHERN IRELAND'S 'TROUBLES'

Since 1921, the six counties of Northern Ireland had enjoyed a large measure of legislative autonomy. The province had its own Parliament, elected by universal adult suffrage, which met at Stormont, on the outskirts of Belfast. While retaining ultimate executive authority and providing subsidies, London's politicians largely left their Belfast counterparts to run their own affairs.

Irish Nationalist hopes at the signing of the 1921 Anglo-Irish Treaty – that partition would prove only a temporary expedient – were quickly confounded. As time passed, the prospect of a united Ireland receded. The promotion of overtly Catholic, culturally Gaelic and anti-British sentiments in the Irish Free State, particularly after Eamon de Valera came to power in 1932, was met in Ulster by a corresponding assertion of British defining characteristics. Despite the presence of a sizeable Catholic minority, Northern Ireland effectively had what its first prime minister, Lord Craigavon, termed 'a Protestant government for a Protestant people'.

Periodic acts of terror by the IRA between 1956 and 1962 entrenched rather than shifted this governing assumption. By 1968, however, a civil rights movement had successfully galvanized the province's Catholic/Nationalist minority in its demands for better housing and an end to the property qualification in local-government elections that had disproportionately reduced their voice in municipal affairs. Rival marches descended into violence. Responding to an appeal by the inspector general of the Royal Ulster Constabulary, and concluding that the Northern Irish authorities were incapable of restoring order in a non-sectarian fashion, Harold Wilson's government sent in British troops in 1969.

The euphemistically named 'Troubles' only escalated and by 1972 British troop deployment had reached 21,000. The Provisional IRA brought terror throughout the province and also to the mainland. Loyalist paramilitaries retaliated with no

greater concern for human life. Support for the IRA swelled on both sides of the border, as well as in the United States, when British paratroopers – in confused and disputed circumstances – shot dead thirteen protesters during a march on 'Bloody Sunday' on 30 January 1972. During the course of that year, almost 500 people were killed in the violence and the IRA detonated 1,300 bombs. When Stormont refused Westminster's request to take over responsibility for law and order, Edward Heath's government responded by suspending Stormont and imposing direct rule from London. Heath's intention was to respect the will of Ulster's majority to remain within the United Kingdom while addressing the underlying problem that the province's Catholics, electorally a permanent minority at Stormont, felt marginalized by existing Northern Irish institutions.

The result was a power-sharing arrangement. In place of direct rule, the province would be governed by an executive, which neither community could dominate, and a legislature, the Assembly (which replaced the suspended Stormont parliament). Using proportional representation, elections to the Assembly in June 1973 returned a majority for the agreement and a power-sharing administration was formed of Unionists, the moderate-nationalist SDLP and the small, non-aligned Alliance Party.

Ominously, the new power-sharing arrangement was opposed by both Sinn Féin (the Provisional IRA's political wing) and the more militant Ulster Unionists, but what tipped the scales against its survival was the next strand of the process. Cross-border rather than cross-community in nature, it was agreed by the British and Irish governments, along with leaders of the Stormont Executive, when they met at Sunningdale, Berkshire, in December 1973. The resulting communiqué announced the establishment of a Council of Ireland, composed of politicians from both Belfast and Dublin, with responsibility for issues of common interest to both the North and the South. The Irish Republic – which still laid constitutional claim to the North – would concede Ulster's right to self-determination and London made clear it would not oppose unification if the North voted for it.

Although the areas of common policy envisaged at Sunningdale were limited, Unionists perceived them as a Trojan horse by which Dublin would increasingly interfere in Ulster politics. The Ulster Unionist Party's governing council voted to withdraw from the agreement and, in the United Kingdom's general election of February 1974, pro-Sunningdale Unionist MPs lost their seats to their opponents. The likelihood, already fatally undermined, that power-sharing could be sustained without the commitment of the Unionist majority was put beyond question in

Northern Ireland's Troubles

1968 A Civil Rights Association campaign is launched against discriminatory policies.

1969 Rioting in Londonderry and Belfast leads to British army troop deployment. The Provisional IRA is formed.

1970 Severe rioting in Londonderry and Belfast. The Nationalist SDLP is formed.

1971 Internment without trial is introduced for those suspected of paramilitary involvement. The Ulster Defence Association (UDA) and its terrorist unit, the Ulster Freedom Fighters, are formed.

1972 On 'Bloody Sunday', in Londonderry, thirteen civilians die from army gunshot wounds during a march. In retaliation, a mob burns down the British Embassy in Dublin. London imposes direct rule upon Northern Ireland. On 'Bloody Friday' the IRA explode twenty-two bombs in Belfast. The British army's 'Operation Motorman' retakes the 'no-go areas' established by republicans.

1973 Elections are held for a Northern Ireland Assembly. The Sunningdale Agreement is signed.

1974 Unionist strikes help bring down the Sunningdale Agreement. Direct rule is reimposed. The IRA bomb the House of Commons and pubs in Guildford and Birmingham.

1975 Internment is ended.

1976 Christopher Ewart-Biggs, the British ambassador to Ireland, is killed. 'Blanket protests' in the Maze prison.

1979 The Irish National Liberation Army (INLA) Republican splinter group murders the Tory politician Airey Neave. Eighteen British soldiers are killed by an IRA bomb at Warrenpoint. The Queen's cousin, Lord Louis Mountbatten, is murdered by the IRA.

1981 Ten republican prisoners die in hunger strikes at the Maze prison. Before his death, the IRA hunger striker Bobby Sands is elected an MP from prison.

1984 The IRA bomb Brighton's Grand Hotel, killing five in an attempt to murder Margaret Thatcher.

1985 The Anglo-Irish Agreement is concluded.

1987 The IRA bomb a Remembrance Sunday service at Enniskillen.

1991 The IRA launch a mortar attack on 10 Downing Street.

1993 The IRA explodes bombs at Warrington and the City of London.

1994 The IRA issues a seventeen-month ceasefire.

1996 The IRA bomb Manchester and London's new financial district at Canary Wharf.

1998 The Belfast Agreement is signed on Good Friday and approved in referenda in both Northern Ireland and the Irish Republic. The 'Real IRA', a dissident Republican group opposed to the peace process, bombs Omagh, murdering twenty-nine civilians.

1999 The Northern Ireland Assembly is re-established.

2001 The RUC is disbanded and replaced by the Police Service of Northern Ireland.

2005 The IRA puts its weapons 'beyond use'.

2007 British army operations in Northern Ireland are wound down. The Northern Ireland Executive is formed.

2010 Despite sporadic violence from splinter republican terror groups, the INLA and the UDA join the list of paramilitary organizations that put their weapons beyond use and the Independent International Commission of Decommissioning is disbanded.

May, when the province was paralyzed by a general strike that led to power cuts and barricades being erected across streets.

The strike was organized by the Ulster Workers' Council, an umbrella movement that included Protestant trade unionists, a the loyalist paramilitary group, the Ulster Defence Association (UDA). Within fourteen days it had achieved its objective and brought down Sunningdale's four-month experiment in power-sharing. Rather than risk all-out insurrection by turning the troops on the strikers in order to restore a system of government that the majority party had rejected, Harold Wilson's administration mothballed Stormont. Direct rule was reimposed from London.

The result was a further twenty-four years of deadlock and violence. Wilson had ordered a study into an alternative strategy, which on 31 May outlined the argument for Northern Ireland's expulsion from the United Kingdom. In this scenario, it would become a self-governing dominion (although, peculiarly, excluded from the Commonwealth), its people still the Queen's subjects but constitutionally severed from Britain in almost every other respect.

The Ulster Unionist leader, Brian Faulkner (above) with the Irish Taoiseach, Lian Cosgrove (below), during the Sunningdale negotiations, December 1973.

Far from being a solution, such a British withdrawal threatened to plunge Ulster into all-out civil war, possibly prompting military intervention by the Republic of Ireland. It was extremely doubtful whether the republic's army, only 12,000 strong, was capable of securing the province, given the likelihood that the attempt would spark an armed uprising by the Unionist majority – as a separate study by the Irish government also concluded.

So Ulster's direct rule from Westminster continued. It was not until the Belfast Agreement of Good Friday 1998 that the process recommenced of restoring devolved government. The Irish government finally renounced its territorial claim to the North, while power-sharing initiatives (cross-community and cross-border) similar to those of 1973, were revived in Ulster. These arrangements had to be halted until the IRA finally declared its terror campaign over in 2005 and put its weapons beyond use. Thereafter, power-sharing began to look as if it might enjoy greater permanence only in 2007 when, improbably, the Democratic Unionist Ian Paisley and Sinn Féin's Martin McGuinness became, respectively, first and deputy first minister. By then, the violence had claimed over 3,500 lives, including more than 1,000 British soldiers and Royal Ulster Constabulary police personnel, and over 1,800 civilians. The 1998 agreement that had laid the ground for ending the Troubles was summed up by the SDLP's Seamus Mallon as 'Sunningdale for slow learners'.

From the Sunningdale Agreement, 1973

5. The Irish Government fully accepted and solemnly declared that there could be no change in the status of Northern Ireland until a majority of the people of Northern Ireland desired a change in that status. The British Government solemnly declared that it was, and would remain, their policy to support the wishes of the majority of the people of Northern Ireland. The present status of Northern Ireland is that it is part of the United Kingdom. If in the future the majority of the people of Northern Ireland should indicate a wish to become part of a united Ireland, the British Government would support that wish. . . .

7. The Conference agreed that a Council of Ireland would be set up. It would be confined to representatives of the two parts of Ireland, with appropriate safeguards for the British Government's financial and other interests. It would comprise a Council of Ministers with executive and harmonising functions and a consultative role, and a Consultative Assembly with advisory and review functions. The Council of Ministers would act by unanimity, and would comprise a core of seven members of the Irish Government and an equal number of members of the Northern Ireland Executive with provision for the participation of other non-voting members of the Irish Government and the Northern Ireland Executive or Administration when matters within their departmental competence were discussed. The Council of Ministers would control the functions of the Council. The Chairmanship would rotate on an agreed basis between representatives of the Irish Government and of the Northern Ireland Executive. Arrangements would be made for the location of the first meeting, and the location of subsequent meetings would be determined by the Council of Ministers. The Consultative Assembly would consist of 60 members, 30 members from Dail Eireann chosen by the Dail on the basis of proportional representation by the single transferable vote, and 30 members from the Northern Ireland Assembly chosen by that Assembly and also on that basis. . . .

8. In the context of its harmonising functions and consultative role, the Council of Ireland would undertake important work relating, for instance, to the impact of EEC membership. As for executive functions, the first step would be to define and agree these in detail. . . . Studies would be directed to identifying, for the purposes of executive action by the Council of Ireland, suitable aspects of activities in the following broad fields:

(a) exploitation, conservation and development of natural resources and the
    environment;

(b) agricultural matters (including agricultural research, animal health and operational aspects of the Common Agriculture Policy), forestry and fisheries;

(c) co-operative ventures in the fields of trade and industry;

(d) electricity generation;

(e) tourism;

(f) roads and transport;

(g) advisory services in the field of public health;

(h) sport, culture and the arts.

It would be for the Oireachtas and the Northern Ireland Assembly to legislate from time to time as to the extent of functions to be devolved to the Council of Ireland. Where necessary, the British Government will cooperate in this devolution of functions. Initially, the functions to be vested would be those identified in accordance with the procedures set out above and decided, at the formal stage of the conference. to be transferred. . . .

10. It was agreed by all parties that persons committing crimes of violence, however motivated, in any part of Ireland should be brought to trial irrespective of the part of Ireland in which they are located. The concern which large sections of the people of Northern Ireland felt about this problem was in particular forcefully expressed by the representatives of the Unionist and Alliance parties. The representatives of the Irish Government stated that they understood and fully shared this concern. Different ways of solving this problem were discussed; among them were the amendment of legislation operating in the two jurisdictions on extradition, the creation of a common law enforcement area in which an all-Ireland court would have jurisdiction, and the extension of the jurisdiction of domestic courts so as to enable them to try offences committed outside the jurisdiction. It was agreed that problems of considerable legal complexity were involved, and that the British and Irish Governments would jointly set up a commission to consider all the proposals put forward at the Conference and to recommend as a matter of extreme urgency the most effective means of dealing with those who commit these crimes. The Irish Government undertook to take immediate and effective legal steps so that persons coming within their jurisdiction and accused of murder, however motivated, committed in Northern Ireland will be brought to trial, and it was agreed that any similar reciprocal action that may be needed in Northern Ireland be taken by the appropriate authorities. . . .

1983

THE NEW HOPE FOR BRITAIN, THE LABOUR PARTY ELECTION MANIFESTO

THE NADIR OF BRITISH SOCIALISM

In the general election campaigns of 1931, 1945 and 1983, the Labour Party promised sweeping nationalization and central planning. The results were decisive: a landslide triumph in 1945 and two landslide humiliations in 1931 and 1983. It was, however, the 1983 defeat that dealt a shattering blow to traditional socialist politics in Britain, leading the Labour politician Gerald Kaufman to dub the party's manifesto of that year 'the longest suicide note in history'.

Labour's defeat was all the more extraordinary given how low the fortunes of Margaret Thatcher's embattled Conservative administration had sunk by 1981. Her strategy to combat the runaway inflation that had bedevilled the British economy over the previous ten years coincided with a worldwide recession. This meant that traditional industries were decimated by a tight monetary squeeze, high interest rates and a strong currency that handicapped exports. Unemployment, which had stood at 1.25 million in May 1979 when Mrs Thatcher was elected, passed the 3 million mark by the beginning of 1983.

At the same time, the Labour Party was engulfed in a bitter internecine fight. Convinced that the parliamentary party and the leadership had failed to deliver effective socialist policies, constituency activists demanded an increased say in determining policy. At the 1980 party conference, they passed motions calling for the transformation of Britain into an isolationist, socialist state. A fortnight later, James Callaghan stood down as leader. In his place was elected Michael Foot, a left-wing intellectual and brilliant orator, whose misfortune it was to look even older and considerably more infirm than his sixty-seven years. In January 1981, Labour lurched further to the Left with the adoption of new rules that handed more power to the party's 'grass roots'. Henceforth, choosing the leader would be assigned to an

electoral college system in which the unions had 40 per cent of the vote, activists 30 per cent and MPs 30 per cent.

The immediate consequence was that some of Labour's most popular moderate politicians – in particular the so-called 'gang of four' of Roy Jenkins, David Owen, Shirley Williams and Bill Rodgers – resigned from the party and formed a new force, the Social Democratic Party (SDP). Sensational by-election victories followed, suggesting that the SDP might, as it claimed, 'break the mould' of British politics, even though its politics – a 'mixed economy' of state-run and private companies, with incomes policies to cap salaries – were essentially those of the 1970s Labour leadership, merely shorn of its trade union ties. In order not to split the middle ground, the SDP formed 'the Alliance' with the Liberal Party.

The Alliance's rapid progress came to a sudden halt in April 1982 when Argentina's right-wing dictatorship seized the British dependency of the Falkland Islands. The ensuing conflict, which ended in the islands' liberation and the downfall of military rule in Argentina, was the first clear evidence for years that Britain's leaders had anything more positive to offer than the orderly management of decline. The resolute approach of Margaret Thatcher had received a vindication in the chilly South Atlantic and, with inflation falling at home and the economy finally beginning to grow again, the Conservatives entered what would be an election year in 1983 with renewed purpose and popularity. The country went to the polls on 9 June.

Offering a refuge for pacifist-inclined idealists, the Labour Party was badly placed to benefit from the resurgent faith in British arms and self-belief unleashed by victory in the Falklands War. With some signs that the worst of the recession was over, increasing numbers of voters seemed prepared to give the hard Thatcherite economic medicine the chance to complete its work, rather than follow the purgative treatment with the risk of returning to rampant inflation and trade union militancy. Instead of adapting to these changing realities, Labour fought the 1983 election campaign on a programme that called for a massive extension of state control over the country.

In accordance with the rules that had been established, the Labour manifesto was drafted by the party's National Executive Committee and presented to the Shadow Cabinet as a *fait accompli*, rather than as a rough copy awaiting discussion and amendment. It promised Britain's unilateral nuclear disarmament and withdrawal from the European Community. Market forces were to be curtailed. Quotas and tariffs would be imposed to restrict imports. Exchange controls were

THATCHER'S REVOLUTION

1979 The Conservatives win the general election with Margaret Thatcher as the UK's first female prime minister. The basic rate of income tax is cut from 33 to 30 per cent and the top rate from 83 to 60 per cent. Exchange controls are abolished. Unemployment runs at 4 per cent (1.4 million), inflation at 13 per cent. Home ownership is at 54 per cent.

1980 The SAS storms the Iranian Embassy to release hostages from terrorists. Unemployment runs at 5 per cent, inflation at 18 per cent.

1981 The Social Democratic Party (SDP) is formed. Serious riots affect Brixton, Toxteth, Southall and other inner-city areas. Unemployment runs at 8 per cent (2.7 million), inflation at 12 per cent.

1982 The Falklands War is won. Unemployment runs at 9 per cent, inflation at 9 per cent.

1983 The Conservatives are returned at the general election. US Cruise missiles are installed at Greenham Common, generating protest. Unemployment runs at 10 per cent, inflation at 5 per cent.

1984 The year-long miners' strike begins. The IRA's Brighton bomb aims to kill Thatcher and her Cabinet. British Telecom is privatized. Unemployment runs at 11 per cent, inflation at 5 per cent.

1985 Riots hit Broadwater Farm estate, London. Unemployment is 11 per cent, inflation is 6 per cent.

1986 The 'Westland Affair' over defence procurement sees Cabinet resignations. British Gas is privatized. Unemployment peaks at 11 per cent (3.2 million people). Inflation runs at 3 per cent.

1987 The Conservatives win an historic third term. Rolls-Royce, British Airways and BAA are privatized. The stock market crashes on 'Black Monday.' Unemployment runs at 10 per cent, inflation at 4 per cent.

1988 The standard rate of income tax is reduced to 25 per cent, the top rate to 40 per cent. Thatcher delivers her Bruges speech condemning European federalism. British Steel is privatized. Unemployment runs at 8 per cent, inflation at 5 per cent.

1989 The Community Charge, soon dubbed the poll tax, is introduced in Scotland (and in England and Wales in 1990). Nigel Lawson resigns as chancellor. Revolutions across Eastern Europe bring down communist regimes and begin the end of the Cold War. Unemployment runs at 6 per cent, inflation at 8 per cent.

1990 Anti-poll tax riots in Trafalgar Square. Geoffrey Howe resigns as leader of the Commons. Thatcher resigns during a damaging leadership election. Unemployment runs at 6 per cent, inflation at 9 per cent. Home ownership is at 65 per cent. A quarter of the population owns shares. Average living standards have increased 30 per cent over the decade.

to be brought back to curb the international flow of capital and the major clearing banks were threatened that if they refused to 'cooperate with us fully . . . we shall stand ready to take one or more of them into public ownership'. Corporatism was to be reintroduced, with a new Department of Economic and Industrial Planning implementing a five-year plan. The limited privatization that had taken place would be reversed. Electronics and pharmaceutical companies were to be largely nationalized along with 'other important sectors, as required in the national interest'.

*Leadership style:
Michael Foot and
Margaret Thatcher
at the Cenotaph
on Remembrance
Day 1981.*

Further expansion of private health care would cease, whilst private schools would be stripped of charitable status and 'integrated' into the local authority sector 'where necessary'. In contrast, trade unions would regain their former powers.

The result was that Labour gained only a little over a quarter of the popular vote, just 2 per cent more than the Alliance (although the first-past-the-post voting system translated this into 209 Labour MPs, with a mere 23 for the Alliance). The Tories won 397 seats. With an overall majority of 144, Margaret Thatcher was free to enact her programme of rolling back state control, taking telecoms, gas and British Airways into the private sector, increasing home ownership with the sale of council houses to their tenants, reducing income tax and defeating the once mighty trade unions. The Labour Party did not return to power for another fourteen years, by which time it, like Britain, had changed markedly.

From *The New Hope for Britain*, 1983

Emergency programme of action

Within days of taking office, Labour will begin to implement an emergency programme of action, to bring about a complete change of direction for Britain. Our priority will be to create jobs and give a new urgency to the struggle for peace. In many cases we will be able to act immediately. In others, which involve legislation, they will take longer to bring into effect. But in all cases we shall act swiftly and with determination.

This is what we plan to do. We will:

Launch a massive programme for expansion. We will:

Provide a major increase in public investment, including transport, housing and energy conservation.

Begin a huge programme of construction, so that we can start to build our way out of the slump.

Halt the destruction of our social services and begin to rebuild them, by providing a substantial increase in resources.

Increase investment in industry, especially in new technology – with public enterprise taking the lead. And we will steer new industry and jobs to the regions and the inner cities.

Ensure that the pound is competitive; and hold back prices through action on VAT, rents, rates and fares.

Introduce a crash programme of employment and training, with new job subsidies and allowances.

Begin to rebuild British industry, working within a new framework for planning and industrial democracy. We will:

Agree a new national economic assessment, setting out the prospects for growth in the economy.

Prepare a five-year national plan, in consultation with unions and employers.

Back up these steps with a new National Investment Bank, new industrial powers, and a new Department for Economic and Industrial Planning.

Repeal Tory legislation on industrial relations and make provision for introducing industrial democracy.

Begin the return to public ownership of those public industries sold off by the Tories.

Give a new priority to open government at local and national levels, and give local communities greater freedom to manage their own affairs. We will also introduce an early Bill to abolish the legislative powers of the House of Lords.

In international policy, we shall take new initiatives to promote peace and development. We will:

Cancel the Trident programme, refuse to deploy Cruise missiles and begin discussions for the removal of nuclear bases from Britain, which is to be completed within the lifetime of the Labour government.

Ban arms sales to repressive regimes.

Increase aid to developing countries towards the UN target of 0.7 per cent.

Re-establish a separate Ministry of Overseas Development.

Take action to protect the status of refugees in Britain.

We will also open immediate negotiations with our EEC partners, and introduce the necessary legislation, to prepare for Britain's withdrawal from the EEC, to be completed well within the lifetime of the Labour government.

A POLICY FOR IMPORTS

But we must also plan ahead so that, as the economy expands, we keep our exports and imports in balance. We must therefore be ready to act on imports directly: first, in order to safeguard key industries that have been seriously put at risk by Tory policy; and second, so as to check the growth of imports should they threaten to outstrip our exports and thus our plan for expansion. We will:

Use agreed development plans, which we shall negotiate with the large companies that dominate our economy, so as to influence their purchasing and development policies. Our aim will be to prevent excessive import penetration and promote our own exports.

Use public purchasing policy to help support our strategy.

Introduce back-up import controls, using tariffs and quotas, if these prove necessary, to achieve our objective of trade balance – upon which sustained expansion depends . . .

PRICES – CONTROLLING INFLATION

The Tories have used mass unemployment to control inflation. We completely reject this approach. We believe it is madness to keep people out of work deliberately. Our priority will be to expand the economy and create jobs. But we are also determined to prevent soaring prices. Expansion will in itself help cut the costs of production and therefore hold back prices. But we will use other measures to help restrain inflation. We will:

Use direct measures of price restraint, such as cutting VAT, and subsidies on basic products, to cut into inflation as and when necessary.

Stop using public sector charges, such as gas prices – up by 116 per cent since 1979 – as a back-door way of raising taxes, as the Tories have done.

Buy our food where it is cheaper, on world markets, following Britain's withdrawal from the EEC.

Give powers to a new Price Commission to investigate companies, monitor price increases and order price freezes and reductions. These controls will be closely linked to our industrial planning, through agreed development plans with the leading, price-setting firms.

Take full account of these measures in the national economic assessment, to be agreed each year with the trade unions. The assessment will also take account of the impact of cost increases on the future rate of inflation.

1991

THE VERDICT IN THE
FACTORTAME (II) CASE

EUROPEAN JURISDICTION AND THE LIMITS
OF BRITISH SOVEREIGNTY

In delivering its verdict in the Factortame case, the European Court of Justice not only overturned the will of the British Parliament, it also gave any individual in any European Union country the right to sue their government for breaching European law. This had profound implications for the sovereignty of Parliament.

Although the judgment's application was universal across the ever-expanding legal competences of the EU, the specific case that established the precedent concerned the fishing industry. In the late 1970s and early 1980s, Spanish fishing boats that had traditionally fished off the coasts of Ireland and the west coasts of England found themselves excluded by the imposition of a fishing exclusion zone designed to deny access to non-members of the European Community (as the EU was then called). Spain did not join the EC until 1985 and in the meantime its fishermen sought to get around the exclusion either by re-registering their Spanish vessels as British ones or by becoming the owners of British vessels. British opposition was initially muted because a rudimentary European Common Fisheries Policy was being established and it was in Britain's interests to demonstrate that its registered fleet landed large catches so that, when formal restrictive quotas were introduced, Britain would be given a large share.

However, following Spain's entry into the European Community and the imposition by Brussels of tight quotas on how much, and what type of, fish each country could catch, British fishermen discovered that a large proportion of their entitlement was effectively being taken by Spanish vessels merely flying a British flag of convenience. Westminster responded in 1988 with the Merchant Shipping Act, which reserved the right to own a British-registered fishing boat

for British citizens, domiciled in the United Kingdom.

Factortame Limited, a Spanish-owned company operating 'British' fishing boats, claimed that the Merchant Shipping Act breached the European law's prohibition of discrimination between member states. The issue was complicated because the whole rationale behind the EU's national fishing quotas was predicated precisely upon recognizing separate national fishing fleets. What was the point of national quotas if there was not a nation-based definition of who was bound by them? The Treaty of Rome did not specify that a member nation no longer had the right to set rules on the entitlement to fly its flag for business purposes.

In June 1990, in what became known as the 'Factortame I' verdict, the European Court of Justice ruled that British courts could not withhold interim relief (such as an injunction) from a British Act of Parliament just because the applicability of European law had not yet been determined. Thus Factortame Limited was granted an injunction against the 1988 Merchant Shipping Act. In July 1991 came 'Factortame II' with the European Court's adjudication on the legality of the 1988 Act. It ruled that member states' rights to set rules on what constituted their national marine area of control did not extend to discriminating against those of a fellow European member state – in this instance, Spain. It therefore declared the Merchant Shipping Act void. 'Factortame III' followed in May 1996 when the European Court ruled that the British government was liable for damages for having steered through a law that the court subsequently deemed illegal. After further legal argument, the government eventually paid up.

It now seemed that, in an area of conflict, the 1972 European Communities Act (which made British law subservient to European Community law) overrode all subsequent legislation. Thus, the ancient notion that no Westminster Parliament could bind its successor was overturned. Nonetheless, a qualification remained. The Factortame case established that the European Court of Justice could strike down British Acts of Parliament that had been originally passed in the belief that they were in keeping with the spirit of European law – in this particular case national fishing quotas. It remained unclear what would happen if a British Act of Parliament was passed that not only broke European law but specifically stated its conscious intention to do so. The implications of the European Union's judiciary attesting that such a firm national declaration was illegal could one day produce a constitutional crisis in Britain.

Judgment of the European Court of Justice, 1991

THE COURT, in reply to the questions referred to it for a preliminary ruling by the High Court of Justice of England and Wales, Queen's Bench Division, by order of 10 March 1989, hereby rules:

1. As Community law stands at present, it is for the Member States to determine, in accordance with the general rules of international law, the conditions which must be fulfilled in order for a vessel to be registered in their registers and granted the right to fly their flag, but, in exercising that power, the Member States must comply with the rules of Community law;

2. It is contrary to the provisions of Community law and, in particular, to Article 52 of the EEC Treaty for a Member State to stipulate as conditions for the registration of a fishing vessel in its national register: (a) that the legal owners and beneficial owners and the charterers, managers and operators of the vessel must be nationals of that Member State or companies incorporated in that Member State, and that, in the latter case, at least 75% of the shares in the company must be owned by nationals of that Member State or by companies fulfilling the same requirements and 75% of the directors of the company must be nationals of that Member State; and (b) that the said legal owners and beneficial owners, charterers, managers, operators, shareholders and directors, as the case may be, must be resident and domiciled in that Member State;

3. It is not contrary to Community law for a Member State to stipulate as a condition for the registration of a fishing vessel in its national register that the vessel in question must be managed and its operations directed and controlled from within that Member State;

4. The fact that the competent minister of a Member State has the power to dispense with the nationality requirement in respect of an individual in view of the length of time such individual has resided in that Member State and has been involved in the fishing industry of that Member State cannot justify, in regard to Community law, the rule under which registration of a fishing vessel is subject to a nationality requirement and a requirement as to residence and domicile;

5. The existence of the present system of national quotas does not affect the replies given to the second question.

1997
CONDOLENCE BOOKS AND POPULAR INSCRIPTIONS TO DIANA, PRINCESS OF WALES

THE DEATH OF PRINCESS DIANA AND THE WEAKENING OF THE NATION'S STIFF UPPER LIP

In the early hours of 31 August 1997, Diana, Princess of Wales, then just thirty-six, died from injuries sustained in a car crash in central Paris. Also killed in the accident were her boyfriend, Dodi Fayed – son of the Egyptian entrepreneur Mohamed Al-Fayed, owner of Harrods department store – and the car's driver, Henri Paul, deputy head of security at the al-Fayed-owned Paris Ritz, where Diana and Dodi had been staying. Diana's life had been a heady mixture of aristocratic privilege and modern celebrity glitz, compassion for the less fortunate and media savviness, mass adulation and personal unhappiness. Her death sparked an outpouring of public emotion so removed from the self-control displayed by her former mother-in-law Queen Elizabeth II and her generation that it seemed as if a social revolution was under way. Some believed the monarchy itself was briefly endangered.

The fact that her fifteen-year marriage to the Prince of Wales had ended in divorce in 1996 had done little to diminish Princess Diana's public profile, either in Britain, where as the mother of Princes William and Harry she could hardly fail to be newsworthy, or in the rest of the world, where she remained a fashion icon on a scale surpassing that achieved by any Englishwoman in history. She had developed from the shy, nineteen-year-old daughter of an earl who married the Prince of Wales in 1981 into a loving mother, a dangerously weight-conscious bulimic and an international superstar. Technically, she had not been the hardest-working member of the royal family, but her stylishness and natural sympathy for others – whether embracing Aids sufferers or campaigning for a worldwide ban of

A page from the Dodi and Diana condolence book at Harrods is depicted in the fourth plate section.

landmines – gave to her engagements and charitable undertakings a frisson that those merely doing their duty could not match.

With the unravelling of her marriage, she launched a media campaign to both put her side of the story and discredit the Prince of Wales, first by providing private briefings to a friendly biographer, Andrew Morton, who turned out the best-selling *Diana – Her True Story*, and then, even more sensationally, by questioning whether her former husband was up to the job of kingship in a carefully choreographed television interview. In the broadcast, she cast herself as a 'queen in people's hearts'. It was a theme that the newly elected prime minister, Tony Blair, embellished when giving his public reaction to her death: 'People everywhere, not just here in Britain, kept faith with Princess Diana. They liked her, they loved her, they regarded her as one of the people. She was the People's Princess and that is how she will stay, how she will remain in our hearts and our memories for ever.'

The royal family was holidaying at Balmoral when the tragedy struck. The queen considered it her first duty to remain on the Scottish estate with her bereaved grandchildren, away from the public glare. The public mood elsewhere in the kingdom switched from grief at the cruel death of a beautiful and well-intentioned young woman to anger at the queen's failure to venture down south and visibly join in the emotional display. Realizing that private reflection was not what the public wanted, Blair was among those who persuaded the queen to make a hasty return to her capital, broadcast an appropriate tribute and ensure that Diana received a full public funeral. These late interventions did much to retrieve the House of Windsor's faltering standing.

Even so, suspicion of 'the Establishment' manifested itself, for a while, in the widespread credence given to a bizarre conspiracy theory in which the accident – caused in reality by a drunken chauffeur trying to shake off motorcycle photographers – had been an assassination carried out by Britain's security services. Resentment was also apparent at the funeral in the burst of applause, first outside and then inside Westminster Abbey, when Diana's brother Earl Spencer delivered a eulogy critical of the royal family's perceived lack of interpersonal skills.

Well over one million mourners gathered in Hyde Park or lined the route of Diana's coffin as it made its way to the Spencer family seat of Althorp in Northamptonshire. Across the world, an estimated 2.5 billion people watched the funeral on television. A sea of floral tributes was laid beyond the gates of Kensington Palace, Diana's former home. Candles were placed next to makeshift shrines, illustrated with cuttings of the princess from glossy magazines. Queues formed to sign books of condolence at St

James's Palace and at other points around the country. The Britain of self-control, of a stiff upper lip, of quiet Protestant understatement appeared to have been replaced by a temperament previously associated with Catholic Latin America. While many rejoiced that the emotionally repressed national caricature was giving way to one newly confident in expressing its feelings, others were aghast at what appeared, rather, to be the symptoms of a collective nervous breakdown.

The days of public mourning for Diana have become an indelible moment of shared national consciousness, like VE-Day or the England football team's 1966 World Cup victory. Measuring the extent to which the event shaped, or exemplified, changes in British society perhaps needs a longer perspective. The style of the public tribute was unprecedented, but its impressive scale needs putting in context. Vast crowds turned out to pay their respects at the state funeral of Field Marshal Earl Haig in 1928, yet his reputation proceeded to diminish almost continuously over the following half-century. At any rate, the damage done to the mystique of monarchy – which, after all, had once been part of Diana's own appeal – was certainly not apparent when, in 2005, joyful nationwide celebrations marked the Queen's Golden Jubilee.

Diana attracted huge crowds all over the world. These admirers are Russian.

1998

THE SCOTLAND ACT AND THE GOVERNMENT OF WALES ACT

A NEW SETTLEMENT FOR THE UNITED KINGDOM, OR THE BEGINNING OF ITS BREAK-UP?

In 1999, the Scottish Parliament was restored, 292 years after it had voted itself out of existence, and Wales gained a democratic national assembly for the first time in its history. What was unclear was whether these developments marked a long-delayed recognition that Scottish and Welsh nationhood could coincide with allegiance to the United Kingdom or whether the new institutions would eventually tear the Union apart.

This was not the first time that home rule for part of the UK had been tried. Between 1921 and 1972, Northern Ireland's internal affairs had been largely determined by its Parliament in Stormont. Yet Ulster was a special case. It was not part of the mainland and its particular sectarian troubles led to its Parliament being suspended. It was supposed to be restored following the 1998 Good Friday Agreement, although it was not until 2007 that the basis for cross-community trust was sufficient to permit Stormont's resumption.

The fact that Wales and Scotland were not just, for administrative purposes, an extension of England had been recognized by the establishment of the Scottish Office in 1885 and the Welsh Office in 1965, with their own secretaries of state, separate bureaucracy and tailored legislation. These arrangements allowed for a devolved approach to implementing policy set by a government answerable to Westminster, but they did not involve Scottish and Welsh politicians taking decisions for which they were accountable to their own legislatures and voters.

The case for devolved authority was attacked on two sides: by those who felt that separate parliaments would create the sort of conflicts with Westminster that could ultimately disunite the kingdom; and by supporters of outright independence, who regarded them as paltry half-measures. The independence movements were led by

Plaid Cymru, the Party of Wales, which was founded in 1925, and by the Scottish National Party (SNP), which was created out of two smaller groups in 1934. Neither party initially attracted widespread support. During the 1950s, the SNP had scarcely more than 1,000 members and, in the 1959 general election, less than 1 per cent of the Scottish vote.

While the extent of public backing for nationalist parties waxed and waned, the principle of devolution *within* the United Kingdom did command support. In 1949, 2 million Scots (almost half the nation's adult population) signed a new 'Covenant', which combined a pledge of loyalty to the British Crown with a request for the restoration of a Scottish legislature. Neither successive Conservative nor Labour governments did much to acknowledge this sentiment, and the 1950s proved to be a period in which Scotland seemed relatively at ease with its existing constitutional arrangements. By the late 1960s, however, endorsement for the SNP was spreading rapidly. The discovery of North Sea oil became the separatists' strongest argument in asserting that a country of only 5 million people could successfully go it alone. In the October 1974 general election, support for the SNP peaked at 30 per cent of the Scottish vote and eleven MPs.

The Labour government of 1974–9 felt compelled to offer devolution (without separate tax-raising powers), but a parliamentary amendment made the adoption of home rule conditional on the support of 40 per cent of the electorate in a referendum. In March 1979, the 'yes' campaign won the most votes, but since the narrow margin of victory equated to only 33 per cent of the Scottish electorate, it failed to clear the qualifying margin. In Wales, the devolutionists were crushed by 956,000 votes to 243,000. The opposition to home rule of Margaret Thatcher and John Major blocked new initiatives between 1979 and 1997.

During this period, the Conservative vote collapsed in Wales and Scotland. Particularly resented was the decision to introduce the ill-fated poll tax to Scotland a year before England. It caused widespread outrage as well as simple refusal to pay it. In 1989, representatives of the Scottish Labour and Liberal parties, together with trade unions, local authorities, churches and other interested entities, met as a 'Constitutional Convention' to draw up fresh proposals for a new Scottish Parliament.

The proposals formed the basis for legislation when Labour won the 1997 general election. Although Tony Blair had little interest in devolving power, he felt unable to dilute the commitment made by John Smith, his Scottish predecessor as Labour leader. Concluding that it was a step towards their goal of independence, the SNP tactically supported devolution when it was proposed in the September

From the Scotland Act and the Government of Wales Act, 1998

SCOTLAND ACT

Part I The Scottish Parliament

(1) There shall be a Scottish Parliament.

(2) One member of the Parliament shall be returned for each constituency (under the simple majority system) at an election held in the constituency.

(3) Members of the Parliament for each region shall be returned at a general election under the additional member system of proportional representation provided for in this Part and vacancies among such members shall be filled in accordance with this Part.

(4) The validity of any proceedings of the Parliament is not affected by any vacancy in its membership.

(5) Schedule 1 (which makes provision for the constituencies and regions for the purposes of this Act and the number of regional members) shall have effect.

Part II The Scottish Administration

(1) There shall be a Scottish Executive, whose members shall be—
    (a) the First Minister,
    (b) such Ministers as the First Minister may appoint under section 47, and
    (c) the Lord Advocate and the Solicitor General for Scotland.

(2) The members of the Scottish Executive are referred to collectively as the Scottish Ministers.

GOVERNMENT OF WALES ACT

Part I The National Assembly for Wales

(1) There shall be an Assembly for Wales to be known as the National Assembly for Wales or Cynulliad Cenedlaethol Cymru (but referred to in this Act as the Assembly).

(2) The Assembly shall be a body corporate.

(3) The exercise by the Assembly of its functions is to be regarded as done on behalf of the Crown. . . .

Part II Assembly functions

21 Introductory

The Assembly shall have the functions which are—
    (a) transferred to, or made exercisable by, the Assembly by virtue of this Act, or
    (b) conferred or imposed on the Assembly by or under this Act or any other Act.

22 Transfer of Ministerial functions

(1) Her Majesty may by Order in Council—

(a) provide for the transfer to the Assembly of any function so far as exercisable by a Minister of the Crown in relation to Wales,

(b) direct that any function so far as so exercisable shall be exercisable by the Assembly concurrently with the Minister of the Crown, or

(c) direct that any function so far as exercisable by a Minister of the Crown in relation to Wales shall be exercisable by the Minister only with the agreement of, or after consultation with, the Assembly.

1997 referendum. This time a simple majority was sufficient and Scotland voted by three to one in favour of a parliament and by two to one that it should also be granted the right to vary income tax by three pence in the pound from the rate set at Westminster. Eight days later, the verdict was far more muted in Wales, with the devolutionists winning by the thinnest of margins, a mere 6,712 votes.

The Scotland Act was largely the work of Blair's secretary of state for Scotland, Donald Dewar (1937–2000). It devolved all competences to Scotland other than those specifically listed as 'reserved' for Westminster. In contrast, the presumption of the Wales Act was that all powers remained at Westminster except those specifically listed as moving to Cardiff. The sixty-member Welsh Assembly, which was not given powers to vary income tax, was primarily concerned with adapting Westminster legislation to Welsh circumstances rather than, as was the case with the Scottish Parliament, instigating its own laws (although Cardiff did gain some primary legislative powers, subject to London's veto, in 2006). In 1999, the Scottish Parliament began sitting in Edinburgh, with Dewar as first minister. Elected by a system of proportional representation that made coalition likely, the Parliament had 129 representatives and enjoyed legislative powers over such domestic affairs as health, education, transport, housing and social security. The commanding heights of economic policy, foreign affairs and defence remained the prerogative of London.

Neither unionists nor separatists imagined that this represented a final and irrevocable settlement. After the SNP formed a minority administration in 2007, they retitled the Scottish Executive in a telling linguistic sleight of hand as the 'Scottish Government' and pursued a legislative and cultural agenda that accentuated the division north and south of the border. Still awaiting a convincing answer was the 'West Lothian question' posed by the pro-Union Scottish Labour MP Tam

Dalyell, who wondered whether it was equitable for Westminster's Scottish MPs to vote on legislation that applied only to England when their English colleagues could not legislate for Scotland. The seemingly obvious solution of excluding the votes of Scottish MPs worked smoothly solely when the government's majority was not dependent on Scottish seats, which historically it often was. It risked legislative confusion, if not havoc, at some stage in the future.

In the past, Britain has always emerged, grumbling yet united, from far more severe trials. In the decades ahead, it will be up to its constituent peoples to decide whether they still believe, as so many of their forebears did, that Britain remains greater than the sum of its parts and an ideal of cooperation worth fighting to preserve.

2002

IRAQ'S WEAPONS OF MASS DESTRUCTION: THE ASSESSMENT OF THE BRITISH GOVERNMENT

TONY BLAIR'S CASE FOR WAR WITH IRAQ

T he most controversial act of British foreign policy since the 1956 Suez Crisis was the decision to join the US invasion of Iraq in 2003. Although it did not provide the only justification for the attack, the government's decision to release an intelligence assessment suggesting that Iraq had the ability to launch weapons of mass destruction (WMD) within forty-five minutes of an order being given was one of the critical influences in persuading the House of Commons to sanction the invasion despite divided public opinion. Too late, the central claims of the report were found to be false.

Following al-Qaeda's terrorist attacks on New York and Washington, which killed 2,976 people on 11 September 2001, President George W. Bush's admin-istration was determined not only to confront the militant Islamist perpetrators of the assault, together with the Taliban government of Afghanistan that had given them shelter, but also to remove another thorn in the side of American foreign policy – the dictatorship of Saddam Hussein in Iraq. In Tony Blair, Bush found the most resolute of allies. British forces joined the American-led invasion of Afghanistan in October 2001.

The plan to occupy Iraq was more controversial, since, despite the country's clear hostility towards the United States and other Western countries, not to mention the viciousness of its ruler, it was not implicated in the September 2001 terrorist outrages. Saddam Hussein had deployed chemical weapons in his war with Iran between 1980 and 1988, but his regime had received a major setback with the American-led coalition's repulsion of his occupation of Kuwait in 1991 and

BLAIR'S BRITAIN

1997 Labour wins the general election with 418 seats, ending eighteen years of Conservative rule. Diana, Princess of Wales, is killed in a Paris car crash. Wales and Scotland vote for devolved powers in referenda. There are about 10 million mobile phone subscriptions in the UK. The average house price is £68,525, the average household debt £16,155.

1998 The Belfast ('Good Friday') Agreement is signed. The Human Rights Act is passed. A national minimum wage is introduced.

1999 The UK joins in NATO airstrikes against Serbia during the Kosovo War. The first elections to the Scottish Parliament and the Welsh Assembly take place. About 20 per cent of households have internet access.

2000 The newly constructed Dome in London is the national focus for celebration – and criticism – during the commemoration of the new millennium. The first directly elected mayor of London, Ken Livingstone, takes office. British troops are sent into Sierra Leone.

2001 Labour wins a second term with 413 seats. The Conservative leader, William Hague, resigns and is replaced by Iain Duncan Smith. British troops join NATO forces in an invasion of Afghanistan following the al-Qaeda terrorist attacks on New York and Washington, DC.

2002 Blair makes the case for invading Iraq with the help of inaccurate intelligence information about Iraq's weapons of mass destruction.

2003 Over 1 million protesters march through London to condemn the proposed war in Iraq. British forces participate in the invasion of Iraq and take control of Basra. Iain Duncan Smith is replaced by Michael Howard as Conservative leader.

2004 The Hutton Report into the suicide of defence analyst David Kelly criticizes BBC journalism and controls. But the Butler report faults British intelligence's contribution in preparation for the Iraq war. The Civil Partnership Act gives same-sex relationships the legal entitlements of marriage.

2005 Labour wins a third term in the general election with 356 seats and a majority reduced to 64. Michael Howard resigns as Conservative leader and is replaced by David Cameron. Fifty-two innocent civilians are killed and hundreds injured in Islamist suicide bomb attacks in London.

2006 The 'cash for honours' investigation looks into the ethics of Labour fund-raising.

2007 The Scottish Nationalist Party (SNP) emerges as the largest party in the 2007 elections for the Scottish parliament. Alex Salmond heads a minority SNP administration. Tony Blair resigns as prime minister and is succeeded by Gordon Brown. Over 60 per cent of households have internet access. There are over 60 million mobile phone subscriptions in the UK. The average house price is £205,102, the average household debt £54,318.

the subsequent international efforts to restrict his war-making potential. When his obstructionism of UN weapons inspectors caused them to abandon their investigative mission in 1998, the assumption remained that he had something to hide. Under threat of military action, Iraq reluctantly allowed back UN inspectors in November 2002. While the inspection team was given wide access, the regime's

failure to respond promptly to some requests played into the hands of those who had decided that regime change in Baghdad could alone solve the problem.

In September, Tony Blair's government had recalled Parliament early from its summer break to discuss the crisis and had issued its intelligence assessment on Iraq's WMD. The report asserted that Saddam's regime still had biological and chemical weapons, some of which could be deployed within forty-five minutes. The report also claimed that Iraq had recommenced work on a nuclear programme and was trying to get hold of uranium from Niger.

It further drew upon various private briefings provided to the Cabinet by its Joint Intelligence Committee (JIC). A furious row later developed over whether the government had strengthened the JIC's language ('sexed up' became the buzz-phrase of the moment) in order to strengthen the case for intervention. This was what the BBC journalist Andrew Gilligan inferred from a private briefing by a government weapons expert, David Kelly. In the subsequent media frenzy following the government's release of his identity, Kelly committed suicide.

Special Relationship: Tony Blair in step with President George W. Bush.

From *Iraq's Weapons of Mass Destruction: The Assessment of the British Government*, 2002

THE CURRENT POSITION: 1998–2002

1. This chapter sets out what we know of Saddam Hussein's chemical, biological, nuclear and ballistic missile programmes, drawing on all the available evidence. While it takes account of the results from UN inspections and other publicly available information, it also draws heavily on the latest intelligence about Iraqi efforts to develop their programmes and capabilities since 1998. The main conclusions are that:

- Iraq has a useable chemical and biological weapons capability, in breach of UNSCR 687, which has included recent production of chemical and biological agents;

- Saddam continues to attach great importance to the possession of weapons of mass destruction and ballistic missiles which he regards as being the basis for Iraq's regional power. He is determined to retain these capabilities; Iraq can deliver chemical and biological agents using an extensive range of artillery shells, free-fall bombs, sprayers and ballistic missiles;

- Iraq continues to work on developing nuclear weapons, in breach of its obligations under the Non-Proliferation Treaty and in breach of UNSCR 687. Uranium has been sought from Africa that has no civil nuclear application in Iraq;

- Iraq possesses extended-range versions of the SCUD ballistic missile in breach of UNSCR 687 which are capable of reaching Cyprus, Eastern Turkey, Tehran and Israel. It is also developing longer-range ballistic missiles;

- Iraq's current military planning specifically envisages the use of chemical and biological weapons;

- Iraq's military forces are able to use chemical and biological weapons, with command, control and logistical arrangements in place. The Iraqi military are able to deploy these weapons within 45 minutes of a decision to do so;

- Iraq has learnt lessons from previous UN weapons inspections and is already taking steps to conceal and disperse sensitive equipment and documentation in advance of the return of inspectors;

- Iraq's chemical, biological, nuclear and ballistic missiles programmes are well-funded.

Certainly, Alastair Campbell, the prime minister's director of communications – famous for being able to put the most favourable 'spin' on any story concerning the Labour government – was involved in the report's presentation. Nonetheless, John Scarlett, the JIC chairman, later gave evidence maintaining that the report was faithful to the briefings the security services had provided.

Whatever view is taken on how the Blair government presented both the report and the case built from it for invading Iraq, the fact remains that the document represented a colossal failing of information assessment by Britain's secret services. The ensuing occupation of Iraq uncovered no WMD, let alone those able to be deployed within forty-five minutes, nor a restarted nuclear programme. The likelihood of Niger successfully delivering uranium to Iraq was discounted.

These disclosures came too late to prevent the invasion. Having failed to secure a UN resolution explicitly endorsing military action, Tony Blair faced the House of Commons on 18 March 2003 and repeated his case, drawing substantively on the JIC's September 2002 report. Impressed by that evidence, Iain Duncan Smith, the leader of the opposition, pledged his party's support on the grounds that 'Saddam Hussein has the means, the mentality and the motive to pose a direct threat to our national security'. Upon these misapprehensions, MPs endorsed the prime minister's actions and voted down an amendment 'that the case for war against Iraq has not yet been established' by 396 to 217. Two days later the invasion began.

The bloody insurgency and the cost, in both human and diplomatic terms, of sustaining a democratic Iraqi state in the chaos that followed Saddam Hussein's overthrow naturally had the most far-reaching effects in the Middle East. In Britain, the consequences were political as well as psychological. There was a widespread – if disputed – claim by the war's opponents that military action was illegal without a specific UN resolution sanctioning it. To this charge was added the accusation that, in basing so much of his case for invasion on the WMD claims, Blair had effectively gone to war on the back of a conscious deceit, rather than merely poor advice. These were grave accusations that Blair and those closest to him strongly refuted when giving evidence to the Chilcot Inquiry in 2010. Yet they were manifestations of growing dissatisfaction not just with the 'New Labour project' but – more alarmingly – with the probity of those in public life more generally. In this sense at the very least, *Iraq's Weapons of Mass Destruction: The Assessment of the British Government* unquestionably had a toxic legacy.

2005

LIFE IN THE UNITED KINGDOM, QUESTION PAPER

TESTING BRITISHNESS

During the early years of the twenty-first century, several research projects were undertaken to track the genetic history of the British people. The preliminary results were surprising. It seemed that around 80 per cent of modern white Britons could trace their genetic make-up all the way back to ancestors who were already settled in the British Isles at the end of the Ice Age – 12,000 years ago.

The findings were particularly startling, not just because they suggested that the political and cultural influence of Anglo-Saxon, Viking and Norman settlers was far greater than their actual numbers, but also for the perspective placed upon more recent immigration. Between the twelfth century and the end of the nineteenth century, the only really huge influx to the mainland came not from abroad but from Ireland, which was at the time of the greatest migration (during and after the Irish potato famine of 1845–51) fully incorporated into the United Kingdom. From beyond the British Isles, the level of migration was continuous but never overwhelming. By 1700, Protestant Huguenots who had escaped religious persecution in France represented about 0.7 per cent of the British population and, a few decades later, the black population was thought to have peaked at about 0.2 per cent of Britons. Indeed, in the early decades of the twentieth century, there were thought to have been scarcely more than 10,000 non-white people in Britain, while the proportion of German and Italian-born residents in the country was put at about 0.2 per cent in 1911. The Jewish community, fleeing first tsarist and then fascist persecution, still represented less than 1 per cent by the end of the 1930s.

The picture began to change more rapidly after the Second World War with large-scale immigration from the 'New Commonwealth' countries of the Caribbean, Africa and the Indian subcontinent. Even so, by the mid-1970s these

'New Commonwealth' immigrants comprised only 3 per cent of the UK population of 55 million. By the 1980s, the majority of them were British-born. It was in the 1990s and, especially, in the first years of the twenty-first century that the most radical change became manifest. By 2006, official net immigration was running at an annual rate of about 300,000 (equivalent to the population of a city the size of Coventry) and one in four children born in Britain had a foreign parent. On top of this, by 2009 there were estimated to be around three-quarters of a million illegal immigrants in the country, all from outside the European Union.

This level of cultural impact was without precedent since the Norman Conquest. Whilst the dramatic influx of workers from Eastern Europe was curtailed by the onset of economic recession in 2008, there were still considerable numbers arriving from other parts of the world. Despite the size – and speed – of the influx, the newcomers were largely welcomed by Tony Blair's government and by businesses keen to tap new talents, filling positions left vacant because of skill shortages among British-born workers as well as ensuring that competitive pressures restrained wage growth. From the arts to the less glamorous jobs, the new arrivals quickly made their mark. Many observers welcomed this new diversity as a source of strength. There was even hopeful talk of creating a British version of the 'American Dream'.

Those more sceptical about the benefits of multiculturalism were less clear that it created a common community, seeing rather a process of atomization and alienation. Indeed, some of the social and religious attitudes introduced with immigration seemed to be at odds with the innate liberalism and tolerance that was supposedly Britain's great appeal. Evidence of divided communities, militant Islamic fundamentalist attitudes (even extending to the planning of Islamist terrorist attacks) and renewed recruiting by racist groups suggested that, for all the achievements, the ideal sometimes fell short of reality. These tensions also triggered reactionary political developments. The belief that Britain had lost control of its borders was among the reasons cited by politicians urging mandatory identity cards and other forms of heightened surveillance.

The governments of Tony Blair and Gordon Brown found themselves simultaneously trying to celebrate the new diversity while searching for ways to channel it towards a common British identity – one that was simultaneously under threat from the re-emergence of Scottish, Welsh and Irish nationalism, recognized by devolution in Edinburgh and Cardiff, and power-sharing in Belfast. Defining a positive British identity was easier said than done. Aspects of British history that might once have been a source of pride, such as an empire that covered a quarter

A selection of sample test questions

1. When will the British Government adopt the euro as the UK's currency?
A 2010
B 2015
C Never
D When the British people vote for it in a referendum

2. What percentage of Christians in the UK are Roman Catholic?
A 10 per cent
B 20 per cent
C 30 per cent
D 40 per cent

3. What type of constitution does the UK have?
A A legal constitution
B A written constitution
C An amended constitution
D An unwritten constitution

4. How might you stop young people playing tricks on you at Hallowe'en?
A Call the police
B Give them some money
C Give them sweets or chocolate
D Hide from them

5. What proportion of the UK population have used illegal drugs at one time or another?
A One quarter
B One third
C One half
D Two thirds

6. Who is the monarch
not allowed to marry?
A Anyone who is not
of royal blood
B Anyone who is not
a Protestant
C Anyone who is
under the age of 25
D Anyone who was
born outside the UK

7. What year did
women in the UK
gain the right to
divorce their husband?
A 1810
B 1857
C 1901
D 1945

8. All dogs in public
places must wear a
collar showing the
name and address
of the owner. Is this
statement true or false?
A True
B False

of the globe, often had a less positive resonance for those who had not been on the side of the conquerors. The same applied to celebrated military victories against European neighbours. In an attempt to define Britishness without offending anyone, the government suggested it was about the spirit of 'fair play', although even this observation implied a certain degree of self-satisfied chauvinism. A 'public consultation' on devising a national motto only managed to provoke derisive suggestions and the widespread reaction that the very idea was distinctly un-British.

One Cabinet minister in particular made constructive efforts to address the future of Britishness: David Blunkett (b. 1947). As a student, he had studied at Sheffield University under the professor of politics there, Bernard Crick (1929–2008). A socialist and constitutional reformer, Crick was the author of *In Defence of Politics* and a strong believer in the active participation of the citizen. Appropriately from this perspective, Britain was nothing if not four nations bound by political institutions. On becoming education secretary in 1997, Blunkett appointed Crick chairman of the Teaching of Citizenship and Democracy in Schools advisory group. The result was that 'citizenship' became part of the school national curriculum. In 2001, Blunkett became home secretary and Crick was again appointed, this time to chair the commission advising on how a test might be devised for those seeking British citizenship.

Previously, the process of British naturalization had been a purely bureaucratic procedure, but, inspired by American practice, the decision was taken to turn it into more of an event, complete with a formal ceremony. The general criteria for applicants included stipulations that they should have lived in Britain for five years (or three years if married to a Briton), be 'of good character', have a basic competency in the English language and pass a citizenship test. The examination was an entirely new initiative in which applicants answered multiple-choice questions on subject matter laid out in a Home Office publication, *Life in the United Kingdom*. Crick had written the history section and, inevitably, immediately drew accusations from professional historians that he had got some of his facts wrong.

Whatever the legacy of the citizenship test, it was clearly the product of a United Kingdom wrestling with a crisis of identity. The prospect of it being torn apart and Balkanized back into its constituent nations has become real for the first time in generations. The very notion of 'British documents' may soon be seen as a dated concept. Yet come what may, those collated in this book represent a rich bequest and, if we are fortunate, may prove an enduring inspiration with which to shape the future.

ACKNOWLEDGEMENTS

A work of this kind is made possible by the custodians of the documents themselves and I would naturally like to thank the keepers and archivists at all the libraries and museums for their help, without which there could have been neither study nor reproduction of the manuscripts in their care. For providing expert knowledge on the extent of collections and the whereabouts of particular documents, I would especially like to thank Professor Richard Aldous, Kate Grimond, Dr Christopher de Hamel, Simon Gough, Dr Peter Jones, Neil Robinson and Robert Seatter. Eamon Dyas and Nick Mays at *The Times* archive must also be thanked for all their wise counsel and forbearance over the years, as must the staff of the London Library for their guidance and assistance.

I am particularly indebted to Anthony Cheetham and Richard Milbank for conceiving this project and to my agent, Georgina Capel, for her zest and stalwart support. At Atlantic Books, Richard Milbank and Sarah Norman have provided invaluable editorial advice, expertise and great professionalism. I should also like to thank Rich Carr, Mark Hawkins-Dady, Celia Levett and Amanda Russell.

For their hospitality and kindness I particularly wish to record my gratitude to Jane Clark at Saltwood and to Mark Craig and Nicole Wright in London. Paul Stephenson has been a source of seasoned sagacity, whether conveyed from long distance or across a dinner table. This book is dedicated to my nephew and godson, Rufus Stewart.

Graham Stewart
Saltwood
Kent

27 June 2010

SELECT BIBLIOGRAPHY

The place of publication is London unless otherwise stated.

THE DARK AGES

GENERAL STUDIES:
Guy de la Bédoyère, *Roman Britain, A New History* (2006); Michael Lapidge et al (eds.), *The Blackwell Encyclopaedia of Anglo-Saxon England* (Oxford 1999); Peter Salway, *Roman Britain* (Oxford 1981); Simon Schama, *A History of Britain: At the Edge of the World? 3000BC–1603* (2000); F. M. Stenton, *Anglo-Saxon England* (Oxford 1971 edn.); Dorothy Whitelock, *English Historical Documents, c.500–1042* (1979 edn.)

SPECIFIC STUDIES:
Robin Birley, *Vindolanda: a Roman Frontier Post on Hadrian's Wall* (1977); Alan K. Bowman, *Life and Letters on the Roman Frontier: Vindolanda and its People* (2003); John Blair, *The Church in Anglo-Saxon England* (Oxford 2005); Michelle Brown, *The Lindisfarne Gospels: Society, Spirituality and the Scribe* (2003); Leo Sherley-Price (trans.), *The Venerable Bede, History of the English Church and People* (1955); Seamus Heaney (trans.), *Beowulf* (1999); Benjamin Thorpe (trans.), *Beowulf* (1889); G. N. Garmonsway (trans.), *The Anglo-Saxon Chronicle* (1953); Alfred P. Smyth, *King Alfred the Great* (Oxford 1995)

THE MEDIEVAL AGE

GENERAL STUDIES:
Robert Bartlett, *England Under the Norman and Angevin Kings, 1075–1225* (Oxford 2000); David C. Douglas and G. W. Greenaway, *English Historical Documents, 1042–1189* (1981 ed); E. F. Jacob, *The Fifteenth Century, 1399–1485* (Oxford 1961); May McKisack, *The Fourteenth Century 1307–1399* (Oxford 1959); Alec R. Myers, *English Historical Documents 1327–1485* (1969); Austin Lane Poole, *From Domesday Book to Magna Carta 1087–1216* (Oxford 1955 edn.); Sir Maurice Powicke, *The Thirteenth Century, 1216–1307* (Oxford 1962 edn.); Michael Prestwich, *Plantagenet*

England 1225–1360 (Oxford 2005); Harry Rothwell, *English Historical Documents 1189–1327* (1975); Simon Schama, *A History of Britain: At the Edge of the World? 3000BC–1603* (2000)

SPECIFIC STUDIES:
Carola Hicks, *The Bayeux Tapestry, the Life History of a Masterpiece* (2006); J. C. Holt, *Magna Carta* (1965); Sir Ivor Jennings, *Magna Carta and its Influence in the World Today* (1965); Richard Vaughan (ed.), *The Illustrated Chronicles of Matthew Paris* (Stroud 1993); John Field, *The Story of Parliament in the Palace of Westminster* (2002); J. R. Maddicott, *Simon de Montfort* (1994); James A. MacKay, *Robert Bruce, King of Scots* (1974); Michael Brown, *The Wars of Scotland, 1214–1371* (Edinburgh 2004); Anthony Kenny, *Wyclif* (Oxford 1985); Tim Card, *Eton Established, a History from 1440 to 1860* (2001); Christopher Brooke and Roger Highfield, *Oxford and Cambridge* (Cambridge 1988); Elisabeth Leedham-Green, *A Concise History of the University of Cambridge* (Cambridge 1996); Christopher Morris, *King's College: A Short History* (Cambridge 1989); Elizabeth Archibald and Ad Putter, *The Cambridge Companion to the Arthurian Legend* (Cambridge 2009); Alan Lupack, *The Oxford Guide to Arthurian Literature and Legend* (Oxford 2005)

RELIGION AND RENAISSANCE

GENERAL STUDIES:
S.T. Bindoff, *Tudor England* (1950); J. B. Black, *The Reign of Elizabeth, 1558–1603* (Oxford 1959 edn.); C. S. L. Davies, *Peace, Print and Protestantism, 1450–1558* (1976); G. R. Elton, *England Under the Tudors* (1955); Douglas Price, *English Historical Documents, 1558–1603* (1966); Simon Schama, *A History of Britain: At the Edge of the World? 3000BC–1603* (2000); C. H. Williams, *English Historical Documents, 1485–1558* (1967); Penry Williams, *The Later Tudors, England 1547–1603* (Oxford 1995)

SPECIFIC STUDIES:

David Daniell, *William Tyndale, a Biography* (New Haven, CT, 1994); Brian Moynahan, *If God Spare My Life: William Tyndale, the English Bible and Sir Thomas More* (2002); C. S. Knighton and D. M. Loades (eds.), *The Anthony Roll of Henry VIII's Navy* (Aldershot 2000); G. W. Bernard, *The King's Reformation, Henry VIII and the Remaking of the English Church* (New Haven, CT, 2005); Diarmaid MacCulloch, *Tudor Church Militant, Edward VI and the Protestant Reformation* (1999); Diarmaid MacCulloch, *Thomas Cranmer, A Life* (1996); Thomas Stuart Willan, *The Early History of the Muscovy Company 1553–1606* (Manchester 1956); Gordon Donaldson, *Mary, Queen of Scots* (1974); Antonia Fraser, *Mary, Queen of Scots* (1969); A.E. MacRobert, *Mary Queen of Scots and the Casket Letters* (2002); Edmund H. Fellowes, *William Byrd* (1948 ed.); Nicholas Canny (ed.) *The Oxford History of the British Empire: The Origins of Empire* (Oxford 1998); *Lawrence James, The Rise and Fall of the British Empire* (1994); John Keay, *The Honourable Company: a History of the English East India Company* (1991)

STUART BRITAIN

GENERAL STUDIES:

Andrew Browning, *English Historical Documents, 1660–1714* (1953); Godfrey Davies, *The Early Stuarts 1603–1660* (Oxford 1959 edn.); Sir George Clark, *The Later Stuarts 1660–1714* (Oxford 1956 edn.); Julian Hoppit, *A Land of Liberty? England 1689–1727* (Oxford 2000); Simon Schama, *A History of Britain: The British Wars 1603–1776* (2001)

SPECIFIC STUDIES:

Nick Groom, *The Union Jack, The Biography* (2006); Anthony James West, *The Shakespeare First Folio: the History of the Book* (2001; 2003); Stanley Wells and Gary Taylor (gen. eds.), *The Oxford Shakespeare, The Complete Works* (Oxford 2005 ed); John Adamson, *The Noble Revolt: The Overthrow of Charles I* (2007); Tristram Hunt, *The English Civil War: At First Hand* (2002); Diane Purkiss, *The English Civil War: A People's History* (2006); A. L. Rowse, *The Regicides and the Puritan Revolution* (1994); C. V. Wedgwood, *The Trial of Charles I* (1964); Austin Woolrych, *Britain in Revolution 1625–1660* (2002); Blair Worden, *The English Civil Wars 1940–1660* (2009); David S. Katz, *The Jews in the History of England, 1485–1850* (Oxford 1994); W. D Rubinstein, *A History of the Jews in the English-Speaking World: Great Britain* (Basingstoke 1996); Bill Bryson (ed.), *Seeing Further: the Story of Science and the Royal Society* (2010); Lisa Jardine, *The Curious Life of Robert Hooke, the Man Who Measured London* (2003); John Miller, *James II, A Study in Kingship* (1978); Edward Vallance, *The Glorious Revolution 1688: Britain's Fight For Liberty* (2006); T. M. Devine, *The Scottish Nation, 1700–2000* (1999); Michael Fry, *The Union: England, Scotland and the Treaty of 1707* (Edinburgh 2007)

HANOVERIAN BRITAIN

GENERAL STUDIES:

D. B. Horn and Mary Ransome, *English Historical Documents, 1714–1783* (1957); Paul Langford, *A Polite and Commercial People, England 1727–1783* (Oxford 1989); Simon Schama, *A History of Britain: The British Wars 1603–1776* (2001); Simon Schama, *A History of Britain: The Fate of Empire 1776–2000* (2002); J. Steven Watson, *The Reign of George III, 1760–1815* (Oxford 1960); *Basil Williams, The Whig Supremacy 1714–1760* (Oxford 1962 edn.)

SPECIFIC STUDIES:

Linda Colley, *Britons: Forging the Nation 1707–1837* (New Haven, CT, 1992); James Boswell, *The Life of Samuel Johnson* (1991 ed.); Henry Hitchings, *Dr Johnson's Dictionary, the Extraordinary Story of the Book that Defined the World* (2005); Jack Lynch (ed.) *Samuel Johnson's Dictionary* (2002); Niall Ferguson, *Empire: How Britain Made the Modern World* (2003); A. J. Youngson, *The Making of Classical Edinburgh* (Edinburgh 1966); James Buchan, *Capital of the Mind: How Edinburgh Changed the World* (2003); Richard L. Hill, *Richard Arkwright and Cotton Spinning* (1973); Steven King and Geoffrey Timmins, *Making Sense of the Industrial Revolution: English Economy and Society, 1700–1850* (Manchester, 2001); Hugh Thomas, *The Slave Trade: the History of the Atlantic Slave Trade* (1997); Steven M. Wise, *Though the Heaven's May Fall: The Landmark Trial that led to the end of*

Human Slavery (2006); Gavin Kennedy, *Adam Smith, a Moral Philosopher and his Political Economy* (2008); P. J. O'Rourke, *On the Wealth of Nations* (2007); *The History of The Times: The 'Thunderer' in the Making* (1935) and successive volumes (now running to seven in total) of the newspaper's official history; Tony Lewis, *Double Century: a Story of MCC and Cricket* (1987); David Underdown, *Start of Play: Cricket and Culture in Eighteenth Century England* (2000); John Major, *More than a Game: the Story of Cricket's Early Years* (2007)

THE YEARS OF REFORM

GENERAL STUDIES:
A. Aspinall and E. Anthony Smith, *English Historical Documents, 1783–1832* (1959); Boyd Hilton, *A Mad, Bad, and Dangerous People? England 1783–1846* (Oxford 2006); Simon Schama, *A History of Britain: The Fate of Empire 1776–2000* (2002); J. Steven Watson, *The Reign of George III, 1760–1815* (Oxford 1960); Sir Llewellyn Woodward, *The Age of Reform 1815–1870* (Oxford 1962 edn.)

SPECIFIC STUDIES:
Janet Todd, *Mary Wollstonecraft, a Revolutionary Life* (2000); Richard Godfrey, *James Gillray: the Art of Caricature* (2001); William Hague, *William Pitt the Younger* (2004); Paul Bew, *Ireland, the Politics of Enmity 1789–2006* (Oxford 2007); Roger J. P. Cain, John Chapman and Richard R. Oliver, *The Enclosure Maps of England and Wales, 1595–1918* (Cambridge 2004); J. M. Neeson, *Commoners: Common Right, Enclosure and Social Change in England, 1700–1820* (Cambridge 1993); W. G. Hoskins, *The Making of the English Landscape* (1955); L. T. C. Rolt, *George and Robert Stephenson: The Railway Revolution* (1960); Wendy Hinde, *Catholic Emancipation: a Shake to Men's Minds* (Oxford 1992); M. D. R. Lays, *Catholics in England 1559–1829 A Social History* (1961); Linda Colley, *Taking Stock of Taking Liberties* (2008); Robert Stewart, *The Foundation of the Conservative Party 1830–67* (1978); Robert Blake, *A History of the Conservative Party from Peel to Major* (1997); Douglas Hurd, *Robert Peel, a biography* (2007); David Jones, *Chartism and the Chartists* (1975)

THE VICTORIAN AGE

GENERAL STUDIES:
R. C. K. Ensor, *England 1870–1914* (Oxford 1936); W. D. Handcock, *English Historical Documents, 1874–1914* (1977); K. Theodore Hoppen, *The Mid-Victorian Generation, England 1846–1886* (Oxford 1998); Simon Schama, *A History of Britain: The Fate of Empire 1776–2000* (2002); A. N. Wilson, *The Victorians* (2002); G. M. Young and W. D Handcock, *English Historical Documents, 1833–1874* (1956); Sir Llewellyn Woodward, *The Age of Reform 1815–1870* (Oxford 1938)

SPECIFIC STUDIES:
Steven Brindle, *Brunel, the Man Who Built the World* (2005); Peter Ackroyd, *Dickens* (1990) and his *Introduction to Dickens* (1991); Michael Leapman, *The World for a Shilling: How the Great Exhibition Shaped a Nation* (2001); Kate Colquhoun, *A Thing In Disguise: The Visionary Life of Joseph Paxton* (2003); Jonathan Glancey, *Lost Buildings: Demolished, Destroyed, Imagined, Reborn* (2008); Geoffrey Green, *The History of the Football Association* (1953); Richard Holt, *Sport and the British, a Modern History* (Oxford 1989)

FROM EMPIRE TO WELFARE STATE

GENERAL STUDIES:
Peter Clarke, *Hope and Glory: Britain 1900–1990* (1996); Simon Schama, *A History of Britain: The Fate of Empire 1776–2000* (2002); G. R. Searle, *A New England? England 1886–1918* (Oxford 2004); Richard Shannon, *The Crisis of Imperialism, 1865–1915* (Oxford 1974); A. J. P. Taylor, *English History 1914–1945* (Oxford 1965)

SPECIFIC STUDIES:
John Charmley, *Splendid Isolation? Britain, the Balance of Power and the Origins of the First World War* (1999); Simon Heffer, *Power and Place: The Political Consequences of Edward VII* (1998); Martin Pugh, *The March of the Women: A Revisionist Analysis of the Campaign for Women's Suffrage, 1866–1914* (2000) and his *The Pankhursts* (2001); David Cannadine, *The Decline and Fall of the British Aristocracy,* (New Haven, CT, 1990);

Roy Jenkins, *Asquith* (1964); John Grigg's *Lloyd George*, vols: II. *The People's Champion 1902–1911* (1978), III. *From Peace to War 1912–1916* (1985) and IV. *War Leader 1916–1918* (2002); Niall Ferguson, *The Pity of War* (1998); Henry Pelling, *A Short History of the Labour Party* (1968 ed.); Sheila Lawlor, *Britain and Ireland 1914–23* (Dublin 1983); J. J. Lee, *Ireland 1912–1985: Politics and Society* (Cambridge 1989); Kenneth O. Morgan, *Consensus and Disunity, the Lloyd George Coalition Government 1918–1922* (Oxford 1979); Niall Ferguson, *Empire: How Britain Made the Modern World* (2003); Judith M. Brown and Wm. Roger Louis (eds), *Oxford History of the British Empire: The Twentieth Century* (Oxford 1999); Tony Judd, *Empire, the British Imperial Experience from 1765 to the Present* (1996); Asa Briggs, *The BBC, the First Fifty Years* (Oxford 1985); Ian McIntyre, *The Expense of Glory: a Life of John Reith* (1993); Philip Ziegler, *King Edward VIII, the Official Biography* (1990); Jonathan Glancey, *Spitfire, the Biography* (2006); John Terraine, *The Right of the Line, the Royal Air Force in the European War, 1939–1945* (1985); R.A.C. Parker, *Chamberlain and Appeasement* (Basingstoke, 1993); John Charmley, *Chamberlain and the Lost Peace* (1989); Graham Stewart, *Burying Caesar, Churchill, Chamberlain and the Battle for the Tory Party* (1999); David Faber, *Munich, the 1938 Appeasement Crisis* (2008); Paul Addison, *The Road to 1945: British Politics and the Second World War* (1975); Kevin Jefferys, *The Churchill Coalition and Wartime Politics, 1940–1945* (Manchester 1995 ed.); Nicholas Timmins, *The Five Giants, A Biography of the Welfare State* (1995); Robin Woolven (int.), *The London County Council Bomb Damage Maps 1939–45* (2005); Angus Calder, *The People's War Britain: 1939–45* (1969); Philip Hoare, *Noel Coward, a Biography* (1995); Sarah Street, *British National Cinema* (1997); Robert Winder, *Bloody Foreigners, The Story of Immigration to Britain* (2004); Eric Richards, *Britannia's Children, Emigration from England, Scotland, Wales and Ireland since 1600* (2004); Peter Hennessy, *Never Again: Britain, 1945–51* (1992); Alan Bullock, *Ernest Bevin*, vol. III (1983);

Ben Macintyre, *For Your Eyes Only: Ian Fleming and James Bond* (2008); Lord Kilmuir, *Political Adventure, the Memoirs of the Earl of Kilmuir* (1964)

ELIZABETH II'S BRITAIN

GENERAL STUDIES:
Peter Clarke, *Hope and Glory: Britain 1900–1990* (1996); Brian Harrison, *Seeking a Role: the United Kingdom 1951–1970* (Oxford 2009); Peter Hennessy, *Having It So Good, Britain in the Fifties* (2006); Dominic Sandbrook, *Never Had It So Good, A History of Britain from Suez to the Beatles* (2005); Dominic Sandbrook, *White Heat, A History of Britain in the Swinging Sixties* (2006); Simon Schama, *A History of Britain: The Fate of Empire 1776–2000* (2002); Alan Sked and Chris Cook, *Post-War Britain: A Political History* (1993 edn.)

SPECIFIC STUDIES:
David Reynolds, *Britannia Overruled, British Policy and World Power in the Twentieth Century* (1991); David Carlton, *Britain and the Suez Crisis* (Oxford 1988); D. R. Thorpe, *Eden: the Life and Times of Anthony Eden* (2003); Ian MacDonald, *Revolution in the Head: The Beatles' Records and the Sixties* (1994); Tim Pat Coogan, *The Troubles: Ireland's Ordeal 1966–95 and the Search for Peace* (1995); J. J. Lee, *Ireland 1912–1985: Politics and Society* (Cambridge 1989); John Campbell, *Edward Heath, a Biography* (1993); Ben Pimlott, *Harold Wilson* (1992); David Butler and Dennis Kavanagh, *The British General Election of 1983* (1984); Kenneth O. Morgan, *Michael Foot, A Life* (2007); Sarah Bradford, *Diana* (2006); T. M. Devine, *The Scottish Nation, 1700–2000* (1999); Con Coughlin, *American Ally: Tony Blair and the War on Terror* (2006); Anthony Seldon, *Blair Unbound* (2007); David Miles, *The Tribes of Britain: Who Are We? And Where Do We Come From?* (2005)

WHERE TO FIND THE DOCUMENTS

The Vindolanda Tablets
British Museum

The Lindisfarne Gospels
British Library

Bedes's *Historia Ecclesiastica Gentis Anglorum*
Among the early copies are those held by the British Library, Cambridge University Library, the Bodleian Library, Oxford and the St Petersburg Public Library, Russia

Beowulf
British Library

The Treaty of Alfred and Guthrum
Corpus Christi College, Cambridge

The Anglo-Saxon Chronicle
The Parker Chronicle is at Corpus Christi College, Cambridge. The Laud (Peterborough) Chronicle is at the Bodleian Library, Oxford. The Abingdon, Canterbury and Worcester Chronicles are at the British Library

The Bayeux Tapestry
Musée de la Tapisserie de Bayeux, Bayeux, France

The Domesday Book
The National Archives

The Assize of Clarendon
Roger of Howden's *Chronica* in the British Library and the Bodleian Library, Oxford

Magna Carta
Four 1215 copies survive: two in the British Library and one each at Lincoln Cathedral and Salisbury Cathedral

Chronicles of Matthew Paris
The *Chronica Majora* is at Corpus Christi College, Cambridge. The *Historia Anglorum* is in the British Library

Medieval parliamentary election writs
The National Archives

The Statute of Rhuddlan
The National Archives

The Declaration of Arbroath
The National Archives of Scotland

Wyclif's Bible
British Library and John Rylands University Library, University of Manchester

Henry VI's charter for Eton College
Eton College

Henry VI's charters for King's College, Cambridge
King's College, Cambridge

Caxton's edition of Malory's *Morte d'Arthur*
British Library

Tyndale's New Testament
British Library

Parliament's petition to the pope
Vatican Archives

The Anglo-Welsh Act of Union
Parliamentary Archives

The Anthony Roll
British Library and Magdalene College, Cambridge

The Book of Common Prayer
British Library

The royal charter of the Muscovy Company
The original document was lost in the Great Fire of London 1666 but a copy of it exists in the London Metropolitan Archives

Foxe's *Book of Martyrs*
British Library

The Thirty-Nine Articles
Corpus Christi College, Cambridge

My Ladye Nevells Book
British Library

The royal charter of the East India Company
British Library

The Elizabethan Poor Law
Parliamentary Archives

The Monteagle Letter and Guy Fawkes's Confession
The National Archives

Union Jack designs
National Library of Scotland

The King James Bible
British Library

Shakespeare's First Folio
British Library

The Petition of Right
Parliamentary Archives

The Scottish National Covenant
The National Archives of Scotland

The record of the Putney Debates
Worcester College, Oxford

The death warrant of King Charles I
Parliamentary Archives

The Instrument of Government
The original document was lost during the Restoration though its contents were published. Text in C. H. Firth, R. S. Rait (eds.), *Acts and Ordinances of the Interregnum, 1642–1660.*

Menasseh Ben Israel's Humble Petition
National Archives

Memorandum of the Royal Society
Royal Society

The Clarendon Code
Parliamentary Archives

The Immortal Seven's Invitation to William of Orange
Text in Sir John Dalrymple, *Memoirs of Great Britain and Ireland*, Appendix I

The Bill of Rights
Parliamentary Archives

John Locke's *Two Treatises of Government*
British Library

The royal charter of the Bank of England
Bank of England

The Act of Settlement
Parliamentary Archives

The Act of Union
Parliamentary Archives; exemplification in the National Archives of Scotland

God Save the King, *Gentleman's Magazine*
British Library

Samuel Johnson's *Dictionary*
British Library

The Declaratory Act
Parliamentary Archives

James Craig's plan for Edinburgh's New Town
National Library of Scotland

Arkwright's water frame patent
The National Archives

The Somerset Judgment
Howell's *State Trials*, British Library

Adam Smith's *The Wealth of Nations*
British Library

First edition of *The Times*
British Library

Marylebone Cricket Club's Code of Laws
The original document was lost after publication. The revised laws of 1795 are in the MCC Library.

Mary Wollstonecraft's *A Vindication of the Rights of Woman*
British Library

The Anglo-Irish Act of Union
Parliamentary Archives

The General Enclosure Act
Parliamentary Archives

James Gillray's *The Plum-Pudding in Danger*
National Portrait Gallery, London

Sketch of *Rocket's* boiler
Science Museum, London

The Catholic Emancipation Act
Parliamentary Archives

The Great Reform Act
Parliamentary Archives

The Tamworth Manifesto
Published in *The Times*, British Library

The People's Charter
British Library

Engine design for SS *Great Britain*
Science Museum

Charles Dickens's *A Christmas Carol*
Morgan Library and Museum, New York

The 'Crystal Palace' design
Victoria & Albert Museum

The Rules of Association Football
Football Association Archives

The Married Women's Property Act
Parliamentary Archives

Charles Booth's poverty maps
British Library

The Anglo-French Entente Cordiale
The National Archives

Nominations for the peerage
Bodleian Library, Oxford

NUWSS 'Fourteen Reasons' appeal
British Library

War recruitment poster
Imperial War Museum, London

Clause IV of the Labour Party Constitution
Labour Party Archives, The People's Museum, Manchester; Passfield Archive, London School of Economics

The Anglo-Irish Treaty
The National Archives

Map of the British Empire
The National Archives

The royal charter of the BBC
BBC Written Archives Centre, Reading

Edward VIII's Instrument of Abdication
The National Archives

Design for the Supermarine Spitfire
Mark I factory drawings at the RAF Museum, Hendon. Mitchell's original Mark I drawings are no longer extant but his chalk drawings for the Prototype are held at the Solent Sky Museum, Southampton. Other material is held in the Supermarine/Vickers-Armstrong Archive at the RAF Museum.

Hitler and Chamberlain's Munich note
The National Archives

The Beveridge Report
British Library

London County Council map of London war damage
London Metropolitan Archives

Brief Encounter film script
British Film Institute

The British Nationality Act
Parliamentary Archives

The North Atlantic Treaty
National Archives, Washington DC, General Records of the U.S. Government

The European Convention on Human Rights
Council of Europe Archives, Strasbourg

Ian Fleming's manuscript for *Casino Royale*
Ian Fleming Will Trust

The Sèvres Protocol
Bodleian Library, Oxford

Department of Education Circular 10/65
Published by Her Majesty's Stationary Office

The Beatles' *Sgt. Pepper* album cover
University of Leeds, School of Music

The Accession Treaty to the EEC
The National Archives

The Communiqué of the Sunningdale Agreement
The National Archives

The New Hope for Britain Labour election manifesto
British Library

Factortame (II) verdict
European Court of Justice

Diana, Princess of Wales condolence books
Althorp House and Harrods

The Scotland Act
Parliamentary Archives

The Government of Wales Act
Parliamentary Archives

Iraq's Weapons of Mass Destruction: The Assessment of the British Government
Published by the Stationery Office

Life in the United Kingdom, question paper
Published by the Stationery Office

INDEX